# Touring Euro[pe]

## Central and South East
## Benelux and Scandinavia

Also available:

© The Caravan Club Limited 2015
Published by The Caravan Club Limited
East Grinstead House, East Grinstead
West Sussex RH19 1UA

General Enquiries: 01342 326944
Travel Service Reservations: 01342 316101
Red Pennant Overseas Holiday Insurance:
01342 336633
Website: www.caravanclub.co.uk
Email: enquiries@caravanclub.co.uk

Editor: Kate Walters
Email: kate.walters@caravanclub.co.uk

Printed by Stephens & George Ltd
Merthyr Tydfil

**ISBN 978-0-9569510-8-3**

# Far and away the best value

## for touring Europe

# Welcome
## to Touring Europe 2015

The Caravan Club has been producing the **Caravan Europe** guides for over 50 years, and in that time there have been a lot of changes in the way people tour on the continent. We know that those who use this guide travel in a wide range of outfits – not just caravans, but motorhomes, trailer tents and tents as well. This, above all else, is the reason for the change in the name of this guide to **Touring Europe**.

The way that people research their trip has also changed considerably. The availability of information, especially online, means that there is far more content accessible than we are able to provide within these books. With this in mind, you will see a change to the introductory chapters - giving you the essential information you need when touring, while directing you to further good sources if you need to delve deeper.

One thing that hasn't changed over the years is our reliance on you, the users of the sites and these guides, to collate the information. The fact that all the entries are from those who stay on these sites makes the guide unique, and we very much appreciate the time and effort you continue to give in contributing to the guides. You can visit www.caravanclub.co.uk/europereport to fill in reports online, or find site report forms at the back of the guide.

I hope the changes will make the guides much easier to use, but we always welcome feedback on the changes or what you would like to see in future editions. Happy touring!

*Kate Walters*

Kate Walters, Editor

# Contents

## How To Use This Guide

## Planning your trip

## Motoring advice

## During your stay

## Continental Campsites

## Site Listings

*See also alphabetical index at the back of the guide*

# How to use this guide

The information contained within *Touring Europe* is presented in the following categories:

## The Handbook

This includes general information about touring in Europe, such as legal requirements, advice and regulations. The Handbook chapters are at the front of the guide and are separated as follows:

| | |
|---|---|
| **Purple section** | Planning your trip - information you'll need before you travel including information on the documents and insurance you'll need, advice on money, customs regulations and planning your channel crossings. |
| **Green section** | Motoring advice - advice on motoring overseas, essential equipment and roads in Europe including mountain passes and tunnels. |
| **Turquoise section** | During your stay - information for while you're away including telephone, internet and TV advice, medical information and advice on staying safe. |
| **Blue section** | Continental Campsites - advice on choosing your site and the differences you might find overseas. |

## Country Introduction

Following on from the Handbook chapters you will find the Country Introductions containing information, regulations and advice specific to each country. You should read the Country Introduction in conjunction with the Handbook chapters before you set off on your holiday.

## Campsite Entries

After the Country Introduction you will find the campsite entries listed alphabetically under their nearest town or village. Where several campsites are shown in and around the same town they will be listed in clockwise order from the north.

To find a campsite all you need to do is look for the town or village of where you would like to stay, or use the maps at the back of each site section to find a town where sites are listed. Where there are no sites listed in a relatively large or popular town you may find a cross reference, directing you to closest town which does have sites.

In order to provide you with the details of as many site as possible in *Touring Europe* we use abbreviations in the site entries.

For a full and detailed list of these abbreviations please see the following pages of this section.

We have also included some of the most regularly used abbreviations, as well as an explanation of a campsite entry, on the tear-out bookmark page.

## Campsite Fees

Campsite entries show high season fees per night for an outfit plus two adults, as at the year of the last report. Prices given may not include electricity or showers, unless indicated. Outside of the main holiday season many sites offer discounts on the prices shown and some sites may also offer a reduction for longer stays.

Campsite fees may vary to the prices stated in the site entries, especially if the site has not been reported on for a few years. You are advised to always check fees when booking, or at least before pitching, as those shown in site entries should be used as a guide only.

## Site Maps

Each town and village listed alphabetically in the site entry pages has a map grid reference

number, e.g. 3B4. The map grid reference number is shown on each site entry. The maps can be found at the end of each country's site entry pages. The reference number will show you where each town or village is located, and the site entry will tell you how far the site is from that town. Place names are shown on the maps in two colours:

**Red** where we list a site which is open all year (or for at least eleven months of the year)

**Black** where we only list seasonal sites which close in winter.

These maps are intended for general campsite location purposes only; a detailed road map or atlas is essential for route planning and touring.

Town names in capital letters (**RED**, **BLACK** or in *ITALICS*) correspond with towns listed on the Distance Chart.

The scale used for the map means that it is not possible to pinpoint every town or village where a campsite exists, so some sites in small villages may be listed under a nearby larger town instead.

*Satellite Navigation*

Most campsite entries now show a GPS (sat nav) reference. There are several different formats of writing co-ordinates, and in this guide we use decimal degrees, for example 48.85661 (latitude north) and 2.35222 (longitude east).

Minus readings, shown as -1.23456, indicate that the longitude is west of the Greenwich meridian. This will only apply to sites in the west of France, most of Spain and all of Portugal as the majority of Europe (including all countries covered in this edition of the guide) are east of the Greenwich meridian.

Manufacturers of Sat Navs all use different formats of co-ordinates so you may need to convert the co-ordinates before using them with your device. There are plenty of online conversion tools which enable you to do this quickly and easily - just type 'co-ordinate converter' into your search engine.

Please be aware if you are using a sat nav device some routes may take you on roads that are narrow and/or are not suitable for caravans or large outfits.

The GPS co-ordinates given in this guide are provided by members and checked wherever possible, however we cannot guarantee their accuracy due to the rural nature of most of the sites. The Caravan Club cannot accept responsibility for any inaccuracies, errors or omissions or for their effects.

# Site Report Forms

With the exception of campsites in The Club's Overseas Site Booking Service (SBS) network, The Caravan Club does not inspect sites listed in this guide. Virtually all of the sites listed in *Touring Europe* are from site reports submitted by users of these guides. You can tell us about great sites you have found or update the details of sites already within the books.

**We rely on you, the users of this guide, to tell us about campsites you have visited**

Sites which are not reported on for five years are deleted from the guide, so even if you visit a site and find nothing different from the site listing we'd appreciate a update to tell us as much.

You will find site report forms towards the back of this guide which we hope you will complete and return to us by freepost (please post when you are back in the UK). Use the abbreviated site report form if you are reporting no changes, or only minor changes, to a site entry. The full report form should be used for new sites or sites which have changed a lot since the last report.

You can complete both the full and abbreviated versions of the site report forms by visiting www.caravanclub.co.uk/europereport.

## Complete site report forms online – www.caravanclub.co.uk/europereport

Please submit reports as soon as possible. Information received by **mid August 2015** will be used wherever possible in the next edition of *Touring Europe*. Reports received after that date are still very welcome and will appear in the following edition. The editor is unable to respond individually to site reports submitted due to the large quantity that we receive.

*Tips for Completing Site Reports*

- If possible fill in a site report form while at the campsite. Once back at home it can be difficult to remember details of individual sites, especially if you visited several during your trip.
- When giving directions to a site, remember to include the direction of travel, e.g. 'from north on D137, turn left onto D794 signposted Combourg' or 'on N83 from Poligny turn right at petrol station in village'. Wherever possible give road numbers, junction numbers and/or kilometre post numbers, where you exit from motorways or main roads. It is also helpful to mention useful landmarks such as bridges, roundabouts, traffic lights or prominent buildings.

We very much appreciates the time and trouble you take submitting reports on campsites that you have visited; without your valuable contributions it would be impossible to update this guide.

## Acknowledgements

The Caravan Club's thanks go to the AIT/ FIA Information Centre (OTA), the Alliance Internationale de Tourisme (AIT), the Fédération International de Camping et de Caravaning (FICC) and to the national clubs and tourist offices of those countries who have assisted with this publication.

# Explanation of a
# Campsite Entry

The town under which the campsite is listed, as shown on the relevant Sites Location Map at the end of each country's site entry pages

Distance and direction of the site from the centre of the town the site is listed under in kilometres (or metres), together with site's aspect

Site Location Map grid reference

Indicates that the site is open all year

Campsite name

Telephone and fax numbers including national code where applicable

Description of the campsite and its facilities

Contact email and website address

Directions to the campsite

⊞ **MUNSTERTAL** *03B4 (1.5km W Rural)* **47.85995, 7.76370**
**Feriencamping Münstertal, Dietzelbachstrasse 6, 79244**
**Münstertal** **[(07636) 7080; fax (07636) 7448; info@**
**camping-muenstertal.de; www.camping-muenstertal.**
**de]** Exit A5 junc 64a at Bad Krozingen-Staufen-Münstertal.
By-pass Staufen & foll Münstertal sps. Site on L 1.5km past
Camping Belchenblick off rd L123. Lge, mkd pitch, shd;
wc; chem disp; mv service pnt; serviced pitches; sauna;
steam rm; solarium; private bathrms avail; shwrs inc; el pnts
(16A) metered; gas; lndtte; shop; rest; snacks; adventure
playgrnd; 2 htd pools (1 covrd); fishing; wintersports nr;
skilift 10km; tennis; horseriding; games area; games rm;
beauty treatments avail; wifi; entmnt; cab TV; some statics;
dogs €3.50; phone; rlwy stn 200m; gates clsd 1300-1430
& 2200-0730; m'van o'night area; adv bkg rec school
hols; quiet; red long stay. CCI. "Superb, well-managed
site; luxurious, clean facs; many activities for all family; gd
walking; vg rest; conv Freiburg & Black Forest." ♦ € 31.55
2011*

Unspecified facilities for disabled guests. If followed by 'ltd' this indicates that the facilities are limited.

The year in which the site was last reported on by a visitor

Campsite address

**BALATONSZEPEZD** *C1* (4km SW Rural) *46.82960,*
*17.64014* **Balatontourist Camping Napfény,**
**Halász út 5, 8253 Révfülöp [(87) 563031; fax**
**464309; napfeny@balatontourist.hu; www.**
**balatontourist.hu]** Take m'way E71/M7 & exit junc 90
along N shore of lake, passing Balatonalmádi & Balatonfüred
to Révfülöp. Site sp. Lge, mkd pitch, pt shd; wc; chem disp;
mv service pnt; baby facs; private san facs avail; shwrs inc;
el pnts (6A) inc; lndtte (inc dryer); shop; supmkt 500m;
tradsmn; rest; snacks; bar; BBQ; playgrnd; paddling pool;
lake sw & beach adj; fishing; watersports; cycle & boat hire;
tennis 300m; horseriding 5km; games area; games rm; wifi;
entmnt; TV rm; 2% statics; dogs HUF900; twin-axles acc
(rec check in adv); phone; adv bkg; quiet; ccard acc; red
low ssn. "Warm welcome; excel, well-organised lakeside
site; gd pitches; gd for families; fees according to pitch
size & location." ♦ 27 Apr-30 Sep. HUF 7150 (CChq acc)
SBS - X06 2011*

GPS co-ordinates – latitude and longitude in decimal degrees. Minus figures indicate that the site is west of the Greenwich meridian

Comments and opinions of caravanners who have visited the site (within inverted commas)

Charge per night in high season for car, caravan + 2 adults as at year of last report

Opening dates

Booking reference for a site the Club's Overseas Travel Service work with, i.e. bookable via The Club.

The site accepts Camping Cheques, see the *Continental Campsites* chapter for details

# Site Description Abbreviations

Each site entry assumes the following unless stated otherwise:

**Level ground, open grass pitches, drinking water on site, clean wc unless otherwise stated (own sanitation required if wc not listed), site is suitable for any length of stay within the dates shown.**

## aspect
**urban** – within a city or town, or on its outskirts
**rural** – within or on edge of a village or in open countryside
**coastal** – within one kilometre of the coast

## size of site
**sm** – max 50 pitches
**med** – 51 to 150 pitches
**lge** – 151 to 500 pitches
**v lge** – 501+ pitches

## pitches
**hdg pitch** – hedged pitches
**mkd pitch** – marked or numbered pitches
**hdstg** – some hard standing or gravel

## levels
**sl** – sloping site
**pt sl** – sloping in parts
**terr** – terraced site

## shade
**shd** – plenty of shade
**pt shd** – part shaded
**unshd** – no shade

## Site Facilities

### adv bkg
Advance booking accepted;
**adv bkg rec** – advance booking recommended

### baby facs
Nursing room/bathroom for babies/children

### beach
Beach for swimming nearby;
**1km** – distance to beach
**sand beach** – sandy beach
**shgl beach** – shingle beach

### bus/metro/tram
Public transport within an easy walk of the site

### chem disp
Dedicated chemical toilet disposal facilities;
**chem disp (wc)** – no dedicated point; disposal via wc only

### CKE/CCI
Camping Key Europe and/or Camping Card International accepted

## CL-type
Very small, privately-owned, informal and usually basic, farm or country site similar to those in the Caravan Club's network of Certificated Locations

## dogs
Dogs allowed on site with appropriate certification (a daily fee may be quoted and conditions may apply)

## el pnts
Mains electric hook-ups available for a fee;
**inc** – cost included in site fee quoted
**10A** – amperage provided
**conn fee** – one-off charge for connection to metered electricity supply
**rev pol** – reversed polarity may be present
(see *Electricity and Gas* in the section *DURING YOUR STAY*)

## Eng spkn
English spoken by campsite reception staff

## entmnt
Entertainment facilities or organised entertainment for adults and/or children

## fam bthrm
Bathroom for use by families with small children

## gas
Supplies of bottled gas available on site or nearby

## internet
Internet point for use by visitors to site;
**wifi** – wireless local area network available

## lndtte
Washing machine(s) with or without tumble dryers, sometimes other equipment available, eg ironing boards;
**lndtte (inc dryer)** – washing machine(s) and tumble dryer(s)
**lndry rm** – laundry room with only basic clothes-washing facilities

## Mairie
Town hall (France); will usually make municipal campsite reservations

## mv service pnt
Special low level waste discharge point for motor caravans; fresh water tap and rinse facilities should also be available

**NH**
Suitable as a night halt

**noisy**
Noisy site with reasons given;
quiet – peaceful, tranquil site

**open 1 Apr-15 Oct**
Where no specific dates are given, opening
dates are assumed to be inclusive, ie Apr-Oct –
beginning April to end October
(NB: opening dates may vary from those shown;
check before travelling, particularly when
travelling out of the main holiday season)

**phone**
Public payphone on or adjacent to site

**playgrnd**
Children's playground

**pool**
Swimming pool (may be open high season only);
htd – heated pool
covrd – indoor pool or one with retractable
cover

**poss cr**
During high season site may be crowded or
overcrowded and pitches cramped

**red CCI/CCS**
Reduction in fees on production of a Camping
Card International or Camping Card Scandinavia

**rest**
Restaurant;
bar – bar
BBQ – barbecues allowed (may be restricted to a
separate, designated area)
cooking facs – communal kitchen area
snacks – snack bar, cafeteria or takeaway

**SBS**
Site Booking Service (pitch reservation can be
made through the Caravan Club's Travel Service)

**serviced pitch**
Electric hook-ups and mains water inlet and grey
water waste outlet to pitch;
all – to all pitches
50% – percentage of pitches

**shop(s)**
Shop on site;
adj – shops next to site
500m – nearest shops
supmkt – supermarket
hypmkt – hypermarket
tradsmn – tradesmen call at the site, eg baker

**shwrs**
Hot showers available for a fee;
inc – cost included in site fee quoted

**ssn**
Season;
high ssn – peak holiday season
low ssn – out of peak season

**50% statics**
Percentage of static caravans/mobile homes/
chalets/fixed tents/cabins or long term seasonal
pitches on site, including those run by tour
operators

**sw**
Swimming nearby;
1km – nearest swimming
lake – in lake
rv – in river

**TV**
TV available for viewing by visitors (often in
the bar);
TV rm – separate TV room (often also a games
room)
cab/sat – cable or satellite connections to pitches

**WC**
Clean flushing toilets on site;
(cont) – continental type with floor-level hole
htd – sanitary block centrally heated in winter
own san – use of own sanitation facilities
recommended

# Other Abbreviations

| AIT | Alliance Internationale de Tourisme |
|---|---|
| a'bahn | Autobahn |
| a'pista | Autopista |
| a'route | Autoroute |
| a'strada | Autostrada |
| adj | Adjacent, nearby |
| alt | Alternative |
| app | Approach, on approaching |
| arr | Arrival, arriving |
| avail | Available |
| Ave | Avenue |
| bdge | Bridge |
| bef | Before |
| bet | Between |
| Blvd | Boulevard |
| C | Century, eg 16thC |
| c'van | Caravan |
| CC | Caravan Club |
| ccard acc | Credit and/or debit cards accepted (check with site for specific details) |
| CChq acc | Camping Cheques accepted |

| | | | | |
|---|---|---|---|
| cent | Centre or central | o'look(ing) | Overlook(ing) |
| clsd | Closed | o'night | Overnight |
| conn | Connection | o'skts | Outskirts |
| cont | Continue or continental (wc) | PO | Post office |
| conv | Convenient | poss | Possible, possibly |
| covrd | Covered | pt | Part |
| dep | Departure | R | Right |
| diff | Difficult, with difficulty | rd | Road or street |
| dir | Direction | rec | Recommend/ed |
| dist | Distance | recep | Reception |
| dual c'way | Dual carriageway | red | Reduced, reduction (for) |
| E | East | reg | Regular |
| ent | Entrance/entry to | req | Required |
| espec | Especially | RH | Right-hand |
| ess | Essential | rlwy | Railway line |
| excel | Excellent | rm | Room |
| facs | Facilities | rndabt | Roundabout |
| FIA | Fédération Internationale de l'Automobile | rte | Route |
| | | RV | Recreational vehicle, ie large motor caravan |
| FICC | Fédération Internationale de Camping & de Caravaning | rv/rvside | River/riverside |
| FFCC | Fédération Française de Camping et de Caravaning | S | South |
| | | san facs | Sanitary facilities ie wc, showers, etc |
| FKK/FNF | Naturist federation, ie naturist site | snr citizens | Senior citizens |
| foll | Follow | sep | Separate |
| fr | From | sh | Short |
| g'ge | Garage | sp | Sign post, signposted |
| gd | Good | sq | Square |
| grnd(s) | Ground(s) | ssn | Season |
| hr(s) | Hour(s) | stn | Station |
| immac | Immaculate | strt | Straight, straight ahead |
| immed | Immediate(ly) | sw | Swimming |
| inc | Included/inclusive | thro | Through |
| indus est | Industrial estate | TO | Tourist Office |
| INF | Naturist federation, ie naturist site | tour ops | Tour operators |
| int'l | International | traff lts | Traffic lights |
| irreg | Irregular | twd | Toward(s) |
| junc | Junction | unrel | Unreliable |
| km | Kilometre | vg | Very good |
| L | Left | vill | Village |
| LH | Left-hand | W | West |
| LS | Low season | w/end | Weekend |
| ltd | Limited | x-ing | Crossing |
| mkd | Marked | x-rds | Cross roads |
| mkt | Market | | |
| mob | Mobile (phone) | | |
| m'van | Motor caravan | | |
| m'way | Motorway | | |
| N | North | | |
| narr | Narrow | | |
| nr, nrby | Near, nearby | | |
| opp | Opposite | | |
| o'fits | Outfits | | |

## Symbols Used

◆     Unspecified facilities for disabled guests check before arrival

⊞     Open all year

\*     Last year site report received (see Campsite Entries in Introduction)

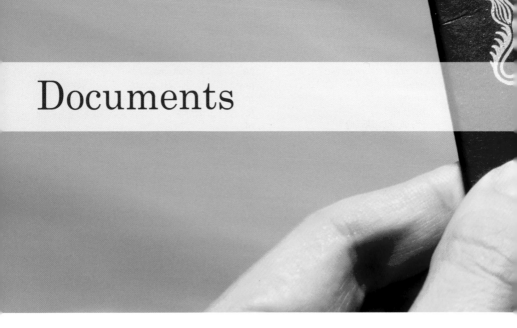

# Documents

## Camping Card Schemes

Camping Key Europe (CKE) is a useful companion for touring in Europe. Not only does it serve as a valid ID at campsites, meaning that you don't have to leave you passport with the site reception, it also entitles you to discounts at over 2200 sites.

CKE also offers Third Party Liability Insurance for up to 6 people travelling in one party, and Personal Accident Cover while on site. Full Terms and Conditions and details of the levels of cover of this insurance are provided with the card.

CKE is available to purchase from The Caravan Club by calling 01342 336633, or is provided free for all members taking out the 'Motoring' level of cover of The Club's Red Pennant Overseas Holiday Insurance.

An alternative scheme is Camping Card International (CCI) which offers similar benefits as CKE.

If you are using a CKE or CCI card as a method of ID at a site, make sure that you retrieve your card on leaving the site. Also check that you have been given your own card instead of someone else's.

See www.campingkey.com or www.campingcardinternational.com for full details of the schemes.

## Driving Licence

A full, valid driving licence should be carried at all times when driving abroad as you must produce it when asked to do so by the police and other authorities. Failure to do so may result in an immediate fine and confiscation of your vehicle(s). If your driving licence is due to expire while you are away it can normally be renewed up to three months before the expiry date - contact the DVLA if you need to renew more than three months ahead.

All European Union countries recognise the pink EU-format driving licence introduced in the UK in 1990, subject to the minimum age requirements (normally 18 years for a vehicle with a maximum weight of 3,500 kg carrying no more than 8 people). However, there are exceptions in some European Countries and the Country Introductions contain specific details. Holders of an old-style green UK paper licence or a licence issued in Northern Ireland prior to 1991, which are not to EU format, should update it to a photocard licence before travelling in order to avoid any difficulties with local authorities. A photocard driving licence is also useful as a means of identification in other situations, e.g. when using a credit card. Remember to carry both the plastic card and its paper counterpart.

Allow enough time for your application to be processed and do not apply if you will need to use your licence in the near future, e.g. to hire a car. Selected post offices and DVLA local offices offer a premium checking service for photocard applications but the service is not available for online applications.

## MOT Certificate

You are advised to carry your vehicle's MOT certificate (if applicable) when driving on the Continent as you may need to show it to the authorities if your vehicle is involved in an accident, or in the event of random vehicle checks. If your MOT certificate is due to expire while you are away you should have the vehicle tested before you leave home.

## Passport

Many countries require you to carry your passport at all times. Enter next-of-kin details in the back of your passport and keep a separate photocopy or record of your passport details. It's also a good idea to leave a photocopy of it with a relative or friend at home.

The following information applies to British passport holders only. For people who's passports are issued by other countries you should contact the local embassy for more information.

### Applying for a Passport

Each person travelling out of the UK (including babies) must hold a valid passport. It is no longer possible to add or include children on a parent's British passport. A standard British passport is valid for ten years, or 5 years for children under 16.

All new UK passports are now biometric passports, also known as e-passports, which contain a microchip with information which can be used to authenticate the holder's identity. When your passport expires and you apply for a new one it will be replaced with a biometric passport.

Full information and application forms are available from main post offices or from the Identity & Passport Service's website, www.

gov.uk where you can complete an online application. Allow at least six weeks for first-time passport applications, for which you may need to attend an interview at your nearest Identity and Passport Service (IPS) regional office. Allow three weeks for a renewal application and the replacement of a lost, stolen or damaged passport.

Main post offices offer a 'Check & Send' service for passport applications. To find your nearest 'Check & Send' post office call 0845 611 2970 or see www.postoffice.co.uk

*Passport Validity*
Most countries in the EU only require your passport to be valid for the duration of your stay. However, in case your return home is delayed for any reason it is a good idea to renew your passport before you travel if there is less than 6 month's validity remaining. Any time left on a passport (up to a maximum of 9 months) will be added to the validity of your new passport.

*Schengen Agreement*
The Schengen Agreement allows people and vehicles to pass freely without border checks from country to country within the Schengen area (a total of 26 countries) . Where there are no longer any border checks you should still not attempt to cross land borders without a full, valid passport. It is likely that random identity checks will continue to be made for the foreseeable future in areas surrounding land borders.

The United Kingdom and Republic of Ireland do not fully participate in the Schengen Agreement.

## Pet Travel Scheme (PETS)

The Pet Travel Scheme (PETS) allows owners of dogs, cats and ferrets from qualifying European countries, to bring their pets into the UK (up to a limit of five per person) without quarantine. The animal must have an EU pet passport, be microchipped and be vaccinated against rabies. Dogs must also have been treated for tapeworm. It also allows pets to travel from the UK to other EU qualifying countries. Some countries may not allow entry to certain types or breeds of dogs and may have rules relating to matters such as muzzling and transporting dogs in cars – check the Country Introductions for any specific details or see www.caravanclub.co.uk/pets for more details. Pets normally resident in the Channel Islands, Isle of Man and the Republic of Ireland can also enter the UK under the PETS scheme if they comply with the rules. Pets resident anywhere in the British Isles (including the Republic of Ireland) are able to travel freely within the British Isles and are not subject to PETS rules.

## Travelling with Children

Some countries require evidence of parental responsibility from single parents travelling alone with children before allowing them to enter the country or, in some cases, before permitting children to leave the country. The authorities may want to see a birth certificate, a letter of consent from the other parent and some evidence as to your responsibility for the child.

If you are travelling with a minor under the age of 18 who is not your own, you must carry a letter of authorisation, naming the adult in charge of the child, from the child's parent or legal guardian.

For further information on exactly what will be required at immigration contact the Embassy or Consulate of the countries you intend to visit before your visit.

## Vehicle Excise Licence

While driving abroad you still need to have current UK vehicle excise licence. If your vehicle's tax is due to expire while you are abroad you may apply to re-license the vehicle at a post office, by post, or in person at a DVLA local office, up to two months in advance.

## Vehicle Registration Certificate (V5C)

You must always carry your Vehicle Registration Certificate (V5C) when taking your vehicle abroad. If yours has been lost, stolen or destroyed you should apply to a DVLA local office on form V62. Call DVLA Customer Enquiries on 0300 790 6802 for more information.

## Caravan – Proof of Ownership (CRIS)

In Britain and Ireland, unlike most other European countries, caravans are not formally registered in the same way as cars. This may not be fully understood by police and other authorities on the Continent. You are strongly advised, therefore, to carry a copy of your Caravan Registration Identification Scheme (CRIS) document.

## Hired or Borrowed Vehicles

If using a borrowed vehicle you must obtain a letter of authority to use the vehicle from the registered owner. You should also carry the Vehicle Registration Certificate (V5C).

In the case of hired or leased vehicles, including company cars, when the user does not normally possess the V5C, ask the company which owns the vehicle to supply a Vehicle On Hire Certificate, form VE103, which is the only legal substitute for a V5C. The BVRLA, the trade body for the vehicle rental and leasing sector, provide advice on hired or leased vehicles - see www.bvrla.co.uk or call them on 01494 434747 for more information.

If you are caught driving a hired vehicle abroad without this certificate you may be fined and/or the vehicle impounded.

## Visas

British citizens holding a full UK passport do not require a visa for entry into any countries covered by this guide. EU countries may require a permit for stays of more than three months and you should contact the relevant country's UK embassy before you travel for information.

British subjects, British overseas citizens, British dependent territories citizens and citizens of other countries may need visas that are not required by British citizens. Again check with the authorities of the country you are due to visit at their UK embassy or consulate. Citizens of other countries should apply to their own embassy, consulate or High Commission for information.

# Insurance

## Car, Motorhome and Caravan Insurance

Insurance cover for your outfit whilst travelling abroad is an absolute essential. Your car or motorhome insurance should cover you for driving in the EU or associated countries, but you should check what you are covered for before you travel. If you are travelling outside the EU or associated countries you'll need to inform your insurer and may have to pay an additional premium.

Make sure your Caravan insurance covers travel outside of the UK, speak to your insurer – most will require the dates of your holiday and it is possible there will be an extra premium to pay.

The Caravan Club's Car, Caravan and Motorhome Insurance schemes extend to provide policy cover for travel within the EU free of charge, provided the total period of foreign travel in any one year does not exceed 270 days for Car Insurance, 182 for Caravan Insurance and 270 days for Motorhome Insurance. It may be possible to extend this period, although a charge may apply.

Should you be delayed beyond these limits speak to your broker or insurer immediately in order to maintain your cover until you can return to the UK.

If your outfit is damaged during loading, unloading or travel on a ferry it must be reported to the carrier at the time the damage occurred. Most insurance policies will cover short sea crossings (up to 65 hours) but check with your insurer before travelling.

For full details of The Caravan Club's Caravan Insurance telephone 01342 336610 or for Car Insurance and Motorhome insurance, telephone 0800 0284809 or visit our website, www.caravanclub.co.uk/insurance.

*European Accident Statement*
Your car or motorhome insurer may provide you with a European Accident Statement form (EAS), or you may be given one if you are involved in an accident abroad. The EAS is a standard form, available in different languages, which gives all parties involved in an accident the opportunity to agree on the facts. Signing the form doesn't mean that you are accepting liability, just that you agree with what has been stated on the form. Only sign an EAS if you are completely sure that you understand what has been written and always make sure that you take a copy of the completed EAS.

## Legal Costs Abroad

If an accident abroad leads to you being taken to court you may find yourself liable for legal costs – even if you are not found to be at fault. Most UK vehicle insurance policies include cover for legal costs or have the option to add cover for a small additional cost – check if you are covered before you travel.

## Holiday Travel Insurance

Having insured your vehicles, there are other risks to consider and it is essential to take out adequate travel insurance. Your vehicle insurance policy won't cover you for all eventualities, such as vehicle breakdown, medical expenses or accommodation. Make sure that the holiday insurance you take out is suitable for a caravan or motorhome holiday.

The Caravan Club's Red Pennant Overseas Holiday Insurance is designed specifically for touring holidays and can cover both motoring and personal use. Depending on the level of cover chosen the policy will cover you for vehicle recovery and repair, holiday continuation, medical expenses and accommodation.

For full details visit www.caravanclub.co.uk/redpennant or call 01342 336633.

Look carefully at the exemptions to your insurance policy, including those relating to preexisting medical conditions or the use of alcohol. Be sure to declare any preexisting medical conditions to your insurer.

*Holiday Insurance for Pets*
Make sure that your pet is also covered if you take them on holiday with you. Some holiday insurance policies, including The Club's Red Pennant, can be extended to cover pet expenses relating to an incident normally covered under the policy – such as pet repatriation in the event that your vehicle is written off.

However in order to provide cover for pet injury or illness you will need a separate pet insurance policy which covers your pet while out of the UK. For details of The Club's Pet Insurance scheme visit www.caravanclub.co.uk/petins or call 0800 015 1396.

## Home Insurance

Your home insurer may require advance notification if you are leaving your home unoccupied for 30 days or more. You may be required to turn off mains services (except electricity), drain water down and have somebody visit the home once a week. Check your policy documents or speak to your insurer or broker.

The Caravan Club's Home Insurance policy provides full cover for up to 90 days when you are away from home (for instance when touring) and requires only common sense precautions for longer periods of unoccupancy. See www.caravanclub.co.uk/homeins or call 0800 028 4815 for details.

*Personal Belongings*
The majority of travellers are able to cover their valuables such as jewellery, watches, cameras, laptops, and bikes under a Home insurance Policy. This includes The Caravan Club's Home Insurance scheme.

## Vehicles Left Behind Abroad

If you are involved in an accident or breakdown abroad which prevents you taking your vehicle home, you must ensure that your normal insurance will cover your vehicle if left overseas while you return home. Also check if you are covered for the cost of recovering it to your home address.

You should remove all items of baggage and personal belongings from your vehicles before leaving them unattended. If this is not possible you should check with your insurer/broker to establish whether extended cover can be provided. In all circumstances, you must remove any valuables and items liable for customs duty, including wine, beer, spirits and cigarettes.

# Customs Regulations

## Caravans and Vehicles

You can temporarily import a caravan, trailer or vehicle from one EU country to another without any Customs formalities. Vehicles and caravans may be temporarily imported into non-EU countries generally for a maximum of six months in any twelve month period, provided they are not hired, sold or otherwise disposed of in that country.

If you intend to stay longer than six months, dispose of a vehicle while in another country or leave your vehicle there in storage you should seek advice well before your departure from the UK.

*Borrowed vehicles*
If you are borrowing a vehicle from a friend or relative, or loaning yours to someone, you should be aware of the following:

- The total time the vehicle spends abroad must not exceed the limit for temporary importation (generally six months).
- The owner of the caravan must provide the other person with a letter of authority.
- The owner cannot accept a hire fee or reward.
- The number plate on the caravan must match the number plate on the tow car.

- Both drivers' insurers must be informed if a caravan is being towed and any additional premium must be paid.

## Currency

Any person entering or leaving the EU will have to declare the money that they are carrying if this amounts to €10,000 (or equivalent in other currencies) or more. This includes cheques, travellers' cheques, bankers' drafts and any cash - notes and coins. This ruling does not apply to anyone travelling within the EU.

For further information contact HMRC Excise & Customs Helpline on 0845 010 9000.

## Customs Allowances

*Travelling within the European Union*
If you are travelling to the UK from within the EU you can bring an unlimited amount of most goods without being liable for any duty or tax, but certain rules apply. The goods must be for your own personal use, which can include use as a gift (if the person you are gifting the goods to reimburses you in any way this is not classed as a gift), and you must have paid duty and

tax in the country where you purchased the goods. If a customs official suspects that any goods are not for your own personal use they can question you, make further checks and ultimately seize both the goods and the vehicle used to transport them. Although no limits are in place, customs officials are less likely to question you regarding your goods if they are under the following limits:

- 800 cigarettes

- 400 cigarillos

- 200 cigars

- 1kg tobacco

- 10 litres of spirits

- 20 litres of fortified wine (e.g. port or sherry)

- 90 litres of wine

- 110 litres of beer

The same rules and guidance limits apply for travel between other EU countries.

*Travelling outside the EU*
There are set limits to the amount of goods you can buy in countries outside of the EU to bring back into the UK. Even within these limits goods must still be for your own personal use. Each person aged 17 and over is entitled to the following allowance:

- 200 cigarettes, or 100 cigarillos, or 50 cigars, or 250g tobacco

- 1 litre of spirits or strong liqueurs over 22 per cent volume, or 2 litres of fortified wine, sparkling wine or any other alcoholic drink that's less than 22 per cent volume

- 4 litres of still wine

- 16 litres of beer

- £390 worth of all other goods including perfume, gifts and souvenirs without having to pay tax and/or duty

- For further information contact HMRC National Advice Service on 0845 010 9000 (+44 2920 501 261 from outside the UK).

# Medicines

There is no limit to the amount of medicines you can take abroad if they are obtained without prescription (i.e. over the counter medicines), but medicines prescribed by your doctor may contain controlled drugs (e.g. those containing morphine). You must obtain a licence if you are leaving the UK for 3 months or more with medication containing a controlled drug. Visit www.gov.uk/travelling-controlled-drugs or tel. 020 7035 0771 for a list of controlled drugs and to apply for a licence.

You don't need a licence if you carry supplies for less than 3 months or if your medication doesn't contain controlled drugs, but you should carry a letter from your doctor stating your name, a list of your prescribed drugs and dosages for each drug. You may have to show this letter when going through customs.

# Personal Possessions

Visitors to countries within the EU are free to carry reasonable quantities of any personal possessions such as jewellery, cameras, and electrical equipment required for the duration of their stay. It is sensible to carry sales receipts for new items in case you need to prove that tax has already been paid.

*Prohibited and Restricted Goods*
Regardless of where you are travelling from the importation of some goods into the UK is restricted or banned, mainly to protect health and the environment. These include:

- Endangered animals or plants including live animals, birds and plants, ivory, skins, coral, hides, shells and goods made from them such as jewellery, shoes, bags and belts.

- Controlled, unlicensed or dangerous drugs.

- Counterfeit or pirated goods such as watches, CDs and clothes; goods bearing a false indication of their place of manufacture or in breach of UK copyright.

- Offensive weapons such as firearms, flick knives, knuckledusters, push daggers or knives disguised as everyday objects.

- Pornographic material depicting extreme violence or featuring children such as DVDs, magazines, videos, books and software.

This list is not exhaustive; if in doubt contact HMRC National Advice Service on 0845 010 9000 or +44 2920 501 261 from outside the UK for more information or, when returning to the UK, go through the red Customs channel or use the telephone at the Red Point and ask a Customs officer. It is your responsibility to make sure that you are not breaking the law. Never attempt to mislead or hide anything from Customs officers; penalties are severe.

## Plants and Food

Travellers from within the EU may bring into the UK any fruit, vegetable or plant products without restriction as long as they are grown in the EU, are free from pests or disease and are for your own consumption. For food products Andorra, the Channel Islands, the Isle of Man, San Marino and Switzerland are treated as part of the EU.

From most countries outside the EU you are not allowed to bring into the UK any meat or dairy products. Other animal products may be severely restricted or banned and it is important that you declare any such products on entering the UK.

For up to date information please contact the Food and Environment Research Agency (Fera) on 0844 248 0071. If you are unsure about any item you are bringing in, or are simply unsure of the rules, you must go to the red Customs channel or use the phone provided at the Red Point to speak to a Customs officer.

# Money

Being able to safely access your money while you're away is a necessity for you to enjoy your break. It isn't a good idea to rely on one method of payment, so always have a backup plan. A mixture of a small amount of cash plus one or two electronic means of payment are a good idea.

Travellers' cheques have become less popular in recent years as fewer banks and hotels are willing or able to cash them. There are alternative options which offer the same level of security but are easier to use, such as pre-paid credit cards.

exchange, some will charge a flat fee and some offer a 'buy back' service. All should stock Euros but during peak holiday times they may be running low so it can be a good idea to pre-order your currency. You should also pre-order any less common currencies. Shop around and compare commission and exchange rates, together with minimum charges.

Banks and money exchanges in central and eastern Europe won't usually accept Scottish and Northern Irish bank notes and may be reluctant to change any sterling which has been written on or is creased or worn

## Local Currency

It is a good idea to take enough foreign currency for your journey and immediate needs on arrival, don't forget you may need change for tolls or parking on your journey. Currency exchange facilities will be available at ports & on ferries but rates offered may not be as good as you would find elsewhere. The Post Office, many high -street banks, exchange offices and travel agents offer commission free foreign

## Foreign Currency Bank Accounts

Frequent travellers or those who spend long periods abroad may find a Euro bank account useful. Most such accounts impose no currency conversion charges for debit or credit card use and allow fee-free cash withdrawals at ATMs. Some banks may also allow you to spread your account across different currencies, depending on your circumstances. Speak to your bank about the services they offer.

## Travel Money Cards

Travel money cards are issued by various providers including the Post Office, Travelex, Lloyds Bank and American Express. For a comparison table see www.which-prepaid-card.co.uk.

They are increasingly popular as the PIN protected travel money card offers the security of Travellers Cheques, with the convenience of paying by card. You load the card with the amount you need before leaving home, and then use cash machines to make withdrawals or use the card to pay for goods and services as you would a credit or debit card. You can top the card up over the telephone or online while you are abroad. Please note that pre-paid cards cannot be used when you are not required to enter a PIN, so cannot be used on the French toll system.

These cards can be cheaper to use than credit or debit cards for both cash withdrawals and purchases as there are usually no loading or transaction fees to pay. In addition, because they are separate from your bank account, if the card is lost or stolen there is less risk of identity theft.

The Caravan Club have partnered with Moneycorp to offer the Explorer prepaid card to members. For more information visit www.caravanclub.co.uk/travelmoney.

## Credit and Debit Cards

Credit and debit cards offer a convenient way of spending abroad. For the use of cards abroad most banks impose a foreign currency conversion charge (typically 2.75% per transaction) which is usually the same for both credit and debit cards. If you use your card to withdraw cash there will be a further commission charge of up to 3% and you will be charged interest (possibly at a higher rate than normal) as soon as you withdraw the money.

If you have several cards, take at least two in case you encounter problems. Credit and debit 'chip and PIN' cards issued by UK banks

may not be universally accepted abroad so check before incurring expenditure.

Contact your credit or debit card issuer before you leave home to let them know that you will be travelling abroad. In the battle against card fraud, card issuers are frequently likely to query transactions which they regard as unusual or suspicious, causing your card to be declined or temporarily stopped. You should always carry your card issuer's helpline number with you so that you can contact them if this happens. You will also need this number should you need to report the loss or theft of your card.

*Dynamic Currency Conversion*

When you pay with a credit or debit card, retailers may offer you the choice of currency for payment, e.g. a euro amount will be converted into sterling and then charged to your card account. You may be asked to sign an agreement to accept the conversion rate used and final amount charged and, having done so, there is no opportunity to change your mind or obtain a refund. This is known as a 'dynamic currency conversion' but the exchange rate used is likely to be worse than the rate offered by your card issuer.

## Emergency Cash

If an emergency or theft means that you need cash in a hurry, then friends or relatives at home can send you emergency cash via money transfer services.

The Post Office, MoneyGram and Western Union all offer services which, allows the transfer of money to over 233,000 money transfer agents around the world. Transfers take approximately ten minutes and charges are levied on a sliding scale.

# Ferries & the Channel Tunnel

## Booking Your Ferry

If travelling in July or August, or peak weekends, such as Easter and half-term, make your reservation as early as possible. Space for caravans and large vehicles is usually limited and cheaper off-peak crossings can fill up quickly. If you need any special assistance or arrangements make sure you request this at the time of booking.

When booking any ferry crossing, make sure you give the correct measurements for your outfit including bikes, roof boxes or anything else which may add to the length or height of your vehicle. If your vehicle is larger than your booking states you may be turned away at boarding.

The Caravan Club is an agent for most major ferry companies operating services. Call The Club's Travel Service on 01342 316 101 or see www.caravanclub.co.uk/ferries to book and for details of special offers, some of which are exclusive to Caravan Club members.

The tables on the following page show current ferry routes from the UK to the Continent and Ireland. Some ferry routes may not be operational all year, and during peak holiday periods the transportation of caravans or motorhomes may be restricted. For the most up-to-date information on ferry routes and prices visit www.caravanclub.co.uk/ferries or speak to The Club's Travel Services team.

## Channel Tunnel

The Channel Tunnel operator, Eurotunnel, accepts cars, caravans and motorhomes (except those running on LPG) on their service between Folkestone and Calais. You can just turn up and see if there is availability on the day, however prices increase as the crossing gets fuller so if you know your plans in advance it is best to book as early as possible.

You will be asked to open your roof vents prior to travel and you will also need to apply the caravan brake once you have parked your vehicle on the train. You will not be able to use your caravan until arrival.

## On the Journey

Arrive at the port with plenty of time before your boarding time. Motorhomes and car/ caravan outfits will usually either be the first or last vehicles boarded onto the ferry. Almost all ferries are now 'drive on – drive off' so you won't be required to do any complicated manoeuvres. You may be required to show ferry staff that your gas is switched off before boarding the ferry.

Be careful using the ferry access ramps, as they are often very steep which mean there is a risk of grounding the tow bar or caravan hitch. Drive slowly and, if your ground clearance is low, consider whether removing your stabiliser and/or jockey wheel would help.

Vehicles are often parked close together on ferries, meaning that if you have towing extension mirrors they could get knocked or damaged by people trying to get past your vehicle. If you leave them attached during the ferry crossing then make sure you check their position on returning to your vehicle.

## Pets on Ferries and Eurotunnel

It is possible to transport your pet on a number of ferry routes to the Continent and Ireland, as well as on Eurotunnel services from Folkestone to Calais. Advance booking is essential as restrictions apply to the number of animals allowed on any one crossing. Make sure you understand the carrier's terms and conditions for transporting pets.

Once on board pets are normally required to remain in their owner's vehicle or in kennels on the car deck and you won't be able to access your vehicle to check on your pet while the ferry is at sea. On longer crossings you should make arrangements at the on-board information desk for permission to visit your pet in order to check its well-being. You should always make sure that ferry staff know your vehicle has a pet on board.

Information and advice on the welfare of animals before and during a journey is available on the website of the Department for Environment, Food and Rural Affairs (Defra), www.gov.uk/defra.

## Gas on Ferries and Eurotunnel

UK based ferry companies usually allow up to three gas cylinders per caravan, including the cylinder currently in use, however some may restrict this to a maximum of two cylinders. Some operators may ask you to hand over your gas cylinders to a member of the crew so that they can be safely stored during the crossing. Check that you know the rules of your ferry operator before you travel.

Cylinder valves should be fully closed and covered with a cap, if provided, and should remain closed during the crossing. Cylinders should be fixed securely in or on the caravan in the position specified by the manufacturer.

Gas cylinders must be declared at check-in and the crew may ask to inspect each cylinder for leakage before travel.

Eurotunnel will allow vehicles fitted with LPG tanks for the purposes of heating, lighting, cooking or refrigeration to use their service, but regulations stipulate that a total of no more than 47 kg of gas can be carried through the Channel Tunnel. Tanks must be switched off before boarding and must be less than 80% full; you will be asked to demonstrate this before you travel. Vehicles powered by LPG cannot be carried through the Channel Tunnel.

Most ferry companies will accept LPG-powered vehicles but you must let them know at the time of booking. During the crossing the tank must be no more than 75% full and it must be turned off. In the case of vehicles converted to use LPG, some ferry companies also require a certificate showing that the conversion has been carried out to the manufacturer's specification.

The carriage of spare petrol cans, whether full or empty, is not permitted on ferries or through the Channel Tunnel. Caravan Club Sites Near Ports.

## Caravan Club Sites Near Ports

If you've got a long drive to the ferry port, or want to catch an early ferry then an overnight stop near to the port gives you a relaxing start to your holiday. The following table lists Caravan Club sites which are close to ports.

Members can book online at www.caravanclub.co.uk or call 01342 327490. If you aren't a Club member you will need to contact the sites directly when they are open.

Please note that Commons Wood, Daleacres, Fairlight Wood, Hunter's Moon, Mildenhall, Old Hartley and Rookesbury Park are open to Caravan Club members only. Non-members are welcome at all the other Caravan Club sites listed below.

| Port | Nearest Club Site and Town | Tel No. |
|------|----------------------------|---------|
| Cairnryan, Stranraer | New England Bay (Drummore) | 01776 860275 |
| | Bearsted (Maidstone) | 01622 730018 |
| Dover, Folkestone, Channel Tunnel | Black Horse Farm* (Folkestone) | 01303 892665 |
| | Daleacres (Hythe) | 01303 267679 |
| | Fairlight Wood (Hastings) | 01424 812333 |
| Fishguard, Pembroke | Freshwater East (Pembroke) | 01646 672341 |
| | Cambridge Cherry Hinton* | 01223 244088 |
| Harwich | Commons Wood* (Welwyn Garden City) | 01707 260786 |
| | Mildenhall | 01638 713089 |
| Holyhead | Penrhos (Benllech) | 01248 852617 |
| | York Beechwood Grange | 01904 424637 |
| Hull | York Rowntree Park | 01904 658997 |
| Newcastle upon Tyne | Old Hartley (Whitley Bay) | 0191 237 0256 |
| Newhaven | Brighton* | 01273 626546 |
| Plymouth | Plymouth Sound | 01752 862325 |
| Poole | Hunter's Moon*, Wareham | 01929 556605 |
| Portsmouth | Rookesbury Park, Fareham | 01329 834085 |
| Rosslare | River Valley, Wicklow | 00353 (0)404 41647 |
| Weymouth | Crossways, Dorchester | 01305 852032 |

*Site open all year*

# Ferry routes and Operators

| Route | Operator | Approximate Crossing Time | Maximum Frequency |
|---|---|---|---|
| **Belgium** | | | |
| Hull – Zeebrugge | P & O Ferries | 12½ hrs | 1 daily |
| **Denmark** | | | |
| Harwich – Esbjerg | DFDS Seaways | 18¼ hrs | 3 per week |
| **France** | | | |
| Dover – Calais | P & O Ferries | 1½ hrs | 22 daily |
| Dover – Dunkerque | DFDS Seaways | 2 hrs | 12 daily |
| Folkestone – Calais | Eurotunnel | 35 mins | 3 per hour |
| Newhaven – Dieppe | Transmanche Ferries | 4 hrs | 2 daily |
| Plymouth – Roscoff | Brittany Ferries | 6 hrs | 2 daily |
| Poole – Cherbourg | Brittany Ferries | 4½ hrs | 1 daily |
| Poole – St Malo (via Channel Islands) | Condor Ferries | 5 hrs | 1 daily (May to Sep) |
| Portsmouth – Caen | Brittany Ferries | 3¾ / 7½ hrs | 4 daily |
| Portsmouth – Cherbourg | Brittany Ferries | 3 / 4½ hrs | 3 daily |
| Portsmouth – Cherbourg | Condor Ferries | 5½ hrs | 1 weekly (May to Sep) |
| Portsmouth – Le Havre | LD Lines | 3¼ / 8 hrs | 2 daily |
| Portsmouth – St Malo | Brittany Ferries | 9 hrs | 1 daily |
| Weymouth – St Malo (via Channel Islands) | Condor Ferries | 9½ hrs | 1 daily |
| **Ireland – Northern** | | | |
| Cairnryan/Troon – Larne | P & O Irish Sea | 1 / 2 hrs | 11 daily |
| Liverpool (Birkenhead) – Belfast | Stena Line | 8 hrs | 2 daily |
| Cairnryan – Belfast | Stena Line | 2 / 3 hrs | 7 daily |
| **Ireland – Republic** | | | |
| Cork – Roscoff† | Brittany Ferries | 14 hrs | 1 per week |
| Fishguard – Rosslare | Stena Line | 2 / 3½ hrs | 3 daily |
| Holyhead – Dublin | Irish Ferries | 1¾ / 3¼ hrs | 4 daily |
| Holyhead – Dublin | Stena Line | 3¼ hrs | 4 daily |
| Holyhead – Dun Loaghaire | Stena Line | 2 hrs | 2 daily |
| Liverpool – Dublin | P & O Irish Sea | 8 hrs | 2 daily |
| Liverpool (Birkenhead) – Dublin | Stena Line | 7 hrs | 2 daily |
| Pembroke – Rosslare | Irish Ferries | 4 hrs | 2 daily |
| Rosslare – Cherbourg† | Irish Ferries | 19½ hrs | 3 per week |
| Rosslare – Cherbourg† | Celtic Link Ferries | 17 hrs | 3 per week |
| Rosslare – Roscoff† | Irish Ferries | 19½ hrs | 4 per week |
| **Netherlands** | | | |
| Harwich – Hook of Holland | Stena Line | 6½ hrs | 2 daily |
| Hull – Rotterdam | P & O Ferries | 10¼ hrs | 1 daily |
| Newcastle – Ijmuiden (Amsterdam) | DFDS Seaways | 15½ hrs | 1 daily |
| **Spain** | | | |
| Portsmouth – Bilbao | Brittany Ferries | 24 hrs | 2 per week |
| Portsmouth or Plymouth – Santander | Brittany Ferries | 24 / 20 hrs | 4 per week |

† Not bookable through the Club's Travel Service.
Note: Services and routes correct at time of publication but subject to change.

# Motoring Advice

## Preparing for Your Journey

The first priority in preparing for your outfit for your journey should be to make sure it has a full service. Make sure that you have a fully equipped spares kit, and a spare wheel and tyre for your caravan – it is easier to get hold of them from your local dealer than to have to spend time searching for spares where you don't know the local area.

If you're a member of The Caravan Club then carry your UK Sites Directory & Handbook with you, as it contains a section of technical advice which may be useful when travelling. If you have any queries you can also contact The Club's free advice service who have information on all things caravanning – you can download free information leaflets at www.caravanclub. co.uk/advice or contact the team by calling 01342 336611 or emailing technical@caravanclub.co.uk.

For advice on issues specific to countries other than the UK, Club members should contact the Travel Service Information Officer, email: travelserviceinfo@caravanclub.co.uk or call 01342 336766.

## Weight Limits

From both a legal and a safety point of view, it is essential not to exceed vehicle weight limits. It is advisable to carry documentation confirming your vehicle's maximum permitted laden weight - if your Vehicle Registration Certificate (V5C) does not clearly state this, you will need to produce alternative certification, e.g. from a weighbridge.

If you are pulled over by the police and don't have certification you will be taken to a weighbridge. If your vehicle(s) are then found to be overweight you will be liable to a fine and may have to discard items to lower the weight before you can continue on your journey.

## Some Final Checks

Before you start any journey make sure you complete the following checks:

- All car and caravan or motorhome lights are working and sets of spare bulbs are packed

- The coupling is correctly seated on the towball and the breakaway cable is attached

- All windows, vents, hatches and doors are shut

- All on-board water systems are drained

- All mirrors are adjusted for maximum visibility

- Corner steadies are fully wound up and the brace is handy for your arrival on site

- Any fires or flames are extinguished and the gas cylinder tap is turned off. Fire extinguishers are fully charged and close at hand

- The over-run brake is working correctly

- The jockey wheel is raised and secured, the handbrake is released.

## Driving in Europe

Driving abroad for the first time can be a daunting prospect, especially when towing a caravan. Here are a few tips to make the transition easier:

- Remember that Sat Navs may take you on unsuitable roads, so have a map or atlas to hand to help you find an alternative route.

- It can be tempting to try and get to your destination as quickly as possible but we recommend travelling a maximum of 250 miles a day when towing. Share the driving if possible, and if you're going a long way then plan in an overnight stop.

- Remember that if you need to overtake a slow moving vehicle or pull out around an obstruction you will not be able to see clearly from the driver's seat. If possible, always have a responsible adult in the passenger seat who can advise you when it is clear to pull out. If that is not possible then stay well back to get a better view and pull out slowly.

- If traffic builds up behind you, pull over safely and let it pass.

- Driving on the right should become second nature after a while, but pay particular attention when turning left, leaving a rest area, petrol station or site, or after a one-way system.

- Stop at least every two hours to stretch your legs and take a break.

## Fuel

Grades of petrol sold on the Continent are comparable to those sold in the UK; 95 octane is frequently known as 'Essence' and 98 octane as 'Super'. Diesel may be called 'Gasoil' and is widely available across Europe.

E10 petrol (containing 10% Ethanol) can be found in certain countries in Europe. Most modern cars are E10 compatible, but those which aren't could be damaged by filling up with E10. Check your vehicle handbook or visit www.acea.be and search for 'E10' to find the publication 'Vehicle compatibility with new fuel standards'.

Members of The Caravan Club can check current average fuel prices by country at www.caravanclub.co.uk/overseasadvice.

Away from major roads and towns it is a good idea not to let your fuel tank run too low as you may have difficulty finding a petrol station, especially at night or on Sundays. Petrol stations offering a 24-hour service may involve an automated process, in some cases only accepting credit cards issued in France.

*Automotive Liquified Petroleum Gas (LPG)*
The increasing popularity of dual-fuelled vehicles means that the availability of LPG – also known as 'autogas' or GPL – has become an important issue for more drivers.

There are different tank-filling openings in use in different countries. Currently there is no common European filling system, and you might find a variety of systems. Most Continental motorway services will have adaptors but these should be used with care – see www.autogas.ltd.uk for more information.

## Low Emission Zones

Many cities in countries around Europe have introduced 'Low Emission Zones' (LEZ's) in order to regulate vehicle pollution levels. Some schemes require you to buy a windscreen sticker, pay a fee or register your vehicle before entering the zone. You may also need to provide proof that your vehicle's emissions meet the required standard. Before you travel visit www.lowemissionzones.eu for maps and details of LEZ's across Europe. Also see the Country Introductions later in this guide for country specific information.

## Motorhomes Towing Cars

A motorhome towing a small A-frame or towing dolly is illegal in most European countries. Motorhome users towing a small car should transport it on a braked trailer so that all four of the car's wheels are off the ground.

## Priority and Roundabouts

When driving on the Continent it can be difficult to work out which vehicles have priority in different situations. Watch out for road signs which indicate priority and read the Country Introductions later in this guide for country specific information.

Take care at intersections – you should never rely on being given right of way, even if you have priority; especially in small towns and villages where local traffic may take right of way. Always give way to public service and military vehicles and to buses and trams.

In some countries in Europe priority at roundabouts is given to vehicles entering the roundabout (i.e. on the right) unless the road signs say otherwise.

## Public Transport

In general in built-up areas be prepared to stop to allow a bus to pull out from a bus stop when the driver is signalling his intention to do so.

Take particular care when school buses have stopped and passengers are getting on and off.

Overtaking trams in motion is normally only allowed on the right, unless on a one way street where you can overtake on the left if there is not enough space on the right. Do not overtake a tram near a tram stop. These may be in the centre of the road. When a tram or bus stops to allow passengers on and off, you should stop to allow them to cross to the pavement. Give way to trams which are turning across your carriageway. Don't park or stop across tram lines; trams cannot steer round obstructions!

## Pedestrian Crossings

Stopping to allow pedestrians to cross at zebra crossings is not always common practice on the Continent as it is in the UK. Pedestrians expect to wait until the road is clear before crossing, while motorists behind may be taken by surprise by your stopping. The result may be a rear-end shunt or vehicles overtaking you at the crossing and putting pedestrians at risk.

## Traffic Lights

Traffic lights may not be as easily visible as they are in the UK, for instance they may be smaller or suspended across the road with a smaller set on a post at the roadside. You may find that lights change directly from red to green, bypassing amber completely. Flashing amber lights generally indicate that you may proceed with caution if it is safe to do so but you must give way to pedestrians and other vehicles.

A green filter light should be treated with caution as you may still have to give way to pedestrians who have a green light to cross the road. If a light turns red as approached, continental drivers will often speed up to get through the light instead of stopping. Be aware that if you brake sharply because a traffic light has turned red as you approached, the driver behind might not be expecting it.

# Motoring Equipment

## Essential Equipment

The equipment that you legally have to carry differs by country. For a full list see the Essential Equipment table at the end of this chapter, or see the Country Introductions of this book for country specific information. Please note equipment requirements and regulations can change frequently. To keep up to date with the latest equipment information please visit www.caravanclub.co.uk/overseasadvice.

## Fire Extinguisher

As a safety precaution, an approved fire extinguisher should be carried in all vehicles. This is a legal requirement in several countries in Europe.

## Glasses

In some countries it is a legal requirement for residents to carry a spare pair of glasses if they are needed for driving, and it is recommended that visitors also comply. Elsewhere, if you do not have a spare pair, you may find it helpful to carry a copy of your prescription.

## Lights

When driving on the Continent headlights need to be adjusted to deflect to the right if they are likely to dazzle other road users. You can do this by applying beam deflectors, or some newer vehicles have a built-in adjustment system. Some modern high-density discharge (HID), xenon or halogen-type lights, may need to be taken to a dealer to make the necessary adjustment. Remember also to adjust headlights according to the load being carried and to compensate for the weight of the caravan on the back of your car. Even if you do not intend to drive at night, it is important to ensure that your headlights are correctly adjusted as you may need to use them in heavy rain, fog or in tunnels. If using tape or a pre-cut adhesive mask remember to remove it on your return home.

Dipped headlights should be used in poor weather conditions and in a tunnel even if it is well lit. You may find police waiting at the end of a tunnel to check vehicles. In some countries the use of dipped headlights is compulsory at all times and in others they must be used in built-up areas, on motorways or at certain times of the year.

*Headlight-Flashing*
On the Continent headlight-flashing is used as a warning of approach or as an overtaking signal at night, and not, as is commonly the case in the UK, an indication that you are giving way. Be more cautious with both flashing your headlights and when another driver flashes you.

*Hazard Warning Lights*
Hazard warning lights should not be used in place of a warning triangle, but they may be used in addition to it.

## Nationality Plate (GB/IRL)

A nationality plate must be fixed to the rear of both your car or motorhome and caravan. Checks are made and a fine may be imposed for failure to display a nationality plate correctly. If your number plates have the Euro-Symbol on them there is no requirement to display an additional GB sticker within the EU and Switzerland. If your number plate doesn't have the EU symbol or you are planning to travel outside of the EU you will need a GB sticker.

GB is the only national identification code allowed for cars registered in the UK. Registration plates displaying the GB Euro-Symbol must comply with the appropriate British Standard.

## Reflective Jackets/Waistcoats

If you break down outside of a built-up area it is normally a legal requirement that anyone leaving the vehicle must be wearing a reflective jacket or waistcoat. Make sure that you jacket is accessible from inside the car as you will need to put it on before exiting the vehicle. Carry one for each passenger as well as the driver.

## Route Planning

It is always a good idea to carry a road atlas or map of the countries you plan to visit, even if you have Satellite Navigation. You can find information on UK roads from Keep Moving – www.keepmoving.co.uk or call 09003 401100. Websites offering a European route mapping service include www.google.co.uk/maps, www.mappy.com or www.viamichelin.com.

## Satellite Navigation/GPS

Continental postcodes don't cover just one street or part of a street in the same way as

UK postcodes. A French five-digit postcode, for example, can cover a very large area.

GPS co-ordinates and full addresses are given for most site entries in this guide wherever possible, so that you can programme your sat nav as accurately as possible.

It is important to remember that sat nav devices don't usually allow for towing or driving a large motorhome and may try to send you down unsuitable roads. Always use your common sense, and if a road looks unsuitable find an alternative route.

Use your sat nav in conjunction with the directions given in the site entries, which have been provided by members who have actually visited. Please note that the directions given in site entries have not been checked by The Caravan Club.

In nearly all European countries it is illegal to use car navigation systems which actively search for mobile speed cameras or interfere with police equipment (laser or radar detection). Car navigation systems which give a warning of fixed speed camera locations are legal in most countries with the exception of France, Germany, and Switzerland where this function must be de-activated.

## Seat Belts

The wearing of seat belts is compulsory throughout Europe and beyond. On-the-spot fines will be incurred for failure to wear them and, in the event of an accident failure to wear a seat belt may reduce any claim for injury. See the country introductions for specific regulations on both seat belts and car seats.

## Spares

### Caravan Spares

It will generally be much harder to get hold of spare parts for caravans on the continent, especially for UK manufactured caravans. It is advisable to carry any commonly required spares (such as light bulbs) with you.

Take the contact details of your UK dealer or manufacturer with you, as they may be able to assist in getting spares delivered to you.

### Car Spares Kits

Some car manufacturers produce spares kits; contact your dealer for details. The choice of spares will depend on the vehicle and how long you are away, but the following is a list of basic items which should cover the most common causes of breakdown:

- Radiator top hose

- Fan belt

- Fuses and bulbs

- Windscreen wiper blade

- Length of 12V electrical cable

- Tools, torch and WD40 or equivalent water repellent/ dispersant spray

*Spare Wheel*
Your local caravan dealer should be able to supply an appropriate spare wheel. If you have any difficulty in obtaining one, The Caravan Club's Technical Department can provide Club members with a list of suppliers on request.

Tyre legislation across Europe is more or less consistent and, while the Club has no specific knowledge of laws on the Continent regarding the use of space-saver spare wheels, there should be no problems in using such a wheel provided its use is in accordance with the manufacturer's instructions. Space-saver spare wheels are designed for short journeys to get your vehicle to a place where it can be repaired and there will usually be restrictions on the distance and speed at which the vehicle should be driven.

## Towbar

The vast majority of cars registered after 1 August 1998 are legally required to have a European Type approved towbar (complying with European Directive 94/20) carrying a plate giving its approval number and various technical details, including the maximum noseweight. Your car dealer or specialist towbar fitter will be able to give further advice.

From 2011 for brand new motorhome designs (launched on or after that date) and 2012 for existing designs (those already being built before 29 April 2011), all new motorhomes will need some form of type approval before they can be registered in the UK and as such can only be fitted with a type approved towbar. This change will not affect older vehicles, which can continue to be fitted with non-approved towing brackets.

## Tyres

Tyre condition has a major effect on the safe handling of your outfit. Caravan tyres must be suitable for the highest speed at which you can legally tow, even if you choose to drive slower.

Most countries require a minimum tread depth of 1.6mm but motoring organisations recommend at least 3mm. If you are planning a long journey, consider if they will still be above the legal minimum by the end of your journey.

*Tyre Pressure*

Tyre pressure should be checked and adjusted when the tyres are cold; checking warm tyres will result in a higher pressure reading. The correct pressures will be found in your car handbook, but unless it states otherwise to add an extra 4 - 6 pounds per square inch to the rear tyres of a car when towing to improve handling. Make sure you know what pressure your caravan tyres should be. Some require a pressure much higher than that normally used for cars. Check your caravan handbook for details.

*Tyre Sizes*

It is worth noting that some sizes of radial tyre to fit the 13" wheels commonly used on older UK caravans are virtually impossible to find in stock at retailers abroad, e.g. 175R13C.

*After a Puncture*

A lot of new cars now have a liquid sealant puncture repair kit instead of a spare wheel. These sealants should not be used to achieve a permanent repair and in some cases have been known to make repair of the tyre impossible. If you need to use a liquid sealant you should get the tyre repaired or replaced as soon as possible.

Following a caravan tyre puncture, especially on a single-axle caravan, it is advisable to have the opposite side (non-punctured) tyre removed from its wheel and checked inside and out for signs of damage resulting from overloading during the deflation of the punctured tyre.

## Winter driving

Winter tyres should be used in severe winter climates and in some countries they are a legal requirement. Winter tyres minimise the hardening effect of low temperatures which can lead to less traction on the road, and to provide extra grip on snow, ice or wet conditions.

Snow chains may be necessary on some roads in winter. They are compulsory in some countries, indicated by a road sign. They are not difficult to fit but it's a good idea to carry sturdy gloves to protect your hands when handling the chains in freezing conditions. Polar Automotive Ltd sells and hires out snow chains (10% discount for Caravan Club members), tel 01892 519933 www.snowchains.com, email: polar@snowchains.com.

## Warning Triangles

In almost all European countries it is a legal requirement to use a warning triangle in the event of a breakdown or accident.

A warning triangle should be placed on the road approximately 30 metres (100 metres on motorways) behind the broken down vehicle on the same side of the road. Always assemble the triangle before leaving your vehicle and walk with it so that the red, reflective surface is facing oncoming traffic. If a breakdown occurs round a blind corner, place the triangle in advance of the corner. Hazard warning lights may be used in conjunction with the triangle but they do not replace it.

## Essential Equipment Table

The table on the following page shows the essential equipment required for each country. The Country Introduction chapters also include details of specific rules for each country. Please note that this information was correct at the time of going to print but is subject to change. For up to date equipment requirements visit www.caravanclub.co.uk/overseasadvice.

| Country | Warning Triangle | Spare Bulbs | First Aid Kit | Reflective Jacket | Additional Equipment to be Carried/Used |
|---|---|---|---|---|---|
| Andorra | Yes (2) | Yes | Rec | Yes | Dipped headlights in poor daytime visibility. Winter tyres recommended; snow chains when road conditions or signs dictate. |
| Austria | Yes | Rec | Yes | Yes | Winter tyres from 1 Nov to 15 April.* |
| Belgium | Yes | Rec | Rec | Yes | Dipped headlights in poor daytime visibility. |
| Croatia | Yes (2 for vehicle with trailer) | Yes | Yes | Yes | Dipped headlights at all times from last Sunday in Oct - last Sunday in Mar. Spare bulbs compulsory if lights are xenon, neon or LED. Snow chains compulsory in winter in certain regions.* |
| Czech Rep | Yes | Yes | Yes | Yes | Dipped headlights at all times. Replacement fuses. Winter tyres or snow chains from 1 Nov - 31st March.* |
| Denmark | Yes | Rec | Rec | Rec | Dipped headlights at all times. On motorways use hazard warning lights when queues or danger ahead. |
| Finland | Yes | Rec | Rec | Yes | Dipped headlights at all times. Winter tyres Dec - Feb.* |
| France | Yes | Rec | Rec | Yes | Dipped headlights recommended at all times. Legal requirement to carry a breathalyser, but no penalty for non-compliance. |
| Germany | Rec | Rec | Rec | Rec | Dipped headlights recommended at all times. Winter tyres to be used in winter weather conditions.* |
| Greece | Yes | Rec | Yes | Rec | Fire extinguisher compulsory. Dipped headlights in towns at night and in poor daytime visibility. |
| Hungary | Yes | Rec | Yes | Yes | Dipped headlights at all times outside built-up areas and in built-up areas at night. Snow chains compulsory on some roads in winter conditions.* |
| Italy | Yes | Rec | Rec | Yes | Dipped headlights at all times outside built-up areas and in poor visibility. Snow chains from 15 Oct - 15 April.* |
| Luxembourg | Yes | Rec | Rec | Yes | Dipped headlights at night and daytime in bad weather. |
| Netherlands | Yes | Rec | Rec | Rec | Dipped headlights at night and in bad weather and recommended during the day. |
| Norway | Yes | Rec | Rec | Rec | Dipped headlights at all times. Winter tyres compulsory when snow or ice on the roads.* |
| Poland | Yes | Rec | Rec | Rec | Dipped headlights at all times. Fire extinguisher compulsory. |
| Portugal | Yes | Rec | Rec | Rec | Dipped headlights in poor daytime visibility, in tunnels and in lanes where traffic flow is reversible. |
| Slovakia | Yes | Rec | Yes | Yes | Dipped headlights at all times. Winter tyres compulsory when compact snow or ice on the road.* |
| Slovenia | Yes (2 for vehicle with trailer) | Yes | Rec | Yes | Dipped headlights at all times. Hazard warning lights when reversing. Use winter tyres or carry snow chains 15 Nov - 15 Mar. |
| Spain | Yes (2 Rec) | Rec | Rec | Yes | Dipped headlights at night, in tunnels and on 'special' roads (roadworks). |
| Sweden | Yes | Rec | Rec | Rec | Dipped headlights at all times. Winter tyres 1 Dec to 31 March. |
| Switzerland (inc Liechtenstein) | Yes | Rec | Rec | Rec | Dipped headlights recommended at all times, compulsory in tunnels. Snow chains where indicated by signs. |

NOTES:
1) All countries: seat belts (if fitted) must be worn by all passengers.
2) Rec: not compulsory for foreign-registered vehicles, but strongly recommended
3) Headlamp converters, spare bulbs, fire extinguisher, first aid kit and reflective waistcoat are strongly recommended for all countries.
4) In some countries drivers who wear prescription glasses must carry a spare pair.
5) Please check information for any country before you travel. This information is to be used as a guide only and it is your responsibility to make sure you have the correct equipment.

* For more information and regulations on winter driving please see the Country Introductions.

# Route planning - North

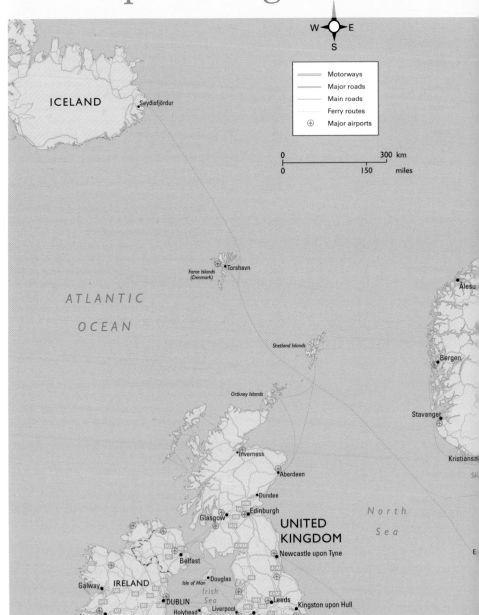

W—⊕—E

**N**
**S**

Motorways
Major roads
Main roads
Ferry routes
⊕ Major airports

0                                    300 km
0                         150         miles

ICELAND    Seyðisfjördur

ATLANTIC

OCEAN

Faroe Islands  •Torshavn
(Denmark)

Ålesu

Shetland Islands

Bergen

Ortkney Islands

Stavanger

•Inverness

Kristiansa

•Aberdeen

•Dundee

•Edinburgh

Glasgow•

North

UNITED
KINGDOM

Sea

•Belfast

•Newcastle upon Tyne

E

Galway•    IRELAND    Isle of Man    •Douglas
                        Irish
•DUBLIN    Sea        ⊕•Leeds
Holyhead•  Liverpool•    Kingston upon Hull
Limerick•              •Manchester ⊕

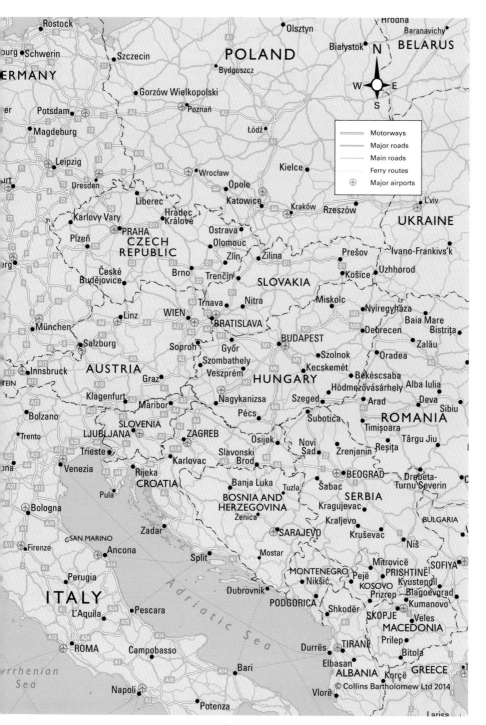

Rostock
Olsztyn
Hrodna
Baranavichy
ourg Schwerin
Szczecin
Białystok N BELARUS
POLAND
ERMANY
Bydgoszcz
W E
er Potsdam
Gorzów Wielkopolski
S
Magdeburg
Poznań
Łódź
Leipzig
Wrocław
Kielce
Motorways
Major roads
urt
Dresden
Opole
Main roads
Liberec
Katowice
Kraków
Rzeszów
L'viv
Ferry routes
Karlovy Vary
Hradec
Králové
Major airports
Plzeň
PRAHA
CZECH
REPUBLIC
Ostrava
Olomouc
UKRAINE
rg
Zlín
Žilina
Prešov
Ivano-Frankivs'k
České
Budějovice
Brno
Trenčín
Košice
Uzhhorod
SLOVAKIA
München
Linz
WIEN
Trnava
Nitra
Miskolc
Nyíregyháza
BRATISLAVA
Baia Mare
Salzburg
Sopron
Győr
BUDAPEST
Debrecen
Bistrița
Zalău
Innsbruck
AUSTRIA
Szombathely
Veszprém
Szolnok
Oradea
TEIN
Graz
Kecskemét
Békéscsaba
Alba Iulia
Klagenfurt
Maribor
HUNGARY
Hódmezővásárhely
Nagykanizsa
Szeged
Arad
Deva
Bolzano
Pécs
Subotica
Sibiu
ROMANIA
Timișoara
Trento
SLOVENIA
LJUBLJANA
ZAGREB
Osijek
Novi
Sad
Zrenjanin
Reșița
Târgu Jiu
Trieste
Slavonski
Brod
ona
Venezia
Rijeka
Karlovac
BEOGRAD
Drobeta-
Turnu Severin
Pula
CROATIA
Banja Luka
Tuzla
Šabac
SERBIA
Bologna
BOSNIA AND
HERZEGOVINA
Kragujevac
BULGARIA
Zenica
Kraljevo
Zadar
SAN MARINO
SARAJEVO
Kruševac
Firenze
Ancona
Niš
Split
Mostar
Mitrovicë
SOFIYA
MONTENEGRO
PRISHTINË
Perugia
Nikšić
Pejë
Kyustendil
Dubrovnik
KOSOVO
Prizren
Blagoevgrad
ITALY
PODGORICA
Shkodër
Kumanovo
L'Aquila
Pescara
SKOPJE
Veles
MACEDONIA
ROMA
Campobasso
Durrës
TIRANË
Prilep
Bitola
Bari
Elbasan
rrhenian
Sea
ALBANIA
Korçë
GREECE
Vlorë
© Collins Bartholomew Ltd 2014
Napoli
Potenza
Larisa

# Route planning - South

# Mountain Passes & Tunnels

## Advice for Drivers

*Mountain Passes*

Mountain passes can create difficult driving conditions, especially when towing or driving a large vehicle. You should only use them if you have a good power to weight ratio and in good driving conditions. If in any doubt as to your outfit's suitability or the weather then stick to motorway routes across maintain ranges if possible.

The tables on the following pages show which passes are not suitable for caravans, and those where caravans are not permitted. Motorhomes aren't usually included in these restrictions, but relatively low powered or very large vehicles should find an alternative route. Road signs at the foot of a pass may restrict access or offer advice, especially for heavy vehicles. Warning notices are usually posted at the foot of a pass if it is closed, or if chains or winter tyres must be used.

Caravanners are particularly sensitive to gradients and traffic/road conditions on passes. The maximum gradient is usually on the inside of bends but exercise caution if it is necessary to pull out. Always engage a lower gear before taking a hairpin bend and give priority to vehicles ascending. On mountain roads it is not the gradient which puts strain on your car but the duration of the climb and the loss of power at high altitudes: approximately 10% at 915 metres (3,000 feet) and even more as you get higher. To minimise the risk of the engine overheating, take high passes in the cool part of the day, don't climb any faster than necessary and keep the engine pulling steadily. To prevent a radiator boiling, pull off the road safely, turn the heater and blower full on and switch off air conditioning. Keep an eye on water and oil levels. Never put cold water into a boiling radiator or it may crack. Check that the radiator is not obstructed by debris sucked up during the journey.

A long descent may result in overheating brakes; select the correct gear for the gradient and avoid excessive use of brakes. Even if you are using engine braking to control speed, caravan brakes may activate due to the overrun mechanism, which may cause them to overheat.

Travelling at altitude can cause a pressure build up in tanks and water pipes. You can prevent this by slightly opening the blade valve of your portable toilet and opening a tap a fraction.

Long tunnels are a much more commonly seen feature in Europe than in the UK, especially in mountainous regions. Tolls are usually charged for the use of major tunnels.

Dipped headlights are usually required by law even in well-lit tunnels, so switch them on before you enter. Snow chains, if used, must be removed before entering a tunnel in lay-bys provided for this purpose.

'No overtaking' signs must be strictly observed. Never cross central single or double lines. If overtaking is permitted in twin-tube tunnels, bear in mind that it is very easy to underestimate distances and speed once inside. In order to minimise the effects of exhaust fumes close all car windows and set the ventilator to circulate air, or operate the air conditioning system coupled with the recycled air option.

If you break down, try to reach the next lay-by and call for help from an emergency phone. If you cannot reach a lay-by, place your warning triangle at least 100 metres behind your vehicle. Modern tunnels have video surveillance systems to ensure prompt assistance in an emergency. Some tunnels can extend for miles and a high number of breakdowns are due to running out of fuel so make sure you have enough before entering the tunnel.

## Mountain Pass Information

The dates of opening and closing given in the following tables are approximate. Before attempting late afternoon or early morning journeys across borders, check their opening times as some borders close at night.

Gradients listed are the maximum which may be encountered on the pass and may be steeper at the inside of curves, particularly on older roads.

Gravel surfaces (such as dirt and stone chips) vary considerably; they can be dusty when dry and slippery when wet. Where known to exist, this type of surface has been noted.

In fine weather winter tyres or snow chains will only be required on very high passes, or for short periods in early or late summer. In winter conditions you will probably need to use them at altitudes exceeding 600 metres (approximately 2,000 feet).

*Converting Gradients*

| | |
|---|---|
| 20% = 1 in 5 | 11% = 1 in 9 |
| 16% = 1 in 6 | 10% = 1 in 8 |
| 14% = 1 in 7 | 8% = 1 in 12 |
| 12% = 1 in 8 | 6% = 1 in 16 |

## Tables and maps

Much of the information contained in the following tables was originally supplied by The Automobile Association and other motoring and tourist organisations. The Caravan Club haven't checked this information and cannot accept responsibility for the accuracy or for errors or omissions to these tables.

The mountain passes, rail and road tunnels listed in the tables are shown on the following maps. Numbers and letters against each pass or tunnel in the tables, correspond with the numbers and letters on the maps.

*Abbreviations*

| | |
|---|---|
| MHV | Maximum height of vehicle |
| MLV | Maximum length of vehicle |
| MWV | Maximum width of vehicle |
| MWR | Minimum width of road |
| OC | Occasionally closed between dates |
| UC | Usually closed between dates |
| UO | Usually open between dates, although a fall of snow may obstruct the road for 24-48 hours. |

# Major Alpine Mountain Passes

| | Pass<br>Height In Metres (Feet) | From<br>To | Max<br>Gradient | Conditions and Comments |
|---|---|---|---|---|
| 1 | **Achenpass**<br>(Austria – Germany)<br>941 (3087) | Achenwald<br>Glashütte | 4% | UO. Well-engineered road, B181/307. Gradient not too severe. |
| 2 | **Albula**<br>(Switzerland)<br>2312 (7585) | Tiefencastel<br>La Punt | 10% | UC Nov-early Jun. MWR 3.5m (11'6") MWV 2.25m (7'6") Inferior alternative to the Julier; fine scenery. **Not recommended for caravans.** Alternative rail tunnel. See *Rail Tunnels* in this section. |
| 3 | **Allos**<br>(France)<br>2250 (7382) | Colmars<br>Barcelonette | 10% | UC early Nov-early Jun. MWR 4m (13'1") Very winding, narrow, mostly unguarded pass on D908 but not difficult otherwise, passing bays on southern slope; poor surface, MWV 1.8m (5'11"). **Not recommended for caravans.** |
| 4 | **Aprica**<br>(Italy)<br>1176 (3858) | Tresenda<br>Edolo | 9% | UC. MWR 4m (13'1") Fine scenery; good surface; well-graded on road S39. Narrow in places; watch for protruding rock when meeting oncoming traffic. Not recommended for caravanners to attempt this pass E or W. Poor road conditions, repairs reduce width drastically. |
| 5 | **Aravis**<br>(France)<br>1498 (4915) | La Clusaz<br>Flumet | 9% | OC Dec-Mar. MWR 4m (13'1"). Fine scenery; D909, fairly easy road. Poor surface in parts on Chamonix side. Some single-line traffic. |
| 6 | **Arlberg**<br>(Austria)<br>1802 (5912) | Bludenz<br>Landeck | 13% | OC Dec-Apr. MWR 6m (19'8"). Good modern road B197/E60 with several pull-in places. Steeper fr W easing towards summit; heavy traffic. **Pass road closed to caravans/trailers.** Parallel road tunnel (tolls) available on E60 (poss long queues). See *Road Tunnels* in this section. |
| 7 | **Ballon d'Alsace**<br>(France)<br>1178 (3865) | Giromagny<br>St Maurice-sur-Moselle | 11% | OC Dec-Mar. MWR 4m (13'1") Fairly straightforward ascent/descent; narrow in places; numerous bends. On road D465. |
| 8 | **Bayard**<br>(France)<br>1248 (4094) | Chauffayer<br>Gap | 14% | UO. MWR 6m (19'8") Part of the Route Napoléon N85. Fairly easy, steepest on the S side with several hairpin bends. Negotiable by caravans from N-to-S via D1075 (N75) and Col-de-la-Croix Haute, avoiding Gap. |
| 9 | **Bernina**<br>(Switzerland)<br>2330 (7644) | Pontresina<br>Poschiavo | 12.50% | OC Dec-Mar. MWR 5m (16'5") MWV 2.25m (7'6") Fine scenery. Good with care on open narrow sections towards summit on S-side; on road no. 29. |
| 10 | **Bracco**<br>(Italy)<br>613 (2011) | Riva Trigoso<br>Borghetto di Vara | 14% | UO. MWR 5m (16'5") A two-lane road (P1) more severe than height suggests due to hairpins and volume of traffic; passing difficult. Rec cross early to avoid traffic. Alternative toll m'way A12 available. |

| Pass / Height In Metres (Feet) | From / To | Max Gradient | Conditions and Comments |
|---|---|---|---|
| ⑪ **Brenner (Europabrücke)** (Austria – Italy) 1374 (4508) | Innsbruck / *Vipiteno/Sterzing* | 14% | UO. MWR 6m (19'8") On road no. 182/12. Parallel toll m'way A13/A22/E45 (6%) suitable for caravans. Heavy traffic may delay at Customs. **Pass road closed to vehicles towing trailers.** |
| ⑫ **Brouis** (France) 1279 (4196) | Nice / *Col-de-Tende* | 12.50% | UO. MWR 6m (19'8") Good surface but many hairpins on D6204 (N204)/S20. Steep gradients on approaches. Height of tunnel at Col-de-Tende at the Italian border is 3.8m (12'4) **Not recommended for caravans.** |
| ⑬ **Brünig** (Switzerland) 1007 (3340) | Brienzwiler Station / *Giswil* | 8.50% | UO. MWR 6m (19'8") MWV 2.5m (8'2") An easy but winding road (no. 4); heavy traffic at weekends; frequent lay-bys. On-going road improvement (2009) may cause delays – check before travel. |
| ⑭ **Bussang** (France) 721 (2365) | Thann / *St Maurice-sur-Moselle* | 7% | UO. MWR 4m (13'1") A very easy road (N66) over the Vosges; beautiful scenery. |
| ⑮ **Cabre** (France) 1180 (3871) | Luc-en-Diois / *Aspres-sur-Buëch* | 9% | UO. MWR 5.5m (18') An easy pleasant road (D93/D993), winding at Col-de-Cabre. |
| ⑯ **Campolongo** (Italy) 1875 (6152) | Corvara-in-Badia / *Arabba* | 12.50% | OC Dec-Mar. MWR 5m (16'5") A winding but easy ascent on rd P244; long level stretch on summit followed by easy descent. Good surface, fine scenery. |
| ⑰ **Cayolle** (France) 2326 (7631) | Barcelonnette / *Guillaumes* | 10% | UC early Nov-early Jun. MWR 4m (13'1") Narrow, winding road (D902) with hairpin bends; poor surface, broken edges with steep drops. Long stretches of single-track road with passing places. **Caravans prohibited.** |
| ⑱ **Costalunga (Karer)** (Italy) 1745 (5725) | Bolzano / *Pozza-di-Fassa* | 16% | OC Dec-Apr. MWR 5m (16'5") A good well-engineered road (S241) but mostly winding with many blind hairpins. **Caravans prohibited.** |
| ⑲ **Croix** (Switzerland) 1778 (5833) | Villars-sur-Ollon / *Les Diablerets* | 13% | UC Nov-May. MWR 3.5m (11'6") A narrow, winding route but extremely picturesque. **Not recommended for caravans.** |
| ⑳ **Croix Haute** (France) 1179 (3868) | Monestier-de-Clermont / *Aspres-sur-Buëch* | 7% | UO on N75. MWR 5.5m (18') Well-engineered road (D1075/N75); several hairpin bends on N side. |
| ㉑ **Falzárego** (Italy) 2117 (6945) | Cortina-d'Ampezzo / *Andraz* | 8.50% | OC Dec-Apr. MWR 5m (16'5") Well-engineered bitumen surface on road R48; many blind hairpin bends on both sides; used by tour coaches. |

| | Pass — Height in Metres (Feet) | From — To | Max Gradient | Conditions and Comments |
|---|---|---|---|---|
| ㉒ | **Faucille** (France) 1323 (4341) | Gex — Morez | 10% | UO. MWR 5m (16'5") Fairly wide, winding road (N5) across the Jura mountains; negotiable by caravans but probably better to follow route via La Cure-St Cergue-Nyon. |
| ㉓ | **Fern** (Austria) 1209 (3967) | Nassereith — Lermoos | 8% | UO. MWR 6m (19'8") Obstructed intermittently during winter. An easy pass on road 179 but slippery when wet; heavy traffic at summer weekends. Connects with Holzleiten Sattel Pass at S end for travel to/from Innsbruck – see below. |
| ㉔ | **Flexen** (Austria) 1784 (5853) | Lech — Rauzalpe (nr Arlberg Pass) | 10% | UO. MWR 5.5m (18') The magnificent 'Flexenstrasse', a well-engineered mountain road (no. 198) with tunnels and galleries. The road from Lech to Warth, N of the pass, is usually closed Nov-Apr due to danger of avalanche. **Not recommended for caravans.** |
| ㉕ | **Flüela** (Switzerland) 2383 (7818) | Davos-Dorf — Susch | 12.50% | OC Nov-May. MWR 5m (16'5") MWV 2.3m (7'6") Easy ascent from Davos on road no. 28; some acute hairpin bends on the E side; bitumen surface. |
| ㉖ | **Forclaz** (Switzerland – France) 1527 (5010) | Martigny — Argentière | 8.50% | UO Forclaz; OC Montets Dec-early Apr. MWR 5m (16'5") MWV 2.5m (8'2") Good road over the pass and to the French border; long, hard climb out of Martigny; narrow and rough over Col-des-Montets on D1506 (N506). |
| ㉗ | **Foscagno** (Italy) 2291 (7516) | Bormio — Livigno | 12.50% | OC Nov-May. MWR 3.3m (10'10") Narrow and winding road (S301) through lonely mountains, generally poor surface. Long winding ascent with many blind bends; not always well-guarded. The descent includes winding rise and fall over the Passo-d'Eira 2,200m (7,218'). **Not recommended for caravans.** |
| ㉘ | **Fugazze** (Italy) 1159 (3802) | Rovereto — Valli-del-Pasubio | 14% | UO. MWR 3.5m (11'6") Very winding road (S46) with some narrow sections, particularly on N side. The many blind bends and several hairpin bends call for extra care. **Not recommended for caravans.** |
| ㉙ | **Furka** (Switzerland) 2431 (7976) | Gletsch — Realp | 11% | UC Oct-Jun. MWR 4m (13'1") MWV 2.25m (7'6") Well-graded road (no. 19) with narrow sections (single track in place on E side) and several hairpin bends on both ascent and descent. Fine views of the Rhône Glacier. Beware of coaches and traffic build-up. **Not recommended for caravans.** Alternative rail tunnel available. See *Rail Tunnels* in this section. |
| ㉚ | **Galibier** (France) 2645 (8678) | La Grave — St Michel-de-Maurienne | 12.50% | UC Oct-Jun. MWR 3m (9'10") Mainly wide, well-surfaced road (D902) but unprotected and narrow over summit. From Col-du-Lautaret it rises over the Col-du-Télégraphe then 11 more hairpin bends. Ten hairpin bends on descent then 5km (3.1 miles) narrow and rough; easier in N to S direction. Limited parking at summit, controlled by traffic lights; caravans are not permitted). There is a single-track tunnel under the Galibier summit. |
| ㉛ | **Gardena (Grödner-Joch)** (Italy) 2121 (6959) | Val Gardena — Corvara-in-Badia | 12.50% | OC Dec-Jun. MWR 5m (16'5") A well-engineered road (S243), very winding on descent. Fine views. **Caravans prohibited.** |

| Pass Height In Metres (Feet) | From To | Max Gradient | Conditions and Comments |
|---|---|---|---|
| 32 **Gavia** (Italy) 2621 (8599) | Bormio Ponte-di-Legno | 20% | UC Oct-Jul. MWR 3m (9'10") MWV 1.8m (5'11") Steep, narrow, difficult road (P300) with frequent passing bays; many hairpin bends and gravel surface; not for the faint-hearted; extra care necessary. Not recommended for caravans. Long winding ascent on Bormio side. |
| 33 **Gerlos** (Austria) 1628 (5341) | Zell-am-Ziller Wald im Pinzgau | 9% | UO. MWR 4m (13'1") Hairpin ascent out of Zell to modern toll road (B165); the old, steep, narrow and winding route with passing bays and 14% gradient is not rec but is negotiable with care. Views of Krimml waterfalls. Caravans prohibited. |
| 34 **Gorges-du-Verdon** (France) 1032 (3386) | Castellane Moustiers-Ste Marie | 9% | UO. MWR probably 5m (16'5") On road D952 over Col-d'Ayen and Col-d'Olivier. Moderate gradients but slow, narrow and winding. Poss heavy traffic. |
| 35 **Grand St Bernard** (Switzerland – Italy) 2469 (8100) | Martigny Aosta | 11% | UC Oct-Jun. MWR 4m (13'1") MWV 2.5m (8' 2") Modern road to entrance of road tunnel on road no. 21/E27 (UO), then narrow but bitumen surface over summit to border; also good in Italy. Suitable for caravans using tunnel. Pass road feasible but not recommended. See *Road Tunnels* in this section. |
| 36 **Grimsel** (Switzerland) 2164 (7100) | Innertkirchen Gletsch | 10% | UC mid Oct-late Jun. MWR 5m (16'5") MWV 2.25m (7'6") A fairly easy, modern road (no. 6) with heavy traffic at weekends. A long winding ascent, finally hairpin bends; then a terraced descent with six hairpins (some tight) into the Rhône valley. Good surface; fine scenery. |
| 37 **Grossglockner** (Austria) 2503 (8212) | Bruck-an-der-Grossglocknerstrasse Heiligenblut | 12.50% | UC late Oct-early May. MWR 5.5m (18') Well-engineered road (no. 107) but many hairpins; heavy traffic; moderate but very long ascent/descent. Negotiable preferably S to N by caravans. Avoid side road to highest point at Edelweissespitze if towing, as road is very steep and narrow. Magnificent scenery. Tolls charged. Road closed from 2200-0500 hrs (summer). Alternative Felbertauern road tunnel between Lienz and Mittersil (toll). See *Road Tunnels* in this section. |
| 38 **Hahntennjoch** (Austria) 1894 (6250) | Imst Elmen | 15% | UC Nov-May. A minor pass; caravans prohibited. |
| 39 **Hochtannberg** (Austria) 1679 (5509) | Schröcken Warth (nr Lech) | 14% | OC Jan-Mar. MWR 4m (13'1") A reconstructed modern road (no. 200). W to E long ascent with many hairpins. Easier E to W. Not recommended for caravans or trailers. |
| 40 **Holzleiten Sattel** (Austria) 1126 (3694) | Nassereith Obsteig | 12.50% | (12.5%), UO. MWR 5m (16'5") Road surface good on W side; poor on E. Light traffic; gradients no problem but not recommended for caravans or trailers. |
| 41 **Iseran** (France) 2770 (9088) | Bourg-St Maurice Lanslebourg | 11% | UC mid Oct-late Jun. MWR 4m (13'1") Second highest pass in the Alps on road D902. Well-graded with reasonable bends, average surface. Several unlit tunnels on N approach. Not recommended for caravans. |

Major Alpine Mountain Passes  51

| Pass Height In Metres (Feet) | From To | Max Gradient | Conditions and Comments |
|---|---|---|---|
| 42 **Izoard** (France) 2360 (7743) | Guillestre Briançon | 12.50% | UC late Oct–mid Jun. MWR 5m (16'5") Fine scenery. Winding, sometimes narrow road (D902) with many hairpin bends; care required at several unlit tunnels near Guillestre. **Not recommended for caravans.** |
| 43 **Jaun** (Switzerland) 1509 (4951) | Bulle Reidenbach | 14% | UO. MWR 4m (13'1") MWV 2.25m (7'6") A modern but generally narrow road (no. 11); some poor sections on ascent and several hairpin bends on descent. |
| 44 **Julier** (Switzerland) 2284 (7493) | Tiefencastel Silvaplana | 13% | UO. MWR 4m (13'1") MWV 2.5m (8'2") Well-engineered road (no. 3) approached from Chur via Sils. Fine scenery. Negotiable by caravans, preferably from N to S, but a long haul and many tight hairpins. Alternative rail tunnel from Thusis to Samedan. See *Rail Tunnels* in this section. |
| 45 **Katschberg** (Austria) 1641 (5384) | Spittal-an-der-Drau St Michael | 20% | UO. MWR 6m (19'8") Good wide road (no. 99) with no hairpins but steep gradients particularly from S. Suitable only light caravans. Parallel Tauern/Katschberg toll motorway A10/E55 and road tunnels. See *Road Tunnels* in this section. |
| 46 **Klausen** (Switzerland) 1948 (6391) | Altdorf Linthal | 10% | UC late Oct–early Jun. MWR 5m (16'5") MWV 2.30m (7'6") Narrow and winding in places, but generally easy in spite of a number of sharp bends; **no through route for caravans** as they are prohibited from using the road between Unterschächen and Linthal (no. 17). |
| 47 **Larche (della Maddalena)** (France – Italy) 1994 (6542) | La Condamine-Châtelard Vinadio | 8.50% | OC Dec–Mar. MWR 3.5m (11'6") An easy, well-graded road (D900); long, steady ascent on French side, many hairpins on Italian side (S21). Fine scenery; ample parking at summit. |
| 48 **Lautaret** (France) 2058 (6752) | Le Bourg-d'Oisans Briançon | 12.50% | OC Dec–Mar. MWR 4m (13'1") Modern, evenly graded but winding road (D1091), and unguarded in places; very fine scenery; suitable for caravans but with care through narrow tunnels. |
| 49 **Leques** (France) 1146 (3760) | Barrême Castellane | 8% | UO. MWR 4m (13'1") On Route Napoléon (D4085). Light traffic; excellent surface; narrow in places on N ascent. S ascent has many hairpins. |
| 50 **Loibl (Ljubelj)** (Austria – Slovenia) 1067 (3500) | Unterloibl Kranj | 20% | UO. MWR 6m (19'8") Steep rise and fall over Little Loibl pass (E652) to 1.6km (1 mile) tunnel under summit. **Caravans prohibited.** The old road over the summit is closed to through-traffic. |
| 51 **Lukmanier (Lucomagno)** (Switzerland) 1916 (6286) | Olivone Disentis | 9% | UC early Nov–late May. MWR 5m (16'5") MWV 2.25m (7'6") Rebuilt, modern road. |
| 52 **Maloja** (Switzerland) 1815 (5955) | Silvaplana Chiavenna | 9% | UO. MWR 4m (13'1") MWV 2.5m (8'2") Escarpment facing south; fairly easy, but many hairpin bends on descent; negotiable by caravans but possibly difficult on ascent. On road no. 3/S37. |

| Pass Height In Metres (Feet) | From To | Max Gradient | Conditions and Comments |
|---|---|---|---|
| (53) **Mauria** (Italy) 1298 (4258) | Lozzo di Cadore Ampezzo | 7% | UO. MWR 5m (16'5") A well-designed road (S52) with easy, winding ascent and descent. |
| (54) **Mendola** (Italy) 1363 (4472) | Appiano/Eppan Sarnonico | 12.50% | UO. MWR 5m (16'5") A fairly straightforward but winding road (S42), well-guarded, many hairpins. Take care overhanging cliffs if towing. The E side going down to Bolzano is not wide enough for caravans, especially difficult on busy days, not recommended for caravans. |
| (55) **Mont Cenis** (France – Italy) 2083 (6834) | Lanslebourg Susa | 12.50% | UC Nov-May. MWR 5m (16'5") Approach by industrial valley. An easy highway (D1006/S25) with mostly good surface; spectacular scenery; long descent into Italy with few stopping places. Alternative Fréjus road tunnel available. See *Road Tunnels* in this section. |
| (56) **Monte Croce-di-Comélico (Kreuzberg)** (Italy) 1636 (5368) | San Candido Santo-Stefano- di- Cadore | 8.50% | UO. MWR 5m (16'5") A winding road (S52) with moderate gradients, beautiful scenery. |
| (57) **Montgenèvre** (France – Italy) 1850 (6070) | Briançon Cesana-Torinese | 9% | UO. MWR 5m (16'5") An easy, modern road (N94/S24) with some tight hairpin bends and with good road surface on French side; road widened & tunnels improved on Italian side, in need of some repair but still easy. Much used by lorries; may be necessary to travel at their speed and give way to oncoming large vehicles on hairpins. |
| (58) **Monte Giovo (Jaufen)** (Italy) 2094 (6870) | Merano Vipiteno/Sterzing | 12.50% | UC Nov-May. MWR 4m (13'1") Many well-engineered hairpin bends on S44; good scenery. **Caravans prohibited.** |
| **Montets** (See **Forclaz**) | | | |
| (59) **Morgins** (France – Switzerland) 1369 (4491) | Abondance Monthey | 14% | UO. MWR 4m (13'1") A lesser used route (D22) through pleasant, forested countryside crossing French/Swiss border. **Not recommended for caravans.** |
| (60) **Mosses** (Switzerland) 1445 (4740) | Aigle Château-d'Oex | 8.50% | UO. MWR 4m (13'1") MWV 2.25m (7'6") A modern road (no. 11). Aigle side steeper and narrow in places. |
| (61) **Nassfeld (Pramollo)** (Austria – Italy) 1530 (5020) | Tröpolach Pontebba | 20% | OC Late Nov-Mar. MWR 4m (13'1") The winding descent on road no. 90 into Italy has been improved but not rec for caravans. |
| (62) **Nufenen (Novena) (Switzerland)** 2478 (8130) | Ulrichen Airolo | 10% | UC Mid Oct-mid Jun. MWR 4m (13'1") MWV 2.25m (7'6") The approach roads are narrow, with tight bends, but the road over the pass is good; negotiable with care. Long drag from Ulrichen. |
| (63) **Oberalp** (Switzerland) 2044 (6706) | Andermatt Disentis | 10% | UC Nov-late May. MWR 5m (16'5") MWV 2.3m (7'6") A much improved and widened road (no. 19) with modern surface but still narrow in places on E side; many tight hairpin bends, but long level stretch on summit. Alternative rail tunnel during the winter. See *Rail Tunnels* in this section. **Not recommended for caravans.** |

| | Pass<br>Height In Metres (Feet) | From<br>To | Max<br>Gradient | Conditions and Comments |
|---|---|---|---|---|
| 64 | **Ofen (Fuorn)**<br>(Switzerland)<br>2149 (7051) | Zernez<br>Santa Maria-im-Münstertal | 12.50% | UO. MWR 4m (13'1") MWV 2.25m (7'6") Good road (no. 28) through Swiss National Park. |
| 65 | **Petit St Bernard**<br>(France – Italy)<br>2188 (7178) | Bourg-St Maurice<br>Pré-St Didier | 8.50% | UC mid Oct-Jun. MWR 5m (16'5") Outstanding scenery, but poor surface and unguarded broken edges near summit. Easiest from France (D1090); sharp hairpins on climb from Italy (S26). **Closed to vehicles towing another vehicle.** |
| 66 | **Pillon**<br>(Switzerland)<br>1546 (5072) | Le Sépey<br>Gsteig | 9% | OC Jan-Feb. MWR 4m (13'1") MWV 2.25m (7'6") A comparatively easy modern road. |
| 67 | **Plöcken (Monte Croce-Carnico)**<br>(Austria – Italy)<br>1362 (4468) | Kötschach<br>Paluzza | 14% | OC Dec-Apr. MWR 5m (16'5") A modern road (no. 110) with long, reconstructed sections; OC to caravans due to heavy traffic on summer weekends; delay likely at the border. Long, slow, twisty pull from S, easier from N. |
| 68 | **Pordoi**<br>(Italy)<br>2239 (7346) | Arabba<br>Canazei | 10% | OC Dec-Apr. MWR 5m (16'5") An excellent modern road (S48) with numerous blind hairpin bends; fine scenery; used by tour coaches. Long drag when combined with Falzarego pass. |
| 69 | **Pötschen**<br>(Austria)<br>982 (3222) | Bad Ischl<br>Bad Aussee | 9% | UO. MWR 7m (23') A modern road (no. 145). Good scenery. |
| 70 | **Radstädter-Tauern**<br>(Austria)<br>1738 (5702) | Radstadt<br>Mauterndorf | 16% | OC Jan-Mar. MWR 5m (16'5") N ascent steep (road no. 99) but not difficult otherwise; but negotiable by light caravans using parallel toll m'way (A10) through tunnel. See *Road Tunnels* in this section. |
| 71 | **Résia (Reschen)**<br>(Italy – Austria)<br>1504 (4934) | Spondigna<br>Pfunds | 10% | UO. MWR 6m (19'8") A good, straightforward alternative to the Brenner Pass. Fine views but no stopping places. On road S40/180. |
| 72 | **Restefond (La Bonette)**<br>(France)<br>2802 (9193) | Barcelonnette<br>St Etienne-de-Tinée | 16% | UC Oct-Jun. MWR 3m (9'10") The highest pass in the Alps. Rebuilt, resurfaced road (D64) with rest area at summit – top loop narrow and unguarded. Winding with hairpin bends. **Not recommended for caravans.** |
| 73 | **Rolle**<br>(Italy)<br>1970 (6463) | Predazzo<br>Mezzano | 9% | OC Dec-Mar. MWR 5m (16'5") A well-engineered road (S50) with many hairpin bends on both sides; very beautiful scenery; good surface. |
| | **Rombo (See Timmelsjoch)** | | | |
| 74 | **St Gotthard (San Gottardo)**<br>(Switzerland)<br>2108 (6916) | Göschenen<br>Airolo | 10% | UC mid Oct-early Jun. MWR 6m (19'8") MHV 3.6m (11'9") MWV 2.5m (8'2") Modern, fairly easy two- to three-lane road (A2/E35). Heavy traffic. Alternative road tunnel. See *Road Tunnels* in this section. |

| Pass Height In Metres (Feet) | From To | Max Gradient | Conditions and Comments |
|---|---|---|---|
| (75) **San Bernardino** (Switzerland) 2066 (6778) | Mesocco *Hinterrhein* | 10% | UC Oct–late Jun. MWR 4m (13'1") MWV 2.25m (7'6") Easy modern road (A13/E43) on N and S approaches to tunnel, narrow and winding over summit via tunnel suitable for caravans. See *Road Tunnels* in this section. |
| (76) **Schlucht** (France) 1139 (3737) | Gérardmer *Munster* | 7% | UO. MWR 5m (16'5") An extremely picturesque route (D417) crossing the Vosges mountains, with easy, wide bends on the descent. Good surface. |
| (77) **Seeberg (Jezersko)** (Austria – Slovenia) 1218 (3996) | Eisenkappel *Kranj* | 12.50% | UO. MWR 5m (16'5") An alternative to the steeper Loibl and Wurzen passes on B82/210; moderate climb with winding, hairpin ascent and descent. **Not recommended for caravans.** |
| (78) **Sella** (Italy) 2240 (7349) | Selva *Canazei* | 11% | OC Dec–Jan. MWR 5m (16'5") A well-engineered, winding road; exceptional views of Dolomites; **caravans prohibited.** |
| (79) **Sestriere** (Italy) 2033 (6670) | Cesana-Torinese *Pinarolo* | 10% | UO MWR 6m (19'8") Mostly bitumen surface on road R23. Fairly easy; fine scenery. |
| (80) **Silvretta (Bielerhöhe)** (Austria) 2032 (6666) | Partenen *Galtur* | 11% | UC late Oct–early Jun. MWR 5m (16'5") Mostly reconstructed road (188); 32 easy hairpin bends on W ascent; E side more straightforward. Tolls charged. **Caravans prohibited.** |
| (81) **Simplon** (Switzerland – Italy) 2005 (6578) | Brig *Domodóssola* | 11% | OC Nov–Apr. MWR 7m (23') MWV 2.5m (8'2") An easy, reconstructed, modern road (E62/S33), 21km (13 miles) long, continuous ascent to summit; good views, many stopping places. Surface better on Swiss side. Alternative rail tunnel fr Kandersteg in operation from Easter to September. See *Rail Tunnels* in this section. |
| (82) **Splügen** (Switzerland – Italy) 2113 (6932) | Splügen *Chiavenna* | 13% | UC Nov–Jun. MWR 3.5m (11'6") MHV 2.8m (9'2") MWV 2.3m (7'6") Mostly narrow, winding road (S36), with extremely tight hairpin bends, not well guarded; care also required at many tunnels/galleries. **Not recommended for caravans.** |
| (83) **Stelvio** (Italy) 2757 (9045) | Bormio *Spondigna* | 12.50% | UC Oct–late Jun. MWR 4m (13'1") MLV 10m (32') Third highest pass in Alps on S38; 40–50 acute hairpin bends either side, all well-engineered; good surface, traffic often heavy. Hairpin bends too acute for long vehicles. **Not recommended for caravans.** |
| (84) **Susten** (Switzerland) 2224 (7297) | Innertkirchen *Wassen* | 9% | UC Nov–Jun. MWR 6m (19'8") MWV 2.5m (8'2") Very scenic and well-guarded road (no. 11); easy gradients and turns; heavy traffic at weekends. Eastern side easier than west. Negotiable by caravans (recommended for small/medium sized only) with care, but not for the faint-hearted. Large parking area at summit. |

| Pass<br>Height in Metres (Feet) | From<br>To | Max<br>Gradient | Conditions and Comments |
|---|---|---|---|
| ⑧⑤ **Tenda (Tende)**<br>Italy – France<br>1321 (4334) | Borgo–San Dalmazzo<br>Tende | 9% | UO. MWR 6m (19'8") Well-guarded, modern road (S20/ND6204) with several hairpin bends; road tunnel (height 3.8m) at summit narrow with poor road surface. Less steep on Italian side. **Caravans prohibited during winter.** |
| ⑧⑥ **Thurn**<br>(Austria)<br>1274 (4180) | Kitzbühel<br>Mittersill | 8.50% | UO. MWR 5m (16'5") MWV 2.5m (8' 2") A good road (no. 161) with narrow stretches; N approach rebuilt. Several good parking areas. |
| ⑧⑦ **Timmelsjoch (Rombo)**<br>(Austria – Italy)<br>2509 (8232) | Obergurgl<br>Moso | 14% | UC mid Oct–Jun. MWR 3.5m (11'6") Border closed at night 8pm to 7am. The pass (road no 186/S44b) **is open to private cars without trailers only** (toll charged), as some tunnels on Italian side too narrow for larger vehicles. Easiest N to S. |
| ⑧⑧ **Tonale**<br>(Italy)<br>1883 (6178) | Edolo<br>Dimaro | 10% | UO. MWR 5m (16'5") A relatively easy road (S42); steepest on W; long drag. Fine views. |
| ⑧⑨ **Tre Croci**<br>(Italy)<br>1809 (5935) | Cortina-d'Ampezzo<br>Auronzo-di-Cadore | 11% | OC Dec–Mar. MWR 6m (19'8") An easy pass on road R48; fine scenery. |
| ⑨⓪ **Turracher Höhe**<br>(Austria)<br>1763 (5784) | Predlitz<br>Ebene-Reichenau | 23% | UO. MWR 4m (13'1") Formerly one of the steepest mountain roads (no. 95) in Austria; now improved. Steep, fairly straightforward ascent followed by a very steep descent; good surface and mainly two-lane; fine scenery. **Not recommended for caravans.** |
| ⑨① **Umbrail**<br>(Switzerland – Italy)<br>2501 (8205) | Santa Maria-im-Münstertal<br>Bormio | 9% | UC Nov–early Jun. MWR 4.3m (14'1") MWV 2.3m (7'6") Highest Swiss pass (S38); mostly tarmac with some gravel surface. Narrow with 34 hairpin bends. **Not recommended for caravans.** |
| ⑨② **Vars**<br>(France)<br>2109 (6919) | St Paul-sur-Ubaye<br>Guillestre | 9% | OC Dec–Mar. MWR 5m (16'5") Easy winding ascent and descent on D902 with 14 hairpin bends; good surface. |
| ⑨③ **Wurzen (Koren)**<br>(Austria – Slovenia)<br>1073 (3520) | Riegersdorf<br>Kranjska Gora | 20% | UO. MWR 4m (13'1") Steep two-lane road (no. 109), otherwise not particularly difficult; better on Austrian side; heavy traffic summer weekends; delays likely at the border. **Caravans prohibited.** |
| ⑨④ **Zirler Berg**<br>(Austria)<br>1009 (3310) | Seefeld<br>Zirl | 16.50% | UO. MWR 7m (23') South facing escarpment, part of route from Garmisch to Innsbruck; good, modern road (no. 171). Heavy tourist traffic and long steep descent with one hairpin bend into Inn Valley. Steepest section from hairpin bend down to Zirl. **Caravans not permitted northbound and not recommended southbound.** |

*Technical information by courtesy of the Automobile Association. Additional update and amendments supplied by caravanners and tourers who have themselves used the passes and tunnels. The Caravan Club has not checked the information contained in these tables and cannot accept responsibility for their accuracy, or for any errors, omissions, or their effects.*

# Major Alpine Rail Tunnels

Before using any of these tunnels, PLEASE READ CAREFULLY THE ADVICE AT THE BEGINNING OF THIS CHAPTER

| | Tunnel | Route | Journey Time | General Information and Comments | Contact |
|---|---|---|---|---|---|
| (A) | **Albula** (Switzerland) 5.9 km (3.5 miles) | **Chur – St Moritz** Thusis to Samedan | 80 mins | MHV 2.85m + MWV 1.40m or MHV 2.50m + MWV 2.20 Up to 11 shuttle services per day all year; advance booking required. | Thusis (081) 2884716 Samedan (081) 2885511 www.rhb.ch |
| (B) | **Furka** (Switzerland) 15.4 km (9.5 miles) | **Andermatt – Brig** Realp to Oberwald | 15 mins | Hourly all year from 6am to 9pm weekdays; half-hourly weekends. | (027) 9277777 www.mgbahn.ch |
| (C) | **Oberalp** (Switzerland) 28 km (17.3 miles) | **Andermatt – Disentis** Andermatt to Sedrun | 60 mins | MHV 2.50m 2-6 trains daily (Christmas-Easter only). Advance booking compulsory. | (027) 9277777 www.mgbahn.ch |
| (D) | **Lötschberg** (Switzerland) 14 km (8.7 miles) | **Bern – Brig** Kandersteg to Goppenstein | 15 mins | MHV 2.90m Frequent all year half-hourly service. Journey time 15 minutes. Advance booking unnecessary; extension to Hohtenn operates when Goppenstein-Gampel road is closed. | Kandersteg (0)900 553333 www.bls.ch/autoverlad |
| (E) | **Simplon** (Switzerland – Italy) | **Brig – Domodossola** Brig to Iselle | 20 mins | 10 trains daily, all year. | (0)900 300300 http://mct.sbb.ch/mct/autoverlad |
| (F) | **Lötschberg/ Simplon** Switzerland – Italy | **Bern – Domodossola** Kandersteg to Iselle | 75 mins | Limited service Easter to mid-October up to 3 days a week (up to 10 times a day) and at Christmas for vehicles max height 2.50m, motor caravans up to 5,000 kg. Advance booking compulsory. | (0)900 553333 www.bls.ch |
| (F) | **Tauerbahn** (Austria) | **Bad Gastein – Spittal an der Drau** Böckstein to Mallnitz | 11 mins | East of and parallel to Grossglockner pass. Half-hourly service all year. | (05) 1717 http://autoschleuse.oebb.at |
| (G) | **Vereina** (Switzerland) 19.6 km (11.7 miles) | **Klosters – Susch** Selfranga to Sagliains | 18 mins | MLV 12m Half-hourly daytime service all year. Journey time 18 minutes. Restricted capacity for vehicles over 3.30m high during winter w/ends and public holidays. Steep approach to Klosters. | (081) 2883737 www.rhb.ch |

NOTES: *Information believed to be correct at time of publication. Detailed timetables are available from the appropriate tourist offices. Always check for current information before you travel.*

# Major Alpine Road Tunnels

Before using any of these tunnels, PLEASE READ CAREFULLY THE ADVICE AT THE BEGINNING OF THIS CHAPTER

| | Tunnel | Route and Height above Sea Level | General Information and Comments |
|---|---|---|---|
| H | **Arlberg** (Austria) 14 km (8.75 miles) | **Langen to St Anton** 1220m (4000') | On B197 parallel and to S of Arlberg Pass which is closed to caravans/trailers. **Motorway vignette required; tolls charged.** www.arlberg.com |
| I | **Bosruck** (Austria) 5.5 km (3.4 miles) | **Spital am Pyhrn to Selzthal** 742m (2434') | To E of Phyrn pass; with Gleinalm Tunnel (see below) forms part of A9 a'bahn between Linz & Graz. Max speed 80 km/h (50 mph). Use dipped headlights, no overtaking. Occasional emergency lay-bys with telephones. **Motorway vignette required; tolls charged.** |
| J | **Felbertauern** (Austria) 5.3 km (3.25 miles) | **Mittersill to Matrei** 1525m (5000') | MVR 7m (23'), tunnel height 4.5m (14'9"). On B109 W of and parallel to Grossglockner pass; downwards gradient of 9% S to N with sharp bend before N exit. Wheel chains may be needed on approach Nov–Apr. **Tolls charged.** |
| K | **Frejus** (France – Italy) 12.8 km (8 miles) | **Modane to Bardonecchia** 1220m (4000') | MVR 9m (29'6"), tunnel height 4.3m (14'). Min/max speed 60/70 km/h (37/44 mph). Return tickets valid until midnight on 7th day after day of issue. Season tickets are available. Approach via A43 and D1006; heavy use by freight vehicles. Good surface on approach roads. **Tolls charged.** www.sftrf.fr |
| L | **Gleinalm** (Austria) 8.3 km (5 miles) | **St Michael to Fiesach (nr Graz)** 817m (2680') | Part of A9 Pyhrn a'bahn. **Motorway vignette required; tolls charged.** |
| M | **Grand St Bernard** (Switzerland – Italy) 5.8 km (3.6 miles) | **Bourg-St Pierre to St Rhémy (Italy)** 1925m (7570') | MHV 4m (13'1"), MWV 2.55m (8'2.5"), MLV 18m (60'). Min/max speed 40/80 km/h (24/50 mph). On E27. Passport check, Customs & toll offices at entrance; breakdown bays at each end with telephones; return tickets valid one month. Although approaches are covered, wheel chains may be needed in winter. Season tickets are available. **Motorway vignette required; tolls charged.** For 24-hour information tel: (027) 7884400 (Switzerland) or 0165 780902 (Italy), www.letunnel.com |
| N | **Karawanken** (Austria – Slovenia) 8 km (5 miles) | **Rosenbach to Jesenice** 610m (2000') | On A11. **Motorway vignette required; tolls charged.** |
| O | **Mont Blanc** (France – Italy) 11.6 km (7.2 miles ) | **Chamonix to Courmayeur** 1381m (4530') | MHV 4.7m (15'5"), MWV 6m (19'6") On N205 France, S26 (Italy). Max speed in tunnel 70 km/h (44 mph) – lower limits when exiting; min speed 50 km/h. Leave 150m between vehicles; ensure enough fuel for 30km. Return tickets valid until midnight on 7th day after issue. Season tickets are available. **Tolls charged.** www.tunnelmb.net |

| Tunnel | Route and Height above Sea Level | General Information and Comments |
| --- | --- | --- |
| (P) **Munt La Schera** (Switzerland – Italy) 3.5 km (2 miles) | **Zernez to Livigno** 1706m (5597') | MHV 3.6m (11'9"), MWV 2.5m (8'2"). Open 24 hours; single lane traffic controlled by traffic lights; roads from Livigno S to the Bernina Pass and Bormio closed Dec-Apr. On N28 (Switzerland). **Tolls charged.** Tel: (081) 8561888, www.livigno.eu |
| (Q) **St Gotthard** (Switzerland) 16.3 km (10 miles) | **Göschenen to Airolo** 1159m (3800') | Tunnel height 4.5m (14'9"), single carriageway 7.5m (25') wide. Max speed 80 km/h (50 mph). No tolls, but tunnel is part of Swiss motorway network (A2). **Motorway vignette required.** Tunnel closed 8pm to 5am Monday to Friday for periods during June and September. Heavy traffic and delays high season. www.gotthard-strassentunnel.ch |
| - **Ste Marie-aux-Mines** 6.8 km (4.25 miles) | **St Dié to Ste-Marie-aux Mines** 772m (2533') | Re-opened October 2008; the longest road tunnel situated entirely in France. Also known as Maurice Lemaire Tunnel, through the Vosges in north-east France from Lusse on N159 to N59. **Tolls charged.** Alternate route via Col-de-Ste Marie on D459. |
| (R) **San Bernardino** (Switzerland) 6.6 km (4 miles) | **Hinterrhein to San Bernardino** 1644m (5396') | Tunnel height 4.8m (15'9"), width 7m (23'). On A13 motorway. No stopping or overtaking; keep 100m between vehicles; breakdown bays with telephones. Max speed 80 km/h (50 mph). **Motorway vignette required.** |
| (S) **Tauern and Katschberg** (Austria) 6.4 km (4 miles) & 5.4km (3.5 miles) | **Salzburg to Villach** 1340m (4396') & 1110m (3642') | The two major tunnels on the A10, height 4.5m (14'9"), width 7.5m (25'). **Motorway vignette required; tolls charged.** |

**NOTES:**

*Dipped headlights should be used (unless stated otherwise) when travelling through road tunnels, even when the road appears well lit. In some countries police make spot checks and impose on-the-spot fines. During the winter wheel chains may be required on the approaches to some tunnels. These must not be used in tunnels and lay-bys are available for the removal and refitting of wheel chains.*

*Much of the information contained in the table was originally supplied by The Automobile Association and other motoring and tourist organisations. Updates and amendments are supplied by caravanners and tourers who have themselves used the passes and tunnels. The Caravan Club has not checked the information contained in these tables and cannot accept responsibility for their accuracy, or for any errors, omissions, or for their effects.*

# Alpine Countries – East

# Keeping in Touch

## Telephones and Calling

Most people need to use a telephone at some point while they're away, whether to keep in touch with family and friends back home or call ahead to sites. Even if you don't plan to use a phone while you're away, it is best to make sure you have access to one in case of emergencies.

### International Direct Dial Calls

International access codes are given in the relevant Country Introduction - first dial the international access code then the local number. If the area code starts with a zero this should be omitted (except in Italy where the full number should be dialled).

Some countries' telephone numbers do not have area codes (e.g. Denmark, Luxembourg, Norway). In these cases you should dial the international access code and the number in full. The international access code to dial the UK from anywhere in the world is 0044.

### Ringing Tones

Ringing tones vary from country to country, so may sound very different to UK tones. Some ringing tones sound similar to error or engaged tones that you would hear on a UK line.

### Phone cards

You can buy pre-paid international phone cards which offer much lower rates for international calls than most mobile phone providers. You load the card with your chosen amount (which you can top up at any time) and then dial an access code from any mobile or landline to make your call. See www.planetphonecards.com or www. thephonecardsite.com for more details.

### Using Mobile Phones Abroad

Mobile phones have an international calling option called 'roaming' which will automatically search for a local network when you switch your phone on. You should contact your service provider to ask about their roaming charges as these are partly set by the foreign networks you use and fluctuate with exchange rates. Most network providers offer added extras or 'bolt-ons' to your tariff to make the cost of calling to/from abroad cheaper.

Storing telephone numbers in your phone's contact list in international format (i.e. use the prefix of +44 and omit the initial '0') will mean that your contacts will automatically work abroad as well as in the UK.

### Global SIM Cards

If you're planning on travelling to more than one country consider buying a global SIM card. This will mean mobile phone can operate on foreign mobile networks, which will be more cost effective than your service provider's roaming charges. For details of SIM cards available, speak to your service provider or visit www.0044.co.uk or www.globalsimcard.co.uk.

You may find it simpler to buy a SIM card or cheap 'pay-as-you-go' phone abroad if you plan to use a mobile phone a lot for local calls, e.g. to book campsites or restaurants. Buying a local SIM or pay-as-you-go mobile may mean that you still have higher call charges for international calls (such as calling the UK). Before buying a different SIM card, check with you provider whether your phone is locked against use on other networks.

### Hands-Free

Legislation in Europe forbids the use of mobile or car phones while driving except when using hands-free equipment. If you are involved in an accident whilst driving and, at the same time, you were using a hand-held mobile phone, your insurance company may refuse to honour the claim.

## Accessing the Internet

### Mobile Internet Costs - Data Roaming

Accessing the internet overseas via your mobile can be very expensive. It is recommended that you disable your internet access by switching 'data roaming' to off, in order to avoid a large mobile phone bill on your return.

### Internet Access

Wi-Fi is available on lots of campsites in Europe, sometimes the cost in included in your pitch fee and other sites charge extra for access. Most larger towns may have internet cafés or libraries where you can access the internet, however lots of fast food restaurants and coffee chains now offer free Wi-Fi for customers and visiting them for a cup of coffee or bite to eat is often the most economical way if you only need access for a short time.

Many people now use their smartphones for internet access or have a dongle – a device which, when connected to your laptop or tablet, allows you to access the internet using a mobile phone network. While these methods are economical in the UK, if you do the same abroad you will be charged data roaming charges which can run into hundreds or thousands of pounds depending on how much data you use. If you plan on using your smartphone or a dongle abroad speak to your service provider before you leave the UK to make sure you understand the costs. There may even be an overseas package that you can add to your plan to make data roaming cheaper.

*Making Calls from your Laptop*

If you download Skype to your laptop you can make free calls to other Skype users anywhere in the world using a Wi-Fi connection. Rates for calls to non-Skype users (landline or mobile phone) are also very competitively-priced. You will need a computer with a microphone and speakers, and a webcam is handy too. It is also possible to download Skype to an internet-enabled mobile phone to take advantage of the same low-cost calls – see www.skype.com.

*Club Together*

If you want to chat to other members either at home or while you're away, you can do so on The Club's online community Club Together.

You can ask questions and gather opinions on the forums, as well as asking for expert advice on a number of caravanning topics. Just visit www.caravanclub.co.uk/together.

## Radio and Television

*Radio*

The BBC World Service broadcasts radio programmes 24 hours a day worldwide and you can listen on a number of platforms: online, via satellite or cable, DRM digital radio, internet radio or mobile phone. You can find detailed information and programme schedules at www.bbc.co.uk/worldservice.

Listeners in northern France can currently listen to BBC Radio 5 Live on either 693 or 909 kHz medium wave or BBC Radio 4 on 198 kHz long wave. Whereas analogue television signals were switched off in the UK during 2012, no date has yet been fixed for the switch off of analogue radio signals.

## Digital Terrestrial Television

As in the UK, television transmissions in most of Europe have been converted to digital. The UK's high definition transmission technology may be more advanced than any currently implemented or planned in Europe. This means that digital televisions intended for use in the UK might not be able to receive HD terrestrial signals in some countries.

## Satellite Television

For English-language TV programmes the only realistic option is satellite, and satellite dishes are a common sight on campsites all over Europe. A satellite dish mounted on the caravan roof or clamped to a pole fixed to the drawbar, or one mounted on a foldable free-standing tripod, will provide good reception and minimal interference. Remember however that obstructions to the south east (such as tall trees or even mountains) or heavy rain, can interrupt the signals. A specialist dealer will be able to advise you on the best way of mounting your dish. You will also need a satellite receiver and ideally a satellite-finding meter.

The main entertainment channels such as BBC1, ITV1 and Channel 4 can be difficult to pick up in mainland Europe as they are now being transmitted by new narrow-beam satellites. A 60cm dish should pick up these channels in most of France, Belgium and the Netherlands but as you travel further afield, you'll need a progressively larger dish. See the website www.satelliteforcaravans.co.uk (created and operated by a Caravan Club member) for the latest changes and developments, and for information on how to set up your equipment.

# Medical Matters

You can find country specific medical advice, including details of any vaccinations you may need from the NHS choices website, www.nhs.uk/healthcare abroad. Your GP surgery should also be able to give you advice on vaccinations and precautions. For general enquiries about medical care abroad you can contact NHS England on 0300 311 22 33 or email england.contactus@nhs.uk.

If you have any pre-existing medical conditions you should check with your GP that you are fit to travel. Ask your doctor for a written summary of any medical problems and a list of medications currently used. This is particularly important for travellers whose medical conditions require them to use controlled drugs or hypodermic syringes, in case customs officers question why you are carrying them.

Always make sure that you have enough of your medication to last the duration of your holiday and some extra in case you are delayed in returning to the UK. Ask your doctor for the generic name of any drugs you use, as brand names may be different abroad. If possible carry a card giving your blood group and details of any allergies or dietary restrictions (translations may be useful for restaurants).

If you have any doubts about your teeth or plan to be away a long time, have a dental check-up before departure. An emergency dental kit is available from High Street chemists which will allow you temporarily to restore a crown, bridge or filling or to dress a broken tooth until you can get to a dentist.

A good website to check before you travel is www.nathnac.org/travel. This website gives general health and safety advice and reports of disease outbreaks, as well as highlighting potential health risks by country.

## European Heath Insurance Card (EHIC)

Before leaving home apply for a European Health Insurance Card (EHIC). British residents temporarily visiting another EU country, as well Norway and Switzerland, are entitled to receive state-provided emergency treatment during their stay on the same terms as residents of those countries, but you must have a valid EHIC to claim these services.

As well as treatment in the event of an emergency, this includes on-going medical care for a chronic disease or pre-existing illness, i.e. medication, blood tests and injections. Apply online for your EHIC on www.ehic.org.uk, call 0845 6062030 or pick up an application form from a post office. An EHIC is required by each individual family member - children under 16 must be included in a parent or guardian's application.

The EHIC is free of charge, is valid for up to five years and can be renewed up to six months before its expiry date. Before you travel remember to check that your EHIC is still valid.

Private treatment is generally not covered by your EHIC, and state-provided treatment may not cover everything that you would expect to receive free of charge from the NHS. If charges are made, these cannot be refunded by the British authorities but may be refundable under the terms of your travel insurance policy.

An EHIC is not a substitute for travel insurance and it is strongly recommended that you arrange full travel insurance before leaving home regardless of the cover provided by your EHIC. Some insurance companies require you to have an EHIC and some will waive the policy excess if an EHIC has been used.

If your EHIC is stolen or lost while you are abroad contact 0044 191 2127500 for help. If you experience difficulties in getting your EHIC accepted, telephone the Department for Work & Pensions for assistance on the overseas healthcare team line 0044 (0)191 218 1999 between 8am to 5pm Monday to Friday. Residents of the Republic of Ireland, the Isle of Man and Channel Islands, should check with their own health authorities about reciprocal arrangements with other countries.

## Holiday Travel Insurance

Despite the fact that you have an EHIC you may incur thousands of pounds of medical costs if you fall ill or have an accident. The cost of bringing a person back to the UK, in the event of illness or death, is never covered by the EHIC. You may also find that you end up with a bill for treatment as not all countries offer free healthcare.

Separate additional travel insurance adequate for your destination is essential, such as The Caravan Club's Red Pennant Overseas Holiday Insurance, available to Club members – see www.caravanclub.co.uk/redpennant.

## First Aid

A first aid kit containing at least the basic requirements is an essential item, and in some countries it is compulsory to carry one in your vehicle (see the Essential Equipment Table in the chapter Motoring – Equipment). Kits should contain items such as sterile pads, assorted dressings, bandages and plasters, antiseptic wipes or cream, cotton wool, scissors, eye bath and tweezers. Also make sure you carry something for upset stomachs, painkillers and an antihistamine in case of hay fever or mild allergic reactions.

If you're travelling to remote areas then you may find it useful to carry a good first aid manual. The British Red Cross publishes a comprehensive First Aid Manual in conjunction with St John Ambulance and St Andrew's Ambulance Association.

## Vaccinations

The Department of Health advises long stay visitors to some eastern European countries to consider vaccination against hepatitis A. Your GP surgery can advise you if this or any other vaccinations are required.

## Accidents and Emergencies

If you are involved in or witness a road accident the police may want to question you about it. If possible take photographs or make sketches of the scene, and write a few notes about what happened as it may be more difficult to remember the details at a later date.

The telephone numbers for police, fire brigade and ambulance services are given in each Country Introduction, however all EU member states the number 112 can be used from landlines or mobile phones to call any of the emergency services.

## Sun Protection

Never under-estimate how ill exposure to the sun can make you. If you are not used to the heat it is very easy to fall victim to heat exhaustion or heat stroke. Avoid sitting in the sun between 11am and 3pm and cover your head if sitting or walking in the sun. Use a good quality sun-cream with high sun protection factor (SPF) and re-apply frequently. Make sure you drink plenty of fluids.

## Tick-Borne Encephalitis (TBE) and Lyme Disease

Hikers and outdoor sports enthusiasts planning trips to forested, rural areas in some parts of central and Eastern Europe should be aware of tick-borne encephalitis, which is transmitted by the bite of an infected tick. If you think you may be at risk, seek medical advice on prevention and immunisation before you leave the UK.

There is no vaccine against Lyme disease, an equally serious tick-borne infection, which, if left untreated, can attack the nervous system and joints.

You can minimise the risk by using an insect repellent containing DEET, wearing long sleeves and long trousers, and checking for ticks after outdoor activity. Avoid unpasteurised dairy products in risk areas. See www.tickalert.org or telephone 01943 468010 for more information.

## Water and Food

Water from mains supplies throughout Europe is generally safe, but may be treated with chemicals which make it taste different to tap water in the UK. If in any doubt, always drink bottled water or boil it before drinking. Food poisoning is potential anywhere, and a complete change of diet may upset your stomach as well. In hot conditions avoid any food that hasn't been refrigerated or hot food that has been left to cool. Be sensible about the food that you eat – don't eat unpasteurised or undercooked food and if you aren't sure about the freshness of meat or seafood then it is best avoided.

## Returning Home

If you become ill on your return home tell your doctor that you have been abroad and which countries you have visited. Even if you have received medical treatment in another country, always consult your doctor if you have been bitten or scratched by an animal while on holiday.

If you were given any medicines in another country, it may be illegal to bring them back into the UK. If in doubt, declare them at Customs when you return.

# Electricity and Gas

## Electricity – General Advice

The voltage for mains electricity is 230V across the EU, but varying degrees of 'acceptable tolerance' mean you may find variations in the actual voltage. Most appliances sold in the UK are 220-240V so should work correctly. However, some high-powered equipment, such as microwave ovens, may not function well – check your instruction manual for any specific instructions. Appliances marked with 'CE' have been designed to meet the requirements of relevant European directives.

The table below gives an approximate idea of which appliances can be used based on the amperage which is being supplied (although not all appliances should be used at the same time). You can work it out more accurately by making a note of the wattage of each appliance in your caravan. The wattages given are based on appliances designed for use in caravans and motorhomes. Household kettles, for example, have at least a 2000W element. Each caravan circuit will also have a maximum amp rating which should not be exceeded.

## Electrical Connections – EN60309-2 (CEE17)

EN60309-2 (formerly known as CEE17) is the European Standard for all newly fitted connectors. However there is no requirement

| Amps | Wattage (Approx) | Fridge | Battery Charger | Air Conditioning | LCD TV | Water Heater | Kettle (750W) | Heater (1kW) |
|------|------------------|--------|-----------------|------------------|--------|--------------|---------------|--------------|
| 2 | 400 | ✓ | ✓ | | | | | |
| 4 | 900 | ✓ | ✓ | | ✓ | ✓ | | |
| 6 | 1300 | ✓ | ✓ | * | ✓ | ✓ | ✓ | |
| 8 | 1800 | ✓ | ✓ | ✓** | ✓ | ✓ | ✓ | ✓** |
| 10 | 2300 | ✓ | ✓ | ✓** | ✓ | ✓ | ✓ | ✓** |
| 16 | 3600 | ✓ | ✓ | ✓ | ✓ | ✓ | ✓ | ✓** |

\*      *Usage possible, depending on wattage of appliance in question*
\*\*    *Not to be used at the same time as other high-wattage equipment*

for sites to replace connectors which were installed before this was standardised so you may still find some sites where your UK 3 pin connector doesn't fit. For this reason it is a good idea to carry a 2-pin adapter. If you are already on site and find your connector doesn't fit, ask campsite staff to borrow or hire an adaptor. You may still encounter a poor electrical supply on site even with an EN60309-2 connection.

*Other Connections*
French – 2-pin, plus earth socket. Adaptors available from UK caravan accessory shops.

German – 2-pin, plus 2 earth strips, found in Norway and Sweden and possibly still Germany.

Switzerland - 3-pin, but not the same shape as UK 3-pin. Adapters available to purchase in Switzerland. Most campsites using the Swiss 3-pin will have adaptors available for hire or to borrow.

If the campsite does not have a modern EN60309-2 (CEE17) supply, ask to see the electrical protection for the socket outlet. If there is a device marked with IDn = 30mA, then the risk is minimised.

## Hooking Up to the Mains

*Connection*
Connection should always be made in the following order:

- Check your outfit isolating switch is at 'off'.

- Uncoil the connecting cable from the drum. A coiled cable with current flowing through it may overheat. Take your cable and insert the connector (female end) into your outfit inlet.

- Insert the plug (male end) into the site outlet socket.

- Switch outfit isolating switch to 'on'.

- Use a polarity tester in one of the 13A sockets in the outfit to check all connections are correctly wired. Never leave it in the socket. Some caravans have these devices built in as standard.

It is recommended that the supply is not used if the polarity is incorrect (see Reversed Polarity overleaf).

If you are in any doubt of the safety of the system, if you don't receive electricity once connected or if the supply stops then contact the site staff.

If the fault is found to be with your outfit then call a qualified electrician rather than trying to fix the problem yourself.

To ensure your safety you should never use an electrical system which you can't confirm to be safe. Use a mains tester such as the one shown above to test the electrical supply. Always check that a proper earth connection exists before using the electrics. Please note that these testers may not pick up all earth faults so if there is any doubt as to the integrity of the earth system do not use the electrical supply.

*Disconnection*

- Switch your outfit isolating switch to 'off'.
- At the site supply socket withdraw the plug.
- Disconnect the cable from your outfit.

Motorhomes – if leaving your pitch during the day, don't leave your mains cable plugged into the site supply, as this creates a hazard if the exposed live connections in the plug are touched or if the cable is not seen during grass-cutting.

## Reversed Polarity

Even if the site connector meets European Standard EN60309-2 (CEE17), British caravanners are still likely to encounter the problem known as reversed polarity. This is where the site supply 'live' line connects to the outfit's 'neutral' and vice versa. You should always check the polarity immediately on connection, using a polarity tester available from caravan accessory shops. If polarity is reversed the caravan mains electricity should not be used. Try using another nearby socket instead. Frequent travellers to the Continent can make up an adaptor themselves, or ask an electrician to make one for you, with the live and neutral wires reversed. Using a reversed polarity socket will probably not affect how an electrical appliance works, however your protection is greatly reduced. For example, a lamp socket may still be live as you touch it while replacing a blown bulb, even if the light switch is turned off.

## Shaver Sockets

Most campsites provide shaver sockets with a voltage of 220V or 110V. Using an incorrect voltage may cause the shaver to become

# Site Hooking Up Adaptor

ADAPTATEUR DE PRISE AU SITE (SECTEUR)
CAMPINGPLATZ-ANSCHLUSS (NETZ)

EXTENSION LEAD TO CARAVAN
Câble de rallonge à la caravane
Verläengerungskabel zum wohnwagen

SITE OUTLET
Prise du site
Campingplatz-Steckdose

MAINS ADAPTOR
Adaptateur Secteur
Netzanschlußstacker

16A 230V AC

hot or break. The 2-pin adaptor available in the UK may not fit Continental sockets so it is advisable to buy 2-pin adaptors on the Continent. Many modern shavers will work on a range of voltages which make them suitable for travelling abroad. Check you instruction manual to see if this is the case.

## Gas – General Advice

Gas usage can be difficult to predict as so many factors, such as temperature and how often you eat out, can affect the amount you need. As a rough guide allow 0.45kg of gas a day for normal summer usage.

With the exception of Campingaz, LPG cylinders normally available in the UK cannot be exchanged abroad. If possible, take enough gas with you and bring back the empty cylinders. Always check how many you can take with you as ferry and tunnel operators may restrict the number of cylinders you are permitted to carry for safety reasons.

The wide availability of Campingaz across Europe means it is worth considering using it while touring overseas. However, prices can vary from country to country, and maximum cylinder sizes are quite limited (2.75kg of gas in a 907 cylinder), making it less practical for routine use in larger vehicles with several gas appliances. A Campingaz adapter is relatively inexpensive, though, and is widely available in the UK.

If you are touring in cold weather conditions use propane gas instead of butane. Many other brands of gas are available in different countries and, as long as you have the correct regulator, adaptor and hose and the cylinders fit in your gas locker these local brands can also be used.

Gas cylinders are now standardised with a pressure of 30mbar for both butane and propane within the EU. On UK-specification caravans and motorhomes (2004 models and later) a 30mbar regulator suited to both propane and butane use is fitted to the bulkhead of the gas locker. This is connected to the cylinder with a connecting hose (and sometimes an adaptor) to suit different brands or types of gas. Older outfits and some foreign-built ones may use a cylinder-mounted regulator, which may need to be changed to suit different brands or types of gas.

*Warnings:*

- Refilling gas cylinders intended to be exchanged is against the law in most countries, however you may still find that some sites and dealers will offer to refill cylinders for you. Never take them up on this service as it can be dangerous; the cylinders haven't been designed for user-refilling and it is possible to overfill them with catastrophic consequences.

- Regular servicing of gas appliances is important as a faulty appliance can emit carbon monoxide, which could prove fatal. Check your vehicle or appliance handbook for service recommendations.

- Never use a hob or oven as a space heater.

The Caravan Club publishes a range of technical leaflets for its members including detailed advice on the use of electricity and gas – you can request copies or see www.caravanclub.co.uk/advice-and-training.

# Safety and Security

EU countries have good legislation in place to protect your safety wherever possible. However accidents and crime will still occur and taking sensible precautions can help to minimise your risk of being involved.

## Beaches, Lakes and Rivers

Check for any warning signs or flags before you swim and ensure that you know what they mean. Check the depth of water before diving and avoid diving or jumping into murky water as submerged objects may not be visible. Familiarise yourself with the location of safety apparatus and/or lifeguards.

Use only the designated areas for swimming, watersports and boating and always use life jackets where appropriate. Watch out for tides, undertows, currents and wind strength and direction before you or your children swim in the sea. This applies in particular when using inflatables, windsurfing equipment, body boards, kayaks or sailing boats. Sudden changes of wave and weather conditions combined with fast tides and currents are particularly dangerous.

## Campsite Safety

Once you've settled in, take a walk around the site to familiarise yourself with its layout and locate the nearest safety equipment. Ensure that children know their way around and where your pitch is.

Natural disasters are rare, but always think about what could happen. A combination of heavy rain and a riverside pitch could lead to flash flooding, for example, so make yourself aware of site evacuation procedures.

Be aware of sources of electricity and cabling on and around your pitch – electrical safety might not be up to the same standards as in the UK.

Poison for rodent control is sometimes used on sites or surrounding farmland. Warning notices are not always posted and you are strongly advised to check if staying on a rural site with dogs or children.

Incidents of theft on campsites are rare but when leaving your caravan unattended make sure you lock all doors and shut windows. Conceal valuables from sight and lock bicycles to a tree or to your caravan.

*Hintersee – Bavaria, Germany*

*Children*

Watch out for children as you drive around the site and don't exceed walking pace.

Children's play areas are generally unsupervised. Check which are suitable for your children's ages and abilities and agree with them which ones they may use. Read and respect the displayed rules. Remember it is your responsibility to know where your children are at all times.

Be aware of any campsite rules concerning ball games or use of play equipment, such as roller blades and skateboards. When your children attend organised activities, arrange when and where to meet afterwards.

Make sure that children are aware of any places where they should not go and never leave children alone inside a caravan.

*Fire*

Fire prevention is important on sites, as fire can spread quickly between outfits. The following fire safety measures should be followed:

- Don't use portable paraffin or gas heaters inside your caravan. Gas heaters should only be fitted when air is taken from outside the caravan.

- Don't change your gas cylinder inside the caravan. If you smell gas (or in the event of a fire starting), turn off the cylinder immediately, extinguish all naked flames and seek professional help.

- Know where the fire points and telephones are on site and know the site fire drill. Establish a family fire drill. Make sure everyone knows how to call the emergency services.

- Where site rules permit the use of barbecues, take the following precautions to prevent fire:

- Never locate a barbecue near trees or hedges. Have a bucket of water to hand in case of sparks.

- Only use recommended fire-lighting materials.

- Do not leave a barbecue unattended when lit and dispose of hot ash safely.

- Never take a barbeque into an enclosed area or awning – even when cooling they continue to release carbon monoxide which can lead to fatal poisoning.

## Swimming Pools

Familiarize yourself with the pool area before you venture in for a swim, especially if you're travelling with children. Check the pool layout – identify shallow and deep ends and the location of safety equipment. Check the gradient of the pool bottom as pools which shelve off sharply can catch weak or non-swimmers unawares.

Never dive or jump into a pool without knowing the depth – if there is a no diving rule it usually means the pool isn't deep enough for safe diving.

For pools with a supervisor or lifeguard, note any times or dates when the pool is not supervised, e.g. lunch breaks or in low season. Read safety notices and rules posted around the pool.

## On the Road

Do not leave valuables on car seats or on view in caravans, even if they are locked. Ensure that items on roof racks or cycle carriers are locked securely.

Beware of a 'snatch' through open car windows at traffic lights, filling stations or in traffic jams. When driving through towns and cities keep your doors locked. Keep handbags, valuables and documents out of sight at all times.

Stowaways in vehicles can be a problem on ferries and Eurotunnel, so check that your outfit is free from unexpected guests at the last practical opportunity before boarding.

If flagged down by another motorist for whatever reason, take care that your own car is locked and windows closed while you check outside, even if someone is left inside.

Be particularly careful on long, empty stretches of motorway and when you stop for fuel. Even if the people flagging you down appear to be officials (e.g. wearing yellow reflective jackets or dark, 'uniform-type' clothing) show presence of mind and lock yourselves in immediately. They may appear to be friendly and helpful, but could be opportunistic thieves. Have a mobile phone to hand and, if necessary, be seen to use it.

Road accidents are a significant risk in some countries where traffic laws may be inadequately enforced, roads may be poorly maintained, road signs and lighting inadequate, and driving standards poor. It's a good idea to keep a fully-charged mobile phone with you in your car with the number of your breakdown organisation saved into it.

## Overnight Stops

Overnight stops should always be at campsites and not at motorway service areas, ferry terminal car parks, petrol station forecourts or isolated 'aires de services' or 'aires de repos' on motorways where robberies and muggings are occasionally reported. If you decide to use these areas for a rest then take appropriate precautions, for example, shutting all windows, securing locks and making a thorough external check of your vehicle(s) before departing. Safeguard your property, e.g. handbags, while out of the caravan and beware of approaches by strangers.

For a safer place to take a break, there is a wide network of 'Stellplätze', 'Aires de Services', 'Aree di Sosta' and 'Áreas de Servicio' in cities, towns and villages across Europe, many specifically for motorhomes with good security and overnight facilities. It is rare that you will be the only vehicle staying on such areas, but avoid any that are isolated, take sensible precautions and trust your instincts. For example, if the area appears run down and there are groups of people hanging around who seem intimidating, then you are probably wise to move on.

## Personal Security

Petty crime happens all over the world; however as a tourist you are more vulnerable to it. This shouldn't stop you from exploring new horizons, but there are a few sensible precautions you can take to minimise the risk.

- Leave valuables and jewellery at home. If you do take them, fit a small safe in your caravan or lock them in the boot of your car. Don't leave money or valuables in a car glovebox or on view. Don't leave bags in full view when sitting outside at cafés or restaurants, or leave valuables unattended on the beach.

- When walking be security-conscious. Avoid unlit streets at night, walk away from the kerb edge and carry handbags or shoulder bags on the side away from the kerb. The less of a tourist you appear, the less of a target you are.

- Keep a separate note of your holiday insurance details and emergency telephone numbers.

- Beware of pickpockets in crowded areas, at tourist attractions and in cities, and be cautious of bogus plain-clothes policemen who may ask to see your foreign currency or credit cards and passport. If approached, decline to show your money or to hand over your passport but ask for credentials and offer instead to go to the nearest police station.

- Laws and punishment vary from country to country so make yourself aware of anything which may affect you before you travel. Be especially careful on laws involving alcohol consumption (such as drinking in public areas), and never buy or use illegal drugs abroad.

- Respect Customs regulations - smuggling is a serious offence and can carry heavy penalties. Do not carry parcels or luggage through Customs for other people and do not cross borders with people you do not know in your vehicle, such as hitchhikers.

The Foreign & Commonwealth Office produces a range of material to advise and inform British citizens travelling abroad about issues affecting their safety - www.gov.uk/foreign-travel-advice has country specific guides.

## Money Security

We would rarely walk around at home carrying large amounts of cash, but as you may not have the usual access to bank accounts and credit cards you are more likely to do so on holiday. You are also less likely to have the same degree of security when online banking as you would in your own home. The following precautions are sensible to keep your money safe:

- Carry only the minimum amount of cash and don't rely on one person to carry everything. Never carry a wallet in your back pocket. Moneybelts are the most secure way to carry cash and passports.
- Keep a separate note of bank account and credit/debit card numbers. Carry your credit card issuer/bank's 24-hour UK contact number with you.
- Be careful when using cash machines (ATMs) – try to use a machine in an area with high footfall and don't allow yourself to be distracted. Put your cash away before moving away from the cash machine.
- Always guard your PIN number, both at cash machines and when using your card to pay in shops and restaurants. Never let your card out of your sight while paying.

- If using internet banking do not leave the PC or mobile device unattended and make sure you log out fully at the end of the session.

## British Consular Services Abroad

British Embassy and Consular staff offer practical advice, assistance and support to British travellers abroad. They can, for example, issue replacement passports, help Britons who have been the victims of crime, contact relatives and friends in the event of an accident, illness or death, provide information about transferring funds and provide details of local lawyers, doctors and interpreters. But there are limits to their powers and a British

Consul cannot, for example, give legal advice, intervene in court proceedings, put up bail, pay for legal or medical bills, or for funerals or the repatriation of bodies, or undertake work more properly done by banks, motoring organisations and travel insurers.

If you are charged with a serious offence, insist on the British Consul being informed. You will be contacted as soon as possible by a Consular Officer who can advise on local procedures, provide access to lawyers and insist that you are treated as well as nationals of the country which is holding you. However, they cannot get you released as a matter of course. British and Irish embassy contact details can be found in the Country Introduction chapters.

# Continental Campsites

The quantity and variety of sites across Europe means you're sure to find one that suits your needs – from full facilities and entertainment to quiet rural retreats. If you haven't previously toured outside of the UK you may notice some differences, such as pitches being smaller or closer together. In hot climates hard ground may make putting up awnings difficult.

Facilities will vary from site to site – in this guide the site listings will give you a good idea of what you can expect to find on each site. In the high season all campsite facilities are usually open, however bear in mind that toilet and shower facilities may be busy. Out of season some facilities such as shops and swimming pools may be closed and office opening hours may be reduced. If the site has very low occupancy the sanitary facilities may be reduced to a few unisex toilet and shower cubicles.

## Booking a Campsite

To save the hassle of arriving to find a site full it is best to book in advance, especially in high season. If you don't book ahead arrive no later than 4pm (earlier at popular resorts) to secure a pitch, after this time sites fill up quickly.

You also need to allow time to find another campsite if your first choice is fully booked.

You can usually book directly via a campsite's website using a credit or debit card to pay a deposit if required. Please be aware that some sites regard the deposit as a booking or admin fee and will not deduct the amount from your final bill.

## Overseas Travel Service

The Caravan Club's Travel Service offers Club members an overseas site booking service to over 200 campsites in Europe. Full details of these sites plus information on Ferry special offers and Red Pennant Overseas Holiday Insurance can be found in the Club's Continental Caravanning brochure – call 01342 327410 to request a copy or visit www.caravanclub.co.uk/overseas.

Overseas Site Booking Service sites are marked 'SBS' in the site listings. Many of them can be booked at www.caravanclub.co.uk. The Caravan Club cannot make advance reservations for any other campsites listed in this guide. Only those sites marked SBS have been inspected by Caravan Club staff.

## Camping Cheques

The Caravan Club operates a low season scheme in association with Camping Cheques, offering flexible holidays. The scheme covers approximately 635 sites in 29 countries.

Camping Cheques are supplied as part of a package which includes return ferry fare and a minimum of seven Camping Cheques. Those sites which feature in the Camping Cheques scheme and which are listed in this guide are marked 'CChq' in their site entries. For full details of the Camping Cheque scheme visit www.caravanclub.co.uk/campingcheques.

## Caravan Storage Abroad

Storing your caravan on a site in Europe can be a great way to avoid a long tow and to save on ferry and fuel costs. Even sites which don't offer a specific long-term storage facility may be willing to negotiate a price to store your caravan for you.

Before you leave your caravan in storage abroad always check whether your insurance covers this, as many policies don't. If you aren't covered then look for a specialist policy - Towergate Bakers (tel: 0800 4961516 or www.towergatebakers.co.uk) or K Drewe Insurance (tel: 0845 408 5929 or www.lookinsuranceservices.co.uk) both offer policies.

## Facilities and Site Description

All of the site facilities shown in the site listings of this guide have been taken from member reports, as have the comments at the end of each site entry. Please remember that opinions and expectations can differ significantly from one person to the next.

The year of report is indicated at the end of each site listing – sites which haven't been reported on for a few years may have had significant changes to their prices, facilities, opening dates and standards. It is always best to check any specific details you need to know before travelling by contacting the site or looking at their website.

### Sanitary Facilities

Facilities normally include toilet and shower blocks with shower cubicles, wash basins and razor sockets. In site listings the abbreviation 'wc' indicates that the site has the kind of toilets we are used to in the UK (pedestal style). Some sites have footplate 'squat' toilets and, where this is known, you will see the abbreviation 'cont', i.e. continental. European sites do not always provide sink plugs, toilet paper or soap so take them with you.

*Waste Disposal*

Site entries show (when known) where a campsite has a chemical disposal and/or a motorhome service point, which is assumed to include a waste (grey) water dump station and toilet cassette-emptying point. Use of the site facilities is very common on continental sites, meaning you may find fewer waste water disposal facilities.

Chemical disposal points may be fixed at a high level requiring lifting of cassettes in order to empty them. Disposal may simply be down a toilet. Wastemaster-style emptying points are not very common in Europe. Formaldehyde chemical cleaning products are banned in many countries. In Germany the 'Blue Angel' (Blaue Engel) Standard, and in the Netherlands the 'Milieukeur' Standard, indicates that the product has particularly good environmental credentials.

## Finding a Campsite

Directions are given for all campsites listed in this guide and most listings also include GPS co-ordinates. Where known full street addresses are also given. The directions have been supplied by member reports and haven't been checked in detail by The Club.

For information about using sat nav to find a site see the Motoring Equipment section.

## Overnight Stops

Towns and villages across Europe may provide dedicated overnight or short stay areas specifically for motorhomes, usually with security, electricity, water and waste facilities. These are known as 'Aires de Services', 'Stellplatz' or 'Aree di Sosta' and are usually well signposted with a motorhome icon.

Many campsites in popular tourist areas will also have separate overnight areas of hardstanding with facilities often just outside the main campsite area. There are guidebooks available which list just these overnight stops, Vicarious books publish an English guide to the Aires including directions, GPS co-ordinates and photographs. Please contact 0131 208 333 or visit their website www.vicariousbooks.co.uk.

For security reasons you shouldn't spend the night on petrol station service areas, ferry terminal car parks or isolated 'aires de repos' or 'aires de services' along motorways.

## Municipal Campsites

Municipal sites are found in towns and villages all over Europe, in particular in France. Once very basic, many have improved in standard in recent years – although you may still find some which are outdated. You can book through the local town halls or tourism office. When approaching a town you may find that municipal sites are not always named and signposts may simply state 'Camping' or show a tent or caravan symbol.

You may sometimes find that these sites are used by seasonal workers, market traders and travellers in low season – where sites try to discourage these visitors you may find that twin-axle or very large caravans aren't accepted or are charged at a much higher rate. If you may be affected check for any restrictions when you book.

## Naturist Campsites

Some naturist sites are included in this guide and are shown with the word 'naturist' after their site name. Those marked 'part naturist' have separate areas for naturists. Visitors to naturist sites aged 16 and over usually require an INF card or Naturist Licence - covered by membership of British Naturism (tel 01604 620361 or www.british-naturism.org.uk).

Alternatively, holiday membership is available on arrival at any recognised naturist site (a passport-size photograph is required). When looking for a site you will find that naturist campsites generally display the initials FNF, INF or FKK on their signs.

## Opening Dates and times

Opening dates (where known) are given for campsites in this guide. However sites may close without notice due to refurbishment work, a lack of visitors or bad weather. Outside the high season it is always best to contact campsites in advance, even if the site advertises itself as open all year.

Most sites will close their gates or barriers overnight – if you are planning to arrive late or are delayed on your journey you should call ahead to make sure you will be able to gain access to the site. There may be a late arrivals area outside of the barriers where you can pitch overnight. Motorhomers should also consider barrier closing times if leaving site in your vehicle for the evening.

Check out time is usually between 10am and 12 noon – advise staff if you will have to leave the site very early for any reason to make sure you can check out before you leave. Sites may also close for an extended lunch break, so if you're planning to arrive or check out around lunchtime check that the office will be open.

## Pets on Campsites

Well behaved dogs are welcome on many sites, although you may have to prove that all of their vaccinations are up to date before they are allowed onto the site. Certain breeds of dogs are banned in some countries and other breeds will need to be muzzled and kept on a lead at all times. A list of breeds with restrictions by country can be found at www.caravanclub.co.uk/pets.

Sites usually charge for dogs and may limit the number allowed per pitch. On arrival make yourself aware of site rules regarding dogs, such as keeping them on a lead, muzzling them or not leaving them unattended in your outfit.

In popular tourist areas local regulations may ban dogs from beaches during the summer. Some dogs may find it difficult to cope with prolonged periods of hot weather if they are used to UK weather. Also watch out for diseases transmitted by ticks, caterpillars, mosquitoes or sandflies to which dogs from the UK have no natural resistance. Consult your vet about preventative treatment before you travel.

Visitors to southern Spain and Portugal, parts of central France and northern Italy should be aware of the danger of Pine Processionary Caterpillars from mid-winter to late spring. Dogs should be kept away from pine trees if possible or fitted with a muzzle that prevents the nose and mouth from touching the ground. This will also protect against poisoned bait sometimes used by farmers and hunters.

In the event that your pet is taken ill abroad a campsite should have information about local vets.

Most European countries require dogs to wear a collar identifying their owners at all times. If your dog goes missing, report the matter to the local police and the local branch of that country's animal welfare organisation.

See the Documents section of this book for more information about the Pet Travel Scheme.

## Prices

Campsite prices per night (for an outfit and two adults) are shown in the site entries. If you stay on site after midday you may be charged for an extra day. Many campsites have a minimum amount for credit card transactions, meaning they can't be used to pay for overnight or short stays. Check which methods of payment are accepted when you check in.

Sites with automatic barriers may ask for a deposit for a swipe card to operate it.

Sites may impose extra charges for the use of facilities such as swimming pools, showers or laundry facilities. You may also be charged extra for dogs, Wi-Fi, tents and extra cars. Often campsites have a daily discounted charge for children, other sites will charge a fixed rate per person, regardless of age.

## Registering on Arrival

Local authority requirements mean you will usually have to produce an identity document on arrival, which will be retained by the site until you check out. If you don't want to leave you passport with reception then most sites will accept a camping document such as the Camping Key Europe (CKE) or Camping Card International (CCI) - if this is known site entries are marked CKE/CCI.

CKE are available for Caravan Club members to purchase by calling 01342 336633 or are free to members if you take out the 'motoring' level of cover from the Club's Red Pennant Overseas Holiday Insurance.

## General Advice

If you've visiting a new site see if it is possible to take a look round the site and facilities before booking in. If your pitch is allocated at check in ask to see it first to check the condition and access, as marked or hedged pitches can sometimes be difficult for large outfits. Riverside pitches can be very scenic but keep an eye on the water level; in periods of heavy rain this may rise rapidly.

*Campsite overlooking Geirangerfjord in Norway*

A tourist tax, eco tax and/or rubbish tax may be imposed by local authorities in some European countries. VAT may also be payable on top of your campsite fees.

Speed limits on campsites are usually restricted to 10 km/h (6 mph). You may be asked to park your car in a separate area away from your caravan, particularly in the high season.

The use of the term 'statics' in the campsite reports in this guide may to long-term seasonal pitches, chalets, cottages, tour operators' fixed tents and cabins, as well as mobile homes.

## Complaints

If a situation arises where you want to make a complaint, take it up with site staff or owners at the time. It is much better to make staff aware of a problem while something could be done to rectify the situation for the rest of your stay than to complain once you are home.

The Caravan Club has no control or influence over day to day campsite operations or administration of the sites listed in this guide. Therefore we aren't able to intervene in any dispute you should have with a campsite, unless the booking has been made through our Site Booking Service - see listings marked 'SBS' for sites we are able to book for you.

## Campsite Groups

Across Europe there are many 'groups' or 'chains' of with sites in various locations all with the same owner. While you may find that sites within a group can be slightly more expensive than independent sites, there are also many benefits to choosing a group campsite.

You will generally find that group sites will be consistent in their format and the quality and variety of facilities they offer. If you liked one site you can be fairly confident that you will like other sites within the same group.

If you're looking for a full facility site, with swimming pools, play areas, bars and restaurants on site you're likely to find these on sites which are part of a group. You might even find organised excursions and activities such as archery on site.

# Austria
## Country Introduction

*Vienna, Austria*

## Welcome to Austria

With breathtaking Alpine scenery, snow-capped mountains and beautiful Habsburg architecture, Austria is a great place to explore and perfect for a walking holiday.

Popular all year round with tourists and sports enthusiasts, the country offers lots of choice and variety. Visit modern cities full of art galleries and culture, or pretty traditional towns with picturesque houses and winding streets.

## Country highlights

Austrian cuisine takes influences from neighbouring Germany and Italy, with hearty stews and snitzel being traditional fare. Typical dishes include Snitzels and hearty soups and stews. Pastries are also a large feature of Austrian meals, with lots of different varieties of sweet or savoury strudels.

Austria holds the most important Schubert festival in the world, the Schubertiade. Attracting culture lovers from far and wide, it is held in Schwarzenberg and Hohenems and has over 70 events.

## Major towns and cities

- Vienna – this historic city is rich in beautiful architecture.
- Linz – a cultural city home to vibrant music and arts.
- Villach – an enchanting Alpine town with a historical centre.
- Innsbruck – an internationally renowned winter sports centre.

## Attractions

- Kunsthistorisches Museum – a fine arts museum full of important antiquities.
- Mariendom Linz – a gothic inspired church with an extraordinary stained glass window.
- Schlossberg Park – a beautiful mountain-top park with stunning views.
- Salzburg's Old Town – teeming with galleries and restaurants.

## Find out more

www.austria.info

Tel: 0043 (0)1 58 86 60 Austrian National Tourist Office

# Country Information

*Population (approx):* 8.2 million

*Capital:* Vienna (population approx 1.7 million)

*Area:* 83,8758 sq km

*Bordered by:* Czech Republic, Germany, Hungary, Italy, Liechtenstein, Slovakia, Slovenia, Switzerland

*Terrain:* Mountainous in south and west; flat or gently sloping in extreme north and east

*Climate:* Temperate; cold winters with frequent rain in the lowlands and snow in the mountains; moderate summers, sometimes very hot

*Highest Point:* Grossglockner 3,798m

*Language:* German

*Local Time:* GMT or BST + 1, i.e. 1 hour ahead of the UK all year

*Currency:* Euros divided into 100 cents
£1 = €1.26, €1 = £0.79 (September 2014)

*Telephoning:* From the UK dial 0043 for Austria and omit the initial zero of the area code of the number you are calling.

*Emergency numbers:* Police 133; Fire brigade 122; Ambulance 144, or dial 112 for any service (operators speak English).

*Public Holidays 2015:* Jan 1, 6; Apr 6; May 14, 25; Jun 4; Aug 15; Oct 26 (National Day); Nov 1; Dec 8, 25, 26.

School summer holidays last the whole of July, August and early September

# Camping and Caravanning

There are approximately 500 campsites in Austria around 150 campsites of which are open all year, mostly in or near to ski resorts.

Casual/wild camping is not encouraged and is prohibited in Vienna, in the Tyrol and in forests and nature reserves. Permission to park a caravan should be obtained in advance from the owners of private land, or from the local town hall or police station in the case of common land or state property.

# Cycling

There is an extensive network of cycle routes, following dedicated cycle and footpaths, such as the 360 km cycle lane that follows the Danube.

Many cities encourage cyclists with designated cycle lanes. A Citybike hire scheme operates in Vienna from more than 60 rental offices situated close to underground/metro stations. For more information see www.citybikewien.at or telephone 0810 500500 in Austria. There are eight signposted mountain bike routes between 10 and 42 kilometres long in the Vienna woods. Cycle helmets are compulsory for children under 12 years, or 15 years in Lower Austria (Niederösterreich).

Bikes may be carried on the roof or rear of a car. When carried at the rear, the width must not extend beyond the width of the vehicle, and the rear lights and number plate must be visible.

# Electricity and Gas

Current on campsites varies between 4 and 16 amps.

Plugs have two round pins and most campsites have CEE connections. Electricity points tend to be in locked boxes, so you will need to check polarity on arrival before the box is locked. Arrangements also need to be made for the box to be unlocked if making an early departure.

Some sites in Austria make a one-off charge for connection to the electricity supply, which is then metered at a rate per kilowatt hour (kwh) The full range of Campingaz cylinders is widely available.

# Entry Formalities

There are no identity checks at the borders with EU countries or Switzerland nor are there Customs controls with EU countries. Checks on goods may still be carried out at the border with Switzerland.

British and Irish passport holders may stay in Austria for up to three months without a visa. Visitors arriving at a campsite or hotel must complete a registration form.

# Medical Services

Minor matters can be dealt with by staff at pharmacies (apotheke). Pharmacies operate a rota system for out of hours access; when closed a notice is often displayed giving the addresses of the nearest open pharmacies.

Free treatment is available from doctors and hospital outpatient departments as long as the doctor is contracted to the local health insurance office (Gebietskrankenkasse). To be covered for hospital treatment you will need a doctor's referral. In-patient treatment will incur a daily non-refundable charge for the first 28 days.
Only a limited amount of dental treatment is covered under the state healthcare system. You will need to present your European Health Insurance Card (EHIC) to receive treatment.

## Opening Hours

Banks – Mon-Fri 8am-12.30pm & 1.30pm-3pm (5.30pm Thu), main branches don't close for lunch; closed Sat/Sun.

Museums – Mon-Fri 10am-6pm (summer), 9am-4pm (winter); Sat, Sun & public holidays 9am-6pm.

Post Offices – Mon-Fri 8am-12pm & 2pm-6pm; city post offices don't close for lunch; in some towns open Sat 9am-12pm.

Shops – Mon-Fri 8am-6pm; some open until 7.30pm Thu; some close 12pm-2pm for lunch; Sat 8am-5pm.

## Safety and Security

Most visits to Austria are trouble-free, but visitors should take sensible precautions to avoid becoming a victim of crime at crowded tourist sites and around major railway stations and city centre parks after dark. Pickpockets and muggers operate in and around the city centre of Vienna.

Drivers, especially on the autobahns in Lower Austria, should be wary of bogus plain clothes police officers. In all traffic-related matters police officers will be in uniform and unmarked vehicles will have a flashing sign in the rear window which reads 'Stopp –Polizei – Folgen'. If in any doubt contact the police on the emergency number 133 or 112 and ask for confirmation. The winter sports season lasts from December to March, or the end of May in higher regions. If you plan to ski contact the Austrian National Tourist Office in London for advice on conditions before travelling, and take local advice throughout your stay.

In most areas children under the age of 15 are legally required to wear a helmet when skiing.

*British Embassy*
JAURESGASSE 12
1030 VIENNA
Tel: (01) 716130
http://ukinaustria.fco.gov.uk/en/
viennaconsularenquiries@fco.gov.uk

There are also Honorary Consulates in Bregenz, Graz, Innsbruck and Salzburg.

*Irish Embassy*
ROTENTURMSTRASSE 16-18, 5th FLOOR
1010 VIENNA
Tel: (01) 7154246
www.embassyofireland.at
vienna@dfa.ie

## Documents

*Driving Licence*
If you hold a UK driving licence which does not bear your photograph you should carry your passport as further proof of identity, or obtain a photocard licence.
*Passport*
You are advised to carry your passport or photocard licence at all times.
*Vehicle(s)*
You should carry your vehicle registration certificate (V5C), insurance details and MOT certificate.

## Money

Cash dispensers (Bankomaten) have instructions in English. Major credit cards are accepted by shops, restaurants, and petrol stations but not as widely as elsewhere in Europe. Small shops and supermarkets, restaurants and hotels may not accept them.

## Motoring in Austria
### Alcohol

The maximum permitted level of alcohol in the bloodstream is 0.049%, i.e. lower than that permitted in the UK. Penalties for exceeding this limit are severe. A lower limit of virtually zero applies to drivers who have held a full driving licence for less than two years.

# Breakdown Service

The motoring organisation, ÖAMTC, operates a breakdown service 24 hours a day on all roads. The emergency number is 120 throughout the country from a land line or mobile phone. Motorists pay a set fee, which is higher at night; towing charges also apply. Payment by credit card is accepted.

Members of AIT and FIA affiliated clubs, such as The Caravan Club, qualify for reduced charges on presentation of a valid Club membership card.

# Essential Equipment

*First aid kit*
All vehicles must carry a first aid kit kept in a strong, dirt-proof box.

*Warning Triangle*
An EU approved warning triangle must be used if the vehicle breaks down, has a puncture or is involved in an accident.

*Lights*
Dipped headlights must be used in poor visibility or bad weather. Headlight flashing is used as a warning of approach, not as an indication that a driver is giving way.

*Reflective Jackets/Waistcoats*
If your vehicle breaks down or you are in an accident you must wear a reflective jacket or waistcoat when getting out of your vehicle (compliant with EU Standard EN471). This includes when setting up a warning triangle. It is also recommended that a passenger who leaves the vehicle, for example, to assist with a repair, should also wear one. Keep the jackets within easy reach inside your vehicle, not in the boot.

*Child Restraint System*
Children under 14 years of age and less than 1.5 metres in height must use a suitable child restraint system for their height and weight when travelling in the front and rear of a vehicle. Children under 14 years aren't allowed to travel in two seater sports cars.

Children under 14 years of age but over 1.35 metres are allowed to use a 3-point seat belt without a special child seat, as long as the seat belt does not cut across the child's throat or neck.

*Winter Driving*
From 1 November to 15 April vehicles, including those registered abroad, must be fitted with winter tyres marked M&S (mud & snow) on all wheels when there is snow or ice on the road. Snow chains are allowed on roads fully covered by snow or ice, as long as road surfaces will not be damaged by the chains. The maximum recommended speed for vehicles with snow chains is generally 50 km/h.

Between 15 November to 15 March vehicles weighing over 3500kg are required to have winter tyres on at least one of the driving axles, regardless of the road conditions. They must also carry snow chains, and use them where road signs indicate that they are compulsory.

It is the driver's legal responsibility to carry the required winter equipment; therefore, it is essential to check that it is included in any hire car.

# Fuel

Most petrol stations are open from 8am to 8pm. Motorway service stations and some petrol stations in larger cities stay open 24 hours. Fuel is normally cheaper at self-service filling stations.

LPG (flüssiggas) is available at a limited number of outlets – a list should be available on www.oeamtc.at.

# Parking

Regulations on the parking of motorhomes and caravans vary according to region, but restrictions apply in areas protected for their natural beauty or landscape and beside lakes.

A zigzag line marked on the road indicates that parking is prohibited. Blue lines indicate a blue zone (Kurzparkzone) where parking is restricted to a period for up to two hours and you need to purchase a voucher (Parkschein) from a local shop, bank or petrol station.

Most cities have 'Pay and Display' machines, parking meters or parking discs, and in main tourist areas the instructions are in English. Illegally-parked cars may be impounded or clamped. Large areas of Vienna are pedestrianised and parking places are limited. However, there are several underground car parks in Vienna District 1.

## Priority

Outside built-up areas, road signs on main roads indicate where traffic has priority or if there are no signs priority is given to traffic from the right.

Buses have priority when leaving a bus stop. Do not overtake school buses with flashing yellow lights which have stopped to let children on and off. Trams have priority even if coming from the left.

In heavy traffic, drivers must not enter an intersection unless their exit is clear, even if they have priority or if the lights are green.

## Roads

Austria has a well developed and engineered network of roads classified as: federal motorways (A roads), expressways (S' roads), provincial (B roads) and local (L roads). There are over 2180km of motorways and expressways.

## Road Signs and Markings

Most signs conform to international usage. The following are exceptions:

Diversions

Street lights not on all night

Tram turns at yellow or red

You may be stopped and fined in Austria for using roads that prohibit trailers and caravans. This is indicated by the below sign:

If there is an additional sign which shows a weight limit, then this indicates the maximum gross vehicle weight of the trailer. You can also find these signs with a length limit.

Some other signs that are also in use which you may find useful Include:

| Austrian | English Translation |
|---|---|
| Abblendlicht | Dipped headlights |
| Alle richtungen | All directions |
| Bauarbeiten | Roadworks |
| Durchfahrt verboten | No through traffic |
| Einbahn | One-way street |
| Fussgänger | Pedestrians |
| Beschrankung für halten oder parken | Stopping or parking restricted |
| Lawinen gefahr | Avalanche danger |
| Links einbiegen | Turn left |
| Raststätte | Raststätte |
| Raststätte Rechts einbiegen | Turn right |
| Strasse gesperrt | Road closed |
| Überholen verboten | No passing |
| Umleitung | Detour |

## Speed Limits

|  | Open Road (km/h) | Motorway (km/h) |
|---|---|---|
| Car Solo | 100 | 130 |
| Car towing caravan/trailer | 80 | 100 |
| Motorhome under 3500kg | 100 | 130 |
| Motorhome 3500-7500kg | 70 | 80 |

*Exceptions*

If the total combined weight of a car and caravan outfit or a motorhome exceeds 3,500 kg the speed limit on motorways is reduced to 80 km/h (50 mph) and on other roads outside built-up areas to 70 km/h (43 mph).

On motorways where the speed limit for solo vehicles is 130 km/h (81 mph) overhead message signs may restrict speed to 100 km/h (62 mph). Between 10pm and 5am solo cars are restricted to 110 km/h (68 mph) on the A10 (Tauern), A12 (Inntal), A13 (Brenner) and A14

(Rheintal). There is a general speed limit of 60 km/h (37 mph) on most roads in the Tyrol, unless indicated otherwise.

The minimum speed on motorways, as indicated by a rectangular blue sign depicting a white car, is 60 km/h (37 mph). A number of towns have a general speed limit of 30 km/h (18 mph), except where a higher speed limit is indicated.

## Traffic Lights

At traffic lights a flashing green light indicates the approach of the end of the green phase. An orange light combined with the red light indicates that the green phase is imminent.

## Traffic Jams

In recent years traffic has increased on the A1 from Vienna to the German border (the West Autobahn). There are usually queues at the border posts with Czech Republic, Slovakia and Hungary. As a result, traffic has also increased on the ring road around Vienna and on the A4 (Ost Autobahn).

Other bottlenecks occur on the A10 (Salzburg to Villach) before the Tauern and Katschberg tunnels, the A12 (Kufstein to Landeck) before the Perjen tunnel and before Landeck, and the A13 (Innsbruck to Brenner) between Steinach and the Italian border. Busy sections on other roads are the S35/S6 between Kirchdorf or Bruck an der Mur and the A9, the B320/E651 in the Schladming and Gröbming areas, and the B179 Fern Pass.

## Violation of Traffic Regulations

Police can impose and collect on-the-spot fines from drivers who violate traffic regulations. For higher fines you will be required to pay a deposit and the remainder within two weeks. An official receipt should be issued. A points system operates which applies to drivers of Austrian and foreign-registered vehicles.

## Motorways

Orange emergency telephones on motorways are 2 km to 3 km apart. A flashing orange light at the top of telephone posts indicates danger ahead.

Whenever congestion occurs on motorways and dual carriageways drivers are required to create an emergency corridor. Drivers in the left-hand lane must move as far over to the left as possible, and drivers in the central and right-hand lanes must move as far over to the right as possible to provide access for emergency vehicles.

*Motorway Tolls – Vehicles under 3,500 kg*
Drivers of vehicles under 3,500 kg using motorways and expressways (A and S roads) must purchase a motorway vignette (sticker). One vignette covers your caravan as well.

Vignettes may be purchased at all major border crossings into Austria and from OeAMTC offices, larger petrol stations and post offices in Austria. A two-month vignette is available for a car (with or without a trailer) or a motorhome at a cost of €24.80. Also available are a 10 day vignette at €8.50 and a one year vignette at €82.70 (2015 tariffs).

Failure to display a vignette incurs a fine of at least €120, plus the cost of the vignette. Credit cards or foreign currency may be used in payment. If you have visited Austria before, make sure you remove your old sticker.

There are special toll sections in Austria which are excluded from the vignette and where the toll needs to be paid at respective toll points. These include A10 Tauern tunnel, A13 Brenner motorway and S16 Alberg tunnel.

*Motorway Tolls – Vehicles over 3,500 kg*
Tolls for vehicles over 3,500 kg are calculated according to the number of axles and EURO emissions category and are collected electronically by means of a small box (called the GO-Box) fixed to your vehicle's windscreen. They are available for a one-off handling fee of €5 from around 220 points of sale – mainly petrol stations – along the primary road network in Austria and neighbouring countries, and at all major border crossing points.

You can pre-load a set amount onto your Go box or pay after you have travelled. Tolls are calculated according to the number of axles on a vehicle; those with two axles are charged between €0.162 and €0.208 per kilometre + 20% VAT, according to the vehicle's emissions rating.

Visit www.go-maut.at to register for the scheme. Telephone 0043 19551266 or email info@go-maut.at for help before you travel, or call 0800 40012400 (from Austria, Germany or Switzerland) or 00800 40012400 from the UK. Operators speak English.

This distance-related toll system does not apply to a car/caravan combination even if its total laden weight is over 3,500 kg, unless the laden weight of the towing vehicle itself exceeds that weight.

*Korridor Vignette*

A special vignette, the 'Korridor Vignette' is required on the A14 in the region of Bregenz. Vehicles up to 3,500 kg without a standard motorway vignette need this special vignette to drive along the 23 km stretch (corridor) between Hohenems (junction 23 on the A14) and Hörbranz (junction 1) at the German border. The vignette is available from petrol stations in the area and at the border and costs €2 for a single journey, €4 return. In addition, separate tolls are payable on many roads and tunnels in mountainous regions.

people travelling as a group by train can buy an Einfach-Raus-Ticket (ERT), which is good for a day's unlimited travel on all Austrian regional trains – see www.oebb.at (English option) for more information or ask at any station.

In Vienna there are travel concessions on public transport for senior citizens (show your passport as proof of age). Buy a ticket from a tobacconist or from a ticket machine in an underground station. Otherwise single tickets are available from vending machines in the vehicles themselves – have plenty of coins ready. Tickets are also available for periods of 24 and 72 hours. Children under six travel free and children under 15 travel free on Sundays, public holidays and during school holidays.

Car ferry services operate throughout the year on the River Danube, and hydrofoil and hovercraft services transport passengers from Vienna to Bratislava (Slovakia) and to Budapest (Hungary).

## Touring

Austria is divided into nine federal regions, namely Burgenland, Carinthia (Kärnten), Lower Austria (Niederösterreich), Salzburg, Styria (Steiermark), Tyrol (Tirol), Upper Austria (Oberösterreich), Vienna (Wien) and Voralberg.

A 10-15% service charge is included in restaurant bills, but it is customary to add a further 5% tip if satisfied with the service.

The Vienna Card offers unlimited free public transport and discounts at museums, restaurants, theatres and shops. The Card is valid for three days and is available from hotels, tourist information and public transport offices; see www.wienkarte.at.

A Salzburg Card and an Innsbruck Card are also available – see www.austria.info/uk or contact the Austrian National Tourist Office for more information.

## Public Transport & Local Travel

All major cities have efficient, integrated public transport systems including underground and light rail systems, trams and buses. Two to five

**ABERSEE** *B3* (1km N Rural) *47.74040, 13.40665* **Seecamping Primus, Schwand 39, 5342 Abersee [06227 3228; fax 32284; seecamping.primus@aon.at]** B158 fr St Gilgen to Strobl. After 3 km turn L. Camp is last but one. Med, mkd pitch, pt shd; wc; chem disp; baby facs; shwrs inc; el pnts (10A); lndtte (inc dryer); shops 300m; playgrnd; beach; sw; games area; wifi; bus 1km; twin axles; Eng spkn; quiet; CCI. "Very helpful owner; beautiful area nr shipping on lake; excel." 26 Apr-30 Sep. € 30.00                    2014*

**ABERSEE** *B3* (2km E Rural) *47.71336, 13.45138* **Camping Schönblick, Gschwendt 33, 5342 Abersee (Salzburg) [(06137) 7042; fax 704214; laimer.schoenblick@aon. at; www.camping-schoenblick.at]** Fr B158 at km 36 dir Schiffstation & site in 1km on L. Med, mkd pitch, pt sl, terr, some hdstg, pt shd; wc; chem disp; shwrs €0.80; el pnts (10A) €1.80; gas; lndtte; shop & 1km; tradsmn; rest, snacks 300m; lake sw adj; 40% statics; dogs €2; quiet; ccard acc; CKE/CCI. "Beautiful, friendly, family-run site nr lakeside opp St Wolfgang town; ferry stn; excel san facs but stretched at busy times; walks & cycle path fr site; vg site." 1 May-15 Oct. € 28.70                    2014*

**ABERSEE** *B3* (1km NW Rural) *47.73656, 13.43250* **Camping Wolfgangblick, Seestrasse 115, 5342 Abersee (Salzburg) [(06227) 3475; fax 3218; camping@wolfgangblick.at; www.wolfgangblick.at]** Fr B158 fr St Gilgen, on ent Abersee turn L at km 34 twds lake. Site in 1km foll sp to site. Med, mkd pich; hdstg, pt shd; wc; chem disp; shwrs €0.70; el pnts (12A) metered; lndtte; shop; rest, snacks; bar; playgrnd; lake beach adj; 50% statics; dogs €2.90; poss cr; Eng spkn; quiet; ccard acc. "Pleasant site; gd, friendly family run site by lake; helpful owners; beautiful scenery; excel for walking & cycling; on bus rte to Salzburg and local vills; poss cr, adv bkg advised." 1 May-30 Sep. € 19.70                    2012*

**ABERSEE** *B3* (1km NW Rural) *47.73910, 13.40065* **Camping Wolfgangsee Birkenstrand, Schwand 4, 5342 Abersee (Salzburg) [tel/fax (06227) 3029; camp@birkenstrand.at; www.birkenstrand.at]** Fr B158 fr St Gilgen, on ent Abersee turn L at km 32 twds lake. Site on both sides of rd in 1km. Med, mkd pitch, pt sl, unshd; wc; chem disp; shwrs €0.70; el pnts (10A) metered; lndtte (inc dryer); shop 100m; rest, bar 100m, snacks; BBQ; playgrnd; lake sw adj; boat & cycle hire; golf 15km; entmnt; TV rm; 20% statics; dogs €3.40; Eng spkn; adv bkg; quiet. "Excel area for walking, cycling; lovely situation; immac site; ACSI card acc." 1 Apr-31 Oct. € 26.60      2013*

**ABERSEE** *B3* (3km NW Rural) *47.73945, 13.40245* **Romantik Camping Wolfgangsee Lindenstrand, Schwand 19, 5342 St Gilgen (Salzburg) [(06227) 32050; fax 320524; camping@lindenstrand.at; www.lindenstrand.at]** Fr St Gilgen take B158 dir Bad Ischl. In 4km at km 32 foll sp Schwand, site on L on lakeside. Lge, mkd pitch, hdstg, pt shd; htd wc; chem disp; serviced pitches; shwrs inc; el pnts (10A) metered; shop; tradsmn; rest 1km; playgrnd; lake adj; watersports; 10% statics; dogs €3.20; phone; bus & boat to local towns & Salzburg; Eng spkn; adv bkg; quiet; ccard acc; red low ssn; CKE/CCI. "Lovely site; rec adv bkg for lakeside pitches." Easter-15 Oct. € 19.00                    2009*

**AFRITZ** *D3* (500m N Rural) *46.73701, 13.76874* **Camping Bodner, Seestrasse 27, 9542 Afritz-am-Zee (Kärnten) [(04247) 2579; fax 29990; office@camping-bodner. at; www.camping-bodner.at]** Fr Villach, take B94 twd Feldkirchen, turn L after 4km onto B98 sp Radenthein. N of Afritz, after Gassen, turn L, site sp. Med, some hdstg, pt sl, pt shd; wc; chem disp; mv service pnt; shwrs €1; el pnts (4-6A) inc; gas; lndtte; shop 1.5km; rest, snacks; bar; BBQ; playgrnd; lake sw adj; sailing; dogs €1.50; quiet. "Family-run site; gd walking country - both mountains & flat." 1 May-30 Sep. € 19.80                    2010*

**ALTAUSSEE** *C3* (1.5km S Rural) **Bauernhofcamping Temel, Puchen 39, 8992 Altaussee (Steiermark) [(03622) 71968]** N fr Bad Aussee dir Altausseer See, site sp. Sm, hdstg, pt sl, unshd; wc; chem disp; mv service pnt; shwrs €0.50; el pnts €2; shop 1.5km; rest 800m; lake sw 800m; dogs €1; quiet. "Well-kept, peaceful site amidst beautiful scenery; friendly owner; idyllic." 1 May-30 Sep. € 13.60                    2009*

⊞ **ALTENMARKT IM PONGAU** *C3* (800m S Rural) *47.37145, 13.41915* **Camping Passrucker, Zauchenseestrasse 341, 5541 Altenmarkt (Salzburg) [(06452) 7328; fax 7821; camping.passrucker@sbg.at; www.camping-passrucker. at]** Exit A10 junc 63 onto B99 to Altenmarkt. In town cent turn R & foll site sp. Med, pt shd; htd wc; chem disp; mv service pnt; baby facs; sauna; solarium; shwrs inc; el pnts (13A) metered; lndtte; shop high ssn; playgrnd; sm pool; fitness rm; skibus; TV rm; 50% statics (sep area); dogs €1.50; Eng spkn; adv bkg; quiet; red long stay; CKE/CCI. "Pretty town in lovely area; gd walking; higher prices in winter; excel san facs; friendly owner." ♦ € 21.00                    2010*

**ASCHACH AN DER DONAU** *B3* (6km N Rural) *48.42026, 13.98400* **Camping Kaiserhof, Kaiserau 1, 4082 Aschach-an-der-Donau (Oberösterreich) [(07273) 62210; fax 622113; kaiserhof@aschach.at; www.pension-kaiserhof. at]** Fr town cent foll site sp. Site adj rv & Gasthof Kaiserhof. Sm, pt shd; htd wc; chem disp; mv service pnt; shwrs; el pnts; lndtte; shop 6km; tradsmn; rest, snacks; bar; playgrnd; 80% statics; poss cr; Eng spkn; ccard acc; red long stay/CKE/CCI. "Beautiful location on Danube." ♦ 15 Apr-30 Sep. € 19.00                    2010*

**ATTERSEE** *B3* (1km S Rural) *47.9121, 13.5307* **Camping Wimroither Mühle, Mühlbach 5, 4864 Attersee (Oberösterreich) [(07666) 7749; fax 07666 7749]** Exit A/E60/ E551 junc 243 twd Attersee. In 2km at town sp turn R to site down unclass rd in 200m. Narr lane. Med, pt sl, pt shd; wc; chem disp; shwrs €1; el pnts (16A) €3.00; lndtte; sm shop & 300m; rest 300m; snacks; lake sw 250m; 60% statics; dogs; poss cr; adv bkg; quiet. "Conv Salzkammergut & Dachstein with lovely scenery." 1 Apr-31 Oct. € 16.00                    2013*

**AUSTRIA**

**ATTERSEE** *B3* (15km S Rural) *47.80100, 13.48266*
**Inselcamping, Unterburgau 37, 4866 Unterach-am-Attersee (Oberösterreich) [(07665) 8311; fax 7255; camping@inselcamp.at; www.inselcamp.at]** Leave A1 at junc 243 St Georgen/Attersee, foll B151 to Unterach fr Attersee vill. Site sp on app to Unterach. Med, pt shd; wc; chem disp; mv service pnt; shwrs €1; el pnts (6A) €2; gas; shop; supmkt nr; tradsmn; snacks; lake sw; shgl beach; 25% statics; dogs €2; clsd 1200-1400; poss v cr; Eng spkn; adv bkg; quiet; CKE/CCI. "Excel site; holiday owner; 5 min walk to attractive town; conv Salzburg & Salzkammergut; lots to see locally; gd boat trips; extra for lakeside pitches - some with boat mooring." 1 May-15 Sep. € 21.00                                        2013*

⊞ **AU** *C1* (500m S Rural) *47.31604, 9.99881* **Camping Köb, Neudorf 356, 6883 Au-im-Bregenzerwald (Voralberg) [(05515) 2331; fax 23314; info@campingaustria.at; www.axtres.net/campingaustria/]** Fr W on B200 fr Dornbirn sp Bregenzerwald, take 2nd turn R after tunnel at end of Au. Site immed on L. NB B200 not open to c'vans Au to Warth. Sm, pt shd; htd wc; chem disp; mv service pnt; shwrs €0.70; el pnts (6A) metered; lndtte; shop 100m; tradsmn; rest, bar 300m; pool 200m; internet; 10% statics; no dogs; phone adj; bus 100m; poss cr; adv bkg; quiet; CKE/CCI. "Mountain scenery; excel, secluded, well-run, family site; helpful owner." € 22.00                                        2009*

**BAD AUSSEE** *C3* (10km NE Rural) *47.63783, 13.90365* **Campingplatz Gössl, Gössl 201, 8993 Grundlsee (Steiermark) [(03622) 81810; fax 81814; office@campinggoessl.com; www.campinggoessl.com]** Fr B145 foll sp to Grundlsee, then along lake to Gössl at far end. Ent adj gasthof off mini-rndbt, site on L. Med; wc; shwrs inc; el pnts (10A) metered + conn fee; lndtte; shop adj; tradsmn; shop, rest, snacks, bar 500m; playgrnd adj; sand beach & lake sw adj; fishing; boating (no motor boats); dogs €1; bus; adv bkg; quiet. "Excel walking cent; scenery v beautiful; local gasthofs vg; daily bus & ferry services; v clean facs." ♦ 1 May-31 Oct. € 27.50                                        2014*

⊞ **BAD GASTEIN** *C2* (3km N Rural) *47.13421, 13.13137* **Kur-Camping Erlengrund, Erlengrundstrasse 6, 5640 Bad Gastein (Salzburg) [(06434) 30205; fax 30208; office@kurcamping-gastein.at; www.kurcamping-gastein.at]** Exit A10/E55 at junc 46 onto B311 thro St Johann to Lend, then S on B167 thro Bad Hofgastein. On N o'skts of Bad Gastein turn L 300m after BP g'ge to avoid narr town rds. Lge, mkd pitch, some hdstg, pt shd; htd wc; chem disp; mv service pnt; serviced pitches; baby facs; shwrs; el pnts (16A) metered; mains gas conn to some pitches; lndtte (inc dryer); shop; tradsmn; rest adj; playgrnd; htd pool; tennis; golf; fishing; ski bus; ski lift 4km; wifi; cab TV; 30% statics; dogs €2.50; adv bkg; quiet; ccard acc; red CKE/CCI. "Excel ski area with over 50 ski lifts & 9 x-country trails." € 25.50                                        2011*

⊞ **BAD GLEICHENBERG** *C4* (3km SE Rural) *46.87470, 15.93360* **Camping Feriendorf in Thermenland, Haus Nr 240, 8344 Bairisch-Kölldorf(Steiermark) [(03159) 3941; fax 288411; camping.bk@aon.at; www.bairisch-koelldorf.at]** Exit A2 at Gleisdorf Süd onto B68 dir Feldbach. Take B66 dir Bad Gleichenberg & at 2nd rndabt turn L, site sp. Med, unshd; htd wc; chem disp; mv service pnt; baby facs; shwrs; el pnts (16A) metered; gas; lndtte (inc dryer); tradsmn; rest, snacks; bar; BBQ; playgrnd; covrd pool; lake sw; tennis 600m; cycle hire; games area; golf 3km; 10% statics; dogs €0.70; adv bkg; quiet. ♦ € 20.00                                        2009*

⊞ **BLUDENZ** *C1* (6km E Rural) *47.14110, 9.92716* **Walch's Camping & Landhaus, Arlbergstrasse 101, 6751 Innerbraz [(05552) 281020; info@landhauswalch.at; www.landhauswalch.at]** Fr A14/S16 E fr Feldkirch dir Arlberg, exit Braz. Site further 2km on L, sp. Med, unshd; wc; chem disp; mv service pnt; baby facs; sauna/solarium; shwrs inc; el pnts (16A) metered + conn fee; lndtte (inc dryer); shop, rest; bar; playgrnd; pool 1km; games rm; wifi; dogs €3.50; bus nr; site clsd Nov; Eng spkn; adv bkg; quiet; CKE/CCI. "Mountain activities & golf avail nrby; vg site; excel facs." ♦ € 24.80                                        2010*

⊞ **BLUDENZ** *C1* (5km SE Rural) *47.14628, 9.90236* **Camping Gasthof Traube, Klostertalerstrasse 12, 6751 Braz (Voralberg) [(05552) 28103; fax 2810340; office@traubebraz.at; www.traubebraz.at]** Site behind Gasthof Traube in middle of Braz vill, which is sp off dual c'way S16. Med, some hdstg, sl, pt shd; htd wc; chem disp; baby facs; sauna; shwrs inc; el pnts (6A) inc (rev pol); lndtte (inc dryer); shop 1km; tradsmn; rest, snacks in gasthof; playgrnd; 2 htd pools (1 covrd); paddling pool; tennis; solarium; ski lift 6km; skibus; golf 1.5km; wifi; entmnt; 40% statics; no dogs; poss v cr; quiet but some rlwy noise; ccard acc; red CKE/CCI. "Clean & tidy, family-run site; poss muddy pitches; conv Liechtenstein." € 25.60                                        2010*

⊞ **BLUDENZ** *C1* (1km S Rural) *47.14651, 9.81630* **Auhof Camping, Aulandweg 5, 6706 Bürs (Vorarlberg) [(05552) 67044; fax 31926; auhof.buers@aon.at; www.buers.at]** Exit A14/E60 junc 59 dir Bludenz/Bürs, then Brand. Site sp in 300m at Zimba Park shopping cent on edge of sm indus est. Med, unshd; htd wc; shwrs inc; el pnts (4A); gas; lndtte; shop & 300m; rest, snacks 300m; some rd noise. "Friendly, tidy, clean site on working farm; conv Arlberg Tunnel, Liechtenstein & mountain resorts; muddy in wet; conv NH for m'way." € 19.50                                        2011*

⊞ **BLUDENZ** *C1* (5km S Rural) *47.14268, 9.77875* **Heidi's Camping, Boden 7, 6707 Bürserberg (Voralberg) [(05552) 65307; fax 053074; info@burtschahof.at; www.burtschahof.at]** Exit A14/E60 at junc 59 twd Bürs/Brand. Site in 4km on L - 10% climb with bends. Sm, mkd pitch, some hdstg, terr, pt shd; htd wc; chem disp; baby facs; fam bthrm; shwrs inc; el pnts (16A) €1.50; lndtte (inc dryer); shop, rest, bar 200m; BBQ; playgrnd; pool; 25% statics; dogs; bus 200m; phone; poss cr; adv bkg; quiet. "CL-type site in lovely situation - worth the climb; sm/med o'fits only - manhandling poss req." € 23.50                                        2010*

**BLUDENZ** *C1* (2km W Rural) *47.16990, 9.80788*
**Terrassencamping Sonnenberg, Hinteroferstrasse 12,
6714 Nüziders (Vorarlberg) [(05552) 64035; fax 33900;
sonnencamp@aon.at; www.camping-sonnenberg.com]**
Exit A14/E60 junc 57 onto B190 N, foll sp Nüziders & foll site
sp thro Nüziders vill. Med, mkd pitch, hdstg, terr, pt shd; htd
wc; chem disp; mv service pnt; shwrs inc; el pnts inc (5-13A)
inc; lndtte (inc dryer); shop 500m; tradsmn; rest, snacks 300m;
bar; playgrnd; wifi; entmnt; TV rm; dogs €3.50; phone; sep car
park; poss cr; Eng spkn; adv bkg; quiet; ccard not acc; red low
ssn/long stay. "Friendly, v helpful owners; superb facs; beautiful
scenery - extra for Panorama pitches at top of site; excel
mountain views; excel walking; lifts to mountains; ltd opening
hrs for recep - use phone at building on L at main ent; no arr
after 2200 hrs but sep o'night area; rec bk in adv in high ssn;
gd for m'vans; highly rec; excel site; gd value." 27 Apr-6 Oct.
€ 37.00                                                    2013*

**BRAZ see Bludenz** *C1*

**BREITENWANG see Reutte** *C1*

**BRIXEN IM THALE see Kitzbühel** *C2*

⊞ **BRUCK AN DER GROSSGLOCKNERSTRASSE** *C2*
(SW Urban) *47.28386, 12.81736* **Sportcamp Woferlgut,
Krössenbach 40, 5671 Bruck-an-der-Grossglocknerstrasse
(Salzburg) [(06545) 73030; fax 73033; info@sportcamp.
at; www.sportcamp.at]** Exit A10 junc 47 dir Bischofshofen,
B311 dir Zell-am-See. Take 2nd exit to Bruck, site sp fr by-
pass, & foll sps thro town to site. Lge, pt shd; wc; chem disp;
mv service pnt; serviced pitches; baby facs; sauna; shwrs inc;
el pnts (10-16A) €2.80 metered + conn fee; gas metered +
conn fee; lndtte; rest, snacks; bar; farm produce; playgrnd;
htd pool; lake sw adj; tennis; indoor play area; games rm;
gym & fitness cent; ski cent; wifi; entmnt; TV; many statics;
dogs €4.50; phone; bus to Zell-am-Zee & glacier; poss cr; Eng
spkn; adv bkg; some rd & rlwy noise; red long stay; ccard acc.
"Extended facs area with R numbered pitches preferable;
excel site for sh or long stay; big pitches; excel mntn walking,
local horse riding; helpful recep; tour ops tents & statics; excel
for young/teenage families; noisy tannoy announcements high
ssn; vg san facs; warm welcome; sm supmkt nrby & plenty of
rests & cafes; excel." ♦ € 35.00                        2012*

See advertisement

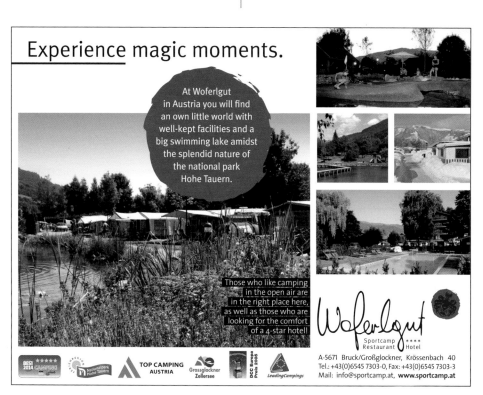

Experience magic moments.

At Woferlgut in Austria you will find an own little world with well-kept facilities and a big swimming lake amidst the splendid nature of the national park Hohe Tauern.

Those who like camping in the open air are in the right place here, as well as those who are looking for the comfort of a 4-star hotel!

Sportcamp Restaurant Hotel ★★★★

A-5671 Bruck/Großglockner, Krössenbach 40
Tel.: +43(0)6545 7303-0, Fax: +43(0)6545 7303-3
Mail: info@sportcamp.at, www.sportcamp.at

**BRUCK AN DER MUR** *C4* (3km W Urban) *47.40311,*
*15.22755* **Camping Raddörf'l, Bruckerstrasse 110, 8600**
**Oberaich (Steiermark) [(03862) 51418; fax 55940; info@**
**gasthofpichler.at; www.gasthofpichler.at]** Fr S6 take
Oberaich exit 4km W of Bruck, Foll site sp (in opp dir to vill of
Oberaich), go under rlwy bdge, turn L at T-junc. Site is 300m
on L at Gasthof Pichler, ent thro car park. Sm, pt shd; wc;
shwrs inc; el pnts (10A) inc; lndtte; shop 3km; rest, snacks; bar;
playgrnd; dogs €2; poss cr; some rlwy noise; CKE/CCI. "Gd
NH; site (10 o'fits max) in orchard at rear of Gasthof; gd rest."
1 May-1 Oct. € 22.00                                    2010*

**DELLACH IM DRAUTAL** *D2* (500m S Rural) *46.73085,*
*13.07846* **Camping Waldbad, 9772 Dellach-im-Drautal**
**(Kärnten) [(04714) 234-18 / (04714) 288; info@camping-**
**waldbad.at; www.camping-waldbad.at]** Clearly sp on B100
& in vill of Dellach on S side or Rv Drau. Med, hdg/mkd pitch,
pt shd; wc; chem disp; mv service pnt; baby facs; shwrs inc;
el pnts (6A); gas; lndtte; shop; rest, snacks; bar; playgrnd;
htd pool complex adj inc paddling pool, waterslide etc; games
area; games rm; entmnt; internet; 5% statics; dogs €2.50; poss
cr; adv bkg; quiet; ccard acc. "Peaceful,wooded site; vg leisure
facs adj." ♦ 1 May-30 Sep. € 37.50                     2013*

⊞ **DOBRIACH** *D3* (1km S Rural) *46.77020, 13.64788*
**Komfort Campingpark Burgstaller, Seefeldstrasse 16,**
**A-9873 Döbriach (Kärnten) [04246 7774; fax 7774426;**
**info@burgstaller.co.at; www.burgstaller.co.at]** Fr on A10/
E55/E66 take exit Millstätter See. Turn L at traff lts on B98 dir
Radenthein. Thro Millstatt & Dellach, turn R into Döbriach,
sp Camping See site on L by lake after Döbriach. V lge, hdg/
mkd pitch, pt shd; wc; chem disp; mv service pnt; baby facs;
sauna; private san facs avail; shwrs inc; el pnts (6-10A) inc; gas;
lndtte; shop; rest, snacks, bar adj; playgrnd; htd pool; lake sw;
boating; solarium; games area; horseriding; cycle hire; cinema;
golf 8km; entmnt; internet; TV; 10% statics; dogs €4; poss cr;
Eng spkn; adv bkg; quiet; red snr citizens/low ssn; CKE/CCI.
"Organised walks & trips to Italy; excel rest; some pitches tight;
fantastic facs." ♦ € 35.00                             2013*

⊞ **DOBRIACH** *D3* (1km SW) *46.76811, 13.64809* **Camping**
**Brunner am See, Glanzerstrasse 108, 9873 Döbriach**
**(Kärnten) [(04246) 7189 or 7386; fax 718914; office@**
**camping-brunner.at; www.camping-brunner.at]**
Fr Salzburg on A10 a'bahn take Seeboden-Millstatt exit bef
Spittal. Foll rd 98 N of Millstattersee to camping sp. Med, pt
shd; wc; chem disp; mv service pnt; fam bthrm; baby facs;
shwrs inc; el pnts (6A) inc; rest, snacks; bar; shop; pool 300m;
playgrnd; tennis; watersports; poss cr; dogs €4.50; adv bkg;
ccard acc; CKE/CCI. "Great site with excel, clean san facs; gd
size pitches; lakeside location; supmkt nrby & rests in vicinity;
superb scenery." ♦ € 55.00                             2013*

**DORNBIRN** *C1* (1.5km SE Rural) *47.39931, 9.75645* **Camping**
**in der Enz, Gütlestrasse, 6850 Dornbirn (Vorarlberg)**
**[(05572) 29119; camping@camping-enz.at; www.**
**camping-enz.at]** Exit A14/E60 for Dornbirn-Sud, foll dir
Ebnit-Rappenlochschlucht gorge for 1.2km, camp sp beyond
cable car base. Med, pt shd; wc; chem disp; shwrs inc; el pnts
(6A) €2.50; lndtte; shop; rest, snacks; playgrnd; lge pool 200m;
cable car stn opp; adv bkg; ccard acc; red CKE/CCI. "Nice site
in attractive location; conv Lake Constance, Bregenz, Lindau;
sep o'night area." 1 Apr-30 Sep. € 17.00               2009*

**DROBOLLACH see Villach** *D3*

⊞ **EBEN IM PONGAU** *C3* (1.5km S Rural) *47.39932,*
*13.39566* **See-Camping Eben, Familie Schneider,**
**Badeseestraße 54, 5531 Eben I Pg [06458 8231 or**
**0664 450 2000; fax 8231; info@seecamping-eben.at;**
**www.seecamping-eben.at]** Head E on A10, take exit 60 -
Eben. Turn L onto B99. R onto Badeseestr. Campsite 800m on
the L. Med, pt shd; htd wc; mv service pnt; baby facs; shwrs
inc; el pnts (16A) inc; lndtte (inc dryer); bar; lake adj; games
area; wifi; dogs; train 800km; adv bkg; quiet. "Helpful owners;
saunas; steam rm; direct access fr mountains; clean & well
organise; gd site." € 25.00                            2014*

**EBERNDORF see Völkermarkt** *D3*

⊞ **EHRWALD** *C1* (1.5km NE Rural) *47.41142, 10.92360*
**Comfort Camping Dr Lauth, Zugspitzstrasse 34, 6632**
**Ehrwald (Tirol) [(05673) 2666; fax 26664; info@**
**campingehrwald.at; www.campingehrwald.at]** On ent
Ehrwald, foll sps Tiroler Zugspitz Camping, turn R immed bef
rlwy bdge (R turn nearest rlwy; do not go under rlwy bdge). Sp
on R 1.5km fr Ehrwald, same rd as for Zugspitzbahn Camping.
Fr Lermoos take 1st L after rlwy bdge. Med, pt sl, pt shd; htd
wc; chem disp; baby facs; shwrs inc; el pnts (4A) metered;
gas; lndtte (inc dryer); shop; tradsmn; rest, snacks; bar; BBQ;
playgrnd; pool 4km; wifi; 50% statics; dogs €2.20; poss cr; Eng
spkn; adv bkg; quiet; red long stay; CKE/CCI. "Excel san facs;
mountain walks, skiing & cycling; conv Innsbruck & Fern Pass; v
beautiful; vg bistro." € 26.00                         2010*

⊞ **EHRWALD** *C1* (4km NE Rural) *47.42689, 10.94093*
**Tiroler Zugspitz Camp, Obermoos 1, 6632 Ehrwald (Tirol)**
**[(05673) 2309; fax 230951; camping@zugspitze-resort.at;**
**www.zugspitze-resort.at]** Foll sp fr Ehrwald to Obernoos
& Zugspitzbahn. Med, mkd pitch, pt terr, pt shd; wc; chem
disp; mv service pnt; baby facs; sauna; shwrs inc; el pnts (16A)
metered; gas; lndtte (inc dryer); shop; tradsmn; rest; playgrnd;
2 pools (1 htd, covrd); paddling pool; games rm; 60% statics;
dogs €4; phone; Eng spkn; adv bkg; quiet; ccard acc; red
CKE/CCI. "Excel site in beautiful location; some awkward,
sm pitches; vg facs; adj cable car to summit Zugspitz." ♦ ltd
€ 32.00                                                2010*

⊞ **EHRWALD** *C1* (2km W Rural) *47.40250, 10.88893* **Happy**
**Camp Hofherr, Garmischerstrasse 21, 6631 Lermoos**
**(Tirol) [(05673) 2980; fax 29805; info@camping-lermoos.**
**com; www.camping-lermoos.com]** On ent Lermoos on
B187 fr Ehrwald site located on R. Med, pt sl, pt shd; htd wc;
chem disp; mv service pnt; shwrs inc; el pnts (16A) metered;
gas (metered); lndtte (inc dryer); shops 200m; rest; playgrnd;
htd pool 200m; tennis; ski lift 300m; wifi; cab TV; 40% statics;
dogs; phone; site clsd 1 Nov-mid Dec; adv bkg; quiet; ccard
acc. "Ideal for walks/cycling; v picturesque; adj park; ask for
guest card for discount on ski lifts etc." € 23.00     2010*

**EISENSTADT** *B4* (10km E Rural) *47.84401, 16.68720*
**Campingplatz Oggau, 7063 Oggau-am-Neusiedlersee
(Burgenland) [(02685) 7271; fax 72714; office@
campingoggau.at; www.campingoggau.at]** Fr N or S exit
A2 at Neustadt Süd, S4 sp Eisenstadt. Foll sps Eisenstadt on S4/
S31, exit at Eisenstadt Süd & foll sps to Rust & Oggau; site sp
thro vill. Lge, hdg pitch, shd; wc; chem disp; mv service pnt;
shwrs €0.80; el pnts (16A) €2; gas; shop; rest, snacks; bar;
playgrnd; pool adj; wifi; 60% statics; dogs; poss cr; adv bkg;
ccard acc. ♦ 1 Apr-31 Oct. € 18.80                    2009*

**EISENSTADT** *B4* (10km E Rural) *47.80132, 16.69185*
**Storchencamp Rust, Ruster Bucht, 7071 Rust-am-
Neusiedlersee (Burgenland) [(02685) 595; fax 5952;
office@gmeiner.co.at; www.gmeiner.co.at]** Fr Eisenstadt
take rd to Rust & Mörbisch. In Rust foll sps to site & Zee;
lakeside rd to ent. Lge, pt shd; wc; chem disp; shwrs inc; el
pnts (16A) €2.30; lndtte; shop; rest, snacks; pool 200m; lake
sw 500m; boating; 60% statics; dogs €2.90; poss cr; quiet. "Nr
Hungarian border; attractive vill with nesting storks." ♦ 1 Apr-
31 Oct. € 20.20                    2012*

**EMMERSDORF AN DER DONAU see Melk** *B4*

**ENGELHARTSZELL** *B3* (500m NW Rural) *48.51238, 13.72428*
**Camp Municipal an der Donau, Nibelungenstrasse 113,
4090 Engelhartszell (Oberösterreich) [(0664) 8708787;
tourismus@engelhartszell.ooe.gv.at; www.engelhartszell.
at]** Fr Passau (Germany) exit SE on B130 along Rv Danube.
Site on L in approx 28km just bef Engelhartszell adj municipal
pool complex. Sm, unshd; wc; chem disp; shwrs; el pnts (6A)
metered; lndtte; tradsmn; snacks; bar; playgrnd; pool adj;
50% statics; bus nr; poss cr; quiet. "Excel, clean, friendly site
on rvside; Danube cycleway passes site." ♦ 15 Apr-15 Oct.
€ 15.00                    2009*

**FAAK/FAAK AM SEE see Villach** *D3*

**FEICHTEN IM KAUNERTAL see Prutz** *C1*

**FELDKIRCH** *C1* (2km NW Urban) *47.25880, 9.58336*
**Waldcamping Feldkirch, Stadionstrasse 9, 6803 Feldkirch
(Vorarlberg) [(05522) 76001-3190; waldcamping@
feldkirch.at; www.waldcamping.at]** Exit A14 at Feldkirch
Nord, strt over next 2 rndabts sp Nofels/
Gisingen, then site sp. Site adj open air pool & leisure cent.
Med, mkd pitch, pt shd; htd wc; chem disp; shwrs inc; el pnts
(6A) €2.20; (poss rev pol); lndry rm; tradsmn; rest 800m; BBQ;
playgrnd; htd pool adj, TV rm; 50% statics; dogs €2.75; bus
200m; poss cr; adv bkg; noise fr adj leisure cent; red CKE/CCI.
"Vg." 1 Apr-31 Oct. € 22.00                    2009*

**⊞ FERLACH** *D3* (500m SW Urban) *46.52166, 14.29222*
**Messeparkplatz Schloss Ferlach, 9170 Ferlach (Kärnten)
[(04227) 4920; office_schloss@ferlach.net; www.ferlach.
at]** Fr B85 foll sp Ferlach, parking sp adj rv (top half of car
park). Sm, hdstg, pt shd; own san rec; chem disp €1; mv service
pnt (water) €1; shop, rest, snacks, bar 500m; quiet. "Free to
stay but €4 parking charge; vg, conv NH for Loibl pass; c'vans
& m'vans acc; pleasant town." € 4.00                    2011*

**FIEBERBRUNN see St Johann in Tirol** *C2*

**FRAUENKIRCHEN** *B4* (6km S Rural) *47.79160, 16.91619*
**Camping Zicksee, 7161 St Andrä-am-Zicksee (Burgenland)
[tel/fax (02176) 2144; info@st.andrae-tourism.or.at;
www.tiscover.com/st.andrae.zicksee]** Fr B51 site sp on
lake 1.5km W of vill of St Andrä. Fr St Andrä foll sp Zicksee,
fork R at junc after rlwy x-ing, site on L. Lge, mkd pitch, some
hdstg, shd; htd wc; chem disp; mv service pnt; baby facs; shwrs
€0.50; el pnts (10A) €1.80 (long cable poss req); gas; lndtte
(inc dryer); shop; tradsmn; rest adj; snacks; playgrnd; lake sw;
fishing; watersports; phone; no dogs; poss cr; quiet; CKE/CCI.
"Excel facs; gd cycling & birdwatching E of lake; remote pt of
Austria; height restriction on ent of 3.20m." ♦ 1 Apr-30 Sep.
€ 18.00                    2011*

**FRAUENKIRCHEN** *B4* (7km W Urban) *47.85424, 16.82665*
**Strandcamping Podersdorf-am-See, Strandplatz 19,
7141 Podersdorf-am-See (Burgenland) [(02177) 2279;
fax 227916; strandcamping@podersdorfamsee.at; www.
podersdorfamsee.at]** Foll sp fr cent of Podersdorf on shore
Neusiedlersee. Lge, mkd pitch, hdstg, pt shd; wc; chem disp;
mv service pnt; shwrs €0.50; el pnts (12A) inc; shop; lndtte;
rest, snacks; playgrnd; lake sw adj; sand beach; windsurfing;
boating; internet; poss cr at w/end; 25% statics; dogs €4.90;
quiet; red CKE/CCI. "Nature reserves & birdwatching lakes to
S; many cycle paths in flat region; gd views fr site; bread baked
daily." ♦ ltd 1 Apr-1 Nov. € 27.00                    2009*

**⊞ FUGEN** *C2* (1km N Rural) *47.35949, 11.85223*
**Campingplatz Hell, Gageringerstrasse 1, 6263 Fügen/
Zillertal (Tirol) [(05288) 62203; fax 64615; info@zillertal-
camping.at; www.zillertal-camping.at]** On A12/E45/E60
exit junc 39 exit onto B169. Site well sp. Med, mkd pitch, some
hdstg, terr, pt shd; wc; chem disp; mv service pnt; sauna; fam
bthrm; shwrs inc; el pnts (10A) metered (long lead poss req);
gas; lndtte (inc dryer); shop; supmkt 500m; rest; snacks high
ssn; bar; playgrnd; htd pool; paddling pool; cycle hire; games
rm; golf 10km; wifi; entmnt; dogs €2.50 (not acc Jul/Aug); Eng
spkn; adv bkg; some rd noise daytime only; red 8+ days; CKE/
CCI. "Wonderful site; superb san facs; lge pitches; friendly,
helpful staff; excel." € 34.00                    2011*

**FURSTENFELD** *C4* (500m W Rural) *47.05631, 16.06255*
**Thermenland Camping, Campingweg 1, 8280 Fürstenfeld
(Steiermark) [(03382) 54940; fax 51671; camping.
fuerstenfeld@chello.at; www.camping-fuerstenfeld.
at]** Exit A2/E59 sp Fürstenfeld onto B65. Site well sp fr town
cent. Med, pt sl, pt shd; wc; chem disp; shwrs inc; el pnts
(10A) €2.30 (poss long lead req); lndtte (inc dryer); shop
500m; tradsmn; rest 1.5km; snacks; bar; pool; paddling pool;
waterslide; rv fishing; golf 5km; entmnt; 25% statics; dogs €2;
phone; quiet; rec CKE/CCI. "Pleasant rvside site; ltd facs but
clean; conv Hungarian border." 15 Apr-15 Oct. € 20.00  2010*

**FUSCH AN DER GLOCKNERSTRASSE** *C2* (S Rural) *47.22452,
12.82658* **Camping Lampenhäusl, Grossglocknerstrsse
15, 5672 Fusch-an-der-Glocknerstrasse (Salzburg)
[(06546) 2150; fax 215302; gasthof@lampenhaeusl.at;
www.lampenhaeusl.at]** E of rd, on S o'skts of Fusch. Sm,
pt shd; wc; shwrs inc; el pnts (16A) €3.80 or metered; lndtte
(inc dryer); shop & 100m; rest, snacks; bar; playgrnd; htd pool
100m; TV rm; 50% statics; phone; bus; Eng spkn; adv bkg;
quiet; ccard acc; red long stay; CKE/CCI. "Vg, clean facs but
stretched if site full; vg site." 10 May-26 Oct. € 17.50   2010*

**FUSCHL AM SEE** *B3* (800m SW Rural) *47.79230, 13.29682*
Camping Seeholz, Dorfsrtrasse 36, 5330 Fuschl-am-See
(Salzburg) [tel/fax (06226) 8310; camping-fuschl@aon.at]
Exit A1 at junc 274 onto B158 dir Hof & St Gilgen. Foll sp to
Fuschl & site. Med, shd; wc; chem disp; shwrs inc; el pnts (8A)
inc (long lead poss req); gas; lndtte; shop; rest, snacks; lake sw
& shgl beach adj; 25% statics; dogs; poss cr; adv bkg; some rd
noise. "Helpful staff; basic, gd san facs; beautiful lake." 1 Apr-
31 Oct. € 23.20                                                    2009*

**GMUND (KARNTEN)** *C3* (8km NW Rural) *46.94950, 13.50940*
Terrassencamping Maltatal, Malta 6, 9854 Malta
(Kärnten) [(04733) 234; fax 23416; info@maltacamp.at;
www.maltacamp.at] Exit A10/E14 onto B99 to Gmünd.
Foll sp Malta & after 6km site sp, on R next to filling stn. Lge,
mkd pitch, terr, pt shd; htd wc; chem disp; mv service pnt;
20% serviced pitches; sauna; shwrs inc; el pnts (10A) inc;
lndtte (inc dryer); sm supmkt; tradsmn; rest, snacks; pizzeria;
bar; BBQ; playgrnd; htd pool; paddling pool; canoeing;
trout-fishing; games area; games rm; tennis; guided walks;
children's mini-farm; wifi; 5% statics; dogs €2.90; phone; poss
cr; adv bkg; quiet; CKE/CCI. "Gmund & gd shopping
towns; Millstättersee 15km, Grossglocknerstrasse 1hr's drive;
magnificant area with rvs, waterfalls, forests & mountains; vg
rest; excel site." ♦ 1 Apr-31 Oct. € 30.00            2012*

**GNESAU** *D3* (2km W Rural) *46.77966, 13.95062* **Camping
Hobitsch, Sonnleiten 24, 9563 Gnesau (Kärnten)**
[(04278) 368; fax 3684; office@camping-hobitsch.at;
www.camping-hobitsch.at] Site sp on B95. Sm, pt shd; wc;
chem disp; shwrs inc; el pnts €2.80; lndtte; shop, rest 2km;
snacks; bar; playgrnd; pool; games area; no statics; dogs
€1.50; Eng spkn; quiet. "Beautiful setting in meadow; excel
san facs; adj to cycle path." 1 May-30 Sep. € 13.30     2010*

**GRAN** *C1* (4km W Rural) *47.50825, 10.49468*
Panoramacamp Alpenwelt, Kienzerle 3, 6675 Tannheim
(Tirol [(05675) 43070; fax 430777; alpenwelt@tirol.com;
www.tannheimertal-camping.com] Fr N leave A7 junc 137
Oy-Mittelberg onto B310 to Oberjoch, then B199 to Tannheim.
Fr S on B198 dir Reutte, turn onto B199 at Weissenbach to
Tannheim. Med, mkd pitch, hdstg, terr, unshd; htd wc; chem
disp; some serviced pitches; baby facs; sauna; shwrs inc; el pnts
(16A) metered; lndtte; shop; tradsmn; rest; bar; playgrnd; pool
4km; lake sw 4km; entmnt; internet; cab TV; 30% statics; dogs
€3.50; ski bus; ski lift 2km; adv bkg; quiet; CKE/CCI. "Excel
site; gd walking, cycling area." ♦ 20 Dec-19 Apr & 1 May-
30 Oct. € 22.00                                               2010*

**GRAZ** *C4* (6km SW Urban) *47.02447, 15.39719*
Stadt-Camping Central, Martinhofstrasse 3, 8054
Graz-Strassgang (Steiermark) [(0316) 697824 or
0676 3785102 (mob); guenther_walter@utanet.at; www.
tiscover.at/campingcentral] Fr A9/E57 exit Graz-Webling,
then dir Strassgang onto B70, site sp on R after Billa supmkt
& filling stn. Med, mkd pitch, some hdstg, pt shd; wc; chem
disp; mv service pnt; shwrs inc; el pnts (6A) inc; gas; lndtte
(inc dryer); supmkt 200m; rest, snacks adj; bar; BBQ; playgrnd;
pool, paddling pool adj; tennis; 80% statics; dogs free; bus
to city; poss v cr; quiet; wifi, "Pleasant, conv site; reg bus
service fr the nrby main rd (no traff noise); free entry to superb
lido (pt naturist); site mngr v helpful." ♦ 1 Apr-31 Oct.
€ 30.00                                                          2012*

**GREIFENBURG** *D2* (1km E Rural) *46.74744, 13.19448*
Fliergercamp am See, Seeweg 333, 9761 Greifenburg
(Kärnten) [(04712) 8666; info@fliegercamp.at; www.
fliegercamp.at] On rd 100/E66, site clearly visible fr rd on app
Greifenburg. Med, mkd pitch, pt shd; htd wc; chem disp; mv
service pnt; baby facs; shwrs inc; el pnts (16A) inc; lndtte; shop
1km; tradsmn; rest, snacks; bar; BBQ; playgrnd; lake sw adj;
dogs; Eng spkn; adv bkg; quiet; CKE/CCI. "Gd cycling; vg site."
♦ 1 Apr-15 Oct. € 18.00                                    2009*

**GREIFENBURG** *D2* (1km W Rural) *46.74805, 13.16416*
Familien-Camping Reiter, Hauzendorf 3, 9761 Greifenburg
(Kärnten) [tel/fax (04712) 389; campingreiter@gmx.at;
www.camping-reiter.at] Fr Greifenburg on B100, site on L.
Sm, pt shd; htd wc; chem disp; baby facs; shwrs €1; el pnts
(10A) metered; lndtte (inc dryer); shop; tradsmn; rest, snacks;
bar; BBQ; playgrnd; htd pool; dogs €1; quiet. "Beautiful area."
1 Apr-15 Nov. € 21.00                                       2011*

> ## "There aren't many sites open at this time of year"
>
> If you're travelling outside peak season
> remember to call ahead to check site opening
> dates – even if the entry says 'open all year'.

**GREIN** *B3* (200m SW Urban) *48.22476, 14.85428*
Campingplatz Grein, Donaulände 1, 4360 Grein
(Oberösterreich) [(07268) 21230; fax 2123013; office@
camping-grein.at; www.camping-grein.net] Sp fr A1 & B3
on banks of Danube. Med, pt shd; wc; chem disp; shwrs inc; el
pnts (6-10A) €3; gas; lndtte; shop adj; rest in vill; snacks; bar;
playgrnd; htd, covrd pool 200m; open air pool 500m; fishing;
canoeing; wifi; 10% statics; dogs €1.50; poss cr; some rd/
rlwy noise; red long stay; CKE/CCI. "Friendly, helpful owner
lives on site; recep in café/bar; vg, modern san facs; lovely
scenery; quaint vill; gd walking; excursions; conv Danube
cycle rte & Mauthausen Concentration Camp." 1 Mar-31 Oct.
€ 32.50                                                           2014*

**GRUNDLSEE see Bad Aussee** *C3*

**HALL IN TIROL** *C2* (500m NE Urban) *47.28423, 11.49658*
Schwimmbad-Camping, Scheidensteinstrasse 26, 6060
Hall-in-Tirol (Tirol) [(05223) 4546475; fax 4546477;
h.niedrist@hall.at; www.hall.ag] Exit A12/E45/E60 at junc
68 at Hall-in-Tirol. Cross rv strt into town & foll camp sp fr 2nd
turn L; site on B171. Diff ent. Med, pt shd; wc; chem disp; mv
service pnt; shwrs inc; el pnts (6A) €2; lndtte; shop high ssn;
supmkt 500m; tradsmn; rest; playgrnd; htd pool adj; tennis;
minigolf adj; wifi; 15% statics; dogs; bus; poss cr; Eng spkn;
adv bkg; some rd noise & church bells; red long stay/CKE/
CCI. "Well-cared for site; friendly welcome; vg, modern facs,
poss stretched high ssn; local excursions, walking; pt of sports
complex; Hall pretty, interesting medieval town; frequent music
festivals; less cr than Innsbruck sites; no twin-axles; walk to
town; conv for m'vans; NB m'vans only 1 Oct-30 Apr for €7.50
per night." ♦ 1 May-30 Sep. € 20.30                    2011*

**HALL IN TIROL** *C2* (5km E Rural) *47.28711, 11.57223*
**Schlosscamping Aschach, Hochschwarzweg 2,
6111 Volders (Tirol) [tel/fax (05224) 52333; info@
schlosscamping.com; www.schlosscamping.com]** Fr A12
leave at either Hall Mitte & foll sp to Volders, or leave at
Wattens & travel W to Volders (easiest rte). Site well sp on
B171. Narr ent bet lge trees. Lge, mkd pitch, pt sl, pt shd; wc;
chem disp; mv service pnt; shwrs inc; el pnts (16A) €2.70 (long
cable req some pitches; adaptor lead avail); gas; lndtte; shop;
tradsmn; 2 supmkts 500m; rest, snacks; bar; BBQ; playgrnd;
htd pool; horseriding, tennis; TV rm; dogs €2.50; phone;
bus 250m; Eng spkn; adv bkg; quiet but church bells, clock
& some rlwy noise at night; red long stay; ccard acc (for 4+
days); CKE/CCI. "Well-run, clean site with vg, modern facs &
helpful management; few water & waste points; grassy pitches;
beautiful setting & views; gd walking/touring; arr early to
ensure pitch." 1 May-12 Sep. € 22.00                        2010*

**HALLEIN** *B2* (3km NW Rural) *47.70441, 13.06868* **Camping
Auwirt, Salzburgerstrasse 42, 5400 Hallein (Salzburg)
[(06245) 80417; fax 84635; info@auwirt.com; www.
auwirt.com]** Exit A10/E55 junc 8 onto B150 sp Salzburg
Süd, then B159 twd Hallein. Site on L in 4km. Med, pt shd;
wc; chem disp; mv service pnt; shwrs €2; el pnts (10A) €3;
lndtte; rest, snacks; bar; playgrnd; paddling pool; wifi; dogs
€2; bus to Salzburg at site ent; poss cr; Eng spkn; adv bkg;
CKE/CCI. "Mountain views; cycle path to Salzburg nr; helpful
staff; v friendly site; gd san facs & rest; conv salt mines at
Hallein & scenic drive to Eagles' Nest; conv for Berchtesgaden;
friendly family owners." ◆ Easter-15 Oct & 1 Dec-7 Jan.
€ 33.80                                                      2014*

**HALLSTATT** *C3* (4km SE Rural) *47.54874, 13.67779*
**Campingplatz am See, Winkl 77, 4831 Obertraun
(Oberösterreich) [(06131) 265; camping-am-see@chello.at;
www.camping-am-see.at]** Fr Hallstatt foll sps for Obertraun.
Site immed on L on ent vill of Winkl. Med, some hdstg, pt
shd; wc; chem disp; mv service pnt; baby facs; shwrs inc; el
pnts (10A) €3 (long lead req); lndtte (inc dryer); shop; supmkt
1.5km; tradsmn; snacks; bar; BBQ; lake sw & shgl beach adj;
wifi; dogs €1.50; Eng spkn; adv bkg; quiet; ccard acc; red
CKE/CCI. "Nr Dachstein ice caves, Hallstatt salt mines, Gosau
valley." 1 May-30 Sep. € 31.50                              2010*

**HALLSTATT** *C3* (500m S Rural) *47.55296, 13.64786*
**Camping Klausner-Höll, Lahnstrasse 201, 4830 Hallstatt
(Oberösterreich) [(06134) 6134/8322; fax 83221;
camping@hallstatt.net; http://camping.hallstatt.net/
home/]** On exit tunnel 500m thro vill, site on R nr lge filling
stn. Med, pt shd; wc; chem disp; shwrs inc; el pnts (16A) €3;
lndtte; shop; rest adj; snacks; bar; playgrnd; pool adj; lake sw;
boat trips; dogs; poss cr; Eng spkn; ccard acc; red long stay/
CKE/CCI. "Excel, level site; gd, clean san facs; chem disp diff
to use; conv Salzkammergut region, Hallstatt salt mines, ice
caves; pretty town 10 mins walk; family run site; relaxed &
friendly; walks; idyllic quiet setting with mountains all around;
cycle path around lake; supmkt 300m." 15 Apr-15 Oct.
€ 27.00                                                     2014*

⊞ **HASELGEHR** *C1* (1km NE Rural) *47.31527, 10.49722*
**Freien-Camping Rudi, Luxnach 122, 6651 Häselgehr
[(05634) 6425; info@lechtal-camping-rudi.at; www.
lechtal-camping-rudi.at]** On rd B198 fr Reutte (N), in
Häselgehr cross rv bdge, turn R bef church. In 100m take R
fork, site on R in 500m. Med, hdstg, unshd; htd wc; chem disp;
mv service pnt; shwrs inc; el pnts (13A) metered; lndtte (inc
dryer); shop 5km; rest 500m; pool 500m; ski lift 5km; skibus;
few statics; dogs €1.50; bus 400m; Eng spkn; adv bkg; quiet;
red long stay; CKE/CCI. "Cycling & x-country skiing fr site;
rafting cent on site; gd." € 20.40                          2010*

**HEILIGEN GESTADE see Ossiach** *D3*

**HEILIGENBLUT** *C2* (2.5km S Rural) *47.02164, 12.86244*
**Camping Möllfluss, Pockhorn 25, 9844 Heiligenblut
(Kärnten) [(04824) 24645; fax 24684; hoopfnstuben@
gmx.at]** On B107 at S end of Grossglockner Pass. Med, pt
shd; htd wc; chem disp; mv service pnt; shwrs inc; el pnts
(16A) metered; gas; lndtte; shop; rest, snacks; bar; playgrnd;
pool; dogs; quiet; ccard acc; red CKE/CCI. "Conv NH bef
x-ing Grossglockner Pass." 1 Jun-15 Oct & 1 Dec-15 Apr.
€ 16.40                                                     2009*

⊞ **HEILIGENBLUT** *C2* (8km S Rural) *46.97908, 12.88574*
**Camping Zirknitzer, Döllach 107, 9843 Grosskirchheim
(Kärnten) [tel/fax (04825) 451; camping.zirknitzer@
utanet.at; http://web.utanet.at/zirknitp]** B107
fr Grossglockner Pass, S thro Heiligenblut dir Winklern &
Lienz, site sp. Sm, pt shd; wc; sauna; shwrs; el pnts (16A)
€2.60; lndtte; shop 500m; tradsmn; rest; bar; playgrnd; pool;
tennis 500m; fitness rm; site clsd Nov & end Apr; adv bkg;
quiet. "Well-run, scenic site; friendly & helpful; gd, modern
san facs; gd walking; conv Grossglockner & Italian border."
€ 15.00                                                     2009*

⊞ **HEILIGENBLUT** *C2* (1km W Rural) *47.03682, 12.83887*
**Nationalpark-Camping Grossglockner, Hadergasse
11, 9844 Heiligenblut (Kärnten) [(04824) 2048; fax
24622; nationalpark-camping@heiligenblut.at; www.
heiligenblut.at/nationalpark-camping]** At S end
Grossglockner. Keep R in Heiligenblut, down hill & foll sp to
site. Med, pt sl, unshd; wc; shwrs inc; el pnts (16-20A) €2.50;
gas; lndtte; shop 500m; rest, snacks; bar; playgrnd; pool
200m; dogs €2; site clsd mid-Oct to end Nov; Eng spkn; quiet;
CKE/CCI. "In Hohe Tauern National Park; sh, steep walk to
vill; gd NH bef/after Grossglockner Pass; v ltd facs low ssn."
€ 19.70                                                     2009*

**HEITERWANG see Reutte** *C1*

⊞ **HIRSCHEGG** *C3* (200m N Rural) *47.02300, 14.95325*
**Campingplatz Hirschegg, Haus No. 53, 8584 Hirschegg
[info@camping-hirschegg.at; www.camping-hirschegg.at]**
Exit A2 junc 224 Modriach N. At T-junc foll sp to Hirschegg &
in cent of vill turn R at petrol stn. Site in 300m on L by fire stn.
Med, hdg/mkd pitch, pt shd; wc; chem disp; shwrs inc; el pnts
(10A) €2; lndtte; shop, rest, bar in vill; playgrnd; pool; lake sw
adj; wifi; 30% statics; dogs €1; adv bkg; quiet. "Excel, family-
run site." € 16.00                                          2009*

**HOPFGARTEN see Wörgl** *C2*

**IMST** *C1* (1km E Rural) *47.23972, 10.7450* **International Camping am Schwimmbad, Schwimmbadweg 10, 6460 Imst (Tirol) [(05412) 66612; camp1@gmx.at; http:// members.aon.at/camp1]** Exit A12/E60 at Imst onto B171 N dir Imst; then exit B171 onto B189; in 500m turn R, then immed L into Schwimmbadweg. Foll camp sps fr by-pass to avoid Imst town & narr rds. Poss easier to foll Schwimbad (sw pool) sps. Med, mkd pitch, pt sl, pt shd; wc; chem disp; shwrs inc; el pnts (6A) €2; gas; lndtte (inc dryer); shop; pool adj; cycle hire; wifi; dogs €1.50; poss cr; Eng spkn; red long stay. "V pleasant in mountain setting; gd walking; helpful owner; ltd san facs low ssn." 1 May-15 Sep. € 18.00          2009*

⊞ **IMST** *C1* (1.5km S Rural) *47.22861, 10.74305* **Caravanpark Imst-West, Langgasse 62, 6460 Imst (Tirol) [(05412) 66293; fax 662319; fink.franz@aon.at; www. imst-west.com]** Fr A12/E60 exit Imst-Pitztal onto B171 N dir Imst. In 1km at rndabt take last exit heading W then immed sharp L opp Citroën dealer into Langgasse. In 750m turn L, site on R. Med, mkd pitch, pt sl, pt shd; wc; chem disp; mv service pnt; shwrs inc; el pnts (6-10A) €3; gas; lndtte; shop 200m; rest 200m; snacks; bar; playgrnd; pool 1.5km; ski lift 2km; free skibus; dogs €2; Eng spkn; quiet. "Gd cent for Tirol, trips to Germany & en rte for Innsbruck; lovely views; clean facs; gd." € 32.60          2013*

**INNSBRUCK** *C1* (11km SE Rural) *47.26002, 11.50509* **Campingplatz Judenstein, Judenstein 42, 6074 Rinn-bei-Innsbruck (Tirol) [(05223) 78098; fax 7887715; camping@ kbrinn.at; www.kbrinn.at/camping]** Exit A12/E60 junc 68 & foll Tulfes sp. Thro Tulfes & 2km onto Rinn, site sp, just bef church with clock. App rd narr & steep in places. Med, hdg/ mkd pitch, pt sl, pt shd; wc; chem disp; mv service pnt; shwrs inc; el pnts (6A) €2; gas; lndtte; shop adj; tradsmn, rest, bar adj; lake sw 5km; golf 1km; cab TV; 50% statics; dogs; Eng spkn; quiet but church bells adj; CKE/CCI. "Gd, clean, well-run site; site yourself; office open evenings; helpful, friendly staff; ample pitches; bus service to area & city cent." 1 May-30 Sep. € 13.00          2011*

⊞ **INNSBRUCK** *C1* (6km SW Rural) *47.23724, 11.33865* **Camping Natterersee, Natterer See 1, 6161 Natters (Tirol) [(0512) 546732; fax 54673216; info@natterersee.com; www.natterersee.com]** App Innsbruck fr E or W on A12 take A13/E45 dir Brenner. Leave at 1st junc sp Innsbruck Süd, Natters. Foll sp Natters - acute R turns & severe gradients (care across unguarded level x-ing), turn sharp R in vill & foll sp to site. Take care on negotiating ent. Narr rds & app. Fr S on A13 Brennerautobahn exit junc 3 & foll dir Mutters & Natters. Med, pt shd, sl, terr; htd wc; chem disp; mv service pnt; baby facs; shwrs inc; el pnts (6A)€3.75; gas; lndtte (inc dryer); shop; rest, snacks; bar; BBQ; playgrnd; lake sw; waterslide; tennis; cycle hire; games area; games/TV rm; wifi; entmnt; no dogs Jul/Aug, otherwise €4.50; bus to Innsbruck; train 2.5km; sep car park high ssn; guided hiking; clsd 1 Nov-mid Dec; poss v cr; Eng spkn; adv bkg; ccard acc; red low ssn; CKE/CCI. "Well-kept site adj local beauty spot; lakeside pitches gd views (extra charge); gd, scenic cent for walking & driving excursions; gd for children; friendly, helpful staff; excel modern san facs; some sm pitches & narr site rds diff lge o'fits; fantastic setting; special shwr for dogs." ♦ € 48.40 SBS - G01          2013*

⊞ **INNSBRUCK** *C1* (5km W Rural) *47.26339, 11.32629* **Camping Kranebittehof, Kranebitter Allee 216, 6020 Innsbruck-Kranebitten (Tirol) [(0512) 279558; fax 579558140; info@camping-kranebitterhof.at; www. camping-kranebitterhof.at]** Fr W fork L after Zirl bef main rd rv bdge, sp Innsbruck & foll B171 for 3km. Fr S on A13 fr border foll dir Bregenz on A12 exit Kranebitten & foll sp to site. Sharp ent on R. Med, mkd pitch, some hdstg, terr, pt sl, pt shd; htd wc; chem disp; mv service pnt; shwrs inc; el pnts (6-10A) inc; lndtte; shop; pizzeria; hiking; ski lift 5km; wifi; 20% statics; dogs; bus; poss cr; Eng spkn; some m'way & airport noise; ccard acc; red low ssn/long stay/CKE/CCI. "Excel, refurbished site in lovely situation; vg, modern san facs; friendly, helpful staff; site easy to find fr m'way, excel rest on site." ♦ € 37.00          2013*

⊞ **INNSBRUCK** *C1* (5km W Urban) *47.25307, 11.32661* **Campingplatz Pizzeria Stigger, Bahnhofstraße 10, 6176 Völs (Tirol) [(0512) 303533; campingvoels@aon.at; www. camping-stigger.at]** Exit A12/E60 at Völs exit & foll site sp. Sm, pt shd; wc; chem disp; mv service pnt; shwrs inc; el pnts inc; lndtte; shop 100m; rest (pizzeria); snacks; bar; pool 200m; bus adj; Eng spkn; ccard acc; CKE/CCI. "Gd; conv Innsbruck." € 28.00          2010*

⊞ **INNSBRUCK** *C1* (8km W Rural) *47.2605, 11.25575* **Farmcamping Branger Alm, Haus Nr 32, 6175 Unterperfuss (Tirol) [(05232) 2209; fax 22094; brangeralm@aon.at; www.brangeralm.at]** Fr A12/E60 exit at Zirl-West, junc 91 & turn R at T-junc on m'way exit & foll sp Unterperfuss. Turn L at next T-junc. Site on R in 2km at ent to vill, immed after church on R. Med, pt shd; htd wc; chem disp; shwrs inc; el pnts (6A) metered; gas; lndtte; snacks; rest adj; bar 1km; pool 3km; ski lift 4km; 90% statics; dogs €1; bus to Innsbruck; Eng spkn; quiet but some rlwy & rd noise. "Excel clean, modern facs; site poss untidy low ssn; if recep not in office, go to rest; vg rest." ♦ € 20.00          2009*

**ITTER BEI HOPFGARTEN see Wörgl** *C2*

⊞ **JENBACH** *C2* (6.4km NW Rural) *47.42156, 11.74043* **Camping Karwendel, 6212 Maurach (Tirol) [(05243) 6116; fax 20036; info@karwendel-camping.at; www. karwendel-camping.at]** Exit A12/E45/E50 junc 39 onto B181. Foll sp Pertisau & Maurach. In 8km (climbing fr a'route turn L at Maurach. Foll rd thro vill, turn L at T-junc, then strt across rndabt twd lake. Site sp past recycling cent. Med, unshd; htd wc; chem disp; shwrs €1; el pnts (10A) €2; lndtte; shop 500m; rest, snacks; bar; playgrnd; lake sw 500m; golf 4km; internet; TV; 80% statics; dogs €2; site clsd Nov; poss cr; quiet. "In open country, glorious views of lake & mountains; diff access lge o'fits; site neglected & rundown." € 35.00          2014*

**KALS AM GROßGLOCKNER** *C2* (7km E) *47.00115, 12.64453* **National Park Camping, Berg 22, A9981 Kals am Großglockner [(043) 4852 67389; info@nationalpark-camping-kals.at; www.nationalpark-camping-kals.at/]** Fr 108 (Leinz - Millersill) take L26 to Kals am Großglockner. Site thro vill in abt 2km well sp. Med; mkd pitch; terr; unshd; htd wc; chem disp;mv service pnt; shwrs; el pnts 10A; lndtte; tradsmn, CKE/CCI, "Excel, brand new purpose built site in Hohe Tauern Nat Park at 1460m; superb san facs." 1 April - 31 Oct. € 22.00          2012*

**KAUMBERG** *B4* (4km E Rural) *48.01958, 15.94335*
**Campingplatz Paradise Garden, Höfnergraben 2, 2572
Kaumberg (Niederösterreich) [0676 4741966 (mob); fax
(02765) 3883; grandl@camping-noe.at; www.camping-
noe.at]** B18 Hainfeld-Berndorf rd, site sp. Med, unshd; htd wc;
chem disp; mv service pnt; baby facs; shwrs inc; el pnts (12A)
€2; gas; lndtte (inc dryer); shop & 4km; rest 1.5km; snacks; bar;
playgrnd; cycle hire; games rm; 60% statics; dogs free; phone;
Eng spkn; adv bkg; quiet; red long stay; CKE/CCI. "Gd walking;
helpful owner; superb san facs; easy access Vienna; lovely rural
area." ♦ 1 Apr-31 Oct. € 22.00                    2011*

**KEUTSCHACH AM SEE** *D3* (3km E Rural) *46.58673, 14.22778*
**Camping Reautschnighof, Reauz 4, 9074 Keutschach-
am-See (Kärnten) [tel/fax (0463) 281106; camping-
reautschnighof@gmx.at; www.camping-reautschnighof.
at]** Exit A2 at Klagenfurt West S to Viktring on S side of
Wörthersee. Foll sp Keutschach & site. Sm, mkd pitch, pt sl,
terr, unshd; wc; chem disp; shwrs €0.50; el pnts (6A) inc; shop
3km; rest 600m; pool 8km; lake sw 200m; dogs €1.50; quiet;
"Lovely rural walks fr area." 1 May-30 Sep. € 20.50      2011*

**KEUTSCHACH AM SEE** *D3* (3km E Rural) *46.58348, 14.22878*
**Camping Reichmann, Reauz 5, 9074 Keutschach-am-See
(Kärnten) [(0699) 1500057; info@camping-reichmann.at;
www.camping-reichmann.at]** Exit A2 at Klagenfurt W onto
B91 S to Viktring. Foll sp Keutschach-am-See, site sp. Lge, pt
sl, pt shd; wc; chem disp; shwrs inc; el pnts (6A) inc; lndtte (inc
dryer); shops 2km; rest, snacks; bar; BBQ; playgrnd; lake sw
adj; fishing; games rm; internet; dogs €1.50; phone; poss cr;
Eng spkn; quiet; ccard acc; red low ssn; CKE/CCI. "Excel." ♦
1 May-20 Sep. € 25.70                              2009*

**KEUTSCHACH AM SEE** *D3* (2.5km S Rural) *46.58472,
14.17225* **Strandcamping Sud, Dobeinitz 30a, 9074
Keutschach-am-See (Kärnten) [(04273) 2773; fax 27734;
info@strandcampingsued.at; www.keutschachsued.at]**
Fr Klagenfurt (N) take rd 91 (E94) sp Loibl Pass & turn R for
Viktring & bypass Keutschach. At Keutschach See turn L off
main rd at rndabt & foll sp past Strandcamping North. Lge,
mkd pitch, some hdstg, pt sl, pt shd; wc; chem disp; mv service
pnt; shwrs inc; el pnts (10A) inc; gas; lndtte (inc dryer); shop;
tradsmn; rest, snacks; bar; BBQ; playgrnd; beach; lake sw adj;
80% statics; dogs €2.30; poss cr; Eng spkn. "Gd walking, sw,
cycling & views." 1 May-30 Sep. € 27.50           2010*

**KEUTSCHACH AM SEE** *D3* (6km SW Rural) *46.57796,
14.14821* **FKK Camping Müllerhof (Naturist), Dobein 10,
9074 Keutschach-am-See (Kärnten) [(04273) 2517; fax
25175; muellerhof@fkk-camping.at; www.fkk-camping.
at]** Exit fr A2 junc 335 sp Velden West dir Velden. In 1km at
rndabt foll sp Keutschach; in 3km turn L at site sp. Or fr Villach,
take B83 E twd Velden. Turn R approx 3km bef Velden sp
Keutschach & foll site sp. Fr Klagenfurt, take B91 S, turn W to
Keutschach. Cont on main rd past vill & foll site sp. Lge, mkd
pitch, some hdstg, pt shd; htd wc; chem disp; mv service pnt;
sauna; baby facs; shwrs inc; el pnts (6A) inc; lndtte (inc dryer);
shops adj; tradsmn; rest, snacks; bar; playgrnd; sw in lake;
games area; games rm; wifi; entmnt; TV; 10% statics; no dogs;
phone; adv bkg; quiet. "Gd for lakes, walks, sailing." 15 Apr-
30 Sep. € 30.00                                   2011*

**KEUTSCHACH AM SEE** *D3* (1km W Rural) *46.59080,
14.16490* **Camping Brückler Nord, Keutschachsee 5, 9074
Keutschach-am-See (Kärnten) [tel/fax (04273) 2384; camp.
brueckler@aon.at; www.brueckler.co.at]** On N point of
Keutschacher See at exit of Reifnitz rd fr Velden-Viktring rd.
Med, pt shd; wc; chem disp; mv service pnt; shwrs inc; el pnts
(6A) €4; lndtte; shop, rest adj; snacks; BBQ; playgrnd; lake sw;
fishing; cycle hire; wifi; 25% statics; dogs €2.50; quiet. "Excel
facs for children." 1 May-30 Sep. € 28.00 (CChq acc)    2009*

⊞ **KITZBUHEL** *C2* (1.5km W Rural) *47.45906, 12.3619*
**Campingplatz Schwarzsee, Reitherstrasse 24, 6370
Kitzbühel (Tirol) [(05356) 62806 or 64479; fax 6447930;
office@bruggerhof-camping.at; www.bruggerhof-
camping.at]** Site sp fr Kitzbühel dir Kirchberg-Schwarzsee.
Lge, pt sl, pt shd; htd wc; chem disp; mv service pnt; fam
bthrm; sauna; shwrs inc; el pnts (16A) metered; mains gas conn
some pitches; lndtte; shop; rest adj; snacks; bar; playgrnd; pool
2km; lake sw 300m; cab TV; 80% statics; dogs €5.50; phone;
bus; poss cr; Eng spkn; adv bkg; ccard acc; CKE/CCI. "Gd
walks, cable cars & chair lifts; vg, well-maintained site; poss
mosquito prob; some pitches in statics area; friendly owner." ♦
€ 34.80                                           2009*

**KLAGENFURT** *D3* (4km W Rural) *46.61826, 14.25641*
**Camping Wörthersee, Metnitzstrand 5, 9020 Klagenfurt
am wörthersee (Kärnten) [(0463) 287810; fax 2878103;
info@campingfreund.at; www.camping-woerthersee.at]**
Fr A2/E66 take spur to Klagenfurt-West, exit at Klagenfurt-
Wörthersee. Turn R at traff lts & immed L at rd fork (traff lts),
then foll sp to site. Lge, shd; wc; chem disp; sauna; shwrs inc;
el pnts (10A) inc; lndtte; shop; rest; playgrnd; sand beach adj;
cycle hire; entmnt; dogs €3.20; 10% statics; bus; quiet; ccard
acc. "V clean facs; local tax €3.50 per visit." ♦ 1 May-30 Sep.
€ 31.00                                           2013*

> ## "That's changed – Should
> ## I let The Club know?"
> If you find something on site that's different from
> the site entry, fill in a report and let us know. See
> www.caravanclub.co.uk/europereport.

**KLOSTERNEUBURG** *B4* (250m NE Rural) *48.31097, 16.32810*
**Donaupark Camping Klosterneuburg, In der Au, 3402
Klosterneuburg (Niederösterreich) [(02243) 25877;
fax 25878; campklosterneuburg@oeamtc.at; www.
campingklosterneuburg.at]** Fr A22/E59 exit junc 7 onto
B14, site sp in cent of town behind rlwy stn. After passing
Klosterneuburg Abbey on L turn 1st R (sharp turn undr rlwy).
Site immed ahead. Med, mkd pitch, pt shd; htd wc; chem disp;
mv service pnt; shwrs inc; el pnts (6-12A) €3; gas; lndtte (inc
dryer); shop; rest 200m; snacks; BBQ; cooking facs; playgrnd;
leisure cent & htd pools adj; cycle & boat hire; tennis; wifi; TV
rm; 5% statics; dogs free; phone; bus; train to Vienna; poss cr;
quiet; ccard acc; red CKE/CCI. "Well-organised, popular site;
vg san facs; helpful staff; sm pitches; conv Danube cycle path
& Vienna; church & monastery worth visit." ♦ 15 Mar-31 Oct.
€ 26.00                                           2012*

⊞ **KOSSEN** *B2* (2.5km W Rural) *47.65388, 12.41544*
**Eurocamping Wilder Kaiser, Kranebittau 18, 6345
Kössen (Tirol) [(05375) 6444; fax 2113; info@eurocamp-
koessen.com; www.eurocamp-koessen.com]** Leave A12 at
Oberaudorf/Niederndorf junc, head E on 172 thro Niederndorf
& Walchsee to Kössen. Strt across at rndabt, in 1km turn R sp
Hinterburg Lift. At next junc turn R & site located after 400m.
Lge, mkd pitch, pt shd; htd wc; chem disp; mv service pnt;
serviced pitches; sauna; solarium; baby facs; shwrs inc; el pnts
(6A) metered + conn fee; gas; lndtte; shop high ssn; tradsmn;
rest, snacks high ssn; bar; playgrnd; htd pool adj; tennis; games
area; golf 2km; entmnt; internet; cab TV; 50% statics; dogs €4;
poss cr; Eng spkn; adv bkg; ccard acc; CKE/CCI. "Lovely site;
excel play area & organised activities; rafting, hang-gliding &
canoeing 1km; excel." € 23.50                           2012*

⊞ **KOTSCHACH** *D2* (800m SW Rural) *46.66946, 12.99153*
**Alpencamp, Kötschach 284, 9640 Kötschach-Mauthen
(Kärnten) [tel/fax (04715) 429; info@alpencamp.at; www.
alpencamp.at]** At junc of rds B110 & B111 in Kötschach turn
W onto B111, foll camp sps to site in 800m on L. Med, mkd
pitch, pt shd; htd wc; chem disp; mv service pnt; sauna; shwrs
inc; el pnts (16A) inc; lndtte (inc dryer); sm shop; supmkt 400m;
rest 100m; snacks; playgrnd; 2 pools (1 htd, covrd); waterslide;
tennis; games area; games rm; boat & cycle hire; tennis 400m;
wifi; TV; dogs €2.50; phone; site clsd 1 Nov-14 Dec; poss cr;
Eng spkn; quiet; ccard acc. "Useful for Plöcken Pass; cycle
tracks on rv bank nrby; vg san facs; friendly, helpful owner; vg
site." ♦ € 27.00 (CChq acc)                            2010*

**KRAMSACH AM REINTALERSEE see Rattenberg** *C2*

**KREMS AN DER DONAU** *B4* (1km SW Urban) *48.40305,
15.59194* **Donaupark-Camping, Yachthafenstrasse
19, 3504 Krems-Stein (Neiderösterreich) [tel/fax
(02732) 84455; donaucampingkrems@aon.at; www.
donauparkcamping-krems.at]** Fr B3 along N of Danube in
Stein, foll site & 'Schiffstation' & camping sps to site on rvside.
Med, unshd; htd wc; chem disp; mv service pnt; shwrs inc; el
pnts (16A) €2; gas; lndtte (inc dryer); shop 500m; tradsmn;
rest adj; snacks; bar; playgrnd 200m; pool 500m; cycle hire;
5% statics; phone; poss v cr; Eng spkn; adv bkg rec high ssn
& pub hols; some rd & rv traffic noise; ccard acc; CKE/CCI.
"Well-run site; excel, clean facs; office open 0730-1000 &
1630-1900; sm pitches; conv Danube cycle rte." 1 Apr-31 Oct.
€ 17.60                                                2009*

**KREMS AN DER DONAU** *B4* (7km SW Rural) *48.38998,
15.51678* **Campingplatz Rossatzbach, Rossatzbach 21,
3602 Rossatz (Neiderösterreich) [(02714) 6317; fax 6249;
gemeinde@rossatz-arnsdorf.at; www.rossatz-arnsdorf.at]**
Exit A1 junc 80 sp Melk & Donau Brücke. Cross Rv Danube &
turn R along Danube L bank. After Dürnstein re-cross Danube
on metal box bdge & turn R sp Melk & Rossatzbach. In 3km
turn 1st R in Rossatzbach vill & foll sp to site in 200m. Sm,
pt shd; htd wc; chem disp; shwrs inc; el pnts (16A) metered;
lndtte; shop 1km; rest, snacks; bar; playgrnd; games area;
20% statics; dogs; poss cr; adv bkg; quiet; CKE/CCI. "Pleasant
site on opp site of Danube to Dürnstein; most pitches on rvside;
interesting area." Easter-31 Oct. € 17.25              2009*

⊞ **LANDECK** *C1* (500m W Urban) *47.14263, 10.56147*
**Camping Riffler, Bruggfeldstrasse 2, 6500 Landeck (Tirol)
[(05442) 64898; fax 648984; info@camping-riffler.at;
www.camping-riffler.at]** Exit E60/A12 at Landeck-West, site
in 1.5km, 500m fr cent on L. Sm, pt shd; wc; chem disp; shwrs
inc; el pnts (10A) €2.70 (poss rev pol); gas; lndtte; shop adj;
snacks, rest adj; playgrnd; pool 500m; cycle hire; dogs free;
poss cr; site clsd May; ccard acc; red CKE/CCI. "Well-kept,
clean, friendly site; sm pitches; narr rds; recep open 1800-2000
low ssn - site yourself & pay later; excel NH." € 23.50    2011*

# "I like to fill in the reports
# as I travel from site to site"

You'll find report forms at the back of
this guide, or you can fill them in online
at www.caravaclub.co.uk/europereport.

⊞ **LANGENFELD** *C1* (400m S Rural) *47.07228, 10.96450*
**Camping Ötztal, Unterlängenfeld 220, 6444 Längenfeld
(Tirol) [(05253) 5348; fax 5909; info@camping-oetztal.
com; www.camping-oetztal.com]** Exit A12 junc 123 at
Ötztal onto B186 dir Sölden. On ent Längenfeld foll sp sports
cent, site on R immed bef bdge over Rv Fischbach. Med,
some hdstg, pt shd; wc; chem disp; mv service pnt; baby facs;
solarium; sauna; shwrs inc (6A) metered; gas; lndtte;
shop adj; rest; bar; playgrnd; htd pool adj; rafting; tennis
500m; wifi; sat TV; 15% statics; dogs €3.10; poss cr; Eng
spkn; quiet. "Gd rest & bar; mountain views; thermal springs,
open air museum & Tirolean folk museum nr; vg site." ♦
€ 22.50                                                2011*

⊞ **LANGENWANG** *C4* (N Rural) *47.56875, 15.62008* **Europa
Camping, Siglstrasse 5, 8665 Langenwang (Steiermark)
[(03854) 2950; fax (02143) 380982394; europa.camping.
stmk@aon.at; www.campsite.at/europa.camping.
langenwang]** Exit S6 sp Langenwang, site sp in town cent.
Sm, hdg pitch, pt shd; htd wc; chem disp; shwrs €0.80; el pnts
(16A) metered; lndtte; shop, rest, snacks; bar 100m; playgrnd
adj; htd, covrd pool 7km; lake sw 4km; ski facs; 30% statics;
dogs; bus; Eng spkn; adv bkg; quiet; red long stay. "Pleasant,
friendly site; family atmosphere; excel facs; peaceful site."
€ 14.80                                                2013*

**LEIBNITZ** *D4* (700m W Urban) *46.77864, 15.52891* **Camping
Leibnitz, Rudolf-Hans-Bartsch-Gasse 33, 8430 Leibnitz
(Steiermark) [(03452) 82463; fax 71491; leibnitz@camping-
steiermark.at; www.camping-steiermark.at]** Fr A9 take exit
Leibnitz onto B74, site not well sp, but nr sw pool, on rvside.
Med, hdg/mkd pitch, pt shd; wc; chem disp; mv service pnt;
fam bthrm; shwrs €1; el pnts (10-16A) €1.80; lndtte (inc dryer);
shop 700m; rest, snacks; bar; playgrnd; pool adj; waterslide; rv
sw adj; tennis; no statics; dogs; Eng spkn; ccard acc; CKE/CCI.
"Gd NH; excel san facs; gd sports & leisure facs; interesting
town." ♦ 1 May-15 Oct. € 15.50                          2009*

**LERMOOS see Ehrwald** *C1*

**LEUTASCH see Seefeld in Tirol** *C1*

**AUSTRIA**

**LIENZ** *C2* (500m S Urban) *46.82255, 12.77111* **Comfort-Camping Falken, Falkenweg 7, 9900 Lienz (Tirol) [(04852) 64022; fax 640226; camping.falken@tirol.com; www.camping-falken.com]** On B100 to town cent, foll sp Tristacher See, site sp adj leisure cent. Med, pt shd; htd wc; chem disp; mv service pnt; baby facs; shwrs €0.75; el pnts (6A) inc; gas; lndtte (inc dryer); sm shop; tradsmn; rest, snacks, bar high ssn; playgrnd; htd, covrd pool 500m; ski lift 2km; ski bus; golf 4km; wifi; TV; 30% statics; dogs €3.50; poss cr; quiet; ccard acc; red long stay. "Gate closes 1300-1500; easy walk to vill with beautiful scenery - nearest site to Lienz; sm pitches; vg site." ♦ 20 Dec-20 Oct. € 27.50                                         2010*

**LIENZ** *C2* (2km SW Rural) *46.81388, 12.76388* **Dolomiten-Camping Amlacherhof, Lake rd 20, 9908 Amlach  Lienz [(04852) 62317 / 69917 62317-1 (mob); fax 62317-12; info@amlacherhof.at; www.amlacherhof.at]** S fr Lienz on B100, foll sp in 1.5km to Amlach. In vill, foll site sp. Med, hdg/mkd pitch, pt shd; htd wc; chem disp; mv service pnt; baby facs; shwrs €0.80; el pnts (16A) metered inc; lndtte (inc dryer); rest 500m; snacks; bar; BBQ; playgrnd; htd pool; tennis; cycle hire; games rm; golf 7km; wifi; TV rm; 5% statics; dogs €2.90; bus adj; site clsd 1 Nov-15 Dec; poss cr; Eng spkn; adv bkg; quiet. "Excel touring cent; many mkd walks & cycle rtes; cable cars, ski lifts 3km; attractive, historic town; excel, scenic site; local taxes €5." ♦ 1 Mar-31 Oct. € 35.40 (CChq acc)      2014*

**LINZ** *B3* (10km E Rural) *48.23527, 14.37888* **Camping-Linz am Pichlingersee, Wienerstrasse 937, 4030 Linz (Oberösterreich) [(0732) 305314; fax 3053144; office@camping-linz.at; www.camping-linz.at]** Exit A1/E60 junc 160; take Enns dir; go L on 1st rndabt; do not go under rndabt thro underpass; site is sp on R. Med, mkd pitch, pt shd; htd wc; chem disp; mv service pnt; shwrs inc; el pnts (6A) inc; gas; lndtte; sm shop & 2km; tradsmn; rest, snacks; bar; cooking facs; lake sw adj; tennis; internet; 40% statics; dogs €1.90; bus; site clsd 1300-1500; poss cr; Eng spkn; adv bkg; some noise fr m'way; red long stay. "Excel modern san facs, well-run, family-run site; friendly staff; gd walks around lake; monastery at St Florian worth visit; conv NH; gd." ♦ ltd 15 Mar-31 Oct. € 26.60                                                            2014*

**LOFER** *C2* (1km S Rural) *47.57500, 12.70804* **Camping Park Grubhof, St Martin 39, 5092 St Martin-bei-Lofer (Salzburg) [(06588) 82370; fax 82377; home@grubhof.com; www.grubhof.com]** Clear sps to camp at ent on rd B311 Lofer to Zell-am-See. Site on L after garden centre. Lge, pt shd; htd wc; chem disp; mv service pnt; baby facs; serviced pitches; shwrs inc; el pnts (10A) €2; lndtte (inc dryer); supmkt 700m; rest; bar; pool 1km; playgrnd; wifi; dogs €3; phone; adv bkg; bus to Salzburg; quiet; ccard not acc; CKE/CCI. "Beautiful scenery; roomy, peaceful site; excel san facs; adult only & dog free areas; sh walk to vill; highly rec; mountain views; some meadowside and rvside pitches; delightful rest/bar." ♦ 1 Jan-23 Mar, 11 Apr-2 Nov, 6 Dec-31 Dec. € 42.80 SBS - G04                                                        2014*

⊞ **LUNZ AM SEE** *B4* (300m E Urban) *47.86194, 15.03638* **Ötscherland Camping, Zellerhofstrasse 23, 3293 Lunz-am-See (Niederösterreich) [tel/fax (07486) 8413; info@oetscherlandcamping.at; www.oetscherlandcamping.at]** Fr S on B25 turn R into Lunz-am-See. In 300m turn L, cross rv & take 1st L, site on L on edge of vill. Sm, hdstg, pt shd; htd wc; chem disp; mv service pnt; shwrs €1; el pnts (16A) inc; lndtte; shop, rest in vill; lake sw 500m; winter skiing; 80% statics; dogs €1; Eng spkn; quiet. "Excel walking; immac facs; vg site on Rv Ybbs & Eisenstrasse." € 15.00                     2009*

**MAISHOFEN see Zell am See** *C2*

**MALTA see Gmünd (Kärnten)** *C3*

**MARBACH AN DER DONAU** *B4* (1km W Rural) *48.21309, 15.13828* **Campingplatz Marbacher, Granz 51, 3671 Marbach-an-der-Donau (Niederösterreich) [tel/fax (07413) 20733; info@marbach-freizeit.at; www.marbach-freizeit.at]** Fr W exit A1 junc 100 at Ybbs onto B25. Cross Rv Danube & turn R onto B3. Site in 7km. Fr E exit A1 junc 90 at Pöchlarn, cross rv & turn L onto B3 to Marbach, site sp. Med, mkd pitch, pt shd; htd wc; chem disp; mv service pnt; shwrs inc; el pnts (16A) €2.50; lndtte (inc dryer); shop 500m; tradsmn; rest 500m; BBQ; rv sw; watersports; tennis 800m; boat & cycle hire; internet; entmnt; 5% statics; dogs €1.90; adv bkg; rlwy & rv noise; ccard acc; red CKE/CCI. "Beautiful, well-managed site; sm, narr pitches; excel facs & staff; gd rst & bar; gd cycling & watersports; v clean facs; gd nh fr m'way or longer stay for touring." ♦ 1 Apr-31 Oct. € 28.00 (CChq acc)                                                        2014*

**MARIAZELL** *B4* (3km NW Rural) *47.79009, 15.28221* **Campingplatz am Erlaufsee, Erlaufseestrasse 3, 8630 St Sebastien-bei-Mariazell (Steiermark) [(03882) 4937; fax 214822; gemeinde@st-sebastian.at; www.st-sebastian.at]** On B20 1km N of Mariazell turn W sp Erlaufsee. Site in 3km on app to lake, turn L thro car park ent to site. Med, pt sl, pt shd; wc; chem disp; shwrs €0.50; el pnts (12A) metered; lndtte; shop 3km; rest, snacks adj; beach nr; bus high ssn; dogs €1.90; quiet. "Cable car in Mariazell; pilgrimage cent; all hot water by token fr owner." 1 May-15 Sep. € 16.30                      2011*

**MATREI IN OSTTIROL** *C2* (500m S Rural) *46.99583, 12.53906* **Camping Edengarten, Edenweg 15a, 9971 Matrei-in-Osttirol (Tirol) [tel/fax (04875) 5111; info@campingedengarten.at; www.campingedengarten.at]** App fr Lienz on B108 turn L bef long ascent (by-passing Matrei) sp Matrei-in-Osttirol & Camping. App for N thro Felbertauern tunnel, by-pass town, turn R at end of long descent, sps as above. Med, pt shd; wc; chem disp; mv service pnt; shwrs €0.50; el pnts (10A); gas; lndtte; supmkt, rest, snacks adj; bar; playgrnd; pool 300m; 10% statics; dogs; bus; poss cr. "Gd mountain scenery; helpful owner; beautiful views; pretty town; some rd noise during daytime." 1 Apr-31 Oct. € 33.60  2014*

**MATREI IN OSTTIROL** *C2* (20km W Rural) *47.01912, 12.63695* **Camping Kals Am Großglockner, Burg 22, 9981 Kals am Großglockner [04852 67389; info@nationalpark-camping-kals.at; www.nationalpark-camping-kals.at]** Fr 108 Matrei in Osttirol to Lienz, exit at Huben onto L26 to Kals. 3km after vill foll sp to Dorfertal. National Park campsite on L. Med, unshd; htd wc; chem disp; mv service pnt; baby facs; shwrs inc; lndtte (inc dryer); shop; tradsmn; rest; wifi; dogs €2.50; ski bus; twin axles acc; Eng spkn; quiet; ccard acc; CCI. "Excel site; excel walking & climbing." ♦ 17 May-13 Oct. € 21.00                    2014*

**MAURACH see Schwaz** *C2*

**MAYRHOFEN** *C2* (1km N Rural) *47.17617, 11.86969* **Camping Mayrhofen, Laubichl 125, 6290 Mayrhofen (Tirol) [(05285) 6258051; fax 6258060; camping@alpenparadies.com; www.alpenparadies.com]** Site at N end of vill off B169. Lge, mkd pitch, hdstg, pt shd; wc; chem disp; mv service pnt; sauna; shwrs inc; el pnts (10A) €2.50 or metered; gas; lndtte; shop 1km; rest, snacks; playgrnd; pool; cycle hire; wifi; 50% statics; dogs €3; site clsd 1 Nov-15 Dec; adv bkg; poss cr; some factory noise; CKE/CCI. "Modern san facs; diff for lge o'fits; nar rds; gd rest." ♦ € 25.00    2012*

> ## "We must tell The Club about that great site we found"
>
> Get your site reports in by mid-August and we'll do our best to get your updates into the next edition.

**MELK** *B4* (1km N Rural) *48.23347, 15.32888* **Camping Fährhaus Melk, Kolomaniau 3, 3390 Melk (Niederösterreich) [tel/fax (02752) 53291; jensch@brauhof-wieselburg.at]** Skirt Melk on B1, immed after abbey at traff lts, turn N on bdge over rv (sp). Site in 700m. Sm, pt shd; wc; shwrs; el pnts (6A) inc; shop & 1km; rest at Gasthaus; snacks; bar; BBQ; playgrnd; fishing; quiet. "Lovely, basic site but adequate; abbey adj & boating on Danube; NB all sites on banks of Danube liable to close if rv in flood." 1 Apr-31 Oct. € 17.60                    2010*

**MELK** *B4* (5km N Urban) *48.24298, 15.34040* **Donau Camping Emmersdorf, Bundesstrasse 133, 3644 Emmersdorf-an-der-Donau (Niederösterreich) [(02752) 71707; fax (2752) 7146930; office@emmersdorf.at; www.emmersdorf.at]** Fr A1 take Melk exit. Turn R, foll sp Donaubrücke, cross rv bdge. Turn R, site 200m on L, well sp. Sm, mkd/hdg pitch, pt shd; wc; chem disp; baby facs; shwrs inc; el pnts (6A) inc; lndtte (inc dryer); shops 300m; supmkt 3km; rest 300m; BBQ; pool 13km; fishing; tennis; cycle hire; games rm; dogs; phone; noise fr rd & disco w/end; ccard acc; CKE/CCI. "Liable to close if rv in flood; clean facs; attractive vill; vg." ♦ 1 May-30 Sep. € 19.00                    2014*

**MELK** *B4* (5km NE Rural) *48.25395, 15.37115* **Campingplatz Stumpfer, 3392 Schönbühel (Niederösterreich) [(02752) 8510; fax 851017; office@stumpfer.com; www.stumpfer.com]** Exit A1 junc 80. Foll sp for Melk on B1 as far as junc with B33. Turn onto B33 (S bank of Danube) for 2km to Schönbühel. Site on L adj gasthof, sp. Sm, pt shd, wc; chem disp; shwrs €0.50; el pnts (10-16A) €2.40 or metered; gas; lndtte; shops 5km; rest, snacks; rv adj; dogs; poss v cr; Eng spkn; adv bkg; ccard acc; red long stay/CKE/CCI. "On beautiful stretch of Danube; arr early for rvside pitch; abbeys in Melk & Krems worth visit; lower end site unrel in wet; helpful staff; vg facs but poss stretched high ssn; cycle path adj." 1 Apr-31 Oct. € 17.40                    2010*

**MILLSTATT** *D3* (2km SE Rural) *46.79581, 13.59768* **Terrassencamping Pesenthein (Part Naturist), Presenthein, 9872 Millstatt (Kärnten) [(04766) 2665; fax 202120; camping-pesenthein@aon.it; www.pesenthein.at]** Exit A10/E55 dir Seeboden & Millstatt. Lake lakeside rd B98 fr Millstatt to Dellach. Site on L just beyond Pesenthein. Lge, mkd pitch, terr, pt shd; htd wc; chem disp; mv service pnt; baby facs; shwrs inc; el pnts (6A) €1.75; lndtte; shop; rest; playgrnd; lake sw & beach adj (via tunnel); TV; 17% statics; dogs free; phone; Eng spkn; adv bkg; quiet; CKE/CCI. "Lovely views over lake; excel facs." 1 Apr-30 Sep. € 25.20    2010*

**MILLSTATT** *D3* (4km SE Rural) *46.78863, 13.61418* **Camping Neubauer, Dellach 3, 9872 Millstatt-am-See (Kärnten) [(04766) 2532; fax 23624; info@camping-neubauer.at; www.camping-neubauer.at]** Exit A10/E55 dir Seeboden & Millstatt. Take lakeside rd B98 fr Millstatt to Dellach, R turn & foll sp camping sp. Med, mkd pitch, some hdstg, terr, pt shd; htd wc; chem disp; baby facs; shwrs inc; el pnts (6A) inc; gas; lndtte (inc dryer); shop; tradsmn; rest adj; snacks; bar; BBQ; playgrnd; lake sw; watersports; tennis; cycle hire; golf 6km; wifi; entmnt; 10% statics; dogs €2; poss cr; no adv bkg; quiet; ccard acc. "Gd touring base; easy access to Italy; superb scenery with lakes & mountains; gd walks; excel facs; boat trips nr; gd rest; steep narr rd's to pitches, tractor avail to help; pt shd on lake pitches." 1 May-15 Oct. € 33.00                    2013*

**MITTERSILL** *C2* (E Rural) *47.27761, 12.49267* **Camping Schmidl, Museumstrasse 6, 5730 Mittersill (Salzburg) [(06562) 6158]** Fr Zell-am-See or Kitzbühel, exit to Mittersill, fr town sq foll camping sp past hospital. Sm, pt shd; wc; chem disp; shwrs €0.60; el pnts (15A) inc; lndtte; shops 1km; rest, snacks 100m; 40% statics; dogs; poss cr; quiet. "Friendly & welcoming; useful stop bef Felbertauern tunnel; conv Krimml waterfall & Grossglockner." 1 May-30 Sep. € 12.00    2009*

**MONDSEE** *B3* (3km N Rural) *47.86640, 13.30621* **Camping Mond-See-Land, Punz Au 21, 5310 Tiefgraben (Oberösterreich) [(06232) 2600; fax 27218; austria@campmondsee.at; www.campmondsee.at]** Exit A1/E60/E55 junc 265 for Mondsee, turn N on B154 dir Strasswalchen. After 1.5km turn L dir Haider-Mühle on narr country rd to site in 2km. Site sp fr B154. Med, mkd pitch, pt sl, pt shd; htd wc; chem disp; shwrs inc; el pnts (16A) €3.20; gas; lndtte (inc dryer); shop; tradsmn; rest, snacks; bar; BBQ; playgrnd; pool; boating; internet; entmnt; dogs €2.90; phone; adv bkg; quiet; red long stay; "Beautiful mountain scenery; spacious pitches; excel new san facs; lovely countryside; serviced pitches avail for extra charge; somewhat isolated & away fr main rd." ♦ 1 Apr-31 Oct. € 19.80                    2011*

**MONDSEE** *B3* (5km SE Rural) *47.82956, 13.36554* **Austria Camp, Achort 60, 5310 St Lorenz (Oberösterreich) [(06232) 2927; fax 29274; camp.mondsee@inode.at; www.oberoesterreich.at/austria-camp]** Exit A1/E55/E60 junc 265 onto B154. In 4km at St Lorenz at km 21.4 turn L onto unclassified rd to site in 600m at lakeside. Fr SW via Bad Ischl, at St Gilgen take Mondsee rd; 500m after Plomberg turn R at St Lorenz; Austria Camp sps clear. Med, shd; wc; chem disp; mv service pnt; sauna; baby facs; shwrs inc; el pnts (6A) €2.90; lndtte (inc dryer); rest, snacks; bar; shop; playgrnd; lake sw; fishing; boat-launch; tennis; cycle hire; golf nr; entmnt; 45% statics; dogs €2.90; poss cr (Jul-Aug); adv bkg; quiet; 10% red CKE/CCI. "Gd, clean san facs; gd rest; friendly, family-run site." ♦ 1 May-30 Sep. € 22.50           2010*

⊞ **MURAU** *C3* (5km W Rural) *47.10791, 14.13883* **Camping Olachgut, Kaindorf 90, 8861 St Georgen-ob-Murau (Steiermark) [(03532) 2162 or 3233; fax 21624; office@olachgut.at; www.olachgut.at]** Site sp on rd B97 bet Murau & St Georgen. Med, pt shd; wc; chem disp; mv service pnt; baby facs; sauna; shwrs inc; el pnts (16A) metered; gas conn; lndtte (inc dryer); shop 2.5km; rest, snacks; bar; playgrnd; lake sw; games area; cycle hire; ski lift 2.5km; horseriding; entmnt; internet; 40% statics; dogs €2.20; adv bkg; quiet. "Rural site nr rlwy." ♦ € 25.00           2012*

**MURECK** *D4* (500m S Rural) *46.70491, 15.77240* **Campingplatz Mureck, Austrasse 10, 8480 Mureck (Steiermark) [(03472) 210512; fax 21056; m.rauch@mureck.steiermark.at]** Fr Graz on A9, turn E at junc 226 onto B69 sp Mureck. NB: Low archway in Mureck. Med, mkd pitch, some hdstg, shd; wc; chem disp; shwrs €0.50; el pnts (10A) inc; lndtte (inc dryer); shops adj; rest, snacks; bar; BBQ; playgrnd; htd pool complex inc waterslide adj; fishing; tennis; cycle hire; games area; wifi; 30% statics; dogs €3.50; phone; adv bkg; quiet; red long stay; ccard acc; red CKE/CCI. "Off beaten track in pleasant country town; pt of leisure complex; gd, modern san facs." ♦ 1 May-15 Sep. € 23.00           2010*

⊞ **MURECK** *D4* (10km W Rural) *46.71611, 15.68277* **Gasthof Dorfheuriger, Unterschwarza 1, 8471 Unterschwarza-Murfeld (Steiermark) [(03453) 21001; dorfheuriger@gmx.net; www.dorfheuriger.eu]** On B69 fr Mureck or exit A9 junc 226 at Gersdorf & take B69 E for 2km. Sm, mkd pitch, unshd; wc; chem disp; mv service pnt; el pnts; rest, bar adj; tennis; wifi; quiet. "Vg NH for m'vans only."           2010*

**NASSEREITH** *C1* (1km N Rural) *47.34043, 10.81585* **Romantik-Camping Schloss Fernsteinsee, Fernsteinsee, 6465 Nassereith (Tirol) [(05265) 5210157; fax 52174; camping@fernsteinsee.at; www.fernsteinsee.at/camping]** 5km S of Fern pass. Immed prior to rd bdge. Ent sp by Hotel - use S ent, not ent by bdge/hotel. Med, pt sl, shd; htd wc; chem disp; sauna; solarium; some serviced pitches; shwrs inc; el pnts (6A) inc; lndtte; shop & 4km; rest 400m; snacks; playgrnd; sw in lake adj; boating; sat TV; dogs €2; quiet; ccard acc. "Immac facs; excel rest; stunning scenery for walking/cycling." ♦ Easter-31 Oct. € 31.00           2011*

⊞ **NASSEREITH** *C1* (1.5km E Rural) *47.30975, 10.85466* **Camping Rossbach, Rossbach 325, 6465 Nassereith (Tirol) [tel/fax (05265) 5154; camping.rossbach@aon.at; www.campingrossbach.com]** On ent vill of Nassereith turn E & foll dir Rossbach/Dormitz, site in 1.5km. Foll sm green sps. Narr app. Med, mkd pitch, pt shd; htd wc; chem disp; mv service pnt; baby facs; shwrs inc; el pnts (6A) inc; lndtte (inc dryer); shop; tradsmn; rest, snacks; bar; BBQ; playgrnd; htd pool; paddling pool; fishing; games rm; ski lift 500m; skibus; TV; 5% statics; dogs €1.50; phone; adv bkg; quiet; CKE/CCI. "Mountain views." ♦ € 19.00           2012*

**NATTERS see Innsbruck** *C1*

⊞ **NAUDERS** *C1* (2km S Rural) *46.85139, 10.50472* **Alpencamping, Bundesstrasse 279, 6543 Nauders (Tirol) [(05473) 87217; fax 8721750; info@camping-nauders.at; www.camping-nauders.at]** On W side of B180 just bef Italian border. Sm, some hdstg, unshd; htd wc; chem disp; baby facs; shwrs €0.50; el pnts €1.90; gas conn & 2km; rest, snacks; bar; no statics; dogs €2; phone; site clsd 1 Nov-19 Dec; poss cr; ccard acc; CKE/CCI. "Conv NH for Reschen pass; gd touring base; excel cycling, walking; excel san facs." € 18.00           2009*

⊞ **NENZING** *C1* (2km SW Rural) *47.18313, 9.68238* **Alpencamping Nenzing, Garfrenga 1, 6710 Nenzing (Vorarlberg) [(05525) 624910; fax 624916; office@alpencamping.at; www.alpencamping.at]** Exit A14/E60 or B190 at Nenzing, foll camping sps thro Nenzing for 3km up Gurtis rd, narr & winding in parts, camp on L sp. When leaving site, vehicles routed away fr Nenzing on sp country rds for 10km back to B190. Lge, mkd pitch, hdstg; terr, pt sl, pt shd; wc; chem disp; mv service pnt; baby facs; sauna; shwrs inc; el pnts (4-12A) metered; gas; lndtte; shop; tradsmn; rest, snacks; bar; playgrnd; htd pool; paddling pool; ski lift 1.5km; games rm; wifi; entmnt; TV; many statics; dogs €4.50; clsd 31 Mar-24 Apr; skibus; poss cr; Eng spkn; adv bkg ess; quiet; 10% red low ssn. "Close to ski school & lifts; gd views & beautiful walks; excel san facs; gd rest; recep poss unmanned in winter - phone box adj; excel." ♦ ltd € 31.00           2011*

*See advert on bookmark*

⊞ **NEUSTIFT IM STUBAITAL** *C1* (E Rural) *47.11076, 11.31021* **Camping Stubai, Stubaitalstrasse 94, 6167 Neustift-im-Stubaital (Tirol) [(05226) 2537; fax 29342; info@campingstubai.at; www.campingstubai.at]** S fr Innsbruck on B182 or A13, take B183 dir Fulpmes & Neustift. Site sp, in vill opp church & adj Billa supmkt. If app via A13 & Europabrucke, toll payable on exit junc 10 into Stubaital Valley. Med, some mkd pitch, pt sl, pt terr, pt shd; htd wc; chem disp; mv service pnt; baby facs; fam bthrm; sauna; shwrs inc; el pnts (6A) €2.90; lndtte; shop; rest, bar adj; playgrnd; htd pool 500m; games rm; 50% statics; dogs €2.60; Eng spkn; adv bkg; quiet but church bells (not o'night) & rd noise fr some pitches; debit cards acc; CKE/CCI; "Friendly, family-run site; pitches nr rv poss flood; recep open 0900-1100 & 1700-1900 - barrier down but can use farm ent & find space; excel mountain walking & skiing." € 33.60           2013*

⊞ **NEUSTIFT IM STUBAITAL** *C1* (6km SW Rural) *47.06777, 11.25388* **Camping Edelweiss, Volderau 29, 6167 Neustift-im-Stubaital (Tirol) [tel/fax (05226) 3484; info@ camping-edelweiss.com]** Fr B182 or A13 exit junc 10 take B183 to Neustift, site on R at Volderau vill. Med, hdstg, unshd; htd wc; chem disp; mv waste; shwrs inc; el pnts (4A) €2; gas; lndtte; shop 6km; tradsmn; rest, snacks; 30% statics; dogs €1.50; phone; bus; quiet. "Excel peaceful site in scenic valley; vg, modern san facs; haphazard mix of statics & tourers; winter skiing." € 20.00         2012*

**NUZIDERS see Bludenz** *C1*

⊞ **OBERNBERG AM INN** *B3* (1km SW Rural) *48.31506, 13.32313* **Panorama Camping, Saltzburgerstrasse 28, 4982 Obernberg-am-Inn (Oberösterreich) [tel/ fax (07758) 30024 / 173 2306 571 (mob); obernberg-panoramacamping@aon.at; http://obernberg-panoramacamping.jimdo.com/]** Exit A8/E56 junc 65 to Obernberg. Then take dir Braunau, site well sp. Sm, hdg pitch, pt sl, pt shd; wc; chem disp; serviced pitches; shwrs inc; el pnts (10A) metered or €2 (poss rev pol); lndtte; shop 200m; rest 400m; pool, tennis 800m; o'night area for m'vans; Eng spkn; adv bkg; quiet. "Friendly, excel sm site; site yourself if office clsd; nr to border; spectacular views; san facs clean; gd walking, birdwatching; network of cycle paths around vills on other side of rv; pleasant walk to town past rv viewpoint." € 24.00         2014*

**OBERSAMMELSDORF see Völkermarkt** *D3*

**OBERTRAUN WINKL see Hallstatt** *C3*

**OBERWOLZ** *C3* (1km E Rural) *47.20076, 14.29296* **Camping Rothenfels (Part Naturist), Bromach 1, 8832 Oberwölz (Steiermark) [tel/fax (03581) 76980 or 0664 1412514 (mob); camping@rothenfels.at; www. rothenfels.at]** Fr E on B96 to Niederwölz, then B75 to Oberwölz. Site sp on edge of town. Med, terr, pt shd; htd wc; chem disp; mv service pnt; shwrs inc; el pnts (6A) inc; lndtte (inc dryer); shop 1km; tradsmn; rest, snacks, bar 1km; tradsmn; playgrnd; rv fishing; games rm; 15% statics; dogs €1; Eng spkn; no adv bkg; quiet; ccard acc; red long stay. "Magnificent setting; Oberwölz worth visit - m'vans use car parks outside gates; clean facs." 1 Apr-31 Oct. € 18.50         2010*

⊞ **OETZ** *C1* (8km S Rural) *47.13533, 10.9316* **Ötztal Arena Camp Krismer, Mühlweg 32, 6444 Umhausen (Tirol) [tel/fax (05255) 5390; info@oetztal-camping.at; www. oetztal-camping.at]** Fr A12 exit junc 123 S onto B186 sp Ötztal. S of Ötztal turn L into Umhausen vill & foll site sp. Med, mkd pitch, pt sl, pt shd; wc; chem disp; shwrs €0.75; el pnts (10A) metered; gas; lndtte; shop 200m; tradsmn; rest; snacks 200m; bar; BBQ; playgrnd; pool 200m; lake sw; internet; dogs €2.60; phone; Eng spkn; adv bkg (dep); quiet. "Well-run site; immac facs; lots of local info given on arr; friendly owners; poss diff pitching on some sh pitches; excel cent for Stuibenfal waterfall (illuminated Wed night high ssn) & Ötztaler Valley; pool & lake sw 200m; wonderful scenery; gd walking fr site." € 22.50         2014*

**OGGAU AM NEUSIEDLERSEE see Eisenstadt** *B4*

**OSSIACH** *D3* (3km E Rural) *46.68558, 14.01233* **Familien-Camping Jodl, Alt-Ossiach 6, 9570 Ossiach (Kärnten) [(04243) 8779; fax 87794; info@camping-jodl.at; www. camping-jodl.at]** Site on S shore of Ossiachersee at E end, fr Feldkirchen take B94 rd in 6km turn S sp Ossiach-Villach, at rd junc turn W, site on R in 1km (approx). Sp at site ent. Fr W on B94 thro Bodensdorf & Steindorf turn S as above. Med, mkd pitch, terr, pt shd; wc; chem disp; mv service pnt; shwrs inc; el pnts inc (16A) inc; lndtte; shop high ssn; tradsmn; supmkt 2km; rest, snacks; playgrnd; shgle beach adj; lake sw; watersports; dogs €3; o'night facs for m'vans; Eng spkn; adv bkg; quiet; red snr citizens; CKE/CCI. "Excel site; beautiful scenery; friendly owners; facs for sm boats; oldest established site on Ossiachersee." 11 Apr-30 Sep. € 26.30         2009*

**OSSIACH** *D3* (1km SW Rural) *46.66388, 13.97500* **Terrassen Camping Ossiacher See, Ostriach 67, 9570 Ossiach (Kärnten) [(04243) 436; fax 8171; martinz@camping.at; www.terrassen.camping.at]** Leave A10/E55/E66 at exit for Ossiachersee, turn L onto B94 twd Feldkirchen & shortly R to Ossiach Süd. Site on lake shore just S of Ossiach vill. Lge, mkd pitch, terr, pt shd; htd wc; chem disp; mv service pnt; baby facs; fam bthrm; shwrs inc; el pnts (4-10A) €3; gas; lndtte; shop; rest, snacks; bar; BBQ; playgrnd; lake sw & beach; watersports; windsurfing; fishing; horse riding; tennis; games area; cycle hire; games rm; cash machine; wifi; entmnt; TV rm; dogs €3; twin-axles acc (rec check in adv); poss cr; clsd 1200-1500 low ssn, parking adj; quiet; ccard acc; red long stay/low ssn; CKE/CCI. "Ideal Carinthian lakes, Hochosterwitz castle & excursions into Italy; beautiful scenery; many activities; excel san facs." ♦ 1 May-29 Sep. € 31.00 SBS - G05         2011*

**OSSIACH** *D3* (4km SW Rural) *46.65321, 13.93344* **Seecamping Berghof, Ossiachersee Süduferstrasse 241, 9523 Heiligengestade (Kärnten) [(04242) 41133; fax 4113330; office@seecamping-berghof.at; www. seecamping-berghof.at]** Exit Villach on rd sp Ossiachersee; take R turn Ossiachersee Süd, site on L bet rd & lake. Lge, terr, pt sl, pt shd; htd wc; chem disp; mv service pnt; serviced pitches; fam bthrm; baby rm; private bthrms avail; shwrs inc; el pnts (10A) inc; gas; lndtte (inc dryer); shop, rest; snacks high ssn; bar; playgrnd; lake beach & sw; sailing; fishing; tennis; games area; cycle hire; golf 10km; wifi; entmnt; 10% statics; dogs €3 (in sep area); phone; poss cr; adv bkg; quiet; red snr citizens/long stay/low ssn. "Excel site; gd cent for excursions to castles & lakes; many sports & activities; extra for lge/lakeside pitches; muddy when wet." ♦ 12 Apr-19 Oct. € 49.70 2014*

**OSSIACH** *D3* (4km SW Rural) *46.65376, 13.93735* **See-Camping Mentl, Süderstrasse 265, 9523 Heiligen-Gestade (Kärnten) [(04242) 41886; fax 43850; camping@mentl. at; www.mentl.at]** Fr A10/E55/E65 turn N onto B94 twd Feldkirchen. Almost immed turn R sp Ossiach, site on L adj lake in 4km. Lge, mkd pitch, terr, pt shd; wc; chem disp; some serviced pitches; baby facs; shwrs inc; el pnts (6A) inc (check pol); lndtte (inc dryer); shops adj; snacks; rest adj; playgrnd; lake sw; watersports; cycle hire; entmnt; no dogs high ssn; poss cr; Eng spkn; adv bkg; quiet; red long stay. "Beautiful setting; gd facs & entmnt for children; helpful staff; excel, modern, clean san facs." ♦ 1 Apr-15 Oct. € 28.80         2010*

**OSSIACH** *D3* (4km W Rural) **Seecamping Plörz, Süduferstrasse 289, 9523 Heiligen-Gestade (Kärnten) [(04242) 41286 or 0676-3221494 (mob); info@camping-ploerz.at; www.camping-ploerz.at]** Fr A10/E55/E65 turn N onto B94 twd Feldkirchen. Almost immed turn R sp Ossiach, site on R just past Camping Mentl. Sm, pt sl, pt shd; htd wc; chem disp; mv service pnt; baby facs; shwrs inc; el pnts (16A) inc; lndtte; shop, rest, snacks, bar nrby; play equipment; lake sw adj; TV rm; dogs €2; phone; Eng spkn; quiet. "Excel sm farm site with gd facs; friendly helpful owners; quiet alt to other busy lakeside sites; lge pitches; v clean facs; cycle paths & gd walks; bus stop at gate; ltd facs for children." Apr-25 Sep. € 25.00          2013*

**PETTNAU** *C1* (500m E) *47.29020, 11.16453* **Camping Tiefental "Roppnerhof", Tiroler Strasse 121, 6408 Pettnau (Tirol) [(0664) 4663003 (mob); tiefental@aon.at; www.camping-tiefental.at]** Leave A12 autoban at junc 101 to join 171 going E twds Zirl and Innsbruck. Site on Tiroler Strabe E end of Unter Pettnau vill. Sm, med pitches, open plan grassy, mkd, pt shd; wc, chem disp, mv service pnt, shwrs; el (13A) €3; lndtte; BBQ; dog €2; twin axle acc; Eng spkn; adv bkg acc; CKE/CCI; "Superb views; walking and cycling in the Inn valley; Innsbruck 25km; excel." ♦ 1 May-30 Sep. € 26.00          2013*

**PETTNEU AM ARLBERG see St Anton am Arlberg** *C1*

**PODERSDORF AM SEE see Frauenkirchen** *B4*

**POYSDORF** *A4* (1km W Urban) *48.66454, 16.61168* **Veltlinerland Camping, Laaerstrasse 106, 2170 Poysdorf (Niederösterreich) [(02552) 20371; fax 37131; veltlinerlandcamping.poysdorf@gmx.at; www.poysdorf.at]** Fr rd 7/E461 at traff lts in Poysdorf turn W onto rd 219 dir Laa an der Thaya. Site sp on R in approx 1km on edge of park. Sm, mkd pitch, some hdstg, terr, unshd; htd wc & shwrs at park adj (key issued); chem disp; mv service pnt; el pnts (6A) €2.20; lndtte; shop 1km; rest; playgrnd; rv sw adj; tennis; 50% statics in sep area; dogs; Eng spkn; quiet. "Gd, under-used site 1 hr N of Vienna; no other site in area; conv Czech border." 1 May-31 Oct. € 12.00          2010*

⊞ **PRUTZ** *C1* (200m E Rural) *47.07955, 10.6588* **Aktiv-Camping Prutz, Pontlatzstrasse 22, 6522 Prutz (Tirol) [(05472) 2648; fax 26484; info@aktiv-camping.at; www.aktiv-camping.at]** Fr Landeck to Prutz on rd B180 turn R at Shell stn over rv bdge, site sp. Med, hdg/mkd pitch, pt shd; htd wc; chem disp; mv service pnt; baby facs; shwrs inc; el pnts (16A) inc; gas; lndtte; shop high ssn; rest, snacks high ssn; bar; playgrnd adj; pool complex in vill; lake sw 1km; cycle hire; internet; TV rm; 20% statics; dogs €3; o'night area for m'vans; site clsd Nov; poss cr; Eng spkn; adv bkg; some rd noise; ccard acc; red low ssn/long stay/snr citizens; CKE/CCI. "Excel, clean facs; gd views; office clsd 1000-1630 - find pitch & pay later; walks & cycle rtes; conv NH en rte Italy & for tax-free shopping in Samnaun, Switzerland; gd site; excel facs; cards given for free bus travel." ♦ € 48.30          2014*

**PURBACH AM NEUSIEDLERSEE** *B4* (1km SE Rural) *47.90958, 16.70580* **Storchencamp Purbach, Türkenhain, 7083 Purbach-am-Neusiedlersee (Burgenland) [(02683) 5170; fax 517015; office@gmeiner.co.at; www.gmeiner.co.at]** Exit A4/E6 junc 43 onto B50 at Neuseidl-am-See to Purbach. Site sp in town nr pool complex. Sm, pt shd; htd wc; chem disp; mv service pnt; baby facs; shwrs inc; el pnts (6A) €2.30; lndtte; shop; rest; bar; BBQ; playgrnd; pools, waterslide adj; games area; 80 statics; dogs €2.90; bus/train 1km; Eng spkn; quiet. "Open field for tourers; excel sw complex adj free with local visitor card + free public transport & red ent to museums etc; modern facs; conv NH." 1 Apr-31 Oct. € 17.50          2010*

⊞ **RADSTADT** *C3* (300m N Rural) *47.38751, 13.46108* **Tauerncamping, Schloss-strasse 17, 5550 Radstadt (Salzburg) [(06452) 4215; fax 42154; info@tauerncamping.at; www.tauerncamping.at]** Exit A10 junc 63 onto B99, site sp in Radstadt. Med, some hdstg, terr, pt shd; htd wc; chem disp; mv service pnt; baby facs; shwrs €1; el pnts (10A) metered; gas; lndtte (inc dryer); shop adj; tradsmn; rest, snacks; bar; BBQ; playgrnd; htd pool; tennis 200m; 50% statics; dogs; poss cr; adv bkg; quiet except church bells. "Conv NH." € 24.80          2010*

## "I need an on-site restaurant"

We do our best to make sure site information is correct, but it is always best to check any must-have facilities are still available or will be open during your visit.

⊞ **RATTENBERG** *C2* (4km N Rural) *47.45670, 11.88084* **Seen-Camping Stadlerhof, Seebühel 15, 6233 Kramsach-am-Reintalersee (Tirol) [(05337) 63371; fax 65311; camping.stadlerhof@chello.at; www.camping-stadlerhof.at]** Exit A12/E45/E60 junc 32 Rattenberg dir Kramsach. At rndabt turn R, then immed L & foll sp 'Zu den Seen' & site sp. Site on L at Lake Krumsee. Lge, mkd pitch, some hdstg, pt sl, pt shd; htd wc; chem disp; sauna; baby facs; shwrs inc; el pnts (10A) inc; gas; lndtte (inc dryer); shops 2km; rest, snacks; bar; BBQ; playgrnd; htd pool; paddling pool; lake sw 200m; fishing; tennis; cycle hire; games rm; wifi; cab TV; 50% statics; dogs €3.50; phone; adv bkg; quiet. "Beautiful, well laid-out site in lovely setting; excel san facs." ♦ € 43.80          2014*

⊞ **RATTENBERG** *C2* (3km NE Rural) *47.46121, 11.9066* **Camping Seeblick Toni, Moosen 46, 6233 Kramsach-am-Reintalersee (Tirol) [(05337) 63544; fax 63544305; info@camping-seeblick.at; www.camping-seeblick.at]** Exit A12/E45/E60 junc 32 sp Kramsach. Foll sps 'Zu den Seen' for about 5km. Drive past Camping Seehof site to Brantlhof site, 3rd site on Reintalersee. Med, mkd pitch, pt shd; wc; chem disp; mv service pnt; baby facs; sauna; serviced pitches; private bthrms avail; shwrs inc; el pnts (10A) €3.50 + conn fee; mains gas conn; lndtte (inc dryer); shop; rest, snacks; bar; playgrnd; lake sw; fishing; cycle hire; games area; games rm; fitness rm; guided walks; x-country skiing; wifi; entmnt; TV rm; 10% statics; dogs €5.50; adv bkg; quiet; ccard acc. "Excel site; lovely lakeside setting; superb san facs, inc for children; excel meals; gd for ski & walking; conv NH fr a'bahn." ♦ € 27.00 (CChq acc)          2009*

**AUSTRIA**

⊞ **RATTENBERG** *C2* (3km NE Rural) *47.46198, 11.90708*
Camping Seehof, Moosen 42, 6233 Kramsach-am-Reintalersee (Tirol) [(05337) 63541; fax 6354120; info@camping-seehof.com; www.camping-seehof.com] Exit A12/E45/E60 junc 32 sp Kramsach, foll sp 'Zu den Seen' for 5km. Site immed bef Camping Seeblick-Toni Brantlhof. Med, mkd pitch, pt shd; htd wc; chem disp; mv service pnt; baby facs; shwrs inc; el pnts (6-13A) €2.80; lndtte; shop; tradsmn; rest, snacks; bar; BBQ; playgrnd; pool; lake sw; cycle hire; gym; solarium; horseriding nr; internet; cab TV; 30% statics; dogs €3.50; phone; poss cr; Eng spkn; adv bkg; quiet; ccard acc; red long stay; CKE/CCI. "Friendly staff; gd views fr some pitches; gd, modern san facs; gd rest; Excel site, local walks, excel museum next door; local taxes €2." ♦ € 41.50        2014*

**REISACH** *D2* (1.5km N Rural) *46.65467, 13.14906*
Alpenferienpark Reisach, Schönboden 1, 9633 Reisach (Kärnten) [(04284) 301; fax 302; info@alpenferienpark.com; www.alpenferienpark.com] Turn E in Kötschach on B111 to Hermagor. At Reisach turn L immed past bdge. Foll sps up hill & across bdge & cont. Bear R up long 1 in 8 slope into wood. Site on L at sp Schonboden. Med, mkd pitch, pt sl, pt shd; htd wc; chem disp; fam bhrm; shwrs inc; el pnts (10A) €2.50; gas; lndtte; shop & 4km; rest, snacks; bar; playgrnd; pool; tennis; some statics; dogs €2; Eng spkn; adv bkg; v quiet. "Friendly site; only suitable sm o'fits." 15 Dec-31 Oct.
€ 20.00        2009*

⊞ **REUTTE** *C1* (600m N Rural) *47.47763, 10.72258*
Camping Reutte, Ehrenbergstrasse 53, 6600 Reutte (Tirol) [(05672) 62809; fax 628094; camping-reutte@aon.at; www.camping-reutte.com] Take Reutte by-pass sp Innsbruck. Enter Reutte at end of by-pass, site sp in 1.5km on L. Med, mkd pitch, some hdstg, pt shd; wc; chem disp; mv service pnt; shwrs €1; el pnts (16A) €2.40; lndtte; shop; tradsmn; rest, snacks; pool adj; ski lift 500m; cab TV; dogs €2; phone; Eng spkn; adv bkg; quiet; ccard acc; CKE/CCI. "Conv for Fern Pass; adj Neuschwanstein Castle; barriers clsd 2100; clean, popular site; excel." € 22.80        2010*

**REUTTE** *C1* (6km SE Rural) *47.47448, 10.78511* **Camping Seespitze, Planseestrasse 68, 6600 Breitenwang (Tirol) [(05672) 78121; fax 63372; agrar.breitenwang@aon.at]** S fr Reutte on by-pass turn L outside town sp Oberammergau/Plansee. Site on L in 5km. Med, pt sl, terr, pt shd; wc; chem disp; shwrs €1; el pnts (12A) metered (long lead poss req) + conn fee; lndtte; shop; tradsmn; rest adj; snacks; bar; playgrnd; lake sw adj; 10% statics; dogs €2.50; Eng spkn; adv bkg; quiet; CKE/CCI. "Beautiful position, mountain scenery; gd walks; v clean san facs; well-maintained site." 1 May-15 Oct.
€ 24.00        2009*

⊞ **REUTTE** *C1* (10km SE Rural) *47.45547, 10.75937* **Camping Heiterwangersee, Fischer-am-See, 6611 Heiterwang (Tirol) [(05674) 5116; fax 5260; hotel@fischeramsee.at; www.fischeramsee.at]** Fr Reutte on B179 dir Ehrwald turn R to Heiterwang, foll sp to Hotel Fischer & to lakeside (1.5km). Med, some hdstg, pt shd; htd wc; chem disp; mv service pnt; sauna; shwrs inc; el pnts (10-16A) metered; lndtte (inc dryer); shop; tradsmn; rest, snacks; bar; lake sw; fishing; boating; ski lift 2km; 70% statics; dogs €2; skibus; poss cr; adv bkg rec high ssn; quiet; ccard acc. "Lovely location; vg san facs." € 29.00        2010*

⊞ **RIED IM OBERINNTAL** *C1* (Rural) *47.05480, 10.65630* Camping Dreiländereck, Gartenland 37, 6531 Ried I O [05472 6025; fax 60254; info@tirolcamping.at; www.tirolcamping.at] Fr Landeck take 180 twd Reschenpass. Exit at Ried & foll sp. Sm, unshd; htd wc; chem disp; mv service pnt; baby facs; shwrs €0.50; el pnts (15A); lndtte (inc dryer); shop 0.1km; tradsmn; snacks; bar; sw adj; wifi; tv rm; dogs €2; bus adj; twin axles; poss cr; Eng spkn; adv bkg; quiet; CCI. "Wellness cent; conv to vill shops; cycle hire; helpful owners; gd clean san facs; adventure sports fac nrby; gd site." € 39.00        2014*

**RINN BEI INNSBRUCK see Innsbruck** *C1*

**RUST AM NEUSIEDLERSEE see Eisenstadt** *B4*

**ST ANDRA AM ZICKSEE see Frauenkirchen** *B4*

⊞ **ST ANTON AM ARLBERG** *C1* (8km E Rural) *47.14809, 10.34668* Arlberg Panoramacamping, Sportranch 45a, 6574 Pettneu-am-Arlberg (Tirol) [(05448) 8352; fax 83524; info@arlberg-panormacamping.at; www.arlberg-panoramacamping.at] Fr S16 exit at E end Arlberg Tunnel sp St Anton. Turn L (E) onto B197/B316 to Pettneu. After 3km at ent to vill, keep R skirting vill. Sportranch 1km on R, ent downhill to L of fire stn. Access only suitable sm/med o'fits. Sm, mkd pitch, pt shd; wc; chem disp; mv service pnt; all serviced pitches; shwrs €1; el pnts (10-13A) €2.50 or metered; lndtte; shop 1km; snacks; rest 500m; bar; games rm; horseriding; Wellness-Park nrby; TV; dogs free; bus; adv bkg; quiet but some rd/rlwy noise; ccard acc; red low ssn/long stay/CKE/CCI. "Clean facs; friendly owner; owner prefers long stay (significant red); geared for winter ssn; gd cent walking, skiing." € 26.00        2010*

**ST GILGEN see Abersee** *B3*

⊞ **ST JOHANN IM PONGAU** *C2* (1km S Urban) *47.34141, 13.19793* Camping Kastenhof, Kastenhofweg 6, 5600 St Johann-im-Pongau (Salzburg) [tel/fax (06412) 5490; info@kastenhof.at; www.kastenhof.at] Take A10 S fr Salzburg onto B311 for Alpendorf. Go over rv & turn L into Liechtensteinklamm twd St Johann, site on L, sp. Med, unshd; htd wc; chem disp; mv service pnt; sauna; shwrs €1; el pnts (15A) metered + €2 conn fee; lndtte (inc dryer); shop; rest, snacks 500m; playgrnd; paddling pool; bus; cab TV; some statics; dogs free; adv bkg; quiet; CKE/CCI. "Conv Tauern tunnel, Grossglockner Hochalpenstrasse, Zell-am-See; gd clean site." € 20.00        2010*

⊞ **ST JOHANN IM PONGAU** *C2* (1km W Urban) *47.34605, 13.19276* Camping Wieshof, Wieshofgasse 8, 5600 St Johann-im-Pongau (Salzburg) [(06412) 8519; fax 8292; info@camping-wieshof.at; www.camping-wieshof.at] On rd B163 dir Zell-am-Zee, past Agip petrol stn, above rd. Med, terr, unshd; htd wc; chem disp; mv service pnt; shwrs €1; el pnts (15A) metered; lndtte; shop 500m; rest adj; playgrnd; golf 6km; 80% statics; dogs; poss cr; Eng spkn; quiet. "Pleasant site; gd views; vg san facs; friendly & helpful owners." € 18.00        2011*

⊞ **ST JOHANN IN TIROL** *C2* (1.5km SW Rural) *47.51078, 12.40888* **Sonnencamping Michelnhof, Weiberndorf 6, 6380 St Johann-in-Tirol (Tirol) [(05352) 62584; fax 625844; camping@michelnhof.at; www.camping-michelnhof.at]** On L of B161 St Johann-Kitzbühel, heading S. Turn L in 2km at sp, fork L after level x-ing. Site on R in 500m. Med, mkd pitch, hdstg, sl, pt shd; htd wc; chem disp; mv service pnt; baby facs; shwrs inc; el pnts (10A) €2.70; lndtte; supmkt 1.5km; rest, snacks; playgrnd; pool 2km; golf 4km; 50% statics; dogs €4; phone; Eng spkn; quiet; CKE/CCI. "Friendly warden; higher prices in winter; vg." ♦ € 18.40                    2009*

## "Satellite navigation makes touring much easier"

Remember most sat navs don't know if you're towing or in a larger vehicle – always use yours alongside maps and site directions.

⊞ **ST MICHAEL IM LUNGAU** *C3* (S Rural) *47.09685, 13.63706* **Camping St Michael, Waaghausgasse 277, 5582 St Michael-im-Lungau (Salzburg) [tel/fax (06477) 8276; camping-st.michael@sgb.at]** Exit junc 104 fr A10/E55, site sp at turn into vill, then on L after 200m bef hill. Sm, pt shd; wc; chem disp; mv service pnt; shwrs inc; el pnts (16A) €3.50 (poss rev pol); gas; lndtte; shop adj; rest, snacks adj; playgrnd; pool adj; ski lift 1km; dogs; poss cr; adv bkg; ccard acc; red CKE/CCI. "Delightful site adj vill; excel san facs (shared with adj sports club); poss full if arr after 6 pm, but o'flow area avail." € 20.00                    2010*

**ST PETER AM KAMMERSBERG** *C3* (2km SE Rural) *47.17905, 14.21671* **Camping Bella Austria, Peterdorf 100, 8842 St Peter-am-Kammersberg (Steiermark) [(03536) 73902; fax 73912; info@camping-bellaustria.com; www.camping-bellaustria.com]** Fr B96 turn N onto L501 into Katschtal Valley dir Oberdorf, Althofen & St Peter-am-Kammersberg. Site sp. Lge, some hdstg, pt shd; wc; chem disp; mv service pnt; baby facs; sauna; hot shwrs; el pnts (16A) inc; lndtte; shop, rest, snacks; bar; playgrnd; htd pool; lake sw; games area; cycle hire; wifi; entmnt; TV rm; 70% statics; dog €2; Eng spkn; adv bkg; quiet. "Superb walking area; excel." ♦ 12 Apr-28 Sep. € 30.00                    2014*

**ST PRIMUS** *D3* (800m N Rural) *46.58569, 14.56598* **Strandcamping Turnersee Breznik, Unternarrach 21, 9123 St Primus (Kärnten) [(04239) 2350; fax 235032; info@breznik.at; www.breznik.at]** Exit A2 at junc 298 Grafenstein onto B70. After 4km turn R & go thro Tainach, St Kanzian twd St Primus. Site is on W side of Turnersee. Lge, mkd pitch, pt shd; htd wc; chem disp; mv service pnt; serviced pitches; baby facs; shwrs inc; el pnts (6A) inc; lndtte (inc dryer); shop; rest; bar; BBQ; playgrnd; lake sw; fishing; tennis 500m; games rm; games area; cycle hire; golf 2km; wifi; entmnt; cinema rm; TV rm; 30% statics; dogs €3.30; adv bkg; quiet; CKE/CCI. "Lovely situation; excel site." ♦ 16 Apr-2 Oct. € 26.60 (CChq acc)                    2009*

**ST VEIT IM PONGAU see St Johann im Pongau** *C2*

⊞ **ST WOLFGANG IM SALZKAMMERGUT** *B3* (2km SE Rural) *47.73063, 13.47795* **Komfortcamping Berau, Schwarzenbach 16, 5360 St Wolfgang-im-Salzkammergut (Oberösterreich) [(06138) 2543; fax 254355; camping@berau.at; www.berau.at]** Turn N off B158 at Strobl at sp for St Wolfgang & foll sps. Easy to miss - look for Gasthaus/Hotel Berau just after soccer field on L. Med, mkd pitch, pt shd; wc; chem disp; mv service pnt; sauna; baby facs; shwrs inc; el pnts (6A) inc; gas; lndtte (inc dryer); shop; tradsmn; rest, snacks; bar; BBQ; playgrnd; lake sw; watersports; cycle hire; wifi; entmnt; dogs €3.10; phone; poss cr; Eng spkn; adv bkg; quiet; ccard acc; red long stay; CKE/CCI. "Immac san facs; excel site." ♦ € 29.00                    2010*

**ST WOLFGANG IM SALZKAMMERGUT** *B3* (1km W Rural) *47.74277, 13.43361* **Seeterrassen Camping Reid, Ried 18, 5360 St Wolfgang/Salzkammergut (Oberösterreich) [tel/fax (06138) 3201; camping-ried@aon.at; www.members.aon.at/camping-ried]** Fr Salzburg take B158 thro St Gilgen dir Bad Ischl. Exit at sp Strobl & foll sp St Wolfgang. Go thro tunnel to avoid town cent, foll rd along lake to site. Sm, pt sl, terr, pt shd; htd wc; chem disp; mv service pnt; baby facs; shwrs €0.80; el pnts (16A) metered; gas; lndtte; shop; tradsmn; rest, snacks; bar; playgrnd; lake sw, fishing, watersports adj; tennis nr; TV rm; 10% statics; dogs €1.80; phone; poss cr; Eng spkn; poss rd noise; ccard not acc; CKE/CCI. "Mountain rlwy stn nr; lake views; gd touring base; easy walk into town; friendly site; v clean san facs." 16 Apr-31 Oct. € 34.00                    2014*

## "There aren't many sites open at this time of year"

If you're travelling outside peak season remember to call ahead to check site opening dates – even if the entry says 'open all year'.

**SALZBURG** *B2* (2km N Urban) *47.82683, 13.06296* **Camping Nord-Sam, Samstrasse 22a, 5023 Salzburg Nord [tel/fax (0662) 660494; office@camping-nord-sam.com; www.camping-nord-sam.com]** Heading E on A1/E55/E69 exit junc 288 Salzburg Nord exit & immed take slip rd on R; then over to L-hand lane for L-hand turn at 2nd traff lts, up narr rd to site, sp. If thro Salzburg foll Wien-Linz sps thro city; turn onto B1 on exit o'skts, camp site posted on L. Med, hdg pitch, hdstg, pt sl, pt shd; htd wc; chem disp; mv service pnt; baby facs; shwrs inc; el pnts (10A) €3; lndtte (inc dryer); shop; supmkt 10m; snacks; playgrnd; htd pool; dogs €3; bus adj; poss cr; Eng spkn; adv bkg ess; rlwy noise; ccard not acc; red long stay/CKE/CCI. "Sm pitches & high hdges; san facs clean but old & stretched when site full; friendly staff; many attractions nrby; site sells Salzburg Card; cycle track to city cent; recep open 0800-1200 & 1600-2030 high ssn." ♦ 1 Jan-6 Jan, 23 Mar-13 Oct, 26 Dec- 31 dec. € 40.00                    2013*

**SALZBURG** *B2* (2km N Rural) *47.82843, 13.05221* **Panorama Camping Stadtblick, Rauchenbichlerstrasse 21, 5020 Salzburg [(0662) 450652; fax 458018; info@panorama-camping.at; www.panorama-camping.at]** Fr A1/E55/E60 exit 288 Salzburg Nord/Zentrum & at end of slip rd turn R & sharp R at traff lts, site sp. If coming fr S, foll ring rd to W then N. Med, mkd pitch, hdstg, terr, pt shd; htd wc; chem disp; mv service pnt; shwrs inc; el pnts (4A) inc (long lead req some pitches); gas; lndtte; shop; tradsmn; rest/café high ssn; bar; wifi; dogs €2; phone; bus to town nr (tickets fr recep); poss cr; Eng spkn; adv bkg; rd noise; ccard not acc - cash only; red 3+ days; CKE/CCI. "Conv a'bahn; views of Salzburg; cycle track by rv to town; Salzburg card avail fr recep; sm pitches - rec phone ahead if lge o'fit; v helpful family owners; vg rest; excel, modern san facs; rec arr early; also open some dates in Dec & Jan; excel; 'Sound of Music' Tour; v conv for Salzburg, gd views; beautiful city; cash only; helpful owner." 1 Jan-8 Jan, 20 Mar-5 Nov, 5 Dec-10 Dec. € 41.00      2014*

**SALZBURG** *B2* (5km SE Urban) *47.78058, 13.08985* **Camping Schloss Aigen, Weberbartlweg 20, 5026 Salzburg-Aigen [tel/fax (0662) 622079; camping.aigen@elsnet.at; www.campingaigen.com]** Fr S leave A10/E55 at junc 8 Salzburg-Süd & take B150 twds Salzburg on Alpenstrasse. Turn R at rndabt dir Glasenbach, then L into Aignerstrasse. 1km S of Aigen stn turn R into Glasenstrasse & foll sps to site. Lge, pt sl, pt shd; wc; chem disp; shwrs inc; el pnts (6-16A) €2; gas; washing machine avail; shop; rest, snacks; bar; bus to town 700m; poss cr; adv bkg; quiet except nr bar/rest; red long stay/CKE/CCI. "Friendly, family-run site; sl pitches v slippery & boggy when wet; excel rest; conv for city, gd walks." 1 May-30 Sep. € 28.00      2014*

**SCHARNSTEIN** *B3* (1.5 km NE Rural) *47.91580, 13.97372* **Almcamp Schatzlmühle, Viechtwang 1A, 4644 Scharnstein [07615 20269; fax 20279; office@almcamp.at; www. almcamp.at]** Fr A1 take exit 207 Vorchtdorf to Pettenbach on the L536. Head twd Scharnstein on 120. Turn R 2km bef vill (dir Viechtwang). Foll sp. Alt take A9, exit 5, dir Scharnstein. Sm, hdg pitch, mkd pitch, hdstg, pt shd; wc; chem disp; mv service pnt; baby facs; shwrs; el pnts (16A); lndtte (inc dryer); shop; rest; bar; BBQ; playgrnd; sauna; games rm; wifi; tv; 10% statics; dogs €1.50; phone; twin-axles acc; Eng spkn; adv bkg; quiet; CCI. "Child friendly; family run site; site by rv, scenic location; gd cycling & walking rtes; htd, excel san facs; excel site." ♦ 12 Mar-31 Oct. € 30.40      2014*

**SCHONBUHEL see Melk** *B4*

⊞ **SCHRUNS** *C1* (1km S Rural) *47.06760, 9.91615* **Camping Zelfen, Zelfenstrasse 79, 6774 Tschagguns (Voralberg) [(0664) 2002326; kunsttischlerei.tschofen@utanet.at; www.camping-zelfen.at]** Fr Bludenz to Schruns. After x-ing rlwy turn R at traff lts, foll rd L in front of Spar. Site on L in 1.6km, sp. Med, pt shd; htd wc; chem disp; shwrs €1; el pnts (6A) inc; lndtte; shop & 1.6km; rest, snacks, bar 1.6km; playgrnd; pool 200m; 50% statics; dogs; phone; poss cr; Eng spkn; adv bkg; quiet; ccard acc; CKE/CCI. "Free sw & children's activities at nrby Activpark; site conv Montafon valley; office open 0800-0900 & 1800-1900 - other times use freephone by office door." € 22.00      2009*

**SCHWAZ** *C2* (6km W Rural) *47.30613, 11.64926* **Alpencamping Mark, Bundesstrasse 12, 6114 Weer (Tirol) [(05224) 68146; fax 681466; alpcamp.mark@aon.at; www. alpencampingmark.com]** Exit A12/E45/E60 junc 61; cont E on B171. Site on R after Weer vill. Ent mkd by flags. Med, hdg pitch, pt shd; htd wc; chem disp; mv service pnt; baby facs; shwrs inc; el pnts (6-10A) €2.70; lndtte (inc dryer); shop 500m; tradsmn; rest, snacks; bar; BBQ; playgrnd; htd pool; lake sw 2km; tennis; horseriding; cycle hire; dogs €3; Eng spkn; adv bkg; quiet; ccard acc; red long stay/CKE/CCI. "Well-maintained site in scenic location; cln pleasant site with nice rest; friendly, welcoming owners & staff; lavish sports facs; gd san facs; nr town of Weer; many local attractions; rec." ♦ 1 Apr-31 Oct. € 21.00      2011*

⊞ **SEEFELD IN TIROL** *C1* (1km N Rural) *47.33661, 11.17756* **Alpin Camp, Leutascherstrasse 810, 6100 Seefeld (Tirol) [(05212) 4848; fax 4868; info@camp-alpin.at; www.camp-alpin.at]** Fr N on B177/E533 turn W into Seefeld. Thro main rd, turn R sp Leutasch, site on L in 2km. Apps fr SE & SW via v steep hills/hairpins, prohibited to trailers. Med, hdstg, pt sl, terr, pt shd; wc; chem disp; mv service pnt; sauna & steambath inc; shwrs inc; el pnts (16A) €2.80 or metered; gas (metered); lndtte; shop & 2km; rest adj; playgrnd; htd, covrd pool, golf 1.5km; cycle hire; wifi; 10% statics; dogs €3; bus to town; site clsd Nov; adv bkg; Eng spkn; quiet; red snr citizens. "Excel site; excel facs; friendly owners; vg walking; delightful setting; ski tows at gate." ♦ € 21.50      2010*

⊞ **SEEFELD IN TIROL** *C1* (8km NW Rural) *47.39832, 11.17941* **Holiday Camping, Reindlau 230B, 6105 Leutasch (Tirol) [(05214) 65700; fax 657030; info@holiday-camping. at; www.holiday-camping.at]** Fr B2 fr Germany & passing S thro Scharnitz on B177 & take minor rd W in 4km sp Leutasch. Foll sps to site approx 11km. Do not use Mittenwald-Leutasch rd, v narr & steep gradients. Rte fr S fr A12 via Telfs not rec for c'vans. Med, unshd; htd wc; chem disp; mv service pnt; private bthrms avail; serviced pitches; sauna; baby facs; shwrs inc; el pnts (12A) €3.20 or metered; gas; lndtte (inc dryer); drying rm; shop; rest, snacks; bar; htd, covrd pool; paddling pool; fishing; tennis; golf driving range; golf 10km; ski lift 3km; skibus; wifi; sat TV each pitch; dogs €3; site clsd 11 Nov-6 Dec; adv bkg; ccard acc. "Gd walking & skiing cent; immac facs; superb location; gd walking, cycling; excel." ♦ € 28.00  2010*

⊞ **SILLIAN** *D2* (2.5km E Rural) *46.74583, 12.46315* **Camping Lienzer Dolomiten, Tassenbach 191, 9920 Strassen-bei-Sillian (Tirol) [(04842) 5228; fax 522815; camping-dolomiten@gmx.at; www.camping-tirol.at]** B100 fr Sillian dir Lienz, turn R after filling stn, over level x-ing, then immed R; site sp. Med, mkd pitch, some hdstg, pt sl, unshd; wc; chem disp; mv service pnt; shwrs inc; el pnts (6A) €2; lndtte; shop, rest 3km; tradsmn; bar; lake sw; ski lift 3km; 25% statics; dogs €2; red long stay. "Informal site; clean facs; helpful staff; mountain views." € 21.00      2010*

⊞ **SOLDEN** *C1* (1km S Rural) *46.95786, 11.01193* **Camping Sölden, Wohlfahrtstrasse 22, 6450 Sölden (Tirol) [(05254) 26270; fax 26725; info@camping-soelden.com; www.camping-soelden.com]** Turn L off main rd at cable car terminal. Turn R at rv & foll narr track on rv bank for about 200m, turn R into site. Med, mkd pitch, pt sl, terr, pt shd; wc; chem disp; mv service pnt; serviced pitches; sauna; shwrs inc; el pnts (10A) metered; gas; lndtte; shop 200m; snacks 500m; rest 20m; playgrnd; gym; wifi; dogs €3; dog-washing facs; site clsd mid-Apr to mid-Jun approx; adv bkg; quiet; Eng spkn; ccard acc. "Excel for touring or climbing in upper Ötz Valley; pitches tight for lge o'fits; superb site; excel san facs." ♦ € 28.00                                                                          2009*

⊞ **SPITAL AM PYHRN** *C3* (3km N Rural) *47.6912, 14.3260* **Campingplatz Pyhrn-Priel, Gleinkerau 34, 4582 Spital-am-Pyhrn (Oberösterreich) [(07562) 7066; pyhrn-priel@aon. at; www.pyhrn-priel.at]** Exit A9 junc 52 - Gleinkerau; cross rndabt on m'way access rd & turn L at T junc; foll sp for approx 500m & turn R to site. Med, unshd; wc; chem disp; shwrs; el pnts (10A) €2.50; lndtte; shop 3km; tradsmn; rest, snacks; bar; playgrnd; pool 3km; 60% statics; dogs €2.20; Eng spkn; adv bkg; quiet; ccard acc; CKE/CCI. "Gd views; walking; para/ hang-gliding school; summer toboggan run; pleasant owners." ♦ € 18.00                                                                          2011*

**SPITTAL AN DER DRAU** *D3* (3km NE Urban) *46.81510, 13.52001* **Strandcamping Winkler, Seepromenade 33, 9871 Seeboden [04 76 28 19 27; fax 76 28 18 22; www. campsite.at]** Leave A10 Villach-Salzburg at Jnc 139 twd Seeboden. Cont along main st across 2 rndabts & turn R down narr rd sp Strandcamping Winkler. Sm, mkd pitch, pt sl, pt shd; wc; chem disp; mv service pnt; shwrs €1; el pnts (16A); lndtte; playgrnd; sw 40m; dogs; twin axles; poss cr; Eng spkn; adv bkg; CCI. "Cycling & walking rtes rnd beautiful Millstätter; gd site." 1 May-1 Oct. € 41.50                                               2014*

**SPITTAL AN DER DRAU** *D3* (500m S Rural) *46.78513, 13.48669* **Camping Draufluss, Schwaig 10, 9800 Spittal-an-der-Drau (Kärnten) [(04762) 2466; fax 36299; drauwirt@ aon.at; www.drauwirt.com]** Exit A10 Salzburg-Villach junc 146 Spittal-Ost. In Spittal foll site & 'Goldeckbahn' sp. Cross bdge & site on L - book in at hotel recep. Site on rvside. Med, pt shd; htd wc; chem disp; shwrs inc; el pnts (10-16A) €3; lndtte (inc dryer); shop in town; rest, bar at hotel; htd, covrd pool 800m; rv fishing adj; boating; tennis; games/TV rm; dogs €1.30; Eng spkn; quiet; red CKE/CCI. "Modern san facs; conv NH." 15 Apr-1 Oct. € 23.30                                            2011*

**STAMS see Telfs** *C1*

**STEYR** *B3* (3km NE Urban) *48.06117, 14.43764* **Camping Forelle, Kematmüllerstrasse 1a, 4400 Steyr-Münichholz (Oberösterreich) [(07252) 78008 or 06764 729445 (mob); fax 78008; forellesteyr@gmx.at]** Fr W on B122 foll camping sp to Amstetten on B115/309 & then 122a to Steyr-Münichholz. Site on Rv Enns. Sm, hdstg, pt shd, unshd; htd wc; chem disp (wc); shwrs inc; el pnts (10A); lndtte; shop 500m; rest, snacks, bar 1km; BBQ; playgrnd; pools 1km; watersports; tennis nr; cycle hire; dogs €2.20; phone; quiet; red long stay; CKE/CCI. "Pleasant rvside site; Steyr interesting, historic town." ♦ 1 Apr-31 Oct. € 31.60                                                2014*

**SULZ IM WIENERWALD** *B4* (500m N Rural) *48.10510, 16.13348* **Camping Wienerwald, Leopoldigasse 2, 2392 Sulz-im-Wienerwald (Niederösterreich) [(0)664 4609796; fax (02238) 8855; ww-camp@aon.at; www.camping-wienerwald.at]** Leave A21/E60 at junc 26 dir Sittendorf, Foll sp to site at Sulz (7km fr m'way). Sm, mkd pitch, pt sl, pt shd; wc; chem disp; mv service pnt; shwrs inc; el pnts (6A) €1.90 (poss long lead req); lndtte; shop, rest in vill; tradsmn; wifi; few statics; dogs €1.20; poss cr; quiet. "Conv Vienna - 25km; gd walks." 15 Apr-15 Oct. € 14.00                                             2010*

⊞ **TELFS** *C1* (8km W Rural) *47.27510, 10.98661* **Camping Eichenwald, Schiess-Standweg 10, 6422 Stams (Tirol) [tel/ fax (05263) 6159; info@camping-eichenwald.at; tirol-camping.at; www.tirol-camping.at]** Exit A12 at exit Stams-Mötz, foll B171 sp Stams. Turn R into vill, site behind monastery nr dry ski jump; steep app. Med, terr, pt shd; htd wc; chem disp; mv service pnt; baby facs; private bthrms some pitches; shwrs inc; el pnts (6A) €2.70; gas; lndtte (inc dryer); shop 400m; rest, snacks; bar; playgrnd; sm htd pool high ssn; tennis 500m; games area; games rm; cycle hire; wifi; TV rm; statics in sep area; dogs €2.50; Eng spkn; adv bkg; quiet but monastery bells & rlwy noise; CKE/CCI. "Beautiful views; friendly owner; vg site; gd rest; san facs v clean." ♦ € 45.00                                                                          2013*

**TRISTACH see Lienz** *C2*

**TULLN** *B4* (2km E Urban) *48.33277, 16.07194* **Donaupark-Camping Tulln, Donaulände 76, 3430 Tulln-an-der-Donau (Niederösterreich) [(02272) 65200; fax 65201; camptulln@ oemtc.at; www.campingtulln.at]** Fr S on A1 take exit 41 sp St Christopher & foll B19 to o'skts of Tulln, then turn R onto B14 Südring. Foll B14 round past commercial areas, eventually over rlwy bdge to T-junc. Turn L into Langenlebarnerstrasse, site on R (if reach BP g'ge you have overshot). Fr N foll B19 across rv on Rosenbrucke (bdge) & cont on B19 to B14 Südring, then as above. Site sp (Camping des ÖAMTC) often shown on local sp or on green sports complex sp. Med, some hdg/mkd pitch, pt shd; htd wc; chem disp; mv service pnt; baby facs; sauna; shwrs inc; el pnts (6A) €3; gas; lndtte (inc dryer); shop; supmkt 1km; rest, snacks; bar; BBQ; playgrnd; pool 400m; fishing, lake sw, water skiing nrby; horseriding 2km; cycle hire; tennis; games rm; wifi; entmnt; recep 0730-1930 high ssn; 20% statics; dogs; bus/train to Vienna; Eng spkn; adv bkg; quiet; ccard acc; red low ssn/CKE/CCI. "Welcome pack; helpful staff; gd base for area; gd walks, cycling, birdwatching; bus/ train to Vienna; poss cr & sm pitches; 15 mins walk to town." ♦ 15 Apr-15 Oct. € 26.50                                               2011*

**UNTERACH AM ATTERSEE see Attersee** *B3*

**UNTERPERFUSS see Innsbruck** *C1*

**UNZMARKT** *C3* (W Rural) *47.19847, 14.44121* **Camping im Freizeitpark, Am Sportplatz 27, 8800 Unzmarkt (Steiermark) [(03583) 2956; www.unzmarkt-frauenburg. at]** W fr Judenburg on B317, site sp opp Agip petrol stn. Sm, terr, pt shd; wc; shwrs inc; el pnts €1.10 (long lead poss req); lndtte; shop 200m; rest; bar; playgrnd; sports field adj; quiet, some rlwy noise. "Gd site, pt of lge leisure complex; recep in café." 1 May-30 Sep. € 10.00                                             2009*

**VELDEN AM WORTHERSEE** *D3* (5km E Rural) *46.61890, 14.10565* **Camping Weisses Rössl, Auenstrasse 47, Schiefling-am-See, 9220 Velden-Auen (Kärnten)** [(04274) 2898; fax 28984; weisses.roessl@aon.at; http:// members.aon.at/weisses.roessl] Fr A2 exit 335 dir Velden. At rndabt bef town fol sp twd Maria Wörth for 9km on S side of Wörthersee. Site on R up hill. Lge, some hdstg, terr, pt sl, pt shd; htd wc; chem disp; mv service pnt; baby facs; shwrs inc; el pnts (16A) inc; gas; lndtte (inc dryer); shop; rest; bar; BBQ; playgrnd; pool; beach & lake sw nrby; TV; dogs; phone; poss cr; Eng spkn; some rlwy noise; CKE/CCI. "Gd." 1 May-30 Sep. € 27.60                               2010*

**VIENNA see Wien** *B4*

**VILLACH** *D3* (8km NE Rural) *46.65641, 13.89196* **Campingbad Ossiachersee, Seeuferstrasse 109, 9520 Annenheim (Kärnten)** [(04248) 2757; fax 275757; office@ camping-ossiachersee.at; www.camping-ossiachersee.at] Fr A10/E55/E66 exit sp Villach/Ossiacher See onto B94. Turn R for St Andrä sp Süd Ossiacher See. Site on L in 300m. Lge, pt shd; htd wc; baby facs; chem disp; mv service pnt; shwrs inc; el pnts (10-16A) inc; lndtte; shop; rest, snacks; bar; playgrnd; lake sw adj; sailing; watersking; tennis; games area; 5% statics; phone; no dogs; barrier clsd 1200-1400; poss cr; adv bkg; quiet; ccard acc. "Well-kept site; handy NH even when wet; Annenheim cable car; Lge level grass pitches." ◆ 27 Apr-30 Sep & 15 Dec-31 Dec. € 45.20                        2013*

⊞ **VILLACH** *D3* (3km SE Rural) *46.59638, 13.89333* **Camping Mittewald, Fuchsbichlweg 9, 9580 Drobollach (Kärnten)** [(04242) 37392; fax 373928; camp.mittewald@gmail.com] Exit A2/E55 sp Villach/Faakersee. At end slip rd turn R onto B84 to Faakersee, site sp on L. Sm, pt sl, pt shd; htd wc; chem disp; shwrs; el pnts (10A); gas; lndtte; shop 3km; rest; bar; playgrnd; some statics; dogs; some Eng spkn; quiet. "Lovely location; extensive grass pitches; excel san facs." ◆ € 29.00      2011*

**VILLACH** *D3* (6km SE) *46.58953, 13.91483* **Wisencamping Marhof, Greutherweg 19, A-9580 Drobollach-Faaker See, Kärnten** [(4254) 2888; office@marhof.at; www.marhof. at] Foll sps in Villach mkd Faaker Nord. Site on N side of rd at vill of Greuth. Sm, pt sl, pt shd; wc htd; chem disp; mv waste; shwrs; el pnts (metered); lndtte; BBQ; tradsmn; playgrnd; pool; dogs €0.70; quiet. "Delightful site; beautiful views; conv for lakes; excel facs; gd cycling/walking area; v peaceful; Eng not spkn; v helpful & friendly owners; excel." 01 Mar-30 Nov. € 28.00                               2011*

**VILLACH** *D3* (8km SE Rural) *46.56986, 13.90701* **Familiencamping Poglitsch, Kirchenweg 19, 9583 Faak-am-See (Kärnten)** [(04254) 2718; fax 4144; poglitsch@ net4you.at; www.kindercamping.at] Exit A11/E61 junc 3 & foll sp for Faakersee. Site in vill, bet church & lake. Med, mkd pitch, pt shd; wc; chem disp; mv service pnt; some serviced pitches; baby facs; shwrs inc; el pnts (10-16A) inc; gas; lndtte (inc dryer); shop; tradsmn; rest, snacks; bar; playgrnd; lake beach & sw; watersports; cycle hire; games area; golf 1km; wifi; entmnt; TV; 15% statics; dogs €3.50; phone; Eng spkn; adv bkg; quiet; CKE/CCI. "Excel, well-run site; friendly owner; quiet imposed after 2300." ◆ 1 Apr-15 Oct. € 27.00 2010*

**VILLACH** *D3* (8km SE Rural) *46.57266, 13.93268* **Strandcamping Gruber, 9583 Faak-am-See (Kärnten)** [(04254) 2298; fax 22987; gruber@strandcamping.at; www.strandcamping.at] When app down Drau Valley fr Lienz foll sp round Villach to Faakersee. This will bring round N of lake to Egg. Site 800m beyond on R. Fr A11/E61 exit junc 3 & foll sps to Faakersee/Egg. Med, shd; wc; chem disp; shwrs inc; el pnts (10A) €2.50; gas; lndtte (inc dryer); shop; rest; playgrnd; lake sw; golf 2km; wifi; 10% statics; dogs €2; poss cr; adv bkg; quiet; ccard acc. "Excel for touring Carinthian Lake District; gd for children; v beautiful situation on lakeside; friendly staff." ◆ 1 May-20 Sep. € 31.00           2010*

**VILLACH** *D3* (9km SE Rural) *46.57416, 13.93694* **Strandcamping Arneitz, Seeuferlandesstrasse 53, 9583 Faak-am-See (Kärnten)** [(04254) 2137; fax 3044; camping@ arneitz.at; www.camping-arneitz.at] On B83 Klagenfurt to Villach at Velden, foll sp to Faakersee. Thro Egg to site on R. Fr Villach foll sp to Faakersee. Clearly sp. Lge, mkd pitch, shd; wc; shwrs inc; el pnts (16A) inc; gas; lndtte (inc dryer); shop; rest, snacks; bar; BBQ; playgrnd; lake sw; tennis; entmnt; internet; TV; dogs free; adv bkg; quiet. "Excel facs, but ltd low ssn." ◆ 1 May-30 Sep. € 32.00                      2010*

**VILLACH** *D3* (10km SE Rural) *46.56828, 13.9293* **Strandcamping Sandbank, Badeweg 3, 9583 Faak-am-See (Kärnten)** [(04254) 2261; fax 3943; info@camping-sandbank.at; www.camping-sandbank.at] Exit A11/E61 junc 3 & foll sp to Faakersee. Site last on R on E side of lake. Med, pt shd; wc; chem disp; serviced pitches; shwrs inc; el pnts (12A) €2.20; lndtte (inc dryer); supmkt 1km; rest adj; snacks; playgrnd; lake sw; tennis adj; games area; golf 15km; entmnt; TV; 10% statics; dogs €1.80; rd/rlwy noise; red snr citizens. "Surcharge for lakeside pitch; boats & surfboards for hire." 1 May-30 Sep. € 25.70                               2010*

⊞ **VILLACH** *D3* (3km NW Urban) *46.61503, 13.80684* **Camping Gerli, Badstrasse 23, 9500 Villach (Kärnten)** [(04242) 57402; fax 582909; gerli.meidl@utanet.at; www. campgerli.com] Fr A10/E55/E66 exit junc 172. Fr rndabt at end of slip rd foll campsite sps. Med, pt shd; wc; some serviced pitches; baby facs; shwrs €0.75; el pnts (4-16A) metered or €2; lndtte (inc dryer); sm shop; rest; playgrnd; paddling pool; lake sw nr; solarium; tennis; entmnt; 20% statics; dogs €1.10; phone; poss cr high ssn; adv bkg; poss noisy; 10% red CKE/ CCI. "Ski lift close by." € 15.70                       2009*

**VOLDERS see Hall in Tirol** *C2*

⊞ **VOLKERMARKT** *D3* (9km S Rural) *46.58376, 14.62621* **Rutar Lido FKK See-Camping (Naturist), Lido 1, 9141 Eberndorf (Kärnten)** [(04236) 22620; fax 2220; fkkurlaub@ rutarlido.at; www.rutarlido.at] Take B82 S fr Völkermarkt to Eberndorf. At rndbt on vill by-pass turn R. Site sp on L. Camp ent in 700m down rd. Lge, pt shd; wc; chem disp; mv service pnt; sauna; shwrs inc; el pnts (10A) inc; gas; lndtte; shop; rest, snacks; playgrnd; 4 pools (1 htd, covrd); paddling pool; shgl beach & lake sw 2km; tennis adj; games area; 30% statics; dogs; o'night area for m'vans; adv bkg; quiet; ccard acc; red CKE/CCI. "Gd family site; v helpful staff; ltd Eng spkn." ◆ € 49.00                               2013*

**VOLKERMARKT** *D3* (6km SW Rural) *46.58613, 14.58080* Terrassencamping Turnersee, 9122 Obersammelsdorf (Kärnten) [(04239) 2285; fax 22854; ferienparadies@ ilsenhof.at; www.ilsenhof.at] Turn off B82 dir Klopeinersee & St Kanzian. Just bef Turnersee foll sp L for site. Med, mkd pitch, some hdstg, terr, pt shd; wc; chem disp; mv service pnt; baby facs; shwrs; el pnts (10A) inc; gas; lndtte (inc dryer); shop 1km; tradsmn; rest 300m; snacks; bar; BBQ; playgrnd; pool; covrd pool 8km; shgl beach & lake sw 500m; 20% statics; dogs €2.90; v quiet; red CKE/CCI. "Excel views of mountains beyond Turnersee." ♦ 1 May-10 Sep. € 27.70          2011*

**VOLS see Innsbruck** *C1*

**WAIDHOFEN AN DER THAYA** *A4* (500m SE Rural) *48.81113, 15.28839* Campingplatz Thayapark, Badgasse, 3830 Waidhofen-an-der Thaya (Niederösterreich) [(02842) 50356 or 0664 5904433 (mob); stadtamt@ waidhofen-thaya.gv.at; www.waidhofen-thaya.at] Site sp fr town cent. Med, pt shd; wc; chem disp; mv service pnt; baby facs; shwrs €0.50; el pnts (10A) €2.30; lndtte; shop, rest, snacks, bar 500m; tradsmn; playgrnd; pool 500m; cab TV; 5% statics; no adv bkg; quiet; CKE/CCI. "Quiet site nr attractive town; recep open 0800-1000 & 1600-1800." ♦ 1 May-30 Sep. € 11.00          2010*

⊞ **WALCHSEE** *B2* (300m W Rural) *47.64881, 12.31433* Sonnencamping Seespitz, Seespitz 1, 6344 Walchsee (Tirol) [(05374) 5359; fax 5845; info@camping-seespitz. at; www.camping-seespitz.at] Exit A93/E45/60 junc 59 onto B172 thro Niederdorf to Walchsee (11km). Site on R by lake after rd on R to Südsee at beginning of Walchsee vill. Lge, pt shd; htd wc; chem disp; mv service pnt; serviced pitches; extra for lakeside pitches; baby facs; shwrs inc; el pnts (6A) €3; gas; lndtte (inc dryer); sm shop; supmkt adj; rest, snacks; bar; playgrnd; lake sw; fishing; boating; games area; 60% statics; dogs €3.50; poss cr; adv bkg; quiet; red CKE/CCI. "Excel; attractive lakeside setting with mountain views; vg san facs." ♦ € 21.00          2010*

## "That's changed – Should I let The Club know?"

If you find something on site that's different from the site entry, fill in a report and let us know. See www.caravanclub.co.uk/europereport.

⊞ **WALD IM PINZGAU** *C2* (1km W Rural) *47.24343, 12.21071* SNP Camping, Lahn 65, 5742 Wald-im-Pinzgau (Salzburg) [(06565) 84460; fax 84464; info@snp-camping. at; www.snp-camping.at] Sp fr both dir on B165 Gerlos-Mittersill rd. Sm, unshd, mkd pitch; wc; chem disp; mv service pnt; shwrs €1; el pnts (10A) €4; gas; lndtte; shop 1km; snacks; bar; playgrnd; pool 1km; site clsd Nov; Eng spkn; adv bkg ess; quiet; ccard acc; red long stay/CKE/CCI. "Gd walks; friendly, helpful owner; gd san facs, bus nrby for Krimul waterfalls." € 30.70          2011*

**WEER see Schwaz** *C2*

**WERFEN** *C2* (2km S Rural) *47.44501, 13.21165* Camping Vierthaler, Reitsam 8, 5452 Pfarrwerfen (Salzburg) [(06468) 57570; fax 56574; vierthaler@camping-vierthaler. at; www.camping-vierthaler.at] Fr A10 exit 43 or 44 sp Werfen/Pfarrwerfen. Turn S onto B159 twd Bischofshofen. After 2km site on L bet rd & rv. Sm, pt shd; wc; chem disp; mv service pnt; shwrs €1.30; el pnts (10-16A) €1.30; gas; lndtte; shop; rest, snacks; playgrnd; htd pool 2km; walking; fishing; rafting; wifi; few statics; dogs free; quiet but some rd & rlwy noise; ccard acc. "Scenic site; friendly owners; Werfen castle & ice caves worth a visit; cycle path; ltd san facs, sometimes stretched." 15 Apr-30 Sep. € 23.50          2014*

**WESTENDORF see Kitzbühel** *C2*

## "I like to fill in the reports as I travel from site to site"

You'll find report forms at the back of this guide, or you can fill them in online at www.caravaclub.co.uk/europereport.

**WIEN** *B4* (8km E Urban) *48.20861, 16.44722* Aktiv-Camping Neue Donau, Am Kleehäufel, 1220 Wien-Ost [(01) 2024010; fax 2024020; neuedonau@campingwien. at; www.campingwien.at] Take A21-A23, exit sp Olhafen/ Lobau. After x-ing Rv Danube turn R, sp Neue-Donau Sud. In 150m turn L at traff lts after Shell g'ge; turn R on A4 turn R onto A23 & take 1st slip rd sp N-Donau after x-ing rv Danube. Lge, unshd; htd wc; chem disp; mv service pnt; 20% serviced pitches (extra charge); shwrs inc; el pnts (16A) €4 (poss rev pol); lndtte; shop; rest, snacks; sm playgrnd; rv 1km; tennis; games area; wifi; dogs €4.50; bus/metro to city 1km; Eng spkn; adv bkg; rd & rlwy noise; ccard acc; red CKE/ CCI. "Conv Vienna; lovely site; excel facs but poss stretched high ssn; poss v cr due bus tours on site; cycle track to city cent (map fr recep); 3 classes of pitch (extra charge for serviced); recep clsd 1200-1430; standard san facs." ♦ 15 Apr-30 Sep. € 44.00          2014*

**WIEN** *B4* (8km S Urban) *48.15065, 16.30025* Camping Wien-Süd, Breitenfurterstrasse 269, 1230 Wien [(01) 8673649; fax 8675843; sued@campingwien.at; www.campingwien. at] A1 fr Linz/Salzburg take A21 at Steinhausl (35km W of Vienna), merges with A2 dir Wien sp A23 Altmansdorf. At end a'bahn turn L dir Eisenstadt/Vösendorf, in 500m turn R at 1st set traff lts into Anton Baumgartnerstrasse. Then turn R at 6th traff lts into Breitenfurterstrasse. Fr N on A22 foll A23 to m'way A2 dir Graz. At junc 5 (Vösendorf) take A21 to junc 36 (Brunn am Gebirge & foll 'Zentrum' sp for 5km. At Merkur supmkt on R, turn R to site. Med, mkd pitch, pt shd; htd wc; chem disp; shwrs inc; el pnts (16A) €4; lndtte; supmkt adj; snacks; playgrnd; no statics; dogs €4.50; bus; metro; Eng spkn; adv bkg; ccard acc; CKE/ CCI. "Gd bus & metro conns to city; sep tent area; v pleasant busy site; gd san facs; conv for Wien; v friendly; recep open 0800-1600." ♦ 1 Jun-31 Aug. € 39.00          2013*

AUSTRIA

**Terrassencamping Schlossberg Itter**

Summer: table tennis, enormous children's playground, heated swimming pool. All pitches with TV connection. Wild water boating.

Winter: only 2 km away from the extended ski area Wilder Kaiser - Brixental with 96 lifts and 250 km of ski fields. Free skibus.

Top quality sanitary block with individual cabines. Sauna hut. Internet corner. WiFi on all pitches. Restaurant.

Fam. Ager • A-6305 Itter • Brixentalerstraße 11 • Tel. 05335/2181 • Fax 05335/2181-21
www.camping-itter.at • E-mail: info@camping-itter.at
GPS: N 47°27'58.60" / E 12°08'22.20"

⊞ **WIEN** *B4* (6km W Urban) *48.21396, 16.2505* **Camping Wien-West, Hüttelbergstrasse 80, 1140 Wien** [(01) 9142314; fax 9113594; west@campingwien.at; www.campingwien.at/ww] Fr Linz, after Auhof enter 3 lane 1-way rd. On app to traff lts get into L hand (fast) lane & turn L at traff lts. At next lts (Linzerstrasse) go strt over into Hüttelburgstrasse & site is uphill. Fr Vienna, foll sp A1 Linz on W a'bahn & site sp to R 100m bef double rlwy bdge. After this turn L on rd with tramlines & foll to v narr section, R at traff lts. Lge, mkd pitch, hdstg, pt shd; wc; chem disp; mv service pnt; shwrs inc; el pnts (16A) €4; lndtte; shop & 2km; tradsmn; snacks; playgrnd; wifi; some statics; dogs €4.50; bus; sep car park; site clsd Feb; poss v cr; Eng spkn; adv bkg; noisy in day but quiet at night; ccard acc; red CKE/CCI. "Rec arr early; gd bus service to U-Bahn & city cent - tickets fr recep + Vienna Card; clean facs, but poss stretched high ssn & ltd low ssn; poss travellers; site poss unkempt low ssn; sm pitches."
€ 41.50                                                          2014*

## "We must tell The Club about that great site we found"

Get your site reports in by mid-August and we'll do our best to get your updates into the next edition.

**WILDALPEN** *C3* (500m N Rural) *47.66673, 14.98692* **Camping Wildalpen, Hopfgarten 239, 8924 Wildalpen (Steiermark)** [(03636) 342; fax 313; camping@wildalpen. at; www.wildalpen.at] On B24 in Wildalpen turn down hill by church, site 500m on R by rv. Med, pt shd; wc; chem disp; mv service pnt; shwrs €0.85; el pnts (12A) inc; rest, snacks & shop in vill; tradsmn; pool 1.5km; tennis; 40% statics; dogs €1; poss cr; adv bkg. "Remote site, cent for white water canoeing instruction; excel for walking, photography, botany, bird life."
♦ 15 Apr-31 Oct. € 17.00                                        2009*

## "I need an on-site restaurant"

We do our best to make sure site information is correct, but it is always best to check any must-have facilities are still available or will be open during your visit.

⊞ **WORGL** *C2* (7km SE Rural) *47.46627, 12.13950* **Terrassencamping Schlossberg-Itter, Brixentalerstrasse 11, 6305 Itter-bei-Hopfgarten (Tirol)** [(05335) 2181; fax 2182; info@camping-itter.at; www.camping-itter.at] E fr Wörgl on B170 twd Kitzbühel. Site sp on L (N) side of rd in 7km, below castle & by rv opp Peugeot g'ge. Fr A12/E45 exit at Wörgl Ost & turn L at 1st T-junc sp Brixental for 4km. Turn R onto B178 at sp Brixental, then L on B170 for Hopfgarten. Med, mkd pitch, terr, pt sl, pt shd; htd wc; chem disp; mv service pnt; baby facs; fam bthrm; sauna; shwrs inc; el pnts (8-10A) €2.80; gas; lndtte (inc dryer); sm shop; tradsmn; rest, snacks; bar; BBQ; playgrnd; htd pool; paddling pool; solarium; canoeing; golf 15km; wifi; cab/sat TV; 25% statics; dogs €3.50; site clsd 15-30 Nov; poss cr; Eng spkn; adv bkg; quiet, but some rlwy noise; ccard not acc; CKE/CCI. "Superb site; highly rec, espec for children; immac pool; easy pitching on flat area but tractor assistance for pitching on steep terrs; luxury san facs; gd winter ski cent with drying rm; practice ski-run on site; gd walks; excursions arranged." ♦ € 26.00
2011*

See advertisement

⊞ **WORGL** *C2* (10km SE Rural) *47.43068, 12.14990* **Camping Reiterhof, Kelchsauerstrasse 48, 6361 Hopfgarten (Tirol)** [(05335) 3512; fax 4145; info@campingreiterhof.at; www. campingreiterhof.at] Fr Wörgl S on B170, thro Hopfgarten, site sp on R dir Kelchsau. Med, mkd pitch, pt shd; htd wc; chem disp; mv service pnt; baby facs; shwrs €1; el pnts (10A) €2.80; lndtte (inc dryer); shop 2km; tradsmn; rest, snacks, bar adj; playgrnd; htd pool 200m; ski lift 2km; free ski bus; wifi; 45% statics; dogs €2.20; poss cr; Eng spkn; adv bkg; quiet but some rd noise; CKE/CCI. "V friendly, v welcoming, helpful staff; immac san facs; excel for families or couples; lge recreation park adj; excel walking & cycling area; excel." ♦
€ 17.80                                                          2011*

⊞ **ZELL AM SEE** *C2 (6km N Rural) 47.37740, 12.79583*
**Campingplatz Bad Neunbrunnen, Neunbrunnen 56,**
**5751 Maishofen (Salzburg) [(06542) 68548; camping@**
**neunbrunnen.at; www.camping-neunbrunnen.at]** Foll
B311 N fr Zell-am-See dir Saalfelden; 500m after Maishofen
turn L bef tunnel & foll site sp. Med, mkd pitch, some hdstg,
unshd; wc; chem disp; mv service pnt; shwrs inc; el pnts (10A)
€2.20; lndtte (inc dryer); shop; tradsmn; rest, snacks; bar;
playgrnd; lake sw; fishing; games rm; winter sports area; wifi;
dogs; quiet; ccard acc;. "Vg, scenic site; cycle & walking tracks
fr site." € 17.00                                                    2010*

⊞ **ZELL AM SEE** *C2 (2km NE Rural) 47.33975, 12.80896*
**Seecamp, Thumersbacherstrasse 34, 5700 Zell-am-See**
**(Salzburg) [(06542) 72115; fax 7211515; zell@seecamp.**
**at; www.seecamp.at]** Fr S end Zellersee take B311 N thro
tunnel sp Zell-am-See Centrum. Cont thro town cent & in
500m turn R over rlwy x-ing sp Thumersbach. Site on R past
yacht club. Med, pt shd, mkd pitch, hdstg; wc; chem disp; mv
service pnt; shwrs inc; el pnts (16A) metered + conn fee €2.50;
metered gas; lndtte; shop (high ssn); tradsmn; rest, snacks;
bar; playgrnd; sand beach adj; lake sw; sailing; watersports;
fishing (free); cycle hire; wifi; dogs €4.30; bus at site ent; poss
cr; Eng spkn; quiet but some rd & rlwy noise; ccard acc; red
low ssn; CKE/CCI. "Lge sports cent nr; lger 'Komfort' pitch
avail for extra; gd, clean san facs; gd walk town cent; site
clsd 1100-1600; ltd pitch care low ssn; mountain views." ◆
€ 29.40                                                              2010*

## "Satellite navigation makes touring much easier"

Remember most sat navs don't know if
you're towing or in a larger vehicle – always
use yours alongside maps and site directions.

⊞ **ZELL AM SEE** *C2 (3km SE Rural) 47.30133, 12.8150*
**Panorama Camp Zell am See, Seeuferstrasse 196, 5700**
**Zell am See (Salzburg) [(06542) 56228; fax 562284; info@**
**panoramacamp.at; www.panoramacamp.at]** S fr Zell
on B311 sp Salzburg (using tunnel). At 3rd rndabt turn L dir
Thumersbach, site on L in 1.5km, sp. Med, hdg pitch, pt shd,
50% serviced pitch; mv service pnt; wc; chem disp; baby facs;
shwrs inc; el pnts (16A) metered + conn fee; lndtte; shop;
tradsmn; playgrnd; lake 300m; wifi; TV; 30% statics; dogs
€3.50; bus; Eng spkn; adv bkg; quiet; red long stay; CKE/
CCI. "Conv Salzburg & Krimml falls; clsd 1200-1330; cycle &
footpaths round lake adj; helpful owners; excel facs; peaceful
site; nicely laid out site with adequate pitches; owners take you
to pitch and make elec conn; shops & rest 500m; pizzas & rolls
fr recep; lovely view of mountains; easy access, peaceful site;
gd facs." € 31.00                                                    2014*

⊞ **ZELL AM ZILLER** *C2 (3km N Rural) 47.26326, 11.8995*
**Erlebnis Camping Aufenfeld, Aufenfeldweg 10, 6274**
**Aschau-im-Zillertal (Tirol) [(05282) 2916; fax 291611;**
**info@camping-zillertal.at; www.camping-zillertal.at]**
Fr A12 turn S at junc 39 Wiesing onto B169. At Kaltenbach
take rd to Aschau, site sp. Lge, mkd pitch, terr, pt shd; htd
wc; chem disp; mv service pnt; serviced pitches; baby rm;
fam bthrm; sauna; shwrs inc; el pnts (6A) €2.30; gas; lndtte
(inc dryer); shop; rest, snacks; bar; playgrnd; htd, covrd pool;
padding pool; lake sw; boating; tennis; games area; skiing;
cycle hire; wifi; entmnt; TV; car wash; 30% statics; dogs
€3.50; phone; train 500m; site clsd Nov; adv bkg rec public
hols & high ssn; quiet; ccard acc. "Excel site; wonderful facs
for children." ◆ € 31.00                                            2011*

See advert on bookmark

## "There aren't many sites open at this time of year"

If you're travelling outside peak season
remember to call ahead to check site opening
dates – even if the entry says 'open all year'.

⊞ **ZELL AM ZILLER** *C2 (500m SE Rural) 47.22830, 11.88590*
**Camping Hofer, Gerlosstrasse 33, 6280 Zell-am-Ziller**
**(Tirol) [(05282) 2248; fax 22488; info@campingdorf.at;**
**www.campingdorf.at]** Fr A12/E45/E60 exit junc 39 onto
B169 dir Zell-am-Ziller. In vill, site on R, sp. Med, mkd pitch, pt
shd; htd wc; chem disp; mv service pnt; baby facs; shwrs inc; el
pnts (10A) €3.50 or metered; gas; lndtte (inc dryer); shops adj;
rest, snacks; bar; BBQ; playgrnd; htd pool; cycle hire; games
rm; wifi; entmnt; dogs €2.50; phone; poss cr; quiet but rd
noise; Eng spkn; adv bkg; debit cards acc; red long stay; CKE/
CCI. "Excel site; clean, well-equipped facs; poss fly problem
high ssn; friendly, welcoming family; some pitches tight for lge
o'fits; gd walking & cycling; owner arranges guided walks; site
discount for funicular; excel." € 48.00 (CChq acc)        2013*

**ZWETTL** *A4 (15km SE Rural) 48.58956, 15.31805*
**Campingplatz Lichtenfels, Friedersbach 69, 3533**
**Friedersbach (Niederösterreich) [(02826) 7492 or**
**0664 5746866 (mob); forstverwaltung@thurnforst.at;**
**www.thurnforst.at]** Fr E on B38 fr Zwettl on app Rastenfeld
look for rv bdge & ruins of castle. Site sp on L. Med, pt shd; wc;
chem disp; shwrs; no el pnts; bar; BBQ; lake sw & shgl beach
100m; games area; 40% statics; dogs; quiet. "Pretty lake
setting; open air concerts in ruins of castle high ssn; friendly
owner; v clean facs." 1 May-10 Oct. € 15.50              2011*

---

France and Andorra
Central and South East Europe, Benelux and Scandinavia
Spain and Portugal

© Collins Bartholomew Ltd 2014

# Belgium
## Country Introduction

*Botanique Public Garden, Brussels*

## Welcome to Belgium

Belgium is a small country with great diversity. The north is a flatland, crisscrossed by canals and dotted with great cultural highlights like Antwerp, Bruges and Ghent. In the south you'll find the rolling hills of the Ardennes region scattered with impressive castles and fortresses.

Belgium's capital city, Brussels, is home to both the European Union and NATO. A cosmopolitan city, it is full of both modern and historical architecture, art galleries, museums and restaurants.

## Country highlights

Belgium is famous for it's high quality confectionery, and you should visit one of the country's expert chocolatiers during your stay. No trip is complete without sampling the Belgian national dish 'moules et frites' (mussels and chips served with mayonnaise). There are several hundred speciality beers on offer such as fruit flavoured, as well as known brands.

Belgium is also big on festivals. One of the most renowned is held in February at Binche, where there's a procession involving more than 1500 extravagantly dressed dancers.

## Major towns and cities

- Antwerp – a large cosmopolitan city, surrounding Belgium's biggest port.

- Ghent – a popular city full of historical landmarks.

- Brussels – the famous capital city of Belgium.

- Bruges – a fairytale medieval town with colourful streets and cobbled lanes.

## Attractions

- Grand-Place Brussels – a beautifully ornate medieval square.

- St Michael's Bridge – the historical entrance to the old medieval centre of Ghent.

- Historic Centre of Bruges – the city centre is surrounded by medieval architecture.

- Botanique Public Garden - in the centre of Brussels, a stunning place to explore and relax.

## Find out more

www.visitbelgium.com

Tel: 0032 (0) 70 22 10 21 Bruxelles Tourist Office

# Country Information

*Population (approx):* 10.4 million
*Capital:* Brussels (population approx 1 million)
*Area:* 30,528 sq km
*Bordered by:* France, Germany, Luxembourg, Netherlands
*Terrain:* Flat coastal plains in north-west; central rolling hills; rugged Ardennes hills and forest in south-east; south and west criss-crossed by canals
*Climate:* Mild winters but snow likely in the Ardennes, cool summers, rain any time of the year; coast can be windy
*Coastline:* 66km
*Highest Point:* Signal de Botrange 694m
*Languages:* Flemish, French, German
*Local Time:* GMT or BST + 1, i.e. 1 hour ahead of the UK all year
*Currency:* Euros divided into 100 cents
£1 = €1.26, €1 = £0.79 (September 2014)
*Emergency numbers:* Police 112, Fire Brigade 112, Ambulance 112.
*Public Holidays 2015:* Jan 1; Apr 6; May 1, 14, 25; Jul 21 (National Day); Sept 27; Nov 1, 11 (Armistice Day); Dec 25.

School summer holidays extend over July and August.

## Camping and Caravanning

There are more than 900 campsites in Belgium, most of which are near the coast or in the Ardennes. Coastal sites tend to consist largely of mobile homes/statics and can be very crowded at the height of the holiday season. A local tourist tax is usually included in the rates charged.

Twin-axle caravans are not permitted on municipal sites in and around Antwerp. Caravans and vehicles longer than 6 metres are prohibited from Liège city centre.

Casual/wild camping is prohibited in Flanders. Elsewhere permission must first be sought from the landowner or police. Camping is not permitted alongside public highways for more than a 24-hour period, nor is it permitted in lay-bys, in state forests or along the seashore, or within a 100 metre radius of a main water point, or on a site classified for the conservation of monuments.

## Cycling

Belgium is well equipped for cyclists, with an extensive network of signposted cycling routes. Cycle lanes are marked on the carriageway by means of a broken double white line or by circular signs depicting a white bicycle on a blue or black background.

Bikes may be carried at the rear of a vehicle as long as its width doesn't extend beyond the width of the vehicle or more than one metre from the rear, and providing the rear lights and number plate remain visible.

## Electricity and Gas

The current on most campsites varies between 4 and 16 amps although on some it is as low as 2 amps. Plugs have two round pins. CEE connections are not yet available at all sites.

Use a mains tester to test a connection before hooking up as problems are more common in Belgium than other EU countries. Issues may include reversed polarity, no earth and/or incorrectly alternating current. If any of these issues are present you shouldn't use the connection.

The full range of Campingaz cylinders are available.

## Entry Formalities

British and Irish passport holders may visit Belgium for up to three months without a visa.

## Medical Services

The standard of health care is high. Emergency medical and hospital treatment is available at a reduced cost on production of a European Health Insurance Card (EHIC). Check whether a doctor you wish to see is registered with the national health service (conventionné/geconventioneerd) or offers private healthcare. You will have to pay for services provided but 75% of the cost of treatment and approved medicines will be refunded if you apply to a local Sickness Fund Office with your EHIC.

At night and at weekends at least one local pharmacy will remain open and its address will be displayed in the window of all local pharmacies.

# Opening Hours

Banks - Open hours vary from one bank to another, however usual open hours are – Mon-Fri 9am-12pm & 2pm-4pm; Sat 9am-12pm (some banks).

Museums – Tue-Sun 10am-5pm; most museums close Monday.

Shops – Mon-Sat 9am-6pm or 8pm (supermarkets); some close 12pm-2pm; most shops closed Sunday.

# Safety and Security

Belgium is relatively safe for visitors but you should take the usual sensible precautions to avoid becoming a victim of muggers, bag-snatchers and pickpockets, especially at major railway stations and on the public transport in Antwerp and Brussels.

Belgium shares with the rest of Europe an underlying threat from terrorism. Attacks could be indiscriminate and against civilian and tourist targets. The area around Brussels hosts a number of international institutions (EU, NATO) which are sensitive locations where you should be vigilant.

*British Embassy*

AVENUE D'AUDERGHEM 10
1040 BRUXELLES
Tel: (02) 2876211
http://ukinbelgium.fco.gov.uk/en/
public.brussels@fco.gov.uk

*Irish Embassy*

CHAUSEE D'ETTERBEEK 180
1040 BRUXELLES
Tel: (02) 2823400
www.embassyofireland.be
brusselsembassy@dfa.ie
There is also an Honorary Consulate in Antwerp

# Documents

*Passport*
You should carry your passport or photocard driving licence at all times as Belgian law requires everyone to carry some form of identification.

*Vehicle(s)*
You should carry your vehicle registration certificate (V5C), insurance details and MOT certificate (if applicable).

# Money

Supermarkets often do not accept credit cards. Cash machines are widespread but may be few and far between outside town centres.

Carry your credit card issuer or bank's 24-hour UK contact numbers in case of loss or theft of your cards. If you have difficulty reporting the theft of your card(s) to your UK bank or credit card company, ask the Belgian group 'Card Stop' to send a fax to your UK company to block your card. Card Stop's telephone number is (070) 344344.

# Motoring in Belgium
# Accidents

The police must be called after an accident if an unoccupied stationary vehicle is damaged or if people are injured. If it isn't necessary to call the police to the scene of the accident you must still report it at the local police station.

# Alcohol

The maximum permitted level of alcohol is 49 milligrams in 100 millilitres of blood, i.e. lower than in the UK (80 milligrams). Penalties for exceeding this limit are severe including suspension of driving licence and a possible jail sentence.

# Breakdown Service

The Touring Club Royal de Belgique (TCB) operates a breakdown service 24 hours a day throughout the country, tel (070) 344777. On motorways, use the roadside telephones called 'telestrade' which are controlled by the police and are situated approximately every 2km. Ask for 'Touring Secours' or, when in the north of the country, 'Touring Wegenhulp'. It will be necessary to pay a fee which is variable depending on the time of day.

## Essential Equipment

*First aid kit*
It is not compulsory for foreign registered vehicles to carry a first aid kit, but it is still recommended.

*Warning Triangle*
An EU approved warning triangle must be used if the vehicle breaks down, has a puncture or is involved in an accident.

*Reflective Jacket/Waistcoat*
If you have broken down or are in an accident where stopping or parking is prohibited, you must wear a reflective jacket or waistcoat when getting out of your vehicle. Passengers who leave the vehicle, for example to assist with a repair, should also wear one. Keep the jacket(s) to hand in your vehicle, not in the boot.

*Child Restraint System*
Children under 1.35m must be seated in a child seat or child restraint when travelling in the front or rear seat of a vehicle. If a child seat/restraint is not available, i.e. when two child restraint systems are being used on rear seats and there isn't enough space for a third to be placed, a child must travel in the back of the vehicle using an adult seat belt. If the child is three years or under they must not travel in a vehicle without being seated in a child seat/restraint.

The child restraint must correspond to the child's weight and be of an approved type. A rear facing child restraint must not be used on a front seat with a frontal airbag unless it is deactivated.

## Fuel

Petrol stations on motorways and main roads are open 24 hours and credit cards are generally accepted. Others may close from 8pm to 8am and often all day Sunday.

LPG, also known as GPL, is widely available at many service stations.

## Parking

Blue zones indicating limited parking are used to denote where vehicles must display a parking disc on Monday to Saturday, from 9am to 6pm. Discs are available from police stations, petrol stations and some shops. Outside blue zones a parking disc must also be used where the parking sign has a panel showing the disc symbol. Parking areas are also regulated by parking meters and if these exist inside a blue zone parking discs must not be used, except if the parking meter or ticket machine is out of action. Illegally parked vehicles may be towed away or clamped.

Do not park in a street where there is a triangular sign 'Axe Rouge/Ax Rode'.

## Pollution

From 1 November to 31 March during levels of high pollution, known as pollution peaks, restrictions are imposed on driving in the Brussels area. There are different levels of restriction, from reduced speed limits to a total ban on driving , depending on the severity of the pollution. When in place restrictions are announced on local media and an electronic sign boards around the city. For more information visit www.brussels.be and search for 'pollution peak'.

## Priority

You should take great care to obey the 'priority to the right' rule which is designed to slow traffic in built-up areas. Drivers must give priority to vehicles joining from the right, even if those vehicles have stopped at a road junction or stopped for pedestrians or cyclists, and even if you are on what appears to be a main road. Exemptions to this rule apply on motorways, roundabouts and roads signposted with an orange diamond on a white background.

Trams have priority over other traffic. If a tram or bus stops in the middle of the road to allow passengers on or off, you must stop.

From 2014 a 'Zip Merging' rule has been in place in Belgium. Where a lane is ending or closed, drivers in that lane must continue to where that lane starts to close up before merging into the open lane. Drivers in the lane which remains open must give way in turn to the drivers merging into their lane.

## Roads

Roads are generally in good condition and well lit, however, some stretches of motorways have poor quality surfacing and signs to advise drivers to slow down. Traffic is fast and the accident rate is high, especially at weekends, mainly due to speeding.

## Road Signs and Markings

Roads signs and markings conform to international standards. A sign has been introduced prohibiting the use of cruise control. This sign will normally only be encountered on motorways where there is a risk of multiple crashes due to congestion or road works. Where this particular sign shows a weight limit, the prohibition applies to drivers of vehicles with a higher maximum permitted weight.

Destination road signs can be confusing to foreigners because a town may be signposted either by its French or its Flemish name, according to the predominant language in that particular area. The most important of these towns are listed below:

| Flemish | French |
| --- | --- |
| Aalst | Alost |
| Aken (Aachen) | Aix-la-Chapelle (Germany) |
| Antwerpen | Anvers |
| Bergen | Mons |
| Brugge | Bruges |
| Brussel | Bruxelles |
| Doornik | Tournai |
| Gent | Gand |
| Geraardsbergen | Grammont |
| Ieper | Ypres |
| Kortrijk | Courtrai |
| Leuven | Louvain |
| Luik | Liège |
| Mechelen | Maline |
| Namen | Namur |
| Rijsel | Lille (France) |
| Roeselare | Roulers |
| Tienen | Tirlemont |
| Veurne | Furnes |

Generally signposts leading to and on motorways show foreign destination place names in the language of the country concerned. e.g. German. Exceptions do occur, particularly on the E40 and E314 where city names may be given in Flemish or French.

Roads with the prefix N are regional roads; those with numbers 1 to 9 radiate from Brussels. Motorways have the prefix A and have blue and white signs. When route planning through Belgium follow the green European road numbers with the prefix E which may be the only road numbers displayed.

Road signs you may see include the following:

You may pass right or left

Cyclists have priority over turning traffic

Cyclists have priority at junction

Use of Cruise Control prohibited

## Speed Limits

| | Open Road (km/h) | Motorway (km/h) |
| --- | --- | --- |
| Car Solo | 90 | 120 |
| Car towing caravan/ trailer | 90 | 120 |
| Motorhome under 3500kg | 90 | 120 |
| Motorhome 3500- 7500kg | 90 | 90 |

Whilst the general speed limit in built-up areas is 50 km/h (31mph), lower limits of 30 km/h (18 mph) or 20 km/h (12mph) may be imposed and indicated by signs in residential areas, town centres and near schools. Brussels city centre is a 30 km/h (18mph) speed limit zone. The start and finish points of these zones are not always clearly marked.

Vehicles over 3,500 kg in weight are restricted to 90 km/h (56mph) outside built-up areas and on motorways.

## Traffic Jams

During periods of fine weather roads to the coast, the Ardennes and around Brussels and Antwerp are very busy on Friday afternoons and Saturday mornings, and again on Sunday evenings.

Other busy routes are the E40 (Brussels to Ostend), the E25 (Liège to Bastogne and Arlon), the E411 (Brussels to Namur and Luxembourg), and the N4 from Bastogne to Arlon around the border town of Martelange caused by motorists queuing for cheap petrol in Luxembourg. Avoid traffic on the E40 by taking the R4 and N49, and on the E411 by taking the N4 Bastogne to Marche-en-Famenne and Namur.

These routes are heavily used and consequently the road surface can be poor.

## Traffic Lights

A green light (arrow) showing at the same time as a red or amber light means that you can turn in the direction of the green arrow providing you give way to other traffic and to pedestrians. An amber light, possibly flashing, in the form of an arrow inclined at an angle of 45 degrees to the left or to the right, shows that the number of traffic lanes will be reduced.

## Tunnels

Three road tunnels go under the River Scheldt at Antwerp. In the Liefkenhoeks tunnel on road R2 to the north of the city a toll of €17.60-19.00 (2014) is levied on vehicles over 2.75m in height. Solo cars are charged €4.95-6.00. The Kennedy Tunnel on road R1 to the south of the city is toll-free but is heavily congested in both directions for much of the day. The smallest tunnel, the Waasland Tunnel is part of the N59a and is also toll-free.

## Violation of Traffic Regulations

The police may impose on-the-spot fines on visitors who infringe traffic regulations such as speeding and parking offences. Penalties may be severe and if you are unable to pay on the spot your vehicle(s) may be impounded or your driving licence withdrawn. Fines can be paid in cash or with a debit or credit card. An official receipt must be issued.

In an effort to improve road safety the authorities have increased the number of speed traps throughout the country in the form of cameras and unmarked police vehicles.

Vehicles of 3,500 kg or over are not allowed to use the left lane on roads with more than three lanes except when approaching a fork in a motorway when vehicles have to move to the left or right lane, depending on their destination.

## Motorways

Belgium has an extensive network of approximately 1,750km of motorways (A roads). Although Belgian motorways are toll free, the introduction of a motorway sticker is planned for 2016.

Service areas usually have a petrol station, restaurant, shop and showers. Rest areas have picnic facilities. For detailed information about the motorway network see www.autosnelwegen.net.

Recent visitors report that some motorways are so heavily used by lorries that the inside lane has become heavily rutted and/or potholed. These parallel ruts are potentially dangerous for caravans travelling at high speed. It is understood that parts of the A2/E314 and A3/E40 are particularly prone to this problem.

## Touring

Flemish is spoken in the north of Belgium, whilst French is spoken in the south. Brussels is bi-lingual. English is widely spoken.

Prices in restaurants are quoted 'all inclusive' and no additional tipping is necessary. Smoking is severely restricted in public places including restaurants and cafés.

Carrier bags are generally not provided in supermarkets, so take your own.

When visiting Brussels visitors may buy a Brussels Card, valid for 24, 48 or 72 hours, which offers free access to virtually every major museum in the city and unlimited use of public transport, together with discounts at a number of other attractions. The pass is available from the tourist information office in the Hotel de Ville and from many hotels, museums and public transport stations. Or buy online from www.brusselscard.be.

# Public Transport

Anyone under the age of 25 years is entitled to free or reduced price travel on public transport in the Brussels region. During periods of severe air pollution public transport in that region is free to all passengers.

Brussels and Antwerp have metro systems together with extensive networks of trams and buses. Tram and bus stops are identified by a red and white sign and all stops are request stops; hold out your arm to signal an approaching bus or tram to stop. Tickets, including 10-journey and one-day travel cards, are available from vending machines at metro stations and some bus stops, newsagents, supermarkets and tourist information centres.

Most of Belgium is well connected by train and most main routes pass through Antwerp, Brussels or Namur. Trains are modern, comfortable and punctual and fares are reasonably priced. Buy tickets before boarding the train or you may be charged a supplement. Eurostar tickets to Brussels allow free, same day transfers to domestic Belgian stations.

Bikes are allowed on some buses in the Flanders area of the country.

Plans are in hand to introduce a unified smart card ticketing system covering all public transport, irrespective of company or mode of transport. This system will use chip cards, card readers and on-board computers.

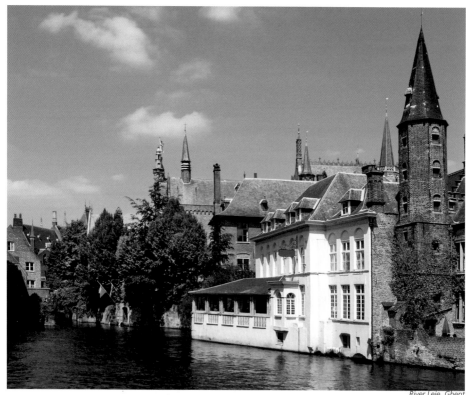

*River Leie, Ghent*

**AALTER** *A2* (1km N Rural) Camping Isabel-Novel, Manewaarde 13A, 9880 Aalter [(09) 3744589; fax 3747515] Fr A10/E40 Ostend-Gent, exit Aalter. Take N44 sp Maldegem. L at 2nd set traff lts (lts are v close together), turn immed R thro indus est. Turn L into narr low at site sp (diff to spot), site 650m on R. Ent to site diff for lge o'fits/m'vans. Med, pt shd; wc; shwrs €0.50; el pnts €1.50; shops 4km; playgrnd; fishing; 50% statics; quiet but rd & rlwy noise; CKE/CCI. "Friendly site; in field adj old residential site; conv NH." 1 Apr-30 Sep. € 12.00                    2010*

**ADINKERKE see De Panne** *A1*

**AISCHE EN REFAIL** *B3* (S Rural) *50.59977, 4.84335* Camping du Manoir de Là-Bas, Route de Gembloux 180, 5310 Aische-en-Refail [(081) 655353; europa-camping.sa@ skynet.be; www.camping-manoirdelabas.be] Fr E411/ A4 exit junc 12 & foll sps to Aische-en-Refail. Site on o'skts of vill. Lge, pt sl, pt shd; wc; chem disp; shwrs €1; el pnts (6A) inc; gas; lndtte; shop; snacks; htd pool; paddling pool; fishing; tennis; games rm; entmnt; 80% statics; dogs; poss cr; Eng spkn; adv bkg; quiet; CKE/CCI. "Friendly staff; site little run down; ltd hot water; basic san facs; some site rds are narr; recep far side of chateau; gd rest & bar." ♦ 1 Apr-31 Oct. € 18.00                    2011*

**AMBERLOUP/STE ODE see Tenneville** *C3*

**ANTWERPEN** *A3* (15km NE Urban) *51.30548, 4.58536* Camping Floreal Club Het Veen, Eekhoornlaan 1, 2960 Sint Job-in't-Goor [(03) 6361327; fax 6362030; het.veen@ florealclub.be; www.florealclub.be] Fr A1/E19 exit junc 4 to Sint Job in't Goor. Strt over traff lts & immed after canal bdge turn L, 1.5km to site alongside canal. Lge, hdg/mkd pitch, pt shd; htd wc; chem disp; mv service pnt; baby facs; shwrs inc; el pnts (10A) inc; lndtte (inc dryer); shop; rest, snacks; bar; playgrnd; tennis; games rm; 80% statics; dogs €3.40; phone; bus 1.5km; Eng spkn; adv bkg; CKE/CCI. "V helpful recep; pleasant site & town; gd cycling along canal; gd NH." 1 Mar-31 Oct. € 25.00                    2010*

⊞ **ANTWERPEN** *A3* (1km NW Urban) *51.23347, 4.39261* Camping De Molen, Thonelaan - Jachthavenweg 6, St Annastrand, 2020 Antwerpen [tel/fax (03) 2198179; info@camping-de-molen.be; www.camping-de-molen. be] Clockwise on ring rd, take 1st exit after Kennedy tunnel, exit 6. R at traff lts, 3rd L where cannot go strt on (rv on R), site on R in 1km on bank of Rv Schelde. On cont Antwerp foll sp Linkeroever, go strt on at 3 traff lts, then turn L & foll camping sp. Fr A14/E17 exit junc 7 & foll sp for Linkeroever Park & Ride until site sp appear, then foll sp. Med, pt shd; wc; chem disp; shwrs; el pnts (10A) €2.50 (poss rev pol) - €25 deposit for adaptor/cable; shops 1km; supmkt by metro; rest adj; pool nr; wifi; bus nrby; metro 1km; poss cr; Eng spkn; adv bkg rec; quiet, but some rv traff noise & poss noise fr local bar; ccard not acc; red low ssn. "Popular site; max 14 nt stay; pedestrian/ cycle tunnel to city cent 1km; gd for rollerblading, cycling; friendly, helpful staff; mosquitoes poss a problem; san facs satisfactory; 30 min walk to city cent." ♦ € 26.00     2014*

⊞ **ARLON** *D3* (2km N Urban) *49.70310, 5.80763* Camping Officiel, 373 Rue de Bastogne, Bonnert, 6700 Arlon [tel/ fax (063) 226582; campingofficiel@skynet.be; www. campingofficielarlon.be] Fr E411 exit junc 31 onto N82 Arlon for 4km, turn twd Bastogne on N4. Site sp on R. Med, pt sl, pt shd; wc; chem disp; fam bthrm; shwrs inc; el pnts (6A) €2.40 (check earth); gas; lndtte (inc dryer); shop 2km; tradsmn; rest, snacks; bar; BBQ; playgrnd; pool; wifi; TV rm; dogs €2; Eng spkn; poss cr; adv bkg; some rd noise; red long stay; CKE/CCI. "Charming, clean site; levelling blocks/ramps req - supplied by site; c'vans tight-packed when site busy; 5km approx to Luxembourg for cheap petrol; Arlon interesting town; vg NH & longer stay; thoroughly rec for stop over; Payment cash only; 3 hardstandings for m'van; new pool (2014)." ♦ € 28.60 2014*

**ARLON** *D3* (7km N Rural) *49.74833, 5.78697* Camping Sud, 75 Voie de la Liberté, 6717 Attert [(063) 223715; fax 221554; info@campingsudattert.com; www. campingsudattert.com] Off N4 Arlon rd on E side of dual c'way. Sp to site fr N4 (500m). U-turn into site ent. Med, hdg/ mkd pitch, some hdstg, pt shd; htd wc; chem disp; shwrs €0.50 (high ssn); el pnts (5-10A) €2.50 (check earth); lndtte; shop; tradsmn; rest, snacks; bar; BBQ; playgrnd; pool; no statics; dogs €2; phone; bus; adv bkg; Eng spkn; quiet, some rd noise; red long stay; CKE/CCI. "Vg, well-organised site; special NH pitches; fishing & walking; peaceful site; v friendly staff; highly rec." 1 Apr-15 Oct. € 25.00                    2014*

**ATTERT see Arlon** *D3*

**AVE ET AUFFE see Han sur Lesse** *C3*

⊞ **AYWAILLE** *C3* (1km E) *50.47633, 5.68916* Domaine Chateau de Dieupart, Route de Dieupart 37, 4920 Aywaille [(042) 631238; fax 462690; info@dieupart.be; www.dieupart.be] Leave E25 at exit 46 Remouchamps/ Aywaille. Turn R at traff lts dir Aywaille, and R by church. Immed L and Rt at Delhaise car park, take ave up to the castle. Site SP. Med, pt sh; wc; chem disp; mv service pnt; shwrs; el pnts (6A) inc; rest; bar; BBQ; playgrnd; wifi; 50% statics; bus 500m, train 1.5km, Eng spkn, adv bkg acc; CKE/CCI, red low ssn; "Nice site by rv; gd walking and cycling; supmkt 300m." ♦ € 23.00                    2013*

⊞ **BASTOGNE** *C3* (500m NE Urban) *50.00340, 5.69525* Camping de Renval, 148 Route de Marche, 6600 Bastogne [tel/fax (061) 212985; info@campingrenval.be; www. campingrenval.be] Fr N leave A26 exit 54, foll Bastogne sp. Fr Marche-en-Famenne dir, exit N4 at N84 for Bastogne; site on L in 150m opp petrol stn. Fr E foll Marche, in 1km site on R opp petrol stn. Med, hdstg, pt sl, terr, pt shd; htd wc; chem disp; baby facs; shwrs inc; el pnts (10A) inc (poss rev pol); lndtte (inc); shops 1km; snacks; BBQ; playgrnd; tennis; games area; wifi; entmnt; 95% statics; dogs €3; site clsd Jan; quiet; ccard acc; red low ssn. "Take care speed bumps; helpful staff; clean san facs but long walk fr tourers' pitches; gd security; facs ltd low ssn; gd NH." € 20.00                    2010*

⊞ **BERLARE** *A2* (1km N Rural) *51.04350, 3.98960* **Camping Roosendael, Schriekenstraat 27, 9290 Berlare-Overmere [(09) 3678742; fax 3657355; hugoscalafilm@skynet.be; www.ideal-caravans.be]** Fr A14/E17 junc 11 onto N449 dir Laarne. At T-junc turn L onto N445 past Overmere & Donk. Approx 2.5km after Overmere at rndabt with Shell g'ge turn R onto N467 past Donkmeer to Berlare. After 1.5km turn L in front of 'Café de Kalvaar', site at end of rd. Med, hdg/mkd pitch, pt shd; htd wc; chem disp; shwrs; el pnts (6A) inc; lndtte; shop, rest, snacks, bar 500m; BBQ; playgrnd; lake beach & sw 500m; fishing 500m; games rm; tennis 500m; many statics; phone; quiet; Eng spkn. "Nice site; lge pitches, mainly sandy soil; warm welcome; clean, modern san facs, but ltd; poss under-used low ssn; local vet comes to site; gd NH." ♦ € 17.00                                    2011*

**BERTRIX** *D3* (2km S Rural) *49.83942, 5.25360* **Ardennen Camping Bertrix, Route de Mortehan, 6880 Bertrix [(061) 412281; fax 412588; info@campingbertrix.be; www.campingbertrix.be]** Exit A4/E411 junc 25 onto N89 for Bertrix & foll yellow sps to site. Lge, mkd pitch, terr, pt shd; htd wc; chem disp; mv service pnt; baby facs; fam bthrm; some serviced pitches; sauna; shwrs inc; el pnts (10A) €4; gas; lndtte (inc dryer); shop high ssn; tradsmn; rest, snacks; bar; playgrnd; htd pool high ssn; paddling pool; tennis; cycle hire; internet; TV rm; 35% statics; dogs €5; poss cr; Eng spkn; adv bkg; quiet; ccard acc; red low ssn/snr citizens; red low ssn/CKE/CCI. "Excel site; scenic location; friendly, helpful owners; gd for families; excel clean facs; gd rest; lg pitches; big pool." ♦ 26 Mar-11 Nov. € 43.00 (CChq acc)                      2013*

**BOUILLON** *D3* (800m S Rural) *49.78247, 5.06212* **Camping Moulin de la Falize, Vieille Route de France 62, 6830 Bouillon [(061) 466200; fax 467275; moulindelafalize@swing.be; www.moulindelafalize.be]** Fr A4 exit junc 25 & foll N89. Turn R dir Bouillon. At end of town 1-way system turn R then immed L up hill, site on L in 800m. Med, pt sl, terr, unshd; wc; chem disp; sauna; shwrs inc; el pnts (6A) inc; lndtte; shop 1km; rest, snacks; bar; BBQ; playgrnd; pool; rv 1km; tennis; fitness cent; entmnt; 95% statics; phone; dogs; quiet; Eng spkn; ccard acc; CKE/CCI. "V ltd touring pitches; steep inclines; conv Orval Abbey, brewery; NH only." 1 Apr-31 Dec. € 17.50                                    2009*

**BOUILLON** *D3* (6km W Rural) *49.79479, 5.01352* **Camp Municipal Halliru, 1 Route de Corbion, 6830 Bouillon [(061) 466009; fax 468048; halliru@bouillon.be; www.bouillon.be]** Fr Bouillon pass under castle, turn L twd Corbion on N810; site on R in 6km. Steep descent into site. Med, pt shd; wc; shwrs €1; shops 1.5km; el pnts (10A) €2.08 (long lead poss req); playgrnd; fishing; 50% statics; dogs; poss cr; phone; quiet. "Peaceful rvside site; conv historic town; fair." ♦ 1 Apr-30 Sep. € 10.42                               2011*

**BREDENE see Oostende** *A1*

**BRUGES see Brugge** *A2*

⊞ **BRUGGE** *A2* (12km NE Rural) *51.28937, 3.33332* **Camping Hoeke, Damse Vaart Oost 10, 8340 Damme [(050) 500496; www.campinghoeke.be]** Fr Brugge ring rd, take minor rd to NE, sp Damme on S side of canal. At Damme, cont by canal to Siphon. Cross canal, turn L in front of cafe, R & cont 4km by canal to Hoeke. Site behind pub building on R bef bdge at Hoeke. Or fr N fr junc N49 & N376 take N49 dir Maldagem for 3.5km. Site sp both sides of canal in Hoeke. Keep canal on R twd Damme, site 300m on L, sp on building. Sm, hdg/mkd pitch, pt shd; wc; chem disp; 10% serviced pitches; shwrs €1; el pnts (6A) inc; gas; shops 4km; rest; bar; BBQ; playgrnd; sand beach 8km; 90% statics; phone; quiet; CKE/CCI. "Picturesque town, conv Bruges fishing in canal; tight access to pitches; charge for all hot water; NH/sh stay only." ♦ ltd 1 Mar-15 Nov. € 16.25                                    2010*

## "That's changed – Should I let The Club know?"

If you find something on site that's different from the site entry, fill in a report and let us know. See www.caravanclub.co.uk/europereport.

⊞ **BRUGGE** *A2* (3km E Urban) *51.20722, 3.26305* **Camping Memling, Veltemweg 109, 8310 Sint Kruis [(050) 355845; fax 357250; info@camping-memling.be / info@brugescamping.be; www.camping-memling.be / www.brugescamping.be]** Exit A10 junc 8 Brugge. In 2km turn R onto N397 dir St Michiels & cont 2km to rlwy stn on R. Turn R under rlwy tunnel & at 1st rndbt take dir Maldegem onto ring rd & in a few kms take N9 sp Maldegem & St Kruis. After 3km at traff lts adj Macdonalds, turn R & immed L sp Camping to site on R in 400m past sw pool. Fr Gent exit E40 sp Oostkamp & foll Brugge sp for 7km to N9 as above. Med, mkd pitch, some hdstg, pt shd; htd wc; chem disp; mv service pnt; shwrs inc; el pnts (6A) inc (poss rev pol); lndtte; shops 500m; rest, snacks; bar 500m; htd pool adj; cycle hire; wifi; 13% statics; dogs €2; bus 200m; poss v cr; Eng spkn; adv bkg ess high ssn; poss noisy at w/ends & rd noise; ccard acc; red low ssn/long stay; CKE/CCI. "Busy site; conv Brugge & ports; red low ssn as no shwrs/rest/bar; friendly, helpful owners; recep open 08:00-22:00 (all day to 2200 high ssn); arr early high ssn to ensure pitch; low ssn site yourself & report to recep; conv Zeebrugge ferry (30mins) & allowed to stay to 1500; bus svrs every 20 mins to Bruges; adv bkgs taken but no pitch reserved; m'van pitches sm, rec pay extra for standard pitch; clean san facs refurbished 2012; cycle rte to Bruges; 35 min walk to Brugge cent; conv bus; nice site; rec." € 35.00                                    2014*

⊞ **BRUGGE** *A2* (500m S Urban) *51.19634, 3.22573* **Motorcaravan Park, Off ring rd R30, Buiten Katelijnevest, Brugge** Exit A10 at junc 7 twd Brugge. After going under rlwy bdge, turn R under ring rd after old bus stn to dedicated mv parking adj coach parking, nr marina. Sm, hdstg, pt shd; chem disp €0.50; el pnts (10A) inc; washrm nr; water €0.50; shop 500m; dogs; noisy; m'vans only; red low ssn. "In great location - gd view of canal, sh walk to town cent thro park; rec arr early high ssn; if full, take ticket & park in coach park opp; NH only." € 22.50                                    2011*

⊞ **BRUGGE** *A2* (9km SW Urban) *51.18448, 3.10445* Recreatiepark Klein Strand, Varsenareweg 29, 8490 Jabbeke [(050) 811440; fax 814289; info@kleinstrand. be; www.kleinstrand.be] If travelling fr W leave A10/E40 at Jabbeke exit, junc 6; turn R at rndabt & in 100m turn R into narr rd. Foll site to statics car pk on L & park - walk to check-in at recep bef proceeding to tourer site in 400m. If app fr E leave A10/E40 at junc 6 (Jabbeke) turn L at 1st rndabt. Drive over m'way twd vill. Turn L at next rndabt & foll site sp into site car pk as above. V lge, hdg/mkd pitch, pt shd; wc; chem disp; mv service pnt; baby facs; shwrs €0.75; el pnts (10A) inc; gas; lndtte (inc dryer); shop & 1km; 2 rests (1 open all yr); snacks; 3 bars; BBQ; playgrnd; paddling pool; direct access to lake sw adj; tennis; fishing; watersports; cycle hire; games rm; wifi; entmnt; TV; 75% statics; dogs €2; no c'vans/m'vans over 12m; bus to Brugge; poss cr with day visitors; Eng spkn; quiet but backgrnd m'way noise; ccard acc; red low ssn/CKE/CCI. "Busy site; vg touring base; lge pitches; wide range of entmnt & excursions; bus to Bruges every 20 mins." ♦ € 38.00 (up to 4 persons) SBS - H15 2014*

See advertisement

**BRUSSELS see Bruxelles** *B2*

**BRUXELLES** *B2* (10km NE Rural) *50.9346, 4.3821* Camping Grimbergen, Veldkantstraat 64, 1850 Grimbergen [(0479) 760378 or (02) 2709597; fax (02) 2701215; camping-grimbergen@webs.com] Fr Ostend on E40/A10 at ringrd turn E & foll sp Leuven/Luik (Liège)/Aachen. Exit junc 7 N sp Antwerpen/Grimbergen N202. At bus stn traff lts turn R twd Vilvoorde N211. Turn L at 2nd traff lts (ignore no L turn - lorries only). Site sp 500m on R. Ent via pool car pk. Med, hdg pitch, pt sl, pt shd; wc; chem disp; shwrs inc; el pnts (10A) €2.50; lndtte; shops 500m; tradsmn; rest adj; pool adj; cycle hire; dogs €1; phone; hourly bus to city 200m; Eng spkn; adv bkg; quiet but some aircraft noise & cock crowing; CKE/CCI. "Well-run, popular site - rec arr early; gd, clean, modern san facs; helpful staff; sh walk to town; train to Brussels fr next vill; red facs low ssn; gates clsd 1130-1400 and 2000 onwards; gd rest by bus stop; conv Brussels; excel san facs; rec; gd NH." ♦ 1 Apr-25 Oct. € 26.00 2014*

**BRUXELLES** *B2* (10km E Urban) *50.85720, 4.48506* **RCCC** de Belgique, Warandeberg 52, 1970 Wezembeek [(02) 7821009; camping.wezembeek@hotmail.com; www. rcccb.com] Leave ringrd RO at junc 2 sp Kraainem turning E. In 600m at rndabt at end of dual c'way take 3rd exit, then 1st L into residential rd. At end turn L, then R at end. Foll rd to crest of hill, site on L, sp. Med, mkd pitch, hdstg, terr, pt sl, pt shd; wc; chem disp; shwrs inc; el pnts (6A) inc (poss rev pol & no earth); gas 3km; lndry rm; shop, rest, snacks 1km; bar; playgrnd; 65% statics; dogs €1; metro nr; gates clsd 1200-1400 & 2200-0800; Eng spkn; adv bkg; some rd & aircraft noise; ccard acc; CKE/CCI. "Poss diff for lge o'fits due narr site ent, v tight corners, raised kerbs; unkempt (2011); poor san facs (2011); gd for metro into Brussels fr Kraainem; welcoming wardens." 1 Apr-30 Sep. € 20.00 2012*

**BURE/TELLIN see Tellin** *C3*

**DAMME see Brugge** *A2*

**DE HAAN** *A1* (2km E Coastal) *51.28330, 3.05610* Camping Ter Duinen, Wenduinesteenweg 143, Vlissegem, 8421 De Haan [(050) 413593; fax 416575; lawrence.sansens@ scarlet.be; www.campingterduinen.be] Exit A10/E40 junc 6 Jabbeke onto N377 dir De Haan. Go thro town dir Wenduine, site on R in 4km. Med, mkd pitch, pt shd; pt terr; htd wc; chem disp; mv service pnt; baby facs; shwrs €1.20; el pnts (6A) inc; lndtte (inc dryer); shop; snacks; bar; BBQ; playgrnd; htd pool 200m; water complex 1km; sand/shgl beach 500m; lake sw adj; fishing, cycle hire 200m; horseriding 1km; golf 4km; wifi; 85% statics; dogs €5.75; phone; tram nrby; poss cr; Eng spkn; adv bkg ess; fairly quiet; CKE/CCI. "Neat, clean, well-managed site; friendly staff; poss long walk to excel san facs inc novelty wcs!; conv ferries, Bruges; excel; hot dish water req tokens, mkt in nrby towns." ♦ 15 Mar-15 Oct. € 40.00 (CChq acc) 2013*

**DE HAAN** *A1* (W Urban/Coastal) *51.26123, 2.99836* Camping 't Rietveld, Driftweg 210, 8420 De Haan [(0475) 669336; camping.rietveld@telenet.be; www.campingrietveld. be] Fr Ostend on N34; fork R onto Driftweg bef golf club dir Vosseslag & Klemskerke, site sp. Sm, unshd, mrkd pitch; htd wc; chem disp; baby facs; shwrs €1.20; el pnts (16A) €1.95; lndtte; shop, rest, snacks, bar in town; playgrnd; sand beach 1km; 80% statics; dogs €1.85; poss cr; Eng spkn; quiet; CKE/ CCI. "Friendly, helpful staff; clean san facs." 1 Apr-15 Oct. € 20.55 2013*

DE PANNE

⊞ **DE PANNE** *A1* (2km W Rural) *51.08288, 2.59094*
Camping Ter Hoeve, Duinhoekstraat 101, 8660 Adinkerke
[(058) 412376; camping.terhoeve@skynet.be; www.
camping-terhoeve.be] Leave Calais-Ostend m'way at junc
1 (ignore junc 1a) dir De Panne. Foll rd past theme park
(Plopsaland), L at filling stn, site 1km on L. Lge, hdg pitch, pt
shd; wc; chem disp; mv service pnt; shwrs inc; el pnts (4A) €2
(poss no earth); lndtte (inc dryer); shop; supmkt 1km; snacks;
playgrnd; beach 2km; 60% statics; no dogs; tram 1km; poss
cr; some daytime noise fr nrby theme park; ccard not acc.
"Nice pitches; friendly, helpful owner; gd, modern san facs;
lge grassed area for tourers & hdstg area for late arr/early
dep; barrier clsd 2200-0800 - go to visitors' car park on R bef
booking in; san facs clsd 1100-1600 low ssn; v busy site high
ssn, phone to check opening times low ssn; conv Dunkerque
ferries & Plopsaland park; tram tickets avail at filling stn; coin
operated dishwash water." € 16.50                    2014*

⊞ **DE PANNE** *A1* (2.3km W Rural) *51.07666, 2.58663*
Familie Camping Kingervreugde, Langgeleedstraat
1, 8660 Adinkerke [(050) 811440; fax 814289; info@
kindervreugde.be; www.familiecamping.net] Leave Calais-
Ostend m'way at junc 1 (ignore junc 1a) dir De Panne. Foll rd
past theme park (Plopsaland), L at filling stn, site 1.3km on L.
Med, hdg pitch, pt shd; htd wc; chem disp; shwrs inc; el pnts
(6A) €2.50; lndtte; shop, rest, snacks, bar 1km; BBQ; playgrnd;
dogs; 50% statics; phone; bus 800m; Ltd Eng spkn; adv bkg;
quiet; ccard not acc; red CKE/CCI. "Conv Dunkerque/Calais
ferries; final appraoch diff for o'fits over 12ft." ♦ ltd 29 Apr-
1 Oct. € 28.00 (3 persons)                    2013*

**DEINZE see Gent** *A2*

**DINANT** *C3* (4km S Rural) *50.22178, 4.92230* Camping Parc
de Vacances Villatoile, Ferme de Pont-à-Lesse, Route
de Walzin, 5500 Anseremme [(082) 222285; fax 227151;
info@villatoile.be; www.villatoile.be] Leave E11 at junc
20 onto N97 dir Philippeville, then onto N94 dir Dinant. At
T-junc facing rv turn L onto N95 to Anseremme. Go thro vill &
turn L just bef rv bdge, site 1.5km on L. NB App rd has v lge,
brick-built speed ramp. Med, pt shd; wc; chem disp; mv service
pnt; shwrs €1.20; el pnts (10A) inc (poss rev pol); gas; lndtte
(inc dryer); shop; tradsmn; rest, snacks; high ssn; bar; playgrnd;
pool 300m; rv sw adj; canoeing; games area; wifi; entmnt;
40% statics; dogs; phone; Eng spkn; adv bkg (winter); quiet;
ccard acc; CKE/CCI. "On loop of Rv Lesse; busy, not particularly
clean site used by canoeists, rock climbers & hikers; extra for
rvside pitch; scenic area; gd san facs; gd walks; hign ssn music
Sat nights; gates locked 2200-0800; poss lge, noisy youth
groups; gd fun for older children otherwise NH only." 1 Apr-
15 Oct. € 17.80                    2010*

**DINANT** *C3* (10km SW Rural) *50.19094, 5.00611*
Camping de la Lesse, Rue du Camping 1, 5560 Houyet
[(82) 666100; fax 667214; lafamiliale@coolweb.be; www.
campingdelalesse.be] S on N95 fr Dinant for about 13km;
turn L onto D929 sp Houyet. Cross rlwy & immed turn L along
Rv Lesse. Lge, pt shd; htd wc; chem disp; shwrs; el pnts (15A)
inc; lndtte; shop 500m; rest, snacks; bar; playgrnd; pool adj;
tennis; kayaking; fishing; 50% statics; dogs €2; train; poss
noisy; CKE/CCI. "Pleasant area for walking/cycling; caves
at Han-sur-Lesse worth visit; basic san facs." 1 Apr-31 Oct.
€ 20.00                    2012*

⊞ **DINANT** *C3* (1.5km NW Urban) *50.27722,
4.89694* Camping Communal Devant-Bouvignes,
1 Quai de Camping, 5500 Dinant [(082) 224002 or
(477) 619873 (mob); fax 224132; devantbouvignes.
dinant@gmail.com; www.dinant.be] Exit E11 junc 20 onto
N936; drive to cent of Dinant (steep descent) to T-junc; turn R
onto N92; cont along rv for 1.5km; site on L after bend. Med,
pt shd; htd wc; chem disp; mv service pnt; baby facs; shwrs €1;
el pnts (16A) €3; lndry rm; supmkt 1km; drinks avail; playgrnd;
rv sw; 50% statics; dogs free; bus at ent; adv bkg; quiet, but
some rd & rlwy noise; ccard not acc. "Excel situation on rv
bank; site undergoing modernisation (2011), inc pitch layout,
when completed it should be excel." € 17.00            2011*

⊞ **DINANT** *C3* (9km NW Rural) *50.33557, 4.99534* Camping
de Durnal - Le Pommier Rustique, Rue de Spontin, 5530
Durnal [tel/fax (083) 699963 / (0475) 407827 (mob); info@
camping-durnal.net; www.camping-durnal.net] Leave
E411 at junc 19. Turn S dir Spontin onto D946, then N937, foll
site sp. Sm, mkd pitch, terr, unshd; wc; chem disp; fam bthrm;
sauna; shwrs inc; el pnts (10A) inc (check rev pol); lndtte (inc
dryer); shop; tradsmn; rest, snacks; playgrnd; games area;
child entmnt high ssn; cab TV; wifi; mainly statics; dogs free;
4 nights for price of 3; Eng spkn; quiet; ccard acc. "Friendly,
helpful owner; well-run, well-maintained site; ltd touring
pitches; sm pitches; conv NH fr m'way; v quiet low ssn; modern
san facs." ♦ 1 Mar-31 Dec. € 27.00                    2013*

# "I like to fill in the reports as I travel from site to site"

You'll find report forms at the back of this guide, or you can fill them in online at www.caravaclub.co.uk/europereport.

⊞ **DOCHAMPS** *C3* (S Rural) *50.23080, 5.63180* Panorama
Campsite Petite Suisse, Al Bounire 27, 6960 Dochamps
[(084) 444450; fax 444455; info@petitesuisse.be; www.
petitesuisse.be] Fr E25, take N89 (La Roche) at Samrée turn
R onto N841 headed twrds Dochamp. Turn R into rd sp Al
Bounire and foll sp to site. Lge, various sizes, mkd pitch, some
hdstg, pt sl, terr, pt shd; 20% statics; htd wc; chem disp; mv
service pnt; shwrs; baby facs; fam bthrm; el pnts (10A) inc;
gas; lndtte (inc dryer); shop; rest, snacks; bar; BBQ; playgrnd;
htd pool; paddling pool; waterslide; tennis; games area; games
rm; wifi; TV rm; adv bkg; 50% statics; dogs €5; bus 8km;
phone; quiet; poss cr; ccard acc; red low ssn/snr citizens; CKE/
CCI. "Gd facs; beautiful spot; busy, popular, excel site." ♦
€ 50.00                    2014*

⊞ **EEKLO** *A2* (7km E Rural) *51.18093, 3.64180* Camping
Malpertuus, Tragelstraat 12, 9971 Lembeke [(09) 3776178;
fax 3270036; campingmalpertuus@telenet.be; www.vkt.
be] Exit A10/E40 junc 11 onto N44 dir Aalter & Maldegem.
Foll sp Eekloo onto N49 & then foll sp Lembeke, site sp. Med,
pt shd; htd wc; chem disp; mv service pnt; shwrs €1; el pnts
(4A) €3; gas; lndry rm; shop 2km; rest 200m; snacks; bar;
85% statics; dogs; phone; bus 300m; Eng spkn; adv bkg;
quiet; 10% red CKE/CCI. "Gd site in lovely area; friendly
staff; entmnt/events at w/end; gd size pitches; gd site." ♦ ltd
€ 15.50                    2011*

⊞ **EREZEE** *C3* (1.5km S Rural) *50.27923, 5.54779* **Camping Le Val de l'Aisne, Rue du TTA, 6997 Blier-Erezée [(086) 470067; fax 470043; info@levaldelaisne.be; www. levaldelaisne.be]** Fr Marche-en-Famenne take N86 dir Hotton. In Hotton cross Rv Ourthe & immed turn R dir Soy & Erezée. In 9km at lge rndabt foll sp La Roche-en-Ardenne, site in 900m on L. Med, hdg/mkd pitch, pt shd; htd wc; chem disp; baby facs; shwrs; el pnts (16A) €3; gas; lndtte (inc dryer); shop 1.5km; rest, snacks; bar; BBQ; playgrnd; htd, covrd pool 10km; lake beach & sw adj; fishing; kayaking; tennis; games area; wifi; entmnt; cab/sat TV; 70% statics; dogs €3; train 8km; phone; poss cr; Eng spkn; adv bkg; quiet; ccard acc; red long stay/low ssn/CKE/CCI. "Beautiful situation; excel, well-maintained facs; friendly, helpful staff; vg, peaceful site." ♦ ltd € 18.00    2010*

## "We must tell The Club about that great site we found"

Get your site reports in by mid-August and we'll do our best to get your updates into the next edition.

**ESNEUX** *C3* (500m N Rural) *50.53941, 5.56986* **Camping Les Murets, Chemin d'Enonck 57, 4130 Hony-Esneux [tel/fax (041) 3801987; lesmurets@skynet.be; www.lesmurets.be]** On rd A26/E25 take exit 41 or 42 dir Esneux. In vill of Méry, directly after green bottle bank turn R over bdge & immed L at end of bdge sp Hony/Hôni. Foll sp Les Murets, under rlwy bdge Les Murets on L. Med, pt shd wc; chem disp; shwrs €0.90; el pnts (4A) inc; gas; shops, rest 500m; tradsmn; supmkt in Méry; BBQ; playgrnd; pool 5km; TV rm; dogs; phone; poss cr; Eng spkn; adv bkg rec high ssn; quiet but some rlwy noise. "Friendly; facs basic but clean; conv touring base." 1 Apr-31 Oct. € 16.80    2009*

⊞ **EUPEN** *B4* (2km SW Rural) *50.61457, 6.01686* **Camping Hertogenwald, Oestraat 78, 4700 Eupen [(087) 743222; fax 743409; info@camping-hertogenwald.be; www. camping-hertogenwald.be]** Fr German border customs on E40 a'bahn for Liège, take 2nd exit for Eupen. In Eupen L at 3rd traff lts & 1st R in 100m. Drive thro Eupen cent, foll sp to Spa. Camping sp immed at bottom of hill, sharp hairpin R turn onto N629, site on L in 2km. Med, unshd; htd wc; chem disp; shwrs inc; el pnts (6A) inc (long lead req & poss no earth); lndtte; shop 2km; rest, snacks; bar; playgrnd; htd, covrd pool 3km; games area; 90% statics; dogs €2; phone; poss cr; Eng spkn; quiet. "Sm tourer area; clean site adj rv & forest; muddy after rain; gd walking & cycling beside rv; conv Aachen." ♦ € 18.00    2011*

⊞ **EUPEN** *B4* (2.5km SW Rural) *50.61250, 6.01128* **Camping Wesertal, Rue de l'Invasion 66-68, 4837 Membach-Baelen [(087) 555961 or 555076; fax 556555; info@wesertal. com; www.wesertal.com]** Fr E40 junc 38 onto N67, turn R at 1st rndabt & foll sp Baelen & Membach, site sp in 7km. Med, shd; htd wc; chem disp; sauna; baby facs; shwrs €1; el pnts (16A) inc (check pol & poss no earth); lndtte; shops 3km; tradsmn; playgrnd; pool 2km; 90% statics; dogs €2; poss cr; Eng spkn; adv bkg; quiet; CKE/CCI. "Site adj rv & forest; friendly welcome; poss run down, scruffy; ltd space for tourers; some pitches well away fr (poss grubby) san facs; NH only." € 19.60    2009*

**FLORENVILLE** *D3* (8km E Rural) *49.69208, 5.40866* **Camping du Faing, Rue du Faing 16, 6810 Jamoigne [(061) 320272; fax 464867]** Exit A4/E25 junc 30 onto N83 W or junc 29 onto N87/N83 thro Tintigny. Site at W end of Jamoigne - track to site adj lge concrete materials depot. Sp diff to spot. Med, pt shd; wc; chem disp; shwrs inc; el pnts inc; lndtte; supmkt in vill; bar; rest; playgrnd; covrd pool & sports adj nr; 80% statics; dogs; phone; quiet; ccard acc. "NH only; san facs need refurb - more facs avail in recep/rest/bar building at site ent." ♦ Mar-Dec. € 22.00    2009*

**FLORENVILLE** *D3* (13km E Rural) *49.6849, 5.5206* **Camping Chênefleur, Norulle 16, 6730 Tintigny [(063) 444078; fax 445271; info@chenefleur.be; www.chenefleur.be]** Fr Liège foll E25 dir Luxembourg. Exit junc 29 sp Habay-la-Neuve to Etalle, then N83 to Florenville. Site sp off N83 at E end of Tintigny vill. Med, pt shd; htd wc; chem disp; shwrs inc; baby facs; el pnts (6-8A) inc; gas; lndtte (inc dryer); shop; tradsmn; rest, snacks; bar; playgrnd; htd pool; paddling pool; games area; cycle hire; wifi; entmnt; dogs €4; Eng spkn; adv bkg; quiet; ccard acc. "Orval Abbey, Maginot Line worth visit; friendly staff; gd, clean site & modern san facs; Well kept site." ♦ 1 Apr-30 Sep. € 32.25 (CChq acc)    2012*

**GEDINNE** *C3* (1km SW Rural) *49.97503, 4.92719* **Camping La Croix Scaille, Rue du Petit Rot 10, 5575 Gedinne [(061) 588517; fax 588736; camping.croix-scaille@skynet. be; www.campingcroixscaille.be]** Fr N95 turn W to Gedinne on N935. Site sp S off vill on R after 1km. Lge, mkd pitch, some hdstg, terr, pt shd; htd wc; chem disp; shwrs inc; el pnts (16A) €1.60; gas; lndtte (inc dryer); snacks; bar; playgrnd; TV; pool; tennis, fishing adj; cycle hire; 75% statics; dogs; poss cr; quiet; ccard acc; CKE/CCI. 1 Apr-15 Nov. € 13.40    2013*

## "I need an on-site restaurant"

We do our best to make sure site information is correct, but it is always best to check any must-have facilities are still available or will be open during your visit.

⊞ **GEEL** *A3* (9km N Rural) *51.22951, 4.97836* **Camping Houtum, Houtum 51, 2460 Kasterlee [(014) 859216; fax 853803; info@campinghoutum.be; www. campinghoutum.be]** On N19 Geel to Turnhout rd 1km bef Kasterlee site sp on R at windmill opp British WW2 cemetery. Foll sps to site 500m on rd parallel to N19, cross next rd, site in 300m. Lge, mkd pitch, pt shd; htd wc; chem disp; shwrs €1; el pnts (4-6A) €2; lndtte; shops adj; snacks; lge playgrnd; pool 2km; adj to rv with boating, canoeing, fishing; tennis & mini-golf 300m; cycle hire; nature trails adj; 60% statics; phone; poss v cr; adv bkg; v quiet; ccard acc; red long stay/ CKE/CCI. "Orderly, attractive site; lots for children all ages." € 20.70    2013*

**BELGIUM**

**GENT** *A2* (10km SW Rural) *51.00508, 3.57228* **Camping Groeneveld, Groenevelddreef 14, Bachte-Maria-Leerne, 9800 Deinze [(09) 3801014; fax 3801760; info@campinggroeneveld.be; www.campinggroeneveld.be]** E or W E40/E10 on Brussels to Ostend m'way exit junc 13 at sp Gent W/Drongen. Take N466 sp Dienze. Approx 1km beyond junc with N437, turn L just after 2nd 70 km/h sp down narr side rd - house on corner has advert hoarding. Site on L opp flour mill. Sm sp at turning. Med, some hdg pitch, pt shd; htd wc; chem disp; mv service pnt; shwrs inc; el pnts (10A) inc (poss no earth); shops 2km; rest (bkg ess), snacks, bar (w/end only low ssn); playgrnd; fishing; entmnt; TV; 40% statics; dogs €2; phone; poss cr; Eng spkn; adv bkg; quiet; red low ssn/long stay; CKE/CCI. "Gd welcome; gd access facs at lower end of site; office open 1800-1900 low ssn but staff in van adj san facs, or site yourself; barrier clsd until 0800; do not arr bef 1400; 1km fr Ooidonk 16th Castle; ok NH; gd site." 1 Apr-31 Oct. € 23.50                    2014*

**GENT** *A2* (3km W Urban) *51.04638, 3.68083* **Camping Blaarmeersen, Zuiderlaan 12, 9000 Gent [(09) 2668160; fax 2668166; camping.blaarmeersen@gent.be; www.blaarmeersen.be]** Exit A10/E40 Brussels-Ostend m'way at junc 13 sp Gent W & Drongen. At T-junc turn onto N466 twd Gent. In 4km cross canal then turn R to site, sp (3 rings) Sport & Recreatiecentrum Blaarmeersen. Fr Gent cent foll N34 twd Tielt for 1km past city boundary & turn L to site; adj lake & De Ossemeersen nature reserve. NB Due to rd layout, rec foll campsing sp on app to site rather than sat nav. Lge, hdg/mkd pitch, pt shd; htd wc; chem disp; mv service pnt; serviced pitch; shwrs inc; el pnts (10A) metered + conn fee €1.25 (poss rev pol); lndtte (inc dryer); shop; tradsmn; rest, snacks; bar; playgrnd; pool & full sports facs adj; lake sw adj; watersports; tennis; frequent bus to Gent; 5% statics; dogs €1.25; phone; bus to town nr; no dep bef 0815 hrs; Eng spkn; rd/rlwy noise; ccard acc; passport req. "Clean, well-organised, busy site; beautiful lake with path around; helpful staff; rest gd value; gd cycle track fr site; cycle into cent avoiding main rd; gd location for walks & activities; poss travellers low ssn; pitches muddy when wet; some m'van pitches sm & v shd; excel." 1 Mar-3 Nov. € 28.00                    2014*

⊞ **GERAARDSBERGEN** *B2* (4km NE Urban) *50.78990, 3.92351* **Camping Domein De Gavers, Onkerzelestraat 280, 9500 Geraadsbergen [(054) 416324; fax 410388; gavers@oost-vlanderen.be; www.degavers.be]** Fr N on A10 exit junc 17; S for 26km on N42 to Geraardsbergen. After level x-ing turn L at traff lts, L at rndabt & foll sp De Gavers for 4.3km. Fr S on N42 foll sp Geraardsbergen to rndabt, turn L then turn R at 2nd traff lts sp De Gavers. Lge, mkd pitch, pt shd; htd wc; chem disp; mv service pnt; baby facs; shwrs €0.50; el pnts (10A) inc (long lead req); lndtte; shop, rest, bar 400m; playgrnd; lake sw & sand beach adj; TV; 80% statics; dogs; phone; train 4km; poss cr; Eng spkn; adv bkg; quiet but some rd noise; ccard acc; red long stay/CKE/CCI. "Sep area for tourers; many leisure facs; excel touring region." € 25.00                    2010*

**GODARVILLE** *B2* (1km S Rural) *50.48794, 4.29318* **Camping Domaine Claire-Fontaine, 11 Ave Clémenceau, 7160 Godarville [(064) 443675; sites.voiesdeau@hainaut.be]** Exit A15/E42 junc 18 onto N59 to Godarville, site sp. Lge, unshd; wc; chem disp; shwrs inc; el pnts (6A) inc; lndry rm; tradsmn; shop 1km; snacks; bar; BBQ; playgrnd; lake sw; games area; 85% statics; dogs; phone; ccard acc; CKE/CCI. "Facs better than 1st impression but avoid san facs nr touring area & avoid area outside barrier; helpful warden; NH only." 1 Mar-31 Oct. € 22.00                    2010*

**GRIMBERGEN see Bruxelles** *B2*

⊞ **HAN SUR LESSE** *C3* (Urban) *50.12727, 5.18773* **Camping Aire Gîte d'Etape, Rue du Gîte d'Etape 10, 5580 Han-sur-Lesse [(084) 377441; gite.han@gitesdetape.be]** Exit A4/E411 junc 23 sp Ave-et-Auffe & Rochefort. Go over 2 rv bdges then immed L & 1st R. Site on L. Sm, hdstg, unshd; wc; mv service pnt; shops, rests etc nr; playgrnd nrby; games area; entmnt; m'van only. "Gd; attendant calls." € 5.00                    2009*

**HAN SUR LESSE** *C3* (Urban) *50.12621, 5.18610* **Camping Le Pirot, Rue Joseph Lamotte 3, 5580 Han-sur-Lesse [(084) 377280; fax 377576; han.tourisme@skynet.be; www.valdelesse.be]** Exit A4/E411 junc 23 sp Ave-et-Auffe & Rochefort. Go over 1st bdge then L immed bef 2nd bdge in Han cent; sh, steep incline. Sm, unshd; wc; chem disp; shwrs inc; el pnts (10A) inc (poss rev pol); lndtte; shop nr; rest, snacks, bar 200m; no statics; dogs; bus adj; poss cr; adv bkg; quiet; ccard acc; CKE/CCI. "Excel position on raised bank of rv; adj attractions & rests; interesting town; helpful staff; basic, dated san facs; conv NH." 1 Apr-15 Nov. € 20.00                    2011*

**HAN SUR LESSE** *C3* (500m S Rural) *50.12330, 5.18587* **Camping de la Lesse, Rue du Grand Hy, 5580 Han-sur-Lesse [(084) 377290; fax 377576; han.tourisme@skynet.be; www.valdelesse.be / www.campingshansurlesse.be]** Site 500m off Han-sur-Lesse main sq adj Office de Tourisme. If app fr Ave-et-Auffe, turn R at Office du Tourisme, take care over rlwy x-ing to site on R in 150m. Med, mkd pitch, pt shd; htd wc; chem disp; shwrs inc; el pnts (3-6A) inc; gas; lndtte; shops, rests 200m; playgrnd; canoeing adj; rv adj; 50% statics; dogs; phone; poss cr; adv bkg ess high ssn via TO; phone adj; noisy; ccard not acc; CKE/CCI. "Gd touring base; undergrnd grotto trip; take care on narr rds to site - v high kerbs; excel; san facs immac; pleasant low ssn." 1 Apr-15 Nov. € 28.80                    2013*

⊞ **HAN SUR LESSE** *C3* (4km SW Rural) *50.11178, 5.13308* **Camping Le Roptai, Rue Roptai 34, 5580 Ave-et-Auffe [(084) 388319; fax 387327; info@leroptai.be; www.leroptai.be]** Fr A4 exit 23 & take N94 dir Dinant. At bottom of hill turn R onto N86. Turn L in vill of Ave, foll sp, 200m to L. Med, mkd pitch, hdstg, pt sl, terr, pt shd; wc; chem disp; mv service pnt; shwrs €0.90; el pnts (6A) €1.80; gas; shop & 5km; tradsmn; snacks; bar; playgrnd; htd pool; TV; 80% statics; dogs €1.50; site clsd Jan; poss cr; Eng spkn; adv bkg; quiet; CKE/CCI. "Some pitches awkwardly sl; generally run down & poor facs; ltd facs low ssn; NH only." € 20.00                    2014*

**HASSELT** *B3* (9km N Rural) *50.99775, 5.42537* **Camping Holsteenbron, Hengelhoefseweg 9, 3520 Zonhoven [tel/ fax 011 817140; camping.holsteenbron@skynet.be; www. holsteenbron.be]** Leave A2 junc 29 twd Hasselt; turn L at 1st traff lts in 1km, foll sp thro houses & woods for 3km. Site is NE of Zonhoven. Med, hdg/mkd pitch, hdstg, pt shd; htd wc; chem disp; shwrs €1; el pnts (6A) inc; lndry rm; snacks; bar; playgrnd; games area; TV; 30% statics; dogs €1; phone; Eng spkn; quiet; CKE/CCI. "Pleasant, happy site in woodland; gd touring base; friendly owners." 1 Apr-13 Nov. € 22.00    2011*

**HOUYET see Dinant**  *C3*

**HUY** *B3* (2km E Urban) *50.5337, 5.2596* **Camping Mosan, Rue de la Paix 3, 4500 Tihange [(085) 231051; fax 251853; ces.huy@skynet.be]** Exit A15 junc 8 & proceed to Huy town cent, then along S bank of Rv Meuse dir Liège for 2km (past bdge on L) beyond town cent. Immed bef lge cooling towers on L, turn R (unmkd). In approx 200m sharp L turn into Rue de la Paix. Site recep at house beyond community cent. Sm, pt shd; wc; chem disp; mv service pnt; shwrs; el pnts inc; shop 1km; adv bkg; ccard not acc. "Fair site; easy access to town; recep opens 1630 - site yourself." 1 Apr-30 Sep. € 15.00    2009*

**JABBEKE see Brugge**  *A2*

**KASTERLEE see Geel**  *A3*

**KEMMEL/HEUVELLAND see Ypres/Ieper**  *B1*

**KNOKKE HEIST** *A2* (500m SE Urban) *51.33530, 3.28959* Camping Holiday, Natiënlaan 70-72, 8300 Knokke-Heist [(050) 601203; fax 613280; info@camping-holiday.be; www.camping-holiday.be] On N49/E34 opp Knokke-Heist town boundary sp. Site ent at side of Texaco g'ge. Med, unshd; wc; chem disp; shwrs inc; el pnts (6A) €1.90 (poss rev pol); sumpkt opp; rest, snacks 500m; playgrnd; beach 1.5km; cycle hire; phone; 60% statics; poss cr; quiet but rd noise. "V clean, tidy site but ltd san facs and waste disp pnts; may need to manhandle c'van onto pitch." ♦ ltd Easter-30 Sep. € 27.00    2012*

**KOKSIJDE** *A1* (500m NE Urban) *51.11105, 2.65215* **Camping De Blekker, Jachtwakersstraat 12, 8670 Koksijde ann Zee [(058) 511633; fax 511307; camping.deblekker@skynet. be; www.deblekker.be]** Fr E40 Brugge-Calais exit dir Veurne & foll sp Koksijde. At rndabt turn R for Koksijde Dorp then Koksijde ann Zee. Site sp on R. Lge, hdg/mkd pitch, pt shd; htd wc; chem disp; mv service pnt; serviced pitches; mv service pnt; baby facs; shwrs €1; el pnts (10A) inc; gas; lndtte (inc dryer); shop 300m; rest, snacks; bar; BBQ; playgrnd; htd, covrd pool 400m; sand beach 1.8km; games rm; TV; 80% statics; no dogs; phone; poss cr; adv bkg; quiet; Eng spkn; ccard acc; CKE/CCI. "Warm welcome; relaxing site; modern san facs but insufficient for size of site." ♦ 15 Mar-15 Nov. € 30.00    2010*

**KOKSIJDE** *A1* (500m SW Rural) *51.11114, 2.67082* **Camping Amazone, Westhinderstraat 2, 8670 Koksijde ann Zee [(058) 513363; fax 522512; info@camping-amazone.com; www.camping-amazone.com]** Fr A18/E40 exit junc 1A dir De Panne, foll sp Koksijde on N8. Pass airfield & turn R to Koksijde, site on L in 500m. Med, mkd pitch, unshd; wc; own san; chem disp; shwrs €1; el pnts (6A) €2; sand beach 1.2km; 80% statics; Eng spkn; quiet. "Ltd touring pitches, but conv NH Dunkerque/Ostend ferries." 1 Apr-30 Sep. € 18.00    2009*

⊞ **KOKSIJDE** *A1* (2km W Rural) *51.10536, 2.62987* **Camping Noordduinen, Noordduinen 12, 8670 Koksijde aan Zee [(058) 512546; fax 512618; roos@campingbenelux.be; www.campingnoordduinen.be]** Exit A18/E40 junc 1a onto N8. Foll sp Koksijde to rndabt, strt over into Leopold III Laan, site on L. Sm, hdg pitch, hdstg, pt shd; wc; shwrs €1; el pnts €2.50; lndtte; supmkt 300m; sand beach 3km; wifi; 80% statics; dogs €2.50; bus 500m; Eng spkn; adv bkg; quiet; CKE/CCI. "Gd site; adj cycle rte to Veurne - attractive, historic town; new san facs closer to pitches (2012)." € 25.00    2012*

**LEMBEKE see Eeklo**  *A2*

**LIEGE** *B3* (10km S Rural) *50.56770, 5.58826* **Camping du Syndicat d'Initiative de Tilff, Rue du Chera 5, 4040 Tilff-sur-Ourthe [(04) 3881883]** Exit m'way at Tilff junc 41 or 42 & foll sp to site. Sm, v sl, pt shd; wc; chem disp; shwrs; el pnts (4A) €2.48; lndtte; shops 500m; playgrnd; pool 2m; poss cr; 95% statics; dogs; quiet; CKE/CCI. "Basic site; ltd space for tourers; NH only." ♦ 1 Apr-31 Oct.    2009*

**LILLE-GIERLE see Turnhout**  *A3*

⊞ **LONDERZEEL** *B2* (2km NE Rural) *51.02194, 4.31926* Camping Diepvennen, Molenhoek 35, 1840 Londerzeel [(052) 309492; fax 305716; info@camping-diepvennen.be; www.camping-diepvennen.be] On A12 exit at Londerzeel, foll sp Industrie Zone & Diepvennen. Foll Diepvennen sp to site. Site on W side of A12. Lge, pt shd; wc; shwrs €1; el pnts €3; lndtte; shop; rest, snacks; playgrnd; pool; fishing pond; tennis; games area; 95% statics; rd noise; red long stay. "Long walk to san facs block; easy access by train to Antwerp & Brussels." ♦ € 18.00    2013*

⊞ **MALMEDY** *C4* (3km E Rural) *50.42008, 6.07059* **Familial Camping, Rue des Bruyères 19, 4960 Arimont-Malmédy [tel/fax (080) 330862; info@campingfamilial.be; www. campingfamilial.be]** Take St Vith rd (N62) out of Malmédy; in 2km over level x-ing turn L in 300m at sp Arimont & 2nd camping sp. Site on L, 1.5km up winding (but easy) hill. Med, pt sl, terr, pt shd; htd wc (some cont); chem disp; mv service pnt; shwrs €1; el pnts inc (4-6A) €2; gas; lndtte (inc dryer); sm shop; tradsmn; rest, snacks; bar; sm pool; playgrnd; games rm; wifi; entmnt; TV; bus 1km; 50% statics; dogs free; phone; site clsd last week Oct to 2nd week Dec; Eng spkn; adv bkg; ccard not acc; CKE/CCI. "Pleasant but untidy site with excel views over hills; gd facs; conv Ardennes, Spa motor racing circuit; lorry noise fr rd to quarry behind site." € 17.50    2011*

**MALONNE see Namur**  *C3*

**BELGIUM**

⊞ **MARCHE EN FAMENNE** *C3* (4km NW Rural) *50.24911, 5.27978* **Camping Le Relais, 16 Rue de Serinchamps, 5377 Hogne [(0475) 423049; info@campinglerelais; www. campinglerelais.com]** Sp fr N4 bet Marche-en-Famenne & Namur. Fr Namur ent immed R under new bdge. Med, pt sl, unshd; htd wc; chem disp; baby facs; shwrs inc; el pnts (10A) €2.50; lndtte; rest, snacks; playgrnd; lake adj; TV; 30% statics; dogs free; adv bkg; some rd noise; CKE/CCI. "V pleasant; gd facs." € 20.00                                     2009*

**MEMBACH-BAELEN see Eupen** *B4*

**MOL** *A3* (5km E Rural) *51.20945, 5.17181* **Camping Zilverstrand, Kiezelweg 17, 2400 Mol [(014) 810098; fax 816685; info@zilverstrand.be; www.zilverstrand.be]** Exit A13 junc 23 dir Geel onto N19 then N71 to Mol, site sp on N712 twd Lommel. Lge, pt shd; htd wc; chem disp; mv service pnt; baby facs; fam bthrm; el pnts (6A) inc; lndtte (inc dryer); shop; tradsmn; rest, snacks; bar; BBQ; playgrnd; htd covrd pool; paddling pool; waterslides; lake sw & beach; tennis 1km; cycle hire; golf 1km; wifi; 60% statics; dogs; adv bkg; quiet. ♦ 22 Apr-31 Oct. € 30.50                                     2011*

⊞ **MUNKZWALM** *B2* (500m E Rural) *50.87573, 3.74058* **Camping Canteclaer, Rekegemstraat 12, 9630 Munkzwalm [(055) 499688; fax 316150; camping. canteclaer@telenet.be; www.campingcanteclaer.be]** Fr A10 exit junc 17 onto N42 S. At junc with N46 turn R & in 7km turn L to Munkzwalm on N415 Noordlaan which becomes Zuidlaan. Turn L again into Zwalmlaan, site by rlwy. Lge, pt shd; wc; chem disp; shwrs €0.75; el pnts (6A) inc; lndtte; shops 1km; rest, snacks; bar; playgrnd; statics; phone; adv bkg; quiet, some rlwy noise; 80% statics. "Sm touring area." € 13.00                                     2009*

**NAMUR** *C3* (11km S Rural) *50.37233, 4.86966* **Camping La Douaire, 43 Rue du Herdal, 5170 Profondeville [(081) 412149]** Fr Namur take N92 S twds Dinant. At approx 8km 100m after rndabt take slip rd sp Profondeville. In 100m turn R into Chemin du Herdal, site on L, narr ent. Med, mkd pitch, sl, pt shd; wc; chem disp; shwrs €1.25; el pnts €3; gas; shop, rest 300m; playgrnd; pool 4km; 95% statics; dogs; quiet. "Conv Namur & Dinant; not suitable twin-axles; only 2 (poor) touring pitches, no hdstg." 1 Apr-15 Oct. € 8.80        2009*

**NAMUR** *C3* (5km SW Rural) *50.44164, 4.80182* **Camping Les Trieux, 99 Rue Les Tris, 5020 Malonne [tel/fax (081) 445583 / 473 810742 (mob); camping.les.trieux@ skynet.be; www.campinglestrieux.be]** Fr Namur take N90 sp Charleroi, after 8km take L fork sp Malonne (camp sp at junc). After 400m turn L at camp sp & site at top of 1 in 7 (13%) hill, approx 200m. To miss steep hill, fr Namur take Dinant (N92) S. In 2km R at camping sp. Take care at hairpin in 200m. Foll site sps. Located up steep, but surfaced rd. Med, mkd pitch, terr, pt shd; htd wc; chem disp; mv service pnt; shwrs €1; el pnts (10A) €2; lndtte; shop; tradsmn; snacks; playgrnd; TV; 50% statics; phone; Eng spkn; quiet; ccard not acc; red low ssn; CKE/CCI. "Friendly owners; pretty site, but steep - take care ent pitch; pitches diff for lge o'fits; basic san facs but clean; NH only." 1 Apr-31 Oct. € 18.00      2013*

**NEUFCHATEAU** *D3* (3km S Rural) *49.83502, 5.41640* **Camping Val d'Emeraude, Route de Malome 1-3, 6840 Neufchâteau [tel/fax (061) 511952; valdemeraude@ skynet.be; www.valdemeraude.be]** Take Florenville rd out of town. In 2km site at lge cream house on L. Sm; pt sl; unshd vlg;mkd pitch; wc; chem disp; shwrs; el pnts €3 (poss rev pol); lndry rm; shop 3km; rest, snacks, bar 1km; BBQ; playgrnd; fishing 500m; pool (child); sw; tv rm; wifi; dogs €1.25; 70% statics; dogs €1.50; phone; bus adj; Eng spkn; adv bkg; quiet but some rd noise; CKE/CCI. "Beautiful setting; gd walks; helpful Eng spkn owner; well-kept, flat pitches; basic, ltd san facs; attractive location; gd NH." ♦ 1 Apr-31 Oct. € 28.00                                     2013*

⊞ **NEUFCHATEAU** *D3* (2.5km SW Rural) *49.83305, 5.41721* **Camping Spineuse, Rue de Florenville, 6840 Neufchâteau [061 27 73  20; fax 27 71 04; info@camping-spineuse. be; www.camping-spineuse.be]** Fr A4/E411 exit junc 26 or junc 27 fr E25 to Neufchâteau. Take N85 dir Florenville, site is 3rd on L. Ent easy to miss. Med, pt shd; htd wc; chem disp; mv service pnt; shwrs free; el pnts (16A) €3; lndtte; shops 1km; tradsmn; rest, snacks; bar; playgrnd; sm pool; wifi; TV; 30% statics; dogs €1.25; phone; Eng spkn; quiet; ccard acc; red low ssn/snr citizens. "Pleasant, pretty site; poss diff lge o'fits if site full; vg san facs; some flooding after heavy rain." € 16.00                                     2013*

**NIEUWPOORT** *A1* (2km E Rural) *51.12960, 2.77220* **Kompascamping Nieuwpoort, Brugsesteenweg 49, 8620 Nieuwpoort [(058) 236037; fax 232682; nieuwpoort@ kompascamping.be; www.kompascamping.be]** Exit E40/ A18 at junc 3 sp Nieuwpoort; in 500m turn R at full traff lts; turn R at rndabt & immed turn L over 2 sm canal bdgs. Turn R to Brugsesteenweg, site on L approx 1km. Fr Ostende on N34 (coast rd) turn L at rndabt after canal bdge as above. V lge, hdg/mkd pitch, some hdstg, pt shd; htd wc; chem disp; baby facs; shwrs inc; el pnts (10A) €2.20; gas; lndtte (inc dryer); shop & 2km; rest, snacks; bar; playgrnd; 2 pools (1 htd, covrd); paddling pool; waterslide; tennis; sports/games area adj; cycle hire; golf 10km; wifi; entmnt; 90% statics; dogs €2.30; poss cr; adv bkg; quiet; red long stay/CKE/CCI. "Well-equipped site; helpful staff; boat-launching facs; sep area for sh stay tourers; v busy w/ends; excel cycle rtes; conv Dunkerque ferry." 1 Apr-14 Nov. € 34.50 (4 persons) (CChq acc)       2012*

See advertisement

⊞ **NIEUWPOORT** *A1* (2km E Rural) *51.13324, 2.76031* **Parking De Zwerver, Brugsesteenweg 16, 8620 Nieuwpoort [(0474) 669526; de_zwerver@telenet.be]** Nr Kompass Camping - see dirs under Kompass Camping. Site behind De Zwerver nursery. Sm, mkd pitch, all hdstg, unshd; wc; mv service pnt €2.50; shwrs & hot water; lndtte; BBQ; playgrnd; m'vans only. "Coin & note operated facs; modern & efficient; walking/cycling dist to town cent & port." ♦ € 0.50 (per hour)                                     2010*

⊞ **OLLOY SUR VIROIN** *C3* (1km SW Rural) *50.06876, 4.59643* **Camping Try des Baudets, Rue de la Champagne, 5670 Olloy-sur-Viroin [tel/fax (060) 390108; masson_p@ yahoo.Fr]** Fr N99 turn to Olloy-sur-Viroin sp Fumay. At end of main street (where Fumay rd turns L) cont strt then R, site sp up fairly steep, narr rd with passing places. Lge, mkd pitch, sl, unshd; wc; chem disp; shwrs inc; el pnts (6A) inc; lndtte; shop, bar 1km; playgrnd; fishing; 80% statics; dogs; bus; Eng spkn; adv bkg; quiet; CKE/CCI. "Gd walking, cycling; steam rlwy in valley; friendly proprietor; vg." ♦ € 18.00            2009*

⊞ **OOSTENDE** *A1* (2km NE Coastal) *51.24882, 2.96710* **Camping 17 Duinzicht, Rozenlaan 23, 8450 Bredene [(059) 323871; fax 330467; info@campingduinzicht.be; www.campingduinzicht.be]** Fr Ostend take dual c'way to Blankenberge on N34. Turn R sp Bredene, L into Driftweg which becomes Kappelstraat & turn R into Rozenlaan. Site sp. Lge, mkd pitch, hdstg, unshd; htd wc; chem disp; mv service pnt; serviced pitches; baby facs; shwrs €1; el pnts (10A) inc (poss no earth); gas; lndtte (inc dryer); shop 500m; rest; snacks, bar adj; BBQ; playgrnd; sand beach 500m; wifi; 60% statics; dogs; phone; security barrier; poss cr; Eng spkn; adv bkg; quiet; ccard acc; red low ssn; CKE/CCI. "Excel site; poss long walk to san facs; take care slippery tiles in shwrs; Bredene lovely, sm seaside town." € 24.00 (4 persons)            2012*

## "Satellite navigation makes touring much easier"

Remember most sat navs don't know if you're towing or in a larger vehicle – always use yours alongside maps and site directions.

⊞ **OOSTENDE** *A1* (4km E Urban/Coastal) *51.24970, 2.96834* **Camping Astrid, Koning Astridlaan 1, 8450 Bredene [(059) 321247; fax 331470; info@camping-astrid.be; www.camping-astrid.be]** Foll tourist sp. Med, unshd; wc; chem disp; serviced pitch; shwrs; el pnts (10A) inc; shops 100m; sand beach adj; cab/sat TV; 80% statics; phone; poss cr; Eng spkn; ccard not acc. "Most sites nrby are statics only; friendly, helpful owners; rec NH; barrier for new arr." ♦ € 29.00       2013*

⊞ **OOSTENDE** *A1* (4km E Rural) *51.24366, 2.98002* **Camping T Minnepark, Zandstraat 105, 8450 Bredene-Dorp [(059) 322458; fax 330495; info@minnepark.be; www.minnepark.be]** Fr Ostend take N34 sp Blankenberge. After tunnel under rlwy turn R sp Brugge. Cross canal & in 300m turn L at filter sp Bredene-Dorp. In 2km immed after blue/white water tower on R, turn L at x-rds. At mini-rndabt turn R passing Aldi supmkt. Site on L after Zanpolder site. Fr A18 exit junc 6 & take N37 sp De Haan. In 5km turn L at rndabt onto N9 sp Oostende. In 5km turn R sp Bredene-Dorp, then R in 2.5km at rndabt into Zandstraat, then as above. V lge, unshd; wc; chem disp; shwrs €1; el pnts (16A) €1 (poss rev pol); lndtte (inc dryer); shops 1km; tradsmn; playgrnd; sand beach 2km; wifi; cab TV; 75% statics; dogs €3; Eng spkn; adv bkg; quiet. "Lge pitches; friendly, helpful staff; warm welcome; excel, well-run site; vg san facs; conv ferries, Bruges & coast." € 30.00            2013*

⊞ **OPGLABBEEK** *B3* (1km S Rural) *51.02825, 5.59745* **Camping Wilhelm Tell, Hoeverweg 87, 3660 Opglabbeek [(089) 854444; fax 810010; receptie@wilhelmtell.com; www.wilhelmtell.com]** Leave A2/E314 at junc 32, take rd N75 then N730 N sp As. In As take Opglabbeek turn, site sp in 1km. Med, mkd pitch, pt shd; wc; chem disp; mv service pnt; shwrs €0.90; el pnts (10A) inc; gas; lndtte (inc dryer); shop high ssn; rest, snacks; bar; BBQ; playgrnd; 2 htd pools (1 covrd); paddling pool; waterslide; tennis; cycle hire; golf 10km; wifi; entmnt; TV rm; 55% statics; dogs €4; phone; adv bkg; red long stay/low ssn; quiet; CKE/CCI. "Nice site; narr ent; superb pools; wave machine; site in nature reserve; helpful staff; San facs dist; bit expensive; not suitable for lge o'fits." ♦ € 32.00            2012*

**OTEPPE** *B3* (1km N Rural) *50.58239, 5.12455* **Camping L'Hirondelle Château, Rue de la Burdinale 76A, 4210 Oteppe [(085) 711131; fax 711021; info@lhirondelle.be; www.lhirondelle.be]** App fr E A15/E42 at exit 8; turn W on N643 for 1.5km; turn at sp on R for Oteppe. In vill 3km pass church to x-rds & R by police stn: site 150m on L. Fr W exit A15 at exit 10 onto N80, turn R onto N652 at Burdinne for Oteppe - easier rte. V lge, pt sl, shd; wc; shwrs €1; el pnts (6A) inc; gas; lndtte; shop; rest, snacks; bar; BBQ; playgrnd; 2 pools; waterslide; tennis; games area; internet; 75% statics; dogs €2.50; poss cr; quiet; ccard acc; red CKE/CCI. "Site in grnds of chateau; excel facs for children; touring pitches at top of site poss diff (steep); gd area for walking, fishing; conv NH; v quiet low ssn." 1 Apr-31 Oct. € 29.00            2013*

**OUDENAARDE** *B2* (12km SW Urban) *50.76250, 3.48719* **Panorama Camping, Boskouter 24, Ruien, 9690 Kluisbergen [(032) 55 38 86 68; info@campingpanorama. be; www.campingpanorama.be]** Fr N8 (Oudenaarde - Berchem) foll sp to Kluisbergen, Ruien. Cont thro Ruien, past church on L turn into Wuipelstraat, then R at rndabt , then L into Boskouter foll sp to site. Med, mkd pitch, pt sl, terr, pt shd; wc; chem disp; shwrs, el pnts; rest, snacks; bar; playgrnd; 90% statics; adv bkg; Eng spkn; CKE/CCI; "Gd site; v sm touring area. Helpful owner; excel cycling and walking fr site." 1 Feb - 30 Nov. € 25.00                    2012*

**OVERIJSE see Bruxelles** *B2*

**PROFONDEVILLE see Namur** *C3*

⊞ **ROCHE EN ARDENNE, LA** *C3* (2km E Rural) *50.17697, 5.59847* **Camping Floréal La Roche, 18 Route de Houffalize, 6980 La Roche-en-Ardenne [(084) 219467; camping.laroche@florealclub.be; www.florealclub. be]** Outside town on N860 dir Houffalize on rvside, sp. V lge, mkd pitch, unshd; htd wc; chem disp; mv service pnt; baby facs; shwrs inc; el pnts (10A) inc; gas; lndtte (inc dryer); shop; tradsmn; rest, snacks; bar; playgrnd; htd pool, paddling pool nr; fishing; tennis; cycle hire; games area; wifi; TV rm; 70% statics; dogs; bus; poss cr; Eng spkn; adv bkg; some rd noise; ccard acc; red long stay/CCI. "La Roche interesting town; vg, well-run, friendly site; lge pitches." ♦ € 20.65     2010*

**ROCHE EN ARDENNE, LA** *C3* (800m S Rural) *50.17465, 5.57774* **Camping Le Vieux Moulin, Rue Petite Strument 62, 6980 La Roche-en-Ardenne [(084) 411507; fax 411080; info@strument.com; www.strument.com]** Off N89 site sp fr La Roche town cent (dir Barrière-de-Champlon), site in 800m. Med, some hdg pitch, pt sl, shd; htd wc; chem disp; shwrs €2; el pnts (6A) €2.50 (poss no earth); gas 800m; lndtte; shops 800m; fishing; canoeing; 70% statics in sep area; dogs €2; poss cr; Eng spkn; adv bkg; quiet;CKE/CCI. "Beautiful site; gd pitches; poss unclean san facs & dishwashing (7/09); poss youth groups; poor security; gd walking (map avail)." Easter-Nov. € 14.00                    2012*

**ROCHEFORT** *C3* (500m E Rural) *50.15801, 5.22606* **Camping Communal Les Roches, 26 Rue du Hableau, 5580 Rochefort [(084) 211900; fax 312403; campingrochefort@ lesroches.be; www.lesroches.be]** Fr Rochefort cent on N86 & turn L at rndabt, then 1st R. Site well sp. Lge, hdg/mkd pitch, hdstg, pt sl, unshd; htd wc; chem disp; mv service pnt; baby facs; serviced pitches; shwrs inc; el pnts (6A) metered; lndtte (inc dryer); shop, rest, bar nrby; BBQ; playgrnd; pool high ssn adj; tennis; games area; games rm; internet; entmnt; TV; 50% statics; dogs; phone; bus 250m; train 2km; Eng spkn; quiet; ccard acc. "Vg, well-managed, refurbished site; gd walking." ♦ 1 Apr-31 Oct. € 25.00                    2012*

**ST VITH** *C4* (9km S) *50.24229, 6.09402* **Camping Hohenbusch, Grufflingen 44, B-4791 Burg Reuland [80 22 75 23; info@hohenbusch.be; www. campinghohenbusch.be]** Fr St Vith take the E421 twds Grüfflingen; site on R of the rd sp. Med, hdg pitch, pt shd; htd wc; chem disp; MV service pnt; baby facs; shwrs (metered); el pnts (6A) €2.50; lndtte; rest; playgrnd; pool; games rm; entmnt; wifi; dogs €2.50. "Eng spkn; v helpful owner; v lge pitches; fully serviced immac modern san facs." 01 Apr-06 Nov. € 22.00                    2011*

**SART LEZ SPA see Spa** *C4*

**SINT JOB IN'T GOOR see Antwerpen** *A3*

**SINT KRUIS see Brugge** *A2*

**SINT MARGRIETE** *A2* (2km NW Rural) *51.2860, 3.5164* **Camping De Soetelaer, Sint Margrietepolder 2, 9981 Sint Margriete [(09) 3798151; fax 3799795; camping. desoetelaer@telenet.be; www.desoetelaer.be]** Fr E on N49/E34 to Maldegem or fr W on N9 or N49 turn N onto N251 to Aardenburg (N'lands), then turn R twd St Kruis (N'lands) - site situated 1.5km strt on fr St Margriete (back in Belgium). Med, mkd pitch, pt shd; wc; chem disp; all serviced pitches; shwrs inc; el pnts (6A) inc; lndry rm; shops 3km; no dogs; Eng spkn; adv bkg; quiet; ccard not acc; CKE/CCI. "Vg, clean site; excel, modern san facs; peace & quiet, privacy & space; highly rec for relaxation; O'fits pitched v close end to end." Easter-15 Oct. € 30.00                    2014*

⊞ **SOUMAGNE** *B3* (1km S Rural) *50.61099, 5.73840* **Domaine Provincial de Wégimont, Chaussée de Wégimont 76, 4630 Soumagne [(04) 2372400; fax 2372401; wegimont@prov-liege.be; www.prov-liege.be/ wegimont]** Exit A3 at junc 37 onto N3 W twd Fléron & Liège. In 500m at traff lts turn L sp Soumagne. In Soumagne at traff lts form R dir Wégimont, site on top of hill on R directly after bus stop. Med, hdg pitch, pt sl, pt shd; htd wc; chem disp; baby facs; shwrs inc; el pnts (16A) inc poss rev pol; shop; rest; bar; communal BBQ; playgrnd; pool adj high ssn; tennis; games area; some entmnt; 70% statics; dogs; bus; site clsd Jan; poss cr; some rd noise; CKE/CCI. "Welcoming site in chateau grnds (public access); clean facs; conv sh stay/NH nr m'way." € 13.50                    2011*

**SPA** *C4* (4km NE Rural) *50.50806, 5.91928* **Camping Spa d'Or (TCB), Stockay 17, 4845(B) Sart-lez-Spa [087 47 44 00; fax 47 52 77; info@campingspador.be; www.campingspador.be]** App fr N or S on m'way A27/E42, leave at junc 9, foll sp to Sart & Spa d'Or. Lge, pt sl, pt shd; htd wc; chem disp; baby facs; shwrs & bath inc; el pnts (10A) €4. (check earth); gas; lndtte; shop high ssn; rest, snacks; BBQ; playgrnd; htd pool; cycle hire; entmnt; 60% statics; dogs €5; poss cr; quiet; ccard acc; red CKE/CCI. "Conv F1 Grand Prix circuit Francorchamps & historic town Stavelot; vg; gd NH." 1 Apr-14 Nov. € 27.50 (CChq acc)                    2013*

**SPA** *C4* (1.5km SE Rural) *50.48559, 5.88385* **Camping Parc des Sources**, Rue de la Sauvenière 141, 4900 Spa [(087) 772311; fax 475965; info@parcdessources.be; www.parcdessources.be] Bet Spa & Francorchamps on N62, sp on R. Med, mkd pitch, pt sl, pt shd; htd wc; chem disp; mv service pnt; baby facs; shwrs €1; el pnts (10A) €2.75; gas; lndtte; shops 1.5km; snacks; bar; playgrnd; pool; dogs €2; 60% statics; phone; poss cr; quiet. "Excel facs, modern lndtte, beautiful location, nr forest; friendly & helpful staff." ♦ ltd 1 Apr-31 Oct. € 30.00                    2013*

---

## "There aren't many sites open at this time of year"

If you're travelling outside peak season remember to call ahead to check site opening dates – even if the entry says 'open all year'.

---

⊞ **STAVELOT** *C4* (3km N Rural) *50.41087, 5.95351* **Camping L'Eau Rouge**, Cheneux 25, 4970 Stavelot [(080) 863075; fb220447@skynet.be; www.eaurouge.eu] Exit A27/E42 junc 11 onto N68 twd Stavelot. Turn R at T-junc, then 1st R into sm rd over narr bdge. Med, mkd pitch, pt sl, pt shd; htd wc; chem disp; mv service pnt; baby facs; shwrs €0.50; el pnts (6-10A) €3 rev polarity; lndtte (inc dryer); shop 2km; tradsmn; snacks; bar; BBQ; playgrnd; games area; archery; wifi; TV; 50% statics; dogs €1; poss cr; Eng spkn; quiet. "Vg rvside site; friendly, helpful owners; twin-axles not acc; conv Francorchamps circuit." ♦ € 25.00                    2013*

⊞ **STEKENE** *A2* (2.5km SW Rural) *51.18366, 4.00730* **Camping Vlasaard**, Heirweg 143, 9190 Stekene [(03) 7798164; fax 7899170; info@camping-vlasaard.be; www.camping-vlasaard.be] Fr N49 Antwerp-Knokke rd, exit sp Stekene. In Stekene, take dir Moerbeke, site on L in 4km. V lge, mkd pitch, unshd; htd wc; chem disp; serviced pitches; shwrs €1.25; el pnts (16A); lndtte; supmkt adj; rest, snacks; bar; playgrnd; pool; games area; 75% statics; poss cr; Eng spkn; poss noisy; ccard acc. ♦ € 16.00                    2009*

⊞ **TELLIN** *C3* (5km NE Rural) *50.09665, 5.28579* **Camping Parc La Clusure**, 30 Chemin de la Clusure, 6927 Bure-Tellin [(084) 360050; fax 366777; info@parclaclusure.be; www.parclaclusure.be] Fr N on A4 use exit 23A onto N899, fr S exit junc 24. Foll sp for Tellin & then take N846 thro Bure dir Grupont vill. At rndabt at junc N803 & N846 take 2nd exit to site, sp Tellin. V lge, mkd pitch, pt shd; htd wc; chem disp; mv service pnt; baby facs; shwrs inc; el pnts (16A) inc (check rev pol); lndtte (inc dryer); shop; tradsmn; rest, snacks; bar; playgrnd; htd pool; paddling pool; rv fishing; tennis; games area; games rm; wifi; entmnt; TV rm; 35% statics; dogs €5; phone; poss cr; Eng spkn; adv bkg; poss noise; ccard acc; red low ssn/CKE/CCI. "V pleasant, popular rvside site; conv m'way; conv for limestone caves at Han-sur-Lesse & gd touring base Ardennes; friendly owners; clean facs; a lovely site; poss noise fr rlwy; wild beavers in adj rv; excel site." ♦ € 55.00 (CChq acc)                    2013*

See advert on bookmark

⊞ **TENNEVILLE** *C3* (1km N Rural) *50.07644, 5.55529* **Camping Pont de Berguème**, Berguème 9, 6970 Tenneville [(084) 455443; fax 456231; info@pontbergueme.be; www.pontbergueme.be] Fr N4 Brussels-Luxembourg fr NW; twd end of Tenneville past g'ge turn R sp Berguème. Almost immed turn L & foll sp to Berguème. Fr SE turn R off N4 50m after x-ing Rv Ourthe & foll sp to Berguème & site in 1.5km. Well sp fr N4. Med, unshd; htd wc; chem disp; baby facs; shwrs; el pnts (4A) inc (poss rev pol &/or earth prob); gas; lndtte; shop; snacks; playgrnd; pool; fishing; canoeing (winter only); wifi; 40% statics; dogs €1.75; phone; Eng spkn; adv bkg; quiet; red CKE/CCI. "Excel site; clean, modern facs." € 16.00        2010*

**TENNEVILLE** *C3* (8km S Rural) *50.02637, 5.51292* **Camping Tonny**, Tonny 35, 6680 Amberloup/Ste Ode [(061) 688285; camping.tonny@skynet.be; www.campingtonny.be] Fr N4 take N826 S; in 4km turn R to Tonny. Site on L. Med, mkd pitch, shd; htd wc; chem disp; mv service pnt; baby facs; shwrs €0.50; el pnts (6-4A) €2.50-3.50; gas; lndtte (inc dryer); ice; tradsmn (high ssn); rest, snacks; bar; BBQ; playgrnd; fishing; games area; games rm; entmnt; TV; 10% statics; dogs €2; bus adj; poss cr; Eng spkn; adv bkg; quiet; CKE/CCI. "Friendly, helpful owners; excel walking & cycling." 15 Feb-15 Nov. € 17.50                    2010*

**TILFF SUR OURTHE see Liège** *B3*

⊞ **TOURINNES LA GOSSE** *B3* (500m SW Rural) *50.77952, 4.73657* **Camping au Val Tourinnes**, Rue du Grand Brou 16A, 1320 Tourinnes-la-Grosse [(010) 866642; info@campingauvaltourinnes.com; www.campingauvaltourinnes.com] Fr N on E40/A3 m'way exit junc 23 onto N25 S dir Hamme-Mille. In Hamme-Mille turn L at traff lts, site on R in 2km. Or fr S on E411/A4 exit junc 8 onto N25 to Hamme-Mille & turn R at traff lts, then as above. Sm, hdg/mkd pitch, shd; htd wc; chem disp; mv service pnt; baby facs; shwrs €0.50; el pnts (10A) €5; lndtte (inc dryer); tradsmn; rest; bar; playgrnd; lake fishing; wifi; some statics; dogs €2.50; Eng spkn; quiet. "Pleasant touring pitches on lakeside (take care goose droppings!); friendly owners; vg, modern san facs; access tight for lge o'fits; airshow 1st w/end July." € 18.00                    2010*

⊞ **TOURNAI** *B2* (2km E Urban) *50.59988, 3.41377* **Camp Municipal de l'Orient**, Jean-Baptiste Moens 8, 7500 Tournai [(069) 222635; fax 890229; campingorient@tournai.be] Exit E42 junc 32 R onto N7 twd Tournai. L at 1st traff lts, foll sp Aquapark, L at rndabt, site immed on L (no sp). Med, hdg pitch, some hdstg, pt shd; htd wc; chem disp; some serviced pitches; shwrs inc; el pnts (10A) inc (poss rev pol/no earth) or metered; gas; lndtte (inc dryer); shops 1km; tradsmn; rest, bar & playgrnd at leisure complex; htd indoor pool adj; leisure cent/lake adj (50% disc to campers); poss cr; Eng spkn; adv bkg ess high ssn; some rd noise daytime & fr leisure cent adj; ccard not acc; CKE/CCI. "Well-kept site in interesting area & old town; facs stretched high ssn, but excel site; take care raised kerbs to pitches; max length of c'van 6.50m due narr site rds & high hdges; helpful wardens; E side of site quietest.; El pnts had no earth on a number of pitches." € 17.50  2014*

**BELGIUM**

⊞ **TURNHOUT** A3 (7km SW Rural) 51.2825, 4.8375
**Recreatie de Lilse Bergen, Strandweg 6, 2275 Lille-
Gierle [(014) 557901; fax 554454; info@lilsebergen.be;
www.lilsebergen.be]** Exit A21/E34 junc 22 N dir Beerse;
at rndabt foll sp Lilse Bergen. Site in 1.5km. Lge, mkd pitch,
shd; htd wc; chem disp; mv service pnt; baby facs; shwrs
€0.20 per min; el pnts (10A) inc; lndtte (inc dryer); shop;
tradsmn; rest, snacks; bar; BBQ; playgrnd; pool; lake sw;
watersports; tennis; cycle hire; games area; wifi; entmnt;
60% statics; dogs €5; phone; sep car park; poss cr; Eng spkn;
adv bkg; poss noisy; ccard acc; red low ssn/CKE/CCI. "Site
sep pt of lge leisure complex; pitches amongst pine trees;
modern san facs, poss streteched high ssn; excel for children/
teenagers." € 26.50 (4 persons) 2011*

⊞ **VEURNE** A1 (500m S Urban) 51.07056, 2.66535 **Aire
Naturelle, Kaaiplaats, 8630 Veurne [stadsbestuur@
veurne.be; www.veurne.be]** M'van parking area sp on inner
ring rd, nr canal quay. No facs & no fee; shops, rest, nrby; busy
in day, quiet at night. 2009*

⊞ **VIELSALM** C4 (Rural) 50.24013, 5.75396 **Camping aux
Massotais, 20 Petites Tailles, Baraque de Fraiture, 6690
Vielsalm [(080) 418560; info@auxmassotais.com; www.
auxmassotais.com]** Exit A26/E25 junc 50 onto N89 dir
Vielsalm. At 1st rndabt turn R onto N30 dir Houffalize. Site on
L in 1km behind hotel. Med, some hdstg, pt sl, pt shd; htd wc;
chem disp; shwrs inc; el pnts (6-16A) inc; lndtte (inc dryer);
tradsmn; rest, snacks; bar; playgrnd; htd pool; internet; TV;
5% statics; dogs; Eng spkn; quiet, but some rd noise; CKE/
CCI. "Special pitches for NH (don't need to unhitch); fair."
€ 15.00 2013*

⊞ **VIRTON** D3 (2km N Rural) 49.57915, 5.54892 **Camping
Colline de Rabais, 1 Rue Clos des Horlès, 6760 Virton
[(063) 571195; fax 583342; info@collinederabais.be;
www.collinederabais.be]** Take junc 29 fr A4/E411 onto
N87, 2km fr Virton turn into wood at site sp. At end of rd
bef lge building turn R, then 3rd turn R at phone box. Lge, pt
sl, terr, pt shd; htd wc; chem disp; mv service pnt; baby facs;
shwrs inc; el pnts (16A) €3; lndtte; shop; tradsmn; rest, snacks;
bar; playgrnd; pool; lake sw, fishing 1km; tennis 1km; cycle
hire; cab TV; 20% statics; dogs €2.50; phone; Eng spkn; adv
bkg; quiet; ccard acc; CKE/CCI. "Pleasant site; gd facs." ♦
€ 24.00 2009*

⊞ **WAASMUNSTER** A2 (1km N Rural) 51.12690, 4.08455
**Camping Gerstekot, Vinkenlaan 30, 9250 Waasmunster
[(0323) 7723424; fax 7727382; maria-lyssens@telenet.be]**
Exit A14/E17 at junc 13 Waasmunster onto N446 S; take 1st L
in 100m into Patrijzenlaan & L again into Vinkenlaan, foll camp
sp. Med, mkd pitch, pt shd; htd wc; chem disp; mv service pnt;
baby facs; shwrs; el pnts (16A) inc; lndtte (inc dryer); shop;
snacks; bar; BBQ; playgrnd; games area; games rm; wifi; TV;
95% statics; phone; poss cr; adv bkg; quiet; ccard acc; CKE/
CCI. "Busy at w/end; water use metered; key req for shwrs;
gd." ♦ € 18.00 2011*

**WESTENDE** A1 (SW Coastal) 51.15787, 2.76060
**Kompascamping Westende, Bassevillestraat 141, 8434
Westende [(058) 223025; fax 223028; westende@
kompascamping.be; www.kompascamping.be]** Exit A18/
E40 junc 4 onto N369/325 dir Westende. Fr Westender
Dorp cent (Hovenierstraat church) turn R in approx 750m into
Beukenstraat, site in 200m, sp. Lge, hdg/mkd pitch, some
hdstg, pt shd; htd wc; chem disp; baby facs; fam bthrm; shwrs
inc; el pnts (10A) €2.40; gas; lndtte (inc dryer); shop; rest,
snacks; bar; playgrnd; sand beach 500m; tennis; games area;
covrd play area; wifi; TV rm; 60% statics; dogs; adv bkg; quiet;
ccard acc. ♦ 1 Apr-14 Nov. € 33.50 (CChq acc) 2009*

**WESTENDE** A1 (3km SW Coastal) 51.15728, 2.76561
**Camping Westende, Westendelaan 341, 8434 Westende
[(058) 233254; fax 230261; info@campingwestende.be;
www.campingwestende.be]** Fr Middelkerke foll N318;
just after Westende vill church take dir Nieupoort, site on
L in 150m. Lge, mkd pitch, unshd; htd wc; chem disp; mv
service pnt; shwrs inc; el pnts (10A) inc; gas; lndtte; shops
adj; rest, snacks; playgrnd; htd pool; sand beach 1km; wifi;
90% statics; dogs €2; bus adj; tram 1km; phone; poss cr; Eng
spkn; quiet; ccard not acc; CKE/CCI. "Sm but tidy touring
area; friendly owners; beach nr; excel cycling; gd." ♦ ltd
1 Apr-14 Nov. € 34.00 2011*

See advertisement on page 135

## "That's changed – Should I let The Club know?"

If you find something on site that's different from
the site entry, fill in a report and let us know. See
www.caravanclub.co.uk/europereport.

⊞ **WESTENDE** A1 (W Coastal) 51.15423, 2.76046 **KACB
Camping Duinendorp, Bassevillestraat 81, 8434 Westende
[(058) 237343; fax 233505; campingkacbwestende@pi.be;
www.kacbcamping.be]** Site clearly sp off N318 in Westende
vill. Fr cent turn R dir Lombardsijde (Beukenstraat). Turn almost
opp TCB site. Lge, unshd; htd wc; chem disp; baby facs; shwrs
inc; el pnts (10A) inc; gas; lndtte (inc dryer); rest, snacks;
bar; playgrnd; sand beach 600m; games area; golf adj; TV;
60% statics; poss cr; adv bkg; quiet; ccard acc; red long stay/
CKE/CCI. ♦ € 28.00 2010*

⊞ **WESTOUTER** B1 (3km SW Urban) 50.78222, 2.74249
**Douve Camping, Bellestraat 58, 8954 Westouter
[(057) 444546; info@douve.be; www.douve.be]** Fr Ypres
take rd SW thro Dikkebus & cont to Mont Noir on Belgium/
France border. Site on L behind Douve Rest & household shop,
at end of main high street. Sm, hdg pitch, sl, pt shd; wc; own
san rec in winter; shwrs €1; el pnts inc (long lead poss req);
rest, snacks; playgrnd; dogs; bus; Eng spkn; quiet. "Conv for
Ypres (14km) & Mont Noir military cemetary; pitch on car park
in winter (no water avail at this time of year); access to pitches
v steep & narr in parts; rough path & 36 steps to facs & chem
disp point; forest walks; gd." € 12.00 2010*

**WEZEMBEEK see Bruxelles** B2

You can now fill in site reports online

**YPRES/IEPER** *B1* (1km SE Urban) *50.8467, 2.8994* **Camping Jeugdstadion, Bolwerkstraat 1, 8900 Leper, Ypres [(057) 217282; fax 216121; info@jeugdstadion.be; www.jeugdstadion.be]** Fr S ent town cent on N336, after rlwy x-ing turn R at rndabt onto ring rd & L at 2nd rndabt (lge, gushing tap in cent). Site in 300m on L, sp fr ring rd. If app town cent fr N on N8 fr Veurne take ring rd N37; at gushing tap rndabt turn L, site in 300m on L, well sp. Fr N38 in Ypres turn off at gushing tap rndabt sp Industrie/Jeugdstadion, take 2nd L, site at end. NB site open all year for m'vans. Med, hdg/mkd pitch, some hdstg, pt sl, pt shd; htd wc; chem disp; mv service pnt; shwrs inc; el pnts (10A) inc (poss rev pol); shop 500m; playgrnd; sports park & pool adj; wifi; statics; dogs €1; poss v cr; Eng spkn; adv bkg rec high ssn; quiet but some noise until evening fr indus unit & fr sports complex adj; ccard acc. "Automatic registration/check out avail when office clsd; peaceful, well-refurbished site conv WW1 battle fields & museums; 10 min walk to Menin Gate for daily Last Post Ceremony; helpful staff; gd, modern san facs; soft grass pitches - ask for one with 'rubber tracks' to avoid sinking; hdstg m'van pitches in sep area like an Aire; site poss v full local public hols; site not fully enclsd; excel site; rec." 1 Mar-12 Nov. € 20.00                                   2014*

**YPRES/IEPER** *B1* (9km SW Rural) *50.7853, 2.8199* **Camping Ypra, Pingelaarstraat 2, 8956 Kemmel-Heuvelland [(057) 444631; fax 444881; camping.ypra@skynet.be; www.camping-ypra.be]** On N38 Poperinge ring rd turn S at rndabt onto N304. Foll sp Kemmel. Site on R in 12km on N edge of Kemmel. Med, mkd pitch, pt sl, pt shd; htd wc; chem disp; shwrs inc; el pnts (6A) inc (poss rev pol); lndtte (inc dryer); sm shop & 1km; tradsmn; rest 1km; bar; playgrnd; 90% statics in sep area; dogs €1.90; Eng spkn; adv bkg; quiet; red CKE/CCI. "Clean, well-maintained site; gd, modern san facs, but ltd; helpful, friendly staff; access to some pitches poss diff; interesting rest in vill; conv for WW1 battlefields; Site clean, ltd san facs, staff friendly & helpful, pitches varied sizes; Site can be noisy due to club house & bar which is nr touring pitches." 1 Mar-30 Nov. € 25.80      2014*

**ZELE** *A2* (4.5km W Rural) *51.05273, 3.97996* **Camping Groenpark, Gentsesteenweg 337, 9240 Zele [tel/ fax (09) 3679071; Groenpark@scarlet.be; www. campinggroenpark.be]** Fr W (Ghent) exit A14 junc 11 onto N449 S & in 2km turn L onto N445. Site in 6km at ent sp to Zele. Sm, mkd pitch, pt shd; htd wc; chem disp; mv service pnt; baby facs; shwrs inc; el pnts (10A) inc; lndtte (inc dryer); shop, rest, bar 1km; snacks; playgrnd; lake sw & sand beach 2km; TV rm; some statics; tram; Eng spkn; adv bkg; quiet; CKE/CCI. "Nr Park & Ride to Ghent; wooded area for tourers; gd; Pleasant site; nice walk around lake." 1 Mar-4 Nov. € 29.00      2013*

**ZONHOVEN see Hasselt** *B3*

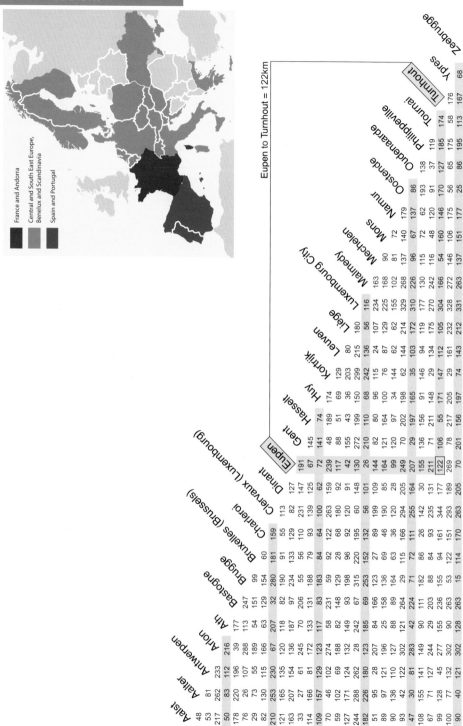

France and Andorra
Central and South East Europe, Benelux and Scandinavia
Spain and Portugal

Eupen to Turnhout = 122km

© Collins Bartholomew Ltd 2014

**Legend:**
- Motorways
- Major roads
- Main roads

- All year site(s)
- Seasonal site(s)
- No sites listed
- 200m +
- 0–200m

# Croatia
## Country Introduction

*Ancient city walls of Dubrovnik*

## Welcome to Croatia

Situated in South East Europe, the Adriatic Coast of Croatia enjoys a Mediterranean climate, with warm dry summers and mild winters. Further inland, the climate is more continental, with hot summers and cold, snowy winters.

Quiet coves and stone built fishing villages keep the country's traditional charm alive in coastal areas. You can also enjoy an active break in Croatia. Plitvice National Park is famous for its beauty, and you can enjoy canoeing, walking and cycling within the park.

## Country highlights

The Adriatic coast offers a wide variety of seafood, try 'Brodet', a traditional Croatian fish stew.

Wine is produced in Dalmatia and Istria and local beers are good and inexpensive. Slivovica, plum brandy, is the local spirit.

Music festivals are big in Croatia. Starting in the summer months, the events attract worldwide acts and visitors from across the globe.

## Major towns and cities

- Zagreb – the capital city is rich in Roman history.
- Split – a city centred on the Roman Palace of the Emperor Diocletian.
- Pula – a port city that has a long tradition of winemaking and fishing.
- Dubrovnik - an enchanting walled city on the Adriatic Coast which is popular with tourists.

## Attractions

- Maksimir Park – an 18th century park that houses the Zagreb city zoo.
- Ancient City Walls of Dubrovnik – walk along the ancient walls and see the stunning views.
- Plitvice National Park – a mountainous park with breathtaking scenery.
- Trsat Castle – an ancient medieval fort with lovely views.

## Find out more

www.croatia.hr

Tel: 0038 5 14 69 93 33 Croatian Tourist Office

# Country Information

*Population (approx):* 4.4 million

*Capital:* Zagreb (population approx 804,000)

*Area:* 56,540 sq km, divided into 20 counties

*Bordered by:* Bosnia and Herzegovina, Hungary, Serbia and Montenegro, Slovenia

*Terrain:* Flat plains along border with Hungary; low mountains and highlands near Adriatic coast and islands

*Climate:* Mediterranean climate along the coast with hot, dry summers and mild, wet winters; continental climate inland with hot summers and cold winters

*Coastline:* 5,835km (inc 4,058km islands)

*Highest Point:* Dinara 1,830m

*Language:* Croatian

*Local Time:* GMT or BST + 1, i.e. 1 hour ahead of the UK all year

*Currency:* Kuna (HRK) divided into 100 lipa; £1 = HRK 9.61, HRK 10 = £1.04 (September 2014)

*Emergency Numbers:* Police 92; Fire brigade 93; Ambulance 94. Or dial 112 and specify the service you need.

*Public Holidays in 2015:* Jan 1, 6; Apr 5, 6; May 1; Jun 4, 22 (Anti-Fascist Resistance Day), 25 (National Day); Aug 5 (Thanksgiving Day), 15; October 8 (Independence Day); Nov 1; Dec 25, 26.

In addition, some Christian Orthodox and Muslim festivals are celebrated locally. School summer holidays take place from the last week in June to end of August.

# Camping and Caravanning

There are more than 150 campsites in Croatia including several well-established naturist sites, mainly along the coast. Sites are licensed according to how many people they can accommodate, rather than by the number of vehicles or tents, and are classed according to a grading system of 1 to 4 stars. There are some very large sites catering for up to 10,000 people at any one time but there are also many small sites, mainly in Dalmatia, situated in gardens, orchards and farms.

Many sites open from April to October; few open all year. They are generally well-equipped.

A tourist tax is levied of between HRK 4 and HRK 7 per person per day according to region and time of year.

Casual/wild camping is illegal and is particularly monitored at beaches, harbours and rural car parks. Most campsites have overnight areas for late arrivals and there are a number of rest areas established along main roads for overnight stays or brief stopovers.

# Electricity and Gas

Current on campsites ranges from 10 to 16 amps. Plugs have 2 round pins. There may not be CEE connections and a long cable might be required.

Campingaz cylinders are not available, so take a good supply of gas with you.

# Entry Formalities

British and Irish passport holders may visit Croatia for up to three months without a visa.

Unless staying at official tourist accommodation (hotel or campsite) all visitors are obliged to register at the nearest police station or town tourist agency within 48 hours of arrival in the country. Campsites and other tourist accommodation should carry out this function for their guests but make sure you check this with them. If you fail to register you may receive a fine or you may even have to leave Croatia.

British citizens intending to stay for an extended period should register their presence with the Consular Section of the British Embassy in Zagreb, tel: (01) 6009100.

# Medical Services

For minor ailments, first of all consult staff in a pharmacy (ljekarna).

Emergency hospital and medical treatment is available at a reduced cost on production of a valid EHIC. You will be expected to pay a proportion of the cost (normally 20%). Only basic health care facilities are available in outlying areas and islands

For information on health risks please visit www.nathnac.org and select Croatia from the country information section of the website.

## Opening Hours

Banks – Mon-Fri 7am-7pm; Sat 7am-1pm.

Museums – Tue-Sun 10am-5pm; most close Mon and some close Sun afternoons.

Post Offices – Mon-Fri 7am-7pm (2pm in small villages), Sat 7am-1pm.

Shops – Mon-Fri 8am-8pm; Sat & Sun 8am-2pm.

## Safety and Security

The level of street crime is low, but you should be aware of pickpockets in major cities, coastal areas (pavement cafés are particularly targeted), and on trains, and take sensible precautions when carrying money, credit cards and passports.

Incidents have been reported of gangs robbing car occupants after either indicating that they are in trouble and require assistance, or pulling alongside a car and indicating that something is wrong with the vehicle. Be extremely cautious should something similar occur.

If you are planning to travel outside the normal tourist resorts you should be aware that there are areas affected by the war, which ended in 1995, where unexploded mines remain. These include Eastern Slavonia, Brodsko-Posavska County, Karlovac County, areas around Zadar County and in more remote areas of the Plitvice Lakes National Park. See the Croatian Mine Action Centre's website at www.hcr.hr/en/protuminUvod.asp for more specific information about mine-affected areas.

Croatia shares with the rest of Europe an underlying threat from terrorism. Attacks could be indiscriminate and against civilian targets, including places frequented by tourists.

*British Embassy*

UL IVANA LUČIĆA 4
HR-10000 ZAGREB
Tel: (01) 6009100
british.embassyzagreb@fco.gov.uk

There are also Honorary Consulates in Dubrovnik and Split.

*Irish Honorary Consulate*

MIRAMARSKA 23 (EUROCENTER)
10000 ZAGREB
Tel: (01) 6310025
irish.consulate.zg@inet.hr

TRUMBICEVA OBALA 3
21000 SPLIT
Tel: (021) 343715
9csain@cpad.hr

## Customs Regulations

*Customs Posts*

Main border crossings are open 24 hours a day.

*Foodstuffs*

Up to 10kg of meat and meat products may be imported into Croatia from EEA countries.

## Documents

*Driving Licence*

All types of full, valid British driving licence are recognised but if you have an old-style green licence then it is advisable to change it for a photocard licence in order to avoid any local difficulties.

*Passport*

You must be able to show some form of identification if required by the authorities and, therefore, should carry your passport or photocard driving licence at all times.

*Vehicle(s)*

Carry your vehicle registration certificate (V5C), insurance details and MOT certificate (if applicable).

*Green Card*

While an International Motor Insurance Certificate (Green Card) is not necessary, you should ensure that your vehicle insurance includes cover for Croatia.

If you are driving to or through Bosnia and Herzegovina (for example, along the 20 km strip of coastline at Neum on the Dalmatian coastal highway to Dubrovnik) you should ensure that you have obtained Green Card cover for Bosnia and Herzegovina. For Club members insured under The Caravan Club's Motor Insurance schemes full policy cover is available for this 20km strip, however you must ask at the time of commencement or renewing your insurance policy for one that specifically covers Bosnia. If you have difficulties obtaining such cover before departure Club members can contact the Club's Travel Service Information Officer for advice, email travelserviceinfo@caravanclub.co.uk. Alternatively, temporary third-party insurance can be purchased at the country's main border posts, or in Split and other large cities. It is not generally obtainable at the Neum border crossing itself.

As an alternative, you can take the ferry from Ploče to Trpanj on the Pelješac peninsula and avoid the stretch of road in Bosnia and Herzegovina altogether. There are frequent ferries during summer months, but be aware that motorhome drivers are sometimes requested to reverse onto them.

## Money

Visitors may exchange money in bureaux de change, banks, post offices, hotels and some travel agencies but you are likely to get the best rates in banks. Exchange slips should be kept in order to convert unspent kuna on leaving the country. Many prices are quoted in both kuna and euros, and euros are widely accepted.

Most shops and restaurants accept credit cards, but VISA is not as widely accepted as other cards. There are cash machines in all but the smallest resorts.

The police are warning visitors about a recent increase in the number of forged Croatian banknotes in circulation, especially 200 and 500 kuna notes. Take care when purchasing kuna and use only reliable outlets, such as banks and cash points.

## Motoring in Croatia
## Accidents

Any visible damage to a vehicle entering Croatia must be certified by the authorities at the border and a Certificate of Damage issued, which must be produced when leaving the country. In the event of a minor accident while in Croatia resulting in material damage only, the police must be called and they will assist, if necessary, with the exchange of information between drivers and will issue a Certificate of Damage to the foreign driver. You should not try to leave the country with a damaged vehicle without this Certificate as you may be accused of a 'hit and run' offence.

Confiscation of passport and a court appearance within 24 hours are standard procedures for motoring accidents where a person is injured.

The Croatian Insurance Bureau in Zagreb can assist with Customs and other formalities following road accidents, tel: (01) 4696600, email: huo@huo.hr or see www.huo.hr.

## Alcohol

The general legal limit of alcohol is 50 milligrams in 100 millilitres of blood, i.e. less than the level in the UK (80 milligrams). For drivers of vehicles over 3,500 kg and for drivers under 24 years of age the alcohol limit is zero. The general legal limit also applies to cyclists.

It is prohibited to drive after having taken any medicine whose side-effects may affect the ability to drive a motor vehicle.

## Breakdown Service

The Hrvatski Auto-Klub (HAK) operates a breakdown service throughout the country, telephone 987 (or 01987 from a mobile phone) for assistance. On motorways use the roadside emergency phones which are placed at 2km intervals. Towing and breakdown services are available 24 hours a day in and around most major cities and along the coast in summer (6am to midnight in Zagreb).

## Essential Equipment

*First aid kit*
All vehicles, including those registered abroad, must carry a first aid kit.

*Lights*
Dipped headlights are compulsory at all times, regardless of weather conditions, from the end of October to the end of March and in reduced visibility at other times of the year. It is compulsory to carry spare bulbs, however this rule does not apply if your vehicle is fitted with xenon, neon, LED or similar lights.

*Reflective Jacket/Waistcoat*
It is obligatory to carry a reflective jacket inside your car (not in the boot) and you must wear it if you need to leave your vehicle to attend to a breakdown, e.g. changing a tyre. It is also common sense for any passenger leaving the vehicle to also wear one.

*Warning Triangle(s)*
All motor vehicles must carry a warning triangle. If you are towing a caravan or trailer you must have two warning triangles.

*Child Restraint Systems*
Children under the age of 12 are not allowed to travel in the front seats of vehicles, with the exception of children under 2 years of age who can travel in the front if they are placed in a child restraint system adapted to their size. It must be rear-facing and the airbag must be de-activated.

Children up to 5 years old must be placed in a seat adapted to their size on the back seat. Children between the ages of 5 and 12 must travel on the back seat using a 3 point seat belt with a booster seat.

*Winter Driving*
It is compulsory to carry snow chains in your vehicle and they must be used if required by the weather conditions (5cm of snow or black ice). The compulsory winter equipment in Croatia consists of a shovel in your vehicle and a set of snow chains on the driving axel.

## Fuel

Petrol stations are generally open from 7am to 8pm, later in summer. Some of those on major stretches of road stay open 24 hours a day. Payment by credit card is widely accepted. LPG (Autogas) is fairly widely available.

## Parking

Lines at the roadside indicate parking restrictions. Traffic wardens patrol roads and impose fines for illegal parking. Vehicles, including those registered outside Croatia, may be immobilised by wheel clamps.

## Roads

In general road conditions are good in and around the larger towns. The Adriatic Highway

or Jadranksa Magistrala (part of European route E65) runs the whole length of the Adriatic coast and is in good condition, despite being mostly single-carriageway. Minor road surfaces may be uneven and, because of the heat-resisting material used to surface them, may be very slippery when wet. Minor roads are usually unlit at night.

Motorists should take care when overtaking and be aware that other drivers may overtake unexpectedly in slow-moving traffic. The standard of driving is generally fair.

## Road Signs and Markings

Road signs and markings conform to international standards. Motorway signs have a green background; national road signs have a blue background.

## Speed Limits

| | Open Road (km/h) | Motorway (km/h) |
|---|---|---|
| Car Solo | 90-110 | 130 |
| Car towing caravan/trailer | 80 | 90 |
| Motorhome under 3500kg | 90-110 | 130 |
| Motorhome 3500-7500kg | 80 | 90 |

In addition to complying with other speed limits, drivers under the age of 25 must not exceed 80 km/h (50 mph) on the open road, 100 km/h (62 mph) on expressways and 120 km/h (74 mph) on motorways.

## Traffic Jams

During the summer, tailbacks may occur at the border posts with Slovenia at Buje on the E751 (road 21), at Bregana on the E70 (A3) and at Donji Macelj on the E59 (A1). During July and August there may be heavy congestion, for example at Rupa/Klenovica and at other tourist centres, and on the E65 north-south Adriatic Highway. This is particularly true on Friday evenings, Saturday mornings, Sunday evenings and holidays. Queues form at ferry crossings to the main islands.

Road and traffic conditions can be viewed on the HAK website (in English), www.hak.hr or tel: (01) 4640800 (English spoken) or (072) 777777 while in Croatia for round-the-clock recorded information.

## Violation of Traffic Regulations

The police may impose on-the-spot fines for parking and driving offences. If you are unable to pay the police may confiscate your passport. Motoring law enforcement, especially for speeding offences, is strictly observed.

## Motorways

There is just over 1250km of motorways, with the major stretches being shown in the table below. Tolls (cestarina) are levied according to vehicle category. Electronic display panels above motorways indicate speed limits, road conditions and lane closures. Information on motorways can be found on www.hac.hr.

*Motorway Tolls*

**Class 1**    Vehicle with 2 axles, height up to 1.3m (measured from front axle) excluding vans

**Class 2**    Vehicle with 2 or more axles, height up to 1.3m (measured from front axle), including car + caravan or trailer, motorhomes and vans.

**Class 3**    Vehicle with 2 or 3 axles, height over 1.3m (measured from front axle), including van with trailer

**Class 4**    Vehicle with 4 or more axles, height over 1.3m (measured from front axle)

Tolls can be paid in cash or by credit card. Details of toll prices can be found in English at www.hac.hr.

## Touring

There are a number of national parks and nature reserves throughout the country, including the World Heritage site at the Plitvice lakes, the Paklenica mountain massif, and the Kornati archipelago with 140 uninhabited islands, islets and reefs. Dubrovnik, itself a World Heritage site, is one of the world's best-preserved medieval cities, having been extensively restored since recent hostilities.

While Croatia has a long coastline, there are few sandy beaches; instead there are pebbles, shingle and rocks with man-made bathing platforms.

The Croatian National Tourist Board operates 'Croatian Angels', a multi-lingual tourist information and advice service available from the end of March to mid-October, tel: 062 999 999 or 00385 62 999 999 from outside Croatia.

Croatia originated the concept of commercial naturist resorts in Europe and today attracts an estimated 1 million naturist tourists annually. There are approximately 20 official naturist resorts and beaches and numerous other unofficial or naturist-optional 'free' beaches. Smoking is prohibited in restaurants, bars and public places. A service charge is general included in the bill. English is widely spoken.

## Public Transport

Many important rail routes are still not electrified and allow only single-track travel, making rail travel slow. By contrast the bus network offers the cheapest and most extensive means of public transport. Buy bus tickets when you board at the front of the vehicle or beforehand from kiosks, and ensure that you validate your ticket once on board. Trams operate in Zagreb and you can buy tickets from kiosks.

Coastal towns and cities have regular scheduled passenger and car ferry services. Most ferries are drive-on/drive-off – see www.jadrolinija.hr for schedules and maps.

Car ferries operate from Ancona, Bari, Pescara and Venice in Italy to Dubrovnik, Korèula, Mali Lošinj, Poreè, Pula, Rijecka, Rovinj, Sibenik, Split, Starigrad, Vis and Zadar. Full details from:

VIAMARE LTD
SUITE 108, 582 HONEYPOT LANE
STANMORE
MIDDX HA7 1JS
Tel: 020 8206 3420

Email: ferries@viamare.com
www.viamare.com

**BANJOLE see Pula** *A3*

**BIOGRAD NA MORU** *B3* (500m N Coastal) *43.96064, 15.42963* **Camping Moče, Put Primorja 8, 23207 Sveti Filip i Jakov [tel/fax (023) 388436; info@camping-moce.com; www.camping-moce.com]** Sp fr rd 8/E65. Sm, pt shd; wc; chem disp; serviced pitches; shwrs inc; el pnts (16A) HRK20; lndtte; shop 100m; rest, bar 200m; playgrnd; shgl beach adj; cab/sat TV; dogs; phone adj; poss cr; Eng spkn; adv bkg; red long stay; CKE/CCI. "CL-type site in garden; excel clean facs; friendly welcome fr owners; beach thro back gate - locked at night." ◆ ltd 1 Apr-15 Oct. HRK 135          2009*

**BIOGRAD NA MORU** *B3* (3km N Coastal) *43.96083, 15.42472* **Camping Đardin, 23207 Sveti Filip i Jakov [(023) 388960; info@camping-croatia.com; www.camping-croatia.com]** S fr Zadar (approx 23km) on E65/rd 8 turn R immed bef lge blue hotels/site sp twd sea. Site on L just bef lane narr. Lge, pt sl, shd; wc; chem disp; shwrs inc; el pnts (10A); gas 500m; lndry rm; shop adj; rest, snacks, bar adj; playgrnd; sand beach adj; watersports; boating; 80% statics; bus; poss cr; Eng spkn; adv bkg; quiet; red CKE/CCI. "In superb position on edge of resort vill; friendly, helpful staff; gd, clean facs." 15 Apr-15 Oct. HRK 138          2010*

⊞ **BIOGRAD NA MORU** *B3* (3km N Coastal) *43.96015, 15.42849* **Camping Filip, Put Primorja 10a, 23207 Sveti Filip i Jakov [tel/fax (023) 389196; auto.kamp.filip@zd.t-com.hr; www.camping-filip-kroatien.de]** S fr Zadar (approx 23km) turn R immed bef lge blue hotels/site sp twd sea. Site on L just past Autocamp Đardin. Sm, hdg pitch, hdstg, pt sl, shd; wc; chem disp; shwrs inc; el pnts HRK23; lndtte (inc dryer); shop 500m; rest, snacks, bar adj; BBQ; cooking facs; playgrnd; beach adj; games area; dogs HRK16; phone; bus nr; Eng spkn; quiet; red long stay. "San facs luxurious & clean; friendly owners; private gate to beach; sh walk to town; excel." 1 May-30 Sep. HRK 148          2010*

**BIOGRAD NA MORU** *B3* (10km NE Coastal) **Autocamp Martin, Sveti Petar na Moru, 23207 Sveti Filip i Jakov [tel/fax (023) 391104]** Fr Zadar on rd 8/E65, lge yellow sp to site. Sm, pt shd; htd wc; chem disp; mv service pnt; shwrs inc; el pnts (16A) inc; supmkt 9km; rest 100m; BBQ; beach adj; dogs HRK10; poss cr; Eng spkn; adv bkg; quiet; CKE/CCI. "Family-run site in unique position - some pitches on purpose-built promontory into sea; friendly welcome; excel, unisex facs; highly rec." HRK 130          2010*

⊞ **BIOGRAD NA MORU** *B3* (6.5km W Coastal) *44.05416, 15.37972* **Autokamp Filko, Aleksandar Colic 23207 Sveti Petar Na Moru [tel/fax 02 33 91 177; www.autokamp-filko.hr; www.info@autokamp-filko.hr]** On D8 bet Zadar & Biograd Na Moru at Sv Petar NM. 1st camp on the R by sea. Sm, pt shd; wc; chem disp; mv service pnt; shwrs; lndtte; rest; bar; shingle beach; wifi; 30% statics; dogs; poss cr; Eng spkn; some rd noise. " Some pitches by water on hdstg with views across to islands; dir access fr rd; ideal low ssn; gd." HRK 170          2014*

⊞ **BOL (BRAC ISLAND)** *C4* (500m W Urban/Coastal) *43.26373, 16.64799* **Camping Konoba Kito, Braćke Ceste bb, 21420 Bol [(021) 635551; www.bol.hr]** Take ferry fr Makarska to Brač & take rd 113/115 to Bol (37km). On o'skrts do not turn L into town but cont twd Zlatni Rat. Pass Studenac sup'mkt on R, site on L. Sm, pt shd; wc; chem disp; shwrs inc; el pnts (16A) HRK20; gas; lndtte; rest; BBQ; beach 500m; TV; some statics; dogs; poss cr; Eng spkn; adv bkg; quiet. "Excel for beaches & boating; gd local food in rest; vg, friendly, family-run site; clean, well-equipped; well worth effort to get there." HRK 141          2010*

**CRES (CRES ISLAND)** *A3* (1km N Coastal) *44.96277, 14.39694* **Camping Kovačine (Part Naturist), Melin 1/20, 51557 Cres [(051) 573150; fax 571086; campkovacine@kovacine.com; www.camp-kovacine.com]** Fr N, foll sp bef Cres on R. Fr S app thro vill of Cres. V lge, pt shd; wc; chem disp; baby facs; shwrs inc; el pnts (12A) inc; lndtte; shop; rest, snacks; playgrnd; beach; watersports; tennis; games area; sep area for naturists; wifi; dogs HRK23; Eng spkn; quiet; ccard acc; red long stay/CKE/CCI. "Site in olive grove; rocky making driving diff, but amenities gd & well-run; welcoming staff; delightful walk/cycle rte to sm vill of Cres; excel site." ◆ 4 Apr-15 Oct. HRK 276          2013*

**DRASNICE see Drvenik** *C4*

## "We must tell The Club about that great site we found"

Get your site reports in by mid-August and we'll do our best to get your updates into the next edition.

**DRVENIK** *C4* (12km NW Coastal) *43.17086, 17.1965* **Camping Dole, 21331 Živogośće [(021) 628749; fax 628750; auto-camp-dole@st.hinet.hr; www.hotelizivogosce.com]** Ent at km post 679 on Adriatic Highway, rd 8/E65, sp. V lge, some hdstg, pt sl, terr, pt shd; wc; chem disp; shwrs; el pnts (10A) HRK32 ; lndry rm; shop; rest, snacks; bar; BBQ; shgl beach adj; tennis; wifi; dogs HRK19; Eng spkn; some rd noise; ccard acc; red CKE/CCI. "Beach slopes steeply; used by school groups; vg." ◆ 1 May-30 Sep. HRK 247          2011*

**DUBROVNIK** *C4* (6km S Rural/Coastal) *42.6240, 18.18856* **Autocamp Kupari, Kupari b.b, 20207 Mlini [(020) 485548; fax 487344; info@campkupari.com; www.campkupari.com]** Fr Dubrovnik along coast rd sp airport & Mlini. Well sp on inland side of rd on ent vill. V lge, hdg/mkd pitch, shd; wc (cont); chem disp; shwrs inc; el pnts (10A) inc; lndtte; shop 200m; rest, snacks, bar, BBQ; shgl beach 400m; internet; entmnt; some statics; dogs HRK23; Eng spkn; adv bkg; some rd noise; ccard acc; CKE/CCI. "San facs need update (2009)." 1 Apr-31 Oct. HRK 136          2009*

**DUBROVNIK** *C4* (7km S Coastal) *42.62471, 18.20801*
Autocamp Kate, Tupina 1, 20207 Mlini [(020) 487006; fax
487553; info@campingkate.com; www.campingkate.com]
Fr Dubrovnik on rd 8 foll sp Cavtat or Čilipi or airport into vill
of Mlini. Fr S past Cavtat into Mlini. Site well sp fr main rd.
Sm, hdstg, pt sl, terr, pt shd; wc; chem disp; shwrs inc; el pnts
(10-16A) inc; lndtte; shop adj; rest, bar adj; BBQ; shgl beach
200m; phone; wifi; bus to Dubrovnik 150m; dogs HRK4; Eng
spkn; adv bkg; some rd noise; red long stay/low ssn; CKE/
CCI. "Family-run site in lovely setting; helpful, hard-working,
welcoming owners; vg clean facs; boats fr vill to Dubrovnik;
long, steep climb (steps) down to beach." 1 Apr-1 Nov.
HRK 143                                                    2012*

## "I need an on-site restaurant"

We do our best to make sure site
information is correct, but it is always best
to check any must-have facilities are still
available or will be open during your visit.

⊞ **DUBROVNIK** *C4* (10km S Coastal) Autocamp
Matkovica, Srebreno 8, 20207 Dubrovnik [(020) 485867;
u.o.matkovica@hotmail.com] Fr Dubrovnik S on coast rd. At
Kupari foll sp to site behind Camping Porto. Sm, mkd pitch,
shd; wc; chem disp; shwrs inc; el pnts (6A) inc; lndtte; supmkt,
rest, snacks, bar 200m; shgl beach adj; wifi; no statics; dogs;
Eng spkn; phone; bus 200m; Eng spkn; no ccard, cash only;
poss traff noise; red low ssn. "Well-kept site; friendly, helpful
owners; san facs old but clean; water bus to Dubrovnik 1km."
HRK 135                                                    2014*

**DUBROVNIK** *C4* (5km NW Urban/Coastal) *42.66191,
18.07050* Autocamp Solitudo, Vatroslava Lisinskog 17,
20000 Dubrovnik [(052) 465010; fax 460199; camping-
dubrovnik@valamar.com; www.camping-adriatic.com/
solitudo-camp-dubrovnik] S down Adriatic Highway to
Tuđjman Bdge over Dubrovnik Harbour. Turn L immed sp
Dubrovnik & in 700m take sharp U-turn sp Dubrovnik & carry
on under bdge. Site on Babin Kuk across harbour fr bdge. Lge,
mkd pitch, hdstg, pt sl, pt terr, pt shd; htd wc; chem disp; mv
service pnt; baby facs; shwrs inc; el pnts (10A) inc (long lead
poss req); lndtte (inc dryer); shop, rest, snacks, bar; BBQ; pool,
paddling pool 200m; shgl beach 500m; tennis; cycle hire;
wifi; no statics; dogs HRK46; twin-axles acc (rec check in adv);
phone; bus 150m; poss cr; Eng spkn; adv bkg; quiet; ccard acc;
red low ssn/CKE/CCI.; "Friendly, clean, well-run, v busy site;
sm pitches poss stony &/or boggy; some lge pitches; levelling
blocks poss req; san facs poss stretched high ssn & dated;
nearest site to city cent; conv Bari ferry; sat nav/map advised
as few sp; site in two parts, upper numbered but not mrkd
and informal, lower numbered and mkd." ♦ 1 Apr-30 Oct.
HRK 366 (CChq acc) SBS - X01                               2013*

**DUGA RESA see Karlovac** *B2*

**FAZANA** *A3* (500m S Coastal) *44.91717, 13.81105* Camping
Bi-Village, Dragonja 115, 52212 Fažana [(052) 300300;
fax 380711; info@bivillage.com; www.bivillage.com]
N fr Pula on rd 21/A9/E751 at Vodnjan turn W sp Fažana.
Foll sp for site. V lge, mkd pitch, pt shd; htd wc; chem disp;
mv service pnt; shwrs inc; el pnts (10A) inc; gas; lndtte (inc
dryer); supmkt; tradsmn; rest, snacks, bar; BBQ; playgrnd; 3
pools; waterslide; shgl/rocky beach adj; watersports; tennis
1km; games area; cycle & boat hire; golf 2km; wifi; entmnt;
30% statics/apartments; dogs HRK37; phone; bus; poss cr; Eng
spkn; adv bkg; ccard acc; red low ssn/snr citizens; CKE/
CCI. "Excel, modern, clean san facs; private bthrms avail; site
surrounded by pine trees; some beachside pitches; conv Brijuni
Island National Park; excel leisure facs for families; vg cycle
paths; no emptying point for Wastermaster; vg." ♦ 1 Apr-
13 Nov.  HRK 263 (5 persons) (CChq acc)                    2010*

**FUNTANA see Poreč** *A2*

**HVAR (HVAR ISLAND)** *B4* (4km N Coastal) *43.18970,
16.42990* Autocamp Vira, Mala Vira b.b, 21450 Hvar
[(021) 741803; info@campvira.com; www.campvira.com]
N fr Hvar town (cent parking area on L) dir Vira, site sp. Med,
mkd pitch, hdstg, pt shd; htd wc; chem disp; mv service pnt;
baby facs; shwrs inc; el pnts (10A); gas; lndtte (inc dryer);
shop; tradsmn; rest, snacks, bar; BBQ; playgrnd; shgl beach;
cycle hire, games area; wifi; entmnt; dogs HRK39; bus; phone;
adv bkg; quiet; red low ssn/long stay. "Excel site; sea views all
pitches; vg san facs; ltd water pnts; rest & bar o'look private
beach; highly rec." 20 Apr-30 Sep.  HRK 267               2011*

**ICICI see Opatija** *A2*

**JELSA (HVAR ISLAND)** *C4* (500m E Coastal) *43.16396,
16.70306* Camping Mina, 21465 Jelsa [(021) 761210; fax
761227; www.tzjelsa.hr] Fr W take main rd 116. After main
town junc ignore sp Hotel Mina & shortly after Autocamp
Holiday turn L (rd passes thro pt of this site) & cont round
bay. Site on R on promontory, sp. Lge, mkd pitch, terr, pt shd;
wc; shwrs; el pnts; lndtte; shop; bar; playgrnd; sand beach
adj; tennis nr; games area; cycle hire; adv bkg; quiet. "Excel
location & lovely vill, but poor facs." 1 May-30 Sep.    2009*

**JEZERA (MURTER ISLAND)** *B3* (800m NW Coastal) *43.79313,
15.62734* Holiday Village Jezera Lovišća, Zaratic 1, 22242
Jezera [(022) 439600; fax 439215; info@jezera-kornati.hr;
www.jezera-kornati.hr] S on main coast rd turn R 4km SE of
Pirovac sp Murter. Foll winding rd into vill & over swing bdge
on island. Foll rd round to R. Site on R in 2km. V lge, pt sl, pt
shd; wc; chem disp; shwrs inc; el pnts (10A) HRK29; shop, rest,
snacks high ssn; bar; playgrnd; shgl beach adj; watersports;
tennis; entmnt; internet; TV rm; 50% statics; dogs HRK46;
quiet; ccard acc; red long stay/CKE/CCI. "Excel site; boat trips
organised fr site; excel rest; lots to do in area." ♦ 26 Apr-
9 Oct.  HRK 212                                             2009*

KARLOVAC *B2* (12km SW Rural) *45.41962, 15.48338*
Autocamp Slapić, Mrežničke Brig, 47250 Duga Resa
[(098) 860601; fax (047) 854700; autocamp@inet.hr;
www.campslapic.hr] Exit A1/E65 junc 3 for Karlovac; strt over
traff lts immed after toll booth sp Split & Rijecka.Take D23 to
Duga Resa; turn L by church in Duga Resa; cont over bdge &
turn R; foll rd keeping rv on your R; cont thro vill of Mrnžnički
Brig in 3km; site sp in another 1km. NB new bdge at Belavici.
Site well sp fr Duga Resa. Sm, mkd pitch, pt shd; wc; chem
disp; shwrs inc; el pnts (16A) HRK20; lndtte (inc dryer); shop
500m; rest, snacks, bar adj; BBQ; playgrnd; rv sw & beach adj;
fishing; canoeing; tennis; games area; cycle hire; wifi; dogs
HRK15; phone; train to Zagreb 500m; Eng spkn; adv bkg; poss
noise fr daytrippers; ccard acc. "Friendly, pleasant, family-
owned site in gd location on rv; lovely area; gd bar/rest; gd
clean facs; lge pitches; long hoses req low ssn; easy drive into
Zagreb; excel; new, superb sans block (2014); rds to site narr."
♦ 1 Apr-31 Oct. HRK 220                                    2014*

KASTEL STARI *B4* (Coastal) *43.55305, 16.34666* Camping
Hrabar, Obala Kralja Tomislava 43, 21216 Kaštel-Stari
[(091) 8998526; ihrabar77@yahoo.com] Fr coast rd 8 turn
twds coast at Kaštel-Stari, site sp. Site approx 18km fr Split.
Med, mkd pitch, pt shd; wc; chem disp; shwrs inc; el pnts;
lndtte; rest, snacks, bar; BBQ; shgl beach adj; dogs; bus 500m;
poss cr; Eng spkn; adv bkg. "Helpful staff; gd cent location
for Split & Trogir; Kaštela area worth exploring." 1 May-
30 Sep.                                                    2010*

KORENICA *B3* (1.5km NW Urban) *44.76527, 15.68833*
Camping Borje, Vranovaca bb, 53230 Korenica
[(053) 751790; fax 751791; info@np-plitvicka-jezera.hr;
www.np-plitvicka-jezera.hr] Exit A1/A6 at Karlovac & take
rd 1/E71 S dir Split. Site on R approx 15km after Plitvička Jezera
National Park, well sp. Med, mkd pitch, sl, pt shd; htd wc;
chem disp; mv service pnt; baby facs; fam bthrm; shwrs inc; el
pnts (10A) inc; gas (1km); lndtte (inc dryer); supmkt 2km; rest,
snacks; bar; BBQ; playgrnd; lake sw nr; TV in adj rest; wifi; dogs
HRK20; twin axles; poss cr; Eng spkn; adv bkg; ccard acc; quiet;
excel; CKE/CCI. "Vg, clean, well-kept, spacious, sloping site
- levelling poss tricky; gd, modern, immac facs; helpful staff;
well run by Plitvicka National Park; excel for visiting the Lakes &
waterfalls; free bus runs to park at 10:30 and returns at 17:30;
mountain views." ♦ 1 Apr-15 Oct. HRK 255               2014*

KRK (KRK ISLAND) *A3* (4km SE Coastal) *45.01638, 14.62833*
Autocamp Pila, Šetalište Ivana Brusića 2, 51521 Punat
[tel/fax (051) 854020; pila@hoteli-punat.hr; www.hoteli-
punat.hr] Take coast rd, rte 2 twd Split. At Kraljevica, turn R
onto rd 103 over Krk toll bdge. Foll sp for Krk, Punat. Site sp at
T-junc after Punat Marina & vill. Lge, pt shd; wc; chem disp; mv
service pnt; baby facs; some serviced pitches; shwrs inc; el pnts
(10-16A) inc; lndtte (inc dryer); shops adj; rest, snacks, cooking
facs; playgrnd; beach adj; fishing; watersports; wifi; entmnt;
TV; 80% statics; dogs HRK32; quiet; ccard acc; red CKE/CCI.
"Well-run, big site; clean facs; gd for families with sm children;
boat hire; boat trips; sm picturesque vill; lots to do; poss cr." ♦
12 Apr-18 Oct. HRK 347                                   2014*

KRK (KRK ISLAND) *A3* (5km SE Coastal) *44.98972, 14.62805*
FKK Camp Konobe (Naturist), Obala 94, 51521 Punat
[(051) 854049; fax 854036; konobe@hoteli-punat.hr;
www.hoteli-punat.hr] Site is approx 30km fr Krk Bdge, sp
fr Krk-Baska rd. Lge, pt shd; wc; mv service pnt; baby facs;
shwrs inc; el pnts (16A) inc; lndtte (inc dryer) shop; rest,
snacks; BBQ; playgrnd; rocky beach adj; watersports; tennis;
wifi; entmnt; 10% statics; dogs HRK23; sep car park; adv bkg;
ccard acc; red CKE/CCI. "Vg san facs; beach with crystal clear
water." ♦ Easter-30 Sep. HRK 225                        2010*

KRK (KRK ISLAND) *A3* (16km SE Coastal) *44.96048,
14.68402* Autocamp Škrila, Stara Baška, 51521 Punat
[(051) 844678; fax 844705; skrila@valamar.com; www.
skrila.hr] Fr Krk E on rd 102, turn S dir Punat & Stara Baška.
Site on R at bottom of hill approx 8km after Punat. Lge,
hdstg, terr, unshd, mkd pitch; wc; chem disp; shwrs inc; el
pnts HRK27; shop; tradsmn; rest; bar; shg beach adj; statics;
dogs 2; poss cr; Eng spkn; quiet. "Approx 50 touring pitches;
friendly, helpful staff; gd security; lovely, isolated position; new
excel san facs (2014) ." 13 Apr-7 Oct. HRK 316          2014*

KRK (KRK ISLAND) *A3* (2km S Coastal) *45.02444, 14.59222*
FKK Camp Politin (Naturist), 51500 Krk [(051) 221351; fax
221246; politin@valamar.com; www.valamar.com] Site
S of Krk town on Baška rd, sp. Lge, unshd; wc; chem disp;
shwrs inc; el pnts (6A) inc; gas; lndtte; shop; rest; playgrnd;
shgl beach; watersports; boat-launching; tennis; entmnt;
dogs HRK33; poss cr; quiet; ccard acc; red INF/CKE/CCI. "Hilly
walk to town; gd renovated san facs." ♦ 24 Apr-9 Oct.
HRK 221                                                 2009*

⊞ KRK (KRK ISLAND) *A3* (800m SW Rural/Coastal)
*45.02246, 14.56210* Autocamp Bor, Crikvenička 10, 51500
Krk [(051) 221581; fax 222429; info@camp-bor.hr; www.
camp-bor.hr] Foll sp to Krk cent. At bottom of hill turn R at
rndabt, site well sp up hill. Med, mkd pitch, hdstg, pt sl, terr, pt
shd/unshd; wc; mv service pnt; shwrs inc; el pnts (10A) HRK33;
lndtte; tradsmn; rest, snacks; bar; shgl beach 800m; cycle
hire; many statics; dogs HRK28; poss cr; Eng spkn; adv bkg;
quiet. "Well-maintained, family-run site, but some pitches bare
earth; close to lovely town & harbour; choice of gd beaches."
HRK 172                                                 2011*

KRK (KRK ISLAND) *A3* (300m W Urban/Coastal) *45.01875,
14.56701* Autocamp Ježevac, Planicka bb, 51500 Krk
[(051) 221081; fax 221137; jezevac@valamar.com; www.
valamar.com] Fr main island rd heading S, app Krk, take 1st
rd on R (W) sp Centar. At rndabt take 2nd exit sp Autocamp.
App to site thro housing estate. V lge, hdstg, pt sl, terr, pt
shd/unshd; wc; mv service pnt; some serviced pitches; shwrs
inc; el pnts (10-16A) inc; lndtte (inc dryer); shop; rest, snacks;
bar; playgrnd; shgl beach adj; watersports; tennis; games area;
wifi; entmnt; dogs HRK34; phone; poss cr; Eng spkn; poss noisy
high ssn; ccard acc; red CKE/CCI. "Conv for touring Krk Island;
pleasant, gd value rest with view of old town; registration fee
payable 1st night; busy site; levelling poss diff for m'vans." ♦
1 Apr-10 Oct. HRK 229                                   2010*

CROATIA

**KRUSCICA** *B3* (5km SE Coastal) **Autocamp Punta Šibuljina, 23245 Trbanj-Šibuljina [tel/fax (023) 658004; info@ campsibuljina.com; www.campsibuljina.com]** On seaward side of E65 in vill. Med, pt sl, shd; wc; chem disp; mv service pnt; shwrs inc; el pnts (10A) HRK16; lndtte; shop 2km; rest 200m; snacks; bar; BBQ; playgrnd; shg beach adj; games area; entmnt; 60% statics; dogs HRK12; phone; bus adj; poss cr; Eng spkn; adv bkg; CKE/CCI. "V friendly welcome; view of Pag & bay; poss untidy site; tired san facs; quiet low ssn; gd." 15 Apr-15 Oct. HRK 106                    2010*

**KUCISTE see Orebič** *C4*

**LANTERNA see Poreč** *A2*

**LOPAR (RAB ISLAND)** *A3* (3km E Coastal) *44.82345, 14.73735* **Hotel Village San Marino, 51281 Lopar [(051) 775133; fax 775290; ac-sanmarino@imperial.hr; www.rab-camping.com]** Fr Rab town N to Lopar, sp ferry. At x-rds turn R sp San Marino, site sp. V lge, mkd pitch, some hdstg, terr, shd; wc (some cont); chem disp; mv service pnt; baby facs; fam bthrm; shwrs inc; el pnts (16A) inc; lndtte (inc dryer); shop, rest, snacks; bar; playgrnd; sand beach adj; watersports; tennis; games area; entmnt; TV; 10% statics; dogs HRK29; phone; bus; poss cr; Eng spkn; adv bkg; ccard acc; red CKE/CCI. "Superb, family site on delightful island; pitches on sandy soil in pine woods." ♦ 1 Apr-30 Sep. HRK 187   2011*

**LOVISTE** *C4* (500m N Coastal) *43.02500, 17.03500* **Autokamp Đenka, 20269 Lovište [(020) 718069; fax 321160; autocamp.denka@hi.t-com.hr; www.camping-denka.com]** Fr Orebič W to Lovište. In vill turn R at T-junc, site along sm rd which runs round bay. Sm, hdstg, terr, pt shd; wc; chem disp; shwrs inc; el pnts (16A); shop, rest, snacks, bar 500m; BBQ; shgl beach adj; dogs; adv bkg; quiet. "Beautiful bay for sw & watersports; gd walks & historical sites; warm welcome; well-maintained site." 1 Jun-15 Oct.          2009*

**LOVRECICA see Umag** *A2*

**LOZOVAC see Sibenik** *B3*

**MALI LOSINJ (LOSINJ ISLAND)** *A3* (2km SW Coastal) *44.53599, 14.45064* **Camping Čikat, Drazica 1, 51550 Mali Lošinj [(051) 232125; fax 231708; info@camp-cikat.com; www.camp-cikat.com]** Sp fr town. V lge, hdstg, terr, shd; wc (some cont); chem disp; mv service pnt; baby facs; shwrs inc; el pnts (16A); lndtte; shop; tradsmn; rest, snacks; bar; playgrnd; shgl beach adj; cycle hire; entmnt; many statics; dogs HRK21; poss cr; adv bkg; quiet; ccard acc; CKE/CCI. "Touring pitches on terr with sea views; gd san facs; easy walk/cycle to attractive town; boat trips & ferry to Zadar daily fr mid-Jun." ♦ 4 Apr-20 Oct. HRK 171                    2009*

**MALI LOSINJ (LOSINJ ISLAND)** *A3* (500m W Coastal) *44.53397, 14.45461* **Kredo Camping & Hotel, Šet. Dr Von M-Montesole 5, Čikat, 51550 Mali Lošinj [(051) 233595; fax 238274; info@kre-do.hr; www.kre-do.hr]** Hotel & site sp on Čikat rd. Med, shd; htd wc; chem disp; mv service pnt; some private bthrms avail; sauna; shwrs; el pnts HRK11; lndtte (inc dryer); shop; supmkt 1.5km; rest, snacks; bar; playgrnd; beach adj; watersports; boat hire; cycle hire; tennis 400m; fitness rm; wifi; TV; some statics; dogs HRK30; adv bkg; quiet. 1 Mar-1 Dec. HRK 217          2010*

**MALI LOSINJ (LOSINJ ISLAND)** *A3* (4km NW Coastal) *44.55555, 14.44166* **Camping Village Poljana, Privlaka 19, 51550 Mali Lošinj [(051) 231726; fax 231728; info@ poljana.hr info@baiaholiday.com; www.baiaholiday. com]** On main island rd 1km bef vill of Lošinj, sp. Two ferries a day fr Rijeka take car & c'van on 2hr trip to island. V lge, pt sl, terr, shd; wc (some cont); chem disp; mv service pnt; baby facs; private washrms avail; shwrs; el pnts (6-16A) inc; gas; lndtte (inc dryer); shop; rest, snacks; bar; playgrnd; shgl beach; watersports; sep naturist beach; tennis; games area; boat & cycle hire; wifi; entmnt; 50% statics; dogs 61; phone; poss cr; adv bkg; quiet; ccard acc; CKE/CCI. "Site in pine forest; sw with dolphins nrby." ♦ 24 Mar-31 Oct. HRK 312     2011*

**MARTINSCICA (CRES ISLAND)** *A3* (500m NW Coastal) *44.82108, 14.34298* **Camping Slatina, 51556 Martinšćica [(051) 574127; fax 574167; info@camp-slatina.com; www. camp-slatina.com]** Fr Cres S on main rd sp Mali Lošinj for 17km. Turn R sp Martinšćica, site in 8km at end of rd. V lge, hdg pitch, hdstg, terr, shd; wc; chem disp; mv service pnt; baby facs; fam bthrm; shwrs inc; el pnts (10A) inc (long lead req); lndtte; shop; rest, snacks; bar; playgrnd; shgl beach adj; boat launching; entmnt; internet; 20% statics; dogs HRK23; phone; poss cr; Eng spkn; adv bkg; quiet; cc acc. "Site on steep slope; newest san facs superb; beautiful island." ♦ 23 Mar-1 Oct. HRK 241                    2013*

**MEDULIN** *A3* (1km S Coastal) *44.80694, 13.95194* **Camp Kažela (Part Naturist), Kapovica 250, 52203 Medulin [(052) 576050; fax 577460; info@campkazela.com]** Fr Pula foll sp to Medulin. In Medulin site on R in 1.5km, sp. V lge, mkd pitch, pt sl, pt shd; wc (some cont) chem disp; mv service pnt; baby facs; shwrs inc; el pnts (10A) inc; gas; lndtte; shop; rest, snacks; bar; playgrnd; paddling pool; rocky beach; tennis; cycle hire; internet; entmnt; TV; 10% statics; dogs HRK31; phone; adv bkg; v quiet; ccard acc; red snr citizens/CKE/CCI. "Well-maintained site with views; sep naturist site & beach." ♦ 3 Apr-9 Oct. HRK 208 (CChq acc)          2009*

## "Satellite navigation makes touring much easier"

Remember most sat navs don't know if you're towing or in a larger vehicle – always use yours alongside maps and site directions.

**MEDVEJA** *A2* (2.5km N Coastal) *45.27080, 14.26897* **Autocamp Medveja, Medveja bb, 51416 Lovran [(051) 291191; fax 292471; medveja@liburnia.hr; www. liburnia.hr or www.camping.hr]** Site Pula-Rijeka rd 21/E751, 2km S of Lovran, well sp. Lge, hdg/mkd pitch, pt shd; wc; chem disp; mv service pnt; baby facs; shwrs; el pnts (10-16A) inc; gas; lndtte (inc dryer); shop adj; rest; snacks adj; bar; playgrnd; shgl beach adj; scuba-diving; games area; wifi; entmnt; 20% statics; dogs; bus adj; poss cr; Eng spkn; adv bkg; quiet, a little rd noise; ccard acc; red low ssn/long stay/CKE/CCI. "Excel for sw & visiting local area - Lovran lovely town; conv for ferry to Cres; gd, modern san facs; various pitch prices." ♦ 1 Apr-15 Oct. HRK 253 (CChq acc)                    2011*

**MLINI see Dubrovnik** *C4*

⊞ **MOLUNAT** *D4* (500m N Coastal) *42.45298, 18.4276*
**Autokamp Monika, Molunat 28, 20219 Molunat [tel/fax
(020) 794557; info@camp-monika.hr; www.camp-monika.
hr]** Site well sp in Molunat off Adriatic Highway E65. Sm, terr,
pt shd; wc (some cont); chem disp; mv service pnt; shwrs inc;
el pnts (6A) HRK27; lndtte; rest, snacks; bar; BBQ; sand beach
adj; internet; dogs HRK8; bus; poss cr; Eng spkn; quiet; red low
ssn. "Gd site close to Montenegro border & in quiet cove; sea
view fr all pitches; owner's wine & olive oil for sale; beautiful
views, v quiet LS; v friendly & helpful owner; highly rec."
HRK 248                                                    2014*

**MURTER see Jezera (Murter Island)** *B3*

**NJIVICE (KRK ISLAND)** *A2* (400m N Coastal) *45.16971,
14.54701* **Autocamp Njivice, 51512 Njivice [(051) 846168;
fax 846185; anton.bolonic@finvestcorp.hr; www.hoteli-
njivice.hr]** 8km S of Krk Bdge on rd 102 turn R to Njivice.
Site not well sp but foll sp to hotel area N of town cent. V
lge, shd; wc (mainly cont); chem disp; mv service pnt; shwrs
inc; el pnts (6-10A) HRK28; shop; rest; bar; shgl/rocky beach
adj; playgrnd nr; wifi; 60% statics; dogs HRK24; phone; bus;
poss cr; Eng spkn; no adv bkg; ccard acc; red CKE/CCI. "Less
cr than other Krk sites; gd facs." ♦ 1 May-30 Sep. HRK 155
(CChq acc)                                                 2010*

**NOVI VINODOLSKI** *A3* (7km NE Coastal) *45.15361, 14.72488*
**Autocamp Selce, Jasenová 19, 51266 Selce [(051) 764038;
fax 764066; kamp-selce@ri.t-com.hr; www.jadran-
crikvenica.hr]** Thro Selce town cent, site is 500m SE of town,
sp. Lge, hdstg, pt sl, terr, pt shd; wc (some cont) chem disp;
mv service pnt; shwrs inc; el pnts (10A) HRK27; lndtte; shop; rest,
snacks; bar; playgrnd; shgl beach adj; TV; statics; dogs HRK17;
phone; poss cr; quiet; ccard acc; red long stay/CCI.
"Wooded site; seaside location; excel facs; helpful staff; Long
stay; blocks & wedges ess; san facs run down & neglected; long
lead rec." ♦ 11 Apr-13 Oct. HRK 221                        2013*

**NOVIGRAD (DALMATIA)** *B3* (N Coastal) *44.18472, 15.54944*
**Camping Adriasol, 23312 Novigrad [(023) 375618; fax
375619; info@adriasol.com or office@adriasol.com; www.
adriasol.com]** Exit A1 at Posedarje & foll sp Novigrad. Site sp
at end of vill. Med, pt shd; wc; chem disp; mv service pnt; baby
facs; shwrs inc; el pnts (16A) HRK31; lndtte; shop 500m; rest,
snacks, bar adj; cooking facs; playgrnd; beach adj; watersports;
cycle hire; games area; internet; some statics; dogs HRK23;
TV; adv bkg; quiet; red CKE/CCI. "Well-positioned site - poss
windy; gd facs; friendly staff; popular level pitches by beach
cost more; freezer avail for camper use; v helpful staff." ♦
1 May-30 Sep. HRK 234                                      2013*

**NOVIGRAD (ISTRIA)** *A2* (4km NW Coastal) *45.34333,
13.54805* **Autocamp Mareda, Škverska bb, 52466
Novigrad [(052) 735291; fax 757035; camping@laguna-
novigrad.hr; www.laguna-novigrad.hr]** Fr Novigrad foll
coast rd dir Umag, in 4km foll sp to L. Lge, mkd pitch, pt
shd; wc (some cont); chem disp; mv service pnt; shwrs inc; el
pnts (10-16A) HRK23; lndtte; shop; rest; bar; BBQ; playgrnd;
shgl beach adj; boat lauch; tennis; entmnt; 50% statics;
dogs HRK35; poss cr; Eng spkn; quiet; ccard acc; red CKE/
CCI. "Peaceful site amongst vineyards; modern, clean san
facs; cheaper, unmkd pitches avail." ♦ 1 Apr-30 Sep.
HRK 194                                                    2009*

⊞ **OMIS** *C4* (8km S Coastal) *43.40611, 16.77777* **Autocamp
Sirena, Četvrt Vrilo 10, 21317 Lokva Rogoznica [tel/fax
(021) 870266; autocamp-sirena@st.t.hr; www.autocamp-
sirena.com]** Thro Omiš S'wards on main coastal rd, site up sm
lane on R immed bef sm tunnel. Med, hdstg, sl, terr, pt shd;
wc; chem disp; mv service pnt; shwrs inc; el pnts (16A) HRK15;
gas; lndtte; shop; tradsmn; rest, snacks; bar; BBQ; shgl beach
adj; watersports; internet; dogs HRK15; phone; bus; poss cr;
Eng spkn; adv bkg; quiet; CKE/CCI. "Enthusiastic, welcoming
staff; improving site; easy access lge o'fits; stunning location
above beautiful beach; excel stop bet Split & Dubrovnik; excel
rest." HRK 206                                             2014*

**"There aren't many sites
open at this time of year"**

If you're travelling outside peak season
remember to call ahead to check site opening
dates – even if the entry says 'open all year'.

⊞ **OMIS** *C4* (1.5km W Coastal) *43.44040, 16.67960*
**Autocamp Galeb, Vukovarska bb, 21310 Omiš
[(021) 864430; fax 864458; camping@galeb.hr; www.
camp.galeb.hr]** Site sp on rd 2/E65 fr Split to Dubrovnik. Lge,
mkd pitch, pt shd; wc; chem disp; mv service pnt; baby facs;
serviced pitches; private bthrms avail; shwrs; el pnts (16A)
inc; gas; lndtte; tradsmn; supmkt adj; rest, snacks; bar; BBQ
(gas, elec); playgrnd; sand beach; watersports; white water
rafting; sports area; tennis; wifi; entmnt;. 50% statics; dogs
HRK33; bus; poss cr; noisy high ssn; ccard acc; red low ssn/
CKE/CCI. "Excel, well-maintained site in gd position; extra
for waterside pitch; clean san facs; suitable young children;
easy walk or water taxi to town." ♦ ltd HRK 289 (CChq acc)
SBS - X02                                                  2012*

**OPATIJA** *A2* (5km S Coastal) *45.30633, 14.28354* **Autocamp
Opatija, Liburnijska 46, 51414 Ičići [(051) 704387; tz-icici@
ri.t-com.hr]** Fr Opatija take Pula rd 66. Site sp on R of rd 5km
after Opatija. Sp fr Ičići. Med, terr, pt shd; wc; chem disp; mv
service pnt; shwrs inc; el pnts (10A); rest, snacks 1km; shgl
beach adj; tennis; dogs; Eng spkn; quiet. "Gd site nr coastal
promenade; diff for lge o'fits without motor mover." 1 May-
30 Sep. HRK 247                                            2013*

**ORASAC** *C4* (500m S Coastal) **Autocamping Peča, Na Przini
38, 20234 Orašac [(020) 891161; info@peca.hr; www.peca.
hr]** Site on L of Split to Dubrovnik rd, on S edge vill Orašac. Sm,
pt shd; wc; chem disp; shwrs inc; el pnts (16A) HRK15; lndry
rm; shop 300m; snacks, bar 600m; shgl beach 600m; dogs;
phone; poss cr; Eng spkn; adv bkg; quiet; ccard not acc; CKE/
CCI. "Excel, well-run, friendly site; clean, modern facs; bus to
Dubrovnik; gd bar/rest at beach - steep climb down." 1 Jun-
30 Sep. HRK 108                                            2010*

CROATIA

ORASAC *C4* (W Coastal) *42.69919, 18.00578* **Autocamp Pod Maslinom, Na Komardi 23, 20234 Orašac [(020) 891169; orasac@orasac.com; www.orasac.com]** On main coast rd, on seaward side. Sp. Sm, hdstg, pt sl, terr, pt shd; wc; chem disp; shwrs inc; el pnts HRK15; sm shop; rest, bar 200m; BBQ; shgl beach 200m; wifi; dogs; bus; Eng spkn; quiet. "Pleasant site, clean facs; vg value for money." 1 May-20 Oct. HRK 87                    2010*

⊞ **OREBIC** *C4* (1km E Coastal) *42.9810, 17.1980* **Nevio Camping, Dubravica bb, 20250 Orebič [(020) 713100; fax 713950; info@nevio-camping.com; www.nevio-camping.com]** Fr N take ferry fr Ploče to Trpanj & take rd 415 then 414 dir Orebič, site sp. Fr S on rd 8/E65 turn W at Zaton Doli onto rd 414 to site. Site ent immed after lge sp - not 100m further on. Sm, terr, pt shd; htd wc; chem disp; mv service pnt; some serviced pitches; baby facs; shwrs inc; el pnts (16A) inc; lndtte (inc dryer); shop 300m; tradsmn; rest, snacks; beach bar; BBQ; cooking facs; pool; dir access to shgl beach; tennis; cycle hire; wifi; TV rm; 40% statics; dogs HRK15-38; Eng spkn; adv bkg; quiet; red low ssn/snr citizens. "Excel new site in gd location; friendly, helpful, welcoming staff; gd views; gd, clean facs; not suitable lge o'fits." ◆ HRK 282                    2013*

OREBIC *C4* (5km W Coastal) *42.97750, 17.12950* **Camping Palme, Kučište 45, 20267 Kučište [tel/fax (020) 719164; info@kamp-palme.com; www.kamp-palme.com]** Fr E thro Orebič on rd 414, site sp. Med, pt sl, terr, pt shd; htd wc; chem disp; mv service pnt; shwrs inc; el pnts (10A) HRK30; gas; lndtte; shop 100m; rest adj high ssn; snacks, bar high ssn; BBQ; shgl beach adj; watersports; boat hire; internet; TV rm; 10% statics; dogs HRK22; bus; poss cr; quiet; red CKE/CCI. "Nice, busy family-run site; beautiful wooded location on coast; friendly owners; excel rest; gd walking; ferry to Korčula; not suitable lge o'fits." HRK 163                    2011*

PAKOSTANE *B3* (4km SE Coastal) *43.88611, 15.53305* **Autocamp Oaza Mira, Ul. Dr. Franje Tudmana 2, 23211 Drage [023 635419; info@oaza-mira.hr; www.oaza-mira.hr]** A1 Karlovac-Split past Zadar, exit Biograd dir Sibenik on coast rd; sp on coastal side of rd; foll sp site after bay. Med, hdstg, terr, pt shd; wc; chem disp; mv serv pnt; baby facs; fam bthrm; shwr; el pnts inc; lndry rm; shop; rest; bar; BBQ; playgrnd; pool; beach adj; games rm; wifi; dogs HRK61; Eng spkn; adv bkg; quiet. "Excel new lovely site in beautiful location; generous pitches; rec using ACSI card; 2 beautiful bays adj to site; highly rec." 1 Apr-31 Oct. HRK 427     2012*

PAKOSTANE *B3* (500m S Coastal) *43.90547, 15.51616* **Autocamp Nordsee, Alojzija Stepinca 68, 23211 Pakoštane [tel/fax (023) 381438; info@autocamp-nordsee.com; www.autocamp-nordsee.com]** Site sp in Pakoštane on rd 8/E65. Med, mkd pitch, terr, pt shd; htd wc; chem disp; mv service pnt; baby facs; shwrs inc; el pnts (16A) HRK23; lndtte (inc dryer); shop 400m; rest, snacks; bar; dir access to beach adj; wifi; 10% statics; dogs HRK23; adv bkg; quiet. "Pleasant, family site." 1 Mar-31 Oct. HRK 196 (CChq acc)     2010*

PIROVAC *B3* (1km N Coastal) *43.82341, 15.65818* **Autocamp Miran, Zagrebačka bb, 22213 Pirovac [(022) 467064; fax 467022; reservations@rivijera.hr; www.rivijera.hr]** Sp on main coast rd NW Šibenik. Site 300m off Adriatic highway. Med, mkd pitch, some hdstg, pt sl, pt shd; wc; shwrs; el pnts (16A) inc; lndry rm; shops & 2km; rest; playgrnd; pool nr; shgl beach; tennis; cycle hire; entmnt; TV; some statics; dogs HRK34; poss cr; quiet; ccard acc. "Ideal for watersports; sm pitches on water's edge." 23 Apr-30 Sep.  HRK 206     2011*

POREC *A2* (10km N Coastal) *45.29728, 13.59425* **Camping Lanterna, Lanterna 1, 52465 Tar [(052) 404 500; fax 404591; lanterna@valamar.com; www.camping-adriatic.com/camp-lanterna]** Site sp 5km S of Novigrad (Istria) & N of Poreč on Umag-Vrsar coast rd. V lge, hdg/mkd pitch, hdstg, pt sl, terr, pt shd; wc; chem disp; mv service pnt; fam bthrm; baby facs; shwrs inc; el pnts (10A); gas; lndtte; supmkts; rest, snacks; bar; BBQ; playgrnd; pool; 2 hydro-massage pools; paddling pool; shgl beach adj; watersports; boat launch; tennis; games area; cycle hire; wifi; entmnt; 10% statics; dogs €5; phone; adv bkg (fee); noise fr ships loading across bay; ccard acc; red CKE/CCI (cash payments only). "V busy, well-run site; excel san facs & leisure facs; although many san facs they may be a long walk; variety of shops; gd sightseeing; extra for seaside/hdg pitch; vg." ◆ 12 Apr-10 Oct. HRK 298 2014*

*See advert on bookmark*

POREC *A2* (5km S Coastal) *45.19313, 13.59670* **Autocamp Bijela Uvala (Part Naturist), Zelena Luguna, 52440 Poreč [(052) 410551 or 410552; fax 410600; reservations@ plavalaguna.hr; www.plavalaguna.hr]** Fr Poreč, take coast rd S to Vrsar, site sp on R. V lge, mkd pitch, some hdstg, pt sl, pt terr, pt shd; wc (some cont); chem disp; mv service pnt; baby facs; fam bthrm; shwrs; el pnts (10A) HRK24; gas; lndtte (inc dryer); shop; rest, snacks; bar; playgrnd; pools; paddling pool; rocky beach; sep naturist beach; watersports; games area; tennis; wifi; entmnt; TV; dogs HRK46; poss cr; Eng spkn; adv bkg; quiet; ccard acc. "Excel touring base Istrian peninsula; clean, tidy, well-run site; friendly staff." ◆ Easter-30 Sep. HRK 230                    2011*

POREC *A2* (5km S Coastal) *45.19193, 13.58916* **Camping Zelena Laguna, 52440 Poreč [(052) 410700; fax 410601; reservations@plavalaguna.hr; www.plavalaguna.hr]** Fr Poreč take rd to Vrsar, site sp on R. V lge, some mkd pitch, hdstg, pt shd; wc; serviced pitches; chem disp; shwrs; el pnts (10A) HRK27; lndtte; shop, supmkt adj; rest, snacks; bar; playgrnd; pool; rocky shgl beach; sep naturist beach; entmnt; dogs HRK46; poss cr; adv bkg; quiet but noisy disco; ccard acc; red long stay/CKE/CCI. "A gd resort site with excel & spotless facs & lge, mainly terr, pitches; gd for touring Istrian peninsula; extra charge if stay fewer than 3 days Jul/Aug; footpath/cycle path to town." ◆ 27 Mar-4 Oct. HRK 203     2011*

**POREC** A2 (7km S Coastal) 45.17693, 13.60053 **Autocamp Puntica, 52452 Funtana [(052) 410102; fax 451044; reservations@plavalaguna.hr; www.plavalaguna.hr]** Fr Koper on rte 2 foll sp to Poreč & Vrsar. 7km S of Poreč, turn R (care needed) 200m past Funtana sp. Site on R in 500m. Narr ent. Lge, sl, pt shd; wc (cont); chem disp; mv service pnt; shwrs inc; el pnts (10A) HRK27; lndtte; shop; rest adj; playgrnd; beach adj; watersports; wifi; 50% statics; dogs HRK32; quiet; red CKE/CCI. "Sep beach for naturists; located on peninsula nr Funtana complex; extra charge if stay fewer than 3 days." ♦ 24 Apr-3 Oct. HRK 171 2010*

**POREC** A2 (7km S Coastal) 45.17453, 13.59213 **Camping Istra Naturist Funtana (Naturist), Ul Grgeti 35, 52450 Funtana [(052) 445123; fax 445306; camping@valamar. com; www.valamar.com or www.camping-adriatic.com]** Fr Poreč S sp Vrsar-Rovinj. After 6km turn R at sp Istra bef Funtana vill. Foll sp to camp in 1km. V lge, hdg/mkd pitch, pt sl, pt shd; wc (some cont); chem disp; mv service pnt; baby facs; fam bthrm; shwrs inc; el pnts (16A) inc; gas; lndtte; shop; rest, snacks; bar; BBQ; playgrnd; shgl beach adj; tennis; games area; boat & cycle hire; wifi; entmnt; TV rm; 10% statics; dogs HRK42; poss cr; Eng spkn; quiet; ccard acc; red low ssn/INF/ CKE/CCI. "Excel site; beaches v rocky." ♦ ltd 16 Apr-3 Oct. HRK 225 2011*

**POREC** A2 (8km NW Coastal) 45.2568, 13.5835 **Naturist-Center Ulika (Naturist), 52440 Poreč (Istra) [(052) 436325; fax 436352; reservations@plavalaguna.hr; www. lagunaporec.com]** Site sp on rd fr Poreč to Tar & Novigrad. V lge, pt sl, shd; wc; shwrs; el pnts (6A) HRK23; lndtte; shop; rest, snacks; bar; playgrnd; pool; shgl & rocky beach; tennis; watersports; entmnt; 9% statics; dogs HRK48; adv bkg; quiet; ccard acc; red INF card/long stay; "Excel site." ♦ 28 Mar-6 Oct. HRK 199 2013*

**PREMANTURA see Medulin** A3

**PRIMOSTEN** B4 (2km N Coastal) 43.60646, 15.92085 **Camp Adriatic, Huljerat b.b, 22202 Primošten [(022) 571223; fax 571360; info@camp-adriatic.hr; www.camp-adriatic.hr]** Off Adriatic Highway, rd 8/E65, sp. V lge, all hdstg, pt sl, pt terr, unshd; wc; chem disp; mv service pnt; fam bthrm; baby facs; shwrs inc; el pnts (16A) inc; gas; lndtte (inc dryer); shop & 2km; rest, snacks; bar; rocky beach adj; boat hire; watersports; diving cent; tennis; games area; wifi; entmnt; dogs HRK32; Eng spkn; quiet; red CKE/CCI. "Gd sea views; excel san facs; some pitches poss diff to get onto; beautiful views fr beach." ♦ 1 May-15 Oct. HRK 305 2010*

**PULA** A3 (7km S Coastal) 44.82048, 13.87852 **Camping Peškera, Indije 73 52100 Banjole/Pula (Istra) [052 573209; fax 573189; info@camp-peskera.com; www.camp-peskera.com]** Fr N take A9 to Pula. Cont on m'way twd Premantura. Exit at Banjole, cont twd Indije. Campsite is 100m after Indije. Sm, pt sl, pt shd; wc; cont; chem disp; mv service pnt; shwrs; supmkt 2km; rest 1km; snacks; bar; shingle beach adj; wifi; dogs HRK15; bus 0.5km; poss cr; Eng spkn; adv bkg; quiet; ccard acc; red low ssn; CCI. "Beautiful situation; helpful & friendly owners; gd clean san facs; vg." ♦ ltd 1 Apr-31 Oct. HRK 219 2014*

**PULA** A3 (8km S Coastal) 44.82012, 13.90252 **Autocamp Pomer, Pomer bb, 52100 Pula [(052) 573128; fax 573062; camp-pomer@camp-pomer.com; www.camp-pomer.com]** Fr N on A9 to Pula, take exit to Pula. At bottom of hill turn L after filling stn & foll dir Medulin/Premantura. In Premantura turn L by Consum supmkt & foll sp to Pomer & site. Med, mkd pitch, terr, shd; wc; chem disp; shwrs; el pnts (16A) HRK21 (long lead poss req); lndry rm; shop; tradsmn; rest, snacks; bar; BBQ; playgrnd; rocky beach adj; fishing; watersports; games area; entmnt; some statics; dogs HRK23; phone; Eng spkn; adv bkg; quiet; red CKE/CCI. "Clean san facs poss stretched high ssn; friendly owner; quiet, relaxing site." 1 Apr-15 Oct. HRK 147 2009*

**PULA** A3 (8km S Rural) 44.82472, 13.85885 **Camping Diana, Castagnes b b, 52100 Banjole [(052) 505630; booking@ camp-diana.com; www.camp-diana.com]** Fr Pula ring rd foll sp Premantura & Camping Indije. Site 1km bef Cmp Indije. Sm, pt sl, pt shd; wc; chem disp (wc); shwrs inc; el pnts (16A) inc; shop 200m; bar; playgrnd; pool; paddling pool; tennis; games area; wifi; no dogs; adv bkg; quiet. "Pleasant site in garden setting; gd range of facs; immac san facs; welcoming family owners." 1 May-1 Oct. HRK 206 2010*

**PUNAT see Krk (Krk Island)** A3

**RABAC** A3 (500m W Coastal) 45.08086, 14.14583 **Camping Oliva, 52221 Rabac [tel/fax (052) 872258; olivakamp@ maslinica-rabac.com; www.maslinica-rabac.com]** On ent Rabac fr Labin, turn R at sp Autocamp; site ent in 500m. V lge, mkd pitch, pt shd; wc (mainly cont); baby facs; shwrs; el pnts (10A) inc (long lead poss req); gas; lndtte (inc dryer); shop 100m; rest, snacks; bar; playgrnd; shgl beach; watersports; boat-launching; sports complex; 30% statics; dogs HRK22; phone; poss cr; adv bkg Aug ess; quiet; ccard acc; red CKE/CCI. "Conv historic walled town Labin; walk along beach to shops & rest." ♦ ltd 21 Apr-6 Oct. HRK 402 (CChq acc) 2013*

**RAKOVICA** B3 (3km S Rural) 44.97340, 15.64789 **Turist Grabovac Camping, Grabovac 102, 47245 Rakovica [(047) 784192; fax 784189; info@kamp-turist.hr; www. kamp-turist.hr]** On main rd 1/E71 S fr Karlovac, site on R, well sp opp Ina petrol stn. Med, hdg/mkd pitch, hdstg, pt sl, pt shd; wc; shwrs inc; el pnts (6-16A) inc (long lead req); shop, rest adj; cycle hire; 20% statics; dogs; bus to National Park adj; Eng spkn; adv bkg; some rd noise; ccard acc; CKE/CCI. "Gd views fr higher pitches; friendly staff; well-maintained site; insufficient facs stretched high ssn; excursions arranged." ♦ 1 Apr-30 Sep. HRK 166 2010*

**RAKOVICA** B3 (7km SW Rural) 44.95020, 15.64160 **Camp Korana, Plitvička Jezera, 47246 Drežnik Grad [(053) 751888; fax 751882; autokamp.korana@np-plitvicka-jezera.hr; www.np-plitvicka-jezera.hr]** On A1/ E59 2km S of Grabovac, site on L. Site is 5km N of main ent to Plitvička Nat Park, sp. Lge, some hdstg, pt sl, pt shd; wc; fam bthrm; own san; chem disp; mv service pnt; shwrs inc; el pnts (16A) inc (poss long lead req); lndry rm; shop; rest, snacks; bar; BBQ; wifi; 10% statics; dogs HRK23; Eng spkn; no adv bkg; ccard acc; CKE/CCI. "Lovely site, v busy; poss long way fr facs; gd san facs but inadequate for size of site; efficient, friendly site staff; poss muddy in wet; bus to National Park (6km) high ssn; new san facs; gd rest." 1 Apr-31 Oct. HRK 259 (CChq acc) 2014*

Tell us about the sites you visit

**RIJEKA** *A2* (9km W Coastal) *45.35638, 14.34222* **Camping Preluk, Preluk 1, 51000 Rijeka [(051) 662185; fax 622381; camp.preluk@gmail.com]** On Rijeka to Opatija coast rd. Sm, shd; wc (some cont); own san; chem disp; shwrs; el pnts (10A) inc; shop; snacks; mainly statics; dogs; bus; poss cr; Eng spkn; rd noise. "NH only; Many statics; facs recently renovated (2012); bus to town; sm beach on site; gd windsurfing." 1 May-30 Sep.  HRK 158                                    2012*

**RIZVANUSA** *B3* (10km W Rural) *44.49580, 15.29165* **Eco Camp Rizvan City, Rizvanuša 1, 53000 Gospić [053 57 33 33; info@adria-velebitica.hr; www.camp-rizvancity.com]** Fr A1 take exit 12 (Gospic). Head 10km E twd Karlobag on highway 25. Turn L off main rd into Vill Rizvanusa. Camp 500m. Sm, pt shd; wc; chem disp; mv service pnt; fam bthrm; shwrs; el pnts (16A); lndtte (inc dryer); tradsmn; BBQ; playgrnd; beach 30km; games area; wifi; dogs; twin axles; Eng spkn; adv bkg; quiet. "Walks, high rope course; quad & jeep safari; archery; paintball; zip line; wall climbing; giant swing; bike trails; vg." ♦ ltd 1 Mar-1 Nov.  HRK 155          2014*

**ROVINJ** *A2* (1km N Coastal) *45.10444, 13.62527* **Camping Valdaliso, Monsena b.b, 52210 Rovinj [(052) 805505; fax 811541; ac-valdaliso@maistra.hr; www.campingrovinjvrsar.com]** N fr Rovinj dir Valalta for 2km, turn W to coast, site sp. Lge, hdg/mkd pitch, some hdstg, pt sl, pt shd; htd wc; chem disp; mv service pnt; baby facs; fam bthrm; shwrs; el pnts (10A) inc; gas; lndtte; shop; rest, snacks; bar; BBQ; playgrnd; shgl beach adj; waterslide; tennis; cycle hire; games area; games rm; wifi; entmnt; sat TV; 10% statics; no dogs; phone; bus; water taxi; Eng spkn; adv bkg; quiet; ccard acc; CKE/CCI. "Pretty site in olive trees; use of all amenities in hotel adj; excel modern san facs; poss waterlogged after heavy rain; excel; facs stretched if site full." ♦ 1 Apr-8 Oct.  HRK 377                                    2014*

**ROVINJ** *A2* (6.9km N Coastal) *45.12287, 13.62970* **Campsite Valalta Naturist (Naturist), Cesta Za Valaltu-Lim 7, 52210 Rovinj (Istra) [052 804800; fax 821004; valalta@valalta. hr; www.valalta.hr]** 7km NW fr Rovinj. Foll signs to Valalta. V lge, hdg pitch, mkd pitch, hdstg, pt shd; wc; chem disp; mv service pnt; baby facs; fam bthrm; shwrs; el pnts (16A); lndtte (inc dryer); shop; rest; snack; bar; BBQ; playgrnd; pool; waterslide; paddling pool; beach; games area; games rm; bike hire; entmnt; wifi; tv; phone; twin axles; Eng spkn; adv bkg; quiet. "Excel site." ♦ ltd 27 Apr-29 Sep.  HRK 450       2014*

**ROVINJ** *A2* (5km SE Coastal) *45.05611, 13.68277* **Camping Veštar, 52210 Rovinj [(052) 829150; fax 829151; vestar@ maistra.hr; www.campingrovinjvrsar.com]** Clearly sp on ent/exit Rovinj dir Pula. V lge, mkd pitch, pt sl, pt shd; wc; chem disp; mv service pnt; baby facs; shwrs inc; el pnts (16A) inc (poss rev pol); gas; lndtte; supmkt; rest, snacks; bar; playgrnd; pool; paddling pool; shgl beach adj; boat & cycle hire; watersports; tennis; internet; entmnt; TV; 20% statics; dogs HRK47; phone; sep naturist beach adj; cash machine; poss cr; Eng spkn; adv bkg; ccard acc; red long stay/snr citizens/CKE/CCI. "Well-run, clean site on beautiful sm bay; coastal cycle track to Rovinj; gd touring base; friendly staff; some lge pitches; ltd el pnts high ssn; extra charge for stay fewer than 3 days." ♦ 25 Apr-3 Oct.  HRK 232                    2009*

**ROVINJ** *A2* (700m NW Coastal) *45.09472, 13.64527* **Autocamp Porton Biondi, Aleja Porton Biondi 1, 52210 Rovinj [(052) 813557; fax 811509; portonbiondi@web.de; www.portonbiondi.hr]** Site sp on ent Rovinj. Lge, pt sl, terr, shd; wc; shwrs inc; el pnts inc; shop adj; rest, snacks; rocky beach nr; watersports; entmnt; dogs HRK24; adv bkg; quiet; ccard acc; red low ssn/ long stay/CKE/CCI. "Gd site within walking dist Rovinj old town; beautiful views; new san facs; sm pitches not suitable lge o'fits; excel rest; 2nd & subsequent nights at red rate." ♦ ltd 15 Mar-31 Oct.  HRK 170      2012*

**ROVINJ** *A2* (4km NW Coastal) *45.10909, 13.61974* **Camping Amarin, Monsena bb, 52210 Rovinj [(052) 802000; fax 813354; ac-amarin@maistra.hr; www.campingrovinjvrsar. com]** Fr town N in dir Valalta, turn L & foll site sp. V lge, mkd pitch, pt sl, pt shd; wc (some cont); chem disp; mv service pnt; shwrs inc; el pnts (10A) inc; lndtte; shop; rest, snacks; bar; playgrnd; htd pool; paddling pool; waterslide; shgl beach adj; sports facs; tennis; cycle hire; entmnt; internet; TV; 30% statics; dogs HRK47; phone; poss cr; Eng spkn; adv bkg; quiet; ccard acc; red low ssn/CKE/CCI. "Excel site; clean, well-maintained san facs & pool; gd entmnt; views of town & islands; lovely situation in pine & olive trees; water taxi to town." ♦ 25 Apr-3 Oct.  HRK 238                                    2011*

**SELCE see Novi Vinodolski** *A3*

**SENJ** *A3* (3km N Urban/Coastal) **Autokamp Škver, Škver bb, 53270 Senj [tel/fax (053) 885266; kamp_skver@yahoo. com]** Fr N on rd 8/E65 on ent town turn R opp petrol stn & cont down narr lane to sea. Site sp bef marina. Sm, mkd pitch, hdstg, unshd; wc; chem disp; shwrs inc; el pnts inc; shops 500m; rest; bar; shgl beach adj; phone; poss cr; Eng spkn; adv bkg; rd noise. "Gd views; harbour & rest nrby."          2009*

## "That's changed – Should I let The Club know?"

If you find something on site that's different from the site entry, fill in a report and let us know. See www.caravanclub.co.uk/europereport.

**SENJ** *A3* (11km S Coastal) *44.98763, 14.91132* **Eurocamp Rača, Rača bb, 53284 Sveti Juraj [tel/fax (053) 883209; info@sojat.net]** On rte 2 Rjeka-Split, well sp fr Senj. Lge, hdstg, pt sl, terr, pt shd; wc; chem disp (wc); shwrs; el pnts; sm shop; rest adj; snacks; bar; shgle beach adj; boat-launching; watersports; diving school; tennis; games area; entmnt; poss cr; some rd noise; CKE/CCI. "In ravine with own beach; beautiful location; ltd facs; conv NH."          2010*

**SENJ** *A3* (6km NW Coastal) *45.04403, 14.87817* **Autocamp Sibinj, Sibinj 9, 51252 Klenovica [(051) 796916; milieijko. tomijanovic@ri.hinet.hr]** Fr Novi Vinodolski, take rd S. In approx 12km site sp. Med, sl, terr, pt shd; wc (male cont); shwrs inc; el pnts (10A); shops, sm bar & rest; private shgl beach adj; some rd noise. "Well-run site; clean facs but in need of modernising; magnificent views; poss open all yr; noisy rd; NH only." 1 May-31 Oct.  HRK 152              2011*

Solaris Aquapark

Wellness & Spa

6 brand new toilets

**Great Resort for a Great Vacation**
Solaris Camping Beach Resort
Šibenik - CROATIA
T. +385 22 361 017
camping@solaris.hr
www.campingsolaris.com

**SIBENIK** *B3* (10km NE Rural) *43.80063, 15.94210* **Camp Krka**, Skocici 21, 22221 Lozovac [(022) 778495; goran.skocic@ si.t-com.hr; www.camp-krka.hr] Exit A1 at junc 22 Šibenik, turn E at T-junc, thro tunnel & site in approx 4km. Fr main coast rd at Sibenik turn N onto rte 33 twd Drniš. After 15km turn L dir Skradin, site sp on L. Med, hdstg, pt shd; wc; chem disp; shwrs; el pnts (16A) HRK23 (poss rev pol; check earth); lndtte; shop 4km; bar; some statics & B&B; Eng spkn; quiet; red low ssn/CKE/CCI. "Pleasant, basic site in orchard; friendly owner; gd modern san facs; conv Krka National Park & Krka gorge; gd; clean new shwr/wc facs (2014); rest, cheap basic food." 1 Apr-30 Oct.  HRK 151                          2014*

## "I like to fill in the reports as I travel from site to site"

You'll find report forms at the back of this guide, or you can fill them in online at www.caravaclub.co.uk/europereport.

**SIBENIK** *B3* (4km S Coastal) *43.69925, 15.87942* **Camping Solaris**, Hotelsko Naselje Solaris, 22000 Šibenik [(022) 364000; fax 364450; info@solaris.hr; www.solaris. hr] Sp fr E65 Zadar-Split rd, adj hotel complex. V lge, hdg/ mkd pitch, pt shd; htd wc; chem disp; mv service pnt in adj marina; sauna; serviced pitches; shwrs inc; el pnts (6A) inc; lndtte; shop adj; rest, snacks; bar; BBQ; playgrnd; pool; paddling pool; waterslide; watersports; tennis; cycle hire; wifi; entmnt; TV; dogs; bus; poss v cr; some rd noise; ccard acc; red long stay/low ssn/CKE/CCI. "Well-situated in olive & pine trees; some pitches adj marina; excel, modern san facs." ♦ 15 Apr-31 Oct.  HRK 225 (CChq acc)                   2012*

See advertisement

**SIBENIK** *B3* (10km S Coastal) *43.65238, 15.95066* **Camping Jasenovo**, Uvala Jasenovo, 22010 Žaborić-Brodarica [(022) 350550; fax 350953; kamp@jasenovo.hr; www. jasenovo.hr] Fr Sibinik S on E65, site well sp on R. Sm, hdstg, pt sl, shd; wc; chem disp; shwrs inc; el pnts HRK23; lndry rm; shop 2km; tradsmn; snacks; bar; shgl beach adj; wifi; dogs HRK31; bus adj; poss cr; Eng spkn; adv bkg; quiet; CKE/CCI. "Vg, family-run site in pine & olive trees; helpful staff; plans to extend." ♦ ltd 1 May-1 Oct.  HRK 168                   2010*

⊞ **SPLIT** *B4* (5km SE Coastal) *43.50501, 16.52768* Camping Stobreč-Split, Sv Lovre 6, 21311 Stobreč [(021) 325426 / (0521) 325452; fax 325452; camping.split@ gmail.com; www.campingsplit.com] Fr N foll E65 & m'way thro Split to sp Stobreč. Site sp R off E65 at traff lts in Stobreč. Lge, mkd pitch, hdstg, pt sl, shd; wc; chem disp; mv service pnt; shwrs; el pnts (16A) inc (long lead poss req); lndtte (inc dryer); shop; rest, snacks; bar; playgrnd; sand beach; games area; wifi; dogs HRK45; bus to Split; poss cr; Eng spkn; some rd noise. "Superb, well-run site in lovely setting with views; helpful, welcoming staff; gd facs; own sandy beach; public footpath thro site; rec arr early to secure pitch; gd value for money; highly rec." ♦ HRK 296 (CChq acc)             2013*

**STARIGRAD (HVAR ISLAND)** *B4* (SW Coastal) *43.18688, 16.58655* Camping Jurjevac, Njiva b b, 21460 Starigrad [(021) 765843; fax 765128; info@hoteli-helios.hr; www. hoteli-helios.hr] Ferry fr Split to Starigrad, fr dock dir Starigrad, site on L in 1km on SW town o'skts. Med, pt shd; chem disp (wc); shwrs inc; el pnts (10A) HRK23; shop 100m; BBQ; rocky beach 300m; watersports; cycle hire; 25% statics; dogs HRK23; phone; bus 500m; poss cr; Eng spkn; adv bkg; quiet; red CKE/CCI. "Gd." 1 May-30 Sep.  HRK 115     2010*

**STARIGRAD PAKLENICA** *B3* (300m S Coastal) *44.28694, 15.44666* Autocamp Paklenica, Dr Franje Tuđjmana 14, 23244 Starigrad-Paklenica [(023) 209050; fax 209073; camping.paklenica@bluesunhotels.com / alan@ bluesunhotels.com; www.bluesunhotels.com] On rd 8/E65 Adriatic H'way at ent to Paklenica National Park in Zidine vill. Hotel Alan is lge, 10-storey block - ent & cont to site. Lge, pt sl, shd; wc; chem disp; shwrs inc; el pnts (16A) inc (long lead poss req); lndtte; shop; rest; bar; playgrnd; pool; adj; paddling pool; beach adj; tennis; games area; cycle hire; wifi; entmnt; TV; 5% statics; dogs HRK37; phone; Eng spkn; poss cr nr shore; adv bkg; ccard acc; red long stay/low ssn/CKE/CCI. "Gd clean facs; conv National Park; excel walking & rockclimbing; use of facs at adj hotel; site muddy when wet; gd res, pleasant helpful staff, san facs being enlarged (2013)." ♦ 1Apr-15 Nov. HRK 329                                2013*

STARIGRAD PAKLENICA *B3* (1km S Coastal) *44.28713, 15.44761* Autocamp Nacionalni Park Paklenica, Dr Franje Tudmana 14, 23244 Starigrad-Paklenica [(023) 369202 or 369155; fax 359133; alan@bluesunhotels.com; www. bluesunhotels.com] On seaward side of rd 8/E65 adj Hotel Alan. Sm, gravel, pt shd; wc (some cont); chem disp; shwrs inc; el pnts (10-15A) HRK16-22; shop adj; rest, snacks adj & 700m; bar; shgl beach; boating; no statics; dogs HRK15; phone; bus; poss cr; ccard acc. "Ent to National Park 2km; hiking; rock-climbing; v pleasant staff; lack of privacy in shwrs." ♦ ltd 1 Apr-15 Nov. HRK 160 2010*

## "We must tell The Club about that great site we found"

Get your site reports in by mid-August and we'll do our best to get your updates into the next edition.

⊞ STARLGRAD PAKLENICA *B3* (1km N Coastal) *44.31340, 15.43579* Auto-Kamp Plantaža, Put Plantaza 2, 23244 Starigrad Paklenica [(038) 23 369131; fax 23 359159; plantaza@hi.t-com.hr; www.plantaza.com/] Fr Rijeka foll M2/E27 coast rd until 1 km N of Steligrad. V Steep pull out of site. Sm, mkd pitch, hdstg, terr, shd; htd wc; chem disp; mv service pnt; child/baby facs; shwrs; el pnts 10A; rest; BBQ; beach; Eng spkn; poss cr; quite; CKE/CCI; ACSI; "V gd site, excel new facs, handy for NP. Shopping for fresh food v ltd locally." HRK 114 2012*

**STOBREC see Split** *B4*

STON *C4* (3km S Coastal) *42.81775, 17.67591* Autocamp Prapratno, Dubrovačko Primorje, 20230 Ston [(020) 754000; fax 754344; dubrovacko-primorje.dd@ inet.hr] SE on Adriatic highway thro Neum. Take R turn after 15km for Ston & Pelješac Island, skirt Ston, up winding hill & after 8.5km turn L on sharp bend, site sp. Easy access due improved rd. Site adj ferry to Korčula. Lge, pt shd; wc; chem disp; mv service pnt; shwrs inc; el pnts (6A) HRK23; shop; rest, snacks; bar; playgrnd; sand beach; tennis; games area; TV; dogs HRK21; poss cr; quiet; ccard acc; red CKE/CCI. "Beautiful setting on gd sand beach; ideal for sailing & watersports; gd san facs; welcoming owner." 15 May-30 Sep. HRK 191 2010*

**SVETI JURAJ see Senj** *A3*

TROGIR *B4* (2km S Coastal) *43.50510, 16.25833* Camping Rožac, Okrug Gornji, 21220 Trogir [(021) 806105; booking@camp-rozac.hr; www.camp-rozac.hr] Fr A8 foll sp Trogir. Cross bdge onto Trogir Island, keep L & cross 2nd bdge to Čiovo Island. Turn R & foll sp Okrug Gornji, site in 1.5km on R. NB Narr app rd to site poss diff lge o'fits. Lge, hdg/mkd pitch, shd; wc; chem disp; mv service pnt; baby facs; shwrs inc; el pnts (16A) HRK27; lndtte (inc dryer); shop 200m; tradsmn; rest, snacks; bar; beach adj; watersports; wifi; entmnt; 5% statics; dogs HRK16; bus to Trogir; adv bkg; quiet, but poss noise fr nrby beach resort; red low ssn/snr citizens. "Pleasant, wooded site on headland; narr app rds - not rec for lge o'fits; gd, modern facs; excel." ♦ 1 Apr-31 Oct. HRK 205 (CChq acc) 2011*

TROGIR *B4* (2km W Coastal) *43.51910, 16.22442* Camping Seget, Hrvatskih Žrtava 121, 21218 Seget-Donji [(021) 880394; kamp@kamp-seget.hr; www.kamp-seget. hr] Exit A1 at junc Prgomet & foll sp Trogir twd coast. Pass under coast rd at Trogir-Seget rd, turn R & site in 300m on L. Fr coast rd going SE take minor rd that runs thro Trogir & Seget Donji. Med, pt sl, pt shd; wc; chem disp; shwrs; el pnts (10A) HRK23; shop on site & 300m; rest 300m; shgl beach adj; dogs HRK12; bus 300m; poss cr; Eng spkn; poss noisy high ssn. "Busy site; old, poor san facs; friendly staff; public access to beach via site; water bus to Trogir fr site; pleasant vill with excel seafood rests etc; mkt in Trogir every day except Sun." ♦ 1 May-31 Oct. HRK 214 2010*

TROGIR *B4* (5km W Coastal) *43.51150, 16.19430* Camping Vranjica-Belvedere, Seget Vranjica bb, 21218 Seget Donji [(021) 798222; fax 894151; vranjica-belvedere@st.t-com. hr; www.vranjica-belvedere.hr] Site clearly sp on coast rd, W of Trogir, 100m bef start of by-pass. Lge, mkd pitch, terr, pt sl, pt shd; wc (some cont); chem disp; mv service pnt; baby facs; private san facs avail; shwrs inc; el pnts (16A) HRK36; lndtte (inc dryer); supmkt; rest, snacks; bar; BBQ; playgrnd; shgl beach adj; watersports; tennis; games area; wifi; entmnt; TV rm; 30% statics; dogs HRK25; phone; bus, water taxi; poss cr; Eng spkn; adv bkg; quiet; ccard acc; red lw ssn/long stay/CKE/CCI. "Beautiful position with views of bay; lovely town; gd facs; vg site; site OK, bit scruffy but clean san facs; v helpful staff." 15 Apr-15 Oct. HRK 303 (CChq acc) 2013*

See advertisement

**TUHELJSKE TOPLICE** B2 (Urban) 46.06583, 15.78513 Camping Terme Tuhelj, Ljudevita Gaja 4, 49215 Tuhelj [(049) 203000; info@terme-tuhelj.hr; www.terme-tuhelj.hr] N fr Zagreb on A2 for approx 24km, exit junc 5 Zabok & foll rds 24/301/205 to sp Tuheljske Toplice. Check in at Hotel Toplice. Sm, pt shd; wc; chem disp; mv service pnt; shwrs inc; el pnts (6A) HRK25; lndry rm; rest, snacks; bar; playgrnd; htd pool; waterslide; paddling pool; thermal spa adj; games area; games rm; wifi; TV; no dogs; phone; bus; Eng spkn; adv bkg; quiet. "Gd, new site (2010); conv Zagreb & gd alt to Zagreb site where poss security probs." ♦ ltd 1 Apr-31 Oct. HRK 200          2010*

**UMAG** A2 (2.5km N Coastal) 45.45055, 13.52265 **Camping Stella Maris**, Savudrijska Cesta b.b, 52470 Umag [(052) 710900; fax 710909; camp.stella.maris@istraturist.hr; www.istracamping.com] Site sp on o'skts of Umag. Lge, pt shd; wc; chem disp; mv service pnt; shwrs inc; el pnts (10A) inc; gas; lndtte; shop; rest, snacks adj; playgrnd; pool 200m; shgl beach; watersports; cycle hire; entmnt; 25% statics; dogs HRK27; m'van o'night area; Eng spkn; adv bkg; ccard acc; red long stay/CKE/CCI. "Gd for touring Istrian peninsula; helpful staff; lge pitches; gd, modern san facs; use of amenities in hotel adj." ♦ ltd 26 Mar-31 Oct. HRK 233          2010*

**UMAG** A2 (10km N Coastal) 45.48550, 13.56523 **FKK Camping Kanegra (Naturist)**, Kanegra b.b, 52470 Umag [(052) 709000; fax 709499; camp.kanegra@istraturist.hr; www.istracamping.com] Fr Trieste foll sp Slovenia, then Umag. Bef Umag foll sp Savudrija, site well sp. Lge, mkd pitch, pt shd; htd wc; chem disp (wc); mv service pnt; baby facs; shwrs; el pnts (10A) inc; gas; lndtte; shop; tradsmn; rest, snacks; bar; playgrnd; beach adj; tennis; watersports; tennis; cycle hire; games area; internet; entmnt; TV; 40% statics; dogs HRK27; phone; poss cr; Eng spkn; adv bkg; quiet; ccard acc; red CKE/CCI. "Clean san facs; excel." ♦ 23 Apr-26 Sep. HRK 233          2010*

**UMAG** A2 (6km S Coastal) 45.39271, 13.54193 **Autocamp Finida**, Križine br 55A, 52470 Umag [(052) 756296; fax 756295; camp.finida@instraturist.hr; www.istracamping.com] Site clearly sp. Lge, mkd pitch, pt sl, pt shd; wc; chem disp; mv service pnt; baby facs; shwrs inc; el pnts (10A) inc; lndtte; shop; rest, snacks; bar; playgrnd; shgl beach adj; cycle hire; TV; 50% statics; dogs HRK25; phone; bus; poss cr; Eng spkn; adv bkg; quiet; ccard acc; red long stay/CKE/CCI. "Gd base for touring Istria; gd, clean, modern facs; lovely site amongst oak trees; friendly staff." 23 Apr-30 Sep. HRK 213          2009*

**UMAG** A2 (8km S Coastal) 45.36540, 13.54473 **Camping Park Umag**, Karigador b.b, 52466 Lovrečica [(052) 725040; fax 725053; camp.park.umag@istraturist.hr; www.istracamping.com] Fr Novigrad, take coast rd N twd Umag. Site in 6km twd sea. V lge, mkd pitch, pt sl, pt shd; wc; chem disp; mv service pnt; baby facs; fam bthrm; shwrs inc; el pnts (6A) inc; gas; lndtte; supmkt; rest, snacks; bar; playgrnd; pools; paddling pool; boat anchorage & own rocky beach adj; tennis; games area; wifi; entmnt; TV; 20% statics; dogs HRK25; m'van o'night area; Eng spkn; adv bkg; ccard acc; red long stay/CKE/CCI. "Excel site for beach holiday; many leisure facs inc dog shwrs! immac san facs; narr site rds; sm pitches & v muddy after rain." ♦ 10 Apr-4 Oct. HRK 293          2010*

**VODICE** B3 (2.5km E Coastal) 43.75268, 15.78981 **Camping Imperial**, Vatroslava Lisinskog 2, 22211 Vodice [tel/fax (022) 454412 or (022) 454488 (LS); reservations@rivijera.hr; www.rivijera.hr] Fr N on E65 pass INA service stn in Vodice, then at rndabt foll Hotel Imperial & site sps. Fr S site sp at ent to town. Med, mkd pitch, terr, pt shd; wc; chem disp; baby facs; shwrs inc; el pnts (16A) inc; shop; rest, snacks; bar; BBQ; playgrnd; 2 pools (1 htd covrd); waterslide; paddling pool; shgl beach adj; fishing; watersports; tennis; cycle hire; games rm; entmnt; internet; 8% statics; dogs HRK54; bus; poss cr; Eng spkn; noisy entmnt; ccard acc; red low ssn/long stay; CKE/CCI. "Vg site." ♦ 22 Mar-9 Nov. HRK 274 SBS - X08   2011*

**VRSAR** A2 (500m N Urban/Coastal) 45.15555, 13.61055 Camping Orsera, 52450 Vrsar [(052) 441330; fax 441010; camping@valamar.com; www.valamar.com] S fr Poreč pass Autocamp Funtana, site on R. V lge, hdg/mkd pitch, pt sl, pt shd; wc; chem disp; mv service pnt; baby rm; fam bthrm; shwrs inc; el pnts (10A) inc; gas; lndtte; shop; rest, snacks; bar; playgrnd; shgl/rocky beach adj; waterslide; boat slipway; watersports; games area; games rm; 15% statics; dogs HRK39; phone; money exchange; poss v cr; Eng spkn; adv bkg rec high ssn; quiet; ccard acc; red CKE/CCI. "Gd situation nr Vrsar vill & harbour; clean san facs; muddy in rain; conv for town; vg." ♦ ltd 1 Apr-3 Oct. HRK 224          2010*

**VRSAR** A2 (2km N Coastal) 45.16505, 13.60796 **Camping Valkanela**, Petalon 1, 52450 Vrsar [(052) 800200; fax 800215; info@maistra.hr; www.campingrovinjvrsar.com] Site sp N of town fr coast rd. V lge, pt sl, terr, pt shd; wc (some cont); chem disp; mv service pnt; fam bthrm; baby rm; shwrs inc; el pnts (6A) inc; gas 1km; lndtte; supmkt; shops; 2 rests; snacks; bar; playgrnd; rocky beach; watersports; tennis; games area; cycle hire; entmnt; TV; 40% statics; dogs HRK50; phone; poss cr; Eng spkn; adv bkg; quiet; ccard acc; red CKE/CCI. "Excel for watersports; vg san facs; vg site for children." ♦ 25 Apr-3 Oct. HRK 275          2013*

**VRSAR** A2 (1km SE Coastal) 45.14144, 13.60196 **Camping Porto Sole**, Petalon 1, 52450 Vrsar [(052) 441198; fax 441830; portosole@maistra.hr; www.campingrovinjvrsar.com] Site sp in dir Koversada. V lge, mkd pitch, hdstg, pt shd; wc (some cont); chem disp; mv service pnt; fam bthrm; baby facs; shwrs inc; el pnts (10A) inc; gas; lndtte (inc dryer); supmkt; rest, snacks; bar; playgrnd; pool; paddling pool; rocky beach adj; watersports; diving school; tennis; games area; cycle hire; wifi; entmnt; TV rm; 20% statics; dogs HRK50; adv bkg req high ssn; quiet; ccard acc; red long stay/CKE/CCI. "Lovely area & site; excel sports facs; easy walk to town cent; vg." ♦ 24 Apr-1 Oct. HRK 239          2010*

**VRSAR** A2 (1km SE Coastal) 45.14233, 13.60541 **Naturist-Park Koversada (Naturist)**, Petalon 1, 52450 Vrsar [(052) 441378; fax 441761; koversada-camp@maistra.hr; www.campingrovinjvrsar.com] Site sp fr Vrsar in dir Koversada. V lge, hdg/mkd pitch, pt sl, terr, pt shd; wc (some cont); chem disp; mv service pnt; baby facs; fam bthrm; shwrs inc; el pnts (10-16A) inc; gas 500m; lndtte; supmkt; shops; rests; snacks; bar; playgrnd; rocky/sandy beach; tennis; games area; diving school; watersports; cycle hire; entmnt; internet; TV rm; 50% statics; dogs HRK46 ; phone; poss cr; Eng spkn; adv bkg; quiet; ccard acc; red long stay/CKE/CCI. "Vg, modern san facs; excel leisure facs; peaceful situation; excel; busy noisy hilly site." ♦ 26 Apr-28 Sep. HRK 214          2013*

**ZADAR** *B3* (3.5km N Coastal) *44.13485, 15.21599* **Autocamp Borik, Majstora Radovana 7, 23000 Zadar [(023) 332074; fax 332065; camp@hoteliborik.hr; www.hoteliborik.hr]** On ent Zadar foll sps to Borik. Site poorly sp. V lge, shd; wc; own san; chem disp; mv service pnt; shwrs; el pnts (10A) inc; shop; rest, snacks; bar; playgrnd; 2 pools (1 htd, covrd) nrby; shgl beach; watersports; tennis; no dogs; phone; bus 450m; Eng spkn; no adv bkg; ccard acc; 10% red CKE/CCI. "Pt of resort complex of 6 hotels; facs poor & some cold water only; poor security; gd sw beach; gd rests nrby; site run down; NH only." ♦ 1 May-30 Sep. HRK 229                2010*

**ZAGREB** *B2* (12km SW Urban) *45.77389, 15.87778* **Camping Motel Plitvice, Lučko, 10090 Zagreb [(01) 6530444; fax 6530445; motel@motel-plitvice.hr]** Site at motel attached to Plitvice services on A3/E70. Access only fr m'way travelling fr N, otherwise long m'way detour fr S. Lge, pt shd; htd wc; chem disp; shwrs inc; el pnts (16A) inc; lndry rm; shop; rest, snacks; bar; tennis; TV; phone; bus to town fr site; m'way noise; ccard acc; red CKE/CCI. "Ask at motel recep (excel Eng) for best way back fr city &/or details minibus to city; Zagreb well worth a visit; site shabby but facs clean & adequate - stretched when site full & in need of update." 1 May-30 Sep. HRK 199  2010*

## "Satellite navigation makes touring much easier"

Remember most sat navs don't know if you're towing or in a larger vehicle – always use yours alongside maps and site directions.

**ZAOSTROG** *C4* (Centre SE Coastal) *43.13925, 17.28047* **Camp Viter, Obala A.K. Miosica 1, 21334 Zaostrog (Dalmatija) [098 704018; fax 021 629190; info@camp-viter.com; www.camp-viter.com]** Foll Camp Viter signs 600m on R after Zaostrog sign. Sm, pt shd; hdstg; wv; chem disp; mv service pnt; shwrs inc; el pnts (16A) HRK25; lndtte (inc dryer); shop, rest, snacks & bar 0.25km; BBQ; beach; wifi; dogs HRK25; twin axles; Eng spkn; adv bkg; Quiet; red low ssn; CCI. "Very helpful, friendly owners; vg." 1 Apr-31 Oct. HRK 195                2014*

**ZAOSTROG** *C4* (1km S Coastal) *43.13133, 17.28751* **Campsite Uvala Borova, Viterska 1, 21334 Zaostrog [tel/ fax 021 629 111 or 099 253 4229 (mob); camp.uvala. borova@gmail.com; www.uvala-borova.com]** On rte 8 fr Split, 1km after Zaotrog on the R. Med, mkd pitch, hdstg, terr, shd; wc; chem disp; mv service pnt; shwrs; el pnts (16A) HRK25; lndtte; rest; bar; BBQ; pool; beach adj; games rm; wifi; tv rm; dogs HRK20; phone; bus; twin axles; Eng spkn; adv bkg; CCI. "Peaceful site with beautiful views of the Croatian coast & mountains; easy walk/cycle into Zaotrog along minor rd; friendly, helpful ownersl vg." ♦ 1 Apr-30 Sep. HRK 165                2014*

**ZATON** *B3* (1.5km N Coastal) *44.22960, 15.17320* **Autocamp Peroš, Put Petra Zoranica 14, 23232 Zaton [(023) 265830; fax 265831; info@autocamp-peros.hr; www.autocamp-peros.hr]** Site sp 16km N of Zadar fr rd 306 dir Nin. Foll sp to Zaton Holiday Vill & fork R to site. Sm, mkd pitch, hdstg, pt shd; wc; chem disp; mv service pnt; shwrs inc; el pnts (16A) inc; lndtte; shop 1.5km; tradsmn; snacks; bar; cooking facs; htd pool; paddling pool; watersports; shgl beach 300m; cycle hire; wifi; TV rm; dogs HRK39 (no Rottweillers or Dobermans); phone; bus 1.5km; Eng spkn; adv bkg; quiet; ccard acc; red low ssn/long stay. "Excel, peaceful, pleasant, family-run site; vg, gd new facs; helpful staff; cycle rtes to local areas of interest; close to sea & gd access to Zadar; friendly owners." 1 Mar-30 Nov. HRK 229 (CChq acc)                2011*

## "There aren't many sites open at this time of year"

If you're travelling outside peak season remember to call ahead to check site opening dates – even if the entry says 'open all year'.

**ZATON** *B3* (1.5km N Coastal) *44.23434, 15.16605* **Camping Zaton, Široka ulica bb, 23232 Zaton [023 280215; fax 280310; camping@zaton.hr; www.zaton.hr]** Site 16km NW of Zadar on Nin rd. Pt of Zaton holiday vill. Wel sp. V lge, pt shd; htd wc; chem disp; mv service pnt; shwrs inc; el pnts (10A) inc; gas; lndtte; supmkt; rest, snacks; bar; playgrnd; pool; paddling pool; sand beach adj; boat hire; watersports; tennis; games area; entmnt; internet; 15% statics; dogs HRK65; phone; adv bkg; quiet; ccard acc; red low ssn; CKE/ CCI. "Excel, well-run, busy site; own beach; excel san facs; cent of site is 'vill' with gd value shops & rests; gd for all ages; nr ancient sm town of Nin, in walking dist; conv National Parks; excel; v expensive outside ACSI discount period but has first class facs and nrby town well worth a visit." ♦ 1 May-30 Sep. HRK 413                2013*

*See advert on bookmark*

**ZIVOGOSCE see Drvenik** *C4*

## "I need an on-site restaurant"

We do our best to make sure site information is correct, but it is always best to check any must-have facilities are still available or will be open during your visit.

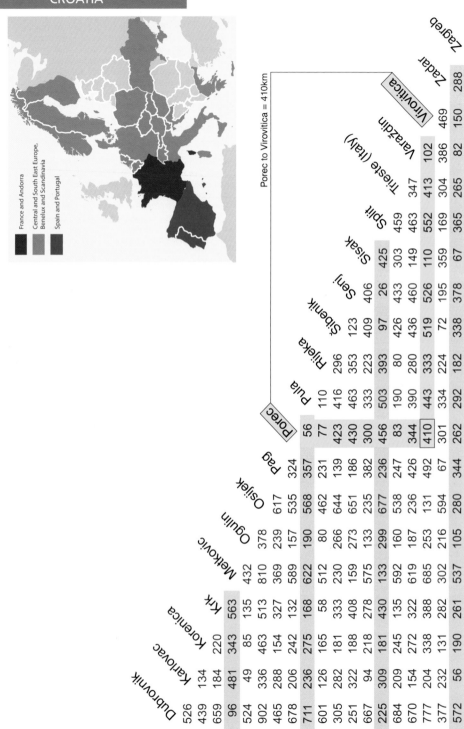

Map legend:
- France and Andorra
- Central and South East Europe, Benelux and Scandinavia
- Spain and Portugal

**Distance chart (km)** — Porec to Virovitica = 410km

| From \ To | Korenica | Krk | Metković | Ogulin | Osijek | Pag | Poreč | Pula | Rijeka | Šibenik | Senj | Sisak | Split | Trieste (Italy) | Varaždin | Virovitica | Zadar | Zagreb |
|---|---|---|---|---|---|---|---|---|---|---|---|---|---|---|---|---|---|---|
| Dubrovnik (Karlovac 526) | 439 | 659 | 96 | 524 | 902 | 465 | 678 | 711 | 601 | 305 | 251 | 667 | 225 | 684 | 670 | 777 | 377 | 572 |
| Karlovac | 134 | 184 |  | 49 | 336 | 288 | 206 | 236 | 126 | 282 | 322 | 94 | 309 | 209 | 154 | 204 | 232 | 56 |
| Korenica |  | 220 | 343 | 85 | 463 | 154 | 242 | 275 | 165 | 181 | 188 | 218 | 181 | 245 | 272 | 338 | 131 | 190 |
| Krk |  |  | 563 | 135 | 513 | 327 | 132 | 168 | 58 | 333 | 408 | 278 | 430 | 135 | 322 | 388 | 282 | 261 |
| Metković |  |  |  | 432 | 810 | 369 | 589 | 622 | 512 | 230 | 159 | 575 | 133 | 592 | 619 | 685 | 302 | 537 |
| Ogulin |  |  |  |  | 378 | 239 | 157 | 190 | 80 | 266 | 273 | 133 | 299 | 160 | 187 | 253 | 216 | 105 |
| Osijek |  |  |  |  |  | 617 | 535 | 568 | 462 | 644 | 651 | 235 | 677 | 538 | 236 | 131 | 594 | 280 |
| Pag |  |  |  |  |  |  | 324 | 357 | 231 | 139 | 186 | 382 | 236 | 247 | 426 | 492 | 67 | 344 |
| Poreč |  |  |  |  |  |  |  | 56 | 77 | 423 | 430 | 300 | 456 | 83 | 344 | 410 | 301 | 262 |
| Pula |  |  |  |  |  |  |  |  | 110 | 416 | 463 | 333 | 503 | 190 | 390 | 443 | 334 | 292 |
| Rijeka |  |  |  |  |  |  |  |  |  | 296 | 353 | 223 | 393 | 80 | 280 | 333 | 224 | 182 |
| Šibenik |  |  |  |  |  |  |  |  |  |  | 123 | 409 | 97 | 426 | 436 | 519 | 72 | 338 |
| Senj |  |  |  |  |  |  |  |  |  |  |  | 406 | 26 | 433 | 460 | 526 | 195 | 378 |
| Sisak |  |  |  |  |  |  |  |  |  |  |  |  | 425 | 303 | 149 | 110 | 359 | 67 |
| Split |  |  |  |  |  |  |  |  |  |  |  |  |  | 459 | 463 | 552 | 169 | 365 |
| Trieste (Italy) |  |  |  |  |  |  |  |  |  |  |  |  |  |  | 347 | 413 | 304 | 265 |
| Varaždin |  |  |  |  |  |  |  |  |  |  |  |  |  |  |  | 102 | 386 | 82 |
| Virovitica |  |  |  |  |  |  |  |  |  |  |  |  |  |  |  |  | 469 | 150 |
| Zadar |  |  |  |  |  |  |  |  |  |  |  |  |  |  |  |  |  | 288 |

You can now fill in site reports online

**Legend**

Motorways
Major roads
Main roads

N
W — E
S

- All year site(s)
- **Seasonal site(s)**
- No sites listed

200m +
0–200m

**Countries and places**

AUSTRIA
SLOVAKIA
HUNGARY
SLOVENIA
BOSNIA-HERZEGOVINA
SERBIA
ITALY
MONTENEGRO

ADRIATIC
SEA

VIENNA
BRATISLAVA
BUDAPEST
Graz
Maribor
Nagykanizsa
LJUBLJANA
Novo Mesto
VARAŽDIN
Tuheljske Toplice
Pécs
ZAGREB
VIROVITICA
Sombor
Trieste
Umag
Opatija
RIJEKA
Novigrad (Istria)
POREČ
Vrsar
Medveja
Njivice
Rovinj
KARLOVAC
SISAK
OSIJEK
Fažana
Rabac
Novi Vinodolski
OGULIN
PULA
Cres
SENJ
Medulin
Martinščica
Lopar
Rakovica
Bihać
Banja Luka
KRK
KRK
CRES
RAB
KORENICA
Mali Lošinj
LOŠINJ
PAG
Rizvanusa
PAG
Kruščica
Starigrad
Paklenica
SARAJEVO
Zaton
ZADAR
Novigrad
(Dalmatia)
Biograd na Moru
Pakoštane
Jezera
Pirovac
MURTER
Vodice
ŠIBENIK
Primošten
Kaštel-Stari
Trogir
SPLIT
Omiš
BRAČ
Bol
Mostar
Starigrad
Drvenik
ADRIATIC
Hvar
Jelsa
Zaostrog
HVAR
Loviste
METKOVIĆ
Orebić
Ston
KORČULA
Orašac
DUBROVNIK
PODGORICA
Molunat

A2 A3 A1/A6 A6 A1 A8 A9 A7 A5 A3

0   50   100   150 kms
0   50   100 mls

© Collins Bartholomew Ltd 2014

# Czech Republic
## Country Introduction

*Bohemian Paradise Nature Reserve, Czech Republic*

## Welcome to Czech Republic

Packed with medieval towns, towering castles, beautiful palaces and charming traditional buildings, the Czech Republic provides an unforgettable holiday. Prague, the capital city, is full of unique architecture and is considered one of the most beautiful cities in Europe.

For a more relaxing stay head to the countryside where the landscape is made up of rolling fields, meadows and forests, a great place for nature lovers. Take some time out to sample the local lifestyle and Czech beer in one of the old medieval inns that can be found in the smaller rustic towns.

## Country highlights

Assorted cold meats, pickles, cabbage, beef, pork and dumplings are national favourites. Beer is regarded as the national drink – there are more than 470 varieties and brewery tours are available.

Prague Spring Festival is an internationally famous celebration of music and takes place in May.

## Major towns and cities

- Prague – the capital and largest city in the Czech Republic.
- Brno – a historical city, full of captivating museums and stunning architecture.
- Liberec – the city contains the stunning towers of Liberec Hall.

## Attractions

- Prague Old Town Square – a lively square surrounded by Baroque styled buildings.
- Znojmo City Walls – take a walk around these historical walls and see the city views.
- Tugendhat Villa – this stunning landmark was built in the early 20th century.
- Prague Castle – a fairy tale castle overlooking the Vltava River.
- Moravian Karst and Caves - interesting natural formations within well lit passage ways.

## Find out more

www.czechtourism.com
Tel:0042 (0)22 4861 578 Czech Republic Tourism

# Country Information

*Population (approx):* 10.1 million

*Capital:* Prague (population approx 1.23 million)

*Area:* 78,864 sq km

*Bordered by:* Austria, Germany, Poland, Slovakia

*Terrain:* Diverse landscape with rolling hills and plains in the west (Bohemia) surrounded by low mountains; higher hills and heavily forested mountains in the east (Moravia)

*Climate:* Temperate continental with warm, showery summers and cold, cloudy, snowy winters

*Highest Point:* Snezka 1,602m

*Language:* Czech

*Local Time:* GMT or BST + 1, i.e. 1 hour ahead of the UK all year

*Currency:* Czech crown (CZK)
£1 = CZK 35, CZK 100 = £2.87 (September 2014)

*Emergency numbers:* Police 158; Fire brigade 150; Ambulance 155 (operators speak English)

*Public Holidays 2015:* Jan 1; Apr 6, 21; May 1, 8 (National Liberation Day); Jul 5, 6 (Johannes Hus Festival); Sep 28 (St Wenceslas), Oct 28 (Independence Day); Nov 17 (Day of Freedom and Democracy); Dec 24, 25, 26.

School summer holidays are from the beginning of July to the end of August.

# Camping and Caravanning

Campsites are divided into four categories from 1 to 4 stars. Normally campsites are open from May to mid September, although some campsites stay open all year. They usually close at night between 10pm and 6am.

Campsites are generally good value and in recent years many have upgraded their facilities. Privacy in the showers may be a problem due to a shortage of, or lack of, shower curtains and only a communal dressing area.

Some sites have communal kitchen facilities which enable visitors to make great savings on their own gas supply.

Motorhomes are recommended to carry a very long hose with a variety of tap connectors. Refill the onboard tank whenever possible as few sites have easily accessible mains water.

Casual/wild camping is not permitted and fines are imposed for violation of this law, especially in national parks. It is prohibited to sleep in a caravan or motorhome outside a campsite.

# Cycling

There are around 2,500 km of cycle tracks, known as Greenways, in tourist areas. A long-distance cycle track links Vienna and Prague and there are many tracks linking the Czech Republic to Austria and Poland. Helmets are compulsory for cyclists under the age of 18.

# Electricity and Gas

Current on campsites varies between 6 and 16 amps. Plugs have two round pins. A few campsites have CEE connections but not many. Reversed polarity may be encountered.

You may find that Campingaz 907 cylinders are available from large DIY warehouses.

# Entry Formalities

British and Irish passport holders may visit the Czech Republic for up to three months without a visa. If intending to stay longer, visitors must register with the police. There are no identity checks at the borders with neighbouring countries and normally it is not necessary for a driver to stop when crossing the border. However, random identity checks may be made at any time at the border or inside the country itself.

# Medical Services

For minor ailments first consult staff at a pharmacy (lékárna) who are qualified to give advice and are sometimes able to sell drugs which are normally only available on prescription in the UK. Language may be a problem outside Prague; if you need particular drugs or a repeat prescription, take an empty bottle or remaining pills with you. For more serious matters requiring a visit to a doctor go to a medical centre (poliklinika) or hospital (nemocnice).

British nationals may obtain emergency medical and hospital treatment and prescriptions on presentation of a European Health Insurance Card

(EHIC). You may have to make a contribution towards costs. Make sure that the doctor or dentist you see is contracted to the public health insurance service, the CMU (most are), otherwise you will have to pay in full for private treatment and for any prescription medicines and the Czech insurance service will not reimburse you. See www.cmu.cz, email info@cmu.cz for advice on healthcare in the Czech Republic.

In parts of the country where few foreign visitors venture, medical staff may not be aware of the rights conferred on you by an EHIC. If you have difficulties contact the British Embassy in Prague.

Outbreaks of hepatitis A occur sporadically, particularly in the Prague and Central Bohemia areas, and immunisation is advised for long-stay visitors to rural areas and those who plan to travel outside tourist areas. Take particular care with food and water hygiene.

## Opening Hours

Banks – Mon-Fri 9am-5pm. Some foreign exchange bureaux's in Prague are open 24 hours.

Museums – Tue-Sun 10am-6pm; closed Monday

Post Offices – Mon-Fri 8am-6pm, some open on Saturday morning; main post office in Prague (Jindrisska Street 14) is open 2am-12am

Shops – Mon-Fri 9am-6pm, small shops usually close at lunchtime; Sat 9am-1pm; some food shops open on Sundays

## Safety and Security

There is a high incidence of petty theft, particularly in major tourist areas in Prague, and pickpocketing is common at popular tourist attractions. Particular care should be taken around the main railway station and on trains and trams, particularly routes to and from Prague Castle where pickpockets may operate.

Beware of fake plain-clothes police officers asking to see your foreign currency and passport. If approached, don't get out your passport. You can call 158 or 112 to check if they are genuine officers, or offer to go to the nearest police station or find a uniformed officer. No police officer has the right to check your money or its authenticity.

If your passport, wallet or other items are lost or stolen you should report the incident immediately

to the nearest police station and obtain a police report. A police station that is used to dealing with foreign travellers and is open 24 hours, is at Jungmannovo Námìstí 9, Praha 1, 24 hour telephone number 974 851 750; nearest metro: Müstek. Any theft of property must be reported in person to the police within 24 hours in order to obtain a crime number.

Seasonal flooding, usually in spring, occurs occasionally.

The Czech Republic shares with the rest of Europe an underlying threat from terrorism. Attacks could be indiscriminate and against civilian targets, including tourist attractions.

*British Embassy*
THUNOVSKÁ 14
118 00 PRAGUE 1
Tel: 257402111
http://ukinczechrepublic.fco.gov.uk/en/
Email: ukinczechrepublic@fco.gov.uk

*Irish Embassy*
VELVYSLANECTVÍ IRSKA
TRŽIŠTĚ 13, 118 00 PRAHA 1
Tel: 257011280
www.embassyofireland.cz
Email: pragueembassy@dfa.ie

## Documents

*Driving Licence*
The Czech Republic authorities require foreign drivers to carry a photocard driving licence. If you still have an old-style driving license you should update it to a photocard before you travel, or obtain an International Driving Permit to accompany your old-style licence. The minimum driving age is 18.

*Passport*
You must have a valid passport to enter Czech Republic. It is recommended that your passport is valid after your planned departure date in case of an unforeseen emergency, which may prevent you from leaving.

British nationals with passports in poor condition have been refused entry so you should ensure that your passport is in an acceptable state.

If you hold a British passport where your nationality is shown as anything other than British Citizen contact the Czech Embassy in London to determine whether you require a visa for entry.

*Vehicle(s)*

Carry your vehicle registration certificate (V5C), insurance details and MOT certificate (if applicable). If you are not the owner of the vehicle you are advised to carry a letter of authority from the owner permitting you to drive it.

## Money

The best place to exchange foreign currency is at banks, where commission rates are generally lower. In Prague some foreign exchange bureaux are open

24 hours. Scottish and Northern Irish bank notes will not be changed. Never exchange money with vendors on the street as notes are often counterfeit.

Credit cards are often accepted in tourist areas. Cash points are widely available but take care using them from a personal security point of view. Many retail outlets accept payment in euros.

## Motoring in the Czech Republic
## Accidents

If an accident causes injury or damage in excess of CZK 100,000 it must be reported to the police immediately. You should wait at the scene of the accident until the police arrive and then obtain a police report. If your vehicle is only slightly damaged it is still a good idea to report the accident to the police as they will issue a certificate which will facilitate the exportation of the vehicle.

## Alcohol

It is prohibited to drink alcohol before or whilst driving. No degree of alcohol is permitted in the blood and driving under the influence of alcohol is considered a criminal offence. This rule also applies to cyclists and horseriders. Frequent random breath-testing takes places and drivers are likely to be breathalysed after an accident, even a minor one.

## Breakdown Service

The motoring organisation ÚAMK provides roadside assistance and towing services 24 hours a day, telephone 1230 or 261104123. Emergency operators speak English. Breakdown assistance is provided for all motorists at a basic cost of approximately CZK 400 for 30 minutes + CZK 24 per kilometre travelled, payable in cash (2014). Extra charges apply at night, at weekends and for towing.

The vehicles used for road assistance are yellow Skodas, bearing the ÚAMK and/or ARC Transistance logos or the words 'Silnični Služba', together with the telephone number of the emergency centre. ÚMAK also uses the services of contracted companies who provide assistance and towing. These vehicles are also marked with the ÚAMK logo and the telephone number of the emergency centre.

## Essential Equipment

*First aid kit*

You are required to carry a basic first aid kit in your vehicle.

*Lights*

Dipped headlights are compulsory at all times, regardless of weather conditions. Bulbs are more likely to fail with constant use and it is recommended that you carry a complete set of spares.

Drivers are required to signal when leaving a roundabout and when overtaking cyclists.

*Reflective Jacket/Waistcoat*

If your vehicle has broken down, or in the event of an emergency, you must wear a reflective jacket or waistcoat on all roads, carriageways and motorways when getting out of your vehicle. Passengers who leave the vehicle, for example to assist with a repair, should also wear one. Jackets should, therefore, be kept inside your vehicle, and not in the boot. These must be of an EU standard EN471.

*Child Restraint System*

Children under 1.5m in height must use a suitable child restraint conforming to ECE standard 44/03 or 44/04. If in the front seat, the restraint must be rear facing with any airbag deactivated.

If there are no seatbelts fitted in the vehicle children over the age of 3 may travel in the rear of the vehicle without a child restraint.

*Warning Triangles*
You must carry a warning triangle, which must be placed at least 100m behind the vehicle on motorways and highways and 50m behind on other roads. Drivers must use Hazard Warning lights in conjunction with the warning triangle.

*Winter Driving*
Winter tyres are compulsory from November to March on all wheels of vehicles up to 3.5 tonnes when there is compacted snow or ice on the road. They are also compulsory whenever the temperature is lower than 4°C and there is a possibility of snow or ice on the road. On roads where there are winter tyres signs (see below) , the regulations apply even if the road surface is free of snow and ice, regardless of the weather.

**Sign for winter tyres (if shown with a line through indicates the end of restriction)**

Vehicles over 3,500 kg must be fitted with winter tyres on the driving wheels or carry snow chains. A full list of roads where this rule applies can be found on www.uamk.cz.

## Fuel

Some petrol stations on main roads, international routes and in main towns are open 24 hours a day. Most accept credit cards.

Diesel pumps are marked 'Nafta'. LPG is called 'Autoplyn' or 'Plyn' and is widely available at many filling stations. A list of these is available from the ÚAMK and a map is available from filling stations, or see www.lpg.cz and click on 'Čerpací stanice'.

## Parking

Vehicles may only be parked on the right of the road. In a one-way road, parking is also allowed on the left.

Continuous or broken yellow lines along the carriageway indicate parking prohibitions or restrictions. Visitors are advised to park only n officially controlled and guarded parking areas since cars belonging to tourists may be targeted by thieves. Illegally-parked vehicles may be clamped or towed away.

Prague city centre is divided into three parking zones: the orange and green zones are limited to two and six hours respectively between 8am and 6pm, and the blue zones are for residents only. Parking meters have been introduced in both Prague and Brno.

## Priority

At uncontrolled intersections which are not marked by a priority road sign, priority must be given to vehicles coming from the right. Where there are priority signs, these may easily be missed and care is therefore needed at junctions which, according to recent visitors, may have no road markings.

Trams turning right have priority over traffic moving alongside them on the right. Drivers must slow down and, if necessary, stop to allow buses and trams to merge with normal traffic at the end of a bus lane. On pedestrian crossings pedestrians have right of way, except if the vehicle approaching is a tram.

## Roads

Czech drivers are sometimes described as reckless (particularly when overtaking) and inconsiderate. Speeding is common and the law on the wearing of seat belts is sometimes ignored.

In general roads are in a good condition and well-signposted. Roads are being upgraded and many have new numbers. It is essential, therefore, to have an up-to-date road map or atlas.

Care is required where roads follow an old route through a village when there may be sudden bends in an otherwise straight road.

## Road Signs and Markings

Road signs and markings conform to international standards. Continuous white lines indicate no overtaking, but are often ignored.

The following road signs may be encountered:

| Czech | English Translation |
|-------|---------------------|
| Bez poplatků | Free of charge (some motorway or express roads) |
| Chod'te vlevo | Pedestrians must walk on the left |
| Dálkový provoz | By-pass |
| Nebezpečí smyku | Danger of skidding |
| Nemocnice | Hospital |
| Objízdka | Diversion |
| Pozor děti | Attention children |
| Průjezd zakázán | Closed to all vehicles |
| Rozsvit' světla | Lights needed |
| Úsek častých nehod | Accident blackspot |
| Zákaz zastavení | Stopping prohibited |

## Traffic Lights

A traffic light signal with a green arrow shows that drivers may turn in the direction indicated by the arrow. If a yellow light in the form of a walking figure accompanies the signal, this means that pedestrians may cross the road and drivers must give them right of way. A green light lit at the same time as a red or yellow light means that drivers may turn in the direction indicated by the arrow on condition that they give way to other traffic and to pedestrians.

An illuminated speed signal indicates the speed at which to travel in order to arrive at the next set of traffic lights when they are green.

## Speed Limits

| | Open Road (km/h) | Motorway (km/h) |
|---|---|---|
| Car Solo | 90 | 130 |
| Car towing caravan/trailer | 80 | 80 |
| Motorhome under 3500kg | 90 | 130 |
| Motorhome 3500-7500kg | 80 | 80 |

Motorhomes over 3,500 kg and cars towing a caravan or trailer are restricted to 80 km/h (50 mph) on motorways and main roads and lower limits in urban areas. Speed limits are strictly enforced and drivers exceeding them may be fined on the spot. Police with radar guns are much in evidence.

The use of radar detectors is prohibited and GPS systems which indicate the position of fixed speed cameras must have that function deactivated.

## Traffic Jams

The volume of traffic has increased considerably in recent years, particularly in and around Prague, including its ring road. Traffic jams may also occur on the E50/D1 (Prague-Mirošovice), the E48/R6 (Prague-Kladno), the E50/D5 (Plzeň-Rozvadov) and on the E50/D1 (Prague-Brno).

Traffic may be heavy at border crossings from Germany, Austria and Slovakia, particularly at weekends, resulting in extended waiting times. Petrol is cheaper than in Germany and you may well find queues at petrol stations near the border. Traffic information can be obtained from the ÚAMK Information Centre, tel 261104333, or from their website www.uamk.cz.

## Violation of Traffic Regulations

The police are authorised to impose and collect on-the-spot fines up to CZK 5,000 and to withdraw a driving licence in the case of a serious offence. An official receipt should be obtained. Efforts are under way to improve enforcement of traffic regulations and a points system has been introduced, together with stricter penalties.

## Motorways

There are approximately 1240 km of motorways and express roads. New sections of motorways are being built and on some motorways junctions are being renumbered to correspond with kilometre markers.

There is a good network of service areas with petrol stations, restaurants and shops, together with rest areas with picnic facilities. Emergency telephones connected to the motorway police are placed at 2 km intervals.

Emergency corridors are compulsory on motorways and dual carriageways. Drivers are required to create a precautionary emergency corridor at least 3 m wide to provide access for emergency vehicles whenever congestion occurs. Drivers in the left-hand lane must move as far over to the left as possible, and drivers in the central and right-hand lanes must move as far over to the right as possible.

*Motorway Tolls – Vignette*
To use motorways and express roads you must purchase a vignette (windscreen sticker) which must be displayed on the right hand side of your windscreen. This is available from post offices, ÚAMK branch offices, petrol stations and border posts where euros may be used in payment. If you have been to the Czech Republic before, make sure you remove your old sticker.

Charges in 2014 (subject to change) are CZK 1,500 for an annual vignette, CZK 440 for one month and CZK 310 for 10 consecutive days. For more information please visit www.motorway.cz/stickers.

*Vehicles over 3,500 kg*
Vehicles over 3,500 kg are subject to an electronic toll (mýto) and vehicle owners must register with the toll-collection service to obtain an on-board device called a Premid which must be fixed on your windscreen inside the vehicle and for which a deposit is required.

Tolls vary according to the emissions category and weight of the vehicle and distance driven. You must be able to show your vehicle documentation when obtaining the device but if your vehicle registration certificate (V5C) does not give an emissions category, then your vehicle will be classified in category Euro 2 for the purposes of this system. For more information please visit www.premid.cz before you travel.

## Touring

It is not necessary to tip in restaurants but if you have received very good service add 10% to the bill or round it up.

Smoking is not permitted in public places (public transport, places of entertainment, etc) and restaurant owners must provide an area for non-smokers.

A Prague Card offers entrance to over 50 tourist attractions and discounts on excursions and activities. It is available from tourist offices, main metro stations, some travel agents and hotels or order online from www.praguecard.com.

German is the most widely spoken foreign language and a basic understanding is particularly helpful in southern Bohemia. However, many young people speak English.

## Public Transport

Prague city centre is very congested, so park outside and use buses, trams or the metro which are efficient and cheap. There are guarded Park and Ride facilities at a number of metro stations around Prague.

Public transport tickets must be purchased before travelling and are available from newspaper stands ('Trafika'), tobacconists, convenience stores and from vending machines at stations. Tickets must be validated before the start of your journey at the yellow machines at metro stations or on board trams and buses, including before boarding the funicular tram at Petřín. Failure to do so may result in an on-the-spot fine.

Take extra care when in the vicinity of tram tracks and make sure you look both ways. Trams cannot stop quickly nor can they avoid you if you are on the track.

As a pedestrian you may be fined if you attempt to cross the road or cross tram tracks within 50 metres of a designated crossing point or traffic lights. You may also be fined if you cross at a pedestrian crossing if the green pedestrian light is not illuminated.

For reasons of safety and economy use major taxi companies wherever possible. If you telephone to order a taxi these companies are usually able to tell you in advance the type, number and colour of the car allocated to you. If you do pick up a taxi in the street always check the per kilometre price before getting in. The price list must be clearly displayed and the driver must provide a receipt if requested.

**BEROUN** *B2* (300m N Urban) *49.96910, 14.07563*
**Autocamping Na Hrázi, Závodí, 266 01 Beroun [tel/fax 311 623 294]** On NE bank of rv, 200m upstream fr bdge dir Krivoklát. Exit D5/E50 junc 14, turn R after uneven level x-ing opp factory, then in 100m L down ul Mostnikovska (turn easy to miss). Med, pt shd; htd wc; shwrs; el pnts (4A) inc (rev pol); lndtte; shop 500m; playgrnd; pool 1.5km; phone; quiet; ccard not acc; CKE/CCI. "Basic san facs; walking dist to rlwy stn to Prague; excel base for Prague & Karlstein; waymkd walks fr Beroun." CZK 180                    2009*

**BEROUN** *B2* (8km NE Rural) *50.0115, 14.1505* **Camping Valek, Chrustenice 155, 267 12 Chrustenice [tel/fax 311 672 147; info@campvalek.cz; www.campvalek.cz]** SW fr Prague on E50; take exit 10 twd Loděnice then N to Chrustenice. Foll sp. Lge, pt shd; wc; chem disp; mv service pnt; shwrs; el pnts (10A) CZK110; lndtte; sm shop & 4km; tradsmn; rest, snacks; bar; BBQ; playgrnd; pool; tennis; entmnt at w/end; TV; 10% statics; dogs CZK45; phone; Eng spkn; adv bkg; quiet; red long stay/CKE/CCI. "Vg location; money change on site; excel rest; metro to Prague at Zličín (secure car park adj)." 1 May-30 Sep. CZK 460                    2010*

⊞ **BESINY** *C1* (500m SW Rural) *49.29533, 13.32086*
**Eurocamp Běšiny, Běšiny 150, 339 01 Běšiny [tel/fax 376 375 0011; eurocamp@besiny.cz; www.eurocamp. besiny.cz]** Fr E53/rd 27 take rd 171 twd Sušice. Site just outside vill on L. Med, unshd; htd wc; chem disp; shwrs; el pnts (6A) inc; lndtte; shop 500m; tradsmn; rest; bar; BBQ; cooking facs; pool; paddling pool; tennis; games area; wifi; 50% statics; dogs; poss cr; adv bkg; quiet; ccard acc; CKE/CCI. "Pleasant setting; nrby vill drab." ◆ CZK 303                    2011*

**BOJKOVICE see Uherský Brod** *C4*

**BOSKOVICE** *C3* (8km NE) *49.50980, 16.77308* **Camping de Bongerd, Benešov U Boskovic C.P. 104. 67953 [tel 516 467 233; campingbenesov@hetnet.nl; www. camping-benesov.nl]** Foll sp fr 373 at E end of Benešov on L. Sm, med, sl, terr, pt shd, wc, chem disp, shwrs, playgrnd, pool, games area, Eng spkn, quiet, CKE/CCI, "V gd site run by helpful talkative Dutch couple. Ent narr unsuitable for lge o'fits." 1 May-20 Sept. CZK 300                    2012*

**BOSKOVICE** *C3* (15km SE Rural) *49.42296, 16.73585*
**Camping Relaxa, 679 13 Sloup [tel 516 435 291; info@ staraskola.cz; www.camprelaxa.cz/]** Fr Boskovice take dir Valchov; at Ludikov head S & onto rte 373 to Sloup. Site sp up track on R. Sm, pt sl, unshd; htd wc; chem disp; shwrs inc; el pnts (6A) inc (poss rev pol); lndry rm; shop, rest 1km; bar; pool 250m; dogs; bus 1km; poss cr; quiet; CKE/CCI. "Conv Moravski Kras karst caves; immed access walking/cycling trails." 1 May-20 Sep. CZK 400                    2012*

**BRECLAV** *D3* (5km NW Rural) *48.78549, 16.82663*
**Autocamp Apollo, Charvátská Nová Ves, 691 44 Břeclav [tel 519 340 414; info@atcapollo.cz; www.atcapollo.cz]** Fr Breclav take Lednice rd. Site is 3km S of Lednice vill. Lge, pt sl, pt shd; wc; chem disp; shwrs inc; el pnts CZK30; shops 3km; rest adj; lake sw 500m; dogs CZK30; bus; poss cr; noisy; CKE/CCI. "Fair sh stay; site in beautiful area; excel cycling & walking; Lednice Castle worth a visit; poss school parties." 1 May-30 Sep. CZK 280                    2009*

**BRNO** *C3* (10km W Rural) *49.20640, 16.41565* **Camping Alpa, Osvobození, 664 81 Ostrovačice [tel 602 715 674 or 728 066 609 (mob); sitar@campalpa.cz; www.campalpa. cz]** Leave E65/E50 exit 178 to Ostrovačice, site well sp. Med, hdg pitch, pt shd; wc; chem disp; shwrs inc; el pnts CZK60; shop, rest 200m; cooking facs; playgrnd; htd, covrd pool 500m; 10% statics; dogs free; phone; Eng spkn; adv bkg; quiet, some rd noise; ccard not acc; CKE/CCI. "If site unattended, site van yourself - owner calls eves; clean facs." 15 Apr-15 Oct. CZK 390                    2010*

**BRNO** *C3* (15km W Rural) *49.21182, 16.40745* **Camping Oáza, Náměstí Viléma Mrštíka 10, 66481 Ostrovačice [tel 606 457 448 / 546 427 552; info@kempoaza.cz; www. kempoaza.cz]** Leave E65/E50 Prague-Brno at junc 178 for Ostrovačice. At T-junc in vill turn L, site on R 100m. Sm, pt sl, pt shd; wc; chem disp (wc); shwrs inc; el pnts (10A) inc; lndtte; shop & 500m; rest 500m; sm pool; playgrnd; phone 500m; quiet; CKE/CCI. "Excel CL-type site, v clean facs; friendly, helpful lady owner; narr, uneven ent poss diff lge o'fits; poss unrel opening dates." 1 May-31 Oct. CZK 310                    2013*

**BRNO** *C3* (12km NW Rural) *49.27618, 16.4535* **Camping Hana, Dlouhá ul 135, 664 71 Veverská Bítyška [tel 549 420 331 or 607 905 801 (mob); camping.hana@ seznam.cz; www.campinghana.com]** On E50 Prague-Brno m'way, exit junc 178 at Ostrovačice & turn N on 386 for 10km to Veverská Bítyška. Site sp bef & in vill. Med, mkd pitch, pt shd; wc; chem disp; shwrs (10A) CZK10; el pnts (10A) CZK40; lndtte (inc dryer); shop; tradsmn; rest in vill 1km; snacks adj; BBQ; cooking facs; wifi; no statics; dogs CZK40; Eng spkn; quiet; twin-axles extra; CKE/CCI. "Peaceful, well-run site; family owned; clean, dated san facs; hot water runs out by evening if site full; gd security; interesting caves N of town; bus/tram/boat to Brno; excel rest in vill; flexible open-closing dates if reserved in adv; helpful, friendly owners; pleasant walk along rv to vill; gd NH; gd site; lg shwrs but communal chnge rm." 1 May-30 Sept. CZK 518                    2013*

**BUCHLOVICE see Uherské Hradiště** *C4*

**BUDISOV NAD BUDISOVKOU** *B4* (500m SE Urban) *49.79089, 17.63668* **Autokemp Budišov, Nábřeží č. 688, 747 87, Budišov nad Budišovkou [tel 556 305 283; autokemp@ budisov.cz; www.autokemp.budisov.cz]** Ent town fr E on rd 443; at T junc turn L sp; foll rd which will take you under rlwy; site on R in 100m. Sm, sl, unshd; wc; shwrs; el pnts (6A) CZK80; shop 500m; rest, snacks; bar; BBQ; playgrnd; pool; wifi; 50% statics; dogs CZK30 (valid vaccination card req); quiet; CKE/CCI. "Space for 20 vans only, with 4 elec pnts; mini-golf onsite & bike hire avail." 01 May-30 Sep. CZK 240                    2011*

**CERNA V POSUMAVI see Horni Plana** *C2*

**CESKA SKALICE see Náchod** *B3*

**CESKE BUDEJOVICE** *C2* (20km N Rural) *49.13701, 14.47413* **Camping Kostelec, Kostelec 8, 373 41 Hluboká nad Vltavou [tel 731 272 098; info@campingkostelec.nl; www. campingkostelec.nl]** Fr České Budějovice N twd Hluboká nad Vltavou, then foll unnumbered rd thro forest to Poněšice & Kostelec for approx 14km. Med, pt sl, terr, pt shd; wc; chem disp; shwrs inc; el pnts (10A) inc; gas; lndtte (inc dryer); shop & 14km; tradsmn; rest, snacks; BBQ (gas/elec); playgrnd; sm pool; fishing; games rm; wifi; entmnt; dogs free; bus adj; poss cr; Eng spkn; adv bkg; quiet; red low ssn; CKE/CCI. "Remote, peaceful site; gd walking; conv Prague, České Budějovice & Český Krumlov." ♦ 30 Apr-15 Sep. CZK 570          2011*

⊞ **CESKE BUDEJOVICE** *C2* (2km S Urban) *48.89633, 14.97818* **Autocamping-Motel Dlouhá Louka, Stromokva 8, 370 01 České Budějovice [tel 387 203 601; fax 387 203 595; motel@dlouhalouka.cz; www.dlouhalouka. cz]** On České Budějovice to Cesky. Krumlov/Linz rd. Site sp on R on o'skts of town. Fr town foll sp for C. Krumlov; after exit ring rd turn R in 300m at motel sp, 60m bef Stromovka site. Can take new ring rd round town. Site next to Interhotel Autocamping Stomovka - foll sp. Med, some hdstg, pt shd; htd wc; serviced pitches; chem disp; shwrs inc; el pnts (10A) inc (rev pol); lndtte (inc dryer); supmkt 1km; rest, snacks, bar high ssn; cooking facs; playgrnd; 10% statics; dogs CZK30; phone adj; poss cr; some Eng spkn; quiet; red low ssn; ccard not acc; CKE/CCI. "Clean facs; supmkt nr; easy walk to interesting town or gd bus service; grassy area rough & uneven - poss diff wet weather; conv Český Krumlov & area; gd cycle paths along rd; gd site; no facs for waste water disp; No curtain or doors on shwrs." 1 Apr-30 Oct. CZK 561          2013*

**CESKY KRUMLOV** *C2* (4km SW Rural) *48.81888, 14.26645* **Caravan Camp Petráškuv Dvur, Topolová 808, 383 01 Prachatice [tel 602 130 418; fax 388 314 125; milan. sebesta@seznam.cz; www.petraskuv-dvur.cz]** Fr Český Krumlov on rd 39 dir Černá for 3km. Take 2nd R after Motorest Krumlov at site sp, then 300m R again for site. Med, pt sl, pt shd; wc; chem disp; shwrs CZK10; el pnts (16A) CZK70; lndtte; shop 3km; rest; bar; games area; wifi; dogs CZK50; Eng spkn; quiet; red long stay; CKE/CCI. "Site yourself if recep clsd; vg san facs; gd & clean; pleasant walk to town, or cycle path." ♦ 1 May-30 Sep. CZK 320          2011*

⊞ **CHEB** *B1* (4km N Rural) *50.11773, 12.32713* **Hotel Jadran Autocamping, Jezerní 84/12, 351 01 Františkovy Lázně [tel/fax 354 542 412 or 603 845 789 (mob); info@ atcjadran.cz; www.atcjadran.cz]** Fr rte 6 turn N dir Libá. After 2km, immed N of new by-pass over bdge, fork L to vill; on o'skirts turn L & foll site/hotel sp, then R in 100m onto narr lane. In 700m turn R. Site in 400m, well sp. Lge, pt shd; wc; mv service pnt; shwrs inc; el pnts (16A) inc (rev pol & long cable req); shop 2km; rest; bar; lake sw; cycle hire; many statics; dogs CZK60; poss noisy w/end; red long stay; CKE/CCI. "Delightful site beside sm lake; many places of interest nr; walk thro woods to beautiful spa town; supmkt on rd to Cheb; run down facs clean, being rebuilt;' rec NH only." CZK 550          2012*

**CHEB** *B1* (5km SE Rural) *50.04931, 12.41326* **Camping am See Václav, Jesenická Přehrada, 350 02 Podhrad [tel/fax 354 435 653; info@kempvaclav.cz; www.kempvaclav.cz]** E fr Cheb on rte 606 sp Praha & Karlovy Vary. After 3km take minor rd to R (70m bef petrol stn) to Podhrad. At Podhrad under rlwy bdge take immed L fork & cont thro houses for 2km (rlwy on R). Site sp fr town on NW shore Lake Jesenice. Fr N on E48/6 exit junc 164 onto rd 606 & foll sp Cheb. Turn L at site sp 150m after petrol stn, foll site sp. Med, pt sl, terr, pt shd; wc; chem disp; shwrs inc; el pnts (16A) inc; lndtte; shop; rest, snacks; bar; playgrnd; beach & lake sw adj; fishing; watersports; games area; TV; wifi; dogs CZK60; poss cr; Eng spkn; adv bkg; quiet but some rlwy noise; red long stay/low ssn; CKE/CCI. "Friendly, improving, spacious, family-run site; well managed & scenic; choose own pitch; gd, clean, modern san facs; boats, pedalos for hire; scenic area; conv Mariánské Lázně, Karlovy Vary, hot springs at Soos." 25 Apr-25 Sep. CZK 735          2011*

⊞ **CHEB** *B1* (9km NW) *50.05258, 12.16572* **Camping Bříza, Bříza 19, 350 02 Briza, Cheb 2 [tel (0420) 773 570 196; campingbriza@gmail.com; www.camping bohemen. com]** Fr W on 303/E48 thro border take the 2nd exit to Leba, travel back down E48 to Bříza, foll sp to site. Sm, various size pitches; wc; green chem disp; shwrs; rest, bar; sw lake; Eng spkn; quiet. "Excel site, lakeside fishing, boat trips, cycling." CZK 500          2012*

**CHOMUTOV** *B1* (1.5km NE Rural) *50.28183, 13.25335* **Autokemp Kamencové Jezero, Tomáše ze Štitného, 430 01 [tel (420) 474 688 029; autocamping@ kamencovejezero.cz; www.kamencovejezero.cz]** Foll site sps in town, look for camp sp on L bet flats. Next sp on R bet more flats. Lge, sl, pt shd; htd wc; snacks; shwrs inc; shop adj; el pnts; beach; lake sw; poss cr; fairly quiet. Site on edge of town with gd bathing facs. Little Eng spkn. "Gd site based in N Czech Rep in v interesting area." 1 May-30 Sept. CZK 160          2012*

**CHRUSTENICE see Beroun** *B2*

**CHVALSINY see Český Krumlov** *C2*

⊞ **DECIN** *A2* (4km W) *50.80101, 14.33389* **Rosalka, Stará Oleška 35, Huntiřov, 405 02 Děčín II [tel 0420 412 513 484; info@rosalka.eu; www.rosalka.eu]** On the E442/13 fr Decin turn L at x-rds in vill of Huntirov, in dir of Stara Oleska, site on R within 2km. Sm, unshd; htd wc; el pnts (16A); chem disp; shwrs, lndtte; rest, bar; BBQ; wifi; dogs €1; bus adj; Eng spkn; adv bkg; quiet; CKE/CCI; ccard not acc; no smoking throughout site; Twin axle acc; "Excel site nr NP attraction; numerous walks & attractions, excel site; welcoming owners; immac facs." ♦ CZK 688          2013*

**DOLNI BREZANY see Praha** *B2*

**DOMAZLICE** *C1* (11km SE Rural) *49.40314, 13.05763*
**Autocamping Hájovna, Na Kobyle 209, 345 06 Kdyně**
**[tel 379 731 233; fax 379 731 595; automotoklub@kdyne.**
**cz; www.camphajovna.cz]** In Kdyně going twd Klatovy on
rd 22, turn L at end of town sq; then 1st R twd cobbled rd (for
300m); site on L in 2km. Med, some hdstg, pt sl, pt shd; wc;
shwrs CZK10; el pnts (10A) inc (poss rev pol); lndtte; shop;
rest adj; playgrnd; pool; TV; some statics; dogs CZK35; phone;
quiet; CKE/CCI. "Hořovský Týn & Domažlice interesting towns;
gd walking; friendly owner; ltd level pitches." 1 May-30 Sep.
CZK 250                                                    2009*

**FRANTISKOVY LAZNE see Cheb** *B1*

**FRYDEK MISTEK** *B4* (1km W Rural) *49.66459, 18.31161*
**Autokemp Olešná, Nad Přehradou, 738 02 Frýdek-Místek**
**[tel 558 434 806; fax 558 431 195; olesna@tsfm.cz; www.**
**katalog-kempu.cz/autokemp-olesna/]** Nr Tesco on S side of
E462/rte 48 on lakeside. Sm, sl, unshd; wc; chem disp; shwrs;
el pnts (10A); shop; rest; bar; cooking facs; fishing; dogs; Eng
spkn; quiet. "Unisex san facs; indiv shwr cabins." 1 May-
30 Sep.                                                    2009*

**FRYDLANT** *A2* (6km SE Urban) *50.90116, 15.14147*
**Rekreační a sportovní areál, Raspenava, U Stadionu 181,**
**46361 [tel 482 360 431; mesto.raspenava@raspenava.cz;**
**www.raspenava.cz]** Ent Raspenava fr E on rd 290, do not
cross rv; turn R round filling stn (dir Nove Mesto Pod Smrkem)
& immed L along R side of rv for approx 500m; site sp on the R.
Sm, pt shd; wc; shwrs inc; el pnts; shop 1km; rest; snacks; bar;
playgrnd; pool; games area; games rm; 50% statics; bus 500m;
train 500m; quiet; CKE/CCI. "In Jizerske Hory mountains area &
close to Polish border; Frydlant has chateau/castle & interesting
cent; sm campsite on a sports cent with pool & hall; only 8 elec
pnts." 1 May-30 Sep.   CZK 200                             2011*

**FRYMBURK** *D2* (800m S Rural) *48.65556, 14.17008*
**Camping Frymburk, Frymburk 20/55, 382 79 Frymburk**
**[tel 380 735 284; fax 380 735 283; info@campingfrymburk.**
**cz; www.campingfrymburk.cz]** Fr Černa on lake, take rd
163 dir Loucovice to site. Fr Český Krumlov take Rožmberk nad
Vltavou rd, turn R at Větřni on rd 162 sp Světlik. At Frymburk
turn L to Lipno then site 500m on R on lake shore. Med, v
sl, terr, pt shd; wc; chem disp; private san facs some pitches;
shwrs CZK15; el pnts (6A) inc; lndtte; shop & 600m; tradsmn
high ssn; rest 200m; snacks; playgrnd; lake sw; fishing;
boating; cycle & boat hire; entmnt & child entmnt high ssn;
wifi; TV rm; some statics; dogs CZK60; poss v cr; adv bkg;
quiet. "Beautiful lakeside site; modern, clean san facs; some
pitches poss tight for lge o'fits; gd rest nrby; helpful Dutch
owners; gd walking; adv bkg rec bef 1st Apr." 25 Apr-1 Oct.
CZK 640                                                    2012*

**HLUBOKA NAD VLTAVOU see České Budějovice** *C2*

**HLUBOKE MASUVKY see Znojmo** *C3*

**HORNI PLANA** *C2* (14km E Rural) *48.74617, 14.11945*
**Autocamp Olšina Lipno, Čkyně 212, 382 23 Černá v**
**Pošumaví [tel 608 029 982 (mob); info@campingolsina.**
**cz; www.campingolsina.cz]** Fr Horní Planá E to Černá v
Pošumaví on rd 39. Cont on this rd 1.5km N to site on lakeside.
Sm, pt shd; wc; chem disp; mv service pnt; shwrs CZK20; el
pnts (6A) CZK80; lndtte; tradsmn; rest, snacks; playgrnd; lake
sw adj; watersports; windsurfing 1.5km; boat & cycle hire;
wifi; 25% statics; dogs CZK60; quiet; CKE/CCI. "Vg; lovely
countryside; welcoming owner; lovely site." ♦ 2 Apr-31 Oct.
CZK 370                                                    2011*

**HRANICE** *C4* (1km SE Rural) *49.54194, 17.74111* **Autocamp**
**Hranice, Pod Hůrkou 2103, 753 01 Hranice [tel/fax**
**581 601 633; autocamphranice@seznam.cz]** Fr Olomouc
head E on rd 35/E442/E462 to Hranice. On app to town turn R
onto E442 sp Valašské-Meziříčí for 2km thro town, sp to site on
R. Site in 500m, turn R then L up steep hill & under rlwy bdge
(3.2m high) to site. Sm, pt sl, pt shd; wc; chem disp; shwrs; el
pnts (10A); lndtte; shops 500m; rest, snacks; bar; cooking facs;
playgrnd; htd pool 1.5km; dogs; poss cr; some rlwy noise; red
CKE/CCI. "Gd 24hr security; lovely site; conv for Helfstýn Castle
& Zbrašov Caves." 1 May-30 Sep.                            2011*

## "That's changed – Should I let The Club know?"

If you find something on site that's different from
the site entry, fill in a report and let us know. See
www.caravanclub.co.uk/europereport.

**JEDOVNICE** *C3* (1km SE Rural) *49.33350, 16.76299*
**Autokemp Olšovec, Havlíčkovo Náměstí 71, 679 06**
**Jedovnice [tel/fax 516 442 216; kemp@olsovec.cz; www.**
**olsovec.cz]** Fr S on rd 373 or fr N on rd 379, site sp on W side
of lake. Med, pt shd; htd wc; chem disp; mv service pnt; shwrs;
el pnts (10A) CZK50; lndtte; shop; tradsmn; rest, snacks; bar;
BBQ; playgrnd; lake sw adj; fishing; TV rm; 25% statics; dogs
CZK50; bus 1km; poss cr; noisy due fairgrnd adj; red CKE/CCI.
"Conv Moravský Kra karst show caves; gd walking/cycling;
lively site." 1 May-30 Sep.   CZK 320                      2010*

**JICIN** *B2* (7.7km NW Rural) *50.47236, 15.31161* **Chatový**
**tábor Jinolice, Jičín Jinolice, 50601 [tel (0420) 493 591 929;**
**jinol.kemp@seznam.cz; www.kempy-ceskyraj.cz]** Fr Jicin
foll rte 35 twrds Turnov. After 6km turn L to Jinolice and foll
sp thro vill. Lge, pt sl, htd wc; shwrs, rest, sw, dogs, TV, sport,
boating, cycling. "In cent of Bohemian Tourist Area." 1 May-
30 Sept. CZK 355                                           2012*

**JIHLAVA** *C3* (6km N Rural) *49.44655, 15.60185*
**Autocamping Pávov, Pávov 90, 586 01 Jihlava**
**[tel 567 210 295; fax 567 210 973; atcpavov@volny.cz]**
Fr D1/E50/E65 exit junc 112 sp Jihlava. Foll sp Pávov & site for
2km. Fr N/S on rte 38, nr a'bahn pick up sp for Pávov. Recep in
adj pension/rest. Med, mkd pitch, unshd; wc; shwrs CZK14; el
pnts (6A); lndtte; shop; rest, snacks; playgrnd; lake sw & beach
adj; fishing; tennis; 30% statics; dogs; m'way noise. "Grand
Hotel in Jihlava gd, friendly rest." 1 May-30 Sep.        2011*

**KARLOVY VARY** *B1* (7km NE Rural) *50.26450, 12.90013*
**Autokamp Sasanka, Sadov 7, 360 01 Sadov [tel/fax
353 590 130 or 603 202 051 (mob); campsadov@seznam.
cz]** Fr Karlovy Vary on rd 13/E442 to Bor, exit to Sadov, site sp.
Med, pt sl, pt shd; wc; chem disp; mv service pnt; shwrs inc; el
pnts (16A) CZK60 (poss rev pol); lndtte; shops 200m; tradsmn;
snacks; bar; playgrnd; wifi; dogs CZK50; poss cr; no adv bkg;
quiet but some rlwy noise; red long stay/CKE/CCI. "Lovely,
well-run site; friendly, helpful staff; modern, clean san facs;
picturesque vill of Loket a must; gd bus service fr vill to Karlovy
Vary; take care height restriction on app to Tesco fr m'way;
rec." 1 Apr-31 Oct.  CZK 380          2011*

**KARLOVY VARY** *B1* (3km S Rural) *50.19558, 12.86282*
**Camping Březová Háj, Staromlýnská 154, 362 15 Březová
[tel/fax 353 222 665; info@brezovy-haj.cz; www.
brezovy-haj.cz]** Fr Cheb-Karlovy Vary R6/E48, turn R on edge
of town onto rd 20/E49 S twd Plzeň. In 7km keep L where rd
goes across dam, site on R. Med, wc; shwrs; el pnts (6A) inc;
rest, bar at hotel adj; games area; adv bkg; quiet. "Ltd space
for c'vans; poss lge, noisy youth groups; some barrack-like
buildings; NH/sh stay only." 1 Apr-30 Sep.  CZK 300    2010*

**KDYNE see Domažlice** *C1*

**KLATOVY** *C1* (9km SW) *49.28177, 13.24003* **Camping
U dvou Orecha, Splz 13 Strážov na Sumava 34024
[tel (0420) 376 382 421; info@camping-tsjechie.nl; www.
camping-tsjechie.nl]** Fr Klatovy twrds Nýrsko on 191, after
Janovice turn L twrds Strážov dir Dešenice, after 3km turn L
twrds Splz -Hajey, site on L. Sm lge pitches, terr, pt shd, wc,
shwrs, lndry rm, shop 4km, bar, wifi, Eng spkn, adv bkg, quiet,
CKE/CCI 10% disc, "Delightful, v gd site, CL type with a warm
welcome fr friendly and helpful Dutch owners." 1 May-1 Oct.
CZK 395                              2012*

**KONSTANTINOVY LAZNE** *B1* (1km N Rural) *49.8869,
12.97168* **Camping La Rocca, 349 52 Konstantinovy Lázně
[tel/fax 374 625 287; laroccacamp@seznam.cz; www.
larocca.cz]** Fr rd 230 turn onto rd 201 to Konstantinovy Lázně
in 18km, site sp. Med, mkd pitch, pt shd; wc; chem disp; mv
service pnt; shwrs; el pnts (4-10A) CZK100; shop adj; rest;
bar; playgrnd; htd pool 100m; paddling pool; games area;
cycle hire; entmnt; 30% statics; dogs CZK50; adv bkg; quiet.
"Friendly, spacious site; conv for spa towns, Pilzen & Tepla
Monastery." ♦ 1 May-30 Sep.  CZK 320          2010*

**KUTNA HORA** *B2* (2.5km NE Urban) *49.96416, 15.30250*
**Autocamp Transit, Malín 35, 284 05 Kutná Hora
[tel 327 523 785; egidylada@seznam.cz; www.transit.zde.
cz]** Fr N on rd 38 fr Kolín, turn R immed after flyover onto rd
No 2 then turn L twrds town, In 1km turn L immed bef rlwy
bdge. Sm, pt shd; wc; chem disp (wc); shwrs inc; el pnts (16A);
shop 1.2km; rest 1km; cooking facs; wifi; TV; dogs free; phone;
bus 800m; Eng spkn;  CKE/CCI. "poss noise fr nrby rlwy; Sw
high ssn; family run; Int UNESCO World Heritage Town; Clean,
well-kept, CL-type site with garden area." 1 Apr-30 Sep.
CZK 390                              2013*

**KUTNA HORA** *B2* (500m NW Urban) *49.95444, 15.26003*
**Camping Santa Barbara, Česká 988, 284 01 Kutná
Hora [tel 327 512 051 or 602 361 330 (mob); info@
santabarbara.cz; www.santabarbara.cz]** Site off minor ring
rd to NW of town, turn uphill (NW) into Ceska Ulice just below
crest, site 200m on on L. Site sp is set back (not easy to see).
Sm, hdg/mkd pitch, pt shd; wc; chem disp; shwrs CZK25; el
pnts (6A) CZK80; lndtte; shop 200m; snacks; bar; htd pool nr;
dogs CZK50; Eng spkn; adv bkg; ccard acc; CKE/CCI. "Nice
shady site; welcoming owner; vg, modern san facs; 5 min
walk to historic cent of Kutná Hora with many attractions;
site locked at night, if locked on arr call for owner." ♦ 1 Apr-
31 Oct.  CZK 370                      2010*

⊞ **KYSELKA** *B1* (2km N Rural) *50.27038, 12.99445* **Camping
Na Špici, Radošov 87, 362 72 Kyselka [tel 353 941 152
or 777 145 710 (mob); fax 353 941 285; naspici@quick.
cz; http://naspici.sweb.cz/naspiciAN.htm]** Fr Karlovy Vary
N on rd 222 along Rv Ohře. Site nr hotel, S of Radošov. Or
take rd 13/E442 fr Karlovy Vary & turn R to Bor. Cont on rd &
cross wooden bdge (max height 3m) & turn R. Site in 500m
on R. Site behind Na Špici Hotel. Med, terr, pt shd; wc; chem
disp; shwrs inc; el pnts (10A); lndtte; shop 500m; rest, snacks;
bar; playgrnd; rv sw adj; rv sports; wifi; TV; 25% statics; dogs
CZK70; phone; bus; site poss clsd mid Jan to mid-Mar & Xmas,
rec phone in adv; Eng spkn; adv bkg; quiet; red long stay; CKE/
CCI. "Vg site in beautiful valley; rest gd value; gd walking & rv
sports; conv Karlovy Vary." ♦ ltd CZK 410          2011*

⊞ **LIBEREC** *A2* (2km NW Rural) *50.7387, 15.1079*
**Autocamp Liberec-Pavlovice, ul Letná, 460 01 Liberec
[tel/fax 485 123 468; info@autocamp-liberec.cz; www.
autocamp-liberec.cz]** App fr W on rte 13, take 1st exit sp
town cent. Foll to rndabt; sp ahead to Pavlovice (site sp after
rndabt). Site on L immed after footbdge. Med, pt shd; wc;
shwrs CZK10; el pnts (10A) CZK80; lndtte; shop 200m; rest;
snacks 200m; playgrnd; pool high ssn; tennis; karting track
adj; dogs CZK50; quiet; red CKE/CCI. "Conv Jizerské Hory
mountains." CZK 290                     2009*

**LIPNO NAD VLTAVOU** *D2* (1km W Rural) *48.63891,
14.20880* **Autocamp Lipno Modřín, 382 78 Lipno nad
Vltavou [tel 380 736 272; camp@lipnoservis.cz]** Site sp on
rd 163 on lakeside. Lge, mkd pitch, unshd; wc; chem disp;
shwrs CZK20; el pnts (6A); lndtte (inc dryer); shop 500m; rest,
snacks; bar; playgrnd; htd pool complex 500m; lake beach &
sw; boat & cycle hire 500m; tennis; games area; wifi; some
statics; dogs CZK41; adv bkg; quiet. "Pleasant, popular site."
♦ 1 Apr-30 Sep.  CZK 450 (CChq acc)          2009*

**LITOMERICE** *A2* (500m SE Urban) *50.53200, 14.13866*
**Autocamping Slavoj, Střelecký Ostrov, 412 01 Litoměřice
[tel 416 734 481; kemp.litomerice@post.cz; www.
autokempslavojlitomerice.w1.cz]** Fr N on rd 15 N of rv make
for bdge over Rv Elbe (Labe) sp Terezín; R down hill immed bef
bdge (cobbled rd), L under rlwy bdge, L again, site 300m on
R bef tennis courts at sports cent beside rv. Fr S on rd 15 turn
L immed after x-ing rv bdge to cobbled rd. Sm, pt shd; wc;
chem disp; shwrs inc; el pnts (8-16A) CZK75; supmkt 1.5km;
rest; pool; tennis; some statics; dogs CZK30; poss cr; Eng spkn;
quiet but rlwy noise; CKE/CCI. "Friendly, family-run site; gd,
modern san facs; vg rest; 10 mins walk town cent; Terezín
ghetto & preserved concentration camp." 1 May-30 Sep.
CZK 300                              2012*

**LITOMERICE** *A2* (3km S Rural) *50.50805, 14.14305*
**Autocamping Kréta, Kréta 322, 411 55 Terezín**
**[tel 416 782 473; camp@terezin-camp.cz; http://autocamp.
kreta.sweb.cz/]** Fr rd 8 (E55) Prague to Lovosice. In Terezín at
L-hand bend turn R at museum & ghetto sp. Take 4th turning
on R (with caution), foll camp sp at T-junc, turn L & immed R,
site on R. Sm, pt shd; wc; own san; shwrs inc; el pnts CZK80;
shop 200m; rest; playgrnd; watersports; some statics; dogs
CZK50; quiet; CKE/CCI. "Basic site & tired facs; no privacy in
unisex san facs; gd rest; ltd space for tourers; historic forts &
Jewish museum in town; fair NH/sh stay when not full." 1 Apr-
30 Sep. CZK 390                                          2010*

**LITOMYSL** *B3* (500m E Urban) *49.86776, 16.32440* **ATC**
**Primátor Camping, Strakovská, 570 01 Litomyšl [tel/
fax 461 612 238 or 732 148 723 (mob); primator@
camplitomysl.cz; www.camplitomysl.cz]** Fr S on E442/35
turn R at sp on edge of town, site on L in 500m. Sm, some
hdstg, sl, pt shd; wc; shwrs CZK10; el pnts (6A) CZK60; lndtte;
shop, rest in town; playgrnd; pool & sports facs 300m; TV;
80% statics; dogs CZK45; Eng spkn; quiet but some rd noise;
CKE/CCI. "Worth visit to Litomyšl - steep walk; easy (paid)
parking in town sq; vg san facs; v sloping site; friendly owner."
1 May-30 Sep. CZK 230                                    2010*

**MARIANSKE LAZNE** *B1* (1.5km SE Rural) *49.94419, 12.72797*
**Camping Stanowitz-Stanoviště, Stanoviště 9, 35301
Mariánské Lázně [tel/fax 354 624 673; info@stanowitz.
com; www.stanowitz.com]** Fr Cheb on rd 215, then rd 230
dir Karlovy Vary/Bečov. Site sp on R after passing under rlwy
bdge. Sm, pt sl, pt shd, some hdstg; htd wc; chem disp; mv
service pnt; shwrs inc; el pnts (16A) CZK90; lndtte; shop &
3km; tradsmn; rest, snacks; bar; BBQ; TV; dogs CZK30; phone;
Eng spkn; ccard not acc; CKE/CCI. "Excel CL-type site with gd
rest; conv spa towns & Teplá Monastery; mkd walks in woods;
helpful staff." ♦ 1 Apr-31 Oct. CZK 539                  2013*

**MARIANSKE LAZNE** *B1* (4km SW Rural) *49.95238, 12.66799*
**Autocamping Luxor, Plzeňská ul, 354 71 Velká Hleďsebe
[tel 354 623 504; autocamping.luxor@seznam.cz; www.
luxor.karlovarsko.com]** Site on E side of rd 21 fr Cheb-
Stříbro at S end of vill. Med, hdstg, pt sl, unshd; wc; chem
disp; shwrs inc; el pnts (10A) inc; shops 1km; rest, snacks; bar;
cooking facs; sm lake 100m; some statics; dogs free; poss cr;
quiet; ccard not acc; CKE/CCI. "Site in woodland clearing; gd,
modern san facs; gd walking; delightful town; grnd poss unrel
in wet." 1 May-30 Sep. CZK 360                           2009*

**MLADA BOLESLAV** *B2* (2km NW Urban) *50.44432, 14.91561*
**Autocamp Škoda, Pod Oborou, 293 06 Kosmonosy
[tel 326 724 134; fax 326 321 344; camp@skskoda.cz;
www.akskoda.cz]** Fr Mladá Boleslav head N to Kosmonosy.
Turn W off main rd in vill cent & foll site sp. Sm, pt sl, pt shd;
wc; shwrs; el pnts inc; lndry rm; rest; cooking facs; games
area; tennis; 70% statics; dogs; quiet. "Fair site; conv Škoda
museum." 1 May-30 Sep.                                   2010*

⊞ **NACHOD** *B3* (8km SW Rural) *50.39866, 16.06302*
**Autocamping Rozkoš, Masaryka 836, 552 03 Česká
Skalice [tel 491 451 112 or 491 451 108; fax 491 452 400;
atc@atcrozkos.com; www.atcrozkos.com]** On rd 33/E67
fr Náchod dir Hradec Králové, site sp 2km bef Česká Skalice
on lakeside. V lge, wc; sauna; baby facs; shwrs; el pnts (16A)
CZK60; lndtte; shop; rest, snacks; playgrnd; paddling pool; lake
sw & beach adj; watersports; windsurfing school; cycle hire;
entmnt; 10% statics; dogs CZK30; poss cr; no adv bkg; ccard
acc. "Lovely countryside." ♦ CZK 290                     2010*

**NEPOMUK** *C2* (1.2km W Rural) *49.48356, 13.53446*
**Autokemping Nový Rybník, Plzeňská 456, 335 01
Nepomuk [tel 371 591 336; kemp@novyrybnik.cz; www.
novyrybnik.cz]** Fr Plzeň foll E49/rd 20 twd Písek. At o'skirts of
Nepomuk turn R onto rd 191 & foll sp. Med, unshd; wc; chem
disp; shwrs; el pnts (10A) CZK70; lndtte; shop; tradsmn; rest,
snacks; playgrnd; lake sw; tennis; boating; cycle hire; wifi; poss
noisy; adv bkg; CKE/CCI. "Gd forest walks." 15 May-30 Sep.
CZK 220                                                  2010*

**NETOLICE** *C2* (1km S Rural) *49.03767, 14.18457*
**Autocamping Podroužek, Tyršova 226, 384 11 Netolice
[tel 338 324 315; post@autocamp-podrouzek.cz; www.
autocamp-podrouzek.cz]** Fr Netolice cent take rd 122 dir
Český Krumlov, site sp on R in 1km adj lake. Med, pt shd; wc;
shwrs CZK5; el pnts CZK85; shop; lndtte; rest; snacks high
ssn & in vill; playgrnd; lake sw; tennis; games area; internet;
some statics; dogs CZK25; quiet; CKE/CCI. "V quiet site;
poss problematic el pnts; modern san facs; conv Kratochvíle
& museum of animated film - delightful." 1 May-30 Oct.
CZK 220                                                  2010*

**NOVE STRASECI** *B2* (4.5km W Rural) *50.17221, 13.83951*
**Camping Bucek, Trtice 170, 271 01 Nové Strašecí
[tel 313 564 212; info@campingbucek.cz; www.
campingbucek.cz]** Site sp fr E48/rd 6, 2km S of Řevničov on
lakeside & approx 40km fr Prague. Med, mkd pitch, pt sl, pt
shd; wc; chem disp; mv service pnt; shwrs inc; el pnts (6A) inc;
lndtte (inc dryer); shop 2km; tradsmn; rest, snacks; bar; BBQ;
playgrnd; htd pool; sw & boating on adj lake; wifi; TV; dogs
CZK60; Eng spkn; no adv bkg; quiet. "Helpful owner; modern
san facs; gd walks in woods." 25 Apr-15 Sep. CZK 400  2009*

**NYRSKO see Klatovy** *C1*

**OPATOV** *C3* (2km S Rural) *49.20888, 15.65611* **Camping
Vidlák, Jur en Lilian Vinke, C.p. 322, 675 28 Opatov na
Morave [tel 736 678 687; campingvidlak@tiscali.cz; www.
campingvidlak.cz]** Fr Prague foll dir Brno (E50, E55, E65), take
exit 112 dir Jihlava; in Jihlava foll E59 dir Znojmo/
Vienna for approx 20km; in Dlouhá Brtnice turn L after first
few houses sp Opatov; in Opatov foll sp for camping. Fr S
(Vienna) drive via Znojmo on the E59 (rd no. 38) dir Jihlava
for approx 50km; turn R dir Třebíč (rd no. 23); in Předín turn
L sp Opatov; in Opatov foll sp for camping. Sm, pt sl, pt shd;
htd wc; chem disp; mv service point; shwrs inc; el pnts (10A)
CZK110; lndtte; BBQ; playgrnd; lake sw; games area; internet;
TV rm; dogs CZK30; bus 1.5km; Eng spkn; adv bkg; quiet; red
low ssn/CKE/CCI. "Well-kept site in picturesque location nr
lake; friendly, helpful Dutch owners; spacious pitches; first class
san facs; bread order during summer months; special m'van
pitches avail; forest walks; cycle rtes for mountain bikes; site is
exceptional." ♦ 15 Apr-15 Sep. CZK 415                  2011*

**ORLIK NAD VLTAVOU** *C2* (7km N Rural) *49.52458, 14.15563* Camping Velký Vír, Kožlí 23, 398 07 Oriik nad Vltavou [tel 382 275 192; fax 382 275 171; obec.kozli@seznam.cz; www.velkyvir.cz] Fr Milevsko head W on rte 19; turn N to Orlik vill; foll camp sp 7km W to Velký Vír. Med, pt sl, unshd; wc; chem disp; shwrs CZK10; el pnts (6A) CZK60; shop; rest, snacks; playgrnd; rv sw adj; tennis; some statics; dogs CZK60; poss v cr; adv bkg; quiet; CKE/CCI. "V quiet site by rv; few el pnts & may not work." 1 May-30 Sep. CZK 310 2009*

**OSECNA** *A2* (1km NE Rural) *50.70428, 14.93898* Camping 2000, Junův Důl 15, 463 52 Janův Důl [tel/fax 485 179 621; camping2000@wanadoo.nl; www.camping2000.com] Fr Liberec on rd 35/E442 turn W sp Ještěd then Osečná. Med, mkd pitch, unshd; chem disp; mv service pnt; wc; shwrs inc; el pnts (6A) inc; lndtte (inc dryer); tradsmn; rest, snacks; bar; cooking facs; playgrnd; pool; paddling pool; waterslide; tennis; horseriding; cycle hire; wifi; TV rm; 5% statics; dogs €2.50; Eng spkn; adv bkg; quiet. "Pleasant site; conv Ještěd Mountains." ♦ 15 Apr-15 Sep. CZK 710 2011*

**OSTROVACICE see Brno** *C3*

**PASOHLAVKY** *C3* (2km E Rural) *48.89914, 16.56738* Autocamp Merkur, 691 22 Pasohlávky [tel 519 427 714; fax 519 427 501; camp@pasohlavky.cz; www.pasohlavky. cz] S fr Brno on E461/rd 52. After Pohořelice take 5km on R, sp. V lge, hdg/mkd pitch, pt shd; wc; chem disp; mv service pnt; shwrs; el pnts inc; lndtte; shop; rest, snacks; bar; BBQ; cooking facs; playgrnd; lake sw & beach adj; watersports; tennis; games area; cycle hire; entmnt; TV rm; some statics; dogs CZK60; phone; poss cr; Eng spkn; adv bkg; ccard acc; CKE/CCI. "Vg; secure, pleasant site." ♦ 1 Apr-31 Oct. CZK 519 2013*

**PLANA** *B1* (5km SW Rural) *49.82043, 12.75463* Camping Karolina, Brod nad Tichou, 348 15 Planá [tel 777 296 990; camping@campingkarolina.com; www.campingkarolina. com] S fr Planá on rd 21 to Brod nad Tichou, site sp 1km SE of Brod. Narr app rd. Med, pt shd; wc; chem disp; shwrs; el pnts (10A) €2.50; lndtte; snacks; bar; BBQ; playgrnd; sm pool; games area; TV; some statics; adv bkg; quiet. "Pretty site; gd walking." 1 May-15 Oct. CZK 413 2009*

**PLUMLOV see Prostějov** *C3*

**PLZEN** *B1* (4km N Rural) *49.77747, 13.39047* Autocamping Ostende, 315 00 Plzeň-Malý Bolevec [tel/fax 377 520 194; atc-ostende@cbox.cz; www.cbox.cz/atc-ostende] Head N fr Plzeň on rd 27 dir Kaznějov; site sp R on o'skts Plzeň. Foll minor rd over rlwy bdge & sharp R bend to site on L. Beware earlier turning off rd 27 which leads under rlwy bdge with height restriction. Med, pt sl, shd; wc; shwrs CZK20; el pnts (10A) poss rev pol CZK140; gas; lndtte; shop; rest, snacks; playgrnd; lake sw; beach adj; entmnt; dogs CZK70; bus to town; poss cr; Eng spkn; no adv bkg; red CKE/CCI. "Pretty, well-run site; bar/rest area untidy - needs upgrade (2009); facs poss gd walk fr c'van area - no shwr curtains; gates not locked at night (2011); cycle rte & walk around lake, site is shabby needs upgrading and thorough cleaning (2011)." 1 May-30 Sep. CZK 719 2013*

**PODEBRADY** *B2* (1km E Rural) *50.13549, 15.13794* Autocamping Golf, U Nové Vodárny 428, 290 01 Poděbrady [tel 325 612 833; ATCAutokemp@gmail.com; www.kemp-golf.cz] Fr D11/E67 (Prague/Poděbrady) take Poděbrady exit N onto rd 32 for 3km; at junc with rte 11/E67 turn W sp Poděbrady (care needed, priority not obvious); site sp on L on E edge of town; site opp town name sp 400m down lane; app fr E if poss. Med, pt shd; wc (own san rec); chem disp; shwrs inc; el pnts (long cable req); snacks; bar; lake 2km; statics; quiet; CKE/CCI. "Conv for touring area; gd supmkt with parking in town; basic site." 1 May-31 Sep. 2010*

**PRAGUE (SEE PRAHA) see Praha** *B2*

## "I like to fill in the reports as I travel from site to site"

You'll find report forms at the back of this guide, or you can fill them in online at www.caravaclub.co.uk/europereport.

⊞ **PRAHA** *B2* (5km N Urban) *50.11715, 14.42775* Autocamp Trojská, Trojská 157/375, 171 00 Praha 7 [tel 233 542 945; autocamp-trojska@iol.cz; www.autocamp-trojska.cz] Fr Plzeň (E50/D5) head into cent to rte D8/E55 sp Treplice. Foll sp N to c sp. Immed after rv x-ing take exit under rte 8 & foll camp sp & site on L. Fr Dresden on E55/D8 foll sp to Centrum. Exit just N of Vltava Rv sp Troja & zoo. R (W) fr exit ramp twd Troja & zoo, turn L at traff lts, site on L in 400m. NB: There are 5 sites adj to each other with similar names. Sm, mkd pitch, shd; wc; chem disp (wc); shwrs inc; el pnts (16A) inc; lndtte; shop; rest, snacks; cooking facs; BBQ; TV; some statics; dogs CZK50; bus for city at ent; tram stop 500m; poss cr; adv bkg; quiet. "Friendly & welcoming; poss diff lge o'fits due trees on site; peaceful, clean & conv site; gd security." CZK 600 2010*

⊞ **PRAHA** *B2* (10km N Rural) *50.15277, 14.4506* Camping Triocamp, Ústecká ul, Dolní Chabry, 184 00 Praha 8 [tel/fax 283 850 793; triocamp.praha@telecom.cz; www. triocamp.cz] Fr N on D8/E55 take junc sp Zdiby, strt on at x-rds to rd 608 dir Praha. Camp sp in 2km on R just after city boundary. Med, pt sl, pt shd; wc; chem disp; mv service pnt; baby facs; shwrs inc; el pnts (6-10A) CZK90; gas; lndtte; shop; rest, snacks; bar; cooking facs; playgrnd; sw 4km; internet; 30% statics; dogs CZK80; phone; bus/tram to city (tickets fr recep); barrier clsd at 2200; poss cr; Eng spkn; rd noise & daytime aircraft noise; ccard acc; red CKE/CCI. "Well-organised, clean, family-run site; excel facs; rec arr early; free cherries in ssn; helpful staff." ♦ CZK 1111 2013*

**PRAHA** *B2* (2km E Urban) *50.53100, 14.28230* Camp Žižkov, Nad Ohradou 2667/17 Praha 3 [tel (0420) 607 296 507; camp.zizkov@gmail.com; www.praguecamping.com] Fr city cent pass main rl'wy stn head E on Husitska then Koněvova, site on L sp. Sm, mkd pitch, pt shd, htd wc; own san rec; mv service pnt, shwrs, el pnts (16A) lndtte, shop 500m, snacks, bar, playgrnd under 5's, games area; wifi; youth hostel, bus/tram adj, Eng spkn, No ccard acc, CKE/CCI."Close to City, cycle path, sports facs." 1 June-30 Sept. CZK 550-1000 2014*

**PRAHA** *B2* (10km E Urban) *50.11694, 14.42361* **Camping Sokol, Národnich Hrdinů 290, 190 12 Dolní Počernice [tel/fax 281 931 112; info@campingsokol.cz; www. campingsokol.cz]** Site sp 400m off main rd 12 to Koíín in vill of Dolní Počernice. Med, pt shd; wc; shwrs inc; el pnts (16A) €4; lndtte (inc dryer); shop; rest, snacks; bar; cooking facs; playgrnd; paddling pool; cycle hire; wifi; some statics; dogs €2; poss cr; Eng spkn; adv bkg; some rd noise; red long stay; ccard acc; CKE/CCI. "Friendly owners; gd, clean facs; excel meals; 1 hr to Prague by public transport." ♦ 1 Apr-31 Oct. CZK 688                                              2010*

**PRAHA** *B2* (18km E Urban) *50.09833, 14.68472* **Camping Praha Klánovice, V Jehličině 391, 190 14 Klánovice [tel 774 553 542; info@campingpraha.cz; www. campingpraha.cz]** Fr Prague ring rd exit at Běchovice onto rd 12 dir Kolin. At Újezd nad Lesy turn L at x-rds twd Klánovice & in approx 3km turn R into Šlechtitelská, site on R in approx 1km. Med, mkd pitch, pt shd; wc; chem disp; mv service pnt; sauna; shwrs inc; el pnts (16A) €4; gas; lndtte (inc dryer); shop; tradsmn; supmkt 3km; rest, snacks; bar; BBQ; playgrnd; pool; paddling pool; cycle hire; games area; games rm; cycle hire; wifi; TV; 50% statics; dogs €2; phone; bus to Prague; poss cr; Eng spkn; adv bkg; quiet. "New site 2010; gd public transport to city; excel site, lge woods for walks and cycling." ♦ 9 Apr-22 Oct.  CZK 688 (CChq acc)                   2012*

**PRAHA** *B2* (10km SE Urban) *50.01271, 14.51183* **Camp Prager, V Ladech 3, Šeberov, 149 00 Praha 4 [tel 244 912 854, 244 911 490 or 603 418 391 (mob); fax 244 912 854; petrgali@login.cz; www. pensioncampprague.com]** Fr W on D1/E50 fr Prague exit 2 sp Praha-Šeberov, turn L at rndabt. Fr SE fr Brno take exit 2A. After traff lts take outside lane & at go strt over at next rndabt & in 700m turn R into V. Ladech. Site L in 100m. Ring bell if gate shut. Site well sp. Sm, pt shd; wc; chem disp; shwrs inc; el pnts (10A) CZK80; shops 500m; games area; games rm; wifi; dog CZK30; bus 100m; metro 1km; Eng spkn; adv bkg; quiet; CKE/CCI. "Gd, secure site in orchard; facs impeccable; helpful & friendly owner; phone ahead to check if open low ssn; flexible opening dates with adv notice; guarded park & ride facs adj Opatov metro stn; bus/metro tickets fr recep; lge o'fits not acc as diff access; excel security; cash payment only." 1 May-30 Sep.  CZK 400                              2012*

> ## "We must tell The Club about that great site we found"
>
> Get your site reports in by mid-August and we'll do our best to get your updates into the next edition.

**PRAHA** *B2* (7km S Rural) *50.03254, 14.40421* **Intercamp Kotva Braník, ul Ledáren 55, 147 00 Praha 4 [tel 244 461 712; fax 244 466 110; kotva@kotvacamp.cz; www.kotvacamp.cz]** Site well sp fr main rd fr Plzeň & fr S ring rd. Med, unshd; wc; shwrs inc; el pnts (10A) inc; lndtte; shop & 500m; snacks; cooking facs; boating; fishing; tennis; games area; wifi; some statics; poss cr; Eng spkn; adv bkg; some rlwy/rd/airport noise; no ccard acc; red CKE/CCI. "Conv Prague - buy tram tickets fr recep; tents & vans pitched v close; 26 steps to wc; site guarded." 1 Apr-31 Oct.         2009*

**PRAHA** *B2* (12km S Rural) *49.95155, 14.47455* **Camping Oase, Zlatníky 47, 252 41 Dolní Břežany [tel 241 932 044; info@campingoase.cz; www.campingoase.cz]** Fr Prague on D1 (Prague-Brno). Exit 12 (Jesenice). Head twd Jesenice on rd 101. In vill turn R then immed L at rndabt dir Zlatníky. At Zlatníky rndabt turn L dir Libeň, site in 500m. Beware 'sleeping policemen' on final app. Med,hdg pitch, pt shd; htd wc; chem disp; mv service pnt; fam bthrm; serviced pitches; sauna; shwrs inc; el pnts (6A) inc (poss rev pol); gas; lndtte (inc dryer); shop; tradsmn; rest, snacks; bar; cooking facs; BBQ; playgrnd; 2 pools (1 htd covrd); paddling pool; fishing lake 1km; horseriding; cycle hire; games area; games rm; wifi; entmnt; sat TV rm; dogs CZK50; no c'vans/m'vans over 12m high ssn; phone; bus, tram to city; metro 10km; Eng spkn; adv bkg; quiet; ccard acc (discount for cash); red low ssn/snr citizens. "Lovely site; v helpful owners; excel, clean san facs; vg pool; swipe card for barrier & all chargeable amenities; well-guarded; bus/train/metro tickets fr recep; rec use metro Park & Ride to city; lge well maintained pitches; excel security." ♦ 25 Apr-14 Sep. CZK 750 SBS - X07                                       2013*

**PRAHA** *B2* (15km S Rural) *49.93277, 14.37294* **Camp Matyáš, U Elektrárny, 252 46 Vrané nad Vltavou [tel 257 761 228 / 777 016073 (mob); fax 257 761 154; campmatyas@centrum.cz; www.camp-matyas.com]** Exit D1 junc 11 onto rd 101 to Dolní Břežany. Turn S thro Ohrobec & foll sp Vrané nad Vltavou, site sp on rvside. Or S fr Prague on rd 4/102, cross Rv Vltava at Zbraslav to Dolní Břežany, then as above. Med, pt shd; wc; chem disp; mv service pnt; shwrs inc; el pnts (10A) CZK120; lndtte; shop & 800m; tradsmn; rest, snacks; bar; cooking facs; playgrnd; paddling pool; rv sw & fishing adj; wifi; dogs free; bus, train to city; Eng spkn; adv bkg; quiet; red low ssn; CKE/CCI. "In lovely location; friendly owners; train & tram service to Prague (1 hr); boat trips on Rv Vltava." 20 Apr-30 Sep.  CZK 550           2013*

⊞ **PRAHA** *B2* (2km SW Urban) *50.05194, 14.40222* **Praha Yacht Club Caravan Park, Cisařská Louka 599, Smíchov, 150 00 Praha 5 [tel 257 318 387 or 060 2343701 (mob); fax 257 318 387; caravanpark.cl@gmail.com; www.volny.cz/convoy]** Fr E50 access only poss fr S by travelling N on W side of rv. After complex junc (care needed), turn sharp R bef Shell petrol stn to Cisařská Island, foll rd to end. Nr C'van Camping CSK. Diff app fr N due no L turns on Strakonická. Sm, pt shd; wc; chem disp; shwrs CZK20; el pnts (16A) CZK95.; shops 1.5km across rv; pool 1km; tennis 100m; dogs CZK57; poss v cr; adv bkg; quiet; ccard acc. "Boats for hire; launch trips on rv; 1 min to ferry & metro to Prague; water taxi fr Prague, book at site recep; helpful staff; friendly, secure site; v basic san facs; excel location; views of city; milk etc avail fr Agip petrol stn on Strakonická." CZK 484                              2013*

⊞ **PRAHA** *B2* (5km SW Rural) *50.01984, 14.35579* **Camping Auto Servis Slivenic, Ke Smíchovu 25, 154 00 Slivenec-Praha 5 [tel/fax 251 817 442; info@camp-autoservis.cz; www.camp-autoservis.cz]** App Prague fr E on E50, turn R into Slivenec, Turn R in vill after pond immed bef shop. Sm, sl, shd; htd wc; chem disp; shwrs; el pnts (10A) inc; lndtte; rest; tram to city; quiet. "Site in garden - recep at back of house; facs old/sparse but clean; sm pitches; conv city cent." CZK 380                                            2012*

**CZECH REPUBLIC**

**PRAHA** *B2* (10km SW Rural) *50.04388, 14.28416* **Camp Drusus, Třebonice 4, 155 00 Praha 5 [tel/fax 235 514 391; drusus@drusus.com; www.drusus.com]** Fr Plzeň take E50/D5 to exit 1/23 Třebonice, then E50 dir Brno. Fr Brno exit E50/D5 at junc 19 sp Řeporyje, site in 2km, sp. Sm, sl, unshd; wc; chem disp; mv service pnt; shwrs CZK20; el pnts (10A) CZK90; gas; lndtte (inc dryer); shop 1.5km; rest; bar; playgrnd; internet; TV; dogs free; 10% statics; bus; Eng spkn; adv bkg; ccard acc; red low ssn/CKE/CCI. "Reg bus service to Prague nrby - tickets fr site; owner v helpful." 1 Apr-15 Oct. CZK 540    2011*

**PRAHA** *B2* (3km W Rural) *50.09890, 14.33569* **Camping Džbán, Nad Lávkou 5, Vokovice, 160 05 Praha 6 [tel 235 359 006; fax 235 351 365; info@campdzban. eu; www.campdzban.eu]** Exit 28 off ring rd onto rd 7 Chomutov-Prague; site approx 4km after airport twd Prague; at traff lts on brow of hill just bef Esso stn on L turn L; take 2nd L & strt on for 600m; site adj go-kart racing. Lge, pt sl, unshd; wc; chem disp; shwrs inc; el pnts (10A) CZK90; lndtte; shop & 2km; rest, snacks; bar; pool & lake 500m; tennis; games area; wifi; dogs CZK60; tram 200m; poss cr; some Eng spkn; ccard acc; red CKE/CCI. "Tram direct to Prague (Republic Sq) 25 mins, tickets at bureau; gd security; long way bet shwrs & wcs; san facs old but clean; communal male shwrs; narr pitches." 1 May-30 Sep. CZK 550    2010*

⊞ **PRAHA** *B2* (5km NW Urban) *50.11694, 14.42361* **Camping Sokol Trója, Trojská 171a, 171 00 Praha 7 [tel/fax 233 542 908 or 283 850 486; tj.sokol.troja @ quick.cz / info@camp-sokol-troja.cz; www.camp-sokol-troja.cz]** Fr Pilsen (E50/D5) head into cent to rte D8/E55 sp Treplice. Foll N to Trója sp. Immed after rv x-ing take exit under rte 8 & foll camp sp & site on L 100m past Autocamp Trojská. Fr Dresden on E55/D8 foll sp to Centrum to Trója exit on R, find camping sp. NB: There are 5 sites adj to each other with similar names. Best app fr Treplice. Med, some hdstg, pt shd; wc; shwrs inc; el pnts (10A) CZK100; lndry service; shop high ssn; rest, snacks; bar; internet; dogs CZK50; poss cr; ccard acc; noise fr bar; red CKE/CCI. "Easy tram transport to city; Trója Palace & zoo 1km; v helpful owner; bar & rest gd value." CZK 590    2013*

**PROSTEJOV** *C3* (8km W Rural) *49.46265, 17.01391* **Autocamping Žralok, Rudé Armády 302, 798 03 Plumlov [tel/fax 582 393 224 / 775 568 378 (mob); atczralok@ seznam.cz; www.camp-zralok.cz]** Fr cent of Prostějov foll sp to Boskovice & thro Čechovice & Plumlov, site clearly sp. Down steep narr lane, cross dam & R to site. Med, sl, unshd; wc; shwrs inc; el pnts (10A) CZK90; long cable req; shop; rest, snacks; paddling pool; 20% statics; dogs CZK35.; quiet; CKE/CCI. "O'looking lake; facs basic but clean; Facs need upgrading; ccards not acc." 1 May-30 Sep. CZK 340    2013*

**PROTIVIN** *C2* (400m S Rural) *49.19038, 14.21723* **Camping Blanice, Celčického 889, 398 11 Protivín [tel 721 589 125; info@campingblanice.nl; www.campingblanice.nl]** Fr E49 take 1st exit Protivin going N or 2nd exit going S. Site sp bef town cent. Sm, mkd pitch, pt shd; wc; chem disp; mv service pnt; shwrs inc; el pnts (8-16A) €3-4.50; lndtte (inc dryer); shop 500m; rest, snacks; bar; playgrnd; wifi; 5% statics; dogs free; train 1km; Eng spkn; adv bkg; quiet but some rlwy noise. "Friendly, peaceful Dutch-run site; easy walk thro fields beside rv into town." 1 Apr-1 Nov. CZK 537    2010*

⊞ **REJSTEJN** *C1* (500m NW Rural) *49.14222, 13.51344* Camping Klášterský Mlýn, Klášterský Mlýn 9, 341 92 Rejštejn [tel 376 582 833; info@klasterskymlyn.nl; www. klasterskymlyn.nl] S fr Susice on rd 169 dir Kašperské Hory for 12 km. In Kašperské Hory turn L onto rd 145 to Rejštejn. In Rejštejn take 1st R, cross bdge & foll site sp. Med, mkd pitch, pt shd; htd wc; chem disp; baby facs; fam bthrm; sauna; shwrs; el pnts (6-16A) CZK100; lndtte; shop; rest, snacks; bar; cooking facs; playgrnd; tennis; games area; cycle hire; fitness rm; wifi; some statics; dogs CZK50; quiet. "Friendly, family-run, renovated site; gd, modern facs; gd touring base." CZK 300 (CChq acc)    2009*

**ROZNOV POD RADHOSTEM** *C4* (1km E Rural) *49.46654, 18.16376* Camping Rožnov, Radhoštská 940, 756 61 Rožnov pod Radhoštěm [tel 571 648 001; fax 571 620 513; info@camproznov.cz; www.camproznov.cz] On rd 35/E442; on E o'skts of Rožnov on N of rd 200m past ent to Camping Sport, take L fork opp Benzina petrol stn (site sp obscured by lamp post. Med, pt shd; htd wc; chem disp; shwrs inc; el pnts (16A) inc; lndtte (inc dryer); shop; tradsmn; rest 300m; snacks; playgrnd; htd pool; tennis; 60% statics; phone; some Eng spkn; no adv bkg; quiet; ccard acc; red CKE/CCI. "Welcoming; gd cooking & washing facs; pitches v close together, but annexe has more space (extra charge); basic, worn san facs; nr open-air museum (clsd Mon); gd walking cent; cycle to town thro park." 1 Apr-15 Oct. CZK 453 (CChq acc)    2011*

**SADOV see Karlovy Vary** *B1*

**SLOUP see Boskovice** *C3*

**"I need an on-site restaurant"**

We do our best to make sure site information is correct, but it is always best to check any must-have facilities are still available or will be open during your visit.

**SOBESLAV** *C2* (3km S Rural) *49.22988, 14.72062* **Autocamp Karvánky, Jiráskova 407/2, 392 01 Soběslav [tel 381 521 003; fax 381 522 011; karvanky@post.cz; www.karvanky.cz]** Site well sp on rte 3/E55. Lge, pt sl, pt shd; wc; shwrs CZK25; el pnts (10A) CZK50; snacks; playgrnd; lake sw; cycle hire; TV; 10% statics; dogs CZK60; phone; rd noise; ccard acc. "Conv NH." 15 May-27 Sep. CZK 170 2009*

**STERNBERK** *B3* (2km N Rural) *49.74800, 17.30641* **Autocamping Šternberk, Dolní Žleb, 785 01 Šternberk [tel 585 011 300; info@campsternberk.cz; www. campsternberk.cz]** Fr Olomouc take rte 46 to Šternberk. At Šternberk go thro town cent & foll sp Dalov, site just bef vill of Dolní Žleb. Or circumnavigate to W on rds 444 & 445, site sp. Med, pt shd; wc; chem disp; shwrs inc; el pnts (10A) CZK60 (poss rev pol); lndtte; shop & 500m; rest 500m; snacks; bar; cooking facs; playgrnd; lake 1km; TV; phone; 30% statics; dogs CZK30; poss cr; adv bkg; quiet; red CKE/CCI. "Gd, clean facs even when full; helpful staff." 15 May-15 Sep. CZK 190    2010*

**STRIBRO** *B1* (16km E Rural) **Transkemp Hracholusky, 330 23 Hracholusky [tel 420 337 914 113 or 420 728 470 650; info@hracholusky.com; www.hracholusky.com]** Fr Ulice bet Stribro & Plzen on rte 5/E50 turn N, sp Plesnice, & foll vill sp to site in 4km at E end of lake. Med, pt sl, unshd; wc; chem disp; shwrs CZK10; el pnts inc (adaptor for hire); rest, snacks; shop 3km; lndtte; shgl beach adj; lake sw; boating; waterskiing; 25% statics; adv bkg; Eng spkn. "Lake steamer trips; gd sh stay/NH; gd location on lakeside; fair site; facs basic." 1 May-31 Dec. CZK 270                    2014*

**STRMILOV** *C2* (1km S Rural) *49.14956, 15.20890* **Autokemp Komorník, 378 53 Strmilov [tel 384 392 468; recepce@ autokempkomornik.cz; www.autokempkomornik.cz]** Sp fr rd 23 at Strmilov. Lge, pt sl, pt shd; wc; chem disp (wc); shwrs CZK20; el pnts (10A) CZK60 (long lead rec); shop; rest, snacks; bar; playgrnd; lake & sand beach adj; 20% statics; quiet; CKE/CCI. "V pleasant setting by lake; clean, modern san facs; gd rest & bar; conv Telč & Slavonice historic towns." ♦ ltd 1 Jun-15 Sep. CZK 300    2009*

⊞ **TABOR** *C2* (5km E Rural) *49.40985, 14.73157* **Autocamping & Hotel Knížecí Rybník, Měšice 399, 39156 Tábor [tel 381 252 546; knizecak@seznam.cz; www. knizecirybnik.cz]** On N side of rd 19 fr Tábor to Jihlava, in woods by lake adj hotel. Lge, hdg/mkd pitch, pt shd; wc; shwrs CZK20; el pnts (6-10A) inc; lndtte; shop & 3km; rest, snacks; bar; lake sw & beach adj; fishing; tennis; some statics; dogs; poss cr; rd noise; ccard acc; CKE/CCI. "Pleasant, lakeside site; modern san facs." CZK 280                    2010*

⊞ **TANVALD** *A2* (2km W Rural) *50.74205, 15.28269* **Camping Tanvaldská Kotlina (Tanvald Hollow), Pod Špičákem 650, 46841 Tanvald [tel 483 311 928; kotlina@ tanvald.cz; www.tanvald.cz]** Fr S on rte 10, in cent Tanvald at rndabt turn foll sp Desnou & Harrachov. In 500m take L fork under rlwy bdge, then immed turn L & foll rd past hospital. Turn R bef tennis courts, site in 600m. Sm, pt shd; wc; chem disp; mv service pnt; shwrs; el pnts CZK30 + metered; lndtte; rest; BBQ; cooking facs; playgrnd; pool in town; games area; entmnt; wifi; dogs CZK20; quiet - occasional motor cycle trials nrby. "Excel." CZK 230                    2012*

⊞ **TELC** *C2* (10km NW Rural) *49.22785, 15.38442* **Camp Velkopařezitý, Řásná 10, 58856 Mrákotín [tel 567 379 449; fax 567 243 719; campvelkoparezity@tiscali.cz; www. campvelkoparezity.cz]** Exit Telč on Jihlava rd; turn L in 300m (sp) & foll sp to site beyond Rásná. Well sp fr Telč. Steep site ent. Sm, pt sl, pt shd; wc; chem disp; shwrs; el pnts CZK100; rest; shop; beach 1km; some statics; dogs CZK30; poss cr. "Friendly atmosphere; poor san facs; gd walking & cycling; Telč wonderful World Heritage site." CZK 270           2010*

**TEREZIN see Litoměřice** *A2*

**TREBIC** *C3* (1.5km W Urban) *49.21671, 15.85904* **Autocamping Třebíč-Poušov, Poušov 849, 67401 Třebíč [tel 568 850 641]** Foll sp for Telč fr town cent. After 3km turn R after 2nd rlwy x-ing, site at bottom of hill. Sm, pt shd; own san rec; shwrs CZK20; el pnts inc; lndry rm; shop 1km; snacks; bar; cooking facs; some statics; dogs; adv bkg; quiet, some rd noise; CKE/CCI. "Excel san facs; cycle rte to town along rv." 1 Jun-30 Sep. CZK 300                    2009*

**TREBON** *C2* (5km SE Rural) *48.96432, 14.93705* **Camping Sever, 37804 Chlum u Třeboně [tel/fax 384 797 189; post@campsever.cz; www.campsever.cz]** S fr Třeboň on E49 dir Vienna, turn L in 5km to Chlum u Třeboně. Site sp thro vill on N side of lake. Med, pt sl, pt shd; wc; chem disp; mv service pnt; shwrs CZK10; el pnts (6A) CZK60; lndtte; shop 300m; tradsmn; rest 300m; snacks; bar; playgrnd; lake sw; fishing; canoeing; games area; cycle hire; golf 15km; wifi; 20% statics; dogs CZK20; phone; bus; adv bkg; quiet; ccard acc; red CKE/CCI. "Lovely situation; excel value site; basic san facs; gd touring base; excel cycling, walking." 9 Apr-31 Oct. CZK 280                    2010*

⊞ **TURNOV** *A2* (5km SE Rural) *50.5580, 15.1867* **Autocamping Sedmihorky, Sedmihorky 72, 51101 Turnov [tel 481 389 162; fax 481 389 160; camp@ campsedmihorky.cz; www.campsedmihorky.cz]** Fr rte 35/ E442 fr Turnov. Turn SW over rlwy x-ing at camping sp S of Sedmihorky. 300m along ave take 1st R. Lge, pt sl, pt shd; wc; chem disp; shwrs CZK10; el pnts (16A) CZK60; lndtte; shop; rest, snacks; bar; playgrnd; lake sw; cycle hire; dogs CZK50; phone; poss cr; Eng spkn; quiet; ccard acc; CKE/CCI. "V beautiful site in National Park, sometimes called Bohemian Paradise; v busy site high ssn; dep bef 1000 otherwise charge for extra day; excel site."♦ 1 Apr-31 Oct. CZK 410     2012*

**UHERSKE HRADISTE** *C4* (16.5km SSE Rural) *48.95000, 17.55000* **Camping Babě hora, Hluk 68725 [tel  581 180; babihora@quick.cz; www.camping-babihora.cz]** Site is 4.5km SE of Hluk on R of minor rd to Boršice u Blantnice. Sm, open grass no mkd pitches, pt sl, unshd; wc; chem disp; shwrs; 50% statics; playgrnd; Eng spkn; quiet. 15 May-31 Aug. CZK 210                    2012*

**UHERSKE HRADISTE** *C4* (10km NW Rural) *49.1186, 17.38038* **Autocamping Velehrad, Velehrad 31, 68706 Velehrad [tel 572 571 183]** Foll rd 428 to Velehrad, site 1km N of vill. Sm, pt sl, pt shd; wc; shwrs inc; el pnts (10A) CZK30; lndtte; shop 1km; rest; bar; playgrnd; tennis; dogs CZK10; adv bkg; CKE/CCI. "Well sp cycle & hiking rtes; Velehrad interesting vill; NH only." 1 May-30 Sep. CZK 200                    2009*

**UHERSKY BROD** *C4* (10km E Urban) *49.04034, 17.79993* **Eurocamping Bojkovice, Štefánikova, 68771 Bojkovice [tel/fax 572 641 717; info@eurocamping.cz; www. eurocamping.cz]** Off E50 at Uherský Brod turn onto rd 495. Find rlwy stn on Bojkovice on rd 495 at SW end of town. Cross rlwy at NE (town) end of stn & foll sp round L & R turns to site. Med, pt sl, terr, pt shd; wc; chem disp; shwrs inc; el pnts (6A) inc; lndry rm; shop; tradsmn; rest, snacks; bar; cooking facs; playgrnd; pool high ssn; paddling pool; games area; entmnt; dogs CZK50; adv bkg; poss noisy. "Gd walking area." 1 May-30 Sep. CZK 520                    2012*

**VELEHRAD see Uherské Hradiště** *C4*

**VRANE NAD VLTAVOU see Praha** *B2*

CZECH REPUBLIC

⊞ **VRCHLABI** *A3* (300m E Rural) *50.62406, 15.64056*
**Euro Air Camp, 54311 Vrchlabí [tel 499 421 292 or
603 235 743 (mob); fax 499 422 179; info@euro-air-camp.
cz; www.euro-air-camp.cz]** E of Vrchlabí on rd 14, site close
to airfield. Med, mkd pitch, pt sl, pt shd; htd wc; chem disp;
mv service pnt; baby facs; shwrs inc; el pnts (16A) inc; lndtte;
shop; rest, snacks; bar; cooking facs; playgrnd; pool high ssn;
lake fishing; tennis 200m; wifi; dogs; Eng spkn; adv bkg; quiet;
ccard acc; red low ssn/CKE/CCI. "Nr Giant Mountains & Polish
border; facs dated but clean; friendly, helpful owners; gd
walking; gliding fr adj grass strip." ♦ ltd CZK 453      2010*

⊞ **VRCHLABI** *A3* (1.5km S Rural) *50.61036, 15.60263*
**Holiday Park Liščí Farma, Dolní Branná 350, 54362
Vrchlabí [tel 499 421 473; fax 499 421 656; info@
liscifarma.cz; www.liscifarma.cz]** S fr Vrchlabí on rd 295,
site sp. Lge, mkd pitch, pt shd; htd wc; chem disp; mv service
pnt; sauna; private bthrms avail; shwrs inc; el pnts (6A) inc;
lndtte; shop 500m; tradsmn; rest; bar; cooking facs; playgrnd;
pool high ssn; canoeing; tennis; games area; cycle hire;
horseriding 2km; golf 5km; entmnt; TV; dogs CZK90; adv bkg;
quiet; ccard acc. ♦ CZK 640      2009*

**ZAMBERK** *B3* (1km E Urban) *50.08638, 16.47527*
**Autocamping Jan Kulhanek, U koupaliště, 564 01
Žamberk [tel 465 614 755; kemp@orlicko.cz; www.
autocamping.cz]** Fr Žamberk centre on rd 11, foll sp. Sm,
pt shd; wc; shwrs; el pnt (16A) CZK70; lndtte; shop 1km;
rest, snacks & bar 200m at sports centre; cooking facs;
playgrnd, pool, games area, games rm at sports centre; TV rm;
50% statics; wifi; dogs CZK50; phone; bus adj; train 1km; Eng
spkn; quiet; CKE/CCI. "Site is pt of sports cent & aqua park
with many diff facs inc mini-golf, volleyball & bowling; site
leaflet avail at recep showing town plans with supmkts & info
office; gd site." 01 Apr-31 Oct. CZK 241      2011*

**ZNOJMO** *C3* (7km N Rural) *48.92018, 16.02588* **Camping
Country, 67152 Hluboké Mašůvky [tel/fax 515 255 249;
camping-country@cbox.cz; www.camp-country.com]** N
fr Znojmo on E59/38 4km; turn E on 408 to Přímětice; then
N on 361 4km to Hluboké Mašůvky. Sharp turn into site fr S.
Med, sl, pt shd; wc; chem disp; shwrs inc; el pnts (16A) CZK80
(long lead poss req); lndtte; shop 500m; rest in ssn; playgrnd;
sm pool; tennis; lake sw 1km; cycle hire; horseriding; TV rm;
20% statics; dogs CZK50; phone 500m; Eng spkn; quiet;
no ccard acc; red CKE/CCI. "Gd, clean, well-manicured site;
v helpful owner & family; not easy to find level pitch; excel
meals." ♦ 1 May-30 Oct. CZK 410      2009*

Tell us about the sites you visit

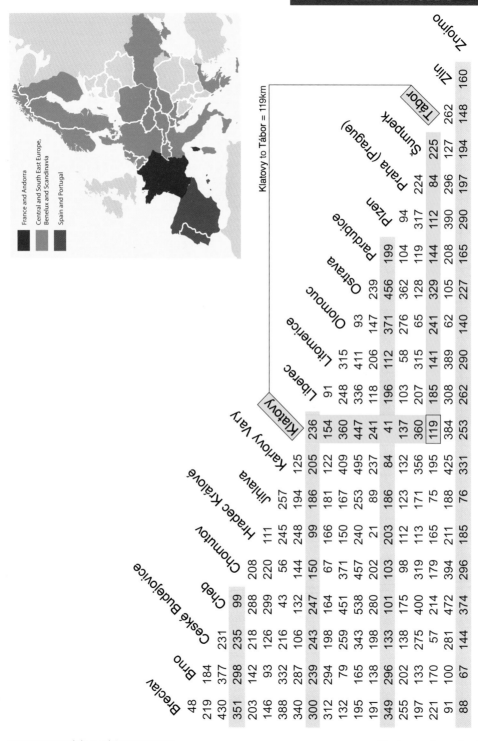

Klatovy to Tábor = 119km

| | Breclav | Brno | Ceské Budejovice | Cheb | Chomutov | Hradec Králové | Jihlava | Karlovy Vary | Klatovy | Liberec | Litomerice | Olomouc | Ostrava | Pardubice | Plzen | Praha (Prague) | Sumperk | Tábor | Zlín |
|---|---|---|---|---|---|---|---|---|---|---|---|---|---|---|---|---|---|---|---|
| Brno | 48 | | | | | | | | | | | | | | | | | | |
| Ceské Budejovice | 219 | 184 | | | | | | | | | | | | | | | | | |
| Cheb | 430 | 377 | 231 | | | | | | | | | | | | | | | | |
| Chomutov | 351 | 298 | 235 | 99 | | | | | | | | | | | | | | | |
| Hradec Králové | 203 | 142 | 218 | 288 | 208 | | | | | | | | | | | | | | |
| Jihlava | 146 | 93 | 126 | 299 | 220 | 111 | | | | | | | | | | | | | |
| Karlovy Vary | 388 | 332 | 216 | 43 | 56 | 245 | 257 | | | | | | | | | | | | |
| Klatovy | 340 | 287 | 106 | 132 | 144 | 248 | 194 | 125 | | | | | | | | | | | |
| Liberec | 300 | 239 | 243 | 247 | 150 | 99 | 205 | 205 | 236 | | | | | | | | | | |
| Litomerice | 312 | 294 | 198 | 164 | 67 | 166 | 181 | 122 | 154 | 91 | | | | | | | | | |
| Olomouc | 132 | 79 | 259 | 451 | 371 | 150 | 167 | 409 | 360 | 248 | 315 | | | | | | | | |
| Ostrava | 195 | 165 | 343 | 538 | 457 | 240 | 253 | 495 | 447 | 336 | 411 | 93 | | | | | | | |
| Pardubice | 191 | 138 | 198 | 280 | 202 | 21 | 89 | 237 | 241 | 118 | 206 | 147 | 239 | | | | | | |
| Plzen | 349 | 296 | 133 | 101 | 103 | 203 | 186 | 84 | 41 | 196 | 112 | 371 | 456 | 199 | | | | | |
| Praha (Prague) | 255 | 202 | 138 | 175 | 98 | 112 | 123 | 132 | 137 | 103 | 58 | 276 | 362 | 104 | 94 | | | | |
| Sumperk | 197 | 133 | 275 | 400 | 319 | 113 | 171 | 356 | 360 | 207 | 315 | 65 | 128 | 119 | 317 | 224 | | | |
| Tábor | 221 | 170 | 57 | 214 | 179 | 165 | 75 | 195 | 119 | 185 | 141 | 241 | 329 | 144 | 112 | 84 | 225 | | |
| Zlín | 91 | 100 | 281 | 472 | 394 | 211 | 188 | 425 | 384 | 308 | 389 | 62 | 105 | 208 | 390 | 296 | 127 | 262 | |
| Znojmo | 88 | 67 | 144 | 374 | 296 | 185 | 76 | 331 | 253 | 262 | 290 | 140 | 227 | 165 | 290 | 197 | 194 | 148 | 160 |

France and Andorra

Central and South East Europe, Benelux and Scandinavia

Spain and Portugal

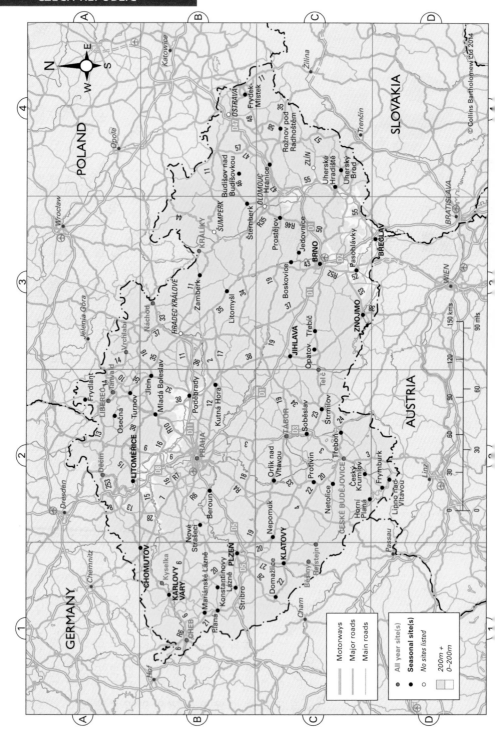

# Denmark
## Country Introduction

*Frederiksberg Castle*

## Welcome to Denmark

Famous for many architectural masterpieces and stunning statues, such as the Little Mermaid in Copenhagen, Denmark is a charming country made up of small islands and green landscapes.

Being a Scandinavian country there are strong links to Viking settlements and the fascinating history that they left behind. As well as some of the most beautiful fairy tale castles which can be found on the different islands.

## Country highlights

Denmark is well known for it's unique cuisine, with fish dishes and smørrebrod (open sandwiches) being local specialities. Visit kros (inns) in the countryside for traditional meals and to sample the national drink - schnapps.

Copenhagen hosts a range of events throughout the year, including Medieval and Beer festivals in May and a summer food festival. Aalborg hosts Northern Europe's largest carnival, with over 25,000 participants, and car enthusiasts shouldn't miss the Classic Race at Aarhus.

## Major towns and cities

- Copenhagen – the dynamic capital city, which is full of amazing architecture.

- Aarhus – this city has a vibrant mix of new and old buildings built around the countries principal port.

- Esbjerg – a seaport town that is popular for its shopping boutiques and old world charm.

## Attractions

- The Church of Our Saviour – Famous for its corkscrew spire, this Copenhagen church offers extensive views of the city.

- Egeskov Castle – Europe's best preserved Renaissance water castle.

- National Open Air Museum – experience life in Denmark through the ages.

- Frederiksberg Park – This romantic landscape garden is designed int he English style.

## Find out more

www.visitdenmark.com

Tel: 0045 (0) 22 88 99 00 Denmark Tourist Office

# Country Information

*Population (approx):* 5.5 million

*Capital:* Copenhagen (population approx 1.2 million)

*Area:* 43,094 sq km (excl Faroe Islands and Greenland)

*Bordered by:* Germany

*Terrain:* Mostly fertile lowland, undulating hills, woodland, lakes and moors

*Climate:* Generally mild, changeable climate without extremes of heat or cold; cold winters but usually not severe; warm, sunny summers; the best time to visit is between May and September

*Coastline:* 7,314km

*Highest Point:* Ejer Bavnehøj 173m

*Languages:* Danish

*Local Time:* GMT or BST + 1, ie 1 hour ahead of the UK all year

*Currency:* Krone (DKK) divided into 100 øre; £1 = DKK 9.38, DKK 10 = £1.07 (September 2014)

*Emergency numbers:* Police 112 (114 for non-urgent calls); Fire brigade 112; Ambulance 112 (operators speak English).

*Public Holidays 2015:* Jan 1; Apr 2, 3, 6; May 1, 14, 25; Jun 5 (Constitution Day); Dec 25, 26.

School summer holidays extend from end June to mid August.

# Camping and Caravanning

Denmark has approximately 500 approved, well-equipped, annually inspected campsites. A green banner flies at each campsite entrance, making it easy to spot. Campsites are graded from 1 to 5 stars, many having excellent facilities including baby-changing areas, private family bathrooms, self-catering cooking facilities and shops. Prices are regulated and there is very little variation.

All except the most basic 1-star sites have water and waste facilities for motorhomes and at least some electric hook-ups. You may find it useful to take your own flat universal sink plug. During the high season it is advisable to book in advance as many Danish holidaymakers take pitches for the whole season for use at weekends and holidays resulting in minimal space for tourers.

A Camping Key Europe (CKE) or Camping Card International (CCI) is required on all classified campsites.

Approximately 190 campsites have a 'Quick Stop' amenity which provides safe, secure overnight facilities on or adjoining campsites, including the use of sanitary facilities. Quick Stop rates are about two thirds of the regular camping rate but you must arrive after 8pm and leave by 10am next morning. A list of Quick Stop sites may be obtained from local tourist offices or downloaded from DK-Camp www.dk-camp.dk.

Casual/wild camping is not allowed and is particularly frowned on near beaches where on-the-spot fines may be incurred.

# Cycling

Although not as flat as the Netherlands, Denmark is very cyclist-friendly and many major and minor roads, including those in all major towns, have separate cycle lanes or tracks. They have their own traffic lights and signals. Cyclists often have the right of way and, when driving, you should check cycle lanes before turning left or right.

In Århus and Copenhagen city centre bicycles are free to use between mid-April and November - you will need to pay a refundable deposit. Simply look for one of the many bicycle racks around the central area; see www.visitcopenhagen.com for more information.

There are many separate cycle routes, including eleven national routes, which may be long distance, local or circular, mainly on quiet roads and tracks. Local tourist offices can provide information. When planning a route, take the (often strong) prevailing westerly winds into account.

*Transportation of Bicycles*

Bicycles may be carried on the roof of a car as well as at the rear. When carried at the rear, the lights and number plate must remain visible.

# Electricity and Gas

Current on campsites varies between 6 and 16 amps, a 10 amp supply being the most common. Plugs have 2 round pins. Some sites have CEE17 electric hook-ups or are in the process of converting. If a CEE17 connection is not available site staff will usually provide an adaptor. Visitors report that reversed polarity is common.

Campingaz 904 and 907 butane cylinders are readily available from campsites, or some Statoil service stations and at camping or hardware shops. If travelling on to Norway, Statoil agencies there will exchange Danish propane cylinders.

## Entry Formalities

Visas are not required by British or Irish passport holders for a stay of up to three months. Visitors planning to stay longer should contact the Danish Embassy in London before they travel - find contact details at www.denmark.org.uk.

## Regulations for Pets

Between April and September all dogs must be kept on a lead. This applies not only on campsites but throughout the country in general.

## Medical Services

The standard of healthcare is high. Citizens of the UK are entitled to the same emergency medical services as the Danish, including free hospital treatment, on production of a European Health Insurance Card (EHIC). Tourist offices and health offices (kommunes social og sundhedforvaltning) have lists of doctors and dentists who are registered with the public health service. For a consultation with a doctor you may have to pay the full fee but you will be refunded if you apply to a local health office if they are registered with the Danish Public Health Service. Partial refunds may be made for dental costs and approved medicines. Prescriptions are dispensed at pharmacies (apotek).

## Opening Hours

Banks: Mon-Fri 10am-4pm (Thu to 6pm). In the Provinces opening hours vary from town to town.

Museums: Tue-Sun 9am/10am-5pm; most close Mon.

Post Offices: Mon-Fri 9am/10am-5pm/6pm, Sat 9am/10am-12pm/1pm/2pm or closed all day.

Shops: Mon-Fri 9am-5.30pm (Fri to 7pm); Sat 9am-1pm/2pm; supermarkets open Mon-Fri

9am-7pm & Sat 9am-4pm/5pm; open on first Sunday of the month 10am-5pm. Most shops close on public holidays but you may find some bakers, sandwich shops, confectioners, kiosks and florists open.

## Safety and Security

Denmark has relatively low levels of crime and most visits to the country are trouble-free. The majority of public places are well lit and secure, most people are genuinely friendly and the police courteous, helpful and often speak good English. Visitors should, however, be aware of the risk of pickpocketing or bag-snatching in Copenhagen, particularly around the central station and in the Christiania and Nørrebro areas, as well as in other large cities and tourist attractions, and should take the usual common-sense precautions. Car break-ins have increased in recent years; never leave valuables in your car.

Denmark shares with the rest of Europe a general threat from terrorism. Attacks could be indiscriminate and against civilian targets in public places, including tourist sites.

*British Embassy*
KASTELSVEJ 36/38/40
DK-2100 Copenhagen Ø
Tel: 35 44 52 00
http://ukindenmark.fco.gov.uk/en

There are also Honorary Consulates in Aabenraa, Åarhus, Fredericia and Herning

*Irish Embassy*
ØSTBANEGADE 21
DK-2100 Copenhagen Ø
Tel: 35 47 32 00
www.embassyofireland.dk

## Documents

*Passport*
Your passport must be valid for the proposed duration of your stay, however in case of any unforeseen delays it is strongly recommended to have a period of extra validity on your passport.

*Vehicle(s)*
Carry your vehicle documentation, including vehicle registration certificate (V5C), certificate of insurance and MOT certificate (if applicable). You

may be asked to produce your V5C if driving a motorhome over the Great Belt Bridge between Funen and Zealand in order to verify the weight of your vehicle. For more information see the 'Motorways' section of this introduction.

The minimum age you can drive, with a valid driver's licence, is 17.

## Money

Some shops and restaurants, particularly in the larger cities, display prices in both krone and euros and many will accept payment in euros.

Travellers' cheques are no longer recommended as it is increasingly difficult to find somewhere to cash them. A pre-paid currency card is an alternative - see www.caravanclub.co.uk/travelmoney for details of the Moneycorp Explorer card.

The major credit cards are widely, but not always, accepted. Credit cards are not normally accepted in supermarkets. Cash machines are widespread. A 5% surcharge is usually applied to credit card transactions. Some banks and/or cash machines may not accept debit cards issued by non-Danish banks.

It is advisable to carry your passport or photocard driving licence if paying with a credit card as you may well be asked for photographic proof of identity. Carry your credit card issuers'/banks' 24-hour UK contact numbers in case of loss or theft of your cards.

## Motoring in Denmark

### Alcohol

The level of alcohol cannot exceed 50 milligrams (0.05%) in 100 millilitres of blood which is lower than in the UK. Drivers caught over this limit will be fined and their driving licence withdrawn. Police carry out random breath tests.

### Breakdown Service

24 hours assistance is available from SOS Dansk Autohjaelp (Danish Automobile Assistance) call Tel: 70 10 80 90.

The hourly charge between Monday and Friday is DKK 638 + VAT and an administration charge;

higher charges apply at night and at weekends and public holidays. On-the-spot repairs and towing must be paid for in cash.

On motorways use the emergency telephones, situated every 2 km, to call the breakdown service. The telephone number to dial in case of an accident is 112.

## Essential Equipment

*Warning Triangle*
An EU approved red warning triangle must be used if the vehicle breaks down, punctures or is involved in an accident.

*Lights and Indicators*
Dipped headlights are compulsory at all times, regardless of weather conditions. Bulbs are more likely to fail with constant use and you are recommended to carry spares.

On motorways drivers must use their hazard warning lights to warn other motorists of sudden queues ahead or other dangers such as accidents.

By law indicators must be used when overtaking or changing lanes on a motorway and when pulling out from a parked position at the kerb.

*Child Restraint System*
Children under three years of age must be seated in an approved child restraint system adapted to their size. Children over three years old and under 1.35 metres in height must be seated in an approved child restraint suitable for both their height and weight. If the vehicle is fitted with an active airbag children must not be placed in the front seat in a rear-facing child seat.

## Fuel

Some petrol stations in larger towns stay open 24 hours a day and they are increasingly equipped with self-service pumps which accept DKK 50, 100 and occasionally DKK 200 notes. Few display instructions in English and it is advisable to fill up during normal opening hours when staff are on hand.

Unleaded petrol pumps are marked 'Blyfri Benzine'. Leaded petrol is no longer available and has been replaced by Lead Replacement Petrol, called Millennium, which contains an additive. The major credit cards are normally accepted.

LPG (Autogas or Bilgas) is available from a handful of BP, OK, Q8, Uno-X, YX, Shell and Statoil service stations – the Danish Tourist Board publishes a list of outlets on its website www.visitdenmark.com.

## Low Emission Zones

Low Emission zones are in operation in many large cities. The rules affect all diesel powered vehicles over 3,500kg, which must meet European Emission Standard 4 (EURO 4). All vehicles over 3,500kg must display an Environmental Zone stocker (Eco-label) You can order the Eco-label online from www.applusbilsyn.dk for DKK 93 or visit a car inspection station in Denmark where the Eco-label will cost DKK 165.

Vehicles which do not meet European Emission Standard 4 are not allowed into the Low Emission Zone. A fine of DKK 15000 (Approximately £1650 in 2014) is payable for non-compliance.

## Parking

Parking prohibitions and limitations are indicated by signs. Hours during which parking is not allowed are displayed in black for weekdays, with brackets for Saturdays and in red for Sundays and public holidays. Parking meters and discs are used and discs are available free of charge from post offices, banks, petrol stations and tourist offices. The centre of Copenhagen is divided into red, green and blue zones and variable hourly charges apply round the clock Monday to Friday (Saturday to 5pm; Sunday and public holidays free). 'Pay and display' tickets may be bought from machines with cash or a credit card. Cars must be parked on the right-hand side of the road (except in one-way streets). An illegally parked vehicle may be removed by the police.

## Priority

At intersections where there are 'give way' or 'stop' signs and/or a transverse line consisting of triangles (shark's teeth) with one point facing towards the driver, drivers must give way to traffic at an intersection. If approaching an intersection of two roads without any signs you must give way to vehicles coming from the right.

Give way to cyclists and to buses signalling to pull out. Motorists should take special care on the Danish islands where many people travel by foot, bicycle or on horseback.

## Roads

Roads are generally in good condition, well-signposted and largely uncongested and driving standards are fairly high.

Caravanners should beware of strong crosswinds on exposed stretches of road. Distances are short; it is less than 500 km (310 miles) from Copenhagen on the eastern edge of Zealand, to Skagen at the tip of Jutland, and the coast is never more than an hour away.

## Road Signs and Markings

Signs directing you onto or along international E-roads are green with white lettering. E-roads, having been integrated into the Danish network, usually have no other national number.

Signs above the carriageway on motorways have white lettering on a blue background. Signs guiding you onto other roads are white with red text and a hexagonal sign with red numbering indicates the number of a motorway exit.

Primary (main roads) connecting large towns and ferry connections have signs with black numbers on a yellow background. Secondary (local) roads connecting small towns and primary routes are indicated by signs with black numbers on a white background. Signs of any colour with a dotted frame refer you to a road further ahead. Road signs themselves may be placed low down and, as a result, may be easy to miss.

'Sharks teeth' markings at junctions indicate stop and give way to traffic on the road you are entering.

General roads signs conform to international standards. You may see the following:

Place of interest

Recommended speed limits

Dual Carriage-way ends

The following are some other common signs:

| Danish | English Translation |
|---|---|
| Ensrettet kørsel | One-way street |
| Fare | Danger |
| Farligt sving | Dangerous bend |
| Fodgægerovergang | Pedestrian crossing |
| Gennemkørsel forbudt | No through road |
| Hold til hojre | Keep to the right |
| Hold til venstre | Keep to the left |
| Omkørsel | Diversion |
| Parkering forbudt | No parking |
| Vejen er spærret | Road closed |

## Speed Limits

| | Open Road (km/h) | Motorway (km/h) |
|---|---|---|
| Car Solo | 80-90 | 110-130 |
| Car towing caravan/trailer | 70 | 80 |
| Motorhome under 3500kg | 80-90 | 110-130 |
| Motorhome 3500-7500kg | 70 | 70 |

Vehicles over 3,500 kg are restricted to 70 km/h (44 mph) on the open road and on motorways. It is prohibited to use radar detectors.

## Traffic Jams

British drivers will enjoy the relatively low density of traffic. At most, traffic builds up during the evening rush hours around the major cities of Copenhagen, Århus, Aalborg and Odense. During the holiday season traffic jams may be encountered at the Flensburg border crossing into Germany, on the roads to coastal areas, on approach roads to ferry crossings and on routes along the west coast of Jutland.

## Violation of Traffic Regulations

The police are authorised to impose and collect on-the-spot fines for traffic offences. Driving offences committed in Denmark are reported to the UK authorities.

## Motorways

There are approximately 1,000 km of motorways, mainly two-lane and relatively uncongested. No tolls are levied except on bridges. Lay-bys with picnic areas and occasionally motorhome service points are situated at 25 km intervals. These often also have toilet facilities. Service areas and petrol stations are situated at 50 km intervals and are generally open from 7am to 10pm.

## Toll Bridges

The areas of Falster and Zealand are linked by two road bridges, 1.6 km and 1.7 km in length respectively.

The areas of Funen and Zealand are linked by an 18 km suspension road bridge and rail tunnel known as the Great Belt Link (Storebæltsbroen), connecting the towns of Nyborg and Korsør. The toll road is part of the E20 between Odense and Ringsted and tolls for single journeys on the bridge are shown in Table 1 below (2014 prices subject to change).

*Table 1 – Great Belt Bridge*

| Vehicle(s) | Price |
|---|---|
| Solo Car up to 6 metres | DKK 230 |
| Car + trailer/caravan | DKK 350 |
| Motorhome (under 3,500 kg) under 6 metres | DKK 220 |
| Motorhome (under 3,500kg) over 6 metres | DKK 335 |
| Motorhome (over 3,500 kg) up to 10 metres | DKK 665 |
| Motorhome (over 3,500 kg) over 10 metres | DKK 1,050 |

You may be asked to produce your Vehicle Registration Certificate (V5C) to verify the weight of your vehicle. Day return and weekend return tickets are also available. For more information see www.storebaelt.dk/english.

The 16 km Øresund Bridge links Copenhagen in Denmark with Malmö in Sweden and means that it is possible to drive all the way from mainland Europe to Sweden by motorway. The crossing is via a 7.8 km bridge to the artificial island of Peberholm, and a 4 km tunnel. Tolls for single journeys (payable in cash, including euros, or by credit card) are levied on the Swedish side, and are shown in Table 2 below (2014 prices subject to change).

*Table 2 – Øresund Bridge*

| Vehicle(s) | Price |
|---|---|
| Solo Car up to 6 metres | € 43 |
| Car + caravan/trailer or motorhome | € 86 |

Speed limits apply, and during periods of high wind the bridge is closed to caravans. Bicycles are not allowed. Information on the Øresund Bridge can be found on www.oeresundsbron.com.

On both the Øresund and Storebælts bridges vehicle length is measured electronically and even a slight overhang over six metres, e.g. tow bars, projecting loads and loose items, will result in payment of the higher tariff.

## Touring

The peak holiday season and school holidays are slightly earlier than in the UK and by mid-August some attractions close or operate reduced opening hours.

Service charges are automatically added to restaurant bills although you may round up the bill if service has been good, but it is not expected. Tips for taxi drivers are included in the fare. Smoking is not allowed in enclosed public places, including restaurants and bars.

The 3,500 km Marguerite Route, marked by brown signs depicting a flower (see below), takes motorists to the best sights and scenic areas in Denmark.

Tourist
Route

A route map and guide (in English) are available from bookshops, tourist offices and Statoil service stations all over Denmark. Stretches of the route are not suitable for cars towing caravans as some of the roads are narrow and twisting.

The capital and major port, Copenhagen, is situated on the island of Zealand. Grundtvig Cathedral, Amalienborg Palace and the Viking Museum are well worth a visit, as are the famous Tivoli Gardens open from mid April to the third week in September and again for a few days in October and from mid November to the end of December (excluding Christmas). The statue of the Little Mermaid, the character created by Hans Christian Andersen, can be found at the end of the promenade called Langelinie. Copenhagen is easy to explore and from there visitors may travel to the north of Zealand along the 'Danish Riviera' to Hamlet's castle at Kronborg, or west to Roskilde with its Viking Ship Museum and 12th century cathedral.

A Copenhagen Card (CPH Card) offers unlimited use of public transport throughout Greater Copenhagen and North Zealand, free entry to over 60 museums and attractions and discounts at restaurants and other attractions. Cards are valid for 24 or 72 hours and may be purchased from selected tourist offices, travel agents, hotels and railway stations or online from www.visitcopenhagen.com. Two children up to the age of nine are included free of charge on an adult card. It is also available to buy and use the Copenhagen Card via a free iPhone app.

National Parks in the country include Thy National Park near Thisted along Jutland's north-west coast, Mols Bjerge National Park in eastern Jutland and Wadden Sea National Park in the south-west of the country.

The Danish Tourist Board publishes a brochure for disabled people travelling in the West Jutland region which contains information about accommodation (including campsites), restaurants, museums, sightseeing, entertainment, events and useful addresses. See www.handicap.dk or write to Turistgruppen Vestjylland, Kirkevej 4, 6960 Hvide Sande, tel 0045 75 28 74 00.

English is widely spoken throughout the country.

## Public Transport

Public transport is excellent and you can buy a variety of bus, train and metro tickets at station kiosks and at some supermarkets. Children under the age of 12 travel free on buses and metro trains in the Greater Copenhagen area when accompanied by an adult. Tickets must be purchased for dogs and bicycles.

Numerous car ferry connections operate daily between different parts of the country. The ferry is a common mode of transport in Denmark and there may be long queues, especially at weekends in summer. The most important routes connect the bigger islands of Zealand and Funen with Jutland using high-speed vessels on day and night services. Vehicle length and height restrictions apply on routes between Odden (Zealand) and Århus and Æbeltoft (Jutland) and not all sailings transport caravans – check in advance.

The Danish Tourist Board can provide general information on car ferry services or contact Scandlines for information on inter-island services including timetables and prices www.scandlines.dk, email scandlines@scandlines.com or telephone 0045 33 15 15 15.

International ferry services are particularly busy during July and August and it is advisable to book in advance. Popular routes include Frederikshavn to Gothenburg (Sweden), Helsingør to Helsingborg (Sweden), Copenhagen to Oslo (Norway), and Rødby to Puttgarden in Germany (this route involves a road bridge which is occasionally closed to high-sided vehicles because of high winds). The ferry route from Copenhagen to Hamburg is a good alternative to the busy E45 motorway linking Denmark and Germany.

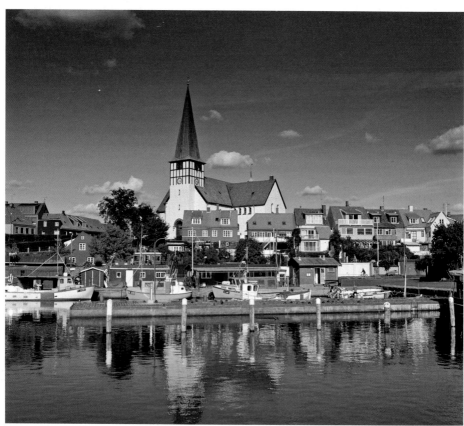

*Roenne Harbor, Bornholm*

**AABENRAA** *B3* (1km W Coastal) *55.02490, 9.41461* **Fjordlyst Aabenraa City Camping, Sønderskovvej 100, 6200 Aabenraa [tel 45 74 62 26 99; fax 45 74 62 29 39; mail(ad) fjordlyst.dk; www.fjordlyst.dk]** Fr S take E45 & exit at junc 72 to Aabenraa. Foll Rd 42 then turn L onto Rd 24. Site sp on R. Med, mkd pitch, sl, terr, pt shd; wc; chem disp; mv service pnt; baby facs; shwrs; el pnts (16A) 35 dkk; lndtte (inc dryer); shop; bar; BBQ; playgrnd; beach 500m; games area; wifi; tv; 10% statics; dogs 10dkk; bus adj; twin axles; poss cr; Eng spkn; adv bkg; quiet; CCI. "Scenic location with views over the bay. Excel facs; friendly staff; some steep slopes on site rds; vg." ◆ ltd 1 Apr-31 Oct. DKK 300          2014*

**AALBORG** *B1* (1.5km W Urban) *57.05500, 9.88500* **Strandparken Camping, Skydebanevej 20, 9000 Aalborg [tel 98 12 76 29; fax 98 12 76 73; info@strandparken.dk; www.strandparken.dk]** Turn L at start of m'way to Svenstrup & Aalborg W, foll A180 (Hobrovej rd) twd town cent. Turn L bef Limfjorden bdge onto Borgergade for 2km, site on R. Fr N turn R after bdge onto Borgergade. Med, shd; wc; chem disp; mv service pnt; baby rm; shwrs DKK10; el pnts (10A) DKK30 (poss rev pol); kiosk & shops 500m; cooking facs; playgrnd; pool adj; TV; some statics; dogs DKK10; phone; bus nr; Eng spkn; acp dogs; poss noisy tent campers high ssn; ccard acc; CKE/CCI. "Gd cent for town & N Jutland; gd security." ◆ 28 Mar-15 Sep. DKK 335          2013*

**AALESTRUP** *B2* (1km E Rural) *56.69166, 9.49991* **Aalestrup Camping, Parkvænget 2, 9620 Aalestrup [tel 98 64 23 86; pouledb@ofir.dk; www.rosenparken.dk]** Fr E45 turn W onto rd 561 to Aalestrup; 500m after junc with rd 13 turn L into Borgergade, cross rlwy line. Site sp. Med, pt shd; wc; shwrs; chem disp; mv service pnt; el pnts DKK25; shop nr; rest, snacks; playgrnd; quiet. "Free entry to beautiful rose garden; gd touring base; friendly staff." 1 Mar-1 Nov. DKK 120  2010*

**AARS** *B2* (1km N Rural) *56.81530, 9.50695* **Aars Camping, Tolstrup Byvej 17, 9600 Aars [tel 98 62 36 03; fax 98 62 52 99; camping@aars.dk; www.aarscamping.dk]** Fr E45 exit junc 33 W to Aars on rd 535. Turn N onto rd 29 (Aggersundvej), site sp. Med, pt sl, pt shd; htd wc; chem disp; mv service pnt; shwrs DKK5; el pnts (16A) DKK30; gas; lndtte; shop; rest, snacks; bar & 1km; BBQ; cooking facs; playgrnd; tennis; horseriding; internet; TV; some statics; dogs; poss cr; Eng spkn; adv bkg; quiet; ccard acc; CKE/CCI. "Vg." ◆ 1 Apr-1 Nov. DKK 150          2011*

**ALBAEK** *C1* (6km N Coastal) *57.64433, 10.46179* **Bunken Camping, Ålbækvej 288, Bunken Klitplantage, 9982 Ålbæk [tel 98 48 71 80; fax 98 48 89 05; dancamp@ mail.tele.dk; www.dancamp.dk]** Site in fir plantation E of A10. V lge, hdg pitch, pt shd; wc; chem disp; mv service pnt; baby rm; fam bthrm; shwrs DKK5; el pnts DKK25 (adaptor on loan fr recep) (poss rev pol); gas; lndtte; shop; cooking facs; playgrnd; sand beach 150m; fishing; boating; TV; dogs DKK15; phone; adv bkg; some rd noise. "Beautiful site in trees; spacious pitches." ◆ 3 Apr-18 Oct. DKK 158          2009*

**ALSGARDE see Helsingør** *D2*

⊞ **ARHUS** *C2* (9km N Rural) *56.22660, 10.16260* **Åarhus Camping, Randersvej 400, Lisbjerg, 8200 Åarhus Nord [tel 86 23 11 33; fax 86 23 11 31; info@aarhuscamping.dk; www.aarhuscamping.dk]** Exit E45 junc 46 Århus N, then to Ikea rndabt. Then foll sp Lisbjerg & head for smoking factory chimney. Site 400m N of Lisbjerg. Med, pt sl, pt shd; wc; chem disp; mv service pnt; baby facs; fam bthrm; shwrs DKK5; el pnts (16A) metered; gas; lndtte (inc dryer); shop; snacks; BBQ; cooking facs; playgrnd; htd pool; beach 9km; games area; golf 10km; wifi; TV rm; 10% statics; dogs DKK10; phone; poss cr; adv bkg; rd noise; red CKE/CCI. "Conv Århus; gd, tidy site; modern san facs; conv for bus into Aarhus, helpful owner." ◆ DKK 293          2013*

**ARHUS** *C2* (5km S Coastal) *56.11030, 10.23209* **Blommehaven Camping, Ørneredevej 35, 8270 Højbjerg [tel 86 27 02 07; fax 86 27 45 22; info@blommenhaven. dk; www.blommehaven.dk]** Fr S on E45 at junc 50 take rd 501 twd Århus. In 10km this becomes 01 ring rd. Take 2nd R Dalgas Ave, at T-junc turn L & immed R into Strandvejen. Site 3km on L in Marselisborg Forest. Lge, hdg/mkd pitch, terr, pt shd; wc; chem disp; mv service pnt; fam bthrm; baby facs; shwrs; el pnts DKK35; lndtte; shop; BBQ; cooking facs; playgrnd; sand beach adj; TV rm; 4% statics; dogs DKK10; phone; bus; Quickstop o'night facs; poss cr; Eng spkn; adv bkg; quiet. "Some pitches sm & bare earth; helpful staff; clean facs; easy reach woods, cliffs & beach; conv for open-air museum." ◆ 21 Mar-18 Oct. DKK 180          2011*

**ASAA** *C1* (SE Urban/Coasal) *57.1460, 10.4023* **Asaa Camping, Vodbindervej 13, 9340 Aså [tel 98 85 13 40; fax 98 85 00 38; info@asaacamping.dk; www.asaacamping. dk]** Fr Aalborg take E45 NE for approx 20km, turn E to Aså at junc 16 onto rd 559, then R onto rd 541, site sp. Lge, pt shd; wc; chem disp; mv service pnt; shwrs; fam bthrm; baby facs; el pnts DKK30; lndtte; shop; snacks; cooking facs; playgrnd; pool; sw 2km; games area; fishing; TV; some statics; dogs free; phone; Eng spkn; adv bkg; red low ssn; quiet; CKE/CCI. "Pleasant location; facs for anglers." ◆ 15 Mar-28 Sep. DKK 180          2011*

**ASSENS** *B3* (12km N Coastal) *55.33400, 9.89002* **Sandager Naes Camping, Strandgårdsvej 12, DK 5610 Assens [tel 45 64 79 11 56; info@sandagernaes.dk; www. sandagernaes.dk]** Fr E20, take exit 57 dir Assens. R at Sandager & foll sp. Med, hdg pitch, mkd pitch, pt sl, pt shd; wc; chem disp; mv service pnt; baby facs; fam bthrm; shwrs DKK5; el pnts (13A); lndtte (inc dryer); shop; snack; bar; BBQ; cooking facs; playgrnd; htd pool; waterslide; paddling pool; beach 0.5km; games area; games rm; wifi; tv rm; 50% statics; dogs; phone; Eng spkn; adv bkg; CCI. "Excel site". ◆ 23 Mar-15 Sep. DKK 330          2014*

**DENMARK**

**ASSENS** *B3* (W Urban/Coastal) *55.26569, 9.88390* **Camping City Camping (formerly Willemoes), Næsvej 15, 5610 Assens [tel 64 71 15 43; fax 64 71 15 83; info@camping-willemoes.dk; www.camping-willemoes.dk]** Site on beach at neck of land W of town adj marina. Med, pt shd; wc; chem disp; mv service pnt; fam bthrm; baby facs; shwrs DKK5; el pnts (10A) DKK30; gas; lndtte; shop; playgrnd; sand beach adj; fishing; watersports; TV; 20% statics; phone; adv bkg; red low ssn. "Pleasant site on beach." ◆ Easter-13 Sep. DKK 155                                    2009*

**AUGUSTENBORG see Sønderborg** *B3*

⊞ **BILLUND** *B3* (2km NE Rural) *55.73131, 9.13565* **FDM Billund Camping, Ellehammers Allé 2, 7190 Billund [tel 75 33 15 21; fax 75 35 37 36; c-billund@fdm.dk; www.billund.fdmcamping.dk]** In vill of Billund take rd twd Grindsted & Vejle. In 1km turn N foll sp to Legoland, site on R. V lge, pt shd; wc; chem disp; mv service pnt; shwrs inc; el pnts (10A) DKK32; gas; lndtte; shop & 2km; rest; bar; playgrnd; pool 500m; games area; internet; TV; some statics; dogs DKK12; phone; Quickstop o'night facs; poss cr; Eng spkn; adv bkg; some aircraft noise; ccard acc; red long stay/CKE/CCI. "Impersonal but excel; open 24 hrs; sh walk to Legoland (free entry for last 90 mins of day)." ◆ DKK 162        2010*

⊞ **BILLUND** *B3* (7km SE Rural) *55.68877, 9.26864* **Randbøldal Camping, Dalen 9, 7183 Randbøl [tel 75 88 35 75; fax 75 88 34 38; info@ randboldalcamping.dk; www.randboldalcamping.dk]** Fr Vejle take Billund rd. After approx 18km take L turn to Randbol & Bindebolle. Foll sp, site located approx 5km on L. Med, pt sl, shd; htd wc; chem disp; mv service pnt; baby facs; fam bthrm; shwrs inc; el pnts (10A) DKK30; lndtte; shop; snacks; cooking facs; playgrnd; lake sw, waterslide & fishing nr; TV; 15% statics; dogs DKK10; phone; poss cr; Eng spkn; adv bkg; quiet; ccard acc. "Wooded site nr rv & trout hatchery; facs stretched high ssn; conv Legoland & Lion Park." ◆ DKK 175                                    2009*

**BINDSLEV** *C1* (4km N Coastal) *57.58994, 10.18716* **Tannisby Camping, Tannisbugtvej 86, 9881 Tversted/Bindslev [tel 98 93 12 50; info@tannisbycamping.dk; www. tannisbycamping.dk]** Fr S on E39 dir Hirtshals, turn R dir Ålbæk & foll sp to Tversted & site. Med, mkd pitch, some hdstg, pt shd; htd wc; chem disp; mv service pnt; baby facs; fam bthrm; private san facs avail; sauna; shwrs inc; el pnts (13A) DKK30; lndtte (inc dryer); shop; tradsmn; BBQ; cooking facs; playgrnd; sand beach 500m; wifi; TV rm; some statics; dogs DKK5; Quickstop o'night facs; Eng spkn; adv bkg; quiet. "Peaceful, friendly site." 1 Apr-26 Sep.  DKK 180        2010*

⊞ **BJERGE** *C3* (3km SW Coastal) *55.56295, 11.16500* **FDM Camping Bjerge Sydstrand, Osvejen 30, Bjerge Sydstrand, 4480 Store Fuglede [tel 59 59 78 03; fax 59 59 37 20; c-bjerge@fdm.dk; www.bjerge.fdmcamping.dk]** E22 to Bjerge. Foll sp Bjerge Systrand on Filipsdalsvej rd, then onto Osvejen rd, site sp. Med, hdg/mkd pitch, pt shd; htd wc; mv service pnt; fam bthrm; shwrs inc; el pnts (6A) DKK30; lndtte; shop, tradsmn high ssn; rest 6km; snacks 300m; playgrnd; sand beach adj; watersports; fishing; internet; TV rm; 50% statics; dogs DKK15; adv bkg; quiet; ccard acc. "Pleasant, peaceful site." DKK 189                                    2009*

**BLOKHUS** *B1* (8km NE Rural) *57.27855, 9.66133* **Jambo Feriepark, Solvejen 60, 9493, Saltum [tel 98 88 16 66]** Take A17/A11 fr Aalborg, L at Saltum Kirke, approx 1.5km, sp on L. Lge, pt shd; wc; chem disp; snacks; shwrs; gas; shops; el pnts; sand beach 1.5km; pool; quiet; lndtte; cook facs; playgrnd; sauna; tennis. ◆ May-15 Sep.  DKK 110        2013*

See advert on bookmark

**BLOMMENSLYST see Odense** *C3*

**BOESLUNDE see Korsor** *C3*

**BOGENSE** *C3* (1.9km SW Coastal/Urban) *55.56144, 10.08530* **Bogense Strand Camping, Vestre Engvej 11, 5400 Bogense [tel 64 81 35 08; fax 64 81 27 17; info@ bogensecamp.dk; www.bogensecamp.dk]** Fr E20 at junc 57 & take 317 NE to Bogense. At 1st traff lts turn L for harbour, site sp at side of harbour. Lge, pt shd; wc; chem disp; mv service pnt; baby facs; fam bthrm; shwrs DKK5; el pnts (12A) DKK35; lndtte; shop on site & 200m; cooking facs; playgrnd; pool; paddling pool; shgl beach adj; TV; some statics; dogs DKK17; phone; adv bkg; quiet; red low ssn; CKE/CCI. "Well-run site; excel facs; interesting sm town 5 mins walk." ◆ 3 Apr-18 Oct.  DKK 250        2009*

> ## "Satellite navigation makes touring much easier"
>
> Remember most sat navs don't know if you're towing or in a larger vehicle – always use yours alongside maps and site directions.

⊞ **BOGENSE** *C3* (1.2km W Coastal/Urban) *55.56770, 10.08336* **Kyst Camping Bogense, Østre Havnevej 1, 5400 Bogense [tel 64 81 14 43; info@kystcamping.dk; www. kystcamping.dk]** Fr E20 at junc 57 take 317 NE to Bogonense, foll sp for harbour, site sp. Lge, mkd, hdg, unshd pitch; wc; chem disp; mv service pnt; child/baby facs; shwrs DKK6; el pnt (16A) DKK35; lndtte; BBQ; cooking facs; playgrnd; pool; beach 200m; games area; games rm; wifi; TV; dogs DKK10; bus 200m. "V gd site; friendly, helpful owners; nice sm town and harbour; ideal cycling." ◆ DKK 285        2012*

**BOJDEN see Faaborg** *C3*

**BORK HAVN** *A2* (2.3km S Coastal) *55.84822, 8.28333* **Bork Havn Camping, Kirkehøjvej 9a, 6893 Bork Havn/Hemmet [tel 75 28 00 37; mail@borkhavncamping.dk; www. borkhavncamping.dk]** Fr Tarm take rd 423 thro Hemmet; 500m bef Nørre Bork turn R to Bork Havn, site on L in town just bef harbour. Lge, mkd pitch, pt shd; htd wc; chem disp; mv service pnt; baby facs; shwrs; el pnts (10A) DKK22; lndtte (inc dryer); shop, rest, snacks, bar adj; cooking facs; playgrnd; htd, cov'rd pool in Tarm; shgl beach 200m; watersports nr; fishing; games rm; TV rm; 25% statics; dogs; Eng spkn; adv bkg; quiet; red low ssn; CKE/CCI. "Conv Esbjerg ferry to UK; excel." 1 Apr-1 Nov.  DKK 144        2010*

**BORRE** *D3* (3km SE Rural) *54.97971, 12.52198* **Camping Møns Klint, Klintevej 544, 4791 Magleby [tel 55 81 20 25; fax 55 81 27 97; camping@klintholm.dk; www. campingmoensklint.dk]** Site nr end of metalled section of rd 287 fr Stege to E of Magleby, site sp. Lge, pt sl, pt shd; wc; chem disp; mv service pnt; shwrs DKK7; el pnts (10A) DKK40; lndtte; gas; shop; rest, snacks; cooking facs; playgrnd; pool; shgl beach 3km; fishing; boating; tennis; games area; cycle hire; wifi; TV; 20% statics; dogs; phone; poss cr; Eng spkn; adv bkg; quiet; ccard acc; red low ssn; CKE/CCI. "150m chalk cliffs adj - geological interest; much flora, fauna, fossils; gd walks; friendly staff; excel facs." 1 Apr-31 Oct. DKK 195          2009*

**BOSORE** *C3* (1km N Coastal) *55.19295, 10.80633* **Bøsøre Strand Feriepark, Bøsørevej 16, 5874 Hesselager [tel 62 25 11 45; fax 62 25 11 46; info@bosore.dk; www. bosore.dk]** Fr Hesselager N on rd 163, site sp. Lge, mkd pitch, pt shd; htd wc; mv service pnt; chem disp; baby facs; fam bthrm; serviced pitches; sauna; shwrs DKK4; el pnts (10A) DKK35; lndtte (inc dryer); shop; rest, snacks; bar; cooking facs; playgrnd; htd, covrd pool; sand beach adj; games area; cycle hire; golf 18km; wifi; entmnt; TV rm; 15% statics; dogs DKK20; phone; poss cr high ssn; red low ssn/snr citizens; Quickstop o'night facs. "Superb san facs; gd facs young children; on-site bakery; swipe card for facs - settle on dep." ◆ 26 Mar-23 Oct. DKK 236          2011*

**BRAEDSTRUP** *B2* (6.3km SSE Rural) *55.93552, 9.65314* **Gudenåcamping Brædstrup, Bolundvej 4, 8740 Brædstrup [tel 75763070; info@gudenaacamping.dk; www. gudenaacamping.dk]** Fr Silkeborg take rd 52 twds Horsens; site sp R off rd 52 approx 4km fr Braedstrup. Sm, mkd pitch, unshd; htd wc; chem disp; MV service pnt; baby facs; fam bthrm; shwrs metered; el pnts (10A) metered; lndtte; tradsmn; rest, snacks; bar; BBQ; playgrnd; pool; games rm; wifi; TV rm; 25% statics; dogs DKK10; adv bking; quiet; CKE/CCI. "Sm, attractive site beside River Gudenå; v well run fam site; fishing fr site; excel san facs." ◆ 08 Apr-25 Sep. DKK 178     2011*

# "There aren't many sites open at this time of year"

If you're travelling outside peak season remember to call ahead to check site opening dates – even if the entry says 'open all year'.

⊞ **BREDERBRO** *B3* (10km W Rural/Coastal) *55.06877, 8.66012* **Ballum Camping, Kystvej 37, 6261 Ballum [tel 74 71 62 63; ballum.camping@bbsyd.dk; www. ballum-camping.dk]** At Bredebro on rd 11 turn W on rd 419 twd coast. Site sp 2km S of Ballum. Med, pt shd; htd wc; chem disp; mv service pnt; shwrs DKK1/min; el pnts (10A) DKK30; lndtte (inc dryer); shop & 2km; tradsmn; rest 1km; playgrnd; sand beach 1km; games area; cycle hire; wifi; 50% statics; dogs DKK10; quiet; CKE/CCI. "Close German border; conv Rømø Island with v lge sand beach; gd birdwatching; immac facs." DKK 136          2010*

**CHARLOTTENLUND see København** *D3*

**COPENHAGEN see København** *D3*

**EBELTOFT** *C2* (5.2km SE Coastal) *56.16775, 10.73085* **Blushøj Camping, Elsegårdevej 55, 8400 Ebeltoft [tel 86 34 12 38; blushoj@mail.dk; http://blushojcamping. dk-camp.dk/]** Head Sw on Rte 21 twds Nørrealle. Turn L onto Nørrealle, go thro 1st rndabt, cont ontosteralle, turn L onto Elsegardevej, turn L then R to stay on same rd. Site will be on R. Lge, mkd pitch, ter, pt shd; htd wc; chem disp; mv service pnt; child/baby facs; fam bthrm; shwrs; el pnts (10A) DKK5; gas; lndtte inc dryer; shop on site & 4km, tradsmn; rest, snacks, bar;BBQ; plygrnd; pool; beach pebble; games rm; internet; wifi; tv rm; dogs free; bus 0.1km; twin axles; Eng spkn; adv bkg acc; ccard acc; CKE; red low ssn; "Fantastic location; number of pitches with sea view; immac facs; friendly owner; highly rec." ◆ ltd 23 Mar-15 Sep. DKK 306          2013*

# "That's changed – Should I let The Club know?"

If you find something on site that's different from the site entry, fill in a report and let us know. See www.caravanclub.co.uk/europereport.

⊞ **EBELTOFT** *C2* (1km W Coastal) *56.20997, 10.67838* **Ebeltoft Strand Camping, Nordre Strandvej 23, 8400 Ebeltoft [tel 86 34 12 14; fax 86 34 55 33; info@ ebeltoftstrandcamping.dk; www.ebeltoftstrandcamping. dk]** Fr N site on R of rd 21 as ent Ebeltoft. Lge, pt shd; wc; chem disp; mv service pnt; fam bthrm; baby facs; shwrs inc; el pnts (10A) DKK30; lndtte; gas; shop; rest 200m; snacks; playgrnd; sand beach adj; wifi; TV; some statics; phone; Eng spkn; ccard acc; red snr citizens; CKE/CCI. "Adv bkg ess 1 Nov-1 Apr as facs open/htd by arrangment only; gd location; 10 mins walk to interesting old town cent; conv Mols Peninsula; excel." ◆ DKK 210          2009*

⊞ **EGTVED** *B3* (1.5km W Rural) *55.60670, 9.27873* **Egtved Camping, Verstvej 9, 6040 Egtved [tel 75 55 18 32; fax 75 55 08 32; post@egtvedcamping.dk; www. egtvedcamping.dk]** Fr junc 63 E20/E45 (Kolding) take rd 176. At Egtved L onto rd 417, site sp on L. Lge, mkd pitch, pt sl, pt shd; wc; chem disp; mv service pnt; baby facs; fam bthrm; shwrs; el pnts (10A) DKK25; gas; lndtte (inc dryer); shop; tradsmn; rest, snacks; cooking facs; playgrnd; htd pool; fishing; games rm; wifi; 60% statics; phone; poss cr; Eng spkn; adv bkg; quiet; ccard acc; CKE/CCI. "Clean san facs; conv Legoland, 20km." ◆ DKK 155          2010*

**ENGESVANG** *B2* (1.5km N Rural) *56.18736, 9.35627* **Bøllingsø Camping, Kragelundvej 5, 7442 Engesvang [tel 86 86 51 44; fax 86 86 41 71; post@bollingso-camping. dk; www.bollingso-camping.dk]** Fr A13 dir Viborg, turn E to N of Engesvang & foll minor rd so Kragelund. Site on L 1km after museum. Med, mkd pitch, pt sl, pt shd; htd wc; chem disp; mv service pnt; fam bthrm; baby facs; shwrs; el pnts (16A) DKK25; lndtte (inc dryer); shop; snacks; rest 3km; cooking facs; playgrnd; pool; paddling pool; games area; lake fishing 250m; TV; 2% statics; dogs DKK10; phone; poss cr; adv bkg; red low ssn; quiet; CKE/CCI. "Conv NH for A13; well-kept family site; clean, dated facs; nr Danish lake district." ◆ 1 Apr-1 Oct. DKK 135          2010*

**DENMARK**

DENMARK

**ERSLEV** *B2* (5km W Coastal) *56.81754, 8.67203* **Dragstrup Camping, Dragstrupvej 87, 7950 Erslev [tel 97 74 42 49; fax 97 74 45 49; dragstrup.camping@mail.dk; www.dk-camp.dk/dragstrup]** Fr Nykøbing (Mors) head NW along rte 26. Turn L level with Øster Jolby sp Hvidberg, foll sp Dragstrup & site - well sp fr rte 26. Lge, mkd pitch, pt sl, pt shd; wc; chem disp; mv service pnt; baby facs; fam bthrm; shwrs DKK5; el pnts (10A) DKK26; lndtte; shop & 5km; tradsmn; BBQ; cooking facs; playgrnd; sand beach 200m; fishing; 20% statics; dogs DKK10; phone; Quickstop o'night facs; Eng spkn; adv bkg; quiet; CKE/CCI. "V attractive site; gd touring base; trout-fishing on site." ♦ 1 Apr-30 Sep. DKK 189 2011*

**ERTEBOLLE see Farsø** *B2*

⊞ **ESBJERG** *A3* (6km NW Coastal) *55.51180, 8.39350* **Ådalens Camping, Gudenåvej 20, Sædding, 6710 Esbjerg Vest [tel 75 15 88 22; fax 75 15 97 93; info@adal.dk; www.adal.dk]** Exit E20 junc 75 & at rndabt take 2nd exit twd Esjberg N. In 5km turn R at major x-rds with traff lts. Turn L at 1st rndabt into Gudenåvej, site sp. Site on R in 300m. Lge, hdg pitch, pt shd; htd wc; chem disp; mv service pnt; serviced pitches; baby facs; fam bthrm; shwrs; el pnts (10A) DKK30; lndtte (inc dryer); shop; cooking facs; playgrnd; htd pool; paddling pool; waterslide; beach 500m; golf 10km; internet; some statics; dogs DKK10; phone; Eng spkn; CKE/CCI. "Gd, clean site & modern facs; excel play areas; friendly, helpful recep; conv ferry to Harwich; worth more than a nights stay, ideal for cycling, lovely quiet site, free dog wash." ♦ DKK 200 2011*

**ESBJERG** *A3* (8km NW Rural/Coastal) *55.54359, 8.33921* **Sjelborg Camping, Sjelborg Standvej 1, Hjerting, 6710 Esbjerg Vest [tel 75 11 54 32; fax 76 13 11 32; info@sjelborg.dk; www.sjelborg.dk]** Fr Esbjerg take coast rd N twds Hjerting & Sjelborg. At T-junc, Sjelborg Vej, turn L & in 100m turn R onto Sjelborg Kirkevej (camping sp); in 600m turn L into Sjelborg Standvej (sp); site on R in 600m. Lge, hdg/mkd pitch, pt shd; wc; chem disp; mv service pnt; shwrs inc; fam bthrm; el pnts (10A)€4.50; lndtte (inc dryer); shop; sand/shgl beach nr; lake adj; fishing; golf 5km; bus to town; phone; adv bkg; quiet. "Excel site in a quiet country setting; superb facs & activities all ages; spacious on edge of conservation area; mkd walks & bird sanctuary; v welcoming & friendly." ♦ 9 Apr-18 Sep. DKK 271 2013*

**FAABORG** *C3* (4km NE Rural) *55.10987, 10.29592* **Diernæs Camping, Bjerregardsvej 1, Diernæs, 5600 Faaborg [tel 62 61 13 76; fax 62 61 13 74; diernaes@dk-camp.dk; www.dk-camp.dk/diernaes]** Fr Faaborg foll sp Diernæs, then site. Med, pt sl, pt shd; wc; chem disp; mv service pnt; baby facs; fam bthrm; shwrs DKK2; el pnts (10A) DKK27; lndtte; shop; cooking facs; playgrnd; pool; TV; quiet. "Faaborg pretty town conv for ferries to nrby islands; site in quiet, isolated area." ♦ 1 May-5 Sep. DKK 150 2009*

**FAABORG** *C3* (6km SE Coastal) *55.06405, 10.31373* **Nab Camping, Kildegårdsvej 8, Åstrup, 5600 Faaborg [tel 62 61 67 79; fax 62 61 67 69; info@nabcamping.dk; www.nabcamping.dk]** Fr Faaborg SE on rd 44 dir Svendborg, turn R after 5km at centre bollards; after 1km turn R onto gravel rd, cont 500m to site. Med, sl, pt shd; wc; chem disp; mv service pnt; baby facs; fam bthrm; shwrs DKK2; el pnts (10A) DKK25; gas; lndtte; shop; rest 1km; snacks; BBQ; playgrnd; sand beach 1km; boating; Wifi; some statics; dogs free; phone; Eng spkn; quiet; ccard acc; red long stay; CKE/CCI. "Superb views over archipelago; conv Egeskov Castle & Gardens; excel site; gd cycling & bird watching nrby; m'vans will need levelling blocks; v quiet, views you dream about." 30 Apr-31 Aug. DKK 190 2011*

**FAABORG** *C3* (10km W Coastal) *55.10568, 10.10776* **Bøjden Strandcamping, Bøjden Landevej 12, 5600 Bøjden [tel 63 60 63 60; fax 63 60 63 63; info@bojden.dk; www.bojden.dk]** Rd 8 W fr Fåborg dir Bøjden/Fynshav, site sp nr ferry. Lge, some hdg/mkd pitch, pt sl, terr, pt shd; htd wc; chem disp; mv service pnt; serviced pitches; baby facs; fam bthrm; shwrs DKK5; el pnts (16A) DKK31; lndtte; shop; rest adj; cooking facs; playgrnd; htd pool & paddling pool; sand beach adj; cycle & boat hire; games rm; golf 12km; entmnt; internet; TV rm; 80% statics; dogs DKK15; sep car park; Eng spkn; adv bkg; ccard acc. "Excel family site with activity cent; blue flag beach; sea views fr pitches; interesting area." ♦ 12 Apr-20 Oct. DKK 460 2014*

⊞ **FAKSE** *D3* (12km E Coastal) *55.23913, 12.23964* **Vemmetofte Strand Camping, Ny Strandskov 1, Vemmetofte, 4640 Fakse [tel 53 71 02 26; fax 53 71 02 59; camping@vemmetofte.dk; www.vemmetofte.dk/camping]** Fr rd E47/E55 turn E on rd 154 to Faske & onto Faske Ladeplads. Head NE for 7km, R for Vemmeltofte-Strand to site in 1.5km. Lge, hdg/mkd pitch, pt shd; wc; chem disp; mv service pnt; baby facs; fam bthrm; sauna; shwrs DKK5; el pnts (10A) DKK30; gas; lndtte (inc dryer); shop; rest, snacks 100m; BBQ; playgrnd; sand beach adj; cycle hire; wifi; 50% statics; dogs DKK20; poss cr; Eng spkn; adv bkg; ccard acc. "Quiet site; Copenhagen 50km; ferry port at Rødby 90km." DKK 159 2010*

**FARSO** *B2* (6km W Rural/Coastal) *56.75751, 9.24267* **Farsø Fjord Camping, Gamle Viborgvej 13, Stistrup, 9640 Farsø [tel 98 63 61 76; fax 98 63 61 73; info@farso-fjordcamping.dk; www.farso-fjordcamping.dk]** Fr Viborg take rd 533 N dir Løgstør. 5km N of junc with 187 turn R, site sp on R in 300m. Med, mkd pitch, unshd; htd wc; chem disp; mv service pnt; fam bthrm; baby facs; shwrs DKK5; el pnts (10A) DKK30; gas; lndtte (inc dryer); sm shop; tradsmn; rest, snacks; playgrnd; sm htd pool; shgl beach adj; TV; some statics; dogs free; phone; Eng spkn; adv bkg; quiet; CKE/CCI. "Gd, clean san facs; well-kept; friendly staff; site only 500m fr fjord edge." ♦ ltd 27 Mar-24 Sep. DKK 128 2010*

**FERRING see Lemvig** *A2*

**DENMARK**

**FJELLERUP** *C2* (2.5km W Coastal) *56.51209, 10.54980* **FDM Camping Hegedal Strand, Ravnsvej 3, 8585 Glesborg [tel 86 31 77 50; fax 86 71 77 40; c-hegedal@fdm.dk; www.hegedal.fdmcamping.dk]** Fr rd 16 turn N onto rd 547 dir Fjellerup. Cont W of Fjellerup to Hegedal, site sp. Med, hdg/mkd pitch, pt shd; htd wc; chem disp; mv service pnt; shwrs; el pnts (6A) DKK32; lndtte; shop; rest 3km; BBQ; cooking facs; playgrnd; sand beach adj; watersports; golf 10km; internet; TV rm; some statics; dogs DKK15; adv bkg; quiet; ccard acc. "Well-maintained family site; gd walking, cycling." ♦ 26 Mar-12 Sep. DKK 184                                                    2010*

⊞ **FJERRITSLEV** *B1* (12km W Rural) *57.10912, 9.09998* **Jammerbugt Camping, Thistedvej 546, 9690 Fjerritslev [tel 98 22 51 36; fax 98 22 55 12; kj@jamcamp.dk; www.jammerbugtcamping.dk]** Fr Ferritslev take rd 569 thro Klim & Vester Torup, site on R 1km beyond Vester Torup. Lge, hdg/mkd pitch, pt shd; htd wc; chem disp; mv service pnt; baby facs; fam bthrm; shwrs; el pnts (16A) DKK32; lndtte; ice; shop; rest, snacks; bar; BBQ; cooking facs; playgrnd; htd pool; paddling pool; sand beach 4km; games area; games rm; internet; entmnt; TV; 80% statics; dogs; phone; bus adj; poss cr; Eng spkn; adv bkg; quiet; CKE/CCI. "Vg; friendly owners." ♦ DKK 144                                                          2010*

⊞ **FREDERICIA** *B3* (6km NE Coastal) *55.6243, 9.8335* **Trelde Næs Camping, Trelde Næsvej 297, Trelde Næs, 7000 Fredericia [tel 75 95 71 83; fax 75 95 75 78; trelde@mycamp.dk; www.mycamp.dk]** Route 28 (Vejle-Fredericia). Fr Vejle take Egeskov exit, then Trelde and Trelde-Næs. Fr Fredericia to Trelde, then Trelde Næs. Lge, pt sl, unshd; htd wc; chem disp; mv service pnt; baby facs; fam bthrm; sauna; shwrs DKK4; el pnts (10A) DKK32; lndtte (inc dryer); shop; snacks; BBQ; cooking facs; playgrnd; htd pool; waterslide; sand beach adj; wifi; TV rm; 10% statics; dogs DKK16; phone; poss cr; adv bkg; quiet; ccard acc; red low ssn. "Vg; friendly; fine views over fjord; conv Legoland & island of Fyn; swipecard for all services - pay on dep." ♦ DKK 405                          2013*

**GILLELEJE** *D2* (12km SW Coastal) *56.09051, 12.14977* **DCU Rågeleje Strand Camping, Hostrupvej 2, 3210 Rågeleje [tel 48 71 56 40; fax 48 71 56 85; raageleje@dcu.dk; www.camping-raageleje.dk]** Fr Gilleleje foll sp to Rågeleje on rd 237. Site on coast rd 2km SW of Rågeleje dir Vejby. Lge, hdg pitch, unshd; wc; chem disp; mv service pnt; shwrs; baby facs; fam bthrm; el pnts (10A) DKK30; gas; lndtte (inc dryer); supmkt; rest 1km; cooking facs; playgrnd; sand beach 300m; wifi; TV; dogs DKK20; phone; poss cr; adv bkg; ccard acc; quiet. ♦ 27 Mar-19 Oct. DKK 193                          2010*

**GIVE see Jelling** *B3*

⊞ **GRAM** *B3* (7km W Rural) *55.28884, 8.94758* **Enderupskov Camping, Ribe Landevej 30, Enderupskov, 6510 Gram [tel 74 82 17 11; fax 74 82 07 82; info@enderupskov.dk; www.enderupskov.dk]** Fr Ribe on rd 24 E twds Gram; site on L of main rd (sp) just bef L turn to Fole. Sm, hdg pitch, pt sl, pt shd; wc; chem disp; mv service pnt; shwrs DKK5; el pnts (10A) DKK20; lndtte (inc dryer); shop & 5km; tradsmn; rest, snacks; bar; playgrnd; fishing; some statics; dogs free; phone; Eng spkn; adv bkg; quiet; CKE/CCI. "Conv stop after Esbjerg for Ribe & sw coast; woodland walks; friendly owner." ♦ ltd DKK 125                                            2009*

**GRENAA** *C2* (2km S Coastal) *56.38957, 10.91213* **Grenaa Strand Camping, Fuglsangsvej 58, 8500 Grenå [tel 86 32 17 18; fax 86 30 95 55; info@grenaastrandcamping.dk; www.grenaastrandcamping.dk]** Fr Grenå harbour foll coast rd due S foll sp. V lge, unshd; wc; chem disp; mv service pnt; fam bthrm; baby facs; shwrs; el pnts (10A) DKK35; gas; lndtte; shop; snacks; playgrnd; pool; solarium; sand beach 250m; entmnt; TV; some statics; dogs DKK30; phone; poss cr; adv bkg; red low ssn; poss noisy high ssn. "Conv for ferries to Sweden; busy site." ♦ 1 Apr-16 Sep. DKK 264                                                    2011*

⊞ **GREVE** *D3* (5km NE Urban/Coastal) *55.59434, 12.34315* **Hundige Strand Familiecamping, Hundige Strandvej 72, 2670 Greve [tel 43 90 31 85; info@hsfc.dk; www.hsfc.dk]** Leave E20/47/55 at junc 27 & foll sp Hundige, cont strt ahead until T-junc with rd 151. Turn L, ent 200m on L. Or leave at junc 22 & foll rd 151 down coast to site on R in 8km. Med, some mkd pitch, terr, pt shd; wc; chem disp; mv service pnt; shwrs; el pnts inc; gas; lndtte; shop; hypmkt 1km; tradsmn; rest, snacks; bar adj; BBQ; cooking facs; playgrnd; sand beach 1km; lge sw stadium 5km; TV; 25% statics (sep area); dogs free; phone; site clsd Xmas & New Year; poss cr; Eng spkn; adv bkg; quiet but some rd noise; ccard acc (surcharge); CKE. "Sh walk to rlwy stn & 15 mins to Copenhagen; friendly, helpful staff; office open morning & eves only low ssn; Site in two parts; v scenic; excel, clean facs." DKK 339                          2013*

**GRINDSTED** *B3* (1km SW Rural) *55.75005, 8.91740* **Grindsted Aktiv Camping, Søndre Boulevard 15, 7200 Grindsted [tel 75 32 17 51; fax 75 32 45 75; grindsted@dk-camp.dk; www.dk-camp.dk/grindsted]** Foll sp on Varde-Vejle rd to site on SW o'skts of town nr open-air pool. Med, hdg pitch, pt shd; wc; chem disp; mv service pnt; fam bthrm; baby facs; shwrs DKK5; el pnts (10A) DKK28; lndtte; kiosk; shops 1km; rest 100m; bar; playgrnd; pool 600m; tennis adj; cycle hire; TV; some statics; dogs DKK15; phone; poss cr w/end; adv bkg; quiet. "Sports complex adj with golf & tennis; clean facs; friendly staff; conv Legoland; gd walking & cycle rtes; nh only, site untidy, rd noise." ♦ 1 Apr-1 Oct. DKK 152                                                    2011*

**GUDHJEM (BORNHOLM ISLAND)** *A1* (2km S Coastal) *55.19566, 14.98602* **Sannes Familiecamping, Melstedvej 39, 3760 Melsted [tel 56 48 52 11; fax 56 48 52 52; sannes@familiecamping.dk; www.familiecamping.dk]** SW fr Gudhjem on rd 158, in 2km site on L. Pass other sites. NB: Bornholm Is can be reached by ferry fr Sassnitz in Germany or Ystad in Sweden. Med, mkd pitch, hdstg, terr, pt shd; wc; chem disp; mv service pnt; sauna; shwrs; el pnts (6A) DKK30; gas; lndtte; shop & supmkt 1km; tradsmn; rest 500m; playgrnd; htd pool; paddling pool; sand beach adj; fishing; fitness rm; cycle hire; wifi; TV rm; 10% statics; dogs; phone; Eng spkn; adv bkg; quiet; ccard acc; CKE/CCI. "Friendly & helpful staff; gd cycle paths in area; bus service fr site." ♦ 1 Apr-18 Sep. DKK 270                                                    2011*

**DENMARK**

**HADERSLEV** *3B* (13.6km S Coastal) *55.15313, 9.49424*
**Vikaer Strand Camping, Dundelum 29, Djernaes, 6100
Haderslev [tel 74 57 54 64; info@vikaercamp.dk; www.
vikaercamp.dk]** Head S on Katsund twrd Lille Klingbjerg,
turn R onto Lille Klingbjerg, turn L onto Højgade, turn R
onto Møllepladsen, turn L to stay on Møllepladsen then take
rte 170 to Diernæs Strandvej for 10.9km, then take 1st R
onto Ny Erlevvej for 450 mtrs, turn L onto Omkørselsvejen/
Rte 170, cont to foll Rte 170 for 8.1km, go throu 1 rndbt,
turn L onto Diernæsvej Strandvej for 2.3km foll Diernæs
Strandvej to Dundelum, turn L onto Diernæs Strandvej, turn R
to stay on same rd, turn R onto Dundelum, turn L to stay on
Dundelum and your dest will be on your R. Lge; mkd pitch;
pt sl; unshd; wc; chem disp; mv service pnt; shwrs; el pnts
(10/16 amps); Indry facs; shop; tradsmn; snacks; playgrnd;
dogs (12DKK); Eng spkn; quiet; CCI. "Super site with many
outlets for children, lovely beach and immac san facs." ♦ ltd
Easter-31 Oct.  DKK 300                        2014*

**HADERSLEV** *B3* (1km W Urban) *55.24431, 9.47701*
**Haderslev Camping, Erlevvej 34, 6100 Haderslev
[tel 74 52 13 47; fax 74 52 13 64; info@haderslev-camping.
dk; www.haderslev-camping.dk]** Turn of E45 at junc 68 sp
Haderslev Cent; turn R onto rd 170. On ent town, cross lake
& turn R at traff lts. Site on R at rndabt in 500m. Med, mkd
pitch, hdstg, pt sl, pt shd; htd wc; chem disp; mv service pnt;
fam bthrm; shwrs; el pnts (16A) DKK25; Indtte (inc dryer); shop
1km; rest, snacks; bar; BBQ; cooking facs; playgrnd; pool 1km;
lake sw 1km; games rm; internet; TV; some statics; phone; bus
1km; Eng spkn; adv bkg; quiet; ccard acc (surcharge); CKE/
CCI. "Gd, well-kept site conv E45; all facs to high standard;
attractive old town." 15 Mar-31 Oct.  DKK 34          2013*

⊞ **HAMPEN** *B2* (1km SE Rural) *56.01433, 9.36365*
**Hampen Sø Camping, Hovedgaden 31, 7362 Hampen
[tel 75 77 52 55; fax 75 77 52 66; info@hampen-soe-
camping.dk; www.hampencamping.dk]** Fr Vejle leave E45
at junc 59 onto rd 13. After approx 35km turn L when app
Hampen at site sp, site on R in 1km. Lge, mkd pitch, pt shd;
htd wc; chem disp; mv service pnt; baby rm; shwrs DKK5; el
pnts (16A) DKK30; gas; Indtte (inc dryer); shop; tradsmn; rest,
snacks; bar; playgrnd; pool high ssn; lake sw 1km; fishing
4km; games area; wifi; entmnt; TV rm; phone; dogs DKK10;
Eng spkn; adv bkg; quiet; ccard acc; CKE/CCI. "Surrounded by
moorland; forests & lakes; conv Legoland (tickets sold) & lake
district; welcoming & friendly." ♦ DKK 149 (CChq acc) 2009*

⊞ **HANSTHOLM** *B1* (4km E Coastal) *57.10913, 8.66731*
**Hanstholm Camping, Hamborgvej 95, 7730 Hanstholm
[tel 97 96 51 98; fax 97 96 54 70; info@hanstholm-
camping.de; www.hanstholm-camping.dk]** Ent town fr S
on rte 26. At rndabt turn R onto coast rd sp Vigsø. Site on L
in about 4km. Lge, hdg/mkd pitch, pt sl, pt shd; htd wc; chem
disp; mv service pnt; baby facs; fam bthrm; sauna; shwrs DKK5;
el pnts (10A) DKK35; gas; Indtte (inc dryer); shop; snacks; BBQ;
playgrnd; htd pool; paddling pool; sand beach 1km; fishing;
horseriding; wifi; TV rm; 30% statics; dogs DKK10; phone; Eng
spkn; adv bkg; ccard acc; CKE/CCI. "Fine view of North Sea
coast; nr wildlife area; gd cycling/walking on coast path; excel,
busy, well-maintained site." ♦ DKK 226          2010*

⊞ **HAVNEBY (ROMO ISLAND)** *A3* (500m N Coastal)
*55.09883, 8.54395* **Kommandørgårdens Camping,
Havnebyvej 201, 6792 Rømø [tel 74 75 51 22; fax
74 75 59 22; info@kommandoergaarden.dk; www.
kommandoergaarden.dk]** Turn S after exit causeway
fr mainland onto rd 175 sp Havneby. Site on L in 8km. V lge,
mkd pitch, pt shd; htd wc; chem disp; mv service pnt; baby
facs; fam bthrm; shwrs; el pnts (10A) DKK25; gas; Indtte; shop;
rest, snacks; playgrnd; htd pool; paddling pool; sand beach
1km; tennis; wellness & beauty cent on site; TV; 30% statics;
dogs DKK15; phone; poss cr; adv bkg; quiet. "Family-owned
site; ferry to German island of Sylt." ♦ DKK 180        2009*

---

## "I like to fill in the reports as I travel from site to site"

You'll find report forms at the back of
this guide, or you can fill them in online
at www.caravaclub.co.uk/europereport.

---

**HEJLSMINDE** *B3* (1km NW Coastal) *55.36847, 9.60097*
**Hejlsminde Strand Camping, Gendarmvej 3, Hejlsminde,
6094 Hejls [tel 75 57 43 74; fax 75 57 46 26; info@
hejlsmindecamping.dk; www.hejlsmindecamping.dk]**
14km NE of Haderslev & 8km E of Christiansfeld. Only site
1km fr harbour at Hejlsminde. Med, mkd pitch, terr, pt shd;
wc; chem disp; mv service pnt; shwrs DKK5; fam bthrm; baby
facs; el pnts (10A) DKK35; gas; Indtte (inc dryer); shop & 1km;
tradsmn; rest 1km; playgrnd; htd, covrd pool; sand/shgl beach
500m; cycle hire; wifi; TV; 40% statics; dogs free; phone; Eng
spkn; adv bkg; quiet; ccard acc; CKE/CCI. "Well-equipped;
friendly owner; excel." ♦ ltd 27 Mar-19 Sep. DKK 209 2010*

**HELNAES BY** *B3* (2km S Coastal) *55.13253, 10.0357* **Helnæs
Camping, Strandbakken 21, Helnæs, 5631 Ebberup
[tel 64 77 13 39; fax 64 77 13 54; info@helnaes-camping.
dk; www.helnaes-camping.dk]** Fr Assens to Ebberup on
rd 323, in town cent foll sp Helnæs island, site sp. Med, hdg/
mkd pitch, htd wc; chem disp; mv service pnt; fam bthrm;
private san facs some pitches; shwrs inc; el pnts (6A) DKK30;
Indtte; shop; tradsmn; rest 900m; snacks; bar; BBQ; cooking
facs; playgrnd; sand beach 300m; fishing; watersports; games
area; wifi; TV rm; 50% statics; dogs free; adv bkg; quiet. 1 Apr-
30 Sep. DKK 166                                2010*

⊞ **HELSINGOR** *D2* (3km NE Urban/Coastal) *56.04393,
12.60433* **Helsingor Camping Grønnehave, Strandalleen
2, 3000 Helsingør [tel 49 28 49 50 or 25 31 12 12; fax
49 28 49 40; campingpladsen@helsingor.dk; www.
helsingorcamping.dk]** Site in NE o'skts of town, twd
Hornbæk. Site nr beach o'looking channel to Sweden on
E side of rd. Foll sps on app or in town (beware: sp are sm
& low down). Med, pt shd; wc; chem disp; mv service pnt;
shwrs DKK5; el pnts (10A) DKK30; Indtte; shop; cooking facs;
playgrnd; htd pool nr; beach; 25% statics; phone; poss v cr.
"10 min walk to Hamlet's castle; 20 min walk to town & stn;
gd train service to Copenhagen; max stay 14 days 15 Jun-15
Aug; Baltic ships w/end mid-Aug; v busy/cr high ssn." ♦
DKK 217                                        2014*

---

**HELSINGOR** *D2* (12km S Coastal) *55.93949, 12.51643* **Niva Camping, Sølyst Allé 14, 2290 Nivå [tel 49 14 52 26; fax 49 14 52 40; nivaacamping@post8.tele.dk; www. nivaacamping.dk]** Take coast rd bet Copenhagen & Helsingør. Fr N foll sp to Nivå, & site 500m fr main rd, sp. Fr S site 2km after vill. Lge, mkd pitch, hdstg, pt sl, pt shd; htd wc; chem disp; mv service pnt; baby facs; fam bthrm; shwrs; el pnts (16A); lndtte (inc dryer); shop; tradsmn; rest 500m, snacks 500m; BBQ; cooking facs; playgrnd; sw beach 800m; fishing adj; games rm; wifi; tv rm; 10% statics; dogs; twin axles; poss cr; Eng spkn; adv bkg; quiet but nr busy rlwy; red snr citizens; ccard acc; CKE/CCI. "Conv Helsingborg ferry, Copenhagen, Kronborg Castle (Hamlet); excel san facs; vg location; v quiet; best site in Zealand; excel help; upper level pitches quietest & coolest if hot." 31 Mar-30 Sep. DKK 240          2014*

**HELSINGOR** *D2* (8km SW Rural) *55.96777, 12.45611* **Højsager Camping, Humlebækvej 31; 3480 Fredensborg [tel 4919 44 48; hojsager@dk-camp.dk; www.hojsager. dk-camp.dk]** Leave E47 at junc 5 sp fredensborg; cont along Humleboekvej Rd; site sp on R. Med, hdg pitch, pt shd; wc; chem disp; shwrs DKK10; el pnts (10A) DKK25; gas; lndtte; shop; BBQ; wifi (ltd); 50% statics; dogs; Eng spkn; adv bkg; quiet. "V conv for Helsingborg-Helsingor ferry & Fredensborg Palace; gd cycle paths adj; basic CL type site; NH/sh stay only; helpful, friendly owner." 1 Apr-30 Sep. DKK 155          2011*

**HELSINGOR** *D2* (10km NW Urban) *56.08104, 12.51348* **Skibstrup Camping, Stormlugen 20, 3140 Ålsgårde [tel 49 70 99 71; fax 49 70 99 61; info@skibstrup-camping. dk; www.skibstrup-camping.dk]** Fr Helsingør take N coast rd to Ålsgårde; then foll site sp. Lge, shd; wc; chem disp; mv service pnt; baby facs; fam bthrm; shwrs; el pnts (10A) DKK35; lndtte (inc dryer); shop 1km; cooking facs; playgrnd; pool; paddling pool; beach 500m; wifi; TV; some statics; dogs free; phone; adv bkg; ccard acc; quiet. "Pleasant site amongst trees; conv for ferry & Copenhagen." ♦ 1 Apr-31 Oct. DKK 155          2010*

## "We must tell The Club about that great site we found"

Get your site reports in by mid-August and we'll do our best to get your updates into the next edition.

**HENNE** *A3* (2.7km NNW Rural) *55.73258, 8.22189* **Henneby Camping, Hennebysvej 20, 6854 Henne [tel 75 25 51 63; fax 75 25 65 01; info@hennebycamping.dk; www. hennebycamping.dk]** Fr Varde on rd 181 & 465 foll sp Henne Strand. Turn R after Kirkeby. Site sp. Lge, hdg pitch, pt shd; htd wc; chem disp; mv service pnt; baby facs; fam bthrm; shwrs DKK2; el pnts (10A) DKK32; gas; lndtte; shop; rest; cooking facs; playgrnd; pool 2.5km; beach 2km; cycle hire; TV rm; some statics; dogs DKK15; poss cr; Eng spkn; quiet; ccard acc; CKE/CCI. "Superb facs; gd, clean site." ♦ 22 Mar-20 Oct. DKK 349          2013*

**HILLEROD** *D2* (500m W Urban) *55.9246, 12.2941* **Hillerød Camping, Blytækkervej 18, 3400 Hillerød [tel 48 26 48 54; info@hillerodcamping.dk; www.hillerodcamping.dk]** Fr Roskilde or Copenhagen on A16 twd Hillerød, take 1st L at traff lts sp Hillerød & Frederiksborg Slot Rv233. Site in town cent, not well sp. Med, pt sl, pt shd; wc; chem disp; mv service pnt; fam bthrm; baby facs; shwrs inc; el pnts (10A) DKK35 (long lead poss req); gas; lndtte; shop, rest nrby; snacks; cooking facs; common/dining rm; playgrnd; cycle hire; TV; phone; bus; train nr; poss cr; Eng spkn; adv bkg; quiet; ccard acc; CCI. "Frederiksborg castle in town cent; gd base for N Seeland; 30 min by train to Copenhagen; v helpful, charming owner; pleasant, well-run site; excel, new san facs 2010; no mkd pitch, but owner positions o'fits carefully; many personal touches - eg courtyard with herbs, fruit trees, candles & torches; best site." 12 Apr-19 Oct. DKK 340          2014*

## "I need an on-site restaurant"

We do our best to make sure site information is correct, but it is always best to check any must-have facilities are still available or will be open during your visit.

**HIRTSHALS** *C1* (5.5km SW Coastal) *57.55507, 9.93254* **Tornby Strand Camping, Strandvejen 13, 9850 Tornby [tel 98 97 78 77; fax 98 97 78 81; mail@tornbystrand.dk; www.tornbystrand.dk]** Take rd 55 fr Hjørring twd Hirtshals. In 12km turn L sp Tornby Strand & Camping, site on L in 200m. Lge, pt shd; wc; chem disp; mv service pnt; baby facs; fam bthrm; shwrs; el pnts (10A) DKK30; gas; lndtte; shops adj; snacks; playgrnd; pool 2km; sand beach 1km; TV; dogs DKK5; phone; some statics; Eng spkn; poss cr; adv bkg; quiet; CKE/CCI. "Useful for ferries to Kristiansand & Arendal." ♦ 1 Apr-1 Oct. DKK 170          2009*

**HIRTSHALS** *C1* (W Urban) *57.58650, 9.94583* **Hirtshals Camping, Kystvejen 6, 9850 Hirtshals [tel 98 94 25 35; fax 98 94 33 43; hirtshals@dk-camp.dk; www.dk-camp. dk/hirtshals]** Located 16km N of Hjørring. Turn L off rd 14 3km SW of Hirtshals & site on L. Fr ferry foll sp town cent, then site sp. Med, terr, unshd; wc; chem disp; mv service pnt; baby facs; fam bthrm; shwrs DKK5; el pnts (10A) DKK30; kiosk; rest 500m; snacks 300m; playgrnd; beach 200m; fishing & sw 200m; cycle hire; TV; dogs DKK10; phone; quiet; red low ssn. "Open site on cliff top; san facs dated; friendly staff; conv ferries; on coastal cycle path; late arr area; busy but efficient." ♦ 26 Apr-15 Sep. DKK 172          2013*

**HJORRING** *C1* (12km W Urban) *57.47375, 9.80100* **Lønstrup Camping, Møllebakkevej 20, Lonstrup, 9800 Hjørring [tel 45 21 44 56 37; loenstrupcamping@mail.dk; www. campingloenstrup.dk]** Fr E39 take Exit 3 dir Hjørring for Rte 35 twd Rte 55. Turn R onto Lonstrupvej. Foll sp to site. Med, mkd pitch, pt shd; htd wc; chem disp; mv service pnt; fam bthrm; shwrs inc; el pnts (10A) 25dkk; lndtte (inc dryer); BBQ; cooking facs; playgrnd; beach 500m; wifi; 30% statics; dogs 15dkk; bus 200m; twin axles; Eng spkn; adv bkg; quiet; CCI. "Vg site; family owned; helpful & friendly; lge units may be tight access; close to sm vill & coast." ♦ ltd 28 Mar-29 Sep. DKK 225          2014*

**DENMARK**

**HOBRO** *B2* (7km NE Rural) *56.65161, 9.86876* **Camping Bramslev Bakker, Valsgård, 9500 Hobro [tel 40 29 52 53; mail@bramslevbakker.dk; www.bramslevbakker.dk]** Fr E45 turn E at junc 34 onto rd 541 dir Hadsund. Foll sp fr Valsgaard, site above fjord at end of rd. Med, hdg/mkd pitch, pt sl, unshd; htd wc; chem disp; mv service pnt; shwrs inc; el pnts (10-16A) DKK23; lndtte (inc dryer); shop 3km; rest adj; BBQ; cooking facs; playgrnd; lake sw & beach 300m; fishing, watersports adj; 80% statics; dogs; phone; poss cr; Eng spkn; quiet; red long stay; CKE/CCI. "In nature reserve." ♦ 15 Apr-2 Oct. DKK 112                                                    2011*

**HOBRO** *B2* (1km NW Urban/Coastal) *56.63589, 9.78109* **Hobro Camping Gattenborg, Skivevej 35, 9500 Hobro [tel 98 52 32 88; fax 98 52 56 61; hobro@dk-camp.dk; www.hobrocamping.dk]** Exit E45 junc 35 dir Hobro. Site sp in 3km. Med, mkd pitch, terr, pt shd; htd wc; chem disp; mv service pnt; baby facs; fam bthrm; shwrs DKK5; el pnts (10A) DKK28; lndtte; shop; snacks; cooking facs; playgrnd; pool; games area; TV; 5% statics; Quickstop o'night facs; Eng spkn; quiet; CKE/CCI. "Excel, clean site; easy walk to town; views over fjord; friendly site; vg playgrnd; Viking sites in area." ♦ 1 Apr-30 Sep. DKK 280                                        2011*

**HOJBJERG see Århus** *C2*

**HOJER** *A3* (4km NW Coastal) *54.98713, 8.66325* **Vadehavs Camping, Emmerlev Klev 1, 6280 Højer [tel 74 78 22 38; fax 74 78 20 58; vadehavscamping@mail.dk; www.vadehavscamping.dk]** Take rd 419 W fr Tønder; on ent Højer turn R sp Emmerlev. In 1.5km turn L at campsite sp to end of rd. Med, hdg/mkd pitch, pt shd; wc; chem disp; mv service pnt; baby facs; shwrs inc; el pnts (10A) DKK25; lndtte (inc dryer); shop high ssn; rest 100m; snacks high ssn; BBQ; playgrnd; pool; beach 200m; fishing; cycle hire; wifi; 30% statics; dogs DKK10; Eng spkn; quiet; CKE/CCI. 26 Mar-24 Oct. DKK 146                                                     2010*

⊞ **HOLBAEK** *D3* (2.5km E Coastal) *55.71799, 11.76020* **FDM Holbæk Fjord Camping, Sofiesminde Allé 1, 4300 Holbæk [tel 59 43 50 64; fax 59 43 50 14; c-holbaek@fdm. dk; www.holbaek.fdmcamping.dk]** Fr Rv21 exit junc 20 (fr N) or junc 18 (fr S) & foll sp to harbour. Turn R (E) at harbour - Munkholmvej. Approx 1.5km along Munkholmvej, after traff lts, turn L into Sofiesminde Allé dir marina. Site on R, close to marina. Lge, hdg/mkd pitch, pt shd; htd wc; chem disp; mv service pnt; baby facs; fam bthrm; sauna; shwrs inc; el pnts (10A) inc; gas; lndtte (inc dryer); shop; rest, snacks; cooking facs; BBQ; playgrnd; htd pool; paddling pool; whirlpool; spa; watersports, fishing, golf nr; games area; games rm; wifi; TV rm; 80% statics; dogs DKK15; no c'vans/m'vans over 10m high ssn; phone; adv bkg; quiet; ccard acc; red low ssn. "Well-run site in attractive position; helpful staff; pitches poss tight lge o'fits; clean san facs; gd walks & cycle tracks." ♦ DKK 328 SBS - H17                                                        2013*

**HOLSTEBRO** *B2* (2km S Rural) *56.34930, 8.64496* **Mejdal Camping, Birkevej 25, 7500 Holstebro [tel 97 42 20 68; fax 97 41 24 92; mejdal@dcu.dk; www.camping-mejdal.dk]** Sp off ring rd A11 & A16, SE of town, sp at km 44. Med, pt sl, pt shd; wc; chem disp; mv service pnt; shwrs inc; fam bthrm; baby facs; el pnts (10A) DKK25; gas; lndtte; shop; rest 2km; playgrnd; fishing; boating; golf 5km; TV; dogs DKK15; phone; adv bkg; ccard acc. "Site adj to lge lake in quiet surroundings, but v cr high ssn; open air museum adj." ♦ 21 Mar-22 Sep. DKK 158                                                     2009*

⊞ **HORSENS** *B2* (4km W Rural/Coastal) *55.85928, 9.91747* **Husodde Camping, Husoddevej 85, 8700 Horsens [tel 75 65 70 60; fax 75 65 50 72; husodde@dk-camp.dk; www.husodde-camping.dk]** Site sp to R of Horsens-Odder rd (451), foll rd to fjord, site sp. Med, mkd pitch, pt sl, pt shd; wc; chem disp; mv service pnt; baby facs; fam bthrm; shwrs DKK5; el pnts (10A) DKK35; lndtte; kiosk & shops 500m; rest, snacks, bar 5km; cooking facs; BBQ; playgrnd; pool 3km; sand beach & fishing adj; TV; 10% statics; dogs DKK10; phone; Eng spkn; quiet; CKE/CCI. "Lovely location; lge pitches; well-maintained, well-managed site; friendly welcome; cycle tracks." ♦ DKK 195                                                          2011*

## "Satellite navigation makes touring much easier"

Remember most sat navs don't know if you're towing or in a larger vehicle – always use yours alongside maps and site directions.

⊞ **HOVBORG** *B3* (700m NW Rural) *55.60900, 8.93267* **Holme A Camping, Torpet 6, 6682 Hovborg [tel 75 39 67 77 / 60 91 86 65 (mob); holmeaacamping@ mail.dk; www.holmeaacamping.dk]** Campsite located besides the 425 Grindsted-Ribe. Well sp after Hovborg. Med, mkd pitch, pt shd; htd wc; chem disp; mv service pnt; child/baby facs; fam bthrm; shwrs inc; el pnts DKK32; gas; lndtte inc dryer; shop 0.5km; tradsmn; rest, snacks, bar 300m; playgrnd; pool;entmnt; wifi; tv rm; dog DKK10; bus 0.5km; twin axles; Eng spkn; ccard acc; CKE; red low ssn; "gd cycling; walking; fishing lakes; 20 min fr Legoland; lovely quiet site; immac facs; friendly helpful owner." DKK 165                         2013*

**HVIDE SANDE** *A2* (4.5km S Coastal) *55.96253, 8.14221* **Camping Holmsland Klit, Tingodden 141, Årgab, 6960 Hvide Sande [tel 97 31 13 09; fax 97 31 35 20; c-holmsland@fdm.dk; www.holmsland.fdmcamping.dk]** Fr Ringkøbing rd 15 then rd 181 twd Søndervig, Hvide Sande & Årgab. Site on R. Med, hdstg, pt sl, unshd; wc; chem disp; mv service pnt; fam bthrm; baby facs; shwrs; el pnts (6-10A) DKK30; gas; lndtte (inc dryer); shop; rest 4.5km; bar; beach adj; playgrnd; fishing; wifi; TV; 20% statics; dogs DKK12; phone; Eng spkn; adv bkg; quiet; ccard acc; red CKE/CCI. "Superb beach; next to 40km cycle track; excel for sm children; Legoland 1 hour; friendly." ♦ Easter-26 Sep. DKK 187 (CChq acc)                                                    2010*

**HVIDE SANDE** *A2* (6km S Coastal) *55.94975, 8.15030* **Nordsø Camping & Badeland, Tingodden 3, Årgab, 6960 Hvide Sande [tel 96 59 17 22; fax 96 59 17 17; info@ nordsoe-camping.dk; www.nordsoe-camping.dk]** Fr E20 take exit 73 onto rd 11 to Varde. Then take rd 181 twd Nymindegab & Hvide Sande. Lge, some hdstg, unshd; htd wc; chem disp; mv service pnt; baby facs; fam bthrm; serviced pitches; sauna; private san facs avail; shwrs inc; el pnts (10A) DKK30; lndtte (inc dryer); shop, rest, snacks; bar; playgrnd; 2 pools (1 htd, covrd); paddling pool; waterslides; sand beach 200m; fishing; tennis; wifi; entmnt; TV rm; 10% statics; dogs DKK20; phone; adv bkg; quiet. "Well-maintained facs; extra charge seaview pitches; vg." ◆ 15 Apr-31 Oct. DKK 199 (CChq acc)                                                    2011*

**IDESTRUP see Nykøbing (Falster)** *D3*

**ISHOJ HAVN see København** *D3*

**JELLING** *B3* (10km NW Rural) *55.83138, 9.29944* **Topcamp Riis & Feriecenter, Østerhovedvej 43, Riis  7323 Give [tel 75 73 14 33; fax 75 73 58 66; info@riisferiepark.dk / info@topcampriis.dk; www.riisferiepark.dk]** Fr S exit E45 at junc 61, turn L & foll rd 28 for approx 8km. Turn R onto rd 441 for 15km, then turn R into Østerhovedvej for 2km & turn L into site. Or fr N on E45 exit junc 57, turn R & foll rd for 25km; turn L & foll 442 for 500m; turn R into Østerhovedvej & cont for 1.5km; turn R into site. Med, pt shd; hdg; mkd; hdstg; wc; chem disp; mv service pnt; serviced pitch; baby facs; fam bthrm; jacuzzi; sauna; shwrs DKK5; el pnts (13A) inc; gas; lndtte (ind dryer); shop; bar; BBQ; playgrnd; htd pool; waterslide; paddling pool; jaccuzi; fishing 3.5km; cycle hire; games rm; child entmnt high ssn; golf 4km; wifi; TV rm; 60% statics; dogs DKK20; no o'fits over 15m high ssn; phone; recep 0800-2200; poss cr; adv bkg; quiet; ccard acc; red low ssn; CKE/CCI. "Attractive, well laid-out, well-run site in beautiful countryside; vg san facs; conv for Legoland, Safari Park, Center Mobilium museum in Billund, lakes & E coast; excel." ◆ 12 Apr-27 Sep. DKK 430 SBS - H11         2014*

## "There aren't many sites open at this time of year"

If you're travelling outside peak season remember to call ahead to check site opening dates – even if the entry says 'open all year'.

**JUELSMINDE** *B3* (1.6km ENE Urban) *55.71330, 10.01562* **Juelsminde Strand Camping, Rousthøjs Allé 1, 7130 Juelsminde [tel 75 69 32 10; fax 75 69 32 28; juelsmin@ image.dk; www.juelsmindecamping.dk]** Nr beach in SE corner of town; site sep fr public beach. Nr ferry terminal to Kalundborg. Lge, hdg/mkd pitch, pt shd; htd wc; chem disp; mv service pnt; baby facs; fam bthrm; shwrs; el pnts (10A) DKK15; lndtte (inc dryer); shop, rest, snacks & bar; cooking facs; playgrnd; sand beach 200m; fishing; boating; wifi; TV; phone; poss cr; dogs DKK10; Eng spkn; adv bkg; quiet; CKE/ CCI. "Conv to town & harbour; poss cr." ◆ 1 Apr-27 Sep. DKK 258                                                    2011*

**JYDERUP** *C3* (1km S Rural) *55.65251, 11.39555* **Skarresø Camping, Slagelsevej 40, 4450 Jyderup [tel 59 24 86 80; fax 59 24 86 81; info@skarresoecamping.dk; www. skarresoecamping.dk]** Approx 25km fr Kalundborg dir Copenhagen rte 23 turn L dir Jyderup. Fr town cent foll sp to site on RV225 dir Slagelse, site on R in 1km. Med, pt sl, pt shd; htd wc; chem disp; mv service pnt; baby facs; fam bthrm; shwrs DKK2; el pnts (10A) metered or DKK30; gas; lndtte (inc dryer); shop; tradsmn; rest 1km; BBQ; cooking facs; playgrnd; lake adj; fishing; cycle hire; games area; wifi; TV rm; 25% statics; dogs free; Eng spkn; adv bkg; quiet. "Pleasant site; gd walks round lake fr site; tourist info fr site office." ◆ 26 Mar-26 Sep. DKK 140                                                    2010*

## "That's changed – Should I let The Club know?"

If you find something on site that's different from the site entry, fill in a report and let us know. See www.caravanclub.co.uk/europereport.

⊞ **KARISE** *D3* (3km S Rural) *55.27086, 12.22281* **Lægårdens Camping, Vemmetoftevej 2A, Store Spjellerup, 4653 Karise [tel 56 71 00 67; fax 56 71 00 68; info@ laegaardenscamping.dk; www.laegaardenscamping. dk]** Turn S off rd 209 in Karise, site sp. Med, hdg/mkd pitch, pt shd; htd wc; chem disp; mv service pnt; shwrs DKK5; el pnts DKK30; lndtte; rest, snacks 1km; playgrnd; beach 3km; TV; 60% statics; dogs DKK10; Eng spkn; adv bkg; CKE/CCI. DKK 150                                                    2011*

**KARREBAEKSMINDE see Næstved** *D3*

**KERTEMINDE** *C3* (1.5km N Coastal) *55.46348, 10.67077* **Kerteminde Camping, Hindsholmvej 80, 5300 Kerteminde [tel 65 32 19 71; fax 65 32 18 71; kerteminde@mycamp. dk; www.kertemindecamping.dk]** On L of coast rd on N o'skts of town on rd 315. Lge, pt shd; htd wc; chem disp; mv service pnt; shwrs DKK6; fam bthrm; baby facs; el pnts (10A) DKK30; lndtte; gas; kiosk; tradsmn; rest 2km; BBQ; cooking facs; playgrnd; beach 100m; watersports; cycle hire; wifi; TV rm; 10% statics; dogs DKK15; phone; poss cr; adv bkg; quiet; ccard acc (surcharge); CKE/CCI. "Excel facs; Viking burial ship in cave nrby." ◆ 27 Mar-24 Oct. DKK 173         2010*

**KOBENHAVN** *D3* (6km N Coastal) *55.74536, 12.58331* **Camping Charlottenlund Fort, Strandvejen 144B, 2290 Charlottenlund [tel 39 62 36 88; fax 39 61 08 16; camping@gentofte.dk; www.campingcopenhagen.dk]** Take København-Helsingør coast rd O2/152, site on seaside 2km N of Tuborg factory. Sm, mkd pitch, few hdstg, shd; wc; chem disp; mv service pnt; shwrs DKK5; el pnts (10A) metered; lndtte (inc dryer); shops 500m; rest, bar adj; cooking facs; sand beach; bus; poss v cr; wifi; Eng spkn; quiet but noisy during mid-summer festivities; ccard acc; CKE/ CCI. "Experimentarium Science Park at Tuborg brewery; in grnds of old moated fort; conv Copenhagen & Sweden; gd facs but inadequate high ssn; friendly staff." ◆ 30 Apr-6 Sep. DKK 260                                                    2014*

---

Site report forms at back of guide                    *Last year of report    **197**

**KOBENHAVN** *D3* (15km N Rural) *55.80896, 12.53062*
**Nærum Camping, Langebjerg 5, Ravnebakken, 2850
Nærum [tel 42 80 19 57; fax 45 80 11 78; naerum@dcu.dk;
www.camping-naerum.dk]** Fr Copenhagen take E47/E55/rd
19 N for 16km, turn W to Nærum at junc 14, over bdge x-ing
m'way & sharp L. Lge, pt sl, pt shd; wc; chem disp; mv service
pnt; shwrs inc; el pnts (10A); gas; lndtte; shop; playgrnd; pool
10km; TV rm; train/bus 500m; poss cr; Eng spkn; adv bkg;
some rlwy & m'way noise; ccard acc; CKE/CCI. "Popular nr
woods; conv Copenhagen & Helsingor; shopping cent nrby
over m'way bdge; gd cycle paths; path fr site for suburban rlwy
to Copenhagen; if arr bet 1200 & 1400 select pitch & report to
office after 1400; facs stretched in high ssn; excel bus service
to Copenhagen." ♦ 21 Mar-19 Oct. DKK 331          2014*

**KOBENHAVN** *D3* (2.7km S Urban) *55.65903, 12.55785*
**City Camp, Fisketorvet/Vasbygade, 1560 København
[tel 45 21 42 53 84; reservation@citycamp.dk]** Fr S on E20,
cont over O2 over 'Sjællandsbroen' to R on Scandiagade, cont
on Vasbygade, turn R at 1st traff lts. Site is behind Fisketorv
shopping cent on 'brown field' site - looks like car park - S of
rlwy line by canal. Suggest phone for dirs. M'vans only. Med,
hdstg, unshd; wc; shwrs inc; chem disp; mv service pnt; el
pnts (16A) DKK35; shops nr; dogs; open 0800 to 2200; poss
cr; Eng spkn; poss noisy. "Conv city cent & Tivoli; boat ride
to cent; facs sufficient but simple; friendly." 29 May-30 Aug.
DKK 225                                            2009*

⊞ **KOBENHAVN** *D3* (9km W Urban) *55.67055, 12.43353*
**DCU Absalon Camping, Korsdalsvej 132, 2610 Rødovre
[tel 36 41 06 00; fax 36 41 02 93; absalon@dcu.dk; www.
camping-absalon.dk]** Fr E55/E20/E47 exit junc 24 dir
København, site on L in 1km, sp. Or fr København foll A156
W for 9km. Sp Rødovre then Brøndbyøster, shortly after this
site sp to R at traff lts; ent on L after 100m down side rd, sp.
V lge, mkd pitch, pt shd; htd wc; chem disp; mv service pnt;
baby facs; fam bthrm; shwrs inc; el pnts (10-16A) DKK30 or
metered + conn fee; gas; lndtte (inc dryer); shop & 500m; rest
2km; BBQ; cooking facs; playgrnd; htd pool 300m; golf 10km;
wifi; TV rm; 10% statics; dogs DKK21; bus/train nr; poss cr;
ccard acc (surcharge). "Well located nr Brøndbyøster rlwy stn
& bus Copenhagen (rail tickets fr recep); some pitches unrel
in wet & dusty when dry; vg, modern san facs; office clsd
1200-1400 low ssn; sep area for c'vans & m'vans; helpful staff;
cycle rte to city; vg; nice site; gd cooking facs; well run." ♦
DKK 331                                            2014*

⊞ **KOGE** *D3* (10km SE Coastal) *55.44601, 12.19240* **Stevns
Camping, Strandvejen 29, 4671 Strøby [tel 60 14 41 54;
info@stevnscamping.dk; www.stevnscamping.dk]** Exit
E20/E55 junc 33 twd Køge. In Køge take rd 209 & 260 to
Strøby. In Strøby turn L onto Strandvejen. Lge, mkd pitch,
unshd; htd wc; chem disp; mv service pnt; fam bthrm; baby
facs; shwrs inc; el pnts (10A) inc; lndtte (inc dryer); shop;
tradsmn; rest, bar 400m; BBQ; cooking facs; playgrnd; htd
pool; paddling pool; shgl beach 400m; wifi; some statics; dogs
DKK10; phone; Eng spkn; quiet; CKE/CCI. "Gd site nr coast &
Koge; access to Copenhagen by public transport." ♦ DKK 240
(CChq acc)                                         2013*

**KOGE** *D3* (1km S Coastal) *55.44561, 12.19280* **Vallø
Camping, Strandvejen 102, 4600 Køge [tel 56 65 28 51;
fax 56 65 10 25; vallo.camp@mail.dk; www.
valloecamping.dk]** Exit Køge head SE on rd 261, sp Store
Heddinge for 500m. Site on R on o'skts of town. Lge, pt sl,
pt shd; wc; chem disp; mv service pnt; shwrs; fam bthrms;
baby facs; el pnts (10A) DKK34; gas; lndtte; shop; cooking
facs; playgrnd; sand beach 500m; TV; phone; poss cr; adv
bkg; quiet. "Poss some traff noise fr boundary rd; DKK100
deposit for card to use facs - automatically deducted; pitches
& san facs run down (Jun 09); excel rlwy links to Copenhagen,
Roskilde & Helsingør 15 mins walk fr site." ♦ 1 Apr-30 Sep.
DKK 168                                            2009*

**KOLDING** *B3* (15km E Coastal) *55.46777, 9.67972* **Gammel
Ålbo Camping, Gammel Aalbovej 30, 6092 Sønder
Stenderup [tel 75 57 11 16; camping@gl-aalbo.dk; www.
gl-aalbo.dk]** Foll rd SE fr Kolding to Agtrup then on to Sønder
Bjert & Sønder Stenderup. Foll site sp thro vill twd coast, site
at end of rd. Med, hdg pitch, some hdstg, terr, pt shd; htd wc;
chem disp; mv service pnt; fam bthrm; shwrs inc; el pnts (16A)
DKK32; lndry rm; shop; cooking facs; shgl beach adj; fishing;
boat hire; skindiving; dogs free; 10% statics; poss cr; Eng spkn;
quiet; CKE/CCI. "Well-kept, relaxing site o'looking Lillebælt."
1 Apr-15 Sep. DKK 168                              2010*

⊞ **KOLDING** *B3* (3km S Urban) *55.46290, 9.47290* **Kolding
City Camp, Vonsildvej 19, 6000 Kolding [tel 75 52 13 88;
fax 75 52 45 29; info@koldingcitycamp.dk; www.
koldingcitycamp.dk]** E45 (Flensbury-Frederikshavn) take exit
65 at Kolding Syd twrds Kolding; at 1st traff lts turn R site
800m on L. Lge, pt sl, pt shd; htd wc; chem disp; mv service
pnt; baby facs; fam bthrm; private san facs avail; shwrs inc;
el pnts (10A) DKK30; gas; lndtte (inc dryer); shop high ssn;
supmkt 800m; tradsmn; rest 3km; BBQ; cooking facs; playgrnd;
htd, covrd pool 3km; lake beach & fishing 5km; tennis; wifi; TV
rm; dogs DKK10; phone; bus to town; poss cr; Eng spkn; adv
bkg; some rd noise; ccard acc; 10% red CKE/CCI. "Friendly & v
quiet; conv NH Legoland; vg san facs; gd site; level pitches; full
kitchen facs." ♦ ltd DKK 294 (CChq acc)            2014*

**KOLLUND see Kruså** *B3*

**KORSOR** *C3* (3km N Coastal) *55.34951, 11.1064*
**Storebælt Camping & Feriecenter, Storebæltsvej 85,
4220 Korsør [tel 58 38 38 05; fax 58 38 38 65; info@
storebaeltferiecenter.dk; www.storebaeltferiecenter.
dk]** Exit E20 junc 43 & foll sp to site on S side of bdge. Lge,
mkd pitch, unshd; htd wc; chem disp; mv service pnt; baby
facs; fam bthrm; serviced pitches; shwrs DKK5; el pnts (10A)
metered + conn fee; lndtte; shop; snacks; bar; cooking facs;
playgrnd; pool; beach adj; games area; games rm; wifi; some
statics; dogs free; bus 1km; Eng spkn; adv bkg; quiet; ccard acc
(surcharge); CKE/CCI. "Some m'way noise; sea views; exposed
site poss v windy." ♦ ltd 1 Mar-31 Oct. DKK 170    2009*

**KORSOR** *C3* (10km SE Rural) *55.28991, 11.2649*
**Campinggaarden Boeslunde, Rennebjergvej 110, 4242 Boeslunde [tel 58 14 02 08; fax 58 14 03 40; info@ campinggaarden.dk; www.campinggaarden.dk]** Take rd 265 S out of Korsør & in 8km, bef Boeslunde at camping sp, turn R. Site on L in 2km. Lge, pt sl, shd; wc; chem disp; mv service pnt; shwrs inc; fam bthrm; baby facs; el pnts DKK30 (long lead poss req); gas; lndtte; shop; bar; playgrnd; paddling pool; beach 1.5km; sat TV; dogs DKK10; phone; poss cr w/ ends; adv bkg; quiet; red CKE/CCI. "Gd size, grassy pitches." ◆ 1 Apr-30 Sep.   DKK 190                                       2009*

⊞ **KRUSA** *B3* (1km N Rural) *54.85370, 9.40220* **Kruså Camping, Åbenråvej 7, 6340 Kruså [tel 74 67 12 06; fax 74 67 12 05; info@krusaacamping.dk; www. krusaacamping.dk]** S on E45, exit junc 75 twd Kruså. Turn L onto rd 170, site on L. Lge, pt shd, pt sl; wc; chem disp; mv service pnt; fam bthrm; baby facs; shwrs DKK5; el pnts (10A) DKK30; gas; lndtte (inc dryer); shop; rest, snacks; bar; cooking facs; playgrnd; htd pool; TV; dogs; phone; rd noise; CKE/CCI. "Gd NH; bus to Flensburg (Germany) 1km fr site; new san facs 2010."  ◆  DKK 338                                        2013*

**KRUSA** *B3* (5km E Coastal) *54.84538, 9.46715* **DCU Camping Kollund, Fjordvejen 29A, 6340 Kollund [tel 74 67 85 15; fax 74 67 83 85; c-kollund@fdm.dk]** Take coastal rd E fr Kruså dir Sønderborg; site on L 500m after Kollund. Med, mkd pitch, pt sl, unshd; wc; chem disp; mv service pnt; shwrs DKK5; el pnts (6A) DKK45; lndtte; shop; rest adj; cooking facs; playgrnd; internet; 40% statics; dogs DKK15; phone; Eng spkn; adv bkg; ccard acc. "Friendly owners; gd." ◆ Easter-14 Oct.   DKK 175                                                    2009*

⊞ **KRUSA** *B3* (5km E Coastal) *54.84231, 9.45896* **Frigård Camping, Kummelefort 14, 6340 Kollund [tel 74 67 88 30; fax 74 67 88 72; fricamp@fricamp.dk; www.fricamp. dk]** Take coast rd 8 fr Kruså dir Sønderborg. Turn R at 2nd set traff lts dir Kollund, site sp on L after 3km. V lge, pt sl, pt shd; htd wc; chem disp; mv service pnt; baby facs; fam bthrm; sauna; shwrs DKK5; el pnts (16A) DKK35; lndtte (inc dryer); shop; snacks; cooking facs; playgrnd; htd pool; paddling pool; games area; cycle hire; wifi; 50% statics; dogs free; phone; poss cr; no adv bkg; quiet. "Conv Sønderborg & fjord." ◆ DKK 241                                                   2010*

**KULHUSE** *D2* (1km S Coastal) *55.93168, 11.90907* **DCU Camping Kulhuse, Kulhusevej 199, 3630 Kulhuse [tel 47 53 01 86; fax 47 53 51 28; kulhuse@dcu.dk; www. camping-kulhuse.dk]** Fr Jægerspris on rd 207 N sp Kulhuse. Well sp on L 1km bef vill. Lge, pt sl, terr, pt shd; htd wc; chem disp; mv service pnt; fam bthrm; baby facs; shwrs inc; el pnts (4A) DKK30; lndtte; shop & 1km; rest 1km; snacks; bar 1km; BBQ; cooking facs; playgrnd; sand beach 500m; TV; 20% statics; dogs DKK20; phone; poss cr; Eng spkn; adv bkg; quiet; CKE/CCI. "Gd children's playgrnd facs; pleasant site." ◆ 24 Mar-21 Oct.   DKK 194                                      2011*

**LAVEN see Ry** *B2*

**LEMVIG** *A2* (12km W Coastal) *56.52608, 8.12633* **Bovbjerg Camping, Julsgårdvej 13, 7620 Ferring [tel 97 89 51 20; fax 97 89 53 43; bc@bovbjergcamping.dk; www. bovbjergcamping.dk]** Fr Lemvig foll rd 181 past Nissum Fjord, take rd to L for Ferring. Site to N of vill. Med, hdg/mkd pitch, pt shd; wc; chem disp; mv service pnt; baby facs; fam bthrm; shwrs DKK2; el pnts (10A) DKK29; lndtte; shop; rest 400m; cooking facs; htd pool; paddling pool; sand beach 300m; cycle hire; golf 13km; TV rm; 30% statics; dogs; phone; Eng spkn; adv bkg; quiet; red long stay/snr citizens; CKE/CCI. "Lge pitches with view." 20 Mar-18 Oct.   DKK 178                     2009*

**LEMVIG** *A2* (3km NW Coastal) *56.56733, 8.29399* **Lemvig Strand Camping, Vinkelhagevej 6, 7620 Lemvig [tel 97 82 00 42; fax 97 81 04 56; lemvig@dk-camp.dk; www.lemvigstrandcamping.dk]** Foll camping sps in Lemvig to site. Med, mkd pitch, unshd; wc; chem disp; mv service pnt; baby facs; fam bthrm; sauna; shwrs DKK2; el pnts (10A) DKK35; lndtte; shop; rest adj; cooking facs; playgrnd; htd, covrd pool; beach 300m; games area; games rm; internet; TV rm; 30% statics; dogs DKK10; phone; adv bkg; ccard acc. "Vg sailing cent; pretty area." ◆ 30 Mar-16 Sep.  DKK 359  2013*

⊞ **LOHALS (LANGELAND ISLAND)** *C3* (1km N Urban) *55.13383, 10.90578* **Lohals Camping, Birkevej 11, 5953 Lohals [tel 58 37 50 80; info@lohalscamping.dk; www. lohalscamping.dk]** On island of Langeland. Cross to Rudkøbing, fr island of Tåsinge, then 28km to N of island (only 1 main rd); site in middle of vill nr ferry to Sjælland Island. Med, shd; wc; chem disp; mv service pnt; baby facs; fam bthrm; shwrs; el pnts (10A) DKK30; gas in vill; lndtte; shop; rest, snacks 200m; playgrnd; htd pool; paddling pool; sand beach 1km; boat & cycle hire; fishing; tennis; games area; TV; some statics; dogs free; phone; adv bkg; quiet. "Conv ferry (Lohals-Korsor) 500m." ◆ DKK 178                                   2009*

**LOKKEN** *B1* (2km N Rural) *57.38580, 9.72580* **Løkken Strandcamping, Furreby Kirkevej 97, 9480 Løkken [tel 45 98 99 18 04; info@loekkencamping.dk]** Head NE on Lokkensvej/Rte 55. At rndabt take 3rd exit onto Harald Fischers Vej. Turn R onto Furreby Kirkevej. Site 1.3km on the L. Med, pt shd; htd wc; chem disp; mv service pnt; fam bthrm; shwrs; lndtte (inc dryer); shops 2km; tradsmn; cooking facs; sand beach adj; tv rm; dogs DKK11; twin axles; Eng spkn; adv bkg; quiet; ccard acc. "Vg site; pitches separated by fences; direct access to sand dunes." 1 May-7 Sep.  DKK 312         2014*

**LOKKEN** *B1* (6km S Coastal) *57.32070, 9.67760* **Grønhøj Strand Camping, Kettrupvej 125, Ingstrup, 9480 Løkken [tel 98 88 44 33; fax 98 88 36 44; info@gronhoj-strand-camping.dk; www.gronhoj-strand-camping.dk]** S fr Løkken on rd 55, sp on rd Grønhøj Strandvej. Lge, unshd; htd wc; chem disp; mv service pnt; serviced pitches; sauna; baby facs; fam bthrm; shwrs DKK5; el pnts (13A) DKK30; lndtte (inc dryer); shop; tradsmn; rest 2km; BBQ; cooking facs; playgrnd; sand beach 700m; tennis adj; games area; wifi; TV rm; 30% statics; dogs; phone; Eng spkn; adv bkg; quiet; ccard acc; red snr citizens. ◆ 15 Apr-18 Sep. DKK 158 (CChq acc)                                             2011*

**DENMARK**

**LUNDEBORG** *C3* (700m N Coastal) *55.14560, 10.78136*
**Lundeborg Strand-Camping, Gammel Lundeborgvej 46, 5874 Hasselager [tel 62 25 14 50; fax 62 25 20 22; ferie@ lundeborg.dk; www.lundeborg.dk]** Fr rd 163 turn E at Oure, site sp fr Lundeborg. Med, pt sl, unshd; wc; chem disp; mv service pnt; shwrs DKK5; fam bthrm; baby facs; el pnts (6A) DKK35; lndtte; shop; cooking facs; playgrnd; beach adj; boat-launching; TV; some statics; dogs DKK15; phone; poss cr; adv bkg; quiet. "Attractive sm fishing vill; pay in adv on arr." Easter-13 Sep. DKK 192                                      2009*

**MALLING** *C2* (5km E Coastal) *56.04122, 10.26390* **Ajstrup Strand Camping, Ajstrup Strandvej 81, Ajstrup Strand, 8340 Malling [tel 86 93 35 35; fax 86 93 15 84; info@ ajstrupcamping.dk; www.ajstrupcamping.dk]** Fr S turn R in Odder off rd 451 sp Sakslid. Foll rd for 8km thro Norsminde, then turn R & foll site sp. Lge, mkd pitch, pt shd; htd wc; chem disp; mv service pnt; baby facs; fam bthrm; private san facs avail; shwrs; el pnts (6A) DKK30; lndtte (inc dryer); shop; snacks; BBQ; cooking facs; playgrnd; beach adj; cycle & canoe hire; wifi; TV rm; 6% statics; dogs DKK10; Eng spkn; CKE/CCI. "Adj to excel cycle track thro forest to Århus." ◆ 15 Apr-23 Oct. DKK 164 (CChq acc)                                      2009*

**MARIAGER** *B2* (750m N Coastal) *56.65424, 9.97500*
**Mariager Camping, Ny Havnevej 5A, 9550 Mariager [tel 98 54 13 42; fax 98 54 25 80; info@mariagercamping. dk; www.mariagercamping.dk]** E fr Hobro on rd 555, do not take R sp Mariager, but on to bottom of hill, turn L at camp sp. Med, mkd pitch, unshd; wc; chem disp; mv service pnt; baby facs; fam bthrm; shwrs DKK2; el pnts (16A) DKK25; gas; lndtte; shop; snacks; playgrnd; sand/shgl beach adj; sea & rv fishing; boat launch; 50% statics; dogs free; phone; Eng spkn; adv bkg; quiet; CKE/CCI. "Beautiful vill with museum & abbey; fjord views fr site; vg facs." ◆ 5 Apr-23 Sep. DKK 178  2009*

**MARIBO** *C3* (500m SW Rural) *54.77260, 11.49463* **Maribo Sø Camping, Bangshavevej 25, 4930 Maribo [tel 54 78 00 71; fax 54 78 47 71; camping@maribo-camping.dk; www. maribo-camping.dk]** Exit E47 junc 48 at Maribo. At rndabt take rd to 'Centrum' strt on into Vesterbrogade; turn R into Bangshavevej & foll site sp. Lge, pt shd; wc; chem disp; mv service pnt; baby facs; fam bthrm; shwrs inc; el pnts (6A) DKK32; lndtte; shop; cooking facs; playgrnd; sand beach & lake adj; internet; TV rm; 30% statics; phone; poss cr; Eng spkn; adv bkg; quiet; CKE/CCI. "Clean facs; 5 mins walk into Maribo; museum adj; helpful staff; useful as NH after ferry fr Puttgarden, Germany; site clsd 1300-1500, site yourself; late arr area avail at night." ◆ 30 Mar-21 Oct. DKK 177    2011*

⊞ **MARSTAL (AERO ISLAND)** *C3* (500m S Urban/Coastal) *54.84666, 10.51823* **Marstal Camping, Eghovedvej 1, 5960 Marstal [tel 63 52 63 69; fax 62 53 36 40; marstal. camping@mail.tele.dk; www.marstalcamping.dk]** Fr Ærøskobing ferry to E end of Ærø Island, thro town of Marstal & turn R at harbour twd sailing club; site adj to club. Med, mkd pitch, pt shd; wc; chem disp; mv service pnt; baby facs; fam bthrm; shwrs DKK5; el pnts (16A) DKK28; lndtte (inc dryer); shop; rest, snacks, bar 500m; BBQ; playgrnd; TV; 10% statics; dogs DKK15; phone; poss cr; adv bkg; poss noisy; ccard acc; red low ssn/CKE/CCI. ◆ DKK 163 (CChq acc)                                      2009*

**MIDDELFART** *B3* (7km NE Coastal) *55.51948, 9.85025* **Vejlby Fed Camping, Rigelvej 1, 5500 Vejlby Fed [tel 64 40 24 20; fax 64 40 24 38; mail@vejlbyfed.dk; www.vejlbyfed.dk]** Exit E20 junc 57 or 58. Site sp in Vejlby Fed, NE fr Middelfart dir Bogense, on coast. Lge, mkd pitch, pt shd; wc; chem disp; mv service pnt; fam bthrm; baby facs; sauna; shwrs DKK6; el pnts (10A) DKK28; lndtte; shop; tradsmn; snacks; bar; cooking facs; playgrnd; htd pool; paddling pool; sand beach adj; boating; fishing; tennis; wifi; 30% statics; dogs DKK15; phone; Eng spkn; adv bkg; CKE/CCI. ◆ 15 Mar-14 Sep. DKK 430   2014*

**MIDDELFART** *B3* (6km SE Rural/Coastal) *55.43995, 9.82464* **Ronæs Strand Camping, Ronæsvej 10, Ronæs Strand, 5580 Nørre Aaby [tel 64 42 17 63; fax 64 42 17 73; campingferie@hotmail.com; www.camping-ferie.dk]** Leave E20 at Nørre Aaby junc 57, take 313 S twd Assens. In 5km turn R (NW) to Udby. In Udby turn L to Ronaes, turn R in vill. Site on L, sp. Med, mkd pitch, terr, pt sl, pt shd; wc; chem disp; mv service pnt; baby facs; fam bthrm; shwrs DKK6; el pnts (10A) DKK30; gas; lndtte (inc dryer); shop; rest 6km; snacks high ssn; playgrnd; sand beach adj; fishing; boat hire & launching facs; cycle hire; wifi; TV; 10% statics; dogs DKK15; phone; Eng spkn; adv bkg; quiet; ccard acc;  CKE/CCI. "Gd for families; vg facs." ◆ Easter-19 Sep. DKK 200       2010*

**MIDDELFART** *B3* (3km SW Rural) *55.51694, 9.68225*
**Gals Klint Camping, Galsklintvej 11, 5500 Middelfart [tel 64 41 20 59; fax 64 41 81 59; mail@galsklint.dk; www. galsklint.dk]** Fr W on E20 take rd 161. At traff lts turn L & cross Little Belt Bdge. In 300m turn R into Galsklintvej & foll sp. Lge, hdg/mkd pitch, pt shd; htd wc; chem disp; mv service pnt; baby facs; fam bthrm; shwrs DKK3; el pnts (16A) DKK28; lndtte; shop; rest, snacks; BBQ; cooking facs; playgrnd; shgl beach adj; fishing; boat hire; 10% statics; dogs; Eng spkn; adv bkg; quiet; ccard acc (surcharge); CKE/CCI. "Site surrounded by forest; gd cycling/walking; vg; well run mod facs shoreside next woodland." ◆ Easter-2 Oct. DKK 200                2012*

**NAERUM see København** *D3*

**NAESTVED** *D3* (6km SW Rural/Coastal) *55.20051, 11.66438* **De Hvide Svaner Camping, Karrebækvej 741, 4736 Karrebæksminde [tel 55 44 24 15; svaner@mail.dk; www. dehvidesvaner.dk]** Fr Næstved take Karrebæksminde rd 265. Site on L 200m after turn for Skælskør. Lge, hdg/mkd pitch, pt sl, pt shd; wc; chem disp; mv service pnt; baby facs; fam bthrm; shwrs inc; el pnts (10A) DKK30; gas; lndtte; sm shop; rest; playgrnd; htd pool; paddling pool; beach nrby; cycle hire; games area; wifi; TV; many statics; dogs DKK10; phone; Quickstop o'night facs; Eng spkn; adv bkg; quiet. "Excel, modern san facs; friendly staff; well situated nr lake." ◆ Easter-16 Oct. DKK 192                                      2009*

**NAKSKOV** *C3* (13km SW Coastal) *54.79180, 10.98110*
**Albuen Strand Camping, Vesternæsvej 70, Ydø, 4900 Nakskov [tel 54 94 87 62; fax 54 94 90 27; mail@albuen. dk; www.albuen.dk]** S fr Nakskov dir Langø. In approx 10km at Ydø, foll sp to site. Lge, unshd; htd wc; chem disp; mv service pnt; baby facs; fam bthrm; shwrs DKK2; el pnts (10A) DKK30; lndtte (inc dryer); shop; tradsmn; cooking facs; playgrnd; htd pool; paddling pool; sand beach adj; cycle hire; games area; wifi; TV rm; 15% statics; dogs DKK20; phone; adv bkg; quiet. ◆ 17 Apr-25 Sep. DKK 200                2010*

**NAKSKOV** *C3* (2.5km W Coastal) *54.83303, 11.09083*
**Hestehoved Camping, Hestehovedet 2, 4900 Nakskov**
**[tel 54 95 17 47; fax 54 95 69 20; hestehovedet@tdcadsl.**
**dk]** Cont on main rd fr Tårs after exit ferry fr Spodsbjerg. Site
sp R after passing town boundary. Med, mkd pitch, pt shd; wc;
chem disp; mv service pnt; baby facs; fam bthrm; shwrs DKK2;
el pnts (10A) DKK27; lndtte; shop 3km; rest 200m; playgrnd;
marina adj; sand beach 250m; cycle hire; TV; 70% statics;
phone; adv bkg; quiet. "Conv for ferry Spodsbjerg-Tårs." ♦
7 Apr-30 Sep. DKK 140                                    2009*

**NEXO (BORNHOLM ISLAND)** *A1* (4km S Coastal) *55.02895,*
*15.11130* **FDM Camping Balka Strand, Klynevej 6,**
**Snogebæk, 3730 Nexø [tel 56 48 80 74; fax 56 48 86 75;**
**c-balka@fdm.dk; www.balka.fdmcamping.dk]** Fr ferry
at Rønne on rd 38 to Nexø, foll sp to site N of Snogebæk.
Lge, mkd pitch, pt shd; htd wc; chem disp; mv service pnt;
baby facs; shwrs inc; el pnts (6A) DKK30; lndtte; shop;
supmkt 500m; tradsmn; rest, snacks 500m; BBQ; cooking
facs; playgrnd; sand beach 200m; fishing 500m; windsurfing
1km; cycle hire; games area; golf 5km; internet; TV; some
statics; dogs DKK15; adv bkg; quiet; ccard acc. "Superb
beach; vg touring base Bornholm Is." ♦ 25 Apr-13 Sep.
DKK 189                                                 2009*

⊞ **NORDBORG** *B3* (4km N Rural/Coastal) *55.07762, 9.71482*
**Augustenhof Strand Camping, Augustenhofvej 30, 6430**
**Nordborg [tel/fax 74 45 03 04; augustenhof@dk-camp.dk;**
**www.dk-camp.dk/augustenhof]** Take rd N out of Nordborg
to Købingsmark. In 1km turn W to Stærbækvej. Cont twd
Augustenhofvej. Turn NW & foll rd to camp nr lighthouse.
Med, mkd pitch, pt shd; htd wc; chem disp; mv service pnt;
baby facs; fam bthrm; shwrs DKK2; el pnts (6-13A) DKK26.50;
gas; lndtte; shop; rest, bar 4km; playgrnd; pool 5km; beach;
boat-launching; TV; 60% statics; dogs DKK9; phone; Quickstop
o'night facs; adv bkg; quiet. "Conv for Nordberg Castle; adv
bkg rec low ssn." DKK 167 (CChq acc)                    2009*

⊞ **NORDSKOV** *C3* (1km N Coastal) *55.60648, 10.62190*
**Fyns Hoved Camping, Fynshovedvej 748, Nordskov, 5390**
**Martofte [tel 65 34 10 14; fax 65 34 25 14; fynshoved@**
**dk-camp.dk; www.fynshovedcamping.dk]** Fr E20 foll sp
N to Kerteminde then take 315 dir Martofte & Nordskov. Or
fr Odense/Nyborg take 165 N to Kerteminde, then as above.
Lge, mkd pitch, pt shd; wc; chem disp; 50% serviced pitches;
mv service pnt; baby facs; fam bthrm; shwrs; el pnts (10A)
DKK30 (long lead poss req); gas; lndtte; shop; tradsmn; rest,
snacks; bar; BBQ; cooking facs; playgrnd; shgl beach adj;
entmnt; TV rm; some statics; dogs; poss cr; Eng spkn; adv bkg;
quiet; ccard acc; CKE/CCI. "Excel scenic, rural area; ideal for
cycling; vg." ♦ DKK 165                                 2010*

**NORRE AABY see Middelfart** *B3*

**NORRE NEBEL** *A2* (6km NW Rural) *55.82675, 8.21552*
**Vesterlund Camping & Café, Vesterlundvej 101, 6830**
**Nørre Nebel [tel 86 85 56 65; mai-britt.schulze@teliamail.**
**dk; www.vesterlundcamping.dk]** Fr rte 181 thro Nørre
Nebel dir Hvide Sande, turn R at site sp in approx 5km, site in
1km on L. Recep in site rest. Med, hdg pitch, pt shd; htd wc;
chem disp; mv service pnt; fam bthrm; shwrs; lndry rm; rest;
cooking facs; playgrnd; few statics; Eng spkn; quiet; CKE/CCI.
"Peaceful, relaxing, well-kept site; helpful owner." 27 Mar-
24 Oct. DKK 150                                         2010*

**NYBORG** *C3* (2km SE Coastal) *55.3042, 10.82461*
**Nyborg Strandcamping, Hjejlevej 99, 5800 Nyborg**
**[tel 65 31 02 56; mail@strandcamping.dk; www.**
**strandcamping.dk]** Exit E20 at junc 44. Turn N, site sp in
1km. Lge, mkd pitch, pt shd; wc; chem disp; mv service pnt;
fam bthrm; baby facs; shwrs DKK9; el pnts (10A) metered;
gas; lndtte; shop; rest 500m; snacks; playgrnd; sand beach
adj; fishing; golf 1km; internet; TV; 50% statics; dogs; phone;
Eng spkn; adv bkg; CKE/CCI. "Conv m'way, rlwy & ferry; excel
views of bdge; gd facs; gd site; well difined pitches next to
beach." ♦ 13 Apr-15 Sep. DKK 342                        2014*

**NYBORG** *C3* (9km S Rural) *55.23693, 10.8080* **Tårup**
**Stand Camping, Lersey Allé 25, Tårup Strand, 5871**
**Frørup [tel 65 37 11 99; fax 65 37 11 79; mail@**
**taarupstrandcamping.dk; www.taarupstrandcamping.dk]**
S fr Nyborg take 163 twds Svendborg; after 6.5km turn L sp
Tårup. In 2.7km turn L sp Tårup Strand. Site 1.5km on R. Med,
mkd pitch, terr; htd wc; chem disp; mv service pnt; fam bthrm;
baby facs; shwrs DKK5; el pnts (6-10A) DKK26; lndtte; kiosk;
playgrnd; shgl beach; lake; TV; 70% statics; games rm; wifi;
phone; dogs; adv bkg; quiet; poss cr high ssn; Ccard acc; CKE/
CCI. "Quiet family site; excel views of bdge; fishing; excel site."
4 Apr-21 Sep. DKK 288                                   2014*

> ## "I like to fill in the reports
> ## as I travel from site to site"
> You'll find report forms at the back of
> this guide, or you can fill them in online
> at www.caravaclub.co.uk/europereport.

**NYKOBING (FALSTER)** *D3* (8km E Coastal) *54.74057,*
*12.02801* **Campinggården Ulslev Strand, Strandvejen**
**3, Ulslev Strand, 4872 Idestrup [tel 54 14 83 50; fax**
**54 14 83 47; ulslev@dk-camp.dk; www.campinggaarden-**
**ulslev.dk]** Foll E55 around Nykøbing to E, at rndabt turn L
twd Horbelev. In 2km turn R & foll sp Ulslev Strand. Fr Gedser
ferry turn R (E) at rndabt on app Nykøbing, then as above.
Lge, mkd pitch, pt sl, pt shd; wc; chem disp; mv service pnt;
fam bthrm; baby facs; sauna; shwrs; el pnts (10A) DKK30; gas;
lndtte; shop; rest; playgrnd; sand beach adj; games area; TV;
20% statics; dogs free; phone; Eng spkn; adv bkg; quiet; ccard
acc; CKE/CCI. "Gd beaches; gd cycling; nr several theme parks;
day ferry to Rostok fr Gedser." 20 Mar-3 Oct. DKK 174  2010*

**NYKOBING (MORS)** *B2* (5km SW Coastal) *56.76435, 8.8148*
**Jesperhus Camping, Legindvej 30, 7900 Nykøbing**
**[tel 96 70 14 00; fax 96 70 14 17; jesperhus@jesperhus.dk;**
**www.jesperhus.dk]** Exit rd 26 at sp Nykøbing Syd (S) & foll sp
to Salling Sund for 1km; foll sp for Billund. Site on R 200m past
Jesperhus Blomsterpark (Flower Park). V lge, hdg pitch, terr,
pt shd; wc; chem disp; mv service pnt; fam bthrm; baby facs;
sauna; shwrs inc; el pnts (6A) DKK40; lndtte (inc dryer); shop;
rest, snacks; bar; cooking facs; playgrnd; htd pools (1 covrd);
waterpark; beach 1km; fishing; tennis; games area; entmnt; TV;
50% statics; dogs DKK30; phone; adv bkg; quiet. "Jesperhus
Blomsterpark (open May-Oct) excel; site vg for families; many
activities." ♦ 26 Mar-25 Oct. DKK 260                   2010*

Check any essential information with the site before you travel          *Last year of report  **201**

**DENMARK**

NYMINDEGAB *A2* (600m S Rural) *55.81263, 8.20001*
Nymindegab Familie Camping, Lyngtoften 12, 6830
Nymindegab [tel 75 28 91 83; fax 75 28 94 30; info@
nycamp.dk; www.nycamp.dk] Clear sp on L of rd 181 at
ent to vill fr Esbjerg & SE via Nørre Nebel. If app fr N, thro vill
& look for Int'l sp on R. Lge, mkd pitch, pt shd; wc; chem disp;
mv service pnt; baby facs; fam bthrm; sauna; shwrs DKK2; el
pnts (16A) DKK25; gas; Indtte; shop; rest 500m; bar; playgrnd;
pool; paddling pool; sand beach 2km; games area; TV; internet;
dogs; phone; adv bkg; poss cr; quiet; ccard acc; red low ssn.
"Adj army firing ranges troublesome at times; helpful visitors."
♦ 1 Apr-27 Sep.  DKK 151                           2009*

NYSTED *D4* (2km SE Coastal) *54.65426, 11.73167* Nysted
Camping, Skansevej 38, 4880 Nysted [tel 54 87 09 17; fax
54 87 14 29; nystedcamping@post.tele.dk; www.nysted-
camping.dk] Foll sp for site in Nysted. Med, mkd pitch, pt
shd; htd wc; chem disp; mv service pnt; baby facs; fam bthrm;
shwrs; el pnts (10A) DKK30; gas; Indtte; shop; snacks; cooking
facs; playgrnd; sand beach adj; cycle hire; games area; TV;
wifi; 10% statics; dogs; phone; site open in winter on request;
adv bkg; ccard acc; red CKE/CCI. "Noisy at w/end; conv for
Rødbyhavn-Puttgarden ferry; castle & vintage car museum in
4km." ♦ Easter-19 Oct.  DKK 150                     2009*

⊞ ODENSE *C3* (4km S Rural) *55.36966, 10.39316* DCU
Camping Odense, Odensevej 102, 5260 Odense
[tel 66 11 47 02; fax 65 91 73 43; odense@dcu.dk; www.
camping-odense.dk] Exit E20 junc 50 foll sp 'centrum'
(Stenlosevej). After rndabt site on L just after 3rd set traff lts.
Ent to R of petrol stn. Lge, pt shd; mkd pitch; htd wc; chem
disp; mv service pnt; fam bthrm; baby facs; shwrs inc; el pnts
(10A) DKK30; gas; Indtte; shop; rest 1.5km; playgrnd; pool; TV
rm; dogs DKK15; phone; bus; Eng spkn; adv bkg; quiet; ccard
acc (surcharge); CKE/CCI. "Hans Christian Andersen's house;
many attractions; excel, friendly, family-run site; busy high ssn
& facs stretched; easy bus access to town cent; lovely, easy
cycle rte into town cent; gd san fac; pitches tight for larger
units." ♦ DKK 336                                  2014*

⊞ ODENSE *C3* (9km W Rural) *55.3894, 10.2475*
Campingpladsen Blommenslyst, Middelfartvej 494, 5491
Blommenslyst [tel/fax 65 96 76 41; info@blommelyst-
camping.dk; www.blommenslyst-camping.dk] Exit E20
onto 161 (junc 53); sp 'Odense/Blommenslyst', site on R after
2km; lge pink Camping sp on side of house. Sm, pt sl, shd;
htd wc; chem disp; mv service pnt; shwrs DKK5; el pnts (4A)
DKK30; Indtte; shop; café 500m; playgrnd; sm lake; some
statics; dogs DKK10; bus; Eng spkn; adv bkg; some rd noise;
CKE/CCI. "Picturesque setting round sm lake; gd, clean facs;
welcoming owners; frequent bus to town outside site; excel."
♦ 5 Jan-20 Dec.  DKK 206                            2013*

⊞ OKSBOL *A3* (1km N Rural) *55.64048, 8.28204* Camp
West, Baunhøjvej 34, 6840 Oksbøl [tel 75 27 11 30; fax
75 27 11 31; info@campwest.dk; www.campwest.dk] N
fr Oksbøl dir Øster Vrøgum & Henne, site sp. Med, hdg pitch,
pt shd; wc; chem disp; mv service pnt; fam bthrm; baby facs;
shwrs inc; el pnts (10A) DKK30; gas; Indtte; shop; playgrnd;
sand beach 12km; TV; dogs free; phone; Quickstop o'night
facs; adv bkg; ccard acc; quiet; CKE/CCI. "Pleasant, rural site;
less cr than beach sites." DKK 174                  2011*

OTTERUP *C3* (6km NE Coastal) *55.56295, 10.45390* Hasmark
Strand Camping, Strandvejen 205, Hasmark Strand, 5450
Otterup [tel 64 82 62 06; fax 64 82 55 80; info@hasmark.
dk; www.hasmark.dk] Exit rd 51 thro Odense onto rd 162
& foll sp Havn Otterup, then dir Hasmark. Site sp. Lge, pt shd;
htd wc; chem disp; mv service pnt; fam bthrm; private san facs
avail; shwrs; el pnts (10A) DKK35; Indtte; shop; rest, snacks;
bar; cooking facs; playgrnd; pool complex; sand beach adj;
games area; cycle hire; golf 15km; wifi; TV rm; 25% statics;
dogs DKK10; adv bkg; quiet. "Pleasant site on superb beach."
♦ 1 Apr-25 Sep.  DKK 175 (CChq acc)                2009*

RAGELEJE see Gilleleje *D2*

⊞ RANDERS *B2* (6km SW Rural) *56.44984, 9.95287*
Randers City Camp, Hedevej 9, Fladbro, 8900 Randers
[tel/fax 86 42 93 61; info@randerscitycamp.dk; www.
randerscitycamp.dk] Take exit 40 fr E45 & turn twd Randers.
Approx 100m fr m'way turn R at traff lts dir Langå. Site clearly
sp in 3km & also sp fr rd 16. Lge, pt shd; wc; chem disp; mv
service pnt; baby facs; fam bthrm; shwrs inc; el pnts (10A)
DKK30; Indtte (inc dryer); shop 2km; cooking facs; playgrnd;
htd pool; fishing; games rm; golf adj; TV; some statics; dogs
DKK10; phone; Eng spkn; ccard acc. "On heather hills with
view of Nørreå valley; rec arr early for pitch with view; golf
course." ♦ DKK 164                                 2010*

⊞ RIBE *B3* (2km SE Rural) *55.3171, 8.7603* Parking
Storkesøen, Haulundvej 164, 6760 Ribe [tel 75 41 04 11;
fax 41 08 57; info@storkesoen.dk; www.storkesoen.dk]
Fr S on rte 11, turn R at 1st rndabt onto rte 24 & R at next
rndabt. Site 100m on R, sp fishing. Fr S on rte 24, at 1st rndabt
after rlwy turn L, site 200m on R. M'vans only - check in at
fishing shop on R. Sm, all hdstg, unshd; wc; own san; chem
disp; shwrs inc; el pnts (5A/16A) inc; fishing shop; snacks; lake
fishing. "Picturesque, quiet site o'looking fishing lakes; walking
dist Denmark's oldest city; m'vans & c'vans acc, site had fire in
Nov and clsd rest, ideal NH." DKK 140             2011*

"We must tell The Club about
that great site we found"

Get your site reports in by mid-August
and we'll do our best to get your updates
into the next edition.

⊞ RIBE *B3* (1km W Rural) *55.34115, 8.76506* Ribe Camping,
Farupvej 2, 6760 Ribe [tel 75 41 07 77; fax 75 41 00 01;
info@ribecamping.dk; www.ribecamping.dk] Fr S foll A11
by-pass W of Ribe to traff lts N of town; turn W off A11 at traff
lts; site 500m on R. Fr N (Esbjerg ferry) to Ribe, turn R at traff
lts sp Farup. Site on R, sp. Lge, pt shd; htd wc; chem disp; mv
service pnt; baby rm; fam bthrm; some serviced pitches; shwrs
DKK8; el pnts (10A) DKK35; gas; Indtte; shop; snacks; cooking
facs; playgrnd; htd pool; games rm; internet; TV; 10% statics;
dogs DKK15; phone; Quickstop o'night facs; poss cr; adv bkg;
quiet; ccard acc (transaction charge); CKE/CCI. "Ribe oldest
town in Denmark; much historical interest; helpful staff; well-
run, friendly site; excel, modern san facs; conv Esbjerg ferry." ♦
DKK 351                                            2014*

**RINGE** *C3* (1km NNW Urban) *55.24024, 10.47439* **Midtfyns Camping, Søvej 30-34, 5750 Ringe [tel 62 62 21 51; fax 62 62 21 54; mfc@midtfyns-frididscenter.dk; www. midtfyns-fritidscenter.dk]** Exit A9 Odense-Svendborg at Ringe N & foll site sp. Register at recep adj sports cent. Med, hdg/mkd pitch, pt sl, pt shd; wc; chem disp; mv service pnt; shwrs; el pnts DKK24; lndtte; shops 500m; rest, snacks; playgrnd; pool; sand beach 20km; tennis; some statics; phone; Quickstop o'night facs; quiet; ccard acc;CKE/CCI. "Egeskov Castle (10km) worth a visit." ♦ 1 May-30 Sep. DKK 157                                        2009*

**RINGKOBING** *A2* (5km E Rural) *56.08856, 8.31659* **Ringkøbing Camping, Herningvej 105, 6950 Ringkøbing [tel/fax 97 32 04 20; info@ringkobingcamping.dk; www. ringkøbingcamping.dk]** Take rd 15 fr Ringkøbing dir Herning, site on L. Med, hdg/mkd pitch, pt shd; wc; chem disp; mv service pnt; shwrs DKK2; el pnts (10A) DKK29; gas; lndtte; shop; sand beach 3km; playgrnd; TV; phone; dogs DKK10; Quickstop o'night facs; poss cr; adv bkg; quiet. "Beautiful site in mixed forest; friendly welcome; excel facs; gd walks; 3km to fjord; 14km to sea." ♦ 1 Apr-30 Sep. DKK 226        2011*

**RINGSTED** *D3* (8km NE Rural) *55.49644, 11.85796* **Camping Skovly, Nebs Møllevej 65, Ortved, 4100 Ringsted [tel 57 52 82 61; fax 57 52 86 25; info@skovlycamping. dk; www.skovlycamping.dk]** Take junc 35 off E20 onto rd 14 N. Turn W at sp in Ortved. Med, hdg/mkd pitch, pt sl, shd; wc; chem disp; mv service pnt; fam bthrm; baby facs; shwrs DKK6; el pnts (6A) metered + DKK15; lndtte (inc dryer); shop; tradsmn; cooking facs; playgrnd; htd pool; paddling pool; games rm; wifi; TV; 50% statics; dogs DKK15; phone; Eng spkn; adv bkg; quiet; ltd facs low ssn; ccard acc (surcharge);CKE/CCI. "Pleasant, wooded site; friendly, family-run, well-organised site; clean san facs; conv Viking Cent & other attractions." 1 Apr-1 Oct. DKK 182        2010*

⊞ **RODBYHAVN** *C4* (5km NE Urban) *54.69873, 11.39218* **Camping Rødby Lystskov, Strandvej 3, 4970 Rødby [tel 54 60 12 16; info@rodbycamping.dk; www. rodbycamping.dk]** Fr N Zeeland or Rødby ferries, foll sps for site in Rødby, NE of town cent. Med, pt shd; wc; chem disp; mv service pnt; baby facs; shwrs inc; el pnts (16A) DKK25; gas; lndtte (inc dryer); shop; cooking facs; playgrnd; beach 4km; TV; 20% statics; dogs free; poss cr; Eng spkn; adv bkg;CKE/CCI. "Clean facs; helpful owner; liable to flooding; sh walk to town cent; conv for ferries." ♦ DKK 150        2010*

**RODOVRE see København** *D3*

**RONNE (BORNHOLM ISLAND)** *A1* (1km S Coastal) *55.08978, 14.70565* **Galløkken Camping, Strandvejen 4, 3700 Rønne [tel 56 95 23 20; info@gallokken.dk; www.gallokken. dk]** Fr Rønne cent foll dir airport, site well sp. Med, hdg/mkd pitch, pt shd; htd wc; chem disp; mv service pnt; baby facs; fam bthrm; private san facs avail; shwrs; el pnts (13A) DKK25; lndtte (inc dryer); shop; tradsmn; supmkt 500m; rest 600m; BBQ; cooking facs; playgrnd; sand beach 200m; tennis 1km; cycle hire; games rm; wifi; TV; some statics; dogs; adv bkg; quiet. "Lovely location; gd, modern san facs." ♦ 1 May-31 Aug. DKK 168        2010*

**ROSKILDE** *D3* (4km N Rural) *55.67411, 12.07955* **Roskilde Camping, Baunehøjvej 7-9, 4000 Veddelev [tel 46 75 79 96; fax 46 75 44 26; mail@roskildecamping. dk; www.roskildecamping.dk]** Leave rd 21/23 at junc 11 & turn N on rd 6 sp Hillerød. Turn R onto rd 02 (E ring rd); then rejoin 6; (watch for camping sp). At traff lts with camping sp turn L twds city & foll site sp. Lge, mkd pitch, pt sl, pt shd; wc; own san; chem disp; baby facs; shwrs DKK6; el pnts (10A) DKK30; gas; lndtte; shop; rest; playgrnd; shgl beach; watersports; games rm; TV; wifi; poss cr high ssn; Eng spkn; adv bkg; quiet; ccard acc (surcharge); CKE/CCI. "Beautiful views over fjord; nr Viking Ship Museum (a must) - easy parking; beautiful cathedral; excel rest & shop open 0800-2000; bus service to stn, frequent trains to Copenhagen; ltd flat pitches; lovely site; new facs block with card for entry (2014)." 31 Mar-23 Sep. DKK 315        2014*

**ROSLEV** *B2* (10km NW Rural/Coastal) *56.74333, 8.86884* **Glyngøre Camping, Sundhøj 20A, Glyngøre, 7870 Roslev [tel 97 73 17 88; fax 97 73 17 99; post@glyngore-camping. dk; www.glyngore-camping.dk]** Site sp fr rd 26 dir Glyngøre, immed S of Sallingsund bdge. Lge, hdg/mkd pitch, pt sl, pt shd; htd wc; chem disp; mv service pnt; baby facs; fam bthrm; shwrs metered; el pnts (16A) inc; lndtte (inc dryer); ice; shop; rest, snacks; bar; BBQ; cooking facs; playgrnd; htd, covrd pool; sand beach 1km; games area; games rm; internet; TV; 30% statics; dogs; phone; Eng spkn; adv bkg; quiet; ccard acc; CKE/CCI. "Excel, welcoming, spacious site in attractive position; gd touring base." ♦ 1 Apr-12 Oct. DKK 202        2010*

**RY** *B2* (1km S Rural) *56.07692, 9.76527* **Holmens Camping, Klostervej 148, 8680 Ry [tel 86 89 17 62; fax 86 89 17 12; info@holmens-camping.dk; www.holmens-camping. dk]** Exit Skanderborg on 445 sp Ry & Silkeborg. In Ry immed after level x-ing turn L on rd sp Øm-Kloster & camping sp. Site on R in 2km. Lge, mkd pitch, pt sl, pt shd; wc; chem disp; mv service pnt; baby facs; fam bthrm; shwrs DKK7; el pnts (6A) DKK28; gas; lndtte; shops 2km; rest 2km; snacks; cooking facs; playgrnd; lake sw, fishing, caneoing & watersports (no windsurfing); TV; 25% statics; phone; Eng spkn; adv bkg; quiet; ccard acc; red long stay. "Ry cent of Danish lake district; vg, well organised site." 1 Apr-15 Sep. DKK 175        2009*

**RY** *B2* (2km NW Rural) *56.10388, 9.74555* **Birkede Camping, Lyngvej 14, 8680 Ry [tel 86 89 13 55; fax 86 89 03 13; info@birkhede.dk; www.birkhede.dk]** Fr S on rd 52 exit onto rd 445 to Ry, then foll sp N on rd dir Laven. Turn R in 1km to site on lakeside. Clearly sp in cent of Ry. Lge, mkd pitch, pt sl, pt shd; wc; chem disp; mv service pnt; baby facs; shwrs DKK6; el pnts (10A) metered + conn fee; gas; lndtte (inc dryer); shop; tradsmn; rest; bar; cooking facs; playgrnd; htd pool; cycle & boat hire; fishing; games rm; golf 10km; wifi; TV rm; no statics; dogs; phone; poss cr; Eng spkn; adv bkg; CKE/CCI. "Gd site." ♦ 11 Apr-21 Sep. DKK 260        2014*

**RY** *B2* (6km NW Rural) *56.12421, 9.71055* **Terrassen Camping, Himmelbjergvej 9a, 8600 Laven [tel 86 84 13 01; fax 86 84 16 55; info@terrassen.dk; www.terrassen.dk]** In Silkeborg take Åarhus rd 15 to Linå. In Linå turn R for Laven. In Laven turn R parallel to lake; site up hill on R in 300m. Sharp turn R into ent. Lge, terr, pt shd; wc; chem disp; mv service pnt; baby facs; fam bthrm; sauna; shwrs DKK7; el pnts (10A) DKK32; gas; lndtte (inc dryer); rest adj; snacks 1.5km; shops adj; playgrnd; htd pool; fishing; lake sw; games area; pet zoo; wifi; entmnt; TV rm; 15% statics; dogs DKK15; phone; poss cr; adv bkg; ccard acc; quiet. "Excel views of lake & woods; British owner." ◆ Easter-26 Sep. DKK 230　　2010*

**RY** *B2* (7km NW Rural) *56.13603, 9.68978* **Askehøj Camping, Askehøjvej 18, 8600 Laven [tel 86 84 12 82; fax 86 84 12 80; askehoj@dk-camp.dk; www.askehoj. dk]** Fr Silkeborg take rte 15 twd Århus. In approx 5km site is sp. Lge, mkd pitch, pt sl, terr, pt shd; wc; chem disp; mv service pnt; shwrs inc; el pnts (10A) DKK30; lndtte; shop & 8km; rest 3km; playgrnd; htd pool; paddling pool; waterslide; some statics; dogs DKK5; poss v cr; Eng spkn; adv bkg; quiet; ccard acc; CKE/CCI. "Excel site in scenic location; rec." ◆ Easter-27 Sep. DKK 185　　2009*

**SAEBY** *C1* (2km N Coastal) *57.35498, 10.51026* **Hedebo Strandcamping, Frederikshavnsvej 108, 9300 Sæby [tel 98 46 14 49; fax 98 40 13 13; hedebo@dk-camp.dk; www.hedebocamping.dk]** Sp on rd 180. Lge, hdg/mkd pitch, unshd; htd wc; chem disp; mv service pnt; baby facs; fam bthrm; shwrs DKK5; el pnts (10A) inc; lndtte (inc dryer); shop; rest, snacks; bar; BBQ; cooking facs; playgrnd; htd pool; beach adj; wifi; 60% statics; dogs; phone; bus adj; poss cr; Eng spkn; adv bkg; quiet; CKE/CCI. 7 Apr-7 Sep. DKK 240　　2009*

**SAKSKOBING** *C3* (750m W Urban) *54.79840, 11.64070* **Saksskøbing Camping, Saxes Allé 15, 4990 Sakskøbing [tel 45 54 70 45 66 / 45 54 70 47 57; fax 54 70 70 90; sax@sport.dk; www.saxcamping.dk]** N fr Rødby exit E47 at Sakskøbing junc 46, turn L twd town: at x-rds turn R. In 300m turn R into Saxes Allé, site sp. Med, hdg/mkd pitch, pt shd; wc; mv service pnt; fam bthrm; baby facs; shwrs; el pnts (6A) DKK30; gas; lndtte; shop; rest adj; cooking facs; sand beach 15km; pool 100m; fishing; phone; adv bkg; quiet. "Conv for Rødby-Puttgarden ferry; gd touring base; excel site in pretty area; v welcoming & friendly." 15 Mar-28 Sep. DKK 194　　2014*

**SILKEBORG** *B2* (10km SE Rural) *56.12468, 9.64015* **Skyttehuset's Camping, Svejbækvej 3, Virklund, 8600 Silkeborg [tel 86 84 51 11; fax 86 84 50 38; mail@ skyttehusetscamping.dk; www.skyttehusetscamping.dk]** Fr S on rd 52 dir Silkeborg turn R onto rd 445 dir Ry. In 5km turn L twd lake, site in 6km, sp. Med, mkd pitch, hdstg, terr, shd; htd wc; chem disp; baby facs; fam bthrm; shwrs DKK6; el pnts (10A) DKK31; lndtte (inc dryer); shop; rest, snacks; bar; playgrnd; lake sw 500m; fishing; canoe & cycle hire; crazy golf; TV; dogs DKK10; phone; Eng spkn; quiet; ccard acc; CKE/CCI. "Campsite marina; sh walk to Denmark's cleanest lake; forest location; vg." ◆ 27 Mar-12 Sep. DKK 183　　2010*

**SILKEBORG** *B2* (1.5km S Rural) *56.15716, 9.56395* **Gudenåens Camping Silkeborg, Vejlsøvej 7, 8600 Silkeborg [tel 86 82 22 01; fax 86 80 50 27; mail@ gudenaaenscamping.dk; www.gudenaaenscamping. dk]** Fr S on Rv52 at rndabt at beg of Silkeborg bypass take rd sp 'Centrum'. Take 1st R to site, sp. Med, mkd pitch, pt sl, shd; htd wc; chem disp; mv service pnt; baby facs; fam bthrm; el pnts (16A) DKK28; lndtte; shop; rest, snacks 500m; BBQ; cooking facs; playgrnd; internet; TV; many statics; dogs free; Eng spkn; adv bkg; ccard acc; CKE/CCI. "Vg site; heavily wooded; easy walk/cycle to Silkeborg; steamer to Himmelbjerget 5 mins fr site." 3 Apr-18 Oct. DKK 283　　2009*

⊞ **SILKEBORG** *B2* (10km W Rural) *56.14869, 9.39697* **DCU Hesselhus Camping, Moselundsvej 28, Funder, 8600 Silkeborg [tel 86 86 50 66; fax 86 86 59 49; hesselhus@ dcu.dk; www.camping-hesselhus.dk]** Take rd 15 W fr Silkeborg twd Herning; after 6km bear R, sp Funder Kirkeby, foll camping sps for several km to site. Lge, mkd pitch, pt shd; wc; chem disp; mv service pnt; shwrs inc; fam bthrm; baby facs; shwrs; el pnts DKK35; gas; lndtte; supmkt; snacks; playgrnd; htd pool; TV; 40% statics; dogs DKK20; phone; adv bkg; quiet; 10% red CKE/CCI. "Great family site; beautiful natural surroundings; 1 hr fr Legoland; busy at w'ends." ◆ DKK 144　　2011*

⊞ **SINDAL** *C1* (1km W Rural) *57.46785, 10.17851* **Sindal Camping, Hjørringvej 125, 9870 Sindal [tel 98 93 65 30; fax 98 93 69 30; info@sindal-camping.dk; www.sindal-camping.dk]** On rte 35 due W of Frederikshavn on S side of rd. Lge, hdg pitch, pt shd; wc; chem disp; mv service pnt; baby facs; fam bthrm; shwrs; el pnts (16A) metered; gas; lndtte; shop; playgrnd; pool; paddling pool; sand beach 11km; golf 3km; TV; dogs DKK10; phone; poss cr; Eng spkn; adv bkg; quiet; CKE/CCI. "Train & bus v conv; lovely beaches 30 mins; excel modern san facs; vg site; helpful owners." ◆ DKK 260　　2013*

⊞ **SKAELSKOR** *C3* (500m W Rural) *55.25648, 11.28461* **Skælskør Nør Camping, Kildehusvej 1, 4230 Skælskør [tel 58 19 43 84; fax 58 19 25 50; kildehuset@cafeer.dk; www.campnor.dk]** Exit E20 junc 42 sp Korsør. Take rd 265 S sp Skælskør, site on L just bef town, nr Kildehuset Rest. Med, mkd pitch, unshd; wc; chem disp; baby facs; fam bthrm; shwrs DKK5; el pnts DKK35; lndtte; shop 1km; rest; bar; cooking facs; playgrnd; shgl beach 2km; TV; phone; Eng spkn; adv bkg; rd noise; ccard acc (surcharge); CKE/CCI. "Lovely location by lake in nature reserve; woodland walks; excel facs; helpful owners." ◆ DKK 150　　2009*

⊞ **SKAERBAEK** *B3* (500m E Rural) *55.16776, 8.78326* **Skærbæk Familie Camping, Ullerupvej 76, 6780 Skærbæk [tel 74 75 22 22; fax 74 75 25 70; skaerbaekfamiliecamping@c.dk; www. skaerbaekfamiliecamping.dk]** On rd 11 fr Ribe to Tønder, site well sp. Med, hdg/mkd pitch, pt shd; htd wc; chem disp; mv service pnt; fam bthrm; shwrs inc; el pnts DKK25; tradsmn; BBQ; cooking facs; playgrnd; games area; wifi; 50% statics; phone; Eng spkn; quiet; CKE/CCI. "Helpful owner; gd tourist info; conv Rømø Island." ◆ ltd DKK 140　　2010*

　　You can now fill in site reports online

**SKAGEN** *C1* (1.5km N Coastal) *57.7319, 10.61458* **Grenen Camping, Fryvej 16, 9990 Skagen [tel/fax 98 44 25 46; info@grenencamping.dk; www.grenencamping.dk]** Site on rd 40, sp 500m after white lighthouse. Lge, hdg/mkd pitch, pt shd; htd wc; chem disp; mv service pnt; baby facs; fam bthrm; shwrs DKK5; el pnts (16A) DKK35; lndtte; shop; rest, snacks, bar 1km; cooking facs; playgrnd; sand/shgl beach adj; cycle hire; TV rm; 50% statics; dogs DKK15; phone; poss cr; Eng spkn; quiet; ccard acc; CKE/CCI. "Immac site nr pretty town; conv Grenen Point where Baltic & North Seas meet; gd cycling; friendly, helpful staff." ♦ 1 Apr-19 Sep. DKK 240                                        2010*

**SKAGEN** *C1* (3km S Rural) *57.71987, 10.53991* **Øster Klit Camping, Flagbakkevej 55, 9990 Skagen [tel/fax 98 44 31 23; skagen-camping@mail.dk]** Fr Albæk on rte 40, site sp to R of rd. Med, mkd pitch, pt shd; wc; chem disp; mv service pnt; baby facs; fam bthrm; shwrs; el pnts; lndtte; shop; rest, snacks; cooking facs; pool; sand beach 2km; TV; 10% statics; phone; Eng spkn; adv bkg; quiet; ccard acc. "Well-run site; clean facs; friendly staff; Skagen worth visit." ♦ Easter-12 Sep. DKK 200                                    2009*

**SKAGEN** *C1* (10km S Rural) *57.65546, 10.45008* **Råbjerg Mile Camping, Kandestedvej 55, 9990 Skagen [tel 98 48 75 00; fax 98 48 75 88; info@raabjergmilecamping.dk; www.990.dk]** Fr rd 40 Frederikshavn-Skagen, foll sp Hulsig-Råbjerg Mile, site sp. Lge, hdg/mkd pitch, unshd; wc; chem disp fam bthrm; shwrs DKK2; el pnts (10A) DKK30; lndtte; rest 1km; snacks; bar; cooking facs; playgrnd; htd pool; paddling pool; beach 1.5km; tennis; cycle hire; golf 1.5km; TV; 25% statics; dogs DKK10; phone; poss cr; Eng spkn; adv bkg; ccard acc; CKE/CCI. "Gd touring base N tip of Denmark; gd cycling." ♦ 24 Mar-30 Sep. DKK 354 (CChq acc)                          2013*

**SKAGEN** *C1* (1.5km NW Coastal) *57.73448, 10.60412* **Poul Eeg Camping, Bøjlevejen 21, 9990 Skagen [tel 98 44 14 70; fax 98 45 14 60; info@pouleegcamping.dk; www.pouleegcamping.dk]** Take rd 40 thro Skagen twd Grenen; by hexagonal white tower on N o'skts turn L; site sh dist on L. Lge, pt shd; htd wc; chem disp; mv service pnt; baby facs; fam bthrm; shwrs DKK5; el pnts (10A) DKK35; lndtte (inc dryer); shop; rest 1km; snacks; cooking facs; playgrnd; beach 1km; cycle hire; wifi; TV rm; some statics; dogs DKK15; phone; poss cr; Eng spkn; adv bkg; ccard acc (surcharge); CKE/CCI. "Excel, well-run, peaceful site & facs; friendly, helpful staff; gd sea fishing & cycling; conv touring base." ♦ 20 Apr-4 Sep. DKK 195                                        2010*

**SKANDERBORG** *B2* (4km SW Rural) *56.02088, 9.89023* **Skanderborg Sø Camping, Horsensvej 21, 8660 Skanderborg [tel 86 51 13 11; fax 86 51 17 33; info@campingskanderborg.dk; www.campingskanderborg.dk]** N on E45 approx 10km beyond Horsens exit junc 54 to Trebstrup on rd 170 to site on R in 5km. Camping sp on R at top of hill after passing lake. Med, pt sl, pt shd; wc; chem disp; mv service pnt; fam bthrm; baby facs; shwrs DKK8; el pnts (6A) DKK25; gas & 5km; lndtte; shop; rest 1km; snacks; cooking facs; playgrnd; lake sw; boating; fishing; TV; some statics; dogs DKK10; phone; poss cr; adv bkg; Eng spkn; quiet; ccard acc. "In Jutland's lake district; clean, pleasant, well-spaced, friendly site in former orchard; friendly, helpful owner; gd touring base." ♦ ltd 16 Apr-26 Sep. DKK 188                      2010*

⊞ **SONDER FELDING** *B2* (500m W Rural) *55.93960, 8.78418* **Sønder Felding Camping & Hytteby, Søndergade 7, 7280 Sønder Felding [tel/fax 97 19 81 89; http://sdrfelding.dk-camp.dk]** Fr rd 12 turn W onto rd 439, site sp. Call at Q8 filling stn to check in. Sm, pt shd; htd wc; chem disp; mv service pnt; shwrs DKK5; el pnts (10A) inc (long lead req); lndtte; shop; rest, snacks; cooking facs; playgrnd; quiet; CKE/CCI. "If not staffed - pay at petrol stn; rvside walk; gd." DKK 126                                      2010*

**SONDER STENDERUP see Kolding** *B3*

**SONDERBORG** *B3* (4.5km NE Rural) *54.93518, 9.84591* **Madeskov Camping, Madeskov 9, 6400 Sønderborg [tel 74 42 13 93]** Exit E45 at junc 75 onto rd 8 to Sønderborg. Turn L at rndabt with tent sp. Med, unshd; wc; chem disp; mv service pnt; baby facs; shwrs DKK4; el pnts (10A) DKK20; lndtte; shop; rest 5km; playgrnd; sw 300m; cycle hire; TV rm; 20% statics; phone; poss cr; Eng spkn; aircraft noise during day; CKE/CCI. "On shores of Augustenborg fiord; under airport flight path." ♦ 15 Mar-18 Oct. DKK 130          2009*

**SONDERVIG** *A2* (750m S Coastal) *56.11179, 8.11680* **Søndervig Camping, Solvej 2, 6950 Søndervig [tel/fax 97 33 90 34; post@soendervigcamping.dk; www.soendervigcamping.dk]** Fr Ringkøbing E on rd 15. At traff lts in Søndervig turn L, site on R in 600m. Lge, hdg/mkd pitch, unshd; htd wc; chem disp; mv service pnt; baby facs; shwrs DKK6; el pnts (10A) DKK30 or metered + conn fee; lndtte (inc dryer); shop; rest, snacks 600m; playgrnd; htd, covrd pool 700m; cycle hire 600m; wifi; TV rm; 10% statics; dogs DKK15; phone; bus 600m; poss cr; Eng spkn; adv bkg; quiet; CKE/CCI. "Excel; gd, modern san facs." ♦ Easter 31 Oct. DKK 177                                      2010*

**SORO** *C3* (1km W Urban) *55.43806, 11.54705* **Sorø Camping, Udbyhøjvej 10, 4180 Sorø [tel 57 83 02 02; fax 57 82 11 02; info@soroecamping.dk; www.soroecamping.dk]** On rd 150 fr Korsør, 300m bef town name board turn L at camping sp, site in 100m on lakeside. Med, pt sl, pt shd; wc; chem disp; mv service pnt; fam bthrm; baby facs; shwrs DKK2 per min; el pnts (10A) DKK30; lndtte; shop; tradsmn; rest 500m; snacks 1km; cooking facs; playgrnd; lake sw adj; fishing; boating; TV; some statics; dogs free; phone; Eng spkn; adv bkg; quiet; ccard acc; CKE or CCI ess. "Conv Copenhagen, friendly owners; busy site; clean facs - up to CC standards." ♦ 1 Mar-31 Oct. DKK 180                          2013*

**SPODSBJERG (LANGELAND ISLAND)** *C3* (1.5km S Rural/Coastal) *54.92317, 10.80479* **Billevænge Camping, Spodsbjergvej 182, 5900 Spodsbjerg [tel 62 50 10 06; fax 62 50 10 46; info@billevaenge-camping.dk; www.billevaenge-camping.dk]** Fr Spodsbjerg ferry turn L into town. Site on L in approx 2km. Med, mkd pitch, pt terr, pt shd; wc; chem disp; mv service pnt; baby facs; shwrs DKK5; el pnts (16A) inc; gas; lndtte; shop; cooking facs; playgrnd; sand/shgl beach 500m; games area; internet; dogs DKK10; Eng spkn; adv bkg; quiet; ccard acc; CKE/CCI. "Helpful owner; gd, clean beach." 1 Apr-21 Oct. DKK 169                2011*

DENMARK

**DENMARK**

**STENBJERG** A2 (500m W Rural) 56.91835, 8.36483 Krohavens Familie Camping, Stenbjerg Kirkevej 21, 7752 Stenbjerg [tel 97 93 88 99; fax 97 93 86 55; stenbjerg@kh-camp.dk; www.kh-camp.dk] On rd 571 fr Snedsted, site sp on ent vill. Med, hdg pitch, unshd; htd wc; chem disp; mv service pnt; fam bthrm; shwrs; el pnts DKK25; lndtte; shop; rest; bar; cooking facs; playgrnd; sand beach 2km; games area; TV; some statics; dogs free; Eng spkn; quiet; CKE/CCI. 1 Apr-1 Oct. DKK 160                                                        2011*

**STOUBY** B3 (3.5km E Rural) 55.70761, 9.84385 Løgballe Camping, Løgballevej 12, 7140 Stouby [tel/fax 75 69 12 00; camping@logballe.dk; www.logballe.dk] N of Vejle turn onto rd 23 dir Juelsminde, thro vill of Stouby, site on R. Med, hdg/mkd pitch, pt sl, pt terr, pt shd; wc; chem disp; mv service pnt; baby facs; fam bthrm; shwrs DKK5; el pnts (6-10A) DKK27; lndtte; shop; tradsmn; snacks; bar; BBQ; cooking facs; playgrnd; pool; paddling pool; beach 6km; cycle hire; games area; TV rm; some statics in sep area; dogs; phone; bus 500m; poss cr; adv bkg; quiet; CKE/CCI. "Excel facs for children." ♦ Easter-4 Oct. DKK 140                                                        2009*

**STOUBY** B3 (4km S Coastal) 55.67674, 9.81319 Rosenvold Camping, Rosenvoldvej 19, 7140 Stouby [tel 75 69 14 15; info@rosenvoldcamping.dk; www.rosenvoldcamping.dk] Exit E45 at junc 59 E twd Daugard & Juelsminde on rd 23. Watch for site sp in approx 20km & turn R to coast, site sp. Med, mkd pitch, unshd; wc; chem disp; mv service pnt; baby facs; fam bhtrm; shwrs DKK6; el pnts (10A) DKK30; lndtte (inc dryer); shop; tradsmn; snacks; BBQ; cooking facs; playgrnd; beach adj; fishing at marina; games area; entmnt; 80% statics; Eng spkn; quiet; ccard acc; CKE/CCI. "Vg site." ♦ 1 Apr-30 Sep.                                                        2009*

**STROBY see Koge** D3

**SVENDBORG** C3 (5km SE Coastal) 55.0537, 10.6304 Svendborg Sund Camping (formerly Vindebyøre), Vindebyørevej 52, Tåsinge, 5700 Svendborg [tel 21 72 09 13 / 62 22 54 25; fax 62 22 54 26; maria@svendborgsund-camping.dk; www.vindebyoere.dk] Cross bdge fr Svendborg (dir Spodsbjerg) to island of Tåsinge on rd 9; at traff lts over bdge turn L, then immed 1st L to Vindeby, thro vill, L at sp to site. Med, pt sl, pt shd; htd wc; chem disp; mv service pnt; fam bthrm; baby facs; shwrs; el pnts DKK30; lndtte; shop; snacks; cooking facs; BBQ; playgrnd; sand beach; cycle & boat hire; entmnt; internet; TV; some statics; dogs DKK10; phone; o'night area; poss cr; adv bkg; quiet; ccard acc; CKE/CCI. "V helpful owners; swipe card for facs; excel touring base & conv ferries to islands; beautiful views; immac, excel site; narr sandy beach." ♦ 11 Apr-28 Sep. DKK 240     2014*

**SVENDBORG** C3 (5km S Rural) 55.03336, 10.61403 Carlsberg Camping, Sundbrovej 19, Tåsinge, 5700 Svendborg [tel 62 22 53 84; fax 62 22 58 11; mail@carlsberg-camping.dk; www.carlsberg-camping.dk] Fr Svendborg cross bdge on A9 S to Rudkøbing. After traffic lts in approx 4km sp camping on E side of rd. Enter sm rd & up steep hill for 300m. Steep & narr app. Med, pt shd; wc; chem disp; mv service pnt; fam bthrm; baby facs; shwrs inc; el pnts (6A) DKK30; gas; lndtte (inc dryer); shop; snacks; playgrnd; htd pool inc; beach 4km; games area; games rm; TV; poss cr; quiet; ccard acc; red low ssn. "Gd facs; scenic area." ♦ 1 Apr-25 Sep. DKK 184                                                        2010*

⊞ **TAPPERNOJE** D3 (500m NE Urban) 55.16568, 11.98195 Heino's Camping, Hovedvejen 47B, Lille Røttinge, 4733 Tappernøje [tel 55 96 53 22; fax 55 96 01 22; www.heinoscamping.dk] Fr E47/55 exit 38 twd coast. Site sp. Med, hdg pitch, pt shd; wc; chem disp; shwrs; el pnts DKK20; lndry rm; shop, rest 500m; playgrnd; sand beach 2km; cycle hire; 10% statics; quiet; CKE/CCI. "Gd size pitches." DKK 100                                                        2009*

⊞ **TARM** A2 (1km S Rural) 55.89309, 8.51278 Tarm Camping, Vardevej 79, 6880 Tarm [tel 97 37 13 30; fax 97 37 30 15; tarm.camping@pc.dk; www.tarm-camping.dk] Fr rd 11 S of Tarm take exit twds Tarm; immed turn R, site on L in 500m, sp. Med, mkd pitch, pt shd; wc; chem disp; mv service pnt; fam bthrm; baby facs; shwrs DKK2; el pnts (10A) DKK30; gas; lndtte; snacks; cooking facs; playgrnd; pool; some statics; dogs; phone; Eng spkn; adv bkg; some rd noise; CKE/CCI. "Friendly & helpul staff; vg." ♦ DKK 130     2011*

**THISTED** B2 (1km N Coastal) 56.95226, 8.71286 Thisted Camping, Iversensvej 3, 7700 Thisted [tel 97 92 16 35; fax 97 92 52 34; mail@thisted-camping.dk; www.thisted-camping.dk] On side of fjord on o'skts of Thisted, sp fr rd 11. Med, pt sl, unshd; wc; chem disp; mv service pnt; baby facs; fam bthrm; shwrs DKK5; el pnts (16A) DKK30; gas; lndtte; shop; rest; cooking facs; playgrnd; pool; TV; Eng spkn; adv bkg; quiet; CKE/CCI. "Attractive views fr some pitches; nice site; well run." ♦ 23 Mar-1 Oct. DKK 280          2013*

**THORSMINDE** A2 (500m N Coastal) 56.37726, 8.12330 Thorsminde Camping, Klitrosevej 4, 6990 Thorsminde [tel 97 49 70 56; fax 97 49 72 18; mail@thorsmindecamping.dk; www.thorsmindecamping.dk] On rd 16/28 to Ulfborg, turn W twd coast & Husby Klitplantage. Turn N onto rd 181 to Thorsminde, 1st turn R past shops, site sp. Lge, unshd; wc; chem disp; mv service pnt; fam bthrm; baby facs; sauna; shwrs; el pnts (10A) DKK30; lndtte; shop; rest; cooking facs; playgrnd; covrd pool; beach 300m; TV; few statics; phone; poss cr; adv bkg; quiet. "Pleasant site; helpful staff; excel sea fishing." ♦ 8 Apr-23 Oct. DKK 200     2011*

**TOFTUM (ROMO ISLAND)** A3 (290m SW Rural/Coastal) 55.16267, 8.54768 Rømø Familiecamping, Vestervej 13, 6792 Toftum [tel 74 75 51 54; fax 74 75 64 18; romo@romocamping.dk; www.romocamping.dk] Cross to Rømø Island on rd 175, turn R at 1st traff lts & turn L in 1km to site, sp. Lge, hdg/mkd pitch, some hdstg, pt shd; htd wc; chem disp; mv service pnt; baby facs; fam bthrm; shwrs; el pnts (10A) DKK30; lndtte; shop; BBQ; cooking facs; playgrnd; sand beach, windsurfing 4km; games area; cycle hire; wifi; TV rm; some statics; dogs; adv bkg; quiet. "Pleasant site." 15 Apr-23 Oct. DKK 152                                                        2009*

**TONDER** B3 (1km E Rural) 54.93409, 8.87957 Tønder Campingplads, Sønderport 4, 6270 Tønder [tel/fax 74 72 35 00; tonder@danhostel.dk; www.tondercamping.dk] W fr junc A8 & A11 twd town, in 800m turn R at camping sp. Ent on L in 100m. Med, hdg/mkd pitch, unshd; wc; chem disp; mv service pnt; shwrs; baby facs; el pnts (10A) DKK30; lndtte; shop 1km; bar; playgrnd; sand beach 10km; TV; 50% statics; dogs DKK10; phone; poss cr; Eng spkn; adv bkg; quiet; CKE/CCI. "Pleasant old town with gd shopping cent; gd site with modern san facs; helpful recep." ♦ 26 Mar-24 Oct. DKK 150                                                        2011*

⊞ **TONDER** B3 (5km W Rural) 54.93746, 8.80008
**Møgeltønder Camping, Sønderstrengvej 2, Møgeltonder,
6270 Tønder [tel 74 73 84 60; fax 74 73 80 43; www.
mogeltondercamping.dk]** N fr Tønder thro Møgeltønder
(avoid cobbled main rd by taking 2nd turning sp Møgeltønder)
site sp on L in 200m outside vill. Lge, mkd pitch; pt shd; htd
wc; chem disp; mv service pnt; baby facs; fam bthrm; shwrs
DKK2 (per 2 mins); el pnts (10A) DKK25; lndtte (inc dryer);
shop; tradsmn; snacks; BBQ; cooking facs; playgrnd; htd pool;
sand beach 10km; internet; TV rm; 25% statics; dogs DKK10;
phone; poss v cr; Eng spkn; adv bkg; quiet; ccard not acc; CKE/
CCI. "Gd cycle paths; beautiful & romantic little vill adj; Ribe
worth visit (43km); friendly owner." ♦ DKK 219          2014*

**ULFBORG** A2 (10km W Coastal) 56.25961, 8.14625 **Vedersø
Klit Camping, Øhusevej 23, Vedersø Klit, 6990 Ulfborg
[tel 97 49 52 02; fax 97 49 52 01; vedersoklit@dk-camp.dk;
www.dk-camp.dk/vedersoklit]** W fr Ulfborg on rd 537, turn
S onto rd 181 & foll site sp. Lge, mkd pitch, pt shd; wc; chem
disp; mv service pnt; fam bthrm; baby facs; shwrs inc; el pnts
(10A) DKK25; lndtte (inc dryer); shop; snacks; cooking facs;
playgrnd; pool; paddling pool; beach 500m; games area; TV;
some statics; dogs DKK10; phone; adv bkg; quiet. ♦ 27 Mar-
26 Sep. DKK 190          2010*

**ULSTRUP** B2 (2.5km W Rural) 56.38678, 9.76341 **Bamsebo
Camping ved Gudenåen, Hagenstrupvej 28, Hvorslev,
8860 Ulstrup [tel 86 46 34 27; fax 86 46 37 18; bamsebo@
dk-camp.dk; www.bamsebo.dk]** Fr W twd Ulstrup on rd
525, turn R at traff lts to Ulstrop, take 1st exit at rndabt at
top of Ulstrup dir Busbjerg, site sp on R in 2km on rv. Med,
hdg pitch, pt sl, pt shd; htd wc; chem disp; mv service pnt;
baby facs; fam bthrm; shwrs; el pnts (16A) DKK30; lndry rm;
shop on site & 2.5km; snacks; playgrnd; htd pool; canoes for
hire; tennis; games area; TV rm; 60% statics; dogs DKK15;
poss cr; Eng spkn; adv bkg; CKE/CCI. ♦ 17 Apr-2 Oct.
DKK 184          2011*

**VAMMEN see Viborg** B2

## "I need an on-site restaurant"

We do our best to make sure site
information is correct, but it is always best
to check any must-have facilities are still
available or will be open during your visit.

⊞ **VEJERS STRAND** A3 (400m SE Urban) 55.61916,
8.13650 **Vejers Familie Camping, Vejers Havvej 15, 6853
Vejers Strand [tel 75 27 70 36; fax 75 27 72 75; ftj@
vejersfamiliecamping.dk; www.vejersfamiliecamping.dk]**
Well sp in Vejers Strand on coast. Lge, hdg/mkd pitch, pt shd;
wc; chem disp; mv service pnt; fam bthrm; baby facs; shwrs
DKK6; el pnts (8A) DKK30; lndtte (inc dryer); shop; rest, snacks;
cooking facs; BBQ; playgrnd; pool; paddling pool; sand beach
1km; fishing; wifi; TV rm; some statics; dogs DKK13; phone;
Eng spkn; some noise fr adj military firing range; CKE/CCI. "Site
open all yr but in winter telephone ahead; gd, modern facs."
DKK 188 (CChq acc)          2010*

**VEJERS STRAND** A3 (8km S Coastal) 55.54403, 8.13386
**Hvidbjerg Strand Feriepark, Hvidbjerg Strandvej 27,
6857 Blåvand [tel 75 27 90 40; fax 75 27 80 28; info@
hvidbjerg.dk; www.hvidbjerg.dk]** Exit rd 11 at Varde on
minor rd, sp Blåvand, turn L at sp to Hvidbjerg Strand 2km;
site 1km on L. V lge, hdg pitch, pt shd; wc; chem disp; mv
service pnt; baby facs; fam bthrm; serviced pitches; shwrs inc;
el pnts (6A) inc; gas; lndtte; supmkt; rest, snacks; bar; cooking
facs; playgrnd; htd, covrd pool; sand beach; tennis; games
area; entmnt; TV; 10% statics; dogs DKK30; phone; adv bkg;
quiet; ccard acc. "Superb facs; excel family site; young groups
not acc." ♦ 7 Apr-22 Oct.  DKK 312          2014*

See advert on bookmark

## "Satellite navigation makes touring much easier"

Remember most sat navs don't know if
you're towing or in a larger vehicle – always
use yours alongside maps and site directions.

**VEJERS STRAND** A3 (1km W Coastal) 55.61998, 8.11931
**Vejers Strand Camping, Vejers Sydstrand 3, 6853
Vejers Strand [tel 75 27 70 50; fax 75 27 77 50; info@
vejersstrandcamping.dk; www.vejersstrandcamping.
dk]** Site at end of rd 431 fr Varde (23km). Lge, unshd; htd wc;
chem disp; mv service pnt; fam bthrm; baby facs; shwrs; el
pnts (10A) DKK28; lndtte (inc dryer); shop; rest, snacks; bar;
cooking facs; playgrnd; beach 250m; TV; phone; 50% statics;
dogs DKK15; adv bkg; quiet but some aircraft noise; ccard
acc. "Pt sheltered in dunes; fine beach." ♦ 1 Apr-16 Sep.
DKK 180          2009*

**VEJLE** B3 (2km NE Urban) 55.7151, 9.5611 **Vejle City
Camping, Helligkildevej 5, 7100 Vejle [tel 75 82 33 35;
fax 75 82 33 54; vejlecitycamping@mail.dk; www.
vejlecitycamping.dk]** Exit E45 m'way at Vejle N. Turn L twd
town. In 250m turn L at camping sp & 'stadion' sp. Med, pt
sl, pt shd; wc; chem disp; mv service pnt; fam bthrm; baby
facs; shwrs DKK5; el pnts (6-10A) DKK30; lndtte; shop on site
& 1km; snacks; cooking facs; playgrnd; sand beach 2km; TV;
dogs DKK5; phone; poss cr; Eng spkn; adv bkg; quiet; 25% red
long stays; ccard acc; red snr citizens. "Site adj woods & deer
enclosure; Quickstop o'night facs; walk to town; conv Legoland
(26km)." ♦ 17 Apr-14 Sep. DKK 150          2009*

⊞ **VIBORG** B2 (10km N Rural/Coastal) 56.53452, 9.33117
**Hjarbæk Fjord Camping, Hulager 2, Hjarbæk, 8831
Løgstrup [tel 86 64 23 09; fax 86 64 25 91; info@hjarbaek.
dk; www.hjarbaek.dk]** Take A26 (Viborg to Skive) to
Løgstrup, turn R (N) to Hjarbæk, keep R thro vill, site sp. Lge,
mkd pitch, terr, pt shd; htd wc; chem disp; baby facs; fam
bthrm; shwrs inc; el pnts metered; gas; lndtte (inc dryer);
shop; rest, bar; cooking facs; BBQ; playgrnd; pool; sand beach
adj; lake fishing; wifi; TV; 3% statics; dogs DKK10; phone;
quiet; Eng spkn; adv bkg; ccard acc; red snr citizens; CKE/
CCI. "Friendly & well-run; gd views; close to attractive vill &
harbour." ♦ DKK 299 (CChq acc)          2014*

Check any essential information with the site before you travel          *Last year of report     **207**

**VINDERUP** *B2* (6.7km ESE Rural) *56.45901, 8.86918* **Sevel Camping, Halallé 6, Sevel, 7830 Vinderup [tel 97 44 85 50; fax 97 44 85 51; mail@sevelcamping.dk; www. sevelcamping.dk]** Fr Struer on rd 513. In Vinderup L nr church then R past Vinderup Camping. Site sp on R on edge of vill. Sm, hdg pitch, pt sl, pt shd; htd wc; chem disp; mv service pnt; baby facs; fam bthrm; shwrs DKK5; el pnts (16A) DKK27; lndtte; shop 100m; cooking facs; rest 1km; snacks; playgrnd; 10% statics; dogs DKK6; Eng spkn; adv bkg; quiet; ccard acc; CKE/CCI. "Family-run site; pleasant, helpful owners; picturesque, historic area." ♦ 1 Apr-30 Sep. DKK 142 2009*

**VIPPEROD see Holbæk** *D3*

⊞ **VORDINGBORG** *D3* (1km SW Urban/Coastal) *55.00688, 11.87509* **Ore Strand Camping, Orevej 145, 4760 Vordingborg [tel 55 77 8822; mail@orestrandcamping. dk; www.orestrandcamping.dk]** Fr E55/47 exit junc 41 onto rd 59 to Vordingborg 7km. Rd conts as 153 sp Sakskøbing alongside rlwy. Turn R at site sp into Ore, site on L. Med, pt shd; wc; chem disp; mv service pnt; baby facs; shwrs; el pnts (6A) DKK30; lndtte; shop; cooking facs; playgrnd; shgl beach adj; phone; adv bkg; poss cr; quiet; Eng spkn; ccard acc. "Gd touring cent; fine views if nr water; interesting old town." DKK 140 2011*

Tell us about the sites you visit

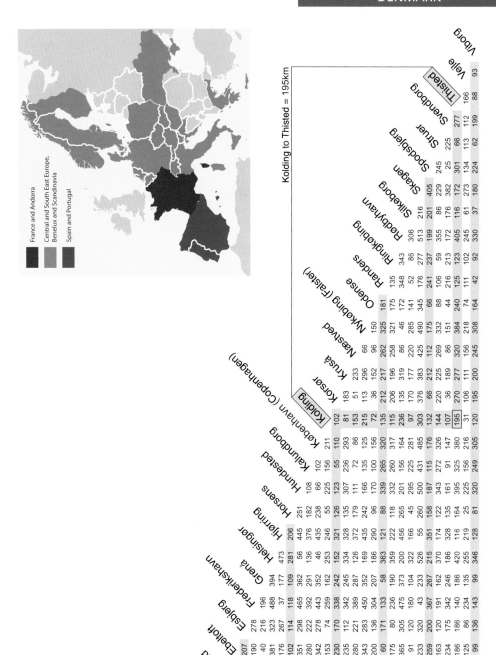

Kolding to Thisted = 195km

*Last year of report  **209**

# Finland
## Country Introduction

*Toolo Bay, Helsinki*

## Welcome to Finland

A popular country to visit in any season, Finland is most famous for Lapland, where visitors can be greeted by Santa all year round.

Most of the country is covered in forests full of wonderful wildlife, a guided tour to try and catch a glimpse of rare wild bears and wolves is not to be missed. The contrast of the cities is quite staggering, with modern museums to colourful night spots and high-end restaurants.

## Country highlights

Finnish cuisine makes simple use of local ingredients, and is a surprising mix of traditional and modern fare. A popular dish is Kalakukko, fish that has been baked into a loaf of bread. Try this with a side of Leipäjuusto, a rich cheese made from goat or reindeer milk.

The Helsinki Festival is the country's biggest annual cultural event. It includes a wide variety of performances, photography and exhibitions shown all over the Capital.

## Major towns and cities

- Helsinki – this capital city has superb museums and historical monuments.
- Lahti – best known for its winter sports, the city has hosted events including the Winter Olympics.
- Oulu – a city that combines nature and traditional culture with modern technology.
- Turku – this city has the Old Great Square where medieval markets are held.

## Attractions

- Espoo Museum of Modern Art – one of the largest art museums in Finland.
- Tampere Cathedral – a beautiful cathedral that also has wonderful paintings on show.
- Temppeliaukio Kirkko – view the stunning copper dome of the 'Church in the Rock'
- Arktikum – a fascinating museum and science centre right on the Arctic Circle.

## Find out more

www.visitfinland.com

Tel: 0035 (0) 82 95 05 80 00 Finnish Tourism

# Country Information

*Population (approx):* 5.3 million

*Capital:* Helsinki (population approx 597,000)

*Area:* 338,145 sq km

*Bordered by:* Norway, Sweden, Russia

*Terrain:* Flat, rolling, heavily forested plains interspersed with low hills and more than 60,000 lakes; one third lies within the Arctic Circle

*Climate:* Short, warm summers; long, very cold, dry winters; the best time to visit is between May and September

*Coastline:* 1,250km (excluding islands)

Highest Point: Haltiatunturi 1,328m

*Languages:* Finnish, Swedish

Local Time: GMT or BST + 2, ie 2 hours ahead of the UK all year

*Currency:* Euros divided into 100 cents; £1 = €1.26, €1 = £0.79 (September 2014)

*Emergency numbers:* Police 112; Fire brigade 112; Ambulance 112 (operators speak English). *Public Holidays 2015:* Jan 1, 6; Apr 3, 6; May 1, 14; Jun 20 (Midsummer's Day); Oct 31 (All Saints); Dec 6 (Independence Day), 25, 26.

School summer holidays from early June to mid-August.

# Camping and Caravanning

There are around 300 campsites in Finland, usually located by a lake or river or on the coast. Of these 200 belong to the Finnish Travel Association's national network. Campsites are graded from 1 to 5 stars according to facilities available. Most have cabins for hire in addition to tent and caravan pitches, and most have saunas.

At some sites visitors who do not already have one must purchase a Camping Key Europe, which replaced the Camping Card Scandinavia (CCS) in 2012. The Camping Key is valid across Europe and you may purchase it for €16 (2014) on arrival at your first campsite or from local tourist offices - for more information visit www.camping.fi.

During the peak camping season from June to mid August it is advisable to make advance reservations. Prices at many campsites may double (or treble) over the midsummer holiday long weekend in June and advance booking is essential for this period. Approximately 70 campsites stay open all year.

Casual/wild camping is not permitted.

# Cycling

Finland is good for cyclists as it is relatively flat. Most towns have a good network of cycle lanes which are indicated by traffic signs. In built up areas pavements are sometimes divided into two sections, one for cyclists and one for pedestrians. It is compulsory to wear a safety helmet

# Electricity and Gas

Current on campsites is usually between 10 and 16 amps. Plugs are round with two pins. Some sites have CEE connections.

Butane gas is not generally available and campsites and service stations do not have facilities for replacing empty foreign gas cylinders. You will need to travel with sufficient supplies to cover your needs while in Finland or purchase propane cylinders locally, plus an adaptor. The Club does not recommend the refilling of cylinders.

# Entry Formalities

Holders of British and Irish passports are permitted to stay up to three months in any six month period in Finland before a visa is required. Campsites, hotels, etc, automatically register their foreign guests with the police within 24 hours of arrival.

# Medical Services

The local health system is good and Finland generally has a high level of health and hygiene. British citizens are entitled to obtain emergency health care at municipal health centres on presentation of a European Health Insurance Card (EHIC). Treatment will either be given free or for a standard fee. Dental care is provided mainly by private practitioners.

There is a fixed non-refundable charge for hospital treatment, whether for inpatient or outpatient visits. Refunds for the cost of private medical treatment may be obtained from local offices of the Sickness Insurance Department, KELA, (www.kela.fi – English option) up to six months from the date of treatment.

Prescribed drugs can be obtained from pharmacies (apteekki), some of which have late opening hours. Some medicines that are available in stores and supermarkets in other countries, such as aspirin and various ointments, are only available in pharmacies in Finland.

## Opening Hours

Banks – Mon-Fri 9.15am-4.15pm.

Museums – Check locally as times vary.

Post Offices – Mon-Fri 9am-5pm. During winter some post offices may stay open until 6pm.

Shops – Mon-Fri 7am/8am/9am-9pm; Sat 7am/8am/9am/10am-6pm; Sun noon-6pm (some supermarkets until 11pm). On the eve of a public holiday some shops close early.

## Safety and Security

The crime rate is relatively low in Finland although the tourist season attracts pickpockets in crowded areas. You should take the usual commonsense precautions to safeguard your person and property.

There is a low threat from international terrorism but you should be aware of the global risks of indiscriminate terrorist attacks which could be against civilian targets in public places, including tourist sites.

*British Embassy*
ITÄINEN PUISTOTIE 17, 00140 HELSINKI
Tel: (09) 22865100  Fax: (09) 22865262
http://ukinfinland.fco.gov.uk
info.helsinki@fco.gov.uk

There are also Honorary Consulates in Åland Islands, Jyväskylä, Kotka, Kuopio, Oulu, Rovaniemi, Tampere, Turku and Vaasa.

*Irish Embassy*
EROTTAJANKATU 7A, FIN-00130 HELSINKI
Tel: (09) 6824240
www.embassyofireland.fi

## Border Posts

The main border posts with Sweden are at Tornio, Ylitornio and Kaaresuvanto. Those with Norway are at Kilpisjärvi, Kivilompolo, Karigasniemi, Utsjoki Ohcejohka and Nuorgam. Border posts are open day and night. The Finnish-Russian border can only be crossed by road at certain official points – contact the Finnish Tourist Board for details.

In order to deter illegal immigrants border guards patrol the area close to the Russian border and it is important, therefore, to carry identification at all times when visiting the region.

## Documents

*Driving Licence/Vehicle(s)*
When driving you should carry your driving licence, vehicle registration certificate (V5C), insurance certificate plus MOT certificate (if applicable).

*Passport*
You should also carry your passport at all times.

## Money

Currency may be exchanged at banks and at bureaux de change.

Major credit cards are widely accepted and cash machines are widespread.

Carry your credit card issuers'/banks' 24-hour UK contact numbers in case of loss or theft of your cards.

## Motoring in Finland
## Accidents

Accidents must be reported to the police and if a foreign motorist is involved the Finnish Motor Insurers Bureau (Liikennevakuutuskeskus) should also be informed. Their address is Bulevardi 28, FIN-00120 Helsinki, tel (09) 40 450 4520, www.lvk.fi./en. At the site of an accident other road users must be warned by the use of a warning triangle.

FINLAND

## Alcohol

The maximum permitted level of alcohol is 50 milligrams in 100 millilitres of blood, i.e. lower than that permitted in the UK (80 milligrams). It is advisable to adopt the 'no drink and drive' rule at all times as anyone exceeding this limit will be arrested immediately and could face a prison sentence. Breath tests and blood tests may be carried out at random.

## Breakdown Service

The Automobile & Touring Club of Finland, Autoliitto, has approximately 300 roadside patrols manned by volunteers and these can be called out at weekends and on public holidays. At other times, or if the Autoliitto patrol cannot be reached, contracted partners will provide assistance. For 24-hour assistance telephone (0)200 8080. Charges are made for assistance and towing, plus a call-out fee.

Emergency telephone boxes are installed around Helsinki, Kouvola, Jamsa, and Rovaniemi, and on the roads Kouvola-Lappeenranta-Imatra-Simpele and Rovaniemi-Jaatila. Drivers are connected to the national breakdown service.

## Essential Equipment

*Lights*
Dipped headlights are compulsory at all times, regardless of weather conditions. Bulbs are more likely to fail with constant use and you are recommended to carry spares.

*Reflective Jacket/Waistcoat*
Pedestrians must wear reflective devices during the hours of darkness (any type of reflector is acceptable). If you get out of your vehicle you are, required to wear one and the standard reflective jacket is probably the best option for driver and passengers.

*Child Restraint System*
Children under the height of 1.35m must be seated in a suitable child restraint.

If there is not a child restraint/seat available children of 3 years or older must travel in the rear seat using a seat belt or other safety device attached to the seat. Unless in a taxi a child under the age of 3 must not travel in a vehicle without a child restraint.

It is the responsibility of the driver to ensure all children under the age of 15 years old are correctly and safely restrained.

*Warning Triangles*
All vehicles must carry a warning triangle and use it when broken down.

*Winter Driving*
Winter tyres are compulsory from 1 December to 28 February. Snow chains may be used temporarily when conditions necessitate.

The main arctic road leads from Kemi on the Gulf of Bothnia through Rovaniemi to the Norwegian border. During the winter, all high volume, main roads are kept open including routes to Norway and Sweden. In total between 6,000 and 7,000km of roads are mainly kept free of ice and snow by the use of salt. Other roads will consist of compacted snow. Drivers should expect winter conditions as early as October.

## Fuel

Petrol stations are usually open from 7am to 9pm on weekdays and for shorter hours at weekends, although a few stay open 24 hours. Their frequency reduces towards the north, so it is advisable not to let your tank run low. Credit cards are accepted at most manned petrol stations. There are many unmanned stations, which have automatic petrol pumps operated with bank notes or credit cards.
It is understood that automatic payment machines at petrol pumps do not accept cards issued outside Finland.

LPG is not available.

## Parking

A vehicle that has been illegally or dangerously parked may be removed by the police and the owner fined. Parking fines may be enforced on the spot, the minimum charge being €10. Parking meters operate for between 15 minutes and four hours; the free use of unexpired time is allowed. In some built-up areas you will need a parking disc obtainable from petrol stations or car accessory shops.

8-14

Restriction applies 8-17 hrs (Mon-Fri) | Restriction applies 8-13 hrs (Sat) | Restriction applies 8-14 hrs (Sun)

In some towns streets are cleaned on a regular basis and road signs indicate which day the cleaning takes place and, therefore, when the street should be kept clear of parked vehicles. Vehicles which cause an obstruction will be removed and drivers fined.

If you have a low emission car you may be entitled to 50% off parking fees in Helsinki. To qualify for this reduction the parking fees must be made by mobile phone and you will need to have obtained a green sticker with the letter 'P' from the Helsinki town authorities, which then needs to be attached to the windscreen. For further information please visit www.easypark.fi or www.nextpark.com.

## Priority

At intersections, vehicles coming from the right have priority, except when otherwise indicated. The approach to a main road from a minor road is indicated by a sign with a red triangle on a yellow background. When this sign is supplemented by a red octagon with STOP in the centre, vehicles must stop before entering the intersection. Trams and emergency vehicles, even coming from the left, always have priority. Vehicles entering a roundabout must give way to traffic already on the roundabout, i.e. on the left.

## Roads

In general there is a good main road system, traffic is light and it is possible to cover long distances quickly, but there are still some gravelled roads in the countryside which have speed restrictions to avoid windscreens being broken by loose stones. During the spring thaw and during the wet season in September, gravelled roads may be in a poor condition. Roadworks take place during the summer months and sections under repair can extend for many miles.

There are large numbers of elk in Finland and they often wander across roads, especially at dawn and dusk. The same applies to reindeer in Lapland. Warning signs showing approximate lengths of danger zones are posted in these areas. If you collide with an elk, deer or reindeer you must notify the police.

The Finnish Transport Agency operates an information service on weather and road conditions, recommended driving routes and roadworks, tel 0295 020 600 or visit www.liikennevirasto.fi.

## Road Signs and Markings

Road markings are generally white. Road signs conform to international conventions. Signs for motorway and end of motorway are on a green background while those for main roads are on a blue background. The following written signs may also be found:

| Finnish | English Translation |
| --- | --- |
| Aja hitaasti | Drive slowly |
| Aluerajoitus | Local speed limit |
| Kelirikko | Frost damage |
| Kokeile jarruja | Test your brakes |
| Kunnossapitotyö | Roadworks (repairs) |
| Lossi färja | Ferry |
| Päällystetyötä | Roadworks (resurfacing) |
| Tulli | Customs |
| Tie rakenteilla | Roadworks (road under construction) |
| Varo irtokiviä | Beware of loose stones |

## Speed Limits

| | Open Road (km/h) | Motorway (km/h) |
| --- | --- | --- |
| Car Solo | 80-100 | 120 |
| Car towing caravan/trailer | 80 | 80 |
| Motorhome under 3500kg | 100 | 100 |
| Motorhome 3500-7500kg | 80 | 80 |

FINLAND

On all roads outside built-up areas throughout the country, other than motorways, differing speed limits between 70 and 100 km/h (44 and 62 mph) apply – except where vehicles are subject to a lower limit – according to the quality of the road and traffic density. Where there is no sign, the basic speed limit is usually 80 km/h (50 mph) on main roads and 70 km/h (44 mph) on secondary roads, whether solo or towing. The road sign which indicates this basic limit bears the word 'Perusnopeus' in Finnish, and 'Grundhastighet' in Swedish.

Reduced speed limits apply during the winter from October to March and these are generally 20 km/h (13 mph) lower than the standard limits. At other times temporary speed limits may be enforced locally.

The maximum speed limit for motorhomes up to 3,500kg is 100 km/h (62 mph).

Recommended maximum speed limits are indicated on some roads by square or rectangular signs bearing white figures on a blue background. The maximum speed limit in residential areas is 20 km/h (13 mph).

Slow moving vehicles must let others pass wherever possible, if necessary by moving onto the roadside verge. Maintain a sufficient distance behind a slow moving vehicle to allow an overtaking vehicle to pull in front.

Radar detectors are prohibited.

## Violation of Traffic Regulations

The police can impose, but not collect, fines when road users violate traffic regulations. Fines should be paid at banks.

## Motorways

There are 700km of motorway (moottoritie) in Finland linking Helsinki, Tampere and Turku. No tolls are levied. There are no emergency phones located on motorways. In the case of breakdown on a motorway drivers of all vehicles must use a warning triangle.

## Touring

Both Finnish and Swedish are official languages. As a result, many towns and streets have two names, e.g. Helsinki is also known as Helsingfors, and Turku as Åbo. Finnish street names usually end 'katu', while Swedish street names usually end 'gatan' or 'vägen'. Swedish place names are more commonly used in the south and west of the country.

Smoking is not permitted in public buildings, restaurants or bars, except in designated smoking zones, nor on public transport.

The Helsinki Card offers free entry to approximately 50 museums and other attractions, and unlimited travel for 24, 48 or 72 hours on public transport, plus discounts for sightseeing, restaurants, shopping, concert tickets, sports, etc. For more information see www.helsinkicard.fi.

The sale of wine and spirits is restricted to Alko shops which are open Monday to Friday until 6pm or 8pm, Saturday until 4pm or 6pm, and closed on Sunday and public holidays. Medium strength beer is also sold in supermarkets and other stores.

A service charge is generally included in most restaurant bills and tips are not expected, but if the service has been good it is customary to round up the bill.

Most lakes are situated in the south east of the country and they form a web of waterways linked by rivers and canals, making this a paradise for those who enjoy fishing, canoeing and hiking. In Lapland the vegetation is sparse, consisting mostly of dwarf birch. Reindeer roam freely so motorists must take special care and observe the warning signs. Rovaniemi is the biggest town in Lapland, just south of the Arctic Circle. It has a special post office and 'Santa Claus Land'.

A number of 'Uniquely Finnish' touring routes have been established including the King's Road along the south coast which takes you through many places of interest including Porvoo, a small town with well-preserved, old, wooden houses, Turku, the former capital, and the famous Imatra waterfall near the southern shore of Lake Saimaa. Swedish influence is evident in this area in local customs, place names and language. These 'Uniquely Finnish' touring routes are marked with brown sign posts; contact the Finnish Tourist Board for more information.

Southern and central Finland are usually snow covered from early December to mid or late April, although in recent years the south coast has had little or no snow. Northern Finland has snow falls from October to May and temperatures can be extremely low. Thanks to the Gulf Stream and low humidity, Finland's winter climate does not feel as cold as temperature readings might indicate but if you plan a visit during the winter you should be prepared for harsh weather conditions.

In the summer many Finnish newspapers have summaries of main news items and weather forecasts in English and radio stations have regular news bulletins in English. English is taught in all schools and is widely spoken.

## The Midnight Sun and Northern Lights

Areas within the Arctic Circle have 24 hours of daylight in the height of summer and no sun in winter for up to two months. There are almost 20 hours of daylight in Helsinki in the summer.

The Northern Lights (Aurora Borealis) may be seen in the arctic sky on clear dark nights, the highest incidence occurring in February/March and September/October in the Kilpisjärvi region of Lapland when the lights are seen on three nights out of four.

## The Order of Bluenosed Caravanners

Visitors to the Arctic Circle from anywhere in the world may apply for membership of the Order of Bluenosed Caravanners which will be recognised by the issue of a certificate by the International Caravanning Association (ICA).

For more information contact David Hirst on tel: 01422 372390, or email: david.hirst118@btinternet.com and attach a photograph of yourselves and your outfit under any Arctic Circle signpost, together with the date and country of crossing and the names of those who made the crossing.

This service is free to members of the ICA (annual membership £20); the fee for non-members is £5. Coloured plastic decals for your outfit, indicating membership of the Order, are also available at a cost of £4. Cheques should be payable to the ICA. See www.icacaravanning.org.

## Public Transport & Local Travel

The public transport infrastructure is of a very high standard and very punctual. You can buy a variety of bus, train, tram and metro tickets at public transport stations, HKL service points, newspaper kiosks and shops all over the country. Single tickets, which are valid for 60 minutes, can be purchased from ticket machines or from bus or tram drivers or train conductors. Tourist tickets valid for one, three or five days can also be purchased from kiosks, ticket machines and from drivers and are valid on all forms of public transport including the Suomenlinna ferry. For a public transport route planner (in English) see http://aikataulut.ytv.fi/reittiopas/en/

Within the Helsinki city area you may hire city bicycles in the summer for a token fee (refundable) from one of 26 Citybike stands.

Vehicle ferries operate all year on routes to Estonia, Germany and Russia and it is now possible to enjoy a visa free ferry trip to St Petersburg for up to 72 hours from Helsinki; see www.visitfinland.com for a link to more information or contact the Finnish Tourist Board.

Internal ferry services (in Finnish 'lossi') transport motor vehicles day and night. Those situated on the principal roads, taking the place of a bridge, are state-run and free of charge. There are regular services on Lake Paijanne, Lake Inari and Lake Pielinen, and during the summer vessels operate daily tours as well as longer cruises through Finland's lake region. Popular routes are between Hameenlinna and Tampere, Tampere and Virrat, as well as the Saimaa Lake routes. Full details are available from the Finnish Tourist Board.

**ECKERO (ALAND ISLANDS)** *A4* (8km SE Coastal) *60.19351, 19.62164* Notvikens Camping, Södra Överbyvägen 239, 22270 Eckerö/Överby [(018) 38020; fax 38329; info@ notviken.aland.fi; www.notviken.aland.fi] Fr Eckerö ferry take rd 1 E & turn R at site sp in hamlet of Överby. Site in 2km. Med, pt sl, pt shd; wc, chem disp, mv service pnt, shwrs €1; el pnts (10A) inc; lndtte; sm shop; rest, snacks; bar; BBQ; cooking facs; playgrnd; sand beach adj; games area; 5% statics; dogs; phone; bus 2km; Eng spkn; adv bkg; quiet; CKE/CCI. "Well-maintained, family-run site in lovely location by long inlet; facs rustic but clean & well-equipped." ♦ ltd 15 May-31 Aug. € 18.00                                    2009*

**FOGLO (ALAND ISLANDS)** *A4* (10km E Coastal) *60.05981, 20.51586* CC Camping, Finholmavägen, 22270 Föglö [(018) 51440; fax 51455; cc.camp@aland.net; http://home. aland.net/cc.camp] Fr ferry at Degerby on Föglö Island foll main island rd E then N. Site sp fr ferry. Sm, pt sl, unshd; htd wc; chem disp; baby facs; shwrs €1; el pnts €3.50; lndtte; shop 10km; rest, snacks; bar; BBQ; cooking facs; playgrnd; shgl beach adj; no statics; dogs; phone; no twin axles; Eng spkn; adv bkg; quiet; CKE/CCI. "Beautiful, quite site on attractive island; gd birdwatching & walks fr site." ♦ 1 Jun-31 Aug. € 10.00                                    2009*

**HAMEENLINNA** *B4* (5km NE Rural) *61.03263, 24.47209* Camping Aulangon Lomäkylä, Heikkiläntie 168, 13990 Hämeenlinna [(03) 6759772; myynti@aulangonlomakyla. fi; www.aulangonlomakyla.fi] E12 exit Hämeenlinna onto rd. Site clearly sp fr Hämeenlinna in Aulanko. Lge, terr, shd; wc; chem disp; mv service pnt; sauna; shwrs inc; el pnts (10A) €5; gas; lndtte; shop; rest, snacks; bar; playgrnd; lake sw & sand beach; cycle hire; tennis; golf course adj; wifi; some statics; poss cr; quiet; ccard acc; red CKE/CCI. "Beautiful location." 1 May-17 Aug. € 20.00                                    2010*

**HANKO/HANGO** *B4* (3km N Coastal) *59.85271, 23.01716* Camping Silversand, Hopeahietikko, 10960 Hanko Pohjoinen [(019) 2485500; fax 713713; info@silversand. fi; www.silversand.fi] Site sp fr rd 25. Lge, shd; wc; chem disp; mv service pnt; sauna; shwrs inc; el pnts (16A) €5; lndtte; shop & 1km; rest 3km; snacks; cooking facs; playgrnd; fishing; boat & cycle hire; games rm; wifi; TV; 10% statics; poss cr; Eng spkn; no adv bkg; ccard acc; red CKE. "Beautiful location on edge of sea in pine forest." ♦ 25 Apr-30 Sep. € 20.00  2009*

⊞ **HELSINKI/HELSINGFORS** *C4* (15km E Coastal/Urban) *60.20668, 25.12116* Rastila Municipal Camping, Karavaanikatu 4, Vuosaari, 00980 Helsinki [(09) 31078517; fax 31036659; rastilacamping@hel.fi; www.hel.fi/rastila] E fr Helsinki on rte 170, over Vuosaari bdge; or get to ring rd 1, turn E dir Vuosaari, site sp. Also sp fr Silja & other ferry terminals & fr rte 170 to Porvoo. Also sp on rte 167. V lge, hdstg, pt shd; wc; chem disp, mv service pnt; sauna, shwrs inc; el pnts (16A) €4.50; lndtte; shops 100m, supmkt 400m; rest, snacks; cooking facs; playgrnd; sand beach 1.2km; wifi; TV & games rm; 10% statics; metro nr; poss cr; Eng spkn; quiet; ccard acc; red long stay/CKE. "Conv Helsinki & district; pleasant site; gd san facs; helpful staff; poss itinerant workers but site clean & tidy; weekly rates avail; best place we stayed at." ♦ € 37.00                                    2014*

⊞ **HOSSA** *C2* (500m NW Rural) *65.44293, 29.55108* Erä-Hossa Camping, Hossantie 278B, 89220 Ruhtinansalmi [(08) 732310; fax 732316; era-hossa@luukku.com; www. hossa.fi] At Peranka on rd 5/E63 Kuusamo to Suomussalmi, turn E onto 9190; at T-junc after 29km turn N on rd 843/9193 sp Hossa; site on L 3km. Med, hdstg, pt shd; wc; chem disp; sauna; shwrs inc; el pnts (10A) inc; lndtte; rest; bar; cooking facs; playgrnd; lake sw adj; boating; fishing; cycle hire; quiet; ccard acc; red CKE/CCI. "Deep in Karelian Forest; lakeside site in holiday cabin complex with cent facs; many hiking & ski trails 4km in National Park." € 21.00                                    2009*

**IISALMI** *C3* (5km N Rural) *63.5947, 27.16165* Camping Koljonvirta, Ylemmäisentie 6, 74120 Iisalmi [(017) 825252; fax 822559; info@campingkoljonvirta.fi; www. campingkoljonvirta.fi] Fr S on rd 5/E63 past Iisalmi, take rd 88 twd Oulu, strt over rndabt, site in 1km on L. Lge, mkd pitch pt sl, pt shd; htd wc; chem disp; mv service pnt; sauna, shwrs inc; el pnts (10A) €5; lndtte; shops adj; rest, snacks; sand beach adj; boating & fishing; poss cr; Eng spkn; quiet; ccard acc; red CKE/CCI. "Vg." ♦ ltd 20 May-30 Sep. € 20.00                                    2011*

**IKAALINEN** *B4* (1.2km NW Rural) *61.77872, 23.0445* Camping Toivolansaari, Toivolansaarentie 3, 39500 Ikaalinen [(03) 4586462; fax 4501206; kylpylakaupunki@ ikaalinen.fi; www.kylpylakaupunki.fi] Fr rd 3/E12 exit twd Ikaalinen cent onto rd 2595 Silkintie. Take 4th L in approx 1km sp Keskusta & foll Vanha Tampereentie thro town cent to lake, site sp on tip of promontory on Kyrösjärvi Lake. Med, pt shd; wc; chem disp; mv service pnt; sauna, shwrs inc; el pnts (16A) €4; lndtte; shops 1km; rest; BBQ; playgrnd; pool nr; sand beach & lake sw; boat hire; tennis nr; games rm; entmnt; TV rm; 5% statics; dogs; boat to hotel 800m; poss cr; Eng spkn; adv bkg; quiet; CKE/CCI. "Vg, attractive lakeside site; friendly, accommodating staff." ♦ 1 Jun-31 Aug. € 18.00      2009*

⊞ **INARI** *B1* (500m SE Rural) *68.90233, 27.0370* Holiday Village/Lomakylä Inari, Inarintie 26, 99780 Inari [(016) 671108; fax 671480; info@lomakyla-inari.fi; www. saariselka.fi/lomakylainari] Fr S on rte 4/E75, site on R app Inari, clearly sp. Fr N on E75 500m past town cent, site on L, sp. Sm, some hdstg, unshd; wc; chem disp; mv service pnt; sauna; shwrs inc; el pnts (16A) inc (long lead poss req); lndtte; shops, rest 500m; snacks; playgrnd; lake sw adj; sand beach adj; motorboat & canoe hire; 40% statics; dogs free; poss cr; no adv bkg; some rd noise; ccard acc; red CKE/ CCI. "Gd for walking; midnight sun cruises on Lake Inari; excel Lapp museum; poss boggy in wet; poss low voltage if site full; some lge pitches suitable RVs & lge o'fits; clean site." € 22.00 (4 persons)                                    2009*

**INARI** *B1* (2km SE Rural) *68.90216, 27.07141* Uruniemi Camping, Uruniementie 7, 99870 Inari [(050) 3718826; pentti.kangasniemi@uruniemi.inet.fi; www.uruniemi. com] N on rte 4/E74, site S of Inari on R, sp. Sm, pt sl, pt shd; wc; sauna; shwrs €0.20; el pnts (10A) €4.50; lndtte; shop on site & 2km; snacks; cooking facs; playgrnd; lake adj; fishing & boating; cycle hire; TV; 10% statics; quiet; ccard acc. "Vg for viewing midnight sun; boggy in wet; slightly makeshift facs." 1 Jun-20 Sep. € 19.00                                    2010*

IVALO *B1* (2km S Rural) *68.64369, 27.52714* **Holiday Village Näverniemi, 99800 Ivalo [(016) 677601; fax 677602]** Sp on W side of rte 4/E75. Lge, unshd; wc; chem disp; sauna; shwrs inc; el pnts (10A) €2.50; lndtte; shop; rest, snacks; playgrnd; lake sw adj; entmnt; TV; adv bkg; quiet; ccard acc.; red CKE/ CCI "Gd cent for birdwatchers; rvside site; reindeer herds nr site; insufficient el hook-ups; helpful, friendly owner; phone ahead early ssn to check open - poss flooding during spring thaw." 1 May-31 Oct.                                   2009*

JUUKA *C3* (5km SE Rural) *63.22607, 29.34165* **Piitterin Lomakylä Camping, Piitterintie 144, 83900 Juuka [(013) 472000; fax 673220; piitteri@piitteri.fi; www. piitteri.fi]** Turn E off R6 just S of Juuka; site in 5km; sp. Med, hdstg, pt shd; wc; chem disp; sauna; shwrs inc; el pnts (15A) inc; lndtte; snacks; BBQ; cooking facs; playgrnd; sand beach adj; lake sw & boating; tennis; some statics; Eng spkn; ccard acc; red CKE. ♦ 1 Jun-15 Aug. € 20.00             2010*

JUVA *C4* (2.5km W Rural) *61.89444, 27.82138* **Juva Camping, Hotellitie 68, 51900 Juva [(015) 451930; camping@juvacamping.com; www.juvacamping.com]** Sp fr x-rds of rds 5 and 14. Sm, hdstg, shd; htd wc; chem disp; mv service pnt; baby facs; el pnts €3; lndtte; shop on site & 700m; rest, snacks; bar 700m; playgrnd; sand beach adj; boat/ canoe hire; games area; internet; some statics; dogs free; Eng spkn; adv bkg; quiet; ccard acc; red CKE. "Vg, well-kept site on lakeside; friendly, helpful staff." ♦ 1 May-31 Oct. € 18.00                                           2009*

⊞ JYVASKYLA *C3* (4km N Urban) *62.25536, 25.6983* **Laajis Camping, Laajavuorentie 15, 40740 Jyväskylä [207 436 436; fax (014) 624888; gasthaus@laajis.fi; www. laajavuori.com]** Well sp fr N on E75 & E63 fr S, site sp adj youth hostel. Med, mkd pitch, hdstg, unshd; htd wc; chem disp; mv service pnt; sauna; shwrs inc; el pnts (16A) inc; lndtte; shop 500m; tradsmn; rest, snacks; cooking facs; htd pool 3km; lake 2km; ski lift/jumps adj; wifi; entmnt; cab TV; dogs; Eng spkn; quiet; red long stay; CKE/CCI. "Facs stretched if site full; c'vans only." ♦ € 29.00                                 2011*

KAMMENNIEMI *B4* (4km NW Rural) *61.65423, 23.77748* **Camping Taulaniemi, Taulaniementie 357, 34240 Kämmenniemi [(03) 3785753; taulaniemi@yritys.soon.fi; www.taulaniemi.fi]** Fr Tampere take rte 9/E63 dir Jyvaskyla. In 10km take rte 338 thro Kämmenniemi. Foll sp Taulaniemi on unmade rd to lakeside site. Sm, pt sl, terr, unshd; htd wc; chem disp; mv service pnt; sauna; shwrs inc; el pnts (16A) €3; lndtte; shop; rest, snacks; cooking facs; playgrnd; sandy beach/lake on site; boat hire; TV; adv bkg; v quiet; CKE/CCI. "Beautiful site." 21 May-13 Sep. € 20.00                     2009*

KARIGASNIEMI *B1* (200m N Rural) *69.39975, 25.84278* **Camping Tenorinne, Ylätenontie 55, 99950 Karigasniemi [(016) 676113; camping@tenorinne.com; www.tenorinne. com]** N of town cent on rd 970 Karigasniemi to Utsjoki. Sm, pt shd; htd wc; chem disp; sauna; shwrs inc; el pnts (16A) €4; lndtte; shop, rest 200m; playgrnd; TV; some statics; no adv bkg; quiet; ccard acc; red CKE/CCI. 5 Jun-20 Sep. € 18.00                                           2010*

KEMIJARVI *C2* (500m SW Urban) *66.71689, 27.41908* **Camping Hietaniemi, Hietaniemenkatu, 98100 Kemijärvi [tel/fax (016) 813640; sales@hietaniemicamping.info; www.hietaniemicamping.info]** In cent of town on lake. Nr x-rds of rte 5 & rte 82, sp. Med; htd wc; chem disp; sauna; shwrs inc; el pnts (16A) inc; lndtte; shop 500m; snacks; bar; playgrnd; pool 1km; fishing; TV; ccard acc; red CKE. "Gd site; helpful staff." ♦ ltd 25 May-31 Aug. € 24.00        2010*

KESALAHTI *D4* (17km N Rural) *62.01883, 29.68420* **Karjalan Lomakeskus Camping, Vääramäentie 147A, 59800 Kesälahti [(013) 378121; fax 378130; info@karjalan-lomakeskus.fi; www.karjalan-lomakeskus.fi]** Fr Kesälähti N on rd 6 to Aittolahti then on rd 4800 for 14km, site sp. Last 400m on narr rd. Med, pt shd; wc; chem disp; mv service pnt; sauna; shwrs inc; el pnts (10A) £3 or metered; lndtte (inc dryer); shop 10km; rest, snacks high ssn; bar; playgrnd; lake sw & sand beach; fishing; tennis; games area; TV; some statics; dogs; no adv bkg; red CKE. 1 May-30 Sep. € 19.00           2009*

KEURUU *B4* (2.5km S Rural) *62.24435, 24.70893* **Camping Nyyssänniemi, Nyyssänniementie 10, 42700 Keuruu [(040) 7002308; leena.ikalainen@nic.fi; www. nyyssanniemi.fi]** Clearly sp W of rd 58 on S o'skirts of Keuruu. Med, some hdstg, pt shd; wc; chem disp; sauna; shwrs inc; el pnts (16A) €5; lndtte; shops in town; snacks; cooking facs; playgrnd; lake sw; boating; wifi; TV; Eng spkn; adv bkg; quiet; ccard acc; red CKE. 20 May-11 Sep. € 21.00        2011*

⊞ KILPISJARVI *A1* (4.6km SSE Rural) *69.01413, 20.88235* **Kilpisjärvi Holiday Village, Käsivarrentie 14188, 99490 Kilpisjärvi [(016) 537801; fax 537803; info@kilpisjarvi. net; www.kilpisjarvi.net]** On main rd 21 almost opp g'ge, in middle of vill, sp. Lge, hdstg, unshd; htd wc; chem disp; baby facs; shwrs €2; el pnts (10A) inc; lndtte; supmkt 100m; rest, snacks; bar; BBQ; cooking facs; bus adj; Eng spkn; quiet. "Gd NH to/fr N Norwegian fjords; access to Saana Fells for gd walking/trekking; winter sports cent." ♦ € 20.00      2011*

KOKKOLA *B3* (2.5km N Coastal) *63.85500, 23.11305* **Kokkola Camping, Vanhansatamanlahti, 67100 Kokkola [tel/fax (06) 8314006; info@kokkola-camping.fi; www. kokkola-camping.fi]** Exit A8 at Kokkola onto rte 749. Site on R, sp fr town. Sm, pt shd; wc; chem disp; mv service pnt; sauna; baby facs; shwrs inc; el pnts €4; shop; snacks; cooking facs; playgrnd; sand beach adj; games area; poss cr; quiet; red CKE. "New owner 2008 - improvements ongoing." 1 Jun-31 Aug. € 20.00                             2009*

KOLI *D3* (7km NE Rural) *63.15028, 29.84301* **Loma-Koli Camping, Merilänrannantie 65, 83960 Koli [(013) 673212; fax 223337; info@lomakolicamping.fi; www. lomakolicamping.fi]** Site 16km off rte 6, down rte 504. 64km N of Joensuu. Lge, pt shd; wc; chem disp; sauna; shwrs inc; el pnts (16A) €3; lndtte; shop; snacks; rest 1km; BBQ; playgrnd; lake sw & sand beach; cycle hire; games rm; TV; some statics; dogs; poss cr; no adv bkg; quiet; ccard acc; red CKE/CCI. 1 Jun-12 Aug. € 12.00                        2009*

FINLAND

FINLAND

**KUOPIO** *C3* (5km S Rural) *62.86432, 27.64165* **Rauhalahti Holiday Centre**, Kiviniementie, 70700 Kuopio [(017) 473000; fax 473099; rauhalahti.camping@kuopio. fi; www.rauhalahti.com] Well sp fr rte 5 (E63). Site 1.5km fr E63 dir Levänen, on Lake Kallavesi. Lge, hdstg, pt sl, pt shd; htd wc; chem disp; mv service pnt; baby facs; sauna; shwrs inc; el pnts (16A) €5; gas; lndtte; shop; rest, snacks; bar; cooking facs; playgrnd; lake sw; boat trips; watersports; TV rm; ccard acc; red CKE/CCI. "Hdstg for cars, grass for van & awning." ♦ 30 May-31 Aug. € 20.00                              2009*

⊞ **KUUSAMO** *C2* (5km N Rural) *66.00143, 29.16713* **Camping Rantatropiikki**, Kylpyläntie, 93600 Kuusamo/ Petäjälampi [(08) 8596000; fax 8521909; myyntipalvelu. tropiikki@holidayclub.fi] Three sites in same sm area on rd 5/E63, sp. Med, pt shd; htd wc; chem disp; mv service pnt; sauna; shwrs inc; el pnts (10A) inc; lndtte; pool in hotel adj; sand beach; lake sw; tennis; cycle hire; internet; dogs; no adv bkg; quiet; ccard acc; CKE/CCI. "Conv falls area; low ssn site recep at hotel 500m past site ent." € 20.00          2009*

⊞ **LAHTI** *C4* (4km N Rural) *61.01599, 25.64855* **Camping Mukkula**, Ritaniemenkatu 10, 15240 Lahti [(03) 7535380; fax 7535381; tiedustelut@mukkulacamping.fi; www. mukkulacamping.fi] Fr S on rte 4/E75 foll camping sps fr town cent. Med, pt shd; htd wc; chem disp; mv service pnt; baby facs; sauna; shwrs inc; el pnts (10A) inc; lndtte; shop 1km; rest, snacks, bar 1km; cooking facs; playgrnd; lake sw; fishing; tennis; cycle hire; internet; TV; no dogs; no adv bkg; quiet; ccard acc; red CKE. "Beautiful lakeside views." ♦ € 22.00                              2009*

**LIEKSA** *D3* (2.5km S Rural) *63.30666, 30.00532* Timitranniemi Camping, Timitra, 81720 Lieksa [(013) 521780; fax 525486; loma@timitra.com; www. timitra.com] Rte 73, well sp fr town on Lake Pielinen. Med, pt sl, pt shd; wc; chem disp; sauna; shwrs inc; el pnts (16A) €4; lndtte; shop; rest 2km; snacks; cooking facs; playgrnd; lake sw; fishing; boat & cycle hire; internet; TV; ccard acc; red CKE/CCI. "Pt of recreational complex; Pielinen outdoor museum worth visit." 15 May-20 Sep. € 20.00                   2010*

**MARIEHAMN/MAARIANHAMINA (ALAND ISLANDS)** *A4* (1km SE Coastal) *60.09079, 19.95038* **Gröna Uddens Camping**, Östernäsvägen, 22100 Mariehamn/ Maarianhamina [(018) 21121; fax 19041; gronaudden@ aland.net; www.gronaudden.com] Sp fr ferry. Lge, sl, pt shd; wc; chem disp; baby facs; sauna; shwrs; el pnts (10A) inc (long lead req); lndtte; shop; rest 1km; snacks; bar; playgrnd; sand beach; watersports; games area; cycle hire; quiet; ccard acc. "Superb natural scenery, worth long haul; unrel in wet; modern san facs but poss long walk." 1 May-17 Sep. € 23.50                              2009*

**MERIKARVIA** *B4* (2km W Coastal) *61.84777, 21.47138* **Mericamping**, Palosaarentie 67, 29900 Merikarvia [tel/ fax (02) 5511283; mericamping.merikarvia@luukka.com; www.mericamping.fi] Fr E8 foll sp to Merikarvia, site sp 2km W beyond main housing area. Med, mkd pitch, unshd; wc; chem disp; mv service pnt; shwrs inc; el pnts €3.50; rest, snacks; beach adj; wifi; some cottages; Eng spkn; quiet; ccard acc; red CKE. "Vg site on water's edge; friendly, helpful staff." € 12.00                              2009*

⊞ **MUONIO** *B1* (5km S Rural) *67.93333, 23.6575* **Harrinivan Lomakeskus**, Harrinivantie 35, 99300 Muonio [016 5300 300; fax 532 750; info@harriniva.fi; www. harriniva.fi] On E8 5km S of Muonio, well sp on R going S. SM, some hdstg, pt sl, pt shd; htd wc; chem disp; shwrs inc; en pnts (16A) €4; shop 5km; rest; bar; BBQ; playgrnd; shingle rv; wifi; twin axles; Eng spkn; adv bkg; quiet; ccard acc; CCI. "Canoe hire for white water rafting; huskies; san facs stretch in high ssn; fair." € 22.00                         2014*

⊞ **NOKIA** *B4* (5km SW Rural) *61.44798, 23.49247* **Camping Viinikanniemi**, Viinikanniemenkatu, 37120 Nokia [(03) 3413384; fax 3422385; info@viinikanniemi.com; www.viinikanniemi.com] SW fr Tampere on rd 12, site well sp. Med, mkd pitch, hdstg, pt sl, pt shd; htd wc; chem disp; mv service pnt; fam bathrm; shwrs inc; el pnts (16A) €5.90-10; gas; lndtte; shop; rest, snacks; bar; BBQ; playgrnd; sand beach & lake sw adj; boat hire; fishing; cycle hire; games area; entmnt; internet; some statics; dogs; Eng spkn; adv bkg; quiet; ccard acc; CKE/CCI. "Excel site; conv Tampere." ♦ € 21.00   2011*

**NURMES** *C3* (4km E Rural) *63.53274, 29.19889* **Hyvärilä Camping**, Lomatie 12, 75500 Nurmes [(013) 6872500; fax 6872510; hyvarila@nurmes.fi; www.hyvarila.com] On rte 73 to Lieksa, turn R 4km fr rte 6/73 junc. Well sp on Lake Pielinen. Check in at hotel. Lge, unshd; wc; chem disp; mv service pnt; sauna; shwrs inc; el pnts (16A) €5; lndtte; shop 2km; rest, snacks; playgrnd; lake sw; tennis; games area; some statics; dogs; quiet; ccard acc; red long stay/CKE/CCI. "Gd base for N Karelia; pt of recreational complex." 15 May-15 Sep. € 19.00                              2009*

⊞ **OULU/ULEABORG** *B2* (2km NW Coastal) *65.0317, 25.4159* **Camping Nallikari**, Leiritie 10, Hietasaari, 90500 Oulu/Uleåborg [(08) 55861350; fax 55861713; nallikari. camping@ouka.com; www.nallikari.fi] Off Kemi rd. Sp fr town & rte 4/E75 fr Kemi. (Do not take Oulu by-pass app fr S). Lge, pt shd; htd wc; chem disp; mv service pnt; sauna; shwrs inc; el pnts (16A) €4.50; lndtte; shop; rest 300m; snacks; bar; BBQ; cooking facs; playgrnd; pool & spa adj; sw 500m; cycle hire; games area; child entmnt high ssn; wifi; TV; 20% statics; dogs; poss cr; no adv bkg; quiet; ccard acc; red CKE/CCI. "Gd cycling; excel modern services block." ♦ € 23.00          2009*

**PELLO** *B2* (1km W Rural) *66.78413, 23.94540* **Camping Pello**, Nivanpääntie 58, 95700 Pello [(016) 512494; fax 515601; era.ahjo@oy.inet.fi] Foll site sp fr town cent. Med, hdstg, pt shd; htd wc; chem disp; mv service pnt; sauna; shwrs; el pnts (16A) inc; lndtte; shop, rest; snacks; playgrnd; rv adj; fishing; boat hire; 30% statics; Eng spkn; quiet; ccard acc. "Rvside pitches avail - insects!" 1 Jun-20 Sep. € 21.00  2009*

**PERANKA** *C2* (2km E Rural) *65.39583, 29.07094* **Camping Piispansaunat**, Selkoskyläntie 19, 89770 Peranka [(040) 5916784] Take rte 5/63 N or S; at Peranka turn E on rd 9190 for 2km; site on R in trees. Sm, hdstg, pt sl, shd; wc; chem disp; sauna; shwrs inc; el pnts (10A) €4; lndtte; shop 2km; snacks; BBQ; cooking facs; playgrnd; lake sw & sand beach adj; fishing; dogs; Eng spkn; quiet; red CKE/CCI. 1 Jun-31 Aug. € 25.00                              2011*

**PORVOO/BORGA** *C4* (2km SE Rural) *60.3798, 25.66673* Camping Kokonniemi, Uddaksentie 17, 06100 Porvoo [(019) 581967; myynti@suncamping.fi; www.fontana.fi] Fr E on rte 7/E18 m'way ignore 1st exit Porvoo, site sp fr 2nd exit. Med, some hdstg, sl, pt sh; wc; chem disp; mv service pnt; sauna; shwrs inc; el pnts (16A) €5; lndry rm; shop, rest 2km; snacks; playgrnd; poss cr; Eng spkn; no adv bkg; quiet; ccard acc; red CKE. "Access to old town & rv walk; conv Helsinki & ferry." 4 Jun-22 Aug. € 19.00                                    2010*

⊞ **PUNKAHARJU** *D4* (9km NW Rural) *61.80032, 29.29088* Punkaharjun Camping, Tuunaansaarentie 4, 58540 Punkaharju [(020) 7529800; fax (015) 441784; punkaharju@fontana.fi] 27km SE of Savonlinna on rte 14 to Imatra, sp on R. V lge, pt shd; wc; chem disp; mv service pnt; sauna; shwrs inc; el pnts (16A) €5; lndtte; shop; rest, snacks; bar; playgrnd; lake sw; waterslide; fishing; tennis; games area; TV; poss cr; no adv bkg; quiet but noise fr bar; ccard acc; red CKE/CCI. "Theme park nrby (closes 15/8); Kerimäki, world's largest wooden church; Retretti Art Cent adj." € 19.00  2009*

**RAUMA** *B4* (2km NW Coastal) *61.13318, 21.4726* Poroholma Camping, Poroholmantie, 26100 Rauma [(02) 83882500; fax 83882400; poroholma@kalliohovi.fi; www.visitrauma.fi] Enter town fr coast rd (8) or Huittinen (42). Foll campsite sp around N pt of town to site on coast. Site well sp. Lge, pt sl, shd; wc; chem disp; sauna; shwrs inc; el pnts (16A) €3; lndtte; shop; snacks; bar; playgrnd; pool 250m; sand beach; dogs; no adv bkg; quiet; ccard acc; red CKE/CCI. "Attractive, peaceful location on sm peninsula in yacht marina & jetty for ferry (foot passengers only) to outlying islands; excel beach; warm welcome fr helpful staff; clean facs." 15 May-31 Aug. € 18.00                                           2009*

**ROVANIEMI** *B2* (500m E Urban) *66.49743, 25.74340* Ounaskoski Camping, Jäämerentie 1, 96200 Rovaniemi [tel/fax (016) 345304] Exit rte 4 onto rte 78 & cross rv. Over bdge turn S on rvside along Jäämerentie. Site on R in approx 500m immed bef old rd & rail bdge, sp. Med, mkd pitch, pt shd, some hdstg; htd wc; chem disp; mv service pnt; baby facs; sauna; shwrs inc; el pnts (16A) €4.90; lndtte; shop; rest 400m; snacks; cooking facs; playgrnd; pool 1km; rv sw & sand beach; wifi; TV rm; poss v cr; Eng spkn; adv bkg; quiet; ccard acc; red CKE/CCI. "Helpful staff; excel site beside rv in parkland; gd facs; suitable RVs & twin-axles; 9km fr Arctic Circle; 6km to Santa Park, 'official' home of Santa; Artikum Museum worth visit; easy walk to town cent." ♦ 25 May-15 Sep. € 24.00                                           2010*

**ROVANIEMI** *B2* (7km E Rural) *66.51706, 25.84678* Camping Napapiirin Saarituvat, Kuusamontie 96, 96900 Saarenkylä [tel/fax (016) 3560045; reception@saarituvat.fi; www.saarituvat.fi] Fr town cent take rd 81, site on R at side of rd on lakeside. NB ignore 1st campsite sp after 2km. Sm, terr, pt shd; htd wc; chem disp; sauna; shwrs inc; el pnts (16A) €5.50; lndtte; shop 4km; rest; bar; BBQ; playgrnd; dogs; Eng spkn; adv bkg; quiet; red CKE/CCI. "Excel; friendly staff; vg base for Santa Park & Vill." 20 May-9 Sep. € 32.50          2014*

**SALO** *B4* (4km SW Rural) *60.36359, 23.06626* Vuohensaari Camping, 24100 Salo [(02) 7312651; fax 7784810] N fr Lahti, foll sp on rd 101 at edge of town. Med, pt sl, pt shd; htd wc; chem disp (wc); shwrs inc; el pnts (16A) inc; lndry rm; shop on site & 4km; snacks; cooking facs; playgrnd; quiet; CKE/CCI. "Lge mkt on Thurs in town." ♦ 1 Jun-30 Sep. € 18.50                                           2009*

**SIMO** *B2* (500m S Rural) *65.65902, 25.06655* Lapin Rinki Camping, Lohitie 14, 95200 Simo [(016) 266444; fax 266044] Fr S just off E75/rd 4 on L, well sp. Sm, pt shd; htd wc; shwrs inc; some el pnts; tradsmn; 50% statics; dogs; poss cr; Eng spkn; quiet; CKE/CCI. "Super NH or longer stay for salmon fishing - rv adj, licence avail." ♦ ltd 20 May-25 Sep. € 14.00                                           2009*

⊞ **SIRKKA LEVI** *B1* (1km W Rural) *67.80407, 24.78827* Muumari Huoneistot & Caravan, Konttisentie 1, 99130 Sirkka-Levi [(016) 644240; www.peak.fi] Fr rd 79 at rndabt in Sirkka take exit W sp for tourist info, then foll site sps. Recep in kiosk by lake. Sm, mkd pitch, pt shd; htd wc; chem disp; shwrs inc; el pnts (10A) inc; lndtte (inc dryer); snacks; bar; BBQ; lake sw 150m; 20% statics; dogs; Eng spkn; quiet; rec CKE. "Gd, friendly site." € 25.00                                           2009*

> ## "There aren't many sites open at this time of year"
>
> If you're travelling outside peak season remember to call ahead to check site opening dates – even if the entry says 'open all year'.

**SUND (ALAND ISLANDS)** *A4* (8km SE Coastal) *60.21252, 20.23508* Puttes Camping, Bryggvägen 40, Bomarsund, 22530 Sund [(018) 44040; fax 44047; puttes.camping@aland.net; www.visitaland.com/puttescamping] N fr Mariehamn on rd 2 for 40+ km, site at Bomarsund fortress ruins. Med, pt sl, pt shd; wc; chem disp; mv service pnt; shwrs €1; el pnts (10A) inc; lndtte; shop; rest, snacks; bar; BBQ; cooking facs; shgl beach adj; cycle hire; games area; 5% statics; dogs; phone; bus adj; Eng spkn; adv bkg; quiet; CKE/CCI. "Basic, but clean & welcoming; vg." ♦ ltd 15 May-11 Sep. € 12.00                                           2009*

**TAMPERE** *B4* (4km S Rural) *61.47183, 23.7390* Camping Härmälä, Leirintäkatu 8, 33900 Tampere [(03) 2651355; fax (09) 713713; myyntipalvelu@lomaliitto.fi; www.lomaliitto.fi] Foll camping sp fr Tampere cent to site on Lake Pyhäjärvi. Lge, pt shd; wc; chem disp; baby facs; sauna; shwrs inc; el pnts (16A) €5.50; lndtte; shop 4km; snacks; playgrnd; sand beach; cycle & boat hire; TV; poss cr; adv bkg; quiet; ccard acc; red long stay; CKE. 13 May-18 Sep. € 24.00          2011*

FINLAND

**TORNIO** *B2* (2.5km S Rural) *65.83211, 24.19953* **Camping Tornio, Matkailijantie, 95420 Tornio [(016) 445945; fax 445030; camping.tornio@co.inet.fi; www.campingtornio. com]** App Tornio on E4 coast rd fr Kemi sp on L of dual c/way; turn L at traff lts then immed R. Site well sp. Lge, pt shd; wc; chem disp; sauna; shwrs inc; el pnts (16A) €4; lndtte (inc dryer); shop 3km; snacks; cooking facs; playgrnd; tennis; cycle hire; TV; quiet; ccard acc; red CKE/CCI. "Poss boggy in wet." ♦ ltd 15 May-30 Sep. € 22.00                                              2013*

⊞ **TURKU/ABO** *B4* (9km SW Rural) *60.42531, 22.10258* **Ruissalo Camping (Part Naturist), Saaronniemi, 20100 Turku [(02) 2625100; fax 2625101; ruissalocamping@ turku.fi]** Well sp fr m'way & fr Turku docks; recep immed after sharp bend in a layby. Med, pt shd, some hdstg; htd wc; chem disp; mv service pnt; sauna; shwrs inc; el pnts (16A) inc; lndtte; shop; rest 200m; snacks; playgrnd; sand beach adj; watersports; games area; wifi; TV; some statics; sep area for naturists; bus; Eng spkn; quiet; ccard acc; red CKE/CCI. "Conv for ferry; modern, clean san facs; ltd el pnts some parts." ♦ ltd € 35.00                                              2014*

⊞ **UUKUNIEMI** *D4* (3.2km NW Coastal) *61.80222, 29.96538* **Papinniemi Camping, Papinniementie 178, Uukuniemi Parikkala 59730, Suomi [(40) 7369852; info@ papinniemicamping.net; www.papinniemicamping. net]** Fr Karelia rd foll sp. Fr S take R Niukkalantie. Fr N take L Uukuniementie. Sm, pt shd; wc; shwrs; el pnts (16A) €4; games area; sauna €15; rest, snacks; BBQ; wifi; bicycles; rowing boats & canoes; "Amazing nature; peaceful beautiful place; lake water so clean." € 33.00                                              2013*

**VAASA/VASA** *B3* (2km NW Coastal) *63.1008, 21.57618* **Top Camping Vaasa, Niemeläntie 1, 65170 Vaasa [(06) 2111255; fax 2111288; info.topcampingvaasa@ aspro-ocio.es; www.topcamping.fi/vaasa]** Fr town cent foll sp to harbour (Satama), site sp. Lge, pt shd; htd wc; chem disp; mv service pnt; baby facs; sauna; shwrs inc; el pnts (10A) €5; lndtte; shop; snacks; bar; playgrnd; cycle hire; TV; 10% statics; dogs; no adv bkg; ccard acc; red long stay/CKE/CCI. ♦ 25 May-10 Aug. € 22.00                                              2009*

**VARDO (ALAND ISLANDS)** *A4* (5km N Coastal) *60.27073, 20.38819* **Sandösunds Camping, Sandösundsvägen, 22550 Vårdö [tel/fax (018) 47750; info@sandocamping. aland.fi; www.sandocamping.aland.fi]** Site sp fr ferry at Hummelvik & fr rd 2. Med, pt sl, pt shd; htd wc; chem disp; mv service pnt; baby facs; shwrs inc; el pnts (10A) €3.50 (long lead poss req); lndtte; shop; rest, snacks; bar; BBQ; cooking facs; playgrnd; sand beach adj; cycle & kayak hire; games area; wifi; 5% statics; dogs; phone; Eng spkn; adv bkg; quiet; CKE/CCI. "Well-run site in beautiful location; excel facs." ♦ ltd 15 Apr-31 Oct. € 14.00                                              2009*

**VARKAUS** *C3* (3km SE Rural) *62.29914, 27.92244* **Taipale Camping, Leiritie 1, 78250 Varkaus [tel/fax (017) 5526644]** Fr rd 5 foll sp Varkaus, site sp on lakeside. Med, pt shd; htd wc; chem disp; mv service pnt; sauna; shwrs inc; el pnts (16A) €3.50; lndtte; shop 1.5km; rest 3km; snacks; playgrnd; lake sw; fishing; games area; cycle hire; TV; adv bkg; quiet; ccard acc. ♦ Jun-Aug. € 16.00                                              2009*

**VIRRAT** *B4* (3km SE Rural) *62.20883, 23.83501* **Camping Lakarin Leirintä, Lakarintie 405, 34800 Virrat [(03) 4758639; fax 4758667; virtain.matkailu@phpoint. net; www.virtainmatkailu.fi]** Fr Virrat on rte 66 twd Ruovesi. Fr Virrat pass info/park & take 2nd L, then 1st L. Site 1.7km on R (poor surface), sp. Med, pt sl, pt shd; htd wc; chem disp; sauna; shwrs inc; el pnts (16A) €3.40; lndry rm; shop in Virrat; snacks; playgrnd; lake sw adj; boating; fishing; 50% statics; Eng spkn; quiet; red CKE. "Beautiful lakeside pitches." 1 May-30 Sep. € 20.00                                              2011*

⊞ **VUOSTIMO** *C2* (1km N Rural) *66.95783, 27.50350* **Camping Kuukiurun, Sodankyläntie, 98360 Vuostimo [(016) 882535; fax 882540; kuukiuru@webinfo.fi; www. kuukiuru.fi]** N fr Kemijarvi on rd 5, site on R of rd leaving Vuostimo adj rv. Sm, mkd pitch, pt sl, unshd; wc; chem disp; sauna; shwrs; el pnts inc; snacks; fishing; boat hire; x-country skiing; TV; many statics; dogs; quiet. "Beautiful, peaceful site; friendly owners." € 20.00                                              2009*

# Germany
## Country Introduction

*Cologne Cathedral, Cologne*

## Welcome to Germany

Situated in the heart of Europe, Germany has plenty of fantastic tourist attractions and unique sights to offer. You can see architectural treasures and fascinating places of natural beauty like the Black Forest.

Rich in culture, Germany has many cities with a wealth of history and beautiful architecture. The countryside offers perfect landscapes for leisurely exploration, and there are plenty of opportunities for sports enthusiasts.

## Country highlights

Traditional German cuisine is characterized by some popular and well known regional delicacies. The most famous include 'Wurst' a variety of sausages made of pork and 'Sauerkraut' - pickled cabbage.

The popular and world famous Oktoberfest in Munich is celebrated with Reinheitsgebot beer. Christmas is a special time to visit Germany, with hundreds of festivals and Christmas Markets springing up across the country.

## Major towns and cities

- Berlin – the capital city has numerous historic buildings and a lively nightlife.
- Cologne – a city full of history and home to the famous Cologne Cathedral.
- Munich – home of the world renowned Oktoberfest, this city also has lots of amazing architecture and art.
- Frankfurt – a modern city known for its futuristic skyline.

## Attractions

- Pergamon Museum – an internationally renowned ancient art museum, full of amazing artefacts.
- Asam's Church – built in the 18th Century the church has an incredibly ornate alter.
- Frankfurter Roemer – the site of the city hall since 1405, this historic building is a beautiful landmark to visit.

## Find out more

www.germany.travel

Tel: 0049 (0) 69 97 46 40 German Tourism Board

GERMANY

# Country Information

*Population (approx):* 81million

*Capital:* Berlin (population approx 3.5 million)

*Area:* 357,050 sq km

*Bordered by:* Austria, Belgium, Czech Republic, Denmark, France, Luxembourg, Netherlands, Poland, Switzerland

*Terrain:* Lowlands in north; uplands/industrialised belt in the centre; highlands, forests and Bavarian alps in the south

*Climate:* Temperate throughout the year; warm summers and cold winters; rain throughout the year

*Coastline:* 2,389km

Highest Point: Zugspitze 2,963m

*Language:* German

*Local Time:* GMT or BST + 1, i.e. 1 hour ahead of the UK all year

*Currency:* Euros divided into 100 cents; £1 = €1.26, €1 = £0.79 (September 2014)

*Emergency numbers:* Police 112; Fire brigade 112; Ambulance 112. Operators speak English

*Public Holidays 2015:* Jan 1, 6; Apr 3,6; May 1, 14, 25; Jun 4; Aug 15; Oct 3, 31; Nov 1, 18; Dec 25, 26.

Public holidays vary according to region. The dates shown here may not be celebrated throughout the country. School summer holidays vary by region but are roughly July to mid/end Aug or Aug to mid Sept.

# Camping and Caravanning

There are approximately 3,500 campsites in Germany, which are generally open from April to October. Many (mostly in winter sports areas) stay open in winter and have all the necessary facilities for winter sports enthusiasts. Sites may have a very high proportion of statics, usually in a separate area. In the high summer season visitors should either start looking for a pitch early in the afternoon or book in advance.

Campsites are usually well equipped with modern sanitary facilities, shops and leisure amenities, etc. Some sites impose a charge for handling rubbish, commonly €1 to €2 a day. Separate containers for recycling glass, plastic, etc, are now the norm.

A daily tourist tax may also be payable of up to €2 or €3 per person per night.

Naturism is popular, particularly in eastern Germany, and sites which accept naturists will generally display a sign 'FKK'.

Many sites close for a two hour period between noon and 3pm (known as Mittagsruhe) and you may find barriers down so that vehicles cannot be moved on or off the site during this period. Some sites provide a waiting area but where a site entrance is off a busy road parking or turning may be difficult.

For a list of small sites (up to 150 pitches) see www.kleincamp.de.

Casual/wild camping is discouraged and is not allowed in forests and nature reserves. In the case of private property permission to pitch a tent or park a caravan should be obtained in advance from the owners, or on common land or state property, from the local town hall or police station.

# Cycling

There is an extensive network of over 40,000 km of well laid-out cycle paths in all regions. Children under eight years are not allowed to cycle on the road. Up to the age of 10 years they may ride on the pavement but must give way to pedestrians and dismount to cross the road. Bicycles must have front and rear lights and a bell.

Cyclists can be fined €25 for using a mobile phone while cycling.

# Electricity and Gas

Current on campsites varies between 2 and 16 amps, 6 to 10 amps being the most common. Plugs have two round pins. Most campsites have CEE connections.

Many sites make a one-off charge – usually €1 or €2 however long your stay – for connection to the electricity supply, which is then metered at a rate per kilowatt hour (kwh) of approximately €0.50-€0.70, with or without an additional daily charge. This connection charge can make one night stays expensive. During the summer you may find only a flat, daily charge for electricity of €2-€5, the supply being metered during the rest of the year.

Campingaz is available and the blue cylinders in general used throughout Europe may be exchanged for German cylinders which are green-grey. At some campsites in winter sports areas a direct connection with the gas mains ring is available and the supply is metered.

## Entry Formalities

British and Irish passport holders may stay in Germany for up to three months without a visa. While there are no Customs controls at Germany's borders into other EU countries, when you enter or leave the Czech Republic and Poland you may still have to show your passport.

## Regulations for Pets

Certain breeds of dogs, such as pit bull terriers and American Staffordshire terriers, are prohibited from entering Germany. There is an exception to this rule, whereby these dogs can be imported for up to 4 weeks with a Certificate of Personality Test, which must be given by a vet on entering Germany. Other large dogs and breeds such as Dobermann, Mastiff and Rottweiler may need to be kept on a lead and muzzled in public, which also means in your car. You are advised to contact the German embassy in London before making travel arrangements for your dog and check the latest available information from your vet or from the PETS Helpline on 0870 241 1710.

## Medical Services

Local state health insurance fund offices offer assistance round-the-clock and telephone numbers can be found in the local telephone directory. EU citizens are entitled to free or subsidised emergency care from doctors contracted to the state health care system on presentation of a European Health Insurance Card (EHIC). Private treatment by doctors or dentists is not refundable under the German health service. You will be liable for a percentage of prescribed medication charges at pharmacies and this is also non-refundable. Pharmacies offer an all-night and Sunday service and the address of the nearest out-of-hours branch will be displayed on the door of every pharmacy.

There is a fixed daily charge for a stay in hospital (treatment is free for anyone under 18 years of age) which is not refundable. If you are required to pay an additional patient contribution for treatment then reduced charges apply to holders of an EHIC. For refunds of these additional charges you should apply with original receipts to a local state health insurance fund office.

## Opening Hours

Banks – Mon-Fri 8.30am-12.30pm & 1.30pm-3.30pm (to 5pm or 6pm on Thurs).

Museums – Daily 10am-5pm/6pm; possibly closed Mon – check locally.

Post Offices – Mon-Fri 7/8am-6/8pm; Sat 8am-12pm.

Shops – Mon-Fri 8/9am-6pm/8pm. Sat 8/9am-12/4pm; in some places bakers are open Sun mornings.

## Safety and Security

Most visits to Germany are trouble free but visitors should take the usual commonsense precautions against mugging, pickpocketing and bag snatching, particularly in areas around railway stations, airports in large cities and at Christmas markets. Do not leave valuables unattended.

Germany shares with the rest of Europe a general threat from terrorism. Attacks could be indiscriminate and against civilian targets in public places, including tourist sites. You should maintain a high level of vigilance at all times.

*British Embassy*
WILHELMSTRASSE 70, D-10117 BERLIN
Tel: (030) 204570,
http://ukingermany.fco.gov.uk/en/

*British Consulates-General*
OststraBe 86, 40210
DÜSSELDORF
Tel: (0211) 94480
MÖHLSTRASSE 5, 81675 MÜNCHEN
Tel: (089) 211090
There are also Consulates or Honorary Consulates in Bremen, Frankfurt, Hamburg, Hannover, Kiel, Nürnberg and Stuttgart

*Irish Embassy*

*Irish Embassy*
JÄGERSTRASSE 51, 10117 BERLIN
Tel: (030) 220720
www.embassyofireland.de
There are also Irish Honorary Consulates in
Frankfurt, Hamburg, Köln (Cologne) and
München (Munich).

## Documents

*Passport*

It is a legal requirement to carry your passport at
all times. German police have the right to ask to
see identification and for British citizens the only
acceptable form of ID is a valid passport.

*Vehicle(s)*

Carry your valid driving licence, insurance and
vehicle documents with you in your vehicle at
all times. It is particularly important to carry your
vehicle registration document V5C, as you will
need it if entering a low emission zone (see later
in this chapter for more information).

If you are driving a hired or borrowed vehicle, you
must be in possession of a letter of authorisation
from the owner or a hire agreement.

## Money

The major debit and credit cards, including American
Express, are widely accepted by shops, hotels,
restaurants and petrol stations. However, you may
find that credit cards are not as widely accepted
in smaller establishments as they are in the UK,
including many shops and campsites, due to the
high charges imposed on retailers, and debit cards
are preferred. Cash machines are widespread and
have instructions in English.

British visitors have been arrested for possession
of counterfeit currency and the authorities advise
against changing money anywhere other than at
banks or legitimate bureaux de change.

Carry your credit card issuers'/banks' 24-hour UK
contact numbers in case of loss or theft of your
cards.

## Motoring in Germany

Roads in Germany are of an excellent standard
but speed limits are higher than in the UK and the
accident rate is greater. Drivers undertaking long
journeys in or through Germany should plan their
journeys carefully and take frequent breaks.

## Accidents

In the event of a road accident the police must
always be called even if there are no injuries.

## Alcohol

The maximum permitted level of alcohol is
50 milligrams per 100 millilitres of blood, i.e.
lower than that in the UK (80 milligrams). For
novice drivers who have held a driving licence for
less than two years, and for drivers under the age
of 21, no alcohol is permitted in the bloodstream.
Penalties for driving under the influence of alcohol
or drugs are severe.

## Breakdown Service

The motoring organisation Allgemeiner Deutscher
Automobil-Club (ADAC) operates road patrols
on motorways and in the event of a breakdown,
assistance can be obtained by calling from
emergency phones placed every 2 km. Members
of clubs affiliated to the AIT or FIA, such as The
Caravan Club, must ask specifically for roadside
assistance to be provided by ADAC as they should
be able to receive assistance free of charge. You
must pay for replacement parts and towing.
ADAC breakdown vehicles are yellow and marked
'ADAC Strassenwacht'.

If ADAC Strassenwacht vehicles are not available,
firms under contract to ADAC provide towing and
roadside assistance, against payment. Vehicles
used by firms under contract to ADAC are marked
'Strassendienst im Auftrag des ADAC'.

On other roads the ADAC breakdown service
can be reached 24 hours a day by telephoning
01802-22 22 22 (local call rates) or 22 22 22 from
a mobile phone.

## Essential Equipment

*First Aid Kit*

Drivers of German registered vehicles must carry
a first aid kit but this is not a legal requirement
for foreign visitors.

*Lights*

Dipped headlights are recommended at all times and must always be used in tunnels, as well as when visibility is poor and during periods of bad weather. Bulbs are more likely to fail with constant use and you are recommended to carry spares.

*Child Restraint Systems*

Children under three years of age must be placed in an approved child restraint and cannot be transported in a vehicle otherwise. Children of three years and over must travel in the rear of vehicles. Children under 12 years old and 1.5 metres in height must be seated in an approved child restraint. If a child restraint is won't fit into the vehicle because other children are using a child restraint, then children of three years and over must use a seat belt or other safety device attached to the seat.

*Winter Driving*

All vehicles, including those registered outside Germany, must be fitted with winter tyres (or all season tyres) during winter conditions, bearing the mark 'M+S' (Mud + Snow) or the snowflake symbol. Failure to use them can result in a fine and penalty points. There must also be anti-freeze in the windscreen cleaning fluid.

The use of snow chains is permitted and for vehicles fitted with them there is a maximum speed limit of 50 km/h (31 mph). In mountainous areas the requirement for chains is indicated by signs.

# Fuel

Most petrol stations are open from 8am to 8pm. In large cities many are open 24 hours. In the east there are fewer petrol stations than in the south and west. Some have automatic pumps operated using credit cards.

LPG (autogas or flussiggas) is widely available. You can view a list of approximately 800 outlets throughout the country, including those near motorways, from the website www. autogastanken.de (follow the links under 'Tanken' and 'Tankstellan-Karte).

On some stretches of motorway petrol stations may be few and far between, e.g. the A45, A42 and A3 to the Dutch border, and it is advisable not to let your fuel tank run low.

# Low Emission Zones

A large number of German cities and towns now require motorists to purchase a 'Pollution Badge' (Umwelt Plakette) in the form of a windscreen sticker in order to enter city centre 'Umwelt' or green zones. The areas where restrictions apply are indicated by signs showing coloured vignettes, the colour of the vignette issued (red, yellow or green) depending on your vehicle's engine type and its Euro emission rating.

You must present your vehicle registration document, V5C, at an 'Umwelt Plakette' sales outlet, which can be found at vehicle repair centres, car dealers, MOT (Tüv) stations and vehicle licensing offices and it is understood that badges are also available from ATU motoring supplies shops. The cost varies between €5 and €10 + VAT and postage.

Failure to display a badge could result in a fine of €40. Enforcement is managed by the police, local authorities and traffic wardens. Older vehicles without a catalytic converter or a particulate filter (generally emission-rated Euro 1) will not be issued with a badge and will not be permitted to enter the centres of those cities and towns participating in the scheme.

Visit www.lowemissionzones.eu or www.umwelt-plakette.de (you may also be able to purchase your badge here before you travel to Germany). Alternatively contact The Club's Travel Service Information Officer (Club members only), email: travelserviceinfo@caravanclub.co.uk.

# Parking

Zigzag lines on the carriageway indicate a stopping (waiting) and parking prohibition, e.g. at bus stops, narrow roads and places with poor visibility, but double or single yellow lines are not used. Instead look out for 'no stopping', 'parking prohibited' or 'no parking' signs.

Except for one-way streets, parking is only permitted on the right-hand side. Do not park in the opposite direction to traffic flow. Parking meters and parking disc schemes are in operation and discs may be bought in local shops or service stations.

## Priority

At crossroads and junctions, where no priority is indicated, traffic coming from the right has priority. Trams do not have absolute priority over other vehicles but priority must be given to passengers getting on or off stationary trams. Trams in two-way streets must be overtaken on the right. Drivers must give way to a bus whose driver has indicated his intention to pull away from the kerb. Do not overtake a stationary school bus which has stopped to let passengers on or off. This may be indicated by a red flashing light on the bus.

Traffic already on a roundabout has right of way, except when signs show otherwise. Drivers must use their indicators when leaving a roundabout, not when entering.

Always stop to allow pedestrians to cross at marked pedestrian crossings. In residential areas where traffic-calming zones exist, pedestrians are allowed to use the whole street, so drive with great care.

## Road Signs and Markings

Most German road signs and markings conform to the international pattern. Other road signs that may be encountered are:

| German | English Translation |
|---|---|
| Einsatzfahrzeuge Fre | Emergency vehicles only |
| Fahrbahnwechsel | Change traffic lane |
| Freie Fahrt | Road clear |
| Frostchaden | Frost damage |
| Gefährlich | Danger |
| Glatteisgefahr | Ice on the road |
| Notruf | Emergency roadside telephone |
| Radweg Kreuzt | Cycle-track crossing |
| Rollsplitt | Loose grit |
| Stau | Traffic jam |
| Strassenschaden | Road damage |
| Umleitung | Diversion |
| Vorsicht | Caution |

Road signs on motorways are blue and white, whereas on B roads (Bundesstrasse) they are orange and black. If you are planning a route through Germany using E road numbers, be aware that E roads may be poorly signposted and you may have to navigate using national A or B road numbers.

Keep distance shown

Street lights not on all night

Lower speed limit applies in the wet

Recommended route on motorways

One way street

Tram or bus stop

## Speed Limits

| | Open Road (kmph) | Motorway (kmph) |
|---|---|---|
| Solo Car | 100 | 130 |
| Car towing caravan/trailer | 80* | 80 |
| Motorhome under 3500kg | 100 | 130 |
| Motorhome 3500-7500kg | 80 | 100 |

* If the combined weight of the car and caravan is over 3500kg then the speed limit is the same as a motorhome over 3500kg

There is a speed limit of 50 km/h (31 mph) in built-up areas for all types of motor vehicles, unless otherwise indicated by road signs. A built-up area starts from the town name sign at the beginning of a town or village.

The number of sections of autobahn with de-restricted zones, i.e. no upper speed limit, is diminishing and the volume of traffic makes high speed motoring virtually impossible. Regulations on many stretches of two-lane motorway restrict lorries, together with cars towing caravans, from overtaking.

Speed cameras are frequently in use but they may be deliberately hidden behind crash barriers or in mobile units. A GPS navigation system which indicates the location of fixed speed cameras must have the function deactivated. The use of radar detectors is prohibited.

A car towing a caravan or trailer is prohibited to 80km/h (50 mph) on motorways and other main roads. You may occasionally see car/caravan combinations displaying a sign indicating that their maximum permitted speed is 100 km/h (62 mph). This is only permitted for vehicles that have passed a TUV test in Germany, who will then need to apply for a sticker at a Zulassungsstelle. The application process can be complicated as some Zulassungsstelles will insist they see a registration certificate for your caravan. Obtaining a 100km/h sticker without a registration certificate is best done in Aachen as they are the only Zulassungsstelle familiar with this process. If you are having difficulty at a different Zulassungsstelle ask them to call the Zulassungsstelle in Aachen to confirm that a registration document is not required.

In bad weather when visibility is below 50 metres, the maximum speed limit is 50 km/h (31 mph) on all roads.

# Towing

Drivers of cars towing caravans and other slow-moving vehicles must leave enough space in front of them for an overtaking vehicle to get into that space, or they must pull over from time to time to let other vehicles pass.

Motorhomes are prohibited from towing a car using an 'A-Frame'. Anyone wishing to do this should put the car on a trailer so that all four wheels of the car are off the ground. Outside built-up areas the speed limit for such vehicle combinations is 80 km/h (50 mph) or 60 km/h (37 mph) for vehicles over 3,500 kg.

# Traffic Jams

Roads leading to popular destinations in Denmark, the Alps and Adriatic Coast become very congested during the busy holiday period of July and August and on public holidays. In those periods traffic jams of up to 60 km are not unheard of.

Congestion is likely on the A3 and A5 north-south routes. Traffic jams are also likely to occur on the A7 Kassel-Denmark, the A8 Stuttgart-Munich-Salzburg and on the A2 and A9 to Berlin. Other cities where congestion may occur are Würzburg, Nürnberg (Nuremberg), Munich and Hamburg. Alternative routes, known as U routes, have been devised; those leading to the south or west have even numbers and those leading to the north or east have odd numbers. These U routes often detour over secondary roads to the following motorway junction and the acquisition of a good road map or atlas is recommended.

ADAC employs 'Stauberater' (traffic jam advisors) who are recognisable by their bright yellow motorbikes. They assist motorists stuck in traffic and will advise on alternative routes.

Upgrading of motorways to Berlin from the west and improvements to many roads in the old east German suburbs may result in diversions and delays, and worsened traffic congestion.

# Violation of Traffic Regulations

Police are empowered to impose and collect small on-the-spot fines for contravention of traffic regulations. Fines vary according to the gravity of the offence and have in recent years been increased dramatically for motorists caught speeding in a built-up area (over 50 km/h – 31 mph). A deposit may be required against higher fines and failure to pay may cause the vehicle to be confiscated.

It is an offence to use abusive language, or make rude gestures in Germany, including to other drivers while driving. It is also an offence to stop on the hard shoulder of a motorway except in the case of mechanical failure - please note that running out of fuel is not classed as a mechanical failure so you may be liable for a fine of up to €20 if you do run out of fuel and stop on the hard shoulder.

It is illegal for pedestrians to cross a road when the red pedestrian light is displayed, even if there is no traffic approaching the crossing. Offenders could be fined and will find themselves liable to all costs in the event of an accident.

## Motorways

With around 12,845 toll free kilometres, Germany's motorways (autobahns) constitute one of the world's most advanced and efficient systems. Together with an excellent network of federal and state highways, it is possible for motorists to reach any destination in Germany quickly and comfortably. For a complete list of autobahns, including the location of all junctions and roadworks in progress, see www.autobahn-online.de.

Some motorways are so heavily used by lorries that the inside lane has become heavily rutted. These parallel ruts are potentially dangerous for caravans travelling at high speed and vigilance is necessary. It is understood that the A44 and A7 are particularly prone to this problem. Caution also needs to be exercised when driving on the concrete surfaces of major roads.

On motorways emergency telephones are placed at 2 km intervals; some have one button to request breakdown assistance and another to summon an ambulance. Other telephones connect the caller to a rescue control centre. A vehicle that has broken down on a motorway must be towed away to the nearest exit.

There are more than 700 motorway service areas offering, at the very least, a petrol station and a restaurant or cafeteria. Tourist information boards are posted in all the modern motorway service areas. Recent visitors have reported an increase in service facilities just off Autobahn exit ramps, in particular with 'Autohof' (truck stops). The facilities at Autohofs are reported to be comparable to service areas, but usually with considerably lower prices.

## Touring

Visitors cannot fail to be impressed by the generally high quality of German food and its regional range and diversity. In the country there is at least one inn – 'gasthof' or 'gasthaus' – in virtually every village. A service charge is usually included in restaurant bills but it is usual to leave some small change or round up the bill by 5-10% if satisfied with the service.

Smoking is generally banned on public transport and in restaurants and bars, but regulations vary from state to state.

The German National Tourist Office (GNTO) produces pocket guides to walking and cycle paths throughout the country, as well an extensive range of other brochures and guides. The individual tourist offices for the 16 federal states can also supply a wealth of information about events, attractions and tourist opportunities within their local regions. Obtain contact details from the GNTO.

Christmas markets are an essential part of the run-up to the festive season and they range in size from a few booths in small towns and villages, to hundreds of stalls and booths in large cities. The markets generally run from mid November to 22 or 23 December.

There are 32 UNESCO World Heritage sites in Germany, including the cities of Lübeck, Potsdam and Weimar, the cathedrals of Aachen, Cologne and Speyer, together with numerous other venues of great architectural and archaeological interest.

The Berlin Welcome Card is valid for 2, 3 or 5 days and includes free bus and train travel (including free travel for three accompanying children up to the age of 14), as well as discounted or free entrance to museums, and discounts on tours, boat trips, restaurants and theatres. It can be extended to include Potsdam and the Museuminsel and is available from tourist information centres, hotels and public transport centres or from www.visitberlin.de. A 3 day museum card – SchauLUST-MuseenBERLIN – is also available, valid in more than 60 national museums in and around the city.

Other cities, groups of cities or regions also offer Welcome Cards, including Bonn, Cologne, Dresden, Düsseldorf, Frankfurt, Hamburg, Heidelberg and Munich. These give discounts on public transport, museums, shopping, dining and attractions. Enquire at a local tourist office or at the German National Tourist Office in London.

## Public Transport

Most major German cities boast excellent underground (U-bahn), urban railway (S-bahn), bus and tram systems whose convenience and punctuality are renowned. On public transport services, pay your fare prior to boarding the vehicle using the automated ticketing machines. Your ticket must then be date stamped separately using the machines onboard the vehicle or at the entry gates at major stops. Daily tickets permit the use of trains, buses and trams. Berlin's integrated transport system extends as far as Potsdam.

A number of car ferries operate across the Weser and Elbe rivers which allow easy touring north of Bremen and Hamburg. Routes across the Weser include Blexen to Bremerhavn, Brake to Sandstedt and Berne to Farge. The Weser Tunnel (B437) connects the villages of Rodenkirchen and Dedesdorf, offering an easy connection between the cities of Bremerhaven and Nordenham. Across the Elbe there is a car ferry route between Wischhafen and Glückstadt. An international ferry route operates all year across Lake Constance (Bodensee) between Konstanz and Meersburg. There is also a route between Friedrichshafen and Romanshorn in Switzerland.

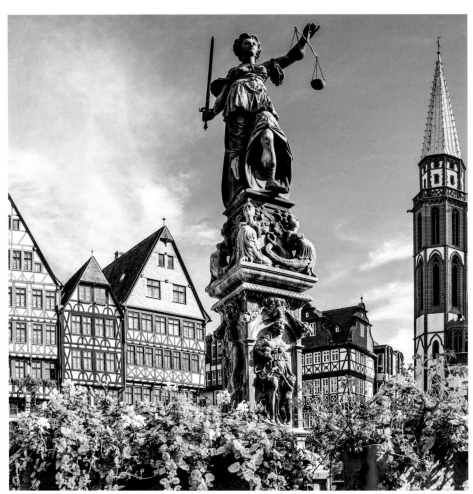

*Old Town, Frankfurt*

⊞ **AACHEN** A4 (15km SE Rural) *50.69944, 6.22194*
Camping Vichtbachtal, Vichtbachstrasse 10, 52159
Roetgen-Mulartshütte [tel/fax (02408) 5131; camping@
vichtbachtal.de; www.vichtbachtal.de] On E40/A44 exit
junc 3 Aachen/Brand onto B258 dir Kornelimünster. In 5km at
R-hand bend turn L sp Mulartshütte. Thro Venwegen. Site ent
on L 50m bef T-junc app Mulartshütte, site sp. Med, pt sl, shd;
wc; chem disp; mv service pnt; shwrs inc; el pnts (16A) €1.50
or metered; lndtte; shop; rest 150m; playgrnd; 80% statics;
site clsd Nov; poss cr; quiet; CKE/CCI. "Sm area for tourers; v
friendly Eng spkn owners; gd site for visiting Aachen; gd walks
adj." € 20.50                                                    2014*

⊞ **AACHEN** A4 (2.3km S Urban) *50.76140, 6.10285*
Aachen Platz für Camping, Branderhoferweg 11, 52066
Aachen-Burtscheid [(0241) 6088057; fax 6088058; mail@
aachen-camping.de; www.aachen-camping.de] Exit A44
junc 2 onto L233 Monschauerstrasse dir Aachen. In 3.8km at
outer ring rd Adenauer Allee L260 turn R, then in 800m L at
2nd traff lts onto Branderhoferweg twd Beverau. Site on R at
bottom of hill. Sm, mkd pitch, hdstg, unshd; htd wc; chem
disp; mv service pnt; el pnts (16A) inc; tradsmn; dogs; shwr
€1 5 mins; bus 500m; poss cr; Eng spkn; no adv bkg; quiet,
but poss noise fr bar. "Nice, clean, well-run municipal site; gd,
modern san facs; max stay 5 nights; excel o'night stop; rec
arr bef 1600 high ssn; ideal Xmas mkts; gd conv site." ♦ ltd
€ 15.00                                                          2013*

⊞ **AALEN** 3D3 (7km SW Rural) *48.78583, 9.98218* Camping
Hirtenheich, Hasenweide 2, 73457 Essingen-Lauterburg
[(07365) 296; fax 251; camphirtenteich@aol.com; www.
campingplatz-hirtenteich.de] Exit A7/E43 at Aalen onto
B29. Site sp beyond Essingen dir Lauterburg. Med, pt sl, unshd;
wc; chem disp; mv service pnt; shwrs inc; el pnts (16A)
metered; lndtte; shop; rest; playgrnd; pool; wintersports; ski
lift 300m; 70% statics; dogs; Eng spkn; quiet; debit cards acc.
"Clean facs; pleasant site." ♦ € 17.50                          2009*

**ABTSGMUND** 3D3 (9km NW Rural) *48.94650, 9.97628*
Camping Hammerschmiede-See, Hammerschmiede
2, 73453 Abtsgmünd [(07963) 369; fax 840032; hug.
hammerschmiede@t-online.de; http://camping.hug-
hammerschmiede.de] Exit B19 (Aalen-Schwabisch Hall) at W
end of Abtsgmünd by-pass dir Pommersweiler. Site sp on lake.
Lge, terr, pt sl, pt shd; wc; shwrs €0.50; el pnts (10A) metered
+ conn fee; gas; shop, rest, snacks 2km; playgrnd; games
area; 60% statics; dogs €1.60; no adv bkg; quiet. "Direct rd
fr Schwabisch Hall, not suitable for lge o'fits; lakeside pitches
long walk to san facs." 1 May-30 Sep. € 11.80                   2009*

⊞ **ACHERN** 3C3 (2km W Rural) *48.64578, 8.03728* Camping
am Achernsee, Oberacherner Strasse 19, 77855 Achern
[(07841) 25253; fax 508835; camping@achern.de; www.
achern.de] Exit A5/E35/E52 junc 53 to Achern, site sp in 1km.
Med, mkd pitch, shd; wc; shwrs €0.50; chem disp; mv service
pnt; el pnts (10A) €2.50; lndtte (inc dryer); shop 2km; rest adj;
BBQ; playgrnd; fishing; lake sw; 80% statics; dogs €3.50; quiet,
but noise nr m'way. "Useful stop for Strasbourg' gd NH". ♦
€ 30.20                                                          2014*

**ADELBERG see Göppingen** 3D3

**AEGIDIENBERG see Bad Honnef** 1B4

**AICHELBERG see Göppingen** 3D3

**AITRACH see Memmingen** 3D4

**AITRANG see Marktoberdorf** 4E4

**ALLENSBACH see Radolfzell am Bodensee** 3C4

⊞ **ALPIRSBACH** 3C3 (1.5km N Rural) *48.35576, 8.41224*
Camping Alpirsbach, Grezenbühler Weg 18-20, 72275
Alpirsbach [(07444) 6313; fax 917815; info@camping-
alpirsbach.de; www.camping-alpirsbach.de] On B294
leave Alpirsbach twds Freudenstadt. 1st site sp on L. Med, pt
shd, serviced pitch; wc; chem disp; mv service pnt; shwrs inc;
el pnts (16A) metered; gas; lndtte; shop; tradsmn; rest, snacks;
bar; playgrnd; tennis; golf 5km; 10% statics; dogs €1; o'night
area for m'vans €10; poss cr; Eng spkn; quiet; ccard not acc;
red long stay/CKE/CCI. "Excel site; helpful, informative &
friendly owner; v gd welcome with free bottle of local beer per
person; immac san facs; gd rest; gd walking; guest card gives
free transport on some local transport; some rvside pitches
shady); metered elect." ♦ € 30.00                               2014*

**ALSFELD** 1D4 (10km W Rural) *50.73638, 9.15222* Camping
Heimertshausen, Ehringshäuserstrasse, 36320 Kirtorf-
Heimertshausen [(06635) 206; fax 918359; info@camping-
heimertshausen.de; www.camping-heimertshausen.de]
Exit A5 junc 3 Alsfeld West onto B49 dir Frankfurt. Turn R in vill
of Romrod to Heimertshausen & L to site. Site also sp fr B62.
Med, shd; wc; chem disp; shwrs €0.55; el pnts (10-16A) €2
or metered; lndtte; shop; rest, snacks; playgrnd; htd pool adj;
dogs €1; 65% statics; clsd 1300-1500 & 2200-0800; o'night
area for m'vans; Eng spkn; adv bkg; quiet; red CKE/CCI.
"Beautiful, wooded area; lovely 'hunting lodge' type cosy rest.
Bar/food open Jul/Aug." 1 Apr-30 Sep. € 27.50                   2012*

⊞ **ALTEFAHR (RUGEN ISLAND)** 2F1 (300m Nw Coastal)
*54.33200, 13.12206* Sund Camp, Am Kurpark 1, 18573
Altefähr [(038306) 75483; fax 60306; info@sund-camp.
de; www.sund-camp.de] Fr Stralsund, cross bdge on B96 to
Rügen Island. Take 2nd turning to Altefähr (fewer cobbles),
after 1km turn R & then L along poor rd to site. Well sp. Med,
mkd pitch, pt shd; wc; chem disp; mv service pnt; shwrs inc; el
pnts (16A) inc (poss rev pol); shops 500m; tradsmn; lndtte; sm
shop; rest 400m; shgl beach 500m; cycle hire; TV; 15% statics;
dogs €2; poss cr; phone; sep car park; quiet; red long stay.
"Conv Rugen Is (walks, cycle tracks, beaches, steam rlwy); easy
walk to vill & harbour; splendid, but busy island; well worth
visit; ferry to Stralsund Altstadt nrby; excel, friendly site; muddy
when wet; gd, clean san facs." € 20.50                          2010*

**ALTENAHR** *3B1* (1km W Rural) *50.51328, 6.98637*
Campingplatz Altenahr, Im Pappelauel, 53505 Altenahr-Altenburg [(02643) 8503; fax 900764; info@camping-altenahr.de; www.camping-altenahr.de] Foll B257 thro narr town cent; site visible on R, on opp bank of Rv Ahr; care needed for lge o'fits over bdge. Lge; wc; shwrs €0.50; el pnts (6A) €3.50; lndtte (inc dryer); shop & 500m; rest, snacks; bar; playgrnd; 30% statics; dogs €1.50; bus; poss cr; some rd & rlwy noise; ccard acc; CKE/CCI. "Clean, friendly, well-kept site amongst vineyards; excel facs; conv for x-country rte Koblenz/Aachen; sh walk to pretty vill." ♦ 1 Apr-31 Oct.
€ 17.00                                              2010*

**ALTENAU see Goslar** *1D3*

⊞ **ALTENBERG** *4G1* (1km W Rural) *50.76666, 13.74666*
Camping Kleiner Galgenteich (Naturist), Galgenteich 3, 01773 Altenberg [(035056) 31995; fax 31993; mail@camping-erzgebirge.de; www.camping-erzgebirge.de] Leave A4 at Dresden-Nord onto B170 sp Zinnwald then Altenberg. On SW side of B170; clearly sp. Lge, pt shd; wc; chem disp; mv service pnt; shwrs €0.50; el pnts (10A) metered + conn fee; lndtte; shop; rest; snacks adj; playgrnd; lake sw & sailing adj; ski lift 500m; 50% statics; dogs €1; poss cr; quiet. "Sep area for naturists." € 18.50        2009*

## "I like to fill in the reports as I travel from site to site"

You'll find report forms at the back of this guide, or you can fill them in online at www.caravaclub.co.uk/europereport.

**ALTENKIRCHEN** *2F1* (2km E Coastal) *54.63157, 13.37250*
Campingplatz Drewoldke, Zittkower Weg 27, 18556 Altenkirchen [038391 12965; info@camping-auf-ruegen.de; www.camping-auf-ruegen.de] Take rd fr Sassnitz to Altenkirchen (L30), site sp on R bef you reach Altenkirchen. Lge, pt shd; htd wc; chem disp; MV service pnt; baby facs; shwrs (metered); el pnts (16A) €2.50; lndtte; shop; tradsmn; rest, snacks; bar; playgrnd; beach adj; dogs €4.50; phone. "Site being updated & has gd modern san facs; site located just outside of Altenkirchen on the Baltic Sea clse to ferry point Sassnitz (plse note there is another place in Germany named Altenkirchen, do not get this confused); gd site." 01 Apr-31 Oct. € 25.40                                    2011*

**ALVERN see Celle** *1D3*

**AMORBACH** *3D2* (7km SW Rural) *49.60730, 9.15876*
Azur Campingpark Odenwald, Siegfriedstrasse 2, 63931 Kirchzell [(09373) 566; fax 7375; kirchzell@azur-camping.de; www.azur-camping.de] Exit A81 at junc 3 Tauberischofsheim onto B27 dir Mosbach. At Walldürn take B47 to Amorbach & turn L dir Kirchzell. Site sp 1km S of Kirchzell dir Amorbach. Lge, hdg pitch, pt shd; wc; mv service pnt; sauna; shwrs; el pnts (10A) €2.80; lndtte (inc dryer); shop; rest, snacks; playgrnd; htd, covrd pool; games area; 60% statics; dogs €3; Eng spkn; adv bkg; quiet; CKE/CCI. ♦ 1 Apr-31 Oct. € 24.00                                        2010*

⊞ **ANNABERG BUCHHOLZ** *4G1* (15km NW Rural) *50.64291, 12.91496* **Camping Greifensteine, 09427 Ehrenfriedersdorf** [(037346) 1454; fax 1218; webmaster@greifenbachstauweiher.de; www.greifenbachstauweiher.de] On B95 S fr Chemnitz turn W at Thum sp Jahnsbach; after 2km at Jahnsbach turn S & site on R after 3km, sp. V lge, pt sl, pt shd; wc; shwrs €0.50; el pnts (10A) €2; lndtte; shop; rest, snacks; bar; playgrnd; pool; lake; boating; windsurfing; cycle hire; 60% statics; dogs €3; Eng spkn; red long stay; CKE/CCI. "Conv for Ore mountains or en rte to Czech Republic; woodland surroundings; friendly staff; excel value." ♦ € 14.00                                          2009*

**ANNWEILER AM TRIFELS see Landau in der Pfalz** *3C3*

**ASBACHERHUTTE see Idar Oberstein** *3B2*

⊞ **ATTENDORN** *3C1* (5km NE Rural) *51.13694, 7.93969* Campingplatz Hof Biggen, Finnentroperstrasse 131, 57439 Attendorn [(02722) 95530; info@biggen.de; www.biggen.de] Exit A55 junc 16 Meinerzhagen onto L539 E dir Attendorn. Thro Attendorn, site sp on Ahauser Stausee, 4km fr Biggesee. Lge, some hdstg, terr, unshd; htd wc (some cont); chem disp; mv service pnt; el pnts (16A); lndtte (inc dryer); shop; tradsmn; rest, snacks; bar; BBQ; playgrnd; games area; games rm; wifi; entmnt; TV; 75% statics; dogs; adv bkg; quiet. "Excel, scenic site." ♦ (CChq acc)          2011*

**AUGSBURG** *4E3* (2km N Rural) *48.43194, 10.92388* **Camping Ludwigshof am See, Augsburgerstrasse 36, 86444 Mühlhausen-Affing** [(08207) 961724; fax 961770; info@bauer-caravan.de; www.bauer-caravan.de] Exit A8/E52 junc 73at Augsburg Ost/Pöttmes exit; foll sp Pöttmes; site sp on L on lakeside. Lge, unshd; wc; chem disp; mv service pnt; shwrs inc; el pnts (6-16A) €3.50 (long cable req); lndtte; supmkt 500m; bar; rest; playgrnd; lake sw; 70% statics sep area; dogs €2; bus; clsd 1300-1500; poss cr; quiet; 10% adv 3+ days; ccard acc; CKE/CCI. "Pleasant site; lge unmkd field for tourers, close to san facs but long walk to recep; both 6A panel & 16A panels for el pnts -16A only accepts German type of plug; beautiful clean, modern facs; nr A8 m'way; conv NH on way to E Italy or gd for a long stay." 1 Apr-31 Oct. € 29.50                                        2014*

⊞ **AUGSBURG** *4E3* (7km N Rural) *48.41168, 10.92371* Camping Bella Augusta, Mühlhauserstrasse 54B, 86169 Augsburg-Ost [(0821) 707575; fax 705883; info@caravaningpark.de; www.caravaningpark.de] Exit A8/E52 junc 73 dir Neuburg to N, site sp. Lge, pt shd; wc; chem disp; mv service pnt; shwrs inc; el pnts (10A) inc; lndry rm; shop; supmkt 4km; rest; snacks & bar adj; playgrnd adj; lake sw & shgl beach adj; boating; 80% statics; dogs €2.55; noise fr a'bahn; ccard acc. "V busy NH; excel rest; camping equipment shop on site; vg san facs but site looking a little run down; cycle track to town (map fr recep); vg; nice lake." € 31.20                                          2014*

**AUGSBURG** *4E3* (10km NE Rural) *48.4375, 10.92916*
**Lech Camping, Seeweg 6, 86444 Affing-Mühlhausen**
**[(08207) 2200; fax 2202; info@lech-camping.de; www.**
**lech-camping.de]** Exit A8/E52 at junc 73 Augsburg-Ost; take
rd N sp Pöttmes; site 3km on R. Sm, mkd pitch, pt shd; htd wc;
chem disp; mv service pnt; shwrs inc; el pnts (16A) €3.60 or
metered + conn fee (poss rev pol); lndtte; shop 300m; supmkt
opp; rest, snacks; bar; playgrnd; lake sw adj; boating; wifi;
adv bkg rec; statics sep area; dogs €3; bus to Augsburg; train
Munich; Eng spkn; some rd noise; ccard acc. "Lovely, well-
ordered site; friendly, helpful owners; excel san facs; gd play
area; deposit for san facs key; camping accessory shop on site;
cycle rte to Augsburg; excel NH for A8; excel site espec lakeside
pitch." ♦ 1 Apr-31 Oct. € 39.50                          2014*

**BACHARACH see Oberwesel** *3B2*

**BAD ABBACH** *4F3* (4.6km W Rural) *48.93686, 12.01992*
**Campingplatz Freizeitinsel, Inselstraße 1a, D93077**
**Bad Abbach [(09405) 9570402; fax 940348; alois.**
**schmidbauer@web.de; www.campingplatz-freizeitinsel.**
**de]** A93 Regensburg, exit Pentling B16 dir twrds Kelheim.
Cont on B16 past Bad Abbach and take next exit R to Poikam/
Inselbad. Over rv and rd round to R past Poikam sp. At junc
turn R sp Inselbad. Site on R. Med, mkd pitches, terr; wc; chem
disp; mv service pnt; baby facs; shwrs; el pnts; lndtte (inc dryer);
tradsmn; café; snack; bar; bbq; cooking facs; playgrnd; sw
400m; cycle hire; wifi; 20% statics; twin axles; Eng spkn; adv
bkg; quiet; CKE/CCI. "New (2014) family run developing site;
vg modern facs; some deluxe serviced pitches avail with supp;
gd area for touring, cycling & walking; nrby lake, sw & thermal
baths; gd rest in vill 1km; train to Regensburg 1km; excel site."
♦ 1 Apr-23 Dec. € 37.00                                 2014*

⊞ **BAD BEDERKESA** *1C2* (1km S Rural) *53.62059, 8.84879*
**Regenbogen-Camp Bad Bederkesa, Ankeloherstrasse 14,**
**27624 Bad Bederkesa [(04745) 6487 or (0431) 2372370;**
**fax 8033; badbederkesa@regenbogen-camp.de; www.**
**regenbogen-camp.de]** Exit A27 junc 5 Debstedt, dir
Bederkesa, site sp. V lge, pt shd; wc; chem disp; mv service pnt;
shwrs inc; el pnts (16A) metered + conn fee; lndtte (inc dryer);
shop 800m; rest, snacks; bar; playgrnd; games area; golf 4km;
wifi; TV; 60% statics; dogs €4; clsd 1300-1500; o'night area
for m'vans; adv bkg; quiet; ccard acc; red long stay/CKE/CCI. ♦
€ 27.00                                                 2013*

**BAD BELLINGEN see Lörrach** *3B4*

**BAD BENTHEIM** *1B3* (2km E Rural) *52.29945, 7.19361*
**Campingplatz am Berg, Suddendorferstrasse 37, 48455**
**Bad Bentheim [(05922) 990461; fax 990460; info@**
**campingplatzamberg.de; www.campingplatzamberg.de]**
Exit A30 ad junc 3 onto B403, foll sp to Bad Bentheim. After sh
incline, passing g'ge on R at traff lts, at next junc turn R round
town to hospital (sp Orthopäde). Turn L & cont past hospital to
rndabt, strt over then 1.5km on L. Sm, mkd pitch, pt shd; htd
wc; chem disp; shwrs inc; el pnts (16A) €2.50; gas; lndtte; shop
2.5km; tradsmn; rest; bar; cooking facs; playgrnd; 50% statics
in sep area; dogs; phone; site clsd 24 Dec-26 Jan; poss v cr;
Eng spkn; adv bkg; quiet; CKE/CCI. "Friendly, helpful owners;
easy drive to Europort & ferries; rlwy museum on Dutch side of
border." ♦ 4 Mar-24 Dec. € 24.50                        2013*

**BAD BREISIG see Remagen** *3B1*

**BAD DOBERAN** *2F1* (5km N Coastal) *54.15250, 11.89972*
**Ferien-Camp Borgerende (Part Naturist), Deichstrasse**
**16, 18211 Börgerende [(038203) 81126; fax 81284; info@**
**ostseeferiencamp.de; www.ostseeferiencamp.de]** In
Bad Doberan, turn L off B105 sp Warnemunde. In 4km in
Rethwisch, turn L sp Börgerende. In 3km turn R at site sp. V
lge, hdg pitch, unshd; wc; chem disp; mv service pnt; baby
facs; fam bthrm; sauna; shwrs inc; el pnts (10-16A) €3; lndtte
(inc dryer) shop; tradsmn; rest, snacks; bar; cooking facs;
playgrnd; shgl beach adj; sep naturist beach; cycle hire; games
area; internet; child entmnt; 10% statics; dogs €4; bus 500m;
phone; o'night area for m'vans; Eng spkn; quiet; red low ssn/
snr citizens; CKE/CCI. "Excel beaches; cycle paths; excel site."
♦ 1 Apr-31 Oct. € 28.00                                 2010*

⊞ **BAD DURKHEIM** *3C2* (2.5km NE Rural) *49.47361,*
*8.19166* **Knaus Campingplatz Bad Dürkheim, In den**
**Almen 3, 67098 Bad Dürkheim [(06322) 61356; fax 8161;**
**badduerkheim@knauscamp.de; www.knauscamp.de]** Fr S
on A61/E31 exit junc 60 onto A650/B37 twds Bad Dürkheim.
At 2nd traff lts turn R, site sp nr local airfield. Fr N on A6 exit
junc 19 onto B271 to Bad Dürkheim. At traff lts after Ungstein
turn L dir Lugwigshafen, at next traff lts turn L, then 1st R.
Site at end of rd. Ent strictly controlled. Site well sp fr all dir
on town o'skts. V lge, mkd pitch, pt shd; htd wc; chem disp;
mv service pnt; child/baby facs; sauna; shwrs inc; el pnts
(16A) €2.50; gas; lndtte (inc dryer); shop; tradsmn; BBQ; rest;
playgrnd; sand beach adj; lake sw adj; tennis; games area;
solarium; TV rm; cycle hire; golf 8km; 45% statics; phone; bus;
m'van o'night facs; poss v cr; quiet but some daytime noise
fr adj sports airfield; Eng spkn; no ccard acc; red long
stay; CKE/CCI. "Well-equipped site in vineyards; sm, well-worn
pitches; some modern san facs - all clean; no access 1300-
1500; gd pool in Bad Dürkheim; wine-fest & wurst-fest Sep
excel; conv NH Bavaria & Austria." ♦ € 27.00            2010*

**BAD DURKHEIM** *3C2* (2km S Rural) *49.43741, 8.17036*
**Campingplatz im Burgtal, Waldstrasse 105, 67157**
**Wachenheim [(06322) 9580-801; fax 9580-899;**
**touristinfo@vg-wachenheim.de; www.wachenheim.de]**
Fr Bad Dürkheim, take B271 S dir Neustadt for approx 2km.
After passing Villa Rustica rest area, turn L for Wachenheim,
then R. Go strt at traff lts, up hill thro vill (narr). Site on L.
Med, hdg/mkd pitch, hdstg, pt shd; wc; chem disp; mv service
pnt; serviced pitches; shwrs inc; el pnts (16A) inc; lndtte (inc
dryer); shop & 1.5km; rest; bar; playgrnd; tennis; golf 12km;
50% statics; dogs €1; poss cr; quiet; CKE/CCI. "Forest walks
in Pfalz National Park; in heart of wine-tasting country; v busy
during wine festival - adv bkg rec; helpful owners; gd facs."
♦ ltd 1 Mar-30 Nov. € 31.00 (3 persons)                 2013*

**BAD EMS** *3B2* (4km E Rural) *50.32773, 7.75483*
**Camping Lahn-Beach, Hallgarten 16, 56132 Dausenau**
**[(02603) 13964; fax 919935; info@canutours.de; www.**
**campingplatz-dausenau.de]** Foll rv E fr Bad Ems twd Nassau
on B260/417. At ent to vill of Dausenau turn R over bdge, site
visible on S bank of Lahn Rv. Med, pt shd; wc; chem disp; mv
service pnt; shwrs €1; el pnts (6-16A) metered + conn fee;
lndtte; shop 400m; rest, snacks; playgrnd; boat-launching;
cycle hire; 40% statics; dogs free; sep car park; poss cr;
adv bkg; rd noise. "Pleasant situation; interesting rv traffic
& sightseeing around Lahn Valley; liable to flood at v high
water." 1 Apr-31 Oct. € 15.00                           2009*

**BAD FEILNBACH see Rosenheim** *4F4*

GERMANY

⊞ **BAD FUSSING** *4G3* (2km S Rural) *48.33255, 13.31440* **Kur & Feriencamping Max I**, Falkenstrasse 12, 94072 Egglfing-Bad Füssing [(08537) 96170; fax 961710; info@ campingmax.de; www.campingmax.de] Across frontier & bdge fr Obernberg in Austria. Site sp in Egglfing. On B12 Schärding to Simbach turn L immed bef vill of Tutting sp Obernberg. Site on R after 7km, sp. Med, pt shd; htd wc; chem disp; mv service pnt; private san facs avail; shwrs inc; el pnts (16A) metered + conn fee; lndtte (inc dryer); shop; rest 300m; snacks; bar; cooking facs; playgrnd; pool 3km; lake sw; fishing; thermal facs in Bad Füssing; tennis 2km; cycle hire; wellness cent; golf 2km; wifi; entmnt; TV; 20% statics; dogs €2; quiet; red CKE/CCI "Gd rest for snacks & meals on site; well managed site; excel clean facs; new indoor thermal bath & outdoor sw pool (2014)." ♦ € 22.60 (CChq acc) 2014*

⊞ **BAD FUSSING** *4G3* (900m NW Rural) *48.35801, 13.30661* **Camping Holmernhof**, Am Tennispark 10, 94072 Bad Füssing [(08531) 24740; fax 2474360; info@holmernhof. de; www.holmernhof.de] Exit A8/E56 junc 118 Pocking. Foll sp Bad Füssing, then sp 'Freibad' & 'Tenniszentrum', site sp. Med, mkd pitch, hdstg, pt shd; wc; chem disp; mv service pnt; baby facs; private bthrms avail; sauna; shwrs inc; el pnts (16A) metered; gas; lndtte (inc dryer); shop; rest adj; snacks; bar; playgrnd; htd pool, tennis 200m; games area; golf 2km; wifi; entmnt; TV; no dogs; phone; o'night area for m'vans; Eng spkn; quiet; CKE/CCI. "Excel site." ♦ € 23.00 2010*

⊞ **BAD GANDERSHEIM** *1D3* (1.5km E Rural) *51.86694, 10.04972* **DCC-Kur-Campingpark**, 37581 Bad Gandersheim [(05382) 1595; fax 1599; info@camping-bad-gandersheim. de; www.camping-bad-gandersheim.de] Exit A7/E45 at junc 67 onto B64 dir Holzminden & Bad Gandersheim. Site on R shortly after Seboldshausen. Lge, pt shd; wc; chem disp; mv service pnt; shwrs €0.50; el pnts (10A) metered + conn fee; lndtte; shop; rest, snacks; playgrnd; pool 1.5km; cycle hire; 40% statics; dogs €1; sep o'night area; poss cr; quiet. "Excel; always plenty of space." ♦ € 28.00 2014*

⊞ **BAD HARZBURG** *2E3* (3.5km W Rural) *51.89158, 10.51100* **Freizeitoase-Harz Camp**, Kreisstrasse 66, 38667 Bad Harzburg-Göttingerode [(05322) 81215; fax 877533; harz-camp@t-online.de; www.harz-camp.de] Fr A395 to Bad Harzburg, foll sp Oker & Goslar. Site on L at traff lts. Lge, hdstg, pt sl, terr, pt shd; wc; chem disp; mv service pnt; fam bthrm; sauna; shwrs €0.50; el pnts (10A) metered + conn fee; gas; lndtte; shop; tradsmn; rest; bar; cooking facs; playgrnd; pool; solarium; games area; entmnt; sat TV; 40% statics in sep area; dogs €2; phone; bus 100m; Eng spkn; no adv bkg; quiet; CKE/CCI. "Friendly owners; excel facs; conv walk to town." ♦ € 18.00 2009*

**BAD HERRENALB see Bad Wildbad im Schwarzwald** *3C3*

⊞ **BAD HONNEF** *1B4* (9km E Rural) *50.65027, 7.30166* **Camping Jillieshof**, Ginsterbergweg 6, 53604 Bad Honnef-Aegidienberg [(02224) 972066; fax 972067; information@ camping-jillieshof.de; www.camping-jillieshof.de] Exit E35/A3 junc 34 & foll sp Bad Honnef. In Himburg bef pedestrian traff lts turn L, then R. Site in 300m. Lge, mkd pitch, sl, pt shd; wc; chem disp; mv service pnt; shwrs inc; el pnts (16A) €2 or metered; shop; playgrnd; pool 9km; fishing; 85% statics; dogs €2; Eng spkn; quiet; red low ssn. "Excel facs; gated." € 17.50 2012*

⊞ **BAD KISSINGEN** *3D2* (500m S Urban) *50.18972, 10.07194* **Campingpark Bad Kissingen**, Euerdorferstrasse 1, 97688 Bad Kissingen [(0971) 5211; info@campingpark-badkissingen.de; www.campingpark-badkissingen.de] Exit A7/E45 junc 96 dir Bad Kissingen. At camping sp take major turn L turn onto B287 immed bef Südbrücke (bdge) - caution tight R-hand bend - take L-hand lane & turn L in cent of this bend. Site on R. Med, pt shd; wc; chem disp; mv service pnt; some serviced pitches; baby facs; shwrs €0.50; el pnts (16A) €2.80; gas; lndtte (inc dryer); shop; rest; playgrnd; adj rv in park; fishing; golf 1km; wifi; some statics; dogs €2.50; adv bkg; quiet; red long stay/CKE/CCI. "Site immac; excel facs; some daytime rd noise; pleasant spa town." ♦ 1 Apr-31 Oct. € 24.50 2010*

⊞ **BAD KOSEN** *2E4* (1.5km S Rural) *51.12285, 11.71743* **Camping an der Rudelsburg**, 06628 Bad Kösen [(034463) 28705; fax 28706; campkoesen@aol.com; www. campingbadkoesen.de] Site sp fr town. Med, pt shd; wc; chem disp; baby facs; shwrs €1; el pnts (16A) metered + conn fee; gas; lndtte; shop 1.5km; tradsmn; rest 1.5km; snacks; bar; playgrnd; 10% statics; dogs €2; o'night area for m'vans; quiet; CKE/CCI. ♦ 1 Apr-1 Nov. € 17.00 2009*

⊞ **BAD KREUZNACH** *3C2* (6km S Rural) *49.80542, 7.84236* **Camping Nahe-Alsenz-Eck**, Auf dem Grün, 55583 Bad Münster-am-Stein-Ebernburg [(06708) 2453; cnae@gmx. de; www.campingplatz-nahe-alsenz-eck.de] Exit A61 junc 51 for Bad Kreuznach, take B48 dir Kaiserslauten thro town. Site well sp on rvside. Med, mkd pitch, pt shd; wc; chem disp; shwrs €0.50; el pnts (10A) metered + conn fee; lndtte (inc dryer); shop 200m; tradsmn; rest 300m; snacks; bar; playgrnd; htd pool 300m; 80% statics; dogs €2.10; clsd 1300-1500; poss cr; quiet; CKE/CCI. "Pleasant spa town; gd facs; sm pitches; gd atmosphere; many long stay residents; site poss muddy in wet & liable to flood." 1 Apr-15 Oct. € 16.00 2010*

⊞ **BAD KREUZNACH** *3C2* (6km NW Rural) *49.88383, 7.85712* **Campingplatz Lindelgrund**, Im Lindelgrund 1, 55452 Guldental [(06707) 633; fax 8468; info@lindelgrund.de; www.lindelgrund.de] Fr A61 exit junc 47 for Windesheim. In cent immed after level x-ing, turn L & pass thro Guldental. Site sp on R in 500m. Sm, some hdstg, terr, pt shd; wc; chem disp; shwrs €0.50; el pnts (10-16A) €2 or metered; tradsmn; rest, snacks; playgrnd; htd, covrd pool 2km; tennis; golf 12km; 60% statics in sep area; dogs €1.50; poss cr; no adv bkg; quiet; red long stay. "Lovely, peaceful site; friendly owner; wine sold on site; narr gauge rlwy & museum adj; gd NH; new san facs (2012) nr touring pitches." 1 Mar-31 Dec. € 24.50 2013*

**BAD LIEBENZELL see Calw** *3C3*

⊞ **BAD MERGENTHEIM** *3D2* (3km SE Rural) *49.46481, 9.77673* **Campingplatz Bad Mergentheim**, Willinger Tal 1, 97980 Bad Mergentheim [(07931) 2177; fax 5636543; info@camping-mgh.de; www.camping-mgh.de] Fr Bad Mergentheim foll B19 S, sp Ulm. After 1km take rd to L (sps). Ent 2.7m. Med, sl, pt shd; wc; chem disp; shwrs inc; el pnts (10A) metered + conn fee or €1.90; gas; lndtte; shop; snacks; playgrnd; htd, covrd pool; paddling pool; tennis; 20% statics; dogs €2.50; bus nr; sep o'night area; quiet; ccard not acc; CKE/CCI. "Nice site; friendly, helpful owner." € 17.00 2013*

GERMANY

⊞ **BAD NEUENAHR AHRWEILER** *3B1* (1km W Urban) *50.53892, 7.09612* **Camping Ahrweiler Am Ahrtor, Kalvarienbergstrasse 1, 53474 Bad Neuenahr-Ahrweiler [(02461) 26539; camping-ahrweiler@online.de; www. camping-ahrweiler.de]** Exit A9 B266 W bet Remagen & Sinzig; then take L84 S to Ahrweiler. Site on S side of city wall sp Nürburgring; after x-ing bdge, sharp R into site on rv bank. Sm, pt shd; wc; shwrs €1; el pnts (16A) €2.50; lndtte (inc dryer); shop, rest, bar 500m; 50% statics on rv bank pitches (rv fast flowing & unfenced); no statics; dogs free; o'night m'van area; Eng spkn; adv bkg; quiet; CKE/CCI. "Excel, modern san facs; interesting walled city; conv for m'way." € 16.50   2010*

**BAD NEUENAHR AHRWEILER** *3B1* (6km W Rural) *50.53400, 7.04800* **Camping Dernau, Ahrweg 2, 53507 Dernau [(02643) 8517; www.camping-dernau.de]** Exit A61 junc 30 for Ahrweiler. Fr Ahrweiler on B267 W to Dernau, cross rv bef Dernau & turn L into Ahrweg, site sp. Sm, some hdstg, shd; htd wc; chem disp; mv service pnt; shwrs €1; el pnts (16A) €2; shops 500m; playgrnd; dogs €1; bus; train; some rlwy noise. "In beautiful Ahr valley - gd wine area; train to Ahrweiler Markt rec; immac, modern san facs; v nice." ♦ 1 Apr-31 Oct. € 17.40   2014*

**BAD PETERSTAL** *3C3* (2km W Rural) *48.42944, 8.18166* **Kurcamping Traiermühle, Renchtalstrasse 53a, 77740 Bad Peterstal-Griesbach [(07806) 8064; fax 910528; camping@traiermuehle.de; www.traiermuehle.de]** Fr French border at Strasbourg take B28 to Bad Peterstal, site sp after Löcherberg site. Sm, unshd; wc; chem disp; shwrs €0.20; el pnts (10-16A) €2 or metered; lndtte (inc dryer); rest 300m; playgrnd; 70% statics; dogs; train 2km; Eng spkn; quiet, but some daytime rd noise; CKE/CCI. "Excel, peaceful site; walking dist to town with rests, shops etc." 1 Apr-31 Oct. € 11.00   2009*

⊞ **BAD PYRMONT** *1D3* (10km S Rural) *51.89800, 9.25533* **Camping Eichwald, Obere Dorfstrasse 80, 32676 Lügde-Elbrinxen [(05283) 335; fax 640; info@camping-eichwald.de; www.camping-eichwald.de]** Fr W 7km after Schwalenberg in dir Höxter turn L at sp Bad Pyrmont & Lügde. In 2km site sp bef vill of Elbrinxen. Fr N take Bad Pyrmont rd to Lugde & foll camp sps. Med, mkd pitch, pt sl, pt shd; wc; chem disp; mv service pnt; sauna; shwrs €0.50; el pnts (16A) €1.50; gas; lndtte; shop 500m; rest; playgrnd; htd pool 400m; 60% statics; dogs €1.30; o'night area for m'vans; poss cr; quiet; ccard acc; CKE/CCI. "Gd for country lovers; pretty site." ♦ € 14.40   2009*

**BAD PYRMONT** *1D3* (10km W Rural) *51.98671, 9.10833* **Ferienpark Teutoburgerwald, Badeanstaltsweg 4, 32683 Barntrup [(05263) 2221; info@ferienparkteutoburgerwald. de; www.ferienparkteutoburgerwald.de]** On B1 bet Blomberg & Bad Pyrmont turn W for 1km to Barntrup & foll sp fr vill cent. Med, some hdstg, terr, pt shd; wc; chem disp; mv service pnt; shwrs inc; el pnts (16A) inc; gas; lndtte (inc dryer); shop, rest, snacks 500m; playgrnd; pool, tennis adj; wifi; 10% statics; dogs €2.25; sep m'van area; adv bkg; quiet; red long stay. "Excel site; vg san facs but poss stretched in high ssn; conv Hameln (Hamelin)." 1 Apr-31 Oct. € 26.50   2010*

**BAD REICHENHALL** *4G4* (2km N Rural) *47.74645, 12.8958* **Campingplatz Staufeneck, Streilachweg, 83451 Piding [(08651) 2134; fax 710450; info@ camping-berchtesgadener-land.de; www.camping-berchtesgadener-land.de]** Exit A8/E52/E60 junc 115 onto B20 for approx 3km, site sp. Cannot ent site fr S, so if coming fr S, turn at m'way junc & return on B20, as above. Med, mkd pitch, some hdstg, pt shd; wc; chem disp; mv service pnt; shwrs €0.50; el pnts (16A) €3 or metered + conn fee; lndtte (inc dryer); shop; supmkt 500m; rest 300m; playgrnd; 30% statics; dogs €1.50; bus; Eng spkn; rest grd CKE/CCI. "Excel views; site clsd 2200-0700; office open am & evenings, site yourself if office clsd; Bad Reichenhall v pleasant; conv Salzburg, Berchtesgaden & Tirol - gd bus service; clean, dated facs; excel walking/cycle tracks; v welcoming - nothing too much trouble; pitches on gravel; fast-flowing rv adj; excel site." 1 Apr-30 Oct. € 20.00   2010*

⊞ **BAD RIPPOLDSAU** *3C3* (8.5km S Rural) *48.38396, 8.30168* **Schwarzwaldcamping Alisehof, Rippoldsauerstrasse 8, 77776 Bad Rippoldsau-Schapbach [(07839) 203; fax 1263; camping@alisehof.de; www.alisehof.de]** Exit A5/E35 junc 55 Offenburg onto B33 dir Gengenbach & Hausach to Wolfach. At end of Wolfach vill turn N dir Bad Rippoldsau. Site on R over wooden bdge after vill of Schapbach. 2 steep passes fr other dir. Med, mkd pitch, pt sl, pt shd; htd wc; chem disp; mv service pnt; 30% serviced pitches; baby facs; fam bthrm; shwrs inc; el pnts (16A) metered + conn fee; gas; lndtte; shop; tradsmn; rest, snacks; bar; playgrnd; pool 2km; entmnt; 20% statics; dogs €2.30; phone; site clsd 1230-1430; poss cr; Eng spkn; adv bkg; quiet; red 7+ nts/CKE/CCI. "Highly rec; clean, friendly site; many gd walks in area; not a NH." ♦ € 35.70   2014*

**BAD SCHANDAU** *2G4* (5km NE Rural) *50.93503, 14.21165* **Panorama-Camping Kleine Bergoase, Oberestrasse 19, 01855 Kirnitzschtal (OT Mittelndorf) [0176 22906538 (mob); fax (035971) 809891; berg-oase@t-online.de; www.panorama-camping.de]** Fr Bad Schandau take rd 154 dir Sebnitz. In 5km at Mittelndorf turn R at end of vill, site sp. Sm, mkd pitch, terr, pt shd; htd wc; chem disp; shwrs €0.50; el pnts (10) metered; shop 5km; tradsmn; rest, snacks, bar 5km; BBQ; pool 5km; spa; wifi; dogs €1.50; bus adj; poss cr; Eng spkn; adv bkg; quiet; CKE/CCI. "Vg site, new in 2009; spectacular views; gd hiking; adv bkg rec - not many pitches; close Czech border, Dresden." Mar-Oct. € 20.00   2011*

⊞ **BAD SCHANDAU** *2G4* (3km E Rural) *50.92996, 14.19301* **Campingplatz Ostrauer Mühle, Im Kirnitzschtal, 01814 Bad Schandau [(035022) 42742; fax 50352; info@ostrauer-muehle.de; www.ostrauer-muehle.de]** SE fr Dresden on B172 for 40km (Pirna-Schmilka). In Bad Schandau turn E twds Hinterhermsdorf; site in approx 3km. Med, terr, pt shd; wc; chem disp; mv service pnt; shwrs €0.50; el pnts (10A) €1.75 + metered; shop; supmkt 4km; rest; sep m'van area; dogs €2; sep car park; quiet; CKE/CCI. "In National Park; superb walking area; rec arr early high ssn; site yourself if office clsd on arr." ♦ ltd € 18.50   2012*

You can now fill in site reports online

GERMANY

⊞ **BAD SEGEBERG** *1D2* (5km NE Rural) *53.96131, 10.33685* Klüthseecamp Seeblick, Stripdorfer Weg, Klüthseehof 2, 23795 Klein Rönnau [(04551) 82368; fax 840638; info@ kluethseecamp.de; www.kluethseecamp.de] Exit A21 junc 13 at Bad Sedgeberg Süd onto B432; turn L sp Bad Sedgeberg; cont on B432 dir Scharbeutz & Puttgarden thro Klein Rönnau, then turn R for site. V lge, pt shd; wc; chem disp; mv service pnt; some serviced pitches; baby facs; sauna; steam rm; shwrs inc; el pnts (16A) inc; gas; lndtte (inc dryer); shop; tradsmn; rest, snacks; BBQ; playgrnd; htd pool; lake sw 200m; fishing; horseriding; tennis; cycle hire; golf 6km; internet; games/TV rm; bus adj; 75% statics (sep area); dogs €2; twin-axles acc (rec check in adv); train to Hamburg, Lübeck; site clsd Feb; poss cr; Eng spkn; adv bkg; quiet; ccard acc; red low ssn/CKE/CCI. "Spacious, well-kept nr lakeside site; relaxing atmophere; lge pitches; helpful staff; gd facs & pool; wide range of activities; gd cycling, walking; conv Hamburg, Lübeck; excel; peaceful 50 min lakeside walk to town." ♦ € 31.60 SBS - G12          2014*

## "We must tell The Club about that great site we found"

Get your site reports in by mid-August and we'll do our best to get your updates into the next edition.

⊞ **BAD SOBERNHEIM** *3B2* (1km S Urban) *49.77861, 7.65861* Reisemobilplatz Am Nohfels, Hömigweg 1, 55566 Bad Sobernheim [(06751) 854611; fax 854626; info@ amnohfels.de; www.amnohfels.de] Exit A6/E31 junc 51 onto B41 Bad Kreuznach-Saarbrücken into Sobernheim. Foll sp 'Freilichtmuseum' & sp with m'van symbol. M'vans only. Sm, pt shd; wc; shwrs inc; el pnts (12A) €2; rest 200m; pool 800m; dogs; adv bkg; quiet. € 7.00          2009*

⊞ **BAD SOBERNHEIM** *3B2* (3km NW Rural) *49.79505, 7.57786* Camping Nahemühle, 55569 Monzingen [(06751) 7475; fax 7938; info@campingplatz-nahemuehle. de; www.campingplatz-nahemuehle.de] On B41 W fr Bad Kreuznach cross rlwy at traff lts & turn R to stadium, site sp. Sm, unshd; wc; chem disp; mv service pnt; sauna; shwrs inc; el pnts (16A) metered + conn fee; lndtte; shop 1.2km; tradsmn; rest, snacks; bar; playgrnd; fishing; horseriding; 60% statics; dogs; Eng spkn; adv bkg; quiet; red CKE/CCI. "Gd cycling area; wine vills." ♦ € 15.00          2009*

⊞ **BAD TOLZ** *4E4* (5km S Rural) *47.70721, 11.55023* Alpen-Camping Arzbach, Alpenbadstrasse 20, 83646 Arzbach [(08042) 8408; fax 8570; campingplatz-arbach@web.de; www.arzbach.de] S fr Bad Tölz on B13. Exit Lenggries, turn R to cross rv & R on Wackersburgerstrasse twds Arzbach; in 5km on ent Arzbach turn L. Site ent past sw pool. Med, pt shd; wc; chem disp; shwrs €1; el pnts (16A) inc; gas; lndtte; shop 4km; tradsmn; rest; snacks 300m; playgrnd; covrd pool; tennis 100m; golf 1km; bus 300m; poss cr; no adv bkg; quiet; CKE/CCI. "Gd walking, touring Bavarian lakes, excel facs & rest; care needed with lge c'vans due trees & hedges." ♦ € 20.00          2012*

⊞ **BAD URACH** *3D3* (2.5km NE Rural) *48.50333, 9.42388* Camping Pfählhof, Pfählhof 2, 72574 Bad Urach [(07125) 8098; fax 8091; camping@pfaehlhof.de; www. pfaehlhof.de] Fr Stuttgart or Reutlingen to Bad Urach & on twd Blaubeuren. 1km after Bad Urach cent nr town exit sp turn L bef long steep climb sp Oberlenningen & Grebenstetten to site on L in 1.6km. Lge, mkd pitch, pt shd; wc; shwrs; chem disp; baby facs; shwrs €0.50; el pnts (16A) metered + conn fee; lndtte; shop 2km; rest; cooking facs; playgrnd; pool 2km; ski lift 8km; 80% statics; dogs €1.65; adv bkg in high ssn rec; quiet; CKE/CCI. "Site admission gives red fees at spa facs; gd rest on site; picturesque sm town; gd walking area; gates close 1300-1500 & 2200-0700; helpful staff." € 16.60          2011*

⊞ **BAD WILDBAD IM SCHWARZWALD** *3C3* (9km E Rural) *48.73745, 8.57623* Camping Kleinenzhof, Kleinenzhof 1, 75323 Bad Wildbad [(07081) 3435; fax 3770; info@ kleinenzhof.de; www.kleinenzhof.de] Fr Calmbach foll B294 5km S. Site sp on R, in rv valley. Fr Bad Wildbad site is on L. Lge, pt sl, pt shd; wc; chem disp; mv service pnt; serviced pitches; sauna; shwrs inc; el pnts (16A) metered + conn fee; gas; lndtte; shop; rest, snacks; playgrnd; 2 pools (1 htd & covrd); cycle hire; ski lift 8km; entmnt; 80% statics; dogs €2.10; o'night area for m'vans; clsd 1300-1500; poss cr; adv bkg; quiet; red long stay. "Nature trails fr site; mountain views; distillery on site; modern san facs; sm pitches." ♦ € 26.40          2012*

See advertisement

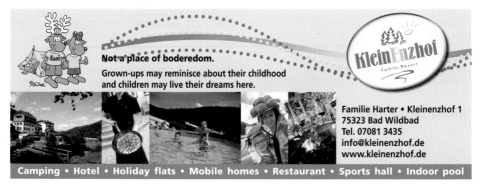

⊞ **BAD WILDBAD IM SCHWARZWALD** *3C3* (4km S Rural) *48.69777, 8.52027* **Camping Kälbermühle, Kälbermühlenweg 57, 75323 Bad Wildbad [(07085) 7322 or 7353; fax 1043; information@kaelbermuehle.de]** Take Enzklösterle rd S fr Bad Wildbad, site sp on rv bank. Med, pt shd; wc; chem disp (wc); shwrs €0.50; el pnts (16A) metered + conn fee; lndtte (inc dryer); playgrnd; 60% statics; dogs €0.80; bus; adv bkg; quiet. "Friendly owners; beautifully kept, peaceful site; superb rest; mkd forest walks; gd; no cc/debit cards." € 22.60                                                     2014*

## "I need an on-site restaurant"

We do our best to make sure site information is correct, but it is always best to check any must-have facilities are still available or will be open during your visit.

⊞ **BAD WILDBAD IM SCHWARZWALD** *3C3* (14km S Rural) *48.66641, 8.46820* **Campingplatz Müllerwiese, Hirschtalstrasse 3, 75337 Enzklösterle [tel/fax (07085) 7485; info@muellerwiese.de; www.muellerwiese. de]** Fr Bad Wildbad take tunnel S; site well sp in vill. Med, hdg/ mkd pitch, pt shd; wc; chem disp; mv service pnt; shwrs €0.50; el pnts (10-16A) €2.50 or metered; gas; lndtte; shop, rest in vill; playgrnd; cab/sat TV; 75% statics; dogs €2; bus; site clsd mid-Nov to 19 Dec; Eng spkn; adv bkg; quiet; CKE/CCI. "Gd walking, cycling in heart of Black Forest; gd local entmnt high ssn; friendly owners; clean but dated facs; vg." € 16.50  2009*

**BAD WILDBAD IM SCHWARZWALD** *3C3* (10km NW Urban) *48.79268, 8.42908* **Campingplatz Jungbrunnen, Schwimmbadstrasse 29, 76332 Bad Herrenalb [(07083) 932970; fax 932971; info@camping-jungbrunnen. de; www.camping-jungbrunnen.de]** On S o'skirts Bad Herrenalb on L564 to Gernsbach & Baden-Baden. Foll sp on L down slope. NB: Rd dist fr Bad Wildbad is much more than crow flies due to no direct rds & inclines. If app fr Gernsbach, pass site & proceed into Bad Herrenalb to rndabt, then return. This avoids diff turn. Med, terr, pt shd; wc; chem disp; shwrs €0.50; el pnts (16A) metered; gas; lndtte; shop; snacks; bar; cooking facs; pool; paddling pool; 60% statics; dogs €1.50; bus; Eng spkn; adv bkg; quiet; "Friendly owner; easy walk into interesting sm town; San facs tired but clean." 1 Apr-31 Oct. € 22.30                                                        2013*

⊞ **BADEN BADEN** *3C3* (1km NW Urban) *48.7720, 8.2215* **Stellplatz, Aumattstrasse, 76530 Baden-Baden [(07221) 275200; info@baden-baden.com]** Exit A5/E35/E52 at junc 51 for Baden-Baden & foll B500 twd cent. Turn R at traff lts into Aumattstrasse, dir 'stadion' (stadium). Make for coach/bus park, site sp. Free, sm parking place for m'vans only; wc; shop 800m; no other facs.                            2010*

**BADENWEILER see Neuenburg am Rhein** *3B4*

⊞ **BAMBERG** *4E2* (5km S Rural) *49.86138, 10.91583* **Camping Insel, Am Campingplatz 1, 96049 Bamberg-Bug [(0951) 56320; fax 56321; buero@campinginsel.de; www.campinginsel.de]** Exit A70/E48 junc 16 or A73 exit Bamberg-Süd onto B22 dir Würzburg. Site on L of rd along Rv Regnitz. Bug sm vill suburb of Bamburg to S of rv. Fr S on A3 exit junc 79 dir Bamberg. In 12km turn L dir Pettstadt; turn R at rndabt, site in 2km. Lge, pt shd; htd wc; baby facs; shwrs inc; chem disp; mv service pnt; el pnts (16A) metered (long lead poss req); gas; lndtte; supmkt 4km; shop; snacks; playgrnd; TV; 20% statics; dogs €1.10; clsd 1300-1500 & 2300-0700; bus to Bamburg; Eng spkn; quiet; ccard not acc; red long stay/ CKE/CCI. "Lovely historic town, Unesco; rvside site; excel cycle facs to town; bus to town €1.50; excel, modern san facs; family run site; gd rest; beautiful walk thro park by rvside." ♦ € 29.50                                                       2014*

**BAUTZEN** *2G4* (2km NE Rural) *51.20194, 14.46083* **Natur & AbenteuerCamping am Stausee Bautzen, Nimschützerstrasse 41, 02625 Bautzen [(03591) 271267 or (035828) 76430; fax 271268; camping-bautzen@web. de; www.camping-bautzen.de]** Exit A4 junc 90 onto B156. Site sp on lakeside. Med, hdstg, pt shd; htd wc; chem disp; mv service pnt; all serviced pitches; baby facs; shwrs inc; el pnts (16A) €2.50 (poss rev pol); lndtte (inc dryer); shop & 2km; tradsmn; BBQ; cooking facs; playgrnd; lake sw & beach adj; watersports; games rm; entmnt; internet; TV; dogs €2.50; phone; bus adj; Eng spkn; adv bkg; quiet; ccard acc; CKE/CCI. "V high quality site; lovely location; Bautzen interesting town; gd cycling & walking; excel." 1 Apr-31 Oct. € 24.50     2010*

⊞ **BERCHTESGADEN** *4G4* (3km NE Rural) *47.64742, 13.03993* **Camping Allweglehen, Allweggasse 4, 83471 Berchtesgaden-Untersalzberg [(08652) 2396; camping@ allweglehen.de; www.allweglehen.de]** On R of rd B305 Berchtesgaden dir Salzburg, immed after ent Unterau; sp. App v steep in places with hairpin bend; gd power/weight ratio needed. Lge, pt sl, terr, pt shd, some hdstg; htd wc; serviced pitches; chem disp; mv service pnt; baby facs; shwrs inc; el pnts (16A) metered + conn fee; lndtte (inc dryer); shop; rest; bar; playgrnd; htd pool; cycles; wifi; entmnt; 20% statics; dogs €2.95 ; bus 500m; ski lift; phone; poss cr; adv bkg rec high ssn; quiet; ccard acc; 10% red CKE/CCI. "Gd touring/ walking cent; wonderful views some pitches; beautiful scenery; Hitler's Eagles' Nest worth visit (rd opens mid-May) - bus fr Obersalzburg; site rds poss o'grown & uneven; steep app some pitches - risk of grounding for long o'fits; friendly, family-run site; excel rest." ♦ € 45.45                            2014*

⊞ **BERCHTESGADEN** *4G4* (11km NW Rural) *47.67666, 12.93611* **Camping Winkl-Landthal, Klaushäuslweg 7, 83483 Bischofswiesen [(08652) 8164; fax 979831; camping-winkl@t-online.de; www.camping-winkl.de]** Fr Munich-Salzburg m'way take rd 20 sp Bad Reichenhall. Where rd turns L, foll rd 20 twd Berchtesgaden. Site on R in 9km. Med, mkd pitch, pt shd; wc; chem disp; some serviced pitches with sat TV; shwrs inc; el pnts (10A) metered + conn fee (poss rev pol); gas; lndtte; shop & 500m; tradsmn; rest; playgrnd; htd pool 3.5km; golf 15km; wifi; 50% statics; dogs €1.50; site clsd Nov; Eng spkn; adv bkg; some rd & rlwy noise; red long stay/CKE/CCI. "Some pleasant, shd pitches adj sm rv; clean san facs." € 21.00                                2009*

⊞ **BERGEN** *1D3* (9km E Rural) *52.80443, 10.10376*
**Camping am Örtzetal, Dicksbarg 46, 29320 Oldendorf**
**[(05052) 3072; www.campingplatz-oldendorf.de]** Fr S, exit
A7/E45 junc 52 dir Celle, in 5km turn L sp Winsen, Belsen &
Bergen. Fr N exit A7/E45 at junc 45 onto B3 to Bergen. Foll rd
to Bergen. In Bergen foll sp Hermannsburg. In about 7km at
T-junc turn R, then 1st L sp Eschede & Oldendorf. In Oldendorf
turn L at 2nd x-rds. Site on R in 1km. Lge, pt shd; wc; chem
disp; shwrs €0.80; el pnts (6A) metered + conn fee; lndtte
(inc dryer); shop 4km; tradsmn; rest 500m; snacks; bar; htd
pool 4km; lake 4km; playgrnd; cycle hire; 40% statics; dogs
€1.50; phone; quiet; CKE/CCI. "Ideal for walking & cycling on
Lüneburg Heath; conv Belsen memorial; welcoming, friendly
owner; peaceful site; barrier clsd 1300-1500." € 15.50 2009*

**BERGWITZ see Lutherstadt Wittenberg** *2F3*

⊞ **BERLIN** *2G3* (15km SW Rural) *52.40027, 13.18055*
**City Campingplatz Hettler & Lange, Bäkehang 9a,**
**14532 Kleinmachnow-Dreilinden [(033203) 79684; fax**
**77913; kleinmachnow@city-camping-berlin.de; www.**
**city-camping-berlin.de]** Fr S exit A115/E51 junc 5 sp
Kleinmachnow, turn L at T-junc & cont to rndabt. Turn L &
foll site sp in 800m. Lge, pt sl, pt shd; htd wc; chem disp; mv
service pnt; baby facs; shwrs inc; el pnts (6A) €2.50; gas; lndtte
(inc dryer); sm shop & 5km; tradsmn; rest, snacks; playgrnd;
lake sw 2km; boats for hire; dogs €2; phone; bus nr; poss v
cr; some Eng spkn; adv bkg; quiet but some barge & rd noise;
CKE/CCI. "Excel location on canal side; immac, modern san
facs; twin-axles by arrangement; gd walking in woods; gd
public transport conv Berlin 45 mins - parking at Wannsee
S-bahn (family ticket avail for bus & train); vg." € 23.00 2013*

⊞ **BERLIN** *2G3* (15km SW Rural) *52.4650, 13.16638* **DCC**
**Campingplatz Gatow, Kladower Damm 207-213, 14089**
**Berlin-Gatow [(030) 3654340; fax 36808492; gatow@**
**dccberlin.de; www.dccberlin.de]** Fr A10 to W of Berlin turn
E on rd 5 sp Spandau/Centrum. Go twd city cent & after 14km
turn R onto Gatowerstrasse (Esso g'ge) sp Kladow/Gatow.
Site 6.5km on L almost opp Kaserne (barracks). Med, pt shd;
htd wc; chem disp; mv service pnt; shwrs inc; fam bthrm; el
pnts (10-16A) metered + conn fee; gas; lndtte (inc dryer);
supmkt 2km; tradsmn; snacks; bar; playgrnd; sand beach 1km;
60% statics; dogs €2; bus at gate; poss cr; Eng spkn; rd noise;
red CKE/CCI. "Excel site; bus tickets fr recep; frequent bus to
Berlin cent at gate; highly rec; excel san facs; bicycles can be
taken on nrby Kladow ferry to Wannsee S. Bahn; gates close
between 1300 & 1500 and at 2200." ◆ € 34.00 2014*

⊞ **BERLIN** *2G3* (10km NW Urban) *52.54861, 13.25694* **City-**
**Camping Hettler & Lange, Gartenfelderstrasse 1, 13599**
**Berlin-Spandau [(030) 33503633; fax 33503635; spandau@**
**city-camping-berlin.de; www.hettler-lange.de]** Fr N on
A111/A115/E26 exit junc 10 sp Tegel Airport & head W on
Saatwinkler Damm. Fr S on A100 exit junc 11 onto Saatwinkler
Damm. Cont 3.2km to traff lts, turn R, then R again immed bef
2nd bdge. Site on island in rv. Med, pt sl, shd; wc; chem disp;
shwrs €1; el pnts (16A) €2; lndtte; shop 2km; tradsmn; rest;
bar; dogs €2; Eng spkn; no adv bkg; aircraft noise; ccard acc;
CKE/CCI. "Conv Berlin; 15 min walk to bus stn; gd location
beside a canal but aircraft noise; gd san facs; NH/sh stay only;
poss to cycle along canal to Potsdam." € 22.50 2014*

**BERNKASTEL KUES** *3B2* (2km NE Rural) *49.96556, 7.10475*
**Camping Rissbach, Rissbacherstrasse 155, 56841 Traben-**
**Trarbach [(06541) 3111; info@moselcampings.de; www.**
**moselcampings.de]** Fr Bernkastel on B53, after Kröv do not
cross Mosel bdge but cont strt on twd Traben, site on R in
1km. NB 20km by rd fr Bernkastel to site. Med, mkd pitch,
pt sl, shd; htd wc; chem disp; mv service pnt; shwrs €0.25/
min; el pnts (16A) €2.50; gas 500m; lndtte; shop & 2km; rest
1km; snacks; BBQ; playgrnd; htd pool adj; boat-launch; wifi;
30% statics; dogs €3.50; phone; quiet. "In lovely position nr
rv; extra for pitches nr rv; well-run site; excel san facs; v gd sw
pools in town; poss flooding at high water; Sept wine fest." ◆
1 Apr-31 Oct. € 16.00 2012*

**BERNKASTEL KUES** *3B2* (2km SW Rural) *49.90883, 7.05600*
**Kueser Werth Camping, Am Hafen 2, 54470 Bernkastel-**
**Kues [(06531) 8200; fax 8282; camping-cueser-werth@**
**web.de; www.camping-kueser-werth.de]** A'bahn A1/48
(E44) exit Salmtal; join rd sp Bernkastel. Bef rv bdge turn L sp
Lieser, thro Lieser cont by rv to ent on R for boat harbour, foll
camping sp to marina. Diff access via narr single-track rd. Lge,
pt shd; wc; chem disp; mv service pnt; shwrs inc; el pnts (16A)
metered; lndtte; sm shop; tradsmn; rest, snacks; playgrnd;
cycle hire; TV rm; 20% statics; dogs €2; bus 1km; poss cr;
Eng spkn; adv bkg; some rd noise & rv barges; 5% red CKE/
CCI. "Excel cent for touring Mosel Valley; Bernkastel delightful
sm town with gd parking, sailing, boat excursions, wine
cent; cycle lanes; site low on rv bank - poss flooding in bad
weather; efficient staff; gd site with excel facs; not rec for NH/
sh stay high ssn as pitches & position poor." ◆ 1 Apr-31 Oct.
€ 18.00 2009*

**BERNKASTEL KUES** *3B2* (4km NW Rural) *49.93736, 7.04853*
**Camping Schenk, Hauptstrasse 165, 54470 Bernkastel-**
**Wehlen [(06531) 8176; fax 7681; info@camping-schenk.**
**de; www.camping-schenk.com]** On Trier/Koblenz rd B53,
exit Kues heading N on L bank of rv & site on R in 4km at
Wehlen, sp. Steep exit. Med, mkd pitch, some hdstg, pt sl,
some terr, pt shd; htd wc; chem disp; mv service pnt; some
serviced pitches; shwrs €0.50; el pnts (16A) metered + conn
fee; gas; lndtte; shops 1km; tradsmn; rest adj; snacks; bar;
playgrnd; pool; 40% statics; dogs; phone; bus; poss cr; Eng
spkn; adv bkg; quiet; CKE/CCI. "In apple orchard on Rv Mosel;
price according to pitch size; friendly owners; debit cards acc;
pool deep - not suitable non-swimmers; poorly ventilated san
facs; rv walks & cycle path to town." ◆ ltd 27 Mar-31 Oct.
€ 25.00 2011*

**BERNKASTEL KUES** *3B2* (10km NW Rural) *49.97972, 7.0200*
**Camping Erden, Moselufer 1, 54492 Erden [(06532) 4060;**
**fax 5294; schmitt@campingplatz-erden.de; www.**
**campingplatz-erden.de]** Exit A1/48 junc 125 onto B50 to
Zeltingen. Cross bdge over Mosel, turn L to Erden, site sp. Med,
pt sl, shd; htd wc; chem disp; mv service pnt; shwrs; el pnts
(16A) metered + conn fee; gas; lndtte; shop nr; tradsmn; rest,
snacks; bar; playgrnd; pool 5km; TV; 90% statics in sep area;
dogs €2; phone; bus; poss cr; adv bkg; rd noise; ccard acc; red
long stay. "Pleasant, less cr site on opp side of rv to main rd;
wonderful setting in scenic area; water point & san facs long
way fr tourer pitches; barrier locked 1300-1500 & o'night." ◆
1 Apr-31 Oct. € 18.00 2013*

**BERNRIED see Deggendorf** *4G3*

---

GERMANY

**BIELEFELD** *1C3* (4km W Rural) *52.00624, 8.45681*
Campingpark Meyer Zu Bentrup, Vogelweide 9, 33649
Bielefeld [(0521) 4592233; fax 459017; bielefeld@
meyer-zu-bentrup.de; www.camping-bielefeld.de] Exit
A2 junc 27 & foll sp Osnabrück on B68; site sp on L - approx
14km fr a'bahn. Lge, pt sl, unshd; wc; chem disp; mv service
pnt; shwrs €0.30/min; el pnts (10-16A) €1; lndtte (inc dryer);
farm shop; tradsmn; bar; cooking facs; playgrnd; games area;
games rm; wifi; 95% statics; dogs €2; quiet; red CKE/CCI. "Vg;
immac, excel san facs; conv for Bielefeld; well maintained." ♦
1 Mar-30 Nov. € 28.00                          2014*

**BINZ** *2G1* (5km NW Coastal) *54.26532, 13.33341*
Wohnmobil-Oase Rügen, Proraer Chaussee 60,
18609 Ostseebad Binz OT Prora [(01577) 428 3715;
info@.wohnmobilstellplatz-ruegen.de] Fr Binz foll coast rd to
Prora, site on L past traff lts. Med, hdstg, pt shd; htd wc; chem
disp; mv service pnt; shwrs, el pnts (16A); lndtte; gas; snacks;
dogs; bus/tram adj; Eng spkn; m'vans only; "V gd site, track to
beach, tradsmn call daily." 23 Mar-20 Oct. € 15.00     2012*

**BINZ (RUGEN ISLAND)** *2G1* (2km NW Coastal) *54.42315,
13.57808* Camping Meier, Proraer Chaussee 30, 18609
Prora [(038393) 2085; fax 32624; info@camping-meier-
ruegen.de; www.camping-meier-ruegen.de] On B96
Stralsund to Bergen cont on 196 to Karow. Turn L on 196a to
Prora, at traff lts turn R onto L29 to Binz. After 1.5km at camp
sp turn R thro wood to site. Med, mkd pitch, pt shd; wc; chem
disp; mv service pnt; shwrs €0.50; el pnts (6A) €2.50; gas 1km;
lndtte; shops 1km; tradsmn; rest; sand beach
500m; tennis; cycle hire; dogs €3.50; phone; Eng spkn; adv
bkg (bkg fee); quiet; red 7+ days; ccard acc (Visa only). "Gd
location for touring Rügen area; gd sandy beach thro woods;
vg rest; vg san facs." ♦  1 Apr-31 Oct. € 23.00     2011*

**BIRKENFELD** *3B2* (1.5km E Rural) *49.65501, 7.18211*
Campingpark Waldwiesen (Naturist), 55765 Birkenfeld
[(06782) 5215; fax 5219; info@waldwiesen.de; www.
waldwiesen.de] Exit A62 junc 4 N to Birkenfeld. Site sp off rd
B41. Med, hdg pitch, pt sl, pt shd; wc; chem disp; mv service
pnt; shwrs inc; el pnts 16A) metered + conn fee; gas; lndtte;
shops 500m; tradsmn; rest 600m; snacks 1km; playgrnd; lake
sw adj; cycle hire; 10% statics; dogs €2.50; adv bkg; quiet;
ccard acc; CKE/CCI. "Sep area for naturists; excel facs for
children; gd base for Saar-Hunsruck area." Easter-14 Oct.
€ 21.75                                         2009*

⊞ **BISCHOFSHEIM** *3D2* (1km SE Rural) *50.39558, 10.02011*
Camping am Schwimmbad, Kissingerstrasse 53,
97653 Bischofsheim [(09772) 1350; fax 931350; info@
rhoencamping.de; www.rhoencamping.de] Fr A7 exit junc
93 at Fulda onto B279 E to Bischofsheim, site sp 1km down
minor rd dir Bad Kissingen. Fr A71 exit junc 25 Bad Neustadt
onto B279 W. Med, hdg/mkd pitch, hdstg, pt shd; wc; chem
disp; mv service pnt; shwrs €0.50; el pnts (16A) metered; gas;
lndtte; shop & 500m; tradsmn; rest, bar 500m; BBQ; playgrnd;
2 htd pools (1 covrd); paddling pool; waterslide; tennis;
solarium; cycle hire; 30% statics; dogs €1; sep m'van area; adv
bkg; quiet; red CKE/CCI. "In cent of Rhon Nature Park, ideal for
walking; ski adj in winter; office hrs 0800-1230 & 1430-1800;
if arr after 1800 phone in adv & ent key will be left for you." ♦
€ 19.50                                         2011*

**BITBURG** *3B2* (9km NE Urban) *50.03750, 6.59111*
Camping Kyllburg, Karl-Kaufmann-Weg 5, D-54655
Kyllburg [65 63 81 33; info@campingkyllburg.de; www.
campingkyllburg.de] Site on E o'skts of Kyllburg on banks
of rv Kyll. App fr W turn R immed after x-ing rv. Ent down hill
on R immed bef sharp LH bend. Steep & narr descent. Med,
unshd; htd wc; chem disp; mv service pnt; baby facs; shwrs
inc; el pnts (16A) €0.80; gas; lndtte; shop 500m; tradsmn; rest,
snacks; bar; BBQ; playgrnd; pool; rv adj; wifi; 30% statics; dogs
€1.80; bus 500m; train 500m; Eng spkn; adv bking; quiet; cc
acc; red low ssn; CKE/CCI. "Gd fr sh stays; 5 sw pool with
waterslide; cycling & walking paths; v gd site." ♦ Mar-Oct.
€ 18.60                                         2011*

⊞ **BITBURG** *3B2* (10km W Rural) *49.95895, 6.42454* Prümtal
Camping, In der Klaus 5, 54636 Oberweis [(06527) 92920;
fax 929232; info@pruemtal.de; www.pruemtal.de] On
B50 Bitburg-Vianden rd. On ent Oberweis sharp RH bend
immed L bef rv bdge - sp recreational facs or sp Köhler Stuben
Restaurant-Bierstube. V lge, pt shd; htd wc; chem disp; shwrs
inc; el pnts (16A) €2.75 or metered; lndtte; shop; rest, snacks;
bar; playgrnd; pool; cycle hire; internet; entmnt; 60% statics;
dogs €2.10; Eng spkn; poss v cr high ssn; adv bkg; ccard acc;
CKE/CCI; "Excel facs; san facs stretched high ssn; vg rest." ♦
€ 26.00                                         2012*

⊞ **BONN** *1B4* (20km S Rural) *50.65388, 7.20111* Camping
Genienau, Im Frankenkeller 49, 53179 Bonn-Mehlem
[(0228) 344949; fax 3294989; genienau@freenet.de] Fr B9
dir Mehlem, site sp on Rv Rhine, S of Mehlem. Med, pt shd;
wc; chem disp; shwrs €1; el pnts (6A) €3 or metered; lndtte;
rest & shop 600m; rest, snacks 1km; 60% statics; dogs €2; bus;
Eng spkn; no adv bkg; some rv & rlwy noise; CKE/CCI. "Excel
site on rv bank; liable to flood when rv v high; nr ferry to cross
Rhine; late arr no problem; san facs up steps but disabled facs
at grnd level; lots to see & do." ♦ € 28.00          2013*

> ## "Satellite navigation makes touring much easier"
>
> Remember most sat navs don't know if
> you're towing or in a larger vehicle – always
> use yours alongside maps and site directions.

**BOPPARD** *3B2* (5km N Rural) *50.24888, 7.62638* Camping
Sonneneck, 56154 Boppard [(06742) 2121; fax 2076;
info@campingpark-sonneneck-boppard.de; www.
campingpark-sonneneck.de] On Koblenz-Mainz rd B9, on W
bank of Rhine, in vill of Spay. Lge, mkd pitch, pt shd; wc; chem
disp; mv service pnt; serviced pitches; sauna; shwrs inc; el pnts
(4A) €2.50; gas; lndtte; shop; rest, snacks; bar; playgrnd; pool
high ssn; shgl beach nr; fishing; crazy-golf; 18-hole golf 2km;
10% statics; dogs €2.40; phone; night watchman; poss cr; Eng
spkn; rlwy & barge noise; CKE/CCI. "V pleasant staff; clean san
facs, poss long way fr pitches; ltd waste water points; extra
for rvside pitch; site poss liable to flood; gd cycle path along
Rhine." ♦ Easter-31 Oct. € 19.60                    2009*

**BORGERENDE see Bad Doberan** *2F1*

⊞ BRANDENBURG AN DER HAVEL *2F3* (6km E Rural) *52.39833, 12.43665* **Camping und Ferienpark am Plauer See, Plauer Landstrasse 200, 14774 Brandenburg [33 81 80 45 44; fax 81 80 46 44; info@camping-plauersee. de; www.camping-plauersee.de]** Fr A2 take 102 to Brandenburg. L onto 1, cont 4km. Just after sign for Plauerhof is a campsite sign. Turn L & foll rd for 1.5km to site on the side of lake. Med, mkd pitch, pt sl, pt shd; wc; chem disp; mv service pnt; fam bthrm; shwrs €1.40; el pnts (10A) €1.90; lndtte (inc dryer); rest; snack; bar; BBQ; playgrnd; games area; cycle hire; 75% statics; dogs; bus 1.5km; Eng spkn; adv bkg; quiet; CCI. "Next to sm lake; boat, cycles & BBQ hire; nr historic town of Brandenburg; vg site." € 17.80        2014*

**BRAUBACH see Lahnstein** *3B2*

⊞ BRAUNEBERG *3B2* (500m W Rural) *49.90564, 6.97603* **Wohnmobilstellplatz Brauneberger Juffer, Moselweinstraße 101, 54472 Brauneberg [6534 933 333; mfrollison@yahoo.co.uk or info@brauneberg.de]** Fr NE of A1 take exit 127-Klausen onto L47 twds Mulheim. Cont onto L158, then turn L onto B53. Supermkt 20m fr site ent which is down side rd twds rv. Sm, hdg pitch, mkd pitch, hdstg, pt shd; chem disp; mv service pnt; el pnts (16A); BBQ; sw 500m; dogs; bus 100m; Eng spkn; quiet. "Gd cycle paths along rv; vg site." € 8.00        2014*

⊞ BRAUNLAGE *2E4* (6km NE Rural) *51.75713, 10.68345* **Campingplatz am Schierker Stern, Hagenstrasse, 38879 Schierke [(039455) 58817; fax 58818; info@harz-camping. com; www.harz-camping.com]** Fr W on B27 fr Braunlage for 4km to Elend. Turn L & cross rlwy line. Site on L in 2km at x-rds. Med, hdstg, pt sl, pt shd; htd wc; chem disp; mv service pnt; shwrs inc; el pnts (6A) €2.60; lndtte; sm shop & 8km; tradsmn; rest 200m; snacks 1km; BBQ; cooking facs; TV; no statics; dogs €1.60; bus at site ent; train 1km; adv bkg; quiet. "Conv & pleasant site in Harz mountains; excel san facs; friendly, helpful owners live on site; sm pitches; vg." € 24.00        2013*

⊞ BRAUNLAGE *2E4* (10km SE Rural) *51.65697, 10.66786* **Campingplatz am Bärenbache, Bärenbachweg 10, 38700 Hohegeiss [(05583) 1306; fax 1300; campingplatz-hohegeiss@t-online.de; www.campingplatz-hohegeiss. de]** Fr Braunlage S on B4 thro Hohegeiss; site sp on L downhill (15%) on edge of town. Med, hdg pitch, mkd pitch, terr, pt shd; htd wc; chem disp; mv service pnt; baby facs; shwrs inc; el pnts (10A); lndtte (inc dryer); shops 500m; rest, snacks; bar; cooking facs; BBQ; playgrnd; htd pool; paddling pool; cycle hire; some statics; wifi; dogs €1.50; Eng spkn; adv bkg; quiet; red snr citizens. "Gd walking; friendly; walking dist to vill; vg." ♦ ltd € 22.50 (CChq acc)        2014*

⊞ BRAUNLAGE *2E4* (1.5km SW Rural) **Camping Hohe Tannen, Am Campingplatz 1, 38700 Braunlage [(05520) 413; fax 417; campingplatz.hohetannen@t-online.de]** Take B27 fr Braulage dir Bad Lauterberg, site sp. Med, mkd pitch, terr, pt shd; htd wc; shwrs inc; chem disp; mv service pnt; el pnts (16A) metered + conn fee; lndtte; shop; rest; snacks 1km; playgrnd; pool; 50% statics; dogs €1.20; ski lift 1km; bus; adv bkg; quiet; red CKE/CCI. "Excel facs, ltd low ssn." € 15.30        2009*

BREISACH AM RHEIN *3B4* (5km E Rural) *48.03104, 7.65781* **Kaiserstuhl Camping, Nachwaid 5, 79241 Ihringen [(07668) 950065; fax 950071; info@kaiserstuhlcamping. de; www.kaiserstuhlcamping.de]** Fr S exit A5/E35 junc 64a, foll sp twds Breisach, then camping sp to Ihringen. At Ihringen site sp dir Merdingen. Fr N exit junc 60 & foll sp. Med, unshd; wc; chem disp; mv service pnt; baby facs; shwrs €0.50; el pnts (16A) metered + conn fee; lndtte; shop 800m; rest adj; snacks; bar; playgrnd; htd pool, tennis adj; golf 8km; 10% statics; dogs €2.50; poss cr; quiet; 10% red long stay/CKE/CCI. "Can get cr in high ssn." ♦ 15 Mar-31 Oct. € 32.00        2014*

## "There aren't many sites open at this time of year"

If you're travelling outside peak season remember to call ahead to check site opening dates – even if the entry says 'open all year'.

BREISACH AM RHEIN *3B4* (2km S Rural) *48.01972, 7.60861* **Campingplatz Münsterblick Breisach, Hochstetterstrasse 11, 79206 Breisach-Hochstetten [(07667) 93930; fax 939393; adler-hochstetten@t-online.de; www.adler-hochstetten.de]** Fr E5/A5 exit 63 sp Breisach. Site sp off B31 rd app Breisach, adj to Gasthof Adler in Hochstetten. Or cross Rv Rhine fr France at Neuf-Brisach on D415. Site sp at Breisach in approx 1km (L of rd). Sm, pt shd; wc; shwrs inc; chem disp; shwrs €0.50; el pnts (10A) metered + conn fee; lndtte; shop 2km; rest; bar; 10% statics; dogs €1.20; poss cr; adv bkg; quiet; red CKE/CCI. "Excel NH; modern, clean san facs; gates clsd 2100." 27 Mar-2 Nov. € 16.30        2009*

BREMEN *1C2* (10km SW Rural) *53.00694, 8.69277* **Campingplatz Steller See, Zum Stellersee 15, 28817 Stuhr-Gross Mackenstedt [(04206) 6490; fax 6668; steller.see@t-online.de; www.steller-see.de]** Exit A1/E37 junc 58a onto B322 sp Stuhr/Delmenhorst. Foll site sp. Lge, unshd; htd wc; chem disp; mv service pnt; baby facs; shwrs €0.50; el pnts (10-16A) metered or €2.50; gas; lndtte (inc dryer); tradsmn; rest, snacks; bar; BBQ; playgrnd; lake sw adj; games area; entmnt; 80% statics in sep area; phone; wifi; poss cr at w/end; adv bkg; poss noisy; no ccard acc; red long stay/CKE/CCI. "Site officially clsd but owner may accommodate you; well-appointed, clean, lakeside site; immac san facs; friendly owners; conv NH fr m'way & for trams to Bremen; some m'way noise; gd space, easy to position; vg." ♦ 1 Apr-30 Sep. € 25.50        2014*

⊞ BREMEN *1C2* (12km SW Rural) *53.01055, 8.68972* **Camping Wienberg, Zum Steller See 83, 28816 Stuhr-Gross Mackenstedt [(04206) 9191; fax 9293; info@camping-wienburg.de; www.camping-wienberg.de]** Exit A1/E37 junc 58a onto B322 sp Stuhr/Delmenhorst. Foll Camping Steller See sp. Lge, mkd pitch, pt sl, hdstg, pt shd; htd wc; chem disp; mv service pnt; baby facs; shwrs €1; el pnts (16A) metered or €3; lndtte (inc dryer); shop; tradsmn; rest, snacks; bar; playgrnd; pool; cycle hire; entmnt; TV; 50% statics; dogs €2; some Eng spkn; adv bkg; rd noise; ccard acc; CKE/CCI. "Helpful staff; basic facs; gd." € 23.70        2011*

⊞ **BREMEN** *1C2* (5km NW Rural) *53.11483, 8.83263*
**Camping am Stadtwaldsee**, Hochschulring 1, 28359
Bremen [(0421) 8410748; fax 8410749; contact@camping-stadtwaldsee.de; www.camping-stadtwaldsee.de] Fr A27 exit junc 18 onto B6. At 1st junc turn R sp University, site on R in approx 2km. Foll 'Campingplatz' sp. Lge, mkd pitch, hdstg, pt shd; htd wc; chem disp; mv service pnt; baby facs; fam bthrm; shwrs inc; el pnts (16A) metered; gas; lndtte (inc dryer); shop; tradsmn; rest, snacks; bar; cooking facs; BBQ; playgrnd; lake sw adj; wifi; some statics; dogs €4; phone; bus 100m; poss cr; Eng spkn; adv bkg; some rd noise; ltd ccard acc; red long stay; CKE/CCI. "Excel, spacious lakeside site; vg san & kitchen facs; cycle path to beautiful city; gd bus service." ♦
€ 47.00                                                    2014*

⊞ **BRETTEN** *3C3* (8km E Rural) *49.03478, 8.83352*
**Stromberg Camping**, Diefenbacherstrasse 70, 75438
Knittlingen-Freudenstein [(07043) 2160; fax 40405; info@strombergcamping.de; www.strombergcamping.de] Take B35 E fr Bretten, foll sp Knittlingen then Freudenstein, site sp in approx 1lm on L. V lge, mkd pitch, pt shd; wc; chem disp; mv service pnt; shwrs inc; el pnts (16A) €1.50 (rev pol); lndtte (inc dryer); shop; tradsmn; rest high ssn; snacks; bar; cooking facs; playgrnd; pool; paddling pool; pony riding; games area; entmnt; 90% statics; dogs €2.50; poss cr; quiet; red long stay; CKE/CCI. "Clsd to vehicles 1300-1500 & 2200-0700; gd touring base for Black Forest; ltd number touring pitches cr nr ent." ♦ € 17.00                                          2010*

# "That's changed – Should I let The Club know?"

If you find something on site that's different from the site entry, fill in a report and let us know. See www.caravanclub.co.uk/europereport.

⊞ **BRIESELANG** *2F3* (500m W Rural) *52.57138, 12.96583* **Campingplatz Zeestow im Havelland**, 11 Brieselangerstrasse, 14665 Brieselang [(033234) 88634; fax 22863; info@campingplatz-zeestow.de; www.campingplatz-zeestow.de] Exit A10/E55 junc 27; turn W dir Wustermark; site on L after canal bdge in 500m. Lge, pt sl, unshd; wc; chem disp; shwrs €1; el pnts (16A) metered; gas; lndtte; shop; rest; bar; 75% statics; dogs €2; bus; poss cr; CKE/CCI. "Gd NH nr a'bahn; facs dated but clean; 13km fr Berlin & 25km fr Potsdam; fair." ♦ ltd € 14.00                  2011*

⊞ **BRUGGEN** *1A4* (2km E Rural) *51.23416, 6.19815*
**Camping-Forst Laarer See**, Brüggenerstrasse 27, 41372
Niederkrüchten [(02163) 8461 or 0172 7630591 (mob); info@campingforst-laarersee.com; www.campingforst-laarersee.com] Exit A92 junc 3 onto B221 to Brüggen. Foll sp Laarer See & site. Sm sp on R. Lge, pt sl, pt shd; htd wc; chem disp; mv service pnt; baby facs; fam bthrm; shwrs €1; el pnts (16A) inc; lndtte; shop 2km; rest, snacks; bar; BBQ; playgrnd; games area; 80% statics; dogs €1; Eng spkn; adv bkg; quiet; CKE/CCI. "Unspoilt area nr pretty town; many leisure amenities nr site - gd for children; vg site." ♦ € 28.00          2012*

**BRUNNEN see Füssen** *4E4*

⊞ **BUHL** *3C3* (5km W Rural) *48.72719, 8.08074* **Ferienpark & Campingplatz Adam**, Campingstrasse 1, 77815 Bühl-Oberbruch [(07223) 23194; fax 8982; info@campingplatz-adam.de; www.campingplatz-adam.de] Exit A5 at Bühl take sp Lichtenau & foll sp thro Oberbruch, then L twd Moos to site in 500m. If app on rd 3 take rd sp W to Rheinmünster N of Bühl. Site sp to S at W end of Oberbruch. Lge, mkd pitch, hdstg, pt shd; serviced pitches; wc; chem disp; mv service pnt; shwrs €0.50; el pnts (10A) €2.20; lndtte; shop; supmkt 1km; rest, snacks; bar; playgrnd; tennis; lake sw; boating; sailing; fishing; entmnt; 60% statics; dogs €2.50; o'night area tarmac car park; extra for lakeside pitches; poss cr; Eng spkn; adv bkg; quiet; ccard acc; red long stay/low ssn; CKE/CCI. "Facs gd, clean; conv for Strasbourg, Baden-Baden & Black Forest visits; if recep clsd use area outside gate; vg; excel camp with own lake; gd rest; friendly staff; handy for m'way but still quiet; o'night tarmac area excel for NH but worth a longer stay." ♦
€ 34.50                                                    2014*

**BULLAY see Zell** *3B2*

**BURGEN** *3B2* (300m N Rural) *50.21457, 7.38976* **Camping Burgen**, 56332 Burgen [(02605) 2396; fax 4919; info@camping-burgen.de; www.camping-burgen.de] Leave A61 at J39; foll B411 twds Dieblich to reach S bank of Mosel; turn L and foll B49 for approx 12km; site on L between rd and rv bef vill. SatNav uses rte thro vill, not suitable. Med, mkd pitch, unshd; wc; mv service pnt; shwrs inc; el pnts (10A) metered + conn fee (poss rev pol); lndtte; gas; shop; rest 200m; snacks adj; playgrnd; pool; boat-launching; entmnt; 30% statics; dogs €2; Eng spkn; some rd, rlwy & rv noise; red CKE/CCI. "Scenic area; ideal for touring Mosel, Rhine & Koblenz areas; gd shop; poss liable to flood; lovely, clean site; gd san facs; rec." 11 Apr-19 Oct. € 30.00 (CChq acc)                               2014*

⊞ **CALW** *3C3* (8km N Rural) *48.77884, 8.73130*
**Campingpark Bad Liebenzell**, Pforzheimerstrasse 34, 75378 Bad Liebenzell [(07052) 935680; fax 935681; campingpark@abelundneff.de] N fr Calw on B463 twd Pforzheim. Site on N edge of Bad Liebenzell on R sp & visible fr rd. Lge, hdg pitch, shd; wc; chem disp; mv service pnt; shwrs inc; el pnts (16A) metered or €2.40; gas; lndtte; shop & 500m; tradsmn; rest, snacks; bar; playgrnd; htd pool adj; waterslide; tennis; 50% statics; dogs €1.50; phone; m'van o'night area; poss cr; adv bkg; poss noisy; ccard acc; red CKE/CCI. "Excel pool complex adj; ltd san facs & site slightly scruffy; popular with young families; lovely area; gd walking." ♦
€ 18.00                                                    2009*

⊞ **CALW** *3C3* (7km S Rural) *48.67766, 8.68990* **Camping Erbenwald**, 75387 Neubulach-Liebelsberg [(07053) 7382; fax 3274; info@camping-erbenwald.de; www.camping-erbenwald.de] On B463 S fr Calw, take R slip rd sp Neubulach to go over main rd. Foll Neubulach sp until camping sp at R junc. Site well sp. Lge, hdg/mkd pitch, pt shd; wc; chem disp; mv service pnt; baby facs; shwrs €0.50; el pnts (10A) metered; lndtte; shop; tradsmn; rest, snacks; bar; playgrnd; htd pool; paddling pool; games area; internet; 60% statics; dogs €2; phone; Eng spkn; adv bkg; quiet. "Gd size pitches; child-friendly site; no vehicles in or out fr 1300-1500; excel." ♦
€ 20.50                                                    2011*

⊞ **CANOW** *2F2* (2km E Rural) *53.19636, 12.93116*
**Camping Pälitzsee, Am Canower See 165, 17255 Canow**
**[(039828) 20220; fax 26963; info@mecklenburg-tourist.**
**de; www.mecklenburg-tourist.de]** Fr N on B198 turn S dir
Rheinsberg to Canow vill, site sp. Lge, pt shd; wc; chem disp;
shwrs €1; el pnts (16A) metered or €3; lndtte; shop high ssn;
supmkt 2km; rest 2m; snacks; bar; playgrnd; lake sw & boating;
50% statics; dogs €2; adv bkg; quiet. "Canow charming vill; vg
touring base for lakes." ♦ € 19.50                       2009*

⊞ **CELLE** *1D3* (10km NE Rural) *52.65305, 10.19361* **Camping**
**Alvern, Beedenbostelerweg 7, 29229 Celle-Alvern**
**[(05145) 6000; schaefer@alvern.com]** NE fr Celle on B191.
After 5km at Garssen turn R onto K29 & foll sp thro Alvern.
Site sp. Med, pt shd; wc; chem disp; shwrs €0.50; el pnts
(10A) inc; lndtte (inc dryer); shop; BBQ; playgrnd; games area;
80% statics; quiet; CKE/CCI. "Gd site; gd cycling tracks."
€ 14.00                                                   2009*

⊞ **CHEMNITZ** *2F4* (10km SW Rural) *50.76583, 13.01444*
**Waldcampingplatz Erzgebirgsblick, An der Dittersdorfer**
**Höhe 1, 09439 Amtsberg [(0371) 7750833; fax 7750834;**
**info@waldcamping-erzgebirge.de; www.waldcamping-**
**erzgebirge.de]** Fr A4 take A72 S & exit junc 15. Foll sp
'Centrum' & join 'Südring' ring rd. Turn onto B174 & foll sp
Marienberg twd junc with B180. Site sp 500m fr junc. Med,
mkd pitch, pt shd; htd wc; chem disp; mv service pnt; baby
facs; shwrs €0.50; el pnts (16A) metered; gas; lndtte; shop;
tradsmn; supmkt 4km; playgrnd; games area; TV rm; dogs
free; bus 1km; Eng spkn; adv bkg; red long stay;
ccard not acc; red long stay/snr citizens/CKE/CCI. "Gd san facs;
relaxing site; gd walking; vg standard of site." € 17.00   2009*

⊞ **CLAUSTHAL ZELLERFELD** *1D3* (4km SE Rural) *51.78490,*
*10.35060* **Campingplatz Prahljust, An den Langen Brüchen**
**4, 38678 Clausthal-Zellerfeld [(05323) 1300; fax 78393;**
**camping@prahljust.de; www.prahljust.de]** Fr Clausthal
turn onto B242 dir Braunlage, in 3km turn R, site sp. V lge,
terr, pt shd; htd wc; chem disp; mv service pnt; baby facs;
sauna; shwrs inc; el pnts (10-16A) metered; gas; lndtte (inc
dryer); shop; tradsmn; rest, snacks; bar; cooking facs; playgrnd;
htd pool; lake sw adj; cycle hire; ski lift 8km; wifi; TV rm;
30% statics; dogs €2; phone; bus 1km; Eng spkn; adv bkg;
CKE/CCI. "Beautiful wooded location adj lake; gd hiking &
cycling; vg." ♦ € 17.40 (CChq acc)                        2010*

⊞ **COBURG** *4E2* (9km SW Rural) *50.19433, 10.83809*
**Campingplatz Sonnland, Bahnhofstrasse 154, 96145**
**Sesslach [(09569) 220; fax 1593; info@camping-sonnland.**
**de; www.camping-sonnland.de]** Exit A73 junc 10 Ebersdorf
onto B303 W. Then at Niederfüllbach turn S onto B4, then
turn W dir Sesslach. Site sp N of Sesslach dir Hattersdorf; turn
R at sp opp filling stn, site in 150m. Med, mkd pitch, some
hdstg, terr, pt shd; htd wc; chem disp; mv service pnt; serviced
pitches; shwrs €1.50; el pnts (16A) metered; lndtte (inc dryer);
shop 300m; rest 400m; BBQ; playgrnd; lake sw; 70% statics;
dogs €1.50; adv bkg; CKE/CCI. "Sesslach unspoilt, medieval,
walled town; site well laid-out." € 18.00                 2012*

**COCHEM** *3B2* (1.5km N Rural) *50.15731, 7.17360*
**Campingplatz am Freizeitzentrum, Moritzburgerstrasse**
**1, 56812 Cochem [(02671) 4409; fax 910719; info@**
**campingplatz-cochem.de; www.campingplatz-cochem.**
**de]** On rd B49 fr Koblenz, on ent town go under 1st rv bdge
then turn R over same bdge. Foll site sp. Lge, mkd pitch, pt sl,
pt shd; wc; chem disp; mv service pnt; shwrs €0.90; el pnts
(10-16A) €2.50 + conn fee (some rev pol); gas; lndtte (inc
dryer); snacks; shops/supmkt, rest nrby; playgrnd; cycle hire;
dogs €3; poss cr; some rd/rlwy/rv noise; red low ssn; CKE/CCI.
"Gd, clean site adj Rv Mosel; pitches tight & poss diff access
fr site rds; gd for children; easy walk along rv to town; train to
Koblenz, Trier, Mainz." 1 Apr-31 Oct. € 17.00            2010*

**COCHEM** *3B2* (5km NE Rural) *50.16861, 7.26555* **Camping**
**Pommern, Moselweinstrasse 12, 56829 Pommern**
**[(02672) 2461; fax 912173; campingpommern@netscape.**
**net; www.campingplatz-pommern.de]** On W edge of vill of
Pommern bet B49 & Rv Mosel. Med, pt shd; htd wc; chem disp;
mv service pnt; baby facs; shwrs; el pnts (16A) metered + conn
fee; gas; lndtte; shop; tradsmn; rest, snacks; bar; BBQ; cooking
facs; playgrnd; htd pool; watersports; games area; internet;
30% statics; dogs €1.60; bus; train adj; poss cr; adv bkg; rd
noise. "Well-kept, friendly site in lovely location; clean, modern
san facs." 1 Apr-31 Oct. € 14.00                          2010*

**COCHEM** *3B2* (10km E Rural) *50.17056, 7.29285* **Camping**
**& Watersports Mosel-Islands, Yachthafen, 56253 Treis-**
**Karden/Mosel [(02672) 2613; fax 912102; campingplatz@**
**mosel-islands.de; www.mosel-islands.de]** Fr Cochem take
B49 to Treis-Karden (11km), cross Mosel bdge bear L then
1st sharp L back under Mosel bdge & parallel with rv. After
300m at bdge over stream turn R then thro allotments. Site
over bdge by boating cent. Fr A61 Koblenz/Bingen a'bahn
descend to rv level by Winningen Valley Bdge, turn L onto B49
(Moselweinstrasse). Do not descend thro Dieblich as c'vans are
prohibited. After 25km; turn R immed bef Mosel bdge & then
as above. Avoid Treis vill (narr with thro traffic priorities). Med,
mkd pitch, pt shd; wc; serviced pitches; shwrs €0.80; el pnts
(6A) metered & conn fee; gas; lndtte; shops 200m; rest; BBQ;
pool 1km; tennis 300m; 50% statics; dogs €4; adv bkg; some
rv & rlwy noise. "Ideal for touring Mosel valley; rv cruising &
historical sites; vg san facs 1st floor; poss midges; gd site." ♦
1 Apr-31 Oct. € 20.00                                     2013*

**COCHEM** *3B2* (6km SE Rural) *50.10999, 7.23542*
**Campingplatz Happy-Holiday, Moselweinstrasse, 56821**
**Ellenz-Poltersdorf [(02673) 1272; fax 962367; www.**
**camping-happy-holiday.de]** Fr Cochem, take B49 S to
Ellenz; site sp on bank of Rv Mosel. Med, pt sl, shd; htd wc;
chem disp; shwrs €1; el pnts (6A) metered; gas; lndtte (inc
dryer); sm shop; tradsmn; rest, snacks; bar; pool 300m; fishing;
watersports; wifi; 70% statics; dogs €1; poss cr; Eng spkn;
quiet but rd & rv noise. "Pleasant situation; gd value rest; clean
facs; conv touring base." 1 Apr-31 Oct. € 15.00          2014*

**COCHEM** 3B2 (7km SE Rural) 50.08231, 7.20796 **Camping Holländischer Hof, Am Campingplatz 1, 56820 Senheim [(02673) 4660; fax 4100; holl.hof@t-online.de; www. moselcamping.com]** Fr Cochem take B49 twd Traben-Trarbach; after approx 15km turn L over rv bdge sp Senheim; site on rv island. Med, mkd pitch, pt shd; wc; chem disp; mv service pnt; baby facs; shwrs €0.85; el pnts (6-10A) metered; lndtte; gas; shop & 1km; tradsmn; rest, snacks; bar; playgrnd; rv sw adj; tennis; wifi at office; 20% statics; no dogs; phone; poss cr; Eng spkn; adv bkg; quiet; debit card acc; red long stay; CKE/CCI. "Pleasant, well-run site; beautiful location; helpful staff; sm pitches on loose pebbles; excel cycle paths; poss flooding when wet weather/high water; poss overcr." ♦ 15 Apr-1 Nov. € 16.20      2012*

**COCHEM** 3B2 (8km SE Rural) 50.13253, 7.23029 **Campingplatz Bruttig, Am Moselufer, 56814 Bruttig-Fankel [(02671) 915429; www.campingplatz-bruttig.de]** Leave Cochem on B49 twd Trier. In 8km turn L over bdge to Bruttig-Fankel. Thro vill, site on R on banks Rv Mosel. Sm, mkd pitch, pt shd; htd wc; chem disp; shwrs €0.50; el pnts (16A) metered; lndtte; snacks; bar; playgrnd; rv sw adj; 50% statics; phone; Eng spkn; quiet. "Pleasant site in pretty vill; gd walking, cycling." Easter-31 Oct. € 14.00      2009*

**COCHEM** 3B2 (6km S Rural) 50.0804, 7.19298 **Campingplatz Nehren, Moselufer 1, 56820 Nehren [(02673) 4612; fax 962825; info@campingplatz-nehren.de; www. campingplatz-nehren.de]** Fr Cochem take B49 twd Bernkastel-Kues site on rv bank at ent to Nehren - 15km by rd. Lge, mkd pitch, pt sl, pt shd; htd wc; chem disp; mv service pnt; shwrs inc; el pnts (6A) €2.20; lndtte (inc dryer); shop; tradsmn; rest 100m; snacks; bar; boat-launching; 40% statics; dogs €1.20; bus adj; poss cr; Eng spkn; adv bkg; quiet; red CKE/CCI. "V pleasant setting; san facs up 2 flights stairs; helpful owners; poss flooding at high water; poss midges; excel cycle paths along Mosel." 1 Apr-24 Oct. € 20.00      2011*

**COCHEM** 3B2 (7km S Rural) 50.09162, 7.16319 **Campingplatz zum Feuerberg, 56814 Ediger-Eller [(02675) 701; fax 911211; prokop@zum-feuerberg.de; www.zum-feuerberg.de]** On A49 fr Cochem to Bernkastel Kues, just bef vill of Ediger on L - 17km by rd. Lge, hdg/mkd pitch, pt shd; wc; chem disp; mv service pnt; shwrs €0.90; el pnts (16A) metered + conn fee; gas; lndtte; shop adj; tradsmn; snacks; bar; playgrnd; pool; boat mooring; cycle hire; internet; 40% statics; dogs €2; phone; bus, train to Cochem; Eng spkn; adv bkg; quiet; CKE/CCI. "Well-kept site in lovely area; charming vill; helpful staff; facs at 1st floor level; gd selection of rests & pubs; rv bus high ssn; gd touring base; gd." 1 Apr-31 Oct. € 16.50      2010*

⊞ **COLBITZ** 2E3 (2km N Rural) 52.33158, 11.63123 **Campingplatz Heide-Camp, Angerschestrasse, 39326 Colbitz [(039207) 80291; fax 80593; info@heide-camp-colbitz.de; www.heide-camp-colbitz.de]** Exit A2/E30 junc 70 onto B189 N dir Stendal. In Colbitz foll sp Angern. Site in 2km. Lge, mkd pitch, pt shd; wc; chem disp; mv service pnt; shwrs inc; el pnts (6-16A) metered + conn fee; gas; lndtte; shop, rest adj; snacks; playgrnd; games area; 20% statics; dogs €2.80; Eng spkn; adv bkg; quiet; ccard acc, red CKE/CCI. "Site on woodland, lge pitches." ♦ € 18.70      2014*

**COLDITZ** 2F4 (2km E Rural) 51.13083, 12.83305 **Campingplatz am Waldbad, Im Tiergarten 5, 04680 Colditz [tel/fax (034381) 43122; info@campingplatz-colditz.de; www.campingplatz-colditz.de]** Fr Leipzig A14 to Grimma, foll B107 to Colditz. Cross rv, foll B176 sp Dobeln. Turn L immed bef town exit sp. Site 1km on R immed after outdoor sw pool, sm sp. App to site narr.On R sp 'sw pool and campsite', immed after sw pool. Med, mkd pitch, pt sl, pt shd; wc; chem disp; mv service pnt; sauna; shwrs €2; el pnts (10A) inc; lndtte (inc dryer); shop 1km; tradsmn; sm rest & 500m; leisure cent/pool adj; 30% statics; dogs €1; phone; quiet but some daytime noise fr leisure cent adj; some Eng spkn; red CKE/CCI. "V nice peaceful site; gd clean facs; gd value; tight turn into site fr narr rd; helpful, friendly manager & staff; 30 mins walk to Colditz Castle; sm rest 200m; new chem point." 1 Apr-30 Sep. € 23.00      2013*

**COLOGNE see Köln** 1B4

## "I like to fill in the reports as I travel from site to site"

You'll find report forms at the back of this guide, or you can fill them in online at www.caravaclub.co.uk/europereport.

**COSWIG** 2G4 (1km W Rural) 51.12055, 13.56388 **Campingplatz am Badesee Coswig-Kötitz, Brockwitzerstrasse 33, 01640 Coswig-Kötitz [(03523) 700220; camping@tw-coswig.de; www. campingplatz-coswig.de]** Exit A4 junc 79 onto S82 dir Meissen for 9km. Pass Autocentre Coswig & under rlwy bdge then in 400m turn L into Brockwitzerstrasse. Foll sp to site. Med, hdg pitch, pt shd; htd wc; chem disp; mv service pnt; serviced pitches; shwrs inc; el pnts (10A) €2.20; lndtte (inc dryer); shop 2km; rest, snacks; bar; BBQ; playgrnd; pool; paddling pool; lake sw adj; games area; 10% statics; dogs €1.70; bus 2km; Eng spkn; quiet; CKE/CCI. "Adj Rv Elbe & cycle path to Dresden & Meissen; gd touring area; easy access to lge pitches." ♦ 1 Apr-31 Oct. € 15.60      2010*

**CREGLINGEN** 3D2 (3.5km S Rural) 49.43945, 10.04210 **Campingpark Romantische Strasse, Münster 67, 97993 Creglingen-Münster [(07933) 20289; fax 990019; camping.hausotter@web.de; www.camping-romantische-strasse. de]** Fr E43 exit A7/junc 105 at Uffenheim. At edge of Uffenheim turn R in dir of Bad Mergentheim; in approx 17km at T-junc turn L for Creglingen, thro vill & then R sp Münster with camping sp - approx 8km further. Site on R after Münster. (Avoid rte bet Rothenburg & Creglingen as includes some v narr vills & coaches). Med, pt shd; 10% serviced pitches; htd wc; chem disp; mv service pnt; baby facs; sauna; shwrs inc; el pnts (6A) €2.20; lndtte (inc dryer); shop; rest, snacks; bar; BBQ; playgrnd; htd, covrd pool; paddling pool; lake fishing; cycle hire; wifi; 20% statics; dogs €1; phone; clsd 1300-1500; poss cr; quiet; debit card acc (surcharge); red CKE/CCI. "Site ent needs care; helpful owner; lovely welcome; excel rest & facs; Romantische Strasse with interesting medieval churches locally; gd cent for historic towns; gd value; facs stretched high ssn; poss long walk fr facs." ♦ ltd 15 Mar-15 Nov. € 32.20  2014*

**DAHME** *2E1* (1.5km N Coastal) *54.24254, 11.08030*
Camping Stieglitz, Im Feriengebiet Zedano, 23747 Dahme
[(04364) 1435; fax 470401; info@camping-stieglitz.de;
www.camping-stieglitz.de] Exit A1/E47 junc 12 at Lensahn
E twd coast. Fr B501 foll sp Dahme-Nord to sea wall, site sp.
Lge, mkd/hdg pitch; pt shd; htd wc; chem disp; mv service
pnt; baby facs; shwrs €0.50; el pnts (16A) €2.60 or metered;
lndtte (inc dryer); shop; tradsmn; rest; playgrnd; sand beach
200m; fishing; watersports; cycle hire; wifi; entmnt; TV rm;
50% statics; dogs (not Jul-Aug) €5; adv bkg; ccard acc; quiet.
"Excel site." ♦ 26 Mar-24 Oct & 5-31 Dec. € 32.50      2013*

**DAHN** *3B3* (500m W Rural) *49.14416, 7.76805*
Campingplatz Büttelwoog, Am Campingplatz 1, 66994
Dahn [(06391) 5622; fax 5326; buettelwoog@t-online.
de; www.camping-buettelwoog.de] Fr rte 10 Pirmasens-
Karlsruhe turn S at traff lts at Hinterweidenthal onto B427 to
Dahn. In Dahn cent turn R, foll Youth Hostel sp; over single
track rlwy & up hill; site on R in 500m, clearly sp opp Youth
Hostel (Jugendherberge). Med, terr, pt shd; wc; chem disp;
mv service pnt; shwrs inc; el pnts (4A) inc (rev pol); gas; lndtte;
shop; tradsmn; sm rest, snacks; bar; playgrnd; covrd pool
adj; cycle hire; 10% statics; dogs €3; Quickstop o'night facs;
poss cr; Eng spkn; adv bkg; quiet; red CKE/CCI. "Welcoming,
informal site; clsd to arr 1200-1400 & 2200-0800; facs dated
& stretched high ssn; picturesque area; gd walks fr site." ♦
15 Mar-4 Nov. € 31.00      2013*

⊞ **DAUN** *3B2* (7km SE Rural) *50.13540, 6.92219* Feriendorf
Pulvermaar, Auf der Maarhöhe, Vulkanstrasse, 54558
Gillenfeld [(06573) 287; info@feriendorf-pulvermaar.
de; www.feriendorf-pulvermaar.de] Fr A1/A48/E44 exit
junc 121 onto B421 dir Zell/Mosel. After approx 5km turn
R to Pulvemaar, site sp nr lakeside. Med, sl, pt shd; wc;
chem disp; shwrs inc; el pnts (16A) metered + conn fee;
lndtte; shop; snacks; BBQ; playgrnd; pool; fishing adj; games
area; 60% statics; dogs €1; Eng spkn; adv bkg; quiet; CKE/
CCI. "Conv Mosel valley & Weinstrasse; attractive site."
€ 17.00      2010*

> ## "We must tell The Club about that great site we found"
> Get your site reports in by mid-August
> and we'll do our best to get your updates
> into the next edition.

⊞ **DAUN** *3B2* (9km NW Rural) *50.25483, 6.77946*
Campingpark Zur Dockweiler Mühle, Mühlenweg,
54552 Dockweiler [(06595) 961130; fax 961131; info@
campingpark-dockweiler-muehle.de; www.campingpark-
dockweiler-muehle.de] Exit A1/A48 at junc 121 onto B421
dir Daun & Gerolstein. Site sp at ent to Dockweiler vill. Lge,
terr, unshd; wc; chem disp; mv service pnt; shwrs €0.50; el pnts
(16A) inc; lndtte; gas; shop 500m; rest high ssn; BBQ; playgrnd;
covrd pool; 60% statics; dogs €2; sep car park; ccard acc; red
long stay/snr citizens; quiet. ♦ € 23.50      2009*

**DAUSENAU see Bad Ems** *3B2*

**DEGGENDORF** *4G3* (1.5km W Rural) *48.83083, 12.94611*
Camping Donaustrandhaus, Egingerstrasse 42, 94469
Deggendorf [(0991) 4324; fax 4349; hirt.hj@t-online.de]
Exit A3 junc 110 onto A92. Exit junc 25 Deggendorf. At N end
of bdge bear R sp Stadtmitte & foll sp 'Festplatz'. Sm, pt shd;
wc; chem disp; shwrs €0.50; el pnts (16A) €1.50; lndtte; rest,
snacks; htd pool 1km; sw 5km; fishing; boating; tennis adj;
60% statics; dogs €1.50; bus; poss cr; some noise fr barges &
rlwy; CKE/CCI. "Gd NH; check earth on el pnts." 1 Mar-31 Oct.
€ 14.50      2009*

⊞ **DEGGENDORF** *4G3* (8km NW Rural) *48.91533, 12.8860*
Campingland Bernrieder Winkl, Grub 6, 94505 Bernried
[tel/fax (09905) 8574; campingland.bernried@vr-web.de;
www.camping-bernried.de] Fr A3/E56 junc 108 or 109 &
foll sp Bernried. Site at S ent to vill. Sm, hdg/mkd pitch, hdstg,
terr, pt shd; htd wc; chem disp; mv service pnt; fam bthrm;
serviced pitches; shwrs; el pnts (10A) metered + conn fee;
lndtte (inc dryer); shop 1km; tradsmn; rest, snacks; bar; BBQ;
playgrnd; tennis; 50% statics; dogs €2.50; adv bkg; quiet; red
long stay. "Excel, well-organised, attractive site in National
Park; gd walking, cycling, skiing; conv Passau, Regensburg;
helpful owner." ♦ € 19.50      2011*

⊞ **DESSAU** *2F3* (5km E Rural) *51.81206, 12.30973*
Campingplatz Adria, Waldbad Adria 1, 06842 Dessau-
Mildensee [(0340) 2304810; fax 2508774; info@cuct.de;
www.cuct.de] Exit A9 junc 10 Dessau-Ost onto B185 dir
Oranienbaum, site sp almost immed on R; down track, on
lakeside. Sm, pt shd; htd wc; chem disp; shwrs €1; el pnts
(16A) €2.50; lndtte; snacks; bar; sand beach & lake sw 150m;
90% statics; no dogs; sep car park; little rd noise. "Excel
touring base; vg." ♦ € 16.00      2009*

**DETTELBACH** *3D2* (6km S Rural) *49.82603, 10.20083*
Camping Katzenkopf, Am See, 97334 Sommerach
[(09381) 9215; fax 6028; www.camping-katzenkopf.
de] Fr A7/E45 junc 101 dir Volkach. Cross rv & foll sp S to
Sommerach, site sp. Fr S exit A3/E43 junc 74 dir Volkach &
foll sp. NB Town unsuitable c'vans; foll site sps bef town ent
(beware - sat nav rte poss thro town). Lge, pt shd; wc; chem
disp; mv service pnt; baby facs; shwrs inc; el pnts (16A) €2.50
or metered; gas; lndtte; shop; rest, snacks; playgrnd; lake sw
& beach; fishing & boating; golf 10km; dogs €2; poss v cr;
no adv bkg; quiet; ccard acc; red low ssn/CKE/CCI. "Beautiful
surroundings; sm pitches; clean, modern facs; m'van o'night
area outside site; barrier clsd 1300-1500; easy walk to
wine-growing vill; gd rest; gd NH nr A3." 1 Apr-25 Oct.
€ 21.60      2012*

**DIERHAGEN STRAND see Ribnitz Damgarten** *2F1*

**DIESSEN** *4E4* (1.5km N Rural) *47.96528, 11.10308* Camping
St Alban am Ammersee, Seeweg Süd 85, 86911 St Alban
[(08807) 7305; fax 1057; ivian.pavic@t-online.de; www.
camping-ammersee.de] Exit A96 junc 29 & foll rd S to
Diessen; site on L 150m after Diessen town sp. Med, unshd;
wc; chem disp; baby facs; shwrs inc; el pnts (16A) inc; lndtte;
rest; lake sw; shgl beach; boating; windsurfing; games rm;
60% statics; dogs €1; train nr; Eng spkn; adv bkg; ccard acc.
"Friendly helpful staff; excel rest; clsd 1200-1400; gd, immac
san facs." ♦ 15 Mar-15 Oct. € 34.00      2013*

**DINGELSDORF see Konstanz** *3D4*

⊞ **DINKELSBUHL** *3D3* (2km N Rural) *49.08194,*
*10.33416* **DCC Campingpark Romantische Strasse,**
**Kobeltsmühle6, 91550 Dinkelsbühl [(09851) 7817; fax**
**7848; campdinkelsbuehl@aol.com; www.campingpark-**
**dinkelsbuehl.de]** On Rothenburg-Dinkelsbühl rd 25. Turn
sharp L at camp sp immed bef rlwy x-ing (at Jet petrol stn) at
N end of town. Site on R in 1km on lakeside. Or exit A7/E43
junc 112; turn R at T-junc. Site well sp. Lge, mkd pitch, terr,
pt shd; wc; chem disp; mv service pnt; baby facs; shwrs inc;
el pnts (16A) metered; gas; lndtte; sm shop; rest, snacks; bar;
playgrnd; lake sw; boating; internet; 40% statics; dogs €1;
phone; dog-washing facs; site clsd 1300-1500 & 2200-0800;
m'van o'night area with el pnts; adv bkg; quiet; 10% red CKE/
CCI. "Pitches poss long way fr san facs; gd, modern san facs;
NH area with easy access; m'van o'night area; close to beautiful
medieval town; quiet, peaceful & well-managed site; excel rest;
gd cycle paths in area; gd." ♦ € 23.00                    2013*

**DOCKWEILER see Daun** *3B2*

⊞ **DONAUESCHINGEN** *3C4* (2km SE Rural) *47.93754,*
*8.53422* **Riedsee-Camping, Am Riedsee 11, 78166**
**Donaueschingen [(0771) 5511; fax 15138; info@riedsee-**
**camping.de; www.riedsee-camping.de]** Fr Donaueschingen
on B31 to Pfohren vill, site sp. Lge, mkd pitch, pt shd; wc;
chem disp; mv service pnt; shwrs inc; el pnts (16A) metered
(check for rev pol); lndtte; shop (inc ltd opening); rest, snacks;
bar; lake sw; boating; tennis; cycle hire; golf 9km; entmnt;
90% statics; dogs €3.50; Eng spkn; ccard acc; CKE/CCI. "Vg
facs; clean, well-run site; sm pitches; site busy at w/end; office
clsd Mon (poss low ssn only); gd value rest; conv Danube cycle
way." ♦ ltd € 19.55                    2011*

⊞ **DONAUWORTH** *4E3* (5km SE Rural) *48.67660, 10.84100*
**Donau-Lech Camping, Campingweg 1, 86698 Eggelstetten**
**[tel/fax (09090) 4046; info@donau-lech-camping.de;**
**www.donau-lech-camping.de]** Fr B2 take Eggelstetten exit
& foll sp to vill. Site immed bef vill on R, foll 'Int'l Camping'
sp. Med, hdg/mkd pitch, hdstg, pt shd; htd wc; chem disp;
mv service pnt; shwrs inc; el pnts (16A) inc (some rev pol);
gas; lndtte; shop adj; tradsmn; rest 200m; bar; playgrnd;
lake sw; boat hire; golf, horseriding & fishing nr; archery; wifi;
80% statics; dogs €2.20; phone; site clsd Nov; Eng spkn; adv
bkg; v quiet; no ccard acc; CKE/CCI. "Superb, well-maintained,
site but poss unkempt & boggy low ssn; ltd area for tourers;
friendly, helpful staff & owner; facs clean but update req;
owner sites vans; conv base for touring Danube & Romantic
Rd; nr Danube cycle way." € 24.00                    2014*

**DORNSTETTEN HALLWANGEN see Freudenstadt** *3C3*

⊞ **DORSEL** *3B2* (1km W Rural) *50.37708, 6.79768* **Camping**
**Stahlhütte an der Ahr, 53533 Dorsel [(02693) 438; fax**
**511; www.campingplatz-stahlhuette.de]** Take B258 SE
fr Blankenheim dir Nürburgring for approx 12km to Dorsel
vill. Site on W side of rd. Med, hdg pitch, pt shd; wc; chem
disp; serviced pitch; shwrs €0.75; el pnts (16A) metered;
lndtte; shop; rest, snacks; bar; playgrnd; cycle hire; golf 10km;
60% statics; dogs €2.50; barrier clsd 1300-1500 & 2130-0730;
ccard not acc; red CKE/CCI. € 20.00                    2009*

⊞ **DORTMUND** *1B4* (10km SE Rural) *51.42078, 7.49514*
**Camping Hohensyburg, Syburger Dorfstrasse 69, 44265**
**Dortmund-Hohensyburg [(0231) 774374; fax 7749554;**
**info@camping-hohensyburg.de; www.camping-**
**hohensyburg.de]** Exit Dortmund a'bahn ring at Dortmund
Sud onto B54 sp Hohensyburg. Foll dual c'way S & strt at next
traff lts. Turn L twd Hohensyburg, up hill to Y junc. Turn L
(camping sp) & cont over hill to Gasthof. Turn R immed bef
Gasthof down narr, steep rd (sharp bends) to site in 100m.
Lge, pt sl, pt shd; wc; chem disp; mv service pnt; shwrs inc;
el pnts (10A) €2.50 or metered; lndtte; shop; rest; playgrnd;
boat launch adj; golf 3km; 80% statics; dogs €3; poss cr; adv
bkg; quiet, but some aircraft noise; "Lovely, friendly site; narr
lane at ent not suitable lge o'fits; excel, clean san facs; gd."
€ 23.00                    2011*

**DORUM** *1C2* (6km NE Coastal) *53.73938, 8.51680* **Knaus**
**Campingpark Dorum, Am Kuterhafen, 27632 Dorum/**
**Neufeld [0049 4741 5020; dorum@knauscamp.de; www.**
**knauscamp.de]** Fr A27 Bremerhaven-Cuxhaven, take exit 4 to
Dorum. Then foll signs to Dorum-Neufeld. Cont over dyke to
harbour, campsite on R. Lge, unshd; wc; chem disp; mv service
pnt; shwrs; el pnts (6A); lndtte (inc dryer); tradsmn; snack;
playgrnd; grass beach adj; bike hire; 40% statics; dogs; bus
0.5km; twin axles; Eng spkn; adv bkg; CCI. "Vg; Temporary
ssnal site; scenic fishing port." 1 Apr-30 Sep. € 41.30
(CChq acc)                    2014*

**DRAGE see Geesthacht** *1D2*

⊞ **DRANSFELD** *1D4* (1km S Rural) *51.49177, 9.76180*
**Camping am Hohen Hagen, Hoher-Hagenstrasse 12,**
**37127 Dransfeld [(05502) 2147; fax 47239; camping.**
**lesser@t-online.de; www.campingplatz-dransfeld.de]** Exit
A7 junc 73 onto B3 to Dransfeld; foll sp to S of town & site.
Lge, mkd pitch, terr, pt shd; htd wc; chem disp; mv service pnt;
baby facs; sauna; shwrs inc; el pnts (16A) metered + conn fee;
gas; lndtte (inc dryer); shop; rest, snacks; BBQ; cooking facs;
playgrnd; htd pool; paddling pool; waterslide; tennis 100m;
games area; wifi; entmnt; 95% statics; dogs €1.50; o'night
area for m'vans; Eng spkn; quiet; ccard acc. "Beautiful area; gd
san facs; diff after heavy rain; helpful staff." ♦ € 17.00 2009*

**DRESDEN** *2G4* (7km N Rural) *51.13833, 13.71861*
**Campingplatz Oberer Waldteich - Dresden Nord,**
**Sandweg, 01471 Volkersdorf [(035207) 81469; fax 81499;**
**kontakt@dresden-camping.com]** Exit A4/E40 junc 81A
(Dresden-Flughafen) onto S81 W - Wilschdorfer Landstrasse.
In approx 600m turn R at x-rds dir Volkersdorf, then L to site
on lakeside, sp. Med, hdg pitch, pt sl, shd; wc; chem disp;
shwrs inc; el pnts (16A) €2.70 or mtrd (poss rev pol); lndtte
(inc dryer); shop; tradsmn; snacks; bar; BBQ; playgrnd; lake
sw; 60% statics; dogs €1; adv bkg; quiet; CKE/CCI. "Gd;
poss cr at w/end; touring pitch at lake v attractive; san facs
v clean but poss a bit distant; little Eng spkn." 1 Apr-31 Oct.
€ 21.50                    2014*

---

DRESDEN *2G4* (17km NE Rural) *51.12027, 13.98000*
Camping- und Freizeitpark Lux Oase, Arnsdorferstrasse
1, 01900 Kleinröhrsdorf [(035952) 56666; fax 56024;
info@luxoase.de; www.luxoase.de] Leave A4/E40 at junc
85 dir Radeberg. S to Leppersdorf, Kleinröhrsdorf. Sp on L
end vill, well sp fr a'bahn. Lge, mkd pitch, pt shd; wc; chem
disp; mv service pnt; fam bthrm; some serviced pitches; baby
facs; sauna; shwrs; el pnts (10A) inc; gas; lndtte (inc dryer);
shop; tradsmn; rest, snacks; bar; BBQ; playgrnd; covrd pool;
beach adj; lake sw adj; fishing; horseriding; cycle hire; games
area; wifi; entmnt; games/TV rm; 30% statics; dogs €3.50;
twin-axles acc (rec check in adv); bus to city; trains 3km; poss
v cr w/end; Eng spkn; quiet; ccard acc; red low ssn/long stay/
CKE/CCI. "Excel site by lake; vg san facs; new luxury san facs
2011; v helpful staff; gd rest; site bus to Dresden Tues - 15
mins walk to reg bus; weekly bus to Prague (in train) & other
attractions in easy reach; new spa 2013." ♦ 1 Jan-31Dec.
€ 33.60 SBS - G14                                    2014*

See advert on bookmark

DRESDEN *2G4* (4.5km S Urban) *51.01416, 13.7500*
Campingplatz Mockritz, Boderitzerstrasse 30, 01217
Dresden-Mockritz [(0351) 4715250; fax 4799227; camping-
dresden@t-online.de; www.camping-dresden.de] Exit E65/
A17 junc 3 onto B170 N sp Dresden. In approx 1.5km turn E
at traff lts sp Zschernitz, site sp. Med, mkd pitch, pt sl, pt shd;
htd wc; chem disp; mv service pnt; baby facs; shwrs €0.50; el
pnts (10A) €2.70; lndtte; shop; rest, snacks; bar; pool; wifi;
bus; quiet; 5% statics; dogs €1; site clsd Christmas to end Jan;
poss cr w/ends; Eng spkn; CKE/CCI. "V conv city cent & buses;
poss muddy after rain; helpful staff; excel; office clsd 1300-
1600 find a pitch and inform recep." ♦ ltd 30 Jan-22 Dec.
€ 25.30                                              2013*

DRESDEN *2G4* (10 km S Rural) *50.59549, 13.52546*
Campingplatz Wostra, At 7 Wostra, 01259 Dresden
[(351) 201 3254; cp-wostra@freenet.de; www.dresden.
de/] Take exit 6 fr E55 Prague-Dresden in dir of Pirna, then
take B172 Dresden-Pirna to Heidenau, foll sp to site. Med; Lge
pitches; pt shd; htd wc; chem dis; shwrs; el pnts (16A); lndtte;
BBQ; cooking facs; htd pool; games rm; bus/tram adj; twin
axles; Eng spkn; ccard acc; CKE/CCI; Red low ssn. "Excel quiet
site." ♦ ltd 1 Apr-31 Oct. € 20.00                  2012*

**DROLSHAGEN see Olpe** *1B4*

DULMEN *1B3* (3km S Rural) *51.78757, 7.27186* **Camping**
**Tannenwiese**, 27 Borkenbergstrasse, 48249 Dülmen
[(02594) 991759; www.camping-tannenwiese.de] Fr A43
take junc 7 Haltern/Lavesum dir Dülmen. In Hausdülmen foll sp
Flugplatz Borkenberge to site in approx 3km. Med, hdg/mkd
pitch, pt shd; wc; chem disp; shwrs €0.50; el pnts (10A) €2.10
or metered; gas; lndtte (inc dryer); shop & 3km; rest 2km;
playgrnd; 80% statics; dogs free; CKE/CCI. "Tidy & tranquil;
lge pitches; gd for families with sm children; away fr main rds;
sep area for tourers." 1 Mar-31 Oct. € 13.20       2010*

DUSSELDORF *1B4* (6km N Urban) *51.30180, 6.72560*
Rheincamping Meerbusch (formerly Azur Campingplatz),
Zur Rheinfähre 21, 40668 Meerbusch [(02150) 911817; fax
707571; info@rheincamping.com; www.rheincamping.
com] Exit A44 junc 28, turn R twd Strümp. Thro vill, turn L at
sp for Kaiserswerth ferry, site on rv. Lge, pt shd; htd wc; chem
disp; mv service pnt; baby facs; shwrs inc; el pnts (10A) €3.20;
gas; lndtte; shop; rest adj; snacks; bar; BBQ; playgrnd; boat
slipway; wifi; 40% statics; dogs €2.80; ferry/tram; site may
flood when rv at v high level; poss cr; Eng spkn; adv bkg; some
rv noise; CKE/CCI. "Pleasant, open site with gd views of rv; all
facs up steps; ferry x-ring rv, then tram/train to Dusseldorf; long
lead req'd; gd NH." 4 Apr-12 Oct. € 36.00          2014*

DUSSELDORF *1B4* (10km SE Rural) *51.19921, 6.88630*
Campingplatz Unterbacher See/Nord, Kleiner Torfbruch
31, 40627 Düsseldorf [(0211) 8992038; fax 8929132;
service@unterbachersee.de; www.unterbachersee.de]
Fr A3 turn W onto A46 dir Düsseldorf/Neuss & exit junc 27
to Erkrath/Unterbach. Foll sp Unterbacher See Nordufer to
harbour, site sp. Lge, pt shd; wc; chem disp; mv service pnt;
sauna; shwrs; el pnts (6A) €2; gas; lndtte; shop 500m; rest
200m; snacks; gas BBQ only; playgrnd; boating & sw in adj
lake; games area; cycle hire; 60% statics; no dogs; poss cr; adv
bkg. "Gd NH; pitches close together & poss cr; gd san facs; gd
rest & lake nrby." ♦ 3 Apr-24 Oct. € 23.50        2009*

# "I need an on-site restaurant"

We do our best to make sure site
information is correct, but it is always best
to check any must-have facilities are still
available or will be open during your visit.

⊞ DUSSELDORF *1B4* (1.5km NW Rural) *51.25225, 6.72813*
Campingplatz Lörick, Niederkasseler Deich 305, 40547
Düsseldorf-Lörick [tel/fax (0211) 591401; duesselcamp@
web.de; www.duesselcamp.de] Fr city take rd 52 to
Monchengladbach & turn R at sp Düsseldorf-Oberkassel &
Düsseldorf-Lörick. Turn L at traff lts, then strt on at next traff
lts. In 1.5km turn R at traff lts (camping sp). Foll cobbled rd to
site. Fr E, cross Theodor Heuss Brücke (bdge) & immed after
bdge fork R then in 1.5km turn R at traff lts, then as above.
Med, shd; wc; snacks; shwrs €1; el pnts (4A) €3; lndtte; shop
2km; 2 pools & lake adj; bus to city nr; poss cr; 10% statics;
dogs €3; noise fr adj airport; CKE/CCI. "Conv NH; ltd facs low
ssn." € 16.00                                       2011*

EBERBACH *3C2* (9km SW Rural) *49.45241, 8.87816*
Odenwald Camping Park, Langenthalerstrasse 80, 69434
Hirschhorn-am-Neckar [(06272) 809; fax 3658; odenwald-
camping-park@t-online.de; www.odenwald-camping-
park.de] Fr Eberbach or Neckargemünd leave B37/45 for
Hirschhorn; foll Int'l Camping sps at Hirschhorn Cent (not
Hirschhorn Ost); site on L in 2km NW of town on Heddesbach
rd L3105. Med, mkd pitch, pt shd; wc; chem disp; mv service
pnt; sauna; shwrs inc; el pnts (6A) €2.50 or metered; gas;
lndtte; shop; rest; bar; playgrnd; htd pool; tennis; cycle hire;
cab TV; 50% statics; dogs €2.50; quiet; ccard not acc; CKE/
CCI. "Friendly, helpful staff; sep area for 20 tourers." ♦ 1 Apr-
4 Oct. € 18.50                                      2009*

**EBERBACH** *3C2* (W Urban) *49.46068, 8.98241* **Campingpark Eberbach, Alte Pleutersbacherstrasse 8, 69412 Eberbach** [(06271) 1071; fax 942712; info@campingpark-eberbach. de; www.campingpark-eberbach.de] Fr Heidelberg-Heilbronn rd B37, ent Eberbach & cross Rv Neckar, turn R at end of bdge. Site 100m on rv bank, sp. Med, pt sl, pt shd; htd wc; chem disp; shwrs €0.50; el pnts (6A) €2.50; lndtte (inc dryer); shops adj; rest; playgrnd; htd pools adj; 10% statics; dogs €2; poss cr w/end; adv bkg; some rd & rlwy noise at night; CKE/CCI. "Rv cruises fr opp bank; ferry adj; annual fair last week Aug; excel cycling; NB - cash only." 1 Apr-31 Oct. € 16.70                2011*

## "Satellite navigation makes touring much easier"

Remember most sat navs don't know if you're towing or in a larger vehicle – always use yours alongside maps and site directions.

**ECHTERNACHERBRUCK** *3A2* (500m E Rural) *49.81240, 6.43160* **Camping Freibad Echternacherbrück, Mindenerstrasse 18, 54668 Echternacherbrück** [(06525) 340; fax 93155; info@echternacherbrueck.de; www.echternacherbrueck.de] Fr Bitburg on B257/E29 site is at Lux'burg border, sp. Fr Trier take A64 dir Luxembourg; exit junc 15 onto N10 to Echternacherbrück; cross bdg dir Bitburg, then 1st L sp camping & foll sp. Lge, pt shd; htd wc; chem disp; mv service pnt; private bthrms avail; baby facs; shwrs inc; el pnts (10A) €2.70 + conn fee; lndtte (inc dryer); shop 100m; rest 100m; snacks; bar; playgrnd; 2 htd pools 400m (1 covrd); paddling pool; waterslide; rv sw & sandy beach adj; tennis 400m; boat & cycle hire; horseriding 4km; games area; wifi; entmnt; TV rm; 30% statics; dogs €4.70; o'night m'van area; Eng spkn; quiet; CKE/CCI. "Poss flooding in v wet weather; excel facs; gd, well-organised site; gd bus service to Luxembourg and Trier; ACSI card acc." ♦ 1 Apr-15 Oct. € 35.00 (CChq acc)                2013*

**ECKERNFORDE** *1D1* (12km NE Coastal) *54.50280, 9.95802* **Ostsee-Camping Gut Ludwigsburg, Ludwigsburg 4, 24369 Waabs** [(49043) 58370; fax 58460; info@ostseecamping-ludwigsburg.de; www.ostseecamping-ludwigsburg.de] Fr Eckernforde take coastal rd NE, sp Ludwigsburg & Waabs. Site sp in approx 12km on R; turn R down single track rd. Site in 2km. Lge, mkd pitch, hdstg, pt shd; wc; chem disp; mv service pnt; baby facs; shwrs; el pnts (16A) €2; lndtte (inc dryer); supmkt; rest; snack; bar; bbq; playgrnd; beach adj; games area; games rm; entmnt; wifi; tv rm; 60% statics; dogs €2-6 (depending on size); twin-axle; Eng spkn; red low ssn; CKE/CCI. "Fishing in lake adj; excel san facs; horseriding & watersports adj; gd walking and cycling rtes nrby; gd site." ♦ ltd 28 Mar-1 Oct. € 26.00                2014*

**EDIGER ELLER see Cochem** *3B2*

**EGGELSTETTEN see Donauwörth** *4E3*

⊞ **EGING AM SEE** *4G3* (1km NE Rural) *48.72135, 13.26540* **Bavaria Kur-Sport-Campingpark, Grafenauerstrasse 31, 94535 Eging** [(08544) 8089; fax 7964; info@bavaria-camping.de; www.bavaria-camping.de] Exit A3 junc 113 at Garham dir Eging, site sp in 4.5km twd Thurmansbang. Med, hdg/mkd pitch, some hdstg, pt sl, terr, pt shd; htd wc; chem disp; mv service pnt; baby facs; shwrs inc; el pnts (16A) €2.50; lndtte (inc dryer); shop; rest; bar; htd pool 700m; lake sw 700m; fishing; tennis; games area; cycle hire; golf 10km; wifi; TV rm; 20% statics; dogs €2.60; Eng spkn; quiet; ccard add; red low ssn/CKE/CCI. "Lovely site nr Bavarian National Park; gd walking/cycling fr site; Wild West theme town, Pullman City, 2.5km; vg NH & longer; adj to Danube llz cycleway and other cycleways." ♦ € 30.00 (CChq acc)                2013*

⊞ **EHRENBERG** *3D1* (500m N Rural) *50.50653, 10.01065* **Rhön Camping Park, An der Ulster 1, 36115 Ehrenberg-Wüstensachsen** [(06683) 1268; fax 1269; info@rhoen-camping-park.de; www.rhoen-camping-park.de] Exit A7 junc 93 at Fulda onto B27 dir Bad Brückenau. In Döllbach turn L to Gersfeld & Ehrenberg. Site on R immed bef vill, well sp. Med, mkd pitch, pt shd; htd wc; chem disp; mv service pnt; baby facs;100% serviced pitches; sauna; shwrs €0.50; el pnts (16A) metered; lndtte; shop; tradsmn; rest 300m; BBQ; playgrnd; sm water theme park; solarium; gym; ski lift 5km; gliding 5km; TV; 25% statics; dogs €2.50; phone; adv bkg; quiet; CKE/CCI. "Gd walking; excel." ♦ € 21.00                2009*

**EHRENFRIEDERSDORF see Annaberg Buchholz** *4G1*

**EISENACH** *1D4* (10km S Rural) *50.90888, 10.29916* **Campingpark Eisenach am Altenberger See, Am Altenberger See, 99819 Wilhelmsthal** [(03691) 215637; fax 215607; campingpark-eisenach@t-online.de; www.campingpark-eisenach.de] Leave E40/A4 at junc 39 Eisenach Ost onto B19 sp Meiningen; site 2km S of Wilhelmsthal, sp. Med, pt sl, pt hdstg, pt shd; wc; chem disp; mv service pnt; serviced pitches; sauna; shwrs metered; el pnts (16A) inc; lndtte; shop; tradsmn; rest, snacks; bar; sm playgrnd; lake adj; boating; 80% statics; dogs €2; bus to Eisenach nr; clsd 1300-1500; site clsd Nov; poss cr; quiet; ccard acc; CKE/CCI. "Helpful staff; conv Wartburg & Thuringer Wald, Bach & Luther houses in Eisenach." 1 Jan-31 Oct, 1 Dec-31 Dec. € 28.00                2013*

**ELBINGERODE see Wernigerode** *2E3*

**ENGEHAUSEN** *1D3* (160m N Rural) *52.68916, 9.69774* **Camping Aller-Leine-Tal, Marschweg 1, 29600 Engehausen** [(05071) 511549; camping@camping-aller-leine-tal.de; www.camping-aller-leine.tal.de] Exit A7/E45 at 'Rasthof Allertal', keep R & at x-rds turn L twd Celle. Site in 800m. Med, mkd pitch, pt shd; htd wc; chem disp; mv service pnt; baby facs; shwrs inc; el pnts (10A) €3; lndtte (inc dryer); supmkt 7km; tradsmn; rest 4km; snacks; bar; playgrnd; rv sw & fishing; games area; games rm; wifi; TV rm; 20% statics; dogs €2.50; Quickstop o'night facs; adv bkg; quiet. "Peaceful site conv m'way." 1 Mar-31 Oct. € 16.50                2009*

**ENZKLOSTERLE see Bad Wildbad im Schwarzwald** *3C3*

**EPPSTEIN NIEDERJOSBACH see Frankfurt am Main** *3C2*

⊞ **ERFURT** *4E1* (10.3km NW) *51.03895, 10.97870*
Campingplatz "Erfurt am See", Steinfeld 4, 99189 Erfurt-
Kühnhausen [(0176) 517 52386; mail@erfurtamsee.de;
www.erfurtamsee.de] Fr A71 take exit 9 twds Kühnhausen.
Turn L onto August-Röbling-Straße. Turn L onto Kühnhäuser
Str, turn R onto Steinfeld, site on L. Med, pt sl, unshd; htd wc;
chem disp; shwrs €0.50; el pnts; lndtte (inc dryer); rest; bar;
beach adj; train 1km; quiet; CKE/CCI. "Basic clean site bet
angling & sw lakes; conv for visiting Erfurt; no laundry rm; gd
site." € 23.00                                               2014*

⊞ **ERKNER** *2G3* (3km S Rural) *52.38530, 13.78160* Camping
Jägerbude, Jägerbude 3, 15537 Erkner [(03362) 888084;
fax 888094; post@spreecamping.de; www.spreecamping.
de] A10/E55 E of Berlin exit junc 7 Freienbrink to Erkner. Site
sp on W side of a'bahn. Lge, hdg/mkd pitch, pt shd; htd wc;
chem disp; mv service pnt; sauna; shwrs €0.50; el pnts (16A)
€3 or metered; lndtte (inc dryer); shop; tradsmn; rest; BBQ;
cooking facs; playgrnd; rv sw; games rm; wifi; few statics; dogs
€2; poss cr; CKE/CCI. "Conv Berlin; some pitches lake view; gd
NH." ♦ € 18.00                                               2010*

**ERLANGEN** *4E2* (7km NW Rural) *49.63194, 10.9425* Camping
Rangau, Campingstrasse 44, 91056 Erlangen-Dechsendorf
[(09135) 8866; fax 724743; infos@camping-rangau.de;
www.camping-rangau.de] Fr A3/E45 exit junc 81 & foll
camp sp. At 1st traff lts turn L, strt on at next traff lts, then L
at next traff lts, site sp. Med, pt shd; htd wc; shwrs inc; chem
disp; el pnts (6A) €3 (long lead poss req); lndtte; shop 2km;
rest, snacks; playgrnd; pool; lake sw; boat hire; dogs €2.50;
gates clsd 1300-1500 & 2200 hrs; poss cr; Eng spkn; adv bkg;
quiet; ccard acc; red long stay/CKE/CCI. "Gd site, espec for
families; clean facs; welcoming & well-run; some sm pitches;
popular NH - overflow onto adj sports field; vg, busy NH; arrive
early; dog wash facs." ♦ ltd 1 Apr-15 Oct. € 28.50     2014*

⊞ **ERNST** *3B2* (800m W Rural) *50.1425, 7.23194*
Wohnmobil Parkplatz, Weingartenstrasse 97, 56814
Ernst [(02671) 980310; fax 980312; info@mosella-
schinkenstube.de; www.mosella-schinkenstube.de] Site
on o'skts of vill behind winery, sp fr B49. Sm, mkd pitch, hdstg,
pt sl, unshd; el pnts inc; shop, rest, snacks, bar adj; bus; poss
cr; no adv bkg; quiet. "Gd NH for m'vans only; drinking water
& rubbish points; pay at nrby butchers (Metzgerei-Gaststätte).
€ 8.00                                                       2011*

⊞ **ESSEN** *1B4* (8km S Urban) *51.38444, 6.99388*
DCC Campingpark Stadtcamping, Im Löwental 67,
45239 Essen-Werden [(0201) 492978; fax 8496132;
Stadtcamping-Essen@t-online.de; www.dcc-
stadtcamping-essen-werden.de] Exit A52 junc 28 onto
B224 S dir Solingen. Turn R bef bdge over Rv Ruhr at traff
lts & immed sharp R into Löwental, site sp. Med, mkd pitch,
hdstg, pt shd; wc; chem disp; mv service pnt; shwrs; el pnts
(16A) metered; gas; lndtte; shop; rest; bar; playgrnd; games
area; games rm; 95% statics; no dogs; phone; poss cr; Eng
spkn; adv bkg; site clsd 1300-1500 & 2130-0700; car park
adj; quiet; no ccard acc. "Rv trips; poss itinerant workers; gd."
€ 16.40                                                      2009*

**ETTENHEIM see Lahr (Schwarzwald)** *3B3*

⊞ **ETTLINGEN** *3C3* (5km SE Rural) *48.91465, 8.45567*
Campingplatz Albgau, Kochmühle 1, 76337 Waldbronn-
Neurod [07243 61849; fax 69887; erwilux@gmx.de; www.
campingplatzstueble-albgau-waldbronn.de] Exit A8/E52 at
junc 42 & foll sp Bad Herrenalb. When rlwy on R, site sp in 4km
on R. Lge, pt shd; wc; own san rec; chem disp; shwrs €0.50;
el pnts (16A) €2.30; gas; lndtte (inc dryer); shop; snacks; bar;
playgrnd; 90% statics; dogs €3; gates locked 1300-1500 &
2200-0700; quiet but poss noisy at w/end & fr rlwy; ccard not
acc. "On edge of Black Forest; footpath walks in vicinity; adj
field for NH; modern san facs; helpful owner; ltd facs in high
ssn." ♦ € 33.60                                              2014*

⊞ **FASSBERG** *1D2* (6km E Rural) *52.87593, 10.22718*
Ferienpark Heidesee (Part Naturist), Lüneburger-
Heidesee, 29328 Fassberg-Oberohe [(05827) 970546; fax
970547; heidesee@ferienpark.de; www.campingheidesee.
com] Leave A7/E45 at exit 44 onto B71. Turn S to Müden, then
dir Unterlüss. Foll site sp. V lge, terr, pt shd; htd wc; chem disp;
mv service pnt; sauna; private bthrms avail; baby facs; shwrs
inc; el pnts (10A) €3; lndtte (inc dryer); gas; shop; tradsmn;
rest, snacks; playgrnd; pool 250m; lake sw; fishing; tennis;
cycle hire; horseriding; games rm; entmnt; 65% statics; dogs
€2; ccard acc; Eng spkn; quiet; CKE/CCI. "Naturist camping in
sep area; long leads maybe req; friendly helpful staff; places
of interest nrby; gd mkd cycling and walking rtes fr site." ♦
€ 21.00 (CChq acc)                                           2014*

⊞ **FELDBERG** *2G2* (2km NE Rural) *53.34548, 13.45626*
Camping am Bauernhof, Hof Eichholz 1-8, 17258 Feldberg
[(039831) 21084; fax 21534; scholverberg@feldberg.
de; www.campingplatz-am-bauernhof.de] Fr B198 at
Möllenbeck turn dir Feldburg, thro Feldburg dir Prenzlau, site
sp. Med, mkd pitch, pt sl, unshd; wc; chem disp; shwrs inc;
el pnts (16A) metered + conn fee; lndtte; shop; tradsmn; rest
800m; snacks; playgrnd; lake sw; fishing; 30% statics; dogs
€3; quiet; CKE/CCI. "Well-situated, vg site among lakes; many
cycle paths in area." ♦ € 18.00                              2011*

> ## "There aren't many sites open at this time of year"
>
> If you're travelling outside peak season
> remember to call ahead to check site opening
> dates – even if the entry says 'open all year'.

**FERCH** *2F3* (3km N Rural) *52.33122, 12.93105* Campingplatz
Neue Scheune, Fercherstrasse 55, Schwielowsee,
14548 Ferch [(033209) 70957; fax 70958; Camping-
Neue-Scheune-Ferch@t-online.de; www.camping-
schwielowsee.de] Exit A10/E55 Berlin ring rd junc 18 twd
Ferch. In Ferch foll sp Petzow & Neue Scheune. Site on L after
stretch of rough cobbles. Sm, pt shd; htd wc; chem disp; shwrs;
el pnts (13A) €2.50; shop 2km; BBQ (gas only); playgrnd;
games area; some statics; dogs €1.10; poss cr; Eng spkn;
adv bkg; quiet; CKE/CCI. "Site on edge woodland on W side
Schwielowsee; helpful staff; conv Potsdam." Easter-31 Oct.
€ 15.00                                                      2009*

⊞ **FICHTELBERG** *4F2* (2.5km N Rural) *50.01673, 11.85525*
Kur-Camping Fichtelsee, Fichtelseestrasse 30, 95686
Fichtelberg [(09272) 801; fax 909045; info@camping-
fichtelsee.de; www.camping-fichtelsee.de] Exit junc 39
fr A9/E51. Foll B303 twd Marktredwitz. After Bischofsgrün take
R turn sp Fichtelberg, site on L in 1km. Lge, mkd pitch, hdstg,
terr, pt sl, pt shd; wc (some cont); chem disp; mv service pnt;
shwrs inc; el pnts (16A) metered + conn fee (poss rev pol);
lndtte; shop 2km; tradsmn; rest 200m; playgrnd; pool 800m;
entmnt; internet; TV; 20% statics; dogs €2.50; dog-washing
facs; phone; site clsd 7 Nov-15 Dec; Eng spkn; ccard acc;
CKE/CCI. "Gd cent for walking in pine forests round lake &
wintersports; peaceful site; barrier clsd 1230-1430; excel san
facs." ♦ ltd € 22.00                                    2009*

⊞ **FINSTERAU** *4G3* (1km N Rural) *48.94091, 13.57180*
Camping Nationalpark-Ost, Buchwaldstrasse 52, 94151
Finsterau [(08557) 768; fax 1062; berghof-frank@berghof-
frank.de; www.camping-nationalpark-ost.de] Fr B12 turn
N dir Mauth. Cont to Finsterau & site 1km adj parking for
National Park. Sm, pt shd; wc; chem disp; shwrs €1; el pnts
(6-16A) metered + conn fee or €2.50; gas; lndtte (inc dryer);
shop 1km; wifi; TV rm; dogs €2; quiet; red CKE/CCI. "Gd
walking & mountain biking; site in beautiful Bavarian forest."
♦ € 17.60                                              2009*

## "That's changed – Should I let The Club know?"

If you find something on site that's different from
the site entry, fill in a report and let us know. See
www.caravanclub.co.uk/europereport.

⊞ **FLOSSENBURG** *4F2* (1.5km N Rural) *49.74457, 12.34414*
Camping Gaisweiher, Gaisweiher 1, 92696 Flossenbürg
[(09603) 644; fax 914666; kontakt@gaisweiher-camping.
de; www.campingauer-hellas.de] Fr A93 to Neustadt.
Take minor rd E thro Floss to Flossenbürg, site sp. Lge, pt sl, pt
shd; wc; shwrs €0.50; chem disp; mv service pnt; el pnts (16A)
metered + conn fee; lndtte; shop; rest, snacks; bar; playgrnd;
sw adj; cycle hire; entmnt high ssn; TV rm; 50% statics; dogs
€2; quiet; CKE/CCI. "Recep 0930-1130, site self other times;
barrier clsd 1300-1500; facs old & dark; gd." € 15.50   2009*

**FRANKFURT** *3C2* (8km NE Rural) *50.81700, 8.46550*
Campingplatz Mainkur, Frankfurter Landstraße 107,
63477 Maintal [(069)-412193; campingplatz-mainkur@t-
online.de; www.campingplatz-mainkur.de] Fr Frankfurt
head NE  B4 and Hanua cross over A661 and cont over 8 sets
of traff lts pass car showrooms and Bauhaus on L.  100m aft
flyover bear R into single track tarmac rd to site.  Sp on B8/
B4. Med, lev, mkd pitch, pt shd; wc; shwrs; lndtte; MV waste
disp; basic shop; bar; BBQ; 35% statics; dogs; bus 3km; adv
bkg; Eng spkn; boating; playgrnd; "Family run site o'looking
rv. Conv for Frankfurt, v gd rec." ♦ ltd 1 Apr-30 Sept.
€ 28.20                                                 2012*

⊞ **FRANKFURT AM MAIN** *3C2* (11km W Rural) *50.1475,
8.36166* Taunuscamp Hubertushof, Bezirkstrasse 2,
65817 Eppstein-Niederjosbach [(06198) 7000; fax 7002;
info@taunuscamp.de; www.taunuscamp.de] Fr A3/E35
exit junc 46 dir Niedernhausen B455 & foll sp for Eppstein
(Niederjosbach). Fr B455 take minor rd K792 x-ing rlwy bef vill,
foll rd & take 1st R into Bezierkstrasse, site on L in 1km. Med,
mkd pitch, terr, pt shd; htd wc; chem disp; mv service pnt;
50% serviced pitch; shwrs inc; el pnts (16A) €2 or metered;
gas; lndtte; shop & 500m; rest 1km; snacks; playgrnd; poss
nr; 60% statics; dogs free; barrier closes 1300-1500; poss cr;
Eng spkn; adv bkg; quiet; ccard acc; red long stay/CKE/CCI.
"Friendly, pleasant site; steep terr diff for underpowered or
long twin-axle o'fits; some sm pitches; excursions arranged."
♦ ltd € 21.00                                           2009*

⊞ **FRANKFURT AM MAIN** *3C2* (5km NW Urban) *50.16373,
8.65055* City-Camp Frankfurt, An der Sandelmühle 35b,
60439 Frankfurt Am Main [(069) 570332; fax 57003604;
info@city-camp-frankfurt.de; www.city-camp-frankfurt.
de] Exit A661 junc 6 dir Heddernheim, site in park, sp. Med,
hdstg, pt shd; wc; chem disp; mv service pnt; shwrs €1.10; el
pnts (10A) €3; gas; lndtte; shop 800m; tradsmn; snacks 800m;
rest 500m; 30% statics; dogs €2.50; poss cr; Eng spkn; poss
noisy; CKE/CCI. "Conv for city via adj U-Bahn (20 min to cent);
clean but dated; v busy when trade fair on; vg for visiting
Frankfurt." ♦ ltd € 28.50                               2013*

**FREIBURG IM BREISGAU** *3B4* (12km NE Rural) *48.02310,
8.03473* Camping Steingrubenhof, Haldenweg 3,
79271 St Peter [(07660) 210; fax 1604; info@camping-
steingrubenhof.de; www.camping-steingrubenhof.de]
Exit A5 junc 61 onto B294. Turn R sp St Peter. Steep hill to site
on L at top of hill. Or fr B31 dir Donaueschingen, after 4km
outside Freiburg turn N sp St Peter; by-pass vill on main rd,
turn L under bdge 1st R. Fr other dir by-pass St Peter heading
for Glottertal; site on R 200m after rd bdge on by-pass.
Med, hdg/mkd pitch, hdstg, pt terr, unshd; wc; chem disp;
mv service pnt; serviced pitches; shwrs €0.50; el pnts (16A);
lndtte (inc dryer); shop & 1km; rest & bar adj; BBQ; playgrnd;
wifi; 70% statics; dogs €2; phone; Eng spkn; adv bkg; quiet;
ccard acc; 10% red long stay; CKE/CCI. "Peaceful site in heart
of Black Forest; wonderful location; pleasant staff; immac
facs; gate clsd 1200-1400 & 2200-0800; v diff to manoeuvre
twin-axle vans onto pitches as narr access paths; pitches are
sm & few for tourers; great site." ♦ ltd 1 Jan-10 Nov, 15 Dec-
31 Dec. € 25.30                                         2014*

⊞ **FREIBURG IM BREISGAU** *3B4* (1km E Rural) *47.99250,
7.87330* Camping Hirzberg, Kartäuserstrasse 99,
79104 Freiburg-im-Breisgau [(0761) 35054; fax 289212;
hirzburg@freiburg-camping.de; www.freiburg-camping.
de] Exit A5 at Freiburg-Mitte & foll B31 past town cent sp
Freiburg, Titisee. Foll camping sp twd Freiburg-Ebnet, nr rocky
slopes on R. Then approx 2.5km on narr, winding rd. Site on
R just after start of blocks of flats on L. Med, pt sl, terr, pt shd;
htd wc; chem disp; mv service pnt; shwrs inc; el pnts (10A)
€2.50; gas; lndtte; sm shop; tradsmn; rest, snacks; bar; BBQ;
playgrnd; pool 500m; cycle hire; internet; 40% statics; dogs
€1; bus 300m/tram; clsd 1300-1500; poss v cr; Eng spkn; adv
bkg; quiet; CKE/CCI. "Pleasant, helpful owner; site clsd 2000 -
ltd outside parking; gd cycle path & easy walk to town; busy in
high ssn; excel san facs; gd value rest." € 31.40      2014*

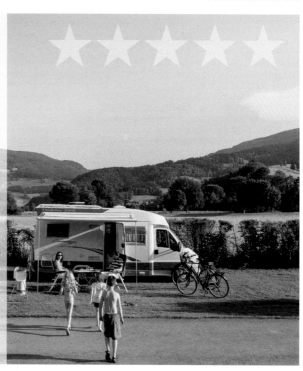
**FREIBURG IM BREISGAU** *3B4* (2.5km E Urban) *47.98095, 7.86666* **Camping Möslepark, Waldseestrasse 77, 79117 Freiburg-im-Breisgau [(0761) 7679333; fax 7679336; information@camping-freiburg.com; www.camping-freiburg.com]** Fr A5 exit junc 62 onto B31 & foll sp Freiburg strt thro city sp Donauschingen. Bef ent to tunnel take L lane & foll site sp (do not go thro tunnel). Site nr Möselpark Sports Stadium. When sps run out, cross level x-ing and turn L. Med, pt sl, shd; wc; chem disp; mv service pnt; sauna; shwrs inc; el pnts (16A) €2.50; lndtte (inc dryer); shop 100m; supmkts 500m; rest adj; playgrnd; htd, covrd pool nr; tennis 1km; cycle hire; wifi; dogs €1.90; tram to city ctr; o'night m'van area; Eng spkn; no adv bkg; noise fr stadium adj; ccard acc; red CKE/CCI. "Conv Freiburg & Black Forest (footpath adj); wooded site easily reached fr a'bahn; clsd 1200-1430 & 2200-0800 - waiting area in front of site; excel, modern san facs; public transport tickets fr recep; parking nr tram stop; v helpful staff; red CC Members." 26 Mar-24 Oct. € 30.00          2013*

⊞ **FREIBURG IM BREISGAU** *3B4* (7km SE Rural) *47.96015, 7.95001* **Camping Kirchzarten, Dietenbacherstrasse 17, 79199 Kirchzarten [(07661) 9040910; fax 61624; info@camping-kirchzarten.de; www.camping-kirchzarten.de]** Sp fr Freiburg-Titisee rd 31; into Kirchzarten; site sp fr town cent. Lge, mkd pitch, pt shd; htd wc; chem disp; mv service pnt; serviced pitches; baby facs; fam bthrm; shwrs inc; el pnts (16A) €2.50 or metered; lndtte; shops 500m; rest adj; snacks; bar; BBQ; playgrnd; 3 htd pools adj; tennis adj; wintersports area; entmnt; 20% statics; dogs €2.50 (not acc Jul/Aug); train 500m; office clsd 1300-1430; Quickstop o'night area; poss cr; Eng spkn; adv bkg (ess Jul/Aug); quiet; ccard acc; red long stay/red low ssn; CKE/CCI. "Gd size pitches; choose pitch then register at office; spacious, well-kept site; excel san facs; gd rest; site fees inc free bus & train travel in Black Forest region; helpful staff." ♦ € 31.50          2014*

See advertisement

**FREIBURG IM BREISGAU** *3B4* (10km NW Rural) *48.06350, 7.81421* **Camping Tunisee, Seestrasse, 79108 Freiburg-Hochdorf [(07665) 2249; fax 95134; info@tunisee.de; www.tunisee.de]** Fr E35/A5 exit junc 61, keep to R lane at traff lts & foll camp sp under 2nd bdge. Site on L; awkward app rd. Lge, mkd pitch, pt shd; serviced pitches; wc; chem disp; mv service pnt; shwrs €0.55; el pnts (16A) €2 or metered; lndtte; shop; rest, snacks; bar; playgrnd; lake sw adj; 75% statics; dogs €1; Eng spkn; some rd noise; red long stay; ccard acc; CKE/CCI. "Pleasant site; conv Freiburg & Black Forest; gd san facs but quite far fr touring pitches; recep clsd 1300-1500." ♦ 1 Apr-31 Oct. € 17.20          2010*

## "I like to fill in the reports as I travel from site to site"

You'll find report forms at the back of this guide, or you can fill them in online at www.caravaclub.co.uk/europereport.

⊞ **FREUDENSTADT** *3C3* (5km E Rural) *48.48011, 8.5005*
**Höhencamping Königskanzel, Freizeitweg 1, 72280
Dornstetten-Hallwangen [(07443) 6730; fax 4574;
info@camping-koenigskanzel.de; www.camping-
koenigskanzel.de]** Fr Freudenstadt head E on rte 28 foll sp
Stuttgart for 7km. Camping sp on R, sharp R turn foll sp, sharp
L on narr, winding track to site in 200m. Fr Nagold on R28,
7km fr Freudenstadt fork L; sp as bef. NB: 1st sharp R turn is v
sharp - take care. Med, some hdg pitch, pt sl, terr, pt shd; wc;
chem disp; mv service pnt; serviced pitch; sauna; shwrs inc; el
pnts (10A) metered; gas; lndtte (inc dryer); shop; tradsmn; sm
rest, snacks; bar; BBQ; playgrnd; htd pool; cycle hire; golf 7km;
ski lift 7km; wifi; 60% statics sep area; dogs €2; phone; site
clsd 3 Nov-15 Dec; Eng spkn; adv bkg (bkg fee); quiet; ccard
not acc; red long stay/CKE/CCI. "Pleasant owners; friendly
welcome; excel shwr facs, inc for dogs; well run family site; hill
top location with gd views of Black Forest; recep clsd 1300-
1400; excel value rest." ♦ € 21.30                    2011*

**FREUDENSTADT** *3C3* (3km W Rural) *48.45840, 8.37255*
**Camping Langenwald, Strassburgerstrasse 167, 72250
Freudenstadt-Langenwald [(07441) 2862; fax 2891; info@
camping-langenwald.de; www.camping-langenwald.de]**
Foll sp fr town on B28 dir Strassbur. Med, terr, pt shd; htd wc;
chem disp; mv service pnt; fam bthrm; serviced pitch; shwrs
inc; el pnts (16A) metered; gas; lndtte; shop; tradsmn; rest,
snacks; playgrnd; htd pool; cycle hire; golf 4km; 10% statics;
dogs €2; Eng spkn; noisy nr rd; ccard acc (not VISA); red
long stay/low ssn/CKE/CCI. "Gd, clean san facs; woodland
walks fr site; gd rest; friendly owners." ♦ 1 Apr-1 Nov.
€ 32.80                                              2014*

**FRICKENHAUSEN AM MAIN** *3D2* (1km W Rural)
*49.66916, 10.07444* **Knaus Campingpark Frickenhausen,
Ochsenfurterstrasse 49, 97252 Frickenhausen/Ochsenfurt
[(09331) 3171; fax 5784; info@knauscamp.de; www.
knauscamp.de]** Turn off B13 at N end of bdge over Rv Main in
Ochsenfurt & foll camping sp. Lge, hdg/mkd pitch, pt shd; wc;
serviced pitches; chem disp; mv service pnt; baby facs; shwrs
inc; el pnts (16A) €2.40 or metered; gas; lndtte; shop; rest high
ssn; bar; playgrnd; htd pool; cycle hire; TV; wifi; 40% statics;
dogs €3; site clsd 1300-1500; Eng spkn; adv bkg; quiet; red
long stay/snr citizens. "Vg, well-managed site on rv island;
excel facs; located on Romantischestrasse with many medieval
vills; v clean, cared for site; gd rest; friendly staff." 31 Mar-
5 Nov. € 35.30                                       2013*

**FRIEDRICHSHAFEN** *3D4* (6km W Rural) *47.66896, 9.40253*
**Camping Fischbach, Grenzösch 3, 88048 Friedrichshafen-
Fischbach [(07541) 42059; fax 401113; info@camping-
fischbach.de; www.camping-fischbach.de]** Take B31
fr Friedrichshafen to Meersburg. Site sp on L at end of vill.
Turning lane avail for easy access off busy rd. Med, mkd
pitch, some hdstg, pt shd; wc; chem disp; mv service pnt;
shwrs €0.50; el pnts (10-16A) €2 (poss rev pol); lndtte (inc
dryer); shop; rest, snacks; bar; lake sw adj; sand beach adj;
40% statics; no dogs; phone; poss v cr; Eng spkn; no adv bkg;
rd noise; CKE/CCI. "Tranquil, relaxing site; some lake view
pitches - worth the extra; excel, clean, modern san facs; ferries
to Konstanz nrby; Zeppelin/Dornier museums nrby; cr; site on
Lake Constance cycle rte." 11 Apr-12 Oct. € 28.60     2014*

**FRIEDRICHSHAFEN** *3D4* (6km NW Rural) *47.66583,
9.37694* **Campingplatz Schloss Helmsdorf,
Friedrichshafenerstrasse, 88090 Immenstaad-am-
Bodensee [(07545) 6252; fax 3956; campingplatz@
schloss-helmsdorf.org; www.schloss-helmsdorf.org]** Site
sp fr B31 bet Meersburg & Friedrichshafen at Immenstaad. Lge,
pt sl, pt shd; htd wc; chem disp; mv service pnt; shwrs €0.50;
el pnts (6A) €2.50; lndtte; shop; rest, snacks; lake beach & sw;
boating; windsurfing; 80% statics; no dogs high ssn; poss cr;
quiet. "Vg, well-run site; gd position on lakeside; gd, clean san
facs; helpful owners; sh walk to lake ferry; gd but expensive."
♦ 30 Mar-14 Oct. € 24.50                             2013*

⊞ **FRIESOYTHE** *1C2* (13km SE Rural) *52.93703, 7.92923*
**Campingplatz Wilken, Thülsfelder Str. 3, 26169 Friesoythe
[04 49 52 61; info@camping-wilken.de; www.camping-
wilken.de]** Fr B72 Cloppenburg-Friesoythe. After 13km turn
L onto Thülsfelder Straße. Site next to Thülsfeld Reservoir on L.
Lge, mkd pitch, hdstg, unshd; htd wc; chem disp; mv service
pnt; shwrs inc; el pnts (16A) inc; lndtte rm; shop; playgrnd;
dogs; quiet. "Excel site for long stay; spacious pitches; v clean
san facs; would rec." € 13.50                         2014*

**FURSTENBERG** *2F2* (1km W Rural) *53.18680, 13.13111*
**Campingplatz am Röblinsee, Röblinsee Nord 1, 16798
Fürstenberg [(033093) 38278; fax 38613]** Fr S on E251/B96,
L turn 500m N of Fürstenburg to N side of lake, site sp. Med,
pt shd; wc; chem disp; mv service pnt; shwrs inc; el pnts (16A)
€1.50 or metered; lndtte; shop 800m; tradsmn; rest 600m;
snacks; lake sw; dogs €1; sep car park high ssn; CKE/CCI.
"Conv for German Lake District & NH to Poland/Baltic Coast."
1 Apr-31 Oct. € 16.00                                2009*

⊞ **FUSSEN** *4E4* (2km N Urban) *47.58222, 10.70083*
**Camper's Stop, Abt-Hafnerstrasse 9, 87629 Füssen
[(08362) 940104; fax 925829; info@wohnmobilplatz.de]**
Foll sp (mv symbol) fr town cent. Fr N or W after junc B310 &
B16 turn R bef chapel (sp), then 2nd L. Fr B17 thro' town, turn
L after chapel. Sm, hdstg, unshd; wc; own san rec; chem disp;
mv service pnt; shwrs €1; el pnts (16A) €2; lndtte (inc dryer);
supmkt 500m; tradsmn; sw adj; sports cent opp (free use of
san facs); wifi; quiet. "Popular site open 24 hrs; warden attends
1700-2100 (site managed fr sports cent); sm pitches; chem
disp & water fr machine during day; full facs open 1900-1000
for NH; conv Neuschwanstein Castle; sh walk to Füssen; m'vans
only; excel." € 11.00                                2010*

⊞ **FUSSEN** *4E4* (2km N Urban) *47.58250, 10.70098* **Caravan
Zentrum Allgäu/Wohnmobilstellplatz, Abt-Hafnerstrasse
1, 87629 Füssen [(08362) 9261097; fax 921291; info@
caravanzentrum-allgaeu.de]** Foll sp (mv symbol) fr town
cent. Fr N or W after junc B310 & B16 turn R bef chapel (sp),
then 2nd L. Fr B17 thro' town, turn L after chapel. This site is
50m bef Camper's Stop. Med, hdstg, unshd; htd wc; chem
disp; mv waste; shwrs €0.50; el pnts (6A) €2; shop 200m;
supmkt 500m; sw 500m; phone; poss cr; quiet. "M'vans only;
excel, clean san facs; gd rest; cycle paths to town, castle & lake;
gd value." € 14.30 (4 persons)                        2011*

FUSSEN *4E4* (6km N Rural) *47.61553, 10.7230* **Camping Magdalena am Forggensee, Bachtalstrasse 10, 87669 Osterreinen [(08362) 4931; fax 941333; campingplatz. magdalena@t-online.de; www.sonnenhof-am-forggensee.de]** Fr Füssen take rd 16 sp Kaufbeuren & Forggensee for 5km; R sp Osterreinen for 500m; L at T-junc foll site sp; site on R in 50m; app rd steep with sharp bends. Site well sp. Med, mkd/hdg pitch, terr, pt shd; wc; chem disp; shwrs €0.50; el pnts (10A) metered + conn fee (poss rev pol); gas; lndtte (inc dryer); shop; tradsmn; rest; bar; playgrnd; beach on lake; sailing; watersports; 40% statics; dogs €3; poss cr; Eng spkn; adv bkg rec; v quiet; CKE/CCI. "Ltd touring pitches; superb views over lake; peaceful; gd site; sm pitches; conv for Zugspitze, Royal Castles, Oberammergau; lakeside cycle track to Füssen & to Neuschwanstein Castle." 1 Apr-31 Oct.
€ 22.00                                            2014*

⊞ FUSSEN *4E4* (5km NE Rural) *47.59638, 10.73861* **Camping Brunnen, Seestrasse 81, 87645 Brunnen [(08362) 8273; fax 8630; info@camping-brunnen.de; www.camping-brunnen.de]** S on rte 17 twd Füssen turn R in vill of Schwangau N to Brunnen; turn R at ent to vill at Spar shop, site clearly sp. Fr Füssen N on B17; turn L in Schwangau; well sp on lakeside. Lge, mkd pitch, hdstg, pt sl, pt shd; wc; chem disp; mv service pnt; serviced pitches; shwrs inc; el pnts (10-16A) metered + conn fee; gas; lndry rm; sm shop; tradsmn; rest/bar adj; playgrnd; sw & yachting in Lake Forggensee adj; beach adj; cycle hire; golf 3km; dogs €4; bus; site clsd 5 Nov-20 Dec; poss cr; Eng spkn; adv bkg; ccard acc; CKE/CCI. "Lovely location, next to lake; o'fits poss tightly packed; steel pegs ess; excel san facs; some pitches cramped; gd for Royal castles; gd cycle rtes; 10% red visits to Neuschwanstein Castle nrby; gates clsd 2200-0700; excel, busy, vg site; handy rest, supmkt & g'ge." ♦  € 46.70                                   2014*

## "We must tell The Club about that great site we found"

Get your site reports in by mid-August and we'll do our best to get your updates into the next edition.

⊞ FUSSEN *4E4* (6km NE Rural) *47.59194, 10.77222* **Camping Bannwaldsee, Münchenerstrasse 151, 87645 Schwangau [(08362) 93000; fax 930020; info@camping-bannwaldsee.de; www.camping-bannwaldsee.de]** On side of B17 rd fr Füssen to Munich & on shore of Bannwaldsee 3km after Schwangau vill. Fr N on B17 5km after Buching vill. Site name only visible at site ent. V lge, mkd pitch, pt sl, pt shd; htd wc; chem disp; mv service pnt; shwrs inc; shop; el pnts (16A) metered + conn fee; lndtte; shop; rest, snacks; bar; playgrnd; lake sw, fishing, boat hire; wintersports area; wifi; entmnt; 30% statics; dogs €3.50; poss cr; poss noisy; red long stay. "Narr site rds & poss diff pitch access; some lge pitches; excel san facs; gd facs young children; gd cycle paths in area." ♦
€ 23.00                                            2009*

⊞ FUSSEN *4E4* (5km NW Rural) *47.60198, 10.68333* **Camping Hopfensee, Fischerbichl 17/Uferstrasse, 87629 Hopfen-am-See [(08362) 917710; fax 917720; info@camping-hopfensee.de; www.camping-hopfensee. com]** Fr Füssen N on B16 twd Kaufbeuren in 2km L on rd sp Hopfen-am-See, site at ent to vill on L thro c'van car park. Lge, mkd pitch, hdstg, pt shd; wc; chem disp; mv service pnt; baby facs; all serviced pitches; sauna; shwrs inc; el pnts (16A) metered; gas; lndtte; shop; rest, snacks; bar; playgrnd; htd covrd pool; shgl beach & lake sw adj; boating & fishing; fitness cent; solarium; wintersports area; entmnt; dogs €4.15; internet; clsd 8 Nov-13 Dec; poss cr; Eng spkn; adv bkg rec high ssn; quiet; ccard not acc; red low ssn; CKE/CCI. "Gd location; excel facs; helpful staff; gd rest on site; no tents allowed except for awnings; tight squeeze in high ssn; vans need manhandling; gd walking & cycling; lakeside pitches rec." ♦  € 33.80                                   2009*

See advert on bookmark

FUSSEN *4E4* (5.5km NW Rural) *47.60883, 10.66918* **Haus Guggemos, Uferstrasse 42, 87629 Hopfen-am-See [(08362) 3334; fax 6765; haus.guggemos@t-online. de; www.haus-guggemos.de]** Fr Füssen take B16 N dir Kaufbeuren; in 2km turn L sp Hopfen-am-See. Drive thro vill; site on R opp lake. Sm, some hdstg, pt shd; terr; wc; chem disp; shwrs inc; el pnts (10A) metered; lndtte; shop 500m; rest, snack & bar 200m; playgrnd; lake sw adj; dogs €2; bus adj; Eng spkn; adv bkg; quiet; CKE/CCI. "Excel, family-run, farm site in beautiful area; views across lake to Alps." 1 Apr-31 Oct.
€ 16.00                                            2013*

**GAIENHOFEN HORN see Radolfzell am Bodensee** *3C4*

**GANDERKESEE** *1C2* (5km W Rural) *53.04666, 8.46388* **Feriencenter Falkensteinsee (Part Naturist), Am Falkensteinsee 1, 27777 Ganderkesee-Steinkimmen [(04222) 8214; fax 1043; campingpark@t-online.de; www. falkensteinsee.de]** Exit A28/E22 junc 18 dir Habbrügge. Site on R in 2km. Lge, pt shd; wc; sauna; shwrs inc; el pnts (16A) €2.50 or metered; lndtte; shop; rest 1km; snacks; playgrnd; lake sw adj; sep naturist beach; golf 8km; 70% statics; dogs €1.50; o'night mv area; quiet; ccard not acc; 5% red CKE/CCI. "Conv Oldenburg & Bremen; gd site." ♦ ltd 1 Apr-15 Oct.
€ 17.00                                            2010*

**GARBSEN see Hannover** *1D3*

⊞ **GARMISCH PARTENKIRCHEN** *4E4* (2km SW Rural) *47.50444, 11.10694* **Alpencamp am Wank, Wankbahnstrasse 2, 82467 Garmisch-Partenkirchen [(08821) 9677805; fax 76866; info@alpencamp-gap.de; www.alpencamp-gap.de]** A9/E533 exit onto B2 to Garmisch. Foll m'van symbol/sp to site. M'vans only. Med, hdstg, terr, unshd; htd wc; chem disp; mv service pnt; shwrs €1; el pnts (16A) metered; gas; lndtte; shop 2km; tradsmn; rest; wifi; dogs; bus to town; Eng spkn; quiet. "M'vans only; v clean facs; view fr all pitches of Zugspitze; excel for walking & winter sports; gd for NH or poss longer; disposal point/water coin operated."
€ 14.00                                            2011*

GERMANY

**GARTOW** *2E2* (5km NW Rural) *53.03972, 11.41583* **Camping Laascher See**, Ortsteil Laasche 13, 29471 Gartow [(05846) 342; pewsdorf@campingplatz-laascher-see. de; www.campingplatz-laascher-see.de] Fr S on B493 to Gartow, turn N on L256 (Rondelstrasse) dir Gartower See & Laasche See, site sp on R. Or E fr Dennenberg on L256 dir Gorleben & Gartow, site sp approx 5km after Gorleben. Med, hdg pitch, pt sl, pt shd; wc; chem disp; mv service pnt; shwrs €0.80; el pnts (6A) inc; lndtte (inc dryer); shop, rest 2.5km; bar; playgrnd; lake sw 300m; 60% statics; dogs €1.50; adv bkg; quiet; CKE/CCI. "Pleasant owners; clean, modern san facs." ♦ 1 Apr-31 Oct. € 16.00                2010*

⊞ **GEESTHACHT** *1D2* (5km SW Rural) *53.42465, 10.29470* Campingplatz Stover Strand International, Stover Strand 10, 21423 Drage [(04177) 430; info@stover-strand. de; www.camping-stover-strand.de] Fr N on A25 to Geesthacht, then B404 dir Winsen to Stove. Site at end Stover Strand on banks of Rv Elbe. Fr S on A7 to Maschen, then A250 to Winsen then B404, as above. V lge, mkd pitch, pt shd; htd wc; chem disp; mv service pnt; baby facs; shwrs €0.50; el pnts (6-16A) €2 or metered; lndtte (inc dryer); shop; rest, snacks; bar; BBQ; cooking facs; playgrnd; rv sw & beach; fishing; watersports; marina; cycle hire; games area; wifi; entmnt; 80% statics; dogs €2; poss cr; adv bkg; quiet; ccard acc; CKE/ CCI. "Excel rvside site; poss cr even low ssn; site clsd 1300-1500; Hamburg Card avail." ♦ € 20.00                2012*

⊞ **GELSENKIRCHEN** *1B4* (Urban) *51.56081, 7.07114* **Mobilcamp Gelsenkirchen**, Adenauerallee 100, 45891 Gelsenkirchen [tel/fax (0176) 78569829; mobilcamp@web. de; www.mobilcamp.de] Fr W exit A2/E34 junc 6, at rndabt at end of sliprd turn R into Emil Zimmerman Allee, then R again. Site on R. M'vans only. Med, pt shd; wc; chem disp; mv service pnt; shwrs €1; el pnts; gas; shop; rest; bar; dogs; Eng spkn; adv bkg; quiet. "Gd NH." € 7.00                2009*

**GEMUNDEN AM MAIN** *3D2* (2km W Rural) *50.05260, 9.65656* **Spessart-Camping Schönrain**, Schönrainstrasse 4-18, 97737 Gemünden-Hofstetten [(09351) 8645; fax 8721; info@spessart-camping.de; www.spessart-camping. de] Rd B26 to Gemünden, cross Rv Main & turn R dir Hofstetten, site sp. Lge, hdg/mkd pitch, some hdstg, terr, pt shd; htd wc; chem disp; mv service pnt; sauna; shwrs €0.50; el pnts (10A) metered + conn €2.15; lndtte (inc dryer); shop & 2km; tradsmn; rest, snacks; bar; playgrnd; children's pool; games area; cycle hire; fitness rm; solarium; TV; 50% static (sep area); dogs €2.80; phone; variable pitch sizes/ prices; poss cr; Eng spkn; quiet; CKE/CCI. "Clean, well-kept, wooded site; interesting towns nrby; excel." ♦ 1 Apr-30 Sep. € 32.25                2014*

**GEORGENTHAL see Ohrdruf** *2E4*

**GERBACH see Rockenhausen** *3C2*

⊞ **GEROLSTEIN** *3B2* (4km NW Rural) *50.23910, 6.61477* **Campingplatz Oosbachtal**, Müllenbornerstrasse 31, 54568 Gerolstein-Müllenborn [(06591) 7409; fax 3635; camping-oosbach@t-online.de; www.camping-oosbachtal.de] Site well sp fr rte 410 Prüm to Gerolstein. Med, pt sl, hdstg, pt shd; wc; chem disp; mv service pnt; fam bthrm; shwrs inc; el pnts (16A) metered or €1.50; lndtte (inc dryer); shop; rest; bar; BBQ; playgrnd; 2 pools (1 htd, covrd); 60% statics; dogs €2; adv bkg; poss cr; Eng spkn; quiet; CKE/CCI. "Scenic area for touring Eifel region; owners friendly & helpful." ♦ € 16.50                2010*

⊞ **GERSFELD (RHON)** *3D2* (1.5km N Rural) *50.46223, 9.91953* **Camping Hochrhön**, Schachen 13, 36129 Gersfeld-Schachen [tel/fax (06654) 7836; campinghochrhoen@ aol.com; www.rhoenline.de/camping-hochrhoen] Exit A7 exit Fulda-Süd S onto B27/B279 to Gersfeld, then B284 sp Ehrenberg, Turn L dir Schachen, foll sp to site. Med, hdg/ mkd pitch, hdstg, pt shd; wc; chem disp; mv service pnt; shwrs €0.60; el pnts (16A) metered; lndtte; shops 1.5km; rest 500m; playgrnd; ski lift 3km; some statics (sep area); dogs free; poss cr; red CKE/CCI. "Conv for gliding & air sports at Wasswerkuppe; friendly." € 18.00                2012*

**GETTORF** *1D1* (6km NE Coastal) *54.47485, 10.02910* **Campingplatz Grönwohld**, Kronshörn, 24229 Schwedeneck [(04308) 189972; fax 189973; info@ groenwohld-camping.de; www.groenwohld-camping. de] Fr A7 exit junc 6 or 8 to Eckernförde, then onto B503, site sp bet km 8.9 & 9. V lge, hdg/mkd pitch, hdstg, pt shd; wc; chem disp; mv service pnt; sauna; shwrs inc; el pnts (10-16A) metered + conn fee; lndtte; shop; tradsmn; rest; playgrnd; beach adj; fishing; sailing; entmnt; 75% statics; dogs €2.10; adv bkg; quiet; ccard not acc; CKE/CCI. "Conv NH; gd, modern facs." ♦ 1 Apr-31 Oct. € 14.00                2011*

**GIESELWERDER** *1D4* (5.5km S Rural) *51.56600, 9.59500* **Camping Weissehütte**, Weissehütte 1, 34399 Oberweser-Weissehütte [(05574) 211939; info@camping-weser.de; www.camping-weser.de] S fr Bad Karlshafen on B80 along W bank of Rv Weser. Site on L. Sm, hdg pitch, pt shd; wc; chem disp; shwrs; el pnts (10A) €2.30; shop 5km; tradsmn; snacks; mainly statics; dogs €1.50; bus adj; Eng spkn; adv bkg; quiet; CKE/CCI. "Gd cycle rtes N & S." € 14.00                2011*

**GIROD see Montabaur** *3C2*

**GLUCKSBURG (OSTSEE)** *1D1* (6km NE Coastal) *54.85901, 9.59109* **Ostseecamp, An der Promenade 1, 24960 Glücksburg-Holnis** [(04631) 622071; fax 622072; info@ ostseecamp-holnis.de; www.ostseecamp-holnis.de] Fr Flensburg on rd 199 turn off thro Glücksburg & further 6km to Holnis. Med, mkd pitch, some hdstg, pt shd; htd wc; chem disp; mv service pnt; baby facs; shwrs inc; el pnts (16A) €3; lndtte (inc dryer); shop; rest 200m; snacks; BBQ; cooking facs; playgrnd; pool; sand beach adj; fishing; windsurfing 1km; cycle hire; wifi; entmnt; 30% statics; dogs €2.50; adv bkg; quiet; CKE/CCI. ♦ 1 Apr-15 Oct. € 20.30 (CChq acc)                2011*

⊞ **GOPPINGEN** *3D3* (7km W Rural) *48.63946, 9.55508*
**Campingplatz Aichelberg, Bunzenberg 1, 73101**
**Aichelberg [(07164) 2700; fax 903029]** Exit E52/A8 junc 58
sp Aichelberg-Goppingen & foll sp to camp site in 1km. Med,
pt shd; wc; chem disp; shwrs inc; el pnts (10A) €2; shop; rest
500m; bar; poss cr; adv bkg; 80% statics; dogs €2; poss cr;
quiet. "Fills up after 1600 hrs but gd overflow field with el
pnts for NH; family-run site; new excel facs; owner helpful."
€ 20.00                                                    2011*

⊞ **GOSLAR** *1D3* (2km S Rural) *51.90113, 10.32743*
**Campingplatz Sennhütte, Clausthalerstrasse 28, 38644**
**Goslar [(05321) 22498; sennhuette@campingplatz-goslar.**
**de; www.sennhuette-goslar.de]** Fr Goslar on B241 twd
Clausthal, Zellerfeld site on R in 2km. Ent thro car pk of Hotel
Sennhütte. Med, pt shd; wc; chem disp; shwrs €0.50; el pnts
(16A) metered + conn fee (poss long lead req); lndtte (inc
dryer); shop; rest; 30% statics; dogs; bus at ent to town; no
adv bkg; noisy nr rd; ccard acc. "Gd NH/sh stay nr beautiful
town." € 15.50                                              2010*

⊞ **GOSLAR** *1D3* (9km S Rural) *51.82166, 10.43722*
**Campingplatz Okertalsperre, Kornhardtweg 2, 38707**
**Altenau [(05328) 702; fax 911708; info@campingokertal.**
**de; www.campingokertal.de]** Fr Goslar B498 S, site on L of
N o'skts of Altenau. Med, hdg/mkd, pt shd; wc; chem disp; mv
service pnt; serviced pitches; shwrs inc; el pnts (16A) metered
+ conn fee; gas; lndtte (inc dryer); shop; tradsmn; snacks; BBQ;
playgrnd; lake sw; shgl beach; watersports; wintersports; ski
lift 2km; games area; games rm; wifi; entmnt; 50% statics (sep
area); dogs €2; adv bkg; Eng spkn; quiet; ccard not acc; red
CKE/CCI. "Beautiful setting 20 mins walk fr cent of Altenau; gd
welcome; sm pitches; excel play area; excel cycle paths around
lake; ltd facs low ssn; excel." ♦ € 16.50                  2010*

⊞ **GOSLAR** *1D3* (7km SW Rural) *51.90110, 10.32724*
**Camping am Krähenberg, Harzstrasse 8, 38685**
**Langelsheim [(05326) 969281; fax 969282; post@**
**campingplatz-Wolfshagen.de; www.campingplatz-**
**wolfshagen.de]** Foll rd 82 W fr Goslar twd Langelsheim.
Turn L to Wolfshagen 1km bef Langelsheim. In Wolfshagen
foll site sp, site in SE corner of vill uphill. Lge, mkd pitch, terr,
pl sl, pt shd; wc; chem disp; mv service pnt; shwrs inc; el pnts
(16A) metered + conn fee; gas; lndtte (inc dryer); shop; rest;
playgrnd; htd pool adj; tennis; horseriding 1km; internet;
75% statics; dogs €1.20; ccard acc; red CKE/CCI. "Gate clsd
1300-1430; shwrs remote (in rest block); lge pitches; charge
for sw pool poss automatically added to bill - check bef dep if
not req; gd." ♦ € 14.20                                     2010*

⊞ **GRAFENDORF** *3D2* (5km E Rural) *50.10678, 9.78241*
**Camping Rossmühle, 97782 Gräfendorf-Weickersgrüben**
**[(09357) 1210; fax 832; www.campingplatz-rossmuehle.**
**de]** Exit A7 junc 96 onto B27 sp Karlstadt. At Hammelburg
foll sps to Gräfendorf & site in 8km on rvside, beyond
Weickersgrüben. Lge, mkd pitch, terr, pt shd; wc; chem disp;
mv service pnt; shwrs €1; el pnts (6-10A) €2; lndtte; shop, rest
high ssn; bar; playgrnd; watersports; fitness rm; cycle & canoe
hire; solarium; entmnt; TV; 50% statics; dogs €2; o'night area
for m'vans; adv bkg; quiet. "Poss liable to flooding after heavy
rain; clean san facs; excel; Cycle rte tourers sep fr statics." ♦
€ 18.00                                                    2012*

**GRAMBIN** *2G2* (700m N Coastal/Rural) *53.75944, 14.01000*
**Campingpark Oderhaff, Dorstrasse 661, 17375 Grambin**
**[tel/fax (039774) 20420; info@campingpark-oderhaff.**
**de; www.campingpark-oderhaff.de]** Exit A20 junc 28 onto
B110 dir Anklam. After approx 23km turn R onto B109 & in
15km turn L in Ducherow onto L31 & foll sp Grambin. Site on
L in 17km. Med, pt sl, pt shd; htd wc; chem disp; shwrs €1; el
pnts (10-16A) €2.50; lndtte (inc dryer); shop 700m; tradsmn;
rest 200m; bar; BBQ; cooking facs; playgrnd; sand beach adj;
games area; 60% statics; dogs €2; bus nr; adv bkg; quiet. "Vg
site; conv day trips Poland & Peenemunde." ♦ 1 Apr-15 Oct.
€ 17.40                                                    2010*

⊞ **GREFRATH** *1A4* (1km N Rural) *51.36492, 6.32328*
**Campingplatz Waldfrieden, An der Paas 13, 47929**
**Grefrath [(02158) 3855; fax 3685; ferienpark@**
**waldfrieden@t-online.de; www.ferienpark-waldfrieden.**
**de]** Fr A40-E34 S to Duisburg; turn S at exit 3 sp Grefrath;
site sp on L in 3km. Lge, hdg pitch, hdstg, pt shd; htd wc;
chem disp; mv service pnt; shwrs; el pnts (10A) metered +
conn fee; gas; lndtte; shop 1.2km; playgrnd; lake sw adj; sw
pools 1.5km; 80% statics; dogs €2; poss cr; Eng spkn; quiet;
CKE/CCI. "Conv NH North Sea ports; WWII cemetaries at
Reichswald; site over-used & weary." € 17.50               2013*

## "I need an on-site restaurant"

We do our best to make sure site
information is correct, but it is always best
to check any must-have facilities are still
available or will be open during your visit.

**GREIFSWALD** *2G1* (8km NE Coastal) *54.12666, 13.52196*
**Campingplatz Loissin (Part Naturist), 17509 Loissin**
**[(038532) 243; fax 725; info@campingplatz-loissin.de;**
**www.campingplatz-loissin.de]** Fr Greifswald E to Kemnitz,
then head N twds Loissin; site on coast N, well sp fr the
vill. Lge, mkd pitch, pt shd; wc; chem disp; mv service pnt;
shwrs €0.50; el pnts (16A) inc; lndtte; shop; rest, snacks; bar;
playgrnd; sand beach adj; sep naturist beach; windsurfing;
games area; cycle hire; internet; entmnt; 40% statics; dogs
€2; clsd 1300-1430 & 2200-0800; adv bkg; quiet; red CKE/
CCI. "Vg site; approx 40km to foot x-ing fr car park to Poland
for shopping; excelsan facs - no toilet paper, main attraction is
immed proximity to sea." ♦ Easter-31 Oct. € 21.00         2011*

⊞ **GREVEN** *1B3* (4km SW Rural) *52.08328, 7.55806*
**Campingplatz Westheide, Altenbergerstrasse 23,**
**48268 Greven [(02571) 560701; kontakt@campingplatz-**
**westheide.de; www.campingplatz-westheide.de]** Exit
A1 junc 76 onto B481 around E side of Greven, then turn L
onto B219 for 2km. Turn R onto L555 Nordwalderstrasse & in
2km at Westerode turn L into Altenbergerstrasse, site on L in
1km. Med, hdg pitch, pt shd; htd wc; chem disp; fam bthrm;
shwrs €0.50; el pnts (16A) metered; lndtte; tradsmn; snacks;
bar; playgrnd; lake & sand beach adj; fishing; games rm;
80% statics; dogs €1; quiet; ccard acc; CKE/CCI. "Gd for sh
stay; walks around lake." € 18.00                          2009*

**GROSS QUASSOW see Neustrelitz** *2F2*

GERMANY

**GROSSENBRODE (FEHMARN ISLAND)** *2E1* (1.5km SE Coastal) *54.36035, 11.08743* **Camping Strandparadies, Südstrand 3, 23775 Grossenbrode [(04367) 8697; fax 999031; camping@strandparadies-grossenbrode.de; www.camping-strandparadies-grossenbrode.de]** Fr E47/ B207 fr Lübeck dir Puttgarden turn R to Grossenbrode & foll 'campingplatz' sp. Turn L after sports hall, foll rd round & turn L into site in front of yellow phone box. Lge, hdg pitch, unshd; wc; chem disp; all serviced pitches; baby facs; shwrs €0.50; el pnts (16A) inc; gas; lndtte; shop, rest, snacks 300m; playgrnd; sand beach 200m; watersports; windsurfing; internet; 75% statics; dogs €2.50; phone; bus; clsd 1300-1500; poss cr; adv bkg; quiet; red long stay. "Superb beach; gd cycle paths; book in after 1800 for special 1 night fee; conv ferries to Denmark & Fehmarn Island; gd for wheelchair users; vg." ♦ 1 Apr-31 Oct. € 21.00                                                  2011*

⊞ **GROSS-SEEHAM** *4F4* (1km S Rural) *47.85166, 11.86222* **Camping Seehamer See, Hauptstrasse 32, 83629 Gross-Seeham [(08020) 396; fax 1400; info@seehamer-see.de; www.seehamer-see.de]** Along W side of A8/E45/E52 a'bahn between juncs 98 Weyarn & 99 Irschenberg exit at km 37 into parking layby; site sp. If fr S take Weyarn exit & in Weyarn turn L opp maypole, site in 4km. Lge, pt sl, unshd; wc; chem disp; mv service pnt; shwrs €1; el pnts (16A) €2; lndtte; shop; rest high ssn; snacks; shop 500m; lake sw; shgl beach; mainly statics; poss cr; no adv bkg; rd noise; red CKE/CCI. "V friendly owner; sm, sep area for tourers." ♦ € 22.00          2009*

**GRUNBERG** *1C4* (1km E Urban) *50.59105, 8.97361* **Camping Spitzer Stein, 35305 Grünberg [(06401) 6553; s.moebus@gruenberg.de; www.gruenberg.de]** Exit A5/E40 junc 7 S to Grünberg. At traff lts turn L onto B49; site in 1km on R. Lge, pt sl, pt shd, some hdstg; wc; chem disp; shwrs €0.50; el pnts (5A) metered + conn fee; lndtte; shop, rest & snacks adj; playgrnd; htd pool adj; golf 8km; 95% statics; poss cr; adv bkg; poss noisy; ccard acc; red CKE/CCI. "Site surrounded by pleasant wooded hills; sm, unmkd area for tourers; interesting old town; OK, busy NH." 1 Mar-31 Oct. € 12.00          2009*

**GUNZBURG** *3D3* (5km S Rural) *48.42688, 10.29842* **Legoland Feriendorf, Legoland Allee 2, 89312 Günzburg [(08221) 700789; fax 700199; info@legoland-feriendorf. de; www.legoland-feriendorf.de]** Exit A8/E52 junc 67 S onto B16. Foll sp Lego-Park & Feriendorf to site. Med, unshd; htd wc; chem disp; mv service pnt; fam bthrm; shwrs; el pnts (16A) inc; lndtte (inc dryer); shop 2km; rest; playgrnd; pool 3km; entmnt; no dogs; adv bkg; ccard acc. "Opening dates/times dependent on Legoland Deutschland adj - www. legoland.de." ♦ 9 Apr-6 Nov. € 42.00 (inc Legoland tickets) (CChq acc)                                                         2009*

⊞ **GYHUM** *1D2* (2km S Rural) *53.19308, 9.33638* **Waldcamping Hesedorf, Zum Waldbad 3, 27404 Gyhum-Hesedorf [(04286) 2252; fax 924509; info@waldcamping-hesedorf.de; www.waldcamping-hesedorf.de]** Exit A1/ E22 junc 49 in dir Zeven. In 1km turn R sp Gyhum & foll site sp to Hesedorf. Med, unshd; htd wc; chem disp; mv service pnt; shwrs; el pnts (16A) inc; lndtte; shop 1km; rest; playgrnd; htd pool 150m inc; wifi; 70% statics (sep area); dogs €0.50; barrier clsd 1300-1500; Eng spkn; quiet; CKE/CCI. "Clean, well-kept site; attractive area; gd rest; lge sep area for tourers." € 20.00                                                         2010*

⊞ **HALBERSTADT** *2E3* (2km NE Rural) *51.90981, 11.0827* **Camping am See (Part Naturist), Warmholzberg 70, 38820 Halberstadt [(03941) 609308; fax 570791; info@camping-am-see.de; www.camping-am-see.de]** Sp on B81 (Halberstadt-Magdeburg). Med, terr, unshd; wc; chem disp; shwrs inc; el pnts (10A) metered + conn fee €2.50 (poss rev pol); lndtte; shop; snacks; pool adj; lake beach & sw adj (sep naturist beach); 75% statics; dogs €2; sep car park; quiet; red CKE/CCI. "Conv Harz mountains & Quedlinburg (770 houses classified as historic monuments by UNESCO); quiet, green site; some individual shwrs; clsd 1300-1500." € 34.00          2013*

⊞ **HAMBURG** *1D2* (1.5km NW Urban) *53.5900, 9.93083* **Campingplatz Buchholz, Keilerstrasse 374, 22525 Hamburg-Stellingen [(040) 5404532; fax 5402536; info@camping-buchholz.de; www.camping-buchholz.de]** Exit A7/E45 junc 26 & foll dir 'Innenstadt' - city cent. Site sp in 600m on L. Sm, hdg/mkd pitch, all hdstg, pt shd; wc; shwrs €1; chem disp; el pnts (16A) €3; lndtte; shop, rest, snacks 200m; bar; 10% statics; dogs €3.80; bus, train nr; poss v cr; adv bkg; rd noise; no ccard acc. "Fair NH nr a'bahn & Hamburg cent; conv transport to city - tickets fr recep; friendly management; sm pitches; busy site, rec arr early; diff access for lge o'fits." ♦ € 34.00                                                         2014*

⊞ **HAMELN** *1D3* (500m S Urban) *52.09638, 9.35805* **Wohnmobilstellplatz Hannes-Weserblick, Ruthenstrasse 14, 31785 Hameln [(05151) 957810; fax 931099; hannes@hwg-hameln.de; www.wohnmobilstellplatz-hameln.de]** Fr B1 to Hameln & foll sp Gewerbegebiet Süd & m'van park. Sm, hdstg; mv service pnt; el pnts (6A) €1; shop 700m; snacks; quiet. "Situated bet buildings of Hameln Youth Training Cent; footpath along Rv Weser to town; m'vans only." € 8.00  2011*

⊞ **HAMELN** *1D3* (1km W Urban) *52.10916, 9.3475* **Campingplatz zum Fährhaus, Uferstrasse 80, 31785 Hameln [(05151) 67489; fax 61167; info@restaurant-athen-hameln.de; www.campingplatz-faehrhaus-hameln. de]** Fr A2/E30 at Bad Eilsen junc 35 onto B83 to Hameln on NE side of Rv Weser; in town foll sp Detmold/Paderborn; cross bdge to SW side (use Thiewall Brücke); turn R on minor rd twd Rinteln; foll site sp. Med, mkd pitch, unshd; htd wc; chem disp; mv service pnt; shwrs inc; el pnts (10-16A) metered; lndtte; supmkt 500m; rest; bar; htd pool high ssn; 40% statics; dogs €1; phone; clsd 1300-1430; quiet; red CKE/CCI. "Picturesque & historic district; open-air performance of Pied Piper in town on Sun to mid-Sep; sm pitches & poss uneven; helpful staff; san facs need update (2012); site poss muddy & untidy; gd cycle paths by rv to town; dog owners - beware owners' own dogs." ♦ ltd € 25.50                                                         2014*

**HAMELN** *1D3* (4km NW Rural) *52.10725, 9.29588* **Camping am Waldbad, Pferdeweg 2, 31787 Halvestorf [tel/fax (05158) 2774; info@campingamwaldbad.de; www. campingamwaldbad.de]** Fr Hameln on B83 dir Rinteln. In approx 10km turn L, cross rv & foll sp Halvestorf & site. Med, pt sl, unshd; wc; chem disp; shwrs €0.50; el pnts (16A) €2; lndtte (inc dryer); shops 2km; snacks; playgrnd; htd pool; paddling pool; 80% statics; dogs free; adv bkg; quiet. "Pleasant site - better than site in Hameln." ♦ 1 Apr-31 Oct. € 15.30  2013*

⊞ **HAMM** *1B3* (10km S Rural) *51.6939, 7.9710* **Camping Uentrop, Dolbergerstrasse 80, 59510 Lippetal-Lippborg [(02388) 437; fax 1637; info@camping-helbach.de; www. camping-helbach.de]** Exit A2/E34 junc 19, site sp; behind Hotel Helbach 1km fr a'bahn. Lge, pt sl, pt shd; htd wc; chem disp; shwrs inc; el pnts (16A) €2; gas; lndtte; shops adj; tradsmn; rest adj; playgrnd; 90% statics; dogs €2; poss cr; Eng spkn; rd noise; ccard acc. "Friendly; gd security; barrier clsd 1300-1500 & 2200-0500; fair NH." € 18.00        2011*

**HAMMELBACH** *3C2* (300m S Rural) *49.63277, 8.83000* **Camping Park Hammelbach, Gasse 17, 64689 Grasellenbach/Hammelbach [(06253) 3831; info@ camping-hammelbach.de; www.camping-hammelbach. de]** Exit A5/E35 exit junc 31 onto B460 E. Turn S in Weschnitz to Hammelbach & foll site sp. Med, hdg pitch, pt shd; htd wc; chem disp; mv service pnt; baby facs; fam bthrm; sauna adj; shwrs inc; el pnts (16A) metered; gas; lndtte (inc dryer); shop 300m; tradsmn; rest, snacks, bar 300m; BBQ; htd pool 300m; wifi; 70% statics; dogs €1.50; bus 300m; poss cr; Eng spkn; adv bkg; quiet; ccard acc; red low ssn; CKE/CCI. "Excel site with views; vg san facs; v pleasant, helpful staff; red for seniors; conv Heidelberg." ♦ 1 Apr-31 Oct. € 16.60        2011*

**HANNOVER** *1D3* (5km NE Urban) *52.45383, 9.85611* **Campingplatz Parksee Lohne, Alter Postweg 12, 30916 Isernhagen [05139 88260; fax 891665; parksee-lohne@t-online.de; www.parksee-lohne.de]** Fr A2 take exit 46 to Altwarmbüchen. Cont onto K114, turn R onto Alter Postweg & foll sp to campsite. V lge, pt shd; htd wc; chem disp; mv service pnt; baby facs; fam bthrm; shwrs inc; lndtte (inc dryer); rest; snacks; bar; cooking facs; 95% statics; dogs; Eng spkn; quiet. "Vg site; next to golf course; excel san facs; narr cobbled rd 1/2 m; under flight path, but quiet at night." ♦ 1 Apr-15 Oct. € 29.60        2014*

⊞ **HANNOVER** *1D3* (7km S Rural) *52.30133, 9.74716* **Campingplatz Arnumer See, Osterbruchweg 5, 30966 Hemmingen-Arnum [(05101) 3534; fax 85514999; info@ camping-hannover.de; www.camping-hannover.de]** Leave A7 junc 59 onto B443 dir Pattensen, then B3 dir Hannover. Site sp in Hemmingen dir Wilkenburg. Lge, hdg/mkd pitch, pt shd; htd wc; chem disp; mv service pnt; baby facs; shwrs €0.50; el pnts (16A) €2.50; gas; lndtte (inc dryer); shop 500m; rest, snacks; bar; cooking facs; playgrnd; lake sw; fishing; tennis; cycle hire; wifi; 95% statics; dogs €1.50; bus to Hannover 1.5km; quiet; CKE/CCI. "Friendly staff; excel, modern, clean san facs; sm area for tourers - gd size open pitches; gd lake sw & boating; insect repellent ess!" € 31.00        2014*

⊞ **HANNOVER** *1D3* (8km S Rural) *52.30447, 9.86216* **Camping Birkensee, 30880 Laatzen [(0511) 529962; fax 5293053; birkensee@camping-laatzen.de; www.camping-laatzen.de]** Fr N leave A7 junc 59 dir Laatzen, turn R, then turn L & site well sp on L after traff lts. Fr S exit junc 60 twd Laatzen, site sp on L on lakeside. Lge, pt shd; wc; chem disp; mv service pnt; sauna; shwrs inc; el pnts (10A) €2.50 (poss rev pol); lndtte; snacks; bar; playgrnd; covrd pool; lake sw & fishing; games area; 60% statics; dogs €2.50; Eng spkn; rd noise; CKE/CCI. "Gd, clean facs; sm touring area; site needs TLC; v helpful staff." ♦ ltd € 27.00        2014*

⊞ **HANNOVER** *1D3* (13km NW Rural) *52.42083, 9.54638* **Camping Blauer See, Am Blauen See 119, 30823 Garbsen [(05137) 89960; fax 899677; info@camping-blauer-see.de; www.camping-blauer-see.de]** Fr W exit A2 at junc 41 onto Garbsen rest area. Thro service area, at exit turn R, at T-junc turn R (Alt Garbson). All sp with int'l camp sp. Fr E exit junc 40, cross a'bahn & go back to junc 41, then as above. Lge, some hdstg, pt shd; htd wc; chem disp; mv service pnt; some serviced pitches; baby facs; shwrs €1; el pnts (16A) €2.70; gas; lndtte (inc dryer); shop; tradsmn; rest, snacks; bar; BBQ; lge playgrnd; lake sw & watersports adj; 90% statics; dogs €2.50; phone; bus to Hannover 1.5km; barrier clsd 2300-0500 & 1300-1500; poss cr; Eng spkn; rd noise; ccard acc; CKE/CCI. "Excel san facs; well-organised site; helpful staff; conv bus/train to Hannover; rec pitch by lake." ♦ ltd € 29.00        2014*

⊞ **HANNOVERSCH MUNDEN** *1D4* (7km SE Rural) *51.39500, 9.72527* **Camping Zella im Werratal, Zella 1-2, 34346 Hannoversch-Münden [(05541) 904711; info@zella-im-werratal.de; www.zella-im-werratal.de]** Exit A7/E45 junc 75 onto B80 dir Hann-Münden. In 4km turn L over rv bdge, site in 1km. Med, pt shd; wc; shwrs €0.60; el pnts (16A) inc; gas; lndtte (inc dryer); shop; tradsmn; rest, bar adj; cooking facs; playgrnd; 30% statics; dogs €2; some train noise; red long stay/ CKE/CCI. "Facs across rd; vg rest; gd NH." € 22.50        2009*

**HANNOVERSCH MUNDEN** *1D4* (2.5km W Rural) *51.41666, 9.64750* **Campingplatz Grüne Insel Tanzwerder, Tanzwerder 1, 34346 Hannoversch-Münden [(05541) 12257; fax 660778; info@busch-freizeit.de; www.busch-freizeit.de]** A7/E45 exit junc 76 onto B496 to Hann-Münden. Cross bdge & site sp on an island on Rv Fulda next to town cent. App over narr swing bdge. Fr junc 75 foll sp to Hann-Münden. At Aral g'ge in town take next L & foll sp to site (sp Weserstein). Med, mkd pitch, pt shd; wc; chem disp; mv service pnt; shwrs €1; el pnts (16A) metered + conn fee; lndtte; shops, rest, snacks, bar 1km; playgrnd; htd pool 1km; wifi; dogs €2; poss cr; Eng spkn; adv bkg; noisy bdge traff; red long stay; CKE/CCI. "Pleasant site on island bordered by rv both sides; historic old town." 30 Mar-15 Oct. € 21.00        2010*

**HASSENDORF see Rotenburg (Wümme)** *1D2*

**HATTINGEN** *1B4* (1km NW Urban) *51.40611, 7.17027* **Camping Ruhrbrücke, Ruhrstrasse 6, 45529 Hattingen [(02324) 80038; info@camping-hattingen.de; www. camping-hattingen.de]** Fr A40 bet Essen & Bochum exit junc 29 dir Höntrop & Hattingen. Foll sp Hattingen on L651 & B1, site sp bef rv bdge. Med, pt sl, unshd; htd wc; chem disp; shwrs €1; el pnts (16A) €3; shop 1km; rest, snacks 1km; bar 800m; BBQ; rv sw adj; canoeing, windsurfing adj; dogs €2; phone; bus, train adj; Eng spkn; adv bkg; quiet; CKE/CCI. "Beautiful rvside setting; plentiful, clean facs; friendly owner; excel cycle tracks." ♦ ltd 1 Apr-10 Oct. € 18.00        2010*

**HAUSBAY see Lingerhahn** *3B2*

**HAUSEN IM TAL** *3C4* (300m E Rural) *48.08365, 9.04290*
Camping Wagenburg, Kirchstr. 24, 88631 Beuron /
i Tal Hausen [(07579) 559; fax 1525; info@camping-
wagenburg.de; www.camping-wagenburg.de] Fr E on
B32 stay on Sigmaringen bypass and take minor rd L227 sp
Gutenstein/Beuron to Hausen, site in vill beside Rv Donau.
Med, hdstg, pt shd; wc; chem disp; mv service pnt; shwrs
€0.50; el pnts (16A) metered + conn fee; lndtte; shop 50m;
tradsmn; rest adj; bar; playgrnd; rv sw adj; tennis 300m; TV; no
statics; dogs €1.50; poss cr; Eng spkn; adv bkg; red long stay.
"Beautiful location in Danube Gorge; friendly, helpful owner;
clsd 1230-1430; poss flooding in wet weather/high rv level;
gd walking/cycling; vg; excel site gd for walking cycling; rv
canoeing." ◆ ltd 10 Apr-3 Oct. € 26.00          2012*

⊞ **HECHTHAUSEN** *1D2* (3km W Rural) *53.62525, 9.20298*
Ferienpark & Campingpark Geesthof, Am Ferienpark 1,
21755 Hechthausen-Klint [(04774) 512; fax 9178; info@
geesthof.de; www.geesthof.de] Site sp on B73 rd to
Lamstedt. Med, hdg/mkd pitch, pt shd; wc; chem disp; mv
service pnt; sauna; baby facs; shwrs inc; el pnts (10A) €2; lndtte
(inc dryer); shop; tradsmn; rest, snacks; playgrnd; 2 pools (1
htd, covrd); paddling pool; waterslide; watersports; fishing;
boat & cycle hire; wifi; entmnt; 60% statics; dogs €2; Eng
spkn; quiet; red 7+ nts. "Superb site with mature trees around
pitches; peaceful surroundings adj to rv, lake & woods; friendly
staff." ◆ € 19.00 (CChq acc)          2010*

**HEIDELBERG** *3C2* (5km E Rural) *49.40175, 8.77916*
Campingplatz Haide, Ziegelhäuser Landstrasse 91,
69151 Neckargemünd [(06223) 2111; fax 71959; info@
camping-haide.de; www.camping-haide.de] Take B37
fr Heidelberg, cross Rv Neckar by Ziegelhausen bdge by sliprd
on R (avoid vill narr rd); foll site sp. Site on R bet rv & rd 1km
W of Neckargemünd site. Lge, unshd; wc; chem disp;
mv service pnt; shwrs €1; el pnts (6A) €2.50 (long lead req);
lndtte (inc dryer); shop 2km; tradsmn; rest, snacks; BBQ;
playgrnd; cycle hire; wifi; 5% statics; dogs €2; bus 1.5km; Eng
spkn; some rd, rlwy (daytime) & rv noise; red CKE/CCI. "Conv
Neckar Valley & Heidelberg; NH/sh stay only." ◆ 1 Apr-31 Oct.
€ 17.80          2011*

**HEIDELBERG** *3C2* (10km E Urban) *49.39638, 8.79472*
Campingplatz an der Friedensbrücke, Falltorstrasse
4, 69151 Neckargemünd [tel/fax (06223) 2178;
j.vandervelden@web.de] Exit Heidelberg on S side of rv
on B37; on ent Neckargemünd site sp to L (grey sp) mkd
Poststrasse; site adj rv bdge. Fr S on B45 turn L sp Heidelberg,
then R at camping sp. Fr A6 exit junc 33 onto B45 sp
Neckargemünd, then as above. Foll sp - do not foll Sat Nav.
Lge, unshd; htd wc; chem disp; mv service pnt; baby facs;
shwrs €0.75; el pnts (6-10A) €5 or metered (poss rev pol);
gas; lndtte; shop; rest adj; snacks; bar; playgrnd nr; pool
adj; kayaking 500m; tennis; wifi; TV rm; dogs €1.50; phone;
transport to Heidelberg by boat, bus & train 10 mins walk
fr site; poss cr; Eng spkn; adv bkg; rd & rv noise; ccard not acc.
"Gd location by busy rv, poss liable to flood; immac, well-run,
relaxing site; ask for rvside pitch (sm) - extra charge; owner will
site o'fits; warm welcome; helpful staff; no plastic grndsheets;
26 steps up to main san facs; gd rvside walks & cycling; TO
500m; gd nh fac, nr ent." ◆ 1 Apr-20 Oct. € 29.50     2014*

⊞ **HEIDENAU** *1D2* (1.5km SW Rural) *53.30851, 9.62038*
Ferienzentrum Heidenau, Minkens Fuhren, 21258
Heidenau [(04182) 4272 or 4861; fax 401130; info@
ferienzentrum-heidenau.de; www.ferienzentrum-
heidenau.de] Exit A1 Hamburg-Bremen m'way junc 46 to
Heidenau; foll sp. Lge, pt shd; htd wc; chem disp; mv service
pnt; sauna; shwrs inc; el pnts (16A) €2 (poss long lead req);
lndtte; shop; rest, snacks; bar; BBQ (sep area); playgrnd; htd
pool; fishing lakes; gd cycling; tennis; games area; internet;
75% statics; no dogs; phone; Eng spkn; quiet; CKE/CCI.
"Pleasant, wooded site; tourers on grass areas by lakes; clean,
modern facs; ltd shop; gd; visa ccards not acc." € 18.50  2012*

**HEIDENBURG see Trittenheim** *3B2*

**HEINSEN see Holzminden** *1D3*

**HELLENTHAL see Schleiden** *3B1*

**HEMMINGEN ARNUM see Hannover** *1D3*

**HEMSBACH see Weinheim** *3C2*

**HENNSTEDT** *1D1* (4km N Rural) *54.31351, 9.18953*
Camping-Ferienpark Eider, Eiderstrasse 20, 25779
Hennstedt-Horst [tel/fax (04836) 611; eidercamping@t-
online.de; www.eidercamping.de] Fr B203 Rendsburg-
Heide rd, turn N in Tellingstedt to Hennstedt, then to Horst.
Site sp on Rv Eider. Med, hdg/mkd pitch, pt shd; wc; chem
disp; shwrs €0.50; el pnts (6A) €1.60; lndtte; shop; rest 4km;
snacks; bar; cooking facs; playgrnd; pool; fishing; boat-
launching; golf 5km; 40% statics; dogs €2; CKE/CCI. 1 Apr-
31 Oct. € 14.50          2009*

**HERBOLZHEIM** *3B3* (500m E Rural) *48.21625, 7.78796*
Terrassen-Campingplatz Herbolzheim, Laue-Dietweg
1, 79336 Herbolzheim [(07643) 1460; fax 913382;
s.hugoschmidt@t-online.de; www.laue-camp.de] Fr E35/
A5 exit 58 to Herbolzheim. Turn R in vill. Turn L on o'skts of
vill. Site in 1km next to sw pool, sp. Med, terr, pt shd; wc;
chem disp; mv service pnt; shwrs inc; el pnts (10A) €2; lndtte;
shop; rest; playgrnd; pool & tennis nrby; 30% statics; dogs €2
(not acc mid-Jul to mid-Aug); o'nights facs for m'vans; clsd
1300-1500; adv bkg; quiet; ccard acc; red long stay; CKE/
CCI; ACSI "Excel friendly, well-maintained site; conv Vosges,
Black Forest & Europapark; gd simple rest, spotless and supmkt
nrby, excel staff; immac grass on firm base." 23 Mar-3 Oct.
€ 30.00          2013*

**HERSBRUCK** *4E2* (3km E Rural) *49.51884, 11.49200* Pegnitz
Camping, Eschenbacherweg 4, 91224 Hohenstadt
[(09154) 1500; fax 91200] Exit A9 junc 49 onto B14 dir
Hersbruck & Sulzbach-Rosenberg. By-pass Hersbruck & after
8km turn L sp Hohenstadt. Bef vill, cross rv bdge & immed turn
R at site sp. Med, pt shd; wc; chem disp; mv service pnt; shwrs
inc; el pnts (10A) inc; gas; lndtte; tradsmn; shop & rest 1km;
cycle hire; 10% statics; trains nrby; Eng spkn; adv bkg; quiet;
CKE/CCI. "Lovely, peaceful, friendly site; Gd walking & cycling
area; helpful owner; v gd san facs; train to Nuremberg; gd; stn
200m." 1 Mar-31 Oct. € 16.00          2014*

HERSBRUCK *4E2* (6km NW Rural) *49.53900, 11.37200*
**Berghof Glatzenstein M'van Parking, Jurastrasse 14,
91233 Weissenbach [(09153) 7906; fax 9229926]** Exit A9/
E51 junc 49 dir Hersbruck. In 2km turn L on minor rd sp
Speikern & Kersbach. Foll sp Weissenbach & Berg Glatzenstein,
up winding rd to Berghof. O'night parking area is opp hotel.
Sm (5 pitches); no facs, no fee on condition have meal in rest;
gd views; m'vans only. May-Sep. € 11.73                    2009*

HIRSCHAU *4F2* (4km E Rural) *49.55608, 12.00634*
**Campingplatz am Naturbad, Badstrasse 13, 92253
Schnaittenbach [tel/fax (09622) 1722; info@campingplatz.
schnaittenbach.de; www.schnaittenbach.de]** On B14
bet Rosenberg & Wernberg, clearly sp in vill. Med, sl, unshd;
wc; chem disp; shwrs inc; el pnts (16A) €1.50 or metered +
conn fee; lndtte (inc dryer); shop 1.5km;tradsmn; rest adj;
playgrnd; pool; games area; 80% statics; quiet; red CKE/CCI.
"Gd NH; scenic area; v pleasant site." ♦ ltd 1 Apr-30 Sep.
€ 17.50                                                    2013*

⊞ HIRSCHAU *4F2* (2km S Rural) *49.53088, 11.96525*
**Camping Monte Kaolino, Wolfgang-Drossbach Strasse
115, 92242 Hirschau [(09622) 81502; fax 81555; info@
montekaolino.eu; www.montekaolino.eu]** Exit A93 junc 27
onto B14, site sp. Med, terr, pt sl, pt shd; wc; chem disp; baby
facs; shwrs; el pnts (16A) metered + conn fee; lndtte; shop
1.5km; rest, snacks; playgrnd; htd pool; paddling pool; games
area; dry-ski & lift; 60% statics dogs €1.50; poss v cr; adv bkg;
quiet; red CKE/CCI. "Vg for children; poss diff access to pitches
for tourers; interesting area." ♦ ltd € 15.00              2009*

**HIRSCHHORN see Eberbach** *3C2*

⊞ **HOF** *4F2* (8km NW Rural) *50.37494, 11.83804* **Camping
Auensee, 95189 Joditz-Köditz [(09295) 381; fax
(09281) 706666; rathaus@gemeinde-koeditz.de; www.
gemeinde-koeditz.de]** Exit A9 at junc 31 Berg/Bad Steben.
Turn R fr m'way & in 200m L to Joditz, foll site sp in vill (1-way
ent/exit to site). Med, terr, unshd; wc; mv service pnt; shwrs; el
pnts (16A) €1.80 or metered; lndtte; shops adj; rest high ssn;
playgrnd; lake sw; fishing; tennis; 75% statics; dogs €1.50; clsd
1230-1500; quiet; red CKE/CCI. € 13.00                     2010*

**HOFHEIM AM RIEGSEE see Murnau am Staffelsee** *4E4*

HOHENFELDE *2E1* (2km N Coastal) *54.38630, 10.49165*
**Camping Ostseestrand, Strandstrasse, 24257 Hohenfelde
[(04385) 620; fax 593846; info@campingostseestrand.
de; www.campingostseestrand.de]** Fr Kiel on B502 dir
Lütjenburg, foll sp to site in Hohenfelde. Med, mkd pitch,
unshd; htd wc; chem disp; mv service pnt; shwrs €0.50; private
san facs avail; el pnts (10A); €2.50; lndtte (inc dryer); shop;
rest, snacks, bar adj; playgrnd; sand beach adj; watersports;
horseriding 2km; golf 5km; internet; TV; 70% statics; dogs €2;
o'night facs for m'vans; adv bkg; quiet; ccard acc. "Pleasant
area of lakes & forests; ltd pitches for tourers; gd, clean san
facs; vg." ♦ 1 Apr-24 Oct. € 19.50                         2009*

**HOHENFELDEN see Kranichfeld** *2E4*

**HOHENSTADT see Hersbruck** *4E2*

⊞ **HOHENSTADT** *3D3* (500m NE Rural) *48.54693, 9.66794*
**Camping Waldpark Hohenstadt, Waldpark 1, 73345
Hohenstadt [(07335) 6754; fax (7335) 184574; camping@
waldpark-hohenstadt.de; www.waldpark-hohenstadt.
de]** Exit A8/E52 junc 60 Behelfs & foll sp to Hohenstadt &
site in approx 5km. Med, some hdstg, pt sl, pt shd; htd wc;
chem disp; mv service pnt; baby facs; shwrs €0.50; el pnts
(16a) €2.50; lndtte (inc dryer); tradsmn; rest, snacks; bar; BBQ;
playgrnd; htd pool; wifi; 75% statics; dogs €1; Eng spkn;
quiet; red low ssn; CKE/CCI. "Gd, peaceful NH to/fr Austria;
handy off A8 - conv for mway; helpful & friendly staff; gd facs;
long walk to shwrs fr tourer parking; lovely site; area ideal for
walking, cycling, climbing, skiing and cross country skiing;
excel." 1 Mar-31 Oct. € 27.50                              2013*

HOLLE *1D3* (4km NE Rural) *52.10285, 10.13877* **Seecamp
Derneburg, 31188 Holle-Derneburg [(05062) 565; fax
8785; info@campingplatz-derneburg.de; www.seecamp-
derneburg.de]** Exit A7/E45 junc 63 at Derneburg onto B6, dir
Hildesheim. Site in 300m. Med, unshd; wc; chem disp; shwrs
€0.50; el pnts (16A) metered; shop high ssn; rest; playgrnd;
lake adj; cycle hire; 50% statics; dogs €2; Eng spkn; ccard acc.
"Quiet site; locked at 2200, barrier key ess after this time;
helpful; gd rest." 1 Apr-15 Sep. € 18.40                   2011*

HOLZMINDEN *1D3* (6km N Rural) *51.88618, 9.44335*
**Weserbergland Camping, Weserstrasse 66, 37649 Heinsen
[(05535) 8733; fax 911264; info@weserbergland-camping.
de; www.weserbergland-camping.de]** Fr Holzminden on
B83 twd Hameln, site sp in Heinsen cent twd rv bank. Med,
pt sl, pt shd; wc; chem disp; sauna; shwrs €0.50; el pnts (10A)
€1.90; gas; lndtte (inc dryer); shop 600m; tradsmn; rest; bar;
playgrnd; htd pool; cycle hire; entmnt in high ssn; 50% statics;
dogs €2; adv bkg; 10% red long stay/CKE/CCI. "Beautiful site
on rv bank; gd san facs; gd area for walking/cycling; gd local
bus service; new owners 2010 & renovations in hand." 15 Mar-
31 Oct. € 15.50                                            2010*

⊞ **HOLZMINDEN** *1D3* (8km SE Rural) *51.77086, 9.54873*
**Campingplatz Silberborn, Glashüttenweg 4, 37603
Holzminden-Silberborn [tel/fax (05536) 664; info@
naturcamping-silberborn.de; www.naturcamping-
silberborn.de]** S fr Holzminden on B497; turn L to Silberborn.
Lge, mkd pitch; pt shd; htd wc; chem disp; baby facs; shwrs
€0.50; el pnts (16A) €2 or metered; gas; lndtte (inc dryer); shop
500m; rest; bar; BBQ; playgrnd; pool; 50% statics; dogs €2;
phone & bus 500m; adv bkg; quiet; red long stay/CKE/CCI. "V
clean, well-kept site; popular with bikers; gd value rest; vg." ♦
€ 17.00                                                    2010*

HOOKSIEL *1C2* (1.5km N Coastal) *53.64100, 8.03400*
**Nordsee Camping Hooksiel (Part Naturist), Bäderstrasse,
26434 Wangerland [(04425) 958080; fax 991475; camp-
hooksiel@wangerland.de; www.wangerland.de]** Site A29
at junc 4 sp Fedderwarden to N. Thro Hooksiel, site sp 1.5km.
V lge, some hdstg, unshd; wc; chem disp; mv service pnt;
baby facs; shwrs inc; el pnts (6-10A) inc; gas; lndtte (inc dryer);
shop; rest, snacks; playgrnd; muddy beach; fishing; sailing;
watersports; games area; cycle hire; wifi; entmnt; 50% statics;
dogs €3.10; naturist site adj with same facs; poss cr; quiet.
"Main san facs excel but up 2 flights steps - otherwise facs in
Portakabin." ♦ 25 Mar-17 Oct. € 21.40                      2010*

**GERMANY**

⊞ **HORB AM NECKAR** *3C3* (4km W Rural) *48.44513, 8.67300* **Camping Schüttehof, Schütteberg 7-9, 72160 Horb-am-Neckar [(07451) 3951; fax 623215; camping-schuettehof@t-online.de; www.camping-schuettehof. de]** Fr A81/E41 exit junc 30; take Freudenstadt rd out of Horb site sp. Med, mkd pitch, pt sl, pt shd; wc; chem disp; shwrs €0.50; el pnts (16A) metered + conn fee; gas; lndtte; shop; rest; playgrnd; htd pool; paddling pool; internet; entmnt; 75% statics; dogs €2; poss cr; adv bkg; quiet. "Horb delightful Black Forest town; site close to saw mill & could be noisy; steep path to town; site clsd 1230-1430." € 17.00          2012*

**HORSTEL** *1B3* (4.5km N Rural) *52.32751, 7.60061* **Campingplatz Herthasee, Herthaseestrasse 70, 48477 Hörstel [(05459) 1008; fax 971875; contact@hertha-see. de; www.hertha-see.de]** Exit A30/E30 junc 10 to Hörstel, then foll sp Hopsten. Site well sp fr a'bahn. V lge, pt sl, shd; wc; chem disp; mv service pnt; baby facs; shwrs €0.50; el pnts (16A) €2.40 or metered + conn fee (poss long lead req); gas; lndtte; shop; rest 2km; snacks; bar; BBQ; playgrnd; lake sw & beach adj; tennis; cycle hire; TV; wifi; 70% statics; no dogs; Eng spkn; quiet; CKE/CCI. "Excel site." ♦ 22 Mar-29 Sep. € 30.70          2013*

⊞ **HOSSERINGEN** *1D2* (1km S Rural) *52.86940, 10.42274* **Campingplatz am Hardausee, Am Campingplatz 1, 29556 Suderburg-Hösseringen [(05826) 7676; fax 8303; info@ camping-hardausee.de; www.camping-hardausee.de]** S fr Uelzen on B4/B191 for 9km to Suderburg & Hösseringen, site sp. Med, pt shd; wc; chem disp; mv service pnt; shwrs inc; el pnts (16A) €2; lndtte; shop (high ssn); rest 1km; snacks; playgrnd; sw 300m; dogs €1.50; quiet. "Ltd touring pitches; excel, clean facs; excel cycling & walking; conv Lüneberg." € 17.00          2009*

**HOXTER** *1D3* (500m E Rural) *51.76658, 9.38308* **Wesercamping Höxter, Sportzentrum 4, 37671 Höxter [(05271) 2589; fax 496335; info@campingplatz-hoexter. de; www.campingplatz-hoexter.de]** Fr B83/64 turn E over rv sp Boffzen, turn R & site sp almost on rv bank. Turn R in 300m at green sp, turn L in car park. Med, pt shd; wc; chem disp; baby facs; shwrs €0.50; el pnts (10-16A) €2; lndtte (inc dryer); shop; rest; playgrnd; internet; child entmnt; 60% statics; dogs €1.50; quiet; red CKE/CCI. "Lge open area for tourers; clsd 1300-1500; spaces beside rv; easy walk along rv to town." 15 Mar-15 Oct. € 14.50          2014*

⊞ **HUCKESWAGEN** *1B4* (3km NE Rural) *51.15269, 7.36557* **Campingplatz Beverblick, Grossberghausen 29, Mickenhagen, 42499 Hückeswagen [(02192) 83389; info@beverblick.de; www.beverblick.de]** Fr B237 in Hückeswagen at traff lts take B483 sp Radevormwald. Over rv & in 500m turn R sp Mickenhagen. In 3km strt on (no thro rd), turn R after 1km, site on R. Steep app. Med, hdstg, pt sl, unshd; htd wc; chem disp (wc); shwrs €1.10; el pnts (10A) metered; shop & 5km; tradsmn; rest; bar; 90% statics; quiet. "Few touring pitches; helpful owners; gd rest & bar; gd touring base; vg." € 15.00          2012*

⊞ **HUNFELD** *1D4* (3.5km SW Rural) *50.65333, 9.72388* **Knaus Campingpark Praforst, Dr Detlev-Rudelsdorff Allee 6, 36088 Hünfeld [(06652) 749090; fax 7490901; huenfeld@knauscamp.de; www.knauscamp.de]** Exit A7 junc 90 dir Hünfeld, foll sp thro golf complex. Med, mkd pitch, pt sl, pt shd; wc; shwrs; chem disp; mv service pnt; el pnts (16A) metered or €2.50; lndtte; shop; tradsmn; playgrnd; pool; fishing; games rm; games area; golf adj; wifi; 40% statics; dogs €2; quiet. "Excel san facs; gd walking/cycling." ♦ € 22.00          2009*

**HUSUM** *1D1* (6km SW Coastal) *54.45557, 8.97224* **Nordseecamping Zum Seehund, Lundenbergweg 4, 25813 Simonsberg [(04841) 3999; fax 65489; info@ nordseecamping.de; www.nordseecamping.de]** L off B5 Heide-Husum at Darigbull sp Simonberg. Site sp. Lge, unshd; wc (htd); chem disp; mv service pnt; baby facs; shwrs inc; el pnts (16A) €2.50; gas; lndtte (inc dryer); shop 6km; tradsmn; rest, snacks; bar; BBQ; playgrnd; mud beach adj; lake sw 300m; wellness cent; golf 10km; 60% statics; dogs €2; poss cr; Eng spkn; quiet; CKE/CCI. "Superb family run site with excel facs; modern air-con san facs; gd value for money; really gd for cycling & bikes avail for hire on site." ♦ 1 Mar-15 Nov. € 22.00          2011*

**IBBENBUREN** *1B3* (3km S Rural) *52.24555, 7.69861* **Camping Dörenther Klippen, Münsterstrasse 419, 49479 Ibbenbüren [(05451) 2553; fax 9615; roesch-ibbenbueren@freenet.de; www.doerenther-klippen.de]** Fr A30/E30 exit junc 11b on B219 dir Greven. Site sp in 1.7km. Sm, hdg/mkd pitch, pt sl, pt shd; wc; chem disp; shwrs inc; el pnts (16A) €2.50 (rev pol); lndtte; rest; bar; pool 5km; many statics; dogs; Eng spkn; quiet but some rd noise; ccard acc; CKE/CCI. "Friendly, gd walking; ltd space for tourers; barrier clsd 2200-0700; site poss unkempt/untidy low ssn; NH only." 1 Mar-31 Oct. € 21.50 (4 persons)          2010*

⊞ **IBBENBUREN** *1B3* (5km S Rural) *52.21829, 7.66502* **Camping Eichengrund, Im Brook 2, 49479 Ibbenbüren [(05455) 521; fax 287]** Exit A30/E30 junc 11b onto B219 dir Greven for 5.8km; site sp on R 200m after x-ing canal bdge. Lge, hdg pitch, pt shd; wc; chem disp; mv service pnt; private bathrms avail; shwrs €0.50; el pnts (16A) €1.50; gas; lndtte; shop; rest; playgrnd; 90% statics; quiet; CKE/CCI. "Excel site; barrier & office clsd 1300-1500; ltd shwrs & san facs." € 14.00          2009*

⊞ **IDAR OBERSTEIN** *3B2* (10km N Rural) *49.80455, 7.26986* **Camping Harfenmühle, 55758 Asbacherhütte [(06786) 7076; fax 7570; mail@harfenmuehle.de; www. camping-harfenmuehle.de]** Fr rte 41 fr Idar twd Kirn, turn L at traff lts at Fischbach by-pass sp Herrstein/Morbach, site 3km past Herrstein vill. Sharp turn to site. Med, pt shd; wc; chem disp; mv service pnt; sauna; shwrs €0.50; el pnts (16A) lndtte; gas; shop; tradsmn; rest, snacks; bar; playgrnd; lake sw adj; fishing; tennis; games area; games rm; golf 10km; internet; TV rm; 50% statics; dogs €2; phone; o'night area for m'vans; adv bkg; Eng spkn; 10% red CKE/CCI. ♦ ltd € 19.00          2009*

**IHRINGEN see Breisach am Rhein** *3B4*

⊞ **ILLERTISSEN** *3D4* (9km S Rural) *48.14138, 10.10665*
Camping Christophorus Illertal, Werte 6, 88486 Kirchberg-Sinningen [(07354) 663; fax 91314; info@camping-christophorus.de; www.camping-christophorus.de] Exit A7/E43 junc 125 at Altenstadt. In cent of town turn L, then R immed after level x-ing. Foll site sp. Lge, pt shd; htd wc; chem disp; sauna; shwrs; el pnts (16A) €2.80 or metered; lndtte; shop high ssn; rest, snacks; playgrnd; covrd pool; lake sw adj; fishing; cycle hire; 80% statics; dogs €3.50; Eng spkn; adv bkg; red CKE/CCI. "Gd site; sm sep area for tourers; excel san facs." € 29.00                                                  2013*

**ILLERTISSEN** *3D4* (1km SW Rural) *48.21221, 10.08773*
Camping Illertissen, Dietenheimerstrasse 91, 89257 Illertissen [(07303) 7888; fax 2848; campingplatz-illertissen@t-online.de; www.camping-illertissen.de] Leave A7 at junc 124, twd Illertissen/Dietenheim; after rlwy x-ing turn R then L foll site sp. Off main rd B19 fr Neu Ulm-Memmingen fr N, turn R in Illertissen, foll sp. Sm, mkd pitch, terr, pt shd; wc; chem disp; mv service pnt; shwrs inc; el pnts (16A) €2 or metered; gas; lndtte; shop & 1.5km; tradsmn; snacks; rest in hotel adj; playgrnd; pool; 65% statics; dogs €2; poss cr; quiet; ccard acc; 10% red CKE/CCI. "Trains to Ulm & Kempten; 20 mins walk to town or cycle track; some pitches poss unrel in wet; site clsd bet 1300-1500 & 2200-0700; obliging owner; conv a'bahn; vg." ♦ 1 Apr-30 Oct. € 19.50                  2009*

**IMMENSTAAD AM BODENSEE see Friedrichshafen** *3D4*

⊞ **IMMENSTADT IM ALLGAU** *3D4* (2.5km NW Rural) *47.57255, 10.19358* Buchers Alpsee Camping, Seestrasse 25, 87509 Bühl-am-Alpsee [(08323) 7726; fax 2956; mail@alpsee-camping.de; www.alpsee-camping.de] Fr Immenstadt, W on B308; turn R dir Isny & Missen. In 1.3km turn L sp Bühl & site sp. Lge, unshd; wc; shwrs inc; el pnts (16A) €2.50 (poss rev pol); gas; lndtte; shop; rest; playgrnd; pool 2km; lake sw adj; ski lift 3km; dogs €3; poss cr; Eng spkn; adv bkg; quiet. "Lake sm but pleasant; gd mountain walks; friendly welcome; excel site, first class facs." € 45.20            2014*

⊞ **INGOLSTADT** *4E3* (3.5km E Rural) *48.75416, 11.46277*
Azur Campingpark Am Auwaldsee, 85053 Ingolstadt [(0841) 9611616; fax 9611617; ingolstadt@azur-camping.de; www.azur-camping.de] Exit A9/E45 junc 62 Ingolstadt Süd, foll sp for camp site & Auwaldsee. V lge, pt shd; wc; shwrs inc; chem disp; mv service pnt; el pnts (16A) €2.80; gas; lndtte (inc dryer); shop 1.5km; rest, snacks; adj; bar; playgrnd; pool 1km; rv beach & sw; fishing & boating; wifi; 50% statics; dogs €3.50; bus; clsd 1300-1500; poss cr; adv bkg. "Basic wooded site by lake; useful NH nr m'way." ♦ ltd € 24.00       2012*

⊞ **INZELL** *4F4* (100m Rural) *47.76722, 12.75341*
Camping Lindlbauer, Kreuzfeldstraße 44, 83334 Inzell [08665 928 99 88; fax 928 99 86; info@camping-inzell.de] Fr A8 exit 112 Traunstein-Siegsdorf. Take B306 twds Inzell. Foll sp in vill to campsite. Med, mkd pitch, hdstg, terr, unshd; htd wc; chem disp; mv service pnt; baby facs; shwrs inc; el pnts (16A); lndtte (inc dryer); shop; rest; snacks; bar; playgrnd; htd covrd pool; games area; wifi; dogs €4; phone adj; bus adj; twin axles; Eng spkn; adv bkg; quiet; red low ssn; CCI. "Excel site; beautiful views; friendly, family run site; excel location for walking & cycling". ♦ € 44.70                             2014*

⊞ **IRREL** *3A2* (700m S Urban) *49.84175, 6.45750*
Campingplatz Südeifel, Hofstraße 19, 54666 Irrel [06525 510; info@camping-suedeifel.de; www.camping-suedeifel.de] Take Irrel exit off B257; site sp. Lge, pt shd; wc; shwrs; el pnts (6A) €2; gas; lndtte; rest; bar; BBQ; playgrnd; wifi; dogs €2; quiet; CKE/CCI. "Cycling in area & walks fr site; pleasant town; tourist info in town; gd site."           2011*

**ISNY IM ALLGAU** *3D4* (8km NW Rural) *47.75400, 10.00432*
Campingplatz am Badsee, Allmisried 1, 88316 Isny-Beuren [(07567) 1026; fax 1092; campingbadsee@t-online.de; www.campingbadsee.de] On Isny-Leutkirch rd turn W on N side of Friesenhofen sp Beuren. In 4km at Beuren turn N onto sm rd sp to site, Badsee & Winnis. Med, pt sl, pt terr, pt shd; wc; chem disp; mv service pnt; baby facs; fam bthrm; shwrs €1; el pnts (16A) metered + €2.50; lndtte; shop high ssn snacks; rest; playgrnd; lake sw & beach; 80% statics; dogs €2.30; clsd 1300-1500; adv bkg. "Isny interesting; excel facs; vg." ♦ 15 Apr-15 Oct. € 18.50                                  2010*

**ISSIGAU** *4F2* (450m S Rural) *50.37413, 11.72103*
Camping Schloss Issigau, Altes Schloss 3, 95188 Issigau [(09293) 7173; fax 7050; info@schloss-issigau.de; www.schloss-issigau.de] Exit A9/E51 junc 31 dir Berg. In Issigau foll sp over bdge to site. Sm, pt sl, pt shd; wc; chem disp; mv service pnt; shwrs inc; el pnts (16A) metered; gas; lndtte; shop 300m; rest, snacks; bar; playgrnd; TV rm; dogs €1.50; phone; Eng spkn; adv bkg; quiet; ccard not acc; CKE/CCI. "Gd walking & cycling; friendly, helpful owners; delightful, well-kept site; vg facs & rest; visit to Mödlareuth worthwhile." 15 Mar-31 Oct & 17 Dec-6 Jan. € 17.50                          2011*

⊞ **JENA** *2E4* (2km NE Rural) *50.93583, 11.60833*
Campingplatz Unter dem Jenzig, Am Erlkönig 3, 07749 Jena [(03641) 666688; post@camping-jena.com; www.camping-jena.com] Exit A4/E40 junc 54 to Jena, then B88 for 4m N dir Naumberg. Turn R just outside Jena at campsite sp, R over blue bdge; site nr sports stadium/sw pool on L, sp. Med, unshd; wc; chem disp; mv service pnt; shwrs inc; el pnts (10A) €2.50 or metered; lndtte; rest 500m; snacks; bar; playgrnd; pool adj; dogs €1; phone; bus 1km; shop 1.5km; some Eng spkn; adv bkg; quiet. "Gd san facs in Portakabin; sh walk to interesting town; gd cycle paths." ♦ ltd € 23.50        2014*

**JESTETTEN** *3C4* (750m SW Urban) *47.64802, 8.56648*
Campingplatz & Schwimmbad, Waldshuterstrasse 13, 79798 Jestetten [(07745) 1220; info@jestetten.de; www.jestetten.de] Site in town on B27 main rd, sp. Sm, pt sl, pt shd; htd wc; chem disp (wc); shwrs inc; el pnts (10A) metered; shop, rest in town; snacks; playgrnd; htd pool; no dogs; bus at gate; train 500m; Eng spkn; adv bkg; quiet. "Gd for walk or train Rhine Falls & Switzerland." ♦ ltd Easter-30 Sep. € 16.60                                              2009*

**JODITZ KODITZ see Hof** *4F2*

GERMANY

⊞ **KALKAR** *1A3* (2km N Rural) *51.76100, 6.28483* **Freitzeitpark Wisseler See, Zum Wisseler-See 15, 47546 Kalkar-Wissel [(02824) 96310; fax 963131; info@wisseler-see.de; www.wisseler-see.de]** Fr A3 take junc 4 onto B67 dir Kalkar & Wissel. Fr Kleve take B57 SE for 8km twd Kalkar, & to Wissel & foll camp sp. V lge, hdg/mkd pitch, pt shd; serviced pitches; wc; chem disp; mv service pnt; shwrs inc; el pnts (16A) inc; lndtte; shop; rest, snacks; pool; playgrnd; beach; watersports; tennis; cycle hire; games area; wifi; entmnt; 75% statics; dogs €2.50; adv bkg;. "Commercialised & regimented but conv NH Rotterdam ferry; gd facs; gd for children & teenagers." ♦ € 24.00          2009*

⊞ **KAMENZ** *2G4* (4km NE Rural) *51.30465, 14.15272* **Campingplatz Deutschbaselitz, Grossteichstrasse 30, 01917 Kamenz [(03578) 301489; fax 308098; info@campingplatz-deutschbaselitz.com; www.campingplatz-deutschbaselitz.com]** Fr Kamenz N on rd S95 dir Wittichenau; at Schiedel turn R twd lake, site sp. Med, pt shd; htd wc; chem disp; mv service pnt; baby facs; fam bthrm; shwrs inc; el pnts (16A) €3; lndtte (inc dryer); shop; tradsmn; snacks; BBQ; cooking facs; playgrnd; lake sw & beach adj; watersports; cycle hire; games area; games rm; 10% statics; dogs; adv bkg; quiet; CKE/CCI. ♦ € 16.00 (CChq acc)          2009*

⊞ **KAPPELN** *1D1* (7km SW Rural) *54.61945, 9.88402* **Campingpark Schlei-Karschau, Karschau 56, 24407 Rabenkirchen-Faulück [(04642) 920820; fax 920821; info@campingpark-schlei.de; www.campingpark-schlei.de]** Exit A7 junc 5 onto B201 dir Kappeln, site sp dir Faulück & Karschau. Lge, mkd pitch, pt sl, unshd; htd wc; mv service pnt; baby facs; shwrs €0.50; el pnts (6A) inc; lndtte (inc dryer); shop; rest, snacks; playgrnd; sand beach & private beach, rv sw adj; fishing; boat & cycle hire; tennis; games area; golf 5km; 70% statics; dogs €2; adv bkg; quiet. "Gd, peaceful site." ♦ € 20.60 (CChq acc)          2011*

⊞ **KARLSHAGEN** *2G1* (1km E Coastal) *54.11769, 13.84477* **Dünencamp, Zeltplatzstraße; 17449 Ostseebad; Karlshagen [038371 20291; camping@karlshagen.de; www.duenencamp.de]** Site sp fr karlshagen along Zeltplatzstrasse. Lge, mkd pitch, pt sl, shd; htd wc; chem disp; MV service pnt; baby facs; fam bthrm; shwrs (metered); elec pnt (16A) €2 (or metered); lndtte; playgrnd; beach adj; dogs €4; phone; Eng spkn; quiet. "Site has direct access to long clean sandy beach; long mains lead may be needed for some pitches; conv for visiting Peenemünde; gd site." € 26.00          2011*

**KARLSRUHE** *3C3* (1.5km E Rural) *49.00788, 8.48303* **Azur Campingpark Turmbergblick, Tiengenerstrasse 40, 76227 Karlsruhe-Durlach [(0721) 497236; fax 497237; karlsruhe@azur-camping.de; www.azur-camping.de]** Exit A5/E35 junc 44 dir Durlach/Grötzingen onto B10 & foll sp to site 3km. Lge, mkd pitch, pt shd; htd wc; chem disp; mv service pnt; baby facs; shwrs inc; el pnts (10A) €3 (long lead poss req); gas; lndtte; shop; tradsmn; supmkt 500m; rest, snacks; bar; playgrnd; 2 pools nr; tennis; entmnt; internet; 20% statics; dogs €3.50; Eng spkn; adv bkg; some rd & rlwy noise; ccard acc; CKE/CCI. "NH conv to a'bahn; adequate san facs; clsd 1230-1400; expensive for average site." ♦ 1 Apr-31 Oct. € 26.50          2012*

⊞ **KASSEL** *1D4* (3.5km S Urban) *51.29055, 9.48777* **Wohnmobilstellplatz Kassel, Giesenallee, 34121 Kassel [(0561) 707707; strassenverkehrsamt@stadt-kassel.de]** Exit A49 junc 5; strt on at traff lts; 1st R sp camping. Site 80m beyond Fulda Camp. Sm, hdstg, unshd; chem disp; mv service pnt; el pnts (10A) metered; dogs; bus adj. M'vans only. "Max stay 3 nights; excel stopover; nice walk along rv & lge park nrby." € 12.50          2014*

⊞ **KASTELLAUN** *3B2* (1.5km SE Rural) *50.06846, 7.45382* **Burgstadt Camping Park, Südstrasse 34, 56288 Kastellaun [(06762) 40800; fax 4080100; info@burgstadt.de; www.burgstadt.de]** Exit A61 junc 42 dir Emmelshausen onto L206/L213 for 1.2km; turn L onto B327; cont for 13.5km to Kastellaun. Site adj hotel on B237. Med, mkd pitch, hdstg, terr, unshd; htd wc; chem disp; mv waste; baby facs; sauna; solarium; shwrs inc; el pnts (16A) metered; lndtte; shop; tradsmn; rest, snacks; bar; BBQ; playgrnd; htd, covrd pool 300m; tennis; cycle hire; riding & kayaking nrby; wifi; no statics; dogs €2; o'night m'van area; Eng spkn; adv bkg; quiet. "Lge pitches; clean site; excel san facs; helpful staff; conv touring base; fitness & beauty cent in hotel adj; excel." ♦ € 20.00          2012*

**KEHL** *3B3* (9km E Rural) *48.54375, 7.93518* **Europa-Camping, Waldstrasse 32, 77731 Willstätt-Sand [tel/fax (07852) 2311; europa.camping@t-online.de; www.europa-camping-sand.de]** Exit A5/E35/E52 at junc 54 almost immed turn R at Int'l Camping sp; foll site sp. Med, some hdstg, pt shd; htd wc; shwrs inc; el pnts (16A) €2.50 (long lead poss req); lndtte (inc dryer); shop & 5km; rest; cooking facs; playgrnd; 30% statics; dogs €2; poss cr; Eng spkn; quiet but some rd noise; ccard acc; red long stay/CKE/CCI. "Easy reach Black Forest & Strasbourg; 1km fr a'bahn exit; well-managed, clean, tidy site; gd san facs; friendly helpful owner; cycle tracks fr site." 1 Feb-30 Nov. € 26.00          2013*

**KEHL** *3B3* (1km S Urban) *48.5615, 7.80861* **DCC Campingpark Kehl-Strassburg, Rheindammstrasse 1, 77694 Kehl-Kronenhof [(07851) 2603; fax 73076; CampingparkKehl@aol.com; www.campingplatz-kehl.de]** Fr A5/E35, take exit 54 onto B28 at Appenweier twd Kehl & foll site sp. Lge, pt shd; htd wc; chem disp; mv service pnt; shwrs €0.50; el pnts (16A) metered + conn fee (long lead poss req); gas; lndtte; shop & 1km; tradsmn; rest, snacks; bar; playgrnd; sw pool adj; wifi; 15% statics; dogs €1; bus 1km; poss cr; Eng spkn; adv bkg; quiet but noise fr adj stadium w/end; ccard acc; red CKE/CCI. "Peaceful site adj Rv Rhine; excel rest & modern san facs; sm pitches; pleasant rv walk & cycle paths to town; barrier clsd 1300-1500." ♦ 15 Mar-31 Oct. € 23.50          2014*

⊞ **KELBRA** *2E4* (2km W Rural) *51.42551, 11.00307* **Seecamping Kelbra, Langestrasse 150, 06537 Kelbra [(034651) 45290; fax 45292; info@seecampingkelbra.de; www.seecampingkelbra.de]** Exit A38 at Berga (bet junc 12 & 14); on app to town turn L at traff lts onto B85 to Kelbra; go thro chicane in vill, then R onto L234/L1040 dir Sonderhausen; site sp. L234 is Langestrasse. Lge, pt sl, unshd; htd wc; chem disp; mv service pnt; shwrs €0.50; el pnts (16A) €2; lndtte; shop; rest, snacks; bar; BBQ (gas/elec); playgrnd; lake sw adj; sand beach 1km; games area; internet; TV; dogs €2; phone; bus adj; poss cr; Eng spkn; adv bkg; quiet; CKE/CCI. "Gd touring base & walking area; boat hire on site; vg." € 15.50          2011*

⊞ **KEMPTEN** *4E4* (24km E Rural) *47.80283, 10.55377*
**Camping Platz Elbsee, Am Elbsee 3, 87648 Aitrang**
**[08 34 32 48; fax 34 31 406; info@elbsee.de; www.elbsee.**
**de]** S on A7. Take J134 dir Marktobedorf on B12. Take exit
twd Unterthingau on OAL10. Turn L on OAL3, cont onto OAL
5. Turn R on Am Elbsee. Foll sp. Lge, hdg pitch, mkd pitch,
hdstg, pt shd; htd wc; chem disp; mv service pnt; baby facs;
shwrs; el pnts (16A); lndtte (inc dryer); shop; rest; snacks; BBQ;
cooking facs; playgrnd; lake adj; games rm; entmnt; wifi; dogs
€4.50; bus 0.75km; twin axles; poss cr; Eng spkn; adv bkg;
quiet;ccard acc; CCI. "Excel site; gd base; many local historical
places & amazing architecture. Camp has much to offer - peace
& quiet, spa art, yoga." ♦ € 34.50                          2014*

⊞ **KEMPTEN (ALLGAU)** *3D4* (6km SE Rural) *47.67485,*
*10.33386* **Camping Öschlesee, 87477 Sulzberg**
**[(08376) 93040; fax 93041; info@camping.oeschlesee.de;**
**www.camping.oeschlesee.de]** Exit A7 at junc 136 Dreieck
Allgäu onto rd 980 dir Lindau/Oberstdorf. Turn L to Sulzberg
in 1.5km, site sp. Lge, some hdstg, pt sl, pt shd; wc; mv service
pnt; shwrs inc; el pnts (16A) €2; gas; lndtte; shop; supmkt 1km;
rest adj; snacks; bar; cooking facs; playgrnd; lake sw 300m; TV;
70% statics; dogs €2; bus 200m; poss cr; Eng spkn; quiet; CKE/
CCI. "Some pitches views of Alps; vg san facs; gd rest 300m;
some pitches diff in wet; gd walks." ♦ € 22.00           2010*

**KIEL** *1D1* (5km N Coastal) *54.41198, 10.18388* **Campingplatz**
**Kiel-Falckenstein, Palisadenweg 171, 24159 Kiel-**
**Friedrichsort [tel/fax (0431) 392078; falckenstein1@aol.**
**com; www.campingkiel.de]** N fr Kiel foll sp to 'Flughafen'
& Friedrichsort on B503. Foll 'Olympiazentrum', site sp. Access
rd narr with bends, but ent gd. Lge, pt sl, unshd; wc; sauna;
shwrs; el pnts (16A) metered + conn fee; gas; lndtte; shop;
rest; bar; playgrnd; pool 1km; shgl beach adj; 60% statics;
dogs €1.90; poss cr; quiet. "Poor san facs; NH only." ♦ 1 Apr-
31 Oct. € 18.50                                              2011*

⊞ **KINDING** *4E3* (5km E Rural) *49.00328, 11.45200* **Camping**
**Kratzmühle, Mühlweg 2, 85125 Kinding-Pfraundorf**
**[(08461) 64170; fax 641717; info@kratzmuehle.de; www.**
**kratzmuehle.de]** Exit A9/E45 junc 58, dir Beilngries. Site sp.
Lge, pt shd; wc; chem disp; mv service pnt; baby facs; some
serviced pitches; sauna; shwrs inc; el pnts (16A) €2.50; gas;
lndtte; shop; rest; cooking facs; playgrnd; lake sw adj & shgl
beach; games area; 40% statics; dogs €2; clsd 1300-1500;
poss cr; adv bkg; 10% red 2+ days; quiet; ccard acc; CKE/
CCI. "Beautiful situation; conv NH for a'bahn; ideal boating
& bathing, public access to lake; poss mosquito prob; helpful
staff." ♦ € 23.50                                           2010*

**KIPFENBERG** *4E3* (500m W Rural) *48.9486, 11.38859* **Azur**
**Campingpark Altmühltal, Campingstrasse 1, 85110**
**Kipfenberg [(08465) 905167; fax 3745; kipfenberg@azur-**
**camping.de; www.azur-camping.de/kipfenberg]** Exit A9/
E45 junc 58 or 59 & foll sp to Kipfenberg, site sp on rvside.
Lge, pt shd; htd wc; mv service pnt; shwrs inc; chem disp; mv
service pnt; baby facs; el pnts (6A) €2.80; gas; lndtte; tradsmn;
shop, rest, snacks 100m; bar; cooking facs; playgrnd; tennis;
fishing; excursions; wifi; TV rm; 20% statics; dogs €3.50; sep
o'night area; quiet; red CKE/CCI. "On edge of attractive old
vill; cent for walking, cycling & canoeing; charming site." ♦
1 Apr-31 Oct. € 23.00                                       2009*

**KIRCHBERG SINNINGEN see Illertissen** *3D4*

⊞ **KIRCHHEIM** *1D4* (5km SW Rural) *50.81435, 9.51805*
**Camping Seepark, Reimboldshäuserstraße, 36275**
**Kirchheim [(06628) 1525; fax 8664; info@campseepark.**
**de; www.campseepark.de]** Exit A7 at Kirchheim junc 87,
site clearly sp. Lge, mkd pitch, pt sl, terr, mkd pitch, pt shd;
htd wc; chem disp; mv service pnt; sauna; shwrs €1; el pnts
(16A) €2.50; metered; gas; lndtte; dishwashers; shop; tradsmn;
rest, snacks; bar; playgrnd; covrd pool; lake sw & sand beach;
tennis; games area; golf 3km; entmnt; 50% statics; dogs €2;
bus 500m; phone; o'night area for m'vans; adv bkg; quiet but
poss noisy high ssn; ccard acc; red long stay/CKE/CCI. "Gd
walking; helpful owner; excel site - leisure facs pt of lge hotel
complex." ♦ € 19.80 (6 people)                              2009*

**KIRCHZARTEN see Freiburg im Breisgau** *3B4*

**KIRCHZELL see Amorbach** *3D2*

## "Satellite navigation makes touring much easier"

Remember most sat navs don't know if
you're towing or in a larger vehicle – always
use yours alongside maps and site directions.

⊞ **KIRKEL** *3B3* (300m W Urban) *49.28175, 7.22860*
**Caravanplatz Mühlenweiher, Unnerweg 5c, 66458 Kirkel-**
**Neuhäusel [(06849) 1810555; fax 1810556; info@camping-**
**kirkel.de; www.caravanplatz-kirkel.de]** Fr A6 junc 7 & fr A8
junc 28, take dir into town & foll sp for 'schwimmbad'. Site on
L past pool, well sp. Med, mkd pitch, hdstg, pt shd; htd wc;
chem disp; mv service pnt; baby facs; shwrs inc; el pnts (10A)
€3 or metered + conn fee (poss rev pol); gas; lndtte (inc dryer);
shop 1km; rest; bar; pool adj; wifi; TV cab/sat; 60% statics;
dogs €1.15; phone; noise fr pool & church bells all night; CKE/
CCI. "Gd welcome; excel area for cycling; site/office clsd 1230-
1500." ♦ € 15.00                                            2010*

**KIRTORF HEIMERTSHAUSEN see Alsfeld** *1D4*

**KITZINGEN** *3D2* (1km SE Urban) *49.73233, 10.16833*
**Camping Schiefer Turm, Marktbreiterstrasse 20, 97318**
**Kitzingen-Hohenfeld [(09321) 33125; fax 384795; info@**
**camping-kitzingen.de; www.camping-kitzingen.de]**
Fr A3 take exit junc 74 sp Kitzingen/Schwarzach or exit 72
Würzburg-Ost, or fr A7 exit junc 103 Kitzingen. Site sp in town
'Schwimmbad'. Med, mkd pitch, pt shd; wc; chem disp; mv
service pnt; shwrs €0.50; el pnts (16A) €2 or metered; gas;
lndtte; shop; supmkt 200m; rest, snacks; pool adj; dogs €1.50;
bus; poss cr w/end & high sn; ccard acc. "Bird reserve; pleasant
town in evening; gd cycling; busy NH high ssn; san facs up
steps; excel Lido adj." 1 Apr-15 Oct. € 18.00              2012*

**KLAIS KRUN see Mittenwald** *4E4*

**KLEIN RONNAU see Bad Segeberg** *1D2*

**KLEINROHRSDORF see Dresden** *2G4*

**KOBLENZ** *3B2* (500m N Urban) *50.36611, 7.60361* Camping Rhein-Mosel, Schartwiesenweg 6, 56070 Koblenz-Lützel [(0261) 82719; fax 802489; info@camping-rhein-mosel.de; www.camping-rhein-mosel.de] Fr Koblenz heading N on B9 turn off dual c'way at sp for Neuendorf just bef Mosel rv bdge; foll sp to Neuendorf vill. Or heading S on B9 exit dual c'way at camping sp (2nd sp) bef Koblenz; fr Koblenz cent foll sp for 'Altstadt' until Baldwinbrücke (bdge); N over bdge instead of foll sp along S bank of Rv Mosel; R after bdge, then foll sp; site on N side of junc Rhine/Mosel rvs. Lge, some hdstg, pt sl, pt shd; wc; chem disp; mv service pnt; shwrs inc; el pnts (6-16A) €2.05 or metered (long lead poss req); lndtte (inc dryer); shop; supmkt 500m; cooking facs; rest, snacks; bar; dogs; poss v cr; Eng spkn; no adv bkg; heavy rv & rlwy noise; no ccard acc; CKE/CCI. "Pleasant, informal site in beautiful location; muddy in wet; staff helpful; no veh acc after 2200; adj ferry to city + easy cycle rte; mkt Sat; sep dog shwr; flea mkt Sun; 'Rhine in Flames' fireworks 2nd Sat in Aug - watch fr site; recently renovated (2013); mv stopover called Knaus Campingpark just outside main gates, basic price €12.50, both sites under same owner." ♦ 1 May-20 Oct. € 33.00        2014*

⊞ **KOBLENZ** *3B2* (8km SW Rural) *50.33194, 7.55277* Camping Gülser Moselbergen, Am Gülser Moselbogen 20, 56072 Koblenz-Güls [(0261) 44474; fax 44494; info@ moselbogen.de; www.moselbogen.de] Fr A61/E31 exit 38 dir Koblenz/Metternich. After 400m turn R at rndabt dir Winningen. Stay on this rd to T-junc in Winningen, turn L dir Koblenz-Güls, site sp on R in 3km. Med, hdg/mkd pitch, pt shd; htd wc; chem disp; mv service pnt; baby facs; fam bthrm; shwrs €0.50; el pnts (16A) €1.50 + conn fee; gas; lndtte (inc dryer); shop 2km; tradsmn; rest 200m; playgrnd; cab/sat TV; 50% statics; dogs €2; phone; poss cr; Eng spkn; adv bkg; rd & rlwy noise; ccard acc; CKE/CCI. "High quality, high-tech san facs; no vehicles 1200-1400; poss subject to flooding; excel." ♦ € 21.00        2012*

**KOBLENZ** *3B2* (9km SW Urban) *50.30972, 7.50166* Campinginsel Winningen (previously Campingplatz Ziehfurt), Raiffeisenstraße 16, 56333 Winningen [(02606) 357 or 1800; fax 2566; ferieninsel-winningen@t-online.de; www.mosel-camping.com] Exit A61/E31 junc 38 to Winningen. In Winningen turn R twrds Cochem B416, then L at sw pool. In approx 100mtrs turn R and then in 700m turn L over bdge to site recep. Lge, pt shd; wc; chem disp; mv service pnt; shwrs €0.90; el pnts (16A) €2.50; lndtte; shop; rest, snacks; playgrnd; pool 300m; rv adj; 50% statics; dogs €3; poss v cr; Eng spkn; no adv bkg; some noise fr rd & rlwy. "Cent of wine-growing country; boat trips avail fr Koblenz; cycle rtes; scenic area; poss flooding if v high water; lively site when busy; gd, modern san facs up steep steps but poss stretched when busy; excel rest; excel site." Easter-1 Oct. € 20.50        2012*

**KOCHEL AM SEE** *4E4* (4km SW Rural) *47.63642, 11.34827* Camping Kesselberg, Altjoch 2 ½, 82431 Kochel-am-See [(08851) 464; mailto@campingplatz-kesselberg.de; www. campingplatz-kesselberg.de] S fr Kochel on Bundestrasse 11. After 3km fork R for Walchensee Kraftwerk, many hairpins, site 150m on R. Med, mkd pitch, pt sl, pt shd; wc; chem disp; mv service pnt; child/baby facs; shwrs €0.50; el pnts (10A) metered; gas; lndtte; shop; rest, snacks; bar; BBQ; lake sw adj; sailing; wifi; 40% statics; dogs €3; poss cr; Eng spkn; adv bkg; CKE/CCI; quiet; red 10+ days. "Friendly site; beautifully situated by Kochelsee; attractive peaceful lakeside site; clean san facs; friendly & helpful staff; vg." 22 Mar-15 Oct. € 29.50        2013*

⊞ **KOLN** *1B4* (3km N Urban) *50.96305, 6.98361* Reisemobilhafen Köln, An der Schanz, 50735 Köln [017 84674591 (mob); info@reisemobilhafen-koeln.de] Fr A1 Köln ring rd exit junc 100 dir Köln 'Zentrum' until reach rv. Turn L & foll sp to site. M'vans only. Sm, mkd pitch, hdstg; own san; mv service pnt; el pnts (10A) €1 for 12 hrs; shop, rest, snacks, bar 500m; dogs; bus, train nr. "Adj Rv Rhine; must have change for elec, water (metered), parking etc; easy access to city cent; site is unmanned." € 10.00        2014*

⊞ **KOLN** *1B4* (10km NE Rural) *50.99551, 7.06021* Camping Waldbad, Peter Baum Weg, 51069 Köln-Dünnwald [(0221) 603315; fax 608831; info@waldbad-camping.de; www.waldbad-camping.de] Exit A3/E35 at junc 24. E for 2km on Willy Brandt ringrd, turn R onto B51 (Mülheimstrasse). In 2.7km turn L into Odenthalerstrasse then foll site sp. Med, pt sl, pt shd; wc; chem disp; mv service pnt; baby facs; shwrs inc; el pnts (10-16A) metered & conn fee; lndtte; shop; rest adj; pool adj; 75% statics; dogs €2; phone; metro to city 10 mins drive; no adv bkg; v quiet. "Close to wildpark, pool & sauna; no ent/exit for cars 1300-1500 & 2200-0700; friendly warden." ♦ € 16.00        2012*

**KOLN** *1B4* (3km SE Urban) *50.90263, 6.99070* Campingplatz der Stadt Köln, Weidenweg 35, 51105 Köln-Poll [(0221) 831966; fax 4602221; info@camping-koeln.de; www.camping-koeln.de] Exit fr A4 (E40) at junc 13 for Köln-Poll-Porz at E end of bdge over Rv Rhine, 3km S of city. At end of slip rd, turn L twd Poll & Köln. Cont about 500m turn L at sp just bef level x-ing, then foll site sp. Narr lane to ent. Lge, pt shd; wc; chem disp; mv service pnt; shwrs €0.50; el pnts (10A) €3.50 (some rev pol & long lead poss req); gas; lndtte; basic shop; tradsmn; snacks; rest 200m; cooking facs; dogs €2.50; phone; trams 1.5km; clsd 1230-1430; poss cr at w/ends; Eng spkn; no adv bkg; some rd & aircraft noise; CKE/CCI. "Tram to city over rv bdge; rural site in urban setting on bank of Rv Rhine & subject to flooding; gd undercover cooking facs; gd refurbished san facs on 1st floor; friendly site; v busy at w/end; rvside cycle track to city." ♦ 28 Mar-15 Oct. € 33.50        2014*

You can now fill in site reports online

⊞ **KOLN** *1B4* (7km SE Rural) *50.8909, 7.02306*
Campingplatz Berger, Uferstrasse 71, 50996 Köln-Rodenkirchen [(0221) 9355240; fax 9355246; camping.berger@t-online.de; www.camping-berger-koeln.de] Fr A4 turn S onto A555 at Köln-Sud exit 12. Leave A555 at Rodenkirchen exit 3. At 1st junc foll site sp to R. Fr A3 Frankfurt/Köln a'bahn, take A4 twd Aachen (Köln ring rd); exit at Köln Sud; foll sp Bayenthal; at lge rndabt turn R sp Rheinufer & R again at camp sp, under a'bahn. App rd narr & lined with parked cars. Lge, pt shd; htd wc; chem disp; mv service pnt; shwrs inc; el pnts (4-10A) €1.50; gas; lndtte; shop; tradsmn; supmkt 1km; rest, snacks; bar; cooking facs; playgrnd; cycle hire; wifi; 80% statics; dogs €1; phone; bus 500m; poss v cr; Eng spkn; no adv bkg; quiet but some noise fr Rhine barges; ccard acc; red long stay; CKE/CCI. "Pleasant, popular, wooded site on banks of Rhine; rvside pitches best; excel rest; helpful staff; gd dog walking; cycle path to city cent; conv cathedral, zoo & museums; don't arr early eve at w/end as narr app rd v busy; pitches poss muddy after rain; san facs up steps - poss clsd 2300-0600; gd site; vr gd facs." ♦ € 30.40      2014*

**KOLPIN see Storkow** *2G3*

⊞ **KONIGSSEE** *4G4* (500m N Rural) *47.59445, 12.98583*
Camping Grafenlehen, Königseer Fussweg 71, 83471 Königssee [(08652) 4140; fax 690768; camping-grafenlehen@t-online.de; www.camping-grafenlehen.de] On B20 fr Berchtesgaden 5km to Königssee. Where car park with traff lts is ahead, turn R sp Schönau, site on R. Lge, terr, pt shd; htd wc; chem disp; mv service pnt; shwrs inc; el pnts (16A) metered; lndtte; shop; rest, snacks; playgrnd; 10% statics; dogs €2; site clsd Nov to mid-Dec; quiet; red CKE/CCI. "Pleasant, quiet site; spectacular views; gd san facs; superb walking; cycle path by rv; gd value rest; 30 mins drive Salzburg Park & Ride; conv Berchtesgaden." € 25.00      2012*

⊞ **KONIGSSEE** *4G4* (1km N Rural) *47.5992, 12.98933*
Camping Mühlleiten, Königsseerstrasse 70, 83471 Königssee [(08652) 4584; fax 69194; info@muehlleiten.eu; www.camping-muehlleiten.eu] On on R of B20 Berchtesgaden-Königssee. Med, unshd; wc; chem disp; shwrs inc; el pnts (16A) €3 or metered; gas; lndtte; shop & 1km; rest adj; snacks; bar; beach 1km; ski lift 500m; golf 6km; entmnt; dogs €2.50; poss cr; quiet; red CKE/CCI. "Beautiful area; friendly staff; excel san facs." € 17.50      2009*

**KONIGSTEIN** *2G4* (1km E Rural) *50.92222, 14.08833*
Camping Königstein, Schandauerstrasse 25e, 01824 Königstein [(035021) 68224; fax 60725; info@camping-koenigstein.de; www.camping-koenigstein.de] Foll B172 SE fr Dresden/Pirna. Site 500m past Königstein rlwy stn. Turn L over rlwy x-ing & R into site ent on Rv Elbe. Med, pt sl, unshd; wc; chem disp; mv service pnt; shwrs €0.80; el pnts (16A) €2.60; gas; lndtte; shop 1km; rest; playgrnd; 15% statics; dogs €3 (not acc Jul/Aug); sep car park & no dogs Jul/Aug; adv bkg; rlwy noise; red 5+ days. "Gd san facs; lovely location nr national parks & Czech border; on Elbe cycle path; frequent trains to Dresden; boat trips; gates clsd 1300-1500; red for 7+ days." ♦ 1 Apr-31 Oct. € 32.00      2013*

⊞ **KONIGSTEIN** *2G4* (2.5km E Rural) *50.91500, 14.10730*
Caravan Camping Sächsische Schweiz, Dorfplatz 181d, 01824 Kurort-Gohrisch [350 21 59107; caravan-camping@web.de; www.caravan-camping-saechsischeschweiz.de] Fr Königstein foll B172 E dir Bad Schandau. Fork R dir Gohrisch for 2.5km, turn L into Dorfplatz & foll site sp. Med, hdg/mkd pitch, hdstg, pt sl, pt shd; wc; chem disp; mv service pnt; baby facs; fam bathrm; sauna; shwrs €0.50; el pnts (16A) metered; lndtte (inc dryer); shop; tradsmn; rest; bar; BBQ; cooking facs; playgrnd; htd, covrd pool 4km; padding pool; games area; cycle hire; wifi; sat/cable TV; 5% statics; dogs €2; bus 500m; Eng spkn; adv bkg; quiet; red low ssn/long stay. "Excel site; gd touring base; interesting area; guided walks." ♦ € 22.00      2012*

**KONIGSWALDE see Annaberg Buchholz** *4G1*

**KONSTANZ** *3D4* (7km N Rural) *47.74596, 9.14701* Camping Klausenhorn, Hornwiesenstrasse, 78465 Dingelsdorf [(07533) 6372; fax 7541; info@camping-klausenhorn.de; www.konstanz.de/tourismus/klausenhorn] Site sp N of Dingelsdorf on lakeside. Lge, mkd pitch, hdstg, pt shd; htd wc; chem disp; baby facs; shwrs €0.50; el pnts (10A) inc; lndtte; shop & 1.5km; rest 800m; snacks; bar; BBQ; playgrnd; shgl beach & lake adj; boating; games area; wifi; entmnt; 50% statics; no dogs; bus 500m; sep car park; poss cr; Eng spkn; adv bkg; quiet; ccard acc; CKE/CCI. "Excel site." ♦ 1 Apr-4 Oct. € 25.50      2009*

**KONSTANZ** *3D4* (10km W Rural) *47.69871, 9.04603*
Camping Sandseele, Bradlengasse 24, 78479 Niederzell [(07534) 7384; fax 98976; beyer@sandseele.de; www.sandseele.de] Clearly sp off B33 Konstanz-Radolfzell rd. Foll sp on island & sm multiple sp. Lge, pt shd; wc; chem disp; mv service pnt; shwrs inc; el pnts (16A) €3; gas; lndtte; shop; rest, snacks; playgrnd; lake sw & beach; watersports; 30% statics; no dogs; sep car park high ssn; poss v cr; poss noisy. "Insect repellent rec, Excel san facs; excel walking & cycling all over island." ♦ 15 Mar-5 Oct. € 26.50      2013*

**KONZ see Trier** *3B2*

⊞ **KORBACH** *1C4* (13km S Rural) *51.17500, 8.89138*
Camping & Ferienpark Teichmann, Zum Träumen 1a, 34516 Vöhl-Herzhausen [(05635) 245; fax 8145; info@camping-teichmann.de; www.camping-teichmann.de] Fr Korbach, take B252 S. In 12m cross Rv Eder. Site in 1km on R by lake. Lge, mkd pitch, pt shd, wc; chem disp; mv service pnt; baby facs; sauna; shwrs inc; el pnts (10A) €2.60; lndtte (inc dryer); shop; rest, snacks; bar; playgrnd; lake sw & beach; boat & cycle hire; tennis; cycle & boat hire; games area; horseriding 500m; wellness cent; winter sports; entmnt high ssn; wifi; TV; 50% statics; dogs €3.60; sep car park; o'night area for m'vans; adv bkg; ccard acc; red CKE/CCI. "Excel family site in lovely situation; friendly, helpful staff; gd walking in area." ♦ € 30.30      2011*

See advert on next page

⊞ **KOTZTING** *4F3* (6km NE Rural) *49.20610, 12.92381* Camping Hohenwarth Fritz-Berger, Ferienzentrum 3, 93480 Hohenwarth [(09946) 367; fax 477; info@ campingplatz-hohenwarth.de; www.campingplatz-hohenwarth.de] Fr Cham, take B85 SW to Miltach, Kötzting & site sp on L on Hohenwarth by-pass. Lge, mkd pitch, some hdstg, unshd; wc; chem disp; mv service pnt; sauna; shwrs inc; el pnts (16A) metered + conn fee; gas; lndtte; shop; tradsmn; rest, snacks; bar; playgrnd; pool; lake sw; ski lift 7km; entmnt; internet; 10% statics; dogs €2; site clsd 5 Nov-10 Dec; adv bkg; quiet; ccard acc; CKE/CCI. "Gd walking & cycling area; office clsd 1200-1400 & 1800-0800; conv NH for Bavaria & Czech Rep." ♦ € 18.00 2011*

⊞ **KRANICHFELD** *2E4* (4km NW Rural) *50.87216, 11.17843* Campingplatz Stausee Hohenfelden, 99448 Hohenfelden [(036450) 42081; fax 42082; info@stausee-hohenfelden. de; www.stausee-hohenfelden.de] Fr A4/E40 take exit 47a S twd Kranichshd. Site clearly sp by lake along rough rd. Lge, sl, pt terr, pt shd; wc; chem disp; mv service pnt; shwrs €0.80; el pnts (10A) €2.60; lndtte (inc dryer); supmkt 3km; tradsmn; snacks; boating; cycle hire; TV; 60% statics; dogs €2.50; no adv bkg; ccard acc; CKE/CCI. "Woodland, lakeside walks; gates clsd 1300-1500 & 2200-0700; poss noisy, scruffy; poss lge youth groups; gd san facs but diff access." ♦ € 17.40 2011*

## "There aren't many sites open at this time of year"

If you're travelling outside peak season remember to call ahead to check site opening dates – even if the entry says 'open all year'.

**KRESSBRONN AM BODENSEE** *3D4* (7km N Rural) *47.63395, 9.6477* Gutshof-Camping Badhütten (Part Naturist), Badhütten 1, 88069 Laimnau [(07543) 96330; fax 963315; gutshof.camping@t-online.de; www.gutshof-camping.de] Fr Kressbronn take B467 to Tettnang & Ravensburg. In 3km immed after x-ing Rv Argen turn R & site sp for approx 3km. V lge, hdg/mkd pitch, pt shd; wc; chem disp; mv service pnt; serviced pitches; baby facs; shwrs inc; el pnts (16A) metered; gas; lndtte; shop; rest, snacks; bar; playgrnd; pool; lake 7km; entmnt; 40% statics; dogs €2; adv bkg; quiet; red long stay; CKE/CCI. "Sep area for naturists; gd facs; v rural site; clean, quiet & pleasant; excel." ♦ 30 Mar-5 Nov. € 27.80 2011*

**KRESSBRONN AM BODENSEE** *3D4* (1km W Rural) *47.58718, 9.58281* Campingplatz Irisweise, Tunau 16, 88079 Kressbronn [(07543) 8010; fax 8032; info@campingplatz-irisweise.de; www.campingplatz-irisweise.de] Fr E or W take exit off B31 bypass for Kressbronn, site well sp. Lge, hdg/ mkd pitch, pt shd; htd wc; chem disp; mv service pnt; baby facs; shwrs inc; el pnts (10A) metered + conn fee; gas; lndtte; shop; rest; bar; BBQ; playgrnd; beach, lake sw adj (sep naturist beach); sailing; watersports; internet; 10% statics; dogs €2; phone; poss v cr; Eng spkn; no adv bkg; quiet; ccard acc; CKE/CCI. "Steamer trips on lake; no car access 2100-0700, park outside site; excel san facs but some dist fr touring pitches; gd." ♦ 8 Apr-15 Oct. € 25.50 2010*

**KROV see Wittlich** *3B2*

**KRUMBACH** *4E4* (4km SW Rural) *48.22720, 10.29280* See Camping Günztal, Oberrieder Weiherstrasse 5, 86488 Breitenthal [(08282) 881870; info@see-camping-guenztal. de; www.see-camping-guenztal.de] W fr Krumbach on rd 2018, in Breitenthal turn S twd Oberried & Oberrieder Weiher, site sp on lakeside. Med, mkd pitch, some hdstg; pt shd; htd wc; chem disp; mv service pnt; baby facs; shwrs inc; el pnts (10A) inc; lndtte (inc dryer); shop 800m; tradsmn; rest 1.5km; snacks; bar; BBQ; playgrnd; lake sw; watersports; fishing; games area; wifi; TV; 30% statics; dogs €2; adv bkg; quiet. ♦ 1 Apr-30 Oct. € 19.50 (CChq acc) 2010*

**KUHLUNGSBORN** *2E1* (600m W Coastal) *54.15137, 11.71947* Campingpark Kühlungsborn, Waldstrasse 1b; 18225 Kühlungsborn [(038293) 7195; fax 7192; info@ topcamping.de; www.topcamping.de] On rd B105 turn N in Neubukow sp Kühlungsborn. In 15km, at W Kühlungsborn stn, rd turns N; foll sp. V lge, pt sl, shd; wc; chem disp; mv service pnt; serviced pitches; baby facs; shwrs; el pnts (16A) inc; lndtte; shop adj; rest, snacks; rest; shop; playgrnd; htd pool 300m; beach (sep naturist beach); sailing; windsurfing; games area; cycle hire; entmnt; TV; 20% statics; dogs €5; poss cr; quiet; ccard acc. "Excel site; upgraded & modernised facs, esp luxurious san facs (even has luxury dog wash!); v clean & well managed; town pleasant, old-fashioned holiday resort." ♦ 30 Mar-26 Oct. € 34.00 2011*

⊞ **KULMBACH** *4E2* (300m NE Urban) *50.11083, 11.46160*
Parkplatz am Schwedensteg, 95326 Kulmbach
[(09221) 95880; fax 958844; touristinfo@stadt-kulmbach.
de; www.stadt-kulmbach.de] Exit A70/E48 junc 24
onto B289 dir Kulmbach Stadtmitte. Foll sp 'Festplatz am
Schwedensteg' to area behind bus & truck park. Sm, hdstg,
unshd; own san; chem disp; mv service pnt; water €1/100
litres; el pnts (16A) metered; shop, rest, snacks, bar 500m;
m'vans only. "Historic town cent." ♦ €3.00          2009*

## "That's changed – Should I let The Club know?"

If you find something on site that's different from
the site entry, fill in a report and let us know. See
www.caravanclub.co.uk/europereport.

**KULMBACH** *4E2* (8km NE Rural) *50.16050, 11.51605*
Campingplatz Stadtsteinach, Badstrasse 5, 95346
Stadtsteinach [(09225) 800394; fax 800395; info@
campingplatz-stadtsteinach.de; www.campingplatz-
stadtsteinach.de] Fr Kulmbach take B289 to Untersteinach
(8km); turn L to Stadtsteinach; turn R at camping sp & foll rd
for 1km. Site also sp fr N side of town on B303. Or fr A9/E51
exit junc 39 onto B303 NW to Stadtsteinach. Med, pt shd; htd
wc; chem disp; mv service pnt; shwrs inc; el pnts (16A) €2.10;
lndtte; shop 600m; rest, snacks; bar; cooking facs; playgrnd;
rv fishing; tennis; cycle hire; games
area; 75% statics; dogs €2; Eng spkn; adv bkg; ccard acc; CKE/
CCI. "Excel site in beautiful countryside; excel, modern facs;
highly rec." ♦ 1 Mar-30 Nov. €29.50          2014*

**LABOE** *1D1* (2km NE Coastal) *54.41399, 10.24846* Camping
Fördeblick, Kreisstrasse 30, 24235 Stein [(04343) 7795;
fax 7790; info@camping-foerdeblick.de; www.camping-
foerdeblick.de] Exit B76/B202 into Kiel & take sp Gaarden-
Ost. Then turn L onto B502 dir Heikendorf. Foll sp Laboe &
Stein. Lge, mkd pitch, pt sl, unshd; htd wc; chem disp; mv
service pnt; baby facs; shwrs inc; el pnts (10A) €2.60; gas;
lndtte; shop; tradsmn; rest, snacks; bar; playgrnd; sand/shgl
beach adj; watersports nrby; games area; golf 5km; wifi;
entmnt; 75% statics (sep area); no dogs; phone; bus 500m;
poss cr; Eng spkn; adv bkg; CKE/CCI. "Facs dated but vg; site
on cliffs, some pitches excel views; narr access lanes to pitches;
pleasant walk into Laboe." ♦ 1 Apr-28 Oct. €26.00     2011*

**LABOE** *1D1* (4km E Coastal) *54.42698, 10.29646* Camping
Oase-Bonanza, Schleusenweg 25, 24235 Wendtorf
[(04343) 9688; fax 9899; camping@camping-oase-
bonanza.de; www.camping-oase-bonanza.de] N fr Kiel
on B502 sp Laboe take turning N sp Stein & Wendtorf. Drive
to end past marina ignoring all sps, site on R behind dyke.
Med, hdg/mkd pitch, pt shd; htd wc; chem disp; mv service
pnt; shwrs €0.60; el pnts (12A) €3; gas; lndtte; shop; supmkt
1km; rest, snacks; bar; playgrnd; sand beach adj (inc naturist);
70% statics; dogs €3; phone; adv bkg; quiet; ccard acc;
CKE/CCI. "Excel cycle paths; friendly owners; excel san facs;
stunning beach." 1 Apr-30 Sep. €20.50          2011*

**LAHNSTEIN** *3B2* (2.5km E Urban) *50.30565, 7.61313*
Kur-Campingplatz Burg Lahneck, Am Burgweg, 56112
Lahnstein-Oberlahnstein [(02621) 2765; fax 18290] Take
B42 fr Koblenz over Lahn Rv, if fr low bdge turn L immed after
church & sp fr there; if fr high level bdge thro sh tunnel turn L
at 1st rd on L sp to Burg-Lahneck - site sp on L. Med, pt sl, pt
shd; wc; chem disp; mv service pnt; shwrs €0.50; el pnts (16A)
metered + conn fee; lndtte; shop; tradsmn; rest; playgrnd;
pool adj; 10% statics; dogs €1; poss cr; Eng spkn; quiet but
distant rlwy noise at night; ccard not acc. "Gd views over
Rhine; scenic area; delightful, helpful owner v particular about
pitching; gd size pitches; immac, well-run site." 1 Apr-31 Oct.
€21.50          2012*

**LAHNSTEIN** *3B2* (8km SE Urban) *50.27393, 7.64098*
Campingplatz Uferwiese, Am Campingplatz 1, 56338
Braubach [tel/fax (02627) 8762; info@campingplatz-
braubach.de; www.campingplatz-braubach.de] Take B42
S twd Rüdesheim. Site behind hotel opp church. Med, shd; wc;
chem disp; shwrs €1; el pnts (16A) €2 (poss rev pol); lndtte;
shop 300m; rest 200m; snacks; bar; 50% statics; dogs €1; bus;
rd & rlwy noise; no ccard acc; CKE/CCI. "Scenic on Rv Rhine;
poss flooding after heavy rain; gd san facs." 15 Apr-25 Oct.
€18.00          2009*

⊞ **LAHR (SCHWARZWALD)** *3B3* (8km SE Rural)
*48.29999, 7.94395* Ferienparadies Schwarzwälder Hof,
Tretenhofstrasse 76, 77960 Seelbach [(07823) 960950;
fax 9609522; camping-rezeption@seelbach.org; www.
campingplatz-schwarzwaelder-hof.de] Fr A5 take exit 56
to Lahr. In 5km turn R twd Seelbach & Schuttertal. Thro town
& site on S o'skts of Seelbach just after town boundary. Med,
mkd pitch, some hdstg, pt sl, terr, pt shd; serviced pitches
(extra charge); wc; chem disp; mv service pnt; shwrs inc; el pnts
(10A) metered + conn fee; gas; lndtte; shop; tradsmn; rest;
snacks 1km; bar; playgrnd; htd pool adj; lake adj; 10% statics;
dogs €3.50; o'night area for m'vans; poss v cr; Eng spkn; adv
bkg ess high ssn; quiet; ccard acc; red CKE/CCI. "Vg touring
base; well-laid out pitches & excel facs; many gd mkd walks; gd
programme of events in Seelbach." ♦ €29.70          2011*

## "I like to fill in the reports as I travel from site to site"

You'll find report forms at the back of
this guide, or you can fill them in online
at www.caravaclub.co.uk/europereport.

**LAHR (SCHWARZWALD)** *3B3* (5km S Rural) *48.24739,
7.82804* Terrassen-Campingpark Oase, Mühlenweg 34,
77955 Ettenheim [(07822) 445918; fax 445919; info@
campingpark-oase.de; www.campingpark-oase.de] Exit
A5/E35 at junc 57a, foll site sp. Lge, shd; wc; shwrs; chem
disp; mv service pnt; baby facs; shwrs €0.50; el pnts (6A) €2;
lndtte; shop; rest, snacks; playgrnd; pool adj; tennis adj; cycle
hire; 30% statics; dogs €1.50; quiet; CKE/CCI. "Modern san
facs; variable pitch size/price; sh walk/cycle track to attractive
town; conv glassworks at Wolfach & House of 1000 clocks nr
Triberg." ♦ ltd 15 Mar-8 Oct. €22.00          2009*

GERMANY

⊞ **LAICHINGEN** 3D3 (2km S Rural) 48.47560, 9.7458 Camping & Freizeitzentrum Heidehof, Heidehofstrasse 50, 89150 Laichingen-Machtolsheim [(07333) 6408; fax 21463; info@heidehof.info; www.camping-heidehof.de] Exit A8 junc 61 dir Merklingen. At T-junc turn R sp Laichingen. In 3km site sp to L. V lge, hdg/mkd pitch, hdstg, pt sl, pt shd, some hdstg; wc; chem disp; mv service pnt; baby facs; fam bthrm; sauna; shwrs inc; el pnts (10-16A) €2 or metered; gas; lndtte; shop; tradmsn; rest; playgrnd; htd pool; cycle hire; 95% statics; adv bkg; red long stay/CKE/CCI. "Blaubeuren Abbey & Blautopf (blue pool of glacial origin) worth visit; sep area for o'nighters immed bef main camp ent - poss unrel when wet; hdstg pitches sm & sl; vg rest; gd NH; clean modern facs; lack of elec boxes; no water taps excep at facs; whole site on uneven sl; arr early to get nr elec." ♦ € 33.00        2014*

**LAIMNAU see Kressbronn am Bodensee** 3D4

**LANDAU IN DER PFALZ** 3C3 (10km W Rural) 49.20138, 7.97222 Camping der Naturfreunde, Victor von Scheffelstrasse 18, 76855 Annweiler-am-Trifels [(06346) 3870; fax 302945; info@naturfreunde-annweiler. de; www.naturfreunde-annweiler.de] Fr Landau take B10 dir Pirmasens, take 1st exit to Annweiler then turn L into vill along Landauerstrasse. Turn L immed after VW/Audi g'ge, site sp. Tight access at ent. Sm, hdstg, pt shd; htd wc; chem disp; mv service pnt; shwrs inc; el pnts (10A) €2; lndtte; shops 500m; rest adj; playgrnd; 80% statics; dogs €2; poss cr; quiet; CKE/CCI. "Friendly, helpful owner poss on site evenings only; immac, modern san facs; ltd space for tourers but adequate facs; vg views across valley & forest; Ent is up steep hill with acute L turn; advise use campingplatz on R." ♦ 1 Apr-31 Oct. € 16.00        2012*

⊞ **LANDSBERG AM LECH** 4E4 (3km SE Rural) 48.03195, 10.88526 DCC Campingpark Romantik am Lech, Pössinger Au 1, 86899 Landsberg-am-Lech [(08191) 47505; fax 21406; campingparkgmbh@aol.com; www.campingplatz-landsberg.de] Not rec to tow thro Landsberg. If app fr S, get onto rd fr Weilheim & foll sp on app to Landsberg. Fr other dir, exit junc 26 fr a'bahn A96 Landsberg Ost, then app town via Muchenstrasse. At rndabt bef town cent, foll sp dir Weilheim, after 400m turn R & foll site sp. Lge, hdg/mkd pitch, pt sl, pt shd; wc; chem disp; mv service pnt; shwrs inc; el pnts (16A) metered (some rev pol); gas; lndtte; shop; rest 2km; snacks; bar; playgrnd; pool 3km; tennis; cycle hire; 65% statics; dogs €1; adv bkg; Eng spkn; quiet; red CKE/CCI. "V pleasant site; excel, clean facs; nature reserve on 2 sides; gd walking & cycling; attractive old town; site clsd 1300-1500 & 2200-0700." ♦ € 17.00        2011*

**LANDSHUT** 4F3 (3km NE Urban) 48.55455, 12.1795 Camping Landshut, Breslauerstrasse 122, 84028 Landshut [tel/fax (0871) 53366; www.landshut.de] Fr A92/E53 exit junc 14 onto B299 dir Landshut N. After approx 5km turn L at int'l camping sp & foll site sp. Med, pt shd; wc; chem disp; mv service pnt; shwrs inc; el pnts (16A) €2.50; lndtte; shop 500m; rest 200m; snacks; bar; BBQ; htd pool 3km; 10% statics; dogs €1.50; poss cr; quiet; CKE/CCI. "Well-run, friendly site; gd san facs; beautiful medieval town & castle - easy cycle rte." ♦ 1 Apr-30 Sep. € 17.00        2009*

**LANGELSHEIM see Goslar** 1D3

**LANGSUR METZDORF see Trier** 3B2

⊞ **LANGWEDEL** 1D1 (1km W Rural) 54.21465, 9.91825 Caravanpark am Brahmsee, Mühlenstrasse 30a, 24631 Langwedel [(04329) 1567; info@caravanpark-sh.de; www.caravanpark-sh.de] Exit A7 at junc 10 dir Tierpark Warder (animal park) & foll site sp to lakeside. Or exit A215 at Blumenthal onto L298 thro Langwedel dir Tierpark Warder, site sp. Med, hdg/mkd pitch, some hdstg, pt shd; htd wc; chem disp; mv service pnt; shwrs inc; el pnts €2.50; lndtte (inc dryer); shop 1km; tradsmn; rest 1km; cooking facs; BBQ; playgrnd; lake sw 100m; fishing; wifi; 80% statics; dogs; adv bkg; quiet. "Peaceful site in nature park; gd; diff access to some pitches for lge o'fits; excel san facs; dedicated hdstg area for campers." ♦ ltd € 20.50 (CChq acc)        2013*

⊞ **LECHBRUCK** 4E4 (2.8km NE Rural) 47.71169, 10.81872 Via Claudia Camping (formerly DCC Campingpark Lechsee), Via Claudia 6, 86983 Lechbruck [(08862) 8426; fax 7570; info@camping-lechbruck.de; www.via-claudia-camping.de] A95 exit junc 10 Murnau/Kochel & then via Murnau, Saulgrub, Steingaden to Lechbruck. Then foll sps. V lge, mkd pitch, terr, pt shd; wc; chem disp; mv service pnt; baby facs; shwrs inc; el pnts (10-16A) €2.65; gas; lndtte (inc dryer); shop; tradsmn; rest; bar; playgrnd; pool 500m; lake beach & sw; watersports; minigolf; volleyball; archery; wifi; entmnt; 50% statics; dogs €3.50; o'night m'van area; Eng spkn; adv bkg; quiet; ccard acc; red CKE/CCI. "Pleasant, peaceful, lakeside site; fac to a high standard; gd welcome; v helpful; cont investment in site fr new owners." ♦ € 24.70        2011*

**LEEDEN see Osnabrück** 1C3

⊞ **LEER (OSTFRIESLAND)** 1B2 (3km W Rural) 53.22416, 7.41891 Camping Ems-Marina Bingum, Marinastrasse 14-16, 26789 Leer-Bingum [(0491) 64447; fax 66405; into-camping-bingum@t-online.de; www.bingumcamper.de] Leave A32/E12 junc 12; site 500m S of Bingum; well sp. Lge, pt shd; wc; chem disp; mv service pnt; baby facs; shwrs €1; el pnts (16A) €2.50 or metered; gas; lndtte (inc dryer); shop 500m; rest, snacks; playgrnd; cycle hire; 65% statics; dogs €3.50; gate clsd 1230-1500; adv bkg; quiet; red long stay/CKE/CCI. ♦ € 20.00        2010*

**LEINATEL see Ohrdruf** 2E4

⊞ **LEIPHEIM** 3D3 (2km W Rural) 48.46566, 10.2035 Camping Schwarzfelder Hof, Schwarzfelderweg 3, Riedheim, 89340 Leipheim [(08221) 72628; fax 71134; info@schwarzfelder-hof.de; www.schwarzfelder-hof. de] Fr A8 exit junc 66 Leipheim onto B10. In Leipheim foll sp Langenau & Riedheim, site sp. Do not confuse with Laupheim 25km S of Ulm on B30. Sm, hdstg, pt shd; htd wc; chem disp (wc); serviced pitches; shwrs inc; el pnts (16A) €2.10 or metered; lndtte; shop 2km; tradsmn; rest 1.5km; snacks; bar; BBQ; playgrnd; 50% statics; dogs €3.20; train 1km; poss cr; Eng spkn; quiet. "Peaceful, farm-based site on site of old quarry; welcoming, helpful owner; lge pitches; vg san facs but ltd; farm animals & riding for children; conv Ulm; recep open 0800-1000 & 1730-2000; poss noisy youth groups; conv NH for m'way." € 18.70        2010*

**LEIPZIG** *2F4* (7km W Rural) *51.38946, 12.15727*
Campingplatz Elsteraue, Delitscherstrasse 68, 06184
Ermlitz [tel/fax (0341) 9121874; ccl-camping@web.
de; www.campingplatzleipzig.de] Exit A9/E51 junc 16
Grosskugel dir Leipzig. Foll sp W to Erlmitz. Site sp (blue sp)
at end of single track, unsurfaced but gd rd. Sm, pt shd;
wc; chem disp; shwrs €0.50; el pnts (16A) €1.50; lndtte;
shop 500m; tradsmn; dogs €1.50; Eng spkn; adv bkg; quiet;
CKE/CCI. "Peaceful; v clean facs; charge for refilling water
tanks & water/waste removal; gd security; cycle rte into
Leipzig; Pleasant site nr rv; conv to town." 15 May-15 Sep.
€ 17.00                                                    2013*

⊞ **LEIPZIG** *2F4* (6km NW Urban) *51.37030, 12.31375*
Campingplatz Auensee, Gustav-Esche Strasse 5, 04159
Leipzig [(0341) 4651600; fax 4651617; info@camping-
auensee.de; www.camping-auensee.de] Fr A9/E51 exit junc
16 onto B6 two Leipzig. In Leipzig-Wahren turn R at 'Rathaus'
sp Leutzsch (camping symbol), site on R in 1.5km, sp. Lge, mkd
pitch, some hdstg, pt shd; htd wc; chem disp; mv service pnt;
shwrs inc; el pnts (16A) €3; lndtte (inc dryer); supmkt 1.5km;
rest, snacks; bar; BBQ; cooking facs; playgrnd; Lake Auensee
500m; TV; dogs €2; phone; bus; tram 1.5km; poss cr; Eng
spkn; adv bkg; ccard acc; CKE/CCI. "Roomy, well-run, clean
site; plentiful san facs; gd size pitches; vg rest; friendly, helpful
staff; 10 mins walk to tram for city cent or bus stop at site ent;
tickets avail fr recep; excel." ◆ € 23.50                 2012*

⊞ **LEMGO** *1C3* (500m S Urban) *52.02503, 8.90874*
Campingpark Lemgo, Regenstorstrasse 10, 32657 Lemgo
[(05261) 14858; fax 188324; info@camping-lemgo.de;
www.camping-lemgo.de] Exit A2 junc 28 onto L712N
to Lemgo; at traff lts turn L following L712; at rnd abt take
Bismarckstrasse exit; at traff lts turn R into Regenstorstrasse.
Site sp. Med, pt shd; wc; shwrs €0.50; el pnts (6A) metered
+ conn fee; lndtte (inc dryer); shop 500m; rest 300m; snacks
500m; playgrnd; pool 200m; wifi; 25% statics; dogs €2; adv
bkg. "Slightly scruffy site but in cent of lovely medieval town;
o'night area for m'vans - modern san facs." € 19.50     2010*

## "We must tell The Club about that great site we found"

Get your site reports in by mid-August and we'll do our best to get your updates into the next edition.

⊞ **LENGERICH** *1C3* (2km W Rural) *52.18854, 7.80439*
Campingplatz auf dem Sonnenhügel, Zur Sandgrube
40, 49525 Lengerich [(05481) 6216; fax 845829; info@
sonnenhuegel-camping.de; www.sonnenhuegel-
camping.de] Leave A1 Lengerich/Tecklenburg, turn R at
bottom of slip rd onto S ring rd; L into Ibbenbüren Str; R &
immed R again into Antruper Str; foll rd under S ring; R into
Sonnenhügeldamm; foll sp. Med, pt shd; wc; chem disp; shwrs
€0.50; el pnts €2 or metered; gas; lndtte; rest 1km; bar; shop;
playgrnd; lake sw adj; fishing; 80% statics; dogs €2; clsd 1300-
1500; Eng spkn; adv bkg; a'bahn noise; ccard acc; CKE/CCI.
"Immac facs; vg value." ◆ € 14.00                          2011*

**LENZEN** *2E2* (5km E Rural) *53.11000, 11.54083*
Naturcampingplatz am Rudower See, Leuengarten 9,
19309 Lenzen [(038792) 80075 or (030854) 4020 (winter);
fax 80076; info@naturcampingplatz.de; www.
naturcampingplatz.de] Fr B195 turn N along S side of
Rudower See, site sp. Site at E end of lake. Med, terr, pt shd;
htd wc; chem disp; fam bthrm; shwrs inc; el pnts (16A) €1.75;
gas; lndtte; shop 4km; tradsmn; rest & bar 2km; snacks;
playgrnd; lake sw adj; boat hire; games area; 20% statics; dogs
€2.50; phone; adv bkg; quiet. "Peaceful site in nature park;
gd facs; helpful owners; gd walking, cycling, birdwatching; gd
NH." ◆ 1 Apr-15 Oct. € 17.00                              2010*

## "I need an on-site restaurant"

We do our best to make sure site information is correct, but it is always best to check any must-have facilities are still available or will be open during your visit.

**LIETZOW** *2G1* (300m N Coastal) *54.48358, 13.50846*
Störtebecker Camp, Gästehaus Lietzow, Waldstraße 59a,
18528 Lietzow [038302 2166; info@lietzow.net; www.
lietzow.net] On rd 96, E22 fr Stralsund to ferry harbour at
Sassnitz; when you arr at Lietzow site sp 'Gästehaus Lietzow'
on RH side of rd; sh, steep incline fr main rd. Med, hdg pitch,
pt shd; wc; chem disp; MV waste; shwrs inc; el pnts inc; gas;
lndtte; tradsmn; rest, snacks; bar; playgrnd; beach 250m; dogs
€2.50; adv bking; CKE/CCI. "Pleasant site, cent for the island,
sightseeing & useful stopover nr ferry point, many mkd cycle
rtes around island." 15 Mar-15 Dec. € 30.50              2013*

**LIMBURG AN DER LAHN** *3C2* (4km SW Rural) *50.38151,
8.00046* Camping Oranienstein, Strandbadweg, 65582
Diez [(06432) 2122; fax 924193; info@camping-diez.
de; www.camping-diez.de] In Diez on L bank of Lahn. Exit
A3 junc 41 Diez or junc 43 Limburg-Süd. Site sp 1km bef
Diez, 8km fr a'bahn. Lge, pt shd; wc; chem disp; mv service
pnt; shwrs; el pnts (6A) inc; gas; lndtte; shop; rest; playgrnd;
children's pool; watersports; cycle hire; 60% statics; dogs; adv
bkg; ccard acc; CKE/CCI. "Pleasant vill; gd rests; hot water
metered; gd NH." ◆ 1 Apr-31 Oct. € 24.85                2014*

**LIMBURG AN DER LAHN** *3C2* (200m W Urban) *50.38916,
8.07333* Lahn Camping, Schleusenweg 16, 65549
Limburg-an-der-Lahn [(06431) 22610; fax 92013; info@
lahncamping.de; www.lahncamping.de] Exit A3/E35 junc
42 Limburg Nord, site sp. By Rv Lahn in town, easy access.
Lge, pt shd; wc; chem disp; mv service pnt; baby facs; shwrs
€1; el pnts (6A) €2.60 (long lead poss req); gas; lndtte; shop;
rest; playgrnd; htd pool 100m; rv sw & fishing; 20% statics;
dogs €1.50; bus; poss v cr; Eng spkn; rd & rlwy noise; red CKE/
CCI. "Busy, well-organised site; sm pitches - some poss diff
to manoeuvre; gd views; friendly staff; poss flooding in wet
weather; sh walk to interesting town; gates clsd 1300-1500;
useful NH." ◆ 28 Mar-27 Oct. € 26.70                     2013*

**GERMANY**

⊞ **LINDAU (BODENSEE)** *3D4* (5km N Rural) *47.58509, 9.70667* **Campingpark Gitzenweiler Hof, Gitzenweiler 88, 88131 Lindau-Gitzenweiler [(08382) 94940; fax 949415; info@gitzenweiler-hof.de; www.gitzenweiler-hof.de]** Exit A96/E43/E54 junc 4 onto B12 sp Lindau. Turn off immed after vill of Oberreitnau twd Rehlings. Site well sp fr all dirs. Lge, mkd pitch, pt sl, pt shd; wc; chem disp; mv service pnt; serviced pitches; baby facs; shwrs inc; el pnts (6A) €2.50; gas; lndtte; shop; rest, snacks; playgrnd; pool; sm boating/fishing lake; lake sw 6km; entmnt high ssn; TV; 50% statics; dogs €2.50; bus 1km; o'night facs for m'vans; Eng spkn; adv bkg; poss noisy high ssn; red long stay; CKE/CCI. "Well-run, busy site in scenic area; gd facs; friendly staff; excel site for children; gd cycling; poss prone to flooding after v heavy rain; pitches poorly maintained; poss cr." ♦ € 33.30                      2014*

**LINDAU (BODENSEE)** *3D4* (4km SE Rural) *47.53758, 9.73743* **Park-Camping Lindau am See, Fraunhoferstrasse 20, 88131 Lindau-Zech [(08382) 72236; fax 976106; info@park-camping.de; www.park-camping.de]** On B31 fr Bregenz to Lindau, 200m after customs turn L to site in 150m; ent could be missed; mini-mkt on corner; ent rd crosses main rlwy line with auto barriers. B31 fr Friedrichshafen, site well sp fr o'skts of Lindau. Lge, mkd pitch, hdstg, pt shd; wc; chem disp; mv service pnt; shwrs inc; el pnts (10A) €1 (long lead poss req); lndtte (inc dryer); sm shop; mini-mkt nr; rest, snacks; playgrnd; shgl beach; lake sw; cycle hire; golf 3km; wifi; entmnt high ssn; 20% statics; dogs €3; m'van o'night area €10; poss cr; Eng spkn; rd & rlwy noise. "Busy site; immac san facs; sh stay pitches poss diff to manoeuvre as v cramped; office/gate clsd 1300-1400; helpful staff; shwr rm for dogs; excel walking in Pfänder area; excel." ♦ 15 Mar-10 Nov. € 26.50      2010*

**LINDENBERG IM ALLGAU** *3D4* (1km S Rural) *47.59789, 9.90047* **Camping Alpenblick, Schreckenmanklitz 18, 88171 Weiler-Simmerberg [(08381) 3447; fax 942195; info@camping-alpenblick.de; www.camping-alpenblick.de]** On S of B308 bet Lindau & Immenstadt. Turn off B308 opp hotels sp 'Schreckenmanklitz. Site in 200m on L, visible fr rd. Diff ent - do not attempt to turn in fr dir Lindau - cont 200m to turning point (mkd 'wendelplatz') & return. Med, mkd pitch, terr, pt shd; wc; chem disp; mv service pnt; shwrs €0.20; el pnts (10A) metered + conn fee; lndtte; shops 700m; tradsmn; rest 800m; snacks; playgrnd; lake sw; 60% statics; dogs €3; adv bkg; quiet; red CKE/CCI. "Pleasant site with gd views fr some pitches; gd san facs; gd." 1 Mar-30 Oct. € 19.50                      2011*

⊞ **LINGERHAHN** *3B2* (1km NE Rural) *50.09980, 7.57330* **Campingpark am Mühlenteich, Am Mühlenteich 1, 56291 Lingerhahn [(06746) 533; fax 1566; info@muehlenteich. de; www.muehlenteich.de]** Exit A61/E31 exit junc 44 to Laudert & Lingerhahn. In Lingerhahn foll sp Pfalzfeld, site sp. Lge, unshd; wc; chem disp; mv service pnt; serviced pitches; baby facs; shwrs inc; el pnts (6A) €2; lndtte; shop; tradsmn; rest, snacks; playgrnd; pool; tennis; entmnt; golf 12km; 75% statics; dogs €3.50; ent clsd 1300-1500 & 2200; poss cr; adv bkg; quiet; 10% red CKE/CCI. "Delightful rest & beer garden; excel site." € 22.50                      2012*

**LIPPETAL LIPPBORG see Hamm** *1B3*

**LIPPSTADT** *1C4* (7km E Rural) *51.70095, 8.40808* **Campingparadies Lippstadter Seenplatte, Seeufer Straße 16, 59558 Lippstadt [02 948 22 53; fax 02948 28 94 14; info@camping-lippstadt.de; www.camping-lippstadt. de]** Turn R off B55 to Lipperode. In town turn R onto Niederdedinghauser. After 2.5km turn L onto Seeuferstraße. Site 200m on R. Sm, mkd pitch, pt shd; wc; chem disp; mv service pnt; baby facs; shwr; el pnts (16A); lndtte (inc dryer); playgrnd; bike hire; 25% statics; dogs €2.50; bus 200m; twin axles; adv bkg; quiet; CCI. " Vg site; fishing in adj lake". ♦ 1 Mar-31 Oct. € 27.00                      2014*

**LOISSIN see Greifswald** *2G1*

**LORCH** *3C2* (5km SE Rural) *50.01820, 7.85493* **Naturpark Camping Suleika, Im Bodenthal 2, 65391 Lorch-bei-Rüdesheim [(06726) 9464; fax 9440; suleika-camping@t-online.de; www.suleika-camping.de]** Site off B42 on E bank of Rv Rhine, 3km NW of Assmannshausen. 3km SE of Lorch foll sp over rlwy x-ing on narr winding, steep rd thro vineyards to site. App poss diff for lge o'fits. Sm, pt sl, terr, pt shd; wc; mv service pnt; serviced pitches; shwrs inc; el pnts (16A) metered + conn fee; lndtte; shop; rest, snacks; playgrnd; cycle hire; dogs €2; poss cr; quiet; sep car park; red CKE/CCI. "Vg site in magnificent setting; excursions by Rhine steamer, local places of interest, wine district; access & exit 1-way system; helpful staff; excel rest." 15 Mar-31 Oct. € 18.00      2010*

⊞ **LORRACH** *3B4* (1.5km N Rural) *47.62461, 7.66275* **Drei-Länder Camp, Grüttweg 8, 79539 Lörrach [(07621) 82588; fax 165034; info@dreilaendercamp.de; www. dreilaendercamp.de]** Exit A98/E54 junc 5. Turn L at 1st traff lts after rv bdge on ent Lörrach & site 100m on L, sp. Med, unshd; wc; chem disp; mv service pnt; baby facs; shwrs €0.60; el pnts (16A) metered + €3 conn fee; lndtte; shop & 300m; rest, snacks; playgrnd; tennis; internet; 30% statics; dogs €3.50; Eng spkn; ccard acc; red CKE/CCI. "Gd facs; lge park adj; clsd 1300-1500; gd NH." ♦ € 24.60      2011*

⊞ **LOWENSTEIN** *3D3* (1km NW Rural) *49.11697, 9.38321* **Camping Heilbronn Breitenauer See, 74245 Löwenstein [(07130) 8558; fax 3622; info@breitenauer-see.de; www. breitenauer-see.de]** Exit m'way A81 (E41) at Weinsberg/ Ellhofen exit & on B39 twd Löwenstein/Schwäbisch Hall; site in approx 8km. V lge, mkd pitch, pt shd; htd wc; chem disp; mv service pnt; baby facs; fam bthrm; shwrs inc; el pnts (16A) €2 or metered + conn fee; gas; lndtte; shop, rest, snacks; bar; playgrnd; lake sw adj; boating; watersports; golf 15km; dog-washing facs; child entmnt high ssn; 50% statics; dogs €5; poss cr; Eng spkn; adv bkg; quiet; ccard acc; 10% red long stay/low ssn; red CKE/CCI. "Lake walks; beautiful location; pleasant site close to A6 & A81; all facs highest quality; some fully serviced pitches; excel." ♦ € 23.50      2013*

⊞ **LUBBEN** *2G3* (8km SE Rural) *51.86965, 13.9799*
Spreewald-Natur-Camping am Schlosspark, Schlossbezirk 20, 03222 Lübbenau [tel/fax (03542) 3533; info@ spreewaldcamping.de; www.spreewaldcamping.de] Leave A13 at junc 9, foll rd 115 into Lübbenau. Site well sp. Med, hdstg, pt shd; wc; chem disp; mv service pnt; shwrs €1; el pnts (16A) metered + conn fee; gas; lndtte; shop; bar; snacks & rest adj; BBQ; canoe hire; cycle hire; dogs €2; phone; poss cr; adv bkg; quiet; CKE/CCI. "Cent of Spreewald nature reserve; Lehde Vill open-air heritage museum 2km; boat trips on Rv Spree in punts; excel walking, cycling, canoeing; highly rec; excel site, gd san facs." ♦ € 19.50                                    2011*

**LUBBEN** *2G3* (500m S Urban) *51.93641, 13.89490*
Spreewald Camping, Am Burglehn 218, 15907 Lübben [(03546) 7053 or 3335 or 8874; fax 181815; info@ spreewald-camping-luebben.de; www.spreewald-camping-luebben.de] Fr N on A13 exit junc 7 at Freiwalde onto B115 twd Lübben. In town cent turn R to stay on B115 sp Lübbenau. Site on L - well sp. Or fr S exit junc 8 onto B87 to Lübben. Cross rlwy, cont along Luckauerstrasse. Turn R at traff lts into Puschkinstrasse, sp Cottbus. Site on L, well sp. Lge, pt shd; wc; chem disp; mv service pnt; shwrs €0.50; el pnts (10A) metered; gas; lndtte (inc dryer); shop 400m; rest; playgrnd; wifi; 20% statics; dogs free; adv bkg; quiet; CKE/CCI. "Excel location; modern, clean facs; excel cycle rtes; adj rv for boating; conv for Berlin." ♦ 15 Mar-31 Oct. € 23.00                2012*

⊞ **LUBECK** *2E2* (3.5km W Rural) *53.86943, 10.63086*
Campingplatz Lübeck-Schünböcken, Steinrader Damm 12, 23556 Lübeck-Schönböcken [tel/fax (0451) 893090; info@ camping-luebeck.de; www.camping-luebeck.de] Fr A1 exit junc 23 for Lübeck-Moisling & foll sp to Schönböcken & then camp sp (not v obvious); turn R at traff lts bef Dornbreite, site in 1km on L. Med, pt sl, unshd; wc; chem disp; mv service pnt; shwrs €0.50; el pnts (6A) €2.50; gas; lndtte; shop; playgrnd; dogs €1; bus to town; wifi; Eng spkn; quiet; CKE/CCI. "Helpful owners; busy site; gd san facs but poss stretched if site full; conv Travemünde ferries; Lübeck interesting town; cycle path to town; vg; some rd noise; nice place." € 24.00        2014*

⊞ **LUNEBURG** *1D2* (4km S Rural) *53.20303, 10.40976*
Camping Rote Schleuse, Rote Schleuse 4, 21335 Lüneburg [(04131) 791500; fax 791695; camproteschleuse@aol.com; www.camproteschleuse.de] Exit A250 junc 4 onto Neu Häcklingen twd Lüneburg. Site sp to R in 300m. Med, pt shd; wc; chem disp; shwrs €0.50; el pnts €2.50 or metered; lndtte; shop; tradsmn; rest adj; snacks; bar; playgrnd; pool; cycle hire; internet; 60% statics; dogs €1; bus fr site ent; clsd 1300-1500; poss cr; Eng spkn; adv bkg; quiet. "Pleasant owners; interesting town." € 19.30                                         2013*

⊞ **LUTHERSTADT WITTENBERG** *2F3* (1.5km S Rural) *51.85465, 12.64563* Marina-Camp Elbe, Brückenkopf 1, 06888 Lutherstadt-Wittenberg [(03491) 4540; fax 454199; info@marina-camp-elbe.de; www.marina-camp-elbe.de] Site on S side of Elbe bdge on B2 dir Leipzig; well sp. Med, pt shd; wc; chem disp; mv service pnt; serviced pitches; baby facs; sauna; shwrs inc; el pnts (16A) metered + conn fee; gas; lndtte (inc dryer); shop 1.5km; tradsmn; BBQ; cooking facs; snacks; marina adj; cycle hire; wifi; TV; dogs €1.50; bus at gate; quiet; ccard acc; CKE/CCI. "Delightful rvside site; excel, modern san facs." ♦ € 23.00                                    2011*

⊞ **LUTHERSTADT WITTENBERG** *2F3* (11km S Rural) *51.79135, 12.56995* Camping Bergwitzsee, Zeltplatz, 06773 Bergwitz [(034921) 28228; fax 28778; info@ bergwitzsee.de; www.bergwitzsee.de] S fr Berlin on B2 thro Wittenberg, then thro Eutzsch, bear R onto B100 into Bergwitz; at cent site is sp, foll to lake, turn R & site ahead. Fr main rd to site thro vill 1.5km, cobbled. Site on lakeside. Lge, shd; wc; chem disp; mv service pnt; shwrs €0.50; el pnts (10-16A) €2; lndtte; shop; tradsmn; rest, snacks; bar; playgrnd; lake sw & sand beach; fishing; watersports; games area; cycle hire; TV; 90% statics; dogs €3; adv bkg rec; red CKE/CCI. "Interesting town - Martin Luther Haus; gd cycling/walking area; quiet, restful site; Lakeside site nr Ferropolis, popular with families." ♦ € 16.30                                           2012*

## "There aren't many sites open at this time of year"

If you're travelling outside peak season remember to call ahead to check site opening dates – even if the entry says 'open all year'.

**MAGDEBURG** *2E3* (12km N Rural) *52.21888, 11.65944* Campingplatz Barleber See, Wiedersdorferstrasse, 39126 Magdeburg [(0391) 503244; fax 2449692; campingplatz@ cvbs.de; www.cvbs.de] Exit A2/E30 junc 71 sp Rothensee-Barleber See; site 1km N of a'bahn. Lge, mkd pitch, pt shd; wc; chem disp; mv service pnt; shwrs inc; el pnts (10A) €2; gas; lndtte; shop; tradsmn; rest, snacks; bar; playgrnd; pool; sand beach adj; lake sw; cycle hire; wifi; 60% statics; dogs €2; poss cr; Eng spkn; no adv bkg; poss noisy w/end; fairly quiet; red long stay/CKE/CCI. "Gd beach & watersports; pleasant site; helpful staff; gd sports facs; gd touring base." ♦ ltd 1 May-30 Sep. € 25.00                                            2014*

**MAINZ** *3C2* (2.5km SE Urban) *50.00296, 8.28556* Camping Internationaler Mainz-Wiesbaden Maaraue, Maaraue 48, 55246 Mainz-Kostheim [(06134) 4383; fax 707137; camping@camping-maaraue.de; www.krkg.de/camping] App fr A671 exit 'Hochheim Süd' foll sp for Kostheim then Int'l camping sp. Med, mkd pitch, pt shd; wc; chem disp; shwrs inc; el pnts (16A) inc; gas; lndtte; shop; rest adj; bar; pool adj; tennis; dogs €3; adv bkg; quiet; ccard not acc; red CKE/ CCI. "Site on island next to Rv Rhine/Maine junc; o'looks city on opp bank; excel for Rhine cruises; gd NH." 1 Apr-31 Oct. € 23.00                                             2009*

⊞ **MALCHOW** *2F2* (5km NE Rural) *53.49216, 12.37412* Naturcamping Malchow am Plauer See, Am Plauser See 1, 17213 Malchow [(039932) 49907; fax 49908; malchow@ campingtour-mv.de; www.campingtour-mv.de] Exit A19/ E55 junc 16 onto B192 dir Schwerin. Turn L at camping sp in 500m down narr lane. Lge, mkd pitch, pt shd; wc; chem disp; mv service pnt; baby facs; shwrs metered; el pnts (10A) €2.50; gas; lndtte; shop; tradsmn; rest; bar; BBQ; cooking facs; playgrnd; sand beach & lake sw adj; 30% statics; dogs €2.90; phone; poss cr; Eng spkn; adv bkg; quiet; CKE/CCI. "Vg NH bet Rostock ferry & Berlin; excel, modern facs; all hot water metered; Malchow swing bdge worth visit." ♦ € 20.20 2011*

GERMANY

⊞ **MALLISS** *2E2* (2km SE Rural) *53.19596, 11.34046*
**Camping am Wiesengrund, Am Kanal 4, 19294 Malliss
[tel/fax (038750) 21060; sielaff-camping@t-online.de;
www.camping-malliss-vp.de]** Sp in Malliss on rd 191
fr Ludwigslust to Uelzen. Sm, pt shd; wc; chem disp; mv
service pnt; shwrs €0.75; el pnts (16A) €2; gas; lndtte; shop
& 2km; tradsmn; rest 2km; snacks; bar; playgrnd; rv sw adj;
watersports; cycle hire; 30% statics; dogs €2.50; phone;
m'van o'night facs; quiet; red CKE/CCI. "Well-run, pleasant,
family site; beautiful surroundings; barrier clsd 1200-1400;
visit Ludwigslust Palace & Dömitz Fortress; vg; Lovely site and v
friendly staff." € 16.50                          2012*

⊞ **MALSCH** *3C3* (2km S Rural) *48.86165, 8.33789*
**Campingpark Bergwiesen, Waldenfelsstrasse 1, 76316
Malsch [(07246) 1467; fax 5762; email@Campingpark-
Bergwiesen.eu; www.Campingpark-Bergwiesen.
eu]** Fr Karlsruhe on B3 thro Malsch vill over level x-ing to
Waldprechtsweier. Foll site sp, take care tight L turn & steep
app thro residential area. Lge, hdg/mkd pitch, hdstg, terr,
pt shd; wc; chem disp; serviced pitches; shwrs inc; el pnts
(16A) metered + conn fee; gas; lndtte; shop 200m; tradsmn;
rest; bar; playgrnd; pool 1km; sw adj; 80% statics; dogs €2;
Eng skn; adv bkg (no fee); quiet; red CKE/CCI. "1st class
facs; well-run site in beautiful forest setting; v friendly site &
owner; not rec for long o'fits or lge m'vans; gd walks fr site."
€ 18.80                                          2011*

**MANDERSCHEID see Wittlich** *3B2*

## "That's changed – Should I let The Club know?"

If you find something on site that's different from
the site entry, fill in a report and let us know. See
www.caravanclub.co.uk/europereport.

**MANNHEIM** *3C2* (3km S Urban) *49.44841, 8.44806* **Camping
am Strandbad, Strandbadweg 1, 68199 Mannheim-
Neckarau [(0621) 8619967; fax 8619968; anfrage@
campingplatz-mannheim.de]** Exit A6 Karlsruhe-Frankfurt
at AB Kreuz Mannheim (junc 27) L onto A656 Mannheim-
Neckarau. Exit junc 2 onto B36 dir Neckarau, site sp. Med, pt
shd; wc; mv service pnt; shwrs €1; el pnts (16A) metered; gas;
lndtte; shop 2km; rest 300m; snacks; shgl beach & rv sw; wifi;
60% statics; dogs €1.50; poss cr; quiet; CKE/CCI. "Some noise
fr barges on Rhine & factories opp; poss flooding at high water;
interesting area." 1 Apr-31 Oct. € 20.00                2009*

**MARBURG AN DER LAHN** *1C4* (1.5km S Urban) *50.80000,
8.76861* **Camping Lahnaue, Trojedamm 47, 35037
Marburg-an-der-Lahn [(06421) 21331; fax 499177; info@
lahnaue.de; www.lahnaue.de]** Site by Rv Lahn, app fr sports
cent. Exit a'bahn at Marburg Mitte & sp fr a'bahn. Med, mkd
pitch, pt shd; wc; chem disp; shwrs inc; el pnts (10A) €2; lndtte
(inc dryer); shops 1km; tradsmn; rest 1.5km; snacks; bar; pool
adj; rv canoeing; tennis, sw & boating nrby; 10% statics; dogs
€2.50; clsd 1300-1500; poss cr; Eng spkn; quiet but mv &
rlwy noise; ccard acc; CKE/CCI. "Busy site; some pitches v narr;
cycle & footpath to interesting town; excel pool adj; gd." ♦
1 Apr-30 Oct. € 27.00                            2013*

**MARKDORF** *3D4* (2km E Rural) *47.71503, 9.40925*
**Camping Wirthshof, Steibensteg 12, 88677 Markdorf
[(07544) 96270; fax 962727; info@wirthshof.de; www.
wirthshof.de]** Take B33 Markdorf to Ravensburg; site on
R sp Camping/Schwimbad/Mini-Golf, in vill of Steibensteg.
Lge, pt shd; wc; mv service pnt; sauna; shwrs inc; el pnts (6A)
inc; lndtte; shop; rest; playgrnd; pool; cycle hire; golf 10km;
entmnt; dogs €4 (reservation req Jul & Aug); clsd 1200-1400;
poss cr; debit cards acc. "Excel; activities for children &
teenagers; gd sightseeing; special pitches for m'vans in quiet
area with el pnts; immac facs; excel rest; helpful owners;
Markdorf vill picturesque; gd walking/cycling rtes; Thurs
mkt; boat trips on Bodensee; gd tourist info; wonderful." ♦
1 Mar-30 Oct. € 27.70                            2009*

See advert on bookmark

⊞ **MARKTHEIDENFELD** *3D2* (3km S Rural) *49.81885,
9.58851* **Camping Main-Spessart-Park, Spessartstrasse
30, 97855 Triefenstein-Lengfurt [(09395) 1079; fax 8295;
info@camping-main-spessart.de; www.camping-main-
spessart.de]** Exit A3/E41 junc 65 or 66 sp Lengfurt. In Lengfurt
foll sp Marktheidenfeld; site in 1km. Lge, pt sl, terr, pt shd; wc;
chem disp; mv service pnt; serviced pitches; shwrs inc; el pnts
(6-10A) €3; lndtte; shop; rest; playgrnd; pool adj; watersports;
50% statics; dogs €2.50; Eng spkn; adv bkg; ccard acc; red
CKE/CCI. "High quality site; vg rest; vg san facs; easy
access A4; sep NH area; helpful owners; access diff parts of site
due steep terrs; busy site; gd facs." ♦ € 32.50       2014*

⊞ **MARKTOBERDORF** *4E4* (6km NW Rural) *47.80285,
10.55360* **Campingplatz Elbsee, Am Elbsee 3, 87648
Aitrang [(08343) 248; fax 1406; info@elbsee.de; www.
elbsee.de]** W fr Marktoberdorf on B472 onto B12. Turn N
foll sp to Elbsee. Fr Kempten E on B12 to Unterthingau N to
Aitrang, site 2km S of vill. Lge, mkd pitch, pt sl, pt shd; htd
wc; chem disp; mv service pnt; serviced pitches; sauna; shwrs
inc; el pnts (16A) metered + conn fee; lndtte (inc dryer); shop;
tradsmn; rest adj; BBQ; playgrnd; lake sw & boating adj;
solarium; cycle hire; wifi; TV rm; 60% statics; dogs €4.50;
phone; o'night facs for m'vans; site clsd 4 Nov-16 Dec; Eng
spkn; adv bkg; ccard acc; red CKE/CCI. "Excel, friendly, family-
owned site; clean, modern facs; gd shwr rm + hairdryer; well
mkd walk signs fr site." ♦ € 24.70                 2011*

⊞ **MEDELBY** *1D1* (300m W Rural) *54.81490, 9.16361*
**Camping Kawan Mitte, Sonnenhügel 1, 24994 Medelby
[(04605) 189391; info@camping-mitte.de; www.
campingkawanmitte.eu]** Exit A7 junc 2 onto B199 dir
Niebüll to Wallsbüll, turn N dir Medelby, site sp. Lge, mkd
pitch, pt shd; htd wc; chem disp; mv service pnt; baby facs;
fam bthrm; sauna; shwrs inc; el pnts (16A) metered; lndtte (inc
dryer); shop; supmkt 600m; rest 600m; snacks; BBQ; cooking
facs; playgrnd; 2 htd pool; games area; fitness rm; cycle hire;
horseriding 600m; golf 12km; wifi; TV rm; 20% statics; dogs
free; adv bkg; quiet; CKE/CCI. "Conv m'way & Danish border;
vg." ♦ € 24.00 (CChq acc)                        2013*

**MEERBUSCH see Düsseldorf** *1B4*

GERMANY

MEISSEN *2G4* (3km SE Rural) *51.13942, 13.49883* **Camping Rehbocktal, Rehbocktal 4, 01665 Scharfenberg-bei-Meissen [(03521) 404827; fax 404828; info@camping-rehbocktal.de; www.camping-rehbocktal.de]** Exit E40/A4 at Dresden Altstadt; foll sp Meissen on B6 to Scharfenberg; site on L opp Rv Elbe. Med, pt sl, pt shd; wc; chem disp; shwrs inc; el pnts (16A) €3; lndtte; shop & 3km; tradsmn; rest adj; snacks; bar; playgrnd; 10% statics; dogs €2; bus; poss cr; no adv bkg; v quiet; CKE/CCI. "In wooded valley opp vineyard; friendly staff; conv Colditz; Meissen factory & museum worth visit; cycle path to Meissen nr." 15 Mar-31 Oct. € 26.00       2013*

**MEISSENDORF see Winsen (Aller)** *1D3*

> # "I like to fill in the reports as I travel from site to site"
> You'll find report forms at the back of this guide, or you can fill them in online at www.caravaclub.co.uk/europereport.

⊞ **MELLE** *1C3* (3km W Rural) *52.22428, 8.2661* Campingplatz Grönegau-Park Ludwigsee, Nemdenerstrasse 12, 49326 Melle [(05402) 2132; fax 2112; info@ludwigsee.de; www.ludwigsee.de] Exit A30/E30 junc 22 twd Bad Essen, site sp on lakeside. Lge, hdg/mkd pitch, pt shd; wc; chem disp; mv service pnt; shwrs €1; el pnts (10A) inc; lndtte; shop 1.5km; rest, snacks; bar; playgrnd; lake sw; games area; cycle hire; internet; entmnt; 80% statics; dogs €2; sep car park; barrier clsd 1300-1500; adv bkg; quiet; ccard acc; red CKE/CCI. "Beautiful & pleasant site; helpful owners; sep area for tourers." € 30.00       2014*

**MEMMINGEN** *3D4* (10km S Rural) *47.94871, 10.08578* **Park-Camping Iller, Illerstrasse 57, 88317 Aitrach [(07565) 5419; fax 5222; info@camping-iller.de; www.camping-iller.de]** Exit A96/E43/E54 junc 11, site in 3km, sp. Or fr Memmingen take rd dir Leutkirch. In Ferthofen vill look for camping sp & turn R after rv bdge. In Aitrach turn R, site 1km on L. Lge, pt shd; htd wc; chem disp; mv service pnt; serviced pitches; baby facs; fam bthrm; shwrs inc; el pnts (10A) €2.50; gas; lndtte (inc dryer); shop; tradsmn; rest 1.5km; snacks; bar; playgrnd; pool; paddling pool; tennis; games rm; internet; 75% statics; dogs €2; o'night area for m'vans; poss cr; adv bkg; quiet; Eng spkn; ccard acc; red snr citizens/CKE/CCI. "Gd family site; helpful staff; gd walking, cycling." ♦ 1 May-15 Oct. € 24.50       2011*

⊞ **MENDIG** *3B2* (2km NNW Rural) *50.38646, 7.27237* Camping Siesta, Laacherseestrasse 6, 56743 Mendig [(02652) 1432; fax 520424; service@campingsiesta.de; www.campingsiesta.de] Fr A61 exit junc 34 for Mendig dir Maria Laach; foll camp sps; site on R in 300m by ent to car park. Med, some hdg pitch, sl, pt shd; wc; chem disp; shwrs inc; el pnts (16A) €1.80; gas; lndtte; tradsmn; rest; bar; playgrnd; sm pool; sw pool 500m; 60% statics; dogs €1.30; poss v cr; Eng spkn; noise fr nrby a'bahn; CKE/CCI. "Useful NH; easy access fr A61; owner helpful in siting NH o'fits; longest waterslide in Europe; gd base for region's castles & wines; friendly owners; spotless site; gd rest; site has so much more to offer than only a NH; v welcoming; vg refurbished; new san facs (2014)." € 24.00       2014*

**MENDIG** *3B2* (4km N Rural) *50.42151, 7.26448* **Camping Laacher See, Am Laacher See, 56653 Wassenach [(02636) 2485; fax 929750; info@camping-laacher-see.de; www.camping-laacher-see.de]** Fr A61, exit junc 34 Mendig. Foll tents sp to Maria Laach. Site on Laacher See. Lge, hdg/mkd pitch, hdstg, pt sl, pt terr, pt shd; htd wc; chem disp; mv service pnt; baby facs; shwrs €0.50; el pnts (16A) metered + conn fee; gas; lndtte (inc dryer); shop; tradsmn; rest, snacks; bar; playgrnd; lake sw; sailing; fishing; wifi; 50% statics; dogs €4; bus 500m; Eng spkn; quiet; adv bkg; ccard acc; CKE/CCI. "Neat, clean, relaxing site; all pitches lake views; busy at w/end; modern, outstanding san facs; gd woodland walks, cycling & sw; excel sailing facs; excel site & rest; close to m'way; rec." ♦ ltd 2 Apr-28 Sep. € 30.50       2014*

⊞ **MESCHEDE** *1C4* (7km S Rural) *51.29835, 8.26425* Knaus Campingpark Hennesee, Mielinghausen 7, 59872 Meschede [(0291) 952720; fax 9527229; hennesee@knauscamp.de; www.knauscamp.de] S fr Meschede on B55 for 7km; at sp for Erholungszentrum & Remblinghausen turn L over Lake Hennesee, site on L in 500m, sp. Lge, mkd pitch, terr, pt shd; wc; chem disp ltd; mv service pnt; sauna; serviced pitches; shwrs inc; el pnts (6A) conn fee; gas; lndtte; supmkt; rest, snacks; bar; playgrnd; lake sw 200m; cycle hire; entmnt high ssn; internet; 60% statics; dogs €3.80; poss cr; adv bkg; Eng spkn; quiet; red CKE/CCI. "Conv Sauerland mountains & lakes; 50m elec cable advisable; vg." € 28.70 (CChq acc)       2012*

**MESENICH see Trier** *3B2*

⊞ **METTINGEN** *1B3* (1.5km SW Rural) *52.31251, 7.76202* Camping Zur Schönen Aussicht, Schwarzestrasse 73, 49497 Mettingen [(05452) 606; fax 4751; info@camping-schoene-aussicht.de; www.camping-schoene-aussicht.de] Exit A30 junc 12 dir Mettingen. Go thro town cent, uphill turn L at traff lts, site sp. Med, hdg/mkd pitch, pt sl, pt shd; wc; chem disp; mv service pnt; shwrs €1.30; el pnts (10A) €3 or metered; lndtte; shop; rest; bar; playgrnd; htd, covrd pool; internet; 50% statics; no dogs; Eng spkn; adv bkg; quiet;CKE/CCI. "Nice, friendly site; gd walking, cycling; easy walk to town; gd facs." € 27.50       2014*

> # "We must tell The Club about that great site we found"
> Get your site reports in by mid-August and we'll do our best to get your updates into the next edition.

**MILTENBERG** *3D2* (500m N Urban) *49.70366, 9.25417* **Camping Mainwiese, 12 Steingasserstrasse, 63897 Miltenberg [(09371) 3985; fax 68723; info@campingplatz-miltenberg.de; www.campingplatz-miltenberg.de]** On B469 to Miltenberg. Cross rv bdge dir Klingenberg. Ent in 200m on R, sp. Lge, unshd; wc; chem disp; mv service pnt; baby facs; shwrs inc; el pnts (16A) €2; lndtte; shop; rest adj; playgrnd; golf 10km; 25% statics; dogs €2; quiet; red long stay. "Poss long walk to san facs." 1 Apr-30 Sep. € 14.50       2009*

**GERMANY**

⊞ **MITTENWALD** 4E4 (4km N Rural) 47.47290, 11.27729
**Naturcamping Isarhorn, Am Horn 4, 82481 Mittenwald
[(08823) 5216; fax 8091; camping@mittenwald.de; www.
camping-isarhorn.de]** E fr Garmisch-Partenkirchen on rd 2;
at Krün turn S on D2/E533 dir Mittenwald. Site on R in approx
2km at int'l camping sp. Ent on R fr main rd. NB: Rd thro to
Innsbruck via Zirlerberg improved & no longer clsd to c'vans
descending S; long & steep; low gear; not to be attempted N.
Lge, pt shd, unmkd, some hdstg; wc; chem disp; mv service
pnt; shwrs €0.50; el pnts (16A) €2.80 or metered; Indtte; shop;
snacks; rest; BBQ; htd, covrd pool 4km; canoeing (white water);
ski lift; tennis; wifi; dogs €2.90; bus adj; site clsd 1300-1500 &
2200-0700; site clsd 1 Nov-mid Dec; Eng spkn; quiet but some
rd noise; ccard acc; red low ssn; CKE/CCI. "Relaxed, secluded
site in pines; mountain views; excel base for walking; cycle
track to attractive town; poss some noise fr nrby military base;
owner v keen on recycling waste; facs gd but insufficient for
size of site; highly rec; new san facs 2013." € 27.50      2013*

⊞ **MITTENWALD** 4E4 (8km N Rural) 47.49040, 11.25438
**Alpen-Caravanpark Tennsee, Am Tennsee 1,82493 Klais-
Krün [(08825) 170; fax 17236; info@camping-tennsee.
de; www.camping-tennsee.de]** N fr Mittenwald on main
Innsbruck-Garmisch rd turn off for Krun, foll Tennsee & site sp.
2km SE of Klais, not well sp. Lge, mkd pitch, hdstg, pt terr, pt
shd; htd wc; chem disp; mv service pnt; 50% serviced pitches;
family & baby facs; shwrs inc; el pnts (16A) metered; gas;
Indtte; shop & 2km; rest, snacks; bar; playgrnd; ski lift 2.5km;
cycle hire; entmnt; dogs €3.30; phone; poss cr; Eng spkn; adv
bkg; ccard acc; CKE/CCI. "Excel area for Bavarian Alps, Tirol;
site clsd Nov-mid Dec; barrier clsd 1200-1500; gd size pitches;
red snr citizens; vg, clean, friendly, family-run site; Price inc use
of tourist buses." ♦ € 49.00      2013*

## "I need an on-site restaurant"

We do our best to make sure site
information is correct, but it is always best
to check any must-have facilities are still
available or will be open during your visit.

⊞ **MITTERTEICH** 4F2 (3km NW Rural) 49.97311, 12.22497
**Campingplatz Großbüchlberg, Großbüchlberg 32, 95666
Mitterteich [09633 40 06 73; fax 40 06 77; camping@
freizeithugl.de; www.freizeithugl.de]** Fr A93 Marktredwitz-
Mitterteich take exit 16 Mitterteich. At xrds in town centre foll
Freizeithugl signs. Turn L after 200m twds Grossbuchberg. Foll
sp. Med, hdg pitch, mkd pitch, hdstg, pt sl, terr, pt shd; htd
wc; chem disp; mv service pnt; baby fasc; fam bthrm; shwrs
inc; el pnts (16A); Indtte (inc dryer); shop; rest; snacks; bar;
playgrnd; wifi; tv rm; dogs €1.50; phone adj; bus adj; twin
axles; poss cr; Eng spkn; adv bkg; quiet; ccard acc; CCI. "Excel
site; superb htd san facs; close to mini-golf, toboggan run, etc;
extensive views; v friendly." ♦ € 25.00      2014*

**MOHNESEE see Soest** 1C4

**MONSCHAU** 3A1 (1.5km SW Rural) 50.54305, 6.23694
**Camping Perlenau, 52156 Monschau [(02472) 4136;
fax 4493; familie.rasch@monschau-perlenau.de; www.
monschau-perlenau.de]** Fr N (Aachen) foll B258 past
Monschau dir Schleiden. Site on L just bef junc with B399 to
Kalterherberg. Steep & narr app. Fr Belgium, exit A3 junc 38 for
Eupen & foll rd thro Eupen to Monschau. Site on rvside. Med,
hdg/mkd pitch, hdstg, pt sl, terr, pt shd; htd wc; chem disp;
mv service pnt; baby facs; fam bthrm; shwrs; el pnts (10-16A)
€2.60 or metered; gas; Indtte; shop; tradsmn; rest, snacks;
bar; BBQ; cooking facs; playgrnd; 20% statics; dogs €2.60;
phone; bus 500m; poss cr; Eng spkn; adv bkg; quiet; red long
stay; CKE/CCI. "Gd touring base for Eifel region; attractive site
beside stream; historic town in walking dist." ♦ 20 Mar-
31 Oct. € 27.60      2013*

⊞ **MONTABAUR** 3C2 (6km SE Rural) 50.43761, 7.90498
**Camping Eisenbachtal, 56412 Girod [(06485) 766; fax
4938]** S on A3/E35 exit junc 41 dir Montabaur; at Girod turn
L to site, well sp. Med, hdg/mkd pitch, some hdstg, pt sl, pt
shd; htd wc; chem disp; mv service pnt; some serviced pitches;
shwrs €0.50; el pnts (4A) inc (poss rev pol); gas; Indtte;
tradsmn; 2 x rest adj; playgrnd; sw 5km; 75% statics; dogs
€2; poss cr; Eng spkn; adv bkg; quiet; red long stay; CKE/CCI.
"Beautiful, well-equipped site in Naturpark Nassau; conv NH
fr a'bahn & worth longer stay; friendly, welcoming staff; gd for
nature lovers & children; gd walking & cycling; adj rest excel;
site clsd 1300-1500 but car park opp; conv Rhine & Mosel
valleys." ♦ € 25.00      2014*

**MORFELDEN** 3C2 (5km SE Rural) 49.94461, 8.60544
**Campingplatz Am Steinrodsee, Triftweg 33, 64331
Weiterstadt [06150 53593; fax 591345; rezeption.
koehres@t-online.de; www.camping-steinrodsee.de]**
Leave A5 twds Darmstadt at exit 25. L at 2nd traff lts onto
L3113. Turn R in 5km & foll signs. Lge, hdg pitch, mkd pitch,
pt shd; htd wc; chem disp; mv service pnt; baby facs; shwrs
inc; el pnts (16A); Indtte (inc dryer); rest; bar; BBQ; playgrnd;
wifi; 60% statics; dogs; bus 2km; twin axles; quiet; CCI. "Vg
site; quiet with some aircraft noise; clean, tidy, well regulated
site; immac san facs; conv for Darmstadt." ♦ 1 Jan-31 Oct.
€ 23.00      2014*

**MORITZBURG** 4G1 (3km S Rural) 51.1450, 13.67444
**Campingplatz Bad Sonnenland, Dresdnerstrasse 115,
01468 Moritzburg [(0351) 8305495; fax 8305494; bad-
sonnenland@t-online.de; www.bad-sonnenland.de]**
Leave A4/E40 exit 80. Turn R sp Moritzburg, foll site sp thro
Reichenberg. Site on L 3km bef Moritzburg. Lge, pt shd; wc;
chem disp; mv service pnt; shwrs (inc); el pnts (16A) €2.50; gas;
Indtte; shop; supmkt 2km; rest, snacks; bar; playgrnd; lake sw
adj; games rm; games area; statics in sep area; dogs €3; bus
to Dresden; quiet; ccard acc; CKE/CCI. "Scenic area; friendly
staff; excel, immac facs; site clsd 1300-1500 & 2200-0700; also
holiday vill with many huts; conv Dresden, Meissen; narr gauge
steam train Dresden-Moritzburg; day trip to Prague; many mkd
walking & cycling rtes in area; Schloss Moritzburg in vill; vg
site." 1 Apr-31 Oct. € 25.70      2014*

**MOSCHWITZ see Plauen** 4F1

**MUDEN AN DER ORTZE see Fassberg** 1D2

⊞ MUHLBERG *2E4* (3km SW Rural) *50.87516, 10.80843*
Campingplatz Drei Gleichen, Am Gut Ringhofen,
99869 Mühlberg [(036256) 22715; fax 86801; service@
campingplatz-muehlberg.de; www.campingplatz-
muehlberg.de] Leave A4/E40 at junc 43 (Wandersleben) S
twds Mühlberg; site well sp in 2km on rd to Wechmar. Med,
hdg/mkd pitch, pt sl, unshd; wc; chem disp; mv service pnt;
shwrs €1; el pnts (16A) €1.80 + conn fee; lndtte; shop 3km;
rest adj; bar; playgrnd; sw adj; 50% statics; dogs €2.20; site
clsd 1300-1500; adv bkg; quiet; CKE/CCI. "Gd facs; helpful
staff; conv a'bahn." ♦ € 16.00                         2011*

**MUHLHAUSEN see Augsburg** *4E3*

## "Satellite navigation makes touring much easier"

Remember most sat navs don't know if
you're towing or in a larger vehicle – always
use yours alongside maps and site directions.

MUNCHEN *4E4* (5km S Urban) *48.09165, 11.54516* Camping
München-Thalkirchen, Zentralländstrasse 49, 81379
München [(089) 7231707; fax 7243177; campingplatz.
muenchen@web.de; www.muenchen.de] Fr S on A95/E533
at end of a'bahn keep strt on (ignore zoo sp). After tunnel exit
R at sp Thalkirchen. Turn L at traff lts & foll sp to camp. If app
fr S on A8/E45 turn L at traff lts at end twd Garmish & strt on
to tunnel, site sp. Fr NW at end of A8 in 200m turn R & foll sp
to zoo (Tierpark). Cont to foll zoo sp until in approx 10km pick
up sp to site. (Zoo on E side of Rv Isar, site on W side.) App fr N
not rec due v heavy traffic. V lge, mkd pitch, pt shd; htd wc;
chem disp; mv service pnt; many serviced pitches; shwrs €1;
el pnts (10A) €2 (long lead req); lndtte (inc dryer); shop; rest
500m; snacks; playgrnd; pool & rv 500m; internet; dogs inc;
phone; bus 100m; poss cr esp Oktoberfest; Eng spkn; quiet;
ccard not acc; CKE/CCI. "Busy site; some m'van/o'night pitches
v sm; bus/U-bahn tickets avail fr recep; cycle track/walk along
rv to town cent, avoiding traffic; helpful staff; san facs clean,
stretched when site full; gd site when visiting Munich." ♦
15 Mar-31 Oct. € 28.00                         2013*

MUNCHEN *4E4* (8km NW Rural) *48.17421,
11.44645* Waldcamping München-Obermenzing,
Lochhausenerstrasse 59, 81247 München [(089) 8112235;
fax 8144807; campingplatz-muenchen@t-online.
de; www.campingplatz-muenchen.de] Foll sp around
Munich ring rd to ent of A8 Munich/Stuttgart a'bahn;
passing m'way ent on L cont on Pippingerstrasse & site on
Lochhausenerstrasse; heavy traff to/fr S of site. Lge, hdg/mkd
pitch, pt shd; htd wc; chem disp; mv service pnt; serviced
pitches; shwrs €1; el pnts (10A) metered; gas; lndtte; shop;
tradsmn; snacks; bar; cooking facs; pool 3km; internet;
10% statics; dogs €1; bus to city 1km, train 2km; poss cr;
Eng spkn; no adv bkg; m'way noise; CKE/CCI. "Pleasant
management; Park & Ride to city 3km; variable size pitches,
some narr, & poss overgrown; v busy & noisy during beer
festival & prices increased." 15 Mar-31 Oct. € 22.00    2009*

⊞ MUNCHEN *4E4* (10km NW Urban) *48.19888, 11.49694*
Campingplatz Nord-West, Auf den Schrederwiesen
3, 80995 München-Moosach [(089) 1506936; info@
campingplatz-nord-west.de; www.campingplatz-nord-
west.de] Fr N exit A99 junc 10 Lugwigsfeld onto B304
S - Dachauerstrasse, sp München. Turn L in approx 800m at
traff lts. Turn R at T-junc to site on R. Med, hdstg, shd; htd
wc; chem disp; mv service pnt; shwrs €1.50; el pnts (10-16A)
€5 or metered; lndtte (inc dryer); shop & 1km; tradsmn; rest
3km; snacks; bar; entmnt; 50% statics; dogs €2; phone; bus
to city; poss cr; Eng spkn; adv bkg; quiet; ccard acc; CKE/CCI.
"Friendly, helpful welcome; enquire about public transport
tickets; ltd facs low ssn; Dachau - pretty town 10km; gd." ♦
€ 24.40                         2014*

⊞ MUNCHEN *4E4* (12km NW Rural) *48.19821, 11.41161*
Campingplatz am Langwieder See, Eschenriederstrasse
119, 81249 München-Langwied [(089) 8641566; fax
8632342; info@camping-langwieder-see.de; www.
camping-langwieder-see.de] Exit A8 junc 80 at Langwieder
See & foll sp Dachau; site within 200m. Fr ring rd A99 junc 8
join A8 to N, then as above. Med, hdstg, pt shd; htd wc; chem
disp; shwrs €0.50; el pnts (10A) metered + conn fee €1; gas;
lndtte; shop; snacks; rest; bar; lake sw adj; 95% statics; dogs
€1.70; poss v cr; Eng spkn; no adv bkg; m'way noise; CKE/CCI.
"Pleasant owners; tourers in a row outside recep area parked v
close together; v sm pitches, mostly on gravel; gd san facs; site
used by workers; easy access to Munich by train fr Dachau; lge
free car park at stn; NH/sh stay only." € 21.50        2011*

**MUNCHSTEINACH see Neustadt an der Aisch** *4E2*

**MUNICH see München** *4E4*

## "There aren't many sites open at this time of year"

If you're travelling outside peak season
remember to call ahead to check site opening
dates – even if the entry says 'open all year'.

⊞ MUNSTER *1B3* (3km SE Rural) *51.94638, 7.69027*
Camping Münster, Laerer Wersuefer 7, 48157 Münster
[(0251) 311982; fax 3833985; campingplatz-muenster@t-
online.de; www.campingplatz-muenster.de] Fr A43 exit
junc 2 or A1/E37 exit junc 78 onto B51 dir Münster then
Bielefeld. On leaving built-up area, turn R after TV mast on
R. Cross Rv Werse & turn L at 1st traff lts, site sp. (Site is also
sp fr Münster S by-pass). Lge, mkd pitch, some hdstg, pt shd;
htd wc; chem disp; mv service pnt; serviced pitches; shwrs
€0.50; el pnts (16A) inc; lndtte; shop; rest, snacks; playgrnd;
htd pool adj; fishing; tennis; cycle hire; wifi; 50% statics; dogs
€3; bus 300m; o'night m'van area; barrier clsd 1300-1500;
poss v cr w/e; Eng spkn; adv bkg; quiet; red CKE/CCI. "Excel;
quiet mid wk; Münster v interesting; radio/tv mast useful
landmark fr S; gd cycle rtes; Vg site, tokens for shwrs; sep
motor parking outside camp; vg; excel for bus to Munster." ♦
€ 28.00                         2013*

⊞ **MUNSTERTAL** *3B4* (1.5km W Rural) *47.85995, 7.76370*
Feriencamping Münstertal, Dietzelbachstrasse 6, 79244
Münstertal [(07636) 7080; fax 7448; info@camping-
muenstertal.de; www.camping-muenstertal.de] Exit
A5 junc 64a at Bad Krozingen-Staufen-Münstertal. By-pass
Stauffen & foll Münstertal sps. Site on L 1.5km past Camping
Belchenblick off rd L123. Lge, mkd pitch, shd; wc; chem disp;
mv service pnt; serviced pitches; sauna; steam rm; solarium;
private bathrms avail; shwrs inc; el pnts (16A) metered; gas;
lndtte; shop; rest, snacks; adventure playgrnd; 2 htd pools
(1 covrd); fishing; wintersports nr; ski lift 10km; tennis;
horseriding; games area; games rm; beauty treatments avail;
wifi; entmnt; cab TV; some statics; dogs €3.50; phone; rlwy stn
200m; gates clsd 1300-1430 & 2200-0730; m'van o'night area;
adv bkg rec school hols; quiet; red long stay/CKE/CCI. "Superb,
well-managed site; luxurious, clean facs; many activities for all
family; gd walking; vg rest; conv Freiburg & Black Forest." ♦
€ 31.55                                                    2011*

**MURNAU AM STAFFELSEE** *4E4* (5km N Rural) *47.70680,
11.21821* Camping Brugger am Riegsee, Seestrasse 1,
82418 Hofheim-am-Riegsee [(08847) 728; fax 228; office@
camping-brugger.de; www.camping-brugger.de] Fr A95/
E533 exit 9 for Sindelsdorf, dir Habach. Foll sp Hofheim & site.
Med, hdg/mkd pitch, hdstg, terr, pt shd; htd wc; chem disp; mv
service pnt; serviced pitches; shwrs €0.50; el pnts (16A) €2.50
or metered; gas; lndtte; shop; snacks; playgrnd; pool 5km; shgl
beach & lake sw adj; boating; windsurfing; tennis 2km; games
area; games rm; internet; entmnt; 60% statics; dogs €2.50;
m'van o'night area; clsd 1230-1430; Eng spkn; adv bkg; quiet;
red long stay; CKE/CCI. "Friendly/helpful owners; beautiful
lake & mountain views; gd, modern facs; excel site; panoramic
pitches get booked up early for the peak ssn." 1 May-1 Oct.
€ 25.00                                                    2011*

---

## "That's changed – Should I let The Club know?"

If you find something on site that's different from
the site entry, fill in a report and let us know. See
www.caravanclub.co.uk/europereport.

---

**MURNAU AM STAFFELSEE** *4E4* (5km NW Rural) *47.69861,
11.15833* Campingplatz Aichalehof, Aichalehof 4, 82449
Uffing-am-Staffelsee [(08846) 211; camping@aichalehof.
de; www.aichalehof.de] N fr Murnau dir Seehausen & Uffing
- Murnaustrasse. In Murnau turn L into Seestrasse to site in
2km. Site on L after sailing club. Or exit A95 junc 9 onto B472
W to Uffing, then as above. Med, pt sl, pt shd; wc; chem disp;
mv service pnt; baby facs; shwrs €0.50; el pnts (10A) €2; lndtte
(inc dryer); shop, rest 2km; snacks; bar; BBQ; playgrnd; lake sw
adj; watersports; fishing; 70% statics; dogs €2; Eng spkn; adv
bkg; quiet; CKE/CCI. "Excel, peaceful, scenic site, cycle/walking
path around lake, steamer on lake, trains and buses fr Uffing."
♦ 1 May-3 Oct. € 21.00                                     2011*

⊞ **NAUMBURG (HESSEN)** *1C4* (800m NW Rural) *51.25070,
9.16060* Camping in Naumburg (formerly Kneipp Kur
Camping), Am Schwimmbad 12, 34311 Naumburg
[(05625) 9239670 / (mob) 0170 4418621; info@camping-
naumburg.de; www.camping-naumburg.de] Exit A44
junc 67 onto B251 thro Istha. At Bründersen foll sp Altenstadt
& Naumburg. Foll int'l camping sp, well sp. Lge, mkd pitch,
terr, pt shd; htd wc; chem disp; mv service pnt; shwrs; el pnts
(16A) €2 or metered (poss rev pol); lndtte; shop; tradsmn;
rest, snacks, bar 800m; BBQ; cooking facs; playgrnd; pool
adj; tennis; horseriding 5km; golf 15km; spa treatments;
30% statics; dogs €2.50; bus 500m; clsd 1300-1500; Eng
spkn; adv bkg; quiet. "Charming site; excel, modern san facs;
spacious pitches; friendly, helpful staff; interesting town;
gd walks fr site; rec; nr pool, smkt, Dambusters Dam; new
management." ♦ € 26.50                                     2014*

NECKARGEMUND see Heidelberg *3C2*

---

## "I like to fill in the reports as I travel from site to site"

You'll find report forms at the back of
this guide, or you can fill them in online
at www.caravaclub.co.uk/europereport.

---

⊞ **NECKARSULM** *3D3* (2km E Urban) *49.18734,
9.24776* Camping Reisachmühle, Reisachmühlweg 6,
74172 Neckarsulm [(07132) 2169; fax 308633; info@
campingplatz-reisachmuehle.de; www.campingplatz-
reisachmuehle.de] Exit A6/E50 junc 37 onto B27 to
Neckarsulm, site well sp nr Aquatoll. Med, mkd pitch, unshd;
wc; chem disp; shwrs inc; el pnts (16A) €2 or metered; gas;
lndtte; shop; rest 500m; playgrnd; 40% statics; dogs €2; some
Eng spkn; CKE/CCI. "Conv NH nr a'bahn; rec arr early high
ssn." € 16.00                                              2011*

**NEEF** *3B2* (200m N Rural) *50.09500, 7.13694*
Wohnmobilplatz Am Frauenberg, Am Moselufer, 56858
Neef [(06542) 21575] Exit A1/E44 junc 125 onto B49 to Neef.
In Neef cross rv bdge, site sp on L beside rv. M'vans only. Med,
pt shd; chem disp; mv service pnt; el pnts (10A) inc; shwrs
400m; rest 100m; tradsmn; some rlwy & rv noise. "Gd; owner
calls am & pm for payment; beautiful location." 1 Mar-30 Oct.
€ 5.00                                                     2013*

**NEEF** *3B2* (4km S Urban) *50.05294, 7.13115* **Bären Camp
Bullay, Am Moselufer 1+3, D-56859 Bullay (Mosel)**
[06542 900097; info@baeren-camp.de; www.baeren-
camp.de] Foll B49 to Alf, cross Moselle bdge to Bullay. Turn
L and drive under the rlwy bdge, foll the rd. At the vill sq turn
into Fährstrasse, drive across Moselle car park past the football
grnd foll sp to site. Sm, mkd pitch, pt shd; htd wc; chem disp;
shwrs; baby facs; lndtte; playgrnd; shop; rest, bar; BBQ; dogs;
Eng spk; poss noisy; CKE/CCI. "Fair site, handy for Mosel
Cycle Rte, diff ent, barrier down rest time." 18 Apr-27 Aug.
€ 21.00                                                    2012*

NEHREN see Cochem *3B2*

**GERMANY**

**NENNIG** *3A2* (1km N Rural) *49.54331, 6.37207* Camping Mosella am Rothaus (formerly Moselplatz), Zur Moselbrücke 15, 66706 Perl-Nennig [(06866) 510 or 26660222 (Lux'bourg); fax 1486; info@mosel-camping.de] Site on bank of Mosel opp Remich (Luxembourg), access on R just bef bdge. Fr Luxembourg cross rv bdge, turn L after former border post, site is ahead, opp Mosel-Camping Dreiländereck. Med, hdg pitch, pt shd; htd wc; chem disp; mv service pnt; shwrs inc; el pnts (10A) inc; gas 1km; shop 500m; rest, snacks; bar; BBQ; 50% statics; dogs; bus 100m; poss cr; Eng spkn; quiet; CKE/CCI. "Lovely site by rv for sh or long stay; helpful, friendly owner; adequate facs; rest adj; rvside pitch sm extra charge; gd touring base." ♦ ltd 1 Apr-15 Oct. € 22.60 2013*

**NENNIG** *3A2* (1km N Rural) *49.54303, 6.37066* Mosel-Camping Dreiländereck, Am Moselufer, 66706 Perl-Nennig [(06866) 322; fax 1005; info@mosel-camping.de; www.mosel-camping.de] Site on bank of Mosel opp Remich (Luxembourg), access on R just bef bdge (fr German side). Fr Luxembourg cross rv bdge, turn L after former border post cont to rv & turn L under bdg; site is ahead. Med, unshd; htd wc; chem disp; mv service pnt; shwrs €1.40; el pnts (16A) inc; lndtte; shops 400m; tradsmn; rest, snacks; bar; BBQ; playgrnd; fishing; cycling; golf 15km; 65% statics; dogs €1; phone; poss cr; adv bkg; quiet; no ccard acc; Eng spkn; 10% red long stay; 5% red CKE/CCI. "Nice site; dishwashing & chem disp adj; ltd facs; conv vineyards, Roman mosaic floor in Nennig; cycle track along rv; sh walk to Remich." 1 Apr-15 Oct. € 23.40 2014*

**NESSELWANG** *4E4* (10km SE Urban) *47.56315, 10.57843* Campingplatz Pfronten, Tirolerstrasse 109, 87459 Pfronten-Steinach [(08363) 377 or 8353] Fr Nesselwang on B309/E532, go thro Pfronten, site on R by 'Osterreich 1km' sp. Med, pt sl, pt shd; wc; chem disp; mv service pnt; shwrs inc; el pnts (10A) €1.40 (poss rev pol); lndtte; shop & 1km; tradsmn; rest 300m; bar; pool 2km; dogs €0.50; phone; no adv bkg; quiet; CKE/CCI. "Gd mountain walks; castles & lakes adj; helpful & friendly staff; no grndsheets allowed, duckboards provided; immac facs." 15 May-27 Sep. € 17.00 2009*

**NESSLBACH** *4G3* (500m NW Rural) *48.69400, 13.11638* Donautal Camping, Schillerstrasse 14, 94577 Nesslbach-Winzer [(08545) 1233 or 0121 or 8225; fax 911562; info@camping-donautal.de; www.camping-donautal.de] Exit A3/E56 junc 112 to Nesslbach. Site adj sports stadium, sp. Sm, mkd pitch, unshd; htd wc; chem disp; mv service pnt; shwrs inc; el pnts (6A) inc; lndtte; shop 100m; tradsmn; rest 300m; snacks 100m; games area; 20% statics; dogs free; quiet. "Adj Danube cycleway; lovely, open site; friendly staff; lge pitches - easy access lge o'fits; ltd san facs but clean; site yourself instructions if site not manned; vg." € 15.00 2013*

**NEUENBURG AM RHEIN** *3B4* (9km E Rural) *47.81000, 7.67694* Feriencamping Badenweiler, Weilertalstrasse 73, 79410 Badenweiler [info@camping-badenweiler.de; www.camping-badenweiler.de] Exit A5 junc 65 at Neuenburg onto B378 dir Müllheim, then L131. Site sp on L bef R turn to Badenweiler. Med, terr, pt shd; htd wc; chem disp; mv service pnt; fam bthrm; shwrs inc; el pnts (16A) metered; lndtte (inc dryer); shop; tradsmn; rest, snacks; bar; playgrnd nr; pool 500m; wifi; no statics; dogs €3; phone; bus 300m; site clsd mid-Dec to mid-Jan; Eng spkn; adv bkg; quiet; red low ssn; CKE/CCI. "Excel, well-managed site; strenuous cycle rides; thermal baths nr." ♦ € 29.00 2009*

**NEUHAUSEN SCHELLBRONN see Pforzheim** *3C3*

**NEUKLOSTER** *2E2* (500m E Urban) *53.86597, 11.69792* See-Camping Neukloster, Bützowerstrasse 27a, 23992 Neukloster [(038422) 20844; fax 20461; info@see-camping-neukloster.de; www.see-camping-neukloster.de] Exit A20 junc 10 or 11 & foll sp Neukloster, then camping sp. Med, pt sl, shd; htd wc; chem disp; shwrs €0.80; el pnts (10-16A) €1.50 (poss rev pol); lndtte; shop 300m; rest 200m; playgrnd; lake adj; 50% statics; dogs €1.50; bus 500m; quiet; CKE/CCI. "Conv touring base; easy walk to town; sep site for m'vans sp in town." ♦ 1 Apr-31 Oct. € 13.50 2010*

**NEUMAGEN DHRON see Trittenheim** *3B2*

**NEUMARKT IN DER OBERPFALZ** *4E3* (4.5km N Rural) *49.32944, 11.42876* Campingplatz Berg, Hausheimerstrasse 31, 92348 Berg [(09189) 1581; fax 412 733; campingplatz-herteis@t-online.de; www.camping-in-berg.de] Exit A3 junc 91 & foll sp Berg bei Neumarkt. In cent of Berg, turn R, site on R in 800m, sp. On ent turn R to tourers area & walk to recep. Med, pt sl, unshd; wc; chem disp; mv service pnt; baby facs; shwrs €0.60; el pnts (20A) €2.50; lndtte (inc dryer); shop 400m; rest 400m; snacks; golf 8km; 60% statics (sep area); dogs €2; Eng spkn; quiet. "Well-run, friendly, family-owned site; excel san facs; sh walk to Berg cent; excel touring base; gd nh fr m'way; pleasant views of countryside; canal walk." € 27.00 2014*

**NEUMUNSTER** *1D1* (2km SW Rural) *54.04636, 9.92306* Familien-Camping Forellensee, Humboldredder 5, 24634 Padenstedt [(04321) 82697; fax 84341; info@familien-campingplatz.de; www.familien-campingplatz.de] Exit A7 junc 14 for Padenstedt, join dual c'way for 1km & turn L sp Centrum. In 1km turn L at traff lts sp Padenstedt for 3km, under m'way. Site on L in vill. Lge, mkd pitch, pt shd; wc; chem disp; mv service pnt; shwrs inc; el pnts (16A) €3 or metered; lndtte; rest 500m; snacks; bar; playgrnd; lake sw; trout-fishing; tennis; games area; 75% statics; phone; poss cr; Eng spkn; some rd noise; CKE/CCI. "Gd NH; conv for trains to Hamburg/Lübeck." ♦ € 26.50 2014*

**NEUNKIRCHEN** *3B2* (3km SE Rural) *49.32777, 7.19416* Camping Volkssonnengarten, Kirkelerstrasse, 66539 Neunkirchen [(0160) 94753613; fax (06821) 24564] Leave A8 at junc 24; N twd Neunkirchen; 1st L (camping sp); next L into Kirkelerstrasse sp Kirkel; sharp turn L immed after passing under a'bahn into rd sp as no thro rd. Med, terr, pt shd; wc; chem disp; shwrs inc; el pnts (16A) metered + conn fee or €1.50; lndtte; shops 600m; rest, snacks; bar; playgrnd; pool adj; paddling pool; tennis 200m;90% statics; dogs €2; phone; clsd 1300-1500; poss cr; some Eng spkn; quiet but some rd noise; red CKE/CCI. "V friendly, helpful staff; tight pitches; adj pool free to campers; gd NH/sh stay." 1 Mar-31 Oct. € 14.50 2009*

**GERMANY**

NEUREICHENAU 4G3 (9km NE Urban) 48.74861, 13.81694
Knaus Campingpark Lackenhäuser, Lackenhäuser
127, 94089 Neureichenau [(08583) 311; fax 91079;
lackenhaeuser@knauscamp.de; www.knauscamp.de]
Leave A3/E56 at junc 14 (Aicha-vorm Wald) & go E for 50km
via Waldkirchen, Jandelsbrunn, Gsenget & Klafferstrasse to
Lackenhäuser. Lge, some hdg/mkd pitch, pt sl, terr, pt shd;
wc; chem disp; mv service pnt; some serviced pitches; baby
facs; sauna; shwrs inc; el pnts (16A) €2.60 or metered; gas;
lndtte; shop; rest, snacks; bar; BBQ; playgrnd; 2 pools (1 htd);
paddling pool; tennis 500m; cycle hire; fishing; horseriding adj;
games rm; entmnt; solarium; hairdresser; internet; games/TV
rm; 40% statics; dogs €2.50; adv bkg; quiet; ccard acc; red low
ssn/long stay. "Lge site with lite waterfalls & walkways; ski lift
on site - equipment for hire; mv service pnt diff to access; excel
shop; 2km to 3 point border with Austria & Czech Republic;
excursions booked; recep clsd 1200-1500 & after 1800." ♦
10 Jan-7 Nov. € 26.00                                    2010*

NEUSTADT 3C2 (7km S Rural) 49.30083, 8.09027
Campingplatz Wappenschmiede, Talstrasse 60, 67487
St Martin [(06323) 6435; cpWappenschmiede@hotmail.de;
www.campingplatz-wappenschmiede.beep.de] Exit A65
at junc 13 or 14 to Maikammer, then foll sp St Martin & site
(blue/white or yellow/brown sp). At end houses take 1st L into
touring area (do not go up hill to statics area). Sm, shd; wc;
chem disp; shwrs €1; el pnts €2; lndtte; supmkt 5km; rest; bar;
playgrnd; 50% statics; dogs; Eng spkn; adv bkg; quiet; red long
stay; CKE/CCI. "Poss long walk to facs; friendly site; St Martin
v picturesque; gd rests; gd walking area." 1 Apr-1 Nov.
€ 20.00                                                  2011*

NEUSTADT AM MAIN 3D2 (2.5km S Rural) 49.91173,
9.59998 Main-Spessart-Camping International, 97845
Neustadt-am-Main [(09393) 639; fax 1607; info@camping-
neustadt-main.de; www.camping-neustadt-main.de]
Exit A3/E41 junc 65 sp Marktheidenfeld. Do not cross bdge
to Marktheidenfeld but turn L up rv sp Lohr. Site on R past
Rothenfels on W bank of Rv Main. Med, mkd pitch, pt shd;
wc; chem disp; mv service pnt; baby facs; shwrs €0.50; el pnts
(16A) metered + conn fee; gas; lndtte (inc dryer); shop; rest
2.5km; snacks; playgrnd; htd pool; paddling pool; boating,
waterskiing & fishing; golf 10km; entmnt; 70% statics; dogs
€2.50; clsd 1200-1400; Eng spkn; adv bkg; quiet but some
rd noise; ccard acc; red CKE/CCI. "Beautiful countryside;
rvside cycle track 500m; sm pitches; excel." 1 Apr-30 Sep.
€ 18.50                                                  2010*

⊞ NEUSTADT AN DER AISCH 4E2 (6km N Rural) 49.64058,
10.59975 Campingplatz Münchsteinach, Badstrasse 10,
91481 Münchsteinach [(09166) 750; fax 278; gemeinde@
muenchsteinach.de; www.muenchsteinach.de] Turn NW
fr rd 470 Neustadt-Höchstadt at camp sp 8km fr Neustadt &
thro Gutenstetten. Int'l camping sp in 5km turn R, foll camp
sp. Lge, unshd; wc; mv service pnt; chem disp; shwrs inc; el
pnts (16A) metered; lndtte (inc dryer); shop, snacks 500m;
pool adj; 60% statics; dogs €2; quiet; red long stay; CKE/
CCI. "Sm touring area; clean facs; site muddy when wet." ♦
€ 11.00                                                  2010*

⊞ NEUSTADT AN DER WALDNAAB 4F2 (500m NW Urban)
49.73750, 12.17222 Waldnaab Camping, Gramaustrasse
64, 92660 Neustadt-an-der-Waldnaab [(09602) 3608; fax
943466; pfoster@neustadt-waldnaab.de; www.neustadt-
waldnaab.de] Exit June 21a onto B15 for 4km S into
Neustadt. Site sp fr N side of vill. Sm, hdg pitch, pt shd; htd
wc; chem disp; mv service pnt; shwrs €0.50; el pnts (16A)inc;
lndtte; supmkt 500m; rest 1km; snacks; bar; playgrnd; pool;
games area; dogs €1.50; quiet. "Helpful owners; clean facs;
excel value for money." € 17.00                          2013*

NEUSTADT IN HOLSTEIN 2E1 (2km E Coastal) 54.09286,
10.82583 Camping am Strande, Sandbergweg 94, 23730
Neustadt-in-Holstein [(04561) 4188; fax (04561) 7125;
info@amstrande.de; www.amstrande.de] Exit A1/E47
junc 13 or 14 for Neustadt; thro Neustadt twd Pelzerhaken
for 2km, site on R past hospital. Lge, hdg/mkd pitch, pt sl,
pt shd; wc; chem disp; mv service pnt; shwrs €0.50; el pnts
(10A) €2; gas; lndtte; shop 100m; rest 200m; playgrnd; sw &
shgl beach adj; watersports; cycle hire; 70% statics; dogs €3;
poss cr; Eng spkn; adv bkg; quiet; ccard acc; CKE/CCI. "Gd
area, gd beaches, & cycling; v pleasant site." ♦ 1 Apr-30 Sep.
€ 18.00                                                  2009*

⊞ NEUSTADT/HARZ 2E4 (2km NW Rural) 51.56897,
10.82836 Campingplatz am Waldbad, An der Burg 3,
99762 Neustadt/Harz [036331 479891; fax 479892; info@
neustadt-harz-camping.de] Fr A38, exit J10 for B243 to
Nordhausen. Turn L onto B4 dir Niedersachswerfen. Turn R
onto L1037, L onto Osteroder Straße and R onto Klostergasse.
Foll sp to campsite. Med, hdg pitch, pt sl, pt shd; htd wc; chem
disp; mv service pnt; shwrs inc; el pnts (10A); lndtte (inc dryer);
tradsmn; snacks; bar; playgrnd; games area; 50% statics; bus/
train 4km; twin axles; adv bkg; quiet; CCI. "Gd site; conv for
Harz; helpful owners; vg san facs." ♦ € 31.00           2014*

⊞ NEUSTRELITZ 2F2 (8km S Rural) 53.30895, 13.00305
Camping- und Ferienpark Havelberge, An der
Havelbergen 1, 17237 Gross Quassow [(03981) 24790;
fax 247999; info@haveltourist.de; www.haveltourist.de]
Fr Neustrelitz foll sp to Userin on L25 & bef Userin turn L sp
Gross Quassow. Turn S in vill at camping sp, cross rlwy line &
rv, sm ent in 1.5km. Site 1.7km S of Gross Quassow twd lake,
sp. Lge, pt sl, pt shd; wc; chem disp; mv service pnt; sauna;
shwrs €0.90; el pnts (10A) €2.90; lndtte (inc dryer); shop adj;
rest high ssn; snacks; bar; playgrnd; lake sw; watersports;
cycle hire; wifi; entmnt & 30% statics; dogs €4.40; quiet.
"Lovely wooded area; poss diff lge o'fits; not rec as NH." ♦
€ 24.60                                                  2010*

⊞ NIDEGGEN 1A4 (2km SW Rural) 50.68530, 6.46966
Campingplatz Hetzingen, Campingweg 1, 52385 Brück
[(02427) 508; fax 1294; info@campingplatz-hetzingen.de;
www.campingplatz-hetzingen.de] Fr Nideggen take rd sp
Schmidt/Monschau, ent 2km on L at R-hand bend on ascent
fr level x-ing. Lge, pt sl; pt shd; wc; chem disp; sauna; baby
facs; shwrs €0.80; el pnts (10-16A) metered; gas; lndtte; shop;
rest, snacks; bar; playgrnd; cycle hire; 75% statics; dogs €2.50;
train 500m; poss cr; Eng spkn; adv bkg; some rlwy noise; red
CKE/CCI. "C'van may need manhandling onto pitch; site in
wildlife reservation." € 16.00                            2009*

NIEDERAU see Meissen 2G4

NIEDERZELL see Konstanz 3D4

Send in your site reports by mid August 2015

NIESKY 2H4 (3km W Rural) 51.30156, 14.80302
Campingplatz Tonschächte (Part Naturist),
Raschkestrasse, 02906 Niesky [(03588) 205771; camping_
tonschacht@gmx.de] Leave A4/E40 at junc 93 onto B115 sp
Niesky; cont on B115 site sp on L; do not go into Niesky but
stay on B115. Lge, shd; wc; shwrs €0.75; el pnts (10A); lndtte;
shop; rest 1km; snacks; playgrnd; games area; 50% statics;
dogs; poss cr. "Conv Polish border x-ing & a'bahn; sep naturist
area." ♦ 15 Apr-15 Oct. € 12.50                    2011*

⊞ NOHFELDEN 3B2 (5km SW Rural) 49.56072, 7.06105
Campingplatz Bostalsee, 66625 Nohfelden-Bosen
[(06852) 92333; fax 92393; campingplatz@bostalsee.
de; www.bostalsee.de] Fr A62 exit junc 3 sp Nohfelden/
Türkismühle & Bostalsee. Turn R & foll camp sp. Site on R
in 1.6km after passing thro vill of Bosen. V lge, mkd pitch,
pt sl, unshd; htd wc; chem disp; mv service pnt; baby facs;
fam bthrm; sauna; shwrs inc; el pnts (16A) €2; lndtte (inc
dryer); shop 1km; rest; snacks adj; playgrnd; lake sw 800m;
watersports; golf 7km; wifi; entmnt; 75% statics; dogs €2;
clsd to vehicles 1300-1500 & 2200-0700; adv bkg; quiet. "Vg
san facs; pleasant lakeside site but poss unrel in wet; spacious,
hdstg pitches; conv NH." ♦ € 20.00                    2012*

NORDEN 1B2 (2km W Coastal) 53.60471, 7.13863 Nordsee-
Camp Norddeich, Deichstrasse 21, 26506 Norden-
Norddeich [(04931) 8073; fax 8074; www.Nordsee-Camp.
de] Off B70 N of Norden. Well sp. V lge, mkd pitch, pt shd;
wc; chem disp; mv service pnt; baby facs; shwrs inc; el pnts
(6A) €2.20; lndtte; shop; rest, snacks; playgrnd; beach 200m;
fishing; cycle hire; internet; entmnt; 25% statics; dogs; €3.80;
ccard acc; red CKE/CCI. "Immac san facs; friendly atmosphere;
day trips to Frisian Islands; excel rest; v gd site." ♦ 8 Mar-
25 Oct. € 20.80                    2011*

## "We must tell The Club about that great site we found"

Get your site reports in by mid-August
and we'll do our best to get your updates
into the next edition.

NORDLINGEN 4E3 (8km SW Rural) 48.82622, 10.40933
Campingplatz Ringlesmühle, 73469 Riesbürg-
Utzmemmingen [(07362) 21377; fax 923516; info@
ringsmuehle.de; www.ringlesmuehle.de] Exit
Nördlingen on B466 dir Ulm. In approx 5km turn R in
Holheim sp Utzmemmingen. Site sp fr B466 500m beyond
Utzmemmingen. Med, pt sl, unshd; wc; chem disp; shwrs; el
pnts (6A) €1.50; BBQ; dogs; quiet. "Beautiful setting, cycle
rte to Nördlingen; relaxed, friendly site; poss w/end rallies."
Easter-31 Oct. € 12.00                    2009*

⊞ NORDLINGEN 4E3 (500m NW Urban) 48.85529, 10.48162
Nördlingen Wohnmobil Stellplatz, Würtzburger Strasse,
Nördlingen Fr Donauwörth foll B25 round Nördlingen. Site
on R, NW of town. Sm, hdstg, unshd; chem disp; mv service
pnt; el pnts €2; dogs; bus/train adj; noisy. " Along main
rd; mvs only, pt of car & coach park; grassy area alongside;
services fr coin operated machines; notice in Eng; easy walk to
cent of lovely town, built on site of ancient meteorite hit; NH
only."                    2014*

⊞ NORTHEIM 1D4 (3.5km NW Rural) 51.72900, 9.98374
Camping Sultmerberg, Am Sultmerberg 3, 37154
Northeim [(05551) 51559; fax 5656; campingplatzmajora@
web.de; www.campingplatzsultmerberg.de] Exit 69
fr A7/E45 onto B3, site sp. Med, pt shd; wc; shwrs inc; el pnts
(10A) €3 or metered + conn fee; lndtte; shop; rest 100m;
snacks; playgrnd; sm pool; 30% statics; dogs €2; poss some
rd & rlwy noise; clsd 1-14 Jan; ccard acc; red long stay/CKE/
CCI. "Delightful, well-kept, woodland site; gd, clean san
facs; superb views Harz mountains; plenty space; conv NH."
€ 21.80                    2010*

NUREMBERG see Nürnberg 4E2

NURNBERG 4E2 (12km WSW Rural) 49.43174, 10.92541
Camping Zur Mühle, Seewaldstraße 75, 90513 Zirndorf/
Leichendorf [(0911) 693801; fax 9694601; camping.
walther@t-online.de; www.camping-zur-muehle.de]
Head W on Adlerstraße twd Stangengäßchen, cont onto
Josephspl, then Vordere Lederg. Cont onto Schlotfegerg then
onto Fürther Tor; Cont onto Dennerstraße then slight R onto
Am Plärrer. Cont onto Rothenburger Str, turn L to stay on
Rothenburger. Turn R twd Seewaldstraße, keep R. Site on L.
Med, mkd pitch, pt shd; htd wc; chem disp; baby facs; shwrs
€0.50; el pnts metered; lndtte (inc dryer); tradsmn; rest; snacks;
bar; bbq; playgrnd; wifi; dogs €2; quiet; ccard acc; CKE/CCI.
"Mastercard acc not Visa; local style rest in traditional building
on site; conv for visiting Nurnberg; vg site." 1 Apr-31 Dec.
€ 24.00                    2014*

⊞ NURNBERG 4E2 (5km SE Urban) 49.42305, 11.12138
Knaus Campingpark Nürnberg, Hans-Kalb-Strasse
56, 90471 Nürnberg [(0911) 9812717; fax 9812718;
nuernberg@knauscamp.de; www.knauscamp.de] Exit
E45/A9 junc 52 or E50/A6 junc 59 dir Nürnberg-Langwasser
heading N, or Nürnberg-Fischbach exit travelling S; foll sp to
'Stadion', turn L. Site ent off wide rd opp Nürnberg Conference
Centre. Lge, pt mkd pitch, pt shd; htd wc; chem disp; mv
service pnt; shwrs inc; el pnts (6-16A) €3 (long cable rec);
gas; lndtte (inc dryer); shop; rest 1km; playgrnd; htd, pool
adj; tennis; wifi; TV; 25% statics; dogs €5 (on request); tram/
metro 1.2km; poss cr; Eng spkn; adv bkg; noise fr rd & poss
fr stadium; red long stay; ccard acc; CKE/CCI. "Friendly, helpful
staff; peaceful, surrounded by trees; san facs poss stretched
high ssn; v quiet midwk low ssn; gd security; office & access
clsd 1300-1500 & 2200-0700; gd cycle rte to town; national
rlwy museum in town worth visit; 1.2km to metro to town
cent; red squirrels on site." ♦ € 40.00                    2013*

⊞ OBERAMMERGAU 4E4 (1km S Rural) 47.58988, 11.0696
Campingpark Oberammergau, Ettalerstrasse 56B, 82487
Oberammergau [(08822) 94105; fax 94197; service@
camping-oberammergau.de; www.campingpark-
oberammergau.de] Fr S turn R off B23, site on L in 1km; fr N
turn L at 2nd Oberammergau sp. Do not ent vill fr N - keep
to bypass. Med, plenty hdstg, hdg/mkd pitch, pt shd; wc;
chem disp; mv service pnt; fam bthrm; baby facs; shwrs inc;
el pnts (16A) metered + conn fee; gas; lndtte (inc dryer); shop
in vill; tradsmn; rest adj; playgrnd; cycle hire; wifi; entmnt;
25% statics; dogs €2; sep car park; bus; poss cr; Eng spkn; adv
bkg ess high ssn; red long stay/low ssn; CKE/CCI. "Plenty of
space; helpful recep; excel san facs; excel rest adj; easy walk to
vill; well run site." ♦ € 38.00                    2014*

⊞ **OBERSTDORF** *3D4* (1km N Rural) *47.42370, 10.27843*
**Rubi-Camp, Rubingerstrasse 34, 87561 Oberstdorf**
**[(08322) 959202; fax 959203; info@rubi-camp.de; www.**
**rubi-camp.de]** Fr Sonthofen on B19, just bef Oberstdorf at
rndabt take exit sp Reichenbach, Rubi. Site in 1km over level
x-ing, 2nd site on R. Med, hdstg, unshd; htd wc; chem disp; mv
service pnt; baby facs; serviced pitches; shwrs inc; el pnts (8A)
metered; lndtte; shop 1km; tradsmn, rest, snacks; bar; BBQ;
playgrnd; skiift 1km; TV; 10% statics; dogs €2.70; phone; bus;
site clsd Nov; Eng spkn; adv bkg; quiet; CKE/CCI. "Well-run,
well-maintained site; immac facs; block paved paths to pitches;
block hdstg with grass growing thro; excel scenery; excel facs."
♦ € 31.20                                                          2011*

⊞ **OBERSTDORF** *3D4* (1.5km N Rural) *47.42300, 10.27720*
**Campingplatz Oberstdorf, Rubingerstrasse 16, 87561**
**Oberstdorf [(08322) 6525; fax 809760; camping-**
**oberstdorf@t-online.de; www.camping-oberstdorf.de]**
Fr B19 dir Oberstdorf, foll site sp. Med, hdstg, pt shd; wc; chem
disp; mv service pnt; serviced pitches; shwrs inc; el pnts (10A)
metered; lndtte (inc dryer); shops 1.5km; tradsmn, rest, snacks;
golf 5km; ski lift 3km; skibus; wifi; 45% statics (sep area); dogs
€0.50; Eng spkn; rd & rlwy noise. "Cable cars to Nebelhorn
& Fellhorn in town; Oberstdorf pedestrianised with elec buses
fr o'skirts; ask for Allgäu Walser card for free local buses &
shop discounts; vg." ♦ € 19.40                                     2010*

**OBERWEIS see Bitburg** *3B2*

⊞ **OBERWESEL** *3B2* (5km N Rural) *50.14188, 7.72101*
**Camping Loreleyblick, An der Loreley 59-33, 56329**
**St Goar-am-Rhein [(06741) 2066; fax 7233; info@camping-**
**loreleyblick.de; www.camping-loreleyblick.de]** Exit A61/
E31sp Emmelshausen junc 42 & foll sp for St Goar; site adj
B9 1km S of St Goar opp Loreley rock on rv bank. Or exit A48
junc 10 dir Koblenz, then B9 St Goar. Lge, pt sl, unshd; htd
wc; chem disp; mv service pnt; shwrs inc; el pnts (6A) €2.50;
gas; lndtte; shop & 500m; tradsmn, rest, snacks, bar adj (hotel
opp); pool 3km; 10% statics; dogs €1.70; phone adj; poss v
cr; wifi; Eng spkn; no adv bkg; much noise fr rlwy 24 hrs, plus
noise fr rd & rv barges; red long stay; CKE/CCI. "Lovely setting
in scenic area; friendly, helpful owner; excel modern san facs,
stretched when site full; pool complex in hills behind; conv
boat trips & car ferry across Rhine 500m; if office clsd site self
& report later; site clsd if rv in flood Dec-Feb; el voltage drops
when site v cr; easy walk to town; castles & museums; wine
cents; chair lift at Boppard; gd range of shops in St Goar." ♦
€ 18.80                                                            2012*

⊞ **OBERWESEL** *3B2* (8km N Urban) *50.15995, 7.70875*
**Camping Loreleystadt, Wellmicher Str 55, 56346**
**St Goarshausen [(06771) 2592; info@camping-loreleyblick.**
**de; www.camping-loreleystadt.de]** Site on B42, E side of
Rhine on N o'sksts of St Goarshausen, sp, but take care not to
overshoot. Med, unshd; wc; chem disp; mv service pnt; shwrs
€0.75; el pnts (10A) metered + conn fee €1.28; rest 200m;
snacks 100m; gas; shop; entmnt; sw in rv; poss cr; adv bkg;
few statics; quiet. "Poss flooding in heavy rain." ♦ 20 Mar-
31 Oct. € 24.00                                                   2013*

**OBERWESEL** *3B2* (600m S Urban) *50.10251, 7.73664*
**Camping Schönburgblick, Am Hafendamm 1, 55430**
**Oberwesel [(06744) 714501; fax 714413; camping-**
**oberwesel@t-online.de; www.camping-oberwesel.de]**
Fr A61/E31 exit sp Oberwesel, site sp on L at ent to sports
stadium, on rvside. Sm, pt shd; wc; chem disp; mv service pnt;
shwrs inc; el pnts (6A) €8.50; supmkt 200m; rest 200m; snacks;
bar; tennis adj; o'night area for m'vans; poss cr; adv bkg;
some rlwy noise; red long stay; CKE/CCI. "Clean, modern san
facs in Portacabins - stretched when site full; rv trips, cycling,
walking." 15 Mar-31 Oct. € 17.00                                  2011*

**OBERWESEL** *3B2* (5km NW Rural) *50.14976, 7.69478*
**Camping Friedenau, Gründelbach 103, 56329 St Goar-**
**am-Rhein [tel/fax (06741) 368; info@camping-friedenau.**
**de; www.camping-friedenau.de]** App on B9 fr Boppard or
Bingen; turn under rlwy bdge 1km N of St Goar; keep L; site
on L in 1km. NB - do not app fr J43 off m'way. Sm, pt sl, shd;
wc; chem disp; mv service pnt; shwrs inc; el pnts (16A) €2.50;
gas; lndtte; shops 1.5km; tradsmn; rest; bar; playgrnd; pool
1.5km; dogs €1; bus; poss cr; Eng spkn; quiet; red CKE/CCI.
"Quieter than other sites in area - uphill fr busy Rhine & resorts;
some pitches uneven & poss diff after heavy rain; vg welcome;
easy walk or cycle to rv town; country walks fr site; relaxed
atmosphere; friendly staff; gd bar/rest; san fac adequate but
needs updating; great views fr Rheinfels Castle." ♦ 15 Mar-
1 Nov. € 27.50                                                    2014*

**OHNINGEN WANGEN see Radolfzell am Bodensee** *3C4*

⊞ **OHRDRUF** *2E4* (8km S Rural) *50.73363, 10.75671*
**Oberhof Camping Lütschesee, Am Stausee 9, 99330**
**Frankenhain [(036205) 76518; fax 71768; info@**
**oberhofcamping.de; www.oberhofcamping.de]** Fr A4/
E40 exit junc 42 onto B247 S twd Oberhof. After approx 25km
at Gasthaus Wegscheide turn L onto forest rd to site. Also
accessible fr B88, sp in vill of Frankenhain via tarmac rd - 5km.
Lge, shd; htd wc; chem disp; mv service pnt; shwrs inc; el pnts
(10A) inc; gas; lndtte (inc dryer); shop; tradsmn; rest 1.5km;
rest, snacks; bar; BBQ; playgrnd; lake sw; boat & cycle hire;
wifi; TV rm; 60% statics; dogs €2; adv bkg; ccard acc; red long
stay/CKE/CCI. "Vg, busy site in heart of Thüringer Forest; excel
san facs; gd walking & cycling." ♦ € 22.00 (CChq acc)  2010*

⊞ **OHRDRUF** *2E4* (6km W Rural) *50.82452, 10.61060*
**Campingplatz Paulfeld, Catterfeld, 99894 Leinatal**
**[(036253) 25171; fax 25165; info@paulfeld-camping.de;**
**www.paulfeld-camping.de]** Fr E exit A4 junc 42 onto B88
sp Friedrichroda & foll sp Catterfeld & site on R. Or fr W exit
junc 41a at Gotha. Take B247 S twd Ohrdruf. After 6km bear
R sp Georgenthal. In Georgenthal vill, bear R onto B88. After
2km site sp L on app Catterfeld vill. Foll rd 2km thro forest to
site, sp. Site approx 12km fr A4. Lge, some hdg, pt shd; chem
disp; mv service pnt; wc; sauna; shwrs €0.80; el pnts (16A) inc;
gas; lndtte (inc dryer); shop; rest, snacks; bar; BBQ; playgrnd;
sm pets corner; lake sw & fishing; solarium; games area; cycle
hire; games rm; internet; 40% statics in sep area; dogs €2;
twin-axles acc (rec check in adv); poss cr w/end; quiet; ccard
not acc; red low ssn/long stay; CKE/CCI. "Excel, well-kept
site; gd access to pitches; helpful staff; clean san facs; gd for
families with young children; woodland walks; conv stop en rte
eastern Europe; happy family site; helpful friendly owners." ♦
€ 26.50                                                          2013*

**OLDENDORF see Bergen** *1D3*

⊞ **OLPE** *1B4* (6km N Rural) *51.0736, 7.8564* **Feriencamp Biggesee - Vier Jahreszeiten, Am Sonderner Kopf 3, 57462 Olpe-Sondern [(02761) 944111; fax 944141; info@ camping-sondern.de; www.camping-biggesee.de]** Exit A45/E41 junc 18 & foll sp to Biggesee. Pass both turnings to Sondern. Take next R in 200m. Ent on R in 100m. NB: Other sites on lake. Lge, mkd pitch, terr, pt shd; wc; chem disp; mv service pnt; baby facs; sauna; shwrs inc; el pnts (16A) inc; gas; lndtte; shop & 6km; rest, snacks; bar; cooking facs; playgrnd; shgl beach & lake sw adj; watersports inc diving; tennis; rollerskating rink; cycle hire; solarium; entmnt; internet; 20% statics; dogs €2.50; poss cr; Eng spkn; adv bkg; quiet; CKE/CCI; "Gd facs; well-organised site; barrier clsd 1300-1500 & 2200-0700; conv Panorama Theme Park & Cologne; vg cycling area; footpaths." ♦ € 30.50                    2014*

⊞ **ORTRAND** *2G4* (2km E Rural) *51.37265, 13.77956* **Ferienpark Dresden, Am Bad 1, 01990 Ortrand [35 75 56 20 00; fax 75 56 20 09; ferienpark-dresden@ themencamping.de; www.themencamping.de]** A13 Berlin-Dresden. Take exit 18 - Ortrand. At rndabt take 2nd exit (L55) & foll signs to camp site 2km. Note tight turn L after passing thro indus units. Med, mkd pitch, unshd; wc; chem disp; mv service pnt; baby facs; fam bthrm; shwrs; el pnts (16A) €2.90; lndtte (inc dryer); shop; tradsmn; rest; bar; BBQ; cooking facs; playgrnd; htd pool; waterslide; paddling pool; games area; games rm; bike hire; entmnt; wifi; tv rm; 30% statics; dogs €2; phone; bus/train 1.5km; twin axles; Eng spkn; adv bkg; quiet; CCI. "Vg site; volleyball; fishing adj; cls to mkd cycle rtes; sep car park with hook-ups for late arrs." ♦ € 35.00      2014*

⊞ **OSNABRUCK** *1C3* (4.5km NE Rural) *52.29181, 8.10593* **Camping Niedersachsenhof, Nordstrasse 109, 49084 Osnabrück [(0541) 77226; fax 70627; osnacamp@aol. com; www.osnacamp.de]** Exit A30/E30 junc 19 onto A11 sp Diepholz. At traff lts (end of m'way) at junc with B51/65 turn L sp Osnabrück & L again at next traff lts into minor rd (Nordstrasse). Site on R in 600m - do not take 1st ent. Fr Osnabrück, take B51/65 sp Diepholz, & turn R at traff lits in approx 4km by TV tower. Sp throughout Osnabrück. Med, mkd pitch, pt sl, pt shd, pt sl; wc; chem disp; shwrs €0.50; el pnts (16A) €2.80 or metered; lndtte (inc dryer); supmkt 2km; rest adj; snacks 1.5km; BBQ; playgrnd; entmnt; 30% statics; dogs; phone; bus; Eng spkn; adv bkg; quiet but some rd noise; CKE/ CCI. "V friendly; spacious pitches with views; mv service pnt outside site & diff to use; excel." € 18.50           2010*

⊞ **OSNABRUCK** *1C3* (11km SW Rural) *52.22944, 7.89027* **Regenbogen-Camp Tecklenburg, Grafenstrasse 31, 49545 Leeden [tel/fax (05405) 1007; tecklenburg@regenbogen-camp.de; www.regenbogen-camp.de]** Exit A1/E37 junc 73 or fr A30/E30 junc 13; foll sp to Tecklenburg, then Leeden & foll site sp. V lge, pt sl, pt shd; wc; chem disp; mv service pnt; serviced pitches; baby facs; shwrs; el pnts (16A) €2.90; lndtte; shop, rest, snacks high ssn; playgrnd; htd, covrd pool; paddling pool; games area; cycle hire; entmnt; 45% statics; dogs €4; o'night area for m'vans open all yr; site clsd 1 Nov-15 Dec; clsd 1300-1500; poss cr; adv bkg; quiet; ccard acc; red CKE/CCI. "Gd views; excel san facs, poss sometimes unclean; gd rest." ♦ € 37.00                                 2013*

**OSTERREINEN see Füssen** *4E4*

**OSTRINGEN** *3C3* (5km SE Rural) *49.20035, 8.76066* **Kraichgau-Camping Wackerhof, Schindelberg 10, 76684 Ostringen-Schindelberg [(07259) 361; fax 2431; info@ wackerhof.de; www.wackerhof.de]** Exit A5 junc 41 Kronau; E on B292 to cent Ostringen 9km; turn SE foll camp sp. Site in 5km. Med, mkd pitch, pt sl, terr, pt shd; wc; chem disp; mv service pnt; shwrs inc; el pnts (16A) metered; gas; lndtte; shop; rest, snacks 5km; playgrnd; 60% statics; rd & rlwy noise; some Eng spkn; 10% red CKE/CCI. "Friendly; gd, clean facs." 25 Mar-15 Oct. € 10.00                           2011*

**OTTERNDORF** *1C2* (4km NE Coastal) *53.82524, 8.87613* **Campingplatz See Achtern Diek, Deichstrasse 14, 21762 Otterndorf [(04751) 2933; fax 3016; campingplatz. otterndorf@ewetel.net; www.otterndorf.de]** Fr Cuxhaven W to Otterndorf on B73. Take 1st L after rlwy to traff lts, turn L twd Müggendorf, foll site sp, site on Rv Elbe. V lge, hdg/mkd pitch, hdstg; wc; chem disp; mv service pnt; baby facs; serviced pitches; shwrs inc; el pnts (16A) €1.80; gas; lndtte; shop 3.5km; rest, snacks, bar adj; playgrnd; pool; sand beach & sw adj; entmnt; 40% statics; dogs €3.50; phone; adv bkg; quiet; ccard acc; red CKE/CCI. "Friendly; efficiently run; easy cycle rtes to town; gd touring cent; site clsd 1300-1500; conv for ferry." ♦ 1 Apr-31 Oct. € 20.00                           2009*

⊞ **PAPENBURG** *1B2* (3km SE Rural) *53.06481, 7.42691* **Camping Poggenpoel, Am Poggenpoel, 26871 Papenburg [(04961) 974026; fax 974027; campingpcp@aol.com; www.papenburg-camping.de]** Fr B70, site sp fr town. Med, pt shd; htd wc; chem disp; mv service pnt; baby facs; shwrs €2; el pnts (10A) €2; lndtte; shop; rest; snacks 1km; bar; playgrnd; lake sw adj; games area; golf 1km; entmnt; cab TV; 40% statics; dogs €2; phone; o'night facs for m'vans; quiet; red long stay/CKE/CCI. ♦ € 19.00               2009*

**PAPPENHEIM** *4E3* (1.8km N Rural) *48.93471, 10.96993* **Camping Pappenheim, Badweg 1, 91788 Pappenheim [(09143) 1275; fax 837364; info@camping-pappenheim. de; www.camping-pappenheim.de]** B2 heading S, site sp after passing thro Weissenburg, on edge of Pappenheim. Med, pt shd; wc; shwrs; chem disp; mv service pnt; el pnts (16A) €2; lndtte; shop; rest 500m; snacks; lake sw; 25% statics; dogs €1.50; quiet. "Mountain views." 1 Apr-25 Oct. € 16.50 2010*

**PASSAU** *4G3* (10km W Rural) *48.60605, 13.34583* **Drei-Flüsse Campingplatz, Am Sonnenhang 8, 94113 Irring [(08546) 633; fax 2686; dreifluessecamping@t-online.de; www.dreifluessecamping.privat.t-online.de]** On A3/E56, junc 115 (Passau Nord); foll sps to site. Med, pt sl, terr, pt shd; wc; chem disp; mv service pnt; 60% serviced pitches; shwrs inc; el pnts (16A) €2.50 or metered; gas; lndtte; shop; rest; BBQ; playgrnd; cov'rd pool May-Sep; dogs €1.50; phone; bus 200m; poss cr; adv bkg; ccard acc; red 5+ days; CKE/CCI. "Interesting grotto on site; gd rest; rec arr early; facs need updating; poor surface drainage after heavy rain; interesting town at confluence of 3 rvs; on Danube cycle way; conv NH fr A3/E56." ♦ 1 Apr-31 Oct. € 35.00                           2014*

⊞ **PEINE** *1D3* (8km NW Rural) *52.35158, 10.12657* **Camping Waldsee, Am Waldsee 1, 31275 Lehrte-Hämelerwald** [(05175) 4767; fax 929025] Exit A2 junc 51 dir Hämelerwald. Thro Hämelerwald, under rlwy bdge. Strt over 1st traff lts, immed L after 2nd pedestrian x-ing in 300m. Site sp. Med, htd wc; chem disp; mv service pnt; shwrs inc; el pnts (10A) inc; lndtte (inc dryer); shop 2km; rest high ssn; snacks; bar; playgrnd; pool 3km; lake sw adj; 5% statics; dogs; Eng spkn; rlwy noise; CKE/CCI. "Woodland site; rather run down (2010) but conv NH." ♦ € 15.00                                         2014*

## "I need an on-site restaurant"

We do our best to make sure site information is correct, but it is always best to check any must-have facilities are still available or will be open during your visit.

⊞ **PETERSDORF (FEHMARN ISLAND)** *2E1* (4km NW Coastal) *54.48760, 11.01858* **Strandcamping Wallnau (Part Naturist), 23769 Wallnau** [(04372) 456; fax 1829; wallnau@strandcamping.de; www.strandcamping.de] Site is to W of Fehmarn peninsula 4km W of Petersdorf, sp. V lge, mkd pitch, pt shd; htd wc; mv service pnt; serviced pitches; sauna; baby facs; shwrs; el pnts (16A) €2.50; gas; lndtte (inc dryer); shop; tradsmn; rest, snacks; bar; BBQ; playgrnd; sand beach adj; sep naturist beach; cycle hire; wellness cent; games area; cycle hire; wifi; entmnt; 50% statics; dogs €5.50; poss cr; adv bkg; quiet; red low ssn. "Nature reserve & bird sanctuary nr; excel for families." ♦ 1 Apr-30 Oct. € 29.80 (CChq acc)                                                      2011*

⊞ **PFALZFELD** *3B2* (1km N Rural) *50.10612, 7.56804* **Country-Camping Schinderhannes, Hausbayerstrasse, 56291 Hausbay** [(06746) 8005440; fax 80054414; info@ countrycamping.de; www.countrycamping.de] Fr A61/ E31 exit junc 43, foll sps for 3km to Pfalzfeld & onto Hausbay, site sp. V lge, mkd pitch, pt sl, terr, pt shd; htd wc; chem disp; mv service pnt; some serviced pitches; baby facs; shwrs inc; el pnts (8-16A) inc; lndtte (inc dryer); shop; rest, snacks; bar; BBQ; playgrnd; htd pool 8km; lake sw; fishing; tennis; internet; entmnt; TV rm; internet; 60% statics; dogs €2; twin axles; Eng spkn; sep NH area; adv bkg; quiet; red CKE/CCI. "Pleasant, peaceful, clean site; spacious pitches, some far fr san facs; helpful, friendly staff; excel, immac san facs; scenic area close Rv Rhine; vg cycle track; conv m'way; excel NH with sep area to stay hitched-on; wonderful touring area; excel." ♦ € 29.00                                                          2014*

⊞ **PFEDELBACH** *3D3* (2km S Rural) *49.15356, 9.49894* **Camping Seewiese, 11 Seestrasse; 74629 Pfedelbach-Buchorn** [ fax (07941) 33827; campingseewiese@t-online. de; www.camping-seewiese.de] Exit A6 junc 40 at Öhringen; foll sp Pfedelbach & Camping. Lge, pt sl, pt shd; wc; chem disp; shwrs inc; el pnts (16A) €2 or metered; gas; lndtte (inc dryer); ice; rest; sacks; bar; BBQ; playgrnd; htd pool; lake fishing; games rm; TV; 90% statics; phone; dogs €1.50; Eng spkn; adv bkg; quiet; CKE/CCI. "Mainly statics, ok NH." ♦ ltd € 19.00                                                       2009*

⊞ **PFORZHEIM** *3C3* (12km SE Rural) *48.81800, 8.73400* **International Camping Schwarzwald, Freibadweg 4, 75242 Neuhausen-Schellbronn** [(07234) 6517; fax 5180; fam.frech@t-online.de; www.camping-schwarzwald. de] Fr W on A8 exit junc 43 for Pforzheim; fr E exit junc 45. In town cent take rd 463 sp Calw, immed after end of town sp take minor rd L thro Huchenfeld up hill to Schellbronn. Site in vill of Schellbronn on N side of rd to Bad Liebenzell - sp at church on R. Lge, pt sl, pt shd; wc; chem disp; mv service pnt; shwrs €0.50; el pnts (17A) €2 or metered; gas; lndtte; shop; rest, snacks; bar; playgrnd; htd pool adj; dance & fitness cent; cycle hire; entmnt high ssn; internet; 80% statics; no dogs; bus; no vehicle access after 2200; poss cr; adv bkg; quiet; red long stay; CKE/CCI. "Scenic area; v clean, well-maintained site; vg san facs; excel rest/takeaway; v rural." ♦ € 18.00       2011*

**PFRONTEN STEINACH see Nesselwang** *4E4*

**PIDING see Bad Reichenhall** *4G4*

⊞ **PIELENHOFEN** *4F3* (1.5km S Rural) *49.05896, 11.95820* **Campingplatz Naabtal, Distelhausen 2, 93188 Pielenhofen** [(09409) 373; fax 723; camping-pielenhofen@t-online. de; www.camping-pielenhofen.de] Exit A3/E56 junc 97 onto B8 dir Etterzhausen. Thro Etterzhausen turn L to Pielenhofen/Amberg. In Pielenhofen turn R over bdge. Med, mkd pitch, pt shd; htd wc; chem disp; mv service pnt; sauna; shwrs €0.50; el pnts (10A) metered + conn fee €0.60; gas; lndtte; sauna/solarium; shop; rest; bar; playgrnd; tennis; cycle hire; skittle alley; summer curling rink; games area; dogs €2.20; 65% statics; Eng spkn; CKE/CCI. "In beautiful valley; helpful warden; v nice site in gd location; liable to flooding; gd rv access for boating; family-run site; lots of facs; spacious pitches; gd rest; conv Regensburg." ♦ € 17.60       2011*

⊞ **PIRMASENS** *3B3* (12km NE Rural) *49.27546, 7.72121* **Camping Clausensee, 67714 Waldfischbach-Burgalben** [(06333) 5744; fax 5747; info@campingclausensee.de; www.campingclausensee.de] Leave a'bahn A6 at junc 15 Kaiserslautern West; S onto B270 for 22km. E 9km on minor rd sp Leimen, site sp. Lge, mkd pitch, pt shd; chem disp; htd wc; mv service pnt; some serviced pitches; shwrs €0.50; el pnts (6-16A) inc; gas; lndtte (inc dryer); shop; tradsmn; rest, snacks; bar; BBQ; playgrnd; lake sw adj; fishing; boating; games/TV rm; quiet; 50% statics; dogs €4.20; no twin-axles; poss cr; Eng spkn; adv bkg; quiet; ccard acc; red low ssn/long stay; CKE/ CCI. "Peaceful situation in Pfalzerwald Park; helpful staff; clean san facs; busy at w/ends; gd walking & cycling; gd." ♦ € 23.50                                                    2009*

**PIRNA** *4G1* (2km N Urban) *50.98169, 13.92508* **Waldcampingplatz Pirna-Copitz, Außere Pillnitzerstrasse 19, 01796 Pirna** [(03501) 523773; fax 571855; waldcamping@stadtwerke-pirna.de; www.waldcamping-pirna.de] Fr B172 fr Dresden to Pirna-Copitz or fr A17/E55. Site well sp. Med, mkd pitch, pt shd; htd wc; chem disp; mv service pnt; baby facs; shwrs inc; el pnts (10A) €3; lndtte; shop 200m; tradsmn; rest 400m; snacks 700m; playgrnd; 20% statics; dogs €2.50; bus 200m; adv bkg; quiet; "Clean, well-run site; modern facs." ♦ 1 Apr-31 Oct. € 31.00  2013*

⊞ **PLAU** *2F2* (3km SE Rural) *53.43832, 12.28699*
**Campingpark Zuruf am Plauer See, Seestrasse 38d,
19395 Plau-Plötzenhöhe [(038735) 45878; fax 45879;
campingpark-zuruf@t-online.de; www.campingpark-
zuruf.de]** N on B103, turn E at x-rds 200m after int'l camping
sp. Site on lakeside. Lge, pt shd; wc; chem disp; mv service
pnt; shwrs €0.80; el pnts (10A) €2.20; lndtte; shop; rest 1km;
snacks; playgrnd; lake sw & beach; watersports; cycle hire;
entmnt; dogs €2.50; adv bkg; quiet; CKE/CCI. "Pleasant,
friendly site; sm pitches, tight access; muddy when wet."
€ 18.00                                                        2010*

**PLAUEN** *4F1* (5km N Rural) *50.53860, 12.18495* **Camping
Gunzenberg Pöhl, 08543 Möschwitz [(037459) 6393; fax
45013; tourist-info@poehl.de; www.camping-poehl.de]**
Exit A72/E441 junc 7 & foll sp for Möschwitz & white sp for
Talsperre Pöhl. V lge, pt hdg/mkd pitch, terr, pt shd; wc; chem
disp; mv service pnt; shwrs inc; el pnts (10A) €2 or metered +
conn fee; lndtte (inc dryer); shop; rest, snacks; bar; playgrnd;
shgl beach & lake sw adj; golf 2km; wifi; entmnt; 60% statics;
dogs €3; clsd 1230-1400; poss cr; quiet; red CKE/CCI. "Excel,
v formal, clean site; helpful, friendly staff." ◆ 26 Mar-2 Nov.
€ 19.00                                                        2012*

**PLON** *1D1* (3km SE Rural) *54.12855, 10.45510* **Campingpark
Augstfelde, Am See, 24306 Augstfelde [(04522) 8128; fax
9528; info@augstfelde.de; www.augstfelde.de]** Fr Plön
on B76 twd Bosau, sp. Lge, mkd pitch, terr, pt shd; htd wc;
chem disp; mv service pnt; baby facs; sauna; private bthrms
avail; shwrs €0.75; el pnts (10-16A) €2.50; gas; lndtte (inc
dryer); shop; rest; snacks 3km; bar; playgrnd; lake sw & sand
beach adj; fishing; boat, canoe & cycle hire; tennis; fitness
cent; games area; golf 100m; wifi; entmnt; 60% statics;
dogs €2; o'night area for m'vans; Eng spkn; adv bkg; ccard
acc; red long stay; CKE/CCI. "Lovely situation; superb sailing,
windsurfing; gd for families; excel." ◆ 1 Apr-24 Oct. € 20.30
(CChq acc)                                                     2010*

**PLON** *1D1* (6km SW Rural) *54.11928, 10.33670* **Camping
Seeblick, Dorfstrasse 59, 24326 Dersau [(04526) 1211; fax
1218; info@camping-dersau.de; www.camping-dersau.
de]** Exit A21/B404 junc 8 dir Plöner See, turn R bef lake to
Dersau, site on L in 2km, sp. Lge, pt sl, unshd; wc; chem disp;
mv service pnt; shwrs inc; el pnts (10-16A) €2 (poss rev pol);
lndtte (inc dryer); shop; rest 200m; snacks; playgrnd; lake sw &
sand beach adj; boating; wifi; 75% statics; no dogs; adv bkg;
quiet; red long stay/low ssn; CKE/CCI. "Excel site bet vill & lake;
gd walks; gd site shop." 1 Apr-25 Oct. € 16.00      2010*

⊞ **PLOTZKY** *2E3* (1.5km N Rural) *52.06249, 11.79998*
**Ferienpark Plötzky, Kleiner Waldsee 1, 39245 Plötzky
[(039200) 50155; fax 76082; info@ferienpark-ploetzky.
de; www.ferienpark-ploetzky.de]** Exit A14 junc 7 onto
B246a dir Schönebeck & Gommern for 13km. Site on L immed
after vill of Plötzky, site sp. Lge, pt shd; htd wc; chem disp; mv
service pnt; private bthrms avail; baby facs; shwrs €1; el pnts
(16A) €2 or metered; lndtte (inc dryer); shop 1.5km; tradsmn;
rest 1.5km; snacks; bar; playgrnd; lake sw; boat & cycle hire;
games area; horseriding; archery; entmnt; internet; TV rm;
70% statics; dogs €2; adv bkg; quiet; ccard acc. "Gd walking,
cycling in wooded area; peaceful, relaxing, well-run site." ◆
€ 17.00                                                        2010*

**POMMERN see Cochem** *3B2*

**PORSTENDORF see Jena** *2E4*

⊞ **PORTA WESTFALICA** *1C3* (2km SW Rural) *52.22146,
8.83995* **Camping Grosser Weserbogen, Zum Südlichen
See 1, 32457 Porta Westfalica [(05731) 6188 or
6189; fax 6601; info@grosserweserbogen.de; www.
grosserweserbogen.de]** Fr E30/A2 exit junc 33, foll sp
to Vennebeck & Costedt. Site sp. Site 12km by rd fr Bad
Oeynhausen. Site sp fr m'way. Lge, mkd pitch, some hdstg, pt
shd; wc; chem disp; shwrs; el pnts (10A) €2.90; lndtte; shop &
5km; tradsmn; rest, snacks; bar; playgrnd; lake sw adj (w/ends
only); fishing; watersports; dogs €1.50; some Eng spkn; adv
bkg; quiet; poss noisy w/end; debit card acc; 10% red CKE/CCI.
"Site in cent of wildlife reserve; v tranquil; gd base Teutoburger
Wald & Weser valley; barrier clsd 1300-1500 & o'night; many
statics; lge area for tourers; gd for families; excel san facs &
rest; shwrs charged to electronic card; level access; highly rec."
◆ Easter-31 Oct. € 25.50                                       2012*

**POTSDAM** *2F3* (8km S Rural) *52.35278, 12.98981*
**Naturcampingplatz Himmelreich, Wentorfinsel, 14548
Caputh [(033209) 70475; fax 20100; himmelreich@
campingplatz-caputh.de; www.campingplatz-caputh.
de]** Exit A10 junc 20 or 23 to Glindow. Take B1 to Geltow,
turn L immed after rlwy x-ring & foll sp Caputh. Lge, shd; htd
wc; chem disp; mv service pnt; shwrs €1; el pnts (10A) €1.50;
lndtte; shop; tradsmn; rest, snacks; bar; sand beach & lake adj;
boat hire; 65% statics; dogs €2; phone; metro 500m; poss
cr; adv bkg; quiet - rlwy noise some pitches; CKE/CCI. "Lovely
position on waterfront; modern san facs; poss haphazard
pitching; cycle rtes & walks." ◆ 1 Apr-31 Oct. € 17.00   2010*

**POTSDAM** *2F3* (8km SW Rural) *52.36088, 12.94663*
**Camping Riegelspitze, Fercherstrasse, 14542 Werder-
Petzow [(03327) 42397; fax 741725; info@campingplatz-
riegelspitze.de; www.campingplatz-riegelspitze.de]**
Fr A10/E55 Berlin ring a'bahn take exit 22 dir Glindow or
Werder exits & foll sp to Werder; then foll B1 for 1.5km twd
Potsdam, R after Strengbrücke bdge twd Petzow. Med, terr,
pt shd; wc; chem disp; mv service pnt; shwrs (metered); el pnts
(16A) €1.80 (poss rev pol & long lead req); lndtte; shop; lge
supmkt 1km; rest, snacks; bar; playgrnd; lake sw & sand beach;
watersports; cycle hire; 50% statics; dogs €2.50, no dogs high
ssn; bus; poss cr; adv bkg; quiet. "Friendly recep; haphazard
pitching; transport tickets fr recep; recep clsd 1300-1500;
bus outside site; Sanssouci visit a must." ◆ 1 Apr-25 Oct.
€ 23.00                                                        2011*

**POTSDAM** *2F3* (10km SW Rural) *52.36055, 13.00722*
**Camping Sanssouci, An der Pirschheide 41, 14471
Potsdam [tel/fax (0331) 9510988; info@camping-potsdam.
de; www.camping-potsdam.de]** Fr A10 Berlin ring rd take
exit 22 at Gross Kreutz onto B1 twd Potsdam cent for approx
17km, past Werder (Havel) & Geltow. Site sp approx 2km
after Geltow immed bef rlwy bdge. Lge, shd; wc; chem disp;
mv service pnt; 50% serviced pitches; baby facs; shwrs inc; el
pnts (6A) inc (poss rev pol); gas; lndtte; shop; tradsmn; rest;
bar; BBQ; playgrnd; covrd pool 200m; lake sw & sand beach
adj; watersports; fishing; horseriding 8km; cycle hire; games
rm; wifi; 25% statics; dogs €4.90; mini-bus to stn; poss cr;
Eng spkn; adv bkg; quiet; ccard not acc; CKE/CCI. "Helpful,
friendly owners; lovely area; sandy pitches; poss diff lge o'fits
manoeuvring round trees; excel clean facs inc music in san facs;
camp bus to/fr stn; gate clsd 1300-1500; gd security; conv
Schlosses & Berlin by rail; excel site and rest; 5 star facs; sm
pitches." ◆ 1 Apr-31 Dec. € 38.40 SBS - G16            2014*

GERMANY

⊞ **POTSDAM** *2F3* (11km W Rural) *52.36002, 12.91677* Camping Glindowsee, Jahnufer 41, 14542 Glindow [(03227) 40855; info@hogab.de; www.hogab.de] Fr A10/ E55 a'bahn exit junc 23 dir Werder. In 4km at beginning of Glindow turn R (S). Thro Glindow, site sp on L. Med, pt shd; htd wc; chem disp; mv service pnt; shwrs inc; el pnts (16A) €3; gas 3km; lndtte; shop 1.5km; rest; bar; BBQ; playgrnd; sand beach & lake sw adj; 80% statics; dogs €1; poss cr; quiet; CKE/ CCI. "Sm grassy area for tourers; gd, clean, modern facs." € 21.00                                                         2010*

⊞ **POTTENSTEIN** *4E2* (2km NW Rural) *49.77942, 11.38411* Feriencampingplatz Bärenschlucht, 12 Weidmannsgesees, 91278 Pottenstein [(09243) 206; fax 880; info@ baerenschlucht-camping.de; www.baerenschlucht-camping.de] Exit A9 junc 44 onto B470 dir Forchheim; cont past Pottenstein; site in 2km on R. Med, pt sl, pt shd; htd wc; chem disp; mv service pnt; baby facs; shwrs €0.50; el pnts (8-16A) €1.90; gas; lndtte; cooking facs; shops 2km; rest; bar; 40% statics; dogs €1.90; poss cr; quiet. "A naturalized quarry surrounded by trees & rocky cliffs; Vg." ♦ € 19.00      2011*

**PREETZ** *1D1* (5km SE Rural) *54.21073, 10.31720* Camp Lanker See, Gläserkoppel 3, 24211 Preetz-Gläserkoppel [(04342) 81513; fax 789939; camp-lanker-see@t-online.de; www.campingplatz-lanker-see.de] Sp off B76 bet Preetz & Plön. Lge, mkd pitch, terr, pt shd; wc; chem disp; shwrs €0.50; el pnts (6A) metered; lndtte; shop; rest; snacks; bar; lake sw; boating; horseriding; some statics; dogs €1; phone; adv bkg; quiet; ccard acc; red low ssn; CKE/CCI. "Barrier clsd 1300-1500 & o'night; gd." 1 Apr-31 Oct. € 22.00      2009*

**PRIEN AM CHIEMSEE** *4F4* (1.5km S Rural) *47.8387, 12.35078* Camping Hofbauer, Bernauerstrasse 110, 83209 Prien [(08051) 4136; fax 62657; ferienhaus.campingpl. hofbauer@t-online.de; www.camping-prien-chiemsee. de] Exit A8/E52/E60 junc 106 dir Prien. Site on L in 3km immed after rndabt. Med, mkd pitch, pt sl, pt shd; wc; chem disp; mv service pnt; shwrs inc; el pnts (16A) metered + conn fee; shop; snacks; playgrnd; pool; lake sw 1km; cycle hire; internet; 50% statics; dogs €2; some rd noise; ccard acc (surcharge); CKE/CCI. "Well-kept site; helpful owners; sm pitches - siting poss diff; pts of site flooded after heavy rain, but some raised pitches; solar htd water; gd." ♦ 1 Apr-30 Oct. € 19.00  2009*

**PRIEN AM CHIEMSEE** *4F4* (2km S Rural) *47.83995, 12.37170* Panorama-Camping Harras, Harrasserstrasse 135, 83209 Prien-Harras [(08051) 904613; fax 904616; info@camping-harras.de; www.camping-harras.de] Exit A8/E52/E60 junc 106 dir Prien. After 2.5km turn R at rndabt sp Krankenhaus & site. Lge, pt shd; htd wc; chem disp; mv service pnt; baby facs; fam bthrm; shwrs €0.80; el pnts (6A) €2 (poss no earth); gas; lndtte (inc dryer); shop; tradsmn; rest; snacks; bar; playgrnd; htd, covrd pool 3km; lake sw; canoeing; boat & cycle hire; golf 3km; wifi; 20% statics; dogs €3.20; poss v cr; Eng spkn; quiet but poss noisy disco at w/end; ccard acc, not at w/ends; CKE/ CCI. "Beautiful, scenic area; on Chiemsee lakeside (extra for lakeside pitches); 15% extra if staying fewer than 4 nights; sm pitches; popular, busy site - rec arr early; modern, clean facs; poor drainage after rain; site rather run down end of ssn." ♦ 1 Apr-31 Oct. € 33.00 (CChq acc)                    2013*

**PRORA see Binz** *2G1*

**PRUCHTEN** *2F1* (800m NW Rural/Coastal) *54.37960, 12.66181* Naturcamping Pruchten, Zeltplatzstrasse 30, 18356 Pruchten [(038231) 2045; fax 038231 66346; info@ naturcamp.de; www.naturcamp.de] Fr Rostock on B105, at Löbnitz take L23 N sp Barth & Zingst to Pruchten & foll site sp. Lge, mkd pitch, pt shd; htd wc; chem disp; mv service pnt; baby facs; shwrs; el pnts (16A) €2; lndtte; shop; tradsmn; rest, snacks; bar; playgrnd; sand beach 500m; games area; horseriding 500m; wifi; 20% statics; dogs €2; m'van o'night area; adv bkg; quiet. "Gd birdwatching, surfing, fishing; vg." 1 Apr-31 Oct. € 26.00                                                2012*

See advertisement

⊞ **PRUM** *3A2* (1.5km NE Rural) *50.21906, 6.43811* Waldcamping Prüm, 54591 Prüm [(06551) 2481; fax 6555; info@waldcamping-pruem.de; www.waldcamping-pruem.de] Site sp fr town cent dir Dausfeld. Med, pt shd; wc; chem disp; mv service pnt; baby facs; shwrs inc; el pnts (10-16A) inc; gas; lndtte (inc dryer); shop; rest 1km; snacks; playgrnd; pool complex adj; tennis adj; cycle hire; ski lift 2km; entmnt high ssn; internet; 60% statics; dogs €1.50; o'night facs for m'vans; poss cr; Eng spkn; adv bkg; quiet; ccard acc; red CKE/CCI. "Pleasant site in lovely surroundings; friendly staff; clean facs; m'van o'night facs; do not arr bef 1900 on Sundays due local rd closures for family cycling event." ♦ € 24.00                                                 2014*

**PUTTGARDEN (FEHMARN ISLAND)** 2E1 (8km SE Coastal) 54.45806, 11.27203 **Camping Klausdorfer Strand, 23769 Klausdorf** [(04371) 2549; fax 2481; info@camping-klausdorferstrand.de; www.camping-klausdorferstrand.de] Fr Puttgarden on minor rd (not main E47) sp Burg, turn L after 6km sp Klausdorf. Foll site sp thro Klausdorf to coast. Lge, hdg/mkd pitch, unshd; htd wc; chem disp; mv service pnt; some serviced pitches; baby facs; fam bthrm; shwrs inc; el pnts (16A) metered or €2; lndtte; shop; rest; playgrnd; sand beach adj; cycle hire; golf 10km; entmnt; 50% statics; dogs €4; phone; poss cr; Eng spkn; adv bkg; quiet; red CKE/CCI. "Conv for ferry to Denmark; excel cycling area; bird sanctuary nr; gd access to pitches; excel." 1 Apr-15 Oct. € 23.00         2011*

**PUTTGARDEN (FEHMARN ISLAND)** 2E1 (1km NW Coastal) 54.5029, 11.21635 **Camping Puttgarden, Strandweg, 23769 Puttgarden** [tel/fax (04371) 3492 or 2185] N on B207/E47, on app Puttgarden ferry terminal take L turn & foll sp Strand to site on R. Med, hdstg, unshd; wc; mv service pnt; shwrs €0.50; el pnts (16A) metered; lndtte; shop; rest, snacks; playgrnd; fishing; sailing; many statics; dogs €1; poss cr; adv bkg; quiet; ccard acc. "Conv NH for ferry to Denmark." 1 Apr-15 Oct. € 18.00         2009*

⊞ **QUEDLINBURG** 2E3 (10.4km SW Urban) 51.75614, 11.04956 **Kloster Camping Thale, Burghardt Wilsdorf, Wendhusenstraße 3, 06502 Thale** [(03947) 63185; info@ klostercamping-thale.de; www.klostercamping-thale.de] Head S twds Steinholzstraße. 1st R onto Steinholzstraße. Bear L onto Stauffenberg-Platz. Turn L onto Weststraße cont onto Wipertistraße for 1.4km then onto Unter der Altenburg. Cont onto K2356, turn L onto Thalener Str. Cont onto L240 then turn L onto L92. After 1.4km turn L onto Schmiedestraße. Then R onto Breiteweg & bear R onto Wendhusenstraße. Site is on LH side. Med, mkd pitch, pt hdstg, pt shd; htd wc; chem disp; mv service pnt; baby facs; shwrs €0.80; el pnts (10A) €2.50; lndtte; shop 0.5km; tradsmn; rest 0.5km; snacks; bar; playgrnd; 10% statics; bus 0.3km; quiet; no ccard acc; CKE/CCI. "San facs excel." € 23.00         2014*

⊞ **RADEVORMWALD** 1B4 (4km NE Rural) 51.18400, 7.31300 **Camping-Ferienpark Kräwinkel, Kräwinkel 1, 42477 Radevormwald** [(02195) 6887899; fax 689597; info@ ferienpark.de] Exit A1 Remscheid onto B229 Radevormwald. In Radevormwald 1st mini island turn R, site on L in 4km. Sm, hdg pitch, terr, pt shd; htd wc; chem disp; shwrs inc; el pnts (20A) inc; rest; bar; playgrnd; lake sw nr; 80% statics; dogs €2; Eng spkn; adv bkg; quiet; CKE/CCI. "Lge pitches; pleasant area; key needed for all facs €10 deposit." ♦ € 15.00         2013*

**RADOLFZELL AM BODENSEE** 3C4 (3km E Rural) 47.73888, 9.00305 **Campingplatz Markelfingen, Unterdorfstrasse 19, 78315 Radolfzell-Markelfingen** [(07732) 10611; fax 10727; info@campingplatz-markelfingen.de; www. campingplatz-markelfingen.de] Fr B33 turn twd Radolfzell. Turn L in 2km at traff lts sp Markelfingen then R at traff lts in Markelfingen. Site sp. Med, hdstg, pt shd; wc; chem disp; shwrs €1; el pnts (10A) metered; lndtte; shop; tradsmn; rest, snacks; bar; BBQ; lake sw & shgl beach; boat launch; 50% statics; dogs €2.30; phone; train adj; poss cr; Eng spkn; quiet; CKE/CCI. "Recep clsd 1230-1400; gd train service to Radolfzell & Konstanz; modern san facs." ♦ 1 Apr-3 Oct. € 18.80         2011*

**RADOLFZELL AM BODENSEE** 3C4 (6km S Rural) 47.68796, 8.99428 **Campingdorf Horn, Strandweg 3-18, 78343 Gaienhofen-Horn** [(07735) 685; fax 8806; campingdorf. horn@t-online.de] Fr Stein-am-Rhein take L192 along N of Untersee for approx 13km. Site on app to Horn vill, sp. Fr Radolfzell, take rd S on E bank of Zellersee, site on L exit Horn vill. Med, pt shd; wc; chem disp; some serviced pitches; shwrs €1; el pnts (16A) metered + conn fee; lndtte; shop; tradsmn; rest; snacks 200m; bar; playgrnd; lake sw; watersports; entmnt; 20% statics; no dogs; bus; phone; sep car park; adv bkg; quiet; ccard acc; red CKE/CCI. "Vg." ♦ 15 Mar-7 Oct. € 26.00         2011*

**RADOLFZELL AM BODENSEE** 3C4 (10km S Rural) 47.65972, 8.93388 **Campingplatz Wangen, Seeweg 32, 78337 Öhningen-Wangen** [(07735) 919675; fax 919676; info@ camping-wangen.de; www.camping-wangen.de] Site in Wangen vill, 5km E of Stein am Rhien. Med, hdstg, pt shd; wc; chem disp; mv service pnt; baby facs; shwrs inc; el pnts (10A) metered + conn fee; lndtte (inc dryer); shop 300m; rest, snacks; bar; BBQ; playgrnd; lake sw & sand beach adj; fishing; games area; wifi; 40% statics; dogs €2 (check with site bef arr to make sure they will acc); phone; twin axles; Eng spkn; adv bkg; quiet; CKE/CCI. "Lovely scenery; site in vill but quiet; helpful recep; gd cycling & sw; lake steamer trips; Stein-am-Rhein 5km; water sports in adj lake." ♦ ltd 3 Apr-3 Oct. € 29.00         2014*

---

## "Satellite navigation makes touring much easier"

Remember most sat navs don't know if you're towing or in a larger vehicle – always use yours alongside maps and site directions.

---

**RADOLFZELL AM BODENSEE** 3C4 (6km SW Urban) 47.72942, 9.02432 **Campingplatz William, 78315 Markelfingen** [(049) 7533 6211; info@campingplatz-william.de; www.campingplatz-william.de] Fr S on A81 at junc 40 take A98 for 9m, at end of m'way turn L, site ent on L in 0.75m. Lge, med mkd pitch, pt shd; wc, chem disp, shwrs; lndtte; gas; rest, snacks, bar; BBQ; playgrnd; beach and sw adj; boat hire; Eng spkn; CKE/CCI and passport. "Gd site; cycle track; modern san facs; some noise fr rlwy." 1 Apr-3 Oct. € 18.00         2012*

**RAVENSBURG** 3D4 (8km SW Rural) 47.73935, 9.47187 **Camping am Bauernhof, St Georg Strasse 8, 88094 Oberteuringen-Neuhaus** [(07546) 2446; fax 918106; kramer@camping-am-bauernhof.de; www.camping-am-bauernhof.de] Fr Ravensburg twd Meersburg on B33. In Neuhaus foll sp on R; site bef chapel. Sm, pt shd; wc; chem disp; shwrs inc; el pnts (10A) €2.50; lndtte inc dryer; shop 300m; BBQ; playgrnd; lake sw,games rm, volleyball,; 20% statics; dogs €2; quiet; CKE/CCI. "CL-type but with full facs inc shwrs for wheelchair users; vg, clean, modern san facs; relaxed atmosphere; gd cycling area; farm with animals, fruit, distillery, herb garden, barn; sm lake on site; pre order fresh rolls/bread daily; excel site." ♦ 23 Mar-15 Sep. € 30.00         2013*

⊞ **REGENSBURG** *4F3* (2km W Rural) *49.02779, 12.05899*
**Azur Campingpark Regensburg**, Weinweg 40, 93049
Regensburg [(0941) 270025; fax 299432; regensburg@
azur-camping.de; www.azur-camping.de] Fr A93/E50 exit
junc 40 Regensburg W, dir Weiden; turn W away fr town onto
dual c'way; R at traff lts, site sp fr next T-junc. Lge, some hdstg,
pt shd; htd wc; chem disp; mv service pnt; shwrs inc; el pnts
(4A) €3 (poss long lead req); lndtte; shop high ssn; supmkt
400m; rest high ssn; bar; playgrnd; covrd pool 300m; cycle
hire; 40% statics (sep area); dogs €3.50; phone; bus at site ent;
o'night area for m'vans; poss cr; quiet; ccard not acc; red CKE/
CCI. "Helpful owner; vg facs; san facs gd & kept cln; lge block
san facs unisex; sm pitches poss diff lge o'fits; cycle path into
town along Rv Danube; gates clsd 1300-1500 & 2200-0800;
gd." ♦ € 29.00                                              2012*

**REINSBERG** *2G4* (750m S Rural) *51.00381, 13.36012*
Campingplatz Reinsberg, Badstrasse 17, 19629 Reinsberg
[(037324) 82268; fax 82270; campingplatz-reinsberg@
web.de; www.campingplatz-reinsberg.de] Exit A4/E40
junc 75 Nossen. Take 1st R to Siebenlehn & foll sp Reinsberg.
In Reinsberg take 1st R sp camping & 'freibad' to site. Med,
pt shd; htd wc; chem disp (wc); shwrs inc; el pnts (16A) €2;
lndtte; sm shop; tradsmn; rest, bar 500m; snacks; playgrnd;
pool & sports facs adj; 40% statics; dogs €2; phone; Eng spkn;
adv bkg; quiet. "Friendly, helpful owner; excel san facs; gd
walking; conv Meissen, Dresden & Freiberg." ♦  1 Apr-31 Oct.
€ 15.00                                                     2010*

⊞ **REINSFELD** *3B2* (1km W Rural) *49.68612, 6.86781* Azur
Campingpark Hunsrück, Parkstrasse 1, 54421 Reinsfeld
[(06503) 95123; fax 95124; reinsfeld@azur-camping.
de; www.azur-camping.de/reinsfeld] Fr A1 exit junc 132
Reinsfeld onto B407; site well sp. Lge, pt sl, pt shd; htd wc;
chem disp; private bthrms avail; shwrs inc; el pnts (10A) €3;
gas; lndtte; shop; rest, snacks; bar; playgrnd; htd pool 200m;
paddling pool; sm lake; tennis; games area; entmnt; TV;
40% statics; dogs €3; clsd 1300-1500; poss cr; Eng spkn; adv
bkg; no ccard acc; red CKE/CCI. "Aircraft exhib worthwhile;
some pitches v muddy in wet weather; scenic area; conv Trier &
Luxembourg." ♦  € 22.00                                     2010*

## "There aren't many sites open at this time of year"

If you're travelling outside peak season
remember to call ahead to check site opening
dates – even if the entry says 'open all year'.

**REIT IM WINKL** *4F4* (5km E Rural) *47.65845, 12.54114*
Camping Seegatterl, Seegatterl 7, 83242 Reit-im-Winkl
[(08640) 98210; fax 5150; info@camping-reit-im-winkl.
com; www.camping-reit-im-winkl.com] On B305, site sp
behind lge car park. Camping sp obscured in vill. Med, pt sl,
unshd; htd wc; chem disp; mv service pnt; sauna; shwrs inc; el
pnts (16A) metered; gas; lndtte (inc dryer); shop; tradsmn; rest,
snacks; BBQ; playgrnd; lake sw & beach 2km; cycle hire; ski lift
fr site; skibus 100m; golf 5km; internet; 50% statics; dogs €2;
adv bkg; quiet. "Gd family site; friendly; excel skiing & walking;
mainly for winter sport users." 1 Dec-31 Mar & 15 May-15 Oct.
€ 20.00                                                     2009*

⊞ **REIT IM WINKL** *4F4* (7.5km NW Rural) *47.73556,
12.41565* Camping Zellersee, Zellerseeweg 3, 83259
Schleching-Mettenham [(08649) 986719; fax 816; info@
camping-zellersee.de; www.camping-zellersee.de] Fr A8
exit junc 109 S sp Reit im Winkel. Just after Marquartstein turn
R onto B307 sp Schleching, site sp just N of Schleching. Med,
mkd pitch, pt sl, terr, pt shd; htd wc; chem disp; baby facs;
shwrs inc; el pnts (16A) metered; gas; lndtte; shop 1.2km;
tradsmn, rest, bar 600m; lake sw; tennis; 50% statics; no dogs;
phone; Eng spkn; adv bkg; quiet; ccard acc; red long stay/CKE/
CCI. "Excel, high quality facs; many footpaths fr site; mountain
views; nr Alpenstrasse." ♦ ltd € 23.00                      2012*

**REMAGEN** *3B1* (7km N Rural) *50.64500, 7.20694* Camping
Siebengebirgsblick, Wickchenstrasse, 53424 Remagen-
Rolandswerth [(02228) 910682; fax (02633) 472008; info@
siebengebirgsblick.de; www.siebengebirgsblick.de] Site
sp close to car ferry to Königswinter, opp Nonnewerth Is. Fr B9,
foll sp to site on rvside. Lge, mkd pitch, unshd; wc; chem disp;
shwrs €0.50; el pnts (8A) metered or €2.50; sm shop 500m;
rest, snacks; bar; playgrnd; TV; 40% statics; dogs €1; Eng spkn;
quiet; red long stay; CKE/CCI. "Extra for pitches on rvside; facs
in Portacabins; minimal rv & rlwy noise; cycle tracks along rv to
Bonn & Remagen; gd NH." 15 Apr-20 Oct. € 17.00             2010*

⊞ **REMAGEN** *3B1* (1km SE Rural) *50.57666, 7.25083*
Campingplatz Goldene Meile, Simrockweg 9-13, 53424
Remagen [(02642) 22222; fax 1555; info@camping-
goldene-meile.de; www.camping-goldene-meile.
de] Fr Köln dir Remagen onto B266; foll sp 'Rheinfähre
Linz'; in Kripp turn L, site sp. Or fr B266 1km beyond Bad
Bodendorf at rndabt take B9 (dir Bonn & Remagen); in 1km
take exit Remagen Süd; foll sp to sports cent/camping. Site
adj Luddendorf Bdge. Fr S on A48 exit junc 10 onto B9 twd
Bonn. Site sp in 22km after junc with B266. Lge, hdg/mkd
pitch, some hdstg, pt shd; wc; chem disp; mv service pnt; some
serviced pitches; shwrs €0.75; el pnts (16A) €2.60 (50m cable
rec some pitches); gas; lndtte; shop (ltd opening); tradsmn;
rest high ssn; snacks; bar; playgrnd; pool adj; cycle hire; wifi;
entmnt; 50% statics; dogs €1.70; m'van o'night area adj; poss
cr; Eng spkn; adv bkg; quiet but some noise fr rlwy across rv;
red CKE/CCI. "Tourers on flat field away fr rvbank; sm pitches
tightly packed in high ssn; gd rest; helpful staff; el pnts up
ladder; access to facs not gd; cycle path along Rhine; site clsd
1300-1500; v gd site." ♦  € 28.40                           2011*

⊞ **RERIK** *2E1* (1.1km NE Urban) *54.11133, 11.63234*
Campingpark Ostseebad Rerik, Straße am Zeltplatz
18230 Ostseebad Rerik [038296 75720; fax 75722; info@
campingpark-rerik.de; www.campingpark-rerik.de] Fr A20
junc 12 to Kröpelin on L12 thro Kröelin twrds Rerik then foll
sps to site. Med, hdg pitch, mkd pitch, pt shd; htd wc; chem
disp; mv service pnt; child/baby facs; shwrs; el pnts (16A);
lndtte; rest; snacks; bar; playgrnd; beach; internet; dogs-€3;
Eng spkn; quiet; ccard acc; "Gd site; new modern facs." ♦
€ 34.00                                                     2014*

**RETGENDORF** 2E2 (750m N Rural) 53.72947, 11.50279 Campingplatz Retgendorf, Seestrasse 7A, 19067 Retgendorf [(03866) 400040; fax 400041; info@camping-retgendorf.de; www.camping-retgendorf.m-vp.de] Exit A241 at junc 4 onto B104 dir Schwerin, in 2km turn N onto lakeside rd dir Retgendorf & Flessenow. On ent Retgendorf, site on L by bus stop. Med, mkd pitch, pt shd; wc; chem disp; shwrs €1; el pnts (10A) €2; lndtte; shop 1km; snacks; bar; lake sw & sand beach adj; fishing; 70% statics; dogs €1.50; phone; quiet; "Views of lake; conv beautiful towns of Schwerin & Wismar; gd cycling area; san facs clean & functional but dated; shwrs lack privacy; staff/ static owners friendly & helpful; lovely peaceful site if prepared to rough it a bit." ♦ ltd 1 Apr-15 Oct. € 15.00                              2013*

**RETGENDORF** 2E2 (3.5km N Rural) 53.75194, 11.49638 Seecamping Flessenow, Am Schweriner See 1a, 19067 Flessenow [(03866) 81491; info@seecamping.de; www.seecamping.de] Exit A14 at junc 4 Schwerin-Nord onto B104 dir Schwerin. In 2km turn R along lakeside sp Retgendorf & Flessenow, site in approx 10km at end of surfaced rd. Med, mkd pitch, pt shd; htd wc; chem disp; mv service pnt; baby facs; shwrs €0.80; el pnts (10A) €2.50; gas; lndtte (inc dryer); shop; tradsmn; snacks; bar; playgrnd; sand beach & lake sw adj; watersports; games area; 35% statics; dogs free; phone; bus adj; quiet; CKE/CCI. "Fair site in gd location." ♦ 1 Apr-31 Oct. € 22.50                              2009*

⊞ **RIBNITZ DAMGARTEN** 2F1 (8km NE Coastal) 54.28194, 12.31250 Camping in Neuhaus, Birkenallee 10, 18347 Dierhagen-Neuhaus [(038226) 539930; fax 539931; ostsee@camping-neuhaus.de; www.camping-neuhaus.de] Exit E55/A19 junc 6 onto B105 N. At Altheide turn N thro Klockenhagen dir Dierhagen, then turn L at camping sp & foll site sp to sea. Med, pt hdg pitch, pt shd; htd wc; chem disp; baby facs; shwrs €0.50; el pnts (16A) €3; lndtte (inc dryer); shop; rest 1.5km; snacks; playgrnd; beach 100m; wifi; 40% statics; dogs €3; adv bkg; quiet; ccard not acc. "Friendly site; vg." ♦ € 26.00                              2009*

**RIBNITZ DAMGARTEN** 2F1 (8km NW Coastal) 54.29188, 12.34375 Ostseecamp Dierhagen, Ernst Moritz Arndt Strasse, 18347 Dierhagen-Strand [(038226) 80778; fax 80779; info@ostseecamp-dierhagen.de; www.ostseecamp-dierhagen.de] Take B105 fr Rostock dir Stralsund. Bef Ribnitz, turn L sp Dierhagen & Wustrow & cont for 5km to traff lts & camp sp. Turn L to site on R in 300m. Lge, pt shd; wc; chem disp; mv service pnt; shwrs €0.50; el pnts (6A) €3; gas; lndtte; shop; supmkt 500m; rest 1km; snacks; playgrnd; sand beach 800m; cycle hire; 20% statics; dogs €2.80; phone; adv bkg (fee); quiet. "Site low-lying, poss v wet after heavy rain; charge for chem disp." ♦ ltd 15 Mar-31 Oct. € 21.50                              2009*

**RIEGEL AM KAISERSTUHL** 3B4 (1.5km N Rural) 48.16463, 7.74008 Camping Müller-See, Zum Müller-See 1, 79359 Riegel-am-Kaiserstuhl [(07642) 3694; fax 923014; info@muellersee.de; www.muellersee.de] Exit A5/E35 at junc 59 dir Riegel, foll site sp. Med, unshd; htd wc; chem disp; mv service pnt; baby facs; shwrs €0.30; el pnts (16A) €2; lndtte; shop in vill; tradsmn; rest, snacks in vill; bar; playgrnd; lake sw adj; no dogs; phone; quiet; redCKE/CCI. "Excel cycle paths in area; excel san facs; gd NH." ♦ 1 Apr-31 Oct. € 16.00 2012*

⊞ **RIESTE** 1C3 (2km W Rural) 52.48555, 7.99003 **Alfsee** Ferien- und Erholungspark, Am Campingpark 10, 49597 Rieste [(05464) 92120; fax 5837; info@alfsee.de; www.alfsee.de] Exit A1/E37 junc 67; site in 10km, sp. V lge, mkd pitch, pt shd; htd wc; chem disp; mv service pnt; baby facs; fam bthrm; shwrs inc; el pnts (16A) metered; lndtte (inc dryer); shop; rest, snacks; bar; playgrnd; lake sw & sand beach adj; watersports; tennis; cycle hire; 50% statics; dogs €3; phone; poss cr at w/end with day visitors; Eng spkn; poss noisy; ccard acc; 10% redCKE/CCI. "Site pt of lge watersports complex; modern san facs; gd for famiies, conv for Osnotbruk old town." ♦ € 39.40                              2014*

See advert on bookmark

⊞ **RINTELN** 1C3 (10km S Rural) 52.05118, 9.10223 Camping Extertal, Eimke 4, 32699 Extertal-Eimke [(05262) 3307; info@campingpark-extertal.de; www.campingpark-extertal.de] Fr Rinteln on B238 S twd Barntrup; about 1.5km S Bösingfeld turn L at sp to site over level x-ing. Sm, mkd pitch, terr, unshd; wc; chem disp; mv service pnt; serviced pitches; shwrs inc; el pnts (16A) €1.50 or metered; lndtte (inc dryer); shop; tradsmn; rest 500m; snacks high ssn; bar; cooking facs; playgrnd; lake sw; games rm; wifi; entmnt; 75% statics in sep area; dogs €1.50; some Eng spkn; quiet; red long stay/CCI. "Excel site; dry & well-drained in v wet weather; all facs clean; forest walks & cycle paths fr site." ♦ € 14.00                              2010*

⊞ **RINTELN** 1C3 (2km W Rural) 52.1865, 9.05988 Camping Doktorsee, Am Doktorsee 8, 31722 Rinteln [(05751) 964860; fax 964888; info@doktorsee.de; www.doktorsee.de] Exit A2/E30 a'bahn, junc 35; foll sp 'Rinteln' then 'Rinteln Nord'. Turn L at traff lts, foll 'Stadtmitte' sp over rv bdge. immed turn R, bear L at fork, site in 1km on R. V lge, pt shd; wc; chem disp; mv service pnt; shwrs inc; el pnts (16A) €1.90; lndtte; shop; rest, snacks; bar; playgrnd; lake sw adj; tennis; cycle hire; entmnt high ssn; 60% statics; dogs €1.60; phone; poss cr; Eng spkn; adv bkg; ccard acc; redCKE/CCI. "NH on hdstg by ent; picturesque town with gd shops; 1 excel san facs block, other run down; pleasant staff." ♦ € 20.00                              2012*

**ROCKENHAUSEN** 3C2 (7km NE Rural) 49.67000, 7.88666 Azur Campingpark Pfalz, Kahlenbergweiher 1, 67813 Gerbach [(06361) 8287; fax 22523; gerbach@azur-camping.de; www.azur-camping.de/gerbach] Fr Rockenhausen take local rd to Gerbach then foll site sp on rd L385. Med, pt shd; wc; chem disp; mv service pnt; baby facs; shwrs inc; el pnts (16A) metered or €2.80; gas; lndtte; supmkt; rest, snacks; bar; cooking facs; playgrnd; pool; paddling pool; tennis; entmnt; 60% statics; dogs €2.80; adv bkg; quiet; redCKE/CCI; "Conv Rhein & Mosel wine regions; gd walking." 1 Apr-31 Oct. € 33.80                              2013*

**RODENKIRCHEN see Köln** 1B4

⊞ **ROSENHEIM** *4F4* (9km N Rural) *47.92518, 12.13571* **Camping Erlensee, Rosenheimerstrasse 63, 83135 Schechen [(08039) 1695; fax 9416; campingplatz-erlensee@t-online.de; www.camping-erlensee.de]** Exit A8 junc 102, avoid Rosenheim town cent by foll B15 sp Landshut. Site on E side of B15 at S end Schechen. Med, pt shd; wc; chem disp; some serviced pitches; shwrs €0.50; el pnts (16A) €2; lndtte; shop 1km; rest; lake sw; 60% statics; dogs €2; poss cr; Eng spkn; adv bkg; quiet; red CKE/CCI. "Pleasant, & simple site; helpful owners; excel facs; mosquito prob." ♦ € 19.40                                                                   2014*

⊞ **ROSENHEIM** *4F4* (12km SW Rural) *47.78978, 12.00575* **Kaiser Camping (Formerly known as Tenda-Park), Reithof 2, 83075 Bad Feilnbach [(08066) 884400; fax 8844029; info@kaiser-camping.com; www.kaiser-camping.com]** Take exit 100 fr A8/E45/E52 & foll sp to Brannenburg. Site in 5km on R, 1km N of Bad Feilnbach. V lge, pt shd; wc; baby facs; shwrs inc; el pnts (16A) €2. or metered + conn fee (poss rev pol); gas; lndtte (inc dryer); shop; rest; playgrnd; htd pool; paddling pool; cycle hire; ski lift 12km; entmnt high ssn; wifi; 80% statics; dogs €3; Eng spkn; adv bkg; quiet. "V busy, clean, well-run site; pleasant, wooded pitches; useful NH; pleasant helpful staff; some of the best san facs; discount vouchers for local shops/rest." ♦ € 35.00                                2014*

⊞ **ROSSHAUPTEN** *4E4* (500m N Rural) *47.65800, 10.71900* **Wohnmobilstellplatz Rosshaupten, Augsburgerstrasse 23, 87672 Rosshaupten [(08367) 913877; fax 913876; info@womomi.de]** Fr N twd Forggensee on B16, site on R immed after taking Rosshaupten exit. Sm, mkd pitch, hdstg, pt shd; htd wc; chem disp; mv service pnt; shwrs €1; el pnts (10A) €2; gas; lndtte; shop, rest, bar 500m; sat TV; dogs; bus; Eng spkn; some rd noise; red long stay. "OK for m'vans but will acc cars/c'vans if site not busy; gd, modern san facs; helpful, friendly owners; c'van dealer/repair on site - can be like parking in a c'van sales yard!; gd location for castles, Forggensee & Austrian border." ♦ ltd  € 9.00 (4 persons)                    2010*

⊞ **ROTENBURG (WUMME)** *1D2* (3km E Rural) *53.06977, 9.49413* **Camping Ferienpark Hanseat, Am Campingplatz 4, 27386 Bothel [(04266) 335; fax 8424; info@campingpark-hanseat.de]** Exit A1 junc 50 Sottrum twd Rotenburg, then take B71 E dir Soltau. Site sp in Bothel. Med, unshd; htd wc; chem disp; mv service pnt; shwrs; el pnts; lndtte (inc dryer); shop; rest, snacks; BBQ; playgrnd; htd pool 100m; lake sw & fishing 1km; tennis; games area; TV rm; 60% statics; dogs €2; adv bkg; quiet; "Gd for NH, a bit run down." ♦ € 21.80                                                                   2013*

**ROTENBURG (WUMME)** *1D2* (8km W Rural) *53.12027, 9.27833* **Camping Stürberg, 27367 Hassendorf [(04264) 9124; fax 821440; campingpark-stuerberg@gmx.de; www.stuerberg.de]** Exit A1/E22 Ottersberg-Rotenburg at Sottrum exit, junc 50. Turn E on B75, site on N side of B75 3km after Sottrum. Fr Rotenburg, take B75 turn S sp Hassendorf; site well sp. Med, pt shd; wc; chem disp; mv service pnt; shwrs inc; el pnts (10A) €2 & metered; gas; lndtte (inc dryer); shop 3km; tradsmn; rest 200m; snacks; bar; playgrnd; pool 3km; 30% statics; dogs €2; Eng spkn; some rd noise; red long stay/ CKE/CCI. "Grassy, open plan pitches; peaceful; pleasant staff; excel, clean facs." ♦ 15 Mar-31 Oct. € 15.00                   2009*

**ROTENBURG AN DER FULDA** *1D4* (1km E Urban) *50.99348, 9.74303* **Camping der Stadt, Campingweg, 36199 Rotenburg-an-der-Fulda [(06623) 5556; petra.reinhardt@ rotenburg.de; www.rotenburg.de]** Fr A4/E40 junc 32 N to Bebra on B27 Kasselerstrasse. Thro Bebra twd Rotenburg on B83; site sp on N side of Rv Fulda. Med, hdstg, pt shd; wc; chem disp; mv service pnt; shwrs inc; el pnts (16A) €2; lndtte (inc dryer); shop; rest 600m; snacks; covrd pool 400m; cycle hire; TV; dogs €0.70; quiet; red CKE/CCI. "Basic facs; few mins walk to town." 1 Apr-15 Oct. € 13.00                  2010*

⊞ **ROTHENBURG OB DER TAUBER** *3D2* (1km S Urban) *49.37083, 10.18361* **Wohnmobil Park (P2), Bensenstrasse, 91541 Rothenburg-ob-der-Tauber [(09861) 404800; fax 404529; info@rothenburg.de]** Exit A7/E43 junc 108. Just S of Rothenburg, foll sp P2 (car park no. 2). M'vans only. Med, mkd pitch, hdstg, pt sl, unshd; wc; chem disp; mv service pnt & water €1; el pnts (metered); shop 500m; rest opp; rd & rlwy noise. "M'vans only; clean, tidy o'night stop; wcs avail in car park; pay at machine; 5 min walk beautiful, interesting medieval town." € 10.00                                          2011*

## "That's changed – Should I let The Club know?"

If you find something on site that's different from the site entry, fill in a report and let us know. See www.caravanclub.co.uk/europereport.

**ROTHENBURG OB DER TAUBER** *3D2* (2km NW Rural) *49.38805, 10.16638* **Camping Tauber-Idyll, Detwang 28, 91541 Rothenburg-ob-der-Tauber [(09861) 3177 or 6463; fax 92848; camping-tauber-idyll@t-online.de; www.rothenburg.de/tauberidyll]** NW on Rothenburg-Bad Mergentheim rd in vill of Detwang. Sp. Site behind inn nr church. Care on tight R turn into ent. Sm, pt shd; htd wc; chem disp; mv service pnt; shwrs inc; el pnts (6-16A) €2 or metered + conn fee; gas; lndtte; shop; rest at inn; cycle hire; dogs €1; bus; poss v cr; Eng spkn; adv bkg. "Church clock chimes each hour; clsd to vehicles 2200-0800; old walled town; gd cent for Romantische Strasse & Hohenlohe Plain; owners helpful; pleasant site; gd san facs; sm c'van pitches at busy times; gd cycle rte along valley." 22 Mar-1 Nov. € 25.60         2013*

**ROTHENBURG OB DER TAUBER** *3D2* (2km NW Rural) *49.38888, 10.16722* **Campingplatz Tauber-Romantik, Detwang 39, 91541 Rothenburg-ob-der-Tauber [(09861) 6191; fax 9368889; info@camping-tauberromantik.de; www.camping-tauberromantik.de]** NW on Rothenburg-Bad Mergentheim rd in vill of Detwang; turn L at camp sp & immed R; site sp fr Rothenburg. Sharp turn into site ent. Med, some hdstg, pt sl, terr, pt shd; htd wc; chem disp; mv service pnt €1; shwrs inc; el pnts (16A) €2.20; gas; lndtte (inc dryer); sm shop; rest nr; snacks; bar; playgrnd; pool 2km; some statics; dogs €1.80; phone; bus adj; poss cr; Eng spkn; adv bkg; ccard acc; quiet, but constant church bells; CKE/ CCI. "Pleasant, gd value site; excel, clean, gd facs; gd sized pitches; picturesque town; gd cycle rte; pleasant atmosphere; gd facs for children; conv NH for Rothenburg, Austria, Italy; Busy over festival w/ends; vg; well managed." ♦ 15 Mar-4 Nov & 30 Nov-7 Jan. € 22.50                      2014*

⊞ **ROTTENBUCH** *4E4* (1km S Rural) *47.72763, 10.96691*
Terrasencamping am Richterbichl, Solder 1, 82401
Rottenbuch [(08867) 1500; fax 8300; info@camping-
rottenbuch.de; www.camping-rottenbuch.de] S
fr Schongau for 10km on B23 dir Oberammergau, site just S of
Rottenbuch. Med, mkd pitch, terr, pt shd; wc; chem disp; mv
service pnt; shwrs inc; el pnts (10A) metered + conn fee; gas;
lndtte (inc dryer); shop; rest 300m; snacks; bar; playgrnd; lake
sw adj; wifi; 40% statics; dogs €2; Eng spkn; adv bkg; quiet;
ccard acc; red long stay/CKE/CCI. "Walks & cycle paths fr site;
local castles, churches & interesting towns; excel facs; friendly,
helpful owners." ♦ ltd € 18.00                    2012*

**RUDESHEIM** *3C2* (500m E Urban) *49.97777, 7.94083*
Camping am Rhein, Auf der Lach, 65385 Rüdesheim-am-
Rhein [(06722) 2528 or 49299 (LS); fax 406783; mail@
campingplatz-ruedesheim.de; www.campingplatz-
ruedesheim.de] Fr Koblenz (N) on B42 pass car ferry to
Bingen on app to Rüdesheim; turn L & over rlwy x-ing, foll
Rheinstrasse & rlwy for 1km; cont under rlwy bdge, turn R sp
to Car Park 6; turn R at T-junc, pass coach park; turn L at x-rds
& foll rd to site on R. When arr via Bingen ferry turn R onto B42
& foll above dir fr level x-ing. Fr S on B42 ent Rüdesheim, turn
L immed after o'head rlwy bdge (2.8m); foll camping sp. Lge,
pt shd; htd wc; chem disp; mv service pnt; baby facs; shwrs
€1; el pnts (10A) inc (poss rev pol & poss long lead req); gas;
lndtte (inc dryer); shop; tradsmn; rest 600m; bar; BBQ (gas/
charcoal); playgrnd; htd pool, paddling pool, tennis adj; cycle
hire; horseriding 4km; no statics; dogs €3; no c'vans/m'vans
over 11m; bus 500m; recep 0800-2200; poss v cr; Eng spkn;
adv bkg; quiet but rlwy & rv traff noise; ccard not acc; CKE/CCI.
"Pleasant, busy, family-run site; busy, well-kept & well-run;
gd facs; poss long walk to water supply; pleasant 1km walk/
cycleway by rv to town; warden sites you & connects elec -
no mkd pitches; perforated grnd sheets only allowed; rallies
welcome; Harley Davidson w/end bike festival in June; shwrs
far; pleasant loc by rv; shops conv." ♦ 1 May-2 Oct. € 27.00
SBS - G08                                          2014*

**RUDESHEIM** *3C2* (3km E Urban) *49.97944, 7.95777*
Camping Geisenheim Rheingau, Am Campingplatz
1, 65366 Geisenheim [(06722) 75600; fax 406655;
campingplatzgeisenheim@t-online.de; www.rheingau-
camping.de] Well sp fr B42, on rvside. Lge, mkd pitch, pt shd;
htd wc; chem disp; baby facs; fam bthrm; shwrs inc; el pnts
(16A) inc; lndtte (inc dryer); shop 2km; rest, snacks; bar; BBQ;
playgrnd; htd pool 1km; games area; 50% statics; dogs €1.50;
phone adj; bus adj; Eng spkn; adv bkg; quiet; CKE/CCI. "Vg
site bet Rv Rhine & vineyards; walks and cycling by rv; lots to
do." ♦ 1 March to 31 October. € 30.30              2013*

⊞ **RUHPOLDING** *4F4* (3km S Rural) *47.7424, 12.66356*
Camping Ortnerhof, Ort 5, 83324 Ruhpolding
[(08663) 1764; fax 5073; camping-ortnerhof@t-online.de;
www.camping-ruhpolding.de] Exit A8/E52/E60 junc 112,
thro Ruhpolding, turn L onto B305 dir Berchtesgaden, site sp.
Med, mkd pitch, some hdstg, unshd; htd wc; chem disp; mv
service pnt; shwrs inc; el pnts (10A) metered + conn fee; lndtte;
shop 1.5km; tradsmn; rest, snacks; playgrnd; pool 3km; ski
lift 3km; skibus; internet; quiet; 30% statics; no dogs; poss cr;
10% red CKE/CCI 2+ nts. "Restful, friendly site in gd location;
helpful recep; sep area for m'vans adj hotel; barrier clsd 1200-
1400." ♦ € 18.50                                   2010*

**SAALBURG** *4F2* (1km N Rural) *50.51542, 11.73072*
Campingplatz Kloster, Klosterstrasse 1b, 07929 Saalburg-
Kloster [tel/fax (036647) 22441; bb@saalburg-ebersdorf.
de; www.saalburg-ebersdorf.de] Exit A9/E51 junc 28 dir
Saalburg. Site sp on lakeside. Lge, pt sl, unshd; wc; chem disp;
mv service pnt; baby facs; shwrs €1; el pnts (10-16A) €1.50;
gas; lndtte (inc dryer); shop 1km; rest, snacks; bar; playgrnd;
lake sw adj; games area; 80% statics; dogs €2; sep car park;
quiet. "Gd." ♦ 1 Apr-31 Oct. € 19.00              2010*

⊞ **SAARBURG** *3B2* (1.5km S Rural) *49.60083, 6.52833*
Campingplatz Waldfrieden, Im Fichtenhain 4,
54439 Saarburg [(06581) 2255; fax 5908; info@
campingwaldfrieden.de; www.campingwaldfrieden.
de] Fr B51/B407 bypass foll sp 'krankenhaus' (hospital). Site
sp off L132. Med, hdg pitch, some hdstg, pt sl, pt shd; wc;
chem disp; mv service pnt; some serviced pitches; shwrs inc;
el pnts (16A) metered; gas; lndtte; shop 600m; tradsmn; rest,
snacks; bar; BBQ; cooking facs; playgrnd; pool 1km; cycle hire;
wifi; TV rm; 60% statics; dogs €2; Eng spkn; adv bkg; quiet;
red low ssn/long stay/CKE/CCI. "Highly rec; helpful owners;
warm welcome; clean facs; pitches poss tight lge o'fits." ♦
€ 24.30                                            2014*

**SAARBURG** *3B2* (4km W Rural) *49.62010, 6.54274* Camping
Landal Warsberg, In den Urlaub, 54439 Saarburg
[(06581) 91460; fax 914646; warsberg@landal.de; www.
landal.de] Fr Trier foll B51 S and turn at rd sp Saarbrücken
at Konz, after 25km on leaving Ayl vill turn R sp Saarburg.
Cont over bdge turn R sp Centre. At rndabt turn L thro cent,
at rndabt L into rd sp Warsburg, after 300m turn L uphill sp
Landal. V lge, mkd pitch, pt sl, pt shd; wc; chem disp; mv
service pnt; baby facs; shwrs inc; el pnts (6A) inc; gas; lndtte;
shop; rest, snacks; bar; BBQ; playgrnd; htd, covrd pool; tennis;
cycle hire; games rm; entmnt high ssn; dogs €3; site clsd
1300-1500; poss noisy, quiet at far end; ccard acc. "Excel; gd
san facs; chem disp diff to use; excel pool; chairlift to attractive
town cent; gd views; many activities all ages." ♦ 3 Apr-9 Nov.
€ 32.00                                            2012*

---

## "I like to fill in the reports as I travel from site to site"

You'll find report forms at the back of
this guide, or you can fill them in online
at www.caravaclub.co.uk/europereport.

---

**SAARLOUIS** *3B2* (1km NW Urban) *49.31833, 6.73972*
Campingpark Saarlouis Dr Ernst Dadder, Marschall-
Ney-Weg 2, 66740 Saarlouis [(06831) 3691; fax 122970;
campsls@aol.com; www.camping-saarlouis.de] Exit A620/
E29 junc 2. Foll sp to city cent. At 500m approx turn L at traff
lts sp 'Schiffanlegestelle'. At 500m approx site on R. Med,
pt shd; wc; mv service pnt; shwrs inc; el pnts (16A) €2.30 or
metered; gas; lndtte; shop 500m; rest, snacks; htd pool 150m;
30% statics; dogs €0.60; adv bkg; quiet; ccard acc; red long
stay/snr citizens/CKE/CCI. "Castles, Roman remains, ruins &
forest rds at Saarland & Saarbrücken; friendly owner; gd rest."
15 Mar-31 Oct. € 18.00                            2011*

**ST GOAR AM RHEIN see Oberwesel** *3B2*

**ST GOARSHAUSEN** *3B2* (5km S Rural) *50.14021, 7.73469* Campingplatz auf der Loreley, Auf de Loreley 5, 56346 Bornich [(06771) 802697; fax 802698; info@loreley-camping.de; www.loreley-camping.de] Fr St Goarshausen on E bank of Rhine, take minor, steep rd to Bornich for 2.5km. Turn R twds Loreley rock, site on L 1km downhill. Med, mkd pitch, pt sl, pt shd; htd wc; chem disp; shwrs inc; el pnts (16A) metered + conn fee; lndtte (inc dryer); shop 2km; tradsmn; rest, snacks; bar; BBQ; playgrnd; htd, covrd pool; wifi; 20% statics; dogs €1.50; Eng spkn; quiet; CKE/CCI. "Lovely, peaceful, spacious site with views of Rv Rhine; gd, clean san facs; gd bar & rest; friendly, helpful owner with fund of local knowledge." 1 Mar-31 Oct. € 19.00      2010*

**ST LEON ROT see Wiesloch** *3C3*

**ST MARTIN see Neustadt** *3C2*

**ST PETER see Freiburg im Breisgau** *3B4*

> ## "We must tell The Club about that great site we found"
> Get your site reports in by mid-August and we'll do our best to get your updates into the next edition.

**SALEM** *3D4* (1.5km E Rural) *47.76926, 9.30693* Gern-Campinghof Salem, Weildorferstrasse 46, 88682 Salem-Neufrach [(07553) 829695; fax 829694; info@campinghof-salem.de; www.campinghof-salem.de] Site well sp on all app to Neufrach on rvside. Med, mkd pitch, pt sl, unshd; htd wc; chem disp; baby facs; shwrs inc; el pnts (16A) €2; gas; lndtte (inc dryer); tradsmn; rest, snacks 2km; bar; BBQ; cooking facs; playgrnd; htd, covrd pool 4km; lake sw nr; tennis; games rm; internet; cab/sat TV; 5% statics; dogs €2 (not Jul/Aug); phone; bus; poss cr; Eng spkn; adv bkg; quiet; ccard acc; CKE/CCI. "Excel touring base for Lake Constance away fr busy lakeside sites; barrier clsd 1230-1500 & 2200-0700; avoid pitches facing recep - noise & dust; gd, clean san facs; friendly, helpful, young owners; gd for families; vg." 1 Apr-31 Oct. € 17.50      2010*

⊞ **SALZHEMMENDORF** *1D3* (6km S Rural) *52.00390, 9.64302* Campingpark Humboldtsee, Humboldtsee 1, 31020 Salzhemmendorf-Wallensen [(05186) 957140; fax 957139; info@campingpark-humboldtsee.se; www.campingpark-humboldtsee.de] E fr Hameln on B1, at Hemmendorf turn S twd Salzhemmendorf & Wallensen, site sp 2.5km SE of Wallensen. V lge, hdg/mkd pitch, pt shd; htd wc; chem disp; mv service pnt; baby facs; shwrs €0.50; el pnts (6A) inc; lndtte (inc dryer); shop & 2km; rest, snacks; cooking facs; playgrnd; pool 3km; paddling pool; lake sw & beach; fishing; boat hire; games rm; entmnt; 60% statics; dogs €2; adv bkg; quiet; ccard acc; red snr citizens/CKE/CCI. "Gd facs for families; Hameln (Hamlin) 30km." € 22.50      2011*

**SCHAPRODE (RUGEN ISLAND)** *2F1* (230m N Coastal) *54.51610, 13.16510* Camping am Schaproder Bodden, Langestrasse 24, 18569 Schaprode [tel/fax (038309) 1234; camping.schaprode@t-online.de; www.camping-schaprode.de] Fr Stralsund on B96 to Rügen Island, N to Samtens then turn N thro Gingst; at Trent turn W to Schaprode; site sp on ent to vill. Lge, mkd pitch, pt shd; wc; chem disp; mv service pnt; shwrs €0.50; el pnts (6A) €1.50; lndtte; shop; tradsmn; rest, snacks; bar; BBQ; playgrnd; sand/shgl beach adj; watersports; cycle hire; 20% statics; dogs €1.25; Eng spkn; adv bkg; quiet; CKE/CCI. "Pleasant beach position; some great pitches; cheerful, family-owned site; trips to island of Hiddensee (nature reserve) - unspoilt island; rec." 1 Apr-31 Oct. € 18.00      2011*

**SCHIERKE see Braunlage** *2E4*

⊞ **SCHILLINGSFURST** *3D3* (1.5km S Rural) *49.27353, 10.26587* Campingplatz Frankenhöhe, Fischhaus 2, 91583 Schillingsfürt [(09868) 5111; fax 959699; info@campingplatz-frankenhoehe.de; www.campingplatz-frankenhoehe.de] Fr A7/E43 exit junc 109; fr A6/E50 exit junc 49. Site situated bet Dombühl & Schillingsfürst. Med, pt sl, pt shd; htd wc; chem disp; mv service pnt; baby facs; shwrs inc; el pnts (16A) €2.50 or metered + conn fee; gas; lndtte; shop; tradsmn; rest; playgrnd; lake sw 200m; wifi; 40% statics; dogs €1.50; phone; poss cr; adv bkg; red long stay/CKE/CCI. "Very clean facs; barrier clsd 1300-1500 & 2100-0700; poss unkempt early ssn (2009); gd cycle paths." ♦ € 16.50      2011*

**SCHILTACH** *3C3* (800m W Urban) *48.29061, 8.33746* Camping Schiltach, Bahnhofstrasse 6, 77761 Schiltach [(07836) 7289; fax 7466; campingplatz-schiltach@t-online.de] Site on B294 sp on ent to vill; short, steep ent & sharp turns. Sm, mkd pitch, pt shd; htd wc; chem disp; mv service pnt; shwrs inc; baby facs; el pnts (16A) metered + conn fee; lndtte (inc dryer); shop 500m; tradsmn; rest 200m; snacks; bar; BBQ; playgrnd; covrd pool 2km; shgl beach adj; 2% statics; no dogs; phone; recep clsd 1230-1430; train 200m; Eng spkn; adv bkg; quiet; CKE/CCI. "Vg, clean, tidy site on rv bank adj indus est; picturesque vill; disused rlwy bdge over pt of site, 2.60m headrm; friendly staff." ♦ ltd 1 Apr-10 Oct. € 15.00      2010*

**SCHLECHING METTENHAM see Reit im Winkl** *4F4*

⊞ **SCHLEIDEN** *3B1* (6km NW Rural) *50.52752, 6.41195* Camping Schafbachmühle, 53937 Schleiden-Harperscheid [(02485) 268; info@schafbachmuehle.de; www.schafbachmuehle.de] Fr Schleiden take B258 twd Monschau. In 3.5km turn R sp Schafbachmühle. Site in 2.5km on L. Med, mkd pitch, hdstg, terr, pt shd; htd wc; chem disp; mv service pnt; baby facs; shwrs €1; el pnts (10A) metered + conn fee; lndtte (inc dryer); shop 800m; tradsmn; rest, snacks; bar; BBQ; playgrnd; games area; 60% statics; dogs €2.20; phone; Eng spkn; adv bkg; quiet. "Tranquil site; gd for touring Eifel, Mosel Valley, Rhine Valley." ♦ € 14.80      2010*

⊞ **SCHLESWIG** *1D1* (7.5km E Coastal) *54.52563, 9.71543* Campingplatz am Missunder Fährhaus, Missunder Fährstrasse 33, 24864 Brodersby [(04622) 626; fax 2543; missunder-faehrhaus@t-online.de; www.missunder-faehrhaus.de] Exit A7 junc 5; take B201 sp Kappeln; in 10km turn R sp Scholderup & Brodersby; foll sp Missunder ferry. Site 100m bef ferry x-ing. Sm, sl, unshd; wc; chem disp; shwrs €1; el pnts (16A) €2.50; rest, snacks & bar adj; sailing & canoeing; dogs; quiet; gd. "Watersports; deposit for wc key; rest rec." € 12.00                                                          2009*

**SCHLESWIG** *1D1* (2km S Rural) *54.50111, 9.57027* **Wikinger Camping Haithabu**, 24866 Haddeby [(04621) 32450; fax 33122; info@campingplatz-haithabu.de; www.campingplatz-haithabu.de] Leave A7/45 N & S junc 6. Travel E two Schleswig & turn R onto B76 sp Kiel & Eckernförde. Site on L in 2km sp. Med, pt shd; wc; chem disp; mv service pnt; shwrs €0.50; el pnts (4A) €2; lndtte; shop 3km; tradsmn; rest, snacks; playgrnd; lake sw adj; boating facs; dogs €2; poss cr; Eng spkn; adv bkg; some rd noise; CKE/CCI. "Lovely site on rv; foot & cycle paths to Schleswig (4.5km) & ferry; gd area for children; Schloss Gottorf worth visit; vg Viking museum adj." 1 Apr-25 Oct. € 18.00                                              2009*

⊞ **SCHLUCHSEE** *3C4* (1km NW Rural) *47.82236, 8.16273* Campingplatz Wolfsgrund, Sägackerweg, 79859 Schluchsee [(07656) 573; fax 7759; info@schluchsee.de; www.camping-schluchsee.de] Site sp fr rd B500 - rec app fr N only. Lge, hdg/mkd pitch, terr, pt sl, pt shd; wc; chem disp; mv service pnt; shwrs inc; el pnts (10A) metered; gas; lndtte (inc dryer); shop 500m; rest, snacks; playgrnd; shgl beach & lake sw 200m; games area; wifi; dogs €1.50; site clsd 1300-1500 & 2200-0800; poss cr; Eng spkn; quiet; ccard acc; red CKE/CCI. "Fishing & sailing on lake adj; wintersports area; gd walking & cycling country with excel views." € 27.50     2011*

⊞ **SCHOMBERG** *3C3* (2km N Rural) *48.79820, 8.63623* Höhen-Camping, Schömbergstrasse 32, 75328 Langenbrand [(07084) 6131; fax 931435; info@hoehencamping.de; www.hoehencamping.de] Fr N exit A8 junc 43 Pforzheim, take B463 dir Calw. Turn R sp Schömberg & foll sp Langenbrand. Med, hdg/mkd pitch, pt sl, pt shd; htd wc; chem disp; fam bthrm; shwrs €0.50; el pnts (10-16A) €3; lndtte; shop 200m; playgrnd; TV; 70% statics; dogs €2; phone; adv bkg; quiet; CKE/CCI. "Clean, well-maintained site in N of Black Forest; vg san facs; no recep - ring bell on house adj site ent; blocks req for sl pitches." € 18.80                           2013*

**SCHONAU (RHEIN-NECKAR)** *3C2* (5km N Rural) *49.46593, 8.80307* **Camping Steinachperle, Altneudorferstrasse 14**, 69250 Schönau-Altneudorf [(06228) 467; fax 8568; campingplatz-steinachperle@t-online.de; www.camping-steinachperle.de] Fr Heidelberg foll B37 alongside Rv Neckar to Neckarsteinach, turn L at traff lts in cent to Schönau, thro Schönau to Altneudorf; site behind Inn Zum Pflug on L thro vill of Altneudorf. Steep ent/exit. Med, hdg pitch, pt sl, pt shd; wc; chem disp; shwrs €0.50; el pnts (16A) metered + conn fee; lndtte (inc dryer); shop; rest, snacks; bar; playgrnd; pool 2km; beach sw 2km; dogs €1.10; phone; Eng spkn; v quiet; CKE/CCI. "Well-kept site; gd san facs but climb to san blocks; gd sized pitches; barrier clsd 1300-1500; ideal for Neckar Valley - rec." 1 Apr-30 Sep. € 16.00                                              2011*

⊞ **SCHONAU IM SCHWARZWALD** *3B4* (800m N Rural) *47.79127, 7.90076* **Camping Schönenbuchen**, Friedrichstrasse 58, 79677 Schönau [(07673) 7610; fax 234327; info@camping-schoenau.de; www.camping-schoenau.de] Fr Lörrach on B317 dir Todtnau for approx 23km. Site thro Schönau main rd on R on rvside, ent thro car park. Narr access diff for l'ge o'fits. Med, hdg pitch, pt shd; wc; chem disp; mv service pnt; baby facs; sauna; shwrs; el pnts inc (16A) (poss rev pol); lndtte; shop 400m; rest; bar; playgrnd; htd pool; sw & watersports adj; tennis; horseriding; cycle hire; 70% statics; dogs €1; adv bkg; quiet; red long stay; CKE/CCI. "Friendly staff; site poss not well-kept; gd walking & cycling; lovely old town." ♦ € 28.20                              2014*

⊞ **SCHONENBERG KUBELBERG** *3B2* (1.5km E Rural) *49.41172, 7.40479* **Campingpark Ohmbachsee, Miesauerstrasse**, 66901 Schönenberg-Kübelberg [(0673) 4001; fax 4002; jungfleisch@campingpark-ohmbachsee.de; www.campingpark-ohmbachsee.de] Exit A6/E50 junc 10 or 11 twd Schönenberg, site sp on Lake Ohmbach. Lge, mkd pitch, terr, pt shd; htd wc; chem disp; mv service pnt; baby facs; sauna; shwrs inc; el pnts (6A) €2.50 or metered; lndtte (inc dryer); shop; rest, snacks; bar; BBQ; cooking facs; playgrnd; htd pool; paddling pool; canoeing; boat & cycle hire; tennis; games area; horseriding 7km; golf driving range; wifi; entmnt; 50% statics; dogs €3; adv bkg; quiet. "Lake views fr some pitches (ltd); excel facs & rest." ♦ € 19.50                                                          2009*

## "I need an on-site restaurant"

We do our best to make sure site information is correct, but it is always best to check any must-have facilities are still available or will be open during your visit.

**SCHORTENS** *1C2* (1km W Rural) *53.55055, 7.93722* **Friesland Camping, Am Schwimmbad 2**, 26419 Schortens [(04461) 758727; fax 758933; info@friesland-camping.de; www.friesland-camping.de] Exit A29 junc 5 onto B210 dir Schortens & Jever. Site on L past Schortens vill. Med, mkd pitch, shd; htd wc; chem disp; mv service pnt; baby facs; serviced pitches; shwrs inc; el pnts (16A) €2.40 or metered; lndtte (inc dryer); shop 800m; snacks; cooking facs; playgrnd; pool; sand beach 15km; lake sw adj; golf 8km; wifi; 20% statics; dogs €3; phone; bus 800m; Eng spkn; adv bkg; quiet; red long stay. "V pleasant site; gd facs; aquapark at Schortens & Jever worth visit; vg." ♦ Easter- 24 Oct. € 20.00                         2010*

**SCHUTTORF** *1B3* (1km N Rural) *52.33960, 7.22617* **Camping Quendorfer See, Weiße Riete 3**, 48465 Schüttorf [05923 90 29 39; fax 90 29 40; info@camping-schuettorf.de; www.camping-schuettorf.de] A1/A30, exit J4 Schüttorf-Nord. Or A31 exit J28 Schüttorf-Ost twds town centre. Foll sp to site. Sm, hdg pitch, mkd pitch, unshd; htd wc; chem disp; mv service pnt; baby facs; fam bthrm; shwrs inc; el pnts (16A); lndtte (inc dryer); shop 2km; tradsmn; snacks; bar; playgrnd; sw adj; games area; dogs €2; bus 2km; twin axles; adv bkg; quiet; ccard acc; CCI. "Excel site; Immac san facs; mostly fully serviced pitches; conv NH for ferries fr Holland; flat cycling & walking." ♦ 1 Apr-31 Oct. € 25.00                                   2014*

**SCHWAAN** *2F2* (2km S Rural) *53.92346, 12.10688*
Camping Schwaan, Güstrowerstrasse 54/Sandgarten 17, 18258 Schwaan [(03844) 813716; fax 814051; info@campingplatz-schwaan.de; www.campingplatz-schwaan.de] Fr A20 exit junc 13 to Schwaan, site sp. Fr A19 exit junc 11 dir Bad Doberan & Schwaan. Site adj Rv Warnow. Lge, mkd pitch, pt shd; htd wc; mv service pnt; sauna; baby facs; shwrs inc; el pnts (16A) €2.20 or metered; lndtte (inc dryer); shop high ssn; supmkt 800m; rest, snacks; bar; cooking facs; playgrnd; canoeing; boat & cycle hire; tennis 700m; games area; wifi; entmnt; TV; 30% statics; dogs €2; site clsd 21 Dec-4 Jan; adv bkg; quiet. "Pleasant rvside site; gd touring base; tight app thro Schwaan town (esp fr N)." ♦ 1 Mar-31 Oct. € 26.50                                    2014*

**SCHWABISCH HALL** *3D3* (2km S Urban) *49.09868, 9.74288*
Camping am Steinbacher See, Mühlsteige 26, 74523 Schwäbisch Hall-Steinbach [(0791) 2984; fax 9462758; thomas.seitel@t-online.de; www.camping-schwaebisch-hall.de] Fr A6/E50 exit junc 43 fr W or junc 42 fr E to Schwäbisch Hall. On ent town foll site sp to Comburg. Turn sharp R after castle at pedestrian x-ing to site. Site well sp. Med, mkd pitch, pt shd; htd wc; chem disp; mv service pnt; shwrs €0.50; el pnts (10A) metered + conn fee; lndtte; shop 3km; rest 200m; snacks; bar; BBQ; playgrnd; cycle hire; 50% statics; dogs €2; clsd 1300-1500; poss cr; Eng spkn; adv bkg; red CKE/CCI. "Lovely well kept idiosyncratic site; friendly; walking dist to interesting medieval town; cycle track to town." ♦ 1 Feb-30 Nov. € 16.70                                    2011*

**SCHWANGAU see Füssen** *4E4*

**SCHWEDENECK see Gettorf** *1D1*

**SCHWEPPENHAUSEN** *3B2* (2km N Rural) *49.9340, 7.79180* Campingplatz Aumühle, Naheweinstraße 65, 55444 Schweppenhausen [06724 602392; fax 601610; info@camping-aumuehle.de] Fr A61 take exit 47 - Waldlaubersheim. Foll signs to Schweppenhausen. Sp to camp site. Med, mkd pitch, pt shd; wc; chem disp; baby facs; shwrs inc; el pnts (10A); lndtte; rest; snacks; bar; playgrnd; 50% statics; poss cr; quiet; CCI. "Gd site; cycle rtes fr site." 1 Apr-31 Oct. € 26.50                                    2014*

⊞ **SCHWERIN** *2E2* (10km N Rural) *53.69725, 11.43715*
Ferienpark Seehof, Am Zeltzplatz 1, 19069 Seehof [(0385) 512540; fax 5814170; info@ferienparkseehof.de; www.ferienparkseehof.de] Take B106 N fr Schwerin for approx 5km: turn R at city boundary & site within 5km at end of vill, sp. Lge, pt sl, pt shd; wc; chem disp; mv service pnt; serviced pitches; shwrs €1; el pnts (4A) inc (poss rev pol); gas; lndtte; shop; rest, snacks; bar; playgrnd, lake sw & sand beach; windsurfing; sailing school; cycle hire; entmnt; 30% statics; dogs €1; poss cr; adv bkg; quiet; ccard acc. "Lge pitches; vg." € 27.00                                    2009*

⊞ **SEEBURG** *2E4* (800m NW Rural) *51.49400, 11.69400*
Camping Seeburg am Süsser See, Nordstrand 1, 06317 Seeburg [(034774) 28281; fax 41757; info@campingplatz-seeburg.de; www.campingplatz-seeburg.de] W fr Halle on B80 twd Eisleben, sp fr Seeburg. Site on N shore of Lake Süsser See. Lge, pt shd; wc; chem disp; shwrs €0.52; el pnts (16A) €1.10; rest 500m; playgrnd; lake sw; fishing; 95% statics; dogs €1.20. "Attractive, busy site by lake; facs old but clean; excel base for medieval towns nr & 'Martin Luther country'; gd; nice site by lake; not many pitches." ♦ € 23.60                                    2014*

**SENHEIM see Cochem** *3B2*

**SESSLACH see Coburg** *4E2*

⊞ **SIGMARINGEN** *3D4* (500m SW Urban) *48.08366, 9.20794* Erlebnis-Camp Sigmaringen, Georg-Zimmererstrasse 6, 72488 Sigmaringen [(07571) 50411; fax 50412; info@outandback.de; www.erlebnis-camp.de] App town fr N or SW, ent town over Danube bdge, turn R into car pk (camp sp). To far end of car park, turn R in front of supmkt & cont on rv bank. Ent camp fr far end. Site adj to stadium by rv, sp fr town. Med, pt shd; wc; chem disp; mv service pnt; shwrs €0.50; el pnts (6-16A) €3; lndtte; shop 300m; tradsmn; rest; snacks 300m; playgrnd; htd pool 300m; cycle hire; internet; 10% statics; dogs €1; CKE/CCI. "On Danube cycle way; gd outdoor activities; lovely site." ♦ € 26.50                                    2014*

⊞ **SIMMERATH** *1A4* (10km NE Rural) *50.62753, 6.3853* Campingplatz Woffelsbach, Promenadenweg, 52152 Woffelsbach [(02473) 2704; fax 929445; www.campingplatz-woffelsbach.de] Fr Simmerath B266 W to Kesternich; L166 to Rurberg; L128 to Woffelsbach; clear sps in vill. Sm, hdstg, terr, unshd; wc; chem disp; mv service pnt; serviced pitches; shwrs €1; el pnts (16A) inc; lndtte; shop adj; rest 200m; snacks 100m; lake sw adj; few statics; no dogs; site clsd Jan; quiet; no ccard acc. "Most pitches with lake views; site rather run down (2010)." € 16.00                                    2010*

⊞ **SIMMERATH** *1A4* (6km SE Rural) *50.56388, 6.33333* Camping Hammer, An der Streng 7, 52152 Simmerath-Hammer [(02473) 929041; fax 937481; info@camp-hammer.de; www.camp-hammer.de] Fr Monschau take B399 N for 5km to Imgenbroich, minor rd E to Hammer. Fr Simmerath take B399 SW for 2km L sp Hammer to site on R in vill. Med, pt shd; htd wc; chem disp; mv service pnt; shwrs €1; el pnts (10A) €3; gas; lndtte; shop & 5km; rest 800m; playgrnd; 60% statics; no dogs; quiet; cash only; CKE/CCI. "Excel rvside site; pleasant bistro; unique san facs! walking area, non-touristy." € 18.00                                    2011*

**SIMONSBERG see Husum** *1D1*

**SIMONSWALD see Waldkirch** *3C4*

**SOEST** *1C4* (10km S Rural) *51.47722, 8.10055* **Camping Delecke-Südufer, Arnsbergerstrasse 8, 59519 Möhnesee-Delecke** [(02924) 5010; fax 1288; info@camping-berndt. de; www.camping-berndt.de] Exit A44/E331 at junc 56 onto B229 sp Korbecke/Möhnesee. Cont to lake, cross bdge. At next junc turn L & site immed on L, sp. Med, hdg pitch, pt sl, unshd; wc; chem disp; mv service pnt; shwrs €1; el pnts (16A) €2.20 + conn fee; tradsmn; snacks; bar; rest 800m; lndtte; shop; playgrnd; lake sw & beach adj; boating; 50% statics; phone; no dogs; poss cr; quiet; clsd 1300-1500 & 2000-0800; Eng spkn; adv bkg; CKE/CCI. "Excel site on boating lake; san facs locked o'night; gd walking & sailing; v busy at w/ends." ♦ 1 Apr-3 Oct. € 22.50                                                     2010*

⊞ **SOLINGEN** *1B4* (5km S Rural) *51.13388, 7.11861* **Waldcamping Glüder, Balkhauserweg 240, 42659 Solingen-Glüder** [(0212) 242120; fax 2421234; info@ camping-solingen.de; www.camping-solingen.de] Exit A1 junc 97 Burscheid onto B91 N dir Hilgen. In Hilgen turn L onto L294 to Witzhelden then R on L359 dir Solingen. Site sp in Glüder by Rv Wupper. Med, hdg/mkd pitch, some hdstg, unshd; htd wc; chem disp; shwrs inc; chem disp; el pnts (6-10A) €3; gas; lndtte; tradsmn; shop 3km; rest adj; snacks; bar; playgrnd; TV; 80% statics; dogs €2.30; bus; Eng spkn; quiet; CKE/CCI. "Beautiful location in wooded valley; clsd 1300-1500; resident owner; excel san facs; easy walk to Burg-an-der-Wupper Schloss - worth visit." € 27.40                         2013*

⊞ **SOLTAU** *1D2* (1.5km N Rural) *53.00075, 9.8366* **Kur & Fereincamping Röders Park, Ebsmoor 8, 29614 Soltau** [(05191) 2141; fax 17952; info@roeders-park.de; www. roeders-park.de] Exit A7/E45 junc 45 onto B3 dir Soltau. Turn L onto B71 in Soltau cent, then R onto B3 sp Hamburg. Site sp on L at town boundary. Med, mkd pitch, pt shd; wc; chem disp; mv service pnt; some serviced pitches; shwrs inc; el pnts (6A) metered + conn fee; gas; lndtte; shop; rest, snacks; playgrnd; cycle hire; 25% statics; dogs €2; office clsd 1300-1500; ccard acc; red CKE/CCI. "Delightful, family-run site; helpful staff; excel rest; vg san facs; gd walking nrby." ♦ € 23.50                                                     2009*

**SOLTAU** *1D2* (13.4km SE Urban) *52.93487, 9.96786* **Südsee Camp, 29649 Wietzendorf** [(5196) 345] Exit a'bahn at Soltau Sud on rte 3 to Celle. After 3km turn L for Wietzendorf. Campsite on L, look for lge flag poles. Lge, pt shd; wc (cont); meals; snacks; shwrs; shop; el pnts; sand beach; lake sw; poss cr; adv bkg; quiet. pony rides, gd walking, all watersports. 22 Dec-Oct. € 23.47     2011*

See advert on bookmark

⊞ **SOLTAU** *1D2* (6km SW Rural) *52.94801, 9.85403* **Freizeithof Imbrock, Imbrock 4, 29614 Soltau** [(05191) 5202; fax 15960; www.camping-imbrock.de] Exit A7/E45 junc 45 Soltau-Süd. Foll sp Soltau then Brock, site sp fr main rd. V lge, pt shd; wc; mv service pnt; baby facs; shwrs €0.50; el pnts (10A) €2; lndtte; shop; rest, snacks; playgrnd; lake sw; tennis; games area; 60% statics; dogs €1.50; quiet. "San facs poss stretched." € 16.00                         2009*

**SOMMERACH see Dettelbach** *3D2*

⊞ **SONTHOFEN** *3D4* (1.5km SW Rural) *47.50636, 10.27353* **Camping an der Iller, Sinwagstrasse 2, 87527 Sonthofen** [(08321) 2350; fax 68792; info@illercamping.de; www. illercamping.de] Clearly sp fr Sonthofen Süd junc on B19; on Rv Iller. Med, mkd pitch, hdstg, unshd; wc; shwrs inc; chem disp; mv service pnt; el pnts (16A) metered; gas; lndtte; shop; rest 200m; snacks; bar; playgrnd; htd pool adj; dogs €2; clsd 1300-1500; some Eng spkn; adv bkg; quiet but some rlwy noise; CKE/CCI. "Scenic wintersports area; gd walking, cycling; excel, well-maintained facs; helpful owner; some rd noise; site quite bare; site designed on feng shui principles!" ♦ € 18.00                                                     2011*

⊞ **SOTTRUM** *1D2* (3km SW Rural) *53.08335, 9.17697* **Camping-Paradies Grüner Jäger, Everinghauser Dorfstrsse 17, 27367 Sottrum/Everinghausen** [(04205) 319113; fax 319115; info@camping-paradies.de; www.camping-paradies.de] Exit A1 junc 50 at Stuckenborstel onto B75 dir Rotenburg. In approx 500m turn R & foll sp Everinghausen. Site in 4km. Med, mkd pitch, unshd; htd wc; chem disp; mv service pnt; baby facs; shwrs €0.15 per min; el pnts (16A) €2.50; lndtte; shop 6km; rest; bar; playgrnd; pool; paddling pool; 30% statics; dogs free; Eng spkn; some rd noise; CKE/CCI. "Excel NH." € 23.50                                             2011*

⊞ **SPANGENBERG** *1D4* (500m SE Rural) *51.11373, 9.67391* **Campingplatz Municipal am Sportplatz, Jahnstrasse 23, 34286 Spangenberg** [(05663) 222; fax 509026; service-center@stadt-spangenberg.de; www.stadt-spangenberg. de] Fr A7 exit sp Melsungen & take B487 to Spangenberg. Site on SE of town, clearly visible fr rd. Narr app. Med, mkd pitch, terr, unshd; htd wc; chem disp; shwrs inc; el pnts (16A) metered; lndtte; supmkt 1km; cooking facs; playgrnd; pool & sports complex adj; 60% statics; dogs; clsd 1300-1500; some rd noise; CKE/CCI. "Historic old town; welcoming staff; gd clean facs; gd walking/cycling; gd NH & longer." ♦ € 16.80                                                     2010*

**SPEYER** *3C3* (2km N Rural) *49.33600, 8.44300* **Camping Speyer, Am Rübsamenwühl 31, 67346 Speyer** [(06232) 42228; fax 815174; info@camping-speyer.de; www.camping-speyer.de] Fr Mannheim or Karlsruhe take rd 9 to exit Speyer Nord dir Speyer. At 3rd traff lts turn L into Auestrasse, then at 2nd rndabt L into Am Rübsamenwühl. Site in 500m. Sm, some mkd pitch; shwrs €1; el pnts €3; supmkt 500m; rest, snacks; bar; playgrnd; lake sw & sand beach; 90% statics; dogs €2; no adv bkg; quiet; red long stay. "Speyer pleasant town, cathedral & Technik Museum worth visit; v basic site; scruffy & not well-kept; fair NH/sh stay." 15 Mar-15 Oct. € 29.00                                                     2014*

⊞ **SPEYER** *3C3* (1km SE Urban) *49.31250, 8.44916* **Camping Technik Museum, Am Technik Museum 1, Geibstrasse, 67346 Speyer** [(06232) 67100; fax 6710 20; info@hotel-speyer.de; www.hotel-speyer.de] Exit A61/E34 at junc 64, foll sp to museum. Med, unshd; htd wc; chem disp; mv service pnt; shwrs inc; el pnts inc (10A); shop 1km; rest, snacks, bar adj; dogs free; phone (hotel); bus; poss cr; Eng spkn; adv bkg. Ccard acc, 3 nights max stay; "Book in at hotel adj; excel museum & IMAX cinema on site; conv Speyer cent; site unkept; excel san facs." ♦ ltd € 22.00                       2014*

GERMANY

⊞ **SPIEGELAU** *4G3* (2km W Rural) *48.91737, 13.33150*
**Camping am Nationalpark, Bergstrasse 44, 94518
Klingenbrunn** [(08553) 727; fax 6930; info@camping-
nationalpark.de; www.camping-nationalpark.de] Fr A3
exit 111 at Hengersberg onto B533 dir Schönberg, turn N onto
B85 (Regen-Passau) & foll sp Klingenbrunn. At T-junc in vill cent
R & bear L in 300m to site on R in 1km. Med, mkd pitch, terr,
pt shd; serviced pitches; mv service pnt; wc; shwrs inc; chem
disp; mv service pnt; el pnts (16A) metered + conn fee; lndtte;
shop 1km; rest; playgrnd; covrd pool; fishing; horseriding 1km;
ski lift 3km; entmnt; 15% statics; dogs €1; site clsd 9 Nov-14
Dec; adv bkg; quiet; ccard acc; red CKE/CCI. "Peaceful, family-
run site." € 13.70                                                    2010*

## "Satellite navigation makes touring much easier"

Remember most sat navs don't know if you're towing or in a larger vehicle – always use yours alongside maps and site directions.

⊞ **STADTKYLL** *3B2* (1km S Rural) *50.33903, 6.53966*
**Camping Landal Wirfttal, Wirfttalstrasse 81, 54589 Stadtkyll**
[(06597) 92920; fax 929250; wirfttal@landal.de; www.
landal.de] Exit A1 onto B51 dir Prüm to Stadtkyll, site well sp
on minor rd to Schüller fr town cent. Fr SE app town on B421
then foll sps. Lge, pt shd; htd wc; chem disp; mv service pnt;
baby facs; sauna; baby facs; shwrs inc; el pnts (8A) inc; gas;
lndtte (inc dryer); shop; rest, snacks; bar; playgrnd; htd pool
adj; paddling pool; waterslides; tennis; games area; horseriding
adj; cycle hire; entmnt; TV; 30% statics; dogs €3; phone; adv
bkg; quiet; ccard acc. "Excel site; all facs htd & clean." ◆
€ 32.00                                                             2009*

**STADTSTEINACH see Kulmbach** *4E2*

⊞ **STAUFEN IM BREISGAU** *3B4* (500m SE Rural)
*47.87194, 7.73583* **Ferien-Campingplatz Belchenblick,
Münstertälerstrasse 43, 79219 Staufen-im-Breisgau**
[(07633) 7045; fax 7908; camping.belchenblick@t-online.
de; www.camping-belchenblick.de] Exit A5/E35 junc 64a
dir Bad Krozingen-Staufen-Münstertal. Avoid Staufen cent,
foll Münstertal sp. Camp on L 500m past Staufen. Visibility
restricted fr Münstertal dir. Lge, pt shd; wc; chem disp; mv
service pnt; baby facs; fam bthrm; sauna; shwrs inc; el pnts
(16A) metered; gas; lndtte (inc dryer); shop; rest 500m;
snacks; bar; BBQ area; sm htd indoor pool; playgrnd, public
pool & tennis nrby over unfenced rv via footbdge; cycle hire;
horseriding 500m; wifi; entmnt; games/TVrm; 60% statics;
dogs €2.50; no c'vans/m'vans over 8m high ssn; phone; no veh
access 1230-1500 & night time - parking area avail; poss cr;
Eng spkn; adv bkg rec holp ssn; some rd & rlwy noise in day;
no ccard acc; red low ssn/CKE/CCI. "Well-run, family-owned
site; some pitches sm; strict pitching rules; beautiful area &
Staufen pleasant town; beware train app round blind corner
at x-ing; gd walking, cycling, horseriding; San facs tired, need
refurbishing (2013); better cheaper sites close by." ◆ € 37.80
SBS - G02                                                          2013*

⊞ **STECHOW** *2F3* (6km N Rural) *52.65472, 12.42972*
**Campingpark Buntspecht Ferchesar, Weg zum Zeltplatz 1,
14715 Stechow-Ferchesar** [(03387) 490072; camping-park-
buntspecht@web.de; www.campingpark-buntspecht.de]
Fr Rathenow NE on B188 to Stechow, then turn L sp Ferchesar
& foll site sp to lakeside. Or fr A10 exit junc 26 sp Nauen &
take B5 for approx 25km to junc with B188 to Stechow. At
Stechow turn R sp Ferchesar then as above. Lge, mkd pitch, pt
shd; htd wc; chem disp; mv service pnt; baby facs; private san
facs avail; shwrs inc; el pnts (16A) €2; lndtte (inc dryer); shop;
tradsmn; rest, snacks; BBQ; cooking facs; playgrnd; lake sw;
fishing; boat, canoe, cycle hire; games area; wifi; 10% statics;
dogs €3.50; Eng spkn; adv bkg; quiet. "Pleasant, peaceful,
family site; gd walking/cycling in area." ◆ 1 Apr-31 Oct.
€ 23.00                                                             2011*

⊞ **STEINENSTADT** *3B4* (190m W Urban) *47.76895, 7.55115*
**Camping Vogesenblick, Eichwaldstrasse 7, 79395
Steinenstadt** [(07635) 1846] Exit A5/E35 junc 65 Neuenburg-
am-Rhein. Turn S at traff lts for Steinenstadt, site sp. Sm,
pt shd; wc; chem disp; mv service pnt; shwrs €0.50; el pnts
(16A) metered; lndtte; shop, rest adj; bar; htd, covrd pool
5km; 20% statics; dogs €1.50; bus nr; poss cr; adv bkg; quiet.
"Peaceful, friendly site; gd cycling beside Rv Rhine; easy access
Black Forest, Freiburg etc; v quiet site and vill; petrol 2km."
15 Mar-31 Oct. € 20.50                                              2012*

⊞ **STOCKACH** *3C4* (4km S Rural) *47.80860, 8.97000*
**Campinggarten Wahlwies, Stahringerstrasse 50, 78333
Stockach-Wahlwies** [(07771) 3511; fax 4236; info@
camping-wahlwies.de; www.camping-wahlwies.de] Exit
A98 junc 12 Stockach West onto B313 to Wahlwies. In vill
turn L immed after level x-ing, site on R bef next level x-ing,
sp. Med, pt shd; wc; chem disp; mv service pnt; shwrs inc; el
pnts (16A) €2; lndtte; shop 1km; tradsmn; rest 1km; snacks;
bar; lake sw 5km; 50% statics; dogs free; phone; poss cr;
Eng spkn; adv bkg rec bank hols; quiet; CKE/CCI. "Pleasantly
situated, friendly, orchard site 6km fr Bodensee; female san
facs inadequate; gd touring cent; gd local train service; excel
cycle tracks." 20 Mar-7 Nov. € 19.30                                2011*

⊞ **STOCKACH** *3C4* (1.5km SW Urban) *47.84194, 8.99500*
**Camping Papiermühle, Johann Glatt Strasse 3, 78333
Stockach** [(07771) 91651333; campingplatz@caramobil.
de; www.caramobil.de/stockach/freizeitpark] Fr Stockach
at junc rndabt of B31 & B313, turn L (E) to Caramobil C'van
Sales Depot. Site adj under same management. Med, mkd
pitch, some hdstg, pt sl, terr, pt shd; htd wc; chem disp; mv
service pnt; shwrs; el pnts (6A) €2; lndtte (inc dryer); shop;
tradsmn; rest adj; snacks; bar; BBQ; playgrnd; 50% statics;
dogs €2.20; phone; bus 200m; poss cr; Eng spkn; adv bkg;
quiet; ccard acc; CKE/CCI. "Sep m'van area adj; v clean facs;
helpful staff; conv location for town; gd walking & cycling; vg
site." ◆ € 19.00                                                    2013*

⊞ **STORKOW** *2G3* (6km NE Rural) *52.29194, 13.98638*
Campingplatz Waldsee, 15526 Reichenwalde-Kolpin [(033631) 5037; fax 59891; mail@campingplatz-waldsee. de; www.campingplatz-waldsee.de] Fr A12/E30, exit junc 3 Storkow. Just bef ent Storkow, turn N twd Fürstenwalde. In 6km turn R leaving Kolpin, site sp. Med, pt sl, pt shd; wc; chem disp; sauna; shwrs €0.50; el pnts (16A) €2; lndtte; shops 2km; rest 6km; rest 6km; snacks; bar; playgrnd; lake sw adj; cycle hire; 60% statics; dogs €1; Eng spkn; adv bkg; quiet; ccard acc; red CKE/CCI. "Gd san facs; haphazard pitching; conv NH en rte to/fr Poland; gd cycling area; Bad Saarow lakeside worth visit; Facs dated (2012); staff friendly." € 16.00                  2012*

**STUHR see Bremen** *1C2*

⊞ **STUTTGART** *3D3* (4km E Urban) *48.79395, 9.21911*
Campingplatz Cannstatter Wasen, Mercedesstrasse 40, 70372 Stuttgart [(0711) 556696; fax 557454; info@ campingplatz-stuttgart.de; www.campingplatz-stuttgart. de] Fr B10 foll sp for stadium & Mercedes museum & then foll camping sp. Access poss diff when major events in park adj. Lge, all hdstg, pt shd; htd wc; chem disp; mv service pnt; serviced pitches; shwrs inc; el pnts (16A) metered + conn fee; lndtte; shop 1.5km; tradsmn; rest; BBQ; playgrnd; pool 2km; dogs €3; bus nr; stn 1.5km; poss v cr; Eng spkn; adv bkg; poss noise fr local stadium; ccard acc; CKE/CCI. "Helpful staff; clean san facs (2010); town cent best by train - tickets fr recep; cycle ride to town thro park; Mercedes museum 15 mins walk; fr Sep site/office open 0800-1000 & 1700-1900 only; site within low emission zone." ♦ € 21.80                  2013*

⊞ **STUTTGART** *3D3* (8km E Urban) *48.83111, 9.32222*
Parkplatz am Hallenbad, An der Talaue, 71332 Waiblingen [(07151) 5001155; parkierungsgesellschaft@ waiblingen.de] Fr N exit A81/E41 junc 16 at Ludwigsburg Süd, foll sp dir Remseck & Waiblingen. Fr S or E on B29 take B14 to Waiblingen town cent. Foll sp sw pool, sports park & parking. M'vans only. Sm, mkd pitch, hdstg, pt shd; wc; chem disp; mv service pnt; water €1/80 litres; el pnts €1/8 hrs; pool; dogs; rd noise. "Fair NH." € 6.00                  2010*

**SULZBERG see Kempten (Allgäu)** *3D4*

⊞ **SULZBURG** *3B4* (1.5km SE Rural) *47.83583, 7.72333*
Terrassen-Camping Alte Sägemühle, Badstrasse 57, 79295 Sulzburg [(07634) 551181; fax 551182; info@camping-alte-saegemuehle.de; www.camping-alte-saegemuehle. de] Exit A5 junc 64b to Heitersheim & Sulzburg. Fr cent of Sulzburg, foll camp sps SE past timber yard on rd to Bad Sulzburg hotel. Sm, mkd pitch, terr, pt shd; htd wc; chem disp; mv service pnt; shwrs inc; el pnts (16A) metered + conn fee; gas 1km; lndtte; shop; tradsmn; rest, snacks, bar 1.5km; BBQ; lake sw adj; 10% statics; dogs €2; Eng spkn; quiet; 10% red CKE/CCI. "Excel san facs - poss long walk; v friendly, helpful owners site van with tractor; restful site in beautiful hilly countryside; gd walking, cycling." € 21.00                  2011*

⊞ **SULZBURG** *3B4* (1km NW Rural) *47.84778, 7.69848*
Camping Sulzbachtal, Sonnmatt 4, 79295 Sulzburg [(07634) 592568; fax 592569; a-z@camping-sulzbachtal. de; www.camping-sulzbachtal.de] Fr A5/E35 exit junc 64a Bad Krozingen onto L120/L123 dir Staufen-in-Breisgau. Cont on L125, site sp on L. Med, mkd pitch, hdstg, terr, pt shd; htd wc; chem disp; mv service pnt; 65% serviced pitches; baby facs; shwrs inc; el pnts (16A) metered; lndtte (inc dryer); shop 1km; tradsmn; snacks; rest 1km; playgrnd; pool; tennis; wifi; 10% statics; dogs €2.60; phone; mv o'night facs; Eng spkn; adv bkg; quiet; ccard acc; red long stay/CKE/CCI. "Gd base for S Black Forest & Vosges; well laid-out site; clean facs; conv m'way; 45 mins to Basel; helpful, pleasant owners; ask about bus/train pass; high standards; well maintained; excel san facs; lge pitches; in wine growing area; excel walks." ♦ € 38.00 (CChq acc)                  2014*

**SUTEL** *2E1* (1km E Coastal) *54.33356, 11.06885*
Campingplatz Seepark Sütel, 23779 Sütel [(04365) 7474; fax 1027; info@camping-seekamp.de; www.seepark-suetel.de] Fr B501 foll sp to Sütel; drive thro vill to beach & site. V lge, mkd pitch, unshd; wc; chem disp; baby facs; shwrs €0.50; el pnts (16A) €2; lndtte (inc dryer); shop, rest 500m; snacks; bar; playgrnd; beach adj; 90% statics; dogs €1.50; quiet; phone; adv bkg; CKE/CCI. "San facs poss inadequate if site full; helpful owner." ♦  1 Apr-3 Oct. € 14.00                  2009*

⊞ **TENGEN** *3C4* (600m NW Rural) *47.82365, 8.65296* **Hegau Familien-Camping, An der Sonnenhalde 1, 78250 Tengen [(07736) 92470; fax 9247124; info@hegau-camping.de; www.hegau-camping.de]** Exit A81 junc 39 thro Engen dir Tengen, site sp. Lge, mkd pitch, hdstg, pt sl, pt shd; htd wc; chem disp; mv service pnt; serviced pitches; baby facs; fam bthrm; sauna; shwrs inc; el pnts (16A) metered or €2; gas; lndtte (inc dryer); shop; supmkt 500m; tradsmn; rest, snacks; bar; playgrnd; htd, covrd pool; paddling pool; lake sw; canoeing; tennis adj; games area; games rm; cycle hire; horseriding 2km; wifi; entmnt; 40% statics; dogs €4 inc dog shwr; bus 500m; clsd 1230-1430; o'night area for m'vans; Eng spkn; adv bkg; quiet; ccard acc; red long stay/low ssn/CKE/CCI. "Site of high standard; fairly isolated; gd family facs; excel." ♦ € 35.00                  2010*

⊞ **TIEFENSEE** *2G3* (700m E Rural) *52.68019, 13.85063* Country-Camping Tiefensee, Schmiedeweg 1, 16259 Tiefensee [(033398) 90514; fax 86736; info@country-camping.de; www.country-camping.de] Site sp fr B158 on lakeside. Lge, hdg/mkd pitch, pt shd; htd wc; chem disp; mv service pnt; sauna; baby facs; shwrs €0.50; el pnts (16A) metered or €2.50; lndtte (inc dryer); shop; rest, snacks; bar; BBQ; playgrnd; lake sw & beach adj (sep naturist area); fishing; games area; internet; TV; 75% statics; dogs €1.50; sep car park; o'night area for m'vans; clsd 1300-1500; poss cr; Eng spkn; adv bkg; quiet; ccard acc; red long stay. "Family-owned site; sep m'van pitches; gd cycling & walking; train to Berlin fr Arensfeldt; working ship lift at Niederfinow; vg." ♦ € 20.00 (CChq acc)                  2012*

**TITISEE NEUSTADT** *3C4* (1.5km SW Rural) *47.88693, 8.13776*
Terrassencamping Sandbank, Seerundweg 9, 79822 Titisee-Neustadt [(07651) 8243 or 8166; fax 8286 or 88444; info@camping-sandbank.de; www.camping-sandbank.de] Fr rte 31 Freiberg-Donauschingen turn S into Titisee. Fork R after car park on R, foll sp for Bruderhalde thro town. After youth hostel fork L & foll sp at T junc. Gravel track to site. Lge, mkd pitch, terr, mainly hdstg by lake; wc (htd); chem disp; mv service pnt; baby facs; shwrs €0.50; el pnts (16A) €1.40; lndtte; shop; rest, snacks; bar; playgrnd; lake sw; boating; cycle hire; 50% statics; dogs €1.50; poss cr; Eng spkn; no adv bkg; quiet but some rlwy noise; ccard acc; red long stay/CKE/CCI. "Ltd touring pitches; steel pegs ess; clean, well-run, well laid-out site in gd position; terr gives gd lake views; helpful owner; gd welcome; larger pitches avail at extra cost; gd touring base for Black Forest; gd walks round lake; lakeside walk into town thru woods (approx 30 mins); ask for Konus card for free travel on local buses; clsd 1200-1400; excel; rd to site tarmaced." ♦ 1 Apr-19 Oct. € 32.40                     2014*

⊞ **TITISEE NEUSTADT** *3C4* (2km SW Rural) *47.88611, 8.13993* Camping Bühlhof, Bühlhofweg 13, 79822 Titisee-Neustadt [(07652) 1606; fax 1827; herta-jaeger@t-online.de; www.camping-buehlhof.de] Take rd 31 out of Freiburg to Titisee; R fork on ent Titisee; bear R to side of lake, site on R after end of Titisee, up steep but surfaced hill, sharp bends. Lge, mkd pitch, pt sl, terr, pt shd; wc; chem disp; mv service pnt; serviced pitch; baby facs; shwrs €0.50; el pnts (16A) €1.80; gas; lndtte (inc dryer); rest 300m; BBQ; playgrnd; htd pool 1km; tennis; 300m fr Lake Titisee (but no access); watersports; wintersports area - ski lift 6km; boats for hire; horseriding; wifi; 30% statics; dogs €2.30; recep 0700-2200; site clsd Nov to mid-Dec; Eng spkn; ccard not acc; CKE/CCI. "Beautiful situation on hillside above Lake Titisee; lower terr gravel & 50% statics; top terr for tents & vans without elec; pitches sm; woodland walks; pleasant walk to town." € 17.00        2014*

⊞ **TITISEE NEUSTADT** *3C4* (2.5km SW Rural) *47.88633, 8.13055* Camping Bankenhof, Bruderhalde 31a, 79822 Titisee-Neustadt [(07652) 1351; fax 5907; info@camping-bankenhof.de; www.camping-bankenhof.de] Fr B31 Frieberg-Donaueschingen, turn S into Tittisee & fork R after car park on R, foll sp Bruderhalde thro town. In 2.5km fork L after youth hostel; foll sp to site in 200m. If app Titisee fr Donausechingen (B31) do not take Titisee P sp exit but exit with int'l camping sp only, then as above. Lge, mkd pitch, hdstg, pt shd; wc; chem disp; mv service pnt; fam bthrm; shwrs inc; el pnts (10A) metered (poss rev pol); gas; lndtte (inc dryer); shop; rest; bar; playgrnd; lake sw adj; cycle hire; wifi; entmnt high ssn; boat-launching 200m; 20% statics; dogs €2.80; shwr inc ; o'night area for m'vans €12; poss cr; Eng spkn; adv bkg; quiet; ccard acc; red CKE/CCI. "Gd walk to town & in forest; lovely scenery; helpful staff; vg san facs; excel rest; most pitches gravel; ask at recep for red/free tickets on public transport; excel, well-run, clean site, some pitches narr." ♦ € 36.00                     2014*

**TITISEE NEUSTADT** *3C4* (3km SW Rural) *47.88996, 8.13273* Natur-Campingplatz Weiherhof, Bruderhalde 26, 79822 Titisee-Neustadt [(07652) 1468; fax 1478; info@camping-titisee.de; www.camping-titisee.de] Fr B31 Frieberg-Donaueschingen, turn S into Titisee & fork R after car park on R, foll sp Bruderhalde thro town. Site on L on lakeside. Lge, shd; htd wc; chem disp; shwrs inc; el pnts (10A) €2.50; lndtte; shop; rest, snacks; bar; playgrnd; pool 1km; lake sw adj; cycle hire; golf 2km; 20% statics; dogs €2; phone; poss cr; quiet; CKE/CCI. "Site in woodland next to the lake; no mkd pitches but ample rm; vg; trip to town along lakeside well worth a visit." ♦ 1 May-15 Oct. € 23.00                     2012*

⊞ **TODTNAU** *3C4* (6km NW Rural) *47.86400, 7.91670* Feriencamping Hochschwarzwald, Oberhäuser Strasse 6, 79674 Todtnau-Muggenbrunn [(07671) 1288 or 530; fax 95190; camping.hochschwarzwald@web.de; www.camping-hochschwarzwald.de] Freiburg rd fr Todtnau past vill of Muggenbrunn; site ent at top end of vill. Med, terr, pt sl, pt shd; htd wc; chem disp; shwrs €0.50; el pnts (10-16A) metered; gas; lndtte; shop; rest, snacks; playgrnd; htd, covrd pool 1km; tennis 1km; sm lake; wintersports; 70% statics; dogs €1.50; sep car park winter ssn; poss cr; quiet; red CKE/CCI. "Beautiful location; gd walking area; sm pitches unsuitable lge o'fits; san facs stretched; helpful staff." ♦ € 16.00        2011*

**TORGAU** *2F4* (1km S Rural) *51.54589, 12.98991* Campingplatz am Grosser Teich, Turnierplatzweg, 04860 Torgau [(03421) 902875; SV_info@torgau.de; www.torgau.de] S on B182 fr Torgau, turn R at site sp onto Tunierplatzweg, site sp on L in 700m. Sm, pt shd; wc; shwrs; el pnts (10A) inc; shop 500m; pool; lake sw; quiet. "Sm, old san facs block, but clean; pleasant hosts; lake famous for rare birds & visiting beavers; conv Elbe cycle path." Mid-Apr to Mid-Oct. € 19.00                     2009*

**TRABEN TRARBACH see Bernkastel Kues** *3B2*

⊞ **TRAUNSTEIN** *4F4* (8km S Rural) *47.81116, 12.5890* Camping Wagnerhof, Campingstrasse 11, 83346 Bergen [(08662) 8557; fax 5924; info@camping-bergen.de; www.camping-bergen.de] Exit A8/E52/E60 junc 110. On ent Bergen take 2nd R turn (sp). Med, mkd pitch, pt shd; wc; chem disp; mv service pnt; shwrs €0.50; el pnts (16A) metered; lndtte; shop on site & 500m; rest 400m; playgrnd; htd pool adj; shgl beach 10km; tennis; 30% statics; dogs €2; site clsd 1230-1500; some Eng spkn; adv bkg; quiet; debit & euro card acc; red long stay; CKE/CCI. "Excel, v clean, pleasant site in beautiful location; helpful owner; when not full owner tries to offer pitches with empty pitches adjoining; conv a'bahn; cable car to Hockfelln." € 22.00                     2014*

⊞ **TRAVEMUNDE** *2E2* (2km SW Rural) *53.94196, 10.84417* Camping Ivendorf, Frankenkrogweg 2, 23570 Ivendorf [(04502) 4865; fax 75516] Fr A1 exit junc 19 take B226 to Ivendorf, then B75 dir Travemünde, site well sp. Med, mkd pitch, pt shd; wc; chem disp; baby facs; shwrs inc; el pnts €3.50 or metered; lndtte (inc dryer); shop; rest 200m; playgrnd; pool 4km; 10% statics; dogs €2; train 2km; poss cr; CKE/CCI. "Sep disabled pitches; conv ferries to/fr Sweden; easy access to Lübeck, a beautiful city." ♦ € 23.00                     2010*

**TREIS KARDEN see Cochem** *3B2*

⊞ **TRENDELBURG** *1D4* (1km S Rural) *51.57250, 9.42416* Campingplatz Trendelburg, Zur Alten Mühle, 34388 Trendleburg [(05675) 301; fax 5888; conradi-camping@t-online.de; www.campingplatz-trendelburg.de] Enter Trendelburg fr Karlshafen on B83 turn R immed bef x-ing Rv Diemel, site on L in 800m. Sm, pt shd; wc; chem disp; baby facs; shwrs €0.50; ; el pnts (16A) metered + conn fee; gas; lndtge; shop; tradsmn; rest, snacks; bar; playgrnd; canoeing in adj rv; tennis; 40% statics; dogs €2.20; poss cr; adv bkg; quiet; 10% red CKE/CCI. "Pleasant, rvside site." ♦ € 12.20    2011*

**TRIER** *3B2* (2km S Urban) *49.74385, 6.62523* **Camping Treviris, Luxemburgerstrasse 81, 54290 Trier [(0651) 8200911; fax 8200567; info@camping-treviris. de; www.camping-treviris.de]** On E side of Rv Mosel on A1/A603/B49/B51 cross to W side of rv on Konrad Adenauerbrücke. Cont in R lane & foll sp Koln/Aachen - Luxemburgerstrasse. In 500m turn R to site, site on R. Well sp fr W bank of rv. Med, mkd pitch, pt shd; wc; chem disp; mv service pnt; baby facs; shwrs inc; el pnts (6A) €2.90; lndtte (inc dryer); shop 500m; tradsmn; rest, snacks; bar; BBQ; playgrnd; dogs €1.30; bus 200m; poss cr; site clsd 1-10 Jan; quiet; ccard acc; CKE/CCI. "Cycle/walk to town cent; m'van park adj open all yr - ltd facs; clean, modern san facs; swipe card for all facs; elec pylon in cent of site; gd touring base; gd sh stay/NH." ♦ ltd 15 Mar-15 Nov. € 29.45    2014*

"There aren't many sites open at this time of year"

If you're travelling outside peak season remember to call ahead to check site opening dates – even if the entry says 'open all year'.

**TRIER** *3B2* (6km SW Rural) *49.70460, 6.57398* **Camping Konz, Saarmünding, 54329 Konz [(06501) 2577; fax 947790; camping@campingplatz-konz.de; www. campingplatz-konz.de]** On B51 S of rv at rndabt just bef rv x-ing, go L & foll sp Camping Konz (not Konz-Könen). Do not go into Konz. Med, mkd pitch, pt shd; wc; mv service pnt; shwrs €1; el pnts metered + conn fee; lndry rm; shops 500m; rest, snacks; playgrnd; watersports; dogs €0.70; Eng spkn; some rd noise. "Conv NH/sh stay for Trier - cycle rte or public transport; facs clean; poss flooding." 15 Mar-15 Oct. € 13.20    2010*

**TRIER** *3B2* (8km SW Rural) *49.70555, 6.55333* **Campingplatz Igel, Moselstrasse, 54298 Igel [(06501) 12944; fax 601931; info@camping-igel.de; www.camping-igel.de]** SW on A49 Luxembourg rd fr Trier; in cent of Ige vill, turn L by Sparkasse Bank, thro narr tunnel (3.6m max height); in 200m turn L along rv bank; site 300m on L; café serves as recep. Med, pt shd; htd wc; chem disp; mv service pnt; shwrs €1; el pnts (6A) €2 (poss rev pol); lndtte; shop in vill; rest; bar; playgrnd; fishing lakes adj; 90% statics (sep area); dogs €2; bus/train to Trier & Roman amphitheatre; poss cr; quiet but some noise fr rlwy & rv barges; CKE/CCI. "Excel, friendly, well-run site; immac san facs; gd rest; ltd touring pitches; rv bank foot & cycle path to Trier; conv Roman amphitheatre in Trier; close to Luxembourg border for cheap petrol; conv for bus into Trier." 1 Apr-31 Oct. € 24.50    2014*

⊞ **TRIER** *3B2* (15km W Rural) *49.75416, 6.50333* Campingplatz Alter Bahnhof-Metzdorf, Uferstrasse 42, 54308 Langsur-Metzdorf [(06501) 12626; fax 13796; info@camping-metzdorf.de; www.camping-metzdorf. de] Fr W leave A64/E44 junc 15 & foll sp Wasserbillig; at T-junc in Wasserbillig turn L onto B49 sp Trier. Ignore campsite in 500m. On ent Germany at end of bdge turn sharp L onto B418 sp Ralingen/Metternich. In 3km turn L sp Metzdorf; in 750m turn L, site in 750m. Fr N (Bitburg) join A64 at junc 3 sp Luxembourg, then as above. Fr SE on A1/E422 join A602 (Trier) & approx 1km past end of a'bahn turn R over Kaiser Wilhelm Bdge sp A64 Lux'bourg) & immed L at end of bdge. In 9km in Wasserbillig turn R under rlwy bdge & keep R on B418 sp Ralingen/Mesenich. In 3km turn L sp Melzdorf, in 750m turn L, site in 750m. Med, pt sl, pt shd; htd wc; chem disp; mv service pnt; shwrs €0.50; el pnts (6-16A) €2 or metered (10A); lndtte; tradsmn; rest; bar; playgrnd; wifi; 75% statics; dogs €1; phone; bus 500m; m'van o'night €9; poss cr; Eng spkn; adv bkg; quiet; ccard not acc; red long stay/low ssn; CKE/CCI. "Rvside location; gd san facs but poss long walk & steep climb; cycle rte to Trier; vg NH." ♦ ltd € 15.00    2009*

⊞ **TRIPPSTADT** *3B2* (1km E Rural) *49.35145, 7.78117* Camping Freizeitzentrum Sägmühle, Sägmühle 1, 67705 Trippstadt [(06306) 92190; fax 2000; info@saegmuehle. de; www.saegmuehle.de] Fr Kaiserslautern take B270 or B48 S for 14km, foll sp Trippstadt. Cont thro vill in dir of Karstal; site sp. Lge, mkt pitch, pt sl, pt terr, pt shd; htd wc; chem disp; mv service pnt; baby facs; fam bthrm; shwrs inc; el pnts (16A) inc; lndtte (inc dryer); shop; rest, snacks; bar; playgrnd; lake fishing; boat & cycle hire; tennis; games area; wifi; entmnt; TV rm; 50% statics; dogs €2.60; site clsd 1 Nov-13 Dec; poss cr; adv bkg; quiet. "Excel walking area; san facs on edge of site nr tents vg & under-used but long way fr pitches; san facs in cent stretched; c'van spares shop/dealer on site." ♦ € 25.70 (CChq acc)    2011*

**TRITTENHEIM** *3B2* (300m N Urban) *49.82472, 6.90305* Reisemobil/Wohnmobilstellplatz (Motorhome Camping), Am Moselufer, 54349 Trittenheim [(06507) 5331; info@ trittenheim.de; www.trittenheim.de] Fr Trier foll B53 dir Bernkastel Kues. Site sp in Trittenheim dir Neumagen-Dhron, on rvside. Sm, hdstg, pt sl, unshd; own san req; chem disp; mv service pnt; el pnts (16A) €2.50; shop, rest, snacks nr; dogs; poss cr; quiet; "M'vans only; pleasant site poss clsd if rv floods; warden calls for payment." 1 Apr-31 Oct. € 5.00    2013*

⊞ **TRITTENHEIM** *3B2* (4km N Urban) *49.84933, 6.89283* Camping Neumagen-Dhron, Moselstrasse 100, 54347 Neumagen-Dhron [(06507) 5249; fax 703290; camping-neumagen@t-online.de; www.campingneumagen.de] On B53 fr Trittenheim twd Piesport. Immed after x-ing rv turn R, then R again sp Neumagen. Site sp in vill on rvside. Med, mkd pitch, pt shd; wc; chem disp; baby facs; shwrs inc; el pnts (6-10A) metered + conn fee; lndtte (inc dryer); shop; rest, snacks; bar; BBQ; playgrnd; boating; 40% statics; dogs free; phone adj; poss cr; Eng spkn; adv bkg; quiet; CKE/CCI. "Gd; site clsd if rv in flood." € 19.30    2010*

GERMANY

**TRITTENHEIM** *3B2* (300m SE Rural) *49.82131, 6.90201*
**Campingplatz im Grünen, Olkstrasse 12, 54349
Trittenheim** [(06507) 2148; fax 992089; cp-trittenheim@t-
online.de; www.camping-trittenheim.de] Foll B53 along
Rv Mosel fr Trier dir Bernkastel Kues; turn R in Trittenheim
at camping symbol sp Leiwen as if to go over rv & site on R
immed bef x-ring rv. Sm, mkd pitch, pt shd; wc; chem disp;
fam bthrm; shwrs inc; el pnts €2.60 or metered + conn fee;
lndtte; shop, rest in vill; 20% statics in ssn; dogs €1.50; recep
clsd 1200-1500; Eng spkn; some rv noise; no ccard acc; CKE/
CCI. "Lovely, quiet site by Rv Mosel o'looking vineyards; boat
trips; beautiful area; excel, clean san facs; mv service pnt
point in adj vills; friendly owner; gd cycle paths; close to vill;
infrequent bus to Trier; interesting area; adv bkg fr March; no
plastic materials on lawns; close to local rests and seasonal boat
cruises." 15 Apr-15 Oct. € 36.00                     2013*

**TRITTENHEIM** *3B2* (3km S Rural) *49.80305, 6.89111*
**Ferienpark Landal Sonnenberg, 54340 Leiwen**
[(06507) 93690; fax 936936; sonnenberg@landal.de;
www.landal.de] Fr Bernkastel Kues or Trier on B53 take bdge
over Rv Mosel to S bank at Thörnich & foll sp Leiwen. Turn R to
top of hill, site sp. Long, winding ascent. Med, mkd pitch, terr,
pt shd; wc; chem disp; mv service pnt; sauna; shwrs inc; el pnts
(6A) inc; gas; lndtte; shop; rest, snacks; playgrnd; htd, cov'rd
pool; tennis; games rm; fitness rm; internet; entmnt; dogs €3;
poss cr; adv bkg; quiet; red CKE/CCI. "Vg family site with rv
views; excel san facs." ♦ 15 Mar-15 Nov. € 46.00     2013*

⊞ **TRITTENHEIM** *3B2* (4km S Rural) *49.79956, 6.92715*
**Campingplatz Moselhöhe, Bucherweg 1, 54426
Heidenburg** [(06509) 99016; fax 99017; dieter@qasem.de;
www.campingplatz-moselhoehe.de] Leave A1/E422 at junc
131, foll sp twd Thalfang. After 4km take 2nd L over bdge sp
Heidenburg (2 hairpin bends). Thro Büdlich to Heidenburg, foll
sp in vill. Med, mkd pitch, terr, unshd; htd wc; chem disp; mv
service pnt; serviced pitch; shwrs inc; el pnts (16A) metered;
lndtte; shops 1km; tradsmn; snacks; rest 200m; bar; games
rm; playgrnd; paddling pool; 25% statics; dogs €1.70; site
clsd mid-Nov to mid-Dec; Eng spkn; adv bkg; quiet; ccard acc;
red long stay; CKE/CCI. "Excel, clean, hilltop site surrounded
by meadows; well-maintained; generous terraces; excel san
facs; water & waste disposal points nr every pitch; wonderful
views; friendly owner; conv Rv Mosel attractions 4km." ♦
€ 26.30                                           2013*

**UBERLINGEN** *3D4* (3km SE Rural) *47.75186, 9.19315*
**Campingplatz Nell, Zur Barbe 7, 88662 Überlingen-
Nussdorf** [(07551) 4254; info@campingplatz-nell.de;
www.campingplatz-nell.de] Exit B31 to Nussdorf. In vill
cent turn L under rlwy bdge at 2nd campsite sp, site on R on
lakeside. Sm, pt shd; wc; chem disp; snacks; shwrs €0.50; el
pnts (6A) metered; lndry rm; shop, rest, snacks, bar 200m;
BBQ; shgl beach & lake sw adj; no dogs; adv bkg; poss cr;
quiet. "Beautifully-kept site; friendly owner; all amenities nr; gd
cycling; excel; lge plots; ltd places for tourers so arrive early."
Easter-20 Oct. € 21.00                            2014*

**UBERLINGEN** *3D4* (2km NW Rural) *47.77081, 9.13813*
**Campingplatz Überlingen, Bahnhofstrasse 57, 88662**
Überlingen [tel/fax (07551) 64583; info@campingpark-
ueberlingen.de; www.campingpark-ueberlingen.de]
Heading SE on B31, bef Überlingen turn R at sp Campingplatz
Goldbach down slip rd; after 1.75km turn R; foll rd parallel
with rlwy; after level x-ing site immed on R by lakeside. Lge, pt
sl, pt shd; htd wc; chem disp; mv service pnt; shwrs €0.50; el
pnts (16A) metered; gas; lndtte; shop; rest, snacks; bar; BBQ;
playgrnd; lake sw & boating adj; 30% statics; dogs €2.50; bus;
ltd Eng spkn; no adv bkg; rd & rlwy noise; red long stay/snr
citizens/low ssn; no ccard acc; CKE/CCI. "Extra for lake pitches;
high ssn poss diff for lge c'vans to manoeuvre; gd rest; strict
rule no vehicles in after 2230; rec arr early to secure pitch."
1 Apr-9 Oct. € 25.00                              2011*

> ### "That's changed – Should I let The Club know?"
> If you find something on site that's different from
> the site entry, fill in a report and let us know. See
> www.caravanclub.co.uk/europereport.

**UBERLINGEN** *3D4* (10km NW Rural) *47.81783, 9.03856*
**Camping See-Ende, Radolfzellerstrasse 23, 78346
Bodman-Ludwigshafen** [(07773) 937518; fax 937529;
info@see-ende.de; www.see-ende.de] Exit A98/E54 junc
12 onto B34, site sp. Med, pt sl, pt shd; wc; chem disp; mv
service pnt; shwrs inc; el pnts (16A) metered + conn fee; gas;
lndtte; shop; rest 1.5km snacks; gas; lake sw & shgl beach;
50% statics; no dogs; Eng spkn; quiet; ccard acc; CKE/CCI.
"Excel position on lake; poor san facs; fair NH." 1 May-30 Sep.
€ 19.50                                           2009*

**UBERSEE** *4F4* (3km N Rural) *47.8412, 12.47166* **Chiemsee-
Campingplatz Rödlgries, Rödlgries 1, 83236 Übersee-
Feldwies** [(08642) 470; fax 1636; info@chiemsee-camping.
de; www.chiemsee-camping.de] Exit A8/E52 junc 108
Übersee, foll sp Chiemseestrand, veer L at wooden sign of sites.
V lge, mkd pitch, some hdstg, pt shd; 50% serviced pitch; htd
wc; chem disp; mv service pnt; shwrs inc; el pnts (16A) metered
+ conn fee; gas; lndtte; shop; rest, snacks; bar; playgrnd; sand/
shgl beach; lake sw; boating; entmnt & dogs €2.50 (July/Aug
by agreement only); phone; train 3km; poss cr w/end; adv
bkg; quiet but some rd noise; "Superb facs; vg for children;
highly rec; extra for lakeside/serviced pitches; vg touring base;
v conv nr A8; cycle track around lake." ♦ 1 Apr-31 Oct.
€ 38.75                                           2013*

**UCKERITZ** *2G1* (1km E Coastal) *54.01666, 14.06833*
**Naturcamping Ückeritz (Part Naturist), Strandstrasse,
17459 Ückeritz** [(038375) 2520; fax 25218;
kv.campingplatz@ueckeritz.de; www.campingplatz-
ueckeritz.de] Sp fr B111. V lge, pt shd; wc; chem disp; mv
service pnt; shwrs €1; el pnts (10A) metered + conn fee; lndtte
(inc dryer); shop; rest, snacks; bar; playgrnd; sand beach (sep
naturist area); games area; cycle hire; 60% statics; dogs €3;
phone; bus 500m; poss cr; adv bkg; poss noisy high ssn. ♦
Easter-31 Oct. € 20.70                            2010*

⊞ UFFENHEIM *3D2* (1km S Rural) *49.52277, 10.12583*
Camping Paradies Franken, Walkershofen 40, 97215
Simmershofen [(09848) 969633; camping-paradies-
franken@web.de; www.camping-paradies-franken.de]
Fr N exit A7 junc 105 Gollhofen or fr on B13 to Uffenheim. In
Uffenheim turn W thro Adelhofen to Simmershofen, then turn
L twd Walkershofen, site sp. Med, mkd pitch, pt shd; htd wc;
mv service pnt; baby facs; shwrs; el pnts inc; lndtte (inc dryer);
shop; tradsmn; rest, snacks; bar; BBQ; playgrnd; htd pool nr;
games area; cycle hire; wifi; some statics; dogs €1.50; adv bkg;
quiet. "Interesting area; gd touring base; gd rest, cycling gd."
♦ € 23.00                                    2012*

UFFENHEIM *3D2* (500m SW Urban) *49.54426, 10.2248*
Naturcamping am Freibad, Sportstrasse, 97215 Uffenheim
[(09842) 1568; fax (09381) 716821; maempel-volkach@t-
online.de] Fr A7/E43 exit junc 105 onto B13 dir Uffenheim,
site sp. Med, hdg pitch, pt shd; wc; chem disp; shwrs inc;
el pnts (16A) €3 or metered + conn fee; lndtte; shops 1km;
tradsmn; rest 300m; snacks; bar; pool adj; dogs €1; adv bkg;
quiet; CKE/CCI. "Charming town; excel site; quite, v friendly CL
type site; gd cycling area." 1 May-15 Sep. € 15.60      2011*

URNSHAUSEN *1D4* (2km NE Rural) *50.74308, 10.20200*
Camping Am Schönsee, Schönsee, 36457 Urnshausen
(Thüringen) [(036964) 7451] Exit B285 at Urnshausen; turn
L sp Schönesee; site in 2km at end of rd/track. Med, sl, pt
shd; wc; chem disp; shwrs €0.50; el pnts inc; shop 2km; rest,
snacks; BBQ (charcoal); playgrnd; lake sw adj; 30% statics;
dogs; bus 2km; adv bkg; quiet. "Rustic site adj sm lakes; basic,
clean san facs; gd walking in woods; gd value; gd." May-Oct.
€ 12.00                                       2009*

URZIG see Wittlich *3B2*

⊞ VLOTHO *1C3* (3km NE Rural) *52.17388, 8.90666*
Camping Sonnenwiese, Borlefzen 1, 32602 Vlotho
[(05733) 8217; fax 80289; info@sonnenwiese.com; www.
sonnenwiese.com] Fr S exit A2 junc 31 to Vlotho; cross rv
bdge (Mindenerstrasse) & in 500m turn R into Rintelnerstrasse
to site - 2 sites share same access. Lge, some hdstg, unshd; htd
wc; chem disp; mv service pnt; baby facs; some serviced pitches
inc private san facs; shwrs inc; el pnts (10A) inc; lndtte (inc
dryer); shop; rest, snacks; bar; BBQ; playgrnd; paddling pool;
lake sw; games rm; wifi; entmnt; cab TV; 75% statics; dogs
€2.20; phone; bus/train 4km; Eng spkn; adv bkg; quiet; CKE/
CCI. "Excel site." ♦ € 30.50                  2014*

VOHL HERZHAUSEN see Korbach *1C4*

WAGING AM SEE *4F4* (1.5km NE Rural) *47.94333,
12.74741* Strandcamping Waging-am-See, Am See 1,
83329 Waging-am-See [(08681) 552; fax 45010; info@
strandcamp.de; www.strandcamp.de] Exit A8 junc 112
to Traunstein, then foll sp to Waging-am-See; in vill site sp
on rd to Tittmoning. V lge, hdg/mkd pitch, pt shd; wc; chem
disp; mv service pnt; some serviced pitches; baby facs; shwrs
inc; el pnts (10A) metered + conn fee; gas; lndtte; shop;
rest, snacks; bar; playgrnd; shgl beach & lake sw adj; sailing;
windsurfing; fishing; tennis; games area; cycle hire; wifi;
entmnt; 30% statics; dogs €2.90 (not acc Jul & Aug); site
clsd 1200-1400; adv bkg; quiet; 10% red long stay; CKE/CCI.
"Excel, clean, family site; gd cycling country; well-equipped
shop." ♦ 1 Apr-31 Oct. € 23.60               2013*

See advertisement

WAHLHAUSEN see Witzenhausen *1D4*

WALDBREITBACH *3B1* (1.5km NE Rural) *50.55389, 7.42518*
Campingplatz Wiedhof, Wiedhof 1, 56588 Waldbreitbach
[(02638) 4258; camping@wiedhof.de; www.wiedhof.
de] Exit A3 junc 36 onto B256 W to Bonefeld, then take
L257 Kurtscheiderstrasse to Niederbreitbach, then L255 to
Waldbreitbach, site sp on rvside. This rte avoids steep hills.
Sm, unshd; wc; chem disp; shwrs; el pnts (10A) inc; lndtte
(inc dryer); tradsmn; snacks; bar; BBQ; playgrnd; fishing; TV;
80% statics; dogs; adv bkg; quiet; CKE/CCI. "Conv A3 m'way;
vg, peaceful site; gd walks, quiet site next to local town."
Easter-30 Sep. € 15.50                        2013*

WALDFISCHBACH BURGALBEN see Pirmasens *3B3*

WALDKIRCH *3C4* (4km NE Rural) *48.10256, 7.99045*
Camping Elztalblick, Biehlstrasse 10, 79183 Waldkirch-
Siensbach [(07681) 4212; fax 4213; elztalblick@t-online.
de; www.camping-elztalblick.de] Exit Waldkirch by B294
NE; within 1km of town cent fork R, sp Siensbach & Camping
2km. After 2km Siensbach vill, turn R into narr rd (camping sp),
site at top of hill with 1 in 7 app. If app fr m'way do not go
into Waldkirch but foll sp to Waldkirch-Siensbach. Med, hdstg,
terr, pt shd; wc; chem disp; mv service pnt; shwrs inc; el pnts
(10A) €2; lndtte; shop; tradsmn; rest, snacks; bar; playgrnd;
golf 2km; TV rm; 70% statics; dogs €1; Eng spkn; quiet; CKE/
CCI. "Wonderful views; friendly, family-run site." 1 Apr-20 Oct.
€ 18.00                                       2009*

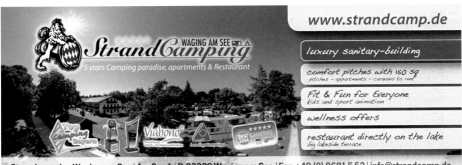

**GERMANY**

**WALDKIRCH** *3C4* (10km NE Rural) *48.10023, 8.05215*
Camping Schwarzwaldhorn, Ettersbachstrasse 7, 79263
Simonswald [(07683) 477 or 1048; fax 909169; evers@
schwarzwald-camping.de; www.schwarzwald-camping.
de] Exit Waldkirch by B294 NE twd Elzach. Turn E dir to
Bleibach/Simonswald onto L173. After 3km turn R at camping
sp & site on R. Sm, mkd pitch, pt sl, pt shd; htd wc; chem disp;
mv service pnt; shwrs €0.50; el pnts (16A) metered or €1.50;
lndtte; shop; tradsmn; rest adj; playgrnd; htd pool 200m;
40% statics; dogs €2.50; phone; bus 500m; sep car park; adv
bkg; quiet; CKE/CCI. "Pleasant owners; vg site amongst fruit
trees; excl base for Black Forest, Freiburg; modern san facs."
1 Apr-20 Oct. € 31.00                                    2011*

⊞ **WALDMUNCHEN** *4F2* (2km N Rural) *49.39598,
12.69913* Camping am Perlsee, Alte Ziegelhütte 6, 93449
Waldmünchen [(09972) 1469; fax 3782; info@see-
camping.de; www.see-camping.de] N fr Cham on B22 to
Schontal, NE to Waldmünchen for 10km. Foll site sp 2km. Med,
hdg/mkd pitch, terr, pt shd; htd wc; chem disp; mv service pnt;
baby facs; shwrs inc; el pnts (16A) metered; lndtte (inc dryer);
shop & 1km; tradsmn; rest, snacks; bar; BBQ; playgrnd; lake sw
adj; watersports; games area; 50% statics; dogs €2; quiet; CKE/
CCI. "Vg san facs; superb site." ♦ € 17.50            2010*

⊞ **WALDSHUT** *3C4* (1km SE Urban) *47.61083, 8.22526*
Rhein Camping, Jahnweg 22, 79761 Waldshut-Tiengen
[(07751) 3152; fax 3252; info@rheincamping.de; www.
rheincamping.de] Site on rvside on E o'skts of vill. Fr N foll
rd 500 in dir Tiengen fr Switzerland, take 1st L after Koblenz
border x-ing & foll site sp. Med, mkd pitch, hdstg, pt shd;
wc; chem disp; mv service pnt; shwrs €0.50; el pnts (16A)
metered + conn fee €1; gas; lndtte (inc dryer); shop; rest,
snacks; bar; pool 200m; paddling pool; rv sw 100m; wifi;
TV; 40% statics; dogs €2; poss cr; Eng spkn; adv bkg;
quiet; debit cards acc; red long stay/CKE/CCI. "Nr Rhine falls at
Schaffhausen; boat for Rhine trips fr site; immac facs; sm, tight
pitches; helpful staff; gd rest; pleasant walk along Rhine; excel;
conv NH mobil park adj." ♦ ltd € 30.40            2013*

⊞ **WALKENRIED** *2E4* (1km NE Rural) *51.58944, 10.62472*
Knaus Campingpark Walkenried, Ellricherstrasse 7,
37445 Walkenried [(05525) 778; fax 2332; walkenried@
knauscamp.de; www.knauscamp.de] A7, exit Seesen,
then B243 to Herzberg-Bad Sachsa-Walkenried, sp. Lge,
mkd pitch, terr, pt sl, pt shd; wc; chem disp; mv service pnt;
sauna; solarium; shwrs inc; el pnts (6-10A) €2.40; gas; lndtte;
shop, rest, snacks; bar; playgrnd; htd covrd pool; games area;
wintersports; entmnt; TV; 20% statics; dogs €1; site clsd
Nov; Eng spkn; adv bkg; quiet; ccard not acc; red long stay/
snr citizens. "Vg rest; lovely old vill; excel site." ♦ € 34.25
(CChq acc)                                          2013*

⊞ **WARBURG** *1C4* (1km E Rural) *51.48600, 9.16590*
Camping Eversburg, Zum Anger 1, 34414 Warburg
[(05641) 8668; www.camping-eversburg.de] Exit A44 junc
65 Warburg; turn R onto B7 twd Kassel; site in approx 4km on
R (tight turn) just aft bdge. Sm, pt sl, unshd; wc; chem disp; mv
service pnt; shwrs €1; el pnts €1.50 or metered (poss long lead
req); gas; lndtte; shops 1km; pool 2km; dogs €1; adv bkg;
quiet; red long stay. "Pleasant town." ♦ € 19.50      2011*

⊞ **WAREN** *2F2* (3.5km S Rural) *53.50025, 12.66525*
Camping Ecktannen, Fontanestrasse 66, 17192 Waren
[(03991) 668513; fax 664675; camping-ecktannen@waren-
tourismus.de; www.camping-ecktannen.de] Exit A19/E55
Berlin-Rostock dir Waren on B192; in Waren foll site sp. Lge,
pt sl, pt shd; wc; chem disp; mv service pnt; shwrs inc; el pnts
(10A) €2.30 (long lead poss req); gas; lndtte; shop; supmkt
2km; tradsmn; rest, snacks; bar; playgrnd; sand beach & lake
sw adj; cycle hire; internet; 10% statics; dogs €2.10; o'night
area; poss cr; quiet; ccard acc; CKE/CCI. "Open plan site
amongst trees; insects poss a problem in spring; gd for cycling;
public transport nrby." ♦ € 17.70                      2011*

**WARNITZ** *2G2* (500m SW Rural) *53.17751, 18.87395*
Camping Oberuckersee, Lindenallee 2, 17291 Warnitz
[(039863) 459; fax 78349; info@camping-oberuckersee.
de; www.camping-oberuckersee.de] Fr A11/E28 exit 7.
Site sp fr Warnitz on lakeside. Lge, pt sl, shd; wc; chem disp;
mv service pnt; shwrs €0.80; el pnts (10A) €2; lndry rm; shop
500m; rest 100m; snacks adj; playgrnd; lake sw & beach;
fishing; boating; cycle hire; TV; 50% statics; dogs €2; clsd
1300-1500; quiet. "Lovely site in pine trees on edge lge lake;
conv NH en rte to Poland; deposit for san facs key; gd cycle rte
nrby." ♦ 1 Apr-5 Oct. € 16.00                          2011*

**WASSENACH see Mendig** *3B2*

---

---

**WAXWEILER** *3A2* (300m N Rural) *50.09270, 6.35866*
Eifel Ferienpark Prümtal, Schwimmbadstrasse 7, 54649
Waxweiler [(06554) 92000; fax 920029; info@ferienpark-
waxweiler.de; www.ferienpark-waxweiler.de] Exit A60/
E42/E29 junc 5 to B410 to Waxweiler. Site sp dir Prüm on
rvside. Med, hdg/mkd pitch, pt shd; htd wc; chem disp; mv
service pnt; sauna; shwrs inc; el pnts (10A) inc; lndtte (inc
dryer); shop; tradsmn; rest 800m; snacks; bar; BBQ; playgrnd;
htd pool adj; paddling pool; waterslide; fishing; tennis; cycle
hire; games area; wifi; entmnt; 50% statics (sep area); dogs
€2.50; Eng spkn; adv bkg; quiet. "V nice site in the valley; v
warm welcome fr staff; lovely pool adj." ♦ 1 Apr-31 Oct.
€ 29.00 (CChq acc)                                    2012*

⊞ **WEBERSTEDT** *1D4* (1.4km SW Rural) *51.10186, 10.50806*
Campingplatz am Tor zum Hainich, Hainichstrasse, 99947
Weberstedt [(036022) 98690; fax (36022) 98691; nh@
camping-hainich.de; www.camping-hainich.de] Leave
B247 Mühlhausen to Bad Langensalza rd at Schönstedt sp
Weberstedt; on entering vill look for sp on L; 1km up cobbled
rd. Med, hdstg, unshd; wc; chem disp; mv service pnt; baby
facs; el pnts (10A) metered; lndtte; sm shop; shop, rest &
bar 1km; playgrnd; cycle hire; horseriding nrby; TV rm; dogs
€1; quiet; ccard acc; CKE/CCI. "Close to Hainich National
Park; modern san facs; recep 0700-1300 & 1500-2200."
€ 14.40                                               2011*

**WEHLEN see Bernkastel Kues** *3B2*

**WEIKERSHEIM** *3D2* (3km S Rural) *49.45640, 9.92565*
Camping Schwabenmühle, Weikersheimer Straße 21,
97990 Weikersheim [07934 99 22 23; fax 99 24 08;
info@camping-schwabenmuehle.de; www.camping-
schwabenmuehle.de] Fr Weikersheim twd Laudenbach, site
on R in 3km. Med, hdg pitch, mkd pitch, hdstg, pt shd; wc;
chem disp; mv service pnt; shwrs; el pnts (16A); lndtte (inc
dryer); bar; playgrnd; bike hire; wifi; dogs €1; twin axles; Eng
spkn; CCI. "Excel; bread can be ordered." ◆ 17 Apr-12 Oct.
€ 32.60                                                    2014*

**WEILBURG** *3C1* (3km SW Rural) *50.4757, 8.23966*
Campingplatz Odersbach, Runkelstrasse 5A, 35781
Weilburg-Odersbach [(06471) 7620; fax 379603; info@
camping-odersbach.de; www.camping-odersbach.de]
Fr Limburg exit B49 sp Weilburg & Bad Homburg, turn S (R)
opp Shell stn at top of hill at Weilburg o'skts. Site on L at foot
of hill in Odersbach. Lge, unshd; wc; shwrs €0.90; el pnts (16A)
metered + conn fee; lndtte; shops at ent; rest 100m; snacks;
bar; playgrnd; pool; paddling pool; boating; cycle hire; golf
8km; 75% statics; dogs €1; poss cr; quiet; ccard acc; CKE/CCI.
◆ ltd 1 Apr-31 Oct. € 23.00                                2014*

**WEIMAR** *2E4* (8km S Rural) *50.92456, 11.34785* Camping
Mittleres Ilmtal, Auf der Butterberge 1, 99438 Oettern
[(036453) 80264; fax 808519; weil-camping@freenet.de;
www.camping-oettern.de] Exit A4/E40 junc 50 & foll B87
to SW to Oettern, take 1st L after narr bdge, site on L in 600m
along narr rd, sp 'Camperbaude'. Med, some hdstg, pt sl, terr,
pt shd; wc; chem disp; shwrs €1; el pnts (16A) €2; tradsmn;
rest, snacks; bar; 50% statics; dogs €2; phone; quiet. "Conv
Weimar & Buchenwald; recep open 0800-1000 & 1700-2000;
welcoming; gd NH/sh stay." 15 Apr-31 Oct. € 14.00    2011*

⊞ **WEINHEIM** *3C2* (4km N Rural) *49.59776, 8.64013*
Camping Wiesensee, Ulmenweg 7, 69502 Hemsbach
[(06201) 72619; fax 493426; familie.herwig@camping-
wiesensee.de; www.camping-wiesensee.de] Exit A5/E35
junc 32; foll sp Hemsbach. On ent vill strt at 1st rndbt & traff
lts, at 2nd rndabt turn L & foll camping sp about 1km. Lge, hdg
pitch, pt shd; wc; chem disp; mv service pnt; serviced pitches;
shwrs €0.60; el pnts (16A) €1.90 or metered + conn fee;
gas; lndtte (inc dryer); shop; rest high ssn; snacks; playgrnd;
htd pool 100m; lake sw; boating; tennis 10m; cycle hire;
golf 12km; 75% statics; dogs €2; Eng spkn; adv bkg rec high
ssn; quiet but some rlwy noise. "Superb facs to CC standard;
friendly welcome; helpful staff; supmkt in walking dist; gd NH
for A5."◆ € 30.00                                          2014*

**WEISSENSEE** *2E4* (1.5km N Rural) *51.20593, 11.06735*
Camping Weissensee, Grünstedterstrasse 4, 99631
Weissensee [(036374) 36936; fax 36937; info@
campingplatz-weissensee.de; www.campingplatz-
weissensee.de] App on B4 fr Erfurt, turn R after Straussfurt
onto B86. Site on R exit Weissensee past lake, clearly sp fr town
cent. Med, unshd; wc; chem disp; mv service pnt; shwrs inc;
el pnts (10A) metered + conn fee; lndtte (inc dryer); shop high
ssn; rest adj; snacks; playgrnd; pool & paddling pool; cycle hire;
wifi; 50% statics; dogs €1; no adv bkg; quiet. 1 Apr-30 Sep.
€ 16.50                                                    2009*

**WENNINGSTEDT see Westerland** *1C1*

**WERDER PETZOW see Potsdam** *2F3*

⊞ **WERNIGERODE** *2E3* (8km S Rural) *51.77586,
10.7965* Camping am Brocken, Schützenring 6, 38875
Elbingerode [(039454) 42589; hobittner@ngi.de; www.
campingambrocken.de] S on B244 fr Werningerode. Turn
R at int'l camping sp at bottom of hill ent Elbingerode. Foll sp
for 1km - take care on app fr N. Lge, mkd pitch, some hdstg,
pt sl, unshd; wc; chem disp; mv service pnt; shwrs €0.50; el
pnts (16A) metered + conn fee (poss rev pol); gas; lndtte; shop;
tradsmn; rest, snacks 100m; playgrnd; pool 200m; dogs €2;
poss cr; adv bkg; quiet; 10% red CKE/CCI. "Lovely, friendly
site; vg facs; easy for c'vans; sep area for m'vans; highly rec;
excel." ◆ € 20.00                                          2011*

⊞ **WERTACH** *4E4* (1km E Rural) *47.60861, 10.41750*
Camping Waldesruh, Bahnhofstrasse 19, 87497 Wertach
[(08365) 1004; fax 706369; info@camping-wertach.de;
www.camping-wertach.de] Fr A7 exit junc 137 at Oy & take
B310 dir Wertach; 2km bef Wertach turn R into Bahnhofstrasse
& foll site sp. Med, mkd pitch, pt sl, pt shd; htd wc; chem disp;
mv service pnt; baby facs; shwrs inc; el pnts (10A) metered;
gas; lndtte (inc dryer); shop, rest, snacks, bar 500m; BBQ;
playgrnd; lake sw 2km; games area; games rm; wifi; TV rm;
50% statics; dogs €2; phone; bus; Eng spkn; adv bkg; quiet;
red long stay; CKE/CCI. "V picturesque area;  friendly site; gd
walks; winter sports site & conv NH in rte Austria/Italy." ◆
€ 14.50                                                    2011*

⊞ **WERTACH** *4E4* (1km E Rural) *47.61030, 10.44618*
International Grüntensee-Camping, Grüntenseestrasse
41, 87497 Wertach [(08365) 375; fax 1221; info@
gruentensee.de; www.gruentensee.de] Exit A7 junc 137
to Nesselwang. Site on rd fr Nesselwang to Wertach, sp. Lge,
terr, pt shd; wc; chem disp; mv service pnt; baby facs; shwrs; el
pnts (10-16A) metered + conn fee; lndtte; shop 2km; tradsmn;
playgrnd; lake sw & beach; watersports; entmnt; golf 4km;
ski lift nr; wifi; 40% statics; dogs €2.50; o'night m'van facs;
adv bkg; quiet; red CKE/CCI. "Excel location; extra charge for
lakeside pitches; gd walking." € 22.00                     2009*

**WERTHEIM** *3D2* (5km E Rural) *49.78097, 9.56553*
Campingpark Wertheim-Bettingen, Geiselbrunnweg 31,
97877 Wertheim-Bettingen [(09342) 7077; fax 913077;
info@campingpark-wertheim-bettingen.de; www.
campingpark-wertheim-bettingen.de] Fr A3/E41 exit junc
66 - 2nd Wertheim exit; then turn off to vill of Bettingen; site
sp. Med, pt sl, unmkd pitch, pt shd; wc; chem disp; mv service
pnt; shwrs €0.50; el pnts (6A) €3.50 (long lead req for rvside
pitches); gas; lndtte (inc dryer); shop; rest, snacks; playgrnd;
htd pool adj; paddling pool adj; waterslide adj; boating; fishing;
cycle hire; 60% statics; dogs €1; poss v cr; adv bkg; red long
stay; Eng spkn; many statics; quiet; ccard acc; red 3+ days;
CKE/CCI. "On bank of Rv Main; conv, popular NH for A3 - rec
arr early; NH tourers on sep, lge, level meadow outside main
site (but within barrier); gd rest; san facs tired, req upgrade
(2014)." ◆ 1 Apr-31 Oct. € 25.00                          2014*

GERMANY

**WERTHEIM** *3D2* (2km NW Urban) *49.77805, 9.50916*
Azur Campingpark Wertheim, An den Christwiesen 35, 97877 Wertheim-Bestenheid [(09342) 83111; fax 83171; wertheim@azur-camping.de; www.azur-camping.de/wertheim] Exit A3/E41 junc 66 onto L2310 thro Wertheim, site on W bank of Rv Main sp dir Bestenheim. V lge, mkd pitch, hdstg, pt shd; htd wc; chem disp; mv service pnt; baby facs; shwrs inc; el pnts (6A) €3; gas; lndtte; shop; supmkt 1km; rest 1km; snacks; bar; cooking facs; playgrnd; htd pool; paddling pool; waterslide; fishing; boat hire; tennis 500m; games area; 30% statics; dogs €3; phone; bus 100m; train 1km; poss cr; adv bkg; Eng spkn; rush hr rd noise; red low ssn/CKE/CCI. "Interesting town in walking dist; helpful staff; gd pitches on rv (extra charge); san facs OK 1 block needs upgrade); site clsd 2200; gd rvside cycle paths; gd." ♦ 1 Apr-31 Oct. € 22.50 (CChq acc) 2011*

**WESTERHEIM** *3D3* (2km SW Rural) *48.51055, 9.60933*
Alb-Camping Westerheim, Albstrasse, 72589 Westerheim [(07333) 6197 or 6140; fax 7797; info@alb-camping.de; www.alb-camping.de] Exit A8/E52 at junc 61 (Merklingen) to Laichingen; turn R to Westerheim; foll camp sp (thro housing estate) for 2km to top of hill. Or exit A8 junc 60 thro Westerheim. V lge, mkd pitch, hdstg, pt sl, pt shd; wc; shwrs inc; chem disp; el pnts (16A) €2.50; gas; lndtte; shop; rest, snacks; playgrnd; 3 free pools; tennis 500m; games area; skibus; entmnt; 80% statics; poss cr with long stay vans; Eng spkn; adv bkg ess high ssn; quiet; no ccard acc; red long stay/CKE/CCI. "Huge, holiday-camp style site; gd walking & touring area; wintersports; ski lift adj; lge pitches; helpful staff; gd facs for children; immac san facs; office clsd 1200-1300 (check-in at bar)." € 20.60 2010*

**WESTERLAND (SYLT ISLAND)** *1C1* (3km N Coastal)
*54.94251, 8.32685* Camping Wenningstedt, Am Dorfteich, 25996 Wenningstedt [(04651) 944004; fax 44740; camp@wenningstedt.de; www.wenningstedt.de] Fr Westerland foll sp to Wenningstedt or List. Site app rd on sharp bend bef Wenningstedt. Lge, pt sl, unshd; wc; chem disp; mv service pnt; baby facs; shwrs inc; el pnts (16A) metered; lndtte (inc dryer); shop; rest; playgrnd; htd, covrd pool; fishing 300m; wifi; entmnt; dogs €3.20; adv bkg; quiet. Easter-31 Oct. € 25.00 2010*

**WESTERSTEDE** *1C2* (1km S Rural) *53.2508, 7.93506*
Camping Westerstede, Süderstrasse 2, 26655 Westerstede [tel/fax (04488) 78234; camping@westerstede.de; www.westerstede.de/camping] Exit E35/A28 junc 6 to Westerstede; turn R dir Bad Zwischenahn on L815 for 1km; then foll L815 to L onto Oldenburgerstrasse (rd conts strt on as L821); in 200m turn L to site. Med, mkd pitch, hdstg, pt shd; htd wc; chem disp; mv service pnt; shwrs inc; el pnts (9A) inc; lndtte; shop 300m; rest; playgrnd; bus; train 400m; poss cr; Eng spkn; quiet; red CKE/CCI. "Pleasant, friendly, relaxing, well-managed site; clsd 1300-1500; sm pitches; outer field cheaper but rd noise & remote fr facs; o'night m'van facs; gd touring base; many cycle paths; gd town for shopping." ♦ € 15.50 2009*

**WETTRINGEN** *1B3* (8km N Rural) *52.27408, 7.3204*
Campingplatz Haddorfer Seen, Haddorf 59, 48493 Wettringen [(05973) 2742; fax 900889; info@campingplatz-haddorf.de; www.campingplatz-haddorf.de] Exit A30 junc 7 at Rheine Nord dir Neuenkirchen. At end city limits turn R dir Salzbergen then L in 4km & foll site sp. V lge, mkd pitch, pt shd; htd wc; chem disp; mv service pnt; shwrs inc; el pnts (16A) metered + conn fee; lndtte (inc dryer); shop; tradsmn; supmkt 10km; rest, snacks; bar; playgrnd; lake sw; fishing; watersports; boat hire; games area; 90% statics; dogs €3; adv bkg; quiet; red CKE/CCI. "Family-friendly site; modern san facs; gd bistro; gd walking/cycling." ♦ € 19.00 2010*

**WIESLOCH** *3C3* (5km SW Rural) *49.28146, 8.58445* Camping St Leoner See, 68789 St Leon-Rot [(06227) 59009; fax 880988; info@st.leoner-see.de; www.st.leoner-see.de] Fr A5/E35 exit junc 39 & turn S onto L 546 for 5km. Thro St Leon-Rot two Reilingen, site sp on R. Avoid Walldorf & Wiesloch. V lge, pt shd; wc; chem disp; mv service pnt; baby facs; shwrs inc; el pnts (6-16A) €2; lndtte; shop; rest, snacks; playgrnd; lge watersports complex inc fishing, windsurfing, waterskiing, skin-diving; lake sw; golf 4km; entmnt; internet; 60% statics; no dogs; phone; sep car park; gates clsd 1300-1500 & 2200-0700; poss cr; Eng spkn; adv bkg; quiet except w/end; ccard acc; red CKE/CCI. "Touring vans on hdstg in mkd bays at ent - no space for chairs, awning, etc - NH only; otherwise gd family site; excel sports/water facs." ♦ € 21.00 2009*

**WIESLOCH** *3C3* (6km W Urban) *49.31643, 8.63481*
Campingplatz Walldorf-Astoria, Schwetzingerstrasse 98, 69190 Walldorf [tel/fax (06227) 9195] Fr A5, exit junc 39 for Walldorf & Wiesloch; take B291/L598 N sp Walldorf Nord; in 2km turn R onto Schwetzingerstrasse; site sp in 250m. Med, pt shd; wc; chem disp; mv service pnt; shwrs inc; el pnts (16A) €2.50; shop; rest; indoor pool 200m; 50% statics in sep area; no dogs; Eng spkn; CKE/CCI. "Vg rest on site; sm zoo & sports complex adj; bus to Heidelberg at gate; gates clsd 1200-1500; excel NH/sh stay; rec arr bef 1700 high ssn; conv for Hockenheim Circuit." ♦ 15 Apr-15 Oct. € 18.00 2009*

**WILDESHAUSEN** *1C2* (4km N Rural) *52.93400, 8.40200* Camping Aschenbake, Zum Sande 18, 27801 Dötlingen [(04433) 333; fax 1531; aschenbeck@nwn.de; www.aschenbeck-camping.de] Exit E37/A1 Osnabrück/Bremen junc 60 dir Wildeshausen. Turn R in traff lts in 800m + foll sp to site in 4km. Single track for last km. Med, hdg/mkd pitch, pt shd; wc; chem disp; shwrs €0.60; el pnts (16A) €2; lndtte; shop; rest, snacks; playgrnd; lake sw & beach adj; dogs €2; quiet. "Walks in woods; office clsd 1300-1500." ♦ € 14.00 2009*

**WILDESHAUSEN** *1C2* (2km W Rural) *52.89916, 8.35444* Camping Auetal, Aumühlerstrasse 75, 27793 Aumühle [(04431) 1851; fax 2203] Exit a'bahn A1/E37 junc 61. Take rd B213 E; site on L in 1.5km. Sm, pt shd; wc; shwrs; el pnts (16A) €1.50; lndtte (inc dryer); rest; bar; BBQ; playgrnd; lake sw adj; CKE/CCI. "Statics site but sm field for tourers; vg rest; NH only." ♦ ltd € 13.00 2012*

WILDESHAUSEN *1C2* (3km W Rural) *52.8995, 8.3281*
Camping Bürgerpark, Aumühle 78A, 27793 Oberhausen
[(04431) 7048812; camp.buergerpark@gmx.de; www.
wildeshausen.de] Exit A1/E37 junc 61 onto B213 dir
Cloppenburg. Site in 300m on R. Med, pt sl, pt shd; wc; chem
disp; shwrs; el pnts (6A) inc; shops 500m; snacks; 50% statics;
adv bkg; quiet but some rd noise. "Fair NH; pleasant, wooded
o'night area; conv for a'bahn; Tourers in sep field, san facs
clean and adequate but dated, Eng spkn, gd for nh." 1 Apr-
30 Sep. € 14.00                                          2013*

WILHELMSTHAL see Eisenach *1D4*

WILLSTATT SAND see Kehl *3B3*

⊞ WILSUM *1B3* (3.5m S Rural) *52.51689, 6.87390*
Wilsumerberge Resort, Zum Feriengebiet 1, 49849 Wilsum
[(05945) 995590; fax 9955899; info@wilsumerberge.nl;
www.wilsumerberge.nl] Site sp on B403. V lge, pt shd; htd
wc; chem disp; mv service pnt; baby facs; shwrs inc; el pnts
(6A) inc; lndtte (inc dryer); shop; rest, snacks; bar; playgrnd;
lake sw; waterslide; fishing; tennis; cycle hire; games area;
games rm; wifi; entmnt; 60% statics; dogs €3; adv bkg; ccard
acc; red low ssn. "Attractive site in forest; extra for serviced
pitches; vg facs, espec for youngsters." ♦ € 22.00    2010*

WINNINGEN see Koblenz *3B2*

⊞ WINSEN (ALLER) *1D3* (1.5km W Rural) *52.67506, 9.89968*
Campingplatz Winsen, Auf der Hude 1, 29308 Winsen
[(05143) 93199; fax 93144; info@camping-winsen.de;
www.camping-winsen.de] Fr A7/E45 exit junc 50 Wietze
onto B214Thro Wietze & in 6km turn L to Oldau & Winsen.
Foll site sp. Med, mkd pitch, pt shd; htd wc; chem disp; mv
service pnt; shwrs inc; el pnts (10-16A) inc; gas; lndtte (inc
dryer); shop; tradsmn; supmkt 1km; rest, snacks; bar; playgrnd;
htd, covrd pool 200m; rv beach adj; wifi; 50% statics; dogs
€2; phone; bus 1km; m'van o'night area; quiet; red CKE/CCI.
"Attractive site; helpful staff; some rvside pitches - poss liable
to flood; easy walk to picturesque town cent; lovely cycle
paths." € 31.00                                          2013*

⊞ WINSEN (ALLER) *1D3* (8km NW Rural) *52.71983,
9.82521* Campingpark Hüttensee, Hüttenseepark 1,
29308 Meissendorf [(05056) 941880; fax 941881; info@
campingpark-huettensee.de; www.campingpark-
huettensee.de] Fr N on A27/A7 exit at Westenholz & cont
twd Westenholz/Ostenholz to Meissendorf, site sp. Fr S exit at
Allertal rest stop twd Celle/Winsen-Aller. Turn L at traff lts &
L again to Meissendorf. Lge, mkd pitch, pt shd; htd wc; chem
disp; mv service pnt; baby facs; shwrs €0.50; el pnts (16A) inc;
lndtte (inc dryer); shop; tradsmn; supmkt 800m; rest, snacks;
bar; playgrnd; lake sw & sand beach; fishing; tennis 500m;
boat & cycle hire; games area; wifi; entmnt; 60% statics; dogs
€2.50; clsd 1300-1500; adv bkg; quiet; ccard acc; red CKE/CCI.
♦ € 24.80 (CChq acc)                                     2011*

⊞ WINTRICH *3B2* (100m E Rural) *49.96541, 7.10537* Mosel
Stellplatz Wintrich, Rissbacherstraße 155, 56841 Traben-
Trarbach [06541 3111; info@moselstellplatz.de; www.
moselstellplatz.de] Fr S of A1 take exit 125 Wittlich-Mitte for
B50 twds Wittlich. Merge onto B49, cont onto L55 to Urzig,
then turn R onto B53 & foll sp to camp. Med, shd; wc; chem
disp; mv service pnt; shwr; el pnts (6A); tradsmn; wifi; dogs;
poss cr; quiet. "Vg site." € 8.00                        2014*

⊞ WISMAR *2E2* (200m N Urban) *53.89388, 11.45166*
Wohnmobilpark Westhafen, Schiffbauerdamm 12, 23966
Wismar [(03841) 706070; info@wohnmobilpark-wismar.
de] Exit A20/E22 junc 8 to cent of Wismar; foll sp to 'hafen',
site sp. Sm, hdstg, unshd; wc; shwrs €1; el pnts (10A) €1 for
8 hrs; shop adj; rest 200m; adv bkg; quayside noise. "Superb
NH in stunning town; m'vans only - no c'vans allowed."
€ 9.00                                                   2011*

⊞ WISMAR *2E2* (5km NW Coastal) *53.93441, 11.37160*
Ostsee Camping, Sandstrasse 19c, 23968 Zierow
[(038428) 63820; fax 63833; info@ostsee-camping.de;
www.ostsee-camping.de] Fr Wismar-Lübeck rd B105/22 to
Gägelow, turn N to Zierow; thro vill to site at end of rd. V lge,
unshd; htd wc; chem disp; mv service pnt; sauna; baby facs;
shwrs €1; el pnts (16A) €2.80; lndtte (inc dryer); shop; tradsmn;
rest, snacks; playgrnd; beach adj; cycle hire; games area;
horseriding adj; wifi; TV; 75% statics (sep area); dogs €2.70;
CKE/CCI. "Busy site in superb location; gd san facs; a first class
campsite." ♦ € 32.30                                     2011*

WITTENBERG see Lutherstadt Wittenberg *2F3*

WITTLICH *3B2* (8km E Urban) *49.97861, 7.00750*
Wohnmobilstellplatz (M'van Park), Moseluferstrasse,
54539 Ürzig [(06532) 954888; info@uerzig-mosel.de] Foll
B50 fr Wittlich, then B53 for 3km along rv bank to Ürzig.
M'vans only, sp. Sm, own san; chem disp; mv service pnt; el
pnts €1.50 (16A); shop 200m; rest, bar 100m; dogs; adv bkg.
1 Apr-5 Nov. € 6.50                                      2009*

⊞ WITTLICH *3B2* (11km E Rural) *49.98986, 7.07780*
Camping Sportzentrum Kröverberg, 54536 Kröv
[(06541) 70040; fax 700444; www.kroeverberg.de] Exit A1/
A48 junc 125; then B49 dir Koblenz; then L62 Ürzig; L in Ürzig
sp Kröv-Bergstrecke up hill (10%) for 2km; foll sp on this rd (do
not go downhill into Mosel Valley). Med, hdg/mkd pitch, terr,
unshd; wc; shwrs inc; chem disp; mv service pnt; el pnts (10A)
metered; gas; lndtte; shop 4km; rest, snacks; playgrnd; games
area; statics; dogs €1.80; quiet; adv bkg. "Friendly site high
above Mosel; lovely scenery; boat trips on Mosel; mkd walks
thro vineyards; excel facs." € 14.00                     2011*

WITTLICH *3B2* (12km NW Rural) *50.09680, 6.79797* Natur-
Camping Vulkaneifel, Feriendorf Moritz, Herbstwiese 1,
54531 Manderscheid [(06572) 92110; fax 921149; info@
vulkan-camping.de; www.vulkan-camping.de] Exit A1/E44
junc 122 dir Manderscheid, then foll sp Daun. Site sp. Med,
mkd pitch, terr, pt shd; wc; chem disp; mv service pnt; shwrs
inc; el pnts (2A) €2.50; lndtte; shop 2km; rest 700m; snacks;
playgrnd; htd pool; games area; 10% statics; dogs €1.50;
o'night m'van area; red CKE/CCI. "Gd walking, cycling; facs
shared with football club." ♦ 1 Apr-31 Oct. € 20.00     2009*

⊞ **WITZENHAUSEN** *1D4* (1.5km N Rural) *51.3499, 9.86916*
Camping Werratal, Am Sande 11, 37213 Witzenhausen
[(05542) 1465; fax 72418; info@campingplatz-werratal.
de; www.campingplatz-werratal.de] Exit A7/E45 junc 75
to Witzenhausen. Cross rv & immed R foll sp rte around town
cent. Site nr rv, sp. Med, unshd; wc; chem disp; mv service pnt;
shwrs €0.70; el pnts (16A) €2.30; lndtte (inc dryer); shop; rest,
snacks adj; playgrnd; htd, covrd pool 200m; cycle hire; wifi;
50% statics; dogs €2.30; red long stay. "Pleasant, family-run
site; poss flooding at high water." € 24.80                2011*

⊞ **WITZENHAUSEN** *1D4* (10km SE Urban) *51.28889,
9.97638* Camping Oase, Kreisstrasse 32, 37318
Wahlhausen [tel/fax (036087) 98671; www.camping-
oase.de] Take B27 dir Wahlhausen, site sp bet Bad Sooden &
Allendorf. Med, pt sl, pt shd; wc; chem disp; shwrs inc; el pnts
(16A) metered; lndtte (inc dryer); shop adj; rest; playgrnd; Rv
Werra nr; dogs €1; adv bkg; quiet. € 14.50                2010*

⊞ **WOLFACH** *3C3* (2km E Rural) *48.29083, 8.27805*
Trendcamping Wolfach (previously named Schwarzwald
Camp Wolfach), Schiltacherstrasse 80, 77709
Wolfach-Halbmeil [(07834) 859309; fax 859310; info@
trendcamping.de; www.trendcamping.de] Fr Wolfach E
5km on B294 dir Schiltach. Site on L opp rv bdge. Med, hdstg,
terr, unshd; wc; chem disp; mv service pnt; serviced pitches;
shwrs; el pnts (16A) metered + conn fee; gas; lndtte; shop;
rest, snacks; playgrnd; wifi; some sat TV; 30% statics; dogs
€2; o'night m'van area; Eng spkn; adv bkg; quiet but some rd
noise; red long stay. "Scenic views across valley; excel, modern,
clean san facs; barrier clsd 1230-1430; NH area for m'vans;
rock pegs req for awning; free bus & train pass for Black Forest;
gd cycling & walking." € 25.00                2012*

⊞ **WOLFACH** *3C3* (5km S Rural) *48.26750, 8.23777*
Campingplatz zur Mühle, Talstrasse 79, 77709 Kirnbach
[(07834) 775; fax 8670975; camping-kirnbach@t-online.de;
www.camping-kirnbach.de] Turn S off B294 dir Kirnbach,
site sp. Steep access. Sm, hdg/mkd pitch, terr; pt sl, pt shd; htd
wc; chem disp (wc); shwrs €0.50; el pnts (16A) metered + conn fee;
lndtte; shop; tradsmn; snacks; bar; BBQ; rv 500m; TV rm; few
statics; no dogs high ssn; phone; quiet. "Pleasant site but not
suitable lge o'fits; poss boggy in wet weather; friendly owners
help with van placing; gd touring base; gd views Black Forest;
gd walks & rests nrby." € 18.00                2009*

⊞ **WOLFSBURG** *2E3* (2km NE Urban) *52.4316, 10.8158*
Camping am Allersee, In den Allerwiesen 5, 38446
Wolfsburg [(05361) 63395; fax 651271; allerseecamping@
gmx.de; www.camping-allersee.de] Turn L over canal, then R past
B188, foll sp VW Autostadt sp. Turn L over canal, then R past
stadium. Med, mkd pitch, hdstg, pt shd; htd wc; chem disp;
shwrs €0.50; el pnts (10A) €2.50 or metered; lndtte; shops
2km; rest; bar; cooking facs; playgrnd; beach adj; lake sw
100m; sailing & canoeing; entmnt; 80% statics; dogs €1; clsd
1300-1500 & 2200-0700; o'night area for m'vans; poss cr;
Eng spkn; adv bkg; quiet, but poss noise fr pop concerts in VW
stadium. "Vg, clean site beside lake; conv VW factory visits
(not w/end or bank hols) - check time of tour in Eng; gd lake
perimeter path adj; friendly, helpful owners; ice rink & indoor
water cent other side of lake." ◆ ltd € 22.00                2011*

⊞ **WOLFSTEIN** *3B2* (2km S Rural) *49.5803, 7.6187*
Azur Camping am Königsberg, Am Schwimmbad
1, 67752 Wolfstein [(06304) 4143; fax 7543; nfo@
CampingWolfstein.de; www.campingwolfstein.de] Exit
A61 at junc 15 Kaiserslauten West onto B270 dir Lauterecken,
site on R 200m bef Wolfstein, sp. Sm, mkd pitch, hdstg, pt sl,
unshd; wc; chem disp; serviced pitches; shwrs inc; el pnts (16A)
€3 + conn fee; lndtte; ice shop 200m; rest; bar; playgrnd; htd
pool adj; games area; wifi; 60% statics; dogs €2.30; poss cr;
adv bkg; site clsd 1300-1500; Eng spkn; quiet; ccard acc; red
snr citizens/CKE/CCI. "Gd." € 22.00                2011*

⊞ **WULFEN (FEHMARN ISLAND)** *2E1* (1km E Coastal)
*54.40611, 11.1772* Camping- und Ferienpark Wulfener
Hals (Part Naturist), Wulfener Hals Weg, 23769 Wulfen
[(04371) 86280; fax 3723; camping@wulfenerhals.de;
www.wulfenerhals.de] Turn off B207/E47 to Avendorf, site
sp. V lge, mkd pitch, shd; htd wc; chem disp; mv service pnt;
serviced pitches; sauna; baby rm; fam bthrm; shwrs; el pnts
(10A) €2.10; gas; lndtte; shop; rest, snacks; bar; playgrnd;
pool; sand beach adj; sailing; watersports; golf adj; wifi;
entmnt; 60% statics; dogs €7.50; phone; adv bkg; ccard acc;
red CKE/CCI. "Excel." ◆ € 39.50                2011*

See advert on bookmark

WURZBURG *3D2* (6km NE Urban) *49.83286, 9.99783*
Camping Estenfeld, Maidbronnerstrasse 38, 97230
Estenfeld [(09305) 228; fax 8006; cplestenfeld@freenet.
de; www.camping-estenfeld.de] Exit A7/E45 junc 101. Foll
sp to Estenfeld & site sp. Sm, some hdstg, pt shd; wc; chem
disp; shwrs €0.75; el pnts (16A) €2.50 or metered & conn fee;
lndtte; shop; tradsmn; rest adj; snacks; bar; playgrnd; some
statics; dogs €1.50; clsd 1300-1500; poss v cr high ssn; Eng
spkn; quiet; red long stay; CKE/CCI. "Helpful owner; clean, tidy
site; rec NH." 15 May-10 Nov. € 26.50                2014*

## "We must tell The Club about that great site we found"

Get your site reports in by mid-August
and we'll do our best to get your updates
into the next edition.

WURZBURG *3D2* (2km S Urban) *49.77973, 9.92636* Kanu-
Club Würzberg, Mergentheimerstrasse 13b, 97082
Würzburg [(09317) 72536; www.kc-wuerzberg.de] Fr A3/
E43 exit junc 70, Heidingsfeld. Turn L onto B19 & foll sp for
Heidingsfeld. Turn R at site sp to cross tram line, sp Zeltplatz.
Site L in 30m on W bank of rv, not well sp. Sm, mkd pitch,
pt shd; wc; chem disp; shwrs €0.50; el pnts €2; shop 1.5km;
rest; bar; 80% statics; bus/tram adj; dogs €1.50; Eng spkn; adv
bkg; CKE/CCI. "Site is private club with ltd touring pitches; gd
access to lovely, historic city; gd cycling by rv; friendly staff; not
suitable lge o'fits due sm pitches & restricted access; long walk
to san facs; adv bkg ess holiday w/ends; attractive quiet site."
Mar-Dec. € 13.00                2011*

⊞ **WURZBURG** *3D2* (4km S Rural) *49.74471, 9.98433* **Camping Kalte Quelle, Winterhäuserstrasse 160, 97084 Würzburg-Heidingsfeld [(0931) 65598; fax 612611; info@ kalte-quelle.de; www.kalte-quelle.de]** Exit A3/E43 at Heidingsfeld junc 70 onto A19 dir Würzburg. Take 1st exit & foll sp Ochsenfurt + camping sp. Site on L in approx 5km. Med, mkd pitch, pt shd; wc; chem disp; mv service pnt; shwrs €1; el pnts (16A) conn fee + €2; lndtte; shop; rest; bar; playgrnd; cycle hire; 50% statics; dogs free; clsd 1330-1430; poss cr; Eng spkn; adv bkg; some rd, rv & rlwy noise; ccard acc; CKE/ CCI. "No doors on shwrs & run down facs, but clean; pleasant situation on rv; NH only; conv Würzburg & Nürnberg; bus to centrum 2km." € 16.00                                2012*

## "I need an on-site restaurant"

We do our best to make sure site information is correct, but it is always best to check any must-have facilities are still available or will be open during your visit.

**WUSTENWELSBERG** *4E2* (500m SE Rural) *50.13750, 10.82777* **Camping Rückert-Klause, Haus Nr 16, 96190 Wüstenwelsberg [tel/fax (09533) 288]** Fr Coburg on B4, turn W at Kaltenbrunn; site sp thro Untermerzbach & Obermerzbach. Or fr B279 fr Bamberg to Bad Königshofen, turn R just S of Pfarrweisch, sp. Sm, pt sl, pt shd, wc; chem disp; shwrs inc; el pnts (16A) metered + conn fee; lndtte; shops 3km; snacks; bar; playgrnd; 50% statics; Eng spkn; adv bkg; quiet; ccard not acc; CKE/CCI. "Many castles nrby; beautiful countryside; super situation." 1 Apr-31 Oct. € 14.00     2009*

**ZELL** *3B2* (1.5km W Rural) *50.03375, 7.17365* **Campingplatz Mosella, 56856 Zell-Kaimt [tel/fax (06542) 41241; info@ capingpark-zell.de; www.campingpark-zell.de]** Fr Cochem S on B49, in Alf take B53 dir Bernkastel-Kues. In Zell site sp to Kaimt. Med, mkd pitch, hdstg, unshd; wc; chem disp; mv service pnt; shwrs; el pnts (16A) inc; gas; lndtte; snacks; playgrnd; watersports; wifi; dogs €1; poss cr; quiet. "Scenic area; v quiet at night; site soggy after rain; excel well kept site, rest and bar being built (2012); cycles and boats for hire." 1 Apr-31 Oct. € 26.50                                2012*

**ZELL** *3B2* (3km NW Rural) *50.05889, 7.13027* **Bären Camp, Am Moselufer 1-3, 56859 Bullay [(06542) 900097; info@ baeren-camp.de; www.baeren-camp.de]** Exit A1 junc 125 at Wittlich onto B49 to Alf. At Alf cross rv to Bullay & foll sp to site. Med, pt shd; wc; chem disp; mv service pnt; baby facs; shwrs €1; el pnts (16A) metered; lndtte (inc dryer); shop; BBQ; playgrnd; dogs €2; Eng spkn; quiet. "Conv Cochem, Bernkastel-Kues; gd cycling along tow-path; extra for rvside pitch." ♦ ltd Easter-1 Nov. € 20.20                    2010*

**ZELL** *3B2* (4km NW Rural) *50.03305, 7.11527* **Camping Moselland, Im Planters, 56862 Pünderich [(06542) 2618; fax 960696; www.campingplatz-moselland.de]** Foll Rv Mosel S fr Zell on B53. In 6km turn R sp Pünderich & site. Turn immed L, then immed R & foll narr rd to site in 1km. Med, mkd pitch, pt shd; wc; chem disp; shwrs €1; el pnts (16A) metered + conn fee; lndtte; tradsmn; rest, snacks; bar; playgrnd; boat-launching; 30% statics; dogs €2; phone; Eng spkn; adv bkg; quiet. "Pleasant rvside site in vineyards & orchards; vg." 1 Apr-31 Oct. € 16.00                                2009*

⊞ **ZEVEN** *1D2* (1.5km NE) *53.30401, 9.29793* **Campingplatz Sonnenkamp Zeven, Sonnenkamp 10, 27404 Zeven [(04281) 951345; fax 951347; info@campingplatz-sonnenkamp.de; www.campingplatz-zeven.de]** Fr A1 exit 47 or 49 to Zeven. Fr Zeven dir Heeslingen/Buxtehude rd, site sp fr all dir twd stadium. Lge, mkd pitch, some hdstg, unshd; htd wc; chem disp; mv service pnt; baby facs; sauna; shwrs inc; el pnts (16A) metered; gas; lndtte (inc dryer); shop; tradsmn; rest, snacks; bar; playgrnd; pool, paddling pool, waterslide & sports facs adj; tennis; cycle hire; games area; games rm; wifi; entmnt; 75% statics; dogs €0.50; phone; Eng spkn; poss cr; adv bkg; ccard acc; quiet; red snr citizens; CKE/CCI. € 22.60                                2011*

## "Satellite navigation makes touring much easier"

Remember most sat navs don't know if you're towing or in a larger vehicle – always use yours alongside maps and site directions.

⊞ **ZIERENBERG** *1D4* (500m E Rural) *51.36809, 9.31494* **Campingplatz Zur Warme, Im Nordbruch 2, 34289 Zierenberg [tel/fax (05606) 3966; campingplatz-zierenberg@t-online.de; www.campingplatz-zierenberg. de]** Exit A44 at junc 67 to Zierenberg. In vill cent foll sp for Freizeit Centrum. Site on R on leaving vill, well sp. Med, mkd pitch, some hdstg, unshd; htd wc; chem disp; shwrs inc; el pnts (16A) €1.70 or metered; lndtte (inc dryer); shop 500m; tradsmn; rest, snacks; bar; playgrnd; covrd pool; fishing; TV; 75% statics; dogs €1.50; poss v cr; Eng spkn; adv bkg; quiet. "Scenic, well-kept site with stream & sm lake adj; clean, modern facs but poss stretched if site full." ♦ € 16.50  2011*

**ZIEROW see Wismar** *2E2*

⊞ **ZINGST AM DARSS** *2F1* (500m W Coastal) *54.44055, 12.66031* **Camping am Freesenbruch, Am Bahndamm 1, 18374 Zingst-am-Darss [(038232) 15786; fax 15710; info@camping-zingst.de; www.camping-zingst.de]** On rd 105/E22 at Löbnitz take rd thro Barth to Zingst; site on coast rd. Lge, mkd pitch, pt shd; wc; chem disp; mv service pnt; shwrs inc; el pnts (16A) metered + conn fee; lndtte; shop; rest, snacks; bar; playgrnd; beach adj; games area; cycle hire; entmnt; 20% statics; dogs €2; sep car park; o'night facs for m'vans; poss cr; adv bkg; quiet; ccard acc; CKE/CCI. "Well-maintained site in National Park; sep fr beach by sea wall & rd; well-maintained; card operated barrier." ♦ € 20.00     2009*

GERMANY

⊞ **ZISLOW** *2F2* (2km N Rural) *53.44555, 12.31083*
Naturcamping Zwei Seen, Waldchaussee 2, 17209 Zislow
[(039924) 2550; fax 2062; info@zwei-seen-naturcamping.
de; www.zwei-seen-naturcamping.de] A19/E55 exit 17 dir
Adamshoffnung. Turn R at x-rds in 4km. Site sp. Also sp fr W
of Stuer on B198. Lge, pt shd; wc; chem disp; mv service pnt;
shwrs €0.50; el pnts (6A) €2; lndtte (inc dryer); shop; tradsmn;
rest, snacks; bar; playgrnd; lake sw; watersports; games area;
cycle hire; wifi; entmnt; 40% statics; dogs €2.50; phone;
poss cr; Eng spkn; adv bkg; quiet; ccard acc; red CKE/CCI.
"Ideal for country lovers; remote spot; vg lakeside pitches." ♦
€ 17.50                                                    2010*

⊞ **ZITTAU** *2H4* (3km S Rural) *50.8943, 14.77005* **See-**
**Camping Zittauer Gebirge, Zur Landesgartenschau 2,**
02785 Olbersdorf [(03583) 69629-2; fax 696293; info@
seecamping-zittau.com; www.seecamping-zittau.com]
Fr Zittau foll Olbersdorfer See sp, site on lakeside. Lge, sl,
unshd; wc; chem disp; shwrs €0.70; el pnts (10A) €2; lndtte
(inc dryer); shop; tradsmn; rest, snacks, bar adj; lake sw adj;
entmnt; 10% statics; dogs €2; Eng spkn; quiet; ccard acc; CKE/
CCI. "Excel san facs; excel base for hill walking; close Polish &
Czech borders." ♦ € 19.00                                 2010*

⊞ **ZORGE** *2E4* (1km NE Urban) *51.64176, 10.65083*
Camping im Waldwinkel, Im Kunzental 2, 37449 Zorge
[(05586) 1048; fax 8113] Fr N via Bad Harzburg, Braunlage,
Hohegeiss, turn L at ent to Zorge vill, site sp dir 'Schwimmbad'.
Fr S on B243, turn N at Bad Sachsa, dir Walkenried & Zorge,
turn R in vill. Med, pt sl, unshd; wc; chem disp; mv service pnt;
shwrs; baby rm; el pnts (16A) metered + conn fee; gas; lndtte
(inc dryer); shop 1km; rest, snacks adj; playgrnd; htd pool
200m; tennis; ski lift 4km; skibus; entmnt; TV; dogs €1; o'night
area for m'vans; adv bkg; quiet; red CKE/CCI. "Beautiful
location." ♦ € 16.00                                       2010*

**ZWEIBRUCKEN** *3B3* (1km E Urban) *49.25368, 7.37736*
Campingplatz Zweibrücken, Geschwister-Scholl-Allee 11,
66482 Zweibrücken [(06332) 482984; info@campingplatz-
zw.de; www.campingplatz-zw.de] Exit A8 junc 32 for
Zweibrücken town cent. Sp infrequent so foll sp to Rosegarten
site beyond show-jumping arena. Turn R at camping sp immed
over bdge. Med, unshd; wc; chem disp; shwrs inc; el pnts (10A)
metered + conn fee; lndtte; shop 300m; rest, snacks; playgrnd;
htd pool 150m; rv & beach adj; cycle hire; wifi; 50% statics;
dogs €1; noisy at w/end; red CKE/CCI. "Poss diff access due
parked cars for sw pool; 15 min walk to town cent; gd NH." ♦
1 Apr-30 Sep. € 22.00                                     2009*

**ZWEIBRUCKEN** *3B3* (3km SW Rural) *49.20638, 7.33111*
Camping Hengstbacher-Mühle, Hengstbacher Mühle
1, 66482 Zweibrücken-Mittelbach [(06332) 18128; fax
904001] Fr A8 exit junc 33 onto B424 sp Zweibrücken-Ixheim
& Mittelbach. At T-junc turn R dir Bitsch & in 50m turn R at
camping sp. Site on L in 4km after end of Mittelbach vill. Sm,
pt shd; wc; chem disp; mv service pnt; shwrs inc; el pnts (15A)
€2.50 or metered (poss rev pol); shops 4km; 70% statics in
sep area; liable to flooding; Eng spkn; quiet. "Friendly owner;
lovely setting; basic site but clean san facs; gd NH; cl type size."
15 Apr-31 Oct. € 13.50                                    2014*

**ZWEIBRUCKEN** *3B3* (11km SW Rural) *49.15888, 7.24388*
Camping am Schwimmbad, Am Campingplatz 1,
66453 Gersheim-Walsheim [(06843) 1030; fax 80138;
freizeitbetrieb@gersheim.de; www.gersheim.de] Fr A8/
E50 exit junc 9 onto B423 dor Blieskastel. In Webenheim turn
L twd Gersheim, after 11km turn L for Walsheim. Site on L
beyond vill. Med, pt sl, pt shd; wc; chem disp; shwrs inc; el pnts
€2 or metered (10A); lndtte (inc dryer); shop in vill; tradsmn;
rest, bar adj; BBQ; htd pool adj; 85% statics; dogs €0.50;
phone; poss cr; adv bkg; quiet; red CKE/CCI. "Helpful warden;
sep area for tourers; pleasant countryside; walking & cycle
paths nr; site barrier clsd 1300-1500 & 2200." ♦ 15 Mar-
15 Oct. € 15.70                                           2014*

You can now fill in site reports online

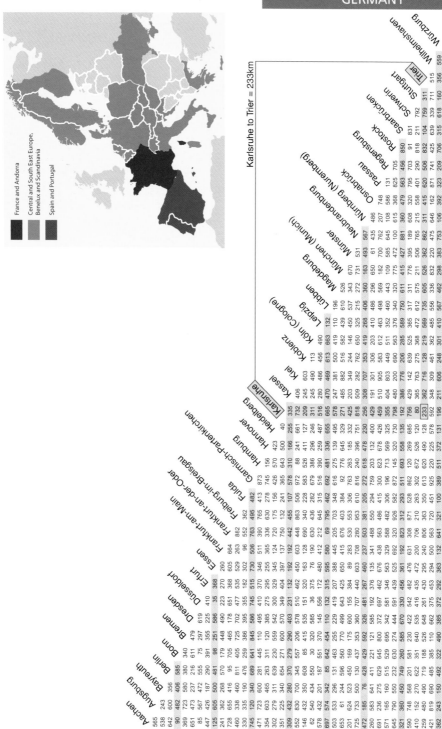

Karlsruhe to Trier = 233km

**Map I**

Legend:
- All year site(s)
- Seasonal site(s)
- No sites listed
- 200m +
- 0–200m

0  20  40  60  80  100 kms

0  10  20  30  40  50  60 mls

© Collins Bartholomew Ltd 2014

NORTH SEA

DENMARK

NETHERLANDS

BELGIUM

HAMBURG

BREMEN

HANNOVER

KASSEL

KÖLN

BONN

DÜSSELDORF

ESSEN

MÜNSTER

OSNABRÜCK

Westerland
Aabenraa
Glücksburg (Ostsee)
Medelby
Kappeln
Husum 201
Schleswig
Eckernförde
Labo
Gettorf
KIE
Hennstedt
Preetz
Langwedel
Neumünster 205
Bad Bramstedt 5
Bad Segeberg
CUXHAVEN
Otterndorf
Dorum
Bad Bederkesa
Hechthausen
Norden
Hooksiel
WILHELMSHAVEN
Schortens
HAMBURG
Geesth
Groningen
Leer (Ostfriesland)
Westerstede
Zeven
Heidenau
Lünebu
Gyhum
Papenburg
Ganderkesee
Sottrum
Rotenburg (Wümme)
Soltau
Friesoythe
Wildeshausen
Emmen
Bergen
Hösseringe
Engehausen
Winsen (All
Celle
Wilsum
Rieste
HANNOVER
Peine
Schüttorf
Mettingen
Bad Bentheim
Hörstel
Ibbenbüren
OSNABRÜCK
Porta Westfalica
Hameln
Enschede
Wettringen
Greven
Lengerich
Melle
Herford
Rinteln
Salzhemmendorf
Arnhem
MÜNSTER
Bielefeld
Vlotho
Lemgo
Bad Pyrmont
Bad Gandersheim
Clausthal-Zellerfeld
Nijmegen
Dülmen
Holzminden
Höxter
Hamm
Lippstadt
Northeim
Gieselwerder
Eindhoven
Gelsenkirchen
Soest
Trendelburg
Dransfeld
Greyrath
Dortmund
Warburg
Hannoversch-Münden
Witzenhause
Brüggen
ESSEN
Meschede
Zierenberg
DÜSSELDORF
Korbach
KASSEL
Solingen
Radevormwald
Naumburg (Hessen)
Spangenberg
Webers
Hückeswagen
Olpe
Rotenburg an der Fulda
Eisenach
Maastricht
KÖLN
Kirchheim
AACHEN
Marburg an der Lahn
Alsfeld
Liège
Nideggen
Urnshause
Monschau
Simmerath
BONN
Bad Honnef
Schleiden
Bad Neuenahr-Ahrweiler
Remagen
Wetzlar
Grünberg
Hünfeld

Map 2

## Map labels

E F G H

**Legend:**
- Motorways
- Major roads
- Main roads

BALTIC SEA

POLAND

CZECH REPUBLIC

Spodsbjerg
Tårs
Rødbyhavn
etersdorf
Puttgarden
FEHMARN
Wulfen
enfelde
Grossenbrode
Sütel
Dahme
Kühlungsborn
Rerik
Bad Doberan
ROSTOCK
Neustadt
Holstein
Trevemünde
Lübeck
Wismar
Neukloster
Retgendorf
SCHWERIN
Blekede
Malliss
Lenzen
Gartow
Altenkirchen
Schaprode
Zingst am Darss
Pruchten
Altefähr
STRALSUND
Ribnitz-Damgarten
Schwaan
Waren
Plau
Malchow
Zislow
Neustrelitz
Fürstenberg
Canow
Lietzow
Binz
RÜGEN
Greifswald
Karlshagen
Ückeritz
Grambin
NEUBRANDENBURG
Feldberg
Warnitz
Swinoujście
Szczecin
Gorzów Wielkopolski
Wolfsburg
Colbitz
Brandenburg an der Havel
Stechow
Brieselang
Potsdam
Ferch
BERLIN
Erkner
Storkow
Tiefensee
Kostrzyn
FRANKFURT AN DER ODER
Swiebodzin
MAGDEBURG
Plötzky
zburg
Halberstadt
Wernigerode
Quedlinburg
aunlage
orge
alkenried
Neustadt
Seeburg
Kelbra
eissensee
Bad Kösen
Weimar
Jena
ERFURT
Mühlberg
Ohrdruf
Kränichfeld
Hohenwarte
Lutherstadt Wittenberg
Dessau
Torgau
LEIPZIG
Meissen
Coswig
Colditz
Chemnitz
Annaberg-Buchholz
Ortrand
Kamenz
Bautzen
Moritzburg
DRESDEN
Pirna
Reinsberg
Königstein
Altenberg
Bad Schandau
Zittau
Zgorzelec
Niesky
Bolesławiec
LÜBBEN
Usti nad Labem

© Collins Bartholomew Ltd 2014

N W E S

Map 3

POLAND

Bolesławiec
Zgorzelec
Niesky
Zittau

CZECH
REPUBLIC

PRAHA

Torgau
LEIPZIG
Kamenz
Bautzen
Meissen
Coswig
Moritzburg
DRESDEN
Reinsberg
Pirna
Bad Schandau
Königstein
Attenberg
Usti nad Labem
Annaberg Buchholtz
Colditz
Chemnitz
Seeburg
Weissensee
Bad Kösen
ERFURT
Weimar
Jena
Gera
Kranichfeld
Ohrdruf
ühlberg
kenried
Kelbra
eberstedt

Plauen
Saalburg
Issigau
Hof
Karlovy Vary
Coburg
stenwelsberg
Zell
Kulmbach
Fichtelberg
Mitterteich
Bamberg
BAYREUTH
Pottenstein
Flossenbürg
Neustadt an der Waldnaab
Plzen
Erlangen
Hersbruck
Hirschau
istadt an der Aisch
NÜRNBERG
Waldmünchen
Klatovy

Neumarkt in der Oberpfalz
Pielenhofen
Kötzting
Pappenheim
Kinding
Kipfenberg
REGENSBURG
Bad Abbach
Spiegelau
Deggendorf
Finsterau
Neureichenau
Nördlingen
Ingolstadt
Donauwörth
Eging am See
Nessibach
Landshut
PASSAU
Bad Füssing
Linz

GSBURG

MÜNCHEN
Diessen
Prien am Chiemsee
Gross Seeham
Rosenheim
Traunstein
Übersee
Waging am See
AUSTRIA
Salzburg
Ruhpolding
Bad Reichenhall
xtoberdorf
Rottenbuch
ibruck
Murnau am Staffelsee
Bad Tölz
Inzell
Berchtesgaden
Rosshaupten
Kochal am See
Reit im Winkl
Königsee
Vesselwang
Oberammergau
Kufstein
ach Füssen
GARMISCH-PARTENKIRCHEN
Mittenwald
Innsbruck

Motorways
Major roads
Main roads

© Collins Bartholomew Ltd 2014

Map 4

# Greece
## Country Introduction

*Ruins in Delfi, Greece*

## Welcome to Greece

Think of Greece and ancient history, idyllic beaches and olive groves come to mind. This is a country with so much to see and do, you'll never feel like you've had enough time to explore.

The mainland has so much history that you'll feel like the whole country is one vast archaeological site. If you get tired of all the cultural highlights there are plenty of beaches and coves to while away some tranquil days.

## Country highlights

Olives and olive oil are the most prominent complement to any Greek dish and are also said to have great health benefits. Another popular food is feta cheese made from sheep or goats milk. The most popular drink in Greece is Ouzo. It can be flavoured with spices such as anise, mint and coriander.

Athens and Epidaurus Festival, which takes place every summer, celebrates the ancient history and customs of the nation.

## Major towns and cities

- Athens – the cosmopolitan capital and largest city of Greece.

- Thessaloniki – a modern metropolis that still has lots of historical buildings and charm.

- Larissa – an ancient city surrounded by some of the most imposing mountains in Greece.

- Chalcis – this amazing city has ancient monuments and a Roman aqueduct.

## Attractions

- The Acropolis Museum – this important museum houses ancient Greek statues and much more.

- Paleochristian and Byzantine Monuments of Thessalonika – stunning architecture of medieval Greece.

- Delphi Theatre – an important site home to the sanctuary and oracle of Apollo.

## Find out more

www.visitgreece.gr

Tel: 0030 (0) 21 03 31 05 29 Greece Tourist Board

# Country Information

*Population (approx):* 10.7 million

*Capital:* Athens (population approx 3.7 million)

*Area:* 721,477 sq km (inc islands)

*Bordered by:* Albania, Bulgaria, Macedonia, Turkey

*Coastline:* 13,676km

*Terrain:* Mainly mountain ranges extending into the sea as peninsulas and chains of islands

*Climate:* Warm Mediterranean climate; hot, dry summers; mild, wet winters in the south, colder in the north; rainy season November to March; winter temperatures can be severe in the mountains

*Highest Point:* Mount Olympus 2,917m

*Language:* Greek

*Local Time:* GMT or BST + 2, i.e. 2 hours ahead of the UK all year

*Currency:* Euros divided into 100 cents; £1 = €1.26, €1 = £0.79 (September 2014)

*Emergency numbers:* Police 100; Fire brigade 199; Ambulance 166. Operators speak English. Dial 171 for emergency tourist police.

*Public Holidays 2015:* Jan 1, 6; Feb 23; Mar 25; Apr 10, 13; May 1; Jun 1; Aug 15; Oct 28; Dec 25, 26.

School summer holidays run from the beginning of July to the first week in September.

# Camping and Caravanning

There are over 340 campsites licensed by the Greek National Tourist Office. These can be recognised by a sign displaying the organisation's blue emblem. Most are open from April until the end of October, but those near popular tourist areas stay open all year. There are other unlicensed sites but visitors to them cannot be assured of safe water treatment, fire prevention measures or swimming pool inspection.

Casual/wild camping is not allowed outside official sites in Greece.

# Electricity and Gas

Usually current on campsites varies between 4 and 16 amps. Plugs have two round pins. There are few CEE connections.

The full range of Campingaz cylinders are available from hypermarkets and other shops, but when purchasing a cylinder you may not be given a refundable deposit receipt.

# Entry Formalities

Visas are not required by British or Irish passport holders for a stay of up to three months. Visitors planning to stay longer should contact the Greek Embassy in London before they travel www.greekembassy.org.uk.

# Medical Services

For minor complaints seek help at a pharmacy (farmakio). Staff are generally well trained and in major cities there is usually one member of staff in a pharmacy who speaks English. You should have no difficulty finding an English speaking doctor in large towns and resorts.

Medications containing codeine are restricted. If you are taking any medication containing it, you should carry a letter from your doctor and take no more than one month's supply into the country.

There are numerous public and private hospitals and medical centres of varying standards. Wards may be crowded and the standards of nursing and after care, particularly in the public health sector, are generally below what is normally acceptable in Britain. Doctors and facilities are generally good on the mainland, but may be limited on the islands. The public ambulance service will normally respond to any accident but there are severe shortages of ambulances on some islands.

Emergency treatment at public medical clinics (yiatria) and in state hospitals registered by the Greek Social Security Institute, IKA-ETAM, is free on presentation of a European Health Insurance Card (EHIC) but you may face a long wait. You will be charged for prescriptions so keep the adhesive labels from the medicines packages in order to claim a refund at an IKA-ETAM office. See www.ika.gr for a list of local offices.

You may consult a doctor or dentist privately but you will have to present your EHIC and pay all charges up front. You can then claim back the charges later from the IKA-ETAM.

If staying near a beach, ensure that you have plenty of insect repellent as sand flies are prevalent. Do not be tempted to befriend stray dogs as they often harbour diseases which may be passed to humans.

## Opening Hours

Banks – Mon-Fri 8am-2pm (1.30pm on Friday); 8am-6pm in tourist areas.

Museums – Check locally for opening hours. Normally closed on Mon or Tues and some bank holidays.

Post Offices – Mon-Fri 8am-2pm; 8am-7pm in tourist areas; many in Athens open Sat mornings in summer.

Shops – Mon-Fri 8am/8.30am/9am-2pm/4.30pm & on some days 5pm-8.30pm; Sat 8.30am-3pm; check locally as hours vary according to season.

## Safety and Security

Normally visits to Greece are trouble-free, but the tourist season results in an increase in incidents of theft of passports, wallets, handbags, etc, particularly in areas or at events where crowds gather. The use of 'date-rape' drugs has also increased. Personal attacks are rare but visitors are advised to maintain the same level of personal security awareness as in the UK.

Take care when visiting well-known historical sites; they are the favoured haunts of pickpockets, bag-snatchers and muggers. Women should not walk alone at night and lone visitors are strongly advised never to accept lifts from strangers or passing acquaintances at any time.

Multi-lingual tourist police operate in most resorts offering information and help; they can be recognised by a 'Tourist Police' badge, together with a white cap band. There is also a 24-hour emergency helpline for tourists; dial 171 from anywhere in Greece.

Certain areas near the Greek borders are militarily sensitive and you should not take photographs or take notes near military or official installations. Seek permission before photographing individuals.

There is a general threat from domestic terrorism. Attacks could be indiscriminate and against civilian targets in public places. Public protests are a standard feature of Greek politics and it is wise to avoid public gatherings and demonstrations. Domestic anarchist groups remain active but their actions are primarily directed against the Greek state.

During especially hot and dry periods there is a danger of forest fires. Take care when visiting or driving through woodland areas. Ensure that cigarette ends are properly extinguished, do not light barbecues and do not leave rubbish or empty bottles behind.

Some motorists have encountered stowaway attempts while waiting to board ferries to Italy from Patras. Keep a watch on your vehicle(s).

In order to comply with the law, always ensure that you obtain a receipt for goods purchased. If you buy pirate CDs or DVDs you could be penalised heavily.

*British Embassy*

1 PLOUTARCHOU STREET
106 75 ATHENS
Tel: (210) 7272600
http://ukingreece.fco.gov.uk

There are also British Consulates/Vice-Consulates/Honorary Consulates in Corfu, Heraklion (Crete), Rhodes. Patras, Thessaloniki and Zakynthos.

*Irish Embassy*

7 LEOF.VAS
KONSTANTINOU, 106 74 ATHENA
Tel: (210) 7232771
www.embassyofireland.gr

There are also Honorary Consulates in Corfu, Crete, Rhodes and Thessaloniki.

## Border Posts

Borders between Greece and Bulgaria and Turkey may be crossed only on official routes where a Customs office is situated. These are usually open day and night. Customs offices at ports are open from 7.30am to 3pm Monday to Friday.

## Documents

*Passport*

Carry your passport at all times as a means of identification.

*Vehicle(s)*

Carry your vehicle registration certificate (V5C), insurance certificate and MOT certificate (if applicable) at all times.

## Money

Major credit cards are accepted in hotels, restaurants and shops and at some petrol stations. They may not be accepted at shops in small towns or villages. There is an extensive network of cash machines in major cities.

Carry your credit card issuers'/banks' 24-hour UK contact numbers in case of loss or theft.

## Motoring in Greece

## Accidents

It is not essential to call the police in the case of an accident causing material damage only, however motorists are advised to call at the nearest police station to give a description of the incident to the authorities.

Whenever an accident causes physical injury, drivers are required to stop immediately to give assistance to the injured and to call the police. Drivers who fail to meet these requirements are liable to imprisonment for up to three years.

If a visiting motorist has an accident, especially one causing injuries, they should inform the motoring organisation, ELPA, preferably at its head office in Athens, on (210) 606880, email: info@elpa.gr, as they should be able to offer you assistance.

## Alcohol

The maximum permitted level of alcohol is 50 milligrams in 100 millilitres of blood, i.e. lower than that permitted in the UK (80 milligrams). A level of 20 milligrams in 100 millilitres of blood applies to drivers who have held a driving licence for less than two years and to motorcyclists. Police carry out random breath tests and refusal to take a test when asked by the police, and/or driving while over the legal limit, can incur high fines, withdrawal of your driving licence and even imprisonment.

## Breakdown Service

The Automobile & Touring Club of Greece (ELPA) operates a roadside assistance service (OVELPA) 24 hours a day on all mainland Greek roads as well as on most islands. The number to dial from most towns in Greece is 10400.

Members of AIT/FIA affiliated clubs, such as The Caravan Club, should present their valid membership card in order to qualify for reduced charges for on-the-spot assistance and towing. Payment by credit card is accepted.

## Essential Equipment

*First Aid Kit*

All vehicles must carry a first aid kit.

*Fire Extinguisher*

All vehicles must carry a fire extinguisher.

*Warning Triangles*

The placing of a warning triangle is compulsory in the event of an accident or a breakdown. It must be placed 100 metres behind the vehicle.

*Child Restraint System*

Children under three years of age must be seated in a suitable and approved child restraint. Children between the ages of 3 and 11 years old that are less than 1.35 metres in height must be seated in an appropriate child restraint for their size. From 12 years old children that are over 1.35 metres in height can wear an adult seat belt.

A rear facing child restraint can be placed in the front seat but only if the airbag is deactivated.

## Fuel

Petrol stations are usually open from 7am to 7pm; a few are open 24 hours. Some will accept credit cards but those offering cut-price fuel are unlikely to do so. In rural areas petrol stations may close in the evening and at weekends, so keep your tank topped up. There are no automatic petrol pumps operated with either credit cards or bank notes.

LPG (autogas) is available from a limited number of outlets.

# Parking

Parking is only permitted in the Athens 'Green Zone' where there are parking meters. Special parking sites in other areas are reserved for short-term parking for tourists.

There may be signs on the side of the road indicating where vehicles should be parked. Parking restrictions are indicated by yellow lines at the side of the road. The police are entitled to remove vehicles. They can also confiscate the number plates of vehicles parked illegally and, while this usually applies only to Greek-registered vehicles, drivers of foreign registered vehicles should nevertheless avoid illegal parking.

Parking is not permitted within three metres of a fire hydrant, five metres of an intersection, stop sign or traffic light, and fifteen metres of a bus stop, tram stop and level crossings.

# Roads

The surfaces of all major roads and of the majority of other roads are in good condition. Some mountain roads, however, may be in poor condition and drivers must beware of unexpected potholes (especially on corners), precipitous, unguarded drops and single-carriageway bridges. Even on narrow mountain roads you may well encounter buses and coaches.

British motorists visiting Greece should be extra vigilant in view of the high incidence of road accidents. Driving standards are generally poorer than in the UK and you may well have to contend with dangerous overtaking, tailgating, weaving motorcycles and scooters, constant use of the horn, roaming pedestrians and generally erratic driving. Greece has one of the highest rate of road fatalities in Europe and overtaking and speeding are common causes of accidents, particularly on single lane carriageways. Drive carefully and be aware of other drivers at all times.

August is the busiest month of the year for traffic and the A1/E75 between Athens and Thessalonika is recognised as one of the most dangerous routes, together with the road running through the Erimanthos mountains south of Kalavrita. Mountain roads in general can be dangerous owing to narrow carriageways, blind bends and unprotected embankments, so keep your speed down on these roads.

You are strongly advised against hiring motorcycles, scooters and mopeds, as drivers of these modes of transport are particularly at risk. The wearing of crash helmets is a legal requirement. Never hand over your passport when hiring a vehicle.

Greece has a high level of pedestrian fatalities. Where there is a shortage of parking spaces drivers park on pavements so that pedestrians are forced to walk in the road. Collisions between pedestrians and motorcycles are common.

# Road Signs and Markings

Road signs conform to international conventions. Motorway signs have white lettering on a green background, signs on other roads are on a blue background. All motorways, major and secondary roads are signposted in Greek and English.

Some open roads have a white line on the nearside, and slower-moving vehicles are expected to pull across it to allow vehicles to overtake.

# Traffic Jams

There is heavy rush hour traffic in and around the major cities and traffic jams are the norm in central Athens any time of day. During the summer months traffic to the coast may be heavy, particularly at weekends. Traffic jams may be encountered on the A1/E75 Athens to Thessalonika road and on the A8/E65 Athens to Patras road. Traffic may also be heavy near the ferry terminals to Italy and you should allow plenty of time when travelling to catch a ferry. Delays can be expected at border crossings to Turkey and Bulgaria.

# Speed Limits

|  | Open Road (km/h) | Motorway (km/h) |
|---|---|---|
| Car Solo | 90-110 | 130 |
| Car towing caravan/trailer | 80 | 80 |
| Motorhome under 3500kg | 80 | 90 |
| Motorhome 3500-7500kg | 80 | 80 |

GREECE

**319**

GREECE

## Violation of Traffic Regulations

The Greek police are authorised to impose fines in cases of violation of traffic regulations, but they are not allowed to collect fines on-the-spot. Motorists must pay fines within ten days, otherwise legal proceedings will be started.

## Motorways

There are over 2,000 km of motorways in Greece. Service areas provide petrol, a cafeteria and shops. The main motorways are A1 Agean, A2 Egnatia, A6 Attiki, A7 Peloponissos, A8 Pathe, A29 Kastorias. For further information visit www.greek-motorway.net.

### Motorway Tolls

Tolls are charged according to vehicle classification and distance travelled. By European standards the tolls are generally quite low. Cash is the preferred means of payment.

### The Egnatia Highway

The 804 km Egnatia Highway (the A2), part of European route E90 linking the port of Igoumenitsa with the Turkish border at Kipoi, has undergone extensive upgrade and improvement in recent years. The route includes many bridges and tunnels with frequent emergency telephones for which the number to call from a landline or mobile phone is 1077. The road provides a continuous high speed link from west to east and will eventually connect with Istanbul. An electronic toll collection system is planned for the future.

### Patras – Antirrio Bridge

A 2.8 km long toll suspension bridge between Rio (near Patras) and Antirrio links the Peloponnese with western central Greece and is part of the A8/E55 motorway. It has cut the journey time across the Gulf of Corinth – formerly only possible by ferry – to just five minutes. Tolls are charged.

### Preveza – Aktio Tunnel

This undersea toll tunnel links Preveza with Aktio near Agios Nikolaos on the E55 along the west coast of mainland Greece and is part of a relatively fast, scenic route south from Igoumenitsa to central and southern regions.

## Touring

Mainland Greece and most of the Greek islands that are popular with British tourists are in seismically active zones, and small earth tremors are common. Serious earthquakes are less frequent but can, and do, occur.

Smoking is prohibited in bars and restaurants. In restaurants, if the bill does not include a service charge, it is usual to leave a 10 to 20% tip. Taxi drivers do not normally expect a tip but it is customary to round up the fare.

The best known local wine is retsina but there is also a wide range of non-resinated wines. Beer is brewed under licence from German and Danish breweries; Ouzo is a popular and strong aniseed-flavoured aperitif.

The major Greek ports are Corfu, Igoumenitsa, Patras, Piraeus and Rhodes. Ferry services link these ports with Cyprus, Israel, Italy and Turkey. The routes from Ancona and Venice in Italy to Patras and Igoumenitsa are very popular and advance booking is recommended.

For further information contact:

VIAMARE LTD
SUITE 108
582 Honeypot Lane
STANMORE
MIDDX
HA7 1JY
Tel: 020 8206 3420, Fax: 020 8206 1332
www.viamare.com
Email: ferries@viamare.com

Some ferries on routes from Italy to Greece have 'camping on board' facilities whereby passengers are able to sleep in their caravan or motorhome. Mains hook-ups are available, together with showers and toilets.

There are 18 World Heritage Sites in Greece (with more under consideration), including such famous sites as the Acropolis in Athens, the archaeological sites at Olympia and Mistras, and the old towns of Corfu and Rhodes.
See www.worldheritagesite.org for more information. When visiting churches and monasteries dress conservatively, i.e. long trousers for men and no shorts, sleeveless T-shirts or short skirts for women.

## Public Transport

Greece has a modern, integrated public transport system, including an extensive metro, bus, tram and suburban railway network in and around Athens – see www.ametro.gr for a metro map. A metro system is under construction in Thessaloniki that is not due for completion until 2018.

Buy bus/tram tickets from special booths at bus stops, newspaper kiosks or from metro stations. A ticket is valid for a travel time of 90 minutes.

Taxis are relatively cheap. All licensed taxis are yellow and are equipped with meters (the fare is charged per kilometre) and display a card detailing tariffs and surcharges. In certain tourist areas, you may be asked to pay a predetermined (standard) amount for a ride to a specific destination.

Taxis run on a share basis, so they often pick up other passengers on the journey.

There are many ferry and hydrofoil services from Piraeus to the Greek islands and between islands.

GREECE

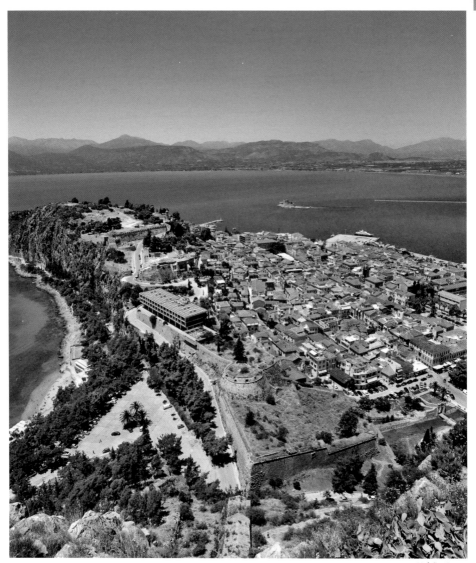

*Nafplio, Greece*

# SITES IN GREECE

⊞ AGIA GALINI (CRETE) *C4 (500m E Rural/Coastal) 35.10004, 24.69514* Camping No Problem!, 74056 Agia Galini [(28320) 91386; www.agia-galini.com] Site sp on Tympaki rd. Sm, mkd pitch, pt shd; wc; chem disp; mv service pnt; shwrs; el pnts (6A) €4; lndtte; shop; tradsmn; rest, snacks; bar; BBQ; pool; paddling pool; sand/shgl beach 500m; wifi; some statics; dogs free; bus 500m; poss cr; Eng spkn; adv bkg; quiet. "Vg, family-run site; gd walks." ♦ € 25.50      2010*

⊞ AGIOI THEODOROI *B3 (8km E Coastal) 37.95212, 23.17868* Camping Glaros, Kineta, 19100 Agioi Theodoroi [(22960) 62805; info@camping-glaros.gr; www.camping-glaros.gr] E fr Korinthos on A8 dir Athens, site sp. Med, pt sl, pt shd; wc; chem disp; shwrs; el pnts; lndtte; shop; rest, snacks; bar; cooking facs; playgrnd; sand beach; internet; some statics; dogs; quiet. "Well-situated for archeological sites; pleasant." (CChq acc)      2011*

AGIOS KONSTANTINOS see Kamena Vourla *B2*

⊞ ALEXANDROUPOLI *C1 (1.5km W Coastal) 40.84679, 25.85614* Camping Alexandroupolis Beach, Makris Ave, 68100 Alexandroupolis [tel/fax (25510) 28735; camping@ditea.gr; www.ditea.gr] Site on coast - after drainage channel, at 2nd set traff lts close together. Lge, hdg/mkd pitch, pt hdstg, shd; wc (some cont); chem disp; shwrs inc; el pnts (8A) €3.60; gas; shop; snacks; bar; playgrnd; sand beach adj; watersports; tennis; games area; wifi; 20% statics; phone; Eng spkn; quiet but cr & noisy high ssn; red CKE/CCI. "Spacious, secure, well-run site; clean, hot shwrs; easy walk to pleasant town cent." € 18.50      2011*

ALISSOS see Patra *A2*

ANTIRRIO see Nafpaktos *B2*

ASSINI see Nafplio *B3*

ATHENS see Athina *B3*

⊞ ATHINA *B3 (16km NE Urban) 38.09944, 23.79166* Camping Nea Kifissia, Potamou 60, Adames, 14564 Athina [tel/fax (210) 8075579 or 6205646; camping@hol.gr; www.camping-neakifissia.gr] Sp both dirs on E75 Athens-Lamia rd. Heading twd Athens exit at sp, to U-turn onto service rd then take 1st L & foll sp. Sm, hdg pitch, hdstg, terr, shd; wc; chem disp; shwrs inc; el pnts (10A) €4; lndry rm; shop 800m; pool high ssn; TV; 50% statics; dogs; phone; bus to metro stn 200m; poss cr; Eng spkn; aircraft, rlwy & rd noise; red CCI. "Conv base for Athens - metro at Kifissia; pleasant, quiet, well-run site; excel pool; clean san facs but tired; helpful recep staff; san facs down 30+ steps." € 43.00      2014*

⊞ ATHINA *B3 (7km NW Urban) 38.00916, 23.67236* Camping Athens, 198-200 Athinon Ave, 12136 Athens [(210) 5814114 or 5814101 winter; fax 5820353; info@campingathens.com.gr; www.campingathens.com.gr] Fr Corinth on E94 m'way/highway, stay on this rd to Athens o'skts; site is approx 4km past Dafni Monastery, set back on L of multi-lane rd, sh dist beyond end of underpass. Go past site to next traff lts where U-turn permitted. Fr N use old national rd (junc 8 if on toll m'way). Med, pt shd; wc (some cont); chem disp; mv service pnt; shwrs inc; el pnts (16A) €4; lndtte; shop, rest high ssn; snacks; bar; internet; TV; dogs; frequent bus to Athens; poss v cr; rd noise; ccard acc; red low ssn. "V dusty but well-managed site; gd san facs but poss insufficient high ssn; helpful staff; bus tickets to Athens sold; visitors rec not to use sat nav to find site, as it misdirects!" € 42.00      2013*

CHRISSA see Delfi *B2*

CORINTH see Korinthos *B3*

DELFI *B2 (7km S Coastal) 38.42502, 22.45824* Camping Ayannis, 33200 Itea-Kirra [(22650) 32555; fax 33870; m.anagnostakos@hotmail.com] App Itea fr Delfi; 1km bef Itea take ring rd sp Desfina; site on R after 4km; ent site on rough track for 200m. Med, pt shd; wc (some cont); chem disp; 100% serviced pitches; shwrs inc; el pnts (6A) inc; gas; lndtte; shop; tradsmn; rest, snacks; bar; BBQ; sm shgl beach adj; Eng spkn; quiet; ccard acc; CKE/CCI. "Friendly owner; conv for Delphi; poss diff access lge o'fits; fair sh stay." 1 May-30 Oct. € 22.50      2010*

⊞ DELFI *B2 (1.5km W Rural) 38.4836, 22.4755* Camping Apollon, 33054 Delfi [(22650) 82762 or 82750; fax 82888; apollon4@otenet.gr; www.apolloncamping.gr] Site on N48 fr Delfi twd Itea & 1st of number of campsites on this rd. Site 25km fr Parnassus ski cent. Med, mkd pitch, pt sl, pt terr, pt shd; wc; chem disp; mv service pnt; shwrs inc; el pnts (16A) €3; gas; lndtte; shop; rest; bar; playgrnd; pool; TV; cycle hire; 30% statics; dogs free; phone; Harmonie Group site; poss cr; adv bkg; ccard acc; red CKE/CCI. "Magnificent views over mountains & Gulf of Corinth; site cooler than some other sites due to its elevation; vg site; popular with groups of students." ♦ € 22.50      2011*

⊞ DELFI *B2 (7km W Rural) 38.47305, 22.45926* Chrissa Camping, 33055 Chrissa [(22650) 82050; fax 83148; info@chrissacamping.gr; www.chrissacamping.gr] 1st site on Itea to Delfi rd, sp. Med, pt sl, terr, shd; wc; chem disp; shwrs inc; el pnts (10A) €4; gas; lndtte; shop; tradsmn; rest, snacks; bar; playgrnd; pools; paddling pool; shgl beach 10km; tennis 300m; games area; wifi; TV rm; adv bkg; quiet; ccard acc; red CKE/CCI. "Excel, scenic site." € 26.00 (CChq acc)      2011*

**DELFI** *B2* (4km NW Rural) *38.47868, 22.47461* **Camping Delphi**, Itea Road, 33054 Delfi [(22650) 82209; fax 82363; info@delphicamping.com; www.delphicamping.com] App fr Itea-Amfissa rd or Levadia; well sp. Med, terr, shd; wc; chem disp; mv service pnt; shwrs inc; el pnts (16A) €3.90; gas; lndtte; shop, rest, snacks high ssn; bar; pool; tennis; wifi; TV; dogs free; phone; bus to Delfi; Sunshine Group site; poss cr; adv bkg; ccard acc; red CKE/CCI. "Visit grotto, refuge of Parnassus; Delfi archaeological sites 3km; friendly, helpful staff; magnificent views; gd pool; tired facs; 20% discount for Minoan Line ticketholders; delightful site; san facs bit tired but clean & tidy; excel site." 1 Apr-31 Oct. € 25.00                    2014*

**DREPANO see Nafplio** *B3*

⊞ **DREPANO** *B3* (12km E Coastal) *37.49710, 22.99028* Iria Beach Camping, Iria Beach 21100, Nafplio [tel/fax 02 75 20 94 253; iriabeach@naf.forthnet.gr; www.iriabeach.com] Fr Drepano head E on Epar. Od. Drepanou-Kantias. Cont onto Kantias-Irion. 800m after Iria Beach Hotel turn R. Site on L after 1.5km. Med, hdstg, shd; wc; chem disp; mv service pnt; baby facs; shwrs; el pnts (16A); lndtte; shop; tradsmn; snack; bar; BBQ; cooking facs; pool; beach adj; wifi; tv; 5% statics; dogs; twin axles; Eng spkn; adv bkg; quiet; CCI. "Opp beach; gd sw; site quiet & relaxing; helpful staff; vg site." ♦ ltd € 33.40                    2014*

**ERETRIA (EVIA)** *B2* (1km W Coastal) *38.39148, 23.77562* Milos Camping, 34008 Eretria [(22290) 60420; fax 60360; info@camping-in-evia.gr; www.camping-in-evia.gr] Fr Chalkida for 20km; ignore any previous sp for Milos Camping. Med, mkd pitch, terr, pt shd; wc; chem disp; mv service pnt; shwrs inc; el pnts (16A) inc; gas; lndtte; shop; rest, snacks; bar; BBQ; playgrnd; shgl beach adj; internet; TV; 50% statics; dogs; phone; Eng spkn; quiet but some rd noise; red CKE/CCI. "Friendly site; excel rest; rather scruffy (5/09) but facs OK." ♦ 10 Apr-30 Sep. € 26.00                    2009*

⊞ **FINIKOUNDAS** *A3* (1km W Coastal) *36.80555, 21.79583* Camping Thines, 24006 Finikoundas [(27230) 71200; fax 71027; thines@otenet.gr; www.finikounda.com] Fr Methoni dir Finikoundas, turn R 1km bef vill, site on L. Sm, hdg/mkd pitch, hdstg, pt shd; wc; chem disp; shwrs inc; el pnts (6-10A); gas; lndtte; shop & 1km; tradsmn; snacks; bar; BBQ; cooking facs; sand beach adj; boat-launching; wifi; TV; no statics; dogs; poss cr; Eng spkn; quiet; ccard acc; red winter long stay; CKE/CCI. "Excel facs; helpful, friendly management; wonderful scenery & beach; lovely vill in walking dist." ♦ € 25.00 (CChq acc)                    2011*

**GERAKINI** *B2* (1.5km SE Coastal) *40.26464, 23.46338* Camping Kouyoni, 63100 Gerakini [tel/fax (23710) 52052; info@kouyoni.gr; www.kouyoni.gr] Take main rd S fr Thessaloniki to Nea Moudania, then turn E twd Sithonia. Site is 18km on that rd past Gerakini on R, past filling stn. Well sp. Med, hdg/mkd pitch, pt sl, shd; wc; chem disp; shwrs inc; el pnts (16A) €3.30; lndtte; shop & 1km; rest, snacks; bar; BBQ; playgrnd; pool; paddling pool; sand beach adj; games area; boat-launching; TV rm; 30% statics; dogs; phone; adv bkg; quiet; red long stay/CKE/CCI. "Gd touring base set in olive grove; friendly owner; gd facs; gd beach; influx of w/enders high ssn." 24 Apr-30 Sep. € 26.00                    2009*

**GIALOVA see Pylos** *A3*

**GIANNITSOCHORI see Kyparissia** *A3*

⊞ **GITHIO** *B3* (4km S Coastal) *36.72847, 22.54215* **Camping Mani Beach**, Mavrovouni, 23200 Githio [(27330) 23450; fax 25451; info@manibeach.grr; www.manibeach.gr] Fr Githio dir Aeropolis, site sp on L on Mavrovouni beach. Lge, hdg/mkd pitch, hdstg, shd; htd wc; chem disp; shwrs inc; el pnts (16A) €4; gas; lndtte; shop; tradsmn; rest, snacks; bar; BBQ; playgrnd; shgl beach adj; games area; wifi; cab TV; 10% statics; dogs; phone; Eng spkn; adv bkg; ccard acc; red long stay/snr citizens/CKE/CCI. "Less cr & noisy than other sites along this rd; set in olive grove; lovely mountain views; conv ferries to Crete; vg." ♦ € 22.00                    2011*

⊞ **GITHIO** *B3* (4km SW Coastal) *36.72913, 22.54519* Gython Bay Camping, 23200 Githio [(27330) 22522; fax 23523; info@gythiocamping.gr; www.gythiocamping.gr] Sp fr Githio town, on E of Githio-Areopolis rd. Med, shd; wc (some cont); chem disp; mv service pnt; shwrs inc; el pnts (16A) inc; gas; lndtte; shop; rest, snacks; bar; playgrnd; beach adj; surfing school; boating; games area; wifi; entmnt; TV; no dogs; poss cr; no adv bkg; quiet; Harmonie Group site; ccard acc; 10% red CKE/CCI. "Facs clean; mv service pnt up ramp - risk of grounding; site in orange grove; ferries to Crete in ssn." ♦ € 24.00 (CChq acc)                    2009*

**HANIA (CRETE)** *C4* (5km W Coastal) *35.51183, 23.98482* Camping Hania, Agii Apostoli, Kato Daratso, 73100 Hania [(28210) 31138; fax 33371; camhania@otenet.gr; www.camping-chania.gr] W fr cent of Hania on main rd to Kissamos. Med, hdstg, pt sl, shd; wc (some cont); chem disp; mv service pnt; shwrs inc; el pnts (16A) inc; gas; lndtte; shop; rest, snacks; bar; BBQ; cooking facs; playgrnd; pool; paddling pool; sand beach 200m; cycle hire; games rm; TV; some statics; dogs; bus; phone; poss cr; Eng spkn; adv bkg; quiet; ccard acc; red long stay; CKE/CCI. "Take care low olive trees; vg." 1 Apr-30 Oct. € 30.00                    2011*

**IERISSOS** *B2* (500m NW Coastal) *40.40369, 23.87608* Camping Ierissos, 63075 Ierissos [(23770) 21130; fax 21132; desa@ierissos.gr] Sp at major x-rds in town cent. Med, mkd pitch, unshd; wc; chem disp (wc); shwrs inc; el pnts (10A) €3.15; lndtte; shop, rest, snacks, bar in town/on beach; BBQ; sand beach adj; 80% statics; dogs; poss cr; Eng spkn; poss noisy high ssn. "Fair sh stay; a few dogs roaming site." 1 May-30 Sep. € 15.50                    2009*

**IGOUMENITSA** *A2* (7km SE Coastal) *39.47437, 20.23919* Camping Kalami Beach, 46100 Plataria [(26650) 71211; fax 71245; info@campingkalamibeach.gr; www.campingkalamibeach.gr] S fr Igoumenitsa on coast rd, turn sharp R at camping sp down lane to sea & site. Site is 4km N of Platariá. Lge, terr, pt shd; wc; chem disp; mv service pnt; shwrs inc; el pnts (10A) €3; gas; lndtte (inc dryer); shop; tradsmn; rest, snacks; bar; BBQ; shgl beach; watersports; games rm; wifi; TV; some statics; dogs; phone; poss cr; adv bkg; quiet but some rd noise; Sunshine Group site. "Access diff for lge o'fits due tight corners & sm pitches; ltd lge pitches & some diff due to trees; pleasant, relaxing site; helpful staff; excel, clean san facs; 20% discount for Minoan Line ticketholders." 20 Mar-31 Oct. € 28.00                    2011*

IGOUMENITSA *A2* (10km S Coastal) *39.46346, 20.26037*
Camping Elena's Beach, 46100 Platariá [(26650) 71031; fax
71414; bteo@altecnet.gr/info@campingelena.gr; www.
epirus.com/campingelena] Sp on Igoumenitsa-Preveza rd,
2km NW of Platariá. Med, hdstg, pt terr, pt shd; wc; chem
disp; shwrs inc; el pnts (5A) inc; gas; lndtte; shop; tradsmn;
rest, snacks; bar; BBQ; playgrnd; shgl beach adj; a few statics;
dogs; phone; bus; adv bkg; quiet; red long stay; CKE/CCI.
"Well-maintained, family-run, friendly site; clean, modern san
facs; beautiful location with pitches next to sea; excel rest; conv
ferries Corfu, Paxos." ♦ 1 Apr-31 Oct. € 33.50      2014*

IGOUMENITSA *A2* (14km S Coastal) *39.44390, 20.25813*
Nautilos Camping, 46100 Plataria [(26650) 71416; fax
71417; wassosf@otenet.gr] S fr Igoumenitsa on coast rd
to Plataria; turn R at end of Plataria Beach; site at top of hill
with flags clearly visible, 2km SW of Plataria. Lge, mkd pitch,
some hdstg, terr, pt sl, shd; wc; chem disp; shwrs inc; el pnts
(16A) inc; gas; lndtte; shop; tradsmn; rest; bar; BBQ; cooking
facs; playgrnd; pool; private beach; tennis; wifi; some statics;
dogs; phone; Eng spkn; adv bkg; quiet; red CKE/CCI. "Helpful
staff; lovely quiet site; picturesque setting." 1 Apr-20 Oct.
€ 27.50      2011*

IOANINA *A2* (1.5km NW Urban) *39.67799, 20.84279*
Camping Limnopoula, Kanari 10, 45001 Ioanina
[(26510) 25265; fax 38060] At Ioanina Nautical Club on
Igoumenitsa rd at W o'skts of town on rd that runs along
lake fr citadel; site well sp fr all dirs. Med, pt shd; wc; chem
disp; shwrs inc; el pnts (10A) inc; gas; lndtte; shop; tradsmn;
rest, snacks, bar adj; BBQ; playgrnd; watersports; dogs free;
phone; Eng spkn; quiet. "Beautiful situation on lake, mountain
views; excel touring base; helpful staff; gd facs; clean; san facs
refurbished to excel standard; may close earlier; adv bkg acc
1-2 days ahead only low ssn; popular with groups low ssn; vg."
1 May-15 Oct. € 28.00      2011*

KALAMBAKA *A2* (2km SE Rural) *39.69017, 21.64564*
Camping International Rizos, Trikala Road, Meteora,
42200 Kalambaka [(24320) 22239; info@
meteorarizoscamp.gr; www.meteorarizoscamp.gr] Site
visible on S of E92 rd. Med, hdg/mkd pitch, pt shd; htd wc;
chem disp; shwrs inc; el pnts (16A); gas; lndtte; shop; rest,
snacks; bar; playgrnd; pool; paddling pool; TV; bus to town;
adv bkg; CKE/CCI. ♦ 1 Apr-31 Oct.      2010*

KALAMBAKA *A2* (2.5km SE Rural) *39.68250, 21.65510*
Camping Philoxenia, 42200 Kalambaka [(24320) 24466;
fax 24944; philoxeniacamp@ath.forthnet.gr] Site on N
side of E92 Trikala rd, behind barrier. Med, some hdstg, shd;
htd wc; chem disp; mv service pnt; shwrs inc; el pnts (6A)
inc; gas; lndtte; shop; tradsmn; rest 1km; snacks; bar; BBQ;
cooking facs; playgrnd; pool; paddling pool; waterslide; cycle
hire; TV; 30% statics; dogs free; poss cr; Eng spkn; adv bkg;
quiet; ccard acc; red CKE/CCI. "Interesting area particularly
during Easter religious festivals." ♦ ltd 1 Mar-30 Nov. € 20.00
(CChq acc)      2011*

⊞ KALAMBAKA *A2* (2km NW Rural) *39.7120, 21.61625*
Camping Vrachos, Meteoron Street, 42200 Kastraki
[(24320) 22293; fax 23134; campingkastraki@yahoo.
com; www.campingkastraki.gr] Fr cent of Kalambaka take
rd at app to vill of Kastraki. Site is 2km N of E92. Med, hdg/
mkd pitch, pt sl, terr, shd; wc; chem disp; mv service pnt;
shwrs inc; el pnts (16A) inc; gas; lndtte; shop; rest, snacks;
bar; BBQ; cooking facs; playgrnd; pool; TV; internet (ltd); dogs
free; phone; poss cr; Eng spkn; adv bkg; Harmonie Group site;
red CKE/CCI. "Friendly management; clean san facs; vg views
fr some pitches; ltd facs open in winter; conv for monasteries."
♦ € 18.00      2011*

**KALIVIA VARIKOU see Plaka Litohorou** *B2*

KAMENA VOURLA *B2* (5km N Coastal) *38.82310, 22.71543*
Venezuela Camping, Paralia, Agios Serafeim; 35009
Malos [tel/fax (22350) 41691; camping@venezuela.gr;
www.venezuela.gr] Fr Lamia on E75, turn L twd Skarfeia &
foll site sp. Fr Athens turn R sp Agios Serafeim, site sp. Med,
hdg/mkd pitch, some hdstg, shd; wc; chem disp; shwrs inc; el
pnts (10A) €4; shop; tradsmn; rest, snacks; bar; cooking facs;
beach adj; wifi; TV; dogs; phone; Eng spkn; adv bkg; quiet;
CKE/CCI. "Conv NH bet Athens & N; peaceful." 1 May-30 Sep.
€ 20.00      2011*

**KARDAMILI see Stoupa** *B3*

⊞ KASSANDRIA *B2* (10km SW Coastal) *39.96416, 23.36472*
Camping Kalandra, 63077 Possidi [(23740) 41345; fax
41123] Fr Thessaloniki foll sp to Nea Moudania, down
peninsula to Kalithea, W to Kassandria, S thro Fourka, W to
Kalandra, fork R to Possidi & foll sps to end of rd. Lge, pt shd;
wc; chem disp; shwrs; el pnts (15A); gas; lndtte; shop; rest,
snacks; bar; sand beach adj; no adv bkg; 40% statics; dogs; red
CKE/CCI. "Quiet but fills up end Jun for Greek hols."      2009*

**KASTRAKI see Kalambaka** *A2*

**KATO ALISSOS see Patra** *A2*

**KATO GATZEA see Volos** *B2*

⊞ KAVALA *C1* (4km SW Urban/Coastal) *40.91573, 24.37851*
Camping Multiplex Batis, 65000 Kavala [(2510) 243051;
fax 245690; nfo@batis-sa.gr; www.batis-sa.gr] On W app
to town on old coast rd, ent on a curving hill. Med, hdg/mkd
pitch, pt sl, shd; htd wc; chem disp; shwrs inc; el pnts (6A)
€4; lndry rm; shop; tradsmn; rest, snacks; bar; pool; paddling
pool; sand beach adj; entmnt; phone; bus; poss cr; Eng spkn;
adv bkg; ccard acc; red CKE/CCI. "Beautiful location but v
developed; conv ferry to Thassos & archaeological sites; clean
facs but site poss unkempt low ssn; vg." ♦ € 26.00      2009*

Tell us about the sites you visit

**KORINTHOS** *B3* (5km W Coastal/Urban) *37.93470, 22.86543* Blue Dolphin Camping, 20006 Lecheon [(27410) 25766 or 25767; fax 85959; info@camping-blue-dolphin.gr; www. camping-blue-dolphin.gr] Best app fr E to avoid town; Fr A8 exit sp Ancient Corinth, then N (R) to T-junc end of rd, W (R) past pipe factory, sp 400m N (R) at bottom of bdge sl. Fr W take exit sp Ancient Corinth after toll point. Fr Old National rd turn N (L) immed over rlwy bdge bef pipe factory. Fr Corinth foll old National rd twd Patras, past pipe factory. Med, mkd pitch, hdstg, pt shd; wc; chem disp; shwrs inc; el pnts (6A) €3.50; gas; lndtte; shop; tradsmn; rest, snacks; bar; BBQ; playgrnd; shgl beach; games area; wifi; TV; dogs; Sunshine Group site; Eng spkn; quiet; ccard acc; red CKE/CCI. "V obliging owners; pleasant site; sm pitches." ♦ 1 Apr-30 Oct. € 22.50    2011*

**KORONI** *B3* (200m S Coastal) *36.79932, 21.95013* Camping Koroni, 24004 Koroni [(27250) 22119; fax 22884; info@ koronicamping.com; www.koronicamping.com] Sp on Kalamata to Koroni rd. Med, mkd pitch, pt sl, terr, shd; wc; shwrs inc; el pnts (6A) €4; lndtte; shop; rest, snacks; bar; cooking facs; pool; sand beach adj; wifi; TV; dogs; phone; site clsd Nov; Sunshine Group site; Eng spkn; red CKE/CCI. "Pleasant site; friendly owners; basic but adequate facs; gd pool; easy walk to lovely fishing vill; dusty in summer." 1 Mar-20 Oct. € 25.00    2009*

**KOS (KOS)** *D3* (3km E Coastal) Kos Camping, 85300 Psalidi [(22420) 29886; fax 29887; grigoris70@hotmail.gr] On Ag Fokas rd fr Kos town, site on R. Only site on island. Med, mkd pitch, pt shd; wc; shwrs inc; el pnts; gas; shop; rest, snacks; playgrnd; shgl beach across rd; tennis; cycle hire; 30% statics; phone; sep car park; poss cr; adv bkg; quiet. 1 May-5 Oct.    2009*

⊞ **KYLLINI** *A3* (10km S Coastal) *37.83828, 21.12972* Camping Aginara Beach, Lygia, 27050 Loutra Kyllinis [(26230) 96211; fax 96271; info@camping-aginara.gr; www.camping-aginara.gr] S fr Patras on E55 twds Pyrgos; exit Gastouni & turn W thro Vartholomio twd Loutra Kyllinis; turn L about 3km bef Kyllinis then foll sps. Lge, hdg pitch, hdstg, pt sl, shd; wc; chem disp; mv service pnt; shwrs inc; el pnts (10A); gas; lndtte; shop; tradsmn; rest, snacks; bar; BBQ; playgrnd; sand/shgl beach adj; watersports; wifi; TV; 25% statics; dogs; phone; Eng spkn; adv bkg; quiet; ccard acc; red CKE/CCI. "Friendly proprietor; excel, modern facs; site on lovely beach; beautiful views." ♦ € 36.00    2014*

**KYLLINI** *A3* (15km S Coastal) *37.88539, 21.11175* Campsite Melissa, 27050 Kastro Kyllinis Ilia [02 62 30 95 213; fax 62 30 95 453; camping_melissa@yahoo.gr] S fr Patras twd Pygros on E55. Turn R twds Lehena after 58km marker. Foll signs to Kastro Kyllinis. Med, hdg pitch, shd; wc; chem disp; mv service pnt; shwrs; el pnts (10A); lndtte; shop; tradsmn; rest; bar; BBQ; cooking facs; playgrnd; beach; wifi; tv; 2% statics; dogs; twin axles; Eng spkn; adv bkg; quiet; CCI. "Great campsite to chill; excel rest, bar & shop; lovely sandy beach; excel sw; fabulous views across the bay." ♦ ltd 1 Apr-31 Oct. € 31.00    2014*

**KYLLINI** *A3* (6km SW Coastal) *37.89944, 21.11666* Camping Fournia Beach, 27050 Kastro-Kyllini [(26230) 95095; fax 95096] W fr Patras on E55, for about 61 km, exit Kyllini/ Zakinthos, turn R & foll sp for 15km to Kastro-Kyllini. Site sp. Med, mkd pitch, pt shd; wc; chem disp; shwrs; el pnts (16A) inc; lndtte; shop; tradsmn; rest; bar; BBQ; playgrnd; sand beach adj; wifi; TV; some statics; dogs; phone; Eng spkn; adv bkg; ccard acc; CKE/CCI. 1 Apr-1 Nov. € 21.30 (CChq acc)    2011*

**KYPARISSIA** *A3* (1km N Coastal) *37.25697, 21.67120* Camping Kyparissia, 24500 Kyparissia [(27610) 23491; fax 24519; info@campingkyparissia.com; www. campingkyparissia.com] S fr Pirgos take R fork on ent Kyparissia, foll sp via beach rd; site in view ahead; fr Pilos turn N on o'skts of town. Med, pt sl; wc; chem disp; mv service pnt; shwrs; el pnts (16A) €3.50; lndtte; shop & 1km; rest, snacks; bar; playgrnd; sand beach; watersports; wifi; TV; dogs free; phone; Eng spkn; Sunshine Group site; quiet; red long stay/CKE/CCI. "Excel, attractive site; friendly staff; ltd number of shd pitches for high o'fits." 1 Apr-20 Oct. € 19.50    2009*

**KYPARISSIA** *A3* (18km N Coastal) *37.39690, 21.67738* Camping Apollo Village, 27054 Giannitsochori [tel/fax (26250) 61200] Fr Pirgos S dir Kyparissia, 11km after Zaharo at sp for Giannitsochori, turn R, cross rlwy line & foll site sp. Lge, shd; wc; chem disp; shwrs inc; el pnts (16A) inc; lndtte; shop; rest, snacks; bar; BBQ; sand beach adj; games rm; TV; 10% statics; dogs; phone; quiet; red long stay; CKE/CCI. "Excel beach." 1 May-31 Oct. € 24.00    2010*

**LECHEON see Korinthos** *B3*

**LEFKADA (LEFKAS)** *A2* (20km S Coastal) *38.67511, 20.71475* Camping Santa Maura, Dessimi, 31100 Vlycho [(26450) 95007; fax 95493; www.lefkada.biz/ campingsantamavra/] Take coast rd S fr Lefkada to Vlycho, turn L for Dessimi, site in 2.5km (after Camping Dessimi). Access via v steep hill - severe gradients both sides. Med, mkd pitch, terr, pt shd; wc; chem disp; mv service pnt; shwrs inc; el pnts (12A) inc; gas; lndtte; shop; rest, snacks; bar; BBQ; sand/ shgl beach adj; TV rm; phone; quiet; CKE/CCI. "Excel site & beach; gd,clean san facs; friendly owners." 20 Apr-20 Oct. € 25.00    2009*

**LEONIDI** *B3* (20km N Coastal) *37.27566, 22.84054* Camping Zaritsi, Paralia Tirou, 22300 Tiros [(27570) 41429; fax 41074; camping@zaritsi.gr; www.zaritsi.gr] Foll main N-S rd down E coast; site immed off this rd on coast 4km N of Tirós, well sp. Steep rd down, but practical for lge o'fits. Site not sp fr S. Med, hdstg, pt shd; wc; chem disp; mv service pnt; shwrs inc; el pnts (16A) inc; gas; lndtte; shop; rest (high ssn); snacks; bar; playgrnd; shgl beach adj; watersports; TV rm; 50% statics; phone; Eng spkn; adv bkg; quiet; no ccard acc; CKE/CCI. "Fine site on exceptionally beautiful Arcadia coast rd; friendly owner; stunning mountain scenery; gd rest." 15 Apr-30 Sep. € 27.00    2009*

GREECE

**METHONI** *A3* (500m E Coastal) *36.81736, 21.71515* **Camp Methoni, 24006 Methoni [(27230) 31228 or 0728 31455]** Fr Pylos on rd 9, strt thro Methoni to beach, turn E along beach, site sp. Med, hdstg, pt shd; wc (some cont); shwrs inc; el pnts (10A) inc; lndry rm; tradsmn; rest, snacks; bar; BBQ; playgrnd; sand beach; dogs; phone; Eng spkn; adv bkg; some rd noise; ccard not acc; CKE/CCI. "Superb Venetian castle; close to pleasant vill; park away fr taverna & rd to avoid noise; excel sw; v dusty site; clean san facs; new owner & undergoing renovations (2013); quiet & gd site." 1 Jun-30 Sep. € 19.00                                                   2014*

**METHONI PIERIAS** *B2* (5km S Coastal) *40.42712, 22.60401* **Hotel & Camping Agiannis, 60066 Methoni-Pierias [(23530) 41216; fax 51840]** Leave E75 Thessaloniki/Athens m'way dir Magrigialos/Methoni, foll sp Camping & Hotel. Med, hdg pitch, pt sl, terr, shd; wc (some cont); chem disp (wc); mv service pnt; shwrs inc; el pnts (6-10A) €3.50 (poss no earth/rev pol); shop; tradsmn; rest high ssn; snacks; playgrnd; pool; sand beach adj; entmnt; TV; 80% statics; dogs free; Eng spkn; red long stay;CKE/CCI. "Friendly family-run site; clean facs; gd touring base; excel rest o'looking beach." 1 May-15 Oct. € 18.00                                                    2009*

## "There aren't many sites open at this time of year"

If you're travelling outside peak season remember to call ahead to check site opening dates – even if the entry says 'open all year'.

⊞ **MIKINES** *B3* (95m E Urban) *37.71922, 227.4676* **Camping Mikines/Mykenae, 21200 Mikines [(27510) 76247; fax 76850; dars@arg.forthnet.gr; www.ecogriek.nl]** In town of Mikines (Mycenae) nr bus stop. On R as heading to archeological site, sp. Sm, mkd pitch, hdstg, pt shd; wc; chem disp (wc); shwrs inc; el pnts (10A) €4.50; lndtte; shops 500m; meals served; dogs; Eng spkn; quiet; CKE/CCI. "Quaint family-run site; v warm welcome; conv ancient Mycenae; friendly staff; vg." ◆ ltd € 21.00                                     2014*

⊞ **MIKINES** *B3* (1km W Rural) *37.71915, 22.74081* **Atreus Camping, Argolida, 21200 Mikines [(27510) 76221; fax 76760; atreus@otenet.gr]** Fr E65 twd Mycenae (Mikines), site on L when heading twd archeological site. Sm, pt shd; wc; chem disp; shwrs inc; el pnts (10A) €4; lndtte; shop; tradsmn; rest; bar; pool; paddling pool; wifi; TV; no statics; Sunshine Camping Group site; Eng spkn; CKE/CCI. "Sm pitches; poss noise fr barking dogs; san facs dated but clean; 2km fr archeological site." € 24.00                                     2010*

**NAFPAKTOS** *B2* (7km SW Coastal) *38.34297, 21.77006* **Camping Dounis Beach, Neromana, 30200 Antirrio [(26340) 31565; fax 31131]** Foll sp to Antirrio off E55 Mesolongi to Nafpaktos rd. Site situated 1.5km E of Antirrio. Med, pt shd; wc; chem disp; mv service pnt; shwrs inc; el pnts (16A) €4; gas; lndtte; shop; rest, snacks adj; playgrnd; shgl beach; entmnt; no dogs; adv bkg; quiet; red CKE/CCI. "San facs in need of upgrade; gd size pitches; ltd facs low ssn; rather run down." 1 May-30 Oct. € 24.50                            2010*

**NAFPLIO** *B3* (10km SE Coastal) *37.53226, 22.89143* **New Triton Camping, Plaka Drepano, 21060 Drepano [(27520) 92128; fax 92121; campnewtriton@yahoo.gr]** E fr Nafplio to Epidhuros; in 5km turn R twds Drepano; in Drepano centre turn R; in one block turn slight L; may not be sp but foll sp for Camping Triton II which is 100m beyond New Triton. Sm, hdg pitch, hdstg, well shd; wc (some cont); chem disp; mv service pnt; serviced pitches; shwrs inc; el pnts (16A) inc; gas 1km; lndtte; shop; rest, snacks; bar; BBQ; cooking facs; beach adj; watersports; games area; wifi; TV; dogs free; poss cr; Eng spkn; CKE/CCI. "Immac site & facs; wheelchair-friendly; excel site." ◆ 1 Apr-31 Oct. € 25.00                     2011*

**NAFPLIO** *B3* (10.6km SE Coastal) *37.58280, 22.86725* **Camping Lido, Sfakes Tolon, 21056 Tolon [(27520) 59396; fax 59596; lidotolo@otenet.gr; www.camping-lido.com]** App Tolon fr Nafplio, site just bef vill on L. Med, pt sl, terr, shd; wc; chem disp; shwrs inc; el pnts (16A); gas; lndtte; shop adj; snacks; sand beach adj; watersports; TV; poss cr; quiet; ccard acc; red CKE/CCI. "Excel beach; easy walk to town - many rests & boat trips; sm pitches; some pitches excel views; newer san facs block gd." 1 Apr-30 Oct. € 26.00                 2010*

⊞ **NAFPLIO** *B3* (12km SE Coastal) *37.53173, 22.89056* **Camping Triton II, Plaka Drepano, 21060 Drepano [(27520) 92228; fax 92510; tritonii@otenet.gr; www.tritonii.gr]** Take rd E fr Nafplio dir Epidavros; after 5km turn R for Drepano vill & foll site sps. Med, hdg/mkd pitch, hdstg, pt shd; wc; chem disp; mv service pnt; baby facs; shwrs; el pnts (6A) inc; lndtte (inc dryer); shop & 1km; tradsmn; rest, snacks; shgl beach adj; tennis; games area; wifi; 30% statics; dogs; phone; Eng spkn; adv bkg (Jul/Aug); ccard acc; red low ssn/long stay; CKE/CCI. "Vg low ssn; excel, clean facs; all supplies in walking dist in vill." € 25.00                            2011*

**NAFPLIO** *B3* (12km SE Coastal) *37.5287, 22.87553* **Kastraki Camping, Kastraki Assinis, 21100 Assini [(27520) 59386 or 59387; fax 59572; sgkarmaniola@kastrakicamping.gr; www.kastrakicamping.gr]** Fr Nafplio take rd to Tolon. Immed after Assini, take L fork sp Ancient Assini. Site 3km on L. Lge, shd; wc; chem disp; mv service pnt; baby facs; shwrs €0.20; el pnts (16A) shared €4; lndtte; shop; rest, snacks; bar; playgrnd; sand beach; tennis; games area; TV; dogs; quiet; red facs low ssn; ccard acc. "Vg location with own private beach & excel facs; day trips to several islands fr Tolón harbour; many pitches too sm for lge m'vans." ◆ 1 Apr-30 Sep. € 34.80                                                  2013*

**NAFPLIO** *B3* (10km S Coastal) *37.53006, 22.86528* **Sunset Camping, 21056 Tolon [(27520) 59566; fax 59195; info@camping-sunset.gr; www.camping-sunset.gr]** Visible on R as app Tolón fr Nafplio, approx 200m bef Tolon. Med, hdstg, terr, pt shd; wc; chem disp; mv service pnt; shwrs inc; el pnts (16A) €4.50; lndtte; shop; tradsmn; rest, snacks; bar; rest; BBQ; cooking facs; playgrnd; sand beach 200m; games rm; wifi; TV rm; some statics; dogs; Eng spkn; adv bkg; quiet; red CKE/CCI. "Lovely seaside site; v friendly; pleasant town." 1 Apr-31 Oct. € 26.50                                                  2010*

NEOS MARMARAS *B2* (12km S Coastal) *40.04252, 23.81391* Camping Stavros, Agia Kyriaki, 63081 Neos Marmaras [tel/fax (23750) 71375; info@campingstavros.gr] Site on W side of Sithonia Peninsular. Fr Nikitas go S thro Neos Marmaras & Porto Carrasi; sp on R on winding rd. Med, shd; wc (some cont); chem disp; mv service pnt; el pnts (10A) €4; gas; lndtte; shop; rest; bar; playgrnd; beach adj; watersports; games area; TV; phone; Eng spkn; adv bkg; quiet. "Excel facs; friendly, helpful management; gd rest & bar; clean, well-run, peaceful site." 1 May-10 Oct. € 22.00                    2009*

**NEOS PANTELEIMONAS see Platamonas** *B2*

⊞ OLIMBIA *A3* (150m S Urban) *37.64518, 21.6228* Camping Diana, 27065 Olimbia [(26240) 22314 or 22945; fax 22425; harmocamp@europe.com; www.campingdiana.gr] Fr E55 Pyrgos to Tripoli rd take exit sp 'Ancient Olympia' & foll site sp. Sm, sl, terr, pt shd; wc; chem disp; shwrs inc; el pnts (16A) €5; gas; lndry rm; shop; snacks; bar; pool; TV; dogs; Eng spkn; adv bkg; quiet but some rd noise; Harmonie Group site; red CKE/CCI. "Pretty site; san facs clean & tidy; helpful & friendly management; closest campsite to archaeological sites; noisy roosters in morning!" € 23.00                    2011*

OLIMBIA *A3* (850m W Rural) *37.64337, 21.61943* Camping Alphios, 27065 Olimbia [(26240) 22951; fax 22950; alphios@otenet.gr; www.campingalphios.gr] Fr E55 Pyrgos to Tripoli rd take exit sp 'Ancient Olympia' & foll site sp. Med, hdg/mkd pitch, hdstg, terr, pt sl, pt shd; wc; chem disp; mv service pnt; shwrs inc; el pnts (16A) inc; gas; lndtte; shop; rest, snacks; bar; BBQ; cooking facs; playgrnd; pool; wifi; TV; quiet; ccard acc. "Superb views fr some pitches; excel pool; v friendly; walking dist to ancient Olympic site." 1 Apr-15 Oct. € 30.30                    2013*

**OLYMPIA see Olimbia** *A3*

PALEA EPIDAVROS *B3* (2km S Coastal) *37.61868, 23.15599* Camping Bekas, Gialasi, 21059 Palea Epidavros [(27530) 41524; fax 41394; info@bekas.gr; www.bekas.gr] S fr Korinthos past Nea (New) Epidavros. Do not take 1st sp to Palea (Ancient) Epidavros but exit R 3km later & foll sp to vill. On ent vill turn sharp R at Bekas sp, site in 1.5km. Med, hdstg, terr, shd; wc; chem disp; mv service pnt; baby facs; fam bthrm; shwrs inc; el pnts (16A) €4; gas; lndtte; ice; shop; tradsmn; supmkt 4km; rest, snacks; bar; BBQ; cooking facs; shgl beach adj; tennis; wifi; TV; 10% statics; dogs free; phone; poss cr; Eng spkn; adv bkg; quiet; ccard acc; red low ssn/long stay; CKE/CCI. "Sheltered beach in beautiful bay; friendly, family-run site in orange grove; some beachfront pitches; excel." 25 Mar-20 Oct. € 23.50                    2009*

PARGA *A2* (3km E Coastal) *39.2822, 20.43478* Enjoy Lichnos Camping, 48060 Lichnos-Parga [(26840) 31371 or 31171; fax 32076; holidays@enjoy-lichnos.net; www.enjoy-lichnos.net] On Igoumenitsa-Preveza rd turn W at sp Parga; sp 3km bef vill, steep app down private rd. Lge, terr, shd; wc; chem disp; shwrs; el pnts (16A) €3.80; lndtte; shop, rest high ssn; snacks; bar; shgl beach; watersports; dogs free; wifi; sep car park; Sunshine Camping Group site; adv bkg; quiet; red CKE/CCI. "Vg facs, excel location; some pitches adj excel beach; water taxis to Parga." 1 May-15 Oct. € 22.00    2011*

PATRA *A2* (19km SW Coastal) *38.14367, 21.58772* Camping Golden Sunset Beach, 25002 Alissos [(26930) 71276; fax 71556; goldensunset@patrascamping.gr; www.patrascampings.gr] 1st site on old national rd W of Patras to Pirgos-Olimbia, sp. Med, pt shd; wc; shwrs inc; el pnts (6A) €4; gas; lndtte; shop; rest, snacks; bar; playgrnd; 3 pools; waterslides; shgl beach; boating; tennis; games area; sat TV; 10% statics; poss cr; Eng spkn; adv bkg; quiet; ccard acc; red long stay; Harmonie Group site. "Helpful management; gd base for tours; site poss clsd Jun-Aug for exclusive use parties of students - phone ahead to check; excel." ♦ 1 May-30 Sep. € 28.00                    2009*

PATRA *A2* (21km SW Coastal) *38.14986, 21.57740* Camping Kato Alissos, 25002 Kato Alissos [(26930) 71249 or 71914; fax 71150; demiris-cmp@otenet.gr; www.camping-kato-alissos.gr] W of Patra on old national rd turn R at Kato Alissos & foll site sp for 600m. Med, shd; wc; chem disp; shwrs inc; el pnts (10A) €4.; lndtte; shop; rest, snacks; bar; cooking facs; playgrnd; shgl beach adj (down 50 steps); watersports; wifi; 10% statics; dogs; phone; bus 1km; Sunshine Camping Group site; poss cr; Eng spkn; adv bkg; quiet; ccard acc; red snr citizens; CKE/CCI. "Clean ltd facs; gd NH." 1 Apr-25 Oct. € 19.00                    2013*

PEFKARI (THASSOS) *C2* (250m W Coastal) *40.61630, 24.60021* Camping Pefkari Beach, 64002 Pefkari [tel/fax (25930) 51190; info@camping-pefkari.gr; www.camping-pefkari.gr] SW fr Thassos port approx 43km to Limenaria, Pefkari is next sm vill. Site well sp in vill. Med, hdstg, pt shd; own san; chem disp; shwrs inc; el pnts (6A) €2.90; lndry rm; shop; rest, snacks; bar; BBQ; sand beach adj; 5% statics; bus 1km; Eng spkn; quiet; CKE/CCI. "Lovely spot; worth putting up with poor, dated san facs; gd local rest; vg; improving site; beautiful; easy walk to Pefkari and Potos; excel on site rest; lovely spot." 1 May-30 Sep. € 27.50                    2014*

PETALIDI *B3* (2.5km N Coastal) *36.98167, 21.92886* Camping Petalidi Beach, 24005 Petalidi [(27220) 31154; fax 31690; info@campingpetalidi.gr; www.campingpetalidi.gr] Turn L off Kalamata-Pylos rd at Rizomylos. Site sp in 2km. Lge, hdstg, pt shd; wc; chem disp; mv service pnt; shwrs inc; el pnts (16A) inc; gas; lndtte (inc dryer); shop; rest, snacks; bar; BBQ; playgrnd; shgl beach adj; watersports; games area; entmnt; TV; dogs; phone; Eng spkn; adv bkg; quiet; red CKE/CCI. 1 Apr-30 Sep. € 23.50                    2011*

⊞ PLAKA LITOHOROU *B2* (6km N Coastal) Camping Stani, 60200 Kalivia Varikou [(23520) 61277] Leave E75 (Athens-Thessaloniki) at N Efesos/Variko, foll sp Varikou & site. Lge, mkd pitch, shd; wc; chem disp; shwrs inc; el pnts; lndtte; shop; rest, snacks; bar; TV rm; dogs; phone; poss cr; CKE/CCI. "Ltd facs low ssn; conv Dion; fair site." € 22.00                    2014*

---

> ## "That's changed – Should I let The Club know?"
>
> If you find something on site that's different from the site entry, fill in a report and let us know. See www.caravanclub.co.uk/europereport.

GREECE

**PLATAMONAS** *B2* (6km N Coastal) *40.01291, 22.59053*
Camping Poseidon Beach, Paralia Pandeleimonas, 60065
Platamonas [(23520) 41654 or 41792; fax 41994; info@
poseidonbeach.net; www.poseidonbeach.net] Exit Katerini
to Larissa toll rd 1/E75 & foll site sp over rlwy line (2km) & turn
L (sp camping), use underpass, turn R at junc, site in 400m.
Lge, hdg pitch, pt shd; wc; chem disp; shwrs inc; el pnts (16A)
€3.50; gas; lndtte; shop; rest; bar; sand beach; TV; 80% statics;
no dogs; bus 1km; poss cr; Eng spkn; quiet; red long stay/
CKE/CCI. "Well-managed site; immac facs; sm pitches & narr
rds may be diff for lge o'fits; vg beach; pleasant area." 1 Apr-
15 Oct. € 23.50                                               2011*

**PLATARIA see Igoumenitsa** *A2*

**POSSIDI see Kassandria** *B2*

**PREVEZA** *A2* (3km NW Coastal) *38.97395, 20.7161* Camping
Kalamitsi Beach, 48100 Preveza [(26280) 23268; fax
28660; kalamitsi_camping@hotmail.com] Fr Preveza on E55
twds Igoumenitsa on L of rd; clearly sp. Best app fr N. Med,
shd; wc; chem disp; shwrs inc; el pnts (16A); gas; lndtte; shop;
rest; bar; playgrnd; pool; beach adj; watersports; wifi; TV; Eng
spkn; adv bkg; quiet; red long stay; CKE/CCI. "Attractive site;
nr archaeological sites; friendly owner; poss diff to manoeuvre
onto pitches high ssn." ♦ ltd 15 Jun-1 Oct. € 26.00     2009*

⊞ **PYLOS** *A3* (5km N Coastal) *36.94784, 21.70635* Camping
Navarino Beach, 24001 Gialova [(27230) 22973; fax 23512;
info@navarino-beach.gr; www.navarino-beach.gr] Fr Pylos
N twds Kiparissia for 5km around Navarino Bay, site at S end
of Gialova vill; sp. Med, some hdstg, pt shd, wc; chem disp; mv
service pnt; shwrs inc; el pnts (16A) €4; gas; lndtte; shop 300m;
tradsmn; rest, snacks; BBQ; cooking facs; playgrnd; beach;
windsurfing, boat-launch; internet; dogs; bus; Eng spkn; adv
bkg; quiet; ccard acc; red long stay; CKE/CCI. "Management
v helpful; gd, clean, modern facs; several rest & shops in easy
walking dist; some pitches on beach; vg." € 32.50     2014*

**PYLOS** *A3* (7km N Coastal) *36.95291, 21.69565* Camping
Erodios, 24001 Gialova [(27230) 28240; fax 28241; info@
erodioss.gr; www.erodioss.gr] Fr N side of Gialova foll sp
'Golden Beach, site sp. Med, pt shd; wc; chem disp; mv service
pnt; baby facs; shwrs; el pnts (10A) €4.50; lndtte; shop; rest,
snacks; bar; cooking facs; playgrnd; beach adj; watersports;
surfing; cycle hire; wifi; sat TV; 10% statics; bus 500m; Eng
spkn; adv bkg; quiet; ccard acc; red long stay/CKE/CCI. "Excel
facs; welcoming; beautiful situation & sea views fr some
pitches; some v lge pitches - can be pre-booked; friendly,
helpful staff." ♦ 1 Apr-31 Oct. € 27.50               2011*

**RAFINA** *B3* (2km N Coastal) *38.03120, 23.99992* Camping
Kokkino Limanaki, 19009 Rafina [(22940) 31604;
fax 31603; info@athenscampings.com; www.
athenscampings.com] On Marathon/Athens rd, 25km
fr Athens turn L sp Rafina 3km; after 1.6km turn L; after 1.2km
thro x-rds & turn L after 200m; site on R in 150m. Med, pt sl,
terr, pt shd; wc (some cont); chem disp; shwrs inc; el pnts (10A)
inc; gas; lndtte; shop; rest, snacks; bar; BBQ; sand beach; dogs;
quiet low ssn; ccard acc. "Site on cliff 100m above sea with
excel mountain & ocean views; some pitches sm & poss diff lge
o'fits." 1 Apr-15 Oct. € 26.00                        2010*

⊞ **RETHYMNO (CRETE)** *C4* (3km E Coastal) *35.36795,
24.51487* Camping Elizabeth, Ionias 84 Terma, 74100
Missiria [tel/fax (28310) 28694; wallydewever@yahoo.
gr; www.camping-elizabeth.com] W fr Iraklio/Heraklion exit
Platanes/Arkadi. Site 1km bef Platanes, on R on sh unsurfaced
rd. Lge, hdg pitch, shd; wc; chem disp; mv service pnt; shwrs;
el pnts (12A) inc; lndtte (inc dryer); shop; tradsmn; rest, snacks;
bar; BBQ; cooking facs; beach adj; wifi; 3% statics; dogs;
phone; bus 500m; poss cr; Eng spkn; adv bkg; quiet; red low
ssn; CKE/CCI. "Gd walking on mkd rtes; gd cycling; excursion
programme; vg." ♦ ltd € 28.20                         2010*

⊞ **RIZA** *A2* (1km NW Coastal) *39.13493, 20.58415* Camping
Acrogiali, Mitos Apostolos, 48100 Riza [(26820) 56382;
fax 56283; campacro@hol.gr; www.camping-acrogiali.
com] Fr S foll E44 N fr Preveza, site sp on L in approx 28km.
Fr N approx 20km S of Igoumenitsa after x-ring rd bdge, start
to climb & at sharp R-hand bend (sign for Riza to L) turn R onto
winding, tarmac rd, downhill to coast. In approx 4km, site on
L. Sm, mkd pitch, shd; wc; chem disp; mv service pnt; shwrs
inc; el pnts (16A) inc; lndtte; shop; rest; bar; BBQ; shgl beach
adj; wifi (in rest); TV rm; 50% statics; Eng spkn; adv bkg; quiet;
ccard acc. "Gd facs & sw; excel, new, modern san facs; pitches
poss a challenge but location of site on beach worth effort!"
€ 20.00 (CChq acc)                                   2011*

**RODA (CORFU)** *A2* (500m W Coastal) *39.78446, 19.78486*
Camping Roda Beach International, 49081 Roda
[(26630) 63120; fax 63081; info@rodacamping.gr; www.
rodacamping.gr] N fr port to join main rd to Palaeokastlitsa.
Turn R for Sidari & foll sp to Roda. Turn L 30m bef rndabt,
200m on R, sp. Med, pt shd; wc; mv service pnt; shwrs inc;
el pnts €3.80; lndtte; shop; rest, snacks; bar; playgrnd; pool;
beach 700m; cycle hire; entmnt; internet; TV; no statics; dogs
free; Eng spkn; some rd noise; red snr citizens/CCI. 15 Apr-
15 Oct. € 22.50                                       2010*

**ROVIES (EVIA)** *B2* (3km N Coastal) *38.83276, 23.19886*
Camping Rovies Beach, 34005 Rovies [(22270) 71120;
info@campingevia.com; www.campingevia.com] Fr N on
ferry fr Glifa to Agiokampos foll coast rd S for 23 km. Med,
hdg pitch, hdstg, terr, pt shd; wc; chem disp; shwrs inc; el pnts
(12A) inc; lndry rm; shop; BBQ; shgl beach adj; 5% statics;
CKE/CCI. "Delightful location; facs dated & plagued by moths
(5/09); many pitches diff for m'vans due low branches; gd."
1 Apr-30 Oct. € 29.00                                 2009*

**SAMI (CEPHALONIA)** *A2* (1km N Coastal) *38.25088,
20.63803* Camping Karavomilos Beach, 28080 Sami
[(26740) 22480; fax 22932; info@camping-karavomilos.
gr; www.camping-karavomilos.gr] Site sp. Lge, hdg/mkd
pitch, pt shd; wc; chem disp; mv service pnt; shwrs inc; el pnts
(16A) inc; lndtte (inc dryer); shop; tradsmn; rest, snacks; bar;
playgrnd; pool; paddling pool; shgl beach adj; wifi; TV rm;
dogs; phone; poss cr; Eng spkn; adv bkg; some rd noise; ccard
acc; red CKE/CCI. "Friendly owner; wonderful scenery; easy
walk to town; v lge o'fits ring ahead for easy access; excel."
1 May-30 Sep. € 28.50                                 2010*

**SARTI** *B2* (12km N Coastal) *40.15233, 23.91293* **Camping Armenistis, Akti Armenistis, 63072 Sarti [tel/fax (23750) 91487; info@armenistis.com.gr; www.armenistis. com.gr]** Fr Nikitas, turn E at junc down E side of Sithonia along coast rd sp Sarti/Sikia; site on E side 28km fr junc; last few km diff driving. Lge, mkd pitch, pt shd; wc; mv service pnt; shwrs inc; el pnts (6A) €3.70; lndtte; shop; rest, snacks; bar; BBQ; playgrnd; beach; games area; entmnt; 30% statics; Sunshine Camping Group site; ccard acc; red CKE/CCI. "Gd location with views of Mount Athos; excel for families." 1 May-15 Sep. € 26.40                                                                2009*

**SISI (CRETE)** *C4* (1.2km W Coastal) *35.30371, 25.50858* **Sisi Camping, 72400 Sisi [tel/fax (28410) 71247; info@ sisicamping.gr; www.sisicamping.gr]** E fr Iraklio/Heraklion on E75, after Malia look for Sisi turn approx 5km after Malia. Site sp. Sm, mkd/hdg pitch, pt shd; wc (cont); chem disp; mv service pnt; shwrs inc; el pnts (10A) €3.50; lndtte; shop 800m; tradsmn; rest 250m; snacks; bar; BBQ; pool; paddling pool; sand beach 1km; watersports; wifi; dogs free; phone; Eng spkn; adv bkg; quiet; red low ssn; CKE/CCI. "Sisi pretty vill; gd touring base attractions & archaeological sites; warm welcome; vg." 1 May-15 Oct. € 23.30                                          2010*

⊞ **SOUNIO** *B3* (5km N Coastal) *37.67620, 24.04884* **Camping Bacchus, Ave Lavrio, 19500 Sounio [tel/fax (22920) 39572; campingbacchus@hotmail.com; www. tggr.com/camping-bacchus]** Site sp on N89 coastal rd at km stone 71. Sm, pt shd; wc; chem disp; shwrs inc; el pnts (6A) €4; gas; lndtte; shop, rest (high ssn); snacks; bar; cooking facs; playgrnd; sand beach adj; fishing, windsurfing nr; TV; 50% statics; phone; Sunshine Group site; quiet; ccard acc; red low ssn. "Basic facs; solar water heating, open air wash basins with cold taps only, no privacy cubicles - not rec in winter (2009); rundown statics (2009); 4.5km fr Temple of Poseidon; easy access coastal walks & views." € 25.50                          2009*

**SPARTI** *B3* (5km W Rural) *37.06941, 22.38163* **Camping Castle View, 23100 Mistras [(27310) 83303; fax 20028; info@castleview.gr]** Fr Kalamata take 1st turning to Mistras, past castle then thro vill dir Sparti. Site in approx 1km on L, well sp. Med, pt shd; wc; chem disp; shwrs inc; el pnts (16A) inc; gas; lndtte; shop; tradsmn; rest, snacks; bar; playgrnd; pool; wifi; TV; some statics; dogs; phone; Eng spkn; quiet; red CKE/ CCI. "Gd clean facs; gd rest; close to archaeological remains; helpful owner." 1 Apr-20 Oct. € 26.00                                  2011*

**STOUPA** *B3* (100m N Coastal) *36.84934, 22.25877* **Camping Kalógria, Barbecer Nicda 29, 24024 Stoupa [(27210) 77319]** S fr Kalamata, turn R at site sp just bef Stoupa, site 200m on L. Med, some hdstg, pt sl, pt shd; wc; chem disp; mv service pnt; shwrs; el pnts (16A) inc; lndtte; shop; tradsmn; rest, snacks, bar 100m high ssn; BBQ; playgrnd; sand beach adj; phone; poss cr; Eng spkn; quiet; CKE/CCI. "Nice location; friendly staff; pitches on loose earth amongst trees; pleasant resort town." ♦ ltd 5 May-31 Oct. € 24.30                                                                    2011*

**STOUPA** *B3* (2km N Coastal) *36.86071, 22.25220* **Camping Ta Delfinia, Neo Proastio, 24022 Kardamili [(27210) 77318; perdikeas@in.gr]** Site sp in lay-by; go thro gate & keep going. Sm, some hdstg, pt sl, shd; wc (some cont); chem disp; shwrs; ltd el pnts (16A) inc; lndtte; shop high ssn; rest 1.5km; snacks, bar high ssn; BBQ; playgrnd; sand/shgl beach adj; wifi; TV; poss cr; Eng spkn; red snr citizens; CKE/CCI. "Friendly welcome; ltd facs low ssn." 1 Mar-31 Oct. € 26.20                              2010*

⊞ **STYLIDA** *B2* (3km E Coastal) *38.89638, 22.65555* **Camping Interstation, Rd Athens-Thessalonika, Km 230, 35300 Stylida [(22380) 23827; fax 23828; interstation@ hotmail.com; www.tggr.com/interstation/]** Fr Lamia take rd E to Stylis; cont for further 3km & site situated to side of dual-c'way opp petrol stn. Med, shd; wc; chem disp; shwrs €0.30; el pnts (16A) €3.60; gas; lndtte; shop, rest high ssn; playgrnd; beach adj; tennis; watersports; TV; entmnt; some statics; no dogs; Eng spkn; adv bkg; quiet but some rd noise; red CKE/CCI. "Day visitors have access to beach via site; do not confuse with Cmp Paras adj - not rec; Sunshine Camping Group site; poss poor san facs low ssn; NH only." ♦ € 22.60                                                                    2009*

**THASSOS (THASSOS)** *C1* (8km S Coastal) *40.72561, 24.7567* **Camping Golden Beach, 64004 Panagia [(25930) 61472; fax 61473; info@camping-goldenbeach.gr; www. camping-goldenbeach.gr]** S fr Thassos to Panagia. Turn L to Hrissi Armoudia & site. Site sp in Panagia. Lge, hdg/mkd pitch, pt shd; wc (some cont); shwrs inc; el pnts €4.30; lndtte; shop; rest adj; snacks; bar; playgrnd; sand beach adj; games area; entmnt; TV; 50% statics; poss cr; Eng spkn; quiet. "Beautiful, long, sandy beach." ♦ 1 May-15 Oct. € 20.00                2011*

**THERMISIA** *B3* (350m SE Coastal) *37.41047, 23.32733* **Hydra's Wave Camping, Thermissia Argolidas, TK 21051 Greece [tel/fax (27540) 41095; info@hydraswave.gr; www.hydraswave.gr]** Fr Kranidi turn E on rd to Ermioni & then foll coast rd dir Póros. Site sp on R after 6km. Med, hdg pitch, shd; wc (some cont); chem disp; shwrs inc; el pnts (16A) €4; lndtte; shop; rest, snacks; bar; playgrnd; shgl beach adj; TV; dogs €2.50; bus 500m; Eng spkn; adv bkg; quiet; ccard acc; CKE/CCI. "Gd cent for Poros, Hydra, Spetses; helpful owner; dated facs but clean; area somewhat run down (2010); OK touring base." 1 Mar-30 Nov. € 21.00                        2010*

**TINOS (TINOS)** *C3* (500m E Coastal) *37.53994, 25.16377* **Tinos Camping, Louizas Sohou 5, 84200 Tinos [(22830) 22344; fax 24373; tinoscamping@thn.forthnet. gr; www.tinos-info.gr/tinoscamping]** Clearly sp fr port. Sm, hdg/mkd pitch, hdstg; shd; wc; chem disp; shwrs inc; el pnts €4.50; lndry rm; shop; rest, snacks; BBQ; cooking facs; sand/shgl beach 500m; dogs; phone; Eng spkn; adv bkg; ccard acc; red long stay/CKE/CCI. "1,600 Venetian dovecots & 600 churches on island; monastery with healing icon." ♦ 1 May-31 Oct. € 21.50                                                        2009*

**TIROS see Leonidi** *B3*

**TOLON see Nafplio** *B3*

⊞ **VARTHOLOMIO** *A3* (8km SW Coastal) *37.83555, 21.13333* Camping Ionion Beach, 27050 Glifa [(26230) 96395; fax 96425; ioniongr@otenet.gr; www.ionion-beach.gr] Fr E55 Patras-Pirgos rd turn W to Gastouni, Ligia & Glifa, then Glifa Beach. Site is 1km SW of Glifa. Med, hdg pitch, hdstg, pt shd; htd wc; chem disp; mv service pnt; serviced pitch; shwrs; el pnts (16A); gas; lndtte (inc dryer); shop in vill; tradsmn; rest, snacks; bar; BBQ; playgrnd; pool; paddling pool; beach adj; watersports; games area; wifi; TV; statics; dogs; Eng spkn; adv bkg; poss noisy; ccard acc; red low ssn; CKE/CCI. "Excel, well-run site; superb facs." ♦ € 27.00  2010*

**VASILIKI (LEFKAS)** *A2* (500m W Coastal) *38.63108, 20.60663* Camping Vasiliki Beach, 31082 Vasiliki [(26450) 31308; fax 31458] On arr in Vasiliki, turn R in 300m, site sp. Med, some hdstg, shd; wc; chem disp; mv service pnt; shwrs; el pnts (10A); gas; lndtte; shop; rest, snacks; bar; BBQ; playgrnd; beach adj; games rm; TV; dogs; phone; poss cr; Eng spkn; red CKE/CCI. "Popular with windsurfers; easy walk to town along beach." ♦ ltd 15 Apr-15 Oct. € 36.00  2011*

**VLYCHO see Lefkada (Lefkas Island)** *A2*

**VOLOS** *B2* (17km SE Coastal) *39.31105, 23.10922* Camping Hellas International, 38500 Kato Gatzea [(24230) 22267; fax 22492; info@campinghellas.gr; www.campinghellas.gr] Fr Volos take coast rd N34 to Kato Gatzea; sp on R immed bef & adj Sikia (Fig Tree) Camping. Med, shd; wc; chem disp; baby facs; shwrs inc; el pnts (16A) inc; gas; lndtte; shop high ssn; tradsmn; rest, snacks high ssn; BBQ; shgl beach adj; boating; cycle hire; internet; 30% statics; dogs; phone; Harmonie Group site; Eng spkn; adv bkg; ccard acc; red low ssn; CKE/CCI. "Excel san facs - poss stretched with site full; friendly, helpful family-run site; great location; vg touring base." ♦ 15 Mar-31 Oct. € 27.50  2010*

**VOLOS** *B2* (17km SE Coastal) *39.31027, 23.10972* Camping Sikia Fig Tree, 38500 Kato Gatzea [(24230) 22279 or 22081; fax 22720; info@camping-sikia.gr; www.camping-sikia.gr] Fr Volos take coast rd S to Kato Gatzea site on R, sp immed next to Camping Hellas. Med, terr, shd; wc; chem disp; mv service pnt; shwrs inc; el pnts (16A) €3; gas; lndtte; shop; rest, snacks; shgl beach; internet; entmnt; 20% statics; dogs; phone; poss cr; Eng spkn; adv bkg; quiet; Sunshine Group site; ccard acc; red long stay/CKE/CCI. "Highly rec; some beautiful, but sm, pitches with sea views; excel, friendly family-run site; v clean; v helpful staff; take care o'hanging trees." ♦ 1 Apr-30 Oct. € 19.00  2011*

**ZACHARO** *A3* (8km S Coastal) *37.41163, 21.66825* Camping Tholo Beach, Tholo, 27054 Zacharo [(26250) 61345 or 33454 (winter); campingtholo@hotmail.com] S fr Pyrgos on E55 dir Kyparissia, 8km S of Zacharo turn R to Tholo. Site sp in 500m on L. Med, shd; wc; chem disp; mv service pnt; shwrs inc; el pnts €4; lndry rm; shop; rest; bar; BBQ; playgrnd; sand beach adj; wifi; TV; no statics; dogs; Eng spkn; adv bkg; quiet; CKE/CCI. "Excel, quiet, clean site; gd, clean san facs; friendly staff; excel sandy beach where loggerhead turtles lay eggs; dolphins off shore; san facs need updating; great location; excel mkt on Tuesdays; Ancient Olympia about an hour's drive ." 1 May-30 Oct. € 32.50  2014*

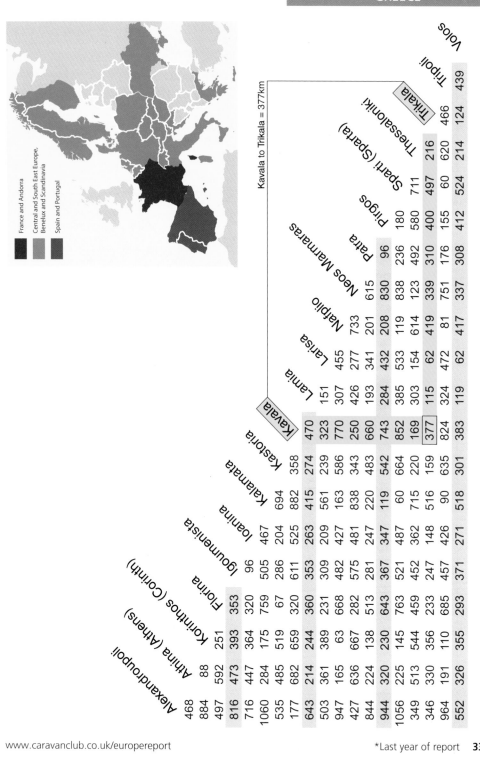

Map legend:
- France and Andorra
- Central and South East Europe, Benelux and Scandinavia
- Spain and Portugal

Kavala to Trikala = 377km

Distance chart (km) — triangular road-distance table:

| To → | Athína (Athens) | Kórinthos (Corinth) | Florina | Igoumenítsa | Ioánina | Kalamáta | Kastoriá | Kavala | Lamía | Lárisa | Náfplio | Neos Marmaras | Patra | Pírgos | Spárti (Sparta) | Thessaloníki | Tríkala | Trípoli | Vólos |
|---|---|---|---|---|---|---|---|---|---|---|---|---|---|---|---|---|---|---|---|
| Trípoli | | | | | | | | | | | | | | | | | | | 439 |
| Tríkala | | | | | | | | | | | | | | | | | | 466 | 124 |
| Thessaloníki | | | | | | | | | | | | | | | | | 216 | 620 | 214 |
| Spárti (Sparta) | | | | | | | | | | | | | | | | 711 | 497 | 60 | 524 |
| Pírgos | | | | | | | | | | | | | | | 180 | 580 | 400 | 155 | 412 |
| Patra | | | | | | | | | | | | | | 96 | 236 | 492 | 310 | 176 | 308 |
| Neos Marmaras | | | | | | | | | | | | | 615 | 830 | 838 | 123 | 339 | 751 | 337 |
| Náfplio | | | | | | | | | | | | 733 | 201 | 208 | 119 | 614 | 419 | 81 | 417 |
| Lárisa | | | | | | | | | | | 455 | 277 | 341 | 432 | 533 | 154 | 62 | 472 | 62 |
| Lamía | | | | | | | | | | 151 | 307 | 426 | 193 | 284 | 385 | 303 | 115 | 324 | 119 |
| Kavala | | | | | | | | | 470 | 323 | 770 | 250 | 660 | 743 | 852 | 169 | 377 | 824 | 383 |
| Kastoriá | | | | | | | | 358 | 274 | 239 | 586 | 343 | 483 | 542 | 664 | 220 | 159 | 635 | 301 |
| Kalamáta | | | | | | | 694 | 882 | 415 | 561 | 163 | 481 | 247 | 347 | 487 | 362 | 516 | 90 | 518 |
| Ioánina | | | | | | 467 | 204 | 525 | 209 | 148 | 427 | 482 | 281 | 367 | 452 | 247 | 96 | 457 | 371 |
| Igoumenítsa | | | | | 96 | 505 | 353 | 263 | 309 | 452 | 668 | 282 | 513 | 233 | 459 | 356 | 233 | 685 | 293 |
| Florina | | | | 353 | 320 | 759 | 67 | 286 | 505 | 282 | 575 | 668 | 281 | 367 | 452 | 160 | 204 | 609 | 255 |
| Kórinthos (Corinth) | | | 251 | 393 | 364 | 175 | 519 | 659 | 244 | 389 | 63 | 667 | 138 | 230 | 145 | 544 | 356 | 110 | 355 |
| Athína (Athens) | | 88 | 592 | 473 | 447 | 284 | 485 | 682 | 214 | 361 | 165 | 636 | 224 | 320 | 225 | 513 | 330 | 191 | 326 |
| Alexandroúpoli | 468 | 884 | 497 | 816 | 716 | 1060 | 535 | 177 | 643 | 503 | 947 | 427 | 844 | 944 | 1056 | 349 | 346 | 964 | 552 |

**GREECE**

- MONTENEGRO
- SERBIA
- KOSOVO
- SOFIYA
- BULGARIA
- Burgas
- Blagoevgrad
- Plovdiv
- SKOPJE
- MACEDONIA
- Edirne
- TIRANË
- Bitola
- 14
- ALBANIA
- KAVALA
- ALEXANDROUPOLI
- FLORINA
- Thassos
- THESSALONIKI
- Pefkári
- THASSOS
- Methoni
- Ierissos
- KASTORIA
- Pierias
- Gerakini
- Gjirokastër
- Plaka Litohorou
- Kassandria
- Sarti
- LEMNOS
- Roda
- Platamonas
- NEOS
- Kalambaka
- MARMARAS
- IOANINA
- LARISA
- IGOUMENITSA
- TRIKALA
- LESBOS
- CORFU KERKIRA
- Parga
- VOLOS
- Riza
- AEGEAN
- Preveza
- 38
- LAMIA
- Stylida
- EUBOEA/ EVIA
- SEA
- TURKEY
- Lefkada
- Kamena
- Rovies
- LEVKAS Vasiliki
- Vourla
- Izmir
- Sami
- Delfi
- Eretria
- CHIOS
- Nafpaktos
- PATRA
- CEPHALONIA
- Agioi
- Rafina
- Kyllini
- Theodoroi
- Vartholomio
- Amaliada
- KORINTHOS
- ATHINA
- ZANTE
- Olimbia
- Mikines
- Palea Epidavros
- PYRGOS
- TRIPOLI
- NAFPLIO
- Sounio
- TINOS
- Zacharo
- Drepano
- Tinos
- Kyparissia
- Thermissia
- CYCLADES
- KALAMATA
- Leonidi
- Pylos
- Petalidi
- SPARTI
- Bodrum
- Methoni
- Stoupa
- Kos
- Finikoundas
- Koroni
- Githio
- KOS
- RHODES
- MEDITERRANEAN SEA
- Hania
- Sisi
- Rethymno
- 90
- Agia Galini
- CRETE

Legend:
- ● All year site(s)
- ● Seasonal site(s)
- ○ No sites listed
- 200m +
- 0–200m

Scale: 0 50 100 150 200 250 kms
0 50 100 150 mls

- Motorways
- Major roads
- Main roads

© Collins Bartholomew Ltd 2014

N W E S

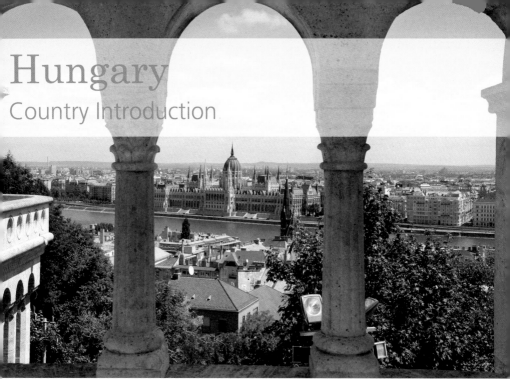

# Hungary
## Country Introduction

*View of Budapest, from Fishermen's Bastion*

## Welcome to Hungary

Hungary is a land of rich heritage. Folk culture is not only preserved in museums, the traditions live on in many of the small villages, kept alive by local communities.

The country has over a thousand thermal water springs and the second largest thermal lake in the world. Visitors travel far and wide to enjoy the many spas and health centres.

Budapest offers panoramic views of the Danube and UNESCO world heritage site in Buda Castle.

## Country highlights

Renowned for its goulash, Hungary is also known for the huge variety of different sausages, salamis, hams and other meat products. The most popular smoked variety is the Csabai sausage. Ground red paprika is a spice used in many dishes.

Perhaps the biggest festival in Hungary, held in the North Obuda, is the Sziget Festival. A huge music event attracting international artists and around 400,000 visitors each year.

## Major towns and cities

- Budapest – the capital city is full of amazing monuments, restaurants and nightlife.

- Debrecen – a cultural city that is famous for its brightly coloured Great Church.

- Pécs – located on the Mecsek mountains, this city has many historical buildings and ancient archaeological sites to visit.

## Attractions

- Zsolnay Museum – the museum houses beautiful displays of porcelain.

- Fisherman's Bastion (Halaszbatya) – this beautiful structure gives great views of Budapest.

- Hortobagy National Park – this large park has natural history and bird watching in its large pleasant grounds.

## Find out more

www.gotohungary.com

Tel: 0036 (0) 14 38 80 80 Tourist Information Service

# Country Information

*Population (approx):* 9.9 million

*Capital:* Budapest (population approx 1.7 million)

*Area:* 93,030 sq km

*Bordered by:* Austria, Croatia, Romania, Serbia, Slovakia, Slovenia, Ukraine

*Terrain:* Mostly flat and rolling plains; hills and low mountains to the north

*Climate:* Temperate, continental climate; cold, cloudy winters; warm, sunny summers; changeable in spring and early summer with heavy rain and storms. The best times to visit are spring and autumn

*Highest Point:* Kekes 1,014m

*Language:* Hungarian

*Local Time:* GMT or BST + 1, i.e. 1 hour ahead of the UK all year

*Currency:* Forint (HUF); £1 = HUF 395, HUF 1000 = £2.52 (September 2014)

*Emergency numbers:* Police 107; Fire brigade 105; Ambulance 104. Operators speak English.

*Public Holidays 2015:* Jan 1; Mar 15 (National Day); Apr 5, 6; May 1, 24, 25; Aug 20 (Constitution Day); Oct 23 (Republic Day); Nov 1; Dec 25, 26.

School summer holidays are from mid-June to the end of August

# Camping and Caravanning

There are approximately 100 organised campsites in Hungary rated from 1 to 4 stars. These are generally well signposted off main routes, with the site name shown below a blue camping sign. Most campsites open from May to September and the most popular sites are situated by Lake Balaton and the Danube. A Camping Key Europe (CKE) or Camping Card International (CCI) is essential.

Facilities vary from site to site, but visitors will find it useful to carry their own flat universal sink plug. There has been much improvement in recent years in the general standard of campsites, but communal changing areas for showers are not uncommon. Many sites have communal kitchen facilities which enable visitors to make great savings on their own gas supply.

Many campsites require payment in cash. Prices have risen sharply in recent years. Therefore, prices in this guide for sites not reported on for some time might not reflect the current prices.

Casual/wild camping is prohibited.

# Cycling

There are approximately 2,000km of cycle tracks, 100km of which are in Budapest and 200km around Lake Balaton. Tourinform offices in Hungary provide maps of cycling routes.

Children under 14 years are not allowed to ride on the road and all cyclists must wear a reflective jacket at night and in poor daytime visibility.

# Electricity and Gas

Current on campsites varies between 6 and 16 amps.

Plugs have two round pins. There are some sites that do not have CEE connections.

Only non-returnable and/or non-exchangeable Campingaz cylinders are available.

# Entry Formalities

British and Irish passport holders may stay for a period of three months without a visa. Your passport needs to be valid for the duration of your stay and it is always recommended when visiting a foreign country to have an additional period of validity on your passport in case of any unforeseen delays. Anyone planning to stay longer than three months should contact the Hungarian Embassy for further information

There are no longer any immigration or Customs checks at borders with other EU countries, i.e. Slovakia, Slovenia and Austria. Border crossings with other countries are generally open 24 hours.

# Medical Services

British nationals may obtain emergency medical and dental treatment from practitioners contracted to the national health insurance scheme, Országos Egészségbiztosítási (OEP), together with emergency hospital treatment, on presentation of a European Health Insurance Card (EHIC) and a British passport. Fees are payable for treatment and prescribed medicines, and are not refundable in Hungary. You may be able to apply for reimbursement when back in the UK.

Pharmacies (gyógyszertár)) are well stocked. The location of the nearest all-night pharmacy is displayed on the door of every pharmacy.

## Opening Hours

Banks – Mon-Thurs 8am-4pm.

Museums – Tue-Sun 10am-6pm; closed Mon.

Post Offices – Mon-Fri 8am-6pm; post office at Budapest open Mon-Sat 7am-9pm.

Shops – Mon-Fri 10am-6pm (supermarkets from 7am-7pm with some grocery stores open 24 hours); open half day Saturdays.

## Safety and Security

Petty theft in Budapest is common in areas frequented by tourists, particularly on busy public transport, at markets and at popular tourist sites. Beware of pickpockets and bag snatchers and leave valuables in your caravan safe.

Do not carry large amounts of cash. Take care when receiving bank notes and change as some that are no longer valid are still in circulation, e.g. HUF 200 notes were withdrawn in 2009. There has been a small number of instances of taxi drivers deliberately passing these notes to tourists. Be aware especially when paying with a HUF 10,000 or 20,000 bank note.

Theft of and from vehicles is common. Do not leave your belongings, car registration documents or mobile phones in your car and ensure that it is properly locked with the alarm on, even if leaving it for just a moment. Beware of contrived 'incidents', particularly on the Vienna-Budapest motorway, designed to stop motorists and expose them to robbery.

Visitors have reported in the past that motorists may be pestered at service areas on the Vienna to Budapest motorway by people insisting on washing windscreens and demanding money.

During the summer season in Budapest, uniformed tourist police patrol the most frequently visited areas of the city. Criminals sometimes pose as tourist police and ask for visitors' money, credit cards or travel documents in order to check them. Always ensure that a uniformed police officer is wearing a badge displaying the word 'Rendörség' and a five-digit identification number, together with a separate name badge. Plain clothes police carry a badge and an ID card with picture, hologram and rank. If in doubt, insist on going to the nearest police station.

There are still occasional incidents of exorbitant overcharging in certain restaurants, bars and clubs in Budapest, accompanied by threats of violence. Individuals who have been unable to settle their bill have frequently been accompanied by the establishment's security guards to a cash machine and made to withdraw funds. Visitors are advised to ask for a menu and only order items which are priced realistically. A five digit price for one dish is too high. Never accept menus which do not display prices and check your bill carefully.

Taxi drivers are sometimes accomplices to these frauds, receiving 'commission' for recommending restaurants and bars which charge extortionate prices to visitors. Never ask a taxi driver to recommend a bar, club or restaurant. If a driver takes you to one or you are approached on the street with an invitation to an unfamiliar bar or restaurant, you should treat such advice with extreme caution.

Do not change money or get involved in any form of gambling in the street; these activities are illegal.

If you need help, go to the nearest police station or to the 24 hour tourist assistance office in Budapest, which is open from 1 June to 1 September at the police headquarters at Teve Utca 6 in District 13, tel (1) 4435259. District police stations in Districts 1, 5, 11 and 14 also have 24 hour tourism desks where complaints can be dealt with and assistance given in English.

There is a low threat from terrorism.

*British Embassy*

HARMINCAD UTCA 6, BUDAPEST 1051
Tel: (1) 2662888
http://ukinhungary.fco.gov.uk

*Irish Embassy*

SZABADSÁG TÉR 7,
BANK CENTRE, GRANIT TOWER, V. FLOOR
1054 BUDAPEST
Tel: (1) 3014960
www.embassyofireland.hu

# Documents

## Passport

Carry your passport at all times. A photocopy is not acceptable.

## Vehicle(s)

Carry your vehicle registration certificate (V5C), vehicle insurance certificate and MOT certificate (if applicable) with you when driving.

# Money

Hungarian currency is available from banks in Austria before crossing the border. For emergency cash reserves, it is advisable to have euros, rather than sterling. Foreign currency is best exchanged at banks as, by law, this is at the rate shown on the banks' currency boards and they are not permitted to charge commission. Private bureaux de change, however, do charge commission, but the rate of exchange may be better.

Credit cards are accepted at many outlets in large towns and cities and cash dispensers, 'bankomats', are widespread even in small towns. There is a high incidence of credit card fraud and payment in cash wherever possible is advisable. Carry your credit card issuers'/banks' 24 hour UK contact numbers separately in case of loss or theft of your cards.

Recent visitors report that some newer types of debit and credit cards issued in the UK do not work in certain cash machines in Hungary. The banks are working on a solution but, in the meantime, if you encounter this problem you should try a cash machine at a different bank. It is possible to obtain cash from post offices with a debit or credit card.

Euros are widely accepted in shops and restaurants frequented by tourists, but check the exchange rate.

When leaving Hungary on the MI motorway (Budapest-Vienna), it is important to change back your forints on the Hungarian side of the border by crossing the carriageway to the left at the designated crossing-point, as visitors report that there are no facilities on the right hand side and none on the other side in Austria.

# Motoring in Hungary

## Accidents

Accidents causing damage to vehicles or injury to persons must be reported to the nearest police station and to the Hungarian State Insurance Company (Hungária Biztosító) within 24 hours. The police will issue a statement which you may be asked to show when leaving the country.

If entering Hungary with a conspicuously damaged vehicle, it is recommended that you obtain a report confirming the damage from the police in the country where the damage occurred, otherwise difficulties may arise when leaving Hungary.

## Alcohol

It is illegal to drive after consuming any alcohol whatsoever.

# Breakdown Service

The motoring organisation, Magyar Autóklub (MAK), operates a breakdown service 24 hours a day on all roads. Drivers in need of assistance should telephone 188 or (1) 3451755 (operators speak English on this number). The number (1) is the area code for Budapest. On motorways emergency phones are placed at 2km intervals.

MAK road patrol cars are yellow and marked 'Segélyszolgálat'. Their registration numbers begin with the letters MAK.

The roadside breakdown service is chargeable, higher charges applying at night. There is a scale of charges by vehicle weight and distance for towing vehicles to a garage. Payment is required in cash.

# Essential Equipment

## First Aid Kit

It is a legal requirement that all vehicles should carry a first aid kit.

## Lights

Outside built-up areas dipped headlights are compulsory at all times, regardless of weather conditions. Bulbs are more likely to fail with constant use and you are recommended to carry spares. At night in built-up areas dipped headlights must be used as full beam is prohibited.

Headlight flashing often means that a driver is giving way, but do not carry out a manoeuvre unless you are sure that this is the case.

*Reflective Jackets/Waistcoats*
If your vehicle is immobilised on the carriageway outside a built-up area, or if visibility is poor, you must wear a reflective jacket or waistcoat when getting out of your vehicle. Passengers who leave the vehicle, for example, to assist with a repair, should also wear one. Keep the jackets inside your vehicle, not in the boot.

In addition, pedestrians and cyclists walking or cycling at night or in poor visibility along unlit roads outside a built-up area must also wear a reflective jacket.

*Warning Triangles*
In the event of accident, it is compulsory to place a warning triangle 100 metres behind the vehicle on motorways and 50 metres on other roads.

*Child Restraint System*
Children under the height of 1.5m must be seated in a suitable child restraint system appropriate for their size in the rear of the vehicle.

If no child restraint is available a child over 3 who is over 1.35m in height may travel in the rear seat with a seatbelt. Children younger or shorter than this may not ever travel without a suitable restraint system in the vehicle.

*Winter Driving*
The use of snow chains can be made compulsory on some roads when there is severe winter weather.

# Fuel

Leaded petrol is no longer available. The sign 'Ólommentes üzemanyag' or 'Bleifrei 95' indicates unleaded petrol. LPG is widely available.

Most petrol stations are open from 6am to 8pm. Along motorways and in large towns they are often open 24 hours. Virtually all petrol stations accept credit and debit cards, possible exceptions being in remote, rural areas.

# Parking

Zigzag lines on the carriageway and road signs indicate a stopping/parking prohibition. Illegally-parked vehicles will be towed away or clamped. On two-way roads, vehicles must park in the direction of traffic; they may park on either side in one-way streets. In certain circumstances, parking on the pavement is allowed.

Budapest is divided into various time restricted parking zones (maximum three hours) where tickets must be purchased from Monday to Friday from a machine. For longer periods you are advised to use 'Park and Ride' car parks located near major metro stations and bus terminals.

# Priority

Pedestrians have priority over traffic at pedestrian crossings and at intersections. They do not have priority on the roadway between central tram loading islands and pavements, and drivers must exercise care on these sections. Major roads are indicated by a priority road ahead sign. At the intersection of two roads of equal importance, where there is no sign, vehicles coming from the right have priority. Trams and buses have priority at any intersection on any road and buses have right of way when leaving bus stops after the driver has signalled his intention to pull out.

# Roads

Hungary has a good system of well surfaced main roads and driving standards are higher than in many other parts of Europe. There are few dual carriageways and care is required, therefore, when overtaking with a right-hand drive vehicle. Extra care is required on provincial roads which may be badly lit, poorly maintained and narrow. In the countryside at night be on the alert for unlit cycles and horse drawn vehicles

# Road Signs and Markings

Road signs and markings conform to international conventions. Square green road signs indicate the number of km to the next town. At traffic lights a flashing amber light indicates a dangerous intersection.

Destination signs feature road numbers rather than the names of towns, so it is essential to equip yourself with an up-to-date road map or atlas. Signs for motorways have white lettering on a blue background; on other roads signs are white and green.

## Speed Limits

| | Open Road (km/h) | Motorway (km/h) |
|---|---|---|
| Car Solo | 90-110 | 130 |
| Car towing caravan/trailer | 70 | 80 |
| Motorhome under 3500kg | 90-110 | 130 |
| Motorhome 3500-7500kg | 70 | 80 |

A speed limit of 30 km/h (18 mph) is in force in many residential, city centre and tourist resort areas.

## Traffic Jams

Roads around Budapest are busy on Friday and Sunday afternoons. In the holiday season roads to Lake Balaton (M7) and around the lake (N7 and N71) may be congested. There are regular traffic hold ups at weekends at the border crossings to Austria, the Czech Republic and Serbia. Motorway traffic information (in English) is available on www.motorway.hu.

## Violation of Traffic Regulations

The police make spot vehicle document checks and are keen to enforce speed limits. They are permitted to impose on-the-spot fines of up to HUF150,000. Credit cards are not accepted for the payment of fines.

## Motorways

All motorways (autópálya) and main connecting roads run to or from Budapest. In recent years the road network has been extended and improved and there are now approximately 900 kilometres of motorway and dual carriageways or semi-

motorways, as listed on the following page. However, most roads are still single carriageway, single lane and care is recommended. The M0 motorway is a 75km ringroad around Budapest which links the M1, M7, M6, M5 and Highway 11. The recently built Megyeri Bridge on the Danube is part of the M0 and its opening has considerably reduced traffic congestion to the north of Budapest.

Emergency corridors are compulsory on motorways and dual carriageways. Drivers are required to create a precautionary emergency corridor to provide access for emergency vehicles whenever congestion occurs. Drivers in the left-hand lane must move as far over to the left as possible, and drivers in the central and right-hand lanes must move as far over to the right as possible.

*Motorway Vignettes*

Approximately 30% of motorways are toll-free; otherwise you must purchase an electronic vignette (matrica) or e-vignette (sticker) before entering the motorway.

They are available online, from motorway customer service offices and at petrol stations. You can pay in forints or by credit card.

Leaflets are distributed to motorists at the border and a telephone information centre is available in Hungary – tel 06 40 40 50 60. Vignettes should only be purchased from outlets where the prices are clearly displayed at the set rates. For full details (in English), including how to buy online and toll-free sections, see www.motorway.hu

When purchasing an e-vignette a confirmation message will be sent or a coupon issued and this must be kept for a year after its expiry date. There is no need to display the vignette in your windscreen as the motorway authorities check all vehicles electronically (without the need for you to stop your vehicle) and verify registration number, category of toll paid and validity of an e-vignette. Charges in forints (2014 charges, subject to change) are as shown below:

| Category of Vehicle | Period of Validity | |
|---|---|---|
| | 1 week | 1 month |
| Vehicle up to 3,500kg with or without caravan or trailer | 2,975 | 4,780 |
| Vehicle between 3,500kg and 7,500kg with or without caravan or trailer | 13,385 | 21,975 |

Since the beginning of 2013 Hungary's State Motorway Management company (AAK) have been imposing on-the-spot fines for motorists who do not have a vignette. Fines amount to HUF 14,875 (around £40) for vehicles under 3,500kg or HUF 66,925 (around £178) for vehicles between 3,500kg and 7,500kg if paid within 30 days. 78% of the motorists fined so far have been foreign nationals, so ensure you have a vignette before travelling on motorways.

## Touring

Hungary boasts eleven World Heritage sites including the national park at Aggtelek which contains Europe's largest cave network, the Christian cemetery at Pécs and the monastery at Pannonhalma. Lake Balaton, the largest lake in Central Europe, attracts lovers of bathing, sailing, fishing and windsurfing. With 200km of sandy shoreline and shallow warm waters, it is very popular with families and easily Hungary's favourite tourist area.

A Budapest Card is available, allowing unlimited travel on public transport for two or three consecutive days, free city walking tours, discounted entry to museums and other attractions, plus discounts on many guided tours, events, shops and restaurants. Cards are available from metro stations, tourist information offices, many travel agencies, hotels, museums and main Budapest transport ticket offices, as well as from the Hungarian National Tourist Office in London. A child under 14 travelling with the cardholder is included free of charge. You may also order online from www.budapestinfo.hu.

A tip of 10-15% of the bill is expected in restaurants. Check your bill first to ensure that a service charge has not already been added.

Take your own supply of plastic carrier bags to supermarkets, as generally they are not supplied.

Hungarian is a notoriously difficult language for native English speakers to decipher and pronounce. English is not widely spoken in rural areas, but it is becoming increasingly widespread elsewhere as it is now taught in schools. German is widely spoken and a dictionary may be helpful.

## Public Transport & Local Travel

Cars are not permitted within the Castle District and on Margaret Island in Budapest. It is advisable to use public transport when travelling into the city and there is an excellent network of bus, tram and metro routes (BKV). All public transport in Hungary is free for over 65, and this also applies to foreign visitors with proof of age (passport).

There are a number of ticket options, including family tickets, 1, 3 and 7 day tickets, and they can be bought at metro stations, ticket machines, tobacconists and newsagents. Validate your bus and metro tickets before use at each stage of your journey and every time you change metro lines at the red machines provided. Tickets are often checked on vehicles or at metro station exits by controllers wearing arm bands and carrying photo ID. For further information on public transport in Budapest see www.bkv.hu

As a general rule, it is better to phone for taxis operated by reputable local companies, rather than flag them down in the street, and always ensure that fares are metered. A tip of approximately 10% of the fare is customary.

Mahart, the Hungarian Shipping Company, operates a regular hydrofoil service from April to October along the Danube between Budapest and Vienna. The journey lasts six hours and covers 288km.

Local companies, Legenda (www.legenda.hu) and Mahart also offer city cruises between April and October, as well as regular trips to tourist attractions outside Budapest, such as Szentendre, Visegrád and Esztergom.

A ferry service takes cars across Lake Balaton from Szántód to Tihany. There are crossings every 10 minutes from June to September and every hour during the low season. Regular bus and train services link the towns and villages along the lakeside.

**AGGTELEK** *A3* (500m NW Rural) *48.47094, 20.49446*
Baradla Camping, Baradla Oldal 1, 3759 Aggtelek [tel/fax
(48) 503000; szallas@anp.hu] Fr Slovakia turn off E571/A50
at Plesivec onto rd 587 S via Dlha Ves to border x-ing. Cont S
for approx 800m & hotel/campsite complex is on L. Fr Miskolc
45km N on rte 26, turn onto rte 27 sp Perkupa then foll sp
Nemzeti National Park & Aggtelek. Site sp in vill. Med, pt sl,
pt shd; wc; shwrs; el pnts (16A) inc; rest, snacks, bar at motel;
BBQ; cooking facs; playgrnd; some statics; quiet. "Gd NH to/
fr Slovakia; ent to lge Barlang Caves system adj; facs poss
stretched high ssn." 15 Apr-15 Oct. HUF 4359          2010*

**ALSOORS see Balatonfüred** *C2*

**BALATONAKALI** *C1* (200m SE Rural) *46.8834, 17.76913*
Balatontourist Camping Strand-Holiday, Strand u 2,
8243 Balatonakali [(87) 544021; fax 544022; strand@
balatontourist.hu; www.balatontourist.hu] Site sp on rte
71 at km 53.6 at E end of Balatonakali. Lge, hdg/mkd pitch, pt
shd; wc; chem disp; mv service pnt; baby facs; private bthrms
avail; shwrs incl; el pnts (6-10A) inc; lndtte; shop high ssn;
rest & 500m; playgrnd; sand beach & lake sw; windsurfing;
watersports; fishing; cycle hire; games area; internet; entmnt;
TV rm; some statics; dogs HUF900; adv bkg; daytime rlwy
noise; ccard acc. "Excel san facs; some lakeside pitches;
cycle track around lake adj." ✦ 2 Apr-10 Oct. HUF 8250
(CChq acc)                                           2010*

**BALATONAKALI** *C1* (300m SW Rural) *46.87939, 17.74190*
Balatontourist Camping Levendula (Naturist), Hókuli u 25,
8243 Balatonakali [(87) 544011; fax 544012; levendula@
balatontourist.hu; www.balatontourist.hu] NE on rte 71
on N shore of Lake Balaton twds Tihany. Site sp on W app to
Balatonakali. Turn R twds lake; go over level x-ing, site ent
on R. Med, mkd pitch, pt shd; wc; chem disp; mv service pnt;
sauna; shwrs incl; el pnts (4A) inc; gas; lndtte (inc dryer); shop;
supmkt 1km; rest, snacks; bar; playgrnd; sand beach & lake sw;
fishing; windsurf school; games area; cycle hire; wifi; TV rm;
dogs HUF950; adv bkg; Eng spkn; quiet at night, train noise
fr early morning; ccard acc; CKE/CCI. "Superb site." ✦ 7 May-
12 Sep. HUF 6800 (CChq acc)                          2010*

**BALATONALMADI** *C2* (1km SW Rural) *47.0205, 18.00828*
Balatontourist Camping Yacht, Véghely Dezső út 18,
8220 Balatonalmádi [(88) 584101; fax 584102; yacht@
balatontourist.hu; www.balatontourist.hu] Fr rd 71, km
post 25.5, site sp at lakeside. Lge, hdg/mkd pitch, pt shd;
wc; chem disp; mv service pnt; shwrs incl; el pnts (4A) inc
(rev pol); lndtte; shop; rest, snacks; bar; playgrnd; beach adj;
watersports; cycle hire; entmnt; TV; 10% statics; dogs HUF990;
Eng spkn; adv bkg; ccard acc; CKE/CCI. "Excel san facs; excel
rest; several sites in close proximity; great site with friendly
owners." ✦ 1 May-15 Sep. HUF 9980          2013*

**BALATONBERENY** *C1* (500m W Rural) *46.71340, 17.31080*
FKK Naturista Camping (Naturist), Hetvezer u.2, 8649
Balatonberény [(85) 377299; fax 377715; bereny@
balatontourist.hu] Fr Keszthely foll rte 71 & rte 76 round SW
end of lake. Lge sp indicates Balatonberény & site. Sps change
fr Naturista Camping to FKK at turn off main rd. Med, hdg/
mkd pitch, pt shd; wc; chem disp; shwrs inc; el pnts (12-16A)
inc; lndtte; shop; tradsmn; rest, snacks; bar; BBQ; direct access
lake sw adj; playgrnd; windsurfing; watersports; games area;
wifi; entmnt; TV; few statics; dogs €2.60; phone; quiet; poss
cr; adv bkg; red INF. "vg site; gd sized pitches; excel san facs."
15 May-15 Sep. HUF 8695          2013*

⊞ **BALATONFURED** *C2* (9km NE Rural) *46.99722,
17.98944* Présház Camping, Présház út 1, 8226 Alsóörs
[(87) 447736] Rd 71 fr Balatonfüred, site just past vill of
Alsóörs on L. Sm, pt sl, pt shd; wc; chem disp; shwrs inc; el
pnts (10A) inc; lake sw 1km; games area; dogs; quiet. "Vg CL-
type site in orchard of wine shop; friendly owner; wine-tasting;
paid in Euros but Forint preferred; sighting of wild boar nrby!"
HUF 4359          2011*

**BALATONFURED** *C2* (1km SW Rural) *46.94660, 17.87590*
Balatontourist Camping Füred, Széchenyi út 24,
8230 Balatonfüred [(87) 580241; fax 580242; fured@
balatontourist.hu; www.balatontourist.hu] Exit M3 or rte
70 on rte 71 sp Balatonfüred. Site sp 1km SW of Balatonfüred
on SE side of rd 71 on N side of lake. V lge, pt shd; htd wc;
chem disp; mv service pnt; baby facs; sauna; shwrs incl; el pnts
(4A) inc; lndtte (inc dryer); shop; rest, snacks; bar; playgrnd;
pool; paddling pool; waterslides; beach & lake sw; watersports;
tennis; cycle hire; wifi; entmnt; TV rm; 10% statics; no dogs;
phone; bus; poss cr; adv bkg; quiet except nr rd; ccard acc; red
low ssn. "Many attractions in this holiday area; lovely lakeside
town; gd facs, but ltd low ssn; prices vary depending on pitch
size; excel." ✦ 22 Apr-2 Oct. HUF 8700 (CChq acc)          2011*

**BALATONKENESE** *C2* (W Rural) Romantik Camping,
Gesztenye Fasor 1, 8174 Balatonkenese [tel/fax
(88) 482360; romantikcamping@invitel.hu] Off rte 71 on
N shore of lake, sp. Med, pt terr, pt shd; wc; shwrs; el pnts
HUF400; lndry rm; shop; snacks; cooking facs; 250m to lake;
quiet. "Reasonable facs; site has potential." Jun-Sep.          2009*

**BALATONSZEPEZD** *C1* (2km NE Rural) *46.8610, 17.67335*
Balatontourist Camping Venus, Halász út 1, 8252
Balatonszepezd [(87) 568061; fax 568062; venus@
balatontourist.hu; www.balatontourist.hu] On rte 71;
site sp at km post 61, over level x-ing into site. Med, pt shd;
wc; chem disp; mv service pnt; shwrs inc; el pnts (4-10A) inc;
lndtte; shop; rest, snacks; playgrnd; beach; watersports; fishing;
games area; dogs HUF750; Eng spkn; noise fr rlwy; ccard acc.
"Excel lakeside position; gd rest; gd value." ✦ 14 May-5 Sep.
HUF 5400          2010*

BALATONSZEPEZD *C1* (4km SW Rural) *46.49771, 17.38404* Balatontourist Camping Napfény, Halász út 5, 8253 Révfülöp [(87) 563031 or (88) 544444 (LS); fax 464309 or (88) 544455 (LS); napfenyj@balatontourist.hu; www. balatontourist.hu] Take m'way E71/M7 & exit junc 90 along N shore of lake, passing Balatonalmádi & Balatonfüred to Révfülöp. Site sp. Lge, mkd pitch, pt shd; wc; chem disp; mv service pnt; baby facs; private san facs avail; shwrs inc; el pnts (6A) inc; lndtte (inc dryer); shop; supmkt 500m; tradsmn; rest, snacks; bar; BBQ; playgrnd; paddling pool; lake sw & beach adj; fishing; watersports; cycle & boat hire; tennis 300m; horseriding 5km; games area; games rm; wifi; entmnt; TV rm; 2% statics; dogs HUF900; twin-axles acc (rec check in adv); phone; adv bkg; quiet; ccard acc; red low ssn. "Warm welcome; excel, well-organised lakeside site; gd pitches; gd for families; fees according to pitch size & location." ♦ 25 Apr-27 Sep.  HUF 9449 (CChq acc) SBS - X06  2012*

BOLDOGASSZONYFA *D2* (1km S Rural) Camping Horgásztanya, Petöfi  út 53, 7937 Boldogasszonyfa [(73) 702003; csukabeno@ciromail.hu; www. horgasztanya.hu] Take rte 67 S fr Kaposvár. Immed after vill of Boldogasszonyfa turn L, site sp on rvside. Sm, hdg pitch, pt sl, shd; wc; chem disp (wc); shwrs inc; el pnts (10A); rest; bar; fishing; quiet;CKE/CCI. "Simple, rural site; conv Pécs & border area; rec use own facs." ♦ ltd 1 May-30 Sep.  2012*

**BOZSOK see Köszeg** *B1*

⊞ BUDAPEST *B2* (10km N Urban) *47.57434, 19.05179* Római Camping, Szentendrei útca 189, 1031 Budapest [(1) 3887167; fax 2500426; info@romaicamping.hu; www. romaicamping.hu] Fr Gyor/Budapest m'way M1/E50 foll rte 11 twd Szentendre/Esztergom for approx 9km. Turn R at site sp. Site adj Római Fürdő rlwy stn. Med, mkd pitch, shd; wc; chem disp; shwrs inc; el pnts (16A) HUF600; lndtte (inc dryer); shop 500m; rest, snacks; BBQ; playgrnd; htd pool; playgrnd; waterslide; TV; dogs HUG590; train 300m; phone; Eng spkn; poss noisy; ccard not acc; CKE/CCI. "V conv for city." HUF 10613  2013*

BUDAPEST *B2* (11km N Rural) *47.6013, 19.0191* Jumbo Camping, Budakalászi út 23, 2096 Üröm [tel/fax (26) 351251; jumbo@campingbudapest.com; www. jumbocamping.hu] Best app fr N on rd 10 or 11. Fr M1 take Zsámbék exit thro Perbál to join rd 10 & turn W twd Budapest. After Pilisvörösvar turn L in 8km sp Üröm Site well sp. Med, hdg pitch, hdstg, pt sl, terr, pt shd; wc; chem disp; shwrs inc; el pnts (6-10A) inc; lndtte; shop 500m; rest 300m; snacks; bar; playgrnd; htd pool high ssn; TV; 10% statics; dogs; bus to Budapest fr vill; Eng spkn; adv bkg; quiet. "Highly rec; v helpful owners; clean, modern facs; immac, family-run site." 1 Apr-31 Oct.  HUF 12453  2012*

⊞ BUDAPEST *B2* (8km E Urban) Camping Arena, Pilisi Str 7, 1106 Budapest [06 30 29 691 29; info@budapestcamping. hu; www.budapestcamping.hu] Leave M0 at exit 60 Kistarcsa & foll Rd 3 twd city centre for 7.5km. Turn L just bef rlwy bdge. Site 200m on R. Sm, hdg pitch, pt shd; wc; chem disp; mv service pnt; shwrs; el pnts (16A); lndtte (inc dryer); cooking facs; wifi; 10% statics; dogs; bus 400m; metro 1km; Eng spkn; adv bkg; CCI. "Some rlwy & aircraft noise; supermkt 400m; shopping arcade 1km; rec all day travel card for metro, trams & busses; vg." ♦ ltd HUF 5800  2014*

BUDAPEST *B2* (3.5km SE Urban) *47.47583, 19.08305* Haller Camping, 27 Haller útca, 1096 Budapest [(20) 3674274; info@hallercamping.hu; www.hallercamping.hu] Fr S on M5 twd Budapest cent. At ring rd foll dir Lagnymanyosi Hid (bdge). Bef bdge by lge shopping cent (Lurdy-Ház) turn R. Site sp. Or fr SE on rd 4 sp airport/Cegléd, turn R 100m bef new church steeple on L, foll sp Haller Piac. Med, hdstg, pt shd; wc; chem disp; mv service pnt; shwrs inc; el pnts (16A) inc; lndtte; lge shoping cent 500m; rest adj; snacks; BBQ; wifi; no statics; dogs free; phone; tram & bus 100m; poss cr; Eng spkn; adv bkg; quiet; red long stay/CKE/CCI. "V friendly; vg security; gd, clean san facs; tram stop opp site; conv for city cent; v helpful staff." ♦ ltd 10 May-30 Sep.  HUF 8985  2013*

⊞ BUDAPEST *B2* (5km NW Urban) *47.51645, 18.9741* Zugligeti Niche Camping, Zugligeti út 101, 1121 Budapest [tel/fax (1) 2008346; camping.niche@t-online.hu; www. campingniche.hu] Fr W approx 12km bef Budapest exit M1/E60/E75 N'wards sp Budakesi. Foll sp Budakeszi & Budapest - bumpy, rough rd. Clear sp for Zugligeti. Or fr W on M1 foll sp Budapest cent & Moszkva Tér. Keep to NW side of Moszkva, site clearly sp. Site nr new Tesco. Sm, terr, pt sl, shd; wc; chem disp; mv service pnt; shwrs inc; el pnts (6A) HUF1200; gas adj; lndtte; shop 700m; rest, snacks; bar; playgrnd; pool 3km; wifi; dogs HUF600; bus to city; Eng spkn; adv bkg; red long stay/ CKE/CCI. "Site converted former tram terminus; gd, modern san facs; ltd facs low ssn; gd security; friendly, helpful owners; buffet breakfast inc in price; pitches for twin-axles (rec check in adv)." ♦ HUF 7390  2011*

> **"I need an on-site restaurant"**
>
> We do our best to make sure site information is correct, but it is always best to check any must-have facilities are still available or will be open during your visit.

BUDAPEST *B2* (12km NW Urban) *47.60451, 19.06931* Mini Camping, Királyok út 307, 1039 Budapest [(6) 302003752] N fr Budapest on rte 11 dir Szentendre, 3.5km past Roman ruins turn R just after Shell stn. Cont E for 1km & turn N at 'give way' sp & site sp. Site in 1.3km (sp poss obscured by trees). Sm, mkd pitch, pt shd; wc; chem disp; shwrs inc; el pnts (10A) inc; lndry rm; shop 300m; rest adj; BBQ; playgrnd; pool 1km; dogs HUF400; boat, bus or tram to Budapest; poss cr; quiet; CKE/CCI. "Gd security; sh walk to Danube; 40 mins by public transport to city cent; helpful staff; quiet, pleasant oasis in scruffy area." 1 May-30 Sep.  HUF 5604  2011*

⊞ BUK *B1* (2.5km E Rural) *47.38433, 16.79051* Romantik Camping, Thermál Krt 12, 9740 Bükfürdö [(94) 558050; fax 558051; info@romantikcamping.com; www. romantikcamping.com] Fr Sopron on rte 84 twd Lake Balaton for approx 45km, foll sp & exit Bükfürdö. After service stn turn R then cont for 5km sp Thermalbad & site. Lge, pt shd; htd wc; chem disp; mv service pnt; shwrs inc; el pnts (10-16A) metered; lndtte; shop; rest; bar 100m; playgrnd; pool high ssn; thermal cent 500m; tennis 500m; cycle hire; entmnt; 10% statics; dogs €2; adv bkg; quiet; ccard acc; red long stay/CKE/CCI. ♦ HUF 5604  2009*

**CEGLED** *B3* (8km W Rural) *47.2009, 19.73553*
Thermalcamping Cegléd, Fürdo út 27-29, 2700 Cegléd
[tel/fax (53) 501177; camping@cegleditermal.hu; http://
cegleditermal.hu] On rd 4/E60 dir Budapest, foll sp thermal
pool & aquapark. Med, hdg/mkd pitch, pt shd; htd wc; chem
disp; mv service pnt; baby facs; serviced pitches; shwrs inc;
el pnts (6-10A) HUF750; lndtte; shop; tradsmn; rest, snacks
100m; cooking facs; playgrnd; htd, covrd pool & spa complex
adj; 30% statics; dogs HUF1000; phone; bus; quiet; ccard acc;
red CKE/CCI. "Highly rec, clean site; superb thermal facs - open
late at night." ♦ 15 Apr-15 Oct. HUF 3400          2010*

**CELLDOMOLK** *B1* (6km W Rural) *47.21466, 17.10043* Vulkán
Resort, Szabadság út 023/2, 9553 Kemeneskápolna
[(95) 446070; fax 446056; info@vulkanresort.com; www.
vulkanresort.com] S fr Sárvár on rd 84, turn L dir Gérce
& Kemeneskápolna, site sp. Sm, mkd pitch, pt shd; htd wc;
chem disp; mv service pnt; sauna; shwrs inc; el pnts (10A)
€3.50; lndtte (inc dryer); supmkt 6km; tradsmn; rest 2km will
deliver; snacks; bar; BBQ; cooking facs; playgrnd; 2 pools (1
htd, covrd); wellness cent; cycle hire; horseriding; wifi; cab TV;
some statics; dogs free; adv bkg; quiet; red CKE/CCI. "Pleasant,
welcoming, peaceful; site in lovely surroundings; gd cycling in
area; a feng-shui site!" ♦ 1 Mar-31 Oct. HUF 6227   2012*

## "Satellite navigation makes touring much easier"

Remember most sat navs don't know if you're towing or in a larger vehicle – always use yours alongside maps and site directions.

**CSERKESZOLO** *C3* (W Urban) *46.86386, 20.2019* Thermal
Camping Cserkeszölö, Beton út 5, 5465 Cserkeszölö
[(6) 56568450; fax 56568464; hotelcamping@cserkeszolo.
hu] On rte 44 bet Kecksemet & Kunszentmárton. Site sp in
Cserkeszölö. Lge, pt shd; htd wc; chem disp; mv service pnt;
sauna; shwrs inc; el pnts (10A) inc; lndtte; shop 200m; rest,
snacks; BBQ; cooking facs; 2 pools (1 htd, covrd); paddling
pool; waterslide; tennis; games area; 10% statics; dogs; phone;
bus 200m; poss cr; quiet; CKE/CCI. "Use of sw pools & thermal
pools inc in site fee; gd." HUF 6226          2011*

**DOMOS** *B2* (500m E Rural) *47.7661, 18.91495* Dömös
Camping, Dömös Dunapart, 2027 Dömös [(33) 482319; fax
414800; info@domoscamping.hu; www.domoscamping.
hu] On rd 11 fr Budapest, site on R on ent Dömös, adj Rv
Danube. Med, hdg pitch, pt shd; wc; chem disp; shwrs inc;
el pnts (10A) HUF950; lndtte (inc dryer); rest, snacks; bar;
cooking facs; playgrnd; pool; paddling pool; wifi; TV rm; dogs
HUF500; phone; bus to Budapest; poss cr; Eng spkn; adv bkg;
some rd & rlwy noise; red long stay/CKE/CCI. "Delightful site
with views Danube bend; spacious pitches - lower ones poss
subject to flooding; excel, clean facs & rest." ♦ 1 May-15 Sep.
HUF 4200          2011*

**DUNAFOLDVAR** *C2* (500m NE Rural) *46.81227, 18.92664*
Kék-Duna Camping, Hösök Tere 23, 7020 Dunafoldvár
[tel/fax (75) 541107; ddifzrt@freemail.hu] Fr rndabt S of
Dunafoldvár turn twd town cent. At traff lts turn R down to
rv, then turn L, under green bdge & foll towpath 300m to site.
Sm, shd; wc; shwrs inc; el pnts (16A) inc; lndtte; shop high
ssn & 500m; rest; BBQ; 2 pools adj (1 covrd); paddling pool;
watersports; fishing; tennis; cycle hire; adv bkg; quiet; 10%
red CKE/CCI. "Pleasant position o'looking Danube; adequate,
clean san facs but dated; gd touring base Transdanubia."
HUF 4100          2010*

**EGER** *B3* (9km N Rural) *47.98935, 20.32951* Öko-Park Panzió
Kemping, Borsod út 9, 3323 Eger-Szarvaskö [tel/fax
(36) 352201; info@oko-park.hu; www.oko-park.hu] Fr Eger
N on rd 25. On app voll 500m fr will name sp, turn R (sp parking)
into car park. Cross sm wooden bdge at back of sq. Sm, hdg/
mkd pitch, pt shd; htd wc; chem disp; baby facs; shwrs inc;
el pnts (16A) inc; lndtte; shop adj, rest, snacks; bar; playgrnd;
wifi; TV; 5% statics; dogs; phone; bus; Eng spkn; adv bkg; rd &
rlwy noise; ccard acc. "Well-laid out; well-managed site; clean
facs; lge o'fits stop in car park & walk in; friendly owner; vg."
♦ 15 Mar-15 Nov. HUF 5600          2010*

**EGER** *B3* (1km SW Urban) *47.89396, 20.36992* Tulipán
Camping, Szépasszonyvölgy 71, 3300 Eger [tel/
fax (36) 311542; info@tulipancamping.com; www.
tulipancamping.com] Enter Eger fr S on rte 25 & foll sp to
site. Med, mkd pitch, pt shd; wc; chem disp; shwrs inc; el pnts
(10A) HUF700; shop 500m; rest; bar; snacks; htd pool; phone;
dogs HUF400; poss cr; Eng spkn; adv bkg. "Clean, modern
san facs; sm pitches; sh walk to local wine cellars; v interesting
town; painting of Council of Trent on library ceiling is a must;
waterlogged after heavy rain; pleasant site." 15 Mar-15 Oct.
HUF 2980          2010*

**ERD** *B2* (2km N Urban) *47.39388, 18.93638* Flamingo
Camping, Fürdö út 4, 2030 Érd [(23) 375328;
flamingocamp@t-online.hu] Fr Vienna on M1, then M0,
exit at Diósd/Érd & foll sp to site on rd 70. Med, pt shd; htd
wc; chem disp; shwrs inc; el pnts (6A) HUF1000; lndtte; shop
200m; rest, snacks; bar; cooking facs; pool high ssn; tennis; TV
rm; few statics; dogs HUF1000; bus 50m; rlwy stn 1km; quiet;
red long stay/CKE/CCI. "Conv Budapest (12km)." 1 Apr-1 Nov.
HUF 5000          2010*

**ESZTERGOM** *B2* (1km W Urban) *47.7910, 18.73165*
Gran Camping, Nagy-Duna Sétány 3, 2501 Esztergom
[(33) 402513; fax 411953; fortanex@t-online.hu; www.
grancamping-fortanex.hu] Fr rte 11 site well sp into town.
Fr cent turn twds Danube along street to old bdge, foll sp
to site on rv bank. Med, mkd pitch, pt shd; wc; chem disp;
shwrs inc; el pnts (20A) HUF400; shop high ssn; tradsmn; rest,
snacks; bar; BBQ; playgrnd; htd pool; rv cruises; tennis; games
area; wifi; 5% statics; dogs HUF500; bus; poss cr; Eng spkn;
quiet; red long stay/CKE/CCI. "Basilica worth a visit; poss youth
groups; gd clean facs." 1 May-30 Sep. HUF 4200   2011*

FERTOD *B1* (5km W Urban) *47.62116, 16.78513* Termál Camping, Fürdö út 1, 9437 Hegykö [tel/fax (99) 376818; termalkemping@freemail.hu; www.termalkemping. hu] Fr Sopron on rd 85 turn N at km 60.2 to Hegykö, site in 4.5km on S side of main rd, sp. Sm, pt shd; wc; chem disp; shwrs inc; el pnts (6A) HUF600; lndtte; shop, rest, snacks 500m; htd, covrd pool 500m; no statics; dogs free; poss cr; ccard acc; CKE/CCI. "Economical NH; excel spa complex adj; Lake Fertöd & Esterházy Palace worth visit." 15 Apr-15 Oct. HUF 2700                                                           2009*

FONYOD *C1* (3km SW Rural) *46.73312, 17.53198* Napsugár Camping, Wekerle út 5, 8644 Fonyód-Bétatelep [(85) 361211; fax 361024; napsugar@balatontourist.hu; www.balatontourist.hu] On NW side of rte 7/E71 on S side of Lake Balaton, sp. V lge, hdg pitch, shd; wc; chem disp; shwrs inc; el pnts (16A) inc; lndtte; shop & 1km; rest, snacks adj; playgrnd; rocky beach adj; 5% statics; dogs; rd & rlwy noise; ccard acc. 1 May-15 Sep.  HUF 5604                      2010*

**GYENESDIAS see Keszthely** *C1*

⊞ **GYULA** *C4* (2km N Urban) *46.64538, 21.29851* Thermál Camping & Motel, Szlésö út 16, 5700 Gyula [(66) 463704; fax 463551; gyulacamping@t-online.hu; www. gyulacamping.hu] Site sp on every app rd to Gyula. Med, some hdstg, shd; wc; chem disp; shwrs inc; el pnts (16A) inc (poss no earth); shop & 500m; lndtte; shop 500m; rest 200m; snacks; cooking facs; thermal baths 1.5km; tennis; dogs HUF500; adv bkg; quiet; CKE/CCI. "Site 5km fr Romanian border."  HUF 4100                                               2010*

⊞ **HAJDUSZOBOSZLO** *B4* (1km E Urban) *47.45756, 21.39396* Thermál Camping, Böszörményi út 35A, 4200 Hajdúszoboszló [tel/fax (52) 558552; thermalcamping@ hungarospa-rt.hu; www.hungarospa.hu] Fr W on rte 4/ E573 thro town, site sp on L. Fr Debrecen, turn R 500m past Camping Hadjdútourist on lakeside. Lge, hdg pitch, pt shd; wc; chem disp; mv service pnt; shwrs inc; el pnts (12A) inc; gas 1km; lndtte; shop, rest high ssn; snacks; BBQ; cooking facs; playgrnd; htd, covrd pool & thermal baths adj; paddling pool; waterslide; TV rm; dogs HUF440; phone; poss cr; Eng spkn; no adv bkg; quiet; ccard acc; red CKE/CCI. "Pleasant site; sm naturist island in lake." HUF 6435                           2010*

**HEGYKO see Fertöd** *B1*

**HEVIZ see Keszthely** *C1*

JASZAPATI *B3* (500m S Urban) *47.50537, 20.14012* Tölgyes Strand Camping, Gyöngyvirág u 11, 5130 Jászapáti [(57) 441187; fax 441008; info@tolgyesstrand.hu; www. tolgyesstrand.hu] Fr Budapest E on M3, exit at Hatvan & take rd 32 to Jászberény then foll rd 31 to Jászapáti. Site sp fr town cent. Med, mkd pitch, pt shd; wc; chem disp; mv service pnt; shwrs; el pnts (10A); lndtte (inc dryer); rest, snacks; bar; playgrnd; 2 pools (1 htd, covrd); tennis 200m; games area; cycle hire; internet; TV rm; some statics; dogs; site clsd 1 Nov to mid-Dec; adv bkg; quiet. "Gd, modern facs." 1 Apr-30 Nov.                                                    2009*

**KEMENESKÁPOLNA see Celldomolk** *B1*

⊞ **KESZTHELY** *C1* (14km N Rural) *46.89442, 17.23166* Camping St Vendal, Fö út Hrsz 192/3, 8353 Zalaszántó [tel/fax (83) 370147; camping.stvendel@freemail.hu; www.szallas.net/st.vendel-camping] Fr N on rd 84 turn dir Bazsi/Hévíz at Sümeg. Site at ent to town. Fr S take Sümeg Hévíz off rd 71 bef Keszthely & foll sp Sümeg & Zalaszántó. Sm, pt shd; htd wc; chem disp; shwrs inc; el pnts (6A) HUF540 long lead poss req'd; lndtte; rest, snacks; bar; BBQ; cooking facs; internet; TV rm; dogs HUF250; quiet; CKE/CCI. "Friendly welcome; gd walking/cycling; conv for thermal lake at Heviz & Lake Balaton but without crowds, noise of lakeside sites; delightful site in orchard - awkward for lge o'fits; spotless facs; lovely peaceful site." HUF 9293                        2013*

KESZTHELY *C1* (1km E Rural) *46.76797, 17.25936* Camping Castrum Keszthely, Móra Ferenc u 48, 8360 Keszthely [(83) 312120; fax 314422; keszthely@castrum.eu; www. castrum-group.hu] Clearly sp W fr Budapest. Fr all other dir take rd 71 out of town; 300m past church turn twd Lake Balaton. Lge, hdg pitch, pt shd; wc; chem disp; shwrs inc; el pnts (6-15A) HUF900; shop & 200m; lndtte; rest, snacks; playgrnd; pool; paddling pool; lake & watersports 300m; tennis; TV; dogs HUF900; phone; poss cr; adv bkg; some rlwy noise. "Attractively laid-out with excel facs; rlwy runs close to site; friendly staff; Festetics Palace & gardens worth visit." ◆ 1 Apr-31 Oct.  HUF 5200 (CChq acc)                   2010*

KESZTHELY *C1* (7km NW Rural) *46.78393, 17.19575* Kurcamping Castrum, Tópart, 8380 Hévíz [(83) 343198; fax 540263; heviz@castrum.eu; www.castrum-group. hu] Fr Keszthely foll sp to Hévíz & site 700m to E, opp Hévíz thermal lake. Lge, mkd pitch, pt shd; htd wc; chem disp; mv service pnt; 20% serviced pitches; shwrs inc; el pnts (6-16A) €3; lndtte; shop; tradsmn; rest; bar; htd pool adj; lake sw adj; sat TV; dogs €4; poss cr; Eng spkn; adv bkg; quiet; CKE/CCI. "Lake fed by hot springs so gd for sw; casino adj; easy cycle ride/walk into lovely spa town & cycle path to Keszthely; excel san facs; excursions Budapest fr gate; v nice site; gd location to explore by foot or bike." 1 Mar-31 Dec. HUF 3113      2013*

⊞ **KOSZEG** *B1* (500m N Urban) *47.39336, 16.54291* Gyöngyvirág Camping, Bajcsy-Zsilinszky út. 6, 9730 Köszeg [(94) 360454; fax 360574; info@ gyongyviragpanzio.hu; www.gyongyviragpanzio.hu] Foll sp in town cent to site adj hotel. Sm, pt shd; htd wc (cont); shwrs inc; el pnts (10A) HUF400; shop 200m; BBQ; playgrnd; quiet; no ccard acc; red low stay. "Superb, welcoming, orchard site; clean, modern facs; site diff in wet weather; access diff lge o'fits; nature reserve adj town; gd walking; sh walk to one of prettiest towns in Hungary." HUF 3300                    2010*

MATRAFURED *B3* (2km N Rural) *47.84416, 19.95725* Mátra Camping Sástó, Farkas út 4, 3232 Mátrafüred [tel/fax (37) 374025; info@matrakemping.hu; www. matrakemping.hu] Take rte 24 N fr Gyöngyös. Site on L 2km after Mátrafüred. Med, some hdstg, pt sl, pt shd; wc; shwrs inc; el pnts (10A) inc; shop, rest, snacks, bar adj; cooking facs; TV; some statics; dogs HUF500; phone adj; poss cr; ccard acc. "Site pt of controlled sports complex; vg secure site." 15 Apr-10 Oct.  HUF 3500                                  2010*

**MEZOKOVESD** *B3* (3km W Rural) *47.7969, 20.5291*
Autóscamping Zsóry, Zsóry-fürdö, 3400 Mezökövesd
[tel/fax (49) 411436; zsoryamping@freemail.hu; www.
zsory-camping.lhcom.hu] Fr W leave M3/E71 at exit Eger/
Füzesabony for 3km N twd Eger. Turn E onto rd 3 sp Miskolc,
site on L in 8km. Lge, hdg pitch, pt shd; wc; chem disp; mv
service pnt; baby facs; shwrs inc; el pnts (16A) HUF550; lndtte;
shop 500m; tradsmn; rest, snacks; bar; cooking facs; playgrnd;
htd, covrd thermal pool 500m; some statics; dogs HUF330;
phone; Eng spkn; quiet; ccard acc; redCKE/CCI. "Thermal
baths adj; helpful staff; nr National Park." 1 May-30 Sep.
HUF 3200                                                2011*

**MISKOLC** *A3* (10km W Rural) *48.09623, 20.62128* Camping
Lillafüred, Erzsébet Sétány 39, 3517 Miskolc-Lillafüred
[(46) 333146; kovatt@lillacamp.hu; http://kovatt.lillacamp.
hu] Fr Miskolc take rd to Lillafüred. After passing under 2 low
bdges (max height 3.4m) site sp on L. Sm, hdg/mkd pitch, pt
shd; wc; own san; chem disp (wc); shwrs inc; el pnts (16A)
HUF500; shop in vill; rest in hotel nrby; cooking facs; dogs;
phone; bus 1km; adv bkg; quiet. "Basic site; gd mkd walks;
friendly owner; not suitable lge o'fits; 1km to narr gauge rlwy;
NH." ♦ ltd 1 May-30 Sep.  HUF 3700              2009*

**MOSONMAGYAROVAR** *B1* (1km E Urban) **Termál Aqua**
**Camping**, Kigyó út 1, 9200 Mosonmagyaróvár [tel/fax
(96) 579168; aquahotel@t-online.hu; www.tha.hu] Foll sp
fr town cent to Termál Hotel Aqua; site in grnds, just behind
lge thermal baths. Sm, hdg/mkd pitch, shd; htd wc; chem
disp; mv service pnt; shwrs inc; el pnts €3; lndtte; shop 1km;
rest, snacks; bar; BBQ; cooking facs; htd, covrd thermal & sw
pool adj; dogs €2; bus, train 1km; phone; Eng spkn; quiet.
"Vg site; price inc ent to thermals & sauna." 1 Apr-30 Oct.
HUF 9028                                                2009*

⊞ **MOSONMAGYAROVAR** *B1* (2km SE Urban) *47.84224,*
*17.28591* Camping Kis-Duna, Gabonarakpart 6, 9200
Mosonmagyaróvár [tel/fax (96) 216433; www.hotels.hu/
kis_duna] Site on L of M1 Mosonmagyaróvár-Györ in grnds
of motel & rest, 15km fr border. Sm, some hdstg, unshd; wc;
chem disp; shwrs inc; el pnts (16A) HUF500; lndtte; shop 1km;
rest; thermal pool 2.5km; TV; dogs HUF500. "Gd, clean, facs;
rest gd but busy; gd alt to Bratislava site (Slovakia); ideal NH."
HUF 3150                                                2011*

**NESZMELY** *B2* (3km E Rural) *47.74421, 18.40258* Éden
Camping, Dunapart, 2544 Neszmély [(33) 474183; fax
474327; eden@mail.holop.hu; www.edencamping.com]
Site sp on rte 10 bet Neszmély & Süttö, on rvside. Lge, hdg
pitch, pt shd; htd wc; chem disp; mv service pnt; baby facs;
shwrs inc; el pnts (6-10A) HUF600; lndtte (inc dryer); shop;
tradsmn; rest, snacks; bar; playgrnd; pool high ssn; rv sw adj;
canoeing; watersports; boat & cycle hire; tennis 3km; games
area; entmnt; excursions; 10% statics; dogs HUF470; phone;
bus 500m; Eng spkn; adv bkg; some rd/rlwy noise; ccard acc;
red CKE/CCI. "V pleasant, tranquil site in gd location; helpful
staff." ♦ 1 Apr-31 Oct. HUF 4310                     2010*

**ORFU** *D2* (1km NW Rural) *46.14638, 18.13750* **Panoráma**
**Camping**, Dollar út 1, 7677 Orfü [tel/fax (72) 378434;
campingorfu@freemail.hu; www.panoramacamping.hu]
Rte 66 fr Pécs dir Kaposvár. In Magyarszék take rd to Orfü &
at lake turn R & foll rd down W side of lake. Site shortly bef
end of lake. Lge, mkd pitch, terr, pt shd; wc; chem disp; shwrs
inc; el pnts (6A) HUF700; lndtte; shop; snacks; playgrnd; pool,
tennis, watersports 1km; lake sw 500m; tennis; cycle hire;
games area; TV; some statics; phone; quiet on higher terr;
ccard acc; 10% red CKE/CCI. "Lovely situation; twin-axles on
lower terr only; site badly in need of refurb; gd base for Pécs."
1 May-30 Sep.  HUF 3900                              2010*

**OZD** *A3* (12km E Rural) *48.21281, 20.40603* Camping
Amedi, Rákóczi út 181, 3658 Borsodbóta [tel/
fax (48) 438468; info@campingamedi.hu; www.
campingamedi.hu] Fr Budapest N on M3/E71, exit at Hatvan
N onto rd 21. At Kisterenye turn R onto rd 23 dir Ózd. In Ózd
foll sp Borsodbóta for 12km to site. Sm, mkd pitch, pt shd;
wc; shwrs inc; el pnts (10A) €3.75; lndtte; supmkt 500m; rest
6km;bar; BBQ; cooking facs; pool; cycle hire; games area;
entmnt; some statics; dogs €2; adv bkg; quiet. "Peaceful,
Dutch-owned site." 15 Apr-15 Oct.  HUF 5448        2010*

**PANNONHALMA** *B2* (500m E Urban) *47.54916, 17.75777*
Panoráma Camping, Fenyvesalja 4/A, 9090 Pannonhalma
[(96) 471240; fax 470561; akosprikkel@axelero.hu] Fr Györ
take rte 82 twd Veszprém. After approx 20km turn L on sm
loop rd to vill of Pannonhalma. Site at top of v steep slope,
low gear needed. Med, hdg pitch, terr, pt shd; htd wc; chem
disp (wc); shwrs inc; el pnts (10A) HUF800; lndry rm; shop
300m; rest in vill; snacks; TV rm; dogs HUF450; adv bkg; quiet;
red CKE/CCI. "Panoramic views; v helpful owners; clean facs;
levelling blocks req; conv for visit to basilica; diff app but site
worth it!" 1 May-15 Sep.  HUF 3500                  2009*

⊞ **PAPA** *B1* (1km NE Urban) *47.33797, 17.47367*
Termál Camping Pápa, Várkert út 7, 8500 Pápa [tel/
fax 36 89 320 735; info@thermalkemping.hu; www.
thermalkemping.hu] Fr 83 exit at Gyori Way. Foll sp. Lge, hdg
pitch, mkd pitch, hdstg, pt shd; htd wc; chem disp; mv service
pnt; baby facs; shwrs; el pnts (16A); gas; lndtte rm (inc dryer);
shop 1km; tradsmn; rest; snacks; bar; BBQ; cooking facs;
playgrnd; htd pool adj; paddling pool; sw thermal adj; games
area; games rm; entmnt; wifi; 20% statics; dogs €2; phone;
bus 500m; twin axles; Eng spkn; quiet; adv bkg; red low ssn;
CCI. "Onsite kids club; boccia; basketball; archery; disco adj;
thermal baths with indoor & outdoor pools, slides; excel; well
managed site; gd area for long stay & touring; very helpful
staff." ♦  HUF 8804                                    2014*

⊞ **PECS** *D2* (1.5km E Urban) *46.08601, 18.26319* Familia
Privat Camping, Gyöngyösi Istvan út 6, 7627 Pécs
[(72) 327034] On rte 6 fr Budapest (N side) well sp fr city
o'skts. Tight ent for lge o'fits. Sm, pt sl, terr, hdstg, pt shd;
htd wc; chem disp; shwrs inc; el pnts (10A) inc (long lead req);
lndtte; shop 800m; adv bkg; quiet. "V congested site; arr early
to ensure pitch; OK NH." HUF 4200                   2010*

**REVFULOP see Balatonszepezd** *C1*

**SAROSPATAK** *A4 (2km NE Rural) 48.33274, 21.58245*
Tengerszem Camping, Herceg Ferenc ut 2, 3950
Sárospatak [(47) 312744; fax 323527; info@tengerszem-camping.hu; www.tengerszem-camping.hu] NW fr Tokaj
on R38; then NE on R37 to Sárospatak; foll camp sp.
Med, hdg pitch, pt shd; wc; mv service pnt; shwrs; el pnts (10A) inc; shop; rest, snacks; playgrnd; pool; tennis; games area; TV; rlwy noise; CKE/CCI. "Refurbished thermal sw baths next door; gd site for mountains." 15 Apr-15 Oct. HUF 4000        2010*

⊞ **SARVAR** *B1 (1km SE Urban) 47.24671, 16.9473* Sárvár
Thermal Camping, Vadkert út 1, 9600 Sárvár [(95) 320292; fax 523612; info@thermalcamping.com; www.thermalcamping.com] E fr Szombathely via rtes 86 & 88. Site on Sopron-Lake Balaton rte 84. Med, some hdstg, pt shd; htd wc; mv service pnt; sauna; baby facs; private san facs avail; shwrs; el pnts (16A) €3; lndtte; shop; tradsmn; rest, snacks adj; BBQ; cooking facs; playgrnd; htd thermal pools adj; paddling pool; waterslide; lake fishing; tennis 500m; wifi; some statics; dogs €2; poss cr; 10% statics; ccard acc; quiet; red long stay; CKE/CCI. "Barrier clsd 1330-1500; free ent to spa & fitness cent adj." ♦ HUF 10274 (CChq acc)        2010*

**SIOFOK** *C2 (5km NE Urban) 46.92838, 18.10245*
Balatontourist Camping Aranypart, Szent László út 183-185, 8604 Siófok [(84) 353399; fax 352801; aranypart@balatontourist.hu; www.balatontourist.hu] Fr Budapest on M7 take exit Siófok onto rd 70. Site sp at Balatonszabadi rlwy stn. V lge, hdg pitch, pt shd; wc; chem disp; mv service pnt; shwrs inc; el pnts (10A) inc; lndtte; shop; rest, snacks; bar; BBQ; cooking facs; playgrnd; lake sw, fishing adj; waterslide; cycle hire; tennis 500m; games area; wifi; entmnt; TV rm; 15% statics; dogs HUF950; phone; poss cr; Eng spkn; adv bkg; quiet; CKE/CCI. "Price varies according to pitch size; well-maintained, attractive site." ♦ 22 Apr-11 Sep. HUF 6700 (CChq acc)        2011*

⊞ **SOPRON** *B1 (7km SE Rural) 47.6525, 16.6575*
Kurcamping Castrum Balf-Sopron, Fürdö Sor 59-61, 9494 Balf [(99) 339124; fax (83) 314422; castrum.sopronbalf@rlan.hu; www.sopron-balf-castrum.hu] On rte 84 S of Sopron turn E sp Balf. In 2km turn N sp Sopron & foll sps. Site at W end Balf vill. Med, hdg/mkd pitch, pt shd; htd wc (cont); chem disp; sauna; shwrs inc; el pnts (6A) HUF800; lndtte (inc dryer); shops 350m; rest 250m; pool & 250m; cycle hire; TV; dogs €2.50; phone; Eng spkn; rd noise; ccard acc; CKE/CCI. "Thermal baths avail; Tesco hypmkt on app to Sopron 6km, with ATM; pitches uneven; ltd facs low ssn & poss unkempt; poss cold shwrs but new owners (2010) plan refurb; site in need of maintenance; overpriced NH." HUF 4730        2010*

**SZENTES** *C3 (1km W Urban) 46.65052, 20.24812* Thermál
Camping Szentes (Szentesi Üdülökozpont), Csallány Gáborpart 4, 6600 Szentes [tel/fax (63) 400123; udulohazak@udulokozpont-szentes.hu; www.udulokozpont-szentes.hu] Fr N fr Csongrád on rte 451, site on R at ent to town in park, int'l camping sp. Sm, pt shd; wc; chem disp (wc); shwrs inc; el pnts (16A) HUF1000; shop 1km; rest, snacks, bar in park; 4 htd pools; tennis; horseriding; dogs HUF600; phone; poss cr; Eng spkn; quiet; ccard acc; CKE/CCI. "Attractive park; thermal pools open to day visitors; helpful staff." ♦ 1 Apr-30 Sep. HUF 4300        2010*

**SZILVASVARAD** *A3 (500m S Rural) 48.09615, 20.38783*
Hegyi Camping, Egri út 36, 3348 Szilvásvárad [tel/fax (36) 355207; hegyi.camping@axelero.hu; www.hegyicamping.com] App fr Eger, site sp just bef vill. Turn R at petrol stn. Med, pt sl, pt shd; wc; chem disp; shwrs inc; el pnts (16A) inc; lndtte; shop 1km; rest; bar; cooking facs; internet; TV; 40% statics; phone; poss noisy; ccard acc; red CKE/CCI. "Lipizzaner horse stud farm nr; conv touring Bükk National Park; conv narr gauge rlwy into Szalajka Valley; gd rests within 10 mins walk; facs inadequate & tired; poss school parties on site; friendly staff." 1 May-15 Oct. HUF 4000        2010*

**SZOLNOK** *B3 (2km SE Urban)* Tiszaligeti Motel & Camping, Tiszaligeti Sétány 34, 5000 Tiszaligeti [tel/fax (56) 424403; tiszaligetimotel@gmail.com; www.tiszaligetimotel.hu] Leave rte 4 onto rd 442 sp Martfü, but foll sp 'Centrum' into Szolnok. Bef bdge look for sps to turn L & foll rd for 800m, site on L. Med, pt shd; wc; chem disp (wc); shwrs inc; el pnts HUF700; shop 2km; rest; BBQ; playgrnd; pool 300m; canoeing, tennis nr; cycle hire; some statics; dogs HUF1500; phone; bus; poss cr; quiet; CKE/CCI. "Pleasant location; vg, modern facs." 1 May-30 Sep. HUF 3200        2009*

**TAHITOTFALU** *B2 (500m E Rural) 47.75117, 19.08043* Duna
Camping, Kemping út 1, 2022 Tahitótfalu [(26) 385216; fax (33) 412294; juhaszjozsef@mailbox.hu] In cent Tahitótfalu at km 30.3 on rte 11 to Budapest, site sp. Med, shd; wc; chem disp; shwrs inc; el pnts (10A) inc; lndtte; shops adj; rest, snacks; bar; BBQ; playgrnd; boating; TV; 20% statics; dogs; poss noisy; ccard acc. "Beautiful situation on Danube bend; Szentendre worth visit; basic site; NH only." 15 Apr-15 Oct. HUF 4359        2009*

**TAKSONY** *B2 (6km S Rural) 47.28711, 19.09990* Camping Rukkel-tó Waterpark, Rukkel-tó 1, 2335 Taksony [(70) 3860852; rukkel@waterpark.hu; www.waterpark.hu] Exit M0/E71 onto rd 51 dir Taksony & Dunavarsány. Waterpark sp 6km S of Taksony dir Bugyi. Med, mkd pitch, pt shd; wc; shwrs; el pnts; lndtte; rest, snacks; bar; playgrnd; pools; waterslides; boat hire; no dogs; quiet. "Clean site adj waterpark; excel." 1 May-7 Sep. HUF 4800        2009*

**TAMASI** *C2 (1km S Urban) 46.62577, 18.28734* Thermál
Camping, Hársfa út 1, 7090 Tamási [tel/fax (74) 471738; camping@tamasistrand.hu; www.tamasikemping.hu] Site & thermal baths sp on rd 65 adj motel. Med, pt shd; wc; shwrs inc; el pnts (10A) HUF575 (long lead req); lndtte; shop 500m; rest 200m; htd pool; dogs HUF67; 10% statics; phone; CKE/CCI. "Security gate; free access to lge thermal pool complex; vg; Perfect location for spa nxt door; nice town and surrounding area." 1 May-15 Oct. HUF 5099        2013*

**TATABANYA** *B2 (12km N Rural) 47.6679, 18.3090* Fényes
Camping, Környei út 24, 2890 Tata [(34) 481208; fax 588144; fenyes@fenyesfurdo.hu; www.fenyesfurdo.hu] Exit junc 67 fr M1 to Tata town cent; foll sp for 3km E to site. Lge, shd; wc; own san rec; shwrs inc; el pnts; shop; rest; playgrnd; 3 pools; games area; dogs HUF500; Eng spkn; CKE/CCI. "Tata interesting town; fair site set in lge park." 1 May-15 Sep.        2009*

TOROKBALINT

**HUNGARY**

⊞ **TOROKBALINT** *B2* (1km S Rural) *47.43305, 18.90027*
Fortuna Camping, Dózsa György út 164, 2045 Törökbálint
[(23) 335364; fax 339697; fortunacamping@axelero.
hu; www.fortunacamping.hu] Fr M1 or M7 take exit for
Törökbálint & foll camp sp to Törökbálint. Leave on rd sp Erd,
rd bends L, go under m'way into vill. At T-junc site sp, turn R,
rd swings L; site ent halfway up hill on L. Med, some hdg pitch,
sl, terr, pt shd, htd wc; chem disp; baby facs; shwrs inc; el pnts
(4-16A) €2; lndtte; shop 1.5km; tradsmn; hypmkt 5km; rest
high ssn; playgrnd; 2 pools (1 htd, covrd); dogs €2; phone; bus
to city 1km; Eng spkn; CKE/CCI. "Friendly, helpful, family-run
site adj vineyards, but untidy; gd, clean san facs; gd security;
variable elec supply & san facs block poss poorly lit; bus/tram
tickets to Budapest fr site; excursions arranged; easy access
Budapest - tickets fr recep; excel rest; ltd facs low ssn." ♦
HUF 5604                                                      2011*

⊞ **TURISTVANDI** *A4* (SW Rural) *48.04710, 22.64300*
Vizimalom Camping, Malom út 3, 4944 Túristvándi
[(44) 721082; turvizimalom@freemail.hu; www.
turvizimalom.hu] Fr Fehérgyarmat foll rd 491 NE for 4km to
Penyige, turn L to Túristvándi. After approx 12km site on R adj
18thC water mill on Rv Túr. Sm, some hdstg, pt shd; wc; shwrs;
el pnts (10A); shop 500m; rest, snacks; bar; BBQ; playgrnd;
canoeing; games area; games rm; TV; internet; dogs; quiet.
"Excel location; no hdstg." HUF 4670              2010*

**UROM see Budapest** *B2*

**VAJTA** *C2* (1km N Rural) *46.72859, 18.65587* **Aucost**
Holiday Parc, Termálsor 1, 7041 Vajta [tel/fax (25) 229700
or 0031 0416 543258 (N'lands); holiday@aucost.nl; www.
aucost.nl] Take rd 63 S fr Cece dir Szekszárd, site on R bef
Vajta. Med, mkd pitch, pt sl, pt shd; wc; chem disp; shwrs
inc; el pnts €1.95; lndtte; shop 1km; tradsmn; rest 1km;
bar; playgrnd; thermal pool; 400m; games rm; internet; TV;
10% statics; dogs €1; Eng spkn; adv bkg; quiet. "Friendly,
helpful Dutch owners; gd birdwatching area; vg site." 18 Apr-
14 Sep. HUF 7472                                          2009*

**ZALAKAROS** *C1* (2km S Rural) *46.53165, 17.12443*
Kurcamping Castrum, Ady Endre út, 8754 Galambok
[tel/fax (93) 358610; zalakaros@castrum.eu; www.
castrum-group.hu] Fr rte 7 N dir Zalakaros, site sp. Med,
hdg/mkd pitch, pt shd; htd wc; chem disp; sauna; shwrs inc;
el pnts (6A) inc; lndtte; shop, rest 1km; snacks; bar; BBQ; htd,
covrd pool; thermal complex 2km; wifi; some statics; dogs;
bus; quiet; ccard acc; CKE/CCI. ♦ 1 Mar-31 Oct. HUF 7783
(CChq acc)                                                2010*

**ZALASZANTO see Keszthely** *C1*

Salgótarján to Tatabánya = 168km

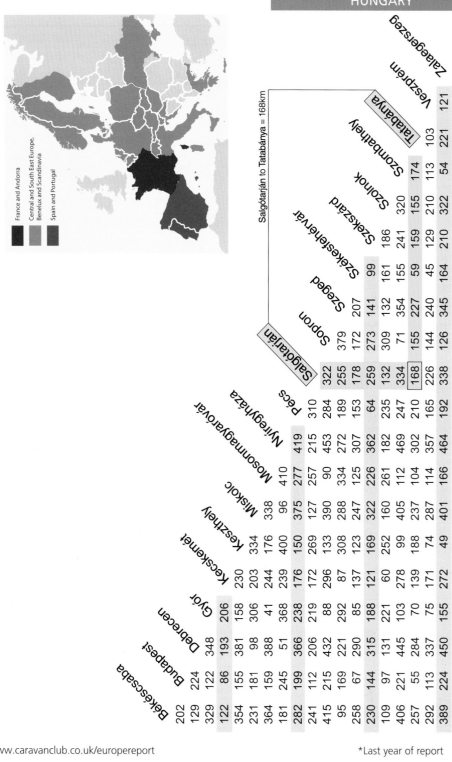

Distance chart (km)

| | Békéscsaba | Budapest | Debrecen | Győr | Kecskemét | Keszthely | Miskolc | Mosonmagyaróvár | Nyíregyháza | Pécs | Salgótarján | Sopron | Szeged | Székesfehérvár | Szekszárd | Szolnok | Szombathely | Tatabánya | Veszprém |
|---|---|---|---|---|---|---|---|---|---|---|---|---|---|---|---|---|---|---|---|
| Budapest | 202 | | | | | | | | | | | | | | | | | | |
| Debrecen | 129 | 224 | | | | | | | | | | | | | | | | | |
| Győr | 329 | 122 | 348 | | | | | | | | | | | | | | | | |
| Kecskemét | 122 | 86 | 193 | 206 | | | | | | | | | | | | | | | |
| Keszthely | 354 | 155 | 381 | 158 | 230 | | | | | | | | | | | | | | |
| Miskolc | 231 | 181 | 98 | 306 | 203 | 334 | | | | | | | | | | | | | |
| Mosonmagyaróvár | 364 | 159 | 388 | 41 | 244 | 176 | 338 | | | | | | | | | | | | |
| Nyíregyháza | 181 | 245 | 51 | 368 | 239 | 400 | 96 | 410 | | | | | | | | | | | |
| Pécs | 282 | 199 | 366 | 238 | 176 | 150 | 375 | 277 | 419 | | | | | | | | | | |
| Salgótarján | 241 | 112 | 206 | 219 | 172 | 269 | 127 | 257 | 215 | 310 | | | | | | | | | |
| Sopron | 415 | 215 | 432 | 88 | 296 | 133 | 390 | 90 | 453 | 284 | 322 | | | | | | | | |
| Szeged | 95 | 169 | 221 | 292 | 87 | 308 | 288 | 334 | 272 | 189 | 255 | 379 | | | | | | | |
| Székesfehérvár | 258 | 67 | 290 | 85 | 137 | 123 | 247 | 125 | 307 | 153 | 178 | 172 | 207 | | | | | | |
| Szekszárd | 230 | 144 | 315 | 188 | 121 | 169 | 322 | 226 | 362 | 64 | 259 | 273 | 141 | 99 | | | | | |
| Szolnok | 109 | 97 | 131 | 221 | 60 | 252 | 160 | 261 | 182 | 235 | 132 | 309 | 132 | 161 | 186 | | | | |
| Szombathely | 406 | 221 | 445 | 103 | 278 | 99 | 405 | 112 | 469 | 247 | 334 | 71 | 354 | 155 | 241 | 320 | | | |
| Tatabánya | 257 | 55 | 284 | 70 | 139 | 188 | 237 | 104 | 302 | 210 | 168 | 155 | 227 | 59 | 159 | 155 | 174 | | |
| Veszprém | 292 | 113 | 337 | 75 | 171 | 74 | 287 | 114 | 357 | 165 | 226 | 144 | 240 | 45 | 129 | 210 | 113 | 103 | |
| Zalaegerszeg | 389 | 224 | 450 | 155 | 272 | 49 | 401 | 166 | 464 | 192 | 338 | 126 | 345 | 164 | 210 | 322 | 54 | 221 | 121 |

France and Andorra

Central and South East Europe, Benelux and Scandinavia

Spain and Portugal

# Italy
## Country Introduction

*Bellagio, Lake Como, Italy*

## Welcome to Italy

From the frantic pace of its cities to the stunning tranquillity of its rolling hills, Italy is a country which evokes a passion for life.

A land of history, culture and fine food, Italy is deservedly included in most lists of must-visit destinations. Touring the country by motorhome or caravan is the perfect way to see the sights at your own pace, enjoying the famous Italian food and hospitality as you go.

## Country highlights

There is much more to Italian cooking than pasta and pizza; try veal dishes, such as saltimbocca or ossobuco, and sample some of the delicious pastries, cured meats, desserts and gelato.

Italian coffee is generally considered to be the best in the world. Also the country is one of the world's largest producers of wine.

Summer in Italy is hot, and many towns put on outdoor festivals of music, dance and shows for both visitors and locals. Often these take place in the local ruins, castles or parks. In some cases the entertainment is free and is well worth investigating.

## Major towns and cities

- Rome – the famous capital city has amazing monuments such as the Colosseum.
- Milan – this city is as famous for its buildings as for its links to fashion.
- Florence – a charmingly small city made up of medieval streets, museums and churches.
- Naples – the city is made up of narrow Roman streets and an 18th century seaside promenade with views of Vesuvius.

## Attractions

- Museo di Castelvecchio Verona – a 14th century castle housing a fine art gallery.
- Milan Cathedral – a breathtaking cathedral with amazing architecture.
- Statue of David – a must-see when visiting Florence, Michelangelo's magnificent marble statue.
- Leaning Tower of Pisa - one of the most remarkable and iconic structures in Italy.

## Find out more

www.enit.it

Tel: 0039 (0) 06 49 711 Italian Tourist Board

# Country Information

Population (approx): 61.7 million

Capital: Rome (population approx 2.7 million)

Area: 301,318 sq km (inc Sardinia & Sicily)

Bordered by: France, Switzerland, Austria, Slovenia

Terrain: Mountainous in the north descending to rolling hills in the centre; some plains and coastal lowlands

Climate: Predominantly Mediterranean climate, alpine in the far north, hot and dry in the south

Coastline: 7,600km

Highest Point: Monte Bianco (Mont Blanc) 4,807m

Language: Italian, German (in the northern Alps)

Local Time: GMT or BST + 1, i.e. 1 hour ahead of the UK all year

Currency: Euros divided into 100 cents; £1 = €1.26, €1 = £0.79 (September 2014)

Emergency numbers: Police 113; Fire brigade 115; Ambulance 118

Public Holidays 2015: Jan 1, 6; Apr 6, 25 (Liberation Day); May 1; Jun 2 (Republic Day); Aug 15; Nov 1; Dec 8 (Immaculate Conception), 25, 26. Each locality also celebrates its patron saint's day, e.g. Apr 25 (Venice), Jun 24 (Florence), Jun 29 (Rome).

School summer holidays run from mid June to mid September

# Camping and Caravanning

There are approximately 2,000 organised and supervised campsites in Italy. They are usually well signposted and are open from April to September. Advance booking is recommended in high season, especially by the lakes and along the Adriatic coast. About 20% of campsites are open all year including some in the mountains and around large towns. Campsites organised by the Touring Club Italiano (TCI) and the Federcampeggio are particularly well equipped.

In general pitch sizes are small at about 80 square metres and it may be difficult to fit a large outfit plus an awning onto a pitch. You will frequently find that hot water is supplied to showers only, for which you will be charged. Published opening and closing dates may be unreliable - phone ahead if travelling during the low season.

It is not compulsory to have a Camping Key Europe (CKE) or Camping Card International (CCI), but it is recommended as a means of identification. If for any reason details are missing from the CKE or CCI a site will insist on holding a visitor's passport instead.

Casual camping is not recommended and is not permitted in national parks or in state forests.

# Motorhomes

Many local authorities permit motorhomes to park overnight in specially designated places known as 'Camper Stops' or 'Aree di Sosta' and a list of their locations and the services provided are contained in a number of publications and on a number of websites including the French 'Guide Officiel Aires de Service Camping-Car' published by the Fédération Française de Camping et de Caravaning, www.ffcc.fr. You will also find a list of 'Camper Stops' on www.turismoitinerante.com (put 'sosta' in the search box).

# Cycling

Transportation of bicycles

An overhanging load must be indicated by an aluminium square panel (panello) measuring 50cm x 50cm with reflective red and white diagonal stripes. The load must not exceed 30% of the length of the vehicle, may only overhang at the rear and the regulation applies to a car or caravan carrying bicycles at the rear or windsurf boards on the roof. A fine may be imposed for failure to display the approved sign which is made by Fiamma and in the UK may be purchased from or ordered through motorhome or caravan dealers/accessory shops. For a list of Fiamma stockists please see www.fiamma.com.

At night outside built-up areas cyclists must wear a reflective jacket and must ride in single file.

# Electricity and Gas

Current at campsites varies between 2 and 16 amps and often it is very low, offering a maximum of only 4 amps across the whole site. Many sites have CEE connections. Plugs have three round pins in line.

Campingaz cylinders are generally available, except in the south of Italy, Sardinia and Sicily where exchange may be difficult outside of marinas and holiday resorts.

## Entry Formalities

British and Irish passport holders may stay in Italy for up to three months without a visa.

## Regulations for Pets

All dogs, including those temporarily imported, must be on a leash at all times. It is advisable to carry a muzzle as the Police/authorities can insist on your dog wearing one if they consider your dog to be dangerous. Some sites and some public transport operators insist that all dogs are muzzled at all times - check local requirements on arrival.

A domestic animal may be transported in a car provided it does not distract the driver. More than one animal may be transported provided they are kept in the rear of the car, separated from the driver by bars, or kept in special cages.

## Medical Services

Ask at a pharmacy (farmacia) for the nearest doctor registered with the state health care scheme (SSN) or look in the telephone directory under 'Unita Sanitaria Locale'. The services of a national health service doctor are normally free of charge.

A European Health Insurance Card (EHIC) entitles you to emergency treatment and medication at local rates and to hospital treatment under the state healthcare scheme. Any charges you do incur are non-refundable in Italy but you may be able to make a claim on your return to the UK. Dental treatment is expensive and you will be charged the full fee.

Emergency services (Guardia Medica) are available at weekends and at night and there are first aid posts at major train stations and airports. Staff at pharmacies can advise on minor ailments and at least one pharmacy remains open 24 hours in major towns.

## Opening Hours

Banks – Mon-Fri 8.30am-1.30pm & 3pm-4pm.

Museums – Tue-Sun 8.30am-6.30pm (check locally as may vary); closed Mon. The Vatican museums and Sistine Chapel are not open to visitors Sun. Visitors under 18 or over 60 are admitted free to State museums on production of a passport.

Post Offices – Mon-Fri 8.30am-2pm/5.30pm, Sat 8.30am-12 noon.

Shops – Mon-Sat 8.30am/9am-1pm & 3.30pm/4pm-7.30pm/8pm. In southern Italy and tourist areas shops may stay open later. There is no lunch time closing in large cities. Shops are closed half a day each week (variable by region).

## Safety and Security

Most visits to Italy are trouble free and, in general, levels of crime are low, but visitors should take care on public transport and in crowded areas where pickpockets and bag snatchers may operate. In Rome take particular care around the main railway station, Roma Termini, and on the bus to and from St Peter's Square. Also take care in and around railway stations in large cities. Be particularly wary of groups of children who may try to distract your attention while attempting to steal from you. Do not carry your passport, credit cards and cash all together in one bag or pocket and only carry what you need for the day. Do not wear expensive jewellery, particularly in the south of Italy.

Take care in bars and don't leave drinks unattended. Recently there have been cases of drinks being spiked. Check prices before ordering food and insist on seeing a priced menu. Be particularly careful when ordering items, such as lobster, which are charged by weight.

When driving in towns keep your car windows shut and doors locked and never leave valuables on display. Around Rome and Naples moped riders may attempt to snatch bags from stationary cars at traffic lights. Always lock your vehicle and never leave valuables in it, even if you will only be away for a short time or are nearby. Avoid leaving luggage in cars for any length of time or overnight.

Increasingly robberies are taking place from cars at rest stops and service stations on motorways. Treat with caution offers of help, for example with a flat tyre, particularly on the motorway from Naples to Salerno, as sometimes the tyre will have been punctured deliberately.

Do not be tempted to enter or bathe in Italy's many fountains – there are heavy fines if you do. Dress conservatively when visiting places of worship, i.e. cover shoulders and upper arms and do not wear shorts. Avoid queues in the peak season by visiting early in the morning.

The authorities are making strenuous efforts to stamp out the illegal production and sale of counterfeit goods. Illegal traders operate on the streets of all major cities, particularly tourist cities such as Florence and Rome. You are advised not to buy from them at the risk of incurring a fine.

Italy shares with the rest of Europe a general threat from terrorism. Attacks could be indiscriminate and against civilian targets in public places, including tourist sites. There continue to be isolated cases of domestic terrorism by extreme left wing and secessionist groups, aimed primarily at official Italian targets.

*British Embassy*
VIA XX SETTEMBRE 80A, I-00187 ROMA RM
Tel: 06 4220 0001
http://ukinitaly.fco.gov.uk/en

*British Consulate-General*
VIA SAN PAOLO 7, I-20121 MILANO MI
Tel: 02 7230 0237
There is also a British Consulates in Naples.

*Irish Embassy*
VILLA SPADA, VIA GIACOMO MEDICI
1 - 00153 ROMA
Tel: 06 5852 381
www.embassyofireland.it
There is also an Irish Honorary Consulate in Milan.

## Foodstuffs

If you are travelling from Croatia you must not import eggs, meat or meat products into Italy.

## Documents

*Driving Licence*

The standard pink UK paper driving licence is recognised in Italy but holders of the old-style green UK licence are recommended to change it for a photocard licence. Alternatively an International Driving Permit may be purchased from the AA, the RAC or selected Post Offices.

*Vehicle(s)*

You must be able to present to the police on demand your vehicle and insurance documents, i.e. vehicle registration certificate (V5C), insurance certificate and MOT certificate (if applicable) and, if you are not the owner of your vehicle(s), authorisation for its use from the owner.

## Money

There are few bureaux de change, so change cash at a bank.

Major credit cards are widely accepted including at petrol stations, but not as widely as in some other European countries. Automatic cash machines (Bancomat) are widespread. Carry your credit card issuers'/banks' 24-hour UK contact numbers in case of loss or theft of your cards.

## Motoring in Italy
### Alcohol

The maximum permitted level of alcohol is 50 milligrams in 100 millilitres of blood, i.e. less than in the UK (80 milligrams). For drivers with less than three years' driving experience, the limit is zero. It is advisable to adopt the 'no drink and drive' rule at all times as penalties are severe.

## Breakdown Service

The motoring organisation, Automobile Club d'Italia (ACI) operates a breakdown service 24 hours a day throughout Italy, including San Marino and Vatican City. Telephone 803116 from a landline or mobile phone. ACI staff speak English. This number also gives access to the ACI emergency information service, operated by multi-lingual staff, for urgent medical or legal advice. You may also use the emergency phones placed every 2km on motorways.

On all roads, including motorways, a charge of €101 is made for assistance and/or recovering a vehicle weighing up to 2,500kg to the nearest ACI garage. Higher charges apply at night, over weekends and public holidays and for towing to anywhere other than the nearest ACI garage. Vehicles over 2,500kg also incur higher charges. Payment is required in cash.

Road police, 'Polizia Stradale', constantly patrol all roads and motorways and can assist when vehicles break down.

## Congestion Charge in Milan

In January 2012 a new congestion charge scheme in Milan was introduced to replace the old Pollution Charge (Ecopass). The new scheme is more restrictive than the old Ecopass scheme. To access the historical centre (Area C) from 7.30am – 7.30pm on Monday, Tuesday, Wednesday and Friday and from 7.30am- 6pm on Thursday you must pay a fee of €5 a day.

You can buy a ticket for entrance from parking meters, newsagents and some ATM points or online at www.areac.it – tickets must then be activated on the day before you plan to drive into the area. You can activate the ticket via text message or telephone. Visit the above website address to find out more. Petrol vehicles classed as Euro 0 and diesel vehicles in classes Euro 0 - 3 are not allowed to enter Area C at all during the above times.

## Essential Equipment

### Lights

It is compulsory for all vehicles to have dipped headlights at all times when driving outside built-up areas, on motorways and major roads, when driving in tunnels and when visibility is poor, e.g. in rain or snow. Bulbs are more likely to fail with constant use and you are recommended to carry spares.

### Reflective Jackets/Waistcoats

If your vehicle is immobilised on the carriageway outside a built-up area at night, or in poor visibility, you must wear a reflective jacket or waistcoat when getting out of your vehicle. This rule also applies to passengers who may leave the vehicle, for example, to assist with a repair. Keep the jackets to hand inside your vehicle, not in the boot.

### Warning Triangle

At night a warning triangle must be used to give advance warning of any vehicle parked outside a built-up area near a bend, or on a hill if rear side lights have failed, or in fog. Place the triangle at least 50 metres behind the vehicle (100 metres on motorways). Failure to use a triangle may result in a fine.

### Child Restraint System

Children travelling in UK registered vehicles must be secured according to legislation in force in the UK.

### Winter Driving

In the area of Val d'Aosta vehicles must be equipped with winter tyres or snow chains must be carried between 15 October and 15 April. This rule may apply in other areas and over other periods as conditions dictate.

## Fuel

Unleaded petrol is sold from pumps marked 'Super Unleaded' or 'Super Sensa Piombo'. Diesel is called 'gasolio' and LPG is known as 'gas auto' or 'GPL'.

Fuel is sold 24 hours a day on motorways but elsewhere petrol stations may close for an extended lunch break and overnight from approximately 7pm. Opening hours are clearly displayed, as are the addresses of the nearest garages which are open.

Major credit cards are accepted, but possibly not in rural areas, so always carry some cash. Look for the 'Carta Si' sign. Recent visitors report that many petrol stations in rural areas and on major routes between towns are now unmanned and automated. Payment may be made with bank notes but the machines will usually only accept credit cards issued by Italian banks.

## Low Emission Zones

Many Italian cities and towns operate low emission zones. They often affect all vehicles, but rules vary from city to city. For more information visit www.lowemissionzones.eu.

## Overtaking

On roads with three traffic lanes, the middle lane is reserved for overtaking, but overtaking is only allowed if a vehicle travelling in the opposite direction is not already in the middle lane.

When pulling out to overtake on motorways check for cars travelling at well over the maximum speed limit of 130km/h (81 mph).

## Parking

In major towns there are parking zones where payment is required and these are indicated by blue road signs. Pay either at a machine with coins or buy a card from local tobacconists or newspaper shops and display it inside your vehicle. Some cities also have green zones where parking is prohibited on working days during the morning and afternoon rush hours.

Parking against the traffic flow and parking on the pavement are not allowed. Illegally parked vehicles may be clamped or towed away.

## Priority

In general, priority must be given to traffic coming from the right except if indicated by road signs. At traffic lights a flashing amber light indicates that traffic must slow down and proceed with caution, respecting the priority rules.

## Roads

The road network is of a high standard and main and secondary roads are generally good. Many main roads are winding and hilly but provide a more interesting route than the motorways. Stopping places for refreshments may be few and far between in some areas.

Standards of driving may be erratic, especially overtaking, and lane discipline poor; some roads have a particularly bad reputation for accidents. Those where special vigilance is called for include the Via Aurelia between Rome and Pisa, which is mostly two lane and is extremely busy at weekends, the A12 to the north with its series of tunnels and curves, the A1 between Florence and Bologna, the Rome ring road, roads around Naples and Palermo, and mountain roads in the south and in Sicily.

## Road Signs and Markings

Road signs conform to international standards. White lettering on a green background indicates motorways (autostrada), whereas state and provincial roads outside built-up areas have white lettering on a blue background. This is a reversal of the colouring used in France and may initially cause confusion when driving from one country to the other.

Other frequently encountered signs include the following:

Snow chains required

Horizontal traffic light

Carabinieri (police)

Ecopass zone (Milan)

| Italian | English Translation |
| --- | --- |
| Attenzione | Caution |
| Autocarro | Lorries |
| Coda | Traffic jam |
| Curva pericolosa | Dangerous bend |
| Destra | Right |
| Deviazione | Diversion |
| Divieto di accesso | No entry |
| Divieto di sorpasso | No overtaking |
| Divieto di sosta | No parking |
| Ghiaia | Gravel |
| Incidente | Accident |
| Incrocio | Crossroads |
| Lavori in corso | Roadworks ahead |
| Pericoloso | Danger |
| Rallentare | Slow down |

| Italian | English Translation |
|---|---|
| Restringimento | Narrow lane |
| Senso unico | One-way street |
| Senso vietato | No entry |
| Sinistra | Left |
| Sosta autorizzata | Parking permitted (times shown) |
| Sosta aietata | No parking |
| Svolta | Bend |
| Uscita | Exit |
| Vietato ingresso veicili | No entry for vehicles |

A single or double unbroken line in the centre of the carriageway must not be crossed.

## Speed Limits

| | Open Road (km/h) | Motorway (km/h) |
|---|---|---|
| Car Solo | 90-110 | 130 |
| Car towing caravan/trailer | 70 | 80 |
| Motorhome under 3500kg | 90-110 | 130 |
| Motorhome 3500-7500kg | 80 | 100 |

Motorhomes over 3,500kg are restricted to 80 km/h (50 mph) outside built-up areas and 100 km/h (62 mph) on motorways.

Speed on some sections of Italian motorways is electronically controlled. When you leave a motorway at a toll booth electronic tills calculate the distance a vehicle has travelled and the journey time. The police are automatically informed if speeding has taken place, and fines are imposed.

In bad weather the maximum speed is 90 km/h (56 mph) on roads outside built-up areas and 110 km/h (68 mph) on motorways.

The transportation or use of radar detectors is prohibited.

## Traffic Jams

During the summer months, particularly at weekends, the roads to the Ligurian and Adriatic coasts and to the Italian lakes are particularly busy, as are the narrow roads around the lakes. Travelling mid week may help a little. Bottlenecks are likely to occur on the A1 north-south motorway at stretches between Milan and Bologna, Rioveggio and Incisa and on the ring road around Rome. Other traffic jams occur on the A14 to the Adriatic coast; on the A4 between Milan and Brescia caused by heavy traffic to Lakes Iseo and Garda; the A11 Florence to Pisa (before the A12 junction); the A12 Rome to Civitavecchia; the A23 Udine to Tarvisio and before the tunnels on the A26 between Alessandria and Voltri.

Italians traditionally go on holiday during the first weekend of August when traffic density is at its worst. Rush hour traffic jams regularly occur on the ring roads for Milan, Rome and Naples.

## Violation of Traffic Regulations

The police may impose on the spot fines, which are particularly heavy for speeding and drink and/or drug related driving offences. Payment is required in cash and a receipt must be given. It can take up to a year for notice of a traffic violation and resulting fine to reach the owner of a foreign registered vehicle.

## Motorways

There are approximately 6,500km of motorway (autostrade) in Italy. Tolls (pedaggio) are levied on most of them.
On some motorways, tolls are payable at intermediate toll booths for each section of the motorway used. On a few others the toll must be paid on entering the motorway.

*Tolls*

**Category A** Cars with height from front axle less than 1.30m.

**Category B** Motor vehicles with 2 axles with height from front axle over 1.30m including motorhomes.

**Category C** Motor vehicles with 3 axles, e.g. car plus caravan.

**Category D** Motor vehicles with 4 axles, e.g. car plus twin-axle caravan.

To calculate the tolls payable and find traffic and motorway services information see www.autostrade.it which allows you to enter your route and class of vehicle.

Tolls can prove to be expensive especially over long distances.

*Toll Payment*

Cash (euro only), debit and credit cards are accepted. Credit cards are also accepted for payment in the Fréjus, Mont-Blanc and Grand St Bernard tunnels. However, visitors advise that on some stretches of motorway automated pay desks which accept credit cards will only do so for solo vehicles. If you are towing a caravan it is advisable to have cash available as you may need to pass through the manned white channel for cash payments.

The prepaid Viacard, available in values of €25, €50 and €75, is also accepted on the majority of motorways and is obtainable from motorway toll booths, service areas and PuntoBlu points of sale along the motorways. The card may be used for any vehicle. When leaving a motorway on which the Viacard is accepted (use the blue or white lanes – do not use the yellow 'Telepass' lanes), insert your entry ticket and card into the machine or give them to the attendant who will deduct the amount due. A Viacard is valid until the credit expires and may be used on a subsequent visit to Italy but cannot be refunded. Viacards are not accepted on Sicilian motorways.

## Touring

Italy's great cities, with their religious, artistic and historic treasures, are high on the short break list and are worthy destinations in their own right. Visitors over 65 often qualify for reduced or free entrance to museums and other attractions, so carry your passport as proof of age.

In Rome an Archaeological Card is available, valid for up to seven days, offering entry (ahead of any queues) to many of the most famous sites, together with discounts on guided tours. The cards are available from participating sites and museums.

Smoking is not permitted in public places including restaurants and bars.

In bars prices shown are for drinks taken standing

at the bar. Prices are higher if you are seated at a table. In restaurants a service or cover charge is usually added to the bill but it is customary to add 50 cents or €1 per person if you are happy with the service provided. Not all restaurants accept credit cards; check before ordering.

The east coast of Italy has many holiday resorts with fine, sandy beaches, from Ravenna, to Pescara and beyond. However, most beaches in Italy are commercially managed and unless a campsite or hotel has its own private beach, be prepared to pay to enjoy a day by the sea. By law a part of every beach must have free access, but usually it is the least attractive part.

Many parts of Italy lie on a major seismic fault line and tremors and minor earthquakes are common. Visitors climbing Mount Etna should follow the marked routes and heed the advice of guides. There is also ongoing low-intensity volcanic activity on the island of Stromboli.

Visitors to Venice should note that parts of the city are liable to flood in late autumn and early spring.

There are more than 40 World Heritage Sites in Italy (more than any other country) including the historic centres of Florence, Siena, Naples, Pienza, Urbino and the Vatican City.

The Vatican museums and Sistine Chapel are closed on Sundays, except on the last Sunday of the month. When visiting art galleries in Florence, in particular the Uffizi and Accademia, you are advised to buy timed tickets in advance, either online or in person. Otherwise you will encounter very long queues.

There are numerous ferry services transporting passengers and vehicles between Italy and neighbouring countries. Major ports of departure for Croatia, Greece and Turkey are Ancona, Bari, Brindisi, Trieste and Venice. Services also operate to Corsica from Citavecchia, Genoa, Livorno, Porto Torres (Sardinia), Santa Teresa di Gallura (Sardinia) and Savona.

For further information contact:

VIAMARE LTD
SUITE 108, 582 HONEYPOT LANE
STANMORE
MIDDX HA7 1JS
Tel: 020 8206 3420, Fax: 020 8206 1332
www.viamare.com
Email: ferries@viamare.com

If you are planning a skiing holiday contact the Italian State Tourist Board for advice on safety and weather conditions before travelling. Off-piste skiing is highly dangerous and all safety instructions should be followed meticulously in view of the dangers of avalanches in some areas.

Italy has introduced a law requiring skiers and snowboarders to carry tracking equipment if going off-piste. The law also obliges children up to 14 years of age to wear a helmet. There are plans for snowboarders to be banned from certain slopes, check local news for updates.

## Public Transport & Local Travel

Traffic is restricted or prohibited at certain times in the historical centre of most Italian cities in order to reduce congestion and pollution levels, and you are advised to use out of centre car parks and public transport. The boundaries of historic centres are usually marked with signs displaying the letters ZTL (zona traffico limitato). A crossed hammer on the sign means the restriction does not apply on Sundays and public holidays. Do not pass the ZTL sign as your registration number is likely to be caught on camera and notice of a fine – or fines if you cross more than one ZTL zone – will probably be sent to your home address. Fines are around €100 each time you enter a ZTL.

In addition many northern Italian regions have banned traffic in town and city centres on Sundays. Buses and taxis are permitted to operate.

Public transport is usually cheap and efficient. All the major cities have extensive bus networks and Messina, Milan, Padova, Rome and Turin also have trams. At present only Rome and Milan have an extensive underground network and Perugia has recently inaugurated a 'minimetro'. Bus and metro tickets cannot be purchased on board and must be obtained prior to boarding from newsagents, tobacconists, ticket kiosks or bars. Books of tickets and daily, weekly and monthly passes are also available for purchase.

Validate your ticket when using public transport at the yellow machines positioned at the entrance to platforms in railway stations, in the entrance hall of metro stations and on board buses and trams. Officials patrol all means of public transport and will issue an on the spot fine if you do not hold a validated ticket. Tickets for buses and the metro tend to be time limited (75 minutes) and it is therefore necessary to complete your journey within the allotted time and purchase a new ticket for any additional travel.

Only use taxis which are officially licensed. They will have a neon taxi sign on the roof and are generally white or yellow. Also ensure that the meter in the taxi has been reset before starting your journey. Fares are quite high and there are additional charges for luggage and pets, at night and on public holidays. A tip is expected (up to 10%) and this is sometimes already added to the fares for foreigners.

Car ferry services operate between Venice and the Lido, the Italian mainland and the Aeolian Islands, Sardinia, Sicily, Elba and Capri, Corsica (France) and on Lakes Maggiore, Como and Garda. Parking in Venice is very difficult; instead park at a mainland car park and use a bus or ferry to the city. However, be aware that thieves may operate in car parks in Mestre. Driving and parking in Naples are not recommended in any circumstances.

Cars towing caravans are prohibited at all times from using the S163 south of Naples because it is narrow and has many bends. Motorhomes are prohibited in summer between Positano and Vietri-a-Mare.

⊞ **ACIREALE (SICILY)** *3C4 (1.5km NE Coastal) 37.62015, 15.17320* **La Timpa International Camping, Via Santa Maria La Scala, 25 -Cap 95024 Acireale (CT)** [095 7648155; fax 7640049; info@campinglatimpa.com; www. campinglatimpa.com] Exit A18/E45 onto rd S114 dir Acireale. Foll sp for Santa Maria La Scala; site on L after 1.5km; steep & diff access rds. Med, pt shd; wc; shwrs free; el pnts (6A) €3.50; lndtte; shop high ssn; rest, snacks; bar; playgrnd; beach adj; 60% statics; dogs €4 (not acc Jul/Aug); sep car park; poss noisy; ccard acc; red CKE/CCI. "Site in orchard, surfaced in black volcanic ash; hot & cold shwrs ; chem displ; trips to Etna; lift down to rocky beach; sh, steep walk to vill & harbour." ◆ € 25.50 *2013\**

⊞ **AGEROLA** *3A3 (2km E Urban)* **Camping Beata Solitudo, Piazza Generale Avitabile 4, San Lazzaro, 80051 Agerola (NA)** [tel/fax 081 8025048; beatasol@tiscalinet.it; www. beatasolitudo.it] Exit A3/S145 at Castellammare-di-Stabia & foll dirs S on S366 to Agerola. Turn L sp San Lazzaro, site in vill sq - narr access rds. Do not app via Amalfi coast rd. Sm, terr, shd; wc (cont); chem disp; mv service pnt; shwrs incl; el pnts (3A) inc; lndry rm; shop, rest, snacks, bar in vill; sm playgrnd; shgl beach 16km; wifi; 70% statics; dogs free; bus adj; poss cr; Eng spkn; adv bkg; quiet; red CKE/CCI. "V access to Amalfi coast via bus; site at 650m - sea views; v helpful owner; bungalows & hostel accomm avail in restored castle building on site; vg but suitable m'vans only." € 20.00 *2009\**

**AGLIENTU (SARDINIA)** *1C4 (6km N Coastal) 41.12701, 9.07071* **Camping Village Saragosa, Pineta di Vignola-Mare, 07020 Aglientu (SS)** [079 602077; fax 602037; info@campingsaragosa.it; www.campingsaragosa.it] Take coastal rd SW fr Santa Teresa Gallura (ferries fr Corsica) to Vignola Mare - approx 20km, site sp. Lge, shd; wc; mv service pnt; shwrs; el pnts (3A) inc; lndtte; shop; tradsmn; snacks; bar; playgrnd; sand beach adj; games area; entmnt; 50% statics; dogs €4; phone; poss cr; Eng spkn; adv bkg; ccard acc; red low ssn. "Direct access to superb beach; some pitches adj beach." ◆ 1 May-30 Sep. € 37.00 *2010\**

⊞ **AGRIGENTO (SICILY)** *3C3 (4km SE Coastal) 37.24395, 13.61423* **Camping Internazionale Nettuno, Via Lacco Ameno 3, San Leone, 92100 Agrigento** [tel/fax 0922 416268 / 0922 416983; info@campingnettuno.com; www.campingnettuno.com] Fr Agrigento to San Leone on SS115, foll rd SE out of San Leone alongside beach until sharp L away fr beach. Turn immed R into lane, site on R. Med, hdg pitch, hdstg, terr, pt shd; wc (some cont); chem disp; mv service pnt; shwrs inc; el pnts (6A) €2.50 (rev pol); gas; lndtte; shop; tradsmn; rest, snacks; bar; BBQ; sand beach adj; wifi; entmnt; TV rm; 15% statics; dogs free; phone; poss cr; adv bkg; ccard acc; red long stay/CKE/CCI. "Bus to temples at Agrigento; peaceful, unspoilt beach; steep slope to pitches - towed c'vans rec to keep to upper levels if poss; gd rest; take care low branches." ◆ ltd € 27.00 *2013\**

⊞ **AGRIGENTO (SICILY)** *3C3 (8km S Coastal/Urban) 37.26936, 13.58299* **Camping Valle dei Templi, Viale Emporium, 92110 San Leone** [tel/fax 0922 411115; info@campingvalledeitempli.com; www. campingvalledeitempli.com] Sp S of Agrigento, foll sp San Leone, site on L bef beach. Lge, some hdstg, pt sl, terr, pt shd; wc; chem disp; mv service pnt; shwrs inc; el pnts (6A) €3; lndtte; shop adj; rest, snacks; bar; beach 800m; tennis; cycle hire; 20% statics; dogs; phone adj; bus; site clsd 8 Dec-15 Jan; poss cr; Eng spkn; adv bkg; ccard acc; red long stay/CKE/CCI. "Gd modern facs; no potable water on site; bus to temples fr site ent." ◆ € 26.50 *2009\**

> **"I like to fill in the reports as I travel from site to site"**
> You'll find report forms at the back of this guide, or you can fill them in online at www.caravaclub.co.uk/europereport.

⊞ **ALBA** *1B2 (1km SW Urban) 44.68507, 8.01019* **Camping Village Alba, Corso Piave 219, San Cassiano, 12051 Alba (CN)** [0173 280972; fax 288621; info@albavillagehotel. it; www.albavillagehotel.it] Fr A21 exit Asti fr onto S231 to Alba ring rd. Take Corso Piave dir Roddi & Castiglione Falletto, site sp (Campo Sportivo) on L - red block. Or fr A6 exit at SP662 & foll sp Cherasco & Marene, then at rndabt foll sp Pollenza, then Roddi. Fr Roddi site sp dir Alba. Med, hdg/ mkd pitch, pt shd; htd wc; chem disp; mv service pnt outside site; shwrs inc; el pnts (16A) €2.50; lndtte; shop 150m; rest; bar; BBQ; htd pool adj; paddling pool; sports cent adj; cycle hire; games area; internet; some statics/apartmnts; dogs free; bus; Eng spkn; adv bkg; quiet; ccard acc; red CKE/CCI. "Excel, friendly, clean site; open country to rear; vg facs; conv Barolo vineyards; attractive town & area." ◆ € 38.00 *2014\**

**ALBENGA** *1B2 (2km E Rural/Coastal) 44.08277, 8.21611* **Camping Baciccia, Via Torino 19, 17023 Ceriale (SV)** [0182 990743; fax 993839; info@campingbaciccia.it; www. campingbaciccia.it] Exit A10 for Albenga, turn L onto SS1 Via Aurelia dir Savona for 3km. Turn L inland at traff lts bef Famiglia Supmkt in Ceriale, site in 200m on L, sp. Med, mkd pitch, pt sl, pt shd; htd wc (some cont); chem disp; mv service pnt; serviced pitches; baby facs; shwrs inc; el pnts (6A) inc; gas; lndtte; shop; supmkt nr; rest, snacks; bar; BBQ; playgrnd; pool high ssn; paddling pool; public shgl beach 600m, private beach nrby; tennis 500m; cycle hire; horseriding 2km; golf 10km; wifi; entmnt; TV rm; 5% statics; dogs €4; bus to private beach; sep car park; poss cr; Eng spkn; adv bkg; quiet; ccard acc; red long stay/low ssn/CKE/CCI. "Family-run site; ltd touring pitches; narr site rds & ent & sm pitches; friendly owners; gd san facs & pool; busy w/ends; lovely pool & café; conv many historical attractions." 01 Apr-3 Nov & 1 Dec-10 Jan. € 50.00 (3 persons) *2013\**

Send in your site reports by mid August 2015

ALBENGA *1B2* (5km NW Rural) *44.08472, 8.21027* **Camping Bella Vista, Via Campore 23, 17030 Campochiesa-d'Albenga (SV) [0182 540213; fax 554925; info@ campingbellavista.it; www.campingbellavista.it]** Exit A10 at Borghetto S Spirito & foll sp Ceriale. In Ceriale turn R at 3rd traff lts, R at next traff lts & foll site sp. Med, hdg/mkd pitch, terr,pt shd; htd wc (some cont); chem disp; mv service pnt; baby facs; shwrs inc; el pnts (3-6A) €2.50 (poss rev pol); lndtte; shop; tradsmn; rest, snacks; bar; BBQ; htd pool; paddling pool; beach 1.5km; games rm; internet; entmnt; 30% statics; dogs €6.50; phone; bus 900m; poss cr; adv bkg; quiet. "Pleasant, friendly, clean, Dutch family-run site; helpful staff; narr site rds; mostly sm pitches; owner will site c'van with tractor on request; poss diff lge o'fits." ♦ ltd 15 Mar-15 Nov & 15 Dec-15 Jan. € 33.50                        2011*

ALBEROBELLO *3A4* (1.5km N Rural) *40.80194, 17.25055* Camping Dei Trulli, Via Castellana Grotte, Km 1.5, 70011 Alberobello (BA) [0804 323699; fax 322145; info@campingdeitrulli.it; www.campingdeitrulli.com] Fr Alberobello, site sp on R. Lift barrier to ent if clsd. Med, mkd pitch, hdstg, pt shd; wc; mv service pnt opp; shwrs €0.50; el pnts (6A) €2.50; shop &1.5km; rest, snacks; bar; 2 pools high ssn; cycle hire; wifi; entmnt; phone; Eng spkn; ccard acc; red long stay/CKE/CCI. "Gd touring base; some pitches sm due to trees; ltd, basic facs low ssn; hot water to shwrs only; site run-down." 1 Apr-30 Sep. € 42.50                        2014*

⊞ ALBEROBELLO *3A4* (1km S Rural) *40.77507, 17.24040* Camping Bosco Selva, 27 Via Bosco Selva, 70011 Alberobello (BA) [080 4323726; fax 4323863; info@ campingboscoselva.it; www.campingboscoselva.it] Sp fr S172/S239 Alberobello ring rd. Med, some hdstg, pt sl, shd; wc; chem disp; mv service pnt; shwrs inc; el pnts (2A) inc; lndtte; shop 1km; rest; bar; wifi; Eng spkn; quiet; red low ssn; CKE/CCI. "In heart of 'Trulli' region of sm beehive-shaped houses; wooded site; friendly owner; vg facs; v nice site; tennis courts; walks in forest adj." € 37.00                        2014*

**ALBINIA see Orbetello** *1D4*

ALGHERO (SARDINIA) *3A1* (1.5km N Coastal) *40.57916, 8.31222* Camping La Mariposa, Via Lido 22, 07041 Alghero (SS) [079 9950480; fax 984489; info@lamariposa. it; www.lamariposa.it] N fr Alghero on coast rd dir Fertilia. Site on L just beyond pool. Lge, pt sl, hdstg, terr, pt shd; wc; chem disp; mv service pnt; shwrs €0.50; el pnts (6-10A) €3; gas; lndtte; shop; rest, snacks; bar; BBQ; private sand beach adj; watersports; cycle hire; games rm; wifi; entmnt; TV; dogs; 20% statics; dogs; bus nr; sep car park; Eng spkn; ccard acc; red CKE/CCI. "Lovely wooded site; gd clean facs; gd security; friendly staff; boat fr Alghero to caves at Cape Caccia or by rd + 625 steps." 1 Apr-15 Oct. € 46.00                        2011*

ALGHERO (SARDINIA) *3A1* (6km NW Coastal) Camping Calik, 07040 Fertilia (SS) [tel/fax 079 930111; info@ campeggiocalik.it; www.campeggiocalik.it] Fr Alghero W on coast rd, site bet rndabt & rv bdge 500m bef Fertilia on R. Med, shd; wc; chem disp; shwrs inc; el pnts (3A); lndtte; shop; rest, snacks; bar; playgrnd; sand beach 200m; entmnt; 50% statics; dogs €3; bus at gate; poss cr; adv bkg; ccard acc. "Well-situated by rv with easy access to beach; cycle track to Fertilia." 15 Mar-30 Sep. € 35.50                        2009*

ALGHERO (SARDINIA) *3A1* (12km NW Coastal) *40.64110, 8.18960* Camping Torre del Porticciolo, Loc Porticciolo, 07041 Alghero (SS) [079 919007; fax 919212; info@ torredelporticciolo.it; www.torredelporticciolo.it] N fr Alghero sp SS127 to Capo Caccia; in 18km site sp R at T-junc then L in 300m. V lge, shd; wc (some cont); private san facs avail; shwrs inc; el pnts (4A) inc; gas; lndtte; shop; rest, snacks; bar; BBQ; playgrnd; sand beach; pool; paddling pool; watersports; tennis; games area; games rm; wifi; entmnt; TV; some statics; dogs €6; quiet; adv bkg; ccard acc; CKE/CCI. "Excel; close to Grotto di Nettuno; beautiful area." 1 May-10 Oct. € 73.00 (CChq acc)                        2011*

**AMEGLIA see Sarzana** *1C2*

⊞ ANGHIARI *1D3* (600m S Urban) *43.53666, 12.05204* Agrturism Vel della Pieve, Via della Fossa, 8 - 52031(AR) [tel/fax 0575 788593; info@agriturismovaldellapieve.it; www.agriturismovaldellapieve.it] Fr N on the SP47 turn L on to Via della Fossa rd to the site. Sm, hdstg, pt shd; htd wc; chem disp; mv service pnt; shwrs; fam bthrm; el pnts (6A) inc; gas 1km; lndtte (inc dryer); shop 1/2km; rest 1/2km; snacks 1/2km; playgrnd; htd pool; wifi; dogs; twin axles; Eng spkn; adv bkg; CKE/CCI. € 25.00                        2013*

⊞ ANTERSELVA DI SOPRA/ANTHOLZ OBERTAL *2E1* (500m NE Rural) *46.86450, 12.10966* Camping Anterselva/ Antholz, Obertal 34, 39030 Anterselva-di-Sopra/Antholz-Obertal (BZ) [0474 492204; fax 492444; info@camping-antholz.com; www.camping-antholz.com] E fr Brunico on S49. Turn N at Rasun & Antholz valley; cont 12km, well sp, app not steep. Site is 2km N of Antholz. Med, pt sl, unshd; htd wc; chem disp; mv service pnt; baby facs; shwrs inc; el pnts (4A) inc; gas; lndtte; shop; rest snacks; bar; playgrnd; tennis 500m; cycle hire; wifi; TV; dogs €3; bus nr; adv bkg; quiet. ♦ € 25.00                        2009*

AOSTA *1B1* (1km N Rural) *45.74666, 7.31897* Camping Ville d'Aoste, Viale Gran San Bernardo 67, Loc Les Fourches, 11100 Aosta (AO) [0165 361360] 1st site on L off old rd fr Aosta to Grand St Bernard tunnel rte S27. Nr Hotel Rayon du Soleil. Sm, pt shd; wc (some cont); chem disp; mv service pnt; shwrs inc; el pnts (4-10A) inc; gas; lndtte; shop; snacks; bar; playgrnd; TV; phone; train at Saraillon; some rd noise; ccard acc; CKE/CCI. "Interesting town with many Roman historic remains; excel mountain views; uncr, even in high ssn; clean & friendly site; unrel opening dates." 9 Jul-31 Oct. € 17.40                        2014*

AOSTA *1B1* (4km E Rural) *45.74088, 7.39355* Camping Aosta, Villaggio Clou 29, 11020 Quart (AO) [tel/ fax 0165 765602; info@campingaosta.com] Site 1km fr Villefranche at Quart on SS26. Med, pt sl, terr, shd; wc (some cont); chem disp; shwrs inc; mv service pnt; el pnts (6A) inc; lndtte; sm shop; supmkt 2km; rest; bar; playgrnd; pool 5km; cycle hire; mainly statics; phone; rlwy noise. "Ltd touring pitches; poorly-maintained site; NH only." 15 May-15 Sep. € 21.00                        2012*

---

Site report forms at back of guide                        *Last year of report    **359**

ITALY

**AOSTA** *1B1* (3km SE Rural) *45.73338, 7.36006* **Camping Les Iles**, Loc Les Iles 17, 11020 Pollein (AO) [tel/fax 0165 53154; camping_les_iles@hotmail.it] Fr N exit A5 Aosta Est sp St Christophe/Pollein, go under a'strada, cross Rv Dora, site sp. Med, pt shd; wc; chem disp; mv service pnt; shwrs; el pnts metered; snacks; bar; playgrnd; tennis; some statics; dogs €3; bus nr; some rd noise; ccard acc; CKE/CCI. "Beautiful location; conv Mont Blanc & St Bernard tunnels." ♦ € 29.00                                          2009*

**AOSTA** *1B1* (4km W Rural) *45.72190, 7.26985* **Camping International Touring**, Fraz. Arensod 10, 11010 Sarre (AO) [tel/fax 0165 257061; campingtouring@libero.it; www.campingtouring.com] Exit A5/E25 Aosta West, site sp fr rd S26. Lge, pt shd; wc (some cont); own san rec; chem disp; mv service pnt; shwrs inc; el pnts (3-6A) €2.80; gas; lndtte; sm supmkt 100m; rest, snacks; bar; playgrnd; pool high ssn; tennis; 10% statics; dogs €1; poss cr; quiet; 10% red CKE/CCI. "Lovely scenery; conv for Val d'Aosta with historical castles; somewhat run down site; NH only." 15 May-15 Sep. € 24.50                                          2009*

## "We must tell The Club about that great site we found"

Get your site reports in by mid-August and we'll do our best to get your updates into the next edition.

**AOSTA** *1B1* (5km W Rural) *45.71706, 7.26161* **Camping Monte Bianco**, St Maurice 15, 11010 Sarre (AO) [tel/fax 0165 258514; info@campingmontebianco.it; www.campingmontebianco.it] Fr A5/E25 exit Aosta W twd Aosta, site on R, well sp. Fr Mont Blanc tunnel on S26 site on R at Sarre 500m past St Maurice sp. W fr Aosta, site on L 100m past boundary sp St Maurice/Sarre, yellow sp. Turn into site poss tight for lge o'fits. Sm, terr, pt shd; wc (some cont); chem disp; mv service pnt; shwrs €0.50; el pnts (6-10A) €2.80; gas; lndry rm; shop adj; supmkt 500m; rest 200m; bar 100m; playgrnd; pool 4km; phone; Eng spkn; adv bkg; quiet; red long stay low ssn; CKE/CCI. "Sm, family-run site set in orchard on rv; friendly, helpful; excel tourist info; beautiful alpine scenery & walks; last tunnel is close to exit when coming fr Mont Blanc do not rely on sat nav to restart in time." 15 May-30 Sep. € 32.00   2014*

**AQUILEIA** *2E1* (300m NE Rural) *45.77786, 13.36943* Camping Aquileia, Via Gemina 10, 33051 Aquileia (UD) [0431 91042; fax 30804; info@campingaquileia.it; www.campingaquileia.it] Fr A4/E70 take Grado/Palmanova exit & foll sp Grado on SS352. Turn L at traff lts at ent to Aquileia. Site in 400m on R. Fr SS14 turn onto SS352, site sp. Med, shd; wc (some cont); chem disp; mv service pnt; shwrs inc; el pnts (6A) inc; lndry rm; supmkt adj; rest, snacks; playgrnd; pool; paddling pool; some statics; dogs €3; bus 300m; quiet; red long stay; ccard acc; CKE/CCI. "Excel site; lge pitches; 10 mins walk thro Roman ruins to magnificent, unique basilica & mosaics; poss noisy concerts July festival week; gd, friendly site; great site." 1 May-30 Sep. € 30.50                2013*

**AQUILEIA** *2E1* (3km S Coastal) *45.72640, 13.39860* **Camping Village Belvedere Pineta**, Via Martin Luther King, 33051 Belvedere-Di-Grado (UD) [0431 91007; fax 918641; info@belvederepineta.it; www.belvederepineta.it] Fr Venezia/Trieste a'strada, exit for Palmanova & foll Grado sp on S352 to Aquileia. Drive thro Belvedere, & site is nr lagoon. Slow app to site due to uneven surface. V lge, mkd pitch, shd; wc; chem disp; mv service pnt; baby facs; shwrs inc; el pnts (3-6A) inc; gas; lndtte (inc dryer); supmkt; rest, snacks; bar; BBQ; playgrnd; pool; paddling pool; waterslide; sand beach adj; watersports; tennis; games area; games rm; cycle hire; excursions; entmnt; golf 5km; 50% statics; dogs €7.50; rlwy stn 10km at Cervignano; adv bkg; quiet; red long stay/snr citizens; CKE/CCI. "Wooded site - poss mosquitoes; steamer trips fr Grado; gd touring base, inc Venice; red for Seniors; excel site with v clean san facs." ♦ 1 May-30 Sep. € 59.00 (CChq acc)     2013*

**ARBOREA (SARDINIA)** *3A1* (2km NW Coastal) *39.81667, 8.55337* **Camping Village S'Ena Arrubia**, Strada Ovest 29, 09092 Arborea (OR) [tel/fax 0783 809011; info@senarrubia.it; www.senarrubia.it] Fr N on SS131 dir Oristano at km 94.5 foll sp Oristano-Sorgono. In 2km foll sp Oristano-Fenosu, then Santa Giusta (Oristano-Sud) to site. Lge, mkd pitch, pt sl, shd; wc; mv service pnt; shwrs inc; el pnts €3; lntte; shop; rest, snacks; bar; BBQ; playgrnd; pool; sand beach nr; lake sw & fishing; watersports; tennis; cycle & boat hire; games area; entmnt; some statics; adv bkg; red snr citizens. "Wooded site; excel touring base; gd modern san facs; cycle rtes." 10 May-30 Sep. € 41.00 (CChq acc)      2011*

**ARCO** *2D1* (6km SSW Coastal) *45.87614, 10.86779* **Camping Bellavista**, Via Gardesana, 31 - Arco [0464 505644; fax 505166; www.camping-bellavista.it] Fr A22 take exit for Roveretto Sud-Lago di Garda; at rndabt take 4th exit twrds Riva Del Garda; in 3km turn L onto SS240. After town cent in 8km take L into site bef lakeside tunnel, just after Lidl supmkt on L. Med, mkd pitch, shd; wc; chem disp; mv service pnt; baby facs; fam bthrm; shwrs; el pnts (3A) inc; lndtte (inc dryer); shop; rest; snack; takeaway; bar; bbq; pool; lakeside beach; cycle hire; wifi; dogs €3.50; phone; public trans 100m; twin axles; poss cr; Eng spkn; noisy (fr deliveries at adj supmkt & busy rd); "V busy but v pleasant site; direct access to beach; excel, immac san facs; vg & reasonable rest; next to supmkt; town cent 5 min walk along lakeside path; vg touring area for northern towns of lake Garda; excel site." ♦ 1 Apr-30 Oct. € 33.50   2014*

**ARCO** *1D1* (1km N Rural) *45.92694, 10.8925* **Camping Arco**, Loc Prabi, Via Legionari Cecoslovacchia 12, 38062 Arco (TN) [0464 517491; fax 515525; arco@arcoturistica.com; www.arcoturistica.com] Fr N foll sp Arco Centre at rndabt at start of ring rd & turn R after x-ing rv bdge. Fr S foll ring rd sp Trento. Turn L at Camping/Prabi (climbing area) sp. Lge, shd; wc (some cont); chem disp; mv service pnt; shwrs inc; el pnts (4A) inc; gas; lndtte; shop; rest 300m; snacks adj; bar; playgrnd; pool adj; tennis; games area; cycle hire; wifi; 10% statics; dogs €4; quiet; ccard acc. "V busy site; v clean." ♦ 21 Mar-8 Nov. € 28.00                        2009*

**ARENZANO see Genova** *1C2*

⊞ **AREZZO** *1D3* (10km SW Rural) *43.44982, 11.78990* Camping Villaggio Le Ginestre, Loc Ruscello 100, 52100 Arezzo [0575 363566; fax 366949; info@ campingleginestre.it; www.campingleginestre.it] Ont A1 sp Arezzo. Foll sp to Battifolle & Ruscello, proceed for 2km to rdbt, turn L to Ruscello and foll signs to site which will be on the L. Med, some hdstg, terr, pt sl, pt shd; htd wc; chem disp; mv service pnt; shwrs inc; el pnts (5-10A) inc; lndtte; shop 500m; rest, snacks; bar; playgrnd; pool; tennis; games area; games rm; 5% statics; dogs; bus; site clsd Jan; poss cr; adv bkg; ccard acc; CKE/CCI. "Pleasant, grassy site with views; friendly owner; gd rest; trains fr Arezzo to Florence, Rome etc; gd touring base." ♦ € 41.00                          2013*

## "I need an on-site restaurant"

We do our best to make sure site information is correct, but it is always best to check any must-have facilities are still available or will be open during your visit.

**ARONA** *1B1* (7km N Rural) *45.81583, 8.54992* Camping Solcio, Via al Campeggio, 28040 Solcio-de-Lesa (NO) [0322 7497; fax 7566; info@campingsolcio.com; www. campingsolcio.com] Foll S33 N fr Arona, thro Meina campsite on R of rd app Solcio; well sp, adj boatyard. Med, mkd pitch, pt shd; htd wc (some cont); chem disp; mv service pnt; baby facs; shwrs inc; el pnts (6A) inc; gas; lndtte (inc dryer); shop & 1km; rest, snacks; bar; BBQ; lake sw & shgl beach adj; fishing; watersports; wifi; entmnt; 40% statics; dogs €7.80; phone; rlwy noise; poss cr; Eng spkn; adv bkg; red low ssn/long stay; CKE/CCI. "Gd site adj lake; some sm pitches; premium for lakeside pitches; gd rest; gd cent for area; conv Stresa; friendly; highly rec; beach has permanent wooden parasols; immac san facs." 8 Mar-20 Oct. € 55.00 (3 persons)          2014*

⊞ **ARONA** *1B1* (2km S Rural) *45.73741, 8.57651* Camping Lago Azzurro, Via Enrico Fermi 2, 28040 Dormelletto (NO) [tel/fax 0322 497197; info@campinglagoazzurro.it; www. campinglagoazzurro.it] Exit A8/A26/E62 dir Castelletto Ticino onto SS33. Site 1km N of Dormelletto, on W shore of lake. Rec app fr Dormelletto, not Arona. Med, hdg/mkd pitch, shd; wc (some cont); mv service pnt; shwrs €0.70; el pnts (3A) €3.50; lndtte; shop; rest 1km; snacks; bar; pool high ssn; tennis; private shgl beach; boating; tennis adj; games area; entmnt; sat TV; 50% statics; dogs €4; phone; poss cr; adv bkg; quiet but motor boats noisy w/end, noisy entmnt high ssn. "Facs stretched high ssn due tented teenage vill on site; sm pitches." ♦ € 29.50                                    2010*

**ARONA** *1B1* (2km S Urban) *45.73648, 8.57564* Camping Röse, Via Fermi 3, 28040 Dormelletto (NO) [0322 497979; fax 498970; info@campingrose.it; www.campingrose. it] Site 2km N of Dormelletto, on W shore of lake. Rec app fr Dormelletto, not Arona. Med, some mkd pitch, shd; wc (some cont); chem disp; shwrs; el pnts (3A) €3; gas; lndtte; shop; rest adj; snacks; bar; playgrnd; beach adj; fishing; watersports; 80% statics; dogs €5; adv bkg; ccard acc; quiet. "Friendly site; inadequate shwrs; lake ferry boats at Arona." ♦ 1 Apr-12 Oct. € 26.00                          2010*

⊞ **ARONA** *1B1* (5km S Rural) *45.72825, 8.57966* Camping Lido Holiday Inn, Via Marco Polo 1, 28040 Dormelletto (NO) [tel/fax 0322 497047; info@campingholidayinn. com; www.campingholidayinn.com] Exit A8/A26/E62 at Castelletto Ticino dir Arona, foll sp Dormelletto. Lido sp on R. Lge, hdg/mkd pitch, pt sl, pt shd; htd wc; chem disp; mv service pnt; baby facs; shwrs inc; el pnts (3A) €4.50; gas; lndtte; shop; tradsmn; rest, snacks; bar; BBQ; playgrnd; pool; lake sw & shgl beach; tennis; golf 8km; 30% statics; dogs €5; phone; train 400m; Eng spkn; adv bkg; quiet; red CKE/CCI. "Ent thro fountain (it stops on ent!)." ♦ € 37.00                          2009*

**ARSIE** *1D1* (1km S Rural) *45.96333, 11.76027* Camping Al Lago, Via Campagna 14, 32030 Rocca di Arsie (BL) [0439 58540; fax 58471; info@campingallago.bl.it; www. campingallago.bl.it] Fr Trento on S47, turn E dir Feltre/ Belluno rd SS50B, take 1st exit after long tunnel. Fr Belluno on S50 & S50B take Arsié exit & foll site sp. Med, pt shd; wc; chem disp (wc); shwrs inc; el pnts (3A) inc; gas 2.5km; shop 3km; rest high ssn; bar; playgrnd; lake sw adj; 15% statics; dogs; phone; poss cr; adv bkg; quiet; ccard acc; CKE/CCI. "Excel, well-run, clean, tidy site in unspoilt area of historical & cultural interest; simple facs, basic but clean; boat hire locally; ent clsd 1400-1530 & 0000-0800; passport req to register." 1 Apr-4 Oct. € 23.00                                    2009*

**ARSIE** *1D1* (3km S Rural) *45.96777, 11.76583* Gajole - Quiet & Lake Camping, Loc Soravigo, 32030 Arsie (BL) [tel/fax 0439 58505; info@campinggajole.it; www.campinggajole. it] Fr S47 take S50bis dir Feltre, Belluno. Turn 1st R after long tunnel, site well sp. Med, hdstg, pt sl, terr, pt shd; wc (some cont); chem disp; mv service pnt; shwrs inc; el pnts (4A) inc; lndtte; shop; snacks; bar; lake sw 200m; 50% statics; dogs; Eng spkn; quiet. "Excel, peaceful site." ♦ ltd 1 Apr-30 Sep. € 22.00                                    2009*

## "Satellite navigation makes touring much easier"

Remember most sat navs don't know if you're towing or in a larger vehicle – always use yours alongside maps and site directions.

**ARZACHENA (SARDINIA)** *1C4* (7km NW Coastal) *41.13156, 9.44064* Camping Centro Vacanze Isuledda, 07020 Cannigione (OT) [0789 86003; fax 86089; info@isuledda. it; www.isuledda.it] Fr S125 foll sp Cannigione, site 3km N of Cannigione, sp on R. V lge, mkd pitch, pt shd; wc (some cont); chem disp; mv service pnt; shwrs; el pnts (4A); lndtte (inc dryer); shop; tradsmn; rest; bar; BBQ; sand beach adj; watersports; boat & cycle hire; fitness/beauty rm; wifi; entmnt; TV; some statics; no dogs; adv bkg; quiet; ccard acc. 1 Apr-30 Oct. € 54.00                                    2011*

⊞ **ASCOLI PICENO** *2E3* (200m Urban) *42.85274, 13.58182* Parking De Gasperc, Viale A De Gasperi, Ascoli Piceno Foll signs in town ctr. Sm, hdstg, unshd; own san rec; shops 200m; train 500. "C'van parking only; NH; historic town." € 1.20                                    2014*

**ASSERGI see Aquila, L'** *2E4*

ITALY

⊞ **ASSISI** *2E3* (1km E Rural) *43.06605, 12.63056* **Camping Fontemaggio**, Via Eremo delle Carceri, 24 Assisi 06081 (PG) [075 813636 or 812317; fax 813749; info@ fontemaggio.it; www.fontemaggio.it] Fr Perugia on S75, turn L onto rd SS147 twd Assisi; keeping Assisi walls on L past coach car park & foll sp to Porta Nuova. In sq at front of gate turn R & foll sp to Eremo delle Carceri, Foligno & Cmp Fontemaggio. Foll sp 1km to sq in front of next gate, turn R (sharp hairpin), site sp 800m on R at gate with narr arch, site 800m on R. Diff long, winding uphill app; recep in hotel. Lge, terr, hdstg, pt shd; htd wc (some cont); chem disp; mv service pnt; serviced pitches; shwrs inc; el pnts (6A) inc (long lead rec); gas; lndry rm; shop (high ssn) & 1km; rest; snacks (high ssn); bar; htd pool 3km; TV cab/sat; some statics; dogs; phone; poss cr; Eng spkn; adv bkg; quiet; ccard acc; CKE/CCI. "Lovely, spacious site in olive grove; views; footpath to attractive town; steep site rds diff when wet; order bread at hotel recep; firefly displays on site; facs tired." ◆ € 25.50                            2013*

**ASSISI** *2E3* (3km W Rural) *43.07611, 12.57361* **Camping Assisi (Formaly Internazionale)**, Via San Giovanni Campiglione 110, 06081 Assisi (PG) [075 816813; fax 812335; info@campingassisi.it; www.campingassisi.com] Fr Perugia SS75 to Ospedalicchio, then SS147 twd Assisi. Site well sp on R bef Assisi. Fr Assisi take SS147 to Perugia. Site on L in 3km adj Hotel Green. Lge, mkd pitch, shd; wc (mainly cont); chem disp; mv service pnt; shwrs inc; el pnts (3A) €2 (rev pol), 6A avail; gas; lndrte (inc dryer); shop & supmkt 3km; rest; pizzeria; bar; playgrnd; pool high ssn; tennis; 40% statics; dogs €2; phone; bus; car wash; poss cr; Eng spkn; adv bkg rec high ssn; quiet; ccard acc; red low ssn; CKE/CCI. "Helpful staff; minibus to Assisi; lovely, tidy, clean site; busy even in low ssn; immac san facs; gd rest; sm pitches; caves at Genga worth visit; excel; 10% red on next site if pt of same chain." ◆ ltd 20 Mar-2 Nov. € 42.00                            2014*

**ASTI** *1B2* (2km NW Rural) *44.94087, 8.18726* **Camping Umberto Cagni**, Loc Valmanera 152, 14100 Asti [0141 271238; info@campingcagniasti.it; www. campingcagniasti.it] Leave A21 at Asti E. Foll sp to Asti. At beg of town cntre with Asti Service Stn on L; turn R foll sp to camping site. Med, pt sl, shd; wc (mainly cont); shwrs; el pnts €3; shop; rest, snacks; bar; games area; entmnt; 50% statics; dogs €2; poss cr & noisy; 10% red CKE/CCI. "Fair NH/sh stay; friendly staff; not suitable lge o'fits; poss travellers; gates clsd 1300-1500." 1 Apr-30 Sep. € 23.50                            2012*

⊞ **AVOLA (SICILY)** *3C4* (4km N Coastal) *36.93631, 15.17462* Camping Sabbiadoro, Via Chiusa di Carlo 45, 96012 Avola (SR) [tel/fax 0931 822415; info@campeggiosabbiadoro. com; www.campeggiosabbiadoro.com] Fr N exit A18/E45 at Cassibile onto S115 dir Avola, site sp in 4km. Last 500m on narr, winding rd. Med, mkd pitch, terr, pt sl, shd; wc; chem disp; mv service pnt; shwrs €0.50; el pnts (2A) €4; lndrte; shop & 2km; snacks; bar; dir access to sand beach; horseriding; wifi; 20% statics; dogs; phone; sep car park Jul-Aug; adv bkg; quiet; ccard acc. "V attractive site with clean, ltd facs; rec visit Noto; well run; poss muddy pitches after heavy rain." € 59.00 (CChq acc)                            2014*

**BAIA DOMIZIA see Marina di Minturno** *2F4*

**BALISIO DI BALLABIO see Lecco** *1C1*

**BARBERINO VAL D'ELSA see Poggibonsi** *1D3*

**BARDOLINO** *1D2* (800m N Rural) *45.5570, 10.7181* Camping Continental, Loc Reboin, 37011 Bardolino (VR) [045 7210192; fax 7211756; continental@campingarda. it; www.campingarda.it/continental] Exit A22/E45 Lago di Garda Sud onto SR249. Site bet km 52/III & 52IV. Lge, shd; wc (some cont); mv service pnt; shwrs inc; el pnts (3A) inc; lndtte (inc dryer); shop; rest, snacks; bar; playgrnd; lake sw & beach adj; car wash; 50% statics; dogs not acc end Jun-end Aug; poss cr; adv bkg; quiet. ◆ 16 Apr-9 Oct. € 33.60                            2011*

**BARDOLINO** *1D2* (1.2km N Rural) *45.56388, 10.71416* Camping La Rocca, Loc San Pietro, Via Gardensana 37, 37011 Bardolino (VR) [045 7211111; fax 7211300; info@ campinglarocca.com; www.campinglarocca.com] Exit A22/E45 Affi/Lago di Garda Sud & foll SR249 sp Bardolino. Camp 1st site on both sides of rd exit town at km 53/IV. V lge, shd; wc (some cont); chem disp; mv service pnt; shwrs inc; el pnts (10A) inc; lndtte; shop; tradsmn; rest, snacks; bar; BBQ; playgrnd; pool; paddling pool; shgl beach adj; lake sw; fishing; cycle hire; TV rm; 15% statics; dogs €5.90; phone; poss cr; Eng spkn; no adv bkg; some rd noise (rd thro site); ccard acc; red CKE/CCI. "Pleasant, popular site; gd views; avoid field nr lake; lakeside walk to Garda or Bardolino 20mins; mkt Thurs Bardolino, Fri Garda; red snr citizens." ◆ Easter-6 Oct. € 52.30                            2013*

> # "There aren't many sites open at this time of year"
>
> If you're travelling outside peak season remember to call ahead to check site opening dates – even if the entry says 'open all year'.

**BARDOLINO** *1D2* (1.5km N Rural) *45.55944, 10.71666* Camping Serenella, Loc Mezzariva 19, 37011 Bardolino (VR) [045 7211333; fax 7211552; serenella@camping-serenella.it; www.camping-serenella.it] Site on R SR249. Lge, pt sl, pt shd; wc; chem disp; mv service pnt; shwrs inc; el pnts (6A) inc; lndtte (inc dryer); shop; rest, snacks; bar; playgrnd; pool; paddling pool; lake sw; boat launching; waterski; games rm; cycle hire; entmnt; 50% statics; no dogs; poss v cr; Eng spkn; no ccard acc. "Bus to Verona; lakeside walk to Garda or Bardolino; excel, clean facs; sm pitches poss diff lge o'fits - check bef pitching; vg supmkt, rest." ◆ ltd 1 Apr-18 Oct. € 36.50                            2009*

**BARDOLINO** *1D2* (500m S Rural) *45.54275, 10.72513* Camping Europa, Loc Mandracci, Via Santa Cristina 12, 37011 Bardolino (VR) [045 7210073; fax 7210073; europa@ campingarda.it; www.campingarda.it] N fr Peschiera on SR249, site on W side of rd opp 2nd Bardolino 50 km/h sp at S of vill, adj lge petrol stn & Hotel du Lac. Med, mkd pitch, pt shd; wc; chem disp; shwrs inc; el pnts (6A) inc; lndtte (inc dryer); shop; rest 500m; snacks; bar; lake sw & watersports adj; TV; 40% statics; no dogs Jul & Aug; adv bkg; rd noise. "Lovely lakeside setting; helpful staff." ◆ 1 Apr-9 Oct. € 32.50  2010*

**BARDOLINO** *1D2* (2km S Rural) *45.52525, 10.72977* Camping Cisano/San Vito, Via Peschiera 48, 37011 Cisano (VR) [045 6229098; fax 6229059; cisano@camping-cisano. it; www.camping-cisano.it] Sites on S boundary of Cisano, on SE shore of Lake Garda. V lge, mkd pitch, terr, sl, shd; wc; chem disp; mv service pnt; shwrs inc; el pnts (4A) inc; gas; lndtte (inc dryer); supmkt; rest, snacks; bar; pool; paddling pool; waterslide; private beach & lake sw adj; waterskiing; windsurfing; canoeing; tennis; games area; cycle hire; entmnt; TV rm; statics; no dogs; Eng spkn; quiet; red low ssn. "Two lovely, clean, lakeside sites run as one - San Vito smaller/ quieter; helpful staff; san facs in need of refurb; some pitches diff access & chocks req; passport req at site check-in; Verona Opera excursions arranged high ssn; gd; v popular; helpful staff; gd walking/cycling; gd rest." ♦ 29 Mar-12 Oct. € 66.00 (CChq acc) 2014*

⊞ **BARDONECCHIA** *1A2* (5km SW Rural) *45.04954, 6.66510* Camping Bokki, Loc Pian del Colle, 10052 Bardonecchia (TO) [tel/fax 0122 99893; info@bokki.it; www.bokki. it] Fr A32 ent Bardonecchia & foll sp Melezet. After Melezet foll rd uphill for 1.5km. Bokki is 2nd site on R. Med, mkd pitch, pt sl, pt shd; htd wc; chem disp; mv service pnt; baby facs; fam bthrm; shwrs inc; el pnts (2A) inc; lndtte; shop 3km; rest, snacks; bar; playgrnd; lake sw adj; TV rm; 95% statics; dogs €1; phone; Eng spkn; adv bkg; quiet; CKE/CCI. "Helpful owners; beautiful location; conv Fréjus tunnel; diff ent to v sm sloping, uneven pitch; no red in low ssn." € 31.00 2014*

**BAROLO** *1B2* (1km W Rural) *44.61246, 7.92106* Camping Sole Langhe, Piazza della Vite e Del Vino, Frazione Vergne, 12060 Barolo (CN) [0173 560510; fax 386819; info@solelanghe.com; www.campingsolelanghe.it] Fr S exit A6 E sp Carru. At Carru turn N onto SP12 & foll sp Barolo. Site sp on ent Barolo. Sm, hdg pitch, pt shd; wc; chem disp; mv service pnt; shwrs inc; el pnts (6A) inc; lndtte; shop; rest; snacks; bar 1km; BBQ; playgrnd; games area; no statics; dogs; Eng spkn; quiet. "Lovely orchard site in cent Barolo wine region; v helpful owner." 1 Mar-30 Nov. € 32.00 2014*

⊞ **BARREA** *2F4* (500m S Rural) *41.74978, 13.99128* Camping La Genziana, Loc Tre Croci 1, 67030 Barrea (AQ) [tel/fax 0864 88101; pasettanet@tiscalinet.it; www. campinglagenzianapasetta.it] Fr S83 to S end Lago di Barrea, thro Barrea S, site immed on L on uphill L-hand bend. Med, mkd pitch, terr, pt shd; wc; chem disp; mv service pnt; shwrs; el pnts (3A) €2.60; lndtte; sm shop; rest 300m; bar; BBQ: playgrnd; sand beach & lake sw 3km; dogs €3; bus; Eng spkn; adv bkg; quiet. "Knowledgeable owner; delightful site but unrel hot water & poor facs; excel area cycling; trekking, skiing; ltd shops Barrea 10 mins walk; conv Abruzzi National Park." € 26.40 2009*

⊞ **BASTIA MONDOVI** *1B2* (1km N Rural) *44.44871, 7.89417* Camping La Cascina, Loc Pieve 3, 12060 Bastia-Mondovi (CN) [tel/fax 0174 60181; info@campinglacascina.it; www. campinglacascina.it] Fr Cuneo on S564 turn R at rndabt adj to Rv Tanaro sp to Bastia Mondovi, site on R in 500m. Lge, pt shd; wc; chem disp; mv service pnt; shwrs; el pnts (6A) €2.50; lndtte; shop; rest 1km; bar; playgrnd; pool; games area; 90% statics; phone; site clsd Sep; poss cr; Eng spkn; ccard acc; CKE/CCI. "Touring vans on edge of sports field; conv wine vills; hot water poss erratic; v busy w/end high ssn." ♦ 01 Jan-02 Sep, 22 Sep-31 Dec. € 35.50 2013*

**BAVENO see Stresa** *1B1*

**BELLAGIO** *1C1* (1.5km S Rural) Clarke Camping, Via Valassina 170/C, 22021 Bellagio, Como [031 951325; info@villa-magnolia.co.uk; www.bellagio-camping. com] Fr Como, on arr in Bellagio foll sp Lecco to R, foll site sps uphill. Narr rds & site ent. Med, terr, pt shd; wc (some cont); chem disp; mv service pnt; shwrs inc; el pnts €2; shop 500m; rest, snacks, bar 1.5km; lake sw 1.5km; no statics; no dogs; ferries, water taxis 1.5km; quiet; wifi; ccards & chq's not acc; "British owner; views over lake; uphill walk fr town to campsite; town is on lakeside; site & app not suitable lge o'fits; no twin-axles; beautiful, peaceful site.basic san facs but clean, friendly owners.; use vehicle ferry fr Cadenabbis or Varenne €20 for m'van & 2 people, then foll dirs." 15 May-15 Sep. € 33.00 2013*

**BELLARIA** *2E2* (3km N Coastal) *44.16606, 12.43563* Camping Delle Rose, Via Adriatica 29, 47043 Gatteo-a-Mare (FC) [0547 86213; fax 87583; info@villaggiorose.com; www. villaggiorose.com] Exit A14/E55 dir Rimini Nord onto S16. Exit S16 at Gatteo a Mare, turn R at junc, over rndabt. Site on L in 100m at km 186. Lge, mkd pitch, shd; wc (some cont); chem disp; mv service pnt; shwrs inc; el pnts (6A) €3; gas; lndtte; shop; rest, snacks; bar; playgrnd; pool; paddling pool; sand beach 300m; games area; entmnt; TV; 30% statics; dogs €8.10 (sm only); free shuttle bus to beach; poss cr; Eng spkn; adv bkg; quiet, some rlwy & rd noise; ccard acc; red CKE/CCI. "Easy reach San Marino & Urbino." ♦ 24 Apr-20 Sep. € 36.00 (CChq acc) 2009*

⊞ **BELLARIA** *2E2* (2km NE Coastal) *44.16076, 12.44836* Happy Camping Village, Via Panzini 228, San Mauro a Mare, 47814 Bellaria (RN) [0541 346102; fax 346408; info@happycamping.it; www.happycamping.it] Fr A14 exit Rimini Nord onto S16 N. Turn off dir San Mauro Mare & Bellaria Cagnona, foll sp Aquabell Waterpark. Over rlwy x-ing, turn R, site on L. Lge, mkd pitch, hdstg, pt sl, pt shd; wc (some cont); chem disp; mv service pnt; baby facs; fam bthrm; shwrs inc; el pnts (8-10A) €3.50; gas; lndtte (inc dryer); shop; rest, snacks; bar; playgrnd; pool; paddling pool; sand beach adj; tennis; games area; games rm; wifi; TV; 40% statics; dogs €6; phone; poss cr & noisy; ltd Eng spkn; adv bkg; red low ssn; CKE/CCI. "Conv Rimini, San Marino; variable size pitches; clean, private beach; pool clsd 1300-1530 & after 1900; lge shopping cent & cinema complex 2km; Bellaria pleasant resort with port & marina." € 39.00 2012*

**BELLARIA** *2E2* (1.5km NW Coastal/Urban) *44.16235, 12.44231* Camping Green, Via Vespucci 8, 47030 San Mauro-Mare (FO) [tel/fax 0541 341225; info@ campinggreen.it; www.campinggreen.it] Exit A14/E55 at Rimini Nord onto S16. Foll sp N to San Mauro-Mare, site sp. Med, shd; wc; chem disp; mv service pnt; shwrs inc; el pnts (6A) €2.50; gas; lndtte; shop 200m; rest 100m; playgrnd; sand beach adj; watersports; cycle hire; wifi; some statics; dogs €4; poss cr; quiet but some rlwy noise. "Excel, family-run, friendly site." ♦ 9 Apr-24 Sep. € 27.50 2011*

**BELVEDERE DI GRADO see Aquileia** *2E1*

ITALY

**BERGAMO** *2C1* (25km N Rural) *45.78866, 9.94705* **Camping La Tartufaia**, Via Nazionale 2519, 24060 Ranzanico al Lago di Endine [tel/fax 39 035 819 259; info@latartufaia.com; www.latartufaia.com] Fr A4 Milan-Venice, exit at Seriate. Take SS42 dir Lovere. Campsite on L past Ranzanico exit. Med, mkd pitch, hdstg, terr, pt shd; wc; chem disp; mv service pnt; shwr; el pnts (6A) inc; gas; lndtte (inc dryer); shop 50m; rest; snacks; bar; BBQ; pool; beach adj; sw adj; games rm; wifi; dogs; bus adj; twin axles; Eng spkn; ccard acc; red low ssn; CCI. "Excel site; beautiful views over lake & mountains; gd bus conns; foothpath around lake; v friendly & helpful owners." ♦ 25 Apr-21 Sep. € 42.50                               2014*

# "That's changed – Should I let The Club know?"

If you find something on site that's different from the site entry, fill in a report and let us know. See www.caravanclub.co.uk/europereport.

**BEVAGNA** *2E3* (3km SW Rural) *42.91236, 12.58622* **Camping Pian di Boccio**, Via Pian de Boccio 10, 06031 Bevagna [0742 360 164; fax 360 391; info@piandiboccio.com; www.piandiboccio.com] Fr Foligno to Bevagna in c'van strt on S316 & turn R after 3km, foll signs. In car - just past Bevagna 1st rd on the R past the bdge. Med, hdstg, terr, pt shd; wc; chem disp; mv service pnt; shwrs; el pnts (6A); lndtte; shop; tradsmn; rest; bar; BBQ; playgrnd; pool; paddling pool; games area; entmnt; wifi; tv rm; 10% statics; dogs; phone; bus 2km; twin axles; Eng spkn; quiet; CCI. "Excel site." ♦ 1 Apr-30 Sep. € 34.50                               2014*

**BIBIONE** *2E1* (6km W Coastal) *45.63055, 12.99444* **Camping Village Capalonga**, Viale della Laguna 16, 30020 Bibione-Pineda (VE) [0431 438351 or 0431 447190 LS; fax 438370 or 0431 438986 LS; capalonga@bibionemare.com; www. capalonga.com] Well sp approx 6km fr Bibione dir Bibione Pineda. V lge, shd; wc (some cont); chem disp; mv service pnt; baby facs (on request); shwrs inc; el pnts (10A) inc; gas; lndtte; shop; rest, snacks; bar; BBQ; playgrnd; pool; private Blue Flag sand beach adj; watersports; fishing; tennis; archery; cycle hire nrby; horseriding 6km; golf 10km; games rm; excursions; various activities; wifi; entmnt; TV; 25% statics; no dogs; no c'vans/m'vans over 10m high ssn; phone; adv bkg; quiet; ccard acc; red low ssn. "Well-organised site; gd for families; extra for pitches on beach; spacious, clean san facs; rest o'looking lagoon; voracious mosquitoes!" ♦ 24 Apr-21 Sep. € 51.80 SBS - Y15                               2011*

**BOBBIO** *1C2* (1.5km S Rural) *44.75340, 9.38456* **Camping PonteGobbo Terme**, Via San Martino 4, 29022 Bobbio (PC) [0523 936927 / 0523 936068; fax 960610; camping. pontegobbo@iol.it; www.campingpontegobbo.com] Heading twd Genova on S45 turn L on long bdge & immed R. Site sp. Lge, pt sl, shd; htd wc (some cont); chem disp; shwrs €0.50; el pnts (4A) €2; gas; shop & 1km; bar; playgrnd; games area; entmnt; TV; 40% statics; phone; sep car park; No dogs; Eng spkn; no adv bkg; quiet; ccard acc; red low ssn/CCI/CCI. "Trout-fishing in rv; gd scenery; lovely town; hot water to shwrs only; rvside walks and cycling." ♦ € 21.50      2013*

**BOGLIASCO see Genova** *1C2*

**BOLOGNA** *1D2* (2km NE Rural) *44.52333, 11.37388* **Centro Turistico Campeggio Città di Bologna**, Via Romita 12/4a, 40127 Bologna [051 325016; fax 325318; info@ hotelcamping.com; www.hotelcamping.com] Access is fr A14 Bologna to Ancona. Leave at junc 7 sp Fiera & Via Stalingrado. Can be accessed fr the parallel 'Tangenziale' at same junc. Sp at 1st junc after toll. Med, mkd pitch, pt shd; htd wc; chem disp; mv service pnt; shwrs inc; el pnts (6A) inc; lndtte (inc dryer); shop; tradsmn; supmkt nrby; rest, snacks; bar; BBQ (charcoal/gas); playgrnd; pool; games rm; wifi; TV rm; dogs €2; no c'vans/m'vans over 15m on hdstg & over 9m on grass; bus to city; site clsd 20 Dec-9 Jan; Eng spkn; adv bkg; some rd & aircraft noise; ccard acc; red low ssn/long stay/ CKE/CCI. "Conv Bologna Trade Fair & Exhibition cent; friendly, helpful staff; excel, clean san facs; excel pool; tourist pitches at rear nr san facs block; gd bus service fr ent into city; access to pitches poss diff lge o'fits; sat nav dir may take you down narr rds; poss lots mosquitoes; excel site." ♦ 26 Jan-19 Dec. € 44.00 SBS - Y14                               2014*

**BOLSENA** *1D3* (2km S Rural) *42.62722, 11.99444* **Camping Village Lido di Bolsena**, Via Cassia, Km 111, 01023 Bolsena (VT) [0761 799258; fax 796105; info@bolsenacamping.it; www.bolsenacamping.it] Fr S on a'strada A1 foll sp Viterbo & Lago di Bolsena, then take SR2 N to site; sp. Fr N exit A1 at Orvieto onto SS71 to Bolsena. At traff lts in cent of town turn L, site on R in approx 2km. V lge, pt shd; wc; chem disp; mv service pnt; private bthrms avail; shwrs €0.50; el pnts (3A) inc (poss rev pol); gas; lndtte (inc dryer); shop; rest, snacks; bar; playgrnd; pool; private sand beach adj; lake sw; watersports; tennis; cycle hire; games area; entmnt; some statics; phone; sep car park; Eng spkn; adv bkg; quiet; ccard not acc. "Beautiful lakeside location; gd size pitches; all facs excel; cycle path around lake to town; sm dogs acc; charge for pool." 20 Apr-30 Sep. € 44.50                               2014*

# "I like to fill in the reports as I travel from site to site"

You'll find report forms at the back of this guide, or you can fill them in online at www.caravaclub.co.uk/europereport.

**BOLSENA** *1D3* (6km W Rural) *42.65340, 11.93120* **Camping Valdisole**, Via Cassia, Km 117, 01023 Bolsena (VT) [tel/ fax 0761 797064 or 03349 952575 LS; valdisolecamping@ virgillio.it; www.campingvaldisole.com] Fr N on A1 exit Orvieta & foll S71 to junc with S74; turn R twd San Lorenzo Nuovo. Then take S2 (Via Cassia) to site on R, 10km after San Lorenzo Nuovo. Fr S exit at Orte onto S204 sp Viterbo, then S2 Via Cassia N dir Montefiascone & Bolsena. Thro town & site approx 500m after g'ge. Lge, mkd pitch, shd; wc (cont); chem disp; shwrs inc; el pnts (8A) inc (check pol); gas; lndtte; shop; tradsmn; rest, snacks; pizzeria adj; bar; BBQ; playgrnd; lake sw & (black) sand beach; fishing; watersports; horseriding 5km; golf 500m; guided walks 5km; wifi; games/TV rm; dogs; Eng spkn; adv bkg rec Jul/Aug; poss noisy high ssn; ccard acc; red low ssn/CKE/CCI. "Beautiful location; charming owners; lge grassed pitches, shd or sunny (poss dusty high ssn); vg san facs; easy transport Rome, Siena & Orvieto; rallies welcome; mkt Tues." ♦ 1 May-30 Sep. € 33.00                               2009*

ITALY

BOLZANO/BOZEN *1D1* (8km S Rural) *46.4300, 11.34305* Camping-Park Steiner, Kennedystrasse 32, 39055 Laives/Leifers (BZ) [0471 950105; fax 593141; info@ campingsteiner.com; www.campingsteiner.com] Fr N take Bolzano/Bozen-Sud exit fr A22/E45 & pick up rd S12 twd Trento to site; site on R on ent Laives at N edge of vill. Fr S leave A22 at junc for Egna onto rd S12 dir Bolzano. Poorly sp. Lge, hdg/mkd pitch, pt sl, shd; htd wc; (some cont) chem disp; mv service pnt; baby facs; shwrs inc; el pnts (6A) inc; gas; lndtte; shop; rest, snacks; pizzeria; bar; playgrnd; 2 pools (1 covrd); cycle hire; wifi; TV; some statics; dogs €5; phone; Eng spkn; adv bkg rec; some rd & rlwy noise; CKE/CCI. "Pleasant, well-run, excel site on edge of Dolomites; attractive pitches; helpful staff; gd, clean, modern san facs; gates clsd 1300-1500 & 2200-0700; beautiful area; vg walking; well stocked shop; highly rec." ♦ 5 Apr-31 Oct. € 52.00          2014*

⊞ BOLZANO/BOZEN *1D1* (2km NW Rural) *46.50333, 11.3000* Camping Moosbauer, Via San Maurizio 83, 39100 Bolzano [0471 918492; fax 204894; info@moosbauer. com; www.moosbauer.com] Exit A22/E45 at Bolzano Sud exit & take S38 N dir Merano (keep L after toll booths). After tunnel take 1st exit sp Eppan & hospital, & turn L at top of feeder rd sp Bolzano. After approx 2km at island past 08 G'ge turn L & foll site sp. Site on R in 1km by bus stop on S38, sp. Med, hdg/mkd pitch, hdstg, pt sl, pt shd; htd wc; chem disp; mv service pnt; serviced pitches; baby facs; shwrs inc; el pnts (5A) inc; lndtte; shop; tradsmn; rest, snacks; bar; playgrnd; htd pool; games rm; cab/sat TV; entmnt; dogs €4; bus; poss cr; Eng spkn; adv bkg; quiet but some rd noise; CKE/CCI. "Popular, well-maintained, attractive site; gd welcome fr friendly owners; pitches narr; excel, modern san facs; gate shut 1300-1500; bus service adj for archaeological museum (unique ice man); gd cent for walks in Dolomites." ♦ ltd € 34.00          2012*

⊞ BOMBA *2F4* (2km W Rural) *42.0175, 14.36138* Campeggio Isola Verde, Via del Lago 2, 66042 Bomba (CH) [0872 860475; fax 860450; isolaverde@tin.it; www. isolaverdeonline.it] Exit A14 at Val di Sangro exit & take SS652 for Bomba. Site clearly sp. Med, some hdstg, terr, pt shd; wc; chem disp; shwrs inc; el pnts (10A) inc; shop; rest, snacks; bar; playgrnd; pool; lake sw & beach; tennis; cycle hire; entmnt; 50% statics; dogs; bus/train 500m; Eng spkn; adv bkg; quiet; ccard acc. "Excel position above lake in beautiful countryside; gd base winter sports; excel rest." € 38.00  2011*

BORGO SAN LORENZO *1D3* (7km SE Rural) *43.93087, 11.46426* Camping Vicchio Ponte, Via Costoli 16, 50039 Vicchio [055 8448306; fax 579405; info@ campingvecchioponte.it; www.campingvecchioponte.it] On SP551 adj to sw pool in Vicchio. Med, pt shd; wc (cont); chem disp; mv service pnt; shwrs inc; el pnts (4A) inc; lndry rm; shop, rest, bar in vill; htd pool adj; dogs; train to Florence 1km; poss cr; Eng spkn; quiet; CKE/CCI. "Simple, municipal site." 1 Jun-15 Sep. € 24.00          2009*

BORGO SAN LORENZO *1D3* (5km W Rural) *43.96144, 11.30918* Camping Mugello Verde, Via Massorondinaio 39, 50037 San Piero-a-Sieve (FI) [055 848511; fax 8486910; mugelloverde@florencecamping.com; www. florencecamping.com] Exit A1 at Barberino exit & foll Barberino sp twd San Piero-a-Sieve & Borgo San Lorenzo. Turn S on S65 twd Florence. Site sp immed after Cafaggiolo. Lge, sl, terr, pt shd; htd wc (some cont); chem disp; mv service pnt; shwrs inc; el pnts (6A) inc; gas; lndtte (inc dryer); shop; rest, snacks; bar; playgrnd; pool (bathing caps req); tennis; cycle hire; wifi; entmnt; 50% statics; bus/train; no adv bkg; quiet; ccard acc; red low ssn; CKE/CCI. "Hillside site; bus to Florence high ssn (fr vill low ssn) or 20 mins drive; hard grnd diff for awnings; poss long walk to recep & shop; helpful, friendly staff; refurbed, gd, clean san facs; avoid early Jun - Italian Grand Prix!." ♦ 15 Mar-30 Oct. € 42.00          2014*

**BOTTAI see Firenze** *1D3*

BRACCIANO *2E4* (3km N Rural) *42.1300, 12.17333* Kwan Village Roma Flash Sporting, Via Settevene Palo 42, 00062 Bracciano [tel/fax 0699 805458 or 3389 951738 LS; info@romaflash.it; www.romaflash.it] Fr A1 exit at Magliano Sabina dir Civita Castellana. Then foll sp Nepi, Sutri, Trevignano & Bracciano. Sp on lakeside rd N of Bracciano. Lge, mkd pitch, pt shd; wc (some cont); chem disp; mv service pnt; baby facs; sauna; shwrs inc; el pnts (6A) inc; lndtte (inc dryer); shop high ssn; rest, snacks; bar; BBQ (charcoal, gas); playgrnd; pool; lake sw & free beach; watersports; fishing; horseriding 4km; tennis; cycle hire; games rm; wifi; entmnt; TV; 5% statics; dogs €5.50; no c'vans/m'vans over 12m; shuttle bus to Bracciano; bus/train to Rome; sep car park; Eng spkn; quiet; ccard acc; red low ssn. "Attractive, well-kept lakeside site; clean, modern san facs; conv Rome." ♦ 1 Apr-29 Sep. € 42.00 (CChq acc) SBS - Y16          2012*

BRACCIANO *2E4* (8km N Rural) *42.14673, 12.26905* Camping Internazionale Lago di Bracciano, Via Del Pianoro 4, 00069 Trevignano-Romano (RM) [0699 85032; fax 826781; robertocarrano@tin.it; www.camping-inter-lagodibracciano.com] Fr SS2 exit at Lake Bracciano & cont twd Trevignano then Anguillara. Site on lakeside at end of lane. Lge, pt shd; wc (some cont); chem disp; mv service pnt; shwrs; el pnts (3-6A) inc; lndtte (inc dryer); shop; rest, snacks; cooking facs; playgrnd; paddling pool; cycle hire; games area; internet; TV rm; 20% statics; dogs €3.70; adv bkg; quiet; ccard acc. "Set in Due Laghi Nature Park; peaceful." 1 Apr-30 Sep. € 28.00          2009*

BRACCIANO *2E4* (1.5km SE Rural) *42.10505, 12.18595* Camping Porticciolo, Via Porticciolo, 00062 Bracciano [06 99803060; fax 99803030; info@porticciolo.it; www. porticciolo.it] Avoid town cent. Fr Rome circular rd take S2 dir Viterbo, then Anguillara & dir Bracciano. Keep to lakeside; at traff lts turn twds town & after rlwy bdge turn immed R & foll site sp. Avoid town cent. Med, hdg/mkd pitch, shd; wc; chem disp; shwrs €0.50; el pnts (3-6A) €3.40-5; lndtte; shop; tradsmn; rest, snacks; bar; playgrnd; shgl beach & lake adj; sand beach 15km; sailing; watersports; wifi; 10% statics; dogs €4.50; sep car park Jul/Aug; site bus to stn; excursions; Eng spkn; adv bkg; quiet; red low ssn/long stay; ccard acc; CKE/ CCI. "Lovely position on lakeside; gd base for touring; frequent trains to Rome fr Bracciano; new, modern san facs; lge pitches; haphazard site layout; vg." ♦ 1 Apr-30 Sep. € 26.00    2010*

**BRESSANONE/BRIXEN** *1D1* (1km SE Rural) *46.73472, 11.64555* Camping Löwenhof, Brennerstrasse 60, 39040 Varna/Vahrn (BZ) [0472 836216; fax 801337; info@ loewenhof.it; www.loewenhof.it] On main Brenner rd SS12 at 481km mark, on R at minor rd junc adj hotel; easily seen fr main rd. Sm, mkd pitch, wc; shwrs inc; el pnts (4A) €2; lndtte; shop & 2km; rest, snacks; bar; htd pool; paddling pool; hotel sauna, solarium, whirlpool & steambaths avail for use; tennis; games rm; cycle hire; dogs €5 (not acc Jul/Aug); poss cr; Eng spkn; adv bkg; quiet but rd noise behind hotel; red low ssn/long stay/CKE/CCI. "Vg." 1 Apr-30 Oct. € 33.00      2009*

**BRIATICO** *3B4* (W Coastal) *38.72378, 16.02538* Villaggio Camping L'Africano, 89817 Briatico (VV) [tel/fax 0963 391150; info@villaggiocampinglafricano.it; www. villaggiocampinglafricano.it] Exit A3/E45 or S18 at Pizzo onto S522 W dir Tropea, site sp. Lge, pt shd; wc; mv service pnt; shwrs inc; el pnts €3; lndtte; shop high ssn; rest high ssn; rest, snacks; bar; pool; paddling pool; sand beach 200m; games area; entmnt; TV rm; some statics; dogs €2; adv bkg; quiet. 1 Apr-31 Oct. € 31.50      2009*

**BRUCOLI (SICILY)** *3C4* (E Coastal) *37.28191, 15.18941* Camping Baia del Silenzio, Campolato Basso, 96010 Brucoli (SR) [0931 981881; fax 982288; www. baiadelsilenzio.net; www.baiadelsilenzio.net] Sp fr Brucoli stn level x-ing, E of rd SS114. Lge, mkd pitch, pt sl, shd; wc (some cont); chem disp; mv service pnt; shwrs inc; el pnts (2A) €8; lndtte; shop; tradsmn; rest, snacks; bar; sm sandy/rocky beach adj; tennis; 20% statics; dogs €5 (not acc Jul/Aug); phone; sep car park high ssn; adv bkg; poss noisy; ccard acc; red low ssn; CKE/CCI. "Clean, well-maintained site with gd facs; conv Siracusa, Catania & Mt Etna." ♦ ltd € 43.00  2009*

**BRUNICO/BRUNECK** *1D1* (10km E Rural) *46.77600, 12.03688* Camping Residence Corones, Niederrasen 124, 39030 Rasun-di-Sotto/Niederrasen (BZ) [0474 496490; fax 498250; info@corones.com; www.corones.com] On SS49 dir Rasun, turn N to site to Antholz, bear L in front of Gasthof, over bdge turn L, site in 400m. Med, pt shd; wc; chem disp; mv service pnt; serviced pitches; sauna; shwrs inc; private bthrms avail; el pnts (3A) metered; gas; lndtte; shop; rest, snacks; bar; playgrnd; htd pool; paddling pool; tennis; games area; cycle hire; solarium; some statics; dogs €4.20; phone; Eng spkn; adv bkg; quiet; ccard acc (poss not in rest); red low ssn. "Gd cent for walking & skiing - outings arranged; superb facs, inc in winter; conv day visit to Dolomites; helpful owner & staff; excel." ♦ 1 Dec-19 Apr & 20 May-25 Oct. € 32.80      2013*

**BRUNICO/BRUNECK** *1D1* (8km W Rural) *46.80805, 11.81305* Camping Gisser, Via Val Pusteria 26, San Sigismondo, 39030 Chienes/Kiens (BZ) [0474 569605; fax 569657; camping@hotelgisser.it; www.hotelgisser.it] On SS49 at 20.8km post in San Sigismondo. Lge, pt sl, pt shd; wc; shwrs inc; el pnts (5A) €2; lndtte; shop 100m; rest, snacks; bar; htd pool; canoeing; dogs €2.50; no adv bkg; quiet. "NH en rte Venice; ltd facs low ssn & basic." 1 May-15 Oct. € 22.00      2009*

**CAGLIARI (SARDINIA)** *3B1* (1km SE Urban) *39.21129, 9.12883* Camper Cagliari Park, 13 Via Stanislao Caboni, 09125 Cagliari [346 7245766 or 070 303147 or 0328 3348847 (mob); fax 070 303147; info@ campercagliaripark.it; www.campercagliaripark.it] Well sp on main rds into Cagliari. Sm, unshd; wc; chem disp; mv service pnt; el pnts (10A) €4; lndtte nr; bus 200m; Eng spkn; CKE/CCI. "Gd secure site; v helpful owner; walking dist historical cent, rests etc; c'vans enquire 1st." € 21.00      2014*

**CALCERANICA AL LAGO see Levico Terme** *1D1*

**CANAZEI** *1D1* (200m E Rural) *46.47326, 11.77586* Camping Marmolada, Via Pareda 60, 38032 Canazei (TN) [0462 601660; fax 601722; campingmarmolada@virgilio. it; www.campingmarmolada.com] On R bank of Rv Avisio on rd S641. Sp fr cent of Canazei. Lge, hdstg, pt shd; wc; chem disp; shwrs; el pnts (4A) €3; lndtte (inc dryer); snacks; bar; BBQ; htd pool adj; 45% statics; dogs €3; winter ski cent; poss cr; Eng spkn; no adv bkg ess high ssn; poss noisy high ssn; ccard acc. "Opp cable car & stn; gd for walking/skiing; excel views all round; vg san facs; 10 min walk to town." € 30.50      2010*

**CANAZEI** *1D1* (2km W Rural) *46.47479, 11.74067* Camping Miravalle, Strèda de Greva 39, 38031 Campitello-di-Fassa (TN) [0462 750502; fax 751563; info@campingmiravalle. it; www.campingmiravalle.it] In vill cent on rte 48 site sp down side rd. Lge, sl, unshd; wc (some cont); chem disp; mv service pnt; baby facs; shwrs inc; el pnts (3A) inc (poss rev pol), extra €2 for 6A; lndtte; shop 100m; rest, snacks; 100m; bar; dogs €4; poss cr; Eng spkn; adv bkg; quiet; ccard acc; CKE/CCI. "Excel facs; conv cable car." ♦ 1 Jun-30 Sep & 1 Dec-30 Apr. € 28.50      2009*

**CANNIGIONE see Arzachena (Sardinia)** *1C4*

**CANNOBIO** *1C1* (200m N Rural) *46.06515, 8.6905* Camping Riviera, Via Casali Darbedo 2, 28822 Cannobio (VB) [tel/ fax 0323 71360; riviera@riviera-valleromantica.com; www.riviera-valleromantica.com] N of Cannobio twd Switzerland on main rd. Over rv at o'skts of town, site ent on R in 30m; sp. Lge, hdg/mkd pitch, shd; wc; chem disp; mv service pnt; private san facs some pitches; shwrs inc; el pnts (4A) €4; gas; lndtte; shop; rest, snacks; bar; playgrnd; private shgl beach & lake sw adj; boat hire; windsurfing; some statics; dogs €4.50; poss cr; adv bkg. "Popular, peaceful, well-maintained site bet rv & lake; extra for lakeside pitch; gd sailing; v helpful staff." ♦ 1 Apr-18 Oct. € 47.00      2013*

**CANNOBIO** *1C1* (500m N Urban) *46.06678, 8.69507* Camping Del Sole, Via Sotto i Chiosi 81/A, 28822 Cannobio (VB) [0323 70732; fax 72387; info@campingsole. it; www.campingsole.it] Fr S fr A26 foll Verbania sp then sp Cannobio or Locarno. Ent vill, over cobbles, 2nd R in 750m. Bef rv bdge immed sharp R under main rd, site on L after quick R turn. Fr N ent Cannobio, 1st L after x-ing rv, then as above. Lge, hdg pitch, pt shd; wc; chem disp; shwrs inc; el pnts (4A) €3; gas; lndtte; supmkt 150m; rest; bar; playgrnd; pool; shgl beach & lake sw 250m; 60% statics; dogs €4; poss cr; Eng spkn; adv bkg; poss noisy; ccard acc; red long stay/low ssn; CKE/CCI. "Attractive vill & lake frontage; friendly, family-run site; poss tight access some pitches; clean facs; lovely pool area." 1 Apr-10 Oct. € 24.00      2009*

Tell us about the sites you visit

CANNOBIO *1C1* (1km N Rural) *46.07791, 8.69345* Villaggio Camping Bosco, Punta Bragone, 28822 Cannobio (VB) [0323 71597; fax 739647; bosco@boschettoholiday.it; www.boschettoholiday.it/bosco] On W side of lakeshore rd bet Cannobio & Swiss frontier. Sh steep app to site & hairpin bend fr narr rd, unsuitable for car/c'van o'fits & diff for m'vans. Med, terr, pt shd; wc; chem disp; shwrs €0.50; el pnts (3A) €3.50; gas; lndtte; shop; BBQ; bar; playgrnd; private shgl beach; lake sw; dogs €3.50; Eng spkn; adv bkg - ess in high ssn; quiet; CKE/CCI. "All pitches with magnificent lake view; beautiful town; hot water to shwrs only." ♦ 1 Apr-30 Sep. € 28.50 (CChq acc) 2011*

CANNOBIO *1C1* (1.5km N Urban) *46.07136, 8.69366* Camping Campagna, Via Casali Darbedo, 20-22 - 28822 Cannobio (VB) [0323 70100; fax 72398 / 0323 71190; info@campingcampagna.it; www.campingcampagna.it] Brissago-Cannobio rd, site on L on ent town. Med, shd; wc; mv service pnt; shwrs inc; el pnts (6-10A) €4.; gas; lndtte; shop; rest, snacks; bar; shgl beach; some statics; dogs €5.; poss cr; Eng spkn; adv bkg; quiet. "Steamer trips on Lake Maggiore; vg Sunday mkt in Cannobio; vg, modern facs; friendly staff; clean; friendly staff; fabulous views of lake." ♦ 15 Mar-15 Nov. € 47.00 2013*

CANNOBIO *1C1* (1.5km SW Rural) *46.05756, 8.67831* Camping Valle Romantica, Via Valle Cannobina, 28822 Cannobio (VB) [tel/fax 0323 71249; valleromantica@ riviera-valleromantica.com; www.riviera-valleromantica. com] Turn W on S o'skirts of Cannobio, sp Valle Cannobina. In 1.5km at fork keep L. Site immed on R. On ent site cont to bottom of hill to park & walk back to recep. Lge, hdg/ mkd pitch, pt sl, terr, pt shd; wc; chem disp; mv service pnt; shwrs inc; el pnts (4-6A) €4.00; lndtte; shop; rest, snacks; bar; playgrnd; pool; golf 12km; 25% statics; dogs €4; adv bkg; quiet. "Vg; some sm pitches; particularly helpful staff; narr site rds poss diff m'vans; masses of flowers; beautiful situation; footpath to town, poss cr high ssn." ♦ 24 Mar-30 Sep. € 32.00 2011*

CA'NOGHERA see Mestre *2E2*

CAORLE *2E2* (3km SW Coastal) *45.57388, 12.81166* Centro Vacanze Pra' delle Torri, Via Altanea 201, 30021 Caorle (VE) [0421 299035; fax 299035; torri@vacanze-natura.it; www.pradelletorri.it] Fr A4 exit dir Santo Stino di Livenze, then foll sp Caorle & Porto Santa Margherita. by-pass town & cont on coast rd. Site clearly sp on L. V lge, shd, mkd pitch, serviced pitch; wc (some cont); mv service pnt; chem disp; baby facs; shwrs inc; el pnts (4-5A) inc; lndtte; shop; snacks; rest; shop; htd pool complex; sand beach; boat hire; windsurfing; tennis; cycle hire; games area; car wash; internet; entmnt; 30% statics; phone; no dogs; poss cr; adv bkg (min 3 nts); quiet; red snr citizens; ccard acc. "Extensive, excel sport & entmnt facs for children; lge water park inc; entmnt inc; excel family holiday cent." ♦ 4 Apr-27 Sep. € 41.80 2009*

CAORLE *2E2* (5km SW Coastal) *45.56694, 12.79416* Camping Villaggio San Francesco, Via Selva Rosata 1, Duna Verde, 30020 Porto-Santa-Margherita (VE) [0421 299333; fax 299284; info@villaggiostrancesco.com; www.villaggiosfrancesco.com] Fr A4/E70 exit Santo Stino di Livenza, then dir Caorle. By-pass town & cont on coast rd, site sp on L. V lge, shd; wc (some cont); chem disp; mv service pnt; baby facs; shwrs inc; el pnts (6A) inc; gas; lndtte (inc dryer); shop; 3 rests; snacks; bar; 5 pools; waterslide; private beach adj; boat hire; windsurfing; waterskiing; tennis; games area; games rm; cycle hire; solarium; internet; entmnt; TV; 60% statics; dogs €3; phone; min 2 nights' stay; poss cr; quiet; ccard not acc; red snr citizens/CKE/CCI. "Excel family facs." ♦ 24 Apr-25 Sep. € 44.60 (CChq acc) 2009*

CAPALBIO *1D3* (8km S Coastal) *42.38086, 11.44660* Campeggio di Capalbio, Strada del Chiarone, Loc Graticciaia, 58010 Capalbio (GR) [0564 890101; fax 890437; mauro.ricci@ilcampeggiodicapalbio.it; www. ilcampeggiodicapalbio.it] Exit SS1 heading S twd Rome at sp Chiarone Scalo twd sea. Cross rlwy, site sp. Lge, mkd pitch, pt sl, shd; wc (some cont); mv service pnt; shwrs; el pnts (3-5A); gas; lndtte (inc dryer); shop; tradsmn; rest, snacks; bar; BBQ; playgrnd; sand beach adj; cycle hire; games area; entmnt; 70% statics; no dogs; sep car park; poss cr; adv bkg; quiet; ccard acc. "narr lanes, diff for lge o'fits without mover." 10 Apr-4 Oct. € 47.00 2011*

CAPANNOLE see Montevarchi *1D3*

CAPO D'ORLANDO (SICILY) *3B3* (1km W Coastal) *38.12866, 14.70936* Camping Santa Rosa, Via Trazzera Marina 761, 98071 Capo-d'Orlando (ME) [0941 901723; info@ campingsantarosa.com; www.agatirno.it/santarosa/] Fr S113 fr Palermo in Capo d'Orlando cross over rlwy line at level x-ing or carry on to end of town & acc 'lungomare' at E end. Site well sp. Med, hdg pitch, pt shd; wc; chem disp; mv service pnt; shwrs inc; el pnts (6A) €3; lndry rm; shop; rest; bar; playgrnd; pool; sand/shgl beach adj; TV rm; 20% statics; phone; poss cr; rec CKE/CCI. "Pleasant, friendly, simple site." 15 Jun-15 Sep. € 27.50 2010*

CAPOLIVERI (ELBA ISLAND) *1C3* (3km NW Coastal) *42.75810, 10.36070* Camping La Calanchiole, Loc Calanchiole, 57031 Capoliveri (LI) [0565 933488; fax 940001; info@lecalanchiole.it; www.lecalanchiole.it] Fr Portoferraio, take rd twd Porto Azzuro & Marina de Campo. Then foll sp Capoliveri, site sp. Lge, mkd pitch, pt shd; wc (some cont); chem disp; mv service pnt; shwrs; el pnts (3A) inc; lndtte (inc dryer); rest, snacks; bar; BBQ; paddling pool; private sand beach; watersports; boat & cycle hire; tennis; wifi; entmnt; some statics; adv bkg; quiet; ccard acc. ♦ 1 Apr-31 Oct. € 53.50 (CChq acc) 2011*

CAPRAROLA *2E4* (4km W Rural) Camping Natura, Loc Sciente Le Coste, 01032 Caprarola (VT) [tel/fax 0761 612347; info@camping-natura.com; www.camping-natura.com] Fr Viterbo take Via Cimina sp Ronciglione. After approx 19km bef Ronciglione turn R sp Nature Reserve Lago di Vico, in 200m turn R, site sp on R in 3km. Med, mkd pitch, pt shd; wc; chem disp; mv service pnt; shwrs; el pnts (4A) €3; shop; rest, snacks; bar; lake sw adj; dogs €3; quiet; red low ssn; ccard acc. "Friendly site; guided walks in nature reserve; run down low ssn & ltd facs." Easter-30 Sep. € 18.00 2012*

**CARLAZZO see Porlezza** *1C1*

**CAROVIGNO** *3A4* (5km N Coastal) *40.76643, 17.67850* Camping Villaggio Lamaforca, SS379, Km 25, Contrada da Mindelli, 72012 Carovigno (BR) [0831 968496; fax 968070; informazioni@lamaforca.it; www.lamaforca.it] Exit SS379 sp Torre Pozella, site sp. Lge, pt shd; wc; mv service pnt; baby facs; shwrs inc; el pnts inc; lndtte; shop; rest, snacks; bar; playgrnd; pool; paddling pool; waterslide; sand beach adj; cycle hire; games rm; TV rm; 70% statics; dogs €2.50; phone; adv bkg; quiet; ccard acc; red low ssn/snr citizens. "Conv Brindisi, Ostuni." ◆ 1 Apr-18 Sep. € 39.00                                2009*

**CASAL BORSETTI see Marina di Ravenna** *2E2*

**CASALBORDINO** *2F4* (7km NE Coastal) *42.20018, 14.60897* Camping Village Santo Stefano, S16, Km 498, 66020 Marina-di-Casalbordino (CH) [0873 918118; fax 918193; info@campingsantostefano.com; www.campingsantostefano.com] Exit A14 Vasto N onto S16 dir Pescara, site at km 498 on R. Med, mkd pitch, shd; wc; chem disp; shwrs inc; el pnts (6A) inc; shop; rest, snacks; bar; playgrnd; pool; paddling pool; beach adj; entmnt; 10% statics; no dogs; Eng spkn; adv bkg; quiet but some rlwy noise; CKE/CCI. "Pleasant, well-maintained, family-run site; sm pitches; beautiful private beach & pool area; gd rest." 24 Apr-12 Sep. € 41.00                                2014*

**CA'SAVIO see Punta Sabbioni** *2E2*

⊞ **CASSA, LA** *1B2* (600m N Rural) *45.18689, 7.51599* Camping Club Le Betulle (Naturist), Via Lanzo 33, 10040 La Cassa (TO) [011 9842962; fax 9842819; info@lebetulle.org; www.lebetulle.org] Exit Turin by-pass at Collegno & foll sp Pianezza. In 200m bear R at traff lts sp San Gillio & La Cassa. In La Cassa foll sp Fiano, site on L. Site is 25km fr Turin cent. Lge, hdstg, pt sl, pt shd; htd wc (some cont); chem disp (wc); baby facs; fam bthrm; shwrs inc; el pnts (16A) inc; lndtte; shop 600m; tradsmn; rest, snacks; bar; playgrnd; pool; TV rm; 90% statics; dogs €2; poss cr; Eng spkn; adv bkg; INF card. "Friendly staff." € 38.00                                2011*

**CASSONE see Malcesine** *1D1*

⊞ **CASTEL DEL PIANO** *1D3* (500m S Urban) *42.88454, 11.53646* Camping Residence Amiata, Via Roma 15, Montoto, 58033 Castel-del-Piano (GR) [0564 956260; fax 955107; info@amiata.org; www.amiata.org] Fr Siena on S223 to Paganico. Turn L (via overpass) twd Castel del Piano. On reaching town, turn R, sp Ospedale (Hospital). Strt over rndabt site on R up hill (1km). Lge, hdg/mkd pitch, hdstg, shd; htd wc; chem disp; mv service pnt; baby facs; shwrs; el pnts (3-6A) inc; gas; lndtte (inc dryer); shop & 1km; tradsmn; rest, snacks; bar; BBQ; playgrnd; pool 3km; games area; solarium; TV rm; some statics; dogs €2.70; poss cr; Eng spkn; adv bkg; quiet; ccard acc; red long stay; red CKE/CCI. "Friendly owners; dated san facs; lovely views; excel touring base medieval towns & vills." ◆ € 22.20 (CChq acc)                                2010*

**CASTELDIMEZZO see Pesaro** *2E3*

**CASTELLAMMARE DEL GOLFO (SICILY)** *3C3* (1km E Coastal) *38.02393, 12.89348* Nausicaa Camping, C/da Spiaggia-Plaia, Loc Forgia, 91014 Castellammare-del-Golfo (TP) [0924 33030; fax 35173; info@nausicaa-camping.it; www.nausicaa-camping.it] Site 1km E fr Castellammare on R of rte 187. Well sp. Awkward ent for lge o'fits as steep ramp. Sm, mkd pitch, hdstg, pt shd; wc; chem disp; shwrs inc; el pnts €3; gas; lndry rm; shop; rest 100m; snacks; playgrnd; sand beach adj; tennis; some statics; ccard acc; CKE/CCI. "Nr Roman temple at Segesta; gd 1st stop fr Palermo if touring historical sites." 1 Mar-31 Oct. € 42.00                                2009*

**CASTELLAMMARE DEL GOLFO (SICILY)** *3C3* (4.5km NW Coastal) *38.05596, 12.83868* Camping Baia di Guidaloca, Corso Garibaldi, 91014 Scopello (TP) [tel/fax 0924 541262 / 0924 32359 / 339 1581927 l/s; giovannitod@libero.it; www.campinguidaloca.com] Fr SS187 foll sp bet km 34 & 33 dir Scopello, site sp on L. Med, pt shd; wc; chem disp; shwrs inc; el pnts (3A) €2.50; shop 2km; rest 2km; snacks; bar; sand beach adj; 10% statics; phone;dogs leashed; bus; sep car park high ssn; poss cr; adv bkg; quiet; CKE/CCI. "Conv Zingaro nature reserve - v beautiful; vg." 1 Apr-30 Sep. € 27.00                                2013*

**CASTELLETTO SOPRA TICINO see Sesto Calende** *1B1*

**CASTELLINA IN CHIANTI see Poggibonsi** *1D3*

## "We must tell The Club about that great site we found"

Get your site reports in by mid-August and we'll do our best to get your updates into the next edition.

**CASTELSANTANGELO SUL NERA** *2E3* (4km S Rural) *42.88223, 13.18181* Camping Monte Prata, Loc. Schianceto, 62030 Castel S Angelo Sul Nera [07 37 97 00 62 or 33 32 95 18 60 (mob); sostare@campingmonteprata.it; www.campingmonteprata.it] Fr SP209 Muccia-Visso. Thro Visso on the Strada Provinciale 134 twds Castelsantangelo Sur Nera. Aft vill slight R onto SP 136. Campsite on L after vill of Gualdo. Med, mkd pitch, hdstg, terr, pt shd; htd wc; chem disp; mv service pnt; shwrs inc; el pnts; lndtte (inc dryer); shop; rest; snacks; bar; BBQ; playgrnd; games area; 0% statics; dogs; Eng spkn; quiet; ccard acc. "Gd site; excel position nr top of Monte Prata; guided walks & other excursions fr site in Nat Park." ◆ 15 Jun-15 Sep. € 29.50                                2014*

⊞ **CASTELVETRANO (SICILY)** *3C3* (12km SE Rural) *37.59764, 12.84269* Camping Maggiolino, Contrada Garroffo, 91022 Marinella di Selinunte (TP) [tel/fax 0924 46044; info@campingmaggiolino.it; www.campingmaggiolino.it] Exit SS115 (Castelvetrano-Sciacca) at sp to Selinunte, site on L bef Selinunte. Sm, pt shd, hdstg; wc; shwrs; el pnts (3A) €2; shop 1km; lndtte; snacks; bar; playgrnd; sand beach 1.5km; tennis; cycle hire; dogs; Eng spkn; quiet; ccard acc; red CKE/CCI. "Ideal for Greek city of Selinunte, temples, etc; not suitable lge o'fits." ◆ € 21.00                                2009*

⊞ **CASTELVETRANO (SICILY)** *3C3* (13km SE Coastal) *37.59571, 12.84139* **Camping Athena, Loc Marinella, Contrada Garraffo, 91022 Castelvetrano (TP) [tel/fax 0924 46132; info@campingathenaselinunte.it; www. campingathenaselinunte.it]** Exit SS115 (Castelvetrano-Sciacca) at sp to Selinunte, site on L bef Selinunte. Sm, some hdstg, pt shd; wc; mv service pnt; shwrs inc; el pnts (10A) inc; lndtte; shop 1km; rest, snacks; bar; BBQ; sand beach 800m; dogs; phone; ccard acc; red CKE/CCI. "Can take lger o'fits than Maggiolino site; conv temples at Selinunte; excel facs; gd rest adj." 2012*

## "I need an on-site restaurant"

We do our best to make sure site information is correct, but it is always best to check any must-have facilities are still available or will be open during your visit.

**CASTIADAS (SARDINIA)** *3B2* (4km E Coastal) *39.24450, 9.56980* **Villaggio Camping Capo Ferrato, Via delle Ginestre, Loc Costa Rei-Monte Nai, 09040 Castiadas (CA) [070 991012; fax 885653; info@campingcapoferrato.it; www.campingcapoferrato.it]** Fr Cagliari take coastal rd E twd Villasimius, then N to Monte Nai, site sp. Or fr Cagliari take S125 to San Priamo, then S to Monte Nai & site. Med, pt shd; wc; chem disp; mv service pnt; shwrs inc; el pnts (2-6A) €2.30-3.40; lndtte; shop; supmkt 500m; rest, snacks; bar; BBQ; playgrnd; sand beach adj; windsurfing 100m; tennis; cycle hire; horseriding 3km; games area; wifi; entmnt; TV; 10% statics; Eng spkn; adv bkg; quiet; ccard acc. "Welcoming, family-run site; might be diff for lge o'fits; Discover Sardinia theme weeks end Jun & beg Sep; conv Capo Carborana Nature Park." 1 Apr-2 Nov. € 44.20 (CChq acc) 2011*

**CASTIGLIONE DEL LAGO** *2E3* (500m N Rural) *43.13460, 12.04383* **Camping Listro, Via Lungolago, Lido Arezzo, 06061 Castiglione-del-Lago (PG) [tel/fax 075 951193; listro@listro.it; www.listro.it]** Fr N A1 Val di Chiana exit 75 bis Perugia, site clearly sp on N edge of town on lakeside. Med, mkd pitch, pt shd; wc; chem disp; mv service pnt; shwrs inc; el pnts (3A) inc (poss rev pol); gas; lndtte; shop & 500m; rest 200m; snacks; bar; playgrnd; pool nr; private sand beach & lake sw adj; tennis nr; cycle hire; poss cr; Eng spkn; adv bkg; rd noise; ccard acc; red long stay/low ssn; CKE/CCI. "On W shore of Lake Trasimeno; facs stretched when site full; v helpful staff; bus to Perugia; rlwy stn 1km for train to Rome; 'tree fluff' a problem in spring." ◆ ltd 1 Apr-30 Sep. € 18.70 2011*

**CASTIGLIONE DEL LAGO** *2E3* (6km N Rural) *43.18028, 12.0163* **Camping Badiaccia, Via Pratovecchio 1, 06061 Castiglione-del-Lago (PG) [0759 659097; fax 659019; info@badiaccia.com; www.badiaccia.com]** Leave A1 m'way at Val-di-Chiana exit & foll sp for Castiglione-del-Lago. Site on L immed past Shell g'ge. Lge, mkd pitch, sl, pt shd; wc (cont); chem disp; mv service pnt; baby facs; shwrs inc; el pnts (4A) inc; gas; lndtte (inc dryer); shop; tradsmn; rest, snacks; bar; BBQ; playgrnd; 2 pools; lake sw; boat & cycle hire; windsurfing; tennis; games area; wifi; 10% statics; dogs €2.50; adv bkg ess; quiet; red 7+ days. "Refurbished san facs; gd site." ◆ 1 Apr-30 Sep. € 25.00 2010*

**CASTIGLIONE DELLA PESCAIA** *1D3* (2km N Coastal) *42.77361, 10.84398* **Camping Maremma Sans Souci, Strada delle Collacchie, Casa Mora, 58043 Castiglione-della-Pescaia (GR) [0564 933765; fax 935759; info@ maremmasanssouci.it; www.maremmasanssouci.it]** Exit SS1 Via Aurelia at Follonica onto SS322, site at km post 12, sp. Lge, mkd pitch, shd; wc; chem disp; mv service pnt; shwrs; el pnts (3A) inc; lndtte; shop; rest, snacks; bar; no BBQ; sand beach adj; TV; dogs €2 (not acc Jun-Aug); phone; sep car park; Eng spkn; adv bkg ess Jul-Aug; ccard acc; red low ssn. "Most pitches diff lge o'fits; lovely location; direct access to beach; poss mosquito problem." ◆ 1 Apr-31 Oct. € 43.00 (CChq acc) 2011*

**CASTIGLIONE DELLA PESCAIA** *1D3* (6km W Coastal) *42.77760, 10.79384* **Camping Village Baia Azzurra, Via delle Rocchette, 58043 Castiglione-della-Pescaia (GR) [0564 941092; fax 941242; info@baiaazzurra.it; www. baiaazzurra.it]** Fr Castiglione della Pescaia on S322, turn L sp Rocchette, site on R in 3km. Med, mkd pitch, shd; wc (some cont); chem disp; shwrs inc; el pnts (3A) inc; gas; lndtte; shop; tradsmn; rest nr; snacks; bar; no BBQ; playgrnd; pool high ssn; paddling pool; private sand beach adj; tennis; cycle hire; wifi; entmnt; TV; 10% statics; dogs €6; phone; sep car park; bus; poss cr; Eng spkn; adv bkg; quiet; ccard acc; red low ssn. "Beautiful location; 24 hr security." ◆ 15 Apr-17 Oct. € 54.00 (CChq acc) 2011*

**CAVALLINO** *2E2* (2.5km S Coastal) *45.45710, 12.50702* **Camping Village Vela Blu, Via Radaelli 10, 30013 Cavallino (VE) [041 968068; fax 5371003; info@velablu.it; www. velablu.it]** Site sp on leaving Ca'ballarin. Lge, mkd pitch, pt shd; wc; chem disp; mv service pnt; 50% serviced pitches; baby facs; shwrs inc; el pnts (6A) inc; lndtte lnc dryer); shop; rest, snacks; bar; BBQ; playgrnd; private beach adj; cycle hire; wifi; entmnt; sat TV; 50% statics; dogs €4.50; phone; poss cr; Eng spkn; adv bkg; ccard acc; red long stay/low ssn; CKE/CCI. "Well-kept site; excel san facs; excel rest; gd facs for children; gd beach; bus/ferry tickets to Venice fr recep; friendly site." ◆ 30 Apr-30 Sep. € 33.00 (CChq acc) 2009*

**CAVALLINO** *2E2* (2.5km S Coastal) *45.46726, 12.53006* **Union Lido Park & Resort, Via Fausta 258, 30013 Cavallino (VE) [041 968080 or 2575111; fax 5370355; info@unionlido.com; www.unionlido.com]** Exit a'strada A4 (Mestre-Trieste) at exit for airport or Quarto d'Altino & foll sp for Jesolo & then Punta Sabbiono; site on L 2.5km after Cavallino. V lge, mkd pitch, shd; htd wc; chem disp; mv service pnt; 60% serviced pitches; baby facs; sauna; shwrs inc; el pnts (6A) inc; gas; lndtte (inc dryer); 30 shops & supmkt; 7 rests; snacks; bars; playgrnd; pools & children's lagoon with slides; dir access private beach; tennis; gym; golf; fishing; boating; horseriding; watersports; cycle hire; skating rink; hairdressers; babysitting; wifi; entmnt; sat TV some pitches; late arr (after 2100) o'night parking area with el pnts; church; banking facs; 1st aid cent; Italian lessons; wellness cent; 50% statics; no dogs; Eng spkn; adv bkg; ccard acc. "Variable pitch size & price; min stay 7 days in high ssn; some pitches soft sand (a spade useful!); many long-stay campers; no admissions 1230-1500 (poss busy w/end); excursions; varied entmnt programme high ssn inc firework displays; well-organised, well-run; clean facs; no need to leave site; worth every penny! excel." ◆ 30 Apr-26 Sep. € 48.00 2010*

See advert on bookmark

ITALY

CAVALLINO 2E2 (5km SW Coastal) 45.45638, 12.4960
Camping Enzo Stella Maris, Via delle Batterie 100, 30010
Cavallino-Treporti (VE) [041 966030; fax 5300943; info@
enzostellamaris.com; www.enzostellamaris.com] Exit A4
at sp for airport. Foll sp Jesolo, Cavallino, Punta Sabbioni rd
SW. Site sp after Ca'Ballarin. Lge, mkd pitch, pt shd; wc; chem
disp; mv service pnt; baby facs; serviced pitches; shwrs inc;
el pnts (6A) inc; gas; lndtte; shop; rest, snacks; bar; no BBQ;
playgrnd; htd pool; sand beach adj; fitness rm; games area;
wifi; entmnt; TV rm; 25% statics; no dogs; phone; clsd 1230-
1600 & 2300-0700; poss cr; Eng spkn; no adv bkg; quiet; ccard
acc; red snr citizens/long stay; CKE/CCI. "Well-run, friendly,
family-owned site; excel facs; beware mosquitoes; indoor htd
pool; wellness cent." ♦ 12 Apr-18 Oct. € 73.60          2014*

CAVALLINO 2E2 (5km SW Coastal) 45.45666, 12.50066
Camping-Village Cavallino, Via delle Batterie, 164 - 30013
Cavallino-Treporti (VE) [041 966133; fax 5300827; info@
campingcavallino.com info@baiaholiday.com; www.
baiaholiday.com] Foll rd Jesolo/Cavallino, lge sp at L turn
into camp. V lge, hdstg, pt shd; wc; chem disp; mv service pnt;
serviced pitches; shwrs inc; el pnts (6A) inc; lndtte; supmkt;
shop; rest, snacks; bar; playgrnd; 2 pools; sand beach adj;
waterskiing; golf 2km; internet; entmnt; 25% statics; dogs
€8; poss cr; adv bkg - ess in high ssn; quiet; red snr citizens.
"Lovely, wooded, well-organised, clean site; gd facs; poss
mosquito prob." ♦ 24 Mar-31 Oct. € 46.20          2011*

CAVALLINO 2E2 (6km SW Coastal) 45.44872, 12.47116
Camping Dei Fiori, Via Vettor Pisani 52, 30010 Cavallino-
Treporti (VE) [041 966448; fax 966724; fiori@vacanze-
natura.it; www.deifiori.it] Fr Lido di Jesolo foll sp to
Cavallino; site on L approx 6km past Cavallino & bef Ca'Vio.
Lge, mkd pitch, shd; wc; chem disp; mv service pnt; serviced
pitch; shwrs inc; el pnts (5A) inc (poss rev pol); gas; lndtte;
shop; supmkt; rest, snacks; bar; playgrnd; pool; sand beach adj;
hydro massage; games area; entmnt; internet; no dogs; Eng
spkn; adv bkg ess Jul/Aug; quiet; ccard acc; red snr citizens/
long stay. "V clean & quiet even in Aug; excel facs & amenities;
conv water bus stop at Port Sabbioni; 3/5 day min stay med/
high ssn; highly rec; excel." ♦ 19 Apr-30 Sep. € 43.50  2009*

CA'VIO see Cavallino 2E2

CAVRIGLIA see Montevarchi 1D3

CECINA 1D3 (5km E Rural) 43.30043, 10.58153 Camping
Valle Gaia, La Casetta, Via Cecinese 87, 56040 Casale-
Marittimo (PI) [0586 681236; fax 683551; info@vallegaia.
it; www.vallegaia.it] Fr Cecina E on S68 foll sp Guardistallo
& Casale Marittimo, site poorly sp - look for Robin Hood rest.
Med, hdg pitch, pt shd; wc; chem disp; baby facs; shwrs inc;
el pnts (6A) inc; gas; lndtte; shop; rest, snacks; bar; BBQ;
playgrnd; 2 pools; tennis; games area; cycle hire; entmnt;
TV rm; 10% statics; dogs €3; phone; poss cr; Eng spkn; adv
bkg; quiet; red CKE/CCI. "Best site in area; scenic location;
gd sized pitches; excel, modern facs; helpful staff; excursions
arranged; conv Siena, San Gimignano, Pisa." ♦ 4 Apr-10 Oct.
€ 29.60                                             2009*

CECINA 1D3 (5km S Rural) 43.25388, 10.55291 Camping Le
Capanne, SS Aurelia, Km 273, 57020 Marina-di-Bibbona
(LI) [0586 600064; fax 600198; info@campinglecapanne.
it; www.campinglecapanne.it] Fr E side of rd SS1 fr La
California to Marina di Bibbona, sp at km 273. Lge, shd; wc
(some cont); chem disp; mv service pnt; shwrs inc; el pnts
(3A) inc; gas; lndtte; shop; rest, snacks; bar; playgrnd; pool;
paddling pool; beach 1.5km; tennis; games area; cycle hire;
entmnt; 10% statics; dogs €8.20; adv bkg; quiet; cc acc; red
low ssn. 24 Apr-30 Sep. € 38.00                    2009*

⊞ CECINA 1D3 (2km W Urban/Coastal) 43.30464, 10.48809
Camping Bocca di Cecina, Via Guado alle Vacche 2, 57023
Marina-di-Cecina (LI) [0586 620509; fax 621326; bocca.
cecina@tin.it; www.ccft.it] Fr Livorno ignore 1st sp to Cecina
Mare Centu. At cent of Marina di Cecina turn R, site bef rv
bdge. Lge, shd; wc; shwrs; el pnts (2A); gas; lndtte; shop; rest
high ssn; snacks; bar; beach; windsurfing; tennis; games area;
many statics; no dogs; sep car park; poss cr; ccard acc. "Lovely
situation." € 29.00                                 2009*

CECINA 1D3 (3km NW Coastal) 43.31850, 10.47440
Camping Mareblu, Via dei Campilunghi, Mazzanta, 57010
San Pietro-in-Palazzi (LI) [0586 629191; fax 629192; info@
campingmareblu.com; www.campingmareblu.com] Fr S
on SS1 exit sp Cecina Nord & foll dir Mazzanta, site sp. Fr N
exit sp Vada then Mazzanta. Lge, hdg/mkd pitch, pt shd; wc
(some cont); chem disp; mv service pnt; shwrs inc; el pnts (3A)
inc; gas; lndtte (inc dryer); shop; tradsmn; rest, snacks; bar;
BBQ (gas only); playgrnd; pool; paddling pool; sand beach adj;
wifi; 10% statics; dogs free (not acc Jul & Aug); phone; sep
car park; ATM; poss cr; Eng spkn; adv bkg; red low ssn; ccard
acc; red CKE/CCI. "Lge pitches; gd facs & pool area; car must
be parked in sep car park; well-organised, friendly site." ♦
26 Mar-15 Oct. € 37.00 (CChq acc)                  2011*

CECINA 1D3 (6km NW Coastal) 43.33206, 10.46021 Camping
Molino a Fuoco, Via Cavalleggeri 32, 57018 Vada (LI)
[0586 770150; fax 770031; info@campingmolinoafuoco.
com; www.campingmolinoafuoco.com] Sp fr SS1 Aurelia
at cent of vill of Vada, adj Camping Rada Etrusca. Lge, shd;
wc (some cont); chem disp; mv service pnt; baby facs; shwrs
inc; el pnts (4A) inc; lndtte (inc dryer); shop; rest, snacks; bar;
BBQ; playgrnd; shgl beach adj; games area; cycle hire; wifi;
30% statics; dogs €2 (not acc Jul/Aug); sep car park; phone;
poss cr; ccard acc; red low ssn. "Pleasant site; helpful staff; gd
san facs." ♦ 2 Apr-16 Oct. € 34.00                 2010*

CEFALU 3B3 (3km W Rural) 38.02700, 13.98247 Camping
Sanfilippo, Ogliastrillo SS113, 90015 Cefalù [tel/fax
0921 420 184; info@campingsanfilippo.com; www.
campingsanfilippo.com] Fr Palermo E twds Cafalu on rd
SS113. Med, mkd pitch, hdstg, terr, shd; wc; chem disp; mv
service pnt; shwrs; el pnts (4A) inc; lndtte; shop; tradsmn;
snacks; BBQ; playgrnd; beach 150m; games area; games rm;
wifi; 50% statics; dogs €3.50; bus 300m; twin axles; poss
cr; Eng spkn; adv bkg; quiet; no ccard acc; CCI. "Vg site." ♦
1 Apr-31 Oct. € 42.50                              2014*

CEFALU (SICILY) *3B3* (3km W Coastal) *38.02703, 13.98283*
Camping Costa Ponente, C de Ogliastrillo, 90015 Cefalù
(PA) [0921 420085; fax 424492] Fr Palermo E twd Cefalù,
on rd SS113 at km stone 190.3, site sp. Lge, hdstg, terr, shd;
wc (some cont); chem disp; shwrs; el pnts rev pol (3A) €5; gas;
lndry rm; shop & 4km; tradsmn; rest high ssn; snacks; bar;
pool; paddling pool; sand beach (down steep steps); tennis;
10% statics; dogs €3.50 (not acc Aug); bus nr; sep car park
(high ssn); poss cr; no adv bkg; poss noisy; ccard acc; 5% red
CKE/CCI. ♦ 1 Apr-31 Oct. € 30.00                    2012*

**CERIALE see Albenga** *1B2*

CERVIA *2E2* (1.5km S Coastal) *44.24760, 12.35901* **Camping
Adriatico**, Via Pinarella 90, 48015 Cervia (RA) [0544 71537;
fax 72346; info@campingadriatico.net; www.
campingadriatico.net] On SS16 S fr Cervia twd Pinarella, turn
L at km post 175, over rlwy line & take 1st R, site sp. Lge, shd;
wc (some cont); chem disp; mv service pnt; baby facs; shwrs
inc; el pnts (6A) inc; lndtte; shop; tradsmn; rest, snacks; bar;
playgrnd; htd pool; paddling pool; sand beach 600m; fishing;
tennis 900m; golf 5km; entmnt; TV rm; 40% statics; dogs
€6; Eng spkn; adv bkg; ccard acc; red CKE/CCI. "V pleasant
site; friendly staff; gd san facs." ♦ 21 Apr-15 Sep. € 34.00
(CChq acc)                                        2010*

**CERVO see Diano Marina** *1B3*

⊞ CESENATICO *2E2* (1.5km N Coastal) *44.21545, 12.37983*
Camping Cesenatico, Via Mazzini 182, 47042 Cesenatico
(FC) [0547 81344; fax 672452; info@campingcesenatico.it;
www.campingcesenatico.com] Travelling S on S16 look for
Esso g'ge on R on app Cesenatico. Take 2nd L after Eng g'ge,
over rlwy x-ing, site on L, sp. V lge, mkd pitch, hdstg, pt shd;
htd wc (some cont); chem disp; mv service pnt; shwrs inc; el
pnts (4A) €3.60; gas; lndtte; shop; snacks; rest; bar; playgrnd;
htd pool; private sand beach adj; tennis; games area; entmnt;
hairdresser; medical cent; wifi; entmnt; TV; 80% statics; dogs
€8.70; phone; poss cr; Eng spkn; adv bkg; ccard acc; red long
stay/low ssn/CKE/CCI. "Many long stay winter visitors; gd
touring base; unspoilt seaside resort with canal (designed by
Da Vinci), port & marina; excel; in easy walking/cycling dist
fr Cesenatico." ♦ € 55.00 (CChq acc)              2014*

CESENATICO *2E2* (2km N Coastal) *44.21584, 12.37798*
Camping Zadina, Via Mazzini 184, 42047 Cesenatico
(FC) [0547 82310; fax 702381; info@campingzadina.it;
www.campingzadina.it] Leave A14 at Cesena Sud; foll sp
Cesenático; after 10.5km turn R at T-junc onto SS16; after
2km fork L over level x-ing; site on L. Lge, mkd pitch, pt terr,
pt shd; wc; chem disp; mv service pnt; shwrs inc; el pnts (6A)
inc; gas; lndtte; shop; rest, bbq; snacks; bar; playgrnd; private
sand beach; entmnt; wifi; fishing; 80% statics; dogs €7; train
1.5km; Eng spkn; sep car park; poss cr; adv bkg; noisy in high
ssn; ccard not acc; red low ssn. "Sea water canal runs thro
site; pitches poss tight lge o'fits; gd." ♦ ltd 20 Apr-21 Sep.
€ 56.00                                          2014*

**CHATILLON see St Vincent** *1B1*

**CHIENES/KIENS see Brunico/Bruneck** *1D1*

CHIOGGIA *2E2* (2km E Coastal) *45.20533, 12.29856*
Camping Adriatico, Lungomare Adriatico 82, 30019
Sottomarina (VE) [041 492907; fax 5548567; info@
campingadriatico.com; www.campingadriatico.com]
Fr rd S309 foll sp for Sottomarina Lido, foll dual c'way on sea
front, site on L. Med, mkd pitch, shd; wc (cont); chem disp; mv
service pnt; some serviced pitches; shwrs inc; el pnts (6A) inc
(some rev pol); gas; lndtte; shop; rest, snacks; bar; playgrnd;
pool; sand beach adj; sailing; watersports; TV; 30% statics;
phone; dogs (not acc Jun-Aug); poss v cr; quiet; some traff
noise; adv bkg; Eng spkn; red long stay; ccard acc; red low ssn;
CKE/CCI. "Water bus to Venice; Chioggia worth visit; money
exchange." ♦ 4 Apr-20 Sep. € 32.50               2009*

CHIOGGIA *2E2* (2km E Urban/Coastal) *45.19027, 12.30361*
Camping Miramare, Via A. Barbarigo 103, 30015
Sottomarina (VE) [tel/fax 041 490610; campmir@tin.it;
www.miramarecamping.com] Fr SS309 foll sp Sottomarina.
In town foll brown sp to site. Lge, mkd pitch, pt shd; wc; chem
disp; mv service pnt; shwrs inc; el pnts (6A) inc; gas; lndtte;
shop; rest, snacks; bar; playgrnd; pool; private sand beach;
games area; wifi; entmnt; TV; dogs €3.50; poss cr; adv
bkg; ccard acc; CKE/CCI. "Busy site - field across rd quieter;
friendly staff; gd entmnt facs for children; cycle tracks to
picturesque Chioggia." ♦ 18 Apr-23 Sep. € 47.20      2013*

---

## "Satellite navigation makes touring much easier"

Remember most sat navs don't know if you're towing or in a larger vehicle – always use yours alongside maps and site directions.

---

CHIOGGIA *2E2* (3km SE Coastal) *45.18138, 12.3075* **Kawan
Village Camping Oasi**, Via A. Barbarigo 147, 30019
Sottomarina (VE) [041 5541145; fax 490801; info@
campingoasi.com; www.campingoasi.com] Exit SS309/
E55 sp Sottomarina, Chioggia & foll Viale Mediterraneo twd
coast. Site sp on R - last one along Via Barbarigo. Med, hdg/
mkd pitch, pt shd; wc (some cont); chem disp; mv service pnt;
baby facs; shwrs inc; el pnts (6A) inc; lndtte (inc dryer); shop;
rest, snacks; bar; BBQ; playgrnd; pool; paddling pool; private
sand beach adj; watersports; games area; tennis; cycle hire;
wifi; entmnt; TV; 50% statics; dogs €3; phone; poss cr; adv
bkg; quiet; ccard acc; red low ssn. "Pleasant, welcoming site;
vg facs; excel beach; water bus to Venice." ♦ 25 Mar-30 Sep.
€ 34.00 (CChq acc)                               2011*

⊞ CHIUSA/KLAUSEN *1D1* (1km N Rural) *46.64138,
11.57361* Camping Gamp, Via Griesbruck 10, 39043
Chiusa/Klausen (BZ) [0472 847425; fax 845067; info@
camping-gamp.com; www.camping-gamp.com] Exit A22
Chiusa/Klausen & bear L at end of slip rd (sp Val Gardena). Site
on L at rd fork 800m, sp. Sm, mkd pitch, pt shd; htd wc; chem
disp; shwrs inc; mv service pnt; baby facs; el pnts (6A) €2.60;
lndtte; shop & 500m; tradsmn; rest, snacks; bar; playgrnd;
pool; table tennis; htd ski & boot rm; internet; sat TV; dogs
€3.50; phone; sep m'van o'night facs; Eng spkn; some rd &
rlwy noise; CKE/CCI. "Excel cent for mountain walks; Chiusa
attractive town; immac facs, sep m'van o'night area." ♦
€ 30.50                                          2011*

---

Check any essential information with the site before you travel          *Last year of report   **371**

**CIRO MARINA** *3B4* (2km N Coastal) *39.38526, 17.14255*
Camping Villaggio Punta Alice, 88811 Ciro-Marina
(KR) [0962 31160; fax 373823; info@puntalice.it; www.
puntalice.it] Fr N on S106 twd Crotone, exit Cirò Marina.
Cross rlwy line, foll site sp thro town (rds narr) to site. Lge, mkd
pitch, pt shd; wc; chem disp; mv service pnt; shwrs inc; el pnts
(6A) inc; lndtte; shop; rest, snacks; bar; playgrnd; pool; private
sand/shgl beach; games area; cycle hire; entmnt; cinema; TV
rm; 50% statics; dogs €5.50; phone; sep car park high ssn;
poss cr; Eng spkn; poss noisy; CKE/CCI. "Vg, clean site; friendly
staff; excel rest." ♦ 1 Apr-30 Sep. € 44.00 (CChq acc) 2010*

**CISANO see Bardolino** *1D2*

**CITTA DI CASTELLO** *2E3* (3km W Rural) *43.45142, 12.22205*
Camping La Montesca, Loc Montesca, 06012 Città di
Castello (PG) [0758 558566; fax 520786; info@lamontesca.
it; www.lamontesca.it] W fr SS3bis on winding rd; foll sp
to town cent then sm brown site sp. Med, hdg/mkd pitch,
terr, pt shd; wc; shwrs; el pnts (6A) inc; lndtte; shop & 3km;
rest, bar high ssn; pool; entmnt; dogs; quiet; red CKE/CCI.
"Superb views; ltd, sm touring pitches, but made welcome;
poor san facs (2009); beautiful town." ♦ 15 Apr-20 Sep.
€ 27.00                                                        2009*

## "There aren't many sites open at this time of year"

If you're travelling outside peak season
remember to call ahead to check site opening
dates – even if the entry says 'open all year'.

**COGNE** *1B1* (3km SW Rural) *45.58764, 7.34157* Camping
Lo Stambecco, Frazione Valnontey, 11012 Cogne (AO)
[0165 74152; infotiscali@campeggiolostambecco.it; www.
campeggiolostambecco.it] On Aosta-Mont Blanc rd (S26)
heading W, after Sarre turn L to Cogne. In Cogne turn R sp
Valnontey (Gran Paradiso). Site on L at ent to Valnontey vill.
Use easier 2nd ent opp car park. Long 10% app fr S26. Med,
pt sl, pt shd; wc (some cont); chem disp; mv service pnt; shwrs
inc; el pnts (3A) €2; gas; lndtte; shop 3km; bar; 20% statics;
Eng spkn; poss cr; quiet; ccard not acc; CKE/CCI. "In
magnificent Gran Paradiso National Park; botanic garden highly
rec; gd facs; excel walks." 20 May-20 Sep. € 22.00      2011*

**COLTANO see Pisa** *1C3*

**COMACCHIO** *2E2* (1km SE Coastal) *44.70130, 12.23810*
Kawan Village Florenz, Via Alpi Centrali 199, 44020
Lido-degli-Scacchi (FE) [0533 380193; fax 313166; info@
campingflorenz.com; www.campingflorenz.com]
Fr a'strade Ferrara-Comacchio take exit dir Porto Garibaldi, site
sp on coast rd. V lge, hdg pitch, pt shd; wc (some cont); chem
disp; mv service pnt; baby facs; shwrs inc; el pnts (3A) inc;
gas; lndtte; shop; rest, snacks; playgrnd; pool; paddling pool;
sand beach adj; beauty cent; cycle hire; games area; golf 5km;
wifi; entmnt; TV rm; 60% statics; dogs €5.90; poss cr; quiet;
ccard acc; red snr citizens; CKE/CCI. ♦ 1 Apr-1 Nov. € 37.60
(CChq acc)                                                    2011*

**COMACCHIO** *2E2* (2km SE Coastal) *44.68944, 12.23833*
Camping Spiaggia e Mare, S.P. Ferrara-Mare 4, 44029
Porto Garibaldi (FE) [0533 327431; fax 325620; info@
campingspiaggiamare.it; www.campingspiaggiamare.
it] Fr a'strade Ferrara-Comacchio take exit dir Porto Garibaldi,
then S on S309 dir Ravenna. In 1km take sliprd on R to Porto
Garibaldi. Strt over traff lts, site on L just bef RH bend. Fr S take
slip rd on R at km 27 sp, then as above. Lge, mkd pitch, pt shd;
wc (mainly cont); chem disp; mv service pnt; shwrs inc; el pnts
inc (6A) inc; gas; lndtte; supmkt; rest, snacks; bar; playgrnd;
2 pools; paddling pool; sand beach adj; watersports; games
area; cycle hire; wifi; entmnt; 50% statics; dogs €6.30; poss cr;
poss noisy; red snr citizens. "Excel beach; excel sw pool; active
fishing port." ♦ 10 Apr-20 Sep. € 38.70                     2009*

**COMO** *1C1* (5km S Urban) *45.78385, 9.06034* International
Camping-Sud, Breccia, Via Cecilio, 22100 Como [tel/fax
031 521435; campingint@hotmail.com; www.camping-
internazionale.it] Fr E to Como, on SS35 Milano rd foll sp
a'strada Milano; site on Como side of rndabt at junc S35 &
S432; ent/exit diff unless turn R. Or take 2nd exit off m'way
after border (Como S), site sp. Med, pt sl, pt shd; wc; shwrs
inc; el pnts (4-6A) €2.50 (rev pol); gas; lndtte; shop; supmkt nr;
rest, snacks; bar; playgrnd; pool; cycle hire; golf 5km; dogs €2;
poss cr; no adv bkg; rd noise; red low ssn; ccard acc. "Conv NH
for m'way." 1 Apr-31 Oct. € 24.00                            2014*

⊞ CORIGLIANO CALABRO *3A4* (7km N Coastal) *39.70333,
16.52583* Camping Onda Azzurra, Contrada Foggia, 87064
Corigliano-Calabro (CS) [tel/fax 0983 851169; info@onda-
azzurra.it; www.onda-azzurra.it] On SS106-bis Taranto to
Crotone rd, after turn off for Sibari, cont S for 6km. Turn L at
4 lge sp on 1 notice board by lge sep building, 2km to site on
beach. Lge, mkd pitch, shd; htd wc; chem disp; mv service pnt;
shwrs inc; el pnts (6-10A) €3-4; lndtte; shop; tradsmn; rest (all
year); snacks; bar; playgrnd; sand beach adj; tennis; cycle hire;
10% statics; dogs €3; adv bkg; ccard acc; red long stay/CKE/
CCI. "Excel, well-run site all ssns - facs open all yr; popular
long stay; clean facs; lge pitches; water not drinkable; v friendly
helpful owner; popular in winter; special meals Xmas/New
Year; site conv Sybaris & Rossano; high standard site; excel
friendly welcome; free acitivities low ssn." ♦ € 45.00     2014*

⊞ CORIGLIANO CALABRO *3A4* (8km N Coastal) *39.68141,
16.52160* Camping Il Salice, Contrada da Ricota Grande,
87060 Corigliano-Calabro (CS) [0983 851169; fax 851147;
info@salicevacanze.it; www.salicevacanze.it] Exit A3 dir
Sibari onto SS106 bis coast rd dir Crotone. At 19km marker
after water tower on L, turn L sp Il Salice - 1.5km to new access
rd to site on L. Site sp easily missed. Lge, mkd pitch, hdstg, pt
sl, pt shd; htd wc (cont); chem disp; mv service pnt; serviced
pitches; baby facs; fam bthrm; shwrs inc; el pnts (3-6A) inc;
gas; lndtte; shop & 2km; rest, snacks; bar; BBQ; playgrnd;
pool; sand beach adj; watersports; tennis; games area; games
rm; cycle hire; TV; 70% statics; dogs €4; phone; poss cr; Eng
spkn; red low ssn; CKE/CCI. "Narr rds thro vill to site - care
needed when busy; v popular, well-run winter destination;
haphazard siting in pine trees; clean, private beach; modern
san facs; ltd facs low ssn; big price red low ssn; scenic area." ♦
€ 48.00                                                        2012*

⊞ **CORIGLIANO CALABRO** (10km N Coastal) *39.69130, 16.52233* **Camping Thurium, Contrada Ricota Grande, 87060 Ricota Grande (CS) [tel/fax 0983 851101; info@ campingthurium.com; www.campingthurium.com]** Exit SS106 at km stone 21. Site sp on gd app rd for 2km. Rd narr and bumpy in places. Do not foll SatNav. Lge, mkd pitches, pt shd; wc; chem disp; mv service pnt; shwrs (€0.35); el pnts inc (3-6A); lndtte (inc dryer); shop; snacks; rest; bar; gas; playgrnd; pool; paddling pool; sand beach adj; tennis; games area; cycle hire; windsurfing lessons; entmnt; wifi; 20% statics; dogs (€4.80); twin axles; Eng spkn; CKE/CCI. "Vg well-run site; site rdways narr on corner, tight for lge o'fits; fair." ♦ ltd € 65.30                                                      2014*

### CORTENO GOLGI see Edolo *1D1*

**CORTINA D'AMPEZZO** 2E1 (1.5km SE Rural) *46.52241, 12.13413* **Camping Rocchetta, Via Campo 1, 32043 Cortina-d'Ampezzo (BL) [tel/fax 0436 5063; camping@ sunrise.it; www.campingrocchetta.it]** Fr Cortina on SS51 dir Belluno & Venice, site sp. Fr Belluno on S51 on app Cortina turn L, brown sp at junc, site sp. Lge, shd; htd wc (some cont); chem disp; mv service pnt; shwrs inc; el pnts (3A) inc; lndtte (inc dryer); shop; rest adj; bar; pool 2km; 10% statics; dogs €1; poss cr; Eng spkn; adv bkg; quiet; ccard acc; red low ssn; CKE/CCI. "Gd, clean facs; 30 min walk to Cortina; mountain views." 1 Jun-20 Sep & 3 Dec-3 Apr. € 26.00          2010*

**CORTINA D'AMPEZZO** 2E1 (3.5km S Rural) *46.51858, 12.1370* **Camping Dolomiti, Via Campo di Sotto, 32043 Cortina-d'Ampezzo (BL) [0436 2485; fax 5403; campeggiodolomiti@tin.it; www.campeggiodolomiti. it]** 2km S of Cortina turn R off S51. Site beyond Camping Cortina & Rocchetta. Lge, mkd pitch, pt shd; htd wc; shwrs inc; chem disp; el pnts (4A) inc (check earth); gas; lndtte; shop; rest 1km; bar; playgrnd; htd pool; games area; games rm; wifi; 10% statics; dogs; phone; bus; poss cr; Eng spkn; no adv bkg; quiet; red low ssn; ccard acc. "Superb scenery in mountains; gd walks; cycle rte into Cortina; helpful owner; beautiful setting; choice of open meadow or shd woodland pitches." ♦ 1 Jun-20 Sep. € 24.00                                         2014*

**COURMAYEUR** *1A1* (6.2km NE) *45.83293, 6.99095* **Campsite Grandes Jorasses, Via per la Val Ferret 53, 11013 Courmayeur (Valle d'Aosta) [0165 869708; info@ grandesjorasses.com; www.grandesjorasses.com]** Foll the brown 'Val Ferret' signs between Courmayeur and the Mont Blanc tunnel, and the campsite is located a few km on the L of the rd. med; hdstg; pt shd; wc; chem disp; mv service pnt; shwrs (50c); lndtte;shop on site; tradsmn; rest;snacks; bar; games rm; wifi; CKE/CCI. "Beautiful site at the foot of Mt Blanc; nature trails thro forest; trekking expeditions arranged; gd rest." ♦ ltd 20 Jun-15 Sep. € 30.00                 2014*

⊞ **COURMAYEUR** *1A1* (6km SE Rural) *45.76333, 7.01055* **Camping Arc en Ciel, Loc Feysoulles, 11017 Morgex (AO) [0165 809257; fax 807749; info@campingarcenciel. it; www.campingarcenciel.it]** Fr A5/E25 take Morgex exit, turn L to vill & foll sp dir Dailley. Site in 1km on L, sp. Fr tunnel take SS25 to Morgex, then as above. Med, terr, pt shd; wc; chem disp; shwrs inc; el pnts (4-6A) €1.50; lndtte; shop; rest, snacks; bar; rafting; mountain climbing; ski lift 8km; ski bus; 30% statics; dogs €1; sep car park; site clsd 6 Nov-8 Dec; poss cr; adv bkg; quiet; ccard acc; red CKE/CCI. "Gd, clean san facs; views Mont Blanc fr some pitches; vg; Views of the mountains marvellous." € 21.50                                          2011*

**CREMONA** *1C2* (1km SW Rural) *45.11978, 10.0088* **Camping Parco al Po, Via Lungo Po Europa 12, 26100 Cremona [0372 21268; fax 27137; campingcr@libero.it; www. campingcremonapo.it]** Exit A21 at Castelvetro or Cremona onto S10 ring rd. Site well sp fr ring rd, adj to sports complex nr rvside. If lost foll sp Paziena, then site, Med, mkd pitch, shd; wc (some cont); mv service pnt; chem disp; shwrs €0.50; el pnts (4A) inc; lndtte; shop 2km; bar; snacks; rest; rv sw 1km; cycle hire; 20% statics; dogs €2; phone; poss cr; adv bkg; ccard acc; some rd noise. "In spacious park; some pitches gloomy due excessive shading; facs old; gates locked 1400-1530; gd rest; interesting town; mosquitoes." ♦ 1 Apr-30 Sep. € 22.00                                                      2011*

**CUGLIERI (SARDINIA)** *3A1* (15km S Rural) *40.07083, 8.49055* **Camping Bella Sardinia - Village Europa, Loc Torre del Pozzo, 09073 Cuglieri (OR) [0785 38058; info@ bellasardinia.it; www.bellasardinia.it]** S fr Olbia on SS131 dir Alghero, foll sp to Caglieri on SS15, then S on SS292, site sp in 15km. Lge, mkd pitch, pt shd; wc (some cont); chem disp; mv service pnt; shwrs; el pnts (3A); lndtte; shop; rest, snacks; bar; BBQ; playgrnd; pool; paddling pool; tennis; games area; games rm; wifi; entmnt; TV; some statics; adv bkg; quiet; ccard acc. "Pleasant, forested site." 9 Apr-15 Oct. € 44.00 (CChq acc)                                                      2010*

**CUNEO** *1B2* (3km SW Rural) *44.36443, 7.51483* **Camping Communale Bisalta, Via San Maurizio 33, 12010 San Rocco-Castagnaretta (CN) [tel/fax 0171 491334; campingbisalta@libero.it]** App Cuneo on S20 fr S fr Col de Tende (France) dir. On o'skts of town turn L at traff lts by cemetary, foll site sp. Lge, shd; wc; chem disp; mv service pnt; shwrs inc; el pnts (3A) inc; lndtte; shop; rest 1km; snacks; bar; BBQ; cooking facs; pool; tennis; cycle hire; 85% statics; dogs; 10% red long stay/CKE/CCI. "Pleasant site; friendly atmosphere; fair facs poss stretched high ssn; gd touring base." ♦ € 21.50                                          2009*

**CUPRA MARITTIMA** *2F3* (1km W Urban/Coastal) *43.02054, 13.84925* **Villaggio Verde Cupra, Via Lazio 26, 63012 Cupra-Marittima (AP) [0735 777411; fax 777666; info@ verdecupra.it; www.verdecupra.it]** Fr N leave A14 dir Pedaso, then S on SS16 in dir Pescara. In 10km site sp in town on R. Med, mkd pitch, pt shd; wc; shwrs inc; el pnts (4A) inc; gas 2km; lndtte; shop; rest, snacks; bar; playgrnd; pool; beach 1km; tennis; cycle hire; entmnt; TV rm; phone; poss cr; some Eng spkn; adv bkg; poss noisy; CKE/CCI. "Helpful owner & staff; quite a climb up a hill to the site." ♦ ltd 1 Apr-31 Oct. € 33.00                                                      2011*

ITALY

**DEIVA MARINA** 1C2 (1km NE Rural) 44.22520, 9.53250
Villaggio Turistico Arenella, Loc Arenella, 19013 Deiva-Marina (SP) [0187 825259; info@campingarenella.it; www.campingarenella.it] Exit A12/E80 Deiva Marina. In approx 6.8km site sp on R, easy access. Med, hdstg, terr, pt shd; wc (some cont); chem disp; mv service pnt; shwrs inc; el pnts (3A) €2; lndtte; shop; rest, snacks; bar; BBQ; beach 2.2km; wifi; 40% statics; dogs; phone; bus to stn (trains to Cinque Terre) high ssn; Eng spkn; adv bkg; quiet; red low ssn/CKE/CCI. "Pleasant site with stream running thro it; helpful staff; vg."
♦ ltd 1 May-31 Oct & 5-31 Dec. € 33.00          2010*

# "That's changed – Should I let The Club know?"

If you find something on site that's different from the site entry, fill in a report and let us know. See www.caravanclub.co.uk/europereport.

⊞ **DEIVA MARINA** 1C2 (3km E Rural) 44.22630, 9.55013
Camping La Sfinge, Loc Gea 5, 19013 Deiva-Marina (SP) [tel/fax 0187 825464; info@campinglasfinge.com; www.campinglasfinge.com] Fr a'strada A12 exit Deiva Marina, site on R in approx 4.5km Med, hdg/mkd pitch, hdstg, terr, pt shd; wc (cont); mv service pnt; chem disp; serviced pitches; shwrs inc; el pnts (3A) inc; gas; lndtte; shop; tradsmn; rest, snacks; bar; playgrnd; shgl beach 3km (free bus high ssn); entmnt; fishing; watersports; trekking; internet; 50% statics; dogs €2; phone; bus to beach/stn high ssn; sep car park; poss cr; Eng spkn; adv bkg ess high ssn; quiet; 10% red 5+ days; red low ssn; ccard acc; 10% red CKE/CCI. "Excel san facs; v popular inc low ssn - rec arr early; gd, clean site; ltd touring pitches & some sm/diff for lge o'fits; conv Genova, Pisa, Portofino, Cinque Terre, marble quarry at Carrara; gd walking." ♦
€ 31.50          2010*

**DEIVA MARINA** 1C2 (3km E Coastal) 44.22476, 9.55146
Villaggio Camping Valdeiva, Loc Ronco, 19013 Deiva-Marina (SP) [0187 824174; fax 825352; camping@valdeiva.it; www.valdeiva.it] Fr A12 exit Deiva Marina, site sp on L in approx 4km by town sp. Med, mkd pitch, hdstg, pt sl, pt shd; wc (some cont); chem disp; shwrs inc; el pnts (3-6A) inc; lndtte; shop; tradsmn; rest, snacks; bar; BBQ; playgrnd; pool; shgl beach 3km; wifi; entmnt; sat TV; 90% statics; dogs; phone; bus to stn; sep car park high ssn; poss cr; Eng spkn; adv bkg ess high ssn; ccard acc; red low ssn; CKE/CCI. "Free minibus to stn - conv Cinque Terre or Portofino; helpful, friendly staff; gd rest; excel walking; v quiet LS & shwrs ltd." 1 Jan-31 Oct & 5 Dec-31 Dec. € 42.80 (3 persons)          2013*

**DEIVA MARINA** 1C2 (1km SE Coastal) 44.21473, 9.51874
Camping Fornaci al Mare, Loc Fornaci, 19014 Framura (SP) [tel/fax 0187 816295] Foll 1-way to L in town, sp La Spezia-A'strada, over narr bdge. Site immed S of rv bdge. Med, pt sl, pt shd; wc (some cont); chem disp; mv service pnt; shwrs €0.50; el pnts (2A) inc; shop, rest, snacks, bar nr; beach adj; 80% statics; no dogs; train nr; phone; poss cr; rlwy noise; CKE/CCI. "Not suitable lge o'fits; v friendly; san facs dated; sh walk to stn for Cinque Terra towns, some railyway noise." ♦ ltd
1 Apr-31 Oct. € 25.00          2011*

⊞ **DEMONTE** 1B2 (1.5km N Rural) 44.32260, 7.29222
Campeggio Il Sole, Frazione Perosa 3/B, 12014 Demonte (CN) [0334 1132724; fax 0171 955630; erikamelchio@virgilio.it; www.ghironda.com] Fr lge town sq on S21 go E for 100m, fork L & in 100m turn L. Pass 2 churches on L, turn L, then R over rv into Via Colle dell'Urtica to N. Foll this rd uphill for 1.2km, turn L at T-junc & in 300m L at T-junc again. Site on R. Town cent side rds v narr with arches & app rd narr & steep in places. Sm, mkd pitch, unshd; wc; chem disp; mv service pnt; shwrs €1; el pnts €2; lndry rm; rest; bar; BBQ; playgrnd; dogs; quiet. "Lovely, peaceful site in mountains; vg value rest." ♦ ltd
€ 17.00          2013*

**DEMONTE** 1B2 (1.5km W Rural) 44.31357, 7.27275 Camping Piscina Demonte, Loc Bagnolin, 12014 Demonte (CN) [338 2464353; fax 011 2274301; info@campingdemonte.com; www.campingdemonte.com] App only fr Borgo on S21, 500m after Demonte turn L, foll sp. Med, pt shd; wc; chem disp; shwrs €0.60; el pnts (6A) €1.50; gas; lndtte; shop, rest 1.5km; bar; pool; 90% statics; dogs €1.60; poss cr; adv bkg; quiet; ccard acc; CKE/CCI. "Gd NH bef Col d'Larche; helpful, friendly owner; gd mountain scenery." 15 Jun-15 Sep.
€ 16.50          2013*

**DESENZANO DEL GARDA** 1D2 (5km SE Rural) 45.46565, 10.59443 Camping San Francesco, Strada V San Francesco, 25015 Desenzano-del-Garda (BS) [030 9110245; fax 9902558; booking@campingsanfrancesco.com; www.campingsanfrancesco.com] E fr Milan on A4 a'strada take exit Sirmione & foll sp twd Sirmione town; join S11 twd Desenzano & after Garden Center Flowers site 1st campsite on R after rndabt; site sp twd lake bet Sirmione & Desanzano. Or fr Desenzano, site just after Rivoltella. Lge, mkd pitch, pt sl shd; wc; chem disp; baby facs; shwrs inc; el pnts (6A) inc; gas; lndtte (inc dryer); shop; rest, snacks; bar; BBQ (charcoal/gas); playgrnd; pool; lake sw & shgl beach; boat hire; windsurfing; sailing; canoe hire; fishing; tennis; games area; cycle hire; golf 10km; wifi; entmnt; TV rm; 50% statics; dogs free; no c'vans/m'vans over 6m high ssn; phone; recep clsd 1300-1500 & no vehicle movement; poss cr; Eng spkn; adv bkg; noisy entmnt high ssn; ccard acc; red low ssn; CKE/CCI. "Lovely lakeside pitches for tourers (extra); muddy if wet; poss diff lge o'fits due trees; helpful staff; well managed site; gd position on edge of lake; handy for local bus; excel site; v clean facs; gd rest." ♦ 1 Apr-30 Sep. € 69.00 (CChq acc)          2014*

**DIANO MARINA** 1B3 (4km NE Coastal) 43.92177, 8.10831
Camping del Mare, Via alla Foce 29, 18010 Cervo (IM) [0183 400130 / 0183 405556; fax 402771; info@campingdelmare-cervo.com; www.campingdelmare-cervo.com] Exit A10/E80 at San Bartolomeo/Cervo onto Via Aurelia. Turn L at traff lts twd Cervo. Sp adj rv bdge. R turn acute - long o'fits app fr NE. Med, hdg/mkd pitch, hdstg, shd; wc; chem disp; baby facs; shwrs; el pnts (6A) €2; gas; lndtte; shop; snacks; shgl beach adj; internet; TV; 40% statics; dogs; phone; Eng spkn; adv bkg rec Jun-Aug; quiet; ccard acc. "Immac site; spacious pitches; friendly, helpful staff; picturesque beach & perched vill (Cervo); easy walk San Bartolomeo; gd mkts; highly rec site; pitches close together; office closes 12:00-15:00" ♦ 23 Mar-15 Oct. € 50.00  2014*

DIANO MARINA *1B3* (4km NE Urban/Coastal) *43.92345, 8.10924* Camping Lino, Via Nazario Sauro 4, 18010 Cervo (IM) [0183 400087; fax 400089; info@campinglino.it; www.campinglino.it] Exit A10 dir San Bartolomeo al Mare. Inside Cervo boundary where main coast rd N bends L to pass under rlwy. Turn R clearly sp. Site ent visible fr rd. Med, mkd pitch, shd; wc (some cont); chem disp; fam bthrm; serviced pitches; shwrs; el pnts (6A) metered; gas; lndtte; shop; rest 100m; snacks; playgrnd; cycle hire; internet; 10% statics; dogs; adv bkg; red low ssn; quiet. "Lge pitches completely shd; vans manhandled onto pitch fr ent; sw & boating for children in lagoon; clean, tidy site, but regimented; minimum stay 3 nights; various pitch sizes & prices; park outside bef checking in as diff to turn once inside site." ♦ 1 Apr-20 Oct. € 43.00 (4 persons)                    2009*

DIANO MARINA *1B3* (4km NE Urban/Coastal) *43.92384, 8.11100* Camping Miramare, Via Nazario Sauro 12, 18010 Cervo (IM) [tel/fax 0183 400285; info@campingmiramare.im.it; www.campingmiramare.im.it] In Cervo where coastal main rd bends L under rlwy bdge, turn R 50m beyond Camping Lino. Sm, mkd pitch, shd; wc; chem disp; shwrs inc; el pnts (4A) €2; lndtte; shop; rest 100m; snacks; bar; shgle beach adj; 10% statics; dogs; phone; poss cr; quiet but some rlwy noise. "Pleasant, family-run site." 1 Apr-3 Oct. € 43.00 (3 persons)                    2010*

> "I like to fill in the reports as I travel from site to site"
> You'll find report forms at the back of this guide, or you can fill them in online at www.caravaclub.co.uk/europereport.

⊞ DIANO MARINA *1B3* (500m W Urban/Coastal) *43.90667, 8.07097* Camping Oasi Park, Via Sori 5, 18013 Diano-Marina (IM) [tel/fax 0183 497062; oasi-park@libero.it; www.oasipark.it] On W o'skts Diano Marina, cross rlwy bdge & immed turn R. Foll rd to L past Camping Marino. In 200m turn L, site 200m ahead. M'vans only. Lge, hdstg, terr, pt shd; wc (cont); own san; chem disp; mv service pnt; shwrs €1; el pnts (8A) €2; gas; lndtte; shop 200m; tradsmn; playgrnd; sand beach 500m; 20% statics; dogs; phone; bus, train 500m; poss v cr; Eng spkn; quiet; ccard acc; CKE/CCI. "Conv pleasant town & gd beaches; helpful owner; awnings not allowed." € 15.00                    2009*

DIMARO *1D1* (1km W Rural) *46.32611, 10.86222* Dolomiti Camping Village, Via Gole 105, 38025 Dimaro (TN) [0463 974332; fax 972000; info@campingdolomiti.com; www.campingdolomiti.com] Site sp on S42 nr rv bdge. Med, terr, pt shd; wc; chem disp; sauna; baby facs; shwrs inc; el pnts (5A) €1.30 or metered; gas; lndtte (inc dryer); shop; rest, snacks; bar; playgrnd; 2 htd pools (1 covrd); tennis; canoeing; cycle hire; ski lift 1.5km; free skibus; mountain biking; extreme sports; wifi; entmnt; TV; 25% statics; dogs €4 (not acc Jul/Aug); sep car park high ssn; gate clsd 1300-1500; quiet; ccard acc; red long stay/CKE/CCI. "Helpful staff; gd facs; some pitches poss diff lge o'fits & m'vans; excel walking." ♦ 20 May-25 Sep & 3 Dec-15 Apr. € 33.40                    2010*

⊞ DIMARO *1D1* (11km W Rural) *46.30980, 10.74010* Camping Cevedale, Via di Sotto Pilla 4, 38026 Fucine-di-Ossana (TN) [tel/fax 0463 751630; info@campingcevedale.it; www.campingcevedale.it] Exit A22 at San Michele sull' Adige onto SS43/SS42 twd Dimaro & Fucine. Foll sp Ossana & site over bdge. Lge, mkd pitch, terr, pt shd; htd wc (some cont); chem disp; mv service pnt; shwrs; el pnts (3A) inc; lndtte (inc dryer); shop 500m; snacks; bar; playgrnd; games area; ski shuttle bus; internet; TV rm; 30% statics; no dogs; adv bkg; quiet; ccard acc. "Excel, clean san facs; beautiful area." ♦ € 32.00 (CChq acc)                    2011*

⊞ DOBBIACO/TOBLACH *2E1* (2km W Rural) *46.73431, 12.19362* Camping International Olympia, Via Pusteria 1, 39034 Dobbiaco/Toblach (BZ) [0474 972147; fax 972713; info@camping-olympia.com; www.camping-olympia.it] Trun off S49 at E end of Villabassa/Niederdorf by-pass, sp 'camping'. Site 1km E of Villabassa. Lge, mkd pitch, pt shd; wc; chem disp; mv service pnt; some serviced pitches; sauna; shwrs inc; el pnts (6A) inc; gas; lndtte; shop; rest, snacks; bar; playgrnd; pool; paddling pool; cycle hire; solarium; ski school; entmnt; TV; 30% statics; dogs €4.50; Eng spkn; adv bkg; quiet; ccard acc; CKE/CCI. "Vg, luxurious facs; magnificent views; cycle tracks; gd walks; sm zoo; excel." ♦ € 31.00                    2010*

⊞ DONNALUCATA (SICILY) *3C3* (2km E Rural/Coastal) Camping Club Piccadilly, Via Mare Adriatico, Contrada da Spinasanta, 97010 Donnalucata (RG) [tel/fax 0932 938704; info@club-piccadilly.it; www.club-piccadilly.it] Site sp fr coast rd bet Donnalucata & Cava d'Aliga. Med, mkd pitch, hdstg, pt shd; wc; chem disp; mv service pnt; shwrs €1; el pnts (6A) €4; gas 2km; lndtte; shop 2km; tradsmn; rest, snacks, 2km bar; playgrnd; htd, covrd pool 15km; sand beach adj; internet; TV rm; dogs €2; poss cr; Eng spkn; adv bkg; red long stay; CKE/CCI. "Gd touring base; excursions to Malta high ssn; v friendly owner sells own wine; lovely quiet seaside site; strongly rec; poss cr in Aug." ♦ € 33.00                    2014*

DORGALI (SARDINIA) *3A2* (7km W Coastal) *40.28486, 9.63370* Camping Villaggio Calagonone, Via Collodi 1, 08022 Cala-Gonone (NU) [0784 93165; fax 93255; info@campingcalagonone.it; www.campingcalagonone.it] Fr S125 turn E twd Cala Gonone, thro tunnel. Site sp on L of main rd. Med, terr, shd; wc; chem disp; mv service pnt; el pnts (6A) €5; shop; rest, snacks; bar; BBQ; playgrnd; pool; sand/shgl beach 400m; tennis; games area; 30% statics; dogs €5; phone; poss cr; adv bkg; ccard acc. "Beautiful situation in pine forest on edge of pretty town; nrby coves & grottoes accessible by boat or on foot." ♦ 1 Apr-3 Nov. € 63.00                    2014*

⊞ EDOLO *1D1* (1.5km W Rural) *46.17648, 10.31333* Camping Adamello, Via Campeggio 10, Loc Nembra, 25048 Edolo (BS) [tel/fax 0364 71694; info@campingadamello.com; www.campingadamello.com] On rd 39 fr Edolo to Aprica; after 1.5km turn sharp L down narr lane by rest; camping sp on rd; diff app. Med, pt sl, terr, pt shd; wc; chem disp; shwrs inc; el pnts (6A) €1.50; lndtte; shop; rest, snacks 1km; bar; 50% statics; dogs €3; poss cr; quiet; no ccard acc. "Useful NH; beautiful mountain site; steep rds all round; v diff app fr W; quiet for couples; nothing for children." ♦ € 27.00                    2011*

ERACLEA MARE see Lido di Jesolo *2E2*

ITALY

⊞ **FALZE DI PIAVE** *2E1* (700m S Rural) **Parking Le Grave,** Via Passo Barca, 31010 Falze-di-Piave (TV) [0339 2348523; fax 0438 86896; belleluigi@libero.it; www.legrave. it] Fr A27 exit Conegliano & turn R onto SP15 then SS13 to Susegana. At Ponte-della-Priula turn onto SP34 to Falze-di-Piave. Fr town cent turn L just past war memorial into Via Passo Barca, site on R. Sm, unshd; no wc or shwrs; chem disp; mv service pnt; el pnts(4A) inc; BBQ; playgrnd; quiet. "CL-type site in delightful area; friendly, helpful owner; gd walking/cycling. Wine tasting last w/end May." € 10.00          2011*

**FERIOLO see Verbania** *1B1*

⊞ **FERRARA** *1D2* (2km NE Rural) *44.85303, 11.63328* Campeggio Comunale Estense, Via Gramicia 76, 44100 Ferrara [tel/fax 0532 752396; campeggio.estense@ freeinternet.it / idem@libero.it] Exit A13 Ferrara N. After Motel Nord Ovest on L turn L at next traff lts into Via Porta Catena. Rd is 500m fr city wall around town; foll brown/yellow sps - well sp fr all dirs. Med, pt shd; htd wc (some cont); chem disp; mv service pnt; shwrs inc; el pnts (6A) €3; lndtte; shops, rest 200m; pool in park nrby; cycle hire; golf adj; some stored c'vans; dogs €1.50; site clsd early-Jan to end-Feb; Eng spkn; quiet; ccard acc €50+; 10% red CKE/CCI. "Peaceful, well-kept, clean site; helpful staff; lge pitches; ltd privacy in shwrs; interesting town; gd cycle tracks round town; rlwy stn in town for trains to Venice; gd NH." ♦ 1 Jan-7 Jan / 22 Feb-31 Dec. € 32.00          2013*

---

**"We must tell The Club about that great site we found"**

Get your site reports in by mid-August and we'll do our best to get your updates into the next edition.

---

**FIANO ROMANO** *2E4* (2km W Rural) *42.15167, 12.57670* Camping I Pini, Via delle Sassete 1/A, 00065 Fiano-Romano [0765 453349; fax 1890941; ipini@camping.it; www.camping.it/roma/ipini] Fr A1/E35 exit sp Roma Nord/ Fiano Romano (use R-hand lane for cash toll), foll sp Fiano at rndabt. Take 1st exit at next rndabt sp I Pini & stay on this rd for approx 2km. Take 2nd exit at next rndabt, L at T-junc under bdge, site sp on R. Med, hdg/mkd pitch, pt sl, terr, pt shd; htd wc; chem disp; mv service pnt; shwrs inc; el pnts (6A) inc (poss rev pol); lndtte (inc dryer); shop; rest, snacks; bar; BBQ; playgrnd; pool; paddling pool; tennis; cycle hire; horseriding nrby; fishing; wifi; entmnt; games rm; TV; 60% statics (tour ops); dogs €2; no c'vans/m'vans over 10m high ssn; phone; bus; poss cr; Eng spkn; adv bkg rec high ssn; quiet, but noisy nr bar; ccard acc; red low ssn/CKE/CCI. "Well-run, clean, excel san facs; helpful, friendly staff; excel rest; access poss diff lge o'fits; kerbs to all pitches; most pitches slope badly side to side req double height ramps; excursions by coach inc daily to Rome or gd train service; super site." ♦ 18 Apr-21 Sep. € 56.00 SBS - Y13          2014*

**FIE/VOLS** *1D1* (3km N Rural) *46.53334, 11.53335* Camping Alpe di Siusi/Seiser Alm, Loc San Constantino 16, 39050 Fiè-allo-Sciliar/Völs-am-Schlern (BZ) [0471 706459; fax 707382; info@camping-seiseralm.com; www.camping-seiseralm.com] Leave Bolzano on SS12 (not A22) sp Brixen & Brenner. After approx 7km take L fork in tunnel mouth sp Tiers, Fiè. Foll rd thro Fiè, site in 3km dir Castelrotto, sp on L. Lge, mkd pitch, hdstg, terr, unshd; htd wc; chem disp; mv service pnt; baby facs; sauna; shwrs inc; el pnts (16A) metered; lndtte; shop; rest, snacks; bar; playgrnd; golf 1km; sat TV; wifi; 20% statics; dogs €4.50; bus; phone; site clsd 5 Nov to 20 Dec; poss cr; Eng spkn; adv bkg; quiet; CKE/ CCI. "Well-organised site with gd views; impressive, luxury undergrnd san facs block; private san facs avail; vg walking/ skiing; an amazing experience; v popular site; efficiently run!" 1 Jan-2 Nov, 20 Dec-31 Dec. € 47.00          2014*

⊞ **FIESOLE** *1D3* (1km NE Rural) *43.80666, 11.30638* Camping Panoramico, Via Peramonda 1, 50014 Fiesole (FI) [055 599069; fax 59186; panoramico@florencecamping. com; www.florencecamping.com] Foll sp for Fiesole & Camping Panoramico fr Florence; site on R. Rd to Fiesole v hilly & narr thro busy tourist area. Lge, terr, pt shd; wc; chem disp; shwrs inc; el pnts (3A) inc; gas; lndtte; shop; bar; rest in high ssn; playgrnd; pool; internet; 20% statics; dogs free; poss cr; Eng spkn; quiet; ccard acc. "Access v diff - more suitable tenters; site soggy in wet; ltd water points; Florence 20 mins bus but 1.5km steep walk to stop; excel views; excel site." ♦ € 38.80          2012*

**FIGLINE VALDARNO** *1D3* (20km SW Rural) *43.53847, 11.41380* Camping Orlando in Chianti, Localita Caffggiolo, 52022 Cavriglia [tel/fax 055 967 422; Info@campingorlandoinchianti.it; www. campingorlandoinchianti.it] Fr A1 Firenze-Roma, exit Incisa. Foll Figline Val d'Arno. Dir Greve in Chianti, exit at Lucolena, then foll signs to 'Piano Orlando Parco Cavriglia'. Med, mkd pitch, hdstg, pt sl, shd; wc; chem disp; mv service pnt; shwrs inc; el pnts (16A); lndtte; BBQ; shop; rest; snacks; bar; pool; 10% statics; poss cr; Eng spkn; adv bkg; quiet; CCI. "Vg site; excel priced rest; rural; v friendly staff." ♦ 12 Apr-19 Oct. € 48.50          2014*

**FIGLINE VALDARNO** *1D3* (2.5km W Rural) *43.61111, 11.44940* Camping Norcenni Girasole Club, Via Norcenni 7, 50063 Figline-Valdarno (FI) [055 915141; fax 9151402; girasole@ecvacanze.it; www.ecvacanze.it] Fr a'strada A1, dir Rome, take exit 24 (sp Incisa SS69) to Figline-Valdarno; turn R in vill & foll sp to Greve; site sp Girasole; steep app rd to site with some twists for 3km. V lge, some hdg pitch, terr, pt shd; wc (some cont); chem disp; mv service pnt; baby facs; private bthrm extra; sauna; shwrs inc; el pnts (6A) inc; gas; lndtte (inc dryer); shop; tradsmn; rest, snacks; bar; BBQ; playgrnd; 2 pools (1 covrd); paddling pool; jacuzzi; tennis; games area; horseriding; cycle hire; fitness cent; games rm; wifi; entmnt; TV; dogs free; twin-axles acc (rec check in adv); stn 1.5km; bus to Florence; excursions; initial cash payment to smart card req for all expenses on site (cash not acc); busy at w/end in ssn; poss v cr; Eng spkn; adv bkg; ccard acc; red low ssn/long stay; CKE/CCI. "Excel, well-run site; some pitches sm; steep rd to site poss diff lge o'fits; steel pegs rec; upper level pool area excel for children; site clsd 1330-1530; poss long walk to san facs block; site hilly; wine tasting trips; gd touring base." ♦ 1 Apr-13 Oct. € 45.50 SBS - Y07          2011*

⊞ **FINALE (SICILY)** *3B3* (500m W Coastal) *38.02305, 14.15388* **Camping Rais Gerbi, di Triscele Tu.Rist Srl - Finale di Pollina (PA) S.S.113km. 172,9 [0921 426570; fax 426577; camping@raisgerbi.it; www.raisgerbi.it]** Direct access fr SS113 immed after bdge W of Finale. Lge, hdg/mkd pitch, mainly hdstg, terr, pt shd; wc; chem disp; mv service pnt; shwrs inc; el pnts (6A) €5.; lndtte; shop; tradsmn; rest, snacks; bar; BBQ; playgrnd; pool; private shgl beach 600m; tennis; games area; cycle hire; horseriding 200m; entmnt; internet; TV rm; 13% statics; dogs free; phone; bus; poss cr; Eng spkn; adv bkg (min 10 day stay); quiet but some rlwy noise; ccard acc; red long stay/CKE/CCI. "Gd touring base Cefalu & N coast; friendly, helpful staff; excel, clean site & facs." ♦ € 41.00    2013*

**FINALE LIGURE** *1B2* (1.5km N Rural) *44.18395, 8.35349* **Eurocamping Calvisio, Via Calvisio 37, 17024 Finale-Ligure (SV) [019 600491; fax 601240; info@eurocampingcalvisio. it; www.eurocampingcalvisio.it]** On SS1 Savona-Imperia, turn R at ent to Finale-Ligure; sp to site in Calvisio vill. Med, hdg/mkd pitch, shd; wc (some cont); chem disp; shwrs €0.50; el pnts (6A) inc; lndtte (inc dryer); shop; rest, snacks; bar; playgrnd; pool high ssn; paddling pool; sand beach 2km; solarium; wifi; entmnt; 80% statics; dogs; sep car park high ssn; poss cr; adv bkg; quiet; ccard acc; red low ssn. "Security guard at night; clean, well-maintained san facs." ♦ Easter- 5 Nov. € 54.50    2010*

⊞ **FIRENZE** *1D3* (3km NE Urban) *43.79066, 11.29005* **Camp & Ostello Municipal Villa di Camerata, Viala Augusto Righi 2/4, 50100 Firenze [055 601451; fax 610300; firenze@ostellionline.org]** Exit a'strada at Firenze Sud. Foll any sp for Fiesole several km fr a'strada. Rd crosses Rv Arno at Ponte G da Verrazzano, then cross rlwy & cont along Via Lungo L'Affrico. Watch for camp sp/Youth Hostel sp (Ostello) on L at rndabt into Viale Augusto Righi. Turn L, site is 50m on R in Youth Hostel grnds. V poor sp around Florence & poss diff to find. Med, pt sl, pt shd; mkd pitch, hdstg; wc; chem disp; mv service pnt; shwrs inc; el pnts (5A) inc; lndtte; shop 700m; rest 700m; snacks; bar; bus; poss cr; Eng spkn; adv bkg; noisy; red CKE/CCI. "Bus to Florence every 20 mins (tickets fr hostel office); access to Youth Hostel facs low ssn; hot water to shwrs only - other san facs basic but clean; gd local rest; poss unkempt low ssn." € 30.00    2009*

⊞ **FIRENZE** *1D3* (3km SE Urban) *43.76183, 11.26801* **Camping Michelangelo, Viale Michelangelo 80, 50125 Firenze [055 6811977; fax 689348; michelangelo@ evacanze.it; www.ecvacanze.it]** Exit a'strada A1/ E35 at Firenze Certosa or Firenze Sud; foll sp for Piazzale Michelangelo; site on L (N) in approx 6km, 200m past Piazzale (lge view point); steep site ent. Lge, some hdstg, pt sl, pt shd; wc (mainly cont); chem disp; mv service pnt; shwrs inc; el pnts (2-5A) inc; gas; lndtte; supmkt high ssn; rest 1km; snacks; bar; playgrnd; cycle hire; golf 10km; wifi; 30% statics; dogs €2; phone; bus; poss v cr; Eng spkn; quiet; ccard acc (€103 min); CKE/CCI. "Views over city fr some pitches; noise fr jukebox & bar at top end of site high ssn; cr, busy, backpacker site but well-run; gd rests walking dist; bus (tickets fr recep); v conv to visit city on foot; arr early for gd pitch; diff sl pitches in wet weather; check for suitable place bef booking in; care using light switches; old san facs in poor condition; few pitches suitable c'vans & most diff for m'vans." € 37.70    2011*

**FIRENZE** *1D3* (12km SE Rural) *43.70138, 11.40527* **Camping Village Il Poggetto, Strada Provinciale Nr1 Aretina Km14, 50067 Troghi [tel/fax 055 8307323; info@ campingilpoggetto.com; www.campingilpoggetto.com]** Fr S on E35/A1 a'strada take Incisa exit & turn L dir Incisa. After 400m turn R dir Firenze, site in 5km on L. Fr N on A1 exit Firenze-Sud dir Bagno a Ripoli/S. Donato; go thro S. Donato to Troghi, site on R, well sp. Narr, hilly app rd & sharp turn - app fr S easier. Lge, hdg/mkd pitch, pt sl, pt terr, pt shd; wc (some cont); chem disp; mv service pnt; baby facs; private san facs avail; shwrs inc; el pnts (7A) inc (poss rev pol); gas; lndtte; shop; tradsmn; rest, snacks; bar; playgrnd; 2 pools; cycle hire; table tennis; internet; 5% statics; dogs €2.20; phone; bus adj; money change; poss cr; Eng spkn; adv bkg ess high ssn; quiet but some m'way noise; red long stay; ccard acc over €200; 10% red CKE/CCI (low ssn). "Superb, picturesque, family-run site in attractive location inc vineyard; clean, modern facs; lovely pool; bus to Florence 45mins - tickets fr recep; trains fr Incisa Valdarno (free parking at stn); excursions; gd rest on site; low ssn offers for long stay (7+ days); vg site; helpful staff; lge o'fits come form S." ♦ 23 Apr-15 Oct. € 48.00    2013*

⊞ **FIRENZE** *1D3* (3km SW Rural) *43.72146, 11.21861* **Camping Internazionale Firenze, Via San Cristofano 2, 50029 Bottai (FI) [055 2374704; fax 2373412; internazionale@florencecamping.com; www. florencecamping.com]** Exit A1/E35 for Firenze/Certosa & foll sp twds Florence. Site well sp in 1.4km. Fairly steep climb on narr, v congested app rd. Med, pt sl, terr, pt shd; wc; shwrs; chem disp; mv service pnt; el pnts (6A) inc (rev pol); gas; lndtte (inc dryer); shop; rest, snacks; bar; playgrnd; pool; internet; entmnt; 50% statics; dogs; bus; poss cr; Eng spkn; rd noise; ccard acc. "Conv Florence, Siena; gates clsd 0000-0700 ; vg, clean facs; friendly recep; touring pitches on hilltop only - levelling poss diff; site diff in wet weather; poss cr." ♦ € 34.00    2011*

**FLORENCE see Firenze** *1D3*

**FOCE DI VARANO see Rodi Garganico** *2G4*

**FOLLONICA** *1D3* (6km E Rural) *42.91291, 10.85253* **Camping Vallicella, Loc Vallicella, 58020 Scarlino (GR) [0566 37229; fax 37232; info@vallicellavillage.com; www. vallicellavillage.com]** Fr E80, S1 Via Aurelia exit for Scarlino-Scalo, foll sp Scarlino & site. Lge, hdg/mkd pitch, terr, pt shd; wc (some cont); chem disp; mv service pnt; baby facs; private san facs avail; shwrs inc; el pnts (4-6A) inc; lndtte (inc dryer); shop; rest, snacks; bar; no BBQ; playgrnd; pool; paddling pool; sand beach 6km; tennis; cycle & boat hire; tennis; archery; horseriding 3km; golf 10km; wifi; TV rm; 40% statics; dogs €4.50; sep car park; adv bkg; quiet; ccard acc. ♦ 23 Apr-1 Oct. € 35.00 (CChq acc)    2011*

⊞ **FOLLONICA** *1D3* (3km NW Coastal) *42.94339, 10.71522* **Camping Parco Vacanze Il Veliero, Isole Eolie, 58022 Follonica (GR) [0566 260099; fax 260100; ilveliero@ sivacanze.it; www.sivacanze.it]** Exit SS1 Follonica Nord S onto SP152 Pratoranieri, site sp. Lge, pt shd; wc; chem disp; mv service pnt; private san facs on pitches; sauna; shwrs; el pnts inc; lndtte; shop; rest, snacks; bar; playgrnd; pool; paddling pool; sand beach 1km; tennis; cycle hire; golf 12km; some statics; adv bkg; quiet. € 50.00    2009*

**FOLLONICA** *1D3* (5km NW Coastal) *42.95029, 10.68681*
Camping Village Pappasole, Loc Torre Mozza, Via di Carbonifera 14, 57020 Vignale-Riotorto (LI) [0565 20414 or 20420; fax 20346; info@pappasole.it; www.pappasole. it] Fr SS1 take Follonica Nord exit onto SS322 & foll sp twd Piombino. After approx 1km turn L twd Torre Mozza onto overpass over m'way. Site in 1km. V lge, hdg/mkd pitch, hdstg, pt shd; wc; chem disp; mv service pnt; baby facs; private san facs + kitchen avail; shwrs inc; el pnts (3-10A) inc; gas; lndtte (inc dryer); shop; rest, snacks; bar; BBQ; playgrnd; pool; sand beach adj; watersports; tennis; cycle hire; games area; wifi; entmnt; 70% statics; dogs €9; phone; poss cr; Eng spkn; adv bkg; rd & rlwy noise & poss noisy at w/end; ccard acc; red long stay/low ssn; CKE/CCI. "Excel site; helpful staff; vg beach; lots of tourist info." ♦ 3 Apr-16 Oct. € 56.50      2010*

**FONDOTOCE see Verbania** *1B1*

⊞ **FORNI DI SOPRA** *2E1* (2km E Rural) *46.42564, 12.56928*
Camping Tornerai, Stinsans. Via Nazionale, 33024 Forni-di-Sopra (UD) [0433 88035] Site sp on SS52 Tolmezzo-Pieve di Cadore rd, 2km E of Forni-di-Sopra (approx 35km by rd fr Pieve-di-Cadore). Sm, pt sl, pt shd; wc (cont); chem disp (wc); el pnts (2A) €1 (extra for 6A) (long lead poss req); 50% statics; dogs €2; poss cr; Eng spkn; quiet; ccard acc. "Conv CL-type site for Forni-di-Sopra chairlift & Passo-della-Mauria; gd san facs." € 20.00      2009*

**FUCINE DI OSSANA see Dimaro** *1D1*

**FUSINA see Venezia** *2E2*

**GALLIPOLI** *3A4* (4km SE Coastal) *39.99870, 18.02590*
Camping Baia di Gallipoli, Litoranea per Santa Maria di Leuca, 73014 Gallipoli (LE) [0833 273210 / 338 8322910 l/s; fax 275405 / 340 7632095 l/s; info@baiadigallipoli.com; www.baiadigallipoli.com] Fr Brindisi/Lecce take S101 to Gallipoli. Exit at sp Matino-Lido Pizzo & foll sp to site, on coast rd bet Gallipoli & Sta Maria di Leuca. V lge, pt shd; htd wc; chem disp; mv service pnt; shwrs inc; el pnts (6A) inc; lndtte (inc dryer); shop; rest, snacks; bar; BBQ; playgrnd; pool; paddling pool; sand beach 800m (free shuttle bus); tennis; games area; wifi; entmnt; excursions; TV rm; statics; dogs (sm only) €3; sep car park; quiet; ccard acc. ♦ 1 Apr-15 Sep. € 64.00 (CChq acc)      2014*

**GEMONA DEL FRIULI** *2E1* (12km NW Rural) *46.32570, 13.06317* Camping Val del Lago, Loc Alesso, Via Tolmezzo 54, 33010 Trasaghis (UD) [0432 979164; fax 979455] Exit A23 sp Gemona-del-Friuli onto S13 N. Foll sp for Alesso, Trasaghis & Lago di Cavazzo. Site adj Camping Lago dei Tre Comuni. Sm, mkd pitch, shd; wc; chem disp; shwrs inc; el pnts inc (poss rev pol); shop 2km; rest, snacks; bar; lake sw adj; statics; dogs €3; Eng spkn; quiet. "Superbly situated; friendly owner; gd facs." 1 Apr-30 Sep. € 24.00      2009*

**GENOA see Genova** *1C2*

**GENOVA** *1C2* (10km E Rural/Coastal) *44.38085, 9.07215*
Camping Genova Est, Via Marconi, Loc Cassa, 16031 Bogliasco (GE) [tel/fax 010 3472053; info@camping-genova-est.it; www.camping-genova-est.it] Sp fr SS1 (Via Aurelia) in both dir. Exit A12/E80 Genova/Nervi exit & foll La Spezia sp to Bogliasco, look for sp on wall on L. V steep narr access, unsuitable without high power/weight ratio. Med, terr, pt shd; wc; mv service pnt; shwrs; el pnts (5A) €2.70; gas; lndtte; shop; rest, snacks, bar high ssn; BBQ; playgrnd; shgl beach 1.5km; dogs €2; bus; sep car park; Eng spkn; quiet; ccard acc. "Narr pitches; manhandling vans poss req; upper facs better than lower; steep footpath to Bogliasco; adv bkg rec during boat show in Oct." 15 Mar-20 Oct. € 25.00      2010*

⊞ **GENOVA** *1C2* (9km W Urban/Coastal) *44.43055, 8.81364*
Camping Villa Doria, Via al Campeggio Villa Doria 15, 16156 Pegli [tel/fax 010 6969600; villadoria@camping.it] Take SS1 coast rd W fr Genova to cent Pegli, past airport thro dock waterfront & look out for brown site sp on R by bus stop at traff lts. Foll narr & steep app to site - care needed. Site sp on wall on R round blind L-hand bend. Or exit A26 sp Pegli, turn W & foll site sp. Sm, mkd pitch, pt sl, unshd; htd wc (some cont); chem disp; mv service pnt; shwrs inc; el pnts (3-10A) inc; gas; lndtte (inc dryer); shop; rest 1km; snacks; bar; playgrnd; beach 1km; solarium; TV; dogs; phone; bus; sep car park; site clsd Jan; poss cr; Eng spkn; ccard acc; CKE/CCI. "Friendly, helpful owner; conv trains to Genoa & La Spezia; not rec for lge o'fits due narr access rd & o'hanging branches; footpath to vill; gd site but needs some TLC." ♦ € 30.00      2010*

⊞ **GENOVA** *1C2* (15km W Coastal) *44.41437, 8.70475*
Caravan Park La Vesima, Via Aurelia, Km 547, 16100 Arenzano (GE) [010 6199672; fax 6199686; info@caravanparklavesima.it; www.caravanparklavesima.it] E of Arenzano on coast rd, clearly sp. Or leave A10 at Arenzano & go E on coast rd. Med, mkd pitch, hdstg, unshd; htd wc (cont); chem disp; baby facs; fam bthrm; shwrs €0.50; el pnts (3A) inc (poss rev pol); gas; lndtte; shop high ssn & 3km; rest, snacks, bar high ssn; private shgl beach adj; 90% statics; no dogs; poss cr; Eng spkn; adv bkg; rd, rlwy noise; CKE/CCI. "Useful low ssn NH/sh stay; gd security; gd, clean san facs; v cr, noisy high ssn; some pitches sm; v gd site" € 32.60      2012*

**GIANO DELL'UMBRIA** *2E3* (1km SW Rural) *42.82932, 12.57178* Camping Pineta Di Giano, Via Monte Cerreto, 25 06030 Giano Dell'Umbria [39 07 42 93 00 40 or 39 34 03 76 23 43; fax 34 92 43 69 72; info@pinetadigiano. com; www.pinetadigiano.com] N fr Spoleto on S418 twds Montefalco. Turn L after Mercatello. Site well sp (brown) to Griano dell'Umbria. Site just outside vill. Sm, mkd pitch, hdstg, terr, shd; htd wc; shwr inc; el pnts (3A); shop 1km; rest; snack; bar; htd pool; 60% statics; dogs; quiet. "Gd site; off beaten track, v quiet in pine forest surrounded by long dist trails; v conv for Spoleto." 1 Apr-30 Sep. € 18.00      2014*

**GIGNOD see Aosta** *1B1*

GIOVINAZZO *2H4* (1km NW Coastal) *41.19167, 16.65769* Camping La Baia, Loc Trincea, 70054 Giovinazzo (BA) [tel/fax 0803 945165; camping.labaia@libero.it; www.campinglabaia.it] Well sp fr S16bis onto S16, then no sp. Turn L at traff lts sp 'Lungomare', then L at end. Cont for 1km, site on L. Med, mkd pitch, some hdstg; pt shd; wc (mainly cont); shwrs €0.50; el pnts (6A) €3; lndtte; shop 1km; tradsmn; snacks; bar; shgl beach adj; 40% statics; dogs €3; poss noisy (rd & disco adj); ccard acc; red CKE/CCI. "Attractive town & close to cathedral town of Trani & 13thC Castel de Monte; no sea views; gd NH." ♦ 1 May-30 Sep. € 26.00        2010*

## "We must tell The Club about that great site we found"

Get your site reports in by mid-August and we'll do our best to get your updates into the next edition.

GIULIANOVA LIDO *2F3* (2.9km N Coastal) *42.77790, 13.95613* Camping Don Antonio (formerly Baviera Holiday Ovest), Lungamare Zara Nord 127, 64022 Giulianova-Lido (TE) [085 8008928; fax 8004420; baviera@camping.it; www.campingbaviera.it] Exit A14/E55 dir Giulianova, site sp at Lido, 2km N of Giulianova, sp adj Camping Holiday. Med, mkd pitch, pt shd; wc; serviced pitches; shwrs inc; el pnts (6A) inc; lndtte; shop, rest, snacks in Cmp Holiday adj; pool; sand beach adj; playgrnd; games area; tennis adj; watersports; entmnt; excursions; sep car park high ssn; statics; dogs free (not acc Jul/Aug); adv bkg; quiet but some rlwy noise; red low ssn/snr citizens; ccard acc; red CKE/CCI. "Excel family site; lots to do in area." ♦ 16 May-13 Sep. € 42.00        2011*

GIULIANOVA LIDO *2F3* (2.9km N Coastal) *42.77790, 13.95588* Camping Village Holiday, Lungamare Zara, 64022 Giulianova-Lido (TE) [085 8000053; fax 8004420; holiday@camping.it; www.villaggioholiday.it] Exit A14/E55 dir Giulianova, site sp at Lido, adj Baviera Camping. Lge, pt shd; wc (some cont); chem disp; mv service pnt; serviced pitches; shwrs inc; el pnts (6A) €1.86; lndtte; supmkt; rest, snacks; bar; playgrnd; pool; sand beach adj; watersports; tennis; games area; entmnt;TV; sep car park; 20% statics; dogs free (not acc Jul/Aug); poss cr; adv bkg; quiet but some rlwy noise & tannoy; ccard acc; red low ssn; red CKE/CCI. "Excel family site; sm pitches; site clsd 1400-1600." ♦ 24 Apr-20 Sep. € 42.00        2009*

GIULIANOVA LIDO *2F3* (500m S Coastal) *42.73510, 13.98095* Camping Stork, Viale Del Mare 11, 64020 Cologna-Spiaggia (TE) [0858 937076; fax 937542; info@campingstork.com; www.campingstork.com] Fr A'strada foll sp on SS80 to Giulianova; at junc with SS16 turn R for 300m, turn L at traff lts, site sp. V lge, mkd pitch, shd; wc; chem disp; mv service pnt; baby facs; shwrs inc; el pnts (6A) inc; lndtte; supmkt; rest, snacks; bar; playgrnd; pool; paddling pool; sand beach adj; watersports; tennis; games area; cycle hire; wifi; entmnt; TV; cash machine; 40% statics; dogs €2.50; phone; sep car park high ssn; adv bkg; ccard acc; red long stay. ♦ 19 Apr-13 Sep. € 38.50 (CChq acc)        2011*

GIUNCUGNANO *1C2* (2km W Rural) *44.20680, 10.23520* Camping Argegna, Via Argegna, 55030 Giuncugnano (LU) [0583 611182; fax 611536; info@toscanacampclub.com; www.toscanacampclub.com] Exit A1 at Aulla. After bdge turn R; at rndabt foll sp Fivizzano. Approx 5km bef Fivizzano turn R onto rd SR445; foll sp Lucca to Carpinelli Pass, site sp in 4km on L - foll rd (approx 4m wide) to site. NB Fr Giuncugnano rte to site narr & winding for 20km; poor surface in parts. Sm, mkd pitch; shd; wc; mv service pnt; shwrs; el pnts €2.20; lndtte; shop; rest, snacks, bar 100m; BBQ; cooking facs; games area; WiFi; TV rm; some statics; dogs; adv bkg; quiet. "Peaceful site in lovely, little-known, interesting area." 1 May-15 Oct. € 26.00        2011*

GLURNS/GLORENZA see Mals/Malles Venosta *1D1*

GRADO *2E1* (2km E Coastal) *45.67848, 13.42021* Camping Al Bosco, Loc La Rotta, 34073 Grado (GO) [043 180485; fax 181008; info@campingalbosco.it; www.campingalbosco.it] Site in dunes E of Grado. App via narr rd, ent 3.6km, sp. Lge, pt shd; wc; shwrs €0.30; el pnts (3A) inc; lndtte (inc dryer); shop; rest, snacks; bar; playgrnd; sand beach 500m; cycle hire; no dogs; poss cr; adv bkg ess Jul/Aug; ccard acc. "Poss long walk to facs; reasonable site." 1 May-15 Sep. € 28.00        2009*

GRAVEDONA *1C1* (3km NE Rural) *46.15438, 9.33701* Camping Le Vele, 244 Via Case Sparse, 22013 Domaso [0344 965049; fax 536107; levele@domaso.it; www.levele.domaso.it] Site sp fr SS340. Med, mkd pitch, pt shd; htd wc; chem disp; mv service pnt; sauna; shwrs inc; el pnts (3A) inc; lndtte (inc dryer); shop nr; rest, snacks; bar; BBQ; playgrnd; htd pool; lake sw & beach adj; watersports; fitness cent; internet; 15% statics; dogs free; bus 200m; adv bkg; ccard acc. "Clean, well-run site; excel san facs; vg situation - direct access to lake; sm pitches." 26 Mar-24 Oct. € 38.00        2010*

GRAVEDONA *1C1* (2km SW Rural) *46.1255, 9.2842* Camping La Breva, Via Cimitero 19, Loc Cossognini, 22014 Dongo (CO) [tel/fax 034 480017; info@campinglabreva.com; www.campinglabreva.com] On E O'skts Dongo on SS340, site sp. Rec app fr Colico - avoid Julier Pass fr N if towing. Med, mkd pitch, some hdstg, pt sl, pt shd; htd wc (some cont); chem disp; mv service pnt; shwrs €0.80; el pnts (6A) €1.50; gas; shop 500m; tradsmn; snacks; bar; BBQ; playgrnd; pool 2km; shgl beach adj; lake sw; 5% statics; no dogs; phone; sep car park; poss cr; Eng spkn; adv bkg; red long stay. "Clean, well-run, family-owned site; v helpful staff; pitches tight for lge o'fits; gd location next to lake; san facs basic diff to fill van with water or empty; elec usage poss poor." ♦ ltd 1 Mar-31 Oct. € 26.00        2011*

GRAVEDONA *1C1* (2km SW Rural) *46.13268, 9.28954* Camping Magic Lake, Via Vigna del Lago 60, 22014 Dongo (CO) [tel/fax 034 480282; camping@magiclake.it; www.magiclake.it] Site sp on S340d adj Lake Como. Sm, pt sl, pt shd; htd wc; chem disp; mv service pnt; baby facs; shwrs inc; el pnts (6A) inc; lndtte; shop adj; tradsmn; snacks; bar; BBQ; playgrnd; lake sw adj; TV; 40% statics; dogs €3; bus 100m; poss cr; Eng spkn; adv bkg; quiet; red long stay; CKE/CCI. "Excel, friendly, family-run site; walk, cycle to adj vills along lake; excel facs; v.clean mod facs, cycle/kayak hire on site, cycle repairs on site." ♦ 8 Apr-11 Oct. € 38.00        2013*

**GROSSETO** *1D3* (10km SW Coastal) *42.71390, 11.00870*
Camping Cieloverde, Via della Trappola 180, 58046
Marina-di-Grosseto (GR) [0564 321611; fax 30178; info@
cieloverde.it; www.cieloverde.it] Fr Grosseto take SS322
twd Marina-di-Grosseto, then twd Principina-a-Mare. Site on
R. V lge, pt shd; wc; private san facs avail; baby facs; shwrs
inc; el pnts (3-6A) inc; lndtte (inc dryer); supmkt; tradsmn; rest,
snacks; bar; BBQ; playgrnd; sand beach 800m (free shuttle);
watersports; tennis 500m; games area; cycle hire; wifi; entmnt;
cinema; TV rm; some statics; adv bkg; ccard acc. "Conv
Maremma Nature Reserve; some pitches for RVs." ◆ 9 May-
20 Sep. € 49.00 (CChq acc) 2009*

**GROSSETO** *1D3* (12km SW Coastal) *42.74598, 10.94936*
Camping Le Marze, Strada Statale 322 della Collacchie,
Le Marze, 58046 Marina-di-Grosseto (GR) [0564 35501;
fax 744503; lemarze@boschettoholiday.it; www.
boschettoholiday.it/lemarze] Fr E80/SS1 S fr Livorno foll
dual c'way round Grosseto by-pass. Leave at 4th exit Grossetto
Sud; cont dir Grosseto for 5km on SP154; look for sp Marina
on L & foll rd for 9km; at traff lts turn R onto SP158 sp
Castiglione-della-Pescia, site on R in approx 5km. Lge, shd; wc
(cont); chem disp; mv service pnt; baby facs; shwrs inc; el pnts
(3A) inc; gas; lndtte (inc dryer); sm shop; rest; pizzeria; bar;
BBQ areas (gas/elec); playgrnd; pool; private beach 1km; cycle
hire; fishing 500m; games rm; cinema; wifi; entmnt; TV; dogs
€4.50; no c'vans/m'vans over 7m; sep car park; 15% statics;
adv bkg; quiet; red facs low ssn; ccard acc; red long stay/low
ssn; CKE/CCI. "Site in pine forest; excel staff; vg san facs; some
pitches uneven & poss tight lge o'tfits, espec when site busy;
free standing pool not suitable unsupervised childen; poss
mosquitoes; excursions Elba, Florence, Rome, Siena." ◆ 1 Apr-
7 Oct. € 49.00 2011*

**GROTTAMMARE see Martinsicuro** *2F3*

**GUBBIO** *2E3* (3.5km SW Rural) *43.32105, 12.56778* Camping
Citta di Gubbio, Frazione. Cipolleto 49, 06024 Gubbio
(PG) [075 9272037; fax 9276620; info@gubbiocamping.
com; www.gubbiocamping.com] Fr E3 take 1st Gubbio exit
onto Gubbio by-pass & take Perugia rd. Fork R in 500m beside
garden cent into narr lane, site 1.5km on R. Fr Perugia on S298
site sp on L 4km bef Gubbio at bottom of hill at Ponte d'Assi,
well sp. Med, pt shd; wc; chem disp; shwrs; el pnts (3A) €3;
lndtte; shop, rest, snacks, bar 3.5km; playgrnd; pool; paddling
pool; tennis; games area; cycle hire; dogs €2.50; phone; Eng
spkn; adv bkg; quiet; red long stay; ccard acc; red CKE/CCI.
"Excel, friendly, spacious site; clean facs; Gubbio sm medieval
city well worth a visit." ◆ 1 Apr-15 Sep. € 29.50 2011*

⊞ **GUBBIO** *2E3* (1.2km W) *43.35213, 12.56704* Camping
Parking Gubbio, Via Bottagnone 06024 Area Communale
P4 [07 59 22 06 93] Head NW on SR298 twrd Via Bruno
Buozzi, at rndbt take 2nd exit onto Viale Parruccini cont for
500m, at rndbt take 1st exit onto Viale Leonardo da Vinci, after
250 mtrs turn L onto Via Botagore. Sm; pt shd; no san facs;
chem disp; mv service pnt; gd NH. "Only campervan parking
allowed; historical town worth a visit." € 5.00 2014*

**IDRO** *1D1* (2km NE Rural) *45.7540, 10.4981* **Azur Ferienpark**
Idro Rio Vantone, Via Vantone 45, 25074 Idro (BS)
[0365 83125; fax 823663; idro@azur-camping.de; www.
idrosee.eu] Fr Brescia, take S237 N. At S tip of Lago d'Idro,
turn E to Idro. thro Crone, on E shore of lake, thro sh tunnel,
site 1km on L, last of 3 sites. Lge, shd; wc; chem disp; mv
service pnt; baby facs; serviced pitches; shwrs; el pnts (6-16A)
€2.50; lndtte; gas; shop; rest, snacks; bar; playgrnd; paddling
pool; tennis; lake adj; boat hire; windsurfing; games area; cycle
hire; internet; entmnt; TV rm; dogs €2.80; phone; poss cr; adv
bkg; quiet; ccard acc; 5% red CKE/CCI. "Idyllic on lakeside with
beautiful scenery; superb san facs; excel." ◆ 20 Mar-31 Oct.
€ 51.80 2013*

**IMER** *1D1* (1km E Rural) *46.14805, 11.79666* Camping
Calavise, Villaggio Sass Maor 36, Loc Pezze, 38050 Imer
(TN) [tel/fax 0439 67468; info@campingcalavise.it; www.
campingcalavise.it] Fr Trento on S47 then N on S50 - take
care as narr in places. Turn R at traff lts in Imer in front hotel
Al Bivio to site in 1km. Med, mkd pitch, terr, pt shd; wc
(mainly cont); chem disp; shwrs inc; el pnts (2A) inc; lndtte;
shop 500m; rest, snacks 1km; bar; playgrnd; pool; wifi; TV rm;
80% statics; dogs €3; bus 1km; poss cr; Eng spkn; adv bkg;
quiet; CKE/CCI. "V helpful owner; beautiful area; excel walking
in National Park; easy 10km cycle track along rv; vg." ◆ 1 Jun-
30 Sep & 8 Dec-30 Apr. € 22.50 2010*

⊞ **IMPERIA** *1B3* (1km SW Coastal) *43.86952, 7.99810*
Camping de Wijnstok, Via Poggi 2, 18100 Porto-Maurizio
(IM) [tel/fax 0183 64986; info@campingdewijnstok.com;
www.campingdewijnstok.com] Exit A10/E80 Imperia W
twds sea, take coast rd SS1 Via Aurelia dir San Remo. At km
651/1 turn dir Poggi, site sp. Med, shd; wc (some cont); chem
disp; shwrs €0.70; el pnts (3A) €2; gas; lndtte; shop 200m;
snacks; bar; shgl beach 500m; wifi; TV; 80% statics; phone;
sep car park; site clsd mid-Dec to mid-Jan; quiet but some rd
noise; ccard acc. "Shabby facs ltd low ssn; sm pitches diff for
lge o'fits; sh walk to town; NH only." ◆ € 25.00 2010*

⊞ **IMPERIA** *1B3* (2km SW Coastal) *43.87152, 8.00362*
Camping Eucalyptus, Via D'Annunzio 32, 18100 Imperia
[tel/fax 0183 61534; info@campingeucalyptus.com; www.
campingeucalyptus.com] Exit A10 Imperia W. Turn L after
tolls. Site well sp. Diff access lge o'fits - rec site ent via 2nd gate
100m beyond 1st. Med, hdstg, pt terr, shd; wc; chem disp;
mv service pnt; shwrs inc; el pnts (6A) €1.50; lndtte; gas; bar;
rest 100m; shop 200m; sand beach 500m; wifi; some statics;
dogs; Eng spkn; red low ssn; CKE/CCI. "Quiet on terr pitches
away fr rd; each pitch set in own garden & site in grnds of villa;
interesting owner; mosquitoes." € 26.00 2010*

⊞ **IMPERIA** *1B3* (2km SW Coastal) *43.87244, 7.99997*
Camping Parco La Pineta, Via Tommaso Littardi 68, 18100
Imperia [0183 61498] Exit A10 Imperia W. Turn L after tolls.
Site well sp. Med, hdstg, terr, pt shd; wc; chem disp; shwrs €1;
el pnts (3A) €2; lndry rm; shop & 200m; rest by beach; sand
beach adj; 95% statics; poss cr; Eng spkn; ccard not acc; quiet.
"Site in grnds of 17thC house; a few sm touring pitches - no
rm for awnings; clean san facs; pleasant owners; smart town
30 mins walk; gd." ◆ ltd € 26.00 2009*

ISEO *1C1* (500m NE Rural) *45.66416, 10.05722* **Camping Iseo, Via Antonioli 57, 25049 Iseo (BS) [tel/fax 030 980213; info@campingiseo.it; www.campingiseo.com]** Fr A4 exit sp Rovato & immed foll brown sp Lago d'Iseo. Site well sp in vill. Med, some hdg pitch, pt shd; wc (some cont); chem disp; mv service pnt; baby facs; fam bthrm; some serviced pitches; shwrs inc; el pnts (6-10A) inc; gas; lndtte; shop; rest 300m; snacks; bar; playgrnd; beach adj; windsurfing; games area; cycle hire; golf 3km (red for campers); wifi; entmnt; some statics; dogs €3.50; phone; poss v cr; Eng spkn; adv bkg; quiet; red CKE/CCI. "V scenic; friendly, welcoming owner; well-organised, smart site; sm pitches; extra for lakeside pitches; well-maintained, clean facs but ltd; cruises on lake; many rests nr; excel; site next to a rlwy line, poss sm noise; sm pitches." ♦ 1 Apr-1 Nov. € 39.00                                      2011*

ISEO *1C1* (500m NE Rural) *45.66388, 10.05638* **Camping Punta d'Oro, Via Antonioli 51-53, 25049 Iseo (BS) [tel/fax 030 980084; info@camping-puntadoro.com; www.puntadoro.com]** Fr Brescia-Boario Terme into Iseo, look for `Camping d'Iseo' sp on corner; after 200m cross rlwy, 1st R to site in 400m on lakeside. Med, pt sl, pt shd; wc; chem disp; mv service pnt; shwrs inc; el pnts (4A) inc; lndtte; shop 500m; rest 500m; snacks; bar; playgrnd; shgl beach; lake sw; boating; golf 6km; wifi; dogs €3.50; poss v cr high ssn; Eng spkn; some rlwy noise; red snr citizens; CKE/CCI. "Strictly-run but friendly site; gd security; beautiful area; friendly family run site cheerful and eager to help." ♦ Easter-19 Oct. € 32.00          2011*

ISEO *1C1* (1km NE Rural) *45.66527, 10.06277* **Camping Quai, Via Antonioli 73, 25049 Iseo (BS) [tel/fax 030 9821610; info@campingquai.it; www.campingquai.it]** Fr Brescia-Boario Terme rd by-passing Iseo, take NE exit; look for 'Camping d'Iseo' sp on corner. After 200m cross rlwy, site sp (sps obscured - go slow). Site adj Punta d'Oro on lakeside. Med, mkd pitch, shd; wc (some cont); chem disp; mv service pnt; shwrs inc; el pnts (4A) inc (poss rev pol); lndtte; shop, rest 1km; tradsmn; snacks; bar; BBQ; playgrnd; shgl beach & lake sw adj; watersports; games area; boat-launching; 25% statics; dogs; phone; bus, train 1km; sep car park; poss cr; Eng spkn; adv bkg; some rd noise; ccard acc; red long stay/snr citizens. "Well-kept; lake views fr some pitches; helpful manager; some noise fr nrby rlwy." ♦ ltd 18 Apr-21 Sep. € 41.00     2014*

ISEO *2F2* (1km E Urban) *45.66700, 10.06766* **Camping Covelo, Via Covelo 18, 25049 Iseo [tel/fax 030 982 13 05; info@campingcovelo.it; www.campingcovelo.it]** Fr A4 Bergamo-Brescia, take exit Palazzolo/SP469. Cont Onto SP12. At rndabt take 2nd exit SPxi. Take 3rd exit at next rndabt and foll sp to camp. Med, pt shd; wc; chem disp; shwrs; el pnts (6A); lndtte (inc dryer); shops; tradsmn; rest; snacks; bar; playgrnd; sw adj; games area; wifi; dogs €3.50; poss cr; Eng spkn; adv bkg; ccard acc. "Excel site; v well run; adj to lake; beautiful views; range of watersports; v helpful staff." 17 Apr-2 Nov. € 40.00                                      2014*

ISEO *1C1* (1.5km W Rural) *45.65689, 10.03739* **Camping Del Sole, Via per Rovato 26, 25049 Iseo (BS) [030 980288; fax 9821721; info@campingdelsole.it; www.campingdelsole.it]** Exit Brescia-Milan a'strada at Rivato-Lago d'Iseo exit & foll sp to Iseo. At complex rd junc with rndabts on Iseo o'skirts, site ent on L (lge sp). Site bet lakeside & rd, bef API petrol stn on R. Lge, mkd pitch, shd; wc; chem disp; mv service pnt; htd private bthrms avail; shwrs; el pnts (6A) inc; lndtte (inc dryer); supmkt; rest, snacks; bar; playgrnd; htd pool; paddling pool; shgl beach & lake sw: tennis; waterskiing; cycle hire; games area; wifi; entmnt; TV rm; 75% statics; dogs €3; sep car park; poss cr; Eng spkn; adv bkg; quiet; ccard acc. "Glorious views; excel facs; well-run, pleasant, popular lakeside site; pitches poss closely packed; ltd waste/water disposal; narr site rds." ♦ 15 Apr-25 Sep. € 41.00 (CChq acc)                     2011*

ISEO *1C1* (1.5km W Rural) *45.65690, 10.03429* **Camping Sassabanek, Via Colombera 2, 25049 Iseo (BS) [030 980300; fax 9821360; sassabanek@sassabanek.it; www.sassabanek.it]** On periphery of Iseo by lakeside. Lge, pt shd; wc (some cont); chem disp; mv service pnt; sauna; shwrs inc; el pnts (3A) inc; gas; lndtte; shop; tradsmn; rest, snacks; bar; BBQ; playgrnd; pool; paddling pool; boating; windsurfing; tennis; cycle hire;TV; 50% statics; no dogs; phone; sep car park; adv bkg; quiet; ccard acc. "Clean facs; sh walk to pretty lakeside & vill; helpful staff; gd NH/sh stay." ♦ 1 Apr-30 Sep. € 35.30                                      2010*

**ISPRA see Sesto Calende** *1B1*

**LAIVES/LEIFERS see Bolzano/Bozen** *1D1*

⊞ **LAVENA** *1C1* (9km SW Rural) *45.95960, 8.86340* **International Camping di Rimoldi Claudio, Via Marconi 18, 21037 Lavena-Ponte-Tresa (VA) [0332 550117; fax 551600; info@internationalcamping.com; www.internationalcamping.com]** On rte S233 going SW into Italy fr Switzerland, turn SE after border twd Lavena-Ponte-Tresa. Going twd Switzerland fr Italy on same rte turn R twd vill. Site sp in vill. Med, pt sl, hdg pitch; pt shd; wc (some cont); shwrs; el pnts (2-6A) €1.50; lndtte; supmkt opp; rest, snacks; bar; playgrnd; sand beach on lake; mainly statics; poss cr; adv bkg; quiet; CKE/CCI; acsi card acc; "On smallest, most W bay of Lake Lugano; excel facs; friendly, helpful staff; wall around site so no lake views." € 40.50                     2013*

LAZISE *1D2* (1.5km N Urban) *45.50807, 10.73166* **Camp Municipale, Via Roma 1,37017 Lazise (VR) [045 7580020; fax 7580549; camping.municipale@comune.lazise.vr.it; www.comune.lazise.vr.it]** N on S249 fr Peschiera, thro Pacengo & Lazise, at rndabt cont on S249 then turn L into Via Roma. Site sp at end of rd. Care req in 100m, sharp R turn; site ent pt hidden. Med, hdg/mkd pitch, pt shd; wc; chem disp; mv service pnt; shwrs inc; el pnts (10A) inc; lndtte; shop 250m; rest, snacks, bar adj; lake sw & beach adj; 5% statics; dogs €3; Eng spkn; quiet; ccard acc. "Gd touring cent; some pitches v muddy; gd, clean facs; friendly staff; avoid arr bef 1500 Wed (mkt on app rd); easy walk along lake to interesting sm town." ♦ ltd 22 Mar-2 Nov. € 32.00                     2012*

**LAZISE** *1D2* (500m S Rural) *45.49861, 10.7375* **Camping Du Parc, Via Gardesana, 110 I, 37017 Lazise (VR)** [045 7580127; fax 6470150; duparc@camping.it / duparc@campingduparc.com; www.campingduparc.com] Site on W side of lakeside rd SR249. Lge, pt sl, hdg pitch, pt shd; wc; chem disp; mv service pnt; shwrs; el pnts (5A) inc (rev pol); lndtte; shop; rest, snacks; bar; playgrnd; pool; waterslides; sand beach & lake sw; watersports; boat & cycle hire; gym; entmnt; 15% statics; dogs €5.70; poss cr at w/end; Eng spkn; adv bkg; red low ssn; ccard acc; red low ssn. "Sh walk to old town & ferry terminal; lovely lakeside position; excel, well-maintained site; vg san facs; gd size pitches, some on lake - long walk to water point; vg pizzeria & pool; quiet low ssn; ideal for families; gd security; Magic of Europe discount; vg." ♦ 12 Mar-31 Oct. € 60.30                                   2013*

**LAZISE** *1D2* (1km S Urban) *45.49722, 10.73694* **Camping Spiaggia d'Oro, Loc Bottona, Via Sentieri 1, 37017 Lazise (VR)** [045 7580007; fax 7580611; info@campingspiaggiadoro.com; www.campingspiaggiadoro.com] Fr A4/E70 exit dir Peschiera & take SR249 N; site sp. Fr Innsbruck on A22 exit Lago di Garda S. At rndabt take SR450 for Peschiera, then in 8km exit to Lazise. V lge, mkd pitch, pt sl, pt shd; wc; chem disp; mv service pnt; shwrs inc; el pnts (3-5A) inc (rev pol on 3A); gas; lndtte; shop & supmkt; snacks; bar; playgrnd; 3 pools; sandy private beach & sw adj; boat hire; dogs €7; quiet; Eng spkn; ccard not acc; CKE/CCI. "Helpful staff; lovely location nr historic walled town; gd facs." ♦ 27 Mar-15 Oct. € 49.40                         2009*

**LAZISE** *1D2* (1.5km S Rural) *45.49277, 10.73305* **Camping La Quercia, Loc Bottona, 37017 Lazise (VR)** [045 6470577; fax 6470243; laquercia@laquercia.it; www.laquercia.it] Exit A22/E45 at Affi/Lago di Garda Sud or exit A4/E70 at Peschiera-del-Garda. Site on SR249, on SE shore of lake. V lge, hdg/mkd pitch, pt sl, shd; htd wc; chem disp; mv service pnt; baby facs; fam bathrm; shwrs inc; el pnts (6A) inc; gas; lndtte (inc dryer); shops; rest, snacks; bar; playgrnd; pool; paddling pool; waterslide; jacuzzi; private sand beach; watersports; tennis; games area; gym; wifi; entmnt; 15% statics; dogs €6.90; phone; vehicle safety checks for cars/m'vans; poss cr; adv bkg. "Superb site for family holidays; many excel sports & leisure facs; some pitches on lakeside; easy walk to town along beach; highly rec." ♦ 1 Apr-4 Oct. € 61.00                 2012*

⊞ **LAZISE** *1D2* (2km S Urban) *45.47912, 10.72635* **Camping Amici di Lazise, Loc Fossalta Nuova, Strada del Roccolo 8, 37017 Lazise (VR)** [045 6490146; fax 6499448; daniela@campingamicidilazise.it] S fr Lazise, immed bef high rest with Greek columns (bef Gardaland) take side rd on R, site on R. Med, pt shd; wc (some cont); chem disp; mv service pnt; some serviced pitches; shwrs inc; el pnts (6A) inc; lndtte; shop; rest; bar; playgrnd; pool; paddling pool; shgl beach 300m; entmnt; 40% statics; dogs €4.50; poss cr; Eng spkn; adv bkg; quiet; red low ssn. "Gd." ♦ € 32.00                            2011*

**LAZISE** *1D2* (2.5km S Rural) *45.4825, 10.72861* **Camping Piani di Clodia, Loc Bagatta, 37017 Lazise (VR)** [045 7590456; fax 7590939; info@pianidiclodia.it; www.pianidiclodia.it] Site on SR249 just bef Camping Fossalta. V lge, mkd pitch, pt sl, terr, pt shd; wc (some cont); chem disp; 25% serviced pitch; shwrs inc; el pnts (10A); lndtte; shop & 2km; rest, snacks; bar; playgrnd; 5 pools; private shgl beach adj; tennis; games area; cycle hire; solarium; 10% statics; dogs €9; bus; Eng spkn; adv bkg; red long stay/low ssn; ccard acc; red low ssn; CKE/CCI. "Excel clean facs; superb pools; ideal for families; v helpful staff; some pitches poss diff lge o'fits." ♦ 24 Mar-14 Oct. € 46.00                        2009*

*See advert on bookmark*

⊞ **LECCE** *3A4* (6km W Rural) *40.36417, 18.09889* **Camping Lecce Namaste, 73100 Lecce** [0832 329647; info@camping-lecce.it; www.camping-lecce.it] Fr Lecce ring rd exit junc 15 W dir Novoli, in 5km immed after (abandoned) sm petrol stn turn R at sp Namaste. App rd to site potholed/gravelled. Site may appear clsd - sound horn for attention. Sm, some hdstg, pt shd; wc; shwrs inc; el pnts (10A) inc; shop 2km; beach 16km; bus to Lecce; quiet. "Gd, clean site but dated facs; conv for Baroque city of Lecce & coast around heel of Italy." € 21.00                                   2014*

**LECCO** *1C1* (5.8km S) *45.81555, 9.39969* **Camping Village Riviera, Via Foppaola 113, 23852, Garlate** [0341 680346; info@campingvillageriviera.com; www.campingvillageriviera.com] Head S on SS36, take exit Pescate/Lecco, cont strt, at rndbt take 3rd exit onto Via Roma, over rndbt, cont onto Via Statale, turn L onto Via Foppaola, dest will be on your L. Sm; Hdg pitch; pt shd; wc; shwrs; chem disp; el pnts (10A); lndtte; playgrnd; games rm; wifi; TV in bar; bus; Eng spkn. "Lake location with free kayak, pedalo, gym, playgrnd and pool." ♦ ltd. € 26.00                       2014*

**LECCO** *1C1* (4km W Rural) *45.81730, 9.34307* **Camping Due Laghi, Via Isella 34, 23862 Civate (LC)** [tel/fax 0341 550101; erealin@tin.it; www.duelaghicamping.com] S side of Lecco-Como rd on lake. Use slip rd mkd Isella/Civate. Turn L at T-junc, then L over bdge; foll v narr app rd to site, sp. Med, pt sl, shd; wc (cont); shwrs inc; el pnts (4A) inc; gas; lndtte; shop; rest, snacks; bar; pool; paddling pool; games area; mainly statics; dogs €3; quiet; Eng spkn. "Unkempt site; gd, modern san facs; app to site is v narr." 1 Apr-30 Sep. € 36.00                                    2014*

**LECCO** *1C1* (9km NW Rural) *45.92138, 9.28777* **Camping La Fornace, Via Giuseppe Garibaldi, 52 23865 Oliveto-Lario (LC)** [tel/fax 031 969553; lafornace@libero.it; www.lafornace.it] Fr Lecco SP583 twd Bellagio. Site on R at '37km' sp. Fr Bellagio on SP583 site on L 100m after Onno boundary sp. V sharp L turn at yellow sp. App diff for lge o'fits; narr app rd. Sm, mkd pitch, hdstg, pt sl, pt shd; wc (male cont); chem disp; mv service pnt; shwrs inc; el pnts (5A) inc; shop; rest, snacks; bar; beach & lake sw adj; games rm; dogs; poss cr; adv bkg; quiet; red low ssn; CKE/CCI. "Peaceful, lakeside site but poss loud music fr bar until sm hours; delightful setting; simple, clean facs." 1 Apr-30 Sep. € 22.00                     2013*

**LENNO see Menaggio** *1C1*

**LEVANTO** *1C2* (1km NE Coastal) *44.17364, 9.62550*
Camping Cinque Terre, Sella Mereti, 19015 Levanto (SP)
[tel/fax 0187 801252; info@campingcinqueterre.it; www.
campingcinqueterre.it] Clearly sp fr cent of Lèvanto. Fr E
turn L off SS1 to Lèvanto, sp Carradano, site on R bef town.
Sm, hdg/mkd pitch, terr, shd; htd wc (mainly cont); chem disp;
mv service pnt; shwrs €2; el pnts (3A) inc; gas; lndtte; shop
500m; tradsmn; rest 500m; snacks; bar; sm playgrnd; shgl/
sand beach 1km; games rm; wifi; TV; no dogs high ssn; sep car
park; bus to beach high ssn; poss cr; adv bkg; quiet; ccard not
acc; red low ssn; CKE/CCI. "Excel, friendly, family-run site; gd,
modern san facs; steep ent, but site level; Quiet and secluded;
helpful staff; Some rd noise; sm pitches." ♦ ltd Easter-30 Sep.
€ 35.00                                                    2013*

⊞ **LEVANTO** *1C2* (4km NE Rural) *44.17561, 9.63665*
Camping San Michele, Localita' Busco, 19015 Levanto
(SP) [tel/fax 0187 800 449; info@campingsanmichele.
net; www.campingsanmichele.net] Head S on SS566 dir
Carrodano Inferiore-Levanto. At 2nd rndabt take 3rd exit, then
turn L onto Localita Albero D'Oro. Campsite on the R after
2.3km. Lge, hdstg, terr, pt shd, wc (cont); chem disp; shwrs;
tradsmn; snacks; bar; scooter hire; poss cr; Eng spkn. "Helpful
staff; fair site; clean but tired facs." € 29.00           2014*

**LEVANTO** *1C2* (1km E Coastal) *44.17505, 9.62289* **Camping
Pian di Picche**, Pian di Picche, 19015 Levanto (SP) [tel/fax
0187 800597; piandipicche@libero.it] Clearly sp fr cent of
Lèvanto. Fr E turn L off SS1 to Lèvanto, sp Carradano, site on R
bef town; adj Camping Cinque Terre. Med, hdg pitch, terr, pt
shd; wc (some cont); chem disp; shwrs €0.50; el pnts (3A) inc;
gas; lndtte; sm shop; tradsmn; rest 200m; bar; BBQ; shgl beach
800m; TV; dogs; sep car park high ssn; Eng spkn; quiet; ccard
acc. "Basic facs; access to site/pitches diff - narr rds; early arr
rec in Aug; conv Cinque Terre vills; friendly, helpful staff." ♦
1 Apr-30 Sep. € 34.00                                      2010*

⊞ **LEVANTO** *1C2* (300m S Coastal/Urban) *44.16656,
9.61366* **Camping Acqua Dolce**, Via Guido Semenza 5,
19015 Levanto (SP) [0187 808465; fax 807365; mail@
campingacquadolce.com; www.campingacquadolce.com]
Site sp fr town cent, app rd to Levanto steep & winding. Site
ent steep. Med, mkd pitch, hdstg, terr, shd; wc (some cont);
chem disp; mv service pnt; serviced pitches; shwrs inc; el pnts
(6A) €2.50; lndtte; shops adj; rest, snacks; bar; playgrnd; pool
250m; sand beach 300m; dogs; phone; sep car park; site clsd
mid-Jan to end Feb; poss cr; Eng spkn; adv bkg; quiet; ccard
acc; red low ssn. "Site ent poss diff; sm pitches; vg, modern
san facs but unisex; o'fits parked v close high ssn; not rec
c'vans over 6m; gd touring base Cinque Terre vills; gd walks
fr site; lovely, clean beach; easy walk to boat terminal & rlwy
stn." ♦ € 46.50                                            2011*

**LEVICO TERME** *1D1* (1km S Rural) *46.00638, 11.28944*
Camping Jolly, Via Pleina 5, 38056 Levico-Terme (TN)
[0461 706934; fax 700227; mail@campingjolly.com; www.
campingjolly.com] Foll sp to Levico fr A22 or SS12 onto SS27;
site sp. Lge, mkd pitch, shd; wc; chem disp; mv service pnt;
serviced pitches; baby facs; shwrs inc; el pnts (6A) inc; gas;
lndtte (inc dryer); shop & 500m; rest 200m; snacks; bar; BBQ;
playgrnd; pool high ssn; paddling pool; shgl beach 200m; golf
7km; internet; entmnt; 30% statics; dogs €5; poss cr; adv bkg;
quiet; red snr citizens. "Health spa nr; vg." ♦ 1 Apr-10 Oct.
€ 38.00                                                    2011*

**LEVICO TERME** *1D1* (1km SW Rural) *46.00392, 11.25838*
Camping Spiaggia, Viale Venezia 12, 38050 Calceranica al
Lago (TN) [tel/fax 0461 723037; info@campingspiaggia.
net; www.campingspiaggia.net] Foll sp to Levico fr Trento;
after exit rd turn L & in 400m turn L foll sp to site. Site after
Camping Jolly on S side of lake. Med, hdg/mkd pitch, pt shd;
wc; chem disp; mv service pnt; private san facs avail; shwrs
inc; el pnts inc; playgrnd; private shgl beach & lake sw (across
rd); some statics; dogs €3; poss cr; Eng spkn; quiet. "Gd site."
10 Apr-15 Oct. € 22.50                                     2009*

**LEVICO TERME** *1D1* (2km W Rural) *46.00444, 11.28527*
Camping Due Laghi, Loc Costa 3, 38056 Levico-Terme
(TN) [0461 706290; fax 707381; info@campingclub.it;
www.campingclub.it] E fr Trento on S47 to Levico Terme;
L at junc & in 100m turn L up Trento slip rd & foll sp to site
immed on R on lake. Lge, pt shd; wc (some cont); chem disp;
mv service pnt; baby facs; sauna; shwrs inc; el pnts (3-6A) inc;
gas; lndtte (inc dryer); shop; rest, snacks; bar; BBQ; htd pool;
paddling pool; shgl beach 500m; tennis; games area; cycle
hire; wifi; entmnt; TV rm; 5% statics; dogs €4; phone; poss cr;
Eng spkn; adv bkg; some rd noise; ccard acc; red long stay/snr
citizens. "Friendly, helpful owner; clean facs; individ washrms
avail; scenic area & pretty town." ♦ 14 Apr-11 Sep. € 34.00
(CChq acc)                                                 2011*

## "I need an on-site restaurant"

We do our best to make sure site
information is correct, but it is always best
to check any must-have facilities are still
available or will be open during your visit.

**LEVICO TERME** *1D1* (5km W Rural) *46.00194, 11.25527*
Camping Al Pescatore, Via dei Pescatori 1, 38050
Calceranica-al-Lago (TN) [0461 723062; fax 724212;
trentino@campingpescatore.it; www.campingpescatore.
it] Exit Trento-Padova rd (SS47) either end of lake for
Calceranica. Turn W in vill over rlwy x-ing & R on to lakeside.
Site sp in 300m. Lge, pt shd; wc; chem disp; mv service pnt;
shwrs inc; el pnts (3A) inc; lndtte (inc dryer); shop; rest, snacks
200m; bar; pool; paddling pool; shgl beach & lake sw adj; wifi;
entmnt; 10% statics; dogs €3; poss cr; quiet. "Vg, modern san
facs; lovely lakeside location; cycle rtes fr site." ♦ 7 May-
11 Sep. € 32.50                                            2011*

**LEVICO TERME** *1D1* (5km W Rural) *46.00458, 11.26034*
Camping Mario Village, Via Lungolago 4, 38052
Caldonazzo (TN) [0461 723341; fax 723106; direzione@
campingmario.com; www.campingmario.com] Exit A22
onto SS47 E. Past Pergine foll sp Calceranica & Caldonazzo.
Site on lakeside. Med, mkd pitch, pt sl, pt shd; wc; chem disp;
mv service pnt; baby facs; shwrs inc; el pnts (6A) inc; gas;
lndtte; shop; rest, snacks adj; bar; playgrnd; pool; solarium;
lake sw; games area; wifi; entmnt; some statics; dogs €3;
phone; poss cr; Eng spkn; adv bkg; quiet; red low ssn. "Lovely
location; mountain views; cycle paths; vg, modern san facs." ♦
1 May- 13 Sep. € 25.00                                     2009*

**LIDO DELLE NAZIONI see Comacchio** *2E2*

**LIDO DI JESOLO** *2E2* (5.8km NE Coastal) *45.52862, 12.69693*
Campsite Parco Capraro, Via Corer 2 ramo, 4 30016 Lido
di Jesolo [0421 961073; fax 362994; info@parcocapraro.it;
www.parcocapraro.it] Fr Jesolo head NE on Via Roma Destra
twrds Via Giotto da Bondone. Cont onto Via Loghetto, then
onto Via Cà Gamba, L onto Via Corer. Site on L. Lge, Pt shd,
wc, chem disp, mv service pnt; baby facs; shwrs; el pnts (16A);
lndtte (inc dryer); shop; rest; café; bar; takeaway; bar; bbq;
playgrnd; htd pool; games rm; bike hire; entmnt; wifi; tv in bar;
dogs; public transport 1km; twin axles; Eng spkn; quiet. "Vg; v
well kept family site; path thro sm pine forest leads to beach &
bus stop to cent of town; vg rest/bar; superb sw pool." 1 Mar-
28 Sep. € 44.40                                                              2014*

**LIDO DI JESOLO** *2E2* (300m W Coastal) *45.48425, 12.58762*
Jesolo International Club Camping, Via Alberto da
Guissano 1, 30017 Lido-di-Jesolo (VE) [0421 971826;
fax 972561; info@jesolointernational.it; www.
jesolointernational.it] Site at W end of Lido-di-Jesolo, twd
Cavallino. V lge, mkd pitch, shd; wc; serviced pitches; chem
disp; mv service pnt; shwrs inc; el pnts (10A); gas; lndtte;
shop; rest, snacks; bar; playgrnd; pool; paddling pool; sand
beach adj; watersports; tennis; boat hire; games area; golf
3km; wifi; entmnt; sat TV; 10% statics; no dogs; site boat to
Venice; sep car par; poss cr; quiet; ccard acc; red long stay/
low ssn. "Superb site; many activities." ♦ 1 May-30 Sep.
€ 50.00                                                                       2010*

**LIDO DI JESOLO** *2E2* (6km NW Coastal) *45.55356,
12.76705* Portofelice Camping Village, Viale dei Fiori,
30020 Eraclea-Mare (VE) [0421 66441; fax 66021; info@
portofelice.it; www.portofelice.it] Exit A4 sp Caorle. In
Caorle foll coast rd S to Eraclea-Mare, site sp. V lge, hdg/mkd
pitch, shd; wc; chem disp; baby facs; some serviced pitches;
shwrs inc; el pnts (6A) inc; gas; lndtte; shop; tradsmn; rest,
snacks; bar; playgrnd; pool; paddling pool; sand beach 400m;
tennis; games area; golf 6km; entmnt; 50% statics; no dogs;
phone; bus; sep car park; poss cr; Eng spkn; adv bkg; ccard acc;
red long stay/snr citizens. "Excel pool complex." ♦ ltd 9 May-
16 Sep. € 41.30                                                              2009*

**LIDO DI SAVIO see Cervia** *2E2*

**LIGNANO SABBIADORO** *2E1* (2km NE Urban) *45.68196,
13.12580* Camping Sabbiadoro, Via Sabbiadoro 8, 33054
Lignano-Sabbiadoro (UD) [0431 71455; fax 721355;
campsab@lignano.it; www.campingsabbiadoro.
it] Fr Latisano strt rd 20km to Lignano. Bear L & foll sp to
Sabbiadoro. After 3km thro pine trees on edge of town turn
R. Rndabt with BP G'ge after 400m. Site opp. V lge, pt shd;
shwrs; wc; el pnts (4A) inc; lndtte; shop; rest, snacks; bar;
playgrnd; htd pool; paddling pool; tennis; cycle hire; games
area; internet; some statics; dogs €2; adv bkg; ccard acc; quiet.
"Vg; fine beach for children 20 mins walk." ♦ 4 Apr-18 Oct.
€ 35.50                                                                       2009*

⊞ **LIVORNO** *1C3* (10km S Coastal) *43.48119, 10.33327*
Camping Village Miramare, Via del Littorale 220, 57100
Antignano (LV) [0586 580402; fax 587462; contact@
campingmiramare.com; www.campingmiramare.com]
Fr Livorno foll SS1 in dir Grosseto/Rome. Site on R just after
2nd rd tunnel. Med, hdg pitch, hdstg, pt shd; wc (cont); chem
disp; mv service pnt; shwrs inc; el pnts (10A) inc; lndtte; shop &
5km; rest, snacks; bar; BBQ; playgrnd; pool; paddling pool; shgl
beach adj; wellness cent; entmnt; internet; TV; 10% statics;
bus; phone; no dogs; quiet but some rlwy noise; adv bkg; Eng
spkn; red long stay; ccard acc. "Extra for beachside pitches; ltd
space/access for twin-axle vans; conv visits Pisa, Siena, Florence
& wine areas; lovely setting." ♦ € 52.00                        2009*

⊞ **LUCCA** *1D3* (800m NW Urban) *43.85000, 10.48583*
Camper Il Serchio, Via del Tiro a Segno 704, Santa
Anna, 55100 Lucca (LU) [tel/fax 0583 317385; info@
camperilserchio.it; www.camperilserchio.it] Sp fr main rds
to Lucca & fr town. Gd access rds. Med, hdg/mkd pitch, hdstg,
pt shd; wc; chem disp; mv service pnt; shwrs inc; el pnts (5A)
inc; lndtte (inc dryer); rest nr; BBQ; playgrnd; pool €5; tennis,
games area opp; cycle hire; wifi; no statics; dogs; bus; poss cr;
adv bkg; quiet but disco noise nrby; "Attractive pitches; mainly
for m'vans - not suitable lge car/c'van o'fits or lge tents; v gd
site." ♦ € 25.00                                                            2012*

## "Satellite navigation makes touring much easier"

Remember most sat navs don't know if you're towing or in a larger vehicle – always use yours alongside maps and site directions.

**LUINO** *1C1* (6km N Rural) *46.04189, 8.73279* Camping Lido
Boschetto Holiday, Via Pietraperzia 13, 21010 Maccagno
(VA) [tel/fax 0332 560250; lido@boschettoholiday.
it; www.boschettoholiday.it/lido] On E shore of Lake
Maggiore on SS394 bet Bellinzona & Laveno. Fr Luino pass
under 2 rlwy bdges & foll sp L twd lake, site clearly sp. Med, pt
shd; wc; shwrs inc; chem disp; shwrs inc; el pnts (3-4A) €3.50;
(poss rev pol); lndtte; shop; snacks adj; playgrnd; lake sw &
beach adj; watersports; some statics; dogs €3; adv bkg; quiet;
ccard acc; CKE/CCI. "Hydrofoil/ferries fr vill to all parts of lake;
trains to Locarno." 1 Apr-30 Sep. € 29.00 (CChq acc)    2011*

**MACCAGNO see Luino** *1C1*

**MAGIONE** *2E3* (10km S Rural) *43.08140, 12.14340* Camping
Polvese, Via Montivalle, 06060 Sant' Arcangelo-sul-
Trasimeno (PG) [075 848078; fax 848050; polvese@
polvese.com; www.polvese.com] Fr A1 exit dir Lake
Trasimeno to Castiglione-del-Lago, then S599 to San
Arcangelo. Med, mkd pitch, pt shd; wc (cont); chem disp;
mv service pnt; shwrs inc; el pnts (10A); gas; lndtte; shop;
tradsmn; snacks; bar; playgrnd; 2 pools; paddling pool; sand
beach adj; watersports; lake fishing; cycle hire; games area;
wifi; entmnt; 40% statics; dogs €2; phone; poss cr; adv bkg;
quiet; red long stay; CKE/CCI. "Gd touring base for Umbria;
lakeside pitches avail; helpful staff." ♦ 1 Apr-30 Sep. € 22.00
(CChq acc)                                                                    2012*

MAGIONE *2E3* (5km SW Rural) *43.12422, 12.16700*
Camping Riva Verde, Loc Trasiemeno, Via Ghandi 5/7,
06063 San Feliciano (PG) [tel/fax 075 8479351; info@
rivaverdecamping.com; www.rivaverdecamping.com] Exit
SS75 at Magione, foll SS599 twd Chiusi. In 4km R on SP316
to San Feliciano & foll to site at N end of vill on lakeside. Med,
shd; wc; shwrs; el pnts inc; shops 1km; bar; rest; BBQ; pool
adj high ssn; lake sw; waterskiing; games area; entmnt; lge
new pool (2011), many statics; no dogs; sep car park; poss
cr; adv bkg; quiet. "Excel for touring Umbria; indiv washrms;
lovely lake views; hot water to shwrs only; diff for lge o'fits." ♦
1 Apr-30 Sep. € 22.00                                    2011*

MAGIONE *2E3* (6km SW Rural) *43.08835, 12.15630* Camping
Villaggio Italgest, Via Martiri di Cefalonia, 06060 Sant'
Arcangelo-sul-Trasimeno (PG) [075 848238 or 848292;
fax 848085; camping@italgest.com; www.italgest.com]
Fr Magione, take SS599 on S edge of Lake Trasimeno; site sp to
R on app to Sant' Arcangelo. Lge, mkd pitch, pt shd; wc (some
cont); chem disp; mv service pnt; baby facs; shwrs inc; el pnts
(6A) inc; gas; lndtte (inc dryer); shop; tradsmn; rest, snacks;
bar; cooking facs; playgrnd; pool; paddling pool; waterslides;
lake sw & private sand beach adj; fishing; watersports; tennis;
boat, cycle hire; games area; games rm; wifi; entmnt; sat TV
rm; 60% statics; dogs €2.50; sep car park; poss cr esp w/end;
Eng spkn; adv bkg (dep); ccard acc; CKE/CCI. "High standard,
well-maintained site; mosquitoes poss a prob; friendly owner;
helpful staff; clean facs; noisy nr disco & recep; quiet low ssn;
highly rec." ♦ 20 Apr-30 Sep. € 28.50 (CChq acc)      2009*

MALCESINE *1D1* (Urban) *45.76583, 10.81096* Camping
Villaggio Turistico Priori, Via Navene 31, 37018 Malcesine
(VR) [045 7400503; fax 6583098; antpriori@katamail.com;
www.appartement-priorantonio.it] Well sp in town cent.
Take care if app fr N. Sm, mkd pitch, hdstg, pt sl, terr, pt shd;
wc; chem disp; shwrs inc; el pnts (3A) inc; lndtte; shop adj; rest,
snacks, bar adj; lake sw & shgl beach 200m; no dogs; phone;
poss cr; some rd noise; adv bkg; Eng spkn; CKE/CCI. "Vg;
conv all amenities & Monte Baldo funicular." 15 Apr-16 Oct.
€ 24.00                                                  2011*

MALCESINE *1D1* (2km N Rural) *45.7850, 10.82027* Camping
Tonini, Via Gardesana 378, Loc Campagnola, 37018
Malcesine (VR) [tel/fax 0457 401341; info@campingtonini.
com; www.campingtonini.com] Site sp on SS249 on
lakeside, sp at gate. Med, mkd pitch, terr, pt sl, pt shd; wc;
chem disp; mv service pnt; shwrs inc; el pnts (6A) €2; lndtte;
sm shop; rest, snacks, bar 2km; shgl beach thro tunnel;
dogs €2; poss cr; Eng spkn; some rd noise; CKE/CCI. "In
beautiful position, walking dist town; gd sized pitches; clean,
modern san facs; gd views; friendly owner; gd cent mountain
walking/biking & windsurfing; excel." ♦ ltd 1 Apr-5 Oct.
€ 25.00                                                  2009*

MALCESINE *1D1* (3km N Rural) *45.78971, 10.82609*
Camping Martora, Campagnola, Martora 2, 37018
Malcesine (VR) [045 4856733; fax 4851278; martora@
martora.it; www.martora.it] On E side of lake on rd SS249
at km 86/11. Ent up concrete rd bet iron gates at 'Prinz Blau'
sp. Med, mkd pitch, pt sl, pt shd; wc; chem disp; shwrs; el pnts
(4A) inc; gas 200m; rest 100m; lake sw, windsurfing adj; wifi;
10% statics; poss cr; adv bkg; quiet. "Lakeside cycle path to
town." 1 Apr-3 Oct. € 27.00                              2011*

⊞ MALCESINE *1D1* (5km S Rural) *45.7300, 10.78333*
Camping Bellavista, Via Gardesana 4, Loc Vendemme,
37010 Cassone (VR) [tel/fax 045 7420244; info@
campingbellavistamalcesine.com; www.
campingbellavistamalcesine.com] 1km S of Cassone on R of
rd SS249. Steep access rd. Lge, terr, pt shd; wc; mv service pnt;
shwrs; el pnts (5A) inc (poss rev pol); gas; lndtte; shop; rest adj;
bar; playgrnd; shgl beach & lake sw; no dogs; poss cr; adv bkg;
quiet. "Ltd facs low ssn; footpath along lake shore; lovely views
over lake; on arr park 20m past STOP sp at recep; v clean san
facs." € 31.00                                           2009*

## "There aren't many sites open at this time of year"

If you're travelling outside peak season
remember to call ahead to check site opening
dates – even if the entry says 'open all year'.

⊞ MALS/MALLES VENOSTA *1D1* (1km S Rural) *46.68416,
10.55055* Mals Camping, Bahnhofstrasse/Via Stazione
51, 39024 Mals (BZ) [0473 835179; fax 845172; info@
campingmals.it; www.campingmals.it] Exit A12 to Landeck.
In Landeck take 1st exit at rndabt over rv bdge, then turn L &
foll sp Reschen Pass. On app Mals do not take any of L turns
into town (v narr streets); stay on main rd until traff lts then
turn R twd stn. Site in 500m on L. Sm, hdg/mkd pitch, terr,
pt shd; htd wc; chem disp; mv waste; shwrs inc; el pnts (16A)
inc; gas; lndtte; shop 500m; tradsmn; snacks; bar; playgrnd;
htd, covrd pool, tennis nr; cycle hire adj; wifi; dogs €3; bus/
train 250m; skibus 100m; Eng spkn; adv bkg; quiet; ccard acc;
CKE/CCI. "Gd walking, cycling area, free ent to local pools; vg,
high-quality, modern site." ♦ ltd € 32.00                2009*

MALS/MALLES VENOSTA *1D1* (3km S Rural) *46.67305,
10.5700* Campingpark Gloria Vallis, Wiesenweg 5, 39020
Glurns/Glorenza (BZ) [0473 835160; fax 835767; info@
gloriavallis.it; www.gloriavallis.it] Sp on rd S41 E of
Glorenza. Med, mkd pitch, terr, unshd; htd wc; chem disp; mv
service pnt; baby facs; shwrs inc; el pnts (10A) inc; gas; lndtte;
shop; tradsmn; snacks; bar; playgrnd; pool 1km; tennis; games
area; entmnt; 5% statics; dogs €4; phone; o'night parking
place for m'vans; Eng spkn; adv bkg; quiet; ccard acc; CKE/CCI.
"Excel mountain views; dog shwr rm; higher prices in winter."
♦ 1 Apr-31 Oct. € 34.80                                  2009*

MALS/MALLES VENOSTA *1D1* (3km S Rural) Stadt-
Camping im Park (Municipal), 39026 Glurns/Glorenza (BZ)
[0473 835160; fax 845767] Fr W (Ofenpass) on rd 28/S41 at
Glorenza take v sharp L turn immed after bdge & bef town
walls. Site 500m along v narr rd, not suitable lge/wide o'fits.
Sp 'MV Parking' fr town but all units acc. NB Height restriction
fr S (S40) 2.8m; fr N (Mals) 3.4m. Sm, pt sl, pt shd; wc; chem
disp; mv service pnt; shwrs €0.50; el pnts (10A) €2.50; shop,
rest, snacks, bar 400m; no statics; dogs; CKE/CCI. "Spacious,
tranquil CL-type site; beautiful views; easy walking, cycling;
attractive medieval town with all facs; v clean san facs; owner
calls in evening." 1 Apr-30 Oct. € 12.00                 2010*

**MANERBA DEL GARDA** *1D2* (1.5km N Rural) *45.56194, 10.56472* Camping La Rocca, Via Cavalle 22, 25080 Manerba-del-Garda (BS) [0365 551738; fax 552045; info@laroccacamp.it; www.laroccacamp.it] Fr Desenzano-Salo rd SS572 turn E at sp Manerba. Site sp fr Manerba. Be careful to head for 'Camping La Rocca' & not 'La Rocca'. Sh, steep app rd, site on R. Lge, pt shd; wc (some cont); chem disp; mv service pnt; shwrs inc; el pnts (4A) inc; shop; rest 200m; snacks; bar; playgrnd; pool & paddling pool; shgl beach & lake sw adj; tennis; games area; cycle hire; wifi; 20% statics; €4.50; adv bkg; quiet; "Excel site & facs; some pitches with lake views, some with low olive trees - care req; amusing, helpful owner; highly rec." 1 Apr-30 Sep. € 35.00          2010*

**MANERBA DEL GARDA** *1D2* (1.5km N Rural) *45.56333, 10.56611* Camping San Biagio, Via Cavalle 19, 25080 Manerba-del-Garda (BS) [0365 551549; fax 551046; info@campingsanbiagio.net; www.campingsanbiagio.net] Fr S572 rd turn E at sp Manerba, site sp 1.5km N fr Manerba. Lge, mkd pitch, hdstg, terr, shd; htd wc; baby facs; shwrs inc; el pnts (16A) metered; lndtte (inc dryer); shop; rest, snacks; bar; BBQ; playgrnd; shgl beach & lake sw; wifi; dogs €5; poss cr; Eng spkn; adv bkg; quiet; ccard acc. "Terr pitches with views over Lake Garda; v clean, modern san facs; easily got twin axle into lge pitch (reserved); excel." ♦ ltd 1 Apr-30 Sep. € 45.00          2011*

**MANERBA DEL GARDA** *1D2* (2km N Rural) *45.56138, 10.55944* Camping Rio Ferienglück, Via del Rio 37 Pianarolli, 25080 Manerba-del-Garda (BS) [0365 551450 summer 0365 551075 winter; fax 551044; info@campingrioferiengluck.com; www.gardalake.it/rioferiengluck] Fr S572 rd turn E at traff lts sp Manerba Centro. At TO turn L down hill & at petrol stn turn R into Viale Degli Alpini. At next rndabt turn L & foll site sp. Site 1.5km N of Manerba opp Hotel Zodiaco. Lge, mkd pitch, pt shd; wc (some cont); chem disp; mv service pnt; shwrs inc; el pnts (6A) €3; gas; lndtte (inc dryer); shop; tradsmn; rest nr; snacks; bar; BBQ; playgrnd; htd pool; paddling pool; shgl beach & lake sw adj; watersports; wifi; some statics; dogs €2; Eng spkn; no adv bkg; quiet; CKE/CCI. "Excel, family-run lakeside site with lge, level, grass pitches; welcoming vill nr; cent for Garda sightseeing; conv for train to Venice & Milan; beautiful area; cr but delightful situation." ♦ 23 Mar-20 Oct. € 40.50    2013*

**MANERBA DEL GARDA** *1D2* (1km SE Rural) *45.53040, 10.55487* Camping Sivino's, Via Gramsci 78, 25080 Manerba-del-Garda (BS) [0365 552767; fax 550678; info@sivinos.it; www.campingsivinos.it] Exit A4/E70 to Desenzano & foll sp dir Salo. In Moniga-del-Garda turn R at traff lts to vill sq & foll sp to Sivino's. Med, mkd pitch, terr, pt shd; wc; chem disp; shwrs inc; el pnts (6A) inc; gas 3km; lndtte; shops 1km; tradsmn; rest, snacks, bar at adj holiday vill; lake sw & shgl beach adj; 5% statics; dogs €8; phone; bus 500m; poss cr; Eng spkn; adv bkg; quiet. "Beautiful site; excel facs; dir access to lake; extra for superior lakeside pitches; noise poss high ssn due parties/discos nrby; this pt of lake poss v windy - extra storm straps ess." ♦ 1 Apr-30 Sep. € 43.00    2009*

**MANERBA DEL GARDA** *1D2* (1km S Rural) *45.53916, 10.55555* Camping Zocco, Via del Zocco 43, 25080 Manerba-del-Garda (BS) [0365 551605; fax 552053; info@campingzocco.it; www.campingzocco.it] Fr Desenzano rd N twd Riva. In 5km take minor rd to Manerba. Shortly after Irish pub turn R dir Moniga-del-Garda, thro vill & foll site sp. Lge, mkd pitch, terr, shd; wc (some cont); some serviced pitches; baby facs; fam bthrm; shwrs inc; el pnts (4A) inc; gas; lndtte; shop; rest; bar; playgrnd; pool; paddling pool; beach & lake sw adj; tennis; games area; wifi; 60% statics; dogs €4; quiet; ccard acc; red long stay/low ssn/CKE/CCI. "Beautiful situation; excel pool complex." ♦ 4 Apr-20 Sep. € 30.60          2009*

**MANERBA DEL GARDA** *1D2* (3km S Rural) *45.52555, 10.54333* Camping Fontanelle, Via del Magone 13, 25080 Moniga-del-Garda (BS) [0365 502079; fax 503324; info@campingfontanelle.it; www.campingfontanelle.it] Exit A4 m'way dir Desenzano del Garda & foll sp Salo. In 10km arr at Moniga del Garda take 2nd exit off 1st rndabt twd Salo, then 1st R into Via Roma sp Moniga Centro. Immed after 'Api' g'ge on L turn R into into Via Caccinelli; at end of this narr rd turn R into Via del Magone; site on L by lake. Access poss diff lge o'fits due narr vill streets. Lge, mkd pitch, sl, terr, pt shd; wc; chem disp; mv service pnt; baby facs; shwrs inc; el pnts (6A) inc; gas; lndtte (inc dryer); shop; supmkt; rest, snacks; bar; BBQ (gas/charcoal only); playgrnd; pool; paddling pool; lake sw & shgl beach; watersports; boat trips; fishing; tennis; golf 5km; horseriding 8km; cycle hire 2km; wifi; entmnt; games/TV rm; 20% statics; dogs €7; no c'vans/m'vans over 6.50m high ssn; phone; poss cr nr lake; Eng spkn; adv bkg; ccard acc; red low ssn/snr citizens; extra for lakeside pitches; CKE/CCI. "Vg site; excursions to Venice, Florence, Verona; friendly, helpful staff; excel san facs; levellers needed all pitches; pitches poss tight lge o'fits due trees; mkt Mon; lovely site." ♦ 18 Apr-26 Sep. € 40.00 SBS - Y01          2011*

**MANERBA DEL GARDA** *1D2* (3.5km S Rural) *45.52006, 10.52945* Camping Piantelle, Via San Michele 2, 25080 Moniga-del-Garda (BS) [0365 502013; fax 502637; info@piantelle.com; www.piantelle.com] Fr Desenzano take SP572 sp Salo. In Moniga turn R twd lake & foll site sp. Lge, hdg/mkd pitch, some terr, pt shd; wc; chem disp; some serviced pitches; el pnts (6A) inc; lndtte; shop; rest, snacks; bar; playgrnd; pool; paddling pool; lake sw & beach adj; watersports; games area; gym; wifi; entmnt; TV; 25% statics; dogs €7.50; extra for lakeside pitches; Eng spkn; adv bkg; quiet; red low ssn/snr citizens. "Friendly, helpful staff; gd touring base; excel, well-kept, well-managed site & facs; sep area for v lge o'fits; site produces own olive oil." ♦ 1 Apr-26 Sep. € 35.00          2009*

⊞ **MANERBA DEL GARDA** *1D2* (2km SW Rural) *45.53186, 10.52741* Camping Trevisago, Via Prato Negro 10, 25080 Moniga-del-Garda (BS) [tel/fax 0365 502252; info@trevisago.com; www.trevisago.com] Fr Desenzano take SP572 sp Salo. In Moniga foll brown sp. Med, hdg/mkd pitch, pt shd; wc (some cont); chem disp; shwrs €1; el pnts (10A) €2.50; lndtte; shop 1km; rest, snacks; bar; playgrnd; pool; paddling pool; lake beach 1km; watersports; TV; 80% statics; dogs €2.50 (not acc mid-July to end Aug); phone; bus 400m; poss cr high ssn w/end; Eng spkn; adv bkg; quiet; CKE/CCI. "Owner v helpful; well-maintained facs; mountain views; gd." € 30.50          2010*

⊞ MANFREDONIA *2G4* (10.5km SSW Coastal) *41.55477, 15.88794* Camping Lido Salpi, SS159 delle Saline Km 6,200, 71043 Manfredonia [tel/fax 0884 571160; lidosalpi@alice.it; www.lidosalpi.it] Head S on A14, exit at Foggia dir Manfredonia/SS89. Take ramp to Manfredonia Sud and cont strt. Turn R onto SS159, site on the R. Sm, mkd pitch, pt shd; wc; chem disp; mv service pnt; shwrs €0.50; el pnts (6A) €2; lndtte (inc dryer); shop; rest; café; bar; bbq; beach; wifi; 10% statics; dogs; ltd bus 0.5km; twin axles; Eng spkn; red low ssn. "V well located for San Giovanni Rotondo & Gargano; gd o'night stop fr A14; some pitches awkward for lge o'fits due to trees & site furniture; gd site." ♦ ltd € 31.00                                                        2014*

MARCIALLA CERTALDO see Poggibonsi *1D3*

MARINA DI BIBBONA see Cecina *1D3*

MARINA DI CAMEROTA *3A4* (4km N Coastal) *40.02650, 15.32583* Camping Nessuno, Via Mingardo 3, 84059 Marina-di-Camerota (SA) [tel/fax 0974 931457; info@villaggionessuno.com; www.villaggionessuno.com] On coast rd N twd Palinuro, site on L 1.5km after series of sh tunnels. NB Height restriction 3.3m & width 2.3m at Lentiscosa. Lge, mkd pitch, pt shd, terr, shd; wc; chem disp; mv service pnt; shwrs inc; el pnts (3A) inc; gas; lndtte; shop & 1km; rest; bar; playgrnd; sand beach adj; games area; cash machine; entmnt; 10% statics; dogs; phone; sep car park; poss cr; Eng spkn; no adv bkg; some rd noise; ccard acc. "On sand in pine forest; dir access to beach; most pitches reasonable size; friendly, helpful staff." ♦ ltd 29 May-5 Sep. € 46.00    2010*

MARINA DI CAULONIA *3B4* (1km NE Coastal) *38.35480, 16.48375* Camping Calypso, Contrada Precariti, 89040 Marina-di-Caulonia (RC) [tel/fax 0964 82028; info@villaggiocalypso.com; www.villaggiocalypso.com] On o'skts of Marina-di-Caulonia on S106. Med, hdg pitch, shd; wc (mainly cont); mv service pnt; chem disp; baby facs; shwrs €0.50; el pnts (2A) €3.50; lndtte; shop; rest, snacks; bar; playgrnd; sand beach adj; games area; tennis 500m; games area; entmnt; TV rm; wifi; 5% statics; dogs €2.50; phone; sep car park high ssn; Eng spkn; ccard acc; CKE/CCI; "Superb sandy beach; gd (if dated) facs; close to early Byzantine church at Stilo & medieval hill vill of Gerace." 1 Apr-30 Sep. € 28.50    2013*

MARINA DI EBOLI see Paestum *3A3*

MARINA DI GROSSETO see Grosseto *1D3*

MARINA DI MASSA *1C3* (1km N Coastal) *44.0250, 10.07388* Camping Giardino, Via delle Pinete 382, Loc Partaccia, 54037 Marina-di-Massa (MS) [0585 869291; fax 240781; info@campinggiardino.com; www.campinggiardino.com] On coast rd bet Marina-di-Massa & Marina-di-Carrara, sp. Lge, shd; wc (some cont); chem disp; mv service pnt; shwrs; el pnts (3A) (check pol); gas; lndtte; shop; rest 200m; snacks; bar; playgrnd; pool adj; paddling pool; sand beach 100m; 50% statics; dogs (not Jun-Aug); phone; sep car park; poss cr; adv bkg; rd noise; ccard acc; red low ssn. "Spacious pitches low ssn; conv NH for A12." ♦ 1 Apr-26 Sep. € 38.00    2010*

MARINA DI MINTURNO *2F4* (6km SE Coastal) *41.20731, 13.79138* Camping Villlago Baia Domizia, Via Pietre Bianche, 81030 Baia-Domizia (CE) [0823 930164; fax 930375; info@baiadomizia.it; www.baiadomizia.it] Exit A1 at Cassino onto S630, twd Minturno on S7 & S7quater, turn off at km 2, then foll sp Baia Domizia, site in 1.5km N of Baia-Domizia. V lge, hdg pitch, shd; wc (some cont); chem disp; mv service pnt; baby facs; shwrs inc; el pnts (3-10A) inc (poss rev pol); gas; lndtte; shop; rest, snacks; bar; 2 pools; sand beach adj; boat hire; windsurfing; tennis; games area; cycle hire; entmnt; TV; no dogs; poss cr; quiet; ccard acc; red low ssn. "Excel facs; 30/7-16/8 min 7 night stay; site clsd 1400-1600 but adequate parking area; top class site with all facs; gd security." ♦ 30 Apr-20 Sep. € 45.40    2009*

MARINA DI MINTURNO *2F4* (3km S Coastal) *41.22891, 13.75482* Camping Golden Garden, Via Dunale 74, 04020 Marina-di-Minturno (LT) [tel/fax 0771 614985; servizio.clienti@goldengarden.it; www.goldengarden.it] S on S7 Via Appia; bef x-ing Rv Garigliano turn R foll N bank of rv almost to mouth. Turn R, site on L in 300m. Or fr Gaeta (16km S) foll old S7 Via Appia, thro Scauri, turn R at traff lts after km 153 sp, Bar Marina on corner, foll sp. Med, mkd pitch, pt shd; wc; chem disp; shwrs inc; el pnts (4A) inc; gas 5km; lndtte; shop 5km; bar; sand beach adj; waterskiing; games area; solarium; entmnt; 50% statics; dogs €5; phone; sep car park; poss cr; Eng spkn; adv bkg; ccard acc; red low ssn. "Gd sand beach; slightly run down area." ♦ 30 Apr-5 Sep. € 35.00    2010*

MARINA DI MONTENERO *2F4* (1km NW Coastal) *42.06500, 14.77700* Centro Vacanze Molise, SS Adriatica, Km 525, 86036 Marina-di-Montenero (CB) [tel/fax 0873 803570; info@campingmolise.it; www.campingmolise.it] Exit A14 at Vasto Sud to SS16 dir S. On R Centro Commerciale Costa Verde, site opp on L. Med, mkd pitch, pt shd; wc (some cont); chem disp; mv service pnt; shwrs inc; el pnts (3A) inc; gas; lndtte; shop opp; tradsmn; rest, snacks; bar; private sand beach adj; tennis; games area; dogs €1; phone; bus; poss cr; Eng spkn; adv bkg; poss noisy high ssn; CKE/CCI. "Excel site; helpful staff; vg beach; Aqualand Water Park nr; Tremiti Isands rec; gd touring base; conv for m'way A14." ♦ 14 May-15 Sep. € 31.00    2011*

MARINA DI PISA *1C3* (6km S Coastal) *43.64720, 10.29603* Camping Village St Michael, Via della Bigattiera 24, 56018 Tirrenia (PI) [050 33103; fax 33041; info@campingstmichael.com; www.campingstmichael.com] Fr A12/E80 exit Pisa Sud & foll sp Tirrenia. In vill turn N twd Marina di Pisa, sp along coast rd to R. Lge, hdg pitch, pt shd; wc (some cont); chem disp; shwrs €0.50; el pnts (3A) inc; gas; lndtte; shop; rest, snacks; bar; playgrnd; private sand beach 600m; games area; golf 1.5km; entmnt; TV; 25% statics; no dogs; bus to Pisa & Livorno 600m; phone; poss cr; quiet; ccard acc. "Nr Livorno for ferries to Sardinia & Corsica; helpful staff." ♦ 1 Jun-15 Sep. € 29.00    2009*

ITALY

ITALY

**MARINA DI RAVENNA** *2E2* (6km N Coastal) *44.55895, 12.27995* **Camping Adria, Via Spallazzi 30, 48010 Casal-Borsetti (RA) [0544 445217; fax 442014; adria@camping.it; www.villaggiocampingadria.it]** Fr Ravenna take SS309 N for 17km, then at km 13 R (E) to sea & Casal-Borsetti & foll camp sp. Lge, pt shd; wc (some cont); chem disp; baby facs; shwrs inc; el pnts (4A) inc; gas; lndtte (inc dryer); shop; tradsmn; rest, snacks; bar; BBQ; playgrnd; pool; paddling pool; private beach 200m; wifi (recep area); entmnt; TV rm; 75% statics; dogs €4; phone; bus; poss cr; Eng spkn; adv bkg; ccard acc; red low ssn; CKE/CCI. "Conv Venice/gd NH bet Ancona & Venice; 1st class beach; new pool complex; many interesting buildings." ◆ 16 Apr-15 Sep. € 30.60 (CChq acc)                    2011*

**MARONE** *1C1* (1km S Rural) *45.73166, 10.09361* **Campeggio Riva di San Pietro, Via Cristini 9, 25054 Marone (BS) [tel/fax 030 9827129; info@rivasanpietro.it; www.rivasanpietro.it]** Site well sp on lakeside on L of SS510 on app Marone dir Pisogne. Turn sharp L, site adj Camping Breda. Med, mkd pitch, pt shd; wc (some cont); chem disp; mv service pnt; baby facs; shwrs inc; el pnts (4A) inc; gas; lndtte; shop; tradsmn; rest, snacks, bar 150m; playgrnd; 2 pools; lake sw; boat hire; windsurfing; canoeing; solarium; cycle hire; 30% statics; dogs €3; sep car park; poss v cr; Eng spkn; adv bkg (ess high ssn); rd/rlwy noise; red long stay; ccard acc; CKE/CCI. "Welcoming, helpful owners; poss v cr & cramped, even low ssn; gd dog exercise area." ◆ ltd 1 May-30 Sep. € 31.00                    2009*

**MARTINSICURO** *2F3* (10km N Coastal) *42.97238, 13.87748* **International Camping Don Diego, Lungomare De Gasperi 124, 63013 Grottammare (AP) [0735 581285; fax 583166; info@dondiegocamping.it; www.campingdondiego.it]** Exit A14/E55 dir Grottammare, site bet San Bernadetto & Grottammare off SS16 coast rd, well sp. Lge, shd; wc (some cont); shwrs inc; el pnts (6A) €3.50; gas; lndtte; shop; rest, snacks; bar; no BBQ; playgrnd; beach adj; games area; internet; entmnt; 50% statics; no dogs; adv bkg; quiet; ccard acc; red low ssn; CKE/CCI. "Gd facs; vg." ◆ 29 May-12 Sep. € 44.50                    2010*

**MASSA LUBRENSE see Sorrento** *3A3*

⊞ **MATERA** *3A4* (2km S Rural) *40.65305, 16.60694* **Azienda Agrituristica Masseria del Pantaleone, Contrada Chiancalata 27, 75100 Matera (MT) [0835 335239; fax 240021; info@agriturismopantaleonematera.it; www.agriturismopantaleonematera.it]** Do not use SatNav. Fr S on SS7 take Matera Sud exit, site 2km on L, not well sp. Opp Ospedale Madonna delle Grazie. Sm, all hdstg, terr, pt shd; wc; chem disp; mv service pnt; shwrs €1; el pnts (16A) inc; rest; bar; BBQ; dogs; Eng spkn; quiet; CKE/CCI. "Conv Matera - World Heritage site; helpful owners provide transport to/fr Matera cent." € 12.00                    2013*

**MATTINATA** *2G4* (2km Coastal) *41.70510, 16.06681* **Camping Mattinata, Contrada Funni, 71030 Mattinata (FG) [tel/fax 0884 550313; mattinata@camping.it]** Exit a'strada A14 at Foggia, sp Manfredonia. Fr Manfredonia on SS89 foll sp to Mattinata. Turn twds sea at km 145.8 & foll sp 'Lido'. Tight turn R into site fr W. Lge, pt shd; wc; shwrs €0.50; el pnts (4A) €2.07; gas; lndtte; shop; snacks; bar; playgrnd; sand/shgl beach adj; watersports; tennis; entmnt; 30% statics; no dogs; sep car park; poss cr; adv bkg; quiet. 25 May-25 Sep. € 39.00 (3 persons)                    2009*

**MAZARA DEL VALLO (SICILY)** *3C3* (1km E Coastal) *37.63630, 12.61722* **Sporting Club Camping, Contrada da Bocca Arena, 91026 Mazara-del-Vallo (TP) [tel/fax 0923 947230; info@sportingcampingvillage.com; www.sportingclubvillage.com]** Site 1km fr S115, clearly sp (brown) fr all dirs. Lge, pt shd; wc (some cont); chem disp; mv service pnt; shwrs inc; el pnts (6A) €5; lndtte; shop; rest, snacks; bar; BBQ; playgrnd; pool; beach 500m; tennis; games area; games rm; entmnt; 5% statics; dogs; bus 500m; dogs €4; poss cr; Eng spkn; red long stay/low ssn; ccard acc; CKE/CCI. "Interesting area." ◆ 1 Apr-1 Oct. € 32.00                    2009*

**MENAGGIO** *1C1* (500m N Rural) *46.02516, 9.23996* **Camping Europa, Loc Leray, Via dei Cipressi 12, 22017 Menaggio (CO) [344 31187; europamenaggio@hotmail.it]** On ent Menaggio fr S (Como) on S240 turn R & foll 'Campeggio' sp along lakeside prom. On ent fr N turn L at 'Campeggio' sp, pass site ent & turn in boatyard. Sm, mkd pitch, terr, pt shd; wc; shwrs €70 for 5 mins; el pnts; shop; rest 300m; snacks; bar; lake sw; boat hire; cycle hire; 80% statics; dogs; poss v cr; Eng spkn; adv bkg; rd noise; CKE/CCI. "V sm pitches cramped high ssn; narr site rds diff for lge o'fits; old-fashioned facs but clean; poor security; helpful owner; m'vans rec to arr full of water & empty of waste; hardly any rd noise, Menaggio delightful place; v friendly." 1 Apr-30 Sep. € 22.50                    2013*

**MENAGGIO** *1C1* (6km S Urban) *45.96937, 9.19298* **Camping La'vedo, Via degli Artigiani 1, 22016 Lenno (CO) [0344 56288; www.campinglavedo.it]** Fr Como foll S340 along W shore of lake, site SE of Lenno 200m fr lake, adj to supmkt. Sm, pt sl, pt shd; wc (cont); chem disp; mv service pnt; shwrs €0.50; el pnts (3A) inc; lndtte; shop adj; rest opp; bar; BBQ; games area; entmnt; 25% statics; dogs; rd noise; CKE/CCI. "Picturesque, friendly site in sm town; basic facs; 15 mins to boat skm for other towns on lake; great care needed on S340 - v narr & busy rd." ◆ 1 Apr-30 Sep. € 20.00                    2013*

⊞ **MENFI (SICILY)** *3C3* (6km S Coastal) *37.56500, 12.96416* **Camping La Palma, Contrada Fiore, Via delle Palme 29, 92013 Menfi (AG) [tel/fax 0925 78392; campinglapalma@libero.it; www.campinglapalma.com]** Foll sp fr SS115 past Menfi to coast. Med, shd; hdstg; wc; chem disp; shwrs; el pnts €4.50; el pnts 16 A; gas; lndtte; rest, snacks; wifi; shop; bbq; playgrnd; sand beach adj; quiet; entmnt; wifi; tv; 10% static; dogs; bus 1.5km; twin axles; poss cr; eng spkn; adv bkg; CKE/CCI. "Lovely, unspoilt quiet beach (blue flag) with dunes; v helpful owner & staff; family run site; excel." ◆ltd € 29.50                    2014*

⊞ **MERANO/MERAN** *1D1* (500m S Urban) *46.66361, 11.15638* **Camping Merano, Via Piave/Piavestrasse 44, 39012 Merano/Meran (BZ) [0473 231249; fax 235524; info@meran.eu]** Exit S38 at Merano Sud & foll rd into town. Brown site sps to Camping & Tennis (no name at main juncs in town cent). Site ent mkd 'Camping Tennis'. Site also sp fr N. Med, hdstg, pt shd; wc; chem disp; mv service pnt; shwrs inc; el pnts (6A) €2.40; shop opp; supmkt 500m; rest, snacks, bar adj; htd pool; tennis adj; no statics; dogs €3.30; phone; poss cr; some rd noise; red long stay days; CKE/CCI. "Sh walk to town cent; fine site surrounded by spectacular mountain scenery; helpful staff; pitches soft after rain; gd clean san facs; helpful staff." € 44.00                    2014*

**MERANO/MERAN** *1D1* (9km S Rural) *46.59861, 11.14527*
Camping Völlan, Zehentweg 6, 39011 Völlan/Foiana
[0473 568056; fax 557249; info@camping-voellan.com;
www.camping-voellan.com] Leave S38 dual c'way (Merano-
Bolzano) S of Merano sp Lana. Drive thro Lana, turn uphill sp
Gampenpass. Turn R sp Foliana/Völlan & foll sp to site. Sm,
mkd pitch, terr, pt shd; wc; chem disp; mv service pnt; some
serviced pitches; shwrs €0.50; el pnts (4A) €2.50; lndtte (inc
dryer); shop; rest 800m; playgrnd; pool; dogs €4m; 10% statics;
dogs €3; phone; Eng spkn; quiet; CKE/CCI. "Long drag up to
site fr Lana, but worth it; beautiful situation o'looking Adige
Valley; excel facs & pool; barriers clsd 1300-1500 & 2200-0700;
v helpful owners." 19 Mar-7 Nov. € 24.00                  2010*

**MESSINA (SICILY)** *3B4* (12km W Coastal) *38.25920,
15.46779* Camping Il Peloritano, Contrada Tarantonia,
Km 28, 98161 Rodia-Messina (ME) [tel/fax 090 348496;
il_peloritano@yahoo.it; www.peloritanocamping.it]
Fr Messina on A20 take exit Villafranca. Turn R onto rd S113 dir
Rodia, site 2km on R. Fr Palermo exit sp Rometta, under m'way
& turn R, site on R in approx 5km. Med, mkd pitch, pt sl, pt
shd; htd wc; chem disp; mv service pnt; shwrs €0.50; el pnts
(6A) €4; gas; lndtte; shop; tradsmn; rest, snacks; bar; playgrnd;
htd, covrd pool; sand beach; wifi; entmnt; excursions; dogs;
phone; bus; poss cr; Eng spkn; adv bkg; quiet; red long stay/
CKE/CCI. "Local bus to Messina; site in olive grove; low trees
& tight ent poss diff lge o'fits; old but clean san facs; conv
Messina ferry; vg." ♦ 1 Mar-31 Oct. € 27.00            2009*

**MESTRE** *2E2* (3km E Urban) *45.48098, 12.27516* Venezia
Camping Village, Via Orlanda 8/C, 30170 Mestre/Venezia
(VE) [041 5312828; fax 5327618; info@veneziavillage.
it; www.veneziavillage.it] On A4 fr Milan/Padova take exit
SS11 dir Venice. Exit SS11 for SS14 dir Trieste & airport. 200m
after Agip g'ge on R watch for sp and take 1st exit R fr rdbt
bet two major dealerships. Keep in R lane all way to site. Med,
mkd pitch, pt shd; wc; chem disp; mv service pnt; shwrs inc; el
pnts (6A) inc (poss rev pol); gas; lndtte (inc dryer); shop high
ssn; rest, snacks; bar; playgrnd; pool 3km; sand beach 6km;
rv sw 2km; wifi; TV; 20% statics; dogs €2; phone; buses to
Venice; poss cr & noisy high ssn; Eng spkn; adv bkg; red long
stay/CKE/CCI. "V conv Venice - tickets/maps fr recep; clean,
well-run site; popular with m'vans; friendly, helpful owners;
pitches poss cramped when site full; mosquitoes; new recep,
bar/rest, shop, wellness area & toilet block (2011); excel."
22 Feb-9 Nov, 26 Dec-31 Dec. € 44.70                2014*

**MESTRE** *2E2* (4km E Urban) *45.48425, 12.28227* Camping
Rialto, 16 Via Orlanda, Loc Campalto, 30175 Mestre
(VE) [tel/fax 041 5420295; rialto@camping.it; www.
campingrialto.com] Fr A4 take Marco Polo Airport exit, then
fork R onto SS14 dir Venice. Site on L 1km past Campalto
opp lge car sales area, well sp. Do not enter Mestre. Med, pt
shd; wc (mainly cont); chem disp; mv service pnt; shwrs inc;
el pnts (15A) €1.50; lndtte; shop; no statics; dogs €3; phone;
wifi; bus to Venice; poss cr; Eng spkn; adv bkg; some rd noise;
red CKE/CCI. "Site in need of refurb but v conv Venice; bus
tickets fr recep; friendly, helpful staff; vg san facs, vg rest; rec."
20 Feb-6 Mar / 1 Apr-20 Oct. € 39.65              2014*

⊞ **MILANO** *1C2* (8km W Urban) *45.47390, 9.08233*
Camping Citta di Milano, Via Gaetano Airaghi 61, 20153
Milano [0248 207017; fax 202999; info@campingmilano.it;
www.campingmilano.it] Fr E35/E62/A50 Tangentiale Ovest
ring rd take Settimo-Milanese exit & foll sp San Siro along
Via Novara (SS11). Turn R in 2km at Shell petrol stn, then R
at traff lts in 500m & L to site in 600m. Site ent at Gardaland
Waterpark, poorly sp. Lge, hdstg, mkd pitch, pt shd; wc; chem
disp; mv service pnt; shwrs inc; el pnts (6A) inc; lndtte; shop
500m; rest, snacks; bar; waterspark adj; dogs €3.50; phone;
bus 500m; poss cr; Eng spkn; no adv bkg; rd, aircraft noise;
disco at w/end & waterpark adj; ccard acc; red low ssn/CKE/
CCI. "Gd san facs; noise fr adj concerts high ssn; conv bus/
metro Milan; properly penned animals for children to enjoy; Gd
security; peacocks roaming site." ♦ € 44.00          2013*

⊞ **MILAZZO (SICILY)** *3B4* (2km N Coastal) *38.26090,
15.24335* Camping Villaggio Riva Smeralda, Strada
Panoramica 64, 98057 Milazzo (ME) [090 9282980; fax
9287791; info@rivasmeralda.it; www.rivasmeralda.it]
Clearly sp in Milazzo; foll sp Capo-di-Milazzo. Diff app. Med,
hdstg, pt sl, terr, shd; wc; chem disp; mv service pnt; shwrs; el
pnts (6A) €3; lndry rm; shop; rest, snacks; bar; BBQ; playgrnd;
paddling pool; rocky beach adj; entmnt; 5% statics; poss cr;
Eng spkn; adv bkg; twin axles acc; poss noisy; CKE/CCI. "Gd

---

## "I need an on-site restaurant"

We do our best to make sure site
information is correct, but it is always best
to check any must-have facilities are still
available or will be open during your visit.

---

base for trips to adj isles; site a bit run down; 1 in 5 sl access to
pitches, ltd turning space; best for sm m'vans; diving cent on
site; excel; v nice site with beautiful views of sea; pitches tight;
extremely helpful owners; €3 a night to leave camper to go to
Aeolian Islands." ♦ € 43.50                         2014*

**MILAZZO (SICILY)** *3B4* (4km N Coastal) *38.26222, 15.24387*
Villaggio Turistico Cirucco, Strada Panoramica 66, Capo di
Milazzo, 98057 Milazzo (ME) [090 9284746; fax 9287384;
info@cirucco.it; www.cirucco.it] Foll Capo di Milazzo sp
fr Milazzo, site sp adj Camping Riva Smeralda. Diff, narr app.
Med, hdstg, pt sl, terr, pt shd; wc; chem disp; mv service pnt;
shwrs inc; el pnts (6A); shop; rest, snacks; bar; playgrnd; private
shgl beach 100m; internet; entmnt; 30% statics; sep car park
high ssn; poss cr; Eng spkn; red long stay. "Insufficient san
facs; private beach down steps; barrier clsd 1400-1600; gd
base Stromboli." 1 Apr-31 Oct. € 35.00              2009*

**MISURINA see Cortina d'Ampezzo** *2E1*

⊞ **MODENA** *1D2* (3km N Urban) *44.65429, 10.86884* Camping International, Via Cave di Ramo 111, 41100 Modena (MO) [059 332252 or 06771259 (mob); fax 823235; info@internationalcamping.org; www. internationalcamping.org] Exit A1/E35/E45 to Modena Nord; after toll stn turn 1st L & immed L again at rndabt, then R; site nr motel rest adj to toll booth. Alt rte fr city cent: take S9 Via Emilia fr cent sp dir Milan; camp sp clear on R of main rd; turn R; foll sp. Med, mkd pitch, pt shd; wc (cont); mv service pnt; shwrs inc; el pnts (6-10A) €3 (poss rev pol); gas; lndtte; ice shop; rest, snacks; bar; playgrnd; pool; dogs €2; phone; poss cr; Eng spkn; rd noise; ccard not acc; CKE/CCI. "Easy to find; poss travellers; parts of site waterlogged after heavy rain; facs clean but inadequate for size of site high ssn; conv for m'way; call mob no, if arr low ssn; mosquitoes NH only." ♦ ltd € 27.00                                                    2009*

⊞ **MODENA** *1D2* (2km SE Urban) *44.61361, 10.94444* Camper Club Mutina, Strada Collegarola 76A, 41100 Modena (MO) [059 4557043; fax 39 1782732524; camperclub.mutina@tiscali.it; www.camperclubmutina. it] Exit A1 Modena Sud onto SP623 dir 'Centro'. In approx 4km site sp on L (also sp Camper Market). Site adj rugby club. M'vans only. Sm, hdstg, unshd; htd wc (cont); chem disp; mv service pnt; shwrs inc; el pnts (6A) inc; gas; lndry rm; BBQ; wifi; bus 1km; vehicle-washing facs; red CKE/CCI. "Vg facs; easy access to Modena; phone first if car+c'van - poss acc, gd security, mini-bus to city, cycle path to city 60m, v friendly site." € 15.00                                                           2011*

**MOLINA DI LEDRO see Pieve di Ledro** *1D1*

## "Satellite navigation makes touring much easier"

Remember most sat navs don't know if you're towing or in a larger vehicle – always use yours alongside maps and site directions.

⊞ **MOLVENO** *1D1* (1km SW Rural) *46.13916, 10.95916* Camping Spiaggia Lago di Molveno, Via Lungolago 25, 38018 Molveno (TN) [0461 586978; fax 586330; info@ campingmolveno.it; www.campingmolveno.it] Fr Molveno head S on W side of lake, 1km on L. Lge, shd, mkd pitch; wc; shwrs inc; chem disp; mv service pnt; el pnts (5A) inc; gas 1km; lndtte; shop; rest, snacks; bar; lake sw; windsurfing; tennis; games area; cycle hire; ski school; hiking; TV; 60% statics; dogs €4; phone; poss cr w/end; Eng spkn; quiet; ccard acc; red low ssn. "Beautiful vill & mountains; well-maintained, high quality, friendly, busy site; clean san facs; vg." € 35.00      2009*

**MONFALCONE** *2E1* (8km SE Coastal) *45.77241, 13.6245* Camping Mare Pineta, Via Sistiana 60/D, 34019 Sistiana (TS) [040 299264; fax 299265; info@marepineta.com; www.baiaholiday.com] Well sp on SS14 on NW o'skirts of Sistiana. V lge, pt sl, terr, shd; wc (mainly cont); mv service pnt; some serviced pitches; shwrs inc; el pnts (3A) inc; lndtte; shop; rest, snacks; bar; playgrnd; pool; beach 600m; tennis; cycle hire; solarium; 30% statics; dogs €8; quiet; ccard acc; red long stay/CKE/CCI. "Free bus to beach; overlkg Adriatic & Bay of Trieste; site tight for lge m'vans." ♦ 01 Apr-15 Oct. € 40.00                                                            2011*

**MONFALCONE** *2E1* (9km SE Rural/Coastal) *45.76742, 13.64214* Camping Alle Rose, Via Sistiana 24/D, 34013 Sistiana (TS) [040 299457] Exit A4 at Sistiana exit & foll sp Sistiana. On app to vill turn R at T-junc, pass supmkt set back on R & look for blue site sp on L bef shops. Narr ent poss diff lge o'fits. Sm, shd, wc (some cont); shwrs; el pnts (6A) inc; gas adj; rest 200m; shgl beach 1km; dogs; bus to Trieste 300m; Eng spkn; quiet. "Shops & rests in walking dist; sand beach at Monfalcone; friendly, helpful owner; lovely spot - like a gd CL." 10 May-30 Sep. € 21.00                                         2010*

**MONIGA DEL GARDA see Manerba del Garda** *1D2*

⊞ **MONOPOLI** *2H4* (5km S Coastal) *40.91333, 17.34387* Camping Atlantide, Contrada Lamandia 13E, 70043 Capitolo Monopoli (BA) [080 801212; fax 4120238; demattia@residenceatlantide.it; www.residenceatlantide. it] On SS379 (Bari-Brindisi coast rd), 3km S of Monopoli, fr SS16 (Adriatica) take exit Capitolo. Lge, mkd hdstg pitch, pt sl, terr, pt shd; wc; chem disp; mv service pnt; serviced pitches; shwrs; el pnts (6A) inc (poss rev pol); lndtte; shop 2km; tradsmn; rest; bar; pool; tennis; games area; rocky waterfront adj; golf 5km; entmnt; 40% statics; dogs €4 on leash (not acc Aug); bus adj; adv bkg; Eng spkn; poss noisy; ccard acc; red low ssn/CKE/CCI. "Friendly owner; gd, clean site; basic facs low ssn; hot water to shwrs only; gd size pitches; disco every Sat high ssn until v late; Conv Roman ruins & UNESCO site; excel seafood rest 1km; site & area highly rec; conv Bari ferries; gd rest." € 41.00                                                          2013*

**MONTECATINI TERME** *1D3* (3km N Rural) *43.90505, 10.79190* Camping Belsito, Via delle Vigne 1/A, Loc Vico, 51016 Montecatini-Terme (PT) [tel/fax 0572 67373; info@ campingbelsito.it; www.campingbelsito.it] Fr Montecatini-Terme foll sp to Montecatini-Alto for 3km; site sp fr rd junc nr vill. NB Steep app with hairpins but OK with care & balanced o'fit. Med, mkd pitch, some hdstg, pt sl, pt shd; wc (some cont); chem disp; mv service pnt; 50% serviced pitch; private bthrms some pitches - extra charge; shwrs inc; el pnts (6A) €1.50 (check pol); lndtte (inc dryer); sm shop; rest; bar; BBQ; playgrnd; htd pool; games rm; internet; TV; 10% statics; dogs; phone; bus; Eng spkn; adv bkg ess; quiet; ccard acc; red low ssn/long stay/CKE/CCI. "Superb, well-kept site; excel facs; beautiful situation in high grnd o'looking Tuscan hills/valleys; helpful staff; conv for Florence, Pisa & Lucca; gate clsd 1300-1500; excel pool & rest; traditional Easter lunch at camp rest was outstanding." ♦ ltd 1 Apr-30 Sep. € 33.00          2011*

MONTESE *1D2* (3km S Rural) *44.25569, 10.93254* Camping Ecochiocciola, Via Testa 80, 41055 Maserno-di-Montese (MO) [059 980065; fax 980025; info@ecochiocciola.com; www.ecochiocciola.com] Exit A1 Modena Sud onto S623 dir Vignola, then rd P4. At Verica turn L to Montese & foll sp 'Chiocciola' to Maserno & site. Med, mkd pitch, pt sl, pt shd; wc (mainly cont); mv service pnt; shwrs inc; el pnts (6A) inc; shop 200m; rest; bar; BBQ; pool high ssn; tennis; games rm; TV; 30% statics; dogs €5; bus 100m; sep car park; site clsd 5 Nov-5 Dec; Eng spkn; quiet; CKE/CCI. "Beautiful setting; friendly owner knowledgeable about local ecology; excel cent for walking; ltd touring pitches suitable sm m'vans only; gd rest." ♦ ltd 4 Apr-2 Nov & Xmas/New Year. € 35.00      2010*

MONTEVARCHI *1D3* (10km S Rural) *43.44500, 11.61855* Camping La Chiocciola, Via G Cesare, 52020 Capannole (AR) [tel/fax 055 995776; info@campinglachiocciola.com; www.campinglachiocciola.com] Exit A1 at Valdarno & foll sp Levane. In Levane strt on at traff lts sp Bucine, site on R in 7km. NB Do not ent Bucine - narr rds. Med, hdg/mkd pitch, terr, pt shd; wc; chem disp; mv service pnt; all serviced pitch; shwrs inc; el pnts (6A) inc; gas; lndtte; hypmkt 13km; tradsmn; rest adj; playgrnd; htd pool adj; statics inc tour ops; dogs €2; poss v cr; Eng spkn; adv bkg (rec book in Jan for Jul/Aug); ccard acc; noise of barking dogs; CKE/CCI. "Excel for Tuscany, Florence & Siena easy drive; vg, clean san facs; lge pitches; site v cr early ssn - rec book mkd pitch; vg pool." ♦ ltd 1 Mar-25 Oct. € 40.00      2011*

MONTEVARCHI *1D3* (12km W Rural) Camping Piano Orlando, Loc Cafaggiolo, 52022 Cavriglia (FI) [tel/fax 055 967422; info@campingchianti.com; www.campingchianti.com] Fr Montevarchi take P408 to Cavriglia & foll sp for Castelnuovo-dei-Sabbiono. Site is 5km W of Castelnuovo, sp. Steep, narr rd. Easier rte on R222, turn E at Greve-in-Chianti & foll sp. Med, mkd pitch, pt sl, shd; wc; chem disp; mv service pnt; shwrs inc; el pnts (3A) inc; gas; lndtte; shop; rest, snacks; bar; pool; 10% statics; dogs; phone; poss cr; Eng spkn; ccard acc. "Site high on Monti di Chianti, surrounded by forests; 500m fr ent of Parco di Cavriglia; gd walking." 1 Mar-31 Oct. € 30.00 (CChq acc)      2009*

⊞ MONTOPOLI IN VAL D'ARNO *1D3* (1km N Rural) *43.67611, 10.75333* Kawan Toscana Village, Via Fornoli 9, 56020 Montópoli (PI) [0571 449032; fax 449449; info@toscanavillage.com; www.toscanavillage.com] Bet Pisa & Florence; exit Fi-Pi-Li dual c'way at Montópoli, foll site sps. Turn L bef Montópoli vill - site well sp. Med, mkd pitch, terr, pt shd; htd wc (some cont); chem disp; mv service pnt; some serviced pitches; baby facs; shwrs inc; el pnts (10A) €2.50; gas; lndtte (inc dryer); shop; tradsmn; supmkt 4km; rest, snacks; bar; BBQ; playgrnd; pool high ssn; cycle hire; golf 7km; wifi; TV rm; 15% statics; dogs; phone; train 3km; poss cr; Eng spkn; adv bkg req; some rd noise; ccard acc; red long stay; CKE/CCI. "Helpful staff; gravel site rds, steep in places; some v sm pitches; spotless facs; gd food in rest; gd pool; well organised; excel for Florence, Pisa & Tuscany; walking dist to Montopoli; beautiful surroundings; reasonably priced rest." ♦ € 43.50 (CChq acc)      2013*

MONZA *1C2* (4km N Urban) *45.62305, 9.28027* Camping Autodromo, Autodromo Nazionale Monza 20900 [tel/fax 039 339 2665523; segreteria@campeggiomonza.it; www.monzanet.it/eng/campeggi.aspx] Fr E exit A4 at Agrate-Brianza; fr W A4 exit Sesto San Giovanni onto S36. Foll sp to Autodromo/Biassono, then to site in Parco Reale complex. NB: Do not go to Monza Centro or exit main rd to Autodromo as no access to site; site clearly sp by g'ge. Lge, shd; wc (cont); own san rec; mv service pnt; shwrs €0.50; el pnts (5A) €6; lndtte (inc dryer); shop; rest adj; snacks; bar; playgrnd; pool adj; games area; 10% statics; dogs; phone; bus to Milan nr; poss cr; Eng spkn; no adv bkg; quiet except during racing. "Day ticket for all transport; bus 200m fr gate to Sesto FC (rlwy stn, bus terminal & metro line 1) - fr there take metro to Duomo; poor facs; NH/sh stay only for racing." ♦ 31 Aug - 9 Sep. € 60.00      2013*

MORGEX see Courmayeur *1A1*

MUGGIA see Trieste *2F1*

⊞ NARBOLIA (SARDINIA) *3A1* (6km W Coastal) *40.06956, 8.48375* Camping Nurapolis, Loc Is Arenas, 09070 Narbolia (OR) [0783 52283 or 348 8080839(mob); fax 52255; info@nurapolis.it; www.nurapolis.it] Fr Oristano take sp to Cuglier on rd SS292i. Site sp fr rd approx 5km fr S. Caterina-di-Pittinura. Lge, pt shd; wc; shwrs; el pnts (3A) €3; gas; shop; rest, snacks; bar; sand beach adj; tennis; entmnt; watersports; dogs; poss cr; adv bkg; ccard acc; red CKE/CCI. "Site in pine forest; many sports, guided walks Easter to Oct; v pleasant owners." ♦ € 26.50      2014*

## "There aren't many sites open at this time of year"

If you're travelling outside peak season remember to call ahead to check site opening dates – even if the entry says 'open all year'.

NARNI *2E3* (6km S Rural) *42.48459, 12.51516* Camping Monti del Sole, Strada Borgaria 22, 05035 Narni (TR) [tel/fax 0744 796336; montisole@libero.it; www.campingmontidelsole.it] Fr Narni on S3 dir Rome, then foll sp Borgheria, R in 1km. Diff rd to site. Med, shd; wc (some cont); chem disp; mv service pnt; shwrs inc; el pnts (5A) inc; lndtte; rest high ssn; snacks; bar; pool high ssn; paddling pool; tennis; games area; 20% statics; no dogs; phone; adv bkg; quiet. "Beautiful wooded site in heart of Umbria; off-the-beaten-track; lge pitches; dated san facs, but clean; friendly, welcoming owner; conv Rome, Perugia, Spoleto." ♦ 1 Apr-30 Sep. € 27.50      2010*

ITALY

⊞ NICOLOSI (SICILY) *3C3* (1km N Rural) *37.62303, 15.00854* Camping Etna, Via Goethe s/n, Monti Rossi, 95030 Nicolosi (CT) [tel/fax 095 914309; campingetna@tiscali. it] Fr Nicolosi on SP92 foll sp Etna Sud, turn L just bef Titanic rest. Site on L in pinewood, sp. Med, mkd pitch, terr, shd; wc; chem disp; mv service pnt; el pnts (6A) inc; lndtte; shop 1km; tradsmn; rest 500m; snacks; bar; BBQ; playgrnd; pool; paddling pool; entmnt; TV rm; 50% statics; dogs; poss cr; Eng spkn; poss noisy; CKE/CCI. "Gd, modern san facs; friendly staff; v conv Etna." ♦ ltd € 23.00                                         2010*

⊞ NICOTERA *3B4* (3km S Coastal) *38.50755, 15.92666* Camping Villaggio Mimosa, Mortelletto, 89844 Nicotera Marina (VV) [tel/fax 0963 81397; info@villaggiomimosa. com] Exit A3/E45 at Rosarno exit. Cross S18 & site sp dir San Ferdinando Porto. Foll sp on SP50 for approx 7km. Sm, mkd pitches, pt shd (reed matting); wc; chem disp; mv service pnt; hot shwrs; el pnts (12A); lndtte; gas; shop; rest, snacks; bar; BBQ; playgrnd; pool; paddling pool; sand beach adj; boat hire; windsurfing; tennis; games area; cycle hire; entmnt; wifi; 40% statics; dogs; twin axles; Eng spkn; CKE/CCI. "Some pitches have tight corners for lge o'fits; gd site." ♦ ltd € 54.00                                         2014*

NORBELLO *3A1* (7km NW Rural) *40.17472, 8.77305* Camping Villaggio Nuragheruiu, Loc Sant' Ignacio, 09070 Norbello [0785 825101; info@nuragheruiu.it; www. nuragheruiu.it] Fr SS131 take Norbello/Sant' Ignacio exit; site in 4km. Lge, mkd pitch, some hdstg, pt sl, pt shd; wc; chem disp; mv service pnt; shwrs inc; el pnts (5A) inc; lndtte; shop; tradsmn; rest, snacks; bar; BBQ; playgrnd; pool; paddling pool; games area; cycle hire; wifi; entmnt; TV; some statics; dogs €3.50; Eng spkn; adv bkg; quiet; ccard acc; red CKE/CCI. "Gd touring base; gd." ♦ 1 May-30 Sep. € 39.00                2010*

⊞ OLIVERI (SICILY) *3B4* (1.5km N Coastal) *38.12913, 15.05813* Camping Villaggio Marinello, Via del Sole, 17 Contrada Marinello, 98060 Oliveri (ME) [0941 313000 / 0941 526038; fax 313702; marinello@ camping.it / villaggiomarinell@gmail.com; www. camping.it/sicilia/marinello / www.villaggiomarinello.it] Exit A20 Falcone dir Oliveri, site well sp. Lge, hdg/mkd pitch, hdstg, pt shd; wc; chem disp; mv service pnt; shwrs inc; el pnts (6A) inc; lndtte; shop; rest high ssn; snacks bar; playgrnd; sand/ shgl beach adj; watersports; tennis; excursions; 20% statics; dogs free (not acc Jul/Aug); phone; train; poss cr; Eng spkn; quiet but some rlwy noise; red CKE/CCI. "Basic, clean, well-managed site; excel but shelving beach; helpful staff." ♦ € 46.00                                         2013*

**OLIVETO LARIO see Lecco** *1C1*

**OLMO, L' see Perugia** *2E3*

⊞ OPI *2F4* (3km E Rural) *41.77914, 13.86282* Camping Il Vecchio Mulino, Via Marsicana, Km 52, 67030 Opi (AQ) [tel/fax 0863 912232; ilvecchiomulino@tiscalinet.it; www. campingvecchiomulino.it] Turn off A1 twd Frosinone, 35km NE on S214 to Sora, 40km E on S509 to Opi, 5km E on S83 twd Villetta Barrea. Site on R. Med, pt shd; htd wc (some cont); chem disp; mv service pnt; shwrs inc; el pnts (8A) inc; lndtte; shop 3km; rest, snacks; bar; BBQ; playgrnd; games area; some statics; dogs; phone; Eng spkn; adv bkg rec Jul/Aug; quiet; ccard acc; CKE/CCI. "Wonderful walking country; excel rest; lovely site but facs stretched if site full." ♦ € 28.50     2010*

ORA/AUER *1D1* (NE Urban) *46.34779, 11.29980* Camping Markushof, Via Truidn 1, 39040 Ora/Auer (BZ) [0471 810025; fax 810603; info@campingmarkushof.it; www.hotelmarkushof.it] Exit A22 at Bolzano Sud onto SS12, then S to Ora. Site on main rd, sp. Sm, mkd pitch, some hdstg, unshd; wc; chem disp; mv service pnt; some serviced pitches; el pnts (16A) inc; lndtte (inc dryer); shop adj; rest, snacks; bar adj; playgrnd; htd pool; paddling pool; some statics; dogs €4; quiet; CKE/CCI. "Pt of hotel complex; excel facs." ♦ 1 Apr-20 Oct. € 27.00                                         2010*

ORBETELLO *1D4* (5.5km N Coastal) *42.46341, 11.18597* Camping Village Obertello, Strada Gianella 166, 58015 Orbetello [0564 820 201; fax 821 198; info@orbetellocampingvillage.it; www. orbetellocampingvillage.it] Fr SS1 Aurelia take exit Albinia. Cont twds Porto Santo Stefano. Campsite on L after 5km. V lge, mkd pitch, hdstg, pt shd; wc; chem disp; mv service pnt; baby facs; shwrs; el pnts (6A); lndtte (inc dryer); shop; rest; snacks; bar; BBQ; cooking facs; playgrnd; htd pool; paddling pool; beach adj; games area; bike hire; entmnt; wifi; tv; quiet; Eng spkn; adv bkg; CCI. ♦ 19 Apr-27 Sep. € 62.00     2014*

ORBETELLO *1D4* (7km N Coastal) *42.49611, 11.19416* Argentario Camping Village, Torre Saline, 58010 Albinia (GR) [0564 870302; fax 871380; info@argentariocampingvillage.com; www. argentariocampingvillage.com] Turn W off Via Aurelia at 150km mark, sp Porto S. Stefano, site on R, clearly sp in 500m. Ignore sps Zona Camping. Lge,mkd pitch; shd; wc; mv service pnt; shwrs inc; el pnts (6A) inc; lndtte; rest, snacks; bar; shop; playgrnd; pool & paddling pool; sand/shgl beach; boat hire; games area; 90% statics; no dogs; phone; sep car park; poss cr; adv bkg; quiet. "Better suited for campervans and tent; San facs due for upgrade; excel rest; easy access to beach." ♦ 1 Apr-30 Sep. € 42.00                                         2012*

ORBETELLO *1D4* (8km N Coastal) Camping Ideal, Via Aurelia, Km 156, 58010 Osa-Fonteblanda (GR) [tel/fax 0564 885379; campingideal@libero.it] S on Via Aurelia fr Grosseto, past Fonteblanda over rlwy bdge at km 157, camp on R of main rd after Hotel & Agip petrol stn. Most N of string of pine-shaded beach-side sites. Lge, shd; wc; mv service pnt; shwrs €0.25; el pnts (4A) inc; gas; lndtte; rest 500m; snacks; bar; sand beach; 95% statics; no dogs; sep car park; poss cr; quiet; ccard acc. "Helpful, friendly staff." Easter-20 Sep. € 22.00                                         2009*

ORBETELLO *1D4* (8km N Coastal) *42.53258, 11.18593* Camping Il Gabbiano, SS Aurelia, Km 154.2, 58010 Albinia (GR) [tel/fax 0564 870202; info@ilgabbianocampingvillage.com; www. ilgabbianocampingvillage.com] On W side of Via Aurelia at km stone 154. Lge, mkd pitch, shd; wc; shwrs inc; el pnts (3A) inc; gas; lndtte; shop; rest, snacks; bar; BBQ; playgrnd; private sand beach adj; entmnt; 90% statics; no dogs Jul/Aug; sep car park high ssn; poss cr; adv bkg; poss noisy; red low ssn. "Vg; v clean facs." ♦ 1 Apr-13 Sep. € 37.50                2010*

**ORIAGO see Venezia** *2E2*

**ORISTANO (SARDINIA)** *3A1* (5km W Coastal) *39.90388, 8.53111* **Camping Spinnaker, Via del Pontile, Marina-di-Torre Grande, 09170 Oristano [0783 22074; fax 22071; info@campingspinnaker.com; www.spinnakervacanze. com]** Fr Cagliari on S131 exit at Sta Giusta & foll sp Oristano & Torre-Grande. Med, mkd pitch, pt shd; htd wc; mv service pnt; baby facs; shwrs €0.50; el pnts €3; lndtte; shop; tradsmn; rest, snacks; bar; BBQ; playgrnd; pool; paddling pool; beach 200m; watersports; fishing; tennis 500m; cycle & boat hire; entmnt; TV rm; some statics; dogs €3; adv bkg; quiet. "Easy access to Sinis Peninsula for birdwatching & Tharros archaeological site." ♦ ltd 1 Apr-30 Sep. € 46.00 (CChq acc)            2009*

**ORTA SAN GIULIO** *1B1* (500m N Rural) *45.80125, 8.42093* **Camping Orta, Via Domodossola 28, Loc Bagnera, 28016 Orta San Giulio (NO) [tel/fax 0322 90267; info@ campingorta.it; www.campingorta.it]** Fr Omegna take rd on SS229 for 10km to km 44.5 sp Novara. Site both sides of rd 500m bef rndabt at Orta x-rds. Recep on L if heading S; poor access immed off rd. Med, pt sl, pt terr, pt shd; htd wc (some cont); chem disp; shwrs €0.20; el pnts (3-6A) €2.50; gas; lndtte (inc dryer); shop; rest 500m; bar; playgrnd; lake sw adj; waterskiing; wifi; dogs €4; Eng spkn; adv bkg; rd noise; ccard not acc; red low ssn. "Popular site in beautiful location; sm pitches; narr site rds & tight corners; arr early for lakeside pitch (extra charge); slipway to lake; friendly, helpful owner; Orta a gem; noise fr Beach Club at night; €4.50 for lakeside pitches." ♦ 1 Mar-31 Dec. € 45.50            2013*

⊞ **ORTA SAN GIULIO** *1B1* (4km N Rural) *45.83117, 8.39664* **Camping La Punta di Crabbia, Via Crabbia 2, 28028 Pettenasco (NO) [tel/fax 0323 89117; infotiscali@ campingpuntacrabbia.it; www.campingpuntacrabbia.it]** Site situated on L (E) of rd 229 fr Omegna to Orta, 1.5km N of Pettenasco. Steep access rd to site. Med, sl, shd; wc (cont); chem disp; mv service pnt; shwrs; el pnts (6A) €2.50; lndtte; ice shop & 3km; rest 700m; snacks; bar; lake adj; windsurfing; solarium; 90% statics; dogs €4; quiet; Eng spkn; ccard not acc; red low ssn. "Gd view of lake fr some pitches but with rd noise; v helpful recep." € 24.00            2009*

**ORTA SAN GIULIO** *1B1* (E Rural) *45.79785, 8.42087* **Camping Cusio Lyons Edda, Via Giovanni Bosco 5, 28016 Orta San Giulio (NO) [tel/fax 0322 90290; cusio@tin.it; www.campingcusio.it]** S fr Omegna, turn L at traff lts (sp Miasino) & site on L in 100m. Access via steep, rough track. Med, pt sl, pt shd; wc; shwrs; el pnts €2.70; gas; lndtte; shop 150m; snacks; bar; sm pool; beach 2km; tennis; games rm; internet; some statics; dogs €3.70; quiet. "Views over Lake Orta; gd, clean facs; conv for walk into town." 1 Apr-30 Nov. € 27.60            2009*

**ORTONA** *2F4* (5km NW Coastal) *42.37623, 14.37394* **Camping Torre Mucchia, Loc Lido Riccio, 66026 Ortona (CH) [0859 196298; taoceti@supereva.it] Exit SS16 at Ortona. In 500m turn sharp L & site sp. Med, shd; wc; shwrs; el pnts inc; gas; lndtte; shops 300m; snacks; bar; sand beach 200m; dogs; sep car park; adv bkg; quiet; CKE/CCI. "Sm, friendly, family-run site but poss scruffy." Easter-15 Sep.            2009*

⊞ **ORVIETO** *2E3* (500m S Urban) *42.72379, 12.13162* **Aree di Sosta Parcheggio Funicolare, Via della Direttissima, 05018 Orvieto (TR) [0763 300161/ 338 6843153 / 328 0644317; renzo. battistelli@hotmail.com; www.orvietoonline.com]** At Orvieto foll sp rlwy stn & funicular parking. Site on L just beyond funicular parking & behind rlwy stn. Foll sp 'Parcheggio Camper'. Sm, mkd pitch, hdstg, unshd; htd wc; chem disp; shwrs inc; el pnts (10A) inc; lndtte (inc dryer); shops 500m; rest, snacks, bar 200m; dogs; phone; bus, train 200m; rlwy noise; CKE/CCI. "M'vans only but c'vans poss acc low ssn; conv A1; gd san facs." ♦ € 15.00            2013*

**OSTRA** *2E3* (200m SW Rural) *43.61032, 13.15351* **Camping 'L Prè, Viale Matteotti 45, 60010 Ostra (AN) [tel/fax 071 68045; info@lpre.it; www.lpre.it]** Exit A14 at Senigallia onto S360. After approx 10km turn R to Ostra. Sp in vill. Sm, terr, pt shd; wc (some cont); chem disp; shwrs inc; el pnts (3A) €2.50; shop 300m; rest 100m; sand beach 10km; games rm; dogs; red long stay. "Gd san facs; v friendly owners; lovely, quiet, simple site with easy access Ancona, Esini Valley; beautiful views over valley; gd for cyclists; gd place to relax after Venice." 1 Apr-30 Sep. € 24.50            2014*

**OSTUNI** *3A4* (9km NE Coastal) *40.76602, 17.65044* **Camping Cala dei Ginepri, Contrada da Montanaro, SS 379, Km 23.500, 72017 Ostuni (BR) [tel/fax 0831 330402; info@ caladeiginepri.com; www.caladeiginepri.com]** Fr SS379 exit Cala dei Ginepri & foll sp to site. Lge, hdg/mkd pitch, shd; htd wc; mv service pnt; htd private san facs on pitches; shwrs inc; el pnts inc; lndtte; shop; rest, snacks; bar; pool; sand beach 700m; watersports; cycle hire; entmnt; TV rm; some statics; adv bkg; quiet. "Gd touring base." 1 May-12 Sep. € 38.00 (CChq acc)            2009*

**OTRANTO** *3A4* (1.5km NW Urban/Coastal) *40.16665, 18.47620* **Camping Mulino d'Acqua, Via Santo Stefano, 73028 Otranto (LE) [0836 802191; fax 802196; mulino. camping@anet.it; www.mulinodacqua.it]** Clearly sp on S611 coast rd. Lge, pt sl, pt shd; wc (cont); chem disp; mv service pnt; baby facs; shwrs €0.50; el pnts (6A) €3; gas; lndtte; shop; rest, snacks; bar; pool; sand beach adj; playgrnd; tennis; games area; cycle hire; entmnt; TV; statics; dogs €6; sep car park; adv bkg; quiet; ccard acc; red low ssn. 21 May-12 Sep. € 56.00 (CChq acc)            2010*

**PACENGO see Peschiera del Garda** *1D2*

**PADENGHE SUL GARDA see Desenzano del Garda** *1D2*

**PAESTUM** *3A3* (5km WNW Coastal) *40.42896, 14.98214* **Campsite Athena, Via Ponte di Ferro, 84063 Paestum [0828 851105; fax 724809; vathena@tiscali.it; www. campingathena.com]** Site 50km S of Salerno. Foll a'strada to Battipaglia onto main rd to Paestum. Head S on SS18. At rndabt take 1st exit onto SP276, then at next rndabt take 1st exit onto Via della Repubblica. Go thro 1 rndabt, turn L onto SP175, at rndabt take 1st exit onto Via Marittima, L onto Via Poseidonia and 1st L onto Via Ponte di Ferro. Site on R. Med, pt shd; wc; chem disp; mv service pnt; shwrs; el pnts (5A); lndtte; shop; rest; snack; takeaway; bar; wifi; dogs; train 2.5km; twin axles; Eng spkn; red low ssn; CKE/CCI. "Gd site, direct access to beach." ♦ ltd 1 Apr-30 Oct. € 51.00            2014*

**PAESTUM** *3A3* (N Coastal) *40.42780, 14.98244* **Camping Villaggio Ulisse, Via Ponte di Ferro, 84063 Paestum (SA) [tel/fax 0828 851095; info@campingulisse.com; www. campingulisse.com]** Foll site sp in cent Paestum, well sp. Lge, unmkd pitch, shd; wc (some cont); chem disp; shwrs inc; el pnts (3A) inc; lndtte; shop; rest, snacks; bar; playgrnd; sand beach adj; games area; 80% statics; dogs; poss cr; quiet; CKE/CCI. "Direct access to beach; gd, clean, friendly site." ♦ 1 Apr-30 Sep. € 35.00                                    2012*

**PAESTUM** *3A3* (9km N Coastal) *40.49248, 14.94196* Camping Villaggio Paestum, Loc Foce Sele, 84025 Marina-Di-Eboli (SA) [tel/fax 0828 691003; info@campingpaestum. it; www.campingpaestum.it] Fr Salerno/Battipaglia foll sp S to Paestum, turn R at site sp, site 150m on L after T-junc with coast rd. Lge, shd; htd wc (some cont); chem disp; mv service pnt; shwrs inc; el pnts (6A) inc; lndtte; shop; rest, snacks; bar; playgrnd; pool; paddling pool; sand beach 300m; tennis; games area; wifi; 50% statics; no lge dogs; phone; poss cr; adv bkg; poss noisy at w/end; ccard acc; CKE/CCI. "Gd rest & pool; sm pitches; Greek temples at Paestum superb." ♦ 15 Apr-15 Sep. € 36.00                                    2010*

# "That's changed – Should I let The Club know?"

If you find something on site that's different from the site entry, fill in a report and let us know. See www.caravanclub.co.uk/europereport.

⊞ **PAESTUM** *3A3* (5km NW Coastal) *40.41330, 14.99140* Camping Villaggio Dei Pini, Via Torre, 84063 Paestum (SA) [0828 811030; fax 811025; info@campingvillaggiodeipini. com; www.campingvillaggiodeipini.com] Site 50km S of Salerno in vill of Torre-de-Paestum. Foll a'strada to Battipaglia onto main rd to Paestum, site sp bef Paestum on rd S18, foll to beach. Med, hdg/mkd pitch, shd; wc (mainly cont); chem disp; mv service pnt; shwrs inc; el pnts (6A) inc; lndtte; shop; tradsmn; rest, snacks; bar; BBQ; playgrnd; private sand beach adj; games area; internet; entmnt; 30% statics; no dogs Jul/ Aug; phone; quiet low ssn; red low ssn; ccard acc; CKE/CCI. "Historical ruins nr; narr access rd fr vill due parked cars; lge O'fits may grnd at ent; some sm pitches - c'vans manhandled onto pitches; pleasant site by beach; gd rest; helpful owner; rec." ♦ ltd € 51.00 (4 persons)          2014*

**PALAU (SARDINIA)** *1C4* (500m N Coastal) *41.18586, 9.37700* Villagio Camping Acapulco, Loc Punta Palau 07020 Palau [0789 709497; fax 706380; info@campingacapulco.com; www.campingacapulco.com] Take rd S133 SE fr Sta Teresa-Gallura (ferry fr Corsica) sp Palau/Olbia, site sp in Palau. Med, mkd pitch, terr, some hdstg, pt shd; wc (some cont); chem disp; shwrs inc; el pnts (4A) €3; lndtte (inc dryer); shop 500m; rest, snacks; pizzeria; bar; BBQ; playgrnd; sand beach adj; boat-launching; watersports; wifi; entmnt; TV; 30% statics; phone; sep car park; Eng spkn; no adv bkg; ccard acc; quiet. "Superb situation; vg Mexican rest; helpful staff; vg site." 1 Mar-31 Oct. € 36.00                                    2009*

**PALAU (SARDINIA)** *1C4* (400m E Coastal) *41.17916, 9.39333* Villaggio Camping Baia Saraceno (Part Naturist), Punta Nera, 07020 Palau (SS) [0789 709403; fax 709425; info@ baiasaraceno.com; www.baiasaraceno.com] Take rd S133 SE fr Sta Teresa-Gallura (ferry fr Corsica) sp Palau/Olbia, site sp dir Capo d'Orso. Lge, mkd pitch, pt shd; wc (some cont); chem disp; mv service pnt; shwrs inc; el pnts (3A) €3; gas; lndtte (inc dryer); supmkt high ssn; rest, snacks; pizzeria; bar; BBQ; playgrnd; beach adj; watersports; boat-launching; wifi; entmnt; 25% statics; no dogs; sep area & beach for naturists; no adv bkg; ccard acc. "Superb situation on water's edge; helpful, friendly staff; vg rest; site busy in ssn; ferry to La Maddalena islands; conv day trips to Corsica." ♦ 1 Mar-31 Oct. € 40.00                                    2009*

**PALAU (SARDINIA)** *1C4* (5km SE Coastal) *41.16116, 9.40300* Camping Capo D'Orso, Loc Le Saline, 07020 Palau (SS) [0789 702007; fax 702006; info@capodorso.it; www. capodorso.it] Site sp on coast rd dir Arzachena. Lge, mkd pitch, pt sl, terr, shd; wc (some cont); chem disp; mv service pnt; shwrs; el pnts (3A) €3; gas; lndtte; shop; rest, snacks; pizzeria; bar; playgrnd; pool; private sand beach adj; boat hire; sailing & diving school; watersports; tennis; cycle hire; games area; games rm; entmnt; TV; 50% statics; dogs; phone; bus (high ssn); extra for pitches adj beach high ssn; sep car park high ssn; poss cr; Eng spkn; adv bkg; quiet; CKE/CCI. "Excel family site in beautiful position; vg facs." 15 May-30 Sep. € 41.00 (CChq acc)                                    2009*

**PALERMO (SICILY)** *3B3* (12km NW Coastal) *38.19686, 13.24455* Camping La Playa, Viale Marino 55 - 90040 Isola delle Femmine (PA) [tel/fax 091 8677001; campinglaplaya@virgilio.it; www.laplayacamping.it] On Palermo-Trapani rd take A29 exit Isola-delle-Femmine & foll sp. Med, hdstg, pt shd; wc; chem disp; mv service pnt; shwrs €0.50; el pnts (6A) inc; gas; lndtte (inc dryer); shop; rest, snacks; bar; BBQ; playgrnd; sand beach adj; dogs; Eng spkn; adv bkg; quiet; ccard acc; red CKE/CCI. "V helpful staff; bus into Palermo hourly; barrier clsd 1400-1600; v clean, well-managed, busy site; Lady mngr well versed on local info." 21 Mar-15 Oct. € 47.00                                    2013*

⊞ **PALMI** *3B4* (4km N Coastal) *38.39194, 15.86555* Camping San Fantino, Via San Fantino 135, Loc Taureana, 89015 Lido-di-Palmi (RC) [tel/ fax 0966 479729 / 334 3015485 (mob); info@ campingsanfantino.it; www.campingsanfantinopalmi. it] Leave A3/E45 at Palmi exit & take S18 N dir Gioia. After 4km turn L sp Taureana, site well sp. Lge, hdstg, terr, shd; wc; chem disp; shwrs; el pnts (4A) €2 (rev pol); gas; lndtte; shop; tradsmn; rest; bar; playgrnd; sand beach 400m; 20% statics; Eng spkn; 20% statics; adv bkg; quiet; CKE/CCI. "Site on cliff top with path to beach; gd views fr some pitches; conv NH bef Sicily ferry; gd rest; rough site rds - care needed; Path to beach locked low ssn." ♦ € 28.00                                    2014*

PASSIGNANO SUL TRASIMENO 2E3 (800m E Rural) 43.18397, 12.15089 Camping La Spiaggia, Via Europe 22, 06065 Passignano-sul-Trasimeno (PG) [075 827246; fax 827276; info@campinglaspiaggia.it; www. campinglaspiaggia.it] Exit A1 at Bettolle-Valdichiana & foll sp Perugia for 30km. Exit at Passignano Est & foll sp to site. Sm, mkd pitch, shd; htd wc (some cont); chem disp; mv service pnt; baby facs; fam bthrm; shwrs inc; el pnts (6A/10A) inc; lndtte; shop 800m; rest, snacks; bar; BBQ; playgrnd; pool; lake & sand beach adj; slip for boats; beach for dogs; nursery; table tennis; games area; cycle hire; wifi; sat TV; no statics; dogs €2; phone; bus/train 800m; poss cr; Eng spkn; adv bkg; quiet; ccard acc; red long stay/low ssn. "Lovely lakeside site; friendly owner; lge pitches; excel san facs but hot water variable; gd rest; interesting lakeside town; 800m fr the historic cent of Passignano; excel touring base for hill towns." ♦ 27 Mar-13 Oct. € 29.00                                    2013*

PASSIGNANO SUL TRASIMENO 2E3 (1km E Rural) 43.18338, 12.15085 Camping Kursaal, Viale Europa 24, 06065 Passignano-sul-Trasimeno (PG) [075 828085; fax 827182; info@campingkursaal.it; www.campingkursaal. it] Fr Perugia on S75 to Lake Trasimeno. Exit at Passignano-Est twd lake; site on L past level x-ing adj hotel, well sp. Med, hdg/mkd pitch, pt sl, pt shd; wc; chem disp; mv service pnt; baby facs; shwrs inc; el pnts (6A) €2 (poss rev pol); lndtte (inc dryer); shop; rest, snacks; bar; playgrnd; pool; private shgl lake beach; cycle hire; wifi; TV; dogs €1.50; phone; poss v cr; Eng spkn; adv bkg ess; some rlwy noise; red low ssn; ccard acc; red CKE/CCI. "Pleasant site in gd position; vg rest; some pitches have lake view; ltd space & pitches tight; gd clean site." ♦ 10 Apr-31 Oct. € 43.00                                    2014*

PASSIGNANO SUL TRASIMENO 2E3 (2km E Rural) 43.18176, 12.16517 Camping Europa, Loc San Donato 8, 06065 Passignano-sul-Trasimeno (PG) [tel/fax 075 827405; info@ camping-europa.it; www.camping-europa.it] Fr A1 E on SS75 bis twd Perugia; exit SS75 at Passignano Est & cont E on smaller parallel rd for 2km. Site on R via subway under rlwy. Med, pt shd; wc (some cont) chem disp; mv service pnt; shwrs inc; el pnts (6A) inc; gas; lndtte; shop; rest, snacks; bar; playgrnd; pool; private sand beach by lake; boat hire; watersports; games area; cycle hire; wifi; 20% statics; bus; Eng spkn; quiet; some rlwy noise; ccard acc. "Well-run, clean, friendly, gd value site; san facs in need of renovation; ltd (plunge-type pool); conv Assisi, Perugia, lake trips to islands." ♦ 28 Mar-10 Oct. € 23.00                                    2009*

PEGLI see Genova 1C2

⊞ PEIO 1D1 (1.5km S Rural) 46.35833, 10.68138 Camping Panoramico Val di Sole, Via Dossi di Cavia, 38020 Peio (TN) [0463 753177; fax 753176; info@valdisolecamping.it; www.valdisolecamping.it] Travelling W fr Dimaro on SS42 twd Tonale Pass, turn R into Val-de-Peio thro Cogolo twd Peio-Fonti. Site in 1.8km on R. Med, mkd pitch, terr, pt shd; htd wc (some cont); chem disp; mv service pnt; baby facs; shwrs inc; el pnts (3A) inc; lndtte (inc dryer); shop; rest 2km; snacks high ssn; bar; playgrnd; 60% statics; dogs €2; phone; bus 300m; site clsd end May & Nov; poss cr Aug; quiet; ccard acc; red CKE/CCI. "Excel for mountain walking in Stelvio National Park." ♦ ltd € 23.50                                    2009*

PERTICARA 2E3 (2km N Rural) 43.89608, 12.24302 Camping Perticara, Via Serra Masini 10/d, 61017 Perticara (PS) [0541 927602; fax 927707; info@campingperticara.com; www.campingperticara.com] Fr A14 at Rimini take S258 to Novafeltria. Foll sp Perticara & site. Steep, hairpins on pt of rte. Med, hdg/mkd pitch, hdstg, terr, unshd; htd wc; chem disp; mv service pnt; baby facs; serviced pitches; shwrs inc; el pnts (10A) inc; gas; lndtte; shop & 2km; tradsmn; rest, snacks; bar; playgrnd; pool; paddling pool; wifi; entmnt; TV rm; 5% statics; dogs; phone; bus; poss cr; Eng spkn; adv bkg; quiet; ccard acc; red low ssn; CKE/CCI. "Clean, well-maintained, scenic site; hospitable Dutch owners; many activities arranged; immac san facs; poss diff egress to SW (hairpins with passing places) - staff help with 4x4 if necessary; rough terrain." 1 May-20 Sep. € 34.00                                    2010*

PERUGIA 2E3 (8km NW Rural) 43.12030, 12.31328 Camping Paradis d'Eté, Colle della Trinita, Strada Fontana 29/H, 06074 Perugia [075 5173121; fax 0755 176056; jnlagu@tin. it; www.wel.it/cparadis] Exit Perugia-Firenze a'strada A1 at Ferro-di-Cavallo exit to N. At traff lts turn L (W) & foll rd parallel to a'strada for approx 1km. Turn R at camp sp, & site 3km up steep hill on R. Sm, pt sl, terr, shd; wc; mv service pnt; shwrs inc; el pnts (6A) €1.50; lndtte; shop; supmkt 3km; snacks; bar; playgrnd; pool; games rm; dogs; bus to Perugia; quiet; ccard acc; CKE/CCI. "Peaceful site; steep incline in & out of site; dated facs, but clean." 1 Mar-31 Aug. € 29.00      2009*

PESARO 2E3 (10km N Coastal) 43.95993, 12.80136 Camping Paradiso, Via Rive del Faro 2, 61010 Casteldimezzo (PS) [tel/fax 0721 208579; info@campingparadiso.it; www. campingparadiso.it] Turn of SS16 at Colombare, turn in vill (by bank). Steep & narr - best turn by church N of vill. Site sp. Med, terr, shd; wc (some cont); chem disp; shwrs inc; el pnts (6A) inc; lndtte; shop; tradsmn; rest adj; snacks; bar; playgrnd; sand & shgl beach adj; internet; 10% statics; dogs €2.50; phone; poss cr; adv bkg; some rlwy noise; red low ssn; ccard acc. "Gd views; beach down v steep cliff rd." ♦ 1 Mar-31 Dec. € 35.50                                    2010*

"I like to fill in the reports as I travel from site to site"

You'll find report forms at the back of this guide, or you can fill them in online at www.caravaclub.co.uk/europereport.

⊞ PESCASSEROLI 2F4 (500m S Rural) 41.79888, 13.79222 Camping Sant' Andrea, Via San Donato, 67032 Pescasseroli (AQ) [tel/fax 0863 912725 / 335 5956029 (mob); info@ campingsantandrea.com; www.campingsantandrea.com] Site sp on R bet Pescasseroli & Opi. If gate clsd ent thro side gate & turn key to open main gate. Sm, mkd pitch, pt shd; htd wc (some cont); chem disp; mv service pnt; shwrs inc; el pnts (10A) inc; shop, rest, snacks, bar in town; playgrnd; statics in sep area; dogs; phone; CKE/CCI. "Beautiful, open pitches in lovely area; clean facs but ltd high ssn." € 15.00        2013*

**PESCHICI** *2G4* (10km E Coastal) *41.94361, 16.04855* Villaggio Camping Internazionale Manacore, 71010 Manacore (FG) [0884 911020; fax 911049; manacore@ grupposaccia.it; www.grupposaccia.it] Coast rd thro town of Peschici to Vieste, site sp. If app fr W, do NOT enter town. Turn R twd Vieste; at rndabt in 2km turn L, sp Manacore. V lge, pt sl, pt shd; wc; chem disp; mv service pnt; shwrs inc; private bthrms avail; el pnts (3A) inc; gas; lndtte; shop; rest, snacks; bar; playgrnd; sand beach; boat hire; windsurfing; tennis; cycle hire; games area; entmnt; 25% statics; dogs; sep car park high ssn; poss cr; no adv bkg; quiet; ccard acc; CKE/ CCI. "Magnificent scenery; excel for boats & sw; excel facs." ♦ 1 May-11 Oct. € 49.00                    2010*

**PESCHICI** *2G4* (5km SE Rural) *41.93815, 16.04963* Camping La Gemma, Loc Baia di Manaccora, 71010 Peschici (FG) [0884 911010; fax 962777; info@la-gemma.it; www. la-gemma.it] Exit A14 at Poggio Imperiale onto SS89 E to Peschici. Turn off & foll sp to Manaccora & site. Med, shd; htd wc; mv service pnt; shwrs; el pnts; lndtte; shop; rest, snacks; bar; playgrnd; pool; paddling pool; sand beach 300m; watersports; fishing; tennis; entmnt; internet; TV rm; some statics; adv bkg; quiet. 1 Apr-1 Oct. € 26.50           2009*

**PESCHICI** *2G4* (1.5km S Coastal) *41.94237, 16.03054* Centro Turistico San Nicola, Punta San Nicola, 71010 Peschici (FG) [0884 964024; fax 964025; sannicola@sannicola.it; www. sannicola.it] Site clearly sp on S89 bet Peschici & Vieste. V lge, mkd pitch, sl, terr, pt shd; wc (some cont); chem disp; mv service pnt; shwrs inc; el pnts (5A) inc; gas; lndtte; shop; rest, snacks; sand beach; windsurfing; tennis; gym; entmnt & some statics; no dogs high ssn; adv bkg; noisy; ccard acc; red long stay/CKE/CCI. "Excel for families; lovely site in beautiful location; surface water on pitches after heavy rain." ♦ 1 Apr-15 Oct. € 37.00                    2009*

**PESCHIERA DEL GARDA** *1D2* (1km N Urban) *45.44780, 10.70195* Camping del Garda, Via Marzan 6, 37019 Castelnuovo-del-Garda (VR) [045 7550540; fax 6400711; info@camping-delgarda.com; www.campingdelgarda.it] Exit A4/E70 dir Peschiera onto SR249 dir Lazise. Turn L in 500m dir Lido Campanello, site in 1km on L on lakeside. V lge, shd; wc (mainly cont); chem disp; mv service pnt; shwrs inc; el pnts (4A) inc; gas; lndtte; shop; rest, snacks; bar; playgrnd; 3 pools; shgl beach; lake sw; tennis; games area; entmnt; 60% statics; no dogs; phone; adv bkg; quiet. "Busy, well-organised site; helpful staff, discount snr citizens." ♦ 1 Apr-30 Sep. € 51.00                    2011*

**PESCHIERA DEL GARDA** *1D2* (1km N Rural) *45.46722, 10.71638* Eurocamping Pacengo, Via del Porto 13, 37010 Pacengo (VR) [tel/fax 045 7590012; info@ eurocampingpacengo.it; www.eurocampingpacengo.it] On SS249 fr Peschiera foll sp to Gardaland, Pacengo in 1km. Turn L at traff lts in cent of vill, site on L. Lge, mkd pitch, sl, pt shd; wc (some cont); chem disp (wc); mv service pnt; shwrs €0.30; el pnts (4A) inc; lndtte; shop & 500m; rest, snacks; bar; playgrnd; pool adj; lake sw, boat-launching adj; entmnt; 25% statics; dogs €2.40; phone; cr; Eng spkn; adv bkg; quiet; CKE/CCI. "Well-equipped site on shore Lake Garda; helpful staff; some sm pitches; espec gd end of ssn; excel rest; conv Verona." ♦ 10 Apr-22 Sep. € 41.60           2014*

**PESCHIERA DEL GARDA** *1D2* (2.5km N Rural) *45.45480, 10.70200* Camping Gasparina, Loc Cavalcaselle, 37014 Castelnuovo-del-Garda (VR) [045 7550775; fax 7552815; info@gasparina.com; www.gasparina.com] On SS249 dir Lazise, turn L at site sp. Lge, mkd pitch, sl, pt shd; wc; chem disp; mv service pnt; shwrs inc; el pnts (3A) inc; gas; lndtte; shop; tradsmn; rest, snacks; bar; playgrnd; pool; lake adj; games area; entmnt; some statics; dogs; poss cr; adv bkg; poss noisy; ccard acc; "Popular, busy site; variable pitch sizes; lake views some pitches; long lead req." 1 Apr-30 Sep. € 35.00                    2013*

**PESCHIERA DEL GARDA** *1D2* (4km N Rural) *45.46472, 10.71416* Camping Le Palme, Via del Tronchetto 2, 37010 Pacengo (VR) [045 7590019; fax 7590554; info@ lepalmecamping.it; www.lepalmecamping.it] A4/E70 exit at Peschiera onto SS249, sp Lazise. Site sp bef Pacengo in approx 5km. Lge, mkd pitch, terr, pt shd; wc; chem disp; serviced pitches; baby facs; shwrs inc; el pnts (6A) inc; lndtte (inc dryer); shop; rest 300m; snacks; bar; playgrnd; htd pool; paddling pool; waterslide; lake sw & shgl beach adj; wifi; 40% statics; dogs €4.60; Eng spkn; adv bkg; ccard acc; red low ssn. "Well-maintained site; excel, clean facs; extra for lakeside pitches; helpful staff; sh walk to vill; 4 theme parks nr; excel." ♦ 1 Apr-25 Oct. € 31.00                    2011*

**PESCHIERA DEL GARDA** *1D2* (700m W Rural) *45.44555, 10.69472* Camping Butterfly, Lungo Lago Garibaldi 11, 37019 Peschiera (VR) [045 6401466; fax 7552184; info@ campingbutterfly.it; www.campingbutterfly.it] Fr A4/ E70 exit twd Peschiera for 2km. At x-rds with bdge on L, strt over & foll rv to last site after RH bend at bottom. Lge, shd; wc (some cont); shwrs; el pnts inc; gas; lndtte; shop; rest, snacks; bar; playgrnd; pool; paddling pool; lake sw; entmnt; 75% statics; dogs €5; poss cr; adv bkg; quiet except w/end; ccard acc. "Busy holiday site; conv town & lake steamers; sm pitches; clean san facs; adv bkg rec." ♦ 09 Mar-10 Nov. € 70.50 (4 persons)              2013*

**PESCHIERA DEL GARDA** *1D2* (1km W Urban) *45.44222, 10.67805* Camping Bella Italia, Via Bella Italia 2, 37019 Peschiera del Garda (VR) [045 6400688; fax 6401410; info@camping-bellaitalia.it; www.camping-bellaitalia. it] Fr Brescia or Verona on SP11 to Peschiera del Garda, site sp on lakeside. Fr Brescia or Verona on A4/E70 exit at Peschiera on to SP11 in dir of Brescia, site on R in about 2km. V lge, slight sl, shd; wc; chem disp; mv service pnt; baby facs; shwrs inc; el pnts (16A); gas; lndtte (inc dryer); shop; 2 rests; snacks; bar; BBQ; playgrnd; pool; paddling pool; waterslides; lake sw adj; windsurfing; tennis; games area; cycle hire; archery; wifi; entmnt; many static tents; no dogs; bus to Verona; poss cr; Eng spkn; adv bkg rec; poss noisy high ssn; red low ssn; CKE/CCI. "Busy, popular site, nr theme park, Aqua World, Verona; suits all ages; v clean; rests gd & gd price; gd recep for satellite & wifi." ♦ 16 Mar-26 Oct. € 81.50                    2013*

**PESCHIERA DEL GARDA** *1D2* (6km W) *45.45120, 10.66557* Camping Wien, Loc. Fornaci, 37019 Peschiera (VR) [045 7550379; fax 7553366; info@campingwien.it] On Verona-Brescia rd (not a'strada) W of Peschiera, turn R at San Benedetto, turn R 400m after traff lts, site has 2 ents 100m apart. Med, mkd pitch, hdstg, pt sl, shd; wc; chem disp; mv service pnt; shwrs inc; el pnts inc (3A); gas; lndtte; ice; shop; tradsmn; rest; snacks; bar; playgrnd; pool; shgl beach adj; games area; entmnt; boating; fishing; 50% statics; dogs; phone; bus adj; Eng spkn; adv bkg; poss cr; quiet; ccard not acc; red long stay; CKE/CCI. "Wonderful pool o'looking Lake Garda; walking/cycle path into town; vg site." ♦ 18 Apr-30 Sep. € 52.00                                    2014*

**PETTENASCO see Orta San Giulio** *1B1*

**PEVERAGNO see Cuneo** *1B2*

⊞ **PIAZZA ARMERINA (SICILY)** *3C3* (4km SE Rural) *37.20239, 14.23155* Camping Agriturismo Agricasale, C da Ciavarini, 94015 Piazza-Armerina (EN) [tel/fax 0935 686034; www.agricasale.it] In Piazza-Armerina town foll sp twd Mirabella but at rndabt with stone cross bear R (red fox sign) & foll red fox down nar rd to wooded site. Park with care. Sm, pt sl, pt shd; wc; chem disp; mv service pnt; shwrs inc; el pnts (4A) inc; lndtte; shop 4km; rest; bar; BBQ; playgrnd; pool; TV rm; dogs; poss cr; Eng spkn; adv bkg; quiet; CKE/CCI. "Excel site close Palazzo Romana mosaics; pony-trekking, archery & other activities high ssn; all inc rate of €50 avail per day inc excel banquet; site run down." ♦ € 15.00      2014*

⊞ **PIENZA** *1D3* (6km E Rural) Camping Il Casale, 64 53026 Pienza (SI) [tel/fax 0578 755109, 333 4250705 (mob); podereilcasale@libero.it] Fr Pienza dir Montepulciano on S146, turn R in 4km onto sm, gritted track sp Monticchiello (sm, brown sp easily missed). Site in 3km on L sp Podereilcasale. Fr Montepulciano dir Pienza rd to L sp Il Borghetto (Fago). Sm, pt shd; pt sl; wc; shwrs inc; el pnts (16A) inc; lndtte; tradsmn; rest; bar; playgrnd; lake adj; dogs; phone; poss cr; Eng spkn; adv bkg; quiet; ccard acc. "8 pitches only for c'vans/mvans; simple farm site; friendly family; price inc breakfast; panoramic views; rec phone to check availability; v friendly owners, site fees inc breakfast." ♦ 1 Apr-15 Nov. € 26.00      2013*

**PIEVE DI LEDRO** *1D1* (Rural) *45.88527, 10.73138* Camping Azzurro, Via Alzer, 38060 Pieve-di-Ledro (TN) [0464 508435 or 591276; fax 508150; info@campingazzurro.net; www.campingazzurro.net] Fr Riva-del-Garda foll sp Val di Ledro on S240. Ent vill on by-pass, at x-rds turn L, site on L in 200m on lakeside. Med, mkd pitch, some hdstg, shd; wc; chem disp; mv service pnt; shwrs inc; el pnts (2-6A) inc; lndtte; supmkt adj; rest 100m; snacks; playgrnd; pool; lake sw; fishing; watersports; internet nr; 50% statics; dogs €5; bus nr; adv bkg; quiet; red low ssn. "Attractive vill; cycle track around lake; friendly staff; well-run site." ♦ 1 May-30 Sep. € 30.00 (CChq acc)      2011*

**PIEVE DI LEDRO** *1D1* (3km E Rural) *45.87805, 10.76777* Camping Al Sole, Loc Besta, Via Maffei 127, 38060 Molina-di-Ledro (TN) [tel/fax 0464 508496; info@campingalsole.it; www.campingalsole.it] Exit A22 at Rovereto S onto SS240 twd Riva-del-Garda then Vall di Ledro & Molina, site sp on Lake Ledro. Lge, mkd pitch, pt shd; wc; shwrs inc; el pnts (3A) inc; lndtte (inc dryer); shop; rest, snacks; bar; playgrnd; pool; lake sw & beach adj; watersports; tennis adj; wifi; entmnt; TV rm; 10% statics; dogs; adv bkg; quiet. "Peaceful site; busy but clean & well-ordered; some lake view pitches; gd outdoor activities." ♦ 1 Apr-30 Sep. € 31.00                                    2010*

**PIEVE DI LEDRO** *1D1* (500m S Rural) *45.88361, 10.73157* Camping Al Lago, Via Alzer 7-9, 38060 Pieve-di-Ledro (TN) [tel/fax 0464 591250; info@camping-al-lago.it; www.camping-al-lago.it] Exit A22 W onto SS240 to Riva-del-Garda, then cont on SS240 to Pieve-di-Lago. Turn L into Via Alzer & foll sp to site (after Cmp Azzurro). Med, mkd pitch, some hdstg, pt shd; wc (some cont); chem disp; mv service pnt; shwrs; el pnts (3A) inc; lndtte (inc dryer); shop 500m; rest 250m; snacks; bar; BBQ; playgrnd; lake sw adj; fishing; tennis; games area; cycle & canoe hire; wifi; entmnt; TV; 10% statics; dogs; Eng spkn; adv bkg; quiet; ccard acc; CKE/CCI. "Vg site; gd walking area." ♦ ltd 2 Apr-10 Oct. € 30.00      2010*

⊞ **PIEVE TESINO** *1D1* (6km N Rural) *46.11361, 11.61944* Villaggio Camping Valmalene, Loc Valmalene, 38050 Pieve-Tesino (TN) [0461 594214; fax 592654; info@valmalene.com; www.valmalene.com] Fr Trento E for 50km on S47. Turn N at Strigno to Pieve-Tesino, site sp. Med, mkd pitch, pt shd; htd wc; mv service pnt; sauna; private bthrms avail; baby facs; shwrs; el pnts inc; lndtte; shop; supmkt 6km; tradsmn; rest, snacks; bar; playgrnd; htd pool; padding pool; tennis; cycle hire; games area; fitness rm; internet; some statics; dogs €4; site clsd Nov; adv bkg rec; quiet; ccard acc. "Gd base for summer & winter hols." ♦ € 27.00      2009*

**PINETO** *2F3* (9km S Coastal) *42.5675, 14.0925* Camping Europe Garden, Via Belvedere 11, 64028 Silvi-Marina (TE) [085 930137; fax 932846; info@europegarden.it; www.europegarden.it] Exit A14/E55 for Atri/Pineto or Pescara N onto coast rd SS16, bet Silvi-Marina & Pineto, turn W away fr coast at Europe Garden at km 5 & site sp. Lge, terr, shd; wc (some cont); mv service pnt; baby facs; shwrs inc; el pnts (5A) €2.50; gas; lndtte; shop; hypmkt 2km; rest, snacks; bar; playgrnd; pool; paddling pool; sand beach adj; tennis; archery; cycle hire; entmnt; 90% statics; no dogs; sep car park high ssn; Eng spkn; adv bkg; ccard acc; red CKE/CCI. "Well laid-out; steep slopes; tractor help for c'vans avail; sm pitches diff for l'ge o'fits; site muddy in wet weather; panoramic views; pleasant staff; conv Appenines, Atri walled town & Abruzzo National Park." 1 May-1 Sep. € 36.50      2009*

**PINZOLO** *1D1* (5km N Rural) *46.18535, 10.78027* Camping Fae', 38080 Sant' Antonio-di-Mavignola (TN) [tel/fax 0465 507178; campingfae@campiglio.it; www.campiglio.it/campingfae] Site well sp on SS239 bet Pinzolo & Madonna-di-Campiglio. Med, mkd pitch, terr, pt shd; htd wc (some cont); chem disp; mv service pnt; shwrs inc; el pnts (6A) inc; lndtte; shop 1km; tradsmn; bar; BBQ; playgrnd; games rm; TV; 40% statics; dogs; bus adj; poss cr; adv bkg; quiet; ccard acc; red low ssn. "Well-run, family owned site; clean san facs; gd walking." ♦ 1 Jun-30 Sep & 1 Dec-30 Apr. € 31.50      2009*

⊞ **PISA** 1C3 (500m N Urban) **Camper Parking, Via Pietrasantina, 56100 Pisa** On Via Aurelia SS1 fork R app Pisa, then turn E approx 1km N of Arno Rv, sp camping. After 1km turn L into Via Pietrasantina. Site on R behind lge Tamoil petrol stn, sp coach parking. Max height under rlwy bdge 3.30m. C'vans acc. Lge, hdstg, unshd; own san ess; mv service pnt; no el pnts; shop; rest, snacks, bar 100m; dogs; bus adj; quiet. "Excel NH; parking within walking dist of leaning tower; water & waste inc; plenty of space; Toilets open at café opp during day." ♦ € 12.00                                                2012*

## "We must tell The Club about that great site we found"

Get your site reports in by mid-August and we'll do our best to get your updates into the next edition.

**PISA** 1C3 (1km N Urban) 43.72416, 10.3830 **Camp Torre Pendente, Viale delle Cascine 86, 56122 Pisa** [050 561704; fax 561734; pisa@campingtorrependente.com; www. campingtorrependente.com] Exit A12/E80 Pisa Nord onto Via Aurelia (SS1). After 8km & after x-ing rlwy bdge, turn L after passing Pisa sp at traff lts. Site on L, sp. Lge, mkd pitch, pt shd; wc; mv service pnt; chem disp; baby facs; fam bthrm; shwrs inc; el pnts (5A) inc (poss rev pol); gas; lndtte (inc dryer); shop; supmkt 400m; rest; pizzeria; snacks; bar; BBQ; playgrnd; pool; sand beach 10km; cycle hire; wifi; TV rm; dogs €1.60; phone; poss cr; Eng spkn; no adv bkg; ccard acc over €100; red long stay; CKE/CCI; "Gd base Pisa; leaning tower 15 mins walk; immac, modern, well-maintained san facs; private san facs avail; pitches typically 45sqm; poss tight lge o'fits due narr site rds & corners; many pitches shd by netting; site rds muddy after rain; friendly staff; excel, well-run site; 300m fr Pisa San Rossore rlwy stn, trains to Lucca etc." ♦ 25 Mar-15 Oct. € 51.00                                                2013*

**PISA** 1C3 (7km S Rural) 43.63083, 10.36277 **Agricampeggio Lago Le Tamerici, Via della Sofina 6, 56121 Coltano (PI)** [050 989007; info@lagoletamerici.it; www.lagoletamerici. it] S fr Pisa on SS1 Via Aurelia, turn L sp Coltano, then Lago Le Tamerici. Or fr S on SS206 foll sp Coltano etc. Sm, hdg/mkd pitch, pt shd; wc; chem disp; mv service pnt; el pnts (10A) inc; lndtte (inc dryer); shop; tradsmn; rest, snacks; bar; BBQ; playgrnd; pool; lake fishing; canoe & cycle hire; games area; adv bkg; quiet."V friendly." ♦ 12 Mar-16 Oct. € 28.00 2011*

**PISOGNE** 1C1 (200m N Rural) 45.80611, 10.1050 **Camping Eden, Loc Goia, Via Piangrande 3/A, 25055 Pisogne (BS)** [tel/fax 0364 880500; info@campeggioeden.com; www. campeggioeden.com] Exit P510 at Pisogne Sud, over rlwy line, site sp. Med, mkd pitch, shd; wc; shwrs inc; el pnts (2A) €1.30; lndtte; shop 200m; rest, snacks 100m; playgrnd; sand beach; watersports; tennis; some statics (sep area); dogs €1.50; adv bkg; quiet. "Lovely, wooded site; excel facs." ♦ 1 May-15 Sep. € 24.50                                                2010*

**PISTOIA** 1D3 (10km S Rural) 43.84174, 10.91049 **Camping Barco Reale, Via Nardini 11, 51030 San Baronto-Lamporecchio (PT)** [0573 88332; fax 856003; info@ barcoreale.com; www.barcoreale.com] Leave A11 at Pistoia junc onto P9 & foll sp to Vinci, Empoli & Lamporecchio to San Baronto. In vill turn into rd by Monti Hotel & Rest, site sp. Last 3km steep climb. Lge, mkd pitch, pt sl, terr, shd; wc; chem disp; mv service pnt; 30% serviced pitch; baby facs; shwrs inc; el pnts (3-6A) inc (poss rev pol); gas; lndtte; shop; tradsmn; rest, snacks; bar; playgrnd; pool; games area; cycle hire; internet; wifi; entmnt; dogs; phone; Eng spkn; adv bkg ess; quiet; red long stay/low ssn; ccard acc; red long stay; CKE/CCI. "Excel site in Tuscan hills; helpful staff; gd touring base; excel mother & baby facs; vg rest; poss diff access some pitches but towing help provided on request; unsuitable lge o'fits; well-organised walking & bus trips; excel pool." ♦ 1 Apr-30 Sep. € 57.40                                                2014*

See advert on bookmark

**PIZZO** 3B4 (6km N Coastal) 38.72213, 16.15104 **Camping Villaggio Pinetamare, 88812 Pizzo (VV)** [0963 264067; fax 534871; info@villaggiopinetamare.it] Exit A3/E45 dir Pizzo. Fr Pizzo go N on S18 twd Santa Eufemia-Lamezia, km 392; site sp. Lge, mkd pitch, hdstg, shd; wc (some cont); chem disp; shwrs inc; el pnts (6A) €3.50; gas; lndry rm; shop; rest, snacks; bar; playgrnd; 3 pools; private sand/shgl beach adj; windsurfing; tennis; entmnt & no dogs; Eng spkn; adv bkg; ccard acc; CKE/CCI. "Vg family site under pine trees." 15 Jun-15 Sep. € 37.00                                                2009*

## "I need an on-site restaurant"

We do our best to make sure site information is correct, but it is always best to check any must-have facilities are still available or will be open during your visit.

**POGGIBONSI** 1D3 (12km N Rural) 43.58198, 11.13801 **Camping Panorama Del Chianti, Via Marcialla 349, 50020 Marcialla-Certaldo (FI)** [tel/fax 0571 669334; info@ campingchianti.it; www.campingchianti.it] Fr Florence-Siena a'strada exit sp Tavarnelle. On reaching Tavernelle turn R sp Tutti Direzione/Certaldo & foll by-pass to far end of town. Turn R sp to Marcialla, in Marcialla turn R to Fiano, site in 1km. NB Some steep hairpins app site fr E. Med, mkd pitch, hdstg, terr, pt shd; wc (some cont); chem disp; mv service pnt; shwrs inc; el pnts (3A) inc; shop, rest, snacks, bar 800m; tradsmn; sm pool; cycle hire; dogs €2; phone; adv bkg; Eng spkn; ccard not acc; CKE/CCI. "Gd tourist info (in Eng); sports facs in area; cultural sites; helpful staff; friendly owner; san facs clean - hot water to shwrs only; 4 excel rests nr; panoramic views; midway bet Siena & Florence; popular site - arr early to get pitch; facs need updating." 25 Mar-4 Nov. € 49.00 (CChq acc)                                                2014*

⊞ POMPEI *3A3* (1km S Urban) *40.74638, 14.48388* Camping Spartacus, Loc Pompei Scavi, Via Plinio 127, 80045 Pompei (NA) [tel/fax 081 8624078; staff@campingspartacus.it; www.campingspartacus.it] Fr N on A3 exit Pompei Ovest. At T-junc turn L & site on R just after passing under rlwy bdge. Fr S exit Pompei Est & foll sp Pompei Scavi (ruins). SatNav may lead to low bdge. Sm, mkd pitch, shd; wc; chem disp; mv service pnt; shwrs inc; el pnts (5A) €2.30.(poss rev pol); gas; lndtte; shop; supmkt 400m; rest, snacks, bar in high ssn; internet; TV rm; poss v cr; Eng spkn; adv bkg; some rd/rlwy noise; ccard acc; red low ssn/CKE/CCI; "Nice, family-run, welcoming site, 50m fr historical ruins; conv train to Naples, boats to Capri; stray dogs poss roam site & ruins; v popular with students high ssn; best of 3 town sites; gd site for exploring area; friendly owners; clean san facs." ♦ € 31.00                                      2014*

PORLEZZA *1C1* (4km E Rural) *46.04074, 9.16827* Camping Ranocchio, Via Al Lago 7,22010 Loc Piano di Porlezza, Carlazzo (CO) [tel/fax 0344 70385; campingranocchio@ngi.it] On main rd bet Menaggio & Porlezza. Ent in vill of Piano on S side. Sp. Steep app in Lugano with hairpin bends; 15% gradient. V narr rd fr Lugano - clsd to c'vans at peak times. Lge, terr, shd, pt sl; wc; chem disp; mv service pnt; baby facs; shwrs €0.50; el pnts inc; gas; lndtte (inc dryer); shop adj; rest 50m; snacks; bar; playgrnd; pool; paddling pool; lake sw & fishing; horseriding 2km; wifi; TV rm; dogs €2; Eng spkn; quiet; CKE/CCI. "Friendly recep; gd for exploring Como & Lugano; steamer trips on both lakes; lovely site; v attractive site; helpful recep; excel corner shop." ♦ 1 Apr-30 Sep. € 32.00          2013*

PORTESE see San Felice Del Benaco *1D2*

PORTO CESAREO *3A4* (6.5km NE Coastal) *40.29077, 17.82711* Camping Porto Cesareo, Via Torre Lapillo-Torre Columena, Km 0.7, 73010 Porto-Cesareo (LE) [tel/fax 0833 565312; info@portocesareocamping.it; www.portocesareocamping.it] S fr Manduria or N fr Nardo on SP359, foll sp Porto Cesareo & site. Med, hdg/mkd pitch, shd; wc; chem disp; mv service pnts; shwrs inc; el pnts (4A) inc; lndtte; shop & 1km; tradsmn; rest, snacks; bar; BBQ; playgrnd; pool; sand beach 400m; cycle hire; games area; wifi; entmnt; TV rm; 15% statics; dogs free; Eng spkn; adv bkg; quiet; ccard acc. "Scenic, well-maintained site; vg, modern san facs; lovely pool; bus transfer to beach - gd snorkelling area; friendly, helpful staff." ♦ 1 Jun-12 Sep. € 32.00          2010*

PORTO RECANATI *2F3* (4km N Coastal) *43.47123, 13.64150* Camping Bellamare, Lungomare Scarfiotti 13, 62017 Porto-Recanati (MC) [071 976628; fax 977586; info@bellamare.it; www.bellamare.it] Exit A14/E55 Loreto/Porto-Recanati; foll sp Numana & Sirolo; camp on R in 4km on coast rd. Lge, unshd; wc; chem disp; shwrs; el pnts (6A) €3; gas; lndtte; shop; rest, snacks; bar; playgrnd; pool; paddling pool; sand & shgl beach (shelves steeply); cycle hire; games area; games rm; entmnt; some statics; no dogs; phone; Eng spkn; ccard acc; red low ssn; CKE/CCI. "V well-run site; NH tarrif of €19 (inc elec) for a pitch at the edge of the site but ok; beach access." ♦ 23 Apr-30 Sep. € 42.50          2011*

⊞ PORTO RECANATI *2F3* (7.7km NW Urban) *43.44155, 13.61446* Area Attrezzata Camper Loreto, Via Maccari, 60025 Loreto [07 19 77 748; info@prolocoloreto.com] Fr A14 S of Ancona, exit at Loreto. Fr town ctr foll sp to campsite. Med, mkd pitch, hdstg, unshd; wc; mv service pnt; shwrs inc; el pnts inc; dogs; quiet. "M'van NH; conv for Basilica, beach & Ancona ferries; clean & well run; occasional c'vans allowed if not busy; vg site." € 12.00          2014*

PORTO SAN GIORGIO *2F3* (1km S Coastal) *43.15905, 13.80823* Camping Spinnaker, Via Campofiloni, Santa Maria-a-Mare 27, 63023 Fermo (AP) [0734 53412; fax 53737; info@vacanzespinnaker.it; www.vacanzespinnaker.it] Exit A14 at junc for Porto-San Giorgio onto S16 S, foll site sp. V lge, mkd pitch, pt shd; wc; chem disp; mv service pnt; baby facs; shwrs inc; el pnts €3; lndtte; shop; rest, snacks; bar; playgrnd; pool; waterslide; sand beach adj; watersports; tennis; games area; cycle hire; entmnt; cash machine; some statics; dogs €3 (sm only); poss cr; adv bkg. 16 May-13 Sep. € 44.00          2009*

PORTO SAN PAOLO (SARDINIA) *3A2* (2km S Coastal) *40.85870, 9.64296* Camping Tavolara, Loc Porto Taverna, 07020 Loiri-Porta San Paolo (SS) [0789 40166; fax 480778; info@camping-tavolara.it; www.camping-tavolara.it] On SS125, sp. Med, hdg/mkd pitch, shd; wc (mainly cont); mv service pnt; shwrs inc; el pnts (3-6A) €3.50; lndtte; shop & 2km; rest, snacks; bar; playgrnd; sand beach 500m; tennis; cycle hire; entmnt; 50% statics; dogs €3; phone; site clsd Dec & early Jan; Eng spkn; adv bkg; ccard acc; red CKE/CCI. "Friendly staff; conv ferries & boat trips." 20 Apr-15 Oct. € 59.50  2014*

PORTO SANTA MARGHERITA see Caorle *2E2*

PORTO TORRES (SARDINIA) *3A1* (7km E Coastal) *40.81607, 8.48541* Camping Golfo dell'Asinara-Cristina, Loc Platamona, 07037 Sorso (SS) [079 310230; fax 310589; info@campingasinara.it; www.campingasinara.it] Foll coast rd SP81 E fr Porto-Torres to site. Sp. Lge, pt shd; wc; mv service pnt; shwrs; el pnts (4A) €4; gas; lndtte; shop; rest, snacks; bar; playgrnd; pool; sand beach adj; tennis; games area; cycle hire; 40% statics; no dogs; sep car park; poss cr; quiet; ccard acc; red long stay/CKE/CCI. "Gd position." ♦ 1 May-30 Sep. € 34.00          2010*

**"That's changed – Should I let The Club know?"**

If you find something on site that's different from the site entry, fill in a report and let us know. See www.caravanclub.co.uk/europereport.

**ITALY**

**PORTOFERRAIO** *1C3* (9km E Rural) *42.80072, 10.36452* Rosselba Le Palme, Loc. Ottone 3, 57037 Elba Portoferraio [0565 933 101; fax 933 041; info@rosselbalepalme.it; www.rosselbalepalme.it] Fr ferry terminal foll signs 'tutti direzioni'. At 3rd rndabt head twds Porto Azzurro. Take L fork to Bagnaia. Site sp. Sm, hdg pitch, terr, pt shd; wc; chem disp; mv service pnt; shwrs inc; el pnts (6A); lndtte rm; shop; rest; snacks; bar; playgrnd; pool; sand beach 0.5km; entmnt; wifi; 80% statics; bus adj; twin axles; Eng spkn; adv bkg; quiet; CCI. "Ferry service fr Piombino every 1/2 hr; statics enhance site facs." 20 Apr-6 Oct. € 72.00                    2014*

⊞ **POZZA DI FASSA** *1D1* (1km SE Rural) *46.42015, 11.70730* Caravan Garden Vidor, Loc Vidor 5, 38036 Pozza-di-Fassa (TN) [0462 763247; fax 764780; info@campingvidor.it; www.campingvidor.it] Exit A22 at Ora/Auer onto SS48 to Pozza-di-Fassa cent, turn R (E) over bdge dir Val di Nicolo, site in 2km on L on rvside. Other rds in area clsd to c'vans. Med, mkd pitch, hdstg, terr, pt shd; htd wc (some cont); chem disp; mv service pnt; baby facs; fam bthrm; sauna; shwrs inc; el pnts (2-16A) metered; gas (fixed supply to some pitches); lndtte (inc dryer); shop; tradsmn; rest adj & 2km; snacks; bar; BBQ; playgrnd; htd pool; paddling pool; sh tennis; cable car 1km; wifi; TV rm; 30% statics; dogs €4.50; phone; site clsd Nov; poss cr; Eng spkn; adv bkg; quiet; ccard acc; CKE/CCI. "Beautiful location; friendly, family-run site; excel views & facs; above hubbub of main valley; gd walking." ♦ € 31.00          2010*

> ## "Satellite navigation makes touring much easier"
>
> Remember most sat navs don't know if you're towing or in a larger vehicle – always use yours alongside maps and site directions.

**POZZA DI FASSA** *1D1* (500m SW Rural) *46.42638, 11.68527* Camping Rosengarten, Via Avisio 15, 38036 Pozza-di-Fassa (TN) [0462 763305; fax 763501; info@ catinacciorosengarten.com; www.catinacciorosengarten. com] Fr S SS48 site sp just after San Giovanni. Lge, hdstg, pt shd; wc; chem disp; mv service pnt; shwrs inc; el pnts (2A) inc (extra for higher amperage); lndtte; shop 500m; rest, snacks adj; bar; pool 300m; ski lift 1km; ski bus; wifi; 30% statics; dogs €4; site clsd Oct; poss cr; Eng spkn; adv bkg ess; quiet; 10% red 14+ days; ccard acc; CKE/CCI. "Superb scenery; helpful staff; luxury san facs; free taxi (2010) to Vigo di Fassa cable car; excel site; v convly sited for access to vill & public transport." 1 Jan-30 Apr, 1 Jun-15 Oct, 1 Dec-31 Dec. € 46.70                    2014*

**PRAIA A MARE** *3A4* (500m S Coastal) *39.88198, 15.78529* International Camping Village, Lungomare F. Sirimarco, 87028 Praia-a-Mare (CS) [tel/fax 0985 72211; reception@ campinginternational.it; www.campinginternational.it] On beach rd just bef rocky island. Lge, hdg/mkd pitch, hdstg, shd; wc (some cont); chem disp; mv service pnt; shwrs inc; el pnts (5A) inc; lndtte; shop, rest, bar high ssn; BBQ; playgrnd; paddling pool; private shgl beach adj; tennis; games area; entmnt; some statics; dogs; phone; rlwy noise; ccard acc; red low ssn. "Welcoming, clean site; hot water to shwrs only." ♦ 23 Apr-30 Sep. € 38.50                    2009*

**PRAIA A MARE** *3A4* (2km S Coastal) *39.87654, 15.78867* Camping Villaggio Turistico La Mantinera, Contrada de Mantinera, 87028 Praia-a-Mare (CS) [0985 779023; fax 779009; lamantinera@tiscali.it; www.lamantinera.it] On old coast rd, exit SS18 at sp to Praia. Fr N thro town on L; fr S immed at bottom of hill on R. Lge, hdg/mkd pitch, shd, all serviced pitches; wc; shwrs inc; el pnts (7A) inc; rest (Jul/Aug); bar; snacks; shop; lndry rm; playgrnd; shgl beach 750m; pool; boat hire; windsurfing; tennis; cycle hire; 30% statics; no dogs high ssn; poss cr; adv bkg; noisy disco & traff; ccard acc; 10% red CKE/CCI. "Indiv tree-lined bays with own water & el pnts; free transport to beach; tours to Naples, Pompei & organised activities." ♦ 30 Apr-30 Sep. € 42.00 (3 persons)        2009*

**PRATO ALLO STELVIO** *1D1* (500m E Rural) *46.61777, 10.59555* Camping Sägemühle, Dornweg 12, 39026 Prato-allo-Stélvio (BZ) [0473 616078; fax 617120; info@ campingsaegumuehle.com; www.campingsaegemuehle. com] Fr rd S40 turn E at Spondigna onto rd S38 dir Stélvio, site sp in vill. Med, hdg/mkd pitch, hdstg, pt sl, pt shd; htd wc; chem disp; mv service pnt; baby facs; fam bthrm; sauna; shwrs inc; el pnts (16A) inc; lndtte (inc dryer); shop 200m; rest; bar; playgrnd; 2 pools (1 htd, covrd); paddling pool; games area; ski lift 10km; skibus; wifi; TV; phone; dogs €4; adv bkg; quiet; 10% red low stay; ccard acc; CKE/CCI. "Excel, well-run site; gd, clean facs; helpful staff; gd walking area in National Park; conv for the reschen pass Austria Italy; all pitches fully serviced." 1 Jan-9 Nov, 16 Dec-31 Dec. € 55.00                2014*

**PRATO ALLO STELVIO** *1D1* (500m NW Rural) *46.62472, 10.59388* Camping Kiefernhain, Via Pineta 37, 39026 Prato-allo-Stélvio (BZ) [0473 616422; fax 617277; kiefernhain@rolmail.net; www.camping-kiefernhain.it] Fr rd S40 turn SW at Spondigna onto rd S38 dir Stélvio, site sp in vill. Lge, mkd pitch, pt shd; wc; chem disp; mv service pnt; baby facs; private bthrms avail; shwrs inc; el pnts (6A) €2.50; lndtte; shop; tradsmn; rest 300m; snacks; bar; BBQ; playgrnd; htd pool; waterslide; sports cent adj; dogs €4; phone; dog shwr; wifi; Eng spkn; adv bkg rec high ssn; quiet; red long stay. "V modern, clean san facs; superb views; facs stretched hg ssn; vg value." ♦ 8 Apr-5 Oct. € 52.50                2014*

**PRECI** *2E3* (2km NW Rural) *42.88808, 13.01483* Camping Il Collaccio, 06047 Castelvecchio-di-Preci (PG) [0743 939005; fax 939094; info@ilcollaccio.com; www.ilcollaccio.com] S fr Assisi on S75 & S3, turn off E sp Norcia, Cascia. Then foll sp for Visso on S209. In approx 30km turn R for Preci, then L, site sp. Rte is hilly. Med, mkd pitch, terr, pt shd; htd wc (some cont); chem disp; mv service pnt; baby facs; shwrs inc; el pnts (6A) inc (long lead poss req); lndtte; shop & 2km; tradsmn; rest, snacks; bar; playgrnd; 2 pools; tennis; games area; horseriding; paragliding; cycle hire; TV rm; 20% statics; dogs; phone; Eng spkn; adv bkg; quiet; ccard acc; red CKE/CCI. "Beautiful views; well-maintained, clean site; pleasant rest; maganificent pool area; sm pitches; gd walking in Monti Sibillini National Park; conv Assisi & historic hill towns." ♦ 1 Apr-30 Sep. € 33.00                    2010*

ITALY

**PULA** *3B1* (4km Coastal) *38.95778, 8.96930* **Camping Cala d'Ostia, Localita Cala d'Ostia, 09010 Pula [39 070 921470; fax 070 921471; info@campingcaladostia.com; www. campingcaladostia.com]** Fr Cagliari, take SS195 past Pula. Foll the rd along the seafront about 1km, sp to site. Lge, pt shd; wc; mv service pnt; fam bthrm; shwrs; el pnts (13A); tradsmn; bar; BBQ; beach; games rm; wifi; dogs; bus adj; twin axles; poss cr; Eng spkn; CCI. "Fair site; busy in high ssn; beautiful coastline; lovely area." ♦ ltd Apr-Sep. € 35.00 2014*

## "There aren't many sites open at this time of year"

If you're travelling outside peak season remember to call ahead to check site opening dates – even if the entry says 'open all year'.

⊞ **PULA (SARDINIA)** *3B1* (4km S Coastal) *38.96779, 8.97799* **Camping Flumendosa, Santa Margherita, Km 33.800, 09010 Pula (CA) [070 9208364; fax 9249282; info@campingflumendosa.it; www.campingflumendosa. it]** Fr Cagliari take SS195 past Pula, sp. Turn L, foll track for 500m to site ent. Med, hdstg, pt shd; wc; chem disp; mv service pnt; shwrs €0.50; el pnts (3A) €3; gas; lndtte; shop; rest 1km; snacks; bar; playgrnd; sand beach; boat & cycle hire; windsurfing; waterskiing; canoeing; golf 4km; 20% statics; dogs €2.50; sep car park; poss cr; Eng spkn; adv bkg; quiet; ccard acc; red low ssn. "Beautiful coastline; excel for children; sand flies abound." ♦ € 27.00 2011*

⊞ **PUNTA BRACCETTO** *3C3* (4km SW Coastal) *36.81661, 14.46895* **Camping Baia Dei Coralli, Punta Braccetto, 97017 Santa Croce Camerina [0932 91 81 92; fax 91 82 82; info@baiadeicoralli.it; www.baiadeicoralli.it]** Fr Agrigento take SS115 twds Sircusa to Gela. Turn L onto SP14, cont onto SP13. At rndabt take 3rd exit onto SP20, R onto SP85, L twd Strada Regionale 25. R onto Strada Regionale 24. Campsite on L. Lge, hdg pitch, hdstg, unshd; wc; chem disp; mv service pnt; shwrs inc; el pnts (6A); lndtte; tradsmn; rest; snacks; bar; BBQ; playgrnd; pool; sand beach; entmnt; wifi; tv rm; dogs; bus; twin axles; Eng spkn; adv bkg; quiet; ccard acc; red low ssn; CCI. "Excel site; v busy in summer." ♦ € 30.00 2014*

⊞ **PUNTA BRACCETTO (SICILY)** *3C3* (Coastal/Urban) *36.81722, 14.46583* **Camping Luminoso, Viale dei Canalotti, 97017 Punta Braccetto - Santa Croce Camerina (RG) [0932 918401; fax 918455; info@campingluminoso. com; www.campingluminoso.com]** W fr Marina di Ragusa on SP80/SC25 coast rd. Site sp. Med, mkd pitch, hdstg, shd; wc; chem disp; mv service pnt; private bathrms avail; shwrs; el pnts (6A) €5; lndtte; shop & 400m; tradsmn; rest; snacks; bar; direct access to private sand beach adj; cycle hire; wifi; child entmnt; TV; dogs free; adv bkg rec high ssn; ccard acc; red low ssn/CKE/CCI. "Well-run site in gd location; easy access to pitches - suitable lge o'fits/m'vans; excel; modern, immac facs; spacious level hdstg pitches; reliable wifi; helpful English manager; direct access to sandy beach; mobile shops call daily; ideal long stay in winter." ♦ ltd € 61.00 2014*

⊞ **PUNTA BRACCETTO (SICILY)** *3C3* (Coastal/Urban) *36.81713, 14.46736* **Camping Scarabeo, Via dei Canaletti 120, Punta-Braccetto, 97017 Santa Croce Camerina (RG) [0932 918096; fax 918391; info@scarabeocamping. it; www.scarabeocamping.it]** W fr Marina di Ragusa on SP80/SC25 coast rd. Site sp. Sm, mkd pitch, hdstg, pt sl, pt shd; wc; chem disp; mv service pnt; private bthrm €4; shwrs €0.60; el pnts (3-6A) €3.50-4.50; lndtte (inc dryer); shop & 4km; tradsmn; rest, snacks 600m, bar nr; BBQ; direct access to sand beach adj; wifi; child entmnt; 5% statics; dogs €2.50; phone; poss cr; Eng spkn; adv bkg; quiet; red long stay; CKE/CCI. "Beautiful situation; well-maintained, friendly, family-run site; gd, clean, modern facs; vg security; friendly, helpful staff; excel." ♦ € 37.50 2011*

**PUNTA MARINA TERME see Ravenna** *2E2*

⊞ **PUNTA SABBIONI** *2E2* (1km Rural) *44.44278, 12.42260* **Al Batèo, via Lungomare Dante Alighieri 19/A, 30013 Cavallino Treporti Venice [040 5301 455 or 041 5301 564; info@albateo.it; www.albateo.it]** Take rd Jesolo to Punta Sabbioni and go to end of the peninsula. Turn L at boat piers and foll rd along side beach. Site 300 on L. Sm, hdg pitch, shd; htd wc; chem disp; mv service pnt; shwrs inc; lndtte; shop; tradsmn; dogs; bus; Eng spkn; adv bkg; quiet. "M'vans only; gd value; Vapporeti to Venice 300m." € 25.00 2014*

## "That's changed – Should I let The Club know?"

If you find something on site that's different from the site entry, fill in a report and let us know. See www.caravanclub.co.uk/europereport.

**PUNTA SABBIONI** *2E2* (2km N Coastal) *45.43773, 12.43881* **Camping Marina di Venezia, Via Montello 6, 30010 Punta-Sabbioni (VE) [041 5300955; fax 966036; camping@marinadivenezia.it; www.marinadivenezia.it]** Exit A4 dir Marco Polo Airport, foll dir Jesolo. At Jesolo where rd splits, bear R dir Cavallino/Punta-Sabbioni. Site well sp. V lge, hdg/mkd pitch, pt shd; wc; chem disp; shwrs inc; el pnts (6A) inc; gas; lndtte; shops & supmkt; rest, snacks; bar; playgrnd; 2 pools; sand beach adj; boat hire; windsurfing; tennis; cycle hire; solarium; games area; 5% statics; dogs €3.50; phone; bus fr site to waterbus to Venice; adv bkg rec; quiet; ccard acc; red low ssn/snr citizen. "Lge pitches; high quality site, wonderfully equipped and well run; min stay 2 nts (7 nts Jul/Aug); excel, clean facs; some pitches avail v lge o'fits; superb pool complex; pleasant, helpful staff; within easy reach of Venice; highly rec." ♦ 16 Apr-30 Sep. € 44.00 2011*

ITALY

**PUNTA SABBIONI** *2E2* (2km NE Coastal) *45.44560, 12.46100* Campéole Camping Ca'Savio, Via di Ca'Savio 77 - 30013 Cavallino Treporti Ca'Savio (VE) [041 966017 / 041 966 570 (mob); fax 5300707; info@casavio.it; www.casavio.it or www.campeole.com] Fr Lido di Jesolo head twd Punta-Sabbioni; at x-rds/rndabt in cent of Ca'Savio turn L twd beach (La Spiaggia) for 800m; turn L into site just bef beach. Or at L turn at rndabt - rd poss clsd at night - cont to Punta-Sabbioni, turn L at sp to beach; L at T-junc, then R at x-rds. V lge, hdg/mkd pitch, shd; wc (some cont); chem disp; mv service pnt; baby facs; shwrs; el pnts (5A) inc (check pol); gas; lndtte (inc dryer); supmkt; rest; pizzeria; snacks; bar; playgrnd; pool; paddling pool; direct access to adj sandy beach; water sports; canoeing/kayaking; games area; archery; cycle hire; wifi; entmnt; games rm; TV; 50% statics; no dogs; no c'vans/m'vans over 7m high ssn; phone; bus to Venice ferry; ccard acc; red low ssn; CKE/CCI. "Well laid-out, well-run, busy site - noisy high ssn; helpful staff; conv Venice by ferry fr Punta Sabbioni; excel, clean san facs; facs ltd low ssn; long, narr pitches; access poss diff lge o'fits; gd supmkt; min 3 nights stay high ssn; barriers clsd 1300-1500." ♦ 26 Apr-27 Sep. € 38.50 (CChq acc) SBS - Y02            2013*

**PUNTA SABBIONI** *2E2* (700m S Coastal) *45.44035, 12.4211* Camping Miramare, Lungomare Dante Alighieri 29, 30010 Punta-Sabbioni (VE) [041 966150; fax 5301150; info@camping-miramare.it; www.camping-miramare.it] Take rd Jesolo to Punta-Sabbioni, pass all camps & go to end of peninsula. Turn L at boat piers & foll rd alongside beach; site 500m on L. Med, hdg/mkd pitch, pt shd; htd wc; chem disp; mv service pnt; shwrs inc; el pnts (6A) inc (rev pol); gas; lndtte; shop; rest & pizzeria adj; playgrnd; internet; statics; dogs €4 (only sm dogs allowed); phone; bus to beach 2km & ferry; min 3 nights stay high ssn; Eng spkn; poss cr; ccard acc (min €100); red low ssn/snr citizens. "Excel, well-organised, family-owned site - 10 mins walk for Venice (tickets fr recep) - can leave bikes at terminal; gd security; helpful, friendly staff; new pt of site v pleasant wooded area; clean facs; poss mosquito problem; superior to many other sites in area; min stay 2 nights Jul/Aug; don't miss camping supmkt on way in - an Aladdin's cave; avoid dep on Sat due traffic; Magic of Italy site; highly rec; reasonable mobile home rentals; excel staff." ♦ 23 Mar-3 Nov

23 Mar-3 Nov. € 47.50            2013*

**PUNTA SABBIONI** *2E2* (700m S Coastal) *45.44141, 12.42127* Parking Dante Alighieri, Lungomare Dante Alighieri 26, 30010 Punta-Sabbioni (VE)  Take rd Jesolo to Punta-Sabbioni, pass all camps & go to end of peninsula. Turn L at boat piers & foll rd alongside beach; site on L just bef Camping Miramare. Sm, pt shd; wc; chem disp; mv service pnt; shwrs inc; el pnts (8A) inc; shop, rest, snacks, bar 500m; bus 500m; dogs; poss cr; Eng spkn; quiet. "M'vans only; friendly, helpful owner; 10 min walk for boats to Venice; vg." € 23.00            2012*

**QUART see Aosta** *1B1*

**RAPALLO** *1C2* (2km N Urban) *44.35805, 9.2100* Camping Miraflores, Via Savagna 10, 16035 Rapallo (GE) [0185 263000; fax 260938; info@campingmiraflores.it; www.campingmiraflores.it] Exit A12/E80 at Rapallo. In 100m fr toll gate sharp L across main rd, sharp L again, site sp 200m on R. Site almost immed beside toll gate but not easily seen. Sp fr town. Med, hdg/mkd pitch, hdstg, terr, pt shd; wc (some cont); chem disp; mv service pnt; shwrs €0.60; el pnts (3A) €1.80; gas; lndry rm; shop 300m; rest 200m; snacks; bar; playgrnd; pool; 10% statics; dogs free; bus 200m to stn & town cent; sep car park; poss cr; rd noise; ccard acc; red low ssn/CKE/CCI. "Excel htd pool adj; gd, modern san facs; grass pitches for tents, earth only for m'vans & c'vans; v noisy & dusty as under m'way; v friendly staff; ferries to Portofino fr town; conv NH; rec phone ahead if lge o'fit." ♦ 1 Mar-31 Dec. € 26.50            2011*

**RAPALLO** *1C2* (2.5km W Urban) *44.35691, 9.1992* Camping Rapallo, Via San Lazzaro 4, 16035 Rapallo (GE) [tel/fax 0185 262018; campingrapallo@libero.it; www.campingrapallo.it] Exit A12/E80 dir Rapallo, turn immed R on leaving tolls. Site sp in 500m on L at bend (care), over bdge then R. Narr app rd. Site sp. Med, hdg/mkd pitch, pt shd; wc (some cont); chem disp; mv service pnt; shwrs inc; el pnts (3A) €2.20; gas; lndtte; supmkt 500m; rest 200m; bar; pool; shgl beach 2.5km; cycle hire; 10% statics; dogs; bus (tickets fr recep); poss cr; Eng spkn; adv bkg; some daytime rd noise; ccard acc; CKE/CCI. "Clean, family-run site; conv Portofino (boat trip) & train to Cinque Terre; beautiful coastlline; shwrs clsd during day but hot shwrs at pool; v busy public hols - adv bkg rec; awkward exit, not suitable for lge o'fits; NH only." 13 Mar-15 Nov. € 32.50            2014*

**RASUN DI SOTTO/NIEDERRASEN See Brunico/Bruneck** *1D1*

**RAVENNA** *2E2* (7km E Coastal) *44.43335, 12.29680* Camping Park Adriano, Via dei Campeggi 7, 48020 Punta-Marina-Terme (RN) [0544 437230; fax 438510; info@campingadriano.com; www.campingadriano.com] Fr S309 Ravenna-Venezia rd foll sp to Lido Adriano. Site at N end of Lido. Lge, shd; wc; chem disp; mv service pnt; shwrs inc; el pnts (5A) inc (poss rev pol/no earth); lndtte (inc dryer); shop; tradsmn; rest, snacks; bar; BBQ; playgrnd; pool; paddling pool; beach 300m; cycle hire; golf 10km; wifi; entmnt; TV rm; 70% statics; dogs €3; bus to Ravenna; ATM; Eng spkn; adv bkg; poss noisy disco; ccard acc; red snr citizens/CKE/CCI. "Site in pine forest; excel san facs; sh walk to beach." ♦ 22 Apr-19 Sep. € 40.00 (CChq acc)            2009*

**RAVENNA** *2E2* (9km E Coastal) *44.43147, 12.30034* Camping Villaggio dei Pini, Via della Fontana, 48020 Punta-Marina-Terme (RA) [0544 437115; fax 531863; villaggiodeipini@gestionecampeggi.it; www.gestionecampeggi.it] Foll sp to Punta Marina fr S67; in cent of Punta-Marina take sm rd S; site at end of rd on L. Lge, pt shd; wc (some cont); chem disp; mv service pnt; shwrs inc; el pnts (5A) inc; gas; lndtte; shop; rest, snacks; bar; playgrnd; beach adj; cycle hire; entmnt; 90% statics; no dogs; phone; clsd 1400-1600 & 0000-0700; poss v cr; quiet; ccard acc. "Conv for mosaics; pitches v sm." ♦ 23 Apr-13 Sep. € 31.30            2010*

Tell us about the sites you visit

RHEMES ST GEORGE *1B1* (Rural) *45.64966, 7.15150*
Camping Val di Rhemes, Loc Voix 1, 11010 Rhêmes-
St George (AO) [tel/fax 0165 907648; info@
campingvaldirhemes.com; www.campingvaldirhemes.
com] Fr S26 or A54/E25 turn S at Introd dir Rhêmes-St George
& Rhêmes-Notre-Dame; site on R in 10km past PO; app is diff
climb with hairpins. Med, pt sl, pt shd; htd wc (some cont);
chem disp; mv service pnt; shwrs; el pnts (2-6A) €2; lndtte
dryer; shop; bar; wifi; Eng spkn; ccard acc; CCI; playgrnd;
10% statics; dogs €2.50; adv bkg; quiet. "Peaceful, family-run
site; nr Gran Paradiso National Park; gd walking; excel." ♦
1 Jun-10 Sep. € 35.60                                    2014*

RICCIONE *2E3* (1km SE Coastal) *43.9850, 12.67916*
Camping Riccione, Via Marsala 10, 47838 Riccione (RN)
[0541 690160; fax 690044; info@campingriccione.it; www.
campingriccione.it] Exit A14/E55 onto SS16 thro Riccione
ignoring numerous other camp sp & look for site sp. Turn L
and site in 150m on R. Lge, shd; wc; mv service pnt; some
serviced pitches; shwrs inc; el pnts (5A) inc; gas; lndtte; shop;
rest, snacks; bar; playgrnd; pool & paddling pool; sand beach
500m; tennis; games area; cycle hire; solarium; wifi; sat TV;
10% statics; dogs (not acc mid-Jul to mid-Aug); poss cr; adv
bkg; traff noise (rd, rlwy & air); ccard acc; redCKE/CCI. "Pitch
acc poss diff due to trees." ♦  18 Apr-21 Sep. € 47.00  2011*

RICCIONE *2E3* (2km S Coastal) *43.98610, 12.68806* Camping
Alberello, Viale Torino 80, 47838 Riccione (RN) [tel/fax
0541 615248; direzione@alberello.it; www.alberello.
it] Exit A14/E55 dir Riccione on SS16. Site is sp off this rd dir
Misano Adriatico, twds sea. Lge, hdg/mkd pitch, shd; wc;
shwrs inc; el pnts (4A) €2.50; gas; lndtte; shop; rest, snacks;
bar; playgrnd; sand beach adj; games area; golf 1km; entmnt;
TV rm; no dogs; car wash; no adv bkg; quiet but rlwy/rd noise.
"Gd for families." ♦  9 Apr-28 Sep. € 32.70            2009*

RIVA DEL GARDA *1D1* (2.5km E Rural) *45.88111,
10.86194* Camping Monte Brione, Via Brione 32, 38066
Riva-del-Garda (TN) [0464 520885; fax 520890; info@
campingbrione.com] Exit A22
Garda Nord onto SS240 to Torbole & Riva; on app to Riva
thro open-sided tunnel; immed R after enclosed tunnel opp
Marina; site ent 700m on R. Med, mkd pitch, terr, pt shd; wc
(some cont); chem disp; mv service pnt; shwrs inc; el pnts (6A)
inc; gas; lndtte; shop; rest 200m; snacks; bar; BBQ; playgrnd;
htd pool; shgl beach & lake sw 500m; watersports; cycle hire;
solarium; wifi; dogs €4; barriers clsd 1300-1500 & 2300-0700;
Eng spkn; adv bkg; quiet; ccard acc;CKE/CCI. "Olive groves adj;
pleasant site with lge pitches; gd, modern san facs." ♦  1 Apr-
30 Sep. € 28.50                                          2009*

⊞ RIZZOLO *1C2* (3km S Rural)  Camping Cascinotta, 29019
Rizzolo (Postal address: San Giorgio-Piacentino (PC))
[0523 530113; fax 0523 530451; rose@cittadellerose.
it; www.cittadellerose.it] Site is 10km S of San Giorgio-
Piacentino on rd fr Rizzolo to Ponte-dell'Ollio. Med, mkd pitch,
pt terr, pt shd; wc; chem disp; mv service pnt; shwrs inc; el pnts
€2; lndtte; bar; BBQ; playgrnd; 5% statics; dogs; adv bkg;CKE/
CCI. "Site attached to religious sanctuary & pilgrimage cent; set
in parkland; vg touring base." € 24.00                  2009*

⊞ ROCCARASO *2F4* (2km NE Rural) *41.84194, 14.10277*
Camping Del Sole, Piana del Leone, Via Pietransieri, 67037
Roccaraso (AQ) [0864 62532 / 0864 62571; fax 619329;
albergodelsole@libero.it; www.villaggiodelsole.com/]
Turn E fr S17 at sp Petransieri & site on R in 2km. Med, pt sl,
pt shd; wc; chem disp; shwrs inc; el pnts inc (poss no earth -
long lead rec); gas; lndtte; shop 2km; rest; bar; playgrnd; sw
2km; ski school; 50% statics; dogs (sm only); bus; quiet; ccard
acc;CKE/CCI. "Excel & conv National Park; ltd facs low ssn;
unrel opening, suggest phone to confirm." ♦  € 26.00  2013*

RODI GARGANICO *2G4* (7.5km E Rural) Camping Village
Valle D'Oro, Via degli Ulivi, Loc Aia del Cervone,
71010 San Menaio (FG) [tel/fax 0884 991580; info@
campingvalledoro.it; www.campingvalledoro.it] Exit A14
at Poggio Emperiate onto S89 E dir Peschici & Vieste thro Rodi
Garganico. At San Menaio turn R twd Vico del Gargano for
4km, site on R, well sp. Sm, terr, pt shd; htd wc; chem disp;
shwrs inc; el pnts (3A) €2.50; lndry rm; shop; rest, snacks;
bar; playgrnd; sm pool; sand beach 4km; games area; dogs;
poss cr; Eng spkn; adv bkg; quiet; red low ssn;CKE/CCI.
"Pleasant site in olive trees away fr busy coastal sites; friendly,
welcoming, helpful owners; vg rest; shuttle bus to beach high
ssn; Vico-del-Gargano interesting town." ♦  ltd 1 Jun-15 Sep.
€ 23.50                                                  2009*

RODI GARGANICO *2G4* (4km W Coastal) *41.91209, 15.72950*
Camping 5 Stelle, C da Pagliai dei Combattenti, Km
34.500, 71010 Foce-di-Varano (FG) [tel/fax 0884 917583;
info@camping5stelle.it; www.camping5stelle.it] Exit A14
at Poggio-Imperiale E twd Vieste. Turn N at Sannicandro & foll
sp Torre-Mileto, Porto-Capoiale & Isola-Varano. Site sp. Lge,
pt shd; wc; chem disp; mv service pnt; private bthrms some
pitches; baby facs; shwrs; el pnts (5A) €2.50; lndtte; shop; rest,
snacks; bar; BBQ; playgrnd; pool; paddling pool; sand beach
adj; lake fishing; tennis; cycle hire; games area; entmnt; TV rm;
20% statics; dogs €3; poss cr; quiet; ccard acc; red low ssn. ♦
1 Apr-30 Sep. € 49.00 (CChq acc)                       2011*

⊞ ROMA *2E4* (8km N Urban) *41.95618, 12.48240* Camping
Village Flaminio, Via Flaminia Nuova 821, 00189
Roma [06 3332604 or 3331429; fax 3330653; info@
villageflaminio.com; www.villageflaminio.com] Exit GRA
ring rd at exit 6 & proceed S along Via Flaminia twd Roma
Centrale. In 3km where lanes divide keep to L-hand lane
(R-hand land goes into underpass). Cross underpass, then
immed back to R-hand lane & slow down. Site on R 150m, sp
as Flaminio Bungalow Village. No vehicular access to site fr S
or exit to N. Lge, pt sl, pt shd; htd wc; chem disp; mv service
pnt; shwrs inc; el pnts (3-12A) inc; gas; lndtte (inc dryer); shop;
supmkt 200m; rest, snacks; bar; playgrnd; pool (sw caps req);
cycle hire; wifi; TV rm; some statics; phone; bus (cross v busy
rd); train nr; site clsd mid-Jan to end Feb; poss cr; no adv bkg;
red long stay/low ssn; ccard acc (min €155). "Well-run site;
excel, clean san facs; poss long walk fr far end of site to ent
(site transport avail); poss dusty pitches; take care sap fr lime
trees; cycle/walking track to city cent nrby; train 10 mins walk
(buy tickets on site); local excursions pick-up fr site (tickets
fr recep). ♦  € 57.00 (CChq acc)                        2013*

---

**ROMA** *2E4* (9km N) *42.00353, 12.45283* **Happy Village & Camping**, Via Prato della Corte 1915, 00123 Roma [06 33626401/ 06 33614596; fax 33613800; info@ happycamping.net; www.happycamping.net] Take exit 5 fr Rome ring rd sp Viterbo. Site sp on ring rd, fr N & S on dual c'way Rome/Viterbo at 1st exit N of ring rd. Lge, pt terr, pt shd; wc; chem disp; mv service pnt; shwrs inc; el pnts (6A) inc; gas; lndtte; shop; rest, snacks; bar; BBQ; playgrnd; pool high ssn; some statics; dogs free; train into Rome; poss cr; adv bkg; poss noisy; ccard acc; red CKE/CCI. "Friendly, busy site in hills; sm pitches; vg rest; mini bus shuttle to train stn; gd site; v nice well kept site." ♦ 1 Mar-6 Jan. € 51.00          2013*

**ROMA** *2E4* (12km N Urban) *42.0102, 12.50368* **Camping Tiber**, Via Tiberina, Km 1.4, 00188 Roma [06 33610733; fax 33612314; info@campingtiber.com; www.campingtiber. com] Fr Florence, exit at Rome Nord-Fiano on A1 & immed after tolls turn S on Via Tibernia, site sp. Fr any dir on Rome ring rd take exit 6 N'bound on S3 Via Flaminia. Site 1km S of Prima Porta. Lge, pt shd; wc; mv service pnt; shwrs inc; el pnts (4-6A) inc (long lead req & poss rev pol); gas; lndtte (inc dryer); shop; rest, snacks; bar; pool high ssn; games area; wifi; some statics; dogs; free bus to metro stn; Eng spkn; quiet; ccard acc; red long stay/CKE/CCI. "Ideal for city by metro (20 mins) & bus; helpful staff; recep 0700-2300; modern san facs; some lge pitches; poss ant/mosquito prob; Magic of Europe discount; perfectly comfortable." ♦ 23 Mar-30 Oct. € 52.00     2013*

**ROMA** *2E4* (10km SW Rural) *41.77730, 12.39605* **Camping Fabulous**, Via Cristoforo Colombo, Km 18, 00125 Acilia (RM) [06 5259354; fax 83517789; fabulous@ecvacanze. it; www.ecvacanze.it] Exit junc 27 fr Rome ring rd into Via C Colombo. At 18km marker turn R at traff lts, site 200m on R. V lge, mkd pitch, pt sl, shd; htd wc; baby facs; shwrs inc; el pnts (6-10A) inc; lndtte; shop; rest, snacks; bar; BBQ; playgrnd; pool; paddling pool; waterslide; sand beach 12km; tennis; games area; entmnt; quiet at night; 80% statics; dogs €1.50; phone; bus on main rd; Eng spkn; adv bkg; ccard acc; CKE/CCI. "Set in pinewoods; gd sh stay." ♦ ltd 12 Mar-31 Oct. € 35.00   2009*

⊞ **ROMA** *2E4* (4km W Urban) *41.88741, 12.40468* Roma Camping, Via Aurelia 831, Km 8.2, 00165 Roma [06 6623018; fax 66418147; campingroma@ecvacenze.it] Site is on Via Aurelia approx 8km fr Rome cent on spur rd on S side of main dual c'way opp lge Panorama Hypmkt. Fr GRA ring rd exit junc 1 Aurelio & head E sp Roma Cent & Citta del Vaticano. In approx 3km take spur rd on R 50m bef covrd pedestrian footbdge x-ing dual c'way & 250m bef flyover, sp camping; site gates on R (S) in 100m. W fr Rome take spur rd 8km fr cent sp camping just after Holiday Inn & just bef Panorama Hypmkt. At top turn L (S) over flyover & immed R sp camping; site gates on L in 200m. V lge, hdstg, terr, pt shd; wc (some cont); baby facs; shwrs inc; el pnts (4-6A) inc; lndtte; supmkt opp; rest, snacks; bar; playgrnd; pool high ssn; games area; wifi; 75% statics; dogs €1.50; bus to city; poss cr; Eng spkn; rd noise; ccard acc; red low ssn/CKE/CCI. "Gd, clean site; excel san facs & pool; friendly staff; popular site - rec arr early; rec not leave site on foot after dark; Rest open all year; conv walk to Hypermkt." ♦ € 55.00          2013*

**ROME see Roma** *2E4*

**ROSETO DEGLI ABRUZZI** *2F3* (3km S Coastal) *42.65748, 14.03568* Eurcamping Roseto, Lungomare Trieste Sud 90, 64026 Roseto-degli-Abruzzi (TE) [085 8993179; fax 8930552; eurcamping@camping.it; www.eurcamping.it] Fr A14 exit dir Roseto-degli-Abruzzi to SS16. At rndabt turn R, next L & under rlwy bdge to promenade. Turn R at sea front, site at end of promenade. Med, shd, hdg/mkd pitch; wc; chem disp; mv service pnt; shwrs inc; el pnts (3A) inc; lndtte (inc dryer); shop; rest, snacks; bar; playgrnd; pool; paddling pool; private sand & shgl beach adj; tennis; cycle hire; games area; wifi; entmnt; 20% statics; dogs €5; poss cr; Eng spkn; adv bkg; quiet but some rlwy noise; red low ssn; CKE/CCI. "Phone to check if open low ssn; gates close 2300; pitches poss flood after heavy rainfall; Roseto excel resort." ♦ 1 May-31 Oct. € 40.50 (CChq acc)          2010*

⊞ **ST VINCENT** *1B1* (10km N Rural) *45.78729, 7.60361* Camping Dalai Lama Village, Loc Promiod, 11024 Châtillon (AO) [0166 548688; fax 549921; info@ dalailamavillage.com; www.dalailamavillage.com] Exit A5/E25 at Châtillon & take R46 N to Antey-St André. In cent of town fork R over sm bdge & climb for approx 5km to site, sp. Care needed lge M'vans. Lge, mkd pitch, pt shd; htd wc; chem disp; mv service pnt; sauna; shwrs inc; el pnts inc; lndtte; rest, snacks; bar; playgrnd; htd, covrd pool; games area; games rm; gym; entmnt; 50% statics; dogs €4; adv bkg; quiet. "Stunning views; superb, peaceful site & san facs; vg bar/rest terr; highly rec; diff narr rd for lge o'fits, 1km single track without passing places, excep views, 80% statics, shwrs not incl or pool/sauna €29 for session." ♦ € 39.00          2011*

⊞ **SALBERTRAND** *1A2* (1km SW Rural) *45.06200, 6.86821* Camping Gran Bosco, SS24, Km 75, Monginevro, 10050 Salbertrand (TO) [0122 854653; fax 854693; info@ campinggranbosco.it; www.campinggranbosco.it] Leave A32/E70 (Torino-Fréjus Tunnel) at Oulx Ouest junc & foll SS24/ SS335 sp Salbertrand. Site sp 1.5km twd Salbertrand at km 75. Fr S (Briançon in France) on N94/SS24 to Oulx cent, foll SS24 thro town & foll sp Salbertrand, then as above. Lge, pt shd; htd wc (mainly cont); chem disp; mv service pnt; shwrs; el pnts (3-6A) inc; gas; lndtte; shop; rest 1km; snacks; bar; playgrnd; tennis; games area; entmnt; 80% statics (sep area); some rd & rlwy noise; ccard acc. "Beautiful setting; excel NH bef/after Fréjus Tunnel or pass to/fr Briançon; gates open 0830-2300; excel, modern, clean san facs; sm pitches; grnd soft in wet - no hdstg." € 29.00          2012*

**SALSOMAGGIORE TERME** *1C2* (3km E Rural) *44.80635, 10.00931* Camping Arizona, Via Tabiano 42, 43039 Tabiano-Salsomaggiore Terme (PR) [0524 565648; fax 567589; info@camping-arizona.it; www.camping-arizona. it] Exit A1 for Fidenza & foll sps for Salsomaggiore fr Co-op supmkt, to Tabiano; sp on S side of rd. Not rec to attempt to find site fr S9 fr Piacenza. Lge, pt sl, shd; wc (some cont); chem disp (wc); mv service pnt; shwrs inc; el pnts (3A) inc (rev pol); lndtte (inc dryer); shop; rest, snacks; bar; playgrnd; 4 pools high ssn; 2 waterslides; jacuzzi; fishing; tennis; games rm; games area; cycle hire; golf 7km; wifi; entmnt; 30% statics; dogs €3; phone; sep car park; bus to Salsomaggiore; phone; quiet; red low ssn; ccard acc. "Vg site; friendly, helpful staff; interesting, smart spa town; excel touring base; gd for families; san facs vg; best campsite shop; vg rest." ♦ 1 Apr-7 Oct. € 47.00          2014*

SALTO DI FONDI see Terracina *2E4*

SAN BARONTO LAMPORECCHIO see Pistoia *1D3*

SAN CANDIDO/INNICHEN see Dobbiaco/Toblach *2E1*

SAN FELICE DEL BENACO *1D2* (1km N Rural) *45.59972, 10.54972* Camping Eden, Via Preone 45, 25010 Portese (BS) [0365 62093; fax 559311; mail@camping-eden.it; www.camping-eden.it] Best app fr Salo (N), foll lakeside twd Porto Portese. Site ent up steep slope on R. Lge, hdg/mkd pitch, hdstg, terr, shd; wc; chem disp; mv service pnt; baby facs; shwrs inc; el pnts (3A) inc; lndtte; shop; rest, snacks; bar; playgrnd; pool; lake sw & shgl beach adj; golf 3km; 85% statics; dogs €10; phone; Eng spkn; adv bkg; quiet; red low ssn/snr citizen; CKE/CCI. "Beach down steep rd opp site; 10 mins walk to boat terminal for lake; steep steps to san facs; manhandling req to get c'vans onto pitches; site not rec lge o'fits." ◆ 11 Apr-27 Sep. € 42.00          2009*

# "I like to fill in the reports as I travel from site to site"

You'll find report forms at the back of this guide, or you can fill them in online at www.caravaclub.co.uk/europereport.

SAN FELICE DEL BENACO *1D2* (1km E Rural) *45.58500, 10.56583* Camping Fornella, Via Fornella 1, 25010 San Felice-del-Benaco (BS) [0365 62294; fax 559418; fornella@fornella.it; www.fornella.it] N fr Desenzano on S572 twd Salo. Turn R to San Felice-del-Benaco, over x-rds & take 2nd R turn at sp to site. R into app rd, L into site. Rd narr but accessible. Avoid vill cent, site sp (with several others) fr vill by-pass just bef g'ge. Lge, pt sl, terr, pt shd; htd wc (some cont); chem disp; mv service pnt; baby facs; shwrs inc; el pnts (6A) inc; gas; lndtte (inc dryer); shop; rest, snacks; bar; BBQ (charcoal); playgrnds; pool; paddling pool; sw & shgl beach on lake; fishing; boat hire & windsurfing; cycle hire; tennis; games area; entmnt; games rm; wifi; entmnt; TV (in bar); 20% statics; dogs €7; no c'vans/m'vans over 7m high ssn; sep car park; recep 0800-1200 & 1400-2000; poss v cr; Eng spkn; adv bkg; quiet; ccard acc; extra for lge pitches & lakeside pitches; red low ssn & snr citizens low ssn; CKE/CCI. "Family-run site in vg location by Lake Garda; park outside until checked in; excel pool; excursions to Venice, Florence & Verona opera; excel rest; gd san facs." ◆ 1 May-20 Sep. € 69.00  SBS - Y11     2014*

SAN FELICE DEL BENACO *1D2* (1km SE Rural) *45.57861, 10.55388* Camping Ideal Molino, Via Gardiola 1, 25010 San Felice-del-Benaco (BS) [0365 62023; fax 559395; info@campingmolino.it; www.campingmolino.it] Site approx 6km S of Salo on W shore of lake. Foll sp Porto & San Felice. Site 1km past San Felice; narr app. Med, mkd pitch, pt shd; wc; chem disp; baby facs; shwrs inc; el pnts (4A) inc; gas; lndtte; shop; rest; bar; playgrnd; shgl beach; boat hire; fishing; 30% statics; no dogs; phone; adv bkg rec; quiet; red low ssn/snr citizens. "Steamer trips on lake; some v sm pitches; excel lakeside rest." ◆ 24 Mar-30 Sep. € 38.60          2009*

SAN FELICE DEL BENACO *1D2* (1km NW Rural) *45.59517, 10.53313* Camping Villaggio Weekend, Via Vallone della Selva 2, 25010 San Felice-del-Benaco (BS) [0365 43712; fax 42196; info@weekend.it; www.weekend.it] Well sp fr Desenzano. Ignore 1st sp San Felice-del-Benaco, turn R at rndabt to vill then 2nd L. Do not app fr Riva-del-Garda end of lake - narr tunnels. Nearest town Salo. Lge, mkd pitch, terr, shd; wc; chem disp; some serviced pitches; baby facs; shwrs inc; el pnts (6A) inc; lndtte (inc dryer); supmkt; rest, snacks; bar; BBQ; playgrnd; pool; paddling pool; waterslide; lake sw & scuba diving; cycle hire; games area; wifi; entmnt; 20% statics; dogs €7.50; poss cr; Eng spkn; adv bkg ess; quiet; ccard acc; red low ssn; CKE/CCI. "Excel, family site in olive grove; excel entmnt; bathing caps req in pool; views of lake & mountains fr some pitches; low branches some pitches diff for m'vans; some sm pitches - lge avail; tight corners poss diff lge o'fits; office clsd 1300-1500." ◆ 16 Apr-25 Sep. € 52.00     2010*

⊞ SAN GIOVANNI ROTONDO *2G4* (700m SE Rural) Aree di Sosta Giovanni di Cerbo, Contrada Coppa Mazzanelle, 71013 San Giovanni-Rotondo (FG) [0882 453900] Fr A14 exit onto SS272 dir San Marco-in-Lamis. Foll sp to San Giovanni-Rotondo. On town o'skts at rndabt turn R dir Foggia. Site on R bef next rndabt - 1km down narr lane. Fr S fr Foggia foll sp Manfredonia then San Giovanni. On o'skts of town turn L at rndabt, site in 50m. Sm, all hdstg, pt sl, unshd; wc; chem disp; mv service pnt; shwrs inc; el pnts (10A) metered (poss rev pol/no earth); shop 500m; rest; bar; htd pool 8km; sand beach 20km; dogs; poss cr; Eng spkn; adv bkg; noisy dogs in area; CKE/CCI. "V popular with m'vanners; off beaten track in scenic area; ltd san facs; minibus to town cent; conv Gargano National Park & Forest of Umbra." ◆ € 15.00          2010*

SAN LORENZO DI SEBATO see Brunico/Bruneck *1D1*

⊞ SAN MARINO *2E3* (4km N Rural) *43.95990, 12.46090* Centro Vacanze San Marino, Strada San Michele 50, 47893 Cailungo, Repubblica di San Marino [0549 903964; fax 907120; info@centrovacanzesanmarino.com; www.centrovacanzesanmarino.com] Exit A14 at Rimini Sud, foll rd S72 to San Marino. Pass under 2 curved footbdges, then 800m after 2nd & 13km after leaving a'strada, fork R. Cont uphill for 1.5km then turn R at Brico building, site sp. Steep long-haul climb. Lge, hdg pitch, hdstg, terr, pt shd; htd wc; chem disp; mv service pnt; serviced pitch; shwrs inc; el pnts (6A) inc (poss rev pol); lndtte; sm shop, rest high ssn; snacks; bar; BBQ; cooking facs; playgrnd; htd pool; paddling pool; tennis; games area; cycle hire; solarium; mini-zoo; wifi; sat TV; some statics; dogs €5; bus; poss v cr; Eng spkn; adv bkg; quiet; red 7+ days; ccard acc; CKE/CCI. "V busy at w/end - rec arr early; superb hill fort town; excel rest & pool; sm pitches; conv Rimini 24km; excel, clean site; bus calls at site ent for San Marino." ◆ € 53.00 (CChq acc)          2014*

SAN MENAIO see Rodi Garganico *2G4*

SAN MICHELE ALL'ADIGE *1D1* (3km S Rural) Camping Moser, Via Nazionale 64, 38015 Nave San Felice (TN) [0461 870248] 12km N of Trento on SS12. Sm, mkd pitch, shd; wc; chem disp; shwrs; el pnts inc; shop in vill; rest; bar; dogs; bus 500m; poss cr; Eng spkn; adv bkg; rd & rlwy noise. "Gd, friendly NH." 1 May-31 Oct. € 18.00          2009*

SAN PIERO A SIEVE see Borgo San Lorenzo *1D3*

⊞ **SAN REMO** *1B3* (2.5km W Coastal) *43.80244, 7.74506* Camping Villaggio Dei Fiori, Via Tiro a Volo 3, 18038 San Remo (IM) [0184 660635; fax 662377; info@ villaggiodeifiori.it; www.villaggiodeifiori.it] Fr A10/E80 take Arma-di-Taggia exit & foll sp San Remo Centro. At SS1 coast rd turn R sp Ventimiglia. At 2.5km look for red/yellow Billa supmkt sp on R; 50m past sp take L fork, site on L in 50m. Fr W on A10 take 1st exit dir San Remo - winding rd. Turn R & site on L after Stands supmkt. Fr Ventimiglia on SS1, 150m past San Remo boundary sp turn sharp R (poss diff lge o'fits) to site. Lge, some hdg/mkd pitch, all hdstg, pt terr, pt shd; htd wc (some cont); chem disp; mv service pnt; baby facs; fam bthrm; shwrs inc; el pnts (3-6A) €4-7; lndtte (inc dryer); supmkt 200m; rest, snacks; bar; BBQ; playgrnd; htd pool; shgl beach adj; tennis; games area; cycle hire; wifi; entmnt; 60% statics; no dogs; train to Monaco & bus San Remo nr; poss cr; Eng spkn; adv bkg rec high ssn; rd & fairgrnd noise; red long stay/low ssn; ccard acc.; CKE/CCI "Gd location; well-kept, tidy, paved site; vg, clean facs; beach not suitable for sw; some pitches superb sea views (extra charge), some sm; lge o'fits not acc high ssn as sm pitches; vg rest; conv Monaco; gates locked at night." ♦ ltd 15 May-15 Oct. € 67.00 (4 persons) 2013*

**SAN ROCCO CASTAGNARETTA see Cuneo** *1B2*

⊞ **SAN VALENTINO ALLA MUTA** *1D1* (500m W Rural) *46.7700, 10.5325* Camping Thöni, Landstrasse 83, 39020 San Valentino-alla-Muta/St Valentin-an-der-Haide (BZ) [0473 634020; thoeni.h@rolmail.net; www.camping-thoeni.it] N twd Austrian border site on L on edge of vill on S edge of Lago di Resia. Sm, pt sl, unshd; htd wc; chem disp; shwrs inc; el pnts (6A) €1.50; shop, rest, snacks, bar 300m; pool 7km; dogs; site clsd Nov; quiet. "Conv sh stay/NH en rte Austria; cycle rte around lake." € 20.50 2010*

**SAN VINCENZO** *1D3* (8km S Coastal) *43.02815, 10.5345* Camping Park Albatros, Pineta di Torre Nuova, 57027 San Vincenzo (LI) [0565 701018; fax 703589; albatros@ camping.it; www.camping.it/toscana/albatros] Fr N exit SS1 San Vincenzo Nord, fr S exit Sud. As app town foll sp Piombino on SP23 Via Della Principessa, just after 7km post turn L on reaching pine wood, site sp. V lge, pt shd; wc; chem disp; mv service pnt; baby facs; shwrs; el pnts (5A) inc; lndtte; gas; shop; rest, snacks; bar; playgrnd; pool complex; sand beach 900m; games area; cycle hire; wifi; entmnt; 40% statics; dogs €3; phone; poss cr; Eng spkn; food music in pool area all day; ccard acc; red low ssn. "Gd, improving, busy site; lge pitches; gd, modern san facs; excel pool complex." ♦ 24 Apr-25 Sep. € 47.70 2010*

⊞ **SAN VITO LO CAPO (SICILY)** *3B3* (1km E Coastal) *38.17395, 12.74795* Camping La Pineta, Via del Secco 88, 91010 San Vito-lo-Capo (TP) [0923 972818; fax 974070; info@campinglapineta.it; www.campinglapineta.it] Foll sp fr town. Lge, mkd pitch, hdstg, pt sl, shd; htd wc; chem disp; mv service pnt; shwrs €0.50; el pnts (6A) €5; lndtte; shop; rest; bar; BBQ; playgrnd; pool; paddling pool; sand beach 1km; cycle hire; games area; wifi; entmnt; 30% statics; phone; site clsd Nov; Eng spkn; ccard acc; red low ssn/CKE/CCI. "Gd, clean site; easy walk to vill." ♦ € 38.00 (CChq acc) 2009*

⊞ **SAN VITO LO CAPO (SICILY)** *3B3* (3km S Coastal) *38.15067, 12.73184* El Bahira Camping Village, Contrada Salinella, 91010 San Vito-lo-Capo (TP) [0923 972577; fax 972552; info@elbahira.it; www.elbahira.it] W fr Palermo on A29 dir Trapani. Exit at Castellammare del Golfo onto SS187, then turn N onto SP16 sp San Vito-lo-Capo. At Isolidda foll site sp. Lge, mkd pitch, shd; wc (some cont); chem disp; el pnts (6A) inc; lndtte; shops; rest, snacks; bar; pizzeria; BBQ; playgrnd; pool (sw caps req); paddling pool; sand/shgl beach adj; watersports; tennis; games area; games rm; entmnt; excursions; TV; some statics; phone; bus nr; sep car park; Eng spkn; ccard acc; quiet; CKE/CCI. "Excel, secure site in vg location; gd facs for families; san facs tired need updating (2014)." ♦ € 55.40 2014*

**SANT' ANTIOCO (SARDINIA)** *3B1* (12km SW Coastal) *39.00691, 8.38752* Tonnara Camping, Cala Sapone, 09017 Sant' Antioco (CA) [0781 809058; fax 809036; mail@campinga-tonnara.it; www.campingtonnara.co.uk] Fr Cagliari take S130 & then S126. Site on W coast of Isola-di-S. Antiocio. Lge, hdg/mkd pitch, shd; wc; mv service pnt; shwrs; el pnts (6A) inc; gas; lndtte; shop; rest; bar; pool; sand/ shgl beach; tennis; games area; scuba-diving school; sep car park; dogs €6; phone; bus 100m; poss cr; adv bkg; quiet; ccard acc; red low ssn. "Delightful, peaceful site in gd location; some narr lanes." 1 Apr-30 Sep. € 49.00 2011*

**SANT' ANTONIO DI MAVIGNOLA see Pinzolo** *1D1*

**SANT' ARCANGELO SUL TRASIMENO see Magione** *2E3*

**SANTA MARIA DI MERINO see Vieste** *2G4*

**SANTA TERESA GALLURA** *1C4* (1km W Urban) *41.21938, 9.18372* Camping Gallura Village, Loc Li Lucianeddi, 07028 Santa Teresa Gallura [078 975 55 80; fax 974 19 32; info@ galluravillage.it] Fr Santa Teresa Gallura on SP90. Site 1km on L. Med, mkd pitch, unshd; wc; chem disp; shwrs inc; shop 0.5km; snacks; rest; bar; playgrnd; pool; paddling pool; games area; entmnt; wifi; bike hire; 50% statics; dogs; Eng spkn; ccard acc. "Fair site; power point at each plot; gd NH for ferry to Corsica." 1 Mar-30 Oct. € 52.00 2014*

⊞ **SARNANO** *2E3* (3km SSW Rural) *43.01743, 13.28358* Quattro Stagioni, Contrada Brilli, 62028 Sarnano [0733 651147; fax 651104; quattrostagioni@camping. it; www.camping4stagioni.it] A14 exit Civitanova Marche. M'way to Macerata as far as Sarnano exit. In Sarnano turn R at sq, foll main rd. Site approx 3km outside Sarnano to the W. Sm, mkd pitch, pt sl, pt shd; wc; chem disp; mv service pnt; shwrs; el pnts; lndtte; shop; rest; café; snack; bar; bbq; playgrnd; pool; paddling pool; games area; wifi; 60% statics; dogs; twin axles; Eng spkn; adv bkg; red low ssn; CKE/CCI. "Fair site." ♦ ltd € 41.00 2014*

**SARRE see Aosta** *1B1*

SARZANA *1C2* (8km S Rural/Coastal) *44.07638, 9.97027* Camping River, Loc Armezzone, 19031 Ameglia (SP) [0187 65920; fax 65183; info@campingriver.com; www. campingriver.com] Exit A12 at Sarzana & foll sp Ameglia & Bocca di Magra on SP432. In 7km turn L into Via Crociata to site (blue sp). Narr app rd with few passing places. Lge, mkd pitch; pt shd; wc (mainly cont); chem disp; mv service pnt; sauna; shwrs inc; el pnts (3-6A) inc; Indtte (inc dryer); supmkt 700m; rest, snacks; pizzeria; bar; playgrnd; 2 pools; paddling pool; beach 2km; rv fishing; tennis 200m; games area; boat & cycle hire; horseriding 200m; golf driving range; wifi; entmnt; TV rm; 50% statics; dogs €3; bus to beach; poss cr; adv bkg; red low ssn. "Gd touring base Cinque Terre; pleasant, helpful staff; vg, well-situated site; gd shop & rest; nice location by rv; dated facs; gd pools." ♦ 12 Apr-4 Oct. € 69.00 (3 persons)                                      2014*

SASSELLO *1B2* (5km NE Rural) *44.49672, 8.52794* Club Naturista Costalunga (Naturist), 17046 Sassello (SV) [tel/ fax 019 720004; info@costalunga.org; www.costalunga. org] Fr A10 exit at Albissola & turn L after toll booth sp Sassello. In Sassello bear R sp Palo & Urbe, in 5km turn L at site sp, site on L in 500m. Sm, hdstg, pt sl, terr, pt shd; wc; chem disp; shwrs inc; el pnts (6A) €3; Indtte; shop 5km; pre-ordered snacks; playgrnd; pool; TV rm; 30% statics; dogs €2; bus 500m; adv bkg; quiet; ccard not acc; red long stay; INF card. "Friendly, helpful owners; views fr some pitches; gd." 1 Apr-30 Sep. € 25.00                                      2011*

⊞ SASSO MARCONI *1D2* (11km SW Rural) Centro Naturista Ca'Le Scope (Naturist), Loc San Martino/La Quercia, 40043 Marzabotto (BO) [tel/fax 051 932328; calescope@virgilio.it; www.calescope.com] Fr A1 exit at Rioveggio, turn R after toll booth. In 200m turn R onto S325 sp Bologna. In 3.5km turn sharp L sp Quercia, chvr to foll rd for 4km (narr & uneven in parts - care req). Turn L at x-rds sp to site, site in 1.5km on L. Med, hdg/mkd pitch, hdstg, pt sl, pt shd; wc (some cont); chem disp (wc); baby facs; shwrs inc; el pnts (6A) €3.15; gas; Indtte; basic shop; tradsmn; rest, snacks; bar; playgrnd; pool; internet; TV rm; 50% statics; dogs; train 6km; poss cr; Eng spkn; adv bkg; quiet; ccard acc; INF card. "Spectacular views over Monte Sole National Park; friendly Dutch owners; site rds steep in parts - care req." € 31.00                                      2011*

SAVONA *1B2* (10km NE Rural) *44.38105, 8.50151* Camping Dolce Vita, Via Riobasco 62, 17040 Stella-San Giovanni (SV) [tel/fax 019 703269 or 03939 836543 (mob); campingdolcevita@libero.it; www.campingdolcevita.it] Foll sp Albisola off Genoa-Savona a'strada, Turn L in town onto rd SS334 dir Sassello. Site in 5km on L on rd twd mountains. Site sp faces S only; if app fr N look for flags. Sm, pt shd; wc; mv service pnt; chem disp; shwrs €1; el pnts (4-8A) €3; gas; Indtte; shop 2.5km; rest, snacks; bar; playgrnd; pool; beach 5.5km; TV; 75% statics; dogs €3; Eng spkn; no adv bkg; quiet; CKE/CCI. "Sm touring pitches unsuitable lge o'fits; v busy at w/end; gd welcome; poss untidy low ssn; gd NH." ♦ 1 Jan-20 Oct. € 31.00                                      2009*

SAVONA *1B2* (1km SW Coastal) Camping Charly, Via Nizza 93/R, Zinola, 17100 Savona (SV) [0198 62265; fax 0192 63427; info@campingcharly.it; www.campingcharly. it] Take SS1 fr Savona twd Sportorno. Site in vicinity of Zinola bet AGIP & BP g'ges on dual c'way. Med, shd; wc; shwrs €0.50; el pnts (5A) inc; shop; snacks; bar; pool; paddling pool; sm sand beach across rd; 50% statics; no dogs; poss cr; Eng spkn; adv bkg; some rd & rlwy noise at night; red low ssn; CKE/CCI. "Hot water to shwrs only." 15 Apr-14 Sep. € 30.00                                      2009*

SAVONA *1B2* (2km SW Coastal) *44.29079, 8.45331* Camping Vittoria, Via Nizza 111/113, Zinola, 17100 Savona (SV) [019 881439; www.campingvittoria.com] Exit Savona heading SW, site on L on seashore immed bef Shell petrol stn behind bar Vittoria. Med, unshd; wc (some cont); shwrs; el pnts €2; shops adj; rest adj; bar; private sand beach adj; 90% statics; poss v cr; Eng spkn; adv bkg; quiet; CKE/CCI. "Excel location with views; busy site; helpful, friendly owner; pitches adj beach; clean, simple facs; ltd sm touring pitches." 1 Apr-30 Sep. € 35.00                                      2013*

**SCARLINO see Follonica** *1D3*

⊞ SECCAGRANDE (SICILY) *3C3* (Coastal) *37.43833, 13.2450* Kamemi Camping Village, Contrada Camemi Superiore, 92016 Seccagrande-di-Ribera (AG) [tel/fax 0925 69212; info@kamemicamping.it; www.kamemicamping.it] Foll sp fr S115 to Seccagrande & site. Med, hdstg, pt shd; wc; shwrs inc; el pnts (6A) €5; Indtte; rest, snacks; bar; playgrnd; 2 pools; sand beach 1km; tennis; games area; entmnt; 40% statics; dogs free; sep car park high ssn; Eng spkn; adv bkg. ♦ € 57.00 (CChq acc)                                      2014*

SENIGALLIA *2E3* (1km S Coastal) *43.70416, 13.23805* Villaggio Turistico Camping Summerland, Via Podesti 236, 60019 Senigallia (AN) [tel/fax 071 7926816; info@ campingsummerland.it; www.campingsummerland.it] Exit A14/E55 onto SS16 to Senigallia S. Site on R after lge car park at side of rd. Lge, shd; wc (cont); mv service pnt; baby facs; shwrs; el pnts (5A) €2.50; gas; Indtte; shop; rest, snacks; bar; playgrnd; 2 pools & paddling pool; beach 200m; tennis; games area; entmnt; TV rm; some statics; no dogs Jul/Aug; sep car park; poss cr; adv bkg. ♦ 1 Jun-15 Sep. € 42.00                                      2012*

SESTO CALENDE *1B1* (1km N Rural) *45.72988, 8.61989* Camping La Sfinge, Via Angera 1, 21018 Sesto-Calende (VA) [0331 924531; fax 922050; info@campeggiolasfinge. it; www.campeggiolasfinge.it] Take rd fr Sesto-Calende to Angera. Site 1km on L bef junc for Sant' Anna. Med, mkd pitch, shd; wc (mainly cont); shwrs; el pnts; gas; Indtte; shop 1km; snacks; bar; playgrnd; pool; boating; games area; 90% statics; dogs €4; poss cr; quiet; ccard acc. "Friendly owners; gd lakeside location; poss mosquitoes; poor facs; lovely pool; excel position for lake Maggiore; within reach of gd shops and rest." ♦ 1 Jan-30 Oct. € 39.00                                      2014*

**ITALY**

**SESTO CALENDE** *1B1* (4km N Rural) *45.74892, 8.59698* **Camping Okay Lido**, Via per Angera 115, Loc Lisanza, 21018 Sesto Calende (VA) [tel/fax 0331 974235; campingokay@camping-okay.com; www.camping-okay.com] Exit A8 at Sesto Calende onto SP69 N dir Angera, site sp. Med, mkd pitch, terr, pt shd; wc; chem disp; mv service pnt; private san facs avail; baby facs; shwrs €0.60; el pnts (6A) €3; lndtte; supmkt 3km; rest, snacks; bar; playgrnd; htd pool; paddling pool; lake sw; watersports; games area; games rm; wifi; entmnt; TV rm; some statics; dogs €5; Eng spkn; adv bkg; quiet. "Friendly, welcoming site; NH pitches by lakeside; gd NH for Amsterdam ferry." ♦ 22 Mar-12 Oct. € 46.00    2014*

**SESTO CALENDE** *1B1* (7.5km N Rural) *45.82712, 8.62722* **International Camping Ispra**, Via Carducci, 21027 Ispra (VA) [0332 780458; fax 784882; info@internationalcampingispra.it; www.internationalcampingispra.it] Site 1km NE of Ispra on E side of lake. Med, pt terr, shd; wc (cont); own san; shwrs €0.20; el pnts (6A) €3; lndtte; shop; tradsmn; rest, snacks; bar; BBQ; playgrnd; pool (sw caps req); beach & lake sw; boating; fishing; games area; TV rm; 90% statics; dogs €6; poss cr; Eng spkn; adv bkg; quiet; red low ssn; CKE/CCI; "Gd views of lake - muddy beach; vg rest; nice, peaceful site; friendly, helpful staff." 16 Mar-1 Nov. € 42.00    2013*

⊞ **SESTO/SEXTEN** *2E1* (3km SE Rural) *46.66806, 12.39935* **Caravan Park Sexten**, St. Josefstr. 54, 39030 Sexten / Moos [0474 710444; fax 710053; info@caravanparksexten.it; www.caravanparksexten.it] Fr S49 take S52 SE fr San Candido thro Sexten & Moos. After sh, steep climb site on W of S52 midway bet Moos & Kreuzberg pass. Lge, mkd pitch, pt sl, pt shd; wc; chem disp; mv service pnt; serviced pitches; sauna; private bthrms avail; shwrs inc; el pnts (16A) metered; gas; lndtte; shop; rest; bar; playgrnd; pool; paddling pool; solarium; tennis; wintersports; internet; entmnt; beauty & wellness treatments; TV; dogs €6; poss cr; Eng spkn; adv bkg ess high ssn; quiet; CKE/CCI. "Excel, clean facs; Waldbad worth visit; rock climbing wall; lovely scenery; mountain walks; v popular & busy site; v well managed & equipped; rest worth a visit." ♦ € 57.00    2014*

See advert on bookmark

⊞ **SETTIMO VITTONE** *1B1* (2.5km N Rural) *45.56474, 7.81668* **Camping Mombarone**, Torre Daniele, 10010 Settimo-Vittone (TO) [0125 757907; fax 757396; info@campingmombarone.it; www.campingmombarone.it] On E side of Ivrea-Aosta rd (SS26), 100m S of Pont-St Martin. Exit A5 at Quincinetto, turn R onto SP69 across bdge, R at end onto SP26 & site on L in 150m. (App fr S, sp at ent but if overshoot go on 100m to rndabt to turn). Tight ent off busy rd. Med, pt sl, pt shd; wc; chem disp; shwrs inc; el pnts (6A) €2.50; lndtte; shop 400m; tradsmn; rest adj; snacks; bar; sm pool; games area; wifi; 80% statics; poss v cr & noisy high ssn; ccard not acc; red CKE/CCI. "Gd base Aosta valley; superb views; Quincinetto medieval vill walking dist; lovely, grassy, well-kept site; ltd space for tourers; v pleasant, helpful owner who speaks gd Eng, friendly welcome; san facs immac; gd NH; rlwy stn nrby." ♦ € 29.50    2014*

**SFERRACAVALLO (SICILY) see Palermo** *3B3*

**SIBARI** *3A4* (4km E Coastal) *39.77944, 16.47889* **Camping Villaggio Pineta di Sibari**, 87070 Sibari (CS) [0981 74135; fax 74302; info@pinetadisibari.it; www.pinetadisibari.it] Exit A3 at Frascineto onto SS106, then exit at Villapiana-Scalo. Site sp on beach. Lge, pt shd; wc; mv service pnt; shwrs inc; el pnts (4A) inc; lndtte; shop; rest, snacks; bar; playgrnd; sand beach adj; tennis; cycle hire; internet; entmnt; TV rm; 20% statics; dogs €5; poss cr; poss noisy; ccard acc. "Vg beach; site in pine forest; noisy bar/music; gd touring base; watch out for low bdge on app." ♦ 17 Apr-22 Sep. € 56.50    2014*

**SIENA** *1D3* (2.5km N Urban) *43.33750, 11.33055* **Camping Siena Colleverde**, Via Scacciapensieri 47, 53100 Siena [0577 334080; fax 334005; info@sienacamping.com; www.campingcolleverde.com] Site sp ('Camping' or symbol) on all app to Siena, foll sp for 'Ospedale' (hospital). Use exit Siena Nord & foll site sp, but take care as some sp misleadingly positioned. Lge, hdg/mkd pitch, hdstg, pt sl, terr, pt shd; htd wc; chem disp; mv service pnt; shwrs inc; el pnts (10A) inc; gas; lndtte; shop; rest, snacks; bar; playgrnd; pool high ssn; wifi; TV rm; dogs; phone; bus; poss cr; Eng spkn; adv bkg; some rd noise; CKE/CCI. "Attractive location; gd views old town wall fr upper pitches (no shade); excel touring base; upgraded site - gd, well kept; modern san facs; easy access by bus to town fr site ent." ♦ 1 Mar-03 Jan. € 49.00    2013*

**SIENA** *1D3* (10km W Rural) *43.2815, 11.21905* **Camping La Montagnola**, Strada della Montagnola 39, 53100 Sovicille (SI) [tel/fax 0577 314473; montagnolacamping@libero.it; www.camping.it/toscana/lamontagnola] Fr N on S2 or S on S223 site well sp fr junc with S73. Avoid Siena town cent. Med, mkd pitch, hdstg, terr, pt shd; wc; chem disp; mv service pnt; shwrs inc; el pnts (6A) inc; gas; lndtte; shop & 5km; rest 800m; snacks; bar; playgrnd; games area; 7% statics; dogs free; phone; bus to Siena; sep car park; poss cr; adv bkg rec; Eng spkn; quiet; ccard acc (over €50); red CKE/CCI. "Super site; sm pitches; sharp stone chippings on hdstg pitches; v clean facs; vg refuge fr summer heat in wooded hills; facs poss stretched high ssn & rubbish bins o'flowing; gd walks fr site (booklet fr recep); Magic of Italy disc, conv bus service to Siena fr site." Easter-30 Sep. € 25.00    2011*

**SILVI MARINA see Pineto** *2F3*

**SINISCOLA (SARDINIA)** *3A2* (7km E Coastal) *40.57853, 9.77306* **Camping Selema**, Thiria Soliana, 08029 Santa Lucia-di-Siniscola (NU) [tel/fax 0784 819068; info@selemacamping.com; www.selemacamping.com] Sp fr coast rd S125. Lge, mkd pitch, pt sl, terr, pt shd; wc; chem disp; mv service pnt; shwrs inc; el pnts (6A) €4.50; lndtte; shop; rest, snacks; bar; playgrnd; pool; paddling pool; sand beach adj; tennis; games area; horseriding; cycle hire; wifi; 30% statics; poss cr; adv bkg; red low ssn; CKE/CCI. "Excel clean facs; site in pine forest; might be diff for lge o'fits if cr." 1 Apr-31 Oct. € 45.50    2011*

⊞ SIRACUSA (SICILY) 3C4 (4km SW Rural) 37.03841, 15.25063 Camping Agritourist Rinaura, Strada Laganelli, Loc Rinaura, SS115, 96100 Siracusa [tel/fax 0931 721224; marinas@sistenia.it] S fr Siracusa on S115 twd Avola. Turn R 300m past Hotel Albatros then immed R after rlwy x-ing. Narr lane to site in 300m. Lge, pt shd; wc; chem disp (wc); shwrs €0.60; el pnts (16A) €3; shop high ssn; rest 2km; bar; playgrnd; sand beach 2km; cycle hire; phone; bus 1km; poss cr; Eng spkn; adv bkg; noise fr nrby hol camp; red long stay/CKE/CCI. "CL-type site in lge orchard; basic but adequate san facs; rather neglected low ssn; helpful owners." ♦ € 27.00          2014*

SIRMIONE 2G2 (3km E Coastal) 45.45738, 10.64025 Tiglio, Loc. Punta Grò, 25019 Sirmione [tel/fax 030 990 4009; info@campingtiglio.it] A4 Milan-Verona, exit S11. 1st exit at rndabt onto SP13. 1st exit at next rndabt. Turn L twds Via San Martino. 1st exit at rndabt onto Via Verona. Foll sp to camp. Lge, mkd pitch, shd; wc; mv service pnt; shwrs inc; el pnts inc (4A); rest; snacks; bar; BBQ; playgrnd; 50% statics; bus adj; twin axles; poss cr; Eng spkn; adv bkg; ccard acc; CKE/CCI. "Gd site; noisy & busy but friendly; on bus rte to Verona." 16 Apr-30 Sep. € 39.00          2014*

SIRMIONE 1D2 (3km S Rural) 45.46845, 10.61028 Camping Sirmione, Via Sirmioncino 9, 25010 Colombare-di-Sirmione (BS) [030 99 04 665; fax 91 90 45; info@camping-sirmione.it; www.camping-sirmione.it] Exit S11 at traff lts sp Sirmione, in 500m R at site sp. Lge, mkd pitch, pt sl, some hdstg, pt shd; wc (cont); mv service pnt; shwrs; el pnts (6A) inc; lndtte; shop; tradsmn; rest, snacks; bar, pool; paddling pool; lake sw; private beach; watersports; games area; 30% statics; dogs; poss cr; adv bkg; quiet; ccard acc. "Excel lakeside site; facs poss stretched when site busy; excel rest, bar, pool & san facs; lovely walk to Sirmione; highly rec." ♦ 25 Mar-5 Oct. € 54.00          2014*

SISTIANA see Monfalcone 2E1

SOLCIO DE LESA see Arona 1B1

SORICO 1C1 (500m E Rural) 46.17152, 9.39302 Camping La Riva, Via Poncione 3, 22010 Sorico (CO) [tel/fax 0344 94571; info@campinglariva.com; www.campinglariva.com] Fr Lecco take SS36 twd Colico & Sondrio. At end of tunnels fork L sp Como & Menaggio. At end of dual c'way turn L onto S340 to Sorico sp Como & Menaggio. Cross bdge & site 500m down lane on L bef cent Sorico, sp Cmp Poncione & La Riva. Easiest app on SS36 on E side of lake (pt dual c'way). Rd on W side narr & congested. Med, mkd pitch, pt shd; wc (some cont); chem disp; mv service pnt; shwrs €0.80; el pnts (6A) inc; gas 50m; lndtte; sm shop; tradsmn; rest nr; snacks; bar; BBQ; playgrnd; pool; sw & rv/lakeside beach adj; canoeing; waterskiing; fishing; cycle & boat hire; games/TV rm; dogs €4 (must be kept on lead); no c'vans/m'vans over 7.50m high ssn; phone; Eng spkn; quiet; 50% statics; red low ssn; CKE/CCI. "Excel, family-run site; gd views of lake & mountains; clean, well-kept & tidy; immac san facs; v warm welcome; less commercialised than some other sites in area; cycle track to vill; poss mosquito problem in Jun; v tidy clean site; friendly helpful owners; rd fr Lugano to Como not adv for c'vans." ♦ 1 Apr-2 Nov. € 54.00 SBS - Y12          2013*

⊞ SORRENTO 3A3 (3km N Coastal) 40.63541, 14.41758 Camping I Pini, Corso Italia 242, 80063 Piano-di-Sorrento (NA) [081 8786891; fax 8788770; info@campingipini.com; www.campingipini.com] S fr Naples on A3; Exit A3 sp Castellammare di Stabia & take SS145 sp to Sorrento; pass thro vill of Meta; site on R immed over bdge; lge sp on main rd. Med, hdg/mkd pitch, pt sl, pt shd; wc; chem disp; mv service pnt; shwrs inc; el pnts (4A) inc; shops 500m; rest, snacks; bar; pool (in winter htd & open fr 8.30-15.00); beach 1km; 50% statics; dogs; bus 50m; Eng spkn; adv bkg; quiet; ccard acc; red long stay/low ssn; CKE/CCI. "Spacious site in mountains bet 2 vills; pool restricted to campers; sh walk to public transport to sites of interest; best site in Sorrento to avoid narr gridlocked rds; old, tired facs (2013); tight narr pitches." ♦ € 47.50          2014*

"We must tell The Club about that great site we found"

Get your site reports in by mid-August and we'll do our best to get your updates into the next edition.

SORRENTO 3A3 (5km NE Coastal) 40.65953, 14.41835 Camping Sant Antonio, Via Marina d'Equa 20/21, Seiano, 80069 Vico-Equense (NA) [tel/fax 081 8028570 / 081 8028576; info@campingsantantonio.it; www.campingsantantonio.it] Fr A3 exit at Castellamare-di-Stabia. Foll sp for Sorrento; app Vico-Equense take L fork thro tunnel; at end of viaduct R to Seiano-Spaggia. Last site of 3 on L down narr twisting rd after 1km (poss v congested). Access to pitches poss diff due to trees. Med, pt sl, shd; wc; chem disp; shwrs €0.50; el pnts (5A) inc; gas; lndry rm; shop; tradsmn; rest, snacks; bar; shgl beach 100m; boat hire; excursions; solarium; some statics; dogs €3 (not allowed Aug); phone; bus adj, train 800m; poss cr; Eng spkn; adv bkg; quiet; ccard acc; 10% red CKE/CCI. "Ideal base Amalfi coast, Capri, Naples; lovely harbour adj; v helpful, friendly staff; bus & train tickets avail fr site; gd rest." ♦ ltd 15 Mar-31 Oct. € 32.50          2013*

SORRENTO 3A3 (5km NE Coastal) 40.66022, 14.42048 Camping Seiano Spiaggia, Marina Aequa, Seiano, 80069 Vico-Equense [tel/fax 081 8028560; info@campingseiano.it; www.campingseiano.it] Fr A3 exit at Castellammare-di-Stabia & foll sp Sorrento. On app Vico-Equense take L fork thro tunnel & turn R at end of viaduct to Seiano-Spiagga. Site on L in 800m. Med, mkd pitch, terr, shd; htd wc; chem disp; shwrs €0.50; el pnts (6A) inc; gas; shop; tradsmn; rest, snacks adj; bar; BBQ; pool 200m; sand/shgl beach adj; no statics; dogs; bus, train to Sorrento nrby; Eng spkn; adv bkg; quiet but some rd noise at front of site; red long stay/CKE/CCI. "Clean, well-maintained site; helpful, welcoming staff; conv sightseeing base." ♦ 1 Apr-30 Sep. € 27.50          2009*

**SORRENTO** *3A3* (5km NE Coastal) *40.65990, 14.42153*
Villaggio Turistico Azzurro, Via Marina Aequa 9, 80066
Seiano-di-Vico-Equense (NA) [081 8029984; fax 8029176;
info@villaggioazzurro.net; www.villaggioazzurro.net]
Fr A3 exit sp Castellammare-di-Stabia, foll sp Sorrento. App
Vico-Equense take L fork thro tunnel. At end of viaduct turn
R to Seiano-Spaggia, Site on L in 800m down steep, narr,
twisting rd - poss congested espec at w/ends & used by buses.
Sm, mkd pitch, shd; wc (some cont); chem disp; mv service pnt;
shwrs €0.50; el pnts (6A) inc; lndtte (inc dryer); shop; tradsmn;
rest, snacks; bar; BBQ; playgrnd; shgl beach 400m; cycle hire;
some statics; dogs; bus to stn high ssn; ferry; Eng spkn; adv
bkg; rd noise; ccard acc; red long stay/CKE/CCI. "Conv Naples,
Pompei etc; v helpful owner; site in orange grove & pitching
poss diff lge o'fits due trees; vg." 1 Mar-1 Dec. € 30.00  2009*

**SORRENTO** *3A3* (10km S Coastal) *40.58389, 14.35220*
Camping Nettuno, Via A Vespucci, Marina-del-Cantone,
80068 Massa-Lubrense (NA) [081 8081051; fax 8081706;
info@villaggionettuno.it; www.villaggionettuno.it]
Fr Castellammare to Sorrento rd, turn L in Meta dir Positano.
Site well sp in dir St Agate, then Marina-del-Cantone. Tortuous
rd to site & steep, diff ent to site. Sm, shd; wc (some cont);
chem disp; mv service pnt; shwrs inc; el pnts (3A) €2.50; gas;
lndtte; shop; rest, snacks; bar; BBQ; shgl/rock beach adj; diving
cent; boat hire; tennis; internet; entmnt; TV rm; some statics;
phone; Eng spkn; quiet; ccard acc. "Lovely situation; sea views
fr some pitches (extra cost); v muddy when wet; san facs need
refurb (2009); ltd/primitive water & drainage facs; coastal
walks; gd public transport; 10% red on next site if pt of same
chain." ♦ ltd 1 Mar-2 Nov. € 32.00  2009*

## "I need an on-site restaurant"

We do our best to make sure site
information is correct, but it is always best
to check any must-have facilities are still
available or will be open during your visit.

**SORRENTO** *3A3* (1.5km SW Coastal) *40.62555, 14.36583*
Camping Nube d'Argento, Via Capo 21, 80067 Sorrento
(NA) [081 8781344; fax 8073450; info@nubedargento.
com; www.nubedargento.it] Exit a'strada for
Castellamare. Foll sp to Sorrento. At 1-way system foll sp out
of Sorrento dir Massa Lubrense on SS148. On exit Sorrento
site ent on R. App diff; rec head approx 500m beyond ent
to wide rd, make 'U' turn & rtn to site. Driving thro town
cent diff. Med, pt sl, terr, pt shd; wc (some cont); chem disp
(wc); mv service pnt; shwrs inc; el pnts (4-6A) inc; gas; lndtte;
shop; rest, snacks; bar; playgrnd; pool; boat hire; entmnt; TV;
15% statics; dogs; phone; bus/train; Eng spkn; no adv bkg;
rd noise; ccard acc; red low ssn/CKE/CCI. "Some excel pitches
with sea views, others v sm; steep, narr rds thro site, obstacles,
o'hanging trees & tight bends - suitable sm o'fits only; pitches
muddy after rain; san facs old & basic; hot water to shwrs only;
site nr sewage plant; friendly & helpful staff; excel rest; sh walk
to town; red facs low ssn." 20 Dec-10 Jan & 15 Mar-10 Nov.
€ 41.00  2010*

**SORRENTO** *3A3* (2km W Coastal) *40.62722, 14.35666*
Camping Villaggio Santa Fortunata, Via Capo 39, 80067
Capo-de-Sorrento (NA) [081 8073579; fax 8073590; info@
santafortunata.com; www.santafortunata.com] Only app
fr a'strada, exit Castellamare. Foll sp into Sorrento then sp
Massa-Lubrense. Site poorly sp fr Sorrento on R, gd wide ent. V
lge, mkd pitch, terr, shd; wc (some cont); chem disp; mv service
pnt; shwrs inc; el pnts (6A) inc; gas; lndtte; shop; rest, snacks;
bar; playgrnd; pool high ssn; internet; entmnt; TV; 50% statics;
dogs free; phone; bus adj; sep car park; poss cr; Eng spkn; red
long stay/CKE/CCI. "Gd facs; pitches sm for lge o'fits (7m+) &
poss dusty; bus fr gate, ticket fr recep; boat trips to Capri fr site
beach; noisy nr rest, disco & 18-30 tours; many scruffy statics;
facs dated; steep access & tight hairpins to some pitches."
♦ ltd 1 Apr-18 Oct. € 38.50  2009*

**SORSO see Porto Torres (SARDINIA)** *3A1*

**SOTTOMARINA see Chioggia** *2E2*

**SOVICILLE see Siena** *1D3*

**SPERLONGA** *2E4* (1km SE Coastal) *41.25514, 13.44625*
Camping Villaggio Nord-Sud, Via Flacca, Km 15.5,
04029 Sperlonga (LT) [0771 548255; fax 557240; info@
campingnordsud.it; www.campingnordsud.it] Site on
seaward side of S213 at km post 15.9. Lge sp visible fr both
dirs. Lge, mkd pitch, hdstg, shd; wc (mainly cont); chem disp;
shwrs inc; el pnts (4A) inc; lndtte; shop, rest high ssn; snacks;
bar; private sand beach; windsurfing; tennis; fitness rm;
games area; entmnt; some statics; no dogs; adv bkg; quiet;
red low ssn. "Mostly statics but great location; pleasant site;
picturesque beach." ♦ 1 Apr-31 Oct. € 48.00  2010*

⊞ **SPEZIA, LA** *1C2* (4km SE Urban) *44.10333, 9.86000*
La Spezia Camper Club, Loc Pagliari, Via Pitelli, 19138
La Spezia [0187 519154; areacampersp@libero.it] Sp to
Camper Area at intersection with Via S Bartolomeo in front
of shipyard S Marco & INMA). Adj to ferry slipway (ferries to
Sardinia, Corsica, Tunisia). Well sp fr SP331. Sm, hdstg, unshd;
wc; water; own san; chem disp; mv service pnt; 24-hr security;
no shwrs or el pnts; bus to town. "Unattractive area & site but
conv NH bef ferry or for Cinque Terre; m'vans only; gd security;
helpful staff; no rest or shops locally; managed by local
ambulance service - voluntary contributions welcome."  2009*

⊞ **SPOLETO** *2E3* (2.2km NE Urban) *47.73820, 12.74312*
Parcheggio a Pagamento "Ponzianina", Via del Tiro
a Segno 12622 [07 43 21 81] Head N on Viale Giacomo
Matteotti twd Viale Martiri della Resistenza, take 1st L onto
Viale Martiri della Resistenza, over rndbt, turn R onto SS418,
turn L onto Piazza Vittoria/SS418 and cont for 81 mtrs; turn R
onto Via Cacciatore delle Alpi cont 350 mtrs; turn L onto Viale
Trento e Trieste, then turn R onto Via del Tiro a Segno after
230 mtrs arrive at your destination sm; no facs; paid parking
site only; "200m escalator to the top of historic town and
Cathedral; gd NH; m'vans only." € 5.00  2014*

**SPOTORNO see Savona** *1B2*

**STELLA SAN GIOVANNI see Savona** *1B2*

You can now fill in site reports online

**STIA** *1D3* (5km N Rural) *43.83028, 11.70061* **Camping Falterona, Loc Montalto, 52017 Stia (AR) [tel/fax 0575 582360; info@campingfalterona.it; www. campingfalterona.it]** E fr Florence on R69 to Pontassieve, then R70 to Poppi. Turn N onto R310 to Stia then foll dir Forli to Papiano & site. Med, some hdstg, terr, pt shd; wc (some cont); chem disp; mv service pnt; shwrs; el pnts (3A) €1.50; shop; tradsmn; snacks; bar; BBQ; playgrnd; sm pool; games area; Eng spkn; quiet. "Beautiful area; vg walking." 29 May-5 Sep. € 21.50                                              2010*

**STRESA** *1B1* (4km NW Urban) *45.91246, 8.50410* **Camping Parisi, Via Piave 50, 28831 Baveno (VB) [0323 924160; campingparisi@tiscalinet.it; www.campingparisi.it]** Exit A26 at Baveno, after x-ing bdge on o'skirts Baveno, turn L off main rd bet Hotel Simplon & Agip g'ge & foll sp. Fr Stresa drive thro Baveno. At end of prom, take R fork at Dino Hotel up a minor 1-way rd (poss congested by parked cars); foll Parisi sp. Med, pt sl, pt shd; wc; chem disp; mv service pnt; shwrs inc; el pnts (6A) €3.50; lndtte; shop; supmkt 500m; rest, snacks 500m; bar adj, playgrnd; lake sw; sm shgl beach adj; boat-launching; fishing; wifi; 10% statics; dogs €4; bus; phone; poss cr; Eng spkn; adv bkg; quiet but w/end evening noise fr adj lido; red CKE/CCI. "Well-managed site on Lake Maggiore; fine views; extra for lakeside pitches; frequent lake steamers nr site; gd rests adj; long hose rec for m'van fill up; sm pitches; busy at w/end; sw in lake - supervise children; many repeat visitors; clean facs; welcoming recep; conv base for visiting Borromeo Islands." ♦ ltd 01 Apr-2 Oct. € 29.00                         2013*

**STRESA** *1B1* (4km NW Rural) *45.91185, 8.48913* **Camping Tranquilla, Via Cave 2, Oltrefuime, 28831 Baveno (VB) [tel/fax 0323 923452; info@tranquilla.com; www. tranquilla.com]** Fr N go into Baveno & turn R 200m past Hotel Splendide; fr S turn L immed after x-ing bdge. Foll brown sp to site up steep hill 1km. Med, hdg/mkd pitch, some hdstg, pt sl, terr, pt shd; wc (some cont); chem disp; mv service pnt; serviced pitch; shwrs inc; el pnts (6A) €2.60; lndtte (inc dryer); shops 1km; rest 400m; bar; shgl lake beach 800m; pool; watersports; cycle hire; entmnt at w/end; 25% statics; dogs €2.50; train to Milan 2km; car wash; Eng spkn; adv bkg; quiet; red long stay/snr citizens/CKE/CCI. "Clean, well-managed, family-owned site; v helpful staff; excel rest; sm pitches; conv Lake Maggiore; day trip by train to Milan; site was clean and comfortable the owner is pleasant and helpful." 15 Mar-15 Oct. € 26.00                                              2011*

**STRESA** *1B1* (6km NW Urban) *45.90323, 8.50807* **Camping Calaverde, Sempione 24, 28831 Baveno (VB) [0323 922721; info@calaverde.it]** Fr Stresa N on S33, site ent on R 100m after 87km post. Tight, concealed ent. Sm, pt shd; wc, chem disp; shwrs inc; el pnts inc; lndry rm; shop opp; bar; lake & private shgl beach adj; quiet but some rd/rlwy noise; Eng spkn; dogs; phone; quiet. "Helpful, friendly owner; clean site; boat-launching; gd size pitches; lake steamer 2km." € 26.00                                              2014*

⊞ **TAORMINA (SICILY)** *3C4* (10km NE Coastal) *37.93159, 15.35560* **Camping La Focetta Sicula, Via Torrente Agro, 98035 Sant' Alessio Siculo (ME) [0942 751657; fax 756708; info@lafocetta.it; www.lafocetta.it]** A'strada fr Messina to Catania, exit Roccalumera. SS114 thro Sta Teresa-di-Riva to vill of Sant' Alessio-Siculo. Sp at beg of vill. NB Many towns poorly sp. Med, mkd pitch, pt shd; wc; mv service pnt; chem disp; shwrs €0.50; el pnts (3A) €3 gas; lndtte; shop; rest, snacks; bar; playgrnd; sand beach; games area; cycle hire; wifi; entmnt; dogs free; sep car park; poss cr; quiet; red long stay/low ssn/CKE/CCI. "Popular winter site; v helpful owner." € 36.50 (CChq acc)                                              2014*

**TAORMINA (SICILY)** *3C4* (12km S Coastal) *37.74928, 15.20616* **Camping Mokambo, Via Spiaggia 211, Fondachello, 95016 Máscali (CT) [095 938731; fax 934369; info@campingmokambo.it; www.campingmokambo. it]** Exit A18/E45 at Fiumefreddo & take S114 sp Catania. In Máscali turn L twd Fondachello. At Fondachello turn R & foll site sp, site 1km on R. Med, pt shd; wc; chem disp; shwrs €0.50; el pnts (3A) €2.80; rest, snacks; BBQ; playgrnd; beach adj; games area; wifi; 10% statics; no dogs Jul/Aug; Eng spkn; quiet; ccard acc; red CKE/CCI. "V pleasant site, gd views Etna; conv beach & Taormina." ♦ 1 Apr-30 Sep. € 25.20            2009*

⊞ **TAORMINA (SICILY)** *3C4* (7km SW Coastal) *37.8047, 15.2444* **Camping Internazionale Almoetia, Via San Marco 19, 95011 Calatabiano (CT) [tel/fax 095 641936; info@campingalmoetia.it; www.campingalmoetia.it]** Exit A'strada dir Giardini Naxos. Turn S onto S114 dir Catania, foll sp L onto Via San Marco, site clearly sp. Med, pt shd; wc (some cont); chem disp; shwrs inc; el pnts (6A) €2.50; gas; lndtte; shop & 1.5km; rest, snacks; bar; BBQ; shgl beach 500m; cycle hire; tennis; canoeing; TV rm; dogs; phone; poss cr; adv bkg; quiet but noise fr bar in eve; red low ssn/long stay; CKE/CCI. "Conv Etna, Taormina; surrounded by orchards; used by tour groups in motor hotels; poss unkempt low ssn.; site well kept low ssn; excel facs; lovely beach nrby." ♦ ltd € 27.00      2012*

**TERLAGO see Trento** *1D1*

⊞ **TERMOLI** *2F4* (6km SE Coastal) *41.93861, 15.08194* **Camping La Pineta, Contrada Ramitelli 5/A, 86042 Campomarino-Lido (CB) [0875 539402; fax 538143; info@ lapinetacamping.it; www.lapinetacamping.it]** Leave A'strada A14 at Termoli onto SS16 dir Foggia. After approx 2km turn sp Lido-di-Campomarino; cross over rlwy bdge twds sea, foll site sp. Lge, pt shd; wc (some cont); shwrs; el pnts (3A) €3; gas; lndtte; shop; tradsmn; rest, snacks; bar; sand beach adj; tennis; games area; entmnt; 80% statics; no dogs Jul/Aug; poss cr; some rd & rlwy noise; red low ssn; CKE/CCI. "Friendly, family-run site; site grubby & gloomy low ssn; tight turns & narr pitches poss diff lge o'fits; pitches boggy after rain; gd san facs; hot water only in shwrs; beach access; v friendly staff; NH only." € 29.00                                              2011*

**TERNI** 2E3 (7km E Rural) 42.54801, 12.71878 **Camping Marmore, Loc Campacci, 05100 Cascata-delle-Marmore (TN)** [tel/fax 0744 67198; camping.marmore @ hotmail. it; www.campinglemarmore.com] E fr Terni on S79 dir Marmore & Rieti. Foll site sp. Med, hdstg, pt sl, shd; htd wc (some cont); chem disp; shwrs inc; el pnts inc; water free; shop on site & 1km; rest; bar; rv sw adj; watersports on lake nrby; games rm; 90% statics; dogs €4; phone; poss cr; Eng spkn; quiet. "Spectacular waterfalls adj & mountain scenery; gd; Casacata Hydro elec, well worth visiting." ♦ 1 Apr-30 Sep. € 25.00                                               2013*

**TERRACINA** 2E4 (4km W Coastal) 41.28285, 13.19610 **Camping Internazionale Badino (Naturist), Via Badino, Km 4.8, Porto Badino, 04019 Terracina (LT)** [tel/fax 0773 764430] Fr Latina on S148 (SS Mediana) foll sp Port Badino & site. Med, mkd pitch, pt shd; wc; shwrs €1; chem disp; el pnts (1.50A) inc; gas; lndtte; shop, rest 100m; bar; sand beach adj; games area; solarium; no dogs Jul/Aug; quiet. ♦ 1 Apr-15 Oct. € 35.00                                       2009*

**TEULADA (SARDINIA)** 3B1 (7km SW Coastal) 38.92669, 8.71153 **Camping Proturismo Portu Tramatzu, 09019 Teulada (CA)** [0709 283027; fax 283828; coop. proturismo@libero.it] Sp fr Teulada on SP71 & fr coast rd. Med, terr, pt shd; wc; mv service pnt; shwrs; el pnts (5A) inc; gas; lndtte; shop; rest, snacks, bar high ssn; BBQ; playgrnd; sand beach adj; games area; entmnt; some statics; dogs €3; sep car park high ssn; Eng spkn; adv bkg; red CKE/CCI. "Vg." ♦ Easter-31 Oct. € 33.00                                       2010*

⊞ **TONARA** 3A1 (200m N Rural) 40.02851, 9.17578 **Camping Sa Colonia, Via Muggianeddu 4, 08039 Tonara (NU)** [03921 282340; info@campingsacolonia.it; www. campingsacolonia.it] Sp rte unsuitable lge car + c'van o'fits or v lge m'vans. Avoid town cent streets - v narr & steep. Med, mkd pitch, terr, shd; wc; chem disp (wc); shwrs; el pnts (5A) inc; shop in town; rest; bar; playgrnd; no statics; Eng spkn; quiet. CKE/CCI. "Mountain scenery; rds gd but steep, twisty & slow." € 15.00      2010*

**TORBOLE** 1D1 (Urban) 45.8725, 10.87361 **Camping Al Porto, Via Al Cor, 38069 Tórbole (TN)** [tel/ fax 0464 505891; info@campingalporto.it; www. campingalporto.it] On ent Tórbole fr S take rd twd Riva-del-Garda for approx 600m. Petrol stn & car park on R, turn L into narr lane after shops; site sp. Med, mkd pitch, pt shd; wc (some cont); chem disp; mv service pnt; shwrs inc; el pnts (5A) inc; lndtte; shops 300m; tradsmn; rest 100m; snacks; bar; BBQ; playgrnd; lake sw & htd beach 100m; watersports; dogs €2.50; poss cr; quiet; red long stay/low ssn; CKE/CCI. "Excel san facs; excel site; secure; helpful staff; vill has many rest & sportling locations." ♦ 14 Mar-2 Nov. € 33.00      2014*

**TORRE DEL LAGO PUCCINI see Viareggio** 1C3

**TORTOLI (SARDINIA)** 3A2 (5km E Coastal) 39.90810, 9.67830 **Camping Orri, Loc Orri, 08048 Tortoli (NU)** [0782 624695; fax 624685; camping.orri@tiscali.it; www. campingorri.it] E fr Tortoli to Arbatax, site sp along coast rd. Med, shd; wc (some cont); chem disp; mv service pnt; shwrs inc; el pnts (4A) €2.50; lndtte; shop; tradsmn; rest, snacks; bar; BBQ; playgrnd; pool; paddling pool; sand beach adj; lake fishing; cycle hire; games area; horseriding 1km; entmnt; TV rm; statics; dogs; adv bkg; quiet; red CKE/CCI. "Eng spkn." ♦ 1 May-20 Sep. € 42.00 (CChq acc)                                    2011*

**TOSCALANO MADERNO** 1D1 (N Urban) 45.63777, 10.61277 **Camping Toscolano, Via Religione 88, 25088 Toscolano-Maderno (BS)** [0365 641584; fax 642519; toscolano@ hg-hotels.com; www.hghotels.com] Site at lakeside bet Gargnano & Maderno. Narr archway on app. Lge, pt shd; wc (some cont); shwrs inc; el pnts (3A) inc; gas; lndtte; shop; rest, snacks; bar; playgrnd; pool; paddling pool; shgl beach & lake sw; tennis; games area; golf 5km; entmnt; 50% statics; dogs €3.50; poss v cr; adv bkg rec. ♦ 1 Apr-30 Sep. € 34.50 2010*

**TRASAGHIS see Gemona del Friuli** 2E1

**TRENTO** 1D1 (12km NW Rural) 46.11111, 11.04805 **Camping Laghi di Lamar, Via alla Selva Faeda 15, 38070 Terlago (TN)** [0461 860423; campeggio@laghidilamar.com; www. laghidilamar.com] Head W fr Trento for 10km on SS45b dir Riva-del-Garda/Brescia. Turn R twd Monte-Terlago; site sp on R. Last section via SS45 v steep. Med, terr, pt shd; wc (some cont); chem disp; mv service pnt; shwrs inc; el pnts (6A) inc; gas; lndtte (inc dryer); shop; rest 100m; rest, snacks; bar; BBQ; playgrnd; pool; lake sw 700m; games area; games rm; cycle hire; wifi; TV; 30% statics; dogs €2.50; phone; Eng spkn; quiet; ccard acc; red snr citizens/CKE/CCI. "Excel site." ♦ 1 Apr-15 Oct. € 27.50                                       2010*

**TREPORTI see Cavallino** 2E2

⊞ **TRIESTE** 2F1 (4km N Rural) **Camping Obelisco, Strada Nuova Opicina 37, 34016 Opicina (TS)** [040 212744; fax 212744; info@campeggiobelisco.it; www. campeggiobelisco.it] Sp fr S58. Med, hdstg, pt sl, terr, shd; wc (cont); own san; mv service pnt; shwrs inc; el pnts €2.50; rest, snacks; bar 1km; playgrnd; 95% statics; dogs €2.50; Eng spkn; quiet; CKE/CCI. "V steep, narr, twisting ent/exit to site - suitable sm c'vans only & diff in wet; excel views Trieste harbour; interesting tram ride into city fr obelisk; demanding up hill walk to top of site, both Turkish & European wcs." € 18.00                                       2011*

**TROGHI see Firenze** 1D3

**TROPEA** 3B4 (7km NE Coastal) 38.70610, 15.97024 **Villaggio Camping Sambalon, Via del Mare, 89868 Marina-di-Zambrone (VV)** [0963 392828; fax 45385; info@sambalon. com; www.sambalon.com] Fr N exit A3 at Pizzo Calabro onto S522 dir Tropea for 20km. Foll sp Marina di Zambrone & site. Med, mkd pitch, some hdstg, pt shd; wc; mv service pnt; shwrs; el pnts; lndtte; shop on site & 1km; rest, snacks; bar; playgrnd; sand beach adj; wifi; entmnt; TV; some statics; dogs; adv bkg; quiet. 1 Jun-30 Sep. (CChq acc)                     2012*

UGENTO *3A4* (6km S Coastal) *39.87331, 18.14261* Camping Riva di Ugento, Loc Fontanelle, 73059 Ugento (LE) [0833 933600; fax 933601; info@rivadiugento.it; www. rivadiugento.it] Fr Bari take Brindisi rd to Lecce, then SS101 to Gallipoli, then SR274 twd Sta Maria di Leuca & exit at Ugento. Turn R at traff lts on SS91, site well sp. V lge, mkd pitch, shd; htd wc (some cont); mv service pnt; shwrs inc; el pnts (3A) inc; gas; lndtte (inc dryer); shop; rest, snacks; bar; BBQ; playgrnd; pool; paddling pool; sand beach adj; watersports; tennis; cycle hire; games area; horseriding 1km; boat & cycle hire; wifi; TV rm; cinema; excursions; 10% statics; no dogs; no adv bkg; ccard acc. "Excel beach; some pitches at water's edge; tranquil site." ♦ 15 May-30 Sep. € 45.00 (CChq acc)                                            2011*

URBINO *2E3* (2.5km E Rural) *43.73055, 12.65710* Camping Pineta, Via Ca' Mignore, 5, 61029 San Donato (PS) [0722 4710; fax 4734; campeggiopinetaurbino@email. it; www.camping-pineta-urbino.it] Site sp fr rndabout just below city walls on S423 fr Pesaro. Med, terr, pt shd; wc (mainly cont); chem disp (wc); shwrs inc; el pnts (4-6A) inc (long lead poss req); lndtte; shop in ssn; tradsmn; supmkt 1km; rest, bar 2km; pool; sand beach 20km; dogs €3; bus to town (ltd); Eng spkn; adv bkg red Jul/Aug; quiet; ccard acc; red long stay/low ssn. "Lovely setting on hill o'looking Urbino; v interesting area; sm, steep, tight pitches unsuitable lge o'fits; tired, old facs poss stretched; gd pool." Easter-30 Sep. € 50.00                                               2010*

⊞ URBISAGLIA *2E3* (6km NE Rural) Centro Agrituristico La Fontana, Via Selva 8, Abbadia-di-Fiastra, 62010 La Fontana (MC) [tel/fax 0733 514002] Fr SP77 turn S to Abbadia-di-Fiastra onto SP78. On reaching Abbadia turn L & immed R, then uphill above Monastery for 2km & foll sp to site on R just after sharp RH bend. Sm, terr, pt shd; wc; chem disp; mv service pnt; shwrs inc; el pnts (6A) inc; rest, snacks; bar; BBQ; playgrnd; sand beach 35km; TV rm. "Fair sh stay/NH; CL-type site on farm; not suitable lge o'fits; attractive countryside; v helpful owners." ♦ € 21.00          2012*

VADA see Cecina *1D3*

VALLECROSIA *1B3* (Coastal) *43.78411, 7.63368* Camping Vallecrosia, Lungomare Marconi 149, 18019 Vallecrosia (IM) [tel/fax 0184 295591; info@campingvallecrosia.com; www.campingvallecrosia.com] Fr SS1 Via Aurelia cont W dir Bordighera & Vallecrosia, foll sp. Site on seafront. Fr A10 exit at Ventimiglia & take SS1 dir San Remo, foll site sp. Do not take m'way exits at San Remo or Bordighera as rds unsuitable c'vans & m'vans. Sm, mkd pitch, hdstg, pt shd; htd wc; chem disp; mv service pnt; shwrs inc; el pnts (6A) €3; lndtte; shop; rest, snacks, bar 200m; playgrnd; shgl beach 100m; wifi; 25% statics; dogs €3; phone; quiet; CKE/CCI. "Lovely, well-spaced site; excel beach opp with beach bar; popular with windsurfers; helpful staff; v clean san facs; longer vans may req manhandling onto mkd pitches; ideal NH bet Italy & France." ♦ 1 Apr-30 Sep. € 30.00                                          2010*

VALLEDORIA (SARDINIA) *1B4* (1km W Coastal) *40.93333, 8.81694* Camping La Foce, Via Ampurias 1, 07039 Valledoria (SS) [079 582109; fax 582191; info@foce.it; www.foce.it] Fr Porto Torres N via Castelsardo to Valledoria, site sp twd sea. Lge, shd; wc (some cont); chem disp; mv service pnt; shwrs inc; el pnts (4A) €1.50; gas; lndtte (inc dryer); shop; rest, snacks; bar; no BBQ; playgrnd; pool; paddling pool; sand beach adj; fishing; canoeing; watersports; tennis; cycle hire; games aea; wifi; 10% statics; dogs €3; sep car park; poss cr; adv bkg; ccard acc. 25 Apr-30 Sep. € 35.00 (CChq acc)                                           2011*

VALSAVARENCHE *1B1* (5km S Rural) *45.54889, 7.21250* Camping Gran Paradiso, Loc Plan de la Pesse 1, 11010 Valsavarenche (AO) [tel/fax 0165 905801; campinggranparadiso@libero.it; www. campinggranparadiso.it] Exit A5 Aosta Ovest onto S26 W dir Monte Bianco. In 3km at Villeneuve turn S & foll sp Valsavarenche for approx 18km. Approx 5km after passing cent of Degioz site sp just bef rd crosses rv. Sm, mkd pitch, terr, shd; wc; chem disp; mv service pnt; fam bthrm; shwrs inc; el pnts (3A) €2; lndtte (inc dryer); tradsmn; snacks; bar; BBQ; cooking facs; games area; games rm; dogs; phone; Eng spkn; adv bkg; quiet. "Well-situated, scenic site for hiking, canyoning, rafting; guided walks; excel." ♦ ltd 1 Jun-30 Sep. € 18.00          2010*

VARIGOTTI see Finale Ligure *1B2*

## "Satellite navigation makes touring much easier"

Remember most sat navs don't know if you're towing or in a larger vehicle – always use yours alongside maps and site directions.

⊞ VENEZIA *2E2* (5km S Coastal) *45.41916, 12.25666* Camping Fusina, Via Moranzani 79, 30030 Fusina (VE) [041 5470055; fax 5470050; info@campingfusina.com; www.campingfusina.com] Exit A4 at sp Ravenna/Chiogga onto SS309 S, & foll sp to site. Take care when turning into rd leading to Fusina as L-hand turning lane used by locals for o'taking. Lge, pt shd; htd wc; chem disp; mv service pnt; shwrs inc; el pnts (6A) inc (poss rev pol); gas; lndtte; shop; rest, snacks; bar; playgrnd; boat hire; games area; wifi; entmnt; TV rm; 50% statics; dogs free; poss cr; no adv bkg; some ship & aircraft noise + noise fr bar & adj indus complex; ccard acc; red CKE/CCI. "Pleasant, busy site; some pitches o'looking lagoon; many backpackers, educational groups & 18-30s; gd san facs; gd public transport/boat dir to Venice; helpful staff; poss mosquitoes; some pitches diff due trees & soft when wet; Magic of Europe discount (ask on arr); ltd facs low ssn & poss travellers." € 47.40                                      2014*

**VENEZIA** *2E2* (12km W Rural) *45.45222, 12.18305* **Camping Serenissima, Via Padana 334/A, 30176 Malcontenta [041 5386498 / 041 921850; fax 920286; info@ campingserenissima.it; www.campingserenissima.com]** Exit A4 at Oriago/Mira exit. At 1st rndabt foll sp Ravenna/ Venezia; at next rndabt take 1st exit sp Padova/Riviera del Brenta (SR11) twd Oriago. Rv on L, site on R in approx 2km. Med, mkd pitch, pt shd; htd wc (some cont); chem disp; mv service pnt; shwrs inc; el pnts (16A) inc; gas; lndtte; shop; supmkt 5km; rest, snacks; bar; playgrnd; pool 3km; sand beach 10km; cycle & boat hire; wifi; 25% statics; dogs free; phone; poss cr; gd Eng spkn; adv bkg; quiet; ccard acc; red snr citizens; CKE/CCI. "Bus to Venice - buy tickets on site; friendly, helpful owners; efficient recep; some sm pitches; excel, v clean san facs; poss mosquitoes; conv Padova; highly rec for Venice." ♦ 14 Apr-7 Nov. € 44.40                                                 2014*

**VENEZIA (VENICE)** See also sites listed under Cavallino, Lido di Jesolo, Mestre and Punta Sabbioni.

**VERBANIA** *1B1* (6km NE Rural) *45.97659, 8.63385* **Camping La Sierra, Corso Belvedere, 337 - 28823 Ghiffa (VB) [0333 7815534; info@campinglasierra.it; www. campinglasierra.it]** Fr Verbania N on SS34 dir Cannobio, site on L just after exit fr Ghiffa. Sm, mkd pitch, hdstg, terr, pt shd; wc; chem disp; shwrs inc; el pnts (6A) inc; lndtte; shop 1km; tradsmn; rest, snacks; bar; BBQ; playgrnd; shgl beach adj; fishing; watersports; 8% statics; dogs €3; bus; phone; poss cr; Eng spkn; adv bkg; rd noise; CKE/CCI. "Vg site; views of lake; steep walk to sans facs fr upper terraces." 1 Mar-1 Nov. € 33.00                                                                2013*

**VERBANIA** *1B1* (4km W Rural) *45.95365, 8.47698* **Camping La Quiete, Via Turati 72, Lago di Mergozzo, 28924 Fondotoce (VB) [0323 496013; fax 496139; info@ campinglaquiete.it; www.campinglaquiete.it]** Exit A26 at Gravellona Toce onto SS34 to Fondotoce, then SP54 to Lago di Mergozzo. Site on E edge Lago di Mergozzo, sp. Lge, mkd pitch, pt shd; wc; chem disp; mv service pnt; shwrs; el pnts (6A) €3; lndtte; shop; rest; bar; lake sw adj; canoing; fishing; windsurfing; games area; games rm; golf 2km; some statics; dogs €5.50; some Eng spkn; adv bkg rec; quiet; ccard not acc. "Lovely site with view of alps & lake; extra for lakeside pitches; friendly, welcoming owner; excel." 1 Apr-30 Sep. € 27.00                                                                2010*

**VERBANIA** *1B1* (6km W Rural) *45.93731, 8.48615* **Camping Conca d'Oro, Via 42 Martiri 26, 28835 Feriolo di Baveno (VB) [0323 28116; fax 28538; info@concadoro.it; www. concadoro.it]** Foll S33 NW fr Stresa, thro Bavena to Feriolo. At traff lts in Feriolo fork R, sp Verbania & in 800m immed over rv bdge, turn R into site. Clearly sp. Lge, mkd pitch, pt sl, shd; wc; chem disp; mv service pnt; shwrs inc; el pnts (6A) inc; lndtte; supmkt; rest, snacks; bar; playgrnd; private sand beach adj; windsurfing; games area; cycle hire; internet; entmnt; 10% statics; dogs €5.00 (not acc Jul/Aug); Eng spkn; adv bkg; quiet; ccard acc; CKE/CCI. "Helpful staff; gd, clean, modern san facs; discount for local services; extra for lakeside pitches; excel site." ♦ 29 Mar-29 Sep. € 48.00                            2013*

**VERBANIA** *1B1* (6km W Urban) *45.93283, 8.48266* **Camping Orchidea, Via 42 Martiri, 28835 Feriolo (VB) [0323 28257; fax 28573; info@campingorchidea.it; www. campingorchidea.it]** Exit A26/E62 sp Baveno onto SS33 dir Verbania. Past traff lts in Feriolo to site on R in 500m. Lge, pt shd; wc; mv service pnt; baby facs; shwrs; el pnts (6A) €2.60; gas; lndtte; shop; rest, snacks; bar; playgrnd; sand beach & lake sw adj; cycle hire; wifi; 25% statics; dogs €5; poss cr; adv bkg ess high ssn; quiet but rd noise; ccard acc. "Beautiful situation at lake end, splendid views; lake shore walk to vill; 3 gd rests in 10 mins walk; boats fr Stresa to Locarno; sm pitches." 1 Mar-1 Oct. € 32.00                                                         2009*

**VERONA** *1D2* (1.5km N Rural) *45.44985, 11.00415* **Camping San Pietro, Via Castel San Pietro 2, 37100 Verona [tel/fax 045 592037; info@campingcastelsanpietro.com; www. campingcastelsanpietro.com]** Exit A4/E70 to San Martino-Buon-Albergo & foll S11 dir Verona cent, site sp adj Castel San Pietro. Sm, mkd pitch, hdstg, shd; wc (cont); chem disp (wc); shwrs inc; no el pnts; lndtte; shop; rest 500m; snacks; bar; BBQ; wifi; no dogs; some statics; bus 1km; no vehicles/o'fits over 7m; adv bkg ess; some rd noise. "Basic site in park, more suited to tents or sm m'vans only - no el pnts; beautiful views over city; easy walk to town cent, but many steps; poor & ltd san facs." ♦ 2 May-30 Sep. € 41.00                             2014*

⊞ **VERONA** *1D2* (1km NE Urban) *45.45150, 10.95456* **Camper Park Verona, Via Eraclea, 37100 Verona [0348 7328589; camperparkverona@libero.it]** Fr W on SR11 Corso Milano, site sp to L behind Esselunga supmkt; sp. Sm, unshd; el pnts; water fill. "New m'van parking area; v conv town cent."                                                           2012*

⊞ **VERONA** *1D2* (10km W Rural) *45.44553, 10.83443* **Camping El Bacàn, Via Verona 11, 37010 Palazzolo di Sona (VR) [348 9317204; fax 045 6080708; info@ el-bacan.it; www.el-bacan.it]** Exit A4 onto A22 N & foll for Brescia (W) on SR11. Site in 7km on R, sp 150m bef site ent. Sm, hdg/mkd pitch, unshd; wc (cont); chem disp; el pnts (16A) inc; lndtte; shop (farm produce); tradsmn; rest, snacks, bar 2km; BBQ; playgrnd; internet; TV; no statics; dogs; bus 1km; Eng spkn; adv bkg; quiet, some rd noise; cc acc; CKE/ CCI. "Charming pleasant friendly site on working farm; conv Verona, Lake Garda; helpful, friendly owner & staff; excel farm shop; highly rec." ♦ € 22.50                                   2014*

**VIAREGGIO** *1C3* (2km S Coastal) *43.85133, 10.25963* **Camping Viareggio, Via Comparini 1, 55049 Viareggio (LU) [0584 391012; fax 395462; info@campingviareggio. it; www.campingviareggio.it]** Fr sea front at Viareggio, take rd on canal sp Livorno; after x-ing canal bdge turn L (but not immed on canal) & 2nd R to site in 2km. Lge, shd; wc (some cont); chem disp; mv service pnt; baby facs; shwrs €0.50; el pnts (4A) (poss rev pol); gas; lndtte; shop; rest; bar; playgrnd; pool €3; beach 800m; games area; TV; internet; phone; dogs €4 (not permitted Aug); adv bkg; quiet; red low ssn/CKE/CCI. "Gd site & facs; hot water to shwrs only; cycle rte/footpath to town." ♦ 1 Apr-4 Oct. € 32.00                                     2014*

VIAREGGIO *1C3* (4km S Rural) *43.82693, 10.27182* **Camping Dei Tigli**, Viale del Tigli 54, 55048 Torre-del-Lago Puccini (LU) [0584 359182; fax 341278; info@campingdeitigli.com; www.campingdeitigli.com] Leave A11/12 at Viareggio, foll rd parallel to a'strada sp Torre-del-Lago-Puccini & after 6km turn R twd Torre. When thro town turn L at traff lts, over rlwy, L at rndabt & foll brown camp sp. V lge, hdg pitch, pt shd; wc; chem disp (wc); shwrs €0.50; el pnts (5A) inc; gas; lndtte; shop; rest, snacks; bar; BBQ; sand beach 1.2km; entmnt; 50% statics; dogs €6 (only small); phone; poss cr w/end; Eng spkn; adv bkg; quiet but poss disco noise high ssn; ccard acc; red long stay/CKE/CCI. "Pleasant, friendly site; facs old but clean; sep area for tourers; cycle path to town cent." 1 Apr-30 Sep. € 35.00 (3 persons) (CChq acc) 2011*

VIAREGGIO *1C3* (5km S Coastal) *43.82920, 10.2727* **Camping Italia**, Viale dei Tigli 52, 55048 Torre-del-Lago Puccini (LU) [0584 359828; fax 341504; info@campingitalia.net; www.campingitalia.net] Fr A12 N exit sp Viareggio, fr S exit Pisa N onto SS1 & turn twd Torre del Lago at S junc, site well sp thro vill. Do not turn L at vill cent but cont for 2km N, then L at rlwy bdge. At rndabt turn L, site on R in 250m. Avoid Viareggio town cent. Med, shd; wc (some cont); chem disp; mv service pnt; shwrs €0.50; el pnts (6A) €1.30; gas; lndtte (inc dryer); shop; rest, snacks; bar; lge playgrnd; pool; sand beach 1.5km; tennis; cycle hire; wifi; entmnt; TV rm; some statics (sep area); no dogs Jun-Aug; sep car park; Eng spkn; adv bkg; noisy w/ends high ssn; ccard acc; red low ssn; "Vg for Lucca - Puccini's birthplace; bus tickets fr site for Pisa & Lucca; some pitches diff for lge o'fits due trees & low branches; gd clean facs; poss problem with mosquitoes." ♦ 16 Apr-25 Sep. € 42.50 2014*

VIAREGGIO *1C3* (6km S Rural) *43.83105, 10.2707* **Camping Europa**, Viale dei Tigli, 55048 Torre-del-Lago Puccini (LU) [0584 350707; fax 342592; info@europacamp.it; www.europacamp.it] Exit A12/E80 at Pisa Nord exit, foll sp dir Viareggio to Torre-del-Lago & turn L. Site well sp fr vill cent. Lge, shd; wc (some cont); shwrs €0.40; el pnts (3A) inc (poss rev pol); gas; lndtte; shop on site & 2km; rest, snacks; bar; playgrnd; pool; paddling pool; sand beach 1km; tennis; games area; cycle hire; entmnt; 50% statics; dogs €2 (not acc Jul/Aug); poss cr; Eng spkn; adv bkg; quiet; ccard acc; red long stay/CKE/CCI. "Excel, clean, tidy site in regional coastal park; facs poss stretched when site full; helpful, friendly staff; poss mosquitoes; 1km to bus to Pisa, Lucca, Florence." ♦ Easter-1 Oct. € 33.00 2011*

**VICCHIO see Borgo San Lorenzo** *1D3*

VICENZA *1D2* (5km E Urban) *45.5175, 11.60222* **Camping Vicenza**, Strada Pelosa 239, 36100 Vicenza [0444 582311; fax 582434; info@campingvicenza.it; www.vicenza.vi.it/camping/] Exit A4 Vicenza Est dir Torri di Quartesole; turn R immed after toll; site on L 300m fr Vicenza exit, hidden behind Viest Quality Inn. Fr city foll sp Padua & a'strada; sp. Med, pt sl, pt shd; wc (some cont); chem disp; mv service pnt; baby facs; shwrs inc; el pnts (3A) inc (rev pol); lndtte; shops 1km; rest, snacks 500m; bar; BBQ; playgrnd; tennis; cycle hire; internet; entmnt; bus; Eng spkn; adv bkg; rd noise; 10% red long stay; ccard acc; red CKE/CCI. "Cycle path to interesting town; poss ant problem; functional site." ♦ ltd 1 Apr-30 Sep. € 32.20 2013*

**VICO EQUENSE see Sorrento** *3A3*

VIESTE *2G4* (2km N Coastal) *41.89901, 16.14964* **Camping Punta Lunga**, Loc Defensola, 71019 Vieste (FG) [0884 706031/ 0884 706032; fax 706910; puntalunga@ puntalonga.com; www.puntalunga.it] N fr Vieste 1.5km fr end of long beach, turn R at traff lts down narr lane. Site sp. Lge, mkd pitch, pt terr, pt shd; htd wc (some cont); chem disp; mv service pnt; baby facs; shwrs inc; el pnts (3-5A) inc; gas; lndtte; shop; rest, snacks; playgrnd; beach adj; windsurfing; canoeing; cycle hire; wifi; entmnt; TV; 15% statics (sep area); no dogs; phone; bus; sep car park; poss cr; Eng spkn; adv bkg; quiet; ccard acc; red low ssn/CKE/CCI. "Friendly, helpful staff; well-run site on lovely cove; tight pitches - beware pitch marker posts; v clean facs; rec use bottled water; beautiful coastal area; gd rest; lovely cove; excel beaches." 30 May-15 Sep. € 49.00 2014*

VIESTE *2G4* (2km S Coastal) *41.85914, 16.17405* **Camping Adriatico**, Lungomare. Enrico Mattei 110, 71019 Vieste (FG) [tel/fax 0884 700954; info@campingadriatico.it; www.campingadriatico.it] S fr Vieste on coast rd SP53, site on both sides of rd. Med, mkd pitch, pt shd; wc (cont); chem disp; mv service pnt; shwrs inc; el pnts (6A) inc; lndtte; shop; tradsmn; rest, snacks; bar; BBQ; playgrnd; sand beach adj; windsurfing; games area; wifi; some statics; phone; bus; poss cr; Eng spkn; adv bkg; red low ssn. "Vg family-run site." ♦ ltd 1 Apr-31 Oct. € 33.50 2014*

**VIGNALE RIOTORTO see Follonica** *1D3*

**VILLANOVA D'ALBENGA see Albenga** *1B2*

## "There aren't many sites open at this time of year"

If you're travelling outside peak season remember to call ahead to check site opening dates – even if the entry says 'open all year'.

⊞ VIPITENO/STERZING *1D1* (S Urban) *46.88737, 11.43098* **Autoporto**, 00098 Vipiteno [0472 760620; info@hotel-brenner.com] S fr Brenner Pass approx 17km, take exit immed bef toll booths Vipiteno & foll sp 'Autoporto'. Site well sp fr toll booth - 500m. Can also be accessed fr SS12. Push button on site barrier if office clsd. Med, hdstg, pt shd; wc; mv service pnt; shwrs; el pnts inc; shop, rest adj. "Excel NH for c'vans or m'vans; conv Austrian border." € 15.00 2009*

VIVERONE *1B2* (3km S Rural) *45.40544, 8.05313* **Camping Internazionale del Sole**, Loc Comuna 45, 13886 Viverone (BI) [tel/fax 0161 98169; www.campeggiodelsole.com] Exit A5/A4 m'way network at junc for Cavaglia/Santhia. Foll S143 to Cavaglia approx 4km. At Cavaglia join S228 for Viverone/Ivrea. Immed after Viverone town sp turn L at rndabt. After 2km site sp strt on past hotel on R, recep on L. Lge, terr, pt sl, pt shd; wc (some cont); chem disp; shwrs €1; el pnts (3A) €1.50; lndtte; shop; rest, snacks; bar; playgrnd; lake sw; boating & fishing in lake; games rm; 90% statics; poss cr; adv bkg; poss noisy; red CKE/CCI. "Conv Aosta Valley, National Park & mountain resorts below Matterhorn; lovely situation by lake but facs minimal for such a lge site, espec low ssn; NH only." 1 Apr-30 Sep. € 21.50 2010*

---

Site report forms at back of guide      *Last year of report   **415**

**VIVERONE** *1B2* (1km SW Rural) *45.41644, 8.04874* **Camping Rocca, Via Lungo Lago 35, 13040 Viverone (BI)** [tel/ fax 0161 98416; laroccaviverone@hotmail.com; www. la-rocca.org] On lakeside sp fr S228. Not well sp. Sm, pt shd; wc (mainly cont); chem disp; mv service pnt; shwrs €0.50; el pnts (2A) €1.80; shop 1km; rest, snacks; bar; playgrnd; lake sw & beach adj; 50% statics; phone; CKE/CCI. "Somewhat tatty (06/09); NH only." ♦ 1 Apr-30 Sep. € 22.00      2011*

**VOLLAN/FOIANA see Merano/Meran** *1D1*

**VOLTERRA** *1D3* (1km NW Rural) *43.41271, 10.8509* **Camping Le Balze, Via di Mandringa 15, 56048 Volterra (PI)** [tel/ fax 0588 87880; campinglebalze@hotmail.it; www. campinglebalze.com] Take Pisa rd (S68) fr town; site clearly sp ('Camping' or symbol) after 1km. Watch out for R turn at sharp L corner. Med, pt sl, terr, pt shd; wc (some cont); chem disp; shwrs inc; el pnts (6A) inc; gas; lndtte; shop; tradsmn; supmkt 300m; rest 150m; bar; pool; paddling pool; dogs free; bus adj; poss cr; Eng spkn; no adv bkg; quiet; ccard acc; CKE/CCI. "Beautifully situated with views of Volterra & hills; gd, modern san facs; select own pitch; easy walk to town; Etruscan walls just outside site; excel site." ♦ 1 Apr-15 Oct. € 38.00      2012*

**ZAMBRONE see Tropea** *1B4*

France and Andorra
Central and South East Europe, Benelux and Scandinavia
Spain and Portugal

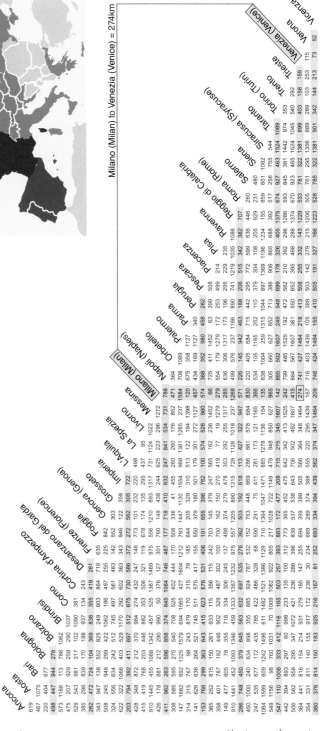

Milano (Milan) to Venezia (Venice) = 274km

Map 1

E F G H

AUSTRIA

terselva di
pra/Antholz Obertal
Dobbiaco/
Toblach
Sesto/Sexten

ORTINA D'AMPEZZO

Forni di Sopra

SLOVENIA

Gemona
del Friuli

13

di Piave

A23

A28
A27

Monfalcone
Aquileia
ignano Sabbiadoro
Bibione
Caorle
Lido di Jesolo
Cavallino
Punta Sabbioni

Grado

TRIESTE

58

Chioggia

Comacchio

Marina di Ravenna

RAVENNA

Cervia
Cesenatico
Bellaria
San
rino
Riccione
Pesaro
icara
SAN
MARINO
Urbino
18
Senigallia
ANCONA
Ostra

Citta di
Castello
Gubbio
ignano sul Trasimeno
Magione
PERUGIA
glione
Assisi
ago
Bevagna
Giano
'Umbria
Preci
vieto

18

Urbisaglia

Sarnano
Castelsantangelo
sul Nera
Ascoli
Piceni

Porto Recanati

Porto San
Giorgio
A14
Cupra Marittima

Martinsicuro

Giulianova Lido
Roseto degli Abruzzi
Pineto

Narni
Terni
A1
Caprarola
Fiano
Romano
racciano
A24
ROMA
Pescasseroli
Opi
Barrea
Roccaraso
Bomba
Casalbordino
A25
Vasto
Marina di Montenero
Termoli
A14

L'AQUILA
A24
PESCARA
Ortona

5

Rodi
Garganico
89
Peschici
Vieste

Terracina
Sperlonga
Marina di
Minturno

Pescasseroli
17
82
5

650
647

San Giovanni
Rotondo
90
FOGGIA
Mattinata
Manfredonia

A1

85
17

17
89

16
A14
98
96
Giovinazzo
BARI
A16
Monopoli

148
156

ADRIATIC
SEA

CROATIA

BOSNIA AND
HERZEGOVINA

SARAJEVO

Split

San Valentino
alla Muta
Mals/Malles
Venosta
38
Prato allo
Stelvio
St Moritz

Vipiteno/Sterzing

Bressanone/
Brixen

Brunico/
Bruneck

Merano/
Meran
Chiusa/
Klausen
Naturno/
Naturns
BOLZANO/BOZEN
Peio
Dimaro

San Michele
All'Adige
Fie/Vols
Canazei
Pozza di Fassa
Ora/Auer

Sorico
38
Edolo
Molveno
Pinzolo
TRENTO
Pieve
Tesino
Imer
Levico Terme

Gravedona
Menaggio
Bellagio

Lecco

Pisogne

Pieve di Ledro
Riva
del Garda

Arco
Torbole
Malcesine

Arsie

Bergamo

Marone
Iseo
Idro

Toscolano-
Maderno
Monza
San Felice del Benaco
Manerba del Garda
Sirmione
DESENZANO
DEL GARDA
A4
Peschiera
del Garda
Lazise
VERONA

Bardolino
VICENZA
A4
A31

C

D

0          50 kms
0          25 mls

A22

A4

Pula

0956951082

Map 2

Map 3

# REGIONS AND PROVINCES OF ITALY

**ABRUZZO**
Chieti
L'Aquila
Pescara
Teramo

**BASILICATA**
Matera
Potenza

**CALABRIA**
Catanzaro
Cosenza
Crotone
Reggio di Calabria
Vibo Valentia

**CAMPANIA**
Avellino
Benevento
Caserta
Napoli
Salerno

**EMILIA-ROMAGNA**
Bologna
Ferrara
Forli
Modena
Parma
Piacenza
Ravenna
Reggio Emilia
Rimini

**FRIULI-VENEZIA GIULIA**
Gorizia
Pordenone
Trieste
Udine

**LAZIO**
Frosinone
Latina
Rieti
Roma
Viterbo

**LIGURIA**
Genova
Imperia
La Spezia
Savona

**LOMBARDIA**
Bergamo
Brescia
Como
Cremona
Lecco
Lodi
Mantova
Milano
Pavia
Sondrio
Varese

**MARCHE**
Ancona
Ascoli Piceno
Macerata
Pesaro e Urbino

**MOLISE**
Campobasso
Isernia

**PIEMONTE**
Alessandria
Asti
Biella
Cuneo
Novara
Torino
Verbano-Cusio-Ossola
Vercelli

**PUGLIA**
Bari
Brindisi
Foggia
Lecce
Taranto

**SARDEGNA**
Cagliari
Nuoro
Oristano
Sassari

**SICILIA**
Agrigento
Caltanissetta
Catania
Enna
Messina
Palermo
Ragusa
Siracusa
Trapani

**TOSCANA**
Arezzo
Firenze
Grosseto
Livorno
Lucca
Massa Carrara
Pisa
Pistoia
Prato
Siena

**TRENTINO-ALTO ADIGE**
Bolzano
Trento

**UMBRIA**
Perugia
Terni

**VALLE D'AOSTA**
Aosta/Aoste

**VENETO**
Belluno
Padova
Rovigo
Treviso
Venezia
Verona
Vicenza

# Luxembourg
## Country Introduction

*Luxembourg City, Luxembourg*

## Welcome to Luxembourg

Officially named the Grand Duchy of Luxembourg, this small country is surrounded by Belgium to the west and north, Germany to the east and France to the south.

Its history is filled with emperors and counts as well as many battles and disputes. Today, the almost fairytale-like castles and fortresses are an impressive reminder of those days, and amidst their lovely natural settings, they make picturesque sights.

## Country highlights

The cuisine is a combination of French, Flemish and German dishes. Specialities include smoked pork with beans, Ardennes ham, sauerkraut, trout and pike. They also have some of the best pastries you're ever likely to eat filled with Luxembourg cheese. Local beers and wines are recommended.

With many events all year round, the Summer in the City festival is one of the popular ones. Based in Luxembourg City, visitors come back to enjoy the free open air concerts, cinemas, markets and street artists.

## Major towns and cities

- Luxembourg City – the capital city has an impressive castle and fascinating history.
- Dudelange – a city known for its cultural galleries and live music festivals.
- Differdange – a historical city is home to the Differdange Castle built in the 14th century.
- Esch-sur-Alzette – this small city is home to the longest shopping street in Luxembourg.

## Attractions

- Musee National de la Resistance – an impressive building housing a variety of exhibits, photography and sculptures.
- Altstadt Vianden – an enchanting medieval small town with narrow lanes and gothic churches.
- Beaufort Castle – walk around the ancient ruins with impressive views.

## Find out more

www.visitluxembourg.lu

Tel: 0035 (0) 24 28 28 21 Luxembourg National Tourist Office

# Country Information

*Population (approx):* 521,000

*Capital:* Luxembourg City (population approx 76,000)

*Area:* 2,586 sq km

*Bordered by:* Belgium, France, Germany

*Terrain:* Rolling hills to north with broad, shallow valleys; steep slope to Moselle valley in south-east

*Climate:* Temperate climate without extremes of heat or cold; mild winters; warm, wet summers; July and August are the hottest months; May and June have the most hours of sunshine.

*Highest Point:* Burgplatz 559m

*Languages:* French, German, Lëtzebuergesch (Luxembourgish)

*Local Time:* GMT or BST + 1, i.e. 1 hour ahead of the UK all year

*Currency:* Euros divided into 100 cents; £1 = €1.26, €1 = £0.79 (September 2014)

*Emergency numbers:* Police 113; Fire brigade 112; Ambulance 112. Operators speak English

*Public Holidays 2015:* Jan 1; Apr 6; May 1, 14, 25; Jun 23 (National Day); Aug 15; Nov 1; Dec 25, 26.

Please note there are other dates such as Luxembourg City Fete and 2 Nov (All Souls Day) which are not official bank holidays but many businesses, banks and shops may be closed. School summer holidays run from mid-July to mid-September

# Camping and Caravanning

There are approximately 120 campsites in Luxembourg; most are open from April to October. Apart from in the industrial south, campsites are found all over the country. The Ardennes, the river banks along the Moselle and the Sûre and the immediate surroundings of Luxembourg City are particularly popular.

Casual/wild camping is only permitted with a tent, not a caravan, but permission must first be sought from the landowner.

# Motorhomes

Many campsites have motorhome amenities and some offer Quick Stop overnight facilities at reduced rates.

# Electricity and Gas

Most campsites have a supply of between 6 and 16 amps and many have CEE connections. Plugs have two round pins. The full range of Campingaz cylinders is widely available.

# Entry Formalities

British and Irish passport holders may stay for up to three months without a visa.

# Medical Services

Emergency medical treatment is available on presentation of a European Health Insurance Card (EHIC) but you will be charged both for treatment and prescriptions. Refunds can be obtained from a local sickness insurance fund office, Caisse de Maladie des Ouvriers (CMO). Emergency hospital treatment is normally free apart from a non-refundable standard daily fee.

# Opening Hours

Banks – Mon-Fri 8.30am-12 noon & 1.30pm-4.30pm.Some stay open to 6pm and open Sat 9am-12 noon.

Museums – Tue-Sun 10am-6pm, Thurs late opening 5pm-8pm (check locally); most close Mon.

Post Offices – Mon-Fri 8am-12 noon & 1.30pm-4.30pm/5pm; the central post office in Luxembourg City is open 7am-7pm Mon to Fri & 7am-5pm Sat.

Shops – Mon-Sat 9am/10am-6pm/6.30pm. Some close for lunch and Mon mornings. Large malls may be open to 8pm or 9pm.

# Safety and Security

There are few reports of crime but visitors should take the usual commonsense precautions against pickpockets. Do not leave valuables in your car.

Luxembourg shares with the rest of Europe an underlying threat from terrorism. Attacks could be indiscriminate and against civilian targets in public places, including tourist sites.

*British Embassy*
5 BOULEVARD JOSEPH II, L-1840 LUXEMBOURG
Tel: 22 98 64
http://www.ukinluxembourg.fco.gov.uk

*Irish Embassy*
Résidence Christina (2nd floor)
28 ROUTE D'ARLON, L-1140 LUXEMBOURG
Tel: 450 6101~
www.embassyofireland.lu

## Documents
*Passport*
When driving it is easy to cross into neighbouring countries without realising it. Although you are unlikely to be asked for it, you must have your valid passport with you.

*Vehicle(s)*
Drivers of foreign-registered vehicles must be able to produce on demand a current driving licence, vehicle registration document (V5C) insurance certificate, insurance certificate and MOT certificate (if applicable).

## Money
The major credit cards are widely accepted and cash machines are widespread. Carry your credit card issuers'/banks' 24-hour UK contact numbers in case of loss or theft of your cards.

## Motoring in Luxembourg
### Alcohol
The maximum permitted level of alcohol is 50 milligrams in 100 millilitres of blood, i.e. lower than that permitted in the UK (80 milligrams). For drivers who have held a driving licence for less than two years the permitted level is 20 milligrams i.e. virtually nil. Breath tests are compulsory following serious road accidents and road offences.

### Breakdown Service
A 24-hour breakdown service 'Service Routier' is operated by the Automobile Club De Grand-Duche de Luxembourg (ACL) on all roads, telephone 26000. Operators speak English. Payment by credit card is accepted.

## Essential Equipment
*Warning Triangle*
A warning triangle must be used if the vehicle is immobilised on the roadway.

*Lights*
The use of dipped headlights in the daytime is recommended for all vehicles.

*Reflective Jacket/Waistcoat*
It is compulsory to wear a reflective jacket when getting out of your vehicle on a motorway or main road. Pedestrians walking at night or in bad visibility outside built-up areas must also wear one.

*Child Restraint System*
Children under the age of 3 years old must be seated in an approved child restraint system.

Children from the ages of 3 to 17 and/or under the height of 1.5m must be seated in an appropriate restraint system. If they are over 36kg in weight they can use a seat belt but only if they are in the rear of the vehicle.

Rear-facing child restraint systems are not allowed on seats with front airbags unless the airbag has been deactivated.

## Tyres
Vehicles are required to have M&S (Mud and Snow) marked tyres fitted when driving in wintery conditions (frost, snow, ice etc.). This regulation applies to all drivers, regardless of where the vehicle is registered.

## Fuel
Petrol stations are generally open from 8am to 8pm with 24 hour service on motorways. Most accept credit cards and many have automatic pumps operated with a credit card.

It is illegal to carry petrol in a can.

LPG is available at a handful of petrol stations – see www.mylpg.eu and use the drop down menu listed under LPG stations.

## Overtaking
When overtaking at night outside built-up areas it is compulsory to flash headlights.

# Parking

Parking is prohibited where there are yellow lines or zigzag white lines. Blue zone parking areas exist in Luxembourg City, Esch-sur-Elzette, Dudelange and Wiltz. Parking discs are obtainable from the ACL, police stations, tourist offices and shops. Parking meters operate in Luxembourg City. The police will clamp or remove illegally parked vehicles.

There are free car parks two to three kilometres outside Luxembourg City and Esch-sur-Elzette from which regular buses leave for the city.

If there is no public lighting when parking on a public road sidelights are required to be switched on.

# Priority

Where two roads of the same category intersect, traffic from the right has priority. In towns give priority to traffic coming from the right, unless there is a 'priority road' sign (yellow diamond with white border) indicating that the driver using that road has right of way.

# Road Signs and Markings

Road signs and markings conform to international standards and are shown in French and German. Traffic lights pass from red immediately to green (no red and amber phase). A flashing amber light allows traffic to turn in the direction indicated, traffic permitting. In Luxembourg City some bus lanes and cycle lanes are marked in red.

# Speed Limits

| | Open Road (Km/h) | Motorway (Km/h) |
|---|---|---|
| Car Solo | 90 | 130 |
| Car towing caravan/trailer | 75 | 90 |
| Motorhome under 3500kg | 90 | 130 |
| Motorhome 3500-7500kg | 90 | 130 |

The top speed of 130 km/h (80 mph) for solo cars is reduced to 110 km/h (68 mph) in wet weather. The speed limit for drivers who have held a licence for less than a year is 90 km/h (56 mph) on motorways and 75 km/h (47 mph) outside built-up areas. In some residential areas called 'Zones de Rencontre' the maximum permitted speed is 20 km/h (13 mph).

# Traffic Jams

Many holidaymakers travel through Luxembourg in order to take advantage of its cheaper fuel. Queues at petrol stations often cause traffic congestion, in particular along the 'petrol route' past Martelange (N4 in Belgium), at Dudelange on the A3/E25 at the Belgium-Luxembourg border, and at the motorway junction near Steinfort on the A6 where waiting cars may encroach onto the hard shoulder.

Other bottlenecks occur, particularly during weekends in July and August, at the junctions on the A1/E44 near Gasperich to the south of Luxembourg City, and the exit from the A3/E25 at Dudelange. To avoid traffic jams between Luxembourg City and Thionville (France), leave the western ring road around Luxembourg and take the A4 to Esch-sur-Alzette and then the D16. When past Aumetz join the N52 which then connects to the A30 to Metz.

The website www.cita.lu provides webcam views of all motorways and information on traffic flow.

# Violation of Traffic Regulations

Police officers may impose on the spot fines for infringement of regulations. These must be settled in cash and a receipt given. Non-residents of Luxembourg are liable to receive penalty points for serious infringements of traffic law.

# Motorways

There are approximately 115km of motorways, all of which are toll-free for private vehicles. Motorway service areas are situated at Capellen on the A6 near Mamer, at Pontpierre on the A4, and at Berchem near Bettembourg on the A3.

Emergency telephones are situated every 1.5km along main roads and motorways and link motorists to the 'Protection Civile'.

## Touring

Luxembourg is the only Grand Duchy in the world and measures a maximum of 81km (51 miles) from north to south and 51km (32 miles) from east to west. The fortifications and old town of Luxembourg City have been designated as a UNESCO World Heritage site.

Smoking is not allowed in bars and restaurants. A service charge is usually added to restaurant bills and it is normal practice to leave a little extra if the service is good.

The Luxembourg Card is valid for one, two or three days, and entitles the holder to free public transport, admission to numerous museums and tourist attractions, and discounts on sightseeing trips. It is available from tourist offices, campsites, hotels, information and public transport offices as well as from participating attractions. You can also buy it online at www.ont.lu.

There are many marked walking trails throughout the country – see www.hiking-in-luxembourg. co.uk for full details. A Christmas market is held in the pedestrianised Place d'Armes in Luxembourg City. Others are held in towns and villages throughout the country.

French is the official language, but Lëtzebuergesch is the language most commonly used. English is widely spoken in Luxembourg City, but less so elsewhere.

## Public Transport & Local Travel

A transport network ticket (billet réseau) is available at railway stations throughout the country and at the airport. It allows unlimited travel on city buses, trains and country coaches for one day (until 8am the next morning) throughout Luxembourg. Public transport maps can be downloaded from the Luxembourg Tourist Office website, www.luxembourg.co.uk.

Luxembourg is a compact city and walking around it is easy and pleasant. It is served by an efficient network of buses. You can buy bus tickets valid either for two hours (billet de courte durée) or one day (billet de longue durée). A discount is offered on a block of 10 tickets. Tickets must be validated at the machines on buses and train platforms. Dogs are allowed free of charge on city buses. People over 65 years of age may qualify for travel concessions; show your passport as proof of age.

**ALZINGEN** see Luxembourg City *C3*

**BERDORF** see Echternach *C3*

**BETTENDORF** *C2* (1.1km SE Rural) *49.87262, 6.22137*
**Camping Um Wirt, 12 Rue de la Gare, L-9353 Bettendorf**
**[tel 808386; fax 26804792; info@campingumwirt.**
**lu; www.campingumwirt.lu]** Foll the N17/N19 Diekirch/
Echternach. Turn R and foll camping signs in Bettendorf. Med,
pt shd or shd; wc; chem disp; shwrs; el pnts (10A); lndtte; rest/
café; bar; playgrnd; rv adj; games area; games rm; entmnt;
wifi; 70% statics; dogs €2.50; Eng spkn; adv bkg; red low ssn;
bowling green; trampoline; tennis court; sports field; "Vg site;
gd walking & cycling; open plan, grassy site." 1 Apr-15 Oct.
€ 25.00                                                    2013*

**BORN SUR SURE** *C3* (200m NE Rural) *49.76081, 6.51672*
**Camping Officiel Born-Sûre, 9 Rue du Camping, 6660**
**Born-sur-Sûre [tel/fax 730144; syndicat@gmx.lu; www.**
**camping-born.lu]** E along E44 sp Trier; leave immed bef ent
Germany. On N10 go N sp Echternach; ignore sat nav & drive
to end of vill, site sp. Med, mkd pitch, pt shd; wc; chem disp;
shwrs inc; el pnts (6A); lndtte; supmkt 8km; tradsmn; rest,
snacks; bar; BBQ; htd pool 8km; fishing; boating; 70% statics;
dogs €2.50; wifi; phone; Eng spkn; adv bkg; some rd noise;
ccard acc; CKE/CCI. "Gd, clean site; all tourers on rvside;
if barrier clsd find contact in bar; excel." ♦ 1 Apr-1 Oct.
€ 16.00                                                    2014*

**CLERVAUX** *B2* (11km SW Rural) *49.97045, 5.93450* **Camping**
**Kaul, Rue Joseph Simon, 9550 Wiltz [tel 950359; fax**
**957770; icamping@campingkaul.lu; www.campingkaul.**
**lu]** Turn N off rd 15 (Bastogne-Ettelbruck) to Wiltz, N to
Ville Basse & Camping. Lge, mkd pitch, unshd; htd wc; chem
disp; mv service pnt; baby facs; fam bthrm; shwrs €0.50; el
pnts (6-10A) €2.50-2.75; gas; lndtte; shop high ssn & 500m;
snacks; playgrnd; pool adj; waterslides; tennis; dogs €1.50;
poss cr; quiet; adv bkg. "Gd site; pitches tight for awnings
if site full; excel san facs & take-away; local children use
playgrnd." ♦ 1 Apr-31 Oct. € 28.00                          2014*

**CLERVAUX** *B2* (200m W Rural) *50.05471, 6.02391* **Camping**
**Officiel Born-Sûre, 33 Klatzewe, 9714 Clervaux**
**[tel 920042; fax 929728; campingclervaux@internet.**
**lu; www.camping-clervaux.lu]** Site sp fr town cent & fr all
dirs at foot of Abbey Hill; some sharp bends. Med, hdg/mkd
pitch, pt shd; htd wc; chem disp; mv service pnt; baby facs;
shwrs €1; el pnts (10A) €2.50; gas; lndtte intmnt; shop &
1km; tradsmn; snacks; BBQ; playgrnd; htd pool; tennis 200m;
games area; internet; TV; 50% statics; dogs €2; phone; poss cr;
Eng spkn; some rlwy noise; CKE/CCI. "Friendly, helpful staff;
pleasant town; gd walking; trains to Liège & L'bourg City; rv
on site unfenced; 5 mins walk town; vg." ♦ 1 Apr-15 Oct.
€ 17.00                                                    2010*

**DIEKIRCH** *C2* (10km E Rural) *49.86852, 6.26430* **Camping**
**de la Rivière, 21 Rue de la Sûre, 9390 Reisdorf [tel/fax**
**836398; campingreisdorf@pt.lu; www.campingreisdorf.**
**com]** Fr Diekirch take N19 (sp Echternach) for 10km to where
rd crosses rv Sûre. Site on L after bdge. Med, mkd pitch, pt
shd; htd wc; chem disp; shwrs €1.10; el pnts (6-10A) metered;
gas; lndtte (inc dryer); shop adj; rest, snacks; bar; playgrnd;
internet; 20% statics; dogs €1.50; bus; poss cr; Eng spkn;
quiet; red CKE/CCI. "Lovely site in beautiful countryside; excel
for walking/cycling; helpful, friendly owners; gd touring base."
♦ ltd Feb - Nov. € 15.00                                   2013*

**DIEKIRCH** *C2* (500m SE Urban) *49.86635, 6.16513*
**Camping de la Sûre, 34 Route de Gilsdorf, 9234 Diekirch**
**[tel 809425; fax 802786; tourisme@diekirch.lu; www.**
**diekirch.lu]** Fr town cent take N14 twds Larochette, then 1st
L after x-ing rv bdge. Well sp. Lge, mkd pitch, pt shd; htd wc;
chem disp; baby facs; shwrs €1; el pnts (10A) €2.50; lndtte;
shop 500m; bar; playgrnd; pool 200m; 50% statics; dogs €2;
m'van o'night area outside gates; Eng spkn; adv bkg; quiet; red
CKE/CCI; ccard acc. "Nice welcome; excel, clean facs; pleasant
rvside site 5 mins walk fr town cent; vg touring base, Battle of
Bulge Museum nrby." ♦ 1 Apr-30 Sep. € 20.50               2012*

# "There aren't many sites open at this time of year"

If you're travelling outside peak season
remember to call ahead to check site opening
dates – even if the entry says 'open all year'.

⊞ **DIEKIRCH** *C2* (500m S Rural) *49.86768, 6.16984*
**Camping op der Sauer, Route de Gilsdorf, 9201 Diekirch**
**[tel 808590; fax 809470; info@campsauer.lu; www.**
**campsauer.lu]** On rd 14 to Larochette, on S o'skts of Diekirch.
1st L after x-ing rv bdge, site well sp on L past Camping de
la Sûre and behind sports facs. Lge, mkd pitch, pt shd; htd
wc; chem disp; shwrs inc; el pnts (6A) €3; gas; lndtte; shop &
400m; tradsmn; rest, snacks; bar; playgrnd; pool 400m; dogs
€2.50; bus 800m; Eng spkn; adv bkg; CKE/CCI. "On banks Rv
Sûre; sh walk/cycle to town; spacious site; friendly owners; ltd
facs low ssn; gd, basic site." € 19.00                     2012*

**ECHTERNACH** *C3* (2km SE Rural) *49.79681, 6.43122*
**Camping Alferweiher, Alferweiher 1, 6412 Echternach**
**[tel/fax 720271; info@camping-alferweiher.lu; www.**
**camping-alferweiher.lu]** Fr S on N10 to ent Echternach turn
R at sp (pictogram fishing/camping) then L at sp to Alferweiher.
Lge, mkd pitch, pt shd; htd wc; chem disp; mv service pnt;
baby facs; shwrs inc; el pnts (10A) €2.75; gas; lndtte; shop;
tradsmn; snacks; bar; playgrnd; cycle hire; TV rm; entmnt; dogs
€2; poss cr; Eng spkn; adv bkg; quiet; CKE/CCI. "Gd walking;
office open 0900-1300 & 1400-1800; if shut site yourself - el
boxes not locked; hot water in individ cubicles in san facs
block only - other basins cold water." ♦ 23 Apr-15 Sep.
€ 20.00                                                    2010*

**LUXEMBOURG**

**ECHTERNACH** *C3* (1km NW Rural) *49.81716, 6.41058*
**Camping Officiel, 5 Rue de Diekirch, 6430 Echternach
[tel 720272; fax 26720747; info@camping-echternach.
lu; www.camping-echternach.lu]** Fr Luxembourg City cont
thro Echternach on N10 sp Diekirch & Ettelbruck. Site clearly sp
on L overlkg rd & rv; diff exit fr site. Lge, hdg/mkd pitch, terr,
pt shd; wc; chem disp; mv service pnt; baby facs; shwrs inc;
el pnts (16A) €2.50; lndtte (inc dryer); shops 500m; tradsmn;
playgrnd; pool; rv/lake sw; fishing; 10% statics; dogs €2; bus to
Luxemb'g City 500m; Eng spkn; adv bkg; some rd noise; ccard
acc; red low ssn. "Music festival Jun/Jul; gd walks; gd rests in
town; rvside cycle path." ♦ 15 Mar-30 Oct. € 17.00    2011*

**ECHTERNACH** *C3* (6km NW Rural) *49.81904, 6.34694*
**Camping Bon Repos, 39 Rue de Diekirch, 6551 Berdorf
[tel 790631; fax 799571; irma@bonrepos.lu; www.
bonrepos.lu]** In cent Echternach at x-rds take Vianden rd, then
in 2km turn L to Berdorf thro vill twds Consdorf. Site nr cent vill
on L adj Camping Belle-Vue. Fr Luxembourg thro Consdorf to
Berdorf, site on R on ent to vill, clearly sp. Med, hdg/mkd pitch,
terr, pt sl, pt shd; htd wc; chem disp; baby facs; shwrs inc; el
pnts (16A) €2.80 (poss rev pol); gas; lndtte; tradsmn; shop adj;
rest & bar 100m; playgrnd; pool 5km; games rm; wifi; TV; no
dogs; bus 100m; Eng spkn; adv bkg; quiet; red long stay; CKE/
CCI. "Clean, tidy site - best in area; clean facs; helpful, friendly
owners; some pitches sm; forest walks fr site; conv for trips to
Germany." 1 Apr74 Nov. € 18.00    2013*

 **ESCH SUR ALZETTE** *B3* (500m E Rural) *49.4846, 5.9861*
**Camping Gaalgebierg, 4001 Esch-sur-Alzette [tel 541069;
fax 549630; gaalcamp@pt.lu; www.gaalgebierg.lu]** Sp
in cent of town, turn L dir Kayl. Under rlwy bdge sharp R, up
steep hill. Lge, hdstg, terr, shd; htd wc; baby facs; shwrs inc; el
pnts (16A) €1.50 but elec for heating metered & restricted in
bad weather; lndtte; shop; snacks; bar; playgrnd; pool 2km; TV
conn all pitches; mainly statics; bus 1km; train to Luxembourg
city; Eng spkn; quiet; ccard acc; CKE/CCI. "V clean san facs; gd
walks; park & sm zoo adj site; well-kept site; poss boggy when
wet." ♦ € 20.75    2013*

**ESCH SUR SURE** *B2* (6km NE Rural) *49.91420, 6.00098*
**Camping Toodlermillen, 1 Op der Millen, 9181 Tadler-
Moulin [tel 839189; fax 899236; keisera@gms.lu; www.
toodlermillen.lu]** Fr Ettelbruck on N15 twd Esch-sur-Sûre,
turn E onto N27 dir Goebelsmühle. Site is 4km on R. Med, mkd
pitch, unshd; htd wc; chem disp; baby facs; shwrs €1; el pnts
(6A) €3; lndtte; shop, rest, bar adj; playgrnd; BBQ; rv fishing;
canoeing; 20% statics; dogs €3; Eng spkn. "V helpful owner;
beautiful area; excel san facs." 15 Apr-15 Oct. € 22.50  2010*

 **ESCH SUR SURE** *B2* (500m E Rural) *49.90693, 5.94220*
**Camping Im Aal, 7 Rue du Moulin, 9650 Esch-sur-Sûre
[tel 839514; fax 899117; camping-im-aal@hotmail.com;
www.camping-im-aal.lu]** Fr N turn R off N15 onto N27
sp Esch-sur-Sûre. Pass thro sh tunnel, site on L in 500m on
banks of Rv Sûre. Lge, hdg/mkd pitch, pt sl, pt shd; htd wc;
chem disp; shwrs inc; el pnts (6A) €2; lndtte (inc dryer); shop
& 500m; tradsmn; bar; playgrnd adj; fishing; 30% statics;
dogs €2; site clsd 1 Jan-14 Feb; Eng spkn; quiet; red CKE/
CCI. "Well-kept, clean site; gd welcome; gd, modern facs;
some rvside pitches; walks along towpath & in woods; gd for
wheelchair users; gd fishing, walking; gd NH & longer." ♦
€ 19.50    2013*

**ETTELBRUCK** *B2* (3km E Rural) *49.85043, 6.13461* **Camping
Gritt, 2 Rue Gritt, 9161 Ingeldorf [tel 802018; fax 802019;
apeeters@pt.lu; www.campinggritt.lu]** On N15 fr Bastogne
turn R at rndabt in Ettelbrück sp Diekirch, go under A7 sp
Diekirch. In 3km at end of elevated section foll slip rd sp
Diekirch, Ettelbrück, Ingeldorf. At rndabt take 2nd exit sp
Ingledorf, site on R over narr rv bdge. Fr Diekirch on N7 fork L
twd Ingeldorf. Site on L over rv bdge. Lge, mkd pitch, pt shd;
htd wc; chem disp; baby facs; mv service pnt; shwrs inc; el pnts
(6A) €2.80; gas; lndtte; supmkt 1.5km; tradsmn; rest, snacks;
bar; BBQ; rv sw 1.5km; fishing, canoe hire, tennis nrby; ltd wifi;
entmnt; games/TV rm; 30% statics; dogs €2; twin-axles acc (for
check in adv); bus/train to Luxembourg City; recep 0900-1800
high ssn; poss cr; Eng spkn; adv bkg; quiet; red for groups;
red low ssn/CKE/CCI. "Peaceful site; helpful, welcoming Dutch
owners; lge pitches with open aspect; gd, modern san facs;
pitching still OK after heavy rain; on banks of Rv Sûre (swift-
flowing & unfenced); gd walking & sightseeing; rest vg; vg
site." ♦ 01 Apr-30 Oct. € 28.40  SBS - H07    2014*

**ETTELBRUCK** *B2* (2km NW Rural) *49.84600, 6.08193*
**Camping Kalkesdelt, 88 Chemin du Camping, 9022
Ettelbrück [tel 812185; fax 813186; kalkesdelt@ettelbruck-
info.lu; www.campingettelbruck.com]** Exit Ettelbrück
on Bastogne rd N15. Site visible as app town; approx 200m
fr town cent fork L into lane, turn R at sp at foot of hill, narr
rd. Site sp fr town. Lge, mkd pitch, terr, pt shd; htd wc;
chem disp; mv service pnt; baby facs; shwrs inc; el pnts (16A)
€2.90; lndtte; shop; rest, snacks; bar; playgrnd; pool 3km;
TV; 15% statics; dogs €2.50; phone; poss cr; Eng spkn; adv
bkg; quiet; CKE/CCI. "Gd, well-maintained, friendly, family-
run site in woods; excel san facs; lge pitches; gd walks; train
to Luxembourg city fr town; excel site." ♦ 1 Apr-2 Nov.
€ 20.00    2013*

 **ETTELBRUCK** *B2* (10km NW Rural) *49.87748, 5.99288*
**Camping Fuussekaul, 4 Fuussekaul, 9156 Heiderscheid
[tel 268888; fax 26888828; info@fuussekaul.lu]** Take N15
fr Bastogne twd Ettelbrück, site 1.5km past Heiderscheid
on R. Lge, pt sl, pt shd; htd wc; chem disp; mv service pnt;
sauna; shwrs €1; el pnts (10A) inc; gas; lndtte; shop high ssn;
rest, snacks; bar; playgrnd; 2 pools; waterslide; lake sw 8km;
tennis; games area; archery; internet; entmnt; 30% statics;
dogs €2; bus; poss cr; adv bkg; quiet; red long stay. "Vg site."
€ 35.00    2009*

**GRAVENMACHER** *C3* (500m NE Urban) *49.68302, 6.44891*
**Camping La Route du Vin, 32 Route de Thionville, 6791
Grevenmacher [tel 750234 or 758275; fax 758666; sitg@
pt.lu; www.grevenmacher.lu]** Fr E44/A1 exit junc 14 onto
N1 to Grevenmacher. After 1km turn R at T-junc opp Esso
g'ge. Site sp in town, ent off rndabt. Med, sl, pt shd; wc; chem
disp; shwrs inc; el pnts (6A) €1.50; shop, rest, snacks 500m;
bar; pool nr; tennis; child entmnt; 60% statics; dogs €1; Eng
spkn; some rd noise; CKE/CCI. "Easy walk to town cent; wine
festival in Sep; pleasant site but rather scruffy (8/09); NH only."
1 Apr-30 Sep. € 11.60    2009*

**HEIDERSCHEID see Ettelbrück** *B2*

**INGELDORF see Ettelbrück** *B2*

Send in your site reports by mid August 2015

⊞ **KAUTENBACH** B2 (N Rural) 49.95387, 6.02730 Camping Kautenbach, An der Weierbaach, 9663 Kautenbach [tel 950303; fax 950093; info@campingkautenbach.lu; www.campingkautenbach.lu] Travelling E fr Bastogne on N84, approx 5km after Luxembourg border take N26 to Wiltz & foll sp to Kautenbach/Kiischpelt. In 10km turn L over bdge into vill, site sp 800m. Lge, mkd pitch, pt shd; htd wc; chem disp; shwrs inc; baby facs; el pnts (6A) inc; gas; lndtte; shop; tradsmn; rest, snacks; bar; BBQ; playgrnd; entmnt; cycle hire; wifi; TV rm; 20% statics; phone; dogs; site clsd 21 Dec-14 Jan; Eng spkn; adv bkg; quiet but some rlwy noise; ccard acc. "Gd for walking & mountain biking; long site along beautiful, secluded rv valley." ♦ € 22.25                2009*

See advertisement

**KOCKELSCHEUER see Luxembourg City** C3

**LAROCHETTE** C3 (1.5km W Rural) 49.78525, 6.21010 Camping Birkelt, 1 Um Birkelt, 7633 Larochette [tel 879040; fax 879041; info@camping-birkelt.lu; www.camping-birkelt.lu] Fr Diekirch take N14 to Larochette; turn R in town on CR118 (N8), foll sp for Mersch. At top of hill foll site sp. Fr Luxembourg take N7 foll sp for Mersch & Ettelbruck (ignore Larochette sp bef Mersch). Turn R bef rv bdge at Mersch onto CR118 & foll rd to o'skts of town. Site on R beyond municipal sports cent - fairly steep, winding app rd. Lge, hdg/mkd pitch, pt sl, pt shd; htd wc; chem disp; mv service pnt; serviced pitch; baby facs; sauna; shwrs inc; el pnts (16A) inc; gas; lndtte (inc dryer); shop; rest, snacks; bar; BBQ (gas/charcoal only); playgrnd; 2 pools (1 htd, covrd); paddling pool; tennis; fitness rm; horseriding; fishing, canoeing, golf 5km; cycle hire; games rm; games area; games rm; wifi; entmnt; TV rm; 50% statics; dogs €2.50; no c'vans/m'vans over 9m; poss cr; Eng spkn; ccard acc; red low ssn; CKE/CCI. "Excel, well-kept, busy site in pleasant wooded hilltop location; friendly, helpful staff; ideal for families; gd san facs; poss stretched high ssn; access poss diff lge o'fits, care req; late arr report to rest/bar; gd bar & rest, open in low ssn; under new ownership." ♦ 15 Mar-1 Nov. € 46.40  (CChq acc) SBS - H08   2014*

## "That's changed – Should I let The Club know?"

If you find something on site that's different from the site entry, fill in a report and let us know. See www.caravanclub.co.uk/europereport.

**LAROCHETTE** C3 (4km W Rural) 49.78521, 6.16596 Europacamping Nommerlayen, Rue Nommerlayen, 7465 Nommern [tel 878078; fax 879678; nommerlayen@vo.lu; www.nommerlayen-ec.lu] N7 Luxembourg to Diekirch. At Mersch N8 E dir Larochette & Nommern. Site is 1km S of Nommern. Lge, hdg/mkd pitch, terr, pt shd; htd wc; mv service pnt; chem disp; baby facs; sauna; shwrs inc; private bthrms avail; el pnts (16A €3.75); gas; lndtte (inc dryer); shop; tradsmn; rest, snacks; bar; playgrnd; htd pool; paddling pool; tennis; games area; games rm; cycle hire; wifi; entmnt; TV; 10% statics; dogs €2.85; phone; Eng spkn; adv bkg; quiet; red low ssn/snr citizens. "Superb site & facs." ♦ 1 Feb-1 Dec. € 40.00                2011*

See advertisement

## "I like to fill in the reports as I travel from site to site"

You'll find report forms at the back of this guide, or you can fill them in online at www.caravaclub.co.uk/europereport.

⊞ **LIELER** B2 (300m W Rural) 50.12365, 6.10509 Camping Trois Frontières, Hauptstroos 12, 9972 Lieler [tel 998608; fax 979184; camp.3front@cmdnet.lu; www.troisfrontieres.lu] Fr N7/E421 turn E sp Lieler, site sp. Med, mkd pitch, pt shd; htd wc; chem disp; mv service pnt: baby facs; shwrs; el pnts (6A) €2.75; lndtte (inc dryer); tradsmn; rest, snacks; bar; playgrnd; 2 htd pools (1 covrd); paddling pool; cycle hire; games rm; games area; wifi; entmnt; TV; some statics; dogs €2.20; adv bkg; quiet. "V pleasant site; gd touring base." € 25.00                2011*

LUXEMBOURG

**LUXEMBOURG CITY** *C3* (4km S Rural) *49.57220, 6.10857*
Camping Kockelscheuer, 22 Route de Bettembourg, 1899
Kockelscheuer [tel 471815; fax 401243; caravani@pt.lu;
www.ccclv.lu/site/index.php/en] Fr N on A6 then A4 exit
junc 1 sp Leudelange/Kockelscheuer, at top of slip rd turn L N4.
After about 1.5km turn R N186 sp Bettemburg/Kockelscheuer
& foll camp sp. Foll sp 'Park & Ride', site is 1st R. Fr S exit
A3 junc 2 sp Bettembourg & Kockelscheuer. In 700m turn R
dir Kockelscheuer & in 3km turn L & foll site sp, rd numberd
CR196. Lge, some hdg/mkd pitch, pt terr, pt shd; htd wc; chem
disp; mv service pnt; shwrs inc; el pnts (10-16A) metered (check
pol); gas; lndtte (inc dryer); shop; tradsmn; rest adj; snacks;
bar; playgrnd; pool 4km; sports complex adj; internet; sat TV;
dogs free; bus to city 400m (tickets fr site recep); office & gates
clsd 1200-1400 & 2230-0700; Eng spkn; adv bkg; some rd &
aircraft noise during day; ccard not acc; low ssn weekly rate
for snr citizens; 10% red CKE/CCI. "Rec arr early afternoon as
popular; well-run, clean, pretty site; helpful, pleasant staff; gd
san facs; pitch access on lower level needs care; gd size pitches
on terr; poss boggy after rain; gd dog walks nrby; useful NH for
Zeebrugge; excel site." ◆ 12 Aprr-31 Oct. € 19.50    2014*

**LUXEMBOURG CITY** *C3* (7km W Rural) *49.63012, 6.04761*
Camping Mamer, 4 Rue de Mersch, 8251 Mamer [tel/
fax 312349; campingmamer@hotmail.com; www.
campingmamer.tk] App Luxembourg on A6/E25. Exit m'way
at Mamer junc on N6. Pass thro Mamer vill, turn L in 1km at
2nd rndabt, site sp. Bef m'way viaduct turn R into site. Med,
pt sl, pt shd; htd wc; chem disp; shwrs inc; el pnts (6A) inc
(poss rev pol); gas; shops 1.5km; hypmkt nr; rest, snacks; bar;
playgrnd; dogs; poss v cr; Eng spkn; adv bkg; CKE/CCI. "V
pleasant site; helpful owners; easy access to city; bus into city
fr hypmkt; o'night/late arr area in gravel car park under m'way
(noisy); poss long walk to facs; many o'nighters." 1 Apr-
30 Sep. € 18.00    2010*

**MAMER see Luxembourg City** *C3*

**NOMMERN see Larochette** *C3*

**OBEREISENBACH** *C2* (1.5m N Rural) *50.01640, 6.13680*
Camping Kohnenhof, Maison 1, 9838 Obereisenbach
[tel 929464; fax 929690; kohnenho@pt.lu; www.
campingkohnenhof.lu] Fr N on N7/E421 turn E onto N10
at Marbourg, foll rd S to Kohnenhof, site sp on rvside. Med,
mkd pitch, pt sl, terr, pt shd; htd wc; chem disp; mv service
pnt; baby facs; shwrs inc; el pnts (6A) inc; gas; lndtte; shop;
tradsmn; hypmkt 10km; rest, snacks; bar; BBQ; playgrnd; htd
pool 12km; rv sw adj; boating; tennis 4km; games area; cycle
hire; golf 18km; wifi; TV rm; 5% statics; dogs €3; phone; poss
cr; Eng spkn; adv bkg rec; red low ssn; CKE/CCI. "Clean site
in lovely setting; gd walking & interesting town; self-operated
ferry on site to cross rv to forest; vg touring base; excel."
20 Mar-9 Nov. € 28.00 (CChq acc)    2011*

**REMICH** See also sites listed under Nennig in Germany,
map ref 3A2.

**REMICH** *C3* (5km S Rural) *49.5106, 6.36302* **Camping Le
Port, 5447 Schwebsange** [tel 23664460; fax 26 66 53 05;
commune@wellenstein.lu/info@camping-port.lu]
Fr Remich take N10 S on W bank of Moselle. Site 1km E of
Schwebsange. Or fr S leave A13 at junc 13 onto N10. Site
sp. Lge, mkd pitch, pt shd; wc; chem disp; mv service pnt;
serviced pitch; shwrs inc; el pnts (10A) inc; gas; lndtte; shop
4km; tradsmn; bar; playgrnd; pool 4km; marina & rv activities;
80% statics; dogs; Eng spkn; poss cr; adv bkg rec high ssn; rd,
rv & port noise; debit cards acc (no ccards); CKE/CCI. "Busy
transit site for Austria/Italy; clean facs; helpful staff; office open
1830-2030; sep area for m'vans on far side of port; red facs
low ssn; gd cycle rtes fr site." ◆ 1 Apr-31 Oct. € 18.00  2014*

**SCHWEBSANGE see Remich** *C3*

⊞ **SEPTFONTAINES** *B3* (4km NE Rural) *49.69274, 5.98514*
Camping Simmerschmelz, Rue de Simmerschmelz 1,
8363 Septfontaines [tel 307072; fax 308210; info@
campingsimmer.lu; www.campingsimmer.lu] Head NE
fr Arlon sp Mersch. In 4km at Gaichel (Bel/Lux frontier) foll
valley of Rv Eisch thro Hobscheid, Septfontaines & in 2km
at rd junc turn R. Site on L in 100m. Or fr E25 m'way exit at
Windhof. Head N to Koerich & onto Septfontaines, as above.
Med, pt sl, pt shd; htd wc; chem disp; shwrs inc; el pnts (6A)
€2.50; gas; lndtte; shop high ssn; snacks; pool high ssn;
TV; 40% statics; dogs €3; phone; Eng spkn; adv bkg; quiet.
"Pleasant site in valley - wet in winter; 1 hdstg pitch; helpful
owner." € 21.00    2009*

Tell us about the sites you visit

**TROISVIERGES** *B2* (500m S Urban) *50.11908, 6.00251* **Camping Walensbongert, Rue de Binsfeld, 9912 Troisvierges [tel 997141; fax 26957799; wbongert@pt.lu; www.walensbongert.lu]** Fr Belgium on E42/A27 exit at junc 15 St Vith on N62 sp Troisvierges. Site sp. Med, hdg/mkd pitch, pt shd; htd wc; chem disp; mv service pnt; baby facs; shwrs inc; el pnts (16A) €2.50; lndtte (inc dryer); shop 500m; tradsmn; rest 500m; snacks; bar; pools adj; paddling pool; tennis; games rm; 10% statics; dogs €2; phone; train 1km; Eng spkn; adv bkg; quiet; ccard acc; red low ssn; CKE/CCI. "Pretty town; gd hiking; charming, helpful owners." ♦ ltd 1 Apr-30 Sep. € 24.70                                              2014*

**VIANDEN** *C2* (SE Urban) *49.93213, 6.21554* **Camping op dem Deich, Rue Neugarten, 9420 Vianden [tel 834375; fax 834642; info@campingopdemdeich.lu; www. campingopdemdeich.lu]** Fr Diekirch take N19 E for 3km. Turn L on N17 to Vianden. Site sp 500m fr town cent twd Bitburg. Lge, mkd pitch, hdstg, unshd; htd wc; chem disp; baby facs; shwrs; el pnts (16A) €2.20; lndtte (inc dryer); shops 500m; BBQ; playgrnd; pool 2km; fishing; games rm; wifi; some statics; dogs €1.50; phone; poss cr; quiet. "Some rvside pitches; excel scenery; sh walk along rv to lovely old town & castle." 1 Apr-11 Oct. € 17.00                                        2010*

**VIANDEN** *C2* (2km S Rural) *49.92673, 6.21990* **Camping du Moulin, Rue de Bettel, 9415 Vianden [tel/fax 834501; info@campingdumoulin.lu; www.campingdumoulin. lu]** Fr Diekirch take N17 dir Vianden. In 8km at Fouhren take rd N17B sp Bettel then sp Vianden. Site on R behind yellow Vianden sp. Lge, mkd pitch, pt shd; htd wc; chem disp; mv service pnt; baby facs; shwrs; el pnts (10-16A) €2.20; lndtte; shop; tradsmn; rest, bar; playgrnd; pool 2km; rv adj; wifi; cab TV; no statics; dogs €1.50; phone; Eng spkn; quiet; CKE/CCI. "Lovely location; spacious pitches, some on rv bank; gd, modern san facs; superb children's san facs." 24 Apr-5 Sep. € 17.00                                         2011*

**WASSERBILLIG** *C3* (Urban) *49.71536, 6.50592* **Camping Schützwiese, 41 Rue des Romains, 6649 Wasserbillig [tel 740543; fax 26 714203; info@camping-schuetzwiese. eu]** Fr A1/E44 exit 14, B49 sp Trier, site sp 150m fr frontier bdge. Med, pt sl, pt shd; wc; chem disp; mv service pnt; shwrs inc; el pnts (6A) €2; shops adj; rest 4km; tennis 500m; 40% statics; dogs €1.50; poss cr; adv bkg ess; quiet. 1 Apr-31 Oct. € 11.50                                    2009*

**WASSERBILLIG** *C3* (2km SW Rural) *49.70241, 6.47717* **Camping Mertert, Rue du Parc, 6684 Mertert [tel/fax 748174]** On E of rte 1 (Wasserbillig-Luxembourg), clearly sp in both dir. Immed R after rlwy x-ing. Site on rv. Med, some mkd pitch, shd; htd wc; chem disp; baby facs; shwrs; el pnts (10A) inc; lndtte; shops 250m; playgrnd; pool 4km; sm boating pond; 70% statics; buses & trains nr; adv bkg; quiet; ccard not acc. "Grassed tourer area open fr Apr, but owner allows pitching on tarmac rd adj office; excel, clean facs; scruffy statics area; recep clsd 1300-1500; vg." ♦ ltd 15 Apr-15 Oct. € 12.50                                         2013*

**WEISWAMPACH** *B2* (500m W Rural) *50.13806, 6.06335* **Camping du Lac, Klackepëtzn, 9990 Weiswampach [tel 9972811; fax 9972812; camping.weiswampach@ pt.lu; http://camping.weiswampach.lu]** Foll N7/E421 fr Luxembourg. Site sp on L 500m fr vill of Weiswampach. Lge, hdg/mkd pitch, terr, pt shd; htd wc; chem disp; mv service pnt; baby facs; fam bthrm; shwrs €0.50; el pnts (10A) €1.90; gas; lndtte (inc dryer); shop; supmkt 1km; rest, snacks; bar; BBQ; cooking facs; playgrnd; lake sw adj; fishing; watersports; entmnt; TV; 50% statics; dogs €1.80; phone; poss cr; Eng spkn; adv bkg; quiet; red long stay/CKE/CCI. "Wonderful site on edge of 2 lakes; gd facs; warm welcome." ♦ 1 Apr-31 Oct. € 16.40                                        2010*

**WILTZ see Clervaux** *B2*

**BELGIUM**

**GERMANY**

Liège

Malmédy

Weiswampach
Troisvierges • Lieler
**CLERVAUX**
N7
Obereisenbach
Bastogne
N15
Kautenbach
Bitburg
Esch-sur-Sûre
Vianden
Bettendorf
Ettelbruck • Diekirch

Larochette
Echternach
Born-sur-Sûre
Wasserbillig
Trier
Septfontaines
A7
N7
N11
Gravenmacher
Arlon
N1
A1
N6
A6
N5
N10
Saarburg
**LUXEMBOURG CITY**
N4
N2
A13
A4
A3
Remich
Longwy
A13
Esch-sur-Alzette

Thionville

**FRANCE**

Motorways
Major roads
Main roads

• All year site(s)
• Seasonal site(s)
○ No sites listed

200m +
0–200m

0    10    20    30    40    50 kms
Metz
0    10    20    30 mls

N
W  E
S

© Collins Bartholomew Ltd 2014

# Netherlands
## Country Introduction

*Amsterdam, Netherlands*

## Welcome to Netherlands

Many tourists come to the Netherlands to visit the beautiful city of Amsterdam. However the Netherlands has plenty to offer outside its capital. The country's flat landscape is perfect for exploring on bike. In the west and north the long coastline is marked by dunes and sandy beaches. During springtime the flower gardens and bulb fields are great attractions.

The country is also known for its world famous painters such as Rembrandt and Van Gogh. Many of their works and others can be found in the numerous museums that make up the old cities.

## Country highlights

A traditional Dutch treat that is popular to try are Poffertjes - a snack similar to pancakes, usually served with butter and icing sugar.

The Netherlands is also renowned for its cheese, for example Gouda, Leyden, and Edam.

The country is also popular for it's many flower festivals, starting with world-renowned Holland Flowers Festival in Feburary.

## Major towns and cities

- Amsterdam – the capital city is full of canals, museums and beautiful buildings.
- The Hague – a popular city with many monuments and a historic district.
- Nijmegen – full of historical buildings, this is one of the three oldest cities in the Netherlands.

## Attractions

- Rijksmuseum in Amsterdam – the largest and most prestigious museum of art and history in the Netherlands.
- Hoge Veluwe – one of the largest nature reserves in the country, also home to the Kröller-Müller Museum.
- Delft City Hall – an imposing Renaissance style building.
- Keukenhof Gardens – the world's largest flower garden is very popular with visitors.

## Find out more

www.holland.com

Tel: 0031 (0) 70 37 05 705 Netherlands Tourism

# Country Information

*Population (approx):* 16.7 million

*Capital:* Amsterdam (population approx 740,000)

*Area:* 41,532 sqkm

*Bordered by:* Belgium, Germany

*Terrain:* Mostly coastal lowland and reclaimed land (polders) dissected by rivers and canals; hills in the south-east

*Climate:* Temperate maritime climate; warm, changeable summers; cold/mild winters; spring is the driest season

*Coastline:* 451km

*Highest Point:* Vaalserberg 321m

*Language:* Dutch

*Local Time:* GMT or BST + 1, i.e. 1 hour ahead of the UK all year

*Currency:* Euro divided into 100 cents; £1 = €1.26, €1 = £0.79 (September 2014)

*Emergency numbers:* Police 112; Fire brigade 112; Ambulance 112. Operators speak English

*Public Holidays 2015:* Jan 1; Apr 5, 6, 27; May 14 , 24, 25; Dec 25, 26

School summer holidays vary by region, but are roughly early/mid July to end August/early September

# Camping and Caravanning

There are approximately 2,500 officially classified campsites which offer a wide variety of facilities. Most are well equipped with modern sanitary facilities and they generally have a bar, shop and leisure facilities.

A number of sites require cars to be parked on a separate area away from pitches and this can present a problem for motorhomes. Some sites allow motorhomes to park on pitches without restrictions, but others will only accept them on pitches if they are not moved during the duration of your stay. Check before booking in.

A tourist tax is levied at campsites of between €0.50 and €1.00 per person per night. It is not generally included in the prices quoted in the Site Entry listings which follow this chapter.

The periods over, and immediately after, the

Ascension Day holiday and the Whitsun weekend are very busy for Dutch sites and you can expect to find many of them full. Advance booking is highly recommended.

Casual/wild camping is prohibited as is overnight camping by the roadside or in car parks. There are overnight parking places specifically for motorhomes all over the country – see the website of the Camper Club Nederland, www.campervriendelijk.nl and look under 'camperplaatsen NL' or write to CCN at Postbus 115, 7480 AC Haaksbergen, tel:(0)634 492 913. Alternatively see www.campercontact.nl or email ccc@campervriendelijk.nl.

Many campsites also have motorhome amenities and some offer Quick Stop overnight facilities at reduced rates.

# Cycling

There are twice as many bicycles as cars in the Netherlands and as a result cyclists are catered for better than in any other country. There are 15,000 km of well-maintained cycle tracks in both town and country, all marked with red and white road signs and mushroom-shaped posts indicating the quickest and/or most scenic routes. Local tourist information centres (VVV) sell maps of a wide range of cycling tours and a cycling fact sheet and maps are available from the Netherlands Board of Tourism in London. Motorists should expect to encounter heavy cycle traffic, particularly during rush hours.

Obligatory separate bicycle lanes for cyclists are indicated by circular blue signs displaying a white bicycle. Small oblong signs with the word 'fietspad' or 'rijwielpad' indicate optional bicycle lanes. White bicycles and dotted white lines painted on the road surface indicate cycle lanes which may be used by motor vehicles providing they do not obstruct cyclists. Cycle lanes marked by continuous white lines are prohibited for use by motor vehicles.

Cyclists must obey traffic light signals at crossroads and junctions; elsewhere, where no traffic lights are in operation, they must give way to traffic from the right.

Cycle tracks are also used by mobility scooters and mopeds. Pedestrians should be especially cautious when crossing roads, especially on zebra crossings. Look out for both cyclists and riders of mopeds, who often ignore traffic rules as well as red lights. In Amsterdam in particular, many cyclists do not use lights at night.

*Transportation of Bicycles*

Bicycles may be carried on the roof of a car providing the total height does not exceed 4 metres. They may also be carried at the rear providing the width does not extend more than 20cm beyond the width of the vehicle.

## Electricity and Gas

Most campsites have a supply ranging from 4 to 10 amps and almost all have CEE connections. Plugs have two round pins.

The full range of Campingaz cylinders is available.

## Entry Formalities

British and Irish passport holders may stay in the Netherlands for up to three months without a visa.

## Medical Services

Pharmacies (apotheek) dispense prescriptions whereas drugstores (drogisterij) sell only over-the-counter remedies, amongst other items. Pharmacies may require a photocopy of the details on your European Health Insurance Card (EHIC). You will need to show your EHIC to obtain treatment by a doctor contracted to the state health care system (AGIS Zorgverzekeringen) and you will probably have to pay a fee. You will be charged for emergency dental treatment. Charges for prescriptions vary. Treatment refunds are obtained from AGIS.

Inpatient hospital treatment is free provided it is authorised by AGIS. Local state health insurance fund offices can give advice on obtaining emergency medical services and provide names and addresses of doctors, health centres and hospitals. Tourist Information offices also keep lists of local doctors.

## Opening Hours

Banks – Mon-Fri 9am-4pm/5pm (some open Sat).

Museums – Tue-Fri 10am-5pm; Sat & Sun 11am/1pm-5pm.

Post Offices – Mon-Fri 9am-5pm; some Sat 9am-12 noon/1.30pm.

Shops – Mon-Fri 8am/8.30am-6pm/8pm; Sat 8am/8.30am-4pm/5pm; late night shopping in many towns on Thursday or Friday to 9pm. Shops close one day or half day in the week in addition to Sunday.

## Safety and Security

In relative terms there is little crime but visitors should take the usual precautions in central Amsterdam (particularly in and around Central Station), in Rotterdam and The Hague. As in many large cities, pickpocketing and bag snatching are more common. Pickpockets operate on trams, especially on numbers 2 and 5 in Amsterdam.

Ensure you keep your valuables safely with you at all times and do not leave them unattended or hanging on the back of a chair. Bicycle theft is a common occurrence in the major cities.

Fake, plain clothes policemen carrying badges are in action pretending to be investigating counterfeit money and false credit cards. Dutch police do not have badges and plain clothes police will rarely carry out this kind of inspection. Always ask for identity, check it thoroughly and do not allow yourself to be intimidated. Call 0900 8844 to contact the nearest police station if you are concerned or suspicious.

Several deaths occur each year due to drowning in canals. Take particular care when driving, cycling or walking alongside canals.

Avoid confrontation with anyone offering to sell you drugs and stay away from quiet or dark alleys, particularly late at night.

There have been incidences of drinks being spiked in city centre locations. Always be aware of your drink and do not leave it unattended. Young women and lone travellers need to be especially vigilant in these situations.

The Netherlands shares with the rest of Europe a general threat from terrorism. Attacks could be indiscriminate and against civilian targets in public places, including tourist sites.

*British Embassy*

LANGE VOORHOUT 10, 2514 ED THE HAAG
Tel: (070) 4270427
http://ukinnl.fco.gov.uk/en/

**NETHERLANDS**

British Consulate-General
KONINGSLAAN 44,1075 AE AMSTERDAM
Tel: (020) 6764343

Irish Embassy
SCHEVENINGSEWEG 112, 2584 AE THE HAGUE
Tel: (070) 3630993
www.embassyofireland.nl
There is also an Irish Honorary Consulate-General
in Rhoon (Rotterdam).

## Documents

*Passport*

Everyone from the age of 14 is required to show
a valid identity document to police officers on
request and you should, therefore, carry your
passport at all times.

*Vehicle(s)*

When driving carry your driving licence, vehicle
registration certificate (V5C), insurance certificate
and MOT certificate, if applicable. If driving a
vehicle that does not belong to you, carry a letter
of authority from the owner.

## Money

Money may be exchanged at main border
crossing posts, major post offices, banks, VVV
tourist information offices and some ANWB
offices. Other bureaux de change may not give
such favourable rates.

The major credit and debit cards are widely
accepted (VISA more widely than others) but
supermarkets will not generally accept credit
cards. As a precaution carry enough cash to cover
your purchases as you may find that debit cards
issued by banks outside the Netherlands are not
accepted. Cash machines are widespread.

## Motoring in the Netherlands

The Dutch drive assertively and are not renowned
for their road courtesy. Pedestrians should be very
careful when crossing roads, including on zebra
crossings.

## Accidents

All accidents which cause injuries or major
damage must be reported to the police. Drivers
involved in an accident must exchange their
identity details and their insurance company
contact information.

## Alcohol

The maximum permitted level of alcohol is
50 milligrams in 100 millilitres of blood, i.e. lower
than that permitted in the UK (80 milligrams).
Penalties for driving under the influence of alcohol
can be severe. A lower level of 20 milligrams
applies to drivers who have held a driving licence
for less than five years. It is wisest to adopt a 'no
drinking and driving' rule.

## Breakdown Service

There are emergency telephones every 2km on
all motorways and they are directly linked to the
nearest breakdown centre.

ANWB, the motoring and leisure organisation,
has a road patrol service which operates 24 hours
a day on all roads. Drivers requiring assistance
may call the 'Wegenwacht' road patrol centre by
telephoning 088 2692888. Alternatively call the
ANWB Emergency Centre on (070) 3141414.
Operators speak English.

Charges apply for breakdown assistance and
towing is charged according to distance and time
of day. Members of clubs affiliated to the AIT/FIA,
such as The Caravan Club, incur lower charges.
Payment by credit card is accepted. In some areas
the ANWB Wegenwacht has contracts with local
garages to provide assistance to its members
and affiliates.

## Essential Equipment

*Lights*

The use of dipped headlights during the day is
recommended.

*Child Restraint System*

Children under the age of 18 years, measuring
less than 1.35m, must be seated in an approved
child restraint adapted to their size (ECE 44/03 or
44/04 safety approved). Children under 3

years old are able to travel in the front if they are seated in a rear facing child seat with the airbag deactivated, and under no circumstances are they allowed to travel in a car with no child restraint system fitted.

## Fuel

Unleaded petrol is available from green pumps marked 'Loodvrije Benzine'. LPG (autogas) is widely available along main roads and motorways.

Petrol stations along motorways and main roads and in main towns are open 24 hours, except in parts of the north of the country where they close at 11pm. Credit cards are accepted but some all night petrol stations only have automatic pumps which may operate with bank notes only.

## Low Emission Zones

Low Emission Zones are in operation in 11 cities in the Netherlands. Restrictions only apply to freight vehicles over 3500kg, however currently all foreign vehicles are able to enter the Low Emission Zone without any restrictions. This may change so check www.lowemissionzones.eu before you travel.

## Parking

Parking meters or discs are in use in many towns allowing parking for between 30 minutes and two or three hours; discs can be obtained from local shops. A sign 'parkeerschijf' indicates times when a disc is compulsory. Paid parking is expensive and there are insufficient parking spaces to meet demand. Clamping and towing away of vehicles are commonplace and fines are high. Check signs for the precise times you are allowed to park, particularly on main roads in Amsterdam.

## Priority

Yellow diamond shaped signs with a white border indicate priority roads. In the absence of such signs drivers must give way to all traffic approaching from the right. At the intersection of two roads of the same class where there are no signs, traffic from the right has priority.

At junctions marked with a 'priority road ahead' sign, a stop sign or a line of white painted triangles ('shark's teeth') across the road, drivers must give way to all vehicles on the priority road, including bicycles and mopeds. Be particularly careful when using roundabouts – on some you have the right of way when on them, but on others you must give way to vehicles entering the roundabout, i.e. on your right.

Trams have priority at the intersection of roads of equal importance, but they must give way to traffic on priority roads. If a tram or bus stops in the middle of the road to allow passengers on and off, you must stop. Buses have right of way over all other vehicles when leaving bus stops in built-up areas.

## Roads

Roads are generally good and well maintained, but are overcrowded and are frequently subject to strong winds. Most cities have a policy of reducing the amount of nonessential traffic within their boundaries. Narrowing roads, obstacles, traffic lights and speed cameras are often in place to achieve this.

## Road Signs and Markings

National motorways are distinguished by red signs, and prefixed with the letter A, whereas European motorways have green signs and are prefixed E. Dual carriageways and other main roads have yellow signs with the letter N and secondary roads are prefixed B.

In general road signs and markings conform to international standards. The following are some road signs which may also be seen:

Cycle path

Cycle route

District Numbers

Hard shoulder open as rush-hour lane

| Dutch | English Translation |
|---|---|
| Afrit | Exit |
| Doorgaand verkeer gestremd | No throughway |
| Drempels | Humps |
| Langzaam rijden | Slow down |
| Omleiding | Detour |
| Oprit | Entrance |
| Ousteek u lichten | Switch on lights |
| Parkeerplaats | Parking |
| Pas op! | Attention |
| Stop-verbod | No parking |
| Wegomlegging | Detour |
| Werk in uitvoering | Road works |
| Woonerven | Slow down (in built-up area) |

A continuous central white line should not be crossed even to make a left turn.

## Speed Limits

| | Open Road (km/h) | Motorway (km/h) |
|---|---|---|
| Car Solo | 80-90 | 120 |
| Car towing caravan/trailer | 80-90 | 90 |
| Motorhome under 3500kg | 80-90 | 120 |
| Motorhome 3500-7500kg | 80 | 80 |

Be vigilant and observe the overhead illuminated lane indicators when they are in use, as speed limits on motorways are variable. Speed cameras, speed traps and unmarked police vehicles are widely used. Radar detectors are illegal, with use resulting in a fine of £430.

Motorhomes over 3,500kg are restricted to 50 km/h (31 mph) in built-up areas and to 80 km/h (50 mph) on all other roads.

Certain sections of motorways have a speed limit of 130 km/h for solo cars. This is indicated by signposts.

The beginning of a built up area is indicated by a rectangular blue sign with the name of the locality in white. The end of a built up area is indicated by the same sign with a white diagonal lines across it.

## Traffic Jams

The greatest traffic congestion occurs on weekdays at rush hours around the major cities of Amsterdam, Den Bosch, Eindhoven, Rotterdam, Utrecht, The Hague and Eindhoven.

Summer holidays in the Netherlands are staggered and, as a result, traffic congestion is not too severe. However during the Christmas, Easter and Whitsun holiday periods, traffic jams are common and bottlenecks regularly occur on the A2 (Maastricht to Amsterdam), the A12 (Utrecht to the German border) and on the A50 (Arnhem to Apeldoorn). Roads to the Zeeland coast, e.g. the A58, N57 and N59, may become congested during periods of fine weather.

Many Germans head for the Netherlands on their own public holidays and the roads are particularly busy during these periods.

## Violation of Traffic Regulations

Police are empowered to impose on-the-spot fines (or confiscate vehicles) for violation of traffic regulations and fines for speeding can be severe. If you are fined always ask for a receipt.

## Motorways

There are over 2,750 kilometres of toll-free motorway. There are rest areas along the motorways, most of which have a petrol station and a small shop. Tolls are charged on some bridges and tunnels, notably the Westerschelde Toll Tunnel. This road tunnel links Terneuzen (north of Gent) and Ellewoutsdijk (south of Goes) across the Westerschelde. It provides a short, fast route between Channel ports and the road network in the west of the country. The tunnel is 6.6km long (just over 4 miles) and the toll (2014) for a car + caravan (maximum height 3m measured from front axle) is €7.45 and for a motorhome €7.45 (height under 2.5m) or €18.20 (height over 3m). Credit cards are accepted. See www.westerscheldetunnel.nl.

# Touring

The southern Netherlands is the most densely populated part of the country but, despite the modern sprawl, ancient towns such as Dordrecht, Gouda, Delft and Leiden have retained their individuality and charm. Rotterdam is a modern, commercial centre and a tour of its harbour – the busiest in Europe – makes a fascinating excursion. The scenery in the north of the country is the most typically Dutch – vast, flat landscapes, largely reclaimed from the sea, dotted with windmills. Some of the most charming towns and villages are Marken, Volendam and Alkmaar (famous for its cheese market). Aalsmeer, situated south of Amsterdam, stages the world's largest daily flower auction.

It is worth spending time to visit the hilly provinces in the east such as Gelderland, known for its castles, country houses and its major city, Arnhem, which has many links with the Second World War. Overijssel is a region of great variety and the old Hanseatic towns of Zwolle and Kampen have splendid quays and historic buildings. Friesland is the Netherland's lake district.

An Amsterdam Card entitles you to free admission to many of the city's famous museums, including the Rijksmuseum and Van Gogh Museum, and to discounts in many restaurants, shops, attractions and at Park & Ride car parks. It also entitles you to discounts on tours as well as free travel on public transport and a free canal cruise. The Card is valid for one, two or three days and is available from tourist information offices, some Shell petrol stations, Canal Bus kiosks, Park & Ride car parks and some hotels. Alternatively purchase online from www.iamsterdamcard.com.

Service charges are included in restaurant bills and tips are not necessary. Smoking is not permitted in bars or restaurants.

Spring is one of the most popular times to visit the Netherlands, in particular the famous Keukenhof Gardens near Lisse, open from 22 March to 20 May in 2012, see www.keukenhof.nl. Visitors enjoy a display of over seven million flowering bulbs, trees and shrubs. Special events take place here at other times of the year, including a National Bulb Market in October.

# Public Transport

There is an excellent network of buses and trams, together with metro systems in Amsterdam (called the GVB), Rotterdam and The Hague. An electronic card 'OV Chipkaart' is gradually replacing the previous system of 'Strippenkaart' which were strips of 15 or 45 tickets valid throughout the country.

OV-Chip cards can be bought at vending machines at stations or ticket offices and on board buses and trams and are available for periods from one hour to seven days allowing unlimited travel on trams, buses and the metro. Children under the age of 12 and people over the age of 65 qualify for reduced fares (show your passport as proof of age). For more information see www.gvb.nl.

Tickets must be validated before travel either at the yellow machines on trams and at metro stations or by your bus driver or conductor.

In Amsterdam canal transport includes a regular canal shuttle between Centraal Station and the Rijksmuseum. A 'circle tram' travels from Centraal Station through the centre of Amsterdam past a number of local visitor attractions, such as Anne Frank's house, the Rijksmuseum, Van Gogh museum and Rembrandthuis.

There are Park & Ride facilities at most railway stations. Secure parking is also offered at 'transferiums', a scheme offering reasonably priced guarded parking in secure areas on the outskirts of major towns with easy access by road and close to public transport hubs. Transferiums have heated waiting rooms and rest rooms as well as information for travellers, and some even have a shop.

Frequent car ferry services operate on routes to the Frisian (or Wadden) Islands off the north west coast, for example, from Den Helder to Texel Island, Harlingen to Terschelling Island and Holwerd to Ameland Island. Other islands in the group do not allow cars but there are passenger ferry services. In the summer island-hopping round tickets are available to foot passengers and cyclists and are popular for exploring the country.

**AARDENBURG see Sluis** *A4*

**AERDT see Zevenaar** *C3*

**ALKMAAR** *B2* (2km N Rural) *52.64200, 4.72390*
**Camping Alkmaar, Bergerweg 201, 1817 ML Alkmaar [(072) 5116924; info@campingalkmaar.nl; www.campingalkmaar.nl]** Fr W ring rd (Martin Luther Kingweg) foll Bergen sp, bear R at T-junc & site 150m on L. Site well sp. Med, mkd pitch, hdstg, pt shd; htd wc; chem disp; mv service pnt; fam bthrm; shwrs €0.50; el pnts (4-10A) inc; lndtte; shop 1km; BBQ; playgrnd; pool adj; sand beach 6km; golf 2km; cab TV; some statics; dogs €3; bus at gate; poss cr; Eng spkn; adv bkg; quiet; ccard acc; red CKE/CCI. "Clean, friendly site; sm pitches; buses to town; 10 mins walk to cent; cheese mkt on Friday in ssn." ♦ ltd 1 Apr-1 Oct. € 25.00                    2009*

**ALKMAAR** *B2* (3km N Rural) *52.69425, 4.77080* **Camping DroomPark Molengroet, Molengroet 1, 1723 PX Noord-Scharwoude [(0226) 393444; fax 391426; info@molengroet.nl; www.molengroet.nl]** Fr Amsterdam, Haarlem take A9 to end at rndabt, then onto Ring Alkmaar & foll sp Schagen. Take N245 sp Schagen (dual carr'way). Exit at km post 25.2 W sp Geestmeerambacht. Site sp on R. Lge, hdg/mkd pitch, unshd; htd wc; chem disp; mv service pnt; baby facs; fam bthrm; some serviced pitches; private san facs some pitches; shwrs inc; el pnts (4-10A) inc; gas; lndtte (inc dryer); shop; rest, snacks; bar; BBQ; htd pool; sand beach 10km; lake sw 300m; entmnt; cycle hire; sat TV; 50% statics; dogs €3; sep car park; free bus to cheese mkt (Fri) & beach (Sat); Holland Tulip Parcs site; adv bkg; quiet; ccard acc. "Located in recreation park with lge lake; site bus to cheese mkt & beach; modern, clean san facs." Easter-31 Oct. € 26.00 (CChq acc)                    2009*

**ALKMAAR** *B2* (5km SW Rural) *52.60649, 4.69016* **Camping Heiloo, De Omloop 24, 1852 RJ Heiloo [(072) 5355555; fax 5355551; info@campingheiloo.nl; www.campingheiloo.nl]** Exit A9 to Heiloo. At 1st traff lts in Heiloo turn L sp Egmond, foll sp to site. Med, pt shd; htd wc; chem disp; mv service pnt; baby facs; shwrs inc; el pnts (4A) inc; lndtte; shop 100m; rest, snacks; bar; playgrnd; htd, covrd pool adj; sand beach 5km; internet; TV; 50% statics; no dogs; train nr; sep car park (extra for car on pitch); Eng spkn; adv bkg; quiet, but occasional aircraft noise; ccard acc (surcharge). "San facs unisex low ssn; Heiloo quiet & untouristy; easy cycling to coast, bulbfields, Alkmaar; gd." ♦ ltd 4 Apr-20 Sep. € 26.75                    2009*

⊞ **ALKMAAR** *B2* (6km SW Rural) *52.63100, 4.69500* **Camping Hoeve Engeland, Egmondermeer 9, 1934 PN Egmond aan den Hoef [(072) 5116370; rus.jan@tiscali.nl]** Take A9 to Alkmaar & take N9 ring rd W. Take 1st L turn after rlwy viaduct at traff lts opp ING bank. Foll sm rd past garden cent, site in approx 250m - sp on gate. Sm, pt shd; htd wc; shwrs inc; el pnts (16A) inc (poss rev pol); beach 8km; bus 1km; poss cr; Eng spkn; adv bkg; quiet. "Friendly, CL-type farm site; clean (ltd) facs; mosquitoes; gd cycling to historic Alkmaar & coastal dunes; Gd cycling area; Friendly helpful owner." 15 Mar-15 Oct. € 15.00                    2013*

**ALMERE** *C3* (2km S Rural) *52.35688, 5.22505* **Camping Waterhout, Archerpad 6, 1324 ZZ Almere [(036) 5470632; fax 5470634; info@waterhout.nl; www.waterhout.nl]** Exit A6 junc 4, site sp fr slip rd on S edge Weerwater. Med, mkd pitch, shd; wc; chem disp; baby facs; fam bthrm; shwrs €0.50; el pnts (10A) inc; lndtte (inc dryer); shop; tradsmn; rest, snacks; bar; playgrnd; sand beach & lake sw adj; entmnt; TV rm; 30% statics; dogs €2.50; phone; bus 200m; poss cr; Eng spkn; adv bkg; quiet; red CKE/CCI. "Well laid-out site; conv Amsterdam by bus or train - 30 mins; Almere ultra-modern city." 4 Apr-19 Oct. € 29.00                    2014*

**AMERSFOORT** *C3* (9km S Rural) *52.07975, 5.38151* **Vakantiepark De Heigraaf, De Haygraeff 9, 3931 ML Woudenberg [(033) 2865066; info@heigraaf.nl; www.heigraaf.nl]** Exit A12 at Maarn junc 21 or junc 22 & foll sp to site on N224, 2km W of Woudenberg. V lge, mkd pitch, pt shd; htd wc; chem disp; mv service pnt; baby facs; shwrs €0.50; el pnts (4-6A) inc; lndtte (inc dryer); shop, rest, snacks; bar; playgrnd; lake sw 150m; wifi; entmnt; 50% statics; no dogs; phone; bus 500m; Eng spkn; adv bkg; quiet. "Vg, well-managed site; modern san facs; well run site, does not accept Visa."♦ 1 Apr-31 Oct. € 20.00                    2012*

**AMSTELVEEN see Amsterdam** *B3*

**AMSTERDAM** *B3* (2.5km N Urban) *52.38907, 4.92532* **Camping Vliegenbos, Meeuwenlaan 138, 1022 AM Amsterdam [(020) 6368855; fax 6322723; www.vliegenbos.com]** Fr A10 Amsterdam ring rd, take exit S116 Amsterdam Noord, at 2nd slip rd turn R sp Noord over rndabt, turn L at next rndabt, then immed sharp R, L onto service rd; site sp. Lge, hdstg, pt sl, pt shd; htd wc; chem disp; mv service pnt; baby facs; shwrs inc; el pnts (6A) inc; gas; lndtte; shop; rest 2km; snacks; bar; pool 1.5km; no dogs; phone; bus to city nr; poss cr; Eng spkn; poss noisy tent campers; ccard acc. "Sm pitches mainly for tents; ltd el pnts; m'vans & c'vans park outside barrier; friendly staff; bus tickets to city cent fr recep; cycle path to city cent via free ferry; modern san facs." ♦ 1 Apr-1 Oct. € 28.50                    2013*

See advertisement

**AMSTERDAM** *B3* (5km N Rural) *52.43649, 4.91445* **Camping Het Rietveen, Noordeinde 130, 1121 AL Landsmeer [(020) 4821468; fax 4820214; info@campinghetrietveen.nl; www.campinghetrietveen.nl]** Fr A10 ring rd exit junc 117. At junc off slip rd turn L dir Landsmeer, site sp. Sm, mkd pitch, mkd pitch; wc; chem disp; mv service pnt; shwrs inc; el pnts (10A) inc; shop, rest, bar 500m; lake sw & fishing; tennis; cycle hire; dogs free; phone adj; bus to Amsterdam 200m; poss cr; Eng spkn; adv bkg; quiet; CKE/CCI. "Vg, pretty lakeside site, like lge CL, in well-kept vill; no recep - site yourself & owner will call; sep field avail for rallies; excel touring base; city 30 mins by bus; san facs inadequate." 1 Mar-30 Nov. € 34.00                    2014*

NETHERLANDS

⊞ **AMSTERDAM** *B3* (3km E Urban) *52.36555, 4.95829*
**Camping Zeeburg, Zuider Ijdijk 20, 1095 KN Amsterdam
[(020) 6944430; fax 6946238; info@campingzeeburg.nl;
www.campingzeeburg.nl]** Fr A10 ring rd exit at S114 &
foll site sps. Lge, unshd; wc; chem disp; mv service pnt; shwrs
€0.80; el pnts (6-10A) inc; gas; lndtte; shop; snacks; cycle hire;
internet; some statics; dogs €3; bus/tram to city nr; poss cr; adv
bkg. "Used mainly by tents in summer, but rest of year suitable
for c'vans; conv city cent." € 28.00                          2011*

**AMSTERDAM** *B3* (10km S Urban) *52.31258, 4.99035*
**Gaasper Camping, Loosdrechtdreef 7, 1108 AZ
Amsterdam-Zuidoost [(020) 6967326; fax 6969369; info@
gaaspercamping.nl; www.gaaspercamping.nl]** Fr A2
take A9 E sp Amersfoort. After about 5km take 3rd exit sp
Gaasperplas/Weesp S113. Cross S113 into site, sp. Lge, hdg/
mkd pitch, some hdstg, pt shd; htd wc; chem disp; mv service
pnt; serviced pitches; shwrs metered; el pnts (10A) €3.50
(care needed); gas; lndtte; shop; rest, snacks; bar; playgrnd;
20% statics; dogs €2.50; metro 5 mins walk (tickets fr site
recep); poss cr; Eng spkn; quiet but some rd & air traffic noise;
CKE/CCI. "Immac site set in beautiful parkland; well-run with
strict rules; night guard at barrier (high ssn); vans must be
manhandled onto pitch (help avail); high ssn arr early to ensure
pitch - no adv bkg for fewer than 7 nights; poss cold shwrs &
ltd shop low ssn; gd security; well run site; conv for metro; adv
bkg rec in high season." 1 Jan-6 Jan, 15 Mar-1 Nov, 27 Dec-
31 Dec. € 33.50                                             2014*

**AMSTERDAM** *B3* (12km SW Rural) *52.29366, 4.82316*
**Camping Het Amsterdamse Bos, Kleine Noorddijk 1,
1187 NZ Amstelveen [(020) 6416868; fax 6402378; info@
campingamsterdam.com; www.campingamsterdambos.
com]** Foll A10 & A4 twd Schiphol Airport. Fr junc on A4 &
A9 m'way, take A9 E twd Amstelveen; at next exit (junc 6)
exit sp Aalsmeer. Foll Aalsmeer sp for 1km bearing R at traff
lts then at next traff lts turn L over canal bdge onto N231. In
1.5km turn L at 2nd traff lts into site. Fr S exit A4 junc 3 onto
N201 dir Hilversum (ignore other camp sps). Turn L onto N231
dir Amstelveen, at rd junc Bovenkirk take N231 dir Schiphol,
site on R in 200m, sp. V lge, pt shd; htd wc; chem disp; mv
service pnt; shwrs €0.80; el pnts (10A) €4.50; gas; lndtte; shop;
supmkt nr; rest, snacks; bar; waterpark nr; wifi; 20% statics;
dogs €3; bus to city; poss cr; Eng spkn; adv bkg; some aircraft
noise; ccard acc; CKE/CCI. "Conv Amsterdam by bus - tickets
sold on site; poss migrant workers resident on site; san facs
stretched high ssn; gd walking & cycling paths; spectacular
daily flower auctions at Aalsmeer; conv bulbfields." ♦ 15 Mar-
31 Oct. € 30.50                                             2014*

**AMSTERDAM** *B3* (10km W Rural) *52.39548, 4.75308*
**Camping Parc Spaarnwoude (formerly Houtrak),
Zuiderweg 2, 1105 NA Halfweg [(020) 4972796; fax
(087) 7844089; info@campinghoutrak.nl; www.
parcspaarnwoude.nl]** Fr A9 dir Haarlem exit onto A200 sp
Halfweg. In 1.5km sp for Spaarnwoude, go L under A200, over
rlwy x-ing & take 4th on L. Site on R in 100m. Fr Amsterdam
foll N202, Spaarnwoude & site sp. Sm, mkd pitch, pt shd; htd
wc; chem disp; mv service pnt; baby facs; shwrs €0.50; el pnts
(6A) €2.20; lndtte; playgrnd; pool 11km; internet; TV; dogs
€5; poss cr; noise fr aircraft. "Under flightpath into Schiphol
airport; min stay 3 nights Aug." 1 Apr-31 Oct. € 17.40  2009*

⊞ **ANNEN** *D2* (3.7km S Rural) *53.03017, 6.73912*
**De Baldwin Hoeve, Annerweg 9, 9463 TB Eext
[05 92 27 16 29; baldwinhoeve@hetnet.nl; www.
baldwinhoeve.nl]** Fr N34 take Annen exit. Turn R onto
Anlooerweg. At rndabt take R dir Eext. Bef underpass take sm
service rd on L to campsite. Sm, mkd pitch, unshd; wc; chem
disp; shwrs; el pnts (10A); BBQ; dogs; bus adj; twin axles; Eng
spkn; adv bkg; poss cr; CCI. "CL type farm site with excel san
facs; friendly owners; some rd noise; horses & other livestock;
lg group accomodation avail; vg." € 51.00                 2014*

**APELDOORN** *C3* (7km N Rural) *52.29066, 5.94520* **Camping
De Helfterkamp, Gortelseweg 24, 8171 RA Vaassen
[(0578) 571839; fax 570378; info@helfterkamp.nl; www.
helfterkamp.nl]** Leave A50 junc 26; foll sp to Vaassen; site
sp on ent to town - 2.5km W of Vaassen. Med, mkd pitch, pt
shd; htd wc; chem disp; baby facs; fam bthrm; shwrs €0.50; el
pnts (16A) metered (poss rev pol); gas; lndtte; shop; playgrnd;
lake sw 1.5km; cycle hire; 40% statics; dogs €1.75; phone;
Eng spkn; adv bkg ess high ssn; quiet; wifi; ccard acc; 10%
red long stay; CKE/CCI. "Excel, immac, well-maintained, busy
site in beautiful woodland area; key for shwrs & hot water; v
friendly owners; conv for Apeldoorn/Arnhem areas & De Hooge
Veluwe National Park; gd walking/cycling." 22 Feb-31 Oct.
€ 33.50                                                    2014*

**APELDOORN** *C3* (13km N Rural) *52.31366, 5.92705*
Recreatiecentrum De Wildhoeve, Hanendorperweg
102, 8166 JJ Emst [(0578) 661324; fax 662965; info@
wildhoeve.nl; www.wildhoeve.nl] Exit 26 fr A50, site
sp 3.5km W of Emst. Lge, mkd pitch, pt shd; htd wc; chem
disp; mv service pnt; serviced pitches; fam bthrm; baby facs;
shwrs; el pnts (6A); gas; lndtte (inc dryer); shop; tradsmn;
rest, snacks; bar; playgrnd; 2 pools (1 htd, covrd); paddling
pool; waterslide; games area; tennis; cycle hire; wifi; TV;
20% statics; no dogs; sep car park; Holland Tulip Parcs site;
adv bkg. ◆ 1 Apr-30 Sep. € 31.75 (CChq acc)          2011*

See advert on bookmark

⊞ **APELDOORN** *C3* (8km S Rural) *52.15096, 6.02197*
Camping De Vinkenkamp, Vinkenkamp 10, 7364 CD
Lieren [(055) 5051253; info@vinkenkamp.nl; www.
vinkenkamp.nl] Exit A1 junc 20 Apeldoorn Sud & foll sp
Loenen-Eerbeek. Site sp. Med, mkd pitch, pt shd; htd wc; chem
disp; mv service pnt; baby facs; shwrs inc; el pnts (6-16A) inc;
gas; lndtte; shop; snacks; bar; playgrnd; entmnt; TV; some
statics; dogs €1.70; Eng spkn; quiet; ccard acc. "Beautiful pt of
Holland; excel site." € 22.50          2010*

**APELDOORN** *C3* (13km SW Rural) *52.15040, 5.74080*
Camping De Harskamperdennen, Houtvester van
't Hoffweg 25, 3775 KB Kootwijk [(0318) 456272;
fax 457695; info@harskamperdennen.nl; www.
harskamperdennen.nl] Exit A1/E30 at junc 17 dir Harskamp,
site sp on L in 6km. Lge, shd; htd wc; chem disp; mv service
pnt; baby facs; shwrs €0.50; el pnts (4-6A) inc; gas; lndtte;
tradsmn; playgrnd; games area; cycle hire; TV; no dogs; phone;
sep car park; quiet; ccard acc. "All pitches in sm glades in
forest; military base nr & explosions heard fr time to time,
otherwise peaceful; neat, tidy site; friendly staff." ◆ 1 Apr-
25 Oct. € 26.00          2009*

**APPELSCHA** *D2* (4.5km SSW Rural) *52.92134, 6.34447*
Boscamping Appelscha, Oude Willem 3, 8426 SM
Appelscha [(0516) 431391; info@boscampingappelscha.
nl; www.campingalkenhaer.nl] A28 junc 31 sp Drachten.
Turn L onto N381. About 13km turn L onto Oude Willem then
take 3rd R, site on L. Lge, mkd pitch, pt shd; wc; chem disp; mv
service pnt; baby facs; shwrs; el pnts (16A); lndtte (inc dryer);
tradsmn; snack; takeaway; playgrnd; paddling pool; wifi;
60% statics; Eng spkn; quiet; CKE/CCI. "Neat, friendly, well run
site; many walking, cycling & riding trails in nrby national park;
vg site." 1 Apr-1 Oct. € 33.50          2014*

**ARNHEM** *C3* (5km W Rural) *51.99365, 5.82203* Camping
Aan Veluwe (formerly De Bilderberg), Sportlaan 1,
6861 AG Oosterbeek [(0224) 563109; fax 563093; info@
aannoordzee.nl; www.aanveluwe.nl] Fr S fr Nijmegen,
cross new bdge at Arnhem. Foll Oosterbeek sp for 5km, cont
past memorial in Oosterbeek, in 1km turn R at rndabt, 500m
L to site. Or fr A50 exit junc 19 onto N225 twd Osterbeek/
Arnhem. In 3km at rndabt turn L, site on L in 500m. Med,
pt sl, pt shd; htd wc; chem disp; shwrs inc; el pnts (16A) inc;
gas; shop; bar; playgrnd; pool 3km; adv bkg; few statics; dogs
€1.80; sep car park; quiet; red for long stays. "Conv Airborne
Museum & Cemetery & Dutch Open Air Museum; sports club
bar open to site guests; shwr facs for each pitch; lovely walks."
29 Mar-13 Oct. € 27.80          2014*

**ARNHEM** *C3* (3km NW Rural) *52.0072, 5.8714* Camping
Warnsborn, Bakenbergseweg 257, 6816 PB Arnhem
[(026) 4423469; fax 4421095; info@campingwarnsborn.
nl; www.campingwarnsborn.nl] Fr Utrecht on E35/A12,
exit junc 25 Ede (if coming fr opp dir, beware unnumbered
m'way junc 200m prior to junc 25). Take N224 dual c'way twd
Arnhem & foll sp Burgers Zoo, site sp. Beware oncoming traff
& sleeping policeman nr site ent. Med, pt shd; htd wc; chem
disp, mv service pnt; baby facs; fam bthrm; shwrs €1; el pnts
(4A) inc; gas; lndtte; sm shop & 3km; tradsmn; rest 1km; BBQ;
playgrnd; internet; 5% statics; dogs €3; phone; bus 100m; poss
cr; Eng spkn; adv bkg; quiet; ccard acc; red long stay/CKE/CCI.
"Excel, spacious, clean, well-maintained, wooded site; san facs
clean; friendly, helpful family owners & staff; airborne museum
& cemetery; cycle rtes direct fr site; conv Hooge Veluwe
National Park & Kröller-Müller museum (Van Gogh paintings);
super site but busy." ◆ ltd 1 Apr-26 Oct. € 28.00          2014*

**ARNHEM** *C3* (5km NW Rural) *52.03192, 5.86652* Droompark
Hooge Veluwe, Koningsweg 14, Schaarsbergen, 6816
TC Arnhem [(026) 4432272 / (088) 0551500; fax 4436809;
hoogeveluwe@droomparken.nl; www.hoogeveluwe.
nl] Fr Utrecht A12/E35, Oosterbeck exit 25 & foll sp for Hooge
Veluwe to site in 4km on R. Lge, pt shd; htd wc; chem disp;
mv service pnt; baby facs; fam bthrm; serviced pitches; shwrs
inc; el pnts (6-16A) inc; gas; lndtte; shop; rest, snacks; bar;
playgrnd; 2 pools (1 htd, covrd); paddling pool; games area;
entmnt; dogs €3.50; 50% static in sep area; sep car park;
some rd noise; poss cr; adv bkg; Eng spkn; ccard acc. "Vg,
espec for children; excel site; lots of facs; helpful staff; care
needed turning into site area; great value; vg clean san facs; gd
rest; conv for Arnhem area, m'way & Ijmuiden ferry port." ◆
28 Mar-26 Oct. € 39.00          2014*

**BARENDRECHT see Rotterdam** *B3*

**BEERZE see Ommen** *D2*

**BEILEN** *D2* (7km S Rural) *52.80166, 6.52501* Camping
De Otterberg, Drijberseweg 36A, 9418 TL Wijster
[(0593) 562362; fax 562941; info@otterburg.nl; www.
otterberg.nl] Take A28 Hoogeveen-Assen exit Dwingeloo/
Wijster. In Wijster turn R & foll sps approx 1.5km dir Dribjer.
Lge, mkd pitch, pt shd; htd wc; fam bthrm; baby facs; chem
disp; shwrs €0.20; el pnts (6A) inc; gas; lndtte (inc dryer); shop;
snacks; rest; playgrnd; pool; tennis; cycle hire; TV; 60% statics;
dogs €3; phone; poss cr; Eng spkn; adv bkg. "Helpful, friendly
site adj National Park; gd, modern san facs." ◆ 1 Apr-1 Oct.
€ 25.00          2010*

**BEILEN** *D2* (2.5km NW Rural) *52.85285, 6.59010* Camping
De Valkenhof, Beilerstraat 13a, 9431 GA Westerbork
[(0593) 331546; fax 333278; info@camping-de-valkenhof.
nl; www.camping-de-valkenhof.nl] Exit A28 junc 30
Beilen, dir Westerbork, site sp to W of Westerbork. Lge,
some hdstg, pt shd; htd wc; chem disp; mv service pnt; baby
facs; fam bthrm; shwrs inc; el pnts (6A) inc; gas; lndtte (inc
dryer); supmkt high ssn; snacks; BBQ; playgrnd; htd pool;
paddling pool; waterslide; games area; cycle hire; wifi; cab TV;
20% statics; dogs €4.35; sep car park; Holland Tulip Parcs site;
Eng spkn; adv bkg; quiet. "Gd walking area." 1 Apr-1 Oct.
€ 25.00          2011*

**BELT SCHUTSLOOT see Meppel** *C2*

**BERG EN TERBLIJT see Valkenburg aan de Geul** *C4*

**BERGEIJK see Eersel** *C4*

**BERGEN OP ZOOM** *B4* (3km NW Rural) *51.51122, 4.31652* **Camping De Heide, Bemmelenberg 12, 4614 PG Bergen op Zoom [(0164) 235659 or 253522; fax 254377; info@ campingdeheide.nl; www.campingdeheide.nl]** Exit A58 at Bergen op Zoom Noord, foll sp to town until De Heide sps are picked up. Lge, hdg pitch, pt shd; wc; chem disp; mv service pnt; baby facs; fam bthrm; serviced pitch; shwrs €0.50; el pnts (4A) €2.50; gas; Indtte; shop; rest, snacks; playgrnd; pool; sand beach 3km; TV; 75% statics; dogs €3; phone; adv bkg; quiet; red snr citizens; CKE/CCI. "Gd NH." ♦ 1 Apr-26 Sep. € 30.00                                                  2009*

**BERLICUM see 'S-Hertogenbosch** *C3*

**BIDDINGHUIZEN see Harderwijk** *C3*

**BILTHOVEN see Utrecht** *B3*

**BLADEL** *C4* (1km S Rural) *51.35388, 5.22254* **Mini-Camping De Hooiberg, Bredasebaan 20, 5531 NB Bladel [(0497) 369619 or 06 54341822 (mob); info@minicampingdehooiberg.nl; www. minicampingdehooiberg.nl]** Exit A67 junc 32 onto N284 to Bladel, turn L at traff lts to Bladel-Zuid, site on L in 2km. Sm, pt shd; htd wc; chem disp; shwrs inc; el pnts (6A) inc; Indtte (inc dryer); no statics; dogs free; bus adj; sep car park; Eng spkn; adv bkg; quiet. "Gd site." ♦ ltd 15 Mar-31 Oct. € 14.00                                                  2009*

**BLADEL** *C4* (2km S Rural) *51.34325, 5.22740* **Camping De Achterste Hoef, Troprijt 10, 5531 NA Bladel [(0497) 381579; fax 387776; info@achterstehoef.nl; www. achterstehoef.nl]** Fr A67 exit junc 32 onto N284 to Bladel, then Bladel-Zuid, site sp. V lge, pt shd; htd wc; chem disp; mv service pnt; baby facs; fam bthrm; private san facs avail; shwrs; el pnts (6A) inc; Indtte (inc dryer); supmkt; rest, snacks; bar; playgrnd; 2 pools (1 htd, covrd); waterslide; tennis; games area; games rm; cycle hire; wifi; entmnt; 70% statics; dogs; adv bkg; ccard acc. ♦ 4 Apr-26 Oct. € 48.40 (CChq acc)                                          2014*

**BOURTANGE** *D2* (W Rural) *53.01014, 7.18494* **NCC Camping 't Plathuis, Bourtangerkanaal Noord 1, 9545 VJ Bourtange [(0599) 354383; fax 354388; info@plathuis. nl; www.plathuis.nl]** Exit A47 junc 47 onto N368 sp Blijham to Vlagtwedde. Turn L onto N365 to Bourtange, site sp on R. Med, pt shd, htd wc; chem disp; mv service pnt; baby facs; fam bthrm; shwrs €0.50; el pnts (6A) inc (extra for 10A); gas; Indtte; shop; tradsmn; snacks; bar; playgrnd; lake sw; fishing; games area; cycle canoe hire; wifi; 50% statics; dogs; phone; bus; adv bkg; quiet; red CC1. "Site adj historic fortress town 2km fr German border; sm marina at ent; pt of site belongs to NCC (CC members welcome at red rates but must phone ahead); gd, clean facs; friendly, helpful owners; vg." ♦ 1 Apr-31 Oct. € 17.50                                                  2010*

**BREDA** *B3* (8km E Rural) *51.58270, 4.90721* **Camping D'n Mastendol, Oosterhoutseweg 7-13, 5121 RE Rijen [(0161) 222664; fax 222669; info@mastendol.nl; www. mastendol.nl]** Take main rd fr Breda twd Tilburg (not m'way). After 9km turn L, on rd sp Oosterhout 9km; camp 500m on L. Lge, pt shd; htd wc; chem disp; mv service pnt; baby facs; shwrs €0.75; el pnts (10A) inc; Indtte; shops 2km; snacks; bar; playgrnd; pool; TV; 90% statics; dogs €3; phone; rd noise; ccard acc. "Conv touring base; pitches in pine woods; friendly staff." ♦ 21 Mar-31 Oct. € 23.00                     2010*

**BREDA** *B3* (10km SE Rural) *51.49334, 4.89964* **Camping RCN De Flaasbloem, Flaasdijk 1, 4861 RC Chaam [(0161) 491654; fax 492054; flaasbloem@rcn.nl; www. rcn.nl/centra/deflaasbloem]** A58 Breda-Tilberg, exit junc 14 for Chaam. Fr vill on Alphen rd, site sp. V lge, mkd pitch, pt sl, pt shd; htd wc; chem disp; mv service pnt; baby facs; fam bthrm; shwrs inc; el pnts (10A) inc; gas; Indtte (inc dryer); shop; supmkt; rest, snacks; playgrnd; 2 pools (1 htd, covrd) lake sw & beach; wifi; TV; 75% statics; dogs €4.75; adv bkg; quiet, but poss noisy w/end; Eng spkn; CKE/CCI. "Cycling cent in flat woodland; many sports facs; many facs for children; well-run site." ♦ 1 Apr-31 Oct. € 28.00                     2010*

**BREDA** *B3* (2.5km SW Rural) *51.56488, 4.69628* **Camping Liesbos, Liesdreef 40, 4838 GV Breda [(076) 5143514; fax 5146555; info@camping-liesbos.nl; www.camping-liesbos.nl]** Fr A16 take exit 16 dir Etten-Leur. Fr A58/E312 take exit 18; site sp. Lge, pt shd; wc; chem disp; mv service pnt; shwrs €0.75; el pnts (6A) inc; gas; Indtte; shop; rest, snacks; bar; playgrnd; pool; paddling pool; tennis; cycle hire; TV; 95% statics; dogs €2.50; phone; poss v cr; quiet; ccard acc. "Narr site rds; sm pitches; v clean san facs; NH only." 1 Apr-1 Oct. € 20.00                                                  2009*

⊞ **BRESKENS** *A4* (3km W Coastal) *51.40360, 3.51310* **Molecaten Park Napoleon Hoeve, Zandertje 30, 4511 RH Breskens [(0117) 383838 or 381428; fax 383550; camping@napoleonhoeve.nl; www.napoleonhoeve. nl]** Fr S on N58 twd Breskens, turn L onto N675 dir Groede. Approx 500m bef Groede turn N onto Noordweg twd coast, then L into Zandertje. Site sp on coast rd. Lge, mkd pitch, unshd; htd wc; chem disp; mv service pnt; baby facs; private san facs avail; shwrs €0.50; fam bthrm; el pnts (10A) inc; gas; Indtte; supmkt; rest, snacks; bar; playgrnd; 2 pools (1 htd, covrd); sand beach adj; sep naturist beach; tennis; cycle hire; entmnt; TV; 60% statics; dogs €3.90; phone; adv bkg; ccard acc. "Friendly, family site; excel facs; gd bar, rest & children's play area." ♦ € 37.00                     2010*

**BRIELLE** *B3* (1km NE Urban) *51.90969, 4.18533* **Camping De Krabbeplaat, Oude Veerdam 4, 3231 NC Brielle [(0181) 412363; fax 412093; info@krabbeplaat.nl; www. krabbeplaat.com]** Exit A15 fr Rotterdam junc 12 onto N57. Foll sp Brielse Maas-Noord, then site sp. Site sp fr N57. Lge, hdg/mkd pitch, pt shd; wc; chem disp; mv service pnt; baby facs; shwrs inc; el pnts (4-10A) inc; gas; Indtte (inc dryer); shop; rest, snacks; bar; playgrnd; rv adj; tennis; games area; cycle & boat hire; wifi; cab TV; 70% statics; no dogs; phone; ferry to Brielle; poss cr; Eng spkn; adv bkg; ccard acc; CKE/CCI. "Gd for families; easy access to rv." ♦ 1 Apr-24 Oct. € 24.00    2010*

**BRIELLE** *B3* (5km NE Coastal) *51.91379, 4.18218* **NCC Camping De Lepelaar, Brielse Veerweg, 3231 NA Brielle [(0181) 417338; www.ncc.nl]** Fr Rotterdam foll A15/N15 W dir Europoort. Exit junc 12 at Brielle, over Hartelkanaal & at end sliprd exit Brielse Maas Noord. Turn L on Staaldiepseweg, in 2.3km L into Brielse Veerweg, sp Voetveer Brielle. Site 2nd on R. Sm, mkd pitch, pt shd; htd wc; chem disp; shwrs inc; el pnts (4A) €2.75; lndtte; shop, rest, snacks, bar 9km; BBQ; playgrnd; lake sw & beach 500m; dogs; phone; poss cr; adv bkg req; quiet; CKE/CCI. "Excel site; CC members welcome, but must pre-book; ferry to Brielle (high ssn) 200m." ♦ ltd 1 Apr-31 Oct. € 10.00                                                           2009*

**BRIELLE** *B3* (700m E Urban) *51.90666, 4.17527* **Camping de Meeuw, Batterijweg 1, 3231 AA Brielle [(0181) 412777; fax 418127; info@demeeuw.nl; www.demeeuw.nl]** On A15/N57 foll sp to Brielle. Turn R after passing thro town gates & foll sp to site. Lge, pt shd; wc; chem disp; mv service pnt; fam bthrm; baby facs; shwrs inc; el pnts (6A) €2 (poss rev pol); gas; lndtte; shop; rest, snacks; bar; playgrnd; pool 2km; sand beach; cycle hire; entmnt; 70% statics; dogs €3.75; phone; Eng spkn; red CKE/CCI. "Historic fortified town; attractive area for tourers; conv Europoort ferry terminal; gd NH/sh stay." 1 Apr-31 Oct. € 22.50                                                           2009*

**BROEKHUIZENVORST See Horst** *C4*

⊞ **BUREN (AMELAND ISLAND)** *C1* (1km N Coastal) *53.45355, 5.80460* **Camping Klein Vaarwater, Klein Vaarwaterweg 114, 9164 ME Buren [(0519) 542156; fax 542655; info@kleinvaarwater.nl; www.kleinvaarwater. nl]** Take ferry fr Holwerd to Nes on Ameland Island. Turn R at rndabt twd Buren & strt on to supmkt. At 3-lane intersection turn L twd beach rd & site. Med, mkd pitch, pt shd; htd wc; chem disp; mv service pnt; baby facs; fam bthrm; shwrs; el pnts (16A); gas; lndtte (inc dryer); supmkt; ATM; rest, snacks; bar; BBQ; playgrnd; htd, covrd pool; paddling pool; waterslide; sand beach 800m; tennis; 10-pin bowling; games area; fitness rm; wifi; entmnt; TV; 75% statics; no dogs; Holland Tulip Parcs site; poss cr; adv bkg; red low ssn. "Nature park adj; site in dunes & forest." ♦                                                           2011*

**BURGH-HAAMSTEDE** *A3* (2.8km NW Coastal) *51.71478, 3.72219* **Camping Ginsterveld, Maireweg 10, 4328 GR Burgh-Haamstede (Zeeland) [(0111) 651590; fax 653040; info@ginsterveld.nl / ginsterveld@ardoer.com; www.ardoer.com/en/camping/ginsterveld]** SP fr Burgh-Haamstede. Foll R107. Lge, pt shd, wc, chem disp, child/baby facs, shwrs el (6A) inc, lndtte, shop, rest, snack bar, take away, BBQ; playgrnd, paddling pool, sandy beach 2km, games area, bicycles, entmnt ssn,wifi, 50% statics, Eng spkn, adv bkg acc, red low ssn, "Excel cycling and walking fr site, vg." ♦ 22 Mar-27 Oct. € 46.00                                                           2013*

⊞ **CALLANTSOOG** *B2* (1.5km NE Coastal) *52.84627, 4.71549* **Camping Tempelhof, Westerweg 2, 1759 JD Callantsoog [(0224) 581522; fax 582133; info@ tempelhof.nl; www.tempelhof.nl]** Fr A9 Alkmaar-Den Helder exit Callantsoog, site sp to NE of vill. Lge, mkd pitch, pt shd; htd wc; mv service pnt; chem disp; mv service pnt; serviced pitches; baby facs; fam bthrm; sauna; private bthrms avail; shwrs inc; el pnts (10A) inc; gas; lndtte; rest, snacks, bar high ssn; playgrnd; htd, covrd pool; paddling pool; sand beach 1km; tennis; games area; gym; cycle hire; wifi; entmnt; sat TV; 50% statics; dogs €3.50; phone; adv bkg. "Superb, well-run site & facs; ACSI Card acc." ♦ € 39.00                                                           2013*

See advert on bookmark

**CALLANTSOOG** *B2* (1.5km NE Coastal) *52.84143, 4.71909* **NCC Camping De Ooster Nollen, Westerweg 8, 1759 JD Callantsoog [(0224) 581281 or 561351; fax 582098; info@ denollen.nl; www.denollen.nl]** N fr Alkmaar on A9; turn L sp Callantsoog. Site sp 1km E of Callantsoog. Lge, mkd pitch, pt shd; htd wc; chem disp; mv service pnt; baby facs; shwrs inc; el pnts (10A) inc; gas; lndtte (inc dryer); shop; rest, snacks; bar; playgrnd; pool 400m; sand beach 1.5km; cycle hire; games area; wifi; entmnt; TV; 40% statics; dogs €3; phone; Eng spkn; adv bkg; quiet; ccard acc; 10% red long stay; CKE/CCI. "Nature area nr; cheese mkt." 1 Apr-31 Oct. € 25.50   2009*

**CHAAM See Breda** *B3*

**DE KOOG See Den Burg (Texel Island)** *B2*

**DE KOOG** *B2* (500m SE Rural) *53.09610, 4.76500* **De Luwe Boshoek, Kamperfoelieweg 3, 1796 MT De Koog [02 22 31 73 90]** Fr ferry take 501 to De Koog. Sp after ref point 17. R at De Zwaluw Hotel. Site on L after 100m. Med, mkd pitch, unshd; htd wc; chem disp; fam bthrm; shwr inc; el pnts (16A); lndtte (inc dryer); shop 0.5km; BBQ; sandy beach 1km; 10% statics; dogs; quiet. "Excel; gd base to stay, bike hire 0.5 km." ♦ 15 Mar-1 Nov. € 129.09                          2014*

**DE VEENHOOP See Drachten** *C2*

**DEIL** *C3* (1km SE Rural) *51.87040, 5.26047* **Camping De Kijfakkers, Hooiweg 6A, 4158 LE Deil [(0345) 651203; fax 651590; famdeheus@kijfakker.nl; www.kijfakker.nl]** Fr A2 exit junc 15 onto N327 E sp Geldermalsen. Turn R at 1st rndabt, L at T-junc into Hooiweg, site on L in 500m, sp. Sm, hdg/mkd pitch, unshd; htd wc; chem disp; shwrs; el pnts (6A) inc; lndtte (inc dryer); shop, rest, snacks, bar 3km; BBQ; pool 2km; TV; dogs €1; bus 3km; poss cr; Eng spkn; adv bkg rec; quiet. "CL-type site on farm (cattle, horses); gd cycling, walking espec along Rv Linge; gd touring base." 15 Mar-31 Oct. € 13.50                                                           2010*

# VERSATILE AND SURPRISING

vakantiepark

verrassend veelzijdig

Korftlaan 5
2616 LJ - Delft
The Netherlands

+31 15 213 00 40
info@delftsehout.nl
www.delftsehout.nl

**DELFT** *B3* (1km E Urban) *52.01769, 4.37945* **Camping Delftse Hout, Korftlaan 5, 2616 LJ Delft [(015) 2130040; fax 2131293; info@delftsehout.nl; www.delftsehout.nl]** Fr Hook of Holland take N220 twd Rotterdam; after Maasdijk turn R onto A20 m'way. Take A13 twd Den Haag at v lge Kleinpolderplein interchange. Take exit 9 sp Delft (Ikea on R). Turn L under m'way (3.2m height limit) & immed R at 1st traff lts; then site sp. Lge, hdg/mkd pitch, some hdstg, pt shd; htd wc; chem disp; mv service pnt; baby facs; fam bthrm; shwrs inc; el pnts (10A) inc; gas; lndtte (inc dryer); shop; rest, snacks; bar; BBQ; playgrnd; htd pool; paddling pool; watersports; fishing nrby; cycle hire; golf 5km; wifi; entmnt; games/TV rm; 50% statics; dogs €3.25; no c'vans/m'vans over 7.50m; phone; bus to Delft; Holland Tulip Parcs site; Eng spkn; some rd noise; ccard acc; red low ssn/long stay/snr citizens/CKE/CCI. "Located by pleasant park; gd quality, secure, busy site with excel facs; helpful, friendly staff; little shade; sm pitches poss diff lge o'fits; excursions by bike & on foot; easy access Delft cent; sm m'van o'night area outside site; mkt Thur; excel; site clean & well maintained; gd rest; vg play areas for kids." ♦ 28 Mar-1 Nov. € 40.30 SBS - H06                          2014*

See advertisement

**DELFT** *B3* (9.4km SW Rural) *51.95450, 4.28833* **Hoeve Bouwlust, Oostgaag 31, 3155 CE Maasland [(0105) 912775; info@hoevebouwlust.nl; www. hoevebouwlust.nl]** Fr Hofh on A20 turn N at junc 7. Go thro Maasland on N468. Site on L in 3km. Sm, hdg pitch, pt shd; wc; chem disp; mv service pnt; shwrs; el pnts; lndtte (inc dryer); rest; café; bbq; playgrnd; wifi; 10% statics; bus adj; twin axles; Eng spkn; adv bkg; CKE/CCI. "Lots of outdoor activities inc tandem, boating & scotters; v friendly & helpful owners; vg site." 1 Apr-31 Oct. € 17.50                          2014*

**DEN BURG (TEXEL ISLAND)** *B2* (6km NW Rural) *53.10346, 4.77107* **Camping Om de Noord, Boodtlaan 50, 1796 BG De Koog [(0222) 327842; fax 327167; info@texelcampings. nl; www.texelcampings.nl]** Fr ferry take rd to De Koog; site sp on R of rd on N of town dir De Cocksdorp. Med, mkd pitch, pt shd; htd wc; mv service pnt; chem disp; fam bthrm; baby facs; private san facs avail; shwrs inc; el pnts (16A) inc; lndtte (inc dryer); playgrnd; pool 1.5km; sand beach 2km; games area; wifi; 10% statics; dogs €4; phone; poss cr; quiet; ccard acc; CKE/CCI. "Excel site adj nature reserve; walks in heathland; conv touring Texel; friendly owners." ♦ 1 Apr-31 Oct. € 38.60                          2010*

**DEN HELDER** *B2* (2km SW Coastal) *52.93672, 4.73377*
Camping de Donkere Duinen, Jan Verfailleweg 616,
1783 BW Den Helder [(0223) 614731; fax 615077; info@
donkereduinen.nl; www.donkereduinen.nl] Fr S turn
L off N9 sp Julianadorp (Schoolweg), strt over at x-rds in
Julianadorp (Van Foreestweg). Turn R at t-junc onto N502, site
on L in approx 4km. Lge, pt shd; wc; chem disp; mv service
pnt; baby facs; shwr inc; el pnts (4-16A) inc; gas; lndtte; shops
3km; playgrnd; sand beach 800m; tennis; cycle hire; wifi;
10% statics; dogs €2.75; poss cr; Eng spkn; adv bkg (fee);
quiet; CKE/CCI; Ccard acc (matercard only). "V helpful owner;
excel walking/cycling; ferry to Texel Is; lge naval museum &
submarine." 17 Apr-3 Sep. € 33.50                    2014*

**DENEKAMP** *D3* (3.5km NE Rural) *52.39190, 7.04890*
Camping De Papillon, Kanaalweg 30, 7591 NH
Denekamp [(0541) 351670; fax 355217; info@depapillon.
nl; www.depapillon.nl] Fr A1 take exit 32 onto N342
Oldenzaal-Denekamp, dir Nordhorn, site sp just bef German
border. Lge, pt shd; htd wc; chem disp; mv service pnt; baby
facs; fam bthrm; shwrs €0.20; el pnts (4A) inc; gas; lndtte;
shop; rest, snacks; bar; playgrnd; 2 pools (1 htd & covrd); lake
sw; tennis; cycle hire; TV; 12% statics; dogs €4.50; phone;
quiet; red long stay/low ssn. "Super, clean site; friendly,
helpful owners; man-made lake." ♦ 1 Apr-1 Oct. € 24.75
2012*

See advert on bookmark

**DEVENTER** *C3* (1.5km W Urban) *52.24992, 6.14634* Camp
Municipal De Worp, De Worp 12, 7419 AD Deventer
[(0570) 613601; deventer@stadscamping.eu; www.
stadscamping.eu] Fr N on N337 on o'skts of Deventer foll
'Centrum' sp to W of town cent. Go over rv bdge on N344
dir Apeldoorn, site immed on R. sp. Or fr A1 exit junc 22 dir
Twello, turn R onto N344, site on L just bef rv bdge on ent
Deventer. Med, pt shd; htd wc; chem disp (wc); baby facs;
fam bthrm; shwrs €1; el pnts (4-6A) €2.50; lndtte; playgrnd;
10% statics; dogs €2.50; phone; Eng spkn; quiet; CKE/
CCI. "Foot passenger ferry over rv to Deventer cent adj site;
lovely, interesting old town; Terwolde windmill worth visit;
refurbished san facs but inadequate if site full." 1 Apr-30 Sep.
€ 16.50                                    2011*

⊞ **DIEREN** *C3* (2.5km NW Rural) *52.06908, 6.07705* De
Jutberg Vakantiedorp, Jutberg 78, 6957 DP Laag-Soeren
[03 13 61 92 20; jutberg@ardoer.com; www.ardoer.com/
jutberg] Fr A12 take exit 27 onto the A348. Turn L on the
N348 into Dieren. Turn L at petrol stn, cont for 2.7km. Foll sp
to site. V lge, mkd pitch, pt sl, shd; htd wc; chem disp; baby
facs; shwrs inc; el pnts (6A); lndtte; shop; rest; snacks; bar;
BBQ; playgrnd; htd covrd pool; games area; games rm; entmnt;
wifi; dogs; Eng spkn; adv bkg; quiet; CCI. "Hugh pitches, fully
serviced; v lively but not noisy; excursions for adults & kids in
summer; wet weather diversions; excel san facs; extensive cycle
paths thro countryside & forest; excel site." € 42.50    2014*

**DIEVER** *D2* (1km N Rural) *52.86684, 6.32004* Camping
Diever, Haarweg 2, 7981 LW Diever [tel/fax
(0521) 591644; camping.diever@hetnet.nl; www.
campingdiever.nl] Fr A32 exit 4 dir Havelte & Diever. In Diever
take dir Zorgvlied/Wateren, site sp. Lge, mkd pitch; pt sl, shd;
htd wc; chem disp; fam bthrm; baby facs; shwrs €0.50; el pnts
(10A) €2.75; gas; lndtte; shop; snacks; playgrnd; pool 5km;
cycle hire; internet; TV; some statics; dogs €2.25; phone; sep
car park; Eng spkn; adv bkg; quiet. "Pleasant, densely wooded
site." 1 Apr-1 Oct. € 16.60                    2009*

**DIEVER** *D2* (1km S Rural) *52.82405, 6.31650* Camping
Wittelterbrug, Wittelterweg 31, 7986 PL Wittelte
[(0521) 598288; fax 598250; info@wittelterbrug.nl;
www.wittelterbrug.nl] N of Meppel on N371 for approx
12km. Site on R over narr canal bdge. Med, hdg pitch, pt
shd; wc; chem disp; mv service pnt; serviced pitch; baby facs;
shwrs €0.60; el pnts (10A) inc; gas; lndtte; shop & 5km; rest,
snacks; bar; playgrnd; covrd pool; paddling pool; cycle hire;
entmnt; TV; 65% statics; dogs €3.60; phone; Eng spkn; adv
bkg; quiet. "Lovely family-run site; facs excel." 1 Apr-31 Oct.
€ 19.50                                    2009*

**DIFFELEN see Hardenberg** *D2*

**DOETINCHEM** *D3* (3km SE Rural) *51.94628, 6.33550*
Camping De Wrange, Rekhemseweg 144, 7004 HD
Doetinchem [(0314) 324852; info@dewrange.nl; www.
dewrange.nl] Leave A18 at exit 4 dir Doetinchem Oost, then
L dir Doetinchem. In 500m turn R at water tower, foll site sp.
Lge, mkd pitch, unshd; htd wc; chem disp; mv service pnt; baby
facs; fam bthrm; shwrs €0.70; el pnts (4-6A) €3; gas; lndtte;
shop; rest, snacks; bar; BBQ; playgrnd; htd pool; paddling pool;
cycle hire; entmnt; TV; 75% statics; dogs €3; phone; sep car
park; poss cr; Eng spkn; adv bkg; quiet; CKE/CCI. ♦ ltd 1 Apr-
31 Oct. € 16.50                                2009*

**DOKKUM** *C2* (E Urban) *53.32611, 6.00468* Camping
Harddraverspark, Harddraversdijk 1a, 9101 XA Dokkum
[(0519) 294445; fax 571402; info@campingdokkum.nl;
www.campingdokkum.nl] Best app fr E fr ring rd N361 onto
Harddraversdijk alongside rv, site sp. Do not app thro town -
narr rds. Med, hdg/mkd pitch, some hdstg, pt shd; wc; chem
disp; mv service pnt; shwrs €0.50; el pnts (6A) €2.50; gas;
lndtte; shop, rest, snacks, bar 400m; tradsmn; playgrnd; tennis;
dogs €2; wifi; Eng spkn; quiet. "Excel location in cent of lovely
town; conv for ferry to Ameland Island (12km)." 1 Apr-31 Oct.
€ 15.00                                    2013*

**DOMBURG** *A3* (1.5km SE Rural) *51.55578, 3.51516*
Camping Westhove, Zuiverseweg 2, 4363 RJ Aagtekerke
[(0118) 581809; fax 582502; westhove@ardoer.com;
www.ardoer.com] Fr Middelburg thro Oostkapelle, site sp on
L twds Domburg. Lge, mkd pitch, pt shd; htd wc; chem disp;
mv service pnt; baby facs; shwrs inc; el pnts (4A) inc; lndtte;
shop; rest, snacks; bar; playgrnd; htd, covrd pool; sand beach
2km; cycle hire; entmnt; TV; 25% statics; dogs (not acc Jul/
Aug); phone; sep car park; Eng spkn; quiet; ccard acc; CKE/CCI.
"Gd pool; easy walk/cycle to Domburg & beach." ♦ 27 Mar-
25 Oct. € 35.00 (3 persons)                    2009*

**DORDRECHT** *B3* (3km SE Rural) *51.80738, 4.71862*
**Camping 't Vissertje, Loswalweg 3, 3315 LB Dordrecht**
**[(078) 6162751; info@campinghetvissertje.nl; www.**
**hetvissertje.nl]** Fr Rotterdam across Brienenoord Bdge foll sp
Gorinchem & Nijmegen A15. Exit junc 23 Papendrecht & turn R
onto N3 until exit Werkendam. Turn R & foll sp 'Het Vissertje'.
Sm, pt shd; wc; chem disp; shwrs €0.50; el pnts (6A) inc; wifi;
20% statics; dogs €1; Eng spkn; quiet; red long stay. "Lovely
site; friendly, helpful manager; modern, clean san facs; gd cycle
rtes nr; vg." 1 Apr-31 Oct. € 22.00                    2014*

⊞ **DORDRECHT** *B3* (8km W Rural) *51.79279, 4.53679*
**Camping De Fruitgaarde, Polderdijk 47, 3299 LL Maasdam**
**[(078) 6765176; www.campercontact.nl]** Exit A16 junc
20 onto N217 W dir Puttershoek & Maasdam thro Kiltunnel
(toll). Fork L onto N491 then foll rd round W side of polder dir
Binnenmaas & Westmaas. Site sp on L, 1km W of Maasdam.
Sm, hdstg, pt shd; htd wc; chem disp; mv service pnt; baby
facs; shwrs inc; el pnts (16A) €2; lndtte; shop 6km; tradsmn;
rest; snacks 1km; bar; playgrnd; pool 4km; sw adj; no statics;
dogs; bus 1km; Eng spkn; quiet. "Site in orchard; helpful
owner; water bus, Kinderdijk windmills, historic towns nrby."
♦ ltd € 14.00                                          2012*

**DRACHTEN** *C2* (4km S Rural) *53.07095, 6.13672* **Camping
Het Koningsdiep, De Mersken 2, 9247 WK Ureterp
[(0512) 381844; info@campinghetkoningsdiep.nl; www.
campinghetkoningsdiep.nl]** Exit A7/E22 at junc 30 onto
N381 dir Oosterwolde. In 1km after Azeven indus est turn
R into Selmien West, then in 1km turn L into Selmien/De
Mersken, site sp. Sm, pt shd; htd wc; chem disp; fam bthrm;
shwrs inc; el pnts (10A) inc; lndry rm; shop 2.5km; rest, snacks,
bar 2.5km; BBQ; horseriding; dogs; Eng spkn; adv bkg; quiet;
CKE/CCI. "Vg, friendly site on working stud farm; gd walking;
gd touring base." ♦ 1 Apr-28 Oct. € 20.00              2009*

**DRACHTEN** *C2* (10km W Rural) *53.12556, 5.98391* **Camping
de Stjelp, It West 48, 9216 XE Oudega [(0512) 372270; fax
371053; stjelp@camping-de-stjelp.nl; www.camping-de-
stjelp.nl]** W fr Drachten on N31. Turn L at Nijega then bear
R to Oudega. Site at W end of vill at bungalow no. 1920.
Sm, mkd pitch, unshd; wc; chem disp; shwrs inc; el pnts (4A)
metered; lndry rm; shop, snacks, bar 1km; BBQ; lake sw &
beach 3km; cycle hire; dogs €1; quiet; CKE/CCI. "Attractive
farm site, friendly owners; conv Friesland canals & lakes; cycle
rtes; vg touring base." ♦ ltd 14 Apr-15 Oct. € 13.60   2011*

**DRACHTEN** *C2* (13km W Rural) *53.09696, 5.94695* **Camping
De Veenhoop Watersport & Recreatie, Eijzengapaed 8,
9215 VV De Veenhoop [(0512) 462289; fax 461057; info@
de-veenhoop.nl; www.de-veenhoop.nl]** Exit A7 junc 28 dir
Nij Beets, foll De Veenhoop sp to site. Or exit A32 junc 13 &
turn W for approx 6km via Aldeboarn. Turn L at Pieter's Rest
to De Veenhoop, site on L bef sm bdge. Med, pt shd; htd wc;
chem disp; shwrs €0.50; el pnts (6-10A) €3; lndtte; shops 5km;
rest 200m; BBQ; sm playgrnd; lake sw; boat hire; 50% statics;
dogs; bus adj; Eng spkn; adv bkg; quiet. "Excel, peaceful,
friendly site; clean & well-maintained; excel sailing, cycling,
walking; well situated for lakes & N N'lands; gd NH." 1 Apr-
31 Oct. € 14.50                                        2010*

⊞ **DRIMMELEN** *B3* (1km E Rural) *51.70690,
4.82290* **Camping Biesbosch Marina, Marinaweg
50, 4924 AD Drimmelen [(0162) 685795; fax
681675; info@campingbiesboschmarina.nl; www.
campingbiesboschmarina.nl]** Exit A59 junc 32 at Made
& foll sp Drimmelen & site. Med, mkd pitch, unshd; htd wc;
chem disp; mv service pnt; baby facs; fam bthrm; serviced
pitches; shwrs inc; el pnts (16A) inc; gas; lndtte (inc dryer);
shop; tradsmn; rest, snacks; bar; BBQ; playgrnd; lake sw & sand
beach; sailing lessons; boat, canoe, cycle hire; games area; wifi;
some statics; dogs €3 (max 1); Holland Tulip Parcs site; adv bkg;
quiet; ccard acc; red long stay. "Superb site; access to all facs
by electronic key; lge, well-drained pitches; excel touring base
& conv NH Hook of Holland." € 30.55                    2009*

**DRONTEN** *C2* (1km W Rural) *52.52099, 5.69189* **Camping en
Horecacentrum 't Wisentbos, De West 1, 8251 ST Dronten
[(0321) 316606; info@wisentbos.nl; www.wisentbos.nl]**
E fr Lelystad on N309, site well sp. Sm, some hdstg, pt shd;
htd wc; chem disp; mv service pnt; baby facs; shwrs €0.50;
el pnts (10A) inc; lndtte; rest, snacks; bar; playgrnd; beach &
fishing lake adj; 80% statics; dogs €1.55; bus adj; Eng spkn;
adv bkg; quiet; ccard acc (not Visa). "Wooded area; friendly,
helpful staff; sep area for m'vans; excel." 1 Apr-31 Oct.
€ 15.00                                                2009*

⊞ **DWINGELOO** *D2* (2km SE Rural) *52.82216, 6.39258*
**Camping De Olde Bârgen, Oude Hoogeveensedijk 1,
7991 PD Dwingeloo [(0521) 597261; fax 597069; info@
oldebargen.nl; www.oldebargen.nl]** Exit A28 Zwolle/Assen
rd at Spier, turn W sp Dwingeloo, site clearly sp, in wooded
area. Sm, mkd pitch, pt shd; wc; chem disp; fam bthrm;
shwrs inc; el pnts (4-6A) inc; lndtte; shop 800m; playgrnd;
pool 1.5km; few statics; wifi; dogs €2; adv bkg; Eng spkn;
quiet; CKE/CCI. "Excel, well-run site on N side Dwingelderveld
National Park; gd for walkers & cyclists; v friendly, helpful
owners; delightful, quiet site." ♦ € 27.75             2014*

**ECHT** *C4* (1km N Rural) *51.09213, 5.91116* **Camping
Marisheem, Brugweg 89, 6102 RD Echt [(0475) 481458;
fax 488018; info@marisheem.nl; www.marisheem.nl]**
Exit A2 Maastricht-Eindhoven junc 45 dir Echt. In Echt foll
sp Koningsbosch, site down side rd on L. Lge, mkd pitch, pt
shd; htd wc; chem disp; mv service pnt; shwrs; el pnts (6-10A)
inc; gas; lndtte; shop; rest, snacks; bar; htd pool; playgrnd;
60% statics; no dogs; quiet; Eng spkn; red low ssn; CKE/CCI.
"Vg, well-organised site; vg pool; helpful staff; gd train service
to Maastricht." 1 Apr-30 Sep. € 31.00 (4 persons)      2011*

⊞ **ECHT** *C4* (2km NE Rural) *51.12075, 5.96888* **Camping
Biej De Vogel, Heinsbergerweg 15, 6065 NK Montfort
[(0475) 541522; info@campingbiejdevogel.nl; www.
campingbiejdevogel.nl]** Exit A2/E25 junc 44 dir Roermond,
turn R to Montfort & go thro town to fork & statue. Turn L
up narr rd, then strt over x-rds, farm approx 1km on L. Sm,
mkd pitch, pt shd; wc; chem disp; shwrs €1; el pnts (10-16A)
€1.75; lndtte; shop 2km; pool 2km; dogs; phone; Eng spkn;
adv bkg; quiet; red long stay. "Excel CL-type site - 15 pitches."
€ 12.00                                                2009*

**EDAM** *B2* (9km S Rural) *52.42787, 5.07387* **Camping-Jachthaven Uitdam, Zeedijk 2, 1154 PP Uitdam [(020) 4031433; fax 4033692; info@campinguitdam. nl; www.campinguitdam.nl]** Fr Amsterdam foll N247 (Amsterdam-Hoorn), at 10km turn R sp Marken/Monickendam across canal. After 5km turn R at camping sp to site on L after 2km. Lge, pt shd; htd wc; chem disp; mv service pnt; baby facs; shwrs €0.90; el pnts (4-6A) inc; gas; lndtte; shop; rest, snacks; bar; playgrnd; pool 5km; paddling pool; sand beach adj; fishing; boating; cycle hire; entmnt; TV; 50% statics; dogs €5; phone; poss cr; Eng spkn; adv bkg; 20% red low ssn; ccard acc; CKE/CCI. "Exposed location low ssn; no water supply nr touring pitches; bus 2km to Amsterdam cent; water taxi to Volendam; excel cycle tracks." 1 Mar-31 Oct. € 23.70    2009*

**EDAM** *B2* (2km NW Coastal) *52.52457, 5.06478* **Camping Strandbad Edam, Zeevangszeedijk 7A, 1135 PZ Edam [(0299) 371994; fax 371510; info@campingstrandbad.nl; www.campingstrandbad.nl]** Foll N247 Amsterdam-Hoorn; after sp for Edam foll site sp. At traff lts in Edam keep on N247 past bus stn on R, then R at next rndabt. Last 100m to site is single track opp marina. Access thro public car park. Lge, pt shd; htd wc; chem disp; mv service pnt; baby facs; fam bthrm; shwrs €1; el pnts (10A) €2.90; gas; lndtte; shop; rest, snacks; bar; playgrnd; pool 3km; paddling pool; sand beach adj; watersports; cycle hire; wifi; TV; 40% statics; no dogs; phone; poss cr; Eng spkn; adv bkg; quiet; ccard acc; red long stay. "Walking dist Edam; landing stage for boats; excel san facs; sm, poss cramped pitches high ssn." 1 Apr-30 Sep. € 20.25    2010*

**EERSEL** *C4* (6km SW Rural) *51.33635, 5.35552* **Camping De Paal, De Paaldreef 14, 5571 TN Bergeijk [(0497) 571977; fax 577164; info@depaal.nl; www.depaal.nl]** Fr A67/E34 Antwerp/Eindoven exit junc 32 sp Eersel & bear R onto N284 & stay in R-hand lane. At rndabt take 1st exit onto Eijkereind. In 500m after rndbt turn L at traffic lts & foll rd around R & L bend. Take R turn sp Bergeijk after lge church (site on sharp L bend). After approx 5km turn L into site rd. V lge, pt shd, htd wc (some cont); chem disp; mv service pnt; baby facs; sauna; fam bthrm; shwrs inc; el pnts (6A) inc; gas; BBQ (gas/charcoal); lndtte (inc dryer); shop; rest & snacks (high ssn); bar; playgrnds; 2 htd pools (1 covrd); paddling pool; sand beach, lake sw 7km; watersports 10km; fishing; excursions; sm children's zoo; tennis; cycle hire; horseriding 500m; wifi; entmnt; games rm/TV rm (sat TV); recep 0900-1800; 10% statics; dogs €5; no c'vans/m'vans over 8m high ssn; no twin-axles; phone; sep cark park; poss cr; ccard not acc; red low ssn. "Excel, family-run site set in woodland; espec gd for young children; lge pitches in groups with sep sm play areas; cent play areas; conv Efteling theme park, Hilvarenbeek safari park, Oisterwijk bird park; mkt Mon & Tue pm." ♦ 1 Apr-25 Oct. € 49.00 SBS - H04    2011*

See advert on bookmark

**EERSEL** *C4* (9km SW Rural) *51.29155, 5.29475* **Camping De Zwarte Bergen, Zwarte Bergendreef 1, 5575 XP Luyksgestel [(0497) 541373; fax 542673; info@zwartebergen.nl; www.zwartebergen.nl]** Fr Eindhoven foll sps to Bergeyk & Luyksgestel; site sp on main rd 2km S of Luyksgestel. V lge, mkd pitch, pt sl, shd; htd wc; chem disp; mv service pnt; some serviced pitches; baby facs; shwrs inc; el pnts (6-16A) inc; gas; lndtte; shop; rest, snacks; bar; playgrnd; pool; paddling pool; 60% statics; phone; sep car park; poss cr & noisy; Eng spkn; adv bkg; CKE/CCI. "Vg; well organised; ample facs but ltd low ssn; welcoming staff." ♦ 1 Apr-30 Sep. € 28.50    2009*

⊞ **EINDHOVEN** *C4* (10km SE Rural) *51.37393, 5.55206* **Camping Heezerenbosch, Heezerenbosch 6, 5591 TA Heeze [(040) 2263811; fax 2262422; info@heezerenbosch. nl; www.heezerenbosch.nl]** Exit m'way A56 at junc 34 & foll sp Heeze. Foll rd to town, site sp fr town limits, 2km W of cent. V lge, pt shd; htd wc (cont); chem disp; mv service pnt; baby facs; shwrs inc; el pnts (4A) inc; gas; lndtte; shop; rest, snacks; bar; playgrnd; pool; waterslide; lake sw adj; tennis; games area; cycle hire; TV; 95% statics; dogs €1.50; phone; adv bkg; quiet; red low ssn. "Low ssn site charges per day, ie 1 night's stay costs 2 days' fees; tourers in open field with elec & water - san facs some dist; helpful, friendly staff; busy, poss noisy site; grnd poss boggy low ssn." € 30.00    2009*

**EINDHOVEN** *C4* (10km S Rural) *51.32887, 5.46160* **Recreatiepark Brugse Heide, Maastrichterweg 183, 5556 VB Valkenswaard [(040) 2018304; fax 2049312; info@brugseheide.nl]** S fr Eindhoven, exit Waalre; take N69 Valkenswaard; drive thro to rndabt, turn L. At next rndabt strt ahead, at next rndabt turn R, foll sp Achel. Site on L in 1km. Lge, mkd pitch, shd; htd wc; all serviced pitches; chem disp; mv service pnt; baby facs; shwrs inc; el pnts (6A) inc; gas; lndtte (inc dryer); shop 2km; tradsmn; snacks; bar; BBQ; playgrnd; htd pool; paddling pool; cycle hire; wifi; entmnt; TV; 40% statics; dogs; phone; Eng spkn; adv bkg (no dep); quiet (can be v noisy w/end); ccard acc; red low ssn. "Excel, friendly site; gd NH en rte Germany." ♦ Easter-31 Oct. € 23.20 (4 persons)    2010*

**ELBURG** *C2* (600m E Rural) *52.44294, 5.84318* **Natuurkamping Landgoed Old Putten, Zuiderzeestraatweg Oost 55, 8081 LB Elburg [(0525) 681938; fax 681325; info@oldputten.nl; www. oldputten.nl]** Fr A28 exit junc 16 dir 't Harde & Elburg. Foll sp on Zuiderzeestraatweg. Sm, mkd pitch, pt shd; wc; chem disp; baby facs; shwrs inc; el pnts (4A) €2; lndtte; shops 500m; pool; tennis; 20% statics; sep car park; phone. 1 Apr-1 Oct. € 16.50    2009*

**ELLEWOUTSDIJK** *A4* (1km W Coastal) *51.38801, 3.82226* **NCC Camping Zuudschorre, P J Israelweg 3, 4437 NE Ellewoutsdijk [(0113) 548598; www.ncc.nl]** Exit A58 junc 35 at 's-Gravenpolder & foll sp S to Ovezande. Turn L dir Oudelande & foll sp Ellewoutsdijk. At statue turn L thro vill onto dyke, turn L & site sp 200m on L. Sm, hdg pitch, pt shd; htd wc; chem disp; shwrs inc; el pnts (4A) €2.75; lndtte; shop & 1km playgrnd; rv sw adj; dogs; bus; quiet. "Lovely setting on Schelde estuary nr charming vill; gd touring base Goes & Middelburg; well-maintained, friendly site; members only - CC members welcome but must pre-book." ♦ ltd 1 Apr-31 Oct. € 10.00    2009*

**EMMEN** *D2* (5km N Rural) *52.82861, 6.85714*
**Vakantiecentrum De Fruithof, Melkweg 2, 7871 PE
Klijndijk [(0591) 512427; fax (0591 513572; info@fruithof.
nl; www.fruithof.nl]** On N34 N fr Emmen dir Borger, turn
R sp Klijndijk, foll site sp. Lge, hdg/mkd pitch, pt shd; htd wc;
chem disp; mv service pnt; serviced pitches; baby facs; fam
bthrm; shwrs inc; el pnts (6A) inc; gas; lndtte; shop & 5km;
rest, snacks; bar; BBQ; playgrnd; htd pool; paddling pool; lake
sw & beach adj; tennis; games area; cycle hire; entmnt; TV;
50% statics; dogs; Eng spkn; adv bkg; red low ssn/long stay;
CKE/CCI. "Excel." Easter-29 Sep. € 27.80          2009*

**EMST see Apeldoorn** *C3*

**ENKHUIZEN** *C2* (800m N Coastal) *52.70888, 5.28830*
**Camping De Vest, Noorderweg 31, 1601 PC Enkhuizen
[(0228) 321221; fax 312211; info@campingdevest.nl;
www.campingdevest.nl]** When N302 turns R at traff lts,
keep strt on to T-junc. Foll site sp to R, site on R in 50m. Sm,
pt shd; wc; chem disp; shwrs; el pnts (4A) inc; sand beach
800m; 25% statics; dogs; poss cr; Eng spkn; adv bkg; ccard
not acc. "Gates clsd 2300-0800; easy walk to town cent; lively
jazz festival last w/end in May; facs old but well-kept - poss
stretched when site full." Easter-30 Sep. € 18.50      2011*

**ENKHUIZEN** *C2* (500m E Coastal) *52.7098, 5.2956* **Camping
Enkhuizer Zand, Kooizandweg 4, 1601 LK Enkhuizen
[(0228) 317289; fax 312211; info@campingenkhuizerzand.
nl; www.campingenkhuizerzand.nl]** Sp in town. Lge, pt
shd; htd wc; chem disp; mv service pnt; baby facs; shwrs inc;
el pnts (4A) inc; lndtte; shop; snacks; playgrnd; htd, covrd pool
adj; sand beach & lake sw; boating; tennis adj; TV; 70% statics;
dogs €3.50; phone; sep car park; poss cr; poss noisy; CKE/CCI.
"Modern san facs; Zuider Zee museum 1km; deer park." ♦
1 Apr-30 Sep. € 23.50                           2009*

⊞ **ENSCHEDE** *D3* (2.5km E Urban) *52.21034, 6.95127*
**Euregio Camping de Twentse Es, Keppelerdijk 200,
7534 PA Enschede [(053) 4611372; fax 4618558; info@
twentse-es.nl; www.twentse-es.nl]** Fr Germany, cross
border at Gronau on B54/N35; twd Enschede. In 2.5km turn
R into Oostweg, then in 2km turn R into Gronausestraat, then
in 800m turn R into Esmarkelaan. Foll rd thro residential area,
turn L at end, site on R. Not rec to foll sat nav due rd building,
rec foll rd signs. Lge, pt shd; htd wc; chem disp; shwrs inc; el
pnts (10A) inc; gas; lndtte; shop; snacks; bar; playgrnd;
pool; paddling pool; games area; cycle hire; wifi; entmnt; TV
rm; 70% statics; dogs free; adv bkg; quiet; ccard acc; red CKE/
CCI. "Excel site; modern facs." ♦ ltd € 27.00         2013*

**ERICHEM see Tiel** *C3*

⊞ **EXLOO** *D2* (2km SE Rural) *52.86841, 6.88496* **Camping
Exloo, Valtherweg 37, 7875 TA Exloo [05 91 54 91 47
or 05 91 56 40 14; info@campingexloo.nl; www.
campingexloo.nl]** N34 fr Groningen, exit Exloo. Turn R after
vill twd Valthe. Site 2km on L. Sm, pt shd; wc; chem disp; mv
service pnt; fam bthrm; shwrs; el pnts (6A); lndtte; BBQ; wifi;
tv rm; dogs €1; twin axles; Eng spkn; adv bkg; quiet; CCI.
"Friendly recreation rm; vg site." € 14.00          2014*

**GENDT** *C3* (S Rural) *51.87599, 5.98900* **Waalstrand
Camping, Waaldijk 23, 6691 MB Gendt [(0481) 421604;
fax 422053; info@waalstrand.nl; www.waalstrand.nl]**
Exit A15 to Bemmel, then Gendt. In Gendt foll sp to site on
Rv Waal. Med, mkd pitch, terr, unshd; wc; chem disp; baby
facs; fam bthrm; el pnts (6A) inc; gas; lndtte; snacks, bar adj;
playgrnd; pool; rv beach adj; tennis; cycle hire; wifi; cab TV inc;
50% statics; dogs €3; poss cr; Eng spkn; adv bkg; quiet but
some noise fr rv traff. "Excel, well-kept site; clean, modern san
facs; interesting rv traff." 1 Apr-1 Oct. € 24.50      2009*

**GIETHOORN see Meppel** *C2*

**GOES** *A3* (6km NW Rural) *51.54200, 3.78000*
**de Heerlijkheid van Wolphaartsdijk - Formaly
Minicamping Janse, Muidenweg 10, 4471 NM
Wolphaartsdijk [(0113) 581584 or 06 12612728 (mob);
fax 581111; info@heerlijkheidwolphaartsdijk.nl; www.
heerlijkheidwolphaartsdijk.nl]** Off N256 Zierikzee to Goes rd
foll sp Jachthaven Wolphaartsdijk. Shortly after vill turn L twd
windmill. Turn R at mini rndabt (ignore camping sp by L turn)
sp Arnemuiden, strt on at next rndabt, then L at next rndabt;
site on L in 1km on lakeside - ent thro farm gate. Sm, hdg
pitch, pt shd; wc; chem disp; shwrs inc; el pnts (6-16A) €2.50;
lndtte; playgrnd; lake sw & beach adj; windsurfing; sailing;
dogs €0.50; bus 1km; Eng spkn; quiet; CKE/CCI. "CL-type,
farm site; modern san facs; friendly owners; bird reserve opp;
excel cycling; rec." 15 Mar-31 Oct. € 24.50          2013*

> ## "There aren't many sites open at this time of year"
>
> If you're travelling outside peak season
> remember to call ahead to check site opening
> dates – even if the entry says 'open all year'.

**GOES** *A3* (7km NW Rural) *51.54685, 3.81339* **Camping
De Veerhoeve, Veerweg 48, 4471 NC Wolphaartsdijk
[(0113) 581155; fax 581944; info@deveerhoeve.nl; www.
deveerhoeve.nl]** Off N256 Zierikzee to Goes rd foll sp
Wolphaartsdijk. Site is last of 3 on this rd. Lge, mkd pitch,
some hdstg, pt shd; htd wc; chem disp; mv service pnt;
serviced pitches; baby facs; fam bthrm; shwrs €0.50; el pnts
(10A) inc; gas; lndtte (inc dryer); shop; snacks; playgrnd; pool
8km; watersports cent adj; windsurfing; sport fishing; diving;
sailing; tennis; games area; cycle hire; wifi; 50% statics; dogs
€4; phone; Holland Tulip Parcs site; poss cr; Eng spkn; adv
bkg ess; quiet; ccard acc; CKE/CCI. "By nature reserve & lovely
lake Veerse Meer." ♦ 1 Apr-30 Oct. € 26.00 (4 persons)
(CChq acc)                                        2009*

**GOOR** *D3* (6km N Rural) *52.29639, 6.61444* **Camping 't
Schuttenbelt, Vloodweg 7, 7468 RS Enter [0547 381472;
schuttenbelt@3onnet.nl]** Leave A1 at exit 28 twds Enter; site
sp bef Enter. Sm, mkd pitch, pt shd; wc; chem disp; baby facs;
shwrs inc; el pnts (10A) inc; lndtte; snacks; bar; BBQ; playgrnd;
pool; entmnt; dogs (extra charge); quiet. "Gd facs with excel
pitches; beautiful cycling & walking; gd site." ♦ 15 Apr-
15 Sep. € 19.00                                  2011*

**NETHERLANDS**

**GORINCHEM** *B3* (4km NE Rural) *51.84524, 5.03995* **Camping Het Lingebos, Haarweg 6, 4214 KL Vuren [(0183) 630631; fax 637185; info@lingebos.nl; www.lingebos.nl]** Exit A15 exit junc 28 Gorinchem E sp Lingebos. Site at end of lge recreation area. Lge, pt shd; wc; chem disp; mv service pnt; baby facs; shwrs inc; el pnts (4A) €2.50; lndtte; sm shop & 4km; tradsmn; rest, snacks; playgrnd; pool 5km; lake sw; fishing; canoeing; cycle hire; games area; few statics; dogs €3.50; phone; sep car park; poss cr; Eng spkn; adv bkg; quiet but some m'way noise; red long stay; CKE/CCI. "Pt grass, pt wooded; paved rdways; muddy when wet; gd rest; excel." ♦ 1 Apr-30 Sep. € 19.00                    2009*

**GORINCHEM** *B3* (10km E Rural) *51.81845, 5.12563* **Camping De Zwaan, Waaldijk 56, 4171 CG Herwijnen [(0418) 582354]** Exit A15 at junc 29 dir Herwijnen. In Herwijnen turn R at T-junc sp Brakel. Turn L in 500m (Molenstraat). At T-junc turn R (Waaldijk), site on L in 150m on Rv Waal. Sm, pt shd; wc; chem disp; shwrs €0.50; el pnts (4A) inc; shop 1km; playgrnd; rv adj; 75% statics; poss cr; adv bkg rec; Eng spkn; quiet but some boat noise; CKE/CCI. "Helpful owners; ltd but clean facs; 66 m fr Amsterdam ferry." 15 Apr-15 Oct. € 13.00                    2012*

⊞ **GOUDA** *B3* (500m E Urban) *52.01226, 4.71544* **Klein Amerika Parking, 2806 Gouda** 500m fr Gouda town cent, sp off Blekerssingel/Fluwelensingel. There are 3 designated parking spaces for m'vans in car park at Klein Amerika supervised by Gouda City Council. Max stay 3 days. Chem disp, water, rubbish bins, all free. Public wc (sm fee). Normal car parking fees applicable. € 7.00                    2009*

⊞ **GOUDA** *B3* (8.5km E Rural) *52.01719, 4.82943* **Camping De Mulderije, Hekendorpsebuurt 33, 3467 PA Hekendorp [(0348) 563233 or 06 20680521 (mob); demulderije@ wxs.nl; www.demulderije.com]** Exit A12 junc 14 Woerden onto N204 S. In 5km turn R to Oudewater N228. Cont dir Hekendorp & in approx 2km site sp on R. Narr rd to site. Sm, hdstg, pt shd; wc; chem disp; shwrs inc; el pnts (6A) inc; lndry rm; shop, rest, snacks, bar 2km; dogs free; quiet. "Vg, clean, friendly site in nature reserve; cycle or boat to Gouda; facs clean attractive position; narr rd to site not suitable for lge o'fits; no passing places; do not use Sat Nav." ♦ ltd € 16.00                    2013*

**GRIJPSKERKE** *A3* (2km E Rural) *51.53200, 3.56700* **Mini-Camping Het Munniken Hof, Jacob Catsweg 4, 4364 TE Grijpskerke [(0118) 591659; fax 594826]** Fr S via Westerschelde Tunnel to Middelburg, N on N57 & foll sp L dir Domburg & Grijpskerke. At vill sp take 1st R (opp windmill). In 300m 1st R, site on R 200m. Sm, pt shd; htd wc; chem disp; shwrs inc; el pnts (6A) inc; lndtte; shop, rest, snacks, bar 1km; playgrnd; sand beach 7km; dogs €0.50; sep car park; poss cr; Eng spkn; adv bkg; quiet. "Pleasant farm site; excel for cyling; vg touring base; v helpful owners." Easter-31 Oct. € 17.50                    2009*

**GROEDE see Breskens** *A4*

⊞ **GROENLO** *D3* (1.5km SE Rural) *52.03680, 6.63185* **Camping Marveld, Elshofweg 6, 7141 DH Groenlo [(0544) 466000; fax 465295; info@marveld.nl; www. marveld.nl]** Fr Groenlo take N319 dir Winterswijk, site well sp. V lge, mkd pitch, pt shd; htd wc; chem disp; mv service pnt; baby facs; fam bthrm; private san facs some pitches; sauna; shwrs €0.20; el pnts (6A) inc; gas; lndtte (inc dryer); shop; tradsmn; rest, snacks; bar; BBQ; playgrnd; htd, covrd pools; paddling pool; lake fishing; cycle hire; games area; wifi; entmnt; TV rm; 60% statics; dogs €2.50; phone; sep car park; Holland Tulip Parcs site; poss cr; adv bkg; Eng spkn; ccard acc (surcharge); CKE/CCI. "Huge leisure complex; something for everyone; immac." € 22.60 (CChq acc)                    2009*

**GRONINGEN** *D2* (2km SW Urban) *53.20128, 6.53577* **Camping Stadspark, Campinglaan 6, 9727 KH Groningen [(050) 5251624; fax 5250099; info@campingstadspark.nl; www.campingstadspark.nl]** Take exit 36-A (dir Drachten) and foll 'Stadspark'. In the park go to the L and foll the sp. Fr Drachten/Winsum, take exit 36. Med, shd; wc; chem disp; mv service pnt; fam bthrm; shwrs €0.45; el pnts (6A) €2.50 (poss rev pol); gas; lndtte (inc dryer); shop in ssn; tradsmn; snacks; bar; playgrnd; pool 3km; cycle hire; internet; TV; 20% statics; dogs €2; phone; sep car park; poss cr; Eng spkn; adv bkg; quiet; ccard not acc. "Municipal site adj parkland with gd sports facs; park & ride into town; plenty of space, tents & vans mixed; extensive cycle paths; car park adj to each set of pitches; gd san facs; well run site; interesting town." 15 Mar-16 Oct. € 28.30                    2014*

**GULPEN** *C4* (2km S Rural) *50.80720, 5.89430* **Panorama Terrassencamping De Gulperberg, Berghem 1, 6271 NP Gulpen [(043) 4502330; fax 4504609; info@gulperberg.nl; www.gulperberg.nl]** Fr Maastricht on N278 twd Aachen. At 1st traff lts in Gulpen turn sharp R & foll site sp for 2km (past sports complex). Narr final app. Lge, mkd pitch, some hdstg, terr, pt shd; htd wc; chem disp; baby facs; fam bthrm; shwrs inc; el pnts (6A) inc; gas; lndtte (inc dryer); shop; tradsmn; rest, snacks; bar; BBQ; playgrnd; pool; paddling pool; cycle hire; games area; wifi; cab/sat TV; 10% statics; dogs €3; phone; Holland Tulip Parcs site; poss cr; Eng spkn; adv bkg; quiet; red snr citizens; CKE/CCI. "Nr 3 nations boundary visitor cent & Maastricht with gd walking/views; mkd cycle rtes & footpaths; modern, clean facs - poss long walk; some tourers sited on top terr - long way fr shop & recep; beautiful views; v popular site, poss cr even in low ssn; excel." 1 Apr-30 Oct. € 25.60 (CChq acc)                    2010*

**GULPEN** *C4* (1.5km SW Rural) *50.80688, 5.87175* **Camping Osebos, Reijmerstokkerdorpsstraat, 6271 PP Gulpen [(043) 4501611; info@osebos.nl; www.osebos.nl]** W fr Gulpen on N278 dir Maastricht in 1km turn L, site sp. Lge, mkd pitch, terr, unshd; htd wc; chem disp; mv service pnt; baby facs; fam bthrm; shwrs inc; el pnts (6A) inc; gas; lndtte (inc dryer); shop; rest, snacks; bar & 1.5km; playgrnd; pool; games rm; entmnt; 20% statics; dogs €3; bus; poss cr; Eng spkn; adv bkg; quiet; red long stay. "Excel, popular site; rec book ahead." ♦ 1 Apr-27 Nov. € 24.00                    2010*

⊞ **HAARLEM** *B3* (2km E Rural) *52.37700, 4.67500* **Camping De Liede, Lieoever 68, 2033 AD Haarlem [(023) 5358666; fax 5405613; kampeerbedrijfdeliede@hetnet.nl; www.campingdeliede.nl]** Fr Amsterdam on A9 foll sp Haarlem onto A200. On A200 at 1st traff lts turn L, then L again, site sp. Med; wc; chem disp; shwrs; el pnts (4A) €3; gas; lndtte; shop; rest; beach 11km; 20% statics; phone; bus 700m; poss cr; Eng spkn; adv bkg; CKE/CCI. "Site in 2 parts both sides of rd."
€ 17.00                                                      2011*

**HAARLEM** *B3* (5km SW Rural) *52.32006, 4.56698*
**Camping Vogelenzang, Tweede Doodweg 17, 2114 AP Vogelenzang [(023) 5847014; fax 5849249; camping@vogelenzang.nl; www.vogelenzang.nl]** Foll site sp on rd N206. V lge, hdg/mkd pitch, pt shd; htd wc; chem disp; mv service pnt; baby facs; shwrs €0.50; el pnts (4A) inc; lndtte (inc dryer); shop; tradsmn; rest, snacks; bar; playgrnd; pools; paddling pool; sand beach 4km; games rm; golf 7km; TV; 50% statics; no dogs; adv bkg; quiet; ccard acc; CKE/CCI. "Gd screening & hedging make site appear much smaller than it is; overflow field has el pnts & wc; gd san facs; vg." ◆ 1 Apr-15 Sep. € 25.25                                      2010*

**HALFWEG see Amsterdam** *B3*

**HARDENBERG** *D2* (1km E Rural) *52.52246, 6.54563* **NCC Camping De Rolle, Grote Esweg 96, 7795 DD Diffelen [(0523) 251556; hardenberg@ncc.nl; www.ncc.nl]** Fr N34 turn S onto N36 dir Almelo. After 5km turn L sp Marienberg, then L in 300m; after x-ring rv take 1st L, site 1km on L, sp. Sm, mkd pitch, pt shd; htd wc; chem disp; shwrs inc; el pnts (4A) €2.75; shop 3km; rest 1km; snacks, bar 3km; playgrnd; htd, covrd pool 8km; dogs; poss cr; adv bkg; quiet. "CC members welcome but must pre-book (phone ahead bet 1700 & 1800); excel walking, cycling country; historic towns in area; v friendly; vg. 1 Apr-31 Oct. € 10.00                          2009*

**HARDERWIJK** *C3* (4km N Rural) *52.38500, 5.62860* **Camping Flevostrand, Strandweg 1, 8256 RZ Biddinghuizen [(0320) 288480; fax 288617; info@flevostrand.nl; www.molecaten.nl/flevostrand]** Foll A28 dir Amersfoort-Zwolle past Utrecht. At junc 13 turn off onto N302 Harderwijk; cont on N302 over lake bdge; turn R onto N306 sp Veluwemeer & 'Walibi World'; foll rd along lakeside for 1.5km to site on R. V lge, mkd pitch, pt shd; htd wc; chem disp; mv service pnt; fam bthrm; baby facs; sauna; shwrs inc; el pnts (6A) inc; gas; lndtte (inc dryer); shop; rest, snacks; bar; BBQ; playgrnds; 2 htd pools (1 covrd); paddling pool; marina; sand beach & lake sw; free sailing & surfing lessons; waterskiing; cycle & boat hire; horseriding; tennis; two theme parks nrby; organised child activities; entmnt; games rm; wifi; TV; 60% statics; dogs €3.90; no c'vans/m'vans over 8.50m high ssn; various pitch prices; phone; sep car park; poss cr; adv bkg; quiet; ccard acc; red low ssn; CKE/CCI. "Full marina facs on Veluwemeer for all types of boating; vg." 1 Apr-1 Nov. € 31.25                        2011*

**HARDERWIJK** *C3* (7km NE Rural) *52.39470, 5.73230*
**Camping De Hooghe Bijsschel, Randmeerweg 8, 8071 SH Nunspeet [(0341) 252406; fax 262565; info@hooghebijsschel.nl; www.molecaten.nl/nl/de-hooghe-bijsschel]** Fr A28/E232 exit junc 14 & turn L at rndabt. Go strt over next 3 rndbts foll sp Nunspeet then turn L at 4th rndabt sp Hulshorst, then R at next rndabt sp Veluwemeer. Site on R after 3km (after sharp L-hand bend). Lge, mkd pitch, pt sl, pt shd; htd wc (some cont); chem disp; mv service pnt; serviced pitches; baby facs; fam bthrm; shwrs; el pnts (6A) inc; gas; lndtte (inc dryer); sm shop; supmkt nr; rest, snacks; bar; BBQ; playgrnd; htd pool; lake sw & sand beach adj; watersports; fishing; tennis; cycle hire; horseriding 2km; wifi; entmnt; games/TV rm; 60% statics; dogs €3.90 (1 only per pitch); no c'vans/m'vans over 7.50m; phone; sep car park; recep 0900-2100 high ssn 0900-1700 low ssn; adv bkg; quiet; ccard acc; red low ssn. "Excel, spacious pitches; shop at w/end only low ssn with ltd stock; rec use new san facs block nr rest/pool; gd walking/cycling & watersports." ◆ 28 Mar-29 Sep. € 34.50
SBS - H05                                                     2014*

**HARDERWIJK** *C3* (8km W Rural) *52.27155, 5.43550* **Camping Flevo-Natuur (Naturist), Wielseweg 3, 3896 LB Zeevolde [(036) 5228880; fax 5228664; info@flevonatuur.nl; www.flevonatuur.nl]** Fr A28 Harderwijk exit junc 13 onto N302, L onto N305, foll sp Zeevolde & site. V lge, mkd pitch, pt shd; htd wc; chem disp; mv service pnt; sauna; shwrs €0.50; el pnts (4A) inc (poss rev pol); gas; lndtte; shop; tradsmn; rest, snacks; bar; htd, covrd pool; lake sw; games area; TV; 50% statics; dogs; phone; sep car park; Eng spkn; adv bkg; red long stay. "Excel pool complex." € 23.40                          2009*

**HARICH see Lemmer** *C2*

⊞ **HARLINGEN** *C2* (9km NE Urban) *53.18979, 5.55392* **Recreatiepark Bloemketerp, Burg J Dijkstraweg 3, 8801 PG Franeker [(0517) 395099; fax 395150; info@bloemketerp.nl; www.bloemketerp.nl]** In Franeker town cent, adj sw pool. Med, hdg/mkd pitch, pt shd; htd wc; chem disp; mv service pnt; baby facs; shwrs €0.50; el pnts (6-10A) inc; lndtte (inc dryer); shop; rest, snacks; bar; playgrnd; pool; cycle hire; sat TV; phone; quiet; Eng spkn; ccard acc; CKE/CCI. "Pleasant site; gd train link to Harlingen." ◆ € 22.50    2010*

**HARLINGEN** *C2* (1km SW Coastal) *53.16253, 5.41653* **Camping De Zeehoeve, Westerzeedijk 45, 8862 PK Harlingen [(0517) 413465; fax 416971; info@zeehoeve.nl; www.zeehoeve.nl]** Leave N31 N'bound at sp Kimswerd. At rndabt turn L under N31 & foll site sp. Site on R in 1.6km. Lge, pt shd; htd wc; chem disp; mv service pnt; baby facs; fam bthrm; shwrs €0.50; el pnts (6A); gas; lndtte (inc dryer); shop 1km; rest, snacks; bar; playgrnd; beach adj; fishing; watersports; cycle hire; games area; wifi; entmnt; TV; 30% statics; dogs €3.50; phone; Eng spkn; ccard acc (surcharge). "Roomy, well-maintained, open site; clean facs; easy walk to town & harbour; interesting area; vg." ◆ 1 Apr-15 Oct. € 21.50                                          2011*

**HATTEM see Zwolle** *C2*

**HEERDE** *C3* (2km SW Rural) *52.37764, 6.00601* **Camping De Klippen, De Klippenweg 4, 8181 PC Heerde [(0578) 696690; fax 560258]** Exit A50 junc 28 or 29 & head twd Heerde. Site sp on ent vill on L. Foll sp to De Klippen & also Mussenkamp site. Med, mkd pitch, pt shd; wc; chem disp; shwrs €0.45; el pnts (4A); lndtte; shops 3km; playgrnd; 60% statics; phone; v quiet; CKE/CCI. "Excel site; immac facs; ltd space for tourers - phone ahead." ♦ ltd 1 Apr-31 Oct. € 11.50                                                    2009*

**HEERENVEEN** *C2* (6km S Rural) *52.90814, 5.91828* **Camping De Frije Fries, Schoterweg 2, 8462 TD Rotstergaast [(0513) 636178 or 06 53367727 (mob); fax 647084; info@ gebrdevries.nl]** Exit A32 at junc 11 onto N924 W. In 2.5km turn L sp Rotstergaast, site on R in 4km. Sm, pt shd; wc; chem disp (wc); shwrs €0.50; lndtte; shop; BBQ; Eng spkn; quiet. "Vg, friendly site; gd cycling." 15 Mar-1 Nov. € 9.50    2009*

**HEERLEN** *C4* (6km SW Rural) *50.85213, 5.93594* **Camping Colmont, Colmonterweg 2, 6367 HE Voerendaal [(045) 5620057; fax 5620058; markpot@colmont.nl; www. colmont.nl]** Fr A76 take exit 6 Voerendaal; foll sp Ubachsberg; site sp. Med, pt sl, pt shd; htd wc; chem disp; mv service pnt; baby facs; shwrs inc; el pnts (4-6A) €2; gas; lndtte; shop; rest, snacks; bar; BBQ; playgrnd; htd pool; games area; cycle hire; TV; 30% statics; dogs €2; phone; poss cr; adv bkg (fee); quiet; CKE/CCI. "Gd size pitches; friendly owner." ♦ 2 Apr-25 Sep. € 19.00                                                        2010*

**HEEZE see Eindhoven** *C4*

**HEILOO see Alkmaar** *B2*

**HELDEN** *C4* (2km E Rural) *51.31813, 6.0235* **Camping De Heldense Bossen, De Heldense Bossen 6, 5988 NH Helden [tel/fax 07 73 07 24 76; heldensebossen@ardoer.com; www.deheldensebossen.nl]** Fr A67 Eindhoven-Venlo, take exit 38 (Helden). Turn R onto N277 twds Maasbreeseweg. Cont onto N562. Fr Helden dir Kessel. Turn L after 1km. Campsite 1km further on. V lge, mkd pitch, pt shd; wc; chem disp; mv service pnt; baby facs; shwrs; el pnts (10A); lndtte (inc dryer); shop; tradsmn; rest; snack; bar; BBQ; playgrnd; htd covrd pool; waterslide; paddling pool; games area; bike hire; wifi; 65% statics; dogs 26DKK; twin axles; poss cr; Eng spkn; adv bkg; CCI. "Excel site." ♦ ltd 29 Mar-26 Oct. € 44.75    2014*

**HELLEVOETSLUIS** *B3* (2km W Coastal) *51.82918, 4.11606* **Camping 't Weergors, Zuiddijk 2, 3221 LJ Hellevoetsluis [(0181) 312430; fax 311010; weergors@pn.nl; www. weergors.nl]** Via m'way A20/A4 or A16/A15 dir Rotterdam-Europoort-Hellevoetsluis; take N15 to N57, exit Hellevoetsluis, site sp. Lge, hdg/mkd pitch, some hdstg, unshd; htd wc; chem disp; mv service pnt; baby facs; shwrs €0.15/min; el pnts (16A) €2.80; gas; lndtte (inc dryer); shop; rest; bar; BBQ; playgrnd; paddling pool; lake fishing; tennis; games area; cycle hire; wifi; TV rm; 60% statics; dogs €1.60; sep car park; Holland Tulip Parcs site; poss cr; Eng spkn; quiet; ccard acc. "Delta works 6km worth visit; bird sanctuary adj; flat site; gd san facs; v friendly, helpful staff; excel rest; gd walking/cycling; excel site; charming helpful owners." ♦ 1 Apr-31 Oct. € 19.50 (CChq acc)                                                        2013*

**HENGELO** *D3* (6km W Rural) *52.25451, 6.72704* **Park Camping Mooi Delden, De Mors 6, 7491 DZ Delden [(074) 3761922; fax 3767539; info@parkcamping.nl; www. parkcamping.nl]** Exit A35 junc 28 onto N346 dir Delden. Fr Delden-Oost, site sp. Site ent is R-hand of 2 via barrier (use intercom on arr.) If you have a high vehicle take the turning after Delden-Oost to avoid low rail bdge (2.3m); turn L immed aft lge rv bdge & foll site sp. Med, mkd pitch, pt shd; htd wc; chem disp; baby facs; fam bthrm; shwrs; el pnts (6-10A) €3.40 (poss rev pol); lndtte; shop & 1km; snacks; bar; playgrnd; pool; tennis; 50% statics; dogs €3.15; poss cr; Eng spkn; adv bkg; quiet. "Ideal for touring beautiful pt of Holland; sports complex adj; pleasant, well-kept site; clean facs." ♦ 1 Apr-1 Oct. € 18.65                                                        2011*

**HERKENBOSCH see Roermond** *C4*

⊞ **HEUMEN** *C3* (1km S Rural) *51.76890, 5.82140* **Camping Heumens Bos, Vosseneindseweg 46, 6582 BR Heumen [(024) 3581481; fax 3583862; info@heumensbos.nl; www. heumensbos.nl]** Take A73/E31 Nijmegen-Venlo m'way, leave at exit 3 sp Heumen/Overasselt. Do not re-cross m'way. After 500m turn R at camp sp. Site on R in approx 1.5km, 1km S of Heumen. V lge, hdg/mkd pitch, shd; htd wc (some cont); chem disp; mv service pnt; baby facs; fam bthrm; shwrs €0.50; el pnts (6A) inc; gas; lndtte (inc dryer); sm supmkt; rest, snacks; bar; BBQ; playgrnd; 2 pools (1 htd); paddling pool; jacuzzi; lake sw, sandy beach 2km; fishing 2km; watersports 6km; tennis; games area; cycle hire; horseriding 100m; activities/entmnt in ssn; wifi; games/TV rm; 60% statics in sep area; dogs €4; no c'vans/m'vans over 14m; eng spkn; adv bkg; quiet; phone; sep car park; extra €3 for m'vans; adv bkg; noise fr bar high ssn; ccard acc; red low ssn; CCI. "Excel, busy, family-run site; modern san facs; lots to do on site & in area - info fr recep; ideal for Arnhem; WW2 museums nr; mkt Sat & Mon in Nijmegen." ♦ € 36.00 SBS - H01                    2014*

**HILVARENBEEK** *B3* (4km N Rural) *51.52839, 5.12398* **Safaripark Beekse Bergen, Beekse Bergen 1, 5081 NJ Hilvarenbeek [(013) 5491100; fax 5366716; info@ beeksebergen.nl; www.safaripark.nl]** Exit A58 m'way junc 10 onto N269, site sp. Lge, pt shd; htd wc; chem disp; mv service pnt; baby facs; fam bthrm; shwrs inc; el pnts (6-10A) inc; gas; lndtte (inc dryer); shop; rest, snacks; bar; BBQ; playgrnds; covrd pool; paddling pool; tennis; games area; cycle hire; internet; entmnt; TV; 30% statics; dogs; phone; adv bkg; ccard acc. "Free ent to adj Safari & Adventure Parks; excel facs; excel value - all sports inc in price." ♦ 1 Apr-15 Oct. € 30.60                                                        2010*

⊞ **HOEK** *A4* (3km W Rural) *51.31464, 3.72618* **Braakman Holiday Island, Middenweg 101, 4542 PN Hoek [(0115) 481730; fax 482077; info@braakman.nl; www. braakman.nl]** Sp fr N61. V lge, mkd pitch, pt shd; htd wc; chem disp; mv service pnt; shwrs €0.50; fam bthrm; baby facs; serviced pitches; el pnts (4A) inc; gas; lndtte; shop; rest, snacks; bar; playgrnd; sub-tropical pool; lake beach; sailing; tennis; squash; internet; cab TV; 50% statics; dogs €5; phone; poss cr; Eng spkn; adv bkg; ccard acc;. "Excel for families; extensive recreation facs; conv Bruges/Antwerp; extra for lake view pitches." € 30.00                                                        2009*

**HOEK VAN HOLLAND** *B3* (1.5km N Urban) *51.98953,
4.12767* **Camping Hoek van Holland, Wierstraat
100, 3151 VP Hoek van Holland [(0174) 382550; fax
310210; info@campinghoekvanholland.nl; www.
campinghoekvanholland.nl]** Fr ferry foll N211/220
Rotterdam. After 2.4km turn L, 50m bef petrol stn on R, sp
'Camping Strand', site 400m on R. Lge, mkd pitch, hdstg,
pt shd; htd wc; chem disp; baby facs; shwrs inc; el pnts (6A)
inc; gas; lndtte; shop; rest, snacks; bar; playgrnd; pool; sand
beach nr; tennis; cycle hire; entmnt; TV; 60% statics; no dogs;
phone; bus; sep car park; poss v cr; Eng spkn; quiet; CKE/CCI.
"Open 0800-2300; modern san facs but poss inadequate when
site full & long walk fr m'van area; conv ferry." ♦ 14 Mar-
11 Oct. € 28.00 (4 persons)                                         2009*

**HOEK VAN HOLLAND** *B3* (2km N Coastal) *51.99685,
4.13347* **Camping Jagtveld, Nieuwlandsedijk 41, KV
2691 'S-Gravenzande [(0174) 413479; fax 422127; info@
jagtveld.nl; www.jagtveld.nl]** Fr ferry foll N211/220 sp
Rotterdam. After 3.2km, turn L at junc with traff lts gantry into
cul-de-sac. Site 200m on L. Med, unshd; wc; chem disp; shwrs
inc; shop; el pnts (16A) poss rev pol €2; gas; lndtte; shop;
snacks; playgrnd; sand beach 400m; entmnt; mostly statics; no
dogs; phone; sep car park; poss cr; Eng spkn; quiet. "Ideal for
ferry port; conv Den Haag & Delft; gd, clean, level, family-run
site; diff when wet; helpful owners; excel 8km long beach."
1 Apr-1 Oct. € 33.50                                                 2014*

**HOENDERLOO See Apeldoorn** *C3*

**HORST** *C4* (10km W Rural) *51.50657, 6.15603* **Recreatiepark
Kasteel Ooijen, Blitterswijckseweg 2, 5871 CE
Broekhuizenvorst [(077) 4631307; fax 4632765; info@
kasteelooijen.nl; www.kasteelooijen.nl]** N fr Venlo on
A72/73 turn R at junc 11 Horst twd Lottum. At T-junc turn L
twd Broekhuizen & Broekhuizenvorst, site sp on R. Lge, hdg/
mkd pitch, pt shd; htd wc; chem disp; mv service pnt; 90%
serviced pitches; baby facs; fam bthrm; el pnts (4-10A) inc; gas;
lndtte; shop; rest, snacks; bar; playgrnd; pool; tennis; games
area; cab/sat TV; entmnt; 30% statics; dogs €1; phone; Eng
spkn; adv bkg; quiet; ccard acc; CKE/CCI. "Gd facs; helpful
staff; special area for families with children; gardens at Arcen
worth visit." ♦ 27 Mar-31 Oct. € 24.55                              2009*

**IJHORST See Meppel** *C2*

**JULIANADORP** *B2* (2km S Coastal) *52.90667, 4.72499*
**Camping 't Noorder Sandt, Noordersandt 2, 1787
CX Julianadorp [(0223) 641266; fax 645600; info@
noordersandt.com; www.noordersandt.com]** On ent Den
Helder on N9 turn L sp Julianadorp. Foll sp to site. V lge, mkd
pitch, pt shd; htd wc; chem disp; mv service pnt; baby facs;
shwrs €0.50; el pnts (10A) inc; lndtte; shop; snacks; playgrnd;
covrd pool; waterslide; sand beach 600m; tennis; games area;
cab TV; 30% statics; dogs €3.50; phone; adv bkg; quiet; ccard
acc; red long stay. "Excel, friendly site; gd for children; excel
pool; breakfast avail & bread baked daily; gd foot & cycle
paths; conv Alkmaar." 28 Mar-25 Oct. € 33.75                        2009*

**KAATSHEUVEL** *B3* (E Rural) *51.66086, 5.05484* **Mini-
Camping De Hoefstal, Horst 7A, 5171 RA Kaatsheuvel
[(0416) 273344; fax 284614; info@dehoefstal.com; www.
dehoefstal.com]** Turn S off A59 at junc 37 Waalwijk & foll
sp Kaatsheuvel & Loonen/Drunense Duinen, site sp. Strt ahead
at windmill, site on L in 250m. Sm, pt shd; wc; chem disp;
shwrs €0.50; el pnts (4A) inc; lndtte (inc dryer); rest; playgrnd;
Eng spkn; poss cr; adv bkg rec; some rd noise. "V clean facs;
friendly, helpful owner; cycle path to Efteling theme park."
1 Apr-31 Oct. € 11.00                                                2009*

**KAATSHEUVEL** *B3* (1km E Rural) *51.66300, 5.07100*
**Boerderij Camping, Van Loon's Hoekske, Van
Haestrechtstraat 17a, 5171 RB Kaatsheuvel [(0416) 335758
or 06 20935679 (mob); vanloonshoekske@kpnplanet.nl;
www.vanloonshoekske.nl]** Exit A59 junc 37 Waalwijk & foll
sp Kaatsheuvel & Park de Loose Drunense Duinen. At windmill
turn L, site 1km on L, sp. Sm, mkd pitch, unshd; wc; chem disp;
shwrs inc; el pnts (10A) inc; BBQ; tradsmn; rest, snacks, bar
1km; playgrnd; Eng spkn; quiet. "Vg CL-type site on working
farm." € 15.00                                                      2009*

**KAMPERLAND** *A3* *51.55446, 3.80483* **Camping Villa
Park de Pardakreek, Havenweg 1, NL 4484, N Beevland
[0113-302051; paardekreek@ardoer.com; www.ardoer.
com/nl/camping/paardekreek]** Take the N256 to Zierikzee,
exit Kortgene foll sps to camp. Med, mkd/ hdg pitch, pt shd;
wc; chem disp; MV service pnt; fam bthrm; child/baby facs;
shwrs; el pnts (16A); lndtte; shop; rest, snacks, bar; BBQ
playgrnd; sw pool; water playgrnd; adj lake; games rm;
wifi; 40% statics; dogs; bus 0.5km; Eng spkn; quiet; CKE/CCI.
"Excel site, boat slipway and storage, adj Lake Veerse Meer,
many places to visit." ♦ 25 Mar-30 Oct. € 35.00                    2012*

**KAMPERLAND** *A3* (500m NW Rural) *51.57902, 3.69795*
**Camping De Molenhoek, Molenweg 69a, 4493 NC
Kamperland [(0113) 371202; molenhoek@zeelandnet.nl;
www.demolenhoek.com]** Site sp fr N255. V lge, mkd pitch,
pt shd; htd wc; chem disp; mv service pnt; baby facs; shwrs
€0.50; el pnts (6A) inc; gas; lndtte (inc dryer); shop; tradsmn;
supmkt 800m; rest, snacks; bar; playgrnd; htd tropical pool
complex; paddling pool; sand beach 2.5km; games area; games
rm; cycle hire; wifi; entmnt; TV; 75% statics; dogs €5; Eng
spkn; adv bkg; quiet. "Excel, spacious, family site; gd, clean san
facs; gd touring base." ♦ 1 Apr-30 Oct. € 34.00                    2010*

⊞ **KATWIJK AAN ZEE** *B3* (500m N Coastal) *52.21137,
4.41019* **Camping De Noordduinen, Campingweg 1,
2221 EW Katwijk [(071) 4025295; fax 4033977; info@
noordduinen.nl; www.noordduinen.nl]** Fr A44 Wassenaar-
Amsterdam, exit 8 Katwijk, onto N206. Leave at Katwijk Noord
(fr S) or Katwijk ann Zee (fr N), R at rndabt & go over 6 sets
of traff lts, immed R then L. Lge, hdg/mkd pitch, terr, unshd;
htd wc; chem disp; mv service pnt; serviced pitches; baby facs;
shwrs inc; el pnts (10A) €4.50 (poss rev pol); lndtte (inc dryer);
shop; tradsmn; rest, snacks; bar; BBQ (gas/elec); playgrnd; 2
pools (1 htd/covrd); paddling pool; sand beach adj; tennis;
wifi; cab TV; 60% statics; no dogs; sep car park; Holland Tulip
Parcs site; poss cr; Eng spkn; adv bkg (dep); ccard acc; red low
ssn/snr citizens. "Friendly, helpful management; clean facs;
gd security; poss cr; 'comfort' pitches avail at extra cost." ♦
€ 31.50 (CChq acc)                                                  2011*

---

Site report forms at back of guide                    *Last year of report    **453**

**KATWIJK AAN ZEE** *B3* (2km SE Rural) *52.19990, 4.45625* **Camping Koningshof, Elsgeesterweg 8, 2331 NW Rijnsburg [(071) 4026051; fax 4021336; info@koningshofholland.nl; www.koningshofholland. nl]** Fr A44 (Den Haag/Wassenaar-Amsterdam) exit junc 7 (Rijnsburg-Oegstgeest). In Rijnsburg cont twd Noordwijk. Foll blue & white sps thro Rijnsburg, across a bdge & then R twd Voorhout. Site in 2km. Lge, hdg/mkd pitch, hdstg, pt shd; htd wc (some cont); chem disp; mv service pnt; baby facs; shwrs inc; el pnts (16A) inc; gas; lndtte (inc dryer); shop; rest, snacks; bar; BBQ; playgrnd; 2 pools (1 htd, covrd); paddling pool; sand beach 5km; fishing; cycle hire; tennis; games rm; wifi; entmnt; TV cab/sat; 20% statics; dogs €3; c'vans/m'vans over 8m high ssn by request; phone; sep car park for some pitches; recep 0900-1230 & 1330-2000 high ssn; Holland Tulip Parcs site; Eng spkn; adv bkg; quiet; red long stay low ssn/snr citizens; CKE/CCI. "Vg, well-run, busy, friendly site; gd for families; excel rest; excel facs & pool; useful tour base for bulb fields; mkt Tues; well maintained; close to beaches and town; rec cash as few cards acc." ♦ 15 Mar-14 Nov. € 35.00 (CChq acc) SBS - H03                    2012*

See advertisement

**KATWIJK AAN ZEE** *B3* (1km S Coastal) *52.19319, 4.38986* **Camping De Zuidduinen, Zuidduinseveg 1, 2225 JS Katwijk [(071) 4014750; fax 4077097; info@zuidduinen. nl; www.zuidduinen.nl]** Fr A44 turn off at junc 8 onto N206 to Katwijk & foll 'Zuid-Boulevard' sps. Site sp. Lge, mkd pitch, unshd; htd wc; chem disp; mv service pnt; baby facs; shwrs inc; el pnts (4A) €3.50; gas; lndtte (inc dryer); shop; tradsmn; snacks; bar; no BBQ; playgrnd; sub-tropical pool 2km in Katwijk; sports & organised activities; tennis nr; cycle hire; wifi; cab TV; tour boats; tourist mkt; 50% statics; no dogs; phone; sep secure car park; adv bkg; quiet; ccard acc; red low ssn/snr citizens. "In dunes conservation area; well-run, peaceful site; excel facs." ♦ 1 Apr-30 Sep. € 32.50 (4 persons)            2011*

**KLIJNDIJK see Emmen** *D2*

**KOOTWIJK see Apeldoorn** *C3*

⊞ **KOUDUM** *C2* (1.5km S Rural) *52.90290, 5.46625* **Kawan Village De Kuilart, De Kuilart 1, 8723 CG Koudum [(0514) 522221; fax 523010; info@kuilart.nl; www. kuilart.nl]** Fr A50 exit sp Lemmer/Balk. Foll N359 over Galamadammen bdge, site sp. Lge, mkd pitch, pt shd; htd wc; mv service pnt; fam bthrm; baby facs; private bthrms some pitches; 90% serviced pitches; sauna; shwrs €0.35; el pnts (6-16A) €1.50-3.60; gas; lndtte (with dryer); supmkt; rest, snacks; bar; playgrnd; 2 pools (1 htd, covrd); waterslide; sailing; watersports; marina; games area; wifi; entmnt; TV & cinema rm; 50% statics; ltd dogs €3.35 (adv bkg rec); phone; sep car park; poss cr; Eng spkn; adv bkg; Holland Tulip Parcs site; CKE/ CCI. ♦ € 26.00 (CChq acc)                    2011*

# A carefree stay in Holland

| CAMPING | CARAVANNING | CHALETS |
| --- | --- | --- |

**KOUDUM** C2 (4.5km S Rural) 52.87526, 5.43887 **Camping Martinus, De Soal 6, 8584 VS Hemelum [tel/fax (0514) 581970 or 06 54632485 (mob); pieterzeldenrust@ wanadoo.nl]** W fr Lemmer or E fr Koudum on N359. Turn L sp Hemelum, thro vill into De Soal rd. Site on R in 1.5km. Sm, pt shd; htd wc; chem disp; shwrs inc; shop 1.5km; rest; no statics; dogs €1.25; Eng spkn; quiet. "Friendly, helpful owners; excel cycling; gd." 1 Mar-31 Oct. € 10.00                2009*

**KRAGGENBURG** C2 (1.5km N Rural) 52.67566, 5.89224 **Camping De Voorst, Leemringweg 33, 8317 RD Kraggenburg [(0527) 252524; devoorst@vdbrecreatie. nl; www.vdbrecreatie.nl]** Exit A6 junc 13 onto N352 sp Nagele & Ens. In Ens turn L at 1st traff lts (still N352) & foll sp Kraggenburg. Site sp at 1st rndabt. Lge, mkd pitch, some hdstg, pt shd; wc; chem disp; mv service pnt; shwrs €0.50; el pnts (4A) inc; lndtte (inc dryer); tradsmn; rest adj; snacks; bar; BBQ; playgrnd; htd pool; paddling pool; waterslide; tennis; games area; cycle hire; wifi; TV; 30% statics; dogs €2; bus; Eng spkn; quiet; CKE/CCI. "Excel." 1 Apr-30 Sep. € 19.00    2010*

**LANDSMEER see Amsterdam** B3

⊞ **LAUWERSOOG** D1 (2km SE Coastal) 53.40250, 6.21740 **Camping Lauwersoog, Strandweg 5, 9976 VS Lauwersoog [(0519) 349133; fax 349195; info@lauwersoog.nl; www. lauwersoog.nl]** Fr N355 Leeuwarden-Groningen rd, take N361 Dokkum exit. Foll rd to Lauwersoog, site sp. V lge, unshd; htd wc; chem disp; mv service pnt; serviced pitches; baby facs; shwrs; el pnts (10A) inc; gas; lndtte (inc dryer); shop; rest, snacks; bar; playgrnd; pool; tennis; cycle hire; wifi; entmnt; TV; 50% statics; dogs €4.75; phone; sep car park; Holland Tulip Parcs site; poss v cr; Eng spkn; adv bkg; quiet; ccard acc; CKE/ CCI. "Excel, well-maintained site; vg rest; gd facs." ♦ € 38.00 (CChq acc)                2014*

**LEEUWARDEN** C2 (5km E Rural) 53.21644, 5.88714 **Camping De Kleine Wielen, De Groene Ster 14, 8926 XE Leeuwarden [(0511) 431660; fax 432584; info@dekleinewielen.nl; www.dekleinewielen.nl]** E fr Leeuwarden on N355 twds Groningen; in 5km look on S side for site sp. Lge, pt shd; htd wc; chem disp; mv service pnt; baby facs; shwrs €0.40; el pnts (4A) €3.25; gas; lndtte; shop; snacks; playgrnd; sand beach; lake sw; watersports; fishing; entmnt; TV; 60% statics; dogs €2.40; phone; adv bkg; some rd noise; ccard acc; CKE/CCI. "Beautiful location; helpful staff; sep area for tourers; vg." ♦ 1 Apr-1 Oct. € 14.65        2009*

**LEEUWARDEN** C2 (5km SW Rural) 53.19484, 5.73785 **Minicamping Van Harinxma, Marssummerdyk 7, 9033 WD Deinnum [0031 (0) 58 215 04 98; Info@minicamping-van-Harinxma.nl; www.minicamping-van-harinxma.nl/]** Fr S: take N31/N32 twrds Leeuwarden. Turn L on N31 sp Harlingen, turn R to Masum-Harlingen, and imm R sp Ritsumazijl. Foll rd turn L at T- junc, then fork L into no thro rd. Site on L. Sm, med, hdg pitch, pt shd; wc; chem disp; shwrs; el pnts ( 6A); lndry; snacks; playgrnd; billiards; tv; dogs; twin-axle; Eng spkn; adv bkgs; CKE/CCI; "V gd; fishing fr site." 15 Mar-15 Oct. € 12.00                2012*

**LEIDEN** B3 (5km N Rural) 52.20984, 4.51370 **Camping De Wasbeek, Wasbeeklaan 5b, 2361 HG Warmond [(071) 3011380; dewasbeek@hetnet.nl]** Exit A44 junc 4 dir Warmond; in 200m turn L into Wasbeeklaan, then R in 50m. Site sp. Sm, pt shd; wc; chem disp; shwrs €0.70; lndtte; shop, rest, snacks, bar 1km; BBQ; pool 2km; sand beach 8km; 40% statics; dogs free; bus 500m; sep car park; Eng spkn; adv bkg; quiet but some aircraft noise. "Attractive, lawned site close to bulb fields; m'vans by arrangement; twin-axles not acc; friendly, helpful staff; gd cycling (track to Leiden); fishing; boating; birdwatching; lovely sm tidy site; nice area." 1 Apr-1 Oct. € 13.50                2014*

**LELYSTAD** C2 (5km SW Rural) 52.48570, 5.41720 **Camping 't Oppertje, Uilenweg 11, 8245 AB Lelystad [(0320) 253693; info@oppertje.nl; www.oppertje.nl]** Exit A6 junc 10 & take Larserdreef dir Lelystad. In 3km turn L into Buizerdweg & foll sp to site. Med, mkd pitch, pt shd; htd wc; chem disp; mv service pnt; baby facs; fam bthrm; shwrs €0.50; el pnts (10A) €3; lndtte; shop 5km; tradsmn; snacks; bar; BBQ; playgrnd; lake sw & beach adj; fishing; 20% statics; no dogs; sep car park; Eng spkn; quiet; red low ssn/CKE/CCI. "Pleasant site in nature reserve; friendly, helpful staff; modern san facs; cycle track adj; excel." ♦ 1 Apr-1 Oct. € 17.00                2010*

**LEMMER** C2 (9km SW Rural) 52.87929, 5.62082 **Camping De Tjasker, Iwert 17, 8563 AM Wijckel [(0514) 605869; info@campingdetjasker.nl; www.campingdetjasker.nl]** Fr Lemmer take N359 sp Balk, in approx 7km turn R at c'van sp. Sm, unshd; wc; chem disp; shwrs inc; el pnts (4-6A) €2.20; lndtte; shops 4km; playgrnd; dogs; sep car park; adv bkg; quiet. "Sm farm site with gd facs; gd for exploring Friesland with easy cycling & walking." 15 Mar-1 Oct. € 10.80    2009*

**LEMMER** C2 (6km NW Rural) 52.89993, 5.64208 **Camping De Jerden, Lytse Jerden 1, 8556 XC Sloten [(0514) 531389; fax 531837; info@campingdejerden.nl; www.campingdejerden.nl]** Exit A6 at Lemmer onto N359 sp Balk. In 9km foll sp Wijckel & Slotten. In 3km turn R into Heerenhoogweg, L into Lytse Jerden, site along canal on L. Sm, hdg/mkd pitch, unshd; htd wc; chem disp; shwrs €0.50; el pnts (16A) €3; lndtte (inc dryer); shop 500m; rest, bar in vill; playgrnd; lake sw 500m; sand beach; boat & cycle hire; games area; dogs €2; phone; adv bkg; Eng spkn; CKE/CCI. "Lovely site in excel position; gd touring base; clean facs; lge pitches." 1 Apr-1 Nov. € 17.00                2009*

**LEMMER** C2 (11km NW Rural) 52.92019, 5.57494 **Camping Zwinzicht, Trophornsterweg 2, 8571 MX Harich [tel/fax (0514) 604512 or 06 12145209 (mob); info@zwinzicht. nl; www.zwinzicht.nl]** Fr N359 turn N dir Balk & Woudsend onto N928. Site sp 2km N of Harich. Sm, hdg/mkd pitch, pt shd; htd wc; chem disp; el pnts (6A) inc; lndtte; shop 2km; rest 1km; BBQ; playgrnd; games rm; no statics; dogs €1.75; sep car park; Eng spkn; quiet; red low ssn. "Vg." 1 Apr-2 Oct. € 14.00                2009*

**LIEREN see Apeldoorn** C3

**LISSE** *B3* (5km S Rural) *52.22175, 4.55418* **Camping De Hof van Eeden, Hellegatspolder 2, 2160 AZ Lisse [(0252) 212573; fax 235200; info@dehofvaneeden.nl; www.dehofvaneeden.nl]** Exit A44 junc 3 & turn N onto N208 dir Lisse. Turn R at rest on R bef 1st set traff lts into narr rd, foll rd to end (under A44) to site. Sm, unshd; wc; chem disp (wc); shwrs €0.50; el pnts (16A) inc; rest; playgrnd; wifi; 90% statics; Eng spkn; rlwy noise. "Gd CL-type site, space for 10 tourers - rec phone or email bef arr; interesting location by waterway & lifting rlwy bdge; conv Keukenhof; helpful owners." 15 Apr-15 Oct. € 17.50 2014*

**LOCHEM** *D3* (2km SW Rural) *52.14251, 6.38210* **Camping Landgoed Ruighenrode, Ploegdijk 2, 7241 SC Lochem [(0573) 253618; fax 253535; info@landgoedruighenrode. nl; www.landgoedruighenrode.nl]** Site sp fr N346 dir Zutphen. V lge, shd; htd wc; chem disp; mv service pnt; baby facs; fam bthrm; shwrs inc; el pnts (4-6A) inc; gas; lndtte (inc dryer); shop; tradsmn; rest; snacks; bar; playgrnd; pool complex 1km; lake sw; tennis; cycle hire; games rm; entmnt; TV; 60% statics; dogs €2; phone; adv bkg; quiet; CKE/CCI. "Pleasant wooded site." 1 Apr-30 Oct. € 25.00 2011*

**LUTTENBERG see Nijverdal** *D3*

**LUYKSGESTEL see Eersel** *C4*

**MAASDAM see Dordrecht** *B3*

⊞ **MAASTRICHT** *C4* (4km E) *50.84399, 5.78307* **Camping Mooi Bemelen, Gasthuis 3, 6268 NN Bemelen [(043) 4071321 or 4072327; fax 4072535; info@ mooibemelen.nl; www.mooibemelen.nl]** A2 as far as Maastricht, turn L at the 1st traff lts and then foll the signs to Bemelen. In Bemelen there are signs to the campsite. Lge, pt shd; wc; chem disp; child/baby facs; el pnts (4A) €4; lndry rm; gas; shop; rest, snacks; htd pool; playgrnd; games area; games rm; dog €4; adv bkg; quiet. "Fine surroundings; gd for children; excel site." € 33.75 2013*

**MAURIK** *C3* (2km NE Rural) *51.97605, 5.43020* **Recreatiepark Eiland van Maurik, Rijnbandijk 20, 4021 GH Maurik [(0344) 691502; fax 692248; receptie@ eilandvanmaurik.nl; www.eilandvanmaurik.nl]** Exit A15 junc 33 at Tiel onto B835 N & foll sp to Maurik & site on rvside. Or exit A2 junc 13 at Culembourg onto N320 to Maurik. Lge, pt shd; htd wc; chem disp; mv service pnt; baby facs; fam bthrm; shwrs €0.50; el pnts (10A) inc; gas; lndtte; shop; rest, snacks; bar; playgrnd; tennis; fishing; watersports; games area; covrd play area; horseriding; entmnt; wifi; TV; 50% statics; dogs €4; Holland Tulip Parcs site; Eng spkn; adv bkg; quiet. ♦ 1 Apr-1 Oct. € 43.00 (CChq acc) 2014*

**MEDEMBLIK** *B2* (1.5km SW Rural) *52.75900, 5.10873* **Camping & Lodge Arado, Brakeweg 61, 1671 LP Medemblik [(0227) 541671; info@arado.nl; www.arado. nl]** Exit A7/E22 junc 11 onto N239 dir Medemblik. Go strt over rndabt & turn R onto N240 dir Enkhuizen. Site on R in 2km. Sm, unshd; wc; chem disp; mv service pnt; el pnts (16A) inc; lndtte; shop 2km; cooking facs; internet; TV; no statics; dogs free; Eng spkn; adv bkg; CKE/CCI. "Vg CL-type site; friendly owners; easy access to pleasant town & yachting harbour; excel san facs; comf lounge." ♦ 1 Mar-1 Dec. € 22.50 2011*

**MEERKERK** *B3* (4km NW Rural) *51.93635, 4.96601* **Camping de Victorie, Broeksweg 75-77, 4231 VD Meerkerk [(0183) 351516 or 352741; fax 351234; info@ campingdevictorie.nl; www.campingdevictorie.nl]** Leave m'way A27 10km N of Gorinchem at junc 25 Noordeloos/ Meerkerk; take N214 twd Noordeloos. Turn R after Noordeloos sp SVR Camping & after 1.5km turn R. After 4km turn L at T-junc, site on L. NB: Not rec to tow thro Meerkerk due narr rds. Med, mkd pitch, pt shd; wc; chem disp; shwrs €0.50; el pnts (4A) inc; gas; lndtte; shop 4km; tradsmn; playgrnd; cycle hire; beach 35km; rv sw 3km; 50% statics; dogs €0.50; Eng spkn; sep car park; quiet; adv bkg; ccard acc; CKE/CCI. "Well-run farm site; HQ of SVR organisation (mem'ship avail); helpful staff; sep areas 60+ & families with children; poss boggy after rain; poss long walk to san facs; gd for touring old world Holland; fruit festival in Tiel mid Sep." 1 Apr-30 Sep. € 10.00 2010*

# "That's changed – Should I let The Club know?"

If you find something on site that's different from the site entry, fill in a report and let us know. See www.caravanclub.co.uk/europereport.

**MEERSSEN** *C4* (1.6km ESE Rural) *50.87851, 5.77112* **Camping Meerssen, Houthemerweg 95, 6231 KT Meerssen [(0433) 654743; fax 654745; info@ campingmeerssen.nl; www.campingmeerssen.nl]** Fr Eindhoven A2, take exit 51, foll Valkenburg sp. Take A79 to Hellen exit 2 Meerssen. L at junc after 400mtrs, site on R. Sm, mkd, pt shd; wc; chem disp; mv service pnt; shwrs inc; el pnts (6A); gas; lndtte (inc dryer); shop 1km; rest 1km; snacks 1km; bar 1km; bbq; wifi; 2% statics; dogs; twin axles; poss cr; Eng spkn; quiet; no ccard acc; red low ssn. "Nice, peaceful & relaxing site; v popular with Dutch people; cent for touring the area; excel site." 1 Apr-30 Sep. € 34.50 2014*

**MEPPEL** *C2* (8km W Rural) *52.69395, 6.08130* **Camping de Kettingbrug, Veneweg 270, 7946 LW Wanneperveen [(0522) 281207; fax 282657; info@dekettingbrug.nl; www.dekettingbrug.nl]** N on A28/A32 & exit junc 3 Meppel N onto N375 dir Giethoorn for approx 8km. Turn R onto N334 after x-ing lifting bdge & look for site sp in approx 4km. Sm, hdg/mkd pitch, pt shd; htd wc; chem disp; shwrs inc; el pnts (10A) €3; gas; lndtte; shop 300m; tradsmn; playgrnd; lake sw & grass beach adj; watersports; statics in sep area across rd; dogs €1.50; bus; phone; poss cr; Eng spkn; adv bkg; quiet. "Excel, family-run site; ltd touring pitches, some on lakeside; gd views; conv Giethoorn by cycle rte." 1 Apr-15 Oct. € 19.00 2010*

**MEPPEL** *C2* (9km W Rural) *52.72164, 6.07484* **Passantenhaven Zuiderkluft, Jonenweg, 8355 LG Giethoorn [(0521) 362312]** Turn off N334 sp Dwarsgracht, over lifting bdge, 1st L over bdge, 1st L again, site on R. Sm, unshd; wc; chem disp; mv service pnt; shwrs €0.50; el pnts (10A) metered; lndtte; drinking water €0.50; Eng spkn; m'vans only; quiet. "Site run by VVV (tourist board) for m'vans only; ltd el pnts; walking dist fr delightful vill on water." € 10.00 2009*

NETHERLANDS

**MEPPEL** *C2* (10km W Rural) *52.67261, 6.05973* **NCC Camping 't Hoogland, Vaste Belterweg 4, 8066 PT Belt-Schutsloot [(038) 3866313; www.ncc.nl]** Exit A32 junc 3 at Meppel Noord onto N375 sp Genemuiden. At T-junc after bdge turn R onto N334 sp Giethoorn, in 2km turn L sp Belt-Schutsloot. In vill turn R into Kerklaan then in 200m L into Belterweg, site on R. Do not app fr W - sharp turn onto narr bdge. Med, mkd pitch, unshd; wc; chem disp; shwrs inc; el pnts (4A) €2.75; lndtte; shop, rest, snacks, bar adj; playgrnd; htd, covrd pool; lake sw adj; boating; watersports; dogs; phone; adv bkg; quiet. "Lovely area; historic towns & vills; friendly staff; CC members welcome but must pre-book." ◆ ltd 1 Apr-31 Oct. € 12.50                                       2009*

**MEPPEL** *C2* (7km NW Rural) *52.72100, 6.06300* **Mini-Camping Van de Werfe Hoeve, Jonenweg 11, 8355 CN Giethoorn [tel/fax (0521) 360492]** In Giethoorn turn L at Smost bdge sp Dwarsgracht & Jonen, immed L to foll rd on L side of canal - narr rd. Site on L in 500m. Sm, unshd; wc; chem disp; shwrs; el pnts (4A) inc; gas 1km; shops 1km; no statics; dogs €0.50; poss cr; Eng spkn; adv bkg; quiet; ccard not acc. "Facs clean; boat hire nrby; gd cycle tracks & footpaths; cycle hire avail locally." € 15.00                                       2009*

**MIDDELBURG** *A4* (5km N Rural) *51.55005, 3.64022* **Mini Camping Hoekvliet, Meiwerfweg 3, 4352 SC Gapinge [(0118) 501615; copgapinge@zeelandnet.nl; www.hoekvliet.nl]** Fr Middleburg turn R off N57 at traff lts sp Veere & Gapinge, site sp after Gapinge vill. Sm, mkd pitch, some hdstg, pt shd; wc; chem disp; mv service pnt; shwrs inc; el pnts (6A) inc; lndtte (inc dryer); BBQ; rest, snacks, bar 2km; playgrnd; sand beach 5km; TV cab; cycle hire; 20% statics; dogs €1; sep car park; Eng spkn; quiet; CKE/CCI. "Superb little (25 o'fits) farm site; excel, modern san facs; helpful owner." ◆ ltd 1 Apr-31 Oct. € 21.00                                       2011*

**MIDDELBURG** *A4* (4km NE Rural) *51.53863, 3.65394* **Minicamping Trouw Vóór Goud, Veerseweg 66, 4351 SJ Veere [(0118) 501373; info@trouwvoorgoud.nl; www.trouwvoorgoud.nl]** Take Veere rd N out of Middleburg. Site on L in 4km, bef lge g'ge, sp 'Minicamping'. 1.5km SW of Veere. Sm, pt shd; wc; chem disp; shwrs inc; el pnts (6A) €1.75; lndtte; playgrnd; sand beach 6km; some statics; dogs €0.80; Eng spkn; quiet. "Excel facs; friendly, tidy, spacious, CL-type site; walking dist Veere." 15 Mar-31 Oct. € 14.00   2010*

**MIDWOLDA** *D2* (1km SW Urban) *53.18900, 6.99053* **Camping de Bouwte, Hoofdweg 20A, 9681 AH Midwolda [05 97 59 17 06; fax 97 59 19 63; info@campingdebouwte.nl; www.campingdebouwte.nl]** Via A7 dir Groningen-Winschoten or via N33 Assen-Delfzil, then onto A7. Exit 45 Scheemda-Midwolda. Foll camping signs. Turn R at traff lts, site on R in 500m. Med, pt shd; wc; chem disp; baby facs; shwrs; el pnts (10A); lndtte (inc dryer); shop; tradsmn; rest; bar; BBQ; playgrnd; sw lake; games area; games rm; bike hire; entmnt; wifi; tv rm; 50% statics; dogs €1.75; phone; bus adj; twin axles; poss cr; Eng spkn; adv bkg; CCI. "Vg walking/cycling area with mkd rtes; horse riding 1km; WWII Museum in vill; watersports on Oldambtmeer 2km; vg site." ◆ 6 Jan-20 Dec. € 24.00                                       2014*

**MONTFORT see Echt** *C4*

⊞ **NIEUWVLIET** *A4* (3km N Coastal) *51.3872, 3.4398* **Vakantiepark De Pannenschuur, Zeedijk 19, 4504 PP Nieuwvliet [(0117) 372300; fax 371415; info@pannenschuur.nl; www.roompotparken.nl/parken/pannenschuur]** Fr Westerschelde Tunnel take N58. Foll sp Groede & Cadzand, thro Groede & in 3km turn R sp Nieuwvliet Strand, foll sp Pannenschuur. V lge, pt shd; htd wc; chem disp; mv service pnt; baby facs; fam bthrm; sauna; shwrs; el pnts (6A) inc; gas; lndtte (inc dryer); shop; rest, snacks, bar; playgrnd; covrd pool; sand beach 500m; tennis; cycle hire; wifi; TV; 70% statics; phone; sep car park; adv bkg; quiet; ccard acc. "V gd touring base for N & S Zeeland, Sluis, Bruges, Ghent." ◆ € 44.45                                       2010*

**NIEUWVLIET** *A4* (1km NW Rural) *51.37425, 3.44862* **Camping De Waag, Sint Jansdijk 8, 4504 PB Nieuwvliet [(0117) 371666; dewaag@zeelandnet.nl; www.campingdewaag.nl]** S fr Westerschelde Tunnel onto N61 & N58 dir Breskens. S of Breskens turn W sp Groede & Cadzand. In 6.5km beyond Groede at 2nd sp Nieuwvliet turn R; foll camp sp to site on R in 1.3km. Med, pt shd; wc; chem disp; baby facs; shwrs €0.50; el pnts (6A) €2.50; lndtte (inc dryer); shop; playgrnd; pool 1.5km; sand beach 1.5km; games area; wifi; entmnt; TV; 40% statics; dogs €1.20; phone; quiet; adv bkg. "Helpful owners; gd for sm children; conv Bruges, Zeeland & Zeebrugge." 23 Apr-1 Oct. € 14.70                                       2010*

**NIJVERDAL** *D3* (1.5km SW Rural) *52.34980, 6.45458* **Camping De Noetselerberg, Holterweg 116, 7441 DK Nijverdal [(0548) 612665; fax 611908; info@camping-noetselerberg.nl; www.camping-noetselerberg.nl]** Exit A1 at junc 28. Foll N347 dir Rijssen - Nijverdal. Turn L at rndabt down Noetselerbergweg, site sp. Lge, hdg/mkd pitch, pt shd; htd wc; chem disp; mv service pnt; fam bthrm; baby facs; shwrs; el pnts (4-6A) inc; gas; lndtte; shop; tradsmn; rest, snacks; bar; playgrnd; 2 pool (1 htd, covrd); cycle hire; entmnt; TV; 30% statics; phone; sep car park; quiet; adv bkg; Eng spkn. "Beautiful area; gd cycle tracks; friendly, helpful staff; excel." ◆ 3 Apr-25 Oct. € 34.00                                       2009*

**NOORD SLEEN see Emmen** *D2*

**NOORDWIJK AAN ZEE** *B3* (2.5km N Rural/Coastal) *52.26817, 4.46981* **Camping De Duinpan, Duindamseweg 6, 2204 AS Noordwijk aan Zee [(0252) 371726; fax 344112; contact@campingdeduinpan.nl; www.campingdeduinpan.nl]** Exit A44 at junc 3 dir Sassenheim then foll sp Noordwijkerhout. At 5th rndabt (Leeuwenhorst Congress building) turn R then L. Site sp. Med, mkd pitch, unshd; htd wc; chem disp; mv service pnt; shwrs €0.50; el pnts (10A); gas; lndtte; rest, snacks, bar adj; playgrnd; pool 2.5km; cycle hire; wifi; 60% statics; phone; sep car park; ccard acc; CKE/CCI. "Conv for tulip fields in ssn." 15 Mar-31 Oct. € 29.50                                       2013*

See advert on next page

NETHERLANDS

**NOORDWIJK AAN ZEE** *B3* (4km N Rural) *52.27102, 4.47686* **Camping De Carlton, Kraaierslaan 13, 2204 AN Noordwijk aan Zee [(0252) 372783; fax 370299; info@ campingcarlton.nl; www.campingcarlton.nl]** Fr N206 take Noordwijkerhout turn off, foll sp to town & drive thru to rndabt. Take R exit sp Congrescentrum Leeuwenhorst, then take 1st L & foll site sp. Med, mkd pitch, pt shd; htd wc; chem disp; mv service pnt; shwrs €0.50; el pnts (4A) inc; lndtte (inc dryer); shops 1km; rest, snacks, bar; playgrnd; pool; cycle hire; TV; 40% statics; phone; sep car park; poss cr; Eng spkn; quiet; ccard acc; CKE/CCI. "Conv Keukenhof; gd clean site; friendly owners." ◆ 1 Apr-1 Nov. € 26.60          2009*

⊞ **NOORDWIJK AAN ZEE** *B3* (2km NE Rural) *52.24874, 4.46358* **Camping op Hoop van Zegen, Westeinde 76, 2211 XR Noordwijkerhout [(0252) 375491; info@campingophoopvanzegen.nl; www. campingophoopvanzegen.nl]** Exit A44 junc 6 dir Noordwijk aan Zee. Cross N206 & turn R in 1km into Gooweg dir Leeuwenhorst. In 1km turn L into Hoogweg & foll sp to site. Med, hdg/mkd pitch, unshd; htd wc; chem disp; mv service pnt; baby facs; fam bthrm; shwrs; el pnts (6A) €2.25; lndtte (inc dryer); shop 2km; playgrnd; sand beach 2.5km; cycle hire; games area; dogs €3; phone; poss cr; adv bkg rec when Keukenhof open; Eng spkn; quiet; ccard acc; CKE/ CCI. "Gd site; modern san facs; conv bulb fields, beaches." € 18.00          2013*

**NOORDWIJKERHOUT see Noordwijk aan Zee** *B3*

**NUNSPEET see Harderwijk** *C3*

⊞ **OIRSCHOT** *C3* (1km N Rural) *51.51684, 5.30854* **Camping De Bocht, Oude Grintweg 69, 5688 MB Oirschot [(0499) 550855; info@campingdebocht.nl; www. campingdebocht.nl]** Fr A58/E312 take exit 8 to Oirschot. Site in 4km on Boxtel rd. Site sp. Med, hdg pitch, shd; htd wc; chem disp; baby facs; shwrs €0.50; el pnts (10A) €3; gas; lndtte (inc dryer); rest, snacks; bar; playgrnd; pool high ssn; paddling pool; cycle hire; wifi; entmnt; TV; 60% statics; dogs €2.50; phone; poss cr; adv bkg; quiet; Eng spkn. "Gd touring base; gd for families; pleasant town." € 21.70          2011*

**OMMEN** *D2* (7km E Rural) *52.51033, 6.51564* **Camping de Roos, Beerzerweg 10, 7736 PJ Beerze-Ommen [(0523) 251234; fax 251903; info@camping-de-roos.nl; www.camping-de-roos.nl]** Fr N34 at Ommen turn S onto N347. Cross rv & immed turn E. Site on L in Beerze. Lge, pt shd; htd wc; chem disp; baby facs; shwrs inc; el pnts (6A) €2.70; gas; lndtte; shop; snacks; playgrnd; lake & rv sw adj; boating; fishing; cycle hire; 10% statics; no dogs; phone; sep car park; quiet; ccard acc; red low ssn. "Excel family site; lots of play space." 2 Apr-3 Oct. € 17.00          2010*

**OMMEN** *D2* (3km W Rural) *52.51911, 6.36461* **Resort de Arendshorst, Arendshorsterweg 3A, 7731 RC Ommen [(0529) 453248; fax (0059) 453045; info@resort-de-arendshorst.nl; www.resort-de-arendshorst.nl]** W fr Ommen on N34/N340 turn L at site sp, then 500m along lane past farm, site on rvside. Lge, mkd pitch, pt shd; htd wc; chem disp; serviced pitches; baby facs; shwrs €0.20; el pnts (10A) inc; gas; lndtte; shop; rest, snacks; bar; no BBQ; playgrnd; pool 3km; paddling pool; sw in canal; games area; cycle hire; TV rm; 50% statics; dogs; phone; Eng spkn; adv bkg (fee); quiet; red 7+ days/snr citizens; CKE/CCI. "Beautiful area; many cycle rtes; gd children's facs." 1 Apr-31 Oct. € 28.50          2009*

**OOSTERBEEK see Arnhem** *C3*

⊞ **OOSTEREND (TERSCHELLING ISLAND)** *C1* (E Rural) *53.40562, 5.37947* **Camping 't Wan Tij, Oosterend 41, 8897 HX Oosterend [(0562) 448522; fax 4433495; info@ wantij-terschelling.nl; www.wantij-terschelling.nl]** Fr Harlingen to Terschelling by ferry. Take rd to Oosterend, site ent on L 250m after vill sp, past bus stop & phone box. Sm, mkd pitch, pt shd; htd wc; chem disp; shwrs €0.50; el pnts (6A) €3 (poss rev pol); lndtte; shop 3km; rest, snacks, bar 100m; cooking facs; playgrnd; sand beach 2km; internet; TV; dogs €1.75; bus adj; Eng spkn; adv bkg; quiet; CKE/CCI. "Gd area for birdwatching; many cycle/foot paths across dunes; horsedrawn vehicles for conducted tours; Elvis memorabilia 2km at Heartbreak Hotel - rest on stilts; excel site." ◆ ltd € 15.00          2010*

**OOSTERHOUT** *B3* (2km NW Rural) *51.65358, 4.82736* **Mini-Camping Vrachelen, Vrachelsestraat 48, 4911 BJ Den Hout [(0162) 454032; fax 430680; jan@pheninckx.nl; www.pheninckx.nl]** Leave A59 at junc 32 S twd Oosterhout West. At 1st rndabt foll sp Oosterhout, at next rndabt turn R sp Den Hout & site. Site on R in 400m. Sm, mkd pitch, unshd; htd wc; chem disp; shwrs inc; el pnts (6A) inc; shop; tradsmn; playgrnd; TV; many statics; poss cr; Eng spkn; quiet; red low ssn; CKE/CCI. "Perfect level lawn in mkt garden; farm produce for sale; v helpful, friendly owners; pitches have hdstg for awnings; highly rec." 15 Mar-1 Nov. € 15.00                    2011*

**OOSTKAPELLE** *A3* (200m W Rural) *51.56253, 3.54627* **Zeeland Camping Ons Buiten, Aagtekerkseweg 2A, 4356 RJ Oostkapelle [(0118) 581813; fax 583771; onsbuiten@ardoer.com; www.ardoer.com/nl/camping/ons-buiten]** Fr Middelburg foll sps to Domburg; Oostkapelle vill 4km bef Domburg, on ent foll 1-way system, foll sps to site, 400m fr cent. Lge, mkd pitch, pt shd (in orchard); htd wc; chem disp; mv service pnt; private bthrms some pitches; baby facs; fam bthrm; shwrs inc; el pnts (6A) inc; gas; lndtte (inc dryer); shop; rest, snacks; playgrnd; covrd pools; sand beach 3.5km; tennis; cycle hire; wifi; entmnt; TV; 10% statics; phone; sep car park; no dogs; adv bkg; quiet. "Friendly staff; ideal for sm children." ♦ 1 Apr-1 Nov. € 40.50                    2010*

**OOSTWOUD see Enkhuizen** *C2*

**OPENDE** *D2* (2km SE Rural) *53.16465, 6.22275* **NCC Camping de Watermolen, Openderweg 26, 9865 XE Opende [tel/fax (0594) 659144; info@campingdewatermolen.nl; www.campingdewatermolen.nl]** Exit A7 junc 32 dir Kornhorn. In Noordwijk turn L at church & in 3 km turn R into Openderweg. Site in 700m on L. Med, hdstg, pt shd; htd wc; chem disp; mv service pnt; fam bthrm; shwrs €0.50; el pnts (16A) €2.50; lndtte (inc dryer); shops 4km; rest; bar; BBQ; playgrnd; pool; lake sw; internet; wifi; tv rm; some statics; dogs €2.50; phone; adv bkg; twin axles; ccard acc; SKE/CCI; quiet. "Friendly owners; pt of site for NCC members - CC members welcome but must book ahead; brilliant site with lakes to walk around & woods; hide for bird watching; excel." 1 Apr-30 Sep. € 33.00                    2014*

**OPENDE** *D2* (3km S Rural) *53.15262, 6.19175* **Camping 't Strandheem, Parkweg 2, 9865 VP Opende [(0594) 659555; fax 658592; info@strandheem.nl; www.strandheem.nl]** E22/A7 Amsterdam to Groningen m'way take Frieschepalen exit 31. Foll N358 to Suirhesterveen; site sp. Lge, mkd pitch, some hdstg, pt shd; htd wc; mv service pnt; chem disp; serviced pitches; some pitches individ san facs; baby facs; fam bthrm; shwrs inc; el pnts (10A) €2.50; gas; lndtte (inc dryer); shop; tradsmn; rest, snacks; bar; playgrnd; pool, covrd pool; sand beach 5km; wifi; entmnt; 30% statics; dogs €4.25; poss cr; Eng spkn; adv bkg; quiet; Holland Tulip Parcs site; CKE/CCI. "Lge pitches; friendly owners; gd well-run site." ♦ 1 Apr-30 Sep. € 25.50 (CChq acc)                    2011*

**OTTERLO** *C3* (2km S Rural) *52.08657, 5.76934* **Camping De Wije Werelt, Arnhemseweg 100-102, 6731 BV Otterlo [(0318) 591201; fax 592101; info@wijewerelt.nl; www.wijewerelt.nl]** Exit A50 junc 22 dir Hoenderlo & N304 to Otterlo. Site on R after Camping de Zanding. Lge, mkd pitch, unshd; htd wc; chem disp; mv service pnt; baby facs; fam bthrm; shwrs inc; el pnts (6-10A) inc; lndtte; shop; tradsmn; rest, snacks; bar; playgrnd; pool; paddling pool; games area; 40% statics; dogs €4; phone; Eng spkn; adv bkg; quiet; ccard acc. "Excel, well-run site; immac san facs; vg for families; conv Arnhem." 27 Mar-31 Oct. € 33.00                    2009*

**OTTERLO** *C3* (1km SW Rural) *52.09310, 5.77762* **Camping De Zanding, Vijverlaan 1, 6731 CK Otterlo [(0318) 596111; fax 596110; info@zanding.nl; www.zanding.nl]** Leave A1 at exit 17 onto N310 thro Otterlo, or junc 19 onto N304. Foll camp sp to site. Fr A50 exit junc 22 dir Hoenderloo & N304 to Otterlo. V lge, mkd pitch, some hdstg, pt shd; htd wc; chem disp; mv service pnt; serviced pitches; baby facs; shwrs inc; el pnts (4-10A) inc; gas; lndtte (inc dryer); rest; shop; playgrnd; lake sw & sand beach; tennis; wifi; entmnt; TV; 45% statics; dogs €3.50; Holland Tulip Parcs site; poss cr; Eng spkn; adv bkg ess hol periods; red low ssn; ccard acc; CKE/CCI. "Peaceful, wooded site; modern, well-organised & well laid-out; friendly, helpful staff; gd for families; excel facs; conv National Park, Kröller Müller museum; excel." ♦ 26 Mar-31 Oct. € 35.00 (CChq acc)                    2011*

**OUDEGA see Drachten** *C2*

**OUDEMIRDUM** *C2* (1.5km N Rural) *52.86005, 5.54450* **Camping De Wigwam, Sminkewei 7, 8567 HB Oudemirdum [(0514) 571223; fax 571725; camping@dewigwam.nl; www.dewigwam.nl]** Exit A6 junc 17 onto N359 to Balk. Approx 3km beyond Balk turn L at sp Oudemirdum & foll site sp in woodland N of vill. Lge, mkd pitch, pt shd; wc; chem disp; baby facs; shwrs €0.75; el pnts (16A) inc; gas; lndtte; snacks; playgrnd; lake sw & sand beach 3km; cycle hire; golf adj; wifi; TV; 60% statics (sep area); dogs €2.70; Eng spkn; quiet; ccard acc; red snr citizens/low ssn. "Close to Ijsselmeer; lge pitches; gd cycling area; easy walk to pleasant vill; charge for all hot water." 1 Apr-1 Nov. € 17.30                    2010*

**OUDEMIRDUM** *C2* (500m NW Rural) *52.85436, 5.53147* **Boskampeerterrein De Waps, Fonteinwei 14, 8567 JT Oudemirdum [tel/fax (0514) 571437; waps@planet.nl; www.dewaps.nl]** Fr Lemmer take N359 twd Balk. In 12km turn L sp Oudemirdum, site sp fr church in vill. Med, hdg/mkd pitch, pt shd; htd wc; chem disp; shwrs inc; baby facs; fam bthrm; el pnts (10A) inc; lndtte; shop 500m; tradsmn; rest, snacks; bar; playgrnd; sand beach 3km; games area; cycle hire; entmnt; 25% statics; dogs €2; phone; Eng spkn; quiet; ccard acc. "In pine forest; excel walks; clean facs; friendly staff." 1 Apr-31 Oct. € 24.30                    2009*

**PANNINGEN** *C4* (3km NW Rural) *51.34894, 5.96111*
Beringerzand Camping, Heide 5, 5981 NX Panningen
[07 73 07 20 95; fax 73 07 49 80; info@beringerzand.
nl; www.beringerzand.nl] Fr A67 exit at junc 38 twd S, dir
Koningslust/Panningen. Site is 3km NW Panningen, down narr
lane thro asparagus fields. Med, mkd pitch, pt shd; wc; chem
disp; mv service pnt; shwrs; el pnts (10A); lndtte (inc dryer);
shop; tradsmn; snacks; bar; BBQ; playgrnd; htd pool; covrd
pool; waterslide; paddling pool; games area; games rm; bike
hire; wifi; dogs €4.85 max 2 per pitch; twin axles acc; Eng
spkn; adv bkg. ♦ 28 Mar-7 Nov. € 45.75          2014*

**PETTEN** *B2* (200m W Coastal) *52.77057, 4.65908* **Camping
Corfwater, Strandweg 3, 1755 LA Petten** [(0226) 381981;
fax 383371; camping@corfwater.nl; www.corfwater.nl]
On a A9 N of Alkmaar, foll sp for Petten. Thro vill, site behind
sea wall. Lge, mkd pitch, unshd; htd wc; chem disp; mv service
pnt; baby facs; fam bthrm; shwrs inc; el pnts (6A) inc; gas;
lndtte; shop; no BBQ; playgrnd; pool 3km; sand beach adj;
20% statics; no dogs; phone; sep car park; Eng spkn; quiet;
ccard acc; CKE/CCI. "Vg site; busy in high ssn." ♦ 1 Apr-
31 Oct. € 26.00          2011*

## "I like to fill in the reports as I travel from site to site"
You'll find report forms at the back of
this guide, or you can fill them in online
at www.caravaclub.co.uk/europereport.

**RAVENSTEIN** *C3* (E Urban) *51.79600, 5.65500* **NCC Camping
De Pollepel, Bleek 5, 5371 AP Ravenstein** [(0486) 413849;
info@ncc.nl; www.ncc.nl] Fr N exit A50 junc 17 dir
Ravenstein, strt on at rndabt into Ravenstein. Fr S exit A50
junc 17 turn R at rndabt into Ravenstein. Foll sp for NCC
camping; pass sm marina on RH side; turn L into Walstraat;
then L immed after car park, site ent 50m thro gates. Sm, mkd
pitch, pt shd; htd wc; chem disp; shwrs inc; el pnts (4A) £2.75;
lndtte; shop, rest, snacks, bar 500m; playgrnd; htd, covrd
pool 4km; rv sw adj; TV rm; train 3km; poss cr; adv bkg; some
rd noise. "Beautiful site; located in cent picturesque fortress
town on Rv Maas; gd cycling, walking; interesting area; CC
members welcome but must phone ahead." 1 Apr-31 Oct.
€ 12.00          2011*

**REEUWIJK see Gouda** *B3*

**RENESSE** *A3* (1km N Coastal) *51.73917, 3.77611*
Camping Duinhoeve, Scholderlaan 8, 4328 EP Renesse
[(0111) 461309; fax 462760; info@campingduinhoeve.
nl; www.campingduinhoeve.nl] On rd 102 fr Renesse to
Haamstede, turn R on ent to Haamstede bef T-junc. Last site
on long picturesque lane. Lge, hdg/mkd pitch, pt shd; htd wc;
chem disp; mv service pnt; baby facs; shwrs inc; el pnts (4-6A)
inc; gas; lndtte; shop; rest, snacks; bar; playgrnd; sand beach
nr; games area; cycle hire; TV; 20% statics; dogs €3.50; poss
cr; adv bkg; quiet; ccard acc. "Charming area; Delta works
worth visit; wide dunes on sea shore." ♦ 1 Feb-31 Oct.
€ 28.20          2009*

**RENSWOUDE** *C3* (2.2km NE Rural) *52.08435, 5.55069*
Camping de Grebbelinie, Ubbeschoterweg
12, 3927 CJ Renswoude [(0318) 591073; info@
campingdegrebbelinie.nl; www.campingdegrebbelinie.
nl] Head NW on Dorpsstraat/N224, at rndabt take 1st exit
onto Barneveldsestraat, turn R onto Bekerweg, R onto
Ubbeschoterweg then turn L. Site on the R. Med, unshd; htd
wc; chem disp; baby facs; fam bthrm; shwrs inc; el pnts; lndtte;
shops 2km; rest 2km; snacks 2km; bar 2km; playgrnd; games
area; internet; wifi; dogs €1.75; bus 2km; Eng spkn; adv bkg;
quiet; CKE/CCI. "Friendly owners; excel cycling with cycle rte
adj; conv for Arnhem & Utrecht; peaceful site on former farm;
in open countryside; excel value for money." 21 Mar-18 Oct.
€ 27.00          2014*

**RETRANCHEMENT see Sluis** *A4*

**RIJEN see Breda** *B3*

**RIJNSBURG see Katwijk aan Zee** *B3*

**ROCKANJE** *A3* (NW Coastal) *51.88000, 4.05422* **Molecaten
Park Waterbos, Duinrand 11, 3235 CC Rockanje**
[(0181) 401900; fax 404233; info@waterboscamping.nl;
www.waterboscamping.nl] Site clearly sp fr Rockanje vill.
Lge, hdg pitch, pt shd; htd wc; chem disp; mv service pnt; baby
facs; private san facs avail; shwrs €0.50; el pnts (6A) inc; lndtte;
shop; rest, snacks; bar; playgrnd; sand beach/dunes 1km;
entmnt; cab/sat TV; 80% statics; phone; no dogs; phone; poss
cr; adv bkg; quiet;CKE/CCI. "Lovely base for Voorne area." ♦
1 Apr-1 Oct. € 19.00          2009*

**ROERMOND** *C4* (4km W Rural) *51.19186, 5.94955*
Resort Marina Oolderhuuske, Oolderhuuske 1, 6041
TR Roermond [(0475) 588686; fax 582652; info@
oolderhuuske.nl; www.oolderhuuske.nl] Exit N280 1km
fr Roermond sp De Weerd & foll sp to Marina Oolderhuuske.
Med, mkd pitch, unshd; htd wc; chem disp; mv service pnt;
baby facs; shwrs inc; el pnts (6A) €2.50; gas; lndtte (inc dryer);
shop; rest, snacks; bar; playgrnd; htd, covrd pool; paddling pol;
lake sw adj; boating; fishing; watersports; tennis; games area;
golf driving range; cycle hire; wifi; 75% statics; dogs €4; Eng
spkn; quiet; red long stay. "Facs v clean; mkt Wed/Sat; gd site
in gd weather." ♦ 1 Apr-31 Oct. € 33.00 (4 persons)   2010*

**ROERMOND** *C4* (15km W Rural) *51.20947, 5.83008* **Camping
Geelenhoof, Grathemerweg 16, 6037 NR Kelpen-Oler
(Limburg)** [(0495) 651858; info@geelenhoof.nl; www.
geelenhoof.nl] 1km S of Kelpen-Oler; bet Roermond &
Weert; exit N280 foll sp; well mkd. Med, hdg/mkd pitch, pt
shd; htd wc; chem disp; mv service pnt; baby facs; shwrs inc;
el pnts (6A) €3; rest, snacks; bar; playgrnd; games area; games
rm; dogs (on request) €2.50; Eng spkn; adv bkg; quiet;CKE/
CCI. "Cars not to be parked with c'van; vg site." 1 Apr-4 Nov.
€ 28.70          2013*

**NETHERLANDS**

**ROOSENDAAL** *B3* (5km SE Rural) *51.49430, 4.48536*
**Camping Zonneland, Turfvaartsestraat 6, 4709 PB Nispen
[(0165) 365429; info@zonneland.nl; www.zonneland.nl]**
Take A58 exit 24 onto N262 dir Nispen. Foll site sps. Lge, some hdstg, shd; wc; chem disp; mv service pnt; shwrs €0.50; el pnts (4-10A) €2; lndtte; shop; supmkt 4km; snacks; bar; pool; playgrnd; entmnt; 80% statics; no dogs; phone; Eng spkn; adv bkg; quiet; ccard acc. 1 Mar-15 Oct. € 19.00          2012*

⊞ **ROTTERDAM** *B3* (2.5km N Urban) *51.93100, 4.44200*
**Stadscamping Rotterdam, Kanaalweg 84, 3041
JE Rotterdam [(010) 4153440; fax 4373215; info@
stadscamping-rotterdam.nl; www.stadscamping-
rotterdam.nl]** Adj to junc of A13 & A20, take slip rd sp Rotterdam Centrum & Camping Kanaalweg sp to site. Dist fr m'way 2.5km with 3 L turns. Lge, pt shd; wc; chem disp; baby facs; shwrs inc; el pnts (6A) €3.75; gas; lndtte; shop; snacks; bar; internet; pool 500m; dogs €2; bus; poss cr; adv bkg; quiet but rds, rlwy adj; ccard acc. "Gd bus service to city cent; few water taps."  ♦  € 34.75          2014*

⊞ **ROTTERDAM** *B3* (12km SE Rural) *51.83454, 4.54673*
**Camping De Oude Maas, Achterzeedijk 1A, 2991
SB Barendrecht [(078) 6772445; fax 6773013; www.
campingdeoudemaas.nl]** Leave A29 (Rotterdam-Bergen op Zoom) junc 20 Barendrecht, foll sp for Heerjansdam, site sp, Fr A16 (Breda-Dordrecht) foll Europort sp, then Zierikzee, Barendrecht, site sp. Lge, pt shd; htd wc; chem disp; mv service pnt; baby facs; fam bthrm; shwrs inc; el pnts (10A) inc; lndtte; shop; snacks; playgrnd; TV; 80% statics in sep area; dogs; phone; quiet; ccard acc. "Excel site on Rv Maas inc sm marina & joins rec park; excel facs; some pitches rough & long way fr facs; ferry fr site in ssn; check recep opening time if planning dep bef midday (espec Sun) for return of deposit & barrier key; entry via new ent past old."  ♦  € 25.00          2012*

> "We must tell The Club about that great site we found"
>
> Get your site reports in by mid-August and we'll do our best to get your updates into the next edition.

**RUINEN** *D2* (2km N Rural) *52.77570, 6.37170* **Camping
Ruinen, Oude Benderseweg 11, 7963 PX Ruinen
[(0522) 471770; fax 472614; info@camping-ruinen.nl;
www.camping-ruinen.nl]** Exit A28 junc 28 sp Ruinen & foll sp to site; narr lanes. Lge, mkd pitch, some hdstg, pt shd; htd wc; chem disp; mv service pnt; baby facs; fam bthrm; shwrs inc; el pnts (6A) inc; gas; lndtte (inc dryer); supmkt high ssn; rest, snacks; playgrnd; htd pool; paddling pool; waterslide; tennis; cycle hire; wifi; entmnt; cab TV; 30% statics; dogs €3.35; sep car park; Holland Tulip Parcs site; Eng spkn; adv bkg; quiet. "V pleasant site."  ♦  1 Apr-1 Oct. € 25.00   2011*

**RUURLO** *D3* (3km SE Rural) *52.06778, 6.50236* **Camping de
Meibeek, Bekkenwal 2,7261 RG Ruurlo [(0573) 491236;
info@campingdemeibeek.nl; www.campingdemeibeek.
nl]** Site on N319, sp. Med, hdg/mkd pitch, pt shd; htd wc; chem disp; mv service pnt; baby facs; shwrs €0.50; el pnts (6A) metered; lndtte (inc dryer); tradsmn; rest, snacks; bar; playgrnd; pool; fishing nr; tennis 3km; golf 10km; games area; wifi; entmnt; 50% statics; dogs; Eng spkn; adv bkg; quiet. "Friendly, enthusiastic young owners; excel." 1 Apr-31 Oct.        2009*

**SCHIMMERT** *C4* (6km N Rural) *50.90746, 5.83122* **Camping
Mareveld, Mareweg 23, 6333 BR Schimmert South
Limburg [(045) 4041269; fax 4042148; info@mareveld.
nl; www.campingmareveld.nl]** A76 exit Spaubeek, turn R twd Schimmert. 2nd on the L in Schimmert. Campsite sp. Sm, pt shd; wc; chem disp; baby facs; shwrs, el (6A) €2.10; rest/café; bar; playgrnd; htd pool; games area; wifi; tv in bar; 80% statics; dog €1.75; poss cr; Eng spkn; adv bkg; popular with families; red low ssn; "Gd cycling and walking fr site; gd site; open plan, grassy site." 1 Apr-31 Dec. € 30.00     2014*

⊞ **SEVENUM** *C4* (5km SW Rural) *51.38310, 5.97590*
**Camping De Schatberg, Midden Peelweg 1, 5975 MZ
Sevenum [(077) 4677777; fax 4677799; receptie@
schatberg.nl; www.schatberg.nl]** Fr A2/A67 exit junc 38 for Helden; foll sp Sevenum & site by sm lake. V lge, shd; htd wc; chem disp; mv service pnt; fam bthrm; baby facs; private san facs some pitches; sauna; shwrs inc; el pnts (6-10A) inc; gas; lndtte (inc dryer); shop; rest, snacks; bar; playgrnd; 2 pools (1 htd, covrd); paddling pool; waterslide; jacuzzi; lake sw & sand beach; watersports; fishing; tennis; games area; cycle hire; entmnt; TV; 60% statics; dogs (in sep area); phone; Holland Tulip Parcs site; Eng spkn; adv bkg; quiet; CKE/CCI. "Excel leisure facs, espec for children; vg site but impersonal; tourers pitched amongst statics; Venlo Sat mkt worth visit."  ♦  € 41.30 (4 persons) (CChq acc)        2011*

**'S-HEERENBERG** *D3* (3km W Rural) *51.87795, 6.21125*
**Camping Brockhausen, Eltenseweg 20, 7039 CV Stokkum
[(0314) 661212; fax 668563; info@brockhausen.nl; www.
brockhausen.nl]** Fr A12 exit junc sp 's-Heerenberg, cont past 's-Heerenberg sp & pick up sp to Stokkum & site on L. Med, mkd pitch, pt shd; htd wc; chem disp; mv service pnt; baby facs; shwrs metered; el pnts (4-6A) inc; lndtte (inc dryer); shop 3km; playgrnd; cab TV; 40% statics; dogs €3.45; Eng spkn; adv bkg; quiet. "V clean, eco-friendly site; facs charged on electronic key; friendly, helpful staff; lovely area walking, cycling; excel."  ♦  1 Apr-31 Oct. € 24.20          2012*

**'S-HERTOGENBOSCH** *C3* (6km E Rural) *51.6938, 5.4148*
**Camping de Hooghe Heide, Werstkant 17, 5258 TC
Berlicum [(073) 5031522; fax 5037351; info@hoogheheide.
nl; www.hoogheheide.nl]** Fr A59/A2 circular rd around 's-Hertogenbosch exit junc 21 dir Berlicum. Foll sp Berlicum & site. Site is NE of Berlicum. Med, mkd pitch, pt shd; wc; chem disp; baby facs; shwrs inc; el pnts (10A) €3; lndtte; shop; snacks; playgrnd; pool; paddling pool; games area; TV; 70% statics; dogs €4.25; phone; poss cr/noisy high ssn; Eng spkn; adv bkg ess; quiet; CKE/CCI. "Nice, peaceful wooded site; narr site rds for lge o'fits; tourers on open field; excel."  ♦ 1 Apr-16 Oct. € 26.50          2010*

**SINT OEDENRODE** *C3* (1km N Rural) *51.57741, 5.44648*
**Camping De Kienehoef, Zwembadweg 37, 5491 TE Sint
Oedenrode [(0413) 472877; fax 477033; info@kienehoef.
nl; www.kienehoef.nl]** Exit A50 junc 9; go twds Sint
Oedenrode; foll sp to Centrum at rndabt; foll sp. Lge, hdg/
mkd pitch, some hdstg, pt shd; htd wc; chem disp; mv service
pnt; fam bthrm; baby facs; shwrs inc; el pnts (6A) inc; gas;
lndtte (inc dryer); shop; rest, snacks; bar; BBQ; playgrnd; htd,
covrd pool; paddling pool; lake sw; fishing; tennis; cycle hire;
wifi; entmnt; TV rm; 50% statics; no dogs; phone; sep car
park; Holland Tulip Parcs site; Eng spkn; adv bkg; ccard acc;
CKE/CCI. "Lovely CL type site; v gd facs; 1.50 miles fr lovely
sm town with plenty of shops & rests." 1 Apr-25 Sep. € 30.00
(CChq acc)                                               2011*

⊞ **SINT OEDENRODE** *C3* (1km N Rural) *51.57800, 5.4400*
**NCC Camping 't Roois Klumpke, Vliegden 1, 5491 VS Sint
Oedenrode [(0413) 474702; www.ncc.nl]** Exit A2 junc 26 to
Sint Oedenrode; site sp on Schijndel rd - 100m bef Camping
Kienehoef turn R onto Vliegden, site 400m on L. Med, mkd
pitch, pt shd; htd wc; chem disp; shwrs inc; el pnts (4A) €2.75;
lndtte; BBQ; Eng spkn; poss cr; Eng spkn; adv bkg; quiet; CKE/
CCI. "Members only - CC members welcome but must pre-
book; shop, rest, snacks avail at Camping de Kienehoef." ♦ ltd
€ 11.00                                                  2009*

**SLUIS** *A4* (400m NE Rural) *51.31395, 3.38863* **Camping
De Meidoorn, Hoogstraat 68, 4524 LA Sluis [tel/fax
(0117) 461662; info@campingdemeidoorn.eu; www.
campingdemeidoorn.eu]** Fr Zeebrugge, ignore 1st turn L to
Sluis, cont to rndabt sp Sluis 1km. At windmill keep R (do not
go to town cent). After LH bend turn R, foll sps. Lge, pt shd;
htd wc; chem disp; mv service pnt; baby facs; shwrs €0.50;
el pnts (6A) €3; gas; shop; rest, snacks; bar; playgrnd; tennis;
TV; 80% statics; dogs €1.75; phone; Eng spkn; red CKE/CCI.
"Bus to Bruges and Breskens fr rear site ent." ♦ 1 Apr-1 Nov.
€ 33.45                                                  2013*

**SLUIS** *A4* (5km SE Rural) *51.28682, 3.43580* **Camping
de Oliepot, Draaibrugseweg 8, 4527 PA Aardenburg
[(0117) 491518; fax 493286; s.van.male@agroweb.nl;
www.oliepot.nl]** Fr Knokke take N376 onto Sluis by-pass
N58; turn R onto N251 Aardenburg. At next rndat in 1km turn
L sp Draaibrug & immed R onto service rd. Site on L in 1km.
Sm, mkd pitch, pt shd; wc; chem disp; shwrs €0.50; el pnts
(4-16A) €1.65-6.30; lndtte; shop 1km; playgrnd; pool 3km;
sand beach 6km; no statics; dogs €1.30; Eng spkn; adv bkg rec
high ssn; quiet; ccard not acc; CKE/CCI. "V well-run site, clean
& tidy; friendly, helpful owners; conv Bruges & Ghent." 1 Apr-
30 Sep. € 11.00                                          2009*

**SNEEK** *C2* (1km NE Urban) *53.03557, 5.67630* **Jachthaven
Camping De Domp, De Domp 4, 8605 CP Sneek
[(0515) 412559; fax 439846; www.dedomp.nl]** Fr cent of
Sneek on Leeuwarden rd, turn R sp De Domp. Med, pt shd;
htd wc; chem disp; mv service pnt; serviced pitches; baby
facs; shwrs €0.50; el pnts (6A) inc; gas; lndtte; rest, snacks;
bar; supmkt nr; playgrnd; boating; sep car park; dogs; adv
bkg; Eng spkn. "Many canals in Sneek; marina on site; easy
walk to pleasant town; gd cycling cent." ♦ 1 Apr-1 Nov.
€ 18.20                                                  2009*

**STADSKANAAL** *D2* (1km W Urban) *52.99079, 6.94159*
**Camping 't Nije Hof, Spoorstraat 29b, 9503 AM
Stadskanaal [599 658 892; info@nijehof.nl; www.nijehof.
nl]** Fr Groningen take exit 44 off A7 Winschoten onto N33
dir Pekela; take N366 dir Stadskanaal & foll this rd until junc
& take exit Stadskanaal (N) onto Van Boekerenweg; drive strt
on for several km and pass hospial; turn L after hospital at
traff lts island onto Handlestraat, which becomes Postraat; rd
alongside canal, turn R over bdge sp Drouwener; take 1st R
into Spoorstraat; pass over rlwy lines and immed sharp L into
site. Sm, pt shd; htd wc; chem disp; baby facs; shwrs inc; elec
pnts inc; lndtte; playgrnd; 15% statics; dogs €1.50; adv bkings;
quiet; CKE/CCI. "Pleasant quiet site; friendly owners; pay on
arr; handy for exploring Dolmen on Dutch/German border."
Apr-Sep. € 17.50                                         2011*

**STEENBERGEN** *B3* (4km NW Rural) *51.60887, 4.27303*
**Camping De Uitwijk, Dorpsweg 136, 4655 AH De Heen
[(0167) 560000; fax 560010; info@de-uitwijk.nl; www.
de-uitwijk.nl]** Fr N259 at Steenbergen turn N onto N257 dir
Zierikzee. In 2km turn N thro De Heen & turn R at T-junc. Site
recep on R, site on L. Do not take c'van to recep, but ent site,
park on R & walk back. Med, mkd pitch, pt shd; htd wc; chem
disp; mv service pnt; baby facs; shwrs inc; el pnts (4-10A) inc;
lndtte (inc dryer); shop 4km; rest, snacks; bar; playgrnd; games
rm; wifi; entmnt; sat TV; 60% statics; dogs €3.20; bus 750m;
poss cr; Eng spkn; adv bkg; CKE/CCI. "Pleasant, well run, quiet
site adj marina; friendly staff; excel; excel cycle rtes; conv for
ferry." 23 Mar-28 Sep. € 30.50                           2014*

**STEENWIJK** *C2* (6km NE Rural) *52.84123, 6.17674* **Camping
de Moesberg, Hoofdweg 14, 8383 EG Nijensleek
[(0521) 381563; fax 383285; info@moesberg.nl; www.
moesberg.nl]** Exit A32 junc 6 at Steenwijk N onto N855 sp
Frederiksoord & Vledder; thro Nijensleek, site on L. Med, mkd
pitch, unshd; htd wc; chem disp; mv service pnt; baby facs;
shwrs; el pnts (10A) inc; lndry rm; shop 2km; rest adj; bar;
playgrnd; pool 3km; wifi; sat TV; 10% statics; dogs; poss cr;
Eng spkn; adv bkg; quiet. "Paved patio area at each pitch;
helpful, friendly owners; gd rest adj." 1 Apr-1 Nov.     2009*

**THORN** *C4* (600m SW Rural) *51.1596, 5.8340* **Camping
Viverjerbroek, Kessenicherweg 20, 6017 AA Thorn
[(0475) 561914; fax 565565; info@campingthorn.com]**
Take junc 41 of A2, foll sp to Thorn. Turn R in vill down
Wilhelminalaan, R into Holstraat, foll rd to site. Sm, hdg/mkd
pitch, pt shd; wc; chem disp; shwrs €1; el pnts (4A) inc (rev
pol); shop 500m; rest; bar; BBQ; lake sw & sand beach 1km;
watersports; boating; 80% statics; dogs; phone; adv bkg;
quiet; CKE/CCI. "Nr attractive vill; conv m'way; site run down
(May 2010); NH only." 1 Apr-30 Oct. € 17.50            2010*

**TIEL** *C3* (4km W Rural) *51.89964, 5.35948* **Camping
de Vergarde, Erichemseweg 84, 4117 GL Erichem
[(0344) 572017; fax 572229; info@devergarde.nl; www.
devergarde.nl]** Exit A15 at Tiel-West junc 32; foll sp Erichem
& site. Lge, mkd pitch, pt shd; htd wc; chem disp; mv service
pnt; serviced pitches; baby facs; fam bthrm; shwrs; el pnts
(10A) inc; gas; lndtte; shop; rest, snacks; bar; playgrnd; htd
pool; fishing; tennis; cycle hire; horseriding; children's farm;
entmnt; internet; TV; 60% statics; dogs €3.75; poss cr; Eng
spkn; quiet; red low ssn; ccard acc; CKE/CCI. "Gd facs." ♦
1 Apr-18 Oct. € 27.50                                    2010*

**TUITJENHORN** B2 (2km E Rural) 52.73495, 4.77612 **Campingpark de Bongerd, Bongerdlaan 3, 1747 CA Tuitjenhorn [(0226) 391481; fax 394658; info@bongerd.nl; www.bongerd.nl]** N fr Alkmaar on N245, exit at Dirkshorn & foll sp to site. V lge, mkd pitch, pt shd; htd wc; chem disp; baby facs; shwrs inc; el pnts (10A) inc; gas; lndtte (inc dryer); shop; rest, snacks; bar; BBQ; playgrnd; 2 htd pools (1 covrd); paddling pool; waterslide; lake fishing; tennis; games area; cycle hire; wifi; entmnt; 60% statics; dogs €1.90; Eng spkn; adv bkg; ccard acc; quiet. "Excel, attractive family site; vg facs." ♦ 8 Apr-30 Sep. € 43.30 (CChq acc) 2014*

**UDEN** C3 (11km E Rural) 51.66309, 5.77641 **Mini Camping Boszicht, Tipweg 10, 5455 RC Wilbertoord [(0485) 451565 / (06) 12957217; fax (0845) 471522; boszicht-wilbertoord@planet.nl; www.boszichtcamping. nl]** Fr 's-Hertogenbosch on N279 dir Helmond. At Veghel turn L onto N265. Bef Uden turn R onto N264 to Wilbertoord in 11km. Sm, hdg/mkd pitch, unshd; wc; shwrs; el pnts (6A) metered; shops; rest in vill; playgrnd; games area; dog €2; quiet; "Family-run farm site in woodland; conv Arnhem, Nijmegen." 20 Mar-19 Oct. € 14.50 2013*

**UITDAM see Edam** B2

## "I need an on-site restaurant"

We do our best to make sure site information is correct, but it is always best to check any must-have facilities are still available or will be open during your visit.

**UTRECHT** B3 (8km NE Rural) 52.13123, 5.22024 **Camping Bospark Bilthoven, Burg van der Borchlaan 7, 3722 GZ Bilthoven [(030) 2286777; fax 2293888; info@ bosparkbilthoven.nl; www.bosparkbilthoven.nl]** Exit A28/ E30 Utrecht-Amersfoort at exit sp De Bilt & strt to Bilthoven. Approx 3km after leaving m'way (400m S of level x-ing) turn R sp De Bospark Bilthoven. At edge of town foll sps twd lge brown tower & golf course. Site on L. V lge, pt shd; htd wc; chem disp; mv service pnt; baby facs; fam bthrm; serviced pitches; shwrs inc; el pnts (4-6A) inc (poss rev pol); gas; lndtte; shop 1km; tradsmn; snacks; bar; playgrnd; htd pool; TV; 60% statics; dogs €3.50; phone; poss cr; Eng spkn; adv bkg; quiet but some noise fr air base. "Helpful management; 20 mins walk to stn for trains to Utrecht cent." ♦ 1 Apr-31 Oct. € 25.75 2012*

**UTRECHT** B3 (10km E Rural) 52.09272, 5.28287 **Camping de Krakeling, Woudensbergseweg 17, 3707 HW Zeist [(030) 6915374; fax 6920707; allurepark@dekrakeling.nl; www.dekrakeling.nl]** Fr A12 exit junc 20 Driebergen/Zeist. In Zeist foll dir Woudenberg, site sp. V lge, hdg/mkd pitch, pt shd; htd wc; chem disp; mv service pnt; baby facs; shwrs €0.50; el pnts (6-10A) €2.50; lndtte; shop; rest, snacks, bar w/end only low ssn; playgrnd; pool 3km; lake sw 5km; tennis; internet free; cab TV; 90% statics; dogs free; phone; adj nature reserve; bus; adv bkg. "Gd touring base Amsterdam/Utrecht; friendly; excel, clean facs; recep open 0900-1700, clsd for lunch." ♦ 28 Mar-29 Sep. € 28.40 2013*

**VAALS** C4 (500m W Rural) 50.78159, 6.00694 **Camping Hoeve de Gastmolen, Lemierserberg 23, 6291 NM Vaals [(043) 3065755; fax 3066015; info@gastmolen.nl; www. gastmolen.nl]** Fr A76 exit at Knooppunt Bocholtz onto N281 SW to join N278, turn L twd Aachen. Site on L just bef 1st rndabt as ent Vaals. Med, hdg/mkd pitch, pt sl, pt shd; wc; chem disp; shwrs €0.50; el pnts (4A) €2.70; lndtte; shops 500m; tradsmn; rest 500m; snacks; playgrnd; 10% statics; dogs €2.70; bus 500m; sep car park; poss cr; Eng spkn; adv bkg rec; quiet; CKE/CCI. "Sm rural site; conv Aachen; vg san facs; diff in wet - tractor avail; mosquitoes; 'Drielandenpunt' 4km, in walking dist (where Netherlands, Germany & Belgium meet); excel." 15 Apr-31 Oct. € 35.50 2014*

**VAASSEN see Apeldoorn** C3

**VALKENBURG AAN DE GEUL** C4 (1.5km N Rural) 50.88013, 5.83466 **Familie Camping De Bron, Stoepertweg 5, 6301 WP Valkenburg [(045) 4059292; fax 4054281; info@ camping-debron.nl; www.camping-debron.nl]** Fr A79 exit junc 4 dir Hulsberg. Take 3rd exit fr rndabt onto N298, across next rndabt, then L onto N584, site sp. Fr A76 exit junc 3 dir Schimmert, foll sp Valkenburg & site. Lge, mkd pitch, pt shd; htd wc; chem disp; mv service pnt; baby facs; shwrs inc; el pnts (4-6A) €3-4.50; lndtte; shop; rest, snacks; bar; playgrnd; pool; games area; cycle hire; entmnt; internet; TV; 30% statics; dogs €3.50; phone; adv bkg; CKE/CCI. "Vg, well laid-out site; gd facs; muddy in wet weather; 2 pools with lots of equipment for kids; statics hidden away in the greenery; helpful staff." ♦ 1 Apr-20 Dec. € 42.50 2014*

**VALKENBURG AAN DE GEUL** C4 (5km E Rural) 50.85042, 5.88120 **Camping Schoonbron, Valkenburgerweg 128, 6305 EA Schin op Geul [(043) 4591209; fax 4591486; info@ schoonbron.nl; www.schoonbron.nl]** E fr Valkenburg on N595 to Schin op Geul. Site opp Camping Vinkenhof, just after Esso g'ge on L. Clearly sp, but ent pt hidden by RH bend in rd. V lge, mkd pitch, pt sl, pt shd; htd wc; chem disp; mv service pnt; baby facs; fam bthrm; shwrs inc; el pnts (4A) inc; lndtte (inc dryer); shop; rest, snacks; bar; playgrnd; covrd, htd pool; games area; wifi; entmnt; TV; 60% statics; dogs €3.25; Eng spkn; quiet; ccard not acc; CKE/CCI. "Clean, modern facs; friendly staff; vg." ♦ 15 Mar-31 Oct. € 24.00 2009*

**VALKENBURG AAN DE GEUL** C4 (3km SE Rural) 50.84990, 5.87320 **Camping Vinkenhof, Engwegen 2A, 6305 PM Schin op Geul [(043) 4591389; fax 4591780; info@ campingvinkenhof.nl; www.campingvinkenhof.nl]** Exit E2 Eindhoven-Maastricht at Meersen/Valkenburg about 6km bef Maastricht; foll rd E to Valkenburg. In town take rd E to Schin op Geul & foll camping sps. Med, mkd pitch, unshd; htd wc; serviced pitches; chem disp; baby facs; serviced pitches; shwrs €0.75; el pnts (6A) inc; gas; lndtte; shop 1km; rest adj; snacks; playgrnd; pool; cycle hire; TV rm; 5% statics; dogs €3; phone; site clsd 20 Dec-14 Jan; Eng spkn; quiet; CKE/CCI. "Gd walking country; well-kept, friendly site." 1 Mar-4 Jan. € 26.50 2010*

**VALKENBURG AAN DE GEUL** *C4* (500m S Urban) *50.85972, 5.83138* **Stadscamping Den Driesch, Heunsbergerweg 1, 6301 BN Valkenburg [(043) 6012025; fax 6016139; info@campingdendriesch.nl; www.campingdendriesch.nl]** Fr A2 dir Maastricht exit sp Valkenburg-Cauberg. Foll sp Valkenburg N590 & take turning sp Sibbe-Margraten. At rndabt foll sp Valkenburg, pass coal mine & turn R in 250m into sm, sl, unmkd ent. Steep turn off main rd into ent. NB L turn into site diff - proceed to rndabt at top of hill & return downhill to site. Med, mkd pitch, hdstg, pt sl, terr, pt shd; htd wc; chem disp; mv service pnt; shwrs €0.70; el pnts (10A) inc; lndtte; shop on site & 500m; rest 500m; snacks; no BBQs; htd, covrd pool 1km; cycle hire; 10% statics; dogs €3; phone; Eng spkn; adv bkg; quiet; ccard acc; CKE/CCI. "Castle & caves adj; other attractions nr; gd Xmas mkts in caves; easy access Maastricht by bus/train; vg." Easter-21 Dec. € 28.00            2009*

**VALKENBURG AAN DE GEUL** *C4* (1km S Rural) *50.85672, 5.81891* **Camping De Cauberg, Rijksweg 171, 6325 AD Valkenburg [(043) 6012344; info@campingdecauberg.nl; www.campingdecauberg.nl]** Exit A79 sp Valkenburg, foll Sibbe & Margraten sp to town cent. Take R fork in town sp De Cauberg, site on R at top of hill just past end Valkenburg sp. Med, mkd pitch, pt sl, shd; htd wc; chem disp; baby facs; shwrs inc; el pnts (10A) inc; lndtte; shop, rest, snacks; playgrnd; htd pool 1km; internet; 10% statics; dogs €3.10; bus; phone; site clsd 1-15 Nov; Eng spkn; adv bkg; quiet; red long stay; CKE/CCI. "Excel pool 1km; excel, modern, clean san facs; friendly, helpful owner; conv Maastricht; many rests, cafes in Valkenburg." 1 Jan-5 Jan 14 Mar-31 Oct & 14 Nov-31 Dec. € 34.00            2014*

**VALKENBURG AAN DE GEUL** *C4* (2km W Rural) *50.86057, 5.77237* **Camping Oriëntal, Rijksweg 6, 6325 PE Berg en Terblijt [(043) 6040075; info@campingoriental.nl; www.campingoriental.nl]** Fr A2/E25 exit onto N278 E & in 1km turn L onto N590 sp Berg en Terblijt & Valkenburg. Cont on N590, site on R in 4km at start of vill Lge, mkd pitch, pt shd; htd wc; chem disp; mv service pnt; serviced pitch inc TV at extra cost; baby facs; serviced pitches (inc cab TV); shwrs; el pnts (6A) inc (poss rev pol); gas; lndtte; shop; rest 500m; snacks; bar; supmkt; playgrnd; htd, covrd pool; paddling pool; games area; wifi; 10% statics; dogs €3.50; phone; bus to Maastricht adj; Eng spkn; adv bkg; quiet; red low ssn; red low ssn; CKE/CCI. "Immac, well-run site; some areas flood in heavy rain; gd entmnt for young children; conv Maastricht." ♦ Easter-30 Oct. € 27.00            2013*

**VALKENSWAARD see Eindhoven** *C4*

**VEERE see Middelburg** *A4*

**VENLO** *C4* (10km N Rural) *51.45989, 6.17120* **Camping Landhuis De Maashof, Veerweg 9, 5973 NS Lottum [07 74 63 19 24; fax 74 63 24 72; info@demaashof.nl; www.demaashof.nl]** Fr A67 Eindhoven - Venlo, take exit 12 onto A73. Then exit 11 twd Horst/Melderslo. Foll sp to Lottum. Foll sp to campsite. Med, pt shd; wc; chem disp; shwr; lndtte; snacks; BBQ; playgrnd; wifi; dogs €1.20; bus 800m; twin axles; poss cr; Eng spkn; adv bkg; quiet; CCI. "Cycling, rv bank walks; rose gdn exhibition in vill; lots of rv traff & ferries; working windmill & castle nrby." 1 Apr-30 Sep. € 20.00            2014*

**⊞ VENLO** *D4* (2km SE Rural) *51.34823, 6.18548* **Camping/Restaurant De Kraal, Kaldenkerkerweg 186, 5915 PP Venlo [(077) 3514116; fax 3546164; kraal@dekraal.nl; www.dekraal.nl]** Fr rndabt by Venlo rlwy stn, take Kaldenkerkerweg SE for 2km; rest adj petrol stn. Sm, hdstg, pt shd; own san; chem disp; mv service pnt; el pnts inc; rest, snacks; bar; adv bkg. "CL-type site behind excel rest; nature park; watersports; walking; cycling; excel NH; m'vans only." € 6.00            2009*

**VENLO** *D4* (3km NW Rural) *51.42029, 6.10675* **Camping Californië, Horsterweg 23, 5971 ND Grubbenvorst [(077) 3662049; fax 3662997; info@limburgsecamping.nl; www.limburgsecamping.nl]** Exit A73 at Grubbenvorst junc 12 dir Sevenum, site sp. Med, pt shd; htd wc; chem disp; mv service pnt; shwrs inc; el pnts (4-10A); lndtte; playgrnd; Eng spkn; quiet. "Pleasant, peaceful, warm welcome; unisex shwrs; CL style site with grass cut reg." 15 Mar-15 Oct. € 26.60            2014*

**VIERHUIZEN** *D1* (500m Rural) *53.36011, 6.29505* **Camping Lauwerszee, Hoofdstraat 49, 9975 VR Vierhuizen [05 95 40 16 57; info@camping-lauwerszee.nl; www.camping-lauwerszee.nl]** Fr A7/E22 Amsterdam-Groningen take exit 33 Oude Riet onto N388 Grijpskerk. Turn L on N355 then R onto N388. 2.5km after Zoutcamp turn L to Vierhuizen. Site on R in 1km. Med, hdg pitch, mkd pitch, pt shd; wc; chem disp; mv service pnt; shwrs; el pnts (6A); lndtte (inc dryer); tradsmn; rest; bar; BBQ; playgrnd; bike hire; wifi; dogs; bus 0.5km; twin axles; Eng spkn; adv bkg; quiet; CCI. "Sep field with lge pitches avail for CC memb at red price; helpful owner; vg." ♦ ltd 1 Apr-1 Nov. € 24.25            2014*

**VLISSINGEN** *A4* (500m N Urban) *51.4684, 3.5546* **Camping De Lange Pacht, Boksweg 1, 4384 NP Vlissingen [tel/fax (0118) 460447; delangepacht@zeelandnet.nl]** Fr E on A58 to Vlissingen, then onto N288 & foll sp Kouderkerke. At rndabt at end built-up area turn L into Lammerenburgweg/Jacoba van Beierenweg then L tinto Vlamingstraat & foll to Boksweg & site. Sm, mkd pitch, pt shd; htd wc; chem disp; shwrs inc; el pnts (4-6A) inc; lndtte (inc dryer); shops 500m; BBQ; sand beach & pool 3km; playgrnd; sand beach 2km; wifi; 40% statics; dogs; phone; sep car park; adv bkg; quiet; CKE/CCI. "Clean, friendly site." 1 Apr-31 Oct. € 20.50            2010*

**VUREN see Gorinchem** *B3*

**WASSENAAR** *B3* (3km E Rural) *52.15269, 4.43361* **Camping Maaldrift, Maaldriftsweg 9, 2241 BN Wassenaar [(070) 5113688; fax 5170980; campingmaaldrift@hotmail.com]** Fr Hoek take N211/E30 to A4, then A12 & N44. Turn 1st L after Wassenaar & immed R onto rd parallel with main rd. Site sp on L in approx 2km. Sm, mkd pitch; wc; chem disp; baby facs; shwrs €0.75; el pnts (6A) €2.25; lndtte (inc dryer); shop; snacks; bar; BBQ; playgrnd; pool 5km; sand beach 8km; 60% statics; dogs €1.25; phone; Eng spkn; quiet. "Excel, quiet base away fr cr commercial sites; narr site rds; lge pitches; clean, modern san facs." 1 Apr-30 Sep. € 16.20            2010*

⊞ **WASSENAAR** B3 (300m NW Rural) 52.14638, 4.38750 **Camping Duinrell, Duinrell 1, 2242 JP Wassenaar [tel/fax (070) 5155147 or (070) 5155255; touroperator@duinrell. nl; www.duinrell.nl]** Fr Rotterdam in dir Den Haag on A13/E19, then on A4/E19 foll sp for Amsterdam. On A4 keep R onto A12 in dir Voorburg/Den Haag. At end m'way turn R onto N44 sp Wassenaar. In 8km turn L at traff lts immed bef Mercedes g'ge, foll site sp. On arr at site foll sp to campsite not coach park. Not rec to arrive mid-afternoon/early evening due to heavy traff leaving amusement park. V lge, hdg/mkd pitch, pt shd; htd wc; chem disp; mv service pnt; baby facs; serviced pitches; sauna; private san facs avail; shwrs inc; el pnts (6A) inc; gas; lndtte (inc dryer); shop; rest, snacks; bar; BBQ; playgrnd; 2 pools (1 covrd); paddling pool; waterslide; sand beach 3km; fishing, horseriding nrby; tennis; cycle hire; free ent adj amusement park; golf 1km; games rm; internet; wifi; entmnt; TV; 30% statics; dogs €6; no c'vans/m'vans over 7.75m high ssn; phone; sep car park for some pitches; poss cr; Eng spkn; adv bkg; quiet; red low ssn/snr citizens; ccard acc. "Popular, busy site; some pitches poss diff access, check bef siting; superb, modern facs; tropical indoor pool; vg security; excel." ♦ € 33.50 SBS - H13                     2011*

*See advertisement*

**WEERSELO** D3 (1km W Rural) 52.36530, 6.84285 **Camping De Molenhof, Kleijsenweg 7, 7667 RS Reutum [(0541) 661165 /661201; fax 662032; info@demolenhof. nl; www.demolenhof.nl]** Exit A1 junc 33 dir Oldenzaal then Tubbergen. At Weerselo, foll site sp. Lge, pt shd; htd wc; chem disp; mv service pnt; baby facs; fam bthrm; shwrs inc; el pnts (10A) inc; gas; lndtte (inc dryer); shop; rest, snacks; bar; BBQ; playgrnd; 2 pools (1 htd, covrd); waterslide; fishing; tennis; covrd play area; cycle hire; golf 10km; wifi; entmnt; TV rm & cab TV to pitches; 25% statics; dogs €3; Holland Tulip Parcs site; Eng spkn; adv bkg; quiet; ccard acc; "Spacious pitches; Spotlessly clean." ♦ 16 Apr-2 Oct. € 39.00 (CChq acc) 2013*

**WEERSELO** D3 (1.5km NW Rural) 52.35930, 6.83740 **Camping De Veldmeijer, Oude Almelosedijk 4, 7595 LJ Weerselo [(0541) 662195; info@develdmeijer.nl; www. develdmeijer.nl]** Exit A1/E30 dir Oldenzaal then N343 dir Tubbergen. After Weerselo foll 'Mini-Camping' sp. Sm, pt shd; htd wc; chem disp; shwrs inc; el pnts (6A) inc; lndtte (inc dryer); shop, snacks 1km; playgrnd; pool nrby; wifi; 25% statics; Eng spkn; adv bkg; quiet. "Welcoming owners; excel facs; lge pitches; gd cycling; vg." ♦ ltd 1 Apr-31 Oct. € 16.00     2009*

**WEERT** C4 (6km SE Rural) 51.22480, 5.79916 **Camping Landgoed Lemmenhof, Kampstraat 10, 6011 RV Ell Limburg [(0495) 551277; fax 551797; info@lemmenhof.nl; www.lemmenhof.nl]** Exit A2 junc 40 dir Kelpen. In 2km at traff lts turn R; in 50m turn R dir Ell. In 2km immed bef vill sp & De Prairie Cafe turn R into Kempstraat, site in 200m. Sm, hdg/mkd pitch, unshd; htd wc; chem disp; shwrs inc; el pnts (10A) inc; lndtte; shop 500m; rest, bar 200m; playgrnd; dogs €0.70; Eng spkn; adv bkg; quiet; CKE/CCI. "Vg; B&B & apartments avail; v friendly helpful owners and friendly local caravaners on site." ♦ 15 Mar-31 Oct. € 18.60                     2013*

**WEIDUM see Leeuwarden** C2

**WESTERBORK see Beilen** D2

⊞ **WEZUPERBRUG** D2 (500m E Rural) 52.84030, 6.72370 **Rekreatiepark 't Kuierpadtien, Oranjekanaal Noordzijde 10, 7853 TA Wezuperbrug [(0591) 381415; fax 382235; info@kuierpad.nl; www.kuierpad.nl]** Fr A28 m'way exit 31 dir Emmen onto N381. Take exit Zweeloo & turn L immed. Go under viaduct twd Wezuperbrug via Wezup. In Wezuperbrug go over bdge, turn R, site sp. V lge, pt shd; htd wc; chem disp; mv service pnt; baby facs; fam bthrm; shwrs inc; el pnts (6A) inc; gas; lndtte (inc dryer); shop; rest, snacks; bar; playgrnd; htd, covrd pool; paddling pool; waterslide; lake sw & boating; tennis; games rm; cycle hire; wifi; entmnt; TV; 30% statics; dogs €5; phone; sep car park; Holland Tulip Parcs site; quiet. "Excel site; great for kids; vg pool & extensive sports facs; can get busy; some pitches diff to access, narr & steep ent to pitch espec nr the water." ♦ € 53.00                     2014*

**WIER** C2 (1km S Rural) 53.25033, 5.62216 **Tuincamping De Brinkhoeve, Gernierswei 19, 9043 VN Wier [(0518) 462287; info@debrinkhoeve.com; www. debrinkhoeve.com]** Exit A31 junc 21 dir Menaldum, then dir St Jacobiparochie. Site on this rd 6km fr Menaldum on Gernierswei, not in Wier. Sp locally as 'Theeschenkerij Wier'. Sm, pt shd; htd wc; chem disp; baby facs; shwrs inc; el pnts (6A) €2; lndtte; tradsmn; rest, snacks; BBQ; playgrnd; no statics; dogs €1.50; bus 50m; poss cr; Eng spkn; adv bkg rec. "Friendly, nothing too much trouble; like a high quality CL; beautiful gardens; cycle rtes adj." 1 Apr-15 Oct. € 17.00                     2011*

**WIERINGERWERF** *B2* (200m N Rural) *52.85757, 5.02361* **Camping Land Uit Zee, Oom Keesweg 12A, 1771 ME Wieringerwerf [tel/fax (0227) 601893; campinglanduitzee@hetnet.nl; www.campinglanduitzee. nl]** Fr A7/E22 exit junc 13 Wieringerwerf & foll site sp N thro town 200m, site on R. Sm, hdg pitch, pt shd; wc; chem disp; mv service pnt; shwrs €0.80; el pnts (6A) €2.25; gas; shop; playgrnd; cycle hire; TV; 10% statics; dogs €1.55; Eng spkn; adv bkg; quiet; CKE/CCI. "Friendly, welcoming owners; gd base for cycling; nrby town Medemblick worth visit; run down statics, unclean facs & travellers (Apr 2010)." 1 Apr-12 Sep. € 11.50                                                                   2010*

**WIJCKEL see Lemmer** *C2*

**WIJSTER see Beilen** *D2*

**WILBERTOORD see Uden** *C3*

⊞ **WINSCHOTEN** *D2* (1km NW Urban) *53.15315, 7.02728* **Stadscamping De Burcht, Bovenburen 46A, 9675 HG Winschoten [(0597) 413290; fax 414467; info@ campingdeburcht.nl; www.campingdeburcht.nl]** Exit E22/ A7 junc 47 Winschoten exit & foll sp to site on edge of town. Sm, hdg pitch, pt shd; wc; chem disp; shwrs inc; el pnts (4A) €2.60; lndtte; shop 500m; playgrnd; pool 1km; 15% statics; dogs €1.50; quiet; CKE/CCI. "Gd site for cyclists; pay site fees on arr; vg NH/sh stay." € 16.00                         2009*

**WOERDEN** *B3* (1km N Rural) *52.09280, 4.88530* **Camping Batenstein, Van Helvoortlaan 37, 3443 AP Woerden [(0348) 421320; fax 409691; campingbatenstein@planet. nl; www.camping-batenstein.nl]** Fr A12 exit junc 14 sp Woerden. Twd cent of town, L at rndabt, R at next rndabt, thro rlwy tunnel. L at traff lts, L again at next traff lts, R at camping sp. Ent narr & sm sp. Med, pt shd; wc; chem disp; mv service pnt; baby facs; sauna; shwrs €0.60; el pnts (6-10A) inc; gas; lndtte (inc dryer); shops 1km; snacks; playgrnd; htd, covrd pool; paddling pool; waterslide; games area; wifi; 75% statics; dogs €1.50; phone; bus 750m; Eng spkn; sep car park; poss cr; adv bkg; quiet but some noise fr pool during day; ccard acc; red long stay; CKE/CCI. "Gd touring base; el conn by site staff only (locked boxes); san facs cramped but gd quality & clean; conv for ferries." 28 Mar-26 Oct. € 30.50                         2014*

**WOLPHAARTSDIJK see Goes** *A3*

**WONS** *C2* (1.5km S Rural) *53.06569, 5.42389* **Mini-Camping DeWeeren, Weersterweg 35, 8747 NR Wons [(0515) 231374 or 06 18498048 (mob); deweeren@hetnet. nl]** Fr A7 junc 16 dir Makkum. Site on L in 2km. Sm, pt shd; htd wc; chem disp; shwrs inc; el pnts (10A) inc; lndtte; shop, rest, snacks, bar 2km; BBQ; playgrnd; cycle hire; dogs €0.50; sep car park; quiet. "Gd." 1 Apr-31 Oct. € 13.50        2009*

**WORKUM** *C2* (3km NE Rural) *52.99216, 5.49391* **Minicamping De Klompen, Nummer 19, 8775 XD Nijhuizum [(0515) 541597; info@minicampingdeklompen. nl; www.minicampingdeklompen.nl]** On N359 thro Workumturn R sp Nijhuizum. In vill turn L & foll site sp to end of rd, 2km. Sm, unshd; htd wc; chem disp; shwrs €0.50; el pnts (10A) €2; lndtte; shop, rest, snacks, bar 3km; BBQ; lake & watersports nr; dogs €1; sep car park; Eng spkn; quiet. "Gd, v hospitable owners; san facs v clean; communal rm if rainy day; peaceful; rural dairy farm." € 14.00                         2011*

**WOUDENBERG see Amersfoort** *C3*

**ZANDVOORT** *B3* (2km N Coastal) *52.40415, 4.55180* **Kennemer Duincamping De Lakens, Zeeweg 60, 2051 EC Bloemendaal aan Zee [(023) 5411570; fax 5411579; delakens@kennemerduincampings.nl; www. kennemerduincampings.nl]** Site sp N of Zaandvoort on coast rd, site in sand dunes. V lge, unshd; htd wc; chem disp; mv service pnt; baby facs; shwrs inc; el pnts (4-10A) inc; gas; lndtte; shop; rest, snacks; playgrnd; pool 4km; sand beach 200m; windsuring 2km; games area; horseriding 300m; internet; TV rm; 50% statics; no dogs; poss cr; Eng spkn; adv bkg rec high ssn; ccard acc; quiet. "V busy May/June public holidays; gd facs; excel walking, cycling fr site; welcoming helpful staff; excel spar shop; gd position in National Park; gd for sightseeing in Amsterdam, Haarlem, Aalsmeer flower mkt as well as outdoor pursuits." ♦ 28 Mar-26 Oct. € 53.00                                                                 2014*

**ZEELAND see Uden** *C3*

⊞ **ZEEWOLDE** *C3* (4km SE Rural/Coastal) *52.30300, 5.53400* **NCC Camping de Distel, Dasselaarweg 53, 3896 LT Zeewolde [(036) 5221575; zeewolde@ncc.nl; www.ncc. nl]** Exit A28 junc 9 at Nijkerk onto N301 sp Zeewolde. After 4km turn R onto N705 dir Zeewolde. After 5.6km turn R sp NCC Camping. In 300m turn R & foll site sp. Site on L at white stones. Lge, mkd pitch, pt shd; htd wc; chem disp; mv service pnt; baby facs; shwrs inc; el pnts (4A) €3; lndtte; shop; playgrnd; sand beach 500m; watersports; dogs; bus 4km; poss cr; adv bkg; quiet, "Warm, friendly atmosphere; members only - open to CC members, but must pre-book; conv Amsterdam 1hr by rd." ♦ € 12.00                                                       2009*

**ZEIST see Utrecht** *B3*

**ZEVENAAR** *C3* (4.5km S Rural) *51.89666, 6.07041* **Camping De Rijnstrangen, Beuningsestraat 4, 6913 KH Aerdt [(0316) 371941; info@derijnstrangen.nl; www. derijnstrangen.nl]** Exit A12 junc 29 onto N 336 Elten & Lobith. At sp Aerdt turn R onto dyke (narr) & cont approx 1.5km to church. Turn L in 100m, site on R (500m W of Aerdt). Sm, pt shd; htd wc; chem disp; mv service pnt; shwrs inc; el pnts (6A) inc; lndtte; shop 2km; TV rm; poss cr; adv bkg; quiet. "Friendly, welcoming owners; gd cycling area; excel; excel heated facs." 28 Mar-28 Sep. € 26.50                         2013*

**ZEVENHUIZEN see Gouda** *B3*

**ZIERIKZEE** A3 (4.8km N Rural) 51.68048, 3.89847 **Mini-Camping Appelgaerd, Zandweg 6, 4321 TA Kerkwerve [(0614) 489332; info@appelgaerd.nl; www.appelgaerd. nl]** Fr Zierikzee take N59 dir Serooskerke. Immed turn R onto Zandwek. Cont for 3km, site on L bef vill of Kerkwerve. Sm, lge, hdg pitch, pt shd; wc; chem disp; mv service pnt; shwrs; el pnts (6A) inc; bbq; playgrnd; beach 4km; wifi; dogs; bus 250m; twin axles; Eng spkn; adv bkg; quiet. "Gd cycling, walking & bird watching area; excel site." ♦ ltd 1 Apr-30 Oct. € 19.75                    2014*

**ZIERIKZEE** A3 (1km NE Rural) 51.65683, 3.91242 **Camping 't Uulof, Zandweg 37, 4301 TA Zierikzee [(0111) 414614; info@tuulof.nl; www.campingtuulof.nl]** SE fr Serooskerke on N59. In 9km just bef traff lts turn L. Site 300m on R; sp fr N59. Sm, pt shd; wc; chem disp; serviced pitches; shwrs €2; el pnts (6A) inc; shop 1km; gas 1km; lndtte; pool 2km; sand beach 13km; 25% statics; dogs €1; Eng spkn; some rd noise; CKE/CCI. "Lovely site on farm - produce avail; excel san facs, pt unisex; helpful, friendly owner; interesting town, steamer trips; easy cycling to town; Peaceful site, friendly & welcoming, lovely home-grown veg." 1 Apr-1 Oct. € 15.50                    2013*

**ZIERIKZEE** A3 (1km S Coastal) 51.64660, 3.91133 **Camping Kloet, Eerst Weegje 3, 4301 SL Zierikzee [(0111) 414214; fax (0114) 421200; info@campingkloet.nl; www. campingkloet.nl]** Fr S on N256 cross Zeelandbrug & turn L onto N59 twd Zierikzee. After rndabt turn L sp 'Parking'. Site on L after 2nd rndabt. Sm, htd pitch, pt shd; wc; chem disp; mv service pnt; shwrs inc; el pnts (4A) inc; lndtte; shop, rest, bar 1km; playgrnd; games rm; TV; no dogs; bus 1km; Eng spkn; adv bkg; quiet; CKE/CCI. "Attractive, historic town in walking dist; excel area for cycling; gd birdwatching." 1 Apr-1 Nov. € 28.00                    2011*

**ZOETERMEER** B3 (2km W Rural) 52.06716, 4.44862 **Camping De Drie Morgen, Voorweg 155, 2716 NJ Zoetermeer [(079) 3515107; fax 3512084; mail@dedriemorgen.nl; www.dedriemorgen.nl]** Fr Den Haag take A12/E30 sp Zoetermeer. Exit junc 6 sp Zoetermeer cent. In 1.5km turn L onto Amertaweg. In 2km foll sp to Mini-Camping. At rndabt turn R onto Voorweg, site on R. Sm, unshd; wc; chem disp; mv service pnt; shwrs inc; el pnts (6A) €1.75; tradsmn; farm shop; playgrnd; dogs; sep car park; Eng spkn; adv bkg; quiet. "A working farm; gd touring base; pleasant staff; peaceful; busy in ssn." 1 Apr-31 Oct. € 14.50                    2013*

**ZUIDWOLDE** D2 (2km S Rural) 52.65822, 6.42726 **NCC Camping De Krententerp, Ekelenbergweg 2, 7921 RH Zuidwolde DR [(0528) 372847; www.ncc.nl]** Fr S fr Zwolle exit A28 junc 22 dir Dedemsvaart. Turn L at Balkbrug onto N48, then L at junc Alteveer-Linde to site. Sm, mkd pitch, shd; htd wc; chem disp; shwrs inc; el pnts (4A) €2.75 (long lead poss req); lndtte; shop, rest, snacks, bar 2km, playgrnd; htd, covrd pool 2km; dogs; bus 200m; poss cr; adv bkg; quiet. "Peaceful site; friendly, helpful staff; CC members welcome; phone ahead bet 1700 & 1800; excel cycling, walking; Zuidwolde beautiful town." 1 Apr-31 Oct. € 11.00        2009*

**ZUNDERT** B4 (5km NW Rural) 51.49492, 4.60208 **Camping Internationaal Priem, Rucphenseweg 51, 4882 KB Zundert [(076) 5972632; fax 5971923; info@internationaalpriem. nl; www.internationaalpriem.nl]** S fr Breda on N263 to Zundert. Take N638 dir Rucphen, camp on S of rd, opp abbey. Sm, hdg pitch, pt shd; wc; chem disp; shwrs €0.50; el pnts (4A) inc; gas; lndtte; rest in ssn; playgrnd; entmnt; TV rm; 75% statics (sep area); dogs €3.50; phone; Eng spkn; adv bkg; quiet; ccard acc; red long stay; CKE/CCI. "Well-established, mature site; friendly." 1 Apr-31 Oct. € 17.50        2009*

**ZWOLLE** C2 (1.5km NE Urban) 52.53690, 6.12954 **Camping De Agnietenberg, Haersterveerweg 27, 8034 PJ Zwolle [(038) 4531530; fax 4542084; info@campingagnietenberg. nl; www.campingagnietenberg.nl]** N fr Zwolle on A28 exit junc 20 Zwolle Oost & turn R at end of slip rd then immed L. In 400m turn L at traff lts into Haersterveerweg & foll site sp. Lge, mkd pitch, pt shd; htd wc; chem disp; mv service pnt; baby facs; shwrs €0.50; el pnts (10A); lndtte; shop; rest, snacks; bar; BBQ; playgrnd; pool; lake beach & sw adj; fishing; tennis; wifi; entmnt; TV; 60% statics; dogs €3.50; Eng spkn; quiet; ccard acc (Mastercard only). "Excel, family site in pleasant area; gd walking, cycling, water recreation; cars parked in sep areas; single track rd to site." 1 Apr-31 Oct. € 26.20        2014*

**ZWOLLE** C2 (5km SW Rural) 52.45566, 6.04016 **Molecaten Park De Leemkule, Leemkuilen 6, 8051 PW Hattem [(038) 4441945; fax 4446280; info@leemkule.ne; www. leemkule.nl]** Exit A50 junc 29 dir Wezep; foll sp Hattem/ Wapenveld, site on L after 3km. Lge, shd; htd wc; chem disp; baby facs; shwrs inc; el pnts (10A) inc; gas; lndtte; shop; rest, snacks; bar; playgrnd; 2 pools (1 htd, covrd); paddling pool; tennis; cycle hire; games area; entmnt; 20% statics; no dogs; phone; sep car park; adv bkg; quiet; ccard acc. 1 Apr-1 Nov. € 25.00        2009*

Legend:
- France and Andorra
- Central and South East Europe, Benelux and Scandinavia
- Spain and Portugal

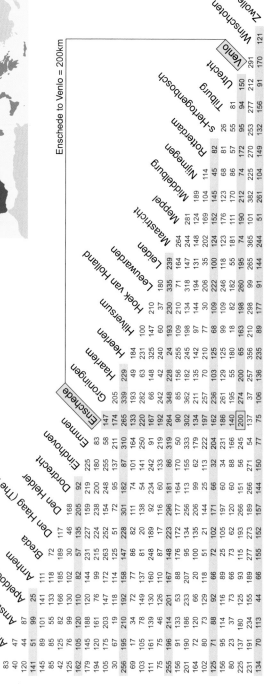

**Enschede to Venlo = 200km**

Distance chart (km) between towns. Origin towns listed alphabetically; distances given to each subsequent town in the list (Amersfoort, Amsterdam, Apeldoorn, Arnhem, Breda, Den Haag (The Hague), Den Helder, Dordrecht, Eindhoven, Emmen, Enschede, Groningen, Haarlem, Heerlen, Hilversum, Hoek van Holland, Leeuwarden, Leiden, Maastricht, Meppel, Middelburg, Nijmegen, Rotterdam, s-Hertogenbosch, Tilburg, Utrecht, Venlo, Winschoten, Zwolle):

**Alkmaar:** 83, 40, 120, 141, 145, 85, 42, 125, 162, 179, 194, 105, 30, 256, 69, 103, 111, 75, 255, 156, 201, 164, 102, 125, 156, 80, 225, 231, 134

(Full matrix of inter-town distances follows in the chart.)

You can now fill in site reports online

- All year site(s)
- Seasonal site(s)
- No sites listed

200m +
0–200m

0    50    100 kms
0    25    50 mls

N
W    E
S

Motorways
Major roads
Main roads

© Collins Bartholomew Ltd 2014

NORTH

SEA

AMELAND    Buren
TERSCHELLING    Lauwersoog
Oosterend    Emden
Vierhuizen    N46
VLIELAND    Wier    Dokkum
LEEUWARDEN    GRONINGEN    Midwolda
Harlingen    N31    Opende    WINSCHOTEN
TEXEL    De Koog    Wons    Drachten    A28    Bourtange
Den Burg    A7    Sneek    A7    Annen    Stadskanaal
DEN HELDER    Workum    Heerenveen    N371    Exloo
Julianadorp    Koudum    A32    Diever    Beilen    Wezuperbrug
Wieringerwerf    Lemmer    Dwingeloo
Callantsoog    Oudemirdum    EMMEN
Petten    Medemblik    Ruinen    Zuidwolde
ALKMAAR    Enkhuizen    Kraggenburg    MEPPEL    A37
Hardenberg
Dronten    ZWOLLE    A28    Ommen    Nordhorn
A9    A7    Edam    Lelystad    Elburg
A6
Zandvoort    AMSTERDAM    Harderwijk    Heerde    Nijverdal    Denekamp
Almere    Weersclo
Noordwijk aan Zee    HAARLEM    Zeewolde    A50    Hengelo
Katwijk aan Zee    Lisse    HILVERSUM    APELDOORN    Deventer    Goor    ENSCHEDE
Wassenaar    LEIDEN    AMERSFOORT    A1    Lochem    Ruurlo
DEN HAAG    UTRECHT    Otterlo    Dieren    Groenlo
Zoetermeer    Woerden    Renswoude    A30    Doetinchem
Delft    Gouda    Maurik    ARNHEM    Zevenaar
HOEK VAN HOLLAND    Meerkerk    Deil    Gendt    's-Heerenberg
Brielle    ROTTERDAM    A2    Tiel    NIJMEGEN    A18
Rockanje    Hellevoetsluis    Gorinchem    Ravenstein    A50    Heumen
DORDRECHT    A16    A27    'S-HERTOGENBOSCH    Wesel
Burgh-Hammstede    N59    Drimmelen    Uden
Zierikzee    Oosterhout    Kaatsheuvel    GERMANY
Oostkapelle    Kamperland    Steenbergen    Roosendaal    BREDA    TILBURG    Sint
Domburg    Goes    Hilvarenbeek    Oirschot    Oedenrode
Grijpskerke    A58    Bergen    Horst
MIDDELBURG    op Zoom    Zundert    Bladel    EINDHOVEN    Sevenum
Vlissingen    Ellewoutsdijk    Eersel    Panningen    VENLO
Nieuwvliet    Breskens    Weert    Helden    Düsseldorf
Sluis    Hoek    Roermond
Antwerpen    Thorn    Echt

Gent

BELGIUM    Schimmert    Köln
Meerssen    HEERLEN
BRUSSEL    MAASTRICHT    Gulpen    Valkenburg aan de Geul
BRUXELLES    Vaals    Aachen

Liege

Newcastle upon Tyne
Hull
Harwich

# Norway
## Country Introduction

*Bergen, Norway*

## Welcome to Norway

Famous for its towering mountains, fjords and sea views, Norway is a hiker's paradise. Seeing the northern lights and midnight sun are popular attractions for tourists who come from far and wide to try and catch a glimpse of these amazing phenomena.

Norway's glaciers stretch out across mountain tops creating memorable photo opportunities.

The country also has a rich heritage. Many museums have displays of old Viking and Sami artefacts.

## Country highlights

Whilst visiting Norway a local delicacy to sample is the sweet brown cheese Brunost. It is traditionally cut into wafer thin slices and eaten on bread, toast or crisp bread.

Cod, salmon, prawns and trout provide the basis for the traditional 'cold table' and reindeer and other game are popular menu choices.

Aquavit is the Norwegian national drink. It is a potato based spirit flavoured with herbs.

## Major towns and cities

- Oslo – the capital city has a combination of urban architecture and outdoor pursuits.
- Arendal – a beautiful town with wooden houses dating back to the 17th century.
- Bergen – surrounded by mountains, this city is full of colourfully painted buildings.
- Drammen – a port and river city that has the oldest surviving brewery in Norway, the Aass.

## Attractions

- Norwegian Aviation Museum – the museum has displays of vintage aircraft.
- Sverresborg Trondelag Folk Museum – an open air museum with beautiful wooden buildings and stone ruins.
- The Royal Palace Oslo – some of the royal rooms are open to the public during the summer season.

## Find out more

www.visitnorway.com

Tel: 0047 (0) 22 00 25 00 Norway Tourist Office

# Country Information

*Population (approx):* 4.7 million

*Capital:* Oslo (population approx 630,000)

*Area:* 385,155 sqkm

*Bordered by:* Finland, Russia, Sweden

*Terrain:* Mostly high plateaux and mountain ranges broken by fertile valleys; deeply indented coastline; arctic tundra in the north

*Climate:* Moderate climate along coastal areas thanks to the Gulf Stream; more extreme inland with snowy/rainy winters; arctic conditions in the northern highlands; summers can be unpredictable and May and June can be cool

*Coastline:* 25,148km (including islands and fjords)

*Highest Point:* Galdhopiggeh 2,469m

*Language:* Norwegian; Sami in some areas

*Local Time:* GMT or BST + 1, i.e. 1 hour ahead of the UK all year

*Currency:* Krone (NOK) divided into 100 øre; £1 = NOK 10.18, NOK 10 = £0.98 (September 2014)

*Emergency numbers:* Police 112, with mobile phone 911; Fire brigade 110; Ambulance 113. From a mobile phone dial 112 for any service.

*Public Holidays 2015:* Jan 1; Apr 2, 3, 6; May 1, 14, 17 (Constitution Day), 25; Dec 25, 26.

School summer holidays run from mid-June to mid-August.

# Camping and Caravanning

There are more than 1,000 campsites in Norway which are classified 1 to 5 stars and which are generally open between June and mid August. A camping guide listing 300 sites is available from the Norwegian Automobile Association, Norges Automobilforbund (NAF), see www.nafcamp.no. The Norwegian Tourist Board also distributes a camping guide free of charge – see www.camping.no. Most 3 star sites and all 4 and 5 star sites have sanitary facilities for the disabled and all classified sites have cooking facilities.

Many sites do not open until mid-June and do not fully function until the beginning of July, particularly if the winter has been prolonged. Sites with published opening dates earlier than June may not open on time if the weather has been

particularly bad and if, for example, there has been heavy rain and flooding near rivers or lakes where campsites are situated. Campsites which are open all year will usually have very limited facilities for most of the year outside the short holiday season.

Facilities vary; in main tourist centres there are large, well-equipped sites with good sanitary facilities, grocery shops, leisure facilities and attendants permanently on duty. Sites are generally maintained to a high standard of cleanliness. In more remote areas, sites are small and facilities can be very simple.

Many small campsites have no chemical disposal point. Roadside notice boards at the entrance to each local area (kommune) indicate campsites, chemical disposal points (normally sited at petrol stations) and other local amenities. These disposal facilities are usually coin-operated and have instructions in English. It is understood that in some areas in the north, there may be no adequate arrangements for the disposal of waste water, either on site or in the immediate area, and you are advised to make enquiries when arriving at a campsite.

The Camping Key Europe, which replaced the Camping Card Scandinavia (CCS) in 2012, may be required at some sites. You can buy the Camping Key Europe on arrival at your first site for around NOK 160, and will be issued with a temporary card. Alternatively, you can order the card before you travel for NOK 130 (2014 prices) from www.camping.no/en/cke and click on 'Bestillig av Kort' where you can then select to view the order form in English. If ordering in advance allow at least three weeks for the card to arrive.

There are many sites on the E6 to the North Cape, seldom more than 30km apart. These sites may be subject to road noise. Caravans are allowed to stay at the North Cape but no facilities are available – see Nordkapp later in this chapter and in the Site Entry listing.

In the short summer season campsites can be crowded and facilities stretched and you are recommended to arrive before 3pm (many sites have a latest arrival time of 4pm) in order to have a better choice of pitches and have the opportunity to erect an awning.

Casual/wild camping is not actively encouraged (and is not permitted for longer than 48 hours in one spot) but the Norwegian 'Right of Access' allows visitors to explore the countryside freely, except for cultivated land, farmland, gardens, nurseries, etc. Off-road driving is not allowed. Visitors must respect nature and take their rubbish away with them when they leave. Open fires (which include Primus stoves) are prohibited in forests or on open land between 15 April and 15 September.

## Motorhomes

Many towns provide parking places for motorhomes close to city centres, known as Bobil Parks, which are open in June, July and August. In general these parking areas provide limited facilities and car and caravan outfits are not permitted. Details, where known, are listed in the Site Entry pages.

Apart from at campsites, motorhome service points are reported to be few and far between and are generally to be found at petrol stations, where water refill may also be available.

## Cycling

Cyclists are fairly well catered for and some areas, such as Vestfold, Rogaland and the Lillehammer area, have a well-developed network of cycle paths. Some old roads have been converted into cycle paths in the mountains and along western fjords. Paths run through magnificent scenery in the Lofoten and Vesterålen Islands in particular, and from Haugastøl in the Hardangervidda National Park to Flåm. A number of tunnels are prohibited to cyclists, but local detours are generally signposted. Information is available at www.cyclingnorway.no

## Electricity and Gas

Campsites usually have a minimum 10 amp supply. Plugs are the continental type and have two round pins plus two earth strips. Some sites do not yet have CEE connections. It is recommended that you take an extension cable of at least 50 metres.

There are often problems with both polarity and the earthing of the electrical supply on some sites. Due to its geology and mountainous nature, Norway's electricity supply network is quite

different from that found elsewhere in Europe. There is no national grid and electricity systems vary from place to place throughout the country. Any polarity testing system is likely to give false readings. It is understood that progress is being made to improve and standardise the electrical supply throughout the country but you should exercise caution and, if in any doubt, ask site staff to demonstrate the integrity of the earthing system before connecting.

Propane gas cylinders are generally widely available from Esso and Statoil petrol stations. You will need to buy an appropriate adaptor, available from camping shops or Statoil garages. AGA AS dealers will allow you to sell back propane cylinders within six months of purchase prior to leaving Norway at approximately 80% of the purchase price. It is understood that Statoil garages no longer buy them back. Some Statoil garages and AGA AS dealers will exchange Swedish Primus propane cylinders for their Norwegian version but will not accept other foreign propane cylinders. There is no refund for the adaptor.

Gas supplies can be conserved by taking advantage of the kitchens and/or cooking facilities available at classified campsites, and using electrical hook-ups at every opportunity.

## Entry Formalities

Holders of British and Irish passports may visit Norway for up to three months without a visa.

## Regulations for Pets

For details of the regulations regarding the import of pets into Norway, see website www.mattilsynet.no (English option) or contact the Norwegian Embassy in London.

## Medical Services

British visitors are entitled to the same basic emergency medical and dental treatment as Norwegian citizens, on production of a UK passport or European Health Insurance Card (EHIC), but you will have to pay the standard fees. Ensure you consult a doctor who has a reimbursement arrangement with the NAV (Norwegian Employment and Welfare

Organisation). Hotels and tourist offices have lists of local doctors and dentists.

You will have to pay in full for most prescribed medicines which are available from pharmacies (apotek). Emergency in-patient hospital treatment at public hospitals, including necessary medication, is free of charge but you will have to pay for out-patient treatment. NAV Health Service Agencies will reimburse any payments that are refundable.

It is recommended to have insect repellent devices as mosquitos and midges may be a nuisance at certain times of the year, especially near lakes.

## Opening Hours

Banks – Mon-Fri 8am-3.30pm and some open until 5pm on Thurs.

Museums – 9am/10am-4pm/5pm; no regular closing day.

Post Offices – Mon-Fri 8am/8.30am-4pm/5pm; Sat 8am-1pm.

Shops – Mon-Fri 9am-4pm/5pm (Thurs until 6pm/8pm); Sat 9am/10am-1pm/3pm. Some supermarkets and shopping centres are open longer and some open Sun.

## Safety and Security

Norway is considered to have lower crime rates than some other European countries, even in the large cities, however you should always take the usual precautions against pickpockets and petty theft, especially in crowded areas. Do not leave valuables in your car.

Following some recent incidents of robbery, the police are warning motorists with caravans, motorhomes and trailers not to stop in lay-bys overnight. The Norwegian Automobile Association, Norges Automobilforbund (NAF), has also sent out warnings to campsites urging campers to be careful.

If you plan to go off the beaten track or out to sea you should take local advice about weather conditions, have suitable specialist equipment and respect warning signs. Because of Norway's northerly latitude the weather can change rapidly, producing sudden arctic conditions on exposed mountains – even in summer. The winter is long

(it can last well into April) and temperatures can drop to minus 25°C and below, plus any wind chill factor.

Norway shares with the rest of Europe an underlying threat from terrorism. Attacks could be indiscriminate and against civilian targets in public places, including tourist sites.

*British Embassy*
THOMAS HEFTYES GATE 8, OSLO
Tel: 23 13 27 00
http://ukinnorway.fco.gov.uk/en/

There are also British Consulates or Honorary Consulates in Ålesund, Bergen, Bodø, Kristiansand, Stavanger, Tromsø and Trondheim.

*Irish Embassy*
HAAKON VIIS GATE 1, N-0244 OSLO
Tel: 22 01 72 00
www.embassyofireland.no

## Customs Regulations

*Border Posts*
Borders with Sweden and Finland may be crossed on all main roads and Customs posts are usually open day and night.

Storskog on the E105, east of Kirkenes, is the only border crossing for tourist traffic from Norway into Russia (visa required).

*Duty-Free Import Allowances*
Norway is not a member of the EU and therefore it is possible to import goods duty-free into the country from the EU. Duty-free allowances are not particularly generous and are strictly enforced. Visitors may import the following:

200 cigarettes or 250gm tobacco

1 litre spirits and 1½ litres wine

or 3 litres wine and 2 litres beer

or 5 litres beer

Goods to the value of NOK 6,000 (including alcohol and tobacco products)

Visitors must be aged 20 years and over to import spirits and 18 years and over for wine, beer and cigarettes.

*Food and Medicines*
Up to 10kg (combined weight) of meat, meat products and cheese can be imported into Norway

from EU countries for personal consumption. The import of potatoes is not permitted but you can take in up to 10kg of fruit, berries and other vegetables. Visitors may only take in medicines for their own personal use with a covering letter from a doctor stating their requirements.

*Money*

Travellers may import or export currency up to the equivalent of NOK 25,000 in Norwegian and/or foreign notes and coins. Any amount above this must be declared to Customs.

*Refund of VAT on Export*

Some shops have a blue and red sign in their window indicating that visitors may, on presentation of a passport, purchase goods free of VAT. For visitors from the UK the purchase price of individual items (exclusive of VAT) must be at least NOK 250. Shop assistants will issue a voucher and on departure from Norway visitors must present goods and vouchers at a tax-free counter situated on ferries, at airports and at main border crossings where a refund of 11-18% will be made.

## Documents

*Vehicle(s)*

Carry your vehicle registration document (V5C), insurance certificate and MOT certificate (if applicable). If driving a borrowed vehicle carry a letter of authority from the owner.

## Money

Norway is expensive; bring or have electronic access to plenty of money, especially if you are intending to eat and drink in restaurants and bars.

Bank opening hours are shorter than in the UK, especially in summer, but cash machines are widespread. Bureaux de change are found in banks, post offices, airports, stations, hotels and some tourist offices.

The major credit cards are widely accepted and may be used at cash machines (minibanks) throughout the country. In remote areas banks and cash machines may be few and far between.

It is advisable to carry your passport or photocard driving licence if paying with a credit card as you may well be asked for photographic proof of your identity.

Carry your credit card issuers'/banks' 24-hour UK contact numbers in case of loss or theft of your cards.

## Motoring in Norway

### Alcohol

Norwegian law is very strict: do not drink and drive. Fines and imprisonment await those who exceed the legal limit of 20 milligrams of alcohol in 100 millilitres of blood, which is considerably lower than that permitted in the UK (80 milligrams), and equates to virtually zero for at least 12 hours before driving. Random roadside breath tests are frequent.

If you are involved in a road accident which causes damage to property or vehicles or injuries you should not drink any alcohol for six hours following the accident as the police may wish to carry out blood alcohol tests.

If purchasing medicines in Norway you should be aware that some containing alcohol should be avoided if you intend to drive. These are marked with a red triangle.

## Breakdown Service

Norges Automobilforbund (NAF) operates a 24-hour breakdown service nationwide. Call 08505 from a landline or 0926 08505 from a mobile phone. Emergency yellow telephones have been installed on difficult stretches of road.

NAF Veipatrulje (road patrols) operates from mid-June to mid-August on difficult mountain passes and in remote areas but in Oslo, Stavanger and Bergen, they operate all year round.

If you're a member of The Caravan Club show your Club membership card in order to benefit from special NAF rates for breakdown assistance. Some breakdown vehicles have credit card payment terminals; otherwise payment for services is required in cash.

## Essential Equipment

*Warning Triangle*

An warning triangle must be used if the vehicle has broken down, punctures or is involved in an accident.

*Lights*

The use of dipped headlights is compulsory at all times, regardless of weather conditions. Bulbs are more likely to fail with constant use and it is recommended that you carry spares.

*Reflective Jacket/Waistcoat*

Owners of vehicles registered in Norway are required to carry a reflective jacket to be worn if their vehicle is immobilised on the carriageway following a breakdown or accident. This legislation does not yet apply to foreign registered vehicles but you are strongly advised to carry at least one such jacket. Passengers who leave the vehicle, for example to assist with a repair, should also wear one.

*Child Restraint System*

Children of four years and under 135cm must be seated in a special child restraint system. If in a rear facing system on the front seat, the airbag must be deactivated. A child between 135-150cm should use a booster seat with an adult seatbelt.

All child restraints must conform to ECE R44-03 or 04 regulations.

*Winter Driving*

Vehicles with a total weight of 3,500kg or more must carry chains during the winter season, regardless of road conditions. Checks are often carried out.

Generally spiked tyres can be used from 1st November to the first Sunday after Easter. In an effort to discourage the use of spiked tyres in Bergen, Oslo and Trondheim a tax is levied on vehicles equipped with them. For vehicles up to 3,500kg the tax is NOK 30 for one day and NOK 400 for a month. For vehicles over 3,500kg the fee is doubled. Daily permits are available from vending machines along major roads into the city marked 'Frisk luft i byen'.

# Fuel

Prices vary not only according to region (they are slightly higher in the north and in mountainous areas) but also according to the manner in which fuel is sold; the lowest currently being self-service prices in Oslo. Prices can also vary on different days and fuel tends to be cheaper on Sunday and Monday. There are automatic petrol pumps where payment is made by credit card or bank notes.

Petrol stations are generally open from 7am to 10pm on weekdays, but may close early. Petrol stations maybe scarce, particularly in the north. In cities some petrol stations remain open 24 hours.

Unleaded petrol is dispensed from pumps marked 'Blyfri'. Not all petrol stations stock diesel. If you fill up with it, ensure that you use the correct pump and do not inadvertently fill with 'Afgift Diesel' (red diesel for agricultural vehicles). LPG is available at a limited number of outlets – see www.visitnorway.com for a list.

# Mountain Passes

If you're visiting in the autumn, winter or spring you should check that any mountain passes you intend to use are open. Some high mountain roads close during the winter, the duration of the closure depending on weather conditions, but many others remain open all year. Other passes may close at short notice or at night or during periods of bad weather.

The Norwegian Tourist Board can provide a list, for guidance purposes, of roads which usually close in winter, or contact the Road User Information Centre (Vegtrafikksentralen) which will provide information about roads, road conditions, mountain passes, tunnels, border crossings, etc. The Centre is open round the clock all year, telephone 02030 within Norway or (0047) 91 50 20 30 from abroad. Alternatively a list of roads that are closed in winter or which have limited accessibility can be found at www.vegvesen.no/en/Traffic and click on Truckers' Guide, or email firmapost@vegvesen.no.

Yellow emergency telephones are installed on mountain passes.

# Parking

A white line on the edge of the carriageway indicates a parking restriction. Do not park on main roads if visibility is restricted or where there is a sign 'All Stans Førbudt' (no stopping allowed). If you do so you may have your vehicle towed away. Parking regulations in towns are very strict and offences are invariably subject to fines. Parking meters and pay and display car parks are in use in the main towns. Free use of unexpired time on meters is allowed.

# Priority

Priority roads (main roads) are indicated by a road sign bearing a yellow diamond on a white background. A black diagonal bar through the sign indicates the end of the priority rule. If you are not travelling on a priority road then vehicles coming from the right have priority. Traffic already on a roundabout has priority and trams always have priority.

Narrow roads have passing places (møteplass) to allow vehicles to pass. The driver on the side of the road where there is a passing place must stop for an oncoming vehicle. However heavy goods vehicles tend to take right of way on narrow roads, especially if travelling uphill, and it may be necessary to reverse to a passing place to allow one to pass.

# Roads

The standard of roads is generally good but stretches of major roads may be bumpy and rutted as a result of use by heavy freight traffic. Caravanners in particular should take care to avoid wheels being caught in ruts.

Some roads are narrow, especially in the mountains, and may not have a central yellow line. State roads are shown in red on maps and are asphalted but may not have kerbs and may, therefore, easily become cracked and rutted. Many roads have barriers mounted close to the side of the road.

Secondary roads have a gravel surface that can be tricky when wet and may be in poor condition for some weeks during and after the spring thaw.

Do not assume that roads with an E prefix are necessarily major roads - sections of the E39, for example, are still single-track with passing places. The E6 road is asphalted all the way to the Swedish border in the south and to Kirkenes in the north. You may encounter reverse camber on both left and right-hand bends.

Some roads in the fjord region have many hairpin bends and can be challenging. Roads may narrow to a single carriageway and single-track bridges often appear without any advance warning.

Gradients on main highways are generally moderate, not over 10%, but the inside of hairpin bends may be much steeper than this. There is a

gradient of 20% on the E68 from Gudvangen (on the southern tip of the Sognefjord) to Stalheim, but a tunnel under the steepest section of the Stalheim road eliminates this difficult section.

Maps showing roads closed to caravans and those only recommended for use by experienced caravanners, together with rest stops, may be obtained from the Norwegian Tourist Board, Norwegian local road authority offices and from the NAF.

Because of the nature of the country's roads – and the beauty of the scenery – average daily mileage may be less than anticipated. Major repairs to roads and tunnels take place during the summer months and traffic controls may cause delays. Ferries make up an integral part of a number of routes, particularly when travelling north along the coast, which also causes slow progress.

Care should be taken to avoid collisions with elk, deer and reindeer, particularly at dawn and dusk. Accidents involving any kind of animal must be reported to the police.

A number of roads are closed in winter, including the E69 to the North Cape, due to snow conditions; some do not open until late May or early June.

# Road Signs and Markings

European highways are prefixed with the letter E and are indicated by signs bearing white letters and figures on a green background, national highways (Riksvei or Stamvei) are indicated by black figures prefixed Rv on a yellow background and local, county roads (Fylkesvei) by black figures on a white background. County road numbers do not generally appear on maps.

Lines in the middle of the carriageway are yellow. Bus, cycle and taxi lanes are marked in white.

Some signs have been introduced, for example a square blue sign showing a car and '2+' in white means that cars carrying more than two people can use bus lanes. Square signs indicate the presence of speed cameras, small rectangular signs indicate the exit numbers on highways and main roads, and a number of triangular signs with a yellow background indicate a temporary danger. Signs advising maximum speeds on bends, obstructions, etc, should be respected.

In addition to international road signs, the following signs may also be seen:

Passing place

Place of intrest

| Norwegian | English Translation |
| --- | --- |
| All stans førbudt | No stopping allowed |
| Arbeide pa vegen | Roadworks ahead |
| Enveiskjøring | One-way traffic |
| Ikke møte | No passing, single line traffic |
| Kjør sakte | Drive slowly |
| Løs grus | Loose chippings |
| Møteplass | Passing place |
| Omkjøring | Diversion |
| Rasteplass | Lay-by |

## Speed Limits

| | Open Road (km/h) | Motorway (km/h) |
| --- | --- | --- |
| Car Solo | 80 | 90-100 |
| Car towing caravan/trailer | 80 | 80 |
| Motorhome under 3500kg | 80 | 90-100 |
| Motorhome 3500-7500kg | 80 | 80 |

Drivers should pay close attention to speed limits, which are in general significantly lower than in the UK. Fines for exceeding speed limits are high and often have to be paid on the spot. Radar detectors are illegal.

In residential areas the speed limit may be as low as 30 km/h (18 mph). Frequent speed controls are in operation. Ramps and speed control bumps are not always signposted.

Vehicles over 3,500kg are restricted to 80 km/h (50 mph) on motorways and highways, regardless of signs showing higher general limits.

## Towing

Drivers of cars and caravans with a combined length of more than 12.4 metres must check from the list of national highways and/or municipal roads may not be allowed on some routes. You can check this information with the Road User Information Centre (Vegtrafikksentralen), tel: 02030 within Norway or (0047) 91 50 20 30 from abroad, www.vegvesen.no/en/Traffic and click on Truckers' Guide, or from the Norwegian Tourist Board or NAF. For a motorhome the maximum length is 12 metres (12.4 metres for those registered before September 1997).

Any vehicle towing must have extended towing mirrors fitted.

Some secondary roads have a maximum width of less than 2.55 metres. If your caravan is wider than 2.3 metres and more than 50cm wider than your car, white reflectors must be mounted on the front of your car mirrors. More information is available from the Road User Information Centre.

It is understood that the Rv55 from Sogndal to Lom and the Rv63 north from Geiranger are not suitable for caravans exceeding 5 metres in length, or those without an adequate power/weight ratio.

## Traffic Jams

Roads in general are rarely busy but the roads in and around the cities of Oslo, Bergen, Kristiansand and Trondheim suffer traffic jams during rush hours and at the beginning and end of the holiday season.
The E6 Oslo-Svinesund road at the border with Sweden and the E18 Oslo-Kristiansand road are generally busy during the June to August holiday period. During the summer you should also expect delays at ferry terminals.

## Tunnels

The road network includes approximately 950 tunnels, most of which can be found in the counties of Hordaland and Sogn og Fjordane in western Norway. Most tunnels are illuminated and about half are ventilated. There are emergency telephones at the entrance to tunnels and inside them. Tunnels also have refuges which can be used by motorists in the event of an emergency.

*Laersdal Tunnel*

The Lærsdal road tunnel links the Rv50 from just east of Aurlandsvangen to the E16 east of Lærdalsoyri, by-passing the ferry link from Gudvangen to Lærsdal. The toll-free 24.5km long tunnel is illuminated and ventilated throughout and has a number of caverns at regular intervals which act as turning points and, it is reported, help dispel any feelings of claustrophobia. An alternative route is to take the Rødnes tunnel and then the Rv53, but this involves a steep climb beyond Øvre Ardal.

*Lofoten and Vesterålen Islands*

The Lofoten Islands can be reached by ferries from Bodø & Skutvik and the Vesteralen Islands can be reached by road (E10) west of Narvik. The individual islands of the Lofoten and Vesterålen groups are connected to each other by bridge or tunnel and the two groups of islands are linked by the E10 Lofast route from Gullesfjordbotn in Vesterålen to Fiskebøl in Lofoten. This route was formerly only possible by ferry.

*Oslo Tunnel*

A 3km long toll-free tunnel runs from east to west Oslo.

# Violation of Traffic Regulations

The police are empowered to impose and collect on-the-spot fines for infringement of traffic regulations.

# Motorways

There are 300km of 4 lane motorways signposted by the prefix A, which are situated around the towns of Bergen and Oslo. In addition there are category B motorways with 2 lanes.

There are normally no emergency telephones on motorways.

# Motorway Tolls

There are many toll roads throughout the country and most have an electronic toll system. Vehicles are categorised as follows:

**Class 1** – Motorcycles

**Class 2** – Car, with or without trailer, with a total weight less than 3,500kg and maximum length of 6m.

**Class 3** – Vehicle with or without trailer and a total weight of more than 3,500kg or between 6m and 12.4m in length.

*Payment*

If you have not registered your credit card under the Visitors' Payment scheme (see below) you would normally pass through tolls in the lanes marked 'Mynt/Coin' or 'Manuell'. You either pay manually or at a coin machine – keep a supply of small change handy as it is understood that the machines do not issue change. Most toll roads have a facility for credit card payment. Drivers of vehicles over 3,500kg must, if there is one, drive through the 'Manuell' lane.

Don't be tempted to pass through unmanned tolls without paying, as checks are made. However, many toll road operators have installed fully automatic toll stations – AutoPASS – where a sign indicates that you should not stop. Drivers without an AutoPASS can stop and pay at a nearby Esso stations (following the 'KR-Service' signs) within three days of being eligible to pay a toll, or they will receive an invoice by post at their home address. This also applies to drivers of foreign-registered vehicles.

*Visitors' Payment*

Alternatively, and more conveniently, there is now a 'Visitors' Payment' system for which you register and pay NOK 300 (vehicles below 3,500kg) or NOK 1,000 (over 3,500kg) by credit card. You specify how long your account is to be operative (maximum three months) and it is then automatically debited when you pass a pay point. Three months after your 'Visitors' Payment' has expired your account will be credited with any balance remaining. See www.autopass.no (English option) for more information and to open an account.

This system means you can drive through all toll roads in the AutoPASS lane and pay automatically at toll stations and pay points where there is no option for manual payment. You do not need an AutoPASS tag which is designed for residents and long-stay visitors and for which you have to enter into a contract.

*City Tolls*

Toll ring roads are in place around major cities charging drivers to take their vehicles into city centres (charge applied one-way only). For example, the toll for the use of the Oslo ring road for an outfit under 6 meters and under 3,500kg is NOK31 whilst an outfit between 6.01-12 meters and over 3,500kg is NOK93 depending on the weight and length of your vehicle (2014).

*Other Tolls*

Because of the mountainous terrain and the numerous fjords and streams, there are many bridges and tunnels where tolls are normally payable. Tunnels may be narrow and unlit and care is needed when suddenly entering an unlit tunnel from bright daylight. Alternative routes to avoid tolls can be full of obstacles which are not marked on a map, e.g. narrow stretches with sharp turns and/or poor road surface, and are best avoided.

*Svinesund Bridge*

There is a 700 metre long bridge linking Norway and Sweden on the E6 at Svinesund (Sweden) – the busiest border crossing between the two countries. Tolls are NOK20 (or SEK equivalent) for vehicles up to 3,500kg and NOK100 (or SEK equivalent) for vehicles over 3,500kgs (2014).

# Touring

International ferry services operate between Norway and Denmark, Germany, Iceland and Sweden. Routes from Harwich to Denmark and Newcastle to the Netherlands are in operation as gateways to Europe and, in addition, a daily overnight ferry service connects Copenhagen and Oslo.

A green 'i' sign indicates a tourist information office which is open all year with extended opening hours in summer, whereas a red sign means that the office is only open during the summer season.

Norwegians take their school and industrial holidays from the middle of June to the middle of August; travelling outside this season will ensure that facilities are less crowded and more economically priced. Winter brings the inevitable snowfall with some of the most reliable snow conditions in Europe. The winter sports season is from November to April.

Alta, on the coast north of the Arctic Circle, boasts the most extensive prehistoric rock carvings in Europe and has been declared a UNESCO World Heritage Site. Other World Heritage Sites include Geirangerfjord, Nærøyfjord, Bryggen in Bergen and the wooden buildings in Røros.

City cards are available for Oslo and Bergen, giving unlimited free travel on public transport, free public parking and free or discounted admission to museums and tourist attractions. They can be bought from tourist information centres, hotels and campsites in or near the city, from some kiosks or online at www.visitoslo.com or www.visitbergen.com.

Wine and spirits are only available from special, state-owned shops (vinmonopolet) usually found in larger towns, and are expensive, as are cigarettes. Beer is available from supermarkets. Smoking in bars, restaurants and public places is prohibited. Tipping is not expected in restaurants.

English is widely spoken, often fluently, by virtually everyone under the age of 60.

# The Midnight Sun and Northern Lights

The best time to experience the midnight sun is early or high summer. The sun does not sink below the horizon at the North Cape (Nordkapp) from the second week in May to the last week in July.

Midsummer Night's Eve is celebrated all over the country with thousands of bonfires along the fjords.

You can hope to see the Northern Lights (Aurora Borealis) between November and February depending on weather conditions. You need to go north of the Arctic Circle, which crosses Norway, just south of Bodø on the Nordland coast. Occasionally the Northern Lights may be seen in southern Norway, again depending on weather conditions.

# North Cape (Nordkapp)

A tunnel links the island of Magerøya, on which the North Cape is situated, to the mainland. There used to be a toll for this crossing, which has now been abolished.

North Cape is open from the beginning of May until the end of September. It is possible to visit in winter; contact the Nordkapp Tourist Office, www.nordkapp.no or tel: (0047) 78 47 70 30.

A charge of NOK 245 per adult and NOK 85 per child (2014) is payable to enter the North Cape Hall area. This is a tourist centre where there are exhibitions, displays, restaurants, shops and a post office, as well as an area of hardstanding for parking. This charge covers a stay of up to 48 hours. More information is given in the campsite entry for Nordkapp or on the website www.nordnorge.com. There are no cash machines at North Cape but credit cards are accepted in shops and restaurants, as are euros and sterling.

The true northernmost point of Norway is in fact at Knivskjellodden on a peninsular to the west of North Cape which is marked by a modest monument and a wooden box where you can record your name in a log book. It is possible to walk the 18km round trip from a car park on the E69 to Knivskjellodden but the walk should not be undertaken lightly. Later you can claim a certificate to mark your achievement from the tourist office in Honningsvåg by quoting the reference number of your signed entry in the log book.

## The Order of Bluenosed Caravanners

Visitors to the Arctic Circle from anywhere in the world may apply for membership of the Order of Bluenosed Caravanners, which will be recognised by the issue of a certificate by the International Caravanning Association (ICA). For further details contact David Hirst on 01422 372390, or email: david.hirst118@btinternet.com and attach a photograph of yourselves and your outfit under any Arctic Circle signpost, together with the date and country of crossing and the names of those who made the crossing. This service is free to members of the ICA (annual membership £20); the fee for non-members is £5. Coloured plastic decals for your outfit, indicating membership of the Order, are also available at a cost of £4. Cheques should be payable to the ICA. See www.icacaravanning.org.

## Public Transport

The public transport network is excellent and efficient with bus routes extending to remote villages. For economical travel buy a 24 hour bus pass (campsites often sell them), valid when stamped for the first time. Many train routes run through very scenic countryside and special offers and discounts mean that train travel is reasonably priced. Only Oslo has a metro system. Trams operate in Bergen and Trondheim.

Using domestic public ferry services is often the quickest way of travelling around Norway and from place to place along the coast and within fjords. Most operate from very early in the morning until late at night. Booking is not normally necessary except in the height of the holiday season when there may be long queues to the more popular destinations. However, internal ferries can be expensive in high season and you may wish to plan your route carefully in order to avoid them.

The ultimate ferry journey is the Norwegian steamer trip (hurtigrute) up the coast from Bergen to Kirkenes. A daily service operates in both directions and the steamer stops at about 30 ports on the way. The round trip lasts eleven days.

The scenic round trip from Bergen or Oslo, 'Norway in a Nutshell', takes you through some of the most beautiful scenery in the country. It combines rail, boat and coach travel on the scenic Bergen railway, the breathtaking Flåm Railway, and takes in the Aurlandsfjord, the narrow Naerøyfjord and the steep Stalheimskleiva. Further details are available from the Norwegian Tourist Board.

You can safely hail a taxi off the street or take one from a taxi stand. Most drivers speak English and all taxis are equipped for taking payment by credit card.

**ALESUND** *1B1* (1km N Coastal) *62.47571, 6.15688* **Ålesund Bobilsenter, Storgata 39, 6015 Ålesund (Møre og Romsdal)** Foll coast to N of town cent & m'van sps; well sp. Sm, hdstg, unshd; wc; mv service pnt; shwrs; el pnts; some traff noise; motor c'vans only Ccard acc. "No on-site warden; site on water's edge adj sea wall; conv town cent; v nice facs in wonderful location." May-Sep. NOK 200        2014*

**ALESUND** *1B1* (1.5km E Urban/Coastal) *62.46986, 6.19839* **Volsdalen Camping, Sjømannsveien, 6008 Ålesund (Møre og Romsdal) [tel 70 12 58 90; fax 70 12 14 94; v.camp@ online.no; www.volsdalencamping.no]** Foll Rv136 two Centrum, ignore 1st camping sp (Prinsen), take 2nd site sp Volsdalsberga to exit R, up slip rd. At top turn L over E136 then immed R, site on L. Sm, mkd pitch, hdstg, terr, unshd; htd wc; chem disp; mv service pnt; shwrs NOK10; el pnts (10A) NOK30 (no earth); gas; lndtte; shop on site & 500m; tradsmn; rest, snacks high ssn; cooking facs; TV rm; 40% statics; dogs; bus 600m; poss cr; Eng spkn; adv bkg; quiet; ccard acc; red long stay. "stunning location; some pitches o'looking fjord; sm pitches not suitable lge o'fits high ssn; 75% travellers; site unkempt; new san facs being built (2013); rec NH; only site for c'van nr Alesund, so adv bkg strongly advised; town 30 min walk." ♦ 1 May-1 Sep. NOK 250        2014*

**ALTA** *2G1* (10km NE Coastal) *70.00000, 23.48283* **Solvang Camping & Ungdomssenter, 9505 Alta (Finnmark) [tel 78 43 04 77; fax 78 44 30 20; post@solvangcamping. no; www.solvangcamping.no]** E along E6 fr Alta dir Rafsbotn, sp. Sm, unshd; wc; chem disp; shwrs; el pnts; lndtte; snacks; cooking facs; beach adj; TV rm; some statics; phone; Eng spkn; adv bkg; quiet; CKE/CCI. "Gd NH in lovely area." 1 Jun-30 Aug.        2009*

⊞ **ALTA** *2G1* (5km S Rural) *69.92904, 23.26136* **Alta River Camping, Steinfossveien 5, 9518 Øvre Alta (Finnmark) [tel 78 43 43 53; fax 78 43 69 02; post@alta-river-camping. no; www.alta-river-camping.no]** Fr E6 (by-passing Alta), take E93 S sp Kautokeino. Site clearly sp on L (opp information board). Med, pt shd; htd wc; chem disp; mv service pnt; sauna; shwrs NOK10; el pnts (10-16A) NOK30; lndtte; shop; cooking facs; playgrnd; ltd wifi; TV; Eng spkn; adv bkg; quiet; ccard acc; CKE/CCI. "Excel facs; o'looks salmon rv; pitches not mkd and close together, some hdstg; elec point poss no earth; facs dated but clean; elec poss no earth." ♦ NOK 279        2014*

⊞ **ALTA** *2G1* (5km S Rural) *69.92735, 23.27075* **Alta Strand Camping & Apartments, Stenfossveien 29, 9518 Øvre Alta (Finnmark) [tel 78 43 40 22; fax 78 43 42 40; mail@altacamping.no; www.altacamping.no]** Fr E6 (W of Alta) take Rv93 S sp Kautokeino. Three sites adj in 3km on L, clearly sp, Strand is last one. Sm, pt shd; htd wc; chem disp; mv service pnt; sauna; shwrs inc; el pnts (10A) NOK40 (poss no earth); lndtte; shop 5km; tradsmn; snacks; bar; BBQ; cooking facs; playgrnd; wifi; some statics; phone; car wash; Eng spkn; adv bkg; ccard acc; CKE/CCI. "Gd for visiting rock carvings; midnight sun visible fr nrby Alta museum; vg." NOK 190        2010*

⊞ **ALVDAL** *1C2* (4km W Rural) *62.13115, 10.56896* **Gjelten Bru Camping, 2560 Alvdal (Hedmark) [tel 62 48 74 44; fax 62 48 70 20; www.nafcamp.com/gjelten-camping]** Fr Rv3 join rd 29 at Alvdal. Cross rv opp general store to site on rv bank. Sm, mkd pitch, pt shd; wc; chem disp; mv service pnt; baby facs; shwrs NOK5; el pnts (10A) NOK40; lndtte (inc dryer); playgrnd; games area; fishing; dogs; Eng spkn; quiet. "V pleasant site; friendly owner." NOK 160        2010*

**AMOT** *1B3* (300m N Rural) *59.5725, 7.99158* **Camping Groven, Ytre Vinje, 3890 Åmot (Telemark) [tel 35 07 14 21; fax 35 07 10 87; grovenc@online.no; www.grovencamping.no]** Fr Åmot take Rv37 N, site 200m on R. Med, terr, pt shd; htd wc; chem disp; mv service pnt; baby facs; sauna; shwrs NOK5; el pnts (10A) NOK30; lndtte; shop; playgrnd; pool 100m; winter skiing; TV rm; phone. "Attractive scenery; walking tours arranged; clean, rustic site." 20 May-1 Oct. NOK 150        2009*

**ANDALSNES** *1B1* (1.5km S Rural) *62.55223, 7.70394* **Åndalsnes Camping & Motell, 6300 Åndalsnes (Møre og Romsdal) [tel 71 22 16 29; fax 71 22 63 60; epost@ andalsnes-camping.no; www.andalsnes-camping.com]** Foll E136 to o'skirts of Åndalsnes. Foll sp Ålesund x-ing rv bdge twd W & L immed. Lge, pt shd; wc; chem disp; mv service pnt; shwrs NOK15; el pnts (10-16A) NOK40 (check earth); lndtte; shop; rest, snacks; fishing; boating; wifi; TV; ccard acc; red CKE/CCI. "Excel facs; rvside, excel mountain scenery; nr Troll Rd & Wall; nice site; grnd can be soft; poss long lead req (poss no earth); gd cent site." ♦ 1 May-30 Sep. NOK 242        2014*

**ANDALSNES** *1B1* (10km S Rural) *62.4940, 7.75846* **Trollveggen Camping, Horgheimseidet, 6300 Åndalsnes (Møre og Romsdal) [tel 71 22 37 00; fax 71 22 16 31; post@trollveggen.com; www.trollveggen.com]** Sp on W side of E136, dir Dombås. Sm, mkd pitch, terr, pt shd; htd wc; chem disp; mv service pnt; baby facs; fam bthrm; shwrs NOK25; el pnts (16A) NOK40; lndtte (inc dryer); kiosk; rest 5km; BBQ; cooking facs; playgrnd; fishing; golf 10km; cycle hire; wifi; statics; dogs; Eng spkn; adv bkg; quiet; ccard acc. "Friendly, family-run site; excel touring base; outstanding scenery; at foot of Trollveggen wall - shd fr late afternoon; ideal site for walking in Romsdal; on Trollsteig classic rte." ♦ ltd 10 May-19 Sep. NOK 258        2014*

**ANDENES (VESTERALEN ISLANDS)** *2F1* (3km S Coastal) *69.30390, 16.06621* **Andenes Camping, Bleiksveien 34, 8480 Andenes [tel 47 41 34 03 88; fax 47 76 11 56 10; camping@whalesafari.no; www.andenescamping.no]** Site on E of Rv82, sp. Sm, some hdstg, unshd; htd wc; chem disp; mv service pnt; shwrs NOK10; el pnts (16A) inc (check earth); shop 250m; cooking facs; sand beach adj; Eng spkn; some rd noise; CKE/CCI. "Nice, sandy beaches; conv whale safari, summer ferry to Gryllefjord & Bleiksøya bird cliff; gd for midnight sun; Beautiful location; whale trips." 1 Jun-30 Aug. NOK 200        2014*

**NORWAY**

**ANDENES (VESTERALEN ISLANDS)** *2F1* (20.2km SW)
*69.20410, 15.84674* **Stave Camping & Hot Pools, Stave
8489 Nordmela [tel 92 60 12 57; info@stavecamping.
no; www.stavecamping.no]** Head S on Storgata/Rv82
twds Stadionveien, cont to foll Rv82, turn R onto Fv976, bear
L onto Laksebakkveien, cont onto Fv976 and arrive at your
destination. sm; pt unshd; htd wc; chem disp; shwr (20 NOK);
el pnts (40 NOK); (16A); nearest shop 18km; cooking facs;
beach adj; wifi; eng spkn; ccard acc. "Excel for midnight sun,
hot tubs 250NOK pn." 17 May-1 Sep. NOK 230      2014*

**ARENDAL** *1B4* (5km SW Rural) *58.42726, 8.72881* **Nidelv
Brygge & Camping, Vesterveien 251, 4817 His (Aust-
Agder) [tel/fax 37 01 14 25; nidelv.c@online.no]** Rv420
fr Arendal, site by bdge over Rv Nidelv. Med, unshd; wc;
chem disp; shwrs NOK10; el pnts NOK35; gas; lndtte; shop;
rest; boating & sw; some statics; bus; Eng spkn; quiet. "Poss
unmanned low ssn." 15 May-15 Sep. NOK 170      2010*

**AURLAND see Flåm** *1B2*

**BALESTRAND** *1B2* (1km S Coastal) *61.20220, 6.53140* **Sjøtun
Camping, 6899 Balestrand (Sogn og Fjordane) [tel/fax
57 69 12 23; camping@sjotun.com; www.sjotun.com]**
Fr Dragsvik ferry or fr W on by-pass; foll int'l site sp. Sm, pt
sl, unshd; htd wc; chem disp (wc); mv service pnt; shwrs inc;
el pnts (16A) NOK25; lndtte; shop, rest, snacks 1km; BBQ;
cooking facs; shgl beach 1km; few statics; dogs; phone; Eng
spkn; adv bkg; quiet; red long stay; CKE/CCI. "Neat, well-kept
site with gd view of Sognefjord; poss diff if wet due grass
pitches." 1 Jun-28 Feb, 15 Apr-1 Oct. NOK 317      2014*

**BALLANGEN** *2F2* (1.5km E Coastal) *68.3383, 16.85776*
**Ballangen Camping, 8540 Ballangen (Nordland)
[tel 76 92 76 90; fax 76 92 76 92; ballcamp@c2i.net;
www.ballangen-camping.no]** Sp on N side of E6 fr Narvik,
beside fjord. Lge, mkd pitch, pt shd; htd wc; chem disp; mv
service pnt; sauna; shwrs inc; el pnts (10A) NOK40; lndtte (inc
dryer); shop, rest, snacks; playgrnd; htd pool; paddling pool;
waterslide; shgl fjord beach; tennis; games area; wifi; TV; some
statics; dogs; Eng spkn; ccard acc; CKE/CCI. "Pleasant site adj
fjord; friendly owners; gd facs - ltd san facs high ssn; gd rest;
foot/cycle path to town." ◆ 14 Mar-1 Oct. NOK 200  2010*

**BARDU see Setermoen** *2F2*

⊞ **BEITOSTOLEN** *1C2* (1km S Rural) *61.24128, 8.92068*
**Beitostølen Hytter & Camping (OP151), Finntøppvegen
2, 2953 Beitostølen (Oppland) [tel 61 34 11 00 or
95 70 35 05; fax 61 34 15 44; info@beitocamp.no; www.
beitocamp.no]** Fr S on Rv51, site on L. Lge, hdstg, pt sl,
unshd; htd wc; chem disp; mv service pnt; sauna; baby facs;
fam bthrm; shwrs NOK10; el pnts (13A) NOK30; lndtte (inc
dryer); shop adj; rest  BBQ; cooking facs; playgrnd; htd, covrd
pool 1km; canoe & cycle hire; wifi; 90% statics (sep area);
dogs; Eng spkn; quiet; ccard acc; CKE/CCI. "Wintersports,
horseriding nrby; gd walking; excel site." ◆ NOK 200  2010*

**BERGEN** *1A3* (6.2 SSE Urban) *60.35405, 5.35962*
**Bergenshallen, Vilhelm Bjerknes Vei 24, 5081 Bergen
[tel 47 55 30 88 50; www.visitnorway.com]** Head SW
on E16/E39. Exit onto E39 twrds Stavanger/Rv580, take exit.
At rndabt take 3rd exit onto Mindeallé. Turn R to stay on
Mindeallé, go thro 1 rndabt, cont onto Rv582. Thro 1 rndabt
then at next rndabt take 2nd exit onto Fv252. Turn R onto
Hagerups vei, cont onto Vilhelm Bjerknes'vei. Turn L and site
is on the R. Sm, hdstg, unshd; own san rec; mv service pnt; el
pnts (on some pitches); dogs inc; train adj. "28 spaces for MV's
only; arrive early; adj to Bergen light Rail - 15 mins to city cent;
only fasc are water, emptying toilet & waste disposal; excel
location for visiting Bergen; no shwrs or wc." 1 May-31 Aug.
NOK 150      2014*

**BERGEN** *1A3* (10km E Rural) *60.37381, 5.45768* **Lone
Camping, Hardangerveien 697, 5268 Haukeland (Horda-
Rogaland) [tel 55 39 29 60; fax 55 39 29 79; booking@
lonecamping.no; www.lonecamping.no]** Fr N on E39
until junc with E16. foll sp Voss to rndabt junc with Rv580 sp
Nesttun. Foll Rv580 S for approx 5km, site sp on L. Fr S on E39
until Nesttun, foll Rv580 N sp Indre Arna for approx 6km, site
sp on R. Recep is sm bureau adj G'ge or, if unmanned, in g'ge.
Do NOT go into Bergen city cent. Site is 20km by rd fr Bergen.
Lge, pt sl, pt shd, some hdstg; wc; chem disp; mv service pnt;
shwrs NOK10 (no earth); el pnts (16A) NOK40; gas; lndtte;
shop; supmkt adj; snacks; playgrnd; lake sw, fishing & boating;
wifi; TV rm; some statics; phone; bus to Bergen; site clsd 5 Nov-
19 Dec & New Year; poss v cr; Eng spkn; quiet; red 3+ days;
ccard acc; CKE/CCI. "Well-organised; helpful staff; peaceful
lakeside setting; superb views; lakeside pitches diff when
wet; bus at camp ent for Bergen (35 mins)." 2 Jan-20 Dec.
NOK 294      2014*

**BERGEN** *1A3* (15km SE Rural) *60.35220, 5.43520* **Bratland
Camping, Bratlandsveien 6, 5268 Haukeland (Hordaland)
[tel 55 10 13 38 & 92 61 52 00 (mob); fax 55 10 53 60;
post@bratlandcamping.no; www.bratlandcamping.no]**
Fr N on E39 until junc with E16, foll sp Voss to rndabt junc with
Rv580 sp Nesttun. Foll Rv580 S for approx 4km; site sp on L.
Fr Voss on E16, emerge fr tunnel to rndabt, turn L onto Rv580.
Then as above. Site 16km by rd fr Bergen. Sm, some hdstg,
unshd; wc; chem disp; mv service pnt; shwrs NOK10; el pnts
(10A) NOK40; lndtte (inc dryer); shop; cooking facs; wifi; TV
rm; 10% statics; bus to Bergen at site ent; poss cr; Eng spkn; rd
noise; ccard acc; CKE/CCI. "Clean, family-run site; gd, modern
san facs; v helpful owners; conv Bergen, nrby stave church &
Grieg's home." ◆ 01 May-15 Sep. NOK 286      2014*

**BERLEVAG** *2H1* (Coastal) *70.85716, 29.09933* **Berlevåg
Camping & Apartments, Havnagata 8, 9980 Berlevåg
(Finnmark) [tel 78 98 16 10; post@berlevag-pensjonat.
no; www.berlevag-pensjonat.no]** Leave E6 at Tanabru, foll
Rv890 to Berlevåg. Site sp at beg of vill. Sm, unshd; htd wc;
chem disp; mv service pnt; shwrs NOK10; el pnts (16A) NOK40;
lndtte (inc dryer); shop 500m; BBQ; cooking facs; playgrnd;
beach; library & lounge; wifi; TV rm; phone; Eng spkn; adv bkg;
ccard acc; CKE/CCI. "Busy fishing port on edge of Barents Sea;
museum, glassworks, WW2 resistance history; v helpful staff
as site is also TO; site will open outside Jun-Sep on request if
contacted ahead; rec arr early; excel site." ◆ 1 Jun-30 Sep.
NOK 160      2009*

**BIRISTRAND see Lillehammer** *1C2*

**BIRTAVARRE** *2G1* (S Rural) *69.49051, 20.82976* **Camping Birtavarre (TR34), 9147 Birtavarre (Troms) [tel/fax 77 71 71 77 07; mail@birtavarrecamping.com; www. birtavarrecamping.com]** On E6 Olderdalen to Nordkjsobotn, sp. Or foll sp fr vill. Med, unshd; wc; chem disp; mv service pnt; baby facs; shwrs NOK10; el pnts NOK45; lndtte; shop 1km; snacks; cooking facs; fjord sw; Eng spkn; some rd noise; ccard acc; CKE/CCI."Basic site; ok for NH." 1 May-15 Oct. NOK 195                                                             2014*

⊞ **BO** *1C3* (5km N Rural) *59.44425, 9.06318* **Bø Camping (TE5), Lifjellvegen 51, 3800 Bø (Telemark) [tel 35 95 20 12; fax 35 95 34 64; bocamping@bo.online.no; www. bocamping.com]** Fr Bø cent on Rv36 dir Folkestad; take rd on L to Lifjell, site sp; 500m fr Bø Sommarland amusement park. Med, hdstg, pt shd; htd wc; chem disp; shwrs; el pnts NOK30; gas; lndtte; snacks; shop; playgrnd; pool; paddling pool; fishing; solarium; TV; 20% statics; phone; poss cr; Eng spkn; adv bkg; ccard acc; CKE/CCI. NOK 180                     2009*

⊞ **BODO** *2F2* (2km SE Rural) *67.2695, 14.42483* **Camping Bodøsjoen, Båtstøveien 1, 8013 Bodø (Nordland) [tel 75 56 36 80; fax 75 56 46 89; bodocamp@yahoo. no; www.bodocamp.no]** Fr E on Rv80 at Bodø sp, turn L at traff lts by Esso g'ge sp airport & camping. L at next rndabt, foll camping sp. Lge, pt sl, unshd; wc; chem disp; shwrs inc; el pnts (10A) NOK20 (no earth); lndtte; shop 1km; rest 2km; beach; bus 1km; boat hire; fishing excursions; bus 250m; Eng spkn; aircraft noise; CKE/CCI. "Conv Lofoten ferry; superb views; midnight sun (Jun-Jul); Mt Rønvik 3.2km fr camp." ♦ NOK 252                                                             2014*

⊞ **BODO** *2F2* (12km SE Coastal) *67.23640, 14.63290* **Saltstraumen Camping, Knapplund, 8056 Saltstraumen (Nordland) [tel 75 58 75 60; fax 75 58 75 40; saltstraumen@pluscamp.no; www.saltstraumen-camping. no]** Fr Bodø take Rv80 for 19km; turn S onto rte 17 at Løding; site sp in Saltstraumen. Site is 33km by rd fr Bodø. Med, hdstg, unshd; htd wc; chem disp; mv service pnt; shwrs inc; el pnts (16A) NOK30; gas; lndtte (inc dryer); shop adj; rest adj; cooking facs; playgrnd; fishing; cycling; boating; TV; phone; poss cr; Eng spkn; quiet; ccard acc; CKE/CCI. "5 min walk to Mælstrom, the 'angler's paradise'; v busy high ssn - rec arr early." ♦ ltd NOK 200                                       2014*

**BOSBERG see Trondheim** *2E3*

**BOVERDALEN see Lom** *1C2*

⊞ **BREMSNES** *1B1* (1.5km S Coastal) *63.08043, 7.59535* **Skjerneset Brygge Camping, Ekkilsøy, 6530 Averøy (Møre og Romsdal) [tel 71 51 18 94; fax 71 51 18 15; info@ skjerneset.com; www.skjerneset.com]** Foll sp to Ekkilsøya Island on Rv64 (off Averøy Island). Site on R over bdge. Sm, some hdstg, pt shd; htd wc; chem disp; mv service pnt; shwrs; el pnts (10-16A) NOK30; lndtte; sm shop; cooking facs; boat hire; fishing; sat TV; apartments to rent; quiet. "Charming, clean site adj working harbour; beautiful outlook; basic san facs; waterside pitches - unfenced deep water in places; museum adj." NOK 150                                       2009*

**BRIKSDALSBRE see Olden** *1B2*

⊞ **BRONNOYSUND** *2E3* (12km SW Coastal) *65.39340, 12.09920* **Torghatten Camping, 8900 Torghatten (Nordland) [tel 75 02 54 95; fax 75 02 58 89; pkha@online. no; www.rv17.no/torghatten-camping/]** Fr Rv17 onto Rv76 to Brønnøysund, foll sp Torghatten. Site at base of Torghatten mountain. Sm, pt sl, unshd; wc; chem disp; mv service pnt; shwrs inc; el pnts (16A) NOK30; lndtte; shop; tradsmn; snacks; bar; playgrnd; sea water pool & beach adj; bus; phone; Eng spkn; quiet. "Take care speed humps in/out Brønnøysund; vg." ♦ ltd NOK 140                                                             2009*

**BUD** *1B1* (500m E Coastal) *62.9040, 6.92866* **PlusCamp Bud (MR11), 6430 Bud (Møre og Romsdal) [tel 71 26 10 23; fax 71 26 11 47; bud@pluscamp.no; www.budcamping.no]** Site on Rv664, sp fr Bud. Med, pt sl, unshd; htd wc; chem disp; mv service pnt; baby facs; shwrs NOK10; el pnts (16A) NOK40; lndtte (inc dryer); shop; snacks; cooking facs; playgrnd; sand beach & sw adj; boat hire; fishing; TV rm; wifi; 50% statics; dogs; Eng spkn; quiet; ccard acc; CKE/CCI. "Waterfront site with beautiful views; 20 min walk to vill shops/rest; gdl facs; gd location for start of Atlantic Highway, National Tourist Rte & for cycling." ♦ 20 Apr-1 Oct. NOK 250                     2014*

**BURFJORD** *2G1* (13km N Rural) *70.02728, 22.08860* **Alteidet Camping, Alteidet, 9161 Burfjord (Troms) [tel 78 48 75 59; fax 77 76 93 51; alteidetcamp@hotmail.com]** On W of E6, midway bet Burfjord & Langfjordbotn. Med, pt sl, unshd; wc; chem disp; baby facs; sauna; shwrs NOK10; el pnts (10A) NOK40; lndtte; kiosk; shops 5km; bar; cooking facs; playgrnd; TV; dogs; phone; poss cr; adv bkg; quiet; Eng spkn. "Attractive by rv & fjord; excel base to visit glacier." 15 Jun-15 Aug. NOK 140                                                             2009*

⊞ **BYGLANDSFJORD** *1B4* (2.5km N Rural) *58.68895, 7.80322* **Neset Camping, 4741 Byglandsfjord (Aust-Agder) [tel 37 93 40 50; fax 37 93 43 93; post@neset.no; www. neset.no]** N on Rv9 fr Evje, thro Byglandsfjord, site on L. Lge, pt sl, unshd; htd wc; chem disp; mv service pnt; fam bthrm; sauna; shwrs NOK5; el pnts (10A) NOK30; gas; lndtte (inc dryer); shop; snacks; rest; BBQ; cooking facs; playgrnd; lake sw & beach adj; fishing; windsurfing; boat & cycle hire; wifi; TV rm; 40% statics; dogs; Eng spkn; adv bkg; quiet; ccard acc. "Wonderful location on lakeside; elk safaris; walks; ww rafting nrby; check elec earth." ♦ NOK 304 (CChq acc)             2014*

**BYRKJELO** *1B2* (3km S Rural) *61.73026, 6.50843* **Byrkjelo Camping & Hytter, 6826 Byrkjelo (Sogn og Fjordane) [tel 91 73 65 97; fax 57 86 71 54; mail@byrkjelo-camping. no; www.byrkjelo-camping.tefre.com]** Fr S site ent on L as ent town, clearly sp. Sm, some hdstg, pt shd; wc; chem disp; baby facs; fam bthrm; shwrs NOK5; el pnts (10A) NOK30; lndtte; shop; snacks adj; rest 500m; cooking facs; playgrnd; htd pool; paddling pool; fishing; cycling; solarium; wifi; 25% statics; phone; Eng spkn; adv bkg; quiet but some rd noise; ccard acc; CKE/CCI. "Horseriding, mountain & glacier walking; excel, well kept site; great facs." ♦ 30 Mar-20 Sep. NOK 190                                                             2014*

---

**DALEN (TELEMARK)** *1B3* (250m S Rural) *59.44223, 8.00758*
**Buøy Camping (TE20), Buøyvegen, 3880 Dalen (Telemark)**
[tel 35 07 75 87; fax 35 07 77 01; info@dalencamping.com;
www.dalencamping.com] Fr E134 at Høydalsmo take Rv45
twd Dalen (approx 20km, 12% gradient). Of fr E134 at Åmot
take Rv38 to Dalen (no gradient). Site in cent of Dalen on Rv45,
well sp. Med, pt shd; htd wc; chem disp; mv service pnt; baby
facs; shwrs inc; el pnts (16A) NOK35; gas; lndtte; shop; rest;
cooking facs; playgrnd; leisure cent 500m; cycle hire; wifi; TV;
60% statics; dogs; phone; Eng spkn; quiet; ccard acc; CKE/CCI.
"Site on island; gd family base; gd walking." 1 May-28 Aug.
NOK 240                                                    2010*

**DALSGRENDA see Mo i Rana** *2F2*

**DOMBAS** *1C2* (6km S Rural) *62.02991, 9.17586* **Bjørkhol
Camping, 2660 Dombås (Oppland) [tel 61 24 13 31; post@
bjorkhol.no; www.bjorkhol.no]** Site on E6. Sm, pt sl, pt
shd; htd wc; chem disp; mv service pnt; shwrs NOK5; el pnts
(10A) NOK40 (long lead poss req); lndtte; shop; rest, snacks,
bar 6km; cooking facs; playgrnd; 10% statics; dogs; phone;
Eng spkn; adv bkg; quiet; CKE/CCI. "A well-kept, friendly,
family-owned, basic site; excel mountain walking in area."
1 May-1 Sep. NOK 150                                        2013*

**DRAMMEN** *1C3* (24.5km SE Coastal) *59.60003, 10.40383*
**Homannsberget Camping, Strømmveien 55, 3060 Svelvik
(Vestfold) [tel 33 77 25 63 / 91 30 98 52 (mob); post@
homannsberget.no; www.homannsberget.no]** Head SW
on E18, take exit 25 twr Svelvik/RV319, at rndabt take 3rd
exit onto E134. At next rndabt take 1st exit onto Bjørnsons
gate/Rv282. Turn L onto Havnegata/Rv319. Cont on Rv319,
go thro 1 rndabt. Site on the L. Med, mkd pitch, unshd; mv
service pnt; shwr 5nok; el pnts; lndtte (inc dryer); shop; bar;
playgrnd; beach adj; games area; wifi; twin axles; poss cr; adv
bkg; quiet; ccard acc; CKE/CCI. "Vg site; train stn within 20
mins; site is also a strawberry farm & orchard." 1 May-1 Sep.
NOK 245                                                    2014*

**EDLAND** *1B3* (5km E Rural) *59.72378, 7.69712* **Velemoen
Camping, 3895 Edland Vinje i Telemark [tel 35 07 01 09 or
90 89 40 49 (mob); fax 35 07 02 15; velemoen@frisurf.no;
www.velemoen.no]** Fr E site on L off E134 bef Edland; Fr W
site is on R, 8km after Haukeligrend on Lake Tveitevatnet. Sm,
pt sl, shd; wc; baby facs; no chem disp/mv service pnt; shwrs;
el pnts; lndtte; shops 1km; cooking facs; playgrnd; lake sw adj;
sat TV; some statics; dogs; Eng spkn; quiet; no ccard acc. "V
helpful owner; immac san facs; beautiful lakeside/mountain
location; on S side of Hardangervidda National Park; on main
E-W rte Oslo-Bergen." ♦ 15 May-1 Oct. NOK 150      2013*

⊞ **EGERSUND** *1A4* (3.5km N Rural) *58.4788, 5.9909*
**Steinsnes NAF Camping, Jærveien 190, Tengs, 4370
Egersund (Horda-Rogaland) [tel 97 40 09 66; fax
51 49 40 73; post@steinsnescamping.no; www.
steinsnescamping.no]** Site located S of Rv44 & on bank of
rv; rv bdge at Tengs Bru. Med, mkd pitch, unshd; wc; chem
disp; mv service pnt; shwrs NOK5; el pnts (4A) NOK35; lndtte;
shops adj; snacks adj; bar 2km; BBQ; playgrnd; sand beach
8km; horseriding school adj; phone; poss cr; Eng spkn; adv
bkg; quiet but some rd noise; ccard acc; CKE/CCI. "Spectacular
rapids 1km (salmon leaping in July); on North Sea cycle rte;
conv ferry to Denmark or Bergen; vg." ♦ NOK 230      2013*

**EIDFJORD** *1B3* (7km E Rural) *60.42563, 7.12318* **Sæbø
Camping (HO11), 5784 Øvre-Eidfjord (Hordaland)
[tel 53 66 59 27 or 55 10 20 48; scampi@online.no; www.
saebocamping.com]** Site N of Rv7 bet Eidfjord & Geilo, 2nd
on L after tunnel & bdge; clearly sp. Med, pt shd; htd wc; chem
disp; mv service pnt; fam bthrm; shwrs NOK10; el pnts (10A)
NOK30 (earth fault); lndtte (inc dryer); shop; tradsmn; rest,
snacks 500m; cooking facs; playgrnd; boating; quiet; CKE/CCI.
"Vg; beautiful lakeside setting; adj to excel nature cent with
museum/shop/theatre; clean san facs; helpful staff; gd location
for walking & cycling." ♦ 1 May-30 Sep. NOK 248      2014*

⊞ **ELVERUM** *1D2* (2km S Rural) *60.86701, 11.55623*
**Elverum Camping, Halvdan Gransvei 6, 2407 Elverum
(Hedmark) [tel 62 41 67 16; fax 62 41 68 17; booking@
elverumcamping.no; www.elverumcamping.no]** Site sp
fr Rv20 dir Kongsvinger. Lge, pt shd; htd wc; chem disp; mv
service pnt; shwrs inc; el pnts (10A) NOK40; lndtte; shop, rest,
snacks, bar 2km; BBQ; playgrnd; 20% statics; phone; dogs;
adv bkg; Eng spkn; quiet. "Vg; museum of forestry adj; rlwy
museum at Hamar (30km)." NOK 200                      2009*

## "Satellite navigation makes touring much easier"

Remember just that sat navs don't know if
you're towing or in a larger vehicle – always
use yours alongside maps and site directions.

**FARSUND** *1A4* (4km S Rural) *58.0663, 6.7957* **Lomsesanden
Familiecamping, Loshavneveien 228, 4550 Farsund
(Vest-Agder) [tel 38 39 09 13; e-vetlan@online.no; www.
lomsesanden.no]** Exit E39 at Lyngdal onto Rv43 to Farsund &
foll camp sps. (NB Rv465 fr Kvinesdal not suitable for c'vans.)
Med, pt shd; wc; chem disp; baby facs; shwrs NOK10; el pnts
(10A) NOK45; lndtte; shop; playgrnd; dir access sand beach
adj; fishing; TV; 95% statics; dogs; Eng spkn; adv bkg rec;
quiet; ccard acc. "Gd site in beautiful location." 1 May-15 Sep.
NOK 185                                                    2009*

⊞ **FAUSKE** *2F2* (12km N Coastal) *67.34618, 15.59533*
**Strømhaug Camping, Strømhaugveien 2, 8226 Straumen
(Nordland) [tel 75 69 71 06; fax 75 69 76 06; mail@
stromhaug.no; www.stromhaug.no]** N fr Fauske on E6, turn
off sp Straumen, site sp. Sm, pt sl, pt shd; htd wc; chem disp;
mv service pnt; shwrs NOK10; el pnts (6-10A) inc; lndtte; shop,
rest, snacks, bar adj; cooking facs; playgrnd; fishing; boating;
TV; Eng spkn; red 7+ days. "Site on rv bank; salmon-fishing in
Aug." ♦ NOK 239                                            2013*

⊞ **FAUSKE** *2F2* (4km S Urban) *67.23988, 15.41961* **Fauske
Camping & Motel, Leivset, 8201 Fauske (Nordland)
[tel 75 64 84 01; fax 75 64 84 13; fausm@online.no]** Fr S
site on R of E6, approx 6km fr exit of Kvenflåg rd tunnel, &
2km bef Finneid town board. Fr N site on L approx 1km after
rv bdge. Sm, pt sl, pt shd; wc; mv service pnt; baby facs; shwrs
NOK10; el pnts (10A) NOK40; lndtte; shop 2km; snacks;
cooking facs; playgrnd; sw 2km; fishing; cycling; wifi; dogs;
poss cr; some Eng spkn; adv bkg; some rd noise; ccard acc.
"Vg; phone ahead low ssn to check open." NOK 165   2009*

**FAUSKE** *2F2* (3km SW Rural/Coastal) *67.24541, 15.3360* **Lundhøgda Camping, Lundeveien, 8200 Fauske (Nordland) [tel 75 64 39 66; fax 75 64 92 49; post@ lundhogdacamping.no; www.lundhogdacamping.no]** Site on Rv80 fr Fauske dir Bodø, sp. Sm, sl, pt shd; htd wc; chem disp; mv service pnt; shwrs NOK10; el pnts (16A) NOK40; lndtte; shops 3km; tradsmn; rest 2km; snacks; cooking facs; playgrnd; beach 300m; cycle hire; TV rm; 40% statics; poss cr; Eng spkn; quiet; ccard acc; CKE/CCI. "On high open grnd on headland but lower slopes boggy; gd views; helpful, friendly staff." 15 Jun-15 Aug. NOK 150                        2009*

⊞ **FJAERLAND** *1B2* (4km N Rural) *61.42758, 6.76211* **Bøyum Camping, 5855 Fjærland (Sogn og Fjordane) [tel 57 69 32 52; fax 57 69 29 57; kfodne@frisurf.no; www.fjaerland.org/boyumcamping]** On Rv5 Sogndal to Skei. Shortly after end of toll tunnel on L, well sp. Sm, pt hdstg, unshd; htd wc; chem disp; mv service pnt; shwrs NOK5-10; el pnts NOK30; lndtte; ltd shop; tradsmn; snacks; cooking facs; playgrnd; wifi; TV rm; 30% statics; phone; poss cr; Eng spkn; adv bkg; quiet; ccard acc; CKE/CCI. "Adj glacier museum, conv for glacier & fjord trips; beautiful location nr fjord (no views); visit Mundal for 2nd hand books; helpful owner; superb, clean site." ♦ NOK 150                        2009*

**FLAKK see Trondheim** *1C1*

**FLAM** *1B2* (8km N Rural) *60.90006, 7.20618* **Lunde Camping, 5745 Aurland (Sogn og Fjordane) [tel 57 63 34 12; fax 57 63 31 65; lunde.camping@alb.no; www.lunde-camping.no]** Fr N exit E16 at rndabt immed after S end of 25km tunnel turn for Aurland. R S exit E16 8km fr Flam at rndabt sp Aurland. Site on S side of rd, sp. Steep ent. Med, pt shd; htd wc; chem disp; mv service pnt; shwrs NOK10; el pnts (16A) NOK30 (rev pol); lndtte; shops 1.4km; cooking facs; dogs; phone; poss cr; Eng spkn; ccard acc; CKE/CCI. "Much quieter than site in Flåm; clean facs; superb setting with views; gd walking." Easter & 1 May-1 Oct. NOK 250                        2011*

**FLAM** *1B2* (400m S Urban) *60.86240, 7.10921* **Flåm Camping, Nedre Brekkevegen 12, 5743 Flåm (Sogn og Fjordane) [tel 57 63 21 21; camping@flaam-camping.no; www.flaam-camping.no]** Fr Lærdal Tunnel cont on E16 thro 2 more tunnels. At end of 2nd tunnel (Fretheim Tunnel) turn L immed to Sentrum. Turn L at x-rds, site on L. Med, hdstg, pt sl, terr, pt shd; htd wc; chem disp; mv service pnt; serviced pitches; baby facs; shwrs NOK10; el pnts (10A) inc; lndtte (inc dryer); shop; supmkt nrby; rest, snacks & bar 500m; BBQ; cooking facs; playgrnd; cycle hire; watersports; boating; fishing; dogs free; no c'vans/m'vans over 8.50m; phone; poss cr; Eng spkn; quiet but noise fr rd & cruise ships during day; ccard acc; red long stay; CKE/CCI. "Well-kept, friendly, busy, family-run site; excel san facs; conv mountain walks, excel location for Flambana rlwy, Aurlandsvangen 7km - gd shops; gd cycling base; excel." ♦ 15 Apr-15 Oct. NOK 312                        2014*

⊞ **FLEKKEFJORD** *1A4* (5km SE Rural) *58.28868, 6.7173* **Egenes Camping (VA7), 4400 Flekkefjord (Vest-Agder) [tel 38 32 01 48; fax 38 32 01 11; post@egenescamping. no; www.egenes.no]** Located N of E39 dir Seland. Med, mkd pitch, pt shd; htd wc; chem disp; mv service pnt; baby facs; shwrs NOK10; el pnts (5A) NOK40; lndtte; shop; snacks; playgrnd; TV; 75% statics; phone; ccard acc; red CKE/CCI. "Ltd facs low ssn; overflow car park area with facs for tourers 0.5km; poss cr; lovely situation." ♦ NOK 250                        2014*

⊞ **FLORO** *1A2* (2km E Coastal) *61.59420, 5.07244* **Pluscamp Krokane (SF15), Strandgt 30, 6900 Florø (Sogn og Fjordane) [tel 57 75 22 50; fax 57 75 22 60; post@ krocamp.no; www.krocamp.no]** On Rv5 Forde to Florø, on ent town turn L at rndabt sp Krokane, then immed R & foll rd to coast. Turn L, pass marina to site, sp. Steep ent/exit. Sm, hdstg, pt sl, pt shd; htd wc; chem disp; mv service pnt; baby facs; fam bthrm; shwrs NOK10; el pnts (10A) NOK30; lndtte; shop 2km; tradsmn; rest, snacks, bar 2km; playgrnd; htd, covrd pool 1km; sand beach adj; boat hire; fishing; internet; 80% statics; phone; bus; Eng spkn; quiet; CKE/CCI. "V sm area for tourers; Florø interesting fishing town with boat trips etc." ♦ NOK 130                        2010*

**FORDE** *1A2* (1.5km NE Rural) *61.44940, 5.89008* **Førde Gjestehus & Camping (SF94), Kronborgvegen 44, Havstad, 6800 Førde (Romsdal Sogn og Fjordane) [tel 46 80 60 00; post@fordecamping.no; www.fordecamping.no]** Site is on NE o'skirts Forde. At rndabt on E39at Havstad foll sp 'Hospital', site on R in 1km; well sp. Med, mkd pitch, some hdstg, pt shd; htd wc; chem disp; mv service pnt; shwrs inc; baby facs; fam bthrm; el pnts (16A) inc; lndtte; shop; rest; cooking facs; playgrnd; rv sw adj; TV rm; some statics; phone; Eng spkn; adv bkg; quiet; ccard acc; CKE/CCI. "Pleasant, peaceful site." ♦ ltd 1 Jan-29 Feb, 15 Apr-1 Oct. NOK 304                        2013*

**FREDRIKSTAD** *1C4* (2km SE Coastal) *59.20116, 10.96263* **Fredrikstad Motel & Camping (OF20), Torsnesveien 16, 1630 Fredrikstad (Østfold) [tel 69 32 03 15; fax 69 32 36 66; eivind.enger@hotelcity.no; www. fredrikstadmotel.no]** Fr S on Rv110 at rndabt bef lge span bdge (TO at bdge) foll sp Gamlebyen/Torsnes, site on L. Or foll brown sps for old city. Med, hdstg, pt sl, pt shd; htd wc; chem disp; baby facs; fam bthrm; shwrs inc; el pnts (10A) NOK50; lndtte; shop; cooking facs; playgrnd; pool 100m; beaches adj; cycle hire; TV; dogs; adv bkg; quiet but poss noise fr late arr fr ferry; CKE/CCI. "Guided tours to craft indus; sh walk to lovely walled city; v cr water festival (2nd w/end July)." ♦ 1 Jun-31 Aug. NOK 200                        2011*

**FREDRIKSTAD** *1C4* (10km SE Coastal) *59.13942, 11.03855* **Bevo Camping, Bevoveien 31, 1634 Gamle Fredrikstad [tel 69 34 92 15; info@bevo.no; www.bevo.no]** Avoid app fr Fredrikstad. Fr E6 junc 4, take RV110 (Fredrikstad) then L on RV111 & L on RV107 (Torsnesveien). Foll signs to campsite. Sm, mkd pitch, pt shd; wc; chem disp; shwrs 10kr; el pnts; lndtte rm; shop; snacks; sw sand beach adj; poss cr; quiet; CCI. "Isolated site on Oslo Fjord; 15 mins to Gamle Frederikstad by car." 28 Apr-8 Sep. NOK 260                        2014*

**FREDVANG (LOFOTEN ISLANDS) see Ramberg** *2E2*

⊞ **GAUPNE** 1B2 (500m S Rural) 61.40056, 7.30076 **Sandvik Camping (SF20), 6868 Gaupne (Sogn og Fjordane)** [tel 57 68 11 53; fax 57 68 16 71; sandvik@pluscamp.no; www.pluscamp.no/sandvik] Site sp N of Rv55 (Sogndal/Lom) after leaving Gaupne. Med, pt shd; htd wc; chem disp; baby facs; shwrs NOK10; el pnts (16A) (poss earth fault); lndtte (inc dryer); shop; snacks; rest 500m; bar; playgrnd; games area; TV; quiet; ccard acc. "Vg; ltd facs early ssn & poss stretched if site full; lovely, peaceful site; gd touring base." ♦ ltd NOK 150 2009*

⊞ **GEILO** 1B3 (1km NE Urban) 60.54251, 8.23495 **Breie Hytter & Camping, Lauvrudvegen 11, 3580 Geilomoen, Geilo** [tel 32 09 04 12 or 97 16 46 01 (mob); fax 32 09 10 44; post@breiehytter.no; www.breiehytter.no] Fr Geilo take RV7 twds Gol & Sundre. Site sp, take R into Lauvrudvegen. Sm, unshd; wc; chem disp; shwr; el pnts inc; shop 1.5km; rest 1.5km; bar 1.5km; 30% statics; quiet; CCI. "Vg for long or sh stays; pleasant, well kep site in residential area; helpful owner." NOK 170 2014*

⊞ **GEILO** 1B3 (400m S Rural) 60.52915, 8.20705 **Geilo Camping, Skurdalsveien 23, 3580 Geilo (Buskerud)** [tel 32 09 07 33; fax 32 09 11 56; post@geilocamping.no; www.geilocamping.no] Fr W on Rv7 at rndabt in town cent turn R (S) onto Rv40 sp Kongsberg, site on R in 300m by rv. Sm, mkd pitch, hdstg, some terr; pt shd; wc; chem disp; shwrs NOK10; el pnts (10A) NOK30; lndtte (inc dryer); shop; tradsmn; snacks; rv beach adj; fishing; 70% statics; bus 300m; Eng spkn; quiet; ccard acc. "Mountain views; walking & fishing cent; poss muddy after heavy rain; san facs tired." NOK 220 2009*

## "There aren't many sites open at this time of year"

If you're travelling outside peak season remember to call ahead to check site opening dates – even if the entry says 'open all year'.

**GEIRANGER** 1B1 (2.9km NNW Rural) 62.11548, 7.18437 **Grande Hytteutleige og Camping, 6216 Geiranger (Møre og Romsdal)** [tel 70 26 30 68; office@grande-hytteutleige.no; www.grande-hytteutleige.no] Head N on Rv63, in 2.3km turn L at the foot of zigzags, then 1st R. Site on the L. Sm, pt sl; htd wc; shwr 15nok; El pnts (16A); lndtte; cooking facs; internet; wifi; Eng spkn; quiet; ccard acc. "Friendly staff; conv for Fjord cruise, vg site." May-Oct. NOK 250 2014*

**GEIRANGER** 1B1 (500m S Rural) 62.09998, 7.20421 **Camping Geiranger, 6216 Geiranger (Møre og Romsdal)** [tel/fax 70 26 31 20; post@geirangercamping.no; www.geirangercamping.no] Site on fjord edge in vill. On Rv63 Eidsdal-Geiranger take lower rd thro vill to site on R & on both sides of rv. Rv63 not suitable for c'vans - steep hill & hairpins, use ferry fr Hellesylt. Lge, pt sl, unshd; wc; chem disp; mv service pnt; shwrs NOK10; ltd el pnts (16A) NOK35; lndtte (inc dryer); tradsmn high ssn; BBQ; cooking facs; playgrnd; wifi; dogs; poss cr; Eng spkn; quiet but noise of waterfall; ccard acc; CKE/CCI; No adv bkgs; "Busy site in superb location, gd touring base, gd boat trips on fjord, facs (inc el pnts) ltd if site full." ♦ 20 May-20 Sep. NOK 1514 2013*

⊞ **GOL** 1C2 (2.5km S Rural) 60.70023, 9.00416 **Gol Campingsenter (BU17), Heradveien 7, 3550 Gol (Buskerud)** [tel 32 07 41 44; fax 32 07 53 96; gol@pluscamp.no; www.golcamp.no] Ent on R of Rv7 fr Gol twd Nesbyen. Lge, pt sl, unshd; htd wc; mv service pnt; baby facs; fam bthrm; sauna; shwrs inc; el pnts (16A) inc; lndtte (inc dryer); gas; shop; supmkt 2km; rest, snacks; bar; cooking facs; playgrnd; htd pool; padding pool; rv sw 2km; games area; wifi; TV rm; poss noisy; ccard acc; CKE/CCI. "Excel; lge extn with full facs across main rd - modern & clean." ♦ NOK 245 (4 persons) 2010*

## "That's changed – Should I let The Club know?"

If you find something on site that's different from the site entry, fill in a report and let us know. See www.caravanclub.co.uk/europereport.

⊞ **GOL** 1C2 (2km W Rural) 60.69161, 8.91909 **Personbråten Camping, 3550 Gol (Buskerud)** [tel 32 07 59 70; leif.personbraten@c2i.net] Fr Gol to Geilo on Rv7, on L on rvside. Med, pt shd; wc; chem disp (wc); shwrs inc; el pnts (10A; lndtte; BBQ; cooking facs; playgrnd; fishing; cycling; rv sw 1km; adv bkg; Eng spkn; CKE/CCI. "On rvside; v pleasant; poss noise fr rd & rv; honesty box if office unmanned; excel NH." 2009*

**GRANLI see Kongsvinger** 1D3

**GRANVIN** 1B2 (2km N Rural) 60.59220, 6.80680 **Camping Espelandsdalen, 5736 Granvin (Hordaland)** [tel 56 52 51 67; fax 56 52 59 62; post@espelandsdalencamping.no; www.espelandsdalencamping.no] Fr Granvin on Rv13, take Rv572 sp Espelandsdalen, narr rd. Sm, pt sl, unshd; htd wc; chem disp; shwrs NOK5; el pnts (10A) NOK35; shops 13km; cooking facs; playgrnd; lake sw; some statics; dogs; adv bkg; quiet. "Ideal for Ulvik & Voss area." 1 May-1 Sep. NOK 130 2009*

⊞ **GRIMSBU** 1C2 (N Rural) 62.15546, 10.17198 **Grimsbu Turistsenter, 2582 Grimsbu (Oppland)** [tel 62 49 35 29; fax 62 49 35 62; mail@grimsbu.no; www.grimsbu.no] On Rv29 11km E of Folldal, well sp. Med, pt sl, pt shd; htd wc; chem disp; mv service pnt; sauna; private san facs avail; shwrs NOK10; el pnts (16A) NOK30; lndtte (inc dryer); shop; rest, snacks; BBQ; cooking facs; playgrnd; lake sw 1.5km; rv fishing; cycle & boat hire; fitness rm; wifi; TV rm; Eng spkn; adv bkg; quiet; ccard acc. "Family-run site; beautiful situation." ♦ NOK 243. (3 persons) (CChq acc) 2014*

⊞ **GRIMSTAD** 1B4 (5km NE Coastal) 58.36888, 8.63722 **Moysand Familiecamping, Moy, 4885 Grimstad (Aust-Agder)** [tel 91 19 75 94; mail@moysand-familiecamping.no; www.moysand-familiecamping.no] Exit A18 junc 78 onto Rv420 E twd Fevik. Foll site sp on rd to Riksveien, site 2km after Riksveien. Lge, mkd pitch, pt shd; htd wc; baby facs; private san facs avail; shwrs; el pnts metered; lndtte (inc dryer); shop; tradsmn; supmkt 5km; rest; BBQ; cooking facs; playgrnd; fishing; boat hire; TV; some statics; dogs; adv bkg; quiet. ♦ NOK 190 2010*

⊞ **GRONG** *2E3* (2km SW Rural) *64.4604, 12.3137* **Langnes Camping, 7870 Grong (Nord-Trøndelag) [tel 47 68 83 33; langnescamping@hero.no; www.nafcamp.com/langnes-camping]** N on E6 turn off S of bdge over rv on by-pass, site sp. Med, mkd pitch, some hdstg, unshd; htd wc; chem disp; mv service pnt; shwrs NOK10; el pnts (10A) NOK35; lndtte (inc dryer); tradsmn; snacks; rest 3km; BBQ; cooking facs; playgrnd; rv sw & beach nr; rv fishing; drying rm for skiers; games area; games rm; wifi; TV; some statics; Quick Stop pitches; Eng spkn; adv bkg; quiet. "Helpful staff; pleasant, family-run site; free phone to owner if site clsd; gd facs." ◆ NOK 140      2011*

**GUDVANGEN** *1B2* (500m SW Rural) *60.87206, 6.82873* **Vang Camping, 5747 Gudvangen (Sogn og Fjordane) [tel 57 63 39 26; fax 41 26 52 12; post@vang-camping. no; www.vang-camping.no]** At S end of of Nærøy Fjord on E16 at edge of vill. Sm, some hdstg, unshd; wc; chem disp/mv service pnt at Shell g'ge 1km; shwrs NOK5; el pnts (16A) NOK30 (poss no earth); lndtte; shop 1km; rest 1km at ferry; Eng spkn; quiet but some rd noise; no ccard acc; CKE/CCI. "Immac site in beautiful valley with waterfalls; spectacular scenery; cruises on adj fjord; bus to Flam." 15 May-15 Sep. NOK 243      2014*

⊞ **GULLESFJORDBOTN (VESTERALEN ISLANDS)** *2F2* (N Coastal) *68.53213, 15.72611* **Gullesfjordbotn Camping, Våtvoll, 8409 Gullesfjordbotn [tel 77 09 11 10; fax 77 09 11 11; post@gullesfjordcamping.no; www. gullesfjordcamping.no]** Fr S on E10 then rd 82. At rndabt just bef Gullesfjordbotn take 2nd exit to site, wel sp. Sm, hdstg, unshd; htd wc; chem disp; mv service pnt; sauna; shwrs NOK10; el pnts (16A) NOK50; lndtte (inc dryer); shop; snacks high ssn; cooking facs; sw & shgl beach adj; fishing; boat hire; phone; poss cr; Eng spkn; ccard acc; CKE/CCI. "On edge of fjord; liable to flood after heavy rain; mountain views; gd san facs; friendly owners." NOK 150      2009*

**HALSA** *2E2* (S Coastal) *66.73930, 13.51661* **Furøy Camping, Furøy 6, 8178 Halsa (Nordland) [tel 75 75 05 25; fax 75 75 03 36; post@furoycamp.no; www.furoycamp.no]** Foll Rv17 S fr Ornes, at Forøy ferry x-ing strt on, foll rd sp to site. Sm, pt sl; htd wc; chem disp; shwrs NOK10; el pnts (16A) NOK25; lndtte; kiosk; shop 1km; rest; bar; BBQ; cooking facs; shgl beach adj; fishing; boat hire; some statics; dogs; phone; Eng spkn; adv bkg; quiet. "Lovely position; arr early for prime pitch, site fills up quickly after 1730 high ssn; archaeological site adj; 15km Svartisen glacier; san facs stretched when site full." ◆ 1 May-30 Sep. NOK 175      2009*

**HAMALVOLL see Os I Osterdalen** *1D1*

**HAMMERFEST** *2G1* (1km E Urban) *70.65890, 23.71335* **Storvannet Camping, Storvannsveien 103, 9615 Hammerfest (Finnmark) [tel 78 41 10 10; storvannet@ yahoo.no]** Descend into & cont thro town. Turn R immed after x-ing rv bdge. Site at top of Storvannet lake nr mouth of Rv Storelva. Sp. Med, some hdstg; pt sl; unshd; htd wc; chem disp; shwrs NOK10; el pnts NOK40; lndtte (inc dryer); shop 3km; rest 3km; BBQ; cooking facs; sw adj; fishing; dogs; poss cr; Eng spkn; quiet; 10% red +3 days; CKE/CCI. "Vg; by attractive lake; 2km out of town." ◆ 1 Jun-15 Sep. NOK 230      2014*

**HAMRESANDEN see Kristiansand** *1B4*

**HARRAN** *2E3* (Rural) *64.55916, 12.48376* **Harran Camping, 7873 Harran (Nord-Trøndelag) [tel 74 33 29 90; harrancamping@gmail.com]** Site E of E6 N of Grong in cent Harran behind Statoil filling stn. Med, pt shd; wc; chem disp; mv service pnt; baby facs; fam bthrm; shwrs NOK10; el pnts (10A) NOK50; gas; lndtte (inc dryer); shop & rest 500m; BBQ; playgrnd; fishing; TV; phone; Eng spkn; quiet but some rd noise. "Pleasant site; lovely location." ◆ 1 May-15 Sep. NOK 150      2009*

⊞ **HARSTAD (VESTERALEN ISLANDS)** *2F2* (5km S Coastal) *68.77231, 16.57878* **Harstad Camping, Nessevegen 55, 9411 Harstad [tel 77 07 36 62; fax 77 07 35 02; postmaster@harstad-camping.no; www.harstad-camping.no]** Sp fr E10/Rv83. Med, pt sl, unshd; wc; chem disp; shwrs NOK10; el pnts (16A) inc; shop; snacks 1km; rest 5km; playgrnd; fishing; boating; quiet; ccard acc; CKE/CCI. "San facs poss stretched high ssn; lovely situation." ◆ NOK 260 (6 persons)      2009*

**HAUGE** *1A4* (4km NE Rural) *58.36166, 6.30944* **Bakkaåno Camping, Bakkaveien, Fidje 4380 Hauge i Dalane (Rogaland) [tel 51 47 78 52 / 930 50 219 (mob); visit@ bakkaanocamping.no; www.bakkaanocamping.no]** Heading E fr Hauge on Rv44, over rv & immed turn L & foll site sp. Site on L, recep on R over golf course at white house. Rd narr. Med, pt shd; wc; chem disp; mv service pnt; shwrs NOK1; el pnts (5A) NOK30; shop; cooking facs; sw & fishing adj; 80% statics; Eng spkn; quiet. "Sep area for tourers; friendly, welcoming owners." ◆ ltd Easter-30 Sep. NOK 220.      2013*

**HAUKELAND see Bergen** *1A3*

⊞ **HEIDAL** *1C2* (10km W Rural) *61.73005, 9.12070* **Jotunheim Feriesenter, N2676 Heidal [tel 61 23 49 50; post@jotunheimenferiesenter.no; www. jotunheimenferiesenter.no]** Fr Rv51 turn E at Randsverk onto rd 267. Site on R in approx 2km. Med, pt sl, pt shd; htd wc; chem disp; baby facs; shwrs NOK10; el pnts (12A) NOK45; lndtte (inc dryer); shop 8km; snacks; BBQ; cooking facs; playgrnd; games area; internet; TV; dogs; Eng spkn; adv bkg; quiet; ccard acc; CKE/CCI. "Beautiful surroundings & walks; friendly owners; vg site." ◆ NOK 190      2010*

**HELLESYLT** *1B1* (E Coastal) *62.08333, 6.87016* **Hellesylt Camping, 6218 Hellesylt (Møre og Romsdal) [tel 90 20 68 85; fax 70 26 52 10; postmottak@ hellesyltturistsenter.no; www.hellesyltturistsenter.no]** Site on edge of fjord, sp fr cent of vill dir Geiranger. Sm, unshd; htd wc; chem disp; mv service pnt; shwrs NOK10; el pnts (10A) NOK30; lndtte (inc dryer); sm shop; supmkt 100m, rest adj; shgl beach; wifi; 40% statics; dogs; Eng spkn; adv bkg; quiet; no ccard acc; CKE/CCI. "Conv ferry to Geiranger; adj fjord surrounded by mountains - great views; gd rest in local hotel; beautiful church nr." ◆ ltd 15 Apr-30 Sep. NOK 140      2014*

**HJERKINN** *1C1* (1.5km E Rural) *62.22148, 9.57801*
**Camping Hjerkinn Fjellstue, 2661 Hjerkinn (Oppland)**
**[tel 61 21 51 00; fax 61 21 51 01; fjellstue@hjerkinn.no;**
**www.hjerkinn.no]** At Hjerkinn on E6 turn E onto Rv29 to
Folldal for 1km. Site at hotel on L. Med, terr, unshd; wc; chem
disp; sauna; shwrs NOK10; el pnts (10A) inc; lndtte (inc dryer);
shop 1.5km; jacuzzi; rest, snacks; bar; horseriding school adj;
wifi; 30% statics; dogs; no adv bkg; quiet; ccard acc. "O'looks
magnificent mountains; walks of historical interest on Old
King's Rd; excel." ♦ 1 Jun-1 Oct. NOK 200          2009*

**HONEFOSS** *1C3* (8km NW Rural) *60.19441, 10.15145*
**Elvenga Camping, Elvengveien 3, 3518 Hønefoss
(Boskerud) [tel 32 14 43 70; fax 32 13 14 27; elvanga-
camp@hotmail.com]** Fr Hønefoss head twds Gol on Rv7; site
on R in approx 10km. Sm, pt shd; wc; chem disp; baby facs;
shwrs NOK10; el pnts NOK30; lndtte (inc dryer); shop; snacks;
bar; playgrnd; TV; Eng spkn; some traff noise; CKE/CCI. ♦ ltd
1 May-15 Sep. NOK 150          2009*

**HONNINGSVAG** *2H1* (7km N Coastal) *71.02625, 25.89091*
**Nordkapp Camping, 9751 Honningsvåg (Finnmark)
[tel 78 47 33 77; fax 78 47 11 77; post@nordkappcamping.
no; www.nordkappcamping.no]** En rte Nordkapp on E69,
site clearly sp. Sm, unshd; htd wc; chem disp; shwrs NOK5; el
pnts (16A) NOK35; lndtte; shop & 10km; snacks; dogs NOK10;
quiet; ccard acc; red CKE/CCI. "Gd." ♦ 1 May-30 Sep.
NOK 180          2009*

**HORTEN** *1C3* (2km S Rural/Coastal) *59.39430, 10.47483*
**Rørestrand Camping, Parkveien 34, 3186 Horten
(Vestfold) [tel 33 07 33 40; fax 33 07 47 90]** Fr Horten
foll Rv19 for 500m S to rndabt, then foll sp. Sm, sl, unshd;
htd wc; chem disp; baby facs; shwrs NOK10; el pnts (10A)
NOK40; lndtte (inc dryer); shop; snacks; playgrnd; games area;
90% statics; dogs; phone; poss cr; Eng spkn; quiet; ccard acc;
CKE/CCI. "Conv NH en rte Oslo; facs stretched high ssn." ♦ ltd
1 May-15 Sep. NOK 205          2010*

**HOVAG see Kristiansand** *1B4*

**IFJORD** *2H1* (Rural) *70.46294, 27.10636* **Nilsen Gjestgiveri &
Camping, Lebesby, 9740 Ifjord (Finnmark) [tel 78 49 98 17
or 90 88 28 14 (mob); fax 78 49 98 57; halvdanhansen@
hotmail.com]** Behind petrol stn at junc of Rv98 and Rv888;
recep in café/petrol stn/shop. Sm, hdstg, pt shd; htd wc; sauna;
shwrs NOK10; el pnts (10A) inc; snacks; wifi; 10% statics.
"Remote area; basic site & facs; conv NH." 1 Jun-31 Aug.
NOK 150          2009*

**INNHAVET** *2F2* (9km S Rural) *67.90305, 15.88076*
**Tømmerneset Camping, Tømmernes, 8260 Innhavet
(Nordland) [tel 75 77 29 55; fax 75 77 29 65; to.ca@online.
no]** Sp on L fr E6 nr Rv835 to Steigen. Med, pt sl, pt shd; wc;
chem disp; mv service pnt; sauna; shwrs NOK10; el pnts (5A)
inc; lndtte (inc dryer); snacks; cooking facs; playgrnd; solarium;
TV; Eng spkn; adv bkg; quiet; CKE/CCI. "Vg; rock carvings adj
to site; museum of Vikings & Iron Age; canoes avail on adj
lake." 1 Jun-31 Aug. NOK 170          2009*

⊞ **JORPELAND** *1A3* (3km SW Rural) *58.99925, 6.0922*
**Preikestolen Camping (RO17), Preikestolvegan 97, 4100
Jørpeland (Horda-Rogaland) [tel 47 48 19 39 50; fax
51 74 80 77; info@preikestolencamping.com; www.
preikestolencamping.com]** Fr S exit Rv13 to Preikestolen
to R, site sp. Rd narr in places, care needed. Med, mkd pitch,
hdstg, unshd; wc; chem disp; mv service pnt; shwrs inc; el pnts
(16A) NOK40; lndtte; shop & 10km; tradsmn; rest, snacks;
bar; playgrnd; rv sw adj; games area; dogs; phone; bus to
Preikestolen parking; poss cr; adv bkg; Eng spkn; quiet; red
long stay; ccard acc; CKE/CCI. "Marvellous views; poss walk to
Pulpit Rock but not easy; conv Stavanger by ferry; excel facs,
esp shwrs; midge repellent ess." ♦ NOK 392          2014*

**KABELVAG (LOFOTEN ISLANDS) see Svolvær** *2F2*

⊞ **KARASJOK** *2H1* (1km SW Rural) *69.46963, 25.48938*
**Camping Karasjok, Kautokeinoveien, 9730 Karasjok
(Finnmark) [tel 78 46 61 35; fax 78 46 66 97;
karasjokcamping@runbox.no/booking@karacamp.no]**
Sp in town; in town & N of rv bdge take Rv92 W dir
Kautokeino, site 900m on L. Sm, pt shd; htd wc; chem disp; mv
service pnt 1km; shwrs NOK5; el pnts (10A) NOK40; lndtte (inc
dryer); shops 1km; playgrnd; wifi; Eng spkn; adv bkg; v quiet;
ccard acc; CKE/CCI. "Youth hostel & cabins on site; gd, clean
site & facs; lge pitches suitable RVs & lge o'fits; sh walk to Sami
park & museum." ♦ NOK 211          2014*

⊞ **KAUTOKEINO** *2G1* (1km S Rural) *68.99760, 23.03662*
**Arctic Motell & Kautokeino Camping, Suomaluodda
16, 9520 Kautokeino (Finnmark) [tel 78 48 54 00; fax
78 48 75 05; samicamp@me.com; www.kauto.no]**
Well sp fr Rv93. Sm, pt sl, unshd; htd wc; shwrs NOK10;
el pnts NOK30; lndtte; shop; rest; 20% statics; poss cr;
Eng spkn; quiet. "No chem disp; Juhls silver gallery worth
visit; gd, friendly site; san facs being improved (2009)."
NOK 180          2009*

⊞ **KILBOGHAMN** *2E2* (3km S Coastal) *66.50667, 13.21608*
**Hilstad Camping, 8752 Kilboghamn (Nordland)
[tel 75 09 71 86; fax 75 09 71 01; post@polarcamp.com/
booking@polarcamp.com; www.polarcamp.com]** N on
Rv17 sp to L just bef Kilboghamn ferry. Sm, hdstg, terr, unshd;
wc; chem disp; shwrs inc; el pnts (10A); lndtte; shop; tradsmn;
rest, snacks; bar; playgrnd; shgl beach adj; fishing; 40% statics;
phone; poss cr; Eng spkn; quiet. "Superb location on Arctic
Circle; ltd san facs in high ssn; fishing/boat trips arranged."
NOK 235          2014*

**KINSARVIK** *1B3* (10km N Rural) *60.44128, 6.77941*
**Ringoy Camping (HO39), 5780 Kinsarvik (Hordaland)
[tel 53 66 39 17; fax 53 66 32 05; torleivr@kinsarvik.
net; www.ringoy-camping.no]** Site on Rv13 halfway bet
Kinsarvik & Brimnes. Do not use 1st access if app fr Brimnes
(v tight turn). Sm, sl, pt terr, unshd; wc; chem disp; mv service
pnt; shwrs NOK10; el pnts (10A) NOK30 (long read req);
BBQ; cooking facs; fishing; boating; dogs; no adv bkg; quiet.
"Delightful meadowland site alongside Hardanger Fjord; no
recep - site yourself, owner calls bet 1900 & 2100." 1 Jun-
15 Sep. NOK 120          2009*

⊞ **KINSARVIK** *1B3* (500m SW Rural/Coastal) *60.37426, 6.71866* **Kinsarvik Camping, RV13, 5780 Kinsarvik (Hordaland) [tel 53 66 32 90; evald@kinsarvikcamping.no; www.kinsarvikcamping.no]** Fr SW edge of vill on rv. At Esso g'ge foll sp uphill fr cent of Kinsarvik. Sm, pt shd; wc; chem disp, mv service pnt at Esso g'ge; baby facs; fam bthrm; shwrs NOK10; el pnts (10A) NOK30 (poss no earth); lndtte; sm shop 400m; snacks; cooking facs; playgrnd; fishing; TV; 80% statics; bus 400m; quiet; CKE/CCI. "Wonderful views over Hardanger Fjord." NOK 284                                    2013*

**KIRKENES** *2H1* (7km S Rural) *69.69911, 29.95000* **Kirkenes Camping, Maggadalen, Ekveien 19, 9912 Hesseng (Finnmark) [tel 78 99 80 28; fax 78 99 23 03; eiri-ols@online.no]** Sp W of Hesseng on E6. Sm, hdstg, pt sl, pt shd; htd wc; chem disp; mv service pnt; shwrs NOK10; el pnts (10A) inc; lndtte (inc dryer); playgrnd; fishing; hiking; TV; some statics; dogs; Eng spkn; CKE/CCI. "Conv for Kirkenes & Russian border; helpful staff; gd site." 1 Jun-1 Sep.  NOK 190    2010*

**KLEPPSTAD (LOFOTEN ISLANDS) see Svolvær** *2F2*

## "I like to fill in the reports as I travel from site to site"

You'll find report forms at the back of this guide, or you can fill them in online at www.caravaclub.co.uk/europereport.

⊞ **KOLVEREID** *2E3* (2km S Coastal) *64.82530, 11.58628* **Kvisterø Kystcamping, 7970 Kolvereid (Nord-Trøndelag) [tel 74 39 67 37; info@kvisteroe.com; www.kvisteroe.com]** Fr Rv17 just N of Foldereid take Rv770 S to Kolvereid. After Kolvereid foll sp ferries (Geisnes/Lund), site sp 1km fr ferries & Hoflesja. Sm, some mkd pitch, some hdstg, unshd; htd wc; chem disp; shwrs inc; el pnts (16A) NOK40; lndtte; shop 1km; snacks; cooking facs; playgrnd; shgl beach adj; fishing; boat hire; games rm; wifi; 40% statics; dogs; phone; Eng spkn; adv bkg; quiet; ccard acc; CKE/CCI. "Vg site; beautiful views." ◆ ltd NOK 150                      2009*

⊞ **KONGSBERG** *1C3* (6km N Rural) *59.71683, 9.61133* **Pikerfoss Camping, Svendsplassveien 2, 3614 Kongsberg (Buskerud) [tel 32 72 49 78 or 91 19 07 41; mail@pikerfoss.no/erikfred@online.no; www.pikerfoss.no]** Fr E134 in Kongsberg turn N bef x-ring rv & go N bet rv (on L) & rlwy line (on R) on Bærvergrendveien. Site on R just after x-ing rlwy line. Sm, mkd pitch, pt shd; htd wc; chem disp; shwrs inc; el pnts (10A) NOK30; lndtte; shop, rest, snacks, bar 6km; playgrnd; 75% statics; Eng spkn; quiet; Ccard acc. "Modern, clean facs; lge pitches; facs stretched high ssn; excel." NOK 160    2014*

**KONGSVINGER** *1D3* (8km SE Rural) *60.11786, 12.05208* **Sigernessjøen Familiecamping, Strenelsrud Gård, Arko-Vegen, 2210 Granli (Hedmark) [tel 62 82 72 05; fax 62 82 72 04; post@golfcamping.no; www.golfcamping.no]** On N side of Rv2 Kongsvinger to Swedish border, well sp. Med, pt sl, pt shd; htd wc; chem disp; baby facs; shwrs inc; el pnts (10A) NOK40; lndtte (inc dryer); playgrnd; lake sw adj; golf adj; wifi; 30% statics; Eng spkn; quiet. "Gd." 1 May-30 Sep. NOK 250                                    2010*

**KOPPANG** *1D2* (1.5km W Rural) *61.57163, 11.01745* **Camping Koppang, 2480 Koppang (Hedmark) [tel 62 46 02 34; fax 62 46 12 34; info@koppangcamping.no; www.koppangcamping.no]** Fr Rv3, 25km S of Atna, turn onto Rv30; site on L soon after Shell stn & immed bef rv bdge. Med, pt sl, pt shd; wc; chem disp; baby facs; shwrs NOK10; el pnts (16A) NOK25; gas; lndtte (inc dryer); shop; snacks; rest 100m; cooking facs; playgrnd; fishing; wifi; TV; some statics; dogs; Eng spkn; adv bkg; quiet; no ccard acc. ◆ ltd 1 May-30 Sep. NOK 175      2010*

**KRISTIANSAND** *1B4* (12km NE Coastal) *58.19011, 8.08283* **Hamresanden Camping, Hamresandveien 3, 4656 Hamresanden (Vest-Agder) [tel 38 14 42 80; fax 38 14 42 81; info@hamresanden.com; www.hamresanden.com]** Fr E18 foll sp Kjevik airport then Hamresanden & site. Lge, pt shd; htd wc; chem disp; fam bthrm; shwrs NOK15; el pnts (10A) inc; lndtte; rest, snacks; bar; cooking facs; playgrnd; htd pool; waterslides; sand beach & sw adj; watersports; tennis; boat & cycle hire; games area; TV; 10% statics; dogs; bus; poss cr; Eng spkn; noise fr airport; ccard acc. ◆ 1 May-30 Sep.  NOK 295      2014*

**KRISTIANSAND** *1B4* (2km E Coastal) *58.14701, 8.0303* **Camping Roligheden, Framnesveien, 4632 Kristiansand (Vest-Agder) [tel 38 09 67 22; fax 38 09 11 17; roligheden@roligheden.no; www.roligheden.no]** Sp fr E18 on N side of town. Lge, pt sl, pt shd; wc; chem disp; mv service pnt; shwrs NOK40; el pnts (25A) NOK40; lndtte; supmkt 400m; rest adj; playgrnd; sand beach adj; 5% statics; bus; poss cr; Eng spkn; quiet; ccard acc; red CKE/CCI. "Conv for ferry & exploring Kristiansand & district; 40 min walk to town; poss travellers; NH/sh stay only; site v run down." 31 May-1 Sep. NOK 260                                    2014*

⊞ **KRISTIANSAND** *1B4* (12km E Rural) *58.12187, 8.06568* **Kristiansand Feriesenter, Dvergsnesveien 571, 4639 Kristiansand (Vest-Agder) [tel 38 04 19 80; fax 38 04 19 81; post@kristiansandferiesenter.no; www.dvergsnestangen.no]** Turn S off E18 jnc 91, 6km E of Kristiansand after Varoddbrua onto Rv401, cont for 5.5km foll sps to site. Rd narr last 3km. Lge, mkd pitch, sl, shd; htd wc; chem disp; mv service pnt; baby facs; shwrs NOK12 pre paid; el pnts (16A) inc; lndtte; shop; snacks; cooking facs; playgrnd; sw in fjord but rocky; fishing; boat hire; TV; phone; poss cr; quiet; ccard acc; CKE/CCI. "Gd NH; conv for ferry (20 mins); beautiful location; helpful, friendly staff." ◆ NOK 417      2014*

⊞ **KRISTIANSAND** *1B4* (16km E Coastal) *58.12551, 8.2310* **Skottevik Feriesenter (AA1), Hæstadsvingen, 4770 Høvåg (Aust-Agder) [tel 37 26 90 30; fax 37 26 90 33; post@skottevik.no; www.skottevik.no]** Fr Kristiansand, take E18 E, turn onto Rv401 twd Høvåg; site sp. Lge, pt shd; wc; chem disp; mv service pnt; private bathrms avail; shwrs NOK10; el pnts (10A) NOK45; gas; lndtte; shop; snacks & bar high ssn; rest 3km; playgrnd; htd pool; paddling pool; beach; 9-hole golf course; wifi; entmnt; poss cr; Eng spkn; adv bkg; quiet; ccard acc; CKE/CCI. "Beautiful area." ◆ NOK 205      2013*

⊞ **KRISTIANSUND** *1B1* (4km N Rural) *63.12543, 7.74106* **Atlanten Motel & Camping, Dalaveien 22, 6501 Kristiansund (Møre og Romsdal) [tel 71 67 11 04; fax 71 67 24 05; resepsjonen@atlanten.no; www.atlanten. no]** Fr Atlantic Rd (Atlanterhavsveien) & Bremsnes-Kristiansund ferry, foll sp on leaving ferry 5km to site. Med, terr, hdstg, pt shd; htd wc; chem disp; mv service pnt; baby facs; shwrs inc; el pnts (6A) NOK40; lndtte; shops; BBQ; cooking facs; playgrnd; pool 300m; shgl beach 2km; dogs; phone; Eng spkn; adv bkg; quiet; ccard acc; CKE/CCI. "Conv Kristiansund & fjords; boat trips to Grip Is with Stave Church; site clsd 20-31 Dec." ♦ NOK 170                                                2014*

**KROKELVDALEN see Tromsø** *2F1*

**KROKSTRANDA** *2F2* (N Rural) *66.46868, 15.08318* **Krokstrand Camping, Saltfjellveien 1573, 8630 Krokstranda (Nordland) [tel/fax 75 16 60 74; toverakvaag@msn.com]** Nr Krokstrand bdge on E6, 18km S of Artic Circle & approx 50km N of Mo i Rana. Med, pt sl, pt shd; htd wc; chem disp; mv service pnt; baby facs; shwrs NOK5-10; el pnts (10A) NOK30; lndtte (inc dryer); shop; rest; snacks bar; cooking facs; playgrnd; fishing; 20% statics; phone; train; Eng spkn; adv bkg; ccard acc; quiet; CKE/CCI. "Conv Polar Circle Cent; gd." 1 Jun-1 Sep. NOK 280      2014*

**KVAM** *1C2* (6km NW Rural) *61.69133, 9.5955* **Kirketeigen Camping (OP18), Bygdahusvegen 11, 2642 Kvam (Oppland) [tel 61 21 60 90; fax 61 21 60 91; post@ kirketeigen.no; www.kirketeigen.no]** On E6, sp fr both dirs. Sm, pt shd; wc; el pnts inc; lndtte; kiosk; games area; covr'd pool, tennis nrby; 80% statics; some rlwy noise. "Conv Peer Gynt rd, war museum." 15 May-1 Sep. NOK 210      2009*

**KVANNDAL see Granvin** *1B2*

**KVISVIKA** *1B1* (8km NE Coastal) **Magnillen Camping, 6674 Kvisvika (Møre og Romsdal) [tel 71 53 25 59; jarl-mo@ online.no; www.magnillen.no]** Fr W turn L off E39 approx 5km after Vettafjellet (N); thro Kvisvika & after another 9km turn L into site; sp. Sm, unshd; wc; chem disp; mv service pnt; serviced pitches; shwrs NOK10; el pnts (10A) NOK30; gas; lndtte; shop 8km; snacks; BBQ; playgrnd; lake sw & sand beach adj; boat hire; 50% statics; Eng spkn; adv bkg; quiet; ccard acc; red long stay; CKE/CCI. "Site adj sm harbour; gd views." ♦ ltd NOK 130                                                2009*

**LAERDALSOYRI** *1B2* (400m NW Rural/Coastal) *61.10056, 7.47031* **Lærdal Ferie & Fritidspark, Grandavegen 5, 6886 Lærdal (Sogn og Fjordane) [tel 57 66 66 95; fax 57 66 87 81; info@laerdalferiepark.com; www. laerdalferiepark.com]** Site on N side of Lærdal off Rv5/E16 adj Sognefjord. Med, unshd; htd wc; chem disp; mv service pnt; baby facs; fam bthrm; shwrs NOK5; el pnts NOK40 (poss no earth); lndtte (inc dryer); shop; supmkt 400m; rest high ssn; snacks; bar; BBQ; cooking facs; playgrnd; shgl beach adj; boat & cycle hire; tennis; games area; games rm; golf 12km; wifi; TV rm; dogs; phone; Eng spkn; quiet; ccard acc; red long stay/ CKE/CCI. "Modern, clean, gd value site; excel san & cooking facs; lovely location adj fjord ferry terminal & nr attractive vill; gd touring base; friendly, helpful owners - will open on request outside dates shown; nice site next to Fjord." ♦ 27 Mar-25 Oct. NOK 291 (CChq acc)                          2014*

**LAKSELV** *2G1* (1km NE Rural) *70.05100, 25.00860* **Solstad Camping, 9700 Lakselv (Finnmark) [tel 78 46 14 04; fax 78 46 12 14]** Fr N thro town & cont on E6, at rndabt take Rv98. Site on R in 500m. Sm, shd; wc; chem disp at Esso g'ge in town; sauna; shwrs inc; el pnts inc; lndry rm; shops 1km; cooking facs; dogs; phone; Eng spkn; quiet; ccard acc. "Poss poor/red facs low ssn; mosquitoes; last site bef Tana Bru; NH only." 30 May-30 Sep. NOK 180                       2009*

**LANGFJORDBOTN** *2G1* (1km S Rural) *70.02781, 22.2817* **Altafjord Camping, 9545 Langfjordbotn (Finnmark) [tel/ fax 78 43 28 24; post@altafjord-camping.no; www. altafjord-camping.no]** On E6, 600m S of exit to Bognelv, site adj to fjord across E6, sp. Dist by rd fr Alta 80km. Med, hdstg, terr, unshd; htd wc; serviced pitches; chem disp; sauna; shwrs NOK5; el pnts (16A); gas; lndtte; shops adj; tradsmn; cooking facs; sand & shgl beach; fjord sw & fishing; cycle hire; TV rm; 50% statics; dogs; phone; poss cr; Eng spkn; no adv bkg; quiet; ccard acc. "Friendly owner; excel views; boat hire; mountaineering." 1 Jun-1 Sep.                      2009*

⊞ **LARVIK** *1C4* (1km S Urban) *59.04902, 10.03330* **Larvic Bobilparkering, Tollerudden, Larvik (Vestfold)** Fr E18 exit at Rv303 twd Larvik. At rndabt take 1st exit onto Strandpromenaden. Sm, hdstg, unshd; el pnts (3A); BBQ; 0% statics; dogs. "Gd; parking lot for M'vans; NH only." NOK 120                                                2014*

**LARVIK** *1C4* (10km S Rural/Coastal) *58.97381, 9.96795* **Kjærstranda Familiecamping, Nalumruta, 3294 Stavern (Vestfold) [tel 33 19 57 50 or 91 77 12 01 (mob); fax 33 19 57 50; kjaerstr@online.no; www.kjarstranda.no]** Fr Larvik W on Rv303 & turn L (S) to Stavern; thro Stavern for approx 6km; then L to Skarabakken; 2nd site on L. Lge, unshd; wc; chem disp; mv service pnt; baby facs; shwrs NOK15; el pnts (8A) NOK45; lndtte (inc dryer); shop 6km; snacks; playgrnd; beach adj; TV; 75% statics; dogs; Eng spkn; CKE/CCI. "Fair sh stay/NH." 1 May-1 Sep. NOK 215      2009*

**LARVIK** *1C4* (10km S Coastal) **Trane Camping, Hummerbakken, 3294 Stavern (Vestfold)** Exit E18 onto Rv303 (Larvik); foll Rv302 (sp Helgeroa); in 13km, turn L onto Rv301 (sp Stavern); in 2km, R nr church (Hummerbakken); site on R in 2km. Sm, unshd; wc; chem disp; shwrs; el pnts (10A); lndtte; playgrnd; 30% statics; phone; Eng spkn; CKE/CCI. "Site yourself if recep clsd." ♦ ltd Jun-Sep.                2009*

⊞ **LARVIK** *1C4* (37.5km SW Coastal) *59.00872, 9.70290* **Rognstranda Camping, Rognsveien 146, 3960 Stathelle (Vestfold) [tel 35 97 39 11 / 92 04 56 61 (mob); post@ rognstrandacamping.no; www.rognstrandacamping.no]** Fr Larvik head SW on E18 for 34km. Turn L onto Tangvallveien, R onto Rognsveien. After 1.4km turn L. Then take 2nd L and 1st R. Site on L. Lge, pt sl, unshd; htd wc; mv service pnt; shwr; el pnts (2 pin); lndtte (inc dryer); shop; sandy beach adj; twin axles; poss cr; Eng spkn; adv bkg; CKE/CCI. "Coastal walks; clean modern facs; 2 areas for sh stay; site popular with MH for NH; vg." NOK 320                                      2014*

⊞ **LAUKVIK (LOFOTEN ISLANDS)** 2F2 (Coastal) 68.38991, 14.42216 Skippergaarden Camping, 8315 Laukvik [tel/ fax 97 10 66 36; laukvikcamping@gmail.com; www. skippergaarden.no] Approx 26km N of Svolvær in Laukvik; sp fr E10. Sm, some hdstg, pt shd; wc; chem disp; mv service pnt; shwrs NOK20; el pnts (16A) NOK25; lndtte; shop, rest 200m; playgrnd; few statics; poss cr; Eng spkn; quiet. "Sh walk to view point for midnight sun; pleasant site with 'local' atmosphere; site in need of attention (2014) but is adequate." NOK 200                              2014*

⊞ **LILLEHAMMER** 1C2 (2km S Urban) 61.10275, 10.46278 Camping Lillehammer, Dampsagveien 47, 2609 Lillehammer (Oppland) [tel 61 25 33 33; fax 61 25 33 65; resepsjon@lillehammer-camping.no; www.lillehammer-camping.no] Exit E6 at Lillehammer Sentrum. Turn 1st R at 1st rndabt, foll rd around Strandtorget shopping cent, cont approx 1.5km along lakeside rd. Med, mkd pitch, some hdstg, unshd; wc; chem disp; mv service pnt; baby facs; shwrs NOK10; el pnts (10A) inc (check earth); gas; lndtte Inc dryer); shop 2km; playgrnd; pool 2km; internet; TV rm; statics; dogs; phone; poss cr; Eng spkn; adv bkg; quiet; ccard acc; red CKE/ CCI. "Excel san facs, site adj Lake Mjøsa; gd views, conv town & skiing areas; site adj to c'van cent, spare parts etc; excel." ♦ NOK 240                              2009*

## "We must tell The Club about that great site we found"

Get your site reports in by mid-August and we'll do our best to get your updates into the next edition.

**LILLESAND** 1B4 (1km E Rural) 58.2560, 8.3896 Tingsaker Familiecamping, Øvre Tingsaker, 4790 Lillesand (Aust-Agder) [tel 37 27 04 21; fax 37 27 01 47; post@ tingsakercamping.no; www.tingsakercamping.no] E18 take 1st R at Texaco petrol stn past turn for Lillesand. Med, pt sl, unshd; htd wc; chem disp; shwrs NOK10; el pnts (10A) NOK35; lndtte; shop; snacks; playgrnd; sand beach; boating; cycle hire; TV; poss cr; adv bkg; quiet; ccard acc. "Gd situation, friendly owner; rather cramped." ♦ 1 May-31 Aug. NOK 255                              2010*

**LOEN** 1B2 (1km SW Rural) 61.86558, 6.83303 Lo-Vik Camping, 6878 Loen (Sogn og Fjordane) [tel 57 87 76 19; fax 57 87 78 11; lo-vik@c2i.net; www.lo-vik.no] On lake side of Rv60. Med, unshd; htd wc; chem disp; shwrs NOK5; el pnts (10-16A) NOK35; lndtte; shop & 300m; tradsmn; rest adj; snacks; playgrnd; pool in hotel opp; sw adj; TV rm; 50% statics; dogs; poss cr; Eng spkn; adv bkg; some rd noise; red long stay; CKE/CCI. "Beautiful views; field adj to fjord exclusively for tourers." ♦ 20 May-15 Sep. NOK 160           2009*

**LOM** 1C2 (300m E Rural) 61.83846, 8.5709 Camping Nordal Turistsenter, 2686 Lom (Oppland) [tel 61 21 93 00; fax 61 21 93 01; booking@nordalturistsenter.no; www. nordalturistsenter.no] In cent Lom at x-rds R of Rv15. Ent by rndabt bet Esso stn & recep. Site at foot of Sognefjell Pass. Med, pt shd; htd wc; chem disp; mv service pnt; baby facs; fam bthrm; sauna; shwrs NOK10; el pnts (10A) (no earth); lndtte; shop adj; rest; snacks adj; bar; cooking facs; playgrnd; TV rm; some statics; dogs; Eng spkn; adv bkg; ccard acc; CKE/ CCI. "Split level site; bottom level quiet; top level adj to recep - often noisy due to rd noise & w/end coach parties; gd, modern san facs; mosquitoes troublesome in hot weather; busy tourist area." 15 May-30 Sep. NOK 328            2014*

**LOM** 1C2 (19km SW Rural) 61.72099, 8.34857 Bøverdalen Vandrerhjem & Galdesand Camping, 2687 Bøverdalen (Oppland) [tel/fax 61 21 20 64] On Rv55 S of junc with Rv15. Site sp in vill just bef Co-op shop. Sm, pt shd, unshd; wc; shwrs; chem disp; el pnts; lndtte; rest; Eng spkn; quiet. "Immac site." Opens May 21. NOK 120                    2009*

**LOM** 1C2 (7.5km NW Rural) 61.8700, 8.45295 Gjeilo Camping, 2690 Skjåk (Oppland) [tel 61 21 30 32; s.gjeilo@ online.no] Site on R of Rv15 fr Lom, sp. Med, pt sl, pt shd; htd wc; chem disp; shwrs NOK5; el pnts (10A) NOK25; lndtte (inc dryer); shop 3.5km; snacks; cooking facs; playgrnd; lake sw & sand beach adj; kayak hire; 20% statics; phone; Eng spkn; adv bkg; quiet; CKE/CCI. "Undulating site on lake; gd." 1 Jun-1 Sep. NOK 120                              2010*

**LOM** 1C2 (12km NW Rural) Storøya Camping, Rv15, 2690 Skjåk (Oppland) [tel 61 21 43 51; post@storoyacamping. com; www.storoyacamping.com] Site clearly sp N of Rv15. Sm, pt shd; htd wc; shwrs; el pnts (10A); some statics; quiet. "Friendly, little site with basic facs; excel san facs (2014)." 15 May-15 Sep. NOK 200                    2014*

**LUSTER see Skjolden** 1B2

**MAJAVATN** 2E3 (500m S Rural) 65.16238, 13.3659 Majavatn Camping, 8683 Majavatn (Nordland) [tel 47 28 94 69; marianne@majavatncamping.no; www. majavatncamping.no] S on E6 fr Trofors for approx 45km, site on R on lakeside. Sm, pt sl, pt shd; htd wc; fam bthrm; shwrs NOK15; el pnts (10A) NOK20; lndry rm; BBQ; cooking facs; lake sw; fishing; boating; Eng spkn; rd & rlwy noise. "Rlwy stn nr; few touring pitches - rec arr early." ♦ ltd 1 Jun-31 Aug. NOK 100                              2009*

**MALMEFJORDEN see Molde** 1B1

**MALVIK** 1D1 (2.5km E Rural) 63.43243, 10.70778 Storsand Gård Camping (ST68), 7563 Malvik (Sør-Trøndelag) [tel 73 97 63 60; fax 73 97 73 46; post@storsandcamping. no; www.storsandcamping.no] On N side of E6 N, site sp. Rec use E6 toll rd fr S, 2nd exit after tunnel. Many lge speed humps on local rd Rv950, care needed. Lge, unshd; wc; chem disp; shwrs NOK10; el pnts (10A) NOK35; lndtte; shop; cooking facs; rest in hotel adj; playgrnd; shgl beach; fishing; games area; TV; some statics; phone; poss cr; rlwy noise. ♦ ltd 1 May-1 Sep. NOK 260                              2011*

NORWAY

⊞ **MALVIK** *1D1* (1.5km W Coastal) *63.44064, 10.63978*
**Vikhammer Camping, Vikhammerløkka 4, 7560**
**Vikhammer [tel 73 97 61 64; vikcampi@online.no; www.**
**vikhammer.no]** E fr Trondheim on E6. Immed bef toll plaza
take ramp sp Vikhammer/Ransheim & turn R, then foll sp
Vikhammer. After approx 6km at traff lts cont strt on Rv950 to
rndabt & take 3rd exit sp motel & site. Fr N exit E6 after airport
sp Hell, then Malvik/Hommelvik. Then take Rv950 to site. NB
Many lge speed humps on Rv950, care req. Sm, terr, unshd;
htd wc; chem disp; mv service pnt; shwrs inc; el pnts (16A)
NOK30; shop 1km; tradsmn; rest; bar; BBQ; wifi; 75% statics;
dogs; phone; bus adj; Eng spkn; adv bkg; rd & rlwy noise; ccard
acc; CKE/CCI. "Insuffiicient san facs; site muddy after rain;
migrant workers in statics." ◆ NOK 258                    2014*

**MANDAL** *1B4* (2.5km N Rural) *58.04213, 7.49436* **Sandnes
Camping, Holumsveien 133, 4516 Mandal (Vest-Agder)
[tel 38 26 51 51; sandnescamping@online.no; www.
sandnescamping.com]** On E39 Kristiansand to Stavanger.
Turn N onto Rv455, site on R 1.4km. Med, some hdstg, pt shd;
htd wc; chem disp; mv service pnt; baby facs; shwrs NOK10;
el pnts (16A) NOK40 (poss rev pol); lndtte; shop, rest, snacks,
bar in Mandal; cooking facs; BBQ; sand beach 2.5km; rv sw
& beach nr; fishing; boating; 5% statics; dogs; wifi NOK20;
phone; Eng spkn; adv bkg; quiet; CKE/CCI. "Excel, well-kept
site; friendly, helpful owners; superb scenery; nature trails thro
adj pine forest; Mandal pretty town with longest sandy beach
in Norway, conv Kristiansand ferry & Lindesnes, Norway's most
S point." ◆ 1 May-1 Sep. NOK 296.                         2014*

**MAURANGER see Odda** *1A3*

⊞ **MAURVANGEN** *1C2* (Rural) *61.48838, 8.84176*
**Maurvangen Hyttegrend Camping, Besseggen Fjellpark,
2680 Maurvangen VÅGÅ (Oppland) [tel 61 23 89 22; fax
61 23 89 58; post@maurvangen.no; www.maurvangen.
no]** At rv bdge turn off Rv51. Foll sp. Med, pt hdstg, pt sl, pt
shd; wc; mv service pnt; chem disp; baby facs; fam bthrm;
shwrs NOK15; el pnts (10A) inc; lndtte; shop; rest, snacks;
BBQ; cooking facs; playgrnd; lake sw 5km; fishing; cycling;
TV; phone; Eng spkn; adv bkg; quiet; CKE/CCI. "White water
rafting; gd views; rd 51 poss clsd Nov to mid-May; gd hillwalking cent." ◆ NOK 180                                  2013*

**MELHUS** *1C1* (7km NW Coastal) *63.32713, 10.21947* **Øysand
Camping (ST38), Øysandan, 7224 Melhus (Sør-Trøndelag)
[tel 72 87 24 15 or 92 08 71 74 (mob); fax 72 85 22 81;
post@oysandcamping.no; www.oysandcamping.no]**
Fr Melhus, N on E6; then L (W) onto E39; site sp. Med, mkd
pitch, unshd; wc; chem disp (wc); shwrs NOK15; el pnts
(10A) NOK50; lndtte; shop; tradsmn; rest, snacks; bar; BBQ;
cooking facs; playgrnd; lake sw, fishing, boating & beach
adj; games area; wifi; statics; dogs; phone; poss cr; Eng spkn;
noise fr daytrippers; ccard acc; red long stay; CKE/CCI. "Fair
site with gd views; facs stretched if full; next to Fjord; beach
open to day trippers; barrier clsd at night." ◆ ltd 1 May-1 Sep.
NOK 240                                                  2014*

**MEVIK see Ornes** *2E2*

**MO I RANA** *2F2* (16km SW Rural) *66.23307, 13.89178*
**Yttervik Camping, Sørlandsveien 874, 8617 Dalsgrenda
(Nordland) [tel 75 16 45 65 or 90 98 73 55 (mob); fax
75 16 92 57; ranjas@online.no; www.yttervikcamping.no]**
Sp S of Mo i Rana, on W side of E6, cross sm bdge over rlwy -
diff for long o'fits. Sm, mkd pitch, hdstg, unshd; htd wc; chem
disp; shwrs NOK5; el pnts (16A) NOK40 (no earth); lndtte; sm
shop; rest; playgrnd; fishing; 50% statics; dogs; poss cr; Eng
spkn; adv bkg; quiet; ccard acc; CKE/CCI. "Pleasant location on
edge fjord; friendly owners; clean, well-run site." 1 Jun-15 Sep.
NOK 180                                                  2010*

⊞ **MOLDE** *1B1* (3.5km E Rural) *62.74258, 7.2333* **Camping
Kviltorp, Fannestrandveien 140, 6400 Molde (Møre
og Romsdal) [tel 71 21 17 42 or 47 90 14 83 05 (mob);
fax 71 21 10 19; kviltorp.camping@online.no; www.
kviltorpcamping.no]** On app fr S, Rv64 (toll) turn L onto E39/
Rv62, site on L, sp. Nr airport. Med, pt sl, pt shd; htd wc; baby
facs; shwrs NOK10; el pnts (10A) NOK35; gas; lndtte; shop
& adj; rest, snacks; playgrnd; pool 3km; fjord sw adj; fishing;
boating; solarium; TV; phone; Eng spkn; aircraft & rd noise;
ccard acc; CKE/CCI. "Conv Molde; adj Romsdal Fjord (some
pitches avail on fjord-side); wonderful mountain views; excel,
clean facs; poor security - site open to rd on 1 side; helpful
owners." ◆ NOK 245                                       2013*

**MOLDE** *1B1* (8.5km S Coastal) *62.81468, 7.22528* **Bjølstad
Camping, 6445 Malmefjorden [tel 71 26 56 56 or
47 23 79 62 (mob); post@bjolstad.no; www.bjolstad.no]**
E fr Molde on E39 turn L by airport & foll Rv 64 N. Turn L sp
Lindset, site on L in 1km. Sm, pt sl, pt shd; wc; chem disp; mv
service pnt; shwrs NOK10; el pnts (10A) NOK30; shop 1km;
BBQ; cooking facs; playgrnd; shgl beach adj; boat hire; dogs;
Eng spkn; quiet. "Vg site on fjord edge; views." 1 Jun-30 Sep.
NOK 170                                                  2009*

**MORGEDAL** *1B3* (Rural) *59.47478, 8.42138* **Morgedal
Camping, 3848 Morgedal (Telemark) [tel 35 05 41 52;
morgedalcamping@kviteseid.online.no; www.
morgedalcamping.no]** W of Seljord, adj E134, sp. Med, pt
shd; wc; chem disp; shwrs NOK10; el pnts (16A) NOK30; lndtte
(inc dryer); shop 500m; BBQ; cooking facs; lake sw & fishing;
boating; 5% statics; dogs; Eng spkn; quiet; CKE/CCI. "Vg
site; conv Heddal stave church; on site lgest wooden bowl in
world!" 14 May-15 Sep. NOK 150                           2009*

⊞ **MOSJOEN** *2E3* (1km S Rural) *65.83453, 13.21971*
**Mosjøen Camping & Hotel, Kippermoen, 8657 Mosjøen
(Nordland) [tel 75 17 79 00; fax 77 17 79 01; post@
mosjoenhotell.no/mosjoen_camping@hotmail.com;
www.mosjoencamping.no]** E6 by-passes town, well sp
on W side of E6 by rndabt. Fr S only mkd by flag 500m bef
rndabt at start Mosjøen bypass. Med, terr, pt shd; htd wc;
chem disp (wc); mv service pnt; shwrs inc; baby facs; el pnts
(10A) NOK30; lndtte; shop 1km; rest, snacks; bar; playgrnd;
pool; bowling alley; entmnt; TV; wifi; dogs; phone; poss cr; Eng
spkn; adv bkg; rd noise; ccard acc; CKE/CCI. "Clean, v basic
san facs; Gd site; gd kitchen facs and san facs, friendly staff."
◆ NOK 264                                                2014*

⊞ **NAMSOS** *2E3* (4km E Rural) *64.47393, 11.57796* **Namsos Camping, 7800 Namsos (Nord-Trøndelag) [tel 74 27 53 44; fax 74 27 53 93; namsos@pluscamp.no; www.pluscamp. no]** Fr Namsen bdge turn E on Rv17. Site on R in 1.5km beside airfield & lake. Sm, hdstg, pt shd; htd wc; chem disp; mv service pnt; fam bthrm; shwrs NOK5; el pnts (16A) NOK35; lndtte; shop; snacks; playgrnd; boating; TV; 60% statics; phone; no dogs; Eng spkn; quiet; ccard acc; CKE/CCI. "Well-equipped site." ♦ NOK 215                          2009*

**NARVIK** *2F2* (1.5km N Rural) *68.4506, 17.45851* **Camping Narvik, Rombaksveien 75, 8517 Narvik (Nordland) [tel 76 94 58 10; fax 76 94 14 20; narvikcamping@ narvikcamping.com; www.narvikcamping.com]** Sp on E6, site by rd. Med, terr, unshd; wc; chem disp; baby facs; fam bthrm; sauna; shwrs NOK20; el pnts (6-10A) inc (no earth); lndtte; shop; rest; BBQ; TV; phone; poss cr; Eng spkn; adv bkg; rd/rlwy noise; ccard acc; red CKE/CCI. "Facs 'tired' & stretched high ssn (may need to share electrics) & poss unkempt; no privacy in shwrs; walk/cycle to town, 20 mins; 3-level site, chem disp 3rd level only; poor NH/sh stay only." ♦ 1 Mar-30 Sep. NOK 211                          2014*

**NES I ADAL** *1C3* (8.5km S Rural) *60.49379, 10.07103* **Sperillen Camping, Skagnes, 3524 Nes I Ådal (Buskerud) [tel/fax 32 14 32 00; sperillc@start.no; www. sperillencamp.no]** Site sp on E15, 45km N of Hønefoss. Med, mkd pitch, unshd; htd wc; chem disp; fam bthrm; shwrs inc; el pnts (10A) NOK40; lndtte; shop; cooking facs; playgrnd; lake sw & beach; 90% statics; poss cr; Eng spkn; quiet; CKE. "Lovely lakesite position; friendly owner; gd facs for children; RVs acc; if coming out of ssn, give 7 days' notice & owner will open site." ♦ 1 May-1 Oct. NOK 200                          2009*

⊞ **NESBYEN** *1C3* (3.5km N Rural) *60.59881, 9.07928* **Sutøya Feriepark, Hallingdal, 3540 Nesbyen (Buskerud) [tel 32 07 13 97; fax 32 07 01 11; sutferie@online.no; www.sutoyaferiepark.no]** On E side of Rv7, sp. Lge, mkd pitch, terr, pt shd; wc; chem disp; shwrs NOK10; el pnts (10A) NOK35; lndtte (inc dryer); sm shop; rest, snacks; playgrnd; rv adj; trout-fishing; skibus; wifi; 40% statics; Eng spkn; quiet; ccard acc; red CKE/CCI. NOK 170 (4 persons)        2009*

⊞ **NESNA** *2E2* (500m N Coastal) *66.20273, 13.02278* **Nesna Feriecamp & Motell, Sjåberget 3, 8700 Nesna (Nordland) [tel 75 05 65 40; fax 75 05 66 97; nesnafer@online.no; www.arctic-circle-coast.no]** Foll rds E12 & Rv17 fr Mo i Rana to Nesna & foll site sp on ent vill. Med, pt sl, unshd; htd wc; chem disp; mv service pnt; shwrs; el pnts (10A); lndtte (inc dryer0; shop high ssn; rest, snacks 200m; cooking facs; playgrnd; pool 300m; beach; waterslide; cycle hire; games area; wifi; TV rm; quiet; ccard acc; CKE/CCI. "Lovely scenery; boat trips to islands & viewing puffins; trip to Træna a must." ♦                          2010*

**NESTTUN see Bergen** *1A3*

**NORDKAPP** *2H1* **See also Skarsvåg.**

⊞ **NORDKAPP** *2H1* (Rural/Coastal) *71.1725, 25.7822* **Nordkapphallen Carpark, 9764 Nordkapp (Finnmark) [tel 78 47 68 60; fax 78 47 68 61; nordkapphallen@rica.no; www.rica.no]** N on E69. Hdstg, pt sl, unshd; wc (0100-1100); own san; rest; bar; shop; 1 Nov-1 Apr private vehicles not permitted - buses in convoy (daily) only. "Max stay 48 hrs; no other o'night or site charges; price inc visit to Nordkapp Cent; no facs; v exposed gravel surface; excel for viewing midnight sun." NOK 235 (per person)                          2010*

**NORDKJOSBOTN** *2G1* (200m S Rural) *69.21623, 19.5553* **Bjørnebo Camping, Sentrumsveien 10, 9040 Nordkjosbotn (Troms) [tel 77 72 81 61]** Fr junc of E6 & E8 (Tromsø) 200m S turn L twd Nordkjosbotn, site 200m on L. Sm, pt shd; htd wc; chem disp; baby facs; shwrs NOK10; el pnts (16A) NOK30; lndtte; shop adj; snacks; bar; playgrnd; TV; dogs; phone; Eng spkn. "Conv for day trip to Tromsø; friendly owners." ♦ 5 Jun-15 Aug. NOK 200                          2014*

**NOTODDEN** *1C3* (1km W Rural) *59.55850, 9.24878* **Notodden Bobilcamp, Nesøya 11, 3674 Notodden** 1km W of Notodden on the E134. Sm, hdstg, pt shd, wc; chemp disp; mv service pnt; shwrs; bus/tram 1km. "City run stop over; low charge for all facs except electric; no one on site, owner calls in evening." NOK 150                          2014*

**NOTODDEN** *1C3* (2.5km W Rural) *59.57105, 9.19851* **Notodden Camping, Reshjemveien 46, 3670 Notodden (Telemark) [tel 35 01 33 10; fax 35 01 85 87; notcamp@ notoddencamping.com; www.notoddencamping.com]** On E134 by airfield. Med, unshd; wc; baby facs; shwrs NOK10; el pnts (10A) NOK30; lndtte; shops adj; snacks; playgrnd; TV; statics; poss cr; Eng spkn; quiet but some airfield noise; red CKE/CCI. "Heddal Stave church 10 mins drive; NH only." ♦ ltd 1 Jul-1 Sep. NOK 230                          2009*

⊞ **ODDA** *1A3* (2km S Rural) *60.0533, 6.5426* **Odda Camping, Jordalsveien 29, 5750 Odda (Hordaland) [tel 41 32 16 10; fax 53 64 12 92; post@oddacamping.no; www.oddacamping.no]** Sp on Rv13; adj sports complex, nr lakeside. Med, pt shd; htd wc; mv service pnt; private san facs avail; shwrs NOK10; el pnts (16A) NOK40; lndtte (with dryer); shop 1km; rest 1km; BBQ; lake fishing; watersports; cycle hire; games area; dogs; Eng spkn; quiet. "Beautiful area; nr Hardanger Fjord; watersports with canoes for hire; owner owns a guesthouse where you can use wifi & organise trips." ♦ NOK 150                          2011*

**ODDA** *1A3* (10km W Rural) *60.11335, 6.26456* **Sundal Camping, Sunndal, 5476 Mauranger (Hordaland) [tel 53 48 41 86; fax 53 48 18 20; sundal.camping@c2i.net; www.sundalcamping.no]** W fr Odda thro Folgefonn Tunnel. Site sp. Or fr ferry at Løfallstrand, take Rv551 approx 22km NE along side of fjord dir Gjerde. Med, pt sl, terr, pt shd; wc; chem disp; mv service pnt; shwrs; el pnts (10A) NOK30; lndtte; shop; rest, snacks; bar; playgrnd; shgl beach adj; fishing; boat hire; games area; 50% statics; poss cr Jul/Aug; Eng spkn; adv bkg; CKE/CCI. "Beautiful location; fisherman's paradise; walk fr site to Bondhus Glacier & Fureberg Waterfall." ♦ ltd 1 Apr-31 Oct. NOK 110                          2009*

NORWAY

**OLDEN** *1B2* (11km S Rural) *61.75823, 6.81173* **Camping Oldevatn, Sunde, 6788 Olden (Sogn og Fjordane) [tel/ fax 57 87 59 15; post@oldevatn.com; www.oldevatn. com]** Turn S off Rv60 in Olden, sp Briksdal, site on R immed after rd crosses lake. Sm, terr, unshd; htd wc; chem disp; mv service pnt; baby facs; fam bthrm; shwrs NOK10; el pnts (16A) NOK30; lndtte; tradsmn; rest 11km; snacks; bar 11km; cooking facs; playgrnd; lake sw & boating; cycle hire; TV rm; few statics; dogs free; phone; bus 50m; Eng spkn; adv bkg; quiet; red CKE/ CCI. "Lovely lakeside setting; 11km fr base of glacier; well-kept, clean site & facs." ♦ 1 May-30 Sep. NOK 200    2010*

**OLDEN** *1B2* (20km S Rural) *61.66513, 6.81600* **Camping Melkevoll Bretun, Oldedalen, 6792 Briksdalsbre (Sogn og Fjordane) [tel 57 87 38 64; fax 57 87 38 90; post@ melkevoll.no; www.melkevoll.no]** Take rte to Briksdal glacier to end of rd. Med, hdg pitch, terr, unshd; htd wc; chem disp; mv service pnt; baby facs; sauna; shwrs NOK10; el pnts (25A) NOK30; lndtte; shop; snacks; cooking facs; playgrnd; internet; phone; Eng spkn; quiet; ccard acc. "Walks to glacier; excel views glaciers some pitches; excel." 15 Apr-15 Oct. NOK 170    2013*

⊞ **OLDERFJORD** *2G1* (1km N Rural) *70.48121, 25.06321* Olderfjord Hotel Russenes Camping, 9713 Russenes (Finnmark) [tel 78 46 37 11; fax 78 46 37 91; olderfj@ online.no; www.olderfjord.no] N fr Olderfjord on E69. Site on L. Med, pt sl, pt shd; wc; shwrs NOK10; el pnts NOK20; gas; lndtte; shop; rest, snacks; cooking facs; playgrnd; beach adj; fishing; boating; TV; bus 500m; Eng spkn; ccard acc; CKE/CCI. "Gd facs but untidy area & poss stretched; space ltd - rec arr early; conv N Cape tunnel." NOK 150    2009*

⊞ **OPPDAL** *1C1* (2km NE Rural) **Solly Camping, Gorsetråket, 7340 Oppdal (Sør-Trøndelag) [tel 72 42 44 16; anug@online.no]** Site sp on E6. Sm, pt shd; wc; chem disp 10km; mv service pnt; shwrs inc; el pnts (10A) inc; lndtte; shop 2km; rest, snacks, bar 2km; BBQ; sm playgrnd; htd pool 2km; games area 1km; internet; TV; dogs; bus nr; train 2km; poss cr; Eng spkn; adv bkg; quiet; CKE/ CCI. "Nr Dovrefjell National Park; rv rafting nrby; gd walking & cycle paths; ski area in winter; v pleasant site; gd NH." NOK 150    2013*

⊞ **OPPDAL** *1C1* (3km NE Rural) *62.61537, 9.74172* **Camping Imi Stølen, 7340 Oppdal (Sør-Trøndelag) [tel 72 42 13 70; fax 72 42 08 70; post@imi-stolen.no; www.imi-stolen.no]** N of Oppdal on E6, site sp on L. Sm, mkd pitch, terr, unshd; wc; baby facs; fam bthrm; shwrs NOK10; el pnts NOK40; lndry rm; shop; snacks; playgrnd; TV; Eng spkn; quiet. ♦ NOK 160    2009*

⊞ **OPPDAL** *1C1* (6.5km S Rural) *62.54779, 9.62911* **Granmo Camping, 7340 Oppdal (Sør-Trøndelag) [tel/ fax 72 42 41 47; grancamp@online.no]** On E6 Oppdal to Dombas rd, well sp by Rv Driva. Med, unshd; htd wc; shwrs; el pnts (10A); lndtte; shop 6km; cooking facs; playgrnd; 15% statics; adv bkg; Eng spkn; quiet; CKE/CCI. "Simple site; pleasant location; friendly staff; gd hillwalking."    2009*

⊞ **ORNES** *2E2* (7km NW Rural) *66.91327, 13.62995* **Reipa Camping, N 8146 Reipa [tel 75 75 57 74 / 95 48 19 53; post@reipacamping.com; www.reipacamping.com]** Head NE on Havneveien twd Chr. Tidemanns vei/Rv17, then turn R onto Havneveien/Fv456. Sm; htd wc; chem disp; mv service pnt; shwrs inc; el pnts inc (16A); playgrnd; internet; wifi; dogs; Eng spkn; adv bkg; ccard acc; CKE/CCI. "Gd NH on classic Rv17." NOK 230    2014*

**OS I OSTERDALEN** *1D1* (2km NE Rural) *62.50430, 11.25938* **Røste Hyttetun & Camping, 2550 Os I Østerdalen (Sør-Trøndelag) [tel 62 49 70 55; fax 62 49 70 86; post@rostecamping.no; www.rostecamping. no]** Sp on Rv30. Sm; wc; chem disp; shwrs NOK10; el pnts NOK40; lndtte (inc dryer); cooking facs; playgrnd; fishing 150m; TV rm; some statics; quiet. NOK 150    2010*

**OS I OSTERDALEN** *1D1* (8km S Rural) *62.44696, 11.11960* **Camping Hummelfjell, 2550 Håmålvoll (Hedmark) [tel 62 49 72 58]** Sp on Rv30. Sm, pt shd; wc; chem disp; baby facs; shwrs NOK10; el pnts NOK35; lndtte; cooking facs; playgrnd; TV rm; quiet. 15 May-15 Sep. NOK 150    2009*

**OSEN** *2E3* (W Coastal) *64.29650, 10.49858* **Osen Fjordcamping, 7740 Steinsdalen [tel 72 57 79 00 or 41 14 68 02 (mob); booking@osen-fjordcamping.no; www.osen-fjordcamping.no]** Fr Rv17 about halfway bet Namsos & Steinkjer take rd 715 W for approx 40km to sea, site sp. Med, unshd; wc; chem disp; sauna; shwrs NOK10; el pnts NOK30; shop, rest in town; tradsmn; playgrnd; beach adj; wifi; 50% statics; dogs; bus adj; Eng spkn; quiet. "Vg." ♦ 1 May-31 Aug. NOK 165    2009*

## "I need an on-site restaurant"

We do our best to make sure site information is correct, but it is always best to check any must-have facilities are still available or will be open during your visit.

⊞ **OSLO** *1C3* (9km N Urban) *59.9623, 10.6429* **NAF Camping Bogstad, Ankerveien 117, Røa, 0766 Oslo [tel 22 51 08 00; fax 22 51 08 50; bogstad@naf.no; www. bogstadcamping.no]** Fr N on E16 cont to E18 & turn E twd Oslo. After approx 7km exit & proceed N twds Røa and Bogstad. Site sp adj Oslo golf club. V lge, some mkd pitch, pt sl, pt shd; htd wc; chem disp; mv service pnt; shwrs NOK10 (swipe card fr recep); el pnts (10A) NOK50 (long lead poss req); lndtte (inc dryer); shop adj; snacks; lake nr; 25% statics; dogs; poss v cr; Eng spkn; adv bkg; bus to Oslo 100m; wifi; ccard acc; CKE/CCI. "Beautiful area with walking trails; avoid area of site with statics & many itinerant workers (behind recep), far end OK with lake views; modern, clean san facs; helpful staff; recep open 24 hrs; conv Oslo cent; bus stop nrby, bus every 10 mins; 30 mins to centre; gd." ♦ NOK 335    2014*

Tell us about the sites you visit

**OSLO** *1C3* (3km SE Urban) *59.8984, 10.7734* **Ekeberg Camping, Ekebergveien 65, 1181 Oslo [tel 22 19 85 68; fax 22 67 04 36; mail@ekebergcamping.no; www. ekebergcamping.no]** Fr Göteborg to Oslo on E6 leave 2km bef Oslo; sp Ekeberg, foll sp to site. Fr S on E6 just after passing thro Oslo ent toll take slip rd sp Ekeberg; camp sp about 6km, up 10% hill. V lge, sl, unshd; wc; chem disp; mv service pnt; shwrs NOK10; baby facs; ltd el pnts (6-10A) inc (long lead poss req & poss rev pol); gas; lndtte (inc dryer); shop; supmkt 1km; tradsmn; rest 200m; snacks; bar; playgrnd; dogs; internet; bus/ tram to city - tickets fr site recep; poss cr; Eng spkn; no adv bkg; ccard acc; CKE/CCI. "Insufficient el pnts & leads running across rds; area without hook-ups flatter & quieter; use san facs block taps for fresh water; easy access to Oslo cent & places of interest; avoid site during annual children's football tournament end Jul/beg Aug - queues for pitches & facs v stretched; poss itinerant workers on site; recep open 0730-2300; helpful staff." ♦ 1 Jun-1 Sep. NOK 355 (4 persons)          2013*

**OSLO** *1C3* (8km S Rural/Coastal) *59.8350, 10.7817* **Oslo Fjordcamping, Ljanbruksveien 1, 1250 Oslo [tel 22 75 20 55; fjordcamping@yahoo.no; www. oslofjordcamping.no]** S on E18 to exit for Rv155 & sp Fjordcamping, site in 100m. Sm, pt sl, pt shd; wc; chem disp; mv service pnt; shwrs inc; el pnts inc (check earth & long lead poss req); lndtte; shop; snacks; BBQ; playgrnd; sand/shgl beach 300m; 20% statics; dogs; phone; bus adj; poss cr; Eng spkn; little rd noise; ccard acc; CKE/CCI. "V easy access to bus to Oslo; gd site but poss run down low ssn & poss travellers; run down, basic san facs; site muddy in wet; NH only." 1 May-30 Sep. NOK 290 (4 persons)          2009*

**OSLO** *1C3* (3km W Urban) *59.91866, 10.67500* **Sjølyst Marina Campervan Parking, Drammensveien 160, Sjølyst Båtopplag, 0273 Oslo [tel/fax 22 50 91 93; post@ bobilparkering.no; www.bobilparkering.no]** Fr E exit E18 at junc after Bygdøy (museums) junc. At rndabt take last exit, go under E18 & into site. Fr W leave E18 at Sjølyst junc, at bottom of slip rd turn R into site. Sm, hdstg, unshd; own san rec; chem disp; mv service pnt; shwrs NOK10; el pnts inc; snacks; BBQ; dogs; bus adj; clsd 2300-0700; Eng spkn; quiet. "Gd, basic site, pt of marina; m'vans only - pay at machine; san facs clsd o'night; 30 min walk city cent." ♦ 1 Jun-15 Sep. NOK 150          2011*

**OTTA** *1C2* (1.5km W Rural) *61.77223, 9.50653* **Otta Camping & Motell, Ottadalen 580, 2670 Otta (Oppland) [tel 61 23 03 09; fax 61 23 38 19; post@ottacamping.no; www.ottacamping.no]** Exit E6 twd Vagamo, 2km; turn L over 2 bdges, then R down track by rv. Med, pt shd; htd wc; chem disp; baby facs; shwrs NOK5; el pnts (10A) NOK30; lndtte; shop; rest 1km; playgrnd; cycle hire; sw; TV; dogs; phone; Eng spkn; adv bkg; rd & rv noise; red low ssn; ccard acc. "Conv for local sightseeing; lovely site; gd facs; gd views of rv." ♦ 1 May-15 Oct. NOK 140          2009*

**OVRE EIDFJORD see Eidfjord** *1B3*

⊞ **PORSGRUNN** *1C4* (4km S Rural) *59.11183, 9.71208* **Camping Olavsberget, Nystrandveien 64, 3944 Porsgrunn (Vestfold) [tel/fax 35 51 12 05]** Leave E18 at Eidanger onto Rv354 N; foll camp sp for 1km; site on L. Fr Porsgrunn foll Rv36 S; just bef E18 junc turn L; foll sp as above. Med, pt sl, unshd; wc; shwrs; el pnts (16A) NOK30 (no earth); lndtte (inc dryer); sm shop; supmkt 1km; snacks; sand beach adj with diving boards; 60% statics; poss cr; rd noise; no ccard acc; clsd 2300-0700; wifi; Eng spkn; CKE/CCI. "Well-run site; public access to beach thro site; gd walks in wood; visits to Maritime Brevik & mineral mine, Porsgrunn porcelain factory & shop, Telemark Canal inc boat tour." ♦ NOK 200          2014*

**RAMBERG (LOFOTEN ISLANDS)** *2E2* (2km W Rural) *68.0975, 13.1619* **Strand & Skærgårdscamping, 8387 Fredvang [tel 76 09 42 33 / 76 09 41 12; fax 76 09 41 12; mail@ fredvangcamping.no; www.fredvangcamp.no]** Foll Fredvang sp fr E10; site sp in vill cent. Sm, unshd; htd wc; chem disp; mv service pnt; shwrs NOK10; el pnts (16A) NOK25; lndtte; kiosk; cooking facs; sand beach adj; boat hire & launching; sat TV; Eng spkn; quiet; CKE/CCI. "View of midnight sun; surrounded by sand beach, sea & mountains; peaceful; gd san facs; friendly." 20 May-31 Aug. NOK 200          2014*

**RAMFJORDBOTN see Sakariasjord** *2F1*

⊞ **RISOR** *1C4* (5km SW Coastal) *58.69083, 9.16333* **Sørlandet Feriecenter, Sandnes, 4950 Risør [tel 37 15 40 80; sorferie@online.no; www.sorlandet-feriesenter.no]** Fr N take E18 to Sørlandsporten then Rv416 to Risør, then Rv411 to Laget. Foll sp Sørlandet. Fr S exit E18 at Tvedestrand & cont to Laget, then foll site sp. Site is 20km by rd fr Risør. Med, mkd pitch, pt shd; htd wc; chem disp; baby facs; private san facs avail; shwrs; el pnts inc; lndtte (inc dryer); shop; supmkt 1km; rest; bar; cooking facs; playgrnd; sand beach; watersports; boat & cycle hire; tennis 1km; fitness rm; games rm; wifi; cab TV; some statics; dogs; adv bkg; Eng spkn; quiet. ♦ NOK 317 (CChq acc)          2014*

⊞ **RISOR** *1C4* (10km W Coastal) *58.72592, 9.07783* **Risør Resort Moen Camping, 4950 Risor [tel 37 15 50 91; fax 37 15 50 92; karen@moen-camping.no; www.moen-camping.no]** Fr E18 S, L onto 416 twds Risor. Site sp on L. Med, unshd; htd wc; baby facs; fam bthrm; shwrs inc; lndtte (inc dryer); snacks; BBQ; cooking facs; playgrnd; sand beach; games rm; wifi; tv rm; 90% statics; dogs; poss cr; Eng spkn; ccard acc; CCI. "Well cared for, popular site; el pnts & water widely spaced; volleyball; boat hire." NOK 400          2014*

⊞ **RISOYHAMN (VESTERALEN ISLANDS)** *2F1* (10km S Coastal) **Andøy Friluftssenter & Camping, Buksnesfjord, 8484 Risøyhamn [tel/fax 76 14 88 04; post@andoy-friluftssenter.no; www.andoy-friluftssenter.no]** Exit E10 onto Rv82 sp Sortland; in 31km at bdge to Sortland do not cross bdge but cont N on Rv82 sp Andenes. Site on R in 38km at Buknesfjord. Sm, hdstg, pt sl, unshd; htd wc; chem disp; shwrs inc; el pnts (10A) NOK50; lndtte; rest, snacks; playgrnd; lake sw; fishing; 50% statics; Eng spkn; adv bkg; quiet; ccard acc; CKE/CCI. "Lake fishing; guided mountain walks; easy access for whale-watching; v clean facs; gourmet meals." ♦ ltd NOK 150          2009*

⊞ **RODBERG** *1C3* (4km S Rural) *60.23533, 9.0040*
**Fjordgløtt Camping, Vrenne, 3630 Rødberg (Buskerud)**
**[tel 32 74 13 35 / 97 15 96 53 (mob); fax 32 74 16 90;**
**info@fjordglott.net; www.fjordglott.net]** Fr Rødberg on
Rv40 dir Kongsberg, take R turn sp Vrenne, cross bdge & foll
sp past power stn. Med, mkd pitch, terr, pt shd; htd wc; chem
disp; 75% serviced pitches; baby facs; sauna; shwrs NOK10;
el pnts (16A) NOK30; lndtte; shop; tradsmn; snacks; playgrnd;
lake sw; fishing; 40% statics; phone; Eng spkn; quiet; ccard
acc; CKE/CCI. "Lovely views of fjord; excel facs; well kept." ◆
NOK 240                                                    2014*

**RODBERG** *1C3* (2km W Rural) **Persgård Camping, Nore**
**og Uvdal, 3630 Rødberg (Buskerud) [tel 32 24 32 54]**
Site fr Rv40. Sm, unshd; wc; chem disp; shwrs NOK10; el
pnts NOK30; sand beach & lake sw adj; 20% statics; quiet.
"Beautiful setting; basic, clean facs; gd." ◆ ltd Jul-Sep.
NOK 100                                                    2009*

**RODBERG** *1C3* (9.2km W Rural) *60.26602, 8.78878* **Uvdal**
**Resort, N-3632 Uvdal (Buskerud) [tel 32 74 31 08; fax**
**99 22 82 10; aud@uvdalresort.no; www.uvdalresort.**
**no]** Fr Rodberg, take Rv40 W for about 9km. Site on R. Sm;
htd wc; chem disp; mv service pnt; shwr 5nok; el pnts (16A)
30nok; lndtte (inc dryer); snacks; playgrnd; games area; Eng
spkn; ccard acc; CKE/CCI. "Family run; level site by rv; fishing &
kayaking; vg site." 1 May-30 Sep. NOK 190              2014*

**ROGNAN** *2F2* (5km S Rural) *67.06150, 15.37120* **Medby**
**Camping, 8250 Rognan (Nordland) [tel 75 69 03 15; fax**
**75 69 07 09]** S on E6, foll sp Medby. Sm, unshd; htd wc; chem
disp; mv service pnt; shwrs inc; el pnts NOK20; lndry rm; shop,
rest, bar, shop 5km; cooking facs; Eng spkn; quiet. "Lovely,
peaceful, CL-type site; gd." 1 Jun-1 Sep. NOK 120     2009*

⊞ **ROLDAL** *1B3* (Rural) *59.83227, 6.81843* **Skysstasjonen**
**Hytter & Camping, Kyrkjevegen 24, 5760 Røldal**
**(Hordaland) [tel 53 64 73 85; fax 53 64 73 44; roldal@**
**roldalstunet.no; www.skysstasjonen.no]** Fr E on E134 turn
L down into vill bef petrol stn. Site ent opp supmkt. Med, some
hdstg, pt sl, pt terr, pt shd; htd wc; chem disp; sauna; shwrs
NOK10; el pnts (10A) NOK35; lndtte (inc dryer); shop adj; rest,
snacks; cooking facs; internet; TV; 50% statics; dogs; phone;
quiet; CKE/CCI. "Vg site in beautiful, sheltered rvside location;
wintersports." ◆ NOK 160                                2009*

⊞ **ROLDAL** *1B3* (1km SE Rural) *59.83103, 6.82888* **Røldal**
**Hyttegrend & Camping, Kyrkjevegen 49, 5760 Røldal**
**(Hordaland) [tel 53 64 71 33; fax 53 64 39 41; adm@**
**roldal-camping.no; www.roldal-camping.no]** Fr E on E134
turn L on ent vill, site sp. Sm, pt shd; htd wc; chem disp; mv
service pnt; baby facs; shwrs NOK10; baby facs; fam bthrm;
el pnts (10A) NOK30; gas; lndtte; shop; snacks; cooking facs;
playgrnd; rv sw adj; wifi; TV rm; 20% statics; dogs; phone; Eng
spkn; adv bkg; ccard acc; red CKE/CCI. "Gd walking, angling."
◆ ltd NOK 206                                            2014*

⊞ **ROLDAL** *1B3* (500m S Rural) *59.83255, 6.82138* **Saltvold**
**Camping, Kirkeveien 34, 5760 Røldal (Hordaland)**
**[tel 53 64 72 45; gulleik@online.no]** Fr W on E134 turn R at
2nd camping sp (immed after 1st camping sp). Site at bottom
of hill just bef stave church. Med, pt sl, unshd; wc; chem disp;
shwrs NOK5; el pnts (10A) NOK40; lndtte; shop, rest, snacks
100m; 20% statics; Eng spkn; quiet; red CKE/CCI. "Mountain
views."  NOK 135 (4 persons)                           2009*

⊞ **ROLDAL** *1B3* (1km SW Rural) *59.83012, 6.81061*
**Seim Camping, 5760 Røldal (Horda-Rogaland) [tel/fax**
**53 64 73 71 / 97 53 35 17 (mob) / 90 91 90 63 (mob);**
**seim@seimcamp.no; www.seimcamp.no]** App fr SW
on E134, site sp at ent town. Turn R off main rd & R again.
Med, pt sl, pt shd; htd wc; chem disp; baby facs; fam bthrm;
shwrs NOK5; el pnts (20A) NOK40; lndtte; shop, rest, snacks,
bar 200m; playgrnd; fishing; boating; dogs; Eng spkn; CKE/
CCI; "Gd walks; beautiful views; prehistoric burial mounds &
museum on site; poss rd noise." ◆ ltd NOK 193          2014*

**"Satellite navigation makes
touring much easier"**

Remember most sat navs don't know if
you're towing or in a larger vehicle – always
use yours alongside maps and site directions.

**ROROS** *1D1* (200m S Urban) *62.57078, 11.38295*
**Idrettsparken Hotel & Camping, Øra 25, 7374 Røros**
**(Sør-Trøndelag) [tel 72 41 10 89; fax 72 41 23 77; ihotell@**
**online.no; www.idrettsparken.no]** Heading twd Trondheim
on Rv30 to Røros cent, turn L at rndabt into Peter Møllersvei,
over rlwy line, L again & foll sp to site. Sm, unshd; htd wc;
shwrs NOK10; el pnts (16A) NOK35; shops & pool nr; quiet.
"Tours of museums & mines; nature reserve & nature park nr;
no chem disp - use dump point at fire stn on Rv30; fair NH."
◆ ltd 1 May-30 Sep. NOK 300                            2014*

**RORVIK** *2E3* (2km N Coastal) *64.8729, 11.2609* **Nesset**
**Camping, Engan, 7900 Rørvik (Nord-Trøndelag)**
**[tel 74 39 06 60]** Fr cent of Rørvik on Rv770, foll sp to site.
Med, hdg pitch, hdstg, pt sl, terr, pt shd; htd wc; chem
disp; shwrs NOK10; el pnts (10A); sw adj; some statics; Eng
spkn; quiet. "Many pitches with fjord view; facs stretched
high ssn; beware of speed bumps on app rd." May-Sep.
NOK 250                                                    2014*

**RUNDE (RUNDE ISLAND)** *1A1* (500m NW Coastal) *62.39717,*
*5.65624* **Runde Camping & Hostel, 6096 Runde (Møre og**
**Romsdal) [tel 90 74 43 43; runde@hihostels.no; www.**
**runde.no]** Fr S via E39 Volda & Ørsta, thro Eiksundsambandet
Tunnel, then 25km by rd to Runde. On reaching Runde Island
turn R along coast, site sp. Fr N take ferry fr Sulesund (nr
Ålesund) to Hareid, then 45km by rd, site sp. Sm, hdstg, unshd;
htd wc; chem disp; shwrs; el pnts (16A); lndtte; shop; snacks
300m; BBQ; cooking facs; wifi; beach adj; dogs; phone; o'night
area for m'vans; Eng spkn; adv bkg; quiet; ccard acc; CKE/
CCI. "Lge bird colonies on island; boat trips organised; helpful
owner." 1 May-30 Sep.                                    2010*

⊞ **RUNDE (RUNDE ISLAND)** *1A1* (3km NW Rural/Coastal) *62.40416, 5.62525* **Camping Goksøyr, 6096 Runde (Møre og Romsdal) [tel 70 08 59 05 or 924 12 298 (mob); fax 70 08 59 60; camping@goksoyr.no; www.goksoeyr-camping.com]** Take causeway/bdge to Runde Island. Turn R off bdge & foll rd round island, thro tunnel. Rd ends 1km after site. Sm, hdstg, unshd; wc; chem disp; mv service pnt; shwrs NOK10; el pnts (16A) NOK30; lndtte; shop; snacks; fishing; cycle hire; phone; Eng spkn; adv bkg; quiet; CKE/CCI. "Excel birdwatching (inc puffins); site on water's edge; boat trips avail; basic facs poss inadequate when site full; owner helps with pitching; vg." NOK 190                          2014*

**RYSSTAD** *1B4* (1km S Rural) *59.0908, 7.5402* **Sølvgarden Feriesenter, 4748 Rysstad (Aust-Agder) [tel 37 93 61 30; fax 37 93 61 09; post@rysstadferie.no; www.rysstadferie.no]** Site sp on E side of Rv9, S of junc of Rv9 & Rv45. Sm, some hdg/mkd pitch, pt sl, pt shd; htd wc; chem disp; shwrs NOK10; el pnts (10A) NOK35; lndtte (inc dryer); shop; tradsmn; rest, snacks; bar; cooking facs; BBQ; playgrnd; rv sw adj; fishing; canoeing; cycle hire; wifi; TV rm; some statics; dogs; phone; Eng spkn; ccard acc; CKE/CCI. "Pleasant site; beautiful setting; modern san facs." ♦ 1 May-1 Oct. NOK 320        2010*

**SAKARIASJORD (RAMFJORDBOTN)** *2F1* (1km NE Rural) *69.51665, 19.24845* **Camping Ramfjord, Sørbotn, 9027 Ramfjordbotn (Troms) [tel 77 69 21 30; fax 77 69 22 60; post@ramfjordcamp.no; www.ramfjordcamp.no]** Approx 27km S of Tromsø on E8, clearly sp. Sm, unshd; wc; chem disp; mv service pnt; baby facs; shwrs NOK5; el pnts (10A) NOK50; gas; lndtte; shop; snacks; cooking facs; playgrnd; shgl beach adj; TV; 75% statics; dogs; phone; poss cr; Eng spkn; adv bkg ess; quiet; ccard acc; red CKE/CCI. "Facs ltd when cr; superb views of fjord; conv Tromsø." ♦ 1 Jun-15 Aug. NOK 170                          2009*

**SALTSTRAUMEN see Bodø** *2F2*

⊞ **SANDANE** *1A2* (1.5km W Coastal) *61.76743, 6.19605* **Gloppen Camping, 6823 Sandane (Sogn og Fjordane) [tel 57 86 62 14; fax 57 86 81 05; post@gloppen-camping.no; www.gloppen-camping.no]** Fr town cent on rd E39 take Rv615 sp Rygg & Hyen. Site on R at fjordside. Med, mkd pitch, hdstg, unshd; htd wc; chem disp; mv service pnt; shwrs NOK10; el pnts (16A) NOK30; lndtte; shop; rest, snacks, bar 2km; BBQ; cooking facs; playgrnd; pool high ssn; beach adj; fishing; boat trips; tennis; golf 3km; TV rm; 70% statics; phone; quiet; ccard acc; CKE/CCI. "Day trips to Briksdal Glacier; gd." ♦ NOK 200                          2011*

**SETERMOEN** *2F2* (20km S Rural) **Solbakken Camping, Sollidveien, Salangsdalen, 9360 Bardu (Troms) [tel 77 18 41 34]** On W side of E6, foll sp up hill. Sm, pt sl, terr, unshd; htd wc; shwrs NOK10; cooking facs; games area; 70% statics; some Eng spkn; quiet. "Poss bleak, windswept but gd views; warden calls evenings; gd NH." May-Sep. 2009*

⊞ **SJOHOLT** *1B1* (9km N Rural) *62.52022, 6.91722* **Camping Ørskog Fjellstova, 6249 Ørskog (Møre og Ronsdal) [tel 70 27 03 03; fax 70 27 00 60; post@fjellstova.no; www.fjellstova.no]** Site sp on E39, 50km E of Ålesund & 25km W of Molde. Med, hdstg, unshd; htd wc; chem disp; shwrs inc; el pnts (10A) NOK30; tradsmn; rest, snacks; BBQ; 5% statics; bus; Eng spkn; quiet; ccard acc. "Dutch owners; gd site mainly for winter use; gd for fishing, cross country, skiing." NOK 150                          2011*

⊞ **SKARNES** *1D3* (5km S Rural) *60.19910, 11.58054* **Sanngrund Camping, Oslovegen 910, 2100 Skarnes (Hedmark) [tel 62 96 46 60; fax 62 96 46 69; booking@sanngrund.no; www.sanngrund.no]** Fr Skarnes foll Rv2 S; site sp on L. Sm, mkd pitch, pt shd; htd wc; chem disp; mv service pnt; baby facs; shwrs inc; el pnts inc; lndtte; shop 10km; rest, snacks; BBQ; cooking facs; playgrnd; rv sw & fishing adj; TV; 50% statics; poss cr; Eng spkn; rd noise; CKE. "Conv NH to/fr Oslo (approx 70km); pleasant rest; fair site." NOK 235                          2010*

**SKARSVAG** *2G1* (1km SW Coastal) *71.1073, 25.81238* **Kirkeporten Camping, 9763 Skarsvåg (Finnmark) [tel 90 96 06 48; fax 78 47 52 47; kipo@kirkeporten.no; www.kirkeporten.no]** Foll E69 fr Honningsvåg for 20km to Skarsvåg junc; site sp at junc & on L after 2km immed bef vill. Sm, hdstg, pt sl, unshd; htd wc; chem disp; mv service pnt; sauna; shwrs inc; el pnts (16A) NOK25; lndtte (inc dryer); rest, snacks; bar; TV; wifi; poss cr; Eng spkn; adv bkg; quiet; ccard acc; CKE/CCI. "Site on edge sm fishing vill 10km fr N Cape, ringed by mountains; exposed location; claims to be world's most N site; helpful, knowledgeable owner; vg rest; clean facs but stretched if site full; poss reindeer on site; highly rec; arr early; work being done to extend camping area (2014)." ♦ 15 May-15 Sep. NOK 220                          2014*

**SKIBOTN** *2G1* (400m N Coastal) *69.39397, 20.26797* **NAF Camping Skibotn, 9143 Skibotn (Troms) [tel 77 71 52 77]** On W of E6 400m N of town. Sm, pt sl, unshd; wc; chem disp; shwrs NOK10 (10 mins); el pnts (10A) NOK25; gas; lndtte; cooking facs; fishing; Eng spkn. "NH only, dir access to beach on fjord; poss traffic noise fr E6." 1 Jun-31 Aug. NOK 200                          2014*

**SKIBOTN** *2G1* (1km S Rural) *69.38166, 20.29528* **Olderelv Camping (TR30), 9048 Skibotn (Troms) [tel 77 71 54 44 or 91 13 17 00 (mob); fax 77 71 51 62; firmapost@olderelv.no; www.olderelv.no]** W of E6 1km N of junc at E8. Lge, mkd pitch, pt sl, pt shd; wc; chem disp; sauna; baby facs; shwrs NOK10; el pnts (10A) inc; lndtte (inc dryer); shop; snacks; cooking facs; playgrnd; solarium; wifi; 80% statics; dogs free; phone; quiet; ccard acc. "Well-maintained & clean; dryest area of Troms; gd walking." ♦ 15 May-15 Sep. NOK 220   2009*

**SKJAK see Lom** *1C2*

NORWAY

**SKJOLDEN** *1B2* (3km NE Rural) *61.48453, 7.6505*
**Vassbakken Camping, RV 55, 6876 Skjolden (Romsdal Sognefjord) [tel 57 68 61 88 or 57 68 67 00; fax 57 68 61 85; info@vassbakken.com; www.skjolden.com/ vassbakken]** Site on Rv55. Sm, pt shd; wc; chem disp; mv service pnt; baby facs; sauna; shwrs NOK10; el pnts (10A) NOK30; lndtte; sm shop & 3km; rest, snacks; playgrnd; lake sw & fishing adj; wifi; TV; phone; Eng spkn; no adv bkg; ccard acc. "Mountain setting; waterfall ad, gd walking & fishing; ltd facs until June." 1 May-20 Sep.   NOK 254          2013*

**SKJOLDEN** *1B2* (1km SE Rural) *61.48977, 7.60709*
**Nymoen Leirplass, 6876 Skjolden (Sogn og Fjordane) [tel 57 68 66 03; fax 57 68 67 33; nymoen@skjolden.com; www.skjolden.com/nymoen]** Fr Sogndal on rd 55 site on R behind petrol stn. Fr Sogndal on exit Skjolden after 2nd bdge site on L. Sm, unshd; wc; chem disp; mv service pnt; shwrs NOK10; el pnts (16A) NOK25; gas; lndtte (inc dryer); shops adj & 500m; cooking facs; lake sw 500m; fishing; poss cr; adv bkg; quiet; ccard acc. "Beautiful situation on lakeside; fine views; walk to vill & Lustrafjorden." 1 May-1 Oct.   NOK 159    2010*

**SNASA** *2E3* (16km SW Rural) *64.17300, 12.09605* **Strindmo Gård Camping, Strindmo, 7760 Snåsa (Nord-Trøndelag) [tel/fax 74 16 39 12]** Fr Snåsa take Rv763 twds Steinkjer; site is sp on L in approx 15km. Sm, hdstg, pt sl, pt shd; htd wc; chem disp; shwrs NOK10; el pnts NOK35; lndtte; cooking facs; playgrnd; rv sw adj; boat & cycle hire; Eng spkn; adv bkg; some rlwy noise; CKE/CCI. "V friendly, welcoming, family-owned site; immac san facs; site has own hydro-elec generating plant open for inspection; midges!" 1 Apr-1 Oct.   NOK 160    2009*

**SOGNDALSFJORA** *1B2* (13km NE Rural) *61.30738, 7.21500*
**Lyngmo Camping (SF16), Lyngmovegen 12, 6869 Hafslo (Sogn of Fjordane) [tel 57 68 43 66; fax 57 68 39 29; lyngmo@lyngmoinfo.com; www.lyngmoinfo.com]** Fr Rv55 Sogndal-Gaupne turn L at sp Galden. Immed turn R at camping sp & foll gravel rd down to site on lakeside. Sm, pt sl, unshd; wc; chem disp; mv service pnt; baby facs; shwrs; el pnts; lndry rm; cooking facs; lake sw & fishing; some statics; phone; Eng spkn; quiet; ccard acc; CKE/CCI. "Beautiful location; steep hill to san facs block." 19 Jun-24 Aug.          2014*

⊞ **SOGNDALSFJORA** *1B2* (3.5km SE Coastal) *61.2118, 7.12106* **Camping Kjornes, 6856 Sogndal (Sogn og Fjordane) [tel 57 67 45 80 / 975 44 156 (mob); fax 57 67 33 26; camping@kjornes.no; www.kjornes.no]** Fr W foll sp in Sogndal for Kaupanger/Lærdal (Rv5) over bdge. Fr E (Rv55) turn L at T-junc with rd 5 over bdge. Site on R; sharp R turn into narr lane (passing places); site ent on R in approx 500m. Med, pt sl, terr, pt shd; wc; chem disp; shwrs NOK10; el pnts (10-16A) NOK30 (no earth); lndtte; shops; rest, snacks 3.5km; cooking facs; playgrnd; beach adj; boat launching; fishing; wifi; some statics; phone; poss cr; Eng spkn; adv bkg; rd noise; ccard acc; CKE/CCI. "Useful for ferries; stunning location on edge of fjord; superb san facs; excel site; v highly rec." ♦ ltd NOK 306          2014*

**SOGNDALSFJORA** *1B2* (1km S Rural) *61.22505, 7.10271*
**Stedje Camping, Kyrkjevegen 2, 6851 Sogndal (Sogn og Fjordane) [tel 57 67 10 12; fax 57 67 11 90; post@ scamping.no; www.scamping.no]** W fr Hella to Sogndal, turn L off Rv55 adj Shell petrol stn, site clearly sp, narr ent. Med, sl, pt shd; htd wc; chem disp; mv service pnt; baby facs; shwrs NOK10; el pnts (16A) NOK40 (check earth); lndtte; shop; snacks; playgrnd; lake sw & beach 500m; watersports; solarium; cycle hire; wifi; TV; Eng spkn; quiet; CKE/CCI. "1st gd site after Sogndal fr E; vg facs; poss poor facs early ssn; poss v diff in wet for lge m' vans; conv visit to 12th C Urnes stave church." ♦ 1 Jun-31 Aug.   NOK 140    2014*

**SOLA** *1A4* (6km W Coastal) *58.86713, 5.56485* **Ølberg Camping & Friområde, Ølberg Havneveg 93, Ræg, 4054 Tjelta [tel 51 65 43 75; post@jarenfri.no; www.jarenfri.no]** Fr Stavanger or Sandnes take rds Rv209 & Rv210 to Sola airport & then foll sps for campsite along Fv380. Med, pt sl, unshd; wc; chem disp; mv service pnt; shwrs NOK10; el pnts (10A) NOK45; lndtte (inc dryer); tradsmn; snacks; BBQ; cooking facs; playgrnd; sand beach adj; games area; cycle hire; 30% statics; dogs free; phone; bus 500m; Eng spkn; adv bkg; quiet; CKE/ CCI. "Adj pretty beach & sm harbour; gd walking & cycling; v relaxed, seaside site; vg, clean & well-run." ♦ ltd 10 May-31 Aug.   NOK 180          2010*

⊞ **SORTLAND (VESTERALEN ISLANDS)** *2F2* (1.5km W Rural) *68.70286, 15.3919* **Camping Sortland & Motel, Vesterveien 51, 8400 Sortland [tel 76 11 03 00; fax 76 12 25 78; hj.bergseng@sortland-camping.no; www. sortland-camping.no]** Exit E10 onto Rv82 sp Sortland; in 31km turn L over bdge to Sortland, L again at end bdge. Site sp in approx 1km immed past church. Foll rd uphill for 1km, site on R. Med, hdstg, pt shd; wc; chem disp; baby facs; fam bthrm; shwrs NOK10; el pnts (16A) NOK30; gas; lndtte; shop; snacks; cooking facs; playgrnd; skiing; cycling; walking; fishing; boating; solarium; gym; wifi; TV; phone; poss cr; Eng spkn; quiet; ccard acc; CKE/CCI. "Basic, clean site; helpful staff; gd base to tour islands; facs stretched when full." NOK 250          2014*

**SORVAGEN (LOFOTEN ISLANDS)** *2E2* (2km N Coastal) *67.90017, 13.04656* **Moskenes Camping, 8392 Sørvågen [tel 99 48 94 05]** Fr ferry turn L, then immed R opp terminal exit, site up sh unmade rd, sp. Med, hdstg, terr, unshd; htd wc; chem disp; mv service pnt; el pnts (10A) NOK10; lndtte; shop 2km; snacks 1km; no statics; Eng spkn; quiet. "Excel NH." May-Sep.   NOK 180          2009*

**SPANGEREID** *1A4* (8km S Coastal) *57.99593, 7.09003* **Lindesnes Camping, Lillehavn, 4521 Spangereid (Vest-Agder) [tel 38 25 88 74 / 91 60 22 76 (mob); fax 38 25 88 92; gabrielsen@lindesnescamping.no; www. lindesnescamping.no]** Fr E39 at Vigeland turn S onto Rv460 sp Lindesnes lighthouse (Fyr). Approx 8km after vill of Spangereid turn L sp Lillehavn, site sp. Sm, pt sl, pt shd; htd wc; chem disp; mv service pnt; shwrs NOK10; el pnts (16A) NOK40; lndtte; tradsmn; BBQ; cooking facs; dogs; phone; poss cr; Eng spkn; adv bkg; quiet; ccard acc; CKE/CCI. "Excel, clean, well-run site; pitches not mkd adv early arr." 1 Apr-30 Sep. NOK 210          2013*

**STABBURSNES see Lakselv** *2G1*

**STAMSUND (LOFOTEN ISLANDS)** *2F2* (6km N Rural/ Coastal) *68.19921, 13.98290* **Brustranda Sjøcamping, Rolfsfjord, 8356 Leknes [tel 76 08 71 00; fax 76 08 71 44; post@brustranda.no; www.brustranda.no]** Take E10 W fr Svolvaer ferry for approx 19km. After 3rd bdge turn L onto Rv815. Site on L in 22km at petrol stn. Sm, pt shd; wc; chem disp; shwrs NOK10; el pnts (10A) NOK40 (poss rev pol); lndtte; shop 16km; snacks; shgl beach adj; sand beach 2km; fishing; boat hire; 30% statics; dogs; Eng spkn; quiet. "Idyllic setting; mountain views; v helpful staff; san facs stretched when site full; highly rec." 1 Jun-31 Aug. NOK 160          2009*

**STAVANGER** *1A3* (2km SW Rural) *58.9525, 5.71388* **Mosvangen Camping, Henrik Ibsens Gate, 4021 Stavanger (Rogaland) [tel 51 53 29 71; fax 51 87 20 55; info@mosvangencamping.no; www.mosvangencamping.no]** Fr Stavanger foll sp E39/Rv510; site well sp. Fr Sandnes on E39 exit Ullandhaug; foll camp sp. Med, some hdstg, sl, pt shd; wc; chem disp; mv service pnt; shwrs NOK10; el pnts (10A) NOK40 (no earth & poss intermittent supply); lndtte (inc dryer); kiosk; shop 500m; rest 1km; cooking facs; playgrnd; lake sw adj; sand beach 10km; dogs; phone; bus; poss v cr; Eng spkn; quiet but some rd noise; ccard acc; CKE/CCI. "Excel for wooden city of Stavanger; easy, pleasant walk to town cent; soft grnd in wet weather; facs well used but clean but stretched when site full; helpful manager; excel rustic type of site; bus to cent nr ent." 1 Apr-1 Oct. NOK 210          2014*

**STAVERN see Larvik** *1C4*

⊞ **STEINKJER** *2E3* (14km N Rural) *64.10977, 11.57816* **Føllingstua Camping, Haugåshalla 6, 7732 Steinkjer (Nord-Trøndelag) [tel 74 14 71 90; fax 74 14 71 88; post@follingstua.no; www.follingstua.com]** N on E6, site on R, well sp. Sm, mkd pitch, hdstg, pt shd; htd wc; chem disp; mv service pnt; shwrs NOK20; el pnts (16A) NOK40; shop 11km; rest, snacks; bar; BBQ; playgrnd; lake & beach adj; fishing; boating; TV rm; 60% statics; dogs; bus 200m; poss cr; adv bkg; quiet. "Excel san facs down 10 steps; some lakeside pitches." ♦ NOK 190          2010*

**STO (VESTERALEN ISLANDS)** *2F1* (N Coastal) *69.01891, 15.12215* **Stø Bobilcamp, 8438 Stø [tel 76 13 25 30; fax 76 13 25 31; loleinan@frisurf.no; www.stobobilcamp. com]** Site sp fr cent of Stø. Sm, hdstg, unshd; htd wc; chem disp; mv service pnt; shwrs NOK10; el pnts (16A) NOK30; shop; rest; cooking facs; fishing; cycle hire; some statics; poss cr; quiet; Eng spkn. "View of midnight sun; 10min walk to whale boat safari; coastal walks, Queen Sonja's walk fr site, v scenic but poss strenuous; facs stretched high ssn; site open to public for parking." ♦ ltd 15 May-1 Sep. NOK 130          2009*

**STOREN** *1C1* (500m E Rural) *63.04465, 10.29078* **Vårvolden Camping (ST17), Volløyan 3A, 7290 Støren (Sør-Trøndelag) [tel/fax 72 43 20 24; varvolden.camping@gauldalen.no]** Leave E6 for Støren & foll site sp. Sm, unshd; htd wc; chem disp; mv service pnt; baby facs; fam bthrm; shwrs; el pnts (16A); lndtte (inc dryer); shop 500m; rest, snacks 1km; cooking facs; playgrnd; 20% statics; dogs; Eng spkn; CKE/CCI. "Vg." ♦ 15 May-1 Sep. NOK 202          2013*

**STOREN** *1C1* (800m E Rural) *63.04083, 10.29333* **Camping Støren, Frøsetøren 1, 7290 Støren (Sør-Trøndelag) [tel/ fax 72 43 14 70; post@storencamping.no; www.gaula.no]** Located at Støren off E6 on sm app rd dir Røros, nr Rv Gaula. Low bdge at ent to site 3.3m. Med, mkd pitch, pt shd; htd wc; chem disp; baby facs; shwrs NOK10; el pnts (10-16A) NOK30; lndtte (inc dryer); shop; snacks; playgrnd; TV; mainly statics; phone. "Gd salmon rv, permit needed." 1 Jun-31 Aug. NOK 125          2010*

**STORFORSHEI** *2F2* (6km N Rural) *66.37946, 14.60366* **Camping Skogly Overnatting, Saltfjellveien 931, Skogly, 8630 Storforshei (Nordland) [tel 97 66 74 68; post@skoglyovernatting.com]** N fr Mo i Rana for 30km, site on L of E6. Sm, hdstg, unshd; htd wc; chem disp (wc); baby facs; shwrs inc; el pnts NOK40; cooking facs; Eng spkn; quiet. "Excel facs; helpful owner." ♦ ltd 1 May-20 Sep. NOK 180          2013*

⊞ **STORJORD** *2F2* (Rural) *66.81317, 15.40055* **Saltdal Turistsenter, 8255 Storjord (Nordland) [tel 75 68 24 50; fax 75 68 24 51; firmapost@saltdal-turistsenter.no; www. saltdal-turistsenter.no]** Site is 35km S of Rognan by-pass on E6, 700m N of junc of Rv77, adj filling stn. Med, mkd pitch, some hdstg, terr, pt shd; htd wc; chem disp; mv service pnt; shwrs NOK10; el pnts (10A) NOK25; lndtte; shop; rest, snacks; BBQ; cooking facs; playgrnd; 99% statics; wifi; phone; Eng spkn; adv bkg; quiet; CKE/CCI. "M'way-style service stn & lorry park; tightly packed cabins & statics; 10 pitches only for tourers; excel rv walks fr site; beautiful area; NH only; secure barrier; clean facs, could be stretched if full." ♦ NOK 263          2014*

**STORSLETT** *2G1* (11km N Coastal) *69.83880, 21.21058* **Fosselv Camping, Straumfjord, 9151 Storslett (Troms) [tel 77 76 49 29; fax 77 76 76 09; fosselv.camping@c2i.net; www.fosselv-camping.no]** Sp fr E6. Sm, pt sl, pt shd; wc; chem disp; mv service pnt; shwrs; el pnts (10A) NOK50; lndtte; cooking facs; playgrnd; shgl beach adj; Eng spkn; rd noise; CKE. "Lovely fjord setting; poss reindeer on site in evening." 10 May-25 Oct. NOK 150          2009*

**STRAUMEN see Fauske** *2F2*

**STRYN** *1B2* (10km E Rural) *61.60008, 6.88866* **Mindresunde Camping (SF43), 6783 Stryn (Sogn og Fjordane) [tel 57 87 75 32 / 41 56 63 16 (mob); fax 57 87 75 40; post@mindresunde.no; www.mindresunde.no]** 2nd site on Rv15 on N side of rd. Sm, mkd pitch, pt sl, unshd; htd wc; chem disp; mv service pnt; baby facs; fam bthrm; shwrs NOK10; el pnts inc (earth prob); lndtte; shop; snacks; playgrnd; shgl beach; TV; car wash; Eng spkn; adv bkg; little rd noise; CKE/CCI. "Well-kept, pleasant site; many pitches on lake; friendly staff; site yourself; vg views; excel facs, conv Geiranger, Briksdal glacier & Strynefjellet summer ski cent; gd walking." ♦ 1 Apr-1 Nov. NOK 220          2014*

**NORWAY**

**NORWAY**

**STRYN** 1B1 (11km E Rural) 61.9314, 6.92121 **Strynsvatn Camping, Meland, 6783 Stryn (Sogn og Fjordane) [tel 57 87 75 43; fax 57 87 75 65; camping@strynsvatn. no; www.strynsvatn.no]** On Rv15 Lom to Stryn, on L. Sm, terr, unshd; wc; chem disp; mv service pnt; sauna; shwrs NOK10; el pnts (10A) inc (poss earth fault); lndtte (inc dryer); shop; snacks; playgrnd; lake adj; TV; 20% statics; Eng spkn; adv bkg; quiet; ccard acc; CKE/CCI. "Superb site; excel facs & v clean, gd views/walking; v friendly owners." ♦ 1 Apr-30 Sep. NOK 210　　　　　　　　　　　　　　2010*

**SVOLVAER (LOFOTEN ISLANDS)** 2F2 (6km SW Coastal) 68.20573, 14.42576 **Sandvika Fjord & Sjøhuscamping (N09), Ørsvågveien 45, 8310 Kabelvåg [tel 76 07 81 45; fax 76 07 87 09; post@sandvika-camping.no; www. sandvika-camping.no]** Sp on S of E10; app lane thro 1 other site. Lge, mkd pitch, terr, unshd; wc; chem disp; mv service pnt; fam bthrm; sauna; shwrs NOK10; el pnts (16A) NOK35 (poss rev pol); lndtte (inc dryer); shop, rest high ssn; snacks; playgrnd; pool; boating; fishing; cycle hire; wifi; TV; phone; bus nr; currency exchange; poss cr; Eng spkn; quiet; ccard acc. "Ideal for trip thro Lofoten Islands; conv Svolvær main fishing port; vg; beautiful views; helpful staff; san facs stretched in high ssn." ♦ 15 Apr-30 Sep. NOK 258　　　　　2014*

**SVOLVAER (LOFOTEN ISLANDS)** 2F2 (15km W Coastal) 68.22356, 14.21471 **Lofoten Bobilcamp, Lyngvær, 8333 Kleppstad [tel 76 07 87 80 or 76 07 87 81; fax 76 07 82 10; post@lofoten-bobilcamping.no; www.lofoten-bobilcamping.no]** On E10 at SW side of island; approx 3km S of Kleppstad. Fr E fr Kabelvåg 13km on E10. Site on L approx 1km after rd turns N. Med, terr, unshd; htd wc; chem disp; mv service pnt; shwrs NOK10; el pnts (10-16A) NOK35; lndtte; shop, rest 10km; BBQ; cooking facs; playgrnd; sand beach adj; boat hire; salmon/trout pond; sat TV; dogs; poss cr; Eng spkn; quiet; red long stay. "Vg; on edge of fjord; facs poss stretched if site full." 1 May-30 Sep. NOK 110　　　　　2009*

**TANA** 2H1 (4km SE Rural) 70.1663, 28.2279 **Tana Familiecamping, Skiippagurra, 9845 Tana (Finnmark) [tel 78 92 86 30; fax 78 92 86 31; tana@famcamp.net]** On ent Tana fr W, cross bdge on E6, heading E sp Kirkenes; site on L in approx 4km. Sm, pt sl, unshd; htd wc; chem disp; mv service pnt; sauna; shwrs inc; el pnts (16A); lndtte (inc dryer); rest; BBQ; playgrnd; Eng spkn; ccard acc; quiet. 1 May-1 Oct.　　　　　　　　　　　　　　2010*

⊞ **TINN AUSTBYGD** 1B3 (1km S Rural) 59.99308, 8.91902 **Sandviken Camping (TE13), 3650 Tinn Austbygd (Telemark) [tel 35 09 81 73; fax 35 09 41 05; kontakt@ sandviken-camping.no; www.sandviken-camping.no]** Site is off Rv364 on L after passing thro Tinn Austbygd. Med, pt shd; htd wc; chem disp; mv service pnt; fam bthrm; sauna; shwrs NOK10; el pnts (10A) NOK35 (check earth); gas; lndtte; shop high ssn; BBQ; cooking facs; playgrnd; lake sw; games rm; games area; boat hire; TV rm; some statics; dogs; phone; poss cr; Eng spkn; CKE/CCI. "Superb, peaceful location at head of Lake Tinnsjø; sh walk thro woods to shops & bank; conv for museum at Rjukan heavy water plant." ♦ NOK 205　　2009*

**TJOTTA** 2E3 (8km N Coastal) 65.82290, 12.41825 **Offersøy Camping, 8860 Tjøtta (Nordland) [tel 75 04 64 11; fax 75 04 63 72; post@kystferie.no; www.kystferie.no]** At end of Rv17 take L & cont 8km. Site well sp. Sm, hdstg, pt sl, pt shd; htd wc; shwrs inc; el pnts NOK40; lndtte; BBQ; cooking facs; playgrnd; beach adj; boat hire & launching; wifi; 80% statics; dogs; poss cr; Eng spkn; quiet. "Conv for ferry; gd." ♦ 15 Jun-15 Aug. NOK 170　　　　2009*

**TJOTTA** (26km N Rural) 65.94685, 12.46261 **Sandnessjøen Camping, Steiro, 8800 Sandnessjøen, Norge [tel 97 56 20 50 / 75 04 54 40; post@ssj.no; www.ssj.no]** Head NW on Rv17 twrds Parkveien. Site is on R. Sm, Pt sl, unshd; htd wc; chem disp; shwrs inc; el pnts; lndtte (inc dryer); bbq; cooking facs; dogs; Eng spkn; some aircraft noise; ccard acc. "Excel san facs; fjord views; gd hiking & fishing; excel site." ♦ 1 May-31 Aug. NOK 250　　　　2014*

**TRETTEN** 1C2 (7km N Rural) 61.38504, 10.26019 **Krekke Camping (OP33), Sør Fåvang, 2634 Fåvang (Oppland) [tel 61 28 45 71; fax 61 28 46 71]** On W side of E6 about 1km N of Mageli Camping, on lakeside. Med, pt sl, unshd; wc; chem disp; mv service pnt; baby facs; shwrs; el pnts inc; lndtte; playgrnd; beach adj; 20% statics; quiet. "Site yourself, warden calls; beautiful views." 1 May-1 Oct.　　　　2009*

**TREUNGEN** 1B4 (15km N Rural) 59.15560, 8.50611 **Søftestad Camping, Nissedal, 3855 Treungen (Aust-Agder) [tel 41 92 76 20]** N fr Kristiansand on Rv41 to Treungen, then alongside E edge of Nisser Water to Nissedal, site sp. Sm, shd; wc; chem disp; baby facs; shwrs 10nok; el pnts (10A) inc; lndtte; BBQ; playgrnd; phone; bus adj; Eng spkn; adv bkg; quiet; red long stay; CKE/CCI. "Close to Telemarken heavy water plant; beautiful alt rte N fr Kristiansand - rd suitable for towed c'vans; gorgeous views over lake." ♦ ltd 1 May-1 Sep. NOK 162　　　　　　　　　　　　　　2014*

**TROGSTAD** 1D3 (6km N Rural) 59.68888, 11.29275 **Olberg Camping, Olberg, 1860 Trøgstad (Østfold) [tel 99 37 45 08; fax 69 82 85 55; froesol@online.no]** Fr Mysen on E18 go N on Rv22 for approx 20km dir Lillestrøm. Site is 2km 2 of Båstad. Sm, hdg pitch, pt shd; htd wc; chem disp; shwrs; baby facs; el pnts (10-16A) NOK35; lndtte (ind dryer); kiosk; snacks; BBQ; playgrnd; pool; beach 3km; fishing; tennis 200m; ice-skating; TV; phone; Eng spkn; adv bkg; quiet; ccard acc; red long stay/CKE/CCI. "Site on lge, working farm with elk safaris; local bread & crafts; farm museum; conv Oslo (40km); v helpful staff; gd for NH or longer." ♦ 1 May-1 Oct. NOK 200　　　　　　　　　　　　　　2014*

⊞ **TROMSO** 2F1 (25km NE Coastal) 69.77765, 19.38273 **Skittenelv Camping, Ullstindveien 736, 9022 Krokelvdalen (Troms) [tel 46 85 80 00; fax 77 69 00 50; post@ skittenelvcamping.no; www.skittenelvcamping.no]** Fr S end of Tromsø Bdge on E8, foll rd sps to Kroken & Oldervik. Site on N side of rd Fv53. Med, some hdstg, unshd; htd wc; chem disp; sauna; shwrs NOK10; el pnts (10A) NOK50; lndtte (inc dryer); shop; tradsmn; snacks; BBQ; playgrnd; htd pool; paddling pool; waterslide; fishing; games rm; wifi; TV; some statics; dogs free; quiet; ccard acc; red CKE/CCI. "Beautiful situation on edge of fjord; arctic sea birds; some facs dated but nice; location o'looking Fjord." ♦ NOK 258　　　2014*

⊞ **TROMSO** 2F1 (2km E Rural) 69.64735, 19.01505 **Tromsø Camping, 9020 Tromsdalen (Troms) [tel 77 63 80 37; fax 77 63 85 24; post@tromsocamping.no; www. tromsocamping.no]** At rndabt on edge of Tromsø take 2nd exit under E8 bdge. Shortly turn R & foll sp. Do not cross narr bdge but turn R then fork L to site. Sm, unshd; wc; chem disp; shwrs inc; mv service pnt; el pnts (10-16A) NOK50; lndtte (inc dryer); shops 1.5km; snacks; playgrnd; wifi; dogs; poss cr; Eng spkn; some noise fr stadium; CKE. "V busy site; facs poss stretched when cr, esp el pnts - improvements in hand; surrounded by fast rv after rain; poss mkt traders on site; rec visit to Arctic church at midnight." NOK 230          2010*

⊞ **TRONDHEIM** 1C1 (1.4km SW Urban) 63.12625, 10.38245 **Parking Øya Stadium, 7030 Trondheim** N on E6, foll sp for St Olevs Hospital. Parking is beyond hospital at side of Øya Stadium running track. Sm. "Free parking; gets busy; MV's only; no facs; o'night parking allowed; 10 min easy walk to cent of Trondheim; excel."          2014*

**TRONDHEIM** 1C1 (10km W Rural) 63.44611, 10.20925 **Flakk Camping (ST19), 7070 Flakk (Sør-Trøndelag) [tel 72 84 39 00; contact@flakk-camping.no; www. flakk-camping.no]** N on E6 to Trondheim cent, then foll sp Fosen onto Rv715 W; site sp & adj Flakk ferry terminal; fr S to Trondheim take Rv707 to site & ferry. Med, pt sl, unshd; wc; chem disp; mv service pnt; baby facs; shwrs inc; el pnts (10A) NOK40 (check earth); lndtte; shop 5km; supmkt 8km; dogs; bus to city; poss cr; Eng spkn; adv bkg; ccard acc; CKE/CCI. "V well-kept site; clean facs; pleasant view over fjord; parts poss muddy after rain; site by ferry terminal (Need to be on R), some ferry noise at night; helpful owner; no earth on elec." ♦ 1 May-1 Sep. NOK 338          2014*

⊞ **TRYSIL** 1D2 (3km N Rural) 61.30400, 12.27459 **Camping Klara, Storvegen, 2420 Trysil (Hedmark) [tel 62 45 13 63; fax 62 45 47 98; klaracamping@trysil.com; www. klaracamping.no]** By Rv26 by Rv Trysilelva, 6km N of Nybergsund, opp hotel. Med, pt sl, pt shd; wc; chem disp; shwrs NOK10; el pnts NOK30; lndtte (inc dryer); shop; snacks; bar; cooking facs; playgrnd; fishing; boating; quiet; CKE/CCI. NOK 170          2010*

**ULSVAG** (2.7km NE) 68.14073, 15.82044 **Sorkil Fjordcamping, Sorkil 8276 [tel 75 77 16 60 / 41 66 08 42 (mob); kontakt@sorkil.no]** Head NE on E6, turn R and destination will be on your R. sm; mkd pitch; pt sl; unshd; htd wc; chem disp; shwr; wc x1; el pnts (16A) €40; lndtte €30; lndry rm; bbq allowed; beach adj; wifi; eng spkn; quiet. "Lovely site S of ferry; adj Fjord excel for midnight sun and fishing." 1 May-30 Sep.          2014*

**ULSVAG** 2F2 (S Rural) 68.11583, 15.86611 **Ulsvåg Camping, 8276 Ulsvåg (Nordland) [tel 75 77 15 73; fax 75 77 12 81; post@gjestgiverinet.net; www.ulvsvag-gjestgiveri.no]** At junc of rd E6 & Rv81 to Skutvik at Hotel Gjestgiveri on N side of junc. Med, hdstg, pt shd; wc; chem disp; mv service pnt; serviced pitches; shwrs NOK5; el pnts (10A) inc; lndtte; shop adj; rest, snacks; bar; shgl beach & lake sw adj; wifi; dogs; poss cr; Eng spkn; adv bkg; quiet; ccard acc; CKE/CCI. "Conv ferries Lofoten Is; beautiful setting & views; gd walking area; useful NH." ♦ ltd NOK 200          2010*

**ULVIK** 1B2 (500m S Rural) 60.56485, 6.90741 **Ulvik Fjordcamping, Sponheim, 5730 Ulvik (Hordaland) [tel 91 17 96 70; post@ulvikcamping.no]** Fr ferry at Bruravik take rd to Ulvik. Site on R in 9km. Fr Granvin, site visible on descending to Ulvik. Sm, pt sl, pt shd; wc; chem disp; shwrs NOK10; el pnts (10A) inc; gas; lndtte; shops 500m; hotel rest adj; snacks; playgrnd; shgl beach; some statics; Eng spkn; adv bkg; quiet; CKE/CCI. "On fjord edge; spectacular scenery; picturesque vill; Osa waterfall 10km, Solsævatnet Lake 10km; immac facs; gd walking; recep in hotel opp." 1 May-31 Aug. NOK 185          2009*

**UTVIKA** 1C3 (Rural) 60.02972, 10.26316 **Utvika Camping (BU14), Utstranda 263, 3531 Utvika (Buskerud) [tel/fax 32 16 06 70; post@utvika.no; www.utvika.no]** Site on loop rd fr E16 N of Nes twd Hønefoss. Site sp but sp opp site ent v sm. Med, pt sl, pt shd; wc; chem disp; baby facs; shwrs NOK10; el pnts (10A) NOK30; lndtte; playgrnd; lake sw adj; cab TV; 50% statics; Eng spkn; quiet. "Conv Oslo (40km) & better than Oslo city sites; busy, friendly site." ♦ 1 May-1 Oct. NOK 225          2009*

**VADSO** 2H1 (15km W Rural) 70.11935, 29.33155 **Vestre Jakobselv Camping, Lilledalsveien 6, 9801 Vestre Jakobselv (Finnmark) [tel 78 95 60 64; s.jankila@imf. no; www.vj-camping.no]** E fr Tana for approx 50km on E6/E75 dir Vadsø, site sp, 1km N of Vestre Jakobselv. Sm, hdstg, pt shd; wc; chem disp; mv service pnt; shwrs inc; el pnts (10A) NOK40; lndtte; shop 1km; rest, snacks; cooking facs; 10% statics; dogs; bus 1km; Eng spkn; quiet; ccard acc; red CKE/CCI. "Conv Vadsø & Vardø - interesting towns." ♦ ltd 15 May-15 Aug. NOK 150          2009*

**VAGAMO** 1C2 (1km S Rural) 61.86465, 9.11438 **Smedsmo Camping, Vågåvegen 80, 2680 Vågåmo (Oppland) [tel 61 23 74 50; fax 61 23 74 14; smedsmo@online.no]** Behind petrol stn on Rv15 twd Lom. Med, pt shd; wc; chem disp; mv service pnt; baby facs; fam bthrm; shwrs NOK10; el pnts (10A) NOK40; lndtte; shop; snacks at g'ge; playgrnd; TV; some statics; dogs; Eng spkn; ccard acc; CKE/CCI. "Gd touring base; pay at petrol stn." ♦ 1 May-30 Sep. NOK 190   2009*

**VALLE** 1B3 (9km N Rural) **Sanden Såre Bobilpark, 4747 Valle (Aust-Agder) [tel 37 93 68 49; td.lunden@online. no; www.setesdal.com]** On Rv9, sp. Sm, mkd pitch, hdstg, pt sl, shd; htd wc; chem disp; mv service pnt; serviced pitches; shwrs inc; el pnts inc; lndry rm; rv adj; TV; quiet. "M'vans & c'vans, but poss diff lge o'fits; honesty box for payment; lovely setting." NOK 150          2009*

⊞ **VANGSNES** 1B2 (N Rural) 61.17483, 6.63729 **Solvang Camping & Motel, 6894 Vangsnes (Sogn og Fjordane) [tel 57 69 66 20; fax 57 69 67 55; post@solvangcamping. com; www.solvangcamping.com]** Site at end of peninsula, on S side of Sognefjord on Rv13, immed overlkg ferry terminal. Sm, sl, pt shd; wc; fam bthrm; baby facs; shwrs inc; el pnts NOK30; lndtte; shops adj & 300m; rest, snacks; bar; playgrnd; pool; lake sw; fishing; boating; TV; some noise fr ferries. "Wonderful views; useful sh stay/NH for x-ing Sognefjord; delightful." NOK 185          2010*

**VANGSNES** *1B2* (3.5km S Rural) *61.14516, 6.62025* **Tveit Camping (SF32), 6894 Vangsnes (Sogn og Fjordane) [tel 57 69 66 00; fax 57 69 66 70; tveitca@online.no; www.tveitcamping.no]** On Rv13; sp. Sm, terr, pt shd; htd wc; chem disp; mv service pnt; baby facs; shwrs NOK10; el pnts (10A) NOK25; lndtte (inc dryer); kiosk; shop, rest, snacks 3.5km; playgrnd; boating; boat & cycle hire; internet; TV; 30% statics; dogs; phone; quiet; red long stay/CKE/CCI. "Sw poss off rocky shore; views of Sognefjord." ♦ 1 May-1 Oct. NOK 160                                                    2010*

⊞ **VASSENDEN** *1A2* (2km SW Rural) *61.48785, 6.08366* **PlusCamp Jølstraholmen, 6847 Vassenden (Sogn og Fjordane) [tel 57 72 89 07; fax 57 72 75 05; jostraholmen@ pluscamp.no; www.jolstraholmen.no]** On R of E39, site is 2km SW of Vassenden at Statoil petrol stn. Med, hdg pitch, terr, pt sl, pt shd; htd wc; mv service pnt; chem disp; baby facs; shwrs NOK6; el pnts (10-16A) NOK40; lndtte (inc dryer); shop; tradsmn; rest, snacks; BBQ; playgrnd; paddling pool; rv & lake sw & fishing; ski lift 500m; cab TV; 70% statics; dogs; Eng spkn; no adv bkg; quiet; ccard acc; red CKE/CCI. "Rv flows thro site; gd facs; friendly site; ltd facs for tourers; NH." NOK 180                                                    2010*

⊞ **VEGA** *2E2* (6.3km SE Rural) *65.64353, 11.95110* **Vega Camping, 8980 Vega [tel 47 94 35 00 80; post@ vegacamping.no; www.vegacamping.no]** Fr Fv90 head NW, take 1st L onto Fv90, turn L twd Fv84, turn R onto Fv84. After 1.6km turn L, then take 2nd L. Site in 450mtrs. Sm, unshd; htd wc; chem disp; shwrs 20NOK; wl pnts (16A) inc; cooking facs; sw lake; 0% statics; dogs; Eng spkn; quiet; cash only. "Island ideal for cycling/walking; Elder Duck cent; beautiful location; excel site." NOK 230          2014*

**VIKEDAL** *1A3* (2km S Coastal) *59.48010, 5.89990* **Camping Søndenaastranden, Søndenå, 5583 Vikedal (Rogaland) [tel 52 76 03 29; fax 53 76 62 63; gunnar@halvorsen-regnskap.no]** Sp on Rv46. Lge, mkd pitch, unshd; wc; chem disp; shwrs NOK10; el pnts (6A); lndtte (inc dryer); shop adj; snacks; bar; cooking facs; playgrnd; shgl beach adj; fishing; boat launching facs; 60% statics; Eng spkn; no ccard acc; CKE/ CCI. 1 Apr-1 Oct.                                            2010*

**VIKERSUND** *1C3* (1km E Rural) *59.97766, 10.02036* **Natvedt Gård & Camping, Øst-Modumveien, 3370 Vikersund (Buskerud) [tel 32 78 73 55; natvedt@frisurf.no]** On Rv35 Hokksund-Hønefoss; in Vikersund R onto Rv284 sp Sylling to site 3km after lake bdge. Clearly sp on L. Med, pt sl, pt shd; chem disp; mv service pnt; shwrs; el pnts (4A) NOK35; lndtte (inc dryer); sm shop on site & 3km; rest 4km; playgrnd; lake sw; phone; poss cr; quiet. "Hilly - not suitable for handicapped." 1 May-15 Sep. NOK 170                                    2010*

**VIKHAMMER see Malvik** *1D1*

**VIKOYRI** *1B2* (W Rural) *61.08416, 6.56786* **Vik Camping, 6891 Vikøyri (Sogn og Fjordane) [tel 57 69 51 25; grolilje@ hotmail.com]** Sp in cent of Vikøyri dir Ligtvor; 67km N of Voss on Rv13. Sm, unshd; htd wc; chem disp; shwrs; el pnts (10A) (no earth); lndtte; shop 200m; dogs; quiet; Eng spkn; CKE/CCI. "Conv for ferry fr Vangsnes, easier access than other sites; gd NH." ♦ 10 May-30 Sep.                                        2009*

**VIKSDALEN** *1A2* (11km S Rural) *61.32628, 6.26926* **Hov Camping, Eldalsdalen, 6978 Viksdalen (Sogn og Fjordane) [tel 57 71 79 37 / 911 88 466 (mob); fax 57 71 79 55; ottarhov@c2i.net; www.viksdalen.no/hov-hyttegrend]** Fr Dragsvik N on Rv13, site is approx 9km S of junc with Rv610, sp. Sm, hdstg, unshd; htd wc; baby facs; shwrs NOK10; el pnts (8-10A); lndtte (inc dryer); shop; tradsmn; playgrnd; fishing; cycle hire; Eng spkn; quiet; ccard acc; CKE/CCI. "Attractive site with boating on lake; wcs by parking area; all other facs 150m; remote area." ♦ 1 Apr-30 Sep. NOK 180                      2013*

**VOSS** *1A2* (300m S Rural) *60.62476, 6.42233* **Voss Camping, Prestegardsmoen 40, 5700 Voss (Hordaland) [tel/fax 56 51 15 97 or 90 18 11 20; post@vosscamping.no; www. vosscamping.no]** Exit town on E16 & camping sp; by lake nr cent of Voss; app fr W on E16, site visible by lake on R; 2nd turn on R in town to site in 300m. Sm, mkd pitch, hdstg, terr, pt shd; htd wc; chem disp; shwrs NOK10; el pnts (10A) NOK45; lndtte; shop 500m; snacks; playgrnd; htd pool; watersports; beach/lake adj; boat & cycle hire; few statics; phone; poss v cr; Eng spkn; no adv bkg; ccard acc; CKE/CCI. "Excel cent for fjords; cable car stn in walking dist; tourist bureau; most pitches hdstg gravel but narr/sm." 1 Jan-1 Oct. NOK 225                                                    2014*

NORWAY

Map 2

*Warsaw Old Town, Poland*

# Poland
## Country Introduction

## Welcome to Poland

Poland has a variety of regions with beautiful landscapes that are dotted with small farms.

A journey through the Polish rural countryside gives you a perfect opportunity to enjoy and absorb its scenery and people.

The cities are full of sightseeing opportunities. Streets crammed with galleries, cafes, pubs and restaurants with some amazing historical buildings in between.

## Country highlights

Polish cuisine is tasty and substantial, with restaurants offering good value. Try the pierogi (savoury ravioli), kalduny (stuffed dumplings) and gołabki (stuffed cabbage rolls). Wódka (vodka) is the national drink.

If you are interested in music, film, dance or art, you are sure to find an event or festival nearby. The Wratislavia Cantans International Festival, which is held in Wrocławs many historical buildings between September and October, if very popular as it celebrates all of the arts.

## Major towns and cities

- Warsaw – the capital and largest city of Poland full of historic landmarks.

- Kraków - one of Polands prettiest cities, retaining old-world ambience and charm.

- Wrocław – a city of stuning architecture, medieval streets and a popular square.

- Katowice – this city is the centre for culture and science with fairs and exhibitions.

## Attractions

- Kraków's Historic Centre – Europe's largest and most historical market square.

- Wrocław Town Hall – an impressive building with numerous carvings and detailed frieze.

- Wieliczka Salt Mine – full of underground lakes, enormous caverns and salt sculptures.

- Malbork Castle – this huge red brick castle from the middle ages is worth exploring.

## Find out more

www.poland.travel

Tel: 0048 (0) 22 53 67 070 Polish Tourist Office

# Country Information

*Population (approx):* 38.4 million

*Capital:* Warsaw (population approx 1.7 million)

*Area:* 312,685 sq km

*Bordered by:* Belarus, Czech Republic, Germany, Lithuania, Russia, Slovakia, Ukraine

*Terrain:* Mostly flat plain with many lakes; mountains along southern border

*Climate:* Changeable continental climate with cold, often severe winters and hot summers; rainfall spread throughout the year; late spring and early autumn are the best times to visit

*Coastline:* 491km

*Highest Point:* Rysy 2,499m

*Language:* Polish

*Local Time:* GMT or BST + 1, i.e. 1 hour ahead of the UK all year

*Currency:* Zloty (PLN) divided into 100 groszy; £1 = PLN 5.22; PLN10 = £1.91 (September 2014)

*Emergency numbers:* Police 997; Fire brigade 998; Ambulance 999.

*Public Holidays 2014:* Jan 1, 6; Apr 6; May 1, 3 (Constitution Day), 25; Jun 4; Aug 15; Nov 1, 11 (Independence Day); Dec 25, 26.

School summer holidays run from the last week of June to the end of August.

# Camping and Caravanning

There are around 250 organised campsites throughout Poland, with the most attractive areas being the Mazurian lake district and along the coast. Campsites are usually open from the beginning of May or June to the middle or end of September, but the season only really starts towards the end of June. Until then facilities may be very limited and grass may not be cut, etc.

You can download details of approximately 160 sites (including GPS co-ordinates) from the website of the Polish Federation of Camping & Caravanning, www.pfcc.eu.

Campsites are classified into two categories. Category one sites provide larger pitches and better amenities, but it may still be advisable to use your own facilities. There are also some basic sites which are not supervised and are equipped only with drinking water, toilets and washing facilities. Sites may be in need of modernisation but, on the whole, sanitary facilities are clean although they may provide little privacy. Some new sites are being built to higher standards. A site may close earlier than its published date if the weather is bad.

Many sites are not signposted from main roads and may be difficult to find. It is advisable to obtain a large scale atlas or good maps of the areas to be visited and not rely on one map covering the whole of Poland.

Casual/wild camping is not recommended and is prohibited in national parks (except on organised sites) and in sand dunes along the coast.

# Cycling

There are several long-distance cycle routes using a combination of roads with light motor traffic, forest trails or tracks along waterways. There are some cycle lanes on main roads where cyclists may not ride two or more abreast.

# Electricity and Gas

The current on most campsites is 10 amps. Plugs have two round pins. There are some CEE connections.

It is understood that both propane and butane supplies are widely available, but cylinders are not exchangeable and it may be necessary to refill. The Caravan Club does not recommend this practice and you should aim to take enough gas to last during your stay. Some campsites have kitchens which you may use to conserve your gas supplies.

# Entry Formalities

British and Irish passport holders may visit Poland for up to three months without a visa. At campsites reception staff should undertake any required registration formalities with local authorities.

# Medical Services

For simple complaints and basic advice consult staff in a pharmacy (apteka). Some English may be spoken. In general, medical facilities are comparatively inexpensive and of a good standard. Medical staff are well qualified. English is not always widely spoken and you may face language difficulties.

You will need a European Health Insurance Card (EHIC) to obtain emergency treatment from doctors, dentists and hospitals contracted to the state health care system, the NFZ. Reimbursements for any charges that you incur can be claimed from the NFZ office in Warsaw. You will have to pay a proportion of the cost of prescriptions, which is not refundable in Poland.

Private health clinics offering a good standard of medical care can also be found in large cities.

## Opening Hours

Banks – Mon-Fri 9am-4pm; Sat 9am-1pm.

Museums – Tue-Sun 10am-5pm; closed Mon.

Post Offices – Mon-Fri 8am-6pm; Sat 8am-2pm (on rota basis).

Shops – Mon-Fri 11am-8pm; Sat 9am-2pm/4pm; food shops open and close earlier; supermarkets open until 9pm/10pm.

## Safety and Security

Most visits to Poland are trouble free and violent crime is rare, but there is a risk of robbery in tourist areas, particularly near hotels, at main railway stations and on public transport. Passengers are most at risk when boarding and leaving trains or trams. Avoid walking alone at night, particularly in dark or poorly-lit streets or in public parks.

Some tourists have been the target of a scam in which men claiming to be plain clothes police officers ask visitors to show their identity documents and bank cards, and then ask for their PIN(s). Although the police are allowed to stop people and request to see identification, under no circumstances should you disclose your bank account details or PIN(s).

Theft of and from vehicles is common so do not leave vehicle documentation or valuables in your car. Foreign registered cars may be targeted, especially in large, busy supermarket car parks.

Cases have been reported of vehicles with foreign number plates being stopped by gangs posing as police officers, either claiming a routine traffic control or at the scene of fake accidents, particularly in rural and tourist areas. If in doubt, when flagged down keep all doors and windows locked, remain in your vehicle and ask to see identification. The motoring organisation, PZM, advises that any car or document inspection performed outside built-up areas can only be carried out by uniformed police officers and at night these officials must use a police patrol car. Although police officers do not have to be in uniform within built-up areas, they must always present their police identity card. More details are available to motorists at Polish road borders.

An emergency helpline has been set up to assist visitors who have been victims of crime or who require assistance tel: 0800 200300 (freephone) or +48 608 599999 (mobile number). The helpline operates from 1 June to 30 September between 10am and 10pm.

Do not leave drinks or food unattended or accept drinks from strangers. There has been a small number of reports of drinks being spiked and of visitors having their valuables stolen whilst drugged.

*British Embassy*

UL KAWALERII 12
00-468 WARSZAWA
Tel: (022) 3110000
http://ukinpoland.fco.gov.uk/en/
There are also Honorary Consulates in Gdansk, Katowice, Kraków, Łódz, Lublin, Poznan, Szczecin and Wrocław.

*Irish Embassy*

UL MYSIA 5, 00-496 WARSZAWA
Tel: (022) 8496633
www.embassyofireland.pl
There is also an Honorary Consulate in Poznan.

## Border Posts

Customs posts are open 24 hours a day throughout the year. Cars crossing the eastern borders, especially to Lithuania and Belarus, are usually intensively scrutinised by the Polish authorities in an effort to combat widespread smuggling of stolen cars. Travellers should ensure all documents are in order.

Borders may be busy at weekends with cross-border shoppers, and it is understood that in particular the crossing from Germany via Frankfurt-on-Oder can be heavily congested on Saturday mornings.

# Documents

## Driving Licence

The standard pink UK paper driving licence is recognised, but if you hold the old style green UK licence or a Northern Irish licence issued prior to 1991 you are advised to update it to a photocard licence in order to avoid any local difficulties.

## Passport

You should carry your passport with you at all times.

## Vehicle(s)

You must carry your original vehicle registration certificate (V5C), insurance documentation and MOT certificate (if applicable) at all times. You may be asked for these if you are stopped by the police and, in particular, when crossing borders. If you do not own the vehicle(s) you will need a letter of authority from the owner, together with the vehicle's original documentation.

# Money

Cash can easily be obtained from ATMs in banks and shopping centres. ATMs offer an English option.

Major credit cards are widely accepted in hotels, restaurants and shops but you may find that supermarkets do not accept them. Take particular care with credit/debit cards and don't lose sight of them during transactions.

Sterling and euros are readily accepted at exchange bureaux but Scottish and Northern Irish bank notes are not generally recognised and you may have difficulties trying to exchange them.

Carry your credit card issuers'/banks' 24-hour UK contact numbers in case of loss or theft of your cards.

# Motoring in Poland

Poland is a major east to west route for heavy

vehicles and driving can be hazardous. There are few dual carriageways and even main roads between large towns can be narrow and poorly surfaced. Slow moving agricultural and horse-drawn vehicles are common in rural areas. Street lighting is weak even in major cities.

Local driving standards are poor and speed limits, traffic lights and road signs are often ignored. Drivers rarely indicate before manoeuvring and you may encounter aggressive tailgating, overtaking on blind bends and overtaking on the inside. Take particular care on national holiday weekends when there is a surge in road accidents.

It is not advisable to drive a right hand drive vehicle alone for long distances or to drive long distances at night. At dusk watch out for cyclists riding without lights along the edge of the road or on its shoulder.

Hitchhikers use an up and down motion of the hand to ask for a lift. This may be confused with flagging down.

# Accidents

A driver involved in an accident must call the police, obtain an official record of damages and forward it to the insurance company of the Polish driver involved (if applicable), for example, the Polish National Insurance Division (PZU) or the Polish Insurance Association (WARTA). Members of AIT/FIA affiliated clubs, such as The Caravan Club, can obtain help from the touring office ('Autotour') of the Polish motoring organisation, Polski Zwiazek Motorowy (PZM), tel: (022) 8496904 or (022) 8499361.

If people are injured, you must call an ambulance or doctor. By law, it is an offence for a driver not to obtain first aid for accident victims or to leave the scene of an accident. In such circumstances the authorities may withdraw a tourist's passport and driving licence, vehicle registration certificate or even the vehicle itself and the penalties can be a prison sentence and a fine.

# Alcohol

There is zero tolerance for drink-driving; the permitted level of alcohol is 20 milligrams in 100 millilitres of blood, which in practice equates to zero. At the request of the police or if an accident has occurred a driver must undergo a blood test which, if positive, may lead to a prison sentence, withdrawal of driving licence and a fine. Penalty points will be notified to the authorities in the motorist's home country.

## Breakdown Service

The toll free telephone number for breakdown assistance throughout the country is 981.

The PZM runs a breakdown service covering the entire country 24 hours a day. Members of AIT and FIA affiliated clubs, such as The Caravan Club, should call the PZM Emergency Centre on (022) 5328433. Staff speak English. Roadside assistance must be paid for in cash.

## Essential Equipment

*Fire extinguisher*
It is compulsory to carry a fire extinguisher on board all vehicles.

*First aid kit*
It is not compulsory to have a first aid kit but it is recommended.

*Lights*
Dipped headlights must be used at all times. Bulbs are more likely to fail with constant use and you are recommended to carry spares. In bad visibility use your horn to indicate that you are going to overtake.

*Warning Triangles*
You must use a warning triangle when a vehicle is stationary on a road in poor visibility (less than 100 metres) and if the vehicle is likely to obstruct traffic. On a normal road the triangle must be placed between 30 and 50 metres behind the vehicle and must be clearly visible to oncoming traffic; on a motorway, it must be placed 100 metres behind the vehicle. Hazard warning lights may be used in addition to, but not instead of, a triangle.

*Child Restraint System*
Children under the age of 12 years old and under the height of 1.5m must use a suitable restraint system that has been adapted to their size. It is prohibited to place a child in a rear facing seat in the front of the vehicle if the car is equipped with airbags.

## Fuel

The usual opening hours for petrol stations are from 8am to 7pm; many on main roads and international routes and in large towns are open 24 hours. Credit cards are widely accepted. LPG (Autogas) is widely available from service stations.

## Parking

There are parking meters in many towns and signs display parking restrictions or prohibitions. There are many supervised car parks charging an hourly rate. Illegally parked cars causing an obstruction may be towed away and impounded, in which case a driver will be fined. Wheel clamps are in use.

Sidelights must be used when parking in unlit streets during the hours of darkness.

## Priority

Priority should be given to traffic coming from the right at intersections of roads of equal importance, however vehicles on rails always have priority. At roundabouts traffic already on a roundabout has priority.

Give way to buses pulling out from bus stops. Trams have priority over other vehicles at all times. Where there is no central reservation or island you should stop to allow passengers alighting from trams to cross to the pavement.

## Roads

All roads are hard surfaced and the majority of them are asphalted. However, actual road surfaces may be poor; even some major roads are constructed of cement or cobbles and heavily rutted. Average journey speed is about 50 km/h (31 mph).

Some roads, notably those running into Warsaw, have a two metre wide strip on the nearside to pull onto in order to allow other vehicles to overtake. Oncoming lorries expect other motorists to pull over when they are overtaking.

Overtake trams on the right unless in a one-way street.

# Road Signs and Markings

Road signs and markings conform to international standards. Motorway and national road numbers are indicated in red and white, and local roads by yellow signs with black numbering. Signs on motorways are blue with white lettering and on main roads they are green and white.

The following road signs may be seen:

| Polish | English Translation |
|---|---|
| Rondzie | Roundabout |
| Wstep szbroniony | No Entry |
| Wyjscie | Exit |

You may also encounter the following:

Paid parking between 7am and 6pm

Residential area- predestrians have priority

Toll road

Rutted road

Winding road

Emergency vehicles

Crossroads and road junctions may not be marked with white 'stop' lines, and other road markings in general may be well worn and all but invisible, so always take extra care.

# Speed Limits

| | Open Road (km/h) | Motorway (km/h) |
|---|---|---|
| Car Solo | 90 | 140 |
| Car towing caravan/trailer | 70 | 80 |
| Motorhome under 3500kg | 90 | 140 |
| Motorhome 3500-7500kg | 70 | 80 |

In built up areas the speed limit is 50 km/h (31 mph) between 5am and 11pm, and 60 km/h (37 mph) between 11pm and 5am. For vehicles over 3,500kg all speed limits are the same as for a car and caravan outfit. In residential zones indicated by entry/exit signs, the maximum speed is 20 km/h (13 mph).

The use of radar detectors is illegal.

# Traffic Lights

Look out for a small, non-illuminated green arrow under traffic lights, which permits a right turn against a red traffic light if the junction is clear.

# Violation of Traffic Regulations

Motorists must not cross a road's solid central white line or even allow wheels to run on it. Radar speed traps are frequently in place on blind corners where speed restrictions apply. Police are very keen to enforce traffic regulations with verbal warnings and/or on the spot fines. Fines are heavy and drivers of foreign registered vehicles will be required to pay in cash. Always obtain an official receipt.

# Motorways and Tolls

There are approximately 1420km of motorways in Poland. Tolls are levied on sections and vary in price, for example, the A1 Rusocin to Nowe Marzy is PLN 41.80 (2014 prices) for a car towing a caravan weighing under 3500kg.

An electronic toll system is in place for vehicles which weigh over 3,500kg, including motorhomes and car and caravan combinations if the total weight is over 3,500kg. These vehicles will need to be equipped with an electronic device called a viaBOX.
Visit www.viatoll.pl/en and select the 'Trucks' option for details of toll costs for motorhomes and car/caravan combinations weighing over 3500kg.

An electronic option is also available for vehicles and car/caravan combinations which weigh under 3500kg - go to the above website and choose the 'Cars' options for details.

There are emergency telephones every 2km along motorways. Recent visitors report that newer stretches of motorway have rest areas with chemical disposal and waste water disposal facilities.

POLAND

## Touring

Poland's climate does not permit the production of wine, the national drinks being varieties of vodka and plum brandy. It is usual to leave a tip of between 10 to 15%.

There are over 9,000 lakes in Poland, mostly in the north. The regions of Western Pomerania, Kaszubia and Mazuria are a paradise for sailing enthusiasts, anglers and nature lovers. In order to protect areas of great natural beauty, national parks and nature reserves have been created, two of the most interesting of which are the Tatra National Park covering the whole of the Polish Tatra mountains, and the Slowinksi National Park with its 'shifting' sand dunes.

There are 13 UNESCO World Heritage sites including the restored historic centres of Warsaw and Kraków, the medieval, walled town of Toruń as well as Auschwitz Concentration Camp. Other towns worth a visit are Chopin's birthplace at Zelazowa Wola, Wieliczka with its salt mines where statues and a chapel are carved out of salt, and Wrocław.

White and brown signs placed strategically in cities and near sites of interest pinpoint architectural and natural landmarks, places of religious worship, etc. Each sign includes not only information on the name of and distance to a particular attraction, but also a pictogram of the attraction, e.g. Jasna Góra monastery. Themed routes, such as the trail of the wooden churches in the Małopolska Region (south of Kraków), are marked in a similar way.

A Warsaw Tourist Card and a Kraków Tourist Card are available, both valid for up to three days and offering free travel on public transport and free entry to many museums, together with discounts at selected restaurants and shops and on sightseeing and local excursions. Buy the cards from tourist information centres, travel agents or hotels.

The Polish people are generally friendly, helpful and polite. English is becoming increasingly widely spoken in major cities.

## Public Transport & Local Travel

For security reasons recent visitors recommend using guarded car parks such as those in Warsaw on the embankment below the Old Town, in the Palace of Culture and near the Tomb of the Unknown Soldier.

Problems have been reported involving overcharging by non-regulated taxi drivers. Use only taxis from official ranks whose vehicles have the name and telephone number of the taxi company on the door and on the roof (beside the occupied/unoccupied light). They also display a rate card in the window of the vehicle. Taxis with a crest but no company name are not officially registered.

There are frequent ferries from Gydnia, Swinoujscie and Gdansk to Denmark, Germany and Sweden. There are no car ferry services on internal waters but passenger services operate along the Baltic Coast, on the Mazurian lakes and on some rivers, for example, between Warsaw and Gdansk.

There is a metro system in Warsaw linking the centre to the north and south of the city. It is possible to buy a daily or weekly tourist pass which is valid for all means of public transport – bus, tram and metro. Buy tickets at newspaper stands and kiosks displaying a sign 'bilety'. Tickets must be punched before travelling at the yellow machines at the entrance to metro stations or on board buses and trams. You will incur an on the spot fine if you are caught travelling without a valid ticket.

AUSCHWITZ see Oświęcim D3

BAKOW see Kluczbork C2

BARANOWO see Poznań B2

BIALOWIEZA B4 (1km W Rural) 52.69395, 23.83088
Camping U Michała (No. 124), ul Krzyże 11, 17-230
Białowieża [(085) 6812703] Exit Bielsk Podlaski onto rd 689;
cont past Hajnówka for 17m; site on R at end of vill. Sm, mkd
pitch, pt shd; wc; chem disp; shwrs inc; el pnts (16A); lndtte;
playgrnd; cycle hire; poss cr; quiet. "Gd san facs." ◆ 15 Apr-
30 Sep. PLN 50                                          2011*

⊞ BIALYSTOK B4 (6.5km N Rural) 53.19364, 23.19364
Camping Hotel Jard, ul Białostocka 94, 16-010 Wasilków
[(085) 7185240; fax 7185511; www.jard.pl] On L of rte 19
when on app Wasilków fr Białystok. Sm, pt sl, pt shd; own
san rec; shwrs inc; el pnts (10A) PLN8; shop 2km; rest; bar;
ccard acc. "Fair NH; simple site - only one for some dist."
PLN 34                                                 2009*

BIELSKO BIALA D3 (1.5km S Rural) 49.78031, 19.05318
Camping Ondraszek (No. 57), ul Pocztowa 43, 43-
309 Bielsko-Biała [(033) 8146425; fax 8143601;
kemping57ondraszek@op.pl; www.tkkfblonia.ovh.org]
Fr E462 ent Bielsk0-Biała & foll sp Szczyrk. Site sp on R after
Park Hotel. Cont uphill to T-junc, L to gates. Site on edge of
town in park. Sm, hdg pitch, pt sl, pt shd; wc; chem disp; mv
service pnt; shwrs inc; el pnts; shops 1.5km; rest adj; bar; BBQ;
playgrnd; pool & sports facs adj; quiet. "Pretty, well-kept site
in woods; daytime noise fr neighbouring sports facs; conv
Oswięcim (Auschwitz)." ◆ 15 Apr-30 Sep. PLN 54    2010*

BIELSKO BIALA D3 (5km SW Rural) 49.78148, 19.02281
Camping Pod Dębowcem (No. 99), ul Karbowa 15, 43-316
Bielsko-Biała [(033) 8216181 or (0604) 144186 (mob); 99@
camping.org.pl; www.camping.bielsko.com.pl] Rd 1/E75
out of Bielsko-Biała to Cieszyn or fr B942 foll sp 'Szyndzielnia'
(cable car) to site. Med, mkd pitch, some hdstg, terr, pt sl,
pt shd; wc; chem disp; shwrs inc; el pnts (6A) PLN10; lndtte;
snacks; bar; BBQ; playgrnd; TV; dogs; no adv bkg; quiet; CKE/
CCI. "Conv Czech border." ◆ 1 May-31 Oct. PLN 48  2010*

BOGACZEWO see Gizycko A3

CHMIELNO see Kartuzy A2

⊞ CZESTOCHOWA C3 (1km W Urban) 50.81122,
19.09131 Camping Oleńka (No. 76), ul Oleńki 10, 42-200
Częstochowa [tel/fax (034) 3606066; camping@mosir.pl;
www.mosir.pl] Fr A1/E75 foll sp Jasna Góra monastery, pick
up sm white camping sp to site. Lge, pt shd; wc; chem disp;
shwrs inc; el pnts (20A); lndtte; shops nrby; rest; bar; playgrnd;
pool 2km; internet; TV; 20% statics; dogs; phone; Eng spkn;
no adv bkg; quiet; ccard acc; red CKE/CCI. "Guided tours;
monastery worth visit; gd NH/sh stay nr Jasna Góra & Black
Madonna painting; poor security; san facs unclean & poorly
maintained (6/09)." ◆ PLN 84                          2009*

DZIWNOW A1 (2km E Coastal) 54.03404, 14.79978 Camping
Wiking (No. 194), ul Wolności 3, 72-420 Dziwnówek
[tel/fax (091) 3813493; camping@campingwiking.pl;
www.campingwiking.pl] Foll rd 102 thro Dziwnówek twd
Dziwnów. Site on R in 400m (past ent to diff site). Med, pt sl,
shd; wc; chem disp; baby facs; shwrs PLN15; el pnts PLN13.50
(poss rev pol); lndtte; shop; rest, snacks; bar; BBQ; playgrnd;
sw & sand beach adj; some statics; dogs PLN7; bus; poss cr;
CKE/CCI. "Fair sh stay/NH; gd security." ◆ 1 May-10 Sep.
PLN 60                                                 2009*

ELBLAG A3 (N Urban) 54.15349, 19.39403 Camping
Elbląg (No. 61), ul Panieńska 14, 82-300 Elbląg [tel/
fax (055) 6418666; camping@camping61.com.pl; www.
camping61.com.pl] Fr rd 7/E77 fr Gdańsk, take slip rd into
Elbląg. At traff lts bdge over canal turn L, site on R, well sp
fr ring rd. Sm, pt shd; wc; chem disp; shwrs; el pnts (16A)
PLN8; lndtte; rest 500m; snacks 400m; playgrnd; wifi; dogs; red
low ssn/long stary/CKE/CCI. "Helpful staff; old san facs clean
but poss stretched high ssn; conv for 'shiplift' canal." 29 Apr-
30 Sep. PLN 51                                        2011*

ELK A3 (500m SW Urban) 53.81545, 22.35215 Camping
Plaża Miejska (No. 62), ul Parkowa 2, 19-300 Ełk
[(087) 6109700; fax 6102223; mosir@elk.com.pl; www.
mosir.elk.com.pl] Fr town cent on rd 16 take rd 65/669 dir
Białystok. After 200m cross rv & immed turn R, site 100m on L.
Sm, mkd pitch, hdstg, pt shd; htd wc; shwrs inc; el pnts (10A)
inc; shop 500m; snacks; bar; cooking facs; lake sw & sand
beach 200m; quiet; CKE/CCI. "Gd security; well-maintained,
clean site adj town cent & attractive lake; gd touring base lake
district." ◆ 1 Jun-1 Sep. PLN 65                      2011*

FROMBORK A3 (1km E Rural/Coastal) 54.35877, 19.69572
Camping Frombork (No. 12), ul Braniewska, 14-530
Frombork [(0506) 803151; kontakt@campingfrombork.
pl; www.campingfrombork.pl] Fr Frombork on rd 504 dir
Braniewo, site on L. Med, pt shd; wc; chem disp & mv service
pnt at car wash; shwrs inc; el pnts inc; lndtte; shop 1km; bar;
BBQ; playgrnd; sand beach 2km; games area; dogs; quiet.
"Pleasant, basic site; san facs tatty but clean (2009); pleasant
countryside." 1 May-30 Sep. PLN 60                   2013*

GAJ see Krakow D3

GDANSK A2 (5km E Coastal) 54.37021, 18.72938
Camping Stogi (No. 218), ul Wydmy 9, 80-656 Gdańsk
[(058) 3073915; fax 3042259; jan@camping-gdansk.pl;
www.kemping-gdansk.pl] E fr Gdańsk on rd 7 (E77) for
approx 2km, then L foll sp for Stogi. Then foll tram rte no. 8
to Stogi Plaza/Beach. Site is 100m fr tram terminus, well sp.
Med, hdstg, wc; chem disp; shwrs inc; el pnts (10-16A) PLN11;
lndtte; shop; snacks; bar; BBQ; playgrnd; sand beach adj;
games area; wifi; 75% statics; tram 100m; poss cr & poss noise
fr school parties; CKE/CCI. "Basic site, more a holiday camp
for school groups; ltd facs low ssn; close to huge, clean beach;
gd security; vg site; sep area for m'vans; san facs upgraded
(2013)." 25 Apr-5 Oct. PLN 89                         2013*

---

POLAND

**GIZYCKO** *A3* (6km SE Rural) *53.96750, 21.77666* **Camping Echo (No. 55), Mazurska 48, 11-511 Rydzewo-Miłki [(087) 4211186; olanowakowska84@gmail.com; www. mazury.info.pl/echo]** Fr Giżycko rd 63 dir Orzysz; in Ruda foll sp to R Rydzewo & site on lakeside. Sm, pt shd; wc; shwrs inc; el pnts (16A) PLN9; lndtte; shop; rest 1km; snacks high ssn; BBQ; sand beach; lake sw; dogs PLN5; Eng spkn; quiet. "Vg; gd, modern san facs; ideal for touring Masurian Lake District." 1 May-30 Sep. PLN 50                                  2010*

**GIZYCKO** *A3* (500m W Urban) *54.03413, 21.76002* **Camping Zamek (No. 1), ul Moniuszki 1, 11-500 Giżycko [(087) 4283410; info@cmazur.pl; www.cmazur. pl]** Fr Olsztyn on rte 59 ent town. After junc with rte 592 fr Kętrzyn bear R to town cent & swing bdge. Site on R bef swing bdge over canal adj Hotel Zamek. NB Swing bdge 2.5T weight & 2m height limit, do not app site thro town. Sm, hdg pitch, pt sl, pt shd; wc; chem disp; shwrs PLN10; el pnts (16A) PLN8; lndtte; shop 500m; rest, snacks; bar; cooking facs; lake 500m; wifi; dogs PLN10; rlwy noise & poss noisy until 2300 as disco adj; CKE/CCI. "Adj boat marina & nr beautiful lakes/ forests." ♦ 1 May-30 Sep. PLN 41                    2011*

⊞ **JELENIA GORA** *C2* (700m SE Urban) *50.89638, 15.74266* **Auto-Camping Park (No. 130), ul Sudecka 42, 58-500 Jelenia Góra [tel/fax (075) 7524525; campingpark@interia. pl; www.camping.karkonosz.pl]** In town foll sp to Karpacz on rd 367. Site 100m fr hotel. Well sp. Med, some hdstg, pt terr, pt shd; wc in recep building; shwrs inc; el pnts (6-10A) PLN10 (poss rev pol); lndtte; shops 100m; rest 200m; snacks; pool, tennis & sports facs 500m; wifi; TV; 20% statics; dogs PLN5; adv bkg; quiet but some rd noise; ccard acc; red CKE/ CCI. "Conv Karkanosze mountains & Czech border; well-run, neat site nr hotel with gd, modern facs; 20 min walk to pleasant town; staff friendly & helpful; conv NH; gd facs." ♦ PLN 40                                              2012*

**JELENIA GORA** *C2* (8km SW Urban) *50.86566, 15.6644* **Camping Słoneczna Polana, ul Rataja 9, 58-560 Cieplici [tel/fax (075) 7552566; info@camping-polen.pl; www. camping-polen.pl]** Fr SW on rd 3/E65 twd Jelenia Góra; after Wojcieszyce, then o'head power lines, turn R to Cieplice & watch for church spire strt ahead. Take care at level x-ing, turn R at T-junc to site on L after 1km where rd crosses stream. Fr N app Jelenia Góra on rd 297 & rd 30, turn R on rd 3/E65 sp Szklarska Poręba. After about 3km app x-rds at Wojcieszyce. Turn L to Cieplice, then as above. Med, mkd pitch, pt shd; wc; chem disp; mv service pnt; shwrs inc; el pnts (6-10A) (adaptors free) PLN10; lndtte (inc dryer); shop 300m; tradsmn; rest, snacks; playgrnd; pool; paddling pool; thermal baths nr; games rm; wifi; sat TV; some statics; dogs PLN5; poss cr; Eng spkn; adv bkg; quiet; ccard not acc; red low ssn/snr citizens; CKE/CCI. "Excel Dutch-run site; barrier clsd 2200-0700; Cieplici attractive spa; v helpful staff; bus stop outside gates." 1 May-30 Sep. PLN 67                                              2013*

**KARPACZ** *D2* (3km N Rural) *50.81110, 15.76836* **Camping Wiśniowa Polana (No. 142), Miłków 40A, 58-535 Młlków [tel/fax (0510) 111415; camping-milkow@karkonosz.pl; www.camping-milkow.karkonosz.pl]** Fr Jelenia Góra to Kowary on rte 367, turn R at junc with rte 366 at Kowary, site on E of Miłków by rv. Med, some hdstg, pt shd; wc; chem disp (wc); mv service pnt; shwrs inc; el pnts (10A) PLN10; lndtte; shop 500m; snacks; bar; BBQ; playgrnd; pool; paddling pool; fishing; games area; internet; no statics; dogs PLN5; quiet; red snr citizens/CKE/CCI. "Well-kept, guarded site & facs; v friendly staff; 7km fr chairlift onto mountain ridge; gd walking - map fr recep." ♦ 1 May-30 Sep. PLN 55                    2013*

⊞ **KARTUZY** *A2* (12km W Rural) *54.31983, 18.11736* **Camping Tamowa (No. 181), Zawory 47A, 83-333 Chmielno [tel/fax (058) 6842535; camping@tamowa.pl; www.tamowa.pl]** Fr Gdańsk take rd 7 & rd 211 to Kartuzy, cont for approx 4km on 211. Turn L for Chmielno; site sp fr vill on lakesite along narr, bumpy app rd. Med, terr, unshd; wc; chem disp; sauna; shwrs PLN2; el pnts (10-16A) inc; shop 1km; snacks; bar; BBQ; playgrnd; lake sw adj; boat & cycle hire; Eng spkn; quiet; CKE/CCI. "Attractive, well-kept site in beautiful location; friendly owner; not suitable lge o'fits; V nice site; little Eng spkn; shop 0.50m." PLN 54                    2012*

**KATOWICE** *D3* (3.5km SE Rural) *50.24355, 19.04795* **Camping Dolina Trzech Statow (No. 215), ul Murckowska 1, 40-266 Katowice [tel/fax (032) 2565939]** Exit A4 at junc Murckowska & foll sp on rd 86 Sosnowiec. In 500m turn R & foll site sp. Med, pt sl, shd; htd wc; shwrs inc; el pnts (16A) PLN2.50/kwh; shop 1km; rest adj; snacks; bar; cooking facs; playgrnd; lake; tennis; dogs PLN5; Eng spkn; adv bkg; quiet; ccard acc; red CKE/CCI. "V clean facs but basic & little privacy; vg." ♦ 1 May-30 Sep. PLN 42                    2010*

**KAZIMIERZ DOLNY** *C4* (2.3km N Rural) *51.33106, 21.95879* **Campsite Pielak, Pulawska 82, 24-120 Kazimierz Dolny (Lubelskie) [(069) 1047409]** Site sp on the S824 300m N of the town. Sm, pt sl, pt shd; wc; chem disp; shwrs; el pnts (16A); lndtte; BBQ; Wifi; bus o'side; "very friendly owners; walking dist to town; close to rv; open grassy site." ♦ ltd 1 May-30 Oct. PLN 61.                            2013*

⊞ **KLODZKO** *D2* (10km W Urban) *50.41502, 16.51335* **Camping Polanica-Zdroj (No. 169), ul Sportowa 7, 57-320 Polanica-Zdrój [(074) 8681210; fax 8681211; polanica@neostrada.pl; www.osir.polanica.net/pl]** Foll sp fr rd 8/E67. Site is 1km N of Polanica-Zdrój. Med, pt shd; htd wc; shwrs inc; el pnts (6A) PLN9.50; shop & 500m; snacks; rest; tennis; many statics adj; dogs PLN5; poss cr; Eng spkn; quiet; ccard acc; CKE/CCI. "Well-run site; clean san facs; helpful warden; easy walk to pleasant spa town - many rests/cafés; wifi free in recep." PLN 49                                  2014*

**KLUCZBORK** *C2* (6km SE Rural) *50.96486, 18.27743* **Camping Bąków (No. 23), ul Kluczborska, 46-233 Bąków [(077) 4180586; osir@kluczbork.pl; www.osir.kluczbork.pl]** On rd 11 Kluczbork to Olesno. Sp on L of rd. Med, mkd pitch, shd; wc; shwrs inc; el pnts (10A) PLN5; lndtte; rest, snacks; bar; playgrnd; pool; TV; 50% statics; quiet; CKE/CCI. "No privacy in shwrs; site poss open outside dates shown; campfires in evening; excel value." 1 May-30 Sep. PLN 23                    2009*

**KOLOBRZEG** *A2* (1km NE Coastal) *54.18131, 15.59338* **Camping Baltic (No. 78), ul 4 Dywizji, 78-100 Kołobrzeg [tel/fax (094) 3524569 or (0606) 411954 (mob); baltic78@ post.pl; www.camping.kolobrzeg.pl]** Nr Solny Hotel on NE edge of town over rlwy x-ing; sp fr rndabt in vill. Med, pt shd; wc; chem disp; mv service pnt; shwrs; shops 500m; el pnts (10-16A) PLN10; shop, rest adj; snacks; bar; playgrnd; sand beach 800m; TV; dogs PLN3; phone; poss cr; Eng spkn; adv bkg; rd & rlwy noise; ccard acc; red long stay/CKE/CCI. "V helpful staff; easy walk/cycle to town; well kept site with spotless facs; easy walk into town." ♦ 15 Apr-15 Oct. PLN 103          2013*

**KRAKOW** *D3* (3km N Urban) *50.09454, 19.94127* **Camping Clepardia (No. 103), ul Pachońskiego 28A, 31-223 Kraków [(012) 4159672; fax 6378063; clepardia@gmail.com; www. clepardia.com.pl]** Fr Kraków cent take rd 7/E77 N twds Warsaw for 3km. Turn L onto rd 79 'Opolska' & foll sp 'Domki Kempingowe - Bungalows'. Fr A4/E40 exit onto E462 then S on rd 79 'Pasternik' thro to 'J Conrada & foll sp. Site is nr lge Elea supmkt & Clepardia Basen (sw pools). Med, mkd pitch, pt shd; wc; chem disp; shwrs inc; el pnts (6A) PLN12; lndtte; supmkt, rest 300m; pool adj; wifi; dogs free; phone; bus nr; poss cr; Eng spkn; no adv bkg; aircraft noise; red low ssn/CKE/CCI. "Busy site with tightly packed pitches - rec arr bef 1700 high ssn to secure pitch; excel, clean, modern san facs; ltd el pnts if site full; muddy in wet weather; friendly, helpful staff; gd security; well maintained." 2 Apr-24 Oct. PLN 70          2014*

**KRAKOW** *D3* (6km S Urban) *50.01546, 19.92525* **Camping Krakowianka (No. 171), ul Żywiecka Boczna 2, 30-427 Kraków [tel/fax (012) 2681135 / (012) 2681417 (phone fax); hotel@ krakowianka.com.pl / hotel@krakowianka.info; www. krakowianka.com.pl]** Exit A4 at Wezel Opatkowice & head N on E77 twd city cent for approx 3km. After passing Carrefour supmkt on R, turn L at next traff lts & foll site sp. Lge, pt shd; wc; chem disp; shwrs; el pnts (16A) inc; lndtte; supmkt 400m; rest 1.5km; snacks; playgrnd; pool adj; games area; TV; some statics; dogs; wifi; phone; tram; car wash. "Ltd, basic facs; conv tram to town; shwrs in hotel v clean & plenty hot water; Gd site; nice snack/bar." 1 May-30 Sep. PLN 50          2013*

**KRAKOW** *D3* (10km S Rural) *49.9625, 19.89277* **Korona Camping (No. 241), ul Myślenicka 32, 32-031 Gaj [tel/fax (012) 2701318; biuro@camping-korona.com.pl; www. camping-korona.com.pl]** Site on E77, well sp fr all dirs. NB dangerous main rd - rec app fr S cont twd Kraków for approx 2km, then turn at x-rds, back to site. When leaving site & travelling N, drive about 5km, take R turn after speed limit warnings, cross rd by bdge, then back N. Med, mkd pitch, terr, pt shd; wc; chem disp; mv service pnt; shwrs inc; el pnts (10-16A) PLN12; lndtte; shop; snacks; bar; BBQ; playgrnd; games area; dogs PLN4; bus to city at gate; poss cr; Eng spkn; adv bkg; rd noise; red long stay/CKE/CCI. "Friendly, family-run site; clean facs need modernising (2010); lower pt of site unrel in wet." ♦ 1 May-15 Sep. PLN 65          2011*

⊞ **KRAKOW** *D3* (4km W Rural) *50.04638, 19.88111* **Camping Smok (No. 46), ul Kamedulska 18, 30-252 Kraków [tel/fax 48 12 429 88 00; info@smok.krakow.pl; www.smok.krakow.pl]** Fr Kraków W ring rd site sp as No 46. Fr S 1st exit immed after x-ing rv onto rd 780 twd Kraków. Med, pt sl, shd; wc; chem disp; mv service pnt; shwrs inc; el pnts (5-10A) PLN12; lndtte; sm shop; supmkt 4km; rest 1km; playgrnd; lake sw & windsurfing 6km; dogs PLN5; poss v cr; some Eng spkn; adv bkg (rec for upper pitches); quiet but some rd noise; red long stay/CKE/CCI. "On rd to Auschwitz; salt mine at Wieliczka; friendly, well-kept site; spotless san facs; lower field (m'vans) poss muddy after rain - tractor tow avail; poss rallies on site; gd tour base; frequent bus to Krakow connects with trams to cent; cycle rte to cent; gd security; tours with pick-up fr site; excel; v helpful and friendly." PLN 85          2014*

**KRETOWINY see Morąg** *A3*

**LEBA** *A2* (Urban) *54.75705, 17.55178* **Camping Marco Polo (No. 81), ul Wspólna 6, 84-360 Łeba [(059) 8662333; marcopolo@leba.info; www.marcopolo.leba.info]** App fr S, foll camping sp L fr main rd. Pass rlwy stn, immed L alongside rlwy, site on R. Med, hdg/mkd pitch, unshd; wc; chem disp; shwrs; el pnts (16A) PLN10; lndry rm; shop; snacks; bar; BBQ; sand beach 700m; games area; some statics; poss cr; Eng spkn; CKE/CCI. "Conv Slowinksi National Park sand dunes." 1 Jun-30 Sep. PLN 44          2010*

**LEBA** *A2* (1.5km Urban) *54.76580, 17.57145* **Camping Przymorze Nr. 48, ul. Nadmorska 9, 84-360 Leba [059 866 5016; fax 866 1304; biuro@camping.leba.pl; www.camping.leba.pl]** Take DW214 dir Leba, at rndabt take 1st exit onto aleja swietego Jakuba. Turn R onto Nadmorska & foll sp to camp. Lge, mkd pitch, pt shd; htd wc; chem disp; mv service pnt; shwrs inc; el pnts; lndtte; shop; rest; BBQ; playgrnd; sandy beach 0.5km; wifi; tv rm; 10% statics; dogs; phone; bus adj; poss cr; Eng spkn; quiet; ccard acc; CCI. "Excel site; shops & rest in walking dist; interesting harbour with fresh fish for sale; windsurfing; lovely sandy beach." ♦ 1 May-30 Sep. PLN 110          2014*

**LEBA** *A2* (500m N Coastal) *54.76150, 17.53833* **Camping Morski (No. 21), ul Turystyczna 3, 84-360 Łeba [tel/fax (059) 8661380; camp21@op.pl; www.camping21. interleba.pl]** N fr Łebork on E214. In Łeba foll sp Camping Raphael & pass rlwy stn on L, over rv bdge twd sea. Site sp. Lge, hdg/mkd pitch, pt shd; htd wc; chem disp; mv service pnt; baby facs; shwrs inc; el pnts (10A) PLN12; lndtte (inc dryer); shop adj; rest; bar; BBQ; cooking facs; playgrnd; sand beach 150m; tennis; wifi; TV; dogs PLN8; phone; poss cr, adv bkg; CKE/CCI. "Nice, well-run site in gd position; modern san facs; pleasant resort; excel; Lacka sand dunes worth a visit." ♦ 1 May-30 Sep. PLN 94 (CChq acc)          2013*

**LEBA** *A2* (500m W Rural) *54.7572, 17.5467* **Camping Rafael (No. 145), ul Turystyczna 4, 84-360 Łeba [(059) 8661972; campingrafael@campingrafael.pl; www.campingrafael.pl]** Fr town cent, site well sp. Med, pt shd; wc; chem disp; shwrs; el pnts (16A) PLN12; lndtte; shop high ssn; snacks; bar high ssn; playgrnd; sand beach 500m; wifi; TV; 5% statics; site open all year for statics, poss also for tourers; dogs PLN5; CKE/CCI. "Nice site, but san facs poor (2011); easy walk to town; conv beaches." 1 Jun-31 Aug. PLN 55          2011*

**LEGNICA** *C2* (10km SE Rural) *51.14216, 16.24006* **Camping Legnickie Pole (No. 234), Ul Henryka Brodatego 7, 59-241 Legnickie Pole [(076) 8582397; fax 8627577; osir.legnica@ wp.pl; www.osir.legnica.pl]** Fr A4/E40 fr Görlitz take exit dir Legnickie Pole/Jawor, foll sp to vill & site. Sharp L turn after leaving main rd. Site sp on S o'skirts of Legnica on E65 & fr m'way. Sm, pt shd; wc; shwrs inc; el pnts (10A) inc; shop 500m; snacks; bar; playgrnd; dogs PLN8; poss cr; no adv bkg; CKE/CCI. "Helpful, friendly welcome; clean, basic facs (hot water to shwrs only); poss diff after heavy rain; gd NH on way S." ◆ 1 May-30 Sep. PLN 53    2013*

**LODZ** *C3* (4km NE Rural) *51.81591, 19.50273* **Camping Na Rogach (No. 167), ul Łupkowa 10/16, 91-527 Łódź [(042) 6306111; hotel.spt@hotel.spt.com.pl; www. hotelspt.com.pl]** Turn L off rte N14 (to Warsaw) 100m bef Peugeot dealer. Site not well sp. Call at adj hotel recep bef ent site. Sm, hdg/mkd pitch, hdstg, unshd; wc; shwrs inc; el pnts (16A) inc; shop opp; playgrnd; rest adj; few statics; dogs PLN6; quiet. "Gd NH; facs run down but clean (2009); o'night coach parties." 15 May-30 Sep. PLN 50    2011*

**LUBLIN** *C4* (7km S Rural) *51.19186, 22.52725* **Camping Graf Marina (No. 65), ul Kręźnicka 6, 20-518 Lublin [tel/fax (081) 7441070; info@graf-marina.pl; www.graf-marina. pl]** Take rd 19 S & cross rlwy line; lge parking area after 1.8km then L after 300m (no sp but leads to Zemborzyce); in 5km cross rlwy then L at T-junc; site on R in 5km on lakeside. Med, hdg/mkd pitch, unshd; wc; own san; shwrs inc; el pnts (10A); shop 3km; rest; sand beach & lake sw adj; statics; Eng spkn; quiet but rd & rlwy noise; CKE/CCI. "Marina adj; sailing; fishing; site run down (early ssn 2011); sodden after rain." 1 May-30 Sep. PLN 71    2011*

**MALBORK** *A2* (1.5km N Urban) *54.04741, 19.03938* **Camping Nogat (No. 197), ul Parkowa 3, 82-200 Malbork [tel/fax (055) 2722413; hotel@osirmalbork.pl; www.osir-malbork.e-tur.com.pl]** Fr Gdańsk on 1/E75 thro Tczew & join rd 22. At Malbork 1st L after main bdge over Rv Nogat. Site adj stadium & Hotel Parkowa. Well sp. Sm, pt shd; wc; chem disp; shwrs inc; el pnts (10A) PLN12; lndtte; supmkt 1.5km; snacks; bar; cooking facs; playgrnd; fishing; canoeing; tennis; games rm; TV; dogs PLN8; phone; quiet; CKE/CCI. "Recep at Hotel Parkowa; gd san facs; excel." ◆ 15 Apr-15 Oct. PLN 56    2011*

**MIEDZYZDROJE** *A1* (1.5km W Coastal) *53.92241, 14.43505* **Camping Gromada (No. 24), ul Polna 134, 72-510 Międzyzdroje [(091) 3280275; fax 3280610; dwgrazyna@ poczta.onet.pl; www.nadmorze.pl/polenamiotowe24]** Fr Świnoujście take rd 3/E65 twd Szczecin. After 12km turn L twd Międzyzdroje. Foll sm camping sp fr town cent. Lge, pt shd; wc; chem disp; shwrs ltd; el pnts (10A) PLN9; lndtte; shop; snacks; bar; BBQ; playgrnd; beach 1km; TV; poss cr; quiet; CKE/ CCI. "Gd NH." 1 May-30 Sep. PLN 49    2009*

**MIELNO** *A2* (500m E Coastal) *54.26272, 16.07245* **Camping Rodzinny (No. 105), ul Chrobrego 51, 76-032 Mielno [(094) 3189385; fax 3475008; recepcja@campingrodzinny. pl; www.campingrodzinny.pl]** Fr Koszalin W on rd 11, turn N onto rd 165 to Mielno turn R at rdbt then 1 1/2 km & foll site sp. Site on L thro narr gate bet gardens - easy to miss. Sm, pt shd, htd wc; chem disp; el pnts (6A) PLN1.50; lndtte; shop; BBQ; cooking facs; playgrnd; sand beach 500m; games rm; internet; some statics; dogs PLN5; poss cr; some Eng spkn; adv bkg; quiet; CKE/CCI. "Easy walk to town; secure, well-kept, family-owned site; gd san facs; Gd site local to beach and shops; friendly owners." ◆ 15 Apr-15 Nov. PLN 88    2013*

**MIKOLAJKI** *A3* (1.5km W Rural) *53.7954, 21.56471* **Camping Wagabunda (No. 2), ul Leśna 2, 11-730 Mikołajki [tel/ fax (087) 4216018; wagabunda-mikolajki@wagabunda-mikolajki.pl; www.wagabunda-mikolajki.pl]** Exit town by rd 16 dir Mrągowo & site sp to L. Med, pt sl, unshd; wc; shwrs inc; el pnts (16A) PLN13; lndtte; shop & 1.5km; rest, snacks; shgl beach 2km; lake sw 400m; games area; TV; 50% statics; dogs PLN2.50; phone; poss cr; adv bkg; quiet; no ccard acc; twin-axles extra charge; red low ssn/CKE/CCI. "Pleasant site nr nice town; san facs adequate but need update (2011); conv Masurian Lakes & historical sites; Vg site; Eng spkn; 10 min walk into town." ◆ 1 May-30 Sep. PLN 82    2013*

**MORAG** *A3* (7km SE Rural) *53.90373, 20.02753* **Camping Kretowiny (No. 247), Kretowiny29, 14-300 Morag [(089) 7582440 / (697) 523402 (mob); pensjonat@narie.pl; www.narie.pl]** Fr cent Morąg foll rd 527 S twd Olsztyn but bef exit town, fork L at sp Żabi Róg/Kretowiny. Site sp on Lake Jezioro Narie. Med, hdg pitch, pt shd; wc; chem disp; shwrs; el pnts (6A) PLN8; lndtte; shop; rest; bar; playgrnd; lake sw; fishing; watersports; tennis; games area; games rm; quiet; CKE/ CCI. "On shore of lge, lovely lake with sw, boating, fishing; pleasant, attractive site." ◆ 1 May-30 Sep. PLN 34    2013*

⊞ **MRAGOWO** *A3* (8km N Rural) *53.94278, 21.32001* **Camping Seeblick, Ruska Wieś 1, 11-700 Mrągowo [tel/ fax (089) 7413155; marian.seeblick@gmail.com; www. campingpension.de]** Fr Mrągowo N on rd 591 dir Ketrzyn, site sp. Med, terr, pt shd; htd wc; chem disp; shwrs inc; el pnts inc; lndry rm; shop 500m; rest; bar; lake sw; boating; tennis; games area; entmnt; quiet. "Gd; gd but ltd san facs; lots for kids to do; shop nrby; little Eng spkn." PLN 50    2012*

⊞ **NIEDZICA** *D3* (2km SE Urban) *49.40477, 20.33411* **Camping Polana Sosny (No. 38), Osiedle Na Polanie Sosny, 34-441 Niedzica [tel/fax (018) 2629403; polana. sosny@narie.pl; www.niedzica.pl]** Rte 969 fr Nowy Targ. At Dębno turn R & foll sp to border (lake on L). At 11km pass castle & 1st dam on L twds 2nd Dunajec dam. Site sp. Sm, mkd pitch, unshd; htd wc; chem disp; shwrs; fam bthrm; el pnts inc; lndttel shop 1.5km; rest adj; snacks; bar; cooking facs; rv adj; watersports; games area; phone; quiet but noise fr dam; adv bkg; quiet; red long stay; CKE/CCI. "Beautiful, well-maintained site in superb location; friendly, helpful staff; clean, modern san facs; excel walks in mountains; 2km to Slovakian border; vg touring base." ◆ PLN 42    2010*

**NOWY SACZ** *D3* (E Urban) *49.61975, 20.71548* **Camping Dom Turysty Nowy Sącz (No. 87), ul Nadbrzeżna 40, 33-300 Nowy Sącz [tel/fax (018) 4415012; apazdyk@gmail. com]** Fr W on rd 28 cross Rv Dunajec & in 2km at rndabt turn L into rd 75. Site on L. Sm, mkd pitch, some hdstg, pt shd; wc; chem disp; shwrs; el pnts (16A); lndtte; shops 1km; snacks; bar; BBQ; quiet; CKE/CCI. "Close to Slovakian border & lakes." ♦ 1 May-30 Sep. PLN 23                                    2010*

**OLSZTYN** *A3* (5km NW Rural) *53.78686, 20.40170* **Agro Camping, ul Młodzieżowa 1, 11-041 Olsztyn [(089) 5238666]** Fr Olsztyn W on rd 16 for approx 5km, turn N thro Łupstych & foll site sp. Sm, pt sl, pt shd; wc; shwr; some Eng spkn; quiet. "Lovely position on Lake Ukiel; CL-type site with facs." 1 May-30 Sep.                              2009*

⊞ **OSWIECIM** *D3* (2km W Rural) *50.02262, 19.19891* **Centre for Dialogue & Prayer in Auschwitz, ul Maksymiliana Kolbego 1, 32-600 Oświęcim [(033) 8431000; fax 8431001; biuro@centrum-dialogu.oswiecim.pl; www.centrum-dialogu.oswiecim.pl]** 700m fr Auschwitz 1 museum car park on parallel rd to S, on forecourt of hotel-like building. Sm, hdstg, unshd; wc; shwrs inc; el pnts inc; shops 2km; rest; BBQ; phone; Eng spkn; rd noise; CKE/CCI. "Conv Auschwitz museum & Auschwitz-Birkenau (3km); clean, modern, site; gd, clean san facs, similar quality to UK CC sites; friendly, helpful staff; v nice site." ♦ PLN 70                          2014*

> ## "We must tell The Club about that great site we found"
>
> Get your site reports in by mid-August and we'll do our best to get your updates into the next edition.

⊞ **OSWIECIM** *D3* (2km W Urban) *50.02895, 19.20054* **Parking Przy Museum Auschwitz, 32-600 Oświęcim** Foll sp to Auschwitz museum fr rd 933. Parking area is on opp side of rd (away fr main car park) by TO. M'vans only. Sm; el pnts (6A) PLN7; shop; rest, snacks; bar; internet; water PLN6; dogs; quiet. "1 night stay only permitted; ltd el pnts; allow 4 hrs for museum tour; basically a big car park with a few elec points; internet at TO or wifi at pizza rest." PLN 40            2014*

**PIECKI**

**PIECKI** *A3* (2km N Rural) *53.77938, 21.33583* **Camping Piecki (No. 269), ul Zwycięstwa 60, 11-710 Piecki [tel/fax (089) 7421025; owpttk@post.pl; www.owpttk.pl]** Site sp bet Mrągowo & Piecki on rd 59. No sps except sm sp at ent. In Masurian Lake District 3km to W of Piecki. NB Ent tight lge o'fits. Med, pt sl, pt shd; wc; chem disp (wc); shwrs inc; el pnts (10A) PLN12; lndtte; shop, rest & snacks 5km; bar; BBQ; playgrnd; lake sw; watersports; games area; TV; 10% statics; dogs PLN10; bus adj; Eng spkn; adv bkg; poss noisy high ssn due school parties; CKE/CCI. "San facs poor; NH only." 1 May-30 Sep. PLN 50                                   2011*

**POLANICA ZDROJ see Kłodzko** *D2*

⊞ **POZNAN** *B2* (4km E Urban) *52.40343, 16.98399* **Camping Malta (No. 155), ul Krańcowa 98, 61-036 Poznań-Malta [(061) 8766203; fax 8766283; camping@malta.poznan.pl; www.poznan.pl]** Fr A2/E30 Poznań bypass leave at rte 2/11 dir Poznań. Turn R at traff lts onto rte 5/E261 sp Malta, Zoo & camping, site sp. Sm, hdg pitch, pt shd; htd wc; chem disp; shwrs inc; el pnts (16A) inc; lndtte; shop; snacks; bar; shop 1km; lake adj; many statics; tram to city; Eng spkn; quiet but loud disco across lake at w/end; ccard acc; red CKE/CCI. "Clean tidy site on lake with sports but poss unkempt pitches low ssn; 6 tram stops to Poznań Sq; vg 24-hr security; helpful staff; site amongst sports facs by lake." ♦ PLN 108            2014*

⊞ **PRZEMYSL** *D4* (1km SW Rural) **Camping Zamek (No. 233), ul.Zamkowa 10, 86-100 Świecie woj. kujawsko-pomorskie [tel/fax (52) 3311726; recepcja@camping-zamek.pl; www.camping-zamek.pl]** Site sp on rd B28. Med, shd; wc; own san rec; shwrs; el pnts (10A) PLN10; shops adj; snacks; fishing; games area; 50% statics; dog PLN 3; phone; quiet; "Interesting town & churches; helpful staff; basic facs; gd pizza rest nrby." PLN 40.                          2013*

**PRZEWORSK** *D4* (1km W Urban) *50.06138, 22.48361* **Camping Pastewnik (No. 221), ul Łańcucka 2, 37-200 Przeworsk [(016) 6492300; fax 6492301; zajazdpastewnik@hot.pl; www.pastewnik.prv.pl]** On N side of N4/E40, sp. Sm, pt shd; wc; shwrs inc; el pnts (10A) PLN10; lndtte; shop adj; rest, snacks; bar; playgrnd; Eng spkn; rd noise; ccard acc; CKE/CCI. "Conv NH/sh stay with motel & rest; Łańcut Castle & Carriage Museum 25km; Elec v dubious, no socket circuit breakers." 1 May-30 Sep. PLN 112     2013*

**ROWY** *A2* (500m W Coastal) *54.65940, 17.04926* **Camping Prymorze (No. 156), ul Bałtycka 6, 76-212 Rowy [tel/ fax (059) 8141940; biuro@przymorze.com.pl; www. przymorze.com.pl]** Fr Ustka on coast rd, site on rd into Rowy. Med, pt shd; wc; shwrs inc; el pnts (16A) inc; lndtte; shop; snacks; bar; cooking facs; playgrnd; pool 300m; TV; dogs 2; phone; quiet. "Sm fishing port; gd facs; helpful staff." ♦ ltd 1 May-31 Aug. PLN 75                               2009*

⊞ **RUCIANE NIDA** *A3* (5km NW Rural) *53.68668, 21.54713* **Camping Nad Zatoka (No. 9), Wygryny 52, 12-220 Ruciane Nida [(087) 4231597 / (502) 328111 (mob); fax 4236342; zbigre@orange.pl; www.ter-lid.com.pl]** Fr rte 58 N onto rd 610 NE twds Piecki for 4km. Turn R for Wygryny 2km, foll sp in vill. Sm, pt sl, unshd; wc; chem disp; mv service pnt; shwrs inc; el pnts (16A) PLN10; lndtte; shop 300m; tradsmn; rest, bar nrby; BBQ; playgrnd; sand beach; lake sw; canoe & cycle hire; dogs PLN6; poss cr; quiet; "Private site in field on lakeside; beautiful scenery; vg san facs; excel." PLN 50         2013*

**RYDZEWO MILKI see Giżycko** *A3*

**SANDOMIERZ** *C3* (400m E Urban) *50.68010, 21.75502* **Camping Browarny (No. 201), ul Żwirki I Wigury 1, 27-600 Sandomierz [(015) 8332703; fax 8323050; wmajsak@ poczta.fm; www.majsak.pl]** Fr S on rd 79, cross rv bdge, site on L. Sm, pt shd; wc; chem disp; mv service pnt; shwrs inc; el pnts (16A) PLN10; lndtte; shop in town; rest nr; bar; BBQ; cooking facs; playgrnd; games rm; dogs; wifi; phone; bus adj; poss cr; Eng spkn; adv bkg; some rd noise; CKE/CCI. "Attractive sm town in walking dist; vg site; helpful staff." ♦ Easter-30 Oct. PLN 42                              2012*

**SIERAKOW** *B2* (2km SE Rural) *52.63324, 16.09870* **Camping Sieraków Owir (No. 109), ul Poznańska 28, 64-410 Sieraków [(061) 2952868; recepcja@owir.sierakow.pl; www.owir.sierakow.pl]** Fr rd 182 in town cent, SE on ul Ponzańska on L, opp hotel. Not well sp. Med, pt sl, shd; wc; chem disp (wc); shwrs inc; el pnts (5A) PLN5; lndry rm; shop 200m; rest 300m; snacks; bar & 300m; htd covrd pool; lake sw & beach 300m; boating; TV rm; 5% statics; phone; poss cr & noisy w/end; CKE/CCI. "Poss pop concerts on beach in summer; gd san facs; site poss diff lge o'fits due tall trees." ♦ 20 Jun-30 Sep.                                                2009*

**SLAWA** *C2* (1km W Rural) *51.88145, 16.05817* **Camping Słoneczny (No. 261), ul Odrodzonego Wojska Polskiego 19, 67-410 Sława [tel/fax (068) 3566452; osir.slawa@ wp.pl; www.osir.slawa.pl]** Site sp on lakeside. Sm, mkd pitch, pt shd; wc; chem disp; el pnts; lndtte; snacks; lake sw; waterslide; fishing; games area; cycle hire; some statics; adv bkg; quiet; CKE/CCI. "Beautiful location; friendly, helpful owners; san facs unclean (6/09)." 1 May-30 Sep. PLN 50                                                   2009*

**SOPOT** *A2* (1.8km N Urban) *54.46136, 18.5556* **Camping Kamienny Potok (No. 19), ul Zamkowa Góra 25, 220-474 and 27-468 Sopot [tel/fax (058) 5500445; kempingnr19@ wp.pl; www.kemping19.cba.pl]** Fr Gdańsk rte 27 twds Sopot. Site on R just behind Shell petrol stn. Fr N on rte 6/E28 turn S at Gdynia, onto new section of E28, for 7.5km. Turn L onto rte 220 by 'Euromarket' for 5km. Turn R onto rte 27 (S) twd Gdańsk & site nr Shell g'ge on opp c'way. Lge, mkd pitch, pt shd; wc; chem disp; shwrs inc; el pnts (2-20A) PLN10; lndtte; shop 500m; snacks; bar; playgrnd; internet; TV; phone; poss cr; rd & rlwy noise; ccard acc; red CKE/CCI. "Pleasant site; friendly & helpful staff; frequent trains for Gdansk 250m; modern, clean san facs; gd security; gd walking/cycling track into town; busy site; upgrades in process (2012)." 1 May-30 Sep. PLN 72                                              2012*

**STEGNA** *A2* (1.5km N Coastal) *54.34186, 19.1176* **Camping Stegna No. 159, ul Morska 26, 82-103 Stegna [(055) 2478303; fax 2478034; camp@camp.pl; www.camp. pl]** Fr Stegna vill on rte 501 turn N at church onto Morska. Site on R, sp. Sm, shd; wc; chem disp; shwrs inc; el pnts (10A) PLN8; lndtte; shop 300m; tradsmn; rest, snacks, bar 100m; playgrnd; sand beach 400m; 10% statics; dogs PLN4; Eng spkn; adv bkg; quiet. "Friendly, family-run site; gd security; gd base Gdansk 30km; rec." 1 May-30 Sep. PLN 56        2009*

**STETTIN see Szczecin** *B1*

**STRZESZYNEK see Poznań** *B2*

**SULECIN** *B1* (3km S Rural) *52.40911, 15.11761* **Camping Marina (No. 50), Ostrów 76, 69-200 Sulęcin [tel/fax (957) 552294 / (171) 3704553; przemyslaw-gula@wp.pl; www.camping-marina.eu]** Cross border fr Frankfurt-an-Oder & take rd 2 to Torzym (35km). In Torzym turn L onto rd 138 dir Sulęcin; thro Tursk & site in 3km. Med, mkd pitch, pt shd; wc; mv service pnt; shwrs; el pnts €2; lndtte; tradsmn; supmkt 4km; snacks; bar; playgrnd; lake sw; fishing; cycle hire; wifi; TV rm; some statics; dogs €1; adv bkg; quiet; red CKE/CCI; "Gd, modern san facs; gd walking/cycling; pleasant, relaxing site; conv Berlin." ♦ 1 Apr-31 Oct. PLN 63                 2013*

**SUWALKI** *A3* (11km NW Rural) *54.0767, 23.0742* **Kajaki Camping Pokoje, 16-412 Stary Folwark 44, Wigry [(087) 5637789; wigry@wigry.info; www.wigry.info]** Fr Suwalki take 653 dir Sejny. In about 11km turn R in Stary Folwark at PTTK sp. Site on R in approx 100m. Sm, unshd; wc; chem disp; shwrs inc; el pnts (10A) inc; lndtte; BBQ; lake sw & kayaking nrby; wifi; Eng spkn; quiet. "Nr lake in National Park; kayaking fr site; vg site." 01 May-30 Sep. PLN 40         2011*

**SWIECIE** *B2* (1km E Urban) *53.40321, 18.45574* **Camping Zamek (No. 54), ul Zamkowa 10, 86-100 Świecie [(052) 3311726 or 604 993 070]** S fr Gdańsk on E75 take rd 1 to Chełmno & Świecie. Cross Rv Wisła & L at x-rds in Świecie cent; site sp at traff lts. Sm, shd; wc; own san rec; shwrs; el pnts (10A); lndtte; shop; bar; playgrnd; games area; dogs; quiet. "In castle grnds (tower visible fr rd); if gate clsd, ring bell on L; new tolet block (2012)." 1 May-15 Sep. PLN 25    2012*

⊞ **SWINOUJSCIE** *A1* (1km N Coastal) *53.91709, 14.25693* **Camping Relax (No. 44), ul Słowackiego 1, 72-600 Świnoujście [(097) 3213912; relax@osir.uznam.net.pl; www.camping-relax.com.pl]** Fr E rd 3/E65 cross rv on free ferry. Fr town cent N for 500m. No vehicle border x-ing fr W. V lge, shd; wc; shwrs inc; el pnts (16A) PLN10; lndtte; shops 500m; snacks; cooking facs; playgrnd; beach 200m; games rm; wifi; phone; quiet; adv bkg; ccard acc. "Nice town; gd beach; gd walking; site popular with families; red snr citizens." PLN 65                                               2012*

⊞ **SZCZECIN/STETTIN** *B1* (7km E Rural) *53.39505, 14.63640* **Marina Camping (No. 25), ul Przestrzenna 23, 70-800 Szczecin-Dabie [tel/fax (091) 4601165; camping.marina@ pro.onet.pl; www.campingmarina.pl]** Fr E28/A6 take A10 sp Szczecin. Immed after rlwy bdge turn R sp Dąbie. At traff lts in cent Dąbie turn L, site on R in approx 2km on lake. Med, pt shd; htd wc; mv service pnt; baby facs; shwrs; el pnts (6A) inc; lndtte (inc dryer); tradsmn; shop 2km; supmkt 3km; rest, snacks; bar; lake sw; boat hire; tennis; games area; dog; wifi; bus to Stettin; poss cr; noise fr late arr & early deps; red CKE/CCI. "Pleasant, lakeside site; clean, modern san facs but inadequate if site full; bus tickets fr recep; helpful staff; vg site on lake side." PLN 106 (CChq acc)                     2014*

⊞ **TARNOW** *D3* (1km N Rural) *50.02320, 20.98813* **Camping Pod Jabłoniami (No. 202), ul Piłsudskiego 28a, 33-100 Tarnów [(014) 6215124; fax 6522933; recepcja@camping. tarnow.pl; www.camping.tarnow.pl]** E fr Kraków on E40, foll sp to Tarnów 'Centrum'. Turn L by Tesco & foll sp to site. Sm, pt sl, pt shd; wc; chem disp; shwrs inc; el pnts (16A) PLN10; lndtte; supmkt 2km; rest, bar 1km; BBQ; playgrnd; pool adj; wifi; TV; poss cr; Eng spkn; some rd noise; red CKE/CCI. "Walk to attractive town; vg site." ♦ ltd PLN 85      2013*

⊞ **TORUN** *B2* (1km S Urban) *53.00138, 18.60472* **Camping Tramp (No. 33), ul Kujawska 14, 87-100 Toruń [tel/fax (056) 6547187; tramp@mosir.torun.pl; www.mosir.torun. pl]** Cross bdge S of town & take 1st L at traff lts, site sp in 500m on rvside. Med, shd; wc; chem disp; shwrs; el pnts (10A) inc; lndtte; shop 500m; rest 1.5km; snacks; bar; games area; some statics; playgrnd; dogs PLN4.50; continual traffic noise & poss noise fr bar; red CKE/CCI. "Noisy, busy site but reasonable; walking dist fr interesting old town across bdge; gd security; NH/sh stay only." ♦ 1 May-30 Sep. PLN 62                        2010*

You can now fill in site reports online

**UCIECHOW** *C2* (1km E Rural) *50.73061, 16.65319*
Camping Forteca, ul. Wroclawska 12, 58-211 Uciechów
(Dolnoslaskie) [(074) 8323008; info@campingforteca.nl;
www.campingforteca.nl] Fr cent of Dzierzoniów foll rd 384
twds Lagiewniki and Wroclaw for 4km. In cent of Uciechow
go ahead at crossrds. After 400m turn R down gravel track
sp to rest and parking. Sm, pt sl; wc; chem disp; child/baby
facs; shwrs; el (16A) 15 ZL; rest, bar; BBQ; lake adj; wifi; 10%
appartments; dog 5 ZL; twin axle; Eng spkn; adv bkg acc; CKE/
CCI; "Pitches surround lake where sw; fishing and boating
permitted; new clean toilet block; helpful, friendly family
owners; lovely peaceful site low ssn; open plan, grassy site."
1 Apr-1 Oct. PLN 88                                    2013*

## "I need an on-site restaurant"

We do our best to make sure site
information is correct, but it is always best
to check any must-have facilities are still
available or will be open during your visit.

**USTKA** *A2* (NE Urban) *54.57655, 16.88088* **Camping Morski**
**(No. 101), ul Armii Krajowej 4, Przewloka, 76-270 Ustka**
**[tel/fax (059) 8144789 or 8144426; cam_mor@pro.onet.**
**pl; www.camping-morski.afr.pl]** Fr Koszalin & Sławno to
łupsk on rd 6/E28 turn L to Ustka. Foll main rd which bears R
& foll camping sp to R. After 200m turn R at rndabt & camp on
L after 300m. Sm, pt shd; wc; shwrs; el pnts (6A) inc; lndtte;
shop 500m; rest adj; snacks; bar; BBQ; playgrnd; beach 1.3km;
tennis; dogs; quiet; red long stay/CKE/CCI. "Seaside resort with
gd shopping & fishing port; vg for children; gd cycling; Gd nh;
30 min walk to town." ♦ 1 May-30 Sep. PLN 60        2013*

**WALCZ** *B2* (12km N Rural) **Camping Zdbice, 78-611 Wałcz**
**[tel/fax (067) 2581677]** Fr N on rd 22 at Szwecja turn R at sp
Zdbice, site sp. Site on L bef vill of Zdbice. Med, pt sl, unshd;
wc; chem disp (wc); shwrs; el pnts; bar; lake sw adj; statics;
quiet. "Pleasant site on lakeside; facs basic but adequate; at
site ent, stop to register & ask owner to open gate at 2nd
ent - main ent has diff turn & overhanging branches; if arr
late - phone number displayed on barrier." 1 May-30 Sep.
PLN 49                                                2010*

**WARSZAWA** *B3* (9km SE Urban) *52.17798, 21.14727*
Camping Wok (No. 90), ul Odrębna 16, 04-867 Warszawa
[(022) 6127951; fax 6166127; wok@campingwok.
warszawa.pl; www.campingwok.warszawa.pl] Fr city cent
or fr W on E30, take bdge on E30 over Rv Wisła to E side of
rv. Then take rte 801 for approx 8km (dual c'way). At rndabt
double back for 600m & take 3rd R into Odrębna. Site 200m
on R. Sm, shd; htd wc; chem disp; mv service pnt; baby facs;
shwrs inc; el pnts (10-16A) PLN15; gas; lndtte; shop 700m; rest
1km; snacks; bar; BBQ; cooking facs; playgrnd; games area;
internet; TV; bus/tram adj; Eng spkn; adv bkg; quiet; ccard acc;
red CKE/CCI. "Lovely little site; v secure; spotless, modern san
facs; helpful staff." 1 Apr-31 Oct. PLN 85            2012*

**WARSZAWA** *B3* (4km W Urban) *52.2144, 20.96575* **Majawa**
Camping (No. 123), ul Bitwy Warszawskiej 19/20, 02-366
Warszawa-Szczęśliwice [(022) 8229121; fax 8237244;
biuro@majawa.pl; www.majawa.pl] Fr W on E30/rd 2
at junc with E67/rd 8 rd goes S thro tunnel under rlwy then
strt on under new over-pass. Site on R in 100m. On E67/rd
8 fr Wrocław app concrete monument 3m high in middle of
tramway; turn L at traff lts. Hotel Vera on R, site on L. Fr cent
of Warsaw, take rd no. 7/8 700m twds Katowice. Not v well sp
fr cent of town. Ent & exit diff due v busy rd. Sm, pt shd; wc;
chem disp; shwrs inc; el pnts (6A) PLN15; lndry rm; shop 300m;
rest 100m; BBQ; tennis; some statics; phone; bus 500m; poss
cr; Eng spkn; quiet; ccard acc; red CKE/CCI. "Easy access to
Warsaw & Royal Castle; gd meals at adj bowling alley or Vera
hotel; poss lge rallies on site; friendly; poor condition but well
positioned to get into city." 1 May-30 Sep. PLN 152    2014*

**WARSZAWA** *3B* (22.5km W) *52.23066, 207.9196* **Campsite**
Kaputy 222, Sochaczewska 222, 05-850 Kreczki,
(Mazowieckie) [(022) 1100061; biuro@camping222.pl;
www.camping222.pl] Head S on SS36, take exit Pescate
twrd Pescate/Lecco/Malgrate/SS583/Bellagio/Calco, cont strt; at
rndbt take 3rd exit via Roma, go throu 1 rndbt; cont onto Via
Statale, turn L onto Via Foppaola, destination will be on your
L. Med; mkd pitch; htd wc; chem disp; mv service pnt; shwr;
el pnts (15 ZL); lndtte; bread on site; Wi-fi (10 ZL); dogs (5 ZL);
public transport adj; eng spkn; quiet; CCI. "fishing lake on sit;,
NH or visit to Warsaw; excel san facs; clean, spacious site and
easy to find." ♦ 15 Apr-31 Oct. PLN 95.00             2014*

## "Satellite navigation makes touring much easier"

Remember most sat navs don't know if
you're towing or in a larger vehicle – always
use yours alongside maps and site directions.

**WEGORZEWO** *A3* (2km SW Rural) *54.18647, 21.77018*
Camping Rusałka (No. 175), ul Lesna 2, 11-600
Węgorzewo [(087) 4272191; fax 4272049; camp.175@
wp.pl; www.cmazur.pl] Fr rte 63 fr Giżycko to Węgorzewo
turn W approx 3km SW of Węgorzewo. Foll sp to site. Lge,
pt shd; wc; chem disp (wc); shwrs inc; el pnts PLN8; lndtte;
shops 2km; snacks; bar; playgrnd; lake sw adj; fishing;
sailing; many statics; dogs; quiet. "Lovely pt of Lake District;
delightful situation; all facs at top of steep hill." 1 May-30 Sep.
PLN 48                                                2012*

**WIELICZKA** *D3* (1.2km E Urban) *49.98273, 20.07611* **Motel**
Camping Wierzynka, ul Wierzynka 9, 32-020 Wieliczka
[tel/fax (012) 2783614; motel@nawierzynka.pl; www.
nawierzynka.pl] Site sp fr E40/rte 4 about 2km fr salt mine.
Sm, some hdstg, pt sl, pt shd; wc; shwrs; el pnts (10A) PLN10
(rev pol); shop 1.5km; rest, snacks; bar; cycle hire; wifi; bus to
Krakow; train 1km; poss cr; Eng spkn; quiet; ccard acc (fee);
CKE/CCI. "10 pitches in pleasant setting; helpful staff; facs
basic but clean; shwrs erratic; 2km fr salt mines; Vg site, local
to salt mines; shwr portacabin, but clean." 1 May-30 Sep.
PLN 80                                                2014*

POLAND

**POLAND**

**WROCLAW** *C2* (5km NE Urban) *51.11722, 17.09138* **Stadion Olimpijski Camp (No. 117), ul Padarewskiego 35, 51-620 Wrocław [tel/fax (071) 3484651]** Fr A4 into Wrocław foll N8 sp Warszawa thro city. On N8 dir Warszawa, pass McDonalds, at fork in rd take Sienkiewicza to end, then Rozyckiego to stadium, site on R. If poss foll sp 'stadion' to camp; head for lighting towers of sports stadium if seen thro trees. Lge, pt shd; wc; shwrs inc; el pnts (16A) PLN7.50; lndry rm; shops, rest adj; snacks; bar; BBQ; playgrnd; pool 700m; 10% statics; dogs; tram nr; phone; poss cr; no adv bkg; poss noise fr stadium; red CKE/CCI. "San facs basic but clean; site in need of modernisation (2010); gd security; v conv for city but NH only; run down but conv for town." 1 May-15 Oct. PLN 72    2014*

⊞ **ZAKOPANE** *D3* (4km N Rural) *49.32415, 19.98506* **Camping Harenda (No. 160), Oś Harenda 51B, 34-500 Zakopane [tel/fax (018) 2014700; harenda51b@gmail. com; www.harenda.tatrynet.pl]** On main rd to Zakopane fr N, after town sp turn R into petrol stn with McDonalds. Cont to R, pass Cmp Ustep on L then turn L over rv bdge to site in 200m on R. Med, pt sl, pt shd; htd wc; shwrs inc; chem disp; mv service pnt; el pnts (10A) PLN10 (long lead req); lndtte; shop 100m; rest; BBQ; playgrnd; dogs; wifi; poss cr; Eng spkn; no adv bkg; some train noise & barking dogs; red CKE/CCI. "Gd views Tatra mountains fr site; superb walking; poss rallies on site; poss unkempt low ssn; laundry done at modest cost; vg rest; rafting (not white water) on Dunajec Rv; Nowy Targ rec; lower site poss muddy in wet weather." PLN 52    2014*

**ZAKOPANE** *D3* (4km N Rural) *49.32208, 19.96555* **Camping Ustup (No. 207), ul Ustup K/5, 34-500 Zakopane-Ustup [(0605) 950007; camping.ustup@gmail.com]** Turn R off Kraków-Zakopane rd 47 at petrol stn/McDonalds just after 1st town sp. Turn R again immed then L sp Cmg Harenda), site on L in 200m. Sm, pt sl, unshd; wc; chem disp; baby facs; shwrs inc; el pnts (10A) inc; shop adj; rest opp; playgrnd; bus to town cent; poss cr; adv bkg; quiet; CKE/CCI. "Ideal cent for Tatra region; mountain views; excel, family-run site; v welcoming, friendly & helpful owner (ltd Eng); vg, clean san facs; grassy pitches; coach tours arranged fr adj g'ge info desk." 1 May-5 Oct. PLN 94    2014*

⊞ **ZAKOPANE** *D3* (1km S Urban) *49.2830, 19.9690* **Camping Pod Krokwia (No. 97), ul Żeromskiego 26, 34-500 Zakopane [tel/fax (018) 2012256; camp@podkrokwia.pl; www.podkrokwia.pl]** Sp fr town cent. Fr N 2nd exit at 1st rndbt; strt over at 2nd rndbt; turn R at 3rd rndabt, then R in 250m. Site on L. Lge, hdstg, pt sl, shd; wc; chem disp; shwrs inc; el pnts (10A) inc; lndtte; shop 500m; rest, snacks; bar nr; BBQ; cooking facs; playgrnd; pool, tennis adj; bus to Kraków; ski slopes & cable cars; rafting on rapids; wifi; TV; dogs PLN5; phone; poss cr; Eng spkn; quiet; CKE/CCI. "Lge tent area; few mkd pitches; poss scruffy low ssn; poor san facs; conv town cent; muddy when set; conv Tatra Mountains; mountain walks; town v touristy; vg loc; ltd facs; free gas stove." PLN 65.4    2012*

⊞ **ZAMOSC** *C4* (2km W Rural) *50.71919, 23.23908* **Camping Duet (No. 253), ul Królowej Jadwigi 14, 22-400 Zamość [tel/fax (084) 6392499; duet@virgo.com.pl; www.duet. virgo.com.pl]** Fr Zamość cent W on rd 74, site on R bef Castorama. Sm, pt shd; wc; chem disp (wc); shwrs inc; el pnts PLN12; shop opp; rest, snacks; bar; pool 150m; some statics; dogs; poss cr; quiet; CKE/CCI. "Walk to attractive town; fair sh stay/NH." PLN 31    2011*

⊞ **ZGORZELEC** *C1* (1km N Urban) *51.15957, 15.00069* **Camping Zgorzelec, ul Lubańska 1a, 59-900 Zgorzelec [(075) 7752436; ardi@op.pl]** Ent Zgorzelec fr Germany & foll rd sp Zagan. Turn L at traff lts at BP g'ge INTO Lubanska rd sp 351 site on R after 560m, bef downwards hill. Only sp is at camp gate. Sm, pt sl, unshd; wc; el pnts inc; CKE/CCI. "Conv NH." PLN 60    2012*

---

> ## "There aren't many sites open at this time of year"
>
> If you're travelling outside peak season remember to call ahead to check site opening dates – even if the entry says 'open all year'.

---

**ZIELONA GORA** *C2* (1km NW Urban) **Leśny Camping (No. 52), ul Sulechowska 39, 65-022 Zielona Góra [tel/fax (068) 3253636; hotel.lesny@op.pl; www.lubtour.pti.pl/ lesny.php]** Fr N on E65 fr Swebodzin, L to cent of town & immed L again. Hotel Lesny is sp. Go to recep for key. Sm, pt shd; wc; chem disp; shwrs; el pnts (10A); lndtte; shop 1km; rest; cooking facs; playgrnd; games area; adv bkg; ccard acc; CKE/CCI. ◆ ltd 1 May-30 Oct.    2010*

**ZLOCIENIEC** *B2* (10km SW Rural) *53.45880, 15.92430* **Inter Nos Island Camping (No. 110), ul Błędno 1, 78-520 Złocieniec [(094) 3631190 or (0602) 554348 (mob); m.moser@inter-nos.pl; www.inter-nos.pl]** Fr Stettin E on rd 10 to Stargard Szczeciński then rd 20 to Drawsko Pomorski. In Drawsko take rd sp Lubieszewo & foll site sps W to lakeside. Access to site on island by ferry. Med, pt shd; wc; chem disp; sauna; shwrs; el pnts €1.50; lndry rm; shop; rest, snacks; bar; BBQ; playgrnd; lake sw & beach; watersports; tennis; cycle hire; horseriding; TV rm; dogs; adv bkg; quiet. "Scenic area." ◆ 1 May-30 Sep. PLN 71 (CChq acc)    2009*

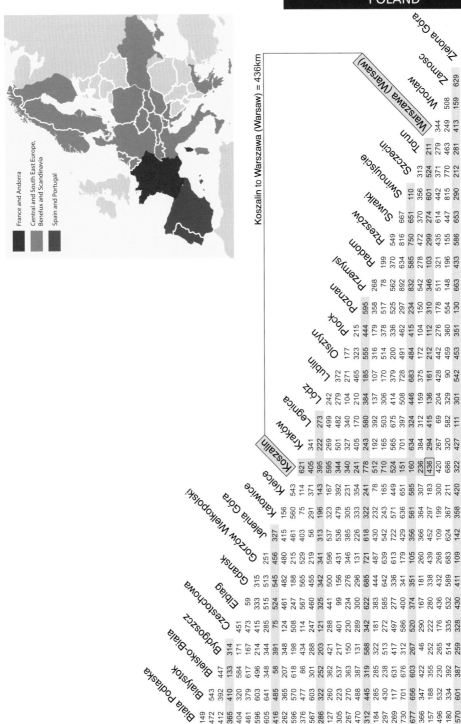

Koszalin to Warszawa (Warsaw) = 436km

POLAND

# Slovakia
## Country Introduction

Spis Castle, Slovakia

## Welcome to Slovakia

Slovakia has one of the highest number of castles and chateaux in the world, ranging from simple ruins to well preserved hilltop castles.

There are numerous thermal springs in Slovakia, popular with both locals and visitors. Many spas have been built around these to provide relaxation and curative therapies.

If you are feeling more adventurous, the country's capital Bratislava is a popular city for tourists.

## Country highlights

Slovakian culture reflects a strong Hungarian influence in terms of food. Assorted cold meats are an important part of the diet. Venison and game, such as duck and pigeon, are plentiful. Southern Slovakia is a wine producing area and Slivovice, a strong plum brandy, is a national favourite.

There are a number of music festivals in Slovkia, Bratislava Jazz Festival being one of them. It takes place in October and attracts a large number of musicians from Europe.

## Major towns and cities

- Bratislava – this capital city has a medieval centre with a hill-top castle.
- Košice – an ancient city has many stunning buildings and an impressive cathedral.
- Prešov – a city of historical architecture, it has many stunning buildings.
- Nitra – an ancient city with a castle and an interesting old town.

## Attractions

- Spis Castle – a 900 years old ruin and one of the biggest castles in Europe.
- Demanovska Cave of Liberty – this cave has impressive halls, stalactites and waterfalls.
- Nitra Castle – a small but stunning castle worth exploring.
- St. Apostle Altar, Church of St. Jacob - a large, ornate and impressive wooden altar.

## Find out more

www.slovakia.travel

Tel:0042 (0) 14 84 13 61 46 Slovakia Tourist Board

# Country Information

Population (approx): 5.4 million

Capital: Bratislava (population approx 424,000)

Area: 49,035 sq km

Bordered by: Austria, Czech Republic, Hungary, Poland, Ukraine

Terrain: Rugged mountains in the centre and north; lowlands in the south

Climate: Continental climate; warm, showery summers; cold, cloudy, snowy winters; best months to visit are May, June and September

Highest Point: Gerlachovský štít 2,655m

Languages: Slovak, Hungarian, German

Local Time: GMT or BST + 1, i.e. 1 hour ahead of the UK all year

Currency: Euros divided into 100 cents; £1 = €1.26, €1 = £0.79 (September 2014)

Emergency numbers: Police 112; Fire brigade 112; Ambulance 112

Public Holidays 2015: Jan 1, 6; Apr 3, 6; May 1, 8 (VE Day); Jul 5 (St Cyril & St Methodius); Aug 29 (Anniversary of Slovak Uprising); Sep 1 (National Day), 15 (St Mary); Nov 1, 17 (Freedom & Democracy Day); Dec 24, 25, 26.

School summer holidays are from the beginning of July to the end of August

# Camping and Caravanning

There are approximately 175 campsites (Kemping or Autocamp) situated near tourist resorts and classified into four categories. Sites are normally open from 15 June until 15 September, although some may open in May and a handful are open all year. The season is slow to get going and sites which claim to open in May may not do so or there may be only minimal facilities.

Campsites' standards are variable and facilities may be basic. Many consist mainly of cabins and chalets in various states of repair, while others form part of the facilities offered by hotels, guest houses or leisure/thermal spa complexes.

Casual/wild camping is not permitted; it is prohibited to sleep in a caravan or motorhome outside a campsite.

Campsite prices and the cost of living in general are still relatively low. Some of the prices shown in the campsite entries that follow have been directly converted from prices previously shown in koruna (crowns) and rounded up. You may find actual prices somewhat higher now that the official currency is the euro. Prices charged include a tourist tax.

# Cycling

There are a number of long distance cycle tracks throughout the country (see www.slovakia. travel for more information) including alongside the River Danube between Bratislava and the Gabčikovo Dam.

Cyclists must ride in single file on the right hand side of the road or may use the verge outside built up areas. Children under 10 years of age may not ride on the road unless accompanied by a person over 15 years of age.

# Electricity and Gas

Usually the current on campsites varies between 10 and 16 amps. Plugs have two round pins. Some campsites, but not all, have CEE connections.

It is not possible to purchase Campingaz International or any other of the gas cylinders normally available in the UK. Sufficient supplies for your stay should be taken with you. Many sites have communal kitchen facilities which enable visitors to make great savings on their own gas supply.

# Entry Formalities

Holders of valid British and Irish passports may visit Slovakia for up to three months without a visa. There are no registration formalities for short stay visitors.

All foreign visitors are required to show proof of medical insurance cover on entry.

# Medical Services

Medical facilities are variable. Whereas the standard of care from doctors is good and medical equipment is constantly improving, many hospitals suffer from a lack of maintenance. The biggest problem you will probably encounter is language, as nurses and ancillary workers may not speak English.

There is a reciprocal health care agreement with the UK for urgent medical treatment and you should present a European Health Insurance Card (EHIC). Emergency treatment is from doctors and dentists contracted to the Slovak health insurance system, but you will be asked for payment and follow on costs could be considerable. Hospital patients are required to make a financial contribution towards costs.

Charges incurred are not refundable in Slovakia.

A 24 hour first aid service exists in all provincial and district towns, as well as in some small communities. For minor ailments, the first call should be to a pharmacy (lekáren) where staff are qualified to give advice and may be able to prescribe drugs normally available only on prescription in the UK.

Hepatitis A immunisation is advised for long stay travellers to rural areas, and those who plan to travel outside tourist areas.

## Opening Hours

Banks – Mon-Fri 8am-3pm/5pm.

Museums – Tue-Sun 10am-5pm; closed Mon.

Post Offices – Mon-Fri 8am-6pm; Sat 8am-1pm.

Shops – Mon-Fri 7am-6pm; Sat 7am-12 noon. Hypermarkets usually open Sun.

Food Shops - Mon-Fri 7am-6pm; Sat 7am-12pm.

## Safety and Security

Most visits to Slovakia are trouble free. However, there is a risk of being a victim of petty theft, particularly in Bratislava, and pickpocketing is common at the main tourist attractions and in some bars where foreigners are easily identified.

When placing your jacket on the back of a chair in a restaurant make sure you don't leave valuables in the pockets. Don't put handbags on the floor or under chairs, where they may be vulnerable to theft. There have been occurrences in Bratislava of visitors being offered 'spiked' drinks and subsequently being robbed.

Visitors entering Slovakia via the border crossings on the D2 and D4 motorways should be extremely vigilant. While you leave your vehicle to buy petrol or a motorway vignette, a tyre may be deliberately damaged. Once you are back on the road and have driven a few kilometres other motorists will flag you down and, under the pretext of offering assistance. In these circumstances you should stay in your vehicle with the doors locked and call the police (dial 112) or the emergency service of the Slovensky Autoturist Klub (SATC) on18124 or (02) 68249211.

Robberies from parked cars are on the increase. Cameras, mobile phones and tablets are as attractive as cash and credit cards; don't leave them or other valuables unattended.

If you intend to ski or hike in the Slovak mountains you are recommended to have sufficient insurance to cover rescue costs should the Slovak Mountain Rescue (HZS) be called out. Take heed of any instructions issued by HZS; if you ignore their advice you may be liable to a heavy fine.

Taking photos of anything that could be perceived as a military establishment or of security interest may result in problems with the authorities.

Slovakia shares with the rest of Europe an underlying threat from terrorism. Attacks, although unlikely, could be indiscriminate and against civilian targets, including places frequented by tourists.

*British Embassy*

PANSKA 16, 81101 BRATISLAVA
Tel: (02) 59982000
http://ukinslovakia.fco.gov.uk/en/

*Irish Embassy*

CARLTON SAVOY BUILDING
MOSTOVA 2, 81102 BRATISLAVA
Tel: (02) 59309611
www.embassyofireland.sk

## Documents
*Passport*

Carry your passport at all times as it is an offence to be without it and you may be fined and held in custody for up to 24 hours. Keep a photocopy of the details page separately. Ensure your passport is in a presentable state as the authorities can refuse you entry if it is worn or damaged or looks as if it may have been tampered with.

### Vehicle(s)

You should carry your vehicle registration certificate (V5C), at all times together with your driving licence, insurance certificate and your vehicle's MOT certificate (if applicable). Fines may be imposed by police patrols if you cannot produce these documents on request.

## Money

Exchange kiosks, although legal, offer poor exchange rates and there is a risk of being robbed by thieves loitering nearby. Scottish and Northern Irish bank notes will not be exchanged in Slovakia.

Cash machines which accept UK debit or credit cards are common but do not rely on finding one in remote areas. Shops, particularly in the main tourist areas, increasingly accept credit cards but are sometimes reluctant to accept cards issued by foreign banks. If you intend to pay for something by card do check first that the shop will accept it and that it can be read. You are also recommended to check your statements carefully for transactions you did not make.

## Motoring in Slovakia

The standard of driving is not high and sometimes aggressive with drivers going too fast, especially in bad weather, pushing into dangerously small gaps, tailgating and overtaking dangerously. Drive defensively and allow yourself more 'thinking time'. Beware particularly of oncoming cars overtaking on your side of the road (especially on bends and hills).

## Accidents

If your vehicle is damaged when you enter Slovakia the border authorities must issue a certificate confirming the visible damage. While in the country if an accident causes bodily injury or material damage exceeding a value of approximately €4,000 it must be reported to the police immediately. If a vehicle is only slightly damaged both drivers should complete a European Accident Report. In the case of foreign motorists driving vehicles registered abroad, it is advisable to report the accident to the police who will issue a certificate which will facilitate the exportation of the vehicle.

## Alcohol

Don't drink and drive. Slovakia has a policy of zero tolerance for drinking or consuming drugs before driving. There is no permitted level of alcohol in the bloodstream. Police carry out random breath tests and you will be heavily penalised if there is any trace of alcohol in your system.

## Breakdown Service

The motoring organisation, Slovensky Autoturist Klub (SATC), operates an emergency centre which can be contacted 24 hours a day by dialling (0)18124 or (02) 68249211. Operators speak English.

## Essential Equipment

### First aid kit

A first aid kit is compulsory in all vehicles.

### Lights

All vehicles must use dipped headlights at all times.

### Reflective Jacket/Waistcoat

If your vehicle is immobilised on the carriageway outside a built up area, or if visibility is poor, you must wear a reflective jacket or waistcoat when getting out of your vehicle. Passengers who leave the vehicle, for example, to assist with a repair, should also wear one.

### Sat Nav/GPS Device

A GPS device must not be placed in the middle of the windscreen. The driver's view must not be impeded.

### Warning Triangles

Carry a warning triangle which, in an emergency or in case of breakdown, must be placed at least 100 metres behind your vehicle on motorways and highways, and 50 metres behind on other roads.
The triangle may be placed closer to the vehicle in built-up areas. Drivers may use hazard-warning lights until the triangle is in position.

In case of breakdown, vehicles left on the edge of the carriageway will be towed away after three hours by the organisation in charge of the motorway or road at the owner's expense.

## Child Restraint System

Children under the age of 12 years and anyone under 1.5m in height must not travel in the front seat of a vehicle. Child restraint seats must be used for any children weighing less than 36kg.

## Winter Driving

In winter equip your vehicle(s) for severe driving conditions and fit winter tyres, which are compulsory when roads are covered in snow or ice. Carry snow chains and use them when there is enough snow to protect the road surface.

## Fuel

Diesel is sold in service stations with the sign 'TT Diesel' or 'Nafta'. LPG is widely available and is sold under the name ECO Auto-gas or ECO Car-Gas – see www.lpg.szm.sk/slovensko_5.pdf for a list of outlets. If driving a vehicle converted to use LPG you must be in possession of a safety certificate covering the combustion equipment in your vehicle.

Some service stations on international roads and in main towns are open 24 hours but in other areas they may close by 6pm. Credit cards are generally accepted. Service stations may be hard to find in rural areas.

## Parking

Visitors are warned to park only in officially controlled parking areas since cars belonging to tourists may be targeted for robbery. There are many restrictions on parking in Bratislava and fines are imposed. Wheel clamps are used in main towns and vehicles may be towed away.

Continuous white/yellow lines along the carriageway indicate that parking is prohibited and broken white/yellow lines indicate parking restrictions.

## Priority

At uncontrolled crossroads or intersections not marked by a priority sign, priority must be given to vehicles coming from the right. Drivers must not enter an intersection unless the exit beyond the crossing is clear.

Drivers must slow down and, if necessary, stop to allow buses and trams to move off from stops and to allow buses to merge with general traffic at the end of a bus lane. A tram turning right and crossing the line of travel of a vehicle moving on its right has priority once the driver has signalled his intention to turn. Trams must be overtaken on the right but do not overtake near a tram refuge.

## Roads

Roads are relatively quiet and are generally well maintained. They often follow routes through towns and villages, resulting in sharp bends and reduced speed limits.

Many main roads, although reasonably good, have only a single carriageway in each direction making overtaking difficult. Road markings may be difficult to see in bad weather.

In winter, north south routes through Slovakia can be challenging as they pass through mountain ranges. The passes of Donovaly (Ružomberok to Banská Bystrica), Veľký Šturec (Martin to Banská Bystrica), and Čertovica (Liptovský Mikuláš to Brezno) are the most frequented. Slow moving vehicles travelling uphill should pull over at suitable stopping places to allow vehicles behind to pass.

## Road Signs and Markings

Road signs and markings conform to international standards. The following signs may also be seen:

| Slovak | English Translation |
|---|---|
| Dialkova premavka | By-pass |
| Hnemocnica | Hospital |
| Jednosmerny premavka | One-way traffic |
| Obchadzka | Diversion |
| Prújezd zakázaný | Closed to all vehicles |
| Zákaz parkovania | No parking |
| Zákaz vjazdu | No entry |

Signs indicating motorways are red and white and signs on motorways or semi-motorways have a green or blue background; on other roads signs have a blue background.

# Speed Limits

| | Open Road (km/h) | Motorway (km/h) |
|---|---|---|
| Car Solo | 90 | 130 |
| Car towing caravan/trailer | 90 | 90 |
| Motorhome under 3500kg | 90 | 130 |
| Motorhome 3500-7500kg | 80 | 90 |

Motorhomes over 3,500kg are restricted to 80/90 km/h (56 mph) on motorways and to 80 km/h (50 mph) on other main roads and dual carriageways. Do not exceed 30 km/h (18 mph) when approaching and going over level crossings.

Speed limits are strictly enforced. The carrying and/or use of radar detectors is prohibited.

# Traffic Lights

A green arrow together with a red or amber light indicates that drivers may turn in the direction indicated by the arrow provided they give way to other traffic and to pedestrians. A green arrow accompanied by an amber light in the form of a walking figure means that pedestrians have right of way.

# Violation of Traffic Regulations

Police are empowered to collect on the spot fines for contravention of driving regulations. An official receipt should be obtained.

# Motorways

There are 432km of motorways. Bratislava has direct motorway connections with Prague and Vienna and a new motorway is planned to connect it with Budapest.

Emergency phones are placed along motorways and callers are connected directly to the police.

Vehicles using motorways and selected highways must display a vignette (windscreen sticker), which may be purchased at border crossings, petrol stations and post offices. Charges for vehicles up to 3,500kg with or without a caravan or trailer are as follows (2014 prices): €10 for a period of 10 days and €14 for one month. Fines are payable for non-display and old stickers must be removed. The road from the Austrian border crossing at Berg to Bratislava is free of charge.

Motorhomes over 3,500kg are considered private vehicles and can buy the above vignettes as long as you are able to show the Vehicle Registration Certificate (V5) and it shows that the vehicle has fewer than 9 seats. Without the V5, drivers of vehicles over 3,500kg must pay motorway tolls by means of an electronic toll collection unit fitted to their vehicle. Tolls vary according to distance driven, vehicle weight and emissions classification. For information see www.emyto.sk or telephone 00421 235 111111.

# Touring

Smoking is not allowed on the premises where food is served and a partial smoking ban is in force in some bars and cafés which have a dedicated area for smokers. A tip of between 5 to 10% is usual in restaurants. It is normal to give taxi drivers a small tip by rounding up fares to the nearest 50 cents.

Mains water is heavily chlorinated and may cause stomach upsets. Bottled water is available.

The highest peaks of the Tatras mountains are covered with snow for approximately four months of the year and offer ample scope for winter sports. There are plenty of cableways and ski-lifts.

There are a number of UNESCO World Heritage sites in Slovakia including the town of Bardejov, the mining centre of Banská Štiavnica, the 'gingerbread houses' of Vlkolínec village, Spiš Castle, wooden churches in the Carpathian mountains and the caves of Aggtelek Karst and Slovak Karst.

Slovakia has over a thousand curative mineral and thermal springs, together with extensive deposits of high quality healing peat and mud reputed to cure a variety of diseases and ailments. Visitors from all over the world attend these spas every year.

The Bratislava City Card valid for one, two or three days, offers discounts and benefits at approximately 60 attractions and at restaurants and cafés. In addition, it offers free access to public transport and a free one hour walking tour of the Old Town. The card can be obtained at tourist information centres, at the central railway station and at hotels.

In general Slovakia does not cater for the physically handicapped. For example, it is normal for cars to park on the pavement and dropped kerbs are perceived as helping drivers to achieve this without damaging tyres or suspension! Public transport invariably requires large steps to be climbed and bus and tram drivers tend to accelerate from stops at great speed, catching passengers by surprise. Access to most buildings is by steps, rather than ramps. However effort is now being taken to make buildings more accessible.

German is the most common second language. English is still not widely understood or spoken.

## Public Transport

From April to September hydrofoil services operate from Bratislava to Vienna and Budapest.

In Bratislava bus, trolley bus and tram tickets are valid for periods of up to 60 minutes, extending to up to 90 minutes at night and weekends. Buy them from kiosks and yellow ticket machines. Alternatively you can buy tickets valid for one or several city zones for a fixed period, e.g. 24, 48 or 72 hours or for seven days. Ensure that you validate your ticket on boarding the bus or tram.

Passengers aged 70 and over travel free; carry your passport as proof of age. You must buy a ticket for dogs travelling on public transport and they must be muzzled. You must also purchase a ticket for large items of luggage. For more information see www.imhd.zoznam.sk/ba.

*Bratislava*

⊞ **BANSKA BYSTRICA** *B2* (7km W Rural) *48.7540, 19.0552*
**Autocamping Tajov, 97634 Tajov [(048) 4197320; kukis@
slovanet.sk; www.velkydvor.sk/en]** Fr Tajov dir Kordíky. Site
well sp 2km NW of Tajov. Sm, pt sl, unshd; htd wc; chem disp;
shwrs inc; el pnts (6-10A) inc; shop; snacks; bar; rest 300m;
playgrnd; wifi; TV; statics; bus; quiet; red CKE/CCI. "Lovely
setting in wooded valley; friendly welcome." € 16.00    2011*

**BRATISLAVA** *C1* (8km NE Urban) *48.18801, 17.18488*
**Autocamping Zlaté Piesky, Senecká Cesta 12, 82104
Bratislava [(02) 44257373 or 44450592; fax 44257373;
kempi@netax.sk; www.intercamp.sk]** Exit D1/E75 junc
sp Zlaté Piesky. Site on S side of rd 61 (E75) at NE edge of
Bratislava. Look for pedestrian bdge over rd to tram terminus,
ent thro adj traff lts. If x-ing Bratislava foll sp for Žilina. In
summer a 2nd, quieter, drier site is opened. For 1st site turn L
when ent leisure complex; for 2nd site carry strt on then turn R.
Med, shd; wc; shwrs inc; el pnts (10A) €3 (long lead poss req);
shop; supmkt (Tesco) 300m; rest, snacks; bar; playgrnd; sw &
pedalos on lake; fishing; tennis; golf 10km; entmnt; dogs €2;
phone; tram to city; poss cr; Eng spkn; v noisy fr adj m'way &
bar; red CKE/CCI. "Basic site on lge leisure complex; no privacy
in shwrs; ltd hot water; muddy in wet; security guard at night &
secure rm for bikes etc but reg, major security problems as site
grnds open to public; helpful, friendly staff; interesting city."
1 May-15 Oct. € 13.20                                    2010*

**BREZNO** *B3* (6km SE Rural) *48.79501, 19.72867* **Camping
Sedliacky Dvor, Hliník 7, 97701 Brezno [(048) 911 078 303;
info@sedliackydvor.com; www.sedliackydvor.com]** Fr cent
of Brezno at traff lts nr Hotel Dumbier take rd 530/72 SE sp
Tisovec. In approx 5km cross rlwy line & ent vill of Rohozná.
At end of vill turn L after Camping sp. Site in 500m. Sm, pt
shd; wc; shwrs; el pnts (10A) €3.25; lndtte; cooking facs; pool;
games area; wifi; dogs €1; Eng spkn; adv bkg; quiet. "Excel site
in lovely orchard setting; welcoming Dutch owners; camp fires
in evening; excel facs." 15 Apr-31 Oct. € 22.50        2013*

**CEROVO** *C2* (8km NE Rural) *48.25228, 19.21783* **Camping
Lazy, Cerovo 163, 96252 Cerovo [(090) 8590837; info@
minicamping.eu; www.campinglazy.eu]** S fr Zvolen on rd
66 dir Krupina. S of Krupina turn L onto rd 526 to Bzovik. After
church in Bzovik turn R sp Kozí Vrbovok, Trpín & Litava. Cont
thro Litava (agricultural co-operative, Družstvo, on R) & cont
for approx 5km to T-junc with bus shelter & turn R. Do not
foll sp Cerovo on R but cont to forest & look out for sm lane
& site sp to R. Sm, pt sl, pt shd; wc; chem disp; shwrs; el pnts
(4-6A) €2.50; lndtte; some statics (equipped tents); dogs free;
quiet. "Site on working farm; ideal for nature lovers, hikers,
dog owners; pleasant, helpful owners; v clean, modern facs."
1 May-30 Sep. € 16.00                                    2013*

**DEMANOVSKA DOLINA see Liptovský Mikuláš** *B3*

⊞ **KOSICE** *B4* (4km SW Rural) *48.68746, 21.25583*
**Autocamping Salaš Barca, Alejová ul, 04001 Košice
[(055) 6233397; fax 6258309; www.autocamping.szm.
sk]** Access only avail E'bound on E571/E50/E58. Fr W foll sp
Miskolc E571/E50/E58. Site on R 2km after clover leaf junc.
Fr N or E foll sp E50/E571 Rožňava W-bound past camp to
clover leaf junc & return E-bound on E571/E50/E58. Fr S (Hung
border) on ent Košice turn L under ring rd sp Spišská Nová Ves
& Rožňava (E571). After approx 2.5km take airport/Rožňava
exit over clover leaf & back down E-bound ringrd (E571). Site
on R. Sm, unshd; wc; shwrs inc; el pnts (10A) inc; shop 1km;
rest; snacks, bar 1km; cooking facs; sand/shgl beach & rv sw
1km; pool 1km; 50% workers' chalets; tram 500m; Eng spkn;
rd noise; CKE/CCI. "Old but clean facs, ltd low ssn; recep sells
tram tickets; 24hr security; gd touring base, but run down
(2009); Košice delightful city." 15 May-15 Oct. € 19.30  2009*

⊞ **LEVOCA** *B3* (3km N Rural) *49.04982, 20.58727*
**Autocamping Levočská Dolina, 05401 Levoča
[(053) 4512705 or 4512701; fax 4513689; rzlevoca@pobox.
sk]** Site on E side of minor rd 533 running N fr E50 at Dolina
to Levočská Dolina. Steep ent; ltd access lge o'fits. Med, sl, pt
shd; wc; chem disp; shwrs inc; el pnts (16A) €3; lndtte; shop
3km; rest, snacks; bar; playgrnd; ski lift 2.5km; TV; dogs €1.50;
Eng spkn; quiet; CKE/CCI. "Diff in wet weather due v sl grnd;
friendly staff; interesting old town; Spišský Hrad castle worth
visit; walks in forests around site." € 15.00            2009*

**LIPTOVSKY MIKULAS** *B3* (6km NE Rural) *49.11108, 19.54608*
**Autocamp Liptovský Trnovec, 03222 Liptovský Trnovec
[(044) 5598459; fax 5598458; atctrnovec@atctrnovec.sk;
www.atctrnovec.sk]** E fr Ružomberok on R18/E50 exit on
R584 to Liptovský Mikuláš. Site on N side of Lake Liptovský
Mara. Med, unshd; wc; chem disp; shwrs inc; el pnts (6A)
€2.50; lndtte; shop; rest, bar in ssn; playgrnd; lake sw; boating;
cycle hire; internet; 10% statics; dogs €2; Eng spkn; quiet; red
CKE/CCI. "Excel; lovely site in beautiful location." ♦ 1 May-
31 Oct. € 13.50                                          2010*

⊞ **LIPTOVSKY MIKULAS** *B3* (10km NW Rural) *49.13608,
19.5125* **Resort Villa Betula (Formerly Penzión), 03223
Liptovský Sielnica [(044) 5598464; fax 5598465;
villabetula@villabetula.sk; www.villabetula.sk]** Fr rd 18/
E50 exit onto R584 to Liptovský Mikuláš, site on N of lake
6km past Autocamp. Med, unshd; wc; chem disp; sauna; baby
facs; shwrs inc; el pnts (10A) inc; rest; bar; playgrnd; lake sw
adj; cycle hire; jacuzzi; wifi; no statics; dogs €7; phone; Eng
spkn; quiet; ccard acc; CKE/CCI. "Family-friendly, gem of a site
in wonderful area of lakes, mountains & forest; welcoming,
helpful owners; v clean & well-kept; vg rest; site at rear of
hotel; excel for long or sh stay." € 27.50               2013*

**LIPTOVSKY SIELNICA see Liptovský Mikuláš** *B3*

**LIPTOVSKY TRNOVEC see Liptovský Mikuláš** *B3*

SLOVAKIA

**NITRIANSKE RUDNO** *B2* (N Rural) *48.80457, 18.47601*
**Autocamping Nitrianske Rudno, 97226 Nitrianske Rudno**
**[(046) 5455403; info@camping-nrudno.sk; www.camping-nrudno.sk]** E fr Bánovce & Dolné Vestenice on rd 50, turn
N onto rd 574. Site on shore of Lake Nitrianske Rudno, sp in
vill. Med, pt shd; wc; shwrs; el pnts €2.50; lndtte; snacks; bar;
cooking facs; playgrnd; lake sw; watersports; games area;
internet; entmnt; some statics; dogs €1; adv bkg; quiet; red
CKE/CCI. "Welcoming, helpful owner; pleasant location."
1 Jun-30 Sep. € 8.70                                        2009*

**PREŠOV** *B4* (600m NE Rural) *49.00386, 21.08145*
**Autokemping A Motorest Kemp, Chminianske Nová Ves,**
**District Prešov 082 33 [0517 795190 / 0905 191056 mob;**
**kemppo@kemppo.sk; www.kemppo.sk]** E fr Prešov on Rte 18/
D1/E50, take exit twd Vit'az/Hrabkov, site on R. Sm pt shd; wc
shwrs inc; gas; el pnts €4; lndtte with campers kitchen; shop,
rest, snacks, bar, BBQ; cooking facs; plygrnd; games area; dog
€2; twin axles acc; Eng spkn; quiet; ccard acc; CKE/CCI. "Site
behind motorest Kemp on Rte 18; recep in rest; 5 chalets for
rent on site; fair site." Feb-Dec. € 15.30                 2014*

**ROZNAVA** *B3* (5km E Rural) **Autocamping Krásnohorské,**
**Hradná 475, 04941 Krásnohorské Podhradie**
**[(058) 7325457; fax 7921332]** E fr Rožňava on rd 50/E571 foll
sp Krásnohorské Podhradie. Site under shadow of castle. Sm,
pt shd; wc; shwrs; mainly huts. "Lovely setting in pine woods;
primitive facs but plenty of hot water; conv for cave visits."
€ 10.00                                                     2012*

## "There aren't many sites open at this time of year"

If you're travelling outside peak season
remember to call ahead to check site opening
dates – even if the entry says 'open all year'.

**SENEC** *C1* (1.5km SE Urban) *48.21386, 17.41088*
**Autocamping Slnečné Jazerá (Die Sonnenseen), Mierové**
**Námestie 19, 90301 Senec [(02) 45924081; fax 45923080;**
**info@slnecnejazerasenec.sk; www.slnecnejazerasenec.**
**sk]** Fr D1/E75 take junc exit for Senec onto rd 503, site sp. Lge,
pt shd; wc; shwrs inc; el pnts (16A) inc; lndtte; shop; supmkts
in town; rest, snacks; playgrnd; aqua park nr; sand beach; lake
sw; boating; tennis; cycling; TV; entmnt; no dogs; phone; bus/
train to Bratislava nr; poss cr; noise fr disco, rd & rlwy. "Gd alt
to Bratislava site." 15 Jun-15 Sep. € 19.30                2011*

**TAJOV see Banská Bystrica** *B2*

**TATRANSKA LOMINICA** *B3* (2.6km S Rural) *49.14974,*
*20.27968* **Camping Rijo (formerly Jupela), Dolny**
**Smokovec, 3705981 Vysoke Tatry [(421) 911 616530;**
**rijocamping@rijocamping.eu; www.rijocamping.eu]**
Fr Tatranska Lominca travel W on 537 take L turn twrds Nova
Lesna. Foll sp to site. Sm, pt shd; wc; chem disp; shwrs; el pnts
16A €3.50; snacks; bar; BBQ; playgrnd; adv bkg. "Beautiful
location nr to mountain torrent. Conv for walking in Takranska;
basic clean san facs; lovely spot; walks and scenice drives."
7 May-16 Sept. € 13.30                                      2013*

⊞ **TATRANSKA LOMNICA** *B3* (2km SE Rural) *49.15830,*
*20.30979* **Intercamp Tatranec, 05960 Tatranská Lomnica**
**[(052) 4467092; hoteltatranec@hoteltatranec.com]** NE
fr Poprad on rd 67, after 8km turn L over level x-ing, thro
Vel'ká Lomnica twds Tatranská Lomnica on rd 540. Site on
L. Lge, pt sl, unshd; wc; chem disp; shwrs inc; el pnts (6A)
inc; lndtte; shop & 4km; rest; bar; playgrnd; wifi; entmnt;
Eng spkn; adv bkg; quiet; red CKE/CCI. "Superb views of
High Tatras; conv cable car, train etc; excel base for walking
& holiday resort; hotel adj; poor, dated facs & ltd privacy."
€ 18.50                                                     2011*

## "That's changed – Should I let The Club know?"

If you find something on site that's different from
the site entry, fill in a report and let us know. See
www.caravanclub.co.uk/europereport.

**TERCHOVA** *B2* (3km W Rural) *49.24779, 18.98866*
**Autocamp Belá, Nižné Kamence, 01305 Belá**
**[(041) 5695135; camp@bela.sk; www.camping.bela.**
**sk]** Fr Zilina foll rd 583 twd Terchová. Site on L 3km after vill
of Belá. Med, pt shd; wc; chem disp; mv service pnt; shwrs
€0.30; el pnts (10A) €3; lndry rm; shop; tradsmn; rest, snacks;
BBQ; cooking facs; playgrnd; tennis; 10% statics; dogs €1; rd
noise. "Delightful rvside site; gd welcome; clean, modern san
facs; conv walking in Malá Fatra mountains." 1 May-15 Oct.
€ 11.50                                                     2011*

**TRENCIN** *B2* (300m N Urban) *48.90011, 18.04076*
**Autocamping Na Ostrove, Ostrov, 91101 Trenčín**
**[(032) 7434013; autocamping.tn@mail.pvt.sk; http://web.**
**viapvt.sk/autocamping.tn]** Fr SW on rd 61/E75 cross rv at
Hotel Tatra, 1st L dir Sihot, go under rlwy bdge. 1st L, then
immed 1st L again, then R at stadium, cross canal to island,
site on L. Sm, unshd; wc; chem disp; shwrs inc; 25% serviced
pitches; el pnts (10A) €3; lndtte; shop in town; snacks; bar;
cooking facs; pool 500m; 90% statics; dogs €1.50; poss cr;
some Eng spkn; some noise fr rlwy & sports stadium; CKE/CCI.
"Popular NH en rte Poland, rec arr early high ssn; on rvside in
run down pt of town adj sports stadium; adj delightful town
with fairy-tale castle; poss waterlogged in wet; facs old but
clean - some lack privacy." 1 May-15 Sep. € 18.00    2013*

**ZVOLEN** *B2* (6km NW Rural) *48.60611, 19.10175* **Autocamp**
**Kováčová, Kúpeľná ul, 96237 Kováčová [(045) 5445220;**
**fax 5445363; recent@recent.sk]** Fr E77/66 dir Banská Bystrica
turn at sp Kováčová. In vill foll site sp. Med, pt sl, pt shd;
wc; chem disp (wc); shwrs inc; el pnts €2.50; lndry rm; shop
500m; snacks; bar; BBQ; cooking facs; htd pool adj; TV rm;
40% statics; Eng spkn; quiet; CKE/CCI. "Clean site but run
down (6/09); friendly owner." 26 May-2 Sep. € 11.40   2009*

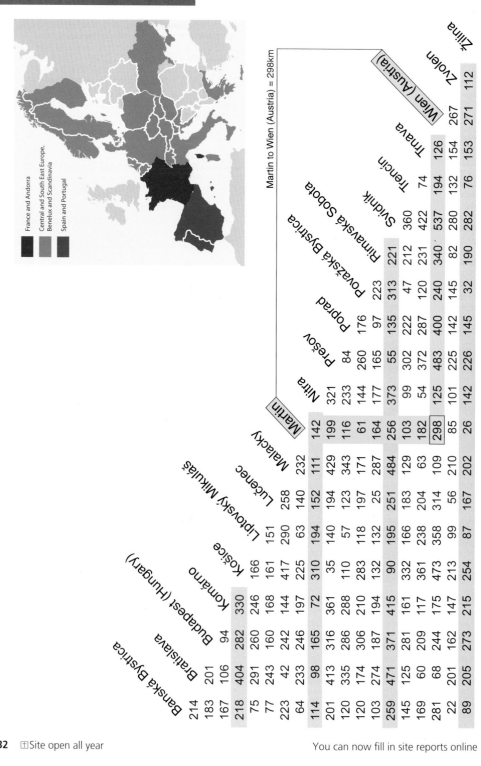

Map legend:
- France and Andorra
- Central and South East Europe, Benelux and Scandinavia
- Spain and Portugal

**Martin to Wien (Austria) = 298km**

Distance chart (km) — lower-triangular reading, each origin to the cities that follow it:

| From \ To | Bratislava | Budapest (Hungary) | Komárno | Košice | Liptovský Mikuláš | Lučenec | Malacky | Martin | Nitra | Prešov | Poprad | Považská Bystrica | Rimavská Sobota | Svidník | Trenčín | Trnava | Wien (Austria) | Zvolen | Žilina |
|---|---|---|---|---|---|---|---|---|---|---|---|---|---|---|---|---|---|---|---|
| **Banská Bystrica** | 214 | 183 | 167 | 218 | 75 | 77 | 223 | 64 | 114 | 201 | 120 | 120 | 103 | 259 | 145 | 169 | 281 | 22 | 89 |
| **Bratislava** | | 201 | 291 | 243 | 42 | 233 | 98 | 413 | 316 | 286 | 306 | 187 | 371 | 281 | 209 | 244 | 162 | 201 | 205 |
| **Budapest (Hungary)** | | | 94 | 282 | 260 | 160 | 242 | 246 | 165 | 371 | 316 | 286 | 306 | 187 | 244 | 162 | 162 | 201 | 273 |
| **Komárno** | | | | 330 | 246 | 168 | 144 | 197 | 72 | 361 | 288 | 210 | 194 | 415 | 161 | 117 | 175 | 147 | 215 |
| **Košice** | | | | | 166 | 161 | 417 | 225 | 310 | 35 | 110 | 283 | 132 | 90 | 332 | 361 | 473 | 213 | 254 |
| **Liptovský Mikuláš** | | | | | | 151 | 290 | 63 | 194 | 140 | 57 | 118 | 132 | 195 | 166 | 238 | 358 | 99 | 87 |
| **Lučenec** | | | | | | | 232 | 258 | 140 | 152 | 194 | 123 | 197 | 25 | 251 | 183 | 204 | 314 | 56 |
| **Malacky** | | | | | | | | 167 | 111 | 429 | 343 | 171 | 287 | 484 | 129 | 63 | 109 | 210 | 202 |
| **Martin** | | | | | | | | | 142 | 199 | 116 | 61 | 164 | 256 | 103 | 182 | 298 | 85 | 26 |
| **Nitra** | | | | | | | | | | 321 | 233 | 144 | 177 | 373 | 99 | 54 | 125 | 101 | 142 |
| **Prešov** | | | | | | | | | | | 84 | 260 | 165 | 55 | 302 | 372 | 483 | 225 | 226 |
| **Poprad** | | | | | | | | | | | | 176 | 97 | 135 | 222 | 287 | 400 | 142 | 145 |
| **Považská Bystrica** | | | | | | | | | | | | | 223 | 313 | 47 | 120 | 240 | 145 | 32 |
| **Rimavská Sobota** | | | | | | | | | | | | | | 221 | 212 | 231 | 340 | 82 | 190 |
| **Svidník** | | | | | | | | | | | | | | | 360 | 422 | 537 | 280 | 282 |
| **Trenčín** | | | | | | | | | | | | | | | | 74 | 194 | 132 | 76 |
| **Trnava** | | | | | | | | | | | | | | | | | 126 | 154 | 153 |
| **Wien (Austria)** | | | | | | | | | | | | | | | | | | 267 | 271 |
| **Zvolen** | | | | | | | | | | | | | | | | | | | 112 |

You can now fill in site reports online

© Collins Bartholomew Ltd 2014

# Slovenia
## Country Introduction

*Preseren Square, Ljubljana, Slovenia*

## Welcome to Slovenia

Slovenia is great for those interested in nature and hikers looking for that perfect view. With soaring Alpine peaks, hills and sparkling lakes and rivers, the countryside has so much to offer.

Even its capital city, Ljubljana, is one of Europe's greenest and is very accessible for foreign visitors. Most of the top attractions are found in a pedestrian only area, which is great for exploring and is also very photogenic along the riverside.

## Country highlights

The cuisine in Slovenia reflects a German influence with Sauerkraut, grilled sausage and apple strudel appearing often on local menus. On the Adriatic coast there are specialities based on fish, lobster and crayfish. Usually served with white wines which are especially good, as are local beers or 'pivo'.

Ljubljana and Bled are at their best during the International Summer Festival, with a number of concerts and theatrical performances on offer.

## Major towns and cities

* Ljubljana – the capital city maintains a small town charm.

* Maribor – a city that has been known for its wine and is surrounded by vineyards.

* Izola – an old Mediterranean town with colourfully painted house and traditions of fishing and wine making.

## Attractions

* Lake Bled – a spectacular lake with the magnificent Julian Alps as a backdrop.

* Franciscan Church –  a beautiful church with a red facade and stunning interior.

* Tivoli Park – home to the botanical gardens and a contemporary history museum.

* Preseren Square – a romantic square is found in the heart of the city of Ljubljana.

## Find out more

www.slovenia.info

Tel: 0038 (0) 61 58 91 840 Slovenian Tourist Board

# Country Information

*Population (approx):* 2 million

*Capital:* Ljubljana (population approx 280,000)

*Area:* 20,273 sqkm

*Bordered by:* Austria, Croatia, Hungary, Italy

*Coastline:* 46.6km

*Terrain:* Coastal strip on the Adriatic; alpine mountains in west and north; many rivers and forests

*Climate:* Mediterranean climate on the coast; hot summers and cold winters in the plateaux and valleys in the east; spring and early autumn are the best times to visit

*Highest Point:* Triglav 2,864m

*Languages:* Slovenian; Serbo-Croat

*Local Time:* GMT or BST + 1, i.e. 1 hour ahead of the UK all year

*Currency:* Euros divided into 100 cents; £1 = €1.26, €1 = £0.79 (September 2014)

*Emergency numbers:* Police 113; Fire brigade 112; Ambulance 112. Operators speak English

*Public Holidays 2014:* Jan 1; Feb 8 (Culture Day); Apr 6, 27; May 1; Jun 25 (National Day); Aug 15; Oct 31 (Reformation Day); Nov 1; Dec 25, 26.

School summer holidays are from the last week in June to the end of August

# Camping and Caravanning

There are approximately 50 organised campsites in Slovenia rated one to five stars. They are usually open from May to October but a few are open all year. Standards of sites and their sanitary facilities are generally good. Campsites on the coast consist mostly of statics and can be overcrowded during the peak summer season. Casual/wild camping is not permitted.

# Cycling

There are some cycle lanes which are also used by mopeds. Cyclists under the age of 15 must wear a safety helmet.

*Transportation of Bicycles*

An overhanging load which exceeds one metre at the rear of a vehicle must be indicated by a red flag or red panel measuring 30cm square. At night the overhanging load must be indicated by a red light and a reflector. Loads may only project rearwards; they must not overhang the sides of vehicles.

# Electricity and Gas

Usually the current on campsites varies between 6 and 16 amps. Plugs have two round pins. Hook-up points on most campsites conform to CEE standards.

Campingaz cylinders cannot be purchased or exchanged. Recent visitors report that it is possible to have gas cylinders refilled at premises on Verovškova Ulica 70, Ljubljana. The company's name is Butan-Plin. However, The Caravan Club does not recommend this practice and you should aim to take enough gas to last during your stay.

# Entry Formalities

All foreign nationals must register with the police within three days of arrival in Slovenia. Campsites carry out registration formalities, but if you are staying with friends or family you or your host will need to visit the nearest police station to register your presence in the country.

British and Irish passport holders may stay in Slovenia for up to three months without a visa. For longer stays contact the Slovenian Embassy for further information.

# Medical Services

British visitors may obtain emergency medical, hospital and dental treatment from practitioners registered with the public health service, Health Institute of Slovenia (HIIS) on presentation of a European Health Insurance Card (EHIC). You will have to make a contribution towards costs which will not be refunded in Slovenia. Full fees are payable for private medical and dental treatment.

Health resorts and spas are popular and the medical profession uses them extensively for treatment of a wide variety of complaints.

## Opening Hours

Banks – Mon-Fri 9am-12 noon & 2pm-5pm; closed Sat/Sun

Museums – Tues-Sun 9/10am-5/6pm. Most closed Mon.

Post Offices – Mon-Fri 8am-6pm; Sat 8am-12 noon.

Shops – Mon-Fri 8am-7pm/9pm; Sat 8am-1pm.

## Safety and Security

Slovenia is relatively safe for visitors but the usual sensible precautions should be taken against pickpockets in large towns and cities.
Do not leave valuables in your car.

Western Slovenia is on an earthquake fault line and is subject to occasional tremors.

If you are planning a skiing or mountaineering holiday, contact the Slovenian Tourist Board for advice on weather and safety conditions before travelling. You should follow all safety instructions meticulously, given the danger of avalanches in some areas. Off-piste skiing is highly dangerous.

There is a low threat from terrorism but attacks could be indiscriminate and against civilian targets, including places frequented by tourists.

*British Embassy*

4TH FLOOR, TRG REPUBLIKE 3, 1000 LJUBLJANA
Tel: (01) 2003910
http://ukinslovenia.fco.gov.uk/en

*Irish Embassy*
POLJANSKI NASIP 6
1000 Ljubljana
Tel: (01) 3008970
www.embassyofireland.si

## Documents
*Driving Licence*
All European countries recognise the EU format paper UK driving licence introduced in 1990. However, it is a legal requirement to show your driving license with a form of photographic identification, such as your passport, if your driving licence does not include a photograph.

*Passport*
Carry a copy of your passport at all times as a form of identification.

*Vehicle(s)*
You should carry your vehicle documentation, i.e. vehicle registration certificate (V5C), insurance certificate, MOT certificate (if applicable) and driver's licence.

If you are driving a hired or borrowed vehicle, you must be in possession of a letter of authorisation from the owner or a hire agreement.

## Money

Cash machines are widespread and the major credit cards are widely accepted. Carry your credit card issuers'/banks' 24-hour UK contact numbers in case of loss or theft of your cards.

## Motoring in Slovenia
### Accidents

Any visible damage to a vehicle entering Slovenia must be certified by authorities at the border. All drivers involved in an accident while in the country should inform the police and obtain a written report (Potrdilo). Drivers of vehicles which have been damaged will need to present this police report to Customs on departure.

## Alcohol

The maximum permitted level of alcohol is 50 milligrams in 100 millilitres of blood, i.e. lower than what is permitted in the UK (80 milligrams). If a driver is under the age of 21 or has held a driving licence for less than three years the permitted level of alcohol is zero. The police carry out tests at random.

## Breakdown Service

The motoring organisation, Avto-Moto Zveza Slovenije (AMZS), operates a 24 hour breakdown service which can be contacted by telephoning 1987. On motorways, using a mobile phone, call the AMZS Alarm Centre in Ljubljana on (01) 5305353 or use the emergency telephones and ask for AMZS assistance.

Charges apply for basic on-the-spot repairs and towing, plus supplements at night, weekends and on public holidays. Credit cards are accepted in payment.

## Essential Equipment

*First aid kit*
Although a first aid kit is not compulsory in all vehicles, it is recommended.

*Lights*
Dipped headlights are compulsory at all times, regardless of weather conditions. Bulbs are more likely to fail with constant use and you are required to carry spares. Hazard warning lights must be used when reversing.

*Reflective Jacket/Waistcoat*
In the event of vehicle breakdown on a motorway, anyone who leaves the vehicle must wear a reflective jacket.

*Child Restraint System*
Children under 12 years of age and under the height of 1.5 metres must use a suitable child restraint system for their size and age.

*Warning Triangles*
Vehicles towing a trailer must carry two warning triangles (single vehicles require only one). In the event of a breakdown to vehicle and trailer combinations, one triangle must be placed at the rear of the towed vehicle and another at the front of the towing vehicle at a distance which ensures maximum safety and visibility.

At night, drivers must always use hazard warning lights or a torch in addition to the warning triangles.

*Winter Driving*
From 15 November to 15 March, and beyond those dates during winter weather conditions (snowfalls, black ice, etc), private cars and vehicles up to 3,500kg must have winter tyres on all four wheels or, alternatively, carry snow chains. Minimum tread depth of tyres is 3mm.

## Fuel

Petrol stations are generally open from 6am to 10pm Monday to Saturday. Many near border crossings, on motorways and near large towns are open 24 hours. Credit cards are accepted. It is understood that few petrol stations sell LPG.

## Parking

Parking meters are used in towns. In city centres white lines indicate that parking is permitted for a maximum of two hours between 7am and 7pm, a parking ticket must be purchased from a machine. Blue lines indicate places where parking is allowed free of charge for up to 30 minutes. Vehicles parked illegally may be towed away or clamped.

## Priority

At intersections drivers must give way to traffic from the right, unless a priority road is indicated. The same rule applies to roundabouts, i.e. traffic entering a roundabout has priority.

## Roads

Slovenia has a well-developed road system, and international and main roads are in good condition. Secondary roads may still be poorly maintained and generally unlit. Minor roads are often gravelled and are known locally as 'white roads'. Road numbers are rarely mentioned on road signs and it is advisable to navigate using place names in the direction you are travelling.

Roadside verges are uncommon, or may be lined with bollards which make pulling over difficult. Where there is a hard shoulder it is usual for slow vehicles to pull over to allow faster traffic to overtake.

The capital, Ljubljana, can be reached from Munich, Milan, Vienna and Budapest in less than five hours. There are numerous border crossings for quick and trouble free entry into Slovenia.

Care should be taken, especially on narrow secondary roads, where tailgating and overtaking on blind bends are not unknown. Drive defensively and take extra care when driving at night. Be prepared for severe weather in winter.

Information on roads may be obtained by telephoning the AMZS Information Centre on (01) 5305300.

# Road Signs and Markings

Road signs conform to international standards. Motorway signs have a green background and national road signs a blue background. On your travels you may see the following signs:

Mountian pass

School area

Toll: Vignette/ card or cash

# Speed Limits

|  | Open Road (km/h) | Motorway (km/h) |
|---|---|---|
| Car Solo | 90-100 | 130 |
| Car towing caravan/trailer | 80 | 80 |
| Motorhome under 3500kg | 90-100 | 130 |
| Motorhome 3500-7500kg | 80 | 80 |

Motorhomes over 3,500kg are restricted to 80 km/h (50 mph) on open roads, including motorways. Other speed limits are the same as for solo cars.

There is an increasing number of areas where speed is restricted to 30 km/h (18 mph) and these are indicated by the sign 'Zone 30'. In bad weather when visibility is reduced to 50 metres the maximum speed limit is 50 km/h (31 mph).

# Traffic Jams

Slovenia is a major international through-route and bottlenecks do occur on the roads to and from Ljubljana, such as the E61/A2 from Jesinice and the E57 from Maribor. Traffic queues can be expected from May to August on the roads around Lake Bled and to the Adriatic and on the E70/A1 motorway near the Razdrto toll station and near Kozina and Koper. Tailbacks also occur at border posts near the Karawanken Tunnel, Ljubelj and Šentilj/Spielfeld particularly at weekends.

The motoring organisation, AMZS, provides traffic information in English – telephone (01) 5305300 or see their website www.amzs.si.

# Violation of Traffic Regulations

The police have powers to stop drivers and levy heavy on-the-spot fines, including penalties for speeding, driving under the influence of alcohol and for using mobile phones without properly installed wireless headsets (bluetooth). Jaywalking is an offence and you could be fined if caught. Fines must be paid in local currency and you should obtain an official receipt.

# Motorways

There are about 620km of motorways (autoceste) and expressways (hitre ceste) with more under construction. For more information about motorways see the website www.dars.si.

There are service areas and petrol stations along the motorways and emergency telephones are situated every 2km.

Emergency corridors are compulsory on motorways and dual carriageways. Drivers are required to create a precautionary emergency corridor to provide access for emergency vehicles whenever congestion occurs. Drivers in the left-hand lane must move as far over to the left as possible, and drivers in the central and right-hand lanes must move as far over to the right as possible.

# Motorway Tolls

Drivers of vehicles weighing up to 3,500kg must purchase a vignette (windscreen sticker) for use on motorways and expressways. Caravans/trailers don't need an additional vignette and the weight of the caravan/trailer isn't taken into account. The vignette is available from petrol stations in Slovenia, neighbouring countries and at border posts. The cost of a 7 day vignette is €15, 1 month is €30 and an annual is €110 (2014 charges). For vehicles over 3,500kg tolls are payable with cash or credit card.

*Karawanken Tunnel*

The 8km Karawanken Tunnel links the E61/A11 in Austria and E61/A2 in Slovenia. The toll is €7.00 for car and caravan or motorhome up to 3,500kg and €10.50 for a motorhome over 3,500kg (2014 charges).

## Touring

A 10% tip is usual in restaurants and for taxi drivers.

The capital, Ljubljana, is a gem of a city with many Baroque and Art Nouveau influences. The works of the world renowned architect Jože Plecnik are among the finest urban monuments in the city. A Ljubljana Card is available for one, two or three days and offers free travel on city buses, tourist boat trips, the city funicular, guided tours and the tourist train to Ljubljana Castle, plus free admission to museums together with discounts at a wide range of shops, restaurants and bars. You can buy the card at the main bus and railway stations, hotels and tourist information centres or from www.visitljubljana.si.

The largest cave in Europe is situated at Postojna, south west of Ljubljana and is a 'must' for tourists. Also worth visiting are the mountains, rivers and woods of Triglav National Park, which covers the major part of the Julian Alps, together with the oldest town in Slovenia, Ptuj, and the city of Maribor. In Lipica guided tours are available around the stud, home to the world famous Lipizzaner horses.

There is a hydrofoil service between Portorož and Venice from April to November.

Slovenian is the official language although Serbo-Croat is widely spoken. Most Slovenians speak at least one other major European language and many, especially the young, speak English.

## Public Transport

There is an extensive bus network in Ljubljana. Buy a yellow 'top-up' Urbana card for a one-off payment of €2 from news-stands, tobacconists, tourist information offices or the central bus station and add credit (between €1 and €50) at the same locations or at the green Urbanomati machines around the city. When boarding a bus simply touch the card to one of the card readers at the front of the bus and €0.80 will be deducted allowing 90 minutes of unlimited travel regardless of how many changes you make. Taxis are generally safe, clean and reliable. Fares are metered. For longer distances ordering a taxi by phone will attract lower rates.

*Soca River, Triglan National Park, Bovec*

**ANKARAN see Koper** *D1*

**BLED** *B2* (4km E Rural) *46.35527, 14.14833* **Camping Šobec,** Šobčeva Cesta 25, 4248 Lesce [(04) 5353700; fax 5353701; sobec@siol.net; www.sobec.si] Exit rte 1 at Lesce, site sp. Lge, pt shd, pt sl; wc; chem disp; mv service pnt; shwrs; el pnts (16A) €3.70 (poss long lead req); Indtte; shop; rest, snacks; bar; playgrnd; rv pool; many sports & activities; cycle hire; internet; TV; wifi; dogs €3.50; bus 2km; Eng spkn; ccard acc; red 7+ days/CKE/CCI. "Excel, tranquil rvside site in wooded area surrounded by rv; friendly staff; lge pitches; clean san facs; gd rest; gd walking/cycling; real camping atmosphere, plenty of space; def rec; beautiful area." ♦ 15 Apr-30 Sep. € 41.25                                                  2013*

**BLED** *B2* (5km SE Urban) *46.34772, 14.17284* **Camping Radovljica, Kopališka 9, 4240 Radovljica** [(04) 5315770; fax 5301229; pkrad@plavalnicklub-radovljica.si] Exit A1/ E61 junc Bled/Bohinj, site in cent of Radovljica bet bus & train stn sp Camping & Sw. Med, pt sl, pt shd; wc; chem disp; shwrs inc; el pnts (16A) inc; shop 500m; rest 300m; snacks adj; bar; playgrnd; pool adj; paddling pool; cycle hire; fitness rm; wifi; 10% statics; dogs; poss cr; quiet; red long stay. "Vg; security gate; vg, clean san facs; gd NH; friendly staff." 1 Jun-15 Sep. € 38.25                                                  2013*

**BLED** *B2* (2km SW Rural) *46.36155, 14.08066* **Camping Bled, Kidričeva 10c, SI 4260 Bled** [04 5752000; fax 5752002; info@camping-bled.com; www.camping-bled. com] Fr Ljubljana take E16/A2 & exit dir Bled/Lesce. At rndabt take 2nd exit for Bled & cont along rd 209. In Bled take rd around lake on L (lake on R), site sp - winding rd. Lge, some mkd pitch, pt sl, pt shd; wc; chem disp; mv service pnt; baby facs; shwrs inc; el pnts (16A) inc (long lead req some pitches - fr recep); gas; Indtte (inc dryer); shop, rest adj; snacks; bar; BBQ; playgrnd; shgl beach; lake sw adj; spa cent nrby; fishing; white water rafting; paragliding; horseriding; cycle hire; games area; wifi; entmnt; games rm; TV rm; dogs €3; twin-axles acc (rec check in adv); m'van & car wash; dog shwrs; bus to Ljubljana adj; Eng spkn; fairly quiet but some rlwy noise; ccard acc; red long stay/low ssn/snr citizens/CKE/CCI. "Beautifully situated nr lake; busy, popular, well-run site; well-drained in bad weather altho lower pitches poss muddy; modern, clean san facs, stretched in ssn; helpful, efficient staff; conv Vintgar Gorge, Bled Castle, Lake Bohinj, Dragna Valley; excel walking/ cycling around lake; excel rest." ♦ 1 Apr-14 Oct. € 25.80 SBS - X03                                                  2013*

See advertisement

⊞ **BOHINJSKA BISTRICA** *B1* (500m W Rural) *46.27438, 13.94798* **Camping Danica Bohinj, Triglavska 60, 4264 Bohinjska Bistrica [(04) 5721702; fax 5723330; info@camp-danica.si; www.camp-danica.si]** Site on o'skts of vill clearly sp. Med, pt shd; wc; chem disp; mv service pnt; shwrs; el pnts (6A) inc (long lead poss req); gas; lndtte; shops 500m; rest, snacks; bar; tennis; entmnt; lake sw 6km; canoe & kayak hire; fly-fishing; wifi; 10% statics; dogs €2; Eng spkn; quiet; ccard acc; red long stay/CCI. "Excel site, spacious, open, attractive site in beautiful valley; gd walking & climbing; gd, clean san facs but poss stretched high ssn; conv bus to Ljubljana & Lake Bohinj." € 38.00                    2014*

> ## "There aren't many sites open at this time of year"
>
> If you're travelling outside peak season remember to call ahead to check site opening dates – even if the entry says 'open all year'.

**BOHINJSKA BISTRICA** *B1* (11km W Rural) *46.27902, 13.83606* **Autocamp Zlatarog, Ukanc 2, 4265 Bohinjsko Jezero [(04) 5723482; fax 5723064; info@aaturizem.com; www.aaturizem.com]** On rte 1 exit at Lesce or Jesenice for Bled & Bohinj. Clearly sp fr Bohinji, further 5km on L side of lake. Lge, some mkd pitch, sl, shd; wc; chem disp; shwrs; el pnts (6A) €5 (long lead req); gas; lndtte; shop adj; rest adj (high ssn); snacks; playgrnd; beach adj; lake sw; 50% statics; dogs €3; bus; sep car park high ssn; Eng spkn; adv bkg; ccard acc; red low ssn/long stay/CCI. "Excel walking, watersports; sm, uneven pitches & rather cramped site, but beautiful lakeside location; facs stretched high ssn; poss long walk to facs; site grnd rough to walk on (2011); poor security low ssn; gd touring base; cable car nr to Mount Vogel." 15 May-30 Sep. € 25.80                    2011*

**BOHINJSKO JEZERO see Bohinjska Bistrica** *B1*

**BOVEC** *B1* (400m E Rural) *46.33659, 13.55803* **Autocamp Polovnik, Ledina 8, 5230 Bovec [(05) 3896007; fax 3896006; kamp.polovnik@siol.net; www.kamp-polovnik.com]** Sp on rd 206 down fr Predil Pass (1,156m - 14% gradient) fr Italy - do not turn into vill. Site 200m after turn to Bovec. Sm, pt shd; wc; chem disp; shwrs €0.50; el pnts (16A) €2.50 (poss rev pol); lndtte (inc dryer); shop adj; rest, snacks; bar; BBQ; tennis; fishing; wifi; poss cr; no adv bkg; quiet; ccard acc; CKE/CCI. "Helpful staff; clean facs; Muddy when wet; friendly staff." 1 Apr-15 Oct. € 30.25                    2013*

**BOVEC** *B1* (7km E Rural) *46.33527, 13.64416* **Camping Soča, Soča 8, 5232 Soča [(05) 3889318; fax 3881409; kamp.soca@siol.net]** Sp on S side of rd 206 in national park, nr turning for Lepena approx 3km bef Soča vill. Lge, pt terr, pt shd; htd wc; chem disp; mv service pnt; shwrs inc; el pnts (6A) inc; lndtte; shop, rest 2km; snacks; bar; BBQ; playrnd; rv & shgl beach adj; TV rm; 50% statics (sep area); dogs €1.00; poss cr; Eng spkn; quiet; red long stay. "Beautiful situation in rv valley; gd, modern san facs; gd walking, rafting; gd touring base Triglav National Park; excel; braziers and wood avail; walking and cycling tracks fr site." ♦ ltd 1 Apr-31 Oct. € 35.20  2013*

⊞ **BREZICE** *C3* (5km S Rural) *45.89138, 15.62611* **Camping Terme Čatež, Topliška Cesta 35, 8251 Čatež ob Savi [(07) 4936700; fax 6207804; info@terme-catez.si; www.terme-catez.si]** Exit E70 at Brežice, foll brown sp to Terme Čatež, then site sp. Lge, mkd pitch, pt shd; htd wc; chem disp; mv service pnt; sauna; baby facs; shwrs inc; el pnts (10A) inc; gas; lndtte (inc dryer); supmkt; rest, snacks; bar; BBQ area; playgrnd; thermal water complex, inc 10 outdoor & 3 indoor pools, waterfalls & whirlpools, etc; paddling pool; fishing; golf 7km; boating; canoeing; tennis; fitness studio; games area; cycle hire; games rm; wifi; entmnt; TV; 50% statics (sep area); dogs €4; poss cr; wifi; Eng spkn; adv bkg; ccard acc; red low ssn; CKE/CCI. "Site in lge thermal spa & health resort; many sports, leisure & health facs; shops 2km; select own pitch - best at edge of site; gd family site; conv Zagreb; san facs dated (2013); not value for money." ♦ € 66.70 SBS - X05    2013*

**CATEZ OB SAVI see Brežice** *C3*

**KAMNIK** *B2* (500m NE Urban) *46.22724, 14.61902* **Kamp Resnik, Nevlje 1a, 1240 Kamnik [(01) 8317314; fax 8318192; info@kampresnik.com; www.kampresnik.com]** Fr Ljubljana foll rd sp Celje then turn N for Kamnik. Fr Kemnik by-pass (E side of rv) bear R thro 2 sets traff lts, site 200m on L just after sports cent - site ent not obvious, turn bef zebra x-ing opp pub. Fr E on rd 414, site sp. Med, pt shd; wc (some cont); chem disp; mv service pnt; shwrs; el pnts (10A) €3; gas; lndtte; shops 500m; rest, snacks 100m; bar; playgrnd; pool adj; thermal spa, golf course nr; 5% statics; dogs; bus; Eng spkn; adv bkg; some daytime rd noise; ccard acc; red CKE/CCI. "Conv Ljubljana & Kamnik Alps; basic, v old facs (2010); friendly staff; pleasant, well-kept NH." 1 May-30 Sep. € 17.00                    2013*

⊞ **KOBARID** *B1* (500m E Rural) *46.25070, 13.58664* **Kamp Koren, Drežniške Ravne 33, 5222 Kobarid [(05) 3891311; fax 3891310; info@kamp-koren.si; www.kamp-koren.si]** Turn E fr main rd in town, site well sp dir Drežnica. Med, pt shd; htd wc (some cont); chem disp; mv service pnt; shwrs inc; el pnts (16A) €4; shop; lndtte; snacks; rest 500m; playgrnd; cycle hire; canoeing; internet; TV rm; dogs €2; Eng spkn; quiet; ccard acc; red low ssn/long stay/CKE/CCI. "Vg, clean facs but stretched; friendly, helpful staff; pitches cramped; pleasant location in beautiful rv valley; excel walk to waterfall (3hrs); WW1 museum in town." ♦ € 23.00                    2011*

**KOPER** *D1* (5km N Coastal) *45.57818, 13.73573* **Camping Adria, Jadranska Zesta 25, 6280 Ankaran [(05) 6637350; fax 6637360; camp@adria-ankaran.si; www.adria-ankaran.si]** Fr A1/E70/E61 onto rd 10 then rd 406 to Ankaran. Or cross Italian border at Lazzaretto & foll sp to site in 3km. Site sp in vill. Lge, mkd pitch, shd; wc; chem disp; mv service pnt; sauna; private san facs avail; shwrs inc; el pnts (10A) €3; lndtte (inc dryer); shop; supmkt adj; rest, snacks; bar; BBQ; playgrnd; 2 pools (1 Olympic-size); waterslide; beach adj; tennis; cycle hire; wifi; entmnt; 60% statics; dogs €4; bus 500m; ccard acc. "Old town of Koper worth a visit; Vinakoper winery rec N of site on dual c'way; poss noisy groups high ssn; insect repellent req; clean san facs but red low ssn; gd rest; vg." ♦ 14 Apr-14 Oct. € 46.00                    2013*

SLOVENIA

⊞ **KRANJSKA GORA** *B1* (12km E Rural) *46.46446, 13.95773* **Camping Kamne, Dovje 9, 4281 Mojstrana [tel/fax (04) 5891105; info@campingkamne.com; www. campingkamne.com]** Sp fr rd 201 bet Jesenice & Kranjska Gora, 2km E of Mojstrana. Do not go thro vill of Dovje. Sm, terr, pt shd; some hdstg; htd wc; chem disp; mv service pnt; shwrs €0.50; el pnts (6A) €2.50-3.50; lndtte (inc dryer); shop 1km; rest 1.5km; snacks; bar; playgrnd; sm pool; fishing; hiking; tennis; cycle hire; TV rm; 10% statics; dogs €2; bus to Kranjska Gora fr site; Eng spkn; quiet but some rd noise; red long stay/CKE/CCI. "Conv Triglav National Park & border; views Mount Triglav; warm welcome; ltd san facs stretched high ssn; friendly helpful staff; gd cycling along old rlwy track." ◆ € 19.00                                                2013*

⊞ **LENDAVA** *B4* (1km S Rural) *46.55195, 16.45875* **Camping Terme Lendava (Part Naturist), Tomšičeva 2a, 9220 Lendava [(02) 5774400; fax 5774412; info@terme-lendava. si; www.terme-lendava.si]** Site well sp, adj hotel complex. Med, pt shd; htd wc; chem disp; mv service pnt; private bthrms avail; sauna; shwrs inc; el pnts (16A) €4.; lndtte; shop 200m; rest, snacks; bar; no BBQ; 2 pools (1 htd, covrd); naturist pool; paddling pool; waterslide; tennis; games area; cycle hire; fitness rm; internet; TV rm; some statics; dogs €3; adv bkg; ccard acc. "Conv Hungarian & Croatian borders; use of spa inc; Unisex san facs." € 45.00                2013*

**LESCE see Bled** *B2*

⊞ **LJUBLJANA** *C2* (5km N Urban) *46.09752, 14.51870* **Ljubljana Resort, Dunajska Cesta 270, 1000 Ljubljana [(01) 5890130; fax 5890129; ljubljana.resort@gpl.si; www. ljubljanaresort.si]** Fr Maribor take A1 twd Ljubljana, at junc Zadobrova take Ljubljana ring rd twd Kranj & exit junc 3 sp Lj - Ježica, Bežigrad. At x-rds turn R twd Črnuče along Dunajska Cesta, turn R 100m bef rlwy x-ing. Fr N (Jesenica/Karawanken tunnel) exit A2/E66 at junc 13 sp Ljubljana Črnuče & foll rd for 3.5km; at rndabt junc with Dunajska Cesta rd turn R (1st exit); site on L in 200m. Lge, hdg/mkd pitch, pt shd; htd wc; chem disp; mv service pnt; shwrs inc; el pnts (10A) €4.50; lndry/dishwash area; lndtte (inc dryer); shop; supmkt 900m; rest, snacks; bar; BBQ (gas/elec, sep area); playgrnd; htd pool complex adj; whirlpools; paddling pool; naturist sunbathing adj pool; rv fishing; tennis; cycle hire; horseriding 500m; archery; fitness club; wifi; entmnt; games rm; some statics; dogs €3; phone; bus to city at site ent (tickets at recep); some rlwy noise; ccard acc; red low ssn/CKE/CCI. "Busy site by rv; gd rest; red facs low ssn; pitches nr hotel poss noisy due late-night functions; some pitches muddy when wet; conv for city; cycle to city cent fr site." ◆ € 57.80                        2014*

⊞ **LUCE OB SAVINJI** *B2* (1km N Rural) *46.36092, 14.73637* **Autocamp Šmica, Luče 4, 3334 Luče [(03) 5844330; fax 5844333; camp.smica@siol.net; www.camp-smica. com]** Fr rd 428, site sp on rvside. Sm, pt shd; wc; shwrs inc; el pnts (16A) €2.50; gas; lndtte; BBQ; playgrnd; tennis; wifi; 5% statics; dogs; phone; bus 400m; poss cr; Eng spkn; adv bkg; quiet; red long stay; CKE/CCI. "Ideal base for mountaineering, hiking, watersports etc; vg." ◆ ltd 1 May-30 Sep. € 13.00                                2009*

⊞ **MARIBOR** *B3* (6km SW Urban) *46.5355, 15.60508* **Camping Centre Kekec, Pohorska ulica 35c, 2000 Maribor [040 665 732; info@cck.si or bernard@cck.si; www.cck. si]** Fr S on A1 exit Maribor Jug; foll rd until you see Bauhaus shopping centre on the R, turn L at this x-rd; turn R after approx 400m; turn L after approx 100m; site on L after approx 3km opp the Merano Hotel. Sm, mkd pitch, hdstg, pt sl, terr, unshd; htd wc; chem disp; MV service pnt; baby facs; shwrs; el pnts (25A) €3; lndtte; rest & bar 250m; BBQ; wifi; dogs €1.50; Eng spkn; adv bkg; ccard acc; CKE/CCI. "Rec for larger o'fits as lge pitches avail but care with narr ent rd; v nice site." € 35.00                                            2013*

**MOJSTRANA see Kranjska Gora** *B1*

**MOZIRJE** *B3* (6km W Rural) *46.30930, 14.91593* **Camping Savinja, Spodnje Pobrežje 11, 3332 Rečica ob Savinji [tel/fax (035) 835472; www.sloveniaholidays.com]** SW fr Velenje for 14km to Mozirje. Then foll sp to Pobrežje for 4km, over bdge. Site is sp in vill down lane opp house no 11. Med, pt shd; wc; chem disp; shwrs; el pnts (16A) €3; lndtte; shop; fishing; dogs €1; quiet; CKE/CCI; "Scenic Savinja & Logarska Dolina valleys; ideal walking & cycling; clean facs; lovely, peaceful, simple site." 1 May-30 Sep. € 12.00     2010*

⊞ **NAZARJE** *B2* (6km W Rural) *46.31166, 14.90916* **Camping Menina, Varpolje 105, 3332 Rečica ob Savinji [(03) 5835027; fax 35835027; info@campingmenina. com; www.campingmenina.com]** Fr rte E57 bet Ljubljana & Celje, turn N twd Nazarje, then dir Ljubno for 3km. Site sp. Med, mkd pitch, some hdstg, shd; wc; chem disp; mv service pnt; shwrs inc; el pnts (6-16A) €3; lndtte (inc dryer); rest, snacks; bar; playgrnd; lake sw adj; cycle hire; wifi; 10% statics; dogs €3; Eng spkn; adv bkg; quiet; red CKE/CCI. "Helpful owners; delightful site in woodland; v ltd facs in winter." € 20.00                                            2010*

**NOVA GORICA** *C1* (8km SE Rural) *45.94182, 13.71761* **Camping Lijak - Mladovan Farm, Ozeljan 6A, 5261 Šempas [(05) 3088557; fax 53079619; camp.lijak@volja. net; www.camplijak.com]** Fr Nova Gorica take rd 444 twd Ljubljana/Ajdovščina. Site on L bef turn-off to Ozeljan. Sm, pt shd; htd wc; chem disp; shwrs inc; el pnts (10A) €3 (poss long lead req); shop 1km; snacks; BBQ; wifi; some statics; dogs €1; phone; bus; Eng spkn; slight rd noise; red low ssn. "Farm site in wine-growing area; weekly wine tasting; hang-gliding area, enthusiasts use site; friendly owner; gd san facs." 15 Mar-31 Oct. € 35.50                                            2013*

**PODCETRTEK see Rogaška Slatina** *B3*

⊞ **PORTOROZ** *D1* (4km NE Coastal) *45.52536, 13.60754* **Autocamp Strunjan, Strunjan 23, 6320 Portorož [(05) 6782076; amd-piran@siol.net; www.amdpiran-drustvo.si]** Fr Koper on rd 111 at 6.5km marker turn R at traff lts sp Strunjan. In 50m turn L, site in L in 200m, well sp. Med, pt shd; wc; chem disp; shwrs inc; el pnts (6A) inc; lndry rm; shop 300m; bar; shgl beach 500m; 95% statics; dogs; phone; bus adj; Eng spkn; rd noise; rec CKE/CCI. "Open all yr for m'vans, but ltd pitches; excel san facs; friendly staff." ◆ ltd € 19.00                                            2010*

SLOVENIA

PORTOROZ *D1* (2.5km S Coastal) *45.50138, 13.59388*
Camping Lucija, Obala 77, 6320 Portorož [(05) 6906000;
fax 6906900; camp@metropolgroup.si; www.
metropolgroup.si] Fr Koper (N) on rd 111, turn R at traff lts in
Lucija. Take next L, then 2nd L into site. Nr Metropol Hotel, site
sp. Lge, pt shd; wc; mv service pnt; serviced pitches; shwrs inc;
el pnts (6-10A) €4.50; lndtte; shop; rest; bar; beach adj; cycle
hire; 60% statics; dogs €5; poss cr; Eng spkn; quiet; ccard acc;
red CKE/CCI. "Conv Piran old town by bike or bus; sea views;
sep area for tourers, extra for beach pitch; sm pitches; vg facs."
♦ 1 Apr-3 Oct. € 33.00                                    2010*

POSTOJNA *C2* (5km NW Rural) *45.80551, 14.20470* Camping
Pivka Jama, Veliki Otok 50, 6230 Postojna [(05) 7203993;
fax 7265348; avtokamp.pivka.jama@siol.net; www.
venus-trade.si] Fr N or S Exit A1/E61 over traff lts, R at
rdbt then bear L at next, foll sp to caves grotto (Postojnska
Jama). Pass caves on R & then foll signs for Predjama Castle.
3km after caves site sp. Narr, winding app rd. Lge, hdstg, pt
sl, terr, hdstg, shd; htd wc; chem disp; mv service pnt; shwrs
inc; el pnts (6A) €3.70 (rev pol); lndtte; shop; rest, snacks;
bar; cooking facs; playgrnd; pool; paddling pool; tennis;
50% statics; dogs; poss v cr; Eng spkn; adv bkg; quiet but noisy
nr sw pool; ccard acc; red low ssn CKE/CCI. "Gd forest site;
gd rest with live Tirolean music; gd san facs; used as transit
to Croatia, open 24 hrs; caves 4km a must visit (take warm
clothing!)." 1 Apr-31 Oct. € 22.80                         2011*

PREBOLD *B3* (N Rural) *46.23832, 15.09266* Camping Park,
Latkova Vas 227, 3312 Prebold [(03) 7001986; info@
campingpark.si; www.campingpark.si] Fr A1/E57 or rd 5
exit at Prebold. Foll site sp for 400m, cross Rv Savinja & site
on L. Sm, shd; htd wc; chem disp; shwrs inc; el pnts (6A) inc;
lndtte; shops 2km; rest; bar; BBQ; games area; some Eng spkn;
adv bkg; quiet; 10% red CKE/CCI. "V pleasant, well-kept site
but ltd facs; pleasant walks by rv; helpful owners own adj
hotel; gd walking & cycling." 1 Apr-31 Oct. € 20.00    2012*

⊞ PREBOLD *B3* (200m N Rural) *46.24027, 15.08790*
Camping Dolina, Dolenja Vas 147, 3312 Prebold
[(03) 5724378; fax 5742591; camp@dolina.si; www.dolina.
si] On A1/E57 turn R 16km fr Celje sp Prebold & foll sp, site on
N edge of vill. Sm, unshd; wc; chem disp; shwrs (inc); el pnts
(6-10A) €3.30; gas; lndtte; shop 400m; rest in hotel 800m; htd
pool; cycle hire; dogs €2; poss cr; quiet; red long stay; CKE/CCI.
"Gd clean facs but no changing area in shwrs; helpful, friendly
owner; conv Savinja valley; gd walking." € 18.50         2010*

⊞ PTUJ *B4* (1km NW Rural) *46.42236, 15.85478* Autokamp
Terme Ptuj, Pot V Toplice 9, 2250 Ptuj [(02) 7494100;
fax 7494520; info@terme-ptuj.si; www.terme-ptuj.si] S
fr Maribor on A4 or rd 1/E59; turn L onto rd 2 sp Ptuj (exit junc
2 fr A4); on app Ptuj foll sp Golf/Terme Camping to L off rd 2;
site after leisure complex on Rv Drava. Diff to find when app
fr SW on rd 432. Med, pt shd; htd wc; chem disp; mv service
pnt; sauna; steam rm; shwrs inc; el pnts (10A) €4; gas; lndtte
(inc dryer); shop 2km; rest, snacks; bar; BBQ; playgrnd; htd;
covrd pools/spa; waterslide; games area; tennis; fitness rm;
cycle hire; golf 1km; internet; statics; dogs €4; phone; weekly
bus to Vienna; poss cr; Eng spkn; red low ssn/long stay/snr
citizens/CKE/CCI. "Helpful staff; clean san facs, poss stretched
high ssn; pitches muddy in wet; superb water park free to
campers; lovely area; castle & monastery in Ptuj old town worth
a visit; new san facs (2013)." ♦ ltd € 58.00              2013*

RECICA OB SAVINJI see Mozirje *B3*

ROGASKA SLATINA *B3* (8km S Rural) *46.16499, 15.60495*
Camping Natura Terme Olimia, Zdraviliška Cesta 24, 3254
Podčetrtek [(03) 8297000; fax 5829024; info@terme-
olimia.com; www.terme-olimia.com] Fr Celje take rte E
dir Rogaška Slatina. Turn S sp Podčetrtek just bef Rogaška.
Site on L (waterchutes) alongside Rv Solta on Croatian border
in approx 10km. Sm, unshd; htd wc; chem disp; mv service
pnt; sauna; shwrs inc; el pnts (10-16A) €3.20; lndtte; shop
high ssn; rest 800m; snacks; bar; playgrnd; 2 htd pools (1
covrd); paddling pool; waterslide; fitness rm; tennis; cycle
hire; horseriding 2km; golf 4km; wifi; TV rm; phone; adv bkg;
ccard acc; red CKE/CCI. "Aqualuna Thermal Pk adj; vg walking
country with wooded hillsides." ♦ 15 Apr-15 Oct. € 32.00
(CChq acc)                                                 2011*

"I like to fill in the reports
as I travel from site to site"

You'll find report forms at the back of
this guide, or you can fill them in online
at www.caravaclub.co.uk/europereport.

SKOFJA LOKA *B2* (10km E Rural) *46.17455, 14.41720*
Camping Smlednik (Part Naturist), Dragočajna 14a,
1216 Smlednik [(01) 3627002; camp@dm-campsmlednik.
si; www.dm-campsmlednik.si] Fr Ljubljana on E61 take
turning W onto rd 413 sp Zapoge & Zbilje. After Valburg & bef
x-ing rv turn R to Dragočajna & site. Lge, terr, pt shd; wc; chem
disp; shwrs inc; el pnts (6-10A) €3-4; shop; snacks; bar; BBQ;
canoeing; tennis; many statics; dogs €1; Eng spkn; quiet; CKE/
CCI. "Pleasant rvside location; steep site; sep sm naturist site;
shwrs poss only warm as solar powered; ltd facs low ssn; poss
muddy when wet." 1 May-15 Oct. € 24.25                  2013*

SOCA see Bovec *B1*

VELENJE *B3* (3km NW Rural) *46.36832, 15.08864* Autocamp
Jezero, Cesta Simona Blatnika 26, 3320 Velenje
[(03) 5866466; mastodontbar@gmail.com] Exit A1/E57
at Velenje & cont to 2nd traff lts, then turn R. Turn L at 3rd
traff lts & foll site sp. Site on lakeside. Med, mkd pitch, pt
shd; wc; chem disp; mv service pnt; shwrs; el pnts (10A) inc;
lndtte; supmkt 2km; rest 300m; snacks; playgrnd; lake sw;
watersports; tennis; games area; fitness rm; internet; some
statics; dogs €1.50; quiet. "Lovely location but nr coal-powered
power stn; poss unkempt low ssn; Velenje coal mining museum
worth visit 1km." ♦ 1 May-30 Sep. € 19.00                2010*

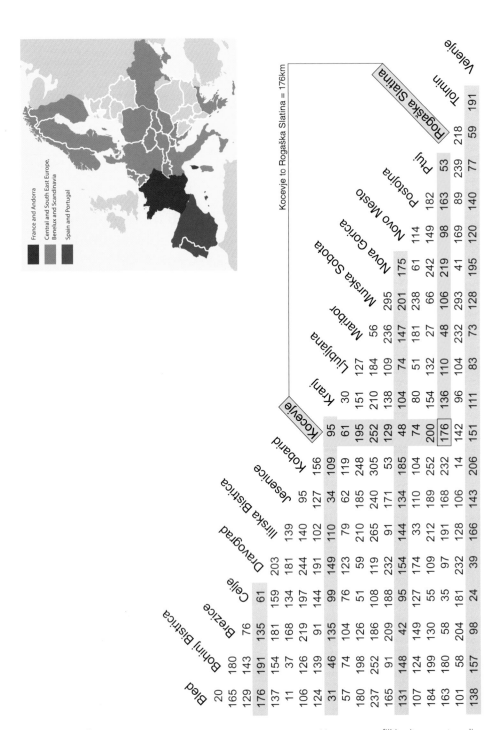

You can now fill in site reports online

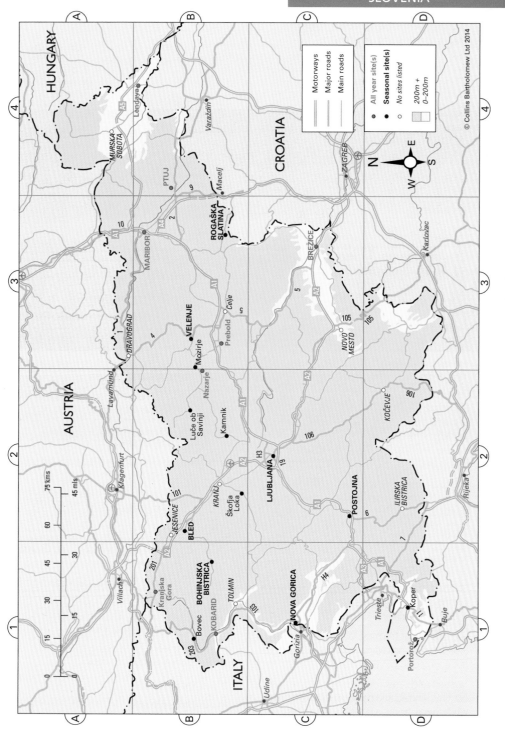

© Collins Bartholomew Ltd 2014

# Sweden
## Country Introduction

*Lupines by a lake, Sweden*

## Welcome to Sweden

Full of beautiful rolling hills and picturesque landscapes, Sweden has some amazing outdoor activities. Visit in winter, when there is skiing and skating, or try cycling, sailing and hiking in the warmer seasons. Sweden has lots to explore for visitors that like the great outdoors.

The country also has a some amazing cities like Stockholm and Gothenburg, as well as the beautiful historic old towns to explore in the same cities.

## Country highlights

Swedish cuisine specialities include crayfish, herring, salmon, eel, reindeer and elk and, of course, the traditional smorgasbord.

Glögg is one of the most famous drinks in Sweden, it is a spiced mulled wine that is served hot during cold winter evenings.

Sweden celebrates The Welcome of Spring, with bonfires, singing and parties, and Midsommar which has dancing, a maypole and lots of good food.

## Major towns and cities

- Stockholm – a beautiful capital city which is the home to the Nobel Prize.

- Gothenburg – a port city that has many historical and cultural buildings.

- Malmö – the historic city has a lively old square called Stortorget.

- Uppsala – home to Scandinavia's largest cathedral of the same name.

## Attractions

- Vasa Museum – home to the most complete and best preserved shipwrecks in the world.

- Botanical Garden (Gothenburg) – beautiful and peaceful garden.

- The Swedish History Museum – a great museum to learn about Vikings.

- Lund Cathedral – a stunning building with lots of historical artefacts to view.

## Find out more

www.visitsweden.com

Tel: 0046 (0) 87 89 10 00 Swedish Tourist Office

# Country Information

*Population (approx):* 9.6 million

*Capital:* Stockholm (population 770,300)

*Area:* 450,000 sqkm

*Bordered by:* Finland, Norway

*Terrain:* Mostly flat or gently rolling lowlands; mountains in the west

*Climate:* Cold, cloudy winters, sub-arctic in the north; cool/warm summers. The best time to visit is between May and September; August can be hot and wet. Be prepared for occasional sub-zero temperatures and snowfalls, even in summer months

*Coastline:* 3,218km

*Highest Point:* Kebnekaise 2,114m

*Language:* Swedish

*Local Time:* GMT or BST + 1, i.e. 1 hour ahead of the UK all year

*Currency:* Krona (SEK) divided into 100 öre; £1 = SEK 11.47, SEK 100 = £8.72 (September 2014)

*Emergency Numbers:* Police 112 (or 11414 for non-emergency calls); Fire Brigade 112; Ambulance 112. Operators speak English

*Public Holidays 2015:* Jan 1, 6; Apr 3, 5, 6; May 1, 14; Jun 6 (National Day), 20 (Midsummer); Oct 10; Dec 25, 26.

School summer holidays are from early June to the second or third week of August

# Camping and Caravanning

Camping and caravanning are very popular but because summer is so short the season is brief and lasts only from May to late August/ early September, although winter caravanning is enjoying increasing popularity. High season on most sites ends around the middle of August when prices and site office opening hours are reduced or sites are closed altogether. There are more than 1,000 campsites of which about 350 remain open during the winter, particularly in mountainous regions near to ski resorts. Those that are open all year may offer fewer or no facilities from mid-September to April and advance booking may be required.

In late June and July advance booking is recommended, especially at campsites along the west coast (north and south of Göteborg), on the islands of Öland and Gotland and near other popular tourist areas.

Approximately 500 campsites are members of the SCR (Svenska Campingvärdars Riksfärbund – Swedish Campsite Owners' Association), which are classified from 1 to 5 stars. Visitors wishing to use these sites must have a Camping Key Europe card. You can buy the Camping Key Europe at campsites for around €20 and you will be given a temporary card, or you can order it in advance from www.camping.se/en for 150 SEK (2014 prices). If ordering in advance you should allow at least 3 weeks for delivery.

Most Swedes use electric hook-ups so caravanners using their battery may obtain a pitch which is on a less congested part of the site. Also aim to arrive by mid afternoon to get a better pitch, since many Swedes arrive late. It is reported that handbasins on sites often do not have plugs so it is advisable to carry a flat universal plug when touring.

Many sites have a 'Quick Stop' amenity which provides safe, secure overnight facilities on, or adjacent to, a site. This normally includes the use of sanitary facilities. 'Quick Stop' rates are about two thirds of the regular camping rate if you arrive after 9pm and leave before 9am.

Casual/wild camping is normally permitted (except in National Parks and recreational areas), however for security reasons it is not recommended to spend the night in a vehicle on the roadside or in a public car park. Instead use the 'Quick Stop' amenity at campsites. In any event local parking rules and signposting should always be observed.

Alternatively there are around 150 organised 'ställplatser' mainly intended for motorhomes but generally car and caravan outfits may also use them for an overnight stay at the discretion of the site's manager. For a list of 'ställplatser' and maps showing their location see www.campinggladje.se/resa.

Most designated rest areas along highways are owned and managed by the Vågverket (Swedish Roads Administration) which, although not officially ranked as 'ställplatser', offer adequate parking space and various facilities for motorhomes staying overnight. A map showing these rest areas is available at local tourist offices.

## Cycling

The network of cycle lanes in Sweden is growing rapidly and many cycle routes are named and signposted. In some cases cycle lanes are combined with foot paths.
See www.svenska-cykelsallskapet.se.

The 'Sverigeleden' cycle trail covers the whole country and connects all major ports and cities. The 190km cycle route along the Göta Canal from Sjötorp on Lake Vänern to Mem on the Baltic coast is relatively flat and hence a very popular route.

The wearing of a safety helmet is compulsory for children up to the age of 15 and is recommended for everyone.

## Electricity and Gas

On campsites the current is usually 10 amps or more and round two-pin plugs are used. CEE connections are becoming standard.

Propane (gasol) is the gas most widely obtainable at more than 2,000 Primus dealers; you will need to buy an appropriate adaptor. It is understood that it is possible to sell back your propane cylinder at the end of your holiday and outlets will also exchange the corresponding Norwegian Progas cylinders. Recent visitors report that major distributors will refill cylinders but they must be of a recognised make/type and in perfect condition. The Caravan Club does not recommend the refilling of cylinders.

Butane gas is available from a number of outlets including some petrol stations. It is understood that Campingaz 904 and 907 cylinders are available but recent visitors report that they may be difficult to find, and virtually impossible in the north of the country. For more information on butane suppliers contact the Swedish Campsite Owners' Association (SCR) by email: info@scr.se

Ensure that you are well-equipped with gas if venturing north of central Sweden as it may be difficult to find an exchange point. Many sites have communal kitchen facilities which enable visitors to make great savings on their own gas supply.

## Entry Formalities

Holders of valid British and Irish passports may visit Sweden for up to three months without a visa.

## Regulations for Pets

In order to protect the countryside and wildlife, dogs are not allowed to run off the lead from 1 March to 20 August and at other times in certain areas.

Dogs travelling directly from the UK and Ireland must be microchipped and have an EU pet passport. For more information please visit www.jordbruksverket.se (english option) and go to the 'Animals' section.

## Medical Services

Health care facilities are generally very good and most medical staff speak English. The general practitioner system does not apply; instead visit the nearest hospital clinic (Akutmottagning or Vårdcentral) and present your passport and European Health Insurance Card (EHIC). You will be charged a fee for the clinic visit (free for anyone under 20) plus a daily standard charge if it is necessary to stay in hospital. These charges are non-refundable in Sweden.

Prescriptions are dispensed at pharmacies (apotek) which are open during normal shopping hours. Emergency prescriptions can be obtained at hospitals. Dental surgeons or clinics (tandläkare or folktandvård) offer emergency out-of-hours services in major cities but you may have to pay the full cost of treatment.

The use of mosquito repellent is also recommended, particularly from mid June to September when mosquitos are most common. Mosquitos are generally more often encountered in the north of Sweden rather than the south.

Visitors to remote areas should consider the relative inaccessibility of the emergency services. In northern Sweden mobile phone coverage does not generally extend beyond main roads and the coast.

## Opening Hours

Banks – Mon-Fri 9.30am-2pm/3pm and until 5.30pm one day a week in larger towns. Many banks do not handle cash after 3pm and some banks will not handle cash at all.

Museums – Tue-Sun 10am-4pm; usually closed Mon.

Post Offices – Post offices no longer exist. Mail is dealt with at local shops, kiosks and petrol stations; opening hours vary.

Shops – Mon-Fri 9am-6pm; Sat 9am-1pm/2pm/3pm; supermarkets may open until 8pm and Sun. Shops generally close early the day before a public holiday.

## Safety and Security

Petty crime levels are much lower than in most other European countries but you should take the usual commonsense precautions. Pickpocketing is common in the summer months in major cities where tourists may be targeted for their passports and cash.

In recent years there have been incidents of 'highway robbery' from motorhomes parked on the roadside, especially on the west coast between Malmö and Gothenburg.

Sweden shares with the rest of Europe an underlying threat from terrorism. Attacks could be indiscriminate and against civilian targets in public places, including tourist sites.

*British Embassy*
SKARPÖGATAN 6-8,115 93 STOCKHOLM
Tel: (08) 6713000
http://ukinsweden.fco.gov.uk/en/
*Irish Embassy*
Hovslagargatan 5, 111 48 STOCKHOLM
Tel: (08) 54504040
www.embassyofireland.se

## Customs Regulations

Visitors arriving from an EU country via a non-EU country (e.g. Norway) may bring quantities of tobacco and alcohol obtained in EU countries, plus the amounts allowed duty-free from non-EU countries. However, you must be able to produce proof of purchase for goods from EU countries and goods must be for your personal use.

## Border Posts

There are approximately 40 Customs posts along the Swedish/Norwegian border. They are situated on all main roads and are normally open Mon to Fri from 8.30am - 4pm/5pm.

Travellers with dutiable goods must cross the land borders during hours when the Customs posts are open. However, travellers without dutiable goods may cross the border outside Customs post opening hours.

The main border posts with Finland are at Haparanda, Övertornea, Pajala and Karesuando.

## Documents

*Driving Licence*
A UK driving licence is only valid when it bears a photograph of the holder, i.e. a photocard licence, or when it is carried together with photographic proof of identity, such as a passport.

## Money

Foreign currency may be exchanged in banks and bureaux de change.

Major credit cards are widely used both for major and minor transactions and cash machines (Bankomat or Minuten) are widespread. It is advisable to carry your passport or photocard driving licence if paying with a credit card as you may be asked for photographic proof of identity.

## Motoring in Sweden

## Accidents

In the case of an accident it is not necessary to call the police unless there are injuries to drivers or passengers and/or vehicles are badly damaged, but drivers are required to give their details to the other persons involved before leaving the accident scene. A driver leaving the scene of an accident without following this procedure may be fined.

If you are involved in an accident with a possible third party claim, you are strongly recommended to report the accident to the national Swedish insurance bureau which will act as claims agent. Contact Trafikförsäkringsforeningen in Stockholm, tel: 08 522 78200, info@ tff.se, www.tff.se.

Accidents involving wild animals (e.g. elk, reindeer, bear, wolf, etc) must be reported to the police immediately by calling 112 or 11414 and the spot where the accident took place must be marked by putting up reflective tape or anything clearly noticeable so that the police can find it easily.

Collisions must be reported even if the animal involved is not injured. After reporting the accident and marking out the place, a driver may leave. Accidents involving smaller animals (badgers, foxes, etc) need not be reported.

## Alcohol

Penalties for driving a motor vehicle under the influence of alcohol are extremely severe. The police carry out random breath tests. If the level of alcohol exceeds 20 milligrams in 100 millilitres of blood a fine will be imposed and driving licence withdrawn. This level is considerably lower than that permitted in the UK (80 milligrams) and equates to virtually zero. A level exceeding 100 milligrams is considered to be severe drink driving for which a jail sentence of up to two years will be imposed and licence withdrawn.

## Breakdown Service

The motoring organisation, Motormännens Riksförbund (known as the 'M'), does not operate a breakdown service. It does, however, have an agreement with 'AssistanceKåren' (a nationwide road service company) which operates a 24-hour, all-year service and can be contacted free on (020) 912912 or 08 6275757 from a foreign-registered mobile phone. Phone boxes are becoming quite scarce and it is advisable to carry a mobile phone. There are normally no emergency telephones along motorways or dual carriageways. Charges for assistance and towing vary according to day and time and payment by credit card is accepted.

## Essential Equipment

### Warning Triangle
It is compulsory for foreign registered vehicles to carry a warning triangle. They should be placed as a distance of 50 meters behind the vehicle on ordinary roads and 100 meters on motorways.

### Lights
Dipped headlights are compulsory at all times, regardless of weather conditions. Bulbs are more likely to fail with constant use and you are recommended to carry spares. Fog lights may be used when visibility is poor but they must not be used together with dipped headlights. Vehicles parked or stopped on a poorly lit road at night, including dawn, dusk and bad weather, must have their parking lights switched on.

### Child Restraint System
Children under the height of 135cm must be seated in a child restraint or child seat. A child aged 15 or over, or 135cm in height or taller, can use normal seat belts in the car.

Children under the height of 140cm are only allowed in the front seat if the passenger seat airbag has been deactivated.

### Winter Driving
The winter months are periods of severe cold and you should be prepared for harsh conditions. The fitting of winter tyres is compulsory for vehicles up to 3,500kg from 1st December to 31st March in the event of severe winter road conditions, i.e. the road is covered with ice or snow, or if the road is wet and the temperature is around freezing point. Trailers towed by these vehicles must also be equipped with winter tyres. Winter tyre regulations do not apply to vehicles over 3,500kg but if summer tyres are used the tread must be at least 5mm deep. These regulations apply to foreign registered vehicles.

## Fuel

Petrol stations are usually open from 7am to 9pm. Near motorways and main roads and in most cities they may remain open until 10pm or even for 24 hours. Outside large towns garages seldom stay open all night but most have self-service pumps (possibly not for diesel) which accept credit cards. In the far north filling stations may be few and far between so keep your tank topped up. Credit cards are accepted.

LPG (known as gasol) is sold at a very limited number of petrol stations mainly located in central and southern Sweden.

## Low Emission Zones

There are Low Emssion Zones (Miljözen) in Sweden. However, at the time of going to print, they only applied to commercial vehicles and do not affect cars or motorhome regardless of size.

Please see www.lowemissionzones.eu for the most up-to-date information.

## Overtaking

Take care when overtaking long vehicles. A typical long-distance Swedish truck is a six-wheeled unit towing a huge articulated trailer, i.e. a very long load.

Many roads in Sweden have wide shoulders or a climbing lane to the right of the regular lane and these permit drivers of slow moving vehicles or wide vehicles to pull over to allow other traffic to pass. These climbing lanes and shoulders should not be used as another traffic lane.

## Parking

Parking meters and other parking restrictions are in use in several large towns. Vehicles must be parked facing the direction of the flow of traffic. Wheel clamps are not in use but illegally parked vehicles may be towed away and, in addition to a parking fine, a release fee will be charged.

In an area signposted 'P' parking is permitted for a maximum of 24 hours, unless otherwise stated.

## Priority

Vehicles driving on roads designated and signposted (with a yellow diamond on an black background) as primary roads always have priority. On all other roads, as a general rule, vehicles coming from the right have priority, unless signs indicate otherwise. This rule is sometimes ignored however, especially by vehicles on roads regarded as major roads but not signposted as such, and care is required.

At most roundabouts signs indicate that traffic already on the roundabout has priority, i.e. from the left.

Give trams priority at all times. Where there is no refuge at a tram stop, you must stop to allow passengers to board and alight from the tram.

## Roads

The condition of national and country roads is good although some minor roads may be covered with oil-gravel only. Road surfaces may be damaged following the spring thaw, and some may be closed or have weight restrictions imposed during that period. Gradients are generally slight and there are no roads that need to be avoided for vehicles towing a caravan.

Road repairs tend to be intensive during the short summer season. Information on major roadworks and road conditions on E roads and major national roads can be obtained from www.trafikverket.se.

There is a good road link with Norway in the far north of Sweden. The Kiruna-Narvik road is open all year from Kiruna to the border. It is a wide road with no steep gradients.

There is generally little or no heavy goods traffic on roads during the Christmas, Easter and midsummer holidays or on the days preceding these holidays so good progress can be made.

## Road Signs and Markings

Road signs and markings conform to international standards. Road markings are white. The middle of the road is indicated by broken lines with long intervals. Warning lines (usually on narrow roads) are broken lines with short intervals which indicate that visibility is limited in one or both directions; they may be crossed when overtaking. Unbroken lines should not be crossed at any time.

National roads (riksvägar) have two-digit numbers and country roads (länsvägar) have three-digit numbers. Roads which have been incorporated into the European road network – E roads – generally have no other national number.

Direction and information signs for motorways and roads which form part of the European road network are green. Signs for national roads and the more important country roads are blue. Signs for local roads are white with black numerals.

In some towns traffic restrictions, including weight restrictions, may apply at certain times and these are signposted. The following are some other signs that you may see:

Passing place

Additional stop sign

Accident

| Swedish | English Tanslation |
|---|---|
| Enkelriktat | One way |
| Farlig kurva | Dangerous bend |
| Grusad väg | Loose chippings |
| Höger | Right |
| Ingen infart | No entrance |
| Parkering förbjuden | No parking |
| Vänster | Left |

## Speed Limits

| | Open Road (km/h) | Motorway (km/h) |
|---|---|---|
| Car Solo | 70-100 | 90-120 |
| Car towing caravan/trailer | 70-80 | 80 |
| Motorhome under 3500kg | 70-100 | 90-120 |
| Motorhome 3500-7500kg | 70-100 | 90-120 |

Speed limits are no longer based on the category of road but on the quality and safety level of the roads themselves. As a result limits may vary from one town to another and along stretches of the same road. It is advisable, therefore, to pay close attention to road signs as speed limits are strictly enforced. If in doubt, or if no speed limit is indicated, you are advised to keep to 70 km/h (44 mph) until you see a speed limit sign.

Outside built-up areas, including expressways, speeds up to 100 km/h (62 mph) may be permitted according to road signs, providing a lower maximum speed is not applicable for certain vehicle categories. Vehicles with trailers must never exceed 80 km/h (49mph). On motorways the maximum permitted speed is 110 or 120 km/h (68 or 74 mph). During the winter a speed limit of 90 km/h (56 mph) is in force on some motorways and dual carriageways. This limit is signposted.

In most residential areas and during certain periods in areas near schools, speed is limited to 30 km/h (18 mph) according to road signs. Periods indicated in black mean Monday to Friday, those in black in brackets mean Saturday and the eves of public holidays, and those indicated in red mean Sunday and public holidays.

Speed limits for motorhomes under 3,500kg and privately registered motorhomes over 3,500kg are the same as for solo cars.

Speed cameras are in use on many roads. The use of radar detectors is not permitted.

## Traffic Lights

A green arrow indicates that traffic may proceed with caution in the direction of the arrow but pedestrians must be given priority. A flashing amber light indicates that a crossing/turning must be made with caution.

## Violation of Traffic Regulations

Police are authorised to impose, but not collect, fines for violation of minor traffic offences which must be paid at a bank, normally within two to three weeks. Fines range from SEK400 to 1,200, but if two or more offences are committed and total fines exceed SEK2,500, the offender will be taken to court. Offences, which may qualify for a fine include driving without lights in daylight, speeding, lack of a warning triangle or nationality plate (GB or IRL) or a dirty or missing number plate.

If a fine is not paid and the driver is a resident of another EU country, notice of the fine will be forwarded to the authorities in the driver's country of residence.
Jaywalking is not permitted; pedestrians must use official crossings.

## Motorways

There are approximately 1,900 kms of motorway and 560 kms of semi-motorway or dual carriageway, all confined to the south of the country and relatively free of heavy traffic by UK standards. No tolls are levied. There are no service areas or petrol stations on motorways; these are situated near the exits and are indicated on motorway exit signs. Please note that there are no petrol stations close to the 110km long Uppsala to Gälve motorway.

## Tolls

Tolls for private vehicles will be introduced in 2014. The Motala by-pass (on road 50m in central Sweden) the toll will be 5 SEK amd for the Sundsvall by-pass (on E4 in northern Sweden) the toll will be 9 SEK.

### Toll Bridges

The Øresund Bridge links Malmö in Sweden with Copenhagen in Denmark and means that it is possible to drive all the way from mainland Europe by motorway. The crossing is via a 7.8 km bridge to the artificial island of Peberholm and a 4 km tunnel. Tolls (payable in cash, including EUR, SEK or DKK or by credit card) are levied on the Swedish side and are as follows for single journeys (2014 prices subject to change)

| Vehicle(s) | Price |
| --- | --- |
| Car, motorhome up to 6 metres | € 49 |
| Car + caravan/trailer or motor caravan over 6 metres | € 98 |

Vehicle length is measured electronically and even a slight overhang over six metres will result in payment of the higher tariff.

Speed limits apply in the tunnel and on the bridge, and during periods of high wind the bridge is closed to caravans. Bicycles are not allowed. Information on the Øresund Bridge can be found on www.oeresundsbron.com.

### Svinesund Bridge

There is a 700 metre long bridge linking Sweden and Norway on the E6, at Svinesund. Tolls are SEK24 (NOK20) for light vehicles and SEK120 (NOK100) for vehicles over 3,500kgs (2014).

## Touring

Ferry services connect Sweden with Denmark, Estonia, Finland, Germany, Latvia, Lithuania, Norway and Poland; some services only operate in the summer. Full details are available from Visit Sweden, www.visitsweden.com. Scheduled car ferry services also operate between the mainland and the island of Gotland during the summer season.

In the south and centre the touring season lasts from May to September. In the north it is a little shorter, the countryside being particularly beautiful at each end of the season. Campsites are most crowded over the midsummer holiday period and during the Swedish industrial holidays in the last two weeks of July and first week of August. Tourist attractions may close before the end of August or operate on reduced opening hours.

Sweden has 14 UNESCO World Heritage sites and 29 national parks which, together with nature reserves, cover eight percent of the country. Information on national parks and nature reserves is available on www.naturvardsverket.se.

Inland, particularly near lakes, visitors should be armed with spray-on, rub-on and electric plug-in insect repellent devices as mosquitoes and midges are a problem.

Discount cards are available in Stockholm and Gothenburg offering free public transport and free admission to many museums and other attractions, plus free boat and canal sightseeing trips. Buy the cards at tourist information offices, hotels, kiosks, some campsites and online – see www.stockholmtown.com or www.goteborg.com.

Local tourist offices are excellent sources of information and advice; look for the blue and yellow 'i' signs. Information points at lay-bys at the entrance to many towns are good sources of street maps.

A good-value 'dagens rätt' (dish of the day) is available in most restaurants at lunchtime. A service charge is usually included in restaurant bills but an additional small tip is normal if you have received good service.

The most popular alcoholic drink is lager, available in five strengths. Wines, spirits and strong beer are sold only through the state-owned 'Systembolaget' shops, open from Monday to Friday and on Saturday morning, with branches all over the country. Light beer can be bought from grocery shops and supermarkets. The minimum age for buying alcoholic drinks is 20 years at Systembolaget and 18 years in pubs, bars and licensed restaurants.

It is not permitted to smoke in restaurants, pubs or bars or in any place where food and drinks are served.

## The Midnight Sun and Northern Lights

The Midnight Sun is visible north of the Arctic Circle from about the end of May until the middle of July.

The Northern Lights (Aurora Borealis) are often visible during the winter from early evening until midnight. They are seen more frequently the further north you travel. The best viewing areas in Sweden are north of the Arctic Circle between September and March.

## The Order of Bluenosed Caravanners

Visitors to the Arctic Circle from anywhere in the world may apply for membership of the Order of Bluenosed Caravanners which will be recognised by the issue of a certificate by the International Caravanning Association (ICA).

For more information contact David Hirst on telephone 01422 372390, or email: david.hirst118@btinternet.com and attach a photograph of yourselves and your outfit under any Arctic Circle signpost, together with the date and country of crossing and the names of those who made the crossing. This service is free to members of the ICA (annual membership £20); the fee for non-members is £5. Coloured plastic decals for your outfit, indicating membership of the Order, are also available at a cost of £4. Cheques should be payable to the ICA. See www.icacaravanning.org.

## Public Transport & Local Travel

Stockholm has an extensive network of underground trains (T-bana), commuter trains, buses and trams. Underground station entrances are marked with a blue 'T' on a white background. You can buy single tickets for one of three zones at the time of your journey, or save money by buying tickets in advance. A discount applies if you are aged 65 or over. Single tickets and prepaid tickets are valid for one hour after beginning your journey. Travel cards offer reduced price public transport throughout the Greater Stockholm area for periods of 1, 3, 7 or 30 days, regardless of zone – see www.sl.se (click on 'Visitor') for details of routes, fares and tickets.

For information on public transport systems in Göteborg and Malmö, see www.vasttrafik.se and www.skanetrafiken.se.

Stockholm is built on an archipelago of islands and island hopping ferries operate all year. You can buy single tickets or an island hopping pass for use on the Waxholmsbolaget and Cinderella fleet of ferries.

Confirm your taxi fare before setting off in the vehicle. Some companies have fixed fares which vary according to the day of the week and time of day. A full price list must be on display. Payment by credit card is generally accepted. It is usual to round up the fare shown on the meter by way of a tip.

Sweden is a country of lakes, rivers and archipelagos and, as a result, there are over 12,000 bridges. Road ferries, which form part of the national road network, make up the majority of other crossings; no bookings are necessary or possible. Most ferries are free of charge and services are frequent and crossings very short.

A congestion charge was introduced in Stockholm in 2007 but drivers of foreign-registered vehicles are exempt from the charge. In some other towns traffic restrictions may apply during certain periods and these are signposted.

When giving directions Swedes will often refer to distances in 'miles'. A Swedish 'mile' is, in fact, approximately ten kilometres. All road signs are in kilometres and so, for example, a distance of 30km to a town, Swedes will tell you it is three miles.

⊞ **AHUS** *2F4* (1km NE Urban/Coastal) *55.94118, 14.31286*
**Regenbogen Camp (L27), Kolonivägen 59, 29633 Åhus**
[(044) 249530; fax 243523; ahus@regenbogen-camp.se;
www.regenbogen-camp.se] Take rd 118 fr Kristianstad SE
twd Åhus. Site well sp fr ent to town. Lge, mkd pitch, hdstg,
pt shd; htd wc; chem disp; mv service pnt; baby facs; sauna;
shwrs inc; el pnts (10A) SEK29; lndtte (inc dryer); shop; rest, bar
500m; BBQ; playgrnd; htd pool 300m; sand beach 150m; some
statics; dogs; site clsd 3 Nov-16 Dec; poss cr; Eng spkn; quiet;
ccard acc; CKE. "Gd base for walking, cycling, watersports;
excel fishing; famous area for artists." ◆ SEK 260       2011*

**ALINGSAS** *2E2* (4km SW Rural) **Lövekulle Camping, 44144**
**Alingsäs** [(0322) 12372; lovekulle@telia.com; www.
lovekulle.com] Foll sp fr E20. Sm, mkd pitch, some hdstg,
unshd; htd wc; chem disp; mv service pnt; shwrs; el pnts
(10A); lndtte; shop; snacks; playgrnd; sw; fishing; games area;
10% statics; Eng spkn; quiet; CKE/CCI. "Pleasant situation by
lake; clean san facs." ◆ 1 May-30 Sep.       2010*

**ALMHULT** *2F3* (2km N Rural) *56.56818, 14.13217* **Sjöstugans**
**Camping (G5), Campingvägen, Bökhult, 34394 Älmhult**
[(0476) 71600; fax 15750; info@sjostugan.com; www.
sjostugan.com] Fr Växjö SW on rd 23, at rndabt turn W to
Älmhult. Fr town cent turn N on Ljungbyvägen, site in 1.5km
on lakeside, well sp. Sm, pt sl, pt shd; htd wc; chem disp; mv
service pnt; baby facs; shwrs; el pnts (10A) SEK40; lndtte (inc
dryer); shop & 1.5km; rest, snacks; bar; cooking facs; playgrnd;
lake & sand beach adj; canoe hire; wifi; some statics; dogs; Eng
spkn; quiet; ccard acc; CKE. "Some lakeside pitches; well-kept
site; 1st Ikea store opened here in 1958; gd." 1 May-30 Sep.
SEK 165       2009*

⊞ **ALVDALEN** *1B4* (W Urban) *61.22789, 14.03007*
**Älvdalens Camping (W2), Ribbholmsvägen 26,**
**79631 Älvdalen** [tel/fax (0251) 12344; kontakt@
alvdalenscamping.se; www.alvdalenscamping.se] Fr S
& Mora take rd 70 N; in Älvdalen, 200m after church turn L
(W) to site; pt of sports & leisure cent; well sp. Lge, hdstg, pt
shd; htd wc; chem disp; mv service pnt; baby facs; fam bthrm;
shwrs inc; el pnts (10A) SEK40; lndtte (inc dryer); shop, rest,
snacks 500m; BBQ; cooking facs; playgrnd; htd, covrd pool,
waterslide, ice rink nr; cycle hire; wifi; TV; dogs; Eng spkn;
quiet; ccard acc; CKE. "Sh walk to town cent; gd facs." ◆
SEK 175       2011*

⊞ **AMAL** *2E2* (1km SE Urban) *59.0465, 12.7236* **Örnäs**
**Camping (P2), Gamla Örnäsgatan, 66222 Åmål**
[(0532) 17097; fax 71624; ornascamping@amal.se; www.
amal.se] Leave rd 45 to Åmål, site sp. Sm, some hdstg, pt
sl, terr, pt shd; htd wc; chem disp; mv service pnt; sauna;
shwrs SEK5; el pnts (10A) inc; lndtte (inc dryer); shop, rest
1km; snacks; bar; playgrnd; sand beach/lake adj; fishing;
tennis; boat & cycle hire; wifi; some statics; dogs; Eng spkn;
red 7 days; ccard acc; CCS. "Gd views Lake Vänern." ◆ ltd
SEK 250       2011*

**ANASET** *1C3* (1km S Rural) *64.26834, 21.04120* **Lufta**
**Camping (AC15), Galgbacken 1, 91594 Ånäset**
[(0934) 20488; fax 20215; info@luftacamping.se; www.
luftacamping.se] Exit E4 at Int'l Camp sp at Ånäset. Site
immed S of Ånäset & 300m W of E4. Med, pt sl, pt shd; htd
wc; chem disp; mv service pnt; sauna; shwrs; el pnts (10A)
SEK50; lndtte; shop 500m; rest, snacks; bar; playgrnd; htd
pool adj; waterslide; games area; cycle hire; fishing; wifi; TV;
some statics; Eng spkn; ccard acc; CKE. "Beautiful setting." ◆
1 May-30 Sep. SEK 130       2009*

**ANGELHOLM** *2E4* (2km W Coastal) *56.2540, 12.8336*
**Råbocka Camping (L12), Råbockavägen 101, 26263**
**Ängelholm** [(0431) 10543 or 430600; fax 16144;
rabockacamping@telia.com; www.rabockacamping.
se] Fr E6 foll sps to Ängelholm, site 2km fr town cent. Lge,
mkd pitch, pt shd; wc; chem disp; mv service pnt; baby facs;
shwrs SEK10; el pnts (10A) SEK50; lndtte; shop; snacks; bar;
playgrnd; sand beach; TV; 10% statics; poss cr; Eng spkn; adv
bkg; ccard acc; CKE. "Excel, busy site; gd beach & nature park
nrby." ◆ 16 Apr-11 Sep. SEK 275       2009*

⊞ **ARBOGA** *2G1* (13km S Rural) *59.28134, 15.90509*
**Herrfallets Camping (U14), 73293 Arboga** [(0589) 40110;
fax 40133; reception@herrfallet.se; www.herrfallet.se]
Foll sp fr E20/E18, turn off at Sätra junc twd Arboga, cross rv.
Foll sp to Herrfallet/Västermo. Med, mkd pitch, pt shd; htd
wc; chem disp; 50% serviced pitches; mv service pnt; baby
facs; sauna; shwrs SEK10; el pnts (10A) SEK40; lndtte (inc
dryer); shop; tradsmn; rest; bar; BBQ; playgrnd; lake sw &
beach; boating; cycle hire; wifi; entmnt; dogs; phone; quiet;
ccard acc; CKE/CCI. "Lovely spot on edge Lake Hjälmaren." ◆
SEK 190       2010*

**ARBOGA** *2G1* (1km SW Rural) *59.38863, 15.82713*
**Krakaborgs Camping, Örebrovägen 2A 24B, 73221**
**Arboga** [(0589) 12670; fax 17425; www.arboga.se] Fr E18
exit sp Arboga. On ent town at rndabt foll site sp, site on L.
Sm, pt shd; htd wc; chem disp; baby facs; shwrs; el pnts (10A)
SEK35; lndtte; shop; snacks; cooking facs; playgrnd; TV; dogs;
phone; adv bkg; quiet. 1 Jun-31 Oct. SEK 150       2009*

**ARJANG** *2E1* (25km SE Rural) *59.30295, 12.44474*
**Camping Grinsby, Grindsbyn 100, Sillerud, 67295 Årjäng**
[(0573) 42022; fax 40175; campgrinsby@telia.com] On E18
SE fr Årjäng & Sillerud, turn L at site sp. Site in 2km on Stora
Bör lake. Med, some hdstg, terr, pt shd; htd wc; chem disp; mv
service pnt; baby facs; shwrs SEK10; el pnts (10A) SEK40; lndtte
(inc dryer); shop; tradsmn; BBQ; cooking facs; playgrnd; sand
beach & lake sw adj; boat & cycle hire; games rm; some statics;
dogs; phone; Eng spkn; adv bkg; quiet; ccard acc; CKE/CCI.
"A 'wilderness' site in beautiful setting; many walking paths;
friendly, helpful staff; vg san facs." ◆ ltd 15 May-31 Aug.
SEK 150       2010*

---

SWEDEN

⊞ **ARJANG** *2E1* (3km S Rural) *59.36756, 12.14036* **Årjäng Camping (S13), Strand Sommarvik, 67291 Årjäng [(0573) 12060; fax 12048; booking@sommarvik.se; www. sommarvik.se]** Foll sp fr E18/rd 172. Site sp in Årjäng. At T-junc foll sp Stubgy & site sp on R 400m up hill, steep in parts but strt. Lge, pt sl, pt shd; htd wc; mv service pnt; baby facs; sauna; shwrs SEK10; el pnts (10A) inc; gas; lndtte (inc dryer); shop; rest, snacks; bar; cooking facs; playgrnd; htd pool high ssn; paddling pool; lake sw & beach; fishing; boating; boat & cycle hire; games area; tennis 1.5km; wifi; entmnt; TV rm; 50% statics; dogs; phone; Quickstop o'night facs; quiet; CKE. "Gd family site." ♦ SEK 200                               2011*

⊞ **ARJEPLOG** *1C2* (1.5km W Rural) *66.05007, 17.86298* **Kraja Camping (BD1), Krajaudden, 93090 Arjeplog [(0961) 31500; fax 31599; arjeplog@kraja.se; www.kraja. se]** NW fr Arvidsjaur thro Arjeplog vill to site on R. Med, pt shd; htd wc; chem disp; baby facs; sauna; shwrs; el pnts (10A) SEK40; lndtte (inc dryer); shop; rest; bar; cooking facs; playgrnd; htd pool; paddling pool; sand beach; lake sw 4km; fishing; boating; TV; many statics; dogs; phone; poss cr; quiet; CKE. "Gd cent for local Lapp area." ♦ SEK 195           2010*

**ASA** *2E3* (S Coastal) *57.34906, 12.12200* **Åsa Camping (N3), Stora Badviksvägen 10, 43031 Åsa [(0340) 219590; info@ asacamping.com; www.asacamping.com]** On E6/E20 S fr Göteborg take exit rd sp Åsa. On app Åsa site sp on R. Med, unshd wc; chem disp; mv service pnt; baby facs; shwrs SEK5; el pnts (10A) SEK40; lndtte (inc dryer); shop & adj; rest; bar; playgrnd; sand beach nr; games area; games rm; golf; fishing; wifi; TV; 80% statics; dogs; phone; adv bkg; quiet; ccard acc; CKE. "Well-organised, family site but dominated by statics; avoid pitches nr access rd & facs block." ♦ 22 Apr-11 Sep. SEK 200                                      2009*

⊞ **ASARNA** *1B3* (9km S Rural) *62.56340, 14.38786* **Kvarnsjö Camp, Kvarnsjö 696, 84031 Åsarna [tel/fax (0682) 22016; info@kvarnsjocamp.com; www.kvarnsjocamp.com]** Fr N on E45 3km after Åsarna turn R onto rd 316 dir Klövsjo. In 8km turn L sp Cmp Kvarnsjö. In 8km cross rlwy, site on L in 1km. Fr S 9km after Rätan turn L dir Klövsjo. In 1.5km bear R at Y-junc site in 4km. Sm, hdstg, terr, unshd; wc; chem disp; mv service pnt; sauna; shwrs inc; el pnts (10A) SEK40; lndtte; shop 16km; no statics; dogs; Eng spkn; adv bkg; quiet. CKE/CCI. "CL-type family-run site o'looking woods & mountains; excel walking, fishing; boating, fresh bread/breakfast in high sssn." SEK 130                                      2011*

**ASKIM see Göteborg** *2E3*

**BARSEBACK** *2E4* (1km W Coastal) *55.77030, 12.92621* **Barsebäckstrand Camping (M19), Kustvägen 125, 24657 Barsebäck [(046) 776079; info@barsebackstrand.se; www. barsebackstrand.se]** Fr S exit E6 junc 23 sp 'Center Syd' & foll sp Barsebäck thro vill. Turn L at T-junc, site in 2km, sp. Fr N exit junc 24 & foll coast rd 'Kustvägen' to site in 5km. Med, mkd pitch, terr, unshd; wc; chem disp; mv service pnt; shwrs inc; el pnts (10A) SEK40; lndry rm; shop 4km; tradsmn; rest, snacks; cooking facs; playgrnd; beach & sw adj; 40% statics; dogs free; poss cr; Eng spkn; adv bkg; quiet; CKE. "Vg site; excel rest." ♦ 26 Apr-1 Sep. SEK 250                              2013*

⊞ **BENGTSFORS** *2E2* (12km SE Rural) *58.95271, 12.25201* **Laxsjöns Camping & Friluftsgård (P3), 66010 Dals Långed [(0531) 30010; fax 30555; office@laxsjons.se; www. laxsjon.se]** Fr Bengtsfors S on rd 172; 4km after x-ing Dalsland Canal at Billingsfors turn L twd Dals Långed; after 1km site on Lake Laxsjön on L; sp. Ent 4.5m. Lge, mkd pitch, pt sl, pt shd; htd wc; chem disp; sauna; shwrs SEK5; el pnts (10A) SEK40; lndtte (inc dryer); shop; rest in ssn; playgrnd; htd pool; lake sw adj; canoe hire; waterskiing; sailing; fishing; bus 200m/1km; Quickstop o'night facs; Eng spkn; adv bkg; quiet; ccard acc; red 7+ days; CKE. "Vg for quiet holiday & watersports; friendly staff; rec." ♦ SEK 190                            2010*

**BERGKVARA** *2G4* (1km E Coastal) *56.39043, 16.09061* **Dalskärs Camping (H15), Dalskärvägen11, 385 40 Bergkvara [(0709) 415567; info@dalskarscamping. se; www.dalskarscamping.se]** Exit E22 in Bergkvara twd Dalskärsbadet, site sp. Med, mkd pitch, pt shd; wc; chem disp; mv service pnt; baby facs; sauna; shwrs SEK5; el pnts SEK40; lndtte; shop; rest; bar; htd pool; paddling pool; sand beach adj; boat & cycle hire; games area; wifi; some statics; dogs free; phone; Eng spkn; quiet; ccard acc. "Gd family site; san facs adequate; excel rest; scenic location." ♦ 24 Apr-11 Sep. SEK 220                                  2013*

⊞ **BOCKSJO** *2F2* (5km NW Rural) *58.68058, 14.59911* **Stenkällegårdens Camping Tiveden, 54695 Stenkällegården [(0505) 60015; fax 60085; stenkallegarden@swipnet.se; www.stenkallegarden.nu]** N on rd 49 fr Karlsborg, turn L at Bocksjö, site sp on L in 2km. Pt of rte single track with passing places. Med, mkd pitch, pt sl, terr. pt shd; htd wc; chem disp; mv service pnt; baby facs; sauna; shwrs SEK10, el pnts (10A) SEK40; lndtte (inc dryer); shop; tradsmn; rest; cooking facs; BBQ; playgrnd; lake sw; fishing; boat hire; TV rm; 30% statics; dogs; site clsd last 2 weeks Apr & 1st 2 weeks Oct; Eng spkn; quiet; ccard acc; CKE. "Gd cycling; mkd walking trails; spacious, sheltered site; clean san facs; skiing on site in winter; Tiveden National Park 5km." ♦ SEK 170                                     2009*

**BOLLNAS** *1C4* (3km E Rural) *61.3475, 16.43245* **Vevlingestrands Camping (X24), Vevlinge 3680, 82150 Bollnäs [(0278) 12684; info@vevlingestrand.com; www. vevlingestrand.com]** Fr Söderhamn take rd 50 twds Bollnäs: turn L at town edge & foll sp for Vevlinge & Segersta. In 600m foll sp Vevlingestrand to site; well sp. Med, mkd pitch, sl, unshd; wc; chem disp; baby facs; shwrs; el pnts (10A) SEK40; lndtte; shop; rest, snacks; cooking facs; playgrnd; lake sw & private beach adj; fishing; games area; Eng spkn; quiet; CKE. "Lovely lakeside setting; pleasant site." 1 May-30 Sep. SEK 150                                2009*

**BORENSBERG** *2G2* (1.5km S Rural) *58.55663, 15.27911* **Strandbadets Camping, 59030 Borensberg [(0141) 40385; info@strandbadetscamping.se; www. strandbadetscamping.se]** Site sp off rd 36. Med, pt shd; wc; mv service pnt; baby facs; shwrs; el pnts (10A) SEK40; lndtte; shop, rest in vill; snacks; cooking facs; playgrnd; lake sw & beach; fishing; few statics; quiet; CKE. "Gd base for Östergötland & Lake Vättern area; cycle rte along Göta Canal." 22 Apr-11 Sep. SEK 190                         2013*

BORGHOLM (OLAND ISLAND) 2G3 (12km S Coastal) 56.7933, 16.5664 Ekerums Camping & Stugor SweCamp (H26), 38792 Borgholm [(0485) 564700; fax 564701; info@ekerum.nu; www.ekerum.nu] Cross land bdge fr Kalmar, turn N, site sp on rd 136 bet Färjestaden & Borgholm. V lge, shd; htd wc; chem disp; mv service pnt; baby facs; shwrs inc; el pnts (10A) inc; lndtte (inc dryer); shop; rest, snacks; bar; cooking facs; playgrnd; 2 htd pools; waterslide; sand/shgl beach adj; fishing; boating; golf 1km; cycle hire; tennis 1km; wifi; TV rm; 20% statics; dogs; phone; Quickstop o'night facs; quiet; CKE. "Excel family site; private san facs avail; Borgholm castle worth visit." ♦ 11 Apr-2 Oct. SEK 300 (CChq acc) 2009*

BROMMA see Stockholm 2H2

BYXELKROK (OLAND ISLAND) 2G3 (1km N Coastal) 57.33013, 17.01211 Neptuni Camping (H41), Småskogsvägen 2, 38075 Byxelkrok [(0485) 28495 or 070 5428495 (mob); neptuni.camping@telia.com; www.neptunicamping.se] Fr S on rd 136 thro Böda, at Byxelkrok turn R past harbour for 200m. Site on R. Med, pt shd; wc; chem disp; mv service pnt; shwrs SEK5; el pnts (16A) SEK40; lndtte (inc dryer); shop; playgrnd; beach adj; games area; dogs; phone; Eng spkn; quiet; ccard acc; CKE. "Conv touring base N Öland, sh walk to harbour, rest & supmkt." ♦ 30 Apr-31 Aug. SEK 170 2009*

DALS LANGED see Bengtsfors 2E2

DEGERFORS 2F2 (1.5km N Rural) 59.25145, 14.4595 Degernäs Camping (T7), 69335 Degerfors [(0586) 44999; reception@degernascamping.se; www.degernascamping.se] Fr rd 204, take rd 243 twds lake, site sp. Med, pt sl, pt shd; htd wc; chem disp; mv service pnt; baby facs; sauna; shwrs inc; el pnts (10A) SEK50; lndtte (inc dryer); shop; rest; snacks 2km; playgrnd; lake beach; fishing; boating; cycle hire; TV; 50% statics; poss cr; no adv bkg; quiet; ccard acc; CKE. ♦ 1 May-18 Sep. SEK 160 2011*

⊞ DEGERHAMN (OLAND ISLAND) 2G4 (12km S Rural) 56.23778, 16.4530 Ottenby Vandrarhem & Camping (H57), Ottenby 106, 38065 Degerhamn [(0485) 662062; fax 662161; info@ottenbyvandrarhem.se; www.ottenbyvandrarhem.se] Rd 36 S to Ottenby, bear R for 4km, site on R at youth hostel. Sm, unshd; htd wc; chem disp; mv service pnt; baby facs; shwrs inc; el pnts (10A) SEK40; lndtte (inc dryer); shop 5km; tradsmn; cooking facs; htd pool; paddling pool; cycle hire; 10% statics; dogs free; phone; quiet; ccard acc. "On edge Ottenby nature reserve; excel walks & birdwatching - ssn geared to bird migration; poss noise fr late arr & early risers as no barrier; World Heritage Site on S pt of island." ♦ SEK 210 2014*

⊞ DOROTEA 1C3 (500m SW Rural) 64.26003, 16.39606 Doro Camping, Storgatan 1A, 91070 Dorotea [(0942) 10238; fax 10779; reception@dorocamp.com; www.dorocamp.com] Site on E side of E45. Med, pt sl, pt shd; wc; chem disp; sauna; baby facs; shwrs inc; el pnts (10A) SEK50; lndtte (inc dryer); shop; snacks; cooking facs; lake sw; playgrnd; fishing; golf; hiking; internet; some statics; site clsd Nov; poss cr; Eng spkn; quiet. ♦ ltd SEK 135 2010*

⊞ ED 2E2 (2km E Rural) 58.89931, 11.93486 Gröne Backe Camping (P8), Södra Moränvägen 64, 66832 Ed [(0534) 10144; fax 10145; gronebackecamping@telia.com] App Ed on rd 164/166, site sp on Lake Lilla Le. Med, pt sl, shd; wc; chem disp; sauna; baby facs; shwrs SEK5; el pnts (10A) SEK40; lndtte (inc dryer); shops, rest, snacks 300m; playgrnd; lake sw; cycle hire; wifi; quiet; ccard acc; CKE. "Excel for boating." SEK 180 2009*

EKSHARAD 2F1 (1km E Rural) 60.1760, 13.5090 Byns Camping (S3), Slätta, 68050 Ekshärad [(0563) 40885; fax 30196; info@bynscamping.eu; www.bynscamping.eu] Turn E off rd 62 at x-rds by church, site sp on rv bank. Sm, pt shd; htd wc; chem disp; baby facs; shwrs SEK5; el pnts (10A) SEK35; lndtte (inc dryer); shop; snacks; cooking facs; playgrnd; cycle hire; phone; v quiet; ccard acc; CKE. "Pleasant site." ♦ 27 May-31 Aug. SEK 140 2010*

⊞ EKSJO 2F3 (1km E Rural) 57.66766, 14.98923 Eksjö Camping (F13), Prästängsvägen 5, 57536 Eksjö [(0381) 39500; fax 14096; info@eksjocamping.se; www.eksjocamping.se] Site sp fr town cent on rd 33 twd Västervik, on lakeside. Med, shd; wc; chem disp; mv service pnt; baby facs; shwrs; el pnts (10A) SEK45; lndtte (inc dryer); shop; rest, snacks; bar; playgrnd; covrd pool 100m; lake sw adj; fishing; boating; cycle hire; wifi; 10% statics; dogs; phone; poss cr; no adv bkg; quiet; ccard acc; CKE. "Gd cent glass region; attractive countryside & old town." ♦ SEK 140 2009*

ELDSBERGA see Halmstad 2E3

⊞ ENKOPING 2H1 (4km S Rural) 59.59334, 17.07146 Bredsand Camping, Falkstigen 1, 74591 Bredsand [(0171) 80011; fax 80095; info@bredsand.com; http://bredsand.com] Fr E18 or rd 55 foll sp to site, well sp on Lake Mälaren. Med, mkd pitch, pt sl, pt shd; htd wc; chem disp; mv service pnt; baby facs; shwrs inc; el pnts (10A) SEK50; lndtte (inc dryer); supmkt 4km; rest, snacks; lake sw & beach adj; 50% statics; dogs; quiet; CKE. "Vg site." SEK 210 2011*

ESKILSTUNA 2G2 (10km N Rural) 59.45138, 16.43700 Mälarbadens Camping (D15), Mälarbadsvägen, 64436 Torshälla [(016) 343187; fax 343559; campingmalarbaden@gmail.com] Fr Eskilstuna on E20 turn N to Torshälla & foll site sp N twds lake. Sm, hdg pitch, pt sl, pt shd; wc; chem disp; baby facs; el pnts (13A) SEK35; lndtte (inc dryer); shop 2km; tradsmn; rest, snacks; cooking facs; playgrnd; lake sw & beach 1km; sports stadium nr; 60% statics; dogs; phone; Eng spkn; adv bkg; quiet; CKE/CCI. "Vg, clean, peaceful site; gd security; gd for children." 1 May-15 Sep. SEK 195 2011*

FALKENBERG 2E3 (10km SE Coastal) 56.8234, 12.60955 Ugglarps Camping (N30), Strandkantsvägen 2, 31169 Ugglarp [(0346) 43889; info@ugglarp.nu; www.ugglarp.nu] Exit E6 junc 48, foll sp Slöinge, then site sp. Lge, mkd pitch, terr, pt shd; htd wc; chem disp; mv service pnt; baby facs; some serviced pitches; shwrs inc; el pnts (16A) inc; lndtte (inc dryer); shop; tradsmn; rest, snacks; bar; BBQ; cooking facs; playgrnd; beach adj; games rm; wifi; 15% statics; dogs; phone; Eng spkn; adv bkg; quiet; red low ssn; CKE. "Gd san facs." ♦ 21 Apr-11 Sep. SEK 340 2011*

**FALKENBERG** 2E3 (3km S Coastal) 56.88315, 12.51495
**Skrea Camping (N12), Strandvägen, 31142 Falkenberg
[(0346) 17107; fax 15840; info@skreacamping.se; www.
skreacamping.se]** Turn off E20/E6 at junc 50 to Falkenberg
S, foll sp Skrea Strand to site. Lge, mkd pitch, pt shd; htd wc;
chem disp; mv service pnt; baby facs; shwrs SEK2; el pnts (10-
16A) SEK45; gas; lndtte (inc dryer); shop & 500m; rest 200m;
BBQ; playgrnd; paddling pool; sand beach 250m; windsurfing;
golf 5km; wifi; entmnt; sat TV; 20% statics; dogs; phone;
Quickstop o'night facs; barrier clsd 2300-0600; poss cr; adv
bkg; ccard acc; CKE. "Vg site; gd san facs." ♦ 20 Apr-4 Sep.
SEK 295                                                    2009*

**FALKENBERG** 2E3 (10km NW Coastal) 56.95551, 12.36641
**Rosendals Camping Morup (N26), Rosendalsvägen
22, 31198 Glommen [(0346) 97300; fax 97302; info@
rosendalscamping.se; www.rosendalscamping.se]** Fr N on
E6 exit junc 52 sp Morup/Glommen. Foll rd to x-rds by school
(ent to Glommen vill). Turn R sp Morup & site on R in 3km at
minor rds. Fr Falkenberg take rd sp Glommen at traff lts nr
docks; foll 11km along coast rd to x-rds at ent to Glommen
vill. Go across x-rds sp Morup & foll rd as above. Med, pt shd;
wc; chem disp; baby facs; sauna; shwrs; el pnts (6A) SEK30;
lndtte (inc dryer); shop; playgrnd; beach 1km; cycle hire;
60% statics; phone; dogs; Quickstop o'night facs; poss cr; ccard
acc; CKE. "Site yourself & owner calls." ♦ 1 Apr-11 Sep.
SEK 190                                                    2009*

⊞ **FALKOPING** 2F2 (1km W Rural) 58.17595, 13.52726
**Mössebergs Camping & Stugby (R7), Lidgatan 4, 52132
Falköping [(0515) 17349; mossebergscamping@telia.
com]** Exit rd 184 at Falköping; foll Int'l Camping sps or sps
to Mösseberg; site also sp fr rds 46 & 47 & in town. Site on
plateau overlkg town. Med, mkd pitch, pt shd; wc; mv service
pnt; baby facs; sauna; shwrs SEK5; el pnts SEK40; lndtte (inc
dryer); cooking facs; shops 1km; playgrnd; pool 400m; lake sw
400m; wifi; some statics; dogs; phone; quiet; ccard acc; CKE.
♦ SEK 150                                                  2009*

**FARJESTADEN (OLAND ISLAND)** 2G3 (1km N Coastal)
56.68681, 16.48253 **Krono Camping Saxnäs/Öland (H25),
Södra Saxnäs, 38695 Färjestaden [(0485) 35700; info@
kcsaxnas.se; www.kcsaxnas.se]** Cross Öland Bdge fr Kalmar
on rd 137, take exit for Öland Zoo/Saxnäs. Site sp. Lge, mkd
pitch, pt shd; wc; chem disp; mv service pnt; baby facs; 25%
serviced pitches; shwrs inc; el pnts (10A) inc (poss rev pol);
lndtte; shop; rest; bar; playgrnd; shgl beach adj; games area;
sat TV inc; some statics; dogs; phone; adv bkg; poss noisy high
ssn; ccard acc; red low ssn; CKE. "Öland is beautiful island with
400 19thC windmills." ♦ 12 Apr-2 Oct. SEK 350      2011*

⊞ **FILIPSTAD** 2F1 (1km N Rural) 59.72035, 14.15899
**Munkeberg Camping (S5), Skillervägen, 68233 Filipstad
[tel/fax (0590) 50100; alterschwede@telia.com; www.
munkeberg.com]** Fr Karlstad take rd 63 to Filipstad. In town
foll sp for rd 246 twd Hagfors, site sp in town. Med, pt sl, pt
shd; htd wc; chem disp; shwrs inc; el pnts (10A) SEK30; lndtte
(inc dryer); shop 1km; snacks; playgrnd; lake sw; boating;
fishing; wifi; some statics; dogs; adv bkg; quiet; CKE/CCI.
"Beautiful lakeside site; gd for touring old mining district." ♦
SEK 160                                                    2009*

**FINNERODJA** 2F2 (5km W Rural) 58.92808, 14.33558
**Skagern Camping (T26), 69593 Finnerödja [tel/fax
(0506) 33040; camp.skagern@telia.com]** S fr Örebro & Laxå
on E20, vill is sp. Med, mkd pitch, sl, pt shd; htd wc; chem
disp; mv service pnt; sauna; baby facs; shwrs; el pnts (10A)
inc; lndtte (inc dryer); shop; tradsmn; BBQ; playgrnd; sand
beach/lake; boat hire; fishing; games area; games rm; wifi; TV;
75% statics; dogs; Quickstop o'night facs; Eng spkn; quiet;
ccard acc; CKE/CCI. "Vg site; levelling blocks req." 1 May-
30 Sep. SEK 230                                           2011*

**FJALLBACKA** 2E2 (3.5km N Coastal) 58.63125, 11.27283
**Långsjö Camping (O12), Långesjö Vikarna 22, 45071
Fjällbacka [(0525) 12116; info@langsjocamping.se; www.
langsjocamping.se]** Exit E6 at junc 103 & foll rd 163 to
Fjällbacka. Site sp in vill, narr ent. Sm, pt shd; wc; chem disp;
mv service pnt; baby facs; shwrs SEK5; el pnts (10A) SEK45;
lndtte (inc dryer); shop; snacks; BBQ; cooking facs; playgrnd;
beach adj; fishing; cycle hire; games area; games rm; wifi;
entmnt; some statics; dogs; poss cr; Eng spkn; quiet; ccard
acc; CKE/CCI. "Gd site; beautiful vill." ♦ 1 May 13 Sep.
SEK 250                                                    2009*

**FROSON see Östersund** 1B3

⊞ **GADDEDE** 1B2 (1km NE Rural) 64.50400, 14.14900
**Gäddede Camping & Stugby, Sagavägen 9,
83090 Gäddede [(0672) 10035; fax 10511; info@
gaddedecamping.com; www.gaddedecamping.se]** On ent
Gäddede cent on rd 342, turn R & site in 500m on R, sp. Med,
mkd pitch, pt shd; htd wc; chem disp; sauna; shwrs SEK5; el
pnts (10A) SEK50; lndtte; shop 500m; rest 100m; playgrnd; htd
pool; paddling pool; canoe hire; fishing; games area; games
rm; TV; 40% statics; dogs; poss cr; Eng spkn; adv bkg; quiet;
ccard acc; CKE/CCI. "Gd touring base 'Wilderness Way'." ♦
SEK 211                                                    2014*

**GAMLEBY** 2G2 (1km SE Coastal) 57.88475, 16.41373
**Hammarsbadets Camping (H2), Hammarsvägen 10, 59432
Gamleby [(0493) 10221; fax 12686; info@campa.se; www.
campa.se]** On E22 Kalmar-Norrköping, foll sp to site 2km
off main rd. Med, mkd pitch, terr, pt shd; wc; chem disp; mv
service pnt; baby facs; sauna; shwrs SEK5; el pnts (10A) SEK45;
lndtte (inc dryer); shop; tradsmn; rest, snacks; bar; playgrnd;
pool; sand beach adj; lake sw; boat & cycle hire; tennis; wifi;
some statics; dogs; phone; Quickstop o'night facs; quiet; ccard
acc; CKE/CCI. "Clean, well-kept, relaxing site." 30 Apr-13 Sep.
SEK 190                                                    2009*

**GAVLE** 2H1 (10km NE Coastal) 60.72946, 17.29145
**Engesbergs Camping & Stugby, Solviksvägen 7, 80595
Gävle [(026) 99025; fax 99347; info@engesbergscamping.
se; www.engesbergscamping.se]** Site sp along coast rd to
Bönan. Lge, pt sl, pt shd; wc; chem disp; mv service pnt; shwrs
inc; el pnts (10A) SEK40 or metered; shop; snacks; playgrnd;
statics; dogs; poss cr; quiet; ccard acc; CKE. "Lovely site, mostly
in trees." ♦ 1 May-1 Oct. SEK 150                         2009*

⊞ **GESUNDA** *1B4* (2km N Rural) *60.90100, 14.58500*
**Solleröns Camping (W60), Levsnäs, 79290 Sollerön**
**[(0250) 22230; fax 22268; info@sollerocamping.se; www.**
**sollerocamping.se]** Fr Gesunda take bdge to Sollerön Island in
Lake Siljan. Site immed on R on reaching island; clearly visible
fr bdge. Lge, pt sl, pt shd; wc; chem disp; mv service pnt; baby
facs; sauna; shwrs inc ; el pnts (10A) SEK30; lndtte (inc dryer);
shop; rest, snacks; bar; playgrnd; lake sw adj; canoe & boat
hire; tennis; wifi; poss cr; adv bkg; quiet; ccard acc; CKE/CCI.
"Beautiful outlook to S across lake; gd base for Dalarna folklore
area; gd site & facs; Every 7th day is free." ◆ SEK 190   2011*

**GLAVA** *2E1* (10km S Rural) *59.4768, 12.68526* **Sölje**
**Camping (S61), Tångeberg, 67020 Glava [(0570) 464141;**
**fax 464142; solje.camping@telia.com]** Fr Arvika take rd 175
S. Just bef Stömne (approx 30km) turn R sp Sulvik. Foll sp at
Sölje x-rds. Sm, pt sl, unshd; wc; chem disp; mv service pnt;
baby facs; sauna; shwrs SEK5; el pnts SEK40; lndtte (inc dryer);
kiosk; cooking facs; playgrnd; lake sw adj, fishing; boat & cycle
hire; games area; wifi; entmnt; some statics; dogs; CKE. "Idyllic
lakeside location; peaceful - a real find." ◆ 1 Jun-31 Aug.
SEK 140                                                                   2011*

**GLOMMEN see Falkenberg** *2E3*

⊞ **GOTEBORG** *2E3* (4km E Rural) *57.7053, 12.0286*
**Lisebergsbyn Camping Kärralund (O39), Olbersgatan 1,**
**41655 Göteborg [(031) 840200; fax 840500; lisebergsbyn@**
**liseberg.se; www.liseberg.se]** Exit E6/E20 junc 71 onto rd
40 E & foll sp Lisebergsbyn, site well sp. Lge, pt sl, terr, pt shd;
wc; chem disp; mv service pnt; fam bthrm; baby facs; shwrs
inc; el pnts (10A) inc; gas; lndtte (inc dryer); shop (open only
once a week low ssn); supmkt nrby; playgrnd; wifi; TV; phone;
tram 400m; poss cr/noisy high ssn; Eng spkn; adv bkg rec;
red low ssn; ccard acc; red low ssn & Sun-Fri; CKE. "Boat trips
arranged; vg, well-run site; low ssn arr early to obtain barrier
key; poss travellers on site; cycle path to Liseberg amusement
park & town cent." SEK 450                                       2013*

**GOTEBORG** *2E3* (15km NW Coastal) *57.7434, 11.7566*
**Göteborgs Camping Lilleby (O40), Lillebyvägen**
**100, 42353 Torslanda [(031) 562240; fax 562246;**
**lillebycamping@gmail.com; www.goteborgscamping.**
**se]** Fr S on E6 pass thro Tingstads Tunnel in Göteborg &
immed turn W onto R155 & foll sp Torslanda. Site sp fr N
on E6; immed S of Kungälv, exit W at sps for Säve; foll sp to
Torslanda; site sp. Med, mkd pitch, pt shd; wc; chem disp; mv
service pnt; shwrs inc; el pnts SEK50; gas; lndtte (inc dryer);
shop; cooking facs; playgrnd; sw at rocky beach 250m with
waterchute; bus adj; poss cr; Eng spkn; poss noisy in ssn; ccard
acc; CKE. "V attractive area; meadowland; clean & pleasant
with gd bus nr ent; avoid arr or dep rush hr - traffic fr Volvo
factory; facs stretched in ssn; friendly, helpful staff." 1 Jun-
28 Aug. SEK 200                                                        2010*

**GOTHENBURG see Göteborg** *2E3*

**GRANNA** *2F2* (9km S Rural) *57.92446, 14.32341*
**Vätterledens Camping (F4), Vättersmålen 7, 56393**
**Gränna [(036) 52167; vatterledenscamping@glocalnet.**
**net; www.vatterledenscamping.se]** Site sp off E4 bet
Jönköping & Gränna, behind a motel. Sm, pt sl, unshd; htd wc;
chem disp; mv service pnt; baby facs; shwrs inc; el pnts (10A)
SEK40; lndtte (inc dryer); rest, snacks, bar 200m; wifi; TV rm;
some statics; Eng spkn; quiet; CKE. "Ltd facs but clean; helpful
owner; pitches waterlogged after rain, but tractor avail; gd
NH." 1 May-14 Aug. SEK 150                                      2011*

**GRANNA** *2F2* (500m NW Rural) *58.02783, 14.45821*
**Grännastrandens Familjecamping (F3), Hamnen, 56300**
**Gränna [(0390) 10706; fax 41260; info@grannacamping.**
**se; www.grannacamping.se]** In cent of Gränna down rd twd
Lake Vättern, sp Visingsö Island. Lge, unshd; wc; chem disp; mv
service pnt; baby facs; shwrs; el pnts (10A) metered + conn fee;
lndtte (inc dryer); shop; rest adj; playgrnd; lake sw & beach;
wifi; sat TV; some cottages; dogs; poss v cr; CKE. "Ballooning
cent of Sweden; Visingsö Island, Brahehus ruined castle, glass-
blowing 3km; vg site; gd location; gd san facs, excel camp
kitchen." ◆ 30 Apr-3 Oct. SEK 260                              2014*

⊞ **GREBBESTAD** *2E2* (1km S Coastal) *58.6832, 11.2625*
**Grebbestads Familjecamping (O10), Rörvik, 45795**
**Grebbestad, Sverige [(0525) 61211; fax 14319; info@**
**grebbestadfjorden.com; www.grebbestadfjorden.com]**
Exit E6 at Tanumshede sp Grebbestad; foll rd thro vill, past
harbour; site on R approx 500m after harbour. Lge, mkd
pitch, pt sl, unshd; wc; chem disp; mv service pnt; baby facs;
sauna; shwrs inc; el pnts (10A) SEK50; lndtte (inc dryer); sm
shop & 500m; snacks; cooking facs; htd pool 1km; sand beach
150m; games area; wifi; mainly statics; phone; dogs; poss cr;
Eng spkn; adv bkg; quiet; ccard acc; CKE. "Well-maintained
site 500m fr busy fishing/yachting harbour; meadowland;
excel mv services; helpful staff; vg facs, lge cr noisy site." ◆
SEK 350                                                                   2013*

**GRYT** *2G2* (2km E Coastal) *58.17378, 16.85228* **KustCamp**
**Ekön (E27), Ekövägen, 61042 Gryt [(0123) 40283; fax**
**12686; ekon@campa.se; www.campa.se]** Exit E2 sp
Valdemarsvik, then rd 212 twd Gryt. Approx 2 km after
Gryt turn R into Ekövägen. Foll site sp. Med, unshd; htd wc;
chem disp; mv service pnt; baby facs; shwrs inc; el pnts (10A)
SEK45; lndtte (inc dryer); shop; rest, snacks; BBQ; cooking
facs; playgrnd; beach adj; canoe & boat hire; games area;
internet; 30% statics; dogs; poss cr; Eng spkn; quiet; ccard
acc; CKE/CCI. "Gd walking & cycling; gd." ◆ 1 Apr-13 Sep.
SEK 160                                                                   2009*

⊞ **HALMSTAD** *2E3* (10km S Coastal) *56.59033, 12.94430*
**Gullbrannagården Camping (N27), 31031 Eldsberga**
**[tel/fax (035) 42180; mail@gullbrannagarden.se; www.**
**gullbrannagarden.se]** Fr S site sp on E6. Lge, pt sl, pt shd;
wc; chem disp; mv service pnt; baby facs; shwrs inc; el pnts
SEK45; lndtte; shop; snacks; cooking facs; playgrnd; sand
beach 500m; games rm; wifi; entmnt; 60% statics; dogs; poss
cr; Eng spkn; adv bkg; quiet. "Christian-run site; church & bible
classes; alcohol discouraged; OK for those of like mind." ◆
SEK 290                                                                   2009*

**HAMBURGSUND** 2E2 (1km S Coastal) 58.54075, 11.28240
**Rorviks Camping, Rorviksangen 15 45747 Hamburgsund
[05 25 33 573; info@rorvikscamping.se; www.
rorvikscamping.se]** Take exit 103 on the E6 (bet Tatum
V-Munkedal). Foll 163 W to Kville. Turn L to Hamburgsund,
cont S 1km. Campsite on R. Lge, mkd pitch, hdstg, pt shd; wc;
chem disp; mv service pnt; fam bthrm; shwr (5kr); el pnts (10A)
inc; lndtte (inc dryer); shop; BBQ; cooking facs; games area;
entmnt; 10% statics; dogs; bus 1km; twin axles; Eng spkn;
adv bkg; CCI. "Quiet, low key site in a great area; vg." 1 May-
31 Aug.  SEK 350                                          2014*

⊞ **HAMMARSTRAND** 1C3 (1km E Rural) 63.12030, 16.34330
**Hammarstrands Camping (Z6), Koppelhällsvägen 18,
84070 Hammarstrand [(0696) 10302; info@goragunda.
com; www.goragunda.com]** Exit rd 87 N twd Hammarstrand
onto rd 323. Cross rv bdge & take 1st R & 1st R again; site
along gravel track in 1km. Sm, pt shd; wc; chem disp; shwrs;
el pnts (10A) SEK30; lndtte (inc dryer); shop 1km; tradsmn;
rest, snacks; bar; cooking facs; playgrnd; htd pool; sand beach
200m; games area; wifi; TV; some statics; dogs free; bus 1km;
Eng spkn; adv bkg; quiet; ccard acc; red long stay; CKE/CCI.
"Pleasant Dutch owners; gd site with basic, clean facs; views
across rv; ideal NH." ♦ ltd SEK 150                      2011*

⊞ **HAPARANDA** 1D2 (15km N Rural) 65.9620, 24.0378
**Kukkolaforsen Camping (BD27), Kukkolaforsen 184,
95391 Haparanda [(0922) 31000; fax 31030; info@
kukkolaforsen.se; www.kukkolaforsen.se]** On rd 99 on
banks of Rv Tornionjoki. Med, pt shd; htd wc; chem disp; baby
facs; sauna; shwrs inc; el pnts (10A) SEK40; lndtte; shop; rest,
snacks; bar; playgrnd; fishing; cycle hire; TV; statics; phone; adv
bkg; ccard acc; CKE. "Friendly staff; rv rapids." SEK 210  2010*

**HARNOSAND** 1C3 (2.5km NE Coastal) 62.64451, 17.97123
**Sälstens Camping (Y21), Sälsten 22, 87133 Härnösand
[tel/fax (0611) 18150; salsten.camping@telia.com]** On Gulf
of Bothnia, E of town & on S side of inlet; exit off E4; foll sp for
Härnösand town cent, then intn'l camping sp; then site. Sm,
mkd pitch, terr, pt shd; htd wc; chem disp; shwrs inc; el pnts
(10A) SEK30; lndtte (inc dryer); shop; playgrnd; beach; wifi; TV;
Eng spkn; quiet; CKE. "Folk museum in town; excl site." ♦ ltd
15 May-31 Aug.  SEK 220                                   2014*

⊞ **HARNOSAND** 1C3 (8km SW Rural) 62.58648, 17.79083
**Antjärns Camping & Stugby (Y28), Antjärn 113, 87191
Härnösand [(0611) 74150; contact@antjarnscamping.
com; www.antjarnscamping.com]** Fr E4 approx 30km N of
Sundsvall, turn R at Antjärns & site sp, site on R in 300m. Sm,
pt sl, unshd; htd wc; chem disp; sauna; shwrs inc; el pnts (10A)
SEK25; lake sw; fishing; wifi; sat TV; dogs; adv bkg; some rd
noise; ccard acc; CKE/CCI. "Beautiful lakeside setting; lovely
town; pleasant owners; immac, modern facs." SEK 160  2009*

**HEBERG see Falkenberg** 2E3

⊞ **HEDE** 2B3 (10km E Rural) 62.40899, 13.67394
**Sonfjällscampen, Hedeviken 753, 84093 Hede [tel/
fax (0684) 12130; info@sonfjallscampen.se; www.
sonfjallscampen.se]** Sp in vill of Hedivikens S of rd 84 on
lakeside. Sm, pt shd; htd wc; chem disp; shwrs; el pnts (10A)
SEK30; lndtte; shops adj; sand beach; fishing; boat hire;
60% statics; adv bkg; quiet; red facs low ssn; ccard acc; CKE.
"Pleasant stay; helpful owner; gd facs; conv Sånfjallet National
Park." SEK 130                                           2009*

**HEDESUNDA** 2G1 (5km SE Rural) 60.35000, 17.02100
**Sandsnäs Camping, Övägen 68, 81040 Hedesunda [tel/
fax (0291) 44123; info@hedesundacamping.se; www.
hedesundacamping.se]** Exit rd 67 L at sp Hedesunda. Foll
camp sp thro Hedesunda; past church, cont about 4km to
Hedesunda Island. Sm, pt shd; htd wc; chem disp; shwrs inc; el
pnts (6A) SEK30; gas; lndtte (inc dryer); shop 3km; rest, snacks;
cooking facs; playgrnd; sand beach & lake sw adj; boat hire;
fishing; TV; poss cr at w/end; Eng spkn; quiet; red 16+ days;
CKE. "Peaceful, lakeside site; organised activities in ssn; helpful
staff." ♦ 15 Apr-15 Nov.  SEK 175                        2010*

**HEDEVIKEN see Hede** 2B3

⊞ **HELSINGBORG** 2E4 (5km S Coastal) 56.0034, 12.7300
**Campingplatsen Råå Vallar (M3), Kustgatan, 25270 Råå
[(042) 182600; fax 107681; raavallar@nordiccamping.se;
www.nordiccamping.se]** Exit E6 into Helsingborg onto rd
111 to Råå, foll sp to camp. Lge, pt shd; htd wc; baby facs;
sauna; shwrs inc; el pnts (10A) SEK50; gas; lndtte (inc dryer);
shop; rest, snacks; bar; playgrnd; pool; paddling pool; sand
beach; fishing; sports cent 2km; golf 5km; wifi; some statics;
phone; Quickstop o'night facs; poss cr; ccard acc; CKE/CCI.
"Excel, secure site with gd facs; friendly staff; excursions to
Copenhagen via Helsingør or Landskrona; town bus excursions
to King's Summer Palace daily; boat trips to glass works at
Hyllinge." ♦ SEK 368                                     2013*

**HJO** 2F2 (600m N Rural) 58.30986, 14.30311 **Hjo Camping
(R11), Karlsborgsvägen, 54432 Hjo [(0503) 31052; fax
13264; campinghjo@hotmail.com; www.hjocamping.
se]** Sp fr town cent on lakeside. Med, mkd pitch; wc, chem
disp; mv service pnt; baby facs; shwrs inc; el pnts (10A) SEK40;
lndtte (inc dryer); shop; bar; cooking facs; playgrnd; htd pool;
lake adj; fishing; games area; wifi; some statics; Eng spkn;
ccard acc; CKE. "Delightful wooden town; gd." 1 Apr-1 Oct.
SEK 180                                                  2010*

**HOGANAS** 2E4 (8km N Rural) 56.27061, 12.52981 **FirstCamp
Mölle (M1), Kullabergsvägen, 26042 Mölle [(042) 347384;
fax 347729; molle@firstcamp.se; www.firstcamp.se]** Site
is S of Mölle at junc of rds 11 & 111, at foot of Kullaberg. Lge,
pt sl, unshd; htd wc; chem disp; mv service pnt; sauna; shwrs
inc; el pnts (10A) inc; lndtte (inc dryer); shop; rest, snacks; bar;
cooking facs; playgrnd; beach 1.5km; fishing; games area;
walking; golf; wifi; entmnt; 10% statics; dogs; Quickstop
o'night facs; Eng spkn; quiet; ccard acc. "Steep slope to san
facs; Krapperups Castle & park sh walk fr site; excel outdoor
activities." ♦ 1 Feb-14 Nov.  SEK 275                    2010*

**HOGANAS** *2E4* (2km S Coastal) *56.18194, 12.55805*
Camping Lerbergets (M2), Lerbergsvägen 108, 26352
Lerberget [(042) 331400; camping@lerberget.se; www.
lerbergetscamping.se] Exit E20 at junc 33 W to Höganäs,
then turn S along coast rd. Site in 2km bef Viken. Med, shd;
wc; chem disp; mv service pnt; baby facs; shwrs inc; el pnts
SEK45; gas; lndtte (inc dryer); shop, rest 1km; playgrnd; sand
beach adj; cycle hire; internet; 80% statics; bus adj; Eng spkn;
quiet; ccard acc; CKE/CCI. "Lovely coast; access to site by
phoning for code to open box with gate-opener (same code for
shwr); gd." ◆ 1 Apr-25 Sep. SEK 200                    2009*

**HOVA** *2chr(160)F2* (6 NE) *58.90998, 14.28995* **Otterbergets
Bad & Camping**, 548 91 Hova [050633 127; info@
otterbergetscamping.com; www.otterbergetscamping.
com] Fr Laxa take E20 rd; site sp approx 4km fr Hova; drive
2 km thro woods to site. Med, mkd pitch, pt shd; wc; chem
disp; baby facs; shwrs (metered); el pnts (10A) SEK 40; lndtte;
snacks; BBQ; playgrnd; sauna; beach adj; 10% statics; poss cr;
Eng spkn; adv bking; quiet; red low ssn. "Attractive site with
private access to lake; events held such as fishing competition
& trade fairs (when site may be busy); v helpful Dutch owners."
◆ 01 May-30 Sep. SEK 190                    2011*

⊞ **HOVMANTORP** *2G3* (SE Urban) *56.7839, 15.13081*
Gökaskratts Campingplats (G11), Bruksallén, 36051
Hovmantorp [(0478) 40807; fax 40822; jonnan.s@live.
se] On Lake Rottnen S of town. Med, mkd pitch, pt shd; htd
wc; chem disp; baby facs; shwrs; el pnts (10A) inc; lndtte (inc
dryer); shop; rest; playgrnd; lake sw adj; fishing; boating; cycle
hire; wifi; TV; 10% statics; phone; Quickstop o'night facs;
poss cr; quiet; ccard acc; CKE. "Conv rlwy stn for Gothenborg/
Kalmar." ◆ SEK 200                    2011*

**HULT** *2G3* (1km N Rural) *57.65583, 15.12435* **Movänta
Camping (F14)**, Badvägen 4, 57592 Hult [(0381) 30028;
fax 30166; info@movantacamping.se; www.
movantacamping.se] Fr Eksjö rd 33 E to Hult, turn L into
vill, foll sp to lakeside. Med, mkd pitch, some hdstg, pt shd;
htd wc; chem disp; mv service pnt; baby facs; shwrs; el pnts
(10A) SEK40; lndtte (inc dryer); shop; snacks; bar; playgrnd;
lake sw adj; fishing; sailing; wifi; TV; some statics; dogs;
phone; Quickstop o'night facs; Eng spkn; quiet; ccard acc;
CKE. "Conv Eksjö & Skurugata canyon." ◆ 29 Apr-25 Sep.
SEK 185                    2011*

⊞ **JARNA** *2H2* (2km E Coastal) *59.09801, 17.64825*
Farstanäs Camping, Farsta 1, 15391 Järna
[(08551) 50215; fax 50650; info@farstanashf.se; www.
vatterledenscamping.se] Exit E4 junc 141 for Järna, E
fr m'way site sp past filling stn about 6km fr exit. Lge, pt sl, pt
shd; wc; mv service pnt; baby facs; shwrs; el pnts (10A) SEK40;
lndtte; shop; rest; snacks; bar; playgrnd; pool; sand beach &
sw; fishing; boat hire; 25% statics; dogs; phone; poss cr; ccard
acc; CKE. "Conv Södertälje & Stockholm on m'way; superb wooded
location." ◆ SEK 250                    2011*

**JOKKMOKK** *1C2* (3km SE Rural) *66.59453, 19.89145*
Jokkmokk Camping Center (BD4), Notudden, 96222
Jokkmokk [(0971) 12370; fax 12476; campingcenter@
jokkmokk.com; www.jokkmokkcampingcenter.com] Sp
fr rd 45. In Jokkmokk take rd 97 E, site in 3km on N side of
rd situated bet rv & rd. Lge, mkd pitch, pt shd; htd wc; chem
disp; mv service pnt; sauna; shwrs inc; el pnts (10A) SEK40
(poss rev pol); lndtte (inc dryer); sm shop & 3km; rest, snacks;
bar; playgrnd; 3 htd pools high ssn; waterslide; lake sw adj;
fishing; cycle hire; internet; some statics; dogs; Eng spkn; adv
bkg; ccard acc; quiet; CKE. "Friendly, clean, well-maintained
site 5km inside Arctic Circle; gd area for Sami culture; excel
playgrnd; lakeside setting, gd pool." ◆ 20 May-31 Aug.
SEK 195                    2011*

⊞ **JONKOPING** *2F3* (2.5km E Urban) *57.7876, 14.2195*
Swecamp Villa Björkhagen (F6), Friggagatan 31,
55454 Jönköping [(036) 122863; fax 126687; info@
villabjorkhagen.se; www.villabjorkhagen.se] Fr N exit
E4 junc 99 or fr S exit E4 junc 98a & foll sp Rosenlund/Elmia
& site sp nr exhibition cent. Site on Lake Vättern. Lge, mkd
pitch, pt sl, pt shd; htd wc; chem disp; mv service pnt; baby
facs; sauna; shwrs inc; el pnts (10A) SEK35; lndtte (inc dryer)
shop; rest; bar; playgrnd; htd, covrd pool complex, waterslide
300m; lake sw 500m; fishing; cycle hire; wifi; entmnt; sat TV;
50% statics; dogs; phone; Quickstop o'night facs; poss v cr;
quiet; ccard acc; CKE. "Gd rest; prone to flooding after heavy
rain; some facs run down & site untidy (2010); site charges
increase considerably during exhibitions & site v full; pitches
well mkd; easy walk into town along sea front." ◆ SEK 265
(CChq acc)                    2014*

**JONKOPING** *2F3* (12km S Rural) *57.66245, 14.18407*
Lovsjöbadens Camping (F7), Hyltena, 55592 Jönköping
[(036) 182010; info@lovsjocamping.se; www.
lovsjocamping.se] Exit E4 at Hyltena, site sp on lakeside. Sm,
mkd pitch, terr, pt sl; wc; chem disp; baby facs; shwrs inc;
el pnts (10-16A) SEK30; lndtte (inc dryer); tradsmn; snacks;
BBQ; cooking facs; lake sw; boat & cycle hire; games rm;
wifi; TV; some statics; dogs; Eng spkn; adv bkg; quiet; ccard
acc; CKE. "V friendly owners; vg site." ◆ 14 May-12 Sep.
SEK 190                    2011*

**KALMAR** *2G3* (2km S Coastal) *56.64975, 16.32705*
Stensö Camping (H12), Stensövägen, 39247 Kalmar
[(0480) 88803; fax 420476; info@stensocamping.se; www.
stensocamping.se] Fr E22 foll sp Sjukhus (hosp) then camping
sp - this avoids town cent. Fr town cent, site sp. Lge, some
mkd pitch, pt sl, shd; wc; chem disp; mv service pnt; baby facs;
shwrs inc; el pnts (10A) SEK40 (check pol); lndtte (inc dryer);
shop; tradsmn; rest; snacks; bar; cooking facs; playgrnd; pool
1km; sand beach adj; fishing; boating; cycling; wifi; some
statics; phone; Quickstop o'night facs; Eng spkn; ccard acc;
CKE. "Conv Öland Island (over bdge); glass factories in vicinity;
walking dist to town; helpful, friendly staff; new clean san facs
(2014); excel." ◆ 27 Mar-30 Sep. SEK 264                    2014*

**SWEDEN**

**KARESUANDO** *1B3* (2km SE Rural) *68.43396, 22.51577*
Karesuando Camping, Laestadiusvagen 185, 98016
Karesuando [(0981) 20139; fax 20381; karesuando.
camping@hotmail.com; www.karesuando.se/foretag/
camping/camping.htm] Travelling N on E45, in town cont
past bdge to Finland onto rd 99 for approx 2km; site on L. App
fr Finland, turn L after x-ing bdge; cont on 99 for 2km. Sm,
unshd; wc; chem disp; mv service point; sauna; shwrs; el pnts
(10A) inc; lndry; cafe; snacks; BBQ; playgrnd; rv adj; games
area; 50% statics; dogs; twin axles; poss cr; Eng spkn; adv
bkg; quiet; CKE/CCI. "Model Sami vill on site; cash point in PO;
poss mosquito prob; canoe hire avail; gd view of midnight sun
on rv; unmkd pitches, fills up quickly." ◆ ltd 15 May-15 Sep.
SEK 200                                                      2014*

**KARLSBORG** *2F2* (1km N Rural) *58.5453, 14.50075*
Karlsborgs Camping (R12), Norra Vägen 3,
54633 Karlsborg [(0505) 44916; fax 44912; info@
karlsborgscamping.se; www.karlsborgscamping.se]
Heading N on rd 49 300m N of Göta canal on L of rd on Lake
Bottensjö. Med, shd; wc; chem disp; mv service pnt; baby facs;
shwrs SEK5; el pnts (10A) SEK40; gas; lndtte (inc dryer); shops
adj; rest, snacks; bar; cooking facs; playgrnd; sand beach on
lake; fishing; boating; wifi; TV; dogs; phone; poss noisy at w/
end; ccard acc; CKE. "Gd touring base in beautiful location; gd
fishing." ◆ 24 Apr-30 Sep. SEK 180                           2010*

**KARLSHAMN** *2F4* (3km SE Coastal) *56.15953, 14.89085*
Kolleviks Camping (K7), Kolleviksvägen, 37430 Karlshamn
[(0454) 19280; fax 16280; kollevik@karlshamn.se; www.
karlshamn.se] Fr E22 dir Karlshamn & Hamnar (harbour), then
site well sp. Med, mkd pitch, pt sl, pt shd; htd wc; chem disp;
mv service pnt; baby facs; shwrs SEK5; el pnts (10A) SEK45;
lndtte (inc dryer); shop; rest, snacks; playgrnd; pool 1km; sand
beach adj; canoeing; 25% statics; Quickstop o'night facs; Eng
spkn; adv bkg; quiet; ccard acc; red long stay/low ssn; CKE.
"Helpful owner; attractive location inc harbour; gd base for
area; ltd facs low ssn; well-kept site; Facs tired, poss stretched
when busy." ◆ 26 Apr-14 Sep. SEK 155                         2012*

**KARLSKRONA** *2G4* (4km N Coastal) *56.20158, 15.60546*
Skönstaviks Camping (K12), Ronnebyvägen,
37191 Karlskrona [(0455) 23700; fax 23792; info@
skonstavikcamping.se; www.skonstavikcamping.se] Rd
15/E22 fr Malmö, camp sp on app to Karskrona. Lge, pt sl,
pt shd; htd wc; chem disp; mv service pnt; baby facs; shwrs;
el pnts (10A) SEK45; lndtte; rest, snacks; bar; shop; playgrnd;
sm sand beach; cycle hire; fishing; boating; wifi; entmnt; TV;
10% statics; dogs; Quickstop o'night facs; quiet; ccard acc;
CKE. ◆ 1 Apr-31 Aug. SEK 225                                 2011*

**KARLSKRONA** *2G4* (2km NE Coastal) *56.1729, 15.5675*
Dragsö Camping (K10), Dragsövägen 14, 37137
Karlskrona [(0455) 15354; fax 15277; info@dragso.se;
www.dragsocamping.se] Foll app to town cent, taking
m'way. At end of m'way foll sp to Dragsö. Site sp - on its own
island. Lge, mkd pitch, pt shd; htd wc; mv service pnt; baby
facs; sauna; shwrs; el pnts (10A) inc; lndtte (inc dryer); kiosk;
supmkt, rest 3km; snacks; bar; playgrnd; beach adj; fishing;
boating; cycle hire; wifi; entmnt; TV rm; some statics; dogs;
Quickstop o'night facs; poss v cr; CKE. "Sea bathing; rocky
cliffs; scenic beauty; gd." ◆ 1Apr-10 Oct. SEK 323          2013*

⊞ **KARLSTAD** *2F1* (6km W Rural) *59.37428, 13.38958* **First
Camp Karlstad-Skutberget (S10), Skutbergsvägen, 65346
Karlstad [(054) 535120; fax 535121; karlstad@firstcamp.se;
www.firstcamp.se]** Sp 1km S of E18, on Lake Vänern, also sp
on rd 61 fr N. Lge, unshd; htd wc; mv service pnt; baby facs;
sauna; shwrs; el pnts (10A); lndtte (inc dryer); shop; rest adj;
snacks; bar; BBQ; cooking facs; playgrnd; sand & shgl beach
500m; fishing; sailing; cycle hire; fitness rm; sport facs adj; wifi;
TV; dogs; Quickstop o'night facs; quiet; CKE. ◆        2011*

⊞ **KARLSTAD** *2F1* (9km W Rural) *59.36233, 13.35891*
Swecamp Bomstad-Badens (S9), Bomstadsvägen 640,
65346 Karlstad [(054) 535068; fax 535375; info@bomstad-
baden.se; www.bomstadbaden.se] Fr E18 on Lake
Vänern. Foll sp thro woods. Lge, pt sl, shd; wc; chem disp; mv
service pnt; baby facs; shwrs SEK10; el pnts (10A) SEK50; lndtte
(inc dryer); shop; supmkt 4km; snacks; bar; BBQ; playgrnd;
pool; sand beach; lake sw; fishing; canoeing; cycle hire; wifi;
entmnt; statics; phone; adv bkg; CKE. "Excel base; beautiful
site in trees; gd walks on mkd trails." ◆ SEK 290           2013*

⊞ **KATRINEHOLM** *2G2* (2km S Rural) *58.9696, 16.21035*
Djulöbadets Camping (D6), Djulögatan 51, 64192
Katrineholm [tel/fax (0150) 57242; djulocamping@
hotmail.com; www.djulocamping.se] At Norrköping on E4
cont twd Stockholm for about 3km, turn L onto rd 55 N twd
Katrineholm. Camping site sp in 2km. Lge, hdstg, pt sl; wc; mv
service pnt; baby facs; shwrs SEK1; el pnts (10A) SEK35; gas;
lndtte (inc dryer); shop 2km; rest 2km; snacks; playgrnd; lake
sw; boating; fishing; games area; cycle hire; wifi; poss cr; adv
bkg; quiet; ccard acc; CKE. "On lakeside in lge park; well-run,
friendly site." ◆ SEK 140                                    2009*

⊞ **KIL** *2F1* (6km N Rural) *59.54603, 13.34145* **Frykenbadens
Camping (S17), Stubberud, 66591 Kil [(0554) 40940;
fax 41010; info@frykenbaden.se; www.frykenbaden.
se]** Fr Karlstad take rd 61 to Kil, site clearly sp on lakeside.
Lge, pt sl, pt shd; wc; chem disp; mv service pnt; baby facs;
sauna SEK5; shwrs; el pnts (10A) SEK40; lndtte (inc dryer);
shop; snacks; bar; playgrnd; lake sw; fishing; boat-launching;
cycle hire; wifi; TV; phone; Quickstop o'night facs; quiet;
adv bkg; CKE. "Very clean, spacious water front site." ◆
SEK 237                                                      2013*

**KINNA** *2E3* (3km SE Rural) *57.47400, 12.70415* **DreamCamp
Hanatorp (P14), Öresjövägen 26, 51131 Örby
[(0320) 48312; fax 49314; info@dreamcamp.se; www.
dreamcamp.se]** 3.2km E of junc rds 41 & 156, site sp 650m
along rd to Öxabäck. Lge, mkd pitch, hdstg, pt shd; wc; chem
disp; mv service pnt; baby facs; shwrs SEK5; el pnts (10A)
SEK40; gas; lndtte (inc dryer); shop; rest, snacks; bar; playgrnd;
htd, covrd pool 8km; lake sw adj; boat & cycle hire; golf 8km;
wifi; TV; 20% statics; dogs; phone; Quickstop o'night facs; adv
bkg; quiet; red long stay; ccard acc; CKE/CCI. "Variable pitch
price; excel." ◆ 21 Apr-18 Sep. SEK 220                      2010*

⊞ **KIRUNA** *1C1* (500m N Urban) *67.8604, 20.2405* **Ripan Hotel & Camping, Campingvägen 5, 98135 Kiruna [(0980) 63000; fax 63040; info@ripan.se; www.ripan.se]** Site sp fr town cent. Med, unshd, mkd pitch, hdstg; htd wc; chem disp; sauna; shwrs SEK20; el pnts (10A) inc; lndtte; shop 500m; rest; bar; playgrnd; htd pool; cab TV; poss cr; quiet; Eng spkn; ccard acc. "No privacy in shwrs; easy walk to town; public footpath thro site (top end) - poss v noisy & disruptive; trips to Kirunavaara Deep Mine fr tourist info office." ♦ SEK 275                                                    2014*

**KLIPPAN** *2F4* (1.5km E Urban) *56.13461, 13.16213* **Elfdalens Camping (L25), Vedbyvägen 69, 26437 Klippan [tel/ fax (0345) 14678; elfdalens.camping@telia.com]** E fr Helsingborg on rd 21. Take E exit to Klippan & foll local sps. Med, pt shd; wc; chem disp; sauna; shwrs inc; el pnts (6A) SEK30; lndtte (inc dryer); shop 300m; snacks; cooking facs; playgrnd; wifi; 5% statics; phone; bus 3km; Eng spkn; quiet; CKE. "Vg, friendly site; gd touring base; gd walking." ♦ 1 Apr-15 Sep.  SEK 130                              2009*

**KOLMARDEN** *2G2* (2km SE Coastal) *58.6597, 16.4006* **First Camp Kolmården (E3), 61834 Kolmården [(011) 398250; fax 397081; kolmarden@firstcamp.se; www.firstcamp.se]** Fr E4 NE fr Norrköping take 1st Kolmården exit sp Kolmården Djur & Naturpark. Site on sea 2km bef Naturpark. Lge, pt terr, pt shd; htd wc; chem disp; mv service pnt; baby facs; sauna; shwrs SEK5; el pnts (10A); lndtte (inc dryer); shop; kiosk; rest, snacks; bar; cooking facs; playgrnd; beach adj; waterslide; boat & cycle hire; entmnt; TV rm; wifi; 10% statics; dogs; phone; ccard acc; CKE. "Gd site; nr to Kilmarden zoo & aquarium; well mkd pitches." ♦ 17 Apr-30 Sep.  SEK 383             2014*

**KUNGALV** *2E2* (1km SE Rural) *57.86211, 11.99613* **Kungälvs Vandrarhem & Camping (O37), Färjevägen 2, 44231 Kungälv [(0303) 18900; fax (303) 19295; info@ kungalvsvandrarhem.se; www.kungalvsvandrarhem.se]** Exit E6 junc 85 or 86 & foll sp Kungälv cent, then sp 'Bohus Fästning'. Site sp. Sm, mkd pitch, some hdstg, shd; htd wc; chem disp; mv service pnt; baby facs; shwrs inc; el pnts (12A) SEK40; lndtte (inc dryer); shop; rest, snacks; bar; gas BBQ; playgrnd; wifi; some statics; dogs; bus adj; Eng spkn; quiet; ccard acc; red long stay; CC1. "Site adj Bonus Fästning (fort) & Kungälv Church (17th C) on rv bank; find pitch & check in at recep 0800-1000 & 1700-1900; door code fr recep for san facs; gd NH." ♦ ltd 15 Apr-30 Sep.  SEK 250       2014*

**KUNGSBACKA** *2E3* (5km SE Rural) *57.42492, 12.15860* **Silverlyckans Camping, Varbersvägen 875, 43433 Fjärås [(0300) 541349; www.silverlyckan.eu]** Exit E6/E20 junc 58 dir Åsa. Site in 400m on L. Med, pt sl, unshd; htd wc; chem disp; mv service pnt (refill only); shwrs SEK5; el pnts (10A) SEK30; lndtte; shop, rest, snacks 3km; cooking facs; playgrnd; htd pool 3km; sand beach 4km; 10% statics; dogs; bus adj; Eng spkn; adv bkg; quiet. "Vg site; rec visit Tjolöholms Slott (castle)." 1 May-15 Sep.  SEK 180                 2014*

**KUNGSHAMN** *2E2* (10km NE Rural/Coastal) *58.37825, 11.33095* **Örns Camping (O67), Håle 2, 45691 Kungshamn [(0523) 34335; fax 34409; kjell.andersson@ornscamping. com; www.ornscamping.com]** Exit E6 junc 101 onto rd 162/171 twd Kungshamn; 7km after Nordens Ark turn L sp Kungshamn S. In 3km turn L twd Bohus Malmön, site on R in approx 2km (thru vill). Lge, mkd pitch, pt shd; wc; chem disp; mv service pnt; baby facs; shwrs SEK5; el pnts SEK50; lndtte (inc dryer); shop; playgrnd; beach adj; wifi; sat TV; statics; dogs; Eng spkn; quiet; ccard acc. "Beautiful area; gd coastal walks, fishing, boating." ♦ ltd 1 May-30 Sep.  SEK 220    2011*

**KVIDINGE see Klippan** *2F4*

**LACKEBY** *2G3* (6km SE Coastal) *56.75718, 16.37700* **Kalmar Camping (H73), Rafshagen 430, 38031 Läckeby [(0480) 60464; fax 60424; info@kalmarcamping.se; www. kalmarcamping.se]** On E22 10km N of Kalmar, turn R approx 500m N of junc with rd 125 to Läckeby & foll sp for Rafshagen & site. Med, mkd pitch, pt sl, pt shd; htd wc; chem disp; mv service pnt; baby facs; shwrs inc; el pnts (10A) SEK40; lndtte (inc dryer); rest, snacks; bar; BBQ; cooking facs; playgrnd; shgl beach adj; fishing; boat hire: games area; TV; some statics; dogs; Eng spkn; quiet; ccard acc. "Gd site; pleasant area; gd cycling area; lakeside site amongst trees, helpful owners, Eng spkn; trips across Oland bdge to island, san facs excel." ♦ 1 Mar-31 Oct.  SEK 210               2011*

**LANDSKRONA** *2E4* (2km N Rural) *55.90098, 12.8042* **Borstahusens Camping (M5), Campingvägen, 26161 Landskrona [(0418) 10837; fax 22042; bengt@ borstahusenscamping.se; www.borstahusenscamping.se]** Exit E6/E20 at 'Landskrona N' & foll sp for Borstahusen 4.5km fr E6/D20. Lge; htd wc; chem disp; shwrs inc; baby facs; el pnts (10A) SEK40; lndtte (inc dryer); shop; snacks 200m; playgrnd; htd pool 2km; tennis; cycle hire; game reserve; golf; wifi; TV rm; 75% statics; phone; poss v cr; ccard acc; CKE/CCI. "Gd pleasant site on edge of Kattegat; sm pitches." ♦ 21 Apr-11 Sep.  SEK 320                                    2014*

**LIDHULT** *2F3* (15km NE Rural) *56.89671, 13.64343* **Lökna Camping & Stugby, Lökna Norregård 8, 34010 Lidhult [(035) 92026; fax 92120; lokna-camping@telia.com; www. loknacamping.com]** Fr rd 25 Ljungby to Halmstad turn N to Odensjö. In Odensjö turn R by church dir Lökna, site in 5km on well-maintained dirt rd, sp. Sm, mkd pitch, hdstg, pt shd; htd wc; chem disp; mv service pnt; sauna; shwrs inc; el pnts (16A) SEK30; lndtte (inc dryer); sm shop; BBQ; cooking facs; playgrnd; lake sw adj; fishing; watersports; some statics; dogs; Eng spkn; adv bkg rec high ssn; quiet; ccard not acc. "Wonderful lake views; excel, relaxing site; no shops nr." 21 Apr-13 Sep.  SEK 200                          2010*

⊞ **LIDKOPING** *2F2* (1km N Rural) *58.51375, 13.14008* **Krono Camping (R3), Läckögaten, 53154 Lidköping [(0510) 26804; fax 21135; info@kronocamping.com; www. kronocamping.com]** On Lake Vänern nr Folkparken, on rd to Läckö; at Lidköping ring rd foll int'l camping sp. Lge, pt shd; serviced pitch; wc; chem disp; mv service pnt; baby facs; some serviced pitches; shwrs inc; el pnts (10A) inc; gas; lndtte (inc dryer); shop; rest 300m; playgrnd; htd pool 300m; lake sw 300m; watersports; wifi; cab TV (via el hook-up); quiet; ccard acc; CKE. "V clean, friendly, well-run site; open pinewoods on lakeside; interesting area." ♦ SEK 360               2009*

**LIMHAMN see Malmo** *2E4*

⊞ **LINKOPING** *2G2* (4km NW Rural) *58.42140, 15.56230*
Glyttinge Camping (E28), Berggårdsvägen 6, 58437
Linköping [(013) 174928; fax 175923; glyttinge@
nordiccamping.se; www.nordiccamping.se] Exit fr E4 sp
Linköping N; foll sp to Centrum & camping sp. Lge, hdg pitch,
pt shd; htd wc; chem disp; mv service pnt; baby facs; fam
bthrm; shwrs inc; el pnts (10A) SEK50; gas; lndtte (inc dryer);
shop; rest; playgrnd; pool adj; cycle hire; fishing; boating;
internet; TV; no statics; Quickstop o'night facs; quiet; ccard
acc; red low ssn; CKE. "Lovely site but inadequate san facs for
size; gd touring base; easy cycle ride to town cent; recep only
mornings only low ssn - no access if arr later than 1pm." ♦
SEK 180                                                    2010*

**LIT** *1B3* (1km E Rural) *63.31928, 14.8651* **Lits Camping/
Little Lake Hill Canoe Centre**, 83030 Lit [(0642) 10247; fax
10103; ove.djurberg@swipnet.se; www.litscamping.com]
On rd 45, sp. Med, pt sl, pt shd; wc; chem disp; mv service pnt;
baby facs; sauna; shwrs inc; el pnts (10A) SEK35; lndtte; shop,
rest 1km; cooking facs; playgrnd; canoeing; fishing; tennis;
cycle hire; wifi; some statics; phone; adv bkg; quiet; ccard acc;
CKE. "Pleasant site, gd alt to cr sites in Östersund high ssn." ♦
29 May-30 Sep.  SEK 155                                    2009*

**LJUNGBY** *2F3* (1km N Urban) *56.84228, 13.95251* **Ljungby
Camping Park**, Campingvägen 1, 34134 Ljungby [tel/
fax (0372) 10350; reservation@ljungby-semesterby.se;
www.ljungby-semesterby.se] Exit E4 at Ljungby N, site sp.
Med, shd; htd wc; chem disp; shwrs inc; el pnts (10A) SEK35;
lndtte (inc dryer); shop; rest (Jun-Aug); playgrnd; htd pool
adj; paddling pool; cycling; poss cr in ssn; ccard acc; CKE.
"Adv bkg ess high ssn; NH only rec low ssn." 1 May-31 Aug.
SEK 215                                                    2009*

**LJUNGBY** *2F3* (14km NW Rural) *56.90406, 13.77996*
SweCamp Sjön Bolmen Camping (G27), Bolmstad Mjälen,
34196 Ljungby [(0372) 92051; fax 92351; swecamp@
bolmencamping.se] Exit E4 at sp Ljungby N, turn L at top of
slip rd & 1st L over E4 sp Ljungby. Foll sp to Bolmsö & site sp
to Sjön Bolmen. Med, mkd pitch, pt shd; htd wc; chem disp;
mv service pnt; baby facs; shwrs inc; el pnts (10A) SEK40;
lndtte; shop; tradsmn; rest; playgrnd; lake sw fr pontoon;
boating; games area; cycle hire; TV; 5% statics; dogs; phone;
poss cr; Eng spkn; quiet; ccard acc; CKE. ♦ 1 Jun-31 Aug.
SEK 210                                                    2011*

⊞ **LJUSDAL** *1B3* (3km W Rural) *61.83894, 16.04059*
Ljusdals Camping (X21), Ramsjövägen 56, 82730
Ljusdal [(0651) 12958; info@ljusdalscamping.se; www.
ljusdalscamping.se] Leave Ljusdal on Rv83 dir Ånge, site on R
in 3km. Med, pt shd; htd wc; chem disp; mv service pnt; sauna;
shwrs inc; el pnts (10A) SEK40; lndtte (inc dryer); tradsmn;
rest, snacks; bar; cooking facs; playgrnd; lake sw & beach adj;
games area; cycle hire; wifi; entmnt; some statics; dogs; Eng
spkn; adv bkg; ccard acc; CKE. ♦ SEK 255            2014*

**LODERUP** *2F4* (5km S Coastal) *55.38181, 14.12795*
Löderups Strandbad Camping (M12), Östanvägen,
27645 Löderup [(0411) 526311; fax 526613; www.
loderupsstrandbadscamping.se] Rd 9 fr Ystad, after
Nybrostrand turn R sp Kaseberga, site sp. Lge, mkd pitch, pt
shd; wc; chem disp; baby facs; shwrs SEK10; el pnts SEK40;
lndtte (inc dryer); shop 400m; rest 1km; snacks nr; playgrnd;
sand beach adj; TV; 50% statics; dogs; phone; quiet; poss cr;
Eng spkn; ccard acc; CKE. "Site in dunes adj nature reserve;
facs poss stretched high ssn; uneven grnd; gd birdwatching,
rambling; nr historical sites." ♦ ltd 21 Apr-27 Sep.
SEK 180                                                    2009*

**LOMMA see Malmö** *2E4*

**LOTTORP (OLAND ISLAND)** *2G3* (3km N Coastal)
*57.17876, 17.03746* **Sonjas Camping (H39)**, John Emils
Gata 43, 38074 Löttorp [(0485) 23212; fax 23255;
info@sonjascamping.se; www.sonjascamping.oland.
com] Fr Kalmar over bdge to Öland Island, take rd 136 N
thro Borgholm. Cont to Löttorp, site sp. Lge, mkd pitch,
pt shd; htd wc; chem disp; mv service pnt; fam bthrm;
baby facs; sauna; shwrs SEK5; el pnts (10A) SEK45; lndtte
(inc dryer); shop; rest, snacks; bar; cooking facs; playgrnd;
htd pool; paddling pool; sand beach adj; fishing; tennis;
cycle hire; wifi; entmnt; 10% statics; adv bkg; quiet. CKE.
"Vg beach; excel family site; vg touring base." ♦ 21 Apr-
4 Oct.  SEK 250 (6 persons)                                2010*

⊞ **LULEA** *1D2* (8km W Coastal) *65.59565, 22.07221*
First Camp Luleå (BD18), Arcusvägen 110, 97594 Luleå
[(0920) 60300; fax 60315; lulea@firstcamp.se; www.
firstcamp.se/lulea] Exit E4 on R 500m N of Luleälv Rv bdge.
Foll sp 'Arcus' (recreation complex). V lge, mkd pitch, pt shd;
htd wc; chem disp; mv service pnt; baby facs; sauna; shwrs inc;
el pnts (10A) inc; lndtte (inc dryer); shop; tradsmn; rest, snacks;
bar; cooking facs; playgrnd; htd pool complex 700m; sand
beach adj; tennis 300m; cycle hire; wifi; TV; dogs; phone; car
wash; Eng spkn; adv bkg; quiet; ccard acc; CKE. "Excel family
site; many sports facs; san facs poss stretched high ssn; suitable
RVs & twin-axles; adj rlwy museum." ♦ SEK 365        2014*

⊞ **MALMO** *2E4* (7km SW Urban) *55.5722, 12.90686*
Malmö Camping & Feriesenter (M8), Strandgatan
101, Sibbarp, 21611 Limhamn [(040) 155165; fax
159777; malmocamping@malmo.se; www.malmo.se/
malmocamping] Fr Öresund Bdge take 1st exit & foll sp
Limhamn & Sibbarp, then int'l campsite sp. Fr N on E6 round
Malmö until last exit bef bdge (sp), then as above. Fr Dragør-
Limnhamn ferry turn R on exit dock. Site in 1km on R, nr sea,
in park-like setting. V lge, pt sl, pt shd; htd wc; chem disp;
mv service pnt; baby facs; shwrs inc; el pnts (10A) inc (poss
rev pol); gas; lndtte (inc dryer); shops; rest, snacks; cooking
facs; playgrnd; pool 400m; sand beach 250m; windsurfing;
cycle hire; wifi; TV rm; phone; bus to Malmo; poss cr; no adv
bkg; quiet; ccard acc; CKE. "Easy cycle to town cent; facs poss
stretched high ssn; v busy city site; well-laid out but poss long
walk to san facs; conv Öresund Bdge." ♦ SEK 290      2010*

⊞ **MALUNG** *2F1* (1km W Rural) *60.68296, 13.70243*
**Malungs Camping (W22), Bullsjövägen, 78200 Malung
[(0280) 18650; fax 18615; campingen@malung.se; www.
malungscamping.se]** Fr Stöllet take rd 45 to Malung, site sp.
Lge, pt shd; htd wc; chem disp; baby facs; shwrs inc; el pnts
(10A) SEK40; lndtte (inc dryer); shop; snacks; playgrnd; pool;
fishing; boating; cycle hire; internet; TV; car wash; Quickstop
o'night facs; quiet; ccard acc; CKE. ♦ SEK 160      2009*

⊞ **MARIESTAD** *2F2* (2km NW Rural) *58.7154, 13.79516*
**Ekuddens Camping (R2), 54245 Mariestad [(0501) 10637;
fax 18601; andreas.appelgren@mariestad.se/ekudden@
nordiccamping.se; www.ekuddenscamping.se]** Fr E20 take
turn off twd Mariestad. At 1st rndabt foll ring rd clockwise
until site sp on Lake Vänern. Lge, shd; wc; mv service pnt;
sauna; shwrs inc; el pnts (10A) SEK40; gas; lndtte (inc dryer);
shop; rest; bar; playgrnd; htd pool; beach; golf 2km; cycle
hire; dogs; phone; Quickstop o'night facs; ccard acc; CKE. "Gd
views fr lakeside pitches; friendly, helpful staff; gd san facs." ♦
SEK 294      2014*

**MARKARYD** *2F3* (500m N Urban) *56.46475, 13.60066*
**Camping Park Sjötorpet (G4), Strandvägen 4, 28531
Markaryd [(0433) 10316; fax 12391; reservation@
sjotorpet-roc.se; www.sjotorpet-roc.se]** E4 fr Helsingborg
(ferry) site is bet E4 N turn to Markaryd & rd 117, sp. Narr app.
Sm, pt sl, pt shd; htd wc; shwrs inc; chem disp; mv service pnt;
baby facs; el pnts (10A) SEK40; lndtte (inc dryer); shop; rest,
snacks; bar; cooking facs; playgrnd; lake sw; fishing; boating;
cycle hire; wifi; some statics; dogs; phone; poss cr; play gnd;
quiet; ccard acc; CKE. "Excel san & cooking facs; well-run site;
helpful staff." ♦ 1 Apr-31 Oct. SEK 210      2011*

**MARSTRAND** *2E2* (1.5km NE Coastal) *57.89380, 11.60510*
**Marstrands Camping (036), Långedalsvägen 16,
44030 Marstrand [(0303) 60584; fax 60440; info@
marstrandcamping.se; www.marstrandscamping.se]** Exit
A6 dir Kungsälv/Marstrand & foll rd 168 to Marstrand. Site
sp on Koön Island. App rd to site v narr. Med, pt sl, pt shd;
htd wc; chem disp; mv service pnt; baby facs; shwrs; el pnts
(10A) SEK45; lndtte; shop; cooking facs; playgrnd; shgl beach;
wifi; TV; 50% statics; dogs; poss v cr; adv bkg; quiet; ccard
acc; CKE. "Ferry to Marstrand Island." ♦ 16 Apr-25 Sep.
SEK 225      2011*

**MELLBODA (OLAND ISLAND)** *2G3* (500m E Coastal)
*57.23891, 17.0698* **Böda Hamns Camping (H43),
Bödahamnsvägen 42, 38074 Mellböda [(0485) 22043;
fax 22457; info@bodahamnsmetup.se; www.
bodahamnsmetup.se]** N fr Borgholm for 52km on rte 136
twd Mellböda & Böda, turn R twd Böda Hamn, site nr harbour.
Lge, mkd pitch, pt shd; chem disp; mv service pnt; shwrs; el
pnts (10A) SEK40; lndtte (inc dryer); shop; rest, snacks; bar;
BBQ; cooking facs; playgrnd; sand beach adj; games area;
wifi; some statics; dogs free; phone; Eng spkn; quiet; ccard
acc. "Sep area of beach for dogs; vg site." ♦ 29 Apr-3 Oct.
SEK 160      2010*

**MELLBYSTRAND** *2E3* (1km N Coastal/Urban) *56.51961,
12.94628* **Marias Camping (N18), Norra Strandvägen 1,
312 60 Mellbystrand [(0430) 28585; fax 27321; info@
mariascamping.se; www.mariascamping.se]** 20km N of
Båstad, exit junc 41 fr E6 W onto rd 24, site sp off coast rd N.
Lge, hdg/mkd pitch, pt shd; htd wc; chem disp (wc); mv service
pnt; baby facs; shwrs; el pnts inc; lndtte (inc dryer); shop; rest,
snacks; bar; cooking facs; playgrnd; sand beach adj; games rm;
internet; TV; dogs; bus 500m; Eng spkn; adv bkg; quiet; CKE.
"Vg site beside dunes; beautiful beach." ♦ ltd 21 Apr-26 Aug.
SEK 320      2013*

⊞ **MELLERUD** *2E2* (4km SE Coastal) *58.68933, 12.51711*
**Mellerud SweCamp Vita Sandar (P13), 46421 Mellerud
[(0530) 12260; fax 12934; mail@vitasandarscamping.
se; www.vitasandarscamping.se]** Fr S on rd 45
take Dalslandsgatan Rd on R & foll sp. Fr N turn L twd
Sunnanåhamn, Vita Sandar. Med, pt shd; htd wc; chem disp;
mv service pnt; sauna; shwrs SEK5; baby facs; el pnts (10A)
SEK50; lndtte (inc dryer); shop; rest, snacks; bar; cooking facs;
playgrnd; htd pool; waterslides; sand beach & lake sw; boat &
cycle hire; fishing; tennis; games area; wifi; TV rm; 20% statics;
dogs; Quickstop o'night facs; poss cr; quiet; ccard acc; red low
ssn; CKE/CCI. "Pleasant family site in pine trees; excel sw." ♦
SEK 420      2013*

# "That's changed – Should I let The Club know?"

If you find something on site that's different from
the site entry, fill in a report and let us know. See
www.caravanclub.co.uk/europereport.

**MELLERUD** *2E2* (2km W Rural) *58.71288, 12.43231* **Kerstins
Camping (P21), Hålsungebyn 1, 46494 Mellerud [tel/
fax (0530) 12715; epost@kerstinscamping.se; www.
kerstinscamping.se]** Fr Mellerud on rd 166 dir Bäckefors &
Ed, site sp. Sm, pt shd; htd wc (cont); chem disp; mv service
pnt; baby facs; shwrs inc; el pnts (10A) SEK45; lndtte (inc
dryer); shop; BBQ; cooking facs; playgrnd; games rm; TV rm;
some statics; dogs; phone; Eng spkn; adv bkg; quiet; CKE.
"Pleasant area; excel." ♦ 3 May-26 Aug. SEK 175      2011*

**MOLLE see Höganäs** *2E4*

**MOLNDAL see Göteborg** *2E3*

⊞ **MORA** *1B4* (500m N Urban) *61.00853, 14.53178*
**Mora Parkens Camping, Parkvägen 1, 79231 Mora
[(0250) 27600; fax 12785; info@moraparken.se; www.
moraparken.se]** Fr SW site sp on rd 45. Or foll sp in town
cent; site in 400m. Recep in adj hotel. Lge, mkd pitch, pt sl, pt
shd; htd wc; chem disp; mv service pnt; baby facs; shwrs inc;
el pnts (10A) SEK; lndtte (inc dryer); shops 500m; rest 300m;
covrd, htd pool; paddling pol; waterslide; fishing; sports facs;
games rm; TV; wifi; some statics; Quickstop o'night facs; Eng
spkn; no adv bkg; quiet; ccard acc; CKE. "Excel site; ltd facs
low ssn & poss unclean; suitable RVs & twin-axles; conv for
bear sanctuary at Orsa." ♦ SEK 165      2009*

**SWEDEN**

**MORBYLANGA (OLAND ISLAND)** *2G3* (1km N Coastal) *56.52163, 16.37725* **Mörbylånga Camping, Kalvhagen 1, 38062 Mörbylånga [tel/fax (0485) 40591; info@ morbylangacamping.se; www.morbylangacamping.se]** Site sp off rd 136 in Mörbylånga. Med, unshd; wc; chem disp; mv service pnt; baby facs; shwrs inc; el pnts SEK40; lndtte; shop; rest, snacks; bar; cooking facs; sand beach adj; fishing; games area; cycle hire; sat TV; some statics; dogs; phone; Eng spkn; red low ssn; ccard acc; CKE. "Pleasant, relaxing, family-run site with open view; unusual & interesting island." ◆ 15 May-1 Oct. SEK 190                2009*

**NJURUNDABOMMEN** *1C3* (5km E Coastal) *62.26828, 17.45181* **Bergafjärdens Camping & Havsbad (Y29), Bergafjärden, 86286 Njurundabommen [(060) 34598; fax 34841; info@bergafjarden.nu; www.bergafjarden.nu]** Clearly sp on E4 at Njurundabommen. Lge, shd; wc; chem disp; mv service pnt; baby facs; shwrs SEK5; el pnts (6A) SEK40; lndtte (inc dryer); shop; snacks; bar; playgrnd; sand beach; lake sw; cycle hire; wifi; TV; some statics; dogs; phone; quiet; ccard acc; CKE. ◆ 9 May-18 Sep. SEK 180               2011*

**NORA** *2G1* (1km N Rural) *59.52576, 15.04386* **Trängbo Camping (T1), 713280 Nora [(0587) 12361; fax 311389; info@trangbocamping.se; www.trangbocamping.se]** Site sp fr sq in cent of town, on rd 244 fr Hällefors to Örebro. Med, pt sl, pt shd; htd wc; chem disp; mv service pnt; baby facs; shwrs; el pnts (10A) SEK35; lndtte (inc dryer); shop & 1km; playgrnd; lake sw; boating; fishing; nature trails; cycle hire; games area; wifi; some statics; ccard acc; quiet; CKE. ◆ 1 May-30 Sep. SEK 190                2011*

**NORA** *2G1* (3km N Rural) *59.5342, 15.0405* **Gustavsberg Camping (Naturist), NF Bergslagens Solsport, 71322 Nora [(073) 6425282; info@gustavsbergscamping.com; www.gustavsbergscamping.com]** Fr Örebro take rd N to Nora, site sp fr Nora cent past Trängbo Camping, just outside vill limits on R. Sm, mkd pitch, pt shd; htd wc; chem disp; fam bthrm; sauna; shwrs inc; el pnts (10A) SEK35; lndtte; shop, rest, snacks, bar 3km; BBQ; cooking facs; playgrnd; lake sw adj; fishing; games area; TV rm; 20% statics; dogs; phone; Eng spkn; adv bkg; quiet; ccard acc; red for INF cardholders. "Gd family site; all facs unisex; many preserved buildings & antique shops in Nora." ◆ 1 Jun-31 Aug. SEK 145                2009*

⊞ **NORDMALING** *1C3* (200m W Rural/Coastal) *63.57546, 19.45881* **SweCamp Rödviken (AC43), Rödviksvägen 93, 91431 Nordmaling [tel/fax (0930) 31250; info@ rundviksrederi.se]** Site off E4, well sp. Med, unshd; wc; chem disp; mv service pnt; shwrs inc; el pnts (16A) SEK45; lndtte (inc dryer); shop; rest; snacks adj; bar; cooking facs; playgrnd; htd pool; paddling pool; sand beach; rv fishing; sports & ice rink adj; cycle hire; some statics; dogs; Quickstop o'night facs; quiet; ccard acc; CKE. ◆ SEK 170                2009*

**NORRFJARDEN** *1D2* (8km SE Rural/Coastal) *65.35521, 21.58571* **Borgaruddens Camping (BD31), Borgaruddsvägen, 94521 Norrfjärden [(0911) 203518; borgarudden.nif@telia.com]** Site on E side of E4. Med, mkd pitch, htd wc; chem disp; mv service pnt; baby facs; shwrs inc; el pnts (10A) SEK40; lndtte (inc dryer); snacks; cooking facs; playgrnd; pool; shgl beach adj; wifi; 10% statics; phone; Eng spkn; quiet; ccard acc; CKE. "Conv unique parish vills Luleå, Piteå & Skellefteå." ◆ 1 Jun-31 Aug. SEK 170                2011*

**NORRKOPING** *2G2* (2km W Urban) *58.59138, 16.14080* **Himmelstalunds Camping (E4), Utställningsvägen, 60234 Norrköping [(011) 171190; fax 170987; info@ norrkopingscamping.com; www.norrkopingscamping. com]** Exit Norrköping S fr E4, foll sp sports cent & site. Lge, pt sl, pt shd; htd wc; chem disp; mv service pnt; baby facs; serviced pitches; shwrs inc; el pnts (10A) SEK40; lndtte (dryer); shop; snacks; cooking facs; playgrnd; htd pool & sports facs 200m; cycle hire; wifi; TV; 10% statics; phone; quiet; ccard acc; CKE. ◆ 15 Apr-15 Oct.  SEK 160               2009*

**NOSSEBRO** *2E2* (500m N Urban) *58.19195, 12.72161* **Nossebrobadets Camping (R22), Marknadsgatan 4, 46530 Nossebro [(0512) 57043; fax 57042; info@nossebrobadet. se; www.nossebrobadet.se]** N fr Alingsås on E20; exit N to Nossebro, site in 16km. Clearly sp. Sm, pt sl, unshd; wc; mv service pnt; sauna; shwrs; el pnts inc; lndtte (inc dryer); shop 500m; playgrnd; 2 pools (1 covrd); fishing; boat hire; sports grnd adj; cycle hire; some statics; dogs; quiet. "Vg NH; stream thro site." ◆ 25 Apr-31 Aug.  SEK 200               2013*

**NYKOPING** *2G2* (8km SE Coastal) *58.71970, 17.09182* **Strandstuvikens Bad & Camping (D10), 61192 Nyköping [tel/fax (0155) 97810; lilian@bissarna.se; www. strandstuvikencamping.com]** On E4 dir Nyköping foll sp town cent then 'Hamnen' (harbour) & turn R onto rd 53 sp Arno. In approx 3km turn L onto minor rd & foll site sp. Med, mkd pitch, pt shd; htd wc; chem disp; mv service pnt; baby facs; fam bthrm; el pnt (10A) SEK50; lndtte; shop; snacks; cooking facs; playgrnd; sand beach adj; TV; some statics; Eng spkn; quiet; CKE/CCI. "Gd site; gd walking, cycling." ◆ 1 May-15 Sep.  SEK 150               2009*

⊞ **NYNASHAMN** *2H2* (1km NW Coastal) *58.90717, 17.93805* **Nicksta Camping (B8), Nickstabadsvägen 17, 14943 Nynäshamn [(08) 52012780; fax 52015317; info@ nickstacamping.se; www.nickstacamping.se]** Fr Stockholm on Rv 73 to Nynäshamn. Foll site sp, turning R at ICA supmkt, then immed L (sp poss cov'rd by hedge.) Med, pt shd; htd wc; chem disp; mv service pnt; baby facs; shwrs inc; el pnts (10A) SEK50; lndtte (inc dryer); shop 700m; snacks; cooking facs; playgrnd; beach adj; waterslide; games area; cycle hire; wifi; some statics; dogs; train 600m; site clsd mid-Dec to mid-Jan; Quickstop o'night facs; Eng spkn; CKE. "Gd site; ferries to Gotland & Poland." ◆  SEK 165               2009*

**OREBRO** *2G2* (1km S Rural) *59.2554, 15.18955* **Gustavsviks Camping (T2), Sommarrovägen, 70229 Örebro [(019) 196950; fax 196961; camping@gustavsvik.com; www.gustavsvik.com]** Foll sp fr E18/E20 & rd 51 to site. V lge, mkd pitch, pt sl, pt shd; htd wc; chem disp; some serviced pitches; mv service pnt; baby facs; fam bthrm; shwrs inc; el pnts (10A) SEK80 inc sat TV (poss rev pol); gas; lndtte (inc dryer); shop; kiosk; rest, snacks; bar; BBQ; cooking facs; playgrnd; 2 pools (1 htd, covrd); waterslide; paddling pool; lake sw & beach adj; golf nr; gym; solarium; wifi; entmnt; cab TV; 10% statics; dogs; phone; bus; Eng spkn; quiet; ccard acc; CKE. "Excel family site; superb facs; gentle stroll to town; v highly rec." ◆ 15 Apr-6 Nov.  SEK 295               2010*

You can now fill in site reports online

⊞ **ORSA** 1B4 (1km W Rural) 61.12090, 14.59890
Orsa SweCamp (W3), Timmervägen 1, 79421 Orsa
[(0250) 46200; fax 46260; info@orsagronklitt.se; www.
orsacamping.se] Sp fr town cent & fr rd 45. V lge, pt shd;
htd wc; shwrs inc; baby facs; sauna; el pnts (10A) SEK50; mv
service pnt; lndtte (inc dryer); shops 500m; rest; bar; cooking
facs; playgrnd; 4 htd pools high ssn; waterslide; sand beach &
lake sw; fishing; canoe & cycle hire; tennis; wifi; entmnt; sat
TV; 5% statics; phone; quiet; CKE. "Excel countryside; bear
reserve 15km; gd general facs but ltd low ssn." ◆ SEK 215
(CChq acc)                                                    2010*

**OSKARSHAMN** 2G3 (3km SE Coastal) 57.2517, 16.49206
Gunnarsö Camping (H7), Östersjövägen 103, 57263
Oskarshamn [tel/fax (0491) 13298; gunnarso@
oskarshamn.se; www.oskarshamn.se] Fr E22 dir
Oskarshamn, site sp on Kalmar Sound. Med, pt shd; htd wc;
chem disp; mv service pnt; baby facs; sauna; shwrs SEK5; el
pnts (10A) SEK35; lndtte (inc dryer); shop; snacks; playgrnd;
2 pools; watersports; wifi; TV; 40% statics; dogs; phone;
adv bkg; quiet; ccard acc; CKE. "Beautiful location; many
pitches with gd views; gd walking/cycling." ◆ 1 May-18 Sep.
SEK 175                                                       2009*

## "I like to fill in the reports as I travel from site to site"
You'll find report forms at the back of this guide, or you can fill them in online at www.caravanclub.co.uk/europereport.

**OSTERFARNEBO** 2G1 (1.5km S Rural) 60.29937, 16.80614
Färnebofjärdens Camping, Berreksvägen 19, 46291
Österfärnebo [0736 505334 (mob); farnebocamping@
hotmail.com; www.farnebocamping.se] Fr rd 67 turn W
at Gysinge onto rd 272 dir Österfärnebo. In 5km turn L sp By
at football grnd, site in 2km, sp. Med, mkd pitch, unshd; wc;
shwrs; el pnts (10A) SEK40; lndtte; lake sw; fishing; boat hire;
20% statics; quiet. "Pleasant site; conv National Park." 1 Jun-
30 Sep. SEK 130                                               2010*

⊞ **OSTERSUND** 2B3 (3km S Rural) 63.15955, 14.6731
Östersunds Camping (Z11), Krondikesvägen
95, 83146 Östersund [(063) 144615; fax 144323;
ostersundscamping@ostersund.se; www.ostersund.se] At
Odensala on lakeside, well sp fr E14. Lge, mkd pitch; pt sl; htd
wc; chem disp; mv service pnt; baby facs; sauna; shwrs SEK5;
el pnts (10A) SEK50 (poss rev pol); lndtte (inc dryer); shop; rest;
bar; cooking facs; playgrnd; pool; paddling pool; tennis; wifi;
cab TV; 80% statics; dogs; phone; poss cr; ccard acc; CKE.
CKE. "Gd NH; v helpful staff." ◆ SEK 278          2013*

⊞ **PAJALA** 1D1 (1.5km SE Rural) 67.20381, 23.4084 Pajala
Camping (BD8), Tannavägen 65, 98431 Pajala [tel/fax
(0978) 74180; pajalacamping@gmail.com] Site sp fr rd 99.
Med, mkd pitch, hdstg, pt shd; htd wc; chem disp; mv service
pnt; baby facs; sauna; shwrs inc; el pnts (10A) SEK30; lndtte
(inc dryer); shop; snacks; cooking facs; playgrnd; tennis; cycle
hire; wifi; TV rm; dogs; bus 1.5km; Eng spkn; adv bkg; quiet;
ccard acc; red long stay; CKE. "Clean, well-presented site;
delightful owner; salmon-fishing in rv in ssn (mid-Jun approx)."
◆ SEK 190                                                     2011*

**RAMVIK** 1C3 (1km S Rural) 62.79911, 17.86931 Snibbens
Camping (Y19), Snibben 139, 87016 Ramvik [tel/fax
(0612) 40505; info@snibbenscamping.com; www.
snibbenscamping.com] Fr E4 15km N of Härnösand;
after high bdge sighted take slip rd dir Kramfors; site sp in
2.5km on L just bef Ramvik. Med, mkd pitch, pt sl, pt shd; htd
wc; chem disp; mv service pnt; baby facs; shwrs inc; el pnts
(16A) SEK20; lndtte (inc dryer); shop 1km; rest, snacks; bar;
cooking facs; playgrnd; lake sw & beach adj; fishing; boat hire;
wifi; TV rm; some statics; bus; poss cr; Eng spkn; quiet; ccard
acc; CKE. "Helpful owners; delightful site with lakeside setting;
v peaceful even when busy; spotless facs & lovely camp kitchen
with seating areas inside & out; conv Höga Kusten suspension
bdge; delightful site in beautiful surroundings." ◆ 6 May-
11 Sep. SEK 212.00                                            2013*

⊞ **RATTVIK** 1B4 (1km N Rural) 60.89103, 15.13115
Enåbadets Camping (W7), Enåbadsvägen 8, 79532 Rättvik
[(0248) 56111; fax 12660; info@enan.se; www.enan.se]
Site sp on N o'skts of town fr Tourist Info board, on rd 70.
Lge, shd; wc; chem disp; mv service pnt; serviced pitches; baby
facs; sauna; shwrs inc; el pnts (10A) SEK50; lndtte (inc dryer);
shop; rest, snacks; bar; cooking facs; playgrnd; pool; lake adj;
wifi; entmnt; TV; 10% statics; phone; poss cr; quiet; ccard acc;
CKE. "Gd base for touring potteries & local vills; wooded." ◆
SEK 190                                                       2010*

**RATTVIK** 1B4 (500m W Rural) 60.88891, 15.10881
Siljansbadets Camping (W8), Långbryggevägen 4, 79532
Rättvik [(0248) 51618; fax 51689; camp@siljansbadet.com;
www.siljansbadet.com] Fr S on rd 70 thro Rättvik. Immed
outside town turn L at rndabt, site sp on Lake Siljan. Height
restriction 3.5m. V lge, mkd pitch, pt shd; wc; chem disp; baby
facs; shwrs inc; el pnts (10A) SEK50; lndtte (inc dryer); shop
& 500m; rest & 500m; bar; cooking facs; playgrnd; lake sw &
sand beach; boat hire; wifi; TV rm; 15% statics; dogs; bus/train;
poss cr; Eng spkn; quiet; ccard acc. "Lovely scenic location;
conv town cent." ◆ 21 Apr-10 Oct. SEK 185          2009*

**RORBACK** 1D2 (Coastal) 65.80030, 22.59516 Rörbäcks
Camping & Havsbad (BD79), Rörbäck 79, 95592 Råneå
[tel/fax (0924) 35047; info@rorbackscamping.se] Off E4
approx 10km SW of junc with E10, at Jämtöfjärden foll sp S to
coast, site well sp. Sm, mkd pitch, hdstg, pt shd; htd wc; chem
disp; serviced pitches; sauna; shwrs inc; baby facs; el pnts (10A)
inc; lndtte; rest, snacks; BBQ; cooking facs; playgrnd; sand
beach adj; fishing; canoe hire; TV; phone; poss cr; Eng spkn;
adv bkg; ccard acc; CKE. "Cosy, clean site on water's edge in a
wood; vg facs." ◆ 1 Jun-31 Aug. SEK 200          2009*

SWEDEN

**SWEDEN**

**ROSTANGA** 2F4 (500m SW Rural) 55.99656, 13.28050
Röstånga Camping (M20), Blinkarpsvägen 3,
26024 Röstånga [(0435) 91064; fax 91652; info@
rostangacamping.se; www.rostangacamping.se] Site sp
in Röstånga along rd 108. Med, pt shd; htd wc; chem disp; mv
service pnt; fam bthrm; baby facs; private san facs avail; shwrs
inc; el pnts (10A) SEK40; lndtte (inc dryer); shop high ssn; rest
300m; snacks; bar; BBQ; cooking facs; htd pool; paddling pool;
waterslide; lake fishing; canoeing; tennis; games area; games
rm; wifi; entmnt; TV rm; 15% statics; dogs; Eng spkn; adv
bkg; quiet; ccard acc; CKE. "Pleasant family site; some pitches
by stream; superb pool; conv Söderåsens National Park." ♦
21 Apr-2 Oct.  SEK 220                              2010*

**ROXENBADEN** 2G2 (S Rural) 58.54135, 15.62292 **Sandviks
Camping, Stjärnorp, 59078 Roxenbaden [tel/fax
(013) 61470; sandvik@caravanclub.se]** Fr E4 Jönköping to
Linköping turn onto rd 36 & foll sp Göta Canal, Berg. Site sp in
Berg & is 3km E of Stjärnorp. Med, mkd pitch, terr, pt shd; wc;
chem disp; shwrs inc; el pnts (10A) SEK50; lndtte (inc dryer);
shop; playgrnd; lake sw & sand/shgl beach adj; 30% statics;
dogs; phone; bus at gate; Eng spkn; quiet; ccard acc; CKE/
CCI. "Well-kept, relaxing site; interesting area; gd walks." ♦
15 Apr-15 Sep.  SEK 180                             2010*

**RYD see Urshult** 2F3

⊞ **SAFFLE** 2F2 (6km S Rural) 59.08326, 12.88616 **Duse Udde
Camping (S11), 66180 Säffle [(0533) 42000; fax 42002;
duseudde@krokstad.se; www.duseudde.se]** Site sp fr rd
45. Med, pt sl, shd; wc; mv service pnt; baby facs; sauna; shwrs
SEK10; el pnts (10A) SEK50; lndtte (inc dryer); shop; rest high
ssn; snacks; bar; playgrnd; watersports; pool 6km; beach; lake
sw; cycle hire; wifi; entmnt; bus; 20% statics; phone; dogs;
Quickstop o'night facs; quiet; ccard acc; red long stay; CKE.
"Place to relax; useful base for Värmland area with nature
walks." ♦ SEK 180                                  2010*

**SALA** 2G1 (6km N Rural) 59.95473, 16.5168 **Silvköparens
Camping (U2), Gamla Riksväg 70, 73397 Sala [tel/fax
(0224) 59003; silvkoparen@caravanclub.se; www.sala.se]**
Site on rd 70 bet Sala & Avesta, sp. Med, pt shd; htd wc; chem
disp; shwrs inc; el pnts (10A); lndtte (inc dryer); shop adj &
6km; snacks; playgrnd; lake sw adj; boating; canoeing; cycling;
TV; some statics; dogs; phone; poss cr; Eng spkn; quiet; ccard
acc; CKE. "Sala silver mine & museum; Sätra Brunn spa; lovely
situation." ♦ 30 Apr-18 Sep.  SEK 205              2011*

**SANDARNE see Söderhamn** 1C4

⊞ **SARNA** 1B3 (1km S Rural) 61.69281, 13.14696
**Särna Camping (W32), Särnavägen 6, 79090 Särna
[(0253) 10851; fax 32055; camping@sarnacamping.se;
www.sarnacamping.se]** Turn R off rd 70 opp fire stn. Med,
terr, pt shd; wc; chem disp; mv service pnt; sauna; shwrs
SEK5; el pnts (10A) SEK35; lndtte (inc dryer); shop, rest, snacks
200m; playgrnd; shgl beach; cycle hire; poss cr; adv bkg;
quiet. "Beautiful setting o'looking lake; pleasant town." ♦
SEK 160                                            2010*

⊞ **SIMRISHAMN** 2F4 (2km N Coastal) 55.57021, 14.33611
**Tobisviks Camping (L14), Tobisvägen, 27294 Simrishamn
[(0414) 412778; fax 412771; hakan@fritidosterlen.se;
www.fritidosterlen.se]** By sea at N app to town. Lge, pt
shd; wc; chem disp; mv service pnt; shwrs SEK1/min; el pnts
(10A) SEK50; lndtte (inc dryer); shop 400m; rest 2km; htd pool;
watersports; TV; phone; ccard acc; CKE. SEK 210       2010*

**SKANOR** 2E4 (2km SE Coastal) 55.39750, 12.86555 **Ljungens
Camping (M9), Strandbadsvägen, 23942 Falsterbo
[(040) 471132; fax 470955; camping@telia.com; www.
mamut.net/ljungenscamping]** Fr E6/E22 exit to W sp
Höllviken onto rd 100. Foll sp Skanör/Falsterbo. Site sp on L
at rndabt at ent to town, dir Falsterbo. Lge, mkd pitch, some
hdstg, pt shd; htd wc; chem disp; mv service pnt; baby facs;
shwrs SEK5; el pnts (10A) SEK40; lndtte (inc dryer); shop;
snacks high ssn; BBQ; cooking facs; playgrnd; sand beach
200m; wifi; TV; 50% statics; dogs; bus; Eng spkn; no adv bkg;
aircraft noise (under flight path Copenhagen airport) ccard
acc; CKE. "Conv Viking Vill museum; nature reserve adj; gd
birdwatching, cycling; vg." ♦ 1 Mayr-1 Oct.  SEK 220  2011*

**SKARHOLMEN see Stockholm** 2H2

⊞ **SKELLEFTEA** 1C2 (1.5km N Rural) 64.76156, 20.97513
**Skellefteå Camping (AC18), Mossgaten, 93170 Skellefteå
[(0910) 735500; fax 701890; skellefteacamping@
skelleftea.se; www.skelleftea.se/skellefteacamping/]** Turn
W off E4; well sp behind g'ge. Also sp as Camping Stugby.
Lge, mkd pitch, pt sl, unshd; htd wc; chem disp; mv service pnt;
sauna; shwrs inc; el pnts (10A) SEK60; lndtte (inc dryer); shop;
rest, snacks 100m; bar 1km; BBQ; cooking facs; playgrnd; htd
pool; waterslide; sand beach 5km; fishing; tennis 150m; cycle
hire; games area; wifi; TV rm; 10% statics; dogs; phone; poss
cr; Eng spkn; quiet; ccard acc; CKE. "Friendly, clean site in pine
trees on sheltered inlet; lge pitches suitable RVs & twin-axles;
Nordanå Cultural Cent & Bonnstan Church Vill in walking dist;
if site clsd book in at Statoil stn 500m S on E4 at rndabt. Exc
san facs, lgr camp kitchen, helpful staff, lge supmkt nrby." ♦
SEK 230                                            2011*

**SKELLEFTEA** 1C2 (7km NE Coastal) 64.77681, 21.11993
**Bovikens Havsbad Camping (AC60), 93140 Skellefteå [tel/
fax (0910) 54000; cecilia@bovikenshavsbad.se; www.
bovikenscamping.se]** Site sp off E4, site in 5km. Med, mkd
pitch, pt shd; wc; chem disp; baby facs; shwrs inc; el pnts;
lndtte (inc dryer); snacks; playgrnd; sand beach adj; tennis
nr; TV rm; some statics; dogs; poss cr; Eng spkn; adv bkg;
quiet; ccard acc; CKE. "Gd family site by secluded beach;
friendly owner; excel birdwatching; avoid shwr cubicles
with elec heaters nr floor level; v nice!" ♦ 16 May-14 Sep.
SEK 360                                            2014*

**SLAGNAS** 1C2 (SE Urban) 65.58458, 18.17284
**Slagnäsforsens Camping, Campingvägen 5, 93091 Slagnäs
[tel/fax (0960) 650093; info@slagnascamping.com; www.
slagnascamping.com]** On rd 45 bet Sorsele & Arvidsjaur,
nr bdge over Skellefteälvan. Sm, pt sl, unshd; wc; chem disp;
sauna; shwrs inc; el pnts (10A) inc; lndtte; shop; rest 700m;
cooking facs; playgrnd; dogs; no adv bkg; quiet; CKE. "Gd."
1 May-30 Sep.  SEK 150                             2009*

**SODERALA see Söderhamn** 1C4

SODERHAMN *1C4* (10km SE Coastal) *61.24843,*
*17.19506* Stenö Havsbad Camping (X9), Stenövägen,
82022 Sandarne [(0270) 60000; fax 60005; steno@
nordiccamping.se; www.nordiccamping.se] Exit E4 at sp
Bollnäs-Sandarne (S of Söderhamn turn), foll sp Sandarne at
Östansjö, turn L at camping sp. Lge, shd; wc; chem disp; baby
facs; mv service pnt; shwrs inc; el pnts (10A) SEK50; lndtte
(inc dryer); shop; rest, snacks; bar; cooking facs; playgrnd;
pool 12km; sand beach; games area; wifi; TV rm; some statics;
phone; bus; poss cr; adv bkg; quiet; ccard acc; CKE. "Adj
nature reserve." ♦ 1 May-31 Oct. SEK 150          2009*

⊞ SODERHAMN *1C4* (10km W Rural) *61.29318, 16.8266*
Moheds Camping (X6), Mohedsvägen 59, 82692 Söderala
[(0270) 425233; fax 425326; info@mohedscamping.se;
www.mohedscamping.se] Take Söderhamn exit fr E4 onto
rd 50 twds Bollnäs; site sp after approx 10km. Med, hdstg,
pt sl, pt shd; wc; chem disp; mv service pnt; sauna; shwrs
SEK5; baby facs; el pnts (10A) SEK35; lndtte (inc dryer); shop;
tradsmn; snacks; bar; playgrnd; pool; lake beach, fishing,
boating & sw adj; tennis; cycling; wifi; TV; many statics; phone;
poss cr; Eng spkn; adv bkg; quiet; ccard acc; CKE. "Skydiving in
nrby airfield; attractive coastline; sh walk to bus to town; busy
site." ♦ SEK 165          2011*

SODERKOPING *2G2* (1km N Rural) *58.49163, 16.30618*
Skeppsdockans Camping (E34), Dockan 1, 61421
Söderköping [(0121) 21630; korskullenscamp@hotmail.
com; www.soderkopingscamping.se] On E22 immed N of
canal bdge. Sm, mkd pitch, unshd; htd wc; shwrs inc; el pnts
SEK40; lndtte (inc dryer); rest & shops 1km; cooking facs; canal
sw; cycle hire; TV; Eng spkn; quiet; ccard acc; CKE. "On side
of Gota Canal with constant boating traffic, but peaceful." ♦
30 Apr-2 Oct. SEK 200          2013*

SODERKOPING *2G2* (SE Urban) *58.4770, 16.33471*
Korskullen Camping (E17), Skönbergagaten 50, 61421
Söderköping [(0121) 21621; korskullencamp@hotmail.
com] On E22 in town cent. Sm, hdg pitch, pt shd; wc; chem
disp; shwrs; el pnts SEK40; lndtte (inc dryer); shop adj; rest;
bar; playgrnd; TV; some statics; dogs; Eng spkn; quiet but some
rd noise; ccard acc; CKE. "Well-maintained san facs." 6 May-
18 Sep. SEK 180          2011*

SOLLENTUNA see Stockholm *2H2*

SOLLERON See Gesunda *1B4*

⊞ SORSELE *1C2* (400m W Rural) *65.53428, 17.52663*
Sorsele Camping (AC21), Fritidsvägen, Näset, 92070
Sorsele [(0952) 10124; fax 10625; info@lapplandskatan.
nu; www.lapplandskatan.nu] N on rd 45/363 fr Storuman to
Arvidsjaur. In Sorsele vill turn W for 500m; site sp. Med, unshd;
htd wc; chem disp; baby facs; shwrs; el pnts (16A) SEK35;
lndtte (inc dryer); shop 200m; playgrnd; pool; beach; canoeing;
fishing; hiking; cycle hire; wifi; TV; some statics; dogs; phone;
poss cr; quiet; ccard acc; CKE. "Nature reserve; interesting
ancient Lapp vill; friendly, welcoming; attractive site." ♦
SEK 183          2014*

STENKALLEGARDEN see Bocksjö *2F2*

STOCKEN *2chr(160)E2* (700m S) *58.14786, 11.42143*
Stocken Camping, 101, 474 92 Ellös [0304 511 00; info@
stocken.nu; www.stocken.nu] Foll rd 160 (sp Orust); at
Varekil turn L onto rd 178 (sp Ellös); in approx 15km turn L
(sp Stocken) & foll sp to site (on L just bef vill). Lge, mkd pitch,
pt sl, unshd; wc; chem disp; MV service pnt; baby facs; shwrs
metered; el pnts (10-16A) metered; lndtte; shop; rest, snacks;
bar; BBQ; playgrnd; beach 500m; games area; games rm; TV;
20% statics; dogs; bus adj; adv bking; quiet; cc acc; red long
stay. "Beautiful coastline; gd walks; vg site." 09 Apr-02 Oct.
SEK 285          2011*

⊞ STOCKHOLM *2H2* (15km N Rural) *59.43821, 17.99223*
Rösjöbadens Camping (B1), Lomvägen 100, 19256
Sollentuna [(08) 962184; fax 929195; info@rosjobaden.
se; www.rosjobaden.se] Take E18 m'way N fr Stockholm, sp
Norrtälje. Pass Morby Centrum on L after 7km. Take Sollentuna
exit, turn L & foll Sollentuna rd 265/262 for approx 5km. At
2nd set of traff lts with pylons adj, turn R on sm rd, clear sp
to site. Lge, pt sl, pt shd; wc; chem disp; mv service pnt; baby
facs; shwrs SEK10; el pnts (10A) SEK45; lndtte (inc dryer);
shops; snacks; playgrnd; fishing; boating; lake sw fr pontoons;
sat TV; some statics; dogs; bus; Quickstop o'night facs; Eng
spkn; quiet; CKE. "Conv Morby Centrum, lge shopping cent,
petrol, metro to city; pleasant walks in woods & lakeside." ♦
SEK 215          2011*

STOCKHOLM *2H2* (10km SW Rural) *59.29558, 17.92300*
Bredäng Camping (A4), Stora Sällskapetväg, 12731
Skärholmen [(08) 977071; fax 7087262; bredangcamping@
telia.com; www.bredangcamping.se] Exit E4/E20 to
Bredäng junc 152 & foll sp to site. Lge, mkd/hdstg pitch
nr ent otherwise grass/unmkd, pt shd; htd wc; chem disp;
serviced pitches; mv service pnt; baby facs; sauna; shwrs inc;
el pnts (16A) SEK40; lndtte; rest, snacks; bar; cooking
facs; playgrnd; lake & beach adj; cycle hire; battery-charging;
metro 700m; Quickstop o'night facs; poss cr; quiet; ccard acc;
red snr citizens/low ssn; "Facs ltd low ssn & poss stretched in
ssn; helpful staff; overspill 3km at Sätra Camping; conv for
Stockholm; shopping cent & metro with free car park about
700m; access to Stockholm also poss by lake steamer fr pier
(high ssn) - 10 min walk; well-run site." ♦ 28 Mar-6 Oct.
SEK 325          2014*

STOCKHOLM *2H2* (2.5km W Urban) *59.32021,*
*18.03198* Långholmens Motorcaravan Park (A11),
Skutskepparvägen, 11733 Stockholm [(08) 6691890; info@
autocamper-stockholm.se; www.autocamper-stockholm.
se] Fr N foll sp Södermalm fr E4. Immed after x-ing Västerbron
(bdge) foll 'Autocamper' sp. Site under S end of bdge. Fr S foll
sp Södermalm, then sp Långholmen S & site. Med, mkd pitch,
hdstg, unshd; wc; chem disp; mv service pnt; shwrs inc; el pnts
(10A) SEK30; lndtte (inc dryer); rest, bar, shop 300m; cycle hire;
TV; adv bkg; Eng spkn; recep open 0700-2200; m'vans only;
security fence; constant rd noise; ccard acc; CKE. "Site under
flyover but conv city cent." 27 May-4 Sep. SEK 190          2009*

⊞ **STOCKHOLM** *2H2* (10km W Rural) *59.33731, 17.90105*
Ängby Campingplats (A3), Blackebergsvägen 25,
16850 Bromma [(08) 370420; fax 378226; reservation@
angbycamping.se; www.angbycamping.se] On E4
fr Stockholm take rd 275 W twd Vällingby. At rndabt turn L
for rd 261 dir Ekerö, then R sp Sodra Ängby, site sp. Med,
mkd pitch, pt sl, pt shd; wc; chem disp; mv service pnt; sauna;
shwrs SEK5; baby facs; el pnts SEK35; lndtte (inc dryer); shop;
rest, snacks; bar; sand beach & lake sw adj; waterslide; tennis;
wifi; cab TV; some statics; dogs; phone; train; poss v cr; Eng
spkn; ltd facs low ssn; ccard acc; CKE/CCI. "Sh walk to metro
stn - 20 mins to city; gd situation; walk/cycle to Drottningsholm
Palace; some sm pitches; poss diff pitching for lge o'fits; lack
of privacy in shwrs; san facs stretched high ssn & need update;
workers living on site; site poss muddy after rain; helpful staff."
♦ SEK 322                                                  2013*

**STODE** *1C3* (200m W Rural) *62.41585, 16.57015* Stöde
Camping (Y39), Kälsta 107, 86013 Stöde [(0691) 10180;
stodecampingstode@hotmail.com; www.stodecamping.
com] Fr S on rd 305 site on L after x-ing rv bdge. Fr Sundsvall
on E14 turn S onto rd 305, site on R after underpass. Sm, mkd
pitch, pt sl, pt shd; htd wc; chem disp; mv service pnt; baby
facs; fam bthrm; el pnts (16A) SEK30; lndtte (inc dryer); shop
500m; snacks; playgrnd; htd pool & sports facs adj; paddling
pool; lake sw adj; fishing; boat hire; tennis; TV rm; some statics;
dogs; phone; Eng spkn; adv bkg; quiet; red long stay; CKE/CCI.
"Well-kept, friendly site." 15 May-30 Oct. SEK 140        2011*

> "We must tell The Club about that great site we found"
> Get your site reports in by mid-August and we'll do our best to get your updates into the next edition.

**STORUMAN** *1C2* (200m NW Rural) *65.10022, 17.11427*
Storumans Camping (AC5), Lokgränd 3, 92331 Storuman
[(0951) 14300; storumanscamping@storuman.se; www.
storuman.se] On Lake Storuman, site sp fr rd 45/E12. Med,
pt shd; wc; chem disp; mv service pnt; sauna; baby facs; shwrs
inc; el pnts (10A) SEK30; lndtte (inc dryer); shop; rest, snacks
200m; playgrnd; lake sw & beach adj; watersports; boat hire;
tennis; cycle hire; TV; quiet; ccard acc; CKE. "Ltd facs low ssn."
♦ 1 Apr-30 Sep. SEK 165                                    2011*

⊞ **STROMSTAD** *2E2* (3km S Coastal) *58.91350, 11.20531*
Camping Lagunen (O3), Skärsbygdsvägen 40, 45297
Strömstad [(0526) 755000; fax 12367; info@lagunen.se;
www.lagunen.se] On Uddevalla rd 176 out of Strömstad. Site
on L. Lge, pt sl, pt shd; wc; mv service pnt; baby facs; shwrs;
el pnts inc; lndtte (inc dryer); shop; rest, snacks; bar; cooking
facs; playgrnd; beach adj; boat & cycle hire; wifi; TV rm; some
statics; dogs; poss cr; adv bkg; quiet; ccard acc; red low ssn.
SEK 280                                                    2013*

⊞ **STROMSTAD** *2E2* (5km S Coastal) *58.9039, 11.20011*
Daftö Feriecenter (O4), Dafter 2511, 45297 Strömstad
[(0526) 26040; fax 26250; info@dafto.com; www.
dafto.com] Fr Uddevalla E6 exit at sp Strömstad, turn L at
sp approx 6km on R. Fr Oslo exit E6 sp Strömstad; foll ring
rd 176 round E side town; foll sp Daftö; site on R. V lge, pt
sl, pt shd; wc; mv service pnt; some serviced pitches; baby
facs; sauna; shwrs inc; el pnts (10A) SEK50; lndtte (inc dryer);
shop; rest, snacks high ssn; bar; cooking facs; playgrnd; htd
pool; sand beach; lake sw; boating; canoeing; fishing; games
area; wifi; entmnt; 15% statics; Quickstop o'night facs; site
clsd Xmas to 8 Jan; poss cr; adv bkg ess in ssn; quiet; ccard
acc; CKE. "Holiday complex with many children's activities;
busy at w/end; quiet during wk; views fr some pitches."
♦ SEK 425 (5 persons)                                      2010*

**STROMSTAD** *2E2* (12km S Coastal) *58.8832, 11.14253*
Bofors Camping (O62), Korsnäs Tjärnö 2821, 45296
Strömstad [(0526) 25036; birgittathyft@hotmail.com;
www.boforscamping.com] Fr S exit E6 L at sp Strömstad;
after 5km turn L at sp Tjarnö 7km (pass Camp Daftö on R);
after 5km turn R at sp Befors Camping 2; site on L. Fr N exit
E6 R of Strömstad; foll as above. Lge, mkd pitch, pt sl, pt shd;
wc; chem disp; shwrs SEK5; el pnts (10A) SEK35; lndtte (inc
dryer); shop; sand beach adj; fishing; boat-launching facs;
wifi; 60% statics; dogs; Eng spkn; adv bkg; quiet; ccard acc.
"Attractive rocky coast with sandy bays; v busy - rec adv bkg."
1 May-15 Sep. SEK 245                                       2011*

**STROMSTAD** *2E2* (4km NW Coastal) *58.95741, 11.14763*
Seläters Camping (O48), Norrkärr, 45290 Strömstad
[(0526) 12290; fax 12238; info@selater.se; www.selater.
se] Exit E6 at sp Strömstad; foll sps to Seläter; site on R. V lge,
mkd pitch, pt shd; wc; mv service pnt; baby facs; shwrs inc; el
pnts (10A) SEK50; lndtte (inc dryer); shop; rest; playgrnd; beach
800m; watersports; tennis 500m; golf 1km; wifi; 10% statics;
bus; phone; dogs; Quickstop o'night facs; CKE. "Pleasant
countryside; well-run site." ♦ 1 Apr-30 Sep. SEK 250  2010*

⊞ **STROMSUND** *1B3* (1km SW Rural) *63.84651, 15.53378*
Strömsunds Camping (Z3), Näsviken, 83324 Strömsund
[(0670) 16410; fax 13705; turism@stromsund.se/
stromsunds.turistbyra@stromsund.se; www.stromsund.
se/stromsundscamping] W of rd 45, over bdge S of main
town on lakeside. Lge, pt sl, pt shd; htd wc; chem disp; mv
service pnt; baby facs; shwrs SEK5; el pnts (10A) SEK30; lndtte
(inc dryer); shop adj; rest, snacks; cooking facs; playgrnd; pool;
paddling pool; fishing; cycle & boat hire; wifi; 10% statics;
dogs; phone; quiet; cccard acc; CKE. "In 2 parts: W side has
main facs but E quieter; go to g'ge adj when site office clsd."
♦ SEK 223                                                  2014*

**SUNDSVALL** *1C3* (4km SE Urban/Coastal) *62.3585, 17.37016*
Fläsians Camping & Stugor (Y26), Norrstigen 15, 85468
Sundsvall [(060) 554475; fax 569601; bernt.ostling@gmail.
com] Clear sps on E4 in both dirs; site on E coast side of rd.
Med, mkd pitch, terr, pt shd; htd wc; chem disp; mv service
pnt; baby facs; shwrs inc; el pnts (10A) SEK35; lndtte (inc
dryer); shop on site & 2km; rest; cooking facs; playgrnd; sand
beach adj; fishing; poss cr; quiet; adv bkg; Eng spkn; ccard
acc; CKE. "Sea view all pitches; gd access even in wet; suitable
RVs & twin-axles; if recep clsd, site yourself & pay later; helpful
staff; some traff noise; sw pools in Sundsvall; clean san facs."
♦ 15 May-31 Aug. SEK 200                                   2013*

⊞ **SVEG** *1B3* (700m S Rural) *62.03241, 14.36496* **Sveg Camping (Z32), Kyrkogränd 1, 84232 Sveg [(0680) 13025; fax 10337; info@svegscamping.se]** Just S of traff lts at junc rds 45 & 84. Opp Statoil at rear of rest, well sp. Med, mkd pitch, pt shd; htd wc; chem disp; shwrs inc; el pnts (16A) SEK25; lndtte (inc dryer); rest, bar nrby; snacks; playgrnd; pool 500m; cycle hire; games area; TV; some statics; dogs; phone; some rd noise; ccard acc; CKE. "Gd for sh stay/NH; many cabins used as long stay family units." SEK 264            2014*

⊞ **TIMMERNABBEN** *2G3* (1.5km S Rural/Coastal) *56.94405, 16.46708* **Camping Timmernabben, Varvsvägen 29, 38052 Timmernabben [(0499) 23809; fax 23871; timmernabben-camp@telia.com]** Turn off E22, site sp. Med, mkd pitch, pt sl, shd; htd wc; chem disp; baby facs; shwrs; el pnts (10A) inc; lndtte (inc dryer); tradsmn; BBQ; playgrnd; shgl beach adj; tennis; games area; internet; Eng spkn; quiet. CKE/CCI. "Tranquil site; delightful views; gd walking & windsurfing; paths on site not wheelchair-friendly."            2009*

*TIVED 2F2* (2km N Rural) *58.79855, 14.5371* **Camping Tiveden (T24), Baggekärr 2, 69597 Tived [(0584) 474083; fax 474044; info@campingtiveden.com; www. campingtiveden.com]** Fr Karlsborg N on rd 202 to Undernäs. Turn R dir Tived, site on L in 2km. Med, mkd pitch, pt shd; wc; chem disp; mv waste; baby facs; shwrs SEK5; el pnts (10A) SEK40; lndtte (inc dryer); shop 2km; snacks; playgrnd; sand beach 15km; lake sw adj; boat & cycle hire; fishing; dogs; some statics; poss cr; Eng spkn; quiet; CKE/ CCI. "Friendly owners; gd walks; conv Tiveden National Park & Göta Canal; excel." ◆ 1 Apr-30 Sep. SEK 145

180            2011*

*TOMELILLA 2F4* (N Urban) *55.54578, 13.95856* **Väla Camping, Folkets Park, Parkgatan 4, 27380 Tomelilla [(0417) 18110; fax 14400; www.tomelilla.se/en/turism/]** Fr Ystad take rd 19 NE to Tomelilla; foll sp in town cent; recep at sw pool kiosk. Sm, mkd pitch, pt sl, pt shd; wc; chem disp; sauna; shwrs; el pnts (10A) SEK30; lndtte; shop & snacks 500m; BBQ; cooking facs; playgrnd; htd pool adj; some statics; dogs; Eng spkn; quiet; CKE. "Well-situated for historic sites, coastal towns; some traff noise at rush hrs." 1 Jun-1 Sep. SEK 125            2009*

*TOREKOV 2E3* (1km N Coastal) *56.43540, 12.63700* **FirstCamp Båstad (L9), Flymossavägen 5, 26093 Torekov [tel/fax (0431) 364525; torekov@firstcamp.se; www. firstcamp.se]** Exit E6 onto rd 115 & head for Torekov, site on R bef Torekov. Lge, pt sl, pt shd; htd wc; chem disp; mv service pnt; baby facs; fam bthrm; sauna; shwrs inc; el pnts (10A); lndtte (inc dryer); shop; rest, snacks; bar; cooking facs; playgrnd; pool; beach adj; fishing; watersports; cycle hire; games rm; golf; wifi; cab TV; 10% statics; bus 800m; poss v cr high ssn; CKE. "Gd sea fishing; pitches cramped high ssn; Båstad picturesque town." ◆ 15 Apr-25 Sep.            2010*

⊞ **TORSBY** *2F1* (20km N Rural) *60.30529, 13.04200* **Abbas Stugby & Camping, Nötön 1, 68594 Torsby [(0560) 30360; fax 30361; info@abbasstugby.se; www.abbasstugby.se]** N fr Torsby on E45 for approx 20km, turn L after Vägsjöfors at site sp. Sm, pt sl, pt shd; htd wc; chem disp; baby facs; shwrs inc; el pnts (10A) SEK40; lndtte (inc dryer); tradsmn; rest, snacks; bar; BBQ; cooking facs; playgrnd; lake sw adj; games area; cycle & boat hire; wifi; entmnt; some statics; dogs; Eng spkn; adv bkg; quiet; ccard acc; CKE. "Vg site." SEK 160            2009*

*TORSBY 2F1* (5km S Rural) *60.09168, 13.03045* **Torsby Camping Svenneby (S21), Bredviken, 685 33 Torsby [(0560) 71095; info@torsbycamping.se; www. torsbycamping.se]** On shore of Lake Fryken, sp fr rd 45. Med; wc; chem disp; mv service pnt; baby facs; sauna; shwrs SEK5; el pnts (10A) inc; lndtte (inc dryer); shop; rest, snacks; bar; playgrnd; lake sw; watersports; wifi; entmnt; TV; 80% statics; dogs; quiet; red long stay; ccard acc; CKE/CCI. 1 May-15 Sep. SEK 260            2014*

**TORSLANDA see Göteborg** *2E3*

⊞ **TRANAS** *2F2* (3km E Rural) *58.03548, 15.0309* **Hättebadens Camping (F1), Hätte, 57382 Tranås [(0140) 17482; fax 68404; hattebaden@tranas.se; www. hattecamping.se]** On W edge Lake Sommen on rd 131, sp. Med, mkd pitch, pt shd; wc; mv service pnt; baby facs; shwrs; el pnts (10A) SEK40; lndtte (inc dryer); sm shop, rest, snacks adj; bar; playgrnd; lake sw; fishing; boating; cycle hire; wifi; 20% statics; dogs; phone; Quickstop o'night facs; Eng spkn; ccard acc; CKE/CCI. "Generous pitches; spacious site; gd, clean facs." ◆ SEK 180            2009*

⊞ **TRELLEBORG** *2E4* (2.5km E Coastal) *55.3638, 13.20933* **Camping Dalabadet, Dalköpingestrandväg 2, 23132 Trelleborg [(0410) 14905; fax 45068]** Bet sea shore & rd 9 (Trelleborg-Ystad), E of town. Foll sp fr town. Med, shd; htd wc; chem disp; mv service pnt; baby facs; sauna; shwrs inc; el pnts (10A) SEK30; lndtte; shop, rest nr; cooking facs; playgrnd; beach; tennis; cab TV; 20% statics; dogs; phone; ccard acc; CKE. "Conv for ferries; gd." ◆ SEK 200            2009*

**TROLLHATTAN** *2E2* (1km N Urban) *58.29206, 12.29848* **Trollhättans Camping Hjulkvarnelund (P7), Kungsportsvägen 7, 46139 Trollhättan [(0520) 30613; fax 32961; folketspark.trollhattan@telia.com; www. trollhattansfp.se/camping/]** Foll rd 45, site sp adj rv/canal. Med, pt sl, shd; wc; chem disp; mv service pnt; baby facs; shwrs inc; el pnts (10A) SEK40; lndtte (inc dryer); shops 1km; playgrnd; htd pool 300m; tennis; cycles; dogs; poss cr; Eng spkn; no adv bkg; some train & rd noise; CKE. "Access to Trollhätte Canal; beautiful, spacious wooded site; easy walk to town & impressive gorge/waterfall; modern, clean san facs poss stretched high ssn." ◆ 2 May-4 Sep. SEK 150            2011*

⊞ **TROLLHATTAN** *2E2* (5km S Rural) *58.23946, 12.23605* **Stenrösets Camping (P25), Assarebo Stenröset 2, 46198 Trollhättan** [(0520) 70710; fax 70811; stenroset.camping@ telia.com; www.stenrosetscamping.se] Site visible & sp fr rd 45. Sm, sl, pt shd; htd wc (cont); mv service pnt; baby facs; shwrs inc; el pnts (10A) SEK30; lndtte (inc dryer); shop; BBQ; cooking facs; playgrnd; wifi; 5% statics; dogs; phone; quiet; Eng spkn; adv bkg; some rd noise; red long stay; ccard acc; CKE. "Helpful owners; conv Göteborg (60km); scenic surroundings & interesting area." ◆ SEK 170        2009*

**TROSA** *2H2* (3km S Coastal) *58.87288, 17.57431* **Trosa Havsbad Camping (D12), Rävuddsvägen 40, 61922 Trosa** [(0156) 12494; info@trosahavsbad.se; www. trosahavsbad.se] Exit E4 at junc 138 onto rd 218 twd Trosa, site sp dir harbour. Lge, pt sl, pt shd; htd wc; baby facs; chem disp; mv service pnt; shwrs; el pnts (10A) SEK40; lndtte (inc dryer); shops 3km; snacks; playgrnd; sand beach; lge sailing marina; fishing; tennis; cycling; wifi; 30% statics; dogs; phone; poss cr; quiet; CKE. ◆ 17 Apr-26 Sep.  SEK 200        2010*

**TYLOSAND see Halmstad** *2E3*

⊞ **UDDEVALLA** *2E2* (8km W Rural) *58.3306, 11.8222* **Unda Camping (O30), Unda 149, 45194 Uddevalla** [(0522) 86347; fax 86392; info@undacamping.se; www.undacamping. se] Exit E6 junc 96 Uddevalla N onto rte 44 twd Uddevalla Centrum. Site sp in 1km on R. Lge, pt sl, pt shd; htd wc; chem disp; mv service pnt; baby facs; sauna; shwrs SEK5; el pnts (10A) SEK50; lndtte (inc dryer); shop; rest; bar; cooking facs; playgrnd; pool; beach sw; fishing; boat & cycle hire; wifi; TV; many statics; phone; o'flow area when full; Quickstop o'night facs; adv bkg; ccard acc; CKE. "Lovely situation in nature reserve; recep hrs erratic low ssn." ◆ SEK 260        2013*

⊞ **UDDEVALLA** *2E2* (15km W Coastal) *58.31470, 11.72310* **Hafsten SweCamp Resort (O28), Hafsten 120, 45196 Uddevalla** [(0522) 644117; fax 644480; info@hafsten. se; www.hafsten.se] Fr S take rd 160 thro Island of Orust, 1km N of bdge turn E at site sp for 4km. Fr N, turn W off E6 at junc 96 onto rd 161 sp Lysekil/Fiskebäcksil, after 8km at Rotviksbro rndabt turn onto rd 160 twd Orust. Turn L (E) in 2km, sp as above. App rd narr with passing places. Lge, pt shd, pt sl, terr; htd wc; chem disp; mv service pnt; baby facs; sauna; shwrs SEK5; el pnts (10A) inc; gas; lndtte (inc dryer); shop; snacks; bar; cooking facs; playgrnd; sand beach adj; fishing; tennis; boat & cycle hire; pedalos; horseriding; wifi; TV rm; 50% statics; dogs; phone; bus 4km; Quickstop o'night facs; poss cr & noisy high ssn; ccard acc; CKE. "Excel location; helpful staff; gd facs block; steel or rock pegs req for awnings; o'flow field used in high ssn - no facs." ◆ SEK 315 (CChq acc)        2009*

**ULRICEHAMN** *2F3* (2km S Rural) *57.77055, 13.40173* **Camping Skotteksgården (P34), Gamla Marbäcksvägen, 52390 Ulricehamn** [(0321) 13184; fax 35185; skotteksgarden@telia.com; www.skottek.cc] On rd 40 take dir Centrum. Foll sp Skotteksgården to Tranemo. Sm, mkd pitch, hdstg, unshd; htd wc; mv service pnt; serviced pitches; baby facs; fam bthrm; sauna; shwrs inc; el pnts SEK45; lndtte (inc dryer); shop on site & 1.5km; rest, snacks; cooking facs; playgrnd; lake sw adj; fishing; cycle & boat hire; 10% statics; dogs; phone; quiet; ccard acc; CKE. "Friendly, helpful owner; cycle path adj." ◆ 15 Apr-15 Oct.  SEK 195        2009*

⊞ **ULRICEHAMN** *2F3* (12km S Rural) *57.67870, 13.37535* **Vegby Camping (P35), Storgatan 2, 52011 Vegby** [(0321) 72912; fax 72562; vegbycamping@hotmail.com; www.vegbycamping.com] Fr Rv 40 at Ulricehamn turn S on rd 157. Turn R at Gällstad & foll sp for Vegby & site. Med, terr, unshd; wc; chem disp; mv service pnt; baby facs; sauna; shwrs inc; el pnts (10A) SEK35; lndtte (inc dryer); shop; snacks; cooking facs; playgrnd; pool nr; lake sw; fishing; wifi; TV; Eng spkn; quiet; ccard acc; red low ssn; CKE/CCI. "Vg site; lake views fr all pitches; cycle rtes nr." SEK 190        2009*

⊞ **UMEA** *1C3* (5km NE Coastal) *63.84210, 20.33815* **FirstCamp Umeå (AC12), Nydalasjön 2, 90654 Umeå** [(090) 702600; fax 702610; umea@firstcamp.se; www. firstcamp.se] Sp fr E4 to N of town on lakeside. Lge, mkd pitch, pt shd; wc; chem disp; mv service pnt; 30% serviced pitches; shwrs inc; el pnts (10A) inc; lndtte (inc dryer); snacks; playgrnd; htd pool complex; waterslide; lake sw 500m; tennis; games area; games rm; wifi; some statics; bus; ccard acc; CKE. "Attractive site; lge pitches suitable RVs & twin-axles; excel service block; conv E4." ◆ SEK 260        2009*

⊞ **UPPSALA** *2H1* (1.5km N Urban) *59.87133, 17.61923* **Fyrishov Camping (C12), Idrottsgatan 2, 75333 Uppsala** [(018) 7274960; fax 244333; info@fyrishov.se; www. fyrishov.se] Exit E4 Uppsala N, in 300m at rndabt foll sp Strangnas, Sala. In 2.25km exit via slip rd sp Bjorklinge, Fyrishov. At rndabt foll sp Fyrishov, in 1.6km at traff lts turn R & immed R. Site in Fyrishov Park adj sw & sports complex. Med, unshd; wc; chem disp; mv service pnt; shwrs SEK5; el pnts (10A) SEK45; lndtte (inc dryer); shop adj; rest adj; snacks; playgrnd; pool adj (sports complex behind pool); bus; poss cr; no adv bkg; ccard acc; CKE. "Within easy access of city cent; fair NH." ◆ ltd SEK 180        2010*

**URSHULT** *2F3* (1km N Rural) *56.54476, 14.80703* **Urshults Camping (G7), Sirkövägen 19, 36013 Urshult** [(0477) 20243; fax 48046; info@urshult-camping.com; www.urshult-camping.com] Rd 30 S fr Växjö, turn W onto rd 120 at Tingsryd. In 10km at Urshult turn R, site sp on lakeside. Med, pt shd; htd wc; chem disp; mv service pnt; baby facs; shwrs; el pnts (10A) SEK45; lndtte (inc dryer); shop; tradsmn; snacks; cooking facs; playgrnd; lake sw adj; 10% statics; dogs; Eng spkn; quiet; CKE. "Well-run site; nr Kurrebo gardens & museum; vg." ◆ 25 Apr-25 Oct. SEK 165        2009*

**URSHULT** *2F3* (10km NW Rural) *56.58466, 14.69491* **Getnö Gård Naturcamping (G24), Lake Åsnen Resort, 36010 Ryd** [(0477) 24011; fax 24049; info@getnogard.se; www. getnogard.se] W fr Urshult on rte 120 to junc with rte 126; turn NW onto rte 126, site in 7km via Ålshult to Getnö Gård. Site on shore Lake Åsnen. Med, mkd pitch, pt sl, pt shd; htd wc; chem disp; mv service pnt; baby facs; shwrs inc; el pnts (10A) SEK45; lndtte (inc dryer); shop; rest, snacks; bar; cooking facs; playgrnd; lake & private shgl beach adj; fishing; canoe hire; some statics; dogs; phone; poss cr; Eng spkn; adv bkg; red long stay; quiet; CKE. "Beautiful location in private nature reserve; well-kept facs." ◆ ltd 1 May-10 Oct.  SEK 195  2009*

You can now fill in site reports online

**VADSTENA** *2F2* (2km N Rural) *58.46448, 14.9334* **Vadstena Camping (E9)**, Vätterviksbadets, 59294 Vadstena [(0143) 12730; info@vadstenacamping.se; www. vadstenacamping.se] On rd 50, 3km N of Vadstena by Lake Vattern. Lge, mkd pitch, pt shd; wc; chem disp; mv service pnt; sauna; shwrs inc; el pnts (10A) SEK50; lndtte (inc dryer); shop; snacks; cooking facs; playgrnd; htd pool 3km; waterslide; sand beach & lake adj; fishing; tennis; wifi; 20% statics; dogs; poss cr; Eng spkn; adv bkg; ccard acc; red low ssn; CKE. "Many local attractions; vg family site; cycle path to town; gd birdwatching nrby." ♦ 29 Apr-11 Sep. SEK 200                    2009*

**VAGGERYD** *2F3* (500m N Rural) *57.50973, 14.1327* **Hjortsjöns Camping (F8)**, Badplatsvägen, 56731 Vaggeryd [(0393) 12262; hjortsjonscamping@vaggeryd.se; www. hjortsjonscamping.com] Site is at E side of lake; take turning at N app to Vaggeryd. Med, mkd pitch, pt sl, pt shd; wc; chem disp; baby facs; shwrs; el pnts (10A) SEK40; lndtte (inc dryer); shop; snacks; cooking facs; playgrnd; lake sw, fishing & boating adj; dogs; phone; quiet; CKE. "Lakeside site with woodland walks; gd touring base." ♦ 16 May-18 Sep. SEK 150   2009*

**VALADALEN See Undersaker** *1B3*

**VANERSBORG** *2E2* (3km N Coastal) *58.4122, 12.3208* **Ursands Camping (P6)**, Ursandsvägen, 46221 Vänersborg [(0521) 18666; ursandscamping@telia.com; www. ursandscamping.se] On rd 45 heading N over rv bdge to site on R in 2km; sp fr bdge. Med, shd; wc; baby facs; mv service pnt; shwrs SEK7; el pnts (10A) SEK40; lndtte (inc dryer); shop high ssn; rest; bar; cooking facs; playgrnd; sand beach & lake sw; fishing; boating; cycle hire; wifi; TV; Quickstop o'night facs; poss cr; adv bkg; quiet; ccard acc; CKE. "Pleasant, family site." ♦ 23 Apr-12 Sep. SEK 205                    2010*

**VARBERG** *2E3* (8km N Coastal) *57.1826, 12.22076* **Kärradals Camping (N7)**, Torpavägen 21, 43295 Varberg [(0340) 622377 / (0708) 975806 (mob); fax 623576; brink@ karradalscamping.se; www.karradalscamping.se] Fr S exit E6 junc 55 Varberg N & foll sp Tångeberg & Kärradal. Fr N exit junc 56 & foll sp Värö & Åskloster, then Kärradal & site. Lge, mkd pitch, pt shd; wc; chem disp; mv service pnt; baby facs; shwrs SEK1; el pnts SEK40; lndtte (inc dryer); shop; rest, snacks; bar; cooking facs; playgrnd; sand beach 500m; games area; cycle hire; wifi; TV rm; 80% statics; dogs; phone; poss cr; Eng spkn; rlwy noise; ccard acc; CKE/CCI. "Rec arrive early afternoon high ssn; o'flow field has minimal san facs, but clean." ♦ 23 Apr-5 Sep. SEK 340                    2013*

**VARNAMO** *2F3* (500m N Rural) *57.19055, 14.04615* **Värnamo Camping (F10)**, Prostsjön, 33183 Värnamo [(0370) 16660; fax 47150; info@varnamocamping.se] Exit E4 Värnamo N, foll site sp. Site is 2km W of E4. Med, pt shd; wc; mv service pnt; baby facs; shwrs SEK5; el pnts (10A) SEK40; lndtte (inc dryer); shop high ssn; tradsmn; rest, snacks 500m; cooking facs; playgrnd; lake sw; fishing; boating; cycling; games rm; wifi; TV; 20% statics; dogs; phone; quiet; red CKE. "NH only; not particularly welcoming." ♦ 1 May-15 Sep. SEK 230                    2010*

⊞ **VASTERVIK** *2G3* (3km SE Coastal) *57.73823, 16.66846* **Camping Lysingsbadets (H3)**, Lysingsvägen, 593 53 Västervik [(0490) 258000; fax 254855; lysingsbadet@ vastervik.se; www.lysingsbadet.se] On coast 3km SE of town. Fr E22 foll sp around S ring rd; on app to Västervik. Site well sp fr E22. V lge, pt shd; htd wc; chem disp; mv service pnt; serviced pitches; sauna; shwrs inc; el pnts (10A) inc; lndtte (inc dryer); shop; 2 rests high ssn; snacks; bar; cooking facs; playgrnd; htd pool; waterslide; sand beach adj; boat & cycle hire; tennis; golf; wifi; entmnt; some statics; dogs; o'night area for m'vans; ccard acc. "Lovely, family site in landscaped, coastal woodland; easy access to islands by wooden footbdge fr site." ♦ SEK 455                    2013*

**VATTERSMALEN See Gränna** *2F2*

**VAXHOLM** *2H1* (2km W Coastal) *59.40508, 18.3047* **Waxholm Strand & Camping (B6)**, Eriksövägen, 18521 Vaxholm [(08) 54130101; info@waxholmstrand.com; www.vaxholmstrand.com] On rd 274 turn R immed after x-ing bdge to Vaxholm Island, foll sp 'Eriksö Camping'. Med, mkd pitch, pt sl, unshd; wc; chem disp; mv service pnt; shwrs inc; el pnts SEK40; lndtte (inc dryer); shop 1km; rest, snacks; playgrnd; sand beach adj; wifi; some statics; dogs; phone; adv bkg; quiet; ccard acc; CKE. "35 mins drive fr Stockholm; boat trips, bike hire, ferry terminal Vaxholm-Stockholm 3.3km." ♦ 30 Apr-25 Sep. SEK 210                    2013*

⊞ **VAXJO** *2F3* (5km N Rural) *56.92216, 14.81905* **Växjö SweCamp Evedal (G16)**, 35263 Växjö [(0470) 63034; fax 63122; evedals.camping@telia.com; www. evedalscamping.com] Sp fr Växjö on E23. Med, pt shd; htd wc; chem disp; baby facs; sauna; shwrs inc; el pnts (10A) SEK50; lndtte (inc dryer); shop; rest adj; playgrnd; sand beach; watersports; cycle hire; wifi; TV; some statics; dogs; quiet; red 7+ days; ccard acc; CKE. "Ideal for children; in lakeside park in cent of glass industry; Kroneberg castle adj; Småland Museum in Växjö." SEK 225                    2011*

**VEGBY See Ulricehamn** *2F3*

**VENJAN** *1B4* (1km E Rural) *60.9537, 13.93021* **Venjans Camping**, Moravägen, 79293 Venjan [(0250) 62310; fax 62350; info@venjanscamping.se; www.venjanscamping. se] Fr E45 turn W 3km N of junc of E45/64. Site in 18km, sp. Sm, mkd pitch, pt shd; htd wc; chem disp; mv service pnt; shwrs SEK5; el pnts (10A) SEK35; lndtte; shop 1km; playgrnd; lake sw & sand beach adj; fishing; boat hire; dogs; phone; Eng spkn; adv bkg; quiet; CKE. ♦ 15 May-1 Sep. SEK 130  2010*

**VILHELMINA** *1C2* (1.5km SE Rural) *64.62131, 16.67846* **Saiva Camping (AC4)**, Baksjön 1, 91231 Vilhelmina [(0940) 10760; info@saiva.se; www.saiva.se] Sp on E site of rd 45. Med, pt shd; htd wc; chem disp; baby facs; shwrs SEK1; el pnts (10A) SEK30; lndtte (inc dryer); shop; snacks; playgrnd; lake beach; tennis; cycle hire; wifi; TV; some statics; dogs; phone; poss cr; quiet; ccard acc; CKE. "Gd; excel san facs in log style cabins, v helpful staff, lovely lakeside setting." ♦ 20 May-1 Oct. SEK 160                    2011*

SWEDEN

⊞ **VILHELMINA** *1C2* (5km NW Rural) *64.64998, 16.59240* Kolgärdens Camping, Lövliden 16, 91292 Vilhelmina [(0940) 10304; kolgarden@vilhelmina.ac; www.kolgarden. se] Site sp fr E45 N of Vilhelmina. Sm, pt shd; htd wc; chem disp; mv service pnt; sauna; shwrs inc; el pnts (10A) SEK35; lndtte; shop 5km; cooking facs; fishing; internet; TV rm; 50% statics; dogs; Eng spkn; quiet. "Wonderful lakeside location; clean san facs; helpful, pleasant owner; highly rec." ♦ ltd SEK 145                                                  2011*

**VINSLOV** *2F4* (500m N Rural) *56.10988, 13.91245* **Vinslövs Camping (L2), Troed Nelsongatan 18, 28834 Vinslöv** [(070) 2077679; info@vinslovscamping.se] Site sp of rte 21. Sm, mkd pitch, pt shd; wc; chem disp; shwrs inc; el pnts (6A) SEK40; lndtte (inc dryer) shop 500m; cooking facs; rest, snacks, bar 500m; playgrnd; htd pool adj; 20% statics; dogs; bus 500m; quiet; CKE. ♦ 1 Apr-30 Sep. SEK 120          2010*

⊞ **VITTSJO** *2F4* (1km N Rural) *56.35106, 13.66541* **Vittsjö Camping, Campingvägen 1, 28022 Vittsjö** [(0451) 22489; v.turistforening@telia.com; www.vittsjocamping.se] Well sp on N edge of vill on rd 117 by Lake Vittsjö, approx 20km N of Hässleholm. Sm, mkd pitch, hdstg, pt shd; htd wc; chem disp; mv service pnt; baby facs; shwrs inc; el pnts (16A); lndtte; shop & 2km; rest 2km; snacks; cooking facs; playgrnd; lake sw adj; cycle hire; wifi; 40% statics; dogs; Eng spkn; quiet; CKE. "Family-run site; security barrier; gd." SEK 160          2010*

**YSTAD** *2F4* (3km E Coastal) *55.43286, 13.8650* **Camping Sandskogens (M15), Österleden, 27160 Ystad** [(0411) 19270; fax 19169; info@sandskogenscamping.se; www.sandskogenscamping.se] On N side of rd 9. Lge, mkd pitch, shd; wc; chem disp; mv service pnt; baby facs; shwrs SEK5; el pnts (10A) SEK40; lndtte (inc dryer); shop; rest 400m; playgrnd; paddling pool; sand beach 100m; wifi; TV; some statics; dogs; phone; no adv bkg; rlwy noise; ccard acc; CKE. "On Baltic coast; cycle path to beautiful town; mkd walks nrby; gd site, well-managed site; extremely helpful Eng spkn staff; high ssn expect queues checking in; CKE card req; metered shwrs; Wallander tv series studios site nr site, tours avail." ♦ 17 Apr-21 Sep.  SEK 325          2014*

SWEDEN

Motorways
Major roads
Main roads

0    50    100    150 kms
0         50         100 mls

● All year site(s)
● Seasonal site(s)
○ No sites listed
  200m +
  0–200m

N
W — E
S

Arctic Circle

NORWEGIAN
SEA

NORWAY

Tynset
Trondheim
Drevsjø
Tælset

Tromsø
Skibotn
Trædal
Narvik
Karesuando
Muonio
KIRUNA
Pajala
Rovaniemi
JOKKMOKK
Størjord
Mo i Rana
95
Arjeplog
97
Rörbäck
Haparanda
TÄRNABY
Sorsele
Slagnäs
Luleå
Norrfjärden
Oulu
Storuman
95
SKELLEFTEÅ
Gäddede
Vilhelmina
DOROTEA
Ånäset
92
Strömsund
UMEÅ
Nordmaling
Lit
87
96
ÖSTERSUND
Hammarstrand
Åsama
86
Ramvik
HÄRNÖSAND
Hede
83
Stöde
SUNDSVALL
Njurundabommen
Sveg
84
Drevsjø
Särna
Ljusdal
GULF
OF
BOTHNIA
Älvdalen
Orsa
Bollnäs
Venjan
Mora
Gesunda
SÖDERHAMN
Rättvik
▼ see map 2
GÄVLE

FINLAND

© Collins Bartholomew Ltd 2014

Map 1

▲ see map 1

Malung
FALUN
BORLÄNGE
Hedesunda
GÄVLE
Kongsvinger
Ekshärad
Österfärnebo
Torsby
64
Glava
Filipstad
63
Kil
KARLSTAD
Nora
Arboga
Sala
UPPSALA
Enköping
77 NORRTÄLJE
76
VÄSTERÅS
Vaxholm
STOCKHOLM
Bengtsfors
Säffle
VÄNERN
Degerfors
ÖREBRO
Eskilstuna
Järna
Nynäshamn
Amål
Finnerödja
Katrineholm
Ed
Hova
Tived
55
Nyköping
Trosa
Mariestad
Bocksjö
Kolmården
Mellerud
Lidköping
Karlsborg
Borensberg
NORRKÖPING
Fjällbacka
Hamburgsund
Vänersborg
Vadstena
Roxenbaden
Söderköping
Trollhättan
SKÖVDE
Hjo
Linköping
BALTIC
Nossebro
Falköping
VÄTTERN
32
Gryt
SEA
Alingsås
Gränna
35
Kungälv
Tranås
Gamleby
GÖTEBORG
27/40
Ulricehamn
JÖNKÖPING
31
Västervik
GOTLAND
Kungsbacka
Eksjö
Hult
Åsa
Kinna
Vaggeryd
Byxelkrok
41
Hillerstorp
Oskarshamn
Mellböda
VARBERG
28
Värnamo
23
Löttorp
Falkenberg
Lidhult
Ljungby
VÄXJÖ
Timmernabben
Borgholm
HALMSTAD
25
Läckeby
ÖLAND
Hovmantorp
Mellbystrand
Älmhult
KALMAR
Färjestaden
Torekov
24
Markaryd
Urshult
Mörbylånga
Höganäs
Vittsjö
Bergkvara
Degerhamn
Ängelholm
Klippan
Karlshamn
HELSINGBORG
Vinslöv
KARLSKRONA
Landskrona
17
Röstånga
Barsebäck
Åhus
KØBENHAVN
DENMARK
MALMÖ
Simrishamn
Skanör
Tomelilla
Ystad
Löderup
Trelleborg
BORNHOLM IS
(Denmark)

0      50      100 kms

0           50 mls

© Collins Bartholomew Ltd 2014

Map 2

# Switzerland
## Country Introduction

*Lavaux Vineyards, Lake Geneva, Switzerland*

## Welcome to Switzerland

What makes Switzerland so popular with tourists is the spectacular mountains, beautiful lakes and clean air. Exploring the wildness of the forests and trekking the surrounding hills make the country an ideal place for those that love the outdoors.

Because Switzerland is a small country, its attractions are close together and can be easily accessed on any type of touring holiday.

## Country highlights

Switzerland's cuisine has a lot of influences from its neighbouring countries. Try its famous Bern, a dish containing a variety of smoked pork, tongue and sausage served alongside sauerkraut, pickled turnips and boiled potatoes. Also popular is the of eating cheese fondue, bread cubes dipped into melted cheese.

For those who enjoy music, film or the performing arts, Switzerland's annual festivals are not to be missed. The Lucerne Summer Festival is the largest classical music event of the country. Leading music performers from across the world convene in Lucerne to celebrate a festival of sound.

## Major towns and cities

- Zürich – many museums and art galleries can be found in this metropolitan city.

- Geneva – part of Lake Geneva, the city is home to the tallest fountain in the world.

- Basel – a cultural city with numerous theatres and museums to explore.

- Lausanne – a hilly city that has a medieval centre and is close to Lake Geneva.

## Attractions

- Chateau de Chillon, Montreux – tour the dungeons and spectacular rooms of this 11th century castle.

- Swiss National Park – home to a variety of wildlife and many walking trails.

- The Rhine Falls – a magnificent waterfall near the town of Schffhausen.

- Mount Pilatus – take a cable car to the top and see the amazing views of the Alps.

## Find out more

www.myswitzerland.com

Tel: 0041 (0) 80 01 00 20 029 Swiss Tourist Office

# Country Information

*Population:* 7.9 million

*Capital:* Bern (population 121,631)

*Area:* 41,293 sq km

*Bordered by:* Austria, France, Germany, Italy, Liechtenstein

*Terrain:* Mostly mountainous; Alps in the south, Jura in the north-west; central plateau of rolling hills, plains and large lakes

*Climate:* Temperate climate varying with altitude; cold, cloudy, rainy or snowy winters; cool to warm summers with occasional showers

*Highest Point:* Dufourspitze 4,634m

*Languages:* French, German, Italian, Romansch

*Local Time:* GMT or BST + 1, i.e. 1 hour ahead of the UK all year

*Currency:* Swiss Franc (CHF) divided into 100 centimes (also called 'rappen' or 'centesimi' in German/Italian areas of the country); £1 = CHF 1.51, CHF 10 = £6.63 (September 2014)

*Emergency numbers:* Police 117; Fire brigade 118; Ambulance 144 or 112 for any service

*Public Holidays 2015:* Jan 1, 2*, 6*; Mar 19*; Apr 3, 6; May 1*, 14, 25; Jun 4*, 29*; Aug 1 (National Day), 15*; Nov 1*; Dec 8, 25, 26, 28

*These public holidays are not necessarily celebrated throughout Switzerland and individual cantons may have additional holidays.

School summer holidays vary by canton but are approximately from early July to mid/end August.

# Camping and Caravanning

There are approximately 340 campsites available to touring caravanners, with around 70 sites remaining open in winter. Some sites may be nearly full with statics, with only a small area for tourers.

There are 29 Touring Club Suisse (TCS) sites and affiliated sites classified into five categories according to amenities available. All TCS campsites have a service station with facilities for emptying sanitary tanks. For further information and current rates see www.reisen-tcs.ch.

The Swiss Camp Sites Association (VSC/ACS) produces a camping and road map covering approximately 180 sites, including charges and classification. See www.swisscamps.ch. To download a guide to more than 40 campsites, including those open in winter, in the Bernese Oberland region of Switzerland see www.camping-bo.ch or write to Camping Berner Oberland, Lehnweg 6, CH-3800 Interlaken, fax 0041 033 8231920.

The Swiss are environmentally conscious with only limited scope for removing waste. Recycling is vigorously promoted and it is normal to have to put rubbish in special plastic bags obtainable from campsites. A 'rubbish charge' or 'entsorgungstaxe' of approximately CHF 3 per person per day is commonly charged.

A visitors' tax, varying according to the area, is levied in addition to the site charges.

The rules on casual/wild camping differ from canton to canton. It may be tolerated in some areas with the permission of the landowner or local police, or in motorway service areas, but local laws – particularly on hygiene – must not be contravened. For reasons of security The Caravan Club recommends that overnight stops should always be at recognised campsites.

# Cycling

Switzerland has 9,000 km of cycle trails, including nine national cycle routes, which have been planned to suit all categories of cyclist from families to sports cyclists. Maps of cycle routes are available from www.schweizmobil.ch. Routes are marked by red and white signs. The problem of strenuous uphill gradients can be overcome by using trails routed near railway lines. Most trains will transport bicycles and often bicycles are available for hire at stations. Switzerland Tourism can provide more information.

Children under the age of 6 may only cycle on the road if accompanied by a person over 16 years of age.

*Transportation of Bicycles*

Bicycles may be carried on the roof of a car providing they are attached to an adequate roof rack and providing the total height does not exceed 4 metres. Bicycles carried on special carriers at the rear of a vehicle can exceed the width of the vehicle by 20 cm on each side, but the total width must not exceed 2 metres. The rear lights and number plate must remain visible and the driver's view must not be obstructed.

## Electricity and Gas

Usually current on campsites varies between 4 and 16 amps. Plugs have two or, more usually, three round pins. Some campsites have CEE connections. Some may lend or hire out adaptors – but do not rely on it – and it may be advisable to purchase an appropriate adaptor cable with a Swiss 3-pin plug. Adaptors are readily available in local supermarkets.

The full range of Campingaz cylinders is available from large supermarkets.

## Entry Formalities

Holders of valid British or Irish passports may enter Switzerland without a visa for a period of up to six months.

## Medical Services

There are reciprocal emergency health care arrangements with Switzerland for EU citizens. A European Health Insurance Card (EHIC) will enable you to get reduced cost for emergency treatment in a public hospital but you will be required to pay the full cost of treatment and apply afterwards for a refund from the Department for Work & Pensions on your return to the UK. Ensure that any doctor you visit is registered with the national Swiss Health Insurance Scheme. Dental treatment is not covered.

You will have to pay 50% of the costs of any medically-required ambulance transport within Switzerland and/or Liechtenstein, including air ambulance. There is a fixed charge for in-patient treatment in a public hospital.

If you are planning to participate in sports activities, such as skiing and mountaineering, your personal holiday insurance should be extended to cover these activities and should also include cover for mountain rescue and helicopter rescue costs.

## Opening Hours

Banks – Mon-Fri 8.30am-4.30pm (some close for lunch; late opening once a week to 5.30pm/6pm in some towns).

Museums – Tue-Sun 10am-5pm; closed Mon; check locally.

Post Offices – Mon-Fri 7.30am-12pm & 13.45pm-6pm (no lunch break in main towns); Sat 7.30am-11am.

Shops – Mon-Fri 8am/8.30am-6.30pm/7pm (closed lunch time) & Sat 8am-4pm/7pm (sometimes lunch time closing); shops close early on the eve of a public holiday. Food shops may be closed on religious and public holidays.

## Safety and Security

Most visits to Switzerland and Liechtenstein are trouble-free and the crime rate is low. However, petty theft is on the increase and you should be alert to pickpockets, confidence tricksters and thieves in city centres, railway stations and other public places.

You should be aware of the risks involved in the more hazardous sports activities and take note of weather forecasts and conditions, which can change rapidly in the mountains. You should be well-equipped; do not undertake the activity alone, study the itinerary and inform someone of your plans. Off-piste skiers should follow the advice given by local authorities and guides; to ignore such advice could put yourselves and other mountain users in danger.

Switzerland and Liechtenstein share with the rest of Europe an underlying threat from terrorism. Attacks could be indiscriminate and against civilian targets in public places, including tourist sites.

*British Embassy*

THUNSTRASSE 50, CH-3005 BERN
Tel: 031 3597700
http://ukinswitzerland.fco.gov.uk/en
*British Consulate-General*

AVENUE LOUIS CASAÏ 58
CH-1216 COINTRIN, GENEVE
Tel: 022 9182300
There are also Honorary Consulates/Vice-Consulates/Consular Agencies in Allschwill (Basel), Lugano, Mollens-Valais, St Légier (Montreux) and Zürich.

*Irish Embassy*
KIRCHENFELDSTRASSE 68, CH-3000 BERN 6
Tel: 031 3521442
www.embassyofireland.ch
There is also an Honorary Consulate in Zürich

## Customs Regulations

*Alcohol and Tobacco*

Switzerland is not a member of the EU and visitors aged 17 years and over may import the following items duty-free:

200 cigarettes or 50 cigars or
250 g tobacco

2 litres of alcoholic drink up to 15% proof
1 litre of alcoholic drink over 15% proof

All goods are duty free up to a total combined value of CHF300, including alcohol and tobacco products.

*Caravans and Motorhomes*

Caravans registered outside Switzerland may be imported without formality up to a height of 4 metres, width of 2.55 metres and length of 12 metres (including towbar). The total length of car + caravan/trailer must not exceed 18.75 metres.

*Food*

From EU countries you may import per person 1 kg of meat and/or meat products (excluding game). This is applicable as of 1st July 2014.

*Refund of VAT on Export*

A foreign visitor who buys goods in Switzerland in a 'Tax-Back SA' or 'Global Refund Schweiz AG' shop may obtain a VAT refund (7.6%) on condition that the value of the goods is at least CHF 300 including VAT. Visitors should complete a form in the shop and produce it, together with the goods purchased, at Customs on leaving Switzerland. See www.globalrefund.com or www.myswitzerland.com.

## Documents

*Vehicle(s)*

Carry your original vehicle registration certificate (V5C), MOT certificate (if applicable) and insurance documentation at all times. Recent

visitors report that drivers may be asked to produce proof of vehicle ownership at the border and failure to do so may mean that entry into Switzerland is refused. If you are driving a vehicle which does not belong to you, you should be in possession of a letter of authorisation from the owner.

## Money

Prices in shops are often displayed in both Swiss francs and euros. Major credit cards are widely accepted, although you may find small supermarkets and restaurants do not accept them. Recent visitors report that some retail outlets may accept only one kind of credit card (MasterCard or VISA), not both, and it may be advisable to carry one of each. You may occasionally find that a surcharge is imposed for the use of credit cards.

Carry your credit card issuers'/banks' 24-hour UK contact numbers in case of loss or theft of your cards.

## Motoring in Switzerland
## Accidents

In the case of accidents involving property damage only, when drivers decide not to call the police, a European Accident Statement must be completed.

In the case of personal injury or of damage to the road, road signs, lights, barriers etc, the police must be called.

## Alcohol

The maximum permitted level of alcohol is 50 milligrams in 100 millilitres of blood, i.e. lower than that permitted in the UK (80 milligrams). A blood test may be required after an accident, and if found positive, the penalty is either a fine or a prison sentence, plus withdrawal of permission to drive in Switzerland for at least two months. Police carry out random breath tests.

## Breakdown Service

The motoring and leisure organisation Touring Club Suisse (TCS) operates a 24-hour breakdown service, 'Patrouille TCS'. To call for help throughout Switzerland and Liechtenstein,

**SWITZERLAND**

dial 140. On motorways use emergency phones and ask for TCS.

Members of clubs affiliated to the AIT, such as The Caravan Club, who can show a current membership card will be charged reduced rates for breakdown assistance and towing, according to the time of day and/or the distance towed. Payment by credit card is accepted.

## Essential Equipment

*Lights*

Dipped headlights are compulsory at all times, even during the day. Bulbs are more likely to fail with constant use and you are recommended to carry spares.

*Nationality Plate (GB or IRL Stickers)*

Strictly-speaking, it is necessary to display a conventional nationality plate or sticker when driving outside EU member states, even when vehicle number plates incorporate the GB or IRL Euro-symbol. However, the Swiss authorities have adopted a commonsense approach and confirm that it is not necessary to display a separate GB or IRL sticker if your number plates display the GB or IRL Euro-symbol. If your number plates do not incorporate this symbol then you will need a separate sticker.

*Warning Triangles*

All vehicles must be equipped with a warning triangle which has to be within easy reach and not in the boot.

*Child Restraint System*

Vehicles registered outside of Switzerland that are temporarily imported into the country, have to comply with the country of registration with regards to safety belt equipment and child restraint regulations. All children up to 12 years of age must be placed in an approved UN ECE 44.03 regulation child restraint, unless they measure more than 150cm and are over seven years old.

*Winter Driving*

Alpine winters often make driving more difficult. You should equip your vehicle(s) with winter tyres and snow chains and check road conditions prior to departure.

A sign depicting a wheel and chains indicates where snow chains are required for the mountain road ahead.

Snow chains are compulsory in areas where indicated by the appropriate road sign. They must be fitted on at least two drive wheels.

## Fuel

Prices of petrol vary according to the brand and region, being slightly cheaper in self-service stations. Credit cards are generally accepted.

On motorways, where prices are slightly higher, some service stations are open 24 hours and others are open from 6am to 10pm or 11pm only, but petrol is available outside these hours from automatic pumps where payment can be made by means of bank notes or credit cards.

There are 42 outlets (August 2014) selling LPG (GPL) – see www.jaquet-ge.ch for a list of outlets and a map showing their location.

## Mountain Roads and Tunnels

One of the most attractive features of Switzerland for motorists is the network of finely engineered mountain passes, ranging from easy main road routes to high passes that may be open only from June to October. In the Alps most roads over passes have been modernised; only the Umbrail Pass, which is not recommended for caravans, is not completely tarred. Passes have a good roadside telephone service for calling aid quickly in the event of trouble.

A blue rectangular sign depicting a yellow horn indicates a mountain postal road and the same sign with a red diagonal stripe indicates the end of the postal road. On such roads, vehicles belonging to the postal services have priority.

During certain hours, one-way traffic only is permitted on certain mountain roads. The hours during which traffic may proceed in either or both directions are posted at each end of the road. The TCS road map of Switzerland, scale 1:300,000, indicates this type of road.

Speed must always be moderate on mountain passes, very steep roads and roads with numerous bends. Drivers must not travel at a speed which would prevent them from stopping within the distance they can see ahead.

When it is difficult to pass oncoming vehicles, the heavier vehicle has priority.

Slow-moving vehicles are required by law to use the lay-bys provided on alpine roads to allow the free flow of faster traffic. This is the case where a car towing a caravan causes a queue of vehicles capable of a higher speed.

## Parking

Parking in cities is difficult and it is worth using the numerous Park & Ride schemes which operate around major towns and cities. Illegal parking of any kind is much less tolerated in Switzerland than in any of its neighbours and fines are common for even minor violations.

Pay and display car parks and parking meters are used throughout the country and permitted parking time varies from 15 minutes to 2 hours. Feeding meters is not allowed. Wheel clamps are not used, but vehicles causing an obstruction may be removed to a car pound.

You may park in a 'blue zone' for limited periods free of charge providing you display a parking disc in your vehicle. These are available from petrol stations, kiosks, restaurants and police stations. Parking in a marked red zone is free for up to 15 hours with a red parking disc obtainable from police stations, tourist offices, etc.

Parking on pavements is not allowed. Do not park where there is a sign 'Stationierungsverbot' or 'Interdiction de Stationner'. Continuous or broken yellow lines and crosses at the side of the road and any other yellow markings also indicate that parking is prohibited.

## Priority

In general, traffic (including bicycles) coming from the right has priority at intersections but drivers approaching a roundabout must give way to all traffic already on the roundabout, i.e. from the left, unless otherwise indicated by signs. However, vehicles on main roads – indicated by a yellow diamond with a white border or a white triangle with a red border and an arrow pointing upwards – have priority over traffic entering from secondary roads.

Please be aware sometimes pedestrians have right of way and will expect vehicles to stop for them.

## Roads

Switzerland has some 72,000 kilometres of well-surfaced roads, from motorways to local municipal roads, all well-signposted. Four-wheel drive vehicles must not be driven off road without the permission of the local authority.

During daylight hours outside built-up areas you must sound your horn before sharp bends where visibility is limited. After dark this warning must be given by flashing your headlights.

Dial the following numbers for information:

162: Weather information

163: Road conditions, mountain passes, access to tunnels and traffic news

187: In winter, avalanche bulletins; in summer, wind forecasts for Swiss lakes

It is also possible to obtain updated information on road conditions via teletext in larger motorway service areas.

## Motorway Tax

To be able to use national roads (motorways and semi-motorways) in Switzerland, motor vehicles and trailers up to a total weight of 3,500kg must have a vehicle sticker (vignette). The ticket is valid for 14 months from 1st December every year and costs CHF40 (2014). An additional fee of CHF 40 is charged for caravans and trailers. The sticker allows multiple re-entry into Switzerland during the period of validity.

If you enter a motorway or semi-motorway without a sticker you will be fined CHF200 and also the cost of the sticker. The stickers can be bought from custom offices, petrol stations or TCS offices in Switzerland or alternatively they can be purchased from the UK before travelling by calling the Swiss Travel Centre on 00800 100 20029.

*Heavy Vehicle Tax*

Vehicles (including motorhomes) over 3,500kg must pay a heavy vehicle tax on entry into Switzerland which is applicable for all roads. This charge applies for every day you are in Switzerland and your vehicle is on the road. For a 10-day pass (valid for a year) you self-select the days that your vehicle is on the road and, therefore, you are not penalised if your motorhome is parked at a campsite and not driven on a public road. This heavy vehicle tax applies to any Swiss road and replaces the need for a motorway vignette. This particular tax is only payable at the border on entry into Switzerland and if there is any doubt about the exact weight of your vehicle it will be weighed. An inspection may be carried out at any time and is likely at the exit border. Failure to pay the tax can result in an immediate fine.

## Road Signs and Markings

Road signs and markings conform to international standards.

White lettering on a green background indicates motorways, whereas state and provincial main roads outside built-up areas have white lettering on a blue background. This is the reverse of the colouring used in France and Germany and may initially cause confusion when driving from one country to the other. Road signs on secondary roads are white with black lettering.

The following are some road signs which you may encounter:

Postal vehicles have priority

Parking disc compulsory

Slow lane

One-way street with a two-way cycle lane

## Speed Limits

|  | Open Road (km/h) | Motorway (km/h) |
|---|---|---|
| Car Solo | 80-100 | 120 |
| Car towing caravan/trailer | 80 | 80 |
| Motorhome under 3500kg | 80-100 | 120 |
| Motorhome 3500-7500kg | 80 | 80 |

The fundamental rule in Switzerland, which applies to all motor vehicles and also to bicycles, is that you must always have the speed of your vehicle under control and must adapt your speed to the conditions of the road, traffic and visibility. On minor secondary roads without speed limit signs speed should be reduced to 50 km/h (31 mph) where the road enters a built-up area. The speed limit in residential areas is 30 km/h (18 mph). Speeding fines are severe.

When travelling solo the speed limit on dual carriageways is 100 km/h (62 mph) and on motorways, 120 km/h (74 mph) unless otherwise indicated by signs. On motorways with at least three lanes in the same direction, the left outside lane may only be used by vehicles which can exceed 80 km/h (50 mph).

Motorhomes with a laden weight of under 3,500 kg are not subject to any special regulations. Those over 3,500 kg may not exceed 80 km/h (50 mph) on motorways.

In road tunnels with two lanes in each direction, speed is limited to 100 km/h (62 mph); in the St Gotthard tunnel and San Bernardino tunnels the limit is 80 km/h (50 mph).

It is illegal to transport or use radar detection devices. If your GPS navigation system has a function to identify the location of fixed speed cameras, this must be deactivated.

## Traffic Jams

Traffic congestion occurs near tunnels in particular, during the busy summer months, at the St Gotthard tunnel on Friday afternoons and Saturday mornings. When congestion is severe and in order to prevent motorists coming to a standstill in the tunnel, traffic police stop vehicles before the tunnel entrance and direct them through in groups.

Other bottlenecks occur on the roads around Luzern (A2) and Bern (A1, A6 and A12), the border crossing at Chiasso (A2), the A9 around Lausanne and between Vevey and Chexbres, and the A13 BellinzonaSargans, mainly before the San Bernardino tunnel.

# Traffic Lights

Outside peak rushhours traffic lights flashing amber mean proceed with caution.

# Violation of Traffic Regulations

The police may impose and collect on-the-spot fines for minor infringements. In the case of more serious violations, they may require a deposit equal to the estimated amount of the fine. Fines for serious offences are set according to the income of the offender. Drivers of foreign-registered vehicles may be asked for a cash deposit against the value of the fine

# Motorways

There are 1,700 km of motorways and dual carriageways. To use these roads motor vehicles and trailers up to a total weight of 3,500kg must display a vignette. Motorists using roads to avoid motorways and dual carriageways may find it necessary to detour through small villages, often with poor signposting. In addition, due to a diversion, you may be re-routed onto roads where the motorway vignette is required.

If you have visited Switzerland before, make sure you remove your old sticker from your windscreen.

There are emergency telephones along the motorways.

# Touring

The peak season for winter sports is from December to the end of April in all major resorts. February and March are the months with the most hours of winter sunshine and good snow for skiing. Summer skiing is also possible in a few resorts. Information on snow conditions, including avalanche bulletins, is available in English from www.slf.ch.

Besides being famous for watches, chocolate and cheese, the Swiss have a fine reputation as restaurateurs, but eating out can be expensive. Local beers are light but pleasant and some very drinkable wines are produced.

There are a number of UNESCO World Heritage Sites in Switzerland including the three castles of Bellinzona, Bern Old Town, the Monastery of St John at Müstair, the Jungfrau, the Aletsch Glacier and the Bietschhoorn region.

Liechtenstein is a principality of 160 sq km sharing borders with Switzerland and Austria. The capital, Vaduz, has a population of approximately 7,000 and German is the official language. The official currency is the Swiss franc. There are no passport or Customs controls on the border between Switzerland and Liechtenstein.

# Public Transport & Local Travel

Some towns are inaccessible by road, e.g. Zermatt and Wengen, and can only be reached by train or tram.

The Swiss integrated transport system is well known for its efficiency, convenience and punctuality. Co-ordinated timetables ensure fast, trouble-free interchange from one means of transport to another. Yellow post buses take travellers off the beaten track to the remotest regions. As far as railways are concerned, in addition to efficient inter-city travel, there is an extensive network of mountain railways, including aerial cableways, funiculars and ski-lifts.

Half-fare tickets are available for attractions such as cable cars, railways and lake steamers. In addition, Switzerland Tourism offers a public transport map and a number of other useful publications. See www.swisstravelsystem.com.

All visitors to campsites and hotels in Interlaken are issued with a pass allowing free bus and train travel in the area.

A ferry operates on Lake Constance (Bodensee) between Romanshorn and Friedrichshafen (Germany) saving a 70km drive. The crossing takes 40 minutes. Telephone 071 4667888 for more information; www.bodensee-schiffe.ch. A frequent ferry service also operates between Konstanz and Meersburg on the main route between Zürich, Ulm, Augsburg and Munich (Germany); information is available on a German telephone number, 0049 7531 8030; www.stadtwerke.konstanz.de. The crossing takes 20 minutes. Principal internal ferry services are on Lake Lucerne between Beckenried and Gersau, www.autofaehre.ch, and on Lake Zürich between Horgen and Meilen, www.faehre.ch. All these services transport cars and caravans.

**AARBURG** *A2* (500m S Rural) *47.31601, 7.89488* **Camping Wiggerspitz, Hofmattstrasse 40, 4663 Aarburg [062 7915810; fax 7915811; info@camping-aarburg. ch; www.camping-aarburg.ch]** Exit A1/A2/E35 junc 46 sp Rothrist/Olten, foll sp to site. Med, mkd pitch, pt shd; htd wc; chem disp; mv service pnt; shwrs CHF1; el pnts (6A) CHF3 (rev pol), long lead req; gas; lndtte; shop; tradsmn; rest 500m; snacks; bar; BBQ; htd pool adj; 25% statics; dogs CHF1; phone; rlwy noise; red CKE/CCI. "Conv Luzern, Zürich, Bern; picturesque, walled town; excel, clean site; friendly warden." 1 May-15 Sep. CHF 29.00                         2012*

**ADLISWIL** *A3* (6.9km S Urban) *47.26384, 8.56056* **Camping Sihlwald, 8135 Langnau-am-Albis [044 7200434; camping. sihlwald@gmx.ch]** Turn off Zürich-Luzern rd Adliswil, site sp on L by Forsthaus rest. Med, pt shd; htd wc; chem disp; shwrs; el pnts inc; gas; lndtte; shop; rest, snacks; bar; playgrnd; pool 4km; dogs CHF4; poss cr; Eng spkn; adv bkg; quiet, but some rd noise; red CKE/CCI. "Pretty setting by rv; conv Luzern, Zürich & Bern; pitches furthest fr rv unrel in wet; excel, clean facs; helpful staff." 15 Apr-15 Oct. CHF 28.00         2009*

**AESCHI see Spiez** *C2*


**AGNO see Lugano** *D3*


⊞ **AIGLE** *C2* (4km NE Rural) *46.34030, 7.01550* **Camping du Soleil, Route du Suchet, 1854 Leysin [024 4943939; fax 4942121; info@camping-leysin.ch; www.camping-leysin. ch]** Take rd 20 Aigle to Le Sépey, exit at Le Sépey for Leysin, 6 hairpin bends to site. On ent vill pass g'ge on L, in 50m turn L into app rd to lge sports cent. In 100m turn R into narr access rd & bear L; site opp Hotel du Soleil. NB: Fr Aigle dist by rd 16km, last 5km up winding, steep but gd rd. Med, pt sl, pt shd; htd wc; chem disp; baby facs; shwrs inc; el pnts (16A) metered (adaptor avail); gas; lndtte (inc dryer); shops, rest nr; bar; BBQ; playgrnd; covrd pool adj; tennis adj; cycle hire; games area; games rm; horseriding, winter & summer skiing; sports cent & skating rink (all year) 100m; TV; many statics; dogs CHF3; quiet; ccard acc; red CKE/CCI. "Mainly winter ski resort but magnificent views; 15 min walk (uphill) to shops etc; conv cablecar; navette 100m; ski & boot rm; friendly, helpful staff; mkt Thu; used by school groups." ◆ CHF 37.00         2011*

**AIGLE** *C2* (1km NW Rural) *46.32385, 6.96206* **Camping de la Piscine, Ave des Glariers 1, 1860 Aigle [tel/fax 024 4662660]** Turn W off N9 (Aigle-Lausanne) at N edge of Aigle, site sp. Foll rd for 400m, site past pool on L. Med, pt shd; wc; chem disp; mv service pnt; shwrs inc; el pnts (4A) CHF3.50 (adaptor avail); gas; lndtte; sm shop; snacks; bar; playgrnd; pool; tennis; fishing; cycle hire; some statics; dogs CHF4; poss cr; Eng spkn; adv bkg; quiet but a little rlwy noise; ccard acc; red CKE/CCI. "V helpful owner; v gd, well-maintained site; pleasant town & gd touring base; outlook on to vineyards; easy flat walk into town, about 10 mins." 06 Apr-30 Sep. CHF 35.00                         2013*

⊞ **ALTDORF** *B3* (1km N Rural) *46.89256, 8.62800* **Remo-Camp Moosbad, Flüelerstrsse 122, 6460 Altdorf [041 8708541; fax 8708161]** Exit A2 at Altdorf junc 36. Foll sp Altdorf to rndabt & turn R. Site 200m on L adj cable car & sports cent. Sm, pt shd; wc; chem disp; mv service pnt; shwrs CHF1; el pnts (10A) CHF3 (adaptor loan); lndtte (inc dryer); shop & 200m; rest; bar; BBQ; public pool, waterslide & rest adj; 80% statics; dogs €1; phone; poss cr; Eng spkn; some rd & rlwy noise; ccard not acc; CKE/CCI. "Ideal windsurfing; useful NH en rte Italy; friendly welcome; excel san facs; excel rest; superb views; gd base for train trip over St Gotthard pass; plenty to see & do in Altdorf; bus & cable car combos avail." CHF 39.00                         2014*

## "I need an on-site restaurant"

We do our best to make sure site information is correct, but it is always best to check any must-have facilities are still available or will be open during your visit.

**ALTDORF** *B3* (5km N Rural) *46.91497, 8.62257* **Camping Windsurfing Urnersee, Unterer Winkel 11, 6454 Flüelen-See [041 8709222; fax 8709216; info@windsurfing-urnersee.ch; www.windsurfing-urnersee.ch]** On N4 & Axenstrasse, site sp on ent Flüelen. Steep app, not rec for lge or heavy o'fits. Med, terr, pt shd; wc; chem disp; shwrs CHF1; el pnts CHF3.50; shop; rest; bar; htd, covrd pool 2km; shgl beach; lake sw; fishing; watersports; cycle hire; tennis; no dogs; poss cr; adv bkg; quiet but some rlwy noise; Eng spkn. "Excel watersports." 1 Apr-30 Oct. CHF 36.00         2011*

**ANDEER see Thusis** *C4*

**ANDELFINGEN** *A3* (500m NE Rural) *47.59698, 8.68376* **TCS Camping Rässenwies, Alte Steinerstrasse 1, 8451 Kleinandelfingen [079 2383535; raessenwies@tcs-ccz. ch; www.tcs-ccz.ch]** On N4 Schaffhausen-Winterthur rd, site well sp in Kleinandelfingen, on Rv Thur. Sm, unshd; wc; shwrs; el pnts CHF3.50; gas; lndtte; shop pool 1km; fishing; dogs CHF3.50; quiet. "Beautiful area; v friendly." 20 Mar-4 Oct. CHF 43.00                         2013*

**ARBON** *A4* (1km W Rural) *47.52449, 9.42049* **Camping Buchorn, Philosophenweg 17, 9320 Arbon [071 4466545; fax 4464834; info@camping-arbon.ch; www.camping-arbon.ch]** Fr N on Kreuzlingen-Romanshorn rd 13, 8km after Romanshorn, site sp at ent to Arbon, on lakeside. Med, pitch, pt shd; wc; chem disp; mv service pnt; baby facs; shwrs; el pnts CHF3; gas; lndtte (inc dryer); sm shop; rest, snacks; BBQ; playgrnd; paddling pool; lake sw; fishing; watersports; boat hire; tennis; games rm; wifi; TV; no dogs; poss cr; adv bkg; quiet but some rlwy noise; ccard acc. "Pleasant location; clean site; helpful owner; steamer trips fr Arbon." ◆ ltd Easter-1 Oct. CHF 38.00                         2010*

**BASEL** *A2* (5km S Urban) *47.49963, 7.60283* **Camping Waldhort, Heideweg 16, 4153 Basel-Reinach [061 7116429; fax 7139835; info@camping-waldhort. ch; www.camping-waldhort.ch]** Fr Basel foll m'way sp to Delémont & exit m'way at Reinach-Nord exit; at top of slip rd, turn R & L at 1st traff lts (about 300m). Site on L in approx 1km at curve in rd with tramway on R, sp. Basel best app off German m'way rather than French. Lge, mkd pitch, pt shd; wc; chem disp; mv service pnt; baby facs; shwrs inc; el pnts (6A) inc; gas; lndtte; shop; tradsmn; rest 500m; snacks; playgrnd; pool; paddling pool; 50% statics; dogs CHF3; tram 500m (tickets fr recep); poss cr; Eng spkn; adv bkg; m'way noise; ccard acc; 10% red CKE/CCI. "Rec arr early in high ssn; helpful staff; gd sized pitches; m'van pitches sm; excel san facs; gates clsd 2200-0700; site muddy when wet; excel art museums in Basel." ♦ 1 Mar-29 Oct. CHF 47.00          2013*

⊞ **BASEL** *A2* (10km S Rural) *47.45806, 7.63545* **TCS Camping Uf der Hollen, Auf der Hollen, 4146 Hochwald [061 7511398; fax 7120240; info@tcscampingbasel.ch; www.tcscampingbasel.ch]** Exit A18 at Reinach-Sud dir Dornach, S thro Dornach dir Hochwald, uphill thro forest to site. Med, mkd pitch, pt shd; htd wc; chem disp; shwrs CHF0.50; el pnts CHF3; lndtte; playgrnd; htd, covrd pool 10km; games area; 90% statics; adv bkg; quiet; red CKE/CCI. "Gd views; peaceful, pleasant site." ♦ CHF 27.00          2010*

**BEATENBERG see Interlaken** *C2*

**BELLINZONA** *C3* (1km N Urban) *46.21186, 9.03831* **TCS Camping Bosco di Molinazzo, Via San Gottardo 131, 6500 Bellinzona [091 8291118; fax 8292355; camping. bellinzona@tcs.ch; www.campingtcs.ch]** Fr A13 exit Bellinzona Nord, foll rd over rv & rlwy bdgs. In approx 200m on R, immed after rd to Gorduno, site sp in 200m down ramp to R just bef Shell g'ge. Med, sl, pt shd; wc; chem disp; mv service pnt; baby facs; shwrs inc; el pnts (6A) CHF4; gas; lndtte (inc dryer); shop; rest, snacks; bar; BBQ; playgrnd; pool; tennis; rv adj; cycle hire; golf; wifi; TV; 20% statics; dogs CHF4; poss v cr; adv bkg; rd & rlwy noise; ccard acc; red CKE/CCI. "Pleasant & attractive city; gd NH en rte Italy; san facs stretched high ssn & site overcr; early arr site yourselves & report later - instructions on barrier." ♦ 1 Apr-9 Oct. CHF 63.00          2013*

**BERN** *B2* (3km SE Rural) *46.93285, 7.45569* **Camping Eichholz, Strandweg 49, 3084 Wabern [031 9612602; fax 9613526; info@campingeichholz.ch; www. campingeichholz.ch]** Exit A1/A12 & take 2nd turn-off sp Bern/Bümplitz dir Belp & airport. Turn L under A12 & foll sp Wabern & site. Lge, hdstg, shd; wc; chem disp; mv service pnt; shwrs CHF3.50; el pnts (rev pol )CHF3.50; gas; lndtte; shop; supmkt nr; rest, snacks; bar; BBQ; playgrnd; pool 2km; fishing; tennis; cycle hire; wifi; tram; poss cr; Eng spkn; adv bkg; poss v noisy; ccard acc. "Walk to Bern by rv (steep climb); clean, modern san facs; helpful staff." ♦ 20 Apr-30 Sep. CHF 44.00          2013*

**BERN** *B2* (10km SW Rural) *46.89301, 7.33408* **Freizeitzentrum Thörishaus, Strandheimstrasse 20, 3174 Thörishaus [031 8890271; fax 031 8890296; sense. giardino@hispeed.ch]** Exit m'way Bern-Fribourg at Flamatt. Strt at 1st rndabt, R at 2nd sp Thörishaus. Site on R in 150m. Med, pt shd; wc; shwrs inc; el pnts (10A) CHF3.50; gas; lndtte; shop; rest, snacks; bar; playgrnd; pool 4km; tennis; fishing; 80% statics; sep car park; Eng spkn; adv bkg; ccard acc; 10% red CKE/CCI. "Conv Bern; gd cycle paths; vg site." ♦ 1 Apr-31 Oct. CHF 26.00          2009*

⊞ **BERN** *B2* (6km NW Rural) *46.96375, 7.38420* **TCS Camping Bern-Eymatt, Wohlenstrasse 62C, 3032 Hinterkappelen [031 9011007; fax 9012591; camping. bern@tcs.ch; www.campingtcs.ch/bern]** Fr E on A1 exit junc 33 sp Bern-Bethlehem; foll sp for Wohlen & site. In 200m turn R at bottom of hill into site on shores Wohlensee. Fr W take Brunnen-Bern exit, then sp to Wohlen. Access for lge o'fits poss diff. Lge, some hdstg, pt shd; htd wc; chem disp; mv service pnt; baby facs; shwrs inc; el pnts (6A) inc; gas; lndtte; shop; rest, snacks; bar; BBQ (charcoal/gas); playgrnd; htd pool; paddling pool; fishing; cycle hire; games area; wifi; entmnt; TV/games rm; many statics; dogs CHF5; no c'vans/m'vans over 8m high ssn; bus to Bern nry; sep car park; poss cr; ccard acc; red low ssn; CKE/CCI. "Recep 0830-1100 & 1700-2000 high ssn, but site yourself; various pitch sizes; clean facs; gd value rest; helpful staff; daily mkt in Bern; 2 supmkt nrby;  excel." ♦ CHF 42.00          2012*

**BERNHARDZELL see St Gallen** *A4*

**BIEL/BIENNE** *B2* (7km SW Rural) *47.10916, 7.01666* **Camping Sutz am Bielersee, Kirchrain 40, 2572 Sutz [032 3971345; fax 3972061; mail@camping-sutz.ch; www.camping-sutz. ch]** Exit A1/E25 Biel cent on rd twd Neuchâtel. Turn L at Biel o'skts, foll sp to Ipsach-Täuffelen along E side of lake. Site sp after Ipsach on R at edge of lake. Lge, unshd; wc; chem disp; baby facs; shwrs inc; el pnts (10A) inc; gas; lndtte; shop; rest 2km; lake sw; fishing; tennis; 90% statics; Eng spkn; adv bkg; quiet; ccard acc. "Gd, modern san facs; extra lge pitches avail; friendly staff; cycle path adj." ♦ 1 Apr-31 Oct. CHF 39.00          2009*

**BIEL/BIENNE** *B2* (10km SW Rural) *47.08556, 7.11726* **Camping Prêles AG, Route de la Neuveville 61, 2515 Prêles [032 3151716; fax 3155160; info@camping-jura.ch; www.camping-jura.ch]** App Biel fr N on rd 6 approx 2km bef town; immed after emerging fr 2nd long tunnel turn R then L sp Orvin. Cont thro Orvin to Lamboing, in Lamboing turn L dir La Neuveville to Prêles. Drive strt thro vill & look out for tent sp beyond vill when descending hill. App fr S on rd 5 poss via Neuveville or Twann but steep climb, tight bends & narr vill streets. Lge, pt sl, shd; wc; chem disp; mv service pnt; baby facs; shwrs CHF0.50; el pnts (10A) CHF3.50; gas; lndtte; sm shop; rest, snacks; BBQ; playgrnd; htd pool; watersports 5km; tennis; cycle hire; horseriding, games rm; entmnt; dogs CHF2; some statics; sep car park high ssn; adv bkg; v quiet; ccard acc; red long stay; CKE/CCI. "Nice scenery & gd views; peaceful site surrounded by woods & meadows; recep clsd 1130-1400 & after 1800." ♦ 1 Apr-15 Oct. CHF 46.00          2012*

**BLUMENSTEIN see Thun** *B2*

**BONIGEN see Interlaken** *C2*

**BOURG ST PIERRE** *D2* (500m N Rural) *45.95265, 7.20740*
**Camping du Grand St Bernard, 1946 Bourg-St Pierre
[tel/fax 027 7871411; grand-st-bernard@swisscamps.ch;
www.campinggrand-st-bernard.ch]** Fr Martigny S to Grand
St Bernard Tunnel. Site well sp in cent of vill. Med, unshd;
wc; chem disp; shwrs; el pnts (4A) CHF3.50; gas; lndtte; shop
200m; tradsmn; rest, snacks, bar adj; htd pool adj; dogs; Eng
spkn; quiet; ccard acc; CKE/CCI. "Conv St Bernard Tunnel; gd
views." 15 May-15 Oct.  CHF 28.00                        2009*

**BOUVERET, LE see Villeneuve** *C1*

**BRENZIKOFEN see Thun** *B2*

**BRIENZ** *B2* (1km SE Rural) *46.75069, 8.04838* **Camping
Seegartli, 3855 Brienz [033 9511351]** Fr Interlaken take N8
sp Luzern/Brienz. Take Brienz exit, ignore sp to site to R & take
L in 1km bef Esso stn, sp Axalp. Site in 500m on R immed after
passing under rlwy. Site on E shore of lake, next to sawmill.
Sm, pt sl, pt shd; wc; chem disp; mv service pnt; shwrs CHF1;
el pnts (10A) CHF3; lndtte; shop; lake sw; watersports; fishing;
tennis; Eng spkn; quiet CKE/CCI. "Beautiful lakeside situation;
well-kept site; friendly owner; lakeside pitches boggy in wet
weather; long hose req for m'van fill-up; arr bef noon in ssn.
No dogs." 1 Apr-31 Oct.  CHF 33.00                       2011*

**BRIENZ** *B2* (1.5km SE Urban) *46.74811, 8.04769* **Camping
Aaregg, Seestrasse 22, 3855 Brienz [033 9511843; fax
9514324; mail@aaregg.ch; www.aaregg.ch]** Fr Interlaken
take N8 sp Luzern/Brienz. Take Brienz exit, ignore sp to site to R
& take L in 1km bef Esso stn, sp Axalp. Site in 500m on R after
passing under rlwy. Site on E shore of lake, next to sawmill.
Med, mkd pitch, hdstg, pt shd; htd wc; chem disp; mv service
pnt; some serviced pitches; shwrs inc; el pnts (10A) CHF5;
lndtte; shop; rest, snacks, bar; pool 500m; lake sw adj; internet;
dogs CHF4; phone; rlwy stn nr; poss cr; Eng spkn; adv bkg rec
(lge dep req); quiet; ccard acc; red long stay/low ssn; CKE/CCI.
"Excel, busy site on lakeside; lakeside pitches sm & poss cr;
ideal touring base; min stay 9 nights on best pitches high ssn;
excel, modern san facs; many attractions nrby." 1 Apr-31 Oct.
CHF 42.00                                               2009*

**BRIG** *C2* (3km E Rural) *46.31500, 8.01369* **Camping Tropic,
Simplonstrasse 11, 3901 Ried bei Brig [027 9232537]** On
Brig-Domodossola rd on Swiss side of Simplon Pass. Fr Brig,
exit Simplon rd at sp Ried-Brig Termen. Site on L in 500m.
Fr Simplon foll sp to Ried-Brig, site in vill. Med, sl, pt shd;
wc; shwrs CHF1; pt sl; gas; lndtte; shop; playgrnd;
pool 2km; TV; Eng spkn; rd noise. "Useful CL-type NH to/fr
Italy; welcoming & helpful owners; superb scenery; san facs
adequate." 1 Jun-15 Sep.  CHF 24.00                     2012*

**BRIG** *C2* (700m S Rural) *46.30838, 7.99338* **Camping
Geschina, Geschinastrasse 41, 3900 Brig [tel/fax
027 9230688; www.geschina.ch]** Foll sps twd Simplon Pass,
site on R at 700m, behind pool at rv bdge. Best app fr Glis.
Med, pt sl, pt shd; wc; chem disp; shwrs; el pnts (10A)
CHF2.50; gas; lndtte; shop; snacks; bar; playgrnd; pool adj;
fishing; dogs CHF2; poss cr; Eng spkn; adv bkg; quiet; red
long stay/CKE/CCI. "Friendly, well-kept, family-run site; vg
san facs; superb mountain & glacier views; ideal for Rhône
Valley & Simplon Pass; sh walk to town." 1 Apr-15 Oct.
CHF 29.00                                               2011*

⊞ **BRUNNEN** *B3* (2km S Rural) *46.99030, 8.63394* **Camping
Ferienhof Rüti, Rüti 4, 6443 Morschach [41 8205309; fax
8205313; info@ferienhof-rueti.com; www.ferienhof-rueti.
ch]** N4/E41 S thro Brunnen tunnel, take next L sp Morschach,
thro vill & site on R bef cable car. Sm, mkd pitch, pt sl, pt shd;
htd wc; chem disp; shwrs inc; el pnts (6a) inc; shop; tradsmn;
BBQ (gas/charcoal); playgrnd; lake sw nrby; games area; games
rm; wifi; TV; dogs; bus adj; Eng spkn; quiet; ccard acc; CKE/
CCI. "Panoramic views; on hobby farm with donkeys, mini-
pigs, hens etc; excel site, quiet." CHF 28.00            2013*

**BRUNNEN** *B3* (1km NW Rural) *46.99775, 8.59346* **Camping
Hopfreben, 6440 Brunnen [041 8201873; www.camping-
brunnen.ch]** A4/E41 exit Brunnen-Nord, dir Weggis, site sp
on lakeside. Med, pt shd; wc; chem disp; mv service pnt; shwrs
CHF1; el pnts (6A) CHF3 (adaptor avail/long cable req); lndtte;
shop; rest 1km; snacks; bar; playgrnd; pool 200m; lake sw
500m; boat launch; cycle hire; 20% statics; dogs CHF3; poss cr
w/end; adv bkg; quiet but some daytime noise fr gravel barges/
lorries adj; CKE/CCI. "Delightful location." 15 Apr-24 Sep.
CHF 39.00                                               2011*

**BRUNNEN** *B3* (1km NW Rural) *47.00076, 8.59149* **Camping
Urmiberg, Gersauerstrasse 75, 6440 Brunnen [tel/
fax 041 8203327; fragen@campingurmiberg.ch; www.
campingurmiberg.ch]** Exit A4 Brunnen Nord dir Weggis. Site
sp opp Urmiberg cable car stn. Med, pt shd; htd wc; chem
disp; shwrs inc; el pnts (10A) CHF2.30; lndtte; shop; tradsmn;
rest, snacks; bar; playgrnd; lake sw adj; 40% statics; dogs
CHF2; phone; poss cr; Eng spkn; adv bkg; quiet. "Peaceful,
clean, family-run site; wonderful views." 1 Apr-15 Oct.
CHF 27.00                                               2013*

**BUCHS** *B4* (450m S Rural) *47.16663, 9.46524* **Camping
Werdenberg, 9470 Buchs [081 7561507; fax 7565090;
verkehrsvereinbuchs@bluemail.ch; www.werdenberg.
ch]** Fr bdge over Rv Rhine at Buchs on rd 16 dir Werdenberg
& Grabs. Turn L at parking/camping sp, thro car park to site.
Sm, unshd; wc; chem disp; shwrs CHF1; el pnts (16A) CHF4;
gas; lndtte (inc dryer); shops nr; htd pool 2km; lake sw adj;
dogs CHF2; adv bkg; quiet but church bells adj every 15
mins. "Vg, attractive setting by lake with views of old town &
castle; friendly owners; gd base for Liechtenstein, Appenzell
& Vorarlberg; walking; plenty of activities mini-golf etc; extra
charge for vans over 5m; gd for families." ♦ 1 Apr-31 Oct.
CHF 34.00                                               2012*

**BULLE** *C2* (6km N Rural) *46.67545, 7.08478* **Camping du
Lac, 1643 Gumefens [026 9152162; fax 9152168; info@
campingdulac-gruyere.ch; www.campingdulac-gruyere.
ch]** Fr S on N12 exit junc 4 for Bulle. At T-junc turn N for Riaz.
Foll rd thro Riaz & Vuippens. Site on R 500m after Gumefens
turning. Fr N exit junc 5 Rossens & foll dir Bulle. In 7km turn
L twd lake & site. Med, mkd pitch, unshd; wc; chem disp; mv
service pnt; shwrs CHF0.50; el pnts (6A) CHF2.50; gas; lndtte;
shop; rest, snacks; bar; playgrnd; private beach; watersports;
cycle hire; 60% statics; no dogs; site open w/ends May & Sep;
Eng spkn; adv bkg; quiet; ccard not acc; red long stay/CKE/
CCI. "Lovely lakeside site, mountain views; helpful owner; sm
pitches not suitable lge o'fits; exit to main rd sh & steep." 1 Jul-
31 Aug.  CHF 27.00                                      2010*

⊞ **BULLE** C2 (8km N Rural) 46.67373, 7.02492 **Camping La Forêt, Route de Montiollin, 1642 Sorens [026 9151882; fax 9150363; info@camping-la-foret.ch; www.camping-la-foret.ch]** Fr S exit N12 Bulle dir Fribourg. In 6km turn L uphill to Sorens & site in 2km on L twd Malessert, sp. Lge, pt sl, pt shd; wc; chem disp; mv service pnt; shwrs CHF1; el pnts CHF3 (adaptor avail); lndtte; shop, rest, snacks; bar; playgrnd; pool; tennis; cycle hire; 80% statics; dogs CHF2; Eng spkn; adv bkg; quiet; red long stay. ◆ CHF 24.00                    2009*

**BUOCHS** B3 (500m N Rural) 46.97950, 8.41860 **TCS Camping Sportzentrum, Seefeldstrasse, 6374 Buochs-Ennetbürgen [041 6203474; fax 6206484; camping.buochs@tcs.ch; www.campingtcs.ch]** Fr W on N2 m'way, exit junc 33 Stans-Süd & bear L. Foll sp Buochs. At 1st x-rds in Buochs, turn L to Ennetbürgen, in approx 1km R twd lake, sp. Fr E exit junc 34 for Buochs, turn L onto Beckenriederstrasse; at x-rds in cent of town turn R dir Ennetbürgen & foll sp as above. Med, mkd pitch, pt shd; wc; chem disp; mv service pnt; shwrs inc; el pnts (4A) CHF3.50 (adaptor avail); gas; lndtte (inc dryer); supmkt adj; tradsmn; rest, snacks; bar; playgrnd; pool adj; lake sw adj; fishing; tennis; cycle hire; games rm; wifi; TV rm; 60% statics in sep area; dogs CHF5; Eng spkn; quiet but some light aircraft noise; ccard acc; red low ssn/CKE/CCI. "Gd NH twd Italy; helpful staff; well-maintained facs; fine views; boat trip tickets sold on site; ferry close by; if recep clsd find own pitch & sign in later; pitches not draining well after heavy rains; v friendly staff; picturesque site." 1 Apr-3 Oct. CHF 62.00          2013*

**BURGDORF** B2 (1.4km SE Rural) 47.05241, 7.63350 **TCS Camping Waldegg, Waldeggweg, 3400 Burgdorf [078 8718780; www.campingtcs.ch]** Exit Bern-Basel N1 m'way at sp Kirchberg. Site in Burgdorf clearly sp. App over narr (2.7m) humpback bdge. Med, pt shd; wc; chem disp; mv service pnt; shwrs inc; el pnts (10A) CHF3; lndry rm; shops 300m; rest 100m; playgrnd; pool 200m; fishing; tennis; golf; wifi; dogs; adv bkg; quiet. "Conv Bern; old town of Burgdorf v interesting; friendly staff; clean san facs; gd NH." 1 Apr-31 Oct. CHF 24.00                    2010*

**CHABLE, LE** D2 (5km S Rural) 46.05488, 7.24563 **Camping La Sasse, Chemin de la Sasse 11, 1947 Champsec [078 8277342; patricia.gabbud@netplus.ch]** Fr Martigny E on rd 21 & cont dir Verbier. Ent Le Châble & turn R at traff lts. Site on R in 5km. Sm, unshd; wc; chem disp; shwrs CHF1; el pnts CHF4; lndtte; shop, rest 1km; bar; 50% statics; adv bkg; quiet. "Rustic site; ltd facs; superb location." 15 May-31 Oct. CHF 20.00                    2009*

**CHAUX DE FONDS, LA** B1 (10km SW Rural) 47.06568, 6.69856 **Camping Lac des Brenets, 2416 Les Brenets [032 9321618; fax 9321639; campinglesbrenets@kfnmail.ch; www.camping-brenets.ch]** Take rd 20 fr La Chaux-de-Fonds to Le Locle, foll sp Les Brenets. Foll twisting rd downhill to lake, turn & ascend to ent site on R. NB Diff L turn on descent. Med, hdstg/grass, terr, unshd; htd wc; chem disp; mv service pnt; shwrs inc; baby facs; el pnts (12A) CHF4; gas; lndtte; shop, rest, snacks, bar high ssn; sm pool; lake sw adj; tennis; 80% statics; dogs CHF3; adv bkg; quiet; Eng spkn; red long stay; ccard acc; CKE/CCI. "Gd site o'looking Lac des Brenets & Rv Doubs; beautiful views; watch/clock museum 3km; friendly owner." ◆ 1 Apr-31 Oct. CHF 36.00    2012*

**CHESSEL see Villeneuve** C1

⊞ **CHUR** B4 (1.5km NW Rural) 46.85605, 9.50435 **Camping Au Chur, Felsenaustrasse 61, Obere Au, 7000 Chur [081 2842283; fax 2845683; info@camping-chur.ch; www.camping-chur.ch]** Site sp fr Chur Süd a'bahn exit, foll sp with tent pictogram (easily missed). Lge, pt shd; htd wc; chem disp; mv service pnt; baby facs; shwrs inc; el pnts (10A) CHF3.50; gas; lndtte; shop, rest 400m; snacks; bar; playgrnd; htd pool 200m; tennis; games area; wifi; TV; 65% statics; dogs CHF3; bus nr; poss cr; Eng spkn; ccard acc; red CKE/CCI. "Well-ordered, clean site; sm area for tourers; sm pitches; gd, modern facs; v soft when wet; helpful, friendly owners; interesting, old town." ◆ CHF 33.00                    2010*

**CLARO see Bellinzona** C3

**COLOMBIER see Neuchâtel** B1

**CORCELETTES LA POISSINE see Yverdon** B1

**CRANS MONTANA see Sierre** C2

**CUGNASCO see Locarno** C3

**CULLY see Lausanne** C1

**CUREGLIA see Lugano** D3

**DISENTIS MUSTER** C3 (2.5km S Rural) 46.69620, 8.85270 **TCS Camping Fontanivas, Via Fontanivas 9, 7180 Disentis-Mustèr [081 9474422; fax 9474431; camping.disentis@tcs.ch; www.campingtcs.ch]** Fr Disentis S twd Lukmanier Pass for 2.5km. Site on L. Lge, pt shd; htd wc; chem disp; mv service pnt; baby facs; shwrs inc; el pnts (6-10A) CHF4; gas; lndtte (inc dryer); shop; rest, snacks; bar; BBQ; cooking facs; playgrnd; pool 2.5km; lake sw; tennis; cycle hire; wifi; TV rm; 25% statics; dogs CHF6; Eng spkn; adv bkg; quiet; ccard acc; CKE/CCI. "Excel san facs; historic old town; gd walks." ◆ 23 Apr-26 Sep. CHF 36.00          2009*

**DUDINGEN see Fribourg** B2

**EGLISAU** A3 (4km W Rural) 47.57900, 8.5817 **TCS Camping Steubisallmend, 8416 Flaach [052 3181413; fax 3182683; camping.flaach@tcs.ch; www.campingtcs.ch]** Fr S (Zürich) on A51 to Bülach at end of m'way, then N4 N to Eglisau. Cross rv & cont twd Schaffhausen. Turn R dir Rüdlingen & Flaach. Site 2km W of Flaach; turn N at Rest Ziegelhütte. Steep access rd needs care. Lge, shd; wc; chem disp; mv service pnt; shwrs inc; el pnts (4A) CHF4; gas; lndtte; shops; rest 500m; snacks; bar; playgrnd; pool; fishing; cycle hire; 75% statics; dogs CHF6; poss cr; Eng spkn; adv bkg; ccard acc; red CKE/CCI. "Well situated on Rv Rhine; lower area subject to flood in wet." ◆ Easter- 4 Oct. CHF 39.00          2009*

**EGNACH see Romanshorn** A4

**ERLACH** *B2* (500m N Rural) *47.04649, 7.09812* **Camping Erlach, Stadtgraben 23, 3235 Erlach [032 3381646; fax 3381656; camping@erlach.ch; www.erlach.ch]** Fr any dir foll sp for sm town of Ins; fr there foll sp Erlach. In Erlach turn L dir Le Landeron, then R twd Hotel du Port; turn L at hotel, site 200m on L by pier. Med, mkd pitch, shd; wc; chem disp; mv service pnt; baby facs; shwrs CHF1; el pnts inc; gas; lndtte (inc dryer); freezer; shop; rest, 200m; snacks; bar; playgrnd; pool 3km; lake sw & beach; tennis; games area; cycle hire; entmnt; TV; 60% statics; dogs CHF3; poss cr; Eng spkn; adv bkg rec; quiet; ccard acc; red CKE/CCI. "Scenic area; gd for walking & sightseeing; pleasure steamers on lake; gd, modern san facs; charming site; sep car park - no cars on pitch." Easter-15 Oct. CHF 42.00                    2012*

## "Satellite navigation makes touring much easier"

Remember most sat navs don't know if you're towing or in a larger vehicle – always use yours alongside maps and site directions.

**ESCHENZ** *A3* (1km S Rural) *47.64467, 8.85985* **Camping Hüttenberg, 8264 Eschenz [052 7412337; fax 7415671; info@huettenberg.ch; www.huettenberg.ch]** Fr Schaffhausen dir Kreuzlingen on rd 13, in Eschenz turn R over level x-ing up hill, site sp. Lge, some hdstg, terr, unshd; htd wc; chem disp; mv service pnt; shwrs inc; el pnts (6-10A) CHF3; lndtte; shop; rest, snacks; bar; playgrnd; pool; paddling pool; internet; 80% statics; dogs CHF3; phone; bus 1km; train 2km; o'night area for m'vans; poss cr; Eng spkn; adv bkg; quiet; ccard acc; red low ssn; CKE/CCI. "Beautiful site with stunning views over Untersee; Stein am Rhein & Rhine Falls a must; gd, modern san facs; ltd space for tourers." ♦ ltd 9 Apr-18 Oct. CHF 33.00                    2009*

**ESTAVAYER LE LAC** *B1* (1.5km NW Rural) *46.86042, 6.86332* Camping La Ferme de la Corbière, 1470 Estavayer-le-Lac [026 6633619; fax 6631638; info@corbiere.ch; www.corbiere.ch] Fr Yverdon foll sp Estavayer-le-Lac. On app Estavayer foll sp Lac de Neuchâtel to pick up site sp. Med, pt shd; wc; shwrs; el pnts (10A) inc (adaptor avail & long lead poss req); shop 3km; BBQ; playgrnd; lake sw adj (steep climb); shgle beach; wifi; dogs; adv bkg; quiet; CKE/CCI. "Delightful, quiet alt to busy lakeside sites; helpful owner; CL-type with basic facs; hostel in farm buidings adj; used by lge youth/school tent groups." CHF 31.00                    2009*

**EVOLENE** *C2* (800m S Rural) *46.11080, 7.49656* **Camping Evolène, 1983 Evolène [027 2831144; fax 2833255; info@camping-evolene.ch; www.camping-evolene.ch]** Fr Sion take rd to Val d'Hérens. As app Evolène take L fork to avoid vill cent. Proceed to Co-op on L, turn sharp R & 1st L to site. Site sp. Sm, unshd; htd wc; chem disp; mv service pnt; shwrs CHF1; el pnts (10A) CHF4.00; gas; lndtte; shop & 400m; rest adj; bar; playgrnd; cycle, x-country ski & snowboard hire; 5% statics; dogs CHF3; Eng spkn; quiet; ccard acc; ACSI; CKE/CCI. "Mountain scenery; well-kept site; vg san facs; attentive owners; sh walk to vill cent, poss cr." 15 May-15 Oct. CHF 43.00                    2012*

**FAIDO** *C3* (1km SE Rural) *46.47165, 8.81705* **Camping Gottardo, 6764 Chiggiogna [091 8661562; fax 8660061; schroeder.camp@vtxmail.ch]** Exit A2/E35 at Faido, site on R in 500m, sp immed bef Faido. Med, terr, pt shd; htd wc; chem disp; shwrs CHF0.50; el pnts (6A) CHF4; gas; lndtte; sm shop & 2km; rest, snacks; bar; playgrnd; sm pool; few statics; dogs CHF2; phone; bus 400m; train 1.5km; poss v cr; Eng spkn; quiet but some rlwy noise; red long stay. "On main rd fr Italian lakes to St Gotthard Pass; interesting vill; poss diff for lge o'fits, espec upper terrs (rec pitch bef white building); excel facs; gd rest - home cooking inc bread, pastries; friendly, helpful staff; access to pitches v ltd in snowy conditions." 1 Mar-1 Nov. CHF 45.00                    2014*

⊞ **FIESCH** *C2* (500m NE Rural) *46.41016, 8.13871* **Camping Eggishorn, Fieschertalstrasse, 3984 Fiesch [027 9710316; fax 9710317; info@camping-eggishorn.ch; www.camping-eggishorn.ch]** Fr N19 turn into Fiesch, site sp in town. Med, mkd pitch, pt shd; htd wc; chem disp; mv service pnt; baby facs; shwrs inc; el pnts (16A) CHF4; gas; lndtte (inc dryer); shop 500m; tradsmn; rest, snacks; bar; BBQ; playgrnd; htd, covrd pool; fishing; games area; games rm; wifi; TV; 25% statics; dogs CHF3; bus, train 600m; poss cr; Eng spkn; quiet; ccard acc; CKE/CCI. "Beautiful situation - views all dirs; cable cars nr for Aletsch glacier; excel walking; well-kept site; highly rec." ♦ CHF 43.00                    2011*

**FILISUR** *C4* (1.5km SW Rural) *46.67176, 9.67408* **Camping Islas, 7477 Filisur [081 4041647; fax 4042259; info@campingislas.ch; www.campingislas.ch]** Fr Tiefencastel take dir Albula. At Filisur foll camping sp. Long, single track rd to site. Med, some hdstg, unshd; htd wc; chem disp; shwrs inc; el pnts (10A) CHF2; gas; lndtte (inc dryer); shop; tradsmn; supmkt 1.5km; rest; bar; BBQ; playgrnd; pool; fishing; wifi; TV; 70% statics; dogs free; phone; train 1.5km; adv bkg; Ccard acc; Eng spkn; quiet. "Gd touring base; informal management; euros acc; Train to Davos free with guest card supplied; excel san facs." ♦ 1 Apr-31 Oct. CHF 52.00                    2013*

**FLAACH see Eglisau** *A3*

## "There aren't many sites open at this time of year"

If you're travelling outside peak season remember to call ahead to check site opening dates – even if the entry says 'open all year'.

**FLEURIER** *B1* (1.4km N Rural) *46.90643, 6.57508* **Camping Val de Travers, Belle Roche 15, 2114 Fleurier [tel/fax 032 8614262; camping.fleurier@tcs.ch; www.camping-val-de-travers.ch]** On Pontarlier (France) to Neuchâtel rd, site sp in Fleurier to L at start of vill. Med, pt shd; wc; chem disp; mv service pnt; shwrs; el pnts (4A) CHF3; gas; lndtte; shop; rest; bar; playgrnd; htd pool 2km; rv fishing; tennis; games area; cycle hire; 15% statics; dogs CHF3; Eng spkn; adv bkg; quiet; ccard acc. "Helpful owners; wild chamois on rocks behind site visible early morning; vg." 17 Apr-26 Sep. CHF 28.00   2009*

**FOREL see Vevey** *C1*

FOULY, LA *D2* (500m N Rural) *45.93693, 7.09548* **Camping des Glaciers, 1944 La Fouly-Val Ferret [027 7831735; fax 7833605; info@camping-glaciers.ch; www.camping-glaciers.ch]** Exit Martigny-Grand St Bernard rd at Orsières. Cont thro Val Ferret to vill of La Fouly. At end of vill turn R, site in 500m. V steep rd for 13km fr Orsières. Lge, terr, pt sl, pt shd; wc; chem disp; mv service pnt; baby facs; shwrs inc; el pnts CHF3.50; gas; Indtte; shop 500m; rest 500m; playgrnd; tennis 300m; games area; fishing; horseriding; wifi; TV; dogs CHF2; Eng spkn; adv bkg; quiet; ccard acc; CKE/CCI. "Lovely site; excel facs; excel walking, climbing cent; lovely views." 15 May-30 Sep. CHF 30.00                                2009*

FRIBOURG *B2* (13km N Rural) *46.87827, 7.19121* **Camping Schiffenensee, Schiffenen 15, 3186 Düdingen [026 4933486; fax 4933474; info@camping-schiffenen.ch; www.camping-schiffenen.ch]** Exit A12 Bern-Fribourg at Düdingen & foll rd for Murten (sp). Ent poss tight lge o'fits. Lge, mkd pitch, pt shd; wc; chem disp; shwrs CHF1; el pnts (10A) CHF3; Indtte; shop; rest, snacks; bar; pool; paddling pool; lake adj; tennis; 80% statics; dogs CHF3; bus; poss cr; Eng spkn; adv bkg; quiet; ccard not acc; CKE/CCI. 1 Apr-31 Oct. CHF 27.00                                2009*

**FRUTIGEN See Kandersteg** *C2*

**GAMPEL See Leuk** *C2*

**GAMPELEN See Neuchâtel** *B1*

GENEVE *C1* (7km NE Urban) *46.24465, 6.19433* **TCS Camping Pointe à la Bise, Chemin de la Bise, 1222 Vésenaz [022 7521296; fax 7523767; camping.geneve@tcs.ch; www.campingtcs.ch]** Fr Geneva take S lakeside rd N5 sp Evian to Vésenaz 4km. Turn L on Rte d'Hermance (D25) at traff lts & foll sp to site in 1km. Med, pt shd; wc; chem disp; mv service pnt; baby facs; shwrs inc; el pnts (4-10A) CHF4.50 (adaptor on loan); gas; Indtte; shop; tradsmn; rest, snacks; bar; playgrnd; paddling pool; lake sw; fishing; cycle hire; wifi; TV; 60% statics; dogs CHF5; bus to Geneva; poss cr; Eng spkn; ccard acc; red CKE/CCI. "Pleasant site; excel lake & mountain excursions; helpful staff; muddy when wet." 1 Apr-3 Oct. CHF 46.00                                2010*

GENEVE *C1* (6km W Rural) *46.20111, 6.06621* **Geneva City Camping (previously Camping du Bois de Bay), 19 Route du Bois de Bay, 1242 Geneve [022 3410505; fax 3410606; info@geneva-camping.ch; www.geneva-camping.ch]** Fr A1 exit sp Bernex, then foll sp to Vernier, site sp. Lge, hdg pitch, pt shd; htd wc; chem disp; mv service pnt; baby facs; shwrs inc; el pnts (6A) CHF4.50; gas; Indtte (inc dryer); shop; tradsmn; snacks; bar; BBQ; playgrnd; tennis 2km; wifi; 40% statics; dogs CHF3.50; bus 2km; Eng spkn; some aircraft noise; ccard acc; red CKE/CCI. "V friendly; modern san facs; park & ride bus to city; don't be put off by indus site outside site." ♦ 1 Mar-31 Dec. CHF 43.00 (CChq acc)         2012*

**GORDEVIO See Locarno** *C3*

**GRAFSCHAFT See Ulrichen** *C3*

GRINDELWALD *C2* (800m SE Rural) *46.62061, 8.04400* **Camping Gletscherdorf, Lochenbodenweg, 3818 Grindelwald [033 8531429; fax 8533129; info@gletscherdorf.ch; www.gletscherdorf.ch]** Exit N6 at Interlaken & then dir Grindelwald. Turn R just after church at end of main rd thro town at sp Gletscher/Schlucht & down steep descent for 500m, camp on R, sharp R turn to ent. Med, mkd pitch, hdstg, pt sl, unshd; wc; chem disp; mv service pnt; shwrs inc; el pnts (10A) CHF4; gas; Indtte; shop; tradsmn; rest 500m; covrd pool 1km; 60% statics; no dogs; poss cr; Eng spkn; adv bkg; quiet; ccard acc; CKE/CCI; "Sh walk to glacier; ideal base for walking; views of Eiger; site yourself & pay later - recep clsd 1000-1730; excel san facs, but ltd; friendly." 1 May-20 Oct. CHF 34.00                                2011*

⊞ GRINDELWALD *C2* (1.5km W Rural) *46.62211, 8.01550* **Camping Eigernordwand, 3818 Grindelwald [033 8534227 or 8553322 winter; camp@eigernordwand.ch; www.eigernordwand.ch]** At 1st rndabt at ent to town turn R, site sp, no. 27. Med, pt sl, pt shd; htd wc; chem disp; mv service pnt; serviced pitch; shwrs inc; el pnts (10A) CHF5 (poss rev pol); gas; Indtte; shop; rest, snacks; bar; playgrnd; pool 1km; games area; TV; 60% statics; no dogs; bus 1km; site clsd mid-Apr to mid-May; higher winter prices; poss cr; quiet; ccard acc; red long stay. "Superb position at base of Eiger N wall; relaxed atmosphere; friendly, helpful staff; uphill walk to town; ski in/ski out; excel." ♦ CHF 34.00                                2010*

⊞ GRUYERES *C2* (4km S Rural) *46.56080, 7.08740* **Camping Haute Gruyère, Chemin du Camping 18, 1667 Enney [tel/fax 026 9212260; camping.enney@bluewin.ch; www.camping-gruyere.ch]** Well sp fr N (Gruyères) but not by name - foll TCS sp, not well sp fr S. Site E of rd fr Bulle to Château d'Oex, 1km S of Enney vill. Beware trains on x-ing at turn in. Med, unshd; htd wc; chem disp; mv service pnt; fam bthrm; shwrs inc; el pnts (6-10A) CHF4.50 (adaptor on loan); Indtte (inc dryer); shops 1km; rest, snacks; bar; playgrnd; lake sw 10km; fishing; cycle hire; entmnt; TV; 50% statics; dogs CHF4; poss cr; adv bkg; quiet; 10% red long stay; ccard acc. "Friendly owners; vg, modern san facs; sm area for tourers; bread baked to order on site; mainly level cycle rte to hill on which Gruyeres sits." CHF 48.00 (CChq acc)         2014*

⊞ GSTAAD *C2* (700m W Rural) *46.48119, 7.27269* **Camping Bellerive, Bellerivestrasse 38, 3780 Gstaad [033 7446330; fax 7446345; bellerive.camping@bluewin.ch; www.bellerivecamping.ch]** App fr Saanen turn R bef Gstaad, sp. Sm, mkd pitch, some hdstg, pt shd; htd wc; chem disp; mv service pnt; shwrs CHF1; el pnts (12A) CHF2.70; gas; Indtte (inc dryer); tradsmn; playgrnd; pool 700m; tennis; fishing; skiing; internet; TV; 60% statics; dogs CHF2.70; Eng spkn; adv bkg; rlwy noise. "Gd touring, walking, wintersports; rvside site; sm pitches; buy Gstaad Card for rd, rail & mountain transport." CHF 29.00                                2011*

**GSTEIG BEI GSTAAD See Gstaad** *C2*

⊞ **GUDO** C3 (1.5km W Rural) 46.17080, 8.93170 **Camping Isola, Via al Gaggioletto 3, 6515 Gudo [091 8593244; fax 8593344; campeggio.isola@ticino.com; www.camping-isola.ch]** Exit A2 at Bellinzona Sud dir Bellinzona (47), turn L at major traff lts sp Locarno. Cross rv and m'way, cont thro Gudo, site on L in 500mtrs, sharp L into site v narr rd, poorly sp. Lge, hdg/mkd pitch, pt shd; htd wc; chem disp; mv service pnt; baby facs; shwrs inc; el pnts (10A) CHF40; lndtte; shop; tradsmn; rest, snacks; bar; playgrnd; htd pool; paddling pool; 95% statics; dogs CHF4; site clsd mid-Dec to mid-Jan; quiet. "Delightful, well-kept site; NH pitches poor with inadequate elec supply; easy access fr main rd; mainly statics creating cr; v sm pitches not suitable for lge o'fits." 15 Jan-15 Dec. CHF 75.00                                              2013*

**GUMEFENS see Bulle** C2

**GWATT see Thun** B2

## "That's changed – Should I let The Club know?"

If you find something on site that's different from the site entry, fill in a report and let us know. See www.caravanclub.co.uk/europereport.

**HASLIBERG GOLDERN** B3 (500m S Rural) 46.73727, 8.19588 **Camping Hofstaff-Derfli, Hoffstatt, 6085 Hasliberg-Goldern [033 9713707; fax 9713755; welcome@derfli.ch; www.derfli.ch]** Fr Brünig pass foll sp for Hasliberg. After cable car at Twing foll rd to Gasthof & turn R down narr rd opp. Site well sp. Sm, mkd pitch, pt shd; htd wc; chem disp; mv service pnt; baby facs; shwrs inc; el pnts (10A) metered; gas; lndtte (inc dryer); shop & 2km; tradsmn; rest, snacks, bar 500m; playgrnd; hot tub; cycle hire; games area; games rm; wifi; TV; 20% statics; dogs CHF2; phone; bus 500m; Eng spkn; adv bkg; quiet. "Excel, beautiful site; vg summer walking/winter sports; gd size pitches." ♦ 15 Dec-30 Apr & 15 May-31 Oct. CHF 34.00                                              2010*

⊞ **HAUDERES, LES** D2 (1.5km N Rural) 46.09303, 7.50560 **Camping Molignon, Route de Molignon 183, 1984 Les Haudères [027 2831240; fax 2831331; info@molignon.ch; www.molignon.ch]** Fr Sion take rd to Val d'Hérens, turn R 2.5km after Evolène. Site sp. Rd fr Sion steep, twisting & narr in places. Med, mkd pitch, terr, pt shd; wc; mv service pnt; chem disp; baby facs; shwrs inc; el pnts (10A) CHF3.80; gas; lndtte; shop; tradsmn; rest, snacks; bar; playgrnd; htd pool; ski lift 3km; TV; 15% statics; dogs CHF3.20; phone; Eng spkn; adv bkg; quiet; ccard acc; red CKE/CCI. "V friendly owner; ideal for mountain climbing & walking; beautiful location." CHF 46.00                                              2014*

**HINTERKAPPELEN see Bern** B2

**HORW see Luzern** B3

**INNERTKIRCHEN** C3 (1km E Rural) 46.70700, 8.24219 **Camping Bauernhof-Wyler, Sustenstrasse 32, 3862 Innertkirchen [033 9718451; camping-wyler@bluewin. ch; www.camping-wyler.com]** App fr Innertkirchen dir Sustenpass, take care hairpin bends. Turn R on ent vill & foll sp. Sm, pt sl, unshd; wc; chem disp; shwrs CHF1; el pnts (10A) CHF2.50 (long lead poss req); lndtte (inc dryer); BBQ; playgrnd; tennis; fishing; games rm; horseriding; 20% statics; dogs CHF2; phone nr; adv bkg; Eng spkn; quiet. "Picturesque location; pleasant owner; CL-type site." ♦ ltd 1 Apr-31 Oct. CHF 27.00                                              2009*

⊞ **INNERTKIRCHEN** C3 (500m S Rural) 46.70669, 8.22619 **Camping Grund, Grundstrasse 44, 3862 Innertkirchen [tel/ fax 033 9714409; info@camping-grund.ch; www.camping-grund.ch]** App fr Susten or Grimsel Pass, turn L at camping sp immed on ent vill. Foll further sp for 1km. Sm, pt shd; htd wc; chem disp; mv service pnt; shwrs CHF1; el pnts (6A) CHF3; gas; lndtte (inc dryer); shops 200m; BBQ; playgrnd; htd covrd pool 6km; tennis; fishing; horseriding; games rm; dogs CHF2; adv bkg; quiet; 10% red long stay. "V helpful & friendly; gd cent for mountains." CHF 29.00                                              2011*

**INNERTKIRCHEN** C3 (1.5km NW Rural) 46.70938, 8.21519 **Camping Aareschlucht, Hauptstrasse 34, 3862 Innertkirchen [033 9715332; fax 9715344; campaareschlucht@bluewin.ch; www.camping-aareschlucht.ch]** On Meiringen rd out of town on R. Sm, pt shd; htd wc; chem disp; shwrs CHF1; el pnts (6-10A) CHF3; gas; lndtte (inc dryer); shop & rests nr; tradsmn; BBQ; playgrnd; pool 5km; games rm; 30% statics; dogs CHF2; adv bkg; Eng spkn; sep car park; quiet, but some rd noise; ccard acc; Red CKE/CCI. "Excel site; clean facs; gd walking; gd touring base Interlaken, Jungfrau region; conv Grimsel & Susten passes; rv walk to town." 1 May-31 Oct. CHF 24.00                                              2011*

## "I like to fill in the reports as I travel from site to site"

You'll find report forms at the back of this guide, or you can fill them in online at www.caravaclub.co.uk/europereport.

**INTERLAKEN** Sites in the Interlaken area are identified by numbers sp fr the N8. Foll the appropriate number to your site as folls: Manor Farm 1, Alpenblick 2, Hobby 3, Lazy Rancho 4, Jungfrau 5, Interlaken-Ost 6, Jungfraublick 7, Oberoi 8, Seeblick 10, Du Lac 15, Bauernhof Wang 19.

⊞ **INTERLAKEN** C2 (5km NE Rural) 46.70761, 7.91330 **Camp au Lac, 3852 Ringgenberg [033 8222616; fax 8234360]** Fr Ringgenberg to Brienz, site sp on R when exit Ringgenberg. Cont under rlwy viaduct to site. Med, pt sl, pt shd; wc; chem disp (wc); mv service pnt; shwrs CHF1; el pnts (6A) CHF3 (long cable poss req); lndry rm; shop & 1km; rest (clsd Mon, Tue low ssn); bar; pool 2km; 25% statics; dogs CHF2; bus; poss cr; Eng spkn; adv bkg; quiet; ccard acc; red low ssn; CKE/CCI. "Excel site; private access to lake; magnificent setting." ♦ CHF 36.00                                              2009*

⊞ **INTERLAKEN (NO. 1)** *C2* (3.5km W Rural) *46.68004, 7.81669* **Camping Manor Farm, Seestrasse 201, 3800 Interlaken-Thunersee [033 8222264; fax 8222279 or 033 8232991; manorfarm@swisscamps.ch / info@ manorfarm.ch; www.manorfarm.ch]** Fr W on A8 exit junc 24 Interlaken West & foll sp Thun & Gunten. At rndabt take 2nd exit twd Thun, sp Gunten; pass Camping Alpenblick on R, then site on L after bdge. V lge, mkd pitch, pt shd; chem disp; mv service pnt; wc; baby facs; serviced pitches; shwrs inc; el pnts (6A) inc (adaptor avail); gas; lndtte (inc dryer); shop; 2 rests adj; snacks; bar; BBQ (charcoal/gas); playgrnd; paddling pool; private beach/lake sw adj; boat & cycle hire; steamer boat trips; excursions; cable car & chairlift nrby; watersports; fishing; golf 300m; horseriding 3km; wifi; entmnt; games/ TV rm; 25% statics; dogs CHF5; c'vans/m'vans over 8m by request; money exchange; variable pitch price; poss cr; Eng spkn; adv bkg (bkg fee); quiet, rd noise some pitches; ccard acc; red low ssn; CKE/CCI. "Site on banks of Lake Thun; excel views; gd sized pitches; helpful staff; immac san facs; excel facs for children; local bus pass provided free; gd walking; if staying on Super pitch, water hose with pressurised valve fitting req; site v easy to find; v pleasant and well looked after; if taking an awning a storm strap req." ♦ CHF 66.00          2013*

**INTERLAKEN (NO. 10)** *C2* (2.8km E Rural) *46.69125, 7.89353* **TCS Camping Seeblick, Campingstrasse 14, 3806 Bönigen [033 8221143; fax 8221162; camping.boenigen@tcs.ch; www.campingtcs.ch]** Fr A8 exit junc 26 Interlaken-Ost dir Bönigen; on ent vill turn L, site sp on Lake Brienz. Med, some hdstg, shd; htd wc; chem disp; mv service pnt; baby facs; shwrs inc; el pnts (6A) CHF4; gas; lndtte (inc dryer); shop; rest 600m; snacks; bar; playgrnd; htd pool, paddling pool 200m; lake sw; fishing; boating; golf 4km; wifi; entmnt; TV rm; 10% statics; dogs CHF5; phone; Eng spkn; quiet; ccard acc; red low ssn/ CKE/CCI. "Ideal for fishing or boating; v helpful owner; clean facs; excel site; friendly owner; excel position walking & cycling into Interlaken." ♦ 28 Mar- 6 Oct. CHF 49.00          2013*

**INTERLAKEN (NO. 15)** *C2* (10km E Rural) *46.71141, 7.96886* **Camping du Lac, Schorren, 3807 Iseltwald [079 3533021; info@campingdulac.ch; www.campingdulac.ch]** Leave N8 at Iseltwald. Site sp fr N8, on Lake Brienz adj hotel. Sm, mkd pitch, terr, unshd; wc; chem disp; shwrs inc; el pnts CHF4.50; lndtte (inc dryer); shop; lakeside rest adj; paddling pool; lake beach & sw 200m; fishing; watersports; mountain biking; internet; TV rm; 80% statics; dogs CHF4; bus 300m; Eng spkn; adv bkg; quiet; red low ssn. "Peaceful site in superb location; friendly owner; vg, modern facs; access poss diff lge o'fits; touring pitches in cent of statics; vg." 1 May-30 Sep. CHF 46.00          2011*

**INTERLAKEN (NO. 19)** *C2* (10km NW Rural) *46.69025, 7.78469* **Camping auf dem Bauernhof Wang, 3803 Beatenberg [033 8412105; fax 8412185; camping-wang@ gmx.ch; www.naturpur.ch/camping-wang]** Exit m'way at junc Unterseen & foll sp to Beatenberg; 300m after church turn L & site sp. GPS rte not rec - use these dirs. Sm, terr, pt shd; wc; chem disp; shwrs inc; el pnts CHF3; lndtte; tradsmn; playgrnd; htd, covrd pool, tennis 1km; wifi; some statics; dogs CHF2; bus 300m; adv bkg; quiet; red low ssn. "Vg, peaceful, beautiful site in superb location; gd san facs; owner helpful; excel hiking country; conv Interlaken." 20 Apr-15 Oct. CHF 31.00          2011*

⊞ **INTERLAKEN (NO. 2)** *C2* (3km W Rural) *46.67969, 7.81764* **Camping Alpenblick, Seestrasse 130, 3800 Unterseen-Interlaken [033 8227757 or 8231470; fax 8216045; info@camping-alpenblick.ch; www.camping-alpenblick.ch]** Fr W on A8 exit junc 24 Interlaken West & foll sp Thun & Gunten. At rndabt take 2nd exit twd Thun, sp Gunten. Site adj Motel Neuhaus & Rest Strandbad on Gunten-Thun rd. Lge, mkd pitch, pt shd; htd wc; chem disp; mv service pnt; baby facs; shwrs inc; el pnts (10A) CHF4.50; gas; lndtte (inc dryer); shop; rest, snacks; BBQ; pool 3km; playgrnd; lake sw adj; watersports; fishing; golf adj; wifi; 30% statics; dogs CHF3; phone; bus fr site ent; stn 3km; Eng spkn; ccard acc (surcharge); red low ssn/long stay/CKE/CCI. "In beautiful situation; mountain views; excel, modern facs; bread baked on site; lake steamers fr hotel opp; gd walks nr; free bus pass to town; cycle rte to Interlaken; CHF1 to fill m'van water tank; adv bkg attracts surchage; site next to shooting club which may be noisy." ♦ CHF 474.00          2014*

**INTERLAKEN (NO. 3)** *C2* (2km W Rural) *46.68400, 7.82961* **Camping Hobby, Lehnweg 16, 3800 Unterseen-Interlaken [033 8229652; fax 8229657; info@campinghobby.ch; www.campinginterlaken.ch or www.campinghobby. ch]** On N8 fr Thun at E end of lake exit junc to Unterseen on rd 70. In 200m past petrol stn, turn L into narr lane; site sp. Site next to Camping Lazy Rancho. Or fr Interlaken turn R by side of Landhotel Golf opp G'ge, foll No.3 sp. Med, pt shd, some hdg pitch; htd wc; chem disp; mv service pnt; baby facs; shwrs CHF0.50; el pnts (10A) CHF4.50 (adaptor avail); gas; lndtte (inc dryer); shop; tradsmn; rest, snacks 400m; BBQ; playgrnd; paddling pool; shgl beach & lake sw 1.5km; golf 1km; wifi; 25% statics; dogs free; Eng spkn; adv bkg; quiet but some noise fr shooting range at w/end; ccard not acc; red low ssn; CKE/CCI. "Gd for touring Interlaken, Jungfrau region & Bernese Oberland; wonderful views of Eiger & other mountains; v clean facs; friendly staff." ♦ 1 Apr-30 Sep. CHF 50.00          2011*

**INTERLAKEN (NO. 4)** *C2* (2.5km W Rural) *46.68555, 7.83083* **Camping Lazy Rancho, Lehnweg 6, 3800 Unterseen-Interlaken [033 8228716; fax 8231920; info@lazyrancho. ch; www.lazyrancho.ch]** Fr W on app to Interlaken, exit A8/ A6 junc 24 sp Interlaken West. Turn L at slip rd rndabt then at rndabt take a sharp R turn (foll camping sp Nos. 3-5); at Migrol petrol stn foll sp for Lazy Rancho 4 (narr rd on L just bef Landhotel Golf); it is 2nd site. Cent of Interlaken best avoided with c'vans or lge m'vans. Rec arr bef 1900 hrs. Med, hdg/ mkd pitch, some hdstg, pt shd; htd wc; some serviced pitches; chem disp; mv service pnt; baby facs; shwrs inc; el pnts (10A) inc (adaptors provided); gas; lndtte (inc dryer); shop; tradsmn; cooking facs; BBQ (charcoal/gas/elec); playgrnd; sm pool; watersports, fishing nrby; cycle hire; tennis 2.5km; horseriding 500m; games rm; wifi; sat TV; 30% statics; dogs CHF3; no c'vans/m'vans over 7.50m high ssn; phone; Eng spkn; quiet but some noise fr shooting range at w/end; ccard acc; red low ssn; CKE/CCI. "Superb views Eiger, Monch & Jungfrau; ideal for touring Interlaken, Bernese Oberland; friendly, caring, helpful owners; sm pitches; recep 0900-1200 & 1330-2100 high ssn; 5 mins to bus stop nr Cmp Jungfrau; ask about Swiss red fare rlwy services - excel value; immac, outstanding, well-maintained site & facs." ♦ 18 Apr-16 Oct. CHF 68.00 SBS - S01          2014*

**INTERLAKEN (NO. 5)** *C2* (2km W Rural) *46.68688, 7.83411* Jungfrau Camp, Steindlerstrasse 60, 3800 Unterseen-Interlaken [tel/fax 033 8225730; info@jungfraucamp.ch; www.campinginterlaken.ch or www.jungfraucamp.ch] Leave N8 at exit Unterseen. In approx 600m turn R at rndabt & foll sp to site. Med, pt shd; htd wc; chem disp (ltd); mv service pnt; baby facs; fam bthrm; shwrs CHF1; el pnts (10A) CHF4; gas; lndtte (inc dryer); shop; rest, snacks; bar; playgrnd; pool; lake sw 1.5km; tennis; 40% statics; dogs CHF4; bus adj; poss cr; Eng spkn; adv bkg; quiet some noise fr shooting range at w/end; red low ssn. "Visits to all Bernese Oberland vills; views of Jungfrau, Mönch & Eiger; town in walking dist; excel, relaxing, well-run site; high standard san facs." 1 Jun-15 Sep. CHF 46.00                                                        2013*

**INTERLAKEN (NO. 6)** *C2* (1.1km N Rural) *46.69256, 7.8689* TCS Camping Interlaken-Ost, Brienzstrasse 24, 3800 Interlaken [033 8224434; fax 8224456; camping. interlaken@tcs.ch; www.campinginterlaken.ch] Exit N8 at Ringgenberg & foll sp for Brienz/Luzern. After viaduct turn L & site sp in 100m. Awkward bends on app. Med, mkd pitch, pt shd; wc; chem disp; mv service pnt; shwrs; el pnts (8A) CHF4; gas; lndtte (inc dryer); shop in ssn; rest; bar; playgrnd; pool 300m; sand beach 2km; wellness facs; wifi; 20% statics; dogs CHF5; train opp; poss cr high ssn; Eng spkn; some rd noise; ccard acc; red CKE/CCI. "Gd cent for Bernese Oberland; excel walking; helpful staff; easy access to town; lively entmnt on lake cruises; concerts." 1 Apr-10 Oct. CHF 44.00      2011*

**INTERLAKEN (NO. 7)** *C2* (2km S Rural) *46.67309, 7.86719* Camping Jungfraublick, Gsteigstrasse 80, 3800 Matten-Interlaken [033 8224414; fax 8221619; info@jungfraublick. ch; www.jungfraublick.ch] Fr E exit N8 after tunnel at Lauterbrunnen-Grindelwald junc 25, head N twd Matten-Interlaken & site 250m on L. Med, mkd pitch, pt shd; htd wc; chem disp; mv service pnt; shwrs CHF0.50; el pnts (6A) inc (poss rev pol); gas; lndtte (inc dryer); shop; BBQ (gas/charcoal); playgrnd; sm htd pool in ssn; lake sw 3km; fishing; rafting; paragliding; canyoning; cycle hire; golf, horseriding 4km; wifi; TV/games rm; 40% statics; dogs CHF3; no c'van/m'van over 7.50m (inc towbar) high ssn; phone; free local bus; poss cr; Eng spkn; adv bkg; some rd/rlwy noise; ccard acc; red long stay/ low ssn; CKE/CCI. "Wonderful views Jungfrau; helpful staff; clean facs; adventure sports adj; excursions, walks & cycle rtes around Interlaken; vg." ♦ 1 May-19 Sep. CHF 53.00 SBS - S04                                                       2014*

**INTERLAKEN (NO. 8)** *C2* (4km S Rural) *46.66161, 7.86500* Camping Oberei, Obereigasse 9, 3812 Wilderswil-Interlaken [tel/fax 033 8221335; oberei8@swisscamps.ch; www.campinginterlaken.ch or www.campingwilderswil. ch] Fr Interlaken by-pass take rd sp Grindelwald & Lauterbrunnen to Wilderswil. Site sp 800m past stn on R in vill. Narr ent. Med, mkd pitch, pt sl, pt shd; htd wc; chem disp; baby facs; shwrs CHF1; el pnts (6A) CHF3; gas; lndtte (inc dryer); shop; rest, snacks; bar; playgrnd; pool 3km; TV rm; dogs CHF2; bus adj, bus/train nr; poss cr; Eng spkn; adv bkg; quiet; ccard not acc; CKE/CCI. "Well-managed, relaxing, family-run site in superb scenic location; helpful owners; grnd sheets supplied if wet/muddy; blocks provided; gd, clean facs; gd touring cent; easy walk to rlwy stn; guest card gives free local train & bus travel; excel rec high ssn; friendly." 1 May-15 Oct. CHF 48.00                                                        2013*

**ISELTWALD see Interlaken** *C2*

⊞ **KANDERSTEG** *C2* (9km N Rural) *46.58188, 7.64150* Camping Grassi, 3714 Frutigen [033 6711149; fax 6711380; campinggrassi@bluewin.ch; www.camping-grassi.ch] Exit rd to Kandersteg at Frutigen-Dorf & in 400m L to site in 500m. Med, pt shd; htd wc; chem disp; mv service pnt; baby facs; shwrs inc; el pnts (10A) CHF3; gas; lndtte; shops; rest 500m; playgrnd; htd covrd pool 1km; fishing; tennis; cycle hire; wifi; TV; 50% statics; dogs CHF1.50; phone; Eng spkn; adv bkg; red long stay. "Walking rte dir fr site to spectacular pedestrian suspension bdge; 10 min walk to town." CHF 41.00                                          2014*

⊞ **KANDERSTEG** *C2* (1.3km NE Rural) *46.49800, 7.68519* Camping Rendez-Vous, 3718 Kandersteg [033 6751534; fax 6751737; rendez-vous.camping@bluewin.ch; www. camping-kandersteg.ch] In middle of Kandersteg turn E dir Sesselbahn Öschinensee; site sp. Med, some hdstg, pt sl, terr, pt shd; htd wc; chem disp; mv service pnt; shwrs CHF1; el pnts (10A) (adaptors avail); gas; lndtte (inc dryer); tradsmn; rest, snacks; bar; BBQ; htd pool 800m; cycle hire; games rm; wifi; dogs CHF3; Eng spkn; adv bkg; quiet; ccard acc; CKE/ CCI. "Excel, well-supervised site; chair-lift adj; excel walking." CHF 49.00                                          2014*

**KRATTIGEN see Spiez** *C2*

> ## "We must tell The Club about that great site we found"
>
> Get your site reports in by mid-August and we'll do our best to get your updates into the next edition.

**KREUZLINGEN** *A3* (8km SE Rural) *47.62182, 9.26602* Camping Ruderbaum, Ruderbaum 3, 8595 Altnau-am-Bodensee [071 6952965; camping@ruderbaum.ch; www. ruderbaum.ch] Fr Kreuzlingen foll main lakeside rd 13 twd Romanshorn. After passing sp for Altnau, at rndabt turn L, cross rlwy, site on L. Lge, pt sl, pt shd; htd wc; chem disp; mv service pnt; shwrs; el pnts CHF3.50; lndtte; shop; tradsmn; rest, snacks, bar adj; shgl beach & lake adj sw; 80% statics; dogs €2.50; train adj; Eng spkn; quiet; some rlwy noise; CKE/CCI. "Sep area for tourers sloping down to lake - poss diff when wet; gd site in beautiful setting; helpful staff; lakeside walks & cycling; landing stage for Lake Constance ships; helpful staff; gd." ♦ 1 Apr-31 Oct. CHF 29.00                       2010*

**LANDERON, LE** *B2* (300m S Rural) *43.05251, 7.06995* Camping des Pêches, Route du Port, 2525 Le Landeron [032 7512900; fax 7516354; info@camping-lelanderon. ch; www.camping-lelanderon.ch] A5 fr Neuchâtel, exit Le Landeron or La Neuveville; foll site sp. Med, mkd pitch, pt shd; wc; chem disp; mv service pnt; 20% serviced pitches; baby facs; shwrs CHF1; el pnts (15A) CHF3.50; gas; lndtte; shop; tradsmn; rest; bar; playgrnd; htd pool 100m; fishing; tennis; cycle hire; TV rm; 60% statics; sep car park; poss cr; Eng spkn; adv bkg; noisy; ccard acc; red CKE/CCI. "Sep touring section on busy site; walks by lake & rv; interesting old town." ♦ ltd 1 Apr-15 Oct. CHF 32.00                                  2009*

Tell us about the sites you visit

**LANDQUART** *B4* (3km E Rural) *46.97040, 9.59620* **TCS**
Camping Neue Ganda, Ganda 21, 7302 Landquart
[081 3223955; fax 3226864; camping.landquart@tcs.ch;
www.campingtcs.ch] Exit A13/E43 dir Landquart, site sp on
rd to Davos. Lge, pt sl, pt shd; htd wc; chem disp; mv service
pnt; fam bthrm; baby facs; shwrs inc; el pnts (6-10A) CHF4;
gas; lndtte (inc dryer); shop; snacks; bar; BBQ; cooking facs;
playgrnd; rv fishing; canoeing; tennis 300m; games rm; cycle
hire; wifi; entmnt; 60% statics; dogs CHF4; rd noise; ccard
acc; red CKE/CCI. "Immac san facs; excel site; v helpful owner
& staff; poss uneven pitches, mainly grass; if recep clsd find
pitch & sign in later; many mkd walks fr site." ♦ 10 Dec-
28 Feb & 19 Mar-17 Oct.  CHF 39.00          2013*

**LANGNAU AM ALBIS See Adliswil** *A3*

**LANGWIESEN see Schaffhausen** *A3*

**LAUSANNE** *C1* (9km E Rural) *46.48973, 6.73786* **Camping
de Moratel, Route de Moratel 2, 1096 Cully [021 7991914;
camping.moratel@bluewin.ch]** Fr Lausanne-Vevey lakeside
rd (not m/way), turn R to Cully; sp thro town; site on R on lake
shore. Ent not sp. Sm, hdg/mkd pitch, hdstg, pt shd; wc; chem
disp; mv service pnt; shwrs inc; el pnts (3-5A) metered (adaptor
provided); gas; lndtte; shop; tradsmn; snacks; bar; pool 3km;
lake sw; fishing; boating; 80% statics; bus, train, ferry; poss
cr; adv bkg; some rlwy noise. "Vg value; attractive, clean site
with beautiful views; rec adv bkg for lakeside pitch; friendly
staff; siting poss diff for lge o'fits; gd location for best pt Lake
Geneva; ex san facs." 20 Mar-20 Oct.  CHF 23.00      2011*

⊞ **LAUSANNE** *C1* (2km W Rural) *46.51769, 6.59766*
Camping de Vidy, Chemin du Camping 3, 1007 Lausanne
(Genferseegebiet) [021 6225000; fax 6225001; info@
clv.ch; www.clv.ch] Leave A1 at Lausanne Süd/Ouchy exit;
take 4th exit at rndabt (Rte de Chavannes); in 100m filter L
at traff lts & foll site sp to L. Site adj to HQ of Int'l Olympic
Organisation, well sp all over Lausanne. Lge, mkd pitch, pt
shd; htd wc (some cont); chem disp; mv service pnt; baby
facs; shwrs inc; el pnts (10A) inc; gas; lndtte (inc dryer); shop;
rest, snacks; bar; BBQ; playgrnd; lake beach adj; watersports;
tennis 1km; cycle hire; sports & recreation area adj; games
rm; wifi; TV; many statics in sep area; recep 0800-2100 high
ssn; dogs CHF2; no c'vans/m'vans over 8m high ssn; bus to
Lausanne 400m; chem disp up steps; Eng spkn; adv bkg;
quiet; ccard acc; CKE/CCI. "Excel lakeside site in attractive
park; friendly staff; sm pitches; gd san facs; gd train service to
Geneva; conv m'way; free bus passes for unltd bus & Metro
tavel in Lausanne; Facs need updating (2013); gd cycling." ♦
CHF 47.00                                  2013*

⊞ **LAUTERBRUNNEN** *C2* (1.1km SE Rural) *46.59100,
7.91311* Camping Schützenbach, Witimatte 204B,
3822 Lauterbrunnen [033 8551268; fax 8551275; info@
schutzenbach.ch; www.schutzenbach.ch] S fr Interlaken,
site sp after Lauterbrunnen. Med, pt sl, terr, pt shd; htd wc;
chem disp; mv service pnt; shwrs CHF0.50; el pnts (15A) CHF4
(poss rev pol); gas; lndtte (inc dryer); shop & 300m; snacks; bar;
playgrnd; pool 400m; fishing; tennis; 60% statics; dogs CHF3;
bus at site ent; rlwy stn nr; site clsd 6 Nov-9 Dec; Eng spkn; adv
bkg; quiet but some noise fr nrby helipad & hostel adj; ccard
acc. "Clean, modern san facs; site used by coach camping
parties & lge groups; friendly owners." CHF 26.00      2010*

⊞ **LAUTERBRUNNEN** *C2* (500m S Rural) *46.58788, 7.91030*
Camping Jungfrau, Weid 406, 3822 Lauterbrunnen
[033 8562010; fax 8562020; info@camping-jungfrau.ch;
www.camping-jungfrau.ch] S o'skirts of Lauterbrunnen sp
at R fork, site in 500m. Lge, some hdstg, terr, pt shd; htd wc;
chem disp; mv service pnt; baby facs; some serviced pitches;
shwrs inc; el pnts (15A) CHF2.50 (metered in winter; poss rev
pol); gas; lndtte (inc dryer); supmkt; tradsmn; rest, snacks; bar;
playgrnd; pool 600m; tennis; cycle hire; wifi; TV; 30% statics;
dogs CHF3; phone; sep car park when site full; ski-bus; ATM;
poss cr; Eng spkn; adv bkg rec; quiet; ccard acc; red/long stay/
CKE/CCI. "Friendly, helpful welcome; fine scenery; rlwy tickets
sold; close to town & rlwy stn to high alpine resorts; ski &
boot rm; rest clsd Sun, Mon in winter; navette inc; some noise
fr helicopter pad & shooting club, top of site quietest; superb
site & facs; clean; shop/rest gd; excel site; lovely views." ♦
CHF 73.00                                  2013*

⊞ **LAUTERBRUNNEN** *C2* (3km S Rural) *46.56838, 7.90869*
Camping Breithorn, Sandbach, 3824 Stechelberg
[033 8551225; fax 8553561; breithorn@stechelberg.ch;
www.campingbreithorn.ch] Up valley thro Lauterbrunnen,
300m past Trümmelbach Falls to ent on R. Med, unshd;
wc; chem disp; mv service pnt; shwrs CHF1; el pnts (10A)
metered; gas; lndtte (inc dryer); shop; rest 200m; BBQ; sm
playgrnd; pool 3km; tennis; fishing; 60% statics; dogs CHF1;
phone; Eng spkn; adv bkg; quiet; red CKE/CCI. "Quiet site in
lovely area; arr early high ssn; fine scenery & gd touring base;
friendly helpful owners; frequent trains, funiculars & cable
cars fr Lauterbrunnen stn (4km); Schilthorn cable car 1.5km;
excel cent for mountain walking & cycling; excel, clean facs."
CHF 38.00                                  2014*

**LAUTERBRUNNEN** *C2* (6km S Rural) *46.54619, 7.90100*
Camping Rütti, 3824 Stechelberg [033 8552885; fax
8552611; campingruetti@stechelberg.ch; www.
campingruetti.ch] Fr Interlaken thro Lauterbrunnen, past
Trümmelbach Falls, site on R at end of valley. Med, pt sl, pt
shd; wc; chem disp; shwrs; el pnts (10A) CHF3; gas; lndtte (inc
dryer); shop, rest, bar 200m; tradsmn; playgrnd; fishing; tennis;
cycle hire; games rm; 10% statics; phone; dogs CHF2.50;
bus 200m; poss cr; Eng spkn; adv bkg rec; quiet; CKE/CCI.
"Frequent buses to Lauterbrunnen stn; gd walking/cycling;
superb site." 1 May-30 Sep.  CHF 31.00        2009*

⊞ **LENK** *C2* (3km S Rural) *46.42819, 7.47788* **Camping
Hasenweide, Hasenweide 1, Oberried, 3775 Lenk im
Simmental [033 7332647; fax 7332973; info@camping-
hasenweide.ch; www.camping-hasenweide.ch]** Take rd S
fr Zweisimmen to Lenk, thro Lenk vill twd Oberreid for 4.5km,
ignore 1st site on R, site at end of rd on L. Sm, pt sl, pt shd;
htd wc; chem disp; shwrs inc; el pnts (6A) CHF3 (poss long lead
req); lndtte (inc dryer); sm shop & 5km; tradsmn; rest adj; BBQ;
games rm; internet; 75% statics; dogs CHF2; phone; bus to
town; site clsd mid-Oct to mid-Nov; Eng spkn; quiet. "Mostly
statics but some rm for tourers, otherwise field outside; poss
long walk to san facs; ideal cent walking & skiing; beautiful
location at foot of waterfall; vg." CHF 30.00     2009*

⊞ **LENZERHEIDE** *C4* (5km S Rural) *46.69873, 9.55813*
**Camping St Cassian, 7083 Lenz bei Lenzerheide**
**[081 3842472; fax 3842489; camping.st.cassian@bluewin.
ch]** Fr Chur exit m'way Chur Süd & foll sp Lenzerheide. 2km
past Lenzerheide site clearly sp on L. Fr S 1km past Lenz on R.
NB Long, hard climb & hairpin bet Lenzerheide & Chur. Med,
hdstg, pt sl, terr, shd; wc; all serviced pitches; mv service pnt;
chem disp; shwrs CHF1; el pnts (10A) CHF3; gas; lndtte; shop
3km; rest adj; playgrnd; lake sw 2km; wifi; 90% statics; dogs
CHF2; phone; poss cr; some Eng spkn; adv bkg; quiet; CKE/
CCI. "Site in conifer woodland; non-glaciated area gd for
walking, touring, mountain biking; mountain views; rec arr
early to secure pitch." ♦ ltd CHF 31.00          2009*

**LENZERHEIDE** *C4* (500m SW Rural) *46.72331, 9.55468* **TCS
Camping Gravas, Voa Nova 6, 7078 Lenzerheide/Lai
[081 3842335; fax 3842306; camping.lenzerheide@tcs.
ch; www.campingtcs.ch]** Exit A13 at Chur-Süd onto rd 3 dir
Lenzerheide (20km). Site sp fr cent of Lenzerheide. Long, hard
climb to site with hairpin. Lge, shd; htd wc; chem disp; shwrs;
el pnts (6-10A) CHF4.50; gas; lndtte (inc dryer); shops adj; pool
1km; lake sw 1.2km; 60% statics; dogs CHF5; poss cr; Eng
spkn; adv bkg; rd noise; ccard acc; CKE/CCI. "Many sports &
activities in Lenzerheide; excel walking; sm pitches." 2 Dec-
11 Apr & 28 May-2 Nov. CHF 35.00          2010*

**LEUK** *C2* (6km N Rural) *46.38119, 7.62361* **Camping
Sportarena, 3954 Leukerbad [027 4701037; fax 4703707;
info@sportarenatop.ch; www.sportarenatop.ch]** Exit A9 at
Susten & foll sp N to Leukerbad, site sp. Med, some hdstg, pt
sl, pt terr, pt shd; htd wc; chem disp; mv service pnt; shwrs inc;
el pnts (10A) CHF5; lndtte; shop 500m; tradsmn; rest, snacks;
bar; BBQ; htd, covrd pool 200m; thermal pools nr; sports cent
adj; games area; TV rm; 20% statics; dogs CHF2; poss cr; Eng
spkn; adv bkg; quiet. "Beautiful situation; pleasant, helpful
staff; attractive little town; cable cars; walks; vg." ♦ ltd 1 May-
31 Oct. CHF 30.00          2012*

**LEUK** *C2* (8km E Rural) *46.30719, 7.76388* **Camping Rhône,
3945 Gampel [027 9322041; info@campingrhone.ch;
www.campingrhone.ch]** Fr rd A9/E62 exit dir Gampel, site
well sp on R bank of Rv Rhône. Lge, pt shd; wc; chem disp;
mv service pnt; baby facs; shwrs inc; el pnts CHF3.20; gas;
lndtte; shop high ssn; rest high ssn; bar; playgrnd; htd pool &
paddling pool; tennis; golf; fishing; 30% statics; dogs CHF3;
poss cr; adv bkg; quiet. "Superb location & touring base; gd
walking, cycling; driest pt of Switzerland." ♦ 1 Apr-31 Oct.
CHF 23.00          2009*

**LEUK** *C2* (1.6km SE Urban) *46.29911, 7.63738* **Camping
Bella-Tola, Waldstrasse 57, 3952 Susten [027 4731491; fax
4733641; info@bella-tola.ch; www.bella-tola.ch]** E fr Sierre
turn R at ent to Susten, after bdge over Illgraben & foll sp for
1.5km. NB Acute turn off main rd; v steep hill & bad rd surface.
Lge, mkd pitch, sl, pt shd; wc; chem disp; mv service pnt;
baby facs; shwrs inc; el pnts (10A) CHF3.60; gas; lndtte; shop;
tradsmn; rest, snacks; bar; BBQ; playgrnd; htd pool; lake sw &
shgl beach; games rm; wifi; TV; 25% statics; dogs CHF2.70;
phone; bus 1.6km; poss cr; adv bkg; noisy at w/end; ccard acc;
red low ssn. 11 May-30 Sep. CHF 49.00          2011*

**LEUK** *C2* (3km SE Rural) *46.29780, 7.65936* **Camping
Gemmi 'Agarn', Briannenstrasse 4, 3952 Susten [tel/fax
027 4731154 or 4734295; info@campgemmi.ch; www.
campgemmi.ch]** Foll A9/E27 SE; then nr Martigny take A9/
E62 to Sierre; then take E62 thro Susten. After 2km, by Hotel
Relais Bayard, take R lane (Agarn, Feithieren), ignoring sp
Camping Torrent, & foll Alte Kantonstrasse sp Agarn. Turn R
at site sp into Briannenstrasse; site in 200m. Med, mkd pitch,
pt sl, pt shd; wc; chem disp; mv service pnt; serviced pitches;
individual san facs some pitches; shwrs inc; el pnts (16A) inc;
gas; lndtte (inc dryer); shop; tradsmn; rest, snacks; BBQ (gas/
elec); playgrnd; pool 600m; golf, tennis, horseriding nrby;
wifi; sat TV; 5% statics; dogs CHF3; no c'vans/m'vans over 9m
high ssn; Eng spkn; adv bkg; quiet; various pitch prices; ccard
acc; red low ssn; CKE/CCI. "Outstanding site; friendly, helpful,
hardworking owners; private bthrms avail; gd stop on way
Simplon Pass; barrier clsd 2200-0800; excel walking; conv A9."
12 Apr-11 Oct.  CHF 40.00 SBS - S12          2011*

**LEUK** *C2* (3.7km SW Rural) *46.30702, 7.61101* **Camping
du Monument de Finges, Alter Kehr 33, 3952 Susten
[027 473 18 27; camping.monument@hotmail.com; www.
campingmonument.ch]** Fr Visp twds Sion, foll E62 (blue sp);
site sp on R approx 3km after passing thro Susten. Lge, hdg,
mkd pitch, pt sl, pt shd; wc; chem disp; shwrs; el pnts (10A);
lndtte; BBQ; playgrnd; pool; 10% statics; dogs; twin axles;
quiet; CKE/CCI. "Lovely, well maintained sw pool; site partly
in pine forest & in lge grassy fields; spacious open pitches;
mountain views; walking tracks fr site; gd site." 1 May-21 Sep.
CHF 50.00          2014*

**LEYSIN see Aigle** *C2*

⊞ **LIGNIERES** *B2* (500m E Rural) *47.08545, 7.07093*
**Camping Fraso Ranch, Chemin du Grand-Marais, 2523
Lignières [032 7514616; fax 7514614; camping.fraso-
ranch@bluewin; www.camping-lignieres.ch]** Fr A5 exit
dir Le Landeron. In Le Landeron turn L sp Lignières. In 5km
(do not go into vill) keep strt to site on R in further 2km. Bef
Lignières keep R & foll camp sp. Lge, pt shd; wc; chem disp;
mv service pnt; baby facs; sauna; shwrs CHF0.50; el pnts (10A)
CHF3.50; gas; lndtte; shop; cooking facs; playgrnd; htd pool;
paddling pool; jacuzzi; tennis; games area; 90% statics (sep
area); dogs CHF1.50; sep car park; site clsd 1 Nov-20 Dec;
gates clsd 1230-1400; Eng spkn; ccard acc; red CKE/CCI. "V
well-organised, tidy site." ♦ CHF 31.00          2009*

**LOCARNO see also sites under Tenero** *C3*

**LOCARNO** *C3* (9km E Rural) *46.16978, 8.91396* **Park-
Camping Riarena, Via Campeggio, 6516 Cugnasco
[091 8591688; fax 8592885; camping.riarena@bluewin.ch;
www.camping-riarena.ch]** Exit A2/E35 Bellinzona-Süd & foll
sp dir airport. Bear R at rndabt & foll site sp to Gudo, site on R
in 2km. Lge, shd; wc; chem disp; mv service pnt; shwrs inc; el
pnts (10A) CHF5 (adaptor avail); gas; lndtte; shop; rest, snacks;
bar; playgrnd; pool & 2 paddling pools; games area; cycle hire;
wifi; snmnt; bbq; Eng spkn; adv bkg; quiet; ccard acc
(CHF100+); red long stay. "Friendly, family-run site; excursions
arranged; gd cycle rtes; gate shut 1300-1500; clean san facs;
dusty site; beware acorn drop September." ♦ 13 Mar-23 Oct.
CHF 47.00          2011*

**LOCARNO** C3 (2km S Urban) 46.15587, 8.80258 **Camping Delta, Via Respini 7, 6600 Locarno [091 7516081; fax 7512243; info@campingdelta.com; www.campingdelta. com]** Fr cent of Locarno make for prom & foll sp to Lido. Site in 400m past Lido on L. Fr Simplon Pass SS337 fr Domodossola to Locarno clsd to trailer c'vans; narr rd with many bends. Site well sp fr m'way. Lge, hdg/mkd pitch, pt shd; wc; chem disp; mv service pnt; shwrs; el pnts (10A) CHF5; gas; lndtte (inc dryer); shop; rest, snacks; bar; playgrnd; pool & lake sw 300m; cycle & kayak hire; fitness rm; wifi; no dogs; poss cr; Eng spkn; adv bkg to end Mar; quiet; no radios or musical instruments allowed; red low ssn/snr citizens. "No access for vehicles 2200-0700; superb location walking dist Locarno; excel facs but long walk fr S end of site; premium for lakeside pitches." 1 Mar-31 Oct. CHF 82.00                    2013*

**LOCARNO** C3 (10km NW Rural) 46.22436, 8.74395 **TCS Camping Bella Riva, 6672 Gordévio [091 7531444; fax 7531764; camping.gordevio@tcs.ch; www.campingtcs. ch]** Fr W end of A13 tunnel under Locarno foll sp Centovalle & Valle Maggia. In 3km turn R to Valle Maggia. Stay on rd which bypasses Gordévio (approx 5km), site on L. Lge, pt shd; wc; chem disp; mv service pnt; baby facs; shwrs; el pnts inc (10A) CHF4.50; gas; lndtte; shop; rest, snacks; playgrnd; pool; rv sw & beach; fishing; tennis; cycle hire; wifi; TV; 30% statics; dogs CHF5; sep car park; poss cr; Eng spkn; adv bkg; quiet; ccard acc; red CKE/CCI. "Attractive region; well-run site; lge tent area adj; Bus to vill nr site." 1 Apr-15 Oct. CHF 54.00    2012*

**LUCERNE see Luzern** B3

## "I need an on-site restaurant"

We do our best to make sure site information is correct, but it is always best to check any must-have facilities are still available or will be open during your visit.

⊞ **LUGANO** D3 (10km N Rural) 46.09036, 8.91626 **Camping Palazzina, La Cuntrada, 6805 Mezzovico [091 9461467; fax 9463061]** Exit A2/E35 at Rivera. R at T-junc dir Lugano; site on L in approx 3.5km. Med, pt shd; wc; chem disp; shwrs; el pnts (10A) CHF4; gas; shop; rest, snacks; bar; playgrnd; pool 1km; TV; 80% statics; dogs CHF2; adv bkg; rd & rlwy noise; ccard acc. "Helpful owner." CHF 34.00              2011*

**LUGANO** D3 (10km N Rural) 46.06921, 8.93675 **Camping Taverne Nord, 6807 Taverne [tel/fax 091 9451198; taverne67@bluewin.ch; http://campeggiotaverne.ch/]** Exit A2/E35 at Rivera or Lugano Nord onto N2. Foll sp for Bellinzona to Taverne. Site ent clearly sp nr long bdge. Med, pt shd; wc; chem disp; mv service pnt; shwrs CHF1; el pnts (6A) CHF4 (poss rev pol); shop; bar; rest 200m; playgrnd; pool high ssn; tennis; 20% statics; dogs CHF2.50; poss cr; adv bkg; rlwy & factory noise; red long stay. "Basic NH site in pleasant situation by shallow stream; Lugano beautiful." 1 Apr-15 Oct. CHF 25.00                    2011*

**LUGANO** D3 (6km S Urban) 45.92861, 8.97670 **Camping Monte Generoso, 6818 Melano [091 6498333; fax 6495944; camping@montegeneroso.ch; www. montegeneroso.ch]** S fr Lugano on N2/E35 m'way; exit immed after tunnel sp Bissone & Chiasso. Cross lake & foll sp Chiasso (blue sps) thro Caroggio. Site on R after rlwy stn. Or fr Como & S on m'way, take exit sp Bissone & Melide bef x-ing lake; foll sp Melano. Med, mkd pitch, pt sl, pt shd; wc; chem disp; shwrs CHF0.50; el pnts (6A) CHF4; gas; lndtte; shop & 1km; snacks; bar; playgrnd; pool 2km; shgl lake beach adj; boating; tennis; games area; boating; TV; 20% statics; dogs CHF5; Eng spkn; adv bkg; 50% statics; quiet but rd & rlwy noise; ccard acc; red low ssn. "Wonderful lakeside location; vg san facs; 500m to rlwy stn for Lugano; gd." 26 Mar-24 Oct. CHF 46.00                    2009*

## "Satellite navigation makes touring much easier"

Remember most sat navs don't know if you're towing or in a larger vehicle – always use yours alongside maps and site directions.

**LUGANO** D3 (15km S Rural) 45.92273, 8.97981 **Camping Paradiso-Lago, Via Pedreta, 6818 Melano [091 6482863; fax 6482602; campingparadiso@bluewin.ch; www. camping-paradiso.ch]** Fr N2/E35 exit after tunnel sp Bissone, foll sp to Bissone. Turn R to site 1km bef Melano, app rd under m'way & rlwy bdges. Lge, mkd pitch, pt sl, pt shd; wc; chem disp; shwrs inc; el pnts (6A) CHF5 inc; gas; lndtte; shop; tradsmn; rest, snacks; bar; BBQ; playgrnd; pool 2km; lake sw adj; watersports; beach; tennis; 40% statics; no dogs; phone; poss cr; adv bkg; rlwy & rd noise; poss noise bar & fr dog-training site adj; ccard acc; CKE/CCI. "Pleasant surroundings; premium for lakeside pitches; sep car park high ssn; excel site; avoid pitches nr office; euros acc mtn rlwy stn 3 miles." 30 Mar-15 Nov. CHF 43.00                    2011*

## "There aren't many sites open at this time of year"

If you're travelling outside peak season remember to call ahead to check site opening dates – even if the entry says 'open all year'.

**LUGANO** D3 (5km W Rural) 45.9927, 8.9006 **Camping Golfo del Sole, 6982 Agno [091 6054802; fax 6054306; info@ golfodelsole.ch; www.golfodelsole.ch]** Exit A2 Lugano Nord & foll sp Ponte Tresa & airport. In Agno at junc, turn R dir Ponte Tresa & Varese. Site sp in 500m, turn L immed bef nightclub. Sm, pt shd; wc; chem disp; shwrs CHF1; el pnts (4A) CHF4 (adaptor avail); gas; lndry rm; shop 500m; playgrnd; lake sw & beach; fishing; tennis; 25% statics; phone; bus/train to Lugano; extra charge for lakeside pitch; poss cr; Eng spkn; adv bkg; quiet. "Beautiful setting; friendly owner." 15 Mar-17 Oct. CHF 38.00                    2009*

⊞ **LUGANO** *D3* (5km W Rural) *45.99534, 8.90845* **Lugano (formerly TCS Camping La Piodella), Via alla Force 14, 6933 Muzzano-Lugano [091 9947788 or 091 9858070 LS; fax 9946708; camping.muzzano@tcs.ch; www.campingtcs.ch/muzzano]** Leave A2 at Lugano Nord & foll sp Ponte Tresa & airport. In Agno turn L at traff island; foll camping sp. In 800m, just after La Piodella town sp, look for sm sp at rd junc with tent symbol & TCS sticker. NB This may appear to direct you to your R but you must make a 180° turn & take slip rd along R-hand side of rd you have just come along - app rd to site. Lge, some mkd pitch, pt shd; wc; chem disp; mv service pnt; baby facs; serviced pitch; shwrs inc; el pnts (10A) inc (long lead poss req - avail fr recep); gas; lndtte (inc dryer); shop & 800m; rest, snacks; bar; BBQ; playgrnd; htd pool & paddling pool; sand beach by lake; watersports; boating & horseriding 6km; fishing; tennis; games area; wifi; entmnt; games/TV rm; some statics; dogs CHF5.50; no cats; no c'vans/m'vans over 7.50m high ssn; sep car park; poss cr; Eng spkn; adv bkg; day/eve aircraft noise; ccard acc; red low ssn/CKE/CCI. "Idyllic location; pitches nr lake higher price; gd welcome; helpful staff; modern san facs; access to pitches poss diff lge o'fits; local train to Lugano 1km, or easy drive; ideal for Ticino Lakes; barrier clsd 1200-1400." ♦ CHF 71.00 SBS - S10                                              2012*

## "That's changed – Should I let The Club know?"

If you find something on site that's different from the site entry, fill in a report and let us know. See www.caravanclub.co.uk/europereport.

**LUGANO** *D3* (6km W Rural) *45.99565, 8.90593* **Camping Eurocampo, Via Molinazzo 9, 6982 Agno [091 6052114; fax 6053187; eurocampo@ticino.com; www.eurocampo.ch]** Exit A2/E34 Lugano N & foll sp airport and Agno. In Agno turn L, then over rlwy x-ing & rnadbt. Turn R down narr lane to site. Lge, pt shd; wc; chem disp; mv service pnt; shwrs; el pnts CHF3.50 (poss rev pol); gas; lndtte; shop; tradsmn; rest; bar; htd pool 200m; paddling pool; lake sw adj; TV rm; 95% statics; dogs free; phone; train 500m; poss cr; Eng spkn; adv bkg; quiet. "Gd site but facs need upgrade; site built in 60's, no changes since; NH only." 1 Apr-31 Oct. CHF 56.00      2014*

**LUGANO** *D3* (6km W Rural) *45.99523, 8.90417* **Camping La Palma, Via Molinazzo 21, 6982 Agno [79 2415343 / 91 6052561; www.lugano-tourism.ch]** N2 exit for Lugano & foll sp airport/camping. Site on L ent Agno. Make U-turn at rndabt & turn R. Narr lane ent. Lge, pt shd; wc (cont); own san rec; chem disp; mv service pnt; shwrs CHF0.50; el pnts (6A) CHF4; gas; lndtte; shop & 1km; rest high ssn & 2km; snacks; bar; BBQ; shgl beach adj; lake sw; TV; 30% statics; dogs CHF4; train; some daytime aircraft noise; CKE/CCI. "Beautiful lakeside location; gd, clean modern san facs; conv Lugano; Swiss adaptor CHF8; friendly, helpful owner; handy for supmkt, bike path and train stn." 18 Apr-1 Nov. CHF 60.00                                    2014*

**LUNGERN see Meiringen** *C3*

**LUTSCHENTAL see Grindelwald** *C2*

⊞ **LUZERN** *B3* (2.5km E Rural) *47.0500, 8.33833* **Camping International Lido, Lidostrasse 19, 6006 Luzern [041 3702146; fax 3702145; luzern@camping-international.ch; www.camping-international.ch]** Fr bdge on lake edge in city cent foll sp Küssnacht & Verkehrshaus. Turn R off Küssnacht rd at traff lts by transport museum (sp Lido), site 50m on L beyond lido parking. Fr A2/E35 exit Luzern Centrum. Lge, mkd pitch, hdstg (mv pitch poss diff), pt shd; htd wc; chem disp; mv service pnt; shwrs inc; el pnts (10A) CHF5 (poss rev pol; adaptors avail); gas; lndtte (inc dryer); shop & 400m; rest 1km; snacks; bar; BBQ; playgrnd; pool adj (May-Sep); lake sw & sand beach adj; boat trips; boat-launch; wifi; 10% statics; dogs CHF4; phone; bus; lake ferry 200m; recep open 0830-1200 & 1400-1800 high ssn; money exchange; poss v cr high ssn; Eng spkn; adv bkg rec; ccard acc; red snr citizens/low ssn/CKE/CCI. "Various sizes/prices pitches; ltd touring pitches cr in peak ssn, early arr rec; recep in bar low ssn; clean, well-maintained facs stretched high ssn; helpful staff; pleasant lakeside walk to Luzern; conv location; excel rest in Wurzenbach; transport museum worth a visit." ♦ ltd CHF 45.00                                                    2014*

**LUZERN** *B3* (8km E Rural) *47.06164, 8.40239* **Camping Vierwaldstättersee, Luzernerstrasse 271, 6402 Merlischachen [041 8500804; fax 8505041; welcome@seecamping.ch; www.seecamping.ch]** Exit A2/E35 junc 26 to Luzern; exit Luzern dir Merlischachen & Küssnacht. Site on R 500m bef Merlischachen on lakeside, well sp. Med, unshd; htd wc; chem disp; mv service pnt; shwrs inc; el pnts (6A) CHF4; gas; shops 500m; rest, snacks, bar & lake sw adj; pool 6km; 10% statics; no dogs; bus adj; phone 500m; Eng spkn; adv bkg; some rd noise; ccard not acc; red long stay/CKE/CCI. "Beautiful lakeside location; wonderful views; excel facs; excel." 1 Apr-30 Sep. CHF 38.00                      2011*

**LUZERN** *B3* (4km S Rural) *47.01201, 8.31113* **TCS Camping Steinibachried, Seefeldstrasse, 6048 Horw [041 3403558; fax 3403556; camping.horw@tcs.ch; www.campingtcs.ch]** Fr A2/E336 exit Horw & foll sp. After x-ing rlwy turn R twd lake in 200m, site sp. Lge, mkd pitch, unshd; wc; chem disp; shwrs (inc) CHF1; el pnts inc (4A) CHF4 (adaptor on loan); gas; lndtte (inc dryer); shop; rest, snacks; bar; playgrnd; lake sw 200m; games rm; 30% statics; dogs CHF5; bus; sep car park; poss cr; Eng spkn; adv bkg; quiet but daytime factory noise; ccard acc; red long stay/CKE/CCI. "Excel facs; beautiful location but car park adj high-rise flats; vg." ♦ 4 Apr-7 Oct. CHF 41.00                                                    2014*

**MARTIGNY** *D2* (500m SE Urban) *46.09788, 7.07953* **TCS Camping Les Neuvilles, Route du Levant 68, 1920 Martigny [027 7224544; fax 7223544; camping.martigny@tcs.ch; www.campingtcs.ch]** Exit A9/E62 dir Grand St Bernard to Martigny. Camping poorly sp fr town; foll Expo sp, ent past cemetary. (SatNav poss inacurate). Lge, mkd pitch, some hdstg, unshd; htd wc; chem disp; mv service pnt; baby facs; shwrs inc; el pnts (6-10A) CHF4.50; gas; lndtte (inc dryer); shop & 500m; tradsmn; rest, snacks; bar; playgrnd; plunge pool; fishing; tennis; cycle hire; wifi; TV rm; 65% statics; dogs CHF5; poss cr; Eng spkn; adv bkg; quiet, but some rd noise; ccard acc; red CKE/CCI. "Excel san facs; conv Valais & Mont Blanc area; Martigny pleasant town; gd cycling." ♦ 1 Apr-31 Oct. CHF 39.00                                      2012*

**MATTEN see Interlaken** *C2*

**MAUR see Zürich** *A3*

**MEIERSKAPPEL** *B3* (1km S Rural) *47.12175, 8.44670*
Campingplatz Gerbe, Landiswilerstrasse, 6344
Meierskappel [041 7904534; info@swiss-bauernhof.ch;
www.swiss-bauernhof.ch] Exit A4/E41 at Küssnacht & foll sp
N to Meierskappel. Bef ent Meierskappel turn L into farm ent
for site (sp.) Med, pt sl, pt shd; htd wc; chem disp; mv service
pnt; baby facs; shwrs inc; el pnts (10A) CHF3.50 (poss rev
pol); lndtte (inc dryer); shop; tradsmn; rest, snacks; bar; BBQ;
playgrnd; htd, covrd pool; wifi; 5% statics; dogs CHF2.50; poss
cr; quiet; CKE/CCI. "Vg, basic farm site with gd facs (unisex);
lge field - choose own pitch; conv Luzerne & Zurich." ♦ ltd
1 Mar-31 Oct.    CHF 24.00                              2010*

⊞  **MEIRINGEN** *C3* (2km S Rural) *46.72538, 8.17088*
Camping Balmweid, Balmweidstrasse 22, 3860 Meiringen
[033 9715115; info@camping-meiringen.ch; www.
camping-meiringen.ch] Turn R off A6 Breinz-Innertkirchen
rd immed after rndabt at BP petrol stn. Site on L after 200m.
Lge, mkd pitch, hdstg, terr, pt shd; htd wc; chem disp; mv
service pnt; 20% serviced pitches; baby facs; fam bthrm;
shwrs inc; el pnts (10A) CHF4.50; gas; lndtte (inc dryer); shops
& 2km; tradsmn; rest, snacks; bar; BBQ; playgrnd; pool; ski
lift 1km; games rm; wifi; TV; 65% statics; dogs CHF2; adv
bkg; quiet; ccard acc; red CKE/CCI. "Ideal base for Sherlock
Holmes fans (Reichenbach Falls) & 3 passes tour; gd cycle track
into town; site unattractive & rather run down (2010)." ♦
CHF 35.00                                               2010*

**MEIRINGEN** *C3* (2km W Rural) *46.73257, 8.17092*
Alpencamping, Brünigstrasse 47, 3860 Meiringen
[033 9713676; fax 9715278; info@alpencamping.ch; www.
alpencamping.ch] Leave A8, then take rd11/6 twd Brünig
Pass. On entering Meiringen, at 1st rndabt foll camp sp L to
site. Med, unshd; htd wc; chem disp; mv service pnt; baby facs;
shwrs inc; el pnts (10A) CHF5.50; gas; lndtte (inc dryer); shop;
tradsmn; rest, snacks nrby; BBQ; cooking facs; playgrnd; pool
nr; internet; entmnt; 30% statics; dogs CHF3; bus 200m; train
1.3km; site clsd Nov; Eng spkn; adv bkg; CKE/CCI. "Meeting
point of alpine passes; friendly, family-run site; excel, modern
san facs; vg walking/cycling; beautiful site with gd views." ♦
1 Jan-31 Oct, 1 Dec-31 Dec.  CHF 55.00                  2014*

⊞  **MEIRINGEN** *C3* (10km NW Rural) *46.78499, 8.15157*
Camping Obsee, Campingstrasse 1, 6078 Lungern
[041 6781463; fax 6782163; camping@obsee.ch; www.
obsee.ch] S fr Luzern on N8 to Sachseln. Exit m'way for rte 4
to Brienz; thro Lungern; R at end of vill & site on R on lakeside.
Best app fr Luzern - turn fr Interlaken diff for lge o'fits. Lge,
pt sl, pt shd; htd wc; chem disp; mv service pnt; shwrs CHF2;
el pnts CHF3; gas; lndtte (inc dryer); shops 1km; rest, snacks;
playgrnd; paddling pool; lake sw; fishing; tennis; games rm;
entmnt; TV; 95% statics; dogs CHF3; poss cr; quiet; Eng spkn.
"Well-kept site in beautiful situation - ski cent; cable rlwy adj;
10 mins walk to vill; sm area for tourers; vg rest; easy access
by rd or train to attractions; Swiss adaptor & poss long lead for
elec." ♦   CHF 42.00                                    2013*

**MELANO see Lugano** *D3*

**MENDRISIO** *D3* (13km NW Rural) *45.88921, 8.94841* TCS
Camping Parco al Sole, Via Ala Caraa 2, 6866 Meride
[091 6464330; fax 6460992; camping.meride@tcs.ch;
www.campingtcs.ch] Fr A2/E35 exit Mendrisio, then foll sp
Rancate & Serpiano. Steep climb. Site on L to S of vill. Med,
some hdstg, pt sl, pt shd; wc; chem disp; mv service pnt; baby
facs; shwrs inc; el pnts (4A) CHF4.50; gas; lndtte (inc dryer);
shop 2km; rest, snacks; bar; playgrnd; htd pool; paddling pool;
fishing lake; wifi; entmnt; TV rm; 20% statics; dogs CHF5;
sep car park; poss v cr; Eng spkn; adv bkg; v quiet; ccard acc.
"Attractive, peaceful setting away fr traffic; Unesco World
Heritage vill; pitches uneven in parts & v sm, some surrounded
by other pitches - make sure you can get off with o'fit; site clsd
to arr 1100-1700; conv Milan by train." ♦  23 Apr-26 Sep.
CHF 37.00                                               2010*

**MERIDE see Mendrisio** *D3*

**MERLISCHACHEN see Luzern** *B3*

**MEZZOVICO see Lugano** *D3*

**MONTANA see Sierre** *C2*

**MORGES** *C1* (1km W Rural) *46.50360, 6.48760* Morges
formerly (TCS Camping Le Petit Bois), Promenade
du Petit-Bois 15, 1110 Morges [021 8011270 or
091 9858070 LS; fax 8033869 or 091 9946708 LS; camping.
morges@tcs.ch; www.campingtcs.ch/morges] Exit A1/
E25 at Morges Ouest, then foll sp to lake. Site well sp on Lake
Léman N shore adj pool. Lge, hdg/mkd pitch, pt shd; wc;
chem disp; mv service pnt; baby facs; shwrs; el pnts (10A) inc
(adaptor/long lead avail); gas; lndtte (inc dryer); shop; rest;
bar; BBQ; playgrnd; htd pool 200m (high ssn) inc; lake sw adj;
watersports; boating; tennis 500m; wifi; entmnt; games/TV rm;
50% statics; dogs CHF3-5; no c'vans/m'vans over 7/8m high
ssn; m'van o'night/late arr area; poss cr; adv bkg; Eng spkn;
quiet, but rd/rlwy noise some pitches; ccard acc; red low ssn/
CKE/CCI. "Pleasant site but sm pitches; pleasant, helpful staff;
clean san facs; vg pool complex nr (high ssn); conv Lausanne,
Geneva & some Alpine passes; tulip festival Apr; easy walk
to town & stn; cycle path around lake; vg." ♦  4 Apr-4 Oct.
CHF 53.00 SBS - S14                                     2012*

**MOSEN** *B3* (200m W Rural) *47.24497, 8.22451* Camping
Seeblick, Seestrasse, 6295 Mosen [tel/fax 041 9171666;
infos@camping-seeblick.ch; www.camping-seeblick.ch]
Fr Lenzburg or Luzern on rd 26 turn E in Mosen at rlwy stn,
immed L into site ent. Med, hdg/mkd pitch, some hdstg, pt
sl, pt shd; wc; chem disp; mv service pnt; shwrs CHF0.50; el
pnts (10A) CHF3; gas; lndtte (inc dryer); shop; rest adj; snacks;
BBQ; playgrnd; lake sw adj; fishing; paddling pool; boating;
games rm; 60% statics; dogs CHF3; poss cr; quiet; red CKE/
CCI. "Pleasant site conv Luzern & Zürich; excel shop & san facs;
helpful owner." ♦  1 Mar-31 Oct.  CHF 27.00             2011*

**MURG** *B3* (300m N Rural) *47.11543, 9.21445* **Camping Murg am Walensee, 8877 Murg [081 7381530; info@camping-murg.ch; www.murg-camping.ch]** Exit A3 junc 47 dir Murg, site sp on lake. Med, pt shd; wc; chem disp; shwrs CHF1; el pnts (10A) CHF3.70; shop & 200m; rest 300m; lake sw & beach adj; 30% statics; dogs CHF4.50; phone; poss cr; adv bkg ess high ssn; quiet. "Spectacular outlook at water's edge; sm pitches; beautiful setting; boat trips adj; cable car 4km; vg." 1 Apr-15 Oct. CHF 49.00                   2014*

**MUZZANO see Lugano** *D3*

**NEUCHATEL** *B1* (7km NE Rural) *47.00198, 7.04145* **TCS Camping Fanel, Seestrasse 50, 3236 Gampelen [032 3132333; fax 3131407; camping.gampelen@tcs.ch; www.campingtcs.ch]** Foll TCS camping sp fr turning off N5 in Gampelen - approx 4km fr vill, on lakeside. V lge, mkd pitch, pt shd; wc; chem disp; mv service pnt; 20% serviced pitch; shwrs; el pnts (4-6A) CHF 3.50-4.50 (adaptor on loan); gas; lndtte (inc dryer); shop; tradsmn; rest; bar; BBQ; playgrnd; htd pool; lake sw & beach; watersports; fishing; tennis; golf; archery; wifi; entmnt; 80% statics; dogs CHF5; wifi; Eng spkn; adv bkg; 10% red 3+ days; ccard acc; CKE/CCI. "In nature reserve; office/barrier clsd 1200-1400; office & shop hrs vary with ssn; gd, modern facs; helpful staff; Euros also acc." ◆ 1 Apr-2 Oct. CHF 48.00                   2012*

**NEUCHATEL** *B1* (9km W Rural) *46.96727, 6.87029* **Camping Paradis-Plage, La Saunerie, 2013 Colombier [032 8412446; fax 8414305; info@paradisplage.ch; www.paradisplage.ch]** Take Lausanne rd out of Neuchâtel; after tunnel exit at int'chge sp Auvenier, Colombier. Foll Colombier sp thro traff lts. Ent L over tram rails past Inn Des Alleens. Lge, shd; wc; chem disp; mv service pnt; shwrs inc; el pnts (10A) CHF4; gas; lndtte; shop; rest, snacks; playgrnd; paddling pool; lake sw; fishing; watersports; tennis; 60% statics; dogs CHF2; adv bkg; some m'way noise; red long stay. "Gd walks/cycling; v pleasant site." ◆ 1 Mar-31 Oct. CHF 41.00                   2009*

**NOVILLE see Villeneuve** *C1*

**OTTENBACH see Zürich** *A3*

**PONTRESINA MORTERATSCH see St Moritz** *C4*

**PRELES see Biel/Bienne** *B2*

**RANDA see Zermatt** *D2*

**RARON see Visp** *C2*

**RECKINGEN see Ulrichen** *C3*

**REINACH see Basel** *A2*

**RINGGENBERG see Interlaken** *C2*

**ROLLE** *C1* (1km N Rural) *46.46192, 6.34613* **Camping Aux Vernes, Chemin de la Plage, 1180 Rolle [tel/fax 021 8251239; reception@campingrolle.ch; www.campingrolle.ch]** Fr A1/E25/E62 exit Rolle, site sp dir Lausanne. Lge, shd; wc; chem disp; mv service pnt; baby facs; shwrs; el pnts (4A) CHF3.50 (loan of adaptor); gas; lndtte (inc dryer); shop; tradsmn; snacks; bar; BBQ; playgrnd; shgl beach & lake sw; boating; watersports; fishing; 20% statics; dogs CHF3; phone; poss cr; Eng spkn; adv bkg; quiet; ccard acc; red long stay/CKE/CCI. "Gd base Geneva, Gruyères, Chillon Castle; attractive site." 1 Apr-1 Oct. CHF 39.00                   2011*

**ROMANSHORN** *A4* (6km SE Rural) *47.53620, 9.39885* **Camping Seehorn (Formerly Wiedehorn), Wiedehorn, 9322 Egnach [071 4771006; fax 4773006; info@seehorn.ch; www.seehorn.ch]** Site is 2km E of Egnach, dir Arbon. Med, pt sl, pt shd,mkd, serviced pitch; wc; chem disp; shwrs inc; el pnts (16A) CHF2.50; gas; lndtte; shop; rest, snacks; bar; playgrnd; fishing; TV; 60% statics; dogs CHF4; phone; sep car park high ssn; adv bkg; quiet; "Direct access Lake Constance; statics sep; V gd facs." 1 Mar-27 Oct. CHF 53.00                   2013*

⊞ **SAANEN** *C2* (500m SE Urban) *46.48738, 7.26406* **Camping Beim Kappeli, Campingstrasse, 3792 Saanen [033 7446191; fax 7446184; info@camping-saanen.ch; www.camping-saanen.ch]** On edge of vill bet rv & light rlwy. Site sp fr town cent. Med, pt shd; htd wc; shwrs CHF0.50; el pnts (6-13A) CHF4; lndtte; shop 1km; playgrnd; pool adj; tennis; fishing; 50% statics; dogs CHF3; site clsd Nov; poss cr; Eng spkn; quiet; ccard acc. "Beautiful walks; neat site; excel, clean facs; buy Gstaad card v.gd value." CHF 36.00                   2012*

**"I like to fill in the reports as I travel from site to site"**
You'll find report forms at the back of this guide, or you can fill them in online at www.caravaclub.co.uk/europereport.

**SAAS FEE** *D2* (2km NE Rural) *46.11368, 7.94136* **Camping Mischabel, Unter den Bodmen, 3910 Saas-Grund [tel/fax 027 9571608; mischabel@hotmail.com]** Fr Visp take Saas Fee rd to Saas Grund & cont twd Saas Almagell for 1.2km. Med, pt shd; wc; chem disp; shwrs inc; el pnts (10A) CHF3; lndtte; shop & 1km; tradsmn; rest, snacks; bar; pool 1km; boating; fishing; TV; no statics; dogs CHF2.50; poss cr; Eng spkn; adv bkg; quiet; CKE/CCI; "Lovely scenery; gd walking; helpful, friendly staff." 1 Jun-30 Sep. CHF 63.00                   2013*

⊞ **SAAS FEE** *D2* (2.5km NE Rural) *46.11150, 7.94238* **Camping Schönblick, 3910 Saas-Grund [tel/fax 027 9572267; schoenblick@campingschweiz.ch]** Fr Visp take Saas Fee rd to Saas Grund & cont twd Saas Almagell for 1.5km. Site on R over rv. Sm, hdstg, unshd; htd wc; shwrs CHF1; el pnts (10A) CHF3; gas; lndtte; shop 1km; rest, snacks; bar; playgrnd; pool 1km; fishing; tennis; winter & summer skiing; horseriding; TV; 25% statics; adv bkg; open Oct-May with adv bkg only; quiet; ccard acc. "Site ideal for walking & mountain scenery; navette 50m; facs ltd low ssn." CHF 64.00                   2013*

**SAAS FEE** *D2* (4.6km NE Rural) *46.11588, 7.93819* **Camping am Kapellenweg, 3910 Saas-Grund [027 9574997; fax 9573316; camping@kapellenweg.ch; www.kapellenweg. ch]** Fr Visp, take Saas Fee rd to Saas Grund, cont twd Saas Almagell, site on R after 1km. Sm, pt sl, pt shd; wc; chem disp; shwrs inc; el pnts CHF3; gas; lndtte; shop & 1km; tradsmn; snacks; golf; fishing; dogs CHF2.50; Eng spkn; red low ssn. "Ideal for walking; family-run site; clean san facs; beautiful scenery; if recep clsd, site yourself; bus or walk (50 mins) into town; excel site." ♦ 1 May-12 Oct. CHF 63.00          2014*

**SAAS GRUND see Saas Fee** *D2*

## "We must tell The Club about that great site we found"

Get your site reports in by mid-August and we'll do our best to get your updates into the next edition.

**ST GALLEN** *A4* (5km N Rural) *47.46191, 9.36371* **Camping St Gallen-Wittenbach, Leebrücke, 9304 Bernhardzell [071 2984969; fax 2985069; campingplatz.stgallen@ ccc-stgallen.ch; www.ccc-stgallen.ch]** Exit A1/E60 St Fiden. L in Wittenbach cent at site sp. Cross Rv Sitter on sharp R bend, turn sharp R at sp. Med, some hdstg, pt shd; wc; chem disp; baby facs; shwrs inc; el pnts (6A) CHF4 (adaptor loan); gas; lndtte (inc dryer); basic shop & 2km; tradsmn; snacks; bar; BBQ; playgrnd; htd, covrd pool nr; canoeing; cycle hire; golf 10km; TV; 30% statics; dogs CHF3; bus; poss cr; Eng spkn; adv bkg; quiet; ccard acc; red CKE/CCI. "Gd base for S shore of Bodensee; pleasant rvside setting; friendly staff." 10 Apr-2 Oct. CHF 28.00          2010*

**ST MARGRETHEN** *A4* (3km N Rural) *47.45114, 9.65650* **Strandbad Camping Bruggerhorn, 9430 St Margrethen [071 7442201; fax 7442757]** Exit N1/E60 dir St Margrethen, site well sp. Med, pt shd; wc; chem disp; shwrs inc; el pnts (10A) CHF2.50 (adaptor avail); gas; lndtte; shop; rest 500m; snacks; playgrnd; 2 pools; lake sw; sports cent adj; tennis; no dogs; poss cr; Eng spkn; adv bkg; quiet; red CKE/CCI. "Picturesque, clean site; vg shwrs; helpful staff." 1 Apr-31 Oct. CHF 34.00          2009*

**ST MORITZ** *C4* (4km NE Rural) *46.50988, 9.87936* **TCS Camping Punt Muragl, Via da Puntraschigna 56, 7503 Samedan [tel/fax 081 8428197; camping.samedan@tcs. ch; www.campingtcs.ch]** Site on S side of rd fr Celerina to Pontresina, adj to rndabt at junc rds 27 & 29. Med, shd; htd wc; mv service pnt; chem disp; shwrs inc; el pnts (6-10A) CHF4 (metered in winter); gas; lndtte; shop; rest 300m; snacks; bar; playgrnd; pool & lake 1km; fishing; tennis; skiing; entmnt; 30% statics; dogs CHF5; adv bkg; quiet; ccard acc. "Excel for mountains & Engadine; close rlwy stns & funicular; walking rtes thro forest; clean, spacious facs; enquire about public transport travel card." 26 Nov-18 Apr & 21 May-10 Oct. CHF 40.00          2011*

**ST MORITZ** *C4* (4.5km S Rural) *46.46132, 9.93568* **Camping Plauns, Via da Bernina, 7504 Pontresina-Morteratsch [081 8426285; fax 8345136; plauns@bluewin.ch; www. campingplauns.ch]** On Bernina Pass rd 4km SE of Pontresina, turn R at camp sp. If app fr St Moritz or Samedan, keep to Pontresina by-pass, do not turn L where sp Pontresina. Lge, pt sl, pt shd; htd wc; chem disp; mv service pnt; shwrs CHF0.50; el pnts (6-13A) CHF3.50 (adaptor avail & long lead poss req); gas; lndtte; shop; rest 1km; snacks; playgrnd; pool 4km; ski lift 3km; ski bus; golf 4km; internet; some statics; dogs CHF4; phone; poss cr; some Eng spkn; adv bkg 2 weeks or more only (non-return fee); quiet; ccard acc; CKE/CCI. "Idyllic site in forest clearing; magnificent scenery; v clean, modern san facs; conv Morteratsch Glacier, Bernina Pass, St Moritz; walking dist rlwy & rest; cable rlwys, funiculars, chair lifts; high walks; glacier excursions." ♦ 25 May-15 Oct & 15 Dec-15 Apr. CHF 38.00          2011*

**SALGESCH see Sierre** *C2*

**SAMEDAN see St Moritz** *C4*

⊞ **SAVOGNIN** *C4* (400m NW Rural) *46.59777, 9.59083* **Camping Julia, Veia Sandeilas 10, 7460 Savognin [081 6841444; camping.julia@savogninbergbahnen.ch; www.savogninbergbahnen.ch]** S on rd 3, clearly sp adj Cube Hotel. Sm, hdstg, unshd; htd wc; chem disp; shwrs inc; el pnts (16A) CHF2.50; lndtte (inc dryer); shop 400m; rest, snacks; bar adj; rv sw & shgl beach adj; 80% statics; dogs CHF1; bus 500m; Eng spkn; adv bkg; quiet; ccard acc; CKE/CCI. "Not particularly attractive site but superb facs; adj chairlift & postbus use free; best for smaller o'fits; gd NH Julier Pass." ♦ CHF 31.00          2010*

## "I need an on-site restaurant"

We do our best to make sure site information is correct, but it is always best to check any must-have facilities are still available or will be open during your visit.

**SCHAFFHAUSEN** *A3* (2.5km SE Rural) *47.68763, 8.65461* **TCS Camping Rheinwiesen, Hauptstrasse, 8246 Langwiesen [052 6593300; fax 6593355; camping.schaffhausen@tcs. ch; www.campingtcs.ch/schaffhausen]** Fr N, S & W on A4/ E41 exit Schaffhausen & foll sp 'Kreuzlingen' on rd 13. Fr E on rd 13 pass under rlwy bdge to Langwiesen about 3km bef Schaffhausen; site sp at Feuerthalen (tent sign only - no site name) down narr rd on L on Rv Rhine. Med, mkd pitch, pt shd; wc; chem disp; mv service pnt; baby facs; shwrs inc; el pnts (4A) inc (adaptor avail); gas; lndtte (inc dryer); shop; rest, snacks; bar; BBQ (gas & charcoal); playgrnd; children's pool; covrd pool 4km; rv beach & sw; fishing; horseriding 3km; wifi; games/TV rm; 30% statics; no dogs; no c'vans/m'vans over 7m high ssn; phone; Eng spkn; adv bkg; quiet but some rd/rlwy noise; ccard acc; red low ssn; CKE/CCI. "Excel site in beautiful location; conv Rhine Falls & Lake Constance; pitches on rvside (rv v fast-moving & unfenced); clean, adequate san facs; grass pitches poss muddy after rain; poss tight access to pitches; gd facs sm children; gd cycling." 24 Apr-7 Oct. CHF 41.00 2012*

**SCHAFFHAUSEN** *A3* (14km SE Rural) *47.66216, 8.84034* **Camping Wagenhausen, Hauptstrasse 82, 8260 Wagenhausen [052 7414271; fax 7414157; campingwagenhausen@bluewin.ch; www. campingwagenhausen.ch]** Turn R off Stein-am-Rhein/ Schaffhausen rd, site sp. Med, pt shd; wc; chem disp; serviced pitches; shwrs CHF1; el pnts (10A) CHF3; gas; lndtte; shop; rest; bar; playgrnd; pool; paddling pool; fishing; games area; TV rm; 80% statics; dogs CHF4; poss cr; Eng spkn; quiet; ccard acc. "Vg; direct access to Rv Rhine; rvside footpath." ♦ 1 Apr-31 Oct. CHF 33.00        2009*

**SCHWYZ** *B3* (5km NW Rural) *47.04761, 8.59173* **Camping Buchenhof, Seebad, 6422 Steinen [041 8321429; www. camping-buchenhof.ch]** Fr N4 exit dir Goldau, then R dir Lauerz. Bef lake take R fork sp Steinen, over m'way bdge; site sp Seebad. Med, mkd pitch, some hdstg, pt sl, unshd; wc; chem disp; shwrs CHF1; el pnts (4A) CHF2; gas; lndtte; shop; rest, snacks; BBQ; playgrnd; lake sw & beach; fishing; boat hire; tennis; 50% statics; dogs CHF2; Eng spkn; quiet but rlwy noise; CKE/CCI. "Mountain scenery; gd facs." ♦ 1 Apr-31 Oct. CHF 44.00        2010*

**SEMPACH** *B3* (1.5km S Rural) *47.12447, 8.18924* **TCS Camping Sempach, Seelandstrasse, 6204 Sempach Stadt [041 4601466 or 091 9858070; fax 4604766 or 091 9946708 LS; camping.sempach@tcs.ch; www. campingtcs.ch/sempach]** Fr Luzern on A2 take exit sp Emmen N, Basel, Bern. Join E35 & cont on this rd to exit at Sempach sp. Site well sp. Lge, mkd pitch, unshd; htd wc; chem disp; mv service pnt; baby facs; private san facs avail; shwrs inc; el pnts (13A) inc (adaptor avail); gas; lndtte (inc dryer); shop; rest; bar; BBQ (gas/charcoal only); playgrnd; paddling pool; shgl beach & lake sw adj; watersports; fishing; golf 5km; cycle hire; tennis; wifi; entmnt; games/TV rm; 60% statics; dogs CHF5; no c'vans/m'vans over 9m high ssn; sep car parks high ssn; poss cr; Eng spkn; adv bkg; quiet; ccard acc; red low ssn/CKE/CCI. "Excel location on Sempacher See, 10 mins drive fr m'way & attractive town; sm pitches; helpful staff; rest & beach open to public; water & bins far fr many pitches; poss tight parking; ltd facs low ssn; lakeside walk to Sempach." ♦ 4 Apr-7 Oct. CHF 56.00 SBS - S08        2011*

**SIERRE** *C2* (2km E Rural) *46.29362, 7.55777* **Camping Bois de Finges, Route du Bois de Finges, 3960 Sierre [027 4550284; fax 4553351]** Exit A9 Sierre-Est dir Sierre, site in 500m E of Rhône bdge. Med, mkd pitch, terr, shd; wc; chem disp; mv service pnt; shwrs; el pnts (4A) CHF3.50; gas; lndtte; shop; snacks; bar; playgrnd; htd pool; tennis nr; lake fishing 1.5km; TV; 10% statics; dogs CHF5; phone; Eng spkn; adv bkg; quiet; red low ssn/long stay; ccard acc. "Lovely wooded site; slopes/terr poss diff; warm welcome." 1 May-30 Sep. CHF 35.00        2011*

**SIERRE** *C2* (3km E Rural) *46.30215, 7.56420* **Camping Swiss Plage, Campingweg 3, 3970 Salgesch [027 4556608 or 4816023; fax 4813215; info@swissplage.ch; www. swissplage.ch]** Fr A9/E62 exit at Sierre, turn L & go over bdge, Foll sp Salgesch & Site. Fr town site well sp. Lge, shd; wc; chem disp; mv service pnt; shwrs CHF1; el pnts (10A) CHF3.60; gas; lndtte; shop; rest, snacks; bar; paddling pool 2km; lake sw; tennis; dogs CHF3.50; Eng spkn; adv bkg ess for long stay; quiet; ccard acc. "Pleasant site in lovely location." Easter-1 Nov. CHF 34.00        2011*

**SIERRE** *C2* (6km NW Rural) *46.30426, 7.48308* **Camping La Moubra, Impasse de la Plage 2, 3962 Crans-Montana [027 4812851; fax 4810551; moubra@campings.ch; www. campingmoubra.ch]** Fr Sierre take rd to Chermignon & Montana. In Montana turn L sp La Moubra; site in 3km by lake. Med, pt shd; wc; mv service pnt; shwrs; el pnts (10A) CHF4; gas; lndtte; rest 300m; snacks; bar; pool 500m; lake sw; tennis; boating; fishing; watersports; golf; 20% statics; dogs CHF3; Eng spkn; adv bkg; quiet; ccard acc. "Ski & boot rm; navette adj; frozen lake - start of x-country skiing; well-maintained site in gd position; lovely situation, suite, E to reach mountain; gd walking & cycling in area." 16 May-15 Oct & 15 Dec-18 Apr. CHF 60.00        2011*

**SILVAPLANA** *C4* (300m SW Rural) *46.45671, 9.79316* **Camping Silvaplana, 7513 Silvaplana [tel/fax 081 8288492; reception@campingsilvaplana.ch; www. campingsilvaplana.ch]** Exit by-pass rd at S junc for Silvaplana (opp camp site). In 100m after g'ge turn R & site sp via underpass, on lakeside. When app fr Julier Pass foll sp for Maloja Pass as above. Lge, pt sl, pt shd; wc; chem disp; mv service pnt; shwrs CHF1.10; el pnts (16A) CHF3.50; gas; lndtte; shop & 300m; playgrnd; pool 3km; lake sw; watersports; fishing; tennis; wifi; many statics in sep area; dogs CHF3; poss cr; Eng spkn; no adv bkg; quiet; ccard acc. "V beautiful location; gd walking; hiking; climbing; vg watersports & windsurfing; excel facs for m'vans; 2.50% surcharge on ccard." 13 May-20 Oct. CHF 45.00        2013*

⊞ **SION** *C2* (3km SW Rural) *46.20578, 7.27855* **Camping du Botza, Route du Camping 1, 1963 Vétroz [027 3461940 or 079 2203575 (mob); fax 3462535; info@botza.ch; www. botza.ch]** Exit A9/E62 junc 25 S'wards over a'bahn. Site adj Vétroz indus est, foll sp 'CP Nr.33'. Lge, mkd pitch, pt shd; wc; chem disp; mv service pnt; baby facs; serviced pitches; shwrs inc; el pnts (10A) CHF3.70; gas; lndtte; shop; tradsmn; rest, snacks; bar; playgrnd; free htd pool high ssn; paddling pool; fishing; tennis; squash; golf 8km; wifi; entmnt; 30% statics; dogs CHF3.50; adv bkg; quiet; ccard acc; red low ssn. "Superb site conv m'way & ski resorts; excel facs; gd security; organised excursions; vg rest; fine mountain views; cycle track along Rhone nrby; some noise fr nrby airport." ♦ CHF 47.00  2014*

**SOLOTHURN** *B2* (1.5km SW Rural) *47.19883, 7.52288* **TCS Camping Lido Solothurn, Glutzenhofstrasse 5, 4500 Solothurn [032 6218935 / 091 9858070 LS; fax 6218939 / 091 9858070 LS; camping.solothurn@tcs. ch; www.campingtcs.ch/solothurn]** Exit A5 dir Solothurn W, cross rv bdge. At traff lts turn L & foll sp to site (new rd 2009). Lge, mkd pitch, pt shd; htd wc; chem disp; mv service pnt; baby facs; 10% serviced pitches; shwrs inc; el pnts (13A) inc; gas; lndtte (inc dryer); shop; tradsmn; rest, snacks; bar; BBQ; cooking facs; playgrnd; htd pool adj; paddling pool; fishing; tennis 200m; cycle & boat hire; golf 100m; games area; wifi; entmnt; games/TV rm; 20% statics; dogs CHF5; no c'vans/m'vans over 12m high ssn; bus 200m; Eng spkn; adv bkg; quiet; ccard acc; red low ssn; CKE/CCI. "Gd touring base by Rv Aare; lge pitches; excel facs; helpful staff; 20 mins walk to picturesque town; excel cycling paths." ♦ 28 Feb-29 Nov. CHF 58.00 SBS - S13        2013*

**SORENS see Bulle** *C2*

⊞ **SPIEZ** C2 (4km SE Rural) 46.65880, 7.71688 **Camping Stuhlegg, Stueleggstrasse 7, 3704 Krattigen [033 6542723; fax 6546703; campstuhlegg@bluewin.ch; www.camping-stuhlegg.ch]** 13km fr Interlaken on hillside on S side of Lake Thun. Advise app fr Spiez. Fr Spiez rlwy stn heading SE turn R over rlwy bdge; foll sp Leissigen & Krattigen for 5km. In Krattigen after modern church turn R (low gear), site 500m on R. To avoid going thro Spiez town, leave Bern-Interlaken m'way at junc 19. Foll dir to Aeschi. At rndabt in Aeschi turn L to Krattigen. Turn L after 1m opp wood yard into Stuhleggstrasse. Site in 300 yds. Lge, pt sl, terr, pt shd; htd wc; chem disp; mv service pnt; baby facs; shwrs CHF1; el pnts (10A) CHF4 (some rev pol); gas; lndtte (inc dryer); sm shop; rest 300m; snacks; bar; playgrnd; htd pool; entmnt; 60% statics; dogs CHF3; sdki bus; phone; site clsd last week Oct to end Nov; adv bkg; quiet; ccard acc; red low ssn/long stay/CKE/CCI. "Excel well-kept, well run site; immac facs; helpful friendly staff; recep clsd 1300-1500; mountain views; gd dog-walking in area; scenic rtes fr site; free bus service with Guest Card; gd rest; bread can be ordered." CHF 43.00          2014*

**SPIEZ** C2 (14km S Rural) 46.65311, 7.70030 **Camping Panorama-Rossern, Scheidgasse, 3703 Aeschi [033 6544377; postmaster@camping-aeschi.ch; www.camping-aeschi.ch]** Leave N6 Thun to Interlaken rd at Spiez junc on main rd, foll sp Spiezwieler. In Spiezwieler turn L at g'ge sp Aeschi. Strt on at x-rds in Aeschi town cent. Site on R immed after fire stn. Med, pt sl, pt terr, pt shd; wc; chem disp; shwrs CHF1; el pnts CHF3 (adaptor avail); lndtte; sm shop & shops 2km; tradsmn; playgrnd; 40% statics; dogs CHF1; bus; quiet; poss cr. "Views of Blümlisalp, Niesen; some cars parked away fr vans due terraces." 15 May-15 Oct.  CHF 30.00  2011*

⊞ **SPLUGEN** C3 (500m W Rural) 46.55003, 9.31662 **Camping auf dem Sand, Untere Allmend, 7435 Splügen [081 6641476; fax 6641460; camping@splugen.ch; www.campingsplugen.ch]** Exit A13/E61 (Chur-San Bernardino) & take slip rd sp Splügen. Foll rd thro vill, site at end. Med, unshd; wc; chem disp; mv service pnt; shwrs inc; el pnts (10A) CHF3; gas; lndtte; shop 800m; playgrnd; tennis; fishing; wifi; 70% statics; dogs CHF3; adv bkg; quiet; red CKE/CCI. "Conv for San Bernardino Tunnel." CHF 45.00          2011*

**STECHELBERG see Lauterbrunnen** C2

**SUMVITG** C3 (500m S Rural) 46.72439, 8.92968 **Camping Garvera, Campadi alla Staziun, 7175 Sumvitg [081 9431922; info@garvera.ch; www.garvera.ch]** Fr Chur on rd 19, site well sp in Sumvitg. Sm, terr, pt shd; htd wc; chem disp; shwrs inc; el pnts (10A) CHF4; lndtte; shop 500m; rest; bar; no statics; dogs CHF4; bus/train adj; Eng spkn; quiet - some daytime rlwy noise; red low ssn. "Excel, clean site; friendly owners; beautiful area; gd walking." ♦ ltd 1 May-18 Oct.  CHF 32.00          2010*

⊞ **SUR EN** B4 (E Rural) 46.81859, 10.36594 **Camping Sur En, 7554 Sur En  (Graubünden) [079 0111147; fax 081 8663767; wb@sur-en.ch; www.sur-en.ch]** Visible in valley fr rd 27. Steep access. Sm, unshd; htd wc; chem disp; mv service pnt; shwrs inc; el pnts (6-10A) CHF3; (long lead poss req; warden has adaptors); lndtte (inc dryer); shop; rest (ccard not acc); snacks; bar; BBQ; playgrnd; sm pool; ski lift 7km; free ski bus; 30% statics in sep area; dogs CHF3; Eng spkn; no adv bkg; quiet; ccard acc (surcharge); CKE/CCI. "Superb facs in out-of-the-way spot; great atmosphere for nature lovers/ walkers/cyclists; gd for dog walking but tick treatment ess." CHF 49.00          2013*

⊞ **SURCUOLM** B3 (500m N Rural) 46.76053, 9.14324 **Panorama Camping Surcuolm, 7138  Surcuolm [081 9333223; fax 9333224; info@camping-surcuolm; www.camping-surcuolm.ch]** Fr N19 to Ilanz & in Ilanz foll sp Valata & Obersaxen. In Valata turn L to Surcuolm, site on L. This is only rec rte - steep climbs. Med, pt sl, unshd; htd wc; chem disp; mv service pnt; shwrs CHF0.50; el pnts (16A) metered (inc dryer); shop; tradsmn; rest, snacks nr; bar; playgrnd; ski lift nr; wifi; 10% statics; dogs CHF3; bus 500m; adv bkg; quiet. "Mountain views; popular winter site; quiet in summer; excel facs." CHF 41.00          2012*

**SURSEE** B2 (1.5km NW Rural) 47.17505, 8.08685 **Camping Sursee Waldheim, Baslerstrasse, 6210  Sursee [041 9211161; fax 9211160; info@camping-sursee.ch; www.camping-sursee.ch]** Exit A2 at junc 20 & take L lane onto rd 24 dir Basel/Luzern. Turn R at traff lts, foll rd 2 turn R at 2nd rndabt dir Basel to site. Med, shd; wc; chem disp; shwrs CHF0.50; el pnts (10A) CHF3; gas; lndtte; shop; tradsmn; rest in town; snacks; bar; playgrnd; lake sw 1.5km; 60% statics; dogs CHF1; poss cr; Eng spkn; quiet but poss noisy at w/end; CKE/CCI. "Pretty site; excel san facs; gd train service to Luzern; sh walk to town cent; popular NH; gd touring base." 1 Apr-30 Sep.  CHF 35.00          2013*

**SUSTEN see Leuk** C2

**SUTZ see Biel/Bienne** B2

**TAGERWILEN** A3 (500m W Rural) 47.65928, 9.12341 **Restaurant Werkhof Oase, Hauptstrasse 12, 8274 Tägerwilen [071 6691717; oasecamping@hotmail.com]** Fr Kreuzlingen take rd 13 twds Schaffhausen. Site on L on o'skirts of Tägerwilen. Sm, hstg, unshd; wc; chem disp; mv service pnt; shwrs inc; el pnts (10A) CHF4; lndtte (inc dryer); shop 3km; rest; snacks; bar; lake sw & beach 2km; wifi; no statics; dogs; Eng spkn; quiet; red low ssn. "Sm m'van site, but c'vans acc if rm; v friendly owners; conv Lake Constance." Jan-Oct.  CHF 20.00          2010*

**TASCH see Zermatt** D2

**TAVERNE see Lugano** D3

---

**TENERO** *C3* (1km E Urban) *46.16921, 8.8538* **Camping Lago Maggiore, Via Lido 4, 6598 Tenero [091 7451848; fax 7454318; info@clm.ch; www.clm.ch]** Fr A2 take Bellinzona S exit & foll sp Locarno. In about 12km take Tenero exit, at end slip rd foll sp to site. C'vans not permitted on rd S337 fr Domodossola to Locarno. If app fr Simplon Pass cont S of Domodossola & take S34 up W shore of lake. Lge, pt shd; wc; chem disp; mv service pnt; shwrs inc; el pnts (adaptor avail) inc; gas; lndtte (inc dryer); shop; tradsmn; rest; bar; BBQ; playgrnd; lake sw, pools for adults & children; watersports; fishing; tennis; TV; no dogs; adv bkg; Eng spkn; quiet; ccard acc. "Beautiful region; extra for pitches nr lake; vg." 15 Mar-31 Oct. CHF 58.00 (5 persons)                    2010*

**TENERO** *C3* (1km SE Rural) *46.17575, 8.84515* **Camping Tamaro, Via Mappo, 6598 Tenero [091 7452161; fax 7456636; info@campingtamaro.ch; www.campingtamaro. ch]** Fr N2 take Bellinzona Süd exit dir Locarno. In about 12km take Tenero exit, at end slip rd foll sp to site. Lge, unshd; htd wc; chem disp; mv service pnt; baby facs; shwrs inc; el pnts (10A) CHF4; gas; lndtte; shops; adv bkg; rest; bar; lake sw; beach; watersports; fishing; tennis; 30% statics; no dogs; phone; bus; boat to Locarno; adv bkg; quiet; Eng spkn; red low ssn/long stay; debit card acc. "Excel site; helpful staff; extra for lakeside pitches; tight corners & high kerbs on site rd - manhandling poss req; ferry to Locarno fr site." ◆ 6 Mar-1 Nov. CHF 56.00                    2009*

⊞ **TENERO** *C3* (500m SW Urban) *46.17292, 8.84808* **Camping Miralago, Via Roncaccio 20, 6598 Tenero [091 7451255; fax 7452878; info@camping-miralago. ch; www.camping-miralago.ch]** Turn L off A13 Bellinzona/ Locarno rd at Tenero & foll camping sp. Med, mkd pitch, unshd; htd wc; chem disp; mv service pnt; baby facs; shwrs CHF1; el pnts (10A) inc; lndtte (inc dryer); shop; tradsmn; rest, snacks; bar; BBQ; playgrnd; htd pool; paddling pool; sand beach & lake sw adj; games area; wifi; dogs CHF3; bus adj; poss cr; Eng spkn; adv bkg; quiet; ccard acc; red low ssn/CKE/CCI. "Beautiful area; ltd facs low ssn; lake steamer pier lakefront camping; sm pitches with no privacy hdgs; fairly new san facs; beautiful location, no rd noise." ◆ CHF 117.00                    2014*

**TENERO** *C3* (1km W Rural) *46.1770, 8.84185* **Camping Lido Mappo, Via Mappo, 6598 Tenero [091 7451437; fax 7454800; camping@lidomappo.ch; www.lidomappo. ch]** Fr A2 take Bellinzona Sud exit & foll sp Locarno. In about 12km take Tenero exit, at end slip rd foll sp to site on lakeside. Lge, shd; htd wc; chem disp; mv service pnt; baby facs; shwrs; el pnts (10A) inc; gas; lndtte (inc dryer); supmkt; tradsmn; rest, snacks; bar; BBQ; playgrnd; lake sw; sand/shgl beach; fishing; boating; watersports; cycle hire; wifi; entmnt; TV; no dogs; phone; adv bkg; poss cr; Eng spkn; quiet, but some noise fr local airfield; ccard acc. "Extra for lakeside pitch; cycle rte to Locarno; v helpful staff." ◆ 14 Mar-31 Oct. CHF 53.00                    2010*

**THORISHAUS see Bern** *B2*

**THUN** *B2* (3km N Rural) *46.81368, 7.60829* **Camping Wydeli, Wydeli 60, 3671 Brenzikofen [031 7711141; fax 7711181; info@camping-brenzikofen.ch; www.camping-brenzikofen.ch]** Fr A6 take Kiesen exit; foll sp Konolfingen-Langnau to Oppligen; site sp. Med, pt shd; wc; chem disp; shwrs; el pnts CHF 2.50; gas; lndtte; shop; rest, snacks; bar; playgrnd; pool; paddling pool; fishing; tennis; horseriding; 60% statics; dogs; Eng spkn; adv bkg. 1 May-30 Sep. CHF 28.00                    2009*

**THUN** *B2* (3km S Rural) *46.72753, 7.62778* **TCS Camping Thunersee, Gwattstrasse 103a, 3645 Gwatt [033 3364067; fax 3364017; camping.gwatt@tcs.ch; www.thunersee. ch]** Fr A6 take Thun-Süd exit & foll sp to Gwatt; on reaching Thun-Speiz main rd turn L, site on R in 500m. Well sp on rte 6 in Gwatt on lake side of rd. Med, unshd, wc; chem disp; mv service pnt; shwrs inc; el pnts (4A) CHF3.50 (adaptor on loan); gas; lndtte; shop; rest, snacks; bar; pool 1km; shgl beach; lake sw adj; watersports; fishing; mooring for boats; tennis; 40% statics; dogs CHF5; bus to Thun; sep car park; poss cr; Eng spkn; adv bkg; quiet; ccard acc; red long stay; red CKE/ CCI. "Walks by lake; mkd cycle ways; superb views; pretty site; office/barrier clsd 1130-1400; helpful management; gd san facs." ◆ 3 Apr-11 Oct. CHF 41.00                    2010*

**THUN** *B2* (5km W Rural) *46.74514, 7.52014* **Camping Restaurant Bad, 3638 Blumenstein [033 3562954; k.wenger@bad-blumenstein.ch; www.bad-blumenstein. ch]** Fr A6 exit Thun Nord dir Wattenwil & Blumenstein; site sp in vill. Sm, pt sl, unshd; wc; shwrs CHF0.50/2mins; el pnts CHF3; rest & bar (Wed-Sun); pool 3km; fishing; wifi; bus, train nr; Eng spkn; adv bkg; quiet; red long stay/low ssn; CKE/CCI. "Basic, CL-type site - v pleasant, but v ltd; gd." 1 May-30 Sep. CHF 25.00                    2009*

**THUSIS** *C4* (500m NE Rural) *46.69945, 9.44547* **Camping Viamala, Pantunweg 1, 7430 Thusis [tel/fax 081 6512472; info@camping-thusis.ch; www.camping-thusis.ch]** Turn off A13 Chur-San Bernardino rd dir Thusis, site well sp. Med, deeply shd; wc; chem disp; shwrs inc; el pnts CHF3; gas; lndtte; shop; rest 500m; snacks; bar; playgrnd; pool adj; tennis; games area; fishing; 20% statics; dogs; phone; Eng spkn; adv bkg; CKE/CCI. "Gd cent for mountains; beautiful situation." 1 May-30 Sep. CHF 27.00                    2010*

⊞ **THUSIS** *C4* (10km S Rural) *46.60580, 9.42630* **Camping Sut Baselgia, 7440 Andeer [081 6611453; fax 6307077; camping.andeer@bluewin.ch; www.campingandeer.ch]** On N edge of vill of Andeer. Exit N13 at Zillis for Andeer; site sp. Med, pt shd; wc; chem disp; shwrs inc; el pnts (10A) CHF3; gas; lndtte (inc dryer); shop; tradsmn; snacks; bar; 2 pools adj (1 htd, covrd); paddling pool; tennis; cycle hire; games rm; wifi; 90% statics; dogs CHF2; site clsd Nov; quiet; ccard acc. "Beautiful location; helpful owner; gd NH." CHF 33.00  2011*

**TRIESEN see Vaduz (Liechtenstein)** *B4*

SWITZERLAND

**ULRICHEN** *C3* (1km SE Rural) *46.50369, 8.30969* **Camping Nufenen, 3988 Ulrichen [027 9731437; info@camping-nufenen.ch; www.camping-nufenen.ch]** On NE end of Ulrichen turn R on Nufenen pass rd. After rlwy & rv x-ing (1km), site on R. Med, pt shd; wc; chem disp; shwrs CHF0.50; el pnts (8A) CHF3.50; lndtte; shop, snacks 500m; tradsmn; rest 1km; pool 6km; tennis 2km; 50% statics; dogs CHF2; phone; poss cr; adv bkg; quiet; red long stay/CKE/CCI. "Pleasantly situated, mountainous site with gd local facs; gd walking; san facs basic but clean; recep clsd 1230-1400." ♦ ltd 1 Jun-30 Sep. CHF 26.00                                   2009*

**ULRICHEN** *C3* (5km SW Rural) *46.46480, 8.24469* **Camping Augenstern, 3988 Reckingen [027 9731395; info@campingaugenstern.ch; www.campingaugenstern.ch]** On Brig-Gletsch rd turn R in Reckingen over rlwy & rv; site sp. Med, unshd; wc; chem disp; mv service pnt; shwrs CHF1; el pnts (10A) CHF4.50; lndtte; shop; rest, snacks; bar; htd pool adj; golf; fishing; 20% statics; dogs CHF2; quiet; red CKE/CCI. "Nr Rv Rhône & mountains." 14 May-16 Oct & 10 Dec-13 Mar. CHF 28.00                                   2009*

**UNTERSEEN see Interlaken** *C2*

**UTTWIL see Romanshorn** *A4*

⊞ **VADUZ (LIECHTENSTEIN)** *B4* (10km S Rural) *47.0866, 9.52666* **Camping Mittagspitze, Saga 29, 9495 Triesen [3923677; info@campingtriesen.li; www.campingtriesen.li]** On rd 28 bet Vaduz & Balzers, sp. Poss diff for lge o'fits. Med, some hdstg, terr, pt shd; wc; chem disp; shwrs inc; el pnts (6A) CHF5; gas; lndtte; shop on site & 3km; rest; beergarden; BBQ; playgrnd; pool high ssn; fishing; fitness trail; many statics; dogs CHF4; poss cr; Eng spkn; quiet; ccard acc. "Pretty site in lovely location; excel touring base; site yourself; recep open 0800-0830 & 1900-1930 only; steep, diff access to pitches & slippery when wet; gd rest." CHF 33.00        2009*

**VALLORBE** *B1* (W Urban) *46.71055, 6.37472* **Camping Pré Sous Ville, 10 Rue des Fontaines, 1337 Vallorbe [021 8432309; yvan.favre@vallorbe.com]** Foll camping sp in town. Med, mkd pitch, pt shd; wc; chem disp; mv service pnt; shwrs inc; el pnts (10A) CHF5; gas; lndtte; rest, snacks adj; bar; playgrnd; htd pool adj; fishing; tennis; games area; 20% statics; dogs; Eng spkn; quiet; red CKE/CCI. "Gd, clean facs; gd size pitches; site yourself if warden absent; conv for Vallée de Joux, Lake Geneva & Jura; views down valley." ♦ 15 Apr-15 Oct. CHF 25.00                           2009*

⊞ **VERS L'EGLISE** *C2* (1km W Rural) *46.35530, 7.12705* **TCS Camping La Murée, 1865 Les Diablerets [079 4019915; dagonch@bluewin.ch; www.camping-caravaningvd.com]** Fr N9 exit Aigle. In 8km at Le Sepey turn R dir Vers-l'Eglise & Les Diablerets; site on R at ent to vill. Med, pt sl, terr; htd wc; shwrs; chem disp; el pnts (6A) CHF3; gas; lndtte; playgrnd; pool 3km; fishing; tennis; wifi; 40% statics; quiet. CHF 21.00                                   2009*

**VESENAZ see Genève** *C1*

**VETROZ see Sion** *C2*

⊞ **VEVEY** *C1* (12km NW Rural) *46.52864, 6.76556* **Camping Les Cases, Chemin des Cases 2, 1606 Forel [021 7811464; fax 7813126; www.campingforel.ch]** Exit A9/E62 Chexbres & foll Lac de Bret & turn L sp Savigny, then immed L. Site 100m on R, 1km S of Forel. Sm, pt sl, unshd; wc; chem disp; mv service pnt; shwrs CHF1; el pnts (13A) CHF4; gas; lndtte; supmkt; rest, snacks; bar; playgrnd; pool; paddling pool; waterslide; fishing; games area; wifi; TV; 75% statics; dogs CHF2; adv bkg; red long stay. "Sep touring area; gd." ♦ CHF 29.00                                   2010*

**VILLENEUVE** *C1* (6km S Rural) *46.38666, 6.86055* **Camping Rive-Bleue, Bouveret-Plage, 1897 Le Bouveret [024 4812161; fax 4812108; info@camping-rive-bleue.ch; www.camping-rive-bleue.ch]** Fr Montreux foll sp to Evian to S side of Lake Geneva. Turn R after sp 'Bienvenue Bouveret'. Foll camp sp to Aqua Park. Site on R approx 1km fr main rd. Lge, mkd pitch, pt shd; wc; chem disp; mv service pnt; shwrs inc; el pnts (10A) CHF4.20 (adaptor avail - check earth); gas; lndtte; rest & snacks adj; shop; playgrnd; pool adj; waterslide; lake sw; watersports; tennis; 20% statics; dogs CHF2.60; wifi; sep car park; adv bkg; quiet; CKE/CCI. "Well-maintained, well-ordered site in lovely setting on lake; friendly staff; water/waste pnts scarce; v gd facs but red low ssn; 15 mins walk to vill with supmkt; conv ferries around Lake Geneva; cars must be parked in sep public car park; gd cyling area; free bicycles for 4 hrs fr vill." 1 Apr-12 Oct.  CHF 50.00                   2014*

> "Satellite navigation makes touring much easier"
>
> Remember most sat navs don't know if you're towing or in a larger vehicle – always use yours alongside maps and site directions.

⊞ **VILLENEUVE** *C1* (4km SW Rural) *46.39333, 6.89527* **Camping Les Grangettes, Rue des Grangettes, 1845 Noville [021 9601503; fax 9602030; noville@treyvaud.com; www.les-grangettes.ch]** Fr N9 Montreux-Aigle rd, take Villeneuve exit, at end slip rd turn N twds Villeneuve. At 1st traff lts turn L to Noville, turn R by PO, site sp. Narr app rd. Med, mkd pitch, unshd; htd wc; chem disp; mv service pnt; shwrs; el pnts (10A) CHF4; lndtte; shop on site & 3km; rest, snacks; bar; pool 3km; lake sw; fishing; boating; 80% statics; dogs CHF3; phone; sep car park; Eng spkn; quiet. "Beautifully situated on SE corner Lake Geneva o'looking Montreux; sep tourer area; poss noisy in hg ssn." ♦ CHF 50.00        2014*

⊞ **VILLENEUVE** *C1* (6km SW Rural) *46.35638, 6.89916* **Camping au Grand-Bois, Chemin au Grand Bois 6, 1846 Chessel [024 4814225; fax 4815113; au.grand-bois@bluewin.ch; www.augrandbois.ch]** Fr N9 Montreux-Aigle, take Villeneuve exit, at end of slip rd turn N twds Villeneuve. At 1st traff lts turn L twds Noville, site on R in 4km. Lge, pt shd; wc; chem disp; mv service pnt; shwrs CHF1; el pnts (10A) CHF3 (adaptor avail); lndtte; shop 3km; tradsmn; playgrnd; htd pool; sand beach 6km; 80% statics; adv bkg; red long stay/CKE/CCI. "Gd cent for Geneva & pt of Alps; clean, peaceful site; poss travellers." ♦ CHF 24.00                                   2009*

**VIRA GAMBAROGNO see Locarno** *C3*

SWITZERLAND

**VISP** *C2* (500m N Rural) *46.29730, 7.87269* **Camping Schwimmbad Mühleye, 3930 Visp [027 9462084; fax 9463469; info@camping-visp.ch; www.camping-visp.ch]** Exit main rd E2 at W end of town bet Esso petrol stn & rv bdge at Camping sp. Site nr pool. Lge, pt shd; wc; chem disp; shwrs; el pnts (13A) CHF3.50; gas; lndtte; shops 500m; tradsmn; snacks; bar; playgrnd; lge pool adj; tennis; fishing; 20% statics; dogs CHF2; Eng spkn; some noise fr rlwy & sometimes rifle range; red long stay/low ssn/CKE/CCI. "Gd for Zermatt & Matterhorn; recep at sw pool ent; gd value espec low ssn; suitable lge o'fits." 10 Mar-31 Oct. CHF 35.00          2013*

## "There aren't many sites open at this time of year"

If you're travelling outside peak season remember to call ahead to check site opening dates – even if the entry says 'open all year'.

**VISP** *C2* (6km W Rural) *46.30280, 7.80188* **Camping Santa Monica, Kantonstrasse, Turtig, 3942 Raron [027 9342424; fax 9342450; santamonica@rhone.ch; www.santa-monica. ch]** Turn R off Sion-Brig rd after Turtig, just after sm rndabt. Lge, pt shd; wc; chem disp; mv service pnt; private san facs avail; shwrs CHF1; el pnts (16A) CHF4; gas; lndtte; shop 250m; snacks; htd pool; tennis; fishing; 50% statics; dogs CHF3.80 (1 only); Eng spkn; adv bkg; quiet, but some rd noise; red low ssn. "Recep clsd lunchtime, but no barrier so site yourself." 10 Apr-18 Oct. CHF 30.00          2009*

⊞ **VISP** *C2* (6km W Rural) *46.30288, 7.79530* **Camping Simplonblick, 3942 Raron [027 9343205; fax 9675012; simplonblick@bluewin.ch; www.camping-simplonblick. ch]** Site on S of rd 9. Fr Visp site past junc to Raron thro g'ge forecourt. Lge, pt shd; wc; chem disp; mv service pnt; el pnts CHF4 (adaptor loan); gas; lndtte; tradsmn; rest; bar; playgrnd; pool; paddling pool; dogs CHF4; Eng spkn; adv bkg; quiet; ccard acc. "Vg rest; friendly, welcoming staff; recep clsd 1200-1500 fr end Aug." CHF 35.00          2011*

**VITZNAU** *B3* (500m SE Rural) *47.00683, 8.48621* **Camping Vitznau, Altdorfstrasse, 6354 Vitznau [041 3971280; fax 3972457; info@camping-vitznau.ch; www.camping-vitznau.ch]** On E edge of Vitznau, sp. Fr Küssnacht twd Brunnen turn L at RC church with tall clock tower. Lge, terr, hdstg, pt shd; wc; chem disp; mv service pnt; shwrs inc; el pnts (15A) CHF4 (adaptors on loan); gas; lndtte; shop & 500m; bar; pool; lake sw & beach 500m; tennis; 40% statics; dogs CHF5; Quickstop o'night facs CHF20; poss cr; Eng spkn; adv bkg rec; quiet; card acc; red low ssn; ccard acc; red long stay; CKE/CCI. "Excel, v clean, family-run site; friendly owner will help with pitching; max c'van length 7m high ssn; sm pitches; some site rds tight & steep; recep closes 1830 hrs; fine views lakes & mountains; many activities inc walking; gd dog-walking; conv ferry terminal, cable cars & mountain rlwy (tickets avail on site); gd saving by using 'tell-pass'; lake steamer to Luzern 500m; gd pool, sm shop." ♦ ltd 27 Mar-17 Oct. CHF 54.00          2013*

**WABERN see Bern** *B2*

**WAGENHAUSEN see Schaffhausen** *A3*

**WALENSTADT** *B3* (1km W Rural) *47.11688, 9.30086* **See Camping, Ziegelhütte, 8880 Walenstadt [081 7351896 or 7351212; fax 7351841; kontakt@see-camping.ch; www. see-camping.ch]** Fr Zürich on A3 turn R at Walenstadt sp, turn L & go thro town. Foll camping sp 2km, turn R into site. Med, pt shd; htd wc; chem disp; mv service pnt; shwrs inc; el pnts (16A) CHF3; lndtte; shop; snacks; playgrnd; lake sw adj; TV; quiet but some train noise; 75% statics; phone; no dogs; sep car park; no adv bkg; Eng spkn; red long stay; CKE/ CCI. "Beautiful area; wonderful lake views." 1 May-30 Sep. CHF 38.00          2010*

⊞ **WILDBERG IM TOSSTAL** *A3* (1km NE Rural) *47.43500, 8.82862* **Camping in der Weid, Wildbergerstrasse, 8489 Wildberg-im-Tösstal [052 3853388; seiler.camping@ bluewin.ch; www.campingwildberg.ch]** Leave N1/E17 at Winterthur-Ohringen to cent Winterthur. Turn R onto N15 sp Turbenthal. Wildberg sp on ent Turbenthal, turn R, site on L in 1km. Steep access rd. Med, hdstg, pt sl, terr, pt shd; htd wc; chem disp; mv service pnt; shwrs CHF0.50; el pnts (6A) CHF1.50; lndtte; shop; tradsmn; rest, snacks; bar; BBQ; playgrnd; pool 2km; paddling pool; games area; TV; 90% statics; dogs CHF2; Eng spkn; adv bkg; aircraft noise. "Gd NH for Zürich; ltd space for tourers; friendly, helpful staff; gd for children." ♦ CHF 26.00          2010*

**WILDERSWIL see Interlaken** *C2*

⊞ **WINTERTHUR** *A3* (3km N Rural) *47.51965, 8.71655* **Camping am Schützenweiher, Eichliwaldstrasse 4, 8400 Winterthur [tel/fax 052 2125260; campingplatz@win.ch; www.campingwinterthur.ch]** Fr A1/E60 exit Winterthur-Ohringen dir Winterthur, turn R & foll site sp, site adj police stn in about 200m. Sm, shd; htd wc; chem disp; shwrs CHF1; el pnts CHF3; gas; lndtte; shops adj; rest; playgrnd; pool 3km; 8% statics; dogs CHF4; phone; poss cr; Eng spkn; some m'way noise; red CKE/CCI. "Helpful owner; office open 1900-2000 to register & pay; find own pitch outside these hrs; sm pitches; NH only." CHF 28.00          2010*

## "That's changed – Should I let The Club know?"

If you find something on site that's different from the site entry, fill in a report and let us know. See www.caravanclub.co.uk/europereport.

**YVERDON** *B1* (2km N Rural) *46.80284, 6.63399* **Camping Le Pécos, Rue du Pécos, 1422 Grandson [024 4454969; fax 4462904; vd24@campings-ccyverdpn.ch; www. campings-ccyverdon.ch]** Foll rd 5 dir Neuchâtel. Site is 800m SW fr Grandson town cent, lakeside site, sp VD24. Med, mkd pitch, hdstg, pt shd; htd wc; chem disp; mv service pnt; baby facs; fam bthrm; shwrs CHF1; el pnts (10A) CHF6 (adaptor avail); gas; lndry rm; shop; rest, snacks; bar; playgrnd; lake sw adj; wifi; 70% statics; dogs CHF3; phone; extra for lakeside pitches; poss cr; Eng spkn; adv bkg; quiet but some rlwy noise; CKE/CCI. "Clean san facs; friendly owners; sm pitches." ♦ 1 Apr-30 Sep. CHF 30.00          2010*

**YVONAND see Yverdon** *B1*

**ZERMATT** *D2* (7km N Rural) *46.06450, 7.77500* **Camping Alphubel, 3929 Täsch (Wallis) [027 9673635; welcome@ campingtaesch.ch; www.campingtaesch.ch]** Turn down R-hand slip rd over level x-ing & bdge after rlwy stn in Täsch, & foll sp to site. S bend bdge poss diff for lge o'fits at app. Med, unshd; htd wc; chem disp; mv service pnt; shwrs inc; el pnts (10A) CHF5 (long lead poss req); lndtte; shops 200m; rest adj; htd pool 1km; tennis; fishing; dogs CHF2; recep clsd 1200-1400; poss cr; Eng spkn; no adv bkg; quiet but rlwy noise; ccard not acc. "Conv for frequent train to Zermatt fr vill; superb scenery & walking; helpful owner; vg, modern san facs; excel." 8 May-14 Oct. CHF 49.00              2013*

## "I like to fill in the reports as I travel from site to site"

You'll find report forms at the back of this guide, or you can fill them in online at www.caravaclub.co.uk/europereport.

**ZERMATT** *D2* (7km N Rural) *46.08600, 7.78219* **Camping Attermenzen, 3928 Randa [027 9672555 or 9671379; fax 9676074; sommercamping@oberwallis.ch or wintercamping@oberwallis.ch; www.camping-randa. ch]** Fr A9/E62 turn S in Visp dir Zermatt. Site on L after approx 30km 2km S of Randa vill bef Tasch. Med, pt sl, unshd; wc; shwrs inc; el pnts (5A) CHF4 (adaptors avail); gas; lndtte; shop; tradsmn; rest, snacks; bar; playgrnd; dogs CHF2; shuttle bus to Zermatt; site clsd Jan; poss cr; Eng spkn; quiet; CKE/ CCI. "Winter c'vanning; main clientele climbers; excel san facs; humourous owner." 15 Jun-15 Sep & 1 Nov-30 Apr. CHF 24.00              2009*

**ZERNEZ** *C4* (500m W Rural) *46.69716, 10.08718* **Camping Cul, 7530 Zernez [tel/fax 081 8561462; info@camping-cul. ch; www.camping-cul.ch]** Fr N foll sp for St Moritz to edge of town, sp thro woodyard to site. Fr S sp on L on reaching town. Med, mkd pitch, pt shd; wc; chem disp; mv service pnt; shwrs inc; el pnts (8A) CHF2.50; lndtte; shop & 500m; tradsmn; rest high ssn; playgrnd; pool in town; 5% statics; dogs CHF2; poss cr; adv bkg; quiet; 10% red CKE/CCI. "Roomy, clean, pretty, well-organised site surrounded by mountains; friendly staff; excel san facs; barrier clsd 1200-1300; conv Swiss National Park & train to St Moritz; conv Livigno (Italy) for tax-free shopping; easy walk into town along Rv Inn & many walking trails." 15 May-31 Oct. CHF 32.00              2009*

**ZUG** *B3* (1km E Rural) *47.17806, 8.49438* **TCS Camping Zugersee, Chamer Fussweg 36, 6300 Zug [041 7418422; fax 7418430; camping.zug@tcs.ch; www.campingtcs.ch]** Fr A4/E41 take A4a Zug-West, site sp on R in 3km on lakeside. Fr Zug take Luzern rd for 2km. Site on L under rlwy. Med, mkd pitch, pt shd; htd wc; chem disp; mv service pnt; shwrs inc; el pnts (4A) CHF4; gas; lndtte (inc dryer); shop; rest, snacks; bar; playgrnd; pool 3km; lake sw; fishing; tennis; games area; cycle hire; 40% statics; dogs CHF5; phone; poss cr; Eng spkn; rlwy noise; ccard acc; red CKE/CCI. "Easy walk to town." 30 Mar-7 Oct. CHF 36.00              2011*

**ZURICH** *A3* (3km S Rural) *47.33633, 8.54167* **Camping Seebucht, Seestrasse 559, 8038 Zürich-Wollishofen [044 4821612; fax 4821660; 2008@camping-zurich.ch; www.camping-zurich.ch]** Fr city foll rd 3 (twd Chur) on S side of lake; foll camping sp. Lge, hdstg, pt shd; wc; chem disp; mv service pnt; shwrs CHF2; el pnts (6A) CHF5; gas; lndtte; shop; tradsmn; rest, snacks; bar; BBQ; playgrnd; pool 3km; lake sw; watersports; fishing; tennis; 80% statics; dogs CHF5; bus; poss cr & noisy; Eng spkn; rd & rlwy noise. "Parking in Zürich v diff, use bus; sm area for tourers; conv NH, v sm pitches." ◆ 1 May-30 Sep. CHF 39.00              2012*

**ZURICH** *A3* (14km SW Rural) *47.27970, 8.39570* **Camping Reussbrücke, Muristrasse 32, 8913 Ottenbach [044 7612022; fax 7612042; reussbruecke8913@bluewin. ch; www.camping-ottenbach.ch]** Exit Basel-Zürich m'way at Lenzburg. Foll sps to Zug/Luzern to Muri. Turn L foll sps twd Affoltern thro Birri. Site on L past rv bdge at Ottenbach. Fr Zürich, take rd to Luzern via Birmensdorf. At Affoltern R sp Muri to site on R in 4.5km at Ottenbach, bef rv bdge. Lge, pt shd; wc; shwrs; chem disp; mv service pnt; el pnts (10A) CHF4; gas; lndtte (inc dryer); shop; tradsmn; rest, snacks; playgrnd; pool; fishing; cycle hire; 75% statics; dogs CHF3.50; poss cr; Eng spkn; adv bkg; quiet; ccard acc; CKE/CCI. "Excel san facs; friendly welcome; in beautiful area; sep car pk partly outside gates." 26 Mar-15 Oct. CHF 34.00              2011*

## "I need an on-site restaurant"

We do our best to make sure site information is correct, but it is always best to check any must-have facilities are still available or will be open during your visit.

⊞ **ZWEISIMMEN** *C2* (1km N Rural) *46.56338, 7.37691* **Camping Fankhauser, Ey Gässli 2, 3770 Zweisimmen [033 7221356; fax 7221351; info@camping-fankhauser. ch; www.camping-fankhauser.ch]** N6 exit Spiez, then foll sp Zweisimmen. On o'skts of town turn L at camping sp immed bef Agip petrol stn, site on L immed after rlwy x-ing. Med, pt sl; htd wc; chem disp; mv service pnt; shwrs CHF0.50; el pnts (10A) CHF3.50 or metered; lndtte; shop 1km; rest, snacks, bar 1km; BBQ; playgrnd; pool 800m; fishing; golf; 90% statics; dogs free; phone; Eng spkn; adv bkg; some rlwy noise & glider tow planes at w/end; CKE/CCI. "Gd NH." CHF 28.00    2011*

⊞ **ZWEISIMMEN** *C2* (1km N Rural) *46.56219, 7.37780* **Camping Vermeille, Ey Gässli 2, 3770 Zweisimmen [033 7221940; fax 7723625; info@camping-vermeille. ch; www.camping-vermeille.ch]** Fr N6 exist Spiez & foll sp Zweisimmen. Pass Camping Fankhauser. Site sp almost opp Aldi supmkt. Med, pt shd; htd wc; chem disp; mv service pnt; baby facs; shwrs; el pnts (10A) CHF3.50; gas; lndtte (inc dryer); shop; rest 300m; snacks; BBQ; cooking facs; playgrnd; htd pool; fishing; tennis; cycle hire; games rm; golf; wifi; TV; 70% statics; dogs CHF2; Eng spkn; adv bkg; quiet; ccard acc; red CKE/CCI. "Well-run site; friendly, helpful staff; clsd 1200-1400; cable car to top of mountains; many walks & excursions; easy walk to vill/rlwy stn; cycle track to vill & up valley." ◆ CHF 33.00              2009*

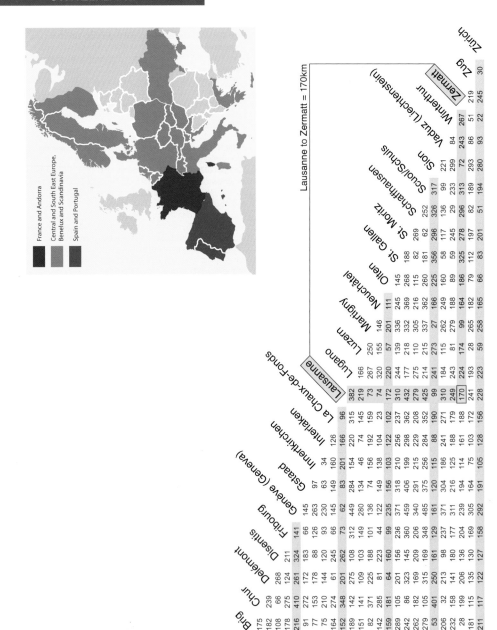

You can now fill in site reports online

# Club Insurance built on firsthand experience

# We've looked closely at our insurances to make sure they meet your needs

## Why choose Club insurance?

- Club know-how ensures great cover
- Created with your touring needs in mind
- Superb value for money
- The aftercare you expect from The Club

*I'm delighted with the service, the premium is very competitive and the online quote system was so easy*

Sara Reynolds, member, Cheshire

## Get peace of mind, get your quote at
## www.caravanclub.co.uk or call

 Caravan Insurance    01342 488209

 Motorhome & Car Insurance    0808 223 4145*

 Overseas Holiday Insurance    01342 488363

Home Insurance    0800 028 48

Pet Insurance    0800 015 13

Mayday UK Breakdown & Recovery    0800 731 01

Motorhome and car insurance new business is not available for drivers aged over 80.

Lines are open Mon-Fri 8.45am-5.30pm (caravan and holiday); Mon-Fri 8.30am-6.00pm & Sat 9.00am-1.00pm (motorhome, car, home & pet); Mon-Fri 8.00am-8.00pm, Sat 9.00am-5.00pm & Sun 10.00am-4.00pm (breakdown). Calls may be recorded. *Freephone numbers above are free to landlines only.

The Caravan Club's Motorhome, Car, Home and Pet insurances are arranged for The Club by Devitt Insurance Services Limited, Insurance Brokers. Mayday vehicle rescue is provided by Green Flag and underwritten by U K Insurance Limited. U K Insurance is authorised by the Prudential Regulation Authority and regulated by the Financial Conduct Authority and the Prudential Regulation Authority. The Caravan Club Limited and Devitt Insurance Services Limited are authorised and regulated by the Financial Conduct Authority.

THE CARAVAI CLUB

# Site Report Form

If campsite is already listed, complete only those sections of the form where changes apply
or alternatively use the Abbreviated Site Report form on the following pages.

*Sites not reported on for 5 years may be deleted from the guide*

| Year of guide used | 20......... | Is site listed? | Listed on page no. .......... | | Unlisted | Date of visit | ......../......../......... |
|---|---|---|---|---|---|---|---|

## A – CAMPSITE NAME AND LOCATION

| Country | | Name of town/village site listed under *(see Sites Location Maps)* | | | | | |
|---|---|---|---|---|---|---|---|
| Distance & direction from centre of town site is listed under *(in a straight line)* | | ...................km | eg N, NE, S, SW | | Urban | Rural | Coastal |
| Site open all year? | Y / N | Period site is open *(if not all year)* | ................../.................. | to | ................../.................. | | |
| Site name | | | | | | Naturist site | Y / N |
| Site address | | | | | | | |
| Telephone | | | Fax | | | | |
| E-mail | | | Website | | | | |

## B – CAMPSITE CHARGES

| Charge for outfit + 2 adults in local currency | PRICE | | EL PNTS inc in this price? | Y / N | Amps ......... |
|---|---|---|---|---|---|

## C – DIRECTIONS

| Brief, specific directions to site (in km) *To convert miles to kilometres multiply by 8 and divide by 5 or use Conversion Table in guide* | |
|---|---|
| GPS | Latitude....................................................*(eg 12.34567)* Longitude....................................................*(eg 1.23456 or -1.23456)* |

## D – CAMPSITE DESCRIPTION

| SITE size ie number of pitches | Small Max 50 | SM | Medium 51-150 | MED | Large 151-500 | LGE | Very large 500+ | V LGE | Unchanged |
|---|---|---|---|---|---|---|---|---|---|
| PITCH size | *eg small, medium, large, very large, various* | | | | | | | | Unchanged |
| Pitch features if **NOT** open-plan/grassy | Hedged | HDG PITCH | Marked or numbered | MKD PITCH | Hardstanding or gravel | HDSTG | Unchanged | | |
| If site is **NOT** level, is it | Part sloping | PT SL | Sloping | SL | Terraced | TERR | Unchanged | | |
| Is site shaded? | Shaded | SHD | Part shaded | PT SHD | Unshaded | UNSHD | Unchanged | | |

## E – CAMPSITE FACILITIES

| WC | Heated | HTD WC | Continental | CONT | Own San recommended | | OWN SAN REC | |
|---|---|---|---|---|---|---|---|---|
| Chemical disposal point | | CHEM DISP | | Dedicated point | | WC only | | |
| Motorhome waste discharge and water refill point | | | | MV SERVICE PNT | | | | |
| Child / baby facilities (bathroom) | | CHILD / BABY FACS | | Family bathroom | | FAM BTHRM | | |
| Hot shower(s) | | SHWR(S) | | Inc in site fee? | Y / N | Price...................*(if not inc)* | | |
| ELECTRIC HOOK UP *if not included in price above* | | EL PNTS | | Price........................... | | Amps........................... | | |
| Supplies of bottled gas | | GAS | | On site | Y / N | Or in .................... Kms | | |
| Launderette / Washing Machine | | LNDTTE | | Inc dryer Y / N | | LNDRY RM *(if no washing machine)* | | |

*You can also complete forms online: www.caravanclub.co.uk/europereport*

CUT ALONG DOTTED LINE

## F – FOOD & DRINK

| | | | | | |
|---|---|---|---|---|---|
| Shop(s) / supermarket | SHOP(S) / SUPMKT | On site | | or | .................. kms |
| Bread / milk delivered | TRADSMN | | | | |
| Restaurant / cafeteria | REST | On site | | or | .................. kms |
| Snack bar / take-away | SNACKS | On site | | or | .................. kms |
| Bar | BAR | On site | | or | .................. kms |
| Barbecue allowed | BBQ | Charcoal | Gas | Elec | Sep area |
| Cooking facilities | COOKING FACS | | | | |

## G – LEISURE FACILITIES

| | | | | | |
|---|---|---|---|---|---|
| Playground | PLAYGRND | | | | |
| Swimming pool | POOL | On site | or ..........km | Heated | Covered |
| Beach | BEACH | Adj | or ..........km | Sand | Shingle |
| Alternative swimming (lake) | SW | Adj | or ..........km | Sand | Shingle |
| Games /sports area / Games room | GAMES AREA | GAMES ROOM | | | |
| Entertainment in high season | ENTMNT | | | | |
| Internet use by visitors | INTERNET | Wifi Internet | | WIFI | |
| Television room | TV RM | Satellite / Cable to pitches | | TV CAB / SAT | |

## H – OTHER INFORMATION

| | | | | | |
|---|---|---|---|---|---|
| % Static caravans / mobile homes / chalets / cottages / fixed tents on site | | | | | ..............% STATICS |
| Dogs allowed | DOGS | Y / N | Price per night ..................... (if allowed) | | |
| Phone | PHONE | On site | Adj | | |
| Bus / tram / train | BUS / TRAM / TRAIN | Adj | or .............. km | | |
| Twin axles caravans allowed? | TWIN AXLES    Y / N | Possibly crowded in high season | | POSS CR | |
| English spoken | ENG SPKN | | | | |
| Advance bookings accepted | ADV BKG | Y / N | | | |
| Noise levels on site in season | NOISY | QUIET | If noisy, why? | | |
| Credit card accepted | CCARD ACC | Reduction low season | | RED LOW SSN | |
| Camping Key Europe or Camping Card International accepted in lieu of passport | CKE/CCI | INF card required (If naturist site) | | Y / N | |
| Facilities for disabled | Full wheelchair facilities | ♦ | Limited disabled facilities | ♦ ltd | |

## I – ADDITIONAL REMARKS AND/OR ITEMS OF INTEREST

| | |
|---|---|
| Tourist attractions, unusual features or other facilities, eg waterslide, tennis, cycle hire, watersports, horseriding, separate car park, walking distance to shops etc | YOUR OPINION OF THE SITE: |
| | EXCEL |
| | VERY GOOD |
| | GOOD |
| | FAIR \| POOR |
| | NIGHT HALT ONLY |

Your comments & opinions may be used in future editions of the guide, if you do not wish them to be used please tick ........

## J – MEMBER DETAILS

| | | | | | |
|---|---|---|---|---|---|
| ARE YOU A: | Caravanner | | Motorhomer | Trailer-tenter? | |
| NAME: | | | MEMBERSHIP NO: | | |
| | | | POST CODE: | | |
| DO YOU NEED MORE BLANK SITE REPORT FORMS? | | YES | | NO | |

Please use a separate form for each campsite and do not send receipts. Owing to the large number of site reports received, it is not possible to enter into correspondence. Please return completed form to:

**The Editor, Overseas Touring Guides, The Caravan Club**
**FREEPOST, PO Box 386, (RRZG-SXKK-UCUJ)**
**East Grinstead RH19 1FH**
(Please use this address only when mailing from within the UK)

# Site Report Form

If campsite is already listed, complete only those sections of the form where changes apply
or alternatively use the Abbreviated Site Report form on the following pages.

*Sites not reported on for 5 years may be deleted from the guide*

| Year of guide used | 20......... | Is site listed? | Listed on page no. ........... | Unlisted | Date of visit | ......./......./......... |
|---|---|---|---|---|---|---|

## A – CAMPSITE NAME AND LOCATION

| Country | | Name of town/village site listed under *(see Sites Location Maps)* | | | |
|---|---|---|---|---|---|
| Distance & direction from centre of town site is listed under *(in a straight line)* | | ...................km | eg N, NE, S, SW | Urban | Rural | Coastal |
| Site open all year? | Y / N | Period site is open *(if not all year)* | ................./................. to ................./................. | | | |
| Site name | | | | Naturist site | Y / N |
| Site address | | | | | |
| Telephone | | Fax | | | |
| E-mail | | Website | | | |

## B – CAMPSITE CHARGES

| Charge for outfit + 2 adults in local currency | PRICE | | EL PNTS inc in this price? | Y / N | Amps ......... |
|---|---|---|---|---|---|

## C – DIRECTIONS

| Brief, specific directions to site (in km) *To convert miles to kilometres multiply by 8 and divide by 5 or use Conversion Table in guide* | |
|---|---|
| GPS | Latitude....................................(eg 12.34567) Longitude....................................(eg 1.23456 or -1.23456) |

## D – CAMPSITE DESCRIPTION

| SITE size ie number of pitches | Small Max 50 | SM | Medium 51-150 | MED | Large 151-500 | LGE | Very large 500+ | V LGE | Unchanged |
|---|---|---|---|---|---|---|---|---|---|
| PITCH size | eg small, medium, large, very large, various | | | | | | | | Unchanged |
| Pitch features if **NOT** open-plan/grassy | Hedged | HDG PITCH | Marked or numbered | MKD PITCH | Hardstanding or gravel | HDSTG | | | Unchanged |
| If site is **NOT** level, is it | Part sloping | PT SL | Sloping | SL | Terraced | TERR | | | Unchanged |
| Is site shaded? | Shaded | SHD | Part shaded | PT SHD | Unshaded | UNSHD | | | Unchanged |

## E – CAMPSITE FACILITIES

| WC | Heated | HTD WC | Continental | CONT | Own San recommended | OWN SAN REC | |
|---|---|---|---|---|---|---|---|
| Chemical disposal point | | CHEM DISP | | Dedicated point | | WC only | |
| Motorhome waste discharge and water refill point | | | | MV SERVICE PNT | | | |
| Child / baby facilities (bathroom) | | CHILD / BABY FACS | | Family bathroom | | FAM BTHRM | |
| Hot shower(s) | | SHWR(S) | | Inc in site fee? | Y / N | Price...................(if not inc) | |
| ELECTRIC HOOK UP *if not included in price above* | | EL PNTS | | Price...................................... | | Amps.......................................... | |
| Supplies of bottled gas | | GAS | | On site | Y / N | Or in ................... Kms | |
| Launderette / Washing Machine | | LNDTTE | | Inc dryer  Y / N | | LNDRY RM *(if no washing machine)* | |

*You can also complete forms online: www.caravanclub.co.uk/europereport*

## F – FOOD & DRINK

| | | | | | |
|---|---|---|---|---|---|
| Shop(s) / supermarket | SHOP(S) / SUPMKT | On site | | or | .................... kms |
| Bread / milk delivered | TRADSMN | | | | |
| Restaurant / cafeteria | REST | On site | | or | .................... kms |
| Snack bar / take-away | SNACKS | On site | | or | .................... kms |
| Bar | BAR | On site | | or | .................... kms |
| Barbecue allowed | BBQ | Charcoal | Gas | Elec | Sep area |
| Cooking facilities | COOKING FACS | | | | |

## G – LEISURE FACILITIES

| | | | | | |
|---|---|---|---|---|---|
| Playground | PLAYGRND | | | | |
| Swimming pool | POOL | On site | or ..........km | Heated | Covered |
| Beach | BEACH | Adj | or ..........km | Sand | Shingle |
| Alternative swimming (lake) | SW | Adj | or ..........km | Sand | Shingle |
| Games /sports area / Games room | GAMES AREA | GAMES ROOM | | | |
| Entertainment in high season | ENTMNT | | | | |
| Internet use by visitors | INTERNET | Wifi Internet | | WIFI | |
| Television room | TV RM | Satellite / Cable to pitches | | TV CAB / SAT | |

## H – OTHER INFORMATION

| | | | | | |
|---|---|---|---|---|---|
| % Static caravans / mobile homes / chalets / cottages / fixed tents on site | | | | ............% STATICS | |
| Dogs allowed | DOGS | Y / N | Price per night ..................... (if allowed) | | |
| Phone | PHONE | On site | Adj | | |
| Bus / tram / train | BUS / TRAM / TRAIN | Adj | or .............. km | | |
| Twin axles caravans allowed? | TWIN AXLES    Y / N | Possibly crowded in high season | | POSS CR | |
| English spoken | ENG SPKN | | | | |
| Advance bookings accepted | ADV BKG | Y / N | | | |
| Noise levels on site in season | NOISY | QUIET | If noisy, why? | | |
| Credit card accepted | CCARD ACC | Reduction low season | | RED LOW SSN | |
| Camping Key Europe or Camping Card International accepted in lieu of passport | CKE/CCI | INF card required (If naturist site) | | Y / N | |
| Facilities for disabled | Full wheelchair facilities | ♦ | Limited disabled facilities | ♦ ltd | |

## I – ADDITIONAL REMARKS AND/OR ITEMS OF INTEREST

| | |
|---|---|
| Tourist attractions, unusual features or other facilities, eg waterslide, tennis, cycle hire, watersports, horseriding, separate car park, walking distance to shops etc | YOUR OPINION OF THE SITE: |
| | EXCEL |
| | VERY GOOD |
| | GOOD |
| | FAIR · POOR |
| | NIGHT HALT ONLY |
| Your comments & opinions may be used in future editions of the guide, if you do not wish them to be used please tick ......... | |

## J – MEMBER DETAILS

| | | | | | |
|---|---|---|---|---|---|
| ARE YOU A: | Caravanner | | Motorhomer | | Trailer-tenter? |
| NAME: | | | MEMBERSHIP NO: | | |
| | | | POST CODE: | | |
| DO YOU NEED MORE BLANK SITE REPORT FORMS? | | YES | | NO | |

Please use a separate form for each campsite and do not send receipts. Owing to the large number of site reports received, it is not possible to enter into correspondence. Please return completed form to:

**The Editor, Overseas Touring Guides, The Caravan Club**
**FREEPOST, PO Box 386, (RRZG-SXKK-UCUJ)**
**East Grinstead RH19 1FH**
(Please use this address only when mailing from within the UK)

# Site Report Form

If campsite is already listed, complete only those sections of the form where changes apply
or alternatively use the Abbreviated Site Report form on the following pages.

*Sites not reported on for 5 years may be deleted from the guide*

| Year of guide used | 20......... | Is site listed? | Listed on page no. ........... | Unlisted | Date of visit | ......../......../......... |
|---|---|---|---|---|---|---|

## A – CAMPSITE NAME AND LOCATION

| Country | | Name of town/village site listed under *(see Sites Location Maps)* | | | |
|---|---|---|---|---|---|
| Distance & direction from centre of town site is listed under *(in a straight line)* | | ...................km | eg N, NE, S, SW | Urban | Rural | Coastal |

| Site open all year? | Y / N | Period site is open *(if not all year)* | ................../.................. to ................../.................. |
|---|---|---|---|

| Site name | | | | Naturist site | Y / N |
|---|---|---|---|---|---|

| Site address | |
|---|---|

| Telephone | | Fax | |
|---|---|---|---|
| E-mail | | Website | |

## B – CAMPSITE CHARGES

| Charge for outfit + 2 adults in local currency | PRICE | | EL PNTS inc in this price? | Y / N | Amps ......... |
|---|---|---|---|---|---|

## C – DIRECTIONS

| Brief, specific directions to site (in km) *To convert miles to kilometres multiply by 8 and divide by 5 or use Conversion Table in guide* | |
|---|---|
| GPS | Latitude.....................................*(eg 12.34567)* Longitude.....................................*(eg 1.23456 or -1.23456)* |

## D – CAMPSITE DESCRIPTION

| **SITE size** ie number of pitches | Small Max 50 | SM | Medium 51-150 | MED | Large 151-500 | LGE | Very large 500+ | V LGE | Unchanged |
|---|---|---|---|---|---|---|---|---|---|

| **PITCH size** | *eg small, medium, large, very large, various* | | | | | | | | Unchanged |
|---|---|---|---|---|---|---|---|---|---|

| Pitch features if **NOT** open-plan/grassy | | Hedged | HDG PITCH | Marked or numbered | MKD PITCH | Hardstanding or gravel | HDSTG | Unchanged |
|---|---|---|---|---|---|---|---|---|

| If site is **NOT** level, is it | | Part sloping | PT SL | Sloping | SL | Terraced | TERR | Unchanged |
|---|---|---|---|---|---|---|---|---|

| Is site shaded? | | Shaded | SHD | Part shaded | PT SHD | Unshaded | UNSHD | Unchanged |
|---|---|---|---|---|---|---|---|---|

## E – CAMPSITE FACILITIES

| WC | | Heated | HTD WC | Continental | CONT | Own San recommended | | OWN SAN REC | |
|---|---|---|---|---|---|---|---|---|---|
| Chemical disposal point | | | CHEM DISP | | Dedicated point | | WC only | | |
| Motorhome waste discharge and water refill point | | | | | MV SERVICE PNT | | | | |
| Child / baby facilities (bathroom) | | CHILD / BABY FACS | | | Family bathroom | | FAM BTHRM | | |
| Hot shower(s) | | SHWR(S) | | | Inc in site fee? | Y / N | Price....................*(if not inc)* | | |
| ELECTRIC HOOK UP *if not included in price above* | | EL PNTS | | | Price........................................ | | Amps........................................... | | |
| Supplies of bottled gas | | GAS | | | On site | Y / N | Or in .................... Kms | | |
| Launderette / Washing Machine | | LNDTTE | | Inc dryer Y / N | | LNDRY RM *(if no washing machine)* | | | |

*You can also complete forms online: www.caravanclub.co.uk/europereport*

CUT ALONG DOTTED LINE

## F – FOOD & DRINK

| | | | | | |
|---|---|---|---|---|---|
| Shop(s) / supermarket | SHOP(S) / SUPMKT | On site | | or | .................. kms |
| Bread / milk delivered | TRADSMN | | | | |
| Restaurant / cafeteria | REST | On site | | or | .................. kms |
| Snack bar / take-away | SNACKS | On site | | or | .................. kms |
| Bar | BAR | On site | | or | .................. kms |
| Barbecue allowed | BBQ | Charcoal | Gas | Elec | Sep area |
| Cooking facilities | COOKING FACS | | | | |

## G – LEISURE FACILITIES

| | | | | | |
|---|---|---|---|---|---|
| Playground | PLAYGRND | | | | |
| Swimming pool | POOL | On site | or .........km | Heated | Covered |
| Beach | BEACH | Adj | or .........km | Sand | Shingle |
| Alternative swimming *(lake)* | SW | Adj | or .........km | Sand | Shingle |
| Games /sports area / Games room | GAMES AREA | GAMES ROOM | | | |
| Entertainment in high season | ENTMNT | | | | |
| Internet use by visitors | INTERNET | Wifi Internet | | WIFI | |
| Television room | TV RM | Satellite / Cable to pitches | | TV CAB / SAT | |

## H – OTHER INFORMATION

| | | | | | |
|---|---|---|---|---|---|
| % Static caravans / mobile homes / chalets / cottages / fixed tents on site | | | | ...............% STATICS | |
| Dogs allowed | DOGS | Y / N | Price per night ................... *(if allowed)* | | |
| Phone | PHONE | On site | Adj | | |
| Bus / tram / train | BUS / TRAM / TRAIN | Adj | or ............. km | | |
| Twin axles caravans allowed? | TWIN AXLES   Y / N | Possibly crowded in high season | | POSS CR | |
| English spoken | ENG SPKN | | | | |
| Advance bookings accepted | ADV BKG | Y / N | | | |
| Noise levels on site in season | NOISY | QUIET | If noisy, why? | | |
| Credit card accepted | CCARD ACC | Reduction low season | | RED LOW SSN | |
| Camping Key Europe or Camping Card International accepted in lieu of passport | CKE/CCI | INF card required *(If naturist site)* | | Y / N | |
| Facilities for disabled | Full wheelchair facilities | ♦ | Limited disabled facilities | ♦ ltd | |

## I – ADDITIONAL REMARKS AND/OR ITEMS OF INTEREST

| | |
|---|---|
| *Tourist attractions, unusual features or other facilities, eg waterslide, tennis, cycle hire, watersports, horseriding, separate car park, walking distance to shops etc* | YOUR OPINION OF THE SITE: |
| | EXCEL |
| | VERY GOOD |
| | GOOD |
| | FAIR   POOR |
| | NIGHT HALT ONLY |
| Your comments & opinions may be used in future editions of the guide, if you do not wish them to be used please tick ......... | |

## J – MEMBER DETAILS

| | | | | | |
|---|---|---|---|---|---|
| ARE YOU A: | Caravanner | | Motorhomer | | Trailer-tenter? |
| NAME: | | | MEMBERSHIP NO: | | |
| | | | POST CODE: | | |
| DO YOU NEED MORE BLANK SITE REPORT FORMS? | | YES | | NO | |

Please use a separate form for each campsite and do not send receipts. Owing to the large number of site reports received, it is not possible to enter into correspondence. Please return completed form to:

**The Editor, Overseas Touring Guides, The Caravan Club**
**FREEPOST, PO Box 386, (RRZG-SXKK-UCUJ)**
**East Grinstead RH19 1FH**
(Please use this address only when mailing from within the UK)

# Site Report Form

If campsite is already listed, complete only those sections of the form where changes apply
or alternatively use the Abbreviated Site Report form on the following pages.

*Sites not reported on for 5 years may be deleted from the guide*

| Year of guide used | 20.......... | Is site listed? | Listed on page no. ........... | | Unlisted | Date of visit | ........./........./......... |
|---|---|---|---|---|---|---|---|

## A – CAMPSITE NAME AND LOCATION

| Country | | Name of town/village site listed under *(see Sites Location Maps)* | | | | | |
|---|---|---|---|---|---|---|---|
| Distance & direction from centre of town site is listed under *(in a straight line)* | | ....................km | eg N, NE, S, SW | | Urban | Rural | Coastal |
| Site open all year? | Y / N | Period site is open *(if not all year)* | ................./.................  to  ................./................. | | | | |
| Site name | | | | | | Naturist site | Y / N |
| Site address | | | | | | | |
| Telephone | | | | Fax | | | |
| E-mail | | | | Website | | | |

## B – CAMPSITE CHARGES

| Charge for outfit + 2 adults in local currency | PRICE | | EL PNTS inc in this price? | Y / N | Amps ......... |
|---|---|---|---|---|---|

## C – DIRECTIONS

| Brief, specific directions to site (in km) *To convert miles to kilometres multiply by 8 and divide by 5 or use Conversion Table in guide* | |
|---|---|
| GPS | Latitude....................................................*(eg 12.34567)* Longitude....................................................*(eg 1.23456 or -1.23456)* |

## D – CAMPSITE DESCRIPTION

| **SITE size** ie number of pitches | Small Max 50 | SM | Medium 51-150 | MED | Large 151-500 | LGE | Very large 500+ | V LGE | Unchanged |
|---|---|---|---|---|---|---|---|---|---|
| **PITCH size** | *eg small, medium, large, very large, various* | | | | | | | | Unchanged |
| Pitch features if **NOT** open-plan/grassy | Hedged | | HDG PITCH | Marked or numbered | MKD PITCH | Hardstanding or gravel | | HDSTG | Unchanged |
| If site is **NOT** level, is it | Part sloping | | PT SL | Sloping | | SL | Terraced | TERR | Unchanged |
| Is site shaded? | Shaded | | SHD | Part shaded | PT SHD | Unshaded | | UNSHD | Unchanged |

## E – CAMPSITE FACILITIES

| WC | | Heated | HTD WC | Continental | CONT | Own San recommended | | OWN SAN REC | |
|---|---|---|---|---|---|---|---|---|---|
| Chemical disposal point | | CHEM DISP | | Dedicated point | | | WC only | | |
| Motorhome waste discharge and water refill point | | | | MV SERVICE PNT | | | | | |
| Child / baby facilities (bathroom) | | CHILD / BABY FACS | | Family bathroom | | | FAM BTHRM | | |
| Hot shower(s) | | SHWR(S) | | Inc in site fee? | Y / N | Price...................*(if not inc)* | | | |
| ELECTRIC HOOK UP *if not included in price above* | | EL PNTS | | Price.......................................... | | Amps.......................................... | | | |
| Supplies of bottled gas | | GAS | | On site | Y / N | Or in ................... Kms | | | |
| Launderette / Washing Machine | LNDTTE | | Inc dryer  Y / N | | LNDRY RM *(if no washing machine)* | | | | |

*You can also complete forms online: www.caravanclub.co.uk/europereport*

CUT ALONG DOTTED LINE

## F – FOOD & DRINK

| | | | | | |
|---|---|---|---|---|---|
| Shop(s) / supermarket | SHOP(S) / SUPMKT | On site | | or | .................. kms |
| Bread / milk delivered | TRADSMN | | | | |
| Restaurant / cafeteria | REST | On site | | or | .................. kms |
| Snack bar / take-away | SNACKS | On site | | or | .................. kms |
| Bar | BAR | On site | | or | .................. kms |
| Barbecue allowed | BBQ | Charcoal | Gas | Elec | Sep area |
| Cooking facilities | COOKING FACS | | | | |

## G – LEISURE FACILITIES

| | | | | | |
|---|---|---|---|---|---|
| Playground | PLAYGRND | | | | |
| Swimming pool | POOL | On site | or ..........km | Heated | Covered |
| Beach | BEACH | Adj | or ..........km | Sand | Shingle |
| Alternative swimming *(lake)* | SW | Adj | or ..........km | Sand | Shingle |
| Games /sports area / Games room | GAMES AREA | GAMES ROOM | | | |
| Entertainment in high season | ENTMNT | | | | |
| Internet use by visitors | INTERNET | Wifi Internet | WIFI | | |
| Television room | TV RM | Satellite / Cable to pitches | TV CAB / SAT | | |

## H – OTHER INFORMATION

| | | | | | |
|---|---|---|---|---|---|
| % Static caravans / mobile homes / chalets / cottages / fixed tents on site | | | | | ..............% STATICS |
| Dogs allowed | DOGS | Y / N | Price per night .................... *(if allowed)* | | |
| Phone | PHONE | On site | Adj | | |
| Bus / tram / train | BUS / TRAM / TRAIN | Adj | or .............. km | | |
| Twin axles caravans allowed? | TWIN AXLES   Y / N | Possibly crowded in high season | POSS CR | | |
| English spoken | ENG SPKN | | | | |
| Advance bookings accepted | ADV BKG | Y / N | | | |
| Noise levels on site in season | NOISY   QUIET | If noisy, why? | | | |
| Credit card accepted | CCARD ACC | Reduction low season | RED LOW SSN | | |
| Camping Key Europe or Camping Card International accepted in lieu of passport | CKE/CCI | INF card required *(If naturist site)* | Y / N | | |
| Facilities for disabled | Full wheelchair facilities  ♦ | Limited disabled facilities | ♦ ltd | | |

## I – ADDITIONAL REMARKS AND/OR ITEMS OF INTEREST

| | |
|---|---|
| *Tourist attractions, unusual features or other facilities, eg waterslide, tennis, cycle hire, watersports, horseriding, separate car park, walking distance to shops etc* | YOUR OPINION OF THE SITE: |
| | EXCEL |
| | VERY GOOD |
| | GOOD |
| | FAIR   POOR |
| | NIGHT HALT ONLY |

Your comments & opinions may be used in future editions of the guide, if you do not wish them to be used please tick ........

## J – MEMBER DETAILS

| | | | | | |
|---|---|---|---|---|---|
| ARE YOU A: | Caravanner | | Motorhomer | | Trailer-tenter? |
| NAME: | | | MEMBERSHIP NO: | | |
| | | | POST CODE: | | |
| DO YOU NEED MORE BLANK SITE REPORT FORMS? | | YES | | NO | |

Please use a separate form for each campsite and do not send receipts. Owing to the large number of site reports received, it is not possible to enter into correspondence. Please return completed form to:

**The Editor, Overseas Touring Guides, The Caravan Club**
**FREEPOST, PO Box 386, (RRZG-SXKK-UCUJ)**
**East Grinstead RH19 1FH**
(Please use this address only when mailing from within the UK)

# Abbreviated Site Report Form

Use this abbreviated Site Report Form if you have visited a number of sites and there are no changes (or only small changes) to their entries in the guide. If reporting on a new site, or reporting several changes, please use the full version of the report form. **If advising prices, these should be for an outfit and 2 adults for one night's stay. Please indicate high or low season prices and whether electricity is included.**

Remember, if you don't tell us about sites you have visited, they may eventually be deleted from the guide.

| Year of guide used | 20.......... | Page No. | .......... | Name of town/village site listed under | | | |
|---|---|---|---|---|---|---|---|
| Site Name | | | | | Date of visit | ....... /....... /........ | |
| GPS | Latitude.........................................................(eg 12.34567) | | | Longitude.................................................(eg 1.23456 or -1.23456) | | | |

Site is in: Andorra / Austria / Belgium / Croatia / Czech Republic / Denmark / Finland / France / Germany / Greece / Hungary / Italy / Luxembourg / Netherlands / Norway / Poland / Portugal / Slovakia / Slovenia / Spain / Sweden / Switzerland

Comments:

| Charge for outfit + 2 adults in local currency | High Season | Low Season | Elec inc in price? | Y / N | ............amps |
|---|---|---|---|---|---|
| | | | Price of elec (if not inc) | | ............amps |

| Year of guide used | 20.......... | Page No. | .......... | Name of town/village site listed under | | | |
|---|---|---|---|---|---|---|---|
| Site Name | | | | | Date of visit | ....... /....... /........ | |
| GPS | Latitude.........................................................(eg 12.34567) | | | Longitude.................................................(eg 1.23456 or -1.23456) | | | |

Site is in: Andorra / Austria / Belgium / Croatia / Czech Republic / Denmark / Finland / France / Germany / Greece / Hungary / Italy / Luxembourg / Netherlands / Norway / Poland / Portugal / Slovakia / Slovenia / Spain / Sweden / Switzerland

Comments:

| Charge for outfit + 2 adults in local currency | High Season | Low Season | Elec inc in price? | Y / N | ............amps |
|---|---|---|---|---|---|
| | | | Price of elec (if not inc) | | ............amps |

| Year of guide used | 20.......... | Page No. | .......... | Name of town/village site listed under | | | |
|---|---|---|---|---|---|---|---|
| Site Name | | | | | Date of visit | ....... /....... /........ | |
| GPS | Latitude.........................................................(eg 12.34567) | | | Longitude.................................................(eg 1.23456 or -1.23456) | | | |

Site is in: Andorra / Austria / Belgium / Croatia / Czech Republic / Denmark / Finland / France / Germany / Greece / Hungary / Italy / Luxembourg / Netherlands / Norway / Poland / Portugal / Slovakia / Slovenia / Spain / Sweden / Switzerland

Comments:

| Charge for outfit + 2 adults in local currency | High Season | Low Season | Elec inc in price? | Y / N | ............amps |
|---|---|---|---|---|---|
| | | | Price of elec (if not inc) | | ............amps |

**Please fill in your details and send to the address on the reverse of this form.**

**You can also complete forms online: www.caravanclub.co.uk/europereport**

| Year of guide used | 20.......... | Page No. | .......... | Name of town/village site listed under | |
|---|---|---|---|---|---|

| Site Name | | | Date of visit | ....... /....... /........ |
|---|---|---|---|---|

GPS    Latitude.................................................(eg 12.34567) Longitude.................................................(eg 1.23456 or -1.23456)

**Site is in:** Andorra / Austria / Belgium / Croatia / Czech Republic / Denmark / Finland / France / Germany / Greece / Hungary / Italy / Luxembourg / Netherlands / Norway / Poland / Portugal / Slovakia / Slovenia / Spain / Sweden / Switzerland

**Comments:**

| Charge for outfit + 2 adults in local currency | High Season | Low Season | Elec inc in price? | Y / N | .............amps |
|---|---|---|---|---|---|
| | | | Price of elec (if not inc) | | .............amps |

---

| Year of guide used | 20.......... | Page No. | .......... | Name of town/village site listed under | |
|---|---|---|---|---|---|

| Site Name | | | Date of visit | ....... /....... /........ |
|---|---|---|---|---|

GPS    Latitude.................................................(eg 12.34567) Longitude.................................................(eg 1.23456 or -1.23456)

**Site is in:** Andorra / Austria / Belgium / Croatia / Czech Republic / Denmark / Finland / France / Germany / Greece / Hungary / Italy / Luxembourg / Netherlands / Norway / Poland / Portugal / Slovakia / Slovenia / Spain / Sweden / Switzerland

**Comments:**

| Charge for outfit + 2 adults in local currency | High Season | Low Season | Elec inc in price? | Y / N | .............amps |
|---|---|---|---|---|---|
| | | | Price of elec (if not inc) | | .............amps |

| Year of guide used | 20.......... | Page No. | .......... | Name of town/village site listed under | |
|---|---|---|---|---|---|

| Site Name | | | Date of visit | ....... /....... /........ |
|---|---|---|---|---|

GPS    Latitude.................................................(eg 12.34567) Longitude.................................................(eg 1.23456 or -1.23456)

**Site is in:** Andorra / Austria / Belgium / Croatia / Czech Republic / Denmark / Finland / France / Germany / Greece / Hungary / Italy / Luxembourg / Netherlands / Norway / Poland / Portugal / Slovakia / Slovenia / Spain / Sweden / Switzerland

**Comments:**

| Charge for outfit + 2 adults in local currency | High Season | Low Season | Elec inc in price? | Y / N | .............amps |
|---|---|---|---|---|---|
| | | | Price of elec (if not inc) | | .............amps |

*Your comments & opinions may be used in future editions of the guide, if you do not wish them to be used please tick* .......

Name .................................................................................

Membership No. ................................................................

Post Code ...........................................................................

Are you a  Caravanner / Motorhomer / Trailer-Tenter?

Do you need more blank Site Report forms?        YES / NO

Please return completed forms to:
**The Editor, Overseas Touring Guides**
**The Caravan Club**
**FREEPOST**
**PO Box 386 (RRZG-SXKK-UCUJ)**
**East Grinstead**
**RH19 1FH**
(Please use this address only when mailing from within the UK)

**You can also complete forms online: www.caravanclub.co.uk/europereport**

# Abbreviated Site Report Form

Use this abbreviated Site Report Form if you have visited a number of sites and there are no changes (or only small changes) to their entries in the guide. If reporting on a new site, or reporting several changes, please use the full version of the report form. **If advising prices,** these should be for an outfit and 2 adults for one night's stay. **Please indicate high or low season prices and whether electricity is included.**

Remember, if you don't tell us about sites you have visited, they may eventually be deleted from the guide.

| Year of guide used | 20......... | Page No. | .......... | Name of town/village site listed under | |
|---|---|---|---|---|---|
| Site Name | | | | Date of visit | ....... /....... /....... |
| GPS | Latitude....................................................(eg 12.34567) Longitude....................................................(eg 1.23456 or -1.23456) | | | | |

Site is in: Andorra / Austria / Belgium / Croatia / Czech Republic / Denmark / Finland / France / Germany / Greece / Hungary / Italy / Luxembourg / Netherlands / Norway / Poland / Portugal / Slovakia / Slovenia / Spain / Sweden / Switzerland

Comments:

| Charge for outfit + 2 adults in local currency | High Season | Low Season | Elec inc in price? | Y / N | ............amps |
|---|---|---|---|---|---|
| | | | Price of elec (if not inc) | | ............amps |

| Year of guide used | 20......... | Page No. | .......... | Name of town/village site listed under | |
|---|---|---|---|---|---|
| Site Name | | | | Date of visit | ....... /....... /....... |
| GPS | Latitude....................................................(eg 12.34567) Longitude....................................................(eg 1.23456 or -1.23456) | | | | |

Site is in: Andorra / Austria / Belgium / Croatia / Czech Republic / Denmark / Finland / France / Germany / Greece / Hungary / Italy / Luxembourg / Netherlands / Norway / Poland / Portugal / Slovakia / Slovenia / Spain / Sweden / Switzerland

Comments:

| Charge for outfit + 2 adults in local currency | High Season | Low Season | Elec inc in price? | Y / N | ............amps |
|---|---|---|---|---|---|
| | | | Price of elec (if not inc) | | ............amps |

| Year of guide used | 20......... | Page No. | .......... | Name of town/village site listed under | |
|---|---|---|---|---|---|
| Site Name | | | | Date of visit | ....... /....... /....... |
| GPS | Latitude....................................................(eg 12.34567) Longitude....................................................(eg 1.23456 or -1.23456) | | | | |

Site is in: Andorra / Austria / Belgium / Croatia / Czech Republic / Denmark / Finland / France / Germany / Greece / Hungary / Italy / Luxembourg / Netherlands / Norway / Poland / Portugal / Slovakia / Slovenia / Spain / Sweden / Switzerland

Comments:

| Charge for outfit + 2 adults in local currency | High Season | Low Season | Elec inc in price? | Y / N | ............amps |
|---|---|---|---|---|---|
| | | | Price of elec (if not inc) | | ............amps |

**Please fill in your details and send to the address on the reverse of this form.**
**You can also complete forms online: www.caravanclub.co.uk/europereport**

CUT ALONG DOTTED LINE

| Year of guide used | 20......... | Page No. | .......... | Name of town/village site listed under | |
|---|---|---|---|---|---|

| Site Name | | | | Date of visit | ....... /....... /........ |
|---|---|---|---|---|---|

GPS    Latitude....................................................*(eg 12.34567)* Longitude....................................................*(eg 1.23456 or -1.23456)*

**Site is in:** Andorra / Austria / Belgium / Croatia / Czech Republic / Denmark / Finland / France / Germany / Greece / Hungary / Italy / Luxembourg / Netherlands / Norway / Poland / Portugal / Slovakia / Slovenia / Spain / Sweden / Switzerland

**Comments:**

| Charge for outfit + 2 adults in local currency | High Season | Low Season | Elec inc in price? | Y / N | .............amps |
|---|---|---|---|---|---|
| | | | Price of elec (if not inc) | | .............amps |

---

| Year of guide used | 20......... | Page No. | .......... | Name of town/village site listed under | |
|---|---|---|---|---|---|

| Site Name | | | | Date of visit | ....... /....... /........ |
|---|---|---|---|---|---|

GPS    Latitude....................................................*(eg 12.34567)* Longitude....................................................*(eg 1.23456 or -1.23456)*

**Site is in:** Andorra / Austria / Belgium / Croatia / Czech Republic / Denmark / Finland / France / Germany / Greece / Hungary / Italy / Luxembourg / Netherlands / Norway / Poland / Portugal / Slovakia / Slovenia / Spain / Sweden / Switzerland

**Comments:**

| Charge for outfit + 2 adults in local currency | High Season | Low Season | Elec inc in price? | Y / N | .............amps |
|---|---|---|---|---|---|
| | | | Price of elec (if not inc) | | .............amps |

---

| Year of guide used | 20......... | Page No. | .......... | Name of town/village site listed under | |
|---|---|---|---|---|---|

| Site Name | | | | Date of visit | ....... /....... /........ |
|---|---|---|---|---|---|

GPS    Latitude....................................................*(eg 12.34567)* Longitude....................................................*(eg 1.23456 or -1.23456)*

**Site is in:** Andorra / Austria / Belgium / Croatia / Czech Republic / Denmark / Finland / France / Germany / Greece / Hungary / Italy / Luxembourg / Netherlands / Norway / Poland / Portugal / Slovakia / Slovenia / Spain / Sweden / Switzerland

**Comments:**

| Charge for outfit + 2 adults in local currency | High Season | Low Season | Elec inc in price? | Y / N | .............amps |
|---|---|---|---|---|---|
| | | | Price of elec (if not inc) | | .............amps |

*Your comments & opinions may be used in future editions of the guide, if you do not wish them to be used please tick .......*

Name ...............................................................................

Membership No. .................................................................

Post Code ..........................................................................

Are you a  Caravanner / Motorhomer / Trailer-Tenter?

Do you need more blank Site Report forms?        YES / NO

Please return completed forms to:
**The Editor, Overseas Touring Guides**
**The Caravan Club**
**FREEPOST**
**PO Box 386 (RRZG-SXKK-UCUJ)**
**East Grinstead**
**RH19 1FH**
(Please use this address only when mailing from within the UK)

**You can also complete forms online: www.caravanclub.co.uk/europereport**

# Abbreviated Site Report Form

Use this abbreviated Site Report Form if you have visited a number of sites and there are no changes (or only small changes) to their entries in the guide. If reporting on a new site, or reporting several changes, please use the full version of the report form. **If advising prices**, these should be for an outfit and 2 adults for one night's stay. **Please indicate high or low season prices and whether electricity is included.**

Remember, if you don't tell us about sites you have visited, they may eventually be deleted from the guide.

| Year of guide used | 20......... | Page No. | .......... | Name of town/village site listed under | |
|---|---|---|---|---|---|
| Site Name | | | | Date of visit | ....... /....... /........ |
| GPS | Latitude....................................................(eg 12.34567) Longitude.....................................................(eg 1.23456 or -1.23456) | | | | |
| Site is in: Andorra / Austria / Belgium / Croatia / Czech Republic / Denmark / Finland / France / Germany / Greece / Hungary / Italy / Luxembourg / Netherlands / Norway / Poland / Portugal / Slovakia / Slovenia / Spain / Sweden / Switzerland | | | | | |
| Comments: | | | | | |

| Charge for outfit + 2 adults in local currency | High Season | Low Season | Elec inc in price? | Y / N | ............amps |
|---|---|---|---|---|---|
| | | | Price of elec (if not inc) | | ............amps |

| Year of guide used | 20......... | Page No. | .......... | Name of town/village site listed under | |
|---|---|---|---|---|---|
| Site Name | | | | Date of visit | ....... /....... /........ |
| GPS | Latitude....................................................(eg 12.34567) Longitude.....................................................(eg 1.23456 or -1.23456) | | | | |
| Site is in: Andorra / Austria / Belgium / Croatia / Czech Republic / Denmark / Finland / France / Germany / Greece / Hungary / Italy / Luxembourg / Netherlands / Norway / Poland / Portugal / Slovakia / Slovenia / Spain / Sweden / Switzerland | | | | | |
| Comments: | | | | | |

| Charge for outfit + 2 adults in local currency | High Season | Low Season | Elec inc in price? | Y / N | ............amps |
|---|---|---|---|---|---|
| | | | Price of elec (if not inc) | | ............amps |

| Year of guide used | 20......... | Page No. | .......... | Name of town/village site listed under | |
|---|---|---|---|---|---|
| Site Name | | | | Date of visit | ....... /....... /........ |
| GPS | Latitude....................................................(eg 12.34567) Longitude.....................................................(eg 1.23456 or -1.23456) | | | | |
| Site is in: Andorra / Austria / Belgium / Croatia / Czech Republic / Denmark / Finland / France / Germany / Greece / Hungary / Italy / Luxembourg / Netherlands / Norway / Poland / Portugal / Slovakia / Slovenia / Spain / Sweden / Switzerland | | | | | |
| Comments: | | | | | |

| Charge for outfit + 2 adults in local currency | High Season | Low Season | Elec inc in price? | Y / N | ............amps |
|---|---|---|---|---|---|
| | | | Price of elec (if not inc) | | ............amps |

**Please fill in your details and send to the address on the reverse of this form.**

You can also complete forms online: www.caravanclub.co.uk/europereport

CUT ALONG DOTTED LINE

| Year of guide used | 20......... | Page No. | .......... | Name of town/village site listed under | |
|---|---|---|---|---|---|

| Site Name | | | | Date of visit | ....... /....... /........ |
|---|---|---|---|---|---|

GPS     Latitude.................................................(eg 12.34567)   Longitude...................................................(eg 1.23456 or -1.23456)

**Site is in:** Andorra / Austria / Belgium / Croatia / Czech Republic / Denmark / Finland / France / Germany / Greece / Hungary / Italy / Luxembourg / Netherlands / Norway / Poland / Portugal / Slovakia / Slovenia / Spain / Sweden / Switzerland

**Comments:**

| Charge for outfit + 2 adults in local currency | High Season | Low Season | Elec inc in price? | | Y / N | ............amps |
|---|---|---|---|---|---|---|
| | | | Price of elec (if not inc) | | | ............amps |

---

| Year of guide used | 20......... | Page No. | .......... | Name of town/village site listed under | |
|---|---|---|---|---|---|

| Site Name | | | | Date of visit | ....... /....... /........ |
|---|---|---|---|---|---|

GPS     Latitude.................................................(eg 12.34567)   Longitude...................................................(eg 1.23456 or -1.23456)

**Site is in:** Andorra / Austria / Belgium / Croatia / Czech Republic / Denmark / Finland / France / Germany / Greece / Hungary / Italy / Luxembourg / Netherlands / Norway / Poland / Portugal / Slovakia / Slovenia / Spain / Sweden / Switzerland

**Comments:**

| Charge for outfit + 2 adults in local currency | High Season | Low Season | Elec inc in price? | | Y / N | ............amps |
|---|---|---|---|---|---|---|
| | | | Price of elec (if not inc) | | | ............amps |

---

| Year of guide used | 20......... | Page No. | .......... | Name of town/village site listed under | |
|---|---|---|---|---|---|

| Site Name | | | | Date of visit | ....... /....... /........ |
|---|---|---|---|---|---|

GPS     Latitude.................................................(eg 12.34567)   Longitude...................................................(eg 1.23456 or -1.23456)

**Site is in:** Andorra / Austria / Belgium / Croatia / Czech Republic / Denmark / Finland / France / Germany / Greece / Hungary / Italy / Luxembourg / Netherlands / Norway / Poland / Portugal / Slovakia / Slovenia / Spain / Sweden / Switzerland

**Comments:**

| Charge for outfit + 2 adults in local currency | High Season | Low Season | Elec inc in price? | | Y / N | ............amps |
|---|---|---|---|---|---|---|
| | | | Price of elec (if not inc) | | | ............amps |

---

*Your comments & opinions may be used in future editions of the guide, if you do not wish them to be used please tick .......*

Name ...............................................................................

Membership No. ................................................................

Post Code ........................................................................

Are you a Caravanner / Motorhomer / Trailer-Tenter?

Do you need more blank Site Report forms?     YES / NO

Please return completed forms to:
**The Editor, Overseas Touring Guides**
**The Caravan Club**
**FREEPOST**
**PO Box 386 (RRZG-SXKK-UCUJ)**
**East Grinstead**
**RH19 1FH**
(Please use this address only when mailing from within the UK)

**You can also complete forms online: www.caravanclub.co.uk/europereport**

# Abbreviated Site Report Form

Use this abbreviated Site Report Form if you have visited a number of sites and there are no changes (or only small changes) to their entries in the guide. If reporting on a new site, or reporting several changes, please use the full version of the report form. **If advising prices,** these should be for an outfit and 2 adults for one night's stay. **Please indicate high or low season prices and whether electricity is included.**

Remember, if you don't tell us about sites you have visited, they may eventually be deleted from the guide.

| Year of guide used | 20......... | Page No. | .......... | Name of town/village site listed under | | |
|---|---|---|---|---|---|---|
| Site Name | | | | | Date of visit | ....... /....... /........ |
| GPS | Latitude...................................................(eg 12.34567) Longitude....................................................(eg 1.23456 or -1.23456) | | | | | |

**Site is in:** Andorra / Austria / Belgium / Croatia / Czech Republic / Denmark / Finland / France / Germany / Greece / Hungary / Italy / Luxembourg / Netherlands / Norway / Poland / Portugal / Slovakia / Slovenia / Spain / Sweden / Switzerland

Comments:

| Charge for outfit + 2 adults in local currency | High Season | Low Season | Elec inc in price? | | Y / N | .............amps |
|---|---|---|---|---|---|---|
| | | | Price of elec (if not inc) | | | .............amps |

| Year of guide used | 20......... | Page No. | .......... | Name of town/village site listed under | | |
|---|---|---|---|---|---|---|
| Site Name | | | | | Date of visit | ....... /....... /........ |
| GPS | Latitude...................................................(eg 12.34567) Longitude....................................................(eg 1.23456 or -1.23456) | | | | | |

**Site is in:** Andorra / Austria / Belgium / Croatia / Czech Republic / Denmark / Finland / France / Germany / Greece / Hungary / Italy / Luxembourg / Netherlands / Norway / Poland / Portugal / Slovakia / Slovenia / Spain / Sweden / Switzerland

Comments:

| Charge for outfit + 2 adults in local currency | High Season | Low Season | Elec inc in price? | | Y / N | .............amps |
|---|---|---|---|---|---|---|
| | | | Price of elec (if not inc) | | | .............amps |

| Year of guide used | 20......... | Page No. | .......... | Name of town/village site listed under | | |
|---|---|---|---|---|---|---|
| Site Name | | | | | Date of visit | ....... /....... /........ |
| GPS | Latitude...................................................(eg 12.34567) Longitude....................................................(eg 1.23456 or -1.23456) | | | | | |

**Site is in:** Andorra / Austria / Belgium / Croatia / Czech Republic / Denmark / Finland / France / Germany / Greece / Hungary / Italy / Luxembourg / Netherlands / Norway / Poland / Portugal / Slovakia / Slovenia / Spain / Sweden / Switzerland

Comments:

| Charge for outfit + 2 adults in local currency | High Season | Low Season | Elec inc in price? | | Y / N | .............amps |
|---|---|---|---|---|---|---|
| | | | Price of elec (if not inc) | | | .............amps |

**Please fill in your details and send to the address on the reverse of this form.**

**You can also complete forms online: www.caravanclub.co.uk/europereport**

CUT ALONG DOTTED LINE

| Year of guide used | 20......... | Page No. | ......... | Name of town/village site listed under | | |
|---|---|---|---|---|---|---|
| Site Name | | | | | Date of visit | ....... /....... /....... |
| GPS | Latitude.................................................(eg 12.34567) | | Longitude.................................................(eg 1.23456 or -1.23456) | | | |

**Site is in:** Andorra / Austria / Belgium / Croatia / Czech Republic / Denmark / Finland / France / Germany / Greece / Hungary / Italy / Luxembourg / Netherlands / Norway / Poland / Portugal / Slovakia / Slovenia / Spain / Sweden / Switzerland

**Comments:**

| Charge for outfit + 2 adults in local currency | High Season | Low Season | Elec inc in price? | Y / N | .............amps |
|---|---|---|---|---|---|
| | | | Price of elec (if not inc) | | .............amps |

| Year of guide used | 20......... | Page No. | ......... | Name of town/village site listed under | | |
|---|---|---|---|---|---|---|
| Site Name | | | | | Date of visit | ....... /....... /....... |
| GPS | Latitude.................................................(eg 12.34567) | | Longitude.................................................(eg 1.23456 or -1.23456) | | | |

**Site is in:** Andorra / Austria / Belgium / Croatia / Czech Republic / Denmark / Finland / France / Germany / Greece / Hungary / Italy / Luxembourg / Netherlands / Norway / Poland / Portugal / Slovakia / Slovenia / Spain / Sweden / Switzerland

**Comments:**

| Charge for outfit + 2 adults in local currency | High Season | Low Season | Elec inc in price? | Y / N | .............amps |
|---|---|---|---|---|---|
| | | | Price of elec (if not inc) | | .............amps |

| Year of guide used | 20......... | Page No. | ......... | Name of town/village site listed under | | |
|---|---|---|---|---|---|---|
| Site Name | | | | | Date of visit | ....... /....... /....... |
| GPS | Latitude.................................................(eg 12.34567) | | Longitude.................................................(eg 1.23456 or -1.23456) | | | |

**Site is in:** Andorra / Austria / Belgium / Croatia / Czech Republic / Denmark / Finland / France / Germany / Greece / Hungary / Italy / Luxembourg / Netherlands / Norway / Poland / Portugal / Slovakia / Slovenia / Spain / Sweden / Switzerland

**Comments:**

| Charge for outfit + 2 adults in local currency | High Season | Low Season | Elec inc in price? | Y / N | .............amps |
|---|---|---|---|---|---|
| | | | Price of elec (if not inc) | | .............amps |

*Your comments & opinions may be used in future editions of the guide, if you do not wish them to be used please tick .......*

Name .................................................................................

Membership No. ................................................................

Post Code .........................................................................

Are you a  Caravanner / Motorhomer / Trailer-Tenter?

Do you need more blank Site Report forms?     YES / NO

Please return completed forms to:
**The Editor, Overseas Touring Guides**
**The Caravan Club**
**FREEPOST**
**PO Box 386 (RRZG-SXKK-UCUJ)**
**East Grinstead**
**RH19 1FH**
(Please use this address only when mailing from within the UK)

**You can also complete forms online: www.caravanclub.co.uk/europereport**

# Index

# Index

PEFC Certified

This product is
from sustainably
managed forests and
controlled sources

PEFC

PEFC/16-33-254      www.pefc.org